THE WYCLIFFE BIBLE COMMENTARY

THE WYCLIFFE BIBLE COMMENTARY

Edited by

CHARLES F. PFEIFFER
OLD TESTAMENT

EVERETT F. HARRISON
NEW TESTAMENT

MOODY PUBLISHERS • CHICAGO

Library of Congress Catalog Card Number: 62-20893

ISBN: 978-0-8024-9695-9

Moody Publishers
820 N. LaSalle Boulevard
Chicago, IL 60610

43 45 47 49 50 48 46 44 42

Printed in the United States of America

PUBLISHER'S PREFACE

(HOW TO USE THIS BOOK)

The Approach

THE *Wycliffe Bible Commentary* is an entirely new commentary on the whole Bible written and edited by a number of scholars representing a wide cross section of American Protestant Christianity. Within the limits of its more than a million and one-quarter words, it attempts to treat the entire text of the Old and New Testaments on a phrase by phrase basis. In addition, summaries of the major sections of each Biblical book generally appear in the text in connection with the main headings in the outline. Thus, the reader is permitted an overview and a detailed discussion of a passage of Scripture at the same time.

In the commentaries on the various books the writers present the results of their own careful, personal Bible study. But also they have preserved some of the best work of the older commentators and have utilized the insights of contemporary scholarship. While they infuse the whole with a fresh spirit, at the same time they manifest their unflinching belief in the divine inspiration of Holy Scripture.

Although the Biblical text used in the preparation of this commentary is that of the King James Version, several of the writers made their own translations of the books on which they worked. Occasionally they use phrases from their own translations in the text of the commentaries. For the convenience of the reader, all Biblical phraseology appears in bold face type, as do all the Biblical verse numbers. In this way numbers of verses are clearly distinguished from points in the outline. In cases in which the writer prefers to employ a reading from some version other than the King James, the source of such phraseology is identified. While the commentaries on the various books emphasize the interpretation of the actual words of Scripture, each is accompanied by a brief introductory discussion of authorship, date of composition, historical background, and the like. To provide the reader with further background information, a brief review of the inter-testamental period has been included.

To improve appearance of the printed page, pronouns referring to deity (which appear in large numbers) are not capitalized, except when capitalization is necessary for clarity of meaning. Also in the interest of typographical appearance, *Lord* and *God,* when they are translations of the Hebrew *YHWH*, are not printed in capitals as in the King James Version. Often the Hebrew *YHWH* is represented by the English *Jehovah*. But in some instances the contributors preferred the spelling of *Yahweh*, which is gaining favor among Biblical scholars.

The basic aim of this volume is to determine the meaning of the text of Scripture. It is therefore, strictly speaking, neither a devotional nor a technical exegetical treatment. It seeks to present the Biblical message in such a way that the serious Bible student will find extensive help within its pages.

The contributors to this commentary represent a total of more than fifteen denominational backgrounds. Among the forty-eight writers are professors in twenty-five schools of Christian higher education. With such a variety of backgrounds, it is to be expected that contributors will differ among themselves in some matters of interpretation. No editorial effort has been made to bring these differences into absolute conformity; writers have been given freedom of expression in such cases. The reader will discover, therefore, some differences in outlook in such instances as parallel passages in the Gospels and in the books of Kings and Chronicles.

Bibliography

Each of the books in this commentary is accompanied by a bibliography. Occasionally, when an author has treated related books (e.g., I, II Peter; I, II Thessalonians; Ezra, Nehemiah, Esther), he has chosen to place all of his bibliographies in one list. In such cases, the reader is directed to the full bibliographical listing.

The fact that a writer has included a given title does not mean that he recommends it as thoroughly conservative or thoroughly accurate. Writers have listed both works which they have referred to and those which will be of use to the reader. In the interests of standardization and economy of space, all annotations which might have classified books according to theological position and usefulness have been omitted.

Because many readers will be interested in knowing about conservative commentaries on the whole Bible or large sections of it, a few of the larger works are listed here. Old favorites are John Peter Lange's *Commentary on the Holy Scriptures* (24 vols.); C. J. Ellicott's *Commentary on the Whole Bible* (8 or 4 vols.); Matthew Henry's *Commentary on the Whole Bible* (6 vols. or 1 vol. abridgement); Jamieson, Fausset, and Brown's *A Commentary Critical, Experimental, and Practical on the Old and New Testaments* (6 vols. or 1 vol. abridgement); Matthew Henry, Thomas Scott, and others, *A Devotional Commentary on the Entire Bible;* and Alexander Maclaren's *Expositions of Holy Scripture* (25 vols.). A newer one-volume commentary that has enjoyed wide usefulness is *The New Bible Commentary*, edited by F. Davidson, A. M. Stibbs, and E. F. Kevan. While no attempt is made here to mention works on individual books of either Testament, it would be too bad to ignore C. H. Spurgeon's great classic on the Psalms, *The Treasury of David* (6 vols.).

More specialized commentaries on one or the other of the Testaments — commentaries which are not too heavily loaded with Hebrew and Greek for the serious student of the English Bible to find them of some use — include the following: C. F. Keil and F. Delitzsch, *Biblical Commentary on the Old Testament* (25 vols.); Marvin H. Vincent, *Word Studies in the New Testament* (4 vols.); A. T. Robertson, *Word Pictures in the New Testament* (6 vols.); and Henry Alford, *The Greek Testament* (4 vols.) or the one-volume *New Testament for English Readers*.

The student who is interested in questions of Biblical introduction, such as authorship, date, occasion for writing, and the like, will find the following four books helpful: Merrill F. Unger's *Introductory Guide to the Old Testament;* Henry C. Thiessen's *New Testament Introduction;* and D. Edmond Hiebert's *Introduction to the Pauline Epistles* and *Introduction to the Non-Pauline Epistles*. An especially useful conservative Bible atlas is *Baker's Bible Atlas,* prepared by Charles F. Pfeiffer; *Unger's Bible Dictionary* and the *New Bible Dictionary* provide information on special problems related to interpretation of Scripture.

Contributors

Genesis: Kyle M. Yates, Sr., Th.D., Ph.D., Professor of Old Testament, Baylor University, Waco, Tex.

Exodus: Philip C. Johnson, Th.D., Professor of Bible, Gordon College, Beverly Farms, Mass.

Leviticus: Robert O. Coleman, Th.D., Assistant Professor of Biblical Introduction, Southwestern Baptist Theological Seminary, Fort Worth, Tex.

Numbers: Elmer Smick, S.T.M., Ph.D., Professor of Ancient Languages, Covenant College and Theological Seminary, St. Louis, Mo.

Deuteronomy: Meredith G. Kline, Th.M., Ph.D., Associate Professor of Old Testament, Westminster Theological Seminary, Philadelphia, Pa.

Joshua: John Rea, A.M., Th.D., Professor of Old Testament, Moody Bible Institute, Chicago, Ill.

Judges: Charles F. Pfeiffer, Th.M., Ph.D., Professor of Old Testament, Gordon Divinity School, Beverly Farms, Mass.

Ruth: Charles F. Pfeiffer (see under Judges).

I and II Samuel: Fred E. Young, B.D., Ph.D., Professor of Old Testament, Central Baptist Theological Seminary, Kansas City, Kan.

I Kings: John T. Gates, S.T.D., Professor of Bible and Philosophy, St. Paul Bible College, St. Paul, Minn.

II Kings: Harold Stigers, Ph.D., Instructor in Ancient Languages, Covenant College and Theological Seminary, St. Louis, Mo.

I and II Chronicles: J. Barton Payne, A.M., Th.D., Associate Professor of Old Testament, Wheaton College Graduate School, Wheaton, Ill.

Ezra, Nehemiah, and Esther: John C. Whitcomb, Jr., Th.D., Professor of Old Testament and Director of Post-Graduate Studies, Grace Theological Seminary, Winona Lake, Ind.

Job: Meredith G. Kline (see under Deuteronomy).

Psalms: Kyle M. Yates, Jr., Th.D., Associate Professor of Old Testament and Biblical Archaeology, Golden Gate Baptist Theological Seminary, Mill Valley, Calif.

Proverbs: R. Laird Harris, Th.M., Ph.D., Professor of Old Testament, Covenant College and Theological Seminary, St. Louis, Mo.

Ecclesiastes: Robert Laurin, Th.M., Ph.D., Professor of Old Testament and Hebrew, California Baptist Theological Seminary, Covina, Calif.

Song of Solomon: Sierd Woudstra, Th.D. pastor, Calvin Christian Reformed Church, Ottawa, Ont., Canada.

Isaiah: Gleason L. Archer, Jr., B.D., Ph.D., Professor of Biblical Languages, Fuller Theological Seminary, Pasadena, Calif.

Jeremiah: John F. Graybill, B.D., Ph.D., Director, Department of Bible and Theology, Barrington College, Barrington, R.I.

Lamentations: Ross Price, M.Th., D.D., Professor of Theology, Pasadena College, Pasadena, Calif.

Ezekiel: Anton T. Pearson, Th.D., Professor of Old Testament Language and Literature, Bethel College and Seminary, St. Paul, Minn.

Daniel: Robert D. Culver, Th.D., Professor of Bible, Northwestern College, Minneapolis, Minn.

Hosea: Charles F. Pfeiffer (see under Judges).

Joel: Derward Deere, Th.D., Professor of Old Testament Interpretation, Golden Gate Baptist Theological Seminary, Mill Valley, Calif.

Amos: Arnold C. Schultz, M.A., Th.D., Professor of Old Testament and Archaeology, Northern Baptist Theological Seminary, Chicago, Ill.

Obadiah and Jonah: G. Herbert Livingston, B.D., Ph.D., Professor of Old Testament, Asbury Theological Seminary, Wilmore, Ky.

Micah: E. Leslie Carlson, A.M., Th.D., Professor of Biblical Introduction and Semitic Languages, Southwestern Baptist Theological Seminary, Fort Worth, Tex.

Nahum: Charles L. Feinberg, Th.D., Ph.D., Dean and Professor of Semitics and Old Testament, Talbot Theological Seminary, La Mirada, Calif.

Habakkuk: David W. Kerr, Th.D., Dean and Professor of Old Testament Interpretation, Gordon Divinity School, Beverly Farms, Mass.

Zephaniah: H. A. Hanke, Th.D., Professor of Bible, Asbury College, Wilmore, Ky.

Haggai: Charles L. Feinberg (see under Nahum).

Zechariah: Charles L. Feinberg (see under Nahum).

Malachi: Burton L. Goddard, Th.D., Director of Library and Professor of Biblical Languages and Exegesis, Gordon Divinity School, Beverly Farms, Mass.

From Malachi to Matthew: Charles F. Pfeiffer (see under Judges).

Matthew: Homer A. Kent, Jr., Th.D., Professor of New Testament and Greek, Grace Theological Seminary, Winona Lake, Ind.

Mark: Donald W. Burdick, Th.D., Professor of New Testament, Conservative Baptist Theological Seminary, Denver, Colo.

Luke: Merrill C. Tenney, Ph.D., Dean of the Graduate School, Wheaton College, Wheaton, Ill.

John: Everett F. Harrison, Th.D., Ph.D., Professor of New Testament, Fuller Theological Seminary, Pasadena, Calif.

Acts: George E. Ladd, B.D., Ph.D., Professor of Biblical Theology, Fuller Theological Seminary, Pasadena, Calif.

Romans: A. Berkeley Mickelsen, B.D., Ph.D., Professor of Bible and Theology, Graduate School, Wheaton College, Wheaton, Ill.

I Corinthians: S. Lewis Johnson, Jr., Th.D., Professor of New Testament Literature and Exegesis, Dallas Theological Seminary, Dallas, Tex.

II Corinthians: Wick Broomall, Th.M., Pastor, Westminster Presbyterian Church, Augusta, Georgia.

Galatians: Everett F. Harrison (see under John).

Ephesians: Alfred Martin, Th.D., Dean of Faculty, Professor of Old Testament Synthesis, Moody Bible Institute, Chicago, Ill.

Philippians: Robert H. Mounce, Th.M., Ph.D., Associate Professor of Biblical Literature and Greek, Bethel College and Seminary, St. Paul, Minn.

Colossians: E. Earle Ellis, B.D., Ph.D., lecturer and writer on the New Testament, currently engaged in research and writing in Germany.

I and II Thessalonians: David A. Hubbard, Th.M., Ph.D., Chairman of the Division of Biblical Studies and Philosophy, Westmont College, Santa Barbara, Calif.

I and II Timothy, Titus: Wilbur B. Wallis, S.T.M., Ph.D., Professor of New Testament Language and Literature, Covenant College and Theological Seminary.

Philemon: E. Earle Ellis (see under Colossians).

Hebrews: Robert W. Ross, Ph.D. candidate, Acting Head, Department of History, Northwestern College, Minneapolis, Minn.

James: Walter W. Wessel, Ph.D., Associate Professor of Biblical Literature, Bethel College and Theological Seminary, St. Paul, Minn.

I and II Peter: Stephen W. Paine, Ph.D., President and Professor of Greek, Houghton College, Houghton, N. Y.

I, II, III John: Charles C. Ryrie, Th.D., Ph.D., Chairman of the Department of Systematic Theology, Dean of the Graduate School, Dallas Theological Seminary, Dallas, Tex.

Jude: David H. Wallace, Th.M., Ph.D., Professor of Biblical Theology, California Baptist Theological Seminary, Covina, Calif.

Revelation: Wilbur M. Smith, D.D., Professor of English Bible, Fuller Theological Seminary, Pasadena, Calif.

Abbreviations

a. Books of the Bible.

1. OT Gen Ex Lev Num Deut Josh Jud Ruth I Sam II Sam I Kgs II Kgs I Chr II Chr Ezr Neh Est Job Ps Prov Eccl Song Isa Jer Lam Ezk Dan Hos Joel Amos Ob Jon Mic Nah Hab Zeph Hag Zech Mal
2. NT Mt Mk Lk Jn Acts Rom I Cor II Cor Gal Eph Phil Col I Thess II Thess I Tim II Tim Tit Phm Heb Jas I Pet II Pet I Jn II Jn III Jn Jude Rev

b. Apocrypha.

I Esd (I Esdras); II Esd (II Esdras); Tob (Tobit); Wisd Wisdom of Solomon); Sir (The Wisdom of Jesus the son of Sirach, or Ecclesiasticus); Bel (Bel and the Dragon); I Macc (I Maccabees); II Macc (II Maccabees)

c. Periodicals, reference works, dictionaries, and versions.

A-S	Abbott-Smith, *Manual Greek Lexicon of the NT*
Alf	Alford's *Greek Testament*
ANET	*Ancient Near Eastern Texts*, ed. by Pritchard
Arndt	Arndt-Gingrich, *Greek-English Lexicon*
ASV	American Standard Version
AV	Authorized Version
BA	*Biblical Archaeologist*
BASOR	*Bulletin*, American Schools of Oriental Research
BDB	Brown, Driver, Briggs, *Hebrew-English Lexicon of the OT*
Beng	Bengel's *Gnomon*
BS	*Bibliotheca Sacra*
BTh	*Biblical Theology*
BV	Berkeley Version
CBSC	Cambridge Bible for Schools and Colleges
Crem	Cremer's *Biblico-Theological Lexicon of NT Greek*
DeissBS	Deissmann, *Bible Studies*
Deiss LAE	Deissmann, *Light from the Ancient East*
EQ	*Evangelical Quarterly*

ERV	English Revised Version (1881)
Exp	*The Expositor*
ExpB	*The Expositor's Bible*
ExpGT	*The Expositor's Greek Testament*
ExpT	*The Expository Times*
HDAC	*Hastings' Dictionary of the Apostolic Church*
HDB	*Hastings' Dictionary of the Bible*
HDCG	*Hastings' Dictionary of Christ and the Gospels*
HERE	*Hastings' Encyclopedia of Religion and Ethics*
HR	Hatch and Redpath, *Concordance to the LXX*
HZNT	*Handbuch zum Neuen Testament* (Lietzmann)
IB	*Interpreter's Bible*
ICC	*International Critical Commentary*
Interp	*Interpretation*
ISBE	*International Standard Bible Encyclopaedia*
JewEnc	*Jewish Encyclopaedia*
JBL	*Journal of Biblical Literature*
JBR	*Journal of Bible and Religion*
JFB	Jamieson, Fausset, and Brown, *A Commentary Critical, Experimental and Practical on the Old and New Testaments*
JNES	*Journal of Near Eastern Studies*
Jos	Josephus' *Antiquities of the Jews, et al.*
JPS	Jewish Publication Society Version of the Old Testament
JQR	*Jewish Quarterly Review*
JTS	*Journal of Theological Studies*
KB	Koehler and Baumgartner, *Lexicon in Veteris*
KD	Keil and Delitzsch, *Commentary on the OT*
LSJ	Liddell, Scott, Jones, *Greek-English Lexicon*
LXX	Septuagint
MM	Moulton and Milligan, *The Vocabulary of the Gr. Test.*
MNT	*Moffatt's New Testament Commentary*
MSt	McClintock and Strong, *Cyclopaedia of Biblical, Theological, and Ecclesiastical Literature*
MT	Masoretic Text
Nestle	Nestle (ed.) *Novum Testamentum Graece*
NovTest	*Novum Testamentum*
NTS	*New Testament Studies*
Pesh	Peshitta (Syriac)
PTR	Princeton Theological Review
RB	*Revue Biblique*
RSV	Revised Standard Version
RTWB	*Richardson's Theological Word Book*

SBK	*Kommentar zum Neuen Testament aus Talmud und Midrasch* (Strack and Billerbeck)
SHERK	*The New Schaff-Herzog Encyclopedia of Religious Knowledge*
ThT	*Theology Today*
Trench	*Trench's Synonyms of the New Testament*
TWNT	*Theologisches Wörterbuch zum Neuen Testament* (Kittel)
VT	*Vetus Testamentum*
Vulg	Vulgate Version
Wett	Wettstein's *Novum Testamentum Graecum*
WC	Westminster Commentaries
WH	Westcott and Hort, *Text of the Greek NT*
WTJ	Westminster Theological Journal
ZAW	*Zeitschrift für die alttestamentliche Wissenschaft*
ZNW	*Zeitschrift für die neutestamentliche Wissenschaft*

d. Others.

A. D.	*anno domini* (in the year of our Lord)
art.	article
B. C.	Before Christ
c.	circa (about)
cen.	century
cf.	*confer* (compare)
ch.	chapter
Com.	*Commentary*
e. g.	*exempli gratia* (for example)
et al.	and others
f., ff.	following
Gr.	Greek
Heb.	Hebrew
i. e.	*id est* (that is)
marg.	margin, marginal reading
MS., MSS.	manuscript, manuscripts
p., pp.	page, pages
pl.	plural
sing.	singular

Transliteration

Hebrew and Greek words have been transliterated according to the following form:

Greek	Hebrew Consonants[1]		Hebrew Vocalization[2]	
α - a	א - ʼ	מ ם - m	בָּה - bâ	בָּ - bo[3]
ᾳ - â	בּ ב - b	נ ן - n	בּוֹ - bô	בֻּ - bu[3]
ε - e	גּ ג - g	ס - s	בּוּ - bû	בֶּ - be
η - ē	דּ ד - d	ע - ʽ	בֵּי - bê	בִּ - bi[3]
ῃ - ê	ה - h	פּ ף - p	בֶּי - bè	בֲּ - bă
ο - o	ו - w	צ ץ - ṣ	בִּי - bî	בֳּ - bŏ
ω - ō	ז - z	ק - q	בָּ - bā	בֱּ - bĕ
ῳ - ô	ח - ḥ	ר - r	בֹּ - bō	בְּ - bᵉ
ζ - z	ט - ṭ	שׁ - sh	בֻּ - bū	בָּה - bāh
θ - th	י - y	שׂ - ś	בֵּ - bē	בָּא - bā'
ξ - x	כּ כ ךּ - k	תּ ת - t	בִּ - bī	בֵּה - bēh
υ - y	ל - l		בַּ - ba	בֶּה - beh
φ - ph				
χ - ch				
ψ - ps				
ʽ - h				

[1]*Dagesh lene* is not indicated. *Dagesh forte* is represented by doubling the letter.

[2]This is an *orthographic equation* and not a scientific representation.

[3]In closed syllables.

Acknowledgments

The Publishers are greatly indebted to the editors of this volume, Dr. Charles F. Pfeiffer and Dr. Everett F. Harrison, and to the contributors, who have given their services so heartily. Especially appreciated is their outstanding co-operation in fulfilling the exacting requirements of a one-volume commentary of this kind. The Publishers also wish to acknowledge the splendid assistance of Dr. John Rea and Mr. Walter Dunnett, of the Moody Bible Institute Faculty, for their editorial help; of Mr. Herbert Klingbeil, director of Moody Correspondence School, for co-ordinating various aspects of the work; and of Dr. Howard F. Vos, textbook editor of Moody Press, for his detailed supervision of the work from its inception to its publication.

CONTENTS

THE OLD TESTAMENT

THE NEW TESTAMENT

THE OLD TESTAMENT

GENESIS

INTRODUCTION

Title. The word Genesis came into English by way of Latin from the Greek. In the Septuagint (LXX), it formed the superscription for the first book of the Bible. The word means "origin, source, or begetting." The Hebrew word *bᵉrʼēshîth*, translated "in [the] beginning," is the first word in the Hebrew Bible. It is frequently used to designate the book of Genesis.

Nature. Genesis is the book of origins. It gives a majestic account of the beginnings of all the Creator brought into being. It answers men's questions concerning the origin of the world, and of plant, animal, and human life. It tells of the establishment of the family, the origin of sin, the giving of the divine revelation, the growth and development of the race, and the inauguration of God's plan to bring about redemption through his chosen people. It presents and illustrates eternal truths, and it resolves enigmas, mysteries, and puzzling situations in the light of God's will for his people. In clear, meaningful language the writer sets forth God's revealed plans and purposes, and the marvels of his dealings with men.

Genesis takes the reader back to the all-important moment of creation when the omnipotent Creator spoke into being the matchless wonders of sun, moon, stars, planets, galaxies, plants, and moving creatures, and the one whom he made in his image. In these fifty chapters the inspired writer unfolds the drama of creation; he tells how sin came stealthily and relentlessly to bring ruin, disfigurement, and death; he reveals the tragic fruits of sin in our first parents' pathetic defeat; and he shows how, later, the accumulated wickednesses of men brought destruction and almost annihilation to human society. In the fresh beginning the writer traces the growth of the new race, and finally the exciting careers of Abraham, Isaac, Jacob, and Jacob's children. The book ends with the death of Joseph in the land of Egypt.

Genesis 1–11 presents the account of man from creation to the beginning of the life of Abraham. Genesis 12–50 recounts God's dealings with his chosen people—Abraham, Isaac, Jacob, Joseph, and their descendants. Throughout the narrative, the author's chief concern is to set forth Jehovah's purpose in creating and providentially guiding such an elect people. Not only Genesis, but the whole Bible shows that through the agency of this people, the Lord sought to reveal his nature and ways to the world, to establish his holy will in the earth, and to bring his "good news" of redemption to all men. Nations and individuals are mentioned and described in the book only as they fit into the Lord's sublime plan and purpose. Sumerians, Hittites, Babylonians, and Assyrians, whenever their history affects that of the chosen people, enter the picture briefly in order to demonstrate God's purpose for the world. At every step, the Spirit sought to make the revelation clear to men of all ages. In the rapidly moving drama, the plan of God was unfolding.

Authorship. It is safe to claim Moses as the responsible author of the book. It is the first book of the Pentateuch, which both Scripture and tradition attribute to Moses. It would be difficult to find a man in all the range of Israel's life who was better qualified to write this history. Trained in the "wisdom of the Egyptians" (Acts 7:22), Moses was providentially prepared to understand available records, manuscripts, and oral narratives. As a prophet to whom was granted the unusual privilege of unhurried hours of communion with God on Sinai, he was well equipped to record for all generations the Lord's portrayal of his activity through the ages. What other individual in all the centuries possessed such powers and such faith, and enjoyed such intimate fellowship with Jehovah?

The discovery in modern times of such ancient records as the Amarna Letters, the Ugaritic (or Ras Shamra) literature, and the clay tablets from Mesopotamia (Mari and Nuzu), has enabled scholars to reconstruct the historical and cultural background of the Biblical record, and to discover what life was like in Egypt, Palestine, and Mesopotamia during the Biblical epoch. Very likely many oral and written records, reaching far back into antiquity, were available to the distinguished Hebrew scholar, whose Egyptian schooling and whose graduate study in the region of Mount Sinai made him aware of significant world movements. According to Jewish tradition, when the great scribe Ezra came back from Babylonia to Jerusalem, bringing the Hebrew manuscripts of the Old Testament, he set to work with prodigious energy preserving, copying, and editing the old materials in his possession.

Genesis and Science. If a student expects to find in Genesis a scientific account of how the world came into existence, with all questions concerning primitive life answered in technical language familiar to the professor or student of science, he will be disappointed. Genesis is not an attempt to grapple with or answer such technical questions. It deals with matters far beyond the realm of science. The author seeks to bring us in touch with the eternal God and to reveal the sacred meaning of his being, his purpose, and his dealings with his creatures as he works out his holy will. This book, so remarkable for its profundity and moral exaltation, its dignity and grandeur, pictures the eternal God at work preparing a place where his beloved creatures can live and grow and reveal the divine glory.

OUTLINE

I. The early beginnings. 1:1–11:32.
  A. The creation. 1:1–2:25.
  B. The temptation and fall. 3:1-24.
  C. The two brothers. 4:1-26.
  D. Seth and his descendants. 5:1-32.
  E. Sin and the Flood. 6:1–8:22.
  F. Noah's later life, and his descendants. 9:1–10:32.
  G. The Tower of Babel. 11:1-32.

II. The patriarchs. 12:1–50:26.
  A. Abraham. 12:1–25:18.
  B. Isaac. 25:19–26:35.
  C. Jacob. 27:1–36:43.
  D. Joseph. 37:1–50:26.

COMMENTARY

I. The Early Beginnings. 1:1–11:32.

A. The Creation. 1:1–2:25. God is the Creator of all things. From the outset in the Book of Genesis, the focus of the strong light of revelation turns upon the Almighty. He is the Beginning, the Cause, the Source of all that is. He brought into being all the things and the persons that were to fit into his plan for the ages. All the matter necessary for his later working, he miraculously created.

1. In beginning *(bᵉrʼēshîth).* The author takes the reader back before time, into the unfathomable reaches of eternity, though language fails him as he seeks to suggest the state of things before time was. He gives no hint of a tangible date for this **beginning.** His account reaches back into the time before the dating of events. **God created.** The sublime certainty of revelation is based on this one mighty assertion. God did it. Nothing more astounding could be declared. *ʼElōhîm* is the usual word for "God" in Hebrew, Aramaic, and Arabic. It is actually plural in form, but it is used with a verb in the singular. Perhaps the plural is best explained as indicating "plenitude of might" or exceptional dignity and unlimited greatness. In this One are united all the powers of eternity and infinity.

Created *(bārāʼ)* is a verb used exclusively of God. Man could not reach up to the powers inherent in this word, for it describes full miracle. By the sovereign, originative power of God something absolutely new was brought into being. **The heavens and the earth.** Here the author focuses interest upon all the areas of the world above, around, and below. In this phrase he includes the completed universe as it was known (or might come to be known) by the Hebrews, and all the raw material needed to make suns, planets, stars, nebulae, galaxies, molecules, atoms, electrons, and all the specific things and beings on the earth.

Men of science reveal that our galaxy

contains more than 100 billion stars, and that our sun is 150 trillion miles from the center of our galaxy. Our galaxy is one of a small cluster of 19 galaxies, the nearest of which is 30 million light years from us (150 million trillion miles). Our research scientists, by using powerful telescopes, have made reasonably sure that there are more than a billion galaxies. They estimate the number of stars in these galaxies as close to 100 quintillion. The candle power of one of the galaxies is equal to that of 400 million suns. As a man looks on this vast creation and compares what he sees with the inspired writer's account of its origin, his heart must be filled with awe. He recognizes the hand of God in the beauty and order of the solar system and in the power at the center of the atom. Whether he looks upon the sun (positively charged), holding the planets (negatively charged), or whether he examines the nucleus (positively charged) at the heart of the atom, holding each electron (negatively charged) in its sway, he senses the wisdom, power, and grandeur of God. In the light of all this, a reverent man bows before his Creator in awe and genuine dedication, and pours out worship, adoration, thanksgiving, and unrestrained praise. The sublime creation of the Lord is that being, greatly beloved, whom he chose to create in his own image.

2. The earth was without form, and void *(tōhû wābōhû)*. The inspired author quickly turns his attention to the earth, for his story has to do with God's plans and provision for human life on this planet. He describes the earth in its unfinished state. There was plenty of material at hand for every work God planned to create, though in a chaotic state—waste, void, dark. Six full creative days were to make phenomenal changes. God's purpose could not be satisfied until his miraculous touch had made something of this chaos. Even darkness (often, in Scripture, associated with evil) was to be made subservient to his will. **The Spirit of God was hovering** *(rûaḥ . . . mᵉrăḥepet)*. The words portray the energy-giving presence of God, swathing and caressing the chaos and unfinished earth as he prepared to complete his creation. Like a devoted mother bird, he moved about, lavishing his love on the newborn world.

3. Then said God, Let be light. The author presents God's first creative word. With unbelievable ease and deliberate consciousness, the omnipotent God brought light into existence. He uttered his word, and instantly his will was accomplished (Ps 33:6,9). Light was God's answer to the dominance of darkness. It was the Lord's first positive move toward completing the full program of creation. Without it, the other steps would have been meaningless. The Apostle John tells us that "God is light" (I Jn 1:5). **4. God saw . . . that it was good.** When the Creator looked upon the product of his will, he found it perfectly complete and admirable; and he was pleased. Seven times this statement is made. Every one of God's creative acts was perfect, complete, pleasing, satisfying. It is good to remember that this was the same light man sees and enjoys today.

5. Evening and morning. In the book of Genesis evening always precedes morning. The creation of light ended the reign of darkness and brought on the first day. Since it was still some time before the creation of the sun and moon, it is incorrect to speak of actual twenty-four-hour days until after that point in the program of the Creator. The reference here is to a day of God, and not to an ordinary day bounded by minutes and hours. The beginning of each act of creation is called morning, and the close of that specific divine act is called evening.

6. A firmament *(expanse)* **in the midst of the waters.** The Hebrew word *rāqîa* represents something beaten out or pressed out so as to extend over a wide surface. The writer suggests here an expanse above the earth, holding vast reservoirs of water to be released for rain.

9. Let the dry land appear. At one stage, water covered everything. On the third day, however, the Lord made the land and the vegetable kingdom. By his divine power he caused the land to emerge from the great mass of waters, and formed the earth (cf. Ps 104:6-8; Job 38:8-11). From the soil, at the express command of God, living vegetation sprang forth, and soon clothed the earth with beauty and provided food for living creatures.

14. Let be lights. Hebrew *mᵉʾōrōt* describes the luminaries or instruments of light. By means of these luminaries, the earth received the light necessary for maintaining life. They were to **rule** over the day and the night (v. 16), to be for signs and seasons, and to give light upon the earth. The account makes it clear that God *made* them and then *set* them in place. According to the divine blueprint, the sun, moon, and stars were all brought into being to carry out his specific will.

20. Let the waters swarm with swarms of living creatures. This verse describes the sudden coming of hosts of winged things and fishes. They were designed to provide another visible demonstration of the Creator's power. With their appearance, there was life on the earth and also activity. And there was, furthermore, an endless succession of living creatures, all made by God's mighty hand. **21. Sea monsters** (AV, *great whales).* Literally, *stretched-out* animals that creep, crawl, or glide upon the earth, in or out of the water, such as, serpents, eels, fish, and dragons. **22.** The Lord breathed his blessing upon these and commanded them to be **fruitful and multiply.** The progress of God's creative activity was upward toward the creation of man.

26. Let us make man. The supreme moment of creation arrived as God created man. The narrative presents God as calling on the heavenly court, or the other two members of the Trinity, to center all attention on this event. Some commentators, however, interpret the plural as a "plural of majesty," indicating dignity and greatness. The plural form of the word for God, *'Elōhîm,* can be explained in somewhat the same way. The Lord is represented as giving unusual deliberation to a matter fraught with much significance.

In our image *(ṣelem),* **after our likeness** *(dᵉmût).* Though these two synonyms have separate meanings, there is here seemingly no effort to present different aspects of God's being. It is clear that man, as God made him, was distinctly different from the animals already created. He stood on a much higher plateau, for God created him to be immortal, and made him a special image of His own eternity. Man was a creature with whom his Maker could visit and have fellowship and communion. On the other hand, the Lord could expect man to answer him and be responsible to him. Man was constituted to have the privilege of choice, even to the point of disobeying his Creator. He was to be God's responsible representative and steward on the earth, to work out his Creator's will and fulfill the divine purpose. World dominion was to be granted to this new creature (cf. Ps 8:5-7). He was commissioned to subdue *(kābash,* "tread upon") the earth, and to follow God's plan in filling it with people. This sublime creature, with his unbelievable privileges and heavy responsibilities, was to live and move in kingly fashion.

31. Very good *(tôb mᵉ'ōd).* When the Lord looked upon the completed result of his creative acts, he expressed peculiar delight and extreme satisfaction. Everything in the universe, from the biggest star to the smallest blade of grass, brought joy to his heart. It was a beautiful symphony. The Creator's satisfaction is here expressed in terse yet vivid language.

2:1,2. Finished *(kālâh)* **. . . . rested** *(shābăt)* **. . . . hallowed** *(kādăsh).* When the Creator had pronounced his approval of everything he had made, including man, the crown of creation, he declared the work finished. For the present, he would undertake no further creation. However, he *sanctified,* or **hallowed,** a day of complete rest. The Hebrew word *shābăt* can be translated "desisted" or "ceased" or "cut off." During this time even God would rest from creative activity (cf. Ex 20:11; 31:17). **3.** The **seventh day** was set apart to be hallowed and honored through the years as a reminder that God had appointed a season of rest, refreshment, and complete cessation of all ordinary work, toil, and struggle.

4. These are the generations *(tôlᵉdôt).* The Hebrew word comes from a verb meaning *to beget or bear children.* It could be translated "begettings." This statement may be a reference to Genesis 1. The LXX translates: *This is the Book of the Genesis.* Some would translate it, *The history of the heavens and the earth.* The offspring of heaven and earth were thus pictured.

Jehovah, the Lord God. For the first time, the name *Yahweh,* or Jehovah (cf. Ex 6:2,3) is presented. Jehovah is the personal covenant God of Israel, who is at the same time the God of heaven and earth. The name connotes the eternal self-existence of the Author of all existence. It is expressive of God's loving-kindness, his grace, his mercy, his lordship, and his eternal relationship to his own chosen ones who are created in his image. Jehovah's special relationship to Israel would be described more distinctly when he would appear at the burning bush near Sinai. Here the Author of life is identified with the divine Creator of Genesis 1.

6. A mist used to go up . . . and wa-

ter. In order to prepare the ground to perform its appointed work, the Creator supplied moisture. The usual translation refers to a very slight drizzle of rain, or a mist. It is possible that the word translated **mist** in the AV *('ēd)* could be translated "river" or "stream." The former is to be preferred. In any event, the **mist** was God's way of working out his will for the soil. Continuous action is expressed.

7. The Lord God formed *(yāṣār)* **man of the dust of the ground.** Again the two names for God are joined in anticipation of the epoch-making event. The word *yāṣār* is used to give the figure of a potter at work, molding with his hands the plastic material he holds (cf. Jer 18:3,4). The same verb is used to picture the shaping of a people or a nation. Man's body was fashioned from the dust of the ground, while his spirit came from the very "breath" of God. He is literally a creature of two worlds; both earth and heaven can claim him. Notice the three statements: **Jehovah formed** *(yāṣār)* **man of the dust . . . Jehovah God breathed** *(nāpaḥ)* **into his nostrils the breath of life . . . man became** *(ḥāyāh)* **a living soul.** The first step was exceedingly important, but the moistened dust was far from being a man until the second miracle was complete. God communicated his own life to that inert mass of substance he had previously created and molded into form. The divine breath permeated the material and transformed it into a living being. That strange combination of dust and deity produced a marvelous creation (cf. I Cor 15:47-49), made in God's own image. As a living being, man was destined to reveal the qualities of the Giver of life.

This language of Scripture does not suggest that man bore physical resemblance to God. Rather, he was made like God in spiritual powers. To him were given the powers to think and feel, to communicate with others, to discern and discriminate, and, to a certain extent, to determine his own character.

8. A garden *(gan)* **. . . in Eden** *(b^e 'ēden).* The author represents God as planting a beautiful garden for his new creatures. The word means an enclosure or a park. The LXX here uses a term that forms the basis for our word "paradise." Man's work in that garden was to exercise dominion while serving – a good combination. The duties probably were rigorous but enjoyable. Eden, or the land of Eden, probably lay in the lower part of the Babylonian valley. Though many rival claims for the location of Eden have been advanced, the evidence seems to point to the area between the Tigris and the Euphrates as the cradle of civilization. The Hebrew word *Eden* probably means "enchantment," "pleasure," or "delight." In this quiet place of indescribable beauty, man was to enjoy fellowship and companionship with the Creator, and to work in accord with the divine blueprint to perfect His will. Magnificent trees furnished sustaining food, but man had to work to care for them. Adequate water supply was ensured by a vast irrigation system, a network of rivers that flowed in and about the garden with its life-giving waters. In order to lead man to full moral and spiritual development, God gave him specific commands and a specific prohibition to govern his behavior. He also gave him the power of choice and set before him the privilege of growing in divine favor. Thus began the moral discipline of man.

18. An help meet for him *('ēzer k^e negdô).* The inspired author indirectly reveals man's natural loneliness and lack of full satisfaction. Though much had been done for him, yet he was conscious of a lack. The Creator had not finished. He had plans for providing a companion who would satisfy the unfulfilled yearnings of man's heart. Created for fellowship and companionship, man could enter into the full life only as he might share love, trust, and devotion in the intimate circle of the family relationship. Jehovah made it possible for man to have **an help meet for him.** Literally, *a help answering to him,* or, *one who answers.* She was to be one who could share man's responsibilities, respond to his nature with understanding and love, and wholeheartedly co-operate with him in working out the plan of God.

21. Deep sleep *(tardēmâ)* **. . . made** her *(bānâ).* Today physicians use various anaesthetics to produce deep sleep. We do not know what means or method the Creator used to induce in Adam such **deep sleep** that he was unconscious of the events. That remains a mystery. Certainly divine mercy was displayed in this miracle. The Eternal was bringing into being not only another individual, but a new one, totally different, with another sex. Someone has said that "woman was taken not from man's head to rule over him, nor from his feet to be trampled upon, but from his side, under his arm, to be protected, and closest his heart, to be loved." She is also represented in the story of creation as wholly dependent upon her husband and not complete without him. Similarly, man is never fully complete without the woman. It is God's will that it should be so. Since woman was formed from man's side, she is bound to him and obligated to be a **help** to him. He is obligated to give her the full protection and devoted shielding of his arm. The two beings make up the completed whole, the crown of creation. The author of Genesis declares that God **builded** *(bānâ)* the rib which he had taken from man into a woman. The hand that had molded clay into the material for the body of man took a part of the living body of man and builded it into the woman.

22. Brought her unto the man. When God was ready with this new creation, he "gave her away" in marriage to her husband, thus establishing the eternally significant institution of marriage. As the Creator instituted marriage, it was a sacred relationship of man and woman, with deep mystery at its center proclaiming its divine origin. The loving heart of God doubtless rejoiced in the institution of a relationship that was to be high, clean, holy, and pleasant for mankind.

23. This is now . . . flesh of my flesh. The man recognized in this new creation a divinely created companion who was fashioned to provide all that his hungry heart would need to carry out God's holy will. **Woman** *('ishshâ)* **. . . man** *('îsh)*. These two Hebrew words are much alike, even in sound. The only difference between them is that the word for "woman" has a feminine ending. More recent lexicons declare that these words are not etymologically related. There is, however, no actual ground for rejecting the earlier view that the word for "woman" is derived from the word for "man."

24. Therefore doth a man . . . cleave *(dābaq)* **unto his wife.** The Creator had established the full basis for monogamous marriage. The great Hebrew commentator, Rashi, declares that these words are a specific comment by the Holy Spirit. The final commentary on the union of man and wife was given by our Lord, when he said: "For this cause shall a man leave his father and mother, and cleave to his wife; And they twain shall be one flesh: so then they are no more twain, but one flesh. What therefore God hath joined together, let not man put asunder" (Mk 10:7-9). God planned that the marriage bond should be forever indissoluble. **Cleave** *(dābaq)* means to "glue himself to" his wife (his own wife). The word for "wife" is singular. The man, who is stronger, is the one who is to **cleave.** The wife will be held when the husband exerts the kind of loving power described in this verse. Love is strong and enduring. "What God hath joined together, let not man put asunder." This is an old statement, but it is truly God's word for all our hearts today, and always.

How remarkable it is that a relationship so accurately described centuries ago by Moses should still be rooted in eternal truth and divine decree! The sacredness of marriage is founded in the very heart of the Scriptures, and eternally underlined as basic by the Holy Spirit. God willed that the beings he created in his image should be his chosen vessels to build a home pleasing to him. In the NT the Spirit reveals: the divinely ordained relationship of man and woman, based on the order of creation; the headship of the family resident in the husband; the eternal sacredness of the marriage vow; the kind of love that should unite husband and wife; and the purity that should characterize those who typify the Bride for whom Christ gave his life.

B. The Temptation and Fall. 3:1-24. The author of Genesis here lists the steps leading to the entrance of sin into the hearts of these divinely created individuals, who had started life with such clean hearts and so much promise. Disobedience and sin becloud the picture. Though these beings were morally upright, they had been given the power of choice; and they were subject to the power of the tempter at any moment. Hence the test was inevitable. The garden was an exquisite creation, filled with plenteous provisions. Man's environment left nothing to be desired. One prohibition, however, had been placed upon the man and woman. Every tree, shrub, and delicacy could be theirs, except the fruit of the "tree of the knowledge of good and evil." This prohibition seems to have produced the atmosphere in which human minds welcome the appeal of the tempter.

1. The serpent *(nāḥāsh)*. The narrative presents the seducer as one of the animals, which was much **more subtil** than the others. The Hebrew word contains the idea of exceptional shrewdness. (Rabbinic legend has it that the serpent walked erect.) He had the power of speech and talked freely with his victim. He was wily, insidious, crafty. Later exegesis will identify the serpent with Satan or the devil. In the light of later Scripture truths, we are justified in concluding that the serpent was a specially chosen instrument of Satan for this test. In Rev 12:9 the tempter is called "the great dragon . . . that old serpent, called the Devil and Satan" (cf. Milton, *Paradise Lost,* Book IX). The word *nāḥāsh,* meaning *to make a hissing sound,* undoubtedly refers to the kind of being known to us as a serpent. Paul declares that Satan fashions himself into "an angel of light" (II Cor 11:14). He chose the craftiest, the most subtle, the most cautious of the animals and took full control of him for his disastrous work. Jesus said of Satan: "He is a liar, and the father thereof" (Jn 8:44, ASV; cf. Rom 16:20; II Cor 11:3; I Tim 2:14; Rev 20:2).

The method of deceit the serpent employed with Eve was to distort the meaning of God's prohibition and then hold it up to ridicule in its new form. The tempter feigned surprise that God should be guilty of issuing such a command. Then he sought to break down the woman's faith by sowing in her mind doubts, suspicions, and false pictures of the Almighty and his motives. It was a deliberate attempt to reflect on God. When faith fails, the sure foundation of moral conduct collapses. It is only a small step from unbelief to sin and disgrace.

2,3. The woman said. To parley with the tempter is always dangerous. Unconsciously, the woman was revealing a willingness to come to terms with the tempter. She did not have the advantage of Jesus' words in Mt 4:10 and James' admonition in Jas 4:7. She was innocent, guileless, and unsuspecting, and no match for the wily antagonist. She was unwilling to stand by and see God misrepresented, and so she courageously attempted to correct the serpent's statement. But she quoted God's prohibition inaccurately, adding the word **touch.**

5. Ye shall be as God (AV, *gods*). Now that Eve had entered into the conversation, the seducer advanced his more powerful argument. He quickly suggested that man's great desire to be on a par with and truly like God had been deliberately thwarted by divine command. He charged the Creator with selfishness and with a malicious falsehood, representing him as envious and unwilling for his creatures to have something that would make them like the omniscient One. (The word *'Elōhîm* can be translated *God* or *gods,* since it is plural. The former is preferred.)

6. The woman saw . . . took . . . did eat . . . gave. The strong verbs tell the story vividly and clearly. Something happened in the thinking of the woman. Gradually the fruit took on new significance. It was attractive to the eye, desirable to the taste, and powerful to give new wisdom. She took a new step into the field of self-deception. She not only wanted food that was delicious and attractive, but she was desirous of power. She believed this fruit would satisfy all her desires. The next step was automatic and immediate. **She took . . . and did eat.** The tempter was not needed after that moment. Eve took up his work and presented the well-recommended fruit to her husband, and **he did eat.**

7. The eyes . . . were opened *(pākaḥ)* **. . . they knew.** The word *pākaḥ* pictures a sudden miracle. The promise of the tempter was fulfilled quickly; instant perception was given. They saw and knew. But what they saw was far different from the rosy picture painted by the serpent. Conscience was rudely awakened. They saw their nakedness, spiritual as well as physical. And then shame and fear were born. When Adam and Eve realized that they were out of touch with God, a terrible loneliness overwhelmed them. Remorse and its inevitable miseries followed. Their loss of faith had subjected them to all these attendant woes. They hastily made **aprons** or *girdles* to provide some measure of concealment as they sought a remedy for their bewilderment, loneliness, and guilt.

8. The voice of the Lord God . . . in the cool of the day. (*Kol,* "voice," is, lit., *sound; lᵉrûaḥ,* "cool," is *wind* or *breeze.)* They might hide from God, but they could not escape him. The loving Creator could not overlook their disobedience, nor could he leave quivering sinners in their poignant need. They were his own. His holiness must come, clothed with love, to seek, find, and judge them. Ordinarily, the approach of God's footsteps brought them joy. Now, terror and dread paralyzed them, though the Lord did not approach in thunder nor call harshly. **9.** It is easy to imagine the sweetness of the divine voice, as it sounded forth through the trees in the stillness of the evening, calling, "Where art thou?" Of course God knew where the man and woman were. But he was appealing to them, seeking through tenderness and love to win a favorable response. And he was seeking to lead the transgressors gently to a full conviction of their sin. Though Justice was dictating the procedure, Mercy was leading. The Judge would render the decision and pronounce the sentence.

12. The woman . . . gave me of the tree, and I ate. God's questions were direct and unusually specific. Instead of making full confession and pleading for mercy, Adam and Eve began to offer excuses and pass the responsibility on to another. The man somewhat recklessly threw a part of the blame back on God—**whom thou gavest . . . me. 13.** The woman, refusing to take responsibility, cast it all on the serpent. The serpent had no way of passing it on. **Beguile**[d] *(hishshîanī).* The verb conveys the idea of deception (cf. Paul's use of this concept in II Cor 11:3; I Tim 2:14).

14. Cursed ***('ārûr)*** **art thou.** The Lord singled out the originator and instigator of the temptation for special condemnation and degradation. From that moment he must crawl in the dust and even feed on it. He would slither his way along in disgrace, and hatred would be directed against him from all directions. Man would always regard him as a symbol of the degradation of the one who had slandered God (cf. Isa 65:25). He was to represent not merely the serpent race, but the power of the evil kingdom. As long as life continued, men would hate him and seek to destroy him.

15. I will put enmity. The word *'êbâ* denotes the blood-feud that runs deepest in the heart of man (cf. Num 35:19,20; Ezk 25:15-17; 35:5,6). **Thou shalt bruise** *(shûp).* A prophecy of a continuing struggle between the descendants of woman and of the serpent to destroy each other. The verb *shûp* is rare (cf. Job 9:17; Ps 139:11). It is the same in both clauses. When translated *crush,* it seems appropriate to the reference concerning the head of the serpent, but not quite so accurate in describing the attack of the serpent on man's heel. It is also rendered *lie in wait* for, *aim at,* or (LXX) *watch for.* The Vulgate renders it *conteret,* "bruise," in the first instance and *insidiaberis,* "lie in wait," in the other clause. Thus, we have in this famous passage, called the *protevangelium,* "first gospel," the announcement of a prolonged struggle, perpetual antagonism, wounds on both sides, and eventual victory for the seed of woman. God's promise that the head of the serpent was to be crushed pointed forward to the coming of Messiah and guaranteed victory. This assurance fell upon the ears of God's earliest creatures as a blessed hope of redemption. An unfortunate translation in the Vulgate changes the pronoun **his** (v. 15c) from the masculine to the feminine, providing spurious support for unfounded claims concerning "the Blessed Virgin Mary."

16. Unto the woman he said. For the woman, God predicted subjection to the man, and suffering. Pregnancy and childbirth would be attended by pain. The word *'asvon* pictures both mental and physical pain. Eve would realize her womanly longings and desires, but not without agony. In other words, as wife and mother, she was to be subject to the discipline of Jehovah. Woman's love and man's lordship are both presented in the vivid description. We cannot *fully* comprehend the nature of such judgments of the Lord.

17. Unto Adam he said. Physical hardship, painful toil, disappointing vexations, and hard struggle were appointed as the lot of the man, who was definitely adjudged a guilty sinner. Formerly the earth had yielded its produce easily and freely to man, in great abundance. Adam had only to "dress" the garden (2:15) in order to enjoy its luscious fruits. But now God pronounced a special curse on the ground. Henceforth it would yield its grains and fruits reluctantly. Man would have to work hard cultivating the soil to make it produce life's necessities. And he would have to wrestle with troublesome thorns and weeds not previously in evidence. Drudgery, difficulties, and weariness would be his daily lot. For Adam, as well as for Eve, sin exacted a heavy toll.

20. Eve ***(ḥawwâ).*** The Hebrew word has to do with life, and the verb to which it is related speaks of living. All life originated with the first woman. She was the mother of each person and, therefore, the mother of each clan and people. In accordance with the divine purpose, life must go on, even though the pronouncement of death had been spoken — **unto the dust thou shalt return** (v. 19).

22-24a. So he drove out ***(gārash)*** **the man.** A necessary and merciful act. The Lord could not allow rebellious man access to the tree of life. With loving care he kept Adam and Eve away from the fruit that would make them immortal and thus perpetuate the terrible condition into which sin had brought them. From the lovely garden he drove them out into an unfriendly wilderness.

24b. Cherubims, and a flaming sword (AV). The Hebrew interpreter, Rashi, claimed that these instruments were "angels of destruction," designed to destroy anyone who sought entrance. Hebrew *kerubim* indicates divinely formed figures that serve as bearers of the deity or as special guardians of sacred things. In one instance they are shown upholding the throne on which God sits. In another, they are used to describe the dread unapproachability of Jehovah. In general, their function seems to be to guard the sacred habitation of God from encroachment or defilement. The tree of life was perfectly safe with the cherubim standing guard at the gate. And sinful man was safe from the harm that could have come to him had he not had the majestic protector. **24c. The flame of a whirling sword** *(mithhapeket)*. The way back into Eden was guarded not only by the cherubim but also by a revolving swordlike flame. This gave further assurance that man would not make his way to the tree of life. Though man's paradise was closed to him because he had become a sinner, Jehovah did not forget his creatures. He had already made provision for their triumphant return.

C. The Two Brothers. 4:1-26.

1. Cain *(Qayin)*. The word **Cain** is usually associated with the Hebrew word *qānâ*, "to acquire" or "to get." The derivation is based on the resemblance of sound, rather than on basic etymology. It might be called a play on words. The actual meaning of the word possibly came through the Arabic ("a lance" or "a smith"). Eve was overjoyed at the birth of her son. She exclaimed, "I have gotten a man." **2. Abel** *(Hebel)*. The name given to the second son indicates "a fleeting breath" or "a vapor." The cognate Accadian word *aplu* means *son*. Abel was the originator of pastoral life, while Cain followed his father in the pursuit of agriculture.

3,4. An offering *(minḥâ)*. Each man brought a special present or gift to Jehovah. No mention is made of the altar or of the place of the religious observance. The *minḥâ*, as the ancients knew it, served to express gratitude, to effect reconciliation with the Lord, and to accompany worship. This account pictures the first act of worship recorded in human history. In each case the worshiper brought something of his own as an oblation to the Lord.

5a. The Lord had respect *(shā'â)*. The gift brought by Cain was not received by the Lord. No reason is given here for the rejection. And the Scripture does not tell us how God indicated his disapproval. It may be that fire fell from heaven and consumed the accepted offering but left the other untouched. Some have thought that Cain's offering was rejected because Cain failed to perform the proper ritual. Others have advanced the idea that the nature of the gifts made the difference – the one being flesh and involving death and bloodshed, the other being vegetable, without bloodshed (cf. Heb 9:22). The author of the Epistle to the Hebrews gives us the inspired explanation of the difference between the offerings: "By faith Abel offered unto God a more excellent sacrifice than Cain . . . God bearing witness in respect of his gifts" (Heb 11:4). This explanation centers upon the difference in spirit manifested by the two men. Because Abel was a man of faith, he came in the right spirit and presented worship that pleased God. We have reason to believe that Abel had some realization of his need for substitutionary atonement. To all appearances both offerings expressed gratitude, thanksgiving, and devotion to God. But the man who lacked genuine faith in his heart could not please God even though the material gift was spotless. God did not **look upon** Cain because He had already looked ***at*** him and seen what was in his heart. Abel came to God in the right attitude of heart for worship and in the only way sinful men can approach a holy God. Cain did not.

5b. Cain's unbridled anger showed itself instantly. Furious wrath blazed out, revealing the spirit that was lodged within the heart. Cain became an enemy of God and hostile to his brother. Thus, wounded pride produced envy and a spirit of revenge. And these brought forth the burning hatred and violence that made murder possible. **6,7a. Countenance fallen . . . . a lifting up.** The heat that blazed within him caused his countenance to "fall." It brought on brooding and an unlovely, morose spirit. Gently and patiently God dealt with Cain, seeking to save the rebellious sinner. He assured him that if he would sincerely repent, he might again lift up his face in happiness and reconciliation. *Nāsā*, "lift up," lends itself to the idea of forgiveness. The merciful Jehovah thus held out to Cain the hope of forgiveness and victory as he faced his momentous decision.

7b. Sin *(ḥatt'at)* **coucheth** *(rābaṣ)*. Close upon that heartening promise, Jehovah uttered a stiff warning, urging the sinner to control his temper and beware lest a crouching beast (sin) spring upon him and devour him. The danger was real. The deadly beast was even at that moment ready to overpower him. God's word demanded instant action and strong effort to repulse the would-be conqueror. Cain must not let these boiling thoughts and impulses drive him to ruinous behavior. God made his strong appeal to Cain's *will*. The will had to be thrown into the struggle to make victory over sin *(ḥatt'at)* complete. It was up to Cain to conquer sin in himself, to control rather than be controlled. The moment of destiny was upon him. It was not too late for him to choose the way of God.

9. Where is Abel thy brother? Failing to gain the mastery over the savage monster, Cain soon found himself at the mercy of a force that controlled him completely. Almost immediately one son became a murderer and the other a martyr. Jehovah came quickly to confront the murderer with a question. Seemingly he hoped to elicit a confession of guilt that could prepare the way for mercy and full pardon. Though Cain had willfully sinned, he found himself pursued by a loving God, rich in grace. **Am I my brother's keeper?** *(shōmēr)* A shameful response to a question from a loving Father! Petulantly, defiantly, Cain made his reply. Sin already had him in the grip of a vise. He renounced the clamant rights of brotherhood. He rufused to show respect to the eternal God. He brazenly leaned back on his own selfish defiance and spoke that which no one should dare to utter.

10. The voice *(qôl)* **of the bloods of thy brother are crying** *(sō'qîm)* **unto me from the ground.** Blood spilled by a murderer, though covered by earth, was crying out to God. Jehovah could hear it, and he understood the meaning of the cry, for he knew of Cain's guilt. How plaintively those **bloods** were crying out for vengeance! The author of Hebrews refers to this experience in the phrase, "the blood of sprinkling that speaketh better things than that of Abel" (12:24).

12. A fugitive *(nā')* **and a wanderer** *(nād)*. The curse pronounced on the murderer involved banishment from food-producing soil to the unproductive desert. The ground, God said, would be hostile to the murderer, so that he could not derive sustenance from tilling the soil. In his search for subsistence, he would become a Bedouin of the waste lands, wandering about in weariness and despair. Insecurity, restlessness, hard struggle, guilt, and fears, were to be his constant "companions." The word for **fugitive** carries the idea of tottering, staggering, stumbling uncertainly along in a fruitless search for satisfaction. It was a dismal, discouraging prospect.

13. My punishment *('ăwōn)*. Though Cain's life was spared, he trembled under the weight of his sin, his guilt, his punishment, and the unending consequences that loomed before him. The Hebrew word *'ăwōn* literally refers to his iniquity, but it also contains the thought of the consequences of his sin. Cain was far more concerned with his sentence than with his sin. **Greater than I can bear.** His bitter cry to God called attention to the unbearable weight of his punishment. It was heavier than he could lift and carry. The Hebrew word *nāsa* carries the ideas of "taking away" (forgiveness) and "lifting up" (expiation). Again, it seems clear that the frightened murderer was thinking of the punishment about to come upon him.

14b. Every one . . . shall slay me. Dread and despondency began to overwhelm the sinful man as he thought of the perils of the desert. He imagined that cruel foes would delight to kill him. He could feel the hot breath of the avenger on his neck. His active conscience was already at work. In his fear, he was sure that certain destruction awaited him, for he felt that he would be completely outside the circle of God's care. **15. A sign** *('ôt)* **for Cain.** But Jehovah, in mercy, assured Cain of his continuing presence and unending protection. He set a **sign** on him—evidently a mark or designation to indicate that Cain belonged to the Lord God and must be spared bodily harm. There is no evidence that the 'mark of Cain' was a sign to announce to the world that he was a murderer. It was, rather, a special mark of loving care and protection. Cain would continue always in the safekeeping of the covenant God. Though a murderer, he was the recipient of God's favor.

16. Land of Nod *(nôd)*. Literally, *land of wandering* or *flight* (cf. 4:12,14).

There is no way to locate this area geographically except to speak of it as being **east of Eden.** Cain was but fulfilling the prediction God made concerning his future existence. Pathetically and stoically he set out into the trackless wastes. The ideas of "flight" and "misery" are discernible in the Hebrew word for **went out.**

17. His wife *('ishtô).* The Book of Genesis does not answer the oft-repeated question: Where did Cain get his wife? It does make it clear that many other sons and daughters were born to Adam and Eve. It also presents the lapse of many years (maybe hundreds of years) before Cain's marriage experience. Since all life came from the first divinely created human pair, it is necessary to conclude that at some time brothers and sisters were married to each other. By the time Cain was ready to set up a home, Adam and Eve had numerous descendants. It is not at all necessary to imagine another race of people already well established in the world. Cain's wife was one of the family of Adam and Eve.

25. Seth *(Shēt).* The divine narrative has preserved the name **Seth** as that of the third son in Adam's line. The Hebrew word shows marked similarity to the word *shāt,* translated "appointed" or "set." In reality, Seth became the one on whom God could depend as the foundation stone for His family. He was "set" or "appointed" to take up the work and mission of Abel. Cain had forfeited his right to carry forward God's sublime hope. Seth would take the burden and the privilege upon his shoulders. Through his line God would perfect His promises.

26. Began to call upon the name of Jehovah. It was a never-to-be-forgotten experience when, under the encouragement of **Enosh** (or Enos), men began to call **upon** (or *with)* the name of Jehovah, the covenant God. Enosh, who was prominent in the line of Seth, was the originator of public prayer and spiritual worship. In it, the ineffable name of the eternal God was used. There was hope for a better day through Seth's descendants.

D. Seth and His Descendants. 5:1-32.

22. Enoch *(Ḥănôk)* **walked with God.** Into a narrative of birth and dreary existence and eventual death, the author suddenly introduces a sublime character, Enoch, who pleased the Lord and lived in his immediate presence. In a deteriorating age, Enoch gave a remarkable demonstration of commendable piety. In thought, word, deed, and attitude he was in accord with the divine will; and he brought joy to the heart of his Maker. The LXX says regarding him: "Enoch was well-pleasing unto God." One striking statement reveals a hint of the beginning of Enoch's walk with God (cf. 22a). It may have been at the moment of the birth of his baby boy, doubtless a high moment in his life, that he set his heart on intimate communion with his God. His close association in such atmosphere brought him heavenly wisdom, which fitted him to understand and appreciate the rich things of God.

24. He was not; for God took him. On account of his genuine piety and his apprehension of divine wisdom, he was lifted from the earth to continue his walk in the sacred regions beyond. His disappearance was sudden and wholly unannounced, and death had nothing to do with it. The LXX says: *He was not found, for God translated him.* "By faith Enoch was translated," says the writer of Hebrews, "that he should not see death, and he was not found, because God had translated him" (Heb 11:5). A beautiful and meaningful miracle was wrought so that the one man who had learned to love God and walk with him might continue in that fellowship without interruption.

E. Sin and the Flood. 6:1 – 8:22.

6:2. The sons of God *(b^e^nê 'Elōhîm)* **. . . daughters of men.** Wickedness was increasing on every hand. Cain's descendants became exceedingly godless and pagan. A powerful race of giants, called "Nephilim," came into prominence. The verb *nāpal,* "to fall," has been considered the source of the noun, and so these gigantic creatures have been thought of as "fallen ones." The reference to the *b^e^nê 'Elōhîm* has occasioned marked differences of opinion among scholars. *'Elōhîm* is plural in form. It is usually translated "God." But it can be translated "gods," as, for instance, when it refers to the gods of the heathen neighbors of Israel. It can, also, denote the heavenly circle of beings in close fellowship with Jehovah, residents of heaven, assigned specific duties as God's assistants (see Job 1:6). In some cases in Scripture "sons of God" may be identified with "angels" or "messengers." Jesus is the Son of God in a unique sense. Believers are called "sons of God" because of their relationship to him. In the OT, however, "sons of God" are a special class of beings that make up the heavenly court.

The reference to the marriages of *b^e^nê 'Elōhîm* to the daughters of men has been dealt with in many ways. To translate it literally would make the passage say that members of the heavenly company selected choice women from the earth and set up marriage relationships with them, literally and actually. This can be the only interpretation of Job 1:6. There, the *b^e^nê 'Elōhîm* were plainly the members of God's heavenly court. S. R. Driver maintains that this is the only legitimate and correct sense that can be accepted. Jesus' reply to the Sadducees, in Mt 22:30, seems to make this view untenable. He said that the angels "neither marry nor are given in marriage." The statement in Gen 6:2 makes it clear that permanent marriage is described. Women were chosen and forced to become parties to the unnatural relationship. Bible students who have rejected this solution have resorted to other explanations. Some have said that a union of Seth's godly line with Cain's godless descendants is described. Still others hold that these words refer to marriage between persons of the upper class of society and those of a lower or less worthy class. In the light of the facts and the accurate rendering of the words of the text, we conclude that some men of the heavenly group (angels or messengers) actually took wives of the earthly women. They used superior force to overpower them, to make the conquest complete. The "sons of God" were irresistible (cf. II Pet 2:4; Jude 6).

3. My spirit *(rûaḥ)* **shall not always strive** *(yādôn)* **with** (or *act in*) **man.** This Hebrew verb may be translated either *strive with* or *abide in.* The first translation would represent God as continually using force on rebellious man to hold him in line and to keep him from utter destruction as a result of his sinful behavior. The second view would represent God as determined to withdraw the vital breath of life from man, with the result, of course, that death would ensue. The Hebrew word *dûn* (or *dîn)* indicates life expressing itself in action or in evidences of power.

In the first interpretation, the **spirit** *(rûaḥ)* is considered an ethical principle used to restrain or to control the created one, the result being ethical behavior. In the other, the **spirit** *(rûaḥ)* is considered a vital principle given to the inanimate bit of clay to provide life, motivation, and power for living. When that *rûaḥ* is withdrawn by the divine hand, judgment is complete. This divine announcement came from Jehovah when he found his creatures dominated by sin. It is God's declaration that he must abandon man to the doom of death. Sin had set in motion that which would guarantee death.

5,6. Wickedness *(rā'āt)* . . . **repented** *(nāḥam)* . . . **grieved** *('āṣăb).* The depravity was widespread. And it was inward, continual, and habitual. Man was utterly corrupt, bad in heart and in conduct. There was no good in him. The whole bent of his thoughts and imaginations was completely out of line with the will of Jehovah. Flesh was on the throne. God was forgotten or openly defied. *Nāḥam* in the niphal form describes the love of God that has suffered heart-rending disappointment. Literally, it speaks of taking a deep breath in extreme pain. God's purposes and plans had failed to produce the precious fruit that he had anticipated, because sinful man had prevented their full fruition. *'Āsăb* in the hithpael form means to pierce oneself or to experience piercing. The statement says, then, that God experienced heart-piercing sorrow as he looked upon the tragic devastation sin had produced. His handiwork had been marred and ruined. Through it all, God's love shone clearly, even when the rumblings of divine judgment began to threaten the people of the earth.

7. Blot out *(maḥâ;* AV, *destroy).* The verb indicates a movement that wipes clean or blots out completely. The operation was designed to destroy every living thing that stood in the way. Full destruction was to be executed. Nothing was to be spared. **8. But Noah found grace** *(ḥēn).* One man of all the countless multitudes then on the earth was fit to receive God's gift of grace. The word **grace** certainly means "favor" or "acceptance," at least, and probably has a much richer meaning. It was love and mercy in action. God's extending grace to Noah signified that there was new life and new hope for mankind in the days ahead.

9. Noah was a righteous man and perfect . . . and Noah walked with God. With these words the author describes three characteristics of a godly life—

justice, purity, and holiness (cf. 6:8—he **found grace in the eyes of the Lord).**

The word **righteous,** from Hebrew *ṣăddîq,* describes Noah's character as it manifested itself in relation to other human beings. "Straightness" or "uprightness" was evident in his behavior. All his conduct revealed this moral and ethical righteousness (cf. Ezk 14:14,20). Hebrew *tāmîm,* **perfect,** describes the perfected product of a wise builder; it is full, complete, and flawless. Viewed objectively, the word *blameless* describes character. In the realm of ethics, the idea of "integrity" comes out as the derived meaning (cf. Job 1:1). The statement, **he walked with God,** opens another area of thought. In walking with God, Noah had displayed a spirit, an attitude, and a character that made him accepted and approved for the most intimate spiritual relationship. He manifested qualities of soul that endeared him to the Lord (cf. Gen 5:22; Mic 6:8; Mal 2:6).

14-16. An ark *(tēbâ).* The English word **ark** came down through the Latin *arca,* "a chest or coffer." The word for the "ark" of the covenant is a different word—*'ārôn. Tēbâ* is probably of Egyptian origin. Noah's ark was very likely a kind of large covered raft built of light resinous wood. With its three floors, it reached up to a total of forty-five feet in height. It was four hundred and fifty feet long and seventy-five feet wide. (The cubit was equal to eighteen inches.) Cells, nests, or small rooms, were built along the sides of the three floors. To make the craft watertight, a powerful **pitch,** or bitumen, was used inside and outside, as a calking compound. The Hebrew word *sōhar* can best be translated a *light* or *window.* This was approximately eighteen inches in height and extended completely around the ark; it admitted light and air.

17-22. Flood *(măbbûl).* This word has no Hebrew etymology. It was used *only* of the deluge of Noah. It may have come from Assyrian *nabalu,* "to destroy." According to the author of Genesis, God's purpose was certainly to bring to an end the living things of his creation. During the 120 years while Noah was completing his work, he was preaching to the people in an urgent effort to cause them to repent. They saw the ark take shape before their eyes while the preacher delivered his sermons. Noah's immediate family, including his wife, his three sons, and their wives, accompanied him into the haven of safety. In obedience to God's command, they took with them representative pairs of all the animals of the earth.

7:11a,b. The fountains of the great deep [were] **broken up** *(bāqa').* Enormous reservoirs of water were stored under the earth. This mighty collection of waters was called *t^e^hôm,* "the great deep" (cf. Gen 1:2). These subterranean waters, confined by creative power on the second day of creation, were unleashed to pour forth in volume and in violence defying description. It was not an ordinary flood, but a giant tidal wave that broke suddenly upon a startled populace. *Bāqa'* indicates a terrestrial convulsion that split asunder every restraining barrier that had existed. It was a tumultuous breaking loose of indescribable destruction. Man cannot imagine the fury and the destructive might of the eruption, nor the awfulness of the display of God's power to destroy sinful beings. The complete corruption of men was far worse than any of us can imagine. The destruction was necessary.

11c,12. The windows of the heavens were opened *(pātaḥ).* In addition to the terrific upheaval from below, the peoples of the earth witnessed the opening of the gates of the mighty reservoirs of waters above the earth. All the stored-up waters burst forth in torrents. Resistlessly and continuously for forty days and forty nights, the gigantic cloudburst poured down upon the earth. The effect of the deluge on men, women, children, animals, and plants, and the earth's surface cannot be completely imagined.

16-18. The Lord shut him in *(sāgar)* **. . . . And the waters prevailed** *(gābar).* In the midst of the raging storm and the flooding torrents, Jehovah, the covenant God, reached out a hand of mercy and shut the door of the ark to keep his people safe. But he poured forth torrents of water to destroy utterly the sinners on earth. The inhabitants of the floating house could ride the waters with a sense of security and safekeeping, for they trusted God. The divine hand that had broken up the deep and opened the windows of the heavens to pour out destruction had also demonstrated God's loving concern for those who were to be the nucleus for his new beginning.

While God's chosen ones nestled safely in the ark, the waters continued to increase and to take over the earth. The verb *gābar* indicates mastery, subjection, and prevailing power. Relentlessly the waters took control and continued to be in command until the high mountains were completely submerged. Again, the majesty, might, and compelling purpose of the Almighty became increasingly apparent. The divine purpose was being worked out in all the earth. God's will was being accomplished.

8:4. The mountains of Ararat. After 150 days, the ark came to rest upon one of the peaks of the high ranges in Armenia. *Urartu,* Accadian cognate of **Ararat,** is used in ancient documents to designate Armenia. The mountain now called Ararat towers to the height of 16, 916 feet.

The Babylonian flood story, a part of the Gilgamesh Epic, relates how its hero, like the Biblical Noah, built an ark, brought into it specimens of the animal kingdom, and, after the flood landed on Mount Nisir east of the Tigris River.

20. Noah builded an altar *(mīzbēaḥ)* **to Jehovah.** As Noah moved out into the bright new day, the most natural thing for him to do was to find a high spot of ground and build a *mīzbēaḥ* It was the first altar built on the cleansed earth. Noah recognized the end of the tragic judgment and the dawning of a new day of hope and promise. Building the altar was his move to pour out to Jehovah praise and thanksgiving.

He **offered up burnt offerings** *('ōlâ).* The word for **burnt offerings** is derived from the verb *'ālāh,* "to go up." The suggestion here is that, as the sacrifice was consumed, the fumes went upward to God, bearing, in a sense, the gratitude and worship of the offerer. It was a truly propitiatory sacrifice (cf. II Sam 24:25), offered in sincere worship, out of deep thankfulness. And so the eternal God was pleased. Noah had found favor in his eyes.

F. Noah's Later Life, and His Descendants. 9:1–10:32.

9:9-15. I established *(mēqîm)* **my covenant . . . . I do set** *(nātan)* **my bow in the clouds.** In solemn manner Jehovah confirmed the covenant promises he had already given. The forming of a covenant involves the solemn binding together of two parties, hitherto free from obligation to each other. God's binding himself to this one family group was a voluntary act of free grace. Noah and his family had done nothing to merit the covenant relation, and God was not obligated to them. Furthermore, this was a covenant with all mankind. By accepting the terms and becoming obedient, man bound himself to his Creator to keep the divine terms and to observe their inner spirit.

The covenant needed to have an outward and visible sign or **token** as a constant reminder of the sacred agreement. This sign *('ôt)* would be a pledge of the inner spiritual bond, guaranteeing its unending reliability. The Hebrew perfect tense can be translated *I have set,* or *I now at this moment do set.* The bow in the cloud was to be the "sign." God could have created the rainbow at that moment and invested it with this meaning. It is probable, however, that he pointed to the bow already in the cloud and indicated that it would now take on new meaning, giving assurance of his mercy and grace; it would be a visible reminder of his love. He said: **I will remember** (v. 15).

18. Shem, Ham, Japheth. The author of Genesis makes it clear that these three sons of Noah became the fathers of the three great families of mankind. **Shem** is named first as occupying the place of leadership and prominence in God's plans for the peoples. The Semites (Shemites) were to be the spiritual leaders of men. God's chosen ones of that line would teach the religion of Jehovah to the world. We know that the Messiah was to come from Shem's descendants. **Japheth** was to be the father of one large branch of the Gentile world. His descendants would scatter far and wide in their search for material gain and power. They would be prosperous and exceedingly powerful. **Ham** was to be the father of the other branch of Gentiles, including Egyptians, Ethiopians, Abyssinians, and kindred groups. His son, Canaan, became the father of the groups called Canaanites, the inhabitants of the land of Canaan, later dispossessed by the Hebrews. The curse pronounced upon Canaan by Noah was not, in any sense, designed as a proof text in slavery or segregation discussions.

10:4. Tarshish. The famed city in Spain to which the Phoenician traders went. Centuries later the prophet Jonah boarded a ship bound for that distant city. The Greeks called it *Tartessus.* **6. Mizraim.** The correct Hebrew word for Egypt, comprising the lower and the upper divisions of that land. The two capitals of Egypt were Memphis and Thebes. **8,9. Nimrod.** Son of Cush. He founded the early Babylonian empire and built the city of Nineveh. He was a mighty hunter and a remarkable leader of armies. His power extended over the cities of Mesopotamia. **11,12. Nineveh.** Known as early as 2800 B.C., it was the center of the powerful Assyrian kingdom, which attained its height under Sennacherib, Esarhaddon, and Ashurbanipal. It was situated on the Tigris River, about 250 miles from the city of Babylon. It was against this stronghold that Jonah and Nahum directed their prophecies.

14. The Philistines (cf. AV *Philistim*) are credited with having given their name to the land of "Palestine." Amos and Jeremiah refer to them as coming from Caphtor. Their five principal cities were Ashdod, Ashkelon, Gaza, Gath, and Ekron. The Philistines continued for centuries to be a thorn in the flesh of the Israelites. **15. Heth.** Ancestor of the Hittites, whose great empire held sway from 1600–700 B.C. The principal cities of the Hittites were Carchemish on the Euphrates and Kadesh on the Orontes. These people settled in the vicinity of Hebron, and witnessed Abraham's purchase of the Cave of Machpelah from Ephron (23:8-10). Esau married into the tribe. The Hittites found their way into the Assyrian and Egyptian inscriptions. Archaeologists have found valuable remains of the civilization of that powerful empire.

21. The children of Eber comprised many different groups among the sons of Shem. The name **Eber** has been associated with the word *Hebrew*, the name by which the Israelites were known by other peoples. They were the ones who possessed the knowledge of the true God. The term "Hebrew" is racial, while "Israelite" is national. In later days, these words were used as synonyms.

22. Aram, or the Aramean or Syrian people, made up the group around and within Damascus. They figured prominently in the history of the people of Israel. The Aramaic language became the language of trade and diplomatic relations. It gradually displaced the Hebrew language until, at the time of our Lord, Aramaic was the language of conversation and writing.

28. Sheba is often mentioned in the OT to denote a wealthy group of people whose principal work was to furnish gold, perfumes, and precious stones for export to Palestine and to Egypt. They are identified with the Sabaeans, who held a prominent place in trade and in governmental achievement. So far as Bible students are concerned, the queen of Sheba was the most famous of the people of Sheba.

29. Ophir was famed for its fine gold. Solomon sent his men along with Hiram's to extract it and to transport it to Palestine. In addition to gold, they found precious metals and gems in great abundance. Soon Solomon's kingdom rivaled all the surrounding lands in wealth. Ophir was probably a seaport on the coast of Arabia. It has been located as far away as the mouth of the Indus. Much of the gold overlay of the Temple of Solomon came from Ophir.

G. The Tower of Babel. 11:1-32.

1,2. The whole earth was of one language. Genesis pictures Noah and his sons coming forth from the ark having one language and one set of words. As the descendants of Noah multiplied, they naturally continued with that same language, since it was sufficient. They lived in and about the Euphrates valley, the locality usually regarded as the cradle of civilization. **Shinar.** The Hebrews used the name Shinar, originally a region in northern Mesopotamia, to designate the whole region of Mesopotamia. Migrating nomads moved along the mountains of Ararat to the well-watered plains of Babylonia.

3,4. Let us build us a city . . . a tower . . . and . . . make us a name. When Noah's eastward-moving descendants had found a spot where they could begin permanent headquarters, they decided to build a city. They would construct a gigantic tower so high that its top would pierce the "vault" above them. This great structure would give them the place of vantage by which they could establish their importance in the eyes of men, and even in God's sight.

The purpose of the undertaking was twofold. First, they wanted to assure themselves of the strength that comes from unity. The city and the tower would tie them into a solid group, so that they might be powerful—even without God's help. They said: **Lest we be scattered.** On the other hand, they were determined to make themselves renowned—**make for ourselves a name.** The sins of self-sufficiency and pride predominated in their thinking. They wanted to make sure that they would not be forgotten. The tower would hold them together and secure their names from oblivion. They defied God and set out to prove their self-sufficiency. Their towering structure would be a monument to their energy, daring, genius, and resources. Many towering cities, such as, Babylon, Sodom, Gomorrah, Sidon, Tyre, and Rome, have proved anything but godly structures. When men spurn God's law and grace, and exalt themselves, catastrophe inevitably falls upon them.

7-9. Confound their language. Jehovah understood the spirit, the motive, and the selfish plans of the rebellious people. Immediately he set out to upset their foolish schemes. The very thing they had sought to avoid came suddenly upon them. God directly intervened to see to it that no one understood the words of the others about him. And he scattered them far and wide. Hebrew *bālal,* "confound," indicates that there was a distinct disturbance that left the people greatly confused. The word **Babel** is translated *Babylon.* The best Hebrew lexicographers claim that it could not have come from the Hebrew *bālal,* to "confuse" or "mix," but that it meant "gate of God." Through a play on words it came to mean "confusion." The Aramaic word *balbel* means "confusion." Alan Richardson reminds us that the bestowal of the gift of tongues at Pentecost (Acts 2:5-11) can be thought of as the reverse of the confusion of tongues at Babel. He says: "When men in their pride boast of their own achievements, there results nothing but division, confusion, and incomprehensibility; but when the wonderful works of God are proclaimed, then every man may hear the apostolic gospel in his own tongue" (*Genesis 1–11*, p. 126).

27. Terah. Son of Nahor (a descendant of Seth) and the father of Abram, Haran, and Nahor. His early home was in Ur of the Chaldees, but he spent the later years of his life in Haran, where he died.

28. Ur of the Chaldees. An ancient city of the early Sumerian kingdom, located about 125 miles from the present mouth of the Euphrates, 100 miles southeast of Babylon, 830 miles from Damascus, and 550 miles from Haran. It was the capital of Sumer. In Abram's day it was a thriving commercial city, with unusually high cultural standards. The buildings of the temple area were most elaborate. The inhabitants worshiped the moon-god, *Sin.* Archaeologists have unearthed fabulous treasures from this old city. The royal cemetery has given up art treasures dated as early as 2900 B.C. The Oriental Institute of Chicago has a plaque from Ur that dates back to 3000 B.C. It was in this ancient world that Abraham was born and grew into manhood. His was a rich heritage.

31. Haran (or *Ḫarran).* An important city in ancient Mesopotamia. It was situated about 550 miles northeast of Ur and 280 miles north of Damascus. Principal routes converged there. Highways to Nineveh, Babylon, and Damascus had their start from it. It was only 60 miles from the stronghold of Carchemish, the capital of the Hittite empire. Haran was one of the chief centers for the worship of *Sin,* the moon-god. Terah and his family moved to Haran, and the record states that Terah died there. Rebekah, the wife of Isaac, and Rachel, the wife of Jacob, grew up in Haran. It still survives as a small Arab village.

II. The Patriarchs. 12:1–50:26.

A. Abraham. 12:1–25:18. In the second principal division of the Book of Genesis, it is evident that in the new order of things God's chosen ones must recognize the direct communication and the direct leadership of the Lord. In chapters 12–50 four characters stand out as men who heard God's voice, understood his directions, and ordered their ways according to his will. The purpose of Jehovah was still to raise up a people who would carry out his will in the earth. In Noah he had made a new start. Shem was the one chosen to carry forward true religion. The Semites (descendants of Shem) were to become missionaries to the other peoples of the earth. In chapter 12 Abram begins to emerge from the line of Shem as Jehovah's chosen representative. On him Jehovah would place the full responsibility of receiving and passing on His revelation for all. From the pagan background of Ur and Haran came forth God's man for the strategic hour of early OT revelation.

1) The Call of Abram. 12:1-9.

1. And Jehovah said. Get thee out of thy country, and from thy kindred, and from thy father's house. The Biblical account makes it clear that before migrating to Palestine, Abram had two homes. He spent his early years in Ur and then a long season in Haran. Each community became his home. He had to leave friends, neighbors, and kindred behind him when he left Ur and still others when he departed from Haran. In each case, the threefold tie of land, people, and kindred was severed. Bishop Ryle says that Abram was commanded "(a) to renounce the certainties of the past, (b) to face the uncertainties of the future, (c) to look for and follow the direction of Jehovah's will" *(Genesis* in the *Cambridge Bible*, p. 155). It was a big demand (cf. Heb 11:8). Severe trials awaited him. This call must have come to him while he still lived in Ur (Acts 7:2). It was renewed many years later in Haran.

Unto the land that I will show thee. Jehovah did not name the land at this time nor describe it. Thus, Abram was to meet a new test of faith. The Lord had found the man for his purpose, one he could subject to heavy strains, a man who would regard the doing of God's will as the one important thing in his life.

2,3. Be thou a blessing *(bᵉrākâ)*. The imperative form actually expresses a consequence—"so that thou shalt be a blessing." This distinguished traveler from polytheistic Mesopotamia had been divinely commissioned to go forth into the midst of utter strangers in some new land. He and his descendants would constitute a channel by which God would bless all the peoples of the world.

I will make of thee a great nation, and I will bless thee, and make thy name great. God strongly fortified Abram with covenant promises of prosperity, plenteous posterity, and greatness. The promise of divine blessing guaranteed Abram everything he could desire. His every need would be supplied. Even hostile neighbors would come to look upon him as the leader of God's people. Through him would come blessings to all the peoples of the earth. And his name would be honored and revered everywhere. Today, Abram is recognized and honored as a "father" by Christians, Jews, and Moslems. God chose Abram and his descendants to bear His Gospel to the world. From the line of Abram, Christ was to come, to fulfill God's purposes. And through "born-again" men and women, His ideals were to find fulfillment. The plan of God was taking shape.

5. The land of Canaan. Abram interpreted the call of God to involve immediate departure for Canaan. How he knew Canaan was his destination is not explained. But God had said: "Get thee out . . . unto a land that I will show thee." So he obeyed. Without hesitation he gathered together his family and set out on a major migration. Seemingly he had no fears, no doubts, no misgivings. He journeyed to Carchemish on the Euphrates and turned south through Hamath to Damascus of Syria. Josephus represents Abram during his stay in that capital city as acting in the capacity of a king over the people of Damascus. The land of Canaan is described in Scripture as comprising all the land from the Jordan to the Mediterranean and from Syria to Egypt. Moab and Edom bounded it on the southeast. In the Bible the word "Canaanites" usually refers to the earliest inhabitants of the land, including any group that lived there before the coming of the Hebrews.

6. Shechem. This ancient city was probably a shrine or sacred place. It was an important settlement at the junction of the main commercial highways. It was situated between Mount Gerizim and Mount Ebal, about forty-one miles north of Jerusalem. In later years, Jacob's well was in the immediate vicinity. In more recent times, Shechem has been called Nablus.

Abram made his way to the **terebinth of Moreh.** This was probably a sacred tree, under which a priest or teacher or soothsayer gave his instruction or teaching. **Moreh** is probably a participle of the verb *yārâ*, "to teach." The oak and the terebinth trees resembled each other. Shechem became Abram's first principal stop in Canaan. Here he received a special message of assurance and promise from the Lord. God gave the land to him as his possession, and promised that his descendants would possess it after him. With warlike tribes on every hand, Abram would find it difficult to establish his claims to the new land. He made a good beginning, however, by immediately setting up an altar and offering sacrifices to Jehovah. As his life in Palestine took shape, he declared his utter dependence upon the Lord and his whole-hearted dedication to him.

8. Bethel *(Bēt-'ēl)*. This ancient sanctuary dates back to the twenty-first century B.C., and is mentioned more often in Scripture than any other city except Jerusalem. It is situated on the road to Shechem, about ten or eleven miles north of Jerusalem. By erecting an altar, the patriarch proclaimed his allegiance to Jehovah, and by pitching his tents, he publicly declared to all observers that he was taking permanent possession of the land. In these two symbolic acts, Abram revealed his resolute faith in the power of Jehovah of hosts to carry out all His promises. The word **Bethel** means, literally, *house of God.* A later narrative indicates that Jacob gave the place that name after his experience with Jehovah there (28:19). Abram **called on the name of Jehovah.** In his act of genuine worship, he used the name Jehovah in the invocation (cf. 4:26).

9. Abram journeyed *(nāsā')* **going toward the Negeb.** *Nāsā'* means to *pluck* or *pull up tent pins.* It refers to Abram's setting out for the south. He pulled up stakes and moved by easy stages. The Negeb, *dry land,* is a definite section of southern Palestine, between Kadesh-barnea and Beer-sheba. In the summer it was dry enough to be a desert, without water or vegetation. With all his flocks and herds, Abram found it necessary to have plenty of water and grass. The Negeb would be of little help to him.

2) The Patriarch in Egypt. 12:10-20.

10. And Abram went down into Egypt to sojourn there. Famines were frequent in Canaan. Nothing could be done to prevent them. The one remedy was to move into Egypt, where the Nile furnished water for cattle and crops. Abram and his large group made their way to Egypt. The Hebrew word *gûr,* **sojourn,** indicates that a temporary residence was anticipated. As soon as the famine had loosed its hold, Abram would be on his way back to Palestine. No evidence is given to help determine which Pharaoh was ruling in Egypt at that time.

11-16. Fear clutched at the heart of the patriarch when he came near to the palace of the monarch. He imagined that the Pharaoh would seek to kill him in order to take Sarai into his harem. Accordingly, Abram devised the plan of passing his wife off as his sister, quieting his conscience meanwhile with the thought that she was his half-sister. It was a shameful expedient to employ. As a result, the mother of future leaders of the Hebrew nation was taken into an Egyptian harem! **17-20.** To settle the whole matter, the Pharaoh was afflicted with plagues until he realized that something was wrong, and drove the visitors from the land. Abram took Sarai, his followers, and his property—greatly increased by his sojourn in Egypt—and made his way back across the miles to the Negeb and on into Canaan. Such behavior as Abram's in Egypt was not at all worthy of the majestic soul of Jehovah's special ambassador to the nations. He would need to grow if he was to approximate the divine blueprint for his life. He needed to go back to Bethel and rebuild the altar of Jehovah.

3) The Parting with Lot. 13:1-18.

1-4. And Abram went up out of Egypt. When the renewal of his fellowship with God had been achieved, Abraham was ready for a new life. He was immensely rich. Cattle, gold, and silver were his in great abundance. His company of followers had increased until a serious problem confronted him. With so many cattle and sheep, he must be able to move quickly to secure sufficient water and grass. **5-8.** Soon Lot's company had difficulty with Abram's band. Hebrew *m'rîbâ,* **strife,** indicates disputing, striving, and contentions. The righteous uncle could not allow such unbecoming conduct to continue. He said: **We are brethren** (v. 8). Behavior like that was unnecessary, unavailing, and wholly out of keeping with God's representatives.

9-13. In the interest of peace and harmony, Abram made the generous suggestion that Lot choose any section of the land he preferred and move in that direction, leaving the rest of the territory to Abram. The selfish and grasping nature of Lot manifested itself immediately; he chose the well-watered valley of the Jordan. There, tropical vegetation abounded under the life-giving waters of the river. The valley *(kikēr)* of the Jordan was large enough and sufficiently fertile to guarantee prosperity and plenty for all the days ahead. However, the cities of Sodom and Gomorrah were included in the area Lot chose, and they were extremely corrupt. How could spiritual religion grow among the thorns of selfishness and corruption in that place? Lot's choice proved to be a disastrous one. **He pitched his tent toward Sodom** (v. 12). At first he *looked toward* Sodom. Then he *pitched his tent toward* Sodom. Later he *dwelt* in Sodom. These are the steps by which the man and his family moved toward certain degeneration and destruction.

14-17. And the Lord said unto Abram . . . Lift up now thine eyes. In this remarkable communication, Lot and Abram are set in direct contrast. The weak, selfish, grasping sinner chose for himself that which he considered the more valuable possession. Jehovah chose for Abram. As a reward for his rare unselfishness, the patriarch received the land of Canaan. God gave him the title deed to the land and invited him to open wide his eyes and feast upon the treasures that stretched out before him in every direction. From the hill near Bethel, he could look upon wonderful panoramas of breath-taking beauty. They were all his! To make the gift more attractive, the Lord promised Abram many descendants, more numerous than the sands of the sea. This prophecy must have amazed the patriarch, who had no son. But he accepted it by faith.

18. **Hebron.** An ancient city in southern Judah, nineteen miles southwest of Jerusalem, at the junction of all the principal highways of the region. It stood out prominently on the landscape, 3,040 feet above sea level. Josephus speaks of it as being more ancient than the city of Memphis in Egypt. He also says that an old oak tree had been there since the creation of the world. Surrounding the city were olive trees, grapes, springs, and wells, and grazing ground. The cave of Machpelah, later bought by Abraham for a tomb for Sarah, was very near. It became the burial place not only of Sarah, but of Abraham, Isaac, Jacob, Rebekah, and Leah.

4) Abram, Lot, Melchizedek. 14:1-24. Instead of living in peace, prosperity, and happiness, Lot and Abram found themselves in the middle of a war. Powerful warring armies from the east invaded the land of Palestine, and wrought much havoc. Abram became deeply involved because of his love for Lot, and soon revealed himself as a warrior to be reckoned with when invaders sought plunder. Lot became a prisoner of war when his city, Sodom, and the neighboring kingdoms were defeated by the invaders. He had invited trouble by choosing to enjoy Sodom's ease and privilege, and by becoming one of the people of that wicked city. Now he found that he had to share the city's danger and tragedy. Abram quickly responded with his 318 men to effect a rescue, and establish himself as a powerful force for righteousness in the land.

1. **Amraphel,** the **king of Shinar.** One of the quartet composing the invading army. **Shinar,** located in northern Mesopotamia, gave its name to the entire area between the Tigris and Euphrates, including Babylonia. Lower Mesopotamia was the center of Sumerian civilization, dating back to about 3500 B.C. **Amraphel** was the king of that region. Until quite recently scholars identified him with Hammurabi, one of the earlier kings of Babylon. However, recent finds among clay tablets have tended to set Hammurabi's date nearer 1700 B.C. Amraphel was king much earlier. **Arioch** was king of **Ellasar,** Babylonian *Larsa,* and probably controlled a much larger region in the southern part of Babylonia.

Chedorlaomer. King of *Elam,* a well-known mountain region near the head of the Persian Gulf. He seemed to be the most powerful of the four kings who made up this expedition. He had established control over the other kings of Babylonia and Palestine. His name *Kudur-Lagamer* means "servant of Lagamer," one of Elam's gods. The capital of **Elam** was Susa. **Tidal,** the other confederate king, was called the king of *Goiim,* i.e., **nations,** or *peoples.* His title may indicate that he was in control of several individual kingdoms, or that he was at the head of a strong band of roving people who were in the business of making raids for plunder.

2. These kings, with their select troops, came from the region beyond Damascus, and swooped down upon the country east of the Jordan as far as the south end of the Sea of Salt. Then they turned northward and moved rapidly up the western side of the Jordan. The decisive battle was fought in the low country below the Dead Sea (the **vale of Siddim,** v. 3), with the five kings of that immediate region who had rebelled against their eastern overlords.

3. **The salt sea** (Dead Sea) is forty-six miles long and nine and one-half miles wide. Since the surface of the water is 1,292 feet below the level of the Mediterranean, and the water is 1,200 feet deep, this sea is the "lowest sheet of water in the world." Its water is five times stronger in saline content than ordinary sea water. Scholars affirm that the ruins of Sodom and Gomorrah lie beneath the waters of the south end of this sea. Admah and Zeboiim (cf. v. 2) were the other cities destroyed by the destructive blast from God's hand. The kings of the east brought decisive defeat upon the assembled fighters and took prisoners and plunder with them as they returned. Lot was among the captured ones.

6. **And the Horites in their Mount Seir.** Archaeology has contributed much to establish the basic historicity of these early narratives. These people, called **Horites,** are now well known as *Hurrians,* a non-Semitic group. Their records, un-

covered at Nuzu by archaeologists, have thrown much light on patriarchal customs. William F. Albright believes that these Hurrians came into prominence as early as 2400 B.C., and became competitors of Hittites and Sumerians for the supremacy in culture and learning. They must have found their way to the region south of the Dead Sea quite early. They were displaced from the region of Mount Seir by Esau's descendants (Deut 2:22).

7. Kadesh *(sanctuary)*. An ancient spot where water trickled from a rock, and judgment issued from a holy man who received divine revelation. It was on the border of Edom, about fifty miles south of Beer-Sheba, and seventy miles from Hebron. Here the Israelites spent a generation waiting for God's command to move forward into Palestine. Miriam was buried at Kadesh, an eleven-day journey from Sinai. **Amalekites.** Rough, predatory marauders who roamed the wilderness area of southern Palestine. They proved a constant menace to the Israelites all the days of the kingdom. In this instance the people of Canaan were severely beaten by the eastern invaders.

10. Bitumen pits (AV, *slime pits*). Pits from which liquid petroleum had been removed. The holes may still have been partially filled with the bubbling liquid. The fighting men, trying desperately to escape the fury of the enemy attack, fell into these holes and were destroyed. It was an hour of disaster for them. The eastern invaders escaped with much plunder and many captives, who would become their slaves.

13. Abram the Hebrew. Quickly the news of the battle reached Abram at Hebron. He had not been involved in the fighting, but since his nephew was a prisoner, he was doubly obligated to attempt a rescue. This is the first use in the Scriptures of the word **Hebrew** *(hā'ibrî)*. The exact derivation of the name is still in dispute. It was used by foreigners in designating descendants of Abraham and the patriarchs. It probably means "a descendant of Eber," or "one from the other side" (of the river). This applies to Abram as one who had migrated from Mesopotamia. Some have identified the Hebrews with the *Habiru*, who came into prominence in archaeology through the Tell el Amarna letters found in Egypt and the Mesopotamian tablets of Nuzu and Mari. The character of these troublesome marauders would not have endeared them to the children of Abram.

14. Hebrew *rîq* (AV, **armed**) describes the rapid, thorough work done by Abram in getting every available man into action at once. It is translated, literally, *drew out*, as a sword from its scabbard. Not a man was left. Three hundred and eighteen men answered the call to follow their honored leader. For an establishment such as the patriarch maintained, it was necessary to have a strong force to count on. Besides these dependable, ready men, Abram took with him troops from the friendly confederates, **Aner, Eshcol,** and **Mamre,** who were loyal to their good friend in the hour of emergency. The fleeing invaders from the east made their way quickly to Dan at the northern boundary of Canaan. The city nestled at the foot of Mount Hermon, some distance northwest of Caesarea Philippi. At that time it bore the name of Leshem or Laish (cf. Jud 18:7). The Danites took it years later and called it **Dan.**

15. Hobah was a city less than fifty miles north of the ancient city of Damascus. After the attack began at Dan, Abram and his fighting men covered one hundred miles in the pursuit of the army of Chedorlaomer. In the surprise attack, they routed the enemy and succeeded in recovering all the booty and the prisoners. Lot was safe again in the keeping of his uncle. And Abram had established his power in Canaan, for surrounding peoples would stand in awe of one who could deliver such smashing blows.

17. Returning to his own district, Abram was met by the king of Sodom, who expressed heartfelt thanks for the notable deliverance. They met at a place called *Shaveh*, or **the king's dale** (AV). The word *shaveh* means "a plain." It was probably near Jerusalem.

18-20. Melchizedek, king of Salem. The name of this mysterious person means either "king of righteousness," or, "my king is righteousness," or, "my king is Zedek." *Zedek* is the Hebrew word for "righteousness," and also the name of a Canaanite deity. Melchizedek was the priest-king of **Salem,** which is a shortened form for *Urusalim*, "city of peace," identified with Jerusalem. The Tell el Amarna tablets identify **Salem** with Jerusalem as early as 1400 B.C. *Shalom* is the Hebrew word for "peace," and Shalem probably was the Canaanite god of peace.

This kindly priest-king, recognizing Abram's nobility and worth, supplied refreshment and sustenance for the weary warrior and his men. These gifts were tokens of friendship and hospitality. Melchizedek praised *El Elyon*, his God (AV,

the most high God) for granting Abram the power to achieve victory. Abram recognized Melchizedek's *'El Elyon* as Jehovah, the God he himself served. The name **God most high** was found in the Ras Shamra documents that date back to the fourteenth century B.C. Evidently Melchizedek had a firm grip on the doctrines of his faith, which were as true and basic as those brought from Babylonia by Abram. Each of these stalwarts had something to give and something to learn. (See Ps 110:4; Heb 5:9,10; 7:1-7 for the development of the concept of the ideal priesthood and the application of this in the Messianic doctrine.) The author of Hebrews declares that Christ was of a priestly order much more ancient than that of Aaron, and therefore his priesthood was superior to the Aaronic priesthood. In further recognition of Melchizedek's priestly standing, Abram brought tithes as a religious offering.

21-24. In dealing with **the king of Sodom,** the patriarch refused to accept for himself the booty gained in the battle. He had waged war not to enrich himself, but to secure the release of Lot. He would not profit in any manner, but would see to it that his allies had a reasonable amount to care for their expenses. Evidently there was nothing little, selfish, or grasping in his character.

5) Abram Promised an Heir. 15:1-21. Throughout his life Abram manifested a strong faith in God. It was easy to let this trust shine forth in hours of triumph. When he remembered God's wondrous promises to him, he took comfort from the declaration that their fulfillment was to be in and through his seed. But when he grew old and saw that the end of his days was near and that he was still childless, he was tempted to be discouraged. His faith in the promises wavered. How could God now fulfill his promises? When would he fulfill them? Abram needed assurance. And so God spoke to him.

1. Fear not . . . I am thy shield, and thy exceeding great reward. First, Abram must put away fear by trusting fully in the Lord. This figure of God as a shield was calculated to give hope, courage, and faith. But defense was not enough. Abram needed to have before his eyes the certainty of a reward that would bring the fullest joys. Perhaps the rendering, *thy reward is to be exceeding great,* is nearer the meaning derived from the text in its context. The two ways of translating these words leave us confused until we see that either way guarantees victory ahead.

2-7. The Lord assured Abram that he was not to look to **Eliezer of Damascus** as his heir, but that a true son of his own begetting would be born to bring a rich fulfillment to every prediction. In moments of peril or despair Abram was to believe in God's protection, God's fulfillment of his promises, and the unlimited number of his descendants. It was a challenge to sublime trust. And Abram was able to believe because he knew the One who had made the promises. He knew that Jehovah could be trusted. Even though no child was in the home, God would yet fill the earth with those who would look back to Abram as father. Trustful surrender to the will of God is the basic element in true religion. **6. He counted it to him for righteousness.** The quality of being right with God is indescribably precious in the Lord's eyes. Abram was justified, i.e., counted righteous, on the basis of his faith.

8-21. Immediately Jehovah was ready to ratify the covenant with the man who had yielded himself to the divine will (cf. Gen 12:1-3). Hebrew *b^erît* is variously translated "covenant," "compact," "solemn agreement," "testament," "treaty." No one of these words brings over into English the full meaning of this solemn transaction. In ancient times men sometimes ratified an agreement or covenant by passing between the parts of a halved, sacrificial animal. This "cutting of the covenant" was not in itself a sacrifice. Rather, it was a sacred ceremony by which the men declared their solemn purpose to keep the agreement. Some Bible students have pointed out that in the instance recorded in Gen 15:8-21, only one symbolic representative of the contracting parties—the **lamp of fire** (AV marg.), or "flaming torch" (cf. Jud 7:16,20), symbol of Jehovah —passed between the halves of the animals. In other words, the covenant in this case was to be kept from the Godward side alone. Only the Lord himself could fulfill its promises. He would make Abram's descendants as numerous as the stars and give them a great land, stretching from the gates of Egypt to the mighty Euphrates.

6) Ishmael. 16:1-16.

1-3. Now Sarai . . . bear him no children. Abram and Sarai had been married for many years. No children had come to brighten the home and to fulfill the wonderful prophecies. Yet Jehovah had been specific in his promise of an heir (cf. 15:4). As the years rolled by, the discrepancy between the promise and the circumstances became more and more baffling. To be childless was a calamity and a disgrace for any Hebrew wife, and it was much worse for Sarai. Both husband and wife must have sought means to help God work out the fulfillment of his promise. They knew the direct teaching of Gen 2:24, and realized that husbands and wives must conform to that high standard. For a man to take a secondary wife or concubine was sinful. Yet, in attempting to provide a way for God to carry out his prediction, Sarai was willing to disregard the divine standard and give her female slave, Hagar, to Abram, in the hope that she might bear a son to the family. **That I may be builded** (Heb. *bānâ,* "built") **by her** (AV marg.), she said. When men and women allow their faith to break down, they resort to human contrivance. The Egyptian slave was brought into Abram's tent that the family might be **built.** But discord and heartache followed as tragic consequences.

4-6a. And he went in unto Hagar. Sarai was acting in thorough accord with the customs of other people in her day (cf. the Nuzu tablets). But Abram and Sarai were expected to hold themselves to a higher standard than that of the people around them. Abram, the friend of God, exercised a richer faith and was bound by a purer code. Nevertheless, he followed his wife's suggestion and took Hagar into his tent. Soon the slave began to despise her mistress. And Sarai became embittered against her maid. All three of the persons in the triangle suffered. Sarai blamed Abram for the whole trouble, but he had only carried out her suggestion. Jealousy changed the atmosphere completely, Peace, harmony, and happiness could not exist in that home. And the home was on the point of breaking up.

6b. Dealt hardly with her. Afflicted her. Hebrew *'ānâ* means to "oppress, depress, afflict." In this case it may mean to "persecute or ill-treat." Sarai may have persecuted Hagar with heavy duties or bodily punishment. Whatever the persecution, it so angered, shamed, or embarrassed her as to drive her from her mistress' presence. Passionate jealousy and bitterness set the two women against each other. And Abram was not much help to either of them. Conditions grew worse by the moment.

7,8. And the angel of Jehovah found her. In desperation Hagar fled in the direction of her homeland, Egypt. She was still legally a slave and had no right to run away. Her situation, however, had become unbearable, and flight seemed to present the only relief. She probably thought she might find peace, rest, and life in her old home country. When she reached **Shur** *(the wall),* she paused before crossing the border. Here the Egyptians maintained a wall or strong line of forts to protect Egypt from invaders from the east. It is mentioned in Egyptian records as early as 2000 B.C.

In the quiet of the wilderness Hagar was confronted by **the angel of Jehovah,** who had come to bring her direction, hope, and peace of mind. This appearance is the first recorded visit of **the angel of Jehovah** to the earth. It was a moment of unusual significance. This "angel" was not a created being, but Jehovah himself, manifesting himself to Hagar. For other uses of this name, see Gen 32:30; Ex 23:20-23; 32:34; I Kgs 19:5,7; Isa 63:9. From these passages it is evident that the "angel" is Jehovah himself, present in time and place. He identifies himself with Jehovah; he speaks and acts with God's authority; he is spoken of as God, or as Jehovah.

9-12. The "angel's" heartening word to Hagar was that she should go back to the hard situation she had left, take up her burden, wait for the fulfillment of the divine plan, and look for the day when her son, **Ishmael,** should become the head of an important tribe. **Ishmael** *(God heareth)* was to be a "wild ass of a man," with strength and daring, and a ferocious disposition. He would live wild and unshackled, in the wilderness, without friends or loyalties. His descendants were destined to grow into a mighty horde of Bedouins, wild, free, treacherous, reckless men, roaming the open spaces of the desert.

13-16. Thou art a God that seeth. Hagar was overjoyed to recognize God in the experience, and to see him to be a gracious, kindly, thoughtful observer of a poor individual in dire need. She responded with reverent faith. The well or spring was named **Beer-lahai-roi.** This name has been variously translated and amended. Perhaps as good a rendering as any is *The well of the living one who seeth me.* Hagar was moved mightily by the realization that she had been in the very presence of the mighty God and that she was still alive. Perhaps the well was in the vicinity of Kadesh (cf. 16:14), about fifty miles south of Beer-sheba. The boy was born, and the name Ishmael was given to him by Abram, then eighty-six years old.

7) New Promises, and Abraham's Response. 17:1-27.

1. I am the Almighty God *('El Shadday).* Thirteen years later God appeared to Abram with a reassurance, a challenge, and a richer promise. He changed Abram's name and that of his wife. He gave specific directions concerning the rite of circumcision. The divine name *'El Shadday,* with its message that, "Nothing is impossible with God, who is all-powerful and all-sufficient," must have brought unusual encouragement to Abram. The word *'El Shadday* evidently calls attention to both of these attributes of God. Early Jewish scholars claimed that it was derived from *sh-da,* meaning, "He who is sufficient." Some scholars derive it from the root *shādad,* "to destroy." Others relate it to the Assyrian word *shādu,* "mountain." The LXX gives us *hikanos,* "sufficient." Perhaps the translator should stay as near the meaning of "all-powerful" as possible, especially since the word *'El* speaks of power. The One who has all power also has all resources to supply every need of his people.

Walk before me, and be thou perfect (AV). Such a God could make such demands. "Walking with God" is described in the narrative concerning Enoch. Now Abram was commanded to make his daily life (thoughts, words, deeds) before God thoroughly pleasing to the all-seeing eye. Hebrew *tāmîn,* **perfect,** carries the sense of "blameless," or "spotless." But it goes beyond that sense in suggesting a well-rounded whole, every area filled out to the full.

3-8. Humbly and reverently Abram fell to the ground to worship. God's patience had brought the patriarch to the right attitude of heart which would make it possible for him to have his name changed, the covenant renewed, and the promises repeated. **Abram,** his name from birth, is usually defined as *exalted father.* The name **Abraham** has no Hebrew meaning, but the new covenant associated with the new name emphasizes the patriarch's world-wide mission as God's representative to the peoples of the earth (cf. Rom 4:16,17). Higher privileges were to bring heavier responsibilities. God promised to give special guidance for each step of the new journey of faith and obedience.

9-14. Circumcised. As a symbol or token of the covenant, Abraham and his descendants were to adopt the rite of circumcision and carefully obey the regulations concerning it. Thus they would give neighboring peoples a perpetual reminder of their dedication and full commitment to Jehovah. Circumcision was not a new rite. Neither was it confined to the Hebrew people. It was widely practiced in many parts of the world, especially in Egypt and Canaan. Assyrians and Babylonians, however, refused to have any part in it. Note that David scornfully refers to Goliath as an "uncircumcised Philistine" (I Sam 17:26; cf. 14:6). God commanded Abraham to seal the covenant between them with the symbol or token of circumcision. Thus it would forever be the "outward and visible sign of an inward and invisible relationship." Every male child of Abraham's household was to experience this divinely commanded rite on his eighth day.

15,16. Sarah. The name *Sarai* had been borne by Abraham's wife for many years. Now God commanded that her name be changed to **Sarah,** *Princess.* It is the feminine form of *sar,* "prince." This new name emphasized the role Abraham's wife was to play in the future, as a mother of nations. Abraham is looked upon as "Father Abraham" by Jews, Mohammedans, and Christians. It would be well to remember that Sarah, too, played a vital part in the drama of the ages.

17-22. Again **Abraham fell upon his face** before the Lord. God had predicted that the long-awaited son would indeed be born to his wife. Although Sarah was ninety years of age, she was yet to have the joy of welcoming a son through whom God's covenant promises would be fulfilled. Abraham had come to look upon Ishmael as his heir and to believe that the golden promises must be fulfilled through him (cf. v. 18). Now he faced the sure word that **Isaac** would be born to be the child of promise. **Abraham . . . laughed** (v. 17). He was overwhelmed. There is no suggestion here of unbelief but rather evidence of wonder and great gladness. Abraham was hardly able to comprehend such an astounding announcement. Hebrew *ṣḥāḥăq* means "to laugh." It is the root verb from which the word **Isaac** is derived.

Compare Sarah's reaction and her laughter in 18:12. There was a decided difference in the causes for laughter in the two instances.

23-27. Abraham was moved by faith and an obedient spirit to carry out the command of God. Immediately he instituted the rite of circumcision throughout his company. Ishmael was among those circumcised. Abraham was obeying God and making himself and his family eligible to fulfill the divine purposes. The Lord's plan to reach and bless all the nations was moving toward fulfillment.

8) Sodom and Gomorrah. 18:1–19:38.

18:1. The terebinths (AV, *plains)* **of Mamre.** The residence of Abraham was in the immediate vicinity of Hebron. Though the Hebrew word *'ēlôn* can be translated "oak" or "terebinth," the latter is probably to be preferred. These trees were the sacred trees of the Canaanite sanctuary of Hebron. The cave of Machpelah was located in the same place. The patriarch was in close touch with the sacred places and hallowed spots. Through the centuries, ancient oaks or terebinths have been identified as dating back to patriarchal times. **Jehovah appeared.** Even though Abraham did not instantly recognize the celestial visitor as the Lord, it soon became clear to him that the chief visitor of the three messengers was Jehovah himself. He was "the angel of Jehovah," who appears several times in the earlier pages of Genesis.

2-5. He ran to meet them . . . and bowed himself toward the ground. Abraham proved extraordinarily hospitable. He did everything for his guests that Oriental hospitality could suggest. His manner was all that could be asked. He made ready to give these heavenly visitors a royal welcome. He invited them to **rest** (AV) or *recline* and **comfort** themselves while the meal was being prepared. Hebrew *ṣā'ād,* **comfort,** means "to strengthen" or "make strong." Both the rest and the food would give "comfort."

6-8. Make ready quickly three measures of fine meal. Abraham and Sarah and Ishmael (**the lad**) went quickly about the task of refreshing the guests. A **measure,** *sĕ'â,* was one third of an ephah, or about a peck and a half. Two Hebrew words, *gĕm'âḥ* and *sōlĕt,* are used to designate the exceptional character of the flour used in making the rolls for the meal. *Ḥem'â,* "curdled milk" mixed with fresh milk, was a refreshing drink served to tired travelers while the more substantial food was being prepared. The **calf** was a rare and added luxury provided for these distinguished visitors.

9-15. The Lord clearly and distinctly declared that a boy would be born to Sarah *when the season comes to life again* (AV, **according to the time of life).** The happy event was only a year away. God had not forgotten his promise but was working toward its miraculous fulfillment. **Was listening** (AV, *heard).* The Hebrew *shōma'at* indicates listening at that moment. **Advanced in years** (AV, *well stricken in age).* From the Hebrew idiom meaning "entered into days." **Sarah laughed.** Sarah laughed in sheer incredulity as she thought how impossible it was for her to bear a child. She here describes herself as *b*ᵉ*lōtî,* "worn out," "withered," "ready to fall apart, as a garment." She remembered that Abraham, too, was old and past the age of parenthood. The divine word assured Sarah and Abraham that nothing is **too hard** (lit., *wonderful)* **for the Lord.** Even if the thing to be done was unusual, extraordinary, or beyond natural behavior, Jehovah was capable of accomplishing it at any time and in any way he chose. "For with God nothing shall be impossible" (Lk 1:37). In the birth of Isaac, as in the birth of Jesus, it was necessary for God to work a miracle.

16-22. Sodom . . . Gomorrah. The two leading cities at the south end of the Dead Sea. The others – Admah, Zeboiim, and Zoar – were to be destroyed along with Sodom and Gomorrah in the conflagration that was to purge the cesspools of iniquity. (Ultimately God spared Zoar as a new home for Lot.) The Scripture clearly indicates that a divine visitation was to bring terrible judgment and doom upon the sinful inhabitants. The cities were about eighteen miles from Abraham's home at Hebron. It was possible for him to see the southern end of the Sea from the immediate vicinity of Hebron.

23-33. In his superb prayer of intercession for the few righteous men in Sodom, Abraham revealed the richer elements of his character – his generosity, sympathy, sensitivity, his concern for righteousness in God and man. He showed that he understood God's willingness to forgive and grant full pardon, and to deal with His creatures, though wicked, in accordance with revealed standards of justice and righteousness. He knew that Jehovah could be depended upon to act in keeping with his holy nature.

When Abraham left off interceding, he had God's promise that He would spare Sodom if as many as ten righteous persons could be found therein. But when the required number could not be found, nothing could avert the catastrophe. Intercessory prayer always brings out the best in men. Their unselfish concern for others shines like a beautiful jewel. In pleading with the Lord, Abraham clearly demonstrated genuine love and concern. And he experienced anew the friendship of God in His willingness to counsel with him and grant him a special revelation before the doom fell.

19:1-3. Lot sat in the gate of Sodom. Lot had achieved some prominence among his fellow citizens in the wicked city. Perhaps his sitting in the gate indicates that he helped mete out justice to the people. But to the heavenly visitors, weak, worldly, selfish Lot must have been a pathetic figure. He immediately volunteered to play the part of a lavish host to the two strangers.

4-22. The tragic experience with the men of the city, at Lot's house, demonstrated that the ugliest situation imaginable prevailed in Sodom. The angels, who had come under divine orders to discover the extent of human depravity there, needed no further disclosure. The vilest, most unspeakable brand of sin was practiced openly and brazenly. The messengers from God had only to pronounce official sentence, give due warning, and seek in every way possible to lead Lot and his reluctant family from the doomed city. Haste was necessary. Unqualified obedience was demanded. Lot sought frantically to warn and persuade those of his own family to leave. But, as the narrative tells us, **he seemed unto his sons-in-law as one who mocked** (*jested*, ASV).

Lot had acted selfishly and foolishly when he had chosen to become a part of Sodom, where his children would be soiled by the city's shame. Though he had attained some measure of prominence among the people, he had never influenced them toward righteous behavior; and so he failed to exert moral leadership in the hour of crisis. His own family, at the end, put no faith in his most urgent warnings. What a striking contrast between the depravity of Lot and the righteous life of Abraham! The members of Lot's family were all corrupt. Not one of them weighed an ounce in the scales of justice and righteousness. When Lot and his wife and two daughters stumbled out of the doomed city, God held back the impending destruction until his messengers could extricate them from the vile grip of Sodom.

23-25. Jehovah rained . . . brimstone and fire. It is well to take this account literally, as recording a definite judgment of the Lord upon people so corrupt that they had no right to live. It was within God's power to produce an earthquake that would open a fissure in the rocks to release stored up gas that would explode and throw immense supplies of petroleum into the air. When all the inflammable stuff was ignited, sheets of literal fire poured back to complete the destruction. Searing flames and black smoke must have covered every area of the city, smothering and consuming every living thing.

26. A pillar of salt. Lot's wife made some effort to escape the impending disaster. But she let her curiosity and her inordinate love for the things of Sodom (as well as for her family, probably) cause her to disobey orders and look back. It was a fatal act. The woman was fixed to the spot, and her body became a **pillar of salt,** covered and encrusted with deposits from the raining brimstone. There it stood for many years, a dreadful warning against disobedience to the specific command of God, and a mute reminder of the Lord's unchanging character. Someone has said: "She stood, a silent sentinel to sordid selfishness." Even to this day pillars and pinnacles of salt are visible in the area south of the Dead Sea. Jesus, seeking to remind his disciples of the tragic consequences of loving mere things, cautioned them to "remember Lot's wife" (Lk 17:32).

27,28. The smoke of the land went up as the smoke of a furnace. Abraham stood on the heights near Hebron and looked upon the inferno in the valley below. He had done all he could to spare Lot and his family. Now he watched the destruction of the four godless cities that had been so insolent in their behavior. Surely the wages of sin is death.

30-38. Two daughters. The closing chapter in the career of Lot is a pitiful one. It describes incestuous relations that we would prefer to forget. The two daughters, brought up in wicked Sodom, stooped low enough to engage in an act that is unspeakably revolting. The result of that deed was the birth of two boys, who became the progenitors of the Moabites and the Ammonites. Lot and his family failed miserably. Disaster, disgrace, despair, and death are written in their epitaph. "Be not deceived; God is not mocked: for whatsoever a man soweth, that shall he also reap" (Gal 6:7).

9) Abraham and Abimelech. 20:1-18. This regrettable episode adds another deplorable line to the picture of the patriarch. Why did he make the same mistake twice? (cf. 12:11-20) Why should God's choice representative err in such a way as to give a pagan king opportunity for a well-deserved rebuke? Through fear and temporary faithlessness, Abraham resorted to falsehood, deceit, and outright misrepresentation.

1. **Abraham . . . sojourned in Gerar. Gerar** was probably five or six miles south of Gaza, and therefore a part of the territory belonging to the Philistines. Some commentators, however, have located it about thirteen miles southwest of Kadesh. **4-6. Integrity of my heart . . . innocency of my hands.** Abimelech, who ruled over the people of Gerar, was unusually honest, ethical, and fair. His claims to **integrity**, i.e., "perfectness" or "sincerity" and **innocency** set him out as a man of high standards. When warned in a dream by Jehovah, he met the difficulty squarely and manfully. He appeared in a better light than God's representative. **7.** Here Abraham is called a **prophet**. As such, he stood in a peculiar relation to the Lord. He had access to God, was protected by divine power, received special revelation, and was obligated to speak for God the message he had received. **9-16.** Abimelech rebuked Abraham, restored Sarah to him, and, in addition, bestowed upon him sheep, oxen, and slaves, and a special treasure (perhaps equal to nearly four hundred dollars); and he assured Abraham of a home in his kingdom. **17,18.** In return, Abraham prayed for the king that the affliction God had sent upon him and his people might be removed. The patriarch departed from Abimelech a wiser, if a sadder, man. He was learning that Jehovah's hand was upon him to fulfill his destiny.

10) Isaac Born; Ishmael Driven Away. 21:1-21.

1-7. Visited. From *pāqăd,* "to visit," in the sense of "bringing a judgment or a blessing." In this case it was a treasured blessing God brought. Divine grace and power wrought the miracle. **Sarah . . . bare Abraham a son in his old age.** True to his promise, God gave a boy to Sarah and Abraham. Every covenant prediction was to have divine fulfillment through this son of Abraham. The father had the joy of naming the lad, and then the privilege of circumcising him when he was eight days old. When Sarah held the babe in her arms, her joy knew no bounds. For many months she had lived for that sacred moment. She said: **God hath made me to laugh** (ASV, *prepared laughter for me);* **everyone that heareth will laugh with me.** For the neighbors, it would be the laughter of good-natured surprise coupled with genuine delight and hearty felicitation. For Sarah, it was the joyous laughter of wondrous realization. She held in her arms God's gift to the world. It was an unforgettable moment of thanksgiving, joy, and sacred dedication.

8. And the child grew. The day for weaning young Isaac, probably when he was three years old, was a big event in the life of all the family. It was an occasion to be celebrated with rejoicing and feasting.

9-11. Soon, however, trouble arose. **Sarah saw the son of Hagar . . . mocking** (AV). Sarah had previously suffered because of Hagar and Ishmael. Now the conflict was renewed when Sarah saw Hagar's son involved in behavior that enraged her. The Hebrew word *mᵉṣaḥēq* is an intensive (piel) form of the verb on which the word *Isaac* is built. It has been translated "mocking," "sporting," "playing," and "making sport." There is no good reason here to introduce the idea of **mocking.** What Ishmael was doing does not matter so much as the fact that it infuriated Sarah. Perhaps she simply could not bear to see her son playing with Ishmael as with an equal. Or it may be that green-eyed jealousy took full control. Sarah may have feared that Abraham, out of love for Ishmael, would give the older lad the prominent place in the inheritance. At any rate, the family life could not go on as it was. Hagar and Ishmael had to go. To drive them out must have been exceedingly **grievous** to Abraham, for he loved the boy, and for years had considered him his heir.

12-14b. Jehovah saved the day for his friend by assuring him that each boy was to have an important place in the future. Abraham was to let Hagar and Ishmael go, as Sarah demanded. In time to come, Ishmael would be the father of a great nation. But Isaac was to be heir of the promises and bring blessing to all the world – **in Isaac shall thy seed be called.** Reluctantly Abraham sent Hagar and Ishmael away toward the wilderness, carrying a goatskin bottle filled with fresh water. It is not clear how old Ishmael was. Careful study of the Hebrew text leaves the student free to think of him as a young adolescent, perhaps about sixteen years of age.

14c-16. Beer-sheba, on the border of Egypt, was about fifty miles south of Jerusalem and twenty-seven miles south of Hebron. For those going southward, it was the last point of any significance in Palestine. In that dry wilderness area, these two travelers could not hope to exist many hours without experiencing extreme thirst. When the water gave out, exhaustion took hold of the boy; and his mother laid him down in the small shade of a shrub to die. But God, in his mercy and love, intervened to bring hope, life, and assurance. **17-19. God heard the voice of the lad.** The Lord provided plenty of fresh, flowing water, and spared the life of the boy. For both mother and son a new day had dawned. **20,21. And God was with the lad.** It was evident that God intended to fulfill his promise regarding this son of Abraham; he would make of him the great nation of Ishmaelites.

11) Abimelech and Abraham. 21:22-34.

When trouble arose (v. 25) between the men of Abraham and those of Abimelech, the two masters agreed to enter into a covenant with each other. First, they straightened out difficulties and rectified injustices. Then Abraham gave gifts to the king to ratify the treaty. In addition to other things, he presented seven ewe lambs to Abimelech. **Thus they made a covenant at Beer-sheba** (v. 32). The similarity of the Hebrew words *sheba'*, "seven," and *shāba'*, "swear," seems to indicate that there is a connection between them. Accordingly, **Beer-sheba** may mean "well of seven" or "well of swearing." The reflexive use of the word for "to swear" means "to seven oneself" or to pledge oneself by seven sacred things. In full commitment to the covenant, Abraham expressed gratitude to the **everlasting God** (*'Ēl 'ōlām*, v. 33). The patriarch would soon march off the map of history, but his God, the unchangeable, Eternal One would remain. Evidently Abraham had made an indelible impression on the pagan king, Abimelech, for in his own way, the king acknowledged his allegiance to the God of Abraham.

12) Abraham and Isaac. 22:1-19. Abraham's supreme test of faith and obedience came after Ishmael had been sent away, when all hopes for the future were lodged in Isaac.

1. God did prove Abraham. Hebrew *nissâ*, **prove** (AV, *tempt*), signifies a testing that would reveal Abraham's faith as nothing else had done. He must give evidence of absolute obedience and unquestioning trust in Jehovah, must even obey blindly, proceeding step by step until the faith stood out as clearly as the noonday sun. Abraham passed through the fiercest fires, stood up under the mightiest pressure, and endured the most difficult strain, to emerge from the trial in complete triumph.

2. No test could have been more severe than the one God now imposed. And no obedience could have been more perfect than Abraham's. When God called, the patriarch responded promptly. Even when he knew what was ahead, he calmly spoke to his servants: "Abide ye here . . . I and the lad will go yonder and worship, and come again to you" (v. 5). His faith in the God who sees and "sees to it" assured him that all would be well. He trusted Jehovah to carry out his promises. "By faith Abraham, being tried, offered up Isaac: yea, he that had gladly received the promises was offering up his only begotten son; even he to whom it was said, In Isaac shall thy seed be called: accounting that God is able to raise up, even from the dead; from whence he did also in a figure receive him back" (Heb 11:17-19). Faith saw beyond the sacrifice and was willing to obey.

Moriah. The place of the sacrifice cannot be positively identified. II Chronicles 3:1 seems to locate it on the site of Solomon's Temple. Tradition has held to this view, and it would be difficult to find a more easily accepted spot. The journey on foot from Beer-sheba must have taken the greater part of three days. **Offer him . . . for a burnt offering.** The Hebrew word used here, *'ālâ*, literally, *lift him up*, signifies the offering of the victim as a whole burnt offering in complete dedication. No reference is made to slaying the boy. The original intention of Jehovah, apparently, was to guarantee the complete offering, but to interfere before the victim was slain. God's purpose, in part, was to present an object lesson depicting his abhorrence of human sacrifice as it was openly practiced by the heathen on all sides.

7,8. As the two trudged along up the side of the mountain, the observant youth asked: **Where is the lamb for a burnt offering?** *How pathetic!* The answer of the father came without delay: **God will provide himself a lamb for a burnt offering.** The verb means "to see." Actually, Abraham was saying that Jehovah was able to *see to* that in his own way. He had within his heart a quiet assurance that God was able to care for such details. Abraham did not know that the boy would be spared the experience of death, but he had the faith to believe that the omnipotent One would provide whatever was necessary in his own way and time. Paul entered into the depths of this truth when he said: "He that spared not his own Son, but delivered him up for us all, how shall he not with him also freely give us all things" (Rom 8:32).

9,10. Everything was in place on the altar. The beloved lad of the promises was bound and prostrate upon the wood he had brought on his own shoulders. The fire was ready. Everything was still and quiet. The sharp knife was unsheathed and lifted high. **12,13.** Suddenly the voice from heaven broke the stillness. God commanded Abraham to lay aside the knife, loose the boy from his thongs, and bring the ram from his place in the thicket. It was Abraham's highest hour. God had tried his heart and was satisfied. Isaac again stood by his father's side, a witness of the Lord's mercy, grace, and provision (cf. v. 14). It is not strange that Jesus should say: "Your father Abraham rejoiced to see my day: and he saw it, and was glad" (Jn 8:56). The man of God returned to Beer-sheba aglow with the sense of the presence of God. He would never be the same again. The great promises had been renewed, and he was assured that the covenant blessings would come upon him and his descendants.

13) Sarah's Death and Burial. 23:1-20.

1,2. Sarah died in . . . Hebron. At the age of 127 Sarah passed away, leaving Abraham bowed in grief. His love for her had been genuine and tender. She was to him "the princess." We may well imagine that during dark hours and happy ones, she had been a steadying prop for his faith and a source of strength in all the journey. They had moved from Beer-sheba to Hebron, a city eighteen miles south of Jerusalem. Isaac was now thirty-seven years old. In his sorrow Abraham revealed something of the dignity of soul that characterizes a strong man of God. Besides wailing and otherwise loudly manifesting his grief, he broke forth into weeping. The Hebrew words for **mourn** and **weep** carry both ideas.

3-20. In due time, however, **he rose up** (AV, *stood up*) from his mourner's place on the ground and went manfully about the business of procuring a burying place and arranging for the funeral. Instead of taking Sarah's body back to Haran or Ur, he chose to find a sepulchre in the land God had given him. He dealt with the native Hittites and bought, at considerable expense, **the cave of Machpelah** so that his family might own a choice burying place for all time to come. In trading with the owners, Ephron and the others, he called himself a **sojourner** and a **settler** in that part of the world, indicating that his origin was foreign and his period of stay in the land uncertain. The children of Heth (Hittites) called him **a mighty prince** (AV) or *a prince of God* (v. 6). They held him in high esteem. Machpelah, a double cave, became the burial place of Sarah, Abraham, Isaac, Rebekah, Jacob, and Leah. In later years it became a Moslem possession, and a mosque was built over it.

14) Eliezer, Isaac, and Rebekah. 24:1-67. The old patriarch was well advanced in years (Heb. *entered into days*). Isaac was still unmarried. Abraham was concerned that his heir find a wife from his own people, instead of from the Canaanites. He chose his trusted servant, Eliezer, to make the long journey to Mesopotamia to find Isaac's bride.

1-9. Abraham said unto his eldest servant . . . take a wife unto my son Isaac (AV). Before Eliezer left, Abraham gave him full directions and demanded from him a sacred vow. Putting a hand under another's thigh was a solemn way of signifying that if the oath were violated, the children, yet unborn, would avenge the act of disloyalty. By means of the oath, the servant would be bound more effectively to secure an acceptable wife for Isaac. Abraham assured him of God's help: **He shall send his angel before thee, and thou shalt take a wife unto my son from thence** (AV).

10-14. And the servant . . . arose, and went . . . unto the city of Nahor. The servant had been promised divine guidance, and he was anxious to be led. A devout man, who sought to know God's will, he prayed fervently and trustfully that minute directions might be given. A mistake, he felt, would be disastrous. Surely Eliezer was God's man for a highly important quest. **The city of Nahor.** Either the city of Haran or a city named Nahor in the vicinity of Haran. **Mesopotamia** is the translation of the Hebrew which might literally be rendered "Aram of the two rivers," i.e., the region of the Tigris and Euphrates river valleys. Bethuel was the father of Laban and Rebekah. His parents were Nahor and Milcah. Abraham was his uncle.

15-28. When the servant met Rebekah at the well, he was convinced that God had answered his prayer and had guided him directly to her. The girl was beautiful and intelligent, and answered precisely to every requirement he had stipulated. So Eliezer presented her with a few preliminary gifts—a ring for the nose and then two bracelets, all showy and extremely valuable. Other gifts were to follow when the family gathered in the tent of Rebekah's mother.

29-31. Laban . . . Eliezer **. . . Rebekah.** Laban betrayed his true character when, upon seeing the expensive ring and bracelets, he decided that nothing should be spared in holding on to Eliezer. He could not fail to be hospitable to a man who could make such gifts. The ornaments were but the beginning. Soon jewels of silver and jewels of gold, and beautiful clothes were bestowed upon Rebekah. And **precious things** (v. 53), special gifts, were presented to the mother and the brother of the bride. In a way these gifts made up for the loss of such a beloved member of the family. The custom of presenting valuable gifts to the members of the bride's family goes back at least as far as the time of Hammurabi (1728–1686 B.C.). Perhaps it came out of the time when the bride was actually purchased.

34-48. Eliezer narrated in some detail the striking fulfillment of his prayer for guidance and assurance. The godly man knew that the Lord had led him and that Rebekah was God's choice for his young master.

49-61. Without waiting for a conference with the selected bride, the other members of the family gave their definite commitment: Rebekah would be Isaac's bride. They were disposed to keep the girl for a while (perhaps for several months), but the maiden, when asked what she preferred, declared her willingness to begin the journey immediately. It was a momentous decision for a girl to make. Her new home was a long way off, and she would probably never see her family again. She was stepping out on faith, even as Abraham had done years before. New life in Canaan was to be her reward.

62-65. Isaac went out to meditate. Isaac was waiting for his bride near Beer-lahai-roi, where Hagar had found hope and cheer and divine direction. Hebrew *sûăḥ,* usually translated **meditate,** has been rendered "walk about," "pray," "wail," "lament," or "moan." Verse 67 may throw some light on its meaning. Isaac needed comforting. It is possible that Sarah had passed away during the absence of Eliezer. The narrative describes Rebekah as literally *leaping down from the camel* in respect for Isaac and proper consideration for his importance. She quickly adjusted her veil, in keeping with accepted rules of etiquette. A betrothed woman remained veiled until the marriage had been consummated. Only then might her husband look upon her face.

66,67. Eliezer gave Isaac a full report of all that had happened on the long journey. Isaac saw that God had led the servant to choose Rebekah and recognized that His will in the matter was to be carried out. He installed Rebekah in Sarah's own tent, and thus she became the first lady of the land. Two verbs stand out in the closing verse of the chapter: **Isaac . . . loved her: and . . . was comforted.** Love came naturally, bringing comfort and joy to Isaac's heart. It was fitting that the lonely soul should find a woman who was lovely and lovable. Isaac's love engendered understanding, considerateness, and gentleness of soul. It was especially good that the young woman, so far from home, was blessed with a husband who truly loved her. The word "comfort" has even deeper overtones when considered in the light of heart and home and marriage. Isaac stood in desperate need of "comfort." Rebekah provided something that had been sadly lacking since the home-going of his mother. Hebrew *nāḥam,* "comfort," actually means to give strength or staying power (cf. Jer 10:4, where the idol builder is said to "*comfort* his idol with nails and with hammers"). The man of quiet, passive, timid faith was joined in marriage to a woman so bold, so adventurous, so ambitious, that she was destined to bring him grief in the years ahead. Yet God was leading, and would use even these imperfect individuals to work out his will for his people.

15) Closing Days of Abraham. 25:1-18.

1-6. Abraham took a wife . . . Keturah. In addition to Sarah and Hagar, Abraham took Keturah as a secondary wife or concubine (I Chr 1:32). This must have occurred many years before the death of Sarah, for several sons are listed. The sons and grandsons of Hagar and Keturah received gifts from the hand of Abraham, but all the property and authority and spiritual possessions went to Isaac, the patriarch's legal heir.

7-10. At the age of 175 Abraham came to the end of his earthly sojourn and expired. He **gave up the ghost.** The expression is derived from Hebrew *gāwa'*, "to breathe out his breath," "to fail," "to sink." Immediately he was **gathered to his father's kin** (literally), and took up his residence in Sheol, the place of departed spirits. He **died in a good old age . . . and full.** A fitting epitaph for a great man of God. His life was truly finished and fully rounded out. He had lived adventurously. He had moved forward in faith along the way pointed out by God. Standing by the sepulchre at the cave of Machpelah were the two sons (v. 9) whom he had loved with unsurpassed affection. Isaac and Ishmael were united in a common grief and a common devotion to the one who had meant most to them. Doubtless Isaac was strengthened in his bereavement by the realization that he stood in the special favor of God and would not have to carry on alone. For he was to be the heir of the rich covenant blessings promised to and through Abraham.

B. Isaac. 25:19–26:35.

1) Isaac and His Family. 25:19-34.

19-23. Sarah, Rebekah, Rachel, and Hannah were all barren, and therefore childless until late in life. It was a tragic experience for each of them. **Isaac entreated the Lord** for Rebekah. The Hebrew verb *'ātar* means "to pray as a suppliant," "to entreat." When it is used in the passive sense, it indicates that the subject has been prevailed upon by means of the praying, and has answered. Isaac prayed fervently for his barren wife, and Jehovah yielded to the entreaty. Rebekah ceased to be sterile, and conceived. Prevailing prayer had been honored by God.

24-34. There were twins in her womb (v. 24). Even before Esau and Jacob were born, they struggled with each other in their prenatal confinement. And they continued the conflict as they grew up. Today their many descendants are passionately striving to gain the advantage over each other in the Middle East. Esau became the hairy man of the field, with little appreciation of spiritual values. He plunged venturesomely along through life, only to find himself defrauded of the best things and checkmated by a cunning supplanter. Jacob derived his inspiration from Rebekah, who stopped at nothing to gain her ends. Isaac was too feeble to keep abreast of underhanded doings or to deal with the combination of Jacob and Rebekah. Esau seemed to be concerned with material matters only. To him, the birthright, which involved both material and spiritual blessings, seemed of little value until he had bargained it away. The birthright was the possession of the first-born. It guaranteed him a more honorable position than his brother's, the best of the estate, and the richest land, as well as the covenant blessings God had promised to Abraham and to his descendants. The birthright was Esau's because God had allowed him to be born first.

Neither Esau nor Jacob showed any commendable interest in spiritual treasures. Each was sordidly selfish and lacked understanding of what behavior would fit a man to be a prince of God. Jacob was ambitious to gather in for himself everything that would give him the pre-eminence. Rebekah supplied the spark and the scheming that secured advantages for her favorite son. He had a long way to go to become the spiritual leader of those who would worship Jehovah. But God was patient; he was not in a hurry; he would train his leader.

Esau made his home in the rocky hills of Edom. Years later his descendants, the people of the nation he founded, would reveal the same type of thinking he had shown and the same profane disregard for the eternal program of Jehovah of hosts. In spite of every discouraging incident, the kingdom of God would move forward toward the fuller realization of the divine purpose.

2) Isaac and Abimelech. 26:1-35.

1. And Isaac went unto Abimelech. Because there was a famine in Canaan, Isaac went to live temporarily in the land of the Philistines. This Abimelech,

king of the Philistines, was not the Abimelech of Abraham's experiences. The name may have been a dynastic name of the rulers in Philistia. **Gerar.** A small settlement on the road to Egypt, about eleven miles southeast of Gaza.

2-5. Isaac was on the verge of deciding to move on to Egypt to seek more plentiful food and pasturage, when Jehovah appeared to him in a special theophany. The Lord warned Isaac not to go to Egypt, and encouraged him to sojourn in Philistia until he could go to dwell in the covenant land. **I will be with thee,** he said, **and will bless thee** (v. 3). At this time Jehovah definitely renewed the promises he had made to Abraham. He clearly explained that he was bestowing those blessings on Isaac because of his father's piety and faithfulness. Abraham had obeyed God's voice and kept his charges, commandments, statutes, and laws. Isaac could take hope and look with assurance for repeated fulfillments of God's promises along the way. And he could count on playing his part in God's plan, already outlined, for witnessing to all peoples.

6-11. She is my sister (v. 7). Isaac revealed something of his human weakness, in Gerar, when he let fear betray him into lying about his wife, Rebekah. Just as Abraham had done on two occasions, Isaac sought to pass his wife off as his sister. When Abimelech observed him indulging in conduct toward Rebekah that was more fitting for a husband than for a brother, he rebuked Isaac sharply for his deception. Again, one who was outside the covenant brought a stinging rebuke to one who should have been above reproach.

12-22. Following this disgraceful episode, Isaac settled down to the kind of prosperous farming that made him the envy of all the surrounding neighbors. Even Abimelech became envious and issued an order that Isaac must leave his territory. The wealthy property owner moved on a short distance to begin life afresh. He found that the natives had stopped up the wells that had been water-giving blessings since Abraham's days. Isaac had his servants reopen all these wells and also dig new ones. Whenever the men dug new wells, the Philistines made much trouble for them. The patriarch named his first new well **'Esek,** *contention,* and the second **Sitnāh,** *enmity.* The third well, which was finished without strife, he called *Reḥōbôt, broad places.*

23-33. Moving on to the vicinity of **Beer-sheba,** Isaac received a special communication from Jehovah assuring him of unusual and continued blessings—**Fear not, for I . . . will bless thee** (v. 24). Now that he was back again in hallowed territory, it was particularly appropriate that he build an altar to Jehovah and thereby announce to all that he was committed to the task set out for him. Isaac began to give evidence of a godly spirit that he had not hitherto revealed so clearly.

C. Jacob. 27:1–36:43.

1) Jacob and Esau. 27:1-46.

1-17. When Isaac was old . . . he called Esau. It is difficult to imagine all the pathos, agony, and cruel disappointment wrapped up in this colorful narrative. The old patriarch, with blinded eyes and a tottering frame, now made plans to give the sacred blessing to his first-born son. But the crafty Rebekah, who listened to his directions to Esau, immediately set about subverting and frustrating his plans. Her favorite son, Jacob, already had the birthright; she was determined that he should receive the oral blessing, too, from the lips of the Lord's representative, so that all would be well with the divine inheritance. She could not risk waiting for God to work out his plans in his own way. So she resorted to the most contemptible deceit to secure the blessing for her younger son.

18-29. And Jacob said . . . I am Esau thy firstborn. Coached by his mother, Jacob came before his old father with deception and lies. He even declared that Jehovah had helped him make his preparations with speed. After lying to his father, he planted a false kiss upon the old man's upturned face.

30-40. And Esau lifted up his voice, and wept (v. 38). The tragedy for Esau was that he was utterly ignorant of the sacredness of the blessing, and only desired the advantages it would give. His deep hurt that Jacob had outwitted him in securing the birthright, his bitter disappointment, his pathetic sobbing, and the burning shame that quickly kindled into intense hatred and desire for revenge are deeply moving.

41-46. Arise, flee thou to Laban. To save Jacob from his brother's revenge, Rebekah found a pretense for sending him away. Which of these three—Rebekah, Jacob, or Esau—was most to be pitied? Their family life was destroyed, and each had to bear lonely hours of separation, disillusionment, and regret. Rebekah would never see her favorite son again, and Jacob would have to face life without father, mother, or brother. And what about God's plans for the kingdom? How could they be worked out in the face of such selfishness, intrigue, and deceit? The Lord of hosts is not to be thwarted by men's opposition, failure, or lack of faith. He is able to make his will prevail in spite of all.

While Isaac moved a little closer to the hour of his death, and Rebekah mourned because of the distressing situation she had precipitated, and Esau thought of revenge, Jacob made his lonely way from Beer-sheba to Padan-aram.

2) Jacob, Laban, Leah, and Rachel. 28:1–30:43.

28:1-5. Isaac **blessed** him, **and charged him . . . . go to Padan-aram** (vv. 1,2). Isaac did not let Jacob go away without a blessing. He spoke in the tone of prophetic utterance, and in beautiful language that reveals his spiritual perception. Jacob was to seek a wife among his relatives in Haran, but he was to be most concerned with entering into the rich inheritance promised to Abraham. Isaac called on *'El Shadday*, **God Almighty** (v. 3), to provide health, prosperity, and keen understanding to equip Jacob for spiritual leadership. He prophesied that if his son would commit his way to the Lord, the blessings God had promised to Abraham would all be his. Through Isaac, God gave Jacob a command, a challenge, an assurance, and direction for the journey.

6-9. Esau observed and listened, then went to Ishmael's house to get for himself a wife of the family line, who would please his parents. Evidently he wanted to make some effort in the right direction. But because he was basically worldly, his career in the land of Edom fell short of behavior that could please the Lord Jehovah.

10-17. Jacob made the journey from Beer-sheba to Luz, about twelve miles north of Jerusalem, where he spent the night. Bethel was in that immediate vicinity. In the night he was honored with a special communication from God, a vision or dream of angels ascending and descending a ladder that reached from earth to heaven. He became aware that there actually is communication between heaven and earth. He recognized in that place that God was by his side, promising him guidance through life, and future greatness. Jehovah said, **I am with thee, and will keep thee . . . and will bring thee again into this land . . . I will not leave thee** (v. 15). What a challenging message! No wonder Jacob exclaimed: **The Lord is in this place . . . . How dreadful** *(awesome)* **is this place!** (vv. 16,17) He was profoundly moved. Perhaps for the first time in his life he was conscious of the presence of God at his side. The voice, the words of hope, the actual presence of *'El Shadday* brought him around to worship and awe and commitment.

18-22. He called the name of the place **Beth-el,** *House of God,* for God was there. To make this a never-to-be-forgotten experience, he set up a stone pillar to indicate that this was a holy spot, a sanctuary where intimate fellowship with God would always be possible (v. 18). Spiritually, he still had a long way to go, but he had made progress in this encounter with God. He also pledged the Lord his life and a **tenth** of all possessions that would become his along the way. But he made this promise conditional: If God would remain with him, keep him in the way, and bring him safely home again, he would carry out his part of the pledge. It was a long step forward. The **stone** *(maṣṣēbâ)* he erected would stand as a permanent reminder of the vow he had made (v. 22).

29:1-12. Then Jacob went on his journey (v. 1). The Hebrew idiom, *lifted up his feet*, tells of the young man's response to the divine encouragement. He was on his way to Padan-aram, seeking his mother's family near Haran. It was difficult to take such a long journey, but Jacob seemed to have no alternative. At last he stood at a well, in the midst of flocks of sheep, with their shepherds waiting for the big stone to be taken from the mouth of the well so that the sheep could be watered. Possibly it was the same well where Eliezer found Rebekah for the young Isaac. Though many years had passed, Laban still lived, as Jacob learned from the shepherds, and his daughter Rachel was the keeper of his flock (v. 6). When Rachel approached with Laban's flock, Jacob stepped forward to remove the big rock and to provide water for the thirsty sheep. Then he kissed his cousin and told her who he was. Deeply moved by all that had befallen him and by this first meeting with kinsfolk, Jacob **lifted up his voice, and**

wept," while Rachel ran to tell Laban that his nephew had arrived.

13,14. Laban, brother of Rebekah, grandson of Nahor, was overjoyed to welcome one of his own bone and flesh. It had been a long time since his sister had ridden away to become Isaac's bride. He gladly received the son of Rebekah into his family circle. Perhaps he remembered the lavish display of wealth brought by Eliezer. Perhaps he was impressed by the strength of the young man, who might become a good shepherd. Almost certainly he considered the possibility of a husband for his daughters. Leah and Rachel were both eligible. Laban never missed an opportunity to drive a hard bargain. The young nephew from the hill country would learn to deal cautiously with him. In fact, Jacob would learn to outwit the chief trickster of all the "children of the East."

15-20. Rachel was unusually beautiful and attractive, and already Jacob was impressed by her. The Scripture says, **Jacob loved Rachel** (v. 18). Leah, the elder sister, was far from beautiful. Her eyes lacked the luster, sparkle, and attractiveness that men admire. Yet Leah was to be established so firmly in sacred history that succeeding generations would have to reckon with her. It would be one of her sons who would be chosen to take his place in the Messianic line. These four—Laban, Jacob, Leah, and Rachel—were to be significant figures in God's dealings with and through his chosen people.

21-30. After toiling seven years for the younger daughter, Jacob was deceived and tricked into marriage with Leah. After the wedding festivities for Leah, Jacob married her younger sister, Rachel, but had to work seven more years as payment for her. Thus he had two wives of equal standing. His burning love for Rachel made his relationship with Leah rather strange and disappointing. Leah must have suffered much from the realization that her husband did not love her. Yet she carried on in the hope that one day Jacob's heart would turn to her.

31-35. At first neither Rachel nor Leah bore Jacob children. In those days, to be barren was regarded as a pathetic situation. However, in time, Jehovah came to Leah's rescue and healed her barrenness, and she became a mother. One after another her sons came, until she had borne six of them. A daughter, Dinah, was added for extra measure. With heart-rending regularity, Leah held out a son with the words: **Now my husband will love me.** But no word of recognition or appreciation came from Jacob. The word for **hatred** *(śānē)* indicates "less affection," or "less devotion." It does not indicate positive hatred.

30:1-13. Rachel also suffered, for her sterile state did not improve, and she was not bearing sons for Jacob. Hebrew *qānē'*, **envied,** has wrapped up within it the feeling of one who has borne about all she can stand. Envy, discontent, petulance marked her voice, her language, and her facial expression. Leah, Rachel, and Jacob were all unhappy. Their domestic trouble and heartache led to words and actions wholly unworthy, unnecessary, and unbecoming. Human attempts to remedy the situation proved unsatisfactory. The giving of **Bilhah** and **Zilpah** as secondary wives to help "build" the family only proved to be hurtful. Sons were born, but hearts were still out of tune and unhappy. Besides Leah's six sons and one daughter (at least), two sons were born to Bilhah and two to Zilpah.

14-24. Rachel sought to use **mandrakes** *(dûdā'îm)* to induce fertility. These mandrakes were popularly called "love apples." Ryle says: "The mandrake is a tuberous plant, with yellow plum-like fruit. It was suposed to act as a love-charm. It ripens in May, which suits the mention (v. 14) of wheat harvest" *(Cambridge Bible, in loco)*. Rachel remained barren in spite of the superstitious charms. The situation was in the hands of the Lord, and he could not honor human attempts to change it. Finally, **God remembered Rachel, and God hearkened to her, and opened her womb. And she conceived, and bare a son . . . and she called him Joseph** (vv. 22-24). In his own good time Jehovah gave his answer. He took away Rachel's **reproach** and filled her with joy and praise.

25-30. Jacob said unto Laban, Send me away, that I may go . . . to my country. When Joseph was born, Jacob had worked out in full his debt to Laban, and he was ready to return to Canaan. Had he gone at that time, he could have taken only his family; he did not own one particle of property. He requested his uncle to let him go home. Laban claimed to have received special knowledge (AV, **learned by experience**), by magic or divination or from his household gods, that he must keep Jacob around to guarantee success and prosperity.

31-36. He offered to let Jacob name his wages. Imagine his surprise when his nephew made him an offer that seemed overwhelmingly in his favor. In Syria the sheep were white and the goats were black, with very few exceptions. Jacob offered to start in business at once, accepting as his the sheep that were not white and the goats that were not black, and leaving the rest to Laban. Thus the two estates would be built up. Laban accepted the offer instantly. He began **that day** by removing to a safe distance every available "off-color" sheep and goat so that Jacob would have nothing with which to start. The separated animals he placed in the keeping of his sons. It was a low, dastardly trick. Laban believed that he had made it impossible for Jacob to win, because he had taken away all of Jacob's capital before the contest began.

37-42. But Jacob was not to be counted out so easily. He installed three devices to outwit his uncle. He set up streaked rods before the ewes at the watering places, that the coloring of the young might be subject to prenatal influence. It is an established fact, declares Delitzsch, that white lambs can be guaranteed by placing a multitude of white objects about the drinking troughs (*New Commentary on Genesis, in loco*). Jacob also separated the spotted and striped lambs and kids from the herd, but kept them in plain view of the ewes, that they might be influenced. His third device was to bring these predetermining influences to bear upon the stronger ewes so that his lambs and kids would be stronger and more virile than the others. Jacob was smart enough to resort to prenatal influence and selective breeding.

43. As a result of these schemes, in a few years Jacob became immensely rich in sheep and goats. Though he had used his head, he would have been the first to declare that the Lord intervened to give him the victory. Jehovah was making it possible for the patriarch to return to the promised land with substance, and become the prince of God, who would do the divine will.

3) Jacob's Return to Canaan. 31:1-55.

1-3. The countenance of Laban . . . was not toward him as before. Finally, the relations of uncle and nephew reached the breaking point. Jacob saw that Laban and his sons felt hostile toward him because of his success. Besides, he had gained enough wealth and possessions to satisfy him. So, when he received direct marching orders from the God of Bethel, he knew it was time to return home. Twenty years had passed, during which time his mother had died. Perhaps Laban would therefore become even more disagreeable. It was the hour for moving out. **4-13.** Jacob explained his decision to his wives, telling them how the **angel of God** had spoken to him in a dream and encouraged him in his purpose. The "angel" had identified himself with the one who had appeared to Jacob at Bethel. He was actually Jehovah himself. **14-16.** Leah and Rachel strongly endorsed Jacob's decision. They knew their father, and they had lost their love and respect for him. They remembered that he had collected fourteen years of work from Jacob without giving them the part that a bride could rightfully expect. **Are we not counted of him strangers?** they said. **For he hath sold us, and hath quite devoured also our money** (v. 15).

17-21. Jacob set his flocks, herds, children, and possessions in readiness for the long journey, and waited until Laban had gone away for a sheepshearing festival. Meanwhile Rachel made sure Jacob's claim to a good share of the birthright by taking the **images** or *t*ᵉ*rāpîm* (cf. Latin *penates*), actually "household gods," highly prized by Laban. Nuzu tablets from the fifteenth century B.C. indicate that possession of the *t*ᵉ*rāpîm* marked a man as the chief heir. Evidently Rachel had not learned to trust in Jehovah to provide for her needs. Jacob had failed to teach his family to trust and worship God with all their hearts. Soon Jacob and his company moved out from Haran, crossed the Euphrates, and journeyed as rapidly as they could toward Canaan. Their immediate goal was the hill country of Gilead on the eastern side of the Jordan River.

22-24. Laban . . . pursued after him. After three days Laban learned of the flight. As soon as he could get his men organized for pursuit, he was on his way to overtake them. Even though it was a journey of three hundred miles, he was able to catch the fleeing group in the hill country of Gilead. On the way, Laban received a strange message from God, a command to abstain from bringing any pressure to bear on Jacob. He was not to speak **either good or bad** to him, i.e., he was not to say anything. (Opposites are frequently used in Scripture to indicate totality.)

25-35. Laban could not be deterred by

divine visitations. He began his remonstrance by expressing his great distress over having his daughters and grandchildren dragged away without suitable farewells. Suddenly he followed with the question: **Why hast thou stolen my gods?** He referred to his *tᵉrāpîm* (v. 30; cf. 19). Evidently Laban was more concerned over losing his images than over losing Jacob's family. Search failed to discover these little "gods," for Rachel had hidden them in the wicker basket that formed a part of the saddle on which she sat. This **camel's furniture** (v. 34) gave an Eastern lady some comfort and privacy as she journeyed.

36-55. Doubtless Jacob found great relief of spirit in replying to Laban. The air was thoroughly cleared, and Laban lost the sting from his tongue. The two men made a covenant with each other, ratifying it and commemorating the event by raising a heap of stones on top of a hill. The heap formed what was called **mizpah** or "outlook point," where a watcher could see the entire country in both directions. It indicated suspicion and lack of trust. By raising such a heap the men signified that they invited Jehovah to sit in the lookout post to keep watch over two people who could not be trusted. God was to be a sentry to watch both Laban and Jacob, in the hope that strife might be avoided. Jacob was bound by the promise to treat Laban's daughters with kindness and consideration. Neither of the parties to the covenant must pass that point on the border to do violence to the other. Neither must ever move to do harm to the other, forever.

4) Jacob's Meeting with Esau. 32:1–33:17.

32:1-5. Jacob went on his way, and the angels of God met him. Both on the way out from Canaan and on the way back, these heavenly messengers came to Jacob to make him conscious of the heavenly presence and to assure him of divine protection. The word **Mahanaim,** *two camps,* describes an inner camp, made up of Jacob's group and an outer company, made up of the messengers of God, the outer company forming a marvelous circle of protection around the travelers. A beautiful picture of security and protection, and serenity of soul! (cf. II Kgs 6:15-17)

6-8. Esau was on his way from Edom, Jacob's couriers informed him, to meet the large company of people arriving from Padan-aram. **Edom** was the land south of the Dead Sea, which is often called **Seir,** or Mount Seir (v. 3) in the Bible. In New Testament times the people of Edom were called Idumaeans. Jacob had much fear in his heart as he remembered Esau's threats of years before and imagined that his brother was making plans to get his revenge. **Four hundred men** under the leadership of the wild man from Edom could be dangerous. Jacob adopted three definite moves to guarantee safety. First, he went to the Lord in humble prayer. Second, he sent lavish presents to Esau to secure his good will. Third, he arranged his families, his possessions, and his fighting men to the best possible advantage, and prepared to put up a good fight if it became necessary.

9-12. In his prayer Jacob reminded the Lord that He had summoned him to make the journey to Canaan and had promised him protection and victory. The prayer was sincere and humble, an earnest entreaty for safety, deliverance, and protection in the emergency that confronted him. Though no word of confession came forth from the petitioner's lips regarding the wrongs he had done to Esau and Isaac, Jacob humbly admitted that he was wholly unworthy of God's favor–literally, **I am less than all** (v. 10). He showed his fear of God and faith in him. He was literally casting himself on the arm of the Lord for victory and deliverance.

13-21a. The **present** (AV), or *gift minḥâ* was an elaborate one, consisting of at least 580 beasts from Jacob's choice herds and flocks. The *minḥâ* was the usual present given to a superior with the intent of securing favor and good will. Jacob said: **I will appease** ***(kipper)*** **him** (v. 20). The word is a significant one in its reference to atonement. Its literal sense is, *I will cover*. By means of the gift, Jacob hoped to "cover" Esau's face so that he would overlook the injury and dismiss his anger. His next word–**so that he will accept me**–is, literally, *so that he will lift up my face*. This is symbolic language, indicating full acceptance after forgiveness. Jacob was exceptionally humble, courteous, and conciliatory in his messages to Esau. He called Esau "my lord," and spoke of himself as "thy servant." He would leave no stone unturned to effect reconcilation.

21b-23. On the night before Esau's arrival, Jacob met the crucial test of his entire life. After seeing his wives and children safely across the Jabbok, he returned to the north bank to be alone in the darkness. The **Jabbok** was a tributary of the Jordan, which joined it about halfway between the Sea of Galilee and the Dead Sea. Today the Jabbok is known as the Zerka.

24-32. There wrestled a man with him until the breaking of the day. In the loneliness of the dark night Jacob was met by a man who wrestled with him. Hebrew *'abaq,* to "twist," or "wrestle," has some connection with the word *Jabbok.* After a long struggle, the unknown visitor demanded that Jacob release him. This Jacob refused to do until the stranger blessed him. The "man" asked Jacob to tell his name, which means *supplanter.* Then the stranger declared that from then on he would have a new name with a new meaning. The word **Israel** can be translated *he who striveth with God,* or *God striveth,* or *he who persevereth*"; or, it may be associated with the word *śar,* "prince." The "man" declared: **Thou hast striven with God . . . and hast prevailed.** It was an assurance of victory in dealing with Esau, as well as assurance of triumphs all along the way. In the titanic struggle, Jacob came to realize his own weakness and the superiority of the mighty One who had touched him. At the moment of yielding, he became a new man, who could receive the blessings of God and assume his place in God's plan. The new name, Israel, suggests royalty and power and sovereignty among men. He was destined to be a God-governed man instead of an unscrupulous supplanter. He had come through defeat into power. All the rest of his life he would be crippled; yet his limp would be a reminder of his new royalty.

Peniel (or *Penuel)* means *face of God.* The *i* and the *u* are mere connecting vowels joining the substantives *pen* and *el.* It is probably to be located up the Jabbok Valley about seven or eight miles from the Jordan. Jacob had seen the face of God and still lived. He would never forget that incredible experience.

33:1-3. Jacob lifted up his eyes, and . . . behold, Esau came. Finally, the moment of meeting arrived. Esau, with his four hundred men, came in sight. With fear and trepidation, and yet with his most engaging manner, Jacob met his estranged brother and prostrated himself before him seven times. Thus, he indicated complete subservience. **4-11.** Esau, in his response, revealed a generous and magnanimous spirit that was almost too good to be true. He had harbored hostility for Jacob, and he had brought four hundred strong men along with him as if he planned to carry out his old threat. But he did not. His heart was changed. God had turned his hatred into magnanimity. He came to meet Jacob with understanding and forgiveness. In the twenty years that had intervened, the controlling hand of God had wrought changes in both men. Now the one who had so recently been humbled before God found his way smoothed out for him.

12-17. Jacob's gift-giving and Esau's eager and affectionate welcome gave evidence that the days ahead could bring new victories for God's kingdom. These men would not fight and kill each other. Although Jacob did not accept Esau's generous offer of protection, nor his urgent invitation to come to Mount Seir, he greatly appreciated his brother's magnanimous spirit. Esau had shown that he could forgive and forget. The brothers parted in peace. At **Succoth** *(booths)* Jacob, with his company, found a home (v. 17). He actually built a house there. Succoth was a magnificent highland site on the eastern side of Jordan and north of the Jabbok.

5) Jacob and His Family at Shechem. 33:18–34:31. Evidence is not conclusive regarding the length of Jacob's stay in Succoth. It may have been a long time. After he had made peace with Esau, he had no occasion to hurry. Before crossing the Jordan, he probably spent several years in the well-watered region to the east of the river.

33:18-20. Crossing the river, he found himself in the vicinity of Shechem, where Abraham had paused on his first journey into the land of Canaan. Shechem was approximately forty-one miles north of Jerusalem, in the valley between Mount Ebal and Mount Gerizim. Jacob's well was there and Sychar was not far away. Jacob bought a parcel of ground in the vicinity of Shechem, and in this way established claim to property in Canaan. He had been commanded to go back to the land of his fathers and to his kindred, probably meaning the vicinity of Hebron. Certainly he should have gone at least as far as Bethel. He was to learn that the people of Shechem would not be a help to his family.

34:1-5. Dinah, a daughter of Jacob and Leah, made a disastrous visit to the near-by city of Shechem. The immature girl had no background of spiritual understanding to sustain her in her hour of need. Shechem, the young son of Hamor, fell desperately in love with her, and soon the tragic consequences were known in Jacob's family. Hebrew *lāqah*, **took** (v. 2), indicates that an irresistible force was used. The word *ānâ*, **defiled** (AV), indicates dishonorable treatment. The poor girl was ruined. Immediately Shechem **spoke to the heart** (v. 3, marg.) of the distressed one he had wronged, seeking to console her. He loved her and wanted her for his wife.

6-12. The word *nᵉbālâ*, **folly**, indicates a shameful, vile, senseless deed that displays utter insensibility in moral behavior. To Jacob and his sons, Shechem's deed was an act of grave immorality, an outrage against decency and family honor. Hamor and Shechem sought to arrange a marriage, since Shechem loved the girl. Jacob was ready to make an agreement with them. The *mōhar*—present to the bride—would be good. The two groups would be bound together so that intermarriage would be legal. **13-24.** However, the sons of Jacob were hotheaded, unyielding, and unscrupulous. Under the guise of requiring religious observance, they made the Shechemites agree to be circumcised. All the men of the tribe submitted to the rite. **25-29.** Then Simeon and Levi led an attack on the city. Jacob's sons cut down all the men while they were incapacitated for fighting, and took away their families and possessions. In the history of the patriarch's family, it is a sordid chapter of passion, cruelty, and disgrace.

30,31. God's chosen people in his holy land had behaved like cruel pagans. Poor old Jacob was distressed. He reminded his sons that they had made it difficult for him to keep the good will of the neighboring peoples. His attitude was unworthy of a man of faith who was God's chosen representative to the peoples of the earth. Selfish fear seemed to be uppermost in his thinking. He did not rebuke his sons for their unspeakable cruelty, nor did he express sorrow because God's honor had been poorly represented. Jacob had spent twenty years in Laban's land, and now probably another ten years at Succoth and Shechem without doing anything noteworthy to prepare his family spiritually for the strong currents of life. He had been too busy building a material empire and gaining worldly advantage to attend to his children's ethical and spiritual foundations. He had yet to reach Bethel. Would it be too late for Dinah and Simeon and Levi and all the others? The story could make even a strong man weep.

6) The Return to Bethel. 35:1-29.

1. Jehovah uttered a solemn command to Jacob to move on to his goal: **Arise, go up to Beth–el, and dwell there: and make there an altar.** Bethel was 1,010 feet higher than Shechem and situated on the road that led to Jerusalem, Bethlehem, and Hebron. Jacob had tarried too long on his way to that holy place. He was now to build an altar there, as Abraham had done on his memorable journey into Palestine. Jacob had set up a *maṣṣēbâ*, i.e., a stone pillar, after his never-to-be-forgotten experience with Jehovah, when he fled toward Haran. This return visit to the holy place would involve a full commitment of his life to the Lord. He had neglected the altar of God. The spiritual emphasis had been absent from his thinking and living.

2-7. Immediately and obediently, Jacob made ready to journey to Bethel. First, he called on his semipagan family to purify themselves (v. 2), to put away all *terāpîm* and visible representations of foreign gods. Then the family of Jacob moved out on their holy pilgrimage to Bethel. The people of the places through which they passed were so awed by **the terror of God** that they did not molest the pilgrims (v. 5). When Jacob came to **Luz,** he knew he was about to walk on holy ground. He erected an altar to Jehovah and called the place **El-beth-el,** *the God of the house of God.*

9-15. Again God appeared to Jacob and assured him that his new name, Israel, would be a constant reminder of his new character, his new relation to Jehovah, and his kingly walk in the divine way of life. He was the heir of the promises made to Abraham. The covenant was still in full force, and it would continue to be binding upon him and his descendants. In speaking with Jacob, God used His name, **God Almighty,** *'El Shadday,* "the all-sufficient One" (v. 11). Jacob could count on *'El Shadday* to supply any and every need, and to give the grace for any emergency.

16-20. Now Rachel, who had provided the inspiration and the love Jacob needed, came to the end of her way. She died in giving birth to her second son, whom she named **Ben-oni,** *son of my sorrow.* But Jacob chose the name **Benjamin,** *son of my right hand.* Rachel must have been buried somewhere south of Bethel, on the road to Hebron (cf. 35:16,19). Bethel was ten miles north of Jerusalem, and Bethlehem was about six miles south of Jerusalem. It is usually concluded that Rachel was buried in the immediate vicinity of Bethlehem. The traditional site is still pointed out to visitors to that city.

27-29. Isaac continued to live until Jacob's return from Haran. From Beer-sheba he had moved to Mamre, very near the old city of Hebron. There Abraham had purchased the Cave of Machpelah for the burial place of Sarah. Now, at the age of 180 years, **Isaac gave up the ghost, and died.** The single Hebrew word *gāwā'* means to "fail," or to "sink down." In the hour of burial, Esau and Jacob stood together at the grave, to honor their father. The brothers were united in a common grief, as Ishmael and Isaac had been at the grave of Abraham.

7) Edom and Its People. 36:1-43. Before recounting the life story of Joseph, the writer of Genesis describes something of the land of Edom and its inhabitants. The original inhabitants of Mount Seir were called Horites or Hurrians. In the course of time, Esau and his descendants took over the territory. Esau became wealthy and possessed much cattle and sheep. The principal cities of the area were Sela, Bozrah, Petra, Teman, and Ezion-geber. The Edomites continued to be hostile to the Israelites throughout OT times (cf. Obadiah, especially vv. 10-15).

D. Joseph. 37:1–50:26.

1) Joseph's Early Experiences. 37:1-36.

1-11. Joseph, the older son of Rachel, was a favorite of his father Jacob. For this and other reasons he became exceedingly unpopular with his brothers. For one thing, he reacted strongly against their unethical and immoral behavior, and frankly reported on them, thus gaining for himself the name of talebearer. To make matters worse, his father made for him royal tunics, with long, flowing sleeves, which set him out from the group as the favored one. The natural inference was that Jacob had chosen Joseph to be the one through whom the divine blessings would flow. Furthermore, Joseph dreamed dreams that pointed to his future outstanding greatness, and he told his dreams to his brothers.

Jacob's sons were incensed to hear from Joseph's lips the announcement that he would rule over them. He, the young favored prince, evidently believed that he was to have the pre-eminence over his entire family. In his guileless talk, he stirred up all the fires of envy and murderous hatred. Yet God did have in mind some wondrous blessings for the lad, as time would reveal. Joseph should have been counseled about the proper way to deal with imperfect creatures who resented his manner and his air of superiority (as they thought). How he needed a wise counselor! Jacob apparently loved him so ardently and so blindly that he could not guide him wisely.

12-28. The brothers harbored malice in their hearts until they determined to get rid of Joseph. They had plenty of time to formulate a plot to accomplish their purpose. From Hebron, where they lived, to Shechem in the north, these men went to find pasture land for their flocks and herds. Jacob sent Joseph to Shechem to visit his other sons and bring him word of their welfare. On arriving in the vicinity of Shechem, Joseph learned that his brothers had moved on to **Dothan,** about fifteen miles farther north. When the brothers saw Joseph coming, they plotted to kill him, though Reuben sought to save the lad's life. Reuben talked the others into putting Joseph into a cistern, hoping to pull him out later. Judah subsequently convinced his brothers that it would be wise to take the boy out of the cistern and sell him to a caravan passing on the way to Egypt. Reuben had planned to take the boy home to his father. Judah planned to save him from starving. As it turned out, Joseph found himself a prisoner of a **company of Ishmaelites** (v. 25) or Midianites. Soon he would be a slave in some Egyptian family. Both Ishmaelites and Midianites were descendants of Abraham. Perhaps the band was made up of men from both these peoples.

29-35. Reuben, the first-born, was directly responsible for the lad to his father. Painfully he and the others faced Jacob with a bloodly coat and a deceitful tale that practically broke the heart of the old patriarch. He was convinced that his favorite son was dead. The one who, in his youth, had been a champion deceiver was now cruelly deceived. His grief knew no bounds. He wailed: **I will go down to Sheol mourning for my son.** Hebrew **Sheol** describes the underground abode of the dead, answering to Greek "Hades." There, according to tradition, disembodied spirits continue to exist in shadowy regions that have no exit and no communication with God or man. It is a mere half existence. Jacob realized that he would be going to Sheol soon, but he had no hope of seeing an end to his poignant sufferings until that hour.

36. The Ishmaelites sold Joseph to **Potiphar**, an official in the court of Pharaoh. Evidently Potiphar was the **chief of the executioners** (marg)) The word probably referred to the work of slaughtering animals for the royal kitchen or perhaps the animals used for sacrifice. The youthful Joseph was appointed steward of Potiphar's residence. He was a long way from home and, seemingly, even farther away from the realization of his heaven-sent dreams of pre-eminence. However, Joseph's God was still working out his purposes and plans. And he was about to use Potiphar and Pharaoh to advance his divine program.

2) Judah and Tamar. 38:1-30. In the midst of the narrative describing Joseph's career in Egypt, the writer of Genesis introduces the account of Judah's shameful involvement among the Canaanites. Judah was the leading member of Jacob's family, one destined to be the channel of all Jehovah's rich promises to and through Abraham to later generations and the world. Judah's name was to be prominent in the Messianic line. David would be one of his honored descendants.

2-11. Judah saw . . . a daughter of a certain Canaanite, whose name was Shuah; and he took her. This sidelight on family life in Canaan reveals to what depths of immorality some, at least, of the Chosen People had fallen. Judah married the daughter of Shuah, a pagan Canaanite, and thus started a chain of sinful events. Two sons, Er and Onan, died without leaving children. Judah promised Tamar, who had been the wife of the brothers, one after the other, that she should have his third son, Shelah, for a husband, when he came of the right age. The family line must not die out.

12-23. In time, when Tamar realized that her father-in-law was not keeping his promise, she took things into her own hands. Pretending to be one of the *kedēshôt* (religious prostitutes), she tricked Judah into having illicit relations with her. **24-26.** When Judah learned that Tamar was with child, he declared her worthy of death, only to find that he was the guilty father of her child. He said: **She hath been more righteous than I** (AV). **27-30.** The account of the birth of the twins, **Perez** and **Zerah,** closes the chapter. The contrast between Joseph and his elder brother would be more sharp when Joseph revealed his behavior in his hour of temptation. Judah needed to become a new man to be pleasing in the Lord's sight.

3) Joseph and the Wife of Potiphar. 39:1-23.

1-6b. And Joseph was brought down to Egypt. When Joseph took up his work at Potiphar's house, he was a slave and an alien. First, he became a personal attendant to the Egyptian officer. When Potiphar found him alert, quick, and trustworthy, and saw that **the Lord was with him** (v. 3), he set him over the entire establishment as his trusted overseer. In his new position Joseph was responsible for every detail of the management of the house, with one exception: As a foreigner, he could not see to the preparation of food (cf. 43:32).

6c. Joseph was unusually attractive. He was like his mother, Rachel, of whom it was said: "Rachel was beautiful and well favored," i.e., "fair in form" and "fair in looks" (cf. 29:17). In addition, Joseph radiated a sweet, clean godliness that made him even more appealing. **7-13.** Potiphar's wife could not resist the temptation to make a conquest of Joseph. Apparently she had nothing to occupy her mind and no principles to undergird her in the hour of temptation. For Joseph, who lived constantly in communion with the holy God, to sin with the woman was utterly out of the question. It would have been sin against God, and unfair to the man who trusted him so implicitly. Even though the temptation came with subtle, sudden, strong appeal, Joseph's victory was assured.

14-20. Frustrated, the temptress became a slanderer. In a rage she went forth to accuse Joseph falsely of evil intent, hoping to stir up sympathy on the part of other servants, and to make her husband angry enough to kill the young man. The circumstantial evidence was strongly incriminating. Potiphar was enraged. However, in spite of the seriousness of the charge, he evidently had some question in his mind about Joseph's guilt, for he did not kill him. Instead, he hurried him off to the **prison** (the "Round House"). This prison was probably a famous round tower or dungeon where prisoners connected with official life were housed. The Hebrew *sōhar,*

prison, may be an attempt to translate an Egyptian word.

In the Egyptian *Tale of the Two Brothers,* there is an interesting parallel to the experience of Joseph. In that story a man who was married lived in the same house with his brother. The wife of the first man accused the younger brother of improper advances. The husband, though enraged, sought to know the truth about the matter. On finding his wife guilty, the husband executed her. This story dates back to the days of Seti II, that is, to about 1180 B.C.

21-23. Life in prison was not desirable, but the narrative declares that **the Lord was with** Joseph. What a difference that made! He was enabled to enjoy comfort and strength.

4) Joseph's Prison Experiences. 40:1-23.

1-4. The butler . . . and . . . baker had offended their lord the king of Egypt . . . And Pharaoh . . . . put them in ward. Even in the prison Joseph could not be kept down. He was given supervision of the prisoners, and **he ministered unto them.** The old dungeon became a different place because of his presence. God was blessing others through Joseph's thoughtfulness and kindness. Potiphar had put him where his remarkable talents could still be felt. The **butler** *(mashgēh),* or *drink-giver,* was a valued member of Pharaoh's household. In Neh 1:11 the word is translated "cupbearer." Nehemiah, who bore that title, was a trusted official in the palace of the Persian monarch. the **baker** *('ōpeh)* was the superintendent of the bakery, responsible for seeing to it that the monarch's food was safe and palatable. These two high officials in the royal household had offended Pharaoh. Pending investigation, they were confined in the same prison to which Joseph had been committed.

5-23. It was the duty of the young Hebrew to wait on these two prisoners. Finding them upset and disturbed, he inquired concerning their needs. They had dreamed dreams that they could not understand. And no official interpreter of dreams was available. Joseph reminded them that God could give the meaning. Then they told him their dreams, and he explained what they signified. The butler would have a pleasant surprise: Within three days he would be granted an official release from prison to go back to his work at the king's side. The baker would be released at the same time, but his head would be severed from his body and his carcass would be hung out in the open to become food for the birds. Joseph made one request of the butler: **Have me in thy remembrance when it shall be well with thee, and shew kindness . . . . and make mention of me unto Pharaoh** (v. 14). Joseph wanted to be free to live and help bring about the full will of God in his life.

5) Joseph and Pharaoh. 41:1-57.

1-8. At the end of two full years . . . Pharaoh dreamed: and, behold, he stood by the river. The king dreamed that he stood by the Nile *(yᵉōr),* the giver of life and refreshment to the ground. (The country depended on the river to provide heaven-sent irrigation year after year.) And he saw seven well-fed cattle grazing in a meadow. Presently seven thin cattle came along and ate up the fatter ones. Again, he saw seven good ears of grain on one stalk, and seven poorer ones appeared and devoured them. These dreams deeply disturbed Pharaoh, especially when no man could be found to interpret them. The **magicians** *(ḥartummîm)* were the sacred scribes who had more knowledge of the occult than any of the other wise men in the realm. But even they were baffled and helpless this time. Their special training in the sacred mysteries proved inadequate for interpreting these dreams. What did it all mean? the king wondered. Who could tell him?

9-24. Suddenly the chief butler remembered Joseph, after having forgotten him for two years, and told Pharaoh of his ability to interpret dreams. Quickly the young Hebrew was summoned. In a brief time he appeared at the palace, shaved and immaculately dressed. Pharaoh said he had heard that Joseph could interpret dreams, but Joseph made it quite clear that the interpretation must come from the Lord: **God shall give Pharaoh an answer of peace** (AV, v. 16).

25-32. Without hesitation and with unusual clearness, the young man revealed to the king that his dreams foretold seven years of plenty, to be followed by seven years of devastating famine. The earlier period of seven years would be a season of fertility and bountiful harvests. The famine years would bring want and suffering and death.

33-36. Look out a man discreet and wise. Joseph went beyond mere interpretation and gave some down-to-earth advice. No time was to be lost. A wise man of superior ability must be found who could supervise agricultural production, gather tremendous stores of grain, and, in due time, make wise disposition of the amassed resources. The position would demand the best man the kingdom could afford.

37-42. Fortunately, Pharaoh was a wise man, for he recognized Joseph as **a man in whom the spirit of God** was (v. 38). He made him the food administrator of Egypt, and appointed him the grand vizier or prime minister. He set him in command over the entire kingdom, next to himself. He had his own signet ring placed on Joseph's hand, as a badge of authority, empowering him to issue official edicts. He had him clothed in special garments reserved for Egypt's mightiest men, and a special distinguished-service chain placed about his neck.

43. Joseph was to ride in a chariot and be regarded as second only to the king. A special official would call out to the people, "*'Abrēk!*" This probably meant, "Pay attention!" or **Bow the knee.** (AV), or something similar. It was to be made clear to all the people that an outstanding man of ability, character, and authority was before them. He was to be in complete control of affairs that meant life or death to multitudes. Privilege and responsibility vied with each other in that moment of recognition and investment. The challenging words of Mordecai to Esther might well have been spoken to Joseph: "Who knoweth whether thou art come to the kingdom for such a time as this?" (Est 4:4, AV).

45,46,50-52. Joseph was **thirty years old when he stood before Pharaoh,** having been in Egypt for twelve or thirteen years. From the prison to the palace in one day was a mighty step. God, who had been with the young man every minute of his life, had provided for this leap. Next, Pharaoh gave Joseph an Egyptian name – **Zaphnath–paa'neah** (which, in the Coptic, according to some scholars, signifies "a revealer of secrets," or, "the man to whom secrets are revealed"; cf. AV marg.). He also gave him a wife named **Asenath,** who was from one of the priestly families, her father being "prince," or **priest of On. On,** a city of culture and religion situated about seven miles north of Cairo, was the center of sun worship. To Asenath and Joseph were born two sons, Manasseh and Ephraim. These boys, some years later, were publicly adopted into the tribe of Jacob, and became heads of two tribes of Israel.

6) The First Visit of the Brothers. 42:1-38.

1-8. And Joseph's ten brethren went down to buy corn in Egypt . . . . But Benjamin . . . Jacob sent not with his brethren . . . lest . . . mischief befall him. When famine became severe in Canaan, and starvation seemed inevitable, Jacob knew that food must be procured elsewhere. He sent his ten sons to Egypt to buy grain. Benjamin he kept at home to be a comfort to him. When the ten brothers presented themselves before the **governor** of Egypt to buy grain, they did not recognize him as their brother. Twelve or more years had elapsed. The slender youth they had sold had grown into a man. He stood before them now as the mightiest figure in the land of Egypt. His language, his dress, his official bearing, and his position did their part in disguising him. But Joseph recognized his brothers at once.

9-12. When he accused his brothers of being spies, he was but calling their attention to the most obvious explanation of their coming. Egyptians realized that their eastern border was especially vulnerable, and so they feared the Asiatic peoples. Joseph accused the ten men of coming to Egypt to discover the weak places in the border defenses in order to give the information to would-be invaders.

13-24. When the men told him of their father and young brother, he demanded proof of their honesty. One of them, he said, must go home to bring the youngest son to Egypt while the others remained in prison. After keeping the men in **ward** for three days, Joseph suggested the easier solution of holding one of them as a hostage while the other nine went home with the grain. **Simeon** was selected to remain in prison (v. 24). He was Jacob's second son, and tradition holds that he was the most cruel of all the brothers.

21-24. In the course of the conversation, Joseph saw that his brothers were greatly concerned and remorseful. He sensed their loyalty to Jacob and their solid family spirit. **He . . . wept** as he thought of the old days and the suffering the men had caused by their hostility and cruelty, and as he recognized their change of heart.

25-38. On the way back to Canaan, one of Jacob's sons made the disturbing discovery that his money was in the top of his grain sack. And when the group reached home and emptied their sacks they found **every man's . . . money** in his sack. They were puzzled and alarmed by the discovery. The mystery of the money, the detention of Simeon, and the news that the Egyptian governor was demanding to see Benjamin—all were too much for the aged Jacob. His grief and fear almost overwhelmed him. And he would not agree to let his youngest son go back with the others to Egypt.

7) Further Experiences with the Brothers. 43:1-34.

1-14. When they had eaten up the corn . . . their father said . . . Go again, buy us a little food (v. 2). The men assured their father that they dared not go to Egypt without Benjamin. Only when Judah offered himself as surety for Benjamin's safety, would Jacob let his youngest go. Judah said: **Send the lad with me . . . . I will be surety for him.** Judah actually pledged his own life to guarantee the safe return of Benjamin (cf. 44:32-34). Surely the sons of Jacob had learned much since the day they had sought to kill Benjamin's brother. When Jacob saw that Benjamin had to go, he directed his sons to prepare a bountiful *minḥâ,* **present** (v. 11), for **the man**—some of the best honey, the choicest fruits, the rarest nuts, and other of the best delicacies of the land. He also directed them to take back double the money they had found in their sacks. No doubt the second portion of money was to be used to pay for the grain they were to purchase this time. Before sending his sons away, Jacob prayed that **God Almighty** *('El Shadday)* might keep them and supply every need (v. 14).

15-34. When they arrived in Egypt, they were startled to find that they were to go to the governor's house to dine. The news puzzled and alarmed them. They feared that some dreadful punishment was to be visited upon them, for they did not know what to expect from the grand vizier of Egypt. When the great man entered the room where they were, they **bowed themselves to him to the earth** in full homage (v. 26). Joseph treated them kindly and graciously, providing a banquet for them, at which he showered extra gifts on Benjamin. He found himself powerfully stirred as he had fellowship with them. It was an occasion the brothers could not forget. They feasted and drank largely. By the time the meal was over, Joseph knew the men much better; he knew that they had changed!

8) Judah's Sacrificial Proposal. 44:1-34. Joseph had one final test for his brothers, one calculated to give him a clear picture of their inner hearts.

1-5. He ordered his steward to prepare the bags of grain as before and place his silver goblet or bowl in the bag Benjamin would be carrying. **Put every man's money in his sack's mouth. And put my cup . . . in the sack's mouth of the youngest.** This goblet was a "divining cup" (cf. v. 5), a prized possession, used for receiving oracles or pictures of coming events. First, water was poured in. Then small fragments of gold, silver, or precious stones were thrown into the water. When the water was shaken slightly, the fragments formed a "picture" or pattern. Skilled users of the device claimed to be able to divine the unknown. It was a class of magic called "hydromancy."

6-13. Joseph had the brothers arrested as they set out on their journey toward Canaan. They protested their innocence and willingly accepted the decision that the guilty person should remain in Egypt as a slave for life. To their amazement, the goblet was found in Benjamin's sack! Brought before Joseph, they were speechless with fear and despair. What could any of them do? Reuben, Benjamin, and the others were silent.

14-34. Then Judah spoke for himself and his brothers in one of the sublime utterances of literature. He offered no excuse, made no denial, but simply pled with the mighty Egyptian official for the life and freedom of Benjamin. Sir Walter Scott called this plea "the most complete pattern of genuine natural eloquence extant in any language." The spirit of self-sacrifice, once so foreign to Judah, shone forth with rare beauty. Judah frankly confessed his own sins and the sins of his brothers. To be sure, they had not stolen the grain money nor the divining cup, but they had committed the black sin of selling their brother into slavery. They had caused Joseph and their father unspeakable grief and anguish. By his references to his father's suffering, Judah revealed himself as one now keenly aware of sacred values and relationships.

The older brother's willingness to become a *substitute* for Benjamin marks him as a great soul. He offered himself as Joseph's servant, and begged that Benjamin and his other brothers might be sent home to bless the heart of the old father. This was the climax of God's dealings with Judah. The Lord had created in him a spiritual champion to represent Him in working out the divine plan.

9) Joseph's Invitation to Jacob. 45:1-28.

1-8. Joseph could not refrain himself . . . . And he wept aloud . . . . And . . . said unto his brethren, I am Joseph. When Joseph could no longer restrain his feelings, he *gave forth his voice in weeping* (literally). In a moment he had disclosed his identity and opened his great heart to his brothers. They, in their confusion and fear, were speechless. But Joseph reassured them. He declared: **God did send me before you to preserve life** (v. 5). He quickly took from their shoulders all the blame for an ugly deed, as he sought to interpret to them the plan and purpose of God. It was his way of centering their attention on the one supreme consideration. The providential purpose was more significant than any minor act of mortal man. That purpose involved preserving alive a remnant who could be used to work out the Lord's will in the earth.

9-24. Joseph urged his brothers to bring their father and come to Egypt to live. He explained that the famine would last five more years, but that in Egypt he could provide a home and unlimited supplies for Jacob and the entire family group. They could settle in **the land of Goshen,** which was about forty miles from the site of present-day Cairo. Situated in the delta of the Nile, this section was the best of the land for herds and flocks. It was near On and also Memphis, where Joseph lived. When the brothers set out for home, he sent wagons along with them for the return trip to Egypt, and filled them with grain, presents, and supplies of all kinds.

25-28. As the old patriarch Jacob listened to his sons' report, **his heart became numb** (*fainted*, AV), for he could not believe the good news about his long-lost son (v. 26). But when he saw the wagons and presents, and heard Joseph's message to him, his spirit revived and he began to look forward to joining his son in Egypt. It was a day of comfort and rejoicing for one who had seen much grief.

10) The Migration to Egypt. 46:1-34.

1-4. Israel took his journey . . . and came to Beer-sheba. Jacob almost certainly was living at Hebron at this time. His first stop on his momentous journey to Egypt was at Beer-sheba. There he offered sacrifices, and there, in a night vision, God spoke to him, encouraging him in his move and assuring him of uncounted blessings. First, he renewed the promise that Jacob's descendants would become a great nation. He made it clear that Egypt was to be the land where this increase would take place. Second, he said: **I will go down with thee,** thus guaranteeing protection and security. Third, he said: **I will . . . bring thee up.** This prediction was destined to be fulfilled after Jacob's death, in the Exodus, when the mighty hand of God would deliver His chosen ones from the power of Egypt and bring them back to Canaan. The declaration that Joseph would **put his hand upon** Jacob's **eyes** was a prophecy that the illustrious son would perform the last rites at his father's death.

5-28. Encouraged by the message from the Lord, Jacob moved out, with his descendants, from Beer-sheba and proceeded on the long journey to the land of Goshen. He chose Judah to go forward in advance of the company (**sent Judah before him . . . to direct his face unto Goshen,** AV), to meet Joseph and complete the arrangements for their entrance into the land.

29,30. The meeting of Jacob and Joseph was a moment of great gladness. Both were too deeply moved to speak. They held each other in a strong embrace for **a good while** (v. 29). When the old patriarch could speak, he said: **Now let me die, since I have seen thy face, that thou art yet alive** (v. 30). He had experienced the topmost joy of life.

31-34. Before Joseph presented his family to Pharaoh, he gave them specific directions about how to reply to the ruler's questions. When asked about their calling, they were to represent themselves as shepherds. Then Pharaoh would likely assign them the land of Goshen as their dwelling place. Goshen would provide excellent grazing for their flocks and herds. They would be together, and therefore well protected from mixing with other peoples.

11) Jacob and Pharaoh. 47:1-12.

1-6. Then Joseph . . . told Pharaoh . . . My father and my brethren . . . are come. The meeting with Pharaoh was memorable. Five of the brothers, chosen for the purpose by Joseph, presented to the ruler their request that Goshen might be allotted to them, since they were shepherds. The king agreed that they should be settled in that area, where grazing was at its best. He also asked Joseph to name some of the best men among them, **men of activity** (v. 6), to be given places of responsibility among his cattlemen. Egypt spent much money and effort in breeding fine cattle.

7-10. The climax of the occasion was Joseph's presentation of his aged father to the king. **Jacob blessed Pharaoh** (v. 7). The word *bārak*, appearing twice, may be translated *saluted*, but the normal and strongly preferred meaning is **blessed.** At that moment the strong man of God stood before the great ruler with dignity and in the consciousness that he himself was the representative of the Almighty *('El Shadday). What could have* been more natural for him than to bestow a heaven-sent blessing on the king of Egypt. He knew that he held a sublime position in God's program. With quiet dignity he spoke the holy blessing upon Pharaoh. Jacob was a special channel of divine blessings, and Pharaoh was the recipient.

When asked his age, the patriarch replied. **The years of my sojourning** *(gûr)* **are an hundred and thirty years** (v. 9). His life had been marked by a series of *wanderings*. It seemed short to him in comparison with the longer lives of Abraham and Isaac.

11,12. The land of Rameses was identical with the land of Goshen. The eastern part of the delta of the Nile comprised an area that included the place of the famous city built by Rameses in a later generation. **Joseph nourished** *(yekalkēl)* **his father.** The particular form of the verb *kûl* used here (the pilpel) may mean "to nourish," "to sustain," or "to protect." It is clear that Joseph did all of these things in providing lavish care and love for Jacob.

12) The Food Administrator. 47:13-27. As the famine conditions grew worse, the Egyptians fell into dire need. The Scripture says, **There was no bread in all the land.** The people came to Joseph seeking food for their families. When their money gave out, they traded their cattle for grain (v. 17). Finally, they had to pledge their lands and their bodies to Pharaoh in order to secure more food (v. 19). Thus, all the lands of the realm, except the holdings of the priests, passed into the hands of Pharaoh. A full-fledged feudal system came into being. The government furnished the people seed, and the people paid 20 per cent of their yield to the state (vv. 23b, 24). It was a distressing situation, but the people agreed to it in order to eat. They said to Joseph: **Thou hast saved our lives . . . we will be Pharaoh's servants** (v. 25). The extreme emergency had made drastic measures necessary. And so the people of Egypt became serfs, and their land became the property of the state.

13) Jacob and the Sons of Joseph. 47:28–48:22.

29,30. And the time drew nigh that Israel must die. Jacob lived his declining years in peace, plenty, and happiness. Before the end of his life he made Joseph promise to take his body back to Canaan for burial. His life had been a tumultuous one; he had wandered far. But he wanted his bones buried beside those of Abraham, Isaac, Sarah, Rebekah, and Leah. The **burying place** mentioned by Jacob was the cave of Machpelah purchased by Abraham at the time of Sarah's death (cf. Gen 23). The body of Jehovah's chosen representative would be laid to rest with those of the other patriarchs. According to the narrative (v. 31), Jacob turned over on his face and stretched out so that his head was at the head of the bed. Thus he humbly and reverently prostrated himself. The other rendering, *bowed himself on the top of his staff*, has nothing to commend it over the Masoretic text.

Before Jacob died, he adopted Joseph's two sons, Manasseh and Ephraim, and thus raised them to the level of his own sons. Therefore, when the promised land was allotted to the tribes many years later, Joseph was represented by two full shares. Thus Rachel became the mother of three tribes in the kingdom of Israel.

48:1-14. Joseph brought his two boys to his father to receive his benediction. He arranged his sons so that Jacob's right hand would rest upon Manasseh, the elder boy, and his left hand upon Ephraim. But though Jacob was old and almost blind, he deliberately corrected the positions by laying his right hand on the head of the younger and his left hand on Manasseh. He knew what he was doing. When Joseph sought to change his father's hands so that Manasseh would receive the chief blessing (according to custom), he was informed that Ephraim was destined to receive it (v. 19). The patriarch's solemn blessing spoken upon the sons of Joseph was as binding as a last will and testament. In it Jacob included a prediction of future prominence for each of the boys, but Ephraim's growth and effectiveness was to be far beyond Manasseh's.

15-22. When the aged man came to pronounce a special blessing upon Joseph, he referred to God in a threefold title: The God of our fathers, the God who shepherded me, and the Angel of deliverance. Thus, the ancestral, the personal, and the redemptive aspects of God were represented. Hebrew *ro'eh* (AV, **fed**) carries the idea of shepherding (cf. Ps 23:1). **The Angel which redeemed me from all evil** (AV, v. 16) identifies this One with the Angel of Jehovah who comforted Hagar (16:7; 21:17) and who warned Abraham of the imminent destruction of Sodom (Gen 18); in other words, this "Angel" was the Lord himself in his OT manifestation. Jacob said that Joseph was to possess the special 'shoulder' *(sh^{e}kem)* or mountain slope of unusual value (AV, **one portion above thy brethren**). This probably refers to the property Jacob had acquired from Hamor, although Genesis 34 shows that Jacob repudiated the manner in which it was first taken. It was probably recaptured by Jacob later from the Amorites (cf. Jn 4:5).

14) The Solemn Blessing. 49:1-27.

1,2. Jacob called unto his sons, and said, Gather yourselves together . . . . and hear. In his farewell address to his sons, Jacob rose to the unusual stature of a prophet speaking in the poetic language of inspiration. He summoned each son in turn to his bedside to hear words of blessing, of censure, or of curse. In each case he singled out some striking trait of character as his appraisal of the man and his family group. Jacob's words constituted a prediction of future developments based on the father's knowledge of the character of each son. The men understood their father's solemn utterances to be significant and determinative predictions.

3,4. Reuben, the first-born of Leah, had enjoyed pre-eminence among his brothers. But he forfeited his natural rights. His place as the favored first-born was given to Joseph. His privileges as priest were to pass to the sons of Levi. His right to be the head of the tribes of Israel, i.e., his kingly right, would go to Judah. Thus Reuben, endowed with dignity, first-born rights, and natural excellencies, would forfeit every place of power and influence because of the instability of his character. His unspeakable sin with Bilhah gave evidence of moral weakness that spelled ruin. His uncontrolled passion (AV, **unstable as water**) is pictured in the Hebrew as "water without restraint pouring down in a foaming torrent" (v. 4). Though capable of dreams and plans and good intentions, he could not be counted on to carry them through to completion.

5-7. Simeon and **Levi,** Jacob's second and third sons by Leah, were brothers in violence. The old father could never forget their cruel massacre of the Shechemites. They revealed their true characters that day, for they violently attacked and destroyed men they had previously made helpless by strategy and deceit. At that time they were censured by their father. Now, as he lay on his death bed, they heard the biting words of his curse: **I will divide them in Jacob and scatter them in Israel** (v. 7b). They were not to have territory they could call their own, but would be dispersed among the other tribes. In Canaan this curse was fulfilled: the Simeonites were swallowed up into the tribe of Judah; the Levites had no territory assigned to them, but served as ministers of the sanctuary and teachers of Israel.

8-10. Judah, Jacob's fourth son by Leah, received the first unqualified praise from the old patriarch. He carried the hope of Israel upon his person. Having neither birthright nor exceptional dignity nor spiritual powers, he would emerge as the powerful leader of a people who could enthusiastically admire and praise him. (Judah means *praise.*) He would be feared by his enemies, for as a lion he would pursue them relentlessly until victory was his. Then, having completed his mission, he would retire to his mountain fastness to rest in the security of a stronghold that none could take. He would grasp in his hand the scepter or baton that would symbolize his mastery in the roles of warrior, king, and judge. Any nation could be happy, secure, and honored with Judah as its head and protector.

11,12. Peace, plenty and prosperity would prevail in Judah's land. The vines would be so flourishing and the grapes so abundant that the conquering rider could fasten his horse's reins to the large branches and enjoy the luscious fruit. The wine would be so plentiful that men could wash their clothes in it, if they chose. The choice grapes would provide the finest sustenance. Judah's eyes would not be red with excessive drinking (**red with wine,** v. 12, AV) but "bright with prosperity" (NBC), and his teeth would be "whiter than milk" (AV, **white with milk**). That is, Judah's land would be divinely blessed.

The phrase, **until Shiloh come,** was spoken by Jacob in the midst of his prophetic picture of Judah's place in the plan of God. For us, the unusual glow of his prediction is greatly enhanced by the fact that from ancient times it has been considered a Messianic message. The Hebrew may be rendered either, **until Shiloh come,** or *till he comes whose it is.* In either rendering the primary reference must be to Judah, but ultimately the Messiah is the true one who should come. In other words, the sovereignty would never depart from Judah until He came who had a right to reign. The prediction, *until he come whose right it is,* is repeated in Ezk 21:27. If this interpretation is correct, then Jacob's words here constitute one of the earliest appearances of the Messianic promise. That which Jacob was enabled to see was a clear picture of Judah's inheritance. But the full realization of God's purposes would not be enjoyed until the ideal ruler, the Messiah, demonstrated perfect sovereignty. Fortunately, the OT presents a distinct line of prophecies—beginning at Gen 3:15 and continuing through the Psalms and the Prophets—regarding Messiah's coming to reign as King of kings. Jacob saw Judah as the father of the royal tribe that would exert power and leadership over all the others. Through catastrophes and difficult times, God would see to it that the scepter would remain in the tribe of Judah until the ideal ruler, the Messiah, would come.

13. Zebulun, Jacob's sixth son by Leah, was to be situated in a place where commercial activity and prosperity would be possible. This may mean that territory along the seacoast was to be allotted to the tribe of Zebulun. Or, it may mean that prosperity would come to the descendants of Zebulun because of their proximity to the Phoenicians, who had unlimited access to the trade routes. Jacob mentions **Sidon** as being there. It is also possible that Jacob's prediction was not fully carried out when the final division of the land was made. In the song of Deborah (Jud 5) the people of Zebulun are warmly commended for their valorous stand against Sisera and his army.

14,15. Issachar, Jacob's fifth son by Leah, is represented as a strong, ox-like lover of rest and quiet. The word *ḥămōr,* literally, *bony ass,* does not refer to the wild, fleet, high-spirited animal that would catch the eye of the onlooker. On the contrary, it designates a powerful beast of burden that submits himself to the galling yoke without complaint in order that he may be free to lie quietly in ease and comfort. Thus Jacob was predicting that the tribe of Issachar would submit to the Canaanite invader, who would fasten the yoke upon them. Instead of fighting, the men of this tribe would submissively allow themselves to become slaves of the peoples of the land. They would prefer shame and slavery to courageous action.

16-18. Dan, the first son of Bilhah, would become a strong defender of his own people. He would plead their cause and defend and help them in their struggle for independence. The tribe would be small, but they would be greatly feared by neighbors who might seek to trample upon them. Jacob called Dan *a horned snake in the path* (AV **a serpent by the way,** v. 17), to cause terror and inflict quick, fatal wounds. Hebrew *nāḥāsh* signifies not only a snake in the grass, but a venomous reptile with deadly fangs. That is, Dan would be exceedingly dangerous to his foes. In later times members of the tribe of Dan fulfilled these words with remarkable accuracy. After a time in their original territory, the Danites moved to the north and occupied the northernmost point in Israel. These people were never distinguished for their spiritual attainments. In 931 B.C. Jeroboam set up a golden calf in Dan to provide opportunity for pagan worship.

19. Gad was the first son of Leah's handmaid, Zilpah. The aged patriarch recognized that the brave, warlike spirit of Gad would be a strong help to his people in the life in Canaan. Jacob predicted that Gad would need all his cunning, courage, and persistence in fighting, because he would be harassed by the continual attacks of desert tribes. Marauding bands would press down upon him. Jacob made use of a play on words—**Gad** meaning a *troop*—to indicate the ferocity and cruelty of the raiders from the desert. He foretold that Gad would be victorious and would be able to drive the enemy away. After the conquest of

Palestine, the tribe of Gad was stationed east of the Jordan.

20. Asher, Zilpah's second son, carried a name meaning *happy*. Jacob pictured him in a fertile field, where wheat and wine and oil would be produced in plenteous measure. He would be prosperous and would gain riches. The delicacies he would produce would be fit for the table of a king. (Even the kings of Tyre and Sidon would desire them.) The tribe of Asher witnessed the fulfillment of that patriarchal prophecy.

21. Naphtali, the second son of Bilhah, would demonstrate a remarkable love of freedom; he was a **hind let loose,** Jacob said. The illustration describes a wild, swift, graceful animal that delights in the freedom provided by wooded hills and open valleys. Naphtali was to have the run of God's great outdoors. **He giveth goodly words** is, perhaps, a reference to the eloquent and helpful discourses that would proceed from the mouths of men of this tribe. Barak, because of his valor, became one of their prize exhibits. In Jud 5:18 we read: "Zebulun and Naphtali were a people that hazarded their lives unto the death."

22. Joseph, the first son of Rachel, received the highest praise of all the sons. A man of vision, of dreams, of moral and spiritual strength, he exemplified all that was best in the realm of OT living. In his several roles as son, brother, slave, and administrator, he demonstrated his superior character through his unwavering loyalty to his God. Jacob called Joseph **a young fruit tree.** Hebrew *parâ* (AV, *fruitful bough)* contains a play on the name "Ephraim." The reference is to a vigorously growing tree or vine, connoting vitality and youthfulness. As a result of being planted by a bubbling fountain (AV, **well**), it would continue to grow and bear fruit. In the dry country, water made the difference between sterility and fruitfulness. Moisture guaranteed fertility. A tree so strengthened could be expected to throw its branches or its tendrils over the wall in giving its plentiful fruit to the peoples of the earth.

23. As a result of this exceptional prosperity, Joseph could expect bitter jealousy and hostility. **The archers** would be busy in their furious attacks. This had been true in Joseph's earlier days, when his brothers, embittered by envy, sought to destroy him. Many years later, in the land of Canaan, the tribes of Ephraim and Manasseh would encounter opposition and persecution. They would have to have a living faith in Jehovah of hosts, who had proved himself the all-sufficient God. Joseph knew him and had leaned on him in every emergency. **Sorely grieved . . . shot at . . . hated,** translate three Hebrew words. *Mārar,* in the piel form, means to "provoke," "embitter," "harass." The use of this piel form, plus the word *rābab* adds to the intensity of the action and speaks of its repeated occurrence. The third word, *sātam,* carries the idea of deep-seated hatred, along with active persecution.

24,25. His bow abode in strength. In Joseph's victories there had been evidences of the firm bow and the agile hands, the special power given by the Lord. Jacob predicted that this same supernatural help could be expected on the hills of Palestine. The word translated *firm* or **abode in strength,** could well be rendered *unmoved, enduring,* or *ever-flowing.* Jacob used the titles, **Mighty One of Jacob . . . the God of thy father,** and **the Almighty** *('El Shadday),* to portray the arm that would be so powerful, so dependable, so quick and agile that no foe could resist it. In simple faith he entrusted the tribe of Joseph into divine hands, and in confident faith he foretold certain victories over the enemies who awaited them. In addition to the special powers in dealing with foes, the descendants of Joseph were assured of bountiful blessings. From above, they would have abundant rain and dew. From beneath, the soil would be supplied with the ingredients that would make for food and harvests. By special divine gift, the fertility among men and animals would provide for the unending fruitfulness of the family.

26. In short, Joseph would always be considered a **prince among his brothers** (AV, *separate from his brethren*). Hebrew *nezîr* indicates "one set apart," or, "one who is separated or consecrated for high duties." The Nazarite was a man who had been given to God and by special vow was irrevocably committed to him. Ephraim, his son, was to have qualities that made for holy dedication to fulfill God's purpose for one who was chosen to put into action the principles so beautifully exemplified by Joseph. He was *the prince* among the tribes of Israel.

27. Benjamin, the younger son of Rachel, was characterized as a fierce, dangerous wolf that could do great damage. The wolf is keen and stealthy in his movements. At night he slips silently among the sheep and makes off with his prize. Hebrew *tāraf* means *to tear into shreds*. The old English word **ravin** means "to prey with rapacity." It speaks of fierce cruelty. The evening wolves could be as savage and destructive in the early morning. At any time they were ready for the fierce business of inhuman behavior. Ehud, Saul, and Jonathan were among the later descendants of Benjamin who gave evidence of their warlike powers. The men of this tribe became famous for their bowmen and their slingers (cf. Jud 5:14; 20:16).

15) Closing Days. 49:28–50:26.

28-33. When Jacob had finished his address of blessing, censure, and curse, he talked to his sons of his approaching death. In his final instructions, he directed his sons to take his body to Canaan for burial. **Bury me with my fathers in the cave,** he said, **that is in the field of Ephron** (v. 29). He reminded them that the family burial place already held the ashes of Abraham, Sarah, Isaac, Rebekah, and Leah. Rachel was buried in a tomb near Bethelehem (cf. 35:19,20). As soon as Jacob had finished his directions, **he gathered up his feet into the bed** and, without a struggle, **yielded up his spirit** *(rûah)* and passed into the presence of those who had already gone into the other world *(Sheol)*. The OT saints were far from the NT conception of life after death, but even in that early day they were aware of some unusual perceptions as they stood in the presence of the deceased members of the family. *Sheol* was the shadowy region where souls that had left the mortal body continued their existence.

50:1-3. Joseph revealed his strong affection for his father in continued emotional demonstration. The other sons, also, probably gave expression to their love. To make certain that Jacob's body was preserved from dissolution for the long journey to Hebron, Joseph called on his servants, the Egyptian physicians, to embalm it, **and the physicians embalmed Israel** (v. 2). The Egyptians were careful to preserve the body of a deceased person so that when the soul returned to take up residence again, the body would be ready for occupation. Egyptian mummies preserved for centuries bear silent witness to the remarkable efficiency of these embalmers. The word *rāphā'* means to "heal" or to "mend," by means of surgery or medicines. Physicians were plentiful in Egypt, and it is possible that they conducted the major part of the embalming. At any rate, Jacob's body was mummified for the journey, and must have been well preserved for the day of burial. **The Egyptians mourned for him threescore and ten days** (v. 3). Perhaps forty days were necessary for the embalming. Additional days were needed to complete the period of mourning, so that seventy days finally passed before the journey to Canaan began. The Egyptian nation, out of respect for Joseph, shared in the mourning.

4-6. In securing official permission to leave the kingdom, Joseph quoted his father's request that he be buried **in my grave which I have digged.** The Hebrew word ***kārâ*** may be translated *dig* or ***buy***. In Deut 2:6 it seems to mean "buy," but in this passage **digged** appears the better translation. Abraham bought the plot of land from Ephron to be used as a burial place for Sarah. There is no reason to object to the idea that Jacob went into the cave and **digged** from the rock his own grave.

7-13. With unusual pomp and display the Egyptian procession moved out from Goshen to make the long journey to Hebron. Chariots and horsemen, along with officials of Pharaoh's court and all the sons of Jacob, made up the funeral company. The Egyptians **wailed there with a very great and sore wailing** (v. 10). The natives marveled at the sight of the large company of mourners; they had never seen anything like it. At the cave of Machpelah **his sons . . . buried him.** Israel had come to the end of his eventful career.

14-21. Joseph, with his brothers, returned to Egypt to take up life again. Immediately fear seized the older sons of Jacob. They thought Joseph might now turn upon them and exact full revenge for their crime of selling him into slavery. They **fell down before his face** (v. 18) in grief, repentance, and entreaty. They begged for forgiveness and mercy. Joseph lovingly reminded them that the hand of God had been in all that had happened, that the Lord had purposed it for good. He assured them of his continued love and promised to provide for their needs during the remaining days of the famine. True to his kindly nature, **he spoke to their hearts** (v. 21; AV, *spake kindly*).

22-26. So Joseph died . . . and he was put in a coffin in Egypt. At the age of one hundred and ten Joseph died, having lived to be Jehovah's representative in a difficult crisis in the life of His chosen people. He exacted a solemn pledge from his brothers that they would keep his body safe until their return to Canaan, and then carry it to his homeland for burial. Cf. Heb 11:22: "By faith Joseph, when his end was nigh, made mention of the departure of the children of Israel: and gave commandment concerning his bones." His body was mummified and placed in a coffin (*'ārôn*) to await the long journey of forty years to Shechem. At the time of the Exodus, that mummy case was kept in the camp as a reminder that God's controlling hand is working out the divine will in all of life's struggles (cf. Ex 13:19).

Genesis closes with the renewal of the Lord's holy promises to his chosen ones and the challenge to move to the fulfillment of divine purposes for Israel. Joseph had gone on. A Pharaoh "who knew not Joseph" would come upon the scene to change the happy relationships provided by Joseph's wisdom, but a Moses would arise to take up the burden of leadership. The eternal Lord would not forget nor fail His people. The rich purposes revealed to the patriarchs would find fulfillment in His own hour.

BIBLIOGRAPHY

ALLEMAN, H. *Old Testament Commentary.* Philadelphia: Muhlenberg Press, 1948.

BENNETT, W. H. *Genesis (The Century Bible).* Edinburgh: T. & T. Clark.

CARROLL, B. H. *Genesis.* New York: Fleming H. Revell Company, 1913.

DELITZSCH, FRANZ. *A New Commentary on Genesis.* 2 vols. Edinburgh: T. & T. Clark, 1899.

DRIVER, S. R. *The Book of Genesis (Westminster Commentary).* London: Methuen, 1948.

ERDMAN, CHARLES R. *The Book of Genesis.* New York: Fleming H. Revell, 1950.

HERTZ, J. H. *The Pentateuch and Haftorahs.* London: Oxford University Press, 1929.

PFEIFFER, CHARLES F. *The Book of Genesis.* Grand Rapids: Baker Book House, 1958.

PIETERS, ALBERTUS. *Notes on Genesis.* Grand Rapids: Wm. B. Eerdmans, 1943.

RICHARDSON, ALAN. *Genesis 1–11.* London: S.C.M. Press, 1953.

RYLE, H. E. *The Book of Genesis.* Cambridge: The University Press, 1914.

SKINNER, JOHN. *Genesis (International Critical Commentary).* New York: Scribner's, 1925.

———. *The Divine Names in Genesis.* London: Hodder and Stoughton, 1914.

EXODUS

INTRODUCTION

Title. The name *Exodus*, a transliteration of the Septuagint (LXX) title *Exodos*, comes to us by way of the Latin Vulgate. The word in Greek means "departure" or "going out." The Hebrew name for the book is simply the first phrase, "These Are the Names," or more commonly, "Names." As a name descriptive of the whole book, *Exodus* is not satisfactory, for the actual departure from Egypt takes up less than half the volume.

Date and Authorship. The Scripture attributes the authorship of Exodus, with the other four books of the Pentateuch, to Moses. Higher criticism has made of these books a compilation of manuscripts, written by various authors from the ninth century to the fifth century B.C. The radical position that denied Moses any part at all in the writing of these books is no longer so widely held as it was a generation ago. Though many liberal scholars still question the Mosaic authorship of the Pentateuch, archaeological discoveries have given scholars of every theological background a higher respect for the historicity of the events it describes.

Historical Background. Exodus takes up the story of the Israelites where Genesis leaves off. The long period between Joseph and Moses is covered with two summary verses, 1:6,7, and then the entirely new situation of the descendants of Jacob is described. The favored guests of the Pharaoh and Joseph have become a nation of slaves, the objects of the fear and hatred of their rulers. As Pharaoh seeks by brutal oppression to control the Hebrews, God acts to deliver them. The deliverer, Moses, is first prepared, and then, in the power of God the great deliverance takes place. Redemption from the power of Egypt is more, however, than just a release from slavery. God has brought the Israelites out of Egypt that he may bring them, as his own prepared people, into the Promised Land. The great theme of Exodus, then, is not simply God's great redemptive act, but also his adoption and constitution of Israel as the people of God. E. E. Flack says, "Exodus is undoubtedly the most significant book dealing with the birth of a nation that has ever been compiled" ("Interpretation of Exodus," *Interpretation*, Jan., 1949). "All subsequent Hebrew history or philosophy of history as reflected in the prophets looked back to the Exodus as the creative act of God which constituted the Hebrews a nation" (Alleman and Flack, *Old Testament Commentary*, p. 207).

The date of the Exodus has been a problem to scholars for centuries, and with the discoveries of modern archaeology, the heat of discussion has increased, though the light of historical fact is still rather dim. The date has been set as early as 1580 B.C. and as late as 1230 B.C. Since the Scripture itself gives very little data for a chronology, it should be kept in mind that the date assigned to the Exodus is not a matter of doctrine, but simply of historical enlightenment. It is commonly thought that the Israelites came into Egypt when their Semitic cousins, the Hyksos, were ruling, possibly around 1700 B.C. If their sojourn in Egypt lasted 430 years (Ex 12:40), then the date of their departure must have been about 1270 B.C. Most of the archaeological evidence we have seems to point to a date some time in the thirteenth century. The builder of Pithom and Raamses (Ex 1:11), Rameses the Great, was ruling at that time. The date determined by excavation for the fall of numerous Canaanite cities, from Lachish to Hazor, is, again, the thirteenth century. The investigations of Nelson Glueck in Transjordan and the Negeb have established the fact that the nations of Moab, Ammon, Edom, and the Amorites were not settled there, ready to contest the advance of Israel, before the thirteenth century (cf. *The Other Side of Jordan* and *Rivers in the Desert*). The chief difficulty with dating the Exodus in the thirteenth century is found in I Kings 6:1. There we read that the Temple was started 480 years after the Exodus, in the fourth year of Solomon. Since the fourth year of Solomon was about 960 B.C., this seems to put the Exodus in the year 1440 B.C.; and this dating conflicts not only with the archaeological evidence but also with the dating gained from Exodus 12:40. A solution for the problem has been suggested by taking the years of I Kings 6 as meaning twelve generations, the actual time being no more than three hundred years. The fact that the exact date for the Exodus cannot be determined, however, does not detract from the historicity of the book nor from its great message of the redemption of God.

OUTLINE

- I. The liberation of Israel. 1:1–18:27.
  - A. Introduction. 1:1-7.
  - B. Bondage in Egypt. 1:8-22.
  - C. Preparation of the deliverer. 2:1–4:31.
    1. Birth and preservation of Moses. 2:1-25.
    2. Call and commission of Moses. 3:1–4:31.
  - D. The mission of Moses to Pharaoh. 5:1–7:7.
    1. Moses' first appearance before Pharaoh. 5:1-23.
    2. The renewed promise and command of Jehovah. 6:1-13.
    3. Genealogy of Moses and Aaron. 6:14-27.
    4. Moses sent back to Pharaoh. 6:28–7:7.
  - E. God's wonders in the land of Egypt. 7:8–11:10.
    1. Divine commission of Moses and Aaron attested. 7:8-13.
    2. The first plague—the Nile turned to blood. 7:14-25.
    3. The second plague—frogs. 8:1-15.
    4. The third plague—lice. 8:16-19.
    5. The fourth plague—flies. 8:20-32.
    6. The fifth plague—murrain. 9:1-7.
    7. The sixth plague—boils. 9:8-12.
    8. The seventh plague—hail. 9:13-35.
    9. The eighth plague—locusts. 10:1-20.
    10. The ninth plague—darkness. 10:21-29.
    11. Announcement of the last plague. 11:1-10.
  - F. The Passover, and the departure of Israel. 12:1–15:21.
    1. The consecration of Israel. 12:1-28.
    2. The tenth plague—God's judgment on Egypt. 12:29-36.
    3. The exodus from Egypt. 12:37–15:21.
       - a. The departure. 12:37-42.
       - b. Further regulations for Passover. 12:43-51.
       - c. Sanctification of the first-born. 13:1-16.
       - d. Passage through the Red Sea. 13:17–14:31.
       - e. The song of Moses. 15:1-21.
  - G. Israel in the wilderness. 15:22–18:27.
- II. Israel at Sinai. 19:1–40:38.
  - A. Establishment of the covenant at Sinai. 19:1–24:11.
  - B. Directions for the sanctuary and the priesthood. 24:12–31:18.
  - C. The covenant broken and restored. 32:1–34:35.
  - D. Building of the sanctuary. 35:1–39:43.
  - E. Erection and consecration of the sanctuary. 40:1-38.

COMMENTARY

I. The Liberation of Israel. 1:1–18:27.

A. Introduction. 1:1-7. These few verses serve to connect Exodus with the narrative of Genesis. After listing those who came down into Egypt with Jacob, the passage quickly moves over many intervening years and resumes the thread of the story in verse 7.

B. Bondage in Egypt. 1:8-22. The period after Joseph died brought a complete change in the condition of the Israelites. From being the favored people of the Semitic Hyksos rulers, they became the feared bondslaves of a new dynasty of native Egyptian kings. Oppressed by their Egyptian masters, the Israelites reached a state of absolute helplessness and despair, when God, in faithfulness to his covenant, redeemed them with mighty power.

8. A new king. The Hyskos invaders controlled Egypt from about 1720 B.C. until 1570. They were driven from the land by Amosis I, the founder of the Eighteenth Dynasty, perhaps the most brilliant age in Egyptian history. After the expulsion of the hated foreign kings, the enmity of the Egyptians was turned against all who had been associated with them, particularly the Hebrews, who were related to the Hyksos both by race and by position. Through the generations that followed, the condition of the Hebrews steadily declined, until we reach the times described here, just before the redemption. **9. More and mightier.** *Too numerous and too strong* (American Trans). **10. Let us deal wisely.** *Take precautions against them* (American Trans.); or, *handle them carefully* (Moffatt). There was a very real danger that the Hebrews, dwelling in Goshen, on the northeast border of the land, might join any invaders that might attack Egypt.

11. Pithom and Raamses. These cities are now located with a considerable degree of assurance at Tell er-Retabeh and at Tanis, both in the Delta region. Tanis is also known in Scripture as Zoan (Num 13:22), and was called Avaris by the Hyksos. Rameses-Tanis, which had been the Hyksos capital, was abandoned after their expulsion. In the Nineteenth Dynasty (1310–1200 B.C.) it was restored, and again became the capital of Egypt. In the providence of God, the only times in the long history of Egypt when the capital was so near the border of the land were the times when Israel was to enter and to depart. **12. They were grieved.** Better, *in dread* (RSV) or *apprehensive* (American Trans.). To the Egyptians there was an element of awe as well as loathing in the increase of the Hebrews, not only because of the danger mentioned in verse 10, but also because of the evidence of God's blessing in their greatly increased numbers.

15. Hebrew midwives. This may mean "Hebrew women" or "midwives of the Hebrew women," i.e., Egyptian women in charge of midwifery for the Hebrews. In either case they were probably the chief midwives, not the only ones. **16. Stools.** *Birth stools* (ASV; lit., *stones*). These were two stones, bricks, or low stools upon which it was the custom for the women to kneel or sit during delivery. **Daughter.** Daughters were spared, since they could be taken and married to Egyptians, thus losing their national identity. This distinction was often made in OT times, not only by the Hebrews but by other nations as well. **19.** The explanation given Pharaoh was only partly true. It is evident from God's rewarding blessing upon the midwives that they themselves took no precautions to prevent the preservation of males.

22. Every son that is born. The LXX, the Targums, and the RSV add the obvious explanatory words, "to the Hebrews."

C. Preparation of the Deliverer. 2:1–4:31. In the fullness of time, when the oppressor was doing his utmost to destroy Israel, God prepared the means of salvation.

1) The Birth and Preservation of Moses. 2:1-25. The exact date of Moses' birth, and the identification of the Pharaoh and his daughter are debatable, but the evidence of God's faithfulness is unmistakable. Upon the ground that there are vague parallels to this narrative in other ancient stories, the IB calls it "a legendary account." Upon this basis almost anything could be called unhistorical.

1. Man of the house of Levi. According to 6:20, this was Amram, who married his father's sister, Jochebed. **2. Goodly.** Hebrews 11:23 attributes this act of Moses' parents to their faith—"because they saw he was a proper child." They took the robust, handsome appearance of the baby as evidence that God had given him for a great purpose.

3. Bulrushes. Probably the papyrus reeds so plentiful in the Nile. **Slime and . . . pitch.** Bitumen and pitch, or asphalt. **By the river's brink.** Very likely the child was placed where the mother knew that the king's daughter was accustomed to bathe (KD). The whole act, including placing the sister to watch, makes it evident that this was not simply abandoning the child to the mercy of the river in a faint hope that he would be rescued. **5.** The bathing may have been an act of worship and the rescue may have been an act of piety rather than of mere pity (Alleman and Flack, *op. cit.*).

9. There was divine irony in this situation in which the destined deliverer was not only preserved but supported by those whom he would one day defeat.

10. Moses. The Hebrew means *drawn*

out, or *drawn forth*. Many critics believe that the Hebrew for Moses (*Mōsheh*) is derived from the Egyptian *mesi*, meaning "to bear." In the process of being born, a child is drawn forth; in this instance the child was called Moses because he was drawn from the water. Some scholars, however, doubt that there is any connection with the Egyptian *mesi*.

11. Looked on. "Contemplated with sympathy" (*Cambridge Bible*). **12.** By this act Moses irrevocably cast in his lot with his brethren (cf. Heb 11:24-26). **14.** Moses had presented himself to his people as their champion, but they were not ready for the redemption, and neither was he. "It was by the staff and not by the sword–by the meekness and not by the wrath of Moses that God was to accomplish the great work of deliverance" (JFB). Acts 7:25 expresses the pathetic thought, "He supposed his brethren would have understood."

15. This thing. It was not so much the murder as the rebellion implicit in it that aroused the anger of Pharaoh (cf. Heb 11:27). **Midian.** The Midianites were a group of tribes descended from Keturah and Abraham (Gen 25:1-4). Although their home seems to have been on the east side of the Gulf of Aqaba, they were a nomadic people and wandered up into Palestine and down into the Negeb and the Sinai Peninsula. According to Ex 3:1, those Moses met must have been dwelling in the vicinity of Mount Sinai. The attempt to confine the Midianites to one area and locate Mount Sinai east of Aqaba (T. Meek, *Hebrew Origins; et al.*) does not agree with Scripture and seems quite unfounded.

16. Priest of Midian. The Scripture does not indicate what god he served. It may indeed have been Jehovah, as some claim, but the words of Jethro in Ex 18:11 sound more like the testimony of a convert. There is absolutely no reason to suppose, as some writers have done, that Moses learned of Jehovah from the Midianites (cf. Meek, *et al.*). **17.** Compassion for the oppressed was a part of Moses' character. **18. Reuel.** The name means *friend of God*. He is also called Jethro (3:1; 4:18). In Num 10:29 the AV translators inconsistently followed the LXX and transliterated the name *Raguel*.

22. Gershom. The name means *a stranger here*. A second son, Eliezer, *God is my help*, is named in 18:3.

23. Process of time. *Course of those many days* (ASV, RSV). According to Acts 7:30, the period was forty years, or one generation. If we take the thirteenth century date for the Exodus, then the king who died would have been Seti I (1319–1301), or possibly Rameses I, the founder of the Nineteenth Dynasty. The new king would have been Rameses II, one of the greatest of all Pharaohs (1301–1234). **24,25.** God had waited long and been silent, but he had never forgotten nor abandoned his people. He **heard . . . remembered . . . . looked** and *knew their condition* (RSV).

2) The Call and Commission of Moses. 3:1–4:31. Trying to redeem Israel in his own way and at his own time, Moses failed. But in God's time he was called upon to deliver in God's way and by God's power.

1. Horeb. Horeb is called **the mountain of God** by anticipation. In the OT Horeb and Sinai are used as equivalent terms, although the former name may refer to the range of mountains and Sinai to a particular peak. It is impossible to know with certainty which of the many peaks, the highest rising to some 8,000 feet, is the place where Moses met God. The tradition, at least 1800 years old, that locates the mount as Jebel Musa, "Mount of Moses," must have some sort of foundation, and the peak called **Horeb** is surely in the vicinity of that "mount." The monastery of St. Catherine is supposed to be on the exact spot of the burning bush! (Cf. further on 19:1) **2.** As Israel was not consumed in her furnace of affliction, so the thorn bush aflame was not consumed, for God was there. **Angel of the Lord.** This was not just *an* angel, but a manifestation of Jehovah himself (v. 4; cf. Gen 16:7; 22:11; 31:11-13; 48:15,16).

7,8. I have . . . seen . . . heard . . . know . . . . am come down to deliver. Not Moses but God was to be the Redeemer. **Milk and honey.** A proverbial expression for great fertility and abundance. **The place of the Canaanites.** God had waited more than four hundred years for a sign of repentance. Now the iniquity of the Amorite nations was full (cf. Gen 15:16).

11,12. Who am I. The confident, impulsive Moses had learned humility; now he had to learn faith. Each of Moses' difficulties was met by assurances from God. **Who am I** was not important, for **I will be with thee.**

14. I am that I am. Other translations of this difficult phrase include: I AM WHO I AM (RSV); *I will be what I will* *be* (Moffatt; Luther); *I am the existing One (Catholic Commentary); I cause to be what comes to pass* (Meek, *op. cit.*, p. 107; and Wm. F. Albright, *From the Stone Age to Christianity*, p. 260). The name expresses "not abstract existence, but active manifestation of existence . . . not what God will be in Himself . . . but what He will approve Himself to others . . . . He will be to Moses and His people what He will be – something which is undefined, but which as His full nature is more completely unfolded, by the lessons of history and the teachings of the prophets, will prove to be more than words can express" *(Cambridge Bible)*. A similar thought is expressed by Keil and Delitzsch: "The question [v. 13] . . . . presupposed that the name expressed the nature and operations of God and that God would manifest in deeds the nature expressed in the name . . . [He] designated Himself by this name as the absolute God . . . acting with unfettered ability and self-dependence." Commenting on the name Jehovah in Gen 2:4, the same scholars say: "He is the personal God in His historical manifestation in which the fullness of the Divine Being unfolds itself to the world . . . the God of the history of salvation. This is not shown in the etymology of the name but in the historical expansion." God, then, revealed himself to Moses not as the Creator-God of power–Elohim, but as the personal God of Salvation, and all that "I am" contains shall be manifested through the ages to come, culminating in him whose "I am" lights the pages of the NT.

15. My memorial. *By this I am to be remembered* (RSV). **16,17. I have surely visited.** The time for the fulfillment of Joseph's promise had come (Gen 50:25).

18. Met with us. Literally, *lighted upon us* in a sudden, unexpected way. **Three days' journey.** Probably a current expression for a considerable distance. "God knew the hard heart of Pharaoh, and therefore directed that no more should be asked at first than he must [either] grant or display the hardness of his heart . . . . It was an act of mercy to Pharaoh, therefore, that the entire departure of the Israelites was not demanded at the very first audience of Moses . . . for, had this been demanded, it would have been far more difficult for him to bend his heart in obedience to the divine will, than when the request presented was as trifling as it was reasonable. And if he had rendered obedience to the will of God in the smaller, God would have given him strength to be faithful in the greater" (KD). **19. No, not by a mighty hand.** *Unless compelled by a mighty hand* (RSV).

22. Borrow. The command was not to **borrow** but to *ask* (ASV, RSV), a request which, under the circumstances, was a demand. Thus the Israelites received a recompense for their years of toil by 'spoiling' the Egyptians.

4:1. They will not believe me. Moses' third difficulty, like the others, was centered in himself. The signs provided by God would not only be a testimony to Israel and Egypt of God's presence with his messenger, but they would also assure and strengthen the faith of Moses. **2-4.** The first sign. The shepherd's rod, surrendered to God, became a sign of power and victory over the enemy. **6,7** The second sign. The defiled, leprous hand of Moses symbolized Israel's own afflicted state, her need of God's cleansing power. **9.** The third sign. **River.** Literally, *the Nile*. As the Nile, the life-stream of Egypt, was in the power of God's messengers, so also were Pharaoh and all his people in Moses' hand.

10. Moses' final difficulty. God makes no mistakes. He had formed Moses; He knew what he was capable of doing. **12. I will be with thy mouth.** "Moses' stammering as God's faithful servant will be adequate enough" (IB). **13. Send, I pray, some other person** (RSV). This last statement of Moses is not as direct a refusal as the RSV translation makes it appear, but it indicates what was behind all the objections. In the weakness of the flesh, Moses simply did not want to go back to Egypt. God stooped to this weakness and provided Aaron as Moses' "prophet." As the story progresses, however, it seems that Moses, with growing courage, more and more took his proper place as leader.

18-31. Moses' return to Egypt. **18.** Since Moses was in the service of Jethro, he had to ask permission to leave. He could not tell his father-in-law the incredible story of the revelation and commission of God, but simply said he wished to go back to see how his brethren were. **20. The rod of God in his hand.** Poor though his outward appearance may have been, he had in his hand the staff before which the pride and might of Pharaoh and all Egypt would bow.

21-23. This is the substance and culmination of God's dealings with Pharaoh.

The hardening of Pharaoh's heart was the divine judgment upon one who had already hardened his own heart against the Lord.

24-26. This passage, which is dismissed by many modern commentators as a curious relic of folklore and superstition, is in fact an illustration of a spiritual law that runs throughout Scripture and history: He who would proclaim God's will to others, must himself be obedient to the express will of God. The sign of circumcision, decreed by God (Gen 17:9-14) had been neglected by Moses until God forcibly reminded him of the obligation by this stroke. **You are my bridegroom in blood by this circumcision** (v. 26; Moffatt). This act of Zipporah, evidently repugnant to her and delayed until it almost cost her husband's life, may have decided Moses to leave her and the children in Midian. Nothing was to hinder his service for the Lord.

D. The Mission of Moses to Pharaoh. 5:1–7:7. Moses and Aaron appeared before Pharaoh to make known God's will. Their request was harshly refused, and the tribulation of Israel was increased by command of the king. Thus the Israelites were brought to their lowest state of helpless despair and suffering in order that the grace and power of God alone might be manifest in their redemption. The genealogies of Moses and Aaron are inserted in this passage to make clear their relationship to Israel as God's accredited leaders.

1) Moses' First Appearance Before Pharaoh. 5:1-23.

1. Hold a feast. This might better be translated, *make a pilgrimage*. The Hebrew *ḥag*, "feast," was accompanied by a pilgrimage (cf. 23:14-17). "The demand presented to Pharaoh on the part of the God of the Israelites . . . appears so natural and reasonable that Pharaoh could not have refused their request if there had been a single trace of the fear of God in his heart" (KD).

2. Who is the Lord? Pharaoh's sneering question was soon to be thoroughly and terribly answered. **4.** Pharaoh considered Moses merely a crafty leader trying to get better working conditions for the Israelites. **Mind your own business** (American Trans.). **5. People of the land.** That is, common workpeople.

6. Taskmasters . . . officers. Egyptian taskmasters dealt with Israelite officers, *shōṭᵉrîm*, perhaps scribes or timekeepers. **7.** The use of chopped straw mixed with the clay increased more than three times the breaking strength of the brick, and Egyptian bricks were usually made this way (cf. BA, xiii, 2). **14.** When the impossible task was not performed, the punishment fell most severely on the Hebrew officers.

16. The fault is in thine own people. "Thou sinnest against thine own people" (LXX). The exact translation and meaning of this text is uncertain, but the Hebrews were undoubtedly defending themselves by placing the blame for their failure where it belonged. **19. In evil case.** The mission of the officers failed to get any relief for the people. **20. They met Moses.** Literally, they *stationed themselves* to meet them. **21. Savour to be abhorred.** "They call upon God to judge whilst by their very complaining they show that they have no confidence in God and His power to save" (KD).

22. Why. How incomprehensible it must have seemed to Moses that God, who had sent him to deliver Israel, had led him, instead, to be the cause of greater suffering.

2) The Renewed Promise and Command of Jehovah. 6:1-13. Critics take this as a parallel account, not a sequel, to the account in Exodus 3–6. Their assumption is quite uncalled for; the promise is affirmed quite differently, and the need for further assurance on the part of Moses is abundantly evident.

1. With a strong hand. *He will be forced* (Moffatt), compelled by God's mighty power. **3. God Almighty.** Hebrew *'El Shaddāi*. The derivation and meaning of *Shaddāi* is uncertain. Probably the translation **God Almighty** is as near as any to the thought contained in the name. It is possible that the name "Jehovah" was not known to the patriarchs, but that is not necessarily the significance of the statement here. God had not revealed himself in his character of "Jehovah" to Abraham as he was now about to do to Israel. As Jehovah, God was now going to redeem the people of Israel (v. 6), adopt them as his people (v. 7), and bring them into the Promised Land (v. 8). By this they would learn the nature of the God who said, **I am Jehovah** (v. 2, ASV).

4,5. The redemption of Israel was based upon the covenant with the fathers and was its fulfillment. **Land of their pilgrimage.** *The land in which they settled as immigrants* (Moffatt). **6. Redeem.** The Hebrew word means "to reclaim, to vindicate the rights." **7. Ye shall know.** One of the great reasons for the Lord's presenting the extraordinary demonstrations of his might, which were to come, was that he might sharply imprint upon the mind and conscience of Israel the fact that he, Jehovah, was God. **9. Anguish of spirit.** Their suffering was too great to be relieved by mere words.

10-13. Moses was charged again to present to Pharaoh the request of the God of Israel. Before the carrying out of this charge is described, the genealogy of Moses and Aaron is given. **Uncircumcised lips** (v. 12). Lips covered as with a foreskin, so that they open and close with difficulty (cf. 4:10).

3) Genealogy of Moses and Aaron. 6:14-27.

14. Fathers' houses. The "house" or "family" descended from a single ancestor. "House" may denote a whole tribe, but usually it indicates the main subdivision or clan. Thus **Hanoch, Pallu, Hezron, and Carmi** were the ancestors, **heads,** of the four main clans of the tribe of Reuben. **18. Amram** the son of Kohath was an earlier ancestor of Amram the father of Moses (v. 20). **27. Moses and Aaron.** As the elder brother (cf. 7:7), Aaron appears first in the genealogy (v. 26); but as the appointed leader, Moses takes precedence when the narrative resumes.

4) Moses Sent Back to Pharaoh. 6:28–7:7. The narrative now resumes as the Lord gives specific directions to Moses concerning his mission.

7:1. Made thee a god. Better, *made thee as God* (ASV, RSV). Moses was given divine authority and power over Pharaoh, while Aaron was commissioned to serve as Moses' prophet or spokesman. This was to be no repetition of the first encounter with Pharaoh. **3. Harden.** *Make obstinate* (American); or *make stubborn* (Moffatt). This is not the usual word for hardening; it is found also in Ps 95:8. **4. Mine armies, and my people.** Better, *my people in their hosts* (Moffatt). **5. Egyptians shall know.** The second great reason for God's display of mighty power. Israel was to know (6:7) by redemption, Egypt by judgment, that **I am Jehovah. 6.** This verse summarizes, and introduces the next major section.

E. God's Wonders in the Land of Egypt. 7:8–11:10. The plagues by which God manifested himself to Israel and Egypt are called by various terms in the Bible: *maggēpâ,* "a severe blow" (9:14), used in I Sam 4:17 for a great defeat in war; *negaʿ* "a heavy touch or stroke" (Ex 11:1), used in Leviticus, chapters 13 and 14, for the stroke of leprosy; *negep* (Ex 12:13), cognate with *maggēpâ,* "a severe blow," used only of the tenth plague, and usually of a calamity inflicted by God in judgment (Josh 22:17). By these awe-inspiring strokes from the hand of God, the people were to be made aware that "I am Jehovah."

The first nine plagues clearly fall into three groups of three each. Numbers one and two, four and five, seven and eight were announced to Pharaoh, beforehand, but three, six, and nine came without warning. The first three fell upon both Israel and Egypt, for both nations had lessons to learn. The last two groups fell upon the Egyptians only, that they might know that God who was caring for Israel was God also in Egypt (Ex 8:22) and greater than all other gods (9:14). The plagues were progressively more severe, the last three almost destroying the land (10:7). The tenth plague is discussed in the next division of the text. It is thus set apart from the others because it was not only the culmination of the judgment and the basis of the redemption, but also because it was a direct visitation from God, not a judgment through secondary causes. The first nine plagues were *natural* wonders, in the sense that they were intensifications of distresses such as were already known in the ordinary course of history. Their severity, and even more, their appearance and disappearance at the word of Moses marked them as miraculous. They had their effect upon the Egyptians not only physically and mentally, but also spiritually. Each plague was directed against some phenomenon of nature worshiped by the Egyptians as in some way related to the gods.

1) Divine Commission of Moses and Aaron Attested. 7:8-13.

9. Prove yourselves by working a miracle (RSV). **11. Wise men . . . sorcerers . . . magicians.** These were not common tricksters, but the highly educated, priestly leaders of Egypt, men of vast influence and skill. Whether they performed their feat by some sort of trick with trained reptiles, or by a Satanically empowered "lying wonder" cannot be determined. In either case the supremacy of Jehovah was demonstrated when their serpents were swallowed up.

13. Hardened. Made strong, firm. Three words are used for the hardening of Pharaoh's heart: *ḥāzaq,* "to be or make strong" (7:13,22; 8:19); *kābēd,* "to be or make heavy, slow to move" (7:14; 8:15,32); and *qāshâ,* "to harden" (only in 7:3). The usual translations obscure the fact that it is always clearly stated when it was God who did the hardening (9:12; 10:1,20,27, *et al.*) and when it was Pharaoh who hardened his own heart. God hardens only "those who begin by hardening themselves. . . . the means by which God hardens a man is not necessarily by any extraordinary intervention on His part; it may be by the ordinary experiences of life, operating through the principles and character of human nature which are of His appointment" *(Cambridge Bible).*

2) The First Plague—The Nile Turned to Blood. 7:14-25.

15. He goeth out unto the water. An act of devotion? If the purpose of Pharaoh's visit was to worship, he would find his very god made loathsome by a greater power. **17. In this thou shalt know.** Pharaoh was now to have the answer to his scornful, "Who is Jehovah?" (5:2). **Turned to blood.** Each year, toward the end of June, when the waters of the Nile begin to rise, they are colored a dark red by the silt carried down from the headwaters. This continues for three months, until the waters begin to abate, but the water, meanwhile, is wholesome and drinkable. The miracle of 7:17-21 involved three elements by which it differed from the accustomed phenomenon: the water was changed by the smiting of Moses' rod; the water became undrinkable; and the condition lasted just seven days (v. 25).

19. Streams. The Nile and its arms. **Rivers** (lit., *their Niles).* Nile canals, irrigation ditches. **Ponds.** Standing lakes formed by the flooding rivers. **Pools** (lit., *every gathering).* Cisterns and reservoirs. **Vessels.** Not a drop was taken up in these vessels that was not contaminated. The listing of all the sources of water makes it evident how completely Egypt was smitten by the plague. **22,23. Magicians . . . did so.** By some means the magicians changed the appearance of some water into that of blood, and Pharaoh's heart **remained hardened** (American), or, *did not heed even this* (Moffatt).

25. Seven days. It has been thought that the first plague may have taken place near the time of the Nile inundation in June. Since the final plague occurred in the spring, it seems that the judgments on Egypt were spread out over most of a year.

3) The Second Plague—Frogs. 8:1-15. There have always been frogs filling the marshes along the Nile. At the word of Moses, however, they appeared in such numbers and so invaded every conceivable place that they became an unbearable nuisance.

7. Magicians did so. Though they did in some way produce more frogs, they were utterly helpless to remove any. **8.** Pharaoh was so discomposed by this repulsive situation that he was ready to promise anything. He had already been forced to acknowledge the God whom he had disdained. **9. Glory over me.** *You may have the honor of saying* (Moffatt). **15. Respite** (lit., *open space).* "As soon as he 'got air' he hardened his heart" (KD).

4) The Third Plague—Lice. 8:16-19. Lice (ASV, AV), gnats (RSV), sand fleas (ERV), and mosquitoes (Moffatt) have all been suggested as the instruments of this plague. Although the exact meaning of the Hebrew word is not known, mosquitoes, which are well known in Egypt, seem to be peculiarly fitting. It is to be noticed that this again was the intensification of a natural experience. The plagues were also intensifying from an inconvenience to a painful affliction.

17. Dust of the earth. "Just as the fertilizing water of Egypt had twice become a plague, so through the power of Jehovah, the soil so richly blessed became a plague to the king and his people" (KD). **19. The finger of God.** The helpless magicians acknowledged that this was supernatural. They did not attribute it to Jehovah, but confessed that it was beyond their mortal powers. The fact that they had duplicated somewhat the earlier plagues, makes their capitulation more striking. Since there is no time limit expressed for this plague, we may assume that it continued for some time.

5) The Fourth Plague—Swarms of Flies. 8:20-32. The second triad of plagues distinguished between Israel and the Egyptians. The confession of the magicians that "a god" had brought these disasters, was now to be enforced and the fact made clear that it was *the* God, Jehovah, that was the cause.

21. Flies. The word denotes some particularly irritating kind of insect, whether flies or gnats. The Hebrew word for "swarm" means *a mixture* and may signify the increase of all kinds of verminous scourges. **22. Sever.** *Set apart* (ASV, RSV). By the fact that Israel would be protected from all the future plagues, it would be made clear whose God was in power. **23. Division** (lit., *redemption*). The separation was a deliverance for Israel. **24. Corrupted.** *Destroyed* (ASV marg.); *ruined* (RSV). The plagues were still increasing in severity; they were now not simply a nuisance, but a danger. The people suffered, the work was hindered, and the whole economy was dislocated.

26. Abomination of the Egyptians. Whether Moses referred to the manner of sacrifice or to the victim, held by the Egyptians to be sacred, the people of Egypt would have regarded the act "as a manifestation of contempt for themselves and their gods" *(Calvin's Commentaries)*. **28.** For the second time Pharaoh gave his permission for the Israelites to leave; but the removal of the plague, in spite of the warning of Moses (v. 29), banished his fear, and he denied the pledge.

6) The Fifth Plague—Murrain. 9:1-7.

3. Camels. This mention of camels has been called anachronistic; but there were camel caravans constantly coming into Egypt, and certainly some Egyptians must have had a vested interest in them. **Murrain.** *Severe plague* (RSV); *deadly pest* (Moffatt). What specific disease this was is not known, but it must have been a severe and deadly epidemic that attacked all kinds of livestock. **6. All the cattle.** As often in Hebrew, the term **all** designates a great number. We say in English, "Everybody is sick," meaning only that sick folk are encountered everywhere. This plague was to come upon those cattle that were in the fields (v. 3).

7) The Sixth Plague—Boils. 9:8-12. Like the third plague this was not announced but simply came as Moses acted.

8. Ashes. Literally, *soot from the kiln.* The kiln was a symbol of the commercial and artistic wealth of Egypt. As disaster had come from the natural resources of the river and the land, so now industry provided the source of new trouble. **9. Boil breaking forth into sores** (RSV). An inflamed painful boil or abscess, breaking into a running sore, exceedingly painful and wretched but not fatal. **10. Stood before Pharaoh.** He took his place before the king so that there might be no question of the source of this new plague. **11.** The magicians not only could not duplicate the plague, but they themselves were in helpless misery. **12.** As the last triad of judgment was about to come, God hardened Pharaoh's heart lest out of sheer human weakness he should surrender before God had accomplished all His will.

8) The Seventh Plague—Hail. 9:13-35.

14. All my plagues upon thine heart. These last plagues would not fall simply as warnings and sufferings, as the others had done. They would "not only strike the head and the arms, but penetrate the very heart and inflict a mortal wound" (Calvin). **15. Cut off from the earth.** Never again did Egypt rise to the height of power and glory reached in this dynasty. **16. For this cause . . . made thee to stand** (ASV). Pharaoh was to experience the power and might of Jehovah, and in his experiences the whole world would learn about the Lord. "As both the rebellion of the natural man against the word and will of God and the hostility of the world power to the Lord and His people were concentrated in Pharaoh . . . (this) should be typical for all times and circumstances of the kingdom of God in conflict with the world" (KD).

17. Exaltest thou thyself. "A peculiar word found only here . . . raisest up thyself as a mound or obstacle against my people" *(Cambridge Bible)*. **19.** Opportunity was now given to those Egyptians who had come to believe in the word of Jehovah to distinguish themselves from those who had not.

23. Hail, thunder, and lightning are not unknown in Egypt, but the terrible fury of such a storm as this had never been known before in all Egypt's long history. **27.** How often a great natural disaster causes even the most ungodly man to cry out in fear and helplessness! Such confessions are not the result of real heart conviction of sin but arise only from the terror of the circumstances. **29,30.** Moses would again manifest Jehovah's supreme control, but he had no illusions concerning the steadfastness of Pharaoh's repentance. It was the terrible storm, not Jehovah, that Pharaoh feared.

31. Flax and . . . barley. Since these ripen in February, the season of year for this plague is fixed. **32. Wheat and . . . spelt** (ASV). Spelt is an inferior kind of wheat; *rye* (AV) was not known in ancient Egypt. These grains ripen about a month after the flax and barley.

9) The Eighth Plague—Locusts. 10:1-20.

2. What things I have wrought. *How I have mocked* (ASV marg.). *How I have made sport* (RSV). God was not amusing himself, but there was divine irony in the fact that the antagonism of Pharaoh was simply leading to the greater manifestation of the glory of Jehovah. **4-6.** That locusts were known and feared for their devastation only made this warning more fearful. Such locust plagues as the Egyptians suffered before would be nothing in comparison with this. **7. Do you not yet understand that Egypt is ruined?** (RSV) Only Pharaoh seemed unaware of the extent of the damage, or insensible to it.

8. Who are they (lit., *who and who*). Who, exactly, shall go? **10.** Pharaoh's answer to the demand that the whole nation depart was at first cynical: "May the Lord be with you if ever I let you go." He hoped, suggests the IB, "that the divine protection on the journey" might be "as non-existent as his permit to go." Then he accused them, "You have some evil purpose" (RSV). **11.** Go then, ye men, for that is what you actually desire. If you are honest, you know that only men are required to sacrifice. **Driven out.** The prolonged interview concluded with this burst of Pharaoh's anger.

13. "The fact that the wind blew a day and a night before bringing the locusts, showed that they came from a great distance, and therefore proved to the Egyptians that the omnipotence of Jehovah reached far beyond the borders of Egypt and ruled over every land" (KD). **16.** The shock of this visitation again brought Pharaoh to his knees, confessing sin and begging for the removal of the plague. **17. This death.** The locusts had all but completely destroyed what was left of the vegetation of Egypt.

10) The Ninth Plague—Darkness. 10:21-29. The ninth plague followed the eighth with no introduction, request, or warning.

21. Darkness which may be felt. Most scholars agree that the darkness was probably caused by the *ḥamsîn,* the fierce sandstorm so dreaded in the East. The hot dry wind, like the blast of a furnace, fills the air with sand and dust, so that the sun is blotted out. The heat, the dust, and the static electricity make conditions almost unbearable physically. Added to this is the effect on mind and spirit of the thick and oppressive darkness. This plague concluded the manifestation of God's wonders and was a forbidding prelude to the final act of judgment. **23. Light in their dwellings.** Miraculous and instructive was the sharp demarcation between Israel and Egypt.

24. Pharaoh almost capitulated. **Only let your flocks . . . be stayed.** Placed in deposit, as it were, as a guarantee of their return. **25. Give us also sacrifices.** That is, you must give us the means of sacrificing, and therefore (v. 26) we must take all our cattle. **28.** To let the whole nation go, with no assurance at all that they would return, was too much for Pharaoh. He terminated not only this interview but also all further interviews with Moses by a threat of death. **29.** God had already informed Moses (11:1) that this was to be the last appeal to Pharaoh, and so Moses responded, **Thou hast spoken well.** Before the prophet departed, however, there was one last message he had to give (11:4-8).

11) Announcement of the Last Plague. 11:1-10. The critical approach to Scripture has made a great deal of unnecessary confusion in determining the proper sequence here. It seems clear that 11:1-3 refers to instructions given previously to Moses, while 11:4-8 is the parting warning to Pharaoh, following 10:29.

1. Thrust you out. The Egyptians would be so anxious for the Israelites to leave that, far from hindering them, they would urge them to go. **2. Ask.** Cf. 3:22. **4. About midnight.** Not midnight of the day in which he was speaking, but midnight of the day appointed byy God (cf. 12:6). **5. All the firstborn.** "The first-born represented the whole race of which it was the strength and bloom" (KD). **7.** Not even the barking of an unfriendly dog would hinder Israel's departure. **8. Get thee out.** Moses' assurance was God's promise (v. 1).

9. Pharaoh shall not hearken. Had Pharaoh listened, even at this extremity, he would still have found a door of hope open; but he would not listen (cf. Mt 23:37).

F. The Passover, and the Departure of Israel. 12:1–15:21.

1) The Consecration of Israel. 12:1-28. "The deliverance of Israel from the bondage of Egypt was at hand; also their

adoption as the nation of Jehovah (6:6,7). But for this a divine consecration was necessary that their outward severance from the land of Egypt might be accompanied by an inward severance from everything of an Egyptian or heathen source. This consecration was to be imparted by the Passover" (KD).

1. In the land of Egypt. The ordinance first given in Egypt would be repeated at Sinai (Lev 23) and on the plains of Moab (Deut 16). **2. This month.** The Hebrew name of the month is *Abib,* meaning "green ears." It corresponds to March-April of our calendar. During the Exile the name *Nisan,* meaning "beginning, opening," came to be used instead. **Beginning of months.** Israel's beginning as the people of Jehovah was to be marked thus on their calendar. The civil year began, as it still does, in the autumn, with the Feast of Trumpets (Lev 23:24; Num 29:1), now called Rosh Hashanah, *Head of the Year*, or New Year. The religious or spiritual year was to begin with the month of Passover, the first month of Israel's new life as a redeemed people.

3. Lamb. *A single head,* either lamb or goat (cf. v. 5). **4.** This was to be a family observance, unless the family was too small. According to rabbinical exegesis, **too little** meant fewer than ten. (Targum Jonathan). **According to his eating.** They were to compute how much each would eat and thus determine whether to unite with other families. **5. Of the first year.** Hebrew, *son of a year.* Rabbis have interpreted this as meaning "as of the first year," i.e., from eight days old. Modern commentators generally take it as meaning a year old. **From the sheep, or from the goats.** Later custom restricted the Passover to lambs.

6. The whole assembly of the congregation, i.e., all at the same time. **In the evening.** Hebrew, *between the evenings*. From very early days opinions have differed as to the exact time of sacrifice. Abn Ezra, the Samaritans, and the Karaites construed it as the time between sunset and complete darkness. The Pharisees held to the traditional explanation that it was from the beginning of lengthening shadows to sunset, approximately 3:00 to 5:00 P.M., and with this the Talmud agrees (Pesahim 61a). This was the usual practice, according to Josephus (*Wars of the Jews,* VI. 9.3). Deuteronomy 16:6 simply says, "at sunset." **7.** The blood was to be sprinkled "on side and lintel, where it might be looked to, not on the threshold to be trodden underfoot" (Jamieson, Fausset, and Brown). By this act both the house and those dwelling in it were to be expiated (by the use of blood and hyssop; cf. Lev 14:4-7; Num 19:1ff.) and consecrated unto God.

8. Roast. The whole animal was to be spitted and roasted over a fire. "Through the unity and integrity of the lamb given them to eat, the participants were to be joined into an undivided unity and fellowship with the Lord who provided them with the meal" (KD). **Unleavened bread.** A memorial of the haste with which they were to leave (v. 34), but also a symbol of their purification and freedom from the world's leaven. **Bitter herbs.** The Mishnah (Pesahim 2:6) mentions lettuce, endive, chicory, snakeroot, peppermint, and dandelion as satisfactory for bitter herbs. This was "to call to mind the bitterness of life experienced by Israel in Egypt, and this bitterness was to be overpowered by the sweet flesh of the lamb" (KD). **9. Sodden.** *Boiled* (ASV, RSV). **With the purtenance.** The inner parts.

11. In haste. In trepidation, mingled hurry and alarm. **Loins girded.** Their long flowing garments were to be bound up so as not to impede progress. **The Lord's passover.** A passover (Heb. *pesah,* LXX *pascha,* and thus English "paschal") to Jehovah; appointed by and kept for him. The etymology of the word is uncertain, but the meaning is made plain by 12:13. God would "leap over," in his judgment, those who had evidenced their faith in him and taken refuge under the blood. **12. Against all the gods.** The Egyptian gods were to be exposed as impotent to defend, and worthless. Moreover, the gods were worshiped in the forms of many of the animals and in the person of Pharaoh himself, and in these representatives the gods themselves were to be smitten.

15-20. Regulations for the Feast of Unleavened Bread. Although these instructions may have been given after the Exodus (cf. v. 17, "have I brought"), the close connection both in meaning and in time between this feast and the Passover explains the inclusion of the regulations here. The unleavened cakes were symbolical of the new life as cleansed from the leaven of a sinful nature. . . . For this reason the Israelites were to put away all the leaven of the Egyptian nature, the leaven of malice and wickedness, and by eating pure and holy bread and meeting for the worship of God to show that they were walking in newness of life. . . . To eat leavened bread at this feast would have been a denial of the divine act by which Israel was introduced into the new life of fellowship with Jehovah" (KD).

15. **First day.** Fifteenth day of Abib. **Soul shall be cut off,** i.e., outlawed or exiled from the community. 16. **Convocation.** *Assembly* (RSV); *sacred gathering* (Moffatt). Necessary work might be done; the day was not as strictly kept as the Sabbath. 17. **Armies.** Better, *hosts* (ASV).

18. **On the fourteenth.** Unleavened bread was to be eaten on Passover on the fourteenth; the Feast of Unleavened Bread started on the fifteenth. 19. **Stranger.** *Sojourner* (ASV, RSV); *resident alien* (Moffatt). One may dwell in the midst of God's people all of one's life and never be an integral part of the company (cf. v. 43).

21-28. Instructions given the elders. The regulations for the Passover, given to Moses by God, were passed on to the representatives of the people. 21. **Draw out,** i.e., out of the folds. 22. **Hyssop.** Though the identity of this plant is disputed, the general opinion is that it was a species of origanum, either marjoram or wild thyme. **Bason.** The vessel in which the blood was caught when the animal was slain. Since the leafy sprig of hyssop was used to sprinkle the blood of a sacrifice for purification, it came to be used figuratively for the purifying itself (cf. Ps 51:7). 23. **The destroyer.** *Destroying angel* (Moffatt). 28. By this act of obedience and faith, the people of Israel made it manifest that they had put their trust in Jehovah; and thus the act became their redemption.

2) The Tenth Plague—God's Judgment on Egypt. 12:29-36. Was this plague, like the others, a heightened and supernaturally directed natural epidemic, or was it more? The repeated stress on its being the work of the Lord (12:12,13,23, 27,29) seems to indicate that it was a direct act of God himself.

29. **The firstborn.** It is usually agreed that this means the eldest son who was not yet himself a father. Otherwise, the first-born of each generation would have died, including, probably, Pharaoh himself. 31. **He called for Moses.** Pharaoh in terror and grief ignored his own threat (10:28). 32. The capitulation was complete. **Bless me.** As you leave, pray for me and this stricken people.

34. **Before it was leavened.** This gives us the natural occasion for the spiritually significant Feast of Unleavened Bread. **Kneadingtroughs.** Literally, *boards,* i.e., shallow wooden bowls. In this case each family carried its kneading bowl bound up in the *śimlâ,* a large square outer garment, often used as a bag for carrying (cf. Ruth 3:15). 36. **Lent unto them.** The Hebrew word for **lent** means "granted, let them have." It does not mean "lend" in the usual sense any more than the Hebrew word in 12:35 means to "borrow" (cf. 3:22; 11:2).

3) The Exodus from Egypt. 12:37–15:21.

a) The Departure. 12:37-42. The exact line of march for the departure from Egypt is still in dispute, but most authorities agree on the identifications made in connection with the following verses. Having assembled the people at Succoth, Moses and Aaron had now to lead them past the barrier of marshes, lakes, and sea that is now the site of the Suez Canal. The way was further determined by the fact that God was to deliver one final blow to Egyptian pride and might.

37. **Succoth.** This is identified as Tell el-Maskhutah, ten miles east of Pithom. This means that after Moses left Pharaoh at Rameses, he came south to the very center of Goshen, there to assemble Israel for the march. **Six hundred thousand.** How to determine the exact number of those involved in the Exodus has long been a problem. It has been pointed out, for instance, that a host of 600,000 men could have overwhelmed Pharaoh's far smaller army by sheer numbers. The question is not whether God could have multiplied the seventy of Jacob's day to over two million, but whether he did. One solution is that the word *'elep,* translated **thousand,** could be translated *clan* or *family,* as it is elsewhere (e.g., Jud 6:15). In that case the total number might well be fifty or sixty thousand individuals. Of one thing we can be sure: God redeemed a great host out of Egypt, miraculously cared for them through forty years in the wilderness, and brought them into the Promised Land. That we do not know the exact number of those involved does not diminish the miracle. 38. **Mixed multitude.** Egyptians and probably other nationalities who had married Hebrews, were seeking escape from bondage or were persuaded that there was some advantage to be gained by being on the side of so powerful a deity as Jehovah.

40. **Four hundred and thirty years.** Genesis 15:13 and Acts 7:6 give the round number, four hundred. Since we

do not know the exact date of the entrance of Israel into Egypt, we can only conjecture the date of departure, but a date near 1300 B.C. seems most reasonable (cf. Introd.). Some conclude that the date was about 1440 on the basis of I Kgs 6:1. **41. Selfsame day.** Cf. 12:17. This was The Day to Israel for generations to come, until a greater Day or a greater Salvation should come. **42. A night to be much observed unto the Lord.** Various translations of this phrase have been offered: *a preservation night of the Lord to bring them out* (KD); *a night of watching was it for Jehovah to bring them out (Cambridge Bible); this same night is a night of watching kept to the Lord by all the people of Israel throughout their generations* (RSV). Perhaps both the ideas expressed in the several translations are implied: the night on which Jehovah watched over his own was to be a watch night for the people of Israel throughout their generations, as a memorial.

b) Further Regulations for Passover. 12:43-51. Such a passage as this is held by critics to be quite out of place here, yet, in fact, it seems most appropriate. It defined, at the very point of action, the exacting requirements that would make the ordinance spiritually significant as well as true to fact in the generations to come.

43-45. Stranger. . . . foreigner . . . hired servant. Only one who was identified with the people of God could have part in this ordinance. This was designed to repel not the foreigner but the unbeliever. Should the alien desire to identify himself in faith with Israel, he was as welcome as one "born in the land" (v. 48). **46.** "In this meal Israel was to preserve and celebrate its unity and fellowship with the Lord" (KD). For this reason the ceremonial unity was not to be broken either by the inclusion of outsiders or by the dividing up of the meal itself. So also the unity of Christ is to be jealously guarded (cf. I Cor 1–3). **49. One law.** Neither natural descent nor association was sufficient. **No uncircumcised person shall eat of it** (v. 48).

c) Sanctification of the First-born. 13:1-16. "If the Israelites completed their communion with Jehovah in the Passover, and celebrated the commencement of their divine standing in the feast of unleavened bread, they gave uninterrupted effect to their divine sonship in the sanctification of the firstborn" (KD). As Egypt was smitten by God in the persons of its first-born, so Israel was consecrated to God in its first-born.

2. Whatsoever openeth, i.e., first opens.

3-10. The law already given Moses (12:15-20) was now proclaimed to the people. **7. Thy quarters.** *Borders* (ASV). **8.** Dedication of the first-born was to be explained generation by generation, as was the Passover (12:26,27). **9. It shall be for a sign.** As other races wore signs, even cuttings and tattoos, to remind them of their god, so this feast was to bring before Israel the remembrance of the redemption of Jehovah. "It was not by mnemonic slips upon the hand and forehead that a law was so placed in the mouth as to be talked of continually, but by the reception of it into the heart and its continued fulfillment" (KD).

11-16. The law of the first-born (cf. 22:29; Deut 15:21,22). **12. Thou shalt set apart** (lit., *cause to pass over* unto the Lord). This is not the usual word for to **set apart,** but the word used to describe the heathen practice of sacrificing children to their gods (II Kgs 16:3; Ezk 20:31). It may be that the Lord purposely used this word to mark the distinction between this dedication and that of the heathen. **13.** The ass was not a sacrificial animal, and so a lamb was to be substituted for it. The first-born of men were to be redeemed by silver, as the people were told later (Num 3:47; 18:16). The obligation for service having been transferred to the Levites as representatives, the people were asked only to acknowledge God's claim upon them. **15.** In this way all that Israel was and all she possessed were continually to be presented to the Lord who had redeemed her.

16. Frontlets. Hebrew *tôtapōt*, the NT "phylacteries." Later Jews literally carried out this exhortation by tying on their foreheads and arms bands to which were attached small leather boxes containing Scripture verses written on parchment. It was God's purpose that the feast and the consecration, not little boxes, should serve as reminders for hand and heart.

d) Passage Through the Red Sea. 13:17–14:31. The description of the journey, started in 12:37, is now continued. There was a good road directly to Palestine, going up the seacoast past Gaza, but this would have taken them past Egyptian fortresses at intervals, and would have required them to do battle, for which they were unprepared both physically and psychologically. God in wise kindness led them up another way.

18. **Wilderness of the Red sea.** Hebrew, *Sea of Suph, Reed Sea.* The mistaken translation, **Red sea,** has given a totally erroneous view of the route of Israel. This is a quite different term from that which designates what we call the Red Sea or the Gulf of Suez. The Reed or Marsh Sea is mentioned in Egyptian writings of the thirteenth century B.C. as being near Rameses. Either Lake Timsah or the southern extension of the present Lake Menzaleh fits the description. These lakes are part of the chain once uniting the Gulf of Suez with the Mediterranean, and are now a part of the Canal. Lake Timsah is nearer Succoth. **Harnessed.** The precise meaning is uncertain. The ASV reads *armed,* and the RSV, *equipped for battle.* **19.** The faith of Joseph was justified (Gen 50:25). **20. Etham.** The location is unknown. **21,22.** These were not two pillars but one, of cloud by day and of fire by night. The Scripture discountenances attempts to explain these guides by natural means (cf. *Cambridge Bible).* The pillar was a real sign of the real presence of Jehovah with his people.

14:1-31. The passage through the Red Sea. "The fact of the passage of the Red Sea can be questioned only by an extreme and baseless scepticism" *(Cambridge Bible).*

2. Turn. *Turn back* (ASV); *wheel around* (Moffatt). **Pi-hahiroth** and **Migdol** are mentioned in Egyptian inscriptions but are not yet identified with certainty. **Baal-zephon.** A Phoenician letter mentions "Baal-zephon and all the gods of Tahpanhes." Tahpanhes is Daphne, the modern Tel Dafneh, located near the southern extremity of Lake Menzaleh, half way between Succoth and Rameses. This explains the words "turn back." Instead of going directly east from Succoth, the Hebrews had turned north again and were now encamped by the marshy lake. This apparent uncertainty in their line of march must have encouraged Pharaoh to believe that the Israelites could find no way across the water barrier and were thus trapped, "wandering aimlessly" (American Trans.). **4. Honoured upon Pharaoh . . . that the Egyptians may know.** The fact that there was one final lesson to be given Egypt explains why God led in this seemingly aimless fashion.

5. Whatever have we done (Moffatt). The departure of Israel was described to Pharaoh as a flight, not a pilgrimage to a place of sacrifice. **7. Captains.** The exact meaning is unknown; some kind of superior officer. **8. With an high hand.** "The high hand of Jehovah with the might which it displayed" (KD). **9. Horsemen.** This is called anachronistic by some, as the Egyptians had no cavalry this early; but the word can just as well mean horsemen in chariots. This possibility is admitted in connection with 15:1 by those who deny it here (cf. *Cambridge Bible).*

12. Let us alone. Humanly speaking, they were faced with certain destruction. How characteristic of human nature is the cry, "Let us alone." We would rather lie supine in sinful bondage than, with the courage of faith, make the effort to follow God into newness of life. **13. Stand still.** Better, *stand firm* (cf. I Cor 15:58 – "Be ye steadfast"). **14.** You have only to stand still (cf. Isa 30:15; Ps 46:10). **15.** Not a reproof but an admonition to act, "Go forward!" **19,20.** Miraculously protected in the rear from the Egyptians by a thick cloud, they were at the same time given a floodlight from the Lord so that they might cross over.

21. The natural force used by God to perform this miracle was the east wind, whether in connection with a strong ebb tide, as some suppose, or not. It is sufficient for us to know that God, at precisely the right moment, caused the ford to be laid bare so that his people might cross; and at exactly the right time brought the waters back, so that the enemy was destroyed. **24. Troubled.** *Threw them into a panic* (Moffatt). **Morning watch,** between 2:00 and 6:00 A.M. **25. Took off their chariot wheels.** *Clogging, binding* (RSV, following LXX, Syriac, and Samaritan versions, rather than the Hebrew). The chariot wheels sank into the sand, which became more marshy by the moment. **27,28.** The waters that had threatened the Israelites in their passage, and, except for God's restraining hand, would have destroyed them, now overwhelmed the Egyptians. "From this manifestation of Jehovah's omipotence, the Israelites were to discern not only the merciful Deliverer but also the holy Judge of the ungodly, that they might grow in the fear of God as well as in the faith which they had already shown" (KD). **31. Believed in.** More than just *believe* (AV), it implies "laying firm hold morally on a person or thing" *(Cambridge Bible).*

e) The Song of Moses. 15:1-21. Although critics recognize this hymn of praise as "one of the finest products of Hebrew poetry" *(Cambridge Bible)*, they usually relegate it to the time of the monarchy. They assume that such great poetry could not have been written as early as Moses! Scripture links this triumphal paean with the song of a greater redemption, as on the shores of the eternal sea, at the final and glorious triumph over all enemies, the redeemed sing "the song of Moses . . . and the song of the Lamb" (Rev 15:3).

1. The horse and his rider hath he thrown into the sea. "Thus briefly but completely is the ruin of the Pharaoh's army described" *(Cambridge Bible)*. **2. I will prepare him an habitation.** The AV follows the Targum. The clause is better rendered *I will praise* (ASV, RSV) or *thank him*. **3. Jehovah is his name.** A taunt to Pharaoh, who had asked, "Who is Jehovah?" **7. Hast overthrown.** The Hebrew is more forceful – "to break in pieces and throw in ruins upon the earth" *(Cambridge Bible)*. **9. The enemy said, I will.** How often the proud purpose of man is thwarted by the power of God (cf. Isa 14:13,14). **Destroy.** Literally, *dispossess, root out*. **10.** "One breath of God was sufficient to sink the proud foe in the waves of the sea" (KD; cf. Ps 46:6). **11. Fearful in praises.** *Terrible in glorious deeds* (RSV); *awe-inspiring in renown* (American).

13. Holy habitation. As a shepherd leads his flock to the fold, so God was leading Israel to His habitation, the Promised Land. **14. Palestina.** Hebrew, *Philistia*. Ironically, the name of the Holy Land most frequently used by us is taken from the name of the bitter enemies of Israel and God. **16. Fear and dread.** Until forty years had passed and Israel had entered the land, the fear of the Lord was upon the Canaanites (cf. Josh 5:1; 2:9,10). **17. The Sanctuary . . . which thy hands have established.** This is the goal, not yet the accomplished fact.

20. Although Miriam was a sister to both, she is ranked with Aaron, not with Moses. **Timbrel.** A tambourine. Dancing was, and still is in the East, the language of religion. **21. Answered.** They sang antiphonally, perhaps the verses of the song of Moses (vv. 1-19).

G. Israel in the Wilderness. 15:22–18:27.

Released from the bondage of Egypt, Israel was now led by the Lord to Mount Sinai. At this stage God's people were a disorganized, quarrelsome, faithless multitude. They had to be molded into a nation, capable of serving him. To this end, everything, including the march to Sinai, was to contribute to their training. The traditional line of march, down the western edge of the peninsula, is still the one most widely accepted by Bible scholars, and the reasonable one. Though the exact places mentioned in Scripture cannot be identified with certainty, the general locations are fairly well established. (For various other routes proposed, cf. Rand McNally *Bible Atlas*).

22. Wilderness of Shur. East of the Suez, in the northwest section of the peninsula. **Shur** means *wall* in Hebrew. In Num 33:8 the area is called "the wilderness of Etham," which is the same name in Egyptian. Possibly it was named for the line of fortifications erected there. **Three days.** In three days the water they carried with them would have been exhausted, even though they had probably gone no more than fifteen miles. **23. Marah.** This is reasonably identified with Ain Hawarah, still a small spring of brackish, unpalatable water. **24. Murmured.** This was the almost automatic reaction of Israel, as it has been the reaction of multitudes of God's people since, to any and every difficulty.

25,26. The search for a natural explanation of this miracle, for some sort of tree that makes bad water good, is quite useless. By this test of Jehovah and proof of his care and power, an ordinance was established for all time–that for the obedient, God would prove to be Jehovah *Rōp'ekā*, "Jehovah that healeth thee." **27. Elim.** About six miles from Ain Hawarah is a beautiful large oasis with plentiful water, Wadi Gharandel, which corresponds to the description of Elim.

16:1. Wilderness of Sin. According to Num 33:10-12, the people of Israel traveled along the seashore, possibly by the regular route to the Sinai mines. They turned in to the Wilderness of Sin at Dophkah. If Dophkah can be identified with Serabit el-Khadem, then the Wilderness of Sin is the plain along the edge of the plateau, called Debbet er-Ramleh. The geographical directions are too slight to give much certainty. **2.** The circumstances and God's provision again combined to prove the faith and obedience of Israel.

7. The glory of the Lord. The eye of faith sees the glory of the Lord in the bread and flesh that he provides. **What are we.** *We do not count; why grumble against us?* (Moffatt) **10. Behold, the glory.**

The unmistakable evidence of God's presence in the fiery pillar authenticated the words of Moses and prepared the people for the more veiled glory of the miracle to come.

14. Small round thing. *Fine flake-like thing* (RSV). **15. It is manna.** From *mān-hû'*, "What is it?" The name **manna** may have arisen from the question, or the similarity in sound may have related the two words. **16. Omer.** About two quarts. **23. Seethe.** Boil. **Sabbath.** This indicates that although the Sabbath was already known, it was not observed in any special way.

31. Manna. There is a species of tamarisk that grows in the Peninsula from which there exudes, perhaps from the puncture of an insect, during summer nights, a liquid which forms small white grains. The Arabs gather this, boil it down, and use it like honey. It has a sweet, aromatic taste. It will keep a long time in a cool place but melts in the sun; it cannot be ground or made into cakes. This resembles but also distinctly differs from the manna of the Bible. The Scripture, not only in its description of the manna, but in its record of marvelous provision for forty years (v. 35) makes it clear that the manna was not a natural phenomenon but a special provision of the hand of the Lord. **Coriander.** A small, grayish-white seed, with a pleasant spicy flavor, used widely as a spice for cooking.

33,34. Before the Lord. . . before the Testimony. That is, before the tables of the Law in the ark. This direction must have been given later, perhaps as the time for the end of the manna drew near. **35.** This need not be taken as meaning that the Israelites ate nothing but manna for forty years. During the stay at Sinai, they may very well have sowed and harvested crops, and they could also have obtained food from time to time from traders.

17:1-7. Water from the rock at Rephidim. From the plateau of the Wilderness of Sin, a series of valleys leads directly to Mount Sinai. One of these, the Wadi Refayid, some claim is the valley of Rephidim.

2. Did chide. *Found fault* (RSV). **Tempt.** Subject to trial. It was unbelief that led them to question the faithfulness of God (v. 7).

6. Horeb is used in Scripture as a term interchangeable with Sinai. It may have a wider reference, to the range of which Sinai is one peak. At Rephidim, then, Israel was close to her immediate journey's end. **Smite the rock.** A natural explanation of this miracle has been offered in that certain rock formations in this area are simply a thin limestone crust which a blow from a rod would break and permit water to come out. The Apostle Paul tells us that "the Rock was Christ" (I Cor 10:4). Whatever means God may have used, the important fact is that it was made manifest to the Israelites that their help came from the Lord. **7. Massah.** *Proving* (AV, *tempted),* from the verb used in 17:2. **Meribah.** *Strife,* translated "chide" in verse 2.

8. Amalek was a tribe, or group of fierce, rapacious nomads, much like the Bedouins of today. Though descended from Esau (Gen 36:12), they were not a part of the nation of Edom. According to Deut 25:18, they had attacked Israel from the rear, making a cowardly assault upon the "faint and weary" stragglers. This explains the severe judgment of Ex 17:14. **9.** This is the first appearance of Joshua, destined to be Moses' great successor. **10. Hur.** Jewish tradition makes him Miriam's husband (Jos *Antiq.* III. 2.4).

11. Commentators, ancient and modern, almost unanimously consider this act of Moses an act of prayer. As such, it expressed an attitude of dependence upon God that determined the outcome of the battle, and it served to demonstrate the reality of this dependence to all the people. "The battle which Israel fought with this foe possessed a typical significance in relation to all the future history of Israel. It [Israel] could not conquer by the sword alone, but could only gain the victory by the power of God, coming down from on high and obtained through prayer" (KD). **13. Discomfited.** *Mowed down* (RSV); disabled, prostrated.

15. Jehovah-nissi. *Jehovah my banner.* **16. The Lord hath sworn.** Literally, *a hand upon,* or *to, the throne of Jehovah.* Some authorities read *nēs,* "banner," instead of *kēs,* "throne," and translate, *a hand upon the banner of the Lord* (RSV); or, *We pledge loyalty to the Eternal's banner* (Moffatt). The AV, ASV rendering hardly suits the context. This should be an oath sworn by Moses, and, as such, an admonition to the people of Israel to pledge themselves to fulfill God's purpose (v. 14).

18:1-27. The visit of Jethro and the appointment of judges. **2. After he had sent her back.** Cf. 4:24-26. **3.** Cf. 2:22. **5. Mount of God.** The sequence of this passage has been questioned because it is not until chapter 19 that Israel is said to have arrived at Sinai. However, since even at Rephidim they could have been said to be at the mountain of God – Horeb (17:6), there seems to be no real problem in the order of the narrative here.

7. Did obeisance. *Bowed down* (Moffatt). The usual Eastern etiquette. **11.** Jethro, in KD is called "the first fruits of the heathen who would hereafter seek the living God." This testimony of Jethro and the subsequent act of worship seem to indicate a conversion experience, and invalidate the theory that it was from Jethro and the Midianites that Moses learned of Jehovah.

15. Inquire of God. The decisions of Moses and the ordinances upon which they were based came ultimately from Jehovah. **18. Wear yourselves out** (RSV). **21. Rulers of thousands.** It is best to take this as meaning "thousands" of families rather than individuals, thus following the natural tribal divisions. Driver finds this plan impractical because a man would be subject to four different judges *(Cambridge Bible)*. But it is assumed that these different categories would function as higher and lower courts. The majority of problems would be solved, as in our own system, by the lowest court, "the rulers of tens."

24. Moses hearkened. Moses has been criticized for this act. However, Jethro conditioned his advice with, "and God command thee so"; and it may be assumed that Moses did inquire of the Lord. Furthermore, there is no record of God's having rebuked Moses. In Deut 1:15 Moses explains how the judges were chosen from leaders, wise and well known, of the various tribes.

II. Israel at Sinai. 19:1–40:38.

The year of sojourn at Sinai accomplished two things: (1) Israel was given the Law of God and instructed in God's ways; and (2) the multitude that had escaped from Egypt was unified into the beginnings of a nation. This period is of the utmost importance for understanding the will and purpose of God as it is revealed in the rest of the OT. This is the heart of what is so frequently referred to throughout Scripture as "the Law." The record of the sojourn at Sinai and the Law given there occupies not only the remainder of Exodus but also the book of Leviticus and the first chapters of Numbers.

The Graf-Wellhausen hypothesis, promulgated in the nineteenth century, that denied even the existence of a Tabernacle, made of these laws simply the reflection of the customs of later centuries. The past half century has seen a reversal of this thinking, so that now practically all scholars are willing to admit that the framework and core of the Law are Mosaic. Critics still insist that the Law, as we now have it, has been modified from the original and edited considerably by later ages. While it is not impossible that later judgments and ordinances are included, those who hold the Law to be a revelation from God accept it in its present form as substantially that which Moses received. Even the critics who theoretically deny this, find it difficult to decide just which of the ordinances are the later ones.

A. Establishment of the Covenant at Sinai. 19:1–24:11. The history of the arrival at Sinai and God's presentation of his covenant is followed by the so-called Book of the Covenant (chs. 20–23), in which the basic code is set forth. Then follows the account of the ratification of the covenant by sacrifice and the sprinkling of blood.

1) Arrival at Sinai and Preparation for the Covenant. 19:1-25.

19:1. The same day. Jewish tradition holds that this was the day of Pentecost, and that the purpose of the Feast of Pentecost was to celebrate the giving of the Law. However, the expression is too general to indicate any particular day. **Wilderness of Sinai.** The southern range of mountains, situated in the wedge of the triangular peninsula, has three summits. The Arabs call the central summit Jebel Musa, the one to the south, Jebel Hum, and the third, Jebel Serbol. Each of these mounts has been claimed as the Sinai of Scripture, but since the fourth century A.D., at least, Jebel Musa has been most widely and consistently held. The *desert* or **wilderness of Sinai** must be a plain near the mountain (v. 2) large enough for Israel to encamp on it. Such a place has been found in er-Raha, to the north of Jebel Musa, or in Wadi es-Sebayeh, to the east. The former is about four hundred acres in extent, quite ample for any number of Hebrews. From er-Raha the Wadi ed-Deir, "Convent Valley," leads to a saddle between Jebel Musa and Jebel ed-Deir, where the famous monastery of St. Catherine is located. The monastery was built by Justinian in 527 A.D. on a site already occupied by a small church identifying the spot where it was believed God had appeared to Moses in the burning bush. The Wadi es-Sebayeh is a long narrow valley, not so commodious as er-Raha, but with easier access to the mountain. It is difficult, if not impossible, to decide which of these peaks and valleys best fits the description given in Scripture.

3. House of Jacob. The name of Jacob recalls the depths from which God had raised them. **4. On eagles' wings.** An allusion to the griffin-vulture, a large majestic bird abundant in Palestine.

5. The covenant was based upon the accomplished fact of the redemption from Egypt, a redemption which Israel had received by faith. "The theocracy established by the conclusion of the covenant was only the means adopted by Jehovah for making His chosen people a royal body of priests; and the maintenance of the covenant was the indispensable subjective condition upon which their attainment of this divinely appointed destiny and glory depended" (KD). We are also to remember that the Law did not disannul the covenant with Abraham (Gal 3:17). "The covenant of law raised itself on the ground of the previous covenant of grace and sought to carry this out to its legitimate consequence and proper fruits" (Patrick Fairbairn, *The Typology of Scripture,* II, 143). **Peculiar treasure.** *My own prized possession* (Moffatt). **6. Priests . . . holy nation.** "As the priest is a mediator between God and man, so Israel is called to be the vehicle of the knowledge and salvation of God to the nations of the earth. . . . He chose Israel as His possession, to make it a holy nation, if it hearkened to His voice and kept His covenant" (KD).

8. All that the Lord hath spoken we will do. The people of Israel unquestionably did not realize all the implications of their vow. Neither does a Christian understand all that is entailed when he presents himself "a living sacrifice" unto God. In both cases there is a response by faith to the express will of God the Redeemer. **9. Believe thee for ever.** The appearance of the Lord would impress the people and at the same time undergird the authority of Moses. **13. Touch it.** Rather, *touch him;* a transgressor was not to be followed onto the mountain, but shot or stoned from a distance. **Trumpet.** Rather, *ram's horn* (Moffatt); this is not the same word as is used in verses 16,19.

16. The vain attempt to determine what kind of phenomenon is described here – earthquake, volcano, or storm – misses the point that whatever these were, they were simply a manifestation of the presence of the Lord. This was not a natural disturbance that convinced a superstitious people that God was near; it was God himself making his presence known.

21. Go down, charge. This is not a confusion of two accounts, but a re-emphasis of the command already given in 19:12. **22. Priests.** Not the Levitical priests, who were not yet appointed, but those who had hitherto discharged the duties of the priestly office according to natural right and custom" (KD).

2) The Ten Commandments. 20:1-20. The Law was not given as a means of salvation. It was given to a people already saved (19:4; 20:2) in order to instruct them in the will of the Lord so that they might fulfill God's purpose for them as "a kingdom of priests and a holy nation" (19:6). The revelation was given "not to give but to guide life" (P. Fairbairn, *The Revelation of Law in Scripture*, p. 274).

The division of the Law into Moral, Social or Civil, and Ceremonial or Religious Laws, while convenient, is misleading. The Law is one, and the whole Law is spiritual, whether dealing with crops or criminals or worship. Calvin's commentary treats all subsequent laws under one or the other of the Ten Commandments. This is eminently justifiable and an excellent illustration of the unity and spirit of the Law. "What is called the ceremonial law, therefore, was in its more immediate and primary aspect an exhibition by means of symbolic rites and institutions of the righteousness enjoined in the Decalogue, and a discipline through which the heart might be wrought into some conformation to the righteousness itself" (Fairbairn, *Typology,* II, 157).

The Decalogue, or *Ten Words* (Deut 4:13) was given directly to all Israel by an audible and terrible voice, the voice of Jehovah, sounding like a trumpet over the multitude (Ex 19:16; 20:18). Overwhelmed by the experience, the people begged that God would speak no more directly, but through Moses. The rest of the Law was then given to Moses as a mediator, but the heart of the Law had already been delivered. The Commandments are repeated, with slight but immaterial variations in Deut 5:6-18. This provides critics with materials for an argument as to the relative age and authenticity of the two records. An attempt has also been made to find a "ritual decalogue" in Exodus 34, but it has not been widely accepted. Although some deny that Moses had anything to do with the Commandments or that they were known to David, Elijah, or even Jeremiah, most modern scholars have come to accept the Biblical statement and believe that the Commandments go back to the days of Moses.

There are different ways of dividing the Commandments. The Lutheran and Roman Catholic churches follow Augustine in making verses 2-6 the first commandment, and then dividing verse 17, on covetousness, into two. Modern Judaism makes verse 2 the first commandment and verses 3-6 the second. The earliest division, which can be traced back at least as far as Josephus, in the first century A.D., takes 20:3 as the first command and 20:4-6 as the second. This division was supported unanimously by the early church, and is held today by the Eastern Orthodox and most Protestant churches.

2. It is important to notice that the basis of God's commandments and the ground of the people's obligation was the fact that Jehovah was their Lord and God who had redeemed them. These injunctions are given to a saved people to teach them how to walk in God's way, but we observe that "nearly all the commandments are couched in the negative form of prohibition, because they presuppose the existence of sin and evil desires in the human heart" (KD).

3. The First Commandment. This is more than just a proclamation of monotheism. It prohibits worshiping or honoring anything before God, in thought or word or deed, "that in all things he might have the preeminence" (Col 1:18). **4-6.** The Second Commandment. This prohibits the creation and use of graven images as objects of worship. But more essentially, it is a reminder that God is a Spirit, not to be conceived of as made in man's image or in that of any other created being. **Visiting the iniquity** (v. 5). The results of sin are seen to affect three or four generations, but God's mercy extends unto thousands. "He does not say He will be faithful or just toward the keepers of His law, but merciful" (Calvin). **Them that love me** (v. 6). "The fountain and origin of true righteousness is expressed, for the external observation of the law would be of no avail unless it flowed from hence" (Calvin). **7.** The Third Commandment. This prohibits the use of God's name "in the service of unbelief and lying" (KD). To substantiate our falsehood by an appeal to God will bring certain judgment. Here also may be found force for the injunction to Christians to "walk worthy of the calling wherewith ye were called" (Eph 4:1), i.e., bear not the name of Christ in vain.

"The first commandment then guards the unity of God, the second His spirituality, and the third His deity or essence. In the first we are forbidden to make God one of many when He is the only One; in the second to liken Him to a corruptible image when He is the incorruptible Spirit; in the third to identify Him in any way with the creature when He is the Creator" (James Murphy, *Commentary on Exodus, in loc.).*

8-11. The Fourth Commandment. The word **sabbath** means, not rest or relaxation, but cessation from labor. The reason for the Sabbath is given objectively here as found in the fact that God ceased from the work of creation on the seventh day. Subjectively, in Deut 5:14,15, there is a reason given in the fact that men need rest. Also the Israelites were reminded thereby that God had redeemed them from the bondage of Egypt to enjoy his rest. The keeping of the seventh day of the week as the Sabbath is not abrogated in the NT, but the Sabbath of the New Creation is most naturally to be celebrated on that day when Christ, having ceased from his finished work, rose from the dead. The apostolic church celebrated both the first and the seventh days, but they soon discontinued the old Hebrew observance.

12. The Fifth Commandment. This command marks a division between the commandments that deal with man's relation to God and those that relate to his fellow man. A man is obligated to honor his parents as he does God, and to assume responsibility for them as he does for his fellow men. **That thy days may be long.** This may be understood as referring both to Israel's sojourn in the land of promise, and also to the life of the individual. Not only in Israel, but in all nations and individual lives, the destruction of the home marks the beginning of the end.

13. The Sixth Commandment. The sanctity of human life is upheld, and murder, for any reason, is forbidden. But this command is wrongly quoted in opposition to capital punishment administered by the state. The judicial taking of life in punishment for crime is authorized in Exodus 21, as well as in Romans 13. On the other hand, it is seldom stressed that this command is applicable to whatever would degrade man and deprive him of the full and rich life it is God's will that he should enjoy.

14. The Seventh Commandment. While this is directed specifically to maintain the purity and sanctity of marriage, it is also applied by Jesus to all sexual immorality of thought as well as deed (Mt 5:27,28). **15.** The Eighth Commandment. The rights of private property are to be respected. **16.** The Ninth Commandment. "Not only is lying prohibited, but false and unfounded evidence in general" (KD). **17.** The Tenth Commandment. Covetousness is "the inordinate desire of unpossessed good" (G. A. Chadwick, *Exodus* in *Expositor's Bible)*. "The most inward of all the commandments, forbidding not an external act, but a hidden mental state, a state, however, which is the root of nearly every sin against a neighbor" *(Cambridge Bible)*. It is basically the sin of Adam and Eve, to desire that which it is not God's will that we have. **20. Fear may be before your faces.** *Keep you from sinning by a steady awe of Him* (Moffatt).

3) The Covenant Constitution. 20:21–23:33. The ordinances next given to Moses and through him to the people have to do briefly with (1) the general form of worship (20:22-26); at some length with (2) social relations and rights of the people (21:1–23:13); and finally with (3) the relation of the people to Jehovah (23:14-33).

Formerly some critics found grounds in these laws for dating this section much later than the time of Moses. Since the discovery of a number of law codes much earlier than the Mosaic—e.g., Babylonian, Assyrian, Hittite, and Sumerian—the practice now is to determine the "dependence" of the Hebrew code upon the earlier ones. That people living in roughly the same era and under similar cultures should require legislation along similar lines is obvious, but this does not constitute dependence. "These laws are not all new, but combined approved customs, already established, with fresh legislation suited to the occasion . . .; foresight also appears in adapting the legislation less to present nomadic conditions than to the proximate settlement in Canaan" *(Catholic Commentary)*. The spirit of the Mosaic law is found in the Ten Commandments. Not only were the people to whom these laws were addressed different from the nations around them, but the underlying assumptions of the laws themselves are radically different.

a) The General Form of Worship. 20:22-26. The command is here emphasized (vv. 22,23) that the God whose presence had been manifested to all Israel was not to be likened to any image produced by man's invention. No elaborate structures were to mark the way of approach of Israel to Jehovah, but a simple altar of earth or of common, unfinished stone (vv. 24-26). This precept does not disagree with later instructions concerning a brazen altar (27:1-9), but deals with a particular situation. Altars were not to be erected everywhere but where "I cause to be remembered my name" (RSV). At such places a simple altar was to be erected, not an ornate shrine. The practical application of the command is found in many places in later history (Jud 6:25,26; Josh 8:30; I Kgs 18:30-32). **Steps** (v. 26). Flowing garments would be lifted by the raised foot and the body would thus be disclosed. Other regulations provide for the priest serving at the larger altar (28:42).

b) Civil and Social Relations. 21:1–23:13.

21:1-11. The Israelite Slave. This law deals only with Hebrew slaves; foreign slaves are treated in Lev 25:44-46. Hebrews could become slaves of their own volition because of poverty or some private disaster. The regulations ensured their being treated as brethren under these circumstances. Some have suggested that these are not so much laws to be enforced as personal rights to be observed (e.g., KD), **Seventh** [year] (v. 2). The sabbatical year, the end of toil (cf. 21:2; 23:10,11). The slave was to go out in the same personal status as he came in (21:3,4). **Unto the judges** (v. 6). *Unto God* (ASV, RSV). Either translation is justified. Although the word is *'Elōhîm,* the customary word for God, the actual transaction undoubtedly took place before judges who acted as representatives of God's righteousness (cf. Ps 82:6; Jn 10:35). **To the door.** He was thus fastened, as it were, to the house forever by the ear, the organ of hearing and obedience.

The ordinance is different for the female slave, who as concubine or even wife would become a part of the master's household (21:7-11). She was protected by three regulations: she could not be sold to a Gentile, to a far different kind of slavery (v. 8); if she had been taken to be espoused to a son, she was to be treated as a daughter (vv. 9,10); if she was not given the food, clothing, and rights of a wife, she was to be set free (v. 11). The father, who because of circumstances was forced thus to dispose of his daughter, was not selling her into cruel bondage, but sending her into a household where she would be as well treated as at home.

12-17. Capital Crimes. The sanctity of life is stressed by these laws against murder, kidnapping, and violence. God curbs the violence of sinful men by this sanction of strict justice. **God deliver him** (v. 13). We would say "accidentally," but to the Hebrew there were no "accidents" in a world where God reigned supreme.

18-32. Bodily Injuries, Whether Inflicted by Man or Beast. Here again the value of an individual in the sight of God is stressed. These also are more in the nature of admonitions than ordinances: injury as the result of a quarrel (vv. 18, 19); injury to a slave (vv. 20,21); injury to a pregnant woman (vv. 22-25). **22. No mischief follow;** i.e., in addition to the loss of her child, no permanent injury to the mother ensues. Verses 23-25 state the *lex talionis* (law of retaliation) so often quoted as typical of the harsh OT laws. It should be noted first that this ordinance is restricted to matters of bodily harm only. Second, its purpose was not to enforce the rule but to check the passionate vengeance that for a slight injury often retaliated with death and destruction. Slaves were to be freed in retribution for a permanent injury (vv. 26, 27). When men suffered injury from animals, the owners were to be held responsible (vv. 28-32).

21:33–22:17. Laws Regarding Property.

33-36. *Injury incurred by animals.* In such cases responsibility was fixed for neglect or failure to take precautions. **Open a pit** (v. 33). This refers to cisterns for the storing of water or grain. "I have been astonished at the recklessness with which wells and pits are left uncovered and unprotected all over this country" (Thomson, *The Land and the Book,* II, 283; cf. I, 89, 90; II, 194; III, 458).

22:1-4. Theft. **Breaking up.** (v. 2). Literally, *digging through.* The usual way of access for a thief was digging through the relatively soft clay walls of the house. **There shall be blood shed for him** (v. 3). *The householder is guilty* (Moffatt). A mortal blow struck in darkness in defense of life and property was excused, but in the light of day, it was reasoned, such violent defense would not be necessary. The life, even of a thief, is of consequence in the eyes of God. **Sold.** Not in punishment but in restitution.

5-17. Loss of value, whether through accident, theft, or other cause. Verses 5 and 6 have to do with restitution for damage done to fields and crops. **To be eaten** may be rendered "to be grazed over" (RSV). Restitution must be made if damage had been done to the field. With slight emendation verse 5 might be read: "If a man shall cause a field or vineyard to be burnt," i.e., to destroy stubble and weeds. Getting out of control, the fire destroys another's field.

Loss or damage to goods left on deposit (vv. 7-13). No bonded warehouses or safety deposit boxes, or even banks were known. If a man had to be absent from home, he entrusted his property to a dependable neighbor. In a sense, this law served as the neighbor's bond. **Stuff** (v. 7). A very general term for a variety of things. **Judges** (v. 8). Cf. 21:6. **Manner of trespass** (v. 9). *Breach of trust* (RSV). **Oath of the Lord** (v. 11). Whether before judges or by oath, disputes were to be settled as before God and in recognition of his law. The Law held a man responsible for things he borrowed or hired (vv. 14, 15).

Seduction (vv. 16, 17). The girl is considered here as part of the family wealth, and the attack is regarded in respect to the loss of value because of the dowry, a considerable item, both then and now in the East. The moral crime is dealt with in Deut 22:22-27. **Dowry.** Better, *marriage price.* It was the price paid by the groom to the parents or family of the bride (cf. Gen 24:53).

22:18–23:9. Moral and Religious Laws. These laws are all based upon the fact that Israel was to be a holy nation unto Jehovah.

18. Witch. *Sorceress* (ASV, RSV). The malignant practice of magic and divination is still a potent force in primitive areas, and even among the superstitious in more enlightened lands. These few words are often quoted and voluminously commented on as a proof that superstitious ignorance is found in the OT, which must therefore not be inspired. These laws have been grossly misapplied, as in the seventeenth century witchcraft trials in New England. The New Testament, it is true, does not contain such laws, because the

Christian economy is not a civil authority as was the Old Testament church. This, however, does not negate the reality of the demonic practices or the validity of the laws against them. **19. Bestiality.** This unspeakable act was in fact a part of some of the degraded religious practices of the day. **20.** Sacrifice to strange gods. **Utterly destroyed.** Literally, *devoted, set apart* unto Jehovah. "By death devoted to the Lord to whom he would not devote himself in life" (KD).

21-27. Humanitarian laws for the protection of the poor, the alien, and the helpless. These admonitions are forgotten by those who think of the Mosaic law as harsh and nationalistic. **I will surely hear** (vv. 22-24). The God who marks the sparrow's fall, will bring due recompense upon the heartless oppressor. **Usury** (v. 25). *Interest.* The lending of money as a commercial transaction is a modern practice and not considered here. Money was loaned as an act of charity to those who were in great need. To charge interest under such circumstances, profiting by another's need, is contrary to all decency. **Raiment** (v. 26). For the poor man who slept in his clothes, the large, rectangular mantle, the only garment worth taking as a pledge, was his only protection at night. **I will hear** (v. 27). God would hear the cry that the hard-hearted creditor ignored (cf. Thomson, I, 54,99; III, 89).

28. Reviling God or the ruler. "Contempt of God consists not only in blasphemies of Jehovah openly expressed, which were to be punished with death (Lev. xxiv. 11 sqq.), but in disregard of His threats with reference to the poorer members of His people (vers. 22-27), and in withholding from them what they ought to receive (vers. 29-31). Understood in this way, the command is closely connected not only with what precedes but also with what follows. The prince (lit., *the elevated one)* is mentioned by the side of God, because in his exalted position he has to administer the law of God among His people" (KD).

29-31. The terms of the covenant emphasized the Israelites' responsibility to the Lord. They were to show themselves holy not only in giving what the Lord required but in abstaining from what was forbidden.

23:1-9. The duty to uphold truth and justice. The Israelites were to walk in integrity and consideration for all men. They were not to bear false witness (v. 1), i.e., **raise a false report** (AV), nor be in any collusion with such as did. **Unrighteous witness.** Literally, *witness of violence.* **Not follow a multitude** (v. 2). A classic condemnation of mob violence. Neither by action nor by word was justice to be perverted because of the pressure of a crowd. **Countenance** (v. 3). To favor or be partial. Some think that this is a scribal error and that "rich" and not "poor" man was meant. But there is need to warn against injustice due to wrongly directed sympathy as well as for other reasons. **Thine enemy's ox** (vv. 4, 5). Not only was their conduct not to be determined by public opinion, the direction taken by the crowd, or compassion for the poor man; but personal antipathy, enmity, and hatred were not to lead them to injustice or churlish behavior (cf. Mt 5:44; Thomson, *op. cit.* III, 345). **Wrest the judgment** (v. 6). *Never tamper with a poor man's rights in court* (Moffatt). This is the converse of the injunction in 23:3.

Keep thee far (v. 7). Have nothing to do with unrighteousness. **I will not justify.** The LXX reads, *Thou shalt not justify.* The Hebrew reading makes the forceful point that to do such a thing puts one in opposition to a holy God who will not justify wickedness. **Blindeth the wise** (lit., *the seeing men)* **and perverteth the causes** (not *words,* AV) **of the righteous.** Again and again God emphasized the Israelites' responsibility for those who were without rights or redress, by recalling their own experiences (**ye know the heart of a stranger,** v. 9) from which only His compassion delivered them.

10-13. A Church Calendar. The responsibilities of worshipers; only brief mention is made here of matters that are treated at length later. Sabbaths, the Year of Rest, and the Day of Rest (vv. 10-12). **Let it rest and lie still.** As the slave was to be released from toil (21:2), so also the land was to rest the seventh year. The poor were permitted to eat of that which grew of itself that year (cf. Lev 25:1-7,20-22; Deut 15:1-18; 31:10-13). **12.** The Sabbath Day. Cf. 20:8-11; 31:12-17; 35:1-3. **That thine ox . . . may rest . . . the son of thy handmaid . . . the stranger.** This adds a humanitarian reason to the religious one given in 20:11, but does not contradict it. **13. In all . . . be circumspect.** Driver *(Cambridge Bible)* thinks this verse is displaced and should follow verse 19. But according to KD, it is a transitional sentence: verse 13a stresses their faithfulness in the laws that deal with their fellow men; and 13b prepares for the laws dealing with their relation to Jehovah.

c) The Pilgrimage Feasts 23:14-19. Though there were other observances to be kept, these three were the great festivals during which all the men of Israel were required to present themselves before the Lord. In them there was a remembrance not only of their redemption, but of God's continual blessing and provision. It has been pointed out that these are not only duties, but rights, "for keeping a feast to the Lord and appearing before Him were both privileges bestowed by Jehovah upon His covenant people" (KD). **14. A feast.** Cf. 5:1. **15. Unleavened bread.** Inseparable, of course, from Passover (cf. chs. 12; 13; Lev 23:5). **None shall appear before me empty.** Gifts were to be brought as evidence of thanks for God's blessings and as tribute to Jehovah their King (cf. Deut 16:16,17). **16. Feast of harvest.** Pentecost (Lev 23:15-22; Num 28:26-31; Deut 16:9-12). **Feast of ingathering.** Tabernacles (Num 29:12 ff.; Lev 23:34-43; Deut 16:13,14). These feasts marked the beginning and ending of the harvest of all the produce of the land.

18,19. Three rules were to be observed in the feasts. (1) Unleavened bread was to be used, not only in the feast of that name, but in all the feasts. (2) **Fat of my sacrifice** was not to remain (cf. 12:10). **Firstfruits.** The withholding of this confession and expression of gratitude brought judgment on Israel again and again (cf. Mal 3:8). (3) **Seethe a kid.** This direction seems oddly at variance with the other regulations, and long caused much speculation by the commentators. Then, in the Ugarit literature discovered in 1930, it was learned that boiling a kid in its mother's milk was a Canaanite practice used in connection with fertility rites *(Birth of the Gods,* 1:14). Israel, by the presentation of the first fruits, acknowledged that blessing came from Jehovah, not from magic.

d) Farewell Exhortation. 23:20-33. The covenant is concluded with these words of promise and warning.

20-22. The Angel of Jehovah. "The name of Jehovah was in this angel; that is to say, Jehovah revealed Himself in Him; and hence he is called in 33:15,16 the face of Jehovah, because the essential nature of Jehovah was manifested in him. This angel was not a created spirit, therefore, but the manifestation of Jehovah Himself" (KD). "The angel is Jehovah Himself in a temporary descent to visibility for a special purpose" (McNeile, *Westminster Commentary).*

23-33. Promise and Warning. God promised to drive out the nations before them and to bless them, providing for their needs and protecting them. The people of Israel, on their part, were to abstain from all idolatry and covenanting with pagan peoples.

Overthrow (v. 24). *Tear down and break down.* **Images.** *Pillars* (ASV). Stones set up near a temple or in a sacred grove, a regular feature of Canaanite worship. **The number of thy days** (v. 26). Both the faithful individual and the faithful nation were promised that they would live out their days. **My fear** (v. 27). The panic of heart that would come to the heathen as the knowledge of God's mighty acts on behalf of Israel became known (Josh 2:11). **Destroy.** Better, *throw into confusion* (RSV). **Hornets** (v. 28). This is hardly to be taken literally, though some do take it so. To determine just what is symbolized here has exercised the ingenuity of generations of commentators. It has been suggested that the hornets represent Egyptians, sickness, natural disasters, *et al.* The suggestion of KD that it was the sting of fear (v. 27) seems a most reasonable idea. After gradually expelling the Canaanites, the people of Israel were to occupy the land (vv. 29, 30). This they signally failed to do (Jud 1; 2). **I will set thy bounds** (v. 31). Only once, under Solomon (I Kgs 4:21), and then only briefly, did Israel achieve these boundaries. **Sea of the Philistines.** The Mediterranean. **Desert.** The wilderness between Egypt and Palestine. **The river.** The Euphrates. **Lest they make thee sin** (vv. 32,33). The destruction of the Canaanites was necessary, and contact with them was forbidden lest they infect the people of God with their sin as with an infectious disease.

4) The Ratification of the Covenant. 24:1-11.

1,2. These two verses are actually the conclusion of the words of the Lord from the preceding chapter. God gave Moses directions in regard to the ratification of the covenant which were distinct from the ordinances to be delivered to all the people. Aaron and his two elder sons, Nadab and Abihu, and seventy of the elders were to worship "afar off" while Moses drew near to the Lord. The rest of the people were not to go up on the mountain at all.

3. Words . . . judgments. Both the positive commands and decisions in regard to particular cases (the contents of 20:22 – 23:33) were delivered to the people. The Decalogue may not have been included, since all Israel had heard this from Jehovah himself. "It was necessary that the people should not only know what the Lord imposed upon them in the covenant about to be made with them, and what He promised them, but that they should also declare their willingness to perform what was imposed upon them" (KD). **4. Altar . . . pillars.** "As the altar indicated the presence of Jehovah, being the place where the Lord would come to His people to bless them (20:24), so the twelve pillars, or boundary stones, did not serve as mere memorials of the conclusion of the covenant, but were to indicate the place of the twelve tribes and represent their presence also" (KD).

5. Young men. These were neither first-born sons nor Aaronic priests, but men chosen by Moses for this particular act, perhaps "as the strongest and most active members of the community" *(Cambridge Bible).* **Burnt . . . peace offerings.** It is significant that no sin offering is described. These were redeemed people, who now, by these sacrifices of dedication and fellowship, were committing themselves and entering into a close and binding communion with their Redeemer. **7. Book of the covenant.** The book written by Moses (v. 4) and containing the laws of 20:22 – 23:33.

8. "In the blood sprinkled upon the altar, the natural life of the people was given up to God, as a life that had passed through death, to be pervaded by His grace; and then through the sprinkling upon the people it was restored to them again as a life renewed by the grace of God . . . . it became a vital power, holy and divine, uniting Israel and its God . . . a transposition of Israel into the kingdom of God, in which it was filled with the powers of God's spirit of grace and sanctified into a kingdom of priests, a holy nation (19:6)" (KD). **Concerning all these words.** *On the basis of all these regulations* (American Trans.).

9-11. The covenant meal was celebrated by Israel in its representatives. **Saw the God of Israel** (v. 10). "We must not go beyond the limits drawn in ch. 33:20-23 in our conceptions of what constituted the sight of God; at the same time we must regard it as a vision of God in some form of manifestation which rendered the divine nature discernible to the human eye. Nothing is said as to the form in which God manifested Himself" (KD).

B. Directions for the Sanctuary and the Priesthood. 24:12–31:18. The covenant having been established, there still remained the necessity "to give a definite external form to the covenant concluded with His people and construct a visible bond of fellowship in which He might manifest Himself to the people and they might draw near to Him" (KD). For this reason Moses was called up into the mountain for a long period. The construction of the sanctuary was not to be left to the devices of men. "The divine directions extended to all the details, because they were all of importance in relation to the design of God" (KD). At the same time, the absence of Moses served as a test of the sincerity of the recent dedication and pledge of the people.

1) Moses' Ascent into the Mountain. 24:12-18.

12. The **tables of stone** were to have inscribed on them the Decalogue (31:18). **Law, and commandments,** including, probably, the instructions *(tōrâ)* for the sanctuary and priesthood, and the laws now in Leviticus and Deuteronomy. **13. Joshua** accompanied Moses onto the mountain, but seems not to have been in the immediate presence of Moses when Jehovah gave the laws. **14. The elders.** Not necessarily just the seventy of 24:1. Aaron and Hur were appointed administrators in Moses' absence.

2) The Offerings To Be Brought for the Tabernacle. 25:1-7.

2. Offering. Literally, *lifted.* A gift lifted from one's possessions and given to the Lord. **3. Brass.** Actually bronze. Modern brass, an alloy of copper and zinc, was not known in the ancient world. Bronze, i.e., copper hardened by tin, was used widely until iron came to be generally used. **4.** The exact shades of the colors mentioned are difficult to determine. **Blue** was nearer purple-blue or violet, while **purple** was a red-purple. Both colors were costly and highly prized for their brilliance. **5. Badgers' skins.** The meaning of the Hebrew word is uncertain, and various interpretations have been offered: *seal* (ASV), *goat* (RSV), *porpoise* (American). A similar Arabic word means "dolphin" or "dugong." Another view is that this is an Egyptian word meaning simply "leather" (Moffatt). *Badger* was suggested by the Talmud, but there is little probability that this was the skin used. **Shittim.** Acacia. Found widely on the Sinaitic peninsula, a very hard and durable wood.

3) Instructions for the Sanctuary. 25:8 – 27:21.

The names given to the structure commonly called the Tabernacle are many. It is called "the tent," usually referring to the outer covering; the "tent of meeting," where God met with his people (27:21); the "tent of the witness" or "testimony," because it contained the ark and the Decalogue (25:16); the "dwelling" and "dwelling of Jehovah" (Num 16:9), or "dwelling of the testimony" (Ex 38:21); and "the sanctuary" or "holy place" (25:8). The names "house" and "temple" (I Sam 1:9; 3:3) are also used, but they refer to a more settled condition of the Tabernacle. The common name is "tent," a term which the English translators exalted to the more high-sounding "tabernacle," following the Vulgate *tabernaculum.*

Although no symbolism is attributed to the Tabernacle in the text, there can be no doubt that it symbolized for Israel, as it does for us, great spiritual truths. It clearly taught the fact of God's presence in the midst of his people At the same time it indicated that he was a holy God in the midst of a sinful people, for the whole arrangement of the Tabernacle made plain that "the way into the holiest was not yet made manifest" (Heb 9:8). With the ark containing the Testimony, it was "an ever present witness to the claims of God and the duty of man" *(Cambridge Bible).*

9. According to all that I show thee. Moses not only received detailed instructions, but he must also have seen a pattern or model. Herein lies the difficulty for us; much that is confusing in the instructions would immediately be made clear if we could only see the model. Therefore, in considering the various speculations as to the exact form and mode of structure for the Tabernacle, we can only attempt to decide which seems the most reasonable.

a) The Ark of the Covenant. 25:10-22.

The ark was an oblong box or chest of acacia wood overlaid with gold. Taking the cubit as approximately eighteen inches long, the ark measured about three feet nine inches long, two feet three inches wide, and two feet three inches deep. Around the top was a crown or molding of gold, forming a rim. At each of the four corners or "feet" (v. 12) there was fixed a ring of gold. Through these rings were slipped gold plated poles or staves by which the ark was carried. The cover of the ark is referred to separately as "the mercy seat" (v. 17) or "the propitiatory." It was a slab of solid gold, fitting the length and width of the ark. Mounted upon the cover were the figures of two cherubim made out of beaten gold. These figures faced each other, with their wings spread as though shadowing the mercy seat. "The gold plate upon the ark formed the footstool of the throne for Him who caused His name, i.e., the real presence of His being, to dwell in a cloud between the two cherubim, above their outstretched wings. . . . Thus the footstool of God became a throne of grace, which received its name *kappōret* or *hilasterion* from the fact that the highest and most perfect act of atonement under the Old Testament was performed upon it" (KD). **16. Testimony.** The Decalogue upon the tables of stone. **18. Cherubim.** Whatever the exact appearance of these figures might have been, they always symbolized the presence of the Lord (cf. Ezk 1:5 ff.; Gen 3:24; II Sam 22:11; Rev 4:6,7).

b) The Table of Shewbread. 25:23-30.

This was a plain table, three feet long, one foot six inches broad, and two feet three inches high, made of wood overlaid with gold. A border or frame about three inches broad **(a handbreadth,** v. 25) ran around the table, either just below the top, as in modern tables, or halfway down the legs, as it appears in the representation on the Arch of Titus. On the four legs were rings of gold for the poles by which the table was carried. The name *shewbread* was first used by Tyndale (A.D. 1526) in translating Heb 9:2, probably following Luther's rendering *schoubrot.* A better translation is *presence bread* (ASV marg.; Moffatt) or *bread of the presence* (RSV). Bread was set on the table in the presence of Jehovah, one loaf for each tribe of Israel. There was thus a continual acknowledgment by Israel that from Jehovah came their daily bread, a symbol of both communion and dependence.

29. Dishes. Large, platter-like dishes to carry the flat loaves of bread. **Spoons.** Rather, *cups* for the frankincense that was to be placed on the bread, identifying it as a sacrifice (Lev 24:7). **Covers.** Chalices or bowls for the wine of the drink offering. **Bowls.** Flagons to pour the wine out in libations.

The loaves of bread were called *bread of the face* (v. 30) because they were to lie on the table before the face of Jehovah as a food offering presented by the children of Israel (Lev 24:7), "not as food for Jehovah but as a symbol of the spiritual food which Israel was to prepare . . . so that the bread and wine, which stood upon the table by the side of the loaves, as the fruit of the labor bestowed by Israel upon the soil of its inheritance, were a symbol of its spiritual labor in the kingdom of God, the spiritual vineyard of its Lord" (KD). The shewbread also reminded the Israelites of their dependence upon Jehovah, from whom came their daily sustenance (cf. Ezk 16:19; Hos 2:8).

c) The Candlestick. 25:31-40.

The only light in the Tabernacle was furnished by the candlestick, or, properly speaking, the lampstand. This consisted of a central shaft from which three branches extended outward and upward from each side; on the tops of the branches and the shaft, lamps were fixed, seven in all. Both stem and branches were decorated at intervals with ornamental work shaped like the calyx and corolla of the almond flower. The size of the lamp is not given in Scripture. Josephus says that it was five feet high and three feet six inches broad. Others infer that it was two feet three inches high and wide, the size of the table of shewbread opposite it. A talent of pure gold, approximately ninety-four pounds, was used to make the lampstand and its various vessels. Apart from its utilitarian function, the lamp stood as a symbol, not only of the light of God by which Israel walked, but of Israel itself, a light in the midst of a dark world, supplied with the oil of the Spirit of God.

31. Shaft, and . . . branches. *Base and shaft* (ASV). **Bowls . . . knops.** *Cups, each with its calyx and petals* (American). The *cup* is the whole flower, the **knop,** the bud with its outer and inner petals. Some have thought that the lampstand was to resemble the almond tree, called the "awakening one" by the Hebrews because of its early blossoming. **37.** A lamp in Bible times was like a saucer with the rim pinched in at one end. It was filled with oil, and a wick was placed in it with one end protruding from the pinched-in part. **Light the lamps.** Actually, "fix on" the lamps to the stand after they had been prepared.

38. Tongs. An instrument, something like tweezers, to draw out the wick. **Snuff dish** (lit., *fire catcher).* A tray for the tongs.

d) The Tabernacle. 26:1-37.

1-6. The Ornamental Curtains that Formed the Tabernacle Itself. There were ten curtains, each forty-two feet long and six feet wide. When fastened together, they formed one great hanging, sixty by forty-two feet. The curtains were beautifully woven tapestries of white linen, and blue, purple, and scarlet fabrics, with figures of cherubim either woven in or embroidered on them. These, mounted on the wooden framework (vv. 15-30), formed the Tabernacle proper. Unless we are to understand that this beautiful work was completely hidden, we must suppose either that the boards of the frame formed hollow squares rather than a solid fence (Kennedy, "Tabernacle," HDB), or else that the curtains hung down inside the frame (James Strong, *The Tabernacle).* Strong believes that they were not used as a tent at all, but hung like curtains on the inside of the frame.

Cunning work (v. 1). Work of the designer or pattern maker. The curtains (vv. 3-6) were fastened together in two sets of three each by means of loops of blue material on the edges, which were coupled together with gold clasps. The two sets were then fastened to each other in the same way, thus making one large curtain. Since the frame of the Tabernacle was forty-five by fifteen by fifteen feet, the sixty-foot curtain must have hung down to the ground in the back (assuming the front left open), and the forty-two-foot width would have reached to within a foot and a half of the ground.

7-14. The Outer Coverings. The tent over the dwelling was made of goats' hair, as Bedouin tents are still made, and probably as the Israelite tents were made then. While the linen curtains formed a beautiful interior, the goats' hair made a serviceable covering outside. This covering was made of eleven curtains, each forty-five by six feet, fastened together by bronze clasps (vv. 10,11) in the same manner as the linen curtains; this formed one great covering sixty-six by forty-five feet. Since the goats' hair curtain was three feet wider than the linen, it must have covered the latter completely on the sides (v. 13). It was six feet longer than the tapestry, and this excess was used by doubling one of the sections over (v. 9) and letting it hang down in front, as a sort of valance to protect the entrance screen. The rest of the excess probably hung down in the back. Any slack in this covering would have been taken up, as in other tents, by the ropes and pegs by which it was stretched out and held. Some think that there may have been a ridgepole to form a peak or gable, but this cannot be determined from the text. Two outer coverings of leather (v. 14; cf. 25:5) covered the woven goats' hair and provided protection from bad weather.

15-30. The Wooden Framework. A framework made of boards or frames of acacia wood plated with gold, each board being fifteen feet long and two feet three inches wide. Kennedy argues that these were open frames rather than solid boards ("Tabernacle," HDB). We do not know the thickness of the boards, but Josephus says that it was three inches (*Antiq.* III. 6.3), which would have made a very substantial and exceedingly heavy fence, rather than simply the sturdy frame that was required. Also, as suggested above, unless we are to think of the tapestry as drapes, the beauty would have been completely hidden by a solid frame. The Scripture does not give us enough detail to enable us to picture the frame exactly. Each board had two tenons (lit., *hands*) projecting beneath (v. 17), which fitted into mortices or sockets in bases of silver (v. 19). The silver bases weighed one talent (ninety-five pounds) each, enough weight to secure the frame quite solidly (38:27). The frames formed the sides and back of the Tabernacle. Twenty boards formed each side, forty-five feet long, and six boards formed the back. At the two corners where side and back met, two extra boards were added in some way for strengthening. Though the exact manner of forming the corners is obscure (v. 24), we know that the extra boards served somehow to buttress the framework. For further strengthening, five bars ran horizontally along each side and the back, fitting into gold rings on the boards. The middle bar ran from end to end (v. 28); the others presumably were shorter, each running perhaps half the length.

Boards (v. 15). *Upright frames* (RSV). **Two tenons . . . set in order** (v. 17). *Two pegs clamped to the foot* (Moffatt). *Each of these two frames forming a double support and running it up to the topmost ring* (v. 24; Moffatt).

31-35. The Veil of the Holy of Holies. The "Dwelling" was divided into two sections, called "the Holy Place" and "the Holy of Holies" or "Most Holy Place." The veil was made of the same richly woven tapestry as the inner curtains. It was hung by gold hooks from four pillars of gilded wood, which were held by tenons in sockets of silver, as were the boards of the framework. **Taches** (v. 33). Hooks or clasps.

36,37. The Entrance Veil. The entrance was covered by a veil of less elaborate workmanship than that of the Holy of Holies, and was hung, like the other, on pillars, fixed into sockets of bronze.

e) The Altar of Burnt Offering. 27:1-8.

This altar was a hollow frame of acacia wood, plated with bronze, seven and a half feet square and four and a half feet in height. At each corner a bronze point (**horns**, v. 2) projected. A grating or network of bronze was placed **under the compass** (v. 5), or ledge of the altar, **even to the midst,** i.e., *reaching half way up* (RSV). Some suppose that this network extended through the altar, forming a grate upon which the sacrifice rested. Others believe that the ledge, supported by the network, ran around the altar and formed a place for the priests to stand on while sacrificing. The latter seems more probable, for it is doubtful that there would have been a fire within the altar itself, as this would soon have charred the wood completely. The bronze altar was probably placed over a mound of earth or stone and the fire laid on top. At the four corners of the ledge were bronze rings, through which bronzed wooden staves were thrust for carrying the altar.

Horns (v. 2). "In these the whole force of the altar was concentrated" (KD). Those who fled for safety to a sanctuary laid hold of the horns of the altar (I Kgs 1:50). The blood of the sacrifice was smeared on the horns (Lev 4:7). As throughout Scripture, "horns" stand for power, it is probable that the horns of the altar symbolized the power of God. **Ashes** (v. 3; lit., *fat*), i.e., the ashes of the burned sacrifice. **Basons** (lit., *tossing vessels*). Large bowls in which the blood was caught and thrown against the sides of the altar.

f) The Court of the Tabernacle. 27:9-19.

A rectangular area, one hundred and

fifty feet long by seventy-five feet wide, surrounded the Tabernacle. It was enclosed by hangings of white linen, seven and a half feet in height, suspended on pillars. There were twenty pillars for each of the longer sides and ten for the shorter ones. The pillars, or poles, were of bronze with capitals of silver (38:17), and were set into sockets or bases of bronze. The curtains were attached to the pillars by means of silver hooks which hooked into the silver fillets or bands of the pillars. Cords and bronze tent pins kept the hangings taut (38:19). The entrance to this court was on the east side. There the hangings extended in for fifteen cubits from each corner, leaving a thirty-foot entrance. The entrance was closed by a screen of tapestry embroidered like the entrance screen of the Tabernacle itself. **Vessels of the tabernacle** (v. 19). Probably the tools used for setting up and taking down the Tabernacle.

20,21. The sanctuary light. Clear olive oil of the first quality, obtained by "beating," i.e., gently pounding the olives in a mortar. Inferior oil was obtained by grinding the pulp that remained. **Evening to morning.** The lamps were kept burning in the Holy Place, before God's testimony, all through the night.

4) The Garments and Consecration of the Priests. 28:1–29:46.

Aaron and his sons were chosen by Jehovah to be the priests, the mediators, of Israel. This was a new ordinance, as were the regulations for the sanctuary and the sacrifices. Critics insist that the restriction of the priesthood to the family of Aaron is a reflection of post-Exilic times. But if there was a Tabernacle, there must also have been a stated priesthood. There is no evidence in any of the later history of Israel that, except for extraordinary circumstances, any but the sons of Aaron ever acted as priests.

a) Directions Regarding the Appointment and Clothing of the Priests. 28:1-5.

b) The Ephod. 28:6-14.

This was the most distinctive part of the high priest's garments. It was a kind of waistcoat or apron, elaborately embroidered. It consisted of two pieces, front and back, joined at the shoulders by straps or **shoulder pieces** (v. 7), and bound around the waist by a girdle that was part of the ephod itself (v. 8). On each shoulder strap was an onyx stone in a setting of gold filigree, upon which were engraved the names of the twelve tribes of Israel, six on each stone. Thus symbolically the priest bore upon his shoulders the burden of all Israel as he represented them before God. The colors and material of the ephod (v. 6) answer to the colors and texture of the sanctuary, thus identifying the sanctuary and the minister. Instead of cherubim, however, the ephod was embroidered throughout with fine gold wire, woven in with the other colors (v. 8). **Curious girdle.** *Skillfully woven band* (ASV, RSV). **According to their birth** (v. 10). In the order of the ages of the ancestral sons of Jacob. **Ouches** (v. 11). *Settings* (ASV); *settings of gold filigree* (RSV).

c) The Breastplate. 28:15-29.

The breastplate or "pouch" of judgment, was a bag of the same material as the ephod. It was made of one piece of material, folded over to form a pouch, nine by nine inches. Fastened into this pouch in settings of gold were twelve precious stones, four rows of three each, upon which were engraved the names of the twelve tribes. The pouch was held to the ephod by means of two chains of gold, which linked into gold rings at the upper corners of the pouch and attached them to the shoulder pieces of the ephod (vv. 22-25). Through other rings at the bottom corners, the pouch was secured to the girdle of the ephod by means of bands of blue lacing (vv. 26-28).

As the high priest ministered in the sanctuary, he bore the burdens and needs of his people not only in the place of strength, upon his shoulders, but also upon his heart, that with wisdom and compassion he might be their mediator before Jehovah (v. 29).

The identity of some of the stones in the breastplate (vv. 17-20) is very uncertain. And since the early translators of the Bible were also uncertain about the identification, their renderings are quite inconsistent. The following identifications represent a consensus of the opinions of modern authorities.

Sardius (v. 17). Possibly carnelian or red jasper. **Topaz.** A yellow or green stone, possibly chrysolite. **Carbuncle.** Emerald or rock crystal. **Emerald** (v. 18). A red stone, obviously not an emerald; either ruby or garnet. **Sapphire.** More likely lapis lazuli than sapphire. **Diamond.** Either the crystal or sardonyx. There is no evidence that the diamond was known in ancient days. **Ligure** (v. 19). A stratified red and white stone, either jacinth or cairngorm. **Agate.** Properly named, a red opaque stone. **Amethyst.** The same clear purple stone we call by this name. **Beryl** (20). Either the same or chalcedony; possibly yellow jasper. **Onyx.** The same as oynx today. **Jasper.** Beryl or green jasper.

The directions for the lower fastening of the breastplate (v. 27) are not clear, but this was probably as explained above. Moffatt translates: *low down on the apron, close to the joining of the shoulder straps and above the artistic ribbon.*

d) **The Urim and Thummim.** 28:30.

The Hebrew words mean *lights and perfections.* The LXX translation is *revelation and truth.* "What the Urim and Thummim really were cannot be determined with certainty, either from the names themselves or from any other circumstances connected with them. Perhaps they were a certain medium given by the Lord to His people through which, whenever the congregation required divine illumination to guide its actions, that illumination was guaranteed; and by means of which the rights of Israel, when called in question or endangered, were to be restored, and . . . this medium was bound up with the official dress of the high priest, though its precise character can no longer be determined" (KD; cf. Num 27:21; I Sam 28:6; Ezr 2:63).

e) The Robe of the Ephod. 28:31-35.

It was woven of one piece of cloth, with armholes but no sleeves. It was put on over the head and probably reached to the knees. Around the edge of the skirt small golden bells alternated with pomegranates of twisted yarn. The pomegranates have been taken as symbols of the Word of God, a sweet and refreshing fruit, and the bells as the sounding forth of this Word (cf. Sir [or Ecclesiasticus] 45:9). **Binding . . . as it were the hole of an habergeon** (v. 32). For **habergeon** the ASV has *coat of mail.* The binding was to keep the edge from fraying. **That he die not** (v. 35). No mere priest was allowed to enter the Holy of Holies, the immediate presence of Jehovah. "This privilege was restricted to the representative of the whole congregation . . . and even he could only do so when wearing the robe of the word of God, as the bearer of the divine testimony upon which the covenant fellowship with the Lord was founded" (KD).

f) The Headdress. 28:36-38.

The headdress of the high priest was a turban of fine white linen (v. 39) upon the front of which was affixed, by means of a band of blue lace, a gold plate on which were engraved the words, "Holy to Jehovah." Thus was the office and person of the high priest marked out by God before the people, until He should come who was Himself holy (cf. Heb 7:26). **Mitre** (v. 37). The AV, ASV term is misleading, as the headdress bore no resemblance to modern conceptions of a mitre. It more likely resembled the common turban of the East. **That Aaron may bear the iniquity** (v. 38). The high priest was exalted into an atoning mediator of the whole nation; and an atoning intercession was associated with his office.

g) **The tunic** (AV, *coat).* 28:39.

The tunic or coat was woven of linen in a check pattern and was worn close to the body, beneath the robe of the ephod. According to Josephus *(Antiq.* III. 7.2), the tunic reached to the feet and had tight sleeves. It was bound about the body with a richly colored sash or girdle embroidered like the tapestries of the sanctuary.

h) Dress of the Ordinary Priests. 28:40-43.

Although they are described as being "for glory and for beauty," these were very simple garments. There was a tunic such as the high priest wore, but of plain color, bound with a sash that is not otherwise described. Upon the head was a cap (RSV), either a band of linen about the head, or, more likely, a skull cap. Beneath the tunic the priests wore linen breeches or drawers. It should be remembered that linen was a costly and highly prized cloth in those days, so that even the least of the priests' garments were made of the finest material. By these garments the priests appointed by Jehovah were officially marked as his representatives. To fail to wear them, and thus approach the Tabernacle (v. 43) as in their own virtue and personal right, was to bring upon themselves judgment and death.

i) The Consecration of the Priests. 29:1-37.

"Although the holiness of their office

was reflected in their dress, it was necessary, on account of the sinfulness of their nature, that they should be sanctified through a special consecration for the administration of their office" (KD). The directions now given for the consecration were carried out in Leviticus 8. Since a full appreciation of the significance of the directions must wait upon a discussion of the sacrificial laws of Leviticus 1–7, it seems best to deal here only with the actual directions and not their spiritual meaning.

1-3. Preparation of the Offerings. Three types of biscuit or **bread** accompanied the offering: ordinary unleavened bread; **cakes,** i.e., unleavened bread mingled with oil; and **wafers,** i.e., very thin cakes anointed with oil (v. 2).

4-9. The Investiture of Aaron and His Sons. The priests were to be washed, dressed, and anointed with oil. Certainly this is a very clear indication of their being cleansed spiritually, clothed with God's righteousness, and empowered by the Holy Spirit.

10-14. The Sin Offering. A bullock was offered as a sin offering for the appointed priests. The men who were a type of the Great Priest to come had first to be cleansed from their own sins (cf. Heb 7:27). **Caul** (v. 13). The appendix or the lobe upon the liver.

15-18. The Ram of Dedication. The ram, wholly burned upon the altar, symbolized the priests, wholly dedicated to God. **Sprinkle** (v. 16). Actually, *toss* or *throw* better represents the Hebrew.

19-28. The Ram of Consecration. The cleansed and dedicated priests, symbolically had communion with their Lord, as they partook of the sacrificed ram. Ears, hands, and feet (v. 20) were dedicated to God to hearken to and obey his word. The cleansing blood and sanctifying oil were sprinkled not only upon the men, but upon their official garments (v. 21), consecrating and empowering them for service.

Rump (v. 22; lit., *fat tail).* The fat-tailed sheep is still bred in Palestine, the tail being considered a special delicacy. **Wave them** (v. 24). The specified portions of the ram and bread were waved, i.e., extended to the altar and then drawn back; this symbolically presented them to God. God's portion (v. 25) was consumed upon the altar. The breast and the thigh of the ram of the installation offering were given to Moses as to the officiating priest (vv. 26-28). Ordinarily, as here ordained, this portion would go to the priest.

29,30. The priestly garments were to be passed on from generation to generation. The installation of priests in succeeding generations was to take seven days, as would this initial consecration (v. 35).

31-34. The Sacrificial Meal. That the priests should partake of the very offering by which they had been atoned for and consecrated, reminds us of Christian communion in the Lamb by whose sacrifice we have been redeemed. **35-37.** Through seven days, the consecration not only of the priests but of the altar of sacrifice was to be carried out.

j) The Morning and Evening Sacrifice. 29:38-42. Daily, morning and evening, on behalf of the whole congregation of Israel, the priests were to offer a lamb, with the accompanying meal and drink offerings. Thus day by day the dedication of all the people was renewed.

k) Promise of Blessing. 29:43-46. In response to such a continual dedication, Jehovah promised his constant presence and blessing. He would dwell in the midst of his people, and the appointed means of mediation – priest, tabernacle, and altar – would be sanctified to him.

5) Concluding Directions in Regard to the Tabernacle. 30:1-38.

a) The Altar of Incense. 30:1-10. This small altar, made of acacia wood plated with gold, is often called the "golden altar" (39:38; 40:5,26; Num 4:11) as contrasted with the brazen altar of sacrifice. It was one and a half feet square and three feet high. Upon the four upper corners were horns. A rim or molding ran around the altar, and beneath this, on the corners, were rings of gold for carrying. The altar was placed in the Holy Place, directly in front of the veil that separated it from the Holy of Holies and the ark. This very close connection between the altar and the ark is apparently referred to in Heb 9:4. (AV erroneously translates *censer.)*

Only incense was to be burned on this altar, and only that mixture prescribed by God (Ex 30:34-38). This altar, the symbol of man's closest approach to God, had also to be cleansed by the atoning blood year by year (v. 10). "The connection between the incense-offering and the burnt-offering is indicated by the rule that they were to be offered at the same time. Both offerings shadowed forth the devotion of Israel to its God, whilst the fact that they were offered every day exhibited this devotion as constant and uninterrupted. But the distinction between them consisted in this, that in the burnt or whole offering Israel consecrated and sanctified its whole life and action, in both body and soul to the Lord, whilst in the incense-offering its prayer was embodied as the exaltation of the spiritual man to God . . . the incense-offering presupposed reconciliation with God. . . . In this respect, the incense-offering was not only a spiritualizing and transfiguring of the burnt-offering, but a completion of that offering also" (KD).

b) The Ransom Money. 30:11-16. Each Israelite, **twenty years old and above** (v. 14) was required to pay a half shekel (about forty cents) to Jehovah as **an atonement for your souls** (v. 15). "It was no ordinary tribute . . . which Israel was to pay to Jehovah as its King, but an act demanded by the holiness of the theocratic covenant. As an expiation for souls, it pointed to the unholiness of Israel's nature, and reminded the people continually, that by nature it was alienated from God, and could only remain in covenant with the Lord and live in His kingdom on the ground of His grace, which covered its sin. It was not till this sinful nature had been sanctified by a perfect atonement, and servitude under the law had been glorified and fully transformed into that sonship to which Israel was called . . . that as children of the kingdom they had no longer to pay this atonement-money for their souls" (KD; cf. Mt 17:25,26). **Every one that passeth among them** (v. 13). *Numbered in the census* (RSV).

c) The Bronze Laver. 30:17-21. The laver was a basin for water, set between the brazen altar and the Tabernacle, in which the priest could wash both hands and feet before entering the Holy Place. No description of the size or shape of the laver is given. By this laver, the need for daily cleansing for those who served the Lord was not simply suggested but demanded (v. 20).

d) The Holy Anointing Oil. 30:22-33. A perfumed oil, mixed according to a specific recipe, was to be prepared for sacramental anointing. To mark the sacredness of that which was set apart unto the Lord, any other use of the oil was forbidden (v. 33). **Pure myrrh** (v. 23). "Flowing" or liquid balsam. **Five hundred shekels.** About sixteen pounds. **Cinnamon.** In those days a rare and costly spice. **Sweet calamus.** An aromatic cane, possibly the same as that which in classical times came from India. **Cassia** (v. 24). A species of cinnamon. In all, about forty-eight pounds of spices, dried and powdered, were mixed with a gallon and a half of olive oil and *blended as by the perfumer* (v. 25, RSV).

e) The Holy Incense. 30:34-38. The incense to be used for worship was also carefully prescribed, and its use for ordinary purposes was forbidden (vv. 37, 38). Thus the fragrance of the holy oil and incense, as it was used in the service of the Tabernacle, was to be unique and unmistakable, a reminder to the people, with every breath they had of it, that God was in their midst. **Stacte** (v. 34; lit., *that which drips*). The word **stacte** is simply a transliteration of the LXX and the Vulgate term. It was a very fragrant kind of myrrh. It has also been identified with the gum of the storax tree, "a beautiful, perfumed shrub, abundant on the lower hills of Palestine" *(Cambridge Bible)*. **Onycha.** This is also a transliteration from the LXX and the Vulgate; it was the powdered shell of a certain mollusc, still gathered and used for incense and perfume. **Galbanum.** A pungent, bitter resin, used also medicinally; it gave sharpness to the other ingredients. **Pure frankincense.** Another gum resin, from trees found in ancient times, chiefly in south Arabia. **Tempered together** (v. 35). Literally, *salted,* either as a symbol of purification or to induce more rapid burning; possibly both reasons. The ingredients were to be mixed together and melted into a solid mass (v. 36). Then small portions would be broken off and beaten into a powder to throw upon the live coals of the altar.

6) The Builders of the Tabernacle. 31:1-11. Two men were named by the Lord to supervise the carrying out of the directions for the Tabernacle. They were men who had been endowed by God with the wisdom and talent necessary for this very thing – Bezaleel of Judah and Aholiab of Dan.

7) The Observance of the Sabbath. 31:12-17. A solemn and repetitive en-

forcement of the Sabbath ordinance, already enjoined in the Decalogue. This observance was to be the peculiar sign of Israel's relation to Jehovah, "By this shall all men know. . . ." It is to be noted that this outward observance, along with other outer signs, such as circumcision, the dietary laws, *et al.*, are specifically translated in the NT into inward, spiritual evidences of discipleship (cf. Rom 2:28,29; Gal 4:9,10; Col 2:16,17). **Surely be put to death** (v. 14). An added sanction to enforce the command (cf. 20:8-11; 23:12).

18. At the conclusion of this long period of instruction, Moses was given the two tables of testimony, inscribed by God himself with the Decalogue.

C. The Covenant Broken and Restored. 32:1–34:35.

The people of Israel found it hard to walk even forty days by faith while their visible leader was gone. They demanded that Aaron produce a tangible sign of God's presence. It is uncertain whether it was the first commandment that was broken, a repudiation of Jehovah as God, or the second, an image demanded to represent Jehovah. In either case, it was a clear and deliberate transgression of the covenant that they had committed themselves to so boldly a few weeks before, a covenant sealed with blood.

1) Israel's Demand for a God. 32:1-6. "They were unwilling to continue longer without a God to go before them; but the faith upon which their desire was founded was a very perverted one, not only as clinging to what was apparent to the eye, but as corrupted by the impatience and unbelief of a natural heart which has not been pervaded by the power of the living God, and imagines itself forsaken by Him whenever His help is not visibly and outwardly at hand" (KD).

1. Gods. The word *'Elōhîm,* though plural, is usually rendered *God,* although it can be and is translated *gods* just as well. In the present instance it is difficult to know how to translate, and the commentators are divided because, as mentioned above, we do not know just what was in the mind of the people. **Delay.** Literally, *cause shame,* i.e., by not returning.

4. These be thy gods. Or, *This be thy God*. **Fashioned it.** The ancient idols were usually made by plating gold or silver upon a wooden center or frame (Isa 40:19,20; 44:12-17; Jer 10:1-9). It is unlikely that Aaron cast a solid gold animal. **Calf.** A young bull. The Egyptian Apis and the Phoenician Baal were both pictured as bulls, a common representation among many peoples of that day for fertility and strength. Whatever the original impulse of the Israelites, the making of the image was the first step on a very slippery path, which led to the eventual identification of Jehovah with the gods of the nations (cf. Isa 40; Jer 10). **6. Rose up to play.** Idolatry was accompanied by sensual, lewd dances which formed a part of the fertility cult.

2) The Sin of Israel Revealed to Moses by God. 32:7-14.

7. Thy people. By this word God seemed to disown Israel. The phrase may have been used (as KD suggests) because they were the transgressors of the covenant of which Moses was the mediator, and so they were particularly his.

10. I will make of thee. "God puts the fate of the nation into the hand of Moses, that he may remember his mediatorial office, and show himself worthy of his calling. This condescension of God, which placed the preservation or destruction of Israel in the hands of Moses, coupled with a promise which left the fullest freedom to his decision . . . constituted a great test for Moses, whether he would be willing to give up his own people, laden as they were with guilt, as the price of his own exaltation. And Moses stood the test. The preservation of Israel was dearer to him than the honor of becoming the head and founder of a new kingdom of God" (KD).

11. Moses pled for Israel in this prayer of intercession because they were **thy people**; because of the great deliverance God had already wrought for them; and lest the Egyptians should mock, misconceiving the reason for the destruction; and finally, he pled the promise made to the fathers.

14. The Lord repented. "God is thus said to 'repent' not because He really changes His purpose, but because He does so apparently, when, in consequence of a change in the character and conduct of men, He is obliged to make a corresponding change in the purpose toward them which He had previously announced, and adopt toward them a new attitude" *(Cambridge Bible).* Keil and Delitzsch mention "the deep spiritual idea of the repentance of God, as an anthropopathic description of the pain which is caused to the love of God by the destruction of His creatures."

3) Moses' Return to the Camp. 32:15-24.

19. The actual sight of the blatant transgression affected Moses more strongly than the report of it could do. Overcome with indignation, he threw to the ground the tablets of stone, the commands of which had already been broken by the hearts and acts of Israel. **20.** The wooden core of the image was burned, the metal pulverized, and the dust of charcoal and gold strewed upon the water. The people were humbled into drinking their own sin.

4) Punishment of the Idolaters. 32:25-29. The Levites may have been involved in the sin of the rest of the people, but if so, there was immediate shame, repentance, and willingness on their part to turn from their idolatry to Jehovah. The stubborn persistence of the others in their sin was made clear by their unwillingness to respond to the call, **Who is on the Lord's side?** (v. 26)

25. Naked. Literally, *broken loose,* i.e., loose from all restraint and from allegiance to God. **27. Sweep the camp from side to side** (Moffatt). "As in every other decimation, the selection must be determined by lot or accidental choice, so here Moses left it to be determined by chance, upon whom the sword of the Levites would fall, knowing very well that even the so-called chance would be under the direction of God. . . . The unresisting attitude of the people generally may be explained partly from their reverence for Moses, whom God had so mightily and marvelously accredited as His servant in the sight of all the nation, and partly from the despondency and fear so natural to a guilty conscience" (KD).

29. Consecrate yourselves . . . even every man upon his son. *Against his son* (ASV; LXX; Vulg.). *You have ordained yourselves . . . each one at the cost of his son* (RSV). "In the cause of the Lord, every one may not spare even his nearest relative, but must deny either son or brother for the Lord's sake" (KD; cf. Deut 33:9; Mt 10:37,38).

5) Moses' Intercession for Israel's Sin. 32:30-35.

30. Peradventure I shall make an atonement. Atonement for sin is a far greater thing than even Moses understood. Only God's Lamb could take away the sin of the world.

32. Blot me . . . out of thy book. "To cut off from fellowship with the living God, or from the kingdom of those who live before God, and to deliver over to death. As a true mediator of his people, Moses was ready to stake his own life for the deliverance of the nation, and not to live before God himself, if Jehovah did not forgive the people their sin" (KD; cf. Rom 9:3). "It is not easy to estimate the measure of love in a Moses and a Paul; for the narrow boundary of our reasoning powers does not comprehend it, as the little child is unable to comprehend the courage of warlike heroes" (Bengel, *Gnomon of the NT).*

33. Whosoever hath sinned. Not even the sacrifice of Moses could take away sin. **34.** "Moses had obtained the preservation of the people and their entrance into the promised land, under the protection of God, through his intercession, and averted from the nation the abrogation of the covenant; but the covenant relation which had existed before was not restored in its integrity. Though grace may modify and soften wrath, it cannot mar the justice of the holy God" (KD).

6) God's Modification of Justice. 33:1-3. The words, **mine Angel shall go before thee** (32:34), are explained here. The statement was a modification of God's judgment upon Israel, but it was still punishment. Jehovah himself, not a mere messenger, had been in their midst before; but now, **I will not go up in the midst of thee** (v. 3).

7) Repentance and Probation of Israel. 33:4-11. The people were beginning to feel the weight of God's judgment, and in sorrow they stripped themselves of all adornment.

7. Tabernacle of the congregation. Critics have gratuitously introduced here a confusion which is not at all in the narrative. This "Tent of Meeting" (RSV) is obviously not the Tabernacle which had been described to Moses but was not yet built. To assume that this tent is the Tabernacle is to judge that generations of Jews and Christians, including the original author or editors of Exodus, have been so incredibly stupid as not to recognize the contradiction. What is stated here is that Moses set up a tent outside the camp, a temporary sanctuary where he met with Jehovah, and to which those who sought the Lord might come. Thus he enforced and illustrated God's judgment that He would not dwell in the midst of Israel. Moses' departure for the tent was marked by all the people (v. 8), and the lesson was firmly driven home that their sins had separated them from their God. This very fact awakened a longing in the hearts of the people (v. 10) that made possible a full restoration.

8) The Reconciliation of Israel to Jehovah. 33:12-23. Moses pleaded that although God had declared that Moses had found grace in His sight, He had not given the assurance that was necessary to carry on this difficult task. Moses also reminded the Lord that, after all, Israel was God's nation. **12. I know thee by name.** I "know thee individually, more intimately than the other Israelites, like a king who knows the names of only such of his servants as he is on intimate terms with" *(Cambridge Bible).* **13. Show me now thy way.** Literally, *make me to know. Show,* in early Modern English meant not only to "let see" but also to "let know" (cf. *Cambridge Bible).* **14.** God promised that he himself, not simply a representative (vv. 1,3), would go up with Israel.

18. Moses was emboldened by this gracious promise to ask an unparalleled favor. "When God talked with him face to face . . . he merely saw a 'similitude of Jehovah,' a form which rendered the invisible being of God visible to the human eye . . . . What Moses desired, therefore, was a sight of the glory or essential being of God, without any figure, and without a veil" (KD). This request was not made from idle curiosity but from "a desire to cross the chasm which had been made by the apostasy of the nation, that for the future he might have a firmer footing than the previous history had given him" (Baumgarten, quoted in KD). **23. Shalt see my back parts.** "So to say, only the afterglow which He leaves behind Him, but which may still suggest faintly what the full brilliancy of His presence must be" *(Cambridge Bible).*

9) The Restored Covenant. 34:1-35.

1-3. God instructed Moses to ascend the mount as before, bringing with him stone tablets to replace those that had been broken.

4-9. The revelation of God's glory to Moses. "What Moses saw we are not told, but simply the words in which Jehovah proclaimed all the glory of His being. . . . 'This sermon on the name of the Lord,' as Luther calls it, disclosed to Moses the most hidden nature of Jehovah. . . . all the words which the language contained to express the idea of grace in its varied manifestations to the sinner, are crowded together here, to reveal the fact that in His inmost being God is love" (KD).

11-26. As Israel was restored to fellowship with Jehovah, two of the leading points of the covenant were stressed, the same two points that the people had ignored in their transgression: a warning against any covenant with the Canaanites; and a reminder of their responsibilities in the worship of Jehovah. **Images . . . groves** (v. 13). *Pillars . . . and asherim* (RSV; ASV). *Asherah*, according to Canaanite mythology, was a goddess, the consort of El. In the OT she appears as the consort of Tyrian Baal, introduced by the Phoenician Jezebel into Israel (I Kgs 18:19). *Asherim,* the plural form, were cult objects erected for the worship of Asherah, probably trees or poles. The *pillars,* or *masseboth,* represented the male deity.

For commentary on verses 18-26, see notes on 13:13,14; 23:12,15-19. **Earing time** (v. 21). Plowing time. The Sabbath was to be observed even at the time when it seemed most necessary to work.

27-35. Moses' return from the mountain. "By the renewed adoption of the nation, the covenant in chap. 24 was *eo ipso* restored; so that no fresh conclusion of this covenant was necessary, and the writing down of the fundamental conditions of the covenant was merely intended as a proof of its restoration" (KD). **29. The skin of his face shone.** The Hebrew word for **shone** is a peculiar one; coming from the word for "horn," it means, literally, *rayed.* Jerome in the Vulgate translated the clause in the light of the basic meaning of the root word – "horned." Hence Moses has often been represented in art with horns coming from his head.

D. The Building of the Sanctuary. 35:1–39:43. These chapters relate in detail the carrying out of the instructions given to Moses (chs. 25–31) for the Tabernacle and its furniture and the garments of the priests. In general the instructions are repeated verbatim, with a few additions for explanation and some omissions or abridgments. There is some difference also in the order of contents (cf. *Cambridge Bible* for a tabular comparison).

1) Materials for the Work Brought by the People. 35:1-35.

1-3. The command to observe the Sabbath was repeated for the people, with the striking addition of the judgment of death upon the Sabbath-breaker (31:15). The reminder at this time was given to restrain the people and make it clear that even in their enthusiasm to build the house of the Lord, they were to rest and wait upon Jehovah one day in seven. The spiritual danger of being an over-industrious "Martha" is always present.

4-9. The invitation was given to the willing-hearted to bring the materials (25:1-8). It should be noticed that there was no pressure put on the people, no constraint or necessity, but a simple announcement of the need was made.

10-19. The **wise hearted** were invited to take part in the work. It is significant that at the very heart of Mosaic legal enactments and activity, there is perfect freedom to will and to do the work of the Lord. **Pins . . . cords** (v. 18). Even to the least item, everything was dedicated to Jehovah. Tent cords are not mentioned in 27:19 but would have been taken for granted.

20-29. Presentation of the Offering. **Every one** (v. 21). Both men and women are mentioned; this was an individual expression of faith and worship. **Bracelets . . . tablets** (v. 22). *Armlets . . . brooches* (ASV, RSV). The precise type of jewelry meant is uncertain. **Offering of gold.** Probably the gold that was not in the form of jewelry. Verses 23,24 describe the particular offering of the men, while verses 25,26 tell of the special contribution of the women, whose particular work was the spinning of coarser materials. The more precious materials came from the rulers (vv. 27,28).

30-35. Moses introduced Bezaleel and Aholiab as God's chosen and specially endowed craftsmen to supervise the work (31:2-5). Their own skills they were to pass on by instructing the others.

2) The Liberality of the People. 36:1-7. The giving exceeded the need. The materials were delivered to Bezaleel and Aholiab, or their assistants, until the amount was so great that the people had to be restrained from further giving.

3) The Execution of the Work. 36:8—38:20. The record of the construction of the Tabernacle follows the account of the instructions almost verbally. This is not useless repetition, but an emphasis upon the fact of Israel's careful adherence to God's word. Without this obedience, no amount of sacrifice and labor would have been acceptable.

8-19. The curtains and coverings of the Tabernacle. Cf. 26:1-14. **20-34.** The framework. Cf. 26:15-30. **35-38.** The veil and screen. Cf. 26:31-37. **38. Chapiters . . . fillets.** Capitals for the pillars, and a band around the pillars just below the capitals (not mentioned in ch. 26). **37:1-9.** The ark of the covenant. Cf. 25:10-20. **10-16.** The table of shewbread. Cf. 25:23-29. **17-24.** The candlestick. Cf. 25:31-39. **25-28.** The altar of incense. Cf. 30:1-5. **29.** The anointing oil and incense, a summary statement of 30:22-38. **38:1-7.** The altar of burnt offering. Cf. 27:1-8.

38:8. The brazen laver. Cf. 30:18-21. The bronze for the laver was provided by the polished metal mirrors of the women. That which once reflected their natural faces was now to be used to remind men of their need of spiritual cleansing that they might reflect the glory of God. **Women . . . which assembled.** Literally, *serving women which served,* possibly for cleaning, or as a choir.

9-20. The court of the tabernacle. Cf. 27:9-19.

4) An Estimate of the Amount of Metal Used. 38:21-31.

The gold amounted to 29 talents, 730 shekels, or about 40,940 ounces troy weight. The silver mentioned was only the atonement money (30:13,14), which amounted to 100 talents, 1,775 shekels, or about 140,828 ounces troy. No account is made of the voluntary gifts of silver. Attempts to value the precious metals used in terms of modern currency do not mean much, as we have no way of knowing the comparable value in that day. It is obvious that the expenditure upon this little sanctuary was enormous, and a monument to the dedication of the people to their God. It is significant that the Tabernacle rested upon, and its curtains were hung upon the silver that was the representative contribution of every man in the congregation of Israel. The Tabernacle stood thus upon the dedication of God's redeemed people. **29-31.** The bronze used weighed about three tons.

5) The Clothing of the Priests. 39:1-31. **2-7.** The ephod. Cf. 28:6-12. **8-21.** The breastplate. Cf. 28:15-27. **22-26.** The robe of the ephod. Cf. 28:31-35. **27-29.** Tunics and other vestments. Cf. 28:39,40,42. **30,31.** The headdress of the high priest. Cf. 28:36-38.

6) The Finished Work Presented to Moses. 39:32-43. As the writer concludes his account of the work, he stresses again, as he has done repeatedly, after the description of each separate piece, that all was done **as the Lord had commanded** Moses.

E. The Erection and Consecration of the Tabernacle. 40:1-38.

1-6. Moses was instructed by Jehovah to set up the Tabernacle and to prepare both the Tabernacle and the priests for God's service. The actual erection is simply stated, the details having already been given, but the recurrent phrase, **as the Lord commanded Moses,** again reminds us of how exactly Israel obeyed the words of the Lord.

17-33. The Tabernacle was set up for use on the first day of the first month (New Year's Day) of the **second year** of the exodus from Egypt.

34-38. The fulfillment of God's commands culminated in the sanctifying by God's visible presence of all that had been dedicated unto him. For Israel and for all ages to come, these chapters clearly teach the lesson that the way of blessing is the way of obedience and faith.

BIBLIOGRAPHY

ALBRIGHT, WM. F. *From the Stone Age to Christianity,* 2nd ed. Garden City, N.Y.: Doubleday and Co., 1957.

CALVIN, JOHN. *Calvin's Commentaries.* Grand Rapids: Wm. B. Eerdmans Publishing Company, reprint, 1948.

CHADWICK, G. A. *Exodus (Expositor's Bible).* New York: Armstrong, 1895.

DRIVER, S. R. *Exodus (Cambridge Bible).* Cambridge: The University Press, 1911.

FAIRBAIRN, PATRICK. *The Typology of Scripture.* Grand Rapids: Zondervan, reprint, n.d.

FILSON, F. V. and WRIGHT, G. E. *The Westminster Historical Atlas.* Philadelphia: Westminster Press, rev. ed., 1956.

KEIL, C. F. and DELITZSCH, F. *Biblical Commentary on the Old Testament, The Pentateuch,* Vols. 1,2. Grand Rapids: Eerdmans, reprint, 1951.

MOOREHEAD, W. G. *Studies in the Mosaic Institutions.* New York: Revell, 1893.

MURPHY, JAMES. *Commentary on Exodus.* Edinburgh: Clark, 1866.

OEHLER, G. *Old Testament Theology.* Grand Rapids: Zondervan, reprint, n.d.

STRONG, JAMES. *The Tabernacle of Israel.* Grand Rapids: Baker, reprint, 1952.

LEVITICUS

INTRODUCTION

Title. The book of Leviticus gets its name from the Vulgate *Leviticus*, derived from *Levitikon*, "pertaining to the Levites," the title it bears in the LXX. To the Jews it was known by its first word, the Hebrew *wayyiqrā'*, "And he called," after the custom of the Jews of naming many Old Testament books by their first word or words. The use of "And" at the beginning of this book does not mean that it forms an appendage to some other segment of Scripture. The thought of Exodus is continued, but the book is a unit and stands by itself. In this regard, note that several other Old Testament books begin with "And" in the Hebrew text, viz., Exodus, Numbers, Joshua, Judges, Ruth, *et al.*

Leviticus presents God's plan for teaching his chosen people how to approach him in a holy manner. Particular emphasis is given to the priestly functions in making this approach to God reverent and holy. Thus the book develops the priestly or "Levitical" office, reference to which we find in the New Testament in Heb 7:11, where the term "the Levitical priesthood" is found.

Date and Authorship. "And they set the priests in their divisions, and the Levites in their courses, for the service of God, which is at Jerusalem; as it is written in the book of Moses" (Ezr 6:18).

Ezra the scribe refers to the scroll of Leviticus in describing the source used in his day to determine proper procedure in dedicating the rebuilt Temple. The book of Leviticus itself continually stresses the role of Moses in recording the regulations given him by God for proper worship in the rites of the Tabernacle. The fact that there would have had to be regulations before there could have been orderly worship by the priests and people demands a central controlling force and a fixed time. We can best understand this as the role of Moses at the establishment of tabernacle worship. The nations of Moses' day had had elaborate, fixed rites of worship long before he came on the scene. There is no need to believe that this fixing of rites in worship of Jehovah was a gradual one of evolution or that the record of Leviticus is a late invention of Ezra's day.

Background Material. The very simplicity of the form of Leviticus has worried its critics. Some see in its second section (chs. 17–27), which describes man's basis for fellowship with God, the later addition of a "Holiness Code." However, shift of emphasis alone may account for the differences between the two main divisions of the book.

One may well say that Leviticus was given us through Moses to anticipate the "eternal sacrifice" – Jesus Christ – of the New Covenant. The book of Hebrews presents this picture of the New Covenant, and Leviticus furnishes the background for the more important aspects of "a priest after the order of Melchizedek." Actually, a study of Leviticus has lasting value only as it points to Jesus Christ – our High Priest.

OUTLINE

I. How one comes to God. 1:1–16:34.
   A. The laws of sacrifice. 1:1–7:38.
      1. The general rules. 1:1–6:7.
         a. Introduction. 1:1,2.
         b. Burnt offerings. 1:3-17.
         c. Meal offerings. 2:1-16.
         d. Peace offerings. 3:1-17.
         e. Sin offerings. 4:1–5:13.
         f. Trespass offerings. 5:14–6:7.
      2. More specific rules about these offerings. 6:8–7:38.

B. The testimony of history. 8:1–10:20.
1. Inauguration of the offerings. 8:1-36.
2. When first offered. 9:1-24.
3. The misuse of offerings (Nadab and Abihu). 10:1-20.
C. The laws of purity. 11:1–15:33.
1. What may be eaten or touched. 11:1-47.
2. Childbirth. 12:1-8.
3. Leprosy. 13:1–14:57.
4. Sexual purity. 15:1-33.
D. The Day of Atonement. 16:1-34.
II. How one keeps in touch with God. 17:1–27:34.
A. The holiness of the people. 17:1–20:27.
1. Concerning food. 17:1-16.
2. Concerning marriage. 18:1-30.
3. Concerning the social order. 19:1-37.
4. The punishments for disobedience. 20:1-27.
B. The holiness of priests and their offerings. 21:1–22:33.
C. The holiness of time. 23:1–25:55.
1. The holy use of days. 23:1-44.
2. The holy use of objects. 24:1-23.
3. The holy use of years. 25:1-55.
D. Promises and warnings. 26:1-46.
E. The making of vows. 27:1-34.

COMMENTARY

I. How One Comes to God. 1:1–16:34.

A. The Laws of Sacrifice. 1:1–7:38.

1) The General Rules. 1:1–6:7.

a) Introduction. 1:1,2.

1. The Lord called unto Moses. The setting is explained in Exodus 40. God speaks to Moses from the **tabernacle,** *'ōhel mō'ēd,* "tent of meeting," i.e., where God meets his people. This was not a meeting place in the sense of the later synagogue, for only priests and Levites were allowed to draw near to it. **2. Offering,** Hebrew *qōrbān,* comes from the root *qrb,* "draw near." It is that with which one draws near to God. A man brought something to prepare him to enter the presence of God. What these offerings were is given in chapters 1 through 7.

b) Burnt Offerings. 1:3-17.

3. If his offering be a burnt sacrifice. The holocaust or burnt offering *('ōlâ)* could consist of a large, male animal, *bāqār* (v. 3), or a small animal, *sō'n* (v. 10). The main thought here is that neither the offerer (cf. chs. 13; 14) nor the offering could be blemished or defiled. The offering was brought to achieve acceptance by God of both offering and offerer. **4. He shall put his hand.** In the Hebrew *(sāmak yādô)* this implies pressing with vigor upon the animal's head. We do not know all the ritual involved, but the intent was probably to show the physical and mental energy involved in the transfer, whatever it implied. The ultimate purpose was atonement or covering *(kappēr)* of sin. **6. He shall flay.** After the victim was bled, the offerer skinned it and divided it at its joints. In later practice (II Chr 29; 35) priests and Levites did the flaying of the carcass.

10. His offering . . . of the flocks. Not only could a large animal be used but also a small one, i.e., a sheep or goat. The same ritual as the above was observed by the offerer and the priests. The added remark is made here that the animal was to be killed on the northern side of the altar.

14. The smallness of the usual fowl necessitated some changes in the ritual used for larger animals. The ritual was handled solely by the priest. **17. A sweet savour.** It smelled good to God; i.e., it pleased him.

c) Meal Offerings. 2:1-16.

1. Meat offering. The word rendered **meat** by the AV is better translated *meal,* though the Hebrew *minḥâ* used here means "a gift or present," and sometimes, "tribute." When used in relation to a sacrifice, it may denote either an animal or a grain offering (as in the case of Abel and Cain, Gen 4). It commonly signifies an offering of grain (in the ear), fine flour, or baked goods. The offering of fine flour, *sōlet,* was mixed with oil, frankincense, and salt. **3. The remnant.** After the priests had burned the fine flour on the altar, the remnant was theirs. It was burned as a memorial, *'azkārâ* – to put God in remembrance (cf. Acts 10:4).

4-10. An oblation. This word is used in the AV to avoid redundance in the usage of "offering." It is the Hebrew *qorbān* (cf. 1:2). This offering could be baked in an oven, in a baking pan or flat plate *(maḥâbat,* v. 5), or in a pot *(marḥeshet,* v. 7). What was left after the ceremony was the priests' for food.

11. No meat offering . . . with leaven. The meal was left unleavened. Nor was honey allowed. Both leaven and honey are subject to fermentation. Leaven as a sign of corruption was used in offerings on heathen altars. Only offerings given to the priests (7:13,14) could contain leaven.

12. First fruits. The *rē'shît,* "first" (fruits), here contrasts with the *bikkûrîm* of verse 14. Both mean the same. The former were not to be offered on the altar, while those mentioned in verse 14 were burned on the altar. **13. Every oblation . . . season with salt.** Salt was considered a precious commodity in the ancient Near East. It was thought of as a necessary adjunct to the food offered to God as well as to that used by man. **14. Green ears of corn . . . corn beaten.** Grain both in the ear and ground *(gereś karmel)* was parched and offered as a memorial, with the remainder going to the priests.

d) Peace Offerings. 3:1-17.

1. Sacrifice of peace offering. Hebrew *zebaḥ shelāmîm* might well be translated, "the sacrifice of unity or completeness." Completeness connotes a close relationship or fellowship between God and man. In ritual this offering was much the same as the burnt offering (ch. 1) except that, while in the former the whole offering was burnt, in the peace offering the worshiper joined the priest in the sacrificial meal of that which remained. In other offerings – meal, sin, and trespass – only the priest partook of this sacrificial meal (cf. 7:11-38). **4. Caul above the liver.** Hebrew *yōteret,* probably "the finger of the liver" *(lobus caudatus).*

6. Of the flock; male or female. A male or female lamb without blemish was the usual sacrifice from the flock, as differentiated from the "herd" (v. 1).

12. If . . . a goat. A goat might also be sacrificed. No fat or blood was to be eaten. No mention is made of an offering of fowls, due, no doubt, to the fact that there would be little left for a sacrificial meal. The poor would have to share the sacrifices from the flock brought by others.

e) Sin Offerings. 4:1–5:13.

2. If a soul sin . . . through ignorance. The Hebrew word *ḥaṭṭā't* may mean either "sin" or "sin offering." This fact may clarify the statement of Paul concerning Christ in II Cor 5:21 a: "He hath made him to be sin (i.e., a sin offering) for us . . ." The sin offering here applies only to those who sin *(bishegāgâ)* "through ignorance," unintentionally. For sin done knowingly (or defiantly), no sacrifice could atone (Num 15:30,31). In this light, consider the lament of the Psalmist (Ps 51) and the cry of the prophets against the sins of the people (e.g., Mic 6:6-8). How much more Christ, our Sin Offering, does for us! (Heb 7:26,27)

3-7. If the priest . . . sin. The anointed or high priest represents the community, and therefore his sin brings guilt on the community. A young bullock without blemish is the offering. The ceremony was much like that of the burnt offering except that the blood was used to sprinkle before the veil of the sanctuary and on the horns of the altar (cf. vv. 14-18).

8-12. And he shall take off . . . all the fat. Note that after the burning of the fat and certain organs on the altar, the carcass was taken to a clean place outside the camp to be burned. Cf. Heb 13:10-13.

13. And if the whole congregation . . . sin. The sin of the congregation of Israel was covered in a ritual much like that used for the sin of the high priest. The ceremony may have varied from the description here, as the account of the ceremony in Num 15:22-26 seems to indicate.

22. When a ruler hath sinned. The ruler, as one anointed of God, is responsible for a godly walk before his people. The sin offering prescribed for the ruler was a male goat. The blood was not brought into the tent of meeting, as in the cases cited above, but put on the horns of the altar of burnt offering and poured out at the base of the altar.

27. And if any one of the common people sin. The private citizen also was accountable to God. He could not hide in the group and feign innocence. He was to bring a female goat or a lamb. The same ritual was used as for the ruler.

5:1-5. Three instances are now given of the bringing of the sin offering. **1. If a soul sin, and hear . . . if he do not utter it.** The first instance is that of a witness who has refused to testify. This is a man who has seen a crime committed or heard something that might help in the solution of a crime. He must pay the penalty for silence if he hides his knowledge. Does not this remind one of the punishment to the Christian for his lack of witness? **2. If a soul touch any unclean thing.** The second instance given is accidental ceremonial defilement. One who accidentally touches an unclean wild or domesticated animal or a creeping thing is liable. The uncleanness of man is also not to be touched. This is further amplified in chapters 12–15. **4. If a soul swear.** The third instance is the case of a man's making a rash oath or vow on any occasion. While the man may not at the moment realize that he has done wrong, he is liable when that truth dawns upon him.

6-13. Various offerings were allowed for expiation. There may be some question as to whether the sin offering and guilt offering (5:14,15) do not overlap. There are, however, some differences which the careful reader will note. A female sheep or goat was to be offered for the sins mentioned in 5:1-4. For those unable to afford an animal, two doves or young pigeons (v. 7) were prescribed. For the very poor a measure of fine flour (v. 11) sufficed.

f) Trespass Offerings. 5:14–6:7.

15. If a soul commit a trespass. The sin offering (ch. 4) stressed the sin of which one became conscious. The trespass or guilt offering emphasized that situation in which one felt guilt but was unable to specify it exactly. Here in the trespass offering *('āshām)* if part of what was due the Lord was withheld – such as a tithe, a double tithe must be paid. Also a ram worth at least two shekels was offered. The act of sin is referred to in the Hebrew word *ma'al,* "deal with deceit."

17. If a soul sin . . . though he wist it not. If one did unwittingly what God had commanded His people not to do, he brought a ram as a trespass offering (as above). But he made no restitution, since the exact sin was unknown. This voluntary offering helped relieve troubled minds and hearts.

6:1-7. If a soul sin, and commit a trespass. This section forms a part of chapter 5 in the Hebrew text. The sin in this case is damage to another's property by fraud or violence. This is a case in which the sin becomes known through confession. The legal aspects of such sins are discussed in Ex 22:7,8.

2) More Specific Rules about These Offerings. 6:8–7:38.

Discussion of the offerings in the prior section was from the viewpoint of the worshiper as he approached the altar with his sacrifice. The point of view now shifts to the priest, as the Law instructs Aaron and his sons in the proper exercise of their office as it had to do with the ritual of sacrifice.

8-13. *Directions for the Presentation of the Burnt Offering.* The offering of two lambs, one at sunrise and the other at sunset (Ex 29; Num 28), was commanded – for all the people – plus the wearing of proper garments by the priests in fulfilling their services.

14-18. *Directions for the Presentation of the Meat (Meal) Offering.* This discussion of the meal offerings is a reiteration of 2:2 ff. The specifications are given for the priests' food from the meal remaining after sacrifice. The court of the tent of meeting is the place of eating.

19,20. A meat offering perpetual. The provision for a perpetual meal offering was made, in which Aaron inaugurated a meal to be continued by his successors. At the time of the second Temple, this offering was made daily. It was wholly burned. No portion was eaten.

24,25. The law of the sin offering. The remainder of this chapter is a discussion of the sin offering as given previously from 4:1 to 5:13.

7:1. The law of the trespass offering. The first ten verses of chapter 7 review the laws relating to the trespass offering given from 5:14 to 6:7. Here, however, more details are given. **2. The place where they kill the burnt offering.** The trespass and sin offerings were to be slain in the same place as the burnt offering (cf. 6:25; 1:11), that is, on the north side of the altar. **6. It shall be eaten in the holy place.** The ritual of the eating of the offering likewise follows that of the sin offering (cf. 6:26,29).

8. The priest shall have . . . the skin. The skin *('ôr)* of the burnt offering was retained by the officiating priest. On the basis of the statement in verse 7, the Mishna extended this privilege to the priests offering both the sin and trespass offerings. **9. And all the meat offering.** The priests were to receive the meal offerings.

11-36. *Directions for the Presentation of the Peace Offering.* The peace offering could be made either as an act of thanksgiving, *tôdâ,* or as a result of a vow, *neder,* or as a freewill or voluntary offering, *nᵉdābâ.*

12. For a thanksgiving. The *tôdâ,* thank offering, was supplemented by three types of cakes prepared with oil. One cake of each type was a heave offering, *tᵉrûmâ,* lifted toward heaven in sight of the congregation and then presented to the officiating priest. **15.** The *tôdâ* must all be eaten on the day of sacrifice, but it was permissible to allow a portion of the *neder* and *nᵉdābâ* to remain and be eaten on the second day. Any portion then remaining was to be burnt.

19. The flesh that toucheth any unclean thing. The sacrificial meat could neither touch anything unclean nor be eaten by an unclean person. That which made an individual unclean is discussed in the laws of purity, chapters 11–15. **22,23. Eat no manner of fat.** Fat and blood were prohibited as items of food. The regulation regarding fat pertained only to the fat portions of sacrificial animals, which were reserved as an offering to God. The restriction was extended to the same portions of fat on animals rendered unsuitable for sacrifice by having died a natural death or having been slain by beasts. Blood of animals and fowls could not be eaten in any form.

28,29. He that offereth . . . shall bring his oblation. The individual making the offering was to bring it to the altar. That portion which served as the wave offering, *tᵉnûpâ,* was lifted and moved toward the altar and then moved away from the altar and given to the priests. The following verses (30-34) tell of those elements of the sacrifice of the peace offering which were to be set aside for the priests.

37. The law of the burnt offering. The last two verses of the chapter conclude the section on the Laws of Sacrifice.

B. The Testimony of History. 8:1–10:20.

1) Inauguration of the Offerings. 8:1-36.

2. Take Aaron and his sons. The background of this material is to be found in Exodus 28; 29, where the procedure for clothing and anointing the priests is given, followed by the sacrifice to be made at the time of their consecration. In Lev 8:1-4 we are told that Moses was to assemble all the required materials, along with the priests, at the door of the tent of meeting in the presence of the people.

8,9. The Urim and the Thummim. The nature of the Urim and the Thummim is not known, nor is their exact significance understood, though indications are that they may have been an early means of determining the will of the Lord (cf. I Sam 28:6; Ezr 2:63; Neh 7:65; and the LXX of I Sam 14:41.

10. The anointing oil. The investiture of the priests with the prescribed garments was followed by the anointing with the holy oil (vv. 10-13,30). The anointing oil *(shemen hammishḥâ)* was symbolic of an enduement with the Spirit of God and the resulting spiritual power (cf. I Sam 16:13; Isa 61:1; Acts 10:38). It likewise set apart the anointed persons and objects, consecrating them for the use of God's work.

14. The bullock for the sin offering. The bull of the sin offering was sacrificed in accordance with Ex 29:10-14. **15. Poured the blood at the bottom of the altar.** The reconciliation *(kapēr)* or atonement (RSV) for the altar was necessary to remove from it the defilement of the priests who made sacrifices upon it. **18. And he brought the ram.** The ram of the burnt offering was sacrificed in accordance with Ex 29:15-18 and Lev 1:3-9, thus implying complete dedication of the priests to the service of the Lord.

22. Brought the other ram. The ram of consecration or "fillings" *(millū'îm)* was sacrificed as in the case of the peace offering, except for the use of the blood, as described in 8:23,24. In this offering, the blood of the ram was placed on certain extremities: the ear hearkening to the Lord's words, the hand performing the Lord's tasks, and the foot hastening on the Lord's errands. **27. He put all upon Aaron's hands.** The "fillings" *(millū'îm)* took place when the elements of the sacrifice were placed in the hands of the participants. The term used for consecration or appointing of the priest was to "fill the hand" (Jud 17:5,12).

31. Aaron and his sons shall eat it. Certain portions of the flesh and bread were to be eaten by the priests. Thus nourishment was provided for them as they observed seven consecutive days wherein the consecration procedure was repeated without their leaving the tent of meeting.

2) When First Offered. 9:1-24.

2. Take thee a young calf. Although Aaron had been consecrated for seven days, during which time the sin offering and the burnt offering had been made repeatedly, more sacrifices were needed. Perfection had not been attained (Heb 10:1-4). Aaron had to make additional sacrifices for himself and, in addition, sacrifices for the people.

22. Aaron lifted up his hand. Before coming down from the ledge which surrounded the altar of sacrifice, Aaron blessed the people with upraised hands. **23. Moses and Aaron went into the tabernacle.** The entrance of Moses and Aaron into the tent of meeting may have been for the purpose of instructing the new high priest in his duties. Coming out of the tent, the mediator of the law of God and the high priest united in a joint blessing of the people. **24. There came a fire out from before the Lord.** The glory of the Lord appeared as a miraculous fire (cf. Ex 3:2-4; 13:21; 19:18, *et al.)* which joined the one already burning on the altar and completed the consuming of the sacrifice. The people responded to the divine manifestation by prostrating themselves in wonder and humility.

3) The Misuse of Offerings (Nadab and Abihu). 10:1-20.

1. And Nadab and Abihu . . . offered strange fire. The strange fire *('ēsh zārâ)* is not explained. The elements used or the procedure followed or both may have been contrary to that prescribed. Whatever their motive and abuse, the act in God's sight was worthy of punishment by death. **3. I will be sanctified.** Improper offering of sacrifice on the part of the priest would detract from the glory of God, and this glory God was determined to maintain.

4. And Moses called. Cf. Ex 6:18,22, 23 for the designated members of Aaron's family. **6. Uncover not your heads** is better read: *Let not the hair of your heads hang loose.* The usual expressions of mourning were denied the high priest and his two remaining sons, in this case lest dissatisfaction with God's judgment be indicated. Rather, they were to remain secluded in the sanctuary while others performed the burials and expressed grief.

9. Do not drink wine nor strong drink. Those consecrated to God's service were to perform their duties with a clear mind, unclouded by alcohol. The presence of this verse here does not necessarily imply, as some believe, that Nadab and Abihu sinned by performing their duties while drunk.

12. Take the meat offering. Moses reviewed with Aaron and his sons the laws concerning the eating of the sacrifices.

16. Behold, it was burnt. The portion of the sin offering which should have been eaten by the priests was burned instead. Aaron's explanation seems to imply that the judgment imposed upon two of his sons indicated that he and his other two sons were themselves not sufficiently free of sin to deserve to eat the designated portion of the sin offering. Moses was satisfied with the explanation.

C. The Laws of Purity. 11:1–15:33.

The means of maintaining and restoring ceremonial cleanness are given in the following chapters. The instructions concern the eating of the flesh of animals, contact with the dead (both human beings and animals), childbirth, and uncleanness of the person, garments, furniture, and houses. Although one important result of all these regulations may have been the preservation of health, this is not the same as stating that preservation of health was the motivation. The laws cannot thus be rationalized. In all ancient nations and religions there is to be found a usually distinct contrast between the cleanness or uncleanness of certain creatures, substances, and situations. There was a propriety connected with some and an impropriety connected with others. No reason for such a designation is assigned and none was apparently needed. Not many of the restrictions apply today, but they can be read with interest and can be recognized as regulations which both helped to maintain Israel's physical health and, at the same time, set her apart as a nation distinct from the idolatrous nations about her.

1) What Might Be Eaten or Touched. 11:1-47.

2. These are the beasts which ye shall eat. Cf. Deut 14:3-8. Although the passage in Deuteronomy lists clean *(ṭāhôr)* as well as unclean *(ṭāmē')* animals, the correspondent Leviticus passage lists only the unclean. The criteria of cleanness, however, are given in both passages: the animal must possess hooves completely severed, and it must also be a ruminant. **5. The coney** *(shāpān)* is a rock rabbit or rock badger, a very timid animal, living in natural caves and rock clefts. Neither the coney nor the hare (v. 6) is actually a ruminant, but the constant movement of the jaws leaves that impression. **8. Of their flesh shall ye not eat.** The unclean animal was not to be eaten, nor was its dead body to be touched (v. 39 includes clean animals that had died of natural causes).

9. These shall ye eat of all . . . in the waters. Cf. Deut 14:9,10. The restrictions in the following verses on creatures living in the water apparently ruled out the eating of all shellfish and eels.

13. These . . . ye shall have in abomination among the fowls. Cf. Deut 14:11-18. Certain fowls are prohibited by name but without naming the factor which disqualified them. Not every fowl mentioned can be identified with certainty. **20.** Cf. Deut 14:19,20. **All fowls that creep, going upon all four** is better rendered: *All winged insects that go upon all fours* (RSV), even though insects actually go upon six legs. **21. These may ye eat of every flying creeping thing.** The cricket (beetle), locust, and grasshopper are here permitted. These are still eaten in many parts of the world today.

24. Whosoever toucheth the carcase of them. Contact with the carcasses of forbidden animals, aquatic creatures, and winged creatures brought defilement until the close of that day, and necessitated the washing of the garments.

29. These also shall be unclean. Additional unclean animals of a smaller size are enumerated. **32. It shall be unclean until the even.** Any object became unclean when it came into contact with the unclean creatures listed, and it had to be washed to be made usable again. **33. And every earthen vessel.** If the object was of pottery, however, washing was insufficient. It was to be destroyed. **36. A fountain . . . shall be clean.** The well or spring had a continual supply of fresh water which tended to purify itself. **39.** Cf. note on verse 8.

44. I am the Lord your God. The motivation for the observance of the restrictions listed above was to be the honoring of God, who had been seen by Israel in mighty acts in their behalf. They were to be a peculiar people, keeping a covenant that would constantly remind them of their relationship to God. Through Jesus Christ it has now been fully revealed that the spirit of an individual determines his obedience (Mt 15:11).

2) Childbirth. 12:1-8.

2. If a woman have conceived. Throughout the chapter it is the woman who is considered unclean, not the new-born child. **3. In the eighth day . . . shall be circumcised.** Cf. instructions in Gen 17:12. This rite was an external sign indicating that a covenant relationship had been established between the individual and the Lord, with all the privileges and responsibilities entailed by such relationship. **4. Shall touch no hallowed thing.** The state of her uncleanness prevented contact with all holy items and prohibited her presence in the house of worship during the designated period. **5. But if . . . a maid child.** The period of uncleanness was twice as long in the case of the birth of a female. This may be attributed to an ancient belief that the period of recovery for the mother was longer in the case of a female child than in the case of a male.

8. If . . . not able to bring a lamb. Mary, Jesus' mother, availed herself of the privilege granted in the case of one of limited means (Lk 2:24).

3) Leprosy. 13:1–14:57.

The condition designated as leprosy *(ṣāra'at)* in this chapter and the next does not in every case refer to the disease known by this name at the present time. On the other hand, true leprosy is most certainly included in the physical irregularities described. With the limitations on diagnosis in the time of Moses, the recorded regulations dealt as effectively as possible with the problems raised by true leprosy and analogous conditions. Isolation and close observation of suspected victims of the disease are no less favored today than they were during that period.

Leviticus 13 deals with the identification of leprosy and analogous conditions in man and his garments. Chapter 14 deals with the purification procedures to be followed when *ṣāraʿat* was observed on man and upon the walls of his house.

13:2. He shall be brought unto Aaron the priest. Aaron or one of his sons was designated to examine the individual suspected of being leprous. If there was a swelling, eruption, or light spot on the skin, it was to be designated leprosy if the hair growing on the mark had become white and if the condition appeared to be deep-seated. If the hair had not changed color and the condition seemed to be superficial, a quarantine for observation purposes was to be imposed. If the condition had not spread in the allotted time, the individual was considered clean; if, however, there was a spreading of the eruption, the condition was pronounced leprosy by the priest.

11. It is an old leprosy. If the priest was able to determine from the appearance of the man that he was suffering from an old case of leprosy, he could be pronounced unclean without quarantine and additional observation.

12. If . . . the leprosy cover all the skin. If the skin disease had spread over the entire body, the man was to be considered clean until raw flesh appeared. He then was to be pronounced unclean. If the raw flesh cleared up, he might be pronounced clean once more. It is not known whether or not this is a reference to true leprosy. **18. The flesh also, in which, . . . was a boil.** A leprous condition might appear at the site of a recently healed boil. If there was doubt as to the certainty of the diagnosis, quarantine and observation were employed. **24. A hot burning.** The site of a burn might also be the point at which leprosy would occur. The priest was to take proper steps to make the correct diagnosis. **29. A plague upon the head or the beard.** If an itch or mange *(neteq)* appeared on the head or in the beard, it was observed by the priest. If after a certain period it did not spread and if it contained no yellow hair, the individual was pronounced clean. A washing was then employed. **35. If the scall spread much.** If, after the washing, the itch appeared to have spread, the man was to be pronounced unclean whether yellow hair was present or not.

38. White bright spots. If a condition of the skin *(bōhaq)* should appear in which the inflammation consisted of dull white spots, no uncleanness would be involved. **40. Whose hair is fallen.** Loss of hair did not of itself imply uncleanness. If, however, the condition was accompanied by an inflamed swelling, one was to be pronounced leprous. **45. The leper in whom the plague is.** The plight of the leper was pitiable. He lived in complete exile outside the city (Num 5:2-4), being regarded as one dead (Num 12:10-12). Since not all skin diseases which brought on such exile were actually leprosy, however, there were apparently those who recovered, were declared clean, and were allowed to return to their places in society.

47. The garment . . . that the . . . leprosy is in. Apparently the reference here is either to a type of mildew or to garments which had been worn by a leper. The former is the more likely. **49. If the plague be greenish or reddish.** If the spots were green or red, the garments were to be put aside for seven days. If the growth had then spread, the material on which it was growing was to be destroyed by burning, because it was a "fretting" growth, i.e., malignant. **54. He shall shut it up seven days more.** If the growth had not spread during the first seven-day period of observation, the garments were to be washed and set aside for seven additional days. **55. Thou shalt burn it in the fire.** If washing did not clear up the growth, the garments were to be burned. To **fret inward** refers to the tendency of the mildew or mold to eat into the leather or fabric, whether it went all the way through or not. **56. He shall rend it out of the garment.** If the spot had grown fainter, the priest was to remove that section of contaminated material from the remainder of the article. **57. Burn that wherein the plague is with fire.** If the removal of the spot did not prevent the spread of the growth, the entire contaminated garment was to be burned. **58. It shall be washed the second time.** If washing removed the growth, the item was to be rewashed and then considered clean.

14:1-57. *Purification of Lepers and Leprous Houses.* The first portion of the chapter (vv. 1-32) is devoted to the purification of the leper. The second portion (vv. 33-57) gives the procedure to be followed in the case of leprosy in houses.

2. He shall be brought unto the priest. When the leper was apparently healed and sought restoration in society, he was to be taken to the priest, who was to meet him outside the city area.

4. Two birds alive. For other references to these birds *(ṣippŏrîm)*, see Gen 15:10, where it is recorded that Abraham used such birds in sacrifice, and Ex 2:21, where Moses' wife is called Zipporah *(ṣippōrâ)*. The species of birds is not designated. The **scarlet** *(shᵉnî tô laʿat)*, literally, "worm-crimson," was likely a small piece of scarlet cloth. **5. The priest shall command that one of the birds be killed.** The blood of the slain bird was to be mixed with water in the earthen vessel. **6. He shall take it . . . and the scarlet.** The scarlet cloth may possibly have been used to tie the cedar wood and hyssop together to be dipped into the blood-water mixture. **7. Shall let the living bird loose.** It may be that as the one bird gave its life as a symbol of and in the place of the leper, the other bird symbolized the man's newfound freedom to return to his place among his people and to the house of worship, from which places he had been excluded. In verse 53 the same ritual is called a "ransom" or "atonement" *(kipper)*.

8. And he that is to be cleansed. The man was not yet allowed to enter the community. After thoroughly washing himself and his garments and removing his hair, he was to remain outside seven additional days. After this time the washing and shaving were to be repeated. **10. And on the eighth day.** On the eighth day he was to bring the elements necessary for a trespass offering, a sin offering, a burnt offering, and a meal offering. The quantity of flour was about three-tenths of a bushel. The **log** contained about a pint of oil.

11. And the priest. The trespass offering was to be made by the priest for the man in the prescribed manner. **15. The log of oil.** The oil, after being sprinkled before the altar to consecrate it to the Lord and sanctify it for further use, was to be used in the same manner as the blood in verse 14. **18. The remnant of the oil.** The remaining oil was to be used for anointing the man's head. **19. The priest shall offer.** The sin offering, burnt offering, and meal offering were all three then made. **21-32.** *Special provision for the poor.* These verses explain how provision was made for those who were unable to provide all the elements designated in 14:10. A reduction was allowed in the cases of the sin offering, burnt offering, and meal offering; but the trespass offering remained the same, viz., one young ram. Verses 23-32 simply repeat the procedure prescribed in verses 11-20 to be observed in the offering of the sacrifices designed to restore the man to a state of cleanness.

34. The plague of leprosy in a house. The presence of a growth on the walls inside a home necessitated examination by a priest. It may have been a species of mold or some form of rot, but it indicated specific action on the part of God and could neither be ignored nor treated without priestly supervision and instruction. Sanitary considerations may have been involved, but the occurrence was not without religious significance as well.

36. Empty the house. Apparently those who lived in the house and the furnishings might possibly be contaminated by that which grew on the walls. Consequently the house was to be vacated prior to the priestly inspection.

37,38. He shall look on the plague. Under certain conditions the house was to be sealed for seven days to observe if the growth spread. If so, the contaminated portions of the walls were to be removed and those sections completely refinished. **43. If the plague come again.** If, however, the growth continued to spread on the walls, more stringent action was to be taken. The entire structure was to be demolished and all the materials disposed of.

46. He that goeth into the house. During the period of observations any person entering the house was to be considered unclean, and proper cleansing measures had to be employed.

48. If the priest shall come in. If after the refinishing of diseased sections the growth did not spread, the house could be considered clean. **49. And he shall take to cleanse the house.** The same sacrificial elements were to be used and the same procedure to be followed in cleansing the house as in the cleansing of the healed leper (vv. 4-7).

4) Sexual Purity. 15:1-33.

2. A running issue *(zāb)*, or "discharge," from the verb *zûb*, "to flow." The discharge **out of his flesh** *(mibbᵉśārô)* is taken to mean from the organs of generation, although the exact nature of the disease discussed is not known. **3. This shall be his uncleanness.** Uncleanness existed whether the discharge was present continually or the condition developed an obstruction that temporarily caused a cessation of the discharge.

4. Every thing . . . shall be unclean. Anyone touching the unclean man, the discharge, or anything upon which he had sat or lain while unclean, had to wash himself and his clothing and be considered unclean until the evening. **11. And whomsoever he toucheth.** If the unclean man touched some person without having washed his hands first, uncleanness would be transferred to the person touched.

13. He shall number to himself seven days. At the conclusion of the disease and after an additional seven days, the man was to wash himself and his clothing and be clean again. **14. And on the eighth day.** Following this procedure, he was to bring two birds to the priest to be offered as a sin offering and a burnt offering. **16. He shall wash all his flesh in water.** Whereas verses 2-15 refer to a diseased condition, verses 16-18 refer to natural secretion. Though the man would be unclean for a time, he did not have to make a sacrifice. The uncleanness prevented participation in the religious services (cf. v. 31).

19. If a woman have an issue. Another natural discharge is discussed in verses 19-24. During the period of a woman's separation, the same regulations applied as in 15:2-10. No need existed in this case for the sacrificial offerings. **25. Beyond the time of her separation.** More in line with verses 2-15 is the diseased condition described in 15:25-30. In this case the woman had to bring two birds to the priest, who offered them for a sin offering and a burnt offering.

D. The Day of Atonement. 16:1-34.

In spite of all the sacrifices made during the year for the members of the congregation of Israel and for the priests themselves, there still remained sins and uncleanness for which atonement had to be made if the right relationship between God and his people was to be maintained. Hence a particular day was inaugurated upon which the ritual performed by the high priest would accomplish the reconciliation of the nation with its God. Hebrews 9 gives the significance of the ceremony to the Christian in such a clear picture that Lev 16 may truly be designated the pinnacle of the OT sacrificial system.

2. Come not at all times into the holy place. Aaron was not to be permitted frequent entrance to the holy place within the veil *(pârōket)*, or "divider," before the mercy seat *(kappōret)*, which is described in Ex 25:17-21. This *kappōret* is from the verb *kāpar,* "to cover, forgive or expiate." Therefore the lid of the ark, or mercy seat, could likewise be called "propitiatory." As prescribed in verses 29,30, the entrance was to be a once-a-year occasion. And it was to be performed only in the prescribed manner.

3. Thus shall Aaron come into the holy place. Since the priest himself needed to be cleansed before he could offer sacrifices for the people, he was to bring a bull for a sin offering and a ram for a burnt offering. From the people (v. 5) he was to take two goats for a sin offering and a ram for a burnt offering, these to be offered for the people. **4. He shall put on the holy linen coat.** After washing himself, the priest was to don the priestly garments. **6. Aaron shall offer his bullock.** The bullock was designated as a sin offering for the priest and his house (cf. v. 11). Contrast with this the description of Jesus in Heb 7:26,27.

7. He shall take the two goats. The two goats, after being "presented before the Lord," were designated by lots for the Lord and for "the scapegoat" *('ăzā'zēl)*. The identity and significance of *'ăzā'zēl* are not given, but it seems clear from the references in this chapter that it was some sort of demon who represented to the Jewish people that which was opposed to Jehovah. It should be noted, however, that whereas one goat was to be sacrificed to the Lord (vv. 9, 15), the other was not to be sacrificed to *'ăzā'zēl* but merely to be released into the wilderness after having first been presented alive before the Lord (cf. vv. 20-22).

Another interpretation of 'ăzā'zēl is that the Hebrew word is an abstract noun meaning "complete removal" (cf. ASV marginal reading). In this view 'ăzā'zēl is formed from an intensive stem of the verb root 'azal found in the cognate Arabic language meaning "to remove." Leviticus 17:7 expressly forbids any further sacrifice to demons. The real function of the live goat is to bear away out of sight all the sins of Israel and to make evident the *effect* of the great work of atonement. This unique ceremony involving the second goat teaches the complete removal of sins atoned for by sacrifice (cf. Ps 103:12; Isa 38:17; 43:25; Jer 31:34; Mic 7:19; Jn 1:29; Heb 9:26).

12. He shall take a censer. The high priest's first entrance into the Most Holy Place was for the purpose of carrying in the censer of live coals and two handsful of incense. **13. The testimony** *(hā'ēdût)* is a term used in reference to the two tablets given Moses on Sinai and subsequently placed in the ark (cf. Ex 25:16; 31:18; 32:15). The cloud resulting from the burning incense was designed, perhaps, to hide from the priest's view the manifestation of God upon the mercy seat in order that he might not die (Ex 33:20).

14. He shall take of the blood. The implication here is that the high priest was to leave the Most Holy Place in order to obtain the blood of the bull, then enter it a second time to sprinkle the blood upon and near the mercy seat as directed. **15. Then shall he kill.** Then he was to go out again, slay the goat of the sin offering for the people, and enter the Most Holy Place a third time, repeating with the blood of the goat the procedure followed in verse 14.

16. He shall make an atonement. Thus the high priest would atone for the sins of the people, and for the related uncleanness of the Holy Place and the Tabernacle, which required a periodic cleansing.

20. He shall bring the live goat. The live goat of verse 10 was to be brought forward, whereupon Aaron would lay both hands upon it and confess over it all the sins of the people of Israel. It was considered that this act symbolized the transference of the sins to the goat, which was then led away into the wilderness and released, presumably to die. It has already been said (v. 8) that *'ăzā'zēl* represented to the Jews the one who was opposed to the Lord. As the first goat was a means of expiation in regard *to the Lord* for the sins of Israel, so the second goat was a means of expiation *to the one who was opposed to the Lord* by returning to him with the goat the sins for which he was responsible. But whereas the goat designated to the Lord was sacrificed, the goat designated to *'ăzā'zēl* was not. Whether, in truth, the second goat was considered to bear *all* the sins (that is, the sins of a high hand as well as the unintentional sins) of the children of Israel is not made clear.

23-25. Aaron shall come into the tabernacle. Aaron was to enter the Tabernacle, remove his linen garments, wash, and put on other clothing. The garments donned at this point are not described, though it is likely that they were the formal clothing of the high priest (cf. Ex 28). He then was to sacrifice on the altar one ram as a burnt offering for the people, after which the fat portions of the sin offerings (cf. Lev 16:11,19) were to be burned.

26. He that let go the goat. The man made unclean by conducting the goat into the wilderness (v. 21) had to wash his clothing and himself before returning to the community. **27. The bullock . . . and the goat . . . shall one carry forth.** The remaining portions of the bullock and goat used in the sin offerings were to be taken from the camp and destroyed by burning. Those performing this act had to wash their clothing and bodies before returning.

29. Ye shall afflict your souls. The perpetual establishment of the Day of Atonement, *yôm hakkippūrîm* (cf. 23: 27), and its observance by the high priest and people follow in the remaining verses of the chapter. The tenth day of the seventh month was designated for the occasion, and on this day the people were to humble *(tᵉ'annû)* themselves and refrain from all work. This humbling or afflicting of one's self was likely performed through fasting (cf. Ps 35:13; Ezr 8:21; Isa 58:3,5), putting into subjection the earthly appetite in order to manifest one's penitence for wrongdoing. **31. A sabbath of rest.** The words *shabbat shabbatôn* mean "a sabbath of solemn rest" (RSV); that is, a *high* sabbath, a *particular* sabbath. **32. And the priest . . . shall make the atonement.** The prescribed ritual was to be followed once each year (v. 34) by the individual then holding the office of high priest. The entire ritual, imperfect and of necessity repetitive as it was, tended only to make the devout long for the coming of the High Priest and Perfect Mediator who should, by one act, fulfill for all time all the requirements necessary to effect perfect reconciliation with the Father.

II. How One Keeps in Touch with God. 17:1–27:34.

Once the desired relationship to God was established, it must be maintained.

The remaining chapters clearly present the way the individual Jew was to walk in order that he might be both different from the heathen and acceptable to the Lord.

A. The Holiness of the People. 17:1–20:27.

1) Concerning Food. 17:1-16.

1. God's instructions were given to Moses and thence to the people through Aaron and his sons.

3. What man soever. All animals to be slaughtered, those suitable for sacrifice, were to be brought to the priest and sacrificed at the door of the tent of meeting. At this time the blood and the fat were to be made a part of a peace offering to the Lord (v. 5). **4. And bringeth it not.** If the command was disobeyed, the man was to be considered to have shed blood wrongly and was to be **cut off from among his people.** The word **cut off** is from the root *krt,* which also means "to root out," "to maim," or "to destroy." There is no certainty as to whether the term implied the death sentence or merely excommunication. Exodus 31:14 seems to imply the death sentence, as both terms are mentioned as the penalty for the same offense.

5-7. They shall no more offer their sacrifices unto devils. The purpose of such severe punishment is given in verses 5 and 7. The animals were to be slain at the door of the tent of meeting rather than to be sacrificed to the "devils" (*śeʿirim).* These creatures, called "satyrs" in the RSV, are referred to in the singular in Lev 4:23 and translated simply "goats." The same term, however, as used in II Chr 11:15; Isa 13:21; 34:14 (in the Isa passages the AV also uses the term "satyr[s]") obviously refers to demons, objects of heathen worship. Apparently some of the idolatry of Egypt which had invaded the ranks of the Jews (Josh 24:14) had been brought from that place at the Exodus. Josephus (*Against Apion.* II. 7) tells of the worship of goats in Egypt. **A statute forever** was adjusted by Moses as reported in Deut 12:15, in anticipation of the entrance into the Promised Land, where the dispersion of the tribes would render such restriction impractical.

9. That man shall be cut off. The penalty for improper offering of any sacrificial animal was designated both for the Hebrews and for the foreigners dwelling among them.

10. That eateth any manner of blood. Neither the Hebrew nor the resident foreigner was to eat any manner of blood. The reasons are given in 17:11. The first was that it was the fluid which carried life through the body, and thus it represented the life or soul (*nepesh*) of the animal. The second was actually the primary reason, with the first simply forming the foundation for the second: Atonement for sins was made by the sacrifice of animals, by offering the life of the animal as a substitution for one's own life; the shedding of blood as the fluid of life was the offering of that portion which most clearly set forth the atonement picture. **13. He shall even pour out the blood thereof.** The blood of all edible game which was slain was to be shed on the ground and not to be eaten.

15. That which dieth of itself. The animal which had died a natural death, or had been slain by other animals, either retained its blood or had shed it in a manner which was ceremonially improper. Thus, even though the animal might ordinarily be considered clean, the nature of its death prevented its being eaten. When through ignorance, or without thinking, such an animal was consumed, the proper purification procedure was to be followed.

2) Concerning Marriage. 18:1-30.

3. After the doings of the land of Canaan. The Hebrew people, chosen by God to be the nation which would produce the Saviour of all mankind, were not to be allowed to indulge in the immoral and idolatrous practices of the people from whom they had just departed nor of the land into which they were soon to march. **4. Ye shall do my judgments.** Rather, they were to walk in the way set for them by their Leader, the Lord God of Israel. And it was with the authority of their Leader and their God that the following commandments were given to them, thus enforcing upon them their covenant obligation. **5. He shall live in them.** The commandments were not given without a promise. The obedient individual would **live.** The same expression is to be found in Ezk 20:11,13,21 without making clear the exact meaning. It is felt, however, that the meaning is to be found in the NT (Lk 20:38; Rom 10:5; Gal 3:12), where the "abundant," "full," or "true" life seems to be signified.

6-15. *Commands Concerning Purity in the Parent-child Relationship.*

6. Near of kin to him. Literally, *flesh of his flesh (shᵉʾēr bᵉśārô),* i.e., blood relation as opposed to relation simply by marriage. **To uncover their nakedness.** Hebrew idiom for having sexual intercourse. This is a prohibition of incest.

7. The nakedness of thy father. These laws were addressed to men. Hence this verse contains a prohibition not against incest between father and daughter, but against incest between son and mother only. The shame brought upon the mother was brought also upon the father. As they were of one flesh (Gen 2:24), any act committed against the mother could be considered to have been likewise committed against the father. **8. It is thy father's nakedness.** Even though a stepmother is not a blood relation, the status of man and wife compelled the same prohibition and for the same reason as in verse 7.

9. The nakedness of thy sister. References to a half sister and a stepsister are found here. **Whether she be born at home, or born abroad** is most likely a reference to whether the girl was a product of a marriage subsequent to or prior to that which produced the son. **10. Thy son's daughter.** Intercourse between father and granddaughter is prohibited. **11. Thy father's wife's daughter.** Again reference is made to a half sister, since a blood relationship exists (see also v. 9).

12,13. Thy father's sister. . . . thy mother's sister. These verses refer to an aunt, sister of either father or mother. **14. Thy father's brother.** Intercourse even with the wife of a paternal uncle is prohibited, since this would bring dishonor upon a blood relation.

15. Thy daughter in law. Dishonor upon a son would result from illicit relations between father and daughter-in-law.

16-18. *Commands Concerning Purity in Other Family Relationships.*

16. Thy brother's wife. The reference is to a sister-in-law. This, however, did not obtain where the deceased brother had left no children. Rather, the man was obliged to marry his brother's widow (Deut 25:5) in order that she might bear a child to preserve the name of the deceased. **17.** Intercourse with both **a woman and her daughter,** or with both a woman and her granddaughter is prohibited. **18. A wife to her sister.** Marriage to two sisters while both were living was prohibited, although the law, it seems, did not prevent marriage to the sister of a deceased wife. Cf. the case of Jacob, Leah, and Rachel (Gen 29:23,30), which shows that the law was not known in earlier times.

19. As long as she is put apart for her uncleanness. Other kinds of impurity and unnatural crimes are mentioned in verses 19-23. During a woman's period of separation, no man was to approach her (cf. 15:24; 20:18).

21. The fire is not in the Hebrew text but is simply an interpolation by the translators, based on such passages as II Kgs 16:3; 17:17; 21:6. Actually, the nature of the dedication that is indicated may have involved both fire and human sacrifice, although such is not stated. Molech was a heathen god who was also called Moloch (Amos 5:26), Milcom (I Kgs 11:33), and Malcham (Zeph 1:5). In I Kgs 11:5 he is called "the abomination of the Ammonites," and in I Kgs 17:7 Solomon is said to have built a high place for him, in the hill that is before Jerusalem." In Jer 32:35 it was at the high places of Baal that Molech was worshiped, thus showing a close relationship between the two gods. By worshiping Molech the children of Israel would profane the name of God. To profane *(ḥillēl)* is "to belittle, defile, make common." It is interesting to note that the Hebrew word is very similar in spelling to another word which means the very opposite *(hillēl),* "to praise, celebrate, glorify."

22. Thou shalt not lie with mankind. The perversions mentioned here and in verse 23 can not produce offspring, and thus they defeat the purpose for which mankind was given such responsibility and capability. This, therefore, is rebellion both against God and against a God-ordered society.

24. Defile not ye yourselves. Cf verse 3. The picture in the remaining verses of the chapter is that of a person, nauseated by the corruption and vileness within, violently expelling from his system that which would only further defile him. By contrast God reminded the people that they were to look to him as their God and to separate themselves *from* the customs of the heathen nations and *unto* him.

3) Concerning the Social Order. 19:1-37.

1,2. This is one of the greatest chapters in the OT. It is a Mosaic anticipation of the very spirit of the Sermon on the

Mount. The contents are closely related to the Ten Commandments with the assertion, **I am the Lord your God,** which frequently recurs as a refrain. The Book of the Covenant (Ex 21–23) likewise reveals several of the commands to be found herein. **Ye shall be holy.** The motive and inspiration for obedience to the commands which follow were to be the holiness of God. The Hebrew people were to measure their own holiness by that of God. Obedience to God's commands would insure that they would remain a separated, peculiar people of God.

3. Ye shall fear every man his mother, and his father. This command may have been placed first in recognition of the truth that, if a child is taught respect for his parents and for God's Day, he will be more likely to have respect for the commandments of his Lord.

4. Turn ye not unto idols. The command to avoid turning to idols (*'ĕlîlîm,* "vanity," "emptiness," "nothing") certainly set them apart from their idolatrous neighbors.

5. Cf. 7:15-18. **Ye shall offer it at your own will** is better translated: *You shall offer it so that you may be accepted* (RSV).

9-18. *Commands Concerning a Man's Dealings with His Neighbor.* Love and generosity were to motivate the course of action to be followed. **9,10. Thou shalt not wholly reap the corners.** Provision for the poor and the sojourner was to be made by allowing some of the crops to remain in the field for them at harvest time (cf. Deut 24:19-21, where olives are included in the commandment). **12. Swear by my name falsely.** To swear by God's name falsely was to do so in order to cheat or defraud another, which act would profane (*ḥālāl,* "discredit, make common") his holy name. **13. The wages of him that is hired.** Prompt payment of wages due was commanded. **14. Thou shalt not curse the deaf.** Ridicule of the deaf and blind was prohibited. Since God knows of each such act, fear of retribution should prevent it. **15. Thou shalt not respect the person of the poor.** There were not to be two standards of justice: one for the rich and one for the poor (cf. Deut 25:13 ff., where two kinds of weights and measures are mentioned). The administration of justice was to be of equal nature to all classes. This was likewise the burden of Amos (see 2:6, 7; 4:1; 5:11,12,24). **16. The blood of thy neighbour.** A man was not to seek the life of his neighbor either by accusation or by silence. **17. Rebuke** (from *yākaḥ)* involved reproving him, telling him where he was at fault. Doing this sincerely would reveal not only a lack of hatred but also a desire for his improvement. A word of rebuke left unsaid might well encourage him to continue in sin, thus bringing sin upon one's self. **18. Avenge, nor bear any grudge.** A man was neither to take vengeance on (*nāqam)* nor bear a grudge against (*nāṭar)* his neighbor. *Nāṭar* means literally *to watch for* and thus to bear malice in the heart towards another. Rather, love towards him was to be the rule (cf. Mt 19:19; 22:39; Rom 13:9; Gal 5:14).

19-25. *Directions for Safeguarding the Moral Order.* According to Keil and Delitzsch, this group of commandments to the Chosen People was designed "to keep the physical and moral order of the world sacred" (KD, *Pentateuch,* II, 421). In verse 19 the people are told that those things which were separated by creation are to remain so. Diverse kinds of animals were not to be allowed to interbreed. Nor were diverse kinds of seeds to be sown together. A cloth consisting of both linen and wool was not to be made.

20. A woman, that is a bondmaid. The fact that the bondmaid, though betrothed, had not been ransomed nor given her freedom would protect her from the death sentence for the sin referred to (cf. 20:10). And the man was to be required to bring a trespass offering to the Tabernacle to gain forgiveness for his sin (vv. 21,22). **23. Count the fruit thereof as uncircumcised.** In the land into which they were to go, they were not to eat fruit from the fruit trees for the first four years. The fruit of the first three years was to be considered unclean or forbidden (RSV), while that of the fourth year was to be dedicated to the Lord as an offering of thanksgiving. **25. In the fifth year.** Eating the fruit in the fifth year was permitted, and in accordance with the obedience of the people, the blessings of the Lord would be upon the future bearing of fruit. The one sanction for the commandment to forbear for four years was not the dedication of fruit to field spirits or fertility spirits but simply, "I am the Lord your God."

26. The first part of this verse is largely a repetition of 17:10 ff. To **use enchantment** and **observe times was to** practice augury and witchcraft (RSV).

27. Ye shall not round the corners of your heads. An ancient Arab religious custom required that the hair and beard be trimmed in such manner. The prohibition of the custom was necessary if the Jews were to be distinguished from the heathen. **28. Cuttings in your flesh.** This prohibited any voluntary disfigurement of the person. Both cutting and tattooing of the body were practiced by the heathen. **29. Do not prostitute thy daughter.** Such action would result in a dissolving of the very heart of society, the home. **30. Ye shall keep my sabbaths.** In honoring the Lord's Day and the Lord's House, the groundwork for a godly nation is laid. **31. Familiar spirits.** Seeking out mediums and wizards would indicate a lack of trust in and dedication to the Lord. **32. The hoary head.** Respect for earthly authority and wisdom is a prerequisite to respect for the judgment and commandments of the Lord.

33. If a stranger sojourn. With God's treatment of the Jews in Egypt as an example, the Jews were likewise to be gracious and kind to the foreigner who came to live among them, loving him as one of themselves (v. 34). **35. Ye shall do no unrighteousness.** Justice and scrupulous honesty were to be the rule in all dealings with one's fellow man.

4) The Punishments for Disobedience. 20:1-27.

3. Given of his seed unto Molech. By such open rebellion on the part of one of the Chosen People, God's house and name would be belittled. **4. Hide their eyes.** If the people did not perform their duty in the carrying out of the death sentence, God would bring judgment upon the man and his family, and all his companions who joined him to play the (spiritual) harlot (from *zānâ*), thus, to apostatize.

6. Familiar spirits. God would deal in like manner with one who turned to mediums or wizards, since this, too, was a form of spiritual adultery. The sentence to be imposed by his fellow man is referred to in verse 27. **7. Sanctify yourselves** *(hitqaddishtem* from *qādash,* "to be holy, consecrated, devoted") can also be rendered *consecrate yourselves* (RSV) or *show yourselves holy.*

9. Cf. Ex 21:17 and Deut 27:16. **His blood shall be upon him** means that the law of blood revenge would not obtain in the case of those who took his life.

10-21. *Review of Some Laws Regarding Sexual Sins.* See chapter 18 for the earlier enunciation of these statutes. Here their punishments are appended.

12. They have wrought confusion *(they have committed incest,* RSV) in that they have rebelled against the divinely created order. **14. Burnt with fire.** Likely, as in Josh 7:15,25, death was not by burning, but destruction of the remains of the executed individual was accomplished by fire. **19. They shall bear their iniquity.** Punishment by the people was not prescribed for the sins encountered in 20:19-21. It appears that God himself would see to the matter. **22. Keep all my statutes.** Since God had separated the Jews unto himself (vv. 24, 26), they were to keep themselves in every way apart from the practices of the heathen who had been cast out of the Land of Promise (v. 23). This Promised Land was to flow "with milk and honey" (v. 24), but it would not retain the Jews if they did not remain a dedicated people (v. 22). They were to be holy because the Lord to whom they belonged was holy.

B. The Holiness of Priests and Their Offerings. 21:1–22:33.

21:1-9. *Instructions to the Priests Generally.*

1,2. None . . . defiled for the dead. Exhibiting external signs of mourning and touching the dead disqualified a priest for performing his priestly duties. Consequently, he was denied this privilege except in the case of his immediate family. **3.** This included a virgin sister who, being still unmarried, had not left the family. It is not known why the wife is not mentioned here, particularly since Ezk 24:15 ff. seems to assume that the prophet would have mourned his wife's death had not the Lord spoken to him on that particular occasion.

4. The meaning of this verse is obscure. **Chief man** *(ba'al)* should in all probability be translated *husband* (RV marg. and RSV) or *lord of the house.* Thus, because of his position in the family and community, the priest should take care not to become defiled, except in the cases permitted above. **5. Make baldness upon their head.** These were signs of mourning among heathen peoples (cf. 19:27,28). They were therefore denied the Jewish priest, who, in offering the "bread *(leḥem;* also translated "meat" and "food" elsewhere) of their God" were not to be in such condition of ceremonial uncleanness that God's name would be profaned (v. 6).

7. Profane *(Hălālâ)* means "a woman who has been defiled" (RSV), an immoral woman. A woman put away from her husband, i.e., a divorced woman, was likewise unacceptable as a wife for a priest.

10-15. *Commands Concerning the High Priest Specifically.*

10-12. Upon whose head the . . . oil was poured. The term **anointing oil,** *shemen hammishḥâ,* comes from the verb, *māshaḥ, meaning* "to anoint or consecrate." The noun *māshîaḥ* is "the anointed one," the Christ, Messiah. A man in the position of high priest was to maintain such purity as would prevent his showing the customary signs of mourning for anyone at all; and he might not leave the sanctuary to participate in mourning, as this would bring defilement upon the Lord's sanctuary.

13. A wife in her virginity. He was to marry only an Israelite virgin. **15. His seed** *(zar'ô,* "posterity") was not to be made unholy by his having contracted an improper marriage, for he was to remember his status of one separated by the Lord to a particular office.

16. The remainder of the chapter is concerned with those imperfections and deficiencies that disqualified a man for exercising the duties of a priest. The general statement made in 21:17 is made specific in 21:18 ff. **18. Flat nose** is better translated more generally a *split* or *mutilated face* (RSV). **Anything superfluous.** Anything beyond that which was normal. **20. A blemish in his eye.** A sight defect. **Scurvy.** An itch.

21. To offer the bread of his God. To offer a sacrifice to God in the role of priest. One with such a blemish might, however, partake of those portions of the sacrifices usually given to the priests (v. 22). He was not to be allowed to perform any priestly function. These restrictions were based on the Hebrew belief that the spiritual nature of a man was reflected in his physical condition. Only one who was physically perfect could be considered of sufficient holiness to perform the functions of a priest.

22:2,3. The holy things consisted of the sacrifices made by the people and offered by the priests. The separation referred to was required during a state of ritual uncleanness. No priest could handle these dedicated gifts while unclean. The portions of the sacrificial food given to the priests were of great importance to them, but they could neither be prepared nor eaten except when the eater was clean. **6.** For the Jew, the new day began at sunset. Therefore, being **unclean until the even** meant being unclean for the remainder of that day—until **the sun is down** (v. 7).

10,11. No stranger *(zār,* "outsider," "layman") could partake of the holy food, but a member of the priest's household, such as a slave, could do so. **12,13.** If **the priest's daughter** married a *zār,* she could not eat of the dedicated food; but if she returned to her father's house as a childless widow or divorcee, she then could do so. **14. These shall he not take.** It is a non-priest to whom reference is here made. Cf. 5:14-16, but in chapter 22 the regulation concerns specifically the eating of the holy food unintentionally by a *zār.*

17-25. *Commands Concerning the Condition of Animals Offered as Sacrifice.* These rules pertain to the payment of vows and freewill offerings (cf. 7:16).

22. A wen. An ulcer or running sore.

23. Any thing superfluous. In the case of a freewill offering an animal might be brought which was not perfectly proportioned; e.g., one part might be longer or shorter than normal. For the fulfilling of a vow, however, such laxity was not permitted. **24. That which is bruised.** The reference here is specifically to castrated animals, the operation having been performed in any of the four ways mentioned. **25. From a stranger's hand.** A foreigner who desired to offer a sacrifice to the Lord had to observe the same rules regarding the quality of the animal as did the Jews.

27. A bullock, or a sheep, or a goat. The animals mentioned were to be at least seven days old before they could be offered as a sacrifice to the Lord. Cf. Ex 22:30. **28. Ye shall not kill it and her young both in one day.** Cf. Deut 22:6. The purpose of this commandment is not clear, but it was perhaps given in order to impress upon the Israelites the importance of keeping sacred the relationship existing between parent and offspring.

29. Cf. 7:15; 19:5,6.

31-33. Concluding exhortation.

C. The Holiness of Time. 23:1–25:55.

1) The Holy Use of Days. 23:1-44.

Certain days and periods were to be dedicated to the Lord. This chapter lists such times.

2. Feasts of the Lord and **my feasts** were those "holy convocations" or religious assemblies set apart by the Lord and dedicated to him for the observance of some particular phase of Israel's religious life. *Mô'ēd,* the word translated "feast," means "an appointed time," "a festival time," "an assembly," and comes from the verb *yā'ad,* "to appoint," "to meet by agreement."

3. The term **sabbath of rest,** *shabbat shabbātôn,* comes from the word *shābat,* which means "to cease," "to rest", "to come to an end." As indicated, the observance of the day presupposes six days of labor. The day of rest is further identified as **the sabbath of the Lord,** i.e., both appointed by and dedicated to him. Its origin, as given in Gen 2:2,3, relates the day to God's creation of the world, places it in an indispensable position in that creation, and makes the observance of it an incontestable imperative. Mark 2:27 can not be used to weaken the imperative. "The sabbath was made for man" because it was an absolute necessity that man have one, and that he observe it in the proper spirit.

5. The first month was Abib (later called Nisan, as in Neh 2:1 and Est 3:7) and corresponded to the latter part of March and the first part of April. The details of the Feast of Passover and the Feast of Unleavened Bread are to be found in Exodus 12. Here only the bare outline is furnished.

6. Unleavened bread is called *maṣṣâ,* with a plural form, *maṣṣôt,* which even today designates the unleavened wafers sold for Jewish observance of this holy time. **7. Servile work** was apparently labor connected with agricultural pursuits and other definite occupations. That preparation of food was permitted is implied in Ex 12:16. **8. An offering made by fire.** Num 28:19 ff. gives the details of the sacrifice.

9-14. *Instructions for the Offering of First Fruits.* Cf. Deut 26:2 ff.

10. When ye be come into the land. This command looked forward to the time when the Israelites would raise crops in the Promised Land. The sheaf, *'ōmer,* was of grain, but it is not specified whether of wheat or barley. The latter is assumed because it was the first ripe. The offering was to be lifted by the priest and moved toward the altar and then moved away from the altar. This constituted waving it. It denoted dedicating it to the Lord and receiving it again. The specific day for the offering, **the morrow after the sabbath** (v. 11), is uncertain, since the seventh day of the week was not the only day called the "sabbath." The Day of Atonement received this designation (16:31; 23:32) regardless of the day of the week on which it occurred. The same is true of the first day of the Feast of Unleavened Bread. It was a day of rest, *shabbāt.* It is most likely that the offering of first fruits was to be brought to the priest on the day after the first day of the Feast of Unleavened Bread. This would place it on the sixteenth day of Abib (cf. v. 6). Thus this feast prefigures the resurrection of Christ as the firstfruits from the dead (I Cor 15:23; Rom 8:29).

13. Two tenth deals referred to two-tenths of an ephah, while a quarter of a hin represented about one and one-half quarts.

15-22. *Instructions for the Observance of the Feast of Weeks.* Cf. Ex 34:22. It was also known as the Feast of Harvest (Ex 23:16). The term "Pentecost," found in Acts 2:1; 20:16; I Cor 16:8, is from the Greek word *pentēkostē,* meaning "fiftieth" (day). The Feast of Weeks was later known as the "Feast of Pentecost."

15. The morrow after the sabbath. See the note on 23:11. **16. Shall ye number fifty days.** In verse 15 the command is to count seven weeks (hence "Feast of Weeks") plus one day ("unto the morrow after the seventh sabbath"), or a total of fifty days. It was to be a **new meat** (meal) offering in that it was to be from the new harvest.

17. They shall be baken with leaven. Cf. note on 23:13. This is the only meal offering to be made with leaven. Very likely it was so made that the produce might be presented to the Lord in the condition in which it would be useful to and enjoyed by the people.

18-20. A burnt offering, a **sin offering,** and **peace offerings** were to be offered at this time. "In this way the whole of the year's harvest was placed under the gracious blessing of the Lord by the sanctification of its commencement and its close; and the enjoyment of their daily food was also sanctified thereby" (KD, *Pentateuch,* II, 444).

22. Thou shalt leave them unto the poor. Cf. 19:9,10. Thanksgiving to the

Lord can frequently best be demonstrated by acts of kindness for the underprivileged.

24,25. In the seventh month. On the first day of the seventh month the Israelites were to observe a day of rest (*shabbāt*), a blowing of the trumpet (likely the ram's horn or *shôpār*), a religious gathering (v. 24), and the offering of a burnt offering. These observances set apart the entire seventh month as a sabbatical month, important not simply because of its numerical order but because of the fact that the month contained the period when Israel received forgiveness for her sins. In OT times the month was called Ethanim (I Kgs 8:2), but it was later called Tishri.

26-32. *Instructions for a Day of Atonement.* Cf. 16:1-34.

27. The day is designated as the tenth day of Ethanim (Tishri). **32.** The Jewish day went from sunset to sunset, thus **from even unto even.**

33-36. *Instructions for the Observance of the Feast of Tabernacles.*

34. Tabernacles. Hebrew *sukkôt*, "booths." This feast was to last for seven days, beginning on the fifteenth day of the seventh month, i.e., five days after the Day of Atonement. **36.** Certain acts, such as the *'ăṣenet* or "solemn assembly," were to be performed on the eighth day, it is true, but these simply provided a closing of the observance. The Feast of Tabernacles (Booths) commemorated the sojourn of the Israelites in the wilderness of Sinai when the Lord brought them out of Egyptian bondage (v. 43).

37,38. These are the feasts of the Lord. This is a concluding statement which looks back to the introduction in 23:4. The preceding verses in the chapter have told of special holy days to be observed in addition to the regular sacrifices, offerings, and holy days indicated elsewhere.

39. Ye shall keep a feast unto the Lord. A fuller description of the Feast of Tabernacles is given in the remainder of the chapter. In Ex 23:16; 34:22 it is called the "Feast of Ingathering" (*ḥag hā'āsip*, from *'āsap*, "to gather or draw together"), and reference is made in this verse to the time when the Israelites shall "have *gathered in* the fruit of the land."

40. Cf. Neh 8:15. **Boughs of goodly trees** were literally, *the fruit* (*pᵉrî;* so RSV), although Keil and Delitzsch hold that "fruit" refers to "the shoots and branches of the trees, as well as the blossom and fruit that grew out of them" (*Pentateuch*, II, 448). The second word translated "boughs" in the AV is from *'ānāp*, which means specifically "sprout" or "branch." It was with the several types of branches here mentioned that the Israelites were to construct the booths of 23:42.

43. I made the children of Israel to dwell in booths. The observance of this special feast was not to remind the people of the privations suffered during the period of desert wandering. It was, rather, to bring to mind the provisions made for their needs by their Creator and Liberator during that most important period of their history, the birth of the Hebrew nation as a result of the direct intervention of the Lord their God.

2) The Holy Use of Objects. 24:1-23. The chapter can be divided into three topics: (1) the oil for the tabernacle lamps (vv. 1-4); (2) the showbread (vv. 5-9); and (3) blasphemy and retaliation (vv. 10-23).

2. Pure oil olive. The oil for the lamps was to be provided by the people to make certain that they would be kept burning at all times. Cf. Ex 27:20,21, where the same instructions are given as appear in verses 2 and 3 here. To obtain this oil, they first pounded the olives or pressed them, to squeeze out their juice. Next they strained the juice to remove the pulp. Then, when the oil rose to the surface of the juice, they skimmed it off. **3. Testimony.** A reference to the Tables of the Law placed in the ark within the veil (Ex 25:16; cf. Deut 31:26. In the former, *'ēdut* is used, as in the Leviticus passage. In the latter, *'ēd* is used. Both mean "witness" or "testimony"). **4. Candlestick.** Better, *lampstand* (RSV), since oil lamps rather than candles were involved.

5. Two tenth deals. Two-tenths of an ephah, as in 23:13,17. This means that each cake or loaf of unleavened bread was to contain about six and one-fourth pounds of flour. **7. The frankincense** was possibly put into small golden cups and placed *with each row* (RSV; cf. Jos *Ant.* iii.10.7), not directly **on the bread.** It was, *with* the bread, to serve as a memorial (*'azkārâ;* cf. note on 2:3), the frankincense itself likely being cast upon the altar fire. **8. Taken from the children of Israel.** As in the case of the oil (v. 2), the showbread was to be provided by the people. **9. And it shall be Aaron's and his sons'.** After the frankincense had been offered by fire to the Lord, the bread was to be eaten by the priests.

10. The son of an Israelitish woman. The son of the Egyptian, accompanied by his Jewish mother, was apparently included among the "mixed multitude" of Ex 12:38. According to Deut 23:7,8, he was likely not considered a part of the "congregation of the Lord." The nature of the quarrel between him and the Israelite is not stated. **11.** The word translated *blasphemed* is from *nāqab* and literally means to "bore, pierce, mark, distinguish, or designate." It does not in itself denote a lack of reverence (cf. Num 1:17, where it is translated "expressed"), but in the context of this passage no doubt is left as to the intended meaning. The Jews later took the word in its general meaning and would not speak the sacred name *Yhwh* at all, substituting for it the word *'Adōnay,* "Lord." **Of the Lord** is not present in Hebrew because it was understood that "the name," *hashshēm,* in this context referred to the Lord. **12. That the mind of the Lord might be shewed them.** No punishment had as yet been specified for blaspheming the name of God.

14. Lay their hands upon his head. Since the sin of the man could have involved the entire community in punishment, what guilt there may have been in the community was transferred to the sinner by the laying on of hands. (Cf. 16:21, where the community sins were symbolically transferred to the "scapegoat".) He was then executed by the people. **15,16.** These verses state the law which was at that time divinely enacted concerning the sin which had been committed. **Shall bear his sin.** Shall bear full responsibility and be subjected to the designated punishment for it.

17-21. *Review of a Group of Previously Enacted Laws.*

For the earlier statement of the laws, see Ex 21:12 ff. The situation in 24:18 is, however, not directly treated in the Exodus passage.

17,18. He that killeth any man is literally, *he that smites the soul (nepesh) of any man.* In verse 18 the same general construction is found: "the one smiting the soul of a beast shall make it good, *soul in place of soul.*" The AV **beast for beast** is preferable to the more literal *life for life* of the RSV (cf. v. 21 a). **19, 20.** Cf. Ex 21:24,25. **Eye for eye, tooth for tooth.** This law of retaliation, *lex talionis,* was mentioned by Jesus Christ in Mt 5:38 ff., when he condemned, not the principle of civil law involved here, but the spirit of retaliation and revenge which was most likely to be found in association with it.

22. Ye shall have one manner of law. The principle mentioned in verse 16 is here stressed. The law was to apply to the foreigner as well as to the Israelite.

3) The Holy Use of Years. 25:1-55. The Sabbatical Year is discussed (vv. 2-7); the observance of the Year of Jubilee is commanded (vv. 8-12); and the effect of the Year of Jubilee upon property (vv. 13-34) and persons (vv. 35-55) is related.

2. Then shall the land keep a sabbath. In 23:3 we learn that a sabbath day was caused to be kept by the people. In this verse it is commanded that the land be allowed to observe a sabbath *(wᵉshābᵉtâ shabbāt)* **unto the Lord. 4. A sabbath of rest unto the land.** Just as the seventh day was designated the sabbath day, so each seventh year was to be a sabbath year, in which neither sowing nor pruning would occur. **5. That which groweth of its own accord.** The owner of the land was not to reap that which grew up of its own accord during the sabbath year. The **undressed** vine is called a *nazir,* the same Hebrew word as for a Nazirite, whose hair was allowed to remain uncut or undressed. **6. The sabbath of the land shall be meat for you.** Instead of the crops being reaped by the owner, they were to provide food for all, rich and poor alike (cf. Ex 23:11).

8,9. After **seven sabbaths of years,** or forty-nine years, Israel was to cause the sound of the horn *(shōpār)* to be heard throughout the land. The blowing of the horn was to take place on the Day of Atonement, and it was apparently at this time that a special year was to begin. **Trumpet of the jubile** is literally, the *horn of shouting,* or "loud trumpet" (ASV). The word translated *jubile* in verse 9 is *tᵉrû'â.* Elsewhere the word "jubile" is from *yôbēl,* a word of uncertain derivation (v. 10 ff.; 27:17-23; Num 36:4; see comment on Josh 6:4). This Hebrew word went into the Vulgate as *Jubilaeus* and thence into English as "jubile" and "jubilee."

10. The fiftieth year presents the difficulty of two successive sabbatical years, the forty-ninth and fiftieth, with the land lying fallow both years. This difficulty has led some to suppose that it may have been so calculated as to make the fiftieth year coincide with the seventh sabbatical year. And the year of "jubile" seems to have commenced on the Day of Atonement, which fell on the tenth day of the seventh month of the Jewish sacred year, Ethanim or Tishri. This seventh month, however, was also the first month of the Jewish civil calendar. This is how a year might be considered to have begun in the seventh month. Another explanation is that the trumpet blast on the Day of Atonement gave six months advance notice of the beginning of the Jubilee Year. However, the inference is that the horn actually ushered in the special year. Insufficient details are furnished to afford a solution to the problem. At least it was to be a year which provided liberty to many who had for a time lived without it. The general statement is made that every man would return to his possession and family, and the statement is more clearly defined in verses 23-34,39-55.

13. Ye shall return every man unto his possession. The first of the two effects of Jubilee Year is stated again generally, and in preparation for the year the instructions of the following verses are given. The basis for these instructions is that the land actually would belong to the Lord rather than to the individual. The Lord would allot the land to the various families, and they could not sell it in perpetuity because it must eventually revert to the family to whom it had been allotted (cf. vv. 23,24).

14-16. Oppress (from *yānâ)* means "to wrong or maltreat" by misrepresenting the value of a piece of land. **According to the number of years.** Since the land belonged to the Lord, only the crops which grew on it could be sold. Therefore the time remaining until the next Jubilee Year had to be considered in the setting of the price for the exchange of all land, since the nearer the exchange occurred to that special year, the fewer crops would remain to be raised before the land reverted to its original Israelite owner.

18,19. When the Israelites kept the Lord's commandments, they were to find themselves dwelling **in safety** *(beṭaḥ,* "security and confidence"). The land was to bear enough so that they should eat their "fill" *(śōba'*, "abundance"). **20-22. What shall we eat the seventh year?** As the Israelites naturally would be concerned lest with the land lying fallow there should be a decrease in harvested crops, God promised that the crops of the sixth year would be sufficient to last until the Sabbatical Year and the Jubilee Year were both completed (vv. 21,22).

24. A redemption for the land. There were several ways in which the land might be redeemed (from *gā'al,* "buy back," "ransom." Boaz performed the duty of a kinsman-redeemer, *gô'ēl,* when he married Ruth. Christ Jesus was our *gô'ēl* at the cross.).

25. If thy brother be waxen poor. Poverty was the only situation which would force an Israelite to sell his land (cf. I Kgs 21:3). In such a case a kinsman-redeemer could come and buy back what had been sold and restore it to its original owner. **26,27. None to redeem it.** If he had no near kinsman to redeem his land and had earned a sufficient amount, he could buy the land back himself by taking into consideration the number of crops still remaining until the Jubilee Year and paying the man for them. **28. Not able to restore it.** If he had neither a kinsman-redeemer nor the ability to redeem the land himself, the land simply reverted to his possession at the arrival of the Jubilee Year. The buyer lost nothing through this arrangement, for he had paid only for the crops to be harvested until the Jubilee Year.

29. If a man sell a dwelling house. In a walled city, if a house was sold and remained in the buyer's possession for a whole year (i.e., without anyone's having redeemed it), it then became the full possession of the buyer (cf. one exception in v. 32). The Jubilee Year did not affect its ownership. **31. The houses of the villages which have no wall.** A house in an unwalled town, however, was subject to the same regulations as the land itself (vv. 25-28). **32-34. The cities of the Levites.** In the case of the Levites, the laws of the Jubilee Year which ordinarily pertained to land applied, instead, only to their houses, whether in a walled city or not. Their land could not be sold at any time.

35-55. The second effect of the Jubilee Year is given in the remaining verses of the chapter.

35-37. Thy brother refers to a fellow Israelite. Loans to needy friends were not to involve interest. Rather, the needy one was to be assisted by being allowed to reside with one of the community and to enjoy the same privileges as a stranger or foreigner who, although he could not own land, was permitted to accumulate property and live in comfort as a free man.

38. I am the Lord your God. As the One who created them, chose them, and delivered them from Egyptian bondage, God was authorized to impose these rules upon the Israelites.

39-43. If thy brother . . . be waxen poor. The Israelite who had to sell himself into bondage to another was not to be a slave laborer, but was to work simply as a hired servant and was to be treated kindly. When the Jubilee Year arrived, he was to be liberated, unless he had renounced his claim to freedom. The contents of these verses do not disagree with Ex 21:2-6, because the Leviticus passage is confined to a discussion of the effect of the Jubilee Year on a man's freedom. If the Israelite sold himself into bondage more than seven years prior to the Jubilee Year, the instructions in Ex 21:2 applied. At any rate, six years was the maximum length of time he could be required to serve before returning with his children to his family and possessions.

44-46. Both thy bondmen, and thy bondmaids. Slave labor was to be restricted to those bought from foreign nations and those foreigners who had settled among the Jews. This category of slaves, *bondman ('ebed,* from *'ābad,* "to serve or work"; cf. *'ōbadyâ,* Obadiah, lit., *servant of the Lord)* and *bondwoman ('āmâ,* "maidservant"), could be passed on to one's children as an inheritance (v. 46).

47-54. And thy brother . . . sell himself. If an Israelite sold himself into the service of a resident foreigner, he could be redeemed by a near kinsman (vv. 48,49; see note on v. 24), or he could redeem himself. Here, too, he would have to consider proper payment for the time remaining until the Jubilee Year, the amount depending on whether there were many or few years left (vv. 50-52).

53. While in service to a resident foreigner, the Israelite was to be treated with consideration, as a hired servant. **54. If he be not redeemed.** His length of service was bound to end free of compensation at the Jubilee Year.

55. They are my servants. The provisions for the Jubilee Year had as their guiding principle the fact that the Israelites were servants of the Lord and could not be sold permanently into the service of another. Likewise, since the land was the Lord's, it must return from time to time to the possession of those Israelites to whom it had been originally allotted.

D. Promises and Warnings. 26:1-46.

After the first two verses, which seem to summarize the first four Commandments, verses 3-13 relate the blessings of obedience, verses 14-39 tell of the punishments for disobedience, and verses 40-45 promise forgiveness upon repentance.

1,2. Ye shall make you no idols. In prohibiting idolatry (v. 1) and requiring the keeping of the Sabbaths (v. 2), the first four of the Ten Commandments can be said to be summarized. **Idols** *('ĕlîlim)* were, literally, *things of nothingness.* **Graven image** *(pesel)* was a carved or cast idol. **A standing image** *(maṣṣēbâ)* was a pillar set upright. **Image of stone** *('eben maśkît)* was a figured stone, or one with an image carved into its face. If idolatry was set aside by the people and if the Lord's Sabbaths were given proper observance, the likelihood of their becoming apostate would be considerably reduced.

3,4. I will give you rain. Obedience to the Lord's commandments would result in improved agricultural conditions within the nation (cf. II Chr 7:14). **5.** They would be able to eat their bread **to the full,** i.e., to the point of complete satisfaction *(śōba';* cf. 25:19). **6. I will give peace in the land.** The safety promised in verse 5 (cf. 25:18,19) is reinforced by the promise of peace *(shalôm),* both mental and national, which would result in the ability to live an abundant life. **7,8. Ye shall chase your enemies.** In the event, however, that war should ensue, they would have complete and easy victory. **10. Because of the new** is apparently *to make way for the new* (RSV), a means of expressing the abundance of provision.

11,12. God would make his **tabernacle** *(mishkān),* i.e., his dwelling place, among them; and they would be continually aware of his presence in their midst. **13. I am the Lord your God.** The gracious deliverance performed by the

Lord only recently would testify to the fact that the promises of the preceding verses could be depended upon.

14,15. If ye will not hearken unto me. The very opposite of the preceding blessings would fall upon Israel if the nation became disobedient and unfaithful. The rebellion is depicted in four ways in the terms **despise, abhor, will not do,** and **break.**

16-39. *The Details of the Curses.*

16. I will even appoint over you terror. Terror would come in the form of disease (**burning ague,** i.e., fever) which would cause life to pine away (AV *cause sorrow of heart* is less accurate). Their enemies would devour their crops, so that seed planting would be useless. **17. I will set my face against you.** Their enemies would so completely overcome them and Israel would be so thoroughly cowed, that they would even run from a nonexistent enemy (cf. v. 36 and Prov 28:1).

18. Seven times or *sevenfold* indicates an even greater intensification of the punishments. This threat is repeated in verses 21,24,28. **19,20. A heaven as iron** would shed no rain and an **earth as brass** could produce no crop.

25. Avenge the quarrel of my covenant. Execute those punishments prescribed for breaking the covenant relationship. **26. And when I have broken the staff.** The supply of bread would be so reduced that one oven would suffice for baking the bread prepared for ten families. Bread would be rationed and, in contrast to the situation in 26:5, that which was eaten would bring no satisfaction. Micklem assumes that, since each house had its own oven, the picture of ten women baking at one oven denotes "the breakup of family life" (Nathaniel Micklem, IB, II, 129). It is more likely, however, that scarcity of food is depicted here rather than dissolution of the home.

29. Ye shall eat the flesh of your sons. The severity of the hunger would result in cannibalism within the family circle (cf. II Kgs 6:28,29; Lam 4:10). **30. Idols.** *Gillûlîm,* from *gālal,* "to roll," was a term of derision, which referred to the objects worshiped as "blocks" or "clods." **32,33. I will bring the land into desolation.** These words look ahead to the time of enemy occupation, and exile.

34,35. Then shall the land enjoy her sabbaths. During the time of exile the land would at last be able to lie fallow, the greed of the people having prevented this earlier. "As the earth groans under the pressure of the sin of men, so does it rejoice in deliverance from this pressure, and participation in the blessed rest of the whole creation" (KD, *Pentateuch,* II, 476).

36,37. I will send a faintness into their hearts. Complete demoralization would be the lot of the exiles (see on v. 17). **38. Shall eat you up** refers both to death at the hands of the enemy and to absorption by them (cf. Num 13:32). **39. Pine away** is from *māqaq,* "to melt or decay." They would suffer not only for their own sins but also for those of their fathers. The word translated **iniquity** *('āwōn)* involves both punishment and sin (cf. Jas 1:15).

40-42. If they shall confess their iniquity. If, however, Israel realized and confessed that her punishment was from God, a deserved and just chastisement for the rebellious and perverse hearts of her people, then God would **remember** the covenant made with the patriarchs.

43. The land . . . shall enjoy her sabbaths. Even though Israel would be made to leave her beloved land, which therefore would lie fallow, and even though she would for a while undergo chastisement for her sin, she would repent and be forgiven, and the covenant would be renewed by the Lord, her Deliverer from Egyptian bondage.

E. The Making of Vows. 27:1-34.

The chapter may be divided into two major portions: vows, 27:1-29, and tithes, 27:30-33. The former consists of instructions on vows concerning (1) persons, verses 1-8; (2) cattle, verses 9-13; (3) houses, verses 14,15; (4) land, verses 16-25; and (5) exceptions to the foregoing instructions, verses 26-29. A vow was never commanded, but, once made, was to be scrupulously kept (Eccl 5:4,5; Deut 23:21-23; Num 30:2). If commutation or redemption (buying off) was to be accomplished, a payment was required. And, according to KD (Pentateuch, II, 480), "the fulfilment of the vow could only have consisted in the payment into the sanctuary of the price fixed by the law."

2. Singular. "Special." A free translation of the passage might be: "When a man makes a special vow, the persons involved shall be reckoned by you as belonging unto the Lord" (Nathaniel Micklem, IB, II, 131).

3-7. And thy estimation. The evaluation of an individual was apparently based on his worth as a laborer for a given period. The value of the shekel at the time is unknown; consequently no attempt will be made to translate the values into modern coinage. They are stated as follows: (1) age twenty to thirty, fifty shekels per man and thirty per woman; (2) age five to twenty, twenty shekels for a boy and ten for a girl; (3) age one month to five years, five shekels for a boy and three for a girl; (4) age over sixty, fifteen shekels for a man and ten for a woman. **8. But if he be poorer than thy estimation.** In case the person making the vow was too poor to provide the designated amount, the fixing of the sum was to be left to the discretion of the priest.

9. And if it be a beast. An animal apparently could not be redeemed for money. **10. He shall not alter it.** Both the animal originally dedicated and the one substituted were to be forfeit.

14,15. And when a man shall sanctify his house. A house that was dedicated to the Lord was evaluated by the priest. If not redeemed, it apparently was to be sold for the good of the sanctuary. If the owner wished to redeem it, he had to add one-fifth to the estimated value.

16. And if a man shall sanctify . . . some part of a field. The value of a field belonging to a man through inheritance was to be reckoned by the amount of seed required to sow it properly. The amount stated here was apparently the estimated value of the crops of such a field for the entire Jubilee period. **17. From the year of jubile.** If the Jubilee period had partly elapsed at the time the field was dedicated, the estimate was to be modified according to the time yet remaining. **19. He shall add the fifth part.** After paying the stated amount, he apparently would continue to hold the field, but would not have the right to sell it. He could redeem it by adding one-fifth to the evaluation. **20,21. It shall not be redeemed any more.** If not redeemed by him before the Jubilee Year, the field would become the property of the priest and would be sold by him.

22,23. A field . . . he hath bought. If the field was his not by inheritance but by purchase, and was dedicated to the Lord, he was to pay all at one time, **in that day,** the value placed upon it by the priest. **24. The field shall return.** According to this verse and to 25:23-28 the land would revert to its hereditary owner at the time of the Jubilee Year.

26. Only the firstling of the beasts. The first-born of clean cattle and sheep belonged to the Lord by law and could not be redeemed. **27. If it be of an unclean beast.** The first-born of an unclean animal dedicated to the Lord was evaluated by the priest and could be redeemed by adding one-fifth to the state value.

28. No devoted thing. Things which were **devoted** (*ḥērem,* under a ban, set apart entirely for the use of the Lord) could not be redeemed. This was different from dedication. An item thus placed under a ban as a result of being vowed to the Lord was to be considered **most holy,** literally, *holiness of holinesses.* It was surrendering something to God in an irrevocable and unredeemable manner. **29. None devoted . . . shall be redeemed.** In certain instances persons could be placed under a ban, and such individuals were to be put to death. It is not likely that this "devoting" was done at the pleasure of just any man. Most probably it was done officially and was used against "those persons who obviously resisted that sanctification of life which was binding upon them" (KD, *Pentateuch,* II, 485).

30. And all the tithe of the land. The tithes belonged to the Lord and were subject to the same redemption rules as the clean beasts that had been dedicated (vv. 9,10). **32. Whatsoever passeth under the rod** refers to the custom of counting animals by causing them to pass in single file out of an enclosure and marking each tenth animal by a rod dipped in a coloring material. **33. It shall not be redeemed.** He was not to substitute another animal for one so designated lest he be required to part with both.

BIBLIOGRAPHY

Barnes, Albert. *Bible Commentary on the Old Testament: Exodus-Ruth.* Grand Rapids: Baker Book House, reprinted 1957.

Bonar, Andrew A. *A Commentary on the Book of Leviticus.* 5th ed. London: James Nisbet & Co., 1875.

Chapman, A. T., and Streane, A. W. *The Book of Leviticus (The Cambridge Bible for Schools and Colleges).*

Cambridge: The University Press, 1914.
ERDMAN, CHARLES R. *The Book of Leviticus*. Westwood, New Jersey: Fleming H. Revell Co., 1951.
GENUNG, GEORGE F. *An American Commentary on the Old Testament: The Book of Leviticus*. Philadelphia: American Baptist Publication Society, 1905.
KEIL, C. F., and DELITZSCH, F. *Biblical Commentary on the Old Testament*. Vol. II: *The Pentateuch*. Translated by James Martin. Grand Rapids: Wm. B. Eerdmans Publishing Co., reprinted 1956.
KENNEDY, A. R. S. (ed.). *Leviticus and Numbers (The New Century Bible)*. New York: Henry Frowde, Oxford University Press, American Branch, n.d.
MICKLEM, NATHANIEL. "The Book of Leviticus," *The Interpreter's Bible*. Edited by George Arthur Buttrick, *et al.* Vol. 2. New York: Abingdon-Cokesbury Press, 1953.
PFEIFFER, CHARLES F. *The Book of Leviticus: A Study Manual (Shield Bible Series)*. Grand Rapids: Baker Book House, 1957.

NUMBERS

INTRODUCTION

Title and Scope of Book. Among the ancient titles given to this book is the one used in our present Hebrew Bibles *bᵉmīdbar,* meaning "in the wilderness." It is taken from a prominent word in the first line, and is quite descriptive of the total contents. The English title has its origin in the Septuagint Version (LXX), whence, through the Vulgate, we get our name Numbers. Only a few chapters (1–4; 26) are given over to numbering (census-taking), while the bulk of the book deals with laws, regulations, and experiences of Israel in the wilderness. We must not, however, underemphasize the significance of two censuses, one taken at Sinai in preparation for the wilderness, the other taken near the Jordan, almost forty years later, in preparation for entering the promised land. One might even say that these censuses break up the book into its two logical divisions. Thus chapters 1–21 begin with a census and cover the years in the wilderness, while chapters 26–36 begin with a census of the new generation and tell of the months before entrance into Canaan. The Balaam story, which separates these two groups of chapters, forms a literary hinge, about which we comment later.

Numbers should not be studied independently of Exodus, Leviticus, and Deuteronomy. For example, Exodus 19:1 tells of Israel's arrival in the wilderness of Sinai in the third month after the Hebrews left the land of Egypt. From the third to the twelfth month they received the Decalogue, instructions for building the Tabernacle, and directions concerning the many details of the sacrificial system set forth in Leviticus. In Numbers, the people of Israel are taught how to function as a camp. Their religious, civil, and military economies are set in order, in preparation for their journeying, worshiping, and conquering as a nation.

Laws and instructions supplementary to the many legal and ceremonial details of Exodus and Leviticus are interspersed throughout the book. The earliest date given in Numbers appears in 9:1, where we are told that in the first month of the second year, the people were given regulations for keeping the first commemorative Passover. Numbers 1:1,2 tells us that Israel, while at Sinai, took a census in the second month of the second year, and received additional instructions, largely ceremonial (chapters 5–10), then left Sinai on the twentieth day of the second month beginning the second year after the Exodus (10:11). Numbers, then, gives the history of Israel's movements from the last nineteen days at Sinai (1:1; 10:11) until the people arrived in the Plains of Moab, east of Jordan, in the fortieth year (Num 22:1; 26:3; 33:50).

The sequence of events in the book of Numbers runs as follows: From Sinai, Israel journeyed north to the Wilderness of Paran. There the spies who brought back an "evil report" instigated a rebellion, and so the people refused to enter the land. Through foolish presumption they suffered defeat at the hands of the heathen, and were turned back to wander in the wilderness thirty-eight more years. At the end of this period, they traveled to the plains of Moab, east of the Jordan, and defeated and occupied all of Trans-Jordan north of the river Arnon. Here they fell into sin with the Moabite and Midianite women and worshiped their gods. Israel, as a new generation, was numbered again, and at the command of God destroyed the Midianites who had so harassed them. Gad and Reuben and the half tribe of Manasseh were given possessions east of the Jordan, and Moses appointed Joshua his successor. From chapter 20 through chapter 36, the book deals with events of the fortieth year (36:13). Because of its many laws and regulations this part has much in common with the book of Deuteronomy.

Date and Authorship. G. B. Gray voices the opinion of a number of higher critics when he says concerning Numbers, "Much that is here related of the age of Moses can be demonstrated to be unhistorical. . . ." (ICC, p. xlii). He admits, however, that some matters presented "are not incompatible with any known historical facts and conditions." In trying to account for the Book of Numbers without admitting its Mosaic authorship, many scholars have proposed that it is a composite of several documents. Most of the book such scholars designate "P" (Priestly) document, which they claim was written not earlier than the sixth or fifth century B.C., *chiefly* by priests of post-Exilic times. They allow that some of Numbers is from "J" and "E", two documents not older than the ninth and eighth centuries B.C. Even these earlier documents, they say, were so far separated from Moses' time and their traditions are so confused that they tell us little about the Mosaic period.

Such a view leaves us with a book written over a half millennium or more of time, by many different authors, editors, and redactors. Numbers, such critics say, is "lacking in unity of religious expression," and it is "impossible to summarize the fundamental ideas, or to point out the religious value of the book, for these are different in different parts" (*ibid.*, p. xlvii). The basic arguments advanced by Gray and others in support of this documentary hypothesis of the origin of the Pentateuch are no longer considered valid by the best source scholars. E. E. Flack in *Interpretation* (1959, XIII, p. 6) says, "The trend in recent thought is to recognize early materials in the Pentateuch and to seek a more satisfactory solution to the problem of literary structure than the documentary theory provides." (See also B. D. Eerdmans, *Oudtestamentische Studien,* Deel VI, 1949). C. H. Gordon in his *"Homer and the Bible" (Hebrew Union College Annual,* Vol. XXVI, 1955) observes that "newly discovered texts show that much of the material ascribed to "P" is very early, even pre-Mosaic." Gordon here accuses advocates of the documentary view of giving hypothetical dates to hypothetical strata (documents) and calling this "historical" criticism. However, recent trends in scholarship have not resulted in any general acceptance of the claims presented in the book (eighty or more times) that "the Lord spake unto Moses" or that "Moses wrote their goings out. . . ." (33:2). One must ask whether pious frauds inserted the words, "The Lord spake unto Moses," to give their literary work a ring of authority. W. F. Albright, the noted archaeologist, pointed out that pious fraud and pseudepigraphy were not common in the pre-Hellenistic Orient.

Indeed, the findings of modern archaeology have forced some scholars to change their attitude about the origin of much of the material in Numbers. Many competent modern archaeologists even depend on the geographical references in the Pentateuch to guide them in their work. As recently as 1959, Nelson Glueck, after many years of fruitful discovery in Bible lands, speaking of the amazing "historical memory" of the Bible, said, "It may be stated categorically that no archaeological discovery has ever controverted a Biblical reference" (*Rivers in the Desert*, p. 31).

The Book of Numbers, along with other books of the Pentateuch, has long posed difficult problems for scholars. But many of the problems have been resolved in the light of recently discovered additional data. For a good example see the comments accompanying Numbers 34:15. The critic's approach to the Scriptures is often negative and destructive, for he begins by ruling out the supernatural. We must come to the text of Numbers with a positive attitude and with faith in the validity of the supernatural. We may be critical of the text and be aware of difficulties in it without closing our minds to its true meaning. In matters involving the supernatural, we must look for the clearest meaning consistent with a historico-grammatical method of interpretation. When the Bible claims that there has been supernatural intervention, we must accept the claim on its own grounds. Where the Bible does not so state, we need not read anything supernatural into the text; for interposition of the supernatural is intended to be the unusual and not the common practice. Hence, what one thinks of the origin of Numbers depends on what philosophical presupposition he assumes. If his basic philosophy is naturalistic, he will conclude that such a supernaturalistic book must be fraudulent and fanciful. But if one believes that the Supreme Being may intervene in the course of human events, he does not find it difficult to view the deliverance of Israel from Egypt as supernatural.

We must recognize, however, that there was an economy of the supernatural. Moses was not always performing a miracle, nor did God dictate every word of the inspired text. The prophet undoubtedly made use of numerous scribes (cf. Num 11:16,25), which explains the use of the third person. God revealed directly to Moses some parts of the book, including the provisions for settlement in the land and the details of ceremonial procedure. But on the other hand, Moses and his scribes probably had access to documents and knew many oral traditions. The Spirit of God kept them from errors of fact, doctrine, or judgment. The account of Balaam and Balak (Num 22–24) is the only passage in the book which is not expressly attributed to Moses and in which Moses is not mentioned.

OUTLINE

Part One: Israel in the Wilderness. 1:1–21:35.
- I. First census in the Wilderness of Sinai. 1:1–4:49.
  - A. Census of Israel's fighting men. 1:1-54.
  - B. Arrangement of the camp. 2:1-34.
  - C. Priestly function of Aaron's sons. 3:1-4.
  - D. Charge and census of Levites. 3:5-39.
  - E. Census of first-born males. 3:40-51.
  - F. Census of Levitical working force, and their duties. 4:1-49.
- II. First priestly scroll, 5:1–10:10.
  - A. Separation of the unclean. 5:1-4.
  - B. Compensation for offenses, and priestly honorarium. 5:5-10.
  - C. A trial of jealousy. 5:11-31.
  - D. Law of the Nazarite. 6:1-21.
  - E. The Priests' blessing. 6:22-27.
  - F. Offerings of the tribal princes. 7:1-89.
  - G. The golden lampstand. 8:1-4.
  - H. Consecration of Levites and their retirement. 8:5-26.
  - I. First commemorative and first supplementary Passover. 9:1-14.
  - J. The cloud over the Tabernacle. 9:15-23.
  - K. The two silver trumpets. 10:1-10.
- III. From the Wilderness of Sinai to the Wilderness of Paran. 10:11–14:45 (cf. 10:12; 13:26).
  - A. Departure from Sinai. 10:11-36.
    1. Order of the march. 10:11-28.
    2. Hobab invited to be guide. 10:29-32.
    3. The ark of the covenant. 10:33-36.
  - B. Taberah and Kibroth-hattaavah. 11:1-35.
    1. Taberah. 11:1-3.
    2. Manna provided. 11:4-9.
    3. Moses' seventy elders as officers. 11:10-30.
    4. Punishment by quails of Kibroth-hattaavah. 11:31-35.
  - C. Rebellion of Miriam and Aaron. 12:1-16.
  - D. The story of the spies. 13:1–14:45.
    1. The spies, their mission and report. 13:1-33.
    2. People disheartened and rebellious. 14:1-10.
    3. Moses' intercession. 14:11-39.
    4. Futile invasion attempt at Hormah. 14:40-45.
- IV. Second priestly scroll. 15:1–19:22.
  - A. Ceremonial details. 15:1-41.
    1. Quantities of meal offerings and libations. 15:1-16.
    2. Cake offerings of the first fruits. 15:17-21.
    3. Offerings for sins of ignorance. 15:22-31.
    4. Punishment of Sabbath-breaker. 15:32-36.
    5. Tassels. 15:37-41.
  - B. The rebellion of Korah, Dathan, and Abiram. 16:1-35.
  - C. Incidents vindicating the Aaronic priesthood. 16:36–17:13.
  - D. Duties and revenues of priests and Levites. 18:1-32.
  - E. The water of purification for those defiled by the dead. 19:1-22.
- V. From the Wilderness of Zin to the steppes of Moab. 20:1–22:1.
  - A. Wilderness of Zin. 20:1-21.
    1. Sin of Moses (around Kadesh). 20:1-13.

2. Request to go through Edom. 20:14-21.
B. The area of Mount Hor. 20:22–21:3.
1. Death of Aaron. 20:22-29.
2. Arad the Canaanite defeated at Hormah. 21:1-3.
C. The journey to the steppes of Moab. 21:4–22:1.
1. Rebellion on the journey around Edom. 21:4-9.
2. Places passed on the march from the Arabah. 21:10-20.
3. Defeat of the Amorites. 21:21-32.
4. Defeat of Og, king of Bashan. 21:33-35.
5. Arrival in the Plains of Moab. 22:1.
Part Two. Foreign intrigue against Israel. 22:2–25:18.
I. Balak's failure to turn the Lord from Israel. 22:2–24:25.
A. Balaam summoned by Balak. 22:2-40.
B. The oracles of Balaam. 22:41–24:25.
II. Balak's success in turning Israel from the Lord. 25:1-18.
A. The Baal-peor sin. 25:1-5.
B. Zeal of Phinehas. 25:6-18.
Part Three. Preparation for entering the land. 26:1–36:13.
I. Second census, in the Plains of Moab. 26:1-65.
II. The law of inheritance. 27:1-11.
III. Appointment of Moses' successor. 27:12-23.
IV. Third priestly scroll. 28:1–29:40.
A. Introduction. 28:1,2.
B. Daily offerings. 28:3-8.
C. Sabbath offerings. 28:9,10.
D. Monthly offerings. 28:11-15.
E. Yearly offerings. 28:16–29:40.
1. Feast of Unleavened Bread. 28:16-25.
2. Feast of Weeks. 28:26-31.
3. Feast of Trumpets. 29:1-6.
4. Day of Atonement. 29:7-11.
5. Feast of Tabernacles. 29:12-40.
V. The validity of women's vows. 30:1-16.
VI. War with Midian. 31:1-54.
A. Destruction of Midian. 31:1-18.
B. Purification of warriors. 31:19-24.
C. Dividing the spoils of war. 31:25-54.
VII. Settlement of two and one-half tribes in Trans-Jordan. 32:1-42.
A. Moses' response to Gad's and Reuben's request. 32:1-33.
B. Cities rebuilt by Reuben and Gad. 32:34-38.
C. Gilead taken by Manassites. 32:39-42.
VIII. The route from Egypt to Jordan. 33:1-49.
IX. Directions for settlement in Canaan. 33:50–35:34.
A. Expulsion of inhabitants, settling of boundaries, division of land. 33:50–34:29.
B. Levitical cities and cities of refuge. 35:1-34.
X. Marriage of heiresses. 36:1-13.

COMMENTARY

Part One. Israel in the Wilderness. 1:1–22:1.

I. First Census, in the Wilderness of Sinai. 1:1–4:49.

The setting of this scene is Sinai, some ten months after Israel arrived there (Ex 19:1). Only nineteen days were left before the cloud would be lifted from the Tabernacle and Israel would start for the Promised Land (Num 10:11). Since the people faced a barren wilderness and stiff enemy resistance, they needed a well-organized camp.

A. Census of Israel's Fighting Men. 1:1-54.

1. And the Lord spake unto Moses. This formula is used over eighty times in the Book of Numbers. It is necessary to assume that the writer of these words was a fraud if this writing did not originate with Moses. **The second month, in the second year.** This was exactly one month after the Tabernacle was set up (Ex 40:1,17). Numbers 7:1 and 9:1,15 refer to the first day of the first month, antedating this opening verse by one month. The priests and the Tabernacle were consecrated in this one month (Ex 40; Lev 8); the princes brought their gifts in this month (Num 7); and the first commemorative Passover took place then (9:1-14).

2. Take ye the sum of all the congregation. The Tabernacle, just completed, became the center of the camp. The army had to be organized and the whole camp arranged and ordered as a religio-civil and military organization; hence a census became a basic necessity. The word *rō'sh,* **sum,** commonly meaning "head," is rendered *number* in I Chr 12:23. Likewise **polls** refers to the actual counting of individuals or heads *(gulgᵉlōt,* "skulls").

3. From twenty years old and upward . . . able to go forth to war. This terminology, used fourteen times throughout the chapter, makes clear that the census had a military purpose. The nonmilitary Levites were to have a separate census (1:47-49; 3:14-51).

5. And these are the names of the men. Attempts to show that the list (vv. 5-15) is "unhistorical" cannot be supported by factual data. Abundant use of the divine name *'ēl* (Eliab, Pagiel, etc.) by no means indicates late authorship (ICC, *Numbers,* pp. 6,7), for the name is freely used in personal names in the Ugaritic texts of about 1400 B.C. Also the compound *Shaddāy* (as in Zurishaddai, v. 6) appears in a personal name on a figurine from the late fourteenth century (Wm. F. Albright, *The Biblical Period,* p. 7).

18. Declared their pedigrees. To the Semitic mind, knowledge of one's genealogy is more important than knowledge of one's birthday or age. Hence we have the long genealogies of the Bible, which were used, eventually, to trace the descent of Messiah through Abraham, Judah, and David, in accordance with the promises of God. **19. So he numbered them.** This verb *pāqad* has a wide area of meaning. Here it means "to pass in review," or "muster," and in this sense, "to number." The much repeated phrases, **by their generations, after their families, by the house of their fathers** (v. 20) indicate what we mean by saying, "by household," "by clans," and "by whole tribes."

46. Six hundred thousand and three thousand and five hundred and fifty. These were the army only, for there were two conditions governing the numbering—the men included were to be over twenty, and they must be able to go forth to war. It has been estimated that from two to three million people—including Levites, aged persons, children, and women—comprised the camp. Scholars unable to accept the supernatural elements of God's dealings with his ancient people claim that five thousand fighting men would be a more reasonable number to expect, and explain this numbering as a misplaced census of a later time. Some say it was David's census of II Sam 24. But there the number of fighting men of Judah alone is 500,000 (II Sam 24:9), while here Judah had only 74,000. In II Sam 24 the term for a soldier is *'îsh ḥayl,* "man of might"; in Numbers it is *kōl yōṣē' ṣābā',* "everyone who goes out with the host."

George E. Mendenhall, in a challenging study (JBL, March, 1958) views the census accounts in Numbers as authentic lists misunderstood by later generations. He points out that such lists appear commonly in early ancient cultures. From the Semitic world, census lists have been discovered from Mari, Ugarit, and Alalakh, ranging in date from the Patriarchal Age to shortly before the time of Moses. The word *'elep,* commonly meaning a thousand, is taken by Mendenhall to mean a tribal unit, probably nonmilitary and comprising far fewer than a thousand men. For example, when the Hebrew lists 46,500 men for Reuben, this would mean forty-six tribal units but only five hundred fighting men. Hence there were 558 such units and 5,550 fighting men. The difficulty with this view is that Num 2:32 gives a total which assumes that *'elep* means "a thousand." But Mendenhall believes that the post-Exilic priests who composed Numbers forced the word to mean "a thousand," not knowing the earlier meaning. Mendenhall correctly observes, in connection with Jud 6:15, that Gideon did consider his thousand *('elep)* to be weak (i.e., not up to full strength), a characteristic of many military units. But then he is forced to regard Ex 18:25 as a spurious verse, because it says, "Moses chose able men . . . and made them . . . rulers of thousands (*'alapîm*), rulers of hundreds, rulers of fifties, and rulers of tens." The present writer believes evidence shows that the term *'elep* designated a military unit (Num 1:16; 31:5,14), but eventually came also to mean a tribal unit of indeterminate number (I Sam 23:23; Mic 5:2). For two to three million people to be sustained in a desert required supernatural intervention. The purpose of the Book of Numbers is to tell us that this is what happened.

B. Arrangement of the Camp. 2:1-34. The order of the march and the arrangement of the camp around the Tabernacle are specified in this chapter.

2. Every man . . . shall pitch by his own standard ("banner"). There were four such banners, marking the four basic encampments about the Tabernacle (vv. 3,10,18,25). There were also other banners marking families, referred to here as the **ensign of their father's house. Far off . . . shall they pitch.** Only the Levites and priests encamped beside the Tabernacle. "The stranger that cometh nigh shall be put to death" (3:10,38). The Tabernacle had to be kept pure from the ceremonial contaminations associated with the daily living of the people. **17. Then the tabernacle . . . shall set forward.** Half of the tribes marched before it and half behind; and when they encamped, the Tabernacle, with its priests and Levites, was in the middle. When the priests and Levites set forward, everyone followed suit and was expected to be **in his place,** literally, *on hand,* by his banner.

34. Israel did . . . all that the Lord commanded. The people obeyed all that God commanded, a marked contrast with the frequent disobedience recorded in this book.

C. Priestly Function of Aaron's Sons. 3:1-4.

1. These also are the generations. This Hebrew idiom is used in Gen 2:4 as a way of introducing the account of creation. This is a transition verse and may be translated: "And this is the story of Moses and Aaron when God spake to Moses on Mount Sinai." **3. Whom he consecrated.** The Hebrew figure of speech translated, literally, *to fill one's hand,* is used to express consecration to a sacred office. The basic idea is not the call to the office but the installation or filling of the office by the one consecrated. **4. Ministered . . . in the sight of Aaron.** Practicing their priestly duties before their father enabled them to learn how to please God in a myriad of ceremonial details that took time and careful practice.

D. Charge and Census of Levites. 3:5-39. Since all first-born sons of Israel were saved from the death angel in Egypt, God declared them hallowed for service in the Tabernacle. Subsequently, however, he provided the Levites to serve in their place. The Levitical branches of Gershon, Kohath, and Merari, having specific duties in the Tabernacle, were encamped adjacent to its three sides. Moses, Aaron, and Aaron's sons camped on the east side of the Tabernacle, in front of the sanctuary. When it was discovered that there were 273 more first-born males than Levites to take their places, the surplus men were redeemed from service by the payment of five shekels of redemption silver apiece.

9. Wholly given unto him. The term *n'tûnim,* "given ones," is repeated for emphasis; hence the translation, **wholly given.** The same root is used later to describe the foreign slaves given to the Levites, who were to perform the most menial of the temple duties (**Nethinims,** I Chr 9:2).

12. I have taken the Levites from among the children of Israel. A separated group, dedicated to serve God through service in the holy Tabernacle, which others were forbidden to approach, on pain of death (1:53; 2:2; 3:10). **Instead of all the firstborn** (cf. v. 41). The preposition *taḥat,* **instead of,** is used often in the OT to express "substitution" (Gen 22:13). The idea of "substitutionary atonement" was a truth long familiar to the Israelites, and was meant by God to prepare them and others for the great First-born among many brethren, the Lord Jesus Christ (Mk 10:45). **13. Mine shall they be. The point here is** not the future tense but the possession of the first-born by the Lord, who redeemed them. The point is made twice again, in verse 41 and in verse 45. The Lord was saying, "They belong to me."

25. The charge of . . . Gershon in the tabernacle . . . shall be the tabernacle, and *(even)* **the tent.** The *tabernacle of an appointed time and place* (*'ōhel mô'ēd*) is reserved as a designation for the entire complex where God alone dwelt and met with his people. The sons of Gershon were in charge of the *'ōhel,* **the tent,** signifying the actual curtains that formed the enclosure.

28. Eight thousand and six hundred. A discrepancy arises when we add together the totals of the three families of Levites. There are three hundred more than the 22,000 given in verse 39. Probably some scribe, by mistake, omitted one letter; instead of writing three *(sh-l-sh)* hundred, he wrote six *(sh-sh)* hundred.

38. Keeping the charge of the sanctuary for the charge of the children of Israel. Better, *preserving the function (mīshmeret) of the sanctuary for the safe-guarding of (mīshmeret;* I Sam 22:23*) the children of Israel.*

E. Census of First-born Males. 3:40-51.

41. And the cattle of the Levites instead of all the firstlings among the cattle of the children of Israel. The first-born cattle of Israel were saved during the Passover in Egypt (Ex 12:29,32); so now the first-born cattle were dedicated to the Lord. The redemption of cattle (Ex 34:20) and the assignment of moral responsibility to cattle (Ex 21:28,29) are not unknown in the Bible. In Jonah 3:7,8; 4:11, it is recorded that God spared the cattle along with the people of Nineveh who repented (cf. Hos 5:6). Among some ancient Semitic peoples (Ugarit), domestic animals were included in census figures as members of the community. While the Hebrews shared this cultural peculiarity, their law strongly opposed the sinful conduct to which such familiarity with animals led the heathen (Lev 18:23,24). In the Hittite Law Code bestiality was permitted with certain animals.

47. The shekel of the sanctuary. The shekel was not a piece of money but a measure of weight. The necessity for standards or official measures of weight is reflected here. Such standard weights bore an official inscription. In a theocratic society the sanctuary provides the standard (cf. Gen 23:16). **49. The redemption money.** Here and in verse 48 **money** for *kesep,* "silver," is not a clear translation. Since coinage was not invented until the sixth century B.C., the commodity silver was an early measure of value; hence it is used to express the Old Testament teaching about atonement. There was atonement silver *(kesep hakkīppūrîm),* as in Ex 30:16, and ransom silver *(kesep happīdyôm),* as in this verse. The greatest measure of value is life itself; therefore the offering of blood, not silver, was the most impressive lesson of man's spiritual indebtedness to God (Lev 17:11).

F. Census of Levitical Working Force, and Their Duties. 4:1-49. On pain of death no one but Aaron and his sons was allowed to see or touch the sacred implements within the sanctuary (vv. 15,19,20). Instructions for proper handling of these **most holy things,** and for covering them (v. 4) are here given. The family of Moses and Aaron (26:58, 59), the Kohathites, were commissioned to carry them, under the direction of Aaron's son, Eleazar (v. 16). The remaining Levitical families were given the less honorable service of caring for the hangings (Gershonites) and the bars and pillars (Merarites). This work was put under the priestly supervision of Aaron's other son, Ithamar. Levites thirty to fifty years old, the actual working force (v. 3), were numbered and found to total 8,580.

4. The most holy things *(qōdesh haqqādāshîm).* The phrase is used to describe the most holy place (Ex 26:34) within the "veil of separation" *(pārōket hammāsāk),* but it is also used for the things of the entire sanctuary.

5. Aaron . . . and his sons . . . shall take down the covering veil. This is the "veil of separation" between the two parts of the Tabernacle—the holy place and the most holy, where the ark of the covenant was kept (Ex 26:31-34).

6. Put thereon . . . badgers' skins. The ASV uses *sealskin,* following an Arabic root similar to the Hebrew *taḥash.* An Egyptian cognate root suggests that this refers to a process like tanning rather than to the skin of a special animal. For protection from the elements, these coverings were customarily used over everything. However, it is to be noted that the ark was to have the **blue** ("violet") cloth placed *over* the skins, not *under* as with the other holy things (vv. 7-10). By such means the ark could be distinguished in the march (cf. 10:33). **Put in the staves.** Literally, *its in-the-hands (baddāyw).* Better rendered, "Set its handles," or "carrying poles."

7. The table of showbread. *The table of the Presence,* i.e., the presence of the Lord. **And covers to cover.** These *qᵉśôt hannāsek* were sacrificial bowls out of which drink offerings were poured. **The continual bread.** Also called *the bread of the Presence* ("showbread"; Ex 25:30), since it was continually kept spread out before the Lord upon the table.

8. A cloth of scarlet. The term *tôla ʿat shānî* indicates the insect or weevil from which the scarlet color was obtained. Another dye, as in **a cloth of blue** *(tᵉkēlet,* "violet"; v. 9) was obtained from a species of shellfish found on the seashores surrounding the Sinai peninsula. Dyeing was a common practice of the Canaanites in the sixteenth century B.C. (W. F. Albright, *Archaeology of Palestine*, p. 96).

20. They shall not go in to see . . . lest they die. In verse 15 the Levitical bearers were warned not to touch any holy thing on pain of death. In verses 17-20 the Lord again warned that the Kohathites could be cut off "from among the Levites" if they became careless handlers of the most holy things. Should they dare even to look for a moment *(kᵉballaʿ=like the time it takes to swallow),* they would die.

23. To perform the service. The Hebrew root *ṣābāʾ* is usually reserved for serving in the army, as in 1:3,30. God is often called the Lord of Sabaoth ("hosts"). By this religious army (see also 1:3) we are reminded of spiritual service in the Church Militant.

37,45,49. According to the commandment of the Lord by the hand of Moses. The word **commandment** is translated "word" in verse 45 and "appointment" in verse 27. It is literally *mouth (peh).* This and the use of the word **hand** *(yad)* provide a fruitful insight. The mouth bespeaks the seat of authority and the hand the means to implement authority. So then the laws were according to God's mouth but by Moses' hand. With delegated authority (by the mouth, appointment; v. 27) Ithamar bore the responsibility for administering (under his hand, vv. 28,33) the service of the sons of Gershon and Merari. Again we are reminded that the Hebrew idiom for "to consecrate" is *to fill one's hand* (3:3).

II. First Priestly Scroll. 5:1–10:10.

Laws about keeping the Passover are dated one month prior to Num 1:1 (see 9:1). This is understandable when we realize that although an over-all chronological order was observed, the materials were arranged and kept together by topics. It is reasonable to assume that the original writings were on scrolls of vellum or papyrus. We have had a census scroll, and now we turn to a scroll in which are gathered additional ceremonial and other hieratic details.

A. Separation of the Unclean. 5:1-4.

2. Put out . . . every leper, and every one that hath an issue, and whosoever is defiled by the dead. According to the directions given here, these three types of unclean persons were to be put outside the camp. But in the three passages dealing more fully with their several defilements (Lev 13; 15; Num 19) only lepers had to be expelled from the camp (Lev 13:46). According to Leviticus 13, a person was not put outside the camp until it was established that he had a real and permanent case of leprosy. As for "one having an issue," Num 5:2 might likewise mean a permanent or long-sustained issue, necessitating expulsion from the camp, while Lev 15 deals only with the temporary type of issue. The third Hebrew idiom refers to "anyone who is unclean because of a person" *(nepesh),* which is usually the expression for defilement by reason of a corpse (Num 9:10; 19:11). This kind of uncleanness did not normally require expulsion from the camp. But, according to 19:20, if the unclean one failed to be properly cleansed, he was to be cut off from the congregation. In short, the three types of uncleanness mentioned here refer to extreme cases in which expulsion from the camp was the only way of preserving the ceremonial purity of the congregation.

B. Compensation for Offenses, and Priestly Honorarium. 5:5-10.

7. He shall recompense his trespass. Hebrew *ʾāshām,* here **trespass,** is the key word of this passage. The term is expressive of an offense for which compensation can be made. These sins are against men, in contrast with sins against God alone. Therefore the AV, which says **sin that men commit** (Num 5:6) should read *sins against man.* This sin, like that dealt with in Lev 5:16, required complete restitution, plus one-fifth the value of the thing compensated for. **8. The ram of the atonement.** The means by which a man's guilt was **expiated** ("cleansed") and hence God's anger against the sinner propitiated ("rendered favorable"). In Lev 5:16 this ram is called "the ram of the trespass offering," which stresses man's offense ("trespass"); while here in Numbers "ram of atonement" stresses God's alienation.

10. It shall be his. If the person to be repaid was deceased and there was no kinsman-redeemer *(gō'ēl)* to receive his recompense, then it was to go to the priest. Verses 9 and 10 make clear that each priest was the sole possessor of whatever he received in this way (Lev 10:12-15).

C. A Trial of Jealousy. 5:11-31. When a wife was suspected by her husband of adultery (there being no witnesses) and she maintained her innocence, she was to be brought to the priest and made to stand before the Lord, who alone could determine her innocence or guilt. The priest was to make her take an oath of innocence and to subject her to an ordeal—the drinking of bitter curse-bringing water made with dust from the floor of the Tabernacle. Her guilt would be determined by certain effects manifested in her body. If there were no telltale effects, she was innocent and was to return to her husband to bear children. A notable example of ordeal for a suspect wife is recorded in Hammurabi's Code (pars. 131,132. ANET, p. 171). We need not assume, with certain 'liberal' scholars, that this "custom of ordeal" among the Hebrews goes back to the remotest period of their history (ICC, p. 46), as if this were a carry-over from pagan beginnings. Nor need we go to the other extreme and ignore the fact that parallels to some Biblical laws have been found in the jurisprudence of certain ancient Semitic peoples (ANET, pp. 163-188). Just as God chose the practice of circumcision, already widely used by pagan peoples (e.g., Canaanites and Egyptians), as an ordinance for his people, so the fact that the Torah was divinely inspired need not rule out Moses' knowledge of his times.

In reality, even pagan ordeal trials had psychological validity, and the principle underlying them is still used in modern crime detection (e.g., the lie-detector). Though the results of the pagan trials were only partially valid, could not similar technique be employed with perfectly valid results under the sovereign providence of the Lord? "This law prescribed no ordeal whose effects were uncertain like the ordeals of other nations, but a judgment of God, from which the guilty could not escape, because it had been appointed by the living God" (KD, *in loco).* It should be added that there was nothing inherent in the dust to cause judgment. Supernatural intervention had to occur in any case.

12. If any man's wife go aside, and commit a trespass against him. Biblical laws express serious condemnation of adultery, in contrast with the lax attitude of Israel's neighbors and their immoral practices (G. E. Wright, *Biblical Archaeology,* pp. 111-119). Strange as this law may seem to us, it helped produce a high level of marital purity in Israel (Lev 20:10).

15. Ephah of barley meal . . . no oil . . . nor put frankincense thereon. Nowhere but here is barley prescribed for a meal offering. Usually fine meal *(sōlet)* was required along with oil and frankincense. The reason for the difference seems to be that the usual meal offering, unlike this one, was a joyous offering, often of the first fruits. The only other dry meal offering was the poor man's sin offering (Lev 5:11). In both cases the dry barley meal bespeaks a sinful and humiliating circumstance. **An offering of memorial, bringing iniquity to remembrance.** The term **remembrance** *(zikkārôn)* actually explains the purpose of this whole unusual procedure. It was not to remind God (ICC, p. 51) but to bring into the open ("make known") whether or not there was a basis for this jealousy. **17. Holy water in an earthen vessel.** Earthen so that it could be broken after the ceremony (Lev 6:28). Water taken from the laver was holy; but since everything in the Tabernacle was holy, the water was rendered impressively more so by the addition of sacred dust. **18. Set the woman before the Lord.** The Lord alone could solve this mystery. For emphasis this is repeated from verse 16. **Uncover the woman's head.** The word *pāra'* means "to unbind the hair," not uncover the head. As one under suspicion, she was deprived of this sign of dignity; her hair was unbound.

23. The priest shall write these curses in a book. This incidental acknowledgment of the use of pen, or brush, and ink fits well for a people who had lived for generations in Egypt, where the scribe's brush had been in constant use since early in the third millennium B.C. **Shall blot.** For the meaning of this blotting of the curse, see verse 24. **24. He shall cause the woman to drink.** This verse anticipates the actual drinking after the priest received the offering (v. 26), but does so because the drinking had to be closely associated with the important detail of "blotting," in verse 23. By this act the very words of the curse were symbolically transferred to the bitter water.

27. Her belly shall swell, and her thigh shall rot. Or, *Her body shall swell, and her thigh shall fall away* (ASV). Though the ASV translation is preferable to that of the AV, it still leaves a question as to what this means. It is obvious that the swelling body may refer to pregnancy. The ICC suggests that the falling thigh means a premature birth (p. 48). The same root *nepel,* "a falling," is rendered *untimely birth* in Job 3:16; Ps 58:8,9; Eccl 6:3. Thigh or loin *(yārēk)* is used similarly as the seat of procreative power, in Gen 46:26 (and elsewhere): "Those that come out of his thigh" (or "loins"). So *her thigh shall fall* could mean "she will give birth." That *nāpal,* "fall," can mean "born" is clear from its usage in Isa 26:18 (ASV, note 17). We would translate this phrase as follows, "Her body shall swell and she shall give birth (or give an untimely birth), and that woman shall become a curse in the midst of her people."

The guilty woman, then, was not made to die, which would have been unjust, since the guilty man went free. However, illegitimate children were not allowed to become a burden to the camp because of God's supernatural intervention in instances like this (cf. Deut 23:2). There is no evidence that this law was practiced at any time except during the period of Moses' leadership.

D. Law of the Nazarite. 6:1-21. God desired that his people should become a "kingdom of priests and an holy nation" (Ex 19:6). Becoming a Nazarite was a step any Israelite man or woman could take toward attaining this ideal. Such a one thereby entered into a condition of life consecrated to God and free from contamination. The high priest, of course, was similarly set apart and purified (Lev 21:10-12). But his condition of life was based on his hereditary office. The vow of the Nazarite was usually undertaken spontaneously, and only for a period of time. The term *nāzîr* means "to separate," and always in this context it means to separate unto the Lord. Two distinct phases of this consecration are set forth here. The first is introduced in Num 6:3, where the devotee is told to separate himself by a certain practice of self-denial. The second phase, prescribed in 6:13-21, is called properly, "the law of the Nazarite." This phase, to be performed at the end of the period of separation, called for an elaborate series of offerings.

A Nazarite was to abstain not only from intoxicants but also from everything that came from the vine (v. 4). Hosea 3:1 (ASV) informs us that raisin (grape) cakes were a feature of luxurious living. I Samuel 25:18,36 tells of the abundant raisins at the home of Nabal, a rich and sensual man. In the spirit of self-denial, luxurious living was to be shunned by a Nazarite. The consecration of a Nazarite, however, was to be most completely symbolized by his wearing his hair uncut (Num 6:5). The Nazarite Samson's hair was a symbol of strength and virility dedicated to God; but when the strong man despised this dedication, he lost his gift of grace. Though such strength was not granted to all Nazarites, all were required, as Samson was, to devote all that they had to the Lord. This is shown by the provision made for Nazarites to vow large gifts as offerings (v. 21).

It was because the Nazarite's hair *(nēzer,* "crown") was consecrated that he had to avoid defilement by the dead. If he became defiled, he was to shave off the defiled hair and start his vow over (v. 12). As a lamb or goat brought for an offering had to be pure, so this "hair offering" had to be pure, for the Nazarite's hair was to become a burnt offering unto the Lord. Hair is representative of life itself, for only a living man produces hair. He offered it, therefore, in place of his own body, as a sign that he himself was a "living sacrifice, holy and well-pleasing to God." It is understandable why Paul (Acts 18:18; 21:24) and James, the elder at Jerusalem (Eusebius *Ecclesiastical History* ii.23), seeing deep spiritual significance in the ancient law of the Nazarite, took Nazarite vows.

The second phase of the law of the Nazarite began at the completion of "the days of his consecration" (Num 6:13). He was to make a sin offering for all his unknown sins, then a burnt offering and a peace offering to symbolize his surrender and worship. At the climax of these ceremonies the devotee was to have his head shaved, and the consecrated hair was to be placed on the coals under the peace offering (vv. 18-20).

2. Shall separate . . . to vow a vow of a Nazarite. The first verb here *(pālā')* means "to do something extraordinary or wonderful" (cf. the same root in an epithet of Messiah in Isa 9:6). Here and elsewhere (Lev 22:21; 27:2; Num 15:3,8) it is used to express the difficult thing of making a solemn vow. The ASV *special vow* is an attempt to show this distinction. Allowance was made also for the devotee to offer something voluntarily, beyond this required minimum (v. 21). **7. The consecration of his God is upon his head.** *Nezer* denotes not merely "consecration" but consecration having to do with the "head," whether a consecrated crown (Ex 29:6; Zech 6:11) or the anointed hair of the high priest (Lev 21:12), or, as here, the "consecrated hair" of the Nazarite (cf. Num 6:19, where the AV inserts the words, "the hair of"). Instead of *his separation unto God* (ASV), read "the consecrated hair of (belonging to) his God is (still) upon his head." **13. Be brought unto the door.** There was no reason why a Nazarite had to "be brought." The grammatical construction of the Hebrew here is unusual; but since there is no reflexive form of this verb, the clause may mean, "He shall bring himself."

21. Besides that that his hand shall get; i.e., the special offerings a Nazarite might vow in addition to what was specified in this law. While this refers to what a man might be able to add to his offering, the same terminology is used for the contribution of the poor man whose hand could not acquire a prescribed offering (Lev 5:11). *According to the vow which he vowed, so he must do.* That is, according to what he promised, he must do. Sometimes another person paid for a Nazarite's vow, as seems to be the case in Acts 21:24.

E. The Priests' Blessing. 6:22-27. This is a beautiful benediction, in the style of excellent Semitic poetry and filled with a message much needed by those facing the uncertainties and hostile forces of wilderness living. It tells of God's goodness in caring for and protecting his people. When an individual or a nation becomes an object of God's favor, distress, famine, peril, or sword only serve to prove how much the Lord loves his own children and how well able he is to deliver them.

23. Bless . . . Israel, saying unto them. The grammar of this sentence has been objected to. However, the famous grammarian, Gesenius, said that the form in question does occur "in the later books of the Old Testament, especially" (Lexicon, par. 113). We now know that Ugaritic texts (c. 1400 B.C.) confirm the construction as an old and much-to-be-expected idiom. **24. The Lord bless thee, and keep thee.** On the one hand God provides all good things for his chosen ones; on the other, he keeps, guards, and protects them from the enemy who would deprive them of good. **25. Make his face shine.** A typical Hebrew expression. When a man's face shines (Prov 16:15), he is filled with happiness; but when his face gathers blackness, it is evident that evil and despair have gripped his soul (Joel 2:6). **26. And give thee peace.** *Shālôm* ("peace") is a comprehensive word, including the concepts of completeness, security, health, tranquillity, contentment, friendship, and peace with God and man.

F. Offerings of the Tribal Princes. 7:1-89. After the entire Tabernacle *('ōhel mô'ēd)* was set up, anointed, and sanctified (see Ex 40:17), the head princes (cf. Num 1:5-16) brought offerings necessary for transporting the Tabernacle. They presented six wagons and twelve oxen to the sons of Gershon (4:24-26) and Merari (4:31,32). (Since the sons of Kohath were forbidden to carry the most holy things on wagons, they suspended them from poles, which they bore on their shoulders). Furthermore, on twelve separate days, the chief princes, each on his own day, brought stores of identical offerings for the dedication of the altar (vv. 11,88). The last verse of this chapter reveals that God communicated with Moses by a voice from above the mercy seat, between the cherubim (cf. Ex 25:22).

1. On the day that Moses had fully set up. This was not a specific day. The meaning is simply that after Moses had completed setting up and anointing, etc., then the princes offered their offerings (see v. 88). **3. Six covered wagons.** The rare Hebrew word used here for wagons is cognate with Akkadian *subbu*, meaning "a cart or litter." The word itself does not specify whether the carts were covered or open.

10. For dedicating of the altar. Critics have insisted on applying this phrase to the Maccabean period, during which the Feast of Dedication originated. They claim that *ḥănukkâ* ("dedication") is a late word. But even they admit (ICC, p. 76) that the root of this word is old, as is seen from its use in the name Enoch (*ḥănōk;* Gen 4:17; 25:4; 46:9) and in the word for Abraham's experienced men (*ḥănîk;* Gen 14:14). Though the word is rare, the Bible shows that it was widely used. King David held a *ḥănukkâ* for his palace, according to the title of **Psalm 30.** Solomon, similarly, dedicated the altar of the Temple (II Chr 7:9). Nehemiah dedicated the wall of Jerusalem (Neh 12:27). And Judas the Maccabee rededicated the Temple after its desecration (I Macc 4:52). In every case the same Hebrew word is used. It is likely that Judas Maccabeus had knowledge of a long *ḥănukkâ* tradition, for his was not a day of innovation.

12. Nahshon . . . of the tribe of Judah. The order in which the princes came, unlike that in Numbers 1, was according to the line of march (ch. 2). **14. One spoon of . . . gold.** A gold saucer (not spoon) filled with incense fits well with the description of the altar of incense in Ex 30:1-10 (cf. Rev 8:3,4).

88. After that it was anointed. A phrase similar to this in 7:10,84—"in the day when it was anointed"—evidently has no reference to a particular day (7:1), but is simply a temporal clause. This verse (88) makes it clear that the dedication of the altar took place sometime following the anointing recorded in Lev 8:11.

89. He heard the voice of one speaking unto him. Moses received divine revelation by conversing with God. A rare use of a Hebrew stem, here, gives a reciprocal meaning, "to converse," to the verb "to speak" (KB, p. 200). The same usage is employed to show that Ezekiel was on speaking terms with God (Ezk 2:1; 43:6; cf. II Sam 14:13). In Mal 3:16 a related verb is used in such a way as to mean "to speak with one another." Thus, "When Moses came in . . . to speak with (God), then he heard the voice making conversation with him from above the mercy seat."

G. The Golden Lampstand. 8:1-4. The details about the lampstand are given elsewhere: in Ex 25:31-40, where it is planned; in Ex 37:17-24, where it is made; in Ex 40:24, 25, where it is actually set up; and in Lev 24:2, where expensive olive oil is prescribed for it. Here in Num 8, we find it in use, shedding its ceremonially sacred light before the Lord continually (cf. Jn 8:12).

7. The seven lamps. Joseph P. Free, in his excavations at Dothan, found a seven-lipped ceramic lamp from early strata, which tends to refute the notion entertained by some scholars that such a lamp was unknown in the time of Moses. **3. He lighted the lamps thereof over against the candlestick.** It is not necessary to add the words "to give light" (ASV; RSV). Translate 8:2,3: "When you set up the lamps on the front of the lampstand, the seven lamps will shine . . . . And Aaron did this; on the front of the lampstand he set up its lamps . . . ."

H. Consecration of Levites, and Their Retirement. 8:5-26. The Levites were to wash their garments and shave their skin, to be sprinkled with holy water, to bring appropriate offerings and gather before the Tabernacle, together with all the congregation. At this time Aaron offered the Levites as living sacrifices (wave offerings) in place of the first-born, whom the Lord, at the time of the Passover in Egypt, purchased to himself for service. Hence the Levites were to be "given ones," wholly dedicated to the service of the sanctuary. Their assigned position, in the immediate vicinity of the Tabernacle and surrounding it, served to guard against violation of the sacred precincts by secular Israelites (v. 19). At age fifty the Levites retired from manual service, which was their main occupation. But they continued to minister in some capacity, perhaps as instructors of the young and in other less strenuous duties.

7. Sprinkle water of purifying. This is called *sin-water (mê ḥaṭṭā't).* As the sin offering was an offering for sin, so this water was for the cleansing of sin. It may be that this water should be identified with the "water of separation" made by use of the ashes of a red heifer and also called *ḥaṭṭā't,* "for sin" (Num 19). **Shave all their flesh.** Since the Hebrew language has another word meaning "to shave bald" (6:9,18), some commentators feel that this means only "to trim the hair" (KD, p. 47). But the command reads, "Let them cause a razor to pass over all their flesh." Certainly this must mean that they were to remove all (ceremonially defiled), **hair, just** as washing was to remove defilement from their clothes and the sprinkling of the "sin water" was to purify their bodies. This ceremonial cleansing not only foreshadowed Christ's spiritual cleansing of the Church (Eph 5:25,26), but also involved the essential element of obedience to God's Word, by which Christ would accomplish the cleansing.

10. The children of Israel shall put their hands upon the Levites. This was done, no doubt, in some representative way, though it is possible that each first-born son actually laid his hand upon one of the Levites. By this act the truth was conveyed pictorially that these Levites were substitutes for the first-born in the service of the sanctuary. The early church continued such well-known practices as the laying on of hands (Acts 6:6; I Tim 4:14).

11. Aaron shall offer (i.e., *wave)* **the Levites . . . for an offering.** In view of the difficulty of determining how the Levites could be "waved" before the Lord, the AV has omitted the full significance of the verb and noun. How thousands of Levites could be waved as a wave offering is only hinted at in verse 13. This technicality, however, is far less important than the meaning of the offering. Some feel that the word may have lost its original significance, so that it now meant simply to offer (Ex 35:22). It seems more likely that the term had a specialized meaning, whether or not the physical procedure of waving was always carried out. It was a "rite in which originally the priest lifted his share of offering and waved it, i.e., moved it toward the altar and back, in token of its presentation to God and its return by him to the priest (BDB, p. 632). Thus the ceremony demonstrated that the Levites belonged to the Lord but were given back to Aaron to minister as living sacrifices in the Tabernacle.

12. The Levites shall lay their hands upon the heads of the bullocks. Again the principle of substitution is the lesson taught. By the substitution of an innocent victim, expiation (atonement) was made *for* ("in behalf of") the Levites. **14. Separate the Levites . . . the Levites shall be mine.** God demands separation of the clean from the unclean, of his people from the heathen and their practices. Here is a truth found in the very warp and woof of Old Testament and New Testament teaching but often neglected by the church. God is holy, and his people are holy, for they belong to him; he therefore makes a division between them and others (Lev 20:26). So Christ came to call men to holiness and thereby make a distinction among people, so that a man's foes may be even those of his own household (Mt 10:34-36).

19. I have given the Levites as a gift. Note the sequence: "I have taken the Levites" (v. 18); "I have given the Levites." The very sequence fulfills the purpose of a *t^enûpâ,* "wave offering". God took and gave back to Aaron these living sacrifices as "given ones." The church likewise speaks of those whom God has "given" to it (cf. Eph 4:11,12), not as its priests but as its ministers, because theirs is the "work of serving, unto the building up of the body of Christ." **To do the service of the children of Israel . . . to make an atonement . . . that there be no plague.** There was only one Servant par excellence who "came not to be ministered unto, but to minister, and to give his life a ransom for many" (Mk 10:45). These servants, like him, were substitutes, taking the place of the children of Israel, by their service making an atonement, providing the ransom that brought deliverance from the wrath of God. **21. Levites were purified.** As the "sin water" (v. 7) and the sin offering were designed to remove sin, this verb from the same root *ḥaṭā'* means *to de-sin oneself,* or better, "to do the things necessary for ceremonial cleansing."

24. From twenty and five years old and upward. This does not agree with 4:35 (and other verses), where the numbering is from thirty years old. Such an obvious difference does not seem to be a textual error. The exacting work of "warring this warfare" (ASV, marg.), in which the mistakes of untrained hands could result in death (II Sam 6:6,7), may well have called for a five-year apprenticeship.

I. First Commemorative and First Supplementary Passover. 9:1-14. The original Passover was observed when Israel came out of Egypt, in the first month, the month of freshly ripened barley *('ābîb).* Now the people celebrated the first Passover *(pesaḥ)* in remembrance of that event, beginning on the fourteenth day of the first month of the second year. The purpose of this section is not to tell about the Passover, but to tell about a provision made for those who were unable to keep the Passover. Hence the section is inserted here, for the keeping of this supplementary Passover began on the fourteenth day of the second month, a month and a half after the opening date of the book. Faithful Israelites who had to isolate themselves seven days because they were defiled by the dead or who were on a journey during the keeping of regular Passover petitioned Moses that they be allowed to make this offering unto the Lord. Moses was instructed by God to make this allowance provided that all who kept the month-late Passover had legitimate reason. God further gave strict warning that any who neglected to keep the Passover in its appointed season should be cut off from the people. It was on the last day of this second-month Passover that the cloud began to rise from the Tabernacle and people began to prepare to journey (10:11).

1. The first month (Ex 12:2; 13:4; Deut 16:1). This month, the time of freshly ripened barley *('ābîb)*, was in the spring, as the Passover is and always has been. After the Exile (587 B.C.), the Israelites gradually adopted the Babylonian calendar, and they have used it since. *Rō'sh Hashānâ* (the present Jewish "New Year") is observed in the fall, following the Babylonian reckoning. While this historical fact is not conclusive, it helps refute the theory that most of Numbers was written by post-Exilic priests. Post-Exilic books of the Bible, like Ezra, Nehemiah, and Esther, show knowledge of the Babylonian calendar. In earlier times the Hebrews numbered their months, instead of naming them, and also used agricultural terms like *'ābîb*, but no cultic terminology (cf. Gezer Calendar, BASOR 92; see also commentary notes on Num 32).

2. Appointed season. This is the same word as is used for the Tabernacle when it is called "the tent of the congregation," meaning the place where the people congregated according to God's instructions at an appointed time. It was around this ritual law of the Tabernacle that the people of Israel carried on their religious life. To break these laws of appointed times and places was paramount to a denial of the Lord and contempt for his revealed message. **3. At even.** Literally, *between the two evenings*. Just as a 'dual' of the word "shine" *(ṣāhar)* refers to that high point of the sun we call noon or midday, so the dual of the word "evening" *('ereb)* refers to that half light we call twilight. Proverbs 7:9 equates this time with twilight in contrast to the middle of the night.

6. The dead body of a man. A most interesting expression in the Hebrew, because the word often rendered "soul" by the AV has here the meaning "corpse." The word *nepesh* is most frequently used in conjunction with the animal functions of the body, the passions, and the appetites, rather than in reference to immaterial existence. In Genesis the animals (2:19), like man (2:7), are called *nepesh ḥayâ*, "living creatures (selves, lives)." And in Deut 12:23,24 *nepesh* is the life principle" that is in the blood (cf. also Prov 12:10; Ex 21:23). The word often stands for one's "self" or "person," and is usually associated with the body. This is true of Ps 16:10, where bodily resurrection—not spiritual immortality—is in view (cf. Acts 2:27-31). In the light of this it is not difficult to see how *nepesh 'ādām*, "the human self," comes to mean a "corpse."

12. Nor break any bone of it. Among the laws of the Passover stands this rather minor detail, which is also enjoined in Ex 12:46. The insignificance of this rule, which is nowhere else mentioned in the OT, gives force to its fulfillment as an evidence that the Christ of Calvary was truly the Passover Lamb of God, which takes away the sin of the world (Jn 19:36).

13. That man shall bear his sin. If he brought the offering of the Lord, that lamb would bear his sin; but if he neglected this offering, he would bear his own sin. Substitutionary atonement is in view, for God's appointed substitute must bear a man's sin if that man would remain an object of divine favor. **14. If a stranger . . . will keep the passover.** Provision was always made for converts (proselytes), but all such had first to become Israelites through the ordinance of circumcision (Ex 12:48,49).

J. The Cloud over the Tabernacle. 9:15-23. The presence of the cloud was no new experience for the Israelites (Ex 13:21, 22). Now that the Tabernacle was erected, the cloud took its position above it. By the movements of the cloud the people were reminded that they were about to journey once again (Num 10:11, 12). (The translators of the LXX stumbled at the redundancy here and left out a few phrases. The repetitive style is not mere literary mannerism, but a way of emphasizing the importance of divine guidance.) To the Israelites the movement of the cloud was the commandment of the Lord. By it they would journey and by it they would encamp. Whether it rested overnight only, or two days, a month or a long time, they had only to rest or go with it, in unquestioning obedience to God. This, in a very short time, they miserably failed to do.

16. So it was always: the cloud covered it. Does this begin a narration of past events or instruction (v. 17) as to how the Israelites should act in the future? Since in Hebrew the tense of verbs is often obscure, let it suffice to say that the verbs of this passage describe a continuous situation. **20. And so it was, when the cloud was a few days upon the tabernacle.** In keeping with the above interpretation, we would translate this verse as follows: "And sometimes the cloud might be but a few days upon the Tabernacle; according to the word of the Lord they would encamp, and then according to the word of the Lord they would journey." **22. Or a year.** Both the AV and the ASV usually translate the Hebrew word for "days" as "a year." Genesis 24:55 shows that this word means a number of days, possibly ten; but usually it means more than a month.

K. The Two Silver Trumpets. 10:1-10. Israel's earlier experience with trumpets is recorded in Ex 19:16-20. There, words of both Canaanite and Phoenician derivation tell of the sound of the ram's horn trumpet that accompanied the terrifying thunders and lightnings on Mount Sinai. Now an entirely new kind of trumpet was prescribed. These *ḥăṣôṣrōt* were silver clarions, depicted in extra-Biblical sources as long straight tubes flared at the end. From this time on, the Hebrews used this particular instrument as a "statute forever," for sacred purposes only (e.g., Num 31:6; II Kgs 12:13; Ezr 3:10). Now God also commanded a variety of signal calls. Two trumpets were to blow together to gather the congregation to the door of the Tabernacle, and one trumpet was to blow for the princes only. Distinction is made in Scripture between merely blowing to gather the people and sounding a blast (alarm) to signal the breaking of camp. The priests were to go forth in battle blasting the trumpets so that Israel "might be remembered before the Lord their God." They also were henceforth to blow in conjunction with feasts, with new moons, and with burnt offerings and peace offerings. The Apostle Paul doubtless had the use of these instruments in mind when he made metaphorical reference to the trumpet in I Cor 14:8.

9. And ye shall be remembered before the Lord your God. Must the Lord be reminded to save his people? The answer is Yes and No. Israel did not conceive of him as a limited deity, whose interest was diverted to other things, or as a god who went to sleep and had to be aroused by the blast of the trumpets. Critics who hold this view appeal to Ps 44:22-24, and quote the words, "Awake, why sleepest Thou, O Lord?" But scrutiny of this psalm shows that it is a complaint to God, who knows the "secrets of the hearts" and who chastens his people. They are in trouble, and he seems to do nothing; hence the feeling of depression comes forth in hyperbolic language. For an account of the use of the trumpets in a time of distress, see II Chr 13:12-15. In battle the people "cried unto the Lord and the priests sounded with the trumpets." Indeed, the trumpets as an "ordinance forever" symbolized dependence on God. Similarly prayer, as a more articulate expression of that dependence, reminds God to bless his people.

III. From the Wilderness of Sinai to the Wilderness of Paran. 10:11–14:45.

Beginning on the twentieth day of the second month of the second year, the tribes set out from Sinai in the order indicated in earlier chapters, and with the cloud proceeding on to the Wilderness of Paran. Time elapsed is not given, but we know the events covered at least a number of months (forty days for the spies and several weeks or months for chapters 10–12). Their route took them by way of Taberah (11:3) and Kibroth-hattaavah (11:35) to Kadesh (13:26).

A. Departure from Sinai. 10:11-36. The order of the march (vv. 11-28), an invitation to Hobab (vv. 29-32), and the importance of the ark (vv. 33-36) constitute the several subjects relating to Israel's taking leave of Sinai.

12. Took their journeys. The Hebrew

would be *broke camp according to their stations* (stages). They were following the procedure outlined in chapter 2. **The cloud rested in the wilderness of Paran.** The verse is a summary statement anticipating their arrival in Paran (cf. v. 33—"the ark . . . went before them . . . three days journey," etc.).

17. The sons of Gershon and . . . Merari set forward, bearing the tabernacle. A slight change from 2:17, where the Levites are said to have traveled in the midst of the host, following the tribes led by Reuben. Verse 21 clears up this point by informing us that the Kohathites, carrying the holy things, traveled in their regular place; while "the sons" of Merari and of Gershon went ahead to set up the Tabernacle and have it ready for the arrival of the holy things (see ASV, 10:21 b). We must remember that there were women, children, and those over fifty in the Levite camps besides the actual burden-bearers. It is likely that only the burden-bearers are meant in verse 17.

21. Bearing the sanctuary. The Kohathites were not bearing the sanctuary but the holy things used in it. The use of *miqdāsh* ("sanctuary") is not improper, for Numbers 18:29 b shows that the word can mean a holy part as well as a holy place, although the latter is indeed its usual meaning. **Against they came.** *Against their coming* (ASV). See comment under verse 17.

25. The rearward of all the camps (ASV). The rearward, ***rear guard*** or (even closer to Hebrew) *gatherer (mᵉʾassēp),* is a word **bearing a tender** connotation. As when a man gathers his neighbor's lost sheep into his own house to restore it, so the Lord gathers us up even when our mother or father forsakes us (Ps 27:10). Or when evil oppression brings on a captivity, the God of Israel not only goes before his people but becomes the "gatherer" ("rear guard") of the strays (Isa 52:12).

29. Hobab, the son of Raguel the Midianite. Moses' "in-laws" are called Midianites in Ex 2:16; 3:1; 18:1, but Kenites in Jud 1:16; 4:11. Both of these are nomadic people who lived adjacent to or even among each other. The term Kenite refers to the roving "smiths," especially coppersmiths from the copper-rich valley of the Arabah. Their presence among the people of Israel fits in with the making of the brazen serpent (Num 21:8,9) and the metal work of the Tabernacle. The intermarriages and long association of these two tribes might make it reasonable for Moses' brother-in-law, Hobab, to be called both Midianite and Kenite. These very Kenites who became a part of Israel continued to be called Kenites and Israelites (I Chr 2:55). It is equally possible that the name Midianite became a generic term for the many camel-riding Bedouins east of the Arabah. The names Ishmaelite and Midianite are used interchangeably in Gen 37:27,28,36. We are also reminded of the camel-riding Midianites who fought Gideon, and the association of the name Midian with both the Edomites (Gen 25:4) and the Moabites (Gen 36:35; Num 22:3,7). **Moses' father-in-law.** *Rᵉʿûʾēl,* may have been the name of the grandfather of this family, or it may be another name for Jethro (cf. Ex 2:18; 3:1). The term *ḥōtēn,* "father-in-law," means any male relative by marriage, so that the words in Jud 4:11 might be translated, "Hobab, the brother-in-law." **We will do thee good: for the Lord hath spoken good concerning Israel.** When the Lord speaks, his word is his promise.

30. I will not go. Hobab was determined to return to his homeland; but Jud 1:16 informs us that Moses persuaded him to come, for it tells us there that he entered Canaan with Israel.

31. Thou knowest how we are to encamp . . . thou mayest be to us instead of eyes. The Jewish Targums and the LXX, interpolating here, represent Moses as pleading with Hobab to serve as guide to Israel, when God had already given a supernatural means of guidance. There is really nothing incongruous in Moses' request, for dependence on God for divine guidance and even for supernatural intervention does not obviate the use of human knowledge when it is available. Hobab knew the wilderness well and could help make both the journeying and the camping easier by pointing out the secrets of the desert.

33. The mount of the Lord. At Mount Sinai God revealed himself as a righteous Sovereign expressing the requirements of his holy will, as well as his wrath against all sin. Though the Mount of the Lord was now behind them, its message (the testimony) remained inscribed on the tablets of stone now kept in the ark. **The ark of the covenant of the Lord.** The ark is often called the ark of the testimony; here it is the ark of the covenant. In Ex 34:28 the covenant is identified with the Ten Commandments. The ark was the abiding place of the Lord and of the tablets of the Law. As such it was a symbol of divine purity. When the high priest approached the ark once a year, it then symbolized the covenant of mercy with a defiled people, who by means of the blood of atonement could be cleansed and so enjoy the benefits of God's favor on them and their children.

34. The cloud of the Lord. With the experience of the Mount of the Lord behind them and the ark before them searching out a resting place, the Israelites also had the sacred cloud over them as a symbol of God's presence. It not only guided but brought comfort and assurance, and possibly provided protection from the elements, especially from the fierce sun, by spreading itself over the entire camp, as is suggested in Ps 105:39 (KD, p. 62).

35. When the ark set forward . . . Moses said. Moses uttered this prayer on the first leg of the journey from Sinai. It became a classic prayer, used, it seems, each time the ark went out (cf. Ps 68:1; 132:8; II Chr 6:41,42). Moses also spoke *for* (in behalf of) *the time of its resting* (Num 10:36). The prayer eloquently teaches the effective working relationship between God and the Church Militant. He goes before her, and the gates of hell cannot prevail against her. He abides in her midst and she is strengthened and becomes a great host.

B. Taberah and Kibroth-hattaavah. 11:1-35. Refusing to be instructed by a minor chastisement at Taberah, the people of Israel allowed the rabble to set them to craving the meat and the succulent fruit and vegetables of Egypt. The anger of the Lord was kindled against them once again, and even Moses fell victim to a feeling of lonely responsibility for these spiritual delinquents. Moses asked the Lord to kill him outright rather than leave the entire burden of rebellious Israel on his shoulders. So God appointed seventy elders to help the prophet bear the burden and gave them the spirit of prophecy. When two elders, not of the seventy, were found exercising the gift of prophecy in the camp, Joshua asked Moses to stop them. This called forth Moses' magnanimous reply: "Would that all the people were prophets, that the Lord would put his spirit upon them." Israel's craving for flesh was satisfied when God sent flocks of quails to eat. Those that lusted ate their fill, and soon afterward a plague broke out among them.

1. And when the people complained. The Hebrew word translated *when* is not temporal. The *as* of the ASV better captures the force of the word. We would translate, "And the people became like murmurers over misfortune, in the ears of the Lord." The idea conveyed is that Israel had no real misfortune over which to complain but murmured, nevertheless, like those who are cursed with actual evil. **The fire of the Lord burnt among them.** Senseless ingratitude in the face of all God's goodness brought a necessary though minor chastisement in the extremities of the camp. They named the place *Taberah*, "burning," which burning may have been a natural phenomenon but was still "the fire of the Lord," sent by God to accomplish his purpose.

2. The people cried . . . Moses prayed . . . the fire was quenched *(abated).* In capsule form we have here the story of God's people for ages to come (cf. Ps 107). Israel failed to learn the lesson of cheerful obedience, and hence went on to harder chastisements as recorded in this and subsequent chapters.

4. The mixed multitude. A nondescript rabble had followed Israel out of Egypt (Ex 12:38). **5. Which we did eat in Egypt freely.** The annual inundation of the Nile made Egypt seem like a garden to Bedouins who lived on the sterile desert. The fruits and vegetables mentioned are still common in modern Egypt and still called by the same Semitic names used in the text. **6. Our soul is dried away.** Again the word for **soul,** *nepesh,* is the seat of animal appetites; it does not designate the spirit (see comment on 9:6). It is translated *appetite* in Prov 23:2 and Eccl 6:7. The people had been so long on a bland diet that they began to crave (lust for) food that would stimulate their salivary glands. **Nothing at all, beside this manna.** This is an exaggeration common to people carried away by self-pity and their animal appetites.

7. The colour of bdellium. Verses 7-9 are a digression on the manna itself. Careful comparison of this description with that in Ex 16:31-36 shows that the only real differences in the two accounts concern color and taste. These differences, far from pointing to different sources, show spontaneity and freedom on the part of the writer, which a redactor would obscure. Both sight and taste are so subjective that the manna could be called white and still be yellowish or pearl (bdellium); and it could taste like honey to one person and fresh oil to another.

12. As a nursing father. The prophet uses a figure here that does not accord well with modern Western ideas of the role of a great national leader. Moses is being neither humorous nor sarcastic with the Lord, but is reminding Him of His sovereignty, for He alone brought this nation into being and promised them a land. Therefore, the Lord alone must bear this baby and sustain it, as a wet nurse carries and feeds a suckling child. **14. I am not able to bear all this people alone.** Moses' human frailty appears here and in the language of verse 15. His words are loaded with intense emotion, for he was at the end of his rope, and he felt that it would be an act of mercy for God to take his life.

16. Gather unto me seventy men . . . elders of Israel. These men became Moses' organizers and secretaries, as is indicated by the word **officers** (*shōṭēr;* cf. Assyrian *shaṭâru,* "to write"). Hence the LXX translates here with the familiar term "scribes" (*grammateis*). They were indeed "officers," but may have contributed to the organization and preservation of the sacred record. These are to be distinguished from the rulers of the thousands and hundreds, etc., of Ex 18:21-27; Num 10:4. **17. Take of the spirit which is upon thee.** Because of Moses' emotional depression, God reserved some of the gift of prophecy to give it to these elders.

18. Sanctify yourselves. Why? Because God was going to do a miraculous work (cf. Josh 3:5). The New Testament counterpart is God's assurance that he will work miracles in hearts. This he does, for example, through his word (and through every means of grace). But unprepared hearts only make a mockery of such a promise. **20. Ye have despised the Lord which is among you.** This was the basic reason for Israel's punishment. The people regretted that they had left a state of bondage for a state of freedom with self-denial. This shows that they were rejecting the promise of God, and therefore God himself.

22. Shall the flocks and the herds be slain for them, to suffice them? "Why should people rich in flocks cry out for flesh?" (ICC, p. 103) Moses' problem was not that of the critical commentary which belittles the account by suggesting that there was inconsistency in the divine economy. Israel's wilderness flocks would soon have been depleted if they had been eaten as daily food. There was undoubtedly some meat consumption (cf. **priests' portions), but this was on** special occasions (festivals), as is still true among the cattle-raising Bedouins.

25. They prophesied, and did not cease. Better, *did not do* (it) *again.* Does this mean that they prophesied only this one time and never again, or that they prophesied on this occasion only once and did not continue (the opposite of the AV translation)? The former view is unlikely in the light of 12:6. The latter view would provide Moses with a corps of inspired secretaries who also assisted in recording and editing the sacred writings (Pentateuch). Exodus 4:16 taken with 7:1 indicates that a part of the Hebrew idea of a prophet (*nâbî'*) was "one who spoke for another." The elders may have had an ecstatic experience; if so, it was only because they were receiving the Word of God.

26. The spirit rested upon them . . . they were of them that were written. Rather than two disobedient members of the seventy who had not gone out with the rest, these were two of the many registered princes-over-the-thousands. This gift upon them was entirely unexpected. **29. Enviest thou for my sake?** Moses showed the true spirit of God-directed leadership. He was not a demagogue, maintaining his position by unworthy means. Wholly desirous that others share in this wonderful gift, he had the corporate good of Israel at heart more than his own position.

31. Went forth a wind. The ICC (pp. 117-119) has a most interesting, largely constructive commentary on verses 31-34. **Two cubits . . . upon the face of the earth.** The phrase makes best sense by taking *'al* ("upon") as "over" or "above" (ASV) the face of the earth, meaning low-flying quails. The RSV uses the word "deep," which is not in the text and is a step backward from AV "high." **32. Spread . . . all abroad . . . round about the camp.** An ancient means of preserving food by sun-drying. **33. Ere it was chewed.** The Hebrew verb does not mean "to chew"; it means "to cut off."

Translate, *ere it ran short.* (The same verb is translated *cut off* in Josh 3:16 and elsewhere.) This does not mean that punishment fell upon the people before they had time to eat any quail, for the Lord had predicted that they would eat flesh for a month (Num 11:19, 20). The idea is that before they had finished eating all the quail, the plague broke out.

35. Kibroth-hattaavah unto Hazeroth. These stations cannot be identified. All that can be said is that Israel was proceeding in a northerly direction from Sinai.

C. Rebellion of Miriam and Aaron. 12:1-16. As high priest, Aaron was a prominent figure in Israel; but he lacked qualities of leadership, and so far as we know he was not granted the gift of prophecy. Using Moses' marriage to an Ethiopian as a pretext to start a whispering campaign against their brother, Miriam and Aaron challenged Moses' sole right to speak for God to the people. God made clear to the rebel couple that Moses was a special instrument of divine revelation, far more intimate with the Almighty than any ordinary prophet. Miriam, as leader in the rebellion (cf. Aaron's weakness in the matter of the golden calf; Ex 32), was smitten with leprosy. Humble repentance by the offenders and gracious intercession by Moses brought healing and restoration, but only after the regular seven days of exclusion for the cleansing of a leper.

1. And Miriam . . . spake against Moses. The Hebrew text makes clear at the opening of the chapter that Miriam was the instigator of this rebellion; for her name is placed before Aaron's, and the verb **spake** carries a feminine inflection. **Because of the Ethiopian.** The circumstance used by the two as a pretext for criticizing Moses was his second marriage. The rest of the chapter reveals that the basic cause for the criticism was jealousy. The Ethiopian woman (Cushite) may have been an Asiatic rather than an African Cushite (cf. Gen 2:13; 10:6-8; Hab 3:7; Herodotus, VII. 70). **2. Hath the Lord . . . spoken only by Moses? The** preposition *b* **(by)** can mean "by means of," "with," or even "out of" Moses (cf. Rom 1:17, *ek,* "out of," quoting Hab 2:4 b). This last rendering is most in keeping with the theme of this passage (Num 12:8), which shows that God chose to communicate with Moses directly, and not indirectly, as he did with other prophets.

3. Moses was very meek. The question is sometimes asked, How could Moses have been truly meek if he sought recognition of his meekness by praising himself? Hengstenberg suggests that Moses' character is not to be measured by that of ordinary men. This chapter itself teaches that the prophet had so intimate a relationship with God that he could speak the truth objectively, as it was revealed to him, even when it regarded his own nature. But the answer may also be that this is the work of a divinely inspired *shōṭēr* (11:16), as were the account of Moses' death and burial and other editorial notes.

6. A prophet among you. The Hebrew says, *If there be your prophet of the Lord, I will make myself known.* The Hebrew is unusual but possible. The grammar represents a survival of a very old form of speech *(Ugaritic Manual,* C. H. Gordon, p. 46). **7. Faithful in all mine house.** God revealed himself to ordinary prophets by secondary means (visions and dreams). But because Moses was *the man of faith* among all the house of Israel, he had a special relationship with the Lord. **8. Mouth to mouth, even apparently, and not in dark speeches.** Not by a vision *(mar'â)* but plainly *(mar'eh);* the meaning being ascertained by the antithetical phrase "not in riddles," for Moses gazed upon the form of the Lord. Aaron knew what this meant, because he himself had had one such experience with Moses (Ex 24:10).

10. Miriam became leprous. She alone was punished, for she was the instigator of this unhappy affair. **12. Of whom the flesh is half consumed.** Aaron was abjectly repentant and pleaded for Miriam's deliverance from the horror of having the leprosy consume her flesh.

13. Heal her now, O God, I beseech thee. Moses' intercession is brief (especially so in Hebrew) but fervent. Twice he interjets *nā,* a particle of entreaty—"O God, please heal her, please." **14. If her father had but spit in her face.** The Lord forgave Miriam and cleansed her of her grievous sin. Spitting in the face was a sign of shame imposed on wrongdoers who had not incurred the extreme discipline of excommunication (Deut 25:9).

T. The Story of the Spies. 13:1–14:45. The spies went forth with orders from Moses to find out whether the land of

Canaan was good or bad, wooded or barren, whether the people were few or many, weak or strong, and whether they were nomads living in tents or inhabitants long settled, having walled fortresses. After a search of forty days, from the Negeb to the border of Hamath, the spies returned. All agreed that the land flowed "with milk and honey," but ten of them were so deeply impressed by the fortresses and the mighty stature of the people that they stirred up a surge of opinion against any attempt to take the land. Only Caleb and Joshua had confidence that, "If the Lord delight in us, then he will bring us into this land, and give it us." The sudden appearance of the glory of the Lord saved the two faithful spies from being stoned. The Lord proposed to Moses that He destroy the people and make of the prophet himself a greater nation. But Moses effectively interceded for Israel. He pled the necessity of upholding God's honor before the heathen, who were sure to say, "The Lord was not able." And he also appealed to God's long-suffering and great mercy. The Lord pardoned the people but also chastised them, declaring that this generation which had murmured and rebelled should not see the Promised Land. The people of Israel, thankful for forgiveness but failing to perceive the full meaning of the promised chastisement, determined now to obey in the matter in which they had disobeyed. Despite Moses' warning, they went up to fight the Amalekites and Canaanites. They were put to rout and beaten back to Hormah.

2. Send thou men, that they may search the land. According to Deut 1:22, God yielded to a request from the people that the land be searched. The Lord did not object to such an intelligent approach. Israel's subsequent lack of faith, however, is even more shameful in the light of the spies' unanimous testimony that the land was fruitful, just as God had promised it would be. **4. And these were their names.** The theory that the unique names in this list fit some other time better than the Mosaic period cannot be proved. The very uniqueness of the names is evidence that they come from the heroic period of Israel's history and are not the product of late authors.

16. Moses called Oshea . . . Jehoshua. Moses added the covenant name of God *(yhwh)* to the name Oshea ("deliverance"). This name for God is translated *Jehovah* in the ASV and in a few places in the AV, but the latter usually renders it LORD. According to Ex 3:14,15, the name designates God as the great "I AM," eternal and personal in his being. It also reminded Israel that he was the Covenant-Maker, who gave the promises to the fathers—Abraham, Isaac, and Jacob. Prefixing this name of the Deity to a personal name was the beginning of a great tradition that kept pace with Israel's increasing contest with the Canaanite deities, especially Baal.

17. Get you up this way southward. They actually went northward, "through the Negeb," or "dry area." *Negeb* is translated "south" because it was south in relation to Caanan. **18. See the land . . . and the people.** This reconnaissance was designed to determine whether or not the land was good, whether the people were strong or weak, and whether they dwelt in walled cities as permanent possessors or in tents as Bedouins. Centuries later, when the Assyrians invented siege warfare, they used massive machinery and an engineering corps to subdue walled cities; and even then it often took years. From the human viewpoint, Israel was to face a formidable foe.

21. Wilderness of Zin unto Rehob, as men come to Hamath. They traveled from an area just north of Kadesh to a town called Rehob, which was near or "in the direction of" the entrance to the ancient kingdom of Hamath, the antiquity of which is reflected in Gen 10:18. **22. Built seven years before Zoan in Egypt.** Zoan was the Greek Tanis, a city in the east part of the Nile delta. As Hebrew Ṣōr became Greek *Tyr*(e), so *Ṣōʿan* became *Tan*(is). **Hebron** played an important role in the life of the patriarchs (Gen 13:18; 23:19), which may make this verse refer to pre-Abrahamic times. The reference, however, may be to the rebuilding of these towns at the time of the Hyksos. The linking of Zoan and Hebron in Hebrew tradition would more likely have occurred after Egypt was under Semitic (Hyksos) rule, especially since Zoan was the capital of Hyksos Egypt and a likely residence of Pharaoh in the time of Moses. **24. Brook Eshcol.** The word for brook is *naḥal,* meaning "a dried river bed." Such 'wadies' often held water beneath the surface long after the rains ceased, and thus contributed to the fruitfulness of the land. Eshcol means "cluster." Some link this name with a ruler who lived in this area at an earlier time (see Gen 14:13).

28. People be strong . . . cities . . . walled. The spies brought back a factual report about the land. With this report or **word** *(dābār,* v. 26) Joshua and Caleb agreed (vv. 26-29). It was the **evil report** *(dibbat,* "a slandering," "a whispering," v. 32) to which they took exception. **30. Caleb . . . said, Let us go up . . . and possess it.** Caleb had confidence in the One who had proved himself thus far. Moses expressed Caleb's characteristic attitude when he said: "The Lord your God . . . he shall fight for you, according to all that he did for you in Egypt . . . and in the wilderness" (Deut 1:30,31). **We are well able to overcome it.** It was after this triumphant expression of faith that the ten spies started their slanderous words **(evil report,** v. 32). This alone is what made them the objects of divine displeasure.

32. Brought up an evil report. The Hebrew says, *They made go out a defamation of the land,* which suggests that they started a campaign of evil-speaking against the two faithful men. **A land that eateth up the inhabitants thereof.** This does not mean that the land was poor – they had shown otherwise – but that many people fought over it because it was such a good land.

33. The giants, the sons of Anak. Some have suggested that the spies imagined there were giants about when they saw great walls, sometimes fifty feet high, and supposed only giants could build them. But the measurements of King Og's iron bedstead given in Deut 3:11 testify to the existence of a race of abnormally large people. Deut 2:10,20 and Gen 14:5 indicate that the "giants" date from as early as patriarchal days, and were given various local designations *(Emims, Zamzumims,* and *Rephaim).* In the Hebrew of Deut 2:11 the Anakim are called *Rephaim* (translated "giants"). Joshua 11:22 tells us that Anakim remained in three of the Philistine cities – Gaza, Gath, and Ashdod (Jer 27:5, LXX). The family of Goliath in Gath may have been descendants of these earlier people, for in II Sam 21:16-22 and I Chr 20:4-8 these Philistine giants are called sons of the *Rāpā'*. The fifteenth century texts from Ugarit mention the Rephaim (C. H. Gordon, *Ugaritic Literature,* pp. 101-103), who probably were not "shades of the dead" but actually these same mighty people (cf. Ugaritic *ilnym* and Hebrew *'ēlîm;* Job 41:17, Heb. Bible; 41:25, Eng.) from the north, whence came iron processing (cf. Og's bedstead).

14:8. If the Lord delight in us, then he will bring us into this land, and give it us. The sinful slander ("evil report") which the ten spies spread among the people accused the Lord himself of wanting to slay them. Note in contrast the wholehearted confidence in the Lord expressed here by Caleb. It was not until Caleb was eighty-five years old (Josh 14:11,12) that, with the same vibrant faith, he dispossessed the Anakim in the vicinity of Hebron. **9. They are bread for us.** The verb *'ākal,* "to eat," also means "to devour," "lay waste," or "destroy" (12:12). The same figure is conveyed here without the verb. **Their defence** *(shadow)* **is departed.** Jonah 4:6 tells how a shadow protected a prophet from the burning heat of the desert sun. When the shadow was removed, Jonah was left exposed and vulnerable (Jon 4:8). But Ezk 31:3,12 shows us that powerful nations are like trees (Num 24:6) under whose shadow other nations are forced to live. When Assyria fell, her shadow, meaning her strength, was dissipated; and other nations no longer were under her power. Thus the text could mean, "Their strength is departed."

15,16. The nations . . . will speak, saying . . . the Lord was not able. The beauty of this passage lies in the fact that Moses was zealous for the Lord's honor and not for his own. While Moses' spirit was wonderful, his argument itself was only partially valid. If God had acted on Moses' advice, he would never have chastened his people, for fear the heathen would misunderstand. The valid part of the argument centers around Moses' confidence that God is able to carry out his promises.

18. The Lord is longsuffering, and of great mercy. This part of Moses' plea is in behalf of the people. The argument now is completely valid, because he states the whole case for God. God is not only of great mercy but is the Just One, who cannot clear the guilty, that is, leave iniquity unpunished. This foundation truth for the teaching of substitutionary blood atonement pervades the whole Bible. God is merciful and does forgive, not by overlooking iniquity but by providing a substitute so that He may be both the Just One and the Justifier of those who believe (Rom 3:21-26). **19.**

As thou hast forgiven. The root meaning of the word *forgive,* "to bear or carry," supports this substitutionary aspect of forgiveness. For God to pardon there must be a sin-bearer.

21. But as truly as I live. This is the introduction to an oath which continues through verse 23. To clarify several points, we offer the following translation: "Surely as I live and as the earth shall be full of the glory of the Lord, none of the men who saw my glory and my signs which I did in Egypt and in the wilderness but who have tried me now tenfold and have not hearkened to my voice, shall see the land which I sware to their fathers." The tenfold trying seems to refer to the ten evil spies.

23,24. Neither shall any of them that provoked me see it but (except) **my servant Caleb.** The verse division in the AV violates the sentence structure. **24. Because he . . . hath followed me fully.** "Follow fully" derives from a root meaning "to fill," and is used to express the consecration of the priest ("fill his hand," 3:3). It also means "to overflow" or "to do anything in abundance without holding back," whether for evil or for good (Job 16:10). Caleb abandoned himself completely to God, who in turn 'abundanced' Caleb by "filling his hand" to do the divine will. A perfect example of consecration! **His seed shall possess it.** This promise was faithfully fulfilled. See Josh 14:6-15.

25. Turn...get you into the wilderness. The command was clear. They had only to obey. **The way of the Red Sea.** The Hebrew *Yam Suph* ("sea of reeds") means the waters of the two gulfs that bound the Sinai peninsula. This "way" is distinguished in Ex 13:17,18 from "the way of the land of the Philistines," which followed the Mediterranean coast.

26. And the Lord spake . . . saying. Verses 26 through 35 form an expanded statement giving the reason for and details of this chastisement. Far from representing a different source document, as some hold, it follows good Semitic literary style in repeating and emphasizing a phase of a larger context (Gen 1,2). **28. Truly as I live.** The oath of 14:21-23 is here repeated in expanded terms that spell out the actual falling of their carcasses in the wilderness and God's fulfilling his promise through their children. The irony of their situation was that in their murmuring they had accused the Lord of making these very children a prey in the wilderness (v. 31). In this chastisement God reminded them of their words, and promised that these same children would inherit the land.

33. Bear your whoredoms. This is a metaphor. Through unfaithfulness, those married to God (believers) committed spiritual adultery, which sin their children bore until the passing of that entire generation. **34. And ye shall know my breach of promise.** The phrase, **breach of promise,** which suggests that God may fail to keep his promise, is an unfortunate translation for a term meaning "rebuke" or "opposition." In 30:5 a verb of this root means "to disapprove," and in 32:7 it means "to discourage." "If God be for us, who can be against us" (Rom 8:31). The converse is the tragic lesson of this verse: When men persist in sinning, God can only oppose, disapprove, and discourage.

36. Who . . . made . . . the congregation to murmur . . . by bringing up (causing to go out) **a slander.** This text, which uses the same word *dibbâ* that is used in Num 13, confirms our interpretation of the "evil report" as slander (13:28,30,32). By a campaign of slanderous words these sinful men turned the entire congregation against the Lord. They now "died by the plague before the Lord" (v. 37).

41. Wherefore now do ye transgress the commandment of the Lord? God had made plain that they must now return to the wilderness (v. 25). Therefore, this attempt to show a belated zeal was ill-advised; for faith is obedience, without which they could not have God's presence or blessing (v. 42).

44. But they presumed to go up. Their former sin was reticent unbelief, shown by their extreme caution and fear (II Tim 1:7). Now they had moved to the other extreme of presumptuous unbelief, demonstrated by their overconfidence and carelessness. The Hebrew root of **presumed,** *'āpal,* is used also in Hab 2:4: "Behold the presumptuous one, his soul is not upright in him; but the righteous one shall live by his faithfulness." The Apostle Paul saw the spiritual truth latent here. The unrighteous man trusts in his own virtue. But true righteousness originates in God's faithfulness and is communicated to man by living, obedient trust, from faith to faith (Rom 1:17).

IV. Second Priestly Scroll. 15:1–19:22.

The main feature of this priestly section is found in chapters 16 and 17, which recount the rebellion of Korah and the consequent triple vindication of the Aaronic priesthood. Gathered around this vindication of Aaron as priest are other details of priestly concern (see outline).

A. Ceremonial Details. 15:1-41. An earlier set of instructions (Lev 2:1-11) regarding meal (cereal) offerings gave no exact quantities. We now have a passage specifying exact proportions (cf. Lev 23:13). Looking forward to the time when the people would eat the food of Canaan, the Lord gave them directions for making a token contribution of the first fruits of their produce (heave offerings). He made provision for forgiveness of sins of ignorance — cases in which either the congregation as a whole or individuals might have transgressed unwittingly — on the ground of burnt offerings accompanied by atonement blood (vv. 22-31; cf. Lev 4). But he also made clear that if a man acted with evil intention *(a high hand),* he must be cut off from the people and bear his own iniquity. One man was stoned to death for despising God's commandment regarding Sabbath observance. Some have attempted to identify this severe judgment with the Sabbath ideas of the Pharisees, against whose misinterpretations Christ spoke. The two situations are not the same. The Pharisees added to Jewish religious law Sabbath regulations not contained in the Old Testament, and so provided loopholes for themselves. The Lord of the Sabbath teaches that the Sabbath law is designed for man's spiritual enjoyment and to satisfy his deepest needs. The Bible nowhere takes a light attitude toward deliberate transgression of any of God's laws. The chapter concludes with a statute of psychological value (Num 15:37-41). The Israelites were to attach tassels made of blue thread to the borders or corners of their garments as a reminder to keep all these commandments (Deut 22:12). This was Israel's "string around the finger."

5. For one lamb. Note that the amounts of mixed oil and flour and of wine for the drink offerings increase with the size of the animal offered: the fourth of a hin of oil and wine with each lamb, a third of each with the ram, but one-half hin with each bullock. This demonstrates a principle underlying all the offerings —that a man is to give according to his ability (Lev 5:7-13).

7. For a sweet (quieting, restful) **savour.** The phrase is used in 15:3,10, 13,14. In Gen 8:20,21 we are told that the Lord smelled the pleasing fragrance of Noah's burnt offering, and it had a favorable effect upon Him. Some dislike the extreme anthropomorphism in this thought. Yet the Bible is filled with such descriptions of God. The expression is no more literal than the words: "And he rode upon a cherub," or, "he did fly upon the wings of the wind" (Ps 18:10). The heathen deity Baal is called "the rider on the clouds" (C. H. Gordon, *Ugaritic Literature,* p. 30), as is also the Lord in Ps 68:4 (RSV). The critic who assumes that this "anthropomorphism" is evidence that Israel's religion was in a primitive stage might as well accuse a modern pastor of idolatry when he prays that God will "lay bare His arm in behalf of His people." In terms of the known, man is made to understand the unknown, in this case God's feeling toward him. By this practical expression, **a sweet savour,** God's people knew that their sacrifices were pleasing to him, much as a pleasant smell was soothing and pleasing to the people themselves.

16. One law . . . for you, and for the stranger that sojourneth with you. Strangers were welcome to "sojourn" with Israel but obligated to worship in God's appointed way, not in their own way. The spiritual decadence of the surrounding peoples was such that the introduction of their religious practices would have defiled the nation.

20. A cake of the first of your dough. The word *'ărîsâ,* translated **dough,** is usually taken to mean "coarse grain." An earlier reference to the offering of first fruits (Lev 23:14) mentions only the waving of a sheaf, accompanied by a meal offering of *sōlet,* "fine flour." The fact that this heave offering of coarse grain is called *t*ᵉ*rûmâ,* "a contribution," indicates that it was for priestly consumption, while the fine flour of Lev 23:13 was to be a fire offering, a pleasing savor unto the Lord.

30. Doeth ought presumptuously *(with a high hand).* Obedient Israel came out of Egypt "with an high hand" (Ex 14:8), with a raised, clenched fist in defiance of Pharaoh. Here arrogant Israel sins with a high hand in defiance of the Lord (cf. Deut 32:27; Isa 10:32).

36. And stoned him with stones, and he died; as the Lord commanded. The lips of Christ described a fate far worse than this for those whose hearts despise the law of God (cf. Mt 18:9). Indeed, this Old Testament event was in reality a merciful lesson. Though such judgment could not change the heart of the one judged, it kept many wayward Israelites from defying God.

39. That ye seek not after your own heart and your own eyes. The tassels reminded them to walk not after their own evil inclinations and desire, but instead to follow the good, health-giving commandments of the Lord.

B. The Rebellion of Korah, Dathan, and Abiram. 16:1-35. Any rebellion of this size has numerous facets and various underlying reasons and grievances. Critics have imagined that the different thought currents here derive from the hypothetical document sources JE and P, and that our story represents the combined accounts of several rebellions during Israel's history. From the text itself, however, we gather that there were both ecclesiastical and civil sides to this rebellion. Korah persuaded fellow Levites and others to join him in seeking the priestly function (vv. 9,10). At the same time, the Reubenites, Dathan and Abiram, turned against Moses because of his seeming failure to provide the fields and vineyards of the Promised Land (v. 14). The thought that they were to spend the rest of their lives in the wilderness must have made rebellion seem like a way out.

Dathan and Abiram refused to come out to the Tabernacle to face Moses but sent a bitter complaint (vv. 12-14). Korah, on the other hand, and his 250 "princes" (not all, but many being Levites; vv. 7,8; 27:3) appeared with censers in hand, to prove that they were holy and could perform this priestly duty. Suddenly the glory of the Lord appeared at the door of the Tabernacle; and the Lord upheld Moses' authority by opening the earth to swallow the three leaders of the rebellion, with their households and possessions (v. 32). A further judgment by fire devoured the company of censer-bearers.

3. Ye take too much upon you. Or, "We have had enough of you." Moses, a little later, threw these very words back at them (v. 7). **All the congregation are holy.** In Ex 19:6 God promised to make Israel a kingdom of priests and a holy nation. But this promise had a condition, "If ye will obey . . . my voice and keep my covenant." For the giving and execution of this covenant divinely appointed mediators were needed. **11. For which cause both thou and all thy company are gathered together against the Lord.** God had already chosen his mediator (v. 5). For Korah and his congregation to question this was to question God. **And what is Aaron.** Aaron's right to be priest did not originate in him.

12. Dathan and Abiram . . . said, We will not come up. The scene shifts to the Reubenites, whose rebellious motives were different from Korah's but whose purpose to overthrow Moses and Aaron was the same. **13. Except thou make thyself altogether a prince over us.** Or, *that you might keep on playing the prince over us.* These men were chafing under the prospect of spending all their lives in the wilderness. They blamed Moses for the defeat at Hormah (14:45). They imagined that he refused to take the ark up with them on that occasion for fear he would lose control over them when they entered the land. **14. Wilt thou put out the eyes of these men?** In line with Prov 30:17 the allusion here is to vultures plucking out the eyes of dead bodies in the wilderness. Had not Moses said that all this generation must die in the wilderness?

19. And Korah gathered all the congregation against them. The Hebrew makes a distinction between **his congregation,** "company," and **the congregation** (cf. v. 9). Korah presented himself as a champion of all the congregation: "Are not all the people holy ones?" (v. 3)

22. The God of the spirits of all flesh. The very evident dualism of spirit and flesh revealed in this phrase gives evidence that this concept was a part of Hebrew religious ideology as early as the time of Moses. 'Liberal' scholarship, however, tends to assign this concept to the late document "P" theology.

24. Get you up from about the tabernacle of Korah, Dathan, and Abiram. It is unlikely that these men had built another tabernacle. The term *mishkan* can refer to any dwelling place or tent (24:5). The mere addition of the Hebrew consonant "yodh" would indicate plural, "tents of." The translators of the LXX either saw this difficulty and left out the names Dathan and Abiram, or worked with a Hebrew manuscript that mentioned only Korah. Our present Hebrew text of 16:32 mentions only Korah as a shortened expression for all three rebels. **27. So they gat up from the tabernacle** (tent) **of Korah.** The people who believed Moses now proved it by their actions. **Dathan and Abiram . . . stood in the door of their tents,** as if to challenge Moses.

28. For I have not done them of mine own mind. Again we see that the quarrel was not with Moses but with God. The Hebrew *lēb*, "heart," is correctly rendered *mind* in the AV; for the heart often meant the intellectual capacities (cf. Hos 7:11, "sense," RSV), while the kidneys, bowels, etc., ("reins," Ps 16:7, and elsewhere) meant the emotional capacities. **30. But if the Lord make a new thing.** Both the verb and the noun are from *bārā'*, "to create"; therefore the *new thing* had to be supernatural, or at least preternatural. **And they go down quick,** i.e., "alive," **into the pit** (Sheol). In the OT the term Sheol rarely means "the place of the departed dead"; here it indicates "the grave."

32. Swallowed them up, and their houses, and all the men that appertained unto Korah, and all their goods. *Bāttêhem* does not mean their **houses** but their *households,* as in 18:31. The rest of the verse differentiates between human possessions (servants) and non-human (animals and goods). This was simply a Hebrew way of saying "everything." However, Num 26:11 informs us that the sons of Korah did not perish with him. Probably Korah's "household" did not include his adult sons who had families of their own.

C. Incidents Vindicating the Aaronic Priesthood. 16:36–17:13. At this point the Hebrew Bible begins a new chapter. Jewish scribes considered the rest of chapter 16 and all of 17 a unit, on the theme of Aaron's sole right as priest. The brazen censers used by the rebels were beaten into covering plates for the altar, as a memorial to perpetuate the exclusive priesthood of Aaron's house. A further overtone of the rebellion appears in a murmuring that blamed Moses for the death of the rebels. God's wrath abated only when Aaron used his censer to make atonement for the people (v. 46). The vindication of Aaron's house culminated in the test of the rods (ch. 17). Of twelve selected rods, one for each tribe, only the rod of Levi, inscribed with Aaron's name, supernaturally blossomed and yielded almonds before the Lord. This rod was to be kept in the ark as a testimony against all future attempts to reject God's choice of the mediatorial family.

37. For they are hallowed. Why were the censers of these evil men counted holy? Because God had a sacred purpose for them. "Because they offered them before the Lord . . . they shall be a sign . . . . a memorial . . . that no stranger, which is not of the seed of Aaron, come near to offer incense before the Lord" (cf. vv. 37-40).

48. And he stood between the dead and the living. A dramatic illustration of Aaron's mediatorial office. Not by virtue of anything in himself (16:5) but only because God had chosen him, did Aaron's incense make an atonement for the people and stay the plague (cf. Heb 5:4-6).

17:4. Before the testimony. The reference is to the ark of the testimony. **Where I will meet with you.** The Hebrew verb for **meet** means "to appoint a time or place." The same root is used for the **tabernacle of the congregation,** *'ōhel mō'ēd,* meaning "the tent of the appointed time and place." The congregation is sometimes called *'ēdâ*, "the company assembled by appointment."

6. Twelve rods. Since one was Levi's (Aaron's) and both Ephraim and Manasseh were constituted as tribes, there would have been thirteen instead of twelve. There were two ways of numbering the tribes so that there would always be twelve. In Num 1:5-15 the sons of Joseph are reckoned as one tribe. In 13:4-15, however, the land and its eventual division is in mind; therefore the tribe of Joseph is divided to give twelve divisions, since Levi was given no inheritance of land. **8. On the morrow.** This limiting of time helps to establish the fact that a true miracle from God took place. **10. Aaron's rod . . . to be kept for a token.** A symbol to teach future generations. Against **the rebels.** The *sons of contention,* or *children of rebellion* (AV marg.). These were men who made their lives miserable and gravely offended God by letting self-pity or some other form of deep unrest seethe in their hearts (v. 12).

12. Behold, we die, we perish, we all perish. A final expression of self-pity from a gainsaying generation closes this chapter and also the report of God's dealings with them. The next words of narration (20:1) describe the closing days of wilderness wandering and the rise of the new generation.

D. Duties and Revenues of the Priests and Levites. 18:1-32. Aaron and the Levites were God's servants appointed to perform the sacred ministry of the sanctuary by which Israel learned of God's holiness (vv. 1-7). None of the house of Levi would receive an inheritance of land; God provided for them by means of the perpetual portion, *ḥāq ʿôlām* (v. 8). This was the priests' part of Israel's offerings. But since not all the tribe of Levi could be supported by portions of offerings, the Levites received the tithe of all Israel's inheritance. And each Levite gave a tenth of his tithe to the priest, just as if he had raised it himself in the field.

1. Shall bear the iniquity of the sanctuary: and . . . of your priesthood. To **bear** *(forgive)* **iniquity** means to cleanse by means of a substitutionary offering. The priests had to make atonement for their own sins (Lev 16:6). Also, since there was always the possibility of the sanctuary's being defiled by someone unwittingly, the holy place itself and the altar had to be cleansed (Ex 29:36, 37; Lev 16:20).

6. To you they are given as a gift for the Lord. They were given to the priests as those who were devoted ("given ones") to serve the Lord. This verse is a key to understanding the Apostle Paul's use of Ps 68:18 in Eph 4:8.

7. As a service of gift. The priesthood was a privileged service, God-given and God-appointed.

8. Heave offerings. These *tᵉrûmōt* were the contributions to the priests and Levites as distinguished from fire offerings, which were expiatory. **By reason of the anointing.** Better rendered, *I have given them for an anointed* (or *consecrated) portion.* **9. Which they shall render** *(return)* **unto me.** The thought is that of returning to God what is his. **10. Every male shall eat it.** The offerings of verse 9 were "most holy"; so only the males partook of them. **11. To thy sons and to thy daughters . . . every one that is clean . . . shall eat of it.** These were not fire offerings for atonement; therefore all the priestly household partook.

16. Those that are to be redeemed . . . This should read, *And his ransom price, beginning at a month old, you shall take, according to your evaluation, starting at five shekels of silver.* Compare Lev 27:1-7 for the varying evaluations according to age and sex. **For the money of five shekels.** There was no money (in our sense) in ancient Israel. The Hebrew text says, *silver, five shekels, which is twenty gerahs* (grains of weight). **19. A covenant of salt for ever.** According to Lev 2:13, every sacrifice was salted. Christ used this thought to describe the eternal verity of hell (Mk 9:49). The salt signified an inviolable covenant between God and the priests.

20. I am thy part and thine inheritance. Their lives were to be spent serving God in the sanctuary. Therefore they were to be physically sustained by the people, who themselves were sustained by God. **24. The tithes . . . which they offer . . . unto the Lord, I have given to the Levites to inherit.** Levites and priests were dependent upon the faithfulness of the people, who in turn enjoyed the good pleasure of their God through careful observance of all the law of the sanctuary

29. Every heave offering *(contribution)* **of** *(due)* **the Lord, of all the best thereof.** The offering due to the Lord (v. 26) was to be from the best of the best. The people gave their best to the Levites, who gave the best of this to the Lord as represented by the priest. **31. It is your reward for** *(in return for)* **your service.** The word *śākār,* "hire," may seem mercenary; but compare Gen 15:1, where God calls himself Abram's *śākār* ("reward").

E. The Water Purification for Those Defiled by the Dead. 19:1-22. Verses 1 to 10 explain how this water was to be prepared, and the rest of the chapter tells how it was to be used. Eleazar, the son of Aaron, was to oversee the slaying of a blemish-free red heifer outside the camp. He was to sprinkle its blood toward the Tabernacle seven times and then burn it entirely, blood included, together with cedar wood, hyssop, and scarlet cloth. The resultant ashes were to be used to make the "water of impurity"; that is, water for removing ceremonial impurity. A person defiled by the dead was to be counted impure for seven days. He was to achieve ceremonial purity by being sprinkled with this water on the third and seventh days. On the seventh day he was to wash his clothes and flesh, and at sundown he would be "clean." One who failed to comply was to be cut off from the congregation as an unclean person.

2. An **ordinance of the law.** What is called here *a teaching statute,* is later called an *eternal* ("perpetual") statute (v. 10). Hence, the dual purpose of this ritual was to teach Israel about the purity of God and to preserve this revelation for future generations. **A red heifer without spot.** Many strained allegorical interpretations of the use of this red heifer have been put forth, wherein each detail, including the color of the animal, is given a spiritual meaning. It is better to regard such a ceremony as one would an artist's painting, recognizing that while the whole conveys a message, the details are insignificant when considered independently. Hebrews 9:13,14 points out the message of this object lesson, which is that God's people need to experience cleansing from impurity. Just as the ashes of the red heifer ceremonially cleansed a defiled Israelite, even so Christ's blood satisfies divine justice, purges a poor sinner's conscience, and restores him to God.

4. Sprinkle of her blood directly before the tabernacle. This was the atoning act that expiated sin and propitiated God (Lev 16:14,15). The life of a pure and innocent victim was substituted for the life of the one defiled. For this reason this is called a sin offering *ḥaṭṭā't* (Num 19:9,17). **9. A clean place,** i.e., ceremonially clean. **For a water of separation.** More correctly *water of impurity,* that which removes impurity. **It is a purification for sin.** The plan of this ritual was to provide a simple way to purify Israelites from a very common defilement. They felt in their consciences the relation between sin and death and the need for deliverance from the curse death represents, the curse of sin.

12. He shall purify himself. As in 8:21, the Hebrew expression is *he shall de-sin himself.* Though it means cleansing, the emphasis is on the defilement, not on the purity, perhaps because one cannot truly be cleansed unless he realizes that sin is sin. **13. Defileth the tabernacle of the Lord.** An Israelite defiled by the dead would pollute everything he touched or came near. This idea of the contagion of ceremonial impurity is stressed in verses 14,15 (cf. Hag 2:13).

16. A dead body, or a bone of a man, or a grave. Anything having to do with death contaminated. The people could not help becoming defiled occasionally; therefore "the water of impurity" was always available. The priest, however, was forbidden to become unclean except when his closest relatives died (Lev 21:1-3). **18. A clean person shall take hyssop.** Any "clean" person could perform this duty; it did not require a priest. The purpose of this provision was to make cleansing from unavoidable contact with the dead readily accessible.

V. From the Wilderness of Zin to the Steppes of Moab. 20:1–22:1.

We may infer from Num 33:36 that at the end of the years of wandering, Israel was at Ezion-Geber, on the northernmost coast of the Gulf of Aqabah. From there they entered the Wilderness of Zin, in which was located the oasis called Kadesh, a term used in 33:36 to designate a wide area. They requested passage through Edom via the ancient trade route, the king's highway, but were refused it. These chapters indicate that Edom, Moab, the Amorites, and the Canaanites controlled many established fortresses in the Negeb and Trans-Jordan. While encamped at Mount Hor, Israel fought and defeated Arad the Canaanite. At this point (21:4) they proceeded south by way of *Yam Suph* (here the Gulf of Aqabah) to avoid a clash with the Edomites. Eventually they traveled north in the Valley of Arabah until they reached the Wadi Zered. They then traversed between Edom and Moab in the Zered Valley, avoiding Moab by going east of it and proceeding northward to the Arnon, then west again to the king's highway. The territory north of the river Arnon, called "the Steppes of Moab," they captured by defeating the Amorite King Sihon, who took it from the Moabites. Additional land east of Jordan they won by conquering Og, king of Bashan. The rest of Numbers (after the Balaam story) is devoted to preparing this new generation for the major conquests west of the Jordan.

A. The Wilderness of Zin. 20:1-21.

1) The Sin of Moses. 20:1-13.

1. Then came . . . Israel . . . into the desert of Zin in the first month. Zin *(Ṣin)* lies between the Ascent of Akrabbim, southwest of the Dead Sea, and Kadesh (20:16; 34:3). Though the year is not mentioned, it must have been the end of the thirty-ninth year or the fortieth year after the Exodus. For they proceeded from Kadesh to Mount Hor (20:22), where Aaron died; and 33:38 tells us that he died in the fortieth year. **5. No place of seed, or of figs, or of vines, or of pomegranates; neither is there any water to drink.** Nelson Glueck's description of the importance of water in the Negeb (*Rivers in the Desert*, pp. 20-25) makes God's sympathetic attitude toward this complaint plausible (p. 16).

8. Speak ye unto the rock . . . and it shall give forth his water. A rock giving forth its water indicates that this water from a rock was somewhat the expected thing. The miracle was in Moses' knowing what rock was ready to give water and in the fact that he needed only to speak to it.

10. Hear now, ye rebels; must we fetch you water. Psalm 106:32,33 gives the divine commentary on these words. The people angered Moses, and "they made his spirit bitter and he spoke words that were rash" (RSV). It was not God but Moses who was angry at the people. Therefore the pronoun **we** was a form of blasphemy. **11. Smote the rock twice.** If Moses had merely spoken to the rock, as the Lord had directed, the miracle would have pointed to the power of God. As it was, Moses took God's place both in word and in deed.

12. Because ye believed me not, to sanctify me in the eyes . . . of Israel (cf. v. 24). Moses' sin was a willful refusal to point away from himself to God's power and thus sanctify the Lord in the eyes of the people. Moses and Aaron shared the chastisement for this sin, for God had said, "Speak ye (plural) unto the rock." After the deed he said, "Ye (plural) shall not bring this congregation into the land." **13. This is the water of Meribah.** The place was not called Meribah after the incident, as Rephidim had been forty years earlier (Ex 17:7); but the water was now called "the water of strife" (*mᵉrîbâ*) because **Israel strove with the Lord.**

2) The Request To Go Through Edom 20:14-21.

14. Moses sent messengers . . . thus saith thy brother Israel. The Edomites were descendants of Esau (Deut 23:7). Moses was being tactful as well as stating the truth. **16. In Kadesh, a city in the uttermost of thy border.** The border of Edom is usually considered to be the western edge of the Valley of Arabah. If present identification for Kadesh at 'Ain Qadeis (or 'Ain el-Qudeirat) is correct, then Edom's border must have extended far into the Negeb. This suggests the extent of Edom's sphere of influence, since actual borders were established only by the control of certain key fortresses. **17. The king's highway.** This was an old caravan route. Long before Moses' day it was used as a major public artery. Verse 19 calls this the public road or the highway (*mᵉsillâ*).

20. Edom came out against him with much people, and with a strong hand. No battle ensued, because God's purpose was not to dissipate Israel's strength here, but to save it for the hard fighting against the Amorites, whose land was needed to secure access to Canaan.

B. The Area of Mount Hor. 20:22–21:3.

1) The Death of Aaron. 20:22-29.

22. Journeyed from Kadesh, and came unto mount Hor. The location of Mount Hor (*Hōr hāhār*) is indefinite. Many think that it is Jebel el-Medhra, which is just east of the Valley of Arabah. Others suggest that some mountain northeast of Kadesh is the place. The latter would fit Moses' description of Edom's sphere of power, since Mount Hor was on the border of Edom (v. 23). Moses, in Deut 1:44, assumes that Seir (a designation for Edom) is in the Negeb, which would fit the view that Edom's border was not confined to Wadi Arabah. The descriptions of Israel's southern border in Num 34:1-5 and Josh 15:1-12 make both Israel's and Edom's border veer away from the Arabah westward, touch Kadesh-barnea, and lead on to the River of Egypt (Wadi el 'Arîsh). **23. Mount Hor, by the coast of the land of Edom.** This does not mean that the mountain was exactly on the border of Edom. It may simply be a way of distinguishing it from the other Mount Hor of 34:8. a number of places were called Kadesh (*sacred*) and had to be distinguished, i.e., Kadesh-barnea, Kedesh-naphtali, and Kadesh on the Orontes.

28. And Moses stripped Aaron of his garments, and put them upon Eleazar. These were the holy garments of Ex 39, the badge of the high priesthood. They had marked Aaron—and now marked Eleazar—as God's chosen mediator, whose ministrations taught the people that God was their almighty and ever-holy Friend.

2) Arad the Canaanite Defeated at Hormah. 21:1-3.

1. Arad the Canaanite, which dwelt in the south (Negeb). The name **Arad** is still used of a mound in the Negeb. A man who could give his name to an area for thousands of years was hardly just a tribal chieftain (Glueck, *Rivers in the Desert*, p. 114). Verses 1,2 do not describe two events separated by hundreds of years, as some think. **By the way of the spies.** "The way of the *'ătārîm*" was possibly the name of a caravan route, since the Arabic equivalent of *'ătārîm* means "the footprints." **3. They utterly destroyed them.** The men of Israel were forced into this battle, for it was not their plan to enter the land from the south. The event became a token of future conquests. The outcome of the last battle God's people had fought thirty-eight years before was sad defeat at a place named Hormah (14:45). Hence there is a play on words in this verse, Hormah being from the same root as the verb "utterly destroy." This may not have been the town of Hormah mentioned in 14:45 (Josh 15:30; Jud 1:17). Perhaps Moses sought to bolster morale by naming this place of victory in remembrance of that place of humiliating defeat by the same enemy.

C. The Journey to the Steppes of Moab. 21:4–22:1.

1) Rebellion on the Journey Around Edom. **21:4-9.**

4. The way of the Red sea. Not the Red Sea as shown on our maps, but *Yam Suph*, meaning "sea where reeds grow," in this case the Gulf of Aqabah. Deuteronomy 2:8 (ASV) calls this "the way of the Arabah," meaning that low plain that gradually ascends from the depths of the Salt Sea to the Gulf. Israel went in this direction, though not necessarily all the way to the sea, to avoid contact with the Edomites.

8. Make thee a fiery serpent. There is no adjective in the Hebrew; the term *śārāp* means a "poison snake." **Every one . . . when he looketh upon it, shall live.** Only those who believed God's promise would act upon the direction and live. Our Lord saw in this not only an illustration of the efficacy of faith in God's word, but an apt object-lesson of his own coming vicarious suffering, when he should be lifted up between heaven and earth (Jn 3:14).

2) Places Passed on the March from the Arabah. 21:10-20.

10. And the children of Israel set forward. Verses 10 to 20 give the names of the places where Israel encamped while traveling north in the Arabah. This itinerary is given more fully in 33:41-49.

14. The book of the wars of the Lord. Here is one of the authentic sources from which Moses and subsequent scribes of Israel obtained information concerning earlier events. **What he did in the Red sea.** These words are a questionable translation of the beginning of a fragment from this ancient source. This first line is obscure because it is broken from its context. The latter part of verse 14 is the more important because it gives the reason for the quotation—to show that the Valley of Arnon was the border of Moab. The two Hebrew words comprising this opening phrase of the quotation may be translated in several ways. The RSV follows the ICC in transliterating the Hebrew as place names—*Waheb in Suphah*. The AV takes the opening words as an Aramaic verbal form (an old Jewish exegesis, followed also by Jerome in the Vulgate). The AV rendering of *sûpâ* as *Red sea* is not likely, since the area in question is adjacent to Moab. The difficult reference to *sûp* in Deut 1:1 (ASV) locates this otherwise unknown place in Trans-Jordan, where Moses gave his last words. The fragment might be translated then as follows:

A portion in direction of Suph:
Even the Arnon wadies,
Even the slope of the wadies
Which turn toward the seat of Ar,
Verily is adjacent to the border of
 Moab.

17. Israel sang this song. The poetic tradition is here reflected. The poets and ballad singers may have passed on some of Israel's history as epic poetry. It is possible that the Book of the Wars of the Lord was a compilation of such poems. That the traditional poetry was very early incorporated in written records is evidenced by the literature from fifteenth century Ugarit. This little fragment, of verse 17, has been called "The Song of the Well." The first line is an introduction or theme line. *With sceptre and with staves* (v. 18, ASV) probably expresses the authority of the nobles, who would direct the digging. However, water often lay very near the surface in a *naḥal*, "wadi," or "dried river bed," so that even a staff thrust into the soil would bring it to the surface (cf. Gen 26:19; II Kgs 3:16-18).

"Spring up, O Well! Sing to it!
A well, the princes dug it,
Even the nobles of the people digged it,
With scepter and with their staves."

18. From the wilderness they went to Mattanah. Most of the place names of verses 18-20 cannot be exactly located. The general direction of the journeying was from the desert east of Moab, in the area north of Arnon, westerly to the height called the Pisgah, which overlooked the waters of the Salt Sea and the wastes of the Wilderness of Jeshimon.

3) Defeat of the Amorites. 21:21-32.

21. Israel sent messengers unto Sihon. Moses' purpose was to gain access to the land west of Jordan. He asked for peaceful passage (vv. 21,22), but Sihon refused (v. 23); and so there was no way to avoid a conflict. **24. The border of . . . Ammon was strong.** The LXX has a better Hebrew text, and correctly reads, *Jazer was the border of the Ammonites* (Josh 13:25; Num 32:1). Our present Hebrew text has lost one letter, an "r." **26. Who had fought against the former king of Moab, and taken all his land . . . even unto Arnon.** This verse, taken with Israel's victory over Sihon, explains the meaning of the poem given in 21:27-30.

27. They that speak in proverbs. These *Mōshᵉlîm* were poets, possibly ballad singers. Baalim oracles are called *mashals* (AV, *maschil*), as are the Proverbs and some didactic psalms (see titles of Ps 32,42,52, and others). According to Num 21:26, Sihon the Amorite had previously destroyed Moab (cf. second and third parallel stanzas below); but verses 21-25 inform us that Israel had destroyed the Amorites (first and fourth parallel stanzas). So the poem is a satiric ode, which says, in substance, "You (Amorites) have beaten them (Moabites), but we (Israelites) have beaten you." Note the strophic balance and the climactic development in this poem. The second and third stanzas have the same structural pattern. The final stanza answers by antithesis what immediately precedes, but actually completes the meaning of the opening stanza.

"Come ye! Heshbon shall be (re)built,
Yea! Let be (re)established the city of Sihon.

For fire has gone out from Heshbon,
A flame from the town of Sihon;
It has devoured Ar of Moab,
The Baals of the high places of Arnon.

Woe to you, O Moab!
You are undone, O people of Kemosh!
(For) he has given his sons as prisoners,
And his daughters into captivity,
(Even) to the Amorite king, Sihon.

But we shot them: Heshbon perished as far as Dibon.
Yea, we devastated (them), until fire spread as far as Medeba."

31. Israel dwelt in the land of the Amorites. All the territory between the rivers Arnon and Jabbok was secured, and in addition, the Ammonite city Jaazer (v. 32) and the kingdom of Og (vv. 33-35); so that Israel controlled the land east of Jordan from the Arnon to Mount Hermon (Deut 3:8). Most of the geographic designations in these verses are well known even to this day.

4) The Defeat of Og. 21:33-35.

33. The king of Bashan went out against them. These verses parallel Deut 3:1-4 almost word for word (except for the change in the personal pronoun). Og's iron bedstead (or sarcophagus) evidently captured Israel's curiosity. The special notice given it here suggests that such use of iron was rare at this time. (In regard to its size, see Deut 3:11; cf. comment on 13:33).

5) Arrival in the Plains of Moab. 22:1.

1. Pitched in the plains of Moab. They encamped at a place called *Shittîm* (25:1), near where the Jordan empties into the Salt Sea. **On this side Jordan by Jericho.** See comment on 34:15.

Part Two. Foreign Intrigue Against Israel. 22:2–23:30.

Chapters 22 to 25 form a literary divider between the two logical halves of the Book of Numbers. Nowhere in chapters 22 to 24 do we have the usual formula, "God said unto Moses," found in every other chapter. This section, like the Book of Job, may have originated outside of Israel. Although we are told (Deut 23:5) that Moses was aware of Balaam's machinations, it is impossible to determine whether this 'foreign' source material became part of the sacred record under Moses' supervision. Numbers 22:4b, which says, **Balak . . . was king of the Moabites at that time,** points to the work of post-Mosaic scribes. The story, then, may have been inserted here, where it fits chronologically and at the same time provides a literary hinge for turning from the old generation to the new, and to a new census and new legislation pointed toward settlement in the land.

Some commentators attempt to reduce the prominence of Balaam, the man, in this story (ICC, p. 316; followed by IB, Vol. 2. pp. 248-263) and to see in it only the larger religio-political concepts of the culture represented. But Balaam is such an integral, strongly etched character that one cannot really appreciate the story without seeking to understand him. Certainly the purpose of the narrative is to show how God protected his people from the evil designs of a pagan monarch and the hidden lusting of an errant prophet. But Balaam's subtle deeds and powerful words make the story a dramatic masterpiece.

Fear was instilled in the heart of Balak, king of Moab, because of Israel's defeat of the Amorites. He sent for Balaam, a popular prophet from northern Mesopotamia, promising him fame and substance in exchange for cursing Israel. Balaam was told by the Lord not to go, and so he refused. When King Balak made greater promises, however, the prophet sought a change of the Lord's mind. The Lord therefore permitted Balaam to set out for Moab. On the way, God sought, through an angel, to communicate to the prophet his displeasure with him. But only Balaam's ass saw the angel of the Lord. The ass eventually spoke and rebuked Balaam for his spiritual blindness. Then the prophet's eyes were opened to see the angel. The Lord permitted Balaam to go on to Moab so that he might openly declare God's purpose to fulfill His ancient promise to Israel. Balak showed Balaam the camp of Israel from three different vantage points in succession, and at each point the prophet uttered a *blessing* on Israel. Balak, in disgust, told Balaam to speak no more. But the prophet continued with even more oracles, in which he predicted not only the future prosperity and power of Israel as a nation, but also the destruction of Moab, Edom, Amalek, the Kenites, and Asshur.

I. Balak's Failure To Turn the Lord from Israel. 22:2–24:25.

A. Balaam Summoned by Balak. 22:2-40.

4. Balak the son of Zippor was king of the Moabites at that time. As a post-Mosaic reference, either the single sentence was added, or it reflects the fact that the whole account was inserted in post-Mosaic times (see above).

5. Pethor, which is by the river of the land of the children of his people. The ICC claims that some editor has confused two different places from a compilation of several stories. The river is the Euphrates; the land is called *'Ăram of the two rivers* in Deut 23:4. This area was just as much the land of the ancestors of Moab through Lot (Gen 19:37) as it was the land of the ancestors of Israel through Abraham. Haran, Lot's father, died in the land of his nativity, in Ur of the Chaldees (Gen 11:28). Some evidence indicates that Ur was possibly a northern Mesopotamian city rather than the ancient Sumerian city of southern Mesopotamia (JNES, XVII, 1958, pp. 28-31, 252). The worship of the Lord by Abraham's family continued, but Lot's descendants, the Moabites and Ammonites, adopted the gods of the people among whom they settled. That there was a prophet of the Lord in the area called *'Ăram Nahărayîm* (Gen 24:10), fits the total Biblical picture.

6. For I wot that he whom thou blessest is blessed. Balaam was apparently a popular prophet and also a prophet of the Lord (Jehovah). Balak therefore sent "fees of divination" (v. 7), with hopes that such a combination of talents would be effective against Israel. Whether Balaam was a true prophet gone astray or a false prophet overpowered by God cannot be known for sure. The comments on him from other places in the OT and NT are consistently derogatory (Num 31:8,16; Deut 23:5,6; Josh 13:22; 24:9; Neh 13:2; II Pet 2:13-15; Jude 11; Rev 2:14). Though some writers have put forth the weak argument that God in Mic 6:5 speaks well of Balaam, really the Lord there speaks well only of His own blessing of Israel through the unfaithful prophet and makes no comment on Balaam's character. In Josh 13:22 Balaam is called a soothsayer *(haqqōsēm)*, and soothsaying was an abomination to the Lord (Deut 18:10). We might compare this prophet with Simon Magus (Acts 8:13-24), a confused believer who sought to combine soothsaying and the power of the Holy Spirit. Numbers 24:1 informs us that Balaam resorted to auguries *(nᵉhāshîm)*.

7. The rewards of divination in their hand. The story shows a marked distinction between the heathen concept that the prophet was a manipulator of the gods and the Hebrew idea that God was a sovereign Determiner of all that came to pass, "who blesses whom he will bless and curses whom he will curse" (v. 6). **18. If Balak would give me his house full of silver and gold, I cannot go beyond the word of the Lord.** Though these were great words, they belied his heart (cf. v. 18). God had spoken, but Balaam was hoping for some change that would make it possible for him to go. And God did allow him to go, to show in a dramatic way His sovereign choice to bless Israel.

22. God's anger was kindled because he went. The use of a participle in the Hebrew suggests the translation, "God's anger was kindled as he was going." Though God had granted Balaam's wish that he might go, His anger arose because the prophet's heart was swayed by his love of "the wages of unrighteousness" (II Pet 2:15). **25. And crushed Balaam's foot against the wall.** The crushing of his foot may be reflected in the word *shepî* (23:3), which, it has been suggested, may come from an Akkadian root, *shēpu*, meaning "with hindered step." The AV renders *shepî*, "a bare height," and the RSV reads, "a high place" (23:3).

28. The Lord opened the mouth of the ass. Did the ass give forth audible sound, or was this merely an experience in the mind of Balaam? The truth is probably to be found on both sides. While the appearance of the angel and the voice of the ass were not hallucinations, it seems that they were seen and heard by Balaam only and not by the others who were present – as was the case several times in the New Testament (Acts 9:7; 22:9; Jn 12:28,29). On the road to Damascus there were physical phenomena which only Paul understood; so Balaam, because of a combination of mental and spiritual distractions, could not see the angel until God opened his eyes. Nor could others have understood the ass unless God had given them this ability.

35. Go with the men. As in 22:20, God told Balaam to go. He was not, therefore, angry because the prophet went but because of his motive for going. Men cannot easily determine the motives of others, but God can. We have the divine commentary in the rest of Scripture to guide us, and Num 31:16 proves that Balaam was reprobate. In addition, the story cannot be understood otherwise, unless we adopt the dubious expedient of claiming that the account is a piecing together of several different stories (cf. ICC).

38. Have I now any power at all to say anything? the word that God putteth in my mouth, that shall I speak. Balaam had not told the Moabites of God's revealed intention to bless Israel. And so the best that can be said for this reply is that it is ambiguous, probably because Balaam was hoping for God to change His mind. Balak assumed, therefore, that Balaam's coming indicated his willingness to curse Israel.

B. The Oracles of Balaam. 22:41–24:25.

Outstanding Semitic linguists see in this poetry a reflection of the Age of Moses. The form of language, the subject matter, technical terms, and proper names all tend to support the view that these are authentic utterances from a poet of the mid-second millenium. Balaam calls each poem a *māshāl*, translated "parable" in 23:7,18; 24:3,15. *Māshāl* cannot be limited to either parable or proverb; rather, it is so broad that it applies to all "Wisdom" literature. Hebrew poetry has as its main feature parallelism of thoughts, lines, and stanzas, in appositional, oppositional, or progressive form. The Balaam oracles display all this, and in addition they have an archaic and often Aramaic flavor, which points to the antiquity and origin (from Aram) of the character who speaks. William F. Albright, who has done definitive, scholarly work on these oracles, says, "There is nothing in the matter of the poems which requires a date in the tenth century or later for original composition" (JBL, Sept., 1944, p. 227). He observes that Balaam's name is characteristic of the second millennium B.C. (2000–1000), and that it has survived in several places, all of which go back to the fifteenth century. Then he states that Balaam was really "a north Syrian diviner from the Euphrates Valley," who "spent some time at the Moabite court . . . became a convert to Yahwehism," and "later abandoned Israel and joined the Midianites in fighting against the Yahwists (Num 31:8,16)" (JBL, Sept., 1944, pp. 232,233). Adequate treatment of the poems would be impossible here. Therefore we offer a private translation which, it is hoped, will clarify some points and illustrate the poetic structure.

First Oracle. 23:7-10.

The poem contains a 1-2-1-2-1 pattern of parallel couplets. The last couplet is a conclusion, expressing the nostalgic thought that Balaam would like to share in Israel's blessing.

7. "From Aram Balak brought me,
The king of Moab from the hills of the east.
'Go, curse for me Jacob,
Go, denounce Israel.'
8. How shall I curse when God has not cursed?
How shall I denounce when God has not denounced?
9. For from the top of the mountains I see,
From hills I do observe.
Lo, a people who dwell alone,
Among the nations they are not reckoned.
10. Who can count the dust of Jacob,
Or number the 'dust' cloud of Israel?
Let me die the death of a just man,
Let my end be like his!"

Second Oracle. 23:18-24.

Balaam here sees the Lord as the One who forces him to bless Israel because He must bring to pass His promised word. The Lord is the source of His people's strength; so no incantation can be effective against them. Balaam concludes by likening Israel to a stalking lion, that catches and devours its prey. In the phrase, **shout of a king (v. 21)**, we follow the LXX, the Targum of Onkelos, and the Samaritan Pentateuch, and translate *royal majesty*.

Introduction

18. "Arise, O Balak, and hearken;
Hear my testimony, O Son of Zippor.

Stanza 1

19. God is not a man, that he should lie,
Nor a human being, that he should repent.
That which he says, will he not do?
That which he decrees, will he not bring to pass?
20. Behold I have learned to bless,
And bless I will, for I cannot do otherwise.
21. Iniquity is not seen in Jacob,
Nor is perverseness evident in Israel.

Stanza 2

The Lord his God is with him,
And royal majesty accompanies him.
22. When God was bringing him out of Egypt,
He had the strength of a wild ox.
23. For there can be no omen against Jacob,
Nor incantation against Israel.
Now it shall be said of Jacob,
Even concerning Israel, 'What has God done!'

Conclusion

24. Lo, a people that arises like a lioness,
Who exalts himself like a lion,
Which does not lie down until it devours the prey,
And licks the blood of the slain."

Third Oracle. 24:2-9.

The two main stanzas of this poem contrast Israel at peace and at war. Among the peoples of the ancient Near East this was a favorite way of depicting a nation. The peace and war standards from the Royal Tombs of Ur (J. Finegan, *Light From the Ancient Past*, Fig. 16) effectively illustrate this custom. The poem also shows symmetry in its opening and closing parallel couplets, which are the only lines using the pronoun "thee" concerning Israel. Though the couplet that ends the first stanza is admittedly difficult, it is clear to this writer that it refers to the boughs of the trees mentioned in the preceding verses. Ezekiel 31 uses the same figure ("the cedar" is Assyria) and the same root, *dālâ*, in reference to boughs of the cedar that grows beside many waters. In Ezk 19 Israel is "a vine beside many waters" and "a devouring lion." The first couplet of the second stanza of this oracle is not found in our Hebrew text but comes from the LXX. It may represent a family of Hebrew manuscripts behind the LXX text that preserved this verse but lost the preceding couplet. This couplet provides a transition between the peace and war stanzas.

Stanza 1

5. "How fair are thy tents, O Jacob,
Thy dwellings, O Israel.
6. Like river valleys that stretch out,
Like gardens beside a river.
Like aloes which the Lord planted,
Like cedars beside the waters.
7. With dew dropping from their boughs,
With their seed being among many waters.

Stanza 2

A man shall proceed from his seed,
And he shall be lord of many nations.
And his kingdom shall be higher than Agag's,
And his dominion shall be exalted.
8. For when God was bringing him from Egypt,
He had the strength of a wild ox.
The nations, his adversaries, he will devour,
Their bones he will break in pieces,
And with his arrows smite through.
9. He crouches, he lies down,
Like a lion, like a young lion.
Who can raise him up?

Conclusion

Blessed is the one blessing thee,
The one cursing thee is accursed."

Fourth Oracle. 24:15-19.

Balaam introduces himself (st. 1) with the same words he used in 24:3,4. The translation of the last words of the opening couplet, "who is true of eye," is upheld by a Phoenician incantation text that uses a similar idiom (Albright, JBL, Sept., 1944). King David is here predicted as that star of Jacob which would crush both Moab and Edom. The translation of the last line as a "remnant of Seir" involves a slight emendation of the text, which the context favors.

Stanza 1

15. "The oracle of Balaam son of Beor,
The oracle of the man who is true of eye.
16. The oracle of the one hearing the words of El,
The one knowing the knowledge of Elyon.
The one being made to see what Shaddai sees,
The one falling and opened of eye.

Stanza 2

17. I see it, but not now,
I behold it, but not nigh.
The star of Jacob shall rule,
The scepter of Israel shall arise,
And shall crush the forehead of Moab,
And tear down the pate of the sons of Sheth.
18. And Edom shall be dispossessed,
Even dispossessed is Seir by his enemies.
19. But Israel shall do mightily;
Dominion shall be exercised by Jacob,
And the remnant of Seir shall he destroy."

Fifth Oracle. 24:20.

The destruction of the Amalekites was particularly a Davidic feat.

Then he saw Amalek . . . and said,
"The first of the nations is Amalek,
But his latter end is eternal destruction."

Sixth Oracle. 24:21,22.

As Albright points out (JBL, 1944, Vol. 63, No. 3, p. 227), the only time the Kenites (metalsmiths) were an autonomous people was in the Mosaic Age, so that the oracle could not have come from the tenth century, as suggested by many. Asshur (v. 22) was the name of an Arab tribe that lived in the same area as the Kenites (cf. Gen 25:3); but it is also the name for the Assyrians. The latter had no contact with the Kenites as a distinct people. A switching of two letters in the word *burned* (AV **wasted**) would make the line read, "Kain (the Kenite) shall belong to *'ēber* ('the Hebrew')." The Kenites were indeed assimilated into Israel, and as part of northern Israel (Jud 4:17; 5:24) were taken into captivity by the Assyrians in 722. However, W. F. Albright takes "Asshur" as a verb, "I gaze"; but this makes little sense even with an emendation.

Then he saw the Kenite and . . . said,
"Enduring is your dwelling place;
Your nest is set in the rock.
Nevertheless Kain (the Kenite) will be burned,
Until Asshur shall take you away captive."

Seventh Oracle. 24:23,24.

We follow Albright in part in the translation of this difficult passage. In the first line we prefer the Aramaic word *ḥayâ*, "to show or make known," to a similar Arabic root meaning "to gather." Albright says the passage refers to the irruption of Mediterranean peoples that brought the Philistines from the Aegean isles into the land of Canaan in stages during the second millennium. The question again arises, Is Asshur the distant Assyrians, or possibly just an Arab tribe related to the Midianites through Abraham's wife Keturah? The latter would fit the view that Balaam was speaking about the early sea peoples from the Aegean world. The former view is variously interpreted to mean (1) Asshur (Syria) of the Seleucids; or (2) Asshur as Persia, and "ships from Kittim" as Alexander the Great (cf. I Macc 1:1).

23. And he took up his parable and said,
"Isles which are known on the side of the north,
24. Even ships from the coast of Kittim,
They shall afflict Asshur,
Even shall afflict his quarter (or, *'ēber*, 'the Hebrew')
And he also shall perish."

II. Balak's Success in Turning Israel from the Lord. 25:1-18.

Numbers 31:16 shows that Balaam, who could not turn God away from the people, succeeded in turning some of the people away from God. The New Testament speaks of "the way of Balaam" (II Pet 2:15), meaning his love of "the wages of unrighteousness" (cf. Num 22–24); and "the doctrine of Balaam" (Rev 2:14), referring to this incident.

A. The Baal-peor Sin. 25:1-5.

2. They called the people unto the sacrifices of their gods. The subject **they** is feminine, referring to the daughters of Moab, with whom the men of Israel committed fornication. Balak, with Balaam's advice (Rev 2:14), used this method to weaken Israel. **3. Joined himself unto Baal-peor.** Possibly Baal of Beth-peor (Deut 3:29; 4:46). In the Baal cult, spring festivals dramatized, in act, the mating of Baal with the goddess of fertility. Archaeological discoveries have revealed that the devotees of Baal practiced prostitution as a part of their worship. This sordid practice was adopted by the Israelites. Legislation against male and female prostitution is given in Deut 23:17. **4. Take all the heads of the people.** Summon the elders to perform judgment. **And hang them up.** That is, the fornicators. The verb is somewhat obscure. It may mean "to slay them." **Before the sun** (ASV) means "openly."

B. Zeal of Phinehas. 25:6-18.

8. He went after the man . . . into the tent. The rare term *qūbbâ*, meaning "vaulted tent," designates the bedchamber where Phinehas caught them in the act (Delitzsch).

11. While he was zealous for my sake. Literally, *zealous with my zeal*. Phinehas had championed God's zealous hatred of sin. Such perfect hatred of sin is behind all the "difficult" plagues and imprecations of the Bible. **13. An everlasting priesthood.** Because of this **covenant of peace** (v. 12), the descendants of Phinehas would become the high priests of Israel (cf. I Sam 14:3; 22:11,20). They continued so throughout the history of the Tabernacle and the Temple.

14. A chief house. The house of a father (AV, marg.), as used in 1:2, and elsewhere, means a subdivision of a tribe. **15. Cozbi, the daughter of Zur.** This man is listed as one of the five kings of Midian. Here he is called "head of a clan." **17. Vex the Midianites.** Slaying of a king's daughter could only mean war. God reminded Israel that they had a righteous reason to be at war with Midian. The Midianites and Moabites were confederates in opposing God's chosen people, both in the hiring of Balaam

(22:4) and in this **matter of Peor** (v. 18).

Part Three. Preparation for Entering the Land. 26:1–36:13.

From this point to the end of Numbers 36, the subject matter is directly connected with Israel's entry into the promised land, a new mustering of the warriors (ch. 26), problems of inheritance by daughters, and the consecration of a successor to Moses (ch. 27), the dividing of the land and various directions for settlement of the land (chs. 32; 34) and the establishment of the Levitical cities (ch. 35).

I. Second Census in the Plains of Moab. 26:1-65.

5. Reuben, the eldest son of Israel. This census, in contrast to the one at Sinai, lists the families of the different tribes with their inheritance in view (cf. Gen 46). **11. The children of Korah died not.** Not all the family of Korah were destroyed. Probably Korah had grown sons, with households of their own, who did not have to share their father's judgment (cf. comment on ch. 16). Some of the sons of Korah became famous in Israel. The prophet Samuel and the singer Heman were among them (I Chr 6:33-37; cf. Ps 88, the title).

51. Six hundred thousand and a thousand seven hundred and thirty. Israel multiplied phenomenally in Egypt (Ex 1:20). Why then, after thirty-eight years of wilderness wandering, did the nation remain approximately the same number as when at Sinai. The answer lies in verses 64,65, which show that only three out of an original 603,550 (Num 2:32) remained alive. Also Israel had been through several serious plagues in this period, the last of which took 29,000 lives. **53. Unto these the land shall be divided.** In addition to supplying information for military purposes, this census was also to provide a basis for dividing the land. The larger tribes were to inherit more land and the smaller less, with the actual placing of tribes to be decided by lot (26:54-56; 33:54).

59. Amram's wife was Jochebed, the daughter of Levi . . . and she bare unto Amram Aaron and Moses, and Miriam. Some suggest that Amram and Jochebed were progenitors but not father and mother of Moses. They say that the genealogy of Kohath, Amram, and Moses is too short for there to have been 8,600 Kohathites (3:27,28) in Moses' day from a month old upward. However, if Moses' father had children by other wives and his uncles each had children by several wives, all of whom had begun another generation (Moses being eighty before he left Egypt), then 8,600 cousins of Moses' age, along with second and third cousins down to those a month old, would not be an unreasonable number to expect.

II. The Law of Inheritance. 27:1-11.

4. Give unto us therefore a possession among the brethren of our father. The Manassite Zelophehad had five daughters and no sons. These daughters pointed out that if they, as daughters, could not inherit land, then their father's inheritance would be lost. God confirmed to Moses the well-known provision by which daughters might inherit land (Josh 17:3-6). But the next in line of inheritance were to be paternal brothers of the deceased, then paternal uncles, and then the nearest kinsman. However, the daughters were to be free to marry, and their children would continue their father's genealogy and inherit his land. Thus was Jair in the line of Manasseh in 32:41 and Deut 3:14 (cf. also I Chr 2:34,35). Similar to this was the law of levirate marriage, by which a widow without children married the nearest kin of her husband, that his name and inheritance might not be cut off. Both of these laws were based on the principle that the land which the Lord gave to a family should never be sold or allowed to pass out of that family (Lev 25:23). The custom of inalienable property is now known to have been in practice long before the time of Moses, as the false adoptions at Nuzu testify (C. H. Gordon, *Old Testament Times,* p. 101). The Hebrews usually followed their ancestral tradition by which an inheritance passed from father to sons (Deut 25:5-10). But in Egypt, where they had spent many years, inheritance passed through mothers. Under an extenuating circumstance, that is what is being allowed in the text.

III. Appointment of Moses' Successor. 27:12-23.

12. Get thee up into this mount Abarim. Abarim was the name of the range that abuts on the geologic cleft which forms the Jordan Valley and the Salt Sea (Num 33:47,48). A part of this range, called Mount Pisgah, had a peak called Nebo, where Moses eventually died (Deut 34:1). Probably the town called Nebo (Num 32:38) gave its name to this prominence. It is evident that in 32:1 the city Jazer gave its name to its area, and for the same reason the people of Tyre were sometimes called Sidonians.

16. The God of the spirits of all flesh. See note on 16:22. **17. Which may go out . . . and . . . in before them.** Hebrew frequently uses antonyms to express totality. Joshua would be the man who could see them through everything. **That the congregation of the Lord be not as sheep which have no shepherd.** Moses had just been reminded that he would not enter the land because of his sin over "the waters of Meribah" in Kadesh. But Moses' spirit was like that of Christ, who without self-pity, though rejected and facing Calvary, was moved with compassion for the multitude and saw them as sheep having no shepherd (Mt 9:36).

18. Take thee Joshua . . . a man in whom is the spirit. The word **spirit** has no article in Hebrew. Though the primary reference here is to Joshua's capacity, he also received divine endowment. The Bible says he "was full of the spirit of wisdom; for Moses had laid his hands upon him" (Deut 34:9). **Lay thine hand upon him.** The laying on of hands as a symbol of the conferring of authority or the imputing of responsibility is ancient Biblical practice. Jacob followed this custom when conveying blessing on Joseph's sons (Gen 48:14). The people of Israel transferred their responsibility by laying hands on the Levites (Num 8:10), and the Levites referred their own guilt to the atonement bullocks by laying on of hands (8:12). The practice was continued in the synagogue and adopted by the apostles (Acts 6:6; I Tim 4:14).

19. Give him a charge in their sight. The Hebrew says *command him.* The command was to all the people as well as to Joshua (see Deut 31). **20. Thou shalt put some of thine honour upon him, that all the congregation . . . may be obedient.** This **honor** was the authority Joshua needed in order to have the respect of the people as their leader. **21. He shall stand before Eleazar . . . who shall ask counsel for him after the judgment of Urim.** Joshua's authority was not to be equal to that of Moses, whose communion with the Lord was direct (Num 7:89; 12:7,8). Joshua would depend upon the use of the *Urim* and *Thummim* (Ex 28:30) by Eleazar the priest. We do not know, today, how the priest used this means of determining God's will.

IV. Third Priestly Scroll. 28:1–29:40.

The two chapters of Num 28; 29, like Lev 23, give the whole ritual year in outline. But here the quantities of offerings are in view, looking forward to Israel's settlement in the land. The months are numbered, and the year is further divided by the observance of a festival at the opening of the seventh month (Num 29:1). The early Hebrew religious calendar was controlled by respect for the agricultural seasons, as is seen from the name of the month Abib, "the first ripe barley" (Ex 13:4), and from the tenth century Israelite tablet, the Gezer Calendar (G. E. Wright, *Biblical Archaeology,* pp. 180,181). Such dependence on solar seasons (Deut 16:9) kept the calendar of the Israelites from revolving, as does the Arab religious calendar today, for the Hebrews put in an extra month when necessary. In these chapters the months (the new moons) are marked by the blowing of silver trumpets, providing a practical means to carry out the ritual year here prescribed. In their rustic simplicity the Hebrews avoided the complicated problems of the Egyptian 365-day calendar, based on observation of stars, which, though sophisticated, was also one-quarter of a day off, and in due time reversed the calendar in relation to the seasons. On the other hand, the Hebrews seem to have borrowed the Egyptian system of numbering the months, while most Semites named their months. Israel did not do this officially, however, until after the Exile, when they adopted the Babylonian designations.

A. Introduction. 28:1,2.

2. My bread for my sacrifices made by fire. God's food here referred to was not that which the priests received as their due, but rather the food that went up in smoke at the fire offerings. The thought is that God eats and drinks with his worshipers, which, far from being a primitive notion, is carried over into the NT in the parallel ordinance of the Lord's table, the Communion.

B. Daily Offerings. 28:3-8.

5. An ephah of flour . . . an hin of beaten oil. The flour was *sōlet,* a fine flour, and the oil was from beaten or crushed olives, very expensive, though prescribed at Sinai and repeated here because the items were specifically for those living a settled life in the land.

C. Sabbath Offerings. 28:9,10.

10. Beside the continual burnt offering. The offerings were cumulative, the Sabbath offering being added to the daily offering, and so on with the rest throughout these two chapters.

D. Monthly Offerings. 28:11-15.

11. In the beginnings of your months (new moons). Since the quantities of offerings is the point stressed, the directions for the blowing of silver trumpets (cf. 10:10) are omitted, though stressed as part of the religious festival in the beginning of the seventh month (29:1). According to 10:10, the trumpets were regularly blown at the new moons. The custom was possibly designed to have civil as well as religious significance for the people. **15. One kid of the goats for a sin offering.** A sin offering was added to care for sins that had not been atoned for during that month.

E. Yearly Offerings. 28:16–29:40.

1) Feast of Unleavened Bread. 28:16-25.

16. The fourteenth day of the first month is the passover. No offering is specified for the Passover, because these instructions are for offerings by the priests. The Passover lamb ceremony was a family affair (Ex 12:3-14,21,22). **17. In the fifteenth day . . . is the feast.** The Feast of Unleavened Bread *(maṣṣôt)* was to be kept from the fifteenth to the twenty-first of the first month (Ex 12:15-17). The first and seventh days were to be sabbaths, when no "servile" work was to be done (Num 28:18,25).

24. The meat (food) **of the sacrifice made by fire . . . shall be offered beside the continual burnt offering.** In addition to the daily offerings, these special ones were to be offered each day of the feast.

2) Feast of Weeks. 28:26-31.

26. When ye bring a new meat (cereal) **offering . . . unto the Lord, after your weeks be out.** Leviticus 23:16 gives the key to understanding these words. On the day following the seven sabbaths after the Feast of Unleavened Bread *(Pentecost,* Gr., "fiftieth day"), the people were to offer a cereal offering of the first fruits. The feast sacrifices to be presented at this time were the same as those offered at the time of unleavened bread. **29. A several tenth deal unto one lamb.** A tenth of an ephah was to be offered along with each lamb. (See the same expression in vv. 13,21).

3) Feast of Trumpets. 29:1-6.

1. In the seventh month, on the first day . . . ye shall have an holy convocation. The new moon of the seventh month was a day of accumulated sacrifices, including the daily sacrifices, the regular new moon sacrifices, plus those that marked the beginning of the second half of the year (cf. Lev 23:24).

4) Day of Atonement. 29:7-11.

7. On the tenth day of this seventh month . . . ye shall afflict your souls. Special mention is made of repentance and soul-searching on this high day when the priest entered within the veil to make atonement for himself and all the people (Lev 16:29-34; 23:26-32).

5) Feast of Tabernacles. 29:12-40.

12. On the fifteenth day of the seventh month . . . ye shall keep a feast. This feast was the climax of the religious year. The attention paid to the offering of bullocks each day indicates the importance of the feast. Seventy bullocks in all were offered, beginning with thirteen on the first day, twelve on the second, and so on, down to seven on the seventh day. Then followed an eighth day sabbath of offerings. All this was in addition to the regular daily offerings. As in the case of the monthly blowing of trumpets (10:10), it is assumed here that such details as dwelling in booths are well known (Lev 23:40-44). Animal sacrifices were multiplied at this season because it was a "feast" *(ḥag)* not a "fast." Except for the Passover and the Day of Atonement, when there was afflicting of souls, the people were in festival mood on their special days. Though some sin offerings were always prescribed, most of these offerings were consecration and thanksgiving offerings.

39. Beside your vows, and your freewill offerings. In addition to presenting the prescribed offerings, the people were always encouraged to take vows of consecration (Num 6) and to make voluntary offerings in gratitude to God for his bounteous provision.

V. The Validity of Women's Vows. 30:1-16.

Every culture devises ways of making human intention binding. In civil matters the Bible world used both the signed document and sworn testimony (oaths). In religious matters people made vows. The unspoken intention was made binding when embodied in speech. Laws regulating vows are taken up in Deut 23; Lev 27; and Num 6; but here special emphasis is laid on the validation of a woman's vow. The Lord directed that a woman's father or her husband was to invalidate her vows if he felt that she was not to be held responsible. He could uphold her vow by his silence or make it invalid by his veto. A father was to have absolute authority over an unmarried daughter in such matters, and a husband over a wife. Women were largely untaught concerning the details of religious ceremony and therefore could make rash pledges (see note on v. 6) or vows harmful to their husbands' households. A disaffected wife might purposely make a vow or pledge that would injure her husband. So his legal ability to invalidate his wife's oath protected his estate, since a vow might include the payment of a large sum. If the vow was the kind that placed an affliction or prohibition on the wife, the husband was free to validate the vow and so share this burden, or to veto it.

5. If her father disallow her. One of the verbs used to express invalidation of a woman's vow is *henî*, "to hinder, restrain, or frustrate." The root, though rare, is used mostly in Numbers and appears in 14:34 (see note), where we are told that, for forty years, God frustrated, or restrained, Israel from entering into the promised land. The same root is also used to describe what the spies did in "discouraging the hearts of the people" (32:7,9). Here in Numbers 30 provision is made for a daughter to be forgiven if she is hindered by her father in fulfilling her vow; and for a husband to "frustrate" the intention of his wife for the good of his household.

6. Or uttered ought out of her lips. The force of this clause is "a rash utterance from her lips." Moses spoke thus rashly at the waters of Meribah (Ps 106:32, 33).

15. If he . . . make them void . . . he shall bear her iniquity. To fail to keep a vow was a sin. If a husband did invalidate his wife's vow, he was to bear her iniquity. That is, he was to meet all ceremonial and legal requirements as if the sin were his own.

VI. War with Midian. 31:1-54.

The Lord commanded the destruction of the Midianites because they were the vile people responsible for the Baal-peor orgy (ch. 25). For light on the degradation of Canaanite worship, see G. E. Wright, *Biblical Archaeology*, pp. 111-119). When the Hebrew warriors returned from the battle, with the Midianite women and children as captives, Moses reminded them that these were the very women of Baal-peor, and that they were morally debased and must die. This seems a cruel judgment, but it was the lesser of two evils. The alternative was to allow the Midianites to live and corrupt Israel, which would have compounded human suffering as well as brought dishonor to God. The Midianite male children were also slain, for if they had been reared among the children of Israel, they would have destroyed the inheritance of Israel's sons. The only ones saved alive were the virgin girls, who could be assimilated into Israel. In later years the same principle was applied in those cases in which non-Israelite women (but never men) became a part of the Messianic line (e.g., Rahab and Ruth).

Nothing is told of the actual fighting with Midian, which indicates that the central purpose of this lengthy chapter is to set forth the law relative to the booty and captives of war. Otherwise the defeat of Midian might have been mentioned in a few verses (cf. the treatment of the victories over Arad, Sihon, and Og; Num 21). This law specified that all booty was to be purified, either by fire or with "the water for impurity" (31:23, ASV; 19:9). Half of the spoil (of captives and animals) was to go to the men of war, and the other half to those who remained behind. Then one five-hundredth of the soldiers' half was to be given to the priests as an offering to the Lord. One fiftieth of that belonging to the rest of the congregation was to be given to the Levites. After the defeat of Midian, the soldiers made a special offering of gold and jewels they had taken. This they turned over to the sanctuary "to make an atonement" for their "souls."

A. Destruction of Midian. 31:1-18.

3. Avenge the Lord of Midian. To **avenge** is "to visit just or merited punishment on a wrongdoer" (Webster). The Lord called on Israel to visit such punishment on Midian. This commandment, however, is no justification for any of the holy wars of the Christian era for the simple reason that in this era there has been no Moses to learn through revelation just when and where the sovereign God wills to avenge himself. **6. Phinehas . . . to the war, with the holy instruments, and the trumpets . . . in his hand.** This use of the Urim and trumpets by the priest in battle (27:21; I Sam 28:6), the unique names of the five kings of Midian (Num 31:8; Jud 21:12), and the taking of the Midianite virgins as wives are all details that run counter to the view advanced by some that the chapter is late Midrash and therefore has little historical value (ICC, p. 418). **17. Kill every male among the little ones.** The Lord, not Moses, bears the responsibility for this slaughter. Had not God described himself as one "visiting the iniquity of the fathers upon the children unto the third and fourth generation of them that hate me"? (Ex 20:5) Refusal to reckon with the prerogative of a righteous Sovereign to judge sin reduces him to something less than sinful man.

B. Purification of Warriors. 31:19-24.

23. Every thing that may abide the fire. In this provision the Lord differentiated between those things that could be purified by fire (metals) and those that could not (people and wooden articles). Everything that could not, including the warriors and their captives, had to be purified with "the water for impurity" made with the ashes of a red heifer according to the law of chapter 19.

C. Dividing the Spoils of War. 31:25-54.

30. One portion of fifty . . . unto the Levites. The Lord required that one five-hundreth of the warriors' half be assigned to the priests as their portion (v. 28). Here one fiftieth of the people's half is designated for the Levites. Multiples of five, it seems, prevailed for tax purposes in the Semitic world. Joseph set up a law in Egypt taxing the Egyptians one-fifth of their yield (Gen 47:26). **32. Six hundred thousand . . . . sheep.** It is claimed that these numbers are too high to be authentic. The census in chapter 1 and that in 26 numbered over 600,000 fighting men in Israel's army. Compare with this David's census of 800,000 fighting men for Israel and 500,000 fighting men for Judah (II Sam 24:9). It is not logical for critics to take David's census seriously but assume that the Mosaic figures are unreliable. The Egyptian culture behind Moses was even more sophisticated than that behind David. There is no evidence to prove that Moses' figures are not correct.

VII. Settlement of Two and One-Half Tribes in Trans-Jordan. 32:1-42.

Reuben and Gad, who had much cattle, seeing that the lands of Jazer and Gilead were good for grazing, asked Moses if they might live there. Moses feared that the settling of two tribes on the east of Jordan might break the morale of the people, as "the evil report" of the spies had done thirty-seven years earlier. He reminded them of the tragic result of their fathers' unbelief at Kadesh. If they now, in turn, he said, avoided facing the enemy, it would bring similar results, and the nation would be destroyed. Reuben and Gad took this advice and willingly offered to fight with their brethren until all were settled in their inheritance, and then return to their homes. To this Moses agreed, with a final warning that to do less would constitute sin. And he added, "Be sure your sin will find you out" (v. 23). The two tribes promised to do as Moses commanded (v. 25). So Reuben, Gad, and half the tribe of Manasseh were given numerous cities in Trans-Jordan. They rebuilt and renamed the cities and provided walled enclosures for their cattle.

A. Moses' Response to Gad's and Reuben's Request. 32:1-33.

1. A very great multitude of cattle. Much of this was cattle that had been acquired through conquest (ch. 31). However, Israel had previously had some cattle in the wilderness, which was not all barren (cf. 20:19). **The land of Jazer, and the land of Gilead.** Jazer was on the border of Ammonite territory (see v. 32; cf. LXX, Num 21:24). Trans-Jordan was divided into two parts, north and south of the river Jabbok

(Josh 12:2). **4. Even the country which the Lord smote.** The land is described not by nonexistent borders but by fortified cities (v. 3) which controlled certain areas. The figure of the Lord smiting the country reminds us of similar figures in the Book of the Wars of the Lord (21:14), which, like the great epic poems, Ex 15, Ps 68, and Hab 3, describes the Lord as a heroic warrior who founds or saves a nation. The same figure is dominant in the apocalyptic literature of the Bible, which describes the Lord's bringing the nation to its ultimate goal (cf. Isa 9:6 – *'El gībbôr,* "the mighty hero").

7. Wherefore discourage ye the heart of the children of Israel. Moses was afraid their proposal might start a wave of complacency among the other tribes, who had yet to face the terrors of an unknown enemy. If a few rested on the laurels of past victory, would not all the others want to do the same? As a leader facing a problem of morale, Moses was justified in this stern treatment of the two tribes. Moses' choice of a verb reminds them of God's rebuke in 14:34 (cf. commentary); and his words stress that incident lest they again fail **wholly** to follow the Lord (32:11-13). The geographic separation of these tribes beyond Jordan eventually produced in them an indifference toward the welfare of the nation that Deborah, in her song, held up to scorn (Jud 5:16,17). Time proved that Moses' fears were well founded.

27. Every man armed for war. The root *ḥālaṣ,* "to gird for battle," is used in 32:17,20,21,27,30, and in 31:3. The hero's belt, *ḥălîṣâ,* with which he girded himself, was standard equipment for every warrior. See II Sam 2:21 (armor-belt) and Jud 14:19 (spoil-belts), which indicate that the stripping off of this girdle from a foe was the symbol of victory over him. Soldier's belts or "girdles" were such commonly accepted pieces of their equipment that in ancient Semitic, Egyptian, and Greek art, not only human but even divine heroes are shown wearing them. In keeping with this custom, the Messiah wears "righteousness as the belt of his waist and faithfulness the belt of his loins" (Isa 11:5). (See C. H. Gordon, "Belt Wrestling in the Bible World," *Hebrew Union College Annual,* Vol. XXIII, p. 131).

30. But if they will not pass over with you armed, they shall have possessions among you in the land of Canaan. In order to secure their possession in Trans-Jordan, they had to be girded for war in the presence of God as Israel crossed the Jordan, thus proving they believed God's promise regarding the land and were willing to trust him for ultimate victory. The tribes that chose to live east of Jordan assisted in the conquest of Canaan, then returned to their own inheritance.

B. Cities Rebuilt by Reuben and Gad. 32:34-38.

34-36. And the children of Gad built . . . fenced cities: and folds for sheep. That is, they rebuilt on top of ruins or simply took over and added to the captured cities. Many of these cities are named in the famous inscription of King Mesha of Moab, dating about 835, where the king of Moab says that "the men of Gad dwelt in the land of Ataroth," etc. The sheepfolds were rough stone enclosures such as are used to this day in the area (cf. Jn 10:1-18).

38. Nebo, and Baal-meon (their names being changed). Nebo may have been named after a Babylonian deity by the same name, while Baal was a popular god of the Canaanite pantheon. The Israelites reacted against giving pagan deities recognition in their own personal and place names. Scribes of later times often changed names that had contained the name of a pagan deity (e.g., in I Chr 8:33,34 two of Saul's sons are called Esh-baal and Merib-baal; in II Sam 4:4,8 they are Ish-bosheth and Mephibosheth).

C. Gilead taken by Manassites. 32: 39-42.

41. And took the small towns thereof, and called them Havoth-jair. The term *havvôt,* translated **small towns,** means "tent villages"; but this only shows that they were at one time such, for Jud 10:4 numbers them at thirty and calls them "cities." While no longer "tent cities," neither were they fortresses, as was Kenath, mentioned in the next verse, where the text speaks of **Kenath and her daughters** (AV, "villages"). The people who worked the fields while living in the hamlets could find refuge behind the walls of the mother city in times of invasion.

VIII. The Route from Egypt to the Jordan. 33:1-49.

Numbers 33 gives the itinerary of Israel's journeys from the day they left Egypt to their arrival on the banks of Jordan forty years later. In verse 2 the writer asserts that Moses wrote these facts according to the commandment of the Lord. The burden of proof rests on those who claim the chapter is a composite of several late documents, for there is no evidence that fraudulent authorship played any part in pre-Hellenistic Hebrew writing.

Nothing is known about that part of the journey outlined in verses 18-30. This passage describes the route during the silent thirty-seven years following the defeat at Hormah (14:15). The chapter does not mention Kadesh at the time the spies were sent out (v. 18). The reason may be that Kadesh is the name of an area as well as a city in the Wilderness of Paran-Sin and that Rithmah was a smaller oasis in the Kadesh area. The encampment covered a large area that could have included both towns (cf. v. 49). Wadi Abu Retemat (cf. Rithmah) is near the 'Ain Qadeis, which modern archaeologists are convinced was near Kadesh-barnea (KD, Vol. III, p. 243).

8. Wilderness of Etham. Called Shur in Ex 15:22. This was an ancient route used by the patriarchs (Gen 16:7; 20:1; 24:62; 25:18; 26:22). **13. Dophkah . . . Alush.** Dophkah is now identified as Serâbit el-Khâdim, an Egyptian mining center (G. E. Wright, *Biblical Archaeology*, p. 64). All the places mentioned in verses 5-12 are found in the Exodus account except Dophkah and Alush. **15. Rephidim.** Identified by archaeologists as Wâdī Refâyid, near Mount Sinai.

31. Moseroth. This is the place where Aaron died, according to Deut 10:6,7. It was near or on Mount Hor. In Deut 10:6,7 there is a different order of these towns, which suggests that this verse (31) speaks of earlier journeying in the area, while verses 37-39 coincide with Deut 10:6,7; Num 20:22-29.

36. Ezion-gaber (Elath). This is Tell el-Kheleifeh on the northern coast of the Gulf of Aqabah, where Solomon's copper refineries have been found. **42. Punon.** Feinan, in northern Edom, mentioned in Byzantine sources, was also a copper-mining center (see G. E. Wright, *Biblical Arch.*, Fig. 35). **43. Oboth.** Identified as 'Ain el-Weiba, on the west side of the Arabah, about thirty miles south of the Salt Sea. **46. Dibon-gad.** Diban, a few miles north of the Arnon. The tribe of Gad inherited it from the Amorites, who had taken it from the Moabites (21:27-30). It later became a capital of Moab, according to the Mesha inscription (835 B.C.).

49. They pitched . . . from Beth-jesimoth even unto Abel-shittim. The extent of Israel's encampment, as may be inferred from the verse, is in keeping with the large numbers given in the census lists.

IX. Directions for Settlement in Canaan. 33:50–35:34.

A. Expulsion of Inhabitants, Setting of Boundaries, Division of Land. 33:50–34:29. The section opens with an introductory formula (33:50), which is repeated in 35:1: "The Lord spoke unto Moses in the plains of Moab by the Jordan at Jericho." Moses instructed Israel to destroy all the stone idols, the molten images, and the high places of heathen worship they would find in Canaan. They were to drive out the pagan inhabitants, for failure to do so would allow these people to become thorns in their sides and would ultimately bring about Israel's own destruction.

Chapter 34 is a description of the ideal borders of the future homeland. Israel did not attain these borders until the time of David and Solomon. Even then they made some of their gains by means of treaty rather than by conquest. The actual dividing of the land into inheritances was to be done, God said, under the supervision of Joshua and Eleazar the priest, with the help of one prince from each tribe.

33:52. Drive out all the inhabitants. Translate: *Dispossess all the inhabitants*. **Destroy all their pictures,** i.e., their *figured stones*. (See W. F. Albright, *The Archaeology of Palestine*, Fig. 27, for Astarte plaques from the Late Bronze Age). **54. Every man's** (family's) **inheritance shall be in the place where his lot falleth.** The size of the inheritance was determined by the size of the tribe, but the position was determined by lot.

34:3. Your south quarter shall be from the wilderness of Zin along by the coast of Edom. This general description, made specific in the next two verses, is proof that Edom's domain included considerable territory west of the Arabah. **4. The ascent of Akrabbim** (Scorpion Pass).

Between this steep rise out of the Arabah and to Kadesh-barnea is the broken hill country called the Wilderness of Zin. Through it the southern border passed and then turned northwest near Kadesh ('Ain Qadeis) to follow Wadi el-'arish, **the river of Egypt** (v. 5), out to the Mediterranean.

7. Your north border: from the great sea ye shall point out for you mount Hor. Except for such outstanding features as Hamath, the sea of Chinnereth (Galilee), and the Jordan, most of the points on the north and eastern borders cannot now be identified with certainty (cf. comment on 20:23).

15. On this side Jordan near Jericho eastward, toward the sunrising. Comments by destructive critics on these words afford an excellent example of how the interpretation of Numbers has been obscured by a negative approach. The ICC claims that "at Jericho" is an unsuitable expression for describing the frontier line of the two and one-half tribes and that the phrase was just mechanically written. Following this view, the IB states that Jericho is described here as eastward, and therefore the sentence was written as from Canaan, and that the mention of Jericho is not exactly a full description of the territory asked for by these tribes. In a number of passages (22:1; 26:3,63; 34:15; 36:13) the phrase used is **Yardēn Yᵉrēho,** "The Jordan of Jericho." Numbers 34:15 and Josh 20:8 say, "Jordan of Jeriocho eastward," and then refer to it as the whole Trans-Jordan. The fact is that the word "Jordan" comes from an East Mediterranean word introduced by the Caphtorim and other Aegean people (Deut 2:23), and meant "the River" in their homeland, Crete (C. H. Gordon, *Old Testament Times,* p. 109 note). Hence these passages all refer to "the River (the Jordan) of Jericho" and all the land east of it. The definite article is used when the word Jordan stands alone, showing that it was a common noun, not a name. It is "The River" of that land, and Jericho was the most commanding fortress in that valley, thus "The River of Jericho."

17. These are the names of the men which shall divide the land unto you. These princes are named in the approximate order of the placement of the tribes in the land, beginning at Judah in the south and proceeding to Naphtali in the north. This seems to indicate that the lots for position (33:54) had already been cast and that these verses did not find their way into the text until after the events of Josh 14:1-5 (the casting of lots).

B. Levitical Cities and Cities of Refuge. 35:1-34. God directed the people to give to the Levites, from their possessions, cities to dwell in and the pasture land around them. Six of these cities were to be "cities of refuge" for manslayers (not murderers). Forty-two other Levitical cities with pasturage were to provide the Levites' living quarters. The manslayer (Deut 19) is defined as one who kills in error and must be protected from the *gō'ēl,* "the kinsman-redeemer," who, among other things, was blood avenger for his slain brother. The protection of the manslayer was a lofty moral principle assuring the administration of justice. A manslayer was to flee to one of these cities and stay there until he stood before the congregation for judgment. The Lord here declared that men who murdered must die, and, in accordance with prevailing custom, the avenger of blood (the kinsman of the slain man) was to slay the murderer. This principle of blood revenge, which is still practiced by Bedouins in the Near East, is upheld in this chapter. It acts as an effective deterrent in communities where there is little or no established central authority. Such was to be the case in Israel for many years, until the rise of the United Monarchy. Even if a man was adjudged an accidental manslayer, the Lord said, he must dwell in the city of refuge until the death of the high priest, after which he might return to his own land. The Lord was careful to point out that murder is premeditated killing; a murderer is a killer guilty of **hatred** or **lying in wait** (ASV, v. 20). Further protection to assure justice required that a man should not be put to death on the testimony of a single witness (v. 30).

5. And ye shall measure. Some claim that the measurements given in this verse leave the city a mere point (IB, Vol. 2, p. 303). Close attention to the Hebrew text shows the following. Verse 4 says, "From the wall of the city verily outward, one thousand cubits." A rather literal rendering of verse 5 would be, "You shall measure from outside with respect to the city, on the east side two thousand cubits." "With respect to the city" could very well mean that this perimeter measurement was in addition to whatever the city measured.

31. Ye shall take no satisfaction for the life of a murderer. That is, no ransom price might be taken to save his life, nor might a manslayer give a ransom to come out of the city of refuge. Since shedding of human blood ceremonially polluted the land in which the Lord dwelt, no offering of animal sacrifice or payment of a price could cleanse the land, but only the blood of the one who had shed blood. This explains the OT concept of blood-guiltiness (Ps 51: 4,14) as an encroachment on God's purity.

X. Marriage of Heiresses. 36:1-13.

Elders from the tribe of Manasseh complained that the legislation given concerning the daughters of Zelophehad (ch. 27) could result in the loss of Zelophehad's portion of their inheritance should his daughters marry outside their tribe. Moses, under divine authority, agreed with this and required that the daughters of Zelophehad marry within their own tribe, Manasseh. The property was inalienable and could not be removed even from tribe to tribe (v. 7). The principle of inalienable property Israel held in common with Near Eastern peoples long before she merged as a nation. The real estate contracts of a fifteenth century north Mesopotamian town, Nuzu, center around this principle (cf. comment on 27:4). It continued to control the thinking of faithful Israelites even in the days of Ahab and Naboth (I Kgs 21:3). Thus these women had to marry their paternal cousins (Num 36: 11), who could have been even second or third cousins.

13. These are the commandments . . . in the plains of Moab. This verse forms a fitting epilogue to Part Three (chs. 26–36), the legislation of which is pointed solely toward Israel's entry into the Land of Promise.

BIBLIOGRAPHY

ALBRIGHT, W. F. "The Oracles of Balaam," *Journal of Biblical Literature*, LXIII (1944), 207-233.

ANDERSON, C. A. "The Book of Numbers," *Old Testament Commentary*. Edited by H. C. Alleman. Philadelphia: Muhlenberg Press, 1949.

BINNS, L. E. *Numbers (Westminster Commentaries)*. London: Methuen and Company, 1927.

EERDMANS, B. D. "Text of Numbers," *Oudtestamentische Studien*. Deel VI. Leiden: E. J. Brill, 1949.

ELLICOTT, C. J. *The Bible Commentary for English Readers*. Vol. I. London: Cassell and Co., Ltd., n.d.

GRAY, G. B. *Numbers (International Critical Commentary)*. 2nd ed. Edinburgh: T. & T. Clark, 1912.

GREENSTONE, J. H. *Numbers with Commentary*. Philadelphia: Jewish Publication Society, 1939.

KEIL, C. F., AND DELITZSCH, F. *The Pentateuch*. Vol. III. Grand Rapids: Wm. B. Eerdmans Publishing Co., reprinted 1956.

KERR, D. W. *Numbers (The Biblical Expositor)*. London: Pickering and Inglis, 1960.

LANGE, J. P. *Numbers (A Commentary on the Holy Scriptures)*. Grand Rapids: Zondervan Publishing House, reprint 1956.

MACRAE, A. A. "Numbers," *The New Bible Commentary*. Edited by F. Davidson, A. M. Stibbs, and E. F. Kevan. Grand Rapids: Wm. B. Eerdmans Publishing Co., 1953.

MARSH, J. "The Book of Numbers," *The Interpreter's Bible*. Vol. 2. New York: Abingdon Press.

MCNEILE, A. H. *Numbers (The Cambridge Bible for Schools and Colleges)*. Cambridge: The University Press, 1911.

MENDENHALL, G. E. "The Census Lists of Numbers 1 and 26," *Journal of Biblical Literature*, LXXVII (1958), 52-66.

NOORDTZIJ, A. *Het boek Numeri*. Kampen: Kok, 1941.

WATSON, R. A. *Numbers (The Expositor's Bible)*. New York: Armstrong & Co., 1903.

DEUTERONOMY

INTRODUCTION

Title. The English title of the book of Deuteronomy is apparently based on the LXX's mistranslation of the phrase, "a copy of this law" (17:18), as *to deuteronomion touto,* "this second law." The Jewish title, *d^e^vārîm,* "words," arises from the custom of using the opening word(s) of a book as its name. Deuteronomy opens with the statement, "These are the words which Moses spake" (1:1a, ASV). Since ancient suzerainty treaties began in precisely this way, the Jewish title draws attention to one of the clues which identify the literary character of this book.

Date and Authorship. The origin of Deuteronomy is of crucial significance in modern higher critical study of the Pentateuch and, indeed, in studies of Old Testament literature and theology in general. According to the older Developmental Hypothesis, Deuteronomy originated in the seventh century B.C. and was the basis for Josiah's reform (cf. II Kgs 22:3–23:25), allegedly in the interests of a centralized cultus (cf. Commentary on Deut 12:4-14). That view in modified forms continues among negative critics; but some would suggest a post-Exilic date, and others trace the Deuteronomic legislation to the early monarchic and even pre-monarchic period. Significant for the dating of the several alleged documents of the Pentateuch is the tendency to explain the supposed conflict of their codes not by resort to a long chronological evolution but by positing different geographic - cultic sources for them. Deuteronomy, in particular, is then traced to a Shechemite sanctuary. Instead of associating Deuteronomy with the first four books of the Pentateuch, one modern approach thinks in terms of a Tetrateuch and of a Deuteronomic literary-historical tradition comprising all the books from Deuteronomy through II Kings.

Current orthodox Christian scholarship joins older Christian and Jewish tradition in accepting the plain claims of Deuteronomy itself to be the farewell, ceremonial addresses of Moses to the Israelite assembly in the plains of Moab. Deuteronomy 31:9 and 24 state that Moses wrote as well as spoke "the words of this law." Some theocratic officer, in all likelihood, completed the document by recording Moses' death (ch. 34) and probably Moses' witness song (ch. 32) and testament (ch. 33). Possibly he also added certain other brief skeletal elements to this legal document.

The unity and authenticity of Deuteronomy as a Mosaic product are confirmed by the remarkable conformity of its structure to that of the suzerainty type of covenant or treaty in its classic, mid-second millennium B.C. form. (See further below and consult Commentary for details. See also M. G. Kline, "Dynastic Covenant," WTJ, XXIII (Nov. 1960), 1, pp. 1-15.)

Historical Occasion. It is only within the framework of the administration of God's redemptive covenant that Deuteronomy can be adequately interpreted. The promises given to the patriarchs and finally and truly fulfilled in Christ had a provisional and typical fulfillment in the covenants mediated to Israel through Moses. In the Sinaitic Covenant the theocracy was established, with Moses as earthly representative of the Lord's kingship over Israel. Then, when the rebellious exodus generation had perished in the wilderness and Moses' own death was imminent, it was necessary to renew the covenant to the second generation. The central, decisive act of the ceremony was the consecration of the servant people by an oath to their divine Lord. In particular, God's reign as symbolically represented in the earthly, mediatorial dynasty must be confirmed by securing from Israel a commitment to obey Joshua as the successor to Moses in that dynasty.

Part of the standard procedure followed in the ancient Near East when great kings thus gave covenants to vassal peoples was the preparation of a text of the ceremony as the treaty document and witness. The book of Deuteronomy is the document prepared by Moses as a witness to the dynastic covenant which the Lord gave to Israel in the plains of Moab (cf. 31:26).

OUTLINE

I. Preamble: Covenant mediator. 1:1-5.
II. Historical prologue: Covenant history. 1:6–4:49.
  A. From Horeb to Hormah. 1:6–2:1.
  B. Advance to the Arnon. 2:2-23.
  C. Conquest of Trans-Jordania. 2:24–3:29.
  D. Summary of the covenant. 4:1-49.
III. Stipulations: Covenant life. 5:1–26:19.
  A. The Great Commandment. 5:1–11:32.
    1. God's covenant lordship. 5:1-33.
    2. The principle of consecration. 6:1-25.
    3. The program of conquest. 7:1-26.
    4. The law of the manna. 8:1-20.
    5. The warning of the broken tablets. 9:1–10:11.
    6. A call to commitment. 10:12–11:32.
  B. Ancillary commandments. 12:1–26:19.
    1. Cultic-ceremonial consecration. 12:1–16:17.
      a. Allegiance to God's altar. 12:1-32.
      b. Resistance to apostasy. 13:1-18.
      c. Filial obligations. 14:1–15:23.
      d. Tributary pilgrimages. 16:1-17.
    2. Judicial-governmental righteousness. 16:18–21:23.
      a. Judges and God's altar. 16:18–17:13.
      b. Kings and God's covenant. 17:14-20.
      c. Priests and prophets. 18:1-22.
      d. Guarantees of justice. 19:1-21.
      e. Judgment of the nations. 20:1-20.
      f. Authority of sanctuary and home. 21:1-23.
    3. Sanctity of the divine order. 22:1–25:19.
      a. The ordinances of labor and marriage. 22:1-30.
      b. The congregation of the Lord. 23:1-18.
      c. Protection for the weak. 23:19–24:22.
      d. Sanctity of the individual. 25:1-19.
    4. Confession of God as Redeemer-King. 26:1-19.
IV. Sanctions: Covenant ratification. 27:1–30:20.
  A. Ratification ceremony in Canaan. 27:1-26.
  B. Proclamation of the sanctions. 28:1-68.
    1. Blessings. 28:1-14.
    2. Curses. 28:15-68.
  C. Summons to the covenant oath. 29:1-29.
  D. Ultimate restoration. 30:1-10.
  E. Radical decision. 30:11-20.
V. Dynastic disposition: Covenant continuity. 31:1–34:12.
  A. Final arrangements. 31:1-29.
  B. The Song of Witness. 31:30–32:47.
  C. Moses' testament. 32:48–33:29.
  D. Dynastic succession. 34:1-12.

COMMENTARY

I. Preamble: Covenant Mediator. 1:1-5.

Ancient suzerainty treaties began with a preamble in which the speaker, the one who was declaring his lordship and demanding the vassal's allegiance, identified himself. The Deuteronomic preamble identifies the speaker as Moses (v. 1a), but Moses as the earthly, mediatorial representative of the Lord (v. 3b), the heavenly Suzerain and ultimate Sovereign of this covenant.

These are the words (v. 1a, ASV). With this introductory formula the extra-biblical treaties began. The site of the covenant renewal ceremony to which Deuteronomy witnesses was the Jordan area in the land of Moab (vv. 1a, 5a; cf. 4:44-46). The time was the last month of the fortieth year after the Exodus (v. 3a), when the men of war of that generation had all perished (2:16), the conquest of Trans-Jordan was accomplished (v. 4; 2:24ff.), and the time of Moses' death was at hand. It was especially this last circumstance that occasioned the renewal of the covenant. God secured the continuity of the mediatorial dynasty by requiring of Israel a pledge of obedience to his new appointee, Joshua (cf. 31:3; 34:9), and a new vow of consecration to himself. The ceremony is described as a declaration or exposition of **this law** (v. 5), since the stipulations occupied so central and extensive a place in suzerainty covenants. The location of this assembly is apparently further described in verse 2b. Although the mention of otherwise unknown localities makes interpretation uncertain, the purpose of the notation in verses 1b,2 seems to be to orient the Moab assembly historically as much as geographically by indicating that it lay at the end of the journey from Horeb via the Arabah wilderness. For Israel, the journey to Canaan by this route proved to be of forty years duration (v. 3), although the original route they followed to Paran was normally only an eleven-day trek (v. 2). At Paran, on the southern border of Canaan, however, Israel had rebelled, refusing to enter the land (Num 12:16ff.), and so that generation was sentenced to die in the wilderness. Now their children had arrived via the Arabah route from "Suph" (presumably the Gulf of Aqabah) for an eastern approach to Canaan through the land of Moab. Both the direction of approach to Canaan and the length of the wanderings spoke of a history of covenant breaking and of postponed inheritance. There is, thus, an interesting contrast between the preamble's look south from Moab into the past of failure and curse and Moses' closing look north from Moab into Israel's future of fulfillment and blessing (Deut 34:1-4).

II. Historical Prologue: Covenant History. 1:6–4:49.

The preamble in the international suzerainty treaties was followed by a historical survey of the relationship of lord and vassal. It was written in an I-thou style, and it sought to establish the historical justification for the lord's continuing reign. Benefits allegedly conferred upon the vassal by the lord were cited, with a view to grounding the vassal's allegiance in a sense of gratitude complementary to the sense of fear which the preamble's awe-inspiring identification of the suzerain was calculated to produce. When treaties were renewed, the historical prologue was brought up to date. All these formal features characterize Deut 1:6–4:49.

The historical prologue of the Sinaitic Covenant had referred to the deliverance from Egypt (Ex 20:2b). Deuteronomy begins at the scene of the Sinaitic Covenant and continues the history up to the covenant renewal assembly in Moab, emphasizing the recent Trans-Jordanian victories. When, still later, Joshua again renewed the covenant to Israel, he continued the narrative in his historical prologue through the events of his own leadership of Israel, the conquest and settlement in Canaan (Josh 24:2-13).

A. From Horeb to Hormah. 1:6–2:1.

6-8. By the end of a year's encampment in the Sinai area, where the covenant was ratified and the Tabernacle established as God's dwelling in Israel, the time had come for the next decisive step in the fulfillment of the promises made to the fathers (vv. 6,8b). The initiative in the advance against the land of promised possession was provided by the Lord's command, **Go in and possess the land** (v. 8; cf. Num 10:11-13). On verse 7b, see Gen 15:18ff.

9-18. With the hour of his death at hand, Moses was concerned to confirm the authority of those who must bear the burden of rule after him. Of primary importance was the succession of Joshua, to which he would presently refer (1:38; 3:21,28), but now Moses reminded Israel of the authorization of other judicial officers. For the original account, see Ex 18:13ff. **10. As the stars of heaven.** The very circumstance that gave rise to the need for these judicial assistants to Moses, namely, the multiplication of Abraham's seed, was itself evidence of the Lord's faithfulness in fulfilling his promises (Gen 12:2; 15:5; etc.), and thus afforded encouragement to Israel to advance in faith to take possession of Canaan (cf. Deut 1:7,8). God's faithful mediator, reflecting the goodness of the Lord, prayed for the full realization of all the promises of the Abrahamic Covenant (v. 11). **17. For the judgment is God's.** This reason for righteous administration of justice was at the same time a reminder of the theocratic nature of the Israelite kingdom, a reminder that God was the Lord who was making covenant anew with them that day.

19-40. Over against the covenant faithfulness of the Lord (cf. 6-18) there had been the infidelity and disobedience of Israel. The fact that the Lord was renewing his covenant against this background of the vassal's past rebellions further magnified his grace and goodness (cf. introductory comments on II. Historical Prologue). The particular sin of the people of Israel recalled on the eve of their conquest of Canaan was their refusal to advance into Canaan when they were first commanded to do so, some thirty-eight years earlier. For the original account, see Numbers 13; 14.

At that time Israel's approach to Canaan was from the south (Deut 1:19). Moses clearly advised them that Canaan was theirs for the taking (vv. 20,21; cf. 7,8; Gen 15:16); yet when so ordered by the Lord (cf. Num 13:1ff.), he consented to Israel's strategy of reconnaissance before attack (Deut 1:22-25). **26,27a. Ye rebelled . . . And ye murmured.** Israel's response to the report of the spies was one of faithless fear and refusal to advance. **27b. He hath brought us forth . . . to destroy us.** Israel's perversity went to the extreme of interpreting their election as an expression of God's hatred of them; he had delivered them from the Egyptians only that the Canaanites might kill them! **29-33.** They could not be dissuaded – **ye did not believe** (v. 32) – from their open revolt against the Lord's covenant program by all Moses' pleas and assurances of God's fatherly and supernatural help, such as they had experienced in Egypt and in the wilderness. **34. The Lord heard . . . and was wroth.** Their unbelief provoked the divine verdict, sealed by an oath, sentencing them to exile from the homeland which they had refused to enter (v. 35), exile unto death in the wilderness (v. 40). **36-38. Save Caleb. . . . Joshua.** In the announcement of judgment there was a manifestation of God's covenant mercy, for not only the godly spies Caleb and Joshua were to be spared to enter Canaan at a later day, but the whole second generation of Israel as well (v. 39). Therein lay the promise of a gracious new beginning – now being fulfilled in the Deuteronomic covenant renewal. **37. The Lord was angry with me.** Israel's rebelliousness became the occasion for a failure on Moses' part to fulfill properly his calling as a type of the messianic mediator who is always submissive to the Father's will (cf. 3:26; 4:21; 32:50ff.). That happened at the return to Kadesh after the thirty-eight years of wandering (cf. Num 20:1ff.), but it is mentioned here because its consequence was the exclusion of Moses along with the older generation from Canaan (cf. v. 35). It was this that necessitated the appointment of Joshua as heir to the mediatorial dynasty – Joshua "shall go in thither" (v. 38) – to lead the spared **little ones** (v. 39) into Canaan.

1:41–2:1. After the people of Israel had capped their revolt against the Lord's will with a presumptuous and disastrous assault on Canaan, in the vain hope of escaping God's verdict against them (1:41-44; cf. Num 14:40ff.), they remained a while in Kadesh (1:46). Then, as God had commanded (1:40; cf. Num 14:25), they wandered unto their wilderness graves (2:1a). So the time was spent in the area to the southwest of the Edomites until the fortieth year (2:1b; cf. 2:14-16).

B. Advance to the Arnon. 2:2-23.

2-8. Cf. Num 20:14-21. **3b. Turn you northward.** The divine mandate to advance on Canaan given a generation earlier (cf. 2:14-16) was now repeated. On the route, apparently around the north of Edom and across the way of the Arabah which leads from the Gulf of Aqabah to the Dead Sea, see Num 20:21ff.; 21:1-12; 33:36-44. Uncertainty as to the route arises from our inability to identify many of the sites, but it is not probable that 2:8 or Num 21:4 suggests a southern detour as far as the Gulf of Aqabah as part of a circuit of Mount Seir. **4. They shall be afraid of you.** Esau's fear of Israel (contrast Gen 32:3ff.) was displayed by his blocking entry into Seir (Num 20:20). **5. Do not contend with them** (RSV). The struggle for the birthright was long since settled; Canaan was Jacob's. Nevertheless, Esau had his possession, too, in Mount Seir (cf. Gen 36), and Israel was forbidden to contend for it. (See Deut 23:7,8 for the relatively privileged position of the Edomites in Israel's assembly.) When the policy dictated by the Lord was followed, the Edomites refused passage through their land, thus compelling Israel to make a circuit about their borders (v. 8; cf. Num 20:14ff.). The Numbers passage does not say that the Edomites refused to sell provisions to the Israelites once it was clear that Israel was content to go around Edom. Moreover, Deut 2:6 and 29 do not clearly state that Edom did sell provisions to Israel. For even 2:29a possibly refers only to the last clause in verse 28 (cf. 2:29b with 23:3,4). Hence there is no contradiction between Numbers and Deuteronomy on this matter. **7. Thou hast lacked nothing.** This verse is one more reminder of God's past benevolences bestowed on Israel even during the execution of his judgment of exile (cf., e.g., 32:1).

9-23. Israel came into contact next with the descendants of Abraham's nephew Lot, the Moabites and Ammonites (Gen 19:37,38). **9. Distress not the Moabites.** Though these groups did not enjoy the Edomites' privilege of entrance into Israel's assembly (23:3ff.), they too had possessions for which Israel was not to contend (cf. 5,19). Each nation had dispossessed a tall Anakim-like people usually known as Rephaim, but called Emim by the Moabites (vv. 10,11) and Zamzummim by the Ammonites (vv. 20,21; cf. Gen 14:5). The tribe of Anak is mentioned in Egyptian execration texts and the Rephaim in Ugaritic administrative texts. **12. The Horites . . . dwelt in Seir beforetime.** In connection with the territorial acquisitions of each nation, it is noted that similarly the Lord had dispossessed the earlier Horite (i.e., Hurrian) population of Seir in favor of the Edomites (cf. 5b,22). Also, in each case one further comparison is made; respectively, the Lord's bestowal of an inheritance on Israel (v. 12b) and the dispossession of the Avvim by the Caphtorim (v. 23). If the notice concerning Israel's inheritance was not appended by some unnamed official, like the one who evidently completed the Deuteronomic document after Moses' death, then it doubtless refers to the conquest of Trans-Jordan.

By all these historical notices the covenant servant Israel was advised that the Lord had a hegemony over the territory about the promised land. In his all-controlling providence he had repeatedly dispossessed great nations—even the Anakim, whose presence in Canaan had frightened Israel into rebellion against the Lord a generation before (cf. 1:28; 2:14,15). And the Lord had done this in behalf of various peoples who enjoyed no such special status of covenant calling as elect Israel enjoyed. With what confidence, therefore, Israel might obey the Lord's summons to **rise up** (v. 13) and cross the mountain torrents of **Zered** and **Arnon** (v. 24), and soon the Jordan (cf. Josh 1:2). See Amos 9:7 for another lesson drawn from such historical data. The Zered marked the southern boundary of Moab, along whose eastern border Israel went, so approaching the frontiers of Ammon, which lay east and north of Moab (Deut 2:18,19; cf. 8b; Num 21:11ff.).

C. Conquest of Trans-Jordan. 2:24—3:29.

Across the Arnon (2:24), Moab's northern boundary, Israel would encounter Amorites. Sihon the Amorite ruled from the Arnon to the Jabbok (2:36; cf. Num 21:24), with his capital at Heshbon (2:26), and Og the Amorite (cf. 3:8) ruled from the Jabbok over northern Gilead and Bashan to Mount Hermon (3:4,8-10; cf. 3:13; Josh 12:5). The Amorites were protected by no such inviolability as the Edomites, Moabites, and Ammonites. The fact that an offer of peace was made to Sihon (2:26) indicates that his land in Trans-Jordania (which had earlier belonged to the Moabites and Ammonites; cf. Josh 13:25; 21:26; Jud 11:13) was not a part of Israel's promised land proper (cf. Deut 20:10). But his people, as a people of Canaan, fell under the *ḥērem* principle (see on 7:1-5; cf. 2:33-35; 3:6; 7:2,16; 20:14-17).

It was indeed the time when the Amorites should have ripened for judgment, which had been set as the hour for Israel's conquest of Canaan (cf. Gen 15:16). With the spread of these Amorites across the Jordan, there was a corresponding extension of the territory that would fall into Israel's possession by conquest. Therefore, a new divine order met Israel at the Arnon: **Begin to take possession and contend** (v. 24, RSV); and a new divine promise: **This day will I begin to put the dread of thee . . . upon the nations** (v. 25). The process of Sihon's fall was much the same as that of the fall of Amenophis II, the Pharaoh of the Exodus. Each was approached with a request to favor the Israelites (vv. 26-29), which he refused, because **the Lord . . . hardened his spirit** (v. 30). Each made a hostile advance against Israel (v. 32) and suffered defeat, as the Lord fought for His people (vv. 31,33ff.). (On 2:29, see comments on 2:2-8.) The upper course of the Jabbok to the east ran north and south, separating Sihon's kingdom from the Ammonites (2:37). **36. The Lord . . . delivered all unto us.** In this victory, the beginning of the dispossession of the Amorites, there were demonstrated the irresistible power and absolute authority of the Lord's dominion exercised over and in behalf of Israel. For the original account of the conquest of Sihon, see Num 21:21ff.; for the conquest of Og, see Num 21:33ff. **3:2. I will deliver him . . . into thy hand.** The advance against Og was also at God's command, accompanied by his promise of success (cf. 2:24,25); and victory was again the gift of the Lord (3:3). **5. Fortified with high walls** (ASV). The height of the enemy's fortifications was not to arouse fear in the armies of the Lord, nor the size of their king (v. 11; cf. 2:11,20). Deuteronomy 3:8-11 summarizes the fruits of Israel's victories at Jahaz (2:32) and Edrei (3:1).

3:12-20. It was given to Moses to see both the beginning of the conquest under his leadership and also the distribution of the tribal allotments. For this latter event, see Numbers 32. **12. This land . . . gave I unto the Reubenites and . . . Gadites.** The tribes of Reuben and Gad took the initiative in requesting the newly conquered land. But when Moses granted the request, he took account of particular triumphs gained in the north by the Manassite families of Machir, Jair, and Nobah (v. 14; cf. Num 32:39-42). To this half tribe of Manasseh was given the territory of Og, i.e., Gilead north from the Jabbok and Bashan (Deut 3:13,15; cf. Josh 13:29-31). To Reuben and Gad was given Sihon's land from the Jabbok in Gilead south to the Arnon, the tribe of Gad being located north of Reuben, with their boundary just above the Dead Sea. Gad also received the Jordan Valley as far as the Sea of Chinnereth (see Deut 3:12,16,17; cf. Josh 13:15-28). **18. Ye shall pass over armed.** The strict condition laid upon the two and a half tribes inheriting land outside of Canaan was that they must first fulfill their responsible share in the conquest of Canaan (Num 32:6-32). Moses' intense concern for this matter emerges again here in the Deuteronomic treaty (vv. 18-20).

21-29. Except for the covenant renewal ceremony itself, the conquest and distribution of the land beyond Jordan eastward brought Moses' work there to an end. **24. Thou hast begun to shew . . . thy mighty hand.** In these achievements the servant of God had witnessed the earnest of Israel's entrance upon its inheritance. But much as he longed to see the fulfillment of God's promises in Canaan itself – **let me go over** (v. 25) –, he was not permitted to pass over the Jordan but only to look across it (v. 27; cf. Num 27:12ff.; Deut 34:1ff.). On 3:26, see 1:37; 4:21,22. Moses' final duty, therefore, was to charge the people to conquer in the name of the Lord (v. 22) and to commission Joshua to lead them in that conquest (vv. 21,28; cf. Num 27:18-23; Deut 1:38; 31:7,8,14,23). The reference to Beth-peor in the identification of the site of these final acts of Moses (Deut 3:29; cf. 4:46) recalls other events that transpired during Israel's encampment there (cf. Num 22-25).

D. Summary of the Covenant. 4:1-49.

The historical prologue closes with exhortation. This is transitional to the following section on the obligations of the covenant relationship. The summons to obedience sounded here is briefly echoed in paragraphs that introduce significant divisions within the stipulations (see 5:1; 6:1; 12:1). Deuteronomy 4 is remarkable in that it embodies, to some extent, all the features which constitute the documentary pattern of ancient suzerainty treaties. Thus, there are: (1) the identification of the author of the covenant as speaker (vv. 1,2,5,10); (2) references to past historical relations; (3) the presentation of the central demand for pure devotion to the suzerain; (4) appeal to the sanctions of blessing and curse; (5) invocation of witnesses (v. 26); (6) the requirement to transmit the knowledge of the covenant to subsequent generations (vv. 9,10); and (7) allusion to the dynastic issue (vv. 21,22). This mingling of the several leading aspects of covenant institution found here and elsewhere throughout the book is explained by the origin of the material in the free oratory of Moses' farewell. Deuteronomy is not a document prepared in the state office with dispassionate adherence to legal form.

Verses **1-8** present a call to wisdom. The statutes that Moses taught Israel were a revelation of the will of God (v. 5). **2. Ye shall not add . . . neither . . . diminish ought.** God's laws must not suffer amendment or abridgment through human legislation (cf. 12:32; Rev 22:18ff.). Man's whole obligation is to heed, and to the obedient Israelites was given the promise of life and rich inheritance – **that ye may live, and . . . possess the land** (v. 1). The fact that, ultimately, piety and prosperity will be united is foreshadowed in the history of the Israelite theocracy, for it symbolizes God's consummate kingdom. Illustrative of this fact was God's recent judgment on Israel for her involvement in the idolatry of the Baal of Peor (v. 3; Num 25:1-9); for those who proved faithful in that temptation were spared the plague of death (Deut 4:4). Understandably, then, obedience to God's law is identified as true wisdom. **7,8. God so nigh. . . . statutes . . . so righteous.** Obedience is the way to the enjoyment of the supreme blessings of the covenant – the nearness of God in saving power, and the knowledge of true righteousness. This light revealed in Israel has indeed become the light of the Gentiles (v. 6b). In this exposition of the way of the covenant as the way of wisdom, the foundation was laid in the Torah for the Wisdom literature which was afterwards to find its place in the sacred canon.

In verses **9-31** the folly of idolatry is declared. As Moses confronted the new generation with the challenge to reaffirm the allegiance their fathers had pledged at Sinai, he was vividly mindful of the fathers' sin of the golden calf, by which they had violated the covenant almost immediately after it had been sealed (cf. 9:7ff.; Ex 32). He therefore stressed the prohibition contained in the second commandment as he contrasted to the way of wisdom and life (Deut 4:1-8) the way of folly and destruction.

10. I will make them hear my words. At Horeb God had revealed to Israel the manner of true worship. That revelation was contained in the covenant which was first orally communicated and then inscribed on the two tables. The preparation of duplicate documents, one for the suzerain and one for the vassal, was the regular procedure in ratifying suzerainty treaties. The fact that the contents of the tables are called the "ten commandments" as well as "covenant" points to the nature of the covenant as a declaration of God's lordship. **12. The Lord spake . . . out of . . . the fire** (see also v. 15). The manner of true worship was also revealed by the very nature of the theophany. For though a voice was heard declaring the words of the covenant, no form of God was seen but only the devouring fire of God's glory. The visible symbols of God's self-revelation thus re-enforced the prohibition of the second commandment.

Israel was to beware of the idolatry of worshiping the work of men's hands – **a graven image** (vv. 16-18,23; cf. 5:8) – but also that of worshiping the work of God's hands, **the host of heaven** (v. 19). The worship of the visible and creaturely was characteristic of the Gentile nations whom God had abandoned to their perverse folly (v. 19b; cf. 29:26; Rom 1:21ff.). **20. To be . . . a people of inheritance.** For Israel to turn aside into idolatry was to prefer the lot of reprobation to her divine election as God's own redeemed and exclusive possession (see also 7:6; 14:2), an exclusive privilege which required an exclusive service and devotion. **23. Take heed unto yourselves.** Prophetically Moses warned that prolonged enjoyment of the blessings of Canaan, blessings denied even to him (vv. 21,22a), would produce the forgetfulness of old age (v. 25; cf. v. 9). Let the Israelites, therefore, recall that the God to whom they had sworn allegiance at Sinai appeared there as a consuming fire (v. 24). If provoked to jealousy by idolatry, he would visit the covenant curses on such folly. And what greater curse than to abandon the repudiators of divine election to the vanity of the idolatry they preferred and to the community of men of like reprobate mind and destiny? (vv. 27,28; 28:64ff.) **29-31. Thou shalt find him, if thou seek him.** Nevertheless, God's covenant is one of salvation, and its fulfillment is guaranteed by the oath of God to the patriarchs. Hence, after Israel's folly and judgment God would grant repentance so that beyond the curse of exile there might arise the blessings of restoration (cf. 30:1ff.).

Verses **32-40** present evidences of true religion. The identity of the Lord as God alone – **none else beside him** (v. 35) – , sovereign Creator of heaven and earth, was evidenced by his wondrous self-revelations in theophany and redemptive miracle (vv. 35,39; cf. Ex 10:2). **32. Ask . . . whether there hath been any such thing.** His glorious acts at Horeb and in Egypt were signs without parallel; no idol of the nations ever thus identified itself. If the purpose of Israel's calling was to bring the people to reverent fear (v. 36) and knowledge of the Lord as God (vv. 35, 39), the source of that calling was found in God's free grace (cf. 9:5). **37,38. Because he loved thy fathers.** Moses traced the deliverance from Egypt and the inheritance of the promised rest (earnest of which was the occupation of Trans-Jordan) to God's sovereign love of the patriarchs, first of all, of Abraham. **39. The Lord he is God.** Moses further pointed to the totality of past miraculous mercies and the sanction of the covenant's future hope (v. 40) as reasons for conscientious reckoning with the claims of the Lord's exclusive deity.

41-43. As part of the historical prologue of the Deuteronomic treaty, the most recent significant event in God's gracious government of Israel is here cited. In obedience to God's direction (cf. Num 35:1,14), Moses appointed three cities of refuge in Israel's Trans-Jordanian inheritance, one each in the southern, central, and northern sectors (cf. 19:1-13).

44-49. This passage is transitional. As a summary of the Trans-Jordanian conquests (vv. 46b-49; cf. 2:32-36; 3:1-17), it serves as a conclusion to the historical prologue. But it is also immediately introductory to the stipulations (vv. 44-46a). The scene of the covenant ceremony and Moses' farewell is precisely set (cf. 1:3-5; 3:29). **46. When they came forth out of Egypt** (ASV) marks the transaction as belonging to the Mosaic era of prolonged journeying from Egypt to the Jordan. The ratifying of this covenant was to be finally concluded in the new era when Israel entered into Canaan under Joshua (cf. 11:29ff.; 27).

III. Stipulations: Covenant Life. 5:1–26:19.

When suzerainty treaties were renewed, the stipulations, which constituted the long and crucial central section of the covenant, were repeated but with modifications, especially such as were necessary to meet the changing situation. So Moses rehearsed and reformulated the requirements promulgated in the Sinaitic Covenant. Furthermore, just as treaty stipulations customarily began with the fundamental and general demand for the vassal's absolute allegiance to the suzerain, and then proceeded to various specific requirements, so Moses now confronted Israel with the primary demand for consecration to the Lord (vv. 5-11) and then with the ancillary stipulations of covenant life (vv. 12-26).

A. The Great Commandment. 5:1–11:32.

The covenant's first and great commandment, the requirement of perfect consecration to the Lord, is enunciated in chapters 5–7, and enforced by divine claims and sanctions in chapters 8–11. These subject divisions are not, however, rigid; the exhortative strand is pervasive. Analyzed in somewhat more detail, this section develops the theme of the great commandment as follows: the Lord's existing claims upon Israel (ch. 5); the challenge of God's exclusive lordship over Israel, expressed as a principle (ch. 6) and a program (ch. 7); warnings against the temptation to autonomy, whether in the form of the spirit of self-sufficiency (ch. 8) or of self-righteousness (9:1–10:11); a call to true allegiance (10:12–11:32).

1) God's Covenant Lordship. 5:1-33.

1. Hear . . . learn . . . keep, and do. This chapter opens and closes (vv. 32,33) with a charge to follow carefully the divine stipulations of the covenant which was in process of solemnization.

2-5. The commitment to which Israel was summoned was to be a renewal of the covenant relationship to the Lord which already obtained. Forty years earlier, at Sinai, God had by covenant ceremony established Israel as his theocratic people (v. 2). That was done in faithfulness to his earlier promises to the patriarchs. **3. Not . . . with our fathers, but with us.** The patriarchal "fathers" (cf. 4:31,37; 7:8,12; 8:18) had died without receiving the promises. But the present generation, with whom the Sinaitic Covenant was established as well as with the older generation that perished in the wilderness (cf. 11:2), was privileged to see the promised kingdom realized. **5. I stood between the Lord and you.** At Sinai, as now, Moses was the mediator between God and Israel, an office the more needful because of Israel's fear of face-to-face confrontation with the fiery theophany (cf. 4:12). If the reporting role of Moses described here does not refer to revelations given after the promulgation of the Decalogue, then statements found elsewhere to the effect that Israel heard God declare the Decalogue (e.g., 4:12; Ex 19:9; 20:19) would mean that God's voice was audible but his words were indiscernible to Israel. However, verse 5 is more likely proleptic, like 22b.

6-22 (Heb. Bible 6-18). From the fact of the Sinaitic Covenant Moses proceeds to its documentary content as inscribed on the duplicate tables (cf. comments on 4:13). While continuing the thought that Israel was already covenantly bound to the Lord, this achieves the additional purpose of incorporating the comprehensive summary of permanent covenant law into the stipulations section of the Deuteronomic renewal document. The Decalogue, being itself not simply a moral code but the text of a covenant, exhibits the treaty pattern as follows: preamble (v. 6a), historical prologue (v. 6b), and stipulations interspersed with curse and blessing formulae (vv. 7-21). **12. Keep the sabbath day to sanctify it.** Most significant of the variations from the form of the Decalogue as presented in Ex 20:2-17 is the new formulation of the fourth "word" or commandment. The sabbatic cycle of life symbolizes the consummation principle characteristic of divine action. God works, accomplishes his purpose, and, rejoicing, rests. Exodus 20:11 refers to the exhibition of the consummation pattern in creation for the original model of the Sabbath. Deuteronomy 5:15 refers to the consummation pattern manifested in redemption, where the divine triumph is such as to bring God's elect to their rest also. Most appropriately, therefore, was the Sabbath appointed as a sign of God's covenant with the people he redeemed from the bondage of Egypt to inherit the rest of Canaan (cf. Ex 31:13-17). The New Testament's association of the Sabbath with the Saviour's resurrection triumph, by which his redeemed, with him, attain to eternal rest, corresponds to the Deuteronomic interpretation of the Sabbath in terms of the progress of God's redemptive purpose.

Other notable Deuteronomic variations in the Decalogue are the reversal of the order of **wife** and **house** in the tenth commandment, and the addition there of **his field** (Deut 5:21). The latter is added because Israel was about to enter upon a settled existence in the land, whereas during the wilderness wanderings such legislation would have been irrelevant. This is a good example of the kind of legislative modification found in ancient secular renewal treaties. **22. These words the Lord spake unto all your assembly.** The uniqueness of the revelation of the ten "words" is underscored in this verse. That revelation alone was spoken directly by God to all Israel; it alone was written by God.

23-27 (Heb. Bible 20-24). Continuing the account of the covenant-making at Sinai, Moses reminded the people of Israel of their former vow to obey God's voice (cf. Ex 20:18-21). Indeed, such had been their fear of God in the presence of his glory that they desired Moses to receive the further revelations of the divine voice for them – **Go thou near, and hear** (Deut 5:27). Such reluctance to experience the presence of God is a far cry from man's original delight in communion with his Creator in the Garden. And therein is exposed the exceeding cursedness of the curse upon sin. There are, of course, ultimate limits to man's qualifications for the vision of God (cf. Ex 33:20). But even though, within those limits, redemptive grace makes possible the enjoyment of a vision of God, fallen man regards the experience as a threat to his life (e.g., Gen. 32:30; Jud 6:22,23). In God's holy presence at Sinai, the Israelites were so keenly conscious of their defilement that they feared to venture further with their unique privilege (cf. Deut 4:33). Nevertheless, their fear was godly, for they acknowledged the God who appeared so terribly on the mount as their God, and committed themselves to do his will.

28-33 (Heb. Bible 25-30). What more stirring memories could Moses have evoked in anticipation of his concluding exhortation to walk in the way of the Lord and of life (vv. 32,33) than these: (1) God's approbation of Israel's previous vow – **they have well said** (v. 28); (2) his fatherly yearning that when the Sinaitic theophany should have ceased, the reverent devotion it had inspired might continue and thus it **might be well with them, and with their children for ever!** (v. 29) This response of the Lord supplements the record of Exodus 20.

In chapter 6 the principle of exclusive devotion to the Lord is enunciated, and with it the corollary prohibition of allegiance to alien deities. Then in chapter 7 the program of conquest is announced for the elimination of foreign gods and their people from the domain of Canaan, the land chosen by the Lord as an earthly type of his eternal and universal kingdom.

2) The Principle of Consecration. 6:1–25.

1-3. The commandments about to be given were the divinely dictated law for the theocratic kingdom as it was soon to be erected in the new paradise land of milk and honey. **3. That it may be well with thee.** Israel's continued enjoyment of a habitation in God's land, like Adam's continued enjoyment of the original paradise, depended on continued fidelity to the Lord. Certain important distinctions are necessary in making such a comparison. Flawless obedience was the condition of Adam's continuance in the Garden; but Israel's tenure in Canaan was contingent on the maintenance of a measure of religious loyalty, which needed not be comprehensive of all Israel nor perfect even in those who were the true Israel. There was a freedom in God's exercise or restraint of judgment, a freedom originating in the underlying principle of sovereign grace in his rule over Israel. Nevertheless, God did so dispense his judgment that the interests of the typical-symbolical message of Israel's history were preserved. (See further the comments on chs. 27–30).

4-9. 4. The Lord is our God, the Lord alone. This confession (various translations of which are grammatically possible) seems best understood as equivalent to the declarations of monotheism in 4:35 and 32:39 (cf. I Chr 29:1). "For though there be that are called gods, whether in heaven or in earth, (as there be gods many, and lords many,) but to us there is but one God, the Father . . . and one Lord Jesus Christ" (I Cor 8:5,6). God is unique; deity is confined to him exclusively. To him alone were the people of Israel to submit in religious covenant, and him they were to serve in the totality of their being, with the intensity of love (Deut 6:5). God's demand of this exclusive and intensive devotion to himself Jesus called "the first and great commandment" (Mt 22:37,38; Mk 12:29,30; cf. Lk 10:25-28). It is the heart principle of all the covenant stipulations. **6. These words . . . shall be in thine heart.** The past mercies of God rehearsed in the historical prologue would prompt such love, and the love would reveal itself in reverent obedience to all God's particular commandments (cf. 11:1,22; 19:9; 30:16; Jn 14:15). These verses are thus the text for all that follows. **7a. Thou shalt teach them . . . unto thy children.** The family character of covenant administration requires that the children be brought under the government of the stipulations (cf. 20 ff.). Day and night the godly are to meditate on God's law (vv. 7b-9; cf. Ps 1:2). Moses was not here making ceremonial requirements, but elaborating with concrete figures the demand for a constant focus of concern on the good pleasure of Israel's Lord. **9. Posts . . . gates.** These words reflect architectural custom in the world of Moses' day. For the figurative use of such language, see Ex 13:9,16. A literal practice of the injunctions of Deut 6:8,9 came into vogue among later Jews in the form of the phylacteries worn on the person (cf. Mt 23:5) and the mezuzah affixed over the doorpost.

10-19. The constant corollary of the demand for loyalty in ancient suzerainty treaties was the prohibition of allegiance to any and all other lords. In Canaan the temptation to idolatry would be fierce, since the claim made for the gods of that region was that they were the bestowers of fertility and abundance in the land. Such is human perversity that Israel, satisfied with the material plenty of a plundered culture, would be inclined to honor the claims of their victims' idols and forget the claims of the Lord who had saved from Egypt and given victory in Canaan (vv. 10-12). **13. Swear by his name.** Such swearing constituted a renewal of the oath of allegiance which ratified the covenant and invoked God as the deity who avenged perfidy. **14. Ye shall not go after other gods.** Thus God explicitly forbade entanglement with the gods of Canaan. He would indeed jealously guard the honor of his name (v. 15). **16. Ye shall not tempt the Lord.** Israel must not, therefore, presume to put God on trial, as at Massah (cf. Ex 17:7), seeking proof of his presence and his power to visit on them the covenant sanctions, whether blessing or curse. Let Israel rather be faithful, and God would faithfully fulfill his good promises (vv. 17-19; cf. v. 10).

20-25. Seeing generations come and go had lengthened Moses' perspective. His interest was not confined to the present assembly of Israel but took in the long future of God's kingdom (cf. v. 2). **20. When thy son asketh.** Crucial to the well-being of the theocracy would be the faithful nurture of the children in the message of God's redemptive actions and purposes for his people. **24. For our good always.** In particular, God's giving of the Law furthered the purposes of mercy by revealing the path of righteousness, to follow which would lead to divine favor and blessing. **25. It shall be our righteousness.** This verse does not present a works principle of salvation. The stress falls on the function of law as disclosing the standard of conduct which is righteous in God's sight, a love for which is prerequisite to beatitude but not the meritorious ground of such a state.

3) The Program of Conquest. 7:1-26.

1-5. In the Book of the Covenant produced at Sinai there was promulgated a program of conquest and extermination against the Canaanite people and cultus (cf. Ex 23:20-33; 34:11-16). Thereby the ancient prophecy in which Noah pronounced Canaan accursed and the servant of Shem (Gen 9:25,26; cf. Gen 10:15-

18; Ex 23:23) would be fulfilled (see, too, Gen 15:16-21). The hour of divine judgment having come, Moses now charged Israel with the execution of that program. Everybody and everything in Canaan that was consecrated to idols rather than to the service of God must be consecrated to the wrath of God.

1. Seven nations (cf. Josh 3:10; 24:11). In such lists elsewhere the number varies from three to ten. The "seven" specified here possibly is a figure for completeness. **2.** The Hebrew root *ḥrm*, translated **utterly destroy** in the major English versions, means primarily *devote* and hence "ban" and "extirpate." The *ḥērem* principle comes to full and final manifestation in the judgments of hell.

Some people take offense at God's command to Israel to exterminate the Canaanites, as though it represented sub-Christian ethics. Actually, they are taking offense at the theology and religion of the Bible as a whole. The New Testament, as well as the Old, warns men concerning the realm of the everlasting ban, where the reprobates, devoted to wrath, must magnify the justice of the God whom they have hated. Since the OT theocracy in Canaan was a divinely appointed symbol of the consummate kingdom of God, there is found in connection with it an intrusive anticipation of the ethical pattern that will obtain at the final judgment and beyond.

Moreover, the extermination of the Canaanites and their cultic installations (**destroy their altars . . . burn their . . . images;** v. 5) was necessary if Israel's calling to positive consecration to God in living service was to be fulfilled. For, because of Israel's frailty, the proximity of the Canaanites would lead to the dissolution of Israel's spiritual distinctiveness (v. 3), to foreign and idolatrous allegiances (v. 4a), and hence to Israel's own destruction (4b). The program of conquest (ch. 7) is thus a consistent application of the principle of consecration (ch. 6; esp. 6:12-15).

6-16. The purposes of Israel's election which were to be protected by the elimination of the Canaanites are here elaborated. **6. Chosen . . . to be a special people.** This recalls Ex 19:5,6, the classic formulation of the unique theocratic status for which Israel was chosen. High calling is attended by temptation to boasting (cf. Moses' concern with this problem in chs. 8–10). Therefore, Israel was reminded to glory only in the name of God. **8. Because the Lord loved you.** In his sovereign love and faithfulness alone was to be found the explanation of Israel's election (4:37), certainly not in the nation's size. For God chose their father Abraham, being only one, and the family of Jacob, which descended into Egypt as only some seventy souls (7:7; cf. 10:22). It followed from the sovereignty of God's grace that Israel had no claims upon him that might encourage carelessness with respect to his covenant demands and sanctions. **9. Keepeth covenant . . . to a thousand generations.** Alluding to the sanction formulae which are affixed to the second commandment, Moses declared that though unmerited grace would be continued to the thousandth generation (5:10), apostate despisers of grace and holiness would discover that the covenant curses were not idle threats (7:9-11). **12. The Lord . . . shall keep . . . covenant.** The faithful might be confident that the covenant blessings were not empty promises (vv. 12-15; cf. Gen 12:2,3; Ex 23:22-31). The God of Israel, the Creator, not Baal, was the bestower of fertility in field, flock, and family (Deut 7:13,14). **15. The Lord will take away . . . all sickness.** It was the Lord who had subjected man to nature's curse for his sin, and he could therefore deliver the Israelites from Egypt's notorious diseases (e.g., elephantiasis, dysentery, and ophthalmia) just as he had rescued them from Egypt's infamous Pharaoh (v. 15; cf. v. 8; Ex 15:26). Verse 16 summarizes, repeating the command and its purpose.

17-26. Though in respect to the privileges of election the Israelites were tempted to vanity, in the face of the responsibility of their commission they would be tempted to timidity (v. 17; cf. Num 13:31ff.). **18,19a. Thou shalt not be afraid.** In answer to any such rising fears Moses reminded them of that wondrous experience in Egypt during their youth when by mighty signs their God saved them. He assured them that this same terrible God was still in their midst to war in their behalf against the Canaanite kings (vv. 19b-24). Whom then should they fear? **20. The hornet** (cf. Ex 23:28; Josh 24:12) is not here a symbol for Pharaoh's power, even though it be so in Egyptian usage. It is, rather, a figure for the terror of God, which, descending on Israel's foes, would produce panic and rout (cf. Deut 7:23). The fact that certain species of hornets in Palestine build nests underground and in rock crevices suggests the appropriateness of the figure to the destruction of Canaanites in hiding. Some would translate *sir'â* not "hornet" but "discouragement." **22. Will put out . . . by little and little.** Cf. Ex 23:29,30; Jud 2:20-23; 3:1,2. God's gradual dispossessing of the Canaanites, designed for Israel's good, was suspended after Israel's post-Joshuan apostasy, as a chastisement. **24. Thou shalt destroy their name.** Reassuring promise turns into renewed imperative in verses 24b-26 (cf. v. 5). To appropriate that which had fallen under God's ban would be to forfeit the status of covenant favor and place oneself under the divine anathema (cf. Josh 7).

Chapters 8–11 set forth the truth that absolute allegiance to the Lord (6:4ff.) meant not only that the Israelites must refrain from simultaneous service to any other god (6:12ff.; 7:1ff.), but also that they might not declare their religious independence. Moses therefore enforced the fundamental obligation of whole-souled devotion to God by warning against the dangers of an autonomous attitude, whether manifested in the spirit of self-sufficiency (ch. 8) or in the spirit of self-righteousness (9:1–10:11). Following the negative warnings, this section concludes with a positive challenge to submit to God's lordship (10:12–11:32).

4) The Law of the Manna. 8:1-20.

The focal point of this chapter is verse 17, with its picture of a future Israel at ease in Canaan, basking in self-congratulation. The recollection of God's providential guidance during the forty years in the wilderness (v. 2ff.) would afford the corrective for such vanity.

1-6. Verse 1 is another introductory summary of the covenant summons and sanctions (see also 4:1; 5:1; 6:1). **2.** So far as the surviving generation was concerned, the wilderness wandering was designed as a period of probation – **to prove thee** – (v. 2b; cf. 13:3) and of necessary instruction (v. 3c). It was a fatherly discipline and contributed to their ultimate blessing (v. 5; cf. 16c). **3. He . . . fed thee with manna.** What is meant by God's humbling Israel (v. 2) is illustrated by reference to his extraordinary provision for every need during the forty years (vv. 3,4; cf. 29:5,6), particularly by means of the manna (see Ex 16, esp. v. 4). Humbling consisted of privation and then the provision of the "What-is-it?," the unknown, supernatural bread of heaven, which compelled the people to recognize their dependence on God (cf. Deut 8:16a,b). Modern naturalistic exegesis identifies the Biblical manna with the honey-like excretions of scale insects found in tamarisk thickets in the Sinai area. Whatever substantive role was or was not played by these excretions, the bread of heaven was, none the less, in its nature and manner of provision, clearly a miraculous product. Moreover, a mere change from one normal, palatable food staple to another, no matter how exotic, would neither have humbled Israel nor taught them the truth which the manna did: **Man doth not live by bread only** (ASV), **but by every word that proceedeth out of the mouth of the Lord doth man live.**

God led Israel into a situation in which life was derived and must be daily sought from a heavenly bread, the fruit of a daily creative exercise of the word of God. This was an effective reminder that the creature does not exist as a self-sufficient being, sustained by the fruits of an earth also existing and producing independently of God. He is ultimately and always dependent on the divine word which called him and his world into being. Furthermore, God purposed to teach Israel that man's life, unlike a beast's, does not consist solely in a physical vitality which bread, whether earthly or heavenly, might sustain. Hence he provided the bread of heaven in such a way as to require an ethical-religious response to his preceptive word. This response was appropriately focused on the observance of the Sabbath, the sign of man's covenant allegiance as well as the recaller of God's role as Creator. The manna thus taught Israel that only as man stands obediently under his Lord's sovereign word, the ultimate source of life, does he find true and lasting life (cf. 30:20).

7-20. 7a. A good land. The recollection of the wilderness lesson was necessary at this point, for God was conducting Israel into a land where the normal products of nature would afford a comparatively luxurious standard of living (vv. 7-10a). **9b. Whose stones are iron.** In the sandstone substratum of Palestine are copper and iron veins, and ancient mining operations have been discovered where this sandstone outcrops in the Arabah. **11. Beware that thou forget not.** Though all these natural products were to be gratefully recognized as the gifts of God just as much as the supernatural manna (v. 10b), luxury and ease would blunt the edge of Israel's awareness of God (vv. 12,13). **14. Thine heart be lifted up.** Pride would suppress the memory of humbler days of slavery, scorpions, and thirst, days when deliverance and survival required divine intervention by hitherto unknown ways (vv. 15,16). Of such denial of their Lord through self-adulation they must beware. The same truth that had to be learned in the former days of empty stomachs would be the relevant truth in the coming days of full stomachs: the source of man's life is the word of God – **he . . . giveth thee power** (17,18a). Israel's beatitude was due solely to God's fidelity to his covenant oath (v. 18b; cf. Gen 15). At the same time the Lord would visit upon covenant-breakers the curses they had invoked. **20. So shall ye perish.** Repudiation of election as the Lord's peculiar possession, and identification with the anathematized Canaanites in their idolatrous iniquity, would result in Israel's identification with the heathen in their doom.

5) The Warning of the Broken Tablets. 9:1–10:11.

For Israel to assume that Canaan was a reward for their righteousness (9:4), would be an even greater contradiction of the realities of the covenant relationship than their boasting that the possession and prosperity of the land were achieved by their might (8:17). The conceit of self-righteousness is an attempt of the sinner lusting after autonomy to free himself from God at that very point where his need of God is most desperate – the need for forgiveness and cleansing. Moses therefore passionately presented the truth that the promises and blessings of the covenant relation were Israel's by virtue of mercy, not of merit.

1-5. The occasion for this admonition was the prospect of Israel's dispossessing a people reputedly invincible in offensive warfare and defended by seemingly impregnable fortifications – **cities great and fortified** (ASV) **up to heaven** (v. 1). On the Anakim and other impressive people, see 1:28; 4:38; 7:1; Num 13:28. The spearhead of Israel's advance, however, was the One who dwelt in the heavens and made the highest mountains of earth his footstool, who was, moreover, a devouring fire (cf. Deut 4:24; 7:17ff.). **4c. For my righteousness.** This is the tragic misinterpretation of the conquest events to which Israel would be prone in defiance of all the obvious historic facts and God's explicit warning to the contrary. The explanation of Israel's triumph could lie only in the wickedness of the Canaanites on the one side (vv. 4c,5) and in God's forgiving grace to Israel on the other (9:6–10:11). For the relationship of the iniquity of the inhabitants of Canaan to the fulfillment of the promises of the Abrahamic Covenant, see Gen 15:16. Archaeological investigation has revealed the abysmal depths of moral degeneration in Canaanite society and religion in the Mosaic age. The way in which Israel's acquisition of their promised land was bound up with the elimination of the Canaanites exemplifies the principle of redemptive judgment. The salvation of the friends of God necessarily involves their triumph over the friends of Satan. From the viewpoint of the elect, the judgment of the latter is a redemptive judgment (e.g., Rev 19:11ff.; 20:9, where the redemption of the elect is consummated by the doom of the Satanic hordes).

9:6–10:11. Israel's self-righteous interpretation of the conquest had been contradicted in advance by all Moses' experience with the nation during the forty years past (vv. 7,24). They had repeatedly shown themselves to be a fractious, covenant-breaking people (vv. 6-17,21-24). They had been spared and preserved in covenant relationship to God only through the Lord's merciful renewal of the broken covenant (10:1-11) in response to the importunate mediatorial intercession of Moses (9:18-20, 25-29).

9:8. In Horeb ye provoked the Lord. The classic example of Israel's faithlessness occurred at the very time the covenant was being solemnized at Horeb (9:8ff.; cf. Ex 32). Israel had just sworn allegiance to God and vowed obedience to his commandments (Ex 24). Indeed, it was while the Lord was in the very process of inscribing the treaty on the duplicate stone documents during Moses' first stay of forty days and nights on the mount that Israel broke the covenant by engaging in idolatry. In that hour the wrath of God blazed and Israel was at the brink of destruction – **Let me alone, that I may destroy them** (v. 14; cf. 19a). So far as merit was concerned, therefore, Israel deserved not to inherit the bounties of Canaan but to fall under the ban along with the dispossessed Canaanites. Moses' treatment of the treaty tablets – **I . . . brake them before your eyes** (v. 17) – and the golden calf (v. 21) was symbolic of the shattering of the covenant. Such ritual procedure is attested in ancient state treaties in connection with a vassal's violation of his oath. **22. And**

at Taberah . . . Massah . . . Kibroth-hatta-avah. Other instances of Israel's provoking God's wrath preceded and followed the day of assembly at Sinai (Ex 17:2-7; Num 11) until their perversity at Kadesh-barnea (Deut 9:23; cf. 1:26ff.; Num 13; 14) brought the verdict of exile unto death upon the older generation.

More than once judgment had been averted through the intercession of Moses. In this aspect of Moses' ministry, more remarkably than in any other, his mediatorship prefigured the antitypical mediatorship of Christ, who also "made intercession for the transgressors" (Isa 53:12). When at Sinai God threatened to blot out Israel and offered to exalt Moses' descendants as a new covenant nation (Deut 9:14; cf. Ex 32:10), Moses faithfully fulfilled his mediatorial office in behalf of Israel rather than grasp at the opportunity to be a second Abraham. In fact, he offered himself as a second Isaac on the altar. Moses pleaded that if there must be a blotting out, rather than being made the one exception to the judgment, he might be blotted out as a means of securing forgiveness for the others (Ex 32:32). He "stood before him in the breach to turn away his wrath lest he should destroy them" (Ps 106:23). The intercession referred to in Deut 9:18,19,25-29 (cf. 10:10) was offered during Moses' second forty days on the mount.

Difficulty has been found in the fact that the content of Moses' prayer, 9:26-29, corresponds to that recorded in Ex 32:11-13, for it has been assumed that the latter refers to Moses' first forty days before God. Actually, Ex 32:11-14 is an introductory summation of the following account, which embraces the second period of forty days. The immediate chronological sequence is from Ex 32:10 to 32:15, as is reflected in Deut 9:14,15. The Exodus narrative from 32:30–34:29 possibly all refers to the second forty days and their sequel, not to preceding events; the arrangement, as often in Hebrew narrative (cf. Deut 9 itself), subordinates strict chronological sequence to topical interests. For **at that time also** (9:19; 10:10), *even at that time* would be better, giving *gam* its more frequent emphatic sense.

God's particular wrath against Aaron, (v. 20), not mentioned in the Exodus account, is cited here to demonstrate how completely devoid of merit Israel was and how dependent on mercy – even their high priest was a brand plucked from the burning! The same truth is apparent from the grounds of Moses' intercession (vv. 26-29). **27. Remember . . . Abraham, Isaac, and Jacob.** He pleaded for a stay of judgment in spite of Israel's stubborn wickedness (v. 27b) and only on the basis of God's interest in his own name among the nations of the earth. God had from of old declared his sovereign purposes of redemptive judgment and had identified that program with his dealings with Israel and Egypt. **28b. Not able to bring them into the land.** If now he destroyed Israel, even though he would not thus violate his covenant and though he would still faithfully fulfill his promises to the patriarchs (cf. 9:14), such a procedure would be liable to misunderstanding. The significance of God's mighty revelation of his name in judgment and salvation at the Exodus would be obscured and the fear of him diminished by contempt for what would be misinterpreted as weakness.

10:1-11. The renewal of the covenant after Israel's idolatry at Sinai was, therefore, due solely to divine grace. Part of the ceremony of renewal was the preparation of the two new treaty tablets. See Ex 34:1-4a, which possibly belongs chronologically between 32:29 and 32:30. Similarly, Deut 10:1a precedes in time 9:18ff. and 9:25ff. There is further disregard of chronological distinctions within 10:1-5, for the mention of the construction of the ark as the depository for the stone tablets is interwoven with the account of the hewing and engraving of this second set of treaty texts. It was actually after the second period of forty days that Moses had Bezalel construct the ark (Ex 35:30ff.; 36:2; 37:1) and it was, of course, some time later that Moses put the testimony in the ark (Ex 40:20) and then put the ark in the Tabernacle (Ex 40:21).

The condensed, summarizing treatment in Deut 10:1-5 reflects the requirement found in the international suzerainty treaties that the duplicate covenant texts were to be deposited in the sanctuaries of the two covenant parties in order thus to be under the surveillance of the oath deities. In the case of God's covenant with Israel, there was but one sanctuary involved, since God, the covenant Suzerain, was also the God who had his sanctuary in Israel. The purpose of 10:1-5 being to state in a comprehensive and general way that God had mercifully reconfirmed the covenant with the rebellious vassals, Moses included the matter of the ark as a familiar and integral element in the standard ratification procedure.

Verses 6 and 7, with which verses 8 and 9 belong materially, constitute a stylistic break. It is uncertain (1) whether this excursus originated as a quotation read from an itinerary in the course of Moses' address, (2) whether he parenthetically inserted it when writing the Book of the Law, or (3) whether someone like the author of Deuteronomy 34 added it. **6. The children of Israel took their journey.** The journey in view is that southward from Kadesh recorded in Num 33:37 (for the particular stations, see Num 33:30-33). **His son ministered in the priest's office** (v. 6c). Verses 6,7 are relevant to the context; for they further enhance the covenant-renewing grace of God by recalling that the Lord re-instituted the priesthood of Aaron of the tribe of Levi and continued it in Aaron's son Eleazer in spite of his anger against the father (9:20). **8. The Lord separated . . . Levi.** Cf. Exodus 28; 29; Num 1:49ff.; 3:9ff.; 4:17ff.; 8:6ff.; 18:20-24. This section may also be regarded as an elaboration of the subject of the covenant tables (Deut 10:8; cf. v. 5). The intercession theme is concluded in 10:10,11. **10. The Lord hearkened unto me.** Cf. 9:18,19. The journey to the promised homeland, of which Israel was so utterly undeserving, was to be resumed because of God's regard for his own name, the name he had taken in oath because he could swear by no higher (10:11; cf. Ex 33:1ff.).

6) A Call to Commitment. 10:12–11:32.

Israel was now confronted with the great decision, the choice between the blessing and the curse (11:26-32). Moses enforced the call to obedience (10:12ff.; 11:1,8,13,18ff.,32) by focusing the eyes of the people on him who addressed to them his covenant as the righteous Judge of heaven and earth (10:12-22), whose impartial judgment Israel had in the past seen irresistibly executed in Egypt and in the wilderness (11:1-7) and should in the future find sovereignly exercised over the land and inhabitants of Canaan (11:8-25).

12-22. 12. And now introduces the conclusion to a major division of the address (cf. 4:1). **Fear the Lord . . . love him.** The basic and comprehensive covenant requirement is here repeated (vv. 12,13,20; cf. 6:5,13,24; Mic 6:8). True fear and true love are complementary and inseparable. They are the response of a true heart to God's majesty and goodness, respectively, and together they are productive of wholehearted service in obedience to all God's good pleasure. **16. Circumcise . . . your heart.** Such genuine devotion can flow only from a heart that has experienced the reality of that qualification which was symbolized in the initiatory sign of the covenant (cf. 30:6; Ex 6:12,30; Lev 26:41; Jer 6:10; 9:25,26). To inspire the fear of the Lord, Moses summoned Israel to behold him as Lord of the cosmos (Deut 10:14), as God above all that be called gods (v. 17a), as righteous Judge (v. 17b), and as Sovereign over history and nature (v. 21). To encourage love toward him, Moses recalled how God had bestowed the privilege of covenant status on Israel's ancestors (v. 15a), fulfilled the patriarchal promises (vv. 15b,21,22), and shown himself a Helper of the helpless (vv. 18,19).

11:1-7. The charge to love the Lord (v. 1) is a connecting refrain in 10:12–11:32. After "And know ye this day" (v. 2), there is a parenthetical remark (see RSV), which notes that the summons to covenantal decision was not addressed to the children born in the wilderness. It was, rather, directed to those who had been born in Egypt and had seen God's great acts of judgment in the past (v. 7). **2.** The object of **know ye is the discipline** (AV, *chastisement*) **of the Lord your God, his greatness,** etc. (RSV). Israel had been disciplined to reverence the Lord as the Judge with whom they had to do by their experience of his judgment on their enemies (vv. 2-4) and themselves alike (vv. 5,6). They knew, therefore, that his judgment was almighty, so that the mightiest on earth could not prevent it; and it was impartially righteous, so that even his covenant people dared not presume upon their election. **6. What he did unto Dathan and Abiram.** See Numbers 16, especially verses 31-33. Moses' silence with respect to the rebel Korah was possibly in deference to the surviving Levitical Korahites (Num 26:11).

8-17. From Israel's future, too, Moses adduced motives for obedience. **8,9. That ye may . . . possess the land . . . and . . . prolong your days.** On the relation of Israel's tenure on the land to her covenant fidelity, see comments on 6:1-3. Unlike Egypt, with its irrigation agriculture, Canaan was clearly dependent for its fruitfulness on the direct blessing of God (vv. 11,12; cf. 8:7ff.); and in that sphere God's righteous judgment with respect to Israel's conduct would be registered (vv. 13-17). **13,14. If ye shall hearken . . . I will give the rain.** Prosperity would depend on proper weather conditions the year around (cf. 12b), especially important being the timely commencement of the rainy season in the fall and the due extension of the latter rains in the spring. The very state of nature would thus constantly serve as a sensitive barometer of Israel's standing before the Lord. Therefore, Israel must be on guard against the spiritual dangers of material abundance (vv. 14b,15). **16. Take heed to yourselves.** For bounty can turn into drought, famine, and death at the mere word of the Lord, the impartial, almighty Judge at whose command even the earth opened its mouth to swallow the Israelites Dathan and Abiram (vv. 15-17; cf. 11:6; 6:11-15; 8:11-20).

18-25. Since the nations, as well as nature, are under the Lord's absolute control, they are another agency in his government of his Israelite vassals. **18. Lay up these . . . words in your heart.** Cf. 6:6-9. Faithfulness from generation to generation would result in the perpetuation of Israel's possession of the promised land **as the days of heaven upon the earth** (v. 21); i.e., as long as the heavens continue above the earth, in short, forever (cf. Ps 72:5,7,17; 89:29). By the same token infidelity must lead to termination of tenure. **22,23. If . . . then.** Success in the stipulated program of conquest (vv. 23-25; cf. 7:1,2,17ff.; 9:1ff.) would depend first and last not on military prowess but on religious commitment. Fulfillment of the great commandment would be blessed with inheritance of the land of promise to its utmost boundaries: from the wilderness of the Sinai peninsula on the south to the Lebanon mountains on the north, and from the Euphrates on the east to the Mediterranean on the west (v. 24; cf. 1:7; Gen 15:18).

26-32. 26. A blessing and a curse. Here is the sum and conclusion of the whole matter (vv. 26-28). The sovereignty of the Lord, declared in the covenant now renewed unto Israel, could be manifested in either blessing or curse (cf. ch. 28; 30:15-20). Israel must decide which it should be. This twofold prospect and its challenge, which Moses placed before Israel **this day** in Moab, would be set before them again by Joshua on the other side of the Jordan in Canaan, that the nation might be careful to obey God and live (11:29-32). The transition from the Mosaic to the Joshuan leadership was thus to be marked by a two-stage renewal ritual, which would exhibit the continuity of the more ultimate divine leadership. This arrangement was the equivalent of measures taken in vassal treaties by human suzerains to guarantee the dynastic succession on their thrones. See Deuteronomy 27 for the more detailed directions concerning the second stage of the ceremony to be conducted on Mount Gerizim and Mount Ebal (cf. Josh 8:30-35).

B. Ancillary Commandments. 12:1–26:19.

Having delineated the inner spirit of theocratic life (chs. 5–11), Moses went on to detail the ordinances and institutions of the theocracy's outward form (chs. 12–26). Chapters 12:1–16:17 are primarily concerned with cultic-ceremonial consecration requirements. Governmental and judicial authority is the subject in 16:18–21:23. The sphere of the mutual relationships of the theocratic citizens is covered by the legislation in 22:1–25:19. The stipulations conclude with ritual confessions of the Lord's dominion and a final declaration of covenant ratification (ch. 26).

1) Cultic - Ceremonial Consecration. 12:1–16:17.

The central interest of the laws of this section was to guarantee a thoroughgoing consecration to the Lord. Governing all the demands for tributary service in tithe (v. 14), first fruits (v. 15), and sacrificial offerings (v. 16) was the law of the central altar, with which this section opens (v. 12). Singleness of devotion to the Lord was safeguarded by the imposition of the severest penalties on all who enticed to or became guilty of apostasy (v. 13).

a) Allegiance to God's Altar. 12:1-32.

1-3. In the land (v. 1; cf. 6:1). In the prophetic perspective of the following stipulations Israel is viewed as already in possession of her inheritance. **Utterly destroy . . . And . . . overthrow** (vv. 2,3). This section connects with the preceding by resuming that part of the mandate of conquest which required the obliteration of Canaanite cultic centers and installations (cf. 7:5,25; Ex 23:24; 34:13). The execution of the program of conquest as a whole would bring the tribes into control of idolatrous shrines throughout the land (cf. Isa 1:29; 57:5; 65:7; Jer 2:20; 3:6; 17:2; Ezk 6:13; 18:6ff.; Hos 4:13; I Kgs 14:23; II Kgs 16:4;

17:10); and these would present a temptation to religious syncretism (Deut 12:29,30). The Israelites would be in danger of adopting abominations like the fiery votive offering of children (v. 31; cf. 18:10; Lev 18:21; II Kgs 16:3; 17:17; 21:6; 23:10; Jer 7:31; 19:5; 32:35). In addition to the punitive purpose of the destruction of Canaanite cultic sites there was, therefore, the preventive design of protecting Israel against ensnarement in the Canaanite cultic rites. The fact that the law of the central sanctuary (Deut 12:4 ff.) is thus introduced (vv. 2,3) and concluded (cf. vv. 29-31) by such references to the Canaanite cultus shows that one purpose of the centralization of Israelite worship, too, was to avoid the contamination of the pure worship of the Lord by idolatrous practices.

The centralization requirement must also be understood in terms of Deuteronomy's nature as a suzerainty treaty. Such treaties prohibited the vassal's engaging in any independent diplomacy with a foreign power other than the covenant suzerain. In particular, the vassal must not pay tribute to any other lord. Similarly, all the requirements and prohibitions of Deuteronomy 12 were calculated to secure for the Lord all Israel's tributary sacrifice and offering. Israel must not pay any sacrificial tribute to other gods, for such an impossible attempt to serve two masters would be rebellion against the great commandment of God's covenant.

In the promised land the law of the central altar would involve both the centralization of the special sacrificial festivals (vv. 4-14) and the decentralization of the common family feasts (vv. 15-28).

4-14. In contrast to the multiplicity of altars among the Canaanites (v. 4), who sacrificed wherever they pleased (cf. v. 13), Israel was to have one central altar, and that at **the place which the Lord your God shall choose** (v. 5). This oneness of the sanctuary corresponded to the oneness of the divine lordship over Israel (cf. 6:4,5).

Modern higher criticism has erroneously held that the concept of the central altar taught in Deuteronomy (or according to some, only in Deut 12:1-7, which is then regarded as a later interpolation) stands in contradiction to other Biblical legislation (see esp., in the Book of the Covenant, Ex 20:24). The Deuteronomic requirement has therefore been judged to be a later modification of earlier, supposedly more lax practice. The book as a whole has been dated in the seventh century B.C. and identified as the law book found in Josiah's day. A more recent approach of critics is to resolve the supposed conflict of codes not by placing them in a chronological sequence across the centuries, but by assigning to each a different geographic-cultic source. Deuteronomy is thought to represent the northern, Levitical outlook, the central sanctuary in view being Shechem. Some critics have even allowed that the centralization law in Deuteronomy might represent a return to an earlier, premonarchical ideal of the amphictyony.

Actually, so far as normative religious practice was concerned, there was nothing essentially new about this law even in Moses' day. In patriarchal times, when a succession of altars was built in the course of the patriarchs' journeyings, there was apparently but one central family altar at any given time. Similarly, in the Sinaitic legislation (Ex 20:24), Israel's place of sacrifice is identified with the central place where God recorded his name (i.e., revealed his glorious nature) by special supernatural theophany, the place of God's visible symbolic dwelling in the midst of his people. The Tabernacle had successively different locations during Israel's wilderness journeyings, but it remained a single sanctuary.

What is new in the Deuteronomic formulation is only the prospect of a stationary location for the sanctuary. Deuteronomy envisages a permanent habitation of God in Israel. **10. When he giveth you rest.** Even this new circumstance must await the attainment of peace and rest (cf. Heb 4:1 ff.), a condition which fully arrived at the OT typical level only in the days of David and Solomon (II Sam 7:1; I Kgs 5:4). Only then did God choose out of all the tribes the city of Jerusalem as the site for his house (I Kgs 8:16,44,48; 11:13,32,36; 14:21; II Kgs 21:7; 23:27), though at the first he had recorded his name temporarily at Shiloh (Jer 7:12; Jud 21:19). Furthermore, the Mosaic law of the central altar, while regulating the prescribed and ordinary sacrificial service of Israel (Deut 12:6,7,11 ff.) as it was to be performed periodically at the three principal festivals, also recognized the possibility of revelatory action of God apart from the central altar and allowed for the specially appointed service and altar (cf. 27:5 ff.). The accent thus falls more heavily on the purity than on the unity of the cultus. Also prominent in Moses' thought of covenant communion with the Lord was the note of joy – **ye shall rejoice before the Lord** (v. 12; cf. v. 7). Love to God expressed in joyful worship was also to find its corollary in love to the brethren, especially in kindness to those who, like the Levites (v. 12; cf. v. 19), were dependent on the generosity, indeed on the piety, of the congregation (cf. Num 18:21; 35:1ff.).

Contrasting the future arrangements with present practice, Moses declared that even under his leadership the Israelites were doing whatever was right in their own eyes (Deut 12:8; cf. Jud 17:6; 21:25). Here at least this expression is not derogatory but apparently indicates simply that there was no need to reckon as yet with distinctions such as that between sacrificial feasts (Deut 12:4-14) and family feasts (vv. 15-28).

15-28. Besides bringing the Israelite tribes into contact with heathen shrines, the inheriting of Canaan would locate the tribal homes at considerable distances from Israel's own central sanctuary (v. 21). If the stipulations of 12:4-14 were to be carried out in that new situation, a distinction had to be made between the slaughtering and eating of animals suitable for a sacrificial feast and those suitable for an ordinary meal; and permission must be granted for the decentralization of the latter. This new provision constituted a modification of the requirements of Lev 17:1ff., which governed the Israelites' consumption of flesh while they were a compact camp about the Tabernacle in the wilderness. **15b. The unclean and the clean may eat of it, as of the gazelle and as of the hart** (RSV; cf. v. 22). Participation in the family feast was not dependent on ceremonial condition (cf. Lev 7:19ff.), and the kind of meat permissible included that which was proper for sacrifice as well as meat like game (cf. Deut 14:5), which was not sacrificially acceptable.

Attached to this permission were certain restrictions. One is the familiar prohibition of blood – **ye shall not eat the blood** (vv. 16,23ff.; cf. Lev 17:10ff.; Gen 9:4). Pouring the blood upon the ground would be a safeguard against pouring it as a sacrifice on some nearby, illegally remaining Canaanite altar. The centralization, during the wilderness journeyings, of the slaughter of all animals fit for sacrifice was explicitly designed to avoid such temptation (cf. Lev 17:7). **17. Thou mayest not eat . . . the tithe,** etc. Another proviso, or better, a clarification of the permission of verse 15, was the reminder that all holy gifts to the Lord must be taken to the place of the central sanctuary which God should choose (see also vv. 26,27). That is, the permission operated within the positive requirements of verses 4-14 (cf. esp. vv. 6,11). The interspersing of exhortations among the stipulations (e.g., vv. 25,28) is one of the identifying marks of the Deuteronomic legislation as treaty stipulations rather than as a legal code.

29-32. On verses 29-31, see comments on verses 1-3. **32. Thou shalt not add thereto, nor diminish from it** (13:1 in Heb. Bible). Repeating essentially 4:2, Moses again declared that the only true standard of ethics and godly service is the revealed will of God – no less, no more.

b) Resistance to Apostasy. 13:1-18.

In the ancient suzerainty treaties it was required of the vassal that he must not connive at evil words spoken against the suzerain, whether they amounted to an affront or to a conspiracy. The vassal must report the insult or the fomenting of revolt. In case of active rebellion, he must undertake military measures against the offenders. Moreover, he must manifest fidelity to his lord in such cases no matter who the rebel might be, whether prince or nearest relative. All of this finds its formal counterpart in Deuteronomy 13. Stylistically the chapter is cast in the casuistic form characteristic of ancient law codes but also of some treaty stipulations. Three cases of rebellion against the Lord are dealt with. The first two relate to the instigation stage, the guilty parties being sign-attested claimants to revelation (vv. 1-5) and the vassal's nearest relative or companion (vv. 6-11). The third case concerns a city that has been enticed to rebel against the Lord and is guilty of serving idol-lords (vv. 12-18).

1-5 (Heb. Bible, vv. 2-6). **1. A prophet, or a dreamer of dreams.** Intimation of the prophetic institution to be established in Israel had already been given. God's self-disclosure to the prophets would be through the media of vision and dream (Num 12:5; cf. Deut 18:15ff.). Even if one with impressive credentials to the effect that he was a channel of revelation (1b,2a) should incite Israel to render allegiance and tribute to other gods (2b; cf. 3b,5b), his counsel must be despised (3a; cf. Gal 1:8,9). **2. And the sign or the wonder come to pass.** Both terms can refer to an event which in itself is either ordinary or extraordinary.

Here they apparently refer to a predicted event, not necessarily miraculous, which comes to pass. The fulfillment of the prediction is then claimed as a sign of genuine prophetic vocation and authority. **Saying** (v. 2) is to be taken with **if there arise** (v. 1). Israel's standard of life and worship was God's revelation through Moses, spoken and written; the fundamental demand thereof was exclusive allegiance to the Lord — **walk after the Lord** (v. 4). In order to test Israel's obedience to that paramount stipulation, God would permit the false prophet to arise (v. 3b). And because the latter would counsel Israel to repudiate that demand, the very essence of the covenant (cf. 6:4,5; Ex 20:3), the ultimate penalty was prescribed for him — **that prophet . . . shall be put to death** (v. 5). Notice the quotations from the preamble and historical prologue of the covenant tablets (cf. Ex 20:2). The execution of the instigator to defection would "burn out" the evil from the midst of Israel, which, if it remained and spread, would result in the burning out of many in Israel (cf. Deut 13:12ff., esp. v. 16; 17:12; 19:11-13; 21:18-21; 22:21-24; 24:7).

6-11 (Heb. Bible 7-12). As effective as the wonder-sign of the speaking serpent, with its oracular declarations, in the case of Eve's seduction was the constraint lent to Eve's subsequent temptation of Adam by his affection for her, the wife of his bosom, beloved as his own soul. **6. If thy brother . . . entice thee secretly.** The subtlety of the temptation in this case contrasts with the public invitation of the false prophet (cf. v. 1ff.) and would make it easy to conceal the dear one's sin and to avoid the judicial responsibility without detection. But, as in the case of the international treaties, any failure to report "evil words" and expose rebellious plots was a breach of God's covenant. **8. Neither shall thine eye pity him.** The call of the covenant is to love the Lord our God though it mean to hate parents and brethren, wife and children, and one's own life also (cf. Lk 14:26). Therefore, that one who was dearest to the covenant servant must be as sternly judged as the false prophet if he or she proposed disloyalty to the Lord. **9. Thou shalt . . . kill him.** For the judicial procedure in view, see 17:7. An important benefit of executing the divine sentence would be the monitory impact on Israel, forestalling further apostasy (v. 11; cf. 17:13; 19:20; 21:21).

12-18 (Heb. Bible, 13-19). If the stipulations of the preceding verses were not vigorously carried out, the rebellion would increase from individual to community proportions, a situation requiring the yet more difficult judicial decision and action prescribed here. **13. Base fellows** (ASV; RSV) and *children of Belial* (AV) are renderings of an expression variously understood as sons of worthlessness or disorder or wickedness or Sheol. This is how God sees those enticers to idolatry who appear to men as impressive prophets or dearest kin. If the verdict of guilt was reached (v. 14), the sentence must be the infliction of the ban (v. 15ff.; cf. comments on 7:1-5). **15. Smite the inhabitants of that city.** By embracing the abomination of Canaan, the Israelite city would become an abomination; it would become like Canaanite Jericho and must share its cursed doom by fire and sword. The divine Suzerain, like the human lords in their ancient treaties, imposed regulations concerning the spoil that would fall into the hands of his vassal on a punitive campaign. In the present instance, the less common demand was made that all the spoil be added to the holocaust by which the accursed city would become a whole burnt offering to the praise of God's justice and wrath. **16. An heap for ever.** Hebrew *tēl* denotes an abandoned mound produced by the accumulated debris of successive occupations of a site. Israel's experience in the case of Achan (Josh 7; 8) exemplified both the danger of violating the law of the spoil in Deut 13:16, 17a and the faithfulness of the Lord to the promise of verses 17b,18.

c) Filial Obligations. 14:1—15:23.

As the people of the Lord, committed to his service and commissioned to remove from their midst all devotees and shrines of idols (chs. 12; 13), Israel was a distinctive nation. That must be manifested throughout the ceremonial dimension of the nation's life. Whether in connection with death (14:1,2) or life (vv. 3-21), the ceremonial practice of the Israelites must reflect their peculiar sanctity. Their sacred consecration was also to be displayed in the consecration of the fruit of their life's labor to the Lord their God (vv. 22-29).

1,2. Ye are the children of the Lord your God. . . . an holy people. Here again the Ex 19:5,6 definition of the theocratic nation is echoed (cf. Deut 7:6), enriched now with the concept of sonship (cf. Ex 4:22). In the OT period the emphasis was on Israel as servant rather than as son, because though the nation of Israel was the son and heir, it was to be under governors until the time appointed of the Father (cf. Gal 4:1ff.). **Ye shall not cut yourselves.** The Israelites were not to mutilate themselves as the heathen commonly did in mourning rites (v. 1b; cf. Lev 19:28; 21:5). The reason assigned is that, as the elect and adopted people of God, they held a holy status. And underlying that reason was the fact that their God is Lord of life and Creator of man in his image.

3-21. 3. Any abominable thing. Ceremonial distinctions may at times appear arbitrary. Such is the case with the classification of clean and unclean meats in these dietary regulations. For although hygienic explanations are apparent in some instances, they are not apparent in all. But the very arbitrariness of these stipulations made them the better tests of submission to the sovereign word of the Lord and more distinctive badges of consecration to him. It reminded Israel that man must live according to every word of God's mouth (cf. 8:3). It is God's creative word that gives to all things their definition and meaning, and man must interpret all things in imitation of the interpretation God assigns them. In this respect the Mosaic dietary rules resembled the probationary proscription of the fruit of the tree of knowledge in Eden or the arrangements for the provision of the manna in the wilderness.

4. These . . . beasts . . . ye shall eat. This section repeats almost verbally Lev 11:2-23. Deuteronomy 14:4b,5 supplements the Levitical formulation and that in a way which reflects the wilderness origin of Deuteronomy. For the habitat of the edible game animals specified was the area of Israel's journeying from Egypt to Canaan, not the wooded hill country of Canaan itself. **21. Any thing that dieth of itself.** This involves a modification of Lev 17:15. The practice mentioned here in verse 21b (cf. Ex 23:19; 34:26) was prohibited because it was a ceremonial custom of the Canaanites.

22-29. 22. Tithe . . . the increase of thy seed. An annual tithe of the produce of the land was to be offered to the Lord in recognition of the fact that the land was his and that he was the bestower of life and fertility. Because of variants between the Deuteronomic and the earlier tithe stipulations (Lev 27:30-33; Num 18:21-32), the erroneous view was developed by the Jews (and has been accepted by many Christian exegetes) that Deuteronomy prescribes a second tithe and, some would say, even a third tithe (cf. Deut 14:28ff.; 26:12-15). Deuteronomy 14 does not, however, necessarily involve any drastic modification of the earlier tithe law. It specifies only an agricultural tithe, though it mentions the firstlings of flock and herd (v. 23; cf. 12:17; 15:19ff.). But even Numbers 18 does not explicitly mention an animal tithe. Only Leviticus 27 does so (cf. II Chr 31:6). It is possibly taken for granted in both Numbers 18 and Deuteronomy 14. According to Num 18:21, "every tithe" (RSV) was given to the Levites. Deuteronomy 14 specifies that except in the third and sixth years (and of course the fallow sabbath year also; cf. Ex 23:11), the offerer might use the tithe—presumably, however, only a small part of it—for a communion feast at the sanctuary.

23. That thou mayest learn to fear the Lord. The purpose of this section is not so much to give a comprehensive statement of the tithe law as to guard tithing procedure from being prostituted to idolatrous ends; that is, to prevent Israel from honoring the Canaanite fertility deities for their harvests. The insistence, therefore, was that all religious ceremony associated with tithing be conducted at the central sanctuary (12:6,11). It is necessary to take account of this particular purpose of these verses when making comparisons with tithing regulations elsewhere. (On the reason for the permission of vv. 24ff., see 12:21.) **28. At the end of three years.** The conjunction of this with the sabbatical legislation of 15:1ff. indicates that such triennial years (called in 26:12 "the year of tithing") were the third and sixth years within the sabbatical-Jubilee cycle.

29. The stranger . . . the fatherless . . . the widow. A minor modification of the agricultural tithe, in keeping with the familiar charitable interest of the Lord in the poor class, which would emerge in the social stratification of life in Canaan, is this inclusion of other dependents along with the Levites in the use of the tithe of the third and sixth years. See Num 18:26-32 for the disposition of these tithes to be made by the Levites.

15:1-23. The main thread of the preceding legislation is picked up again in the law of the firstlings in 15:19-23 (cf. 14:23). Meanwhile, verses 1-18 elaborate the subject of love toward needy brethren, which came up in the exposition of tithing procedure (14:27ff.). Specifically, these stipulations deal with the remission of debts (vv. 1-11) and the manumission of bond servants (vv. 12-18). A further element of continuity is found in the sabbatical framework for this program of mercy (cf. 14:28).

1-11. 1. At the end of every seven years. This refers to the sabbatical year which ended each seven-year period within a Jubilee cycle (cf. 14:28). The institution of the year of release was established in the Book of the Covenant (Ex 23:10,11) and expounded in the Levitical instructions (Lev 25:2ff.). **2. The Lord's release.** Hebrew *shᵉmiṭṭâ*, "release," comes from a root meaning *to let fall*. In Ex 23:11 it is applied to the land in the sense of lying fallow. Hence the year of release is "a sabbath of rest unto the land" (Lev 25:4). Here it is applied to debts in the sense of remission. Many have interpreted this as a one-year moratorium on the creditor's collection of debts. However, the fact that the seventh year of release and the Jubilee year of liberty belonged to one symbolical unit indicates that a permanent cancellation of debts is meant. The crowning Jubilee Sabbath simply carried the principle further to a restoration of personal freedom and a return of real estate. At each level the sabbatical release was a renewal of the Lord's original deliverance of the covenant people from bondage and a reinstatement of the families in their original inheritance. Agreeably, the Sabbath itself is associated with the Lord's deliverance of his needy, crying people from bondage (cf. Deut 5:14,15). The release of the seventh year was the Lord's, though his mercy was manifested through the philanthropy of his servants. It was designed to refurbish the theocratic symbol of the kingdom of God periodically by a fresh realization of the saving and restoring grace of the Lord which was experienced so abundantly at the beginning of Israel's theocratic life. At the same time it pointed prophetically to the future redemptive action of God, anticipating the Messianic reign of mercy to the poor and helpless (cf. Ps 72). This consummation prospect is always present in sabbatical symbolism. **4. But there will be no poor among you** (RSV). The need for such charity, as is parenthetically observed (vv. 4-6), would be obviated by the absence of any poor in Israel, if such faithfulness were always manifested as to warrant the bestowal of the covenant blessings in richest measure. As a matter of fact, however, for want of fidelity in Israel, the poor would always be present (v. 11; cf. Mk 14:7). **9. Beware** [lest] . . . **thine eye be evil against thy poor brother.** Such, indeed, were the sinful propensities of even the covenant people that they must be warned lest this septennial provision of mercy to the poor become an occasion for oppressing them in the intervening periods. The practice of observing a year of release seems to some financially infeasible (which is one reason why some commentators interpret the release as a temporary suspension of debt). But the people of faith were called upon to recognize that within the peculiar covenantal arrangements of God with the theocratic nation, obedience to this stipulation was a guarantee of prosperity — **for this thing the Lord . . . shall bless thee** (v. 10; cf. Lev 25:20,21). That the Scriptures do not recommend this as a normative policy outside the OT theocratic community of Israel is evident even from the exceptive clause in Deut 15:3a. The **foreigner** (v. 3a) is not, like the "sojourner" or "stranger who is within thy gates," a permanent member of the community, but one temporarily visiting for commercial purposes or the like.

12-18. 12. Thou shalt let him go free. Though septennially structured, this law, unlike 14:28,29 and 15:1-11, does not refer to the regular sabbatical units within a Jubilee cycle but to a seven-year period beginning whenever an individual Hebrew became an indentured servant. This provision for manumission was also contained in the Book of the Covenant (Ex 21:2-6), and it finds a counterpart within the Levitical legislation concerning the Jubilee year (Lev 25:39-55; cf. Jer 34:14). **Or an Hebrew woman.** The inclusion of Hebrew women, possibly implicit in Ex 21:2-6 (cf. Ex 21:7-11, which deals with the special case of the concubine-maidservant) becomes explicit here. As in the release of debt, so in the release of the slave, the limits of application were the Israelite brotherhood.

In view of the contrast instituted between the "brother" and the "foreigner" in this context and the identification of the Hebrew servant as a brother (Deut 15:12), the theory which regards the "Hebrew servant" as a "foreign servant" must be judged erroneous. According to that theory, what Ex 21:6 and Deut 15:17 allow for a Hebrew servant, Lev 25:44-46 forbids for an Israelite. But Leviticus 25 refers to a compulsory, rigorous slavery, while the Hebrew servant passages refer to a voluntary, agreeable service. The stipulation of a Jubilee manumission in Lev 25:40,41 supplements the Hebrew servant's right of seventh-year release as a special boon when the Jubilee arrived before his seventh year of service. **16. If he say . . . I will not go away.** This supplementary right, like that of release in the seventh year, was subject to the servant's further right to voluntary lifelong service of a beloved master (cf. Ex 21:5,6). In the Deuteronomic reformulation of this provision, it becomes more liberal (15:13,14) and various inducements to obedience are cited (vv. 15,18).

19-23. The subject of firstlings mentioned in 14:23 (cf. 12:6,17) is now resumed. Earlier legislation on the subject is found in Ex 13:2,11-16; 22:29,30; 34:19,20; Lev 27:26,27; Num 18:15-18. The Deuteronomic treatment is not exhaustive but designed only to clarify the relevance of the law of the central altar (Deut 12) to the administration of the law of firstlings within the anticipated circumstances of the tribes dispersed and exposed to the dangerous influences of local Canaanite shrines. Thus the new formulation refers to a fact not noted in previous legislation, namely, that the offerer and his household were to participate in the sacrificial meal accompanying the presentation of firstlings. **20. Thou shalt eat it before the Lord.** Clearly, that is mentioned here in order to press the requirement that all sacred feasting must take place at the central sanctuary (12:6,17), even though in Canaan common feasts would be permitted elsewhere (12:15ff.). There is no necessary contradiction between the assignment of the firstlings to the priests and their families (Num 18:15-18) and this sharing of the offerer's family in the sacrificial meal. See 14:23-27 for a similar situation with respect to the disposition of the tithes. **Year by year.** Annual offering was substituted for eighth-day offering (cf. Ex 22:30) for the same reason that eating of flesh at home was henceforth to be allowed (Deut 12:21). On verse 21a, see Lev 22:19ff.; Deut 17:1. Observe again the concern to show the relevance of the fundamental legislation of Deuteronomy 12 to this particular matter of the firstlings (15:22,23; cf. 12:15,16,22ff.).

d) Tributary Pilgrimages. 16:1-17.

The section which began at 12:1 concludes with commandments concerning the three annual pilgrimages to the central sanctuary: the feasts of Passover and Unleavened Bread (16:1-8), Weeks (vv. 9-12), and Tabernacles (vv. 13-15). For the earlier legislation, see chiefly Exodus 12; Leviticus 23; Numbers 28 and 29. Our comments here are largely devoted to features peculiar to the Deuteronomic formulation and problems raised thereby. The sabbatical scheme is again present (cf. Deut 14:28–15:18), for the entire religious calendar of feasts was sabbatically patterned. Still prominent is the concern with the way in which the contemplated divine choice of a permanent sanctuary site in the midst of an extensive land must modify previous ceremonial practice. Note the repeated use of the formula for the central altar (16:2,6,7, 11,15,16). Because Deuteronomy is a covenant-renewal document presupposing earlier covenant stipulations as still valid, except as it expressly modifies them, it condenses and omits much while giving new emphasis to features affected by the introduction of "the place which the Lord shall choose." Recognition of this should have prevented many of the higher critical allegations of contradiction between Deuteronomy and other Pentateuchal legislation. Viewed as a suzerainty treaty, Deut 16:1-17 corresponds to the customary demand that the vassal appear annually before the suzerain with the stipulated tribute. Beginning with verse 18 there is a new section principally concerned with the administration of justice.

The Passover. 16:1-8. **1. The month of Abib.** See Ex 12:1,6; 34:18. **The passover.** This term is used in these verses as comprehending both the Passover proper and the following seven-day Feast of Unleavened Bread (cf. v. 3, noting that the antecedent of "therewith" is **passover**). Consequently, this Passover sacrifice might be taken from both flock and herd (v. 2), whereas for the Passover proper, a lamb was prescribed (Ex 12:3ff.). For the sacrifices referred to in Deut 16:2, see the account of the celebration in II Chr 30:22ff. and 35:7ff., and note the use there of the term "passover offerings," literally, *passovers,* for sacrifices from the herd. **3. The bread of affliction** recalled the oppressive circumstances in the house of bondage, especially Pharaoh's opposition to Israel's departure, which compelled them to make hasty preparations for flight. On verses 3,4a, see Ex 12:15,18-20; 13:3,6,7; 23:15; 34:18; Lev 23:6. On verse 4b, see Ex 12:10; 23:18b; 34:25b; Num 9:12. On verse 8, see Ex 12:16; Lev 23:7,8; Num 28:18,25.

4. In order to designate more specifically the Passover proper, Moses calls **it the flesh, which thou sacrificedst the first day at even.** The references to the "passover" immediately after that designation (vv. 5,6) are also evidently to be taken in that narrower sense. **7a. Roast and eat it** (AV, ASV). The RSV unnecessarily creates a conflict with Ex 12:9 by translating the verb *bāshal* as "boil." It is only an additional specification like "with water" or "in pots" that definitely gives this Hebrew verb the meaning "boil" (cf. Ex 12:9; II Chr 35:13b). When further defined by "with fire," *bāshal* clearly signifies "roast" (see II Chr 35:13a). By itself it is ambiguous. This ambiguity in Deut 16:7 is due to the fact that the manner of preparing the sacrifice for eating had already been established and was not Moses' present concern. He was, rather, emphasizing the point that this feast must take place at the central sanctuary. Only after the observance of the complete feast, both preparation and participation, might the worshipers depart from the sanctuary to their living quarters. **7b. Unto thy tents.** The ambiguity of this expression (which would here refer to the pilgrims' temporary quarters in the holy city) is also attributable to Moses' overriding interest in the idea of the central altar. Preparation of the sacrifice at the sanctuary was a modification of the observance of the first Passover in Egypt, when the blood was applied to the individual homes in the absence of a centralized cult and altar.

The Feast of Weeks. 16:9-12. On the subject of this section, see the earlier prescriptions in Ex 23:16; 34:22; Lev 23:15ff.; Num 28:26ff. **10a. The feast of weeks** (cf. Ex 34:22) was also called "feast of harvest" (Ex 23:16) and "day of the firstfruits" (Num 28:26). In later times it received the Greek name *Pentecost* because of the way its date was calculated, namely, fifty days from a set starting point (Lev 23:16). That point is here described in general terms as the beginning of the grain harvest (Deut 16:9). There was no need for greater precision because the exact date had already been given in Lev 23:10ff. It was the second day of the Feast of Unleavened Bread, the day of the offering of the sheaf of the first fruits of the grain harvest. This was the "morrow after the sabbath" (Lev 23:15), for the first day of Unleavened Bread was a day of rest. Following this reckoning, the NT Pentecost event fell on a Saturday. The seven weeks between the Passover and Harvest pilgrimages allowed time for the completion of the grain harvest. **10b. Freewill offering** (cf. Num 29:39; Lev 23:38). This feast was one of joy – joy in the Lord, who had brought his people unto their fruitful paradise land (Deut 16:10c,11; cf. 12:7,12,18; 16:14,15) – joy in the Lord who had delivered from bondage (v. 12), and thus a joy to be shared with all the poor within the covenant family (v. 11b).

The Feast of Tabernacles or *Booths.* 16:13-15. Parallel legislation is in Ex 23:16; 34:22; Lev 23:33ff.; Num 29:12ff. **13. The feast of tabernacles** or ***booths*** (RSV) is also called the "feast of ingathering" (in Exodus). Like the Feast of Unleavened Bread, it lasted a week, i.e., from the fifteenth to the twenty-first of the seventh month. It was followed by an octave sabbath day (Lev 23:36,39). The name Tabernacles reflects the custom of dwelling in booths during the festival, which served as a memorial of life in the wilderness (cf. the use of unleavened bread). The name "Ingathering" indicates that this feast was the culmination of the agricultural year, when vintage as well as grain had been harvested. In the year of release, when there was no harvest, this feast was the occasion for the significant public reading of the text of the covenant (Deut 31:9-13). Once again, the point of the formulation was to enforce the law of the central sanctuary – **the place which the Lord shall choose** (v. 15). Here, too, joy and love are the marks of covenant life and worship (v. 14).

16, 17. Cf. Ex 23:17; 34:23. This concluding summary turns all eyes again to the central sanctuary (v. 16a) and brings into relief the character of the pilgrimages as tributary trips to the throne of the God-King (v. 16b). **17. According to the blessing of the Lord.** Cf. I Cor 16:2.

2) Judicial-Governmental Righteousness. 16:18–21:23.

This section contains a series of stipulations concerning theocratic government, with primary emphasis on the judiciary. Israel must add to cultic holiness political-judicial righteousness. Between the governmental and the cultic there was a unity of ultimate authority, since the Lord was both God and King in Israel. Consequently, all theocratic institutions, unlike those in the ordinary state, were confessionally religious, and there was an extension of cultic practice beyond the sanctuary into the administration of government. Moreover, because all theocratic law, moral and civil as well as cultic, was comprehended in the covenant stipulations of the Lord which were written in the covenant document, and because that Book of the Law was committed to the priests at the central sanctuary to be guarded and expounded by them, the priesthood possessed the dominant judicial voice (cf. 21:5), at least until the beginning of the monarchy (cf. 17:9,10). In addition to their knowledge of the written law, the priests had access by Urim and Thummim to direct divine verdicts. That would afford to the priests a more ultimate role, even though kings became more prominent in the judicial process. Abroad in the land the oracular voice of the divine King enthroned in the sanctuary was increasingly revealed to and through the prophet. But while prophets registered the Lord's unsought judgments upon the vassal people and leadership, the judicial functioning of the priest related to litigation instituted by one Israelite vassal against another or to legal investigations initiated within the Israelite community.

a) Judges and God's Altar. 16:18–17:13.

18-20. During the wilderness journeyings Moses, the mediator, had been Israel's chief judge, while assistant judges appointed from the tribes handled the ordinary cases (cf. 1:12ff.; Ex 18:13ff.). That arrangement was now modified to meet the new conditions of life in Canaan. **18. In all thy gates.** The judicial districts there were to be the towns rather than tribal-genealogical divisions. The natural leaders of the local council of elders would probably be the judges and assistant officers who are in view here (cf. 19:12). In this introduction to the subject, the emphasis falls, however, not on the organizational structure of the judicatories but on the demand for justice in administering the law of the Lord – **thou shalt not wrest judgment** (vv. 19,20; cf. Ex 23:3,6,8). Even in the codes and epics of Israel's heathen neighbors the virtue of justice in leaders is an often reiterated ideal.

16:21–17:1. The interlocking of cultic and governmental processes (cf. introductory comments on 16:18–21:23 above) explains the appearance of cultic proscriptions among the judicial regulations. These verses propound in concrete fashion the regulative religious principles found in the first three laws of the Decalogue, which were to characterize judicial procedure. First, the authority of the Lord alone must be consulted (vv. 21,22; cf. 17:8-10). This is expressed negatively in the prohibition of idolatrous appeal for oracular decision (18:9-14). **21. Asherah** (RSV; *grove*, AV), the Canaanite goddess, had as one significant epithet, "Asherah of deposits, goddess of oracles" *(Keret*, 201,202). The cultic Asherah and pillar were apparently, then, symbols associated with judicial procedure, specifically, the giving of oracular verdict (cf. Prov 16:10). Such a role was played by images of gods in Egypt, especially in the New Kingdom. Second, the cultic aspect of judicial procedure must be characterized by the same reverence for the Lord's holy name that was required in all Israel's cultic service – **Not sacrifice . . . any bullock, or sheep, wherein is blemish** (17:1; cf. 15:21; 21:1ff.; Lev 22:17ff.).

17:2-7. Beginning here, rules of evidence and judgment are presented. The particular case of apostasy which is cited (vv. 2,3) is simply illustrative of cases requiring capital punishment as the verdict. Concrete rather than abstract formulation of principles is a feature of the Deuteronomic legislation. For the stipulations concerned with apostasy as such, see Deut 13 (cf. Ex 22:20). The selection of this particular illustration is appropriate, for it underscores the contextual emphasis on the exclusive lordship of God in the judicial process. **2. In transgressing his covenant.** The prohibition of foreign allegiance is the recurring, basic prohibition of the covenant. **3. Which I have not commanded.** The first person reminds us that Moses spoke as the mouth of the Lord (cf. 1:3; 7:4). The central point is the demand that justice be safeguarded by a conscientiously thorough investigation (v. 4; cf. 13:14) and insistence on adequate evidence (vv. 6,7; cf. 19:15). A minimum of two witnesses was required (see also Num 35:30), and their confidence in their own testimony was to be evidenced by their assuming the dread responsibility of delivering the first and quite possibly lethal blows in the execution of the condemned (cf. 13:9). This measure also prevented secret accusation in prosecution of private quarrels. **5. Bring forth . . . unto thy gates.** The execution occurred outside the camp (cf. Lev 24:14; Num 15:36; Heb 13:12).

8-13. Moses perpetuated in modified form the system of lower and higher judicatories which had been instituted at Sinai (Ex 18:13ff.). During the wanderings, both Moses, the final arbiter, and the body of judges assisting in less weighty matters held court in the vicinity of the sanctuary. Since, however, the lower courts would henceforth be decentralized and located throughout the towns of Israel (Deut 16:18), it was now specified that the higher tribunal was to continue at the central sanctuary — **the place which . . . thy God shall choose** (v. 8) — , a reminder that he who dwelt at the sanctuary was Israel's supreme Judge. This arrangement was designed in the first instance for the premonarchial period, but it could be continued after the rise of a king in Israel (cf. 14ff.; II Chr 19:8ff.).

8a. **A matter too hard for thee.** Any variety of case that proved too difficult (lit., *too wonderful;* cf. Job 42:3) for the local court would come under the jurisdiction of the court at the central sanctuary (cf. 19:16-18). The latter was not a court of appeal, however. 9. **The priests . . . the judge.** The central judicature consisted of a plurality of both priests and judges (19:17), but each of these groups had its individual head, viz., the high priest (cf. 17:12) and a "chief justice." The formulation is not specific enough to determine from this ordinance the exact division of responsibility between priest and judge (cf. II Chr 19:11). Apparently verdicts might be announced by either priest or judge (Deut 17:12). 12. **The man that . . . will not hearken . . . shall die.** Since the decision was in either case delivered by the representative of the Lord, any failure to comply was rebellion against him and rendered the offender liable to the death penalty. Indeed, these representatives of the Lord, as the official agents of his judgment, are denominated *'ĕlōhîm*, "gods" (AV, "judges") in Ex 21:6; 22:8,28 (in the latter, note the parallelism with "ruler of thy people"). On Deut 17:13, see 13:11.

b) Kings and God's Covenant. 17:14-20.

Like the law of the stationary sanctuary, this law envisages not the immediate but the more distant future. Though the establishment of a monarchy is presented not as imperative but as permissive, that is sufficient to show that a monarchy as such need not be antithetical to the principle of theocratic government (cf. Gen 17:6,16; 35:11; 49:10). All depended on the kind of monarchy that should emerge. If the king conformed to the spirit of the present provision, ruling under the Lord and by the covenant law, he would actually enrich the OT's symbolic prefiguration of the Messianic reign. It was the indifference of Israel to the religious requisites for a theocratic king that accounted for Samuel's opposition to their request for a king (cf. I Sam 8:4ff.). It is noteworthy that in the secular suzerainty treaties, a similar oversight of the vassal's choice of king is exercised.

The main insistence of this passage, which lays the legal-covenantal foundation for the later monarchy, is that even when dynastic kingship will have replaced charismatic judgeship, the kings, too, must subject their life and reign, particularly their judicial activity, to God's covenant (vv. 18-20). The judicial supremacy belonged to the Lord, whose law was under the guardianship of the priests (v. 18; cf. 11). 15. **Whom the Lord thy God shall choose.** The divine choice of a king to sit on the throne of the Lord (cf. I Chr 29:23) was revealed through a prophet (cf. I Sam 10:24; 16:12ff.). **One from among thy brethren.** He was to be a fellow covenant servant. In this respect the king would be like his Messianic antitype. The restrictions of verses 16,17 reflect conditions in the royal courts of the nations around Israel. In some of these, the king was a god; in Israel, God was King (cf. Ex 15:18; 19:5,6; Deut 33:5; Jud 8:23). On 16b, see Ex 13:17; 14:13; Deut 28:68. In the wilderness, the Israelites longed for the agricultural produce of Egypt (Num 11:5,18,20; 14:4). Confronted by empires in which horses were a source of economic and military strength, they would lust for the Pharaoh's famed horses and chariots (cf. Isa 30:2; I Kgs 10:28,29), forgetting the import of their election and deliverance from Egyptian bondage. For the Solomonic violation of these restrictions, see I Kgs 10:26ff.; 11:1ff. 18. **A copy of this law.** A duplicate copy of the suzerainty treaty was provided for each vassal king. The Lord's copy, here regarded as the original and standard, was deposited at the central sanctuary (31:9). On verses 19,20, cf. 31:12,13. David manifested the conformity of his spirit to this covenantal law of kingship by his psalmodic response to it (see Ps 1) and by locating his throne site near the central sanctuary at the place which God had chosen.

c) Priests and Prophets. 18:1-22.

Responsibility was laid upon Israel for

the support of the priestly ministers of God whose administrative assignments are cited in the preceding and following contexts (vv. 1-8). Then Moses enjoined the elimination of all false oracular claimants, including the false prophet (vv. 9-22). In that connection, he set forth the institution of the true prophets (v. 15ff., rounding out the treatment of theocratic leaders (judge, 16:8; king, 17:14ff.; priest and Levite, 18:1ff.), which is appropriately incorporated into this section of legislation dealing with the official administration of righteousness in theocratic life.

1-8. 1. The priests the Levites. Deuteronomy uses this designation seven times, and seven times simply "priest(s)." **And all the tribe of Levi.** The and is interpretive, since in Hebrew the construction is one of simple apposition. This interpretation is grammatically acceptable (cf. 17:1) and consistent with the representation in the rest of the Scriptures, according to which all the priests were descended from Levi but only Aaronite Levites were priests. The RSV translation, *that is, all the tribe of Levi,* foists on Deuteronomy the view that all Levites were priests and thereby creates a conflict between it and the other Biblical legislation. Deuteronomy itself conveys a distinctly different image of each group: the priests are the altar ministers of the central sanctuary, who enjoy a position of supreme honor and authority; the Levites are everywhere functional subordinates and social dependents. Priests and Levites did share the commission of instructing Israel in the Law (33:10a; Lev 10:11; II Chr 15:3; 17:8,9; 30:22; 35:3). **1a. No part nor inheritance.** That is, they would have no unified tribal territory (cf. 10:9; 12:12; 14:27,29). As compact formulations serving the purposes of treaty renewal, the Deuteronomic stipulations assume the validity of the more minute regulations given earlier, unless, of course, they expressly modify them. So here, verses 1b,2 allude to legislation like that of Num 18:20ff.; Lev 2:3; 7:6-10,28ff.

2. The Lord is their inheritance. The Lord chose the Levites as his first-born consecration portion of Israel (v. 5; cf. Num 3:5-13) and then gave himself to them as their portion. The latter was expressed in their participation in Israel's offerings to him. The arrangement was symbolic of the great covenantal truth that the Lord was Israel's God and Israel was the Lord's people.

3. The priest's due. It is a question whether this verse further defines the fire offerings and **inheritance** (e.g., first fruits, tithes) of verses 1,2, or appoints certain additional portions. In the former case, there is a modification of earlier law, for the specific parts here assigned to the priests are not those detailed in Lev 7:29ff. If this is correct, an explanation of the modification of the earlier right shoulder requirement might well be that the right shoulder was the portion given to Canaanite priests — as has been disclosed by the discovery of a pit connected with a Canaanite temple and filled with right shoulder bones. Assuming verse 3 to be supplementary to earlier legislation, some have held that the reference is not to sacrifice but to animals slaughtered at home (cf. the terminology in Deut 12:15,21). Such a provision would prevent the serious diminution of priests' revenue, which would otherwise be the effect of removing this considerable share of butchery from the category of sacrifice. Another and more tenable explanation of 18:3 interpreted as a supplementary provision is that it refers not to the peace offerings proper but to certain other sacred meals eaten at the sanctuary, whether generally festive, or, as the present context might suggest, associated with judicial procedure. In verse 4, the fleece supplements earlier requirements (cf. Num 18:12).

6. If a Levite come from any of thy gates. The priests' cities were near Jerusalem, but those of the Levites were farther afield (see Josh 21). Verses 6-8 guaranteed the rights of all Levites against any restrictive tendencies of vested priestly interests at the central sanctuary. The charity towards the Levites required of Israel in general was required of the priests too.

9-22. If Israel desired further revelation of the will of the Lord in addition to that expressly written in the Law of Moses, the means of Urim and Thummim was available to their priests. Beyond that, the initiative in revelation lay with God, who would raise up prophets and speak through them (v. 18). The Israelites must be satisfied with and submissive to that revelation (vv. 15-19). If they deemed Moses and the prophets inadequate, then even a voice from the dead would not help. Allegedly oracular sources, such as flourished among the Canaanites, must be shunned (vv. 9-14). And a presumptuous prophet, speaking as from the Lord, indeed, every false prophet, must be exterminated (vv. 20-22).

9. Thou shalt not learn to do . . . abominations. All occult superstitions – divination, sorcery, spiritualism (vv. 10, 11) – were **abominations** (vv. 9,12) to the Lord and invited the sentence of the ban (cf. comments on 7:1ff.). Pagan magic was identified with pagan religion, and therefore its practice would be rebellion against the demand of the Lord's covenant for Israel's loyalty – **thou shalt be perfect** (v. 13).

15. A Prophet from the midst of thee . . . like unto me. This figure of the prophet, like certain others in the OT (e.g., the seed of the woman, the son of David, the servant of the Lord, the son of man) has both a corporate and an individual significance. The collective sense (i.e., the whole institution of OT prophecy) is clearly required, for the problem of distinguishing true and false prophets is broached in this connection (vv. 20-22), and this "prophet" is presented as the legitimate counterpart to the oracular institutions of Canaan (vv. 9-14). Moreover, within the structure of Deuteronomy, this is the section which deals with the several theocratic offices, and the prophetic office is not elsewhere formally instituted (cf. Lk 11:50,51). At the same time, this passage was interpreted by Jesus and the apostles as pointing to Messiah (see especially Acts 3:22, 23; cf. Jn 5:43; 12:48,49; Mt 17:5). Jesus was the antitypical prophet whom the OT prophetic institution foreshadowed. The prophetic office was a mediatorial function and so, in measure, an extension of the mediatorial office of Moses – **like unto me** (cf. Num 12:6,7). It was given to Israel in response to the request made at Horeb for a mediator of divine revelation (Deut 18:16ff.; cf. 5:23ff.

20a. The prophet, which shall presume to speak a word in my name. Such a one was a more subtle menace than the Canaanite soothsayer or the Israelite dreamer of dreams, sign-attested, who enticed to other gods (v. 20b; 13:1ff.). And he was to receive the same treatment as these (v. 20c; cf. v. 12; 13:5). Identifying him was more difficult (v. 21), but he would be exposed by the failure of his verifiable predictions (v. 22).

d) Guarantees of Justice. 19:1-21.

The theme of judicial justice is continued with stipulations calculated to secure a fair trial and a true verdict. Asylum was provided for the manslayer lest the wrath of the avenger prevent sober adjudication (vv. 1-13). Tampering with evidence was prohibited (v. 14). Adequate and honest testimony was required (vv. 15-21). These measures served justice by protecting the innocent, but justice was also to be satisfied by the pitiless punishment of the guilty (vv. 11-13, 19-21).

Judicial Asylum. 19:1-13. **2,3. Thou shalt separate three cities. . . . that every slayer may flee thither.** The land west of Jordan is in view, for, as stated at the conclusion to the historical prologue (4:41-43), Moses had already appointed the three cities of refuge east of Jordan. Joshua's role in completing this appointment of refuge cities is a mark of the functional and dynastic oneness of Joshua with Moses (cf. Josh 20).

6. One function of the kinsman-redeemer was to be the **avenger of the blood** (Gen 4:10ff.). This institution was not necessarily the mark of an ethically primitive society; rather, it was a mark of a less complex and less centralized form of government. Ideally, the **avenger** was to act out of passion for justice. However, because of the possibility of his acting out of mere passion, his office, while continued, was wisely controlled in the new, more highly centralized government of Israel established by Deuteronomy. The control was achieved by exploiting and expanding the institution of asylum early associated with the altar (cf. Gen 4:15; Ex 21:14b).

The germ of this was contained in the Sinaitic Book of the Covenant (Ex 21:12-14), and it was fully expounded in Num 35:9-34. Certain refinements are added in Deuteronomy 19 (cf. 3a, 8, 9 and 12), particularly with reference to Israel's future growth in Canaan. In Numbers, the term "cities of refuge" is applied to these cities which afforded protection to the fleeing manslayer not guilty of premeditated murder (vv. 4,5). Just as the geographical separation of the tribes from the central altar in Canaan required a decentralization of animal slaughter (12:15ff.), so it required a decentralization of asylum. The fact that the cities of refuge were Levitical cities (cf. Josh 20:7ff. and 21:1ff.) indicates, however, that, unlike animal slaying conducted apart from the central altar, the decentralized asylum did not lose its ceremonially sacred character. Note, too, the integration of this provision with the life of the high priest (Num 35:25). The cities of refuge were, then, extensions of the altar as a place of asylum. All this contributes further to the emphasis of this section of laws on the judicial importance of the priesthood and the central altar. Since the altar was the Lord's dwelling place, one can see in these laws of asylum the Deuteronomic equivalent of the extradition stipulations which figure prominently in the international suzerainty treaties.

9. Then shalt thou add three cities more. Moses looked beyond the near future and the selection of the three western cities to a more remote future, when Israelite expansion – in accordance with the divine promise (1:7; 11:24; 12:20) – would necessitate nine instead of six cities of refuge. There is no historical notice of compliance with this command.

12a. The elders of his city. These local authorities had the responsibility for innocent blood shed in their vicinity (see also 21:3ff.), and were therefore given a role in satisfying the cry of that blood for justice (cf. v. 13), but without abrogating the ancient right of the individual avenger (12b). The trial itself was conducted before "the congregation" (Num 35:12,24), i.e., publicly, but whether in the locality of the homicide or in the city of refuge is not clear. Joshua 20:4 (cf. v. 6) mentions a trial, at least provisional, which was to be held at the latter.

The Law of Landmarks. 19:14. This verse deals with what was, in effect, a violation of the ninth commandment, as do also verses 16-21. **Thy neighbour's landmark.** The value of boundary marks as evidence in property litigation is apparent. Their inviolability was protected by severe sanctions in the various ancient legal codes, and by curses against molesters inscribed on the landmarks themselves (cf. 27:17). Stones several feet high (*kudurru,* in Akkadian), marked the boundaries of royal grants. The fact that the inheritance of Israel and of each individual Israelite was such a royal grant from their divine King would add to the culpability of any who should tamper with the landmarks that would be established by the earliest generations after the conquest – **they of old time.**

The Law of Witnesses. 19:15-21. **15. At the mouth of two . . . or . . . three witnesses.** This verse stipulates as a general principle of administration in criminal cases the law of witness which had earlier been enunciated for capital cases (17:6; Num 35:30). Deuteronomy 19:16-21 deals with the perjured witness, that is, with the violation of the ninth commandment in court (see 5:20; Ex 20:16; 23:1). **16. A false witness.** He is thus designated in view of the outcome; but from the standpoint of the local judges it is not clear whether he or the defendant is the liar. It is precisely because of this difficulty that the case was to be referred to the central court (cf. 17:8-13). **18. Diligent inquisition** (cf. 13:14; 17:4). There was to be no resort to ordeal, as in some such cases in the legal practice of Israel's neighbors. **21. Life for life.** The penalty for perjury, however, was to be set according to the principle of the *lex talionis* (Ex 21:23ff.; Lev 24:17ff.), which was almost universally followed. That principle was not a license to vengeance but a guarantee of justice. Note again the pre-eminence of the priest in judgment (Deut 19:17).

e) Judgment of the Nations. 20:1-20.

Theocratic justice must be exercised in the prosecution of war beyond Israel's borders as well as in the administration of criminal law within the land. Here, again, a hegemony of priest and cult appears in the judicial process (v. 2ff.). Just as the cities of refuge were an extension of the asylum aspect of the altar throughout the land (cf. 19:1ff.), so the consecrated military campaign against the foreign foe was the just and holy judgment of the sanctuary – or better, of the Lord – abroad in the earth (vv. 1b,4,13a). While all Israelite military operations sanctioned by the Lord were theocratic judgments, and the adversary always assumed the character of enemy of God's kingdom, a distinction was made between wars waged against the Canaanite nations and those against nations very far off (v. 15ff.). The programmatic mandate of Deuteronomy 7 concentrated on the former; the present stipulations center on the latter. In the extra-biblical suzerainty treaties, too, the vassal's military activities and share of the spoil were carefully regulated and the suzerain promised support if needed.

1. The Lord . . . is with thee. The memory of God's almighty exploits in establishing the theocracy, and the assurance of his presence in the midst of his people even as they waged the wars of the Lord were to confirm their faith when they faced superior hosts and military technology. As for horses and chariots, let Israel sing anew the Song of the Sea: "The Lord is a man of war . . . . Pharaoh's chariots and his host hath he cast into the sea . . . the horse and the rider hath he thrown into the sea . . . the Lord shall reign for ever and ever" (Ex 15:3a, 4a, 21b, 18). **2. The priest shall approach and speak.** In the ancient world, priests and interpreters of omens were regular members of military staffs (cf. Num 10:8,9; 31:6; I Sam 7:9ff.). The function of the Israelite priest was not analogous to that of a modern army chaplain. He rather represented the sanctuary in the name of which the Israelite host advanced; he consecrated the battle to the glory of the Lord of hosts and of his covenant kingdom. On verse 4, see 23:14; I Sam 14:18; II Sam 11:11.

The situation envisaged in verses **5-9** is that of the early days in Canaan before there would be a regular army with foreign mercenaries as an elite corps. **5. The officers.** The militia of the tribes was to be levied by tribal officers (cf. 1:15). The Assyrian, Shamshi-Adad, in his military correspondence, commands those in charge of the levy: "The chief whose forces are not turned out in full and who leaves one man behind will incur the disfavor of the king" (Mari, I, 6:18ff.). Since, however, in the wars of the Lord, victory came not by the might of Israel's hosts, recruiting was made so free of compulsion that only conscience fortified by faith in the Lord as the Giver of victory (v. 4) compelled enlistment. (For striking historic exemplification of the principle, see Jud 7:2,3). **8. Lest his brethren's heart faint.** The Homeric epics depict demoralized troops weeping like calves and wailing like children for home. Such behavior in the Israelite army would disgrace the name of the Lord before the heathen. The types of exemption cited in verses 5-7 were evidently not novel in Israel (cf. the Sumerian poem, "Gilgamesh and the Land of the Living," 49ff.; The Ugaritic poem, *Keret,* 101ff.). Jesus insisted (Lk 14:18ff.) that such excuses as availed for exemption from military service might not prevent a man's responding promptly to His invitation to salvation. (On v. 6, cf. Lev 19:23ff.; on v. 7, cf. 24:5.)

10. Proclaim peace unto it. Such an offer was expressly forbidden in the conflict with the cities of Canaan (7:2ff.). The identification of God's kingdom with the earthly kingdom of Israel brought an OT anticipation of the final judgment which is to overtake those who remain outside the redemptive kingdom of Christ. This OT judgment, however, could not be executed universally. For then the age of grace for the Gentiles would have been prematurely terminated, and the promise that Israel should be a blessing to all the nations through the Messiah (Gen 12:3) would have been nullified. Therefore, the typology of final judgment was strictly applied only in warfare against nations within the boundaries claimed by God for his typical kingdom (Deut 20:16-18; cf. 7:2ff.). **15. The cities . . . far . . . from thee.** Beyond those boundaries the typology of judgment was tempered by the principles that govern the customary relations of ordinary nations (vv. 10-15), yet not so that the religious significance of the encounter of an ancient nation with God's Kingdom Israel was lost. Consequently, in Israel's offer of peace (v. 10) and in the submission of the Gentile city as a covenant tributary to the Lord (v. 11) there was imaged the saving mission of God's people in this world (cf. Zech 9:7b, 10b). The judgment of those who refuse to make their peace with God through Christ was exhibited in the siege, conquest, and punishment of the unsubmissive city (Deut 20:13), even though, as observed above, this did not amount to a strict application of the *ḥērem* (ban), nor was it even as severe treatment as was customary in ancient warfare (vv. 14,19,20). **19b. The tree . . . is man's life.** These words, placed in parenthesis in the AV, are obscure; but the AV seems to translate the end of the verse more accurately than the ASV and the RSV.

f) Authority of Sanctuary and Home. 21:1-23.

This chapter concludes the commandments concerned with governmental authority. Since all such authority is an extension of the authority of the individual family head (see the fifth commandment), these final stipulations on this subject appropriately concern the exercise of authority within the home. There are sanctions imposed to enforce this authority (vv. 18-21), and there are regulations to insure a just exercise of it (vv. 10-17). The opening verses prescribe judicial procedure in cases in which penal justice cannot be satisfied because the identity of the offender is not known (vv. 1-9). The provisions are such as to demonstrate further the orientation of all theocratic government to the sanctuary. Similarly, the closing stipulation insists that cultic-ceremonial law be respected in the administration of criminal law (vv. 22,23). The theocratic altar and the theocratic court were two manifestations of the justice of the theocratic King, the holy One who chose a dwelling place in Israel.

Corporate Community Responsibility. 21:1-9. **2. Thy elders and thy judges.** The members of the local judiciaries (see 16:18) were to determine which city must bear the responsibility. **3. The city which is nearest** (ASV). This principle of corporate community responsibility in cases of undetected criminals appears also in the Code of Hammurabi. Laws 23 and 24 of that Code require the nearest city to make restitution in cases of robbery and to compensate with one mina of silver the family of someone slain. **The elders of that city** (cf. 19:12), as the representatives of the whole population, were to conduct the ceremonial execution (3b,4). This ritual was to be under the jurisdiction of **the priests** (5a). **5b. By their word shall every controversy and every stroke be tried** (cf. 17:8,10). Here is a clear affirmation of the ultimate judicial authority vested in the priesthood. The priests' function in the case at hand was to be purely judicial, for the slaying of the heifer (v. 4b) would not be a cultic sacrifice, but a judicial execution. That it was not an altar sacrifice is evident from the mode of execution (cf. Ex 13:13). Since it was only a ceremonial execution, with the heifer regarded as a substitute for the unknown murderer, there was no actual satisfaction of justice. **9. So . . . put away the guilt . . . from among you.** The ritual served to preserve the ceremonial status of those involved as sacramentally qualified covenant members (vv. 8,9). In so doing, it prophetically prefigured (as would an altar sacrifice) the vicarious execution of the Messianic Servant of the Lord for the blood-guiltiness of his people. Not only men, but the blood-stained land participated in the symbolical defilement; and its defilement, too, was, after a figure, purged by the judicial ritual (cf. Num 35:33). In this there was a reminder that perfect righteousness must at last pervade the totality of God's kingdom. Another by-product of this ritual requirement would be the preservation of peace by the elimination of possible misunderstanding that might spark inter-city strife if the kinsman of the slain were rashly to pursue his role of avenger.

Limits of a Husband's Authority. 21:10-14. This first of three stipulations concerned with the authority of the head of the household (cf. vv. 15-21) deals with the limits of the husband's authority over his wife. The case of a captive woman (vv. 10,11; cf. 20:14; contrast 7:3) is used as a case in point for establishing the rights of the wife, perhaps because the principle would obviously apply *a fortiori* in the case of an Israelite wife. On the purificatory acts of verses 12b, 13a, which signified removal from captive-slave status, compare Lev 14:8; Num 8:7. On the month's mourning, see Num 20:29 and Deut 34:8. This period would provide for the achieving of inward composure for beginning a new life, as well as for an appropriate expression of filial piety. **14. Thou shalt not sell her.** A wife might not be reduced to slave status, not even the wife who had been raised from slave status. Though the particular illustration of the captive wife is peculiar to Deuteronomy, the same principle is expressed in the Book of the Covenant, where the case of the Israelite bondmaiden is cited (Ex 21:7-11). **Then thou shalt let her go whither she will.** The severance of the marriage relationship is mentioned here only incidentally to the statement of the main principle that a man's authority did not extend to the right of reducing his wife to a slave. The dissolution of the marriage would have to be accomplished according to the laws of divorce in the theocracy (cf. Deut 24:1-4). Not the divorce was mandatory, but the granting of freedom in case the man should determine to divorce his wife according to the permission granted by Moses because of the hardness of their hearts (cf. Mt 19:8).

Limits of a Father's Authority. 21:15-17. This stipulation circumscribed the authority of the father over his sons specifically with respect to the rights of the first-born. The particular illustration involves another situation within the Mosaic economy which was merely tolerated, namely, polygamy. Where polygamy was practiced, the problem cited (v. 15) would have been common (cf. Gen 29:30ff.; I Sam 1:4ff.). **17c. The right of the first-born is his.** The right of primogeniture included a property inheritance share double that of other sons. The principle here enforced is that parental authority is not absolute. A father's mere personal preference did not justify disregard of the divinely sanctioned customary rights of those who were under his parental authority.

Judgment of a Rebellious Son. 21:18-21. If misuse of authority produced tyranny, disrespect for proper authority would produce anarchy, the very contradiction of the covenant order as a manifestation of God's lordship. Parental authority, in particular, had been ordained of God to represent divine authority and to be the cornerstone of all human government and societal order. Therefore, while it was necessary to protect those under the authority of a household head from the arbitrary abuse of his authority (vv. 10-17), it was also necessary to fortify that authority against the spirit of lawlessness in a generation of Belial (v. 20). It is here enforced by the ultimate sanctions of theocratic law (v. 21; Ex 21:15,17; Lev 20:9; Deut 27:16). **18. Though they chasten him** (ASV). Chastening was to be the limit of the parents' own application of judicial sanctions. Beyond that, the judicial process must be conducted by the elders at the gate (v. 19), that is, by the local theocratic judicatory (cf. 16:18ff.).

Disposition of a Criminal's Corpse. 21:22,23. The preceding law had proceeded from parental to official judicial authority and had prescribed the death penalty. The present case takes the judicial process a step beyond the execution, to the exposure of the corpse as a monitory, public proclamation of the satisfaction of justice. The principle being exemplified is that all theocratic law administration must operate in the service of covenant religion. **23. He that is hanged is accursed of God.** The condemned will have been guilty of offenses declared accursed in the covenant sanctions. As one executed, he would visibly embody the curse of God poured out. And as a human carcass exposed to birds and beasts of prey (cf. II Sam 21:10), the man hanged on a tree would be an expression of the ultimate in the curse of God on the fallen race (cf., e.g., Rev 19:17ff.). In this conclusion to the series of stipulations wherein God demands a perfect judicial righteousness and the satisfaction of every claim of justice, if need be through a vicarious sufferer, the New Testament believer is reminded of him who was accursed of God to redeem his people from the law's inexorable curse (Gal 3:13).

3) Sanctity of the Divine Order. 22:1–25:19.

Love for God requires reverence for the divine ordinances at the various levels of creation and in the various spheres of human activity. The covenant servant must respect the sanctity of the orders of nature (22:5-12), marriage 22:13-30; Heb. Bible 23:1), and the theocratic kingdom (23:1 [Heb. Bible 23:2]–25:12). With the partial exception of the natural order, the area in view is that of the mutual relationships of the covenant servants. This whole section, therefore, is bounded by laws which clearly express the basic principle that the same loving regard must be shown for one's neighbor's interests as for one's own (22:1-4; 25:13-16). The extra-biblical suzerainty treaties also regulated the relationships of the lord's vassals to one another.

a) The Ordinances of Labor and Marriage. 22:1-30.

1-4. Similar legislation is found in the Book of the Covenant (Ex 23:4ff.). There, it is in the midst of laws aimed at securing an honest administration of justice. The law of God must be obeyed by a man even in his secret actions which are beyond the detection of God's human agents of law enforcement. Deuteronomy 22:1-4 might thus well serve as an appendix to the preceding section on the enforcement of theocratic law. The reminder is provided that God's requirements concerning our relations with our neighbor are truly fulfilled only when we act in a spirit of love that goes beyond merely keeping within the law, to avoid punishment, and positively seeks the welfare of others as though it were our own. This law of love is the essential principle which the following stipulations apply in the particular life situations of the covenant people.

5-12. Man must be mindful that, in all the use he makes of this world, he is God's steward. Various regulations were therefore prescribed for the Israelites which would continually remind them, as they pursued the cultural program of God's kingdom (cf. Gen 1:28), that the world is the Lord's, for he is its Maker. Man is indeed set as king over the earth, with the whole order of nature under his dominion; but man's rule is a vice-regency in the Creator's name. Human authority must therefore be exercised according to the pattern God appoints. It is this fundamental principle which underlies the opening requirement of this section that the distinction between man and woman should not be blurred by the one's appropriating the characteristic articles of the other (Deut 22:5). God created them male and female, with distinctive natures and functions; specifically, in the divinely established order of authority, man is the head of the woman as together they reign over the earth. The Lord created the various "kinds" in the vegetable and animal kingdom (Gen 1:11ff.). Israel was so to treat these "kinds" that they would be preserved in their distinctive natures (Deut 22:6,7,9-11; cf. Lev 19:19). **8. Bring not blood upon thine house.** Of special significance in the natural order of creation is the lifeblood of man. Carelessness with respect to it shows a want of neighborly love and of respect for God. It therefore incurs guilt before the Creator even when accidents resulting from such carelessness receive no human redress. **12. Make thee fringes.** Like the other stipulations in this section, the final regulation, which required the appendage of tassels to the outer garment, was designed to provide a special reminder of God's suzerainty over Israel (cf. Num 15:37-41).

13-30. The laws of the preceding verses were to regulate the creation ordinance of labor; the laws of this section were designed to govern the creation ordinance of marriage. The sanctity of the divine institution of the family is thus the interest of the present provisions. **13,14. If any man take a wife . . . and bring up an evil name upon her.** The case is that in which a husband brings an allegation of unchastity against his bride, whether falsely (vv. 13-19) or justly (vv. 20,21). In the first instance, the malicious accuser was to suffer corporal punishment (v. 18; cf. 25:1-3), pay compensation to his father-in-law for defaming his house (v. 19a), and retain his wife without ever being permitted to divorce her (v. 19b). In the second case, the guilty bride who had "wrought folly" was to suffer death by stoning before the disgraced house of her father. In societies where such evidence was legally decisive, it was customary after the consummation of the marriage to keep the tokens of the bride's virginity (v. 17). (On the judicial responsibility of the elders, see 19:12; 21:2-6,19,20; 25:7-9. On adultery, punishable by death, see 5:18; Lev 18:20,29; 20:10.)

Verses **23-29** concern the seduction of unmarried girls, whether betrothed (vv. 23-27) or unbetrothed (vv. 28,29). If the girl was betrothed, the apprehended man was to be stoned to death. The same penalty befell the girl if their sexual intercourse occurred in the city (vv. 23,24); but not if the circumstances permitted the reasonable assumption that she had been forced – **there is in** [her] **no sin worthy of death** (vv. 25-27). The seducer of an unbetrothed virgin was obliged to take her as wife, paying the customary bride price and forfeiting the right of divorce (vv. 28,29). Probably the father's rights mentioned in Ex 22:17 continued to have precedence. On Deut 22:30, see Lev 18:6ff.; 20:11ff.; Deut 27:20ff. This single prohibition represents, as it recalls, the whole list of forbidden degrees of affinity.

The theme of chapters **23–25** is the sanctification of the theocratic kingdom. Israel must respect the sanctity of the congregation of the Lord as such (23:1-18; Heb. Bible, 2-19); the sanctity of special classes of God's servants, particularly the needy (23:19 [Heb. Bible, 20] – 24:22); and the sanctity of every citizen of the theocracy as an individual bearer of God's image (25:1-12).

b) The Congregation of the Lord. 23:1-18.

1-8. The sacredness of the congregation of the Lord was signified by the exclusion from participation in the official theocratic assembly of those disqualified in various ways. The disqualification might be physical (vv. 1,2) or ethnic and historical (vv. 3-8). Excluded were the eunuch (v. 1) and the **bastard** (v. 2) together with his descendants – **even to his tenth generation,** i.e., indefinitely (cf. v. 3). The eunuch's condition was a mutilation of the divinely given nature (cf. 14:1). The bastard was the issue of a repudiation of the divinely appointed ordinance. Possibly the *mamzēr,* translated **bastard,** was, more precisely, one born of an incestuous union (cf. 22:30). Such exclusions from privilege point to the importance in covenant administration of the marriage design of securing a godly seed. Nevertheless, even in OT days such physical disability was an obstacle only to external privilege, not to the spiritual realities of salvation. In NT times such disabilities no longer enter into consideration even in the external administration of the church (cf. Isa 56:4,5; Acts 8:27,28). The same is true of the cases of disqualification mentioned in Deut 23:3-8.

4a. Because they met you not with bread and . . . water. Although the Ammonites and Moabites were begotten in incest (cf. v. 2; Gen 19:30ff.), the reason assigned for their debarment is that they were unwilling to show hospitality to the people of God on their wilderness journey from Egypt to their homeland (cf. Deut 2:18ff.,29), and even attempted offensive action against Israel – **hired . . . Balaam . . . to curse thee** (4b; cf. Num 22–25). The divine curse is the portion of those who would curse the covenant people, according to God's promise to Abraham (Gen 12:3). Hence, theocratic Israel might not enter into covenantal alliance with these accursed would-be cursers (Deut 23:6). **7. Thou shalt not abhor an Edomite . . . an Egyptian.** In the case of the Edomites and Egyptians exclusion was again the rule because of their past enmity (cf. the Egyptian oppression, Ex 1:8ff., and Edomite opposition, Num 20:18ff.), but it was modified (Deut 23:8; cf. Ex 20:5), in the one case, because of ties of Abrahamic kinship (cf. Gen 36:1ff.) and, in the other, because of hospitality shown to Abraham and Jacob's family when distressed by famine (Gen 12; 42–47).

9-14. 9. Keep thee from every wicked thing. The military camp of Israel engaged in the wars of the Lord was an extension of the theocratic kingdom and must be characterized by that same sanctity which marked the settled community. **14. Thy God walketh in the midst of thy camp.** In war, as in peace, God was present among his people, and his name must be hallowed. Physical cleanliness was the appropriate symbol of the holiness of the covenant relationship. (On vv. 10,11, cf. Lev 15:16).

15-18. These verses present further examples of what might and might not be deemed compatible with sacred membership in the congregation of the Lord. **15. The servant which is escaped.** This law relates to foreign runaway slaves. On the giving of asylum to the refugee, compare the extradition laws in the secular treaties. **17. Whore . . . sodomite.** These were female and male religious prostitutes, as indicated by the Hebrew terms, which are the feminine and masculine forms of a root meaning "sacred." The law relates to native Israelites devoted to cultic prostitution. The abominable rites of the pagan fertility cults are in view. **18. The price of a dog.** On **dog**, another name for a male prostitute, see Rev 22:15. One could not satisfy the holy demands of God's covenant by hiding sin under religious hypocrisy. Lest the rules given in Deut 23:3-8 leave the false impression that ethnic considerations were paramount, it was made clear by these two further rules, the one welcoming the foreigner and the other excluding certain Israelites, that mercy and morality were the vital principles of covenant administration.

c) Protection for the Weak. 23:19–24:22.

Respect was to be shown to all those dignified by the status of covenant servant to the Lord. This section of stipulations was designed to guarantee this sanctity of the theocratic citizen by regulations which assured peace, prosperity, and liberty within the covenant commitment to all God's people, but especially to those classes whose welfare was jeopardized by various circumstances. The legislation seems to be arranged in groups corresponding to laws six through ten in the Decalogue, but in a slightly different order, as follows: laws of property (23:19-25), of family (24:1-5), of life (24:6-15), of justice (24:16-18), and of charity (24:19-22).

Laws of Property. 23:19-25. **19. Not lend upon usury to thy brother.** Impoverished Israelites were protected from exploitation at the hands of their richer brethren by the prohibition of interest on loans granted to them (cf. Ex 22:25; Lev 25:35ff.; Deut 15:1ff.). Interest might be exacted from foreigners (a **stranger**, v. 20), however, because the loans made to them would not be for the relief of destitution but for business capital to be employed by these traveling merchants for profitable enterprise. **22. If thou . . . forbear to vow.** Beyond the specified tributary demands of the covenant Lord, the property of the vassal was at his own disposal. This right was not intended, however, to discourage the free expression of religious love and gratitude, nor did it provide escape from the obligation of a voluntary vow once made. Reverencing his own holy name, God would not encourage a sense of carelessness or impunity in those who made solemn commitments to him (vv. 21,23; cf. Lev 27; Num 30:2ff.). **24.** The law of crops (vv. 24,25) provided such liberty as to satisfy the principle of brotherly hospitality, but prohibited the changing of liberty to license in violation of the property rights of the theocratic citizen.

Laws of Family. 24:1-5. Divorce as permitted in the Mosaic Law (cf. Lev 21:7,14; 22:13; Num 30:9), because of the hardness of the Israelites' hearts (Mt 19:8; Mk 10:5), endangered the dignity of women within the theocracy. Hence, easy abuse of the permission was forestalled by circumscribing it with technicalities and restrictions (Deut 24:1-4). The RSV is correct in regarding verses 1-4 as one sentence, with 1-3 the condition and 4 the conclusion. The AV is liable to the interpretation that divorce was mandatory in the situation described. Actually, what was mandatory was not divorce, but (if divorce was resorted to) a legal process which included four elements. (a) There must be a serious cause for the divorce. The exact import of the words **some uncleanness** (v. 1; cf. 23:14) is uncertain. Adultery is not meant, for the law prescribed the death penalty for that (22:13ff.; Lev 20:10; cf. Num 5:11ff.). (b) A writ of separation was to be placed in the woman's hand for her subsequent protection. The preparation of this legal instrument implies the involvement of (c) a public official who might also have to judge of the adequacy of the alleged grounds of divorce. (d) The man must give her a formal dismissal – **send her out of his house** (v. 1). The main point of the present law, however, was that a man might not remarry his wife after he divorced her if she had meanwhile remarried, even though her second husband had divorced her or had died. With respect to the first husband, the remarried divorcee was **defiled** (v. 4). Such was the abnormality of this situation, tolerated in OT times but abrogated by our Lord in the interests of the original standard (Mt 19:9; Mk 10:6-9; cf. Gen 2:23,24). **5. He shall be free at home one year.** Further respect was shown for the sanctity of the family relationship and especially for the welfare of the woman within it by granting a year's exemption from public services to the newly married man, that his bride might be gladdened by his presence.

Laws of Life. 24:6-15. The concern of these stipulations was the life of God's people and things essential to the preservation of their life. Safeguards were afforded to the dignity and peace of the needy, in particular, for the Lord delights to be the Help of the helpless, and would have his people to be of like mind. **7. Maketh merchandise of him.** Traffic in human life was forbidden under penalty of death (cf. Ex 21:16). Respect for the whole community's life and health demanded careful attention to the divine prescriptions for dealing with the disease of leprosy (Deut 24:8; cf. Lev 13; 14), the seriousness of which was evidenced by Miriam's experience (Deut 24:9; cf. Num 12:10ff.). **10. When you make your neighbor a loan** (RSV). Though interest on loans to Israelite neighbors was forbidden (23:19,20), a pledge might be taken as security; but even this was not to be acquired in such a way as to prejudice the dignity, let alone the life, of the debtor. Men were not to be deprived of articles indispensable to life and health. In this category were the millstone (v. 6), the quadrangular mantle used as cover in sleeping (vv. 10-13; cf. Ex 22:26,27), and the day laborer's wages (Deut 24:14,15; cf. Lev 19:13). **15. Lest he cry against thee unto the Lord.** In the secular suzerainty treaties, too, complaints of one vassal against another were to be adjudicated by the suzerain.

Laws of Justice. 24:16-18. Justice must be dispensed to each Israelite in accordance with truth. **16. Every man . . . for his own sin.** The guilty individual alone was to be punished, and not innocent members of his family (cf. II Kgs 14:6). There is no contradiction between this and the divine judgment as described in the Decalogue (Deut 5:9; Ex 20:5), for the latter does not say that God afflicts the innocent. Those who share in the visitation of judgment upon the fathers' iniquities are such as share also in the fathers' hatred of God. On the other hand, there is no repudiation of the principle of the corporate responsibility which obtains in certain group situations. **17. Stranger . . . fatherless . . . widow.** Even the most helpless classes were to enjoy justice and be guaranteed all their legal rights. On the familiar appeal to the Exodus (v. 18), see 22; 15:15.

Laws of Charity. 24:19-22. The spirit of charity, negatively required in the tenth commandment, was to be the governing spirit of theocratic life. Once again the poor were to be the beneficiaries. Cf. Lev 19:9,10; 23:22.

d) Sanctity of the Individual. 25:1-19. Verses 1-12, the final laws on the sanctification of the kingdom (23:1–25:12), guarded the sanctity of man as individual image-bearer of God. Verses 13-19 conclude the laws of reverence for the natural, family, and theocratic orders (vv. 22-25) as they began (cf. 22:1-4), with the golden rule principle.

1-12. The just punishment of the guilty was to be so dispensed that his individual human dignity was honored (vv. 1-3). The principle of the sanctity of the individual god-like creature was thus enforced at the point where such respect might most plausibly seem to have been forfeited. Contrary to the sentence division in the AV, the conclusion does not begin until verse 2 (so RSV). Unbecoming public degradation was to be prevented by several precautionary measures. The punishment of the criminal must be preceded by a trial and sentence, and must be personally supervised by the judge. The stripes were to be scrupulously counted – **Forty stripes he may give him, and not exceed** (v. 3) – and not applied at random, as to an animal, or with the abandon of anger, unmindful that the judgment was the Lord's. The severity of the scourging was to be proportionate to the gravity of the offense, yet in no case to exceed forty stripes. **4. Thou shalt not muzzle the ox . . .** The positive counterpart to the prohibition of dishonoring a man in spite of his evil works is the requirement that he receive all proper honor for his good works. This verse, probably a proverbial expression, seems even here to have the force given it by Paul in I Cor 9:9 and I Tim 5:18.

The covenant servant is an immortal being with a stake, even beyond death and the grave, in that future blessedness of God's kingdom which was promised in the Covenant of Redemption to believers and their seed after them (vv. 5-10). **6. That his name be not blotted out of Israel** (ASV). Witness was to be borne to this dignity of the servant-son of God by the perpetuation of his name in a covenant seed dwelling in his inheritance within the OT typical kingdom. As an application of this, the Deuteronomic Covenant adopted a form of the widespread practice of levirate marriage, whereby there devolved upon the brother of a man who died childless the duty of raising up an heir to the dead by his widow – **the firstborn . . . shall succeed in the name of his brother.** This requirement constituted an exception to the prohibition in Lev 18:16; 20:21. For Biblical examples of this or similar practice, see Genesis 38 and the Book of Ruth. The levirate duty is limited in Deuteronomy to situations in which brothers shared the same estate (25:5a), and even then it was not compulsory – **My husband's brother refuseth** (v. 7). Failure to comply, however, betrayed a want of fraternal affection and was publicly stigmatized (vv. 8-10). On the transfer of the sandal for confirming legal transfer of right or property, see Ruth 4:7. In view of the provision of Num 27:4ff., there would be no need for the levirate marriage if the deceased had daughters. Hence the AV seems preferable to the RSV in rendering in Deut 25:5 – **no child** rather than *no son.* Verses 11,12, also are concerned with the dignity of the individual and indeed precisely with his dignity as God's covenant servant, who in his circumcision bears in his body the sign of the covenant. The reference to the organ of reproduction might account for the immediate conjunction of this prohibition with the law of levirate marriage. That the act forbidden includes contempt for the covenant sign and not just indecency is suggested by the apparent similarity in the nature of the punishment and the sign, both involving a mutilation of the body. Weight is added to this interpretation by the fact that apart from this case, only the *lex talionis* (19:21) calls for such penal mutilation.

13-19. 15. Thou shalt have a perfect and just weight. Neighbor must be loved as self (vv. 13-16); therefore, business with one's neighbor was not to be conducted with two sets of measuring standards, the large for receiving, the small for dispensing (cf. Amos 8:5). This law somewhat expands Lev 19:35,36, especially by the appended blessings and curses of the covenant. While this law of love sums up the requirements for inter-theocratic relationships dealt with in the immediately preceding sections of stipulations, no repudiation of the mandate of conquest (cf. Deut 7; 20:16,17) is intended (25:17-19). Nor is there any contradiction between the two. For though God requires love of neighbor, those who set themselves to destroy the people of the typical OT theocratic kingdom removed themselves from the neighbor category, just as those doomed with Satan in eternal perdition are not the neighbors of the inhabitants of the heavenly theocracy. On the charge to exterminate Amalek, see Ex 17:8-16. Taken together, the laws of love and hate amount to the single requirement to love God, and consequently to love whom he loves and hate whom he hates.

4) Confession of God as Redeemer-King. 26:1-19.

The long stipulations division (chs. 5–26) draws to a close with the liturgies for two cultic confessions (vv. 1-11; 12-15) and a declaration of the ratification of the covenant (vv. 16-19).

3. The country which the Lord sware . . . to give us. The Israelite servants of the Lord were to make continual thankful confession that their goodly inheritance in Canaan was the gift of God's redemptive grace in fulfillment of his oath to the patriarchs. They were to confess his continuing lordship and to express their consecration by a tributary offering of the first fruits. On the law of first fruits, see 18:4; Ex 23:19; 34:26; Num 18:12ff. Elements of first-fruit offering are found in connection with each of the annual feasts (Deut 16). For example, at the Feast of Unleavened Bread a sheaf of first fruits was waved (Lev 23:10ff.). Also, the Feast of Weeks was called "the day of firstfruits" (Num 28:26; cf. Ex 23:16; 34:22) and two first-fruit loaves were offered at it (Lev 23:17); and the first fruits of wine could not be offered until the Feast of Tabernacles, when the vintage had ripened. If "all the fruit of the earth" (Deut 26:2) indicates the end of the harvest season, then the Feast of Tabernacles must have been the occasion for the presentation of this basket of first fruits at the central altar. Grammatically, verse 2 can be understood as describing either all the first fruits of the ground or only a token basket thereof. In the case of agricultural first fruits, the amount is nowhere specified. Since first fruits were assigned to the priests (Num 18:13,14), the reference to the sacred feast which the offerer was to enjoy after this ritual – **Thou shalt rejoice in every good thing . . . the Lord . . . hath given** (v. 11; cf. 12:6,7,11,12, 17,18; 16:11,14) – indicates that the basket represented only a token of the first fruits (see comments on 14:22ff.; 15:20), at least if this feast was provisioned out of the first fruits. That, however, is uncertain. The Israelite must confess that the theocratic calling of his people could not be attributed to their might (v. 5ff.; cf. 7:7,8; 8:17,18). **5b. A wandering Aramean** (AV, *Syrian)* **was my father** (RSV). Hebrew *'ôbēd* connotes the ideas of "lost" and "in peril" (cf. AV, *ready to perish)*. The reference is to Jacob. He is called **Aramean** because the patriarchal origins were geographically, though not racially, Aramean, and because Jacob himself sojourned in Aram-naharaim during the period of the birth of his sons, the future tribal fathers of Israel. **7,8. The Lord heard . . . brought us forth.** The commemorative recital of God's redemptive acts in exodus and conquest was Israel's confessional Amen to God's own recital of his favor to the nation in the historical prologue of the covenant. Verse 10b does not describe a new step in the ritual of the first-fruits offering (in contradiction of v. 4); it is, rather, a summarizing conclusion.

12-15. The dependence of Israel on the Lord for continuing prosperity was to be expressed in a special triennial service of petition for his favorable attention and blessing. (On the tithing regulations, see the comments on 14:22ff.). **13. Before the Lord thy God.** This direction probably refers to the central sanctuary. If so, then the emphasis on the completion of the tithing process (vv. 12,13) suggests that the Feast of Tabernacles was the occasion. This liturgy may have followed immediately upon that of the presentation of the basket of first fruits (vv. 1-11). **15. Look down . . . and bless . . . Israel.** The avowal of obedience to all the tithing prescriptions (vv. 13,14) as the preliminary to this petition for divine blessing recalls the fact that God declared the latter to be contingent on the former (14:28,29). The worshiper must affirm that his tithe had not been exposed to ceremonial defilement, particularly, the uncleanness associated with mourning for the dead (v. 14; cf. Lev 22:3ff.; Num 19:11ff.; Hos 9:4).

16-19. The central act in the ceremony of covenant ratification was the oath of allegiance which the vassal took to his lord in response to the declaration of the covenant stipulations and sanctions. Israel had taken such an oath after the reading of the Book of the Covenant at Sinai (Ex 24:7), and now Israel must do the same in the plains of Moab, as is reflected in these verses (see also Deut 29:10-15). **16. Do them with all thine heart.** The Lord demanded covenantal consecration. The people of Israel avowed that they submitted to the Lord as their God, who was to be obeyed according to all his holy will – **to walk in his ways** (v. 17). The Lord graciously acknowledged them as his people (v. 18a) and guaranteed the blessings of the covenant to the faithful (vv. 18b,19; cf. 7:6; 14:2; Ex 19:5,6).

IV. Sanctions: Covenant Ratification. 27:1–30:20.

The fourth standard division in the ancient suzerainty treaties was the curses and blessings, the woe and weal sanctions of the covenant. In Deuteronomy this section is found in chapters 27–30. While 26:16-19 forms a conclusion to the stipulations, it also introduces the element of covenant ratification, the nucleus around which the curses and blessings of these chapters cluster. The ratification of the new covenant which Moses was making with the second generation was to unfold in two stages. That was customary procedure in securing the throne succession to the appointed royal heir. When death was imminent, the suzerain required his vassals to pledge obedience to his son; then, soon after the son's accession, the vassals' commitment was repeated. Similarly, Moses and Joshua formed a dynasty of mediatorial representatives of the Lord's suzerainty over Israel. Hence the succession of Joshua, which symbolized the continuing lordship of Israel's God, was ensured by the oath elicited from Israel before Moses died, and again later by a ratification ceremony after Joshua's accession. The pronouncing of curses and blessings is prominent in each of these ratification rituals.

The sanctions section of Deuteronomy opens with the curses and blessings to be used at the second stage of the ratification (ch. 27), then returns to the immediate situation and the solemn sanctions of the initial stage of ratification (chs. 28–30). When Deuteronomy is considered as the finished legal documentary witness to the covenant, no difficulty need be felt with the position assigned to the directions of chapter 27. On the other hand, the connection between the end of chapter 26 and the beginning of chapter 28 is so smooth as to suggest the possibility that chapter 27 may not have intervened at this precise point in the progress of the ceremony in Moab. Similarly, in the original flow of Moses' oration, Deuteronomy 30 might have followed immediately upon the end of chapter 28.

A. Ratification Ceremony in Canaan. 27:1-26.

Moses prescribed the ceremony for the second stage of the covenant renewal, to be conducted in Canaan (vv. 1-8). The re-establishment of the covenant was proclaimed (vv. 9,10). A charge was given concerning the recital of blessings and curses in the later ceremony (vv. 11-26). For the historical performance of what is here prescribed, see Josh 8:30-35. For an anticipation of these instructions among the Deuteronomic stipulations, see Deut 11:26-30.

1-8. 1. To promote respect for the appointed authorities, Moses associated with himself in this solemn hour **the elders of Israel** and the priests (cf. v. 9). **2. Set thee up great stones, and plaister them.** Covenant consecration must be an act of intelligent, informed faith and devotion. Therefore, the content of the covenant was to be published preparatory to its ratification by the people. That was one purpose of writing the covenant on the plastered stones, an Egyptian technique, as is confirmed by the fact that in the historical fulfillment Joshua read this law to the people (Josh 8:34). Comparable were Moses' reading of the Book of the Covenant to Israel at the ratification of the Sinaitic Covenant and the proclamation of the Deuteronomic Covenant in the plains of Moab. The fact that durable stones were selected invites comparison with the two stone tables of the law written by the finger of God and suggests that a further purpose was to provide a symbolic witness to the permanence of the covenant (cf. Deut 31:26; Josh 24:26,27). **3. All the words of this law.** This refers to the Deuteronomic Covenant, the part, "law," being taken to represent the whole. The ceremonial feast was another recognized symbolic method by which people ratified treaties. That is the significance of the peace offerings and the associated joyous meal (v. 7; cf. Ex 24:11).

The final ratification was to be carried out after Moses' death, when Israel under Joshua was in Canaan (v. 2a). Its setting was to be the impressive one of the adjacent mountains, Ebal and Gerizim, between which lay Shechem (v. 4; cf. vv. 12,13). There is no record of a military effort having been necessary to take that area of Canaan. The essential element of the ceremony would be Israel's self-consecration to the covenant Lord. The burnt offerings (v. 6) symbolized such consecration. To similar effect was the series of self-maledictory oaths (v. cf. 15ff.).

5. There shalt thou build an altar. For the purpose of the sacrificial offerings, a special altar was to be erected on Ebal. It may be that the mount of cursing was selected because the Mosaic economy, in its distinctive emphasis, was a ministration of death and condemnation (cf. II Cor 3:7-9), though, like a schoolmaster, conducting men to the grace of Christ. Or possibly the altar was to be erected on Ebal because the peace of the covenant was to come through the infliction of the curses on the Redeemer-Servant, sacrificed for the sins of God's people. The altar was to be made of unhewn stones, in accordance with the requirement of the Book of the Covenant (Ex 20:25). Clearly the Deuteronomic law of the permanent central altar was not intended to be a repudiation of the altar law of the Book of the Covenant. Nor was the principle of the centralization of the altar so absolutely restrictive that there might not be the special altar for extraordinary occasions (see on 12:4-14).

9,10. In the midst of the instructions concerned with the later stage in the renewal process, a solemn reminder was given that the covenantal engagement had already, on the day of the Deuteronomic proclamation, been entered upon.

11-26. Six tribes descending from Jacob's wives Leah and Rachel were to stand on the slopes of the mount of blessing and two of similar descent – the tribe of Reuben, who forfeited the birthright by the sin of incest (Gen 49:4; cf. Deut 27:20), and the tribe of Zebulun, Leah's youngest son – were to join the four tribes descending from the handmaids on the mount of cursing (vv. 12,13). Whether the two sets of tribes were to fulfill their respective roles unto curse and blessing simply by having either curse or blessing formulae directed toward them, or by themselves reciting or at least assenting to one or the other is not stated. In chapter 28 there appear matching sets of six blessings (vv. 3-6) and six curses (vv. 16-19); it seems difficult to dissociate these from the present two sets of six tribes. Joshua apparently read Deuteronomy 28 before all the assembly of Israel as part of the entire renewal treaty (cf. Josh 8:34,35).

The ark of the covenant and the Levitical priests were to be stationed between Ebal and Gerizim (Deut 27:14; cf. Josh 8:33). They must lead Israel in the oath of ratification, consisting in a series of twelve self-maledictions (Deut 27:15-26). The repeated **Cursed be** identifies the covenant-breaker's fate with that of the serpent (cf. Gen 3:14). The **Amen** response was the customary formula of assent (cf. Num 5:22; I Kgs 1:36; Neh 5:13; 8:6; Ps 72:19). The fact that only curses and not blessings are given in this passage indicates that this is not the detailed account of the curse and blessing proclamation by the two pairs of six tribes mentioned in Deut 27:12,13. A similar indication is the fact that verses 15-26 were to be addressed to and receive response from all the Israelites (v. 14). This section rather describes a separate feature of the covenant ceremony, the actual oath, which characteristically took the form of provisional self-maledictions, but not benedictions. In contrast to the curses in chapter 28, the several members of this series differ not in variety of curse but in kind of sin. The area of transgression covered is that of secret sins likely to escape human detection and punishment (note esp. 27:15,24; cf. Job 31:24ff.) and, therefore, peculiarly the judicial province of God as divine Witness to the oath. Those are imprecated who secretly violate God's demands for respect to himself (v. 15), to rightful authority (v. 16), to truth (vv. 17-19), to family (vv. 20-23), to human life (vv. 24,25), and, in sum, to God's covenant (v. 26).

B. Proclamation of the Sanctions. 28:1-68.

Returning to the first stage of the ceremony of covenant renewal, Moses pronounced its sanctions. In the corresponding section of the Sinaitic Book of the Covenant (Ex 23:20-33), the blessings predominated. Now, the forty years' history of Israelite apostasy having intervened, Moses' emphasis falls heavily on the curses; thus, blessings (Deut 28:1-14) and curses (vv. 15-68). This emphasis was anticipated in the promises and threats of a similar section in Leviticus (ch. 26), written after Israel's earliest rebellion against the Sinaitic Covenant. The remarkable preview in Deuteronomy 28–30 of Israel's history, especially of the far-off exile, has been a major stumbling-block to the recognition of the Mosaic origin of this document by naturalistic higher criticism.

1) Blessings. 28:1-14 (cf. 7:12ff.; 11:13ff.; 22ff.).

1. If thou shalt hearken diligently. Although Israel's inheritance and continued enjoyment of the promises was not a matter of legal merit, there was a connection between the nation's corporate piety and her prosperity. For the OT theocratic kingdom prefigured the consummate kingdom of God, in which righteousness and glory are to be united. Accordingly, to keep the message of the typical-prophetic picture clear, God allowed the Israelites to enjoy the blessings of the typical kingdom only as they, and especially their official representatives, exhibited an appropriate measure of the righteousness of the kingdom. Since any righteousness that Israel possessed was a gift of grace from the God of her salvation, the principle which informs Deuteronomy 28 has no affinities with a religion of works-salvation (see on 6:1-3). Verses 3-6 present six blessings which are paralleled by six curses in 16-19. (On the apparent use of these at the later ceremony in Canaan, see comments on 27:12,13.) The blessings depict a comprehensive fullness of beatitude. The paired opposites, for example, express totality (cf. vv. 3,6). What was concisely presented in liturgical formulae in the six beatitudes is elaborated in verses 7-14. The arrangement of the blessings is chiastic: thus, foreign relations (vv. 7 and 12b,13); domestic affairs (vv. 8 and 11,12a); and in the center position, relationship to the Lord (vv. 9, 10).

If Israel would obey the Lord, she would come out on top in every military and commercial encounter with other nations. Within the kingdom there would be abundance of the earth's goodness. Canaan would truly be a paradise flowing with milk and honey. Of primary import, Israel would prosper in her relationship to her covenant Lord. That is the secret of all beatitude, for his favor is life. From the manifest tokens of God's favor to Israel, all the earth would recognize that **the name of the Lord is called upon thee** (v. 10). That is, it would be clear that God's covenant was established with Israel and that he, the Suzerain, was Israel's Owner and Defender (cf. Isa 63:19; Jer 7:10,11; 15:16). Once and again the prerequisite covenant loyalty is recalled (Deut 28:9b, 13b,14).

2) Curses. 28:15-68.

Banishment from the promised inheritance was the extreme of malediction. It signified the loss of God's special presence and favor, loss of the appointed sacramental access to him on his holy hill of Zion, and loss of status as the people of God's kingdom. In this long section of curses, therefore, siege and exile repeatedly appear as the climax of woe. There is a series of parallel pictures of the disastrous future looming before this nation so prone to unfaithfulness (vv. 20-26,27-37,38-48,49-57,58-68). The first three and the last of these pictures culminate in the doom of conquest by the enemy, with its dreadful sequel (vv. 25,26; 36,37; 48; 63-68); the fourth is completely devoted to that accursed event (vv. 49-57). This extended description of particular evils follows an introductory, ritualistic formulation of the covenant's curse sanctions (vv. 15-19).

15-19. Verse 15 corresponds to verses 1,2, and 16-19 are the counterpart to 3-6. The vengeance of the covenant (cf. Lev 26:25) would overtake the oath-violating people even within the asylum of their inherited paradise land. Without holiness no man can abide where God reveals his glorious presence, and there is no respect of persons with him.

20-26. 20. Thou hast forsaken me. Such was the essence of Israel's sin – violation of the first commandment of the covenant. **The Lord shall send.** It was the right and duty of the forsaken Lord himself, the One to whom and by whom Israel swore the covenant oath, to avenge the oath. Whatever the human or earthly origin of the several curses, the Lord was their ultimate Author. **Until thou be destroyed** (cf. vv. 24,45,51,61). It is repeatedly stated here that the final issue of the various types of curses – epidemic (vv. 21,22a), drought (vv. 22b-24), and war (vv. 25, 26) – would be nothing short of Israel's destruction (vv. 20-22,24,26). **24. The rain of thy land powder and dust.** The sirocco would fill the air with sand and dust. Verse 25 is the reversal of verse 7 (cf. Lev 26:17). **26. Thy carcase . . . meat unto all fowls . . . and . . . beasts.** The curse principle is essentially the prostration of man under the sub-human realms over which God appointed him in the beginning as king. Hence, the Scripture depicts the doom of rebel mankind as an eschatological feast in which slain men are devoured by birds and beasts (cf. Ps 79:2; Ezk 39:4,17ff.; Rev 19:17,18).

27-37. Vexation and frustration characterize the curses of this section. Observe the references in almost every verse either to the utter impotence of the Israelites to cope with their afflictions or to their helplessness in the face of oppression. God created man as one who, entering into the program of His kingdom, might rejoice to follow the divine sabbatic pattern of labor crowned with the joy and satisfaction of consummation. But accursed Israel's undertakings in the areas of marriage and labor would be rewarded always and only with failure. Instead of attaining to the sabbath joy of accomplishment, the people of Israel would be driven mad with the vanity and frustration of their exertions (vv. 28,34). The contents of verses 27-35 are chiastically arranged: (a) incurable disease (v. 27); (b) madness (v. 28); (c) continual oppression (v. 29); (d) frustration (vv. 30-32); (c) continual oppression (v. 33); (b) madness (v. 34); (a) incurable disease (v. 35). The similarities to the calamities of Job are noteworthy.

The section ends (vv. 36,37) with the curse of conquest by a foreign nation – **which neither thou nor thy fathers have known** – which was anticipated in verses 32,33. God would afflict the apostates by abandoning them to their own reprobate mind and worship of idols (v. 36; cf. v. 64; 4:27). In idolatry man substitutes subservience to creatures beneath him for self-consecration to the Suzerain above him. In so doing man seals his own helplessness in sin; for, cutting himself off from the Lord-Protector, the Rock who delights to deliver the helpless, he looks in vain to a covenant lord weaker than himself. The essential nature of the curse principle once more finds expression in this worship rendered by man to the sub-human over which the Creator made him king. **37. Thou shalt become . . . a byword.** Israel, heir of the promise that all nations would be blessed in her, would become proverbially identified with cursedness by all peoples.

38-48. The curses of 28:38-42 are the opposite of the blessings of verses 8,11ff. **38,39. The locust. . . . worms.** The crop pests, another sector of man's erstwhile total dominion (cf. Gen 1:26), in effect would make the Israelites their servants, who must labor to feed them. On 28:41, see verse 32. **43. Thou shalt come down very low.** Here the beatitude of verses 12b,13 is reversed. In verses 45-48 there is a summation of the preceding threats of curse, both as to cause (cf. v. 20) and as to result. The cause would be Israel's breaking of the covenant oath; the result would be that Israel would suffer the full vengeance of the covenant to the extremity of exile's devastation. **46b. And upon thy seed for ever.** If this threat means more than that the climactic OT exile-judgment of Israel would serve as a perpetual sign of God's covenant vengeance, if a perpetual divine cursing of Israel is predicted, then Moses here warns of that which Paul declares to have become a fixed decree (I Thess 2:16). The punishment (Deut 28:48) was to fit the crime (v. 47). Israel's curse-yoke (v. 48) would amount to a return to the status from which God had called her in covenant love (cf. Lev 26:13). Though Moses does not at this point detract from the impressiveness of these curses by any qualifications, elsewhere he proclaims the triumph of covenant grace through the restoration of an elect, repentant remnant (Deut 4:29ff.; 30:1ff.).

49-57. What had constituted the climax in each of the preceding series is the exclusive subject of this fourth prophetic picture of Israel, overtaken by the covenant curse. With unsparing vividness Moses exposes the appalling distress and degradation to which this people, once the head of the nations, would be reduced when caught in the curse of siege. **49. A nation . . . from far . . . as swift as the eagle flieth.** The barbarian invader from afar, descending on Israel like a vulture on its prey, would be unpitying in its rapacity (vv. 50,51). But the inhumanity of the enemy warrior would pale beside that of even the tenderest Israelite mother, turned cannibalistic in the horror of the siege (vv. 52-57; cf. Lev 26:29; Lam 4:1-10). **51-53. The fruit of thy land. . . . the fruit of thine own body.** The passage contrasts the natural appetite of the barbarian and the unnatural lust of the Israelites. There would be no refuge from the siege anywhere in the land (vv. 52a,c,55,57) for those who had put their trust in human defenses rather than in God, their true Refuge. Old Testament history witnessed successive executions of this curse, and it was finally exhausted in the Fall of Jerusalem in A.D. 70.

58-68. 58. If thou wilt not observe . . . this law. In this closing paragraph Moses harks back to the conditional form with which the pronouncing of the curses began (cf. v. 15), for in the day of assembly in Moab the decision between the curses and the blessings was still to be made by Israel. To avoid the curses the people of Israel must obey the stipulations of this covenant document out of true reverence for the Lord who had revealed his glory and fearful works in saving them from Egypt. **62,63. Ye shall be left few in number. . . . and . . . be plucked from off the land.** Disobedience would bring loss of the blessings promised in the Abrahamic Covenant, namely, the multiplication of the people and the possession of a homeland. In place of the blessings would be every possible extraordinary and persistent affliction (vv. 59-61). **64. The Lord shall scatter thee among all people.** Prophetically following the besieged and conquered people into their exile (vv. 64-67), Moses catches with a few strokes all the pathos of unbelieving, homeless Israel down through the centuries – once the people of God, but become in their exile like unto the heathen, without Christ, having no hope, without God in the world (Eph 2:12). By repudiating their election and covenant calling, in virtue of which they had been delivered from Egyptian slavery to become God's theocratic sons, the people of Israel were doomed to fall back into a worse Egyptian bondage (v. 68), into bondage to Satan and sin, death and Hell.

C. Summons to the Covenant Oath. 29:1-29.

In a direct, personal appeal to the generation standing before him, Moses confronted them with the central purpose of the ceremony of this great day (vv. 10-15). This central demand for the oath of allegiance, which reflects the over-all pattern of the suzerainty treaty, is preceded by a reminder of the Lord's past works of salvation (vv. 2-9) and followed by a warning that the curses of the covenant would be visited on an unfaithful nation throughout their generations (vv. 16-29).

1. (Heb. Bible 28:69). Though some, following the Hebrew arrangement, regard this as a subscription, and it would indeed be an accurate description of what preceded, it is probably to be understood as a superscription. On the relation of verses 1 and 2, compare the similar sequence from 4:45 to 5:1. There is essential continuity in God's Covenant of Redemption from Genesis through Revelation. Nevertheless, the successive administrations of that Covenant, as it is repeatedly renewed by divine grace, are to be distinguished. The covenant made in Moab renewed the one made at Sinai, which renewed the covenant God made with Abraham, which renewed the covenant He made with Adam (cf. Gen 3:15; Deut 5:2,3).

2-9. The mercy and the miracle of the deliverance from Egypt and the passage through the wilderness should have opened the eyes of this generation to the supreme wisdom of giving themselves in wholehearted love to so great and gracious a Lord. (On vv. 5,6, see 8:2ff.; on vv. 7,8, see 2:30ff.; 3:1ff.) **4. Not given . . . an heart to perceive.** But the simplest spiritual knowledge is beyond the perception of man the sinner unless the Spirit of God grants him understanding as a sovereign gift of grace. This people, so signally favored as to have lived forty years in the atmosphere of supernatural providence, lacked that necessary gift (cf. 9:7,24). **9. Keep . . . the words of this covenant.** The responsibility for this spiritual dullness was Israel's, and by this reproof the people were incited to a better response to their Lord. The imperceptible way in which the appeal of Moses becomes the direct appeal of the Lord (v. 5ff.; cf. 7:4; 11:15; 17:3; 28:20) evidences the reality of the supernatural revelation which came through Moses, God's mediator.

10-15. The central act of covenant ratification and its significance are here declared. The terms of verses 10,11 indicate the solemnly formal nature of the assembly and stress the fact that the entire covenant community was present for participation in the oath. Women and children, non-Israelites (cf. Ex 12:38; Num 10:29; 11:4), and servants (Deut 29:11c; cf. Josh 9:21) were included. **12. Enter into . . . covenant of the Lord** (RSV). The Hebrew phrase, found only here, means literally, *pass over into,* or *pass through.* According to the latter translation, the expression might derive from a ceremony of oath-taking like that in Gen 15:17,18. The equating of the Lord's covenant with his oath (Deut 29:12) is a significant index to the nature of the covenant as an instrument of God's rule whereby he secures the commitment of a people to his service. **13. That he may establish thee.** This verse is to the same effect, but it shows, too, that God's establishment of covenant relationship with man is not a humiliating subjugation but an act of redemptive favor. It fulfills the promise and oath in which the children of God have found hope and consolation (cf. Heb 6:17,18). **15b. And also with him that is not here with us this day.** This means that there was to be genealogical continuity to the covenant. Such is the case not because salvation is an inalienable family heirloom but because God is faithful to his promise to extend his covenant mercies to the thousandth generation of those who love him and because covenant administration respects parental authority (vv. 14,15). Accordingly, the covenant with its sacramental sign of consecration is administered to believers together with their children.

16-29. For (v. 16) and **lest** (v. 18) both assume some antecedent thought. The idea to be supplied is probably that of the call to faithful allegiance which was presented in the preceding section. Thus: (Remember, O Israel, that the Lord is your God), **for,** as you well know, the temptation to idolatry comes to you from all the surrounding nations—**ye have seen their abominations** (vv. 16,17). (Remember), **lest** idolatry take root among you and you reap a bitter, poisonous harvest (v. 18; cf. Heb 12:15). The danger figuratively depicted in verse 18b is developed in verses 19-28 – the root in verses 19-21 and the bitter fruit in verses 22-28. **19b. To the sweeping away of**

moist and dry alike (RSV). The reference of this proverbial phrase is to plants; watered and thirsty plants means all plants. It continues the figure of verse 18b, warning again that if idolatry took hold in Israel, its ultimate issue must be deadly, indeed must be the ruin of the entire people. This thought is resumed in 29:22ff. As for the individual who would hypocritically mouth the self-maledictory oath of the covenant (v. 19b), the Lord would not hold him guiltless for having taken his name in vain. Though the individual might think himself hidden in the assembled host of Israel and suppose his hypocrisy concealed within his own heart, the Lord, the avenging divine Witness of the oath, would single him out and mercilessly pour on him all the curses he had idly invoked. On verse 20b, see Rev 22:18,19. Abruptly changing his standpoint to the future (Deut 29:22) beyond the desolation of the theocracy and the Exile (v. 28), which he had before threatened in the covenant curses, Moses again traced the cause of Israel's fall to her having forsaken the covenant by transferring her allegiance to idol god-kings (vv. 25-28). **24. Wherefore hath the Lord done thus . . . ?** He used the device of a dramatic dialogue of Israelites and foreigners standing amid the charred ruins of the theocratic land, a former paradise turned, like the cities of the plain, into a barren waste by the fury of God's judgment (v. 23). **29. Those things which are revealed belong unto us and to our children for ever.** Attention to the Lord's revealed demand for consecration is the life business of his servants (cf. 30:11ff.), not lusting after knowledge of divine mysteries (cf. Gen 3:5).

D. Ultimate Restoration. 30:1-10.

Beyond the curse of exile opened the prospect of restoration (vv. 1-10; cf. 4:29-31; Lev 26:40-45). The redemptive program is not to be frustrated by the fall of those who were of Israel yet were not faithful Israelites. An obedient remnant together with the remnant of the Gentiles will be restored to the covenant Lord in his glorious kingdom. Of this ultimate restoration, the OT return from Babylonian exile was typical. The one vast complex of typical and antitypical restoration is embraced in this prophetic blessing of Moses. The section of the treaty concerned with covenant ratification (Deut 27–30) closes with the call for decision, in which Moses reminded the people of Israel that they could not plead ignorance of God's demands (vv. 11-14) and warned them that the alternatives set before them in the covenant curses and blessings were those of life and death (vv. 15-20).

1-10. In 28:64ff. Moses portrayed the hopelessness of unbelieving Israelites in their dispersion among the nations. **1. When all these things are come upon thee.** Here he looked beyond the Exile, indeed beyond all the curse and blessing described hitherto in these covenant sanctions, and extended to his people the hope of restoration, the hope of a new covenant. **2. Shalt return unto the Lord.** The way into this new beatitude would be the way of a renewed and true consecration to the Lord against whom Israel had rebelled (cf. v. 10). **6-8.** The origin of that repentance and heart-love for the Lord would be in a divine work of qualification – **the Lord . . . will circumcise thine heart.** What had been externally symbolized in circumcision, the OT sacrament of consecration, would be spiritually actualized by the power of God (cf. 10:16; Jer 31:33ff.; 32:39ff.; Ezk 11:19; 36:26,27).

As the development of this theme in the prophets shows, the renewal and restoration which Moses foretold is that accomplished by Christ in the New Covenant. The prophecy is not narrowly concerned with ethnic Jews but with the covenant community, here concretely denoted in its OT identity as Israel. Within the sphere of the New Covenant, however, the wall of ethnic distinctions disappears. Accordingly, the Old Testament figure used here of exiled Israelites being regathered to the Lord in Jerusalem (Deut 30:3b,4; cf. 28:64) finds its chief fulfillment in the universal NT gathering of sinners out of the human race, exiled from Paradise, back to the Lord Christ enthroned in the heavenly Jerusalem. **3a. Turn thy captivity** (AV), or *turn thy turning*, refers to a radical change of condition. **9. The Lord . . . will make thee plenteous in every work.** Along with the spiritual gifts of regeneration, conversion, and sanctification by which the rebels are transformed into faithful servants, the Messiah will give them a new world of prosperity and peace as their inheritance (vv. 3a,5,9; cf. 28:4,62). The restored theocratic kingdom in Canaan is used as a typical figure for the anti-typical reality, the eternal kingdom of God in the renewed universe. That will be secured by a divine judgment, for while the people of God are to inherit the earth, their enemies will be plagued with every curse

(v. 7). The Messianic salvation is, thus, a new exodus and conquest, a renewal of the covenant mediated through Moses and Joshua, first at Sinai and afterwards in Moab and at Ebal and Gerizim.

E. Radical Decision. 30:11-20.

11-14. The Lord did not require of Israel something incomprehensible or unattainable (v. 11). Israel's duty was not hidden at some inaccessible height (v. 12) or beyond some insuperable barrier (v. 13). Note Paul's similar use of these proverbial questions in Rom 10:5,6. **14. The word is very nigh unto thee.** There are the secret, incomprehensible things which belong to God (cf. 29:29a; Ps 131:1), but the covenant demand is one of the revealed things given to God's people to be obeyed (cf. 29:29b; 6:6,7; 11:18,19; 31:19). As Job affirmed, exhaustive knowledge is the possession of God alone, but to man God assigns, as his portion of wisdom, the fear of the Lord, which is the way of the covenant (Job 28, esp. v. 28).

15-20. Moses concluded his setting forth of the covenant blessings and curses with an appeal of memorable simplicity and sublimity. He reminded Israel that in her experience as a kingdom, blessing and obedience would be inseparable, as would also rebellion and the curse (vv. 16-18). **15. Life and good . . . death and evil.** The issue was as clear and radical as life and death (cf. 19b). To love the Lord, obey him, and remain loyal to him – that was their life (v. 20; cf. 6:1-5). **19. I call heaven and earth to witness against you this day** (ASV; RSV). One of the standard divisions in the secular suzerainty treaties was that containing the invocation of the gods of the Lord and vassal as the divine witnesses of the covenant oath. It is significant that the Deuteronomic treaty contains at least a rhetorical parallel to that feature (cf. 4:26; 31:28; 32:1). The Lord was, of course, the divine Witness as well as the Suzerain of this covenant. Over and over again Moses traced the work of salvation which God was accomplishing through him to the promises sworn unto Abraham (v. 20c).

V. Dynastic Disposition: Covenant Continuity. 31:1–34:12.

This final section of the covenant document has as its unifying theme the perpetuation of the covenant relationship. Of special importance is the subject of the royal succession, which is also prominent in the extra-biblical suzerainty treaties (cf. above, the introduction to IV. Sanctions). This succession is provided for by the appointment and commissioning of Joshua as dynastic heir to Moses in the office of mediatorial representative of the Lord (ch. 31). The testamentary assignment of kingdom inheritance to the several tribes of Israel (ch. 33) reckons with the status of all God's people as royal heirs. Included also are two other standard elements in the international treaties. One is the invocation of covenant witnesses, here represented chiefly by the Song of Witness (ch. 32). The other is the directions for the disposition of the treaty document after the ceremony (31:9-13). By way of notarizing the document, an account of the death of Moses is affixed at the end (ch. 34).

A. Final Arrangements. 31:1-29.

A series of charges was given by Moses, all concerned with carrying on the covenant and its program: to all the people (vv. 1-6), to Joshua (vv. 7,8), and to the priests (vv. 9-13). Then in a theophanic revelation at the sanctuary (vv. 14,15), the Lord instructed Moses concerning a Song of Witness for future Israel (vv. 16-22), and also commissioned Joshua to his imminent command (v. 23). Finally, Moses again commanded the priests concerning the disposition of the documentary witness to the covenant and concerning the assembling of the people to hear the Song of Witness (vv. 24-29).

1-6. On Moses' age (v. 2a), see Ex 7:7; Deut 29:5. **2b. I can no more go out and come in.** Though Moses was still competent in terms of individual daily life (cf. 34:7), he had lost the stamina necessary to shepherd the whole flock of Israel and in particular to lead the campaign of conquest lying before the nation (cf. Num 27:16ff.). On Deut 31:2c, see 3:23ff.; 4:21,22; Num 20:12. The Lord, with Joshua as his new mediatorial representative, would continue and complete in Canaan the conquest already successfully begun under Moses in Trans-Jordan (vv. 3-6). With such leadership assured, Israel must execute the mandate of conquest (cf. 7:1ff.) with strength and courage (v. 6; cf. vv. 7,23; 20:3,4; 31:7,23; Josh 1:6ff.).

7,8. At the command of God Joshua had already been ordained by Moses before Eleazar and the congregation as the new leader of Israel (Num 27:18-23; Deut 1:38). **8. The Lord . . . will be with thee.** Repeating the promise of the divine presence (cf. Josh 5:13ff.) just made to all the people (Deut 31:3-6), Moses publicly charged Joshua to complete the mission of conducting Israel into its inheritance.

9-13. Moses assigned the priests and elders the duty of regularly republishing the law of the covenant. The effect of this was to associate the priests and elders with Joshua in the responsibility of rule and in the esteem of Israel. More important, all the covenant people, together with all human authorities in the covenant community, were placed under the lordship of the Giver of the law. **9a. Moses wrote this law.** This is a clear statement of obvious import for higher critical investigations (cf. v. 24). Though the writing is mentioned at this juncture, it is probable that the official covenant document, or at least the main part of it, had been prepared earlier. The delivery of the law to the priests and elders referred to here (9b), if it is to be distinguished from that mentioned in verses 24ff., may have been simply a symbolic transfer of the responsibility of enforcing the covenant law as described in verses 10-13.

In the suzerainty treaties of the nations, directions were included for reading them to the vassal people at regular intervals, from once to thrice annually. **11. Thou shalt read this law before all Israel.** In Israel there was to be a constant proclamation of the will of the Lord through the service of the cult and in time through the ministry of prophets. Parents, too, were charged with the faithful instruction of the covenant children in the commandments of the Lord (see e.g., 6:7,20ff.). Hence the septennial reading of the Law to Israel (v. 10) at the Feast of Tabernacles (cf. 16:13ff.) in the year of release (cf. 15:1ff.) was intended not as the sole means of teaching the people of Israel their covenantal obligations but as an especially impressive reminder, at this time of sabbatical renewal and consummation, of the need for an ever fresh self-consecration by the servants of the Lord if they would enjoy full covenant blessing.

14-23. Joshua, like Moses (cf. Ex 3:1–4:17), was personally commissioned by the Lord himself. This was the chief and stated purpose for the summoning of Moses and Joshua into the presence of the heavenly Suzerain, who then spoke with them face to face as a man speaks to his friend (Deut 31:14,15; cf. Ex 33:9,11; Num 12:5). The words of the divine revelation (Deut 31:23) were simply a direct statement of the charge – **Be strong** – and promise – **I will be with thee** – given mediately through Moses (vv. 7,8) and a confirmation of Joshua's public ordination (Num 27:18-23).

On this occasion the Lord also confirmed Moses' dark prophecies of Israel's future infidelity and God's wrath against them – **this people will . . . forsake me, and break my covenant** (v. 16ff.). In particular, the Lord directed Moses to teach Israel a song that would be a witness for Him against them when they broke the covenant (v. 19ff.). Israel's lusting after idol-gods, her spiritual whoredom (v. 16; cf. Ex 34:15,16), because of the abominable rites of the Canaanite fertility cult which would ensnare her, would involve carnal prostitution as well. The inclination to ignore the Lord would be most evident when the people of Israel would become secure and prosperous in their land (Deut 31:20; cf. 6:10ff.; 8:12ff.; 32:15). **17. I will forsake them.** Such would be the inevitable consequence of Israel's forsaking the Lord. Without God's protection the nation would fall victim to many evils and so be made painfully aware that **our God is not among us** (v. 17b). Lest the Israelites should then recall the divine promise not to forsake them (cf. v. 6) and impute unrighteousness to him, God appointed for them the Song of Witness, which places the promised blessings and the threatened curse in their proper perspective within the covenant. This song would proclaim the perfect righteousness of God and convict the Israelites of the justice of their afflictions (cf. 32:4,5). It was only because of the pure grace of God that Israel might even enter the land of promise, for the Lord was fully aware of the pride and rebellion in their hearts before he led them across the Jordan, 31:21b. Verse 22 anticipates 31:30–32:47.

24-29. As a complementary covenant witness along with the song, the treaty document was to be preserved **by the side of the ark of the covenant** (v. 26; cf. 9ff.). This requirement and the similar disposition of the two Sinaitic tables accorded with contemporary practice (see comments on 10:1-11). Possibly it was one of the priests into whose hands the Deuteronomic treaty was now entrusted (v. 25) who affixed the record of Moses' death, or indeed everything from this point to the end. This official may have had some further but minor part in bringing the rest of the document into its final form. **27. Ye have been rebel-**

lious . . . how much more after my death? The foreknowledge of God just revealed to Moses (cf. v. 21) was now the foreknowledge of Moses. In these instructions to the priests, all the treaty witnesses are brought together. The Song of Witness about to be recited to assembled Israel included at the same time an invocation of heaven and earth as witnesses (v. 28). The force of the witness was primarily against the people of Israel in view of their foreseen provocations (v. 29).

B. The Song of Witness. 31:30–32:47.

30. According to Moses' directions (v. 28), Israel was assembled, and Moses, together with Joshua (32:34), the old and new representatives of the Lord, proclaimed the song (Deut 32).

In its general structure this poetic song follows the pattern of the Deuteronomic treaty. After the invocation to the witnesses to give ear (vv. 1-3), the Suzerain is identified in preamble-like fashion as God of truth and as Israel's Father (vv. 4-6). Then the historical prologue of the treaty finds its counterpart in a recital of the special favor shown to Israel by the Lord hitherto (vv. 7-14). Next, the treaty stipulations are reflected upon in the condemnation of Israel's rebellion against the Lord in favor of new gods (vv. 15-18). The consequence of this covenant breaking is the heaping of the curses upon them (vv. 19-25). Yet, as is also asserted in the blessing and curse section of the treaty, beyond the final curse lies the prospect of covenant renewal accomplished through a redemptive judgment in which God will avenge his servants upon their enemies; such is the closing theme of the song (vv. 26-43).

a) Invocation. 32:1-3.

1. The address to heaven and earth must be understood as a summons to them to be witnesses of the covenant, since Moses had just stated that precisely that was the purpose of assembling Israel to hear the song (cf. 31:28). **2.** The way of the covenant and the way of wisdom are united here as Moses identifies this song as **my doctrine** (AV), or, *my teaching* (RSV), a word common in the Wisdom literature. The song presents true wisdom because its theme is the fear of the Lord, great God of Israel (v. 3).

b) Preamble. 32:4-6.

The song is a theodicy (cf. comments on 31:19ff.). **4.** With that in view, the identification of the Lord is in terms of his perfect justice. **The Rock.** This epithet contemplates God as the reliable refuge of his people (cf. vv. 15,18,30). The Hebrew *ṣûr,* as thus used of God, may derive from a root meaning "mountain" (cf. Ugaritic *ǵwr).* In contrast to God's righteousness stands the perversity of the Israelites, these "sons of God" (cf. Deut 32:6,18ff.; 14:1; Ex 4:22ff.) who were actually *his not-sons* (32:5a, lit.; cf. "not-god" (v. 21) and "not-people" (v. 21). This introduces the main burden of the song, namely, that Israel's sin provided a completely adequate explanation of all the evil that would overtake them. **6. O foolish people and unwise.** In keeping with the wisdom motif, sin is regarded as foolishness (cf. vv. 28,29). **Is not he your father, who created you?** (RSV) The reference is to the Lord's forming Israel into the theocratic people by election and redemptive calling out of Egypt.

c) Historical Prologue. 32:7-14.

7a. Remember the days of old. So begins the historical prologue section of the song. The fact that verse 8 refers to divine providence as far back as the events of Genesis 10 and 11 explains the historical perspective of Deut 32:7a. **8. He set the bounds . . . according to the number . . . of Israel.** As Paul teaches that Christ rules over all things for the benefit of his church, so Moses affirms that the Lord took special interest in the geographical needs of Abraham's numerous seed in his providential government of all nations (cf. Gen 10:32), for Israel was his elect people (Deut 32:9; cf. 7:6; 10:15). According to a reading supported by the LXX and the Qumran fragments, "sons of God" would replace **children of Israel.** Those who prefer this reading appeal to the mythical tradition that El, head of the Canaanite pantheon, had seventy sons, and to the fact that there are seventy nations mentioned in Genesis 10; and they conclude that this numerical correspondence is referred to in Deut 32:8. Similarly, Jewish commentators, following the Masoretic text, saw a correspondence of the seventy nations of Genesis 10 to the seventy Israelites of Gen 46:27.

Having arranged for Israel's inheritance in Canaan from the days of old, the Lord was, in the days of Moses, conducting them into the possession of its rich goodness (Deut 32:10-14). **10. He found him.** The Lord, coming to seek and to save that which was lost, found homeless Israel helpless in the desert. **As the apple of his eye.** He cherished his people as jealously as does a man that which is most precious to him, or as an eagle cherishes its young (v. 11). The figure might be interpreted of the deliverance from Egypt as well as of the guidance of Canaan. **12b. There was no foreign god with him** (ASV, RSV). Since the Lord was Israel's sole benefactor, their subsequent shift of allegiance to foreign gods (v. 15ff.) was manifestly without excuse. **13a. He made him ride on the high places of the earth.** In the Lord's strength Israel advanced in majestic triumph through Trans-Jordan (cf. 2:31ff.) and over mountainous Canaan to feast on all the choicest offerings of field and flock (vv. 13b,14).

d) Record of Rebellion. 32:15-18.

As their Suzerain, the Lord demanded, primarily, perfect and exclusive loyalty. Like an unruly beast, Israel, fattened in rich pasture, refused to submit. **15. Jeshurun,** *the upright,* is here used reproachfully. In their arrogant contempt for the Rock of their salvation, the people of Israel paid their sacrificial tribute to phantom no-gods. **17a.** *They sacrificed to demons which were no gods* (RSV), from whom they had received nothing and of whom hitherto they had never even heard. So unspeakable was their ingratitude, that they preferred such new god-kings to the Rock who had shown to them the love of both father (v. 18a) and mother (v. 18b).

e) Curses on the Covenant-Breakers. 32:19-25.

In the Sinaitic Covenant, attached to the stipulation forbidding rival image-gods, was the warning: "I the Lord your God am a jealous God" (5:9; Ex 20:5). God responds to unfaithfulness in the covenant relationship with something akin to the fiery conjugal zeal of a man whose spouse has been unfaithful (Deut 32:21, cf. v. 16). The law prescribed death for the adulteress. The covenant curses threatened Israel with extinction if she played the harlot with the no-gods of Canaan (cf. 31:16ff.). From the fire of divine jealousy there is no escape; it burns unto **the depths of Sheol** (32:22, RSV), the place of the dead. **19,20. He abhorred them. . . . And he said, I will hide my face.** Applying the *lex talionis* principle, God would reject Israel and remove his protection from them. He would incite jealousy in Israel by means of a no-people (v. 21; cf. Eph 2:12). That is, he would grant to a people that had not known his covenant favor to triumph over his **children in whom is no faithfulness** (v. 20b, ASV and RSV).

23. I will heap evils upon them (ASV). In verses 23-25 the covenant curses, especially pestilence, famine, and the sword, the terrors which come with the climactic curse of siege and exile, are threatened (cf. ch. 28). Therein would lie the triumph of the no-people. As a result of siege, Israel would be removed from God's kingdom and become herself a no-people (cf. Hos 1:9). In the further unfolding of redemptive revelation God was to promise a renewal of his mercy whereby the no-people would become again "my people" (cf. Hos 1:10; 2:23). And Paul has interpreted that as fulfilled in the coming of Gentiles as well as Jews into the New Covenant in Christ Jesus (Rom 9:25,26). In that connection Paul also gives a turn to the idea of Israel's jealousy at the favor shown by God to the Gentiles (Rom 11:11ff.; cf. 10:19). The Mosaic Song of Witness itself anticipates the redemptive mercy and blessing that lie beyond the predicted cursing of Israel (see Deut 32:26-43).

f) Blessings Through Redemptive Judgment. 32:26-43.

Attention is now focused upon the enemy nation which would mercilessly smite both infant and hoary head. **27. Our hand is high.** Lest the enemy misinterpret its victory over Israel and withhold from the Lord the honor due Him (cf. Isa 10:5ff.), He would limit the enemy's slaughter of Israel (Deut 32:26). From the viewpoint of the covenant curses, this would be a stay of God's vengeance against Israel. The preservation of a remnant from annihilation is thus rooted in God's jealousy for his own glory. At the same time, the ultimate vindication of his people, which the preservation of a remnant provides for, arises from God's compassion for them (v. 36). **29a. If they were wise, they would understand this** (RSV). The foolish enemy should have known that their easy victory over Israel, the covenant protectorate of the Suzerain of heaven and earth, must be due to his displeasure with Israel (vv. 19ff.,30). Verse 31 is a parenthetical interjection of Moses, enforcing the cogency of 32:30 by eliminating the possibility that the enemy's god had wrought victory for him. On verse 31b, see Ex 14:25; Num 23 and 24; Josh 2:9,10; I Sam 4:8; 5:7ff.; Dan 4:34ff. **29b.** Furthermore, if the enemy were wise, **they would discern their latter end** (RSV). This theme is continued in verse 32ff. Their arrogance would turn to trembling if they realized that the God of Israel, who had judged even his own people in fiery wrath, would certainly judge them also with strict justice (v. 34) for their depravity and cruelty (vv. 32,33). The greatest evil of the enemy nation would be that it was at enmity with the people of God. For though in this it would be the rod of God's anger against Israel, its own motives and purposes would be quite different (cf. 27b; Isa 10:7ff.). **35,36a.** Hence God's judgment of the enemy would be an act of **vengeance** and vindication in behalf of **his people . . . his servants.** So the song returns skillfully to its main theme of Israel and the covenant sanctions, and intimates that ultimate blessing will follow the penultimate curse.

For NT quotation of 32:35,36, see Rom 12:19 and Heb 10:30. **36b. Their power is gone.** Only when his people would be as helpless as when first he found them (v. 10) would God intervene in redemptive judgment. Forgiveness, however, was to be granted only as they were confronted with their sin (vv. 37,38) and so were led to godly sorrow and repentance and to trust in the Lord as their true and only Rock. **39. I kill, and I make alive.** Promising to come in judgment as the Saviour of his servants, the Lord identifies himself as God alone and absolutely sovereign (cf. v. 12; 4:35,39; 5:6a; Isa 43:11-13). **40. I lift up my hand to heaven.** As the Lord added oath to promise in the Abrahamic Covenant, so also he did in this New Covenant, swearing by himself, for there is no other (cf. Isa 45:22,23; Heb 6:13), that his judgment would be terrible against those who hate him (Deut 32:41,42; cf. v. 35; Isa 63:1ff.). In verse 42, the third clause completes the first; the fourth, the second. **43.** The song concludes with the prospect of jubilation over the judgment of God which involves both retribution upon the enemy and expiation of all guilt within the kingdom of God. Since the **nations** universally are called upon to participate in the joy of God's salvation, the horizon of this hope is clearly the Messianic age, when all the nations of the earth will find blessing in the seed of Abraham.

44-47. The commissioning of Joshua and the instructions concerning the Song of Witness were joined in the special revelation at the sanctuary (31:14-23), and significantly Joshua was associated with Moses in proclaiming the song to Israel (32:44). Moses sealed the recital with a final appeal to the covenant community to cultivate in its successive generations fidelity to the covenant, which in its summarization in the song was a witness for God to Israel (v. 46). The conclusion to the sanctions (30:15ff.) is echoed in the warning that this was a question of Israel's very life (32:47).

C. Moses' Testament. 32:48–33:29.

48-52. Cf. 3:27; Num 27:12-14. **48. That selfsame day.** It was toward the close of the day of the renewal ceremony (cf. 1:3-5; 27:11; 31:22) that Moses ascended **this mountain of the Abarim, mount Nebo** (49a, RSV), there to die. On Aaron's death on Mount Hor, see 10:6; Num 20:22ff.; 33:37,38. **51. Because ye trespassed.** On the sin which disqualified Moses for entrance into Canaan, see 1:37; 3:26; 4:21; Num 20:10ff.; 27:14. The performance of this command is described in Deut 34:1ff.

In the ancient Near East, a dying father's final blessings spoken to his sons were an irrevocable legal testament, accepted as decisive evidence in court disputes. In the case of the Biblical patriarchs, the authority and potency of their last blessings derived from the Spirit of prophecy in them, speaking in the testamentary form (cf. the cases of Isaac, Gen 27, and Jacob, Gen 49). As spiritual and theocratic father of the twelve tribes, Moses pronounced his blessings on them just before he ascended the mount to die (Deut 33:1), and thus his words constitute his testament. In so far as Deuteronomy was a dynastic guarantee, Joshua as Moses' successor was the heir of the covenant. It was also true, however, that all the Israelites were God's adopted sons, and thus heirs of the blessings of His kingdom which were being dispensed through His servant Moses. It is impossible simply to equate the covenantal and testamentary forms without a drastic impoverishment and distortion of the covenant concept. But to the extent that the blessings promised in God's redemptive covenant are not inheritable apart from the promisor's death, that covenant does include as one of its features the testamentary principle.

Moses' poetic testament contains three parts: (a) an introduction, describing the glory of the Lord as he declared his kingship in the giving of his theocratic covenant to Jeshurun (vv. 2-5); (b) the blessings of the tribes, these being in the form of prayers, doxologies, imperatives, and predictions (vv. 6-25); and (c) a conclusion, extolling God, the majestic Protector of Jeshurun (vv. 26-29). (For a useful study of textual problems in this chapter and a new translation see F. M. Cross and D. N. Freedman, "The Blessing of Moses," JBL 67 (1948), 191-210.)

1) Introduction. 33:2-5.

The appearing of the Lord as King of Kings to proclaim his covenant was in radiant, sunrise-like glory over the eastern mountains of the Sinai peninsula (v. 2a; cf. the similar poetic descriptions of the desert theophany in Jud 5:4ff.; Ps 68:7ff.,17ff.; Hab 3:2ff.). **2b.** In attendance upon the King at his advent was a heavenly host of **holy ones** (ASV and RSV; cf. Ps 68:17; Zech 14:5; Acts 7:53; Gal 3:19; Heb 2:2). Probably nearer than the AV to the true sense of verses 2d,3 is the translation by Cross and Freedman: *At his right hand proceeded the mighty ones, yea, the guardians of the peoples. All the holy ones are at thy hand, they prostrate themselves at thy feet, they carry out thy decisions.* As the Lord's earthly representative, Moses gave God's covenant with its kingdom promises to Israel (v. 4), and by the covenant ceremony the Lord's theocratic kingship over Israel was ratified (v. 5).

2) The Blessings of the Tribes. 33:6-25.

Moses first blessed the sons of Jacob's wives, then the sons of the handmaids. Though Jacob announced first-born Reuben's loss of the rights of primogeniture, both he and Moses began their testaments with him (cf. Gen 49:3,4). **6. Let Reuben live.** Moses prayed that Reuben might not suffer tribal extinction. **7. Bring him unto his people.** The blessing for royal Judah (Leah's fourth son) is, in effect, the prayer that Jacob's prophetic blessing on him might be fulfilled (cf. Gen 49:9-12), that Judah might be enabled to accomplish the kingly task of conquering the adversaries and thence return to his people to receive their obedience. In the testament of Jacob, Simeon and Levi (second and third sons of Leah) were rebuked and scattered in Israel (Gen 49:5-7). Historically, Simeon was early absorbed by Judah (cf. Josh 19:2ff.). Moses omitted Simeon from the separate blessings (the number twelve being then obtained by the division of the Joseph tribe). But he invested Levi's distribution throughout Israel (cf. Josh 21:1-40) with a new significance. **9b. They have . . . kept thy covenant.** Levi had displayed the devotion to the Lord requisite for the priestly office in the testing at Sinai (Ex 32:26-29). On the events at Massah and Meribah (Deut 33:8b), the beginning and end of God's trial of Israel (cf. 8:2ff.), see Ex 17:1-7; Num 20:1-13; Deut 6:16; 9:22; 32:51. Upon this tribe was conferred the honor of the priesthood in the family of Aaron, with its privileges of receiving special divine revelation (33:8a), teaching the covenant law (v. 10a), and officiating at the altar (v. 10b). Levi's blessing fittingly closes with the prayer that his priestly ministry in behalf of the covenant people may prove efficacious (v. 11).

Having dealt with royal and priestly tribes, Moses turned to Benjamin (younger son of Rachel). **12c. He shall dwell between his shoulders.** To Benjamin was allotted Jerusalem on the border of Judah, site of the Lord's sanctuary and throne (cf. Gen 49:27; Josh 15:8; 18:16). The use of the term "shoulder" in the latter passages (RSV) to denote Jerusalem's elevated situation supports the view that the Lord is the subject of **dwell.** On **the beloved of the Lord,** see Jer 11:15; Ps 60:5. Adjoining Benjamin in the blessing (Deut 33:13-17) and in territorial inheritance was Joseph (Rachel's older son). The double portion, the right of the first-born forfeited by Reuben, had been given to Joseph (Gen 48:22) in that his two sons enjoyed separate tribal status. Moses now confirmed the pre-eminence which Jacob gave Ephraim over Manasseh (Deut 33:17; cf. Gen 48:14ff.). Again like Jacob, Moses blessed Joseph with military power and abundance of the choicest gifts of the earth (cf. Gen 49:22-26). **16.** The source of all Joseph's prowess and prosperity was in the **favor of him that dwelt in the bush** (RSV; cf. Ex 3:2ff.). A slight change in the text would substitute "Sinai" for **bush.** Zebulun and Issachar (sixth and fifth sons respectively of Leah) are here united in their blessing (Deut 33:18,19; cf. Gen 49:13-15). Their special portion was to be the treasures of the sea, secured apparently by trade with those laboring in and along the Mediterranean and the Sea of Chinnereth. Their inheritances were near but not on these waters (cf., however, Gen 49:13). **19a. They shall call the people unto the mountain.** This seems to indicate that their commercial successes would be thankfully acknowledged in true worship.

The tribe of Gad (first son of Leah's

handmaid Zilpah) had chosen **a commander's portion** (v. 21a, RSV) as their inheritance in Trans-Jordan, the first fruits of the conquest (vv. 20,21a). Then they faithfully joined their brethren in the conflict for their portions in Canaan (v. 21b). Like Shem's blessing (Gen 9:26), Gad's is couched in doxology (cf. Gen 49:19). In energetic strength the tribe of Dan (elder son of Rachel's handmaid Bilhah) was to be like the lions of Bashan (Deut 33:22; cf. Gen 49:17). It was to the area of Bashan that an expedition of Danites migrated from their earlier territory on the southern coast (Jud 18). The Lord's favor on Naphtali (Bilhah's younger son) was to be shown in the remarkable fertility and beauty of his inheritance, especially its southern portion on the shores of Chinnereth (Deut 33:23; cf. Gen 49:21). **24a. Blessed above sons be Asher** (RSV). This tribe of Zilpah's younger son was situated on Israel's northwest border, a fertile land adjoining Naphtali (v. 24b; cf. Gen 49:20). **25. As thy days . . . thy strength.** Moses' prayer was that Asher's protection might be constantly strong.

3) Conclusion. 33:26-29.

26a. There is none like unto God, O Jeshurun (RSV). As in the introduction (vv. 2-5), Moses here extols the true Giver of the blessings of this testament. The establishment of the covenant was celebrated in the introduction, but here the Lord is praised as Israel's Defender and Benefactor in the subsequent conquest (v. 27) and settlement in the paradise land (v. 28). On verse 26b, see Ps 18:10; 68:33. On 27a, see the Mosaic Psalm 90:1,2. **29. Who is like unto thee, O people saved by the Lord.** The uniqueness of Israel's beatitude arises from the uniqueness of Israel's Saviour-Lord (cf. v. 26a). **Your enemies shall come fawning to you** (RSV). All must acknowledge Israel's supremacy.

D. Dynastic Succession. 34:1-12.

A testament is of force only after the death of the testator. So the Deuteronomic Covenant in its testamentary aspect (cf. comments introd. to ch. 33) would not become operative until after the death of Moses. Only then would Joshua succeed to the role of vicegerent of God over Israel, and only then under the leadership of Joshua could the tribes, according to the declarations of the Lord, enter into their inheritance in Canaan. It was, therefore, appropriate that the Deuteronomic treaty should close with the record of Moses' death, which in effect notarizes the treaty. That the testamentary significance of Moses' death is in view is evidenced by the accompanying attention given to the land of Israel's inheritance and to Joshua's accession to the royal mediatorship of the covenant. Verses 1-8 record Moses' death and verses 9-12, Joshua's succession to Moses. The account resumes the narrative of 32:48-52.

1-8. 1a. Moses went up . . . unto mount Nebo (ASV). Moses walked alone the ascent of no return, away from the promised land to the top of the mountain ridge on the west of the plains of Moab, opposite Jericho, to Mount Nebo. The panorama of Israel's sworn inheritance is described as it appeared looking first towards the northeast, thence westward and south, back to the plain stretching between Jericho and Moses. **2. The Western Sea** (RSV); i.e., the Mediterranean, lying beyond the hills of Judah, is not naturally visible from Nebo. **4b. Thou shalt not go over thither.** Cf. 1:37; 3:26; 4:21,22; 32:52. Though not now able to enter the land, Moses beheld its northern mountain peaks, on one of which he, with Elijah, was afterwards to stand and speak with the Mediator of the New Covenant concerning the exodus he must accomplish at Jerusalem before he might cross over into the heavenly inheritance (cf. Mt 17:3; Mk 9:4; Lk 9:30,31). It was necessary for Jesus to die before entering his rest, because he was the true Mediator who came to reconcile his sinful people unto God; Moses must die without entering the typical rest because as the OT mediator he had by official transgression disqualified himself for completing the mission which prefigured that of the sinless Son of God. Unlike Moses, who after his death was succeeded by Joshua (Deut 33:9), the Messianic Mediator would succeed himself after his death because it was not possible that death should hold him. **7. Nor his natural force abated.** Moses, though 120 years of age (cf. 31:2; Ex 7:7), did not expire of old age, but by the command of God, who by His sovereign word creates and destroys (Deut 34:5). On the location of Moses' burial (v. 6), see 3:29; 4:46. On its sequel, see Jude 9.

9-12. 9a. Full of the spirit of wisdom. Joshua had been ordained as the dynastic heir by the bestowal of the charismatic gifts of this dynasty, pre-eminently the gift of governmental wisdom (cf. Num 27:18ff.; Deut 31). **9b. Israel heark-**

ened unto him. True to their oath of obedience to the Lord's will, sworn in the Deuteronomic ceremony (cf. 26:17; 29:12), Israel assented to the accession of Joshua. **10. Whom the Lord knew face to face.** Though successor to Moses, Joshua was not his equal. With Moses God conversed directly (Ex 33:11; Num 12:8), but Joshua must discover the will of God through priestly mediation (Num 27:21). By the signs of victory over Jordan's waters and Canaan's hosts, Joshua was attested as the successor of Moses, who had triumphed over Pharaoh's hosts and the waters of the sea. But none was like Moses in the fullness of his revelation of the Lord's redemptive might (Deut 34:11,12).

BIBLIOGRAPHY

Driver, S. R. *A Critical and Exegetical Commentary on Deuteronomy (International Critical Commentary).* New York: Charles Scribner's Sons, 1895.

Keil, C. F. *Commentary on the Pentateuch.* Vol. III. Edinburgh: T. & T. Clark, 1880; Grand Rapids: Wm. B. Eerdmans Publishing Company, reprinted 1949.

Manley, G. T. *The Book of the Law.* Grand Rapids: Wm. B. Eerdmans Publishing Company, 1957.

Reider, J. *Deuteronomy.* Philadelphia: The Jewish Publication Society of America, 1937.

Wright, G. E. "The Book of Deuteronomy," *The Interpreter's Bible.* Vol. 1. New York: Abingdon Press, 1953.

JOSHUA

INTRODUCTION

Title. The first book of *The Prophets*, the second great division of the Old Testament canon, is named after its principal character, Joshua. There is no ancient Jewish tradition or manuscript evidence that this book ever formed a unit with the five books of *The Law* to form a so-called Hexateuch (see E. J. Young, *Introduction to the Old Testament*, pp. 157 ff.).

Authorship and Date. The book appears to be a literary unit, composed by a single author, not based upon two or more primary sources, as some have asserted, which were edited and re-edited for many centuries. While Joshua himself had certain documents written (18:9; 24:26), he cannot have been the author of the entire book bearing his name. It records his death (24:29,30), and events which did not occur until after his death: conquest of Hebron by Caleb (15:13b, 14; cf. Jud 1:1,10,20), of Debir by Othniel (Josh 15:15-19; cf. Jud 1:1,11-15), and of Leshem by the Danites (Josh 19:47; cf. Jud 17; 18) at a time after idolatry was tolerated in Israel (but cf. Josh 24:31). These events probably took place before the oppression by Cushan, or during the Judgeship of Othniel (Jud 3:8-11), about 1370–1330 B.C.

On the other hand, the author was an eyewitness of many of the events described (e.g., Josh 5:1,6). Rahab was still living at the time of writing (6:25). The book must be pre-Solomonic (16:10; cf. I Kgs 9:16); pre-Davidic (Josh 15:63; cf. II Sam 5:5-9); earlier than the twelfth century, when Tyre gained the ascendancy over Sidon, for the Phoenicians are here still called Sidonians (Josh 13:4-6); and it must have been written before 1200 B.C., after which more Philistines invaded Palestine, for the Philistines were not yet a menace in Joshua's time (see Commentary on 13:2 b-4 a).

It seems most likely that Joshua was written during the Judgeship of Othniel (c. 1370–1330. See Commentary on 1:4). The far greater familiarity with the concerns of the tribe of Judah (cf. the detailed account of the southern campaign, 10:1-23; the interest in Caleb and Othniel, 14:1-15; 15:13-19; the lengthy list of the borders and towns of Judah, 15:1-63) indicates that the author may have resided within Judah. He only very sketchily traces the borders of the important Joseph tribes even though within them lay Shiloh (16:1–17:11). If he lived in Judah, it is understandable that he listed the geographical areas of that territory first without qualifying his terms (11:16). Since there is repeated mention of the fact that no territory was given to the tribe of Levi (13:14,33; 14:3,4; 18:7), perhaps he was a priest (see J. J. Lias, "Joshua," *Pulpit Commentary*, III, xi, xii).

Purpose and Value. The purposes of the book are to continue the history of Israel begun in the Pentateuch and to demonstrate God's faithfulness to his covenants with the patriarchs and the theocratic nation by settling the tribes in their promised homeland (11:23; 21:43-45). Furthermore, God's holiness is seen in his judgment upon the iniquitous Canaanites and in his insistence that Israel, in fighting this holy war, must put away everything evil. A third aspect of God's relation to man evidenced in the book is God's salvation. The very name "Joshua," the Hebrew form of Jesus, means "Jehovah is salvation." Thus the redemptive history of Israel's entering and possessing Canaan illustrates the Christian's spiritual experience of conflict, victory, and blessing in heavenly spheres (Eph 1:3; 2:6; 6:12) through the mighty power of God (Eph 1:19,20; 6:10). In Hebrews 4 the rest in Canaan from vain wilderness strivings is set forth as typical of our present spiritual rest in the finished work of Christ and in his continual intercession to enable us to conquer self and Satan.

Historical Background. The data for determining the historical setting of the Exodus and the Conquest are supplied by the Biblical records and archaeological research. The patriarchs sojourned in Canaan during what archaeologists call the Middle Bronze Age (2100–1550). Joseph probably rose to power during Egypt's Twelfth Dynasty. Then the new king who rose against *(qûm ʿal)* Egypt and who knew not Joseph (Ex 1:8) was undoubtedly a Hyksos ruler in the Nile Delta region. Since the Hyksos afflicted the Israelites, forcing them to build Pithom and Raamses (Ex 1:11), Israel did not flee Egypt when native Egyptians thrust out the Hyksos about 1570 B.C. The Pharaohs of the Eighteenth Dynasty (whose capital was Thebes, but who had subsidiary palaces at Memphis, Heliopolis, and probably Bubastis) continued to enslave the Israelites until Moses finally led them into Sinai, about 1447 B.C. (cf. I Kgs 6:1), during the reign of Amenhotep II (1450–1423). Joshua must have led Israel into Canaan about 1407, during the Late Bronze Age (1550–1200). The tribal allotments were made about 1400, and Joshua lived until 1390 or later. An alternate view dates the Exodus during the reign of Pharaoh Rameses II shortly after 1300 B.C. Those who hold this view take the 480 years of I Kgs 6:1 as a round number for twelve generations.

By the time of the Israelite invasion of Canaan, Pharaoh Amenhotep III (1410–1372) was losing interest in his Asiatic holdings, so that most of the petty kings of Palestine and Syria soon revolted from Egypt or refrained from paying their tribute. The cuneiform letters found in 1887 at Tell el-Amarna in Egypt, the site of the capital of Amenhotep's son Akhenaten (1380–1363), are the royal archives of these two rulers. The majority were written by vassal princes in Palestine and Syria during the period 1400–1360, pleading for help from the Pharaoh against neighboring city-states or against the Habiru. Usually the term *Habiru* (or *ʿApiru)* designates mercenary troops. In this case it designates troops hired from Syria by the Canaanite princes rebelling against Egypt. Thus the silence in Joshua concerning Egypt may be explained by the fact that Egypt had a weak foreign policy from Amenhotep III until Seti I (1313–1301), the next Pharaoh to march into Palestine. Even then the Egyptians avoided the mountains and took the coastal route when campaigning against the Hittites in Syria.

By the period of Joshua and the Judges, the Canaanite religious observances had degenerated to the most sordid licentiousness and brutality – as we learn from the Ras Shamra (Ugaritic) tablets and the extant relics of fertility cult practices unearthed at Beth-shan, Megiddo, etc. The immoral character of the Canaanite deities led their devotees into the most demoralizing rites of the ancient Near East, such as sacred prostitution of both sexes, serpent worship, and infant sacrifices. Since such religious practices were spiritually and morally contaminating, one can readily see why God commanded Israel to exterminate the Canaanites. Thus they and their cities were to be devoted to destruction lest the religious life of the Israelites be endangered through contact with such idolatrous peoples. W. F. Albright strikingly explained the issues involved when he wrote:

> It was fortunate for the future of monotheism that the Israelites of the Conquest were a wild folk, endowed with primitive energy and ruthless will to exist, since the resulting decimation of the Canaanites prevented the complete fusion of the two kindred folk which would almost inevitably have depressed Yahwistic standards to a point where recovery was impossible. Thus the Canaanites, with their orgiastic nature-worship, their cult of fertility in the form of serpent symbols and sensuous nudity, and their gross mythology, were replaced by Israel, with its nomadic simplicity and purity of life, its lofty monotheism, and its severe code of ethics *(From the Stone Age to Christianity,* p. 281).

OUTLINE

- I. Entrance into the Promised Land. 1:1–5:12.
  - A. God's commission to Joshua. 1:1-9.
  - B. Joshua's mobilization for crossing the Jordan. 1:10-18.
  - C. Mission of the spies. 2:1-24.
  - D. Crossing of the Jordan. 3:1–5:1.
  - E. Renewal of circumcision and Passover observance. 5:2-12.
- II. Conquest of the Promised Land. 5:13–12:24.
  - A. Appearance of the divine Commander-in-chief. 5:13–6:5.
  - B. The central campaign. 6:6–8:29.
    - 1. Capture of Jericho. 6:6-27.
    - 2. Repulse at Ai because of Achan's sin. 7:1-26.
    - 3. Second attack and the burning of Ai. 8:1-29.

C. Establishment of Israel's covenant as the law of the Land. 8:30-35.
D. The southern campaign. 9:1–10:43.
1. Treaty with the Gibeonite tetrapolis. 9:1-27.
2. Destruction of the Amorite coalition. 10:1-43.
E. The northern campaign. 11:1-15.
F. Summary of the conquest. 11:16-23.
G. Appendix: Catalogue of the defeated kings. 12:1-24.
III. Apportionment of the Promised Land. 13:1–22:34.
A. God's command to divide the land. 13:1-7.
B. Territory of the Trans-Jordanic tribes. 13:8-33.
C. Beginning of the division of Canaan. 14:1-15.
D. Territory of the tribe of Judah. 15:1-63.
E. Territory of the Joseph tribes. 16:1–17:18.
F. Territories of the seven remaining tribes. 18:1–19:51.
G. Inheritance of Levi. 20:1–21:42.
1. Appointment of cities of refuge. 20:1-9.
2. Assignment of cities to the Levites. 21:1-42.
H. Summary of the conquest and apportionment. 21:43-45.
I. Appendix: Departure of the Trans-Jordanic tribes. 22:1-34.
IV. Final summons to covenant-loyalty in the Promised Land. 23:1–24:33.
A. Joshua's farewell address to the leaders of Israel. 23:1-16.
B. Renewal of the covenant commitment at Shechem. 24:1-28.
C. Appendix: Death of Joshua and subsequent conduct of Israel. 24:29-33.

COMMENTARY

I. Entrance into the Promised Land. 1:1–5:12.

A. God's Commission to Joshua. 1:1-9. At the close of the Pentateuch the death of Israel's outstanding leader and lawgiver and Jehovah's faithful servant is recorded. The Israelites were still encamped east of the Jordan. God's inspired history of his chosen people now continues.

1. The Lord spake unto Joshua . . . Moses' minister (cf. Ex 24:13; Num 27:18-23; Deut 1:38; 31:23). Whereas Moses, whom Joshua had served as chief assistant or officer, had previously given a charge to him, now God spoke directly to him to assume command of the Israelites. While probably not "mouth to mouth" (Num 12:8), this revelation must have come almost immediately after Moses died, in order to maintain the continuity of God's theocratic rule. The Lord gave Joshua four specific orders: (1) go over Jordan; (2) be strong . . . ; (3) cause this people to inherit; (4) observe to do according to all the Law. **2. Arise, go over this Jordan.** Up! prepare to cross over into Canaan. The Jordan was now at flood stage (3:15). **The land which I do give.** *I am giving* (Heb. participle), or, *I am about to give*.

3. As I said unto Moses. See Deuteronomy 11:23-32. They actually had to occupy the territory in order to receive it from God, as Christians must claim and appropriate their spiritual blessings in Christ (Eph 1:3). **4. This Lebanon.** According to the LXX, Anti-Lebanon, of which range Mount Hermon, perhaps visible from a height above Abel-shittim, is the southernmost peak. **The land of the Hittites.** This phrase is not in Deut 11:24; the LXX omits it here. In 1407 B.C. the Hittite emperors had not yet overrun Syria; their supremacy between the Euphrates and the Mediterranean began thirty to fifty years later, under King Suppiluliumas. If this phrase is genuine in the original manuscript, then the book of Joshua was not written before about 1350 B.C.

5. I will not fail thee. Literally, *I will not drop, abandon thee* (cf. 10:6, "drop not," or "slack not, thy hand"); LXX, *I will not leave thee in the lurch*. **6. Be strong and of a good courage** (cf. 1:7a, 9). God's second order, so necessary to a warrior, was, *Be strong and resolute, inflexible;* LXX: *Behave like a man.* **For unto this people . . . the land.** Literally, *for thou shalt cause this people to inherit the land,* God's third command to Joshua. Canaan was promised in the Abrahamic covenant (Gen 15:16-21).

7. Observe to do according to all the law. The fourth command was to keep watch or be careful to practice the whole Mosaic law, not merely the letter of the Law, but the spirit of it as well (cf. Mt 5:27,28, etc.). **8. Meditate therein day and night.** *Hāgâ*, "recite in an undertone." The LXX uses *meletáō*, denoting the meditative pondering and audible practice of orators. Joshua's courage, hope of victory, and wisdom necessary for success were dependent upon his constant attention and inflexible adherence to the written Law (*tôrâ*, "instruction, teaching").

9. Have not I commanded thee? The invasion which Joshua was about to lead was unmistakably ordered by God. Hence, Joshua was no desert chieftain or tribal sheik raiding Palestine, as the kings of the Midianites and Amalekites did later on (Jud 6—8). He was simply the field general taking orders from his Commander-in-chief (Josh 5:14) in a holy war of extermination of wicked, God-rejecting peoples.

B. Joshua's Mobilization for Crossing the Jordan. 1:10-18. Rested after the rigorous conquest of Trans-Jordan, the Israelites were far better organized and disciplined than they had been forty years previously.

10. The officers of the people. The term *shoṭᵉrîm* (Ex 5:6-19; Deut 1:15; I Chr 27:1) designates the scribes of the muster roll, corresponding to today's adjutants or staff officers who issue the administrative orders of a command. **11. Victuals.** Provisions. Since other food was now available, no longer were they to depend on manna alone; and soon it was to cease altogether (5:11,12). They could forage in the fields of ripening grain in the Jericho oasis. God does not support his people in idleness. **Within three days.** Literally, *within yet three days ye are going to be passing over this Jordan,* i.e., beginning the march which will take you across Jordan. Probably the same three days that the spies were away (2:22), but not the three days of 3:2. **13. Remember the word.** The proposal made by Moses in Num 32 (cf. Deut 3:12-21).

14. Armed. Literally, *in five parts* — van, rear, body, two wings; i.e., "in battle deployment." **All the mighty men of valour.** Joshua permitted the eastern tribes to send their best troops (4:13), so that a majority remained to protect their families and their flocks. **16-18.** The ready response of the Trans-Jordanian tribes enabled the Israelites to invade Canaan with a united front, so necessary for both the military and the spiritual morale of God's people.

C. Mission of the Spies. 2:1-24. Having some firsthand knowledge of Canaan from his own spying experience thirty-eight years before, Joshua, in executing the divine orders, prudently sent spies to Jericho, the key fortress of the entire southern Jordan Valley. Two immediate difficulties faced him: how to overcome the hostile Canaanites on the western bank; and how to cross the Jordan at flood stage (cf. 3:15; I Chr 12:15. Not all could swim it as the spies must have done).

1. Shittim is identified by Nelson Glueck with Tell el-Hammam on Wadi Kefrein, in the foothills of the eastern edge of the Jordan Valley (Num 25:1; 33:49). **Secretly, saying.** This mission was carefully concealed, even from the Israelites, lest the circulation of an unfavorable report should dishearten the people (cf. Num 13:28—14:4). **Came into an harlot's house, named Rahab.** Josephus and many writers since his time have argued that Rahab was an innkeeper. But the Hebrew word *zônâ,* the Greek *pornē* in the LXX, and Heb 11:31 and Jas 2:25 all definitely class her as a common harlot (not a *qᵉdēshâ,* a temple- or cult-prostitute). Did the spies spot her walking the street toward evening (cf. Prov 7:9-12) and follow her to her house, as detectives today may visit places of ill fame, where they may overhear the secrets of criminals? Or, guided entirely by the Lord, did they merely "happen upon" the house of this one prepared beforehand by the Spirit? Her house was probably built against the western city wall, her rear window overlooking the mountain (Josh 2:15,16); hence her house was some distance from the one city gate of Jericho, which opened upon the fine flowing well just to the east of the city mound. Rahab's calling implied far less deviation from the accepted standard of morality in her environment than it does with us. Furthermore, she also engaged in the honest occupation of linen weaving and dyeing. Her harlotry is mentioned to bring into bold relief God's mercy in giving her faith and in sparing her (cf. Mt 21:32; Lk 15:1).

2. The king of Jericho. In the Late Bronze Age every important city of Canaan was the center of a city-state and had its king. **4,5.** Rahab's expedient lie was a sin of weakness in one whose conscience was just beginning to be awakened out of heathen darkness. A man of developed faith learns to answer without lying (e.g., Gen 22:7,8). In Oriental ethics, guarding one's guest as an act of hospitality is one of the highest virtues. As for the charge that she was betraying her king, a new allegiance to the heavenly

King was developing in her heart. Thus she concealed the spies, though at greatest risk to herself. **6. The stalks of flax** were the stems, three or four feet long, spread out to dry on the flat roof (cf. Deut 22:8) after being retted (soaked) in water for several weeks. The flax bolled (ripened) early in March, when barley was in the ear (Ex 9:31,32).

9-11. Rahab revealed the priceless information that panic (as sung by Moses in Ex 11:15,16; as promised by God in Deut 2:25) had spread throughout the vicinity of Jericho. Her testimony (Josh 2:11b) is remarkable coming from the lips of a sinful woman in an idolatrous, polytheistic society. The Israelite leaders themselves did not always speak so monotheistically (see 24:14,15; I Kgs 18:21). The same evidence that convinced Rahab served only to harden her fellow-countrymen.

12. The translation **shewed you kindness** does not give the proper connotation. The word *ḥesed* basically refers to an unwritten promise, agreement, or covenant (as differentiated from the more formal *bᵉrît*, "covenant," inaugurated by a ceremony; Gen 15:7-18). In the desperate pact between Rahab and the spies, it is evident by the oaths sworn that neither party was acting out of pure sympathy and loving-kindness. More literally, she said: "Now then, swear to me by Jehovah that as I have made a *ḥesed*-agreement with you, ye also will make a *ḥesed*-agreement with my father's house, and give to me a pledge of (your) faithfulness." The pledge was the oath with which they were to confirm their loyalty to the agreement; it is given by them in verse 14.

14. The spies answered: "Our lives to die instead of yours (if we are faithless); if ye (you and your relatives) do not report this our mission, then it shall be, when Jehovah gives us the land, that we shall keep the *ḥesed*-agreement and faithfulness with thee." **15. A cord.** *Ḥebel,* a rope (II Sam 17:13; Jer 38:6-13). **16. And she said.** Better, *Now she had said.* No doubt they exchanged parting instructions (vv. 16-21 a) before the spies climbed through the window, lest they be discovered while still talking. **18. This line of scarlet thread.** A cord *(tiqwâ;* cf. Song 4:3) made of scarlet yarn which they spotted in Rahab's house, to be tied in the window *through* (not **by**) which she let them down. It was to enable the attacking Israelites to identify her house.

22. The mountain. Limestone cliffs 1500 feet high, with many caves, a half mile west, at the edge of the Jordan Valley. These cliffs are only eight or ten miles north of the caves where the Dead Sea Scrolls were discovered. **23, 24.** Probably before the dawn of 3:1 the spies reported to Joshua the dispirited condition of the Canaanites, thus giving him the answer to his first problem. They properly fulfilled their task without trying to give advice as to the attack (cf. 7:2,3).

D. Crossing of the Jordan. 3:1–5:1. Crossing the Jordan into Canaan was a major crisis of faith. Nearly forty years before, Israel had faced the same crisis, but had failed. To escape into Sinai via the Red Sea took a measure of faith; but to invade Canaan via the Jordan and thus become committed, without possibility of retreat, to the struggle against armies and chariots and fortified cities demanded supreme faith in the living God (3:10). Here a whole nation took the step to hazard their lives (cf. Acts 15:26) in total commitment to the Lord.

1. Came to Jordan. As soon as the spies reported, Joshua was reassured that God was working. Though not yet knowing how to get across the river, in faith he moved camp near to the edge of the *Zor,* the narrow depression 150 feet deep in which the waters flooding the "jungle of the Jordan" (Jer 12:5; 49:19 RSV) were contained.

1) Final Preparations for Crossing the River. 3:2-13. At the end of the third day, the ninth of Nisan (cf. 4:19), the people received instructions (3:2-4) for a new manner of marching, since the pillar of cloud would no longer guide them. **The priests the Levites.** The priest Levites, Levites who were priests, not Kohathites (Num 4:15), would carry the ark, because this was to be a solemn and extraordinary occasion (cf. Josh 6:6; I Kgs 8:3-6). The people were to spread around the ark at a radius of 3,000 feet, so that all might see the guiding symbol of Jehovah's presence more readily, "for ye have not marched in this manner heretofore" (Josh 3:4 b). **5. Sanctify yourselves.** They needed to consecrate themselves with outward purification and inward devotion to God, because he was about to perform miracles among them, giving the first public evidence of his presence with Joshua (3:7), and because they were entering upon a holy war (Num 31:24).

7. This day. That night, after the new Hebrew day began at sundown, the Lord honored Joshua's faith by revealing to him the means of passage. Then he could announce to the nation just how they were to cross the river (3:9-13). This was to insure that after the event they would know that their crossing was not a coincidence but that a Being of life, power, and activity was defending them and working for them. **11.** This verse, taken literally, indicates that the ark containing the written Law definitely represented God to the Israelites: *Behold the ark of the covenant! The Lord ('ădôn) of all the earth is about to proceed before you into the Jordan.*

2) Passage of All the People. 3:14-17. Early the next morning the entire nation crossed over, all in one day, for they hasted (4:10), undoubtedly hundreds or thousands abreast. There is no need to search for two differing accounts of the crossing when various statements in chapter 4 are properly interpreted. *The waters . . . from above . . . stood* (v. 16). This difficult verse may best be explained by translating literally: *The waters coming down from above stopped; they rose up as one heap very far at Adam, the town which is on the side of* (i.e., on the same side of the Jordan as) *Zarethan. And those coming down* (to the Jordan in other streams south of Adam) *toward the sea of the Arabah, the Salt Sea, were wholly cut off.* Adam may be identified with Tell ed-Damiyeh just south of the junction of the Jabbok and the Jordan, about fifteen miles upstream from the crossing area. The waters may have been dammed up as far as Zarethan (Tell es-Sa'idiyeh), twelve miles further north. A landslide of high (150 feet) marly cliffs of the Zor in the vicinity of Adam may have blocked the river (which happened about 1266 A.D., and more recently; according to Garstang, in 1927 the river was thus blocked for over twenty-one hours). Nevertheless, God wrought a great miracle: other streams had to be blocked as well; the waters stopped and returned (4:18) almost *immediately;* and the soft river bottom was dry at once; furthermore, the stopping of the water took place at flood time.

3) The Crossing Commemorated and Completed. 4:1-18. Before the priests bearing the ark could leave their post, stones for two cairns were collected, and one of these was erected where the priests stood in the river.

1. That the Lord spake. Rather, *that as the Lord had spoken.* The repetition of the divine command—undoubtedly given at the time of 3:7,8, for Joshua had already appointed the twelve men (3:12)—is made here to introduce the account of its execution.

5. This verse may be translated, *Proceed to the presence* (i.e., the vicinity) *of the ark of Jehovah your God, to the midst of the Jordan, and take up each of you a stone upon his shoulder . . .* Joshua and the twelve appointees may have remained on the eastern bank until the multitude had crossed. **6,7.** The heap of stones was to be a witness to God's power and faithfulness in bringing all Israel back to the Promised Land (cf. 4:21-24). Both the OT and archaeology testify to the frequent use of single standing stones *(maṣṣēbôt)* and cairns as memorials to commemorate theophanies (Gen 28:18; 35:14), vows or covenants (Gen 31:45-53; Josh 24:26), supernatural events (I Sam 7:10-12), or even relatives or tribes (Gen 35:20; Ex 24:4). An altar, since it was built of unhewn stones (Ex 20:25), could serve a similar purpose (Isa 19:19; Josh 22:10, 26-34; cf. Gen 12:7; 26:24, 25; 35:1,3,7; Ex 17:15; Deut 27:1-8; Josh 8:30-35).

9. Joshua set up twelve stones in the midst of Jordan on the very spot where the priests had stood. This spot must have been on the eastern brink, where they first stepped into the flood waters, for neither 3:17 nor 4:9,10 indicates that they had proceeded any farther into the river. Hence the cairn must have been readily visible during most of the year. Note that the two sets of twelve stones bore witness to the fact that *all twelve* tribes were in the wilderness together and entered Canaan at once.

10. And the people hasted and passed over. This statement explains in retrospect (i.e., *had hasted)* how the priests were able to stand patiently. **12,13.** The men of the Trans-Jordanian tribes, unencumbered by families and possessions, had led the crossing (1:12-18). **14. The Lord magnified Joshua** as the divinely chosen leader by enabling him to take the people safely across (cf. 1:5,17; 3:7).

15-18. This passage gives a fuller account of 4:11. Translate 4:15 as follows: *For the Lord had spoken to Joshua . . .*

4) The Erection of the Monument at Gilgal. 4:19–5:1. The first encampment of the Israelites in Canaan, and their headquarters for the conquest of the land, was at Gilgal, two or three miles northeast of Jericho, near Khirbet el-Mefjir. As

on the opposite shore, here the stones were set up in a memorial cairn, each being too small to be an individual standing stone *(maṣṣēbâ)*. The name *Gilgal*, however, which means "circle," evidently belonged to the site already, for Moses seems to have known it (Deut 11:30). Perhaps to mark a cult burial site, as at Stonehenge or Mycenae, the Canaanites had formerly installed sculptured stones in a circle near Gilgal (Jud 3:19, RSV), so that the Israelites established there a memorial to Jehovah to counteract idolatrous practices.

19. The tenth day of the first month. Abib (Ex 13:4) or Nisan (Neh 2:1), our March-April, 1407/6 B.C. They reached their camp just in time to select the Passover lamb (Ex 12:3) to be slain on the fourteenth day (cf. Josh 5:10), the providence of God arranging that exactly forty years after leaving the land of enslavement they should enter the land of promise.

23. As the Lord your God did to the Red Sea. These are the two crowning proofs of Jehovah's power and mercy in the history of the Israelite nation, never forgotten by the psalmists and prophets (Ps 66:6; 74:13,15; 114:3,5; Isa 50:2; Hab 3:8). **24. That all the peoples of the earth may know the hand of Jehovah, that it is mighty** (ASV). This purpose was strikingly fulfilled as soon as the various peoples of the land of Canaan heard the news (5:1). They had probably relied on the swollen Jordan to act as a sure, if temporary, barrier. But when they learned that it had been completely dried up, their morale utterly collapsed before so incontestable a proof that the Jehovah of the invaders was an actual, living, mighty God.

E. Renewal of Circumcision and Passover Observance. 5:2-12. Circumcision and observance of the Passover marked the final stages in God's preparation of his chosen people for the Holy War. Because the inhabitants of Canaan were terror-stricken, Joshua could afford to let his warriors be immobilized a few days by circumcision, the prerequisite to the Passover feast (Ex 12:44,48).

2. Sharp knives. Literally, *knives of flint*, not of bronze; although stone cutting tools were no longer in common use. But the use of flint knives for this ritual seems to have been demanded (cf. Ex 4:25). Egyptian art depicts the survival of this custom, undoubtedly because of religious conservatism. **Circumcise again . . . the second time.** The command did not require the older men, born in Egypt, to undergo the operation again; rather, the men of Israel, as a whole, were now to return *(shûb)* to their former circumcised condition as a people in covenant relation with Jehovah. **The second time** may merely emphasize the word *shûb*, "again" (Keil); or it may indicate a general circumcising on some previous occasion, as before the Passover of Num 9:5, since a mixed multitude accompanied the camp (Jamieson in JFB). The people had not purposely neglected the rite since Sinai, but apparently God had prohibited its practice because the nation was under his judgment. The people had rebelled against Jehovah repeatedly, had practiced idolatry, and had refused to enter the land (Num 14:1-10) promised them in the Abrahamic covenant (Gen 15:18; 17:8); hence they were forbidden to place on their children the sign of the Abrahamic covenant, which in spirit and in reality they had broken.

9. The reproach of Egypt does not refer to the reproach or taunts heaped upon Israel by the Egyptians, nor to the misery the Israelites endured as slaves in Egypt, but to the suspension of the Abrahamic covenant agreement of which circumcision was the sign. The word *ḥerpâ*, "reproach," often refers to the condition of shame, disgrace (cf. Gen 34:14 for the disgrace of uncircumcision). Even though delivered from the land of Egypt and united with God by covenant at Sinai, nevertheless the Israelites abrogated the Abrahamic covenant (conditional upon *faith* in Jehovah) and the Mosaic covenant (conditional upon *obedience* to Jehovah) by their desire for the idolatrous Egyptian worship (Ex 32; Josh 24:14; cf. Ezk 20:5-9; 23:3,8; Acts 7:39-42) and pleasurable things of Egypt (Ex 16:3; Num 11:5,18; 14:2-10; 16:13). Recognizing their apostasy, Moses exhorted the Israelites to repent before Jehovah, employing the figure of circumcision (Deut 10:16). When by faith the people of Israel crossed into their promised land and showed their willingness to re-accept God's covenant terms by submitting to circumcision, then the shame of their idolatry and lustfulness stemming from Egypt was finally rolled away. **Called Gilgal.** A new signification of "rolling" was attached by Israel to the old name, which probably had meant "circle" (see notes on Josh 4:19–5:1).

10. Kept the passover. This is only the third recorded Passover; the second (Num 9:5) was held on the first anniversary of the institution. For many years the people had not been in covenant relation with God, and so could not keep the Passover (see Amos 5:25,26). **11. Old corn of the land.** The yield or produce of the land, eaten in the form of their unleavened bread (Ex 12:14-20), and parched or roasted heads of barley (cf. Lev 2:14; Ruth 2:14), which were also unleavened food and easily prepared. Since barley was available from the harvest then in progress in the Jericho oasis, from that day the gift of manna entirely ceased (Ex 16:35).

II. Conquest of the Promised Land. 5:13–12:24.

A. Appearance of the Divine Commander-in-chief. 5:13–6:5. As Jehovah had spoke to Joshua to prepare him for the first great event – the passage of Jordan, so now He appeared to him to reassure and instruct him for the second great enterprise – the subjugation of Canaan. Recognizing the strategic necessity of the capture of Jericho to the Israelites (any retreat across Jordan was cut off), Joshua had gone to reconnoiter the bastion himself, perplexed because of its seeming impregnability (6:1).

13. A man . . . with his sword drawn. Not a mere vision, but an actual appearance of the preincarnate Son of God himself – a theophany (cf. Gen 18:33; 32:24-30; Ex 3:2-6). The Angel of Jehovah appeared in the character most adapted to the circumstances of his people: to Moses, as Israel's Saviour, suffering with his own (Ex 3; Isa 63:9); to Joshua, as Israel's Commander, leading his army with sword drawn, ready to judge Canaan. As Wm. G. Blaikie comments (Exp B): "The Captain of the Lord's host had drawn His sword from its scabbard to show that the judgment of that wicked people was to slumber no more."

14. One may translate the Man's reply: *Nay, for it is I; as General-of-the-Army-of-Jehovah have I now come.* In fulfillment of his promise to Moses (Ex 33:14), God manifested his presence with Israel not as a mere ally but as their leader. It was *his* war, for the iniquity of the Amorites was now full (Gen 15:16; Deut 9:5; 18:12); and the Israelites were only a division of his great army, along with his angels (Ps 148:2) and forces of nature (Josh 10:11-14; Jud 5:20). Thus Joshua immediately perceived he was but the Captain's servant. The account of the conquest (Josh 6–11) makes clear that Joshua's military strategy was divinely directed. There were three campaigns in the conquest. Brought by the Lord against the center of the land, Israel first captured Jericho and Ai, thus securing the passes to the Central Ridge and driving a wedge between the northern and southern sections of Canaan. The second campaign in the south then conquered the Amorite coalition, and the third, the northern confederacy. **15. The place whereon thou standest is holy.** Compare Ex 3:5. This spot in defiled Canaan was sanctified by the presence of the holy God.

6:1. Straitly shut up. The Hebrew expresses the fact that the defenders had shut the gate, and Jericho was shut in, beleaguered by the Israelites. This verse is a parenthesis introduced to explain the immediate situation of Jericho to the reader, followed by God's orders to Joshua (6:2-5). **2. I have given into thine hand Jericho.** Jehovah, Joshua's Commander, promised the divine, supernatural destruction of Jericho as the earnest of the capture of all Canaan. Joshua therefore no longer needed to devise any plan to take Jericho.

3. Ye shall compass. The execution of this command in absolute silence, but for the trumpets (6:8), could not but produce ridicule among the enemy, and so would be a discipline of humiliation for the Israelites. The brilliance of faith on the part of Joshua, priests, and people shone for a week at its brightest in all of Israel's history (cf. Heb 11:30). **4. Seven trumpets of rams' horns.** Literally, *seven jubilee trumpets.* Hebrew *yôbēl* ("ram's horn"), of uncertain derivation, is first used in Ex 19:13, even before the references to the year of jubilee (Lev 25:8-54; 27:17-24; Num 36:4); it seems to have a religio-ceremonial significance, announcing the arrival of Jehovah as King, whether to his people to complete his covenant or proclaim release and liberty, or to his enemies to judge and smite them. The "trump of God" (I Thess 4:16) will have this dual purpose in announcing Christ's second advent. Seven priests bearing seven trumpets for seven days signified that the judgment would be complete.

B. The Central Campaign. 6:6–8:29.

First Jericho in the Jordan Valley, then Ai on the Central Ridge had to be taken.

1) Capture of Jericho. 6:6-27. The archaeological evidence from Jericho (Tell es-Sultan) is not clear concerning the capture of this stronghold by Joshua. Miss Kathleen Kenyon's expedition (1952–1958) demonstrated that the parallel fortification walls (built of mud bricks and fallen outwards) which John Garstang excavated (1930–1936) and dated to the Late Bronze Age (1500–1200 B.C.), actually belonged to a time much earlier than the days of Joshua. In tombs west of the town, however, Garstang discovered 320 Late Bronze Age objects, including two scarab seals of Amenhotep III (1410–1372 B.C.), as well as Late Bronze potsherds in the fosse and on the mound, especially in debris underlying the isolated "Middle Building" (which Garstang attributed to Eglon; see Jud 3:12-30). Thus he confirmed occupation of the site in Joshua's day. Garstang and Kenyon (who did find a small Late Bronze floor level with an oven and juglet)would essentially agree that the previous city, inhabited by the Hyksos, was destroyed and burned around 1560 B.C. Then the mound lay vacant for about 150 years. Since most of the typically fifteenth century forms of pottery are lacking, reoccupation must have taken place about 1410. Probably the Late Bronze Age Canaanites reused the Hyksos rampart, upon which they built their own mud brick wall. The reason not more Late Bronze pottery has been found may be that the city was reoccupied such a short time before its destruction in 1407. In addition, one must take into account the completeness of the destruction (Josh 6:21,24) and the exposure of most of this stratum to erosion for the following five centuries, until Hiel rebuilt Jericho (I Kgs 16:34).

In this portion we see the triumph of faith. Israel was doing *God's* work in *his* way, no matter how foolish the marching must have seemed (cf. I Cor 1:25).

8. The ark of the covenant of the Lord followed them. Mentioned nine times in 6:6-13, the ark surely symbolized to Israel that Jehovah was with them and leading them in this strange maneuver. **15.** On that day they compassed the city seven times. One can easily walk around the nine-acre mound in fifteen or twenty minutes.

17. Accursed. *Ḥērem,* LXX *anathema,* translated in 6:21 "utterly destroyed." *Ḥērem* was anything irrevocably devoted to one's God, because it was hostile to theocracy by its having been sacred to or associated with another deity (Deut 7:25,26; 20:17,18; Moabite Stone, line 17). To prevent its being put to common use, the object (at times) or person (always) was banned and doomed to destruction (Ex 22:20; Lev 27:29; Deut 13:15-17; I Sam 15:3, 21) by divine sentence pronounced by God's duly appointed leader. Certain possessions (Lev 27:21,28) or captured objects (Josh 6:19), however, could be banned and dedicated to sacred use in the sanctuary or by the priests (Num 18:14; Ezk 44:29). In the case of Jericho alone, the city with all its contents was completely devoted to Jehovah (nothing could be considered as booty for the people; but cf. Deut 2:35; Josh 8:27; 11:14) as the first fruits of the land, for a sign that they would receive all Canaan from him. Thus the destruction was not due to lust for blood. **18.** Translate: *But ye, keep altogether from the devoted portion, lest ye covet* (so the LXX and 7:21) *and take some of the devoted portion, and place the camp of Israel in the devoted status, and* (thus) *bring trouble upon it.*

20. The wall fell down flat. Literally, *the wall fell in its place;* i.e., it collapsed – except for the portion by Rahab's house. Whether an earthquake was used by God or not, it was a miracle of timing and completeness.

22-25. Joshua acted honorably in accordance with the agreement made by the spies with Rahab (2:12-21). Rahab and her kindred had to be placed outside the Israelite camp in order that they, as heathen, might be cleansed from the defilement of their idolatries and the men might be circumcised. The required time may have been seven days (Num 31:19).

26. The curse was a prohibition against refortifying Jericho, not against inhabiting the site (cf. Josh 18:21; Jud 3:13; II Sam 10:5). It was fulfilled during the reign of Ahab, when Hiel rebuilt the walls at the cost of (not *in)* his two sons (I Kgs 16:34).

2) Repulse at Ai Because of Achan's Sin. 7:1-26. Ai stood about two miles east of Bethel, at the eastern edge of the Central Ridge, close to Beth-aven (7:2). French excavations (1933–1935) at et-Tell, the site usually identified with Ai, revealed a gap (c. 2000–1200

B.C.) in its occupation, showing that et-Tell was not occupied when Joshua entered Canaan. Seemingly the evidence from et-Tell favors its being identified as Beth-aven, *house of idolatry,* for pagan temples stood on its summit in the third millennium; and a small settlement existed there again up to the time of Saul, perhaps beginning in the fourteenth century by the time of the author of Joshua (cf. 18:12; I Sam 13:5; 14:23). Later, Hosea applied the name Beth-aven to nearby Bethel (Hos 4:15; 5:8; 10:5). Probably et-Tell is not to be identified with Ai. The long-denuded ruins of Ai may well lie under the present village of Deir Dibwan immediately southeast of et-Tell. Aiath (Isa 10:28) sprang up later, at Khirbet Haiyan, less than a mile south of Deir Dibwan, and was the post-Exilic Ai or (Aramaic) Aija (Ezr 2:28; Neh 7:32; 11:31). Whatever its exact location, in Joshua's day Ai was a fortified city, distinct from Bethel, and having its own king. It was a place of strategic importance, commanding the main route from Gilgal to the region of Bethel.

This chapter reveals how the faith of a body of God's people is undermined and disabled by the spreading effects of secret compromise on the part of a single member. Sin lurks in the very shadow of faith's victory; like leaven, it soon contaminates the whole. Also, Joshua is exhibited as the spiritual guide who drew forth, with mingled sweetness and severity, the sinner's confession (Josh 7:19,20), so that the nation might repudiate the sin and be delivered from the anathema now upon it.

1. Committed a trespass in the accursed thing. Literally, *committed a breach of faith in regard to the devoted portion,* for this was a crime against the covenant law. One transgressor against the *ḥērem* (curse) on Jericho brought the guilt and punishment of such treachery upon the whole nation. This verse anticipates the narrative in order to give the reason for the reverse.

2. Viewed. *Spied out.* The spies erred in estimating the size of Ai's population (8:25; see comment on 2:23,24). **5. Shebarim.** The *broken places* (i.e., defiles) in the cliffs, associated with the next gorge north of the famous one at Michmash (I Sam 14:4,5). Thirty-six Israelite fighting men were slain as they were ignominiously routed and tried in panic to reach the descending trail on the south rim of the wadi.

6-9. As a great general, Joshua was despondent about such loss of morale near the beginning of the war. Momentarily forgetting his own commission (1:5), he feared that God had forsaken Israel. Most of all, he feared the revival of hope among the Canaanites and the dishonoring of God's character (cf. 4:24; Num 14:15,16; Deut 9:28). **10-15.** Jehovah replied that the reverse was owing not to His unfaithfulness but to Israel's sin (cf. Isa 59:1,2). He revealed the reality or perversity of sin (Josh 7:10,11), its result or defeat (7:12), and its remedy or removal (7:13,14).

16-18. The offender, Achan, was identified by the sacred ritual of drawing lots, perhaps inscribed potsherds, from a jar (cf. I Sam 10:20-24; 14:41,42; Prov 16:33). This was the method to be used in apportioning the land among the tribes (Num 26:55). **19. Give . . . glory.** By means of this solemn adjuration to tell the truth before God, Joshua commanded Achan to make full confession (cf. Jn 9:24). **Make confession.** Literally, *render praise;* through a confession Achan was to give the omniscient Jehovah praise for bringing the secret to light and to acknowledge that the judgment was just.

21. A goodly Babylonish garment. Literally, *one beautiful mantle of Shinar,* a robe from North Syria (cf. Amarna Letter No. 35, line 49) probably woven with gold threads, thus devoted to God's treasury. **Two hundred shekels of silver.** Lumps or rings of silver, measured by weighing. **A wedge of gold.** A "tongue" or ingot of gold, about ten inches long, one inch wide, and one-half inch thick, such as Macalister unearthed at Gezer. A similar wedge is indicated in Amarna Letter No. 29, line 39.

24-26. Achan, in stealing devoted objects, placed himself in the devoted status, i.e., under the doom of destruction. Whoever touches *ḥērem* becomes *ḥērem* and thus devoted to death (cf. I Kgs 20:42). Achan's entire household, including his children, was cursed with him (cf. Deut 13:12-17). Living under the same tent, they could not but be accomplices. Infamous persons were often buried under a pile of stones (Josh 8:29; II Sam 18:17). **The valley of Achor** *(Troubling,* Josh 7:25), on the northern boundary of Judah (15:7), is probably Wadi Qelt, a mile south of Jericho.

3) Second Attack and the Burn-

ing of Ai. 8:1-29. As soon as Israel's crime had been judged by Achan's death, the Lord restored His favor and Israel's faith was re-empowered. **1,2.** Now God was ready to lead Joshua, for he was now willing to listen to *His* plan.

3-9. The men of the first ambush were sent by night to take a position back of some knoll behind the city on its west and be ready to rush into the city to set it on fire when the main army would draw out the defenders. The number, **thirty thousand mighty men of valour** (8:3), seems impossibly large for an ambush that was to hide so near the city. R.E.D. Clark has suggested that in certain passages (e.g., I Chr 12:23-27; II Chr 13:3,17; 17:14-19) the Hebrew word *'elep,* translated **thousand,** has the meaning of "chief," "officer," a synonym for the **mighty men of valour** ("The Large Numbers of the Old Testament," Victoria Institute paper for May, 1955). Thus Joshua would have selected thirty officers or chief warriors, each a valiant hero, to go on this commando-like mission.

10-17. Remaining that night in Gilgal, Joshua mustered *(wayyipqōd,* "numbered") the army early next morning and advanced with the men the thirteen to fifteen miles up to Ai (climb of 3,200 feet). He had the main army encamp in plain view across a valley north of Ai. Then he sent another ambush of about 5,000 men (here a full detachment, not specified as "mighty men of valour") to cut off any reinforcements for Ai that might come from Bethel. (Josh 8:17 and 12:16 b indicate that these 5,000 were kept busy killing Bethelites. The fighting potential of Bethel was thus neutralized, making it unnecessary for Israel to capture that city until much later; Jud 1:22-26.) Joshua spent. the night in the valley at the forward outpost to be ready to lead the assault in the morning.

14. At a time appointed, before the plain. Better, *to the appointed place in the direction of the Arabah* (Jordan Valley), where the men of Ai had successfully routed the Israelites previously. **18. Stretch out the spear.** Joshua's signaling weapon actually was his scimitar *(kîdôn),* the large blade more readily reflecting the gleaming sun to the thirty men hidden in ambush.

23,29. The king of Ai, as a greater criminal, was reserved for ignominious execution and burial under the direct supervision of his enemy's leader. For the divine command regarding the suspending or impaling of a criminal's body on a stake – a widely-practiced ancient custom – see Deut 21:22,23.

C. Establishment of Israel's Covenant as the Law of the Land. 8:30-35. Instead of capitalizing on the victory at Ai, Joshua did the militarily foolish thing – he stopped to make a divinely ordered pilgrimage (Deut 11:26-30; 27:2-13). God would protect them while the whole nation worshiped in the area so sacred to the patriarchs. Either Joshua led the people north some twenty miles from Bethel to Shechem, along the approximate route of the present Jerusalem–Nablus road, through wooded mountains (cf. Josh 17:18) almost devoid of ancient sites, except for Shiloh, which Israel later founded; or, more likely, since the women and children accompanied the army, he took the easier route from Gilgal up the Jordan Valley and Wadi Far'a opposite the Jabbok.

To reach the huge natural amphitheater formed by large curved bays, one on the side of each mountain, facing each other, the Israelites had to pass the fortress of Shechem guarding the entrance to the valley, less than a mile to the east. This city must have been in friendly hands (see 20:7; 24:1). Several of the Amarna Letters declare that around 1380 B.C. Lab'ayu, the prince of Shechem, was in league with the invading *'Apiru.* In this case the Israelite Hebrews may be referred to under the stigma of *'Apiru.* The reason for such friendship between Shechemites and Israelites may be that residing in Shechem were some descendants of Jacob who had left Egypt in small numbers before the oppression (e.g., I Chr 7:24, where a daughter or granddaughter of Ephraim returned to Canaan to build Beth-horon generations before Joshua's day).

30. In mount Ebal. At the foot of this landmark in the center of Canaan. Ebal, the higher of the two hills (3,085 feet high), is designated rather than Gerizim (2,890 feet high). Even though Moses had first given orders (in Deut 27:2-4,8) about inscribing the Law on great plastered stones, and then orders about sacrificing on an altar of unhewn stones (Deut 27:5-7; cf. Ex 20:25), the religious ceremony would logically have started with the sacrifices (cf. Ex 24:4-8), necessary because the covenant was being established for the *first* time in *Canaan.*

32. Upon the stones. Not those of the

altar but large pillars, such as the seven-foot-high stele of the famous Code of Hammurabi, with its 3,654 lines of text. According to Deut 27:2-4,8, these stones were to be plastered to receive the inscription. The Egyptians often white-washed stone before writing or painting on it in black ink. Several stelae, about eight feet tall and whitewashed, were found at Byblos in conjunction with a temple dated about 200 B.C. We can only speculate about how much of the Mosaic law was inscribed upon the plastered stones, very possibly Deut 5–26, however. The Behistun Rock inscriptions are about three times as long as Deuteronomy.

33-35. With the officials standing around the ark near the altar, halfway between the mountains and the tribes on the slopes, according to Deut 27:11-26, Joshua had the Law proclaimed to the nation. It was in keeping with the divine purpose for the conquest of Canaan that the Law should be set up in the heart of the country to be thenceforward the law of the land, and that Israel should renew her covenant vows to Jehovah her God. See Ex 24:4,7; II Kgs 23:2; Neh 8,9 for similar public readings of the Law. See comments on Joshua 24.

D. The Southern Campaign. 9:1–10:43. After returning to Israelite headquarters at Gilgal in the Jordan Valley, Joshua was soon called upon to fight against the Amorite city-states which controlled South Canaan. While the kings of 9:1,2 may unanimously have planned to unite, they never succeeded in joining hands to oppose the invading Israelites. The defection of the Gibeonites may explain the collapse of a united effort, so that only five cities in the south and a large confederacy in the north did battle with Joshua.

1) Treaty with the Gibeonite Tetrapolis. 9:1-27. Faith is endangered when God's people fail to refer every decision to him (cf. 9:14). Today, Christians need to be aware of the stratagems of our arch-deceiver (II Cor 2:11).

3. Gibeon. Probably the modern el-Jib (six miles north-northwest of Jerusalem, six and one-half miles southwest of Ai), this large town was the head of an independent republic ruled by elders rather than by a king (9:11; 10:2). In 9:7 its inhabitants are called "Hivites"; here, and in Gen 34:2, the LXX reads, "Horites," who may be identified with the Hurrians. These were a dominant ethnic element in the Near East (c. 2300–1200), spreading so rapidly in Canaan in the sixteenth and fifteenth centuries that one of the Egyptian names for Palestine was *Ḥuru.*

a) Deception of the Gibeonites (vv. 4-15). Craftily pretending to be envoys of a far-off country, as if from across the Jordan (for they claimed to have known about Sihon and Og, but did not mention Jericho and Ai. See 9:10), a group of Gibeonites perpetrated their hoax upon Joshua by means of their old sacks and mended wineskins, patched sandals and threadbare clothing, and dry, crumbled bread. God allowed the Israelites to let people at a considerable distance submit and pay tribute to them, but he ordered them to wipe out completely cities belonging to the peoples of Canaan (Deut 20:10-18). Convinced when they ate of the Gibeonites' stale provisions (which very act of eating, by ancient Oriental custom, established a more or less enduring friendly relationship), the leaders of the congregation made a formal covenant-treaty (*b*ᵉ*rît*) with them. "The Israelites were guilty of excessive credulity and culpable negligence, in not asking by the high priest's Urim and Thummim the mind of God, before entering into the alliance" (Jamieson in JFB; cf. Num 27:21).

b) Discovery of the Stratagem (vv. 16-21). Three days later, when the Israelites somehow heard that their new vassals dwelt in their vicinity, they set out at a normal pace to deal with the deceivers. Besides Gibeon, their towns were **Chephirah** (Tell Kefîreh, four and one-half miles west-southwest of el-Jib, less than two miles north of Abu Ghosh), Beeroth (probably el-Bîreh, a town today on the Jerusalem – Nablus road, four and one-half miles north-northeast of el-Jib, and **Kirjath-jearim** (Tell el-Azhar, with Late Bronze sherds, immediately west of Abu Ghosh, a town five miles southwest of el-Jib). Beeroth was only three miles west of Ai, in sight of the Israelites as they passed by Bethel! Because the covenant was ratified in the holy name of Jehovah, it was sacred; hence the leaders dared not break their treaty oath and bring God's wrath upon themselves (cf. Ezk 17:12-19). God judged Israel in the days of David for Saul's disregard of this oath (II Sam 21:1-6).

22-27. The reason for the decision of the princes in 9:21 is here given in detail: *For Joshua had called for them . . .* **23. There shall none of you be freed from being bondmen.** Literally, *There shall not be cut off from you a slave.* You will never cease to be or to furnish slaves, to act as wood-choppers and water-carriers for the Tabernacle (Deut 29:11). Joshua not improperly called this structure **the house of my God**; it was termed "temple" *(hêkal)* in Eli's time (Sam 1:9). Actually, it was Joshua's curse, not God's. Because they were assigned to perpetual service in God's house, He blessed them. For the protection of Gibeon the Lord performed a great miracle (Josh 10:10-14), and in later years the Tabernacle was pitched there (II Chr 1:3). For sixty-seven years or more God let the ark of the covenant remain at Kirjath-jearim (I Sam 7:1,2; II Sam 6:2,3). Because Joshua *made* (from *nātan,* "to give") them to be hewers of wood, etc. (Josh 9:27), later they were called the Nethinim *(ones given* to the Temple service; I Chr 9:2; Ezr 2:43,58; 8:20) and were brought back from the Exile along with the priests and Levites by God's providential hand.

2) Destruction of the Amorite Coalition. 10:1-43. The king of Jerusalem, closest to the Gibeonite tetrapolis, assumed leadership in gathering allies to punish the Hivite cities for their defection and to prevent the Israelites from occupying them.

1. Adoni-zedek is nearly synonymous with Melchizedek (Gen 14:18), both fairly common names or titles of the Jebusite kings. The Jebusites (Josh 15:63) were a racial mixture of Amorites, Hittites (i.e., non-Indo-European Hattians), and Hurrians, as Ezk 16:3 and the name Araunah (Hurrian word for "the king") in II Sam 24:18,23 indicate. Adoni-zedek must have been a predecessor of Abdi-heba, the ruler of Jerusalem in the Amarna Letters. Meredith Kline has argued clearly (in his articles on the Habiru in WTR, XIX, XX) that in general the Habiru ('Apiru) mercenaries with their chariots, filtering in from Syria to aid the Canaanite kings revolting from Egypt, cannot have been identified with nor have included (except possibly around Shechem) the Israelites invading en masse from Trans-Jordan to destroy the Canaanites and build a nation.

According to the Amarna Letters, by 1375 B.C. there were only four main independent city-states in southern Palestine – Jerusalem, Shuwardata, Gezer, and Lachish (the latter two both hostile to Jerusalem). Jarmuth and Eglon were governed by Egyptian officials. In Joshua's time, however, counting Jericho, Ai, Bethel, Gibeon, and the cities of the other South Canaanite kings of Josh 12:9-16, there were nearly twenty city-states. But before the Amarna period Israel had gobbled up many of these and left the others suspicious of one another. **3. Hebron.** The ancient town evidently was on Jebel er-Rumeidi, just west of the present city, nineteen miles south of Jerusalem. **Jarmuth.** Khirbet Yarmûk, sixteen miles west-southwest of Jerusalem. **Lachish.** Tell ed-Duweir, twenty-seven miles southwest of Jerusalem. **Eglon.** Perhaps Tell el-Ḥesi, over seven miles west of Lachish.

a) The Battle of the Unique Day (vv. 6-21). The historical importance of this victory has been compared with that of the Battle of Marathon (Blaikie). When the Gibeonites appealed urgently for help, the Israelites were covenant-bound (see comment on 24:1) to come to their defense. Encouraged by the Lord (10:8; cf. 1:5), Joshua led a forced moonlight march from Gilgal of at least twenty-five miles, perhaps up the Jericho-Jerusalem route, in order to cut off retreat to this the nearest of the Amorite strongholds (Maunder, in ISBE). He was able to surprise the besieging Amorites at daybreak and to slaughter them from Gibeon northwestward via **Beth-horon** to the Shephelah. The Amorites kept fleeing southwestward along the valleys separating the foothills from the Central Ridge, to **Azekah** (Tell ez-Zakarîyeh, which guards the Valley of Elah, about three miles west of Jarmuth) and **Makkedah** (possibly Khirbet el-Ḥeishum, two miles northwest of Jarmuth), as they tried in vain to reach Jarmuth (10:3), about twenty miles on foot from Gibeon.

The Lord increased the panic (10:10) by sending a storm of deadly hailstones upon the Amorites as they were fleeing the two miles down the sloping trail along the ridge between Beth-horon the Upper (alt. 2,022 feet) and Beth-horon the Lower (1,210 feet). Verses 12-14 do not describe an incident subsequent to the events of verses 10,11; rather, they are part of an extract (10:12-15) from the Book of Jashar introduced to render more vivid the circumstances behind God's raining down the hail. Similar to the Book of the Wars of Jehovah (Num 21:14-18), the Book of Jashar was a collection of songs, interspersed with explanatory historical notices, in praise of the heroes of Israel; the songs must have been progressively accumulated (cf. II Sam 1:18).

The usual interpretation of the miracle described herein is that God prolonged the daylight **about a whole day** (v. 13) to enable the Israelites to complete their pursuit of the enemy. However, if the sunlight was extended for ten, twelve, or more hours, so that the entire ancient Near East could have observed the phenomenon — a more spectacular miracle than the crossings of the Red Sea and the Jordan River — then it seems strange that only one other reference to the event (Hab 3:11) is to be found in the OT. God does not display his miraculous powers recklessly; instead he unleashes his strength only in sufficient measure to achieve his desired goal, only in sight of those who thus can be taught to recognize him if they will. What Joshua deemed necessary for his pursuing troops, already tired from their all-night climb, was relief from the merciless sun in the cloudless summer sky. (Up to this episode the conquest of Canaan moved so rapidly, after Passover at Gilgal, that only a few months need have elapsed.) For the sunshine to cease in the dry season would have been miracle enough. God answered above all that Joshua could ask or think by sending not only the desired shade to refresh His army but also a devastating hailstorm to crush and delay His enemies. Any storm from grain harvest on through the summer months was considered a judgment from God (see I Sam 12:17).

The true explanation of this miracle, told in ancient, Oriental, poetic style, tends to confirm the idea that Joshua was looking for relief from the sun. The word *dôm*, translated **stand thou still** (v. 12b), means basically "be dumb, silent, or still"; and then "rest" or "cease" from usual activity, as in Job 30:27; 31:34; Ps 35:15; 37:7; Lam 2:18. Robert Dick Wilson demonstrated that the root *dm* in Babylonian cuneiform astronomical texts meant "to be darkened." Thus the sun is spoken of as "dumb" when not shining, as in Dante's *Inferno*, line 60; the "words" or "speech" of the sun is its world-wide shining, its universal heat (Ps 19:2-6). Likewise the synonym *'āmad*, translated **stayed** (v. 13a) and **stood still** (v. 13b) frequently has the sense of "cease" (Gen 30:9; II Kgs 4:6; Jon 1:15). Joshua 10:12-14 may then be translated: "Now Joshua spoke to Jehovah, in the day that Jehovah gave the Amorites over to the sons of Israel; and he said before the eyes of Israel,

'O sun, be dumb at Gibeon,
and thou moon, in the Valley of Ajalon.'
And the sun was dumb and the moon ceased (shining),
until the nation took vengeance on its enemies—
Is it not written in the Book of Jashar —
For the sun ceased (shining) in the midst of the sky,
and (i.e., although) it did not hasten to set about a whole day.
And there was no day like that before it or after it,
that Jehovah hearkened to the voice of a man;
for Jehovah was fighting for Israel."

Evidently Joshua made his request when the sun was rising over Gibeon to his east and the moon was setting in the Valley of Ajalon (Wadi Selman, which emerges from the mountains a mile south of Lower Beth-horon) before they had pursued as far as Upper Beth-horon. Thus he prayed *prior* to the hailstorm.

15. Unless, following the LXX, we omit this verse entirely, it must be the conclusion of the condensed account from the Book of Jashar. For according to the main account, Joshua made camp at Makkedah (10:21) and did not return to Gilgal until he had finished this campaign (10:43).

b) The Five Kings Hanged (vv. 22-27). Probably it was on the day after the long one that Joshua had the kings dragged from the cave where they had hidden (10:16-27). **24. Put your feet upon the necks.** The ancient symbol of complete subjugation, pictured often on the monuments of the kings of Egypt and Assyria, here to be acted out by Joshua's field commanders (cf. I Kgs 5:3; Ps 8:6; 18:38-40; Isa 49:23).

c) The Conquest of Southern Palestine (vv. 28-43). At this stage Joshua's method of warfare seems to have been a series of lightning-like raids against key Canaanite cities, with the purpose of destroying the fighting ability of the inhabitants, not necessarily of actually capturing and occupying the cities attacked (10:19,20). When the king of Gezer and his troops were destroyed (10:33; 12:12), Joshua did not go against that city (16:10). The same was true of Bethel (see comment on 8:10-17). At the end of the campaign he returned with his entire army to Gilgal (10:

43), leaving no garrisons; and so Hebron and Debir had to be recaptured later (15: 13-17). Therefore Yehezkel Kaufmann, of the Hebrew University, has termed Joshua's campaigns "wars of destruction and extermination, not of occupation by immediate settlement" *(Biblical Account of Conquest of Palestine*, p. 86).

Since Joshua did not spend enough time at any one city to employ siege tactics (10:31-35) – although concerning sieges Moses had instructed Israel (Deut 20:10-20)–it seems probable that he did not attempt to storm the city walls and certainly not the inner citadels. The mighty army of Thutmose III finally captured Megiddo only after a siege of seven months. There is no report of further divine intervention as at Jericho, whose defenses Israel could not have hoped to destroy by frontal attack. Therefore Joshua must have concentrated on the surrounding dependent towns–**all the cities thereof** (Josh 10:37,39), and the residential section of each main city below and outside of the fortifications. To get an opportunity to kill the king and defenders, Joshua no doubt depended on their making a sortie, as at Ai; or he may have expected their previous battle losses and broken morale to make their resistance negligible. This theory of Joshua's military tactics seems to be confirmed by 11:13, "But none of the cities that stood on their mounds *(tēl)* did Israel burn, except Hazor only." Hence most of these cities could have been quickly resettled by Canaanites, perhaps even by those who survived in the citadel of each town; later, the separate tribes had to reduce them one by one during the period of the Judges (cf. Jud 1).

31. Lachish. The Late Bronze Age city on Tell ed-Duweir was burned about 1230 B.C., perhaps by Pharaoh Merneptah, but certainly not by Joshua (cf. 11:13). The end, however, of the earliest of three successive shrines built in an earlier fosse outside the city wall may give evidence of Joshua's raid. This "Temple I" belonged to the fifteenth century. **38. Debir.** Also named Kirjath-sepher (15:15) and Kirjath-sannah (15:49). Kyle and Albright located Debir at Tell Beit Mirsim, but archaeological evidence at that site does not harmonize with the fifteenth century date of the Exodus. J. Simons suggests instead Khirbet Terrameh (five miles southwest of Hebron) with neighboring springs at noticeably different altitudes, as "the upper and lower springs" of 15:19 *(The Geographical and Topographical Texts of the Old Testament*, p. 282).

40. Read: *So Joshua smote the whole land, the mountain ridge and the Negeb and the Shephelah and the steep slopes* . . . The Negeb is the desert region of South Palestine; the Shephelah is the foothills between the Central Ridge and the Philistine Plain; the steep slopes *(hā'ăshēdôt)* are those descending from the Central Ridge to the Dead Sea. **41. Goshen.** A town (15:51) in the southernmost mountains of Judah, used along with **Gibeon** to delineate the south-north extent of this campaign.

E. The Northern Campaign. 11:1-15. Reports of the Israelite victories in the south alarmed the North Canaanite kings. Summoned by Jabin, king of Hazor (see 11:10b), they joined forces and encamped at the waters of Merom. Meanwhile Joshua and the Israelite soldiers were marching unopposed up the lonely west side of the Jordan Valley. Beth-shean (17:16) may have had only a garrison at this time (Amarna Letter No. 289). Other towns, farther north, allied with Jabin were left undefended. Thus Joshua's rapier-like thrust caught the confederates completely off guard.

1. Jabin *(the intelligent one).* Another king bearing the same dynastic name or hereditary title ruled Hazor in the days of Deborah and Barak (Jud 4:2). It is rash to assert that the two stories are merely varying accounts of the same event. **Hazor** (Tell el-Qedah, nearly five miles southwest of Lake Huleh) in the Late Bronze Age covered over 170 acres and had a probable population of 40,000. It was by far the largest and most famous city of that time in Palestine. Its last phase has been dated archaeologically to the thirteenth century B.C.; the destruction discovered by the excavators must be that alluded to in Jud 4:24. Since the ruins reveal continuous Canaanite occupation from the twentieth century through the thirteenth, Canaanites must have rebuilt the city shortly after Joshua burned it (Josh 11:11). **Madon.** Qarn Hattin *(the horns of Hattin)* on the heights west of Tiberias. **Shimron.** Or Shim'on (so the LXX, Amarna Letter No. 255, and Egyptian ostraca), four miles west of Nazareth. **Achshaph.** Tell Keisan in the Plain of Acco.

2. Read: "And to the kings who were to the north in the hill country (i.e., Upper Galilee), and in the Arabah south of (or, near) Chinneroth (i.e., the Plain of Gennesaret, Mk 6:53), and in the Shephelah (i.e., the foothills between Samaria and Carmel, including Megiddo and Taanach; cf. Josh 11:16), and in the Hills-of-Dor region to the west (low dune-like coastal hills are prominent between Dor and Athlit" – Baly, pp. 24, 132). **Chinneroth.** Tell el-'Oreimeh, captured by Thutmose III, two miles southwest of Capernaum. **3. The Hivite under Hermon in the land of Mizpeh.** Hurrian settlements at the western foot of Mount Hermon in the Valley of Lebanon (the southern part of the Lebanese Beqa', containing the Leontes River; cf. 11:17; Jud 3:3). **The valley of Mizpeh** (11:8) contains the uppermost headwaters of the Nahr el-Hasbani, a source of the Jordan. Mizpeh and Baal-gad (11:17) were side by side, about twenty-three miles east of Sidon.

5. The waters of Merom. Not Lake Huleh. The LXX has *Marrōn*. Very likely it was on the small plain by the copious spring between the modern towns of Meirôn and Safed, about six miles southwest of Hazor; a wadi from the spring flows nine miles southward into the Sea of Galilee at Chinneroth.

6. How graciously God encouraged Joshua to attack the seemingly invincible foe in His strength the next day! The Israelites may have bivouacked on the Plain of Gennesaret that night. God commanded them to hamstring the horses and burn the chariots of the Canaanites, lest Israel put confidence in superior military weapons rather than in him (cf. Deut 17:16; Ps 20:7; Isa 31:1). Furthermore, to employ such equipment would have required a professional army like the *Maryannu* class among the Canaanites (cf. I Sam 8:11,12). Later, worship of Assyrian deities in Jerusalem involved idolatrous horse-and-chariot rituals (II Kgs 23:11). **8. Great Zidon.** The larger, mainland city of Sidon opposite the islets with the island-city of Little Sidon (cf. Taylor Prism of Sennacherib). **Misrephoth-maim.** Khirbet el-Mushreifeh, just south of the promontory known as "the ladder of Tyre." Thus the enemies fled northward, westward, and northeastward (see comment on 11:3).

11. With the edge of the sword. Literally, *to the mouth of the sword,* i.e., to the hilt. The short thrusting sword *(ḥereb),* the chief weapon of the Israelites, had a bronze blade ten or twelve inches in length protruding from a hilt often fashioned like a lion's head with open mouth (cf. Rev 19:15). The handle of Ehud's *ḥereb* had two mouths, with an over-all length of eighteen inches (Jud 3:16. See BASOR, No. 122, pp. 31ff.). Joshua's army also used the scimitars (Josh 8:18; see comment), bows and arrows (24:12), and undoubtedly slings with stone balls (Jud 20:16), thrusting spears or lances (Num 25:7,8), and hurling javelins (I Sam 18:10,11).

F. Summary of the Conquest. 11:16-23. "The battles of Beth-horon and Merom were decisive, and the power of the Canaanites to resist the invaders was shattered. All organized resistance was broken **And the land rested from war** (v. 23) in the sense that no more pitched battles were required" (Blair, NBC, p. 232). But these battles, plus the mopping-up operations or guerrilla fighting, took "a long time" (11:18), about seven years, according to 14:7,10. Courage and perseverance were both essential in possessing all the land (cf. 13:1; 23:5-13), in capturing the isolated strongholds (cf. 15:63; 17:12,16-18; Jud 1). This wearisome activity became the oft neglected responsibility of the individual tribes.

16. The mountain of Israel. The highest mountain in all Canaan (hence, in all Israel) is 3,963 feet high. It is Jebel Jermaq, just west of Meiron. This term, therefore, is not necessarily evidence of Joshua's having been written during the divided monarchy.

17. Mount Halak, that goeth up to Seir. Jebel Halaq *(the bald mountain),* the ridge up which the Maaleh-acrabbim *(Ascent of the Scorpions,* "Scorpion Pass"; 15:3; Num 34:4) zigzagged from Wadi Fiqreh, twenty-three miles southeast of Beersheba. **Seir,** the homeland of the Edomites before the monarchy, was in the Central Negeb, west of the Arabah, between Kadesh-barnea and Scorpion Pass (see Josh 15:1,21). Thus Israel had to go southward from Kadesh-barnea and Mount Hor to Ezion-geber in order to circumvent Seir, before marching northward up the Arabah toward Moab (Num 21:4; Deut 2:1-4,8). **20. Harden their hearts.** An expression revealing the sovereign working of God in confirming the hearts of unrepentant men in their obstinacy before judging them (cf. Ex 4:21; 7:13,14; 9:12; 14:17; Isa 6:10; Jn 12:40; II Thess 2:10-12).

21,22. The Anakim. Joshua nearly exterminated these people, who were either a branch of a race of giants *('Ănāqîm,* "long-necked ones," i.e., tall), or immigrants from Anaku, a land in the Aegean area mentioned in a cuneiform tablet from Asshur. Possibly the Anakim are mentioned in an Egyptian execration text (ANET, p. 328). They inhabited southern Canaan, especially Hebron (Deut 2:10, 11,20,21; Josh 14:12,15; 15:13,14). Only in Gaza, Gath, and Ashdod did some remain, the ancestors of Goliath, *et al.* (II Sam 21:16-22). Perhaps they are specially mentioned here because they were the men who had terrified the spies of Israel over forty years before (Num 13:22-33).

G. Appendix: Catalogue of the Defeated Kings. 12:1-24.

1) Those East of the Jordan. 12:1-6. The territories of Sihon and Og, conquered under Moses, are delineated. See Num 21; Deut 2:24–3:17.

2) Those West of the Jordan. 12:7-24. The thirty-one kings conquered by Joshua either on his three campaigns, or in subsequent isolated battles, were autonomous princes of city-states with only local authority. The Amarna Letters written by such petty rulers to the Pharaohs of Egypt about 1400–1360 B.C. also reveal numerous city-states in Syria and Palestine. It is not claimed that Israel occupied the cities of all these kings. The topographical divisions of 12:7,8 are those of 10:40; 11:16,17.

3) Kings in Southern Canaan. 12:9-16.

4) Kings in Northern Canaan. 12:17-24. **Tappuah** (v. 17 a) is more likely the town named in 16:8; 17:7,8, at the site of Jiljuliyeh, three and one-half miles north of Antipatris by Wadi Kanah, than the Tappuah of 15:34, probably Beit-Nettif east of Azekah. **Hepher** (v. 17 b) may be et-Tayibeh, about ten miles west of Samaria, on the Via Maris, the Mediterranean Trunk Road used so often by the Egyptian military expeditions. The route ran along the eastern edge of the Plain of Sharon, which in those days was swampy and heavily wooded. **Aphek** (v. 18 a; I Sam 4:1; 29:1) is Ras el-ʿAin (Antipatris; see Acts 23:31), nine miles east of Joppa, at the headwaters of the River Yarkon (Josh 19:46), captured by Thutmose III and Amenhotep II. **Lasharon** (v. 18b). In the LXX 12:18 reads, *The king of Aphek of the Sharon;* hence only one king is mentioned here. **Shimron-meron** (v. 20 a), according to the LXX, represents two kings —the king of Shimron (11:1) and the king of Marōn (11:5). Thus, with only one king indicated in 12:18 and three in 12:20, the full number of thirty-one kings is maintained. **The king of the nations of Gilgal** (v. 23 b) is unintelligible as it stands. In the LXX we read, *The king of the Goyim of Galil.* This is most likely a reference to Harosheth-of-the-Gentiles *(Goyim)* of Jud 4:2, a city in the region of Galilee, probably inhabited by some of the Sea Peoples coming from the Aegean Sea area. **Tirzah** (v. 24) is most likely the early capital of the Northern Kingdom (I Kgs 14:17; 15:21,33; 16:6-23), provisionally located at Tell el-Farʿah, six miles northeast of Shechem. This king either heeded Jabin's call (Josh 11:1-3), or was attacked on Joshua's return march from Hazor, or was killed subsequently in an isolated battle.

III. Apportionment of the Promised Land. 13:1–22:34.

This large section of Joshua sets forth in geographical detail the assignment of land made to each tribe, with the boundaries of the tribe's future possessions and usually with an enumeration of the towns contained therein. As Kaufmann has argued, the distribution of the land was an act of national policy made by the tribes which conquered Canaan, begun while the Israelites were still in their base camp at Gilgal (*op. cit.*, p. 25).

It is important to recognize that the tribes had not yet colonized their portions when these lists were drawn up. In actuality, the Danites did not permanently settle their appointed territory; Ephraim did not conquer or settle Gezer (16:3,10; 21:21); and the Benjamites never conquered or enjoyed sole occupation of Jerusalem, although this city was assigned to Benjamin (18:28). Furthermore, the fact that Ophrah and Ophni, towns belonging to Benjamin (18:23,24), were three to four miles north of the border in Ephraim, points to an early period before there was tribal friction. Thus the lists of the tribal territories cannot be lists of the cities and districts of the kingdoms of Judah and Israel either at the time of Josiah (so Alt, Noth, Mowinckel) or at the time of Jehoshaphat (so Cross, Wright, Albright, in regard to Josh 15:21-62; JBL, LXXV, Sept., 1956, 202-226). Many of the cities and their villages listed in these chapters were not conquered by the Israelites for centuries. And some of the town sites listed may then have been uninhabited by Canaanites and not settled by Israelites for a long time after the distribution of the land.

Reuben, Gad, and the half-tribe of Manasseh already had had their territories assigned to them by Moses in Trans-Jordan (Num 32:1-42; Josh 13:8-33). The return of their warriors after helping to conquer Canaan is described in chapter 22. In fulfillment of the tribal blessings pronounced by Jacob (Gen 49) and Moses (Deut 33), the main division of the Promised Land was between the tribes of Judah and Joseph; the divinely governed allocation made to the other tribes depended on this basic division.

The tribe of Judah was allotted territory in southern Canaan because with Judah was associated Caleb, who claimed Hebron for his inheritance (14:12-15). The tribe of Simeon later was given its share within Judah because "the part of the children of Judah was too much for them" (19:9). The descendants of Joseph —Ephraim and the other half-tribe of Manasseh—received central Canaan (Samaria), evidently because Shechem had been assigned to Joseph by Jacob (Gen 48:21,22; Josh 24:32). Shiloh, where the Tabernacle was stationed (18:1), was in Ephraim's territory, this strategic site in the hill country being chosen for its defensibility and its centrality for all the tribes.

Between Judah and Ephraim, land was later allotted to Benjamin (18:11-28), and, westward to the Mediterranean, to Dan (19:40-48). The remaining tribes—Zebulun, Issachar, Asher, and Naphtali – at the same time drew lots for territory north of Manasseh in the regions of Jezreel and Galilee (19:10-39). In addition to the tribal allotments, cities of refuge and cities for the Levites were assigned (20:1—21:42). The method of apportioning the land for the last seven tribes was by casting lots before the Lord (18:6; see comment on 7:16-18). The sections, with their borders, undoubtedly were predetermined to run along natural lines of defense by a special committee selected to describe the remaining land (18:4-9). The partitioning of the land was no simple task, but a complex one, that demanded careful direction and a considerable amount of time.

A. God's Command To Divide the Land. 13:1-7.

1. Joshua was old and stricken in years. Better, *Joshua had aged and was advanced in years,* for since he was nearly one hundred and ten years old in 23:1 (see 24:29), he must have been ninety or one hundred years old here. The apportioning, as well as the subjugation, of the land had been included in the commission to Joshua (1:6). Hence, his aging supplied a special reason for entering on the immediate discharge of that duty – namely, to allocate Canaan among the tribes of Israel, not only the parts already conquered but also those still to be subdued (Jamieson in JFB). Joshua had to be content to see the task of conquest the Lord had committed to him remain unfinished, in order that God might develop the energy and courage of each particular tribe. The peoples and areas still to be overcome are itemized (13:2-6).

2 b-4 a. Translate and punctuate: *all the regions of the Philistines and of the Geshurites (from the Shihor, which is this side of Egypt, northward to the border of Ekron it is reckoned as Canaanite; there are five tyrants of the Philistines, those of Gaza, Ashdod, Ashkelon, Gath, and Ekron), and of the Avvim in the south; all the land of the Canaanites and the cities that belong to the Sidonians.* Only here in Joshua are the Philistines mentioned; for this people from Crete ("Caphtor," Amos 9:7) did not invade Palestine in force until after 1200 B.C., according to Egyptian records. In Josh 11:22 it is the Anakim, not the Philistines, who inhabit the later Philistine cities of Gaza, Gath, and Ashdod. The Philistines are not listed in 12:8 among the inhabitants of the land. They were still confined to the coastal area of the Negeb (Ex 13:17), near the Shihor (Wadi el-Arish), in the same region where the Philistine forerunners were found in the Patriarchal period (Gen 21:32; 26:1). They were classed on an equality with the Geshurites (I Sam 27:8) and the Avvim (Deut 2:23). Their forerunners may well have been Minoan (Cretan) merchants, who were establishing trading colonies around the Mediterranean Sea as early as 2000 B.C. *Philista* is mentioned as a precinct in Crete on the Phaistos Disk, dated about 1450 B.C. (JNES, XVIII (1950, 224-227). In the light of the foregoing evidence, Josh 13:3 is perhaps an early scribal notation to inform us that the domain of the five Philistine lords *(seren,* Jud 16:5; I Sam 5:8) in Joshua's day still belonged to the Canaanites.

B. The Territory of the Trans-Jordanic Tribes. 13:8-33.

8. With whom. God's command to Joshua ends with 13:7; this verse literally begins, *With him* (i.e., with the other half-tribe of Manasseh) *the Reubenites and the Gadites had received their inheritance.*

C. Beginning of the Division of Canaan. 14:1-15.

1) Introduction. 14:1-5. The inheritance of each tribe was designated by lot, according to Num 34:16-29. In the apportionment, the Levites were not considered as one of the twelve tribes, "for the priesthood of Jehovah [was] their inheritance" (Josh 18:7), yea, even God himself (13:33; Deut 18:1,2).

2) Caleb and His Promised Inheritance. 14:6-15. Caleb, the grand old man of Judah, the outspoken minority leader of the twelve spies (Num 13:30), came humbly to Joshua at Gilgal to request his promised tract of land (Num 14:24, 30; Deut 1:36). Notice that no rivalry existed between these two.

6. Caleb the son of Jephunneh the Kenezite. Before the Exodus Caleb's father, a non-Israelite, had married a daughter of Hur of the clan of Chelubai (Caleb) in the tribe of Judah (I Chr 2:9, 18,19,50). She bore to Jephunneh his first son, to whom was given her family name, Caleb. This youth inherited the prerogatives of her clan, and eventually became a chief of her tribe. Caleb's relative, Othniel (Josh 15:17), is called a son of Kenaz (I Chr 4:13,15), i.e., a Kenizzite. The Kenizzites (Gen 15:19) were one of the tribes in the Negeb and Mount Seir. Related to the Kenites, they were perhaps skilled copper workers of the copper-rich Arabah.

8. Caleb is an outstanding example of a godly believer. Because he **wholly followed the Lord,** God kept him physically strong and courageous to the age of eighty-five. He claimed a glorious inheritance – Hebron, near which Abraham had tented and died – and was eager to fight to overcome the Anakim, illustrative to us of inward sins and outward temptations. In capturing Hebron he rendered the whole nation valuable service; later he willingly yielded his city to the Levites and lived in the suburbs (21:12).

D. Territory of the Tribe of Judah. 15:1-63.

1) The Border of Judah. 15:1-12. The southern border went from the southern shallow bay (*lāshōn*, lit., "tongue") of the Dead Sea below the el-Lisan peninsula, along Wadi Fiqreh, southward of the Ascent of the Scorpions (see comment on 11:17), along Wadi Murrah through the Wilderness of Zin, south of Kadesh-barnea, curving northwestward through several other oases to Wadi el-Arish and the Mediterranean.

The northern border began in the east at the mouth of the Jordan, ran northwestward through two small campsites with wells (**Beth-hogla, Beth-arabah**) to the western escarpment of the Jordan Valley at the Wadi Qelt (**Valley of Achor**), where stood the boundary stone of Bohan. It ascended the north bank of Wadi Qelt, turning toward another **Gilgal** (*G^elîlôt*, 18:17) near the Ascent of Blood (not far from the present Good Samaritan Inn on the Jerusalem-Jericho road) on the south side of Wadi Qelt (*the river*). It went on to **En-shemesh** (the Spring of the Apostles, east of Bethany), then over the Mount of Offense to **En-rogel** (the well south of Jebus-Zion, at the juncture of the Kidron and Hinnom Valleys, I Kgs 1:9). From immediately south of Jerusalem the border ascended the **valley of Hinnom** (Aramaic *Ge-henna*) to the height (at the present railroad station) separating it from the northern end of the Vale of Rephaim (**valley of the giants**; see II Sam 5:18,22). Thence the border turned northwestward to the spring of the **water of Nephtoah** (Josh 15:9; 'Ain Lifta) and followed the course of the modern Jerusalem-Jaffa highway to **Kirjath-jearim** (see comment on 9:16-21; cf. 15:60; I Chr 13:6). West of that town the border turned southward through Seir (*Sōrēs*, LXX 15; 59 a; modern Sarīs), entered the Valley of Sorek (Jud 16:4, Wadi es-Surar) north of **Chesalon,** and went down to **Beth-shemesh** (Ir-shemesh, 19:41; Tell Rumeileh, probably unoccupied then, between Levels IV a and IV b, since it is not mentioned in chapter 10 nor in 15:33-36 nor in the Amarna Letters). It continued past **Timnah** (Tell el-Batashi, five miles down Wadi es-Surar from Beth-shemesh) to the shoulder of the hill north of **Ekron** (Khirbet el-Muqanna) on the south slope of the wadi as it leaves the Shephelah. The border curves in the wadi past **Shicron** (Tell el-Ful, three and one-half miles northwest of Ekron) on the north bank, passed along to **mount Baalah** (19:44; Mughar, a steep slope two miles northwest of Shicron), on to Jabneel (Jamnia, Yavneh)' and to the mouth of the wadi at the sea (Y. Aharoni, "The Northern Boundary of Judah," PEQ, 1958, pp. 27-31).

This method of delineating borders – proceeding in order by topographical land-marks, from town to mountain to town to river, etc. – is almost exactly paralleled at this same period in history in the agreement defining boundaries accorded by the Hittite king Suppliuliuma to Niqmadu of Ugarit, ruler of a vassal city-state on the Syrian coast (Claude Schaeffer, *Le Palais Royal d'Ugarit*, IV, 10-18).

2) The Possessions of Caleb and Othniel. 15:13-20. This bit of narrative is repeated in Jud 1:10-15,20. **17. Othniel.** For his subsequent career as Judge, see Jud 3:9-11. **19. A blessing.** Here the *b*ᵉ*rākâ* is a tangible gift, as in Gen 33: 11; I Sam 25:27; II Kgs 5:15. **Given me a south land.** Here it is best to retain the original meaning of *negeb* and translate, *for thou hast set me in arid land.* Kirjath-sepher is on the northern fringe of the Negeb. **Springs of water.** *The gullōt* more likely are either cisterns or reservoir-pools formed by damming wadis. Ruins of ancient dams may still be seen in the Negeb.

3) The Cities of Judah. 15:21-63. The cities are listed by twelve districts according to their location within four geographical areas.

a) Cities in the Negeb (vv. 20-32). **Beersheba** (v. 28) was the principal city of the Negeb in ancient times, as it is also in modern times. The next name, **Bizjothjah,** probably should be read, with the LXX, *and her daughters* (i.e., villages). While some of the place names may be combined **(Hazor-ithnan,** v. 23; **Hazor-hadattah** and **Kerioth-hezron,** v. 25; **Ain-rimmon,** v. 32), there are nevertheless more than **twenty and nine.** Either the number twenty-nine is a copyist's error, or names originally placed in the margin were afterwards interpolated into the text.

A comparison of Josh 15:21-32; 19:1-8; I Chr 2; 4 with the second half of the campaign list of Pharaoh Shishak (II Chr 12:2-12) discovered at Karnak, reveals that few of the eighty-five place names listed by Shishak in the Negeb and adjoining areas are found in the Joshua passages; whereas many appear as personal or clan names in the later genealogical lists of I Chronicles 2 and 4. Therefore the lists of towns in Joshua belong to a time *before* the descendants of Judah and Simeon began to occupy the Negeb and to give their names to new settlements that were in existence by the time of Shishak (see Benjamin Mazar, "The Campaign of Pharaoh Shishak to Palestine," Supplement to *Vetus Testamentum,* IV, 59-66).

b) Cities in the Shephelah (vv. 33-47). Four districts are included in the region of the foothills, although in the fourth (vv. 45-47) lie cities in the coastal plain only theoretically under control of Judah (11:22; 13:2,3). **36. Gederah and Gederothaim.** Read with the LXX, *Gederah and her sheepfolds,* making fourteen cities in all.

c) Cities in the Hill Country (vv. 48-60). Six districts are included in the region of the Central Ridge, the fifth appearing in a verse in the LXX between verses 59 and 60, omitted from the Masoretic text by an ancient copyist. Among the eleven towns listed are Tekoa, Bethlehem, and Etam (cf. II Chr 11:6).

d) Cities in the Wilderness (vv. 61, 62). This is the inhospitable Wilderness of Judea, sloping down to the Dead Sea. Since **Beth-arabah** (15:6; 18:22) is near Jericho, the next three or four towns may have been near the mouth of the Jordan or along the western shore of the Dead Sea north of **En-gedi,** rather than in the Buqei'ah, an elevated valley above and southwest of Qumran. **63.** Neither Judah nor Benjamin could drive out **the Jebusites** from their fortified city on Zion (see Jud 1:21); but men of Judah did capture and burn the unwalled residential area on the southwest hill (Jud 1:8), and dwelt there with Jebusites before David took the stronghold (II Sam 5:6,7).

E. Territory of the Joseph Tribes, 16:1–17:18. This was drawn as one allotment and afterwards divided between Ephraim to the south and the half-tribe of Manasseh to the north. The territory of Ephraim is outlined first because, although that tribe was smaller (Num 26:34,37), Jacob had granted the birthright to Ephraim (Gen 48:9-20).

1) The Southern Border (of Ephraim). 16:1-4. From the Jordan, past Naarath (16:7) at the springs just north of **Jericho** ('Ain Duq and 'Ain Nu'eimeh), into the hill country to the south of **Bethel-Luz** (v. 2), the border went unto the domain of **Beth-horon** the Lower (v. 3), down the Valley of Ajalon past **Gezer,** and along the extension of that wadi to the Mediterranean just north of Joppa. Theoretically at least, Dan was to possess the towns around Joppa and the Yarkon River (19:45,46).

2) Territory of Ephraim. 16:5-10. From the Yarkon the western border followed the shore north to **Michmethath** (v. 6. LXX: *Ikasmon;* probably Tell Arshuf, six and one-half miles north of the Yarkon, where there was an ancient anchorage). The northern border with Manasseh turned southeastward from

Shechem (the central point; cf. Sarid as central point in Zebulun's southern border, 19:11,12) **unto Taanath-shiloh** (six miles east-southeast of Shechem in Wadi Kerad – next valley south of Wadi Far'a) and down Wadi Kerad east of **Janohah** (16:7; Khirbet Janun, seven miles southeast of Shechem) to **Ataroth,** somewhere near the high hill with the Hasmonean fortress of Alexandrium (Qarn Sartabeh; see comment on 22:10-34) overlooking the Jordan Valley. The northern border traveled westward down the **river Kanah** from its headwaters near Shechem (see comments on 17:7-9) to Jiljuliyeh, the **Tappuah** of 16:8; 17:7,8; 12:17. From that town the border went northwestward along an ancient course of the Kanah to Michmethath. (See Eva Danelius, "The Boundary of Ephraim and Manasseh in the Western Plain," PEQ, 1957, 1958.) The stronghold **Gezer** (cf. 10:33) was finally captured by a Pharaoh of Egypt, who presented it to his daughter as a dowry when she married Solomon (I Kgs 9:16).

3) Clan Divisions of the Territory of Manasseh. 17:1-6. **1.** Translate: *There was* (also) *a lot* (in Canaan) *for the tribe of Manasseh, for he was the first-born of Joseph.* (Now) *Machir the first-born of Manasseh, the father* (i.e., lord, owner) *of* (the land of) *Gilead, because he was a man of war, had Gilead and Bashan.* **2-6.** The fact that the ten portions allotted to the clans of Manasseh in Canaan were actually established is attested many centuries later by the Samaria ostraca, dated about 770 B.C. These records of tax payments in kind from various clan districts, discovered in the palace of Jeroboam II, include the name of **Abiezer** (as a district; cf. Jud 6:34; 8:2), **Helek, Shechem, Shemida, Noah,** and **Hoglah** (see Num 26:28-34; 27:1-11; 36:1-13).

4) The Holdings of Manasseh in Canaan. 17:7-13. **7.** The seacoast of Manasseh stretched from Shihor-libnath, the creek-boundary with **Asher** just south of Dor (19:26), to **Michmethath** (16:6). This site **lieth before** (or, is opposite) **Shechem** (*'al-pᵉnê Shᵉkem*) in the sense that, looking eastward from Michmethath across the Sharon Plain, one can see the valley of Shechem between the round hills of Ebal and Gerizim (G. A. Smith, *The Historical Geography of the Holy Land,* p. 119). **8. The land** or fields **of Tappuah** were on the north bank of the River Kanah in Manasseh, although Tappuah itself was south of the river in Ephraim. **9. These cities of Ephraim.** Eva Danelius (*op. cit.,* 1958, pp. 135-142) has proposed to read *'ārîm hā'ēlleh* as *'ārîm ha'ela,* and following the LXX (Margolis' edition), to translate: "The 'Arim (equivalent to Arabic *Ḥaram,* a secluded, holy area) of the terebinth belongs to Ephraim among the cities of Manasseh." For the sacred place with its oak or terebinth near Shechem, see 24:26 and the comment on 24:25-28. Thus Shechem, the city of refuge, was considered as in Mount Ephraim (20:7).

11. Even three countries. Read *(and the) three heights,* i.e., Mount Tabor, the Hill of Moreh, and either Mount Carmel or Mount Gilboa (Baly, *The Geography of the Bible,* pp. 173,174). The northern border with Asher and Issachar was less well defined because Manasseh, the stronger tribe, was allotted the resisting Canaanite fortresses. "This fact would manifestly tend to produce a *solidarity* among the several tribes, and to prevent disunion by creating common interests. The interest of the stronger tribes would be served by completing the conquest of the territory assigned to the weaker" (C. H. Waller, *A Bible Commentary for English Readers,* p. 142). Excavation reveals that Canaanite Megiddo did not fall to Israel until the latter half of the twelfth century B.C.

12,13. But the Canaanites would dwell in that land. That is, they were determined to remain in that region. Manasseh could not drive them out. Jamieson suggests that "indolence, a love of ease; perhaps a mistaken humanity, arising from a disregard or forgetfulness of the Divine command, a decreasing principle of faith and zeal in the service of God, were the causes of their failure" (JFB, p. 154).

5) The Demand of the Joseph Tribes for More Land. 17:14-18. Joshua demonstrated tact and firmness in dealing with his own tribesmen. He did not grant them an additional allotment, but encouraged them to clear the trees and settle the forested hill country. That the Central Ridge was once heavily forested is attested by acorns and terebinth seeds and deer antlers found in many excavations and a wild boar's tooth at Gezer, as well as cypress and pine lumber in King Saul's fortress at Gibeah (Tell el-Ful). While the Canaanites occupied the best

land– **the Valley of Jezreel** (v. 16)–and possessed superior military equipment–chariots armed with projecting iron blades, no doubt obtained at this early time from the Hittites in Asia Minor–, the mountains of Ephraim and Manasseh were very sparsely settled around 1400 B.C. Except for Shechem and Tirzah, there are singularly few Late Bronze I sites of Canaanite fortified towns or villages between Bethel and Ibleam. From that whole area Shechem may be the only town whose name is found in the Amarna Letters. Even Dothan, captured by Thutmose III about 1479 B.C., is not mentioned in Joshua or Judges or in the Amarna Letters. So this large site probably was vacant in 1400 B.C. A little later settled sites increased rapidly in the hill country, as the Israelites learned the knack of digging cisterns and lining them with waterproof lime plaster to store rain water (Albright, *Archaeology of Palestine,* p. 113). Thus a reason exists for the lack of town lists in Joshua 16 and 17.

F. Territories of the Seven Remaining Tribes. 18:1–19:51.

1) The Tabernacle Pitched at Shiloh and the Lots Cast There. 18:1-10. For a common sanctuary the Israelites chose an abandoned Middle Bronze Age town site in Ephraim because of its central location with respect to all the tribes (Seilûn, ten miles north-northeast of Bethel, eleven miles south of Shechem). The Tabernacle served as the nucleus of Israel's amphictyonic organization before the nation desired to have a kingdom. The town must have been named *Shiloh* by Joshua after the Messianic usage of that title in Gen 49:10, since the ark, symbolizing God's presence was to remain there. While the selection of Shiloh and the consequent assembling of the nation there had necessarily interrupted the process of assigning portions to the last seven tribes, these tribes, on their part, were slack in going out to conquer the remaining land in Canaan. Joshua had to commission a twenty-one-man reconnaissance expedition to describe the land in seven parts.

2) Territory of Benjamin. 18:11-28. The hand of God is evident in the drawing of the lot for Benjamin. This tract of land between the Judahites and the Josephites both served to fulfill Deut 33:12 by placing the ultimate temple site in Benjamin, and secured a tie to unite Israel by making Benjamin the link between the two most powerful and naturally rival tribal groups. Joseph and Benjamin were sons of the same mother, and the Rachel tribes marched together from Sinai (Num 10:22-24); while it was Judah who offered himself as hostage in Benjamin's stead (Gen 43:8,9; 44:18-34).

3) Territory of Simeon. 19:1-9. By giving Simeon land in the southern section of the inheritance of Judah, God began the fulfillment of Jacob's curse with respect to Simeon (Gen 49:7). The Simeonites were separated from their marching campanions, Reuben and Gad (Num 10:18-20), who had already rejected Simeon and chosen, instead, to settle Trans-Jordan along with the Manassites.

4) Territory of Zebulun. 19:10-16. A landlocked district in Lower Galilee including the NT Nazareth. Divine wisdom placed the Leah tribes, Zebulun and Issachar, to the north of the Rachel tribes in order to cement the union of all Israel. Judah, Issachar, and Zebulun encamped together in the wilderness (Num 2:3-7; 10:14-16). These ties persisted for centuries. Mary and Joseph, for instance, both of the tribe of Judah, dwelt in the old territory of Zebulun. Also, only the Zebulunites named a town **Bethlehem** (Josh 19:15) after the one in Judah.

5) Territory of Issachar. 19:17-23. The territory stretching from Mount Tabor on the west to the southern tip of the Sea of Galilee and including in its area the Valley of Jezreel.

6) Territory of Asher. 19:24-31. The coastal region from Mount Carmel north, theoretically at least, to Tyre and Sidon. Inscriptions of Seti I (c. 1310 B.C.) and of Rameses II contain references to a territory of a people called *'Asaru,* corresponding to the hinterland of southern Phoenicia, thus indicating that Asher had begun to settle there by the end of the fourteenth century.

7) Territory of Naphtali. 19:32-39. Eastern Upper and Lower Galilee. Y. Aharoni of Israel, who has made an archaeological survey in Upper Galilee, has discovered evidence of numerous small settlements, close together, which he attributes to the Israelites and some of which he says began in the fourteenth century ("Problems of the Israelite Conquest in the Light of Archaeological Discoveries," *The Holy Land, Antiquity and Survival,* II (1957), 146-149. See also in *Journal of Semitic Studies,* IV (July,

1959), 279, 280, B.S.J. Isserlin's review of Aharoni's report in Hebrew).

8) Territory of Dan. 19:40-48. To strengthen further the union of Israel, God separated Dan from his brother Naphtali, both sons of Bilhah (Gen 30:5-8) and from his wilderness campmates, Naphtali and Asher (Num 10:25-27), by locating Dan between Benjamin and the Mediterranean. For this reason, when part of the territory of Dan was lost to the Amorites in the Philistine Plain (Jud 1:34), some of the Danites apostatized and migrated northward and captured Leshem near the northern part of Naphtali (Jud 17; 18). That migration necessarily occurred before the rise of Aramean city-states in that area in the twelfth century (cf. II Sam 10:6), probably during the Judgeship of Othniel (Jud 3:11; 18:28,30), about 1370—1330 B.C.

9) The Conclusion of Dividing the Land. 19:49-51. Joshua was willing to wait until the last for a possession—**Timnath-serah** (Khirbet Tibneh, eleven miles west-southwest of Shiloh, seventeen miles southwest of Shechem) in the mountainous district of Ephraim, his tribe.

G. Inheritance of Levi. 20:1—21:42.

1) Appointment of Cities of Refuge. 20:1-9. All of these six cities were Levitical towns, probably considered as a sacred oblation (*tᵉrûmâ,* Ezk 45:1) to Jehovah for use of his Levites, and therefore God's property, where manslayers could be placed under the protection of divine grace (see Num 35:9-34; Deut 4:41-43; 19:1-13). The cities of refuge were established to protect from the ancient right of vendetta (blood revenge) the manslayer who had killed a person accidentally, without premeditation. Arriving at the nearest asylum, the manslayer presented his case at the gate, the ancient law court (cf. Deut 21:19; 22:15). Later he was brought to stand trial before the congregation of the community nearest the scene of the crime. If acquitted, he was returned to the refuge city until free to return home at the death of the high priest. That death meant a change of priestly administration and acted as does our statute of limitations (see comment on 24:33).

2) Assignment of Promised Cities to the Levites. 21:1-42. The fulfillment of Num 35:2-8. See also I Chr 6:54-81. While these cities with pasturage (**suburbs**) were allocated in anticipation of complete subjugation of the land (**Gezer,** Josh 21:21, not in Israelite hands until Solomon's reign; for **Taanach,** v. 25, and **Nahalal,** v. 35, see Jud 1:27-30), yet for the most part the Levites had occupied their towns by the time of David (I Chr 13:2). This distribution among the other tribes achieved a fulfillment of Jacob's curse on Levi as well as Simeon (Gen 49:5,7 b). But God overruled in the case of Levi's descendants to preserve their identity because of their having stood with Moses in a crucial hour (Ex 32:26) and because of the righteous action of Phinehas in regard to Zimri (Num 25). Neither Shiloh nor any Ephraimite cities were given to the priests; all the priestly cities were assigned in Judah and Benjamin so as to fall ultimately within the kingdom of Judah, of which the capital would be Jerusalem, Zion, the city of God (Ps 48). Thus we see that God *intended* the conquest to be completed rapidly and Jerusalem to be the seat of his sanctuary centuries before David (cf. Josh 9:27). But Israel's repeated apostasy in the period of the Judges prevented the execution of God's perfect will.

H. Summary of the Conquest and Apportionment. 21:43-45. This is the key passage of the book, emphasizing the theme of God's faithfulness in keeping his promises to Joshua (1:5-9; cf. Ps 44:2,3). In harmonizing these general statements with Israel's failure to subdue Canaan, remember God's provision for taking over the land gradually (Ex 23:29,30; Deut 7:22-24).

I. Appendix: Departure of the Trans-Jordanic Tribes: 22:1-34. An incident concerning the two and a half tribes subsequent to the campaigns and distribution of the inheritances is related to demonstrate further God's providential care in maintaining harmony within Israel (cf. 22:31). This chapter reopens the question of whether these tribes were in God's will in settling east of Jordan. Many scholars have blamed Reuben, Gad, and the half tribe of Manasseh for choosing their inheritance in Trans-Jordania. But C. H. Waller has argued that this view is historically incorrect: "God delivered the land of Sihon and Og to Israel; someone must inherit it. Again, the true eastern boundary of Palestine is not the Jordan, but the mountain range of Gilead, which parts it from the desert which lies beyond. Really the two and a half tribes were as much in Palestine as the rest . . . ." (*op. cit.*, p. 153).

1-9. Joshua dismissed the eastern tribes with a blessing. He acknowledged that they had fulfilled their obligations to Moses and to himself (Num 32:20-33; Josh 1:16,17). **5.** Note the six one-syllable infinitives in English, all basic principles for a godly life before the Lord.

10-34. Returning home from Shiloh, the two and one-half tribes erected an altar in the western region of the Jordan Valley, perhaps somewhere near Qarn Sartabeh (see comment on 16:5-10), overlooking the ford at Adam leading to the Jabbok Valley. **10. A great altar to see to.** A large altar to cause one to look, to draw attention. Thus it served well as a testimony (**witness,** 22:27,28) to all generations that the eastern tribes had a portion in the Lord and in Israel. But it was a needless and presumptuous deed; God's method to preserve unity was to have all the tribes gather thrice yearly around the altar at *Shiloh* (Ex 23:17).

11. An altar . . . at the passage of the children of Israel. RSV: *An altar at the frontier of the land of Canaan, in the region about the Jordan, on the side that belongs to the people of Israel* (i.e., to the nine and one-half tribes). **13.** Instead of immediately waging war (22:12) on the basis of Lev 17:8,9; Deut 12:4-14; 13:13-18, the western tribes wisely and providentially sent a delegation headed by Phinehas, the zealous son of the high priest, who once before had stemmed the tide of apostasy when Israel had turned to Baal-peor (Josh 22:17; Num 25). He restored the eastern tribes "in the spirit of meekness" or gentleness, so necessary in Christian workers (Gal 6:1; Mt 18:15). **16. Trespass.** Treachery, faithless act. This word is also used of the sin of Achan (22:20; cf. 7:1), which had almost ruined the whole nation.

22. The Lord God of gods. The combination and repetition of the three divine names, *El, Elohim, Jehovah* (cf. Ps 50:1, ASV), form a solemn and majestic oath pronounced by the accused in their denial of the charge of rebellion and treachery. **Save us not this day.** An excited imprecation, addressed directly to God, in the midst of their affirmation.

30. It pleased them. The action of the eastern tribes seemed perfectly honorable to the deputies. No underlying condemnation of the Trans-Jordanic tribes is set forth by the inspired author. Nevertheless, this departure from God's plan for centralized worship later resulted in apostasy, seen in their refusal to come to Deborah's aid (Jud 5:15 b-17 a).

IV. Final Summons to Covenant-loyalty in the Promised Land. 23:1–24:33.

A. Joshua's Farewell Address to the Leaders of Israel. 23:1-16. The book of Joshua opens with God's commissioning Joshua to assume command; it closes with Joshua's exhorting the nation to complete the conquest of the land. From ten to twenty years must have elapsed since the apportionment of the tribal territories, when Joshua's age first began to tell on him (see notes on 13:1). In those intervening years he observed Israel's growing complacency and tendency to compromise with the heathen, while his own infirmity prevented his taking further personal leadership in the military reduction of the Canaanite centers of resistance. While God did not intend that anyone should succeed him as central commander, had he failed by not training tribal leaders to carry on the fight? Now as he felt death approaching, he had to use his remaining strength to stir up Israel to renewed faithfulness to Jehovah and obedience to the covenant.

1,2. Translate and punctuate: *And it came to pass a long time afterward, when the Lord . . . enemies round about, and Joshua was old and advanced in years* (lit., *days*), *that Joshua called for all Israel: for their elders, . . .* First he summoned the *leaders* of the nation, probably to Shiloh, where the Tabernacle was (18:1), in order to warn them most earnestly of the dangers of apostatizing from Jehovah.

3-5. First, he encouraged them to review what God had done for them and also His promises to thrust out the heathen nations. **6-11.** Secondly, he pleaded (the imperative or jussive form of command is not used) with them to be very resolute in following the Law, as he had been (1:7), lest they mix and associate with the unexpelled idolatrous Canaanites. He urged them to continue to *stick devotedly* (**cleave,** 23:8) to Jehovah their God and to love him (cf. Ex 20:6)—"for the Lord your God, he it is that fighteth for you, as he hath promised you." **Cleave unto the Lord** is the OT way of saying, "Abide in Christ" (cf. Jn 15:1-10).

12,13. Thirdly, he strictly forewarned them of the consequences of intermarrying with their neighbors (prohibited in Ex 34:12-16; Deut 7:3), for such association would lure the Israelites into the snare of the fertility cults and react as a whip on their sides and as rankling thorns in their eyes (cf. Num 33:55). Likewise *we* must not make peace with any lurking habits of sin in our lives. **14-16.** In closing, he summed up his thoughts, emphasizing the curse that would follow transgressing the covenant, basing his threats upon Lev 26:14-33; Deut 28:15-68; etc.

B. Renewal of the Covenant Commitment at Shechem. 24:1-28. As a direct result of his meeting with the leaders, Joshua called the entire nation to Shechem to re-establish once again the covenant as the foundation of their relationship with Jehovah. Twenty years or so had passed—the momentous period of the subjugation and settlement of Canaan, and inclusion of new peoples (e.g., the Gibeonites) in the Hebrew Commonwealth. As Moses had done after the wilderness wandering (Deut 30:15-20), so now Joshua asked the tribes solemnly and formally to pledge anew their covenant allegiance to their God—not at Shiloh but at Shechem, for near the latter was an ancient shrine or holy place of the Hebrews (see comment on 24:26). Here God had first promised Canaan to Abram; here that patriarch erected his first altar in the land (Gen 12:6,7). Here also Jacob had built an altar (Gen 33:20) and called upon his household to put away their idols (Gen 35:1-4). Near here Joshua himself had on a former occasion led in the covenant-establishment ceremony (Josh 8:30-35).

George E. Mendenhall has lucidly revealed the nature of the covenant and covenant-renewal in Israel in the time of Moses and Joshua (*Law and Covenant in Israel and the Ancient Near East*, pp. 24-44). In form, the Mosaic covenant seems closest to the suzerainty treaty by which a great monarch obligated his vassals to serve him in faithfulness and obedience. Such treaties are found in the international covenants of the Hittite Empire with its vassal states, 1450–1200 B.C., but nowhere later than toward the close of the second millennium B.C. Both the Mosaic covenant and the suzerainty treaty are essentially unilateral. "The stipulations of the treaty are binding only upon the vassal, and only the vassal took an oath of obedience" (Mendenhall, p. 30). While the vassal was obliged to trust in the benevolence and protective support of the monarch, the latter maintained "his sole right of self-determination and sovereignty" (*ibid.*) by not binding himself to specific obligations. In the case of the Mosaic covenant, the Israelites and the mixed multitude (cf. Num 11:4) stood in the position of the vassal peoples, while Jehovah was their divine sovereign. Thus God employed a standard form of covenant known in western Asia at that time.

The covenant mediated by Moses is nowhere proclaimed as an everlasting covenant; hence it had to be renewed periodically—at least every generation. Similarly, since the Hittite treaties "were not regarded as binding in perpetuity from the first, a renewal of the covenant would be from time to time necessary" (*ibid.*, pp. 40,41), as with the heir following the death of the vassal king. Likewise there was to be periodic public reading of the covenant, both in the Hittite Empire and in Israel (see note on 8:33-35). The vassal was required to appear or present himself before the ruler once a year to pay tribute (cf. 24:1 b; Deut 16:16).

Most of the elements found in the Hittite treaty texts can be detected in this covenant renewal at Shechem, as shown in the following outline:

1) Preamble. 24:2 a. **Thus saith the Lord God of Israel.** This statement identifies the Author of the covenant in his relationship to his vassal people.

2) Historical Prologue. 24:2 b-13. This section describes in detail the previous relations between the sovereign and the subjects. "In the suzerainty treaties great emphasis is placed upon the benevolent deeds which the Hittite king has performed for the benefit of the vassal . . . . They are emphatically not stereotyped formulas, . . . but are rather such careful descriptions of actual events, that they are a most important source for the historian" (*ibid.*, p. 32). In the historical prologue the monarch always speaks in the "I-thou" form of address, directly to the vassal. Thus in this section it is not Joshua but Jehovah speaking, sketching his theocratic dealings with Israel from his call of Abraham to the Conquest.

2 b. On the other side of the flood. Literally, in *Beyond-the-River*, the district north and east of the Euphrates River, including Haran (cf. II Sam 10:16; I Kgs 14:15; II Kgs 17:6; Isa 7:20). Ur of the Chaldees may well have been a town in the Armenian mountains north of Haran rather than the Sumerian city near the Persian Gulf (see Cyrus Gordon, "Abraham and the Merchants of Ura," JNES, January, 1958). **Terah . . . Abraham . . . Nachor.** Only two of Terah's three sons are mentioned, those who were the ancestors of Israel—Nachor as grandfather of Rebekah and great-grandfather of Leah and Rachel.

7. Since this ceremony was obviously a renewal of the covenant, mention of the original covenant made at Sinai is omitted, perhaps for the sake of brevity. But that covenant is definitely mentioned in the near context (23:16).

12. The hornet. Probably a figurative expression for the panic-producing power of God that overwhelmed Sihon and Og (see Ex 23:27-30; Deut 7:20), rather than a veiled reference to the armies of Pharaoh (see Garstang, *Joshua-Judges*, p. 259), which never pillaged southern Gilead and Moab.

3) The Stipulations. 24:14-24. As in Hittite suzerainty treaties, the first obligation was prohibition of other foreign alliances outside the Hittite Empire, so also "the first obligation of the covenant [of Jehovah] was to reject all foreign relations—i.e., with other gods, and by implication, with other political groups" (Mendenhall, *op. cit.*, p. 38). This primary duty was required of Israel by Joshua, as we learn from 24:14,15,23; and the record of the acceptance of this covenant-obligation by the people rather than the complete text of the formal covenant-renewal, is interposed for the sake of brevity. Furthermore, since it was a renewal of the Mosaic covenant rather than a new covenant, no other stipulations needed to be listed. Probably such local peoples as the Gibeonites and the inhabitants of Shechem (see remarks on 8:30-35) also became "vassals" of Jehovah by giving up **the gods of the Amorites** (24:15; cf. I Kgs 18:21).

4) The Deposit of the Covenant. 24:25-28. Even among the Hittites the treaty was considered as being under the protection of the deity and "was deposited as a sacred thing in the sanctuary of the vassal state" (*ibid.*, p. 34). Likewise, **Joshua wrote these words in the book of the law of God** (24:26; cf. I Sam 10:25), which was deposited by (AV, *in)* the side of the ark of the covenant (Deut 31:24-27). Also he inscribed the statute (s) of the covenant-renewal on a large stele, which he set up beneath the oak or terebinth tree belonging to the sacred place of Jehovah near Shechem (see note on Josh 17:9). This tree is mentioned in Gen 12:6 (lit., *the terebinth of the teacher* for "the plain of Moreh"; cf. 35: 4. In the case of the covenant ceremony of Josh 8:30-35, the curses and blessings formula was pronounced, another regular feature of the Hittite treaties.

C. Appendix: Death of Joshua, and Subsequent Conduct of Israel. 24:29-33. Joshua must have been held in high esteem at the time of his death, for the effect of his godly influence is stated in 24:31—**Israel served the Lord all the days of Joshua, and all the days of the elders that overlived Joshua,** whom he had exhorted so forcefully, according to chapter 23. **32.** The burial of Joseph's remains (cf. Gen 50:25,26; Ex 13:19) may have taken place long before the death of Joshua, but inspired authorship "placed the account of it here, symbolizing at the close the message of the whole book of Joshua—the faithfulness of God" (Blair, in *The New Bible Commentary*, p. 235). **33.** The death of the high priest **Eleazar,** son and successor of Aaron, is recorded along with the death of Joshua, successor of Moses, to indicate the close of the era (cf. 20:6 and comment on 20:1-9).

BIBLIOGRAPHY

AHARONI, YOHANAN. "The Northern Boundary of Judah," *Palestine Exploration Quarterly*, XC (1958), 27-31.

ALBRIGHT, WILLIAM FOXWELL. *From The Stone Age to Christianity*. 2d ed., with a new introduction. (Doubleday Anchor Books). Garden City, N.Y.: Doubleday & Co., 1957.

——. *The Archaelogy of Palestine*. 3rd ed. revised. Hammondsworth: Penguin Books, 1956.

BALY, DENIS. *The Geography of the Bible*. New York: Harper & Bros., 1957.

BLAIKIE, WILLIAM GARDEN. *Joshua. (The Expositor's Bible.)* Edited by W. Robertson Nicoll. Grand Rapids: Wm. B. Eerdmans Publishing Company, reprinted 1947.

BLAIR, HUGH J. "Joshua," *New Bible Commentary*. Edited by Francis Davidson, A. M. Stibbs, and E. F. Kevan. Grand Rapids: Eerdmans, 1953.

BRIGHT, JOHN. "Joshua," *The Interpreter's Bible*. Edited by George Arthur Buttrick. Nashville: Abingdon-Cokesbury Press, 1953.

CLARK, R. E. D. "The Large Numbers of the Old Testament," *The Victoria Institute*. Paper read at the 930th general meeting on May 6, 1955.

DANELIUS, EVA. "The Boundary of Ephraim and Manasseh in the Western Plain," *Palestine Exploration Quarterly*, LXXXIX (1957), 55-67; XC (1958), 32-43; 122-144.

FAY, F. R. "Joshua," *Lange's Commentary on the Holy Scriptures*. Translated by Philip Schaff. Grand Rapids: Zondervan Publishing House, n.d.

GARSTANG, JOHN. *Joshua-Judges: the Foundation of Bible History*. New York: Richard R. Smith, Inc., 1931.

JAMIESON, ROBERT. "Joshua," *A Commentary Critical and Explanatory on the Old and New Testaments*. By Robert Jamieson, A. R. Fausset, and David Brown. Grand Rapids: Wm. B. Eerdmans Publishing Co., reprint.

KAUFMAN, YEHEZKEL. *The Biblical Account of the Conquest of Palestine*. Jerusalem: Hebrew University Magnes Press, 1935.

KEIL, CARL FRIEDRICH. "Joshua," *Joshua, Judges, Ruth. Biblical Commentary on the Old Testament*. By Keil and Delitzsch. Grand Rapids: Wm. B. Eerdmans Publishing Co., reprinted 1950.

KLINE, MEREDITH G. "The Ha-bi-ru—Kin or Foe of Israel?" *Westminster Theological Journal*, XIX (1956), 1-24; 170-184; XX (1957), 46-70.

LIAS, J. J. "Joshua," *The Pulpit Commentary*. Edited by Spence and Exell. Vol. III. Grand Rapids: Wm. B. Eerdmans Publishing Co., reprinted 1950.

MAUNDER, E. W. "Beth-horon, the Battle of," *International Standard Bible Encyclopedia*, I, 446-449.

MENDENHALL, GEORGE E. *Law and Covenant in Israel and the Ancient Near East*. Pittsburgh: The Biblical Colloquium, 1955.

SIMONS, J. *The Geographical and Topographical Texts of the Old Testament*. Leiden: E. J. Brill, 1959.

WALLER, C. H. "Joshua," *A Bible Commentary for English Readers*. Edited by C. J. Ellicott. Vol. II. London: Cassell & Co., n.d.

WILSON, ROBERT DICK. "What Does 'The Sun Stood Still' Mean?" *Princeton Theological Review*, XVI (1918), 46-47.

YOUNG, EDWARD J. *An Introduction to the Old Testaments*. Grand Rapids: Wm. B. Eerdmans Publishing Co., 1949.

JUDGES

INTRODUCTION

Title. The book of Judges receives its name from the leaders *(shōpᵉṭîm)* who delivered Israel from a series of foreign oppressions during the period between the death of Joshua and the beginnings of the monarchy.

The term *shôpēṭ* has a wider connotation than the English term "judge" can convey. In ancient Carthage and Ugarit it was used to describe civil magistrates, or heads of state. The Canaanite literature from ancient Ugarit uses the expression *shptn,* "our judge," in parallel relation to *mlkn, "our king," (Ba 'al* V, v, 32). The Biblical period of the *shōpᵉṭîm* must be distinguished from that of the kings, however. During the time of the Judges a definite antimonarchal feeling existed (cf. Jud 9:8-15), although external pressures from prospective invaders caused the people eventually to demand a king (I Sam 8). Judges were Spirit-endowed men, raised up of God and empowered by him to meet specific crises in Israel's history. God himself was looked upon as Israel's King (I Sam 8:7), although the sin of the people frequently reduced this ideal rule to a state of anarchy (Jud 21:25). The Judges exercised authority under God in both military and civil matters, rendering legal decisions when called upon to do so (4:4,5).

In Judges 11:27 the God of Israel is called *hashshōpēṭ,* "The Judge." God's "judgments" *(mishpāṭîm)* form a part of that instruction which is known as the law *(tôrâ)* of Jehovah (cf. Ps 19:9; 119:7).

Date and Authorship. Like other of the Old Testament historical books, the book of Judges is anonymous. Internal evidence, however, helps us to determine the approximate time of its composition. The destruction of Shiloh is presupposed (18:31). The words, "In those days there was no king in Israel" (17:6), suggest a date during the monarchy. The fact that Jebusites are mentioned as still in Jerusalem (1:21) implies a date before the capture of Jebus during the reign of David. Similarly the mention of Gezer (1:29) implies a date before Pharaoh gave that city as a wedding gift to Solomon (I Kgs 9:16).

Internal evidence thus suggests a date for Judges during the early days of the monarchy (c. 1050–1000 B.C.), either during the days of Saul or early in the reign of David. The Talmud *(Baba Bathra,* 14 b) and early Christian tradition ascribe its authorship to Samuel. Although evidence does not warrant a positive conclusion concerning the writer of the book of Judges, it does indicate that the book was written by a contemporary of Samuel. The author probably made use of both oral and written source material, but the book, in the form in which we have it, exhibits a unity that argues against any complex scheme of compilation.

Historical Background. The generation that entered Canaan under Joshua had accomplished much by way of occupying strategic sites and settling the tribes in their assigned portions. The work of conquest and occupation, however, was far from complete. Important Canaanite strongholds had been bypassed by Joshua, and so the individual tribes were expected to fight to occupy their assigned territories (Josh 13:1-7).

OUTLINE

I. Introduction. 1:1–2:5.
   A. Political background of the period of the Judges. 1:1-36.
   B. Religious background of the period of the Judges. 2:1-5.

II. History of the Judges. 2:6–16:31.
   A. Israel's failure to subdue the enemy nations. 2:6–3:6.
   B. The oppressors and the deliverers of Israel. 3:7–16:31.
      1. Cushan-rishathaim's oppression ended by Othniel. 3:8-11.
      2. Eglon's oppression ended by Ehud. 3:12-30.
      3. Israel delivered from the Philistines by Shamgar. 3:31.
      4. Oppression by Jabin and Sisera ended by Deborah and Barak. 4:1–5:31.

5. Midianite oppression ended by Gideon. 6:1–8:35.
6. The usurpation of Abimelech. 9:1-57.
7. Tola's Judgeship over Israel. 10:1,2.
8. Jair's Judgeship. 10:3-5.
9. Ammonite oppression ended by Jephthah. 10:6–11:40.
10. War between the Gileadites and the Ephraimites. 12:1-7.
11. Judgeship of Ibzan. 12:8-10.
12. Elon's Judgeship. 12:11,12.
13. Abdon's Judgeship. 12:13-15
14. Samson and the Philistines. 13:1–16:31.

III. Lawless conditions during the period of the Judges. 17:1–21:25.
  A. The idolatry of Micah and the Danite migration. 17:1–18:31.
  B. The crime at Gibeah and the war against Benjamin. 19:1–21:25.

COMMENTARY

I. Introduction. 1:1–2:5.

A. Political Background of the Period of the Judges. 1:1-36.

During Joshua's lifetime Canaan was occupied and divided among the Israelite tribes. Substantial pockets of resistance remained, however. The presence of enemy peoples in the midst of Israelite territory and the strength of opposition from without produced the political situation described in the book of Judges.

After the death of Joshua. Cf. Josh 1:1. As the death of Moses marked the end of Israel's wilderness wandering, so the death of Joshua marked the end of the first phase of the conquest of Canaan. **Who shall go up?** Included in the allotments made by Joshua was much territory still unconquered. The tribes were expected to occupy the territories assigned to them. **The Canaanites.** The term is sometimes used of all the inhabitants of Canaan without regard to racial origin. The area occupied by Canaanites at this time is delineated in Jud 1:9.

2. Judah had been assigned the territory west of the Dead Sea and south of Jerusalem (Jebus), the territory known as Judea in NT times (Josh 15:1-63). **I have delivered the land into his hand.** God's purpose is stated as an accomplished fact. The assurance of success is stated as an inducement to activity. **3. Judah said unto Simeon his brother.** Jacob had declared that the tribes of Simeon and Levi would be scattered in Israel (Gen 49:5-7). Joshua did not assign a specific territory to Simeon but permitted the Simeonites to settle in the portion assigned to Judah (Josh 19:9). Thus Simeon was virtually incorporated into the tribe of Judah.

4. Perizzites are thought to have been an aboriginal people of different race from the Canaanites. They were settled in Canaan before Abraham arrived (Gen 13:7). **5. Adoni-bezek** means "lord of Bezek." He had subdued seventy petty kings and cut off their thumbs and great toes (1:7). Physical mutilation disqualified a person from holding either religious or civil office (Lev 21:16-24; contrast I Sam 9:2; 16:12). Adoni-bezek was similarly mutilated by his Israelite captors (Jud 1:6).

8. Fought against Jerusalem. Although temporarily taken, Jerusalem was not held permanently by Israel until the time of David (cf. 1:21; II Sam 5:6-9). During the Amarna Age (c. 1400–1360 B.C.) the city was known as *Urusalim,* and was one of the most important Canaanite city-states.

9. In the mountain, and in the south, and in the valley. These terms explain much of the geography and history of Palestine. The mountain, or "hill country," was first taken and longest held by Israel. Important cities of the Judean mountains include Jerusalem (2,593 feet above sea level) and Hebron (3,040 feet above sea level). The **south** refers to a specific area known as the Negeb or Negev. This semidesert country begins a few miles south of Hebron. Beersheba serves as the principle city of the Negev in modern times as it did in antiquity. **Valley** should be rendered *lowland,* or transliterated as *Shephelah.* It is the term used for the foothills lying between the coastal plain and the Judean mountain range. During the period of the Judges the Philistines occupied the coastal plain, the Israelites occupied most of the Judean mountains, and the Shephelah was the scene of constant fighting between the two.

When the Israelite tribes settled in Canaan, they were subject to the temptations of Canaanite religion. Religious prostitution and the sacrifice of infants to Molech were among the degrading practices that confronted them in their new home. They often forgot their covenant with God at Mount Sinai. When they lapsed into idolatry, God chastised them by delivering them over to their enemies. When, in a spirit of repentance, they prayed for mercy, help came in the person of a 'Judge' who was raised up by God to save His people from their oppressors. The periods of Israel's faithfulness to God were of short duration, however. The pattern of apostasy, defeat, repentance, prayer for deliverance, and victory through a Spirit-endowed Judge is frequently repeated. A series of such episodes forms the major portion of the book of Judges.

10. And Judah went against the Canaanites that dwelt in Hebron. The ancient city of Hebron was located about 20 miles south of Jerusalem, in the highest part of the mountains of Judah, 3,040 feet above sea level. Abraham had sojourned in the vicinity of Hebron (Gen 13:18; 35:27), and the patriarchal burial ground was located there (Gen 23:2-20). In anticipation of the conquest, Hebron was assigned to Caleb (Num 14:24), who subsequently occupied it by right of conquest (Josh 15:13,14). The earlier name of Hebron was Kirjath-arba ("fourfold city" or "tetrapolis"). A man named Arba is described as "the greatest man among the Anakim" (Josh 14:15). He probably took his name from the city which he founded. **And they slew Sheshai, and Ahiman, and Talmai.** Caleb and the detachment of Judean warriors who attacked Hebron were successful in destroying its armed forces and occupying the city. The three names of those killed are Aramaean, suggesting that the city was occupied by tribes related to the people who later had a powerful kingdom with Damascus at its capital.

11. And from thence he went against the inhabitants of Debir. Debir, also known as Kirjath-sepher, is believed to be identified with the mound now called Tell Beit Mirsim, thirteen miles southwest of Hebron. This mound was excavated in 1926 and the following years by an expedition directed by Melvin G. Kyle and William F. Albright. A royal scarab of the Egyptian Pharaoh, Amenhotep III, found there suggests that Egyptian control of the city continued into the fourteenth century B.C. Above the remains from the Late Bronze Age, the excavators found a burned layer, on top of which were Israelite remains. The name **Kirjath-sepher** is usually interpreted to mean *city of* (the) *book*. The name **Debir** seems to be related to a Hebrew root meaning *to say*. In all probability ancient Kirjath-sepher was a town noted for its possession of an oracle.

12. And Caleb said, He that smiteth Kirjath-sepher, and taketh it, to him will I give Achsah, my daughter, to wife. The promise of a daughter in marriage as a reward for an act of bravery is a common motif in the Bible (cf. I Sam 17:25) and in secular literature. Here it is implied that the captured city as well as the daughter would be given to the victor. **13. Othniel, the son of Kenaz, Caleb's younger brother.** Grammatically the words can mean that Othniel was either Caleb's nephew or his younger brother. **Took it;** i.e., captured Debir.

14. She moved him to ask of her father a field. After the marriage, Achsah persuaded her husband to permit her to ask a field of her father. **15. And she said unto him, Give me a blessing;** i.e., a present (cf. Gen 33:11; Josh 15:19; II Kgs 5:15). **For thou hast given me a south land** might better be rendered, *Thou has put me in the Negev region.* She desired a **blessing** to compensate for the arid surroundings of the Judean Negev.

And Caleb gave her the upper springs and the nether springs. Achsah requested *Gūllōt-māyim*, perhaps a place name, translated "springs of waters." Caleb gave her *Gūllōt-'illît* and *Gūllōt-tahtît*, doubtless also place names commonly rendered "upper springs" and "nether springs." The excavators of Tell Beit Mirsim suggest that the "wells" were shafts giving access to the ground water, a number of which have been found in this region. A mile below, and two miles above Tell Beit Mirsim such wells have been discovered. Others, however, identify the wells given to Achsah with the springs above and below the road at the Seil ed-Dilbeh, five and three-quarters miles southwest of Hebron, on the way to Beersheba. This is one of the best-watered valleys in southern Palestine. The possession of these springs was of great importance, and the record here given would indicate to all concerned the claim that Achsah and her descendants had on the wells. J. Simons *(The Geographical and Topographical Texts of the Old Testament,* p. 382) rejects the Tell Beit Mirsim location of ancient Debir, suggesting Khirbet Terrameh because of its proximity to these wells.

16. And the children of the Kenite, Moses' father in law. The Kenites were related to the Israelites through Moses' marriage to Zipporah (Ex 2:21; Jud 4: 11). They preserved their identity, yet remained friendly to the Israelites as late as the time of David (I Sam 30:29). **Went up out of the city of palm trees,** i.e., Jericho, **into the wilderness of Judah, which lies in the south of Arad.** Tell 'Arad is a barren-looking height seventeen miles south of Hebron. The Masoretic text continues, **and they went and dwelt among the people.** We later learn that the Kenites were settled among the Amalekites (I Sam 15:6). It has been suggested that the words **the people**—*hā-'ām*—result from the loss of the latter part of the word *Amalekite* in pre-Masoretic manuscript history. The original would have read, "and they went and dwelt among the Amalekites."

17. And Judah went with Simeon his brother. The tribe of Judah co-operated with the tribe of Simeon in the destruction of **Zephath,** possibly Tell es-Sab'a. **Hormah.** In this passage there is interesting interplay between two different meanings of the one Hebrew root. The same root that produces the noun *ḥērem,* meaning that which is devoted to or sacred to the gods of the non-Israelites and hence offensive to the God of Israel, also produces the verbal *ḥāram,* which means "destroyed." God had said that the Canaanite cities were to be "utterly destroyed" (Deut 7:2). Zephath had been a pagan city, "devoted" *(ḥērem)* to the pagan gods. At the command of the Lord it was "devoted" to him; that is, devoted to destruction, destroyed *(ḥāram).* It was renamed *Hormah,* which means *utter destruction.* **18. Also Judah took Gaza . . . and Askelon . . . and Ekron.** These were the principal Philistine cities south of Joppa. The historian goes on to state that the tribe of Judah was able to drive out the inhabitants of the mountains, but that the chariots of iron used by the inhabitants of the valley formed an insuperable obstacle to conquest. Since the cities of Gaza, Askelon, and Ekron were firmly in Philistine hands at a later date, any victories on the coastal plain at this time were temporary in nature. The Iron Age began in Palestine during the twelfth century B.C. The Hittite monopoly of iron was broken about 1200 B.C. and David's conquest of the Philistines marked the beginning of the use of iron as a common commodity in Israel.

20. And they gave Hebron unto Caleb, as Moses said. Because Caleb had proved himself to be a man of faith when the majority of the spies brought an evil report, God had promised a blessing for him (Num 14:24; Deut 1:36). Although Hebron was given to Caleb, he had the responsibility of occupying it. To do so he had to drive out "the three sons of Anak." The expression **sons of Anak** means *men of* (long) *neck,* i.e., men of great height, or giants. **21. And the children of Benjamin did not drive out the Jebusites.** The Jebusites of Jerusalem did not capitulate before the forces of Benjamin or Judah, their northern and southern neighbors, until Joab, David's general, took the city by stealth (II Sam 5:6-9).

22. And the house of Joseph, the tribes of Ephraim and Manasseh, **they also went up against Bethel.** Bethel was twelve miles north of Jerusalem, eighteen miles south of Shiloh. Excavations at the site of Bethel reveal burned brick, ash-filled earth, and charred debris, evidence of the thorough destruction of the Canaanite predecessor of Israelite Bethel, the city mentioned more often in Scripture than any other except Jerusalem. **25. He showed them the entrance into the city.** The Joseph tribes promised to show mercy to a man they chanced to see in the vicinity of Bethel on condition that he show them the entrance into the city. He did so, and was permitted to escape to the **land of the Hittites** (v. 26), probably a reference to northern Syria, which was reckoned as part of the Hittite "sphere of influence." The great Hittite Empire was centered in Asia Minor. The escapee from Bethel built a city which he named Luz, the earlier name of Bethel (cf. Gen 28:19).

27. Neither did Manasseh drive out . . . Beth-shean . . . Taanach . . . Dor . . . Ibleam . . . Megiddo. A string of fortified Canaanite cities divided north Israel into two parts. Beth-shean is at the eastern end of the Valley of Esdraelon, where it joins the Jordan Valley. It was occupied by Egyptian garrisons until the time of Rameses III (1198–1167 B.C.). Ibleam, Taanach, and Megiddo overlooked the Plain of Esdraelon from the south. Dor was on the Mediterranean coast, south of Mount Carmel. **28. When Israel was strong . . . they put the Canaanites to tribute.** The history of Israel during the time of the Judges alternated between periods of strength and periods of weakness. The Canaanites were never expelled, but they were reduced to slave status during periods of Israelite strength.

29. Neither did Ephraim drive out the Canaanites that dwelt in Gezer. Gezer is located eighteen miles northwest of Jerusalem, where it guards a pass from Joppa to Jerusalem. Entrenched behind walls fourteen feet thick, the Gezerites were able to resist Israelite dominance. The city became part of Solomon's kingdom only when it was given to him as a wedding gift by the Egyptian Pharaoh (I Kgs 9:16).

30. Neither did Zebulon drive out the inhabitants of Kitron, nor . . . of Nahalol. These cities in Zebulon have not been positively identified. **31. Neither did Asher drive out the inhabitants of Accho, . . . Zidon . . . Ahlab . . . Achzib . . . Helbah . . . Aphik . . . Rehob. Accho** is now known as Acre. It is located north of the Carmel Ridge, opposite the city of Haifa on the Bay of Acre. **Zidon** was the Phoenician city famed in Homeric literature as a center of art and culture. In later times it took a place second to Tyre. **Ahlab** has not been identified, but **Achzib** was located about ten miles north of Accho. **Helbah** has been identified with Mahalliba of the Assyrian monuments, located northeast of Tyre. **Aphik** may be Tell Kurdaneh, about six miles southeast of Accho. **Rehob** has been identified with Tell Berweh, a well-watered site seven miles inland from Accho. The Phoenicians were never dispossessed by the Israelites. Both David and Solomon had friendly relations with Hiram of Tyre. **33. Neither did Naphtali drive out the inhabitants of Beth-shemesh, nor . . . of Beth-anath.** Both of these places appear to have been shrines to Canaanite deities, the first to the sun-god, and the second to the popular Canaanite goddess of fertility and war, the sister and consort of Baal. It has been suggested that Beth-shemesh is another name for Kadesh-naphtali. Beth-anath may be modern el-Ba'neh, twelve miles east of Acre.

34. And the Amorites forced the children of Dan into the mountain. The Amorite is here synonymous with the Canaanite. The term appears in Assyrian documents as a designation of people from the west (of Mesopotamia). The Danites appear to have pushed into the lowlands, where they were checked and pushed back into a small district around Zorah and Eshtaol (Jud 13–16). Because this territory was too small, the main body of the tribe migrated to Laish, at the headwaters of the Jordan, which they renamed *Dan* (Jud 18).

35. But the Amorites would dwell in mount Heres in Aijalon, and in Shaalbim. Heres means "Sun Mountain" and is doubtless the equivalent of Beth-shemesh (Josh 15:10) and Ir-shemesh (Josh 19:41). The site, known today as 'Ain-shems, is located on the south side of the Wadi Surar, opposite Zorah. **Aijalon** was located in the valley that bears the same name, fourteen miles from Jerusalem. It appears in the Amarna Letters (fourteenth century B.C.) as *Aialuna*. **Shaalbim** appears in Josh 19:42 as *Shaalabbin*. It may tentatively be identified with Selbit, three miles northwest of Aijalon. The Joseph tribes did not drive out the Amorites from these sectors, but they did gain control over their territory. **36. And the coast of the Amorites was from the going up to Akrabbim, from the rock, and upward.** The **Ascent of Akrabbim** *(scorpions)* leads up from the level of the southern end of the Dead Sea to that of the hill country of southern Judah. It forms the northern border of the Wilderness of Zin and also, in Bible times, it served as the boundary between Edom and Judah. Amorites occupied the territory north of the Ascent of Akrabbim at the period described in Judges 1. The reference to **the rock** (Hebrew, *sela'*) should probably be interpreted as a proper name, *Sela* or *Petra*, the capital city of the Edomites. Petra was built in a valley surrounded by rocky cliffs, and its houses were partly hewn out of the natural rock. The Edomites were driven out of their mountain strongholds by the Nabataean Arabs, c. 300 B.C. (cf. Obadiah's prophecy).

B. Religious Background of the Period of the Judges. 2:1-5.

Although Israel had experienced the power of God during the period of the exodus from Egypt and the conquest of Canaan, they soon forgot the covenant they had made with God at Sinai. Idolatry was tolerated among them, and intermarriage with the Canaanites became commonplace.

1. An angel of the Lord came up from Gilgal to Bochim. The **angel of the Lord** was a theophany, an appearance of God in a form perceptible by the human senses. Such a manifestation had been seen by Hagar (Gen 16:7-12) and Moses (Ex 3:2-6). **Bochim** was probably located between Bethel and Shiloh, some twenty miles from the Dead Sea. **I made you to go up out of Egypt.** God identified himself as the One who has met the needs of his people in the hour of distress. His mercies should have elicited a grateful response. **2. Ye have not obeyed my voice.** God had been faithful to his covenant, but Israel had forgotten her pledge of obedience to the Law given through Moses at Sinai. **3. I will not drive them out from before you.** Israel had compromised her loyalty to God by her idolatry. The Lord declared that the inhabitants of Canaan would not be completely driven out, and that they would prove a snare to Israel. These words anticipate the history of the time of the Judges, when a series of oppressors subdued Israel. The gods of Canaan served as a temptation to the tribes to forget the God of Israel.

4. The people lifted up their voice, and wept. The message of the Angel of the Lord was one of judgment. Subsequent history indicates that the weeping was superficial, for Israel was not deterred from idolatrous practices. **5. They called the name of that place Bochim** *(weepers).* Scripture frequently associates place names with significant episodes (cf. Bethel, Gen 28:16-19; Mahanaim, Gen 32:2; Gilgal, Josh 5:9).

II. History of the Judges. 2:6–16:31.

A. Israel's Failure to Subdue the Enemy Nations. 2:6–3:6.

Under Joshua the initial phase of the conquest of the land was accomplished. The land was divided among the tribes, but it was necessary for the Israelites to occupy the territory assigned to them.

7. The people served the Lord all the days of Joshua, and all the days of the elders that outlived Joshua. The generations of Joshua and his immediate successors remained true to the Lord because of their association with **the great works of the Lord, that he did for Israel.** These words form a transition from the account of Joshua's conquest of Canaan to the history of the Judges. They parallel the words of Josh 24:28-31. **8. And Joshua . . . died, being an hundred and ten years old.** An hundred and ten years is the ideal length of life, according to the Egyptian papyri and stelae. Joseph is said to have had the same life span (Gen 50:26). Moses lived a decade longer (Deut 34:7). **9. And they buried him in the border of his inheritance in Timnath-heres. Timnath-heres,** *portion of the sun,* is also rendered "Timnath-serah," *double portion* (Josh 19:50; 24:30). The traditional site is at Tibneh, seventeen miles northwest of Jerusalem.

10 b. There arose another generation after them, which knew not the Lord. The new generation forgot the mercies of God to Israel and the nation's covenant to obey the Law of the Lord. **11. And the children of Israel . . . served the Baalim.** Baal was a fertility-god, whose worship was thought to bring productivity to mankind, animal life, and the produce of the field. Since Baal was worshiped in local manifestations (Baal-peor, Baal-gad, Baal-zeboul, etc.), the plural **Baalim** is used. **13. And they forsook the Lord, and served Baal and Ashtaroth.** The **Ashtaroth** were the female counterparts to the Baalim. Ashtoreth was the Canaanite equivalent to Babylonian Ishtar, the goddess of love and fertility.

14. And the anger of the Lord was hot against Israel. Idolatry was regarded as a breech of covenant, and it involved immoral rites incompatible with the holiness God demanded of his people. **They could not any longer stand before their enemies.** The God of Israel was not powerless to protect his people from their spoilers. In the exercise of his government, however, he chose to use Israel's enemies as a means of chastening the rebellious people.

16. The Lord raised up judges. The punishment for idolatry was designed to bring Israel back to God. The Lord answered the penitential prayers of his people in their hours of distress, and raised up **judges,** i.e., saviours or deliverers. **17. And yet they would not hearken unto their judges, but they went a whoring after other gods.** The ministry of the Judges had no lasting effect upon Israel. The Book of Judges records an unvarying cycle in which Israel repeatedly relapsed into idolatry. The fertility cult provided the language used in describing apostasy. Unfaithfulness to God is described as adultery. **18. And when the Lord raised them up judges, then the Lord was with the judge.** The Lord enabled the Judges to lead the people of Israel victoriously against their foes. Both the victories and the defeats recorded in the book of Judges are interpreted as acts of God. **19. When the judge was dead . . . they returned, and corrupted themselves.** A strong Judge could influence the people for God during his lifetime. The Judges did not form a dynasty, however. At the death of a Judge, the people tended to lapse into idolatry again.

21. I also will not henceforth drive out any from before them of the nations which Joshua left when he died. The *status quo* was to be maintained. Israel would not be forced out of Canaan, but neither would the Canaanites who were not destroyed by Joshua be dispossessed.

22. That through them I may prove Israel. From one point of view, Israel's failure to drive out the Canaanites was a means God used to chasten his people for their idolatry. It was also a means of testing Israel's faithfulness to him. **23. Therefore the Lord left those nations, without driving them out hastily.** The conquests by Joshua took place over a relatively short period of time. The further conquests which led up to the monarchy of David and Solomon took a much longer time.

3:1. The nations which the Lord left. Those that had not been conquered by Joshua could not be dislodged by the generations of the Judges. **2. To teach them war.** The presence of the enemy among the tribes of Israel helped train the Israelites in the art of warfare. **3. Five lords of the Philistines.** The Philistines seem to have migrated to Palestine from Crete and neighboring islands. Leadership was vested in the **lords** of Ashdod, Ashkelon, Ekron, Gath, and Gaza. **All the Canaanites.** Important Canaanite strongholds were situated in the Valley of Esdraelon. **The Sidonians.** Inhabitants of the Phoenician city-state of Sidon. The term can refer to the Phoenicians as a people. Subsequently the city of Tyre took the place of leadership.

The Hivites that dwelt in mount Lebanon. Hivites were probably a branch of the Horites, or Hurrians, who established the kingdom of Mitanni in upper Mesopotamia about 1500 B.C. Horites spread rapidly in Canaan during the fifteenth and fourteenth centuries. One of the Egyptian words for Canaan is Huru-land. **From mount Baal-hermon unto the entering in of Hamath.** Baal-hermon may be identical with Baal-gad at the foot of Mount Hermon (Josh 11:17; 12:7). It was the northern limit of Joshua's conquest and is thought to have been on the western side of Mount Hermon. Hamath was a town on the Orontes River, about 150 miles north of Dan. The word translated **entering in** *(lᵉbô)* may conceal the name of a town, *Lebo of Hamath,* identified with modern Lebweh in the Beqa'a Valley, which separates the Lebanon Mountains from the Anti-Lebanon ranges. This was Hivite territory during the period of the Judges.

6. And they took their daughters to be their wives. Not only did the Israelites share the land with the tribes that had not been dispossessed by Joshua, but they intermarried with them and adopted their religious customs and beliefs.

B. The Oppressors and the Deliverers of Israel. 3:7–16:31.

After a general introduction which describes life during the period of the Judges, we are given a series of specific episodes. In each instance we read of Israel's idolatry, with its subsequent chastisement.

1) Chushan-rishathaim's Oppression Ended by Othniel. 3:8-11.

8. He sold them into the hand of Chushan-rishathaim. The first oppressor bore a name that means *doubly wicked Chushan.* This may be an epithet assigned to the man by his enemies. It is also possible that the word **rishathaim** is a Hebraized form of a foreign word, perhaps a place name. Chushan came from Mesopotamia, or, as the Jewish Publication Society version transliterates the Hebrew, *Aram-naharaim.* During the time of the Judges, the Hittites overran Mitanni, the state which served as a buffer in northern Mesopotamia between the Hittite and Assyrian kingdoms. During this time Canaan was nominally subject to Egypt. Chushan may have been an obscure Hittite prince who wished to challenge Egyptian power in Canaan. An alternate view suggests that Chushan was from Edom rather than from Aram. The two words look very much alike in Hebrew, and the proximity of Edom to the tribe of Judah is a point in favor of this interpretation. According to those who read *Edom* for **Aram,** the designation **Naharaim** is a later interpolation. Extensive military campaigns were carried on throughout the Fertile Crescent as early as the time of Sargon of Akkad (c. 2400 B.C.), so that a Mesopotamian origin for Chushan cannot be dismissed on a priori grounds. He is not mentioned elsewhere in the Bible, nor in extra-Biblical sources.

9. The Lord raised up . . . Othniel, the son of Kenaz. Othniel has already been introduced (1:13-15). Here he is termed a **saviour** (cf. AV marg.), which is a synonym for a "Judge." He saved his people from the oppression of Chushan.

11. The land had rest forty years. From the victories over Chushan until Othniel's death, Israel was free from foreign domination. The term **forty years** is a round number. Many scholars suggest that it represents a generation.

2) Eglon's Oppression Ended by Ehud. 3:12-30.

12. The Lord strengthened Eglon the king of Moab against Israel. After the death of Othniel, idolatry again became rampant among the Israelite tribes. The leader of the second oppression came from Moab, the land east of the Dead Sea and south of the Arnon River. **13. And he gathered unto him the children of Ammon and Amalek.** The Ammonites were settled east and north of Moab, from the Arnon to the Jabbok. Sihon, king of the Amorites, had been defeated by Israel in this area before the conquest of Canaan. The nomadic Amalekites were bitter foes of Israel from the battle at Rephidim, on the way to Sinai, to their final destruction in the days of Hezekiah (I Chr 4:43). **And possessed the city of palm trees.** Eglon and his confederates invaded Canaan by the same route that Joshua had used earlier. They crossed the Jordan and captured **the city of palm trees,** or Jericho. The city destroyed by Joshua had occupied a strategic position, and evidently another city was built in the same area a short time after its destruction. The text implies a battle for the "city of palm trees" before it was occupied by Eglon and his allies.

15. The Lord raised them up a deliverer, Ehud the son of Gera, a Benjamite, a man lefthanded. The Benjamites seem to have had a tendency to be left-handed (Jud 20:16), and in at least one instance they are described as being ambidextrous (I Chr 12:2). **By him the children of Israel sent a present unto Eglon.** The **present** was doubtless the tribute demanded of Israel by the Moabite oppressors.

16. But Ehud made him a dagger which had two edges, of a cubit length. Ehud provided himself with a sword with which he intended to kill the Moabite king. **18. He sent away the people that bare the present.** Ehud dismissed the large retinue of men who had accompanied him. Since tribute was paid in silver, gold, cattle, and other bulky materials, it required a large number of men to bear it. By dismissing the men, Ehud allayed any suspicion of evil intent. **19. But he himself turned again from the quarries that were by Gilgal.** The word translated **quarries** *(p^e^sîlîm)* is usually rendered *graven images,* and the LXX so renders it here. After dismissing his retinue, Ehud turned back to address the king again. **I have a secret errand unto thee, O king.** A message was sent to Eglon requesting a private audience. The implication was that the errand was of such import that it could not be entrusted to a minor courtier.

20. And he was sitting in a summer parlour. Eglon was in his *ʿălîyâ* when Ehud approached. The *ʿălîyâ* was an additional story raised above the flat roof of the house at one corner. It usually had just one room, with latticed windows on all sides to provide ventilation. The *ʿălîyâ* was the coolest room in the house. **And Ehud said, I have a message from God unto thee.** Ehud's words implied that he was the bearer of a message from the God of Israel to the Moabite king. Some commentators paraphrase the message: "I have God's business with you, a divine commission to execute you." **and he [Eglon] arose out of his seat.** The Moabite king presumably arose as a sign of reverence for the divine oracle. This may have been planned by Ehud so that he might get within striking distance of Eglon.

21. And Ehud put forth his left hand, and took the dagger from his right thigh, and thrust it into his belly. Ehud's plan was successful. Without arousing suspicion, he approached the king, then suddenly drew his weapon and murdered the oppressor of Israel. **22. And the haft also went in after the blade.** The blow was quick and forceful. Ehud left the weapon in the wound. **And the dirt came out.** Such a wound in the abdomen forced out the excrement. This is the most natural interpretation, and it is physiologically correct.

23. Then Ehud went forth through the porch. The *misd^e^rôn,* translated **porch,** through which Ehud escaped, cannot be positively identified. The word appears only once in Scripture.

24. Surely he covereth his feet in his summer chamber. The servants of Eglon evidently saw Ehud leave. As there had been no disturbance, they had no reason to be suspicious. They did not intrude on Eglon's privacy, assuming that he was caring for his personal needs. To "cover the feet" is a euphemism for "to relieve one's self." **25. And they tarried till they were ashamed.** They waited until they saw that they were mistaken. **They took a key, and opened.** The type of lock used in Biblical times was common in Palestine until quite recently. A bolt was shut by hand. A number of pin tumblers dropped into corresponding holes in the bolt and locked it. The key, used for unlocking only, was usually a flat piece of wood with pins at one end corresponding in number and position to the tumblers of the lock. The length corresponded to the depth of the bolt. The bolt was undercut so that the key could be slipped lengthwise under it until the pins lifted the tumblers and allowed the bolt to be pushed back.

26. And Ehud escaped . . . unto Seirath. By the time Eglon's servants discovered his dead body, Ehud had reached the edge of the highlands of Ephraim. The exact location of Seirath is not known. **27. He blew a trumpet in the mountain of Ephraim.** The trumpet called men to battle (cf. I Sam 13:3,4). The mountains of Ephraim comprise the central mountain range of Palestine from the Plain of Esdraelon south to the environs of Jerusalem. **28. And they went down after him, and took the fords of Jordan toward Moab.** The Israelites rallied to the call of Ehud. They seized the fords of the Jordan which would be used by the fleeing Moabites (cf. Josh 2:7; II Sam 19:15). **29. And they slew of Moab at that time about ten thousand men.** Although properly regarded as a round number, the **ten thousand men** must have been a serious loss to Moab. Moabite power over Israel was effectively broken.

30. The land had rest fourscore years. Cf. 3:11. Nothing is said of the Judgeship of Ehud after his victory over the Moabites. We read, however, of eighty years (two generations) during which the land was free from invasion.

3) Israel Delivered from the Philistines by Shamgar. 3:31.

And after him was Shamgar the son of Anath. Shamgar is a foreign (Hurrian) name. Anath was the name of the Canaanite goddess of sex and war, sister of Baal. Hence, **son of Anath** may be interpreted to mean "the warrior." Shamgar is mentioned in 5:6 as living in days when Israel's foes had gained undisputed control over the land. He probably was a contemporary of Deborah and Barak. **Which slew of the Philistines six hundred men with an ox goad.** This is the first of two Philistine oppressions during the time of the Judges. The second (13:1–16:31) is described in the account of Samson. Shamgar is known for but one episode. Using an ox goad, he killed six hundred Philistines. The ox goad might have been as long as eight feet. At one end it had a spike, and on the other a chisel-shaped blade, which was used in cleaning the plow. When necessary, the ox goad could serve as a substitute for a spear. **And he also delivered Israel.** The usual time references are not given in the case of Shamgar. He probably should be thought of as a heroic individual who defeated Israel's enemies rather than as a ruler over Israel during the time of the Judges.

4) Oppression by Jabin and Sisera Ended by Deborah and Barak. 4:1–5:31.

4:1. And the children of Israel again did evil in the sight of the Lord when Ehud was dead. During the lifetime of Ehud, Israel remained true to the Lord. Subsequently, however, a fresh outbreak of idolatry ushered in another period of oppression.

2. The Lord sold them into the hand of Jabin, king of Canaan, that reigned in Hazor. The earlier oppressions were from outside the land of Canaan. Jabin, however, a Canaanite ruler, led an uprising against the Israelites who, under Joshua, had dispossessed them. Hazor was the most important stronghold in northern Canaan. **The captain of whose host was Sisera, which dwelt in Harosheth of the Gentiles.** Sisera's home, *Hărōshet haggôyim,* is modern Tell 'Amar, located at the place where the Kishon River passes through a narrow gorge to enter the Plain of Acre. It is about ten miles northwest of Meggido.

3. He had nine hundred chariots of iron. See 1:19, where the Philistines are similarly described as possessing chariots of iron. These were most formidable war equipment to the Israelites, who had not yet entered the Iron Age. **Twenty years he mightily oppressed the children of Israel.** For half a generation Israel was oppressed by the Canaanites, who used their strategic locations in the Valley of Esdraelon as vantage points from which to expand their holdings.

4. And Deborah, a prophetess, the wife of Lapidoth, she judged Israel at that time. Deborah is described as both a prophetess and a Judge. At a time of despair she aroused her people to fight.

5. And she dwelt under the palm tree of Deborah. Instead of **dwelt** we might read *sat*. Part of Deborah's responsibility as a Judge was to sit as arbitress in the settlement of disputes. The particular tree associated with her Judgeship was **between Ramah and Beth-el.** Ramah was in Benjamin, north of Jerusalem. This is the area in which Samuel subsequently judged Israel (I Sam 7:16).

6. And she sent and called Barak the son of Abinoam out of Kedesh-naphtali. Kedesh-naphtali was a City of Refuge (Josh 20:7; cf. 12:22). This was the part of Israel closest to the Canaanite oppressors. **Go and draw toward mount Tabor.** Barak was ordered to muster the armies of Israel at Mount Tabor, in the northeastern part of the Plain of Esdraelon. **7. And I will draw unto thee to the river Kishon, Sisera . . . and I will deliver him into thine hand.** Deborah spoke as a prophetess. God promised through her to bring destruction to Sisera's armies.

8. If thou wilt go with me, then I will go. Barak wanted the assurance that the prophetess would accompany him, thus insuring success in battle. **9. And she said, I will surely go with thee . . . the Lord shall sell Sisera into the hand of a woman.** Deborah promised to accompany Barak, but she declared that a woman would be the heroine. This anticipates the part played in the defeat of the Canaanites by Jael, the wife of Heber. **10. And Barak called Zebulon and Naphtali to Kedesh.** The two northern tribes had the responsibility of meeting the threat from Sisera.

11. Now Heber the Kenite, which was of the children of Hobab, the father-in-law of Moses. The sacred historian provides some background material concerning the Kenites. They appear to have been nomadic smiths whom Moses first met during his sojourn in the desert before he became leader of the Exodus. Heber had separated himself from the main body of his tribe and had settled near Kedesh.

12. And they showed Sisera that Barak the son of Abinoam was gone up to mount Tabor. Sisera, being informed of Barak's movements, assembled his forces, including the nine hundred iron chariots, and marched from Harosheth to the Kishon. **14. So Barak went down from mount Tabor, and ten thousand men after him.** Assured by Deborah that God was about to bring a great victory to Israel, Barak and his ten thousand men sallied forth against the Canaanite army in the valley. **15. And the Lord discomfited Sisera.** The Canaanites were panic-stricken. The sudden onslaught of the Israelite army and the storm that caused the Kishon to overflow its banks (5:21) forced the Canaanites to flee from their chariots, which they left mired in the valley.

17. Sisera fled away on his feet to the tent of Jael the wife of Heber the Kenite. With the rest of his army destroyed, Sisera's prime concern was to save his own life. **For there was peace between Jabin the king of Hazor and the house of Heber the Kenite.** Sisera had reason to think that he would be safe if he reached the house of Heber. Evidently the Canaanites had not oppressed the nomadic Kenites in their midst, and the Kenites had not taken part in the Israelites uprising against them.

18. And Jael went out to meet Sisera, and said unto him, Turn in, my lord. Jael offered the hospitality of her tent to the frightened Sisera. Whether or not she invited him into her tent in order to kill him is a matter of inference. **She covered him with a mantle.** The exact meaning of the word rendered **mantle** is uncertain. It may also be rendered *tent curtain*. **19. She opened a bottle of milk, and gave him drink, and covered him.** Sisera asked for water, but Jael opened the lamb or goatskin bottle in which milk was kept and poured him a bowlful. **20. Stand in the door of the tent.** Sisera had reason to suspect that the Israelites would pursue him. He asked Jael to tell them that he was not in her tent. Her acts of hospitality led him to feel that he could trust her.

21. Then Jael, Heber's wife, took a nail of the tent . . . and smote the nail into his temples . . . . So he died. Among the Bedouins it is the responsibility of the women to pitch the tents, and this may have been true in antiquity. The tent pin and the mallet that Jael used were probably of wood. Sisera, exhausted from his difficult escape, was sound asleep, and Jael considered this her opportunity to kill the enemy of Israel. Some commentators suggest that Jael was not sympathetic with the neutrality of her husband (4:17), and that her actions toward Sisera were motivated by her loyalty toward Israel. Whether or not her murder of Sisera was premeditated is beside the point, as far as the record in Judges is concerned. From the

Israelite point of view, she was a heroine for bringing death to Sisera. **22. And, behold, as Barak pursued Sisera, Jael came out to meet him.** Jael brought Barak the good news that the Canaanite captain was dead.

23. So God subdued on that day Jabin the king of Canaan before the children of Israel. Scripture does not abstract God from historical processes. The act of Jael is described, but the victory is ascribed to God. The attitude toward history throughout the Bible is consistent. God allows the heathen to chasten his people, and God raises up deliverers to save them. Cause and effect is meaningful at the historical level, but God is seen as the Power behind all that takes place, good or bad. It is not necessary to justify Jael's act. Even wicked deeds are represented in Scripture as furthering God's ultimate purposes (cf. Acts 2:23, 24; Ps 76:10).

5:1. Then sang Deborah and Barak. The account of the defeat of Sisera is given in two recensions, one in prose (Jud 4), and the other in poetry (Jud 5). Most critical authorities ascribe very great antiquity to the Song of Deborah, dating it near the events it describes.

2. Praise ye the Lord for the avenging of Israel, when the people willingly offered themselves. The ode commences with an exhortation to praise the Lord. The words that immediately follow have been interpreted in varying ways. One rendering preserves the parallelism of the original: *For the leading of the leaders in Israel, for the volunteering of the people.* Quite different is the translation: *For that they let the long hair go loose in Israel.* The latter suggests either that Israel became practically a nation of Nazarites, or that they enjoyed the freedom and strength with which the long hair of the Nazarite was associated. **3. Hear, O ye kings; give ear, O ye princes.** The rulers of the nations are urged to consider the mighty acts of the God of Israel.

4. Lord, when thou wentest out of Seir, when thou marchedst out of the field of Edom. In contrast to the fertility-gods of Canaan, the God of Israel was associated with the arid regions of the south, particularly Sinai and Horeb. As he had entered into covenant with his people at Sinai, and as he had provided for them during the wilderness wandering, so now he is pictured as coming out of Seir and Edom to deliver his people from their oppressors. **5. The mountains melted from before the Lord.** The RSV renders this, *The mountains quaked before the Lord.* Moore prefers *The mountains streamed,* which is comparable to the RV *flowed down.* The picture is of God setting forth from his abode to assist his people in the conflict with Sisera. All nature was convulsed as God acted in power. The imagery is poetic and is designed to impress upon the mind of the reader the awesomeness of the Divine activity. **Even that Sinai.** The Israelites doubtless associated Sinai with the theophany to Moses and the giving of the Law. There Israel entered into covenant with God. Here God is pictured as coming from the south, even Sinai, to deliver his people.

6. The highways were unoccupied, and the travellers walked through byways. The Canaanites had secured control of the main roads throughout the land, so that the Israelites who had to travel used the byways, literally, *crooked paths,* the circuitous bypaths unfrequented by the enemy. **7. The inhabitants of the villages ceased.** Peasants deserted their villages for the protection of the walled cities. Others (e.g., Jew. Pub. Soc. vers.) suggest the rendering, *The rulers ceased in Israel.* **Until that I, Deborah, arose.** The verb may be either the first person or the second person, feminine, with an archaic ending. Most recent translations render, *Until that thou didst arise, Deborah* (JPS; similarly RSV). **A mother in Israel.** The phrase occurs in II Sam 20:19, where it denotes a city.

8. They chose new gods. These words have puzzled Biblical scholars. Their most obvious meaning is that Israel, devoid of help from God, turned to idolatry. Some commentators make God the subject, reading, *God ('Ĕlōhîm) chose something new* (so the Peshitta and the Vulgate). Others translate *'Ĕlōhîm* as *judges,* although such a usage is foreign to the Book of Judges. It seems best to render the words as in the AV, seeing in them a description of the apostasy of the people of Israel and their desperate attempt to gain help from idols. **Then was war in the gates.** Raids of the enemy reached the very gates of the Israelite cities. **Was there a shield or spear seen among forty thousand in Israel?** Either the Israelites were unarmed, or they feared to let their arms be seen by the enemy.

9. My heart is toward the governors of Israel, that offered themselves willingly among the people. The poet expresses gratitude for the leaders of Israel who proved faithful in a time of crisis.

10. Ye that ride on white asses. All classes of people had reason to be thankful. The rich merchants and the nobility rode on white asses. **Ye that . . . walk by the way.** The poorer classes had to journey on foot in carrying on their business. **11. There shall they rehearse the righteous acts of the Lord.** Some expressions in this verse are obscure to the modern reader. Albright suggests that at the signal of the cymbals between the drum beats, the people were to repeat the words of praise. In the AV, interpretive words are supplied in italics: *They that are delivered;* i.e., **from the noise of archers**—implying that enemy archers are meant. Keil and Delitzsch translate: *With the voice of the archers among drawers of water, there praise ye the righteous acts of the Lord.* This presupposes a scene of victory in which the warriors, having returned from the field of battle, mingle among the women at the watering-troughs, recounting to them the victories wrought by God.

12. Awake, awake, Deborah. These words form an introduction to the second part of the song, which describes the conflict and victory. **13. Then he made him that remaineth have dominion.** The people of the Lord, thought of as but a remnant, would rule the mighty. The RSV renders it: *Then down marched the remnant of the noble.* **14. Out of Ephraim was there a root of them against Amalek.** The RV renders it: *Out of Ephraim came down they whose root is in Amalek;* i.e., Amalekite nomads had invaded central Canaan. **Out of Machir came down governors.** Machir was a branch of the tribe of Manasseh. The part of Manasseh that settled west of the Jordan took part in the conflict.

16. Why abodest thou among the sheepfolds? Certain of the tribes did not take part in the battle against the Canaanites. They are the subject of a series of taunts. **17. Gilead abode beyond Jordan.** No help came from the two and one-half tribes which settled east of the Jordan. Similarly, Dan, Asher, Zebulon, and Naphtali are chided for their indolence.

19. The kings came and fought. After the account of the attitude of the tribes, the poet describes the battle itself. Sisera led a confederacy of kings against Israel. **In Taanach, by the waters of Megiddo.** Taanach, located five miles southeast of Megiddo, commands one of the passes to the Plain of Esdraelon. The **waters of Megiddo** are the Kishon and its tributaries. **They took no gain of money.** This may be interpreted as a taunt, in which case it would assert that the campaign was profitless. It may also refer to the kings who, in their eagerness to fight against Israel, did not accept the pay of hirelings.

20. The stars in their courses fought against Sisera. The God of Israel intervened on behalf of his people. The very forces of nature itself were arrayed against the Canaanite. **21. The river of Kishon swept them away.** In this area the Kishon is not normally a dangerous stream. At the critical moment of battle it swelled into a torrent that rendered the Canaanite chariots useless. **22. Then were the horsehoofs broken.** The JPS renders, *Then did the horsehoofs stamp;* i.e., stamp the earth in their efforts to escape.

23. Curse ye Meroz. The town of Meroz did not join the Israelites in their attack upon the Canaanites. Its site is unknown. Some think it was located along the route of Sisera's flight, and that its inhabitants failed to capture him. The curse on Meroz may be contrasted with the blessing on Jael. **24. Blessed above women shall Jael the wife of Heber the Kenite be.** In contrast to the cowardice of the men of Meroz, the devotion of Jael stands out in bold relief. **Blessed above women** is a Hebrew superlative, meaning, "Most blessed of women."

25. Water he asked, milk she gave him. The pronouns effectively identify the characters in the story, Sisera and Jael. **She brought forth butter in a lordly dish.** The word *hem'â*, rendered **butter** in the AV, was artificially soured milk. It was made by shaking milk in the skin bottle in which it was stored, and fermenting it with the stale milk adhering to the skin from previous use. The beverage is still prepared by Bedouin Arabs (cf. C. M. Doughty, *Arabia Deserta*, I, 325). The **lordly dish** would have been a dish of large size, a vessel fit for a lord.

26. She put her hand to the nail. The prose account in 4:21 helps explain the action. Jael took the tent pin in her left hand and the mallet in her right hand, and so smote the sleeping Sisera. The act was one of bravery in that she risked her own life to kill Israel's enemy. Had Sisera awakened, Jael would have been at his mercy. **27. At her feet . . . he fell down dead.** The falling need not imply that Sisera was in an upright position when he was smitten. The poet is describing the result of the blow of Jael. The fact that Israel's enemy had been killed was an occasion for rejoicing, and the poet almost gloats over Jael's triumph. The fact that the powerful Sisera was killed by a woman was a particular occasion for rejoicing.

28. The mother of Sisera looked out at a window. The scene – a most human one–now shifts to Sisera's home. Sisera's mother was concerned about her son. She wondered why he was late in returning from battle. **29. Her wise ladies answered.** The women of rank who were with her attempted to encourage her. They were "wise" but in this instance did not know the truth. **30. Have they not divided the prey.** It takes some time to divide the spoils of war. The victorious army must make proper distribution. They killed the men, divided the women among the warriors (**to every man a damsel or two**), and distributed the spoil itself at the behest of the victor. This was the normal practice in ancient warfare. The strong irony of the present reference is that Sisera was not sharing such fruits of victory, but was a corpse at the foot of a woman, his murderess.

31. So let all thine enemies perish, O Lord. The poet suddenly breaks off his graphic description of Sisera's fate with a prayer to God. May all of God's enemies perish as Sisera perished. Conversely, **let them that love him be as the sun when he goeth forth in his might.** The sun, annihilating the darkness of night by its invincible power, is here symbolic of the strength of those blessed by God. **And the land had rest forty years.** The destruction of Sisera brought relief to the harassed Israelites. For a generation Israel was free from outside interference.

5) Midianite Oppression Ended by Gideon. 6:1–8:35.

6:1. The Lord delivered them into the hand of Midian. The cycle of sin, punishment, and deliverance was repeated. The Midianites were nomads who dwelt in the region east and southeast of the Dead Sea. Their genealogy is traced through Abraham's concubine, Keturah (Gen 25:1,2). **2. Because of the Midianites the children of Israel made them the dens which are in the mountains, and caves, and strong holds.** The Midianite raids were so effective that the Israelites had to resort to caves and mountain retreats as places of refuge.

3. When Israel had sown . . . the Midianites came up, and the Amalekites, and the children of the east. Associated with the Midianites were the Amalekites (cf. 3:13) and the **children of the east,** a general term for the nomads of the Syrian desert. **4. And they encamped against them.** In typically nomad fashion they settled temporarily in the land, using it as pasture for their herds and flocks, and taking its produce for themselves. Israel was powerless to interfere with these Bedouin movements. **5. Both they and their camels were without number.** The use of the domesticated camel made possible, for the first time, raids involving long distances. The Bible refers to camels earlier in the Patriarchal Age (Gen 24:10 ff.), but this is the first reference to an organized raid in which camels were used.

8. The Lord sent a prophet unto the children of Israel. The Midianite oppression brought the people to the place where they cried out to God for deliverance. A prophet appeared in their midst who reminded them of God's merciful deliverance of his people from Egypt, and their subsequent disobedience.

11. And there came an angel of the Lord. The message to Israel came from a prophet, but the call to Gideon came from **the angel of the Lord.** The definite article should be inserted, as in the RV and the RSV. As in 2:1-5, this may best be understood as a theophany–an appearance of God himself to Gideon. **And . . . Gideon threshed wheat by the wine press, to hide it from the Midianites.** Read with the RSV: *Gideon . . . was beating out wheat in the wine press.* Gideon, along with his fellow Israelites, had to work in secret lest the Midianites seize the grain. Within the confines of a wine press only a small amount of wheat could be threshed at a time. This was an act of desperation.

12. The Lord is with thee, thou mighty man of valour. The message of the angel of the Lord seemed to be a mockery, for Gideon felt powerless to meet the need of his people. **13. Oh my Lord, if the Lord be with us, why then is all this befallen us?** The power of Israel's enemies seemed to show that God was not with his people. Gideon asked concerning the miracles of the past, and wondered why he did not see them in his generation.

14. Go in this thy might, and thou shalt save Israel from the hand of the Midianites. Although Israel was weak before her foes, God promised Gideon might to deliver his people. **15. Wherewith shall I save Israel?** Israel's leaders uniformly exhibited a spirit of humility before God (Ex 3:11; Isa 6:5; Jer 1:6). Gideon protested that his situation in life precluded his being a leader in Israel. **17. Show me a sign that thou talkest with me.** Gideon wanted a supernatural act performed in his presence to confirm the fact that this was indeed a message from God.

19. And Gideon went in, and made ready a kid. This was to serve as the offering *(minḥâ)* which he desired to present to his guest (6:18). The terminology is purposely ambiguous. In one sense Gideon prepared such food as he might normally set before a guest whom he wished to honor. Such food, however, might also serve as an offering to God. A sign that God had accepted the offering would validate the message that was a source of bewilderment to Gideon. **20. Take the flesh and the unleavened cakes, and lay them upon this rock.** The angel gave orders for setting out the food on an improvised altar. **21. There rose up fire out of the rock, and consumed the flesh and the unleavened cakes.** This was the mark of divine acceptance (Lev 9:24; I Kgs 18:38), the kind of sign for which Gideon had asked.

22. Alas, O Lord God! Gideon was frightened because he had seen **the** (not *an)* angel of the Lord. Jehovah had said to Moses: "There shall no man see me and live" (Ex 33:20). When the Angel of the Lord disappeared, Gideon feared that the theophany was an omen of impending death. **23. And the Lord said unto him, Peace be unto thee; fear not: thou shalt not die.** God assured Gideon that he was not to die. The message of the angelic Visitor was validated, and Gideon would prove a "mighty man of valour." **24. Then Gideon built an altar there.** He built the altar to commemorate God's message to him. *Shālôm* is the Hebrew word for "peace." The altar was still standing at the time the Book of Judges was written.

25. Take thy father's young bullock. Since idolatry was the prevailing sin of Israel, Gideon was commanded to show his loyalty to Israel's God and his abhorrence of the Baalist cult. Gideon was to take a bullock for the worship of the Lord. Then he was to destroy the altar of Baal and cut down the *Asherah* (AV **grove**) which was beside it. This **grove** represented the female element in the fertility cult and consisted of a wooden post, or a stump of a tree, which was set up beside the altar of Baal. **26. Build an altar unto the Lord thy God upon the top of this rock.** Gideon was to build an altar to the God of Israel and use the wood of the *Asherah* in the preparation of his sacrifice.

27. Then Gideon . . . did as the Lord had said unto him. Ten men were associated with Gideon in this act, which was carried out at night as a precaution against meeting opposition from the Israelites who were sympathetic with Baal worship. **29. And they said one to another, Who hath done this thing?** On the next day the villagers were incensed over an act which they interpreted as sacrilege. **31. Will ye plead for Baal?** When the men demanded that Gideon be killed for his act of desecration, Joash, his father, sprang to his defense. He said, **If he be a god, let him plead for himself.** In other words, a god who cannot defend himself is not worthy of the devotion of his people. This was the import of the assertion of Joash, who further threatened death to any who would espouse the cause of Baal.

32. He called him Jerubbaal. This was an alternate name for Gideon. It is here interpreted as meaning, "Let Baal strive *(yārêb Ba'al).* It thus serves as a kind of motto for the adversaries of Baalism. Subsequently the name Jerubbesheth was substituted for Jerubbaal (II Sam 11:21), just as Ishbosheth (II Sam 2:8) replaced Eshbaal (I Chr 8:33). The term *ba'al* in the earliest stratum of Hebrew life was synonymous with *ădōnāy*. Both terms meant "lord" or "master" and could be used of Israel's God. After the period of conflict with the Phoenician Baal cult, the word became synonymous with idolatry. The word *bōshet*, "shame," was considered a suitable substitute for the Baal component in personal names.

33. Then all the Midianites . . . pitched in the valley of Jezreel. The valley extends from Mount Carmel to the Jordan valley. One branch passes between Mount Tabor and the Hill of Moreh, and another between the Hill of Moreh and Mount Gilboa. Because Jezreel leads into the heart of Palestine, it has been a battleground throughout history. **34. But the Spirit of the Lord came upon Gideon.** Literally, *clothed Gideon* (JPS version). God's spirit enveloped Gideon so that he became the instrument used of the Spirit in accomplishing the divine purpose. **And Abiezer was gathered after him.** Gideon's clan, the Abiezrites, were the first to rally to his side. Manasseh, Asher, Zebulon, and Naphtali subsequently aided Gideon in his campaign against the Midianites.

37. Behold, I will put a fleece of wool in the floor. Gideon again sought a sign by which he might know whether or not to expect victory in battle. He placed a fleece on the threshing-floor and declared that he would be assured of victory if he found the fleece wet with dew but the surrounding ground still dry. **38.** On the morrow he found the fleece wet with dew, and he **wringed the dew out of the fleece, a bowlful of water.** To make doubly certain, he proposed that on the next day the fleece be dry but the ground about covered with dew. The double sign, which precluded naturalistic interpretations, was evidence to Gideon that God would bring victory to him and his army.

7:1. Then Jerubbaal, who is Gideon, . . . rose up early, and pitched beside the well of Harod. The Spring of Harod may be ʽAin Jalûd, located at the foot of Mount Gilboa. The Israelites under Gideon encamped there, and the Midianites settled across the valley at the Hill of Moreh, four miles away.

2. The people that are with thee are too many. A large army might have given rise to a measure of *self*-reliance. God desired to teach his people the necessity of trusting in him. **3. Whosoever is fearful and afraid, let him return.** In the first stage of reducing the size of the army, each individual was permitted to leave of his own volition. About two-thirds of the army left, but there were still too many men for God's purpose.

4. Bring them down unto the water, and I will try them for thee there. A further division took place at the water, where the men used two different methods of drinking. Those who bowed on their knees to drink were dismissed, whereas those who lapped with their tongues **as a dog lappeth** (v. 5) were kept in Gideon's army. The latter seem to have taken water in their hands (v. 6) and stood upright while lapping the water. Men drinking thus would be prepared for sudden attack. Josephus interprets this passage differently: Those who lapped were the greatest cowards in the army, for they were afraid to drink in the usual manner in the presence of the enemy. God, according to this view, showed his grace in using the worst men of the army to defeat the Midianites! The passage, however, does not pass moral judgment on the two groups, but does suggest the means by which the numbers were reduced so that God's grace might be made manifest. **7. By the three hundred men that lapped will I save you.** God planned to manifest his grace in using a small army to defeat Israel's enemy.

9. Arise, get thee down unto the host. The command implies an immediate attack. During the Exodus spies were sent from Kadesh-barnea (Num 13) to spy out the land of Canaan. And Joshua sent spies to Jericho before he attacked it (Josh 2). Gideon, however, was to attack the Midianites at once. **10. But if thou fear to go down, go thou with Phurah thy servant down to the host. Phurah** (also written Purah) was the page, or armor-bearer, of Gideon. In spite of God's promise, Gideon must have felt some hesitation in leading an army against the enemy. He had never led an army before, and his men were untrained and inexperienced.

11. And thou shalt hear what they say. The fears of the Midianites would prove a source of encouragement to Gideon. **Afterward shall thy hands be strengthened.** God would use these experiences to prepare Gideon to lead Israel to victory.

12. And the Midianites . . . lay . . . in the valley like grasshoppers. This verse is an example of the use of hyperbole in Scripture. Compared with the three hundred men in Gideon's army, the Midianites and their allies seemed to be an innumerable host. They are here likened to an army of grasshoppers that invades an area, devours all the vegetation, and leaves desolation in its wake. **13. There was a man that told a dream unto his fellow.** Dreams were considered to contain revelations of the future. The Midianite dreamed that a cake of barley bread tumbled upon the tent of Midian and destroyed it. Barley was the cheapest grain in Palestine, and its use here may underscore the poverty of Israel. The dream was interpreted as evidence that God was about to use Israel to destroy the hosts of Midian. Gideon, having learned of the fear in the hearts of the Midianites, returned confidently to his camp and prepared for the attack.

16. And he divided the three hundred men into three companies. Gideon deployed his forces in such a way as to simulate an attack from three sides at the same time. The actual method used by Gideon was a kind of psychological warfare. He made use of horns (Heb. *shôpārôt*, "rams' horns"), empty pitchers, and torches. The pitchers were to conceal the lights until the right moment. Gideon wished to stage a surprise attack. In the midst of the night the Midianites would be awakened by the sound of the horns and at the same time would see sudden bursts of light in the darkness. Gideon thus expected, with God's help, to throw the enemy camp into consternation.

19. In the beginning of the middle watch. The night was divided into three watches of four hours each, the first beginning at 6:00 P.M. **They blew the trumpets, and brake the pitchers.** The sound of the horns would signal the call to battle. The breaking of the pitchers would simulate the clash of arms. As the Midianites awoke, each would think that the battle had already begun. **20. The sword of the Lord and of Gideon.** The war cry added to the sound of the *shôphārim* and the breaking of pitchers to strike panic among the Midianites. The RSV reads, *A sword for the Lord and for Gideon.*

22. And the Lord set every man's sword against his fellow. In the confusion, the Midianites and their allies began attacking one another. Gideon's army was comparatively weak, but the enemy army put itself to rout. The Israelites followed up their advantage and pursued the enemy. **And the host fled to Beth-shittah. Beth-shittah** *(house of acacia)* was located somewhere between the Valley of Jezreel and Zererah in the Jordan Valley. Some scholars equate Zererah with Zarethan (Josh 3:16). **As far as the border of Abel-meholah, by Tabbath. Abel-meholah** *(field of dancing)* has been identified by Nelson Glueck with Tell-el-Maqlûb in the Jordan Valley. Others prefer a site on the west side of the Jordan about twelve miles south of Beth-shean. It is best known as the birthplace of the prophet Elisha. **23. And the men of Israel . . . pursued after the Midianites.** The victory of Gideon's three hundred men served as the cue for a general campaign to rid the land of the Midianites.

24. Take before them the waters unto Beth-barah and Jordan. It was Gideon's purpose to cut off the escape routes in order to bring about the destruction of the enemy. **Beth-barah** may be located south of Beth-shean, facing the Wadi Fāra'a. **25. And they slew Oreb upon the rock Oreb, and Zeeb they slew at the winepress of Zeeb.** The names mean *raven* and *wolf* respectively. Names were given to the places to commemorate the victory over these Midianite princes. **And brought the heads of Oreb and Zeeb to Gideon.** As trophies of victory, the heads of the Midianite princes were taken to Gideon.

8:1. And the men of Ephraim . . . did chide with him sharply. The Ephraimites were angered that Gideon had not enlisted their aid earlier in the battle with the Midianites. Since the victor divided the spoil, they suspected Gideon of trying to deprive them of the spoils of war. **2. Is not the gleaning of the grapes of Ephraim better than the vintage of Abiezer?** Gideon's reply stands in marked contrast to that of Jephthah (12:1-6). He assured the men of Ephraim that theirs was the greater accomplishment. Ephraim had taken the Midianite chieftains, whereas the clan of Abiezer (Gideon's clan) had only performed a preparatory function. Gideon's soft answer satisfied the Ephraimites.

4. And Gideon came to Jordan. Gideon and his band of three hundred pursued the Midianite kings, Zebah and Zalmunna, across the Jordan. **5. Give, I pray you, loaves of bread.** Gideon and his army passed through Succoth, east of the Jordan, north of the Jabbok. Since the army was weakened through hunger, Gideon asked the men of Succoth for loaves (lit., *circles)* of bread. The officials of the city chose to go their separate way, with no concern for the welfare of their brethren in Canaan. They taunted Gideon, asking him if Zebah and Zalmunna were already in his hands that he made such a demand. Gideon threatened to punish the men of Succoth after his defeat of the Midianite kings, and then he moved on. **8. And he went up thence to Penuel.** At Penuel, east of Succoth, Gideon made the same request and received a similar answer. The men of Penuel prided themselves upon their tower, which served as a stronghold during periods of attack. Gideon threatened to destroy the tower on his return **in peace** – that is, as victor over the Midianites.

10. Now Zebah and Zalmunna were in Karkor. The place is not identified. Its name means *soft, even ground.* **11. And Gideon went up by the way of them that dwelt in tents.** The Midianites were escaping into the desert area, which was populated only by tent-dwelling nomads. They did not expect Gideon to pursue them that far. **On the east of Nobah and Jogbehah. Jogbehah** can be identified with Jubeihat, fifteen miles southeast of Penuel. **The host was secure.** The Midianites thought they were sufficiently far removed from Gideon's men to relax their guard. They fancied themselves secure, and so were surprised by Gideon. **12. He . . . took the two kings of Midian . . . and discomfited all the host.** When the kings were captured, fresh terror fell upon the Midianite armies.

13. And Gideon . . . returned . . . before the sun was up. Read with the RSV, *returned . . . by the ascent of Heres*. Somewhere along the route he met a youth from whom he received information concerning the officials and elders of Succoth. **14. He described unto him the princes of Succoth.** Read instead: *And he wrote down for him the princes of Succoth*. Writing was widely known by the time of the Judges. Our first written documents antedate 3000 B.C. Documents from Ras Shamra (ancient Ugarit) in Canaan date from the fifteenth century B.C. **16. With them he taught the men of Succoth.** See 8:7, Gideon's threat: "When the Lord has given Zebah and Zalmunna into my hand, I will flail your flesh with the thorns of the wilderness and with briers." Although the exact form of punishment is not certain, Gideon recompensed the men of Succoth for their refusal to help him. **17. And he beat down the tower of Penuel, and slew the men of the city.** This, too, was in accord with the earlier threat (8:9).

18. What manner of men were they whom ye slew at Tabor? Literally, *Where are they* . . . ? The question implies that Gideon knew that Zebah and Zalmunna had killed his brothers. The reply was in the form of arrogant flattery: "They were just such men as you, men of kingly figure" (ICC). **19. If ye had saved them alive, I would not slay you.** By slaying his brothers, the Midianites imposed the duty of blood-revenge on Gideon (Deut 19:6). Gideon explained that they were his full brethren, i.e., not only of the same father but of the same mother as well. **20. And he said unto Jether his firstborn, Up, and slay them.** This would have added to the humiliation of the Midianite kings. The boy did not draw his sword, however.

21. Rise thou, and fall upon us. With haughty spirit the Midianites challenged Gideon to slay them himself. Gideon slew Zebah and Zalmunna without further delay. **And took away the ornaments that were on their camels' necks.** The collars of the camels had metal, moon-shaped ornaments (Hebrew *śaharon)* attached to them. The word is related to the Aramaic and Syriac word for "moon" *(śahar)*. Such ornaments were also worn by men (8:26) and women (Isa 3:18). They were doubtless originally amulets used to bring good luck or ward off evil spirits.

22. Rule thou over us, both thou, and thy son. Gideon had proved himself a man endued with the spirit of God in bringing victory over the Midianites. His people were ready to make him king. This is the first recorded attempt to establish a hereditary monarchy in Israel. Gideon's refusal is consistent with his recognition of the kingship of the Lord, the theocratic ideal stressed throughout the Book of Judges.

24. Give me every man the earrings of his prey. Having refused the kingdom, Gideon made a request for himself. He asked the warriors to give him the rings they had taken from the fallen Midianites. **27. And Gideon made an ephod thereof.** About seventy pounds of gold was thus provided (8:26), and this was fashioned into an **ephod.** The exact nature of the ephod is uncertain. It was the name given to a part of the attire of the high priest (Ex 28:4). On occasion it was consulted as a source of divine guidance (I Sam 23:9-12; 30:7,8). Perhaps for this reason it developed into an object of idolatry. It is possible that Gideon had an idol made, wearing an ephod similar to that worn by the high priests. **And all Israel went thither a whoring after it.** Gideon's ephod became an object of idolatry. Its erection marks the tragic end of the career of a truly great man. Gideon and his family suffered as a result of it. In 9:5 we read of the death of most of Gideon's sons because of the desire of one, Abimelech, to be king. This tragedy may be traced to the idolatry that resulted from the construction of Gideon's ephod.

28. And the country was in quietness forty years. The victory over the Midianites brought about a generation of peace for the Israelites. **29. And Jerubbaal, the son of Joash, went and dwelt in his own house.** Gideon appears to have retired from his active pursuits a number of years before his death. **31. And his concubine that was in Shechem, she also**

bore him a son. In addition to the seventy sons of his wives, mention is made of Abimelech, the son of a concubine, because of the attempt he was to make, after the death of Gideon, to have himself recognized as Israel's king (9:1 ff.).

33. The children of Israel turned again . . . and made Baal-berith their God. A specific Baal is mentioned as the object of idolatry after the death of Gideon. **Baal-berith** had a shrine at Shechem (9:4). His name means *Lord of the covenant,* a possible reference to a confederation of city-states that looked to Shechem as their leader. The fact that Israel had entered into a *bᵉrît,* or covenant, with God at Sinai may have encouraged some to equate the Israelite with the Canaanite *bᵉrît*. Scripture makes it clear, however, that men cannot make such an equation without incurring the wrath of Israel's God.

6) The Usurpation of Abimelech. 9:1-57.

1. And Abimelech . . . went to Shechem unto his mother's brethren. As the son of a concubine, Abimelech was considered a part of the family of his mother. Among the early Arabians, a concubine or secondary 'wife' stayed with her own clan and was visited by her 'husband' from time to time. The children of the union belonged to the wife's clan. Abimelech, the son of a concubine, had close relations with the family of his mother. He sought their help in supporting his claims to the throne. **2. Remember also that I am your bone and your flesh.** Abimelech implied that all of the sons of Gideon were ambitious to rule. Dissention among them would certainly have harmful consequences for the people subject to them. It would be best to dispose of them all, said Abimelech, in favor of his own rule. Since his mother was from Shechem, he could claim a blood kinship with the Shechemites. Thus he appealed to local pride in the suggestion that he be named ruler.

3. They said, He is our brother. The men of Shechem were convinced that their loyalty should be expressed toward Abimelech. **4. And they gave him . . . silver out of the house of Baal-berith.** In antiquity, temples were frequently the centers of great wealth. People brought gifts to the temples, and public funds were frequently kept there for safekeeping. The seventy pieces of silver given to Abimelech was not a large sum, but it represented the backing of the men of Shechem for Abimelech's cause. **Abimelech hired vain and light fellows** (AV, *persons)* Abimelech found a group of scoundrels who were willing to do anything for a little silver.

5. And he went unto . . . Ophrah, and slew his brethren. Only Jotham, Gideon's youngest son, escaped the carnage. The detail that they were killed **upon one stone** suggests a parallel to animals offered in sacrifice on a stone altar. The brethren were not slain in battle, but were formally executed.

6. And all the men of Shechem . . . and all the house of Millo . . . made Abimelech king. Millo may be the name of the citadel, or fortress, at Shechem. We should probably read *Beth Millo,* for the **house of Millo. By the plain of the pillar that was in Shechem.** It was appropriate that Abimelech be proclaimed king at a spot with religious associations. The coronation took place *by the terebinth of the pillar*. Jacob had buried the idols which his family had gathered under a tree at Shechem (Gen 35:4), and there Joshua had set up a monument as a witness to the covenant between God and Israel (Josh 24:26).

7. And . . . Jotham . . . went and stood in the top of mount Gerizim. A triangular rock platform projects from the side of Gerizim, which forms a natural pulpit overlooking Shechem. The voice of a person speaking on Gerizim can be heard as far as Mount Ebal, across the valley in which Shechem is located. Jotham, the only surviving brother of Abimelech, chose this site as the spot from which he could address the men of Shechem.

8. The trees went forth . . . to anoint a king. Jotham chose to instruct the people by means of a parable. He sought to show that only base individuals desire to lord it over others. Those with worthwhile occupations are too busy to seek to become kings.

9. The olive tree said . . . Should I leave my fatness? Groves of olive trees flourish in the area around Shechem. Olive oil was used as an unguent on the skin and for ceremonial purposes when priests or kings were anointed. It was burned to provide illumination, and used as an article of food corresponding to our butter. The olive tree could not be persuaded to leave its important work in order to be a king. **11. The fig tree said . . . Should I forsake my sweetness?** The fig tree was the commonest fruit tree of Palestine. Figs were not a delicious luxury, as they are in some parts of the world, but one of the food staples of the country. **13. The vine said . . . Should I leave my wine, which cheereth God and man?** *'Ĕlōhîm* may be rendered **God** or *gods*. In this context Jotham appears to refer to religious libations offered to the gods, during which wine was poured either over the sacrifice or on the ground beside the altar. The grape was highly esteemed in Israel, as in the Mediterranean world in general. The vine could serve no higher function than to produce grapes. **15. The bramble said unto the trees . . . come and put your trust in my shadow.** As the last alternative, the trees approached the thorn bush, or bramble, which could be seen clinging to the rocks in the neighborhood of Shechem. The bramble ironically said, **Put your trust in my shadow**, an obvious absurdity. With a feeling of self-importance, it threatened to **devour the cedars of Lebanon** if the other trees did not accord it due deference. The dry thorn often was the starting place for destructive fires. Moore, in ICC notes, "Those who made the thorn king over them put themselves in this dilemma: if they were true to him, they enjoyed his protection, which was a mockery; if they were false to him, he would be their ruin."

16-20. If ye have done truly and sincerely . . . rejoice ye in Abimelech . . . but if not, let fire come out from Abimelech. Jotham made a pointed application to his parable. The men of Shechem may have felt that they had done well in forgetting all that Gideon had done for them and supporting the murderer of his sons. If so, Jotham said, "Much happiness may you have in this bramble-king of yours." (Moore) However, Jotham warned, such may not have been the case. Not only would this bramble-king prove destructive to the men of Shechem, but the men, in turn, would **devour Abimelech. 21. And Jotham . . . went to Beer.** Jotham managed to escape beyond the reach of Abimelech's vengeance. **Beer** means *well*, and there were many places in Palestine bearing that name. Some commentators suggest Beer-sheba as the place of retreat. El-Bireh, between Shechem and Jerusalem, is another possibility.

23. God sent an evil spirit between Abimelech and the men of Shechem. When Abimelech had reigned three years, he and the men of Shechem developed a spirit of animosity one to the other. The Scripture often accounts for such attitudes by the working of God in human affairs (cf. I Sam 16:14; I Kgs 22:21). The principle of divine retribution is evident throughout the Book of Judges. Here we are told how Abimelech fell prey to treachery, even as he had treacherously killed his brothers. **25. And the men of Shechem set liers-in-wait for him in the top of the mountains.** The ambush established by the men of Shechem would have successfully deprived Abimelech of tribute and other tolls that he might have collected from caravans using the important routes through Shechem.

28. And Gaal . . . said, Who is Abimelech . . . ? In the celebration of the vintage, Gaal led the Shechemites in cursing Abimelech and fomenting rebellion against his rule. He spoke as a Canaanite rather than as an Israelite, urging the people to **serve the men of Hamor the father of Shechem** (cf. Gen 33:19). He thus urged the people to reject the "modern" Israelite rule of the house of Gideon and revive the ancient Shechemite aristocracy.

31. They fortify the city against thee. Zebul warned Abimelech of the activities of the rebels. Instead of **fortify**, however, read *incite*, with the RSV. Abimelech evidently had appointed Zebul as governor of Shechem while he, personally, dwelt at Arumah (9:41). Where the AV reads that Zebul sent messengers **privily**, the JPS version reads *in Tormah*, which is another form of the place name, Arumah. **34. And Abimelech rose up . . . and they laid wait against Shechem in four companies.** Abimelech took Zebul's advice and organized his forces to end the rebellion of Gaal (cf. 7:16; I Sam 11:11; 13:17).

36. Behold, there come people down from the top of the mountains. When Gaal saw the movement of men in the mountains, he spoke of it to Zebul, who mocked him for thinking the shadows of the mountain to be men. Zebul implied that Gaal was frightened as the result of a guilty conscience. **37. See there come people down by the middle of the land, and another company come along by the plain of Meonenim.** The first company appeared to come from the **middle**, literally *the navel*, of the land. This was doubtless the central hill in the district. Another came from **Elon-meonenim**, meaning *the terebinth of the diviners*. This may be equated with the terebinth of verse 6.

38. Where is now thy mouth? Zebul now openly taunted Gaal for his boastful renunciation of Abimelech. **39. And Gaal went out before the men of Shechem, and fought with Abimelech.** Gaal rallied his forces, but it was too late to repulse Abimelech. **41. And Zebul thrust out Gaal and his brethren.** The revolt of Gaal was ended and its leader expelled from Shechem. Gaal doubtless became a scapegoat for the Shechemites, who would have blamed him for the unsuccessful revolt.

43. And he [Abimelech] **rose up against them, and smote them.** As the Shechemites left their city, Abimelech personally directed his forces against them. It is not clear whether the men of Shechem were going out to their field for normal agricultural pursuits or on missions of plunder, as in 9:25. **45. And Abimelech . . . took the city, and slew the people . . . therein.** Abimelech showed no mercy to the men of Shechem. To make sure that no trouble would ever again come from that source, he **beat down the city, and sowed it with salt.** Salt ground, in Hebrew, is equivalent to desert. It was Abimelech's purpose to render the very soil of Shechem sterile. Nevertheless, Shechem became an important center during the days of the Israelite kingdom (I Kgs 12:1). It was rebuilt and fortified by Jeroboam (I Kgs 12:25).

46. And . . . the men of the tower of Shechem . . . entered into an hold of the house of the god Berith. Shechem was a walled city, with an outlying tower that served as additional defense. The god **Berith**, or *El-Berith*, is to be identified with Baal-berith (9:4). Since his temple was located near the tower, the men of the tower fled to the temple for refuge. **48,49. And Abimelech . . . and all the people that were with him . . . . cut down every man his bough.** Abimelech decided to burn down the temple that served as a stronghold for the men of the tower of Shechem. He ordered his men to follow him to a near-by mountain, where they cut down branches from trees to serve as kindling wood for the burning of the temple. About a thousand men and women perished in the flames.

50. Then went Abimelech to Thebez. Thebez may be modern Tubas, situated about thirteen miles north of Shechem. The inhabitants of Thebez probably had joined in the revolt that centered in Shechem. **51. But there was a strong tower within the city.** The tower of Shechem was outside the city, that of Thebez, within. After Abimelech took the city, he had to take the stronghold within it.

53. And a certain woman cast a piece of a millstone upon Abimelech's head. The victorious Abimelech was suddenly stopped by a woman. Her weapon was the upper, movable stone of a hand mill. Such stones were eight to ten inches long and several inches thick. Hurled from the height of the tower, this **piece of a millstone** proved an effective weapon. **54. Draw thy sword, and slay me.** A warrior's honor demanded that he die in battle like a man. Death at the hands of a woman was regarded as utter disgrace. Abimelech asked his armor-bearer to slay him, which the young man did.

55. And when the men of Israel saw that Abimelech was dead, they departed every man unto his place. The army of Abimelech is designated as **the men of Israel.** The rebellion of the Shechemites can be interpreted as a Canaanite rebellion against the Israelites. Although Abimelech had initially gained his rule on the basis of the support of the men of Shechem, his relationship to Gideon made him acceptable to many in Israel. The Shechemite support of Gaal may be considered as a nationalistic movement with anti-Israelite overtones.

57. And all the evil of the men of Shechem did God render upon their heads. Both the destruction of Shechem and the death of Abimelech are interpreted as just punishment for the crimes perpetrated against Gideon's family. **Upon them came the curse of Jotham.** Compare 9:20. The men of both Shechem and Abimelech were "devoured" as Jotham had prophesied.

7) Tola's Judgeship over Israel. 10:1,2.

1. And after Abimelech there arose to defend Israel Tola the Son of Puah. Tola was one of the minor Judges of whom we know little. His mission, like that of the other Judges, was *to save (lᵉhôshîaʿ)* Israel. A son of Issachar bore the name of **Tola** (Gen 46:13). He is mentioned as the founder of a clan (Num 26:23). **Tola** and **Puah** seem to have been common names in the tribe of Issachar. **He dwelt in Shamir in mount Ephraim.** There was another Shamir in Judah (Josh 15:48). This Shamir was probably in the neighborhood of Jezreel.

8) Jair's Judgeship. 10:3-5.

10:3. And after him arose Jair, a Gileadite. Jair was the name of one of Manasseh's sons (Num 32:41), and the Judge came from the tribe of Manasseh. **4. And he had thirty sons that rode on thirty ass colts.** This is mentioned as an indication of the rank and prominence of the sons. The ass was highly esteemed as a riding beast (Jud 1:14; I Sam 25:20). **And they had thirty cities, which are called Havoth-jair.** The *hawwōt* were originally groups of Bedouin tents. The term came to be applied to more permanent settlements. Each of Jair's sons was associated with a Gileadite village that bore the name of Jair. **5. And Jair died and was buried in Camon.** Camon may be modern Kumem, east of the Jordan, between the Jarmuk and the Jabbok.

9) Ammonite Oppression Ended by Jephthah. 10:6–11:40.

6. And the children of Israel did evil . . . and served Baalim. Contact with surrounding nations brought to Israel the temptation to adopt the social and religious customs of their neighbors. The Baalim and the Ashtaroth had been a recurring temptation (cf. 2:11,13). Now mention is made of numerous other gods: **the gods of Syria** (including Hadad or Rimmon); **the gods of Zidon,** particularly the Phoenician Baal, whose worship rivaled that of Israel's God in the days of Ahab and Jezebel; **the gods of Moab** (including Chemosh); **the gods of the children of Ammon** (including Molech); and **the gods of the Philistines** (including Dagon and Baal-zeboul, renamed Baal-zebub).

7. And . . . the Lord . . . sold them into the hands of the Philistines, and into the hands of the children of Ammon. Mention of the Philistines and the Ammonites is introductory to the Samson story (13:1–16:31) as well as to the Judgeship of Jephthah (11:1-40). **8. They vexed and oppressed the children of Israel.** For eighteen years the Ammonites oppressed those Israelites settled in Gilead. **9. The children of Ammon passed over Jordan to fight also against Judah.** Like the Moabites, who earlier took the same route (3:12,13), the Ammonites made destructive raids into Judah.

10. We have sinned against thee. In their time of oppression the children of Israel acknowledged their sin against God. By worshiping Baalim, they had broken the covenant; and so they interpreted the power of their enemies as the chastening hand of God. **11,12. Did not I deliver you?** No doubt a prophet or some other spokesman was raised up by God to remind the people of past deliverances. Not only did God bring his people from Egypt, but he also delivered them **from the Amorites** (Num 21:21-35), **from the children of Ammon** (Jud 3:13), **from the Philistines** (Jud 3:31), **the Zidonians** (no specific reference, probably included in the oppression of Jabin, Jud 4:2,3), **the Amalekites** (allied with Eglon, Jud 3:13), **and the Maonites** (LXX, *Midianites;* no specific reference). **14. Go and cry unto the gods which ye have chosen.** Since Israel had rejected the Lord, His spokesman ironically urged them to look for help to the gods they had chosen to serve.

15. The children of Israel said unto the Lord, We have sinned. Confession of sin was the turning point for Israel. **Do thou unto us whatsoever seemeth good unto thee.** They threw themselves on the Lord's mercy. **16. And they put away the strange gods.** Confession of sin was accompanied by renunciation of the cause of offense. **And his soul was grieved for the misery of Israel.** God could no longer stand aloof and allow the enemy to oppress his people (cf. Isa 63:9 a).

17. Then the children of Ammon were gathered together and encamped in Gilead. And the children of Israel assembled themselves together and encamped in Mizpeh. The two armies confronted one another. Israel was at Mizpeh *(watchtower),* which may be the place where Jacob and Laban made their covenant (Gen 31:46-49). **18. What man is he that will begin to fight against the children of Ammon?** The Gileadites needed a leader to direct the campaign against their Ammonite oppressors. This forms an introduction to the story of Jephthah.

11:1. Now Jephthah the Gileadite was a mighty man of valour. The words describe him as a great warrior (cf. Gideon, 6:12; Kish, I Sam 9:1; Naaman, II Kgs 5:1). He was, however, **the son of an harlot,** which gave him inferior status within the family. **2.** (They) **thrust out Jephthah.** The legitimate sons of Gilead called Jephthah **the son of a strange woman,** and sought to have him disinherited. **3. Then Jephthah . . . dwelt in the land of Tob.** Tob was probably northeast of Gilead. Later the men of Tob were allied with the Ammonites in their war with David (II Sam 10:6-8). It was a kind of frontier district, where men like Jephthah could lead a lawless existence on the fringes of society. **And there were gathered vain men to Jephthah, and went out with him.** Jephthah and his companions were esteemed **vain** (*rêqîm,* "empty"), i.e., wild and reckless, in contrast to 'respectable' members of society.

5. The elders of Gilead went to fetch Jephthah. When war broke out between the Ammonites and the Gileadites, the latter thought of Jephthah as a potential leader. **7. Why are ye come unto me now when ye are in distress?** Jephthah reproached the delegation of Gileadites for not helping him in his time of need. They had cast him out, confident of their own prowess. Now they came to him, asking help. **8. Be our head over all the inhabitants of Gilead.** The men gave no answer to Jephthah's complaint, but they were ready to give him absolute power if he would help in the time of need. **11. Then Jephthah went with the elders of Gilead, and the people made him head.** After receiving the assurance that his sovereignty would be recognized after the removal of the Ammonite threat, Jephthah accepted the offered position. The choice was approved by the people (cf. Saul, I Sam 11:15; Rehoboam, I Kgs 12:1; Jeroboam, I Kgs 12:20).

12. And Jephthah sent messengers unto the king of the children of Ammon. As official leader of Gilead, Jephthah sent messengers to the Ammonite leaders to ask a reason for attacks on Israelite territory. **13. Because Israel took away my land when they came up out of Egypt.** The disputed territory was bounded by the Arnon on the south and the Jabbok on the north, and it extended westward to the Jordan. This land had been the kingdom of Sihon at the time of the entrance into Canaan, and Sihon had wrested it from Moab (Num 21:26). Ammonites and Moabites, who were confederate during the time of Jephthah, felt that they had a claim to this forfeited territory.

15. Israel took not away the land of Moab, nor the land of the children of Ammon. Jephthah rejected the charge. Israel had been careful to request permission of the kings of Edom and Moab before passing through their lands. Permission was not granted, and so Israel scrupulously avoided touching the borders of Edom and Moab. When Sihon, king of the Amorites, at Heshbon refused permission for Israel to pass through his country, however, a battle was fought at Jahaz. The God of Israel gave his people victory over Sihon, and "Israel possessed all the land of the Amorites" (v. 21).

24. Wilt not thou possess that which Chemosh thy god giveth thee to possess? Jephthah argued that a people should be expected to occupy territory given them by their god. One such method of assigning territory was through victories given by a people's god on the field of battle. The people of Chemosh would, of course, occupy the territory Chemosh had enabled them to conquer. Since Israel's God had given his people land by right of conquest, it was to be expected that they would occupy it. The Moabite Stone attributes the victories of Moab to the favor of Chemosh, and the victories of Israel over Moab to the anger of Chemosh. Strictly speaking, Milcom (or Molech) was the god of Ammon and Chemosh the god of Moab. Moab and Ammon, descended from the same father, Lot, had much in common; and both Jephthah and the Ammonite king treated them as one people. A confederacy may be the historical justification for this terminology. Jephthah's *ad hominem* argument does not mean that the Israelites of his day actually believed in the power of Chemosh. Considering his own background and his subsequent conduct, Jephthah himself may have had such concepts, however. There was a strong tendency to make the God of Israel merely one of the gods who should be recognized.

25. Art thou any . . . better than Balak? The Moabite king, Balak, did not contest Israel's possession of the lands north of the Arnon. Although he called in a soothsayer to pronounce a curse on Israel, Balak never ventured to meet Israel in battle. Did the present king of Ammon think himself better able than Balak to subdue Israel? **26. While Israel dwelt in Heshbon . . . and in Aroer.** Aroer, the southernmost city of Israel east of the Jordan, was located on the banks of the Arnon. Jephthah implied that the Moabites, by failing to make a claim at the time Israel occupied the kingdom of Sihon, tacitly recognized that the territory was not theirs. **27. The Lord the Judge be judge this day between the children of Israel and the children of Ammon.** Jephthah summarized his defense. Israel had done no wrong. For three centuries (a round number), the right of Israel to its Trans-Jordanian cities had been recognized. If Ammon now insisted on battle, the outcome could be left in the hands of Israel's God.

29. Then the Spirit of the Lord came upon Jephthah. Jephthah was not a mere opportunist. He was empowered by God to lead the Gileadites to victory over their oppressors. We read of a series of journeys made by Jephthah. He **passed on to Mizpah of Gilead** (RSV), where the Israelite camp was located, and then moved against the Ammonites. **30. And Jephthah vowed a vow unto the Lord.** The form taken by Jephthah's vow is reminiscent of his half-heathen background. He vowed to offer as a burnt offering whatever first came out of the door of his house to meet him when he returned as victor from the Ammonite war. **33. And he smote them from Aroer, even till thou come to Minnith, even twenty cities.** Jephthah was victorious in his campaign. This **Aroer** is not the town on the Arnon (v. 26) but another town of the same name, east of Rabbath-ammon (Josh 13:25). **The plain of the vineyards** is a place name, *'Abēl k^e^rāmîm.*

34. And, behold, his daughter came out to meet him. Perhaps Jephthah expected a servant to appear first. The remembrance of his vow and the sight of his daughter changed the joy of the victor to the sorrow of a father about to lose his only child. **35. I have opened my mouth unto the Lord, and I cannot go back.** To Jephthah the vow was sacred, and it had to be carried out. Human sacrifices were forbidden in Israel, but Jephthah had lived on the fringes of society, where heathen ideas prevailed.

37. Let me alone two months. Jephthah's daughter submitted to the demands of the vow without flinching. She requested a two-month period during which she might **bewail** [her] **virginity** with her companions. She regarded her coming death as a double tragedy: Not only was she to become a burnt offering, but she must die childless, not having been married. **39. She returned unto her father, who did with her according to his vow.** After the two-month period, Jephthah fulfilled his vow. Although some commentators suggest that her perpetual virginity would have been a fulfillment of the vow, the text seems to leave no doubt that Jephthah's daughter died at the hands of her father.

10) War Between the Gileadites and the Ephraimites. 12:1-7.

12:1. And the men of Ephraim gathered themselves together. As the Ephraimites had resented Gideon's apparent neglect of them (8:1), so they were offended that Jephthah had apparently neglected them in his battle with the Ammonites. They assembled and crossed the Jordan, going toward Zaphon (AV, *northward)*, a place on the east side of the Jordan, near Succoth. In a hostile spirit they demanded that Jephthah account for his failure to enlist their aid. **2. When I called you, ye delivered me not out of their hands.** Jephthah insisted that he had asked help of the Ephraimites to meet the Ammonite oppressions, but that they had failed to respond.

4. Then Jephthah gathered together all the men of Gilead. They had been dismissed after the victory over Ammon, but the threat of civil war was justification for a fresh call to arms. **Ye Gileadites are fugitives of Ephraim.** The taunt of the Ephraimites has been variously interpreted. It suggests that the tribes in the Trans-Jordan area—those that traced their descent from Joseph—were deserters from Ephraim and Manasseh.

5. And the Gileadites took the passages of Jordan. The Gileadites succeeded in defeating the Ephraimites and seizing the Jordan fords in order to prevent their escape. **6. Say now Shibboleth.** The word **shibboleth** *(an ear of corn)* served as a password because it contained a consonant which was not pronounced in the Ephraimite dialect. The Ephraimites pronounced the word *sibboleth* and thus identified themselves to the Gileadites. The existence of distinct dialects of Hebrew during the period of the Judges is consistent with the concept of tribal rather than national consciousness that appears throughout the book.

7. And Jephthah judged Israel six years. Six eventful years ended with Jephthah's death. The place of his burial is not definitely known. The Hebrew text simply reads, *He was buried in the cities of Gilead.* Some manuscripts of the LXX read *Mizpeh of Gilead.*

11) Judgeship of Ibzan. 12:8-10.

8. And after him Ibzan of Bethlehem judged Israel. The only things told concerning **Ibzan** are the places of his birth and burial and the size of his family. Bethlehem in Judah is probably meant, although many commentators suggest Bethlehem in Zebulun, about seven miles west-northwest of Nazareth. Ibzan seems to have made it a practice to strengthen his political ties by marrying his children into families at a distance from Bethlehem.

12) Elon's Judgeship. 12:11,12.

11. And after him Elon, a Zebulonite, judged Israel. Only the name of the Judge, his birthplace, burial place, and the length of his rule are given. The consonants of **Aijalon** (v. 12), the vocalized reading of Elon's burial place, are identical with the name of the Judge. The place may simply have been named Elon. Its location is not known.

13) Abdon's Judgeship. 12:13-15.

13. And after him Abdon the son of Hillel. Abdon is termed a Pirathonite, i.e., a resident of Pirathon in Ephraim, probably Fer'ata, six miles southwest of Shechem. He is known for his family of forty sons and thirty grandsons (AV, *nephews*), who rode on seventy saddle asses. As noted in 10:4, this was a mark of high rank. **15.** His burial took place **in the hill country of the Amalekites,** a name suggestive of Amalekite occupation (cf. 3:13; 5:14).

14) Samson and the Philistines. 13:1—16:31.

13:1. And the children of Israel did evil again in the sight of the Lord. The recurring idolatry forms the setting for a period of oppression by the Philistines which lasted a full generation (forty years). The career of Samson belongs to this time.

2. And there was a certain man of Zorah, of the family of the Danites, whose name was Manoah. Zorah was a border city between Dan and Judah, seventeen miles west of Jerusalem. Manoah and his wife had not been blessed with a child, which was an occasion of grief to them. **3. And the angel of the Lord appeared unto the woman.** The wife of Manoah received an angelic annunciation. In Scripture such annunciations are associated with the births of important personages, notably, Isaac and John the Baptist. **5. Thou shalt conceive . . . . the child shall be a Nazarite.** Special precautions had to be taken concerning the mother's diet. Numbers 6:2-21 prescribes the laws for the Nazarite. Regarded as dedicated to God, he must be kept pure of possible defilement. **He shall begin to deliver Israel out of the hand of the Philistines.** Other Judges would bring about complete deliverance. The promised child would **begin to deliver.** The Philistine threat continued until the time of David.

6. His countenance was like the countenance of an angel of God, very terrible. The angelic messenger inspired awe and reverence, not terror. **8. Let the man of God . . . come again unto us.** When Manoah received the report of the annunciation to his wife, he desired further instruction concerning the treatment to be accorded the child to be born.

15. Let us detain thee until we shall have made ready a kid. The angel reappeared to Manoah's wife, who sought her husband, and both heard substantially the same directions concerning the care of the child. Manoah sought to detain the stranger in order to show him proper hospitality. **16. Though thou detain me, I will not eat of thy bread.** In 6:18-22, Gideon prepared food for one whom he later recognized as the Angel of the Lord. The food was then converted into an offering. Here the Angel tells Manoah that he will not eat, and that burnt offerings must be made to the Lord. **17. What is thy name?** Manoah asked his strange guest his name, in order that he might subsequently accord it due honor. **18. Why askest thou thus after my name, seeing it is secret?** (AV marg., *wonderful)* The Angel declared that his name was ineffable, beyond human capacity to hear and understand.

19. So Manoah took a kid with a meat offering, and offered it upon a rock unto the Lord: and the angel did wonderously. A burnt offering and a meal offering were offered unto the Lord. Manoah and his wife watched the angel as he "did wonderously." **20. The angel of the Lord ascended in the flame of the altar.** As the smoke of the sacrifice ascended heavenward, the Angel seemed to mount up with it until Manoah and his wife could no longer see him.

21. Then Manoah knew that he was an angel of the Lord. Read *the* angel of the Lord. Manoah may have had some question concerning this mysterious visitor, but the peculiar ascent with the flame from the altar provided positive identification. **22. We shall surely die, because we have seen God.** Cf. Gideon's similar reaction (6:22). **23. If the Lord were pleased to kill us, he would not have received a burnt-offering and a meat-offering at our hands.** The acceptance of the sacrifice and the strange announcement were evidence that God was not ill-disposed toward Manoah and his wife.

24. And the woman bare a son, and called his name Samson. The words of the Angel came true. A son was born and named **Samson,** meaning *sun.* Just across the valley from Manoah's home was Beth-shemesh, the shrine town of the sun-god. Although Manoah was not an idolator, he may have given his son a name that was common in the community. **25. And the Spirit of the Lord began to move him at times in the camp of Dan between Zorah and Eshtaol.** Samson became a leader endued with the Holy Spirit. The place of his activity was the Valley of Sorek.

14:1. And Samson went down to Timnath. Timnath was located about three miles southwest of Beth-shemesh, on the border of Judah's territory. At this time it seems to have been occupied by the Philistines, for Samson decided that he wanted to marry a Philistine girl whom he met in Timnath. **2. Get her for me to wife.** Marriages were negotiated by the parents (cf. Gen 21:21). 3. Manoah was disturbed that his son should ask to marry a Philistine girl, but Samson insisted that he wanted to marry the young lady of his choice: **Get her for me; for she pleaseth me well.**

4. It was of the Lord. The sacred historian views the demand of Samson in the light of its results. Samson's parents could not foresee that their son's desire to marry a woman of the "uncircumcised Philistines" would actually result in the destruction of many of Israel's enemies. The words, **he sought an occasion against the Philistines,** may refer to God or Samson. In view of the theological nature of the earlier statement, it seems best to take this as a statement that God, through Samson's proposed marriage, was seeking to bring about the defeat of the Philistines.

5. Behold, a young lion roared against him. Samson was on his way back to Timnath, with his parents, when a full-grown lion cub attacked him. With his bare hands, Samson tore the lion limb from limb. The source of this physical strength, according to the Scripture, was the Spirit of the Lord, who empowered the young man in the emergency. **8. He turned aside to see the carcase of the lion.** On another trip along the same road, Samson observed that there was a swarm of bees and some honey in the carcass of the lion. Bees will not approach a putrid carcass. In a hot, dry climate, however, the moisture may be dried from a dead body in a very short time. The lion's carcass had quickly dried up, and when Samson next passed along the road, it already contained a hive of bees, with their honey. **9. And he took thereof in his hands.** Read rather, *He scraped it out into his hands.* That was a violation of the Nazarite code, which forbade contact with a carcass. This may be the reason why Samson did not tell his parents where he found the honey.

10. And Samson made there a feast. He made the feast at the bride's home. Samson's father was present, but the other guests were all Philistines.

12. I will now put forth a riddle unto you. Riddles served as a form of entertainment. At a later time, the queen of Sheba came to test Solomon's wisdom with riddles (I Kgs 10:1). In this case, Samson limited the time for solving the riddle to the week of wedding festivities. As a wager, he offered to provide thirty linen garments *(sādîn)* and thirty festive garments *(ḥălîpâ),* one for each of the companions, if the men could solve his riddle. If they failed to do so, they were expected to give him the same. The *sādîn* was a garment made of fine linen, rectangular in shape, which was worn as an undergarment next to the skin or as an outer robe to cover other clothing. The *ḥălîpâ* was a garment worn on festive occasions instead of everyday clothing. **14. Out of the eater came forth meat, and out of the strong came forth sweetness. Meat** is used in the sense of "food." The RSV renders it:

> "Out of the eater came something to eat.
> Out of the strong came something sweet."

Without the clue of the slain lion and the swarm of bees, the guests could not solve Samson's riddle.

15. Entice thy husband, that he may declare unto us the riddle. The Philistines appealed to their countrywoman, Samson's wife, to find the secret. They made it clear that failure to come to their aid would result in her death by burning. In 15:6 such a burning is carried out. **17. She wept before him the seven days.** According to the Hebrew text the Philistines tried to solve the riddle in three days (v. 14), appealed to Samson's wife on the seventh day (v. 15), and she "wept before him the seven days" (v. 17). The LXX and Syriac versions place the appeal to Samson's wife on the fourth day. Rashi suggested that the **seven days** actually meant the days of the week that remained. **On the seventh day . . . he told her.** The entreaty and tears so weakened Samson that he told his wife the answer to the riddle. **18. If ye had not ploughed with my heifer, ye had not found out my riddle.** The use of the term **heifer** was a scornful allusion to the wife who had betrayed her husband's secret.

19. He went down to Ashkelon, and slew thirty men of them, and took their spoil, and gave changes of garments unto them which expounded the riddle. Samson paid his 'companions' with garments taken from thirty men whom he killed in Ashkelon, twenty-three miles away on the Mediterranean coast. Thereupon Samson **went up to his father's house.** The wedding festivities lasted for seven days, but the marriage itself was not consummated until the seventh day. On the day on which it was to have been consummated, Samson's companions presented the solution to his riddle, which proved their complicity with his wife. Samson, thereupon, returned home to Timnath without consummating the marriage. **20. But Samson's wife was given to his companion.** Samson's flight left the bride without a husband to consummate the marriage, which would have disgraced the girl. The marriage was consummated, however, with Samson's **companion** or "best man" taking the bride.

15:1. Samson visited his wife. Samson, bringing a kid as a present, visited his wife when his anger had abated. Her father, however, would not allow the young man to enter the inner chamber, and informed him that the girl had been given to the best man. He offered Samson the younger sister of his 'wife,' with the added suggestion that she was the fairer of the two. **4. And Samson went and caught three hundred foxes.** Feeling himself justified in taking vengeance on the Philistines, Samson caught three hundred foxes (or jackals; the two animals are frequently confused), joined them in pairs by their tails, and tied to the tails torches saturated with oil. Then he lighted the torches with fire and released the foxes into the Philistines' grain fields. The result was destruction to the grain and to the olive orchards of the Philistines. **6. And the Philistines came up, and burnt her and her father with fire.** The Philistines placed the blame for the outrage on Samson's wife and her family, and retaliated accordingly.

7. Though ye have done this, yet will I be avenged of you. The destruction of the family of Samson's wife was not a proper recompence to Samson. **8. And he smote them hip and thigh with a great slaughter.** The idiom, literally *leg on thigh,* apparently means a complete overthrow. On Babylonian cylinder seals, Gilgamesh is represented as using this device in wrestling. **He went down and dwelt in the top of the rock Etam.** This was probably located near the town of Etam in Judah, about two miles southwest of Bethlehem.

9. Then the Philistines went up. From the Philistine Plain the Philistines **went up** to the Judean highlands in search of Samson, that they might punish him.

11. Then three thousand men of Judah . . . said to Samson, Knowest thou not that the Philistines are rulers over us? Samson was a Danite, and the men of the tribe of Judah felt no obligation to protect him. The fact that **three thousand men** were sent to Samson is an indirect tribute to his reputation for strength. Judah recognized that the Philistines held the country tributary, and resented the acts of Samson, which were in the nature of rebellion. **12. We are come down to bind thee.** The men of Judah felt an obligation to their Philistine overlords to capture Samson and turn him over to them. Samson did not resist their purpose to deliver him to the Philistines, but he asked them to swear that they would not personally attack him. If they had attacked him, Samson would have had to defend himself, and in so doing he would have had to shed the blood of Israelites. Though Samson had no scruples about killing Philistines, he did not wish to kill his fellow Israelites.

13. And they bound him with two new cords. When the men of Judah pledged that they would not personally attack Samson, he permitted himself to be bound. The **new cords** were chosen for their strength. It would not have been thought expedient to bind Samson with cords that had been used before, or that were old and brittle. **14. And when he came unto Lehi, the Philistines shouted. Lehi** was occupied by the Philistines. The men of Judah took their prisoner there, and the Philistines rejoiced at the sight of their assailant being brought to them in fetters. While Samson's enemies were shouting in triumph, **the Spirit of the Lord came mightily upon** the captive, and he broke the cords that bound him. For him they seemed as easy to break as flax that has caught fire.

15. And he found a new jawbone of an ass...and took it and slew a thousand men therewith. The moment of Philistine triumph was turned into one of disaster. Samson grabbed the first weapon at hand, a new (literally, *fresh)* jawbone of an ass. With it he attacked his enemies and slew a thousand of them. **16. With the jawbone of an ass, heaps upon heaps.** Samson's song of triumph is in the form of poetry. The day of Philistine victory had been turned into a victory for the Israelite champion. Since he was alone in the conquest, he had to compose and sing his own song of triumph. **17. He . . . called that place Ramath-lehi;** i.e., *the hill of the jawbone.*

18. And he was sore athirst. After the exertion of killing a thousand Philistines, Samson grew thirsty; and he felt that his weakened condition would make him a prey for the other Philistines, who would seek to avenge the death of their countrymen. In his distress he called upon the Lord. **19. But God clave an hollow place . . . and there came water thereout.** The noun *maktēsh,* translated **hollow place,** denotes a round, deep basin. It was used for a "mortar" (cf. Prov 27:22). In this **hollow place** God caused water to spring forth as a means of quenching the thirst of Samson. **He called the name thereof En-hakkore.** *The Spring of the Caller* was the name given to a spring in the vicinity of Lehi at the time the book of Judges was written. *Qôrē',* "the caller," is the Hebrew name for the partridge. The spring may have been known as "Partridge Spring" as well as "Spring of the Caller."

20. And he judged Israel in the days of the Philistines twenty years. This forms a conclusion to the story of Samson's victory over the Philistines at Lehi. The fact is mentioned again in 16:31.

16:1. Then went Samson to Gaza and saw there an harlot. Samson's physical strength had as its counterpart his moral weakness. At Gaza, in the Philistine country, two miles from the Mediterranean coast, Samson fell under the control of another evil woman. **2. And it was told the Gazites.** The men of Gaza learned that their enemy was somewhere within the city. They did not attempt to search the city by night in order to find him, but they set a watch and determined to kill him in the morning. **3. And Samson . . . arose at midnight, and took the doors of the gate of the city . . . and carried them up to the top of an hill that is before Hebron.** Here again stress is placed on the physical prowess of Samson. He was able to lift the gates of the city, with their posts and the bar which fastened them, and carry them forty miles, to the vicinity of Hebron.

4. He loved a woman in the valley of Sorek, whose name was Delilah. This is the final episode in the life of the mighty Samson. Again he was in love with a Philistine woman. Much of Samson's life was spent in the Valley of Sorek, now known as the Wadi es-Surar, which starts fifteen miles west of Jerusalem and runs toward the coastal plain.

5. Entice him, and see wherein his great strength lieth. The Philistine leaders saw an opportunity to gain an advantage over Samson through his affair with Delilah. They requested her to discover, literally, *by what means his strength is great.* If she could tell them the means whereby Samson could be humbled, each of the lords of the Philistines promised to pay Delilah eleven hundred pieces of silver.

6. And Delilah said . . . Tell me, I pray thee, wherein thy great strength lieth. Three times she asked the question and three times Samson gave wrong answers. In his first answer Samson said, **If they bind me with seven green withs that were never dried, then shall I be weak, and be as another man** (v. 7). Thereupon, either while he was sleeping or in playfulness, Delilah bound him with the fresh bowstrings (AV, *green withs)* provided by the Philistines. **9. The Philistines be upon thee, Samson.** In the inner room of the house were Philistines, ready at the call of Delilah to take Samson. After he was securely bound, Delilah uttered the words, **The Philistines be upon thee, Samson;** whereupon Samson **brake the withs,** as **a thread of tow is broken when it toucheth the fire.** The bowstrings were broken, and the secret of Samson's strength was still undisclosed. It is presupposed in the subsequent parts of the story that the Philistines did not rush upon Samson at the word of Delilah. They appear to have waited to see whether or not the cords held.

10. And Delilah said . . . Behold, thou hast mocked me. Delilah pretended to be hurt at Samson's failure to tell her the truth. Urging him again to give the secret of his strength, she drew from him a second explanation: **If they bind me fast with new ropes that never were occupied, then shall I be weak, and be as another man** (v. 11). The pattern was repeated. Delilah bound him with new ropes, and cried out, **The Philistines be upon thee, Samson** (v. 12). Again, however, Samson showed his power, for **he brake them from off his arms like a thread.**

13. And Delilah said . . . Hitherto thou hast mocked me, and told me lies. A third time, however, Samson gave an erroneous answer. He said, **If thou weavest the seven locks of my head with the web . . .** Then, it is presumed (although not expressed in the text), Samson would be rendered weak like other men. Thereupon Delilah fastened her piece of weaving in the loom and began to weave Samson's hair into her work as she would have done with ordinary threads. In this instance Samson was approaching the truth, for the loss of his hair would have resulted in the loss of his strength. When, however, Delilah said, **The Philistines be upon thee, Samson** (v. 14), Samson awakened from sleep and, as he arose from the couch, he pulled the posts of the loom out of the ground by the hair of his head, which was still fastened in the loom.

15. And she said . . . How oanst thou say, I love thee, when thine heart is not with me? Delilah **pressed him daily with her words** (v. 16), insisting that if there were real affection between the two, there would be no reluctance to divulge secrets. **17. He told her all his heart.** Samson explained the Nazarite vow (cf. Num 6:2-21) and declared plainly, **If I be shaven, then my strength will go from me, and I shall become weak, and be like any other man.** Thereupon Delilah called for her Philistine companions. While Samson was asleep on Delilah's knees, one of the Philistines shaved off his seven locks. A fourth time Delilah cried out, **The Philistines be upon thee, Samson** (v. 20), but this time the Israelite strong man was powerless before his enemies. It is part of the tragedy of the story that **he wist not that the Lord was departed from him.**

21. But the Philistines took him, and put out his eyes, and brought him down to Gaza, and bound him with fetters of brass; and he did grind in the prison house. The Philistines mutilated their enemy by blinding him. Then they chained him to the mill in the prison-house, where he was forced to perform menial labor. While he was in the prison, however, **the hair of his head began to grow again.** The process was slow, but it meant that Samson's strength would ultimately be restored.

23. Then the lords of the Philistines gathered . . . to offer a great sacrifice to Dagon their god. Dagon is known to have been one of the gods of the Canaanite pantheon at Ugarit. He was adopted by the Philistines after their settlement in Palestine. They ascribe their victory over Samson to the power of Dagon (v. 24). **25. Call for Samson, that he may make us sport.** While the Philistines were celebrating, Samson was grinding at the mill. In the midst of the merriment, however, they asked that Samson be brought to the temple, probably in order that they might gloat over his humbled condition.

26. Suffer me that I may feel the pillars. Samson was brought into the temple. There he requested permission of the youth who was guiding him to **lean upon** the pillars that held up the temple roof. In the design of the temple, two middle columns supported the roof of the hall where the more distinguished people were assembled. The hall opened to a great court. The crowds would sit or stand on the roof above the hall; from there they could overlook the great court where Samson was forced to provide entertainment. On his request, Samson was led from the court to the supporting pillars of the adjacent hall. If these pillars should be removed, the crowd on the roof would come crashing down on the heads of the dignitaries below, killing many from both groups.

28. And Samson called unto the Lord. Scripture does not present Samson as a model of piety. His downfall is attributed, in the Bible, to his sinfulness. Yet the humiliation he experienced at the hands of the Philistines seems to have made him conscious of his God-given mission. Even here, however, his prayer was for vengeance on the Philistines because of the loss of his eyes. **30. And Samson said, Let me die with the Philistines.** Exerting all his might, the strong man pushed on the two middle supporting pillars (v. 29) until they gave way, and the roof of the temple came crashing down. This brought about the death of the Philistine lords and nobles, and doubtless many of the 3,000 men and women spectators on the roof also died.

31. Then his brethren . . . took him . . . and buried him . . . in the burying place of Manoah his father. Samson had brought about the death of a host of the Philistines, Israel's inveterate enemy. He had not removed the Philistine threat, but he was honored for his peculiar accomplishments. His body was removed from Gaza and given honorable burial in the family burial plot. The Samson story concludes with the statement, **And he judged Israel twenty years** (cf. 15:20). The words may be loosely interpreted to mean that for about two decades he obtained security for Israel by keeping the Philistines from attacking the covenant people.

III. Lawless Conditions During the Period of the Judges. 17:1–21:25.

A. The Idolatry of Micah, and the Danite Migration. 17:1–19:31.

17:1. And there was a man of mount Ephraim, whose name was Micah. The chronology of the story of Micah is not certainly known. The account serves as a part of an appendix to the Book of Judges, preserving certain episodes that do not form a part of the history of the Judges, properly so called. Rabbinical commentators placed the story of Micah in the age of Othniel (3:8-11). Its position following the story of Samson is accounted for by the fact that it deals with Danites, the tribe from which Samson originated. **2. The eleven hundred shekels of silver that were taken from thee.** Micah had stolen eleven hundred pieces of silver from his mother. She, not realizing that her son was the thief, had pronounced a curse on the one who had taken the money. Micah doubtless feared the power of his mother's curse, and so confessed that he had the silver. The fact that the amount was **eleven hundred shekels of silver** has led some commentators to identify Micah's mother with Delilah (cf. 16:5). There is not sufficient evidence, however, to take this view seriously.

3. I had wholly dedicated the silver unto the Lord. Micah's mother determined that the money should be used for religious purposes. By so doing, she doubtless expected to avert the curse upon her son. She determined to make **a graven image and a molten image,** actually one image consisting of carved wood overlaid with silver. **5. And the man Micah had an house of gods.** The JPS version reads, *an house of God,* and the RSV renders, by way of interpretation, *a shrine.* Micah's mother provided the necessary silver; a **founder** (AV, v. 4) or *silversmith* (RSV), did the work; and Micah provided the shrine in which his idol was kept. To complete the equipment of the shrine, Micah **made an ephod, and teraphim, and consecrated one of his sons, who became his priest.** The **ephod** and **teraphim** served as additional idols (cf. 8:27; 18:24). **6. In those days there was no king in Israel.** These words serve as an explanation for the anarchy that allowed such irregularities to take place. The words imply that the author lived during the monarchy, when such lawlessness was not permitted.

7. And there was a young man out of Bethlehem-judah . . . who was a Levite, and he sojourned there. The young Levite from the area of Bethlehem in Judah was residing in the neighborhood of Micah, in Mount Ephraim. When Micah learned that the Levite was not employed (v. 9), he urged him to become his private family priest. He made an offer. **10. Dwell with me, and be unto me a father and a priest, and I will give thee ten shekels of silver by the year, and a suit of apparel, and thy victuals.** The Levite thought the offer a good one, and accepted it. **13. Then said Micah, Now know I that the Lord will do me good, seeing I have a Levite to my priest.** Micah had prepared for the externals of worship. He had his idols, his shrine, and a Levite employed and ordained as priest. Superstition, not faith, however, marked his attitudes toward life. The spiritual content of religion was completely lacking.

18:1. And in those days the tribe of the Danites sought them an inheritance to dwell in. The Danites, whose assigned land was occupied by the powerful Philistines, found themselves cramped for living space in the territory west of Judah. **2. And the children of Dan sent . . . five men . . . to spy out the land.** Five spies were sent in search of new territory that could be made a homeland for the Danites. On their way northward they came to the house of Micah in Mount Ephraim (17:1-13).

3. They knew the voice of the young man, the Levite. The Levite who was serving as Micah's priest had evidently met the Danite spies on some previous occasion. **5. Ask counsel, we pray thee, of God.** The Danites requested the Levite to ascertain the success of their mission.

They assumed that a priest with his ephod could serve as a kind of fortune-teller. **6. Go in peace: before the Lord is your way wherein ye go.** The Levite brought an encouraging report. He indicated that the expedition could expect the blessing of the Lord.

7. Then the five men . . . came to Laish. Laish, or Leshem, is the town at the north of the land occupied by the ancient Israelites. After it was conquered by the Danites, it became known as Dan. The spies found that Laish was a town with no strong internal government, far removed from the Phoenicians of Zidon, and having no treaties with neighboring tribes that might be expected to give the Danites trouble in the event of an attack.

9. Arise, that we may go up against them. The spies brought back a good report, suggesting that the Danites should possess Laish. **11. And there went from thence . . . six hundred men.** The Danite expedition included six hundred warriors, their wives, children, and possessions. **12. And they went up, and pitched in Kirjath-jearim. Kirjath-jearim** *(city of forests)* is a journey of two or three hours from Eshtaol. In the days of the conquest, Kirjath-jearim was one of the cities of the Gibeonite confederacy (Josh 9:17). The name of the Danite settlement near Kirjath-jearim was Mahaneh-dan *(the camp of Dan).*

13. And they . . . came unto the house of Micah. The five spies told the expedition about the Levite who served in the house of Micah and about the cult objects the Ephraimite had in his private shrine (v. 14). After giving the conventional greeting (v. 15), while the six hundred warriors stood by, the five men who had been spies entered the shrine and took the image, the ephod, and the teraphim (cf. 17:4,5). They then persuaded (or forced) the Levite to accompany them (18:19), assuring him that it was better to serve as priest to an entire tribe rather than to one family only. Having accomplished their mission at Micah's house, the Danites prepared to move on (v. 21).

22. The men that were in the houses near to Micah's house . . . overtook the children of Dan. Micah and his neighbors overtook the Danites and challenged them for stealing Micah's priest and cult objects. **25. Let not thy voice be heard . . . lest angry fellows run upon thee.** The Danites threatened the neighbors of Micah with death if they attempted to rescue the threatened cult objects. Micah and his companions were forced to return home without their stolen property (v. 26).

27. And they . . . came unto Laish, and they . . . burnt the city with fire. The Danites came upon the inhabitants of Laish, killed them with the sword, and burned their city. The distance of the city from Zidon, and its lack of allies rendered it defenseless (v. 28). The Danites subsequently rebuilt the city, named it Dan, and occupied it.

30. And the children of Dan set up the graven image. Micah's idol was set up in a shrine in the city of Dan. A line of priests who traced their origin to **Gershom, the son of Moses** officiated in the Danite sanctuary. The AV reading, *Gershom, the son of Manasseh,* is based on a scribal convention devised by the ancient scribes to remove the name of Moses from association with idolatry. Jonathan may have been the name of the Levite first mentioned in 17:7. The priesthood of Jonathan and his sons is said to have lasted **until the day of the captivity of the land.** On the basis of verse 31 the "captivity" is interpreted by some as a reference to the exile of the ark from Shiloh (I Sam 4:11). Others suggest that it refers to the deportation of the people of Northern Galilee by Tiglath-pileser (II Kgs 15:29). **31. And they set . . . up Micah's . . . image . . . all the time that the house of God was in Shiloh.** For a time Shiloh was the religious capital of Israel (I Sam 1:3), but the Danites maintained their own idolatrous worship. Dan continued as a center of idolatry after the disruption of Solomon's kingdom. Jeroboam set up golden calves at Bethel and Dan (I Kgs 12:29).

B. The Crime at Gibeah and the War Against Benjamin. 19:1–21:25.

19:1. There was a certain Levite . . . who took to himself a concubine. The story of the crime at Gibeah is prefaced by the note that **there was no king in Israel.** In those lawless times when in theory God was king, but in practice men did what was right in their own eyes, a Levite from the hill country of Ephraim, in the central highlands, took a concubine from Beth-lehem-judah.

2. And his concubine . . . went away . . . unto her father's house. The cause of the difficulty as given in the AV is that she **played the whore against him.** The RSV, following the LXX and Old

Latin, reads, *she went away from him,* i.e., deserted him. Moore, in the ICC, reads that she *was angry with him.*

3. And her husband arose, and went after her. The husband followed his wife **to speak friendly unto her** (AV), literally, *speak unto her heart* (cf. Hos 2:14). He was warmly welcomed by the young lady's father, who entertained him for three days (v. 4). On the fourth day, the Levite and his concubine prepared to leave, but the father was reluctant to let them go. They remained until the fifth day (v. 8).

10. But the man would not tarry that night. Resisting the further entreaty of his father-in-law, the Levite and his concubine headed northward. They passed Jerusalem, known as Jebus because of the Jebusites who lived there. Because it was a city of non-Israelites, the Levite refused to pass the night at Jebus, but insisted on passing on toward Gibeah, a city of the tribe of Benjamin (v. 12).

15. And they turned aside . . . to lodge in Gibeah. Expecting hospitality in the city of Gibeah, the Levite was disappointed. He waited in the public square, inside the gate of the city, but no man of Gibeah offered hospitality.

16. And, behold, there came an old man from his work out of the field. Hospitality was finally offered from a man of Mount Ephraim who sojourned in Gibeah. Again the lack of hospitality of the men of Gibeah is underscored. **18. I am now going to the house of the Lord.** The Levite identified himself to the man who showed an interest in helping him. The words, **the house of the Lord,** are taken to mean Shiloh or Bethel (cf. 20:18,26). The RSV follows the LXX in reading, *I am going to my home.* **21. So he brought him into his house.** The elderly sojourner in Gibeah offered the Levite hospitality, suggesting that he would care for all of the wants of his guest (v. 20).

22. Certain sons of Belial beset the house round about. The vice of the men of Gibeah is comparable to that of the Sodomites. They desired carnal relations with the Levite. As Lot offered his daughters under similar circumstances (Gen 19:8), so here the host offered his own daughter and the Levite's concubine as a means of protecting his guest (v. 24). **25. So the man took his concubine, and brought her forth unto them.** The Levite offered his concubine as a means of saving himself. The act cannot be justified. Abraham was willing to sacrifice Sarah to save himself under similar circumstances (Gen 12:10-20). The Levite's concubine was abused all night.

27. And her lord rose up . . . and, behold, the woman his concubine was fallen down at the door of the house. After her harrowing night experience, the concubine made her way to the house, seeking a place of safety. She died, however, outside the house of her host. **29. He took a knife, and laid hold on his concubine.** When the Levite saw what had had happened, he placed the dead body of his concubine on an ass and took it to his home. There he divided the corpse into twelve pieces and sent them to the various parts of Israel (cf. I Sam 11:7). All agreed that no such atrocity had taken place since the exodus from Egypt (v. 30).

20:1. Then all the children of Israel went out. The Israelites prepared for war. They assembled at Mizpeh, a central point in the tribe of Benjamin. Except for the men of Jabesh-gilead (21:8), all Israel was represented. **3. Now the children of Benjamin heard that the children of Israel were gone up to Mizpeh.** Gibeah was about three miles from Mizpeh. The Benjamites determined to defend the inhabitants of Gibeah.

4. And the Levite . . . answered . . . I came into Gibeah. The Levite recounted the events that led up to the death of the concubine, and declared his reason for sending parts of the dead body throughout Israel. Then he asked counsel of the assembled company. **8. We will not any of us go to his tent.** The united tribes determined to punish the men of Gibeah, and laid out a plan of action. They decided to **go up by lot against it** (v. 9). A lot could be used in determining who should first attack Gibeah. Here, however, it seems to have been used to determine the tenth of the fighting force which should be deployed to serve as the commissariat. A large army requires men responsible for securing provisions (v. 10).

12. And the tribes of Israel sent men through all the tribe of Benjamin, saying, What wickedness is this that is done among you? The other tribes judged that Benjamin had permitted an atrocity not consistent with the moral stature of Israel as a whole. They asked that the offenders be turned over to them for punishment. The purpose of this was to **put away evil** (v. 13, AV) **from Israel.** In the Jewish liturgy the verb translated **put away** is used of the complete removal of leaven on the eve of Passover. The Israelites desired "to extirpate" evil from their corporate life by punishing the offenders. **14. But the children of Benjamin gathered themselves together . . . to go out to battle against the children of Israel.** The men of the small tribe of Benjamin felt able to defend themselves against the rest of the tribes. They mustered an army, including **seven hundred chosen men, lefthanded** (vv. 15,16; cf. 3:15). The Benjamites were skillful as archers and slingers (cf. I Chr 12:2).

18. And the children of Israel . . . asked counsel of God. The Israelites consulted the oracle at Bethel to determine who should first go to battle with the Benjamites. Judah was designated as the tribe to lead the assault. Israelite troops prepared to assault Gibeah (v. 20), but they were massacred by the forces of Benjamin that sallied forth from the city (v. 21). After regrouping their depleted forces, Israel again asked counsel of the oracle of the Lord: **Shall I go up again to battle against the children of Benjamin my brother?** When the Lord gave an affirmative answer (v. 23), Israel prepared for a second attack. **25. And Benjamin went forth against them out of Gibeah the second day.** A second time the Benjamites defeated the forces of the other tribes.

26. Then all the children of Israel . . . came unto the house of God. The RSV reads *came to Bethel*. Bethel means *house of God*. The question of interpretation, here, concerns the location of the "house of God." Was it at Shiloh or at Bethel? From the days of Joshua to those of the priest Eli, the ark was located at Shiloh (Josh 18:10; I Sam 1:3). This does not, however, rule out the possibility of a shrine at Bethel during the time of the Judges. The Israelites wept, fasted, and offered suitable sacrifices. When the priest Phineas went before the Lord and asked whether or not the battle should be resumed, he received the answer: **Go up; for tomorrow I will deliver them into thine hand** (v. 28).

29. And Israel set liers-in-wait round about Gibeah. In their third battle with the Benjamites, the Israelites used strategy that had been used successfully by Joshua at Ai (Josh 8:4-29). They drew the Benjamites out of Gibeah to fight an Israelite army, while a group of **liers-in-wait** watched for the strategic moment to move into the city. In the initial phase of the battle, the Benjamites, thinking themselves successful, said, **They are smitten down before us, as at the first** (v. 32). The Israelites, however, were acting in accord with their strategy. They said, **Let us flee, and draw them from the city unto the highways.** The line of the Israelites was re-formed at Baal-tamar, a place otherwise unknown. **33. And the liers-in-wait of Israel came forth out of their places, even out of the meadows of Gibeah.** The RSV follows the LXX and the Vulgate in reading *their place west of Gibeah*, as the source whence the ambush came. The JPS version transliterates it as *Maareh-geba*. The place served as a hiding place for the ambush.

37. And the liers-in-wait . . . rushed upon Gibeah. The city was undefended while its armies were pursuing the apparently retreating Israelites. The men of the ambush entered Gibeah without battle and announced their presence there by starting a great fire (v. 38). When the Israelites, in feigned retreat, spied the smoke of the fire (v. 40), a pre-arranged signal (v. 38), they turned upon the Benjamites (v. 42) and slew them within sight of their burning city. Eighteen thousand valiant Benjamites were killed (v. 44). **45. And they turned and fled . . . unto the rock of Rimmon.** A group of six hundred Benjamites found a place of refuge at the rock of Rimmon, about four miles east of Bethel (v. 47), where they remained four months. The other Benjamites, with their cities and property, were destroyed.

21:1. Now the men of Israel had sworn in Mizpeh. After the slaughter of the Benjamites, the Israelites faced a new problem. Almost the entire tribe of Benjamin had been destroyed, and the other tribes had vowed not to allow their daughters to marry the few remaining Benjamites. How was the tribe of Benjamin to be preserved?

5. Who is there . . . that came not up with the congregation unto the Lord? Seeking some means of preserving the tribe of Benjamin from extinction, the Israelites sought to determine if there were any who had not assembled with them at Mizpeh. They had vowed that any who refused to come to Mizpeh should be put to death. Upon inquiry it was discovered that Jabesh-gilead had not responded to the appeal to come to the assembly (v. 8). Thereupon twelve thousand men were sent against Jabesh-gilead with the command to kill the males and the married women, but to bring back the virgins to the camp at Shiloh (vv. 10-12).

13. And the whole congregation sent some to speak to the children of Benjamin that were in the rock Rimmon. The Benjamites that were left were assured of the peaceful intent of the Israelites, and the virgins from Jabesh-gilead became wives to four hundred of them (v. 14).

16. How shall we do for wives for them that remain? In view of the oath that had been taken not to give wives to the Benjamites and the desire to preserve Benjamin from extinction, some means had to be found to provide wives.

19. Behold, there is a feast of the Lord in Shiloh yearly. A way of evading the oath was discovered. During an annual feast at Shiloh, the young ladies of the city would be seen in their dances (v. 21). The Benjamites were instructed to **Go and lie in wait in the vineyards** (v. 20) until they saw the maidens. Then they could come out from hiding and **catch . . . every man his wife.** The Benjamites would thus have wives, and the Israelites would not have violated their oaths, for they would not have 'given' their daughters to the Benjamites. If complaints came from the relatives of the girls involved (v. 22), the Israelites indicated that they would intercede on behalf of the Benjamites. **23. And the children of Benjamin did so.** Wives were thus secured for the Benjamites, who then returned home and rebuilt the cities that had been destroyed in the war.

24. And the children of Israel departed . . . every man to his tribe. The assembly of Israelites was dispersed after the matters pertaining to the Benjamites were properly cared for. The book closes with the reminder that these sad episodes took place during the time when **there was no king in Israel: every man did that which was right in his own eyes** (v. 25). Though the hand of God can be traced throughout the history of the Judges, human failure stands out in bold relief.

BIBLIOGRAPHY

Burney, C. F. *The Book of Judges.* 2nd ed. London: Rivingtons, 1930.

Cohen, A. *Joshua and Judges (Soncino Bible).* London: Soncino Press, 1950.

Cooke, G. A. *The Book of Judges (The Cambridge Bible).* Cambridge: Cambridge University Press, 1913.

Garstang, John. *Joshua-Judges.* London: Constable & Co., 1931.

Keil, C. F. and Delitzsch, F. *Joshua, Judges, Ruth. (Biblical Commentary on the Old Testament).* Grand Rapids: Wm. B. Eerdmans, reprinted 1950.

Moore, George Foot. *A Critical and Exegetical Commentary on Judges (The International Critical Commentary).* New York: Scribner's, 1901.

Myers, Jacob M. "The Book of Judges," *The Interpreter's Bible.* Vol. 2. New York: Abingdon Press, 1953.

Simpson, C. A. *Composition of the Book of Judges.* Oxford: Blackwell, 1957.

RUTH

INTRODUCTION

Title. The Book of Ruth is named after its heroine, a Moabitess who, after the death of her husband, journeyed to Bethlehem with her widowed mother-in-law. Ruth occupies an important place in Israelite history because she became the ancestress of King David (Ruth 4:18-22) and of Jesus (Mt 1:1,5).

Date and Authorship. The date of composition of the Book of Ruth is unknown. Biblical scholars find some clues to the time of composition within the book itself. Since David is mentioned in the book (4:17,22), it could not have been written before the tenth century B.C. The writer found it necessary to explain certain customs which he regarded as archaic (4:6-8), a fact which indicates that the book was written some years after the customs fell into disuse.

How much later than the time of David the Book of Ruth was written is a matter of conjecture. Although some scholars date it as late as the fourth century, many others insist on a pre-Exilic date. Robert Pfeiffer notes, "The general character of the Hebrew vocabulary and syntax, the use of ancient idiomatic expression current in the best prose of the Old Testament . . . , and the classical purity of style could be adduced in favor of an early date" (*Introduction to the Old Testament*, p. 718). He prefers a date about 400 B.C., however, and suggests that a gifted writer from a later period might have patterned his work after earlier models.

Edward Young, calling attention to the absence of Solomon's name in the genealogy, suggests that since a later writer would have extended his genealogy beyond the time of David, the book was probably written some time during the reign of David (*Introduction to the Old Testament*, p. 358).

The Talmud (*Baba Bathra,* 14 b) attributes the authorship of Ruth to Samuel, a view which is no longer held by either Jewish or Christian scholarship. As in the case of other Old Testament historical books, we cannot assign a known author to Ruth. That does not, of course, detract from the spiritual value and literary beauty of this episode from the time of the Judges, which an unknown Jewish author has preserved.

Use of Book. In the Jewish liturgy the scroll of Ruth is read on Pentecost.

Historical Background. The period of the Judges was one of turbulence and unrest. Tribal jealousies and foreign oppressions weakened the Israelites politically, and idolatry sapped the moral strength of the people who had experienced the power of God at the time of the Exodus. The story of Ruth, however, presents a different side of life during the period of the Judges. Here we read of the joys and sorrows of a godly family from Bethlehem. Ruth, the Moabitess, who became a worshiper of Israel's God, exhibited a faith and loyalty at that time rare in Israel. After the sorrow of losing her first husband, Ruth returned to Bethlehem with her mother-in-law and was happily married to Boaz. In this way she became an ancestress of King David.

OUTLINE

I. The family of Elimelech migrates to Moab. 1:1-5.

II. Elimelech's widow and daughter-in-law return from Moab. 1:6-18.

III. Naomi and Ruth arrive at Bethlehem. 1:19-22.

IV. Ruth gleans in the fields of Boaz. 2:1-23.

V. Ruth finds a redeemer. 3:1-18.

VI. Boaz marries Ruth. 4:1-17.

VII. Ruth becomes an ancestress of David. 4:18-22.

COMMENTARY

I. The Family of Elimelech Migrates to Moab. 1:1-5.

1. In the days when the judges ruled. The Book of Ruth presents a contrast to the turbulent events described in Judges. There we read of apostasy and oppression, intertribal jealousy and civil war. Here we are reminded of God's providential dealings in the life of one family, of the sorrows of that family, and of the way the Lord's purposes found fulfillment through a Moabitess who became the ancestress of King David, and of the Saviour (cf. Mt 1:5).

There was a famine in the land. Rainfall in Palestine is never plentiful, and quite frequently it is insufficient to provide adequately for the basic crops. Famines took place during the lifetimes of Abraham (Gen 12:10), David (II Sam 21:1) and Elijah (I Kgs 17:1). **In the country of Moab.** Moab was a son of Lot, the evil fruit of the incestuous relation of Lot with one of his daughters (Gen 19:36,37). Moabites had hired Balaam to curse Israel (Num 22:1-8), during Israel's pilgrimage to Canaan. Under normal circumstances Moabites were barred from participation in the national, corporate life of Israel (Deut 23:3-6). There were friendly relations between some individual Israelites and Moabites, however. When fleeing the wrath of Saul, David found a friend in the king of Moab (I Sam 22:3,4).

2. Mahlon and Chilion. The names of the two sons of Elimelech and Naomi are expressive of physical weakness. Mahlon means "sickly" and Chilion, "wasting." As a matter of fact they did not live long after settling in Moab. **4. They took them wives.** The sons of Elimelech and Naomi settled in Moab and married. There is no specific condemnation of these marriages, although they would surely have been frowned upon by the orthodox in Israel. **5. The woman was left.** During the ten years' sojourn in Moab, the husband and two sons of Naomi died. All that were left of the once happy family were three women – Naomi and her two daughters-in-law, Ruth and Orpah.

II. Elimelech's Widow and Daughter-in-law Return from Moab. 1:6-18.

6. She had heard . . . how that the Lord had visited his people. While in Moab, Naomi learned that the famine had ended in Bethlehem. Being a widow with family ties there, she prepared to return home. **7. Her two daughters-in-law with her.** The girls were so attached to their mother-in-law that they wished to leave their own country and go to Bethlehem. **8. Go, return each to her mother's house.** Naomi thought it would not be wise for the girls to leave Moab, their native land. She commended them for their loyalty to their dead husbands and to herself, and urged them to stay in their homeland. **9. Each of you in the house of her husband.** Naomi thought that the girls would wish to remarry. As they had been faithful in times of adversity, she prayed that God would grant them days of prosperity and blessing in second marriage.

10. Surely we will return with thee unto thy people. It was a tribute to the godly character of Naomi that her daughters-in-law were prepared to leave their own land to go with her to Judah. **11. Why will ye go with me?** According to the principle of levirate marriage, the next brother (or, as we note later, kinsman) was expected to marry the childless widow of his deceased brother. The first child of the second marriage was accounted to the deceased brother, and that child carried on the family name and inherited the property as if he had been the child of the deceased man. Naomi asked, **Are there yet any more sons in my womb?** She implied that she could not hope to be the mother of sons who could later marry the two Moabitish widows.

14. But Ruth clave unto her. Ruth would not be dissuaded. She had determined to abide with Naomi whatever the consequences, and she became the ancestress of David as a result of her choice. Though the character of Orpah suffers by contrast with that of Ruth, no word of reproach is intended for her. She acted on the advice of Naomi and returned to Moab, thereby dropping out of the Biblical record. **16. Whither thou goest, I will go.** This section of Ruth is esteemed one of the most touching passages of literature. Ruth renounced all that she could be expected to hold dear in Moab and voluntarily chose to go to Judah and there begin an entirely new life with her mother-in-law. This choice had religious as well as cultural overtones, as we see from the words – **thy God** [shall be] **my God.** In Moab Ruth would have been expected to worship

Chemosh (Num 21:29). In going to Judah, however, she would worship the God of Israel. It was a testimony both to her deceased husband and to her mother-in-law that Ruth was willing to entrust herself to the God whom they worshiped. **17. The Lord do so to me, and more also.** Ruth in these words solemnly affirmed her desire to be loyal to Naomi as long as she lived. Her words imply a solemn vow, which may be paraphrased, "May a severe judgment fall on me if I am not true to my vow."

18. She saw that she was stedfastly minded to go with her. Ruth's words expressed a love and loyalty that the older woman could not reject, and a determination that made Naomi give up urging her to return to Moab.

III. Naomi and Ruth Arrive at Bethlehem. 1:19-22.

19. So they two went . . . to Bethlehem. When Naomi and Ruth arrived in the city, they caused quite a stir. **Is this Naomi?** the people asked, expressing surprise. Naomi and Elimelech had left with their happy family; now Naomi's very appearance bore testimony to the hardship and sorrow she had experienced.

20. Call me not Naomi, call me Mara. Naomi means *pleasant,* whereas Mara means *bitter.* Naomi said, in effect, that the experiences in Moab had brought such grief into her life that she could no longer bear the name Naomi. **The Almighty hath dealt very bitterly with me.** Naomi recognized that the tragedies of her life were not accidents but that the hand of God had been in each of them. God is the Almighty, the One who controls all the circumstances of life. He is not powerless in the presence of evil, but remains the sovereign God, who can make all things work together for the good of his children (Rom 8:28). Although Naomi did not rise above the feeling of grief as she arrived at Bethlehem, her recognition that God is almighty offered a ray of hope. **21. The Lord hath brought me home again empty.** The very tragedies of her life she traced to God's sovereign will. Paul said he knew how "to be abased" and how "to abound." Naomi thought of her poverty as the result of God's providential dealings in her life. Although "empty," Naomi thankfully recognized that the Lord had brought her home.

22. They came to Bethlehem in the beginning of barley harvest. Famine was over and the beginning of harvest was a good time to return home. The Moabite experience had proved tragic, but the fields of Bethlehem were now full.

IV. Ruth Gleans in the Fields of Boaz. 2:1-23.

1. Naomi had a kinsman . . . and his name was Boaz. The kinsman is described in the AV as **a mighty man of wealth,** translating a phrase that usually signifies *a mighty man of valour,* i.e., a brave warrior. Here the expression seems to convey the idea of the finest manly qualities.

2. Let me . . . go to the field, and glean . . . corn. According to Mosaic law the poor were entitled to gather the grain that fell from the hands of the reapers (Lev 19:9; 23:22; cf. Deut 24:19). **Corn** here signifies *grain.* It is barley that is meant (cf. Ruth 1:22). **3. Her hap was to light on a part of the field belonging unto Boaz.** She had not determined to go to a particular field, but "happened" to go to the field of Boaz. What appeared to be an accident is seen in the light of the whole story to be the providence of God.

5. Whose damsel is this? Boaz noted the presence of a stranger in his field. Her appearance and dress were different from those of the girls he usually saw gleaning behind his reapers. **6. It is the Moabitish damsel.** The reply was almost derogatory: "It is that foreigner who came back with Naomi from Moab!" **7. She came, and hath continued even from the morning until now.** Ruth had asked permission to glean in the field of Boaz. When the overseer of the reapers gave her permission to do so, she worked diligently. **She tarried a little in the house.** These words probably refer to the time she spent in the hut erected in the field for rest and refreshment. The Hebrew text implies that Ruth spent a little time there, although the LXX translates, *She has not rested (even) a little.* The Vulgate reads, *She has not returned home (even) for a short time.*

8. Abide here fast by my maidens. The maidens followed the reapers in the field, in order to bind the sheaves. Boaz suggested that Ruth should remain in his field with them. There is a tacit assumption that he would provide for her needs. **9. Have not I charged the young men that they shall not touch thee?** Boaz directed his workers to keep Ruth from harm. She was further instructed to drink of the water provided for the workers in Boaz' field.

10. Why have I found grace in thine eyes? Ruth was moved by these acts of kindness on the part of Boaz. Her very question showed a spirit of humility and self-effacement.

11. It hath fully been shewed me. Boaz had inquired about Ruth and learned of her faithfulness to her mother-in-law. Leaving the land of one's nativity was considered a real sacrifice. **12. A full reward be given thee of the Lord God of Israel.** Boaz recognized that he alone could not adequately repay Ruth for her faithfulness. He prayed that Ruth might be abundantly rewarded by the Lord. **Under whose wings thou art come to trust.** Ruth had found a place of refuge in Israel's God. As a hen gathers her young under her wings to protect them from harm, so God protects those who come to him for safety.

13. Thou hast comforted me. Ruth had been deeply stirred by the remarks of Boaz. She felt herself unworthy of his acts of kindness. **Though I be not like unto one of thine handmaidens.** She regarded herself as inferior to the girls who worked for Boaz – perhaps because of her poverty, her Gentile nationality, and her heathen background. His kindness to the others was understandable. His kindness to her was pure grace.

14. At mealtime come thou hither. Boaz invited Ruth to take a place of honor at mealtime. He made it a point to see that she had plenty to eat.

15. Let her glean even among the sheaves. Normally the gleaners took only the grain that had not been bound in sheaves. Boaz, however, made special provision for Ruth. **16. Let fall also some of the handfuls of purpose for her.** JPS reads, "Pull out some for her." The reapers were told to provide in a special way for Ruth (without her knowing it). She had the legal right to take all that was accidentally left behind. The reapers saw to it that an abundance of grain was left for her.

17. She . . . beat out that she had gleaned. When the quantity of grain was small, it was beaten by means of a stick to separate the grain from the chaff. **And it was about an ephah of barely.** This amounted to approximately three pecks, dry measure. It was enough to support Ruth and Naomi for about five days. **18. Her mother-in-law saw what she had gleaned.** Naomi was doubtless surprised at the amount of barley Ruth brought home. **She . . . gave to her that she had reserved after she was sufficed.** Ruth brought her mother-in-law the food she had left after she had eaten her own meal.

19. Where hast thou gleaned today? Surprised at the amount of grain, Naomi asked concerning the field where Ruth had worked. **The man's name . . . is Boaz.** Boaz was both a wealthy landowner and a close relative of Naomi. As such he could be expected to buy for the family its rightful land (Lev 25:25) and look after the helpless members of the family.

20. Blessed be he of the Lord, who hath not left off his kindness to the living and to the dead. By caring for the widow of Mahlon, Boaz was providing for the dead as well as showing kindness to the living. **22. It is good, my daughter, that thou go out with his maidens.** "If Boaz desires to treat you kindly, do not go elsewhere," Naomi advised. "Accept his generosity and remain with his maidens." **23. Unto the end of barley harvest and of wheat harvest.** Throughout the harvest season Ruth continued to work with the maidens by day and to return to the home of her mother-in-law each evening.

V. Ruth Finds a Redeemer. 3:1-18.

3:1. Shall I not seek rest for thee. Rest here is equivalent to marriage. Naomi felt that Ruth should not remain a poor gleaner in the fields. Since Ruth had no mother (in Judah, at any rate), Naomi determined to take the initiative to arrange a marriage. **2. Is not Boaz of our kindred?** Naomi, mindful of the levirate marriage customs, determined to approach Boaz. **Behold, he winnoweth barley tonight in the threshing floor.** Boaz spent the night at the threshing floor to avail himself of the breeze that enabled him to winnow. The grain was thrown into the air, and the breeze carried away the chaff. It is possible also that Boaz spent the night there to guard the grain from thieves.

3. Get thee down to the floor. The record is clear that both Naomi and Ruth had the purest of motives in their plans. Although Ruth had been kindly treated by Boaz, he had made no suggestion concerning marriage. Naomi now planned a way by which Ruth might be able to meet Boaz alone. **4. Thou shalt go in, and uncover his feet, and lay thee down.** Under usual circumstances this would have been interpreted as an immoral act. The integrity of both Ruth and Boaz, however, was such that Naomi felt free to suggest it.

9. Spread therefore thy skirt over thine handmaid; for thou art a near kinsman. The custom of a man's placing a corner of his garment over a maiden as a token of marriage is known among the Arabs.

10. Thou followedst not young men, whether poor or rich. A tradition states that Boaz was eighty years old when he married Ruth. She is here commended for not seeking the company of the youthful men who, presumably, would have been more attractive to her. **11. All the city of my people doth know that thou art a virtuous woman.** The term translated **virtuous** when used of a man describes strength, bravery, and manliness. The RSV renders it here *a woman of worth*. All qualities which are admirable in a woman were found in Ruth, according to this testimony.

12. There is a kinsman nearer than I. Boaz was only a nephew of Elimelech, whereas a brother was still living. Although desirous of assuming the responsibility of the *gô'ēl* (i.e., "redeemer") himself, Boaz insisted on allowing the man with the closest relationship to decide whether or not he wished to assume the responsibilities. **13. If he will not do the part of a kinsman to thee, then will I do the part of a kinsman to thee.** The closer relative should have first opportunity, but Boaz expressed a willingness to act as *gô'ēl* if the close relative chose not to do so. The *gô'ēl* was a protector responsible to redeem family property that had been alienated.

14. She rose up before one could know another. This is not the "know" of sexual intercourse, but another verb meaning *discern*. The RSV reads, *before one could recognize another*. The Hebrew idiom says, "Before man could recognize his neighbor," i.e., before morning. **Let it not be known that a woman came into the floor.** Though no overt sin had been committed, Boaz was concerned lest people misunderstand the presence of Ruth at the threshing floor. **15. He measured six measures of barley, and laid it on her.** The barley may have been sent to Naomi in recognition of her responsibility for Ruth's action. Probably Ruth carried the barley on her head, as is customary in the East.

VI. Boaz Marries Ruth. 4:1-17.

4:2. And he took ten men of the elders of the city. Later Judaism considered ten men as the quorum required for a synagogue. Ten also were required among the Jews for the marriage benediction. **3. Naomi . . . selleth a parcel of land, which was our brother Elimelech's.** The context implies that **selleth** means "intends to sell" or "has offered for sale" (cf. v. 5). It was the concern of the community that a family be preserved from extinction. For this reason the problems of Naomi and Ruth were matters of community interest.

4. I thought to advertise thee. Literally, *uncover thine ear*. RSV, *I thought I would tell you of it*. **If thou wilt redeem it, redeem it.** The near kinsman was legally informed of his right of redemption. **I will redeem it.** He assumed that the property belonged solely to Naomi, and that his duty would end with the purchase of the field from her.

5. What day thou buyest the field . . . thou must buy it also of Ruth the Moabitess . . . to raise up the name of the dead upon his inheritance. Both the alienation of land and the extinction of a family were to be prevented by the law of the *gô'ēl*. The *gô'ēl* would not come into possession of the land himself, but would hold it in trust for his son by Ruth, who would inherit the name and patrimony of Mahlon (her first husband). **6. I cannot redeem it.** This would involve financial loss to the purchaser. The prospective *gô'ēl* would **mar** his **own inheritance** by spending money on land that would belong not to him but to a son of Ruth. The Targum suggests that the relative was already married, but this would not have relieved him of obligation.

7. This was the manner in former time in Israel. The explanation implies that at the time of writing this custom was no longer practiced. **A man plucked off his shoe, and gave it to his neighbor.** This was a symbolic act of transfer. The man who took off his shoe renounced any legal rights he had in the matter. The custom is mentioned in the Nuzu tablets (Ernest R. Lacheman, "Notes on Ruth 4:7,8," JBL, LVI [1937], 53-56).

8. Buy it for thee. The next of kin said to Boaz, *Buy it for yourself* (RSV). Boaz had earlier made it clear that he would do so if the next of kin did not choose to accept the responsibility of the *gô'ēl*.

9. I have bought all that was Elimelech's, and all that was Chilion's and Mahlon's, of the hand of Naomi. Boaz publicly stated that he had taken possession of the property and assumed the responsibility for Naomi and Ruth. **10. Ruth the Moabitess . . . have I purchased**

to be my wife. The verbs translated **bought** (v. 9) and **purchased** (v. 10) may simply mean "obtain." Boaz took Ruth in levirate marriage **that the name of the dead be not cut off,** i.e., to perpetuate the family of Mahlon. **From the gate of his place.** The gate of an Oriental city was the city hall, the place of government and authority.

11. The Lord make the woman . . . like Rachel and like Leah . . . and do thou worthily in Ephratah, and be famous in Bethlehem. Rachel and Leah were the wives of Jacob. The witnesses expressed their prayer that Boaz would be rewarded with a family comparable to that of Jacob (or Israel). Ephratah is the name given to the region in which Bethlehem is located. **Be famous.** Literally, *Call a name*. The elders and people expressed a wish for children who would be reckoned descendants of Boaz. **12. Let thy house be like the house of Pharez.** Pharez was the offspring of a Canaanite (Gen 38:2,29). The girl Tamar took into her own hands the law of *gō'ēl* after the death of two husbands. In the disguise of a harlot she enticed Judah into a sinful relationship which produced twin boys – Pharez and Zarah.

13. So Boaz took Ruth . . . and she bare a son. The marriage was blessed of God. In characteristic Biblical teaching **the Lord gave her conception.** Children are looked upon as a sacred trust from the Lord.

15. He shall be unto thee a restorer of thy life. As Naomi's sons were dead, she had no hope of continuing her family line. Ruth's marriage and the son she bore brought the hope of a new family in Israel. **Thy daughter-in-law . . . is better to thee than seven sons.** Seven sons would be indicative of the blessing of God (cf. I Sam 2:5; Job 1:2). Naomi, however, had a daughter-in-law in whose child she found consolation for the loss of her own sons. **16. Naomi took the child . . . and became nurse unto it.** This is often interpreted as an adoption ceremony.

VII. Ruth Becomes an Ancestress of David. 4:18-22.

17. They called his name Obed: he is the father of Jesse, the father of David. Obed means "worshiper," "servant," or "slave." It is often combined with the names of the God of Israel or of pagan gods, as in Obadiah, Obed-edom, Ebednego, and Abdullah.

18. The generations of Pharez. Pharez was a son of Judah (Gen 46:12). **20.** At the time of Moses, **Nahshon** served as head of the house of Judah (Num 1:7; 7:12,17; 10:14). **Salmon** in the form "Salma" (as used in the Hebrew of Ruth 4:20) occurs in I Chr 2:51,54 as "the father of Bethlehem," doubtless an allusion to the people who settled there, including Boaz.

BIBLIOGRAPHY

Bettan, Israel. *The Five Scrolls.* Cincinnati: Union of American Hebrew Congregations, 1950.

Cook, G. A. *The Book of Ruth (The Cambridge Bible).* Cambridge: Cambridge University Press, 1913.

Keil, C. F. and F. Delitzsch. *Biblical Commentary on the Old Testament: Joshua, Judges, Ruth.* Grand Rapids: William B. Eerdmans (reprint), 1950.

Macdonald, D. B. *The Hebrew Literary Genius.* Princeton: Princeton University Press, 1933.

Rowley, H. H. "The Marriage of Ruth," *The Servant of the Lord and Other Essays on the Old Testament.* London: Lutterworth Press. First published in *Harvard Theological Review,* XL (1947).

Slotki, J. R. *The Five Megilloth.* Edited by Abraham Cohen. London and Bournemouth: The Soncino Press, 1952.

Smith, Louise Pettibone. "The Book of Ruth," *The Interpreter's Bible.* Vol 2. New York: Abingdon Press, 1953.

Watson, Robert Addison. *Judges and Ruth (The Expositor's Bible).* New York: A. C. Armstrong and Sons, 1899.

FIRST AND SECOND SAMUEL

INTRODUCTION

Title. The title of these two books comes from the name of the key figure in the opening chapters of I Samuel. The Hebrew word *Samuel* has had many interpretations. However, the meaning first suggested by the German Hebrew scholar, Gesenius, "The Name of God," still seems to hold first place among Biblical scholars.

Date and Authorship. As is the case with many other Old Testament books, the date for the writing of I and II Samuel is not certainly known. Part of the difficulty in determining the date lies in the fact that most portions of the two books deal with events that occurred after Samuel's death. The early part of I Samuel could have been written about 1000 B.C., the remainder some thirty to fifty years later. Although the Talmud ascribes the authorship of the books to Samuel, it is likely that the prophet wrote only those sections that deal with the history of Israel prior to his retirement from public office. One suggestion, an intriguing one, is that Abiathar wrote much of I and II Samuel, especially those parts that treat of the court life of David. Abiathar was intimately associated with the rise and fortunes of the great king of Israel in that he spent some time with David in his exile. Also, he came from a priestly family and thus had access to the art of writing and record-keeping. Another suggestion is that one of the sons of the prophets from one of the schools founded by Samuel carried on the history of Israel begun by his master.

Historical Background. The call of Samuel to be the prophet and judge of Israel formed a strong turning point in the development of the Old Testament kingdom of God. In the period of transition from leadership by divinely chosen judges to the monarchy, Samuel had the tremendous task of directing the rebuilding of social and religious unity. He was God's instrument for establishing the kingdom of Israel in this great national crisis, second only in importance to the Exodus experience. Samuel's task was to lead Israel out of the period of the Judges and into that of the kings.

He finished the work of the Judges, not by the physical might of his arm alone, but by the spiritual power of his word and prayer. He also laid the foundation of the prophetic office and developed it to the level of the priesthood and the kingship. From his time on, the prophets sustained and fostered the spiritual life of the nation and were the instruments through whom God's will was communicated to ruler and to people.

OUTLINE

- I. The life and ministry of Samuel. 1:1–7:17.
  - A. The birth and childhood of Samuel. 1:1–4:1a.
  - B. The capture and return of the ark. 4:1b–7:1.
  - C. The victory over the Philistines. 7:2-17.
- II. The life and ministry of Saul. 8:1–14:52.
  - A. Israel's request for a king. 8:1-22.
  - B. Political life of Saul. 9:1–12:25.
  - C. War of independence. 13:1–14:52.
- III. The life and early ministry of David. 15:1–II Sam 20:26.
  - A. Saul rejected by Samuel. 15:1-35.
  - B. David anointed to be king. 16:1-13.
  - C. David in the court of Saul. 16:14–19:17.
  - D. David in exile. 19:18–31:13.

E. David, king at Hebron. II Sam 1:1–4:12.
F. David, king at Jerusalem. 5:1–8:18.
G. Court life of David. 9:1–20:26.
IV. The last days of David. 21:1–24:25.
A. The famine. 21:1-14.
B. Heroic exploits. 21:15-22.
C. David's psalm. 22:1-51.
D. David's testament. 23:1-7.
E. Heroic exploits. 23:8-39.
F. Census and plague. 24:1-25.

COMMENTARY

I. The Life and Ministry of Samuel. 1:1–7:17.

A. The Birth and Childhood of Samuel. 1:1–4:1a.

1:1. A certain man of Ramathaim-zophim. The LXX reads, *a man from Arimathea* (cf. Mt 27:57), *a Zuphite.* **Ramathaim,** *Twin Heights,* is the dual form of *Ramah,* "high." According to this book, Ramah was the birthplace (1:19), residence (7:17), and burial place (25:1) of the prophet Samuel. It is usually identified with Beit Rima, a village on the western edge of the central highlands of Palestine, twelve miles northwest of Bethel and twelve miles west of Shiloh. Zuph was an ancestor of Elkanah (v. 1), and Ramah, Samuel's home (1:19), lay in the land of Zuph (9:5). Hence, Ramah may be the abbreviated name for Ramathaim-zophim. **An Ephrathite.** Elkanah (and hence Samuel) was a Levite (see I Chr 6:33) living in Ephraimite territory. This was not unusual, since the Levites had no tribal territory but dwelt among the tribes in specified cities.

2. Two wives. Polygamy, at variance with the ideal of marriage (Gen 2:24), was practiced by Abram, Jacob, Gideon, David, and Solomon. This bigamous marriage (probably in accord with Deut 21:15-17), was undoubtedly caused by a childless first marriage. No moral blame is here attached to Elkanah's marriages. **Hannah,** or *Grace,* was also the name of Anna the prophetess (Lk 2:36), and of the mother of the Virgin Mary (according to a tradition), and of the sister of Queen Dido of Carthage, niece of Queen Jezebel. **Peninnah,** "Coral," or "Pearl," may be compared to *Margaret,* which means "pearl."

3. The Lord of hosts. A title for God, the leader of the earthly hosts (armies) of Israel (Ex 7:4; Ps 44:9), and the commander of the heavenly hosts, either (a) celestial bodies, such as the sun, moon, and stars, or (b) celestial beings. This title attached to the divine name Jehovah, occurring for the first time in the OT in Samuel, proclaims his universal sovereignty. **In Shiloh.** Shiloh continued to be the religious center of the nation until after the loss of the ark of the covenant in the disastrous battle of Ebenezer. Nob then replaced Shiloh as the religious center. Jeremiah points to the desolation of Shiloh as the standing witness of God's judgment: "Go ye now unto my place which was in Shiloh, where I caused my name to dwell at the first, and see what I did to it for the wickedness of my people Israel" (Jer 7:12,14). **The two sons of Eli, Hophni and Phinehas.** Both names are Egyptian. **Hophni** means *tadpole,* and **Phinehas** – *the negro.*

4. Offered. His sacrifice was a thank offering, for it was only of the thank offering that the worshipers partook (Lev 7:11-18). Part of the animal was offered in sacrifice to God, and the remainder was consumed by the worshipers in a simple communion service. **5. Unto Hannah he gave a worthy portion.** Most commentaries accuse Elkanah of favoritism toward Hannah. This misconception arose in the translation of the Geneva Bible of 1560, which reads, *a worthy portion,* based on the Targum translation of the difficult Hebrew word *'apāyīm* ("two-faced"?) as *choice.* The LXX reads *'epes-kî,* "but," suggesting that Elkanah gave Hannah but one portion, although he loved her. The favoritism of Elkanah consisted not in his showing discrimination at the dinner table but in his loving Hannah more than he loved Peninnah.

6. And her adversary also provoked her. *Kā'as,* the word for "provoke," denotes the feeling aroused by some unmerited treatment. It is used of God's feeling at the triumph of the enemies of Israel (Deut 32:27). **To make her fret.** Literally, *cause her to thunder.* The word *ra'am* means to stir up inwardly, to excite, put into inward commotion. Later, the Syriac Version read this word to mean "lament, complain, murmur." **8. Better to thee than ten children** (AV, *sons*). Ten is a round number used to express a large number. "Am I not better to you than a large family?" is the meaning.

9. Eli the priest belonged to the family of Ithamar, fourth son of Aaron. The duty of the members of this family was to care for the physical property of the Tabernacle. Just when the high priestly succession passed to Eli's family is unknown. Some scholars feel that the Shiloh temple was an abortive attempt by the family of Ithamar to usurp control of the high priesthood. Others feel that the high priestly line of Eleazar became decadent or may even have died out, and hence this office was transferred to the most promising section of the family. **Temple of the Lord.** Literally, *palace of the Lord*. *Hêkal* is a loan word from Sumerian *É-gal*, "the big house." Originally it was used to denote the palace of the king, while later it was used to signify the temple of the deity. The Tabernacle is called "the palace of Jehovah," not on account of the magnificence and splendor of the building, but because it was the dwelling place of Jehovah of Hosts, the God-King of Israel (cf. Ps 5:7).

10. Bitterness of soul. Elisha uses the expression, "her soul is bitter," in describing to his servant, Gehazi, the distress of the wealthy woman of Shunem at the death of her young son (II Kgs 4:27). The phrase used of Hannah conveys the idea of mental embitterment, deep disappointment. **11. She vowed a vow.** Her vow was twofold: (a) lifelong Levitical service; (b) life membership in the guild of the Nazarites. Neither of these positions was necessarily permanent among the Hebrews. A Levite served until the age of fifty; the Nazarites' vow was for a specific period of time (see Num 6:2 ff. for the law of the Nazarite). Samson, Samuel, and John the Baptist were dedicated to perpetual Nazaritehood from birth.

13. Her lips moved, but her voice was not heard. Silent prayer did not characterize early Hebrew praying. Hannah's unusual type of prayer caused Eli to think her drunk. **16. Daughter of Belial.** Belial is used in post-biblical literature as a surrogate for Satan. Here it means a "base woman."

17. The God of Israel grant thee thy petition. Jewish commentators offer an alternative reading which makes Eli predict that God will give Hannah a son. The Hebrew text implies a pious wish, not a prophetic prediction. **18. Went her way.** The LXX reads, *went to her lodging chamber and ate*. Both the AV and the LXX imply that Hannah interrupted her meal to pray for a son.

19. They rose up . . . early, and worshipped. This custom of rising early for prayer is attested of the Essenes at Qumran. **The Lord remembered her.** The suggestion here is that the direct action of the Lord was required in conception. From this idea it was but a step to the belief that a large family was a reward for virtue, and that barrenness was a sign of sinful conduct.

20. When the time was come. Explained by the Jewish commentator, Kimchi (d. 1235), as "at the end of the period of gestation." It is better understood as "at the coming round of the new year," i.e., at the next season for Elkanah's annual pilgrimage. **Samuel.** Some derive his name from *sh^e^mû'a-'ēl*, "heard of God"; others, from *sh^e^mû-'ēl*, "his name is mighty." Derivation from "the name of God," as first put forth by Gesenius, is preferable, however. Two other persons in the OT have the name of Samuel (Num 34:20; I Chr 7:2).

21. And his vow. Perhaps Elkanah joined Hannah in making vows to the Lord. The LXX reads, *vows*, and adds that on this occasion he paid "all the tithes of his land" (cf. Deut 12:26,27). Following Josephus, it has been suggested that the Hebrew copyist omitted what the LXX had recorded because of the improbability of a Levite's paying tithes. However, Josephus does describe Elkanah as a Levite, and according to Num 18:26 ff. and Neh 10:38, the Levites did pay tithes. **22. Until the child be weaned.** According to II Macc 7:28, Hebrew women suckled their children for three years. **23. The Lord establish his word.** God had not yet revealed himself to Hannah. Perhaps Eli's words to her (v. 17) caused them to think that God had spoken in the birth, and so they anticipated his further word. The Syriac and the LXX read, *thy word*, as Elkanah's expression that Hannah was to fulfill her vow in due time.

24. Three bullocks. The two bulls, according to Ehrlich, were gifts to Eli, and one was sacrificed (v. 25). Keil suggests that all three were offered, one for the vow of the child, one for the annual burnt offering, and one for the annual thank offering. The LXX reads, *a three-year-old bull*. **26. That stood by thee.**

Prayer was offered (a) standing, as by Hannah and Abraham (Gen 18:22); (b) kneeling, as by Solomon (I Kgs 8:54), and Daniel (Dan 6:10); or (c) prostrate, as by Moses and Aaron (Num 16:22), and Jesus (Mt 26:39). **28. I have lent him to the Lord. Lent** is a poor word to describe Hannah's gift of Samuel to the service of the Lord in the Shiloh temple. It carries the idea of temporal action, while here the dedication is complete and irrevocable.

2:1. Mine horn is exalted in the Lord is a picture of the wild ox with head carried high in the confidence of strength. **My mouth is enlarged over mine enemies** refers to a gesture of gaping still used in the Middle East to show derision and contempt.

2. None holy as the Lord. It is the holiness of the Lord that makes him other than man, transcendent. This transcendence is in terms of degree rather than of remoteness. **Rock like our God. Rock** is a frequent metaphor to express the strength and permanence of the Lord. Rocks, as capable of easy defense, were often used as places of refuge. The strength of God is a place of refuge (Ps 91:1,2).

3. By him actions are weighed. With this figure of the balance as the means of testing human worth (Prov 16:2; Dan 5:27), we may compare the familiar illustration from the Egyptian Book of the Dead, representing the heart of the deceased being weighed in a scale against the symbol of Truth and Right before the deceased is admitted to the realm of Osiris. The text to which the Hebrew part refers, however, is applied to this life. **4. Bows of the mighty men are confounded.** Apart from Jer 51:56, *ḥatat* is not used to denote the breaking of outward things, but the breaking of men. **6. He bringeth down to the grave, and bringeth up.** Although this may refer to the resurrection of the dead, it is generally understood to convey the idea that the issues of life and death are in the hand of God; and it may refer to a man's being brought to the point of death but spared.

8. Out of the dust . . . from the dunghill. The town dump was the place where beggars slept at night and where they asked for alms by day. This verse shows God's treatment of the weak and needy. As the human judge is in duty bound to give judgment in favor of the widow, the orphan, the foreigner, and the poor (Isa 1:17; Jer 5:28), so God, the divine Judge, gives judgment in favor of the helpless (Ps 43:1; Isa 11:3,4). Thus, his righteousness becomes a synonym for salvation (Isa 46:13; 51:4-8). **The pillars . . . are the Lord's.** That is, the princes or governors. The Lord has set men in places of authority and has **set the world upon them,** i.e., he has laid the government of world kingdoms upon their shoulders (cf. Gal 2:9, where men are called "pillars").

9. His saints *(ḥasidîm).* The Hebrew word *ḥăsîdāw* is best rendered "loyalty in love." It conveys the idea of loyalty to an agreement. The best example in human affairs is faithfulness to the marriage vow – loyalty and love. *Ḥăsîdaw* is often translated "mercy," "kindness," or "loving kindness." It is the root of *Ḥasidîm,* "the pious ones." **10. His king . . . his anointed.** This is the first reference in the OT to the king as the anointed of the Lord. Later, in the eschatological thought of Judaism, this expression became the characteristic title of the expected Deliverer, the Messiah or the Christ, who would alleviate world troubles in a Messianic era.

11. Did minister unto the Lord. To serve in the presence of the Lord denotes to perform the duties of priests or Levites in connection with the worship of God. In such service Samuel took part as he grew up, under the superintendence of Eli and according to his instructions.

13-17. The priests' custom. That which is justified by precedent. Actually, the precedent is seen in the law of Deut 18:3 and Lev 7:31-34. The sons of Eli were guilty of a twofold sin: (a) instead of taking only their allotted portion, they took all the fork would hold; and (b) they took their share before the fat and blood were offered in sacrifice to the Lord. Apparently the priests did not accept invitations to every family meal but wanted prize cuts sent to their homes. To make sure of getting these prime cuts, they insisted that their servants get the best pieces before the offerings were made.

18. Girded with a linen ephod. The **ephod** was a scanty garment (II Sam 6:14) worn by inferior priests, Levites, judges, and eminent persons for religious purposes. It is not to be confused with the ephod used in divination. Although the Egyptian priests also wore linen garments *(ipd),* it is not certainly known that their dress influenced that of the Hebrew priests. **19. A little coat.** The Hebrew *me'il* denotes a kind of long loose robe worn by kings (I Chr 15:27), prophets (I Sam 15:27), men of position (Job 2:12), and women of rank

(II Sam 13:18). It had a hole for the head, and slits in the sides for the arms to come through, but no sleeves. It was worn as an outer garment over the tunic.

21. Grew. The same verb is used of Moses (Ex 2:10ff.). It may denote mental and moral advancement as well as physical growth.

22. The women that assembled at the door. Exodus 38:8 mentions these women "in service." Some think that the two sons of Eli introduced the cultic prostitution of Canaan into the Shiloh temple. Others think that these women were nursery attendants for small children like Samuel.

24. People to transgress. The LXX reads, *so that the Lord's people do not worship;* i.e., refuse to attend the services because the leaders are immoral.

25. If a man sin against the Lord. When a man has a complaint against another, the matter can be decided by God through his representative, the judge (Ps 82:3), or by the sacred lot in the hand of the priest. But in a case in which God is the plaintiff, there can be no reference to a disinterested party, and the crime incurs the direct vengeance of heaven. **Because the Lord would slay them.** Cf. the language of Ex 4:21 and Josh 11:20, where we read that the Lord hardened the hearts of Pharaoh and the Canaanites; and I Sam 16:14, where it is said that "an evil spirit from the Lord troubled Saul." Yet we are assured that "the Lord delighteth in mercy" (Mic 7:18), and "hath no pleasure in the death of him that dieth" (Ezk 18:32). This coexistence of mercy and judgment in the Divine will (Ex 34:6,7) is a mystery that transcends our comprehension. But it must be carefully noted that it was not until Pharaoh had turned a deaf ear to repeated warnings, not until the Canaanites had polluted themselves with intolerable abominations, that God hardened their hearts. Only when Eli's sons had ignored and defied His laws did He determine to slay them.

27. A man of God. The song of Hannah and the prophecy of the man of God are the only recorded instances of prophecy since the days of Deborah in the early period of the Judges. **The house of thy father.** That is, Aaron. Although the genealogy of Eli is nowhere given in the OT, the chronicler states (I Chr 24:3) that one of Eli's descendants was one "of the sons of Ithamar," the fourth son of Aaron. Also, the name of Eli's son Phinehas is another link connecting him with the family of Aaron (Ex 6:23,25).

28. To burn incense was to sprinkle a powder over live coals and thus create an aroma. Canaanites, Hebrews, Greeks, and Romans all used this feature in the worship of deity.

29. Wherefore kick ye. The figure is that of a pampered and intractable animal (Deut 32:15). **31-35.** Verse 31 refers to the massacre of the priests at Nob; verses 32,33 to the deposition and consequent poverty of Abiathar; verse 35 to the rise of Zadok to the high priesthood. Ezekiel, in his vision of the new Temple, saw the sons of Zadok as the true priests. **36.** Some modern scholars find in this verse a picture of the straits to which the priests of the local sanctuaries were reduced when the latter were abolished by the reform of Josiah.

3:1. The child Samuel. According to Josephus, Samuel had just completed his twelfth year when the Lord spoke to him. It was also at the age of twelve that the child Jesus went up to Jerusalem with his parents (Lk 2:42). **The word of the Lord was precious.** The rarity of revelation made the few occurrences prized possessions. **No open vision.** The revelation was in the form of a word "seen" by the prophet (cf. Isa 2:1 – "The word that Isaiah the son of Amoz *saw*"). The LXX implies that there was no publicly recognized prophet whom the people could consult, and no recipient of divine revelation.

3. Ere the lamp of God went out in the temple. Since the candlestick (seven-branched) was filled with just enough oil to burn through one night (Lev 24:2,3), the time of Samuel's call was undoubtedly the early morn. **And Samuel was laid down.** Samuel slept somewhere near the ark, in a cell for the ministering priests. The word **temple** took in all the area. Hence, Samuel did not sleep by the ark but in a cell in the temple area. **4. The Lord called Samuel.** Modern Moslems still believe that God speaks in visions to those who sleep in the sanctuary. Keret, too, in the Ugaritic Epic, received a revelation in the sacred tent.

11. I will do a thing. This, according to Rashi and Kimchi, means the capture of the ark. However, it may have been intended to be more comprehensive and to include the defeat of Israel, the death of Eli and his sons, the capture of the ark, and the desolation of the sanctuary. **The ears . . . shall tingle.** This expressive phrase occurs two other times (II Kgs 21:12; Jer 19:3), in reference to the destruction of Jerusalem by Nebuchadnezzar.

13. He restrained them not. Either he did not rebuke them severely enough (2:23,24); or (according to Kimchi), he rebuked them too late, when he was old and his rebuke ineffective. Men of God, whose duty it is to admonish others regarding their sinful behavior, often fail to notice the presence of sin in the lives of those nearest to their hearts. Paul's insistence that religious leaders must be home leaders, is appropriate. **14. The iniquity . . . shall not be purged with sacrifice nor offering for ever.** No sacrifice, animal or vegetable, would cause God to turn from his decision to end the dynasty of the house of Eli. The sins of Eli's sons could be forgiven, but their office of priesthood was forever gone.

15. Opened the doors. This was a part of the regular duties of a temple servant. He also lighted the evening lamps and led the semiblind Eli to his posts. The Tabernacle in the wilderness had a curtain at the entrance; the temple at Shiloh had folding doors. **17. God do so to thee, and more also, if thou hide any thing.** An imprecation connected with the slaying of an animal at the taking of an oath. The parties involved prayed that the fate of the victim might be theirs should the oath be violated.

20. From Dan even to Beer-sheba. Equivalent to "from Maine to California." **Dan** was the northernmost point in Israel. It stood on a hill from which the main source of the Jordan takes its rise. **Beer-sheba** was the southernmost point in Israel, a favorite haunt of Abraham. Because of the present division of the city of Jerusalem into Jewish and Arab sections, modern Beer-sheba may soon become the capital of the new State of Israel. Beer-sheba is centrally located in the Negev, the most undeveloped area with potential in modern Israel. **Samuel was established.** He was accredited, approved. The implication of this verse is that men from all parts of Israel came to consult Samuel at Shiloh.

B. The Capture and Return of the Ark. 4:1b–7:1.

1. The Philistines were the sole non-Semitic inhabitants of Palestine. They came from Caphtor (Amos 9:7; Jer 47:4,5; Deut 2:23), which has usually been identified with Crete. Some scholars believe these Philistines were the displaced persons uprooted by the Achaean invasion of ancient Greece, the Aegean Islands, and the coast of Asia Minor in the 1200's. The Philistines were organized under five lords, each of whom controlled one of their five chief cities – Ashdod, Ekron, Askelon, Gaza, and Gath. Their centers lay in the path of conquering armies; and so, eventually, the Philistines pass off the scene of Israel's history, except in their bequeathing to the land of Israel the name Palestine. The earlier Philistine population in Canaan during the patriarchal times was swelled by these displaced persons. **2. In the field.** The battle took place in open country, probably in the Plain of Sharon, where the Philistines had the advantage with their chariots (13:5; II Sam 1:6). The Israelites held their ground but suffered serious loss of men.

3. Let us fetch the ark of the covenant . . . that . . . it may save us. The ark preceded Israel at the crossing of the Jordan and at the battle of Jericho. It symbolized the presence and power of Jehovah, and the elders believed that apostasy could be rectified by the presence of the divine symbol. They could not distinguish between the ark as the symbol of God's presence and the actual presence of God. **4. Which dwelleth between the cherubims. Between** is missing in the Hebrew, and the LXX reads *on.* Dibelius theorized that the ark was a throne borne by cherubim, stylized on the sides of the box.

5. A great shout. This may have been the war cry of Num 10:35 – "Rise up, Lord, and let thine enemies be scattered; and let them that hate thee flee before thee." **6. In the camp of the Hebrews. Hebrews** was the name used of the Israelites by foreigners and by the Israelites of themselves when speaking to foreigners. It may be from *'ēber,* "beyond," originally applied to Abraham as coming from beyond the Euphrates (Josh 24:2ff.). Or it may be a patronymic from Eber (Gen 10:21,24), signifying the descendants of Eber.

10. There fell of Israel thirty thousand footmen. Some say this figure is a military exaggeration of losses; some, that it includes all losses (men and beasts of war); some, that thirty thousand men lost the battle; others, that close combat and poison-tipped arrows produced huge losses. Herodotus and Josephus attest the vast mortality that frequently marked the battles of antiquity. **11. Were slain.** For an account of this national disaster, see Ps 78:60ff.

12. A man of Benjamin. There is a rabbinic tradition that this **man** was Saul and that he rescued the tables of the Law from Goliath, who in turn walked off with the ark of the Lord. **Clothes rent.** Rending one's clothes and putting earth or ashes on one's head were the universal signs of mourning for the dead, or for a national calamity (Josh 7:6; II Sam 15:32).

13. Eli sat . . . by the wayside watching. Eli had gone to the gate of the city to wait for news of the battle. The messenger, in his anxiety to bring the news, hastened past the blind old man at the city gate and had to return to him to render an account of the battle. **All the city cried out.** Most of the men of Shiloh had been killed.

17. This well illustrates the climactic style of the Biblical writer. The four items – Israel's flight, the general massacre, the death of Eli's sons, and the capture of the ark – are presented in order of increasing significance for the old priest.

19. She bowed herself. In some parts of the East, parturient women give birth to their offspring in a standing position; in others, they bring forth kneeling, as is still the custom in Ethiopia. **21. Departed.** The Hebrew word expresses much more. It is an ominous word, meaning, *is gone into exile.* The ark had gone into a foreign land. It is probable that this victory of the Philistines was followed by the desolation of Shiloh. Though the historical books are silent about this tragedy, it was still far from forgotten in Jeremiah's day (7:12,14; 26:6). **Ichabod.** Hebrew *'îkābôd*—"Where is the glory?" Glory has a variety of meanings in Hebrew. It may mean "weight," used metaphorically to denote worth or prestige. Such "glory" may be evidenced in riches (Ps 49:16,17), in a crown (Job 19:9), in gorgeous vestments (Ex 28:2). The glory of a forest is its trees; of a nation, its people. "Glory" is also used as a surrogate for God. Here it means, "Where is God?" The Hebrews often failed to distinguish between the presence of God and the religious symbols for his presence. God was where the holy objects were. When the ark was taken, God was regarded as absent from Israel. In subsequent years, Israel's prophets insisted that God was with his people as truly in the hour of chastisement as at the time of blessing.

5:1. Ashdod was thirty-three miles west of Jerusalem, strategically located on the high road from Syria to Egypt. It had been assigned to Judah (Josh 15:47). Sargon of Assyria captured it in 711 B.C., and in 630 B.C. it withstood an Egyptian siege for twenty-nine years. It was finally destroyed by Jonathan the Maccabee (I Macc 10:84).

2. Dagon. Perhaps from *dag*, "fish," or from *dāgān*, "corn." A fish-god, represented by a figure with the head and the hands of a man and the body of a fish, was worshiped in Syria and is depicted on an Assyrian bas-relief. On the other hand, the Philistines in the rich wheat belt of the Shephelah had worshiped a grain-god imported from the Euphrates Valley. This god was Dagon, who is mentioned in the Ras Shamra tablets as the father of Baal. A temple to Dagon existed in Ashdod until the time of the Maccabees (I Macc 10:83ff.). The depositing of a trophy in this temple of Dagon was not unique. In the Gezer sanctuary was found a sacred stone carried from Jerusalem after a military victory. Also, the Hammurabi stele was carried away by the Elamites and erected in Susa. **4.** The Philistines were victorious over the Hebrews, but not over Jehovah. "The idols shall be moved at his presence" (Isa 19:1). **5. Tread on the threshold.** The practice of jumping over the threshold and not stepping on it was perhaps an ancient custom (cf. Zeph 1:9). The Targum paraphrases this, "who walk in the customs of the Philistines."

6. He destroyed. When applied to men, as in Mic 6:13, the word signifies "to make desolate" not only by diseases but also by withdrawal or diminution of the means of subsistence. **8. Lords.** *Seren* is used only of the five Philistine city rulers. It may be an Achaean word which the Philistines retained when they adopted the Semitic vocabulary. It is related to the Greek *tyrannos*, ("tyrant") in form and function. The Greeks may have borrowed it from their Aegean forebears. **Gath** means *wine press.* It was captured by David (I Chr 18:1), fortified by Rehoboam (II Chr 11:8), taken by Hazael (II Kgs 12:17), then retaken by Uzziah and dismantled (II Chr 26:6). It is mentioned in Amos 6:2 as an example of fallen greatness. Goliath lived there (I Sam 17:4), as also did David, for a while, when fleeing from Saul.

11. For there was a deadly destruction, is used regarding the tumult of a routed army (Deut 7:23; Isa 22:5). **12.** The longer the Philistines refused to recognize the supremacy of Jehovah, the heavier became the plagues. This increasing severity also characterized the plagues inflicted on Egypt in Pharaonic times.

6:2. Diviners. Isaiah 2:6 mentions the

fame of the Philistine diviners. **3. Send it not empty.** In all religions offerings are regarded as a necessary part of worship. These offerings could be in the form of animal or vegetable sacrifices, or in cash. **6. Harden.** This same word is used of the hardening of Pharaoh's heart in Ex 7:14; 8:15,32.

7. A new cart. Likewise our Lord rode on an ass whereon never man sat (Mk 11:2); his body was placed in Joseph's new tomb, wherein never man before was laid (Mt 27:60). From the evidence of archaeology, this was undoubtedly a two-wheeled cart similar to those seen in Europe today. **8. In a coffer.** The word *'argāz* occurs only here. The RSV reads, *in a box;* the AV, *in a coffer.*

12. The kine took the straight way to . . . Beth-shemesh. Since the natural thing for a cow to do is to go directly to her calf, the obvious conclusion was that the animals were controlled by a supernatural power. Compare with this the sign to Gideon, in Judges 6, which consisted in phenomena contrary to expectations. **13. Reaping their wheat harvest in the valley.** At such times in Bible lands, the whole village goes forth to the field.

14. A burnt offering. The cart and oxen, having been used for a sacred purpose, were holy and could not be used for secular purposes, but must be offered in sacrifice. The Talmud and various Jewish commentators explain this offering by stating that, after the desolation of Shiloh, sacrifices were permitted at 'high places.' As there was no central sanctuary, the law of Deut 12:10ff. was temporarily suspended.

19. Fifty thousand and threescore and ten men. Some manuscripts mention only the seventy. How the fifty thousand got into the text is unknown. **20. This holy Lord God.** Their action illustrates man's desire to free himself from the burden of God's presence instead of seeking to fit himself for it. **21. Kirjath-jearim.** *The city of thickets.* In Josh 15:60 it is called Kirjath-baal, indicating possibly the presence of a sanctuary there. Earlier it was a city in the Gibeonite league.

C. The Victory over the Philistines. 7:2-17.

3. The . . . Ashtaroth. The Hebrew plural of *Ashtoreth,* the name of the goddess whom the Babylonians called *Ishtar* and the Greeks, *Astarte* (31:10). She was one of the oldest and the most widely distributed of Semitic deities. Among the western Semites she was the goddess of fertility and sexual relations. Hence, rites of a most licentious character were associated with her worship. The name of the goddess was most probably pronounced *Ashtart* in Palestine (hence the Gr. form), while the traditional form, *Ashtoreth,* was an intentional deformation from the vowels of *bosheth* ("shame") given in the pronunciation of this goddess' name. **4. Baalim.** Baal was the supreme male deity of the Phoenician and Canaanite nations. In the Ras Shamra inscriptions he is known as the son of Dagon and the heir to the throne of El. He was a fertility-god whose domain was in the sky, from where he fertilized the land and thus controlled nature. The cult of Baal was in vogue when Israel entered Canaan, and its many similarities to the Hebrew worship of Jehovah made for a hasty syncretism on the part of many Israelite communities. The ministry of Elijah and Elisha was directed against the worship of Baal, and even some kings joined the crusade.

5. Mizpeh. Mizpeh was the meeting place of the national assembly on two other important occasions – when war was declared on Benjamin (Jud 20), and when Saul was elected king (I Sam 10:17). Two identifications have been suggested: Nebi Samwil, a height about five miles north of Jerusalem, the traditional residence of Gedaliah, the governor of Judah appointed by Nebuchadnezzar (II Kgs 25:23), and the scene of another day of national humiliation under Judas the Maccabee (I Macc 3:44ff.); and Mount Scopus, the broad ridge immediately northeast of Jerusalem. Because of the similarity of meaning between Mizpeh – *watch tower,* and Scopus – *watchman,* some have favored the latter site. **I will pray for you.** Samuel was both the child of prayer and a man of prayer (8:6; 12:19,23). In Jer 15:1, Moses and Samuel are cited as men of prevailing prayer.

6. Poured it out. The pouring of water as a sign of penitence is attested only in this passage. The nearest parallel was the pouring out of water from the pool of Siloam within the temple area on the last day of the Feast of Tabernacles in memory of the gift of water from the rock in the Exodus. **Judged.** His function was twofold – civil and military. As civil judge, he did what Moses did – judged "between one and another," and made them "know the statutes of God, and his laws" (Ex 18:16). As military judge, he did what Othniel, Ehud, Barak, and

Gideon had done before him – organized and marshaled the people for effective resistance to their oppressors and led them to victory.

14. Amorites. In several passages in the Bible the name Amorite *(Westerner)* is used loosely of the original inhabitants of Canaan in general. Hammurabi was a famous Amorite.

16. In circuit. Samuel voluntarily performed the functions of an itinerant judge for the convenience of the people residing in different districts of the country, and for the adjustment of all controversies. **Gilgal.** After the destruction of Shiloh, Gilgal seems to have become one of the principal centers of the religious and civil life of the nation. There Samuel held assizes, the national assembly was convened (11:14), and the army was mustered (13:4). The remoteness of this place from the Philistines may have been the reason for the choice. **17. And there he built an altar.** This deviation from the law of Deut 12:5,13 was probably occasioned by the public disorder of that period and the destruction of both the Tabernacle and its altar. Samuel, being a pious man, was desirous of animating his devotions by prayer and sacrifice. Jehovah sanctioned the erection of this altar by accepting the person and service of the worshiper.

II. The Life and Ministry of Saul. 8:1–14:52.

A. Israel's Request for a King. 8:1-22.

3. Took bribes. Samuel failed to learn from the lesson of Eli and his sons. **5. Make us a king.** The institution of the monarchy involved the separation of the civil from the religious leadership. And this in turn meant that Israel now began to have a political history independent of her religious history, and therefore, of her true calling. Israel was called to religious leadership of the world, and the verdict of history is on the side of those who regarded her entry into world politics as a fundamental mistake.

6. The thing displeased Samuel. The elders (v. 4) gave Samuel two reasons for their request: the maladministration of justice by Samuel's sons in the Beer-sheba court; and the need for a war leader (v. 20). Samuel was personally affected by the request. To be told, after a lifetime of service, that his sons were unworthy to succeed him was most distressing. And to be superseded by another after years of faithful service was a terrific blow to his sensitive spirit.

11. The manner of the king. The demands which the king would make are enumerated: military service, forced labor on royal lands and in the royal arsenal, service in the royal kitchen, appropriation of land to reward the king's ministers, taxation, and confiscation of slaves for the king's work. **13. To be confectionaries.** That is, those who make compounds of spices and perfumes. **15. Tenth.** This is the only reference in the OT to the exaction of tithes by the king. However, in the East it was not unusual for the revenue of the sovereign to be derived in part from tithes, as, for example, in Babylon and Persia.

21. He rehearsed them. "Rehearse" is derived from Old French *rehercier,* "to harrow over again." Samuel once more went over the matter as a farmer harrows again a plot before planting it.

B. Political Life of Saul. 9:1–12:25.

9:1. A mighty man of power. Or, a man of great wealth (cf. II Kgs 15:20). **2. Whose name was Saul.** Saul occurs as the name (a) of an Edomite prince (Gen 36:37,38); (b) of a son of Simeon (Gen 46:10); (c) of a Kohathite Levite (I Chr 6:24); (d) and, in the NT, of Saul of Tarsus (Acts 7:58). **Young man.** *Bāḥûr* in Hebrew means a man in the prime of life. Saul was not a teen-ager, for he had a young son, Jonathan, at this time.

4. Mount Ephraim. This was an extended tour. **Shalisha** and **Shalim** are unidentified. **6. All that he saith cometh surely to pass.** This was one of the tests of a true prophet. A second test was that the teaching of the prophet must be in keeping with the faith of Israel (cf. Deut 18:21,22; 13:1-3).

11. Going out to draw water. The customary duty of the young women of the village, practiced yet today. The time was evening (cf. Gen 24:11). One well or spring supplied the entire village. **12. In the high place. High place** does not mean a height or hill, necessarily; but throughout it signifies a place of prayer or sacrifice. **13. He doth bless. He** is emphatic. Samuel must be present to offer the prayer of blessing before the participants engaged in the sacred meal. Such a blessing of the sacred meal is not mentioned elsewhere in the OT. The priestly blessing on the meal is seen in Qumran literature and in the Lord's Supper.

15. Told Samuel in his ear. Literally, *had uncovered his ear,* a figure of speech said to be derived from the practice of one's pushing aside another man's hair or the corner of his turban in order to whisper a secret into his ear.

19. Go up before me. Permitting a person to go in front was a way of showing great esteem. The Mishnah says that Elkanah was "a fool," for he walked behind his wife! **All that is in thine heart.** May we not suppose that Saul at his plough, like Joan of Arc with her flock, had been brooding over the oppression of his country by the Philistines, and cherishing a vague but real desire to liberate his people?

22. Into the parlour. Connected with the high place was a banqueting hall, in which the sacrificial feast was held. In later times this word was used of the chambers in the temple area used for the residence of priests and Levites. **23,24. The portion.** In Levitical law, this was the priests' portion. Josephus calls it "the royal portion." **25. Samuel communed with Saul upon the top of the house.** The flat roof was used for relaxation. Probably Saul slept there. The content of Samuel's conversation was the deep religious and political degradation of Israel, the oppression of the Philistines, the causes of the inability of the Israelites to meet their problems, the necessity of a national revival, and the need for a leader entirely devoted to the Lord and His program.

10:1. And kissed him. This was an evidence of Samuel's personal affection for Saul, for kissing is nowhere an act expressive of fealty to a king. Bowing expressed one's loyalty to the crown. **Anointed.** Anointing was not a peculiarly Israelite ceremony. It was practiced in Canaan before the Israelite invasion (Tel el Amarna Letters 37, line 6) and in Egypt, where kings were regularly anointed. Originally the fat of an animal was used in the ceremony of anointing; later the oil of olives was used. Some think the custom of anointing started in the belief that the anointing infused the strength of the animal into the king. However, to a Hebrew, anointing signified that the power of God was infused into the person of the one anointed. Anointing is still part of the ceremonial of coronation in England, as well as in many other countries.

2. Thou shalt find. Samuel gave to Saul a sign the fulfillment of which would confirm the divine nature of his call to kingship. **3. The oak** (AV, *plain)* **of Tabor** is supposed by some to be identified with the tree of Deborah, between Ramah and Bethel (Jud 4:5).

5. The hill of God. Or *the Gibeah of God. Gibeah* is used to denote the bald, rounded hills of central Palestine. **Garrison** may be the Philistine officer (13:3) placed in the city to maintain Philistine harmony and to collect tribute. **Company of prophets.** This is the first mention of a prophetic guild in the OT. The main interest of these prophets was to uphold the pure religion of the Lord against any syncretism with the fertility cult of Canaan. Some scholars have felt that Samuel was responsible for introducing the prophetic guilds. **Psaltery . . . tabret . . . harp.** The psaltery was an instrument of ten strings, shaped like a wine bottle and played by the fingers. Tabrets were drums or tambourines, usually played by women. The harps were played with plectra.

9. God gave him another heart. The Spirit of God changed his character into headstrong courage and endowed him with the qualities needed for kingship.

20. The tribe of Benjamin. Benjamin was a favorite son of Jacob and the only son of the twelve born in Palestine proper. The temple area was near the territory of Benjamin and Judah. **22. The stuff.** The baggage of those assembled. Many had come from afar and had brought their own provisions. **23. He was higher than any.** Physical stature was desirable for leadership. Perhaps it was an aid in war, both offensive and defensive, inasmuch as a tall man makes a good fighter and can easily be seen by those who follow him. Goliath was tall; Xerxes stood out above his men. Samuel also saw physical qualification in the eldest son of Jesse and was prepared to make him his choice for king. **24. God save the king.** Literally, *Let the king live!* This expression is still in common use in England.

25. The manner of the kingdom. As Moses had written the law for the *community* of Israel, so Samuel now wrote the constitution of the theocratic kingdom. This constitution has never been located. It would be interesting to read the rules and regulations set forth by Samuel. **In a book.** That is, in a scroll. The book form came into use much later. This scroll was deposited in a high place at Mizpeh.

26. Whose hearts God had touched. Probably these were the men who formed Saul's cabinet. They went home with Saul to Gibeah, where from his farm he ruled as a gentleman farmer. The ruins of the estate of Saul, about four miles north of Jerusalem, have been the subject of much excavation. It is possible to see from Gibeah across the valley to Nebi Samuel (Mizpeh), one of the stations for Samuel's ministry. **27. The children of Belial.** An opposition party formed early. Samuel describes the members as sons of Belial, i.e., "hellions." Their refusal to present gifts according to custom was ignored by the magnanimous Saul, and his spirit of generosity "got him off to a good start."

11:1. The Ammonite. The Ammonites, who were related to Israel through Lot (Gen 19:38), lived a Bedouin type life in the territory east of Gilead. **2. Thrust out . . . right eyes.** The savage character of the Bedouin Ammonites is attested by Amos 1:13. The loss of the right eye was intended to disable a man for war, since his left eye was usually covered by his shield. Similarly, the amputation of a man's thumbs and great toes (Jud 1:7,8) was designed to incapacitate him for the use of the bow and to destroy his swiftness of foot.

5. Saul came after the herd. In view of the opposition to Saul's election (10:27), Kimchi thinks that he refrained, for the time being, from exercising his rule and went back to farming. It is likely that Saul ruled Israel from the farm as a matter of choice. **7. Hewed them in pieces.** The severe threat of Saul, along with his power to carry it out, put "the fear of God" into all Israelite farmers. A volunteer program swamped the draft board!

11. In three companies. Saul used the strategem of Gideon (Jud 7:16). With a forced overnight march, he surprised the Ammonites in the early morning hours and threw consternation and confusion into their hosts.

12:3. Witness against me. Samuel's argument is concerned with his conduct as a judge. A bribe is the price of a life. Normally it means that blood money is offered to the relatives of a murdered man on condition that they forego the right of blood revenge. Here it was a bribe offered to a judge to persuade him to acquit a murderer or to hinder the execution of justice in some manner. **4. Thou hast not.** Samuel's political and religious life was audited and found to be in good order.

7. The righteous acts of the Lord. Those acts whereby he vindicates the helpless in delivering them from their enemies. It is this same saving power of God, directed against sin rather than against human enemies, of which Paul speaks when he declares that the righteousness of God is revealed in the Gospel (Rom 1:17).

9. He sold them. God's abandonment of the people of Israel to their foes is described under the figure of a sale, just as the deliverance of Israel is called redemption or buying back. **Hazor . . . Philistines . . . Moab.** These were the three chief oppressors of Israel during the period of the Judges. **11. Bedan** does not occur in the list of the judges. **Bedan** and *Barak* are almost identical in Hebrew. The Septuagint, Syriac, and Arabic all read *Barak*. Moreover, in Heb 11:32, Gideon, Barak, Samson, and Jephthah are named together, as is the case here. In addition, the mention of Sisera in I Sam 12:9 makes it almost a necessity to read *Barak* here.

17. Thunder and rain. Jerome's testimony (that of an eyewitness), "I have seen rain in the end of June, or in July, in Judea," is borne out by modern travelers. But while unseasonal storms have occurred in Palestine, the evidence of divine intervention in this case is seen in the specific timing of the storm.

23. I should sin. Samuel regarded failure to pray for Israel as a personal sin against God. Prayer for one's nation remains an obligation for a believer.

C. War of Independence. 13:1–14:52.

13:1. Saul reigned one year. The Hebrew of this verse is very difficult to translate. The age of Saul at his accession and one of the two numbers representing the length of his reign have fallen out of the text. It is natural to assume that as David and Solomon reigned forty years, Saul also reigned forty years. Ishbosheth, his son, was also forty years old when he took office and is not mentioned among the sons of Saul in 14:49. One suggested way to read this difficult verse is, "Saul was___years old when he began to reign, and he ruled ___and two years over Israel."

2. Michmash is a village nine miles north of Jerusalem. **Jonathan** in Hebrew means *Jehovah has given;* it may be compared with the Greek *Theodore,* "gift of God." **3. Garrison.** The Hebrew ***n^esîb*** may mean "the resident" or "political officer" of the Philistines. The assassination of this representative of Philistine rule was the signal for revolt.

13. Thou hast done foolishly. Saul's sin was not his sacrificing. David and Solomon offered sacrifices without being censured. His sin was disobedience to a particular command of Samuel to wait seven days. It was Saul's impatience that brought censure. One can well understand his human tendency toward fear when, on the one hand, he saw his army fleeing at the least opportunity, and on the other, he saw the Philistines massing their chariotry and manpower. However, man's extremity always has been God's opportunity. Israel won wars not with numerical superiority but with men of dedicated valor. Samuel had believed Saul could provide this type of courage and was discouraged at the king's lack of faith in the hour of crisis. The single failure of a great man brought an end to the hope of a lasting dynasty. Leaders must not fail. Men who fail in the hour of decision prove faithless to the sacred trust and stand condemned before a holy God. **14. A man after his own heart.** This was the ideal for future leaders (cf. Jer 3:15).

17. The spoilers came. That is, bands sent out to ravage the country immediately concerned in the insurrection. The word "spoiler" is the term used of the destroying angel of Ex 12:23.

21. Yet they had a file for the mattocks. Literally, *And the price of the filing was a pim for the mattocks.* Hebrew weights discovered at Lachish and elsewhere were marked with the word *pîm.* A pîm weighed approximately two-thirds of a shekel. The Philistines controlled the rights to metallurgy and thus held a distinct advantage over the Hebrews in technological warfare. The Iron Age, which came in around 1200 B.C., began to displace the bronze weapons and implements. Since weapons of iron could easily pierce helmets of bronze, they thus nullified the bronze instruments of warfare. The Philistines were known for their interest in iron, and their control of its use kept the Hebrews in subjection.

14:10. Come up unto us, would be a sign to Jonathan of the cowardice of the Philistines, since it would betray their lack of courage to leave their positions to attack the Hebrews.

13. They fell before Jonathan. Apparently the Philistines, surprised by Jonathan's sudden appearance, fled without their weapons. Jonathan easily overtook them and cut them down. It was the function of the armorbearer to kill outright those whom his master had struck down. **15. There was trembling.** The activity of Jonathan started a panic among the Philistines. *A very good trembling,* literally, *a trembling of God,* implies that there was also an accompanying earthquake.

16. The watchmen of Saul. These were the army scouts stationed on an adjoining hill. **17. Number now.** The term used for muster or parade of troops for inspection. **18. Bring hither the ark.** The LXX reads *ephod.* The ephod was the usual organ of divination, and the ark was at this time in Kirjath-jearim. Some have used this passage to suggest that there were several arks in use among the tribes. Perhaps the LXX preserves the true reading, since it would take some time to go to Kirjath-jearim to secure the ark.

19. Withdraw thine hand. Saul feared that by delaying the attack he would lose the advantage of the general confusion in the Philistine camp. Here again Saul displayed lack of patience in determining the will of God.

29. My father hath troubled the land. Troubled is not a good translation for this ominous term, earlier used of the trouble brought by Achan upon Israel (Josh 7:25), by the daughter of Jephthah upon her father (Jud 11:35), and by Elijah upon Ahab (I Kgs 18:17). The Hebrew word means "to make turbid," "to destroy the happiness of." **31. From Michmash to Aijalon.** The route was substantially the same as that by which Joshua chased the Canaanites (Josh 10:10). It was a distance of some twenty miles.

35. Saul built an altar. Apparently at that time the right to sacrifice was not restricted to priests, whose particular function was to use the ephod in interpreting the sacred lot. Saul undoubtedly built other altars, since this was **the first altar that he built.**

43. Lo, I must die. The ban of Saul was as much reverenced as the vow of Jephthah (Jud 11:35). But Jonathan's life, unlike that of Jephthah's daughter, was important to the whole nation, and Saul found that his power was very strictly limited by the popular will. **45. The people rescued.** Hebrew, *ransomed.* This does not mean that another person was killed in Jonathan's place. The ransom paid might be the life of an animal or a sum of money (Ex 12:21-23; 13:11-15; 30:12-15).

47. He vexed them. The disastrous ending of the life of Saul must be viewed in proper perspective. The earlier part of his reign was a series of successes, both against local enemies and against far-flung outposts in the north and in the southeast. To the end, Israel was contented with his rule, and the nation remained faithful to his dynasty even after his death.

49. Ishui is taken by most commentators to be Ishbosheth. Others say it refers to Abinadab (31:2; I Chr 10:2).

III. The Life and Early Ministry of David. I Sam 15:1–II Sam 24:25.

A. Saul rejected by Samuel. 15:1-35.

2. Amalek. The Amalekites, who were descendants of Esau (Gen 36:12), were constant enemies of Israel. They attacked the Israelites at Rephidim in the neighborhood of Sinai and killed the stragglers on the exodus from Egypt. A nomadic people, they were found in a number of locations in Palestine. They were not exterminated by Saul. A remnant survived until the time of Hezekiah (I Chr 4:43), when they were destroyed by a band of Simeonites in the region of Mount Seir. Saul's campaigning against Amalek was to secure the support of Judah against the Philistines, since the Amalekites were on the flank of Judah. **3. Utterly destroy.** Literally, *devote* (to Jehovah). The first idea of *hērem* is that the object is dedicated to Jehovah, and so forbidden to common use. Cities, persons, animals, possessions, and precious objects could be devoted in this manner. We meet with the same idea in "harem" (the women's apartment), and the *haram* (the sacred enclosure at Mecca), in that these, too, were set apart from secular use.

6. The Kenites. The services of Jethro the Kenite to the Israelites in the period of wanderings led to a firm alliance between Israel and the Kenites. These people had accompanied Israel to Jericho, and then gone to dwell with the Amalekites in the desert south of Judah. Famous among the Kenites was Jael, whose husband, Heber, had migrated to north Palestine (Jud 4:11; 5:24). And the Rechabites, who belonged to this tribe (I Chr 2:55), long preserved the nomadic habits of their ancestors (Jer 35:7-10).

7. Shur means *wall*. The name may have been derived from a wall or line of fortifications which anciently defended the northeast frontiers of Egypt. **8. Agag** is found elsewhere only in Num 24:7. It may possibly have been a hereditary title, like *Pharaoh* among the Egyptians and *Abimelech* among the Philistines.

11. It repenteth me. In the language of the OT, God is said to "repent" when a change in the character and conduct of those with whom he is dealing leads to a corresponding change in his plans and purposes toward them. His repentance is not to be understood as his regretting his action, nor is it a sign of changeableness. His promises and threats are often conditional (Jer 18:8-10). **12. He set him up a place.** That is, a monument to commemorate his victory. **To Gilgal.** In the same place where Saul's kingdom had been confirmed (11:14), it was to be taken from him. And where the warning regarding the consequences of disobedience had been uttered (13:13,14), the sentence on disobedience had been pronounced.

15. Saul said . . . the people spared the best . . . Saul, like Aaron at Sinai (Ex 32:22), and Adam and Eve in Eden (Gen 3), tried to shift the personal responsibility to others. Samuel now realized that Saul was not a leader, but the tool and slave of the people. **17. Little in thine own sight.** These were Saul's words about himself when Samuel first told him of God's plans for his kingship. A curious tradition in the Targum here is that Saul's elevation was a reward for the courage of the tribe of Benjamin at the passage of the Red Sea, when they sought to pass over first.

23. Rebellion . . . witchcraft. Both are forms of apostasy, the one being denial of God's authority, the other a recognition of supernatural powers distinct from God. **24. I have sinned.** Saul's penitence was not genuine. He still attempted to shift the blame to the people. His main concern was his fear that the breach between Samuel and himself might become a public scandal and weaken his authority. Notice that Saul **feared the people** instead of fearing Jehovah, and **obeyed their voice** instead of obeying the voice of Jehovah.

32. Agag came unto him delicately. By a slight emendation some read, *came in fetters*. Others, by a clever emendation, read, *came in backwards*. Some think he was doing the dance of death. The Hebrew word is quite uncertain of meaning.

B. David Anointed To Be King. 16:1-13.

2. Take an heifer with thee. It may be inferred from the command that Samuel was in the habit of holding religious gatherings in different provincial towns from time to time. **4. The elders . . . trembled.** Perhaps they looked upon Samuel as the judge who had come to their city to hold court and to punish their offenses (7:16).

7. The height of his stature. Saul's height was one of his qualifications, and Samuel looked upon the height of Eliab and was misled.

12. He was ruddy. Usually this designates the red hair and fair skin regarded as beautiful in southern countries, where the hair and the complexion are generally dark. However, *'admônî,* "ruddy," may refer to the youth's physical prowess. David and Esau are the only two in the OT referred to by this term. Perhaps the word "warrior" would be a better translation than ruddy. **13. In the midst of his brethren.** Probably they understood by the anointing that David would become a disciple of Samuel, or in time might become a prophet in Samuel's stead, as later Elisha became the ministering servant of Elijah. *David* occurs often in the Mari tablets as *dawid-um* and may be a title, such as Captain or Sergeant. The Jewish etymology is that it is from *dôd,* "love," and that he was the beloved of God.

C. David in the Court of Saul. 16:14–19:17.

15. An evil spirit from God. Apparently a gloomy, suspicious melancholy, bordering on madness, affected the mind of Saul. To the Hebrew, every visitation, alike of good and evil, was directly from God (Amos 3:6). **16. He shall play . . . thou shalt be well.** The powerful influence exerted by music upon the state of mind was well known even in the earliest times; so that the wise men of ancient Greece recommended music to soothe the passions, to heal mental diseases, and even to check tumults among the people. **18. A son of Jesse . . . cunning in playing.** The qualifications of David were that he was first-rate. He was good looking. He knew music, and he was a skilled warrior. He was quick to learn and to comprehend. And the Lord was with him. Everything that a king needed for success David had.

21. Stood before him. As a Levite *stood before* the congregation to perform his duties, so David *stood before* Saul in the capacity of a court minister.

17:1. Socoh is the modern Shuweikeh, some fourteen miles west of Bethlehem. The name *Socoh* has been found on jar handles in the neighborhood. **2. Valley of Elah.** Elah means "oak" or "terebinth." The area probably received its name from a distinctive tree that flourished in the region.

4. Six cubits and a span. A cubit is approximately eighteen inches, a span about nine inches. Goliath stood nine feet and nine inches tall. He was a survivor of the ancient race of Anakim, a remnant of which found refuge in Gaza, Gath, and Ashdod, when Joshua "cut them off" (Josh 11:21,22) from the mountains of Judah. **5. Coat of mail.** This piece of armor, made of overlapping plates of metal, protected the body down to the knees. Armor of this kind is represented on the Assyrian sculptures. **6. Brass.** Apart from the javelin, all of Goliath's defensive weapons were of bronze, while those used for attack were iron. **7. One bearing a shield.** This was an attendant who carried a large shield and went before the warrior to protect his whole body.

8. Am not I a Philistine. The Targum of Jonathan states that Goliath went on to boast that it was he who had killed Hophni and Phinehas and carried the ark to the house of Dagon, and on many occasions had slaughtered Israelites. **10. That we may fight together.** Many battles in ancient times were decided by a contest between two warriors. Achilles and Hector agreed to a duel to settle the Trojan War. Goliath proposed that the differences between Israel and Philistia be settled by himself and an Israelite warrior.

15. Went and returned. He went from Saul to feed his father's sheep in Bethlehem, so that he was not in the permanent service of Saul, but at that very time was with Jesse. **17. Parched corn.** The words describe grain plucked just as it was ripening, and roasted in a pan or on an iron plate. Arabs still eat "parched corn" as an important element in their diet. **18. Take their pledge.** Bring back from them some proof that he had fulfilled his mission.

25. Free from forced labor and contributions (cf. 8:11).

28. Few sheep in the wilderness. Wilderness is unfenced range land suitable for grazing cattle, as distinguished from arable land. **Naughtiness.** Cf. Eliab's anger with the hatred of Joseph's brethren for him (Gen 37). Apparently Eliab was unaware of Samuel's having anointed David to succeed Saul, or else he interpreted the anointing to mean that David was to become a servant of Samuel.

34. There came a lion, and a bear. A frequentative imperfect—"From the Lebanon at times descended the bear; from the Jordan ascended the lion." The Syrian bear is said to be especially ferocious, and appears to have been more dreaded than the lion. David had had many harrowing experiences but had been victorious in preserving the flock of his father from the evil beasts. Now he assured Saul that he could protect the flock of God from this uncircumcised Philistine. Faith in past events lends a believer courage to trust in the power of God to meet the crises of the present.

38. Saul armed David. The fact that David tried on the armor of Saul indicates that he approximated the height of Saul. If this is the case, the taunts of Goliath concerning the abilities of the "youth" are more sharply barbed than is commonly supposed.

40. His staff. Probably the common walking stick still seen in the Middle East, used to aid one in walking and to ward off ferocious dogs. **His sling.** In all ages the sling has been the favorite weapon of the shepherds of Syria. The Benjamites were especially expert in its use; even the left-handed could sling stones "at an hair [breadth] and not miss" (Jud 20:16).

54. Brought it to Jerusalem. Jerusalem was still a non-Hebrew city (II Sam 5:4ff.). A little later we find the sword of Goliath at Nob (21:9), and hence some think Nob is intended here. Others think David brought the head of Goliath to Jerusalem at a later period. However, Josh 15:63 and Jud 1:8 show that Hebrews did live at Jerusalem. It was the citadel on Mount Zion that was in the control of the Jebusites.

18:1. And Jonathan loved him as his own soul. Each found in the other the affection that he did not find in his own family. **Knit** is the same Hebrew word used in Gen 44:30 to express Jacob's love for Benjamin. Rare natures, like that of Jonathan, seldom attain to the highest place, and records of their lives are all too few. But as they pass through the world, they strengthen man's faith in humanity, and they leave behind them a fragrance that endures. **4. Jonathan . . . gave . . . to David.** Cf. the exchange of armor between Glaucus and Diomede when they met before Troy and thus confirmed the pledge of old family friendship (Homer *The Iliad* VI. 230). Jonathan, the son of the king, gave all the material gifts; David, the poor man's son, gave but love and respect. One is reminded of the gift of God's Son to poverty-stricken humanity. Perhaps this accounts for Paul's designation of himself as the slave of Christ.

7. Played. This word is used of festive sports, and especially of festal dancing (I Chr 15:29). Some women performed mimic dances while others sang in alternate choruses. **11. The javelin.** Saul, it seems, held the javelin in his hand as a scepter, according to an ancient custom.

18. My father's family means a group of families united by blood ties, moving and acting together, and forming a unit smaller than the tribe, but larger than that of a single family.

21. A snare. The Hebrew word suggests the idea of the trigger of a trap with bait laid upon it. It is also used metaphorically, as here, of that which allures a person to destruction.

25. Dowry. Some payment was made to the father by the prospective bridegroom. Service might be rendered instead of payment in money (Gen 29:20). The same custom prevailed among the ancient Greeks (Homer *The Iliad* XVI. 178; *The Odyssey* VIII. 318), Babylonians, and Assyrians, and it still survives in the East.

19:12. Through a window. The house of Michal was apparently situated on a wall. Cf. the escape of the spies from Jericho (Josh 2:15) and of Saul from Damascus (Acts 9:25). **13. Teraphim** (AV, marg.). Michal, like Rachel, probably kept teraphim in secret because of barrenness (Gen 31:19). **14. He is sick.** Josephus relates that Michal placed a still-moving goat's liver in the bed to make the messengers believe that there was a breathing invalid beneath.

D. David in Exile. 19:18–31:13.

18. Naioth. Somewhere in Ramah, whether a building or a district, is uncertain. Naioth means *dwellings,* and may be the college or common residence of the society of prophets Samuel gathered round him at Ramah.

24. The prophets. From this passage we learn that there was a company of prophets at Ramah, under the superintendence of Samuel, whose members lived in a common building, and that Samuel had his own house at Ramah (7:17ff.), although he sometimes lived in Naioth. The origin and history of these schools are obscure. According to 3:1, before the call of Samuel as a prophet, the prophetic word was rare in Israel, and prophecy was not widespread. There is little doubt that these unions of prophets arose in the time of Samuel, and were called into existence by him. The only uncertainty is whether there were other such companies in different parts of the land besides the one at Ramah. These unions may have grown until the time of Elijah and Elisha. They arose only in Israel, not in Judah. If these schools came from Samuel, it seems strange that there were none in Judah.

20:1. What is mine iniquity? and . . . my sin. Or, my deviation from the right path, and my failure. **3. But a step.** Jewish commentaries here refer to the **step** David took in avoiding Saul's spear. **5. The new moon.** For the observance of new moon festivals in Israel, see II Kgs 4:23; Isa 1:13; Amos 8:5. It was not merely a religious festival (Num 10:10; 28:11-15), but also a civil festival. Apparently it was used as an opportunity for religious instruction (II Kgs 4:23). David, as a member of the royal household, was expected to be present at the new moon sacrificial meal.

15. Thou shalt not cut off thy kindness. Jonathan, who was David's brother-in-law, surmised that his friend would succeed Saul upon the throne. Therefore he requested that when David's enemies were destroyed – especially, in accordance with Oriental custom, the family of his predecessor – his own relationship with David's house might not be forgotten or disowned.

20. I will shoot. No suspicion would be aroused by Jonathan and his bow, since he was a warrior and presumably went out often for archery practice. This was a prearranged agreement in case spies were around. **22. The Lord hath sent thee away.** When Jacob's sons sent their younger brother to Egypt, God was in the plans for Joseph's life. So now God was sending David away to prepare him in the tough discipline of life for the leadership of Israel.

25. The king sat. Saul occupied the place of honor, with his back to the wall opposite the entrance. Jonathan was opposite him, Abner and David to his right and left. Apparently these four sat alone at a round table; so David's absence was conspicuous. **26. He is not clean.** Persons who were ceremonially unclean were excluded from participating in a religious festival. The presence of the Deity in the sacred festivals necessitated ritual and moral purity on the part of the participating members.

27. David's place was empty. The king knew that uncleanness could not be the reason for his second absence, since the impurity Saul had in mind lasted only until sunset (Lev 15:16). **29. My brother, he hath commanded me.** The eldest brother, who acted then as the head of the family, arranged the sacrificial meal. This implies that Jesse was well advanced in years.

30. To thine own confusion. Either Saul was disclaiming Jonathan and suggesting that people would think he was the fruit of an adulterous union; or he was telling Jonathan that his mother would some day become the wife of the new king! **31. Nor thy kingdom.** Saul evidently suspected David as his rival who would either wrest the government from him, or, at any rate, after his death, from his son.

38. Jonathan cried after the lad. These words, spoken to the boy, were really intended for David's ears. **41. Fell on his face.** In token of reverence and loyalty to the king's son. An Oriental, upon meeting a superior, knelt down and touched the ground with his forehead.

21:1. Nob was at that time a priests' city (22:19), where stood the Tabernacle and where the legal worship was carried on. According to Isa 10:30,32, it was between Anathoth and Jerusalem, about one mile north of Jerusalem, on a ridge from the brow of which one can see the temple area.

5. The vessels. Ewald understood this to refer to the young men's bodies, as in I Thess 4:4. The men were ceremonially clean; so they were fit to partake of holy things. Ahimelech departed from the Levitical law and observed the higher commandment of love to a neighbor (Lev 19:18). When Mk 2:26 assigns this action to the days of Abiathar, the high priest, the statement rests upon the copyist's memory, in which Ahimelech is confounded with his son Abiathar. It is also possible that the son acted as coadjutor to his father, as Eli's sons apparently did (cf. I Sam 4:4).

6. The shewbread. So called because it was solemnly placed as an offering in the presence of Jehovah. A golden table for the shewbread in Solomon's Temple is mentioned in I Kgs 7:48; and the form of the table, as it existed in Herod's Temple, is preserved in the sculptures on the Arch of Titus at Rome. The shewbread was renewed every Sabbath, and the loaves that remained were to be eaten by the priests in the Holy Place. Jesus referred to this incident (Mt 12:3,4; Mk 2:25,26; Lk 6:3-5), to show that when moral and ceremonial obligations come into conflict, the ceremonial gives way to the moral. The high priest was bound to preserve David's life, even at the expense of a ceremonial rule.

7. Doeg may have entered the service of Saul after the Israelite campaign against Edom (14:47). Maybe a vow, suspicion of leprosy, or some other impurity kept him at the sanctuary.

10. Achish. Or, *Abimelech* (AV, marg.). The headnote to Psalm 34 refers to the king of Gath by this standing title, "Abimelech." **11. In dances.** They danced in circles as they sang. Whether the Philistines intended by these words to describe David as a hero, or to point him out to their prince as a dangerous man cannot be ascertained from these words; nor can the question be decided with certainty at all. **13. Scrabbled.** Made meaningless marks. The LXX reads, *beat* or *drummed,* from a word which sounds like (but is not written like) the Hebrew for "scrabble."

22:1. They went down. That is, from their home to Bethlehem. The whole clan apparently joined David in exile. In the East it is not uncommon for a whole family to be put to death for the fault of one member, and the massacre at Nob showed David's family what they might expect.

5. This **Gad** is here mentioned for the first time. He later became David's seer (II Sam 24:11). He rebuked David for his sin of the census and wrote a history of the reign of David (I Chr 29:29). From II Chr 29:25 it appears that he was concerned with the arrangement of the temple service.

6. Now Saul abode. Here is a vivid description of an ancient council, such as met to deliberate on affairs of state and to administer justice. **7. Ye Benjamites** shows how isolated the tribes still were, and that for the most part Saul was surrounded by members of his own tribe. **Will the son of Jesse give.** Saul had no palace and no elaborate court. His men were strictly Benjamites. He implied that David would be as narrow in his tribal affiliations. However, as it turned out, David went the other way and risked losing the loyalty of Judah.

18. That did wear a linen ephod. The word rendered **wear** always means "to lift up," "to carry." So, Doeg slew on that infamous day eighty-five ephod-bearing men, priests of full status, each qualified to give oracles by the use of the ephod. **19. The edge of the sword.** Literally, *according to the mouth of the sword.* The ancients designed a sword to resemble an animal, with the blade of the sword representing a tongue and the two sides of the haft resembling lips. In the madness of his self-willed fury, Saul wreaked upon an innocent city, within the confines of his own tribe, the vengeance he had failed to execute upon a guilty heathen nation at the command of God (15:3).

20. Abiathar, one of the sons of Ahimelech, probably left in charge of the sanctuary at Nob, escaped the massacre and fled with the sacred ephod (23:6) to David at Adullam. He shared in all David's wanderings and was made by him joint priest with Zadok. Later he backed Adonijah's quest for the throne and was deported by Solomon to Anathoth. Jeremiah may have been a descendant of this family.

23:1. Keilah was a city in the Shephelah, a place of importance in the time of Nehemiah (Neh 3:17,18). It is mentioned in the Tell el Amarna letters as *Kila.* Today it is a city of ruins, but the terraced hillsides bear testimony to its grain-growing capacity, which the Philistines envied. **They rob.** The Philistines used this method to reduce Israel to submission by starvation. In the East, to this day, the main source of food supply remains — bread.

9. Secretly practised. From *hārash,* "to fabricate," "to forge." It is a metaphor derived from the working of metal.

14. In the wilderness. The wild uncultivated tract lying between the mountains of Judah and the Dead Sea. It begins in about the longitude of Maon and Carmel and becomes wilder and more desolate as it descends toward the Dead Sea. In Josh 15:61,62 six cities are mentioned as existing in this desolate region. David's chief abode was Ziph, which lay about halfway between Hebron and Carmel, in one of the many caves of this limestone rock region. **15. Ziph in a wood** is a conspicuous mound, 2,882 feet above the sea, four miles southeast of Hebron, on a plateau of red, rolling ground. The plateau is mostly bare, though partly covered with wheat and barley. It is broken, here and there, by limestone scarps partly covered by scrub, and it is honeycombed by caves, which commence near Hebron.

16. Jonathan . . . went to David. The humility and unselfish love of Jonathan are apparent in this passage. However, it was doubtless well ordered by God's good providence that Jonathan's noble sentiments were not subjected to the unnatural strain of such a situation. Jonathan died a soldier's death, fighting gallantly for his country, before anything happened to disturb the perfect beauty of his friendship for David.

19. The Ziphites. The reason for the Ziphites' betrayal was either their zeal for Saul or the fact that David levied protection money against them as he did against Nabal (ch. 25).

24. In the plain. The word *'ărābâ* usually denotes the depressed locality around the Dead Sea, the desert tract which extends along the valley of the Jordan from the Dead Sea to the Sea of Galilee, now called El Ghor. This word is also applied to the valley between the Dead Sea and the Gulf of Akaba, to which alone the name is now given by the Arabs.

29. En-gedi is a well watered spot on the east edge of the desert of Judah. It is six hundred feet above the Dead Sea, and from the limestone rock a copious stream plunges toward the sea. There are five or six waterfalls en route, the stream skipping like a goat from one ledge to another; hence the name "The Fountain of the Kid." In the days of Abraham, the city of Hazezon-tamar stood on this site. Engedi is still an oasis in the limestone desert, and though palm trees and vineyards have vanished, the petrified leaves found there and the terraces cut in the hills attest its ancient fertility. A small Jewish kibbutz (farm) is at present located at Engedi.

24:2. The rocks of the wild goats. The cliffs near Engedi, where the wild goats still climb the rocky fastnesses. **3. The sheepcotes.** Rough stone walls built at the entrances to the caves to protect the sheep from wild beasts and to serve for shelter in case of bad weather. Thomson says that there is scarcely a cave in the land but has such a cote in front of it. **4. The skirt of Saul's robe.** Saul had probably laid aside his robe upon entering the cave. This enabled David to cut off a piece of it unobserved.

25:1. Samuel died; . . . all the Israelites . . . lamented. This was like our flying the flag at half-mast in tribute to a national figure. All Israel sent delegates to the funeral service. And Samuel was laid to rest in the family estate at Ramah, the city of his birth, judgeship, and death. **Paran** was the desert that separated Palestine from the Sinai Peninsula.

2. A man in Maon. Nabal's home was in Maon, and his place of business was about a mile north of Carmel. **3. Nabal.** The name means *fool.*

7. We hurt them not. David contrasted the strict discipline maintained by him with the usual license of similar roving bands, and asked that some acknowledgement of this should be made by the wealthy farmer. This species of "protection money" is regularly levied at the present day by the Bedouins living on the borders of the desert and the cultivated land. In return for gifts, they guarantee the protection of life and property in these notoriously insecure districts.

10. Many servants. David's retinue included many runaway slaves, as well as men who had abandoned the service of Saul. Nabal looked upon David as a mere runaway slave. **11. My water.** Water is a precious article in these dry lands.

13. David . . . girded on his sword. David's wrath was an outburst of sinful passion, unseemly in a servant of God. By carrying out his intention, he would have sinned against the Lord and against his people. But the Lord preserved him from this sin. Just at the right time, Abigail, the intelligent and pious wife of Nabal, heard of the affair and was able to appease the wrath of David by her immediate and kindly interposition.

14. He railed. Literally, *he flew at them.* It is the same word as *'ît,* "fly," from which *'ayit,* "a bird of prey," and Greek *aetos,* "eagle," are derived. **18. Clusters of raisins.** The vineyards near Hebron still produce the largest and best grapes in all the country; and the finest of them are dried as raisins.

25. Nabal . . . folly. The Hebrew words for "fool" and "folly" denote not mere stupidity, but moral perversity. *Fool* is an inadequate rendering. The word in Hebrew suggests one who is insensible to the claims both of God and of man, and who is consequently at once irreligious and churlish. **28. A sure house.** Abigail was as certain of David's rise to kingship as was Rahab certain of Israel's conquest of Canaan (Josh 2:9-13). In spite of David's misfortunes at court, the average citizen expected his tide to turn. Many looked upon him in his exile as the hope of Israel.

29. Bound in the bundle of life. This saying has long been applied to life beyond the grave, and its initial Hebrew letters are today found on almost every Jewish tombstone. This beautiful metaphor is taken from the custom of binding up valuable things in a bundle to prevent their being injured. The figure is that of a precious jewel carefully tied up (Gen 42:35). The converse follows in the prayer that the lives of David's enemies might be cast away like the stones from a sling. **31. Shed blood causeless.** Abigail's argument was that any shedding of blood at this point would work against David's program. It would start a blood feud among the clans of Judah that would involve men David needed to support his bid for kingship. David had only Judah to back him in the quest for the throne. In addition, Abigail argued, David's conscience would trouble him if blood flowed needlessly.

39. Communed with Abigail. This is a technical expression for asking one's hand in marriage (cf. Song 8:8). **43. Also took.** David married Ahinoam, mother of Amnon, before he married Abigail. In the lists of David's wives, Ahinoam is always mentioned first. **44. Gallim** is mentioned in the neighborhood of Anathoth in Benjamin (Isa 10:30).

26:6. The Hittite. The Hittites are mentioned repeatedly in the OT as one of the nations to be driven out of Canaan. Their empire, centered in Asia Minor, came to an end about 1200 B.C. Subsequently, powerful Hittite city states maintained themselves in northern Syria, notably at Carchemish on the Euphrates and Kadesh on the Orontes. These were destroyed by the Assyrians in the eighth century. **Abishai** saved David's life in one of the Philistine wars (II Sam 21:17), was implicated in the murder of Abner (II Sam 3:30), shared in the command of the army (II Sam 10:10), and remained faithful to David in Absalom's rebellion.

8. Let me smite him. David's generosity toward Saul is contrasted, in this passage, with Saul's murderous hatred of him. Saul had attempted to transfix David with his javelin. Now Abishai wanted to transfix Saul with his spear. But David refused to let him touch the Lord's anointed.

12. A deep sleep. This was a slumber so profound and unnatural that it was regarded as sent directly from the Lord. The same term is used of the sleep of Adam while the Lord created Eve from a rib taken from Adam's side.

19. Let him accept an offering. The idea here is that if it was the Lord's prompting that led Saul to pursue him, David would seek God's pardon by a suitable expiatory offering. David recognized the legitimacy of Saul's intention but offered to atone for any sin on his part. This was going more than halfway. The second half of the verse suggests that possibly men were seeking to set up human barriers between Saul and David. If this was the case, David pled for their just punishment. **Go, serve other gods.** It was the custom for a person to adopt the gods of the land to which he went. Ruth volunteered to accept Jehovah in Palestine in place of Chemosh in Moab. David felt that Israel was literally driving him from the worship of Jehovah to that of foreign gods. **20. Let not my blood fall to the earth.** No Hebrew wanted to die outside the land of Israel.

27:5. A place in some town. In a district of his own, David could observe his own religious rites as a worshiper of Jehovah and not be under the constant surveillance of the king.

10. The south. The Negev. Literally, *the dry country*. It was the name of the waterless district to the south of Jerusalem, between the hills of Judah and the actual desert. The various regions of **the south** were known as: the Negev of Judah, including the cities mentioned in Josh 15:21-32; the Negev of the Jerahmeelites; the Negev of the Kenites; the Negev of the Cherethites; the Negev of Caleb; and the Negev of Arad.

28:2. Thou shalt know. David's reply was ambiguous. The words, **what thy servant will** (AV, *can*) **do,** contained no distinct promise of faithful assistance in the war with the Israelites. The expression **thy servant** was simply the ordinary form for speaking of oneself to a superior. **Keeper of mine head.** Perhaps this incident caused David later to hire mercenary troops for his bodyguard.

3. Familiar spirits. The term *yiddeʿōnîm* means those in touch with the diviner. One who divined by the *yiddeʿōnîm* consulted only the particular spirit which was his familiar. From Isa 8:19; 19:3 it may be inferred that the oracles were uttered in a squealing voice, by means of ventriloquism.

4,5. They pitched in Gilboa. . . . greatly trembled. Saul may have camped on the same ground where Gideon and his men camped. The spring by which Gideon pitched is called "the well of Harod" (Jud 7:1, AV), i.e., *the Spring of Trembling*. Saul camped beside the same spring and "trembled greatly."

7. Endor was long held in memory by the Jewish people as connected with the great victory of Deborah and Barak over Sisera and Jabin. The distance from the slopes of Gilboa to Endor is seven or eight miles, over difficult ground. On the bleak northern slope of Jebel Duhy (the Little Hermon), the name still lingers, attached to a once considerable but now deserted village. The rock of this mountain village is hollowed into caves, one of which contains a little fountain and may well have been the scene of the incantation of the witch. **8. They came . . . by night.** It was a perilous journey of seven or eight miles, part of which skirted the Philistine encampment.

11. The question whether the woman really possessed the power of communion with the spirits of the dead, or had deluded herself into believing that she had such power, or was simply a deliberate impostor, is answered differently by different writers. That the spirit of Samuel actually appeared was the view of the ancient rabbis. This is attested in the LXX translation of I Chr 10:13b – "And Samuel the prophet made answer to him"; and by Ecclesiasticus 46:20. The same view was held by Justin Martyr, Origen, and Augustine. Tertullian and Jerome maintained that the appearance of Samuel was a diabolical delusion.

12. **Thou art Saul.** With the apparition of Samuel, the woman, either by the fact of Samuel's appearance, or by her intensified perception in the state of clairvoyance, recognized that it was Saul who sought her help. It is difficult to understand why she had not recognized the tallest of all the Israelites before. Perhaps the darkness hid him from her view.

15. **Disquieted me.** The more modern orthodox commentators are almost unanimous in the opinion that the departed prophet did really appear and announce the coming destruction of Saul and his army. They hold, however, that Samuel was brought up not by the magical arts of the witch, but through a miracle wrought by the omnipotence of God. Earlier orthodoxy looked upon this appearance as a spectre, an apparition or delusion. 16. **Is become thine enemy.** This word for **enemy** is an Aramaic form, found only in one or two other places in Hebrew. The LXX renders this, *has come to be on the side of thy neighbor:* the Vulgate, *has passed over to thy rival;* the Targum, *has become the help of man who is thine enemy.* The LXX reading is preferred.

20. **Along on the earth.** Literally, *the fullness of his stature.* Exhausted as he was by fasting, Saul fainted from the shock of hearing his doom pronounced. 23. **The bed.** Probably the platform running along the wall, which in the East serves for a seat by day and a bed by night.

29:2. **The lords of the Philistines** were the supreme civil authorities, but they were not army commanders. This division of civil and military authority predates the Roman system of government division of power.

30:1. **On the third day.** From the probable site of Aphek in the Sharon to the probable site of Ziklag is about seventy miles. David and his men must have returned by forced marches. 2. **The women captives . . . carried away.** The captives were intended for sale as slaves in the markets of Egypt.

9. **Brook Besor.** This may be the Wadi esh-Sheri'ah, four or five miles south of the proposed site of Ziklag. The Hebrew word for brook is *nahal,* which means a ravine, or the bed of a torrent, with a stream at the bottom. 10. **Were so faint.** From the forced march from Aphek to Ziklag, and the immediate pursuit without rest. The warriors were "dead beat." (The word **faint** is used here and in verse 21 with a noun meaning "a corpse.")

13. **My master left me.** The life of a sick slave was of little more importance than that of a crippled horse. 14. **Cherethites** were possibly connected with Crete (Caphtor), the country from which the Philistines were believed to have come (Amos 9:7). **Coast of Judah.** The eastern portion of the Negev belonged to Judah. One part of it belonged to the family of Caleb, and was called Caleb's Negev (25:3; cf. Josh 15:13).

20. **David took all the flocks and the herds.** David's motive in choosing the sheep and oxen for himself is evident from verses 26-31. They were the most acceptable presents he could make to his friends in Judah in exchange for security from the men of Saul and to promote his cause in their midst. 24. **They shall part alike.** According to Polybius (X. 16.5), Scipio, after the sack of New Carthage, directed the tribunes to divide the booty in equal portions to all, including the reserves, the guards of the camp, and the sick.

28. **Siphmoth** is not elsewhere mentioned, but Zabdi, the Shiphmite (I Chr 27:27), who was over David's wine cellars, was evidently a native of the place. 31. **Hebron** was known in the days of Abraham as Kirjath-arba. Today it is called El-Khalil, "The Friend," an abbreviation for "the city of the Friend of God," and is the Mohammedan title for Abraham (cf. II Chr 20:7; Isa 41:8; Jas 2:23).

31:1. **In mount Gilboa.** Four memorable battles were fought in this area:

a. The battle of Kishon, in which Deborah and Barak defeated the hosts of Sisera (Jud 4:15; 5:21).
b. The battle of Jezreel, in which Gideon's three hundred defeated the vast hordes of the Midianites (Jud 7).
c. The battle of Mount Gilboa, recorded here.
d. The battle of Megiddo, in which

Josiah, king of Israel, lost his life fighting against Pharaoh-nechoh (II Kgs 23:29).

3. **He was sore wounded.** The LXX and the Vulgate read, *he was wounded in the abdomen*. The story does imply a wound that prevented his escape. 4. **Abuse me.** This same word is used anthropomorphically of Jehovah's treatment of the Egyptians (Ex 10:2). **Saul took a sword.** There are only four examples of suicide in the Bible, those of Ahithophel (II Sam 17:23), Zimri (I Kgs 16:18), Judas (Mt 27:5), and Saul, here. 5. **Died with him.** Had David continued in his office of minister to Saul, he would probably have perished in this battle. God, however, had stationed him in a place of safety, though at the time it seemed one of great peril.

9. **They cut off his head.** Probably in retaliation for the treatment given Goliath (17:54). 10. **The house of Ashtaroth.** This has generally been supposed to be the famous temple of the Phoenician goddess Ashtart at Ascalon, mentioned by Herodotus (I. 105) as the most ancient of all temples of the Greek Aphrodite. However, in the excavations of the University Museum of Philadelphia at Bethshan, two important temples built by Ramses II have been discovered, one of Ashtoreth, and one of Resheph. It was probably in this temple of Ashtoreth that Saul's head was placed.

12. **Burnt them.** Perhaps they feared that the Philistines would remove the bodies and add further insult. However, cremation, except in the case of criminals (Josh 7:25), was not a Hebrew practice. It was practiced by the Philistines and may have been borrowed by the men of Jabesh-gilead. 13. **Buried.** Saul was a hero of tragedy in the classical sense of the term. He had some good features, such as courage, generalship, modesty, and generosity. But he did not have single-minded tenacity; that was his 'tragic flaw.' Even his pursuit of David was at times halfhearted. He lacked the greatness of the later David. Nevertheless, here, in an exquisite elegy, David laments him as a great figure.

E. David, King at Hebron. II Sam 1:1–4:12.

9. **Slay me.** This account is at variance with the account of the death of Saul in I Sam 31:3ff. It is unlikely that Saul would have been leaning on his spear, unattended by Israelite warriors, as the Philistine chariots charged him, and had to call on a stranger who just happened to be passing by. The story was faked, in part, by the Amalekite in hope of obtaining a better recompense from David. The man probably had found Saul after he had died but before the Philistines returned to strip the slain. **Anguish is come upon me.** The Hebrew word for **anguish** has been variously translated "giddiness" "dizziness," "anguish," and "cramps." The Jewish commentators read, "cramps have seized me and I can't defend myself." 10. **Bracelet.** In the Assyrian sculptures, warriors are often depicted wearing such ornaments. They were really armlets worn on the upper part of the arm.

12. **They mourned . . . for Saul.** The only deep mourning for Saul was by the person he had hated most and persecuted for so many years, even to the time of his death. Compare the weeping of Jesus over the fall of Jerusalem, even when it was about to destroy him.

13. **A stranger.** This is the technical term for a foreigner living in Israel and enjoying protection but not full civil rights. He did receive the benefit of the law of the Sabbath rest (Deut 5:14), but he was expected to adopt the religion of his community if he wanted to participate in the religious festivals. The **stranger** is mentioned, along with the widow and the orphan, in special legislation. Blood feuds, adventure, and discontent may have necessitated the origin of this institution in Israel.

15. **Fall upon him.** This just punishment of the Amalekite precluded any untrue accusations by David's political opponents that he might have had a part, directly or indirectly, in the death of Saul. Though David had numerous opportunities to slay Saul, he always regarded him as the Lord's anointed.

17. **Lamented.** A technical term. According to custom, the lament for the dead was chanted by professional mourners (II Chr 35:25), usually women (Jer 9:17). Here David, himself, lamented the death of Saul and Jonathan. 18. **The use of** (AV marg., *ode of*) **the bow.** This is probably the record of David's custom of teaching military music to develop martial spirit. **The book of Jasher** is mentioned in Josh 10:13 and I Kgs 8:53 (LXX). It was a history of the wars of Israel ("Jeshurun"; Deut 32:15).

20. **The daughters of the Philistines.** The rejoicing of the daughters of the Philistines refers to the custom of employing women to celebrate the victories of their nation by singing and dancing (I Sam 18:6). 21. **Not . . . anointed with**

oil. The shield of Saul is pictured by David as lying upon the mountains, no longer polished and ready to be worn in action, but cast aside as worthless, and neglected. In ancient times, shields, whether made of leather or of metal, were oiled to keep them in good condition.

22. The bow of Jonathan. Jonathan was celebrated for his use of the bow, while Saul was known for the use of the sword. **Returned not empty.** The figure underlying the passage is that of the arrow drinking the blood of the slain, and of the sword devouring their flesh (Deut 32:42). **23. Lovely . . . not divided.** Notwithstanding their difference in character, David pays tribute to both as courageous and of good character. Jonathan remained loyal to his father in spite of his own love for David and Saul's enmity toward the younger man. **Eagles . . . lions.** The light motion or swiftness of an eagle (Hab 1:8) and the strength of a lion were the leading characteristics of the great heroes of antiquity. **24. Scarlet . . . gold.** These were the ordinary ornaments of a Hebrew woman (cf. Jer 4:30).

2:1. Hebron really means *brotherhood* (cf. v. 3, **cities of Hebron,** i.e., a federation of cities). It is now called *El Khalil* ("the friend"), a contraction for *the city of the friend of God,* viz., Abraham. It served as the center of the league or confederation of the clans of Judah and Caleb and those associated with them. It is approximately twenty miles south of Jerusalem, in the region famed in antiquity for its fertile vineyards.

7. Be ye valiant. In sending this royal message, David was doubtless actuated by motives of policy as well as by gratitude. Here, for the first time, he claimed to be Saul's legitimate successor and expressed hope for the loyal support of the men of Gilead.

8. Mahanaim. *Twin camps,* situated on the eastern side of the Jordan, not far from the ford of the Jabbok, was an important place for the execution of Abner's plans, partly from its historical associations (Gen 32:2,3), and partly from its strategic geographic situation. **10. Ishbosheth** was originally *Ishbaal.* Hebrew names were often compounded with *ba'al,* the title of the Canaanite god of fertility. Since the word was peculiarly associated with the low standards of Canaanite sex morality and baseness in worship, this practice was later discontinued. Later editors substituted *bosheth,* "shame," for *ba'al.* Another view of the meaning of *Ishbaal* is that it comes from the Ugaritic *it-ba'al* and means "Baal lives."

13. The pool of Gibeon, six miles northwest of Jerusalem, is known as *el-Jib.* Recent excavations have turned up more than twenty jar handles with the name of the city, Gibeon, inscribed on them. **14. And play before us.** No other example of a war game exactly like this unusual one has ever been found.

23. The hinder end of the spear was pointed so that it might be stuck into the ground. This explains the fact that the spear passed through the body. **32. The sepulchre of his father.** Zeruiah was the mother of the three brothers (cf. 17:25). We do not know why they were called by their mother's name. Perhaps their father had died early. Or, perhaps the fact that Zeruiah was in the immediate family of David accounts for this usage.

3:3. Chileab is called "Daniel" in I Chr 3:1, and therefore he probably had two names. **Geshur.** This marriage with a foreign princess may have been prompted by the desire to secure an ally in the neighborhood of Ishbosheth's capital.

13. Bring Michal. The return of Michal has been viewed by some as a political move to enlist the support of the Benjamites. By others it is taken as a sign of David's undying affection for his first wife. According to the law of Deut 24:1-4, David could not legitimately receive back his wife after her marriage to Paltiel. Jewish commentators explain that David had fled from Saul's home on the night of his marriage. Others say that Paltiel's marriage with Michal was never consummated. The latter seems very unlikely in the light of verse 16.

22. Joab . . . Abner. Abner was doomed as long as there was a Joab. Sooner or later their paths must cross. It is difficult to understand why David tried, in the interests of the state, to sacrifice Joab in the political treaty with Abner. **27. Aside in the gate.** The most public spot in the city is not the place for a "quiet word" with anyone! The LXX reads, *to the side of the gate,* in a retired corner. The motive for Joab's action was blood revenge, to avenge the death of his brother at the hand of Abner (3:30). Underlying this duty to avenge was perhaps jealousy, or a mistaken zeal for what Joab considered to be the best interests of the king.

39. Too hard for me. David organized six hundred malcontents, dealt harshly with the Amalekites (II Sam 1), put to death the men who murdered Ishbosheth

(II Sam 4), but failed to act in the case of Joab's misdeeds. David washed his hands and left the family of Joab to the judgment of God.

4:2,3. Beerothites fled. The Beerothites (Gibeonites, Josh 9:17,27) were expelled by Saul (II Sam 21:1,2) and fled to Gittaim. Their town, Beeroth, passed into the possession of Benjamin. Beeroth is generally identified with el Bireh, a village nine miles from Jerusalem, on the road leading to the north.

5. On a bed at noon. This is the siesta, from twelve till three or four o'clock. At this hour his guard would likewise have been asleep, or at least insufficiently alert. **6. Fetched wheat.** Their ruse to gain entrance to the house is an old one – the delivery man approach. The LXX has an altogether different rendering: *And, behold, the woman who kept the door of the house was winnowing wheat, and she slumbered and slept; and the brothers Rechab and Baanah escaped notice.* This also explains how it was that they were able to enter unnoticed.

F. David, King at Jerusalem. 5:1–8:18.

5:2. Feed. To act as a shepherd. This became a technical term for a ruler (Jer 3:15). The figure is developed in Ezekiel 34. **3. Made a league.** It is regrettable that we do not have the terms of agreement in the covenant with Israel. Apparently they included equal rights with the tribe of Judah.

6. The Jebusites. In Jud 19:10 and I Chr 11:4,5, the city of Jerusalem was called Jebus. The Tel el Amarna letters (c. 1400 B.C.) refer to it as *Uru-salim* ("city of peace"). The inhabitants were of an Amorite-Hittite background (cf. Ezk 16:3,45). For their defense they relied upon the unusual natural advantages of their citadel, which stood upon Mount Zion, a mount shut in by deep valleys on three sides. In their haughty self-assurance they boasted that they did not need to employ healthy and powerful warriors to resist David's men, since their blind and lame could successfully withstand an Israelite attack.

7. David took . . . Zion. The capture of Jerusalem marks a most important point in the history of Israel. Hitherto, the national life had had no real center. The residence of a judge, a prophet, or a king served as a temporary rallying place, such as the "palm tree of Deborah," Shiloh, Mizpeh, Gibeah (of Saul), Nob, or Hebron. From this time, the center was fixed, and, at least for the southern kingdom, all the other cities grew less and less important in comparison with the new capital. Jerusalem's position, however, in the midst of the rocky, barren ridge running down central Palestine made it always more suitable for a fortress than for a wealthy commercial capital, such as Solomon tried to make it.

8. Getteth up to the gutter. Archaeological discovery has provided an attractive identification of this gutter (RSV, *watershaft)* with the shaft that leads down through the rock on which the city is built to a pool fed by the Virgin Spring opposite the village of Siloam. **9. Millo.** The word apparently means *filling* and may denote a mound or a rampart of earth, or a building constructed for the purpose of filling a large hole in the earth. This type of construction was found at several Hyksos centers, e.g., Avaris in Egypt and Hazor in Palestine. It resembled a corral in appearance. **Inward** is literally *toward the house* and means northward in the direction of the Temple. This expression was probably a note by a scribe after the Temple was built.

11. Tyre. One of the two great cities of the Phoenicians, famous for its commerce, craftsmen, and wealth. It was situated midway between Carmel and Beirut.

20. Baal-perazim. An ancient Canaanite name meaning *the Lord of breaking forth*, indicating the local nature-deity or baal, who was supposed to dwell in the fountain. The image is that of waters breaking through a dam. **21. Left their images.** They had probably taken them to the war – as the Israelites took their ark – to serve as an auxiliary force.

23. Mulberry trees. The LXX reads, *pear trees.* The Hebrew word *bākā'*, according to Abulfadl, is the name given in Arabic to a shrub that grows at Mecca. It resembles the balsam, except that it has longer, larger leaves and its fruit is more nearly round. If a leaf is broken off from a twig, a white pungent sap, like a white tar, flows out. This feature, in all probability, gave rise to the name *bākā'*, "weeping."

6:2. Baale of Judah. Cf. I Chr 13:6. The idiom means *Lords of Judah.* These were the leading members of the land of Judah. Cf. the Baal Schechem – Judges 9. Traditionally the term has been regarded as a place name – Baale of Judah. **3. The ark . . . upon a new cart.** Jewish commentators point out that the ark and the holy vessels should have been borne only upon the shoulders of the Levites (Num 3:31; 7:9).

7. **Anger of the Lord was kindled.** The sin of Uzzah arose from the fact that the ark was not carried by Levites, as God had directed (Num 4, espec. v. 15). 10. **The Gittite.** The later tradition (I Chr 15:18) makes him a Levite. If this is correct, he probably came from Gath-rimmon, a Levitical city (Josh 21:25).

13. **Six paces.** After they had proceeded six paces safely, they knew that the journey to Jerusalem had the sanction of God.

14. **Girded with a linen ephod.** Probably David wore only the linen ephod. Hence the contempt of Michal, who saw the kingship degraded by religious ritual. Some feel that her jealousy for the house of Saul, or her desire to lead the procession as did Miriam the prophetess, sister of Moses (Ex 15), caused her to despise David. 18. The fact that David wore an ephod, offered sacrifices, and pronounced the blessing, shows that the priesthood was not confined strictly to the Levite class.

23. **No child.** David thus inflicted on Michal the greatest disgrace that could befall an Eastern woman when he became permanently estranged from her.

7:14. **His father . . . my son.** In Heb 1:5 these words are applied to Christ. God's covenant with David is a guarantee that His purpose to bring to mankind a righteous king would surely be fulfilled. Solomon, David's son and successor, brought an immediate and partial fulfillment to the promise. Solomon was not, however, the righteous king whose dominion would endure forever. David's "greater Son," Jesus, was the long awaited Messiah of Davidic lineage who was in the fullest sense also the Son of God.

18. **Sat before the Lord.** Not in a chair, but back on his heels, with his head erect, in the manner of a modern Muslim at prayer.

8:1. **Metheg-ammah** means *bridle of the mother* (city). In I Chr 18:1 this is equated with Gath, which may have been the control station for the five Philistine cities. David's capture of his city of political asylum and the home of his first victim, Goliath, indicated to the Israelites both his ability and his nationalistic spirit. 2. **Measured them with a line** may mean that he spared the little ones but killed the adults whose height approximated the length of two cords. 3. **Zobah** was a Syrian kingdom, whose territory seems to have lain north of Damascus and not far from the Euphrates. 8. **Exceeding much brass.** It is said that the Egyptians of the Eighteenth and Nineteenth Dynasties got so much copper from Syria that they gave up working the mines at Mount Sinai in the south. 10. **Joram his son.** The king's son was his ambassador.

17. **Zadok . . . Ahimelech . . . priests.** Zadok may have been priest under Saul. Abiathar served under David while the latter was in flight from the court of Saul. David solved the resulting difficulty by dividing the office between them. But for the prompt action of Joab, he would probably have divided the command of the army between Joab and Abner. **Seraiah** was the secretary of state, rather than a military officer responsible for raising and mustering the troops; for the technical expression for mustering the people was not *sāpar* (the verb form from which the noun scribe is derived) but *pāqad*.

18. **Cherethites and the Pelethites.** It is well known that at all times kings and princes have preferred to commit the protection of their person to foreign mercenaries rather than to home guards. Rulers feel that they have all the surer pledge of the guards' devotion in the fact that the men do not spring from the nation, and are more dependent upon the ruler alone. David had received a hospitable reception in the land of the Philistines and perhaps met with many loyal friends there. **Chief rulers.** Literally, *priests*. Just what the duties were which they discharged is far from clear. Zadok and Abiathar were the priests for the nation, and it is evident from 20:26 and I Kgs 4:5 that these "priests" stood in some special relation to the king. Accordingly, Ewald conjectures that they were his domestic priests. In Egypt, the king's confidential advisers are said to have been chosen from among the priests, and it is this view of the functions of these two men which is taken in Chronicles.

G. Court Life of David. 9:1–20:26.

9:10. **Eat bread.** A general expression here meaning to have all the necessaries of life provided.

10:4. **Shaved . . . the one half of their beards.** Even today cutting off a person's beard is regarded by the Arabs as a great indignity, quite equal to that of flogging and branding among ourselves. Many would rather die than have their beards shaved off. The insult was still further increased by the cutting short of the long dress that covered the limbs, and thus exposing the lower part of the body. **5. Jericho** was halfway between Amman and Jerusalem. **12. Be of good courage.** We learn from this that a man should not depend on miracles, but should first strive as far as he can to save himself, and then rely on God's help.

11:1. Rabbah is modern Amman (Philadelphia in Hellenistic times), about twenty miles east of the Jordan at the head of the Wadi Amman.

3. Eliam and **Ammiel** (or *Bath-sheba,* AV) have the same signification. The difference consists simply in the transposition of the component parts of the name. **4. She came in.** Although David is held responsible for the sin, Bath-sheba was not without blame. She came at his request, seemingly without hesitation, and offered no resistance to his desires (at least as far the the record is concerned). The fact that she was bathing in the uncovered court of a house in the heart of a city, into which anyone could look down from the roofs of neighboring houses or from higher ground, does not say much for her modesty, even if she had no ulterior motive, as some commentators suggest. However, this does not excuse David from the enormity of his transgression against the Lord's statutes and against one of his top fighting men.

16. Joab, as a general who was not accustomed to spare human life, served his lord faithfully in this matter, with a view to having his own interests served at another time. **21. Thy servant Uriah the Hittite is dead** might be interpreted as meaning that it was without Joab's command, or in opposition to it that Uriah went so far with his men, and he was therefore chargeable with his own death and that of the other warriors who had fallen.

27. Mourning was past. The ordinary mourning period was seven days. Whether widows mourned longer, we do not know. David promptly took Bath-sheba as his wife, so that she might be married to him as long as possible before the birth of the child. He hoped thus to forestall any suspicions of premarital relations that might otherwise arise.

12:6. Restore . . . fourfold. The fourfold restitution corresponds to the provisions of the law of Ex 22:1. **13. I have sinned against the Lord.** Sin has two results — it separates a man from God, and it produces evil effects in the world. The first of these can be canceled by forgiveness, but the second remains. The tragedy of human history is that the evil effects of sin are not always nor wholly borne by the sinner.

23. I shall go to him. Cf. Job's "the house appointed for all living" (Job 30:23). Something of the Hebrew idea of conscious existence in the next life may be implicit in the common expression, "he was gathered to his fathers." Perhaps by this reference David merely meant that the child could not return to life and activity, but he himself would some day join his son in death.

24. Solomon. The name means *peace.* Perhaps the conferring of this name signified that David was now at peace with God. Another view is that Solomon was born at the end of the hostilities with Ammon and when the peace was declared. Solomon was his royal name. **25. Jedidiah** *(beloved of the Lord)* was his family name. It was quite common in Judah for the king to possess two names. **By the hand of Nathan.** Some think that Nathan served as the royal tutor of Solomon.

27. The city of waters. "Waterfort" — the work defending the water supply of the royal city. Polybius, in his account of the siege of Rabbath-Ammon by Antiochus Epiphanes, says the Syrian king succeeded in stopping the water supply and forced the garrison to surrender the city proper, which was built on the high ground above. **31. The children of Ammon.** David put them to hard labor, not to torture. To a Bedouin this type of punishment was extreme cruelty.

13:1. Absalom . . . Tamar . . . Amnon. Absalom and Tamar were David's children by Maacah, the daughter of the king of Geshur (3:3); Amnon was David's son by Ahinoam the Jezreelitess (3:2). The case of Abram and Sarai shows that marriage between the children of the same father by different mothers was sanctioned by early Hebrew custom, though forbidden by the Levitical legislation (Lev 18:9). **2. Thought it hard.** He had few opportunities to see the unmarried members of the royal harem, probably none to see Tamar alone.

6. Let Tamar . . . come. It is evident that the king's children lived in different houses. Probably each of the king's wives lived with her children in one particular compartment of the palace. **A couple of cakes.** The Hebrew word used for **cakes** is from the root *lbb,* "heart." Perhaps these were heart-shaped cookies. Also, there may be a play on words in the use of this term.

13. He will not withhold. The Law forbade this type of marriage (Lev 18:9), but it may not have been strictly observed at this time. The Talmud overcomes the difficulty by assuming that Tamar was of illegitimate birth.

18. A garment of divers colours. This was also said of the coat of Joseph. The famous tableau of Beni Hasan (Egypt) shows that the typical dress of nomads in patriarchal Palestine was a many-colored garment. However, none of the garments in this tableau are ankle or wrist length. This feature is distinct in the case of Joseph and Tamar, and signifies something special. **20. Tamar remained desolate.** It cannot be proved that *shōmēm,* "desolate," ever meant single or solitary. However, this is the usual interpretation.

21. David . . . was very wroth. He was content merely to be angry, since he himself had been guilty of adultery. However, his lack of appropriate action stemmed from his indulgent affection toward his son and his habitual failure to discipline members of his family.

27. He let Amnon . . . go with him. Since Absalom had shown no sign of desiring revenge, David reluctantly permitted Amnon to attend the party. **29. His mule.** This is the first mention of a mule in the Bible. The horse was used mainly for drawing war chariots; the ass was the mount of royalty (I Kgs 1:33). According to the law of Lev 19:19, the breeding of hybrids was forbidden.

14:1. Joab thought Absalom had the best chance to succeed to the throne. And he felt that if he could put Absalom in the position to succeed to the throne, Absalom in turn would cancel the threat of judgment hanging over him. **2. Tekoah.** Joab grew up in the vicinity of Tekoah, about six miles south of Bethlehem. He may have known this woman from earlier days.

7. Not leave . . . name nor remainder. The extinction of a family was the most dreaded of all misfortunes. The institutions of concubinage and levirate marriage were both instituted to forestall this possibility. The birth of a son to carry on the family name was regarded as most important. **9. The iniquity be on me.** From the woman's answer we infer that David had put her off with a promise because he saw that if he defended the guilty son, he would become involved in his guilt. The mother pleaded for the king's help and offered to bear personally any guilt.

10. Bring him to me. David empowered the woman to bring her prosecutors into the royal presence. **11.** The woman asked David to take an oath to this effect before she applied her story to the situation of Absalom's predicament.

12-20. The woman placed David in the position of her imaginary prosecutors. What they could do to her family by cutting off the only heir, David was doing to the people of God by punishing Absalom for a crime he had committed in the heat of human anger and in his desire to render justice for the dishonor done to his sister, Tamar.

25. His beauty. David was also known for his handsome appearance. Absalom sheared his head yearly and weighed the hair according to a metric system introduced into Palestine. There may have been religious significance in this act. **27.** The LXX adds a note that this second Tamar became the wife of Rehoboam, the son of Solomon, and bore him Abia. According to I Kgs 15:2, Maachah the daughter of Solomon married Rehoboam.

15:1-6. Absalom began a vigorous campaign to win the loyalty of the tribes. His method was to meet persons in the gate, the court of ancient Israel, find out their native cities, suggest to them his interest and availability, and hope that they would return to their district and become ambassadors for his cause.

7. Hebron still bore a grudge against David because he had removed the seat of government to Jerusalem. Also, the allied clans of the Negev, through whose good offices David first mounted the throne, were jealous of the northern tribes — now the dominant partner in the united kingdom — because of their power and influence with the king. **12. Ahithophel the Gilonite.** Giloh was six or seven miles northwest of Hebron. Ahithophel was the grandfather of Bath-sheba (11:3; 23:34). His espousal of Absalom's cause is usually attributed to a desire to avenge the disgrace David had brought upon his family, as well as the murder of Uriah.

14,15. Let us flee. David's decision to abandon Jerusalem has been a constant puzzle to historians. Some have supposed that his courage failed temporarily; some, that he had valid grounds for suspecting the loyalty of the population, perhaps still predominantly Jebusite; others, that he wished to spare the city the horrors of a siege; and still others suppose he argued that, if the revolt prospered in the north while Absalom was marching on him from the south, he would be caught in Jerusalem as in a trap. The fact that David's loyal followers did not question his decision indicates that his decision was not based on cowardice but upon the cold calculation of an experienced military specialist.

18. Gittites. These were the men who had gathered around David on his flight from Saul and emigrated with him to Gath. Afterward they lived with him in Ziklag, and eventually followed him to Hebron and Jerusalem. In all probability, they formed a separate company of well trained veterans, or a kind of bodyguard, in Jerusalem and were well known as the Gittites.

21. In death or life. Ittai's reply is magnanimous in light of the apparent hopelessness of David's cause. Ittai felt undying gratitude to David for his benefactions in earlier days.

23. The brook Kidron is the well-known valley east of Jerusalem. The road taken was probably the one on the south slope of the Mount of Olives, the same which is still traveled to Jericho and the Jordan Valley.

24. Zadok means *righteous*. This family of priests won out over the house of Abiathar (of the line of Eli) in the reign of Solomon. The New Testament Sadducees claimed descent from the house of Zadok.

16:1. Mephibosheth was the lame son of Jonathan to whom David had shown kindness for the sake of his love for Jonathan. **3. The kingdom of my father.** According to Ziba, Mephibosheth believed that the internal struggle within the house of David would enable the house of Saul to regain the throne. This would give Mephibosheth, the sole heir to the throne, the opportunity to assume the leadership of Israel. Ziba's story was an outright fiction, by means of which he hoped to get a grant from the estate of Mephibosheth.

6. He cast stones. This is still done as a sign of anger or insult. **7. Thou man of Belial.** A most degrading epithet; it means, "You are a good-for-nothing."

9-14. David regarded the cursing of Shimei as ordained of God. He felt that if he suffered it silently, God would reward him ultimately. His generous spirit was taxing, however, to his soldiers, who saw in the curses not the will of God but the slanderous remarks of a dissatisfied citizen. **Dead dog** (v. 9). An epithet of disdain. **Take off his head.** That is, decapitate him. Cursing the king was a capital crime.

16. God save the king was a cry of respect for the royal personage. The usual explanation is that it means, "May the king live for a long time!" The repetition of this phrase by Hushai expressed his feigned enthusiasm for the new regime.

21. Go in unto thy father's concubines. Ahithophel advised Absalom to assume the right to the throne through a public seizure of the royal harem. This was the custom employed in ancient times to demonstrate possession of the throne. It was not actually viewed with abhorrence by the Israelites, whose feelings on such matters were blunted by the practice of polygamy. Following this counsel would cause an irreparable breach between father and son. Ahithophel's advice was to run every risk in this adventure.

17:4. The saying pleased Absalom. He thought the advice of Ahithophel was excellent. If David had been attacked that very night, he would have been but twelve or fifteen miles from the capital, without food and ammunition, and with his forces in a serious state of disorganization. The rebellion of Absalom would have secured its objective and David would have met with certain defeat. Apparently Ahithophel's plan was to quickly surround the forces of David and create such a panic that all would flee, making it possible to slay only David. This would make it easier to win over the remnant of David's cohorts.

8. Chafed in their minds. Hushai's argument was that David's men would fight like a cornered bear. The Syrian bear is said to be particularly ferocious. The Septuagint adds, "and like a savage sow in the plain," which is more like the Greek than the Hebrew and must have been added by a later writer.

12. We will light upon him. The verb is used of swarms of locusts (Ex 10:14) or flies and bees settling down (Isa 7:18, 19). **13. We will draw it into the river.** Hushai said that the city in which David might hide would be completely destroyed. Most cities were built on hills, and the penalty of a conquered city was to be treated as is expressed in the words of Mic 1:6: "I will pour down the stones thereof into the valley."

17. En-rogel. Perhaps the fuller's spring, mentioned in I Kgs 1:9. It was in the valley of the Kidron, below the village of Silwan, near the junction of the valleys of Kidron and Hinnom. It served as a landmark on the boundary between Judah and Benjamin. **A wench.** Literally, *a maidservant*. The definite article in the Hebrew may denote simply the maid chosen for the task, or it may denote a particular servant – taken from the household of one of the priests—who could be entrusted with the mission. She could go to the fountain for water without exciting suspicion, since the drawing of water was carried on mainly by women.

19. Ground corn. This was bruised or husked wheat or barley, which the people prepared by pounding it in a mortar.

23. Hanged himself. The number of suicides in the Bible is extremely few. The care with which Ahithophel prepared himself and his family and the burial in the family plot indicate that this suicide was not frowned upon. Ahithophel had worked himself into a difficult predicament. If Absalom had been victorious, Ahithophel would have had to give way to Hushai; if David had been victorious, Ahithophel would have been called to account for his advice concerning the proposed capture of David. The people knew his precarious position and understood the thinking of a hopelessly defeated man. It may be noted that the suicide of Ahithophel did not exclude him from regular burial in the family sepulchre.

24. To Mahanaim. This was originally the headquarters of Ishbosheth's kingdom. It was selected by David for his headquarters in view of its strong position among the Trans-Jordan cities and because of its lesser disaffection. This city was significant in patriarchal days and was the scene of one of Jacob's stops on his return to Palestine to meet with his brother Esau. At this place Jacob saw in a vision the divine messengers encircling and protecting his camp, and he named it **Mahanaim** *(Twin Camps)*.

25. Abigail the daughter of Nahash. According to Jewish tradition **Nahash** is another name for Jesse. Others feel that Nahash was the first husband of Jesse's wife.

29. Butter. Curdled milk is probably meant. It is called *leben* by modern Arabs and is greatly esteemed as a refreshing drink.

18:1. David numbered the people. This means not merely that he counted his forces but that he mustered and reviewed them. **And set captains.** This was the usual military arrangement, and it corresponds to the civil arrangement suggested by Moses in Ex 18:25. It is interesting that David gave one third of the army to Ittai, a man of Gath, who had proved loyal to the cause of the king in the exile.

5. Deal gently for my sake with the young man. Apparently David still looked upon Absalom as but a boy. He treated the rebellion as a youthful escapade which he could forgive rather easily. However, Joab and the army regarded the insurrection as having serious portents.

8. The wood devoured. The usual explanation is that a great multitude perished in the pits and precipices. Apparently, because of the nature of the ground, more were slain in the pursuit through the forest than in the battle itself. **9. A mule.** To ride a mule was a mark of royalty (I Kgs 1:33,38). This mule may have belonged to David. **His head.** The tradition that Absalom was caught by his hair comes from Josephus.

10-13. The man who saw Absalom hanging by his head reproved Joab for suggesting that he should have slain Absalom and claimed Joab's reward for the deed. However much the captain of David's forces might wish for Absalom's death, the man suggested, when faced by the king, who had ordered the troops to deal gently with Absalom, he would not be able to stand up for the slayer.

17. A great pit. This may have been a cave or an unused cistern. Some think the heaping of stones on Absalom's grave was symbolic of the stoning which was the legal penalty due a rebel son (Deut 21:20,21). It is still a custom in the East for passers-by to cast stones on the grave of a criminal. **18. The king's dale.** "The King's Vale" is given as an alternate name for the vale of Shaveh in Gen 14:17 (ASV). Here the King of Sodom met Abraham. The location of the valley is unknown. The Tomb of Absalom still to be seen in the Kidron Valley is of Roman making and is most likely of a later tradition. **Absalom's place.** That is, a monument. Whether it was a column, an obelisk, or a monolith cannot be determined.

23. Ahimaaz . . . overran Cushi. The route taken by Cushi was the shorter route, but it led over hill and dale. The route taken by Ahimaaz lay along the bed of the Jordan River valley and could be traversed more quickly.

19:4. The king covered his face. This was the customary way of expressing one's grief. The muffled head marked the grief which shut one from the external world. Perhaps it symbolized the sorrow unto death that David felt for his son Absalom. His vocal expression suggested to the people that the king wished that he might die and be with Absalom. In a sense the covered head of David symbolized the shroud of Absalom's burial. Veils worn by mourning widows are a modernization of this old custom. However, the suggestion in modern mourning is that one desires to be alone as one grieves. For the same reason, at funerals the members of the immediate family are seated in a separate room.

5. **Thou hast shamed . . . thy servants.** The severe military discipline of Joab hindered his understanding the grief of a father for his son. David viewed the events as they related to himself, and felt keenly the loss of his son Absalom. Joab viewed the same events in the light of their meaning to the people of Judah and the family of David. He urged the king to conceal his personal feelings in the best interests of the political situation. Joab feared the reaction of the populace to the expressed sentiment of David for Absalom. Consequences more serious than Absalom's rebellion might follow if the mob were stirred to anger by their king's lack of appreciation for their bravery on his behalf. **7. Speak comfortably.** Literally, *speak to the heart*. Speak in a friendly way, encouraging them and appeasing their discontent. This expression is used often in the OT.

9. **All the people were at strife.** The short-lived rebellion had failed to gain its objective, and the element of discontent spread throughout the country. The movement to restore David to power was not unanimous. Some felt that he had lost his ability to rule; others looked upon him as having earned the right to rule by his past service.

11. **The elders of Judah.** These were the men who could win the tribe of Judah back to the cause of David. Their reticence derived from the fact that Judah had played a prominent part in the insurrection. David commissioned the religious leaders, Zadok and Abiathar, to make his appeal to Judah through the tribal elders. The text of their message is too brief to disclose what approaches these two religious delegates made. Perhaps they reminded the elders of the movement of Israel to restore David and hinted that there might also be a movement started to make a northern city the capital instead of Jerusalem. David had once before moved his capital from Hebron to Jerusalem, and another move could happen again. David's action in turning to his own tribe was natural and essential in his return to power. However, some have looked upon his conciliatory action toward Judah as a deed breeding fresh rebellion.

13. **Say ye to Amasa . . . thou be . . . captain.** This course of action was a bold stroke of military policy to secure the loyalty of the general of the rebel army. By so doing, David hoped to secure the allegiance of the rebel army and at the same time to demote Joab for his murder of Absalom. The move has been questioned as hardly prudent, for Joab was not the type of man to acquiesce quietly, nor had the loyalty of Amasa been proved. **20. The house of Joseph.** The ten tribes of Israel were distinguished from Judah by the title of the most powerful tribe among them – Ephraim, son of Joseph. **24. Neither dressed . . . nor trimmed . . . nor washed.** The neglect of his appearance was the outward sign of extreme grief. **29. Thou and Ziba divide the land.** It is not known whether David was making a compromise to keep the family of Ziba and Mephibosheth friendly to his cause, or whether he decided this on the spot because he did not have time to investigate the claims of both parties. **37. Behold thy servant Chimham; let him go over with . . . the king.** Cf. I Kgs 2:7. Josephus says that he was Barzillai's son.

20:1. **He blew a trumpet.** Sheba, a worthless son of the family of Becher, the second son of Benjamin, blew the trumpet to call Israel to revolt from the house of David. This rebellion was perhaps engendered by the traditional hostility between the house of Saul and the house of David, the Benjamites and the Judahites. Sheba was interested in wresting the power from Judah and regaining it for Benjamin. In his call to revolt, **Every man to his tents, O Israel,** he employed the words used in the successful rebellion led by Jeroboam (I Kgs 12:16). The meaning is: "Men, let's turn in our uniforms and K rations and return to the farms, and I shall head up a resistance group to secure better portions for us all." The use of **tents** is strange in that Israel had long since left the nomadic form of life for the settled life of Canaan. The terminology of the past culture persists in every society, and Sheba was using a cliché that had propaganda and sentimental value.

3. **Living in widowhood.** These were the ten women whom Absalom had violated in broad daylight as a signal to Israel that he had taken over the throne. David could not return these women to the royal harem, nor did he wish to do so. Instead, he made provision for their support and declared them to be widows for the remainder of their natural life.

This action of David had in it the elements of both generosity and tragedy. Life in a king's harem carried with it the possibility of dire consequences as well as the reward of luxurious living. These women were confined in order to protect David from further embarrassment or predicament in regard to them. They were accorded the right of support because their violation was perpetrated by Absalom and was not initiated as a harem intrigue to overthrow the ruling king.

5. He tarried longer than the set time. Was Amasa, cousin of Joab, whom Absalom had appointed captain of his host, lacking in initiative; or was the assembling of the army a more difficult task than David had expected? It is probable that some men questioned the strength of David's return to power, while others resented the change of generals, preferring Joab to Amasa. David had already promised Amasa the position of Joab (19:13,14). Perhaps Amasa's delay was the result of military and political hindrances set up by those who questioned the wisdom of David's rash promises.

6. David said to Abishai. David still superseded Joab by giving the orders to Joab's brother. However, once the campaign was under way, Joab, with Abishai's consent, resumed his place as commander-in-chief.

9. To kiss him. Laying hold of the beard to kiss is still customary among the Arabs and the Turks as a sign of friendly welcome. **10. Amasa took no heed to the sword.** This part of the text is quite difficult to translate accurately, and hence the nature of Joab's treachery is difficult to ascertain. Joab, it seems, had a second weapon concealed under his military cloak, while he openly wore another sword in its sheath. Presumably he deliberately let fall the sword he wore openly to banish any doubt or suspicion from the mind of Abishai.

14. Unto Abel, and to Beth-maachah. As is seen in verses 15,18, this should be read, *Abel of Beth-maachah*. It is also known as "Abel-maim" *(meadow of waters)* in II Chr 16:4. This town fell to the forces of Ben-hadad of Syria (I Kgs 15:20) and afterward to the Assyrian Tiglath-pileser. The mention of Maachah may suggest a connection with the Syrian kingdom of that name (10:6). Its location is about twelve miles north of Lake Huleh and four miles west of Tell el Kadi (Dan) at the site of the village of Abil. **15. They cast up a bank against the city.** The purpose of this mound was to enable them to reach the highest point of the wall in order to break down the wall and force an entrance. This type of warfare is depicted on the bas-reliefs of the siege of Lachish.

17. Hear the words of thine handmaid. The woman went on to suggest to Joab that before he began the siege and possible destruction of the town, he should ask the inhabitants of Abel whether or not they intended to fight for Sheba and his cohorts. This was to be done, according to the legislation of Deut 20:10ff. Her second implication was that Joab ought to have taken into consideration the peaceableness and fidelity of the citizens of Abel and not to destroy peace-loving citizens and members of the nation of God. She was indeed a wise woman and in sympathy with the wise woman of Tekoa, who undertook to spare needless bloodshed. Compare, too, the intercession of Abigail in the cause of the farm families of Carmel and vicinity. Women have generally pled the cause of peace and argued for peaceful arbitration to avert bloodshed. Ecclesiastes (lit., *The Preacher)* said that wisdom is better than strength, and perhaps used this incident for his reference in Eccl 9:13-16.

22. Every man to his tent. This is a satirical commentary on the rebellion of Sheba. He had called for Israel to secede from the union of Israel and Judah, and had lost his head as a result. The men of Judah returned to their tents, while Sheba's forces were scattered. The way of the sword can lead to dire consequences.

24. Adoram was over the tribute. Rather, he was over the labor gangs raised under the system of forced labor. He held this office until the reign of Rehoboam (I Kgs 4:6; 12:18).

IV. The Last Days of David. 21:1–24:25.

A. The Famine. 21:1-14.

1. A famine. Ezekiel 14:21 lists the sword (war), famine, the noisome beast, and pestilence as the four sore (heavy) judgments of God for the sins of Jerusalem. In I Kgs 8:35-37, Solomon refers to the cloudless heaven that could bring famine as the result of the sins of his people. The precise time of this famine is not given. "In the days of David" could refer to any time during his lengthy reign. Some would place it after David's acquaintance with Mephibosheth (cf. v. 7), but before Absalom's rebellion.

It is for Saul. Saul, it seems, refused to recognize the treaty made by Joshua with the Gibeonites (Josh 9), and, in his zeal for his own people, put some of these Amoritic remnants to death. This constituted the breaking of a covenant and was to be reckoned as unexpiated murder, which, according to Deut 21:7-9, defiled the land.

3. Wherewith shall I make the atonement. David asked the Gibeonites what they would accept as settlement for their injury. The literal meaning of the Hebrew verb for "to make atonement" is *to cover*. This "covering" was intended to hide the offense from the eyes of the offended party, and to withdraw the guilt of the offender from the gaze of a God who avenged the wrong. The atonement could be made by a settlement in money, which gave rise to the expression, "blood money," or by the application of the law of revenge. If the latter method had been used in this case, David could have given the Gibeonites the same number of men Saul had executed. These could have been men in disfavor at the court of David or men chosen by lot. However, the Gibeonites would not be satisfied with anything less than revenge on the family of Saul. They accused Saul of trying to exterminate them (an ancient policy used to invalidate the law of revenge). They wanted to see his descendants dealt with exactly as he had sought to deal with them (cf. v. 5). This demand for exact justice was in keeping with the legislation of Num 35:31,32, which insists upon a strict regard for human life. The payment of money by the murderer to the family of the murdered was a dangerous precedent, which could be abused by the rich. Men with money could "beat the rap."

6. Seven men. Seven may have been the exact number of Gibeonites executed by Saul; or, more likely, it was a sacred number, the men being chosen to be executed in a solemn ritual "unto the Lord." This execution, however, was not like a sacrifice to entreat God for rain, but was a case of judicial retribution.

8. Rizpah. A concubine of Saul. Ishbosheth once accused Abner of having illicit relations with Rizpah in an attempt to assume the throne of Saul in his (Ishbosheth's) place. This accusation led to Abner's transferring his loyalty to the house of David. **Sons of Michal** presents a problem. According to the Biblical record, Michal died childless as a result of her estrangement from David. Her attitude toward her husband in his dealings with the priesthood and the ark of the covenant brought about strained relations. He did not divorce her, but assigned to her a special house and had no further marital relations with her. The Targum recognized the problem here and suggested that Michal raised the five sons of her deceased sister Merab, whom Merab had born to Adriel. **The Meholathite.** That is, of Abel-meholah, a town in the Jordan Valley, near Beth-Shan, famous as the birthplace of Elisha (I Kgs 19:16).

10. Rizpah . . . took sackcloth, and spread it . . . upon the rock. Rizpah took cloth, made a tent, and stood watch from April to October, till the fall rains came and she knew that the sin of Saul's household had been expiated and that no further claim would be made on the lives of her family. It was contrary to the law of Deut 21:23 to permit a body to hang over night, but this law was set aside in the present case.

13. And they gathered the bones of them that were hanged. David was touched by the maternal devotion of Rizpah. To show that he had no personal hostility toward the house of Saul, he disinterred the remains of Saul and Jonathan from the graves given them by the men of Jabesh-gilead and gave them decent burial in their home sepulchre at Zelah. This place is enumerated among the towns of Benjamin in Josh 18:28, but it has not yet been identified. Beih Jala near Bethlehem has been suggested, but this is in Judah, not Benjamin. It is strange that Saul's burial was not at Gibeah, his birthplace.

B. Heroic Exploits. 21:15-22.

16. The sons of the giant. The word for **sons** is used in Num 13:22,28 of the sons of Anak, the giants of the land in the period of the Conquest. The Hebrew for **giant**, *Rapha*, is not a name of an individual. It is a collective, used of the Rephaim, a giant race that inhabited Palestine in primitive times and gave to a valley near Jerusalem the name "Valley of Rephaim." The Vulgate has *Arapha*, from which comes *Harapha*, the name of the giant introduced in Milton's *Samson Agonistes*. **17. Quench . . . the light of Israel.** This was a metaphor for changing the light of prosperity for the darkness of calamity. In modern parlance, these men wanted David to carry the torch for Israel.

19. Elhanan . . . slew the brother of Goliath. The brother is missing in the Masoretic Text. It is added on the basis of the parallel account in I Chr 20:5. Some commentators suppose that the Samuel account preserves the older tradition and that only later was the slaying of Goliath attributed to David. There is no serious difficulty, however, in supposing that there was another man of great stature called Goliath besides the one slain by David. There is another Elhanan of Bethlehem mentioned in II Sam 23:24. Some (cf. Targum and Jerome) have tried to identify Elhanan *(the one whom God shows favor)* with David. But there is no strong evidence to support this idea.

20. Six fingers . . . six toes. This was not an unusual deformity in ancient times, nor is it in modern times. Pliny mentioned such a peculiarity in his *Natural History*. According to Lev 21:18, one with such a deformity was excluded from the temple service.

C. David's Psalm. 22:1-51.

3. My salvation. Salvation in OT thought was often seen in physical deliverance from the power of enemy forces.

6. The snares of death. The fortunes of David brought him on a number of occasions to dangerous places. Many times there was only a step between him and death. In all his life he saw the hand of God protecting him from serious harm.

7. Out of his temple. The Lord as king ruled in the heavens and there was his temple. The Solomonic Temple was to become the earthly symbol of the heavenly authority of God in the national destiny of Israel.

17. He drew me. Same root as the name *Moses*. As Moses was taken out of the waters of the Nile, so David was taken out of the **great** *(many*, AV) waters of tribulation.

D. David's Testament. 23:1-7.

1. The sweet psalmist of Israel. David is remembered for many things. He was not only the patron of synagogue and church choir music, but was the favorite of the song writers of Israel. They loved him for the music that came from the inner depths of his soul. His last words were in poetic form, expressing the glory of God in the ruling of a righteous king.

4. As the light. David saw in the good king the welcome response of the nation to true leadership. It was as welcome as the morning sun and as refreshing as the rains in their seasons.

5. An everlasting covenant. The Lord is a covenant-making God. Covenants in the Bible include those made both with individuals and with nations. With every covenant was implied the duty of loyalty to the terms of the covenant. Although Israel failed to keep her part of the covenant, she was to learn that God was ever faithful.

17. He would not drink it. The magnanimous spirit of a warrior is seen in David's respect for the courage of the three mighty men who braved the armies of the Philistines to bring the cool water to David. A well in modern Bethlehem is pointed out to tourists as the well of David.

E. Heroic Exploits. 23:8-39.

18. Joab is not mentioned. Either he is in a class by himself or the disgrace of killing Absalom, and siding with the unsuccessful claimant (I Kgs 1:7) caused his name to be stricken from the honor roll. He served well, was loyal in a dog-like devotion, yet was without honor. The stories of these heroic figures are often paralleled in the Iliad and Odyssey and in personal exploits in the wars of Egypt and Mesopotamia. In the latter stories it is usually the heroic king or pharaoh who is commemorated; in Homer and in the OT, the heroic figures come from the ranks.

F. Census and Plague. 24:1-25.

1. He moved David. The Chronicler (I Chr 21:1) refers the inciting of David to Satan. From the Biblical viewpoint, all things have their ultimate source in God. Even the wrath of man, and Satan, ultimately further the divine purposes. **Go, number Israel and Judah.** Censuses in the Middle East always have been frowned upon, for the purposes of counting the people were to determine tax proportions and to conscript for war service.

14. Let us fall . . . into the hand of the Lord. The religious insight in this passage is very great indeed. Angry deities in pagan religions were to be appeased quickly and offenders were to keep out of the way of offended deities. David knew that his overt act was sinful and that he was endangering the nation with the righteous anger of God in judgment. However, he also knew his God as a forgiving Lord, plenteous in mercy toward all who repent. He saw more mercy in God than in the hand of man. Sinners in the hands of an angry God have more reason for hope than does offending man in the clutches of an offended society.

16. The Lord repented him of the evil. Repentance on the part of man involves a turning about in a new attitude toward God. Repentance on the part of God is a change of approach toward man on the basis of man's changed attitude toward God. **The threshing floor of Araunah.** Araunah was known as a Jebusite, one of the original inhabitants of the city of Jerusalem. His name indicates a Hurrian origin, or at least a Hurrian title. Many believe that this threshing floor is to be identified with the rock formation preserved under the Dome of the Rock, on or near the site of Solomon's Temple.

BIBLIOGRAPHY

CAIRD, GEORGE B. "Samuel," *Interpreter's Bible*. Vol. 2. New York: Abingdon-Cokesbury Press, 1953.

DEANE, W. J. *Samuel and Saul: Their Lives and Times*. New York: Fleming H. Revell Co., n.d.

DRIVER, S. R. *Notes on the Hebrew Text and the Topography of the Books of Samuel* (2nd ed.). Oxford: Clarendon Press, 1913.

GOLDMAN, S. *Samuel*. London: The Soncino Press, 1951.

KEIL, C. F., and DELITZSCH, F. *Samuel*. Edinburgh: T. & T. Clark, 1872.

KIRKPATRICK, A. F. *I, II Samuel (The Cambridge Bible for Schools and Colleges)*. Cambridge: The University Press, 1930.

SMITH, H. P. *Samuel (International Critical Commentary)*. Edinburgh: T. & T. Clark, 1899.

FIRST AND SECOND KINGS

INTRODUCTION

Title. The books now known as I and II Kings were so named from their contents. In the Septuagint (Greek version of the OT) the original Hebrew Kings is regarded as a continuation of the material in the book of Samuel. It is divided into two parts and is entitled The Third and Fourth Kingdoms. Jerome, though retaining this division in his Vulgate, called the two parts simply, The Book of the Kings.

The two books obviously form one whole, covering Israel's history from the monarchy under Solomon to the nation's dissolution under Zedekiah. They deal with the fortunes of the nation of Israel under the covenant with the Lord, pointing out the sins of the kings who broke the covenant and brought about the deportation of Israel and Judah.

Date and Authorship. II Kings closes with the release of Jehoiachin from prison in the thirty-seventh year of his imprisonment – about 562/561 B.C. The book could not have been completed before this date, nor later than 536 B.C., the year of the return from Babylon, since it says nothing of that event. As this book is a unit and not the product of several hands of successive dates, it is to be dated in the period about 562–536 B.C.

Since the release of Jehoiachin would have been of significance only to Jews of the Babylonian captivity, we would conclude that I and II Kings were written by some Jewish captive living in the area of Babylon.

Sources. The author states plainly that he had sources for his history: (1) Acts of Solomon (I Kgs 11:41). (2) See references to the chronicles of the kings of Judah (e.g., I Kgs 14:29), and the chronicles of the kings of Israel (e.g., I Kgs 14:19). Sources for the history of the kings of Judah are never mixed with those for the history of the kings of Israel. Therefore we know that each of the above was a separate, distinct document. The citations from these works show that they contained much more material than is given in Kings.

Specific authors of the firsthand sources are cited for us in the parallels in I and II Chronicles: *Nathan* the prophet, *Ahijah* the Shilonite, and *Iddo* (II Chr 9:29); *Shemaiah* the prophet and *Iddo* the seer (II Chr 12:15); *Iddo* the prophet (II Chr 13:22); *Isaiah* the prophet (II Chr 26:22; 32:32); *Jehu* (I Kgs 16:1). Because the sources are thus strictly prophetical matter, not mere annals, we have here a forthright record of the deeds of the kings. No royal annalist would have dared to publish such incriminating facts about David or Jeroboam I as are here given.

Aim and Purpose. Though the author's chief concern is with the Davidic monarchy, he first treats a matter of secondary interest – the kingdom in Israel. Then he returns to the account of the Davidic monarchy. While the people knew the prophetical sources of this history, the sources were too numerous, voluminous, and cumbersome to display readily to the people the will of God; hence Kings was written.

Using extracts from the various sources, the author develops the history of the elect nation in respect to the covenant of Jehovah (Ex 19:3-6). They were to have no gods but the Lord (Ex 20:2-6). Idolatry and image worship are regarded in these books as the worst of all sins, which, continued and repeated, brought about Israel's deportation. The language of these books can be said to be 'Deuteronomic' because Deuteronomy speaks in much the same way against the same sins condemned in I and II Kings. The author of Kings holds up the history of Israel and Judah before the captives to teach them that the only way to freedom is to repent of idolatry, return to God, keep the covenant, and trust in the divine promises. He seeks to awaken in them a conviction of the truth of this teaching and to strengthen them in this conviction.

In respect to the covenant the prophets were God's messengers to remind the people of its provisions, and his instruments to oversee its implementation. It was their mission to seek by means of warnings, threats, and promises to obtain adherence to it (cf. Jer 7:13; 11:1-8). In these books, kings are pronounced good or bad as they adhered to or departed from the covenant.

Historical Background. The Israelites were the first people of antiquity to develop a true historiography. Other nations, such as Assyria, Babylonia, and Egypt, composed annals, but only the Hittites among the Gentile nations attempted historical writings.

In David's day Egypt's power had waned and Assyria was weak; hence there were impotent nations on both of Israel's frontiers. However, Assyria soon awakened under Tiglath-pileser III (also called Pul, II Kgs 15:19; 745–727 B.C.). In 721 B.C. Samaria fell under the attack of Shalmaneser and Sargon. Later, under Sennacherib, Assyria invaded Judah and took many cities but failed to take Jerusalem because of the rear-guard threat of Egypt. Esarhaddon and Ashurbanipal extended Assyrian hegemony to Egypt.

In Josiah's time Pharaoh-necho went up to help Assyria against Babylon at Carchemish, but the two allies were defeated. Shortly, the victorious Nebuchadrezzar invaded Palestine, and on his third attack against Jerusalem, plundered and destroyed the city, carrying the people off to final captivity (586 B.C.).

Chronology. The reader is referred to the following publications for the chronology of the period of I and II Kings: BASOR, 100 (Dec., 1945); 130 (Apr., 1953; 141 (Feb., 1956); 143 (Oct., 1956); E. R. Thiele, *The Mysterious Numbers of the Hebrew Kings* (Chicago, 1951); E. R. Thiele, "The Question of Co-regencies Among the Hebrew Kings," *A Stubborn Faith*, ed. E. C. Hobbs (Dallas, 1957).

OUTLINE

I. The united kingdom from Solomon to Rehoboam. I Kgs 1:1–11:43.
   A. Solomon's ascension to the throne. 1:1–2:46.
      1. Adonijah's aspiration to the throne defeated. 1:1-53.
      2. Last words and death of David. 2:1-11.
      3. Solomon's disposal of aspirants to the throne. 2:12-46.
   B. The wisdom and wealth of Solomon. 3:1–4:34.
      1. Solomon's marriage to Pharaoh's daughter. 3:1.
      2. Solomon's worship and vision. 3:2-15.
      3. Solomon's wisdom displayed. 3:16-28.
      4. Organization of the empire. 4:1-28.
      5. Summary of Solomon's wisdom. 4:29-34.
   C. Solomon's building activity. 5:1–9:28.
      1. Preparation for building the Temple. 5:1-18.
      2. Construction of the Temple. 6:1-38.
      3. Solomon's palace and other buildings. 7:1-12.
      4. The furnishings of the Temple. 7:13-51.
      5. The dedication of the Temple. 8:1-66.
      6. Ratification of the Davidic covenant. 9:1-9.
      7. Summary of Solomon's building activities. 9:10-28.
   D. The Golden Age of Solomon. 10:1-29.
      1. The visit of the Queen of Sheba. 10:1-13.
      2. The glory and power of Solomon's empire. 10:14-29.
   E. Solomon's apostasy, decline, and death. 11:1-43.
      1. Solomon's unfaithfulness to God. 11:1-13.
      2. Adversaries and impending division. 11:14-40.
      3. Solomon's decease. 11:41-43.

II. The divided kingdom, from Rehoboam to the fall of Israel. I Kgs 12:1–II Kgs 17:41.
   A. Early antagonism between Israel and Judah, from Jeroboam to Omri. 12:1–16:28.
      1. The rupture of the kingdom. 12:1-33.
      2. The reign of Jeroboam I, and his death. 13:1–14:20.
      3. Judah under Rehoboam, Abijam, and Asa. 14:21–15:24.
      4. Israel under Nadab, Baasha, Elah, Zimri, and Omri. 15:25–16:28.

B. From Ahab to the ascension of Jehu. I Kgs 16:29–II Kgs 9:10.
  1. Beginning of Ahab's reign in Israel. 16:29-34.
  2. The ministry of Elijah, to the call of Elisha. 17:1–19:21.
  3. Later years of Ahab's reign, and his death. 20:1–22:40.
  4. Judah under Jehoshaphat. 22:41-50.
  5. Israel under Ahaziah and Joram. I Kgs 22:51–II Kgs 1:1.
  6. Later ministry of Elijah, to his translation. 1:2–2:11.
  7. Introduction of Elisha. 2:12-25.
  8. Jehoram's expedition against Moab. 3:1-27.
  9. Prophetic ministry of Elisha. 4:1–8:15.
  10. Reigns of Jehoram and Ahaziah in Judah. 8:16-29.
  11. Jehu made king in Israel. 9:1-10.

C. From Jehu to the destruction of Israel. 9:11–17:41.
  1. Jehu's reign. 9:11–10:36.
  2. Athaliah of Judah. 11:1-20.
  3. Judah under Jehoash. 11:21–12:21.
  4. Israel under Jehoahaz and Jehoash. 13:1-25.
  5. Judah under Amaziah and Azariah. 14:1-22.
  6. Reign of Jeroboam II over Israel. 14:23-29.
  7. Reign of Azariah over Judah. 15:1-7.
  8. Reigns of Zechariah, Shallum, Menahem, Pekahiah, and Pekah in Israel. 15:8-31.
  9. Judah under Jotham and Ahaz. 15:32–16:20.
  10. Destruction and captivity of Israel. 17:1-41.

III. The kingdom in Judah to the final destruction of the nation of Israel. 18:1–25:30.

A. The kingdom under Hezekiah. 18:1–20:21.
  1. Hezekiah's reforms. 18:1-12.
  2. Deliverance from Sennacherib's two invasions. 18:13–19:37.
  3. Hezekiah's illness and recovery. 20:1-11.
  4. Embassy of Merodach-baladan. 20:12-19.
  5. Hezekiah's death. 20:20,21.

B. The reigns of Manasseh and Amon. 21:1-26.
  1. The iniquity and death of Manasseh. 21:1-18.
  2. The sins and death of Amon. 21:19-26.

C. Reform in Judah and Israel under Josiah. 22:1–23:30.

D. The last days of Judah. 23:31–25:26.
  1. Reign and deportation of Jehoahaz. 23:31-34.
  2. Jehoiakim's reign and Nebuchadrezzar's invasion. 23:34–24:7.
  3. Jehoiachin's reign and his captivity. 24:8-16.
  4. Reign of Zedekiah. 24:17-20.
  5. Siege and fall of Jerusalem. 25:1-21.
  6. The puppet governor, Gedaliah. 25:22-26.

E. Epilogue. The release of Jehoiachin. 25:27-30.

COMMENTARY

I. The United Kingdom from Solomon to Rehoboam. I Kgs 1:1–11:43.

A. Solomon's Ascension to the Throne. 1:1–2:46.

1) Adonijah's Aspiration to the Throne Defeated. 1:1-53. **1. Now king David was old.** David's many misfortunes at the hand of Saul before he came to the throne, and his forty-year reign over Israel had left their indelible impressions upon him. Yet, before death overtook him, the warrior-poet-king reached the age of seventy years (II Sam 5:4), which his own writings had marked out as the ultimate bound of life. The final blow that hastened the old man's death was Absalom's rebellion (II Sam 15:1–19:10). **And they covered him with clothes.** *Beḡādîm* designates bedclothes, not garments. They took the simplest precautionary measure to sustain the old man in his physical declension, which, however, did not aid the ailing monarch. **2. Wherefore his servants said unto him.** The suggestion of the servants that a maiden be found for the king to restore his lost vitality and to provide him warmth was an accepted medical prescription even down to the Middle Ages.

No immoral connotation should be read into this rather strange-sounding practice.

3. So they sought for him a young maiden. She was chosen for virginity and beauty. **Abishag,** of Shunam, a city of Issachar in the plain of Jezreel, at the foot of Mount Hermon, the lesser. **4. And ministered to him: but the king knew her not.** That is, did not enter into sexual relations with her. Abishag assumed somewhat the role of a practical nurse to the dying David.

5. Then Adonijah the son of Haggith exalted himself. His rebellion was expressed in the determined words – **I will be king.** In his turbulent life David had previously experienced rebellion on the part of another son, Absalom. Adonijah, whose mother was Haggith, was David's fourth son. Perhaps Adonijah believed that as the eldest living son of David he had right to the throne. But if so, he ignored the theological implications of God's having already chosen Solomon, David's son through Bath-sheba, wife of Uriah the Hittite (II Sam 12:24). **6. And his father had not displeased him at any time.** From this it may be inferred that Adonijah was allowed to go unchecked and undisciplined.

7. And he conferred with Joab . . . and with Abiathar. Joab was the son of Zeruiah, David's sister, the brother of Abishai and Asahel. He seems to have resided in Bethlehem. As chief-in-command of David's army, he proved himself a brilliant military strategist, valiant in battle, though not above cruelty and actual treachery in certain instances. His chief military accomplishments were the capturing of Jerusalem and the siege of Rabbah, of the Ammonites. Because he had needlessly shed the blood of Abner and Amasa, Solomon ordered Benaiah to put him to death. At his own request Joab was slain beside the altar of God in the Tabernacle, where he had taken refuge. **Abiathar** was the only priest who had escaped the brutal vengeance Saul took on the priestly order at Nob for extending aid to David. After fleeing to David, he had become spiritual adviser and friend to the fugitive warrior. Up to this point Abiathar had remained true to the king personally, but now he joined in the conspiracy of Adonijah against Solomon. His subsequent penalty was not the execution he deserved, but expulsion from the priesthood by Solomon.

8. But Zadok the priest . . . Nathan the prophet . . . were not with Adonijah. Zadok had joined David at Hebron immediately after Saul's death (I Chr 12:28), accompanied him on his flight from Jerusalem during Absalom's insurrection, and acted as the king's spy (II Sam 15:24-29; 17:15). **Nathan.** See I Kgs 1:11.

9. Adonijah slew sheep and oxen and fatlings by the stone of Zoheleth. As a pretender to the throne, Adonijah wished to be thought munificent. Therefore, in anticipation of his coronation, he gave this royal feast to those concerned. **The stone of Zoheleth;** i.e., *the serpent's stone* (RSV), or "the steep rocky corner of the southern slope of the Valley of Hinnom, which casts so deep a shade." The place has been identified with the Wadi el Rubab. **En-rogel.** "Fountain of the treaders," or "the foot fountain." Here the fullers cleaned garments by treading them in the waters of the spring. This site has been identified as the "Well of Job" (more likely Well of Joab), situated below the junction of the Kidron Valley with the valley of Hinnom, 550 feet below Mount Zion. **10. But . . . Benaiah . . . and Solomon his brother, he called not.** Benaiah, son of Jehoiada the high priest (I Chr 27:5), native of Kabzeel, head of David's police force, valiant in battle against man and beast, remained faithful to Solomon. Hence he was not summoned in the rebellion of Adonijah. Solomon, son of David through Bath-sheba, the legitimate and God-appointed heir to the throne, naturally was not summoned to Adonijah's feast.

11. Then **Nathan spake unto Bath-sheba . . . saying.** Nathan the prophet first appears in Scripture to announce to David that he must defer building the Temple (II Sam 7). Later he appears to reprove David for his double sin of murder and adultery in the matter of Uriah the Hittite (II Sam 12; Ps 51). Nathan now secured the kingdom to David's son Solomon by exposing Adonijah's machinations to the proper authorities, in this case Bath-sheba. **12,13.** Nathan urged Bath-sheba to appeal directly to the king to name his successor before his death. **14. Behold, while thou yet talkest . . . I . . . will come in.** That is, I will appear in order to verify your words before David, to show that you are not a victim of fright or imagination. The news of Adonijah's rebellion now fell upon David's ears, apparently for the first time. **20. The eyes of all Israel are upon thee.** Bath-sheba appealed to David to make a forthright and immediate declaration.

22. True to his promise, Nathan put in an appearance to support Bath-sheba's account of Adonijah's rebellion, which otherwise might have appeared to the monarch as an exaggerated report. **23-27.** Nathan repeated substantially the same story that David had just learned from Bath-sheba's lips.

28. Call me Bath-sheba. In Oriental fashion Bath-sheba had discreetly withdrawn when Nathan entered, but now she was recalled to hear the king make his official pronouncement. **29. And the king sware, and said, As the Lord liveth.** By the sacred name of Jehovah, the king swore that Solomon, Bath-sheba's son, should indeed be appointed legitimate successor to his throne. All debate was thus ruled out of order. **31. Then Bath-sheba bowed with her face to the earth.** She thus conveyed her gratitude for the decision of her husband and monarch, who had thus granted her request.

32,33. Cause Solomon . . . to ride . . . and bring him down to Gihon. This command to Zadok, Nathan, and Benaiah spelled the collapse of Adonijah's plot, for the coronation of the rebel's half brother Solomon was about to begin. The king gave specific instructions for the ceremony of crowning. David's own mule was to be used, the royal mule, to signify that Solomon was the king's chosen one. **34. Anoint him there king over Israel.** Both king and priest in Israel were inducted into office through the rite of anointing, in contradistinction to the prophet, who held a non-anointed office. The blast of the trumpets was to announce to the people that Solomon had now legally taken the throne of his father, even before the latter's death. **Long live king Solomon** (ASV, RSV), a pious combination of a cheer and a prayer for the longevity and prosperity of the reign of the new monarch.

36. And Benaiah . . . answered the king, and said, Amen. Benaiah gave his acquiescence and his promise of obedience to all that David had stated in relation to the crowning of Solomon.

38. The Cherethites, and the Pelethites, went down. The royal bodyguard thus carried out the instructions of the king to the most minute detail. **Gihon** situated in the Kedron Valley just below the eastern hill (Ophel), was an intermittent spring which was at that time Jerusalem's chief source of water. **39. And Zadok the priest took an horn of oil.** Zadok, the custodian of the sacred Tent, repaired to it to bring forth the material symbol of God's invisible anointing (cf. II Sam 6:17). **40. And all the people . . . rejoiced with great joy.** With a new and promising king on the throne, a new and promising era stretched out before Israel. Behind lay memories of great conquests under David; ahead lay a future of peace and expansion.

41-48. And Adonijah and all the guests that were with him heard it. These verses relate the collapse of Adonijah's conspiracy to seize the throne. **49. And all the guests of Adonijah were afraid.** They feared, with reason, that they would be regarded as traitors against the state, and be summarily dealt with.

50. And Adonijah feared because of Solomon. Forsaken and bereft of those who shortly before had called themselves his friends, Adonijah fled in very terror of his life to seek asylum in the sanctuary of the Tabernacle. **51. And it was told Solomon, saying, Behold, Adonijah feareth.** In Oriental practice, an insurgent like Adonijah would have been severely punished, if not put to death. However, Solomon dealt mercifully with him, remitting the death penalty and placing him under watchful observation, thus setting the pattern for his magnanimous rule. Not until Adonijah committed another act of perfidy was his judgment pronounced. **53. So king Solomon sent, and they brought him down from the altar.** Solomon respected the sanctuary of the altar. Only one who was proved to be a murderer was to be removed from the altar without mercy. Adonijah professed to submit to Solomon and obey his rule. Had his submission been genuine, his subsequent life would have been more peaceful and his story far happier.

2) Last Words and Death of David. 2:1-11.

1-4. Now the days of David drew nigh that he should die. This may have been an extended period of months. The words do not necessarily refer to immediate death. **2. I go the way of all the earth.** David's charge to Solomon may be regarded as twofold: (1) an exhortation to obey the law of Jehovah (vv. 3,4); (2) an admonition to deal wisely with David's enemies and friends, according to their deserts (vv. 5-9).

5,6. David specifically instructed Solomon to liquidate the king's enemies, i.e., Joab and Shimei. The critics claim that David's instructions concerning these men were a "piece of Oriental cruelty." However, it should be noted that the inflicting of penalties upon them was not due merely to David's personal desire for vengeance. Joab, captain of the host, was guilty of a double murder – the slaughter of Abner, a deed of deepest treachery (II Sam 3:27), and the slaying of Amasa, son of Jether (II Sam 20:10). Joab was rightfully accused by David of committing acts of war in times of peace. He therefore must die at once. Observe the picturesque figure of speech of the bloody girdle and shoes (I Kgs 2:5).

7. But show kindness unto the sons of Barzillai. Barzillai, the aged man, had sustained David in his flight from his son Absalom (II Sam 19:31ff.). Without this assistance David might have succumbed to starvation in the wilderness.

8. And, behold, there is with thee Shimei . . . who cursed me (ASV). During the rebellion of Absalom, Shimei came out to meet the fleeing king, cursing as he came and flinging dust and stones at David and his entourage (II Sam 16:5-13). After the rebellion had been repressed, Shimei sued for pardon. And David did pardon him as far as execution of punishment was concerned. There are two leading interpretations of David's charge to Solomon to "hold him not guiltless" (I Kgs 2:9). The one, attributing superstition to David, takes the view that the king, as a typical Oriental, feared the curse. The most effective way to remove the curse, according to the prevailing mode of thinking, was to remove the one who had uttered it, and thus render it inoperative. The other, more feasible interpretation is that since Shimei, as a Benjamite, stemmed from the neighborhood of the erstwhile king Saul, David feared that this man, once his protective custody was withdrawn, would again strike at the throne. Moreover, before actual penalty was imposed, Solomon gave Shimei a reprieve conditioned on obedience.

10. Buried in the city of David. Jerusalem, the precincts of Mount Zion (Acts 2:29). The city David had wrested from the Jebusites and claimed for his capital became the burial ground for the great king. Though David was born in Bethlehem, Jerusalem henceforth was to be designated the **city of David. 11. David reigned over Israel . . . forty years.** There is no particular chronological problem involved here. David died at the age of seventy, having reigned forty years. He had reigned seven years over the Hebron area, a small southerly sector, and he had sat upon the throne of all Israel for thirty-three years (1010–971 B.C.).

3) Solomon's Disposal of Aspirants to the Throne. 2:12-46.

Execution of Adonijah. 2:13-25.

13-17. And Adonijah . . . came to Bath-sheba. He approached Solomon's mother with a seemingly harmless but really insidious request. He said, in effect, "Let Abishag be given to me." This young girl had attended David in his declining state. The unsuspecting mother saw nothing perverse in this request, but simply an "affair of the heart," and readily agreed. **19. Bath-sheba therefore went unto king Solomon.** She innocently became a go-between for Adonijah. With great courtesy the king received his mother . . . until she placed the request before him.

22. Why dost thou ask Abishag . . . for Adonijah? The mental acumen of Solomon penetrated the plot. Even though David had not 'known' Abishag, she was nevertheless considered an inheritor. With her would go the rights to the throne. Having once failed in an abortive attempt to seize the kingdom, Adonijah now sought in a more subtle way to gain his objective. This time he would not be pardoned. **25. And king Solomon sent . . . Benaiah.** Adonijah had failed to appreciate mercy; therefore relentless judgment fell.

Demotion of Abiathar. 2:26,27.

26. Unto Abiathar . . . said the king, Get thee to Anathoth (v. 26). Abiathar, a descendant of Aaron through Eli, was removed from his priestly office and sent back in disgrace to his home village. The reason for Abiathar's punishment, as stated by Solomon, was that he had participated in Adonijah's rebellion. Though expelled, he was not executed, because he had remained faithful to David in the rebellion of Absalom (II Sam 15:24ff.).

The Death of Joab. 2:28-35.

28. And Joab fled unto the Tent of Jehovah, and caught hold on the horns of the altar (ASV). Solomon now began to carry out the orders of his deceased father regarding his enemies. The Tabernacle was located at Gibeon (see 3:4), whither Joab fled, knowing that his doom was sealed. However, not even the sanctuary of the altar could afford refuge for the willful murderer.

33. So shall their blood rest upon their own head forever. The king was giving concrete evidence as to the justice of the sentence. The words of the 'benediction' following imply that once bloodguilt was removed from the throne, it would then stand in a position of blessing before God. After the execution had taken place, Joab was interred in his own house. The old general was not dishonored after all. To be buried on one's own property was a mark of distinction, as in the case of Samuel the prophet (I Sam 25:1) and other outstanding personalities. Joab's dwelling was east of Bethlehem, in the wilderness of Judea.

35. And Zadok the priest did the king put in the room of Abiathar. After the replacement of Joab by Benaiah, Zadok succeeded Abiathar. The appointment of Zadok was fraught with serious consequences, for from then on, the priesthood was subject to the political maneuvers of the state.

The Punishment of Shimei. 2:36-46.

36-41. And the king sent and called for Shimei (see 2:8,9). Next in order for Solomon to deal with, in accordance with David's charge, was Shimei. The king commanded him to build a house in Jerusalem, and to remain within the limits of the city. **The brook Kidron** divided the tribe of Judah from the tribe of Benjamin. Shimei was from the latter tribe. He was thus forbidden to return to his own tribe (v. 37). Shimei agreed to the terms and promised obedience (v. 38). Though placed under rigid surveillance, and knowing the punishment, he broke the conditions of his reprieve by leaving Jerusalem to seek two of his servants who had fled to Gath, a city of the Philistines (vv. 39,40).

42. And the king sent and called for Shimei. It is implied here that his every movement was reported to Solomon. Whether or not Solomon's infliction of the death penalty was fully justified is debatable. At least the monarch read into Shimei's disobedience the most pernicious motives, and punished him with death. Solomon had now completed the charge made to him by his father. It would have been well for Solomon if he had been as zealous in adhering to the Lord his God (cf. 2:3) as he was in completing this charge. **45. And king Solomon shall be blessed.** Solomon congratulated himself that with the death of Shimei, the curse placed upon David directly and himself indirectly would now be removed.

46. And the kingdom was established in the hand of Solomon. With all threats removed, Solomon could settle down to a peaceful and prosperous reign.

B. The Wisdom and Wealth of Solomon. 3:1–4:34.

1) Solomon's Marriage to Pharaoh's Daughter. 3:1.

And Solomon made . . . alliance with Pharaoh king of Egypt. This alliance was made through marriage. The exact identity of this Pharaoh is a matter of controversy. He was either the last Pharaoh of the Twenty-first Dynasty or the first of the Twenty-second. Archaeology may yet add more light on this. And he **brought her into the city of David,** i.e., Jerusalem. Popular feeling would have been against a pagan queen's living in the dwelling place of the ark. Solomon's marriage was a political move. This short section may be somewhat out of chronological order.

2) Solomon's Worship and Vision. 3:2-15.

2. Only the people sacrificed in the high places. There is no particular blame charged to the people for their various sanctuaries. This was an anachronistic practice handed down from the period of the Judges. *Bamôt* **(high places)** is from the ancient Canaanite word for an "elevated platform on which cultic objects were placed" (Albright). These **high places** were viewed as sacred to the worship of the Canaanite deity. During the earlier years of Solomon's reign, the "Bamoth" were dedicated to the worship of the God of Israel only and were located at Gibeon. **4. And the king went to Gibeon to sacrifice there.** Prior to the erection of the Temple, **Gibeon** of Benjamin (a possession since the days of Joshua, and the last resting place of the Tabernacle) was the center of worship.

5. In Gibeon the Lord appeared to Solomon in a dream by night. God revealed himself to Solomon. Solomon's mind had probably been lifted to a high state of religious fervor, approaching ecstasy. In this state revelations were often accorded (cf. Isa 6:1-3). **And God said, Ask what I shall give thee.** The God of heaven bent down to grant the supplication of a man. Within the bounds of reason, Solomon could have obtained whatever he wished.

6. Thou hast showed unto . . . David my father great lovingkindness (AV, *mercy).* Solomon acknowledged the Lord's kindness to his father. **7. I am but a little child.** Solomon was about twenty years of age when he ascended the throne. In relation to the magnitude of the task, he felt his own immaturity. **9. Give thy servant, therefore, an understanding heart.** *Lēb shōmēa'*, "a hearing heart," a heart inclined to do thy will. **That I may discern between good and bad.** Here the words **good** and **bad** are used in a judicial sense. The thrust of Solomon's prayer is that he might judge the people in equity and truth.

10-15. And the speech pleased the Lord. God congratulated Solomon because he had requested the highest prize. He had petitioned for the supreme good, the acquisition of wisdom, in comparison with which all other blessings are vain and futile. Many other gifts he might have requested would have been entirely justifiable, but the supplication for wisdom surpassed them all. The Wisdom literature of Solomonic and post-Exilic days bears testimony to the high desirability of wisdom (Prov 8:11-36; Eccl 12:9-11).

3) Solomon's Wisdom Displayed. 3:16-28.

16. Then came there two women, that were harlots. Solomon's wisdom was soon given a pragmatic test. Some critics have regarded this as a fictional incident designed to embellish Solomon's prayer. However, the marks of authenticity are upon it. The problem posed for the youthful monarch to adjudicate was a knotty one: Which woman was the mother of the dead infant and which was the mother of the living infant? Each claimed the living child as her own. Solomon, with a flare for the dramatic, appealed to the sympathies of the real mother by suggesting that the living child be divided between the two women. The woman whose claims were false, not recognizing the intent of the suggestion, all too readily fell into the carefully constructed trap. The mother whose maternal instincts were stirred within her, quickly voiced vehement protest. Solomon accorded the custody of the child to her.

4) Organization of the Empire. 4:1-28.

1. So king Solomon was king over all Israel. This verse takes us back to a time prior to the division of the kingdom. The tribes that formerly often warred and clashed with one another were now united under one head and living in a state of prosperity and happiness (see v. 20).

2-6. And these were the princes which he had. There follows a listing of the priest[s], princes, and other high officials of the royal court. In the light of verse 4, "the priest" of verse 2 refers to Zadok, while Azariah occupied the position of scribal recorder. **Azariah the son of Zadok.** The identity of this man is a controversial problem. Following Unger (Merrill Unger, *Bible Dictionary*) we identify said Azariah with the grandson of Zadok, son of Ahimaaz, who immediately followed his own grandfather (I Chr 6:8,9). In other words, the Azariah, grandson of Zadok, of I Kgs 4:2 and the Azariah, son of Nathan, of 4:5 can not refer to the same individual. Although the term "the priest," *hākkōhen*, is attributed to both individuals, in 4:2 it is apparently employed in the strict or religious sense, to specify a minister; while in verse 5 it is used in a more secular sense, to specify an *officer*.

7-19. And Solomon had twelve officers over all Israel. The names that follow constitute a listing of Solomon's officers, and to all intents and purposes they are unidentifiable. It is of interest to observe that the services of the officers were arranged on the basis of the calendar year of twelve months, each officer being responsible for his particular month.

20. Judah and Israel were many, as the sand. This verse sketches in miniature the picture of a happy, prosperous people. The wars of David were in the past; the sore conflicts of division were yet mercifully hidden in the future.

21. And Solomon reigned . . . from the river . . . unto the border of Egypt. Solomon's kingdom extended from the Euphrates to the land of Egypt. All of the smaller kingdoms in between had by this time become vassals to Solomon. It might seem impossible that with two such strong contending powers as Egypt to the south and Assyria to the north it would be possible to build so large an empire, but such was the case at the beginning of Solomon's reign. At this time, the kingdom of Egypt was ruled by the weak and inglorious Twenty-first Dynasty; and the power of Assyria was in a state of decline. **24. On this side the river.** Better, *beyond the river*. **Tiphsah,** or *Thapsacus*, a most important crossing point on the Euphrates. Perhaps no more is implied here than that Solomon had free and unrestricted usage of this great center of trade upon the Euphrates River.

26. Much of Solomon's wealth was invested in "horse flesh" (see I Kgs 9:19, especially in the light of archaeological information).

5) Summary of Solomon's Wisdom. 4:29-34.

29. And God gave Solomon wisdom . . . and largeness of heart. Largeness of heart is from a Hebrew term meaning *breadth of mind*. **30. And Solomon's wisdom excelled the wisdom of all the children of the east.** This wisdom is concerned with mundane affairs, rather than with spiritual realities. Unfortunately we know nothing of these wise men whom Solomon exceeded in wisdom. **32. And he spake three thousand proverbs.** By common consent the Wisdom literature contained in Proverbs and Ecclesiastes is traditionally ascribed to the pen (or penmen) of Solomon. The literary production of the reigning son of David was little short of prodigious. **34. And there came of all people to hear the wisdom of Solomon.** The writer here expresses himself in hyperbole. He means that Solomon's court was open to all, and that as a wise man he attracted many important and influential visitors (cf. ch. 10).

C. Solomon's Building Activity. 5:1–9:28.

1) Preparation for Building the Temple. 5:1-18.

1. And Hiram king of Tyre sent his servants unto Solomon. Hiram (c. 970–937 B.C.) had been a friend of David. After David had conquered the stronghold of Zion, he made a permanent treaty of peace with the king of Tyre. Hiram had assisted David in his public works by sending to Jerusalem laborers and cedar wood from the Lebanon Mountains (II Sam 5:11; II Chr 2:3,4). Now Hiram guaranteed his continued aid and goodwill to Solomon by a trade agreement, stipulating that in exchange for Tyrian wood and stone, Solomon would furnish him with agricultural products (II Chr 2:3ff.). A temporary rift in the friendship occurred when Solomon turned twenty of the cities in Galilee over to Hiram in exchange for some large shipments of gold, and Hiram found the cities displeasing (I Kgs 9:11-14). However, the rift was subsequently healed, and the two kings engaged in profitable trade with each other (10:22). Hiram assisted Solomon materially in the construction of the Temple.

3. Thou knowest how that David my father could not build an house. Solomon assumed that Hiram knew about his father's earnest desire to erect a house for the service of God, and about God's denying the wish on the ground of David's having been a man of war. Solomon now announced his intention of carrying forward the plans, and solicited Hiram's aid. He painted for the king of Tyre a picture of the favorable conditions in his own land which would contribute to his ability to perform the task.

6. Now therefore command . . . that they hew me cedar trees out of Lebanon. While the western slopes of the Lebanon Mountains must have been extensively covered with cedars in Solomon's day, only a few hundred of these trees remain today. Having taken hundreds of years to grow, these trees were valuable for building purposes because of the beauty of the wood and its extreme bitterness, which repelled insects and worms, and therefore it did not decay as rapidly as other woods.

7. When Hiram heard the words of Solomon . . . he rejoiced greatly. Hiram's response was enthusiastic. He pledged that he would perform all that Solomon had requested. The lumber would be carried from the forest to the sea, and from there it would be floated by rafts along the Mediterranean coast to a designated port of reception.

11. Solomon gave Hiram twenty thousand measures of wheat. An estimated 130,000 bushels of wheat, as well as 120 gallons of pure olive oil were the agricultural products Solomon sent to Tyre in exchange for the material provided by Hiram. This is indeed a good example of a "gentleman's trade agreement." Solomon was exercising caution that his "good should not be evil spoken of." This was on a year-by-year arrangement.

13. And king Solomon raised a levy out of all Israel. There is no contradiction between this and 9:22, as the Israelites were free when their period of service expired, while the Canaanites became permanent slaves. The men were arranged in shifts. While 10,000 men would be working in Lebanon for a month, the other 20,000 would be at home tilling the soil. **14. Adoniram** (or, Adoram), who was placed over the corvee, came to be thoroughly detested (12:18). In addition, Solomon had 70,000 transporters and 80,000 stonecutters working in the mountains to the north. It appears that all the able-bodied males, except the members of the royal court, were engaged in some employment concerned with the construction of the Temple.

17. And they hewed out great stones . . . to lay the foundation (ASV). The term **foundation** refers both to the foundation of the Temple proper and to that of its related structures. **18. Stonesquarers.** *Gebalites, men from Gebal* (modern Byblos, thirteen miles north of Beirut).

2) Construction of the Temple. 6:1-38.

a) Introduction. 6:1.

1. In the four hundred and eightieth year after the children of Israel were come out of . . . Egypt, in the fourth year of Solomon's reign. This introduction, as scholars agree, presents one of the most acute problems in OT chronology. The work proper upon the Temple is said to have begun 480 years after the Exodus. This brings up the thorny problem of the date of the Exodus. There are two main systems of dating this event, one assigning it an early date and the other giving it a late date. To employ round figures for the sake of convenience, the first system dates the departure from Egypt about 1440 B.C., while the second system dates it about 1250–1225 B.C., or nearly two centuries later. The earlier date is in substantial agreement with Gen 15:13; Ex 12:40,41, and Jud 11:26, where Jephthah indicates that Israel had been in Canaan 300 years.

Solomon ascended the throne about 963 B.C. The fourth year of his reign, in which he began to build the Temple, was probably about 959 B.C. This verse must be understood to favor the earlier dating of the Exodus. The city of Raamses (Ex 1:11), which the children of Israel are said to have built for Pharaoh, would then be considered a later name for the older city of Zoan or Avaris. The entrance of the patriarchs into Egypt would have been about 1870 B.C., a date which allows for the 400 years in Egypt. The Pharaoh of the Exodus may then be identified with Amenhotep II, who commenced his reign about 1447 B.C. There is evidence that his eldest brother died and did not succeed his father. It seems that, in the light of present knowledge, the early date is to be preferred. It should be pointed out that on this basis Garstang's date for the fall of Jericho, about 1400 B.C., becomes feasible. **In the month Zif, which is the second month.** Later called Iyyar, the month of flowers, our May.

b) General Plan and Measurements of the Temple. 6:2-10.

We here come to a rather detailed description of the erection of the Temple. **2. And . . . the length thereof was threescore cubits.** In modern measurements this building was an estimated ninety feet long, thirty feet wide, and forty-five feet high. In addition, there was a porch which added another thirty feet to the length.

4. And for the house he made windows. The windows, or *frames,* present a slight difficulty. It is thought that they were unmovable in their construction and designed to let air and light filter through, but that they could not be lowered or raised, as our ordinary windows can be.

5. And against the wall of the house he built stories (*floors,* AV marg.). Hebrew *yāṣiw'a;* AV *chambers.* These are best understood as side rooms, or cells, which were reserved for the priests. **6.** And **the nethermost story** (AV *chamber*) **was five cubits broad.** The lowest cell was seven and a half feet wide, the middle one nine feet, and the highest ten and a half feet. A triple-decker arrangement, with connecting stairs is here outlined.

7. And the house . . . was built of stone made ready at the quarry (ASV). The stones were prepared at the quarry so that no tool or iron would have to be used on the premises of construction. Solomon is known to have possessed a quarry on the outskirts of Jerusalem.

8. The door for the middle side-chambers was in the right side of the house (ASV). There was one main entrance to the side rooms of the priests.

c) God's Charge to Solomon. 6:11-13.

11. And the word of Jehovah came to Solomon (ASV). The Lord once more reaffirmed his conditional covenant with Solomon: namely, that if the king would obey God's commandments, God would confirm the Davidic covenant, and would honor Solomon's house by manifesting His own august presence there. That this promise was indeed conditional was demonstrated by the subsequent history of Judah at the time of the division of the kingdom (ch. 12). As for the Temple itself, it was destroyed in 586 B.C. by the Babylonian army (II Kgs 25:8,9).

d) The Finishing and Ornamentation of the Temple. 6:14-38.

14. So Solomon built the house, and finished it. The Temple was constructed of stone, overlaid with cedar wood. One of the critical barbs directed against the OT is the assertion that structures of such complexity were not known as early as the time of Solomon. However, archaeological findings at Megiddo have shed light upon the problem. Excavations by the University of Chicago have turned up fragments of mud brick together with wood ashes from the superstructure of a large building of the Solomonic era. A piece of charred wood from these remains was subjected to chemical analysis and found to be cedar. The evidence indicated that the superstructure was built with a half timber, half stone type of structure, similar to that of the courts of Solomon, which were made of rows of hewn stones and cedar beams. This type of construction is thought to be of Hittite origination (see J. P. Free, *Archaeology and Bible History*, p. 168).

The details which follow are to be viewed as further description of the house now regarded as completed.

16. And he built twenty cubits on the hinder part of the house (ASV). The rear room of the house is called here the oracle or the most holy place, commonly designated as the Holy of Holies. It was thirty feet (twenty cubits) long, thirty wide, and thirty high (6:20). Thus the entire Temple building contained two main rooms, (1) the Holy of Holies and (2) the Holy Place before it, sixty feet long (6:17), reminiscent of the arrangement of the Tabernacle. Sliding doors separating the two chambers replaced the former curtain (6:31,32).

18. And there was cedar on the house within (ASV). From the floor to the ceiling, the entire interior of the Temple was covered with cypress boards, so that the stone construction was hidden. The decoration of this section of the Temple, which consisted of cedar wood carved in gourds and open flower designs, must have been very beautiful.

19. And he prepared an oracle in the midst of the house within (ASV). **Oracle** is a technical designation for the ark of the covenant, and for the room or chamber containing it. **23. And in the oracle he made two cherubim of olive-wood** (ASV). In this building Solomon carried out the general plan of the ancient Tabernacle. He introduced new figures of the cherubim overshadowing the ark. These cherubim were made of olive wood overlaid with gold and stood fifteen feet high. Their wings, each seven and a half feet long, formed an arch over the ark. The dimensions of the ark are not here recorded, but see Ex 25:10,11.

29. And he carved all the walls . . . with carved figures. The carvings represented angelic figures, palm trees, and open flowers.

In the exterior court were placed the large altar of burnt offering, the lavers, and the bronze sea.

31. And for . . . the oracle he made doors of olive-wood (ASV). These appear to have been sliding doors. They were decorated with the same carved figures as the walls. The entrance to the Temple proper was flanked with doorposts of olive wood and two doors decorated to match those between the Holy Place and the Holy of Holies.

37,38. These verses give the dates of the commencement of the house and of its completion, a period spanning seven years, from the fourth to the eleventh year of Solomon's reign. This was a comparatively short time for a building of such magnificent structure. It should be remembered that: (1) much of the preparation had been completed even before Solomon's time; (2) the building though highly ornate was comparatively small; (3) a huge personnel was employed in the task. The present writer sees no censure implied in the statement that it took Solomon thirteen years to build his own house, but simply a matter of fact.

3) Solomon's Palace and Other Buildings. 7:1-12.

1. But Solomon was building his own house thirteen years. The length of time consumed was nearly double the period involved in building the Temple. But note that no extensive preparations had been made for the palace, and no great urgency beset its construction. **2. He built . . . the house of the forest of Lebanon.** At this point, the original Hebrew is somewhat obscure. The expression *kol betho* **(all his house,** v. 1) is capable of several renderings. It is possible to view Solomon's buildings, exclusive of the Temple, as one great structure. It is also possible to regard these buildings, including the Temple, as four distinct but closely connected structures. The four would be – (1) Solomon's Temple, (2) his private palace, (3) the Hall of Cedars (armory for defense), (4) the throne room for judgment. **10. The foundation was of costly stones.** These stones measured from twelve to fifteen feet in length.

4) The Furnishings of the Temple. 7:13-51.

a) Hiram, the Workman from Tyre. 7:13,14.

13. And king Solomon sent and fetched Hiram out of Tyre. Hiram or *Huram* was half Jewish, having a Tyrian father, but a Jewish mother of the tribe of Naphtali. An apparent contradiction arises between this verse and II Chr 2:14, where Hiram's mother is said to have come from the tribe of Dan. The solution may be quite simple, for the one verse may refer to her place of birth and the other to her place of residence. Some commentators assume that there were two Hirams who were artisans, but this is not likely. **14. A worker in brass . . . filled with wisdom, and understanding.** The brass should be rendered *copper* or *bronze.*

b) The Bronze Pillars. 7:15-22.

For he cast two pillars of brass (v. 15). Cf. II Chr 3:15-17; Jer 52:21-23. The pillars flanking the entrance to the court were fifty-two feet high, with the crown or capital measuring seven and one-half feet. They appear to have been for ornamentation only. Around the top each had decorative chains from which pomegranates were suspended. They were given the names, **Jachin,** *He shall establish,* and **Boaz,** *In it is strength* (v. 21). Some have discerned in these names a cryptogram for the words, "In the name of Jehovah will the king rejoice."

c) The Sea and the Laver. 7:23-39.

And he made a molten sea (v. 23). The sea, a huge, perfectly round, basin-like construction of bronze or copper, for the use of the priests, measured fifteen feet from brim to brim, seven and one-half feet high, and forty-five feet in circumference. It rested on twelve oxen, three facing in each direction of the compass. The sea and its lavers, it seems, were portable. Archaeological findings have helped to make understandable an otherwise difficult passage regarding the wheeled carriages for the ten lavers (7:38).

d) Hiram's Work Summarized. 7:40-47.

40. So Hiram made an end of doing all the work that he wrought for king Solomon in the house of Jehovah (ASV). The making of the bronze altar is not mentioned, although the existence of the altar is assumed in 8:64.

In addition to the lavers and the sea, Hiram's work included the lamp stands, the table of showbread, the pots and the shovels, and the other necessary equipment. No estimate is given of the weight of the bronze utilized.

5) The Dedication of the Temple. 8:1-66.

a) The Ark Brought to the Temple. 8:1-11.

1. Then Solomon assembled the elders of Israel, and all the heads of the tribes. The king was about to hold a service for the dedication of the Temple. As a prelude to this service, the ark was brought up to be enshrined in its new location. The actual dedicatory services were held approximately eleven months after the completion of the Temple. The position of the German OT scholar, Ewald, that the building was dedicated a month prior to its completion, is untenable. In the days previous, the abode of the ark had been the city of David, or Mount Zion (II Chr 6:5-7). The actual transfer of the ark was accompanied by a reverential but joyous procession.

5. Sacrificing sheep and oxen, that could not be . . . numbered for multitude. The act of sacrificing, in the theology of Israel, must be regarded not merely as a "penitential rite," but also as an act of thanksgiving and rejoicing. Such a great occasion seemed to call for a multiplicity of sacrifices. The season chosen for this event was Ethanim, the earlier name for the month Tishri, October-November.

6. And the priests brought in the ark of the covenant of the Lord unto his place. From David's first bitter experience in moving the ark, Solomon had learned God's proper order of procedure (II Sam 6:6ff.). He therefore entrusted the management of the ark to the divinely appointed stewards, the Levites. **9. There was nothing in the ark save the two tables of stone, which Moses put there at Horeb.** In Heb 9:4 two other articles are mentioned as being in the ark, i.e., the pot of manna and Aaron's flowering rod. The seeming discrepancy between the OT (I Kgs 8:9) and the NT in this connection may arise from the fact that the Hebrews verse refers to an earlier period, perhaps to Mosaic times.

b) Solomon's Sermon. 8:12-21.

The Lord said that he would dwell in the thick darkness. The speaker focused his hearers' thoughts on the divine condescension. The point of the sermon, beyond all reasonable question, was that the all-powerful God of heaven was willing to take up His abode, in protective presence and power, in the house that Solomon had now erected for His glory and honor. Magnificent and glorious as the house was to be reckoned among men, Solomon rightly and humbly realized that it was as nothing compared with the glory of heaven, the dwelling place of God. **17. It was in the heart of David.** The "princely preacher" was not unmindful of the debt of gratitude he owed his father.

c) Solomon's Prayer of Dedication. 8:22-61.

22. And Solomon stood before the altar of the Lord. In the similar account in II Chr 6:12-42, a note is added indicating that a special scaffold had been erected for this purpose. This prayer of Solomon may be regarded as containing seven rather distinct petitions. The king asked for: (1) God's continued presence and protection (I Kgs 8:25-30). (2) Condemnation of the wicked and vindication of the righteous (vv. 31,32). (3) Deliverance from the enemy upon confession of sin (v. 33). (4) Divine succor in days of calamity (vv. 35-40). (5) Divine help for the devout foreigner (vv. 41-43). (6) Victory in future battles (vv. 44,45). (7) National forgiveness (vv. 46-53).

In this prayer, the theology of Solomon rises to great heights. The critical allegation (based upon an evolutionary hypothesis) that the theology of Israel was not fully molded until the times of the "Second Isaiah," the "Great Unknown," is here by Solomon's words definitely confounded. The immanence, yet transcendence of the Deity is upheld. **23. Mercy.** Hebrew *ḥesed* implies covenantal love, the kind of love that is expressed in the covenant between God and his people. Solomon prayed on this occasion for a continuance of this covenantal love. The terms of fulfillment of this love are set forth upon the grounds of obedience and faith. Through David's line, the promises culminated in his great son, the Lord Jesus Christ.

27. But will God indeed dwell on the earth? The account in II Chr 6:18 contains the variation *dwell with men on the earth?* This slight divergence is followed by the LXX. Although in this prayer the note of grace is by no means concealed, the emphasis is still upon the attribute of justice (v. 31 ff.).

37. If there be in the land famine . . . pestilence, blasting, mildew. Blasting is blight. The conditions here envisioned are those caused by drought or war, or the invasion of locusts and caterpillars, plagues to which Biblical lands are ever prone. These afflictions are here viewed as intensified above the normal course of events as disciplinary measures. Solomon, however, recognized that the primary need was not the removal of these obnoxious creatures, but the remission of sin (v. 39).

41-43. Moreover, concerning the foreigner . . . Hear thou. Contrary to critical allegations, the people of Israel were commanded to love the **foreigner** (AV *stranger)*, remembering that they were once foreigners in the land of Egypt. To be sure, the God-fearing foreigner, or proselyte, is here in mind.

47. Yet if they shall bethink themselves in the land whither they were carried captives. Here Solomon seems to have exercised the prophetic gift of insight into the future. Peering down the long corridors of time, he seemingly foresaw the Babylonian captivity centuries ahead. It is significant that the builder of the Temple was given a vision of its eventual downfall, which occurred in 586/585 B.C., when Nebuchadnezzar destroyed both city and Temple. Not merely is the captivity of the nation thus foreshadowed, but also its subsequent restoration.

54. And it was so, that when Solomon had made an end of praying. This and the ensuing verses bring us to the benediction. For some reason this brief, but important addition is omitted in the corresponding account in II Chronicles. The benediction, by which the people were subsequently dispersed, was already a very old feature of Hebrew liturgy (cf. Num 6:23-26).

d) Solomon's Sacrifices. 8:62-66.

62. And the king, and all Israel with him, offered sacrifice before the Lord. Although the figures given – 22,000 oxen and 120,000 sheep – for the number of sacrifices offered seem high, they are not to be regarded as impossible, especially when one considers the magnitude of this event.

65. So Solomon held the feast at that time, and all Israel with him (ASV). The feast of dedication was followed by the Feast of Tabernacles, a regularly scheduled event, which commemorated the years of wandering. Its observance on this occasion must have held special significance for Israel. **From . . . Hamath unto the brook** (AV *river)* **of Egypt.** Though the exact boundaries designated by this phrase are controversial, the sense is clear enough. The celebration was observed by people from all over the land, from north to south.

66. On the eighth day he sent the people away. Seven days had been consumed in spiritual service centering around the dedication and the following feast. The people now left for their farms and villages, with a new sense of the divine destiny of the kingdom upon them.

6) Ratification of the Davidic Covenant. 9:1-9.

1-3. The Lord appeared to Solomon the second time. This chapter is concerned with promise and warning. The Lord's first appearance to Solomon had occurred at Gibeon (cf. 3:4,5). **4. If thou wilt walk . . . in uprightness.** Comparison of this passage with II Chr 7:12-22 reveals some interesting variations in the terms on which revival was conditioned: "And as for thee, if thou wilt walk before me." God held up the example of David, a godly father, as a bright and shining standard for the monarch. It is deeply significant that no great moral scandal is connected with the name or reign of Solomon, yet he never attained to the high spiritual character of his father, and at best died under the displeasure of the Lord. The promise is therefore to be viewed as conditional.

6. But if ye . . . turn from following me. The announced penalty was twofold: (1) the kingdom would cease; (2) the Temple, in which both king and people took such pardonable pride, would be leveled to the ground. The subsequent history of Israel fully established the validity of this prophetic warning. After the destruction of the Temple in 586/585 B.C., at the hand of the Babylonians, never again – neither at the time of the restoration, nor yet under Herod the Great – did it attain to its old glory. The cause of Israel's falling away was idolatry. It is noteworthy that Solomon, to whom the warning was given, was soon to be guilty of this very offense (11:4,5). **7. And Israel shall be a proverb and a byword among all people.** This prophetic warning looks even beyond the captivity, and envisions the later rejection of Israel for her repudiation of Jesus the Messiah. **8. Hiss.** Literally, *whistle*. The passer-by, observing the devastation of the Temple, would whistle in surprise and awe.

7) Summary of Solomon's Building Activities. 9:10-28.

a) Hiram's Dissatisfaction. 9:10-14.

12. And Hiram came out from Tyre to see the cities which Solomon had given him. In exchange for the material aid from Tyre, Solomon had agreed to give Hiram twenty cities in northern Galilee. It has been suggested that the Israelitish treasury was at this time short of funds and that therefore these cities were given in lieu of cash settlements. They comprised the area later known as "Galilee of the Gentiles" (Mt 4:15). **13. Cabul.** Unproductive land or marsh land. **14. Sixscore talents of gold.** An estimated $3,500,000. There is some ambiguity in this passage; evidently not all the details of the transaction between the two men are here recorded.

b) Solomon's Conscriptions. 9:15-28.

15. And Megiddo. Solomon's stables at Megiddo used to be regarded by 'liberal' scholars as purely fictional. But "the excavation of Megiddo by the University of Chicago has revealed a section of extensive stone stables from the level of Solomon's time" (Free, *op. cit.*). This stable was large enough, it is estimated, to house from 300 to 500 horses. And it accords very well with the details given here.

24. But Pharaoh's daughter came up out of the city of David. She was taken from Mount Zion because of her heathen religious background, lest she give offense to the pious people of Israel. **Millo.** Better, *the Millo*. Possibly, the fortification covering the breach David had made in the old wall of the Jebusites (cf. 11:27; II Sam 5:9).

25. And three times in a year did Solomon offer burnt offerings. Though Solomon's heart was not right in the sight of God, he nonetheless kept up the outward ceremony prescribed by Mosaic law (Ex 23:14-17). **So he finished the house.** This last clause may be regarded as a final sweeping statement of recapitulation.

26. And king Solomon made a navy of ships in Ezion-geber. Ezion-geber, Solomon's seaport, was situated on the eastern arm of the Red Sea, near Eloth, Israeli Eilat. Archaeology has again confirmed the historicity of the Biblical record in this regard. In 1938 and 1939, under the direction of Nelson Glueck, excavators unearthed a compact but important town at the site of Ezion-geber. Glueck discovered there the smelting furnaces that were used to produce the copper for Solomon's trade. The city of Ezion-geber has often been styled the "Pittsburgh" of Biblical times. **28. And they came to Ophir.** Solomon's merchant marine extended its navigation as far as Ophir. This is generally conceded to have been in southwestern Arabia, but some scholars, on the basis of the cargo mentioned in 10:22, locate it in India.

D. Golden Age of Solomon. 10:1-29.

1) The Visit of the Queen of Sheba. 10:1-13.

1. And when the queen of Sheba heard of the fame of Solomon. The queen of Sheba has been identified as the ruler of the Sabeans (Job 1:15), who inhabited Arabia Felix, or the greater part of the territory of the Yemen. In Biblical times it was considered royal sport for rulers with a reputation to test each other's abilities. The primary purpose of the queen's visit was to find out whether Solomon's pretensions to wisdom were equaled by his performance. All claims that she came from Ethiopia should be regarded as purely legendary. **2. And she came to Jerusalem with a very great train.** In conformity with ancient (and present) diplomatic protocol, the queen presented to the ruler of Israel costly gifts. **3. And Solomon told her all her questions.** Her curiosity was in no way disappointed. The actual wisdom of Solomon fully matched his pre-established reputation. The Sabean people over whom the queen ruled were governed by priest-kings (Ps 72:10). No doubt the queen took back to her native land glowing reports of Solomon's wisdom.

6. And she said . . . It was a true report that I heard. The queen confessed that she had thought the reports greatly exaggerated. Now she admitted that the half had not been told to her. Her astonishment arose not only from what she heard from the king's lips, but from what she saw with her own eyes. **9. Blessed be Jehovah thy God, who delighted in thee** (ASV). Considering the speaker, this statement was not inconsistent with polytheism. The queen was now willing to admit the existence of the God of Israel on the level of other deities. To press this to mean that she had become a proselyte to the Hebrew faith would be claiming too much (Mt 12:42). **10. And she gave the king an hundred and twenty talents of gold.** An estimated $3,500,000, a costly gift from an opulent queen! This was in addition to the precious stones and spices.

11. Moreover, the fleet of Hiram . . . brought gold from Ophir (RSV). The insertion relative to Hiram at this point indicates that at this time Solomon negotiated a trade agreement with the Tyrians in the interest of his visitor.

13. And king Solomon gave unto the queen of Sheba all her desire. The queen after being "wined and dined" and given many gifts, now turned homeward. No doubt the queen had reason to feel that her diplomatic mission had been highly successful.

2) The Glory and Power of Solomon's Empire. 10:14-29.

18-20. Moreover the king made a great throne of ivory, and overlaid it with the best gold. Throne. A high bench, or chair, denoting royalty. Solomon's throne was of special proportions. It was approached by means of six steps, flanked with twelve lions, six on either side, presumably representing the twelve tribes. The throne was a symbol of justice, rulership, and judgment. **19.** The Hebrew words for **round** (AV, ASV) and **calf** (RSV) are formed from the same consonants; only their vowel markings are different. Those who translate *calf* in this verse, take the word to signify that there was a figure of a calf behind the throne. If this is true, we may see the ugly figure of calf worship casting its shadow across the theism of Israel (12:28ff.).

Verses **23-29** constitute a recapitulation of Solomon's wealth and wisdom. **So king Solomon exceeded all the kings of the earth for riches and for wisdom** (v. 23). The court of Solomon was ever open to receive both native and foreign admirers. The reputed wisdom of Solomon, plus the grandeur of his public buildings, including the Temple, inevitably attracted many visitors. **And Solomon gathered together chariots and horsemen** (v. 26). It has been said that little things portray the true character of a man more certainly than great ones. A casual reader might see little significance in the king's assembling horses. However, the Mosaic law, in anticipation of the monarchy, particularly forbade the king of Israel to amass horses from Egypt (Deut 17:16). The fact that Egypt has not been known for breeding horses presents some difficulty here. The horses may have been bred in Cilicia, and Egypt may have been the trader. The Hittites and Syrians also supplied the market. Some take the Hebrew word translated "Egypt" as, in reality, a place in Cilicia – Musr.

E. Solomon's Apostasy, Decline, and Death. 11:1-43.

1) Solomon's Unfaithfulness to God. 11:1-13.

1. But king Solomon loved many foreign women. He disobeyed the Mosaic regulations for the king prophetically viewed in the Deuteronomic code in regard to the multiplication of horses (Deut 17:16), of foreign women (17:17), and of gold (17:17). Although the three sins of this monarch, taken separately or even weighed together, may not be nearly as glaring as the one great sin of his father, yet, they were sins that drew his heart away from the living God. Furthermore, there is no written indication that he ever repented of them. **2. For surely they will turn away your heart after their gods.** The reason given for the prohibition of mixed marriages was that they would lead to idolatry, into which Solomon was about to fall. For a great ruler to maintain seven hundred wives and three hundred concubines was quite in keeping with the fashion of typical Oriental courts. The more dwellers in the harem, the greater the ruler. Perhaps Solomon's great sin was not so much sexuality as it was simply the desire to be thought great.

4. For it came to pass, when Solomon was old. We see here the sad picture of Solomon's forsaking God and turning to idolatry to please his pagan wives. **5. Ashtoreth.** The goddess of the Zidonians, a Canaanite deity connected with the fertility cult. The name is cognate with the Babylonian *Ishtar,* the goddess of sexual love, maternity, and fertility (Unger, *op. cit.).* This goddess is among the best known of the fertility cult goddesses. **Milcom the abomination.** Another form of *Malcham,* sometimes identified with *Molech* or *Moloch,* the chief god of Moab and Ammon. So ensnared in the practice of idolatry did Solomon become that he built a high place for this evil deity. The worship of Molech was stringently prohibited by law (Lev 18:21; 20:1-5). Molech demanded the rite of human sacrifice, especially of little children. His worship was utterly desecrated by the good king Josiah. **6. And Solomon did** that which was **evil.** The particular evil of idolatry; the general evils of greed, love of luxury, and oppression of his people. **7. Then did Solomon build an high place for Chemosh.** The national deity of the Moabites. Chemosh was "twin brother" to Moloch of the Ammonites—equally cruel, licentious, and vulgar in his demands. **The mount** (AV *hill)* **that is before Jerusalem.** Identified tentatively as the Mount of Olives.

9-13. And the Lord was angry with Solomon, because his heart was turned. We now hasten toward the division of the kingdom. God announced to Solomon the extent of the divine chastisement. The kingdom was to be rent and divided; Israel would lose her political unity. Solomon's sun, which had risen in such splendor, was now about to set behind the darkest clouds. However, David was still to have a lamp in Israel (cf. v. 36). Not yet would the kingdom be totally taken away.

2) Adversaries and Impending Division. 11:14-40.

14-28. And Jehovah raised up an adversary unto Solomon (ASV). Although the division of the kingdom did not occur until after the king's death, Solomon was to experience punishments, as God, in His displeasure, raised up external and internal enemies against him. Three strong adversaries arose:

(1) Hadad, a prince of the royal house of Edom, had escaped Joab's massacre and fled with some of his followers to Egypt, where he was treated kindly by the Pharaoh. Now, apparently for no valid reason but through the providential leading of God, he requested and obtained permission from Pharaoh to return home. Back in Israel, he proved to be a thorn in the side of Solomon (vv. 14-22).

(2) Rezon of Damascus, the son of Eliada, after the defeat of his master, Hadadezer (II Sam 8:3-8,10), became a freebooter with a party of bandits that harassed the countryside. Shortly after David's death he seized the city of Damascus, no doubt by a surprise attack. From this position Solomon could not expel him. Little by little Rezon became an increasing threat as he dominated the trade routes to the East (vv. 23-25).

(3) Jeroboam, the son of Nebat, of the tribe of Ephraim, became the internal adversary of Solomon. A young man of considerable ability and talent, he soon attracted the attention of the king (v. 28), who made him overseer of his public works.

29. And it came to pass . . . that the prophet Ahijah the Shilonite found him. On leaving Jerusalem one day, the young Jeroboam was suddenly accosted by Ahijah, the prophet (first introduced here), who symbolically made known to him his future. The prophet took hold of the new garment he himself was wearing and tore it into twelve pieces. Giving the young man ten pieces and retaining two, he announced that God was about to rend the kingdom of Solomon similarly, giving ten tribes to Jeroboam and leaving only two for the house of David.

31. And he said to Jeroboam, Take thee ten pieces. In the light of prophecy, Jeroboam was already viewed as the leader of the new state of Israel formed in disciplinary judgment for Solomon's sins. **32. But he shall have one tribe for my servant David's sake.** The pronoun "he" doubtless refers to the house of Solomon, i.e., Rehoboam and his descendants. The one tribe, Benjamin, faithfully adhered to the house of David. The two tribes are viewed as one; hence, in reality, no tribe is missing here. **33. Because that they have foresaken me, and have worshipped Ashtoreth . . . Chemosh . . . Milcom.** A specific reason given for the impending division is that they had fallen into idolatry – a sin, which, despite the severity of God's judgment, continued to plague both kingdoms until they went into captivity.

34. Howbeit I will not take the whole kingdom out of his hand. Despite the unfaithfulness of men, God was faithful in preserving the seed of David "until he come whose right it is; and I [God] will give it him" (Ezk 21:27; Mt 1:1; Rom 1:3). **36. And unto his son will I give one tribe, that David my servant may have a light.** Literally, *that there may be a light to my servant David.* God's purpose would be carried out despite Solomon's disobedience. The house of David would be disciplined but not destroyed. Solomon indeed had proved to be a sinner; yet through the line of David, Christ, the Saviour of sinners, should appear.

38. And it shall be, if thou wilt hearken. Not only did God pledge himself to be faithful to the house of David, but he also promised, conditionally, to extend his mercies to Jeroboam – **I will . . . build thee a sure house, as I built for David.** How different might have been the personal history of Jeroboam, as well as the subsequent history of his kingdom, if he had obeyed the Lord's voice! This man, however, gained the unenviable epithet, "who caused Israel to sin." Though the prophecy of Ahijah was not immediately fulfilled, all that he foretold came to pass in due time.

40. Solomon sought therefore to kill Jeroboam. Though the prophetic announcement was made in secret, it seems that Jeroboam could not wait for God's time but began to plot against Solomon. The king, therefore, sought to slay him on the ground of supposed treachery. Jeroboam was forced to flee to Shishak (Sheshonk) of Egypt until the death of Solomon.

3) Solomon's Decease. 11:41-43.

41. The rest of the acts of Solomon. The book of the acts of Solomon mentioned here is quite evidently a manuscript no longer extant, to which the author of the book of Kings had access. Thus we are led to the rather tragic end of a life once so promising. **42. And the time that Solomon reigned . . . was forty years.** The actual time of Solomon's reign was forty-two years, though part of this must be reckoned as the time of his coregency with David.

43. And Rehoboam his son reigned in his stead. Rehoboam reigned over all Israel a very short time. The seeds of division planted in the time of Solomon now came to full bloom.

II. The Divided Kingdom, from Rehoboam to the Fall of Israel. I Kgs 12:1–II Kgs 17:41.

A. Early Antagonism Between Israel and Judah, from Jeroboam to Omri. 12:1–16:28.

1) The Rupture of the Kingdom. 12:1-33.

a) The Petition of the Malcontents. 12:1-20.

The immediate natural cause for the impending disruption of the kingdom was the heavy taxation brought about through the vast expenditures of Solomon (cf. II Chr 10). The unseen cause was the divine discipline.

1. And Rehoboam went to Shechem: for all Israel were come to Shechem to make him king. Rehoboam, who is the only son of Solomon mentioned in Scripture, had doubtless been appointed by his father to succeed him. **Shechem.** A town in Ephraim, rather than the capital city, was the rallying point.

2. When Jeroboam . . . heard it, he returned out of Egypt. No doubt it was through spies that Jeroboam, who was in exile (11:40), heard of the impending coronation of Rehoboam. Thereupon, he hastily returned to Israel to bid for the kingdom. Upon his arrival, the people made him their spokesman to voice their varied and many grievances. The people requested the new king to ease their burdens. **4. Thy father made our yoke grievous.** No doubt this is an abridgment of the people's petition, giving its essence. The petition asked primarily for a lightening of the economic load, but perhaps it also had in view political and social oppression.

5. And he said unto them, Depart yet for three days. The king's request that he be allowed time to think over their petition seemed reasonable. From that which follows, however, it seems that the verdict was already determined. **6. And king Rehoboam consulted with the old men.** The elders of the court advised Rehoboam to speak in the language of diplomacy, to admit the validity of the complaints and to promise reformation in due time.

8. But he forsook the counsel of the old men... and consulted with the young men. The advice of Rehoboam's young counselors was exactly the reverse of that proposed by the older, wiser men. **10. Thus shalt thou speak unto this people.** Their advice to him was to assume a threatening, undiplomatic attitude, to show the people that he knew of the plottings behind his back, and to warn them that each complaint would be regarded as a treacherous act.

14. Whips . . . scorpions. A "whip" was a plain leather strap. A "scorpion" was a whip with barbed points or tips of steel imbedded in it, used in the castigation of slaves. Hence the speech was highly insulting. Not only did Rehoboam threaten the people with heavier burdens than they had known before, but he indicated that he was about to treat them as a nation of slaves. It should be said in favor of Rehoboam that his treatment of those who remained faithful to the Davidic house was much more moderate than the speech suggests. This attitude, however, the people could not foresee, and so the rift became unbridgeable. **15.** So **the king hearkened not unto the people.** The hidden motif is given in the following clause: **For it was a thing brought about of Jehovah** (ASV). The words of the prophet Ahijah concerning the division of the kingdom must be fulfilled. The decrees of God, though originated in eternity, are culminated in history.

16. What portion have we in David? Thus the suzerainty of the Davidic house was repudiated by the majority of Israel. With these words, they turned their backs on their heritage to seek out new paths with their newly chosen leader, Jeroboam, the son of Nebat.

17. But as for the children of Israel which dwelt in the cities of Judah, Rehoboam reigned over them. In fulfillment of God's promise that David would "have a light alway . . . in Jerusalem" (11:36, AV), the southern Hebrews that dwelt in Judea remained faithful, while the northern ones went their separate way. Rehoboam's attempt to exercise dictatorial powers had failed.

18. Then king Rehoboam sent Adoram . . . and all Israel stoned him to death. Not fully realizing that the break between the two nations was final and decisive, Rehoboam unwisely sent his officer, Adoram, to Israel to conscript labor. The reaction of Jeroboam's people was swift and terrible: they killed the luckless overseer. **King Rehoboam made haste to mount his chariot** (RSV). It seems that Rehoboam himself narrowly escaped the same fate.

b) Civil War Averted. 12:21-24.

Rehoboam . . . assembled all . . . which were warriors, to fight (v. 21). Rehoboam's thought was to invade the northern tribes to bring them back into subjection to his rule. Shemaiah, the prophet, intervened with a message from God urging him not to go to war and declaring that such a course would only end in his defeat. To his credit, in this instance, he obeyed the voice of the Lord and disbanded the army.

c) Northern Kingdom Set Up. 12:25–32.

25. Then Jeroboam built Shechem in the hill-country of Ephraim (ASV). In this passage we discover what preliminary steps Jeroboam took to establish his new kingdom. He chose Shechem for his capital. In reality, three capitals arose in the north – first Shechem, then Tirzah, and later Samaria, which eventually became the permanent capital.

26. And Jeroboam said in his heart, Now shall the kingdom return to the house of David. This may be viewed as Jeroboam's first act of infidelity to Jehovah. He had already been given assurance that the Lord would build him a sure house. But because he did not trust God's word, he resorted to this measure of religious apostasy – the religious as well as political separation of the two kingdoms. **28. Whereupon the king took counsel, and made two calves of gold.** Two calves (bulls of gold), replacing the cherubim of the mercy seat. Though Jeroboam may not have intended to establish actual idolatry, he thus set the general tenor of spiritual declension. W. F. Albright (*From the Stone Age to Christianity*, p. 299) builds a good case, on archaeological grounds, in support of the theory that the golden bulls were not really images of Jehovah, but formed the visible pedestal upon which the invisible god of Israel stood. But even such use of images was a throwback to the idolatry of the Canaanites or of Egypt, and it was roundly condemned by the prophets Hosea and Amos (Hos 8:5,6; 13:2,3). **30. And this thing became a sin.** Even though it might be insisted, for the sake of the argument, that Jeroboam erected these calves in honor of Jehovah, it is still evident that as far as the people were concerned, the images rapidly became idols.

31. And he made houses of high places, and made priests from among all the people (ASV). The second step which Jeroboam took to weaken the religious ties between northern and southern Israel was to infiltrate non-Levites into the priesthood. The Mosaic law specified that none should attend holy ordinances except men from this tribe.

32. And Jeroboam ordained a feast in the eighth month. This was actually the Feast of Tabernacles, which according to the Law was to be held in the seventh month (Lev 23:24ff.), Jeroboam changed the time to the eighth month. These three measures weakened the ties between the tribes and widened the gulf religiously.

2) The Reign of Jeroboam I, and His Death. 13:1–14:20.

a) The Divine Judgment Pronounced. 13:1-10.

1. And, behold, there came a man of God out of Judah. An unnamed prophet, bearing the simple designation, **a man of God,** came from Judah to Bethel, one of the two centers of Jeroboam's calf worship, to administer a stinging rebuke and to announce doom. **2. Behold, a child shall be born unto the house of David, Josiah by name.** This is one of the most remarkable instances in the OT of prophecy demonstrating God's omniscience. This forecast is on a level with the Isaianic prophecy regarding Cyrus (Isa 45:1ff.). Because this forecast is so remarkable, 'liberal' Biblical critics have sought to reduce it to an *ad hoc* status. However, to regard this as a historical insertion, coming to pass after the day of King Josiah, is utterly to fail to understand the true genius of prophecy. For the remarkable fulfillment of this prediction see II Kgs 23:15-20. **3. And he gave a sign.** The rending of the altar may be regarded as confirmation of the prophetic utterance. It is apparent that there is an immediate as well as a long range manifestation of the divine displeasure.

4. When the king heard the saying . . . he . . . put forth his hand (ASV). Thoroughly angered, Jeroboam stretched out his hand to order the prophet's arrest. Before the wicked order could be carried out, however, the king's hand was withered (Heb., **dried**), that is to say, paralyzed to the extent that he could not draw it in again. The vengeful king now cried for mercy (v. 6). In answer to the prophet's prayer, Jeroboam's hand was restored.

7. Come home with me. Jeroboam's invitation may have been designed to serve a twofold purpose: it may have been in the nature of an apology for attempting arrest; and it may have been a device for warding off or at least softening the judgment pronounced upon the royal household. **8. If thou wilt give me half thine house, I will not go in with thee.** True to his divine instructions, the prophet declined on the ground that it had been expressly forbidden him to eat bread or to drink water in Bethel. Such social intercourse might well have created the impression in the minds of the people that the judgment pronounced by the prophet had either been averted or at least mitigated. **10. So he went another way.** The prophet now sought his homeward way. So far he had acted in strict obedience to the divine command.

b) Seduction of the Man of God by the Old Prophet. 13:11-32.

11-14. Now there dwelt an old prophet in Beth-el. What the king, with all his riches, fame, and glory, could not accomplish in the life of the man of God, a believer obviously not having "the mind of the Spirit," was now able to accomplish. The sons of the old prophet at Bethel told their father about the prophecy that had been made against Jeroboam. Acting upon their report, the old prophet went forth to seek the man of God, and he found him under the oak or terebinth tree.

15. Come home with me, and eat bread. The Oriental is known for his hospitality to a much more marked degree than is his Occidental brother. Besides wishing to show hospitality, perhaps the old prophet wanted to learn more exactly about this wonderful and unusual prophecy. **16. I may not return with thee, nor go in with thee.** As the prophet had declined Jeroboam's invitation, so now he at first refused the invitation of his fellow prophet on the ground of God's prohibition (v. 17).

18. I am a prophet also as thou art; and an angel spake unto me. . . . But he lied unto him. The prophet from Bethel pretended that he had received divine orders countermanding those previously given the younger prophet. We do not know why he lied. **19. So he went back with him.** He disobeyed the divine command. A practical lesson to be learned is that the advice of other men, no matter if they are Christian friends, should not be substituted for the clear call of duty within our own hearts.

20. And it came to pass, as they sat at the table. The prophet who had been willing to assume the role of the tempter, now, by God's urgency, assumed the more difficult role of the announcer of punishment. The prophet's penalty for disobedience was to be death. This prophecy came to pass almost immediately.

24. And when he was gone, a lion met him by the way. Lions still prowled the forest around Bethel and once in a while accosted an unwary traveler. However, in order that it might be known that this was indeed a supernatural judgment and not simply an unfortunate accident, the lion, after slaying the prophet, did not harm or tear his body, nor did he even kill the meek donkey upon which the prophet had been riding, but calmly stood at attention, as if by divine arrest. **26. It is the man of God, who was disobedient unto . . . the Lord.** Though the lying prophet suffered no corporeal punishment, his pangs of conscience must have been severe when he realized that he had brought about the death of a man by urging him to pursue a course of disobedience.

28. And he went and found his body cast in the way. The supernatural character of the story is apparent throughout. We are accustomed to think of miracles being acts or tokens of great healing and benefit, but we must remember that there are miracles of discipline as well. **29-32. And the prophet took up the body of the man of God.** The corpse of the disobedient prophet was not to be left uncared for but given honorable burial. The last tribute that could possibly be paid by one prophet of God to another was thus touchingly performed. With bitter lamentations the old prophet from Bethel laid his brother prophet to rest in his grave. Perhaps a twofold source of grief may be seen here: (1) He had contributed to the death of the first prophet, though perhaps quite unwittingly. (2) At that time the nation could ill afford to sacrifice any of its godly men. The old prophet, with bowed head, lamented not only the sorrowful fate of his brother prophet, but also the miserable state of the divided kingdom as a whole. He acknowledged that the words spoken by the deceased prophet would be fulfilled in due season.

c) Jeroboam's Persistence in Evil. 13:33,34.

33. After this thing Jeroboam returned not from his evil way. These strange, portentous happenings, terrible as they were, did not deter the king from pursuing the wicked ways he had chosen. He repeated rather than repented of the three initial sins which at the beginning began to draw the northern kingdom down the pathway of spiritual declension. **34. And this thing became sin unto the house of Jeroboam, even to cut it off.** The root spiritual cause of the declension and final fall of the house of Jeroboam is given here. Various political and sociological conditions, and even international relations, might be cited as reasons for the destruction of Jeroboam's line. Nevertheless, the destruction stemmed directly from the king's disobedience to the command of the holy God. Therefore, we judge those scholars to be wrong who excuse, if not defend, Jeroboam's calf worship on the ground that he was simply worshiping the true God of Israel in another fashion.

d) Further Doom and Woes Pronounced Against Jeroboam. 14:1-14.

1. At that time Abijah the son of Jeroboam fell sick. This Abijah should not be confused with Rehoboam's son of the same name, who succeeded his father on the throne of Judah. This sickness of the child was not one of the many misfortunes of life to which all human beings are prone, but rather a disciplinary act of God. Jeroboam, first king of the northern union, had failed to hear God's "more tender solicitations"; so now the Lord struck directly at his most precious possession, his young son. **2. And Jeroboam said to his wife, Arise, I pray thee, and disguise thyself.** With these words the writer introduces the king's plot to deceive the prophet Ahijah and yet learn the future. Jeroboam reasoned that if the prophet perceived the identity of the inquirer, he would be sure to deliver a message of judgment and doom. **Shiloh.** The former central sanctuary and previous dwelling place of the ark. The town had now become the dwelling place of Ahijah, the prophet, who originally had predicted Jeroboam's rise to power (I Kgs 11:26-40).

4. But Ahijah could not see; for his eyes were set by reason of his age. The prophet, now deprived of his sight through extreme age, yet kept his ears attuned to the voice of God, ready to receive messages from the outer world. **5. Behold, the wife of Jeroboam cometh to inquire** (ASV). The ungodly queen thought within herself that the ruse would be quite adequate to deceive the prophet. She had no idea that the "God before whom all things are open" had already gone before her to appraise his servant of her coming and of the message he was to deliver to her.

6. When Ahijah heard the sound of her feet . . . he said, Come in, thou wife of Jeroboam. Disguised, discovered, and doomed. Not only the veil upon her face, but the draperies on her heart were penetrated. Her most wicked intentions as well as her nature were now laid bare. Hypocrisy and sham will always meet with the severe displeasure and judgment of our Lord. **7. Go, tell Jeroboam, Thus saith the Lord God of Israel.** Ahijah, with bold strokes, now proceeded to tell of the king's anointing, of God's conditional promise, of His grace in placing Jeroboam over the tribes of the north. He then sharply reminded Jeroboam, through his wife, of his apostasy and serious idolatry, culminating in the worship of the golden calves. Therefore, he must expect punishment.

10. Therefore . . . I will bring evil upon the house of Jeroboam . . . every manchild (ASV). The kingdom of Israel would be depopulated of its male children either by captivity or by death. **11. Him that dieth.** Their bodies were to be devoured by dogs and wild birds of prey – the worst disgrace that could befall a Semite. **12. When thy feet enter into the city, the child shall die.** Thus doom was pronounced in the most awesome way against Jeroboam's household. Even the most calloused in heart are touched by the death of a little child, especially of one in line for the throne. But the decree was to be put into effect speedily. Jeroboam's wife would never again see her son alive. He was to lie still in death as her feet passed over the threshold of the capital city. In contradistinction to his father, he would be given honorable burial.

e) The Captivity Foreseen. 14:15-19.

15. For Jehovah will smite Israel . . . and will scatter them beyond the River (ASV). This is a long-range prediction of the captivity yet to come. When Samaria fell in 722 B.C., the northern kingdom experienced this bitter fate at the hands of the Assyrians. And when Jerusalem fell in 586/585 B.C., the southern kingdom underwent deportation at the hands of the Babylonians. The ground given for such chastisement was Israel's incurable idolatry.

17,18. And Jeroboam's wife arose . . . and came to Tirzah. These verses recount the tragic sequel to Ahijah's prediction. As the prophet had foretold, the child much loved by the populace at large was wept and mourned as his body was laid in the tomb.

f) Jeroboam's Continued Apostasy and His Death. 14:20.

And he slept with his fathers. For supplementary facts the reader is referred to the account in II Chr 13:15-20. However, this reference may be regarded as a convention or formality, since the accounts in I Kings concerning Jeroboam are much fuller than those in Chronicles.

3) Judah under Rehoboam, Abijam, and Asa. 14:21–15:24.

a) Rehoboam of Judah. 14:21-24.

21,22. And Rehoboam the son of Solomon reigned in Judah. The historical scene now shifts toward the south as the fortunes of the house of David are delineated. Rehoboam reigned one year as co-regent with his father and sixteen years in his own right. Though his reign was free from the worship of the golden calves, yet spiritual declension and moral delinquency characterized its downward course.

Idolatry, and that in gross form, had become the order of the day. **23. High places** (Heb. *bāmôt*). Places of elevation which though not necessarily idolatrous in character, readily yielded themselves to this type of worship. The **pillars** (Heb. *maṣṣēbôt;* AV, *images*). Stones placed on end representing the male counterpart of the Canaanitic deity. The **Asherim** were poles representing the female side of the deity. Compare the *groves* of the AV. The licentious worship of Canaan infiltrated the worship of Judea. **24. And there were also sodomites in the land.** Thus, the whole ugly picture of idolatry is now filled in. **Sodomites.** Male prostitutes, reserved for sexual purposes in connection with religious worship. As in the land of Canaan, the Israelites had failed to exterminate this idolatrous practice. Now it had become a snare and a trap to them.

b) The Invasion of Shishak. 14:25-28.

25. In the fifth year of king Rehoboam . . . Shishak king of Egypt came up against Jerusalem. Shishak. *Sheshonk* of Egyptian records (945–924 B.C.), the founder of the Twenty-second Dynasty. This was the first serious foreign invasion of Israelite territory since the days of Saul. In the temple of Karnak, in a relief picturing the victory of Egypt over Judah, Shishak boasts of the trouble he made for the Judean king. A briefer, more sober account is given in the Bible, wherein it is honestly admitted that Shishak despoiled the beautiful Temple of Solomon before he agreed not to pillage Jerusalem fully.

c) Death of Rehoboam. 14:29-31.

29. The rest of the acts of Rehoboam, and all that he did. Once more the reader is referred to the fuller account in II Chr 12:13-16. This reign had been characterized by tension and frequent outbreaking of warfare between the divided tribes, once so strongly united under one glorious head, David.

d) Abijam of Judah. 15:1-8.

1. Now in the eighteenth year of king Jeroboam . . . began Abijam to reign over Judah (ASV). He reigned three years, 913–911 B.C. **2. And his mother's name was Maachah, the daughter of Abishalom. Maachah** was the queen mother. **Abishalom. The longer form for** *Absalom*. **3. And he walked in all the sins of his father, which he had done before him.** For a fuller account of the reign of Abijam, see II Chr 13:1-22. Abijam (or Abijah) fashioned his life after Rehoboam's ungodly and wicked example. **His heart was not perfect.** An expression used to indicate that Abijam was sadly lacking in devotion and fidelity toward God.

4. Nevertheless for David's sake. Verses 4 and 5 set forth God's kindness and fidelity. Despite the continued iniquity of Abijam, the Lord did not withdraw his mercy from these people of Judah. For the meaning of the **lamp**, see 11:36.

6. And there was war between Rehoboam and Jeroboam. Warfare continued to plague and scourge the divided kingdom. **7. Now the rest of the acts of Abijam.** A somewhat more pious portrait of Abijam is given in II Chronicles. Particularly, in the oration Abijam made against Jeroboam, he seems to evidence some faith in Jehovah. Perhaps Abijam, like many others, could preach better than he could practice.

e) Asa and His Reforms. 15:9-15.

It is heart-warming and refreshing to observe the young king breaking away from the evil tradition of the two preceding kings and determining to do what was right in the eyes of the Lord, as did David his 'father.'

9,10. In the twentieth year of Jeroboam . . . reigned Asa over Judah. And his mother's name was Maachah. Abijam and Asa may have been brothers. It is more likely that we should understand **mother** to mean "grandmother" here, in accordance with Semitic usage.

11-15. And Asa did that which was right. Having set his heart on following God's will, Asa first eradicated idolatrous practices and personnel from the kingdom. Especially, he removed the sodomites (14:24). Asa did not limit his reform to strangers, but extended it into his own family. He even removed Maachah from the position of queen, because she had introduced idolatry into the land. The young king next hewed down his grandmother's graven images and burned them by the brook Kidron. This was the swiftly flowing winter brook to the northeast of Jerusalem, the "Cedron" (AV), which Jesus crossed on the night of his agony in Gethsemane (Jn 18:1).

f) War with Baasha of Israel. 15:16-22.

16. And there was war between Asa and Baasha. Baasha declared war upon his neighbors. The threatening, hostile gesture Baasha made was to fortify Ramah, a stronghold four or five miles north of Jerusalem. This was regarded as a very warlike act.

18. Then Asa took all the silver and the gold that were left in the treasures of the house of the Lord. By these means and with this gift, Asa sought the favor of **Ben-hadad** of Syria. Ben-hadad **I, it** seems, assumed the throne of Syria in 890 B.C. Later, King Ahab went to war against Ben-hadad. **20. And Ben-hadad hearkened unto king Asa, and sent the captains of his armies against the cities of Israel** (ASV). The cities here mentioned, which Ben-hadad took, were towns in the general environs of the Sea of Galilee.

21. And it came to pass, when Baasha heard thereof, that he left off building of Ramah. Frightened by the news of the coming of powerful Syrian assistance to Asa, Baasha retired to his own capital city of Tirzah. **22. And king Asa built with them Geba . . . and Mizpah.** Geba of Benjamin is identified with *Jeba'*, near *Mikmash*. Asa took the material Baasha had collected, ostensibly for defense against him, and utilized it for a new fortress of his own.

g) Death of Asa. 15:23,24. **And Asa slept with his fathers, and was buried . . . and Jehoshaphat his son reigned in his stead.** The good Asa was followed by his godly son, Jehoshaphat (873–848), who had been co-regent with him for three years.

4) Israel under Nadab, Baasha, Elah, Zimri, and Omri. 15:25–16:28.

a) Nadab of Israel. 15:25,26.

25. And Nadab . . . began to reign over Israel. The historian here picks up an incident that was occurring in the north. Nadab (910–909), the wicked son of Jeroboam, son of Nebat, came to the throne. It must be remembered that while some eight dynasties were succeeding each other in northern Israel, to the south in Judah but one dynasty, the Davidic house, held sway.

26. And he (Nadab) **did** that which **was evil in the sight of the Lord.** Nadab had a short reign, variously estimated as lasting from one to one and a half years.

b) Baasha's Conspiracy and Reign. 15:27–16:7.

27. And Baasha the son of Ahijah, of the house of Issachar, conspired against him. The dynasty of the house of Jeroboam was coming to an inglorious end, while Baasha's dynasty, which was likewise to be brief, was coming to the fore. **29. As soon as he was king, he smote all the house of Jeroboam . . . even as Ahijah the prophet had predicted.** Thoroughly, ruthlessly, Baasha proceeded to destroy Nadab's house. The judgment of God was thus speedily executed against the wicked dynasty of Israel. Nevertheless, Baasha paid no heed to the precepts and law of God, but walked in the same evil way as did those before him. Civil conflict continued between the two nations (v. 32).

34. And he did evil in the sight of the Lord, and walked in the way of Jeroboam. Though Baasha had extirpated the house of Jeroboam, he most unfortunately had not abolished his sins, either from the kingdom in general or from his own life in particular.

16:1. Then the word of the Lord came to Jehu the son of Hanani against Baasha, saying. Though the Northern Kingdom was unfaithful to the Lord God of Israel, God still extended mercy to her by warning her of coming judgment. **2. Forasmuch as I exalted thee out of the dust, and made thee prince over my people.** Baasha was to be properly chastised. The reason for this was that, although chosen of God to rule over His people Israel, he had lightly esteemed his sacred vocation. He had clung to the sins of Jeroboam, the son of Nebat, who "made Israel to sin." **3. Behold, I will utterly sweep away Baasha and his house** (ASV). A similar threat had been made against the house of Jeroboam by the prophet Ahijah (14:10,11). As Baasha had chosen to share in the iniquity of the house of Jeroboam, so likewise was he to share in the severe penalty thereof, even to being devoured by dogs.

6. So Baasha slept with his fathers. The reign of Baasha was brought to an ignoble end, and Baasha was succeeded by his son Elah. We may consider Elah but a duplicate of his father. On the basis of verse 7 it appears that the prophetic ministry of Jehu continued throughout Elah's reign. Blessed is the king whose prophet is his counselor, but cursed is he who heeds not his prophet.

c) Elah of Israel. 16:8-10.

8. In the twenty and sixth year of Asa king of Judah began Elah the son of Baasha to reign. Elah's reign (886–885 B.C.), a brief and unhappy one, lasted just one year and ended in a violent death. Zimri, one of the captains of Elah's own guard, conspired against him and slew him.

9. Now **he was in Tirzah, drinking himself drunk in the house of Arza.** Elah and Belshazzar had at least this in common: they were both slain while drinking themselves drunk. **Arza.** The prefect of his palace, who arranged for the drinking bout and was doubtless a party to the conspiracy. **10. And Zimri went in and smote him.** Thus the third dynasty came to the throne of Israel – if, indeed, a line that ruled for only seven days can be dignified with the name of dynasty.

d) Zimri of Israel. 16:11-20.

11. When he began to reign . . . he slew all the house of Baasha. In fulfillment of the words of the prophet Jehu, Zimri destroyed not only the relatives but also the friends of his predecessor (vv. 12,13).

15. In the twenty and seventh year of Asa king of Judah did Zimri reign seven days in Tirzah (885 B.C.). The shortest reign of any of the kings of Israel or Judah – one brief week! **17. And Omri went up from Gibbethon, and all Israel with him, and they besieged Tirzah.** News traveled a good deal more slowly then than it does in our day, but finally word about Zimri's treachery reached the ears of the people at Gibbethon. Led by Omri, they marched upon Tirzah, the capital. **18. When Zimri saw**

himself besieged by the forces of Omri, he retired within the castle, shut the doors behind him, and burned himself and his castle to the ground. **19. For his sins which he sinned in doing evil in the sight of the Lord.** The ultimate ground for Zimri's terribly swift end is thus set forth. Divine judgment had been visited upon him.

e) Omri of Israel. 16:21-28.

21. Then were the people of Israel divided into two parts. A second schism now occurred. For a time it appeared that the nation of Israel might be divided into three parts instead of two. For now the people of the north formed themselves into two equal blocks, the one espousing the cause of Omri, the other championing the cause of Tibni. **Tibni** is identified only by name. **22. But the people that followed Omri prevailed against the people that followed Tibni . . . so Tibni died, and Omri reigned.** Omri did not come into possession of the throne of Israel immediately but rather was obliged to contend for it. According to Josephus (*Antiq.* VIII. 12.1) Tibni was slain by his opponents. But this meaning is not necessarily contained in the words **so Tibni died.** It is to be taken that the latter met his death in the fierce engagements that followed the schism, five years later.

23. In the thirty and first year of Asa king of Judah began Omri to reign over Israel. Omri (880–874) was in many ways an able ruler. The blot upon his character is that he departed not from the sins of Jeroboam. **24. And he bought the hill Samaria of Shemer for two talents of silver.** Upon this hill he established a fortified city, and named it after the former owner of the hill, Shemer. No doubt the desolation wrought by Zimri's fire was one of the factors that made a new capital highly desirable, if not absolutely necessary. **28. So Omri slept with his fathers, and was buried in Samaria.** His new capital marked his burial ground.

B. From Ahab to the Ascension of Jehu. I Kgs 16:29–II Kgs 9:10.

1) Beginning of Ahab's Reign in Israel. 16:29–34.

29. And in the thirty and eighth year of Asa king of Judah began Ahab the son of Omri to reign over Israel. Ahab (874–853 B.C.), in many respects an able ruler, was plagued not only with the sins of Jeroboam but also with the idolatrous practices of the princess whom he married. **30. And Ahab the son of Omri did that which was evil in the sight of Jehovah above all that were before him** (ASV). This is the historian's sober evaluation of the infamous career of Ahab.

31. He took to wife Jezebel the daughter of Ethbaal king of the Zidonians. This marriage was doubtless mainly a political maneuver, based on the ancient treaty of peace made between Israel and Zidon under the leadership of Solomon. And Ahab may have thought that he was partially justified in this union. However, the cruel, licentious worship of Baal so permeated the worship of Tyre and Sidon that its infiltration into Israel through Jezebel was inevitable. The term **Baal,** the Hebrew word for "lord" and "master," was employed more or less indiscriminately for a number of national gods. The Baal of Tyre, however, was Melkarth, the Tyrians' chief god. Jezebel played the role of chief priestess of the Tyrian Baal. Melkarth was the kind of god that required the burning of innocent children as oblations upon his altar. One of the underlying reasons why Baal was worshiped was that he was believed to be lord of the land. To induce him to send rain upon the earth, fertility cult practices were engaged in and sacrifices were offered. Perhaps there was some excuse for Jezebel, who was born and reared as a heathen princess, to follow such a religion. But there was absolutely no justification for Ahab's letting his wife introduce this heinous religion into the life of Israel.

32. And he reared up an altar for Baal . . . in Samaria. Samaria, the capital city of the Northern Kingdom, now became one of the centers of Baal worship. **33. And Ahab made the Asherah** (AV, *a grove).* According to G. Ernest Wright, Jezebel may have conceived of the asherah as representing not merely Baal worship but the wife of Baal.

34. In his days did Hiel the Bethelite build Jericho. The ancient city of Jericho, ruined by the Israelites in the days of Joshua, was now rebuilt, with the result that the curse pronounced against it by Joshua (Josh 6:26) came to pass. An older view is that Hiel actually offered up his two sons as "foundation sacrifices." According to a newer view, the lives of the boys were cut off as a divine visitation upon Hiel for his disobedience in restoring the city God had cursed.

2) The Ministry of Elijah, to the Call of Elisha. 17:1–19:21.

a) Drought Predicted by Elijah. 17:1-8.

17:1. And Elijah the Tishbite . . . said unto Ahab. Like the coming of a meteor flashing across the dark, midnight sky, so was the coming of Elijah in the darkness of Israel's spiritual night. With the arrival of Elijah, the process of direct revelation, suspended since the days of Joshua, commenced again. By substituting Baal worship for the worship of Jehovah in Israel, Jezebel had challenged the existence of the living God. God's answer to Baal worship was his mighty prophet, Elijah *(my God is Jahweh* or *Jehovah)* the Tishbite. Tishbe was in Gilead, between the Jarmuk and Jabbok Rivers in Trans-Jordan. **As the Lord God of Israel liveth, before whom I stand.** With this introductory formula, Elijah announced that discipline was about to fall upon Ahab and Jezebel in particular, and upon the land of Israel. The punishment was to be in the form of a drought of three years and six months duration. Note the appropriateness of this punitive measure. The people of Israel had turned from Jehovah to the folk gods of the Baalim, the gods of the fertility cult. They needed to be reminded that Jehovah, the God of Israel, controls the elements and hence all fertility and life. Therefore rain was to be withheld from the land. **2,3. And the word of the Lord came unto him, saying, Get thee hence, and turn thee eastward.** That is, eastward from Samaria, toward the Jordan. The **brook Cherith** is one of several brooks that empty into the Jordan. Though its exact identification is unknown, tradition locates it at Wadi el Kelt. This location constituted a suitable hiding place from the wrath of Ahab and Jezebel; and it also afforded Elijah sustenance in famine, as he was to drink of the brook and be fed twice daily by ravens.

b) Elijah at Zarephath. 17:9-24.

9. Arise, get thee to Zarephath. After the water of the brook had been depleted, God commanded his servant Elijah to proceed to the city of Zarephath, where a widow woman had been commanded to sustain him. **Zarephath** (in the LXX, *Sarepta)* was a small village situated on the Mediterranean Sea between Tyre and Sidon.

10. So he arose and went. Upon his arrival he was greeted by the sight of a widow preparing her last meal for herself and her son. His request for water, though reasonable under ordinary circumstances, may have been designed as a test of faith. As the woman was about to oblige the prophet with a drink, he also asked her for a morsel of bread (v. 11).

12. And she said, As the Lord thy God liveth, I have not a cake. She thus revealed that she recognized the stranger as a prophet of God. At the same time she invited a divine curse upon herself if the words she was about to utter were not true, i.e., that she and her son were about to eat their last meal.

13. And Elijah said unto her, Fear not; go and do as thou hast said. By her obedience in feeding the prophet, the woman exchanged the uncertain for the certain, famine for plenty, death for life. **14. The jar of meal shall not waste.** The prophetic words of assurance given by the man of God were the woman's criterion for conduct, as with unquestioning obedience she carried out the command of the prophet. For a Gentile woman, her faith is unsurpassed. Our Lord's endorsement of this widow is found in Lk 4:26.

16. The jar of meal wasted not. It is worse than useless to try to assign some natural cause for the woman's unfailing supply of oil and flour. The ministry of Elijah was marked by miracles. In this case God intervened supernaturally to preserve the lives of this woman, her family, and the prophet.

17. And it came to pass after these things, that the son of the woman . . . fell sick. In ancient days sickness was regarded as a visitation of God to call sin to remembrance (v. 18). Elijah's actions here prove that this sickness was not a judgment because of sin. **20,21.** Taking the dead child, the prophet retired to his bedchamber, where he called upon God to restore life.

22. And the Lord heard the voice of Elijah. The confident belief of Elijah carried with it the certainty of being heard. This is the first genuine, indisputable instance of the resurrection of the dead in the OT. **24. And the woman said to Elijah, Now by this I know that thou art a man of God.** All her fears and doubts were dissipated. Elijah's claims as a prophet were established.

c) Elijah's Meeting with Obadiah. 18:1-16.

1. The word of the Lord came to Elijah in the third year. The year of the sojourn at Zarephath was accomplished, and Elijah returned to show himself to Ahab. The famine was now most acute. So dire and devastating had been its effects upon the vegetation of Israel that the cattle could no longer find grazing spots. So Ahab set out in search of possible pasture land. Hoping against hope, he sent his servant Obadiah one way, while he himself went another.

7. And as Obadiah was in the way, behold, Elijah met him. The length of the famine, according to Lk 4:25 and Jas 5:17, was three years and six months. When that time had elapsed, God told Elijah to show himself to Ahab. **Obadiah.** The governor or steward of Ahab's castle, a God-fearing man, not to be confused with the author of the book Obadiah. It was this steward who had concealed a hundred prophets of God from the wrath of Jezebel (v. 4). The slaughter referred to in verse 4 is mentioned again in 18:13, but not elsewhere. Jezebel had been doubly irked, first because of the famine, and second, because of her inability to lay hands upon Elijah. So she had vented her wrath upon the luckless heads of the prophets of Jehovah.

8. Go, tell thy lord, Behold, Elijah is here. With these dramatic words Elijah announced his determination to appear before the king.

9-16. And he said, Wherein have I sinned (ASV). Obadiah protested that the bearing of such news to Ahab might well cost him his life, especially if the Spirit of God carried Elijah away. His fears were not altogether groundless, as may be learned from II Kings 2, where we read that Elijah was carried into the other world in a fiery chariot. However, the prophet assured the fearful Obadiah that he would indeed confront Ahab that very day.

d) The Contest upon Carmel. 18:17-40.

Ahab Confronted by Elijah. 18:17-20.

17. Is it thou, thou troubler of Israel? (ASV) Ahab's conduct was more childish than vicious, as he petulantly accused the man of God of bringing trouble upon the land. Elijah met Ahab's insinuating remarks forthrightly by casting the challenge back into his face. **18.** He reminded the king that it was not he, Elijah, who had been the troubler, but **thou, and thy father's house, in that ye have forsaken the commandments of Jehovah, and thou hast followed the Baalim** (ASV).

19. Mount Carmel. A mountain range of surpassing beauty, consisting of many peaks intersected by hundreds of larger and smaller ravines. It extends about thirteen miles in a southeasterly direction, and at its western end drops off sharply into the Mediterranean, near Haifa. On one of the promontories Elijah chose to stage the "battle of the gods," between the gods of the heathen Phoenicians, represented by the Baalim, and the living God, Jehovah. It is probable that the prophet selected this spot first for its natural geographic prominence, but also because it was debated ground between Israel and Phoenicia, and because the Canaanites believed Mount Carmel was the especial dwelling place of the gods. If this interpretation be correct, Elijah, like saints before and after him, dared to do battle with "the spirit of wickedness in high places," even from the heights of Carmel itself. So confident was he of the outcome that he made it as difficult as possible for himself and for his cause to win, yet defied Baal to be the victor.

Elijah's Challenge to Israel. 18:21-24.

21. And Elijah came near unto all the people. After gathering the people of Israel together, Elijah issued his challenge to them. **How long halt ye between two opinions?** (AV). Rather, *How long go ye hobbling between the two forks of the road?* Whichever translation one takes, the meaning is crystal clear. The issue was before them. A clear decision must be made. If Baal was to be god, Jehovah must be renounced. If Jehovah was to reign as God, Baal and all his worship must be forever abandoned. Many in Israel were probably tempted to compromise. Elijah, with whom no compromise was possible, saw clearly the radical character of the two issues and called for a definite decision. Such men always enjoy the blessings of God despite temporary unpopularity with the masses.

Elijah's Proposal to Jezebel's Prophets. 18:25-35.

25. And Elijah said unto the prophets of Baal, Choose you one bullock for yourselves. Following the ominous silence of the people, Elijah proceeded with his proposal, as simple as it was direct. The two opposing factions (450 Baal worshipers; one representative of the worship of Jehovah) were each to make ready a sacrifice, erecting an altar and laying out the prepared sacrificial animals. Only the fire would be missing. The test was clear and unequivocal — "The God that answereth by fire, let him be God" (v. 24).

26. And they . . . called on the name of Baal from morning even until noon. With increasingly frantic measures, the worshipers of Baal tried to coax the lord of the atmosphere to answer by fire, in accord with the agreed stipulation.

27. Elijah mocked them. These words, which on the surface may appear amusing, were spoken with the deepest irony and sarcasm. In mocking mood, Elijah suggested that their god Baal might be sleeping or off on a hunt. **28. And they cried aloud, and cut themselves . . . with knives and lancets.** They worked themselves into an ecstasy of frenzy. Such a condition is not unknown even today among certain of the dervish dancers. To make Baal more propitious, they did not hesitate to mutilate their own bodies till the blood gushed forth. But despite their most frantic endeavors, there was no answer, for they called to deaf ears.

30. And Elijah said . . . Come near unto me. Confidently, with calm assurance, the prophet now proceeded to call upon the one true God of Israel. To build his altar, he selected twelve stones — one for each of the tribes of Israel. Though politically and socially divided, in the mind of God they were still one people, with one Lord and one Messianic expectation. Therefore, Elijah erected the altar with just twelve stones, as a testimony unto and against them. Round about the altar he next constructed a trench large enough to hold two measures, that is two bushels of seed.

35. And the water ran round about the altar; and he filled the trench also with water. The arrangements for the sacrifice being completed, Elijah made the strange request that the altar be soaked with water three times, until the trench was filled to overflowing. This was to prove the absolute validity of the miracle about to follow. Elijah insisted on making the test as difficult as possible for God to meet, that the answer might stand out in clearer, sharper contrast to the impotency of Baal and his prophets.

Elijah's Prayer and Its Answer. 18:36-39.

36,37. O Jehovah, the God of Abraham, of Isaac, and of Israel (ASV). The extreme brevity, though absolute sincerity, of Elijah's prayer is striking when compared with the frenzied crying, leaping, and dancing of the Baal worshipers. The prophet simply reminded God that he had not invented this seemingly strange procedure, but had carried it out by the divine command.

38. The fire of Jehovah fell, and consumed the burnt offering (ASV). So intense was the divine fire, that it devoured the stones of the altar and even licked up the super-abundance of water in the trench. The intervention of the supernatural in response to the believing faith and prayer of the prophet of God now settled the matter. **39.** The people, recalling the terms of the spiritual duel, cried out, **The Lord, he is the God.**

40. Take the prophets of Baal; let not one of them escape. Elijah's slaying of the prophets of Baal has been a point of contention for critics. Let it be remembered that this killing was in reprisal for the slaying of Jehovah's prophets by Jezebel, and that death was the penalty prescribed by God for worshiping idols (Deut 13:13-15). **Kishon.** A rivulet that rises on Mount Tabor and flows down into the Mediterranean. Beside this brook Elijah slew the priests of Baal.

e) The End of the Drought. 18:41-46.

41. Get thee up, eat and drink. That the people might know that the drought was not merely an unfortunate coincidence of nature, but had come particularly as a disciplinary measure, it now ended as it had begun — at the command of a man of God (Jas 5:18).

43. And said to his servant, Go up now, look toward the sea. The sea was the Mediterranean. The dazzling waters could be plainly seen from the heights of Carmel. Six times the servant of Elijah was sent to the top of the mountain to detect the coming of the rain. Each time he was disappointed. **44.** But the seventh time he returned with the report, "There arises a cloud as small as a man's hand." **45a.** The heavens grew black with clouds and wind. The cloud "as small as a man's hand" rapidly increased till the heavens were covered with blackness. Lightning darted, serpent-like, and thunders rolled in the deep ravines of Carmel as the earth, long parched, awaited the welcome rain.

45b. Jezreel, located on the spur of Mount Gilboa, was the winter capital of Ahab. **46. And the hand of the Lord was on Elijah; and he . . . ran before Ahab.** Elijah's celebration of the triumph of God. Well it was for him that he did not know what severe testings lay immediately ahead.

f) Elijah's Flight to Horeb. 19:1-18.

1. And Ahab told Jezebel all that Elijah had done. When Jezebel received the news of the slaying of her prophets, her fury knew no bounds. Her reputation as priestess of Baal worship was at stake. **2. Then Jezebel sent a messenger unto Elijah.** Jezebel doubtless meant every word of her threat and intended to punish Elijah severely. The essence of her ominous message was that as he had done to her prophets, she would do next day to him. **3. And . . . he arose, and went for his life . . . to Beer-sheba.** The southernmost city of Judah. Elijah fled from the Northern Kingdom into the more friendly kingdom of Jehoshaphat. He went not merely to Judah proper but even "to the end of civilization"—to Beer-sheba.

4. But he himself went a day's journey into the wilderness. That is, into the Negeb, to the south of Judah. Not allowing himself the comfort of a city, obviously for fear of detection by one of Jezebel's spies, he retreated into the wilderness. Here, in absolute discouragement, not realizing that God was working out his providential design, Elijah requested that he might die. **Juniper tree.** The broom brush tree, under which Elijah found refuge and solitude. **5. Behold, then an angel touched him.** God's tender care of his overwrought prophet is here evident. The emotional experiences through which the prophet had so recently passed had left their marks upon him.

8. And he arose . . . and went . . . unto Horeb the mount of God. Strengthened by the miraculous provisions, Elijah retired to Horeb, a mountain in Arabia in the vicinity of Mount Sinai (Ex 3:1; 33:6). **The mount of God.** That is, the mount on which the Law had been given to Moses (Ex 19:20). **9a. And he came thither unto a cave, and lodged there.** It was a far cry from the mountain-top experience of Mount Carmel to the cave experience among the rocky cliffs of Horeb. He at whose prayer God moved the elements, now hid from the rage of a woman. However, he was not destined to spend the rest of his days as a fugitive, hunted by Jezebel and Ahab. Baal had been defeated; Jehovah was upon the throne. And God had not yet finished with Elijah; he still had work for him to do.

9b. What doest thou here, Elijah? A divine challenge as well as an interrogation. **10. And he said, I have been very jealous for the Lord God of hosts.** In solitude and loneliness he bewailed his fate before the Lord. Had these words not been uttered in a state of emotional distress, they would have been inexcusable. But God deals tenderly with his overwrought children. The prophet's words taken at face value—which indeed they cannot be—practically accuse God of infidelity. **I, even I only, am left.** See Paul's comment on this experience (Rom 11:2-4).

12. After the fire a still small voice. Hebrew, *a sound of gentle stillness.* In sharp contrast to the tremendous manifestations of nature that moved so catastrophically before the presence of the Lord, the Lord himself now quietly spoke. The *sound of gentle stillness* summoned Elijah from the cave of his hiding to stand face to face with God.

15-18. And the Lord said . . . Go, return . . . to the wilderness of Damascus. God now gave Elijah a threefold commission: (1) to anoint Hazael king over Syria (cf. II Kgs 8:7-15); (2) to anoint a new king for Israel, Jehu son of Nimshi (cf. II Kgs 9:1-10); (3) to appoint his own successor, Elisha the son of Shaphat. These three individuals, though differing in vocation and character, would yet be united in the humbling and desecrating of the house of Ahab.

g) The Anointing of Elisha. 19:19-21.

19. So he departed thence, and found Elisha the son of Shaphat. **Elisha** means, literally, *My God is salvation.* The exact whereabouts of Elisha at the time of his call is not given, though his home was in Abel-meholah, the northern part of the Jordan valley. Elijah cast his mantle over him, a symbolic act signifying that the power and authority of Elijah, the retiring prophet, were about to rest upon the younger prophet, Elisha.

20. Let me, I pray thee, kiss my father and my mother. We may wonder at Elijah's rough response to a seemingly reasonable request until we remember that Oriental farewells sometimes occupy days and even weeks. **21. And he returned from following him.** Despite the rebuff of verse 20, the younger man was permitted a brief adieu to his family and friends. The feast prepared for the occasion was no doubt in honor of the elder prophet, Elijah, as well as in the nature of a farewell.

Then he arose, and went after Elijah, and ministered unto him. The first commission given on Horeb to Elijah was now completed. It provided for the continuation of the prophetic ministry in the person of Elisha, son of Shaphat, after the assumption of Elijah.

3) Later Years of Ahab's Reign, and His Death. 20:1–22:40.

a) War with Syria—The Siege of Samaria. 20:1-21.

1. And Ben-hadad the king of Syria gathered all his host together. Ben-hadad.

A titular rather than a personal name. Ben-hadad I, renewing the struggle against Israel, now chose to besiege the capital city of Samaria. **2. And he sent messengers to Ahab.** He offered conditions of peace which proved quite unacceptable to Israel. **3.** At first Ben-hadad demanded Ahab's wives and children and his silver and gold. Ahab reluctantly agreed to surrender them. Then Ben-hadad made further unjust demands. **6.** He declared that he would also send his servants to search the king's private dwelling and take away whatever was desirable. Ahab answered with a diplomatic note couched in terms of Oriental courtesy but rejecting this demand.

7. Then the king of Israel called all the elders. The king stated to them the unjust demands of the Syrian oppressor, Ben-hadad. A dilemma confronted them: (1) Should they refuse these unjust demands and thus prolong the siege? Or, (2) should they acquiesce and permit this brigand, who called himself a king, to pillage their city? **8. And all the elders . . . said unto him, Hearken not.** The representatives of the people stood behind the king's decision. **9. Wherefore he said unto the messengers of Ben-hadad, Tell my lord the king.** Using the deferential language of a skilled diplomat, Ahab rejected the terms of surrender.

10. The gods do so unto me, and more also. The arrogant boast of the Syrian monarch was that there were more soldiers under arms with him than there were handfuls of dust in the land of Samaria – an Oriental exaggeration for the number of soldiers led by him and by the thirty-two kings (v. 1; otherwise unspecified) allied with him. **11. Let not him that girdeth on his armor boast himself as he that putteth it off.** An Oriental maxim meaning, *Let not the one who inaugurates a fight boast prematurely of the victory.*

12. When Ben-hadad heard this message, as he was drinking . . . he said . . . Set yourselves in array. Drunkenness often creates a false sense of assurance, as exhibited by the attitude of Ben-hadad. **The pavilions.** Tents, the huts of the Syrian army. **Set yourselves in array** (AV, ASV). *Take your positions* (RSV). *Attack* (Berkeley Vers.). So Ben-hadad gave the order for the commencing of the battle.

13. And, behold, there came a prophet unto Ahab. The prophet, here unnamed, directed Ahab's attention to the great multitude that confronted him, not however, to discourage but to encourage him. **Behold, I will deliver it into thy hand this day.** The somewhat surprising promise of God's deliverance was grounded not upon Ahab's fidelity but simply on God's love-care for His people.

14. After learning that he should conduct the battle, Ahab called the army together, about 7,000 men. **16.** Then he struck strategically at noon, the traditional time of repose, when Ben-hadad and his associates were in their tents drinking. By this surprise attack, Ahab threw the Syrian army into confusion and utterly routed them. **20.** Ben-hadad escaped on his horse. But his army was decimated.

b) The Warning of the Prophet. 20:22-30.

22. And the prophet came to the king. God warned Ahab that however glowing the victory had been, it was not the end of the struggle. Ben-hadad would renew his effort.

23. Their gods are gods of the hills. These words betray the Syrians' lack of knowledge regarding the omnipresence of God. The deities of the Syrians were gods of the valley; therefore Ben-hadad's servants suggested that they renew the conflict in the valley. This insinuation about Israel's "gods" was to be sternly corrected in the minds of the Syrians by Jehovah himself (v. 28). **26. At the return of the year . . . Ben-hadad mustered the Syrians.** No doubt it was at the coming of spring that the contest was renewed. **Aphek.** Hebrew, *a fortress.* There are at least four places given the name **Aphek.** It appears that this one was a city on the plateau east of the Sea of Galilee, where disaster befell Ben-hadad.

28. And there came a man of God. Because the Syrians had thought of Israel's God as limited to the hills, they were to learn that Jehovah's power is everywhere.

29. And they pitched one over against the other seven days. The precise reason for the delay in battle is not given. Perhaps they were assaying one another's position by means of spies. On the seventh day hostilities broke out. It was the Syrians – much to their surprise – and not the Israelites who were defeated and devastated. Ben-hadad escaped and concealed himself in a secret chamber of the city.

c) Ben-hadad Spared by Ahab. 20:31-34.

31. Behold now, we have heard that

the kings of . . . Israel are merciful. In Oriental warfare, the victory was not complete until the leader, in this instance Ben-hadad, was executed. The servants of Ben-hadad advised him to throw himself upon the mercy of Ahab. It should be noted that the mercy of the kings of Israel was greater than that of the kings of the enemy nations surrounding them. **32. So they girded sackcloth on their loins. Sackcloth** and **ropes** were signs of penitential submission. Flattered by the Syrians' compliance, Ahab consented to let Ben-hadad live. **He is my brother.** These words imply a disposition to enter into a covenant.

33. Now the men observed diligently, and hasted to catch it (ASV). Trained in the technique of discerning the capricious royal will, the servants regarded the query of Ahab as a good omen and hastily laid hold upon it. Thus Ahab bound himself by an oath to save Ben-hadad's life. This was not only the greatest injustice to his own subjects but open opposition to God, who had foretold the victory and had delivered the enemy into his hands (Keil and Delitzsch, p. 267). **34. The cities which my father took . . . I will restore.** Instead of seizing the opportunity to crush Syria once for all, Ahab permitted Ben-hadad, under the terms of this agreement, to depart in peace. **So he made a covenant with him, and sent him away.** No doubt Ahab spared Syria so that it might serve as a buffer between Israel and the rising power of Assyria.

d) A Prophet's Rebuke. 20:35-43.

35. And a certain man of the sons of the prophets said. The institution of the schools of the prophets was well established in Israel by this time. **Smite me, I pray thee. And the man refused.** The prophet wished to deliver a sermon of rebuke in a parable. He therefore requested his associate to smite him. The second prophet, however, refused and for punishment was slain by a lion (v. 36). **37.** The prophet requested another associate to smite him. This time the request was granted; the third prophet smote the first and wounded him.

38. So the prophet departed, and waited for the king by the way. Disguised, the prophet awaited the coming of the king in order to deliver the message of censure from the Lord. **39. And as the king passed by, he cried unto the king.** In parabolic form, the prophet now set forth a hypothetical situation, which Ahab, not recognizing the prophet's identity, took as actual. The prophet said that a soldier of Israel, an enemy prisoner of war, had been placed in his charge with the stipulation that if the prisoner should escape, he, the imagined soldier, must forfeit his own life, or give a talent of silver ($2,000). **40.** Almost without hesitation, Ahab returned a verdict of guilty, and told the disguised prophet that he must choose between the alternatives of punishment.

41. And he hasted, and took the headband away from his eyes (ASV). The disguise being removed, Ahab recognized the 'soldier' to be a prophet of God. The prophet now turned the verdict of Ahab against the king himself. The prisoner of war committed to his hands had been Ben-hadad. Just as the king had judged the 'soldier' negligible in allowing the prisoner to escape, so the prophet condemned the king on the same charge. **42. Thus saith the Lord, Because thou hast let go out of thy hand a man.** This verse is not given to teach Christian morality in the event of a situation involving prisoners of war. Rather, the spiritual principle set forth is that believers must not extend toleration, even in the name of mercy, to the forces of Satan. It had lain within the power of Ahab to end forever the life and death struggle between Syria and Israel. Now with Ben-hadad free, the struggle would continue, with disastrous results.

43. And the king of Israel went to his house heavy and displeased. Ahab retired to Samaria in a truculent and melancholy mood. It would go ill with any individual who, even through no fault of his own, crossed Ahab's dark pathway, as is shown in chapter 21.

e) Ahab, Jezebel, and Naboth's Vineyard. 21:1-16.

1. Naboth the Jezreelite had a vineyard . . . hard by the palace of Ahab. Naboth is nowhere else referred to except in this chapter. He was a God-fearing Jew, possessor of a vineyard in Jezreel which adjoined the winter palace of King Ahab. **2. And Ahab spake unto Naboth . . . Give me thy vineyard.** Ahab had, of course, legal and moral right to try to purchase the vineyard from Naboth. His great transgression lay in his failing to respect the right and privilege of his neighbor to refuse his offer. The Bible knows nothing of the hideous political doctrine that the individual exists for the state. Ahab made a business proposition to his neighbor, offering to pay for the property in currency or to exchange vineyard for vineyard.

3. The Lord forbid it me. Naboth refused, on religious grounds, to sell Ahab the vineyard because God had forbidden the Jews to sell their paternal inheritance (Lev 25:23-28; Num 36:7ff.). **4. And Ahab came into his house heavy and displeased.** In sullen, childish mood the king returned to his castle, dejected over Naboth's refusal of his offer.

7. And Jezebel his wife said unto him. Noticing Ahab's petulant mood, Jezebel induced him to tell her the cause of his troubles. Her response was cynical and edged with iron: **Dost not thou rule Israel?** In other words, Are you not in supreme authority? What right has one of your subjects to deny you anything you wish? We have already observed that Jezebel was a woman with no conscience. Ahab, pleased with his wife's interest, failed to note the ominous character of her words: **I will give thee the vineyard of Naboth.**

8. So she wrote letters in Ahab's name. That is, letters bearing the royal insignia. **9. Set Naboth on high among the people.** A technical phrase meaning to bring him to trial. The verdict was predetermined. This was a mock trial with a mere semblance of justice. That it might appear, however, in the sight of the people as a legal trial, two witnesses were produced, as provided for by the Law (Deut 17:6,7); but they were false. The technical accusation was not merely that Naboth had opposed the king, but that he had blasphemed the Divine name, a sin of which Jezebel herself was notoriously guilty. The penalty for such a crime, when a man was justly convicted, was stoning (Lev 24:16; Jn 10:33). After the victim had succumbed, it was customary to raise a pile of stones over his grave as a testimony to the manner of his death and the reason for it.

11. And the men of his city, even the elders and the nobles . . . did as Jezebel had sent unto them. There are always men ready to sell their testimony for money and to alter it to suit the evil purposes of the one who hires them. Compare the witnesses at the trial of Jesus (Mt 26:60,61). **13. Then they carried him forth out of the city, and stoned him.** Naboth was executed for a crime he never committed. And the God of all justice had observed the wicked act. Soon Ahab and Jezebel were to stand before the bar of eternal justice, to receive righteous judgment. When Ahab knew Naboth was dead, he promptly claimed the vineyard (v. 16).

f) Elijah's Rebuke. 21:17-29.

17. And the word of the Lord came to Elijah the Tishbite. The God of truth and right, who had seen the criminal act, now sent his prophet with the message of doom. Note that in the Divine estimate, Ahab was equally guilty with Jezebel. **19. Hast thou killed, and also taken possession?** The shadow of justice and of inevitable doom now fell across the house of Ahab.

20. Hast thou found me, O mine enemy? Ahab's ejaculation revealed his dismay; he realized that his sin had found him out. Too late did he learn that God has set our secret sins in the light of his countenance (Ps 90:8). **And he answered, I have found thee.** Elijah boldly replied to Ahab's despairing question, then proceeded to pronounce judgment. Ahab had become the hopeless slave of sin, as is implied by the prophet's explanation: **Because thou hast sold thyself to work evil in the sight of the Lord** (AV).

21. Behold, I will bring evil upon thee. The curse pronounced against Ahab is identical with that uttered against the house of Jeroboam and against Baasha (14:10,11; 16:3,4). **23. The dogs shall eat Jezebel by the rampart of Jezreel.** For the terrible fulfillment of this prophecy, see notes on II Kgs 9:30-37. Because of his belated repentance, Ahab was given a little respite.

25. But there was none like unto Ahab, which did sell himself to work wickedness. This is the sober estimation of the historian as to the life, reign, and character of Ahab, son of Omri of Israel. Once again we note the striking but terrifying figure of Ahab selling himself as a slave to an evil master for the purpose of material gain. **Whom Jezebel his wife stirred up.** Being married to an evil companion, the daughter of the king of Tyre, Ahab chose the course of least resistance. The two principal sins of Ahab denounced in the Scripture were mercenary - mindedness and idolatry — two very closely connected evils.

27. And it came to pass, when Ahab heard those words, that he rent his clothes. Sincerely repentant, Ahab now donned sackcloth and ashes and **went softly** before the Lord. This was not repentance unto life but a temporary turning from sin, to soften the inevitable temporal vengeance. **29. Seest thou how Ahab humbleth himself before me?** Even a temporary token repentance, as here, will move God to mercy. The mercies of the Lord are infinite. The fullness of the Divine curse was not executed upon Ahab as it was upon Jezebel, who showed no sign of repentance.

g) The Battle of Ramoth-gilead and the Defeat of Ahab. 22:1-4.

1. And they continued three years without war between Syria and Israel. The renewal of hostilities was brought about this time by the alliance between the north and the south, between Ahab and Jehoshaphat. The two allied Israelitish nations now took up the offensive against Ben-hadad. **2. In the third year . . . Jehoshaphat the king of Judah came down to the king of Israel.** For a full account of the reign of the godly Jehoshaphat of Judah (co-regent 873–870 and sole ruler 870–848 B.C.), read II Chr 17:1–21:1. For political purposes, Jehoshaphat of the line of David now disregarded the vast moral and religious gulf separating the two kingdoms and made affiliation with the Northern Kingdom, headed by Ahab, son of Omri.

3. Know ye that Ramoth in Gilead is our's. Ramoth-gilead, one of the chief cities of the tribe of Gad, was east of the Jordan. It is now identified as Tell Rāmîth in north Trans-Jordan (Glueck). The immediate objective of the projected offensive warfare was the recapturing of the city of Ramoth-gilead. **4. And he said unto Jehoshaphat, Wilt thou go with me to battle.** Ahab seemed glad enough to welcome the assistance of the South in the contemplated project.

h) False Prophecy Versus True Prophecy. 22:5-18.

5. Jehoshaphat, as a truly God-fearing king, showed some understandable misgiving about the oncoming battle and wished not only the assurances of Ahab but the blessing of Jehovah from the mouth of His prophet.

6. Then the king of Israel gathered the prophets together, about four hundred men. These four hundred are not to be identified with Jezebel's four hundred prophets of Baal, whom Elijah had already slain. These men were ostensibly prophets of the Lord, as Jehoshaphat's willingness to seek their counsel shows. But they were untrue to their calling and willing to bend their message to the whims and wishes of the wicked king. **And they said, Go up; for the Lord shall deliver it into the hand of the king.** They realized that this was the message the king wanted most to hear, but their assurance of victory was too facile for Jehoshaphat.

7. And Jehoshaphat said, Is there not here a prophet of the Lord. The king of Judah was justifiably suspicious of the glib assurances of the prophets. He therefore insisted that the advice of one more prophet be sought. **8. There is yet one man, Micaiah the son of Imlah . . . but I hate him.** Micaiah is the longer form of *Micah* (not to be confused with the prophet in Isaiah's day whose book bears his name). Josephus and the rabbinical scholars have imagined that Micaiah was the unnamed prophet who had condemned Ahab for setting Ben-hadad free (20:35ff.). Ahab himself declared that he hated Micaiah because the prophet never prophesied good of him but always evil. **And Jehoshaphat said, Let not the king say so.** Thus the king of Judah overruled the objections of Ahab and insisted that Micaiah be called.

10. And the king of Israel and . . . the king of Judah sat each on his throne, arrayed in their robes. Before Micaiah arrived there was a very interesting interlude. Another false prophet, Zedekiah, the son of Chenaanah, stepped forward to make his prophecy. Displaying two symbolic iron horns, he predicted that the two kings would push the Syrians as if with horns until they were consumed. This Zedekiah is therefore to be reckoned among the false prophets. **13. And the messenger that went to call Micaiah said . . . speak that which is good.** In the name of diplomacy and good will, but obviously not in the name of veracity, the messenger sent to summon Micaiah pled with him to bring his message into conformity with the others; that is, to break his established reputation of being the purveyor of bad news and for once speak encouraging words to the allied kings. **14. And Micaiah said, As Jehovah liveth, what Jehovah saith unto me, that will I speak** (ASV). Here was a prophet who was above mercenary considerations, who would not 'tailor' his message to suit the situation. He bore the Lord's message, and that only would he declare. This prophet would not compromise himself as Zedekiah and the others had so willingly done.

15. The king said unto him, Micaiah, shall we go against Ramoth-gilead . . . ? The king, most likely, was Ahab, who was more or less in charge of the proposed expedition. The same question was put to Micaiah as had been put to the others: Should they or should they not proceed to battle? **Go, and prosper.** Micaiah's tone of voice and his manner doubtless betrayed the fact that he was speaking in irony – that he meant just the reverse of what he said.

16. And the king said unto him, How many times shall I adjure thee. Fully realizing that Micaiah had spoken sarcastically, Ahab now besought him under oath to tell the truth. The time for mockery had passed; the time for sober dealing had come. **17. And he said, I saw all Israel scattered upon the hills, as sheep that have no shepherd.** A picture of hopelessness, confusion, and despair. The shepherd and leader, Ahab, was to be destroyed and the people scattered (Ezk 34:5; Zech 13:7). The meaning of Micaiah's prophecy was clear: Desist from making war against Syria.

18. Did I not tell thee that he would prophesy no good . . . ? Thus childishly did Ahab dismiss the sober warning of the man of God.

i) Micaiah's Vision. 22:19-28.

19. I saw the Lord sitting on his throne. For one brief moment the curtain of eternity was lifted and Ahab was given a glimpse behind the scene. There Jehovah sits in majesty, the unseen Lord of history. The message of doom previously spoken by the prophet Elijah was about to be fulfilled. Both the Testaments teach that evil and good spirits are under the authority of God. **22. I will be a lying spirit.** The method by which Ahab was to be deceived was through the spirit of deception about to take possession of the prophets. Ahab would listen to their counsel, giving no heed to the true prophet Micaiah, that the purpose of God might be fulfilled. **23.** The sending of the evil spirit is to be regarded as done by the permissive will of God instead of by his direct will. Let it be remembered that Ahab had had ample chance to know truth through Elijah, but had stubbornly resisted it.

24. But Zedekiah . . . went near, and smote Micaiah. Zedekiah, the false prophet, struck Micaiah with the open hand, an act regarded by all Orientals as the greatest of insults. **25. Behold, thou shalt see in that day.** In response to Zedekiah's insult and insinuation that Micaiah was guilty of trying to create fear where there was no cause to fear, the prophet of God quickly replied that the day was coming soon when Zedekiah and all the false prophets would hide themselves in terror in a secret place. This would be when Israel was defeated and Ahab was dead. Then Zedekiah and all would know the truth.

26. And the king of Israel said, Take Micaiah, and carry him. Micaiah the true prophet was thus placed under arrest for telling the truth. We can only hope that someone thought to set him free when the king did not return.

j) The Lord's Warning Spurned. 22:29-33.

29. So the king of Israel and Jehoshaphat . . . went up to Ramoth-gilead. Despite the advice of the prophet of God, the two kings still chose to follow their own inclinations.

30. And the king of Israel said . . . I will disguise myself. Despite his bold front, Ahab secretly feared that Micaiah was telling the truth. He, therefore, suggested that Jehoshaphat should dress in his regal robes (perhaps a special uniform), but that he himself should dress like an ordinary soldier. The good Jehoshaphat did not perceive that he was being involved in trickery – trickery that nearly cost him his life.

31. But the king of Syria commanded. Ahab did not know that he had become the personal target of Ben-hadad and his men. The king of Syria, it seems, did not care if everyone else escaped uninjured so long as he could have the king of Israel slain. In view of the fact that Ahab had recently spared Ben-hadad's life, this was gross ingratitude. Perhaps Ben-hadad justified his conduct on the ground that Ahab was a violator of the peace treaty, for Ahab had renewed the war. **32. When the captains of the chariots saw Jehoshaphat.** When the archers caught a glimpse of the royal robes, they naturally drew the conclusion that the wearer was King Ahab, their target. **And Jehoshaphat cried out.** Perhaps he uttered a brief but earnest prayer for deliverance. **33.** In any event, the Syrians detected that he was not the man they were after, and they withdrew.

k) The Death of Ahab. 22:34-40.

34. And a certain man drew a bow at a venture. The Hebrew for **at a venture** means *in his simplicity*, i.e., without taking specific aim. The mathematical probability that the arrow would find its right target was extremely low. Yet directed by the judgment of the Lord, it found its mark. **35,36.** Though Ahab was struck and mortally wounded, he did not die immediately; he lingered, suffering, while the battle raged.

37. So the king died . . . and they buried the king in Samaria. Jezebel was to be eaten by the dogs, but Ahab, because of his temporary repentance, was allowed honorable burial. To a Jew, the worst punishment that could befall a man was not to be buried.

38. And they washed the chariot (ASV; *And they washed his armor,* AV). This clause presents a textual problem, since the Hebrew consonantal form can be translated *and the harlots washed themselves there*. Though it may be argued that the best reading is the former, let it be remembered that in the Mosaic law dogs and harlots are placed within the same category. The dogs came to lick up Ahab's blood; the harlots came to wash. Perhaps a double curse was thus enacted to show the extreme displeasure of God against a man who had so despised his word.

39. The ivory house which he made. Through archaeological investigation, Ahab's ivory palace has come to light in Samaria. The remains of this structure reveal that the walls were faced with white marble, giving the appearance of ivory. In addition to this there were numerous plaques, panels, and pieces of furniture decorated with ivory. Thus in a double sense Ahab's palace may be called an "ivory house."

40. So Ahab slept with his fathers; and Ahaziah . . . reigned. Ahaziah succeeded his father on the throne of Israel.

4) Judah under Jehoshaphat. 22:41-50.

41. Jehoshaphat . . . began to reign over Judah. With this and the following verses a brief synopsis of the reign of Jehoshaphat is given. Three chief facts stand out: he was co-regent with his father Asa; he was in almost all respects a godly man; his main mistake was that he aligned himself with Ahab of Israel (II Chr 17:1–21:1).

5) Israel under Ahaziah and Joram. I Kgs 22:51–II Kgs 1:1.

The Reign of Ahaziah. 22:51–1:1.

51-53. Ahaziah . . . began to reign over Israel. Ahaziah's reign (853–852 B.C.), despite its brevity, was characterized by extreme iniquity. The new king was very different from his contemporary to the south. A brief alliance was made between them, which was rapidly dissolved when the ships of Jehoshaphat were broken at Ezion-geber because of the displeasure of the Lord (cf. II Chr 20:37).

1:1. Then Moab rebelled. This verse properly goes with I Kgs 22:51-53, forming the conclusion to that passage. Rebellion frequently broke out at the death of a reigning monarch. Mesha, king of Moab, as archaeologists have discovered, has left an inscription (known as the Moabite Stone) describing his successful revolt against Ahab because of the Israelite king's "oppression" of Moab.

6) Later Ministry of Elijah, to His Translation. 1:2–2:11.

This section, which includes the account of King Ahaziah's attempt to capture Elijah and the death of the king, teaches several important lessons. It shows that it is fatal to forsake God, that it is necessary to honor his prophet, and that there is power and protection only in obedience to the God-given prophetic word.

2. Ahaziah . . . was sick. Ahaziah's illness arose from his having fallen out the window of the roof chamber. **Go, enquire of Baal-zebub.** According to the Ugaritic alphabetic cuneiform tablets, this name is to be spelled *Baal-zebul*. Possibly the spelling was changed by some copyist to make the name ridiculous. The former means *Baal of the fly*. The latter means *Baal of the dwelling,* i.e., the Canaanite life-god, the chief Canaanite deity. Ahaziah had tried to syncretize Baal worship with the worship of Jehovah. Elijah here proves Baal to be powerless. Ahab on his part had broken the covenant by introducing Baal worship, substituting idolatry for the worship of the Lord. Ahaziah's request for an oracle was a challenge to the God of Israel. **Whether I shall recover of this disease.** Protracted illness had resulted from the fall, arousing the king's concern and leading him to ask for the oracle.

3. The angel of the Lord said. Genesis 22:15,16 makes the "angel of the Lord" and the Lord the same. God took up the challenge. **Is it not.** The idolatry of the people had shut God out of their hearts. **4b. Thou . . . shalt surely die.** An adverse oracle indicated that open sin and deliberate defection from God must end in death.

4c. Elijah departed. Elijah went to meet the king's messengers. **5. The messengers turned back unto him.** The messengers had met Elijah and, at his message, at once turned back **to him,** i.e., to Ahaziah – to Samaria. Idolatry had so beclouded their hearts that they did not recognize God's intervention through Elijah. **6. There came a man.** The dumbfounded messengers faithfully repeated

Elijah's words to Ahaziah. **7. What manner of man.** Not having forgotten the adventures of Ahab with Elijah, Ahaziah conjectured that Elijah was active again. **8. It is Elijah the Tishbite.** The description of Elijah confirmed his conjecture. Elijah's garb was characteristic of the preachers of repentance. A ministry of repentance was most apropos at this time of apostasy in Israel (cf. Mk 1:6,7).

9. Then the king sent. The second phase of this contest between the Lord and Baal now began. Ahaziah moved to punish Elijah's insult. **Thou man of God . . . Come down.** The address was scornful. The soldier did not understand that the treatment dishonored the covenant by dishonoring God's prophet. **10. And Elijah answered.** And should be read *But,* since this verse stands in contrast to verse 9. The captain's contempt was to result in death. All too often does the "world" regard the servants of God in the same manner. Sin and worldly might blind men's eyes. **Fire from heaven . . . consumed him.** The Lord God confirmed Elijah's word and proved himself the victor in the conflict.

11. Another captain of fifty. In the second attempt to take Elijah, the king compounded his sin by adding the word **quickly. 12.** See verse 10. Sin was not yet vanquished in these people. **13,14. Came and fell on his knees.** The third captain, whether or not he realized the significance of the happenings, was convinced of the prophetic standing and power of Elijah and treated him with respect. He said, in effect, "I am only the king's servant, doing my duty; so please honor me in this and come before the king." **15. The angel . . . said unto Elijah.** The king's power was vain. Elijah was not to fear Ahaziah, because the Lord would defend his prophet. **16. And he said unto him.** Elijah repeated the earlier message given to the messengers.

17. So he died. God's word is never spoken in vain (see E. R. Thiele, *Mysterious Numbers of the Hebrew Kings,* p. 61). **Jehoram reigned in his stead . . . because he had no son.** A brother (cf. 8:16) ascended the throne (cf. 3:1; I Kgs 22:51). Ahaziah's reign of slightly more than a year was too short a time for him to beget an heir. **Second year of Jehoram.** Jehoram of Israel became king in the eighteenth year of Jehoshaphat and the second year of Jehoram, kings of Judah. At this time there was a co-regency in Judah (cf. 3:1. See Introd., *Chronology).*

Elijah's Translation. 2:1-11. See 6) above, Later Ministry of Elijah, etc.

1. And it came to pass. For the time of this event see I Kgs 22:51; II Kgs 3:1; 1:17. Elijah's translation obviously occurred after the death of Ahaziah. **By a whirlwind.** Retrospective insertion. Only the possibility of Elijah's translation was known at this time (2:3,5). **Elijah went with Elisha from Gilgal.** The Hebrew says *went down.* This Gilgal is higher than Bethel, and is in Ephraim near Shiloh, the modern Jiljiliyeh. In Amos 4:4 and Hos 4:15 it is named, along with Bethel, as a seat of false worship of God. **2. Tarry here.** In spite of the exhortation, Elisha declared that he would go with Elijah, who was now to visit the three schools of the prophets to strengthen them against inroads of Baal worship. The existence of these schools indicates that the prophets were organized into a type of guild.

Elijah now began to test Elisha's personal call to the prophetic office. **3. Sons of the prophets . . . at Beth-el.** Students and followers of God's prophets, exercising teaching ministries under them. **Knowest thou . . . ?** God had revealed to Elijah that he was soon to depart. And Elijah had made known the revelation in order to prepare both Elisha and the sons of the prophets for his going. **Take away thy master from thy head.** Elisha was to lose his teacher and leader. **Hold ye your peace.** That is, "Yield to God's will; do not add to my burden of sadness." We should not try to retain those whom God calls away, but rejoice in their entrance into his presence. **4.** See verse 2 for the same request and answer. **5. At Jericho.** See verses 1-3. At this point it appears that God definitely purposed to present Elisha as Elijah's successor (cf. v. 3), qualified to lead in withstanding false worship and in halting its spread among the people. **6.** Cf. verses 2,4. Elisha's constancy was made evident. See 9 below for what must have been growing in his mind.

7. Fifty men . . . stood to view afar off. A number of the sons of the prophets followed after the two and observed the happenings at Jordan, probably from a bluff above them. **8. Elijah took his mantle.** The call of Elisha (I Kgs 19:19) had made Elijah's mantle a symbol of the prophetic office; here it was a symbol of God's power (cf. Moses' rod, Ex 17:9).

9. Ask what I shall do for thee. Elijah opened the door to the prophetic succession. **A double portion.** Comparison with Deut 21:17 indicates that Elisha was asking to be the heir – successor. See Heb 3:5,6 for training in "sonship" to qualify for holding an office in question. **10. A hard thing.** The boon requested was not Elijah's to give. **If thou see me . . . taken from thee.** The sign by which Elisha would know that his request was granted. If Elisha would have the courage to face Elijah's translation, and the spiritual understanding to know the meaning of the older man's going, he would be the successor.

11. As they still went on. As they walked on across and beyond Jordan. The **whirlwind** (storm, *seʿārâ,* with dark clouds and lightning), and the fiery chariot and horses were symbols of Jehovah's power in battle (cf. Isa 31:1; 34:8,9; Ex 14:9,17; I Kgs 10:29; Ps 104:3,4). Elijah went up in the storm in the presence of the Lord, *not* in the chariot. See also Mal 4:5,6; Mt 11:14.

7) Introduction of Elisha. 2:12-25. Elisha was presented as God's prophet appointed to follow Elijah. His was a teaching ministry, designed to show the practicality of following the Lord and to demonstrate that Baal could not fulfill the needs of the people.

12. And Elisha saw. This was evidence that Elisha was chosen. **My father.** Elisha spoke thus as successor to Elijah. **The chariot of Israel, and the horsemen thereof.** The chariot was the mightiest weapon then known, symbolic of God's supreme power. Elisha was speaking of Elijah as the prophetic instrument through which God's power was operating on behalf of the truth in Israel. For Israel's defense lay in the Lord alone, and her idolatry was a rejection of her defense. This divine power could help the people keep the covenant. **Saw him no more.** Elijah disappeared completely. **Took hold of his own clothes, and rent them.** Elisha thus expressed his sincere grief at Elijah's departure. **13. He took up also the mantle.** The dropped mantle was to be one more confirmation of Elisha's succession (see v. 15). **14. Where is the Lord God of Elijah?** See Jer 2:6-8 for the same question, which the people had failed to ask in faith. Elisha was not being impertinent; he was praying, in effect: "Here is thy opportunity to show forth thy great power in thy obedient servant."

15. And when the sons of the prophets . . . saw him. Still watching, they saw Elisha use the cloak. **The spirit of Elijah doth rest on Elisha.** Elisha had been granted the same gifts Elijah had, as evidence of his having been anointed to the prophetic office. **16-18. Let them . . . seek thy master.** The sons of the prophets did not realize that Elijah's departure was permanent. Their persistent demands to send out a search party brought grudging consent. When their search proved fruitless, they had to accept the fact that Elisha was now *the* prophet of the Lord.

19. The men of the city said... Behold . . . the water is evil (AV, *naught).* The pleasant situation of Jericho was deeply marred by the poor water. Translate, . . . *but the water is evil – and the land – causing miscarriage.* They regarded the bad water, which they drank, as responsible for miscarriages. The principal spring by the *ancient* site of Jericho is sweet and pure, while the others are brackish. **20. Bring me a new cruse.** God's work must be performed through new – uncontaminated – vessels. **Put salt therein.** Salt cleanses and preserves. Here it is a symbol of the purifying, preserving power of God. **21. I have healed these waters.** The sign and symbol of the healing was the salt cast therein. **22. The waters were healed unto this day.** God sought to testify of his power to heal from sin and preserve through faith. The purification was permanent; the water from this spring remains good to this day (see on v. 19). Even so God's work of grace in us is permanent, our only sure foundation for building pure lives.

23. He went up . . . unto Beth-el. Elisha's first 'official' visit, as successor to Elijah, to Bethel (cf. vv. 2,3), the seat of the calf worship of Jeroboam (I Kgs 12:29). **Little children.** Rather, *young men (neʿārîm qeṭannîm,* plu.) not irresponsible babes. Both Solomon (I Kgs 3:7) and Jeremiah (Jer 1:6,7) are called *naʿar* (sing.) These were young people, morally responsible. **Go up, thou bald head.** They echoed the words of the sons of the prophets to Elisha: "The Lord will take away [up] thy master" (vv. 3,5). They meant: "Ascend, that we may be rid of thee [and may continue unreproved in our wicked ways]!" A bald or shaven head was the mark of a leper and denoted disgrace (Isa 3:17). While Elisha was probably not yet bald, the epithet shows that the youths considered him as an "outcast," like a leper. They despised God's prophet. **24. Cursed them in the name of the Lord.** Their scorn was a dishonor to God. Hence the promise of divine judgment. They broke the divine covenant by ridiculing its overseer. **Two she bears . . . tare forty and**

two. Breaking the covenant brings punishment. The size of the group suggests that the taunting was prearranged.

25. After completing his business with the sons of the prophets, **he went . . . to mount Carmel,** for quiet and rest to prepare for the work ahead. **He returned to Samaria.** Elisha returned to the scene of his future, significant labors in behalf of Israel.

8) Jehoram's Expedition Against Moab. 3:1-27. Jehoram's campaign against Moab demonstrates how utterly abominable heathen religion was to God. The outcome was an object lesson to Israel showing her why she should turn from her idolatry. Nevertheless, she did not turn from it.

1. Jehoram . . . began to reign . . . the eighteenth year of Jehoshaphat. See 3:1; 1:17 for double dating his accession. This indicates a co-regency of Jehoshaphat and Jehoram in Judah (see Thiele, *op. cit.*, p. 61ff.). **2. He wrought evil,** etc. Jehoram did not sin as Ahab did; but he broke the covenant, for **he cleaved unto the sins of Jeroboam** (v. 3). For Jeroboam's evil way, see I Kgs 12:26-33; 13:33; II Kgs 10:29.

4. Mesha king of Moab. The Moabite Stone describes the length of Moab's subjection to Israel (see ANET, "Moabite Stone"). **Rendered.** *Used to pay,* designating tribute status. **A sheepmaster.** Moab abounded in sheep-raising. The number of sheep noted designates the annual tribute. **5. Rebelled.** Mesha considered Israel weakened enough, after Ahab's death, for Moab to attempt to gain her freedom. See II Chronicles 20 for a previous Moabite invasion of Judah, when the Moabites were destroyed, and Moab was left too weak to repel the alliance. **6. King Jehoram . . . mustered all Israel** (ASV). Mesha's revolt consisted in refusing the tribute. Jehoram, therefore, mustered his troops to collect it. **7. Sent to Jehoshaphat.** The fact that Jehoram sought an alliance with Jehoshaphat indicates that he needed to cross Judean territory in order to advance against Moab. This in turn indicates that Mesha had strengthened his northern border. If Jehoram could gain Jehoshaphat, he would also gain Edom, which was now under Judah. Jehoshaphat forgot that alliances with those who sin against the Lord are forbidden to believers. **8.** The route chosen by Jehoshaphat passed along the west side of the Dead Sea and around its southern end.

9. Seven days' journey. Having left Jerusalem and met and joined Edom on the way, they wandered about seeking Mesha, and finally ran short of water. **10.** Jehoram's impiety led him to blame God for the disaster facing them. **11,12. A prophet of the Lord.** Jehoshaphat rejected Jehoram's opinion. **Here is Elisha.** It seems that Jehoram did not know of Elisha's presence. **The word of the Lord is with him.** Elisha was known by reputation. Dire straits now forced them to go to him. **13,14. Get thee to the prophets of thy father.** See verses 2,3. Elisha rejected all recourse to his office that savored of heathen belief in the magical. **Nay.** See on verse 10 above. If it had not been for the presence of Jehoshaphat, Elisha would have made no response to such impiety. Meeting with the leader of northern idolatry was nerve-racking. **15. Bring me a minstrel.** To play hymns that he might be brought into a proper disposition to hear the Lord's word. **The hand of the Lord.** God answered by foretelling the success of the campaign. He would use it to show his people the abominable aspect of heathen worship.

16. Make this valley full of ditches. The valley was the Zered, present Wadi el Hesa, Moab's southern boundary. **17. Not see . . . rain; yet that valley shall be filled.** Rain water from the upper hills would fill the ditches. The miracle lay in the timing. **18. Will deliver the Moabites.** Confirmation that Jehovah was doing this. **19. Smite every fenced city.** Destruction was to be thorough.

20. When the meat *(meal)* offering was offered. The water, arriving at the time of the love offering in the Temple, spoke of God's love, and thus foreshadowed the conclusion of the expedition. **By . . . Edom.** See verse 17. **21. The Moabites . . . stood in the border.** Moab mustered its troops against the invasion. **22,23. In the morning.** On the same morning that the water appeared. **Red as blood.** Due to its muddy color and to the morning sun's rays. The Moabites, eager for booty, concluded that their enemies had killed each other off. **24. When they came to the camp . . . the Israelites rose up.** The Israelites surprised the attackers from an apparently empty camp. **They went forward.** The prediction of their conquest began to be fulfilled. **25. Beat down the cities.** Such destruction represented the ordinary war policy of that time, now called a "scorched earth" policy. **Kir-haraseth.** The only city not taken, the present el Kerak. Standing on an eminence at the end of a narrow defile, it resisted attack by slingers on surrounding heights.

26. With great boldness Mesha personally led a sortie of seven hundred Moabite swordsmen; however, this attempt failed. **Unto the king of Edom.** Mesha evidently expected him to be a weak link or a less zealous soldier than the others. **27. Took his eldest son.** The king of Moab desperately sought to induce his god to give victory. To heathen peoples, adversity was a sign that their god was angry. The sacrifice of the first-born was not too great a price to pay for a god's favor. **Upon the wall.** In Israel's sight, to cause Israel to fear Chemosh, the Moabite god, and therefore withdraw. **Great indignation in Israel** (not *against*, as in the AV). The Hebrew preposition *'al* here indicates that Judah and Israel were indignant because of this abominable act (cf. Lev 18:21; 20:3). **They departed . . . returned.** Israel, Judah, and Moab broke off the engagement and returned to their land, their moral sensibilities profoundly shocked. The author seems to be asking: If Israel was so deeply moved in this case, why was she not shocked enough to forsake her own idolatry? But idolatry continued in Israel and in Judah.

9) The Prophetic Ministry of Elisha. 4:1–8:15. Elisha's prophetic ministry was intended to show that there is no need, personal or national, that God cannot meet, that all events are in his hands, and that he cares for his people.

a) Elisha and the Widow in Debt. 4:1-7.

1. A certain woman of the wives. The presence of married men among the sons of the prophets indicates that the prophets were not monks. **Did fear the Lord.** He had been a faithful servant of God. **Creditor is come.** The fact that sons were sometimes demanded as payment for debts is frequently indicated in cuneiform records. **2. Not anything . . . save a pot of oil.** Elisha was about to reveal to the woman the living and loving God. The oil was olive oil. **3. Go, borrow . . . vessels.** For the coming abundant provision. **4. Shut the door . . . pour.** To exclude interruption during the filling process, which was to be done in God's presence. **6. The oil stayed.** God's provision exactly meets our capacity and need. **7. Told the man of God.** She sought further instruction. **Sell . . . pay the debt.** The debt could now be paid without the loss of needed sons. **The rest.** To sustain them until the boys should find work.

b) Elisha and the Woman of Shunem. 4:8-37.

8. Shunem. Present *Sôlem*, near Jezreel. **As oft as he passed.** The woman observed Elisha on his frequent trips. **9. Holy man.** A real, not merely a so-called, man of God. **10. Let us make a . . . chamber.** A weatherproof room on the flat top of the house, provided with true regard for his character.

12. Gehazi. In trying to make some return to the woman for her hospitality, Elisha used Gehazi to avoid embarrassing her. **13. I dwell among mine own people.** She explained that her life was contented and undisturbed. She had not extended hospitality to them for gain. **14. What then is to be done for her?** The woman had left them. Elisha questioned Gehazi. **No child, and her husband is old.** She desired a son, but her husband was too old to fulfill her wish. **16. Thou shalt embrace a son.** The woman was called back and promised a son. **Nay, my lord.** This was the cry of a heart weary with hoping. Such a fulfillment she could not expect. Her protest meant, "Don't joke with me!" **17. Bare a son.** God alone can revive and give life. Such blessings he grants to those who keep his covenant.

18. The child . . . went out to his father. The ensuing event occurred during harvest, the warmest time of the year. **19. My head.** Probably he suffered a sunstroke. **20. Brought him to his mother, he . . . died.** The Lord was about to demonstrate again the impotence of Baal. **21. Laid him on the bed of the man of God.** She committed him to Elisha, the only one who could help her in this deep trouble. **22. Called unto her husband.** She requested of her husband the help of a young man and an ass, probably because they had only two asses, both in use. **23. Wherefore wilt thou go . . . today?** There were no annual or other religious affairs to occasion the visit. **It shall be well.** Hebrew, *Peace.* She simply urged him not to worry. God's prophet was her only help.

25. Behold . . . that Shunammite. Elisha saw her as she approached Mount Carmel. **26.** He instructed Gehazi to ascertain her trouble. But she put off the servant, preferring to tell Elisha. **27. Caught him by the feet.** Her anguish could no longer be held in. **Let her alone.** "Let her collect herself before telling me." **The Lord hath hid it.** Elisha was unaware of the child's death. On infrequent occasions, God prepared his prophet beforehand, but not usually. **28. Do not deceive me.** "I did not ask for a child. If I be given a son only to see him die, it would have been better never to have had one."

29. Gird up thy loins. Elisha made Gehazi his deputy. To lay the rod, a symbol of God's power, upon the child's head was to arrest the oncoming death. Elisha believed the child was not dead. **30. I will not leave thee.** That is to say, "This is not enough." **He . . . followed her.** Elisha perceived that the case was serious. **31. But there was neither voice, nor hearing.** Elisha had no authority to depute to another the power God had given him. Hence Gehazi could do nothing. Elisha had been hasty in instructing his servant. **32. When Elisha was come . . . the child was dead.** Elisha now understood completely the woman's grief. **33. Shut the door.** Following the example of Elijah, his "master," Elisha sought quiet for prayer to God. **Prayed.** He asked the Lord to restore life to the boy. **34. Flesh . . . waxed warm.** The preceding actions were symbolic of what was desired, and constituted an extension of the prophet's prayer, which was now being answered. **35. Walked.** Elisha, greatly moved, waited for God's answer. **36. Call this Shunammite.** The Lord was about to show his grace and mercy (cf. Ps 4:3; 25:10). God does reward believers for their faith and trust, but he punishes idolaters and terminates their lives.

c) Elisha and the Deadly Gourds. 4:38-41.

38. Came again to Gilgal. On one of his circuits. **Set on the great pot, and seethe pottage.** Elisha at mealtime used the dearth to teach the sons of the prophets that he who lives in God's presence need not regard the "dearth." **39. Gather herbs.** Our "greens." **Wild vine . . . wild gourds.** Wild cucumbers, egg-shaped gourds having a bitter taste and producing colic and violent diarrhea when eaten. The young man mistook them for the edible variety (cf. Num 11:5). **40. Death in the pot.** The familiar bitter taste warned them. They assumed that it was another similar plant, the colocynth, which also was poisonous and bitter tasting. **41. Bring meal . . . he cast it into the pot.** By casting in ordinary and wholesome food, Elisha demonstrated God's power to remove evil. The Lord by faith can remove the evil in us.

d) Elisha and the Multiplying Loaves. 4:42-44.

42. A man from Baal-shalisha. Or *Beth-shalisha,* "House of Three Valleys" (I Sam 9:4), near Gilgal. The gift met the need of the prophets. **Firstfruits.** See Num 18:13; Deut 18:4. Lacking priests and Levites in Israel, he kept the spirit of the ordinance. These may well have been Israel's "priests and Levites." **43. Give the people.** The prophet recognized and accepted the food as God's provision for the people, rather than for himself and his servant. **They shall eat, and shall leave thereof.** There would be enough and to spare. Thus the Lord demonstrated that his power and provision will always be sufficient and may exceed our needs, and thus he assures us that we need not slow up in opposing evil nor in seeking to root it out.

e) Conversion of Naaman. 5:1-27.

1. Naaman, captain of the host. The public phase of Elisha's ministry now began. Naaman's position enhanced the importance of the event. **A leper.** In Syria, leprosy caused only physical incapacity to perform required duties; Naaman as a leper won no further victories for Syria, and this caused genuine concern. **2. Brought away captive out of . . . Israel a little maid.** A note on God's providence. **3,4. Would God my lord were with the prophet.** Her thought was: There is a living God in Israel who can heal. **One went in, and told his lord.** Her words were reported to the king. **5,6. I will send.** The king promptly sent to the king of Israel, because it was believed that he could gain anything he desired of Elisha, "his" prophet. The message went to the wrong person, for the Lord wished the healing to be a public matter. Apparently a truce existed between Syria and Israel. **8. He shall know that there is a prophet in Israel.** That is, "Do not fear that war shall erupt because of your inability to heal Naaman. Almighty God will deliver Naaman." In face of fear we must remember, "Lo, I am with you alway" (Mt 28:20).

9,10. Elisha sent a messenger . . . saying, Go and wash in Jordan. Elisha remained inside to emphasize to Naaman that neither wealth (v. 5) nor position (v. 1) could buy healing. The washing in Jordan emphasized God's power to heal. **11,12.** Naaman almost lost the blessing through pride. Humility and faith bring deliverance, however, to all (Mt 18:3). **13. How much rather.** If we don't obey God in small things, how can we expect him to bless us with great things? **14. His flesh came again.** Healing was obtained through obedience, on the seventh dip.

15. Now I know. Naaman learned that there was a God in Israel by doing His commands. Thus he was persuaded that Jehovah was God alone, and his own Lord (v. 17). **16. I will receive none.** The Lord wants no payment but the loving obedience of redeemed souls. **17. Earth.** Naaman desired the earth as a remembrance of his "blessing." **18,19. Pardon thy servant in this thing.** Naaman was not to be regarded as worshiping the god [Hadad] **-Rimmon. Go in peace.** Naaman showed a tender conscience about appearing to worship idols, and he received assurance that God understood his heart. However, we are to beware of oft exposure to weakening environment lest we overestimate our powers of resistance.

20,21. Gehazi . . . said, i.e., thought in his heart. **Is all well?** Gehazi's haste made Naaman think he had brought misfortune on Elisha. **22-24. My master.** Gehazi was blind to the fact that great harm would be done to the witness of the Lord through his covetousness. **Bestowed them.** Gehazi took something of "this Syrian," then hid his ill-gotten gains. **25-27. Thy servant went no whither.** Gehazi lied to hide his sin. **Is it a time** . . . "This is the worst possible time to receive gold . . ." Gehazi hoped, through Naaman's largess, to buy the things enumerated. **Shall cleave unto thee.** "If you buy these, you also buy Naaman's leprosy." Naaman had become an Israelite, but Gehazi became a pagan through sin (cf. Mt 6:31-34). Naaman's conversion was to show the Israelites how easily the Lord could turn the hearts of their adversaries and thereby make them worshipers of Jehovah, fellow believers with the Jews themselves.

f) Recovery of the Borrowed Axe. 6:1-7.

1. The place where we dwell . . . is too strait. Through increase of believers, need arose for larger quarters. Elisha's ministry was bearing fruit. Our good works should draw others to the fellowship of the saints. **3. Go with thy servants.** They expressed a sincere desire for Elisha's presence. **5. It was borrowed.** This reflects their simple ways and their poverty. **6,7. The iron did swim.** God's faithful ones may experience his deliverance in seemingly small matters. Sometimes deliverance comes by extraordinary interposition, as is shown by the following incident.

g) The Conqueror Frustrated. 6:8-23. The fact that God could maneuver the Syrians so easily was to teach Israel that the Lord could protect them as well as help them control their sin.

8. The king of Syria warred against Israel. Translate: *The king of Syria, being at war with Israel.* War now existed between Israel and Syria (see 5:5,6). **My camp.** Rather, we should expect, "we shall set an ambush." Theodotion reads, *conceal yourselves.* **9. Thither the Syrians are come down.** The Syrians had set a trap. The Hebrew for **are come down** is inexplicable. The context demands a meaning like "concealed." **10. Saved himself.** The king of Israel saved himself several times through Elisha's warning. **11. Will ye not.** "One of you betrays my plans to Israel." How else could they have been known? **12. Elisha . . . telleth . . . the words that thou speakest in thy bedchamber.** The Lord told Elisha. And the Syrians knew through their own spies that Elisha had this uncanny foreknowledge.

13. That I may . . . fetch him. The king of Syria, wanting to put a stop to Elisha's works, compassed Dothan (v. 14) to get him. **15. Alas . . . how shall we do?** *Sight* looks to appearances, and fears; while *faith* (v. 16) looks to God, and the soul is at peace. **17. The mountain was full of horses and chariots.** God's powerful protection was made evident (cf. Ps 34:7). **18. Smite . . . with blindness,** i.e., lack of recognition. Elisha and his servant had gone **down to him,** i.e., to the Syrian host. The Lord rendered the Syrian army powerless, to show to all that any whom he protects cannot be taken (see on v. 7 above).

19,20. I will bring you to the man whom ye seek. Elisha's words imply a question on the part of the Syrians: "Where is Elisha?" But his answer, **This is not the way, neither . . . the city,** was to spare Dothan, and to lead the Syrians to Samaria, where he restored their powers of recognition. Elisha desired to confound further attacks. **21. Shall I smite?** The king of Israel, recognizing that the circumstances were unusual, did not order the customary execution of prisoners of war (Deut 20:13). Actually, these were the Lord's prisoners. "This is not actually a case of war," Elisha replied, in effect. **22. That they may . . . go to their master.** Syria was to know that she could do nothing to Israel, whose guardian was God. **23. The bands . . . came no more.** Syrian incursions ceased for some time.

h) Ben-hadad's Profitless Siege of Samaria. 6:24–7:20.

This was the Ben-hadad of I Kgs 20, and of II Kgs 8:7, identified as Ben-hadad I. There were not two kings of the same name, as some scholars have formerly held. His inscription on the stele dedicated to the god Melkart has been reliably dated about 850 B.C. (BASOR, 87, p. 23ff.; 90, p. 30ff.). Hence his reign extended from before the thirty-sixth year of Asa (873/872 B.C.; II Chr 15:19) to shortly before 841 B.C., when Shalmaneser, as he records, attacked Hazael of Damascus. A minimum reign of thirty-two years and possibly more than forty is not unlikely, when we consider that Asa and Joash reigned forty years each, Uzziah fifty-two, and Manasseh fifty-five years.

24. Ben-hadad . . . besieged Samaria. See commentary on 6:7. The famine (cf. Lev 26:26-29; Deut 28:51-53) and siege were designed to punish the people for violating the covenant (cf. I Kgs 11:38 for normal covenant requirements). This was at least Ben-hadad's second siege of Samaria (see I Kgs 20). **25. Ass's head.** The siege caused high prices even for defiling food. **Dove's dung.** If bird dung had been eaten, it would not have been dove's dung only; hence, the meaning is, a small grain. The Arabs speak of a certain plant *(herba alcoli)* as "sparrow's dung." The **cab** *(qab)* is a measure. **27. Whence shall I help thee?** "The stores are exhausted. Except Jehovah help you, whence shall I?" **28. Give thy son.** Idolatry stooped so low as to ask royalty to enforce a cannibalistic contract.

30. He rent his clothes . . . sackcloth. Because he wore **sackcloth** underneath his garments, as a symbol of repentance, he thought Elisha should have put an end to the suffering of the people, the continuation of which was now so shockingly revealed to him. **31. If [his] head . . . shall stand on him this day.** Enraged by the woman's crime, he vowed vengeance upon Elisha for having deceived him, as he supposed (cf. 6:21,22). **32. Son of a murderer.** An epithet. Possibly it designates Jehu as the king's father. But more likely it indicates that Joram's attitude was that of an unrepentant murderer. **33. He said.** The king, having changed his mind (cf. v. 31), overtook the messenger and acknowledged that this evil (affliction) was of the Lord. **What should I wait.** "The end is here. Is there no hope?" The king came to the right attitude for God to deliver, and so must we. **7:1. Hear ye the word of the Lord.** Upon the king's repentance (6:33), Elisha gave the ready answer that the next day there would be deliverance, with plenty of food at low prices. **2. If the Lord would make windows in heaven.** The **noble** (lit., *third officer*. See Thiele, *Mysterious Numbers,* p. 114. Cf. v. 11) expressed unbelief and scorn at such a possibility.

3. Four leprous men. Nobody now brought them food. **4. Let us fall unto . . . the Syrians.** Death either by starvation or at the hands of the Syrians faced them, but there was a chance that it was not so certain in the latter case. **5. Behold, there was no man there.** God used the speculative reasonings of despised outcasts to discover Samaria's deliverance. **6. Made . . . the Syrians to hear a noise of chariots.** God used sound produced in unknown ways to deceive and frighten away the besiegers. It may have been wind rushing through mountain defiles. **Hittites . . . Musrians.** Not Egyptians, as in the AV. Muṣri is in Syria (I Kgs 10:28). Shalmaneser III enumerates Muṣri among his adversaries at Qarqar in 853 B.C. (see ANET, Shalmaneser, ii. 78-102, note on Muṣru). Hittites as mercenary bands were common and available, though their empire had long since fallen. Egyptian mercenaries were neither common nor available.

8. These lepers came. Naturally their first thought was to satisfy their hunger. **9. We do not well.** If they delayed till the morning, they would be held guilty of not feeling concern for the besieged. **10. No man there.** They told first the essential item — that the soldiers had fled. Then they told of the provisions and the tents, all which was immediately reported to the king.

11,12. I will now shew you. The king, so soon forgetting Elisha's promise, suspected a plot by which Samaria would open its gates to its destruction. **13. Let some take.** "Don't be hasty; let's find out. In any case, death awaits inside or out; and if not, deliverance is the quicker." **15. They went after them unto Jordan.** And they found conclusive evidence of Syrian flight.

16. So a measure . . . for a shekel. Elisha's prediction as to the plenty was fulfilled. **17. The king appointed** "the third officer" to keep order in the gate — the market place. Such a functionary was often needed. **Trode upon him.** This scoffer was trampled to death under the feet of hunger-driven people scrambling for food. **18-20.** Elisha's prediction concerning food and the unbelieving lord is here recalled. Its fulfillment was perfectly natural, perfectly inevitable.

i) The King's Regard for Elisha. 8:1-6. In spite of the king's high regard for Elisha, shown by this incident, he still did not forsake his sins; for the next paragraph (vv. 7-15) indicates that judgment was to come.

1. Now Elisha had spoken (ASV), serves as introduction to what follows. The exact time of the incident is indeterminate. **Arise.** Elisha's warning was one more testimony to the fact that God cares for those who trust in Him. Evidently the woman was a widow by now, for it was she whom Elisha told to leave and it was she who "cried" for restoration of her properties when she returned. **3.** When **the woman returned,** she found others dwelling in her holdings. **4. Tell me.** The king desired to know of the less-known acts of Elisha. **5. The woman** came in – in God's providence. **6. Restore.** The king was carried away by the story of the raising of her son. He gave more than she asked. This king could have been either Ahaziah or Joram, both of whom "did evil" (I Kgs 22:51,52; II Kgs 3:1,2).

j) Hazael's Usurpation of Ben-hadad's Throne. 8:7-15.

7. The man of God is come hither. Elisha was well known in Syria. The prediction of I Kgs 19:15 waited till now for accomplishment. The change of kings in Syria had been of less importance to Elijah than the destruction of Baalism, against which he moved at once. Now Elisha's visit points up the judgment to come upon Israel through the agency of Hazael because she persisted in her sinful ways (see I Kgs 19:17; II Kgs 8:12). Hazael's rise to the kingship is told to complete the picture. **9. Forty camels' burden** denotes a usual gift made by heathen people to their gods when an oracle was desired. **10. Thou mayest certainly recover.** Translate: "Go say to him (as thou intendest to do), 'Thou shalt surely live'; however, the Lord has shown me that he shall surely die (by your hand)." **11. He** [Hazael] **was ashamed.** Knowing the heart of Hazael, Elisha stared sternly at him till the Syrian's thoughts were revealed by his shamefacedness. **The man of God wept.** He foresaw what cruelties Hazael would wreak on Israel (II Kgs 10:32; 13:3,4,22) despite his protestations of humility – "Am I a dog" – and denial – "Do not think I want to be king" (8:13) – in the same breath. Elisha only repeated the fact that Hazael would be king. **15. Laid** (AV, *spread)* **it on his face.** Hazael smothered the king to make it appear that he died a natural death. Then he usurped the throne, and thus fulfilled Elisha's words and his own ambition. Shalmaneser III (860–825 B.C.) of Assyria says of him: "Hazael, son of a nobody, seized the throne" (David D. Luckenbill, *Ancient Records of Assyria and Babylonia,* Vol. I, Sec. 681). In other words, Hazael was not of the royal line.

10) Reigns of Jehoram and Ahaziah in Judah. 8:16-29. The brief history of Jehoram and Ahaziah is included to show how Baal worship and its attendant sins came into Judah.

16. In the fifth year . . . Jehoram the son of Jehoshaphat . . . began to reign (cf. II Kgs 3:1). Jehoram began a co-regency with his father (see Thiele, *op. cit.,* pp. 54,65). **18. For the daughter of Ahab was his wife.** She was the source of Jehoram's sins. Athaliah brought Baal worship into Judah, which accelerated the downward course of the nation and was a major factor in its ruin (II Chr 21:5-7). **19,20. Yet the Lord would not destroy. . . . In his days . . .** Although Judah had plunged deep into sin, neither the dynasty nor the kingdom would now come to an end. Yet, Judah would pay dearly in the loss of once-subject principalities, such as Edom (vv. 20-22a) and Libnah (v. 22b). **21. Zair.** Probably to be read *Se'ir.* That is, Edom. (See v. 21 for the area of campaign to support the reading of *Se'ir).* **22b. Libnah,** which was near Philistia, was possibly incited by the Philistines (cf. II Chr 21:16). Sin causes immeasurable loss. **25. Did Ahaziah . . . begin to reign.** In 842 B.C. (see Thiele, *op. cit.,* pp. 63,64). **26,27. His mother's name was Athaliah. . . . And he walked in the way of . . . Ahab.** Athaliah handed on Ahab's sins to Ahaziah. "Evil communications corrupt good manners." She was the granddaughter (descendant), not the **daughter** of Omri; a tribute to Omri. In II Chronicles 21 Ahaziah's name is spelled Jehoahaz, but it is the same name. *Ahaz* is the verbal part of the name, to which is prefixed the divine name *Jah,* spelled *Jeho,* and *iah* is added at the end. The ascension of Ahaziah marked the turning point in Judah, from which she never recovered. **28. He went with Joram.** Here was the immediate cause that led Ahaziah to his death (cf.

9:16), which fell as a judgment on the "house of Ahab."

11) Jehu Made King in Israel. 9:1-10.
1. Elisha . . . called one of the sons of the prophets (ASV). The cup of iniquity of the house of Ahab was now full, and the judgment of I Kgs 21:21-24 was about to fall. The next events occurred during Joram's convalescence. **Ramoth-gilead.** Joram and Ahaziah had joined together in an attempt to wrest this place from Syria. Their attempt brought the necessary military strength and disposition of personages into proper setting for the accomplishment of God's purposes. **3. Thus saith the Lord, I have anointed thee king.** Jehu was the second of the two agencies – the prophets Elijah and Elisha being the first – by which the Lord sought to make his will known. If the first and gracious ministry of chastisement was not heeded, the second ministry, of judgment, must follow. **5. Behold, the captains of the host were sitting.** The reference to "the house" (v. 6) indicates that Ramoth-gilead had been taken. **Jehu said.** Jehu answered as spokesman, signifying that he was the chief. Jehu, it appears, was highly regarded by the others, probably because he had distinguished himself in the capture of Ramoth, while Joram had left the scene of battle to recuperate from wounds. **6. Poured the oil.** Signifying divine appointment either to the kingship or as a special servant of the Lord. Jehu was appointed to both offices for a single purpose (see vv. 6,7). **7. Smite the house of Ahab.** The commission given covered the whole house (v. 8). **9. Like the house of Jeroboam . . . and . . . the house of Baasha.** See I Kgs 15:29; 16:11. **10. He . . . fled.** A predictive act indicating the swiftness and awfulness of the destruction to follow.

C. From Jehu to the Destruction ol Israel. 9:11–17:41.

Because idolatry threatened to destroy all remaining good influences in Israel and to invade Judah and so destroy the whole nation, the house of Ahab was marked for extinction.

1) Jehu's Reign. 9:11–10:36.

In conformity with the divine principles regarding judgment of sin, as set forth in Deuteronomy, Jehu became the executioner of the wrath of God on the chief sinners in Israel – Ahab and his wicked descendants.

11. Is there peace? *Is all well?* (AV) The question concerned conditions in Israel. **Mad fellow.** The epithet conveys their impression of his behavior. **Ye know.** Jehu implied that they had sent the prophet-disciple "with a view to proposing that he lead an attempt to revolt." Their reply, "tell us now," revealed their honesty. So Jehu revealed the story. **13.** Translate: *Took every man his garment and spread it upon the way to the stairs and blew. . . .* They laid an impromptu carpet for his on-the-spot coronation.

14. Now Joram had defended (AV, *kept*). After Joram had taken Ramoth, the Syrians had attacked him there, and wounded him in battle. **Kept Ramoth-gilead.** As an outpost against raids by Hazael. **15. Let none go forth** – to divulge plans to Joram. **17. A watchman . . . said, I see a company.** Joram's unpreparedness facilitated the swift execution of judgment (cf. v. 10; **he fled**). **18. Turn thee behind me.** Jehu retained the two messengers to avoid any "leak" to Joram. The act was reported to Joram. **20. The driving of Jehu . . . he driveth furiously.** The driving was said to resemble the furious pace customary to Jehu. Joram now feared for the situation in Gilead. **21. Make ready.** To meet the possible bad news. **22. Is it peace.** That is, Was the Gilead campaign successful? **What peace . . . ?** Jehu played upon the word **peace,** reminding Joram that there was no "peace" to him who partook of Jezebel's sins of idolatry and witchcraft (cf. Ex 22:18; Deut 18:10). Jehu condemned Jezebel as the founder and patroness of idolatry in Israel. **23. Treachery.** Joram did not perceive God's judgment. **24. Between his arms,** i.e., between his shoulders. Jehu felled Joram as he turned and fled. **25. The portion of the field of Naboth.** The **burden** was that he should suffer death by judgment. And the fulfillment of the prediction rightfully took place near Naboth's vineyard (cf. vv. 21,23,25). This incident stands out as showing the Lord's power to use our actions to fulfill his will. Hence it shows, too, that he could have destroyed his nation Israel even though they thought that not probable.

27. When Ahaziah . . . saw. Ahaziah foresaw the doom awaiting him as a descendant of Ahab (cf. I Kgs 21:21). **Smite him also. . . . at the going up to Gur.** Jehu gave orders to his men to pursue Ahaziah, while he himself set out for Jezreel to find Jezebel. He estimated that the men would overtake him in the pass of Gur near Ibleam.

30. **Jezebel heard . . . painted her face.** Jezebel knew for what purpose he had come. 31. **Had Zimri peace . . . ?** "You Zimri! you regicide!" She sought to stop Jehu by reminding him of the quick overthrow and death of Zimri. 32. **Who is on my side?** Jehu called on the onlookers to take sides on the issue. **Eunuchs.** These probably signaled to Jehu as allies. 33. **They threw her down . . . and he,** i.e., the chariot horses, **trode her under foot. 34. Go . . . bury her.** After he had eaten, he belatedly remembered that Jezebel was a princess. **36.** In **Jezreel shall dogs eat the flesh of Jezebel.** So signally and by the carelessness of Jehu was the prediction of the Lord concerning Jezebel fulfilled. **37. They shall not say.** Jezebel would have no grave at all but would be as offal.

10:1. And Ahab had seventy sons. Cf. verses 2,3. All Ahab's male descendants are meant. Jehu intended to obliterate all the house of Ahab. He was now beginning to visit judgment on Israel as a nation. For Israel to lose this family would be to lose the entire line of one of her most able kings. However, what Jehu did in dispatching these people and the worshipers of Baal was condemned by Hosea (1:4), for Jehu acted in a spirit of bloodthirstiness, greed, and ambition. **3. Look even out . . . set him on his father's throne, and fight.** Jehu proposed settling affairs by means of a gladiatorial contest (cf. II Sam 2:11-17), a common means of settlement of disputes in the ancient Near East. Guilt or fear usually worked to the advantage of the winner. **5. We are thy servants.** Fear brought quick acquiescence. Though they favored the old regime (v. 4), they renounced any intent to revolt. **6. The heads of . . . your master's sons.** The elders were required to execute judgment on sin. **7. Seventy persons.** Specifically, the ones demanded (cf. I Kgs 21:21,22). **8. They have brought. . . . Lay ye them.** Jehu's request was fulfilled. **9. Ye be righteous.** That is, "Ye are just; so judge for yourselves." He sought to give the impression that he had nothing to do with this massacre, alleging that, although the seventy died by their act, yet they died because of the sentence of Elijah's prediction.

12. He . . . came to Samaria. After all effective opposition had ceased. **13. Who are ye?** Cf. II Chr 22:8. These were cousins of Ahaziah's sons. They knew nothing of the revolution. **14. Take them alive.** To eliminate them also. **Slew them.** Jehu eliminated them to prevent their leading a counterrevolution.

15. Jehonadab's ascending into Jehu's chariot signified that he accepted Jehu as a servant of Jehovah, hence an adversary of Ahab. As an adversary of Ahab, he led the religious community in worshiping Jehovah. Jehu used him to sanction his actions in Samaria. Josephus reports that Jehonadab praised Jehu's action.

18. Jehu shall serve him [Baal] **much.** Jehu allayed the people's suspicions by pretending to worship Baal. This act, which was one of his falsehoods, showed his bloodthirstiness. **19-22. Call unto me all the prophets of Baal. . . . But Jehu did it in subtilty.** Jehu planned a trap. The garments (v. 22) were to make it easier to identify the priests of Baal. Gathering them in the outer-court confines of the Temple (v. 21) made it easier to effect their death. **23. Search.** Only the priests of Baal were to be put to death. Jehu intended to break the power of Ahab's dynasty completely by removing these adherents, and he hoped at the same time to gain the support of those loyal to Israel's God, thus securing his own position.

25. Translate: **When they had completed preparations for the sacrifice, Jehu said . . .** Jehu did not participate in the sacrifice. To do so would have been fatal to his attempt to win the favor of the faithful Israelites. **Go in.** Only the execution of the priests of Baal could adequately serve the requirements of justice and God's holiness. **27,28. They brake down.** Jehu destroyed the cult center to bring the cult to an end.

29,30. Howbeit from the sins of Jeroboam . . . Jehu departed not. Jeroboam had "broken the covenant" by leading Israel into the worship of the calves of Bethel and Dan. Jehu continued this sin. For this act of Jehu, Israel went into captivity. Thus Jehu destroyed the value of his work. His dynasty was military, not religious. **32. The Lord began to cut Israel short.** In Jehu Israel had her last chance. Her lack was that Jehu's reforms ended in his revival of the "sins of Jeroboam." The "cutting off" was the loss of territory to Hazael (v. 33).

2) Athaliah of Judah. 11:1-20.

The sin of Athaliah brought about her death, but God preserved the line of the house of David, in conformity with II Sam 7:28,29.

1. And when Athaliah . . . saw that

her son was dead. Cf. II Chr 22:10-12. Like many other Oriental usurpers, she attempted to eliminate any and all claimants to the throne. **2. Jehosheba.** Half sister to Ahaziah (II Chr 22:11), the wife of Jehoiada. **Nurse.** Wet nurse; Joash was an infant.

4. And the seventh year. See II Chr 23:1ff. for the gathering of an alliance of five hundred lifeguards and the Levites in a covenant with Jehoiada about Joash, probably at one of the three annual feasts. Verses **5-8** describe the groups of the lifeguard of the king as Jehoida prepared to move Joash from the Temple to the throne. One third of those who came on duty on the Sabbath were to be divided into three parts: one band was to stand guard at the king's house – the palace; another was to guard the palace exit – the gate Sur; and the third was to guard the approach and the gate to the king's house. The two thirds released on the Sabbath were to guard the Temple and Joash with closed ranks, and to slay any that pierced their **ranges** *(ranks).* **10. To the captains . . . did the priest give . . . spears and shields.** Jehoiada armed the soldiers on the day appointed to set Joash on the throne. **11,12.** Joash was crowned by the Lord's officer (the priest). **The testimony.** At least the Decalogue (Ex 25:21; 16:34). Cf. Deut 17:19. The presence of the multitude indicates that the coronation occurred on a feast day. The people signified their approval by clapping their hands.

13. And when Athaliah heard. Noise of this degree did not normally occur at the change of the palace guard or the course of priests. Athaliah had only to see Joash standing in the king's place *('al hā'amôd)* to realize the intent of the assemblage. See II Chr 23:13; Ezk 46:2; (cf. II Chr 6:13 for the concept of the place reserved for the king). Her cry of **Treason** (v. 14), presumes the presence of her own bodyguard, whom she now ordered to take the boy Jehoash and his supporters. **15. Have her forth.** Jehoiada acted first and commanded that Athaliah be taken and executed. Bracketed between ranks, she was led out and executed in the palace horse gate. Jehoiada's faithfulness prevented the politically expedient policy of Jehoshaphat from resulting in the extinction of David's line. However, the priest's act only put off Judah's final downfall.

17. And Jehoiada made a covenant . . . The covenant of Mount Sinai, broken by the sins of Athaliah, Ahaziah, and Jehoram. Joash accepted this "testimony," by which he would govern as God's viceroy, agreed to by the people. This **is** the **covenant.** The destruction of the **house of Baal** (v. 18), in Jerusalem, which necessarily followed their renewing the covenant, occurred after Jehoash had been placed on the throne (v. 19). The order is logical, for verse 18 follows verse 19 in time, while verses 19,20 refer to events under the regime of Jehoash. **18. And the priest appointed officers.** Jehoiada installed the priestly courses in the Temple (cf. I Chr 25; II Chr 23:18).

3) Judah Under Jehoash. 11:21–12:21. Emphasis is here laid upon the renewing of the covenant under Jehoash, requiring the cleansing of the Temple and its restoration to the worship of Jehovah. The calamities that came upon him reflect the principle of Gal 5:17.

12:1. This section should begin with 11:21 in accordance with the normal formula used in regard to a king's life and reign. **Jehoash began to reign.** For the time of this event see Thiele, *Mysterious Numbers,* p. 66. **2. Jehoash did right . . . all his days wherein Jehoiada . . . instructed him.** Jehoash walked with the Lord only as long as Jehoiada lived (II Chr 24:17-25). He lacked personal conviction of the truth. **3. High places:** See I Kgs 22:43; II Kgs 12:3; 14:4; 15:4; II Chr 15:17; 20:33. Not idolatrous high places but illegal centers of Jehovistic worship. Notice I Kgs 3:2. Only two kings of Judah, Hezekiah (II Kgs 18:4) and Josiah (23:8), removed the high places. One of the evil effects of this worship on the high places was that it divided Judah's spiritual vision; and thus it contributed materially to the nation's fall.

4. Jehoash said to the priests. As the final stage of the renewal of the covenant with Jehovah, it was necessary to repair those sections of the Temple that had fallen into a state of dilapidation during the reign of Athaliah (cf. II Chr 24:6,7). Two classes of offerings are cited: (1) payment in fulfillment of a vow (Lev 27:2), the amount fixed by the priest, actually an assessment of persons (Lev 27:8) for the support of the Temple; and (2) **the money coming into one's heart** (II Kgs 12:4b) – a freewill offering to Jehovah. Translate: **All the money regarding dedicatory matters, which is brought . . . the pieces of silver** (not coinage) **used in business, the silver of one's valuation . . .** Jehoash simply asked that temple funds be used for the Temple. **The money of every one that passeth.** Pieces of silver sheet, of definite weight, used in business. Coined money did not occur until the Exile.

6. In the three and twentieth year . . . had not repaired. Instructions were not followed, possibly because the total temple income was insufficient to support the Levites. Previous idolatry under Athaliah had discouraged giving by the people. **7. Receive no more money.** Jehoash commanded that they cease receiving these monies from the worshipers. **8. The priests consented.** For practical reasons, new arrangements were divised to collect repair money, in which process the priests were eliminated.

9. Jehoiada . . . took a chest. II Chronicles 24:8 (RSV) says "outside the gate"; here it says, **beside the altar.** The chest may have been first beside the altar, later outside the gate, for easier access. **10. The king's scribe and the high priest came up.** The work was under the direction of the king in co-operation with the high priest (cf. v. 8). **13. There were not made . . . bowls of silver.** II Chronicles 24:14 states what was done with the *residue* from repairs. There is no contradiction here. **16. The trespass money** (cf. Num 5:8,9; Lev 5:16). These being the "cost of sin," they could not be brought into the Temple.

17. Hazael king of Syria went up. For the sin of Jehoash as the cause of invasion, see II Chr 24:15-22. The exaction of ransom is to be regarded as a judgment on Jehoash and on Judah for their sin (see II Chr 24:18b). **20. His servants . . . made a conspiracy.** Joash died because he had had Zechariah, grandson of Jehoiada, slain (II Chr 24:25). **21. Jehozabad.** "Zabad" in II Chr 24:26 was written in error for Zachar, contracted from Jehozachar.

4) Israel Under Jehoahaz and Jehoash. 13:1-25. This section demonstrates how insidiously sin entrenches itself and spreads in spite of repeated efforts to eradicate it.

1. In the three and twentieth year of Joash. The nonaccession year method of dating was employed, reducing this twenty-third year to the actual twenty-second, the first year of Jehoahaz, with his seventeenth year the thirty-eighth of Joash (21 + 17 = 38; see Thiele, *op. cit.*, pp. 37,38, chart, op. p. 74). **2. Followed the sins of Jeroboam.** The covenant of God remained broken under this king (see also 10:29).

3. The Lord . . . delivered them into the hand of Hazael king of Syria – for the sins enumerated in verse 2 above. For the loss of the territory east of Jordan, see II Kgs 10:32. These new losses were now in the territory west of Jordan, thus an advance on the former chastisements. For several years Hazael was occupied with incursions by Shalmaneser III, but after that ruler's death, he was free to turn his oppressive activities toward Israel. **All their days**; i.e., the days of Jehoahaz (cf. vv. 22,25). **4. And Jehoahaz besought the Lord.** Jehoahaz' extremity (v. 7) forced him to seek the Lord, who sent deliverance for the sake of the oppressed people. **5. The Lord gave Israel a saviour.** He came after Jehoahaz died (see v. 22 below). **6.** The people continued to practice the **sins of . . . Jeroboam,** thus continuing the broken covenant. Jehoahaz' "repentance" was only mental; he did not return to the covenant. **7. Neither did he leave.** See verse 4. The **he** is the Lord.

10. Began Jehoash the son of Jehoahaz to reign. This was in 798 B.C. (see Thiele, *op. cit.*, p. 67). **11. He did evil.** Though Baalism was rooted out, there was, however, no real return of Israel to the Lord under Jehoash, for the calves of Dan and Bethel were still worshiped. The "sins of Jeroboam" had now become permanently enshrined in the hearts of the people.

14. Now Elisha was fallen sick. This incident is related here, with following verses 22-25, because of the needs of topical outline. This was at least forty-five years after the accession of Jehu (cf. 10:36; 13:1). Elisha's sickness was serious enough to bring a visit from Jehoash of Israel to his bedside (13:14-19 falls in the period of 13:10-13). **The chariot of Israel.** Jehoash meant to say, "When you go, whence will wisdom and deliverance come?" **15. Take bow and arrows.** The means of victory and method of assurance for Jehoash. **17. Thou shalt smite** is a specific promise of deliverance by the Lord in fulfillment of the promise of verse 4. **18. Take the arrows.** Compare the last clauses of verses 17 and 19. Jehoash lacked faith and *tireless zeal* to persevere in trusting the Lord for the *utter rout* of Syria. He was told (v. 18) to **shoot the arrows to the earth.** That is, "Lay your enemies in the dust." **19. Five or six times.** Until they were vanquished.

20. And Elisha died. The words form a transition to the next event. **21. He revived, and stood up.** The dead man was restored to life because the Lord wrought a miracle as confirmation of His promise of deliverance to Jehoash.

22. The words, **But Hazael . . . oppressed Israel,** resume the theme of verse 3. **23. And the Lord was gracious** resumes the theme of 4a. Although Hazael had almost ruined Israel, the Lord did not as yet permit the destruction of the nation, because of his covenant with Abraham. **24. Hazael . . . died.** A first step in the promised deliverance. **25. Took again . . . the cities.** These were on the east side of Jordan (cf. 10:32,33). These cities had been taken by Hazael, leaving only the west side of Jordan for Jehoahaz. **Three times.** Cf. v. 19.

5) Judah Under Amaziah and Azariah. 14:1-22. Amaziah's record tells the story of how an arrogant heart lifted up in pride is abased, and how the Lord brings judgment upon the sin of arrogant pride.

1. In the second year of Joash . . . reigned Amaziah . . . king of Judah. This was 797/796 B.C. (See on 13:1 for the chronology of the period, and Thiele, *Mysterious Numbers,* p. 68ff.) **3. He did right . . . yet not like David his father** [=ancestor]. For the account of how Amaziah failed to follow David, see II Chr 25:14ff. He later began to worship Edomite gods brought back from his campaign in Edom. He followed in the steps of his father Joash (3c). **5,6. He slew his servants.** Amaziah did not follow the Oriental custom of slaying the conspirators and their children; he slew only the conspirators, in conformity with Deut 24:16. *Note:* The citation from **the law of Moses** is evidence that Deuteronomy is not a late composition, as the higher critics hold. **7. And took Selah by war. Selah** is ancient Petra. He also took its gods to Jerusalem and worshiped them (cf. II Chr 25:14ff.). This describes an unprovoked act of war on Edom, showing Amaziah's arrogance and cruelty. It was one more step down in Judah's progression to her final destruction.

8,9. Amaziah sent messengers. His arrogance led him into trouble with Israel, because of his worship of Edomite gods. In the flush of victory over Petra, Amaziah challenged Jehoash of Israel to war: **Come, let us look one another in the face.** Josephus *(Antiq.* lx. 9. 2) says that Amaziah demanded submission, or war would result (see also II Chr 25:13). **The thistle . . . sent to the cedar.** Jehoash was the cedar; Amaziah was the thistle. Amaziah's challenge was presumptuous and arrogant. Jehoash had smitten Syria and measured her. Verses 11-14 describe the defeat of Judah, the partial destruction of Jerusalem, and the taking of hostages – all because Amaziah worshiped Edomite gods (II Chr 25:20). Amaziah himself was taken captive (II Kgs 14:13), for he had rejected the prophet's counsel to repent (II Chr 25:15,16).

17-20. Amaziah . . . lived after . . . Jehoash . . . fifteen years. See Thiele, *Mysterious Numbers,* pp. 68-72. Jeroboam II had a co-regency of twelve years with Jehoash (cf. 14:23; 15:1); Azariah had a co-regency of twenty-four years with Amaziah (cf. 15:1,8; 14:23). Azariah was elevated to the throne, then, in the fifth year of Amaziah, probably because the people were dissatisfied with Amaziah's wanton expedition against Israel and its result (see ch. 19). Amaziah fled to **Lachish,** a former royal city, a fortress offering refuge, to avoid capture by the conspirators. Situated near Judah's southern boundary, it offered quick escape to other countries, and possible safety. **Slew him there.** Possibly the people of Lachish did not help the king to defend himself.

21. Now the people . . . had taken Azariah. See verses 13,19; cf. II Chr 26:1,2. The sameness of these passages in Kings and Chronicles, when compared with II Kgs 15:1-7, indicates that Uzziah placed more emphasis on conquest than on ridding Judah of the divisive high places (cf. II Chr 26:11ff.). **Azariah** means (He whose) *help is Jah.* His other name, *Uzziah,* means, "My strength is Jah." **22. Elath.** The event is important; see 15:1-7.

6) Reign of Jeroboam II over Israel. 14:23-29. This account of the reign of Jeroboam II shows (1) how Jeroboam broke the covenant (for only the king's relation to the covenant was important); and (2) how Jehovah's promise to Jehoash (cf. 13:17) was fulfilled.

23. Fifteenth year of Amaziah. Amaziah and Uzziah were co-rulers; so Jeroboam's ascension to the throne is reckoned in terms of the king of Judah first in order (see vv. 17-20). **24. He did evil.** Jeroboam continued the breaking of the covenant, the worship of the calves of Dan and Bethel (cf. 10:29). **25. Hamath.** Not the city but the area (see I Kgs 8:65; Amos 6:2,14; cf. II Kgs 23:33; 25:21). Jeroboam II was an able administrator and general. **Jonah.** An incidental prediction of Jonah the prophet, not contained in the Book of Jonah but dating the prophet's time – 780 B.C. **26. The Lord saw.** Cf. 13:23. Testimony is given to the faithfulness of God that it might turn men's hearts to God.

7) Reign of Azariah over Judah. 15:1-7. The importance of Uzziah's reign lies in his failure to eliminate the worship in the high places, which divided the religious unity of the people, contrary to Deut 12:1-5,14; 16:16.

1. The twenty and seventh year of Jeroboam. See on 14:17. **3. Did right.** He followed the early life of his father Amaziah. **5. The Lord smote the king.** Uzziah intruded into the priest's office (II Chr 26:17ff.), and for this he was smitten with leprosy (cf. Num 12:10; Deut 24:8,9; II Sam 3:29; II Kgs 5:27). Azariah's lack of spiritual insight, revealed in allowing the high places to continue, contributed to his grasping after control of the priesthood (cf. II Chr 26:16,17).

8) Reigns of Zachariah, Shallum, Menahem, Pekahiah, and Pekah in Israel. 15:8-31. The lack of information about the activities of these men is intentional, to show how their despising the covenant hastened the fall of Samaria, now in its final dissolution.

8. Thirty and eighth year of Azariah. See on 14:17ff. Zachariah continued to break the covenant by maintaining the nationally divisive and idolatrous worship of the calves of Dan and Bethel. **10. Before the people.** Zachariah was assassinated publicly. Lack of retaliation by the people indicates that they had sunk far down in their sins. **12. This was the word.** Zachariah was the fourth descendant of Jehu, the last of that line to hold the throne (cf. 10:30).

13. Shallum . . . began to reign. The rapid succession of murders amply illustrates the pitiful condition of the kingdom. **14. For Menahem . . . smote Shallum.** The **for** refers to the shortness of Shallum's reign. Menahem, the commander in chief, according to Josephus (*Antiq.* ix. 11. 1), quartered in Tirzah, hearing of the assassination, marched against Shallum, defeated and slew him, then ascended the throne himself. Menahem's action was based on the facts that the Israelite kingdom was a military monarchy, that Shallum was a usurper, and that when the Jehu line died out, the throne would go to the commander in chief of the army. **16. Menahem smote Tiphsah.** Not the Tiphsah (Thapsacus) on the Euphrates, but the one near Tirzah; Assyria would have stopped any such action at the former. Refusal to recognize him as king arose here, and his ferocious deeds were intended to warn and demoralize his opposition. There was no spiritual vitality left to oppose him.

17. In the nine and thirtieth year. Zachariah ascended the throne in Uzziah's thirty-eighth year, and the reigns of the two kings Zachariah and Shallum bridged over into his thirty-ninth year. **18. He did evil.** See on verse 8. **19. Pul the king of Assyria.** This is Tiglath-pileser III, who had another name, Pul (*Pulu* of the Assyr. inscriptions. See JNES, III (July, 1944), pp. 137-186. See also, Thiele, *Mysterious Numbers,* pp. 76,77). This first Biblical reference to the Assyrians reveals Assyria on the march, on her road to empire. Assyria became the great power in the Near East. The empire fell about 611 B.C. Tiglath-pileser says: "Terror overwhelmed him [Menahem], like a bird alone he fled, and submitted to me. To his place I brought him back and . . . silver . . . I received . . . his tribute" (Luckenbill, *Anc. Rec.,* Vol. 1, para. 815). Menahem fled; but he was captured, set up as a puppet, and forced to pay tribute – **a thousand talents of silver.** The date is approximately 743 B.C. (see Thiele, *op. cit.,* p. 98).

23. In the fiftieth year of Azariah . . . Pekahiah . . . began to reign. Pekahiah's two-year reign coincided with Azariah's last two years, overlapping with his fiftieth year (see Thiele, *op. cit.,* pp. 73,74). **24. He did evil.** Cf. on verse 8. His evil was that he followed in the sins of Jeroboam. **25. Pekah . . . conspired.** Pekah was an adjutant of Pekahiah, a captain of fifty men of the king's bodyguard. The fact that the bodyguard, instead of protecting the king, helped Pekah slay him, shows how the bonds of discipline, order, fidelity, and obedience had dissolved. Therefore the Lord had a "controversy with the inhabitants of the land" (Hos 4:1,2). **27. In the two and fiftieth year.** Pekah took the throne of Israel in Uzziah's last year. Correlation of all references to Pekahiah, Uzziah, Jotham, Ahaz, and Hoshea reveals the startling fact that Pekah usurped the years of Menahem and Pekahiah (see Thiele, *op. cit.,* p. 102ff.; also pp. 133,134). **28. He did evil.** See on verse 8. Pekah perpetuated the sins of Jeroboam, thus breaking the covenant. It appears that the captivity by Tiglath-pileser was a judgment on the sins of Pekah.

29. In the days of Pekah . . . came Tiglath-pileser. These activities occurred before 732 B.C., when Tiglath, as we learn from data in the *Eponym Chronicle,* placed Hoshea on the throne of Israel. This deportation became the beginning of the end of Israel, foretold by a long line of prophets. Tiglath-pileser III (745–727 B.C.) had made Menahem a vassal (see Luckenbill, *Anc. Rec.,* Vol. I, para. 816). He **took . . . and carried them captive.** The first of two deportations of Israel, the second being by Shalmaneser V in 723/722. This was in fulfillment of Deut 28:36. **Ijon.** In Naphtali. See I Kgs 15:20. **Abel-beth-maachah.** See II Sam 20:14,18. **Janoah.** Also in Naphtali, probably near the first two. **Kedesh.** To the northwest of Lake Huleh. **Hazor** has been excavated by Yigael Yadin [see BA, XIX, No. 1 (Feb., 1956); XX, No. 2 (May, 1957); XXI, No. 2 (May, 1958); XXII, No. 1 (Feb., 1959)]. **30. Hoshea . . . made a conspiracy against Pekah.** Tiglath-pileser says, "I placed Ausi (Hosea) over them as king." What happened was that Hosea had to have his usurpation of the throne approved by Tiglath.

9) Judah Under Jotham and Ahaz. 15:32–16:20.

32. The second year of Pekah. Cf. 15:5; II Chr 27:1-9. Jotham had a co-regency with Uzziah, 751/750 to 740/739, and four years' co-regency with Ahaz, 736/735–732/731 B.C. (cf. Thiele, *Mysterious Numbers,* p. 116ff.). He actually began to rule in the second year of the reign of Menahem (II Kgs 15:17). **33. Sixteen years.** See on verse 37. **34. He did according to all that his father Uzziah had done,** except that he did not enter the sanctuary (II Chr 26:16), i.e., did not usurp priestly functions. **35. High places.** Jotham let the divisive high places continue (see on 12:3). **He built the upper** (AV, **higher**) **gate** (cf. Ezk 9:2; on the north side of the Temple). He rebuilt it. The verse speaks of **high places** and the *upper* or **higher** gate, from which juxtaposition of words the conclusion is to be drawn that Jotham constructed the gate to attract the people to the Temple so that they would offer their sacrifices there.

37. In those days. In the days of Jotham. **Rezin . . . Pekah.** Syria and Israel were now seeking to force Jotham into the pro-Assyria camp (cf. Thiele, *op. cit.,* p. 117). Ahaz was brought to the throne, and Jotham is credited with only sixteen years (15:33), due to popular resentment of his (Jotham's) anti-Assyria policy. See also on verse 32.

16:1. In the seventeenth year. See on 15:32. **2,3. Ahaz . . . walked in the way of the kings of Israel** (cf. II Chr 28:1-4, esp. 3,4). Ahaz broke the covenant of the Lord. He lived as the kings of Israel lived, and made images of Baal to worship (cf. Ex 20:3). **Made his son to pass through the fire.** Numbers 31:23 indicates that this means a literal burning. He made of his children a burnt sacrifice to Baal (II Chr 28:3). This was one of the sins for which Israel was deported (see on 17:17).

5. Then Rezin . . . and Pekah. See on verse 37. Now the peoples of Syria and Canaan were resisting Assyria's advance, and this was an attempt to force Ahaz to join the movement. Thus the Lord used circumstances to chastise Ahaz, bringing these forces against him because of his sins. For the deliverance proffered by the Lord, see Isaiah 7. Ahaz was defeated by Pekah, however, because he had no faith (Isa 7:4,9b, 11,12), and many of his people were taken captive (II Chr 28:5-8). **6. Rezin . . . recovered Elath** [from Judah] **to Syria.** A further punishment for Judah for her sins. **7. So Ahaz sent.** Cf. Isa 7:17. Assyria would ultimately plunder the land even if the appeal was made. When Syria fell, Judah lost her buffer against Assyrian invasion. **Thy servant.** The price for help from Assyria was vassalage. **8. Ahaz took the silver and gold.** He did not heed Isaiah's promise. He could not believe! **9. The king of Assyria . . . went up against Damascus.** Tiglath took Damascus, but he also afflicted Ahaz. II Chronicles 28:20 says, "It did him [Ahaz] no good."

10. And king Ahaz . . . saw an altar (in Damascus). Ahaz went to express his obedience to Tiglath for his continued favor, but the altar became one more sin by which he turned away from God. **11.** Note the apostasy of Urijah the high priest, who by his actions, broke the covenant. **12. The king saw the altar . . . and offered thereon.** Ahaz found the altar ready (cf. v. 10) – the original Solomonic altar having been pushed aside to the north side – and he made his sacrifices thereon. **15. To enquire by.** Translate: "Will be to me for deliberation;" i.e., "I will make further arrangements about it after deliberation." The Solomonic altar did not please Ahaz after he had seen the altar in Damascus. He sinned against the Lord by having removed the altar made according to the

Lord's instruction and placed there by His direction. God's appointed instruments are not to be tampered with. **17,18.** Ahaz made further depredations upon the temple furnishings, stripping them of valuable ornamentation for fear of (not **for,** i.e., for the benefit of) the king of Assyria. He guarded against exciting the cupidity of Tiglath-pileser, should he come into Jerusalem.

10) Destruction and Captivity of Israel. 17:1-41.

1. In the twelfth year. See on 16:1-4; 15:27–31. **2. Not as the kings of Israel . . . before him.** Chronicles is silent on the manner of difference. It was only in his "walk"; he perpetuated Jeroboam's sins. **3. Against him came up Shalmaneser.** See 15:30. Tiglath-pileser III had died in 727 B.C. Hoshea became vassal to Shalmaneser. He was to pay tribute annually. About his sixth year, Hoshea sought independence from Assyria. He conspired against Shalmaneser by forming an alliance with So of Egypt, and he stopped paying the tribute. Thus, naturally, arose the attack against Israel, and her fall.

5. The king of Assyria . . . besieged it [Samaria] **three years.** Time here is inclusive; parts of years are considered as whole years (cf. 18:9,10 for the exact time). **6. King of Assyria took Samaria.** For the belief that this was Shalmaneser V and not Sargon II, see J. P. Free, *Archaeology and Bible History,* pp. 199,200. **Carried Israel away into Assyria.** Not Assyria as such, but the empire. **In Halah** and on the **Habor.** Cf. I Chr 5:26. The **Habor** is the river Khabur, which empties into the Euphrates. **Gozan** is the present Tell Halaf (Assyr. *Guzanu*). **Cities of the Medes.** The area northeast of Nineveh. (See *Natl. Geog. Mag.* map: "Bible Lands and the Cradle of Western Civilizations.") Transportation of peoples was now the accepted norm for controlling subject nations.

7. And it came to pass when the children of Israel. The conclusion is in 17:18: **Therefore the Lord.** Verses 8-12 contain a list of sins – specifications for judgment. Who **had brought them up out of . . . Egypt.** The people of Israel sinned against their Saviour. They were ungrateful, unthankful wretches, covenant-breakers and rebels. **8. And walked in the statutes of the heathen . . . and of the kings of Israel.** Their sins fell into two categories – the idolatries of the Canaanites, and the worship of the golden calves. **9. They covered over the Lord their God with words which were not right.** By idolatrous ways and deeds they so denied the Lord that he could no longer be seen or recognized. **From the tower.** No place escaped from this idolatry. Images and statues of Astarte were set up in the **groves** (v. 10), and the **incense** of worship was burned before them (v. 11), as in the practices of the heathen. **12. Logs** (AV, *idols*). *Idols* made of wood, stone, metal, or clay (Deut 29:17); a contemptuous term indicating their utter helplessness. **They served,** i.e., worshiped them.

13. The Lord testified against them. Verses 13-17 review the dealings of the Lord with Israel. The writer shows how God, in his faithfulness, supplemented the prohibitions of the Law with direct warnings by his prophets, exhorting the people of Israel to turn away from their idolatry. Note that in 17:13 Judah also is brought into the account, for this was written after the fall of Judah. Yet they did not hear, following the example of their fathers. **14. That did not believe.** This was the willful act of rebellious hearts, hardened necks. **15. Followed vanity.** "Their whole life had a worthless aim." **16. They left all the commandments of the Lord their God, and made them molten images, even two calves, and asherah** (not *a grove;* the goddess Astarte), **and worshipped all the host of heaven.** The instruments and objects of worship – idols and the stellar deities of Assyria – are enumerated, all strictly prohibited in Deut 4:14-19. **17. Caused their sons . . . to pass through the fire.** The burnt offering of children is prohibited in Deut 18:10,11, as are all forms of soothsaying.

18. Therefore the Lord . . . removed them. God's wrath was provoked, and he punished them by deportation; Judah alone was left. The fact that these sins broke the covenant is the only reason for their deportation. **19-23.** These verses describe the utter rejection of Israel, and though Judah was left, yet she, too, was unfaithful. Verse 19 intimates that she was to share Israel's fate. **20. And the Lord rejected all the seed of Israel.** God delivered them up to judgment because Israel *in toto* broke the covenant. This was, therefore, written after the fall of Judah. **21. For he rent Israel from the house of David.** The Lord did not intend to have the national division result in sin such as is here described (cf. I Kgs 11:37ff.). **22,23.** The thought is: "Though I separated the two peoples, yet Jeroboam led the people into sin, and they consented to be led down the road of sin to final destruction."

Verses 24-41 tell of the transplantation of people from various countries to the land of Israel. **24. The king of Assyria brought.** Shalmaneser died during or just after the siege of Samaria, and Sargon II (722–705) may have been the one who repeopled the land after Israel's deportation. Ezra 4:2 indicates that there was a later transplantation under Esar-haddon (681–668). If this first action also was by Esar-haddon, then the land must have remained waste at least forty-one years. To repeople it just after Samaria's fall was to put into effect a sensible program for producing revenue. **Men from . . . Cuthah.** Josephus identifies these with the Kosseans who lived northeast of Susa (*Antiq*. ix. 14. 3; x. 8. 7). **Ava.** The "Ivvah" of 18:34; 19:13, between Anah and the Habur on the Euphrates. **Hamath.** A city in Syria, on the Orontes. **Sepharvaim.** Sippar on the Euphrates, above Babylon. **Samaria.** First application of this name to the land of Israel. **25. The Lord sent lions.** The lapse of time after the deportation and before the colonists' arrival gave time for the lions to multiply, and God used their natural incursions to humble the people. **26. The nations . . . know not the manner of the God . . . therefore he hath sent lions among them.** A superstitious analysis on the part of these people, but a true one. It formed the basis for their appeal for saviour priests. **27.** Their request implied in verse 26 was heeded. **28. Then one of the priests . . . carried away from Samaria** was sent. He came back to Bethel, seat of Jeroboam's calf worship, and taught the people "how" they should fear the Lord. **29-32.** The result was a mixture of pagan religion and the worship of Jehovah, which was worse than out-and-out paganism. **33. Feared the Lord.** An impure "fear," since they **served their own gods,** as the previous Israelites had done.

Verses **34-41** present an analysis of the peoples' actions in relation to the Lord's commands. Verse 34 indicates that mixed religious practices continued to the day of the writing of Kings. Verses 35-39 constitute a long quotation put together from Ex 20:5,7; 22:11; 6:6; 20:23; Deut 4:34; 5:15; 13:5; 28:14, etc. Here the Lord again points to his works among them to delineate the awful heinousness of their sins.

37. Which he wrote for you. This is a clear reference to the fact that Exodus and Deuteronomy were written by Moses and could not have been composed at a later date. If these books were done at a later date, as the critics hold, how could God have deported his people for sinning against his commandments and statutes? **40. They did not hearken.** They includes both the Israelites and the colonists. They continued in their old sins. **41.** This verse is a summary of events up to the time of writing of the record which was the author's source.

III. The Kingdom in Judah to the Final Destruction of the Nation of Israel. 18:1–25:30.

A. The Kingdom Under Hezekiah. 18:1–20:21.

1) Hezekiah's Reforms. 18:1-12. Hezekiah is the Lord's illustration of a righteous king who trusted in him. Coming at the time of Israel's downfall and the nation's darkest hour, he was given to the people by God to bring home to them their true destiny and character, and to demonstrate that God's ways are pure goodness and truth to such as keep his covenant and testimony. During Sennacherib's first campaign, in 701 B.C., Hezekiah trusted in allies; in the second campaign, about 688 B.C., he depended on the Lord. Judah's king was growing in the area of faith and trust in God.

1. In the third year of Hoshea. This is the last co-ordination in Kings of Judean reigns with Israelite reigns. Other historical data help to establish the proper chronological sequence hereafter. **2. He reigned twenty and nine years.** Hezekiah reigned twenty-nine years. In addition, he held a regency with Ahaz, deduced as follows. Nebuchadrezzar II destroyed Jerusalem on July 19, 586 B.C. (BASOR, 143, pp. 46,47). The reigns of Manasseh (55 years), Amon (2 years), Josiah (31 years), Jehoahaz (3 months), Jehoiakim (11 years), Jehoiachin (3 months), and Zedekiah (11 years) total 110 years. Adding 110 to 586 B.C. gives us 696 B.C. as the date for Manasseh's accession. This does not, however, allow for Hezekiah's additional fifteen years after 701 B.C. (see on ch. 20). The gap of five years (701-696) deducted from fifteen leaves ten years unaccounted for. These must have been a period of coregency with Manasseh. (See below on each of the forenamed kings.) However, Hezekiah's accession is set at 715 B.C. But he is said to have been ruling in the fourth and sixth years of Hoshea, which indicates that he had a co-regency with Ahaz of twelve years minimum (see on 18:13). Ahaz is said to have been twenty years old when he came to the throne (II Kgs 16:2), and he reigned sixteen years. Hence he must have been thirty-six in 715 B.C. In the third year of Hoshea, Hezekiah came to the throne (see on 18:1), which would have been 729/728 (incl. reckoning). Ahaz would, then, have been twenty-three years old, and Hezekiah would have been twelve, which would make Ahaz eleven when Hezekiah was born, and that is too young. It becomes clear that the age twenty at which Ahaz is said to have come to the throne was his age at the beginning of his co-regency with Jotham. The statement that he reigned sixteen years must refer to the period of his independent reign (see Thiele, *op. cit.*, p. 133). According to this reckoning he died at age forty. And he must have been only fifteen years old when his son Hezekiah was born. Such early parenthood is not infrequent in Middle East countries. **3. He did right.** The life of Hezekiah is assessed in regard to his relation to the covenant of Jehovah; he fulfilled it.

4. He removed the high places. See the full account in II Chr 29–31. In II Kgs 18:22 these are places of worship – devisive worship of Jehovah (see on 12:3). Hezekiah and Josiah are said to have been "like David" in that they tolerated no divisive worship. **Brake . . . the brasen serpent . . . Moses had made.** This most distinctive item had become an object of idolatry, and therefore it was destroyed by Hezekiah in spite of its origin and veneration. **5. After him was none like him,** in trust in and obedience to Jehovah, for (v. 6) **he . . . departed not from following him. 7. The Lord was with him** signifies God's favor to the obedient. **He rebelled against the king of Assyria.** Hezekiah reversed Ahaz' policy of submission to Assyria. **8. He smote the Philistines.** Evidence that the Lord was with him.

9-12. These verses present a review of the fall of Israel, filled into Judean annals according to the synchronistic pattern of the author. Though the event recorded came before Sennacherib's first invasion, it is mentioned here to remind the people of what trouble rebellion against the Lord can cause.

2) Deliverance from Sennacherib's Two Invasions. 18:13–19:37.

a) First Invasion of Judah by Sennacherib. 18:13-16. For chronology see on verse 1. Sennacherib was a son of Sargon II, and he reigned 705–681 B.C. Verses 13-16 summarize his first campaign into Judah, in 701 B.C. (17ff. refers to a later campaign, c. 688). Though Hezekiah reversed Ahaz' policy of submission to Assyria, the desertion of Judah's allies forced him to submit (Luckenbill, *Anc. Rec.*, II, par. 240; cf. II Kgs 18:14). Hezekiah collected the tribute by stripping the Temple (vv. 15,16). The fact that Sennacherib received the tribute in Nineveh (Luckenbill, *ibid.*), indicates that Hezekiah gave it on condition that the Assyrians would withdraw from Judea.

b) The Second Campaign. 18:17-25. The point of this account is that the Lord provides deliverance in response to true faith. The time of the second campaign, which took place thirteen or fourteen years after the events of verses 13-16, is determined by the date of Tirhakah, king of Ethiopia (19:9). An article in BASOR (130, pp. 8,9) indicates that Tirhakah did not become co-regent until 690/689 B.C. Since his birth occurred in 711/710, it would have been impossible for him to lead Egyptian forces in 701 at the age of nine years.

17. Tartan. Field marshal. **Rabsaris.** Head of the eunuchs, i.e., of the palace servants, generally eunuchs. **Rab-shakeh.** Chief cupbearer. **Conduit of the upper pool.** It extended from Gihon (II Chr 32:30; I Kgs 1:33) to the field of the clothes-washers – **fullers. 18. When they had called to the king.** The delegation wished to speak to Hezekiah. But he, observing protocol, sent officials ranking on their level. Verses 19-25 constitute a message of heathen effrontery to Jehovah.

19. Thus saith the great king. So styled because he ruled over other kings. **What confidence.** Confidence here means "thing depended on." His question expresses his astonishment in view of the conquests of Assyrian might. **20. Thou sayest . . . vain words.** Just so much "talk." **On whom dost thou trust.** Rabshakeh supposed this whom to be Egypt (v. 21). Evidently Sennacherib supposed that Hezekiah had made an alliance with Pharaoh (cf. v. 22; 19:1ff.). However, the Philistines of Ekron called for Tirhakah to help them (Luckenbill, *Anc. Rec., loc. cit.*). **22. Whose altars Hezekiah hath taken away.** These Assyrians interpreted Hezekiah's cleansing the land of idols as sacrilege rather than obedience.

He had acted in direct opposition to heathen practices and beliefs. Sennacherib was attempting to turn the populace toward himself and so weaken the defenses of Hezekiah. **23. Give pledges** should read *make a bargain.* Note the sarcastic insinuation that Hezekiah did not have even this many horsemen. Hezekiah, however, had chosen other means of defense. **24. How then wilt thou turn away.** "You can't, therefore, oppose the least of Sennacherib's captains." **25. Am I now come up without the Lord.** "The Lord has sent me to destroy the land." Only to chastise the land, however, as events showed. It is true that God uses foreign nations to chastise his people (see 19:25).

c) The Embassy's Attempt to Persuade the People. 18:26-37. **26. Speak . . . in the Aramaic tongue** (AV, *Syrian language).* To prevent further effect on the people, the officials of Judah requested that any further conversation be conducted in the Aramaic language, which was rapidly becoming the lingua franca of the ancient world. It was already the language of diplomacy, but it was not yet generally known by the people. **27. Hath he not sent me to the men . . . on the wall.** Hezekiah's defenders. **That they may eat.** "By refusing to surrender you will subject your people to the terrible famine of a long siege." **28.** In the **Jews' language;** i.e., Hebrew. He addressed his strongest appeal to the populace. **29,30. Deceive.** Hezekiah's exhortation to them to trust the Lord, he said, would lead them astray, for neither Hezekiah nor Jehovah could deliver them. **31. Make an agreement.** That is, "Make peace with me," or, "Surrender"; for he says **come out to me. Eat ye.** A temporary promise. They would be transported to a "better" land. **32. That ye may live.** "You can live only through surrender and deportation." It was the confident expectation of Sennacherib that they would surrender, and this would demonstrate Assyrian might.

Verses **33-35** show how the Assyrians misunderstood the power and purpose of their previous conquests. Rabshakeh was ignorant of the fact that the Lord often selects certain nations for subjection and others for deliverance.

34. Hamath. See on 17:24. **Arpad.** The present Tell Erfad, thirteen miles north of Aleppo. **Hena** and **Ivah** were in the general area of the North Euphrates, east of Hamath. For the others see on 17:24ff.

35. Who are they among all the gods. See on verse 33.

36. The people held their peace. See Isa 36:21. Both the people and Hezekiah's ministers refused to answer. Hezekiah intended God to reply. **37. Clothes rent.** Because of sorrow for blasphemies against Jehovah.

d) Hezekiah's Appeal to the Lord. 19:1-19. **1. When king Hezekiah heard . . . he . . . covered himself with sackcloth.** A sign of penitence. Hezekiah considered the invasion to be a chastisement. The king prayed and also sought God's answer from the prophet Isaiah. He had learned to trust the Lord completely. He had forsaken the practice of worldly alliances. God alone was to lead and deliver. See 3) below. **3. A day of distress . . . chastisement . . . disdain** (not *blasphemy*, as in the AV). The **distress** (AV, *trouble)* of the people was the chastisement of invasion by their enemies. **The children.** The people were in great peril, but their feeble efforts to effect deliverance might destroy all. **4. It may be.** Hezekiah expressed hope that the Lord would take notice of the blasphemy.

6. Be not afraid. Isaiah spoke first to remove fear, declaring that, as Sennacherib had made Hezekiah fear, likewise a message from his capital would make him fear. **7.** As he intended Jerusalem's fall, so would he fall in his own land (see v. 37).

8-13. So Rab-shakeh returned. He withdrew because Jerusalem was too strongly fortified. **Lachish.** A sculpture excavated at Nineveh pictures Sennacherib seated before Lachish, receiving its tribute. **9. When he heard.** Sennacherib heard of the advance of Tirhakah, king of Egypt (see BASOR, 130, p. 8ff.). See comment on 18:17. This occurred after 688, toward the end of Hezekiah's reign. **He sent messengers.** Sennacherib sought to subdue Hezekiah by fear and thus gain Jerusalem without a fight. **10. Let not thy God . . . deceive thee.** Sennacherib now attributed the "deception" to the Lord. In this he reached the apogee of blasphemy and sealed his doom (cf. v. 7). **11. Thou hast heard.** "Take note of my previous conquests" (cf. 18:34). None of these cities is mentioned in the first three campaigns. If this attack had occurred after the capture of these cities, Sennacherib would not have failed to mention them. Hence this must refer to a later, unrecorded campaign (see Luckenbill, *Annals of Sennacherib,* p. 29). The cities not previously mentioned are: **Gozan** – Assyrian *Gazanu,* modern Tell Halaf, on the Habur, east of Haran, which dates back to the fifth millennium B.C.; **Haran** – ancient Haran, on the Balikh river; **Rezeph** – Assyrian *Rasapa,* probably present Rusafah, or Risafe, northeast of Palmyra; **Eden** – the *Bit-Adinni* of the Assyrian inscriptions, a small kingdom athwart the Euphrates, west of the Balikh River; **Thelasar** – probably in the same area. **13. The king of the city** should read, *the king of La'ir,* since this city is now known as the Assyrian city of Lahiru (see BASOR, 141, p. 25; Luckenbill, *Anc. Records,* Vol. II, para. 252. Cf. II Kgs 18:34). Sennacherib lists more cities, etc., to heighten the effect of the message.

14. When Hezekiah had received the letter . . . and had read it. The significance of this incident lies in what Hezekiah did with the message. **Spread it before the Lord.** He handed over the letter to the Lord, so to speak, leaving Him to punish the blasphemy of it. **16.** The words, **Bow down thine ear . . . open . . . thine eyes,** express most earnest appeal for God's help and his most specific attention. God is glorified when we cast ourselves thus so completely on his power and mercy. **17,18. Of a truth.** Hezekiah admitted the truth of the claims of Sennacherib (vv. 12,13). At the same time he recognized that the Assyrian had been successful not because the gods of wood and stone were powerless, but because the Lord was working in human history.

e) The Deliverance of Jerusalem. 19:20-37. **20. Thus saith the Lord God.** The answer came quickly, probably by Eliakim and Shebna (v. 2). The first part of the answer (vv. 21-28) was directed to Sennacherib. **21. The virgin . . . daughter.** That is, Jerusalem yet unconquered and unconquerable by Sennacherib. **Hath despised thee.** Isaiah, anticipating the deliverance of the city, represents Sennacherib's boastful threats as evoking only scorn and ridicule. "She bobs (AV, **wags**) the head at thy retreating figure, departing in shame and discomfiture." Sennacherib was to lose his entire army. **22. Whom hast thou reproached.** Reviling the Lord was Sennacherib's folly. **23. With the multitude of my chariots.** Sennacherib boasted of transient earthly might. **Come up.** Perfect tense. The Lord reveals Sennacherib's thought that he was invincible and could not be turned from his purpose. **Lebanon** is Judah, its **summit** (AV, *height)* is Jerusalem, its **fir trees** are the princes of Judah, and its **lodgings** and **forest** are the palaces of Mount Zion (cf. Jer 22:6,7,23; Ezk 17:3). **24. I have digged,** etc., continues the same idea in another figure. **25. Hast thou not heard.** Now the Lord God speaks of his own deeds and shows that Sennacherib is a thief who has laid claim to the deeds of another, and that he will certainly be punished. **Thou shouldest be.** Sennacherib was but the instrument, and should fear lest he fall as other arrogant sinners had fallen. **26. Therefore their inhabitants were of small power.** Not because their gods were weaker than those of Assyria, but because the Lord had empowered Sennacherib for His own purposes. **Grass on the roof** (AV, *house tops)* withers because of lack of soil. **Grain** (AV, *corn)* **blasted in the germ** is grain prone to decay that fails to germinate. These comparisons illustrate and confirm Sennacherib's failure. **27. But I know thy abode.** God knows a man's heart and his determining thoughts (Ps 139:1-4). **Rage.** Violent hate, positive animosity (cf. vv. 23,24). Here it forms the ground for Jehovah's vengeance. **28. I will put my hook in thy nose.** Sennacherib would most surely be turned away from his purposes, as surely and shamefully as he had led away his captives.

The second section of the Lord's answer to Sennacherib is addressed to Hezekiah (vv. 29-31). **29. And this is the sign to thee.** This description of the three years' cycle of crops indicates that Isaiah was prophesying in a sabbatical year, which means that there would be no crop the next year. The **sign** was that the "aftergrowth" of the sabbatical year would remain to them. That is, Sennacherib's host would not be around to despoil the "aftergrowth." It would be left for the Jews to gather. See Leviticus 25. **30. The remnant . . . shall yet . . . bear fruit.** Jerusalem would escape destruction. And the population left from the invasion would be greatly increased. **31. The zeal of the Lord.** Cf. Zech 4:6b.

Through the prophet Isaiah, God predicted the collapse of Sennacherib's siege. **32. He shall not come into this city.** The invincible siege tactics of the Assyrians would not be used against Jerusalem. The Lord would take the king of Assyria back by the way he came, fruitless and defeated. **34. For mine own sake**; i.e., to rebuke Sennacherib's boasting. **For my servant David's sake.** In order that David's house might endure for a while longer as a testimony to God's sure promises to David.

35. That night . . . the angel of the Lord . . . smote . . . the Assyrians. Compare verse 7. Herodotus records an Egyptian tradition which may describe physical means God used to destroy Sennacherib's army: "Mice ate up the quivers." Presumably the mice came carrying bubonic plague. The plague, incubating in the soldiers, reached killing fever stage on the night when the city had been promised relief, and it slew them in their sleep. God orders events to coincide with his will. The event occurred after Rab-shakeh withdrew from Jerusalem and found Sennacherib at Libnah. **36. Sennacherib . . . departed, and went and returned.** He fled to Nineveh because of possible action from Egypt. **Dwelt at Nineveh** indicates that he undertook no further campaigns to the west (cf. Luckenbill, *Annals of Sennacherib*, p. 17). **37. His sons smote him.** Sennacherib died as the result of a palace intrigue (cf. v. 7). Esarhaddon (681–668 B.C.), states (Luckenbill, *Anc. Rec.*, Vol. II, pars. 501,592) that his brothers slew Sennacherib in a plot to gain the throne. Ashurbanipal (688-626 B.C.) states (*ibid.*, Vol. II, par. 795) that he slew those who slew Sennacherib, his grandfather.

3) Hezekiah's Illness and Recovery. 20:1-11.

1. In those days. The days of the first invasions of Sennacherib. Comparison of the order of 18:1–20:19 with that of Isa 36:1–40:1 indicates that Isaiah's record became the source for this account. It is evident that the two accounts have different purposes. In Isaiah the purpose is to show that only the Lord can comfort his people; in Kings it is to show that Judean kings who follow Hezekiah's policy of worldly alliances assure Judah's fall. **Thus saith the Lord.** Succeeding events show that the pronouncement of death was conditional. **2. He turned his face to the wall.** Hezekiah communed alone with God. **3. I have walked before thee in truth.** Hezekiah prayed for length of days, such as is promised to those who walk uprightly (Prov 10:27). Assuming that his works were done in obedience to God's commands, why then, must he die? Compare Hezekiah's testimony in Isa 38:10-20. Hezekiah wanted time to establish his moral reforms more firmly among the people. **4. The middle city** (AV, *court*). The area of the castle, Mount Zion. The Lord answered quickly. **5. I have heard thy prayer.** He promised healing. From Isa 38:17,18 it appears that there was some reason why Hezekiah should be chastised, most probably because of shameful lack of faith under Sennacherib's first invasion, when Hezekiah made allies of the Arabs (Luckenbill, *Annals of Sennacherib*, p. 33). At this point he was not a notable example of one who trusted and obeyed God. **6. I will add.** God purposed that Hezekiah should yet show what true faith is. The words, **I will deliver thee and this city,** place the illness during the first invasion by Sennacherib. **I will defend.** See 19:34,35. **7. Take a lump of figs.** The ancients believed that a fig poultice would heal boils. The exact cause of Hezekiah's illness is not known. Perhaps the **boil** was symptomatic.

God graciously gave the king a sign that he would certainly be healed. **8. What is the sign.** For the natural sequence of events read the verses in this order – 6,8,11,7. Hezekiah desired an external or "second" witness to relieve his anxiety and strengthen his faith. **The third day.** His recovery was to be rapid. **9. Shall the shadow . . . go back ten degrees?** Hezekiah chose the reversal as the strongest, most positive proof of the Lord's promise.

4) The Embassy of Merodach-baladan. 20:12-19.

12. Merodach-baladan *(Marduk-Apal-iddin)* was twice king of Babylon (722–710, 703–702). He was dethroned the first time by Sargon about 710 B.C., but later regained the throne. The second time he was defeated and dethroned by Sennacherib, along with his ally Elam (see Luckenbill, *Annals of Sennacherib*, p. 24) in his first campaign, 703 B.C. The embassy of 20:12 came in Hezekiah's fourteenth year (since fifteen years are added) during the course of Sennacherib's first invasion (see on v. 6). Merodach sought to make an ally of Hezekiah (see Jos *Antiq*. x. 2. 2). Hezekiah had not yet forsaken his practice of making alliances. He was yet to do so before the second invasion, and thus to be a true man of faith. Merodach's embassy probably came in 700 B.C. **13. Hezekiah hearkened . . . shewed them all the house of his precious things.** Translate **hearkened** as *welcomed*. Josephus (*Antiq*. x. 2. 2) indicates that Hezekiah showed his treasuries to prove he was an able ally. Evidently the tribute he yielded to Sennacherib in 701 had not too badly depleted his reserves.

14. Then . . . Isaiah . . . said unto him. Isaiah, who understood the ulterior motive of the embassy, called Hezekiah to account and warned him of the consequences. Compare II Chr 32:31. **17,18. Which thy fathers have laid up. . . . And . . . thy sons . . . shall they take away.** Hezekiah's vanity was an example of that vanity and faithlessness that would bring about Judah's fall. Hezekiah forsook faith in the Lord of hosts and trusted in his own means (II Chr 32:25). **19. Then said Hezekiah . . . Is it not good, if peace and truth be in my days?** This was not a confession of sin. It was an expression of the "peace in our time" policy, that short-sighted attitude that shows little concern for those on whom coming catastrophe shall fall. Therefore Isaiah could only turn to Jehovah and cry out, "Comfort ye, comfort ye my people" (Isa 40:1). Only after the predicted destruction would there come an end to Israel's sin of apostasy, and only then would true peace endure.

5) Hezekiah's Death. 20:20,21.

20. The building activities of Hezekiah are here summarized (cf. II Chr 32:27-30). **21. Hezekiah slept with his fathers.** The important acts of Hezekiah's life have been told. Now we must turn to the next figure who illustrates that vanity and pride which forwarded Judah's downfall.

B. The Reigns of Manasseh and Amon. 21:1-26.

1) The Iniquity and Death of Manasseh. 21:1-18.

a) Manasseh's Wickedness. 21:1-9.

1. Manasseh was twelve years old when he began to reign. See on 18:1-3. Manasseh had a co-regency of ten years with Hezekiah (cf. Thiele, *Mysterious Numbers,* p. 155). **2. He did that which was evil.** Manasseh, following the wicked kings of Israel, broke the covenant. **3a. He built . . . again the high places** and erected altars for Baal. **3b-5.** He reintroduced the Assyro-Chaldean star worship and erected altars for **all the host of heaven** in the forecourts of the Temple. **6.** He even offered his son as a burnt offering, and made use of **soothsaying** and **communion with evil spirits,** all as though he intended to **provoke** the Lord **to anger. 7. Grove.** Rather, image of Astarte, bloodthirsty female deity. This act was the chief sin by which Manasseh repudiated and broke the covenant of the Lord. **9. More evil than did the nations.** He worshiped more and different gods than the heathen Canaanites did.

b) Jerusalem's Final Doom Pronounced. 21:10-16.

11,12. Because Manasseh . . . hath done these abominations. Manasseh's deliberate sins would destroy the nation and take it into captivity. **His ears shall tingle.** The news of Judah's devastation, like a harsh musical note, would jar and shake all who heard. **13. I will stretch.** God's righteousness had measured Samaria and required its fall. **16. Manasseh shed innocent blood,** that of God's prophets. This made his deportation inevitable (II Chr 33:11).

c) Manasseh's Death. 21:17,18. **Buried . . . in the garden of Uzza.** Because he was considered unworthy of burial with the kings.

2) The Sins and Death of Amon. 21:19-26.

19. Amon was twenty and two years old when he began to reign. See 18:1-3. **20. He did evil in the sight of the Lord.** He broke the covenant, following his father (v. 21). **22. He forsook the Lord.** Therefore Jehovah forsook him; so death resulted. **23. The servants of Amon . . . slew** him. Court officials made a conspiracy which died in its inception, for **the people . . . slew all them** (v. 24), and **made Josiah . . . king.** Josiah could thus not have been co-regent; see on 18:1-3.

C. Reform in Judah and Israel under Josiah. 22:1–23:30. The discovery of the book of the Law stimulated wide reforms of a temporary nature only. There was not sufficient time for Josiah's reforms to root out deep-seated sin.

1. Josiah was eight . . . when he began to reign. Josiah was too young for a co-regency (see Thiele, *op. cit.,* p. 154). **2. He did right.** He kept the Lord's covenant. The reason is given in II Chr 34:3: he sought the Lord in his eighth year, and this gave him direction in his eighteenth year.

3. In the eighteenth year. Cf. II Chr 34:8. The affairs of this year concern the restoration of Judah's covenant relation with the Lord. The juxtaposition of these verses with verse 2 indicates that this was the result of Josiah's seeking God. **4. Sum the silver.** The first step in restoring Judah's covenant relation with God was to obtain money to repair the Temple (cf. II Chr 34:9).

8. Hilkiah . . . said . . . I have found the book of the law. The Torah, the five books of Moses (cf. Deut 31:24-26). **10. Delivered me a book.** Shaphan turned to the important matter last. What he read (v. 8) and what he read to the king (v. 10) were no doubt the same; both he and Hilkiah must have desired more thorough reforms. **11. When the king had heard . . . he rent his clothes.** Possibly the portion read was Lev 26, or Deut 28:15ff. The Lord combined various circumstances to turn Josiah's heart toward reform. **13. Enquire of the Lord.** "Go find out if these imminent judgments can be stayed." **14. Huldah.** The nearest source of answer from Jehovah.

16,17. I will bring evil . . . because they have forsaken me . . . burned incense unto other gods. They broke the covenant by according worship to other gods. God's wrath would **not be quenched,** but it would fall upon Judah in later times. **20. Thine eyes shall not see all the evil . . .** to come. Because of his good works (v. 19).

The second step in restoring Judah's covenant relation with God was to renew the covenant (23:1-3). **23:1. They gathered . . . the elders of Judah and of Jerusalem.** The spiritual rulers must take part and leadership. **2. Both small and great.** All classes of people were to take part in restoring the covenant relation. **He read . . . all the words of the book of the covenant.** See Deut 31:24-26. Josiah read the covenant of the Lord. Cf. Josh 23:6; 24:22-25. **3. The king . . . made a covenant before the Lord . . . And all the people stood to the covenant.** All participated in the restoration.

The third step was to eradicate the idolatry in Judah (vv. 4-20). **4. Bring forth out of the temple.** Josiah removed defiling idols, and had them burned (cf. Deut 7:25; 12:3). God's Temple is for him alone. **5. Put down the idolatrous priests.** "Sacerdotal functionaries" who led the people in idolatry were removed so that the Levites might be restored. **To the planets.** Zodiacal worship. **6. Grove.** Figure of Astarte. These items indicate the scope of Judah's idolatry. **8. Brought all the priests . . . from Geba to Beer-sheba** away from the high places. That is, he caused divisive worship to cease throughout all Judah and Benjamin. **9. Came not . . . but they did eat of the unleavened bread.** Divisive worship deprived them of the right to Levitical service but did not deprive them of sustenance. **10. Defiled Topheth.** By burning human bones there (cf. vv. 16-18). **11. Took away the horses.** Sun worship was removed. **12. The altars . . . of the upper chamber of Ahaz.** Used for astral worship. **13,14. Mount of corruption.** On the Mount of Olives. For the origin of the name, see I Kgs 11:7.

King Josiah also abolished idolatry in Israel. **15. Altar . . . at Beth-el.** He rooted up the fountainhead of the idolatry by which Israel had broken the covenant (cf. I Kgs 12:28; 13:1; Amos 3:14; 6:10,13; Jer 48:13). **16. Polluted it.** By burning human bones upon it to profane it for use in the eyes of the idolater. **17. What grave stone** (AV, *title*) **is that.** This is Josiah's connection with I Kgs 13:2. **19,20. Josiah sacrificed** (AV marg.) these high priests to the Mosaic law which forbade idolatry.

The king next replaced sin with positive worship of Jehovah (vv. 21-23). He led his people in an observance of the Passover, the central reminder of the covenant (cf. II Chr 35:1-19). **22.** The words, **such a passover,** indicate the circumstances and strictness of the observance, surpassing that of Hezekiah.

24. Josiah extended his reforms to every house, **that he might establish** (AV, *perform*) **the words of the law.** Pure homes form the basis of a pure society. **25. Like unto him was there no king.** He carried out the Law more exactly and faithfully than other reformers did.

26. But Josiah's good deeds could not deliver Judah (cf. II Kgs 22:16-20). **27. I will remove** confirms the prediction of II Kgs 20:17 and adds to it. Removal of God's name guaranteed Jerusalem's fall.

29. Pharaoh-nechoh (609-594) **went up to** (not *against*, as in AV) **the king of Assyria . . .** to help him against Nabopolassar, king of Babylon (see BASOR, 143, p. 25; D. J. Wiseman, *Chronicles of Chaldean Kings*, p. 19). **At Megiddo.** On the normal line of march to Syria. Babylon was not stopped, because Josiah's effort weakened Necho and thus facilitated fulfillment of II Kgs 20:17.

D. The Last Days of Judah. 23:31–25:30.

1) The Reign and Deportation of Jehoahaz. 23:31-34.

See 18:1-3 for chronology. His having been made king by the people precludes the possibility of a co-regency (cf. Jer 22:11). **32. He did evil.** He broke the covenant. **33. Nechoh took him captive at Riblah,** whither he was summoned for that purpose (Jos *Antiq*. x. 5. 2).

2) Jehoiakim's Reign and Nebuchadrezzar's Invasion. 23:34–24:7.

34. Nechoh made Eliakim . . . king by right of conqueror, having slain Josiah. **35. Jehoiakim** paid tribute to Nechoh in order to remain king. **37. He did evil.** See on verse 32. **24:1. Nebuchadnezzar . . . came up** in 604 B.C., summoning the kings of Hattu land (Palestine-Syria) to pay tribute (see Wiseman, *op. cit.*, p. 28; BASOR, 143, pp. 24,25). The proper spelling of the name is Nebuchadrezzar. **Jehoiakim became his servant three years.** That is, until 601, when he rebelled, yielding to the pro-Egypt party, but submitting and paying the tribute when Nebuchadnezzar came into the land the same year. **2. The Lord sent against him bands.** Bands of Arabs, and others, who vented their spite against Nebuchadrezzar on Jehoiakim, **to destroy** Judah, i.e., to contribute to her fall (cf. 20:17; 23:27; Wiseman, *op. cit.*, p. 32). **3,4.** These bands acted **at the commandment of the Lord . . . for the sins of Manasseh** (20:17) and **for the innocent blood** he shed (21:16). **5. The rest of the acts.** Cf. II Chr 36:8a. See Introduction, *Sources*. Cf. Jer 22:19 for his ignominious end. **7. King of Egypt came not again any more out of his land.** Nebuchadrezzar now controlled Egypt's former possessions in Palestine and Syria, down to the Wadi Arish, the **river** bordering **Egypt.**

3) Reign and Captivity of Jehoiachin. 24:8-16.

8. Jehoiachin was eighteen years old . . . reigned . . . three months (and ten days; cf. II Chr 36:9a). See 18:1-3. No co-regency is involved (see Thiele, *Mysterious Numbers*, p. 154). **10. At that time.** Cf. II Chr 36:10, "at the turning point of the year," i.e., Tishri (Sept.-Oct. See BASOR, 143, pp. 24,25). **The servants of Nebuchadnezzar . . . came up.** He called out his army in Kislev (Dec.), 598 B.C., *after Jehoiakim had died.* And he took Jerusalem on 15/16 March, 597 B.C. (Wiseman, *op. cit.*, p. 33), when Jehoiachin was king. **12. Jehoiachin . . . went out.** He hoped to keep his rulership by surrendering. **The king . . . took him** to deport him, for he was too badly infected by pro-Egypt influences to be a good vassal. **Eighth year of his reign.** Nisan 10 (April 22), 597 B.C. (Thiele, *op. cit.*, p. 163). **15. He carried away Jehoiachin to Babylon.** Ration tablets from Babylon for Jehoiachin and five sons have been found (see BA, Dec., 1942, pp. 49-55). **16. All the men of might . . . and apt for war.** Specific classifications of those listed in verse **14.**

4) Reign of Zedekiah. 24:17-20.

17. Made Mattaniah . . . king. An uncle of Jehoiachin (cf. Jer 22:30). Matthew records Christ's legal line through Jehoiachin; Luke traces his actual line through Nathan and Mary. Jeremiah's prediction was fulfilled. However, Jehoiachin was still regarded as king of Judah (II Kgs 25:27). **Zedekiah.** A third son of Josiah, Jehoiachin's uncle, brother of Jehoahaz (23:31). Note that Jer 52:1-34 (lacking II Kgs 25:22-26) and II Kgs 24:18–25:30 (lacking Jer 52:28-30) reveal a common source. **19. Did . . . evil.** He broke the covenant. **20. Through the anger of the Lord.** The sins of Judah reached a climax under Zedekiah and brought on her fall under a judgment previously pronounced (20:17; 23:27).

5) Siege and Fall of Jerusalem. 25:1-21.

1,2. In the ninth year . . . tenth month . . . tenth day. January 15, 588 B.C. (BASOR, 143, p. 23). **Came . . . against Jerusalem.** Because Zedekiah broke his oath of allegiance. **Unto the eleventh year.** The siege lasted one year, five months, and twenty-nine days (cf. Jer 37:5,11 for a break in the siege due to a campaign against Egypt; Wiseman, *op. cit.*, p. 30). **3,4. On the ninth day.** The people were weakened through famine, and the city fell. **A breach was made** (ASV). On July 19, 586. **6. They . . . brought him** (Zedekiah) **. . . to Riblah.** (See Jer 39:2-5 for evidence that Nebuchadrezzar's generals took Jerusalem.) Zedekiah was judged as a rebel. **7. Slew the sons.** To put an end to his intractable dynasty. **Put out the eyes of Zedekiah** because he would not do the Lord's will.

Verses **8-17** record the destruction of Jerusalem. **8. In the fifth month,** i.e., four weeks after the breach. **Nineteenth year.** Not to be confused with an eighteenth year, but the actual nineteenth year of Nebuchadrezzar (according to BASOR, 143, p. 26, it was Aug. 15, 586 B.C.; cf. Thiele, *op. cit.*, p. 164). **Nebuzar-adan** [chief executioner] **burnt the house of the Lord . . . the king's house. . . . And all the army . . . brake down the walls.** The destruction of Jerusalem as a resistance fortress fulfilled the forecasts of 20:17; 23:27.

The Babylonians lost no time in liquidating the resistance leaders. **18-21. The captain of the guard took Seraiah,** an ancestor of Ezra (Ezr 7:1) **and Zephaniah,** probably the son of Maaseiah (II Kgs 23:4; cf. Jer 21:7; 24; 25; 29) **and the three keepers** or guards, one at each temple gate, heads of soldiery: **And . . . an officer . . . over the men of war, and five men,** chief royal officers, **and threescore men** who were leaders in the revolt. All were taken **to Riblah** to Nebuchadrezzar. The words **smote . . . slew** denote the power and vigor with which Nebuchadrezzar finished the nation.

6) The Puppet Governor, Gedaliah. 25:22-26.

22. As for the people that remained in the land . . . he made Gedaliah . . . ruler. Gedaliah was a friend of Jeremiah (39:14); he was, therefore, pro-Babylon and for that reason was made governor. **23. Captains of the armies.** Or, of the *fields* (cf. Jer 52:7). Gedaliah, following the words of the Lord, advised cooperation with Assyria (II Kgs 25:24). **25. But . . . Ishmael.** Gedaliah, refusing to believe the warning concerning him (Jer 40:14), lost his life (Jer 41:2). Because Ishmael was of royal blood, he thought he should govern. **26. And all the people . . . came to Egypt.** These were of the pro-Egypt party, the party that helped bring down Judah.

E. Epilogue. The Release of Jehoiachin. 25:27-30.

27. In the seven and thirtieth year. The thirty-seventh year of his captivity, but the twenty-seventh day of the twelfth month of Evil-merodach's accession year. If this had been Jehoiachin's thirty-seventh year only, Evil-merodach's accession year would not have been mentioned. According to Thiele (*op. cit.*, p. 165), it was March 21, 561 B.C. **Did lift up the head.** Cf. Gen 40:13. Jehoiachin had been imprisoned after his deportation, and Evil-merodach released him. **28,29. Set his throne above . . . changed his prison garments.** His change was permanent. **Did eat bread . . . before him all the days of his life.** Because Jehoiachin was so treated, there was hope for restoration of the nation to its land.

BIBLIOGRAPHY

BURNEY, C. F. *Notes on the Hebrew Text of the Kings*. Oxford: The Clarendon Press, 1903.

FINEGAN, JACK. *Light From the Ancient Past*. Princeton: Princeton University Press, 1946.

FREE, J. P. *Archaeology and Bible History*. Wheaton, Ill.: Van Kampen Press, 1950.

GORDON, CYRUS H. *Introduction to Old Testament Times*. Ventnor, N. J.: Ventnor Publishers, 1953.

HONOR, L. L. *Sennacherib's Invasion of Palestine*. New York, 1926.

KRAELING, E. *Aram and Israel*. (Columbia University Oriental Series, Vol. 13.) New York: Columbia University Press, 1918.

LANGE, JOHN PETER. *The Books of Kings (A Commentary on the Holy Scriptures)*. Translated, edited, etc., by W. G. Sumner. New York: Charles Scribner's Sons, 1903.

LUCKENBILL, DAVID DANIEL. *Ancient Records of Assyria and Babylonia*. 2 vols. Chicago: University of Chicago Press, 1926.

———. *The Annals of Sennacherib*. Chicago: University of Chicago Press, 1924.

MCCOWN, C. C. *The Ladder of Progress in Palestine*. New York: Harper & Bros., 1943.

OLMSTEAD, A. T. *History of Assyria*. New York: Charles Scribner's Sons, 1923.

———. *History of Palestine and Syria to the Macedonian Conquest*. New York: Charles Scribner's Sons, 1931.

———. *Western Asia in the Days of Sargon of Assyria*. Lancaster, Pa.: Press of the New Era Printing Co., 1908.

———. "Western Asia in the Reign of Sennacherib," *Annual Report*, American Historical Association. Washington, 1913.

OPPENHEIM, BARON VON. *Tell Halaf, A New Culture in Oldest Mesopotamia*. New York and London: Putnam & Sons, 1933.

PARKER, R. A., and DUBERSTEIN, W. J. *Babylonian Chronology, 625 B.C.—A.D. 75*. Providence, R.I.: Brown University Press, 1956.

PAYNE, J. BARTON, *An Outline of Hebrew History*. Grand Rapids: Baker Book House, 1954.

PRITCHARD, JAMES B. (ed.). *Ancient Near Eastern Texts*. Princeton: Princeton University Press, 1955.

REED, W. L. *The Asherah in the Old Testament*. Fort Worth, Tex.: Texas Christian University Press, 1949.

ROGERS, ROBERT W. *Cuneiform Parallels to the Old Testament*. New York: Eaton & Mains, 1912.

THIELE, EDWIN R. *Mysterious Numbers of the Hebrew Kings*. Chicago: University of Chicago Press, 1955.

WISEMAN, D. J. *Chronicles of Chaldean Kings (626–556 B.C.) In the British Museum*. London: British Museum, 1956.

UNGER, MERRILL F. *Archaeology and the Old Testament*. Grand Rapids: Zondervan Publishing House, 1956.

FIRST CHRONICLES

INTRODUCTION

(for both I and II Chronicles)

Title. In the Hebrew Bible, the books of Chronicles are entitled *dibrê hay-yāmîm,* "The affairs (lit., *the words)* of the days." Other historical journals, which are now lost, such as the *"Dibrê hay-yāmîm* of King David" (I Chr 27:24), employed this same terminology. The name therefore signifies "The Annals," or, as suggested by Jerome, one of the Church Fathers, "The Chronicles," which became the designation of the books in English. The books of I and II Kings mention similar annals entitled *"Dibrê hay-yāmîm* of the kings of Israel" (e.g., I Kgs 14:19), or "of Judah" (I Kgs 14:29). Such citations, however, cannot refer to the present books of Chronicles, which were not written until one hundred years after Kings, but suggest other lost books, contemporary chronicles of Israelitish history.

Chronicles once existed as a single composition. The current division into two parts arose in the Greek translation, which was made some time before 150 B.C., though it now appears in all Bibles, including the printed editions of the Hebrew. In the original arrangement of the canon, moreover, Chronicles stands at the end of the Old Testament. Thus Christ in Lk 11:51 spoke of all the martyrs from Abel, in the first book (Gen 4), to Zechariah, in the last (II Chr 24).

Date and Authorship. The Chronicles do not state when, or by whom, they were written. The books record events down to Cyrus' decree of 538 B.C., which permitted the Jews to return from exile (II Chr 36:22). Their genealogies, moreover, mention King Jeconiah's grandson Zerubbabel (I Chr 3:19), who led the Jews in the return of 537. They then outline Zerubbabel's family down through two grandsons, Pelatiah and Jeshaiah (3:21), or to approximately 500 B.C. Four names follow, of men whose exact relationship to the king Jeconiah is not given in the text. But the family of the last of these, a certain Shecaniah (3:21), is traced down through seven great-great-grandchildren (3:24). Thus, if Shecaniah were of the same period as King Jeconiah, who was born in 616, these four additional generations would again bring us to approximately 500 B.C. as the earliest possible date for the composition of Chronicles, on the basis of the internal evidence.

The origin, however, of Chronicles is strongly suggested by its close relationship with another part of the Old Testament, namely the Book of Ezra, which describes the events from the decree of Cyrus down to 457 B.C. Hebrew tradition affirms that Ezra wrote Chronicles as well as Ezra, a conclusion confirmed by the modern scholarship of William F. Albright (JBL, 40 (1921), pp. 104-124); and the books do have the same style of language and type of contents. This is apparent from such matters as the frequent lists and genealogies, the similar stress upon ritual, and their common devotion to the law of Moses. The closing verses, moreover, of Chronicles (II Chr 36:22,23) are repeated as the opening verses of Ezra (1:1-3 a). This seems to indicate that Ezra and Chronicles were originally one consecutive history, composed by Ezra at about 450 B.C. The very fact that II Chronicles breaks off in the middle of Cyrus' decree suggests that when Ezra was inspired to incorporate his book of Chronicles as the concluding portion of the Old Testament, he was thus deliberately guiding his readers back to his book of Ezra. This latter half of his original writing seems already to have been placed by God in the canon of Scripture so as to continue the historical record of the books of Kings. Then, since Ezra is separated from Chronicles in the Hebrew arrangement by Nehemiah's autobiography, which mentions the king Darius II who began to reign in 423 B.C. (Neh 12:22), we may date the incorporation of Chronicles and the close of the Old Testament canon at about 420 B.C.

If Ezra the scribe (Ezr 7:6) was the writer of Chronicles, his "scribism" may well account for the detailed acknowledgments of historical sources in these books. These sources include the writings of such early prophets as Samuel, Nathan, Gad (I Chr 29:29), Ahijah, Iddo, Shemaiah (II Chr 9:29; 12:15), Jehu the son of Hanani (20:34), and such later ones as Isaiah (32:32) and Hozai (33:19, ASV). The chronicler's major reference work was "The book of the kings of Judah and Israel" (16:11; 25:26, etc.), with "The commentary (Hebrew *midrash*) of the book of the kings" (24: 27). But though I and II Chronicles often follow I and II Kings closely, our books of Kings cannot be the source here intended. For verses such as I Chr 9:1 and II Chr 27:7 refer to "The book of the kings" for additional data on certain genealogies or wars about which nothing further actually appears in our canonical books. This major reference must have been a larger court record, now lost, which also incorporated some of the prophetic writings, as Jehu's (II Chr 20: 34) or Isaiah's chapters 36–39 (II Chr 32:32). From this source both Kings and Chronicles then drew (cf. Isa 36–39 with II Kgs 18:13–20:19 and II Chr 32).

Occasion for Writing. Ezra's zeal for the establishment of the law of Moses (Ezr 7:10) led him in 458 B.C. to return from Babylon to the Jewish community in Palestine. He took immediate measures to restore the temple worship (Ezr 7:19-23,27; 8:33,34) and to eliminate the mixed marriages that a number of the Jews had contracted with pagan neighbors (Ezr 9–10). In light of the wide powers granted Ezra by the Persian king (Ezr 7:18,25), he seems to have been the one who commenced the rebuilding of Jerusalem's fortifications (Ezr 4:8-16). It was not until Ezra was joined by Nehemiah in 444 B.C. that the walls were actually reconstructed (Ezr 4:17-23; Neh 6:15,16) and the Mosaic law was fully recognized (Neh 8). But that the chronicler's purpose was to stimulate this rebuilding of the theocracy is evidenced by the features of the book itself.

In comparison with the parallel histories in Genesis, I and II Samuel, and I and II Kings, the books of Chronicles, with their goal of maintaining racial and religious purity, are weighted with genealogies (e.g., I Chr 1–9). Again, because of their goal of preserving a proper priesthood and worship, they devote greater emphasis to the law of Moses, to the Temple (I Chr 22), and to the ark, the Levites, and the singers (I Chr 13; 15; 16). They omit the detailed activities of the kings (II Sam 9; I Kgs 3:16-28) and also extensive narratives of the prophets (as I Kgs 17–22: 40; or II Kgs 1:1–8:15). This characteristic stress on priesthood seems to account for the books' position in the third (non-prophetic) division of the Hebrew canon, separated from I and II Samuel and I and II Kings, whose moralistic emphases place them with the prophets in the second division. Finally, the books' goal of providing encouragement for those who had been disillusioned by post-Exilic hardships explains their rehearsals of Judah's former, God-given victories (II Chr 13;14;20;25). This goal also explains the omission from I and II Chronicles of David's earlier lack of success (II Sam 1–4), his later sins and defeats (II Sam 11–21), Solomon's failures (I Kgs 11), and indeed the whole inglorious history of the northern kingdom of Israel.

Because of these features, most of today's non-evangelical critics of the Old Testament reject I and II Chronicles as being a propaganda work of fifth century Levites, with extensive (and conflicting) revisions as late as 250 B.C. (so Adam C. Welch, Robert Pfeiffer, and W.A.L. Elmslie). The book, it is argued, cannot reflect authentic history but simply invents "what ought to have happened" (IB, III, 341). Its large figures, such as the 1,000,000 invading Ethiopians (II Chr 14:9), are subject to particular ridicule. Legitimate explanations, however, are forthcoming in such cases (see below, or Edward J. Young, *An Introduction to the Old Testament*, pp. 388-390). This censure, moreover, is based upon liberalism's previous rejection of the Mosaic authorship of the Pentateuch, the rituals of which receive validation throughout the Chronicles record. Disbelieving criticism is thus compelled in advance to deny the historicity of the book. Yet excavations at ancient Ugarit have confirmed the authenticity in Canaan of just such elaborate rituals, and in the very century that Moses was leading Israel out of Egypt (J. W. Jack, *The Ras Shamra Tablets: Their Bearing on the Old Testament*, p. 29 ff.). Albright has noted how many of the historical statements found uniquely in I and II Chronicles have been established by archaeological discoveries (BASOR, 100 (1945), p. 18). Furthermore, it is significant that while the books of Chronicles stress the bright side of Jewish history, they do not deny the failures. They rather assume such prior knowledge on the part of their readers (as in I Chr 22:8; 28:3), and they go on to emphasize, for example, the more encouraging *second* anointing of Solomon (I Chr 29:22) or the more exemplary *first* ways of David (II Chr 17:3). The prophetic judgments of I and II Kings and the priestly hopes of I and II Chronicles are both true and both necessary. The morality of the former is fundamental, but the redemption of the latter is the more distinctive feature of Christian faith.

OUTLINE

I. Genealogies. 1:1–9:44.
  A. Patriarchs. 1:1-54.
  B. Judah. 2:1–4:23.
    1. The clan of Hezron. 2:1-55.
    2. The family of David. 3:1-24.
    3. Other clans of Judah. 4:1-23.
  C. Simeon. 4:24-43.
  D. Trans-Jordan tribes. 5:1-26.
  E. Levi. 6:1-81.
  F. Six other tribes. 7:1–8:40; 9:35-44.
    1. Summaries. 7:1-40.
    2. Benjamin. 8:1-40; 9:35-44.
  G. Jerusalem's inhabitants. 9:1-34.
II. The reign of David. 10:1–29:30.
  A. Background: the death of Saul. 10:1-14.
  B. David's rise. 11:1–20:8.
    1. David established in Jerusalem; his heroes. 11:1–12:40.
    2. The ark sought. 13:1-14.
    3. Independence from the Philistines. 14:1-17.
    4. The ark brought to Jerusalem. 15:1–16:43.
    5. Nathan's prophecy. 17:1-27.
    6. Conquests and administration. 18:1-17.
    7. Victories over Ammon. 19:1–20:3.
    8. Philistine wars. 20:4-8.
  C. David's latter days. 21:1–29:30.
    1. The census. 21:1-30.
    2. Temple preparations. 22:1-19.
    3. Levitical organization. 23:1–26:32.
    4. The civil organization. 27:1-34.
    5. Final words. 28:1–29:30.

COMMENTARY

I. Genealogies. 1:1–9:44.

A. Patriarchs. 1:1-54. This first chapter summarizes the development of the human race. It begins with Adam and follows his genealogical descent through Abraham to Jacob and Esau. Its purpose is to define the place of God's chosen people in world history. Branches of the human race remote from Israel are therefore dismissed with but brief mention, if noticed at all; while those more closely related to Israel are treated in greater detail. Most of the material is drawn directly from the records of Genesis.

4. Noah. The chronicler expects his readers to understand that Shem, Ham, and Japheth are the three sons of Noah, and not successive generations (Gen 5).

5. The sons of Japheth. Verses 5-23 reproduce the table of Genesis 10, with but minor differences of spelling. The Japhethites include such peoples of Europe and northern Asia as Javan (Ionia, the Greeks), Gomer (the Cimmerians of the Russian plains), Tubal and Meshech (the ancient Tabali and Mushki of the Turkish plateau), and Madai (the Medes, of Iran).

8. The sons of Ham. Ham's descendants occupy Africa: Put (Libya), Mizraim (Egypt), and Cush (Ethiopia). But Ham also settled in southwest Asia: Canaan (Palestine), and the Cushite Nimrod in Babylonia (cf. Gen 10:10; and note how the second river of Eden borders "Cush," 2:13).

17. The sons of Shem. After the earth was divided (v. 19), which probably refers to the confusion of languages at Babel (Gen 11:1-9), the Semites stayed closest to mankind's home in central Asia, though ranging from Lud (Lydia, of Asia Minor) and Aram (Syria) to Elam (north of the Persian Gulf). From Arphaxad came Eber (i.e., "Hebrew"), the ancestor of Abram and other unsettled peoples, known in ancient history as the Khabiru or Apiru. **Uz, Hul, Gether,** and **Meshech** were sons of Aram (Gen 10:23). **27. Abram; the same is Abraham.** His descent is drawn from Gen 11:10-26, and the change of his name is described in 17:5. **28. The sons of Abraham.** Though Isaac is named here, verses 28-33 deal with the descendants of Abraham by his subordinate wives, **Hagar** and **Keturah** (v. 32; see Gen 25:1-4, 12-16). The chronicler mentions these nomadic Arabian descendants before he turns to Sarah's son Isaac, who was the child of promise.

35. The sons of Esau. Then, of Isaac's twin sons, Esau and his Edomite offspring are briefly listed, before Jacob and the Israelitish people, who are the theme of I and II Chronicles, are introduced. Verses 35-54 summarize the table of Genesis 36 with but scribal variations in spelling. **36. Timna** was not a son of Eliphaz, but his mistress, and a daughter of Seir (v. 39). She bore Amalek (Gen 36:12), and her name was attached to a district in Edom (v. 51). **38. Seir** was of the "Horites" (Gen 36:20), or Hurrians, an important ancient people, some of whom had settled in Edom before the arrival of Esau (Deut 2:12,22). **42. Uz.** Job, who was from this man's area (Job 1:1), may thus have been an early Edomite descendant of Esau (cf. Lam 4:21). Compare Esau's son Eliphaz, father of Teman (v. 36), after whom Job's friend, Eliphaz the Temanite (Job 2:11), may have been named.

51. Hadad died also. His death is not mentioned in the corresponding section of the Pentateuch (Gen 36:39), probably because he was a contemporary of Moses, but had, of course, long been dead at the time of Ezra and the composition of the Chronicles. **The dukes of Edom.** These were tribal leaders, or "chiefs" (ASV).

B. Judah. 2:1–4:23. The land occupied by the Jews who returned from Exile consisted primarily of the territories of Judah and Benjamin. The leading elements, moreover, in Ezra's community were likewise drawn from these two tribes (Ezr 1:5; 10:9), of which the former southern kingdom had been composed. In his attempt, therefore, to establish national purity, the chronicler's major emphasis rested upon Judah (most of chapters 2–4) and Benjamin (much of 7–9). It was Judah that was particularly prominent (Ezr 4:4,6), from whom the very name "Jew" is derived.

1) The Clan of Hezron. 2:1-55. Of the five sons of Judah, the first two died without issue. Pharez, however, who was the fourth, produced Hezron, under whose headship were included some of the leading elements of Judah's later population. This chapter therefore moves rapidly to this grandson of Judah and concentrates upon the relationships within his clan. Some names are of whole communities, descended from Hezron, as Kirjath-jearim and Bethlehem (vv. 50, 51). **4. Tamar.** The details on Judah, Tamar, Er, and Onan are found in Genesis 38.

6. The sons of Zerah. These appear to be five later descendants, mentioned because of their importance: **Zimri,** who produced the Carmi of the next verse, is called Zabdi in Josh 7:1; the other four "Ezrahites" (Zerah) were famous for wisdom (I Kgs 4:31) and composed Ps 88; 89, but are not to be confused with Ethan and Heman, musicians of David, who were from Levi, not Judah (I Chr 15:15).

7. Achar, the troubler of Israel. His transgression occurred under Joshua at Jericho. See Josh 7, where the name is *Achan.*

10. Of the five sons of Hezron, **Ram** is listed first, being the ancestor of the royal family of David (vv. 10-17; cf. Ruth 4:18-22). **15. Ozem the sixth.** A seventh son is mentioned in I Sam 16:10; 17:12, but not named. He may have died in childhood. **16. Zeruiah and Abigail** were half-sisters of David, by a different father (II Sam 17:25). Their sons were famous soldiers under their half-uncle, David (see II Sam 3:10,20; 19:13). **18.** The branch of **Caleb** (cf.

v. 42), or Chelubai (v. 9), **son of Hezron,** is next traced (vv. 18-20, 42-55). He is not to be confused with Caleb, the faithful spy (4:15), who came three hundred years later. **20. Bezaleel** became the chief craftsman in building the Tabernacle (Ex 31:1,2). **23. The towns of Jair.** See Num 32:41,42; Deut 3:14. Then read with the ASV, *Geshur and Aram took the towns* . . .

25. The descendants of **Jerahmeel the firstborn of Hezron** (vv. 25-41) occupied an extensive area in the Negeb, or south country of Judah (I Sam 27:10; 30:29). **35. Sheshan gave him his daughter,** probably Ahlai (v. 31).

42. The sons of Mareshah (a variant of Mesha?) **the father of Hebron.** Read, from the Hebrew (KD), *and Mareshah also had Abi-Hebron.* **47. Jahdai**['s] exact relationship to the preceding has been lost. **49. The daughter of Caleb, Achsa,** was actually a distant descendant of this Caleb, son of Hezron, and an immediate daughter of Caleb the faithful spy, son of Jephunneh. She is famous as the bride of Othniel, given him because of his conquest of Debir (Josh 15:15-19; Jud 1:11-15).

50. The sons of Caleb the son of Hur. Read, "The (grand)sons of Caleb (were): the son of Hur, (namely) Shobal, etc." **Ephratah** is Caleb's wife, Ephrath (see v. 19). **55. Kenites** of the family of Hobab, brother-in-law of Moses, became incorporated by marriage or adoption into the tribe of Judah (Jud 1:16). J(eh)onadab, a later descendant of **Rechab,** was noted as a reformer and prohibitionist. To prevent his family's corruption, he maintained the primitive forms of nomadic life (II Kgs 10:15-28; Jer 35).

2) The Family of David. 3:1-24. This chapter traces the royal house of Judah from David, its founder, down to about 500 B.C. Under the Persians the Jewish community was permitted no king, and indeed prophecy had stated that no purely human descendant of David would ever again occupy the throne of Israel (Jer 22:30). Post-Exilic interest, however, still centered in this family. For not only did the house of David furnish civic leaders (Zech 12:7,8), including Zerubbabel, the governor of the early restoration, but through this house there would arise Israel's ultimate hope. They looked for that greater Son of David, a man, but more than a man, God's "fellow" (Zech 13:7). Through this Messiah, the Deity pierced (Zech 12:10), would come redemption (Zech 13:1) and the kingdom of God on earth (Zech 14:9).

1. The second Daniel is known as Chileab in II Sam 3:3. **5. Bath-shua** is elsewhere called Bath-sheba. This list of sons appears with minor variants in 14:4-7 and II Sam 5:14-16. It was Solomon whom God selected to succeed David (I Chr 22:9), rather than one of the older sons, at least three of whom were murdered in family feuds. **6. Elishama and Eliphelet.** Rather read, *Elishua and Elpalet* (as in 14:5); they would not have had the same names as their brothers in verse 8. **9. Tamar their sister.** See II Sam 13 for the account of how she was raped by Amnon and avenged by Absalom.

10. Abia. Elsewhere in Chronicles the AV renders this name Abijah. **15. Shallum** is also called Jehoahaz (II Kgs 23; II Chr 36; cf. Jer 22:11). He was, in fact, older than Zedekiah (II Kgs 24:18), but had an inferior length of reign. **16. Jeconiah** is also called Coniah (Jer 22:24, 28; 37:1) and Jehoiachin (II Kgs 24; II Chr 36). **Zedekiah** was **his son** only in the loose Hebrew usage of son for "successor" or "relative." Actually, he was his uncle (v. 15).

17. Assir is probably not a proper noun and should be rendered, *the captive* (ASV). **Salathiel** must have been simply a legal (adopted) son, for Lk 3:27 notes his true father to have been a certain Neri.

19. Zerubbabel is often reckoned as a son of Pedaiah's brother Salathiel (or Shealtiel; see Hag 1:1,12; Ezr 3:2; Mt 1:12; Lk 3:27), perhaps by the custom of the levirate, if it be assumed that Salathiel died without seed (cf. Deut 25:5-10). Zerubbabel was a leader in the return of the Jews to Palestine after the Exile, 538 B.C. (Ezr 2:2; 3:2).

21. Rephaiah, Arnan, Obadiah, and **Shechaniah.** The exact connection of these four with Jeconiah does not appear. If they were brothers, the fifth generation would again bring the line to about 500 B.C., some time before Ezra and the compilation of the Chronicles. See above, Introduction, *Date.*

3) Other Clans of Judah. 4:1-23. Verses 1-7 provide a supplement to the genealogies of Hezron in chapter 2. The clan relationships of the ten leaders listed in verses 8-20 are unclear in the text,

either because of gaps in the records available to Ezra or because of subsequent corruption in copying. Verses 21-23 outline the clan of Judah's third son, Shelah.

1. The sons of Judah. But they are by no means brothers (see above, 2:4-7,50). **2. Reaiah the son of Shobal** is called Haroeh in 2:52, to which this verse constitutes a supplement; as do, also, verses 3,4 to 2:19,50; and verses 5-7 to 2:24. 8. The exact connections of **Coz, Jabez** (v. 9), **Chelub** (v. 11), **Kenaz** (v. 13), **Meonothai** (v. 14), **Jehaleleel** (v. 16), **Ezra** (v. 17), **Hodiah** (v. 19), **Shimon,** and **Ishi** (v. 20) within the tribe of Judah are not given.

9. Jabez and **sorrow** are associated in Hebrew, *Ya'ăbes* and *'oṣeb;* and the name is rendered, *He causes sorrow.* But Jabez' prayer of faith (v. 10) brought blessing instead of *'oṣbî* ("grieving me").

13. Othniel, son of Kenaz. This Kenizzite was adopted from his wilderness people (Gen 15:19; 36:42) into Israel, tribe of Judah, and became the first of the Judges (Jud 3:9,10). **14. Charashim** means *engravers.* **15. Caleb the son of Jephunneh** was Othniel's (considerably) older brother (Jud 1:13; cf. Josh 14:6) and the faithful spy (Num 13; 14). **17. And she bare.** That is, Mered's Egyptian wife, Bithiah (v. 18). **18. For, his wife Jehudijah bare,** read with the RSV, *But his Jewish wife bore . . .* **19. For, The sons of his wife Hodiah,** read with the ASV, *The sons of the wife of Hodiah.*

23. The Hebrew words for **plants and hedges** are better taken as place names: *Netaim and Gederah.* **These were the potters . . . they dwelt with the king.** Archaeology has demonstrated the existence of hereditary guilds of potters during the divided kingdom (930–586 B.C.), with royal patronage, and using regular jar-stamps from generation to generation (R. A. Stewart Macalister, *Palestine Exploration Fund Quarterly Statement* (July and Oct., 1905), pp. 244,245,328,329).

C. Simeon. 4:24-43. Simeon, with Levi, was scattered among the tribes because of the massacre of Shechem (Gen 34:24-30; 49:5-7). Specifically, Simeon was made to inherit the southwestern corner of Palestine and virtually merged with Judah (Josh 19:1-9; cf. Jud 1:3). After the division of the kingdom, however, elements of Simeon either moved to the north, or at least adopted its religious practices (cf. the mention of Beer-sheba in Amos 5:5, etc.), and were counted with the ten northern tribes (II Chr 15:9; 34:6). **Others carried on** a semi-nomadic life in such isolated spots as they could seize, examples being the two migrations noted in verses 34-41 and 42,43.

24. The sons of Simeon. This genealogy enlarges on the family of Simeon as outlined in Gen 46:10; Ex 6:16; Num 26:12-14. **31. Their cities unto the reign of David.** After the Philistine wars, certain of Simeon's towns, as Ziklag (v. 30), became Judean (I Sam 27:6).

40. They of Ham. Probably Canaanites, Hamitic in descent (1:8). **41. And the habitations.** Read, *And the Meunim* (ASV), an Edomite tribe (cf. II Chr 26:6; 20:1 note). **43. Amalekites that were escaped.** Both Saul and David had devastated these ancient enemies (I Sam 14:48; 15:7; II Sam 8:12).

D. Trans-Jordan Tribes. 5:1-26. Just prior to the conquest of Canaan, Israel had been forced to engage in battle with the nations lying east of the Jordan (Num 21:21-35). Upon their defeat, Moses had granted their territories to the tribes of Reuben (I Chr 5:1-10) and Gad (vv. 11-17) and to half of the tribe of Manasseh (vv. 23,24). This chapter is based both on pre-Exilic records and on what may have been a post-Exilic census (v. 7). It describes their lands and clan genealogies, their early faith that gave them a great victory over the Ishmaelites (vv. 16-22), and their later apostasy that caused their exile to Assyria (vv. 25,26).

1. Reuben . . . defiled his father's bed. With Bilhah (Gen 35:22; 49:4). **His birthright was given to . . . Joseph,** as the first son of Rachel, the wife whom Jacob **(Israel)** loved. **2. Judah prevailed.** As predicted by Jacob (Gen 49:8,9) and fulfilled in David (II Sam 5:1-3), the precursor of Jesus Christ (Mt 1:6). **3. The sons of Reuben.** This section enlarges on his family as noted in Gen 46:9; Ex 6:19; Num 26:5-7. **4.** Which of the preceding four was **Joel's** father is not stated.

6. Tilgath-pilneser (-pileser) III of Assyria took the border tribes captive in 733 B.C. (vv. 22,26; II Kgs 15:29), eleven years before the fall of Samaria to Shalmaneser V (or possibly to his successor, Sargon II).

16. Suburbs. Rather, *pasturelands.*

17. Jotham and **Jeroboam** II reigned 751–736 and 793–753 B.C. respectively.

19. Hagar was the mother of Ishmael, the ancestor of **Jetur, Nephish,** and other Arabian tribes (Gen 25:15).

26. Pul was the name of Tiglath-pileser prior to his accession. Therefore read, "God stirred up the spirit of Pul, even the spirit of . . . "

E. Levi. 6:1-81. Though both Simeon and Levi had been cursed to a tribal scattering among Israel (Gen 34:24-30; 49:5-7), Levi's subsequent devotion (Ex 32:26-28) converted this dispersion into one of blessing and religious leadership (Deut 33:8-11). Ezra himself was a Levitical priest and proud of his genealogy (Ezr 7:1-5); and the post-Exilic community centered about the services of the tribe of Levi (cf. Ezra's concern for their presence, 8:15-20). An authentic genealogy, however, was essential for Levitical standing (cf. Ezr 2:59-63); hence the significance of this chapter. It enlarges on the family of Levi as noted in Gen 46:11; Ex 6:17-19; Num 3:17-20; 26:57-62, and includes the high-priestly line (vv. 3-15,49-53), the three clans of Levi (vv. 16-30), the Levitical singers (vv. 31-48), and the scattered territories assigned to Levi (vv. 54-81). See also chapters 23–26.

3. Nadab and Abihu were killed in the wilderness for sacrilege and left no children (Lev 10:1,2; Num 3:4).

4. Eleazar, Phinehas (I), **Abishua.** The relatively short list of high priests that follows cannot be complete for the 860 years between the Exodus and the fall of Jerusalem. It does not include the descendants of Ithamar, who held office under the last Judges and the early kingdom: Eli, Phinehas II, Ahitub I, Ahimelech I (= Ahijah), Abiathar, and Ahimelech II (I Sam 14:3; 22:20; II Sam 8:17); or certain other high priests: Amariah II (II Chr 19:11), Jehoiada (II Chr 22:11), Zechariah (?) (II Chr 24:20), Urijah (II Kgs 16:10), Azariah III (II Chr 31:10), and Meraioth (I Chr 9:11).

8. Zadok (I) was high priest under David and Solomon, 970 B.C. **10. Azariah** (II) . . . **in the temple.** This may refer to his resisting Uzziah's attempt to take over priestly functions, 751 B.C. (II Chr 26:17). **13. Hilkiah** was the high priest who discovered the book of the Law given by Moses, thus causing Josiah's reformation of 621 B.C. (II Chr 34:14).

16,17,20,43. Gershom is the Gershon of verse 1 and elsewhere.

22. Amminadab is apparently another name for Izhar (vv. 18,38). **Korah** was swallowed by the earth for rebelling against Moses (Num 16:32). **25.** The names that follow indicate that this must be **Elkanah** II, the son of Shaul (v. 24) and great-great-great-great grandson of Ebiasaph (vv. 36,37), not Elkanah I, the brother of Ebiasaph, just mentioned in 6:23. **Ahimoth,** the son (not brother) of **Amasai,** is also called Mahath (v. 35). **26.** This is Elkanah (III), son of Ahimoth (v. 25). **Zophai, Nahath,** and **Eliab** (v. 27) are Zuph, Toah, and Eliel (vv. 34,35). **27.** This **Elkanah** (IV) is the famous Levite from Mount Ephraim, husband of Hannah and father of Samuel (I Sam 1:1). **28. Vashni.** Hebrew for *and the second.* This verse should therefore read, "The firstborn, Joel; and the second, Abiah," Joel's name being supplied from verse 33 and I Sam 8:2.

32. Tabernacle of the congregation. *Tent of meeting.* The place where God met the people, and only secondarily, the people each other (cf. Ex 29:42,43). **42, 44. Ethan** and **Kishi** are also called *Jeduthun* (25:1) and *Kushaiah* (15:17).

54. The Hebrew for **castles** means "encampments" or "settlements." **Theirs was the lot.** The first lot in the 1400 B.C. distribution of the land (Josh 21:10). The following verses on the Levitical cities compare with Josh 21:3-40. **56. They gave to Caleb.** As promised by Moses and Joshua (Josh 14:6-15). **57. The city of refuge.** On these six cities see Num 35; Deut 19:1-10; Josh 20. **60. Thirteen cities.** Only eleven have been named in our present text, but the others are to be supplied from Joshua 21. **61. Cities** were **given out of the half tribe of Manasseh,** and also out of Ephraim and Dan (cf. v. 66 and Josh 21:5).

F. Six Other Tribes. 7:1–8:40; 9:35-44. Although Judah and Benjamin (with Levi) dominated post-Exilic Israel, the other tribes that had once composed the northern kingdom were not unrepresented. Many had fled to Judah with the fall of Samaria in 722 B.C. (I Chr 9:1; II Chr 30:1,2; cf. 34:6); and others regained their place among God's people during the exile of 586–538 (cf. Ezk 37:15-23), and returned with the rest under Zerubbabel and Ezra (Ezr 6:17; 8:35; cf. the Anna of the tribe of Asher in Lk 2:36). The so-called lost ten tribes, and their genealogies, were matters of personal involvement for a number of Ezra's contemporaries!

1) Summaries. 7:1-40. On the basis of Genesis 46 and Numbers 26, I Chronicles 7 outlines the significant clans of six tribes: Issachar (vv. 1-5), Benjamin (vv. 6-12), Naphtali (v. 13), Western Manasseh (vv. 14-19), Ephraim (vv. 20-29), and Asher (vv. 30-40). The chronicler thus makes no mention of either Dan or Zebulun. Attempts have been made to account for this on grounds of textual corruption, but it may merely have been that these tribes had little significance to the society of Ezra.

1. The sons of Issachar. These verses expand the data of Gen 46:13 and Num 26:23-25.

6. The sons of Benjamin . . . three. There were others as well (see 8:1). These paragraphs supplement and provide slight variants to Gen 46:21 and Num 26:38-41. **12. Ir** = Iri (v. 7), and **Aher** may perhaps be identified with Ahiram (Num 26:38).

13. The sons of Naphtali. These verses repeat Gen 46:24 and Num 26:48-50, with but minor differences of spelling. The names are of grand-**sons of Bilhah,** the maid of Rachel and mother of Naphtali (Gen 30:3-8).

14. The sons of Manasseh; Ashriel. This man was a great-grandson of Manasseh through Machir and Gilead. For the more complete records of western Manasseh, see Num 26:29-34; Josh 17:2-5. **15. The second,** many generations later, **was Zelophehad,** who **had daughters** that inherited on an equality with males (Num 26:33; 27:1; 36:2). **19. Shemidah** was another great-grandson of Manasseh through Machir and Gilead.

20. The sons of Ephraim. These verses enlarge on Num 26:35-37. **21. Men . . . born in that land,** in Canaan, **came down** to Goshen, on the border of Egypt toward Palestine, where the Israelites had settled under Joseph. **23. Beriah, because it went evil.** The Hebrew words are *b^erîʿâ* because *b^erāʿâ*. **27. Non.** The name of J(eh)oshua's father is usually spelled Nun. **28.** For **Gaza,** which is too far from Ephraim, read rather "Ayyah."

30. The sons of Asher. These verses enlarge on Gen 46:17 and Num 26:44-47.

34,35. Shamer and **Helem** appear as Shomer and Hotham (?) in verse 32.

38,39. Jether and **Ulla** appear as Ithran and Ara in verses 37 and 38.

2) Benjamin. 8:1-40; 9:35-44. This section constitutes a major supplement to 7:6-12, as well as to Gen 46:21 and Num 26:38-40. For the tribe of Benjamin not only produced the family of King Saul, that was prominent for many generations (8:33-40; 9:39-44), but also ranked second to Judah itself in post-Exilic Jewish society (Neh 11:4,7,31,36).

6. Neither **Ehud's** ancestry in Benjamin, nor that of **Shaharaim** (v. 8), is preserved. **7. Naaman, Ahiah,** and particularly **Gera,** were the ones who took away Ehud's descendants, Uzza and Ahihud, in this undated captivity. **8. Shaharaim . . . sent them away.** That is, he divorced his two wives, an early example of moral deterioration within Israel.

17,18. Meshullam and **Ishmerai** may be variants for Misham and Shemed (v. 12). **21. Shimhi** is probably a variant for Shema (v. 13). **27. Jeroham** may be identified with Jeremoth (v. 14).

29. The father of Gibeon: Jehiel (9:35; or, as in I Sam 9:1; 14:51, Abiel). **32. Mikloth** was Jehiel's youngest son (9:37,38).

33. Ner, Jehiel's fifth son (9:36), was grandfather to Saul, the first king of Israel (1050–1010 B.C.), and father to Abner, Saul's military commander and uncle (I Sam 14:50,51). **Abinadab** = Ishui (I Sam 14:49). **Esh-baal.** *Man of Baal,* seems to have been the original name of Ish-bosheth (II Sam 2:8); but in Samuel *bōshet,* "shame," is substituted for the name of the shameful idol. Saul, however, may not have had the idol Baal in mind when he named his son, but simply the Hebrew word *baʿal,* "master." The name would then mean, "man of the Master," perhaps referring to God. **34.** Similarly, **Merib-baal,** "hero of Baal," or "a warrior is Baal," is styled Mephibosheth in Samuel, or *one who scatters (?) shame* (II Sam 4:4).

G. Jerusalem's Inhabitants. 9:1-34. After a transitional verse (9:1) that serves as a conclusion to the genealogies of Israel (I Chr 2–8), this section moves to an enumeration of the inhabitants of Jerusalem, prior to the city's capture and destruction in 586 B.C. It consists primarily of a listing of certain heads of large family groups or clans that once lived in the capital: clans of Judah (vv. 4-6); of Benjamin (vv. 7-9); of the priests (vv. 10-13); of the Levites in general (vv. 14-16); and of the porters or temple gate-keepers (17-19a). This is followed by a description of the duties of the Levites (19b-33). A knowledge of these constituent elements in the population of pre-Exilic Jerusalem was of prime significance in Ezra's subsequent campaign to restore legitimate theocracy to Judah. An attempt, however, is often made to equate this material with the later listing, found in Neh 11:3-24, of Jerusalem's *post*-Exilic groups. But despite a similarity in over-all arrangement, the specific differences between these two lists are pronounced; and only by a forced rendering of I Chr 9:2 (as for example in the RSV) can the plausibility of the later dating of I Chronicles 9 be sustained.

1. **The book of the kings.** This refers to some court record, now lost; see above, Introduction, *Authorship*.

2. **The first inhabitants.** This must refer to Israel's population before the carrying away of 586, just mentioned. **Nethinims** means *given ones*. They were temple slaves, such as the men of Midian (Num 31:47, in context) and of Gibeon (Josh 9:23, in context), organized into a distinct group by David (Ezr 8:20).

3. The scattered individuals and families of **Ephraim, and Manasseh** are not mentioned in the lists that follow, which are limited to the heads of larger family groups or clans. **5. The Shilonites.** Read, *Shelanites*, that is, of Shelah. These, with Pharez and Zerah, constituted the three clans of Judah (Num 26:20).

10. Jedaiah, Jehoiarib, and Jachin appear to be names of the second, first, and twenty-first respectively, of the twenty-four priestly courses established by David (I Chr 24:7-18), rather than of individuals. **11. Azariah** (IV) . . . **the ruler of the house of God,** was high priest in about 600 B.C., shortly before the Captivity (6:13). **12. Adaiah** was a **son of Malchijah,** David's fifth course (24:9); and **Maasiai . . . of Immer,** the sixteenth (24:14).

14. Merari was one of the three clan-founding sons of Levi. **15,16. Asaph** and **Jeduthun** were two of David's chief musicians, 1000 B.C.

18. Porters in the companies . . . of Levi means, "the gate-keepers for the stations of the Levites," as they had once encamped about the Tabernacle (Num 3:23,29,35,38). **19. Shallum,** the porter, was a **son of Korah;** for though Korah himself was destroyed, his clan continued as an important part of the Kohath division of Levi (see above, 6:22 and its note). **The tabernacle** refers to David's tent form of God's house (16:1), prior to the construction of the permanent Temple. **20.** The office of porter thus dates back to **Phinehas the son of Eleazar,** who was the son of Aaron and his successor as high priest in the wilderness. **21. Zechariah** had served as porter under David (26:2). **22. Samuel's** interest is illuminated by his having served as a porter in his youth (I Sam 3:15). With **David** came the final organization of the porters.

31. The things that were made in the pans. The flat cakes used in the "meat" (meal) offerings. **32. The shew bread.** The bread set out in rows on the golden table, symbolizing the communion of the redeemed with God (Lev 24:5,6).

33. These are the singers refers to the men of verses 15,16; even as verse 34 summarizes the whole section.

The rest of this chapter, 9:35-44, is practically identical with 8:29-38 (which see), except for minor matters, such as the spelling of names. It serves to introduce the record of the end of Saul's reign (ch. 10, following).

II. The Reign of David. 10:1–29:30.

A. Background: The Death of Saul. 10:1-14. The chronicler's interest centers in King David. He was both the founder of the royal dynasty of Judah and a heroic example of the success that will crown the endeavors of those who trust in God, in Ezra's time, or in any other. But to establish the background of David, the chronicler connects the genealogy of Benjamin (just given in I Chr 8; 9:35-44) with the historical disaster that precipitated David's rise to the throne, namely the death of his Benjamite predecessor, King Saul. I Chronicles 10 is directly parallel to I Samuel 31, though there is some difference in the choice of the details described. The chapter is a historical demonstration of how failure results when the Lord is forsaken (vv. 13,14).

1. The Philistines fought against Israel. The Philistines were a Hamitic, but non-Canaanitish, people descended from Mizraim (Egypt) through Casluhim (Cyrene) and Caphtor (Crete; see I Chr

1:8-12; Amos 9:7). Some came early to Palestine, "Philistine land," and were encountered by Abraham, 2050 B.C. (Gen 21:32; cf. 26:14). Before 1400 they had occupied the southern coast from Egypt to Ekron (Deut 2:23; Josh 13:2,3). They were not conquered by Joshua (Josh 13:2,3; Jud 3:3), and Judah held their cities only temporarily (Jud 1:18). Shamgar's victorious skirmish, about 1250 B.C. (Jud 3:31), shows at the same time Israel's material inferiority to the Philistines. With the fall of Crete to the general barbarian movements, 1200 B.C., the "remnant of Caphtor" (Jer 47:4) reinforced the older Minoan Philistines.

But while their advance on Egypt was broken in 1196 as a consequence of the crushing defeat of the "Pulesti" by Ramses III, yet these sea people reconsolidated and, in three waves, almost overwhelmed Israel. The first wave, 1110–1070 (Jud 10:7; 13:1; I Sam 4), was broken by Samuel at the second battle of Ebenezer (I Sam 7:13); and the second, about 1055–1048, by Saul at the battle of Michmash (14:31). I Chronicles 10 is dated in 1010 B.C., the inauguration of their third and last great oppression.

1. Israel . . . fell down slain in mount Gilboa, southwest of the Sea of Galilee, at the head of the Valley of Esdraelon, through which the Philistines were able to penetrate into the interior and to the Jordan (cf. I Sam 31:7).

2. The sons of Saul. See 8:33, and its notes, on Saul's family. **5. Saul was dead.** In II Sam 1:6-10, the story reported to David differs from this Scriptural record of Saul's death. The unscrupulous Amalekite who did the reporting seems simply to have discovered and plundered Saul's body and then fabricated his tale of murder, hoping for reward. **6. All his house died.** I Samuel 31:6 says, "all his men;" i.e., those who immediately surrounded him in the battle. There were others, both of his sons and his troops, that managed to survive (II Sam 2:8; 21:8).

9. They stripped him, and took his head, etc. Despite the Philistines' attainments in material culture, "Philistine" has become a byword for barbarism and cruelty. **10. In the house of Dagon,** a Philistine idol (I Sam 5:2-5). I Sam 31:10 adds that they fastened his body to the wall of Bethshan, a leading city that fell to them between Mount Gilboa and the Jordan.

11. The men of **Jabesh-gilead,** in Trans-Jordan, were still loyal to Saul after his great deliverance of them forty years before (I Sam 11:1-11). **12. Oak.** The Hebrew *'ēlâ* refers to a "large tree." I Sam 31:13, however, specifies the species as that of a tamarisk.

13. The word of the Lord he kept not. He disobeyed Samuel (I Sam 13:8,9; 15:2,3); **and he asked counsel of . . . a spirit,** through the witch at Endor (I Sam 28).

B. David's Rise. 11:1–20:8. Upon the death of Saul in 1010 B.C., David was anointed in Hebron as king over the tribe of Judah (II Sam 2:4). But his bid for the national kingship (II Sam 2:5,6) was rejected, as Saul's son, Ish-bosheth, was set up over the northern and eastern tribes (II Sam 2:8,9). The chronicler, however, disregards this inglorious seven and one-half year period (II Sam 5:5) of disputed succession, civil war, and Philistine domination (cf. II Sam 3;4), and moves directly to the events of David's establishment over all Israel (1003 to about 995 B.C.). I Chronicles 11:1–20:3 thus parallels and amplifies II Sam 5–10 (omitting ch. 9, David's personal kindness to Mephibosheth). It describes his capture of Jerusalem, to become "the city of David," his political capital, together with his military supporters (chs. 11–12). It recounts his winning of independence from the Philistines (ch. 14) and his centralizing of worship by his installation of the ark in Jerusalem, which thus became Israel's religious capital as well (chs. 13; 15; 16). It records the advance of his armies, victorious in every direction (chs. 18–20).

The climax appears in God's prophecy through Nathan (ch. 17): "I have been with thee whithersoever thou hast walked, and . . . I will subdue all thine enemies" (17:8,10). For this message of hope applies not only to David, but to "My people Israel . . . . for a great while to come" (17:9,17); to the struggling community of Ezra; to the church of that greater Son of David, of whom God said, "He shall be my Son" (17:13); and to the kingdom, which is yet to be consummated, of the Messiah, whose "throne shall be established for evermore" (17:14).

1) David Established in Jerusalem; His Heroes. 11:1–12:40. After his anointing as king over all Israel (11:1-3), David's first undertaking was to secure

the fortress of Jerusalem (vv. 4-9). This afforded him not only an impregnable citadel but also a neutral site, on the border between Judah and the north, for the capital of his reunited nation. The chronicler then enumerates David's heroes, "the Three" (vv. 10-19), the two commanders (20-25), and "the Thirty" (26-47), following with a description of the military officers and units that had flocked to his standard in exile and had been largely responsible for his elevation to the kingship (I Chr 12). This last section is found only in Chronicles, though chapter 11 has a close parallel in II Sam 5:1-10; 23:8-39.

11:3. They anointed David king . . . according to the word of the Lord. Twenty years previously Samuel had consecrated David through the true anointing of God (I Sam 15:28; 16:1-13), and the tribes at last recognized both his personal worth and his divine appointment. But David **made a covenant,** establishing a "constitutional" monarchy, unique in the ancient Near East. For the only effective curb upon despotism is the believer's commitment to the kingship of God. (Contrast even weak Ahab's religious scruples, I Kgs 21:3,4, with Jezebel's more "natural" course, vv. 7-10).

4. Jerusalem, which is Jebus. This ancient city-state had been known as "Salem" to Abraham (Gen 14:18) and as "Urusalim" to the Egyptians at the time of the conquest (in the Amarna letters of about 1400 B.C.). Jerusalem had been a center of Canaanitish resistance against the Hebrews (Josh 10:1-5). Joshua had defeated its army and executed its king (12:7,10), and the tribe of Judah had overrun its defenses in an initial attack (Jud 1:8). But for almost 400 years Judah had been unable either to win the city or to drive out its Jebusite inhabitants (Josh 15:63; Jud 1:21; 19:10-12); hence their overconfidence (I Chr 11:4; cf. II Sam 5:6).

6. He shall be chief and captain. David may have made this offer in the hope of by-passing Joab, his efficient but uncontrollable general in Judah (cf. II Sam 3:39), and promoting someone else to the rank of commander of the armies of united Israel. But Joab **went up first,** using a *ṣinnôr,* "hook," or scaling ladder (II Sam 5:8). The ASV translates "watercourse," which corresponds to the Jebusite tunnel archaeologists found cut down through the rock under the city, evidently used for drawing up water in case of siege.

8. Millo means *filling* and may have been a fortress constructed to fill a gap in the defenses (cf. R. A. Stewart Macalister, *A Century of Excavation in Palestine,* p. 106).

10. The mighty men are included at this point because of their influence in David's rise to power. Part of this list —through verse 41 a—is also found, with variants in spelling, etc., as one of the appendices to II Samuel (23:8-39). Twelve of the heroes appear also in a list of the commanders of the twelve corps of David's armed forces (I Chr 27). **11. The captains.** The Hebrew text reads "the Thirty" (cf. ASV), which may have been the initial number in this "legion of honor" of David. Actually listed are thirty-seven (II Sam 23:39), including the outstanding Three and the two commanders, plus sixteen more (I Chr 11:41 b-47), apparently subsequent additions to the original group.

13. The text of I Chronicles is defective at this point. On the basis of II Sam 23:9-11 the following restoration should be made: **The Philistines . . . gathered together to battle,** "and the men of Israel were gone away: He arose and smote the Philistines until his hand was weary, and his hand clave unto the sword: and the Lord wrought a great victory that day; and the people returned after him only to spoil. And after him was Shammah the son of Agee the Hararite. And the Philistines were gathered together into a troop," **where was a parcel of ground . . .** The most distinguished "Three" thus consisted of Jashobeam, Eleazar, and Shammah.

15. The Philistines encamped in the valley of Rephaim, southwest of Jerusalem. This refers to their first campaign against David (14:8,9), even before his capture of the city. David thus resorted to his old outlaw refuge of Adullam (cf. I Sam 22:1; II Sam 5:21).

20. David's half-nephew **Abishai** had commanded with Joab against Abner (II Sam 2:24) and later led divisions in the wars against the Ammonites (II Sam 10:10), Absalom (II Sam 18:2), and Sheba (II Sam 20:6). His heroism with David in Saul's camp is recorded in I Sam 26:6,7. **21. Of the three, he was more honorable than the two.** Read, "Over the Three he was doubly honored"

(KD), being made their commander, even though not attaining to their specific acts of heroism. **22. Benaiah** was appointed commander of the professional Cretan and Philistine troops that made up David's guard (18:17). He became Solomon's leading general (I Kgs 4:4). **23. A weaver's beam** refers to the heavy shaft of a loom, that holds the threads taut.

26. Asahel was killed when pursuing Abner in David's war against Ish-bosheth (II Sam 2:18-23). **34.** Instead of **the sons of Hashem,** read the name of one man, *Bene-hashem*. **41. Uriah the Hittite,** the husband of Bath-sheba, was murdered by order of David, who was trying to cover up his adultery with Uriah's wife (II Sam 11).

12:1. Ziklag was the town on the Judean border over which David had been appointed by Achish, the Philistine king of Gath (I Sam 27:5-7). **2.** ***Even* of . . . Benjamin.** Some of Saul's own tribesmen recognized the divine appointment of David.

4. Among the thirty, and over the thirty. Though not a member of this select group, Ismaiah was worthy of even greater recognition. **6. The Korhites** (Korahites, ASV). Descendants of Korah, who rebelled against Moses (see notes on 6:22 and 9:19). These five must, therefore, have been from the tribe of Levi rather than from the tribe of Benjamin, as were the rest of the list, though probably they were residents of Benjamite territory.

8. The Gadites . . . separated themselves, leaving their Trans-Jordanian homes, and perhaps breaking with their fellow tribesmen who yet followed Saul. **The hold** may refer to the Cave of Adullam (11:15). **13. Jeremiah** in the Hebrew is *Jeremiahu,* distinct from the Jeremiah of verse 10. **15. The first month** was March/April, the time of the spring flood (Josh 3:15; 4:19), which made their action all the more outstanding.

18. The Spirit came upon, literally, *clothed Himself with,* Amasai (as in Jud 6:34; II Chr 24:20). Amasai's devotion to David is expressed in the form of Hebrew poetry and may be rendered:

We belong to you, O David;
We are with you, son of Jesse!
Peace, yes, perfect peace go with you;
Peace bless him who fights for you,
Because your God does lend you aid!
The Berkeley Version

19. He came with the Philistines against Saul. See I Samuel 29 for the description of this event. **21. The band of rovers** suggests the group from Amalek that had plundered David's city of Ziklag in his absence (I Sam 30). **22. Like the host of God.** That is, "like a very great army" (cf. I Chr 9:19). The same phrase is used for cedars (Ps 80:10).

23. They **came to David to Hebron.** The total of almost 350,000, from all areas of Palestine, gives some idea of the enthusiasm with which David's rule was received. **27.** This **Jehoiada** seems to have been Benaiah's father (11:22; 27:5). **28.** This may have been the **Zadok** who was the colleague of Abiathar and his successor as high priest. **31.** The western **half** of the **tribe of Manasseh** is intended (cf. v. 37).

2) The Ark Sought. 13:1-14. The primary goal of Ezra was to lead his people into an enthusiastic commitment to the faith and practices of the law of Moses (Ezr 7:10). The chronicler therefore records David's next act, his attempt to conduct the ark of the Lord into Jerusalem. This project sprang from David's sincere piety and his desire to worship in the presence of his God (vv. 3,8). And even its temporary frustration served to underline the necessity of reverence for divine revelation (vv. 9-13). Conformity, however, to the law of God produces blessing (v. 14). Except for minor variants, II Sam 6:1-11 parallels I Chronicles 13.

2. The phrase, **our brethren that are left,** reflects the seriousness of the great Philistine oppression, 1010–1003 B.C. (cf. 16:35).

3. Bring again the ark. The ark, or chest, was the most holy object in the ritual of Moses, a sacramental symbol of the presence of God himself (v. 6; Ex 25:22; cf. I Sam 4:7). But Israel came to believe in an inherent association of the divine presence with the ark. In order to show the falsity of this superstitious notion of a magical "God in a box," the Lord allowed the ark to be captured by the Philistines at the disastrous first battle of Ebenezer, about 1090 B.C. (1 Sam 4:10,11). The lesson learned, however, God resumed his manifestations of power from the ark; the smitten people, both of Philistia and of the Jewish town of Beth-shemesh, had banished its fearful presence; and it had rested for over eighty years in the house of Abinadab in Kirjath-jearim, or Baalah (I Sam 7). **We inquired not at it in the days of Saul.** The one exception is noted in I Sam 14:18; and even there the ark may not have been actually employed but only asked for.

5. Shihor is the stream bed that marks the southwestern border of Palestine (Josh 13:3). **All Israel.** II Samuel 6:1 specifies a total of thirty thousand chosen men.

7. Uzza and Ahio were descendants of Abinadab (II Sam 6:3). **9. Chidon.** A variant name, "Nachon," appears in II Sam 6:6. **10. He died before God.** Such severity served the purpose of emphasizing for all future generations the necessity for reverence and conforming obedience toward God's sacred objects. Two distinct transgressions combined to produce the situation: (1) the ark should not have been mounted on a cart in the first place, but carried by hand (Num 4:15; the Philistines had indeed used a cart, but that had been in ignorance, I Sam 6:11); and (2) it should not have been touched: even its authorized carriers, Levites of the clan of Kohath (which Uzza and Ahio are not known to have been), had been warned against this on pain of death (Num 4:15). Uzza's intentions, however, were good; and his individual salvation was not necessarily involved.

11. David was displeased. Literally, *angry*, a natural response, because he himself was largely responsible. But his anger turned rapidly to fear (v. 12). **Perez-uzza.** *The outbreak of Uzza.* **14. Obed-edom,** though coming from the area of Gath, was a Levite of the family of Korah in the clan of Kohath (26:1,4) and so met the requirement for a caretaker of the ark.

3) Independence from the Philistines. 14:1-17. I Chronicles 14 parallels II Sam 5:11-25. After summarizing David's royal establishment (vv. 1-7), the chronicler turns to David's chief international problem, that of domination by Philistia (vv. 8-17). In his flight from Saul, David had become a vassal of the Philistines (I Sam 27:1–28:2); and, during his years at Hebron, which coincide with their third great oppression (1010–1003 B.C.; see I Chr 10, introd.), he was still doubtless considered a Philistine client-king. His accession, however, over united Israel posed a threat that Philistine power could not ignore. Their attack was launched immediately (I Chr 14:8), even before his capture of Jerusalem (ch. 11; see v. 15, note). But by his reliance upon divine strength, David was able to beat off two invasions and to secure his nation's independence. The lesson is one of permanent validity for the believer: "God is gone before thee to smite the host of the Philistines!" (v. 15).

1. Hiram sent . . . timber. Years later Hiram supplied Solomon in the same way (II Chr 2:3), for even paganism may render service to the people of God.

3. But David took more wives, a thing which was prohibited by the Law (Deut 17:17) and led to calamity (II Sam 5: 13-16; 11:27). **4. These are . . . his children.** The same list appears, with minor variants, in 3:5-8. **7. Beeliada,** *The Master knows,* was later changed to *Eliada,* "God knows," to avoid the idolatrous implications of **Beel,** *Baal* (cf. 8:33 note).

9. The Philistines . . . spread themselves, more accurately, *raided,* **in the valley of Rephaim,** southwest of Jerusalem (Josh 15:8). This is perhaps the Valley of "Weeping," Hebrew *bākā'*, balsam tree (cf. v. 15). **11. Baal-perazim** = *Master of the break-throughs.* **12. Their gods.** David's men took them away (II Sam 5:21) and **burned** them **with fire,** as required by the Law (Deut 7:5,25).

15. A sound of going (marching) **in the tops of the mulberry** (balsam) **trees.** This was a miraculous sound (cf. II Kgs 7:6), signaling David to spring his ambush. **16. He smote the . . . Philistines . . . to Gazer** (Gezer, on the border), thus expelling them from Israelitish territory.

4) The Ark Brought to Jerusalem. 15:1–16:43. In the days of Ezra, Jerusalem was more important religiously than politically (and indeed it has been so ever since). The chronicler therefore resumes his narrative (see ch. 13) of the induction of the ark into Jerusalem, the accomplishment of which brought about a permanent centralization of the religion of Israel within the walls of David's new capital. Chapters 15; 16 considerably amplify the parallel description found in II Sam 6:12-20. For they list the king's elaborate preparations (I Chr 15:1-15) to forestall any tragedy such as marred his previous attempt and to insure an appropriate retinue of singers (vv. 16-24); they quote David's model psalm of thanksgiving, that was used at

the installation of the ark in its tent (16:7-36); and they explain the Levitical organization that he established for the preservation of a regular ministry at the Jerusalem sanctuary (vv. 4-6, 37-42).

15:1. He prepared a place for the ark. The reports of God's blessings on Obed-edom (II Sam 6:12) had revived David's desire for the presence of the ark. **2. None ought to carry the ark . . . but the Levites.** David thus recognized his previous errors (see 13:10, note).

7. Gershom. Read Gershon, as in 6:1 and elsewhere (though cf. 6:16,17). **8-10. Elizaphan, Hebron,** and **Uzziel.** These are family subdivisions within the first named Levitical clan of Kohath (v. 5; Ex 6:18,22).

12. Sanctify yourselves. By the prescribed ritual washings and the avoidance of ceremonial defilement (Ex 19:10,14, 15; Lev 11:44). **16. Cymbals, sounding.** Literally, *ones which cause* (men) *to hear* (cf. v. 19, etc.). That is, the cymbals marked the time by sounding clear and loud. **18. Obed-edom, and Jeiel.** Azaziah (v. 21) should probably be added. **20. Aziel.** A shortened form of Jaaziel (v. 18). **On Alamoth.** In the soprano register (?). **21. On the Sheminith to excel.** In the base register (lit., *the eighth*, or lower octave?), for leading off. **Obed-edom** the Gittite was, by position, a porter or gate-keeper (vv. 18, 24). But, for his faithful ministry (13:14), he, with Jeiel, was rewarded with the post of bass harpist in the procession, a position subsequently made permanent (16:5,38). Berechiah and Elkanah then took over the "door-keeping" en route (15:23). **24. The priests did blow with the trumpets.** This was a function reserved to them (Num 10:8; cf. I Chr 16:6). **Jehiah** is probably the Jeiel of verses 18,21, and 16:5.

25. David . . . went . . . with joy. He seems to have composed Psalm 24 for this occasion, "Lift up your heads, O ye gates; and the King of glory shall come in." **26. They** (the whole company) **offered seven bullocks and seven rams.** II Samuel 6:13 records only David's offering, of one each. **27. An ephod.** A surplice, or cape, worn in worship (Ex 28:6; I Sam 2:18). David, in his enthusiastic devotion (cf. II Sam 6:14), seems to have removed his outer garment. Contrast the rigid, unsympathetic reaction of David's queen, Michal the daughter of Saul (v. 29; II Sam 6:20-23).

16:3. A flagon of wine. Translate rather, *a cake of raisins* (ASV).

4. He appointed . . . Levites to minister. This was by divine command (II Chr 29:25) and marked the establishment of regular Levitical singers, who soon became an important part of Hebrew public worship, much stressed in Chronicles. **5. Asaph the chief.** David thus elevated Asaph over Heman, who had apparently been the first choice of the Levites (15:17). Asaph and his descendants subsequently composed twelve of our inspired psalms (Ps 50 and 73–83). **Jeiel** (first time) is the same as Jaaziel (15:18).

7. David delivered first this psalm. The following model song that David provided them consists, with slight modifications, of Ps 105:1-15; Ps 96; and Ps 106:1,47,48. All three psalms are listed anonymously in the Psalter, but on the basis of David's use of them here, it would appear that he is indeed their author. **Into the hand of Asaph.** Thus many of David's psalms include in their titles, "To the chief musician."

12. Remember his marvellous works. Psalm 105, is one of the Psalter's great historical surveys of God's faithfulness. **15. Be ye mindful . . . of his covenant,** or *testament* (Heb., *b^erît*). This was God's legal instrument of redemption, by which he granted men reconciliation with himself, on condition of their exercising sincere faith in his promise (Gen 15:6). First revealed in Eden to fallen Adam (Gen 3:15), it was confirmed to Abraham and his chosen seed (Gen 17:7,8; Ex 19:5,6; Gal 3:29). Its ultimate effectuation was contingent upon the death of Jesus Christ, the divine testator (Heb 9:15-17), a fact symbolized under the anticipatory older testament by the shedding of sacrificial blood (Ex 24:6-8; Heb 9:18-22).

20. They went from nation to nation, having been promised Palestine, but not yet having received it (Heb 11:9). **22. Mine anointed.** Set apart by My Spirit (cf. I Sam 16:13). **My prophets.** Abraham was a recipient, though not a regular proclaimer, of God's revelations. He was thus designated a prophet at the time of God's protecting him against Abimelech, king of Gerar (Gen 20:7). Other patriarchs, however, did make specific prophecies (e.g., Jacob, Gen 48:19). Psalm 105:16-45 then continues Israel's history through the greater vindication of the Exodus; but at this point David shifted to the second of his compositions, Psalm 96.

29. Worship the Lord in the beauty of holiness. More accurately, *in holy array* (ASV). **Come before him.** This is particularly appropriate because the divine presence rested over the ark (Num 7:89). **33. He cometh to judge the earth.** An expression of Israel's developing hope in the glorious (second) coming of Jesus the Messiah (cf. Gen 49:10; Num 24: 17; I Sam 2:10; Ps 2). **35. Deliver us from the heathen.** An applicable prayer in light of the Philistine oppression just passed (cf. 13:2, note).

36. This verse is based on the conclusion of Psalm 106, which is also the closing doxology of Book IV of the Psalter (Ps 90–106). Thus it appears that David composed Psalm 106 with the purpose of concluding this collection of psalms (cf. v. 13 in his Ps 41, which closes the Davidic Book I of the Psalter). **The people said, Amen,** meaning, *firm, steady.* **Amen** may thus be rendered, "True indeed!" **And praised the Lord.** "Praise the Lord" is in Hebrew, *Hallelu-ya.*

37. The ark of the covenant. For the ark of God's presence was the symbol of his redemptive testament, with its promise, "I am the Lord your God" (v. 14; cf. v. 15 note; Gen 17:7,8). **38. Jeduthun.** The Hebrew text reads *Jedithun,* who is not to be confused with Jeduthun, the chief singer of the clan of Merari. Obed-edom's family was of Kohath (26:1,4). **To be porters.** Obed-edom was thus confirmed in his double position (see 15:21, note). **39. The tabernacle** of Moses remained, as a separate sanctuary, at **the high place . . . Gibeon** (II Chr 1:13) until Solomon's construction of the Temple (I Kgs 8:4). **41. His mercy,** Hebrew, his *ḥesed,* the basic meaning of which is, his loyalty to the provisions of the convenantal relationship (cf. Gen 21:23; Ps 136:10).

5) Nathan's Prophecy. 17:1-27. Chapter 17 (paralleling II Sam 7) is the climax of I Chronicles and explains the abiding significance of David and his career. Dated in about 995 B.C., after the cessation of the wars chronicled in chapter 18 (see 17:8; cf. II Sam 7:1), it commences with David's desire to build a permanent temple for the ark. But though God forbade David to construct His house (vv. 1-6), He promised to establish David's house (vv. 7-15). Just as God had prospered David personally, so He would prosper his kingdom. In the immediate future David's seed (Solomon) would construct God's Temple (vv. 11,12). In the more distant future David's seed (Jesus Christ) would combine in his person both human sonship and the Sonship of God (v. 13), and would some day set up on this earth the Kingdom of God forever (v. 14). David then breaks forth in praise to God for His incredible grace (vv. 16-27).

1. Nathan the prophet later rebuked David's sin (II Sam 12), aided Solomon (I Kgs 1:10,11), and recorded source material drawn upon in the Chronicles (I Chr 29:29; II Chr 9:29). **2. Do all that is in thine heart.** This was Nathan's personal, non-inspired reaction, prior to his receiving God's true word (v. 3).

4. Thou shalt not build. David's ruthless warfare (cf. II Sam 8:2) had disqualified him (I Chr 22:8; 28:3). **5. I have not dwelt in a house.** Except for the building briefly erected at Shiloh (I Sam 3:3), only to be destroyed by the Philistines after the first battle for Ebenezer (Jer 7:12).

7. I took thee from the sheepcote. From the sheepfold. Better, *the pasture* (RSV marg.; cf. I Sam 16:11). **9. I will ordain . . . and will plant them, and they shall dwell . . . and shall be moved no more.** The Hebrew suggests, and context prefers, the past tense: "I have ordained . . . and have planted them so that they dwell . . . and are moved no more" (KD). **As at the first.** When Israel was oppressed in Egypt. **10. The Lord will build thee a house.** Not a building, like the "house" David wished to build for God, but a dynasty (cf. v. 25).

12. He shall build me a house. This was fulfilled by Solomon (II Chr 3;4). But the promise, **I will stablish his throne for ever,** carries us forward to the ultimate successor to the throne of David, Jesus Christ (Lk 1:32,33). Christ set up his kingdom (in men's hearts) at his first coming (Lk 17:21; Dan 2:44 a), though its imposition over the world awaits his second coming (Lk 17:24; Dan 2:44b). **13. I will be his father, and he shall be my son.** This refers to the deity of Jesus Christ (Heb 1:5; cf. Ps 2:7,12; Acts 13: 33; Heb 5:5) and not to Solomon (cf. I Chr 22:10 note). It was necessary that Christ combine in his person perfect humanity and full deity (Mt 22:12-45; Phil 2:9), that he might make a true substitution for sinful man (I Pet 2:24; Heb 2:17,18) and yet restore us to God the Father (Jn 1:18; 14:6). With the words, **I will not take my mercy away from him,** Nathan returns to David's more immediate successors (cf. the context in the parallel passage, II Sam 7:14,15), who would not be overthrown as was **him that was before thee,** namely Saul.

16. David . . . sat before the Lord. In the tent sanctuary he had erected for the ark (16:1). **17. A man of high degree.** The text is somewhat uncertain, but it reflects David's amazement at his own exaltation from humble beginnings (v. 7).

22. Thine own people . . . and thou . . . their God. This is the central promise of God's reconciling covenant (cf. 16:14, 15), from Genesis (17:7) to Revelation (21:3).

6) Conquests and Administration. 18:1-17. This section closely parallels II Samuel 8 and establishes the proposition that "the Lord prospered David whithersoever he went" (vv. 6,13): in the west, against Philistia (v. 1); in the east, against Moab (v. 2); north, against Syria (vv. 3-11); and south, against Edom (vv. 12,13). A concluding paragraph surveys David's administrative officers (vv. 14-17).

1. Now after this. An introductory formula, indicating no more than a logical succession of topics. In point of time, chapter 18 precedes chapter 17 (cf. 17:8), just as chapter 19 (cf. these same introductory words in 19:1) must precede 18 (v. 3). **Gath** was one of the five "mother cities" of the Philistines (II Sam 8:1, ASV). **2,6. Gifts.** Tribute. **3. Hadarezer.** Better, *Hadadezer* (II Sam 8:3). The **king of Zobah,** an Aramean territory lying northeast of Damascus and south of Hamath. **Went to stablish his dominion.** This was the second defeat of these Syrians (Arameans), the full account being found in the next chapter (19:6-19). **The river Euphrates.** Considerably further north and east. Hadadezer had summoned reinforcements from this area (19:16). **4. He houghed,** i.e., hamstrung, **all the chariot horses,** to insure peace.

8. Tibhath and **Chun.** These, and some of the names that follow, have variant forms in the corresponding verses (II Sam 8:8-10). **Brass.** *Neḥoshet,* "bronze." **Wherewith Solomon made the brazen sea** (cf. v. 11). The vast resources that David furnished for Solomon's Temple are outlined in 22:2-5,14,15.

12. Abishai . . . slew of the Edomites . . . eighteen thousand. The title to Ps 60 names Joab as David's "chief of staff" (cf. II Sam 8:13,16; I Kgs 11:15,16), and cites a variant figure of 12,000.

16. Abimelech. Rather, *Ahimelech* (24:3; II Sam 8:17). **Shavsha.** Seraiah (II Sam 8:17).

17. The Cherethites and the Pelethites were David's Cretan and Philistine guard, the Philistines having come originally from Caphtor (Crete; cf. I Chr 10 notes). During the periods of their domination over Israel they had utilized Hebrews as troops (I Sam 14:21; 28:1). But David's victories in 1003 had reversed the situation, and the Philistines were now found in his employ.

7) Victories over Ammon. 19:1–20:3. One of David's last (about 995 B.C.) and most desperate international struggles arose in connection with two campaigns against the Ammonites, a people kindred to Israel and inhabiting an area to their immediate east in Trans-Jordan. The chronicler details this specific instance of God's care for his own (19:13), including: (1) the causes of the conflict (19:1-5); (2) Joab's victorious campaign against the double army of the Ammonites and their mercenary Syrian allies (vv. 6-15); (3) David's crushing of an attempted Syrian counterattack (vv. 16-19); and (4) Joab's second campaign, which resulted in the destruction of the Ammonite state. These records, except for their omission of David's crime with Bath-sheba, are parallel to II Sam 10–12.

19:1. After this. See 18:1, note. **The children of Ammon.** Descendants by incest from Abraham's nephew Lot (Gen 19:36-38). They had repeatedly ravaged the neighboring territories of Israel in the chaotic days of the Judges (Jud 3:13; chs. 10; 11; I Sam 11:1), but had been first repelled and then subdued by Saul (I Sam 11:11; 14:47). **2. His father Nahash showed kindness.** This could hardly be the same Nahash Saul had battled fifty-five years before (I Sam 11), but may have been a son, who aided David against Saul. Compare David's help from the king of Moab (I Sam 22:3). **4. Hanun . . . shaved them.** II Samuel specifies, "Shaved off the one half of their beards" (10:4), a most shameful deed in the Orient (v. 5), and one that reaped heavy punishment (20:3).

6. A thousand talents of silver. Each talent weighed about seventy-five pounds avoirdupois, or ninety-two pounds troy weight, the total value being well over $2,000,000. **Mesopotamia.** The area between the Tigris and the Euphrates rivers provided the later reinforcements v. 16). It probably included the Beth-rehob mentioned in II Sam 10:6,8 (cf. Gen 36:37). **Syria-maachah** was southwest of Zobah (see 18:3 note), between Damascus and Galilee. **7. Thirty and two thousand chariots.** Add "horsemen, and footmen" (cf. v. 18; II Sam 10:6). **The king of Maachah and his people.** II Samuel 10:6 specifies one thousand men. They **pitched before Medeba.** A Trans-Jordanian city in northern Reuben, southwest of the Ammonite border. **9. The gate of the city;** i.e., of their capital, Rabbah (cf. v. 15; 20:1).

13. Behave . . . valiantly . . . and let the Lord do that which is good. One's utmost effort, combined with implicit faith (cf. Phil 2:12,13).

15. Joab came to Jerusalem. It seems to have been too late in the year to undertake a siege (see 20:1).

16. Beyond the river. On the eastern side of the Euphrates (18:3). **17. They fought.** At Helam (II Sam 10:16,17), near Hamath in the Orontes Valley (I Chr 18:3), the northern border of Zobah. **18. Seven thousand men . . . in chariots.** The parallel account (18:4) correctly defines these as "horsemen," since the total of captured chariots was only one thousand. The figures in the Hebrew text of Samuel (but not in the LXX, which agrees with Chronicles) have been corrupted into the less likely proportion of "seven hundred" (II Sam 8:4) horsemen ("men of chariots," II Sam 10:18). **Forty thousand footmen** (not "horsemen," II Sam 10:18) seems likewise to be a textual corruption of the original figure of twenty thousand (II Chr 18: 4). The total of the initial force is given as thirty-two thousand (19:7).

19. The servants of Hadadezer included his client-kings (II Sam 10:19).

20:1. At the time that kings go out. Spring of the following year, after the rainy season. **David tarried at Jerusalem.** At this point occurred the scandalous affair of David's adultery with Bath-sheba and his murder of her heroic husband, Uriah (II Sam 11:2-27), which the chronicler thus suggests to his readers, without retracing the sordid details.

2. David took the crown. After reaching Rabbah for its final capitulation (II Sam 12:27-29). **Their king.** Hebrew *malkām.* Compare "Malcham" (Zeph 1:5) and "Milcom" (I Kgs 11:5,33), names of the leading Ammonite idol. **Found . . . to weigh a talent of gold** (see 19:6, note). It could not have been worn regularly by a man. **There were precious stones in it.** Better, *a precious stone. A singular stone* (RSV). **3. And he cut** (them) **with saws.** Hebrew, *way-yā'sar.* This word should be corrected to a form very similar to it in the original, *way-yā'sem.* Read, "And he put (them to work) with saws," etc. David could be ruthless (cf. II Sam 8:2), but he was not cruel. **Harrows.** Better, *picks.* II Samuel adds, labor "in the brickkiln" (12:31).

8) Philistine Wars. 20:4-8. The chronicler concludes his analysis of the period of David's rise with a survey of certain outstanding incidents that occurred in battle with the Philistines. They follow the first Philistine wars (14:8-17), but they precede the God-given rest from foreign enemies granted David about 995 B.C. (17:8; II Sam 7:1). They are included, with minor variants, within the appendix of II Samuel (in 21:15-22) and may be associated with the campaigns outlined in I Chr 18:1.

4. After this. See 18:1, note. Gezer (II Sam 21:18, "Gob") was the border city to which the Philistines had been forced back after David's wars of independence (14:16 note). **Sibbechai** was one of "the Thirty" heroes (11:29) and commander of David's eighth corps (27:11). **Of the children of the giant.** Hebrew, *Rephaim,* an ancient people (Gen 14:5), noted for their large size. Except for the kingdom of Og in Bashan, the Rephaim had died out by the time of Moses (Deut 3:11). **5. The brother of Goliath,** who was slain by David (I Sam 17). A slight textual corruption causes the parallel passage (II Sam 21:19, ASV) to read as though Elhanan slew Goliath himself! **A weaver's beam.** See 11:23, note.

C. David's Latter Days. 21:1—29:30. David's sin with Bath-sheba precipitated a chain of crimes (cf. Amnon's license, as "king's son," II Sam 13:4), that centered about Prince Absalom and occupied the space of a full eleven years

(II Sam 13:23,38; 14:28; 15:7, variant reading), or from approximately 990 to 979 B.C. Such unenlightening conduct, however, contributed little to Ezra's purpose of embodying in the men of his own day the piety that characterized David at his best. Most of the events recorded in II Sam 11–19, accordingly, find no counterpart in the chronicler's work (cf. Introduction, *Occasion for Writing*). With these must also be included the revolt of Sheba (II Sam 20); so that it is not until about 975 B.C., in the latter years of David's life, that the historical analysis of Chronicles is resumed. It then traces the course of David's census (I Chr 21), which resulted in the revelation of the site for the Temple and the preparations for its building (ch. 22). The results of David's organizational genius, in the spheres both of religious (chs. 23–26) and of civil administration (ch. 27), are outlined, followed by his final charges to the people to be faithful to their God (chs. 28–29). Only chapter 21 has a direct parallel elsewhere in Scripture.

1) The Census. 21:1-30. While the cause for David's census lay in Israel's provocation of God (II Sam 24:1), and while the king's own insistence upon a census was equally sinful (v. 3 note); yet David's subsequent repentance was not only exemplary in every way (vv. 8,13,17,24), but it became, also, the means of God's designating the spot for the high altar of sacrifice, within the Temple that would soon thereafter be erected in Jerusalem. The chronicler therefore retraces these events, which form likewise the concluding chapter to the appendix of II Samuel (ch. 24).

1. Satan . . . provoked David. Because of the devil's antipathy **against Israel** and, ultimately, against the God of Israel (cf. Job 1:11; 2:5). The parallel record (II Sam 24:1) goes deeper and shows that Satan was but an instrument of God, being used to execute punishment on Israel for their sins, presumably their revolts against David, God's anointed, that terminated only with Sheba's death prior to 975 B.C. (cf. Job 1:12; 2:6; I Kgs 22:22,23). **3. A cause of trespass to Israel.** Not that there was anything inherently wrong in a census (cf. Num 1:1,2; 26:1,2); but in this case David seems to have been seeking his security in the strength of his armies (v. 5) rather than by faith in the promises of God (compare 27:23 and Ps 30:6; see I Chr 22:1, note).

4. Joab . . . went throughout all Israel. II Samuel 24:5-8 notes that it took about ten months, and outlines his route of travel. **5. Of Israel one million one hundred thousand . . . and in Judah four hundred and seventy thousand.** II Samuel 24:9 gives the round figure for Judah of 500,000 and limits Israel's census to 800,000 valiant men.

9. Gad, David's seer, counseled him wisely on several occasions (I Sam 22:5; II Chr 29:25), and later composed one of the literary sources of the Chronicles (I Chr 29:29). **12. Three years of famine.** So also in the LXX of II Sam 24:13. The Hebrew text of this parallel passage, however, reads "seven years," a less likely figure in light of the other "three unit" alternatives. **Pestilence . . . and the angel of the Lord.** Compare similar instances of divine punishment in I Sam 6:3-6; II Kgs 19:35. **13. David said unto Gad.** The king's submission to the voice of God through the prophet is noteworthy (cf. II Sam 12:13). **14. There fell of Israel seventy thousand.** An appropriate punishment, since David's sin seems to have involved reliance upon numerical military strength. **15. Ornan.** "Araunah" in II Samuel 24. **17. These sheep.** Scripture frequently compares leader and people to shepherd and flock (11:2; Ps 23). David's self-sacrificing spirit is commendable, though this was not a case of the nation's suffering simply for her leader's sin (v. 1 note).

23. The oxen were used to pull the wooden threshing sledges over the grain. **24. Burnt offerings without cost.** Even so, God finds no pleasure in the man who yields him only what involves no sacrifice. He asks of us our whole life (Rom 12:1; cf. Lk 21:1-3). **25. Six hundred shekels of gold.** Worth about $5000. II Sam 24:24 notes a small amount of silver paid first for the threshing floor itself.

26. He answered him from heaven by fire. God similarly inaugurated others of his places of sacrifice (Lev 9:24; II Chr 7:1). **29. The tabernacle . . . at Gibeon.** See 16:39, note.

2) Temple Preparations. 22:1-19. An effective stimulus for future devotion to the post-Exilic Temple lay in the example of consecration furnished by David, as he made the preparations for its pre-Exilic prototype (cf. chs. 28;29). The

chronicler therefore takes joy in recounting David's own efforts (vv. 2-5) and the exhortations by which he encouraged his son Solomon (vv. 6-16) and the leaders of Israel (vv. 17-19) to the prosecution of this holy task.

1. This is the house of the Lord. Ornan's threshing floor on Mount Moriah, on which site the Temple was soon to be built by Solomon (II Chr 3:1). It thus appears that Psalm 30, which is stated to be by David, and yet was used "at the dedication of the house (temple)" (ASV), belongs historically at this point. Its fifth and sixth verses well summarize David's experiences of I Chronicles 21. **2. David** gathered **together the strangers,** Hebrew, *gērîm,* "resident aliens." Cf. similar "construction drafts" by Solomon (II Chr 2:17,18; 8:7,8). This parallels the employment of the conquered Canaanites as the "Nethinim," temple slaves (I Chr 9:2, note). **5. Solomon . . . is young and tender.** He was apparently David's fourth son by Bath-sheba (3:5). Thus, if born in 990 B.C., he would have been twenty at his accession. **8. The word of the Lord came to me.** Brought by Nathan before Solomon's birth (17:4). Thou **hast made great wars.** It is not that war may not be necessary and right (cf. 14:10; 19:13). But David had gone too far; he had been guilty of needless bloodshed (e.g., II Sam 8:2). **9. For his name shall be Solomon.** Hebrew, *peaceful.* **10. He shall build an house for my name . . . and I will establish the throne of his kingdom.** A direct quotation from 17:12-14, Nathan's prediction that Solomon would build the Temple. The middle clauses, however, **I will be his father, and he shall be my son,** refer to Christ (17:13). Scripture seems to have included them here simply as means of associating the relevant passages that precede them and follow them. Compare the inclusion of Acts 2:19,20 in the total citation that extends from Acts 2:17 to 21, as an example of a similar sandwich-structure quotation.

14. In my trouble. By my hard labor. David's resources came to exceed those of his proverbially wealthy son (II Chr 9:13). **A hundred thousand talents of gold, a million talents of silver** (RSV) = 9,200,000 and 92,000,000 pounds troy weight, respectively. Its value by modern standards would be $6,000,000,000, and its equivalent in ancient purchasing power was far greater! **16. Of the gold . . . there is no number.** "Of men for the gold-work . . . there is no number." **17. The princes of Israel.** National and tribal leaders, not necessarily of royal blood (so in 23:2, etc.). **19. Bring the ark . . . into the house.** David's original project would thus be accomplished (chs. 13; 15; 16; 17).

3) Levitical Organization. 23:1–26:32. One of David's most lastingly significant contributions to posterity lay in the arrangements that he made for the ministry of the tribe of Levi. The genius he displayed in the organization of the Levites helped preserve the Levitical services under his successors, provided the administrative force for the revival of the Mosaic theocracy under Ezra (see chapter 6, introd.), and continued to serve as the basis for Israel's religious organization on into NT times. David's fundamental policy was one of separating the 38,000 Levites of his day into four operational groups (23:3-5). After an outline of the Levitical clans and families (vv. 7-23) and a brief survey of their duties (vv. 24-32), these four groups are enumerated: 24,000 who "set forward the work of the house of the Lord" (ch. 24), under whom were included the priestly family of Aaron (24:1-19) and the other Levites who assisted them (vv. 20-31); 4,000 who served as singers (ch. 25); 4,000 "porters" or door-keepers, under whom were included the temple treasurers (26:1-28); and finally 6,000 "officers and judges," who were engaged in "the outward business over Israel" (26:29-32). The priests, the temple Levites (?), and the singers were further organized within themselves into twenty-four "courses" each, whose rotation could be coordinated into periods of monthly service.

23:1. David was . . . full of days (cf. v. 27; 26:31). He was seventy years old in 970 B.C. (II Sam 5:4). **He made Solomon . . . king.** The disputed succession and the ruthless consolidation that followed upon Solomon's rise to power (I Kgs 1;2) are passed over by the chronicler as unworthy of comment.

3. They **were numbered from the age of thirty years and upward** (see v. 24, note) and, presumably, under fifty years (Num 4:3). **5. Instruments which I made.** The king had inventive genius in this area that was long remembered (Amos 6:5). **6. The sons of Levi.** Compare the lists in 24:20-30; 6:16-30, and the other Biblical references cited in the introduction to chapter 6. Minor variants exist in the spellings, and in some other details.

7. Laadan and Shimei . . . These are listed not to provide a complete genealogy but rather to establish the major clans of Levi, out of which the Davidic organization was formed. **8. The chief was Jehiel.** Jehiel was the ancient Levite who founded this chief family. The individual "chiefs" who headed up David's courses are listed in 24:20-30. **9. This Shimei** is apparently not the same as the Shimei son of Gershon listed in verses 7,10. It is likely that both this second Shimei and Laadan were sons of Libni, the older son of Gershon and brother of Shimei (6:17). Thus the clans of Gershon totaled nine—six for Laadan and three for Shimei (on the basis of the combining of Jeush and Beriah, v. 11).

14. The man of God. Moses' distinctive title (Deut 33:1; Ps 90, title). Moses ranks as one of the greatest human figures in the whole OT (Deut 34:10-12).

22. Their brethren (cousins) **took them** in marriage, according to the Mosaic law for the preservation of family property (Num 36). This gave the clan of Merari four divisions (one for Mahli and three for Mushi), making then, with the nine each of Gershon and Kohath, twenty-two Levitical divisions, plus the Aaronic priests.

24. The age of twenty years and upward. But in verse 3, it is thirty years and upward. Moses had likewise taken the census of Levites aged thirty and above (Num 4:3), but later included in the work those twenty-five and upwards (8:23-26). The explanation for David's further lowering of the age limit appears to have been the lessening physical demands of the service (v. 26), plus the increasing man-power needs that would arise with the new Temple. **25. That they may dwell in Jerusalem for ever.** Rather, *and he dwelleth in Jerusalem for ever* (ASV).

29. For the showbread. Cf. 9:32 note. **Flour for meat offering.** Better, *meal offering* (ASV). This was the one major form of sacrifice that did not employ flesh (Lev 2). **That which is fried.** Literally, *that which is mixed* (with oil).

30. Every morning . . . and at even. The times of the two regular daily sacrifices (Ex 29:38,39). **31. And to offer all burnt sacrifices.** Connect with verse 30 and read, *to stand . . . at even and for all offering of burnt sacrifices.* Only the priests could actually officiate at the altar. **The set feasts,** observed annually, were five: Passover, Pentecost, Trumpets, the Day of Atonement, and Tabernacles (Lev 23). The first, second, and last required pilgrimage to the central sanctuary (Ex 23:14-17; Deut 16:16).

24:1. The sons of Aaron. For the priestly family, compare 6:3-15 and the accompanying notes.

3. David, ***with Zadok and Ahimelech*** (ASV), **distributed them. Ahimelech** II was the son of Abiathar (v. 6) and grandson of Ahimelech I, who had been high priests in the earlier days of David.

4. Sixteen and **eight.** The twenty-four priestly courses (23:6) continued as the basis for rotating the priestly duties down into NT times. Although some of these courses died out or had to be consolidated with others, new ones were formed to take their places. In the return from exile, 538 B.C., four registered courses were represented, David's second, third, and sixteenth, and a new course, Pashur (Ezr 2:36-39); and by 520 B.C. twenty-two were again in operation (Neh 12:1-7; cf. vv. 12-21; 10:2-8).

10. The eighth to Abijah. This was the course to which Zacharias, father of John the Baptist, belonged (Lk 1:5).

20. The rest of the sons of Levi. The courses that follow (vv. 20-30) are those of the Levitical temple assistants that correspond to the priestly courses. The first nine (vv. 20-25) equal the nine family divisions (23:12-20) that arose from the four sons of Levi's son Kohath: **Amram,** Izhar, Hebron, and Uzziel. For each course, e.g., **Shubael** (or Shebuel, 23:16), there is given the chief in the time of David, e.g., **Jehdeiah,** except for the chiefs of Hebron, whose names may have been lost to Ezra. **22. Shelomoth.** Or, Shelomith (23:18).

26. The courses of **the sons of Merari** (vv. 26-30) include four that correspond to the four family divisions (23:21-23), though the only chief's name to appear is Jerahmeel (24:29), for the combined Mahlite group of Eleazar and Kish (cf. 23:22). **The sons of Jaaziah.** This Jaaziah is contextually distinguished from **Mahli** and **Mushi,** the actual sons of Merari, and may have been a later Merarite, the numerical strength of whose descendants had grown to the point of separate recognition as courses by David.

31. They **likewise cast lots over against**

. . . the sons of Aaron; that is, the abovementioned chiefs of the non-Aaronic Levites. If the nine divisions of Gershon from the preceding chapter (23:7-11) be included as courses, and if Jaaziah's sons Beno (or *Bani;* cf. LXX and ICC) and Shoham, Zaccur, and Ibri (24:27), be considered as representing two separate courses, with their chiefs, then the total of the twenty-two Levitical divisions (23:22 note) would provide twenty-four courses of approximately one thousand men each, to correspond to the twenty-four courses of the priests.

25:1. David . . . set apart for the service *certain* (ASV) **of the sons of Asaph.** These arrangements were, by divine command, mediated to David through the prophets Nathan and Gad (II Chr 29:25). **Asaph . . . Heman, and . . . Jeduthun,** belonging respectively to the Levitical clans of Gershon, Kohath, and Merari (6:33-47), had been appointed chief musicians at the time of the entrance of the ark into Jerusalem (16:5, 41).

2. Asaph . . . prophesied. Many of the OT prophecies are in poetic form (cf. the musical prophets of I Sam 10:5); and, correspondingly, much of the poetry is of a prophetic nature (cf. v. 4 note). Specifically, Asaph and his descendants composed Ps 50 and 73–83. **3.** After the name **Jeshaiah** insert "Shimei" (v. 17), to make the required total of six.

4. Starting with the sixth son, **Hananiah,** these names, when translated from the Hebrew, form the following prayer of Heman about his work as a prophet-singer:

(6th) 'Be gracious, oh Lord, (7th) be Thou gracious unto me! (8th) My God, Thou; (9th) I've praised (10th) and exalted for helping; (11th) Though sitting forlorn, (12th) I've proclaimed (13th) highest (14th) visions.

5. Heman the king's seer in the words of God. He may have been responsible for some of the psalms (42–49; 84; 85; 87; 88) composed by his Korahite clan (6:33-38). **Sons . . . to lift up the horn.** That is, Heman's horn (power): God blessed him with a numerous family. **Three daughters.** Women, too, had a part in the musical service (Ps 68:25).

8. They cast lots. To determine the arrangement of the courses under the twenty-four sons of Asaph, Heman, and Jeduthun. **The teacher as the scholar.** The division seems to have included all 4,000 of the singers (23:5) and not just the 288 master musicians.

11. Fourth . . . Izri; i.e., **Zeri** (v. 3). Compare similar spelling variants for the leaders of the seventh, eleventh, thirteenth, and fifteenth courses.

26:1. The porters served as gatekeepers (v. 13) and as guards over temple property in general (v. 20, note). **Korhites** = descendants of Korah, the notorious Levite who rebelled against Moses (see on 6:22; 9:19). **Kore's** father **Asaph** was Ebiasaph (9:19), not the famous musician Asaph, who belonged to the clan of Gershon. Korah, and these porters who were his descendants, belonged to the clan of Kohath.

4. Obed-edom. The Levite who had received God's blessing for keeping the ark after the death of Uzza (13:13,14). He held the double appointment of both singer and temple guard (see on 15:21; 16:38).

10. Hosah was appointed at the same time as Obed-edom (16:38). That original number of 68 gate-keeping guards had, at this point, increased to 93 (18, 62, and 13), who constituted the leaders for the total group of 4,000 porters (23:5). Indeed, by the time Jerusalem fell in 586 B.C., the number had risen to 212 (9:22).

13. They cast lots, not for periods of service, as in the previous allotments, but for places of service. **14. Shelemiah.** Or, "Meshelemiah," as in verse 1 and elsewhere. **15. The house of Asuppim** (cf. v. 17). Literally, *the storehouse* (ASV). **16. Shuppim** is not otherwise known but was probably, like Hosah, a gate-keeper of the clan of Merari. **The causeway** going up moved from the western, lower city, through the Tyropeon Valley, to the higher elevation of the Temple. **17,18. Eastward were six,** etc. A total of twenty-four leaders of guards(?) (cf. v. 10, note) were thus on duty at one time. **18. Parbar.** The form is uncertain, perhaps a colonnade or court.

20. Of the Levites, Ahijah was over the treasures. The porters' "office of trust" included the treasurerships (9:26, ASV). But **Ahijah** (Heb. text, *' ḥ y h)* is otherwise unknown; and it may be better to read with the LXX, *The Levites, their brethren, were over the treasures. Their brethren* (Heb. *'ḥyhm)* would then be Jehieli's Laadanites, over the temple treasury (vv. 21,22), and Shelomith's Amramites, over the dedicated gifts (vv. 23-28).

22. Jehieli. *A man of Jehiel.* Jehiel, Zetham, and Joel were, in fact, all sons of Laadan; but Jehiel was the accepted leader over his two brothers (23:8). **23. The Amramites,** etc. The divisions of the clan of Kohath. **24. Shebuel the son of Gershom** (23:16; 24:20). He had been chief treasure-officer under his grandfather, **Moses.** But **Shelomith** (v. 25) the descendant of Gershom's brother **Eliezer,** held the position under David (v. 26). **26. Treasures of the dedicated things.** See 18:11 and II Chr 5:1 for David's devotion in this regard.

29. Izharites and Hebronites (vv. 30-32). These Levites of the clan of Gershon, provided 4,400 (1,700 plus 2,700) of the 6,000 **officers and judges** (23:4). Moses had first issued the natural directive that the Levites, who taught the word of God (Deut 33:10), should be entrusted with its interpretation in judgment (Deut 17:9; cf. II Chr 19:8,11; Neh 11:15). **32. Reubenites, the Gadites, and the half tribe of Manasseh.** That is, the part of Israel that lay east of the Jordan.

4) The Civil Organization. 27:1-34. The flourishing state of Israel under David was a far cry from the impoverished Jewish subprovince that existed in the days of Ezra. Although this outline of the glories of a past administration was without political relevance to the returned exiles (as it is to us!), it nevertheless must have thrilled Ezra's people (as it does us) with the truth that visible political rewards are included in God's decree for his faithful servants (cf. Rev 2:26). I Chronicles 27, accordingly, surveys: David's military system of twelve army corps, each with its commanding officer, its complement of 24,000 men, and its term of one month's active duty per year (vv. 1-15); his regional organization by tribal areas, each with its tribal prince (vv. 16-25); and his central administration of "cabinet" executives and officials over the royal property (vv. 25-34).

2. Over the first course . . . was. The "lieutenant generals" who commanded the twelve army corps were all distinguished military figures (cf. I Chr 11, with the occasional variant spellings of their names). **Jashobeam.** The first of "the Three," the outstanding heroes (11:11). **3.** Jashobeam was **of the children of Perez,** one of the two chief clans of the tribe of Judah (2:4).

4. The second corps, **Dodai,** the second of "the Three" (11:12). **Of his course was Mikloth also the ruler.** His "executive officer."

5. The third corps, **Benaiah** (11:22-25), **the son of Jehoiada the priest** (ASV; see on 12:27). This was the commander of the Cretan guard (18:17, note). **6. Benaiah . . . was . . . above the thirty.** See notes on 11:11,21; 12:4.

7. The fourth corps, **Asahel.** The first of "the Thirty," the heroic "legion of honor." He was killed in the war against Abner early in David's reign (11:26, note). **8. The fifth** corps, **Shamhuth the Izrahit.** Shamhuth was "of Zerah" (i.e., a Zarhite, vv. 11,13), the other chief clan of Judah (cf. v. 3). He was a member of "the Thirty" (11:27). **9. The sixth** corps, etc. The remaining seven commanders were also members of "the Thirty" (11:28-31). **15. Heldai** was **of** the descendants of **Othniel,** the first of the Hebrew Judges (Jud 1:13; 3:9-11).

17. Hashabiah and **Zadok** the priest. Two princes were thus appointed for Levi, while the princes for the tribes of Gad and Asher were either unknown to Ezra, or perhaps their names were lost from the text by later scribal error. **18. Elihu, . . . of the brethren of David.** Elsewhere called Eliab (2:13). **21.** For **Benjamin, Jaasiel the son of Abner,** who was the famous general and uncle of King Saul of Benjamin (26:28; I Sam 14:50; cf. I Chr 8:33; 9:39).

23. God **would increase Israel like to the stars.** The promise given more than one thousand years before, to Abraham (Gen 22:17). David, therefore, did not order a *total* numbering of the people, which would have left the impression of questioning this prophecy. He had, however, apparently through a lack of faith in God's power to protect his kingdom, taken a sinful census of the men of fighting age (21:1-8).

28. The low plains. Hebrew, *Shephelah.* The piedmont area between the Philistine coastal plain and the inland Judean hills.

32. Also Jonathan. This list of high officials supplements the earlier "cabinet" presented in 18:15-17 and II Sam 20:23-26. **34. After Ahithophel was Jehoiada.** Ahithophel deserted David for Absalom (II Sam 15:12,31; 16:20-23); but, when thwarted by Hushai, **the king's companion** (ASV, *the king's friend,* an official cabinet post; II Sam 15:32-37; 17:1-16), he committed suicide (II Sam 17:23).

5) Final Words. 28:1–29:30. This passage resumes the record of David's last assembling of the leaders of Israel (v. 1 parallels 23:2), 970 B.C. (23:27; 26:31). His purpose had been not simply to place the Levitical organization on a permanent footing (chs. 23–26) but also to insure his nation's commitment to the erection of the Jerusalem Temple. David therefore charged both the people (28:2-8) and his son Solomon (vv. 9,10) with dedication to this holy task. Then, after presenting his son with the inspired written plans for the Temple and its services (vv. 11-19), he again charged him to be faithful (vv. 20,21). Turning to the national leaders, David next appealed to them for an all-out effort of giving for the Temple (29:1-5). The assembly rose to the challenge (vv. 6-9), and David praised God for their bounty (vv. 10-22). Solomon was then confirmed on the throne of his father, and David passed to his eternal reward (vv. 22-30).

28:2. The footstool of our God suggests the golden plate, or "mercy seat" (v. 11), that covered the ark, and above which the cloud of God's glorious presence appeared (Ex 25:20,21; II Sam 6:2; 22:11). **3.** Thou **hast shed blood** (cf. 22:8, note). David had earlier spoken of these same matters with Solomon privately (22:7-16).

4: God . . . chose me . . . to be king over Israel for ever. His dynasty, culminating in Christ, would be eternal (17:11). **Chosen Judah . . . to make me king.** For this progressively narrowing choice, see Gen 49:8-10; I Sam 16:1-13; I Chr 22:9,10. **5. The throne of the kingdom of the Lord over Israel. Earth's** rulers are but ministers, deputies of God (29:23; I Sam 12:14; Rom 13:1-6). **6. I have chosen him to be my son, and I will be his father.** See on 22:10.

9. Serve him with a . . . willing mind. The spirit of this pious charge parallels David's similar admonition in I Kgs 2:2-4.

11. The place of the mercy seat. See on verse 2. **12. The pattern . . . by the Spirit** (cf. v. 19). The plans for the Temple were divinely inspired, just as had been those of Moses' Tabernacle before it (Ex 25:9,40; 27:8). For the very items of furniture and their arrangement were typical of the way in which salvation would ultimately be accomplished by Christ (Heb. 8;9, especially 8:5). **18. The chariot of the cherubim.** Not the cherubim on the ark (see v. 2, note), but the larger cherubim that overshadowed this whole "seat" of God (II Chr 3:10-12; cf. Ezk 1:5-26).

29:1,2. Solomon . . . is yet young and tender, and . . . I have prepared. Thoughts similar to those expressed by David when he commenced the temple preparations (22:5,14, notes). **3. Over and above all** that he had prepared (22:14,15). The following was an additional gift, from David's personal resources. **4. Three thousand talents of gold** from **Ophir** (the best quality) **and seven thousand . . . of . . . silver** (cf. 19:6; 22:14, notes) are worth about $1,100,000,000 and $16, 000,000 respectively, though its purchasing power in ancient times would have been much greater. **5. To consecrate his service.** Literally, *to fill his hand.* The phrase is a technical one. It was used when candidates were ordained to the priesthood. Our gifts should be equally "devoted."

7. Gold, five thousand talents. About $185,000,000. **Ten thousand drams** *(darics,* ASV). Persian gold coins worth about $5.00 each. The chronicler used the daric to evaluate this offering in 970 B.C., even though coinage was actually unknown to David. **Ten thousand talents of silver and eighteen thousand of brass** (bronze). That is, 920,000 and 1,656,000 pounds troy weight, respectively. **One hundred thousand talents of iron** equals 3,750 tons. Iron was then a much rarer commodity than it is today. **8. Jehiel the Gershonite.** The chief temple treasurer (26:21,22). **9. They offered willingly.** Willingness is the attitude that God loves (II Cor 9:7) and that should characterize all our giving.

10. God of Israel. Israel here is the patriarch Jacob (Gen 32:28). **11. Thine is the kingdom.** From these praises come the words placed at the end of the Lord's Prayer in the AV (Mt 6:13). **14. Of thine own have we given thee.** This is the basis of "stewardship": that everything we have and are is from God, being simply held in trust by us, and that it should therefore be used for him (Lk 17:10).

20. They **worshipped the Lord, and the king.** "To worship," as used here, means to "prostrate oneself." Thus it may be performed either to God or to a man. **21. And sacrifices in abundance for all Israel.** Probably peace offerings, on which the people feasted, as the Lord's guests (Lev 7:15; cf. Ex 24:11).

22. They made Solomon . . . king the second time (parallels 23:1). The chronicler thus makes no attempt to conceal, but rather suggests to his readers, the inglorious incident (which he does not relate) of Solomon's first proclamation as king under pressure of a plot to have him displaced (I Kgs 1:39). Confirmatory rites were of value, particularly when there had been such a disputed succession (cf. I Sam 10:24 and 11:14,15 on Saul). **And Zadok.** His anointing as high priest was similarly confirmed; for David's other priest, Abiathar, had disqualified himself in the plots (I Kgs 1:7; cf. 2:26).

24. All the sons . . . of . . . David, submitted themselves, *particularly* Adonijah, Solomon's older brother, who had attempted to usurp the throne (I Kgs 1:53).

28. He died . . . full of . . . honour. I Kings qualifies this generalization with certain specific matters of a less complimentary nature (1:1-4,15; 2:5,6,8,9).

BIBLIOGRAPHY

Evangelical Studies

Beecher, Willis J. "Chronicles," *The International Standard Bible Encyclopaedia*. Edited by James Orr. Vol. I, 1939.

———. *Reasonable Biblical Criticism*. Philadelphia: The Sunday School Times Co., 1911.

Boyd, J. Oscar. "An Undesigned Coincidence," *The Princeton Theological Review*, III (1905), 299-303.

Crockett, Wlliam Day. *A Harmony of the Books of Samuel, Kings, and Chronicles*. Grand Rapids: Baker Book House, 1951.

Ellison, H. L. "I and II Chronicles," *The New Bible Commentary*. Edited by Francis Davidson, A. M. Stibbs, and E. F. Kevan. Grand Rapids: Wm. B. Eerdmans Publishing Co., 1953. Pp. 339-364.

Keil, C. F. *The Books of the Chronicles*. Grand Rapids: Wm. B. Eerdmans Publishing Co., 1950.

Macmillan, Kerr D. "Concerning the Date of Chronicles," *The Presbyterian and Reformed Review*, XI (1900), 507-511.

Zockler, Otto. *The Book of Chronicles (Lange's Commentary)*. New York: Charles Scribner's Sons, 1876.

Other Studies

Albright, William F. "The Date and Personality of the Chronicler," *Journal of Biblical Literature*, XL (1921), 104-124.

Curtis, Edward L., and Madsen, Albert A. *A Critical and Exegetical Commentary on the Books of Chronicles (The International Critical Commentary)*. New York: Charles Scribner's Sons, 1910.

Elmslie, W. A. L. *The Books of Chronicles. (The Cambridge Bible for Schools and Colleges)*. Cambridge: The University Press, 1916.

———. "The First and Second Books of Chronicles," *The Interpreter's Bible*. Vol. 3. New York: Abingdon Press, 1954.

Harvey-Jellie, W. R. *Chronicles (The Century Bible)*. Edinburgh: T. C. and E. C. Jack, 1905.

Slotki, I. W. *Chronicles* (Soncino Books of the Bible). London: The Soncino Press, 1952.

SECOND CHRONICLES

OUTLINE

(For introductory comments see Introduction to First Chronicles)

- I. The reign of Solomon. 1:1–9:31.
  - A. Solomon's inauguration. 1:1-17.
  - B. Solomon's temple. 2:1–7:22.
    1. Preparations. 2:1-18.
    2. Construction. 3:1–4:22.
    3. Deication. 5:1–7:22.
  - C. Solomon's kingdom. 8:1–9:31.
    1. Its achievements. 8:1-18.
    2. Its splendor. 9:1-31.
- II. The kingdom of Judah. 10:1–36:23.
  - A. The division of the kingdom. 10:1–11:19.
  - B. The rulers of Judah. 12:1–36:16.
    1. Rehoboam. 12:1-16.
    2. Abijah. 13:1-22.
    3. Asa. 14:1–16:14.
    4. Jehoshaphat. 17:1–20:37.
    5. Jehoram. 21:1-20.
    6. Ahaziah. 22:1-9.
    7. Athaliah. 22:10–23:21.
    8. Joash. 24:1-27.
    9. Amaziah. 25:1-28.
    10. Uzziah. 26:1-23.
    11. Jotham. 27:1-9.
    12. Ahaz. 28:1-27.
    13. Hezekiah. 29:1–32:33.
    14. Manasseh. 33:1-20.
    15. Amon. 33:21-25.
    16. Josiah. 34:1–35:27.
    17. Jehoahaz, Jehoiakim, Jehoiachin, and Zedekiah. 36:1-16.
  - C. The Exile. 36:17-23.

COMMENTARY

I. The Reign of Solomon. 1:1–9:31.

A. Solomon's Inauguration. 1:1-17. Prior to his own death, King David had placed his son on the throne of Israel and made sure that the nation's leaders "pledged their allegiance to King Solomon" (I Chr 29:24). However, the brilliant reign of Solomon received its inauguration with God's appearing to him at Gibeon (II Chr 1:1-13). This incident, more than any other in all history, confirms the Biblical teaching that, "If any of you lack wisdom, let him ask of God . . . and it shall be given him" (Jas 1:5). With it, therefore, the chronicler opens the second half of his great study. He thus parallels I Kgs 3:4-15, though he omits Gibeon's immediate validation in Solomon's decision over the children of the two harlots (I Kgs 3:16-28), as being of limited, personal interest. He substitutes, rather, its later economic validation, as seen in Israel's national prosperity (II Chr 1:14-17, a passage paralleled in I Kgs 10:26-29).

1. The Lord . . . magnified him. This resumes the thought of I Chr 29:25.

3. The high place that was at Gibeon. This city was seven miles northwest of Jerusalem. By Solomon's time, Gibeon, with **the tabernacle of . . . the Lord** (I Chr 16:39), and Jerusalem, with the ark of God (II Chr 1:4), were the only legitimate places for divine sacrifice (see I Kgs 3:2; cf. the principle of centralized worship, where God was revealed, in Ex 20:24; Deut 12:5). Other high places, even if used in the name of Israel's God Jehovah *(Yahweh)*, were contaminated by association with Baal worship and were under God's ban (Num 33:52; Deut 12:2). Solomon's sin began, in fact, with his recognition of the high places, plural (I Kgs 3:3). **4. The ark . . . had David brought up. See** I Chr 13;15;16.

7. God . . . appear[ed], in a dream (I Kgs 3:5,15; cf. I Sam 28:6). **8. Thou hast shewed great mercy. Mercy** (ḥesed) here means "faithfulness" (see on I Chr 16:41). **9.** For God's **promise unto David** see I Chr 17:11-14. It included the establishment of David's seed upon his throne and the erection of the Temple in Jerusalem. **A people like the dust of the earth.** God had thus fulfilled exactly his earlier promise to Abraham (Gen 13:16). **10. Give me . . . wisdom.** Solomon's own prayer corresponded to that which his father David had wished for him (I Chr 22:12).

12. Wisdom . . . is granted unto thee. Solomon's factual knowledge was limited by his cultural environment; but his "wisdom," his ability in the application of knowledge, has never been surpassed (I Kgs 3:12). **And I will give thee riches, and wealth, and honour** (cf. I Chr 29:25). "Seek ye first the kingdom of God and his righteousness, and all these things shall be added unto you" (Mt 6:33).

14. The existence of Solomon's **chariot cities** (cf. 9:25) has been remarkably confirmed by archaeology. The excavation of Megiddo, southeast of Mount Carmel, has revealed one extensive stone stable capable of housing about four hundred horses (William F. Albright, *The Archaeology of Palestine*, p. 124).

15. Sycomore trees . . . in the vale. This verse parallels 9:27. Cf. I Chr 27:28, note. **16. And linen yarn.** The Hebrew says, actually, "and of *qᵉwē*," i.e., Cilicia, a northern source of supply for horses (cf. 9:28). **17. A chariot for six hundred shekels of silver, and an horse for an hundred and fifty.** A shekel was about two-fifths of an ounce. The cost would therefore be about $500 and $125 respectively, by present standards, though ancient purchasing power was far greater. So the law forbade excess in such matters (Deut 17:16), the very sin into which Solomon's prosperity led him.

B. Solomon's Temple. 2:1–7:22. The greatest productions of Solomon were his inspired books (Prov, Eccl, Song, and possibly Job) and his magnificent Temple. For us today, the former possess the greater significance. But for Ezra, living at a time when the "God-breathed" writings of the OT canon came to an end (II Tim 3:16; see above, Introduction, *Date)*, but when the Temple was concentrating in itself the very means of access to God, the latter became, understandably, his primary concern, the event that for him overshadowed all others in the career of Solomon. For the Temple, like the Tabernacle before it, symbolized the presence of the reconciled God in the midst of the people he had redeemed (II Chr 7:1,2; Ex 29:45,46). It constituted their way of salvation, anticipating with its sacrifices the Lamb of God, who would "tabernacle" amongst us to take away the sin of the world (Jn 1:14 [ASV marg.], 29). And it typified the glorification that awaits men in the heavenly presence of God himself (Ex 24:18; Heb 9:24). The chronicler therefore devotes six of his nine Solomonic chapters to the Temple: the preparation for it (II Chr 2); its construction (chs. 3; 4); and its dedication (chs. 5–7). These sections form an amplified parallel to I Kgs 5; 6; 7:13–8:66.

1) Preparations. 2:1-18. The major planning for the Temple had already been accomplished by David: designing the architecture, gathering the supplies, and enlisting the personnel (I Chr 22; 28; 29). It remained for Solomon to organize his labor force (II Chr 2:2, 17,18). His wisest move, however, was to seek the aid of Hiram king of Tyre, David's friend (cf. v. 12) for the provision of an experienced superintendent of construction, and a supply of the matchless timbers from Lebanon (vv. 3-10). A suitable contract was quickly negotiated (vv. 11-16).

2. Threescore and ten thousand men to bear burdens, etc. (parallels vv. 17, 18). These 153,600 drafted laborers consisted of aliens resident in Israel, as had already been determined by David (I Chr 22:2, note). Solomon also levied 30,000 men out of Israel, to work in shifts of 10,000, each man to serve one month out of three (I Kgs 5:13,14).

3. Huram the king. Read *Hiram* (i.e., Ahiram), as in I Kings, II Samuel, and I Chronicles. **Of Tyre.** On the Mediterranean coast, north of Israel. Tyre possessed the best harbor in the area, and its Phoenician inhabitants were noted for their mercantile ability. **Didst deal with David.** See I Chr 14:1.

4. To burn before him sweet incense. This was done twice daily on the incense altar (Ex 30:6-8). **Shewbread, burnt offerings . . . feasts.** Cf. on I Chr 9:32; 23:30,31. **6 Heaven . . . cannot contain him** (cf. 6:18; Acts 7:48, 49). Solomon thus recognized from the first that God's localized presence in the Temple was a gracious condescension on His part and constituted no limitation upon the otherwise omnipresent God (cf. on I Chr 13:3).

7. Send me . . . a man cunning to work. Solomon, in fact, hired a number of experienced Phoenicians to assist the less highly skilled Palestinians (I Kgs 5:6,18), to the lower culture of whom archaeology bears witness. **8. Send me . . . cedar trees.** The fragrant cedars of Lebanon, famed throughout antiquity, were resistant to rot and superior to any timber native to Israel. Today only a scattering of the trees survives. **Fir trees.** The Phoenician juniper, a tree similar to the cypress. **Algum** (almug) **trees.** Sandalwood, a foreign import from Ophir (9:10), used for ornamental woodwork and in musical instruments (I Kgs 10:12).

10. To . . . the hewers (cf. I Kgs 5:6) **. . . measures** (Hebrew, *kōr*) **. . . and . . . baths.** About ten bushels and ten gallons each, respectively. Solomon also sent a smaller, but annual, supply to Hiram (I Kgs 5:11). Such payments, which were specified by Hiram (I Kgs 5:6), constituted a heavy drain on the economy of Israel. When prolonged, because of Solomon's private building projects (II Chr 2:1,12; cf. I Kgs 7:1-12), they exhausted the kingdom (cf. I Kgs 9:10,11).

11. The Lord hath . . . made thee king, etc. Though these may have been sincere acknowledgments, they seem rather to represent words carefully chosen by a practical business man.

13. Of Huram my father's. Rather, *even Huram, my father* (ASV marg.). Hiram (cf. I Kgs 7:13) is entitled **father** as a token of his master craftsmanship. **14. Son of a woman of . . . Dan,** a widow who lived in Naphtali (I Kgs 7:14). **Purple** was the deep red dye obtained from the murex **shellfish, known** as "royal purple" because of its scarcity and costliness. **16. Joppa** served as the port of inland Jerusalem. Between the cities lay some thirty-five miles of rugged, hilly terrain.

18. Three thousand and six hundred alien **overseers.** There were also 250 Israelites (8:10); total, 3,850 overseers (equals the 3,300 lower, plus 550 higher, overseers of I Kgs 5:16; 9:23).

2) Construction. 3:1–4:22. To the men of Ezra's day, the form of the Solomonic Temple both witnessed to the glory of Israel in the past, and exhibited a structural ideal toward which they might pattern the restoration of their own sanctuary. For men of all time, however, the main features of Solomon's Temple, like those of the Mosaic Tabernacle, which was placed within it (I Kgs 8:4) and upon which it was modeled, furnish typical illustrations of undying significance, created, as they were, by the divine Architect to depict the changeless truths of the Gospel. II Chronicles 3 (generally parallel to I Kgs 6) describes the building as a whole; and chapter 4 (parallel to I Kgs 7) describes its furnishings. The latter, with the exception of the altar of incense and the most holy ark, show considerably more elaboration than the corresponding pieces in the Tabernacle of Moses.

3:1. Mount Moriah. The summit on which Abraham had been willing, almost 1,100 years before, to sacrifice his son Isaac (Gen 22:2). **In the threshingfloor of Ornan.** See I Chr 21:18–22:1. **2. In the . . . second month,** April/May, **in the fourth year,** which ran from the fall of 967 to the fall of 966. The date is therefore 966 B.C. (cf. Edwin R. Thiele, *The Mysterious Numbers of the Hebrew Kings*, pp. 30,31).

3. These are the things wherein Solomon was instructed. Better, *These are the foundations which Solomon laid* (ASV). **Cubits after the first measure.** The earlier, or sacred, measure ran about three inches longer than the ordinary cubit of approximately eighteen inches. **Threescore cubits** by **twenty cubits** is therefore about one hundred and five feet by thirty-five feet rather than ninety by thirty. This was just double the surface dimensions of the Tabernacle. **4. The height an hundred and twenty** cubits. This eastern vestibule was therefore in the form of a great tower, over two hundred feet high. **5. The greater house,** or Temple proper, corresponded to the outer room of the Tabernacle, the Holy

Place. Compare the "most holy house," literally, the *holy of holies* (v. 8). **Fir tree.** Cf. 2:8, note. Cedar also was used (I Kgs 6:9).

6. Gold of Parvaim came, probably, from a mine in southeastern Arabia. The expenditure for this overlaying of the entire house was enormous, but see I Chr 22:14; 29:4,7. **7. The posts.** *The thresholds* (ASV). **Cherubim** were angelic creatures, symbolic of the presence of God, sovereign and transcendent (v. 14, note; Gen 3:24). They appeared normally in human form, but winged (Ezk 1:5,6). The attempt of 'liberal' criticism to relate the cherub to the mythological sphinx is without Biblical foundation. Palm trees and flowers were also depicted in the carvings (I Kgs 6:29). **8. Gold . . . six hundred talents** (see I Chr 19:6, note), worth about $22,000,000. **9. The nails,** for fastening the sheets of gold to the walls, weighed **fifty shekels of gold** (see 1:17). They were worth $640.

11. Wings of the cherubims, twenty cubits long. These are not to be confused with the cherubim on the ark, but were two great, gold-plated figures of olive wood (I Kgs 6:23) that filled "the most holy house" (II Chr 3:8) and, side by side, overshadowed the ark.

14. The veil (see Ex 26:31-33) sealed off from mankind the Most Holy Place with its awesome presence of God. The veil was thus emblematic of the truth that the way to God was not yet clear (Heb 9:8) and would not be until Christ should take out of the way the anticipatory forms of the older testament (Mt 27:51).

15. The **two pillars** stood free, in front of the Temple. **Thirty and five** is either a corruption for eighteen (the two are easily confused in the Hebrew), or a representation of the length of the original casting. Each pillar measured eighteen cubits long if an attachment for **the chapiter**[s], **the ornamented capitals**, is included. The existence of such ornamental pillars, or obelisks, at ancient temples has been confirmed repeatedly by archaeology. **17. Jachin.** *It establishes.* **Boaz.** *In it is strength.*

4:1. The new, larger **altar of brass** (bronze) was the first object encountered in the temple court, demonstrating that God may be approached only through sacrifice, the substitutionary and testamentary death of Christ (Heb 8:2,3; 9:12).

2. The **molten sea** taught the necessity of purity (Ex 30:21), and it points to the washing of regeneration and sanctification in Christ (Tit 3:5; Heb 9:10). **A line of thirty cubits did compass it.** Only approximately, for the diameter was ten cubits. **3. Under it.** Under the brim was **the similitude of oxen . . . ten in a cubit.** The reference, if not a copyist's error in Chronicles, must be to the round-shaped heads of oxen; for I Kgs 7:24 reads "knops," i.e., gourd-shaped ornaments. **5.** A capacity of **three thousand baths** is too great for these dimensions. It must be a textual corruption for two thousand (I Kgs 7:26), or about twenty thousand gallons (cf. II Chr 2:10 note). This huge reservoir, then, supplied the ten smaller lavers on their wheeled bases (vv. 6,14; I Kgs 7:27-39). Archaeological confirmation for the latter has been found in excavations at Cyprus (cf. the plates in C. F. Burney, *Notes on the Hebrew Text of Kings).*

7. Compared with the Tabernacle's one "candlestick" (really, a lampstand), the Temple was equipped with **ten candlesticks** of the same **form** *(prescription).* They symbolized the perfection (seven fold) with which God's Church must shine for him (Lev 24:3), through the oil of the Holy Spirit (cf. Zech 4:2-6). They thus seem to typify the light and truth that should shine in the Christian (Mt 5:14) through the priestly ministration of Christ (Lev 24:4; Jn 8:12).

8. Ten tables likewise replaced the one, though it seems that only one table at a time was used to hold the showbread (13:11; 29:18). The tables symbolized the believer's re-established harmony and sustaining communion with God (Lev 24:8; cf. Ex 24:11), and may have been a type and pledge of that closer fellowship that will exist in the heavenly and eschatological Kingdom of God (Lk 14:15).

9. The court of the priests, and the great court. This was an advance over the Tabernacle with its single court. The desire for efficiency suggested that an inner and higher (more visible) area be constructed, in which the priests could perform their sacred duties (I Kgs 6:36; Jer 36:10). But this very distinction (cf. II Kgs 23:12) gave tangible expression to the fact that under the older testament there did not yet exist that universal priesthood of believers which was to come, when through Christ all should have direct access to the Father (Jer 31:34; Heb 4:14-16).

11. Huram. Not the king, but the master craftsman (2:13,14). **12. The pommels** were the bowl-shaped, net-covered, lower sections of the capitals, above which rose the crowns, like opened lilies (I Kgs 7-17-20). **16. Huram his father.** See 2:14, note. **Of bright brass.** Of polished bronze. **17. Zeredathah.** Or, Zarthan (I Kgs 7:46). It lay east of the Jordan and about halfway between Galilee and the Dead Sea. The **clay ground** was suitable for great metal moulds.

21. The flowers served as ornaments on the lampstands (Ex 25:33). **22. The doors . . . were of** carved olive **wood,** overlaid with **gold** (3:7; I Kgs 6:31-37). These protected **the entry of the house,** the holy place, and provided a barrier, in addition to the veil, for the sealing off of **the most holy place** (see 3:14, note).

3) Dedication. 5:1–7:22. The significance of the Temple is made explicit in the ceremonies that accompanied its dedication. After assembling the representative leaders of Israel, Solomon first designated his Temple to be the lineal successor to Israel's previous sanctuaries by installing within its Most Holy Place the ark of God's testament (5:1-10). God then confirmed the reality of his localized dwelling within the Temple by filling the house with the *Shekinah,* the cloud of his glory (vv. 11-14). Solomon, in adoration, gave a brief testimony to God's faithfulness (6:1-11). This was followed by a longer prayer of dedication, calling upon the Lord to intervene in behalf of the people of Israel when they should submit their petitions toward His presence in the Temple (vv. 12-42). This, too, was confirmed as God sent fire from heaven upon the new altar and thus instituted two weeks of great dedicatory sacrifices and of feasting (7:1-10). Later, after Solomon had built his own palace, the Lord appeared to the king by night and reaffirmed His promises, on condition that Israel prove faithful, but threatened exile and the Temple's destruction in case the nation turned apostate (vv. 11-22). These chapters correspond closely to I Kgs 8:1–9:9.

5:1. The things David . . . had dedicated. See I Chr 18:11; 22:14; 26:26; 29:2-5. Some treasures must have remained, even after the tremendous outlay for the Temple.

2. To bring up the ark . . . out of the city of David. Solomon had it transported from the old citadel of Zion to the ridge of Moriah, which lay north of the former city wall. **3. The seventh month.** September/October. The dedication did not take place until *after* the work was completed (v. 1) in the eight month (Oct./Nov.) of Solomon's eleventh year, or 960 B.C. (cf. 3:2, note). So the Temple was not dedicated until eleven months had passed, that is, in 959 B.C., **in the** annual **feast** of Tabernacles (cf. 7:8-10).

4. The Levites took up the ark. Solomon took the added precaution (cf. on I Chr 13:10) of employing priests within Levi for this work (v. 7; I Kgs 8:3). **5. And the tabernacle.** This was brought from Gibeon (cf. 1:3, notes). **6.** The **multitude** of the sacrifices followed David's more modest precedent (I Chr 15:26).

7. The oracle of the house. Oracle (Heb., *d^e^bîr)* is a technical term for **the most holy place** (cf. 4:20). **Under the wings of the cherubims.** See 3:11, note. **9. There it is unto this day.** Not until Ezra's day, but until the day of the written source being quoted (cf. 9:29; I Kgs 8:8). **10. Nothing in the ark save the two tables.** By this time the golden pot of manna (Ex 16:32-34) and Aaron's rod (Num 17:10,11; Heb 9:4) had disappeared. **The Lord made a covenant.** The two stone tables of the Decalogue expressed the moral fruitage expected of the people whom God had already redeemed (Ex 20:2; cf. 19:4-6). They were therefore called "the testimony" (Ex 25:16,21) to the redemptive covenant (testament).

11. They **did not then wait by course.** Members from all the twenty-four courses (I Chr 24:3-19) assisted on this important occasion. The normal rotations in service could come later! **13. His mercy** (Heb., *ḥesed).* That is, his faithfulness. See I Chr 16:41, note. **14. The cloud . . . the glory of the Lord.** This represented the presence of the divine Angel of God, the pre-incarnate appearance of Christ (Ex 14:19; 23:20-23). It had first guided the people out of Egypt (Ex 13:21,22) and had then filled the Mosaic Tabernacle (Ex 40:34,35). In the days just before the Exile, Israel's sin drove this cloud from earth (Ezk 10:18,19). It was later called the "shekinah," God's "dwelling." It marked Christ's first coming (Mt 17:5); and it will herald his glorious second advent (Rev 1:7; 14:14; cf. R. E. Hough, *The Ministry of the Glory Cloud).*

6:1. The Lord . . . would dwell in the thick darkness. That is, covered by cloud in the darkness, first of Sinai (Ex 19:9; 20:21), and then of the veiled Most Holy Place of the Tabernacle (Lev 16:2). **2. Thy dwelling for ever.** There was, indeed, the condition that Israel must be faithful (7:20; Mt 23:37,38). But Christ will yet reign on Zion (Mt 23:39; Rom 11:26), in the final, new Jerusalem (Rev 21:2).

4. God **fulfilled that which he spake . . . to . . . David;** i.e., that the Temple would be built and David's dynasty established (v. 10; I Chr 17). **6. I have chosen Jerusalem** (I Chr 22:1) **that my name might be there.** That is, his very presence (Deut 12:5,7). **11. The ark, wherein is the covenant.** See 5:10, note.

13. Upon a **scaffold** (platform) **Solomon . . . kneeled down** (cf. I Kgs 8:54). The king thus publicly acknowledged that he, too, was but God's servant, administering a kingdom not his own (I Chr 28:5).

14. Keepest covenant, and showest mercy *(hesed;* cf. on 5:13; I Chr 16:41). Synonymous expressions. God's gracious testament, through the death of Christ, is the source of all blessings, both for us and for those who "received the promise of inheritance under the first testament" (Heb 9:15). **Unto thy servants.** Faith must always be manifested by obedience (v. 16; Jas 2:17-26). **18. The heaven of heavens** (i.e., highest heaven) **cannot contain thee.** See 2:6, note.

20. Prayer **toward this place.** It became the practice of devout Jews to pray literally in the direction of Jerusalem (Dan 6:10). The emphasis here, however, should be on true heart commitment to the God of special revelation, who has ordained the Jerusalem sanctuary to depict his redemptive work in Christ (cf. introd. to chs. 5–7). **21. Hear thou . . . from heaven,** God's ultimate dwelling place (Ps 11:4; Hab 2:20), and **forgive.** The following seven petitions may be summarized by I Jn 1:9, "If we confess our sins, he is faithful . . . to forgive . . . , and to cleanse us . . . ."

22. (1) If an oath is **laid upon him to make him swear.** Testimony in doubtful cases was confirmed by an oath at the sanctuary (Ex 22:10,11; Lev 6:3-5). God is petitioned to intervene for the maintenance of justice. **24.** (2) Defeat and exile **before the enemy** were occasioned by sin (Lev 26:17,33; Josh 7:11,12). **26.** (3) **When . . . there is no rain.** The phenomena of nature may have moral causes. Certainly Israel suffered drought in times of apostasy (I Kgs 17:1; Lev 26:19). **28.** (4) **If there be dearth.** Plagues of various sorts were likewise caused by sin (Lev 26:16,20,25,26), for God knows the hearts of men (v. 30; cf. I Sam 16:7). **32.** (5) **Concerning the stranger . . . if they come and pray.** The Temple was to be "an house of prayer for all people" (Isa 56:6-8). Israel's very election had as its goal the universal knowledge of God (v. 33; Gen 12:3; Eph 2:11,12). **34.** (6) **If thy people go out to war.** God will fight for his own, who cry unto him in the battle (14:11,12; I Chr 5:20). **36.** (7) **There is no man which sinneth not.** Here is expressed the consistent Biblical teaching of man's total depravity (cf. Jer 13:23; 17:9; Eph 2:3). **If . . . they carry them away captives.** The exile and restoration of Israel had been predicted as early as Moses (Lev 26:44,45); and all was fulfilled, just as Solomon had prayed (II Chr 36:16,22,23).

41. Arise, O Lord God, into thy resting place (cf. Num 10:35). These final verses quote Ps 132:8-10, which is anonymous but was probably written by David on the occasion, analogous to this, of his installing the ark in the Jerusalem tent (I Chr 16). **42. Turn not away the face;** i.e., reject not the prayers **of thine anointed.** That is, of Solomon himself, because of the **mercies** *(hesed),* faithful acts, **of David.**

7:1. Fire came down from heaven. In this same way God had inaugurated sacrifice at the Mosaic Tabernacle (Lev 9:24) and at the Davidic altar on Moriah (I Chr 11:26). **3. And all . . . Israel saw . . . the glory of the Lord upon the house.** God thus gave a greater manifestation of what he had already revealed to his priests within the Temple (5:13, 14); and Solomon added his own blessing upon the congregation (I Kgs 8:55-61).

5. Twenty and two thousand oxen, and an hundred and twenty thousand sheep. I Kings 8:63 confirms these staggering figures and defines them as "peace offerings," hence eaten by the people (cf.

on I Chr 29:21). It supplied them for the fifteen days of feasting (II Chr 7: 9,10). **7. The fat of the peace offerings.** Choice token portions were presented to God on the altar, prior to the feasting of the people (Lev 3). For **the burnt offerings, and the meat** (meal) **offerings,** see, respectively, Leviticus 1 and 2.

8. Solomon postponed the dedication for many months (cf. on 5:3) that it might coincide with **the** great harvest **feast** of Tabernacles. Israel gathered **from . . . Hamath** on the Orontes, in the far north toward the Euphrates River, to **the river of Egypt,** Shihor (I Chr 13: 5), the southwestern border toward Egypt. **10. On the three and twentieth day of the seventh month he sent the people away.** The special seven-day dedication feast had lasted from the eighth day to the fourteenth day (v. 9), including the great Day of Atonement on the tenth (Lev 16). This then was followed by the regular Feast of Tabernacles from the fifteenth to the twenty-second (i.e., the "eighth" day of II Chr 7:9; cf. Lev 23:33-36).

11. Solomon finished . . . the king's house. His own palace. Thirteen additional years have thus passed (I Kgs 7: 1; 9:10), bringing us to Solomon's twenty-fourth year, 946 B.C.

12. The Lord appeared to Solomon. This was his second revelation to Solomon (I Kgs 9:2), the first having been at Gibeon (II Chr 1:3-13). **13. If I shut up heaven,** etc. God thus specifically answered Solomon's earlier petitions (vv. 15,16; cf. 6:22-39). **14. If my people . . . shall humble themselves . . . and turn from their wicked ways; then will I . . . heal their land.** This great verse, the best known in all Chronicles, expresses as does no other in Scripture God's requirement for national blessing, whether in Solomon's land, in Ezra's, or in our own. Those who believe must forsake their sins, turn from the life that is centered in self, and yield to God's word and will. Then, and only then, will heaven send revival. **16. That my name may be there for ever.** See on 6:2,6.

18. Then will I stablish the throne of thy kingdom. This quotes I Chr 17:12, 14, but makes explicit the divine condition of faithful obedience. **19. But if ye . . . shall go and serve other gods.** Solomon and his successors did serve other gods (I Kgs 11:1-8; II Chr 36: 16), and their unfaithfulness led to the very results he had himself anticipated (vv. 20-22; cf. 6:36; 36:17-20).

C. Solomon's Kingdom. 8:1–9:31. Just as the chronicler's appraisal of David's kingdom provided encouragement for the post-Exilic community, because of its demonstration of God-given power; so his description of Solomon's kingdom furnishes a correspondingly effective exhibition of the glory that follows upon service to God. Specifically, Chronicles concludes its record of Solomon with an outline of the achievements of his administration (II Chr 8) and with illustrations of the splendor that surrounded his throne (ch. 9). This material agrees closely with that found in Kings except that it intentionally omits, as less edifying, or even detrimental to Ezra's theocratic goal, the details of Solomon's autocratic officialdom (I Kgs 4), the extravagances of his extensive palace (I Kgs 7:1-12), the idolatry that eventuated from his gross polygamy (I Kgs 11:1-8), and the resultant political deterioration that plagued his latter years (11:9-40).

1) The Achievements of Solomon's Kingdom. 8:1-18. II Chronicles 8 parallels I Kings 9, outlining the success achieved by Solomon: in his expansion and military endeavors (vv. 1-6); in his organization of manpower (vv. 7-10); in his regulation of public worship (vv. 11-16); and in his commercial ventures (vv. 17,18).

1. At the end of twenty years. That is, in 946 B.C. (see 7:11, note). **2. Cities which Huram had restored to Solomon.** This reference assumes, without comment, the sordid record of I Kgs 9:11-13. The record tells how Solomon had to give up some twenty non-Israelite cities in Galilee to Hiram king of Tyre, apparently because Hiram foreclosed on Solomon's unpaid building debts. In the transaction Hiram was actually cheated, as the territory was greatly impoverished. Hence Solomon, it seems, was forced to take back the territory. After this he did effect some development of the region by causing **the children of Israel to dwell there.**

3. He went to Hamath-zobah, and prevailed against it, perhaps for breaking the peace of I Chr 18:10. Thus the only recorded campaign of Solomon resulted in his conquest of the kingdom of Hamath, which bordered upon the already occupied kingdom of Zobah (see comment on I Chr 18:3). **4. He built Tadmor in the wilderness.** This is the oasis of Palmyra, 150 miles northeast of Damascus, and the half-way point on the caravan route to the Euphrates River. Tadmor controlled the trade on this desert cut-off to Babylon, producing in Roman times the fabulous state of Queen Zenobia. Some texts of I Kgs 9:18 (cf. ASV) present the less desirable reading, *Tamar,* which was a city in the far south of Judah.

5. The two **Beth-horon**[s] controlled an important pass northwest of Jerusalem leading down to the port of Joppa. **6. Baalath** may have been in the vicinity of Beth-horon. Other cities are listed in I Kgs 9:15-17. **Chariot cities.** See on 1:14.

8. Solomon compelled the Canaanites **to pay tribute** and (cf. I Kgs 9:15,21) conscripted them for labor as well (cf. II Chr 8:9 and I Chr 22:2, note). **10. Chief . . . officers, two hundred and fifty.** Cf. the five hundred and fifty of I Kgs 9:23; but see II Chr 2:18, note.

11. Early in his reign Solomon had married **the daughter of Pharaoh** (I Kgs 3:1). Such an alliance, even with Solomon's contemporary, Hor-Psibkhannu, the last Pharaoh of the weak Twenty-first Dynasty, built prestige. But this woman's Egyptian idolatries led to eventual apostasy in Israel (I Kgs 11:1; cf. 11:8; Ezr 9:1), though at this point Solomon retained enough sensitivity to remove her residence from **the places** that **are holy.**

13. The **certain rate** of sacrifices had been prescribed by Moses (Lev 23:37).

17. Ezion-geber and . . . Eloth (Elath). Ports at the northern end of the Gulf of Aqaba, which provided Solomon with strategic access southward into the Red Sea. Archaeology has shown them also to have been centers of Solomon's copper smelting industry (Nelson Glueck, *The Other Side of the Jordan,* chs. 3,4). **18.** The copper then provided an export product to exchange for the gold from **Ophir,** on the southwestern coast of the Arabian Peninsula, or perhaps the eastern shores of Africa. **Huram sent him . . . ships, and servants that had knowledge of the sea.** That is, the Tyrians constructed ships with materials sent to Ezion-geber and then guided the less experienced Israelites in their navigation, making one trip every three years (9:21). Solomon thus gained a total of **four hundred and fifty talents of gold** (420 is the textual variant of I Kgs 9:28), or over $15,000,000.

2) The Splendor of Solomon's Kingdom. 9:1-31. Our Lord Christ spoke of "Solomon in all his glory" (Mt 6:29); and II Chr 9 (paralleling I Kgs 10) presents a variety of historical data that illustrate the splendor of Solomon: the visit he received from the queen of Sheba (vv. 1-12); the revenue he gathered, and the shields, the throne, and the equipment it produced (vv. 13-21); and the extent of his fame and power (vv. 22-28). A concluding summary is then given for Solomon's reign as a whole (vv. 29-31).

1. The Semito-Hamitic kingdom of **Sheba** (I Chr 1:9,22), lying at the southern point of the Arabian Peninsula, was noted for its commerce in gold and spice. Its queen visited Solomon, perhaps for trading purposes (cf. II Chr 8:18), but also to test his God-given wisdom (I Kgs 10:1) with **hard questions.** The Hebrew is *ḥîdôt,* "riddles" (as in Jud 14:12); and their exchange is a familiar Arabic custom to the present day. **4. The sitting of his servants.** The high officials at his table. **His ascent** suggests the processional of the royal party for temple worship. **6. The half . . . was not told me.** See verse 23, and 1:12 note. **8. God** made **thee king, to do . . . justice.** This had been the purpose of Solomon's wisdom from the first (1:10, 11). **9. An hundred and twenty talents of gold.** Well over $4,000,000.

10. The servants . . . of Huram . . . brought algum trees. See on 2:8 and 8:18. **11. Terraces.** Hebrew *m^e sillôt,* "highways." Perhaps a flight of stairs (cf. I Kgs 10:12, ASV marg.).

12. Solomon gave her **all her desire.** I Kings 10:12 notes this as over and beyond his regular kingly hospitality.

13. Six hundred and three score and six [666] talents of gold per year. About $25,000,000. **14. Chapmen** (traders). Literally, *the men of the caravans.* **Governors of the country.** Vassal princes in neighboring lands.

15. Each of the **two hundred targets** (large shields, covering the body) was plated with **six hundred shekels** (about 240 ozs.) of **gold,** worth approximately $7,600. The three hundred smaller shields (v. 16) had half this value each (in I Kgs 10:17, by a different standard, "three pounds," Heb. *mānîm;* cf. HDB, IV, 903). **16. The house,** or palace, **of the forest of Lebanon** (in Jerusalem) received its name from its rows of cedar pillars (I Kgs 7:2-5). **18.** The **stays** of Solomon's throne; i.e., its arm rests. **21.** Solomon's ships **went to Tarshish.** Literally, *were goers of Tarshish.* Not that they went to Tarshish (Tartessus, on the Mediterranean coast of Spain), for they navigated in the Red Sea (8:17,18), but that they were large ships, like those that were built to sail to Tarshish.

24. Harness. Hebrew *nesheq,* "armor." **25. Four thousand stalls for horses** (cf. on 1:14,17). I Kings 4:26 reads, erroneously, "forty thousand."

26. He reigned . . . from the river. The Euphrates (I Kgs 4:21,24). He thus occupied the limits of what God had promised to Abraham (Gen 15:18). **29. Written in the book . . . in the prophecy . . . in the visions.** See Introduction, *Authorship.* I Kings 11:41 refers to another source, "The book of the acts of Solomon."

II. The Kingdom of Judah. 10:1–36:23.

A. The Division of the Kingdom. 10:1–11:19. "Our God is marching on!" Humanly speaking, the three-stage course of the Kingdom of Judah—its division from the majority of Israel, its succession of diversely-minded rulers, and its final demise in exile—was one of stark tragedy. Even the prophetic author of I and II Kings, writing near the close of the Exile, could salvage from it only the moral vindication of Jehovah, rendering to His faithless people according to their deeds (II Kgs 17:7-23; 24:1-4). But the chronicler, writing after the restoration of 536 B.C., was inspired to see that behind the four centuries of decline in Judah moved the hand of God, sovereignly accomplishing his own plans in history. This is clear, even in the chronicler's analysis of the initial division, 930 B.C. Rehoboam's resistance to reform and the subsequent rebellion against him (II Chr 10) were "brought about of God" (10:15, ASV), and his attempt to resubdue northern Israel was blocked by the word of the Lord (11:1-5). But the result was a separation of the godly from the apostate north (11:6-22), "so they strengthened the kingdom of Judah" (v. 17). Note that II Chr 10 and 11:4,13-17, correspond to I Kgs 12, through II Chr 11:5-12,18-23 is without parallel.

10:1. Solomon's son **Rehoboam went to Shechem.** This city, which was thirty miles north of Jerusalem, was a center for the northern tribes. David's dynasty had been divinely appointed (I Chr 17:14), but each ruler was yet subject to popular confirmation (II Chr 10:4). Rehoboam could reign only as a "constitutional" servant (v. 7) under God (cf. on I Chr 11:3). **2. Jeroboam** had already been anointed of God for kingship over ten-twelfths of Israel (I Kgs 11:26-40); hence the necessity for his flight **from the presence of Solomon** into Egypt.

4. Thy father made our yoke grievous. Solomon had indulged in sinful extravagance at the expense of his people (cf. Deut 17:17,20). **9. That we may return answer.** Rehoboam thus early in his reign identified himself—we—with the insolent autocracy of the generation raised in Solomon's luxury. **15. The cause** (Heb. *n^e sibbâ,* "the turn of affairs") **was of God,** who had ordained Israel's division, through his prophet **Ahijah the Shilonite,** in punishment for Solomon's lapse into idolatry (I Kgs 11:29-33).

16. What portion have we in David? Such a rebellious spirit, however, against the divinely ordained dynasty was equally condemnable (13:5-7). **Every man to your tents** (cf. II Sam 20:1). The geographical isolation arising out of life upon Palestine's broken terrain was, in itself, conducive to political disruption. **17. Israel . . . in . . . Judah.** The more pious of Israel, who had become attached to Judah, remained faithful to Rehoboam (cf. 11:3).

18. Hadoram. *Adoniram* (I Kgs 4:6; 5:14) **was over the tribute.** Hebrew *mas,* the conscripted labor gangs. He was probably one of the most hated men in Israel, an embodiment of autocracy. **19. Israel rebelled.** I Kings 12:20 describes how the northern tribes confirmed Jeroboam as their king. Chronicles, however, concentrates on the faithful remnant and dismisses the history of northern Israel from this point on.

11:1. Judah and Benjamin. As had been prophesied by Ahijah (I Kgs 11:31,32), these two tribes continued loyal to the Davidic dynasty (II Chr 11:3, 12; cf. on I Chr 4:24-43).

2. Shemaiah was the prophet, or **man of God,** who counseled Rehoboam after his later lapse (12:5-7) and who composed one of the source-records of his reign (12:15). **3. All Israel in Judah and Benjamin** are defined in I Kgs 12:

23 as "the remnant," the pious survivors out of the larger apostate group (Lev 26:39,44; Isa 10:20-23). **4. This thing is done of me.** See 10:15, note.

5. Rehoboam . . . built cities. Forbidden to repossess Israel, he prepared defenses for the territory left to him, a necessary move in light of the constant warfare that followed (12:15). The cities listed (vv. 6-10) lie to the south and the west, located there, apparently, because of the Egyptian danger (cf. 12:2-4).

14. Jeroboam . . . had cast off the Levites (cf. I Kgs 12:31), as a part of his general policy of alienating his people from religious dependence upon Jerusalem (I Kgs 12:26-28). **And his sons** (successors). The migration of the faithful to Judah was thus a process that continued down through the years. **15. He ordained him priests . . . for the devils.** Hebrew *sᵉʿîrîm*, "he-goats" (as inhabiting ruins; Isa 13:21; 34:14). Far from being mythological "satyrs," as claimed by 'liberal' criticism, the *sᵉʿîrîm* appear to have been simply goat idols, used in conjunction with the golden **calves . . . he had made** (cf. Lev 17:7). **17.** But sinful as were Jeroboam's substituted idolatries, they did serve, in God's providence, to gather the pious to the south (vv. 13,16) and so **strengthened the kingdom of Judah.**

18. Abihail was the wife of **Jerimoth** and mother of **Mahalath,** not a second wife of Rehoboam (cf. ASV). **21. Maachah** (Michaiah, 13:2) must have been Absalom's grand-**daughter,** through his daughter Tamar, the wife of Uriel (13:2; cf. II Sam 14:27; 18:18). **He took eighteen wives.** Rehoboam thus willfully disregarded both the law of God (Deut 17:17; Lev 18:18; cf. John Murray, *Principles of Conduct,* Appendix B) and the disastrous precedent of his father. **23. He dealt wisely.** By delegating to his sons authority in the national defense, and by providing them with substance and with wives (ASV); but also by dispersing them, to insure the undisputed succession of Abijah, the designated heir (v. 22).

B. The Rulers of Judah. 12:1–36:16. The nineteen men and one woman who occupied David's throne from 930 to 586 B.C. ranged in character from the strongest and best to the weakest and worst. The fate of any nation is determined in large part by the caliber of its leadership, and this was markedly so in Israel, where God's intervening hand was more clearly manifest than elsewhere. The chronicler thus encourages the men of his day to consecration by demonstrating from God's miraculous past deliverances of Judah how "faith is the victory" that can overcome the world (II Chr 20:20). Yet at the same time, and from the same historical data, he admonishes them against compromise with the world, against indifference to the Law, and against deviation from the Lord. For the fundamental pattern of Judah's history is one of religious deterioration. Sin becomes so ingrained that even a Josiah cannot reverse the downward trend: "The wrath of the Lord arose against his people, till there was no remedy" (36:16). God *can* cast off his people whom he foreknew! At points, II Chr 12:1–36:16 corresponds closely to I Kgs 14:22–II Kgs 24:20. Much of the content of Kings, however, is omitted, e.g., the lives of the prophets, and, indeed, the whole history of northern Israel (cf. Introduction, *Occasion for Writing).* But for Judah, the chronicler supplies thrilling examples of faith and of deliverance that are without parallel in the more summary account of Kings.

1) Rehoboam. 12:1-16. Solomon's son succeeded to the throne in 930* B.C. and reigned until 913 B.C. II Chronicles 12 takes up Rehoboam's rule with his establishment (v. 1), after the division of Solomon's kingdom had assumed permanency (chs. 10; 11). It describes his punishment for departure from the Law (vv. 1-6), and then his restoration upon submission to God (vv. 7-12). A summary of his seventeen-year reign concludes the section (vv. 13-16). A shorter, but parallel, account occurs in I Kgs 14:21-31.

1. Rehoboam . . . forsook the law. By turning to the immoralities and polytheism of the native Canaanites (I Kgs 14:23,24; 15:12). This was the determining cause for Shishak's invasion (v. 2). **2. In the fifth year, 925* B.C., Shishak . . . came up.** This campaign of Sheshonk I, energetic founder of the Twenty-second Dynasty of Egypt, has been confirmed by his list of conquered Palestinian cities, engraved on the walls of the temple of Amon at Karnak. This list shows that he

The * indicates a possible occurrence in the closing months of the preceding year; see Edwin R. Thiele, *The Mysterious Numbers of the Hebrew Kings,* p. 55.

plundered northern Israel as well as Judah. **3. Lubim** (ASV). Libyans of North Africa. The **Sukkiim** remain unidentified.

5. Shemaiah. See 11:2, note. **7. They humbled themselves** and were delivered (v. 12), thus illustrating a standing principle (I Pet 5:6), though Rehoboam seems not to have taken the experience to heart (II Chr 12:14). **8. That they may know my service.** Compared with the service exacted by the world. How much better to submit to God! (Mt 11:28-30) **9. Shishak . . . carried away also the shields of gold.** See 9:15, note. **10. Instead of which king Rehoboam made shields of brass** (bronze). Faithlessness reduced him to imitations of the glory that once was his. **11. The guard . . . brought them again,** replacing them after their use.

12. In Judah things went well. Literally, *there were good things*. True consecration did continue. **13. The Lord . . . put his name there,** i.e., in Jerusalem. See 6:6, note. **15. The book . . . of Iddo . . . concerning genealogies.** Its content may have been largely genealogical.

2) Abijah (Abijam, I Kgs 15:1). 13:1-22. The three-year reign of Rehoboam's son Abijah, 913–910* B.C., was occupied primarily by his war with Jeroboam (cf. I Kgs 15:6,7). Moreover, while the outline in I Kgs 15:1-8 gives no detail on this conflict, the parallel account in II Chronicles 13 reveals both Abijah's bravery against odds, springing from trust upon the God whose law he obeyed (vv. 1-12), and his glorious victory that resulted (vv. 13-21). "Judah prevailed, because they relied upon the Lord God of their fathers" (v. 18).

2. His mother's name . . . was Michaiah (Maachah); see 11:21, note.

3. Four hundred thousand against **eight hundred thousand.** Abijah was badly outnumbered. The historicity of these figures, confessedly high for such limited areas, is vouchsafed by I Chr 21:5 (cf. its accompanying note). This was an all-our attack. **4. Mount Zemaraim.** The town of Zemaraim lay within the territory of Benjamin (Josh 18:22); so this battlefield must have been on the border between the kingdoms of **Ephraim** (Israel) and Judah.

5. God . . . gave the kingdom . . . to David, and his descendants (I Chr 17:14), **by a covenant of salt,** meaning, of permanence (cf. Lev 2:13). Salt is noted as a preservative.

7. Children of Belial (Heb., *worthlessness*). By NT times, but not here, Belial had come to refer specifically to Satan (II Cor 6:15). **When Rehoboam was young.** His actual age was forty-one (II Chr 12:13); but he was **tender** (weak)-**hearted,** i.e., immature in his understanding and experience. **8. Golden calves . . . for gods.** 'Liberal' criticism minimizes Jeroboam's apostasy by assuming his calves to have been, like the ark, but "pedestals" for the invisible presence of Jehovah. But those who were contemporaries understood these calves as molten images of other gods (cf. I Kgs 12:28; 14:9).

10. The Lord is our God. This ringing affirmation is modified by the fact that Abijah "walked in all the sins of his father" (note his polygamy, v. 21, and see on 12:1). His faith fluctuated; for "his heart was not perfect with the Lord his God, as the heart of David" (I Kgs 15:3). **11.** Daily **sacrifices and sweet incense,** and **the shewbread.** See notes to 2:4; 4:1,8; I Chr 9:32; 23:30. **The candlestick** *(lampstand)*. Solomon's Temple had ten such lampstands (4:7; cf. the accompanying note), one of which was doubtless *the* original lampstand of Moses. **12. Priests with . . . trumpets to cry alarm.** To call God to their rescue (v. 14; Num 10:9).

15. God smote Jeroboam. Whether through direct supernatural intervention, or through the courage of His encircled people, is not stated. **17.** The slaughter of **five hundred thousand** chosen men, over half the army, was a staggering loss for the relatively small nation of Israel (cf. v. 20).

19. Abijah **took . . . Beth-el,** near the border between Benjamin and Ephraim, the very seat of Jeroboam's calf worship (I Kgs 12:29,33), though the idol was likely removed before the city's capture. **Jeshanah . . . and Ephrain** (Ephron) were four miles north and northeast of Beth-el respectively. **20. The Lord struck him.** The details of Jeroboam's death in 910 B.C., three years after Abijah's, are not elsewhere elaborated.

22. The story of the prophet Iddo. The Hebrew word used here for **story** is *midrash*, a "commentary," perhaps on the official court record (cf. 24:27).

3) Asa. 14:1–16:14. These three chapters (amplifying I Kgs 15:9-24) describe the four outstanding events of Asa's long reign, 910*–869* B.C.: (1)

the first reform, during his ten years of peace (14:1-8); (2) the victory over Zerah the Ethiopian in 896* B.C. (14:9-15); (3) the second reform, that came as a result (ch. 15); and (4) the hostile reaction of Baasha of Israel, 895 B.C., that induced a series of religious deviations on the part of Asa (ch. 16). Asa was, nevertheless, the most righteous monarch yet to arise in Judah after the division of Solomon's kingdom (I Kgs 15:11).

14:1. The land was quiet ten years. That is, until the invasion of Zerah in 896 (see 15:19, note). This peace, which was God's reward for Asa's first reform (vv. 5-7), may be traced back, in part, to Abijah's crushing defeat of northern Israel (13:17,20).

3. He took away . . . the high places (see 1:3, note), in obedience to Deut 12:2,3; but it appears that the people continued to resort to them, despite the royal abolition (15:17). **The images** (Heb., *maṣṣēbôt)* were Canaanitish stone pillars (ASV), thought to contain the local fertility-gods, the Baalim. The term **groves** (Heb., *'ăshērîm)* refers, actually, to Baal's goddess-consort Asherah, believed to reside in a wooden pole beside the stone pillar. Both, when carved, became idols (cf. I Kgs 15:12). **5.** The **images** are now known, from archaeology, to have been incense-stands (William F. Albright, *Archaeology and the Religion of Israel,* pp. 215,216).

7. While the land is yet before us. Free from enemies. **8. Of Judah, three hundred thousand** spearmen with **targets** (heavy shields covering the entire body); **of Benjamin, two hundred and fourscore thousand** [280,000] bowmen with lighter **shields.** These large figures must have included the whole population capable of bearing arms.

9. There came out against them Zerah the Ethiopian. Hebrew, *Cushite.* This may represent an attempt by Osorkon I, second Pharaoh of the Twenty-second Dynasty in Egypt, to duplicate the invasion and pillage of his predecessor, Sheshonk (see on 12:2). The results, however, against pious Asa, were quite opposite! **An host of a thousand thousand.** This is a round figure; but it does indicate a vast assemblage, far outnumbering the forces of Asa. **10. They set the battle in array . . . at Mareshah.** In the valley that marks the entrance into the hills, half way between Gaza and Jerusalem. This was one of the cities Rehoboam had fortified in anticipation of just such an attack (11:9).

11. It is nothing with thee to help . . . them that have no power. Asa's position was hopeless. But for God, the humanly impossible is as nothing (Gen 18:14); and Asa had the faith to rest on God and to expect the impossible (cf. Mk 9:23). **12. The Lord smote the Ethiopians** (cf. v. 13). Again the details are not furnished (see on 13:15).

13. Asa . . . pursued them unto Gerar, even south of Gaza, on their flight back to Egypt. **That they could not recover.** Literally, *so that they had no revival* (KD). Israel experienced no more trouble from Egypt for 170 years, until the Twenty-fifth Dynasty (II Kgs 17:4). **15. They smote also the tents of cattle;** that is, of the Philistinized cattle herders in the area.

15:1. Azariah, and **Oded** (cf. v. 8), are unknown but for this prophecy. **2 If ye seek him,** etc., was David's admonition to Solomon (I Chr 28:9); and Azariah proceeds to illustrate this truth from Israel's past history. **3. Israel hath been** (better, *was,* ASV) **without the true God.** Probably referring to the chaotic days of the Judges (cf. Jud 21:25). **And . . . a teaching priest.** One of the major priestly functions was to teach the *Law* (Lev 10:11). **4. When they in their trouble did turn unto the Lord . . . he was found of them.** Cf. Judges 2:18. **5. There was no peace.** Cf. Judges 5:6.

8. Asa . . . put away the abominable idols, and also the sexual immoralities that accompanied Canaanitish worship (I Kgs 15:12). **9.** The fact that many **fell to him out of Israel** illustrates God's purpose in dividing Solomon's kingdom, that the "remnant" might be preserved (cf. on 11:3,14). But it also explains the acts of reprisal taken by Baasha of Israel soon thereafter (16:2). **Out of Simeon.** See on I Chr 4:24-43.

10. They gathered in the third month of the fifteenth year, May/June, 895 B.C., perhaps for the Feast of Weeks (Pentecost), one of the three annual pilgrimage feasts (cf. I Chr 23:31, note; Lev 23:15-21). This was the year following Zerah's attack (II Chr 15:19, note), since the pursuit and the occupation of the surrounding territories (14:13-15) must have consumed several months.

12-15. They entered into a covenant. Hebrew, "the" covenant. God's one great, everlasting testament (cf. I Chr 16:15, note) for the redemption of his people. The following are among its noteworthy, changeless features: (1) Objective redemption, as expressed by the phrase **God of their fathers** (v. 12). Cf. verse 15, "He was found of them." God enters into a saving relationship with his elect (Gen 17:7; Jer 31:34; Jn 17:6). (2) Man's subjective responses of faith and obedience (v. 13). **Seek the Lord God of Israel** (cf. v. 15; Gen 15:6; Ex 19:5; Lk 13:3; Jn 3:16). Conformity was here enforced on pain of **death** (cf Deut 17:2-6); for, after all, it is better for a man to be restrained in this life than for him, or others who may be affected by him, to be lost for eternity (Deut 13:12-15; Mk 9:43-48). (3) The inheritance of reconciliation (v. 15): **The Lord gave them rest.** Here an immediate rest from their enemies. But the testamental **rest** involves, in its fullness, all the joys of redeemed life in the present (Ps 103), of heaven beyond the grave (Ps 73:23-26; Heb 4:9-11), and of the ultimate kingdom of God upon earth (Rev 20:6; 22:5).

16. Maachah was **the mother of** Asa's father Abijah (cf. 11:21; 13:2, notes), and so technically the queen-grandmother. Since she must have been an influential figure at the court, Asa is to be commended for placing faith above family in her removal (cf. Deut 33:9; Mt 10:37). **An idol in a grove.** Literally, *a horrible thing for Asherah* (see on 14:3). Whatever her object of worship may have been, he burned **it at the brook Kidron,** the sharp valley between the eastern wall of Jerusalem and the Mount of Olives. **17. But the high places were not taken away.** This describes the sad historic fact, not the king's personal intention (see on 14:3).

18. He brought into the Temple (cf. I Chr 18:11; 26:26-28) **the things that his father . . . and that he . . . had dedicated,** including spoils of Jeroboam (13:19) and of Zerah and his allies (14:13-15). **19. There was no more war unto the thirty-fifth year.** The Hebrew text lacks the word **more** and should be rendered, *There had not been war until the thirty-fifth year, which had reference to Asa's reign.* The war was that with Zerah in 896, which was the thirty-fifth year after the division of the kingdom (cf. 16:1). It could not refer to the thirty-fifth of Asa's own reign, since he warred with Baasha before his twenty-sixth (I Kgs 15:16,33; cf. Thiele *Mysterious Numbers,* pp. 57-60).

16:1. In the thirty-sixth year, 895 B.C. (cf. on 15:19), after the assemblage of May/June (15:10), **Baasha came up.** In 909 B.C. Baasha had overthrown the dynasty of Jeroboam I and usurped the kingship of Israel (I Kgs 15:27-29). Having been at odds with Asa from the first (I Kgs 15:16), and having been aroused by the defection among his people to the southern king (II Chr 15:9), he advanced southward, probably recapturing Beth-el (cf. 13:19), and fortified **Ramah,** thus blockading Jerusalem only five miles further south.

2. Asa brought out silver and gold (all there was, I Kgs 15:18) out of the Temple. He thus sacrificed the results of his own piety (II Chr 15:18) and of God's blessing (14:12-14) to induce a pagan king, **Ben-hadad** (I) of Damascus, to perform a deed of perfidy (v. 3) in order to achieve his and Judah's "protection"! But see Jer 17:5. **3. There is a league.** Read with ASV margin, *Let there be a league.* **As there was between my father and thy father.** That is between Abijah and Tabrimon (I Kgs 15:18) the son of Hezion (Rezon[?], the adversary of Solomon and the founder of the Kingdom of Damascus; I Kgs 11:23-25). Damascus switched allies at convenience.

4. Ben-hadad's armies **smote Ijon, and Dan, and Abel-main** (Abel-beth-maachah, I Kgs 15:20), **and all the store cities** (I Kgs specifies Cinneroth, the plains of northwestern Galilee) **of Naphtali,** all in the far north of Israel. This attack on Baasha's rear compelled him to abandon his southern operations against Asa. **6.** Asa Built **Geba and Mizpah, east** and west of Ramah, respectively (cf. Jer 41:9).

7. Hanani the seer. Father to Jehu, the seer of Asa's son Jehoshaphat (19:2; 20:34). **Therefore is the host** (army) **of . . . Syria escaped.** For they, as Baasha's allies (v. 3), would presumably have joined with Israel in attacking Judah, and God would have delivered over the entire force to Asa. **8. The Ethiopians and the Lubims.** See 14:9,11; cf. 12:3, notes. **9. The eyes of the Lord run to and fro.** No problem can arise for God's people of which he is not aware, or from which he will not deliver (cf. Rom 8:32). **Whose heart is perfect.** Hebrew *shālēm,* "whole." God protects those who are "wholeheartedly" devoted to him. **Henceforth thou shalt have wars** (cf. I Kgs

15:32). The very Syrians whose attacks Asa had initiated later brought Judah to her knees (II Kgs 12:17,18).

10. Asa . . . put him in a prison house. Literally, *the house of stocks.* This is the first recorded persecution of a prophet, but many such followed (cf. I Kgs 22:27; Mk 6:17,18). **And Asa oppressed some of the people.** One sin leads to another.

11. The book of the kings of Judah and Israel is not our I and II Kings, but some court chronicle, now lost (see Introduction, *Authorship).* **12. In the thirty and ninth year of his reign, 871* B.C., he sought not to the Lord but to the physicians** (pagans?). Medicine is God's gift, but it is the Creator of medicine who gives healing (II Kgs 20:7; cf. vv. 2,3). **14. Buried him in his own sepulchres.** This clarifies the general statement of I Kgs 15:24 that he "was buried with his fathers in the city of David." **A great burning,** of the spices (not cremation), was made in his honor (cf. Jer 34:5).

4) Jehoshaphat. 17:1–20:37. His regnal years extended from 872* to 848 B.C. (see 17:7, note). Like father, like son! As Asa had accomplished the first reform, so Jehoshaphat removed idolatry, taught God's Law, and strengthened his kingdom, 866 B.C. (II Chr 17); but even as Asa had entered into unholy alliances, so Jehoshaphat allied himself with Ahab of Israel and became involved in the near-fatal campaign of Ramoth-gilead, 853 B.C. (ch. 18). Again, just as the prophet Azariah had admonished Asa and brought about his second reformation, so Jehu the son of Hanani led Jehoshaphat to a further reform in religion and in the administration of justice (ch. 19). Finally, as Asa had faced hordes from the southwest, so Jehoshaphat, with trust in the Lord, met and overcame the multitudes from the east (20:1-30). A final passage summarizes Jehoshaphat's reign and describes the failure of his commercial alliance with Israel (20:31-37). Of these divisions, only chapters 18 and 20:31-37 find real parallels in I Kings (ch. 22).

17:1. Jehoshaphat . . . strengthened himself against Israel. Godless Ahab, second king of the dynasty of Omri, was now ruling in Samaria; hostility between the two kingdoms continued. **2. Asa had** taken **cities of Ephraim.** Not simply the threatening outpost of Ramah (see on 16:1), but others as well (15:8).

3. In the first ways of . . . David. The chronicler thus by implication confesses that David's later ways were less exemplary (cf. II Sam 11–21). The **Baalim.** Hebrew plural. For "the Baals" were multifold, each field, even, having its own fertility-spirit. **4. The doings of Israel** included Jereboam's innovations in the priesthood and calendar as well as his calf worship (I Kgs 12:28-33). **6. He took away the high places and groves** (Asherah-poles; see on 14:3). Cf. I Kgs 22:46; though this official act, like that of Asa before him (II Chr 15:17), was not popularly sustained (20:33).

7. In the third year of his reign. That is, of his sole reign, or 866* B.C. A comparison of II Kgs 3:1 and 8:16 indicates that Jehoshaphat's full reign of twenty-five years (II Chr 20:31) must have commenced three years prior to his father's death, or in 872*. A co-regency was, perhaps, made necessary by Asa's illness, which became increasingly serious in the following year (16:12, note). **He sent to . . . Benhail . . .** Read simply, *He sent Ben-hail,* etc. (ASV). These are the names of the princes. **To teach.** Jehoshaphat realized that the teaching of God's Book (v. 9) is the work of *all* leaders, who are of the faith (cf. Mt 28:20), not just of professional Levites and priests (Deut 33:10; Lev 10:11). **9. They . . . went about,** like the traveling exhorters and evangelists of the NT (cf. III Jn 7,8).

12,13. He built . . . castles . . . . and had much business. Literally, *fortified places* and *work* (and the property gained thereby).

14. Of Judah . . . Adnah . . . and with him . . . three hundred thousand . . . Jehoshaphat's three Judean armies thus totalled 780,000, as compared with 500,000 in the time of David (II Sam 24:9). He also commanded the services of the two Benjamite armies of 380,000. These are very large figures, the muster doubtless including all his citizenry (cf. II Chr 14:8). **19. These,** the five army commanders, **waited on the king.** Portions of their troops would then have been stationed **in the fenced cities. 18:1.** In about 865 B.C. (cf. the age of his son's son, Ahaziah, at his accession in 841; II Kgs 8:26), or after sixty-five years of hostility between northern Israel and Judah, **Jehoshaphat . . . joined affinity with Ahab** (cf. v. 3; I Kgs 22:44). This included the marriage of Jehoshaphat's son Jehoram to Athaliah, the daughter of

Ahab and Jezebel (II Chr 21:6), an alliance which was to have disastrous results for Judah (22:10). This alliance may have been furthered by the threat of Assyrian power, against which a coalition of western states, including Damascus and Israel, fought a drawn battle in 853 at Qarqar on the Orontes River.

2. Go up . . . to Ramoth-gilead. This key city on the caravan route at the edge of Trans-Jordanian Israel had been seized by Syria (16:4, or II Kgs 20:38); but Ahab may have felt that Damascus had been sufficiently weakened by her losses at Qarqar to permit of its recapture at this time (853 B.C.).

4. Enquire . . . of the Lord. Jehoshaphat had already committed himself (v. 3), but he retained enough piety to realize his need of divine guidance, though he neglected the guidance after it was given (v. 29). **5. Of prophets four hundred men.** These men from Ahab's court spoke in the name of the Lord (in his corrupted golden calf form), but falsely (v. 22) with whatever message was calculated to please (v. 12; Mic 3:5,11). Jehoshaphat put little faith in them (v. 6). **7 Micaiah,** who is known only from this incident, **never prophesied good** unto Ahab. The true prophet was, in fact, distinguished by the fact that he faithfully warned Israel of the results of her sin (Jer 23:22; Mic 3:8).

9. A void (open) **place.** Hebrew *a threshing floor.* **At . . . the gate,** the traditional place of judgment (cf. Ruth 4:1). **10. He made . . . horns of iron.** Symbols of victory (Deut 33:17), but perhaps superstitiously believed to possess magical power, too.

13. What my God saith . . . I speak (cf. Num 24:13). God's revelations were objectively distinguished, by genuine prophets, from the thoughts and desires of their own hearts (Jer 14:14). **14. Go ye up, and prosper.** He spoke in mockery, as his tone of voice must have made clear (cf. v. 15).

16. These have no master (cf. Num 27:16,17). He thus predicted Ahab's death (II Chr 18:24), and his people's release **in peace** (v. 30). **18. The host** (army) **of heaven . . . on his right.** That is, angels. Cf. the "sons of God" (Job 1:6). **19. Who shall entice Ahab.** God may work through his spirits to incite evil men to manifest their sin and thus be led to punishment or to repentance (cf. I Sam 16:14,15; 18:10,11). **20. There came out a spirit.** Hebrew, *the* (well-known) *spirit,* Satan (Job 1:6-12). Micaiah assumed in his hearers a knowledge of the Book of Job (already written down in the days of Solomon?).

23. Zedekiah . . . smote Micaiah. This act was proof that the Spirit of God was not with Zedekiah (Jas 3:17). **Which way went the Spirit . . . from me.** The false prophet brazenly asserted that a prophecy contrary to his own could not be of the Spirit. **24. Thou shalt . . . hide thyself.** The fulfillment of this forecast is unrecorded, but the prophecy may refer to the punishment meted out to the false prophets by Ahab's family, after the king's death.

25. The order, **Carry him back,** implies that Micaiah was already in prison at the time; cf. Asa's precedent (16:10). **26. With bread of affliction.** Short rations. **27. Hearken, all ye people.** Hebrew plural, *peoples.* Micaiah summoned all nations to be his witnesses.

29. I will disguise myself. Ahab sought this futile means to avert God's decree (v. 16). **30. Fight . . . only with the king of Israel.** If he could be taken, the battle would be won (cf. II Sam 21:17). **31. They compassed about him.** Jehoshaphat would then and there have reaped the fruit of his sinful alliance had not **the Lord helped him. 33. A . . . man drew a bow at a venture.** Hebrew, *in his unsuspectingness.* But there is no *chance* with God (Prov 16:33). **Between the joints of the harness.** The Hebrew suggests, "between the links of mail below, and the breastplate"; i.e., in the abdomen.

19:1. Jehoshaphat . . . returned . . . in peace, thus fulfilling the last detail of Micaiah's prophecy (see 18:16, note). **2. Jehu the son of Hanani** had condemned the dynasty of Baasha of Israel some twenty-five years before (I Kgs 16:1). **Shouldest thou . . . love them that hate the Lord?** Not that the Christian should not have a compassionate love for the lost (Mt 5:44), but that he must not compromise his stand for God (Ps 139: 21,22) or **help the ungodly** with co-operation (II Jn 10,11; Rom 16:17). **Therefore is wrath upon thee** (ASV). It had been upon him (18:31) and would be (20:1,37; 22:10). Jehoshaphat, however, humbled himself before the prophet (cf. 12:6), as his father Asa had not humbled himself before Jehu's father Hanani (16:10). **3. The groves.** See on 14:3. **6. Ye judge . . . for the Lord.** Good government springs from submission to the Lord (see I Chr 11:3, note). **7. Nor respect of persons, nor taking of gifts.** The servant of God must be impartial, and he must accept no bribes.

8. In the **Jerusalem** central court of appeal, he **set . . . Levites . . . for . . . judgment;** see on I Chr 26:29. **10. Between blood and blood.** Cases of bloodshed. **Warn them.** A judge is chargeable to God for his actions, for which **wrath** may **come upon** him (cf. Ezk 33:6). **11. Matters of the Lord . . . the king's matters.** In the Pentateuch, religious and civil, ceremonial and moral law are inseparable. The distinction that is here first made (though based on Deut 17:9, 12) became clarified in later prophetic thought (Isa 1:11-17; Amos 5:21-24).

20:1. Other beside the Ammonites. The Hebrew, *mēhāʿammônîm,* is quite likely a scribal corruption of *mēhammᵉʿûnîm,* "of the Mehunim," a people from Mount Seir in Edom, farther south (cf. vv. 10, 22,23). **2. From beyond the** (Dead) **sea on this side Syria** (Aram). Read *Edom,* which is a very slight scribal change in the consonantal Hebrew, and which agrees with the geography of **En-gedi,** on the western side of the Dead Sea. **3. Jehoshaphat . . . proclaimed a fast.** Fasting was a sign of grief (Jud 20:26) and was not a regular feature of pre-Exilic Hebrew religion (unless implied in Lev 16:29-31). But from Samuel's time on, it had been employed to emphasize the sincerity of the prayers of God's people when Israel faced special needs (I Sam 7:6; cf. Acts 13:2).

5. The new court was an innovation of Solomon's in building the Temple (see on 4:9). Perhaps it had recently been restored by Jehoshaphat (cf. 17:12). **9. If, when evil cometh.** The king was quoting from Solomon's plea (6:28-30; cf. 7:13-15). **10. Whom thou wouldest not let Israel invade** (Deut 2:4). Jehoshaphat thus called on God to honor Israel's former obedience, as well as His own gracious promise (II Chr 20:11). **12. We have no might . . . but our eyes are upon thee.** Here was faith like that of his father Asa (see on 14:11).

14. Jahaziel . . . of the sons of Asaph seems to have been inspired by God's Spirit to compose Psalm 83 on this occasion (see especially vv. 2,6-8 of the psalm). **15. The battle is not yours, but God's.** Cf. I Sam 17:47. **16.** From a point seven miles north of En-gedi, **the cliff** (*ascent,* ASV) **of Ziz** wound inland to the valley of Berachah (v. 26). **17. Stand ye still, and see the salvation of the Lord.** Cf. Ex 14:13. **20. The wilderness of Tekoa** lay south of Bethlehem, toward Hebron. **Believe in the Lord your God, so shall ye be established.** Cf. Mk 9:27. **21. Singers . . . went out before the army,** as had the arks of God and the priestly trumpeters at Jericho (Josh 6:9). **Praise the beauty of holiness.** Cf. I Chr 16:29, *in holy array* (ASV). **22. The Lord set ambushments.** Perhaps marauding Seirites, for note the way in which the forces then turned on the men of Seir (v. 23). **23. Every one helped to destroy another.** As in the triumph of Gideon (Jud 7:22). **26. Berachah** (see v. 16) means *blessing* in Hebrew.

33. The high places were not taken away. See on 17:6. **34. The book of Jehu . . . who is mentioned in the book of the kings.** Rather, *which is inserted in the book* (ASV; cf. on 32:32).

35. Jehoshaphat . . . join[ed] himself with Ahaziah, the son of Ahab, who reigned in Israel, 853–852 B.C. **36. Ships in Ezion-gaber.** See on 8:17,18. **To go to Tarshish.** That is, of the sort that could go to Tarshish (cf. on 9:21). Their destination was, in fact, Ophir (I Kgs 22: 48). **37. Eliezer** is otherwise unknown. **The ships were broken.** God will not honor compromising alliances.

5) Jehoram. 21:1-20. He reigned from 848 to 841 B.C. II Chronicles 21 is a commentary on the man who married the daughter of Ahab and Jezebel, and who walked in their ways (v. 6). It describes Jehoram's viciousness and his apostasy (vv. 1-11), but also God's condemnation upon him through the prophet Elijah, and the failures, both national and personal, that overwhelmed him as a result (vv. 12-20). The former verses represent an expansion of II Kgs 8:16-24, though the latter are without Biblical parallel, except for Jehoram's death notice.

1. Jehoshaphat slept with his fathers . . . And Jehoram . . . reigned. This was 848 B.C. Actually, Jehoram had been an associate on the throne since 853* (cf. II Kgs 3:1 with 1:17; II Chr 17:7, note; and Thiele, *Mysterious Numbers,* pp. 64, 65). **2.** The second **Azariah** is *Azariahu* in Hebrew. **3.** Jehoshaphat **gave** to his six younger sons **gifts,** etc., following the prudent policy of his great-grandfather Rehoboam (see on 11:23). **4. Jehoram . . . slew all his brethren,** and others.

Having accepted the godless standards of his wife Athaliah, he apparently assumed (falsely, v. 13) that his brothers would act with similar ruthlessness toward him, if given the opportunity.

7. The Lord would not destroy the house of David. It was this same divine reticence that had preserved the southern kingdom to Rehoboam, after Solomon's sin (I Kgs 11:12,13). The term **covenant,** Hebrew *bᵉrît,* does not occur in God's promise in I Chr 17. But that this was indeed one of the manifestations of God's redemptive testament is confirmed in a number of other passages (cf. II Sam 23:5; Isa 55:3).

8. "Because he had forsaken the Lord" (v. 10), **Edom revolted** (ASV) from the rule of its Hebrew governors (I Kgs 22:47). Moab, to the north of Edom, had already established its independence (II Kgs 1:1). **9.** After being **compassed . . . in** (almost overwhelmed), **Jehoram . . . smote the Edomites,** at Zair (I Kgs 8:21; possibly Zior (?), a few miles south of his father's victory-site of Berachah; II Chr 20:26). He failed, however, to quell the Edomitic uprising as such (v. 10). This campaign thus corresponds closely to Israel's unsuccessful attempt to resubdue Moab shortly before (II Kgs 3:3-27). **10. Also . . . Libnah.** A Philistinized city north of Gath.

11. Jehoram **made high places,** the very shrines his fathers had tried with such difficulty to eradicate (see on 14:3; 17:6). While the Canaanitish worship thus introduced did involve obscenities (cf. I Kgs 22:46), the **fornication** concerned here is that of Israel's faithlessness toward Jehovah, her divine Husband. For Moses and the prophets, idolatry was "whoredom" (II Chr 21:13; cf. Lev 20:5; Num 25:1,2).

12. The last recorded act of **Elijah** took place in 852 (II Kgs 1:3,17). But his translation may not have occurred until after Jehoram's crimes of fratricide, following his accession as sole monarch in 848 (II Kgs 3:3 need not require an earlier date). Elijah was, however, probably gone by the time of the delivery of his letter, so that its sentences of doom came almost as a voice from the dead.

16. The Arabians, that were near the Ethiopians (Heb. *Cushites),* may have been nomads from the borderlands between Philistia and Egypt (cf. on 14:9).

19,20. The **sore disease** of which Jehoram died appears to have been a violent form of dysentery. He died, moreover, without mourners—**no burning** (cf. 16:14, note); and was buried in dishonor, apart from **the sepulchres of the kings** (cf. 24:25).

6) Ahaziah (841 B.C.). 22:1-9. These verses furnish a historical demonstration of how, in God's providence, the results of a sin may bring about that very sin's punishment. In the case of Ahaziah it was the evil alliance of Judah with Israel that brought about the king's death (vv. 4,7), after a reign of only a few months. The events through which this came about are explained in the more detailed, parallel passage of II Kgs 8:25–10:14.

1. The inhabitants of Jerusalem made Ahaziah . . . king. This popular intervention suggests a succession that was disputed (cf. II Kgs 23:30), perhaps by the king's own mother, the ruthless Athaliah (cf. II Chr 22:10). **The band of men . . . had slain all** Jehoram's older sons. See 21:17 (Jehoahaz is but a variant form of Ahaziah). **2. Forty and two years old** is impossible (cf. 21:5). It is probably a copyist's error for twenty-two (I Kgs 8:26). **He reigned one year,** and for only one part of it (cf. II Kgs 8:25; 3:1; and note that Ahaziah's death was simultaneous with that of J(eh)oram of Israel). **Athaliah** was **the daughter of Omri,** meaning, one of his dynasty. Specifically, she was a granddaughter (cf. 21:6; I Kgs 16:29). **3. His mother was his counsellor.** Further testimony to the dominating influence of this evil woman (cf. 21:6; 21:4 note). **To do wickedly.** Athaliah patronized the Phoenician Baal worship of her mother Jezebel (cf. 23:17).

5. Twelve years after the death of Ahab at **Ramoth-gilead** in 853 B.C. (18:34). Ahab's second son, Joram, had recaptured the city, apparently emboldened by the murder of Ben-hadad and the succession of **Hazael** as new king in Damascus (II Kgs 8:7-15). Hazael, however, reattacked Ramoth-gilead (cf. II Kgs 9:14,15) and in the fighting **smote** and wounded **Joram. 6.** Joram **returned to . . . Jezreel** at the head of the Valley of Esdraelon, site of Ahab's palace (I Kgs 21:1), from **Ramah** (i.e., Ramoth-gilead, v. 5). **Azariah is** *Ahaziah* in the more correct MSS.

7. The details of how the Lord had **anointed** Jehu **to cut off the house of**

Ahab appear in II Kings 9. **8.** Only after Ahaziah's death (v. 9) did Jehu slay **the sons of the brethren** (v. 1) **of Ahaziah** (cf. II Kgs 10:12-14). They could not have been more than little children (cf. II Chr 21:5). **9.** After the murder of his uncle Joram by Jehu, **Ahaziah** fled southward and **hid in Samaria.** He was then **brought . . . to Jehu,** who fatally wounded him near Ibleam (between Jezreel and Samaria), whence he fled northwest to Megiddo and died (II Kgs 9:27). Ahaziah's servants carried him to Jerusalem (II Kgs 9:28) and **buried him.**

7) Athaliah (841–835 B.C.). 22:10–23:21 (paralleling II Kgs 11). Jehoshaphat's alliance by marriage with the house of Ahab led in the end to the almost total extinction of the dynasty of David and to the official paganizing of Judah. For the queen-mother Athaliah, after the death of her one remaining son, Ahaziah, proceeded to slaughter her own princely grandchildren in order to usurp the throne herself, and to entrench the Baal worship of her mother Jezebel as the state religion of Judah. There remained, however, a one-year-old son of Ahaziah, Joash, who was protected by the high priest Jehoiada (II Chr 22:10-12). Finally, after six years, Jehoiada engineered a revolt that brought about the coronation of Joash (23:1-11), the death of Athaliah (vv. 12-15), and the extirpation of her false worship (vv. 16-21).

22:11. Jehoshabeath (Jehosheba, II Kgs 11:2) **the daughter of the preceding king,** Jehoram, and sister of Ahaziah *(ibid.)* hid her infant nephew **Joash . . . in a bedchamber,** the room, that is, in which the mattresses and bedding were stored. He was later removed to the Temple (v. 12) by the high priest Jehoiada, her husband, who was many years her senior (cf. 24:15).

23:1. II Kings 11:4 explains that **the captains of hundreds** were the officers of the Carites (cf. the Cherethites, I Chr 18:17 note) and other elements of the royal guard. **2.** The gathering of **the Levites . . . and the chief of the fathers** must have been done with secrecy, since the uprising caught Athaliah wholly off-guard (v. 13). **3.** They **made a covenant with the king.** With Jehoiada, that is, as the king's protector (cf. v. 1; II Kgs 11:4). Here is another instance of **the requirement** of popular confirmation, that played so prominent a part in the history of Israel's royal succession (cf. I Chr 11:3; II Chr 10:1, notes).

4. A third part . . . entering on the sabbath. At this time there was a changing of the Levitical courses that were on active service in the Temple (I Chr 24:4,20, notes). Of those coming on duty, one **third** were to be at **the doors** of the Temple, "behind the guard" to "keep the watch of the house" (II Kgs 11:6) and thus prevent the entrance of unauthorized, non-Levitical personnel (v. 6). **5.** A second **third** were to be **at the king's house** in the Temple (cf. 22:12; not Athaliah's palace, which remained open; cf. 23:12). The remaining **third** were to be **at the gate of the foundation** (i.e., the gate of Sur; II Kgs 11:6), a temple gate of uncertain location. **8. With them that were to go out on the sabbath.** The two companies of Levites going off duty were not **dismissed,** but kept watch about the king (II Kgs 11:7), equipped with the temple weapons (II Chr 23:9).

10. He set all the rest of the **people,** the non-Levitical chiefs (v. 2) and such of the royal guard as were considered faithful by the five covenanted commanders (v. 1; II Kgs 11:6,11), with their **weapon**[s], in ranks in the temple court (v. 5). **11.** They gave Joash **the testimony,** perhaps the book of the Law of Moses, that was to guide his conduct in office (Deut 17:18,19).

14. Jehoiada . . . brought out (rather, *commanded,* II Kgs 11:15) **the captains,** to have Athaliah **forth of the ranges.** That is, to march her out of the holy Temple between the armed ranks, and to slay any of her followers who might attempt a rescue.

16. With the political revolution came the corresponding religious revival, that king, priest, and citizenry, all **should be the Lord's people.** This included the reaffirmation of "constitutional" monarchy under God by king and people (v. 3). **17.** They **slew Mattan.** This was the fate required by God's Word for those who lead others into false religion (Deut 13:5-10). And they re-established the true worship, as it had been under David (v. 18).

8) Joash (835–796 B.C.). 24:1-27. The reign of Joash serves as an epitome of the whole history of Judah. In its earlier part, Joash lived righteously, honoring the Lord and caring for the Temple, with its sacrifices that depicted

God's eternal plan of salvation (24:1-14). Yet in its later part, he forsook both the Lord and His Temple (vv. 15-19), murdered the prophet who rebuked him, the son of the very priest who had established and guided him (vv. 20-22), suffered a humiliating subjugation to Hazael of Damascus (23,24), and died weakened by wounds and slain for his crimes (vv. 25-27). This chapter provides an amplified parallel to II Kgs 12 (Joash = Jehoash).

2. Joash did that which was right, except that he did not accomplish the removal of the high places (14:3, note; II Kgs 12:3). **All the days of Jehoiada;** that is, until some years after 813 B.C. (v. 14; cf. II Kgs 12:6). But after the death of his great protector he fell into sin (vv. 17,18).

4. After the temple vandalism of Athaliah's sons (v. 7), **repair** had become necessary for **the house of the Lord. 5. Gather . . . money.** Hebrew, *silver.* Coinage did not arise until the Exilic period. But **the Levites hastened it not,** not only because men become used to things 'the way they are," but because the priests too easily exhausted receipts on current operating expenses and their own support (II Kgs 12:7; Num 18: 19).

6. The collection *(tax,* ASV) **of Moses.** II Kings 12:4 specifies the sources of revenue: (1) "the dedicated things," of "every one that passeth the account," i.e., the half-shekel collected in censuses (Ex 30:14; Mt 17:24); (2) of the evaluation "that every man is set at," in substitutionary redemptions, three to fifty shekels (Lev 22:1-8; Num 18: 15,16); (3) and of the voluntary gift "that cometh into any man's heart." **7. Baalim.** Plural. See on 17:3.

8. They (Jehoiada; II Kgs 12:9) **made a chest,** with a receiving slot in the cover *(ibid.).* The priests had agreed to give up both the collecting and rebuilding work (II Kgs 12:8), their needs being met by "the money for the trespass-offerings, etc." (v. 16, ASV; Lev 5:16). **And set it without at the** south **gate;** that is, on the right-hand side of the altar (II Kgs 12:9). **9. They made a proclamation.** For the necessary boost in receipts (cf. v. 5, note). **13. They set the house of God in** its proper **state,** for none of the gifts was used for holy equipment (II Kgs 12:13) until the repair work was finished (II Chr 24:14). II Kings 12:15 stresses also the honesty and faithfulness of **the workmen.**

16. They buried him . . . among the kings, an honor that contrasts with Joash's fate (v. 25). Jehoiada was son-in-law to Jehoram (22:11).

17. The princes of Judah, to whom **the king hearkened,** were the class most attracted by the materialism of Baal worship (v. 18; cf. Zeph 1:8) and were the most punished later (v. 23). **18. Groves.** Asherah poles (see on 14:3).

19. God **sent prophets and they testified against them.** Some of the earlier ones, e.g., Shemaiah and Jehu, had been heeded (11:2; 12:5; 19:2); but the later ones, e.g., Hanani, Micaiah, and now Zechariah (v. 20; 16:7; 18:16), were increasingly not heeded.

20. The Spirit . . . came upon, literally, "clothed himself with," **Zechariah** (cf. I Chr 12:18, note). **22. Joash . . . remembered not** Jehoiada's **kindness** (Heb. *ḥesed,* "faithfulness"; cf. I Chr 16:41, note). He owed his throne and very life to the priest's loyalty (II Chr 23). Zechariah's martyrdom was cited by Christ as the final instance in the OT canon (Hebrew book order) of the gross perversity of Israel (Lk 11:51). **Lord look upon it, and require it.** This prayer of imprecation, rather than of forgiveness (cf. Lk 23:34; Acts 7:60), was justified by the official positions of both the killer and the killed. God's name was at stake, and vengeance did follow (II Chr 24:24,25).

23. The host (army) **of Syria . . . sent all the spoil to their king,** together with tribute that Joash stripped from the Temple. This included all that had been accumulated since the days of Asa (cf. 16:2 note; II Kgs 12:18), whose sin thus reaped its final reward (cf. II Chr 16:9, note). **24.** A great Judean army fell to **a small company of** [Syrian] **men,** just as Moses had predicted (Lev 26:17; the opposite of v. 8). **25.** The Syrians **left him in great diseases** (Heb., *severely wounded)* and **his own servants . . . slew him on his bed** in the house of Millo (II Kgs 12:20; perhaps this parallels I Chr 11:8, see note). II Kings 12:21 describes his burial as "with his fathers in the city of David," which is here confirmed, but with the specification that it was **not in the sepulchres of the kings** (cf. on v. 16). **26.** Variant forms of **Zabad,** etc., occur in II Kgs 12:21.

27. The burdens laid upon him may refer to prophetic threatenings (v. 19). **The story,** Hebrew *midrash,* "commentary," of **the book of the kings,** suggests some interpretation of this more basic source (cf. on 13:22; and Introduction, *Authorship).*

9) Amaziah (796–767 B.C.). 25:1-28. Apart from an introduction on Amaziah's succession (25:1-4) and a conclusion on his death (vv. 25-28), the chronicler's record of the reign of Amaziah centers about two wars and the historical lessons to be gained therefrom: (1) his reconquest of Edom, through obedience to the Lord (vv. 5-16); and (2) his subsequent defeat by northern Israel, in punishment for idolatries adopted after his earlier victory (vv. 17-24). The chapter closely parallels II Kgs 14:1-20, except for the detailed review of the Edomitic war, which receives only brief mention in II Kings (v. 7).

2. He did the **right,** but **not with a perfect heart.** See below; and the high places were not taken away (II Kgs 14:4; cf. v. 3). **4.** He slew his father's murderers (24:26), but **not their children;** for he honored Moses' commandment (Deut 24:16).

5. Because of losses such as those of Joash (24:23), his **three hundred thousand . . . men** are considerably under the totals of Asa and Jehoshaphat (see on 14:8; 17:14); but they were **choice** *(chosen,* ASV). **6. He hired also an hundred thousand . . . out of Israel for an hundred talents of silver,** or over $200,000. But no purchased alliance with sinners such as the Ephraimites could have God's blessing (v. 7; cf. on 16:2), and his is the final decision (vv. 8,9). **10.** So **Amaziah** sent them **home again,** placing his trust in God, as had his fathers (cf. on 14:11; 20:12).

11. Seir (Edom) had enjoyed fifty years of independence from Judah (cf. 21:8) but was now resubjugated, with wanton cruelty (v. 13). **The valley of salt,** located at the south end of the Dead Sea (?), had been the scene of David's former victory over Edom (I Chr 18:12). Amaziah eventually captured the Edomite capital city of Selah (Petra; II Kgs 14:7).

13. The Ephraimite **soldiers . . . which Amaziah sent back,** plundered the northwestern Benjamite (frontier) **cities of the** kingdom of **Judah . . . and smote three thousand** citizens **of them.** The attempt to hire these mercenaries thus brought about its own punishment (v. 5; cf. 22:1-9, introductory note). **14.** He **burned incense.** Rather, *He made offerings* to them.

15. The futility of **gods . . . which could not deliver their own people** should have been obvious, but still today men worship matters that are known to be unsatisfying. **16. Forbare.** Amaziah's mistreatment of the prophet at least went no further than threats (contrast 24:21).

17. Let us look (AV, *see)* **one another in the face.** Amaziah's victory over Edom emboldened him to challenge the far mightier forces of Israel. This was senseless pride, as the northern ruler **Joash** (Jehoash, II Kgs 14, 798–782 B.C.) himself proceeded to point out in his fable (II Chr 25:18,19). **21. They saw one another** (fought, v. 17) **at Beth-shemesh,** due west of Bethlehem, in **Judah** on Amaziah's own picked ground. **23.** Jehoash **brake down . . . four hundred cubits** (200 yds.) of **the wall of Jerusalem from the gate of Ephraim,** on the north side of the city, toward Ephraim, **to the** northwest **corner gate. 24.** With **the gold,** he took **Obed-edom,** the family of Levitical porters and singers (cf. I Chr 26: 4-8), and other **hostages.**

27. As a further divine punishment (cf. v. 20), this disaster may then have precipitated **a conspiracy against** Amaziah and the accompanying elevation of his sixteen-year-old son Uzziah to the co-regency (and actual rule) in 790* B.C. (26:1). For while Amaziah died in 767, the twenty-seventh year of Jeroboam II (II Kgs 15:1), the latter's death in 753, fourteen years later (II Kgs 14: 23) is called the "thirty-eighth" year of Uzziah (II Kgs 15:8). Amaziah's fatal flight **to Lachish** (25 miles southwest of Jerusalem on the route to Egypt) in 767 may thus have sprung from an attempted recovery of the throne (cf. Thiele, *Mysterious Numbers,* pp. 71,72). **28. The city of Judah.** The city of David (II Kgs 14:20).

10) Uzziah (790*–739* B.C.). 26:1-23. The career of Uzziah ("Azariah" in I Chr 3:12, and predominantly in II Kgs) exhibits a certain parallelism to the career of his father Amaziah and his grandfather Joash. That is, the chronicler evaluates the earlier part of Uzziah's long reign as one of piety and of corresponding prosperity (II Chr 26: 1-15); but its latter part, as marked by religious deviation, which resulted in

his affliction with leprosy, his banishment from the palace, and eventually his death (vv. 16-23). His failure, however, was less than the crimes of his fathers; and his achievements mark him as one of the great kings of Israel, though the parallel passages in II Kings (14:21,22; 15:1-7) provide only the formal summary of his reign.

1. Uzziah, . . . sixteen years old in 790, must have been born when his father was only fifteen (cf. on 25:1). Early marriages of this sort are not uncommon in the East. **2. He built Eloth** (Elath; cf., on 8:17) **after . . . the king** had died, in 767. This confirms the hypothesis of Uzziah's accession some time prior to the death of his father Amaziah (cf. on 25:17).

4. He did the right; though the high places remained (cf. 25:2; II Kgs 15:4) and Israel's moral and spiritual condition suffered decay (cf. Hosea and Amos) beneath the surface prosperity (next note). **5. Zechariah, who had understanding in the visions of God.** Other MSS read, *who instructed* (him) *in the fear* **of God.** This prophet, though seemingly well known to Ezra, cannot be identified today. **God made him to prosper.** The period of Jeroboam II and Uzziah, or the four decades from 790–750 B.C., constituted Israel's "Indian summer" (vv. 8,15), when the Assyrians had destroyed her Syrian enemies on the northern borders (cf. II Kgs 12:17-19; 13:3-5) but had not yet begun their own destruction of the Hebrew states (cf. II Kgs 15:19ff. and the concern suggested by Isa 6:1). **6.** Uzziah's subjugation of **Gath** reduced henceforth, the major Philistine cities from five to four (cf. Zeph 2:4). **7. The Arabians of Gur-baal, and the Mehunims** seem to have been nomadic enemies along Judah's southeastern border (cf. on 20:1; I Chr 4:41).

9. The corner gate and **the valley gate** and **the turning** were located at northwest, west, and east (Neh 3:19-25) points of the wall, respectively. **10. The desert.** That is, arid south Judah. **The low country.** The Shephelah (see on I Chr 21:28). **And . . . the plains.** *The tableland* (ASV marg.) of Trans-Jordan, formerly under Ephraimitic control, but apparently reconquered by Uzziah from Ammonites who had occupied it (v. 8).

11. Maaseiah the officer (ASV). Hebrew *shôṭēr,* "adjutant," the scribal or mustering officer (Ex 5:6). **13.** Uzziah's army of 307,500 fighting men was approximately the same size as Amaziah's army (25:5, note). **14. Habergeons.** *Coats of mail* (ASV).

16. Uzziah's burning **incense** not simply usurped an exclusively priestly function (v. 18; Ex 30:7,8) but implied his claim to the Canaanitish office of divine-priest-king (see Gen 14:18; cf. Num 12:10). **17.** The **Azariah** who withstood Uzziah is probably Azariah II (cf. I Chr 6:10. **21. Uzziah . . . dwelt in a several house.** Literally, *a house set apart,* a modified form of the required quarantine (Lev 13:46). **Jotham** thus assumed the co-regency **over the king's house.** The date was 751* B.C.; for Jotham's twentieth year (II Kgs 15:30) was Ahaz's twelfth (II Kgs 16:1), which is 732* (cf. II Kgs 18:10).

22. Isaiah wrote **the acts of Uzziah,** even as he did those of Hezekiah (cf. on 32:32). **23.** Because Uzziah was leprous, he was buried **in the field of the burial,** not in the sepulchres of the kings (cf. 24:25).

11) Jotham (751*–736 B.C.). 27:1-9. Jotham was a king whose righteousness was rewarded (vv. 2,6) but whose reign so overlapped with the reigns of other rulers as to grant him but little independent notice. The few verses of II Chronicles 27 elaborate the bare summary of II Kgs 15:32-38 only to the extent of mentioning a victory he sustained over the Ammonites and of itemizing the resultant tribute (II Chr 27:5,6).

1. He reigned sixteen years. The words, "in the twentieth year of Jotham" (II Kgs 15:30) seem to mark a theoretical point of time, used because Jotham himself had not yet been discussed, let alone his successor. **2. The people did yet corruptly,** sacrificing to idols on the high places, etc. (II Kgs 15:35; cf. Isa 1–6, which belongs to this period).

3. He built the high (upper) **gate,** on the northern side of the Temple (23:20; Jer 20:2), **and on the wall of Ophel,** the northern part of the original city of David, south of the Temple (II Chr 33:14).

5. An hundred talents of silver. More than $200,000 (cf. 25:6), and **ten thousand measures.** Hebrew *kōr* designates a measure of about ten bushels capacity. **7. All his wars.** Jotham was probably the actual commander of the alliance conceived by his quarantined father Azariah (cf. 26:21), who is mentioned in the Assyrian annals (but not in Scripture) as overcome by Tiglath-pileser III about 743 B.C. (see Thiele, *Mysterious Numbers,* pp. 78-98).

8. **He . . . reigned sixteen years.** But after eight years, in 743*, his son Ahaz was associated with him on the throne (see on 26:21), perhaps because of the defeat by Tiglath-pileser (cf. v. 7; 28: 5, notes; II Kgs 15:37).

12) Ahaz (743*–728* B.C.). 28:1-27 (paralleling II Kgs 16, with changes and additions). Ahaz was one of the weakest and most corrupt of the twenty rulers of Judah. Both II Kings and II Chronicles discuss his reign in two stages: (1) his religious apostasy and resultant subjection to Syro-Ephraimitic attack (II Chr 28:1-7); and (2) his subsequent defensive capitulation to Assyria, which led him into even further corruption because of his involvement in the idolatries of his new masters (vv. 16-27). Between these, the chronicler inserts a paragraph telling how the prophet Oded delivered a company of Jewish captives from the hands of Ephraim (vv. 8-15), which is not mentioned in II Kings.

1. Ahaz's accession to co-regency in 743 B.C. when **twenty years old** (cf. on 27:8), indicates that his father was aged thirteen at his son's birth (27:1; but cf. on 26:1).

2. **Baalim** (plural). See on 17:3. **3. He burnt incense.** Rather, *made offerings* (vv. 4,25, also). **The valley of (the son of) Hinnom** (Heb. *gê'hinnōm)* marked the southern boundary of Jerusalem and became noted as the scene of atrocious pagan practices (33:6). It was later defiled by Josiah when he converted it into a city dump (II Kgs 23:10), the perpetual fires of which became a symbol for hell, Gehenna (Mk 9:43, ASV marg.). **He . . . burnt his children.** The Canaanitish practice of child sacrifice had been forbidden to Abraham (Gen 22:12) and was made a capital offense under Moses (Lev 20:1-5). **4. High places.** See on 14:3.

5. **God delivered him** over to **the king of Syria. . . .** and **the king of Israel,** Rezin and Pekah (752–732 B.C.), respectively. They may have turned on Judah because of the failure of Azariah's alliance (see on 27:7) and the sufferings they had then experienced at the hands of the victorious Assyrians (II Kgs 15:19; cf. v. 37). They besieged, but were unable to capture, Jerusalem (II Kgs 16:5; Isa 7:1), though Rezin did take Elath (II Kgs 16:5; cf. II Chr 26:2; 8:17 note).

9. **Oded,** who is otherwise unknown, reminded the Ephraimites that those who serve as God's punitive instruments must not exceed their divinely appointed mission (cf. Isa 10:5-19). Their own standing, moreover, was far from secure (II Chr 28:10). **15.** They **gave them to eat,** etc., following the OT standard of showing love, even to the enemy (Ex 23:4; Prov 24:17; 25:21; cf. Mt 5:44).

16. In 734 B.C. **Ahaz** threw himself on the "mercy" of the Assyrians, asking them **to help him.** Isaiah had tried to prevent this, as a breach of trust in the Lord (cf. 16:2,9; 25:6,10, notes). Ahaz's cry, moreover, was unnecessary (Isa 7:4-9); it put Judah under the iron heel of Tiglath-pileser (vv. 20,21); it caused Israel's deportation to Assyria—three and one-half tribes in 733 B.C. (II Kgs 15:29), the rest eleven years later (II Kgs 17:6); and it led in 701 to Judah's own devastation by the armies of Sennacherib (II Kgs 18:13). **17. Again the Edomites** smote **Judah,** for Edom was ever ready to capitalize on Judah's distress (cf. 20:22; 21:8). This attack may have then provoked the prophecies of Obadiah (cf. v. 11) and Joel (cf. 3: 19). **18. The Philistines also.** See Joel 3:4. **Low country.** The Shephelah (see on I Chr 21:28).

23. **The gods of Damascus, which smote him** (cf. II Kgs 16:10-13). Reference is to the gods of the Assyrian monarch, who had now become king of Syria II Kgs 16:9). Homage to his gods was doubtless included as part of the price of Ahaz's fealty. **24. He shut up the doors** of the Temple, not simply advocating the Assyrian and other religions, but specifically displacing the true (cf. II Kgs 16:14-18).

27. **They brought him not into the sepulchres of the kings.** For harmonization with II Kgs 16:20, see II Chr 24: 25b (cf. 21:19b), notes. **Hezekiah . . . reigned in his stead.** Popular dissatisfaction with Ahaz seems to have forced Hezekiah to assume rule in 728* (cf. II Kgs 18:9,10), three years prior to his official inauguration (and the death of Ahaz?) in 725* (see on II Chr 32:1).

13) Hezekiah (725*–696* B.C.). 29:

1–32:33. Hezekiah's piety and strength of character were the antithesis of his father's apostasy and surrender to expediency. Whereas Ahaz had converted Jerusalem into a shrine for idolatry and its accompanying immoralities, Hezekiah purified the Lord's Temple of its pollutions (II Chr 29), celebrated a solemn Passover (ch. 30), and campaigned far and wide to stamp out the idolatrous high places and to establish pure religion (ch. 31). Then in politics, whereas Ahaz had short-sightedly capitulated to Assyria, Hezekiah planned and fought for Judah's ultimate welfare and freedom, not always wisely, but with eventual success (ch. 32). The parallel passages in II Kings touch only briefly on Hezekiah's religious reforms (18:1-6) but furnish a more detailed record of his political dealings (18:7–20:21) than is found in the single chapter of II Chronicles 32.

29:2. He did right. Of particular note was his "trust in the Lord," so that among "all the kings of Judah there was none like him before or after" (II Kgs 18:5; cf. Isa 26:3,4).

3. The first year of his reign must refer to that which followed his accession to sole rule in 725* B.C. (see on 30:1), rather than to the time of his rise into power three years earlier (see on 28:27); otherwise Ahaz would have been eleven, rather than fourteen at Hezekiah's birth (cf. 26:1). The first month would then be March/April, 724. **He . . . opened the doors** of the Temple, shut by the apostate Ahaz (vv. 6,7; 28:24), **and repaired them,** which included overlaying with gold (II Kgs 18:16). **4. The east street** (*broad place,* ASV). The wide space in front of the Temple (Ezr 10:9).

5. Sanctify now yourselves (v. 15, also). See on I Chr 15:12. **9.** The punishments experienced by sinful Judah had included **captivities** to Damascus, Samaria, Edom, and Philistia (28:5,8,17,18). **11. The Lord hath chosen you,** Levites (v. 4; cf. Num 3:5-13), **to . . . burn incense.** Rather, *to make offerings,* which was, specifically, the priestly function (v. 21).

12. Kohath, Gershom, and Merari were the three clans of Levi (I Chr 6:1). **13.** Separate mention is given to the family of **Elizaphan,** who had been prince of Kohath in the days of Moses (Num 3:30; cf. I Chr 15:8). **Asaph,** Heman, and Jeduthun (v. 14) had founded the three families of singers (I Chr 25). **15.** The king's commandments were **by the words of the Lord,** conforming, that is, to the inspired Mosaic Law (cf. Deut 12:2-4).

16. The priests . . . brought out all the uncleanness. Not just dirt accumulated by neglect, but Ahaz's filthy idolatries and their equipment (cf. II Kgs 16:15). **To the brook Kidron.** Where Asa had burned the queen-grandmother's abominations (see on 15:16). **19. Ahaz . . . did cast away** (discard), and even partially destroy, the Lord's vessels (28:24; II Kgs 16:17). **21.** For the **sin offering** and its ritual, see Lev 4:1–5:13.

23. They laid their hands upon them [the **he goats**], thus designating them as substitutes for their own lives and transferring their sins to them (Num 27:18-21; cf. 8:18,19). The goats were symbols of Christ's dying in the sinner's place (II Cor 5:21). **24. The priests killed them . . . to make an atonement.** The Hebrew for **atonement,** *kippēr,* means to "appease" or "pacify" (Gen 32:20; Prov 16:14), to avert punishment by paying a ransom (KB, p. 452). Israel was saved through such anticipations of the death of Christ on the cross, who endured the wrath of God for us (Mk 10:45; Rom 3:25). **For all Israel.** Cf. Lev 4:13; 16:30.

27. For the **burnt offering.** See Leviticus 1. **The song of the Lord** suggests the Psalms, used since David's time (I Chr 16) in worship. **31. As many as were of a free heart** brought **burnt offerings,** which were wholly consumed on the altar. These contrast with the more numerous thank, or peace offerings ("consecrated things," v. 33), which were largely eaten by the sacrificers in a feast that followed (see on I Chr 29:21).

34. The subordinate **Levites were more upright . . . than the priests** (cf. 30:3; and Uriah's apostasy, II Kgs 16:11). This was just the opposite of what might have been expected (cf. Ezk 48:11). But true faith is often found among the humble, while historically professional religious leaders have been least willing to submit to Christ and to the Word (cf. Jn 7:48). **35. The** choice **fat of the peace offerings** was presented to God on the altar before the people feasted (cf. v. 31, note; Lev 3).

36. They **rejoiced** over what **God had prepared** for (ASV) **the people,** for in the final analysis all spiritual triumphs are gifts of God's grace (30:12; I Kgs 18:37; Acts 11:18).

30:1. Hezekiah sent . . . to Ephraim and Manasseh to come to Jerusalem. Such an action would have been impossible at any prior point in the history of northern Israel (cf. vv. 5,26; I Kgs 12:27,28). But now Hoshea's capital had been under Assyrian siege for several months (II Chr 30:6; II Kgs 17:5), and the northern king was powerless to interfere. The Assyrians, furthermore, would encourage anything that suggested defection from him.

2. The passover in the second month (April/May, 724) was one month late, but the delay was justified by Mosaic precedent (Num 9:10,11), when circumstances made it necessary, as they did at this time (cf. II Chr 29:17). **3. At that time,** the fourteenth day of the first month (29:3,17), **the priests had not sanctified themselves** (see 29:34 and I Chr 15:12, notes). But repentance followed (v. 15). **5. They had not done it of a long time.** Rather, *in great numbers* (ASV), i.e., as a united kingdom.

8. Enter into his sanctuary. The Passover was one of the three annual pilgrimage feasts, that required every male's presence at the Temple (Deut 16:16). **9. Your** exiled **brethren . . . shall find compassion** and **shall come again,** as Moses had predictively promised (Lev 26:40-42).

10. They laughed them to scorn. Human depravity is so complete as to render men unapproachable, even when on the brink of disaster (cf. Amos 4:10; Rev 9:20).

13. The feast of unleavened bread ran for seven days after the Passover itself (Lev 23:5,6), as a reminder to Israel both of their hasty departure from Egypt and of their perpetual need for separation from sin (Ex 12:11,34; I Cor 5:7). **14.** They **cast them into the brook** (stream-bed) **Kidron.** See 29:16; 15:16 note.

15. They killed the passover lamb, as a memorial of God's past deliverance of Israel from the last plague in Egypt (Ex 12:27) and as a symbol of his continuing claim over sinners, which would be met by the future substitutionary death of Christ, the Lamb of God (Ex 13:15; I Cor 5:7). **16. The priests sprinkled the blood** of the Passover lambs upon the altar, as they **received** it from **the Levites.** It was normally presented directly by the head of each household (cf. Lev 1:11).

17. But **the Levites** had to kill and **sanctify them** (the lambs), because **many in the congregation . . . were not sanctified.** That is, they were **not clean** (as in Num 9:6); and the value of the sacrifice as a propitiation of God depended on its typifying the perfect ransom of Christ (Heb 9:14). **18. Yet did they eat.** Hezekiah's prayer of intercession made it possible for them to share to this extent in the Passover. For if they were true in heart (v. 19), they could on this first occasion be **pardon**[ed] ("healed," v. 20) for a failure in outward conformity.

22. The Levites that taught the good knowledge of the Lord. Rather, *that had good understanding in the* (musical) *service of Jehovah* (ASV). Similarly, not **making confession;** but *giving thanks* (ASV marg.).

24. For Hezekiah . . . did give . . . a thousand bullocks, etc. The quantity of these peace offerings contributed to the decision to extend the week of feasting! (cf. on 29:31; I Chr 29:21)

27. The priests . . . blessed the people, as Moses had directed (Num 6:23-27).

31:1. They **cut down the groves.** See on 14:3. **And threw down the** local **high places** (see 1:3, note), whether of Baal, or of Jehovah worshiped in this Baal pattern. Hezekiah was also forced to destroy Nehushtan, the brazen serpent of Moses, because it had been perverted into an object of idolatry (II Kgs 18:4). **In Ephraim also.** For some had repented of their two centuries of apostasy (30:11), while the obdurate were powerless to act (30:10,11, notes).

2. Hezekiah appointed the courses of the priests. That is, he re-established the orderly administration of worship first set up by David (cf. on 23:17; I Chr 24,25). **3. The king's portion . . . for the burnt offerings.** This responsibility of providing for the national worship had been set forth in detail by Moses (Num 28; 29). **For the morning and evening burnt offerings . . . and for the set feasts.** See on I Chr 23:30,31. **4. The portion of . . . the Levites** (v. 5) consisted primarily of the "firstfruits" (Ex 23:19; Num 18:12) and of tithes from the other tribes (Lev 27:30-33; Num 18:21-24). The Levites could devote themselves to God's work unhindered by secular pursuits only if they received these "portions" regularly (cf. Neh 13:10).

6. The tithe of holy things may be a general term for the token percentages of certain offerings that became the property of the priests (Num 18:6; cf. Lev 6:16–7:36). **7. In the third month** (May/June), the season of the Feast of Pentecost and the grain harvest (Ex 23:16a), **they began . . . , and finished in the seventh month** (Sept/Oct), the time of the Feast of Tabernacles and the ingathering of the fruit and vine harvests (Ex 23:16b). **10. Azariah** III (v. 13; cf. I Chr 6:4, note) is probably not the Azariah (II) who resisted Uzziah (II Chr 26:17) almost thirty years before.

12. Over which Cononiah . . . was ruler. David had first organized **the dedicated things** under Levitical porter-treasurers (I Chr 26:20,26, notes). **14. To distribute the oblation of the Lord.** He assigned these additional **freewill offerings** and **most holy things** (e.g., the specified parts of the guilt offerings; Lev 6:17) to their legitimate priestly recipients (Lev 7:14; cf. 6:29). **15. In the cities of the priests** (v. 19). These had been named and distributed by Joshua (Josh 21:9-19).

16. Beside the males, from three years old and upward . . . that entere[d] **into the house.** From this early age, priests' sons must have accompanied their fathers in the service, and so received their portions directly, in the Temple. **17.** The revived Levitical distributions gave renewed, practical significance **to the genealogy. Twenty years old and upward.** See on I Chr 23:24. **18. They sanctified themselves in holiness.** Kore and his associates faithfully discharged a touchy task!

21. In every work, Hezekiah was whole-heartedly committed to **the law** of Moses, **and prospered.** Cf. II Kgs 18:6,7.

32:1. After these things. In 715 B.C. Ashdod, and other Palestinian states, rebelled against Assyria. They were urged on by Shabaka of the Twenty-Fifth Dynasty in Egypt (i.e., "So," II Kgs 17:4) and Marduk-pal-iddina of Babylon (see on II Chr 32:25,31). But in 711 B.C. Ashdod was resubdued, Hezekiah yielded to the will of God and submitted (Isa 20), and the Assyrian ruler Sargon II called himself the "subjugator of Judah, whose situation is far away" (cf. Isa 10:28-32; Mic 1:9). This was in the fourteenth year of Hezekiah, calculated back from the known accession of his son Manasseh in 696* B.C. But with Sargon's death in 705, Hezekiah let himself become involved in plots with Egypt (Isa 30:1-5; 31:1-3). He disregarded the counsel of Isaiah and assumed the leadership of a western revolt against Assyria, and he even imprisoned the Philistine king of Ekron, who refused to cooperate (II Kgs 18:8). Then in 701 **Sennacherib,** the son of Sargon, **came** against **Judah.** These two attacks are summarized without differentiation in II Kgs 18:13. Compare the description in II Chr 32:24-26 of Hezekiah's sickness in 711 B.C. after the account, in verses 1-23, of Sennacherib's invasion of 701 B.C. Sennacherib **encamped against the fenced cities,** and **thought to win them.** And he did win them, except for Jerusalem (II Kgs 18:13; Isa 36:1).

4. They **stopped . . . the brook.** Probably the Gihon (v. 30, note). **5. . . . built up all the wall and repaired Millo** (see on I Chr 11:8). His efforts, however, were criticized by Isaiah (Isa 22:9,10), because Hezekiah had disobeyed God (Isa 22:11) by relying on the arm of Egypt (Isa 30:7; 31:1-3; cf. II Chr 16:2-9; 25:6, notes) rather than upon the Lord (Isa 30:15,16). As a result, Sennacherib boasts that he "shut up (the king) like a caged bird inside Jerusalem." And Hezekiah was forced to capitulate and pay huge indemnities to Sennacherib, including the very gold with which he had adorned the Temple earlier in his reign (see on II Chr 29:3; II Kgs 18:14-16). These facts are assumed without comment in Chronicles but are confirmed in detail by Sennacherib's own annals, plus further data on the defection of Hezekiah's Arabian mercenaries and the release from Jerusalem and reinstatement of the king of Ekron. Sennacherib claims further to have taken captive over 200,000 from Judah, which serves to explain Isaiah's subsequent messages of comfort for a ravaged country (Isa 40:1) and of hope for its deported people (Isa 43:6,7).

9. After this. That is, after Hezekiah's surrender of the stipulated tribute. Sennacherib's annals, with understandable diplomacy, say nothing of the events beyond this point. But the fact is that the treacherous Assyrian now renewed his demands upon prostrate Hezekiah. He **laid siege against Lachish,** twenty-five miles southwest of Jerusalem, and sent **his servants,** including the "tartan," his military commander, **to Jerusalem.** But the very insolence of the message that follows (cf. II Kgs 18:17-25) provided justification for the stirring hope just expressed by Hezekiah (II Chr 32:7,8; cf. v. 11). **12. Hath not . . . Hezekiah taken away his high places . . . ?** Sennacherib hoped to capitalize on any popular dissatisfaction with Hezekiah's reforms (31:1). **14.** More to the point was his blasphemy of Jehovah, as no more **able to deliver** than had been the false **gods of those nations** already conquered by Assyria (cf. v. 19; Isa 10:15).

16. His servants **spake yet more** (vv. 18,19), as recorded in II Kgs 18:27-35. **17. He wrote also letters,** having had to withdraw his troops to meet the advance of an Egyptian force under Tirhakah, younger brother of Shabaka and later Pharaoh (cf. II Kgs 19:9-13).

20. Hezekiah . . . and . . . Isaiah . . . prayed. See II Kgs 19:1-7,14-34 for these heart-searching pleas and ringing affirmations of faith. **21. An angel . . . cut off all the mighty men of . . . Assyria,** 185,000 in one night. The suggestion has been made that a rodent-carried plague struck down the Assyrians. This theory is based on an Egyptian legend that Hezekiah owed his victory over Sennacherib to field mice that ate up the Assyrians' equipment (Herodotus *Histories* II. 141). But the intensity of the disaster points to a supernatural agency. This event ranks with Israel's crossing of the Red Sea as one of the great historical examples of God's intervention to save his people. **So he returned** and was slain (II Kgs 19:35-37).

24. In those days. Fifteen years before his death (II Kgs 20:6), or 711 B.C., his fourteenth year. **Hezekiah . . . prayed** (cf. 16:12, note; II Kgs 20:2,3). "The prayer of faith shall save the sick" (Jas 5:15). **And he** (God) **spake** in deliverance **unto him** (II Kgs 20:4-6) and **gave him a** confirmatory **sign,** the miracle of the shadow that regressed (II Kgs 20:8-11). **25. But** Hezekiah's **heart was lifted up.** See on verse 31. **Therefore there was wrath.** Isaiah's threat of subsequent exile to Babylon (II Kgs 20:16-18; cf. Mic 3:12). **26. Hezekiah humbled himself . . . so that it came not** in his days. See II Kgs 20:19; Isa 39:8.

30. To provide a permanent supply of water within the walls of Jerusalem, **Hezekiah** brought down **the upper watercourse of Gihon** by tunneling a passageway 1,700 feet long through solid rock. In 1880, archaeological confirmation of this engineering feat was provided by the discovery of the dedicatory "Siloam inscription," in old Hebrew, inscribed by the very engineers who constructed the tunnel.

31. The ambassadors of . . . Babylon were sent by Marduk-pal-iddina (the Merodach-baladan of Isa 39:1,2; cf. II Kgs 20:12,13), not simply to inquire about Hezekiahs' sickness and about the miraculous sign of his recovery, but also, presumably, to arrange practical measures against Sargon's attack of 711 B.C. The embassy thus served **to try** Hezekiah's relative reliance upon man or God. The fact that the test demonstrated the former was the cause of Isaiah's wrath (v. 25).

32. The vision of Isaiah . . . , in the book of the kings (ASV). Isaiah 36–39 was incorporated into the common source from which Kings and Chronicles both drew (cf. Introduction, *Authorship*). **33. The chiefest** *(the ascent,* ASV) **of the sepulchres** may identify some more elevated position, used when the lower tombs had all become occupied.

14) Manasseh (696*–641* B.C.). 33:1-20. It was Manasseh more than anyone else who brought about the destruction of the Kingdom of Judah (II Kgs 23:26; 24:3). This evil son of a godly father was granted the longest reign of any Hebrew king. But he squandered most of it in the seduction of his people to paganism, religiously, and in a renewed subservience to Assyria, politically (II Chr 33:1-10, paralleling II Kgs 21:1-18). In his final years, personal distress did bring him to repentance, though too late to have much national effect (II Chr 33:11-20; there is no corresponding narrative in Kings).

3. He built again the high places . . . for Baalim, and made groves. See 14:3; 17:3, notes. **And worshipped all the** starry **host of heaven** (cf. II Kgs 23:10, 11). This ancient form of idolatry (Deut 4:19) which was a particular sin of the astrology-minded Assyro-Babylonians, must have received stimulus in Judah by Manasseh's resubmission to Assyria in 676 B.C., when Sennacherib's son Esar-haddon advanced westward against Egypt. **4. In Jerusalem shall my name be for ever** (cf. v. 9). See on 6:2,6. **5. The two courts.** See on 4:9.

6. He caused his children to pass through the fire in the valley . . . of Hinnom, as had Ahaz (28:3, notes). **And used enchantments** (soothsaying), etc., attempting to communicate with the dead by means of spiritists, which Scripture condemns as opposed to true faith in God (Ex 22:18; Deut 18:10-12). **Familiar** (knowing) **spirit**[s] meant originally "ghosts," supposedly having superhuman knowledge; but it came to be applied to "mediums." Manasseh also practiced tyranny, shedding "innocent blood very much" (II Kgs 21:16).

8. God would no **more remove . . . Israel from out of the land . . . , so that** *(if only*, ASV) **they will take heed** to his commands. See on 7:14,19. **10. The Lord spake,** through "his servants the prophets," threatening their destruction (II Kgs 21:10-15), **but they would not hearken.**

11. The king of Assyria . . . took Manasseh among the thorns. Rather, *with hooks* (ASV marg.). **To Babylon.** Perhaps in 648 B.C., when Ashurbanipal overcame a four-year revolt led by his brother in that city. Egypt (Dynasty XXVI) had taken this opportunity to throw off the Assyrian yoke; and Manasseh might have attempted the same, with less success. **12. In affliction, he . . . humbled himself.** God sometimes has to drive men to their conversion (cf. Acts 9:3-5).

14. Gihon . . . and **Ophel.** See notes on 27:3; 32:30. **To . . . the fish gate.** In the north wall (Neh 3:3). **17. Nevertheless the people did sacrifice still in the high places.** A half century of paganism could not be overcome by a half-dozen years of reform. **Yet unto the Lord** (Jehovah, *Yahweh*) **. . . only.** This was still contrary to the Mosaic law of the central sanctuary (see on 1:3) and must actually have accomplished little more than to apply a new name to the old Baal worship.

18,19. His prayer (cf. vv. 12,13) is now lost. "The Prayer of Manasses" in the Apocrypha, the title of which is based upon this reference, was composed shortly before the time of Christ. **The sayings of the seers.** Rather, *the history of Hozai* (ASV), an unknown prophet.

15) Amon (641*–639* B.C.). 33:21-25. Amon was the unhappy product of his father's pagan life, not of his pious death. This brief summary of his reign closely parallels II Kgs 21:19-26 and notes the immediate relapse of Judah to the pre-conversion religion of Manasseh. In two years Amon died at the hands of his own courtiers.

22. Amon sacrified unto all the carved images which Manasseh . . . had made. Either their removal had not involved their destruction (v. 15), or the concentration of Manasseh's reformation in Jerusalem had left available his more scattered idolatries (cf. v. 17).

16) Josiah (639*–608). 34:1–35:27. Josiah was Judah's last good king, and in some respects her greatest (see on 34:2). For it was his reformation of 621 B.C. that did more than all else to restore Israel's commitment to God's Book; and it was loyalty to this same written word that provided the glimmer of hope for Judaism during the Exile (cf. Dan 9:2), in its precarious restoration (Ezr 7:10; Mal 4:6), and throughout the centuries down to the coming of Christ (Mt 5:17,18). II Chronicles 34,35 analyzes Josiah's earlier reforms (34:1-7); the great reformation of his eighteenth year, which began with the temple repairs, during which the crucial book of the Law was discovered (34:8-33); the king's solemn Passover, that followed (35:1-19); and his tragic death (35:20-27). The first and third of these topics are little more than touched on in the parallel section in II Kgs 22:1–23:30, while other matters (see II Chr 34:33, note) receive a correspondingly greater emphasis.

2. He did right (see on 29:2), particularly in his devotion to "all the law of Moses," so that "like unto him was there no king before him or after" (II Kgs 23:25).

3. The eighth year. That is, 631 B.C., when Josiah was sixteen years old. **And in the twelfth year.** Or, 627. This second date falls within the time of chaos that was caused by an eruption of nomadic horsemen from the north over most of the Near East (628–626 B.C.). These Scythian hordes wrought terror in the hearts of complacent Jews (Jer 6:22-24; Zeph 1:12); and, while never raiding much beyond the coastal plain, where they were finally stopped by the Egyptians, they did render Judah a twofold service: (1) they precipitated the calls of Jeremiah (Jer 1:2) and Zephaniah the prophet (cf. Zeph 1:1?), as well as the 627 B.C. stage of Josiah's revival, which went far beyond a mere "foxhole" religion (II Chr 34:3-7); and (2) they swept away the Assyrian imperial domination, that had throttled Judah for the half-century preceding (v. 6; cf. 33:3, note).

4. The images (in v. 7, "the idols"). Incense stands (see on 14:5). **6. Simeon.** See on I Chr 4:24-43. **Even unto Naphtali,** in Galilee. Josiah had thus recovered most of the formerly Assyrian province of northern Israel (vv. 7,9).

9. The Levites that kept the doors had gathered money, after the example of Joash and his chest (II Kgs 12:9). **12. The men did the work faithfully,** with no audit needed (II Kgs 22:7), as under Joash (II Kgs 12:15).

14. Hilkiah . . . found a (Heb., *the*) **book of the law of the Lord.** It is also called "the book of the covenant" (v. 30), which suggests Exodus 19–24; while the curses it contained (II Chr 34:24) and the law of the central sanctuary (II Kgs 23:8,9) imply respectively Leviticus 26 or Deuteronomy 28 and 12:5-13, etc. The book was probably the official scroll of the Pentateuch, usually kept by the side of the ark (Deut 31:25,26) but misplaced during the previous administrations, when the ark had been moved about (II Chr 35:3). **Given by** (lit., *by the hand of*) **Moses.** Though not all the Pentateuch claims to have been written down, or even spoken by Moses (cf. Deut 34), the Biblical witness is clear that all its contents belongs to a historical time no later than that of the writer (Deut 4:2; 12:32) and was composed under his directing authority (cf. Christ's own belief, Jn 7:19; Lk 24:44). Our Lord, as if in anticipation of the present widespread denial of the Mosaic authorship of the Pentateuch, stated explicitly that those who refuse to believe Moses' words could not consistently accept His own (Jn 5:47).

19. He rent his clothes. Rendered distraught by threats such as those in Lev 26:32,33 and Deut 28:36 (see II Chr 34:21,24,27), "written concerning us" (II Kgs 22:13). **20. Asaiah a servant of the king's.** Rather, *the servant* (ASV). This was a specific position, high in government. **Abdon the son of Micah.** II Kings 22:12 has the variant forms, "Achbor the son of Michaiah." **22. Huldah the prophetess.** Discrimination on the ground of sex was foreign to the spirit of the OT (cf. Jud 4:4; II Sam 20:16). Restriction of women, e.g., to a separate court in the Temple, arose only with the perversions of inter-Testamental Judaism. **She dwelt . . . in the college.** Hebrew *mishneh,* "the second (quarter)" of the city.

24. I will bring evil. The Lord would not "turn from the fierceness of his great wrath, because of all the provocations (of) Manasseh" (II Kgs 23:26). **28. Neither shall thine eyes see all the evil.** Postponements of divine wrath because of humble repentance had been granted to Hezekiah (32:26) and even to Ahab (I Kgs 21:29) before him.

30. The covenant (v. 31) is the instrument God uses for the redemption of his elect people. This refers to the "older testament" (cf. I Chr 16:15 and II Chr 15:12-15). **31. The king stood in his place.** "At his pillar" (23:13; II Kgs 23:3).

33. Josiah took away all the abominations. For detail on his thorough removal of idolatry—with its accompanying sexual immoralities—, of high place worship, and of spiritism, see II Kgs 23:4-14,24. **Out of all the countries that pertained to . . . Israel** (see v. 6). The king destroyed Jeroboam's altar at Beth-el, together with the other high places of the former Northern Kingdom, slaying such of the priests as remained (II Kgs 23:15-20). **All his days they departed not from following God.** The testimony, however, of Jeremiah, who supported Josiah's reformation (Jer 11:1-5), shows that for many the **following** was one of external compliance, and not of the heart (Jer 11:9-13).

35:1. Josiah kept a passover. This confirmation of Josiah's reform sprang likewise from his obedience to the re-established Law, "as it is written in this book of the covenant" (II Kgs 23:21). **The first month.** Of the same great eighteenth year (v. 18), 621 B.C.; compare Hezekiah's having had to postpone his passover to the second month (30:2). **3. Put the holy ark in the house which Solomon . . . did build.** In the dark days of Manasseh and Amon, the ark seems to have been removed by faithful Levites and carried elsewhere for its protection (cf. 33:7-17; 28:24). **4. After your courses, according to . . . David.** See on I Chr 24:4,20. **And according to . . . Solomon.** See 8:14. **6. Prepare your brethren.** Josiah thus provided against the sort of confusion that had arisen under Hezekiah a century before (cf. on 30:16-18). **7. Three thousand bullocks** (cf. vv. 8,9,13b). The flocks had been for paschal lambs, but these must have served as peace offerings for feasting in the days of unleavened bread that followed (cf. 30:24; I Chr 29:21, notes).

12. They removed the burnt offerings. That is, they separated certain choice parts of the passover lambs **to offer unto the Lord** (v. 14), apparently after the pattern of the peace offerings (Lev 3). The people then roasted and ate the Passover itself (per Deut 16:7). **17. And the feast of unleavened bread.** See on 30:13. **18. There was no passover like** it, since **the days of Samuel.** II Kings 23:22 adds, "from the days of the judges." That is, Josiah's feast met the Biblical standards as had no others since those of Moses and Joshua.

20. After all this; i.e., in 608 B.C. (Thiele, *Mysterious Numbers,* pp. 158-160). **Necho (II) king of Egypt came up.** The Pharaohs of the Twenty-sixth Dynasty made an active bid to succeed to the rule of the Assyrian empire. Nineveh fell in 612; and the Egyptians opposed Babylon's claim to the spoil by going up "on behalf of [not, *against*] the king of Assyria, to the river Euphrates" (II Kgs 23:29), at the westernmost point of which lay the key city of *Carchemish.* **21. I come not against thee.** Necho wished merely to march along the Palestinian coast, so as to meet **the house wherewith I have war,** namely the Babylonian army under the crown-prince Nebuchadr(n)ezzar. **God commanded me to make haste.** This was probably no more than diplomatic doubletalk on Necho's part (cf. on 2:11; 32:12).

22. Josiah, like Ahab, **disguised himself** for protection against his fate (cf. 18:29, note). For though this fact might have come as a surprise to the Pharaoh, **the words of Necho** were **from the mouth of God.** For the Lord's insistent message to Judah had been that she must rely upon Him and avoid involvement in international "power politics" (cf. on 16:9; 28:16; 32:1,5). **Megiddo** marked the strategic pass in the ridge between the coastal plain and the valley of Esdraelon to the northeast. It has been the scene of key battles from the fifteenth century B.C. right down to World War I. The final battle of the age, against Christ at his second advent, will be joined at "Armageddon" (Rev 16:16), i.e., *the mountain of Megiddo.*

25. Jeremiah lamented for Josiah, whom he held in high regard (Jer 22:15,16). **Written in the lamentations.** These dirges are not to be confused with Jeremiah's later laments over Jehoiachin (Jer 22:10-30) or over Jerusalem's fall (Lam).

17) Jehoahaz, Jehoiakim, Jehoiachin, and Zedekiah (608–586 B.C.). 36:1-16. In signal contrast to the godliness and strength of character of their father, these last kings of Judah, three sons and one grandson of Josiah, exhibited a moral incapacity that brought what remained of the kingdom of Israel to its inglorious end. Jehoahaz' displacement from the kingship marked the end of independent government in Judah (36:1-4); Jehoiakim's regime saw the establishment of Babylonian domination (vv. 5-8); Jehoiakim's son, Jehoiachin, reaped the fruit of his father's rebellion (vv. 9,10); and Zedekiah heedlessly touched off the final revolt through infidelity to his suzerain, Nebuchadrezzar, who thus became God's instrument for bringing destruction upon a faithless people (vv. 11-16). These paragraphs are an abbreviated parallel of II Kgs 23:31–24:20.

2. Jehoahaz was twenty and three, younger than Jehoiakim, who succeeded him (v. 5). But though "he did that which was evil" (II Kgs 23:32), the people of the land, the free citizens (II Chr 36:1), seemingly saw more hope in him than in his elder brother. **He reigned three months,** or just until Necho found opportunity to replace him (cf. 35:20, 21). **3.** Necho imposed indemnities of **an hundred talents of silver and a talent of gold** (cf. 25:6; 27:5), about $220,000, plus $35,000 (cf. I Chr 19:6, note). **4. He turned his name** from Eliakim, *God raises up,* **to Jehoiakim,** *Jehovah (Yahweh) raises up,* showing Necho's willingness to tolerate the religion of the Jews. More significantly, this control over the king's name demonstrated Necho's control over his person (see on 6:6). **Necho took Jehoahaz . . . to Egypt,** where he died (II Kgs 23:34; cf. Jer 22:10).

5. Jehoiakim . . . reigned eleven years, 608–598 B.C., **and did evil.** He taxed the land for tribute to Pharaoh (II Kgs 23:35), while living in luxury himself (Jer 22:14,15); he perverted justice and oppressed the poor (Jer 22:13,17); and he persecuted the prophets who reproved him (cf. II Chr 35:8,16, below; Jer 26:21-24; 32:36).

6. Against him . . . Nebuchadnezzar (more correctly, Nebuchadrezzar, II Kgs 24:1, Hebrew text) **came up.** In the spring of 605 the Babylonians won a decisive victory over Necho at Carchemish (see on 35:20; Jer 46:2). The Egyptians, as a result, were driven back within their own borders; and Palestine was left in the hands of Nebuchadrezzar (II Kgs 24:7). The conqueror proceeded to bind Jehoiakim **in fetters, to carry him** captive, though the threat seems to have been sufficient without taking him bodily **to Babylon.**

7. Nebuchadnezzar also carried off temple vessels, and also an initial captivity of select Jewish hostages, including Daniel (cf. Dan 1:1-3). This began the seventy years of Babylonian exile, 605–536 B.C. (Jer 29:10). The authenticity of this Palestinian campaign of 605, once widely questioned by disbelieving OT critics, was strikingly confirmed by the publication in 1956 of two Babylonian tablets of Nebuchadrezzar's reign. On these Nebuchadrezzar states that he conquered "the whole land of Hatti" [the western Fertile Crescent including Palestine] in the summer of 605 and "took heavy tribute of Hatti to Babylon" (cf. J. B. Payne, "The Uneasy Conscience of Modern Liberal Exegesis," *Bulletin of the Evangelical Theological Society,* I:1 Winter, 1958), 14-18).

8. The rest of the acts of Jehoiakim. After serving Nebuchadrezzar three years (until 602), he rebelled (II Kgs 24:1,2) but died before his full punishment could **fall.**

9. Jehoiachin was eight years old, rather, "eighteen years old," according to other MSS (cf. II Kgs 24:8; **and he reigned three months and ten days,** from December 598 to March 16, 597, according to the new Nebuchadrezzar texts (v. 7, note). **10. Nebuchadnezzar . . . brought him to Babylon,** 597 B.C., along with a second deportation, which included Ezekiel and 10,000 of the backbone of Jewish society (cf. II Kgs 24: 10-16). **And made Zedekiah his brother** (uncle, II Kgs 24:17) **king.**

12. He **humbled not himself before Jeremiah.** Zedekiah first disregarded Jeremiah's messages (Jer 34:1-10), then inquired of the prophet (Jer 21), and finally pleaded with him for help (Jer 37), but never submitted to his requirements. Zedekiah was a weak man, pliable to the schemes of the vicious nobles that had been left to him (Jer 38:5). **13. He . . . rebelled against . . . Nebuchadnezzar,** at the instigation of Hophra (588–567 B.C.), Pharaoh of the Twenty-sixth Dynasty in Egypt (cf. Ezk 17:15; Jer 37:5). He **made him swear.** Zedekiah had been bound as a vassal to Nebuchadrezzar by oath; thus his faithlessness became his undoing (Ezk 17:13-19).

C. The Exile. 36:17-23. Chronicles is essentially a book of encouragement. The chapters on Judah's rulers record great triumphs, vindications of men's faith in God, even in the midst of the nation's general deterioration. Then, having demonstrated that God can and will cast off his people for their disobedience (36: 17-21, paralleling II Kgs 25 in brief summary), the chronicler goes on to intimate that out of the ruins are to arise a rejuvenated land, a recommissioned Temple depicting God's changeless salvation, and a refined and therefore restored people (II Chr 36:22,23, paralleling Ezr 1:1-3a). For the Exile was not a permanent defeat but, ultimately, a triumph of God's providence. History is a process, not of disintegration, but of sifting and selection. When the dross, therefore, is removed, a faithful remnant is disclosed (cf. on 10:9; 11:3): "The Lord his God be with him! Let him go up!" (II Chr 36:23).

17. The Lord **gave them all into the hand** of the Chaldeans. See II Kgs 25:1-21 for the details of Jerusalem's fall and pillage and the third, great deportation, 586 B.C. (cf. II Chr 36:7,10, notes). **20. Them that had escaped from the sword.** II Chronicles omits, as irrelevant to the final destiny of Judah, any account of the regathering under Gedaliah and the flight of the remnant to Egypt (II Kgs 25:22-27); of the small, fourth deportation of 582 B.C. (Jer 52:30); and of "the poorest of the land" that remained scattered in Palestine (II Kgs 25:12, ASV). Archaeology has demonstrated Judah's thorough depopulation at this time. He **carried . . . away to Babylon,** as **servants.** After certain initial discouragements (Ps 137) and oppressive service (Isa 14:2,3), some Jews gained favor and status (cf. II Kgs 25:27-30). The worldly ones grew indifferent and drifted away (cf. Ezk 33:31,32), but the godly gained in spiritual maturity (cf. Dan 1:8; Est 4: 14-16; Neh 1:4).

21. To fulfill the word of the Lord . . . land had enjoyed its sabbaths . . . seventy years (RSV; cf. v. 7, note), presumably making up for a half-millennium of neglected sabbatic years (Gustav Oehler, *Theology of the Old Testament,* p. 343; cf. Lev 25:1-7; 26:34).

22. In 538 B.C. **Cyrus king of Persia**

overthrew Nabonidus and his son Belshazzar, the last native Babylonian rulers (Dan 5). His policy of religious conciliation and of restoration for exiles has received full archaeological confirmation from the inscriptions of Cyrus himself. (On the correspondence of this material with Ezr 1:1-3a, see Introd., *Authorship*).

23. All the kingdoms of the earth hath the Lord (Jehovah) **given me.** Such diplomatic language (cf 35:21, note) meant nothing to Cyrus; of his words to a Babylonian audience, "Marduk, king of the gods [the leading deity of Babylon, but not of Persia!] . . . designated (me) to rule over all the lands." But Cyrus was in fact an instrument of God's providence (Isa 44:28–45:5).

BIBLIOGRAPHY

For bibliography see under I Chronicles.

EZRA

INTRODUCTION

Title. The Book of Ezra, like Ruth, Job, Esther, and others, is named after its principal character. The Jews considered it to be one book with Nehemiah (cf. Talmud, Masoretic text, Josephus), but the repetition of Ezra 2 in Nehemiah 7 indicates that the two books were originally distinct works. In the LXX, Ezra and Nehemiah are called Esdras B, to distinguish them from an apocryphal book, Esdras A (which contains II Chr 35:1 through Ezra, plus Neh 8:1-12, with variations and additions).

Date and Authorship. Although the author is not mentioned, and the narrative appears in both first and third persons, it is highly probable that Ezra himself wrote the book, using various decrees, letters, and genealogies as his original sources. Some Babylonian documents used a similar form of narration; so the change of persons is not a conclusive argument against his authorship. Nor can the fact that he refers to himself as "a ready scribe in the law of Moses" (7:6) be used as an effective argument to the contrary (cf. Num 12:3).

Since Ezra lived to the time of Nehemiah (Neh 8:1-9; 12:36), he had plenty of time to finish his book between April of 456 B.C., when the events of Ezra 10:17-44 took place, and the summer of 444 B.C., when Nehemiah arrived in Jerusalem from the Persian court. Robert Dick Wilson ("Ezra-Nehemiah," ISBE, II, 1083) pointed out that the Hebrew of Ezra resembles that of Daniel, Haggai, and Chronicles much more than that of Ecclesiasticus (written about 180 B.C.), and the Aramaic portions of Ezra (4:7–6:18; 7:12-26) are very similar to the Aramaic of the Elephantine papyri of the fifth century B.C.

Historical Background. The Book of Ezra records the fulfillment of God's promise to the nation of Israel through Jeremiah to bring them back to their land after seventy years of captivity. Through the protection and help of three Persian kings (Cyrus, Darius, and Artaxerxes), and the leadership of such great and godly Jews as Zerubbabel, Joshua, Haggai, Zechariah, and Ezra, the second Temple was completed and true worship restored in Jerusalem.

The first six chapters of the book cover events during the first two or three years of the reign of Cyrus (538–530 B.C.) and the first six years of the reign of Darius I (521–486 B.C.). The last four chapters (plus 4:7-23) record events during the first part of the reign of Artaxerxes I (464–423 B.C.). No mention is made of Cambyses (530–522 B.C.) or of Smerdis (522 B.C.), and only one verse (4:6) mentions Xerxes (486–465 B.C.). Thus, although eighty important years of Achaemenid Persian history are spanned by the Book of Ezra, practically nothing is said of the fifty-eight-year period between 515 B.C. and 457 B.C., during which time the Persians made two great but futile efforts to conquer Greece, and the events of the book of Esther occurred.

As the scene opens in Ezra 1, the Jews have just seen the overthrow of the hated Neo-Babylonian Empire, in 539 B.C., by Cyrus the Persian. And Daniel has just been put into a place of honor by Darius the Mede, whom Cyrus appointed to rule over the Neo-Babylonian territories (Dan 5:30–6:3).

OUTLINE

I. The exiles' return from Babylon. 1:1–2:70.
   A. The decree of Cyrus. 1:1-4.
   B. Preparations for the journey. 1:5-11.
   C. Those who returned. 2:1-70.
II. Temple building begun. 3:1–4:24.
   A. The altar and the foundation. 3:1-13.
   B. Opposition to the work. 4:1-24.

III. The building completed. 5:1–6:22.
 A. Work resumed. 5:1-5.
 B. Tatnai's letter to Darius. 5:6-17.
 C. Decrees of Cyrus and Darius. 6:1-12.
 D. The Temple finished. 6:13-22.
IV. Ezra's journey to Jerusalem. 7:1–8:36.
 A. Ezra introduced. 7:1-10.
 B. Letter of Artaxerxes to Ezra. 7:11-28.
 C. The journey to Jerusalem. 8:1-36.
V. The great reformation. 9:1–10:44.
 A. The tragic report and Ezra's prayer. 9:1-15.
 B. The abandonment of mixed marriages. 10:1-17.
 C. List of those with foreign wives. 10:18-44.

COMMENTARY

I. The Exiles' Return from Babylon. 1:1–2:70.

A. The Decree of Cyrus. 1:1-4. God fulfilled his promises to Israel through Jeremiah that the Captivity would last only seventy years. When that period ended, he raised up Cyrus the Persian to conquer the Babylonians, who had enslaved the Israelites. One of Cyrus' first public acts as the new king of Babylon was to encourage the Jews to return to Palestine to rebuild the ruined house of Jehovah.

1. Now in the first year of Cyrus. These words, and those that follow, to the middle of verse 3, are identical with those that conclude II Chronicles. The two books are thus connected by a common link. It is quite possible that Ezra wrote I and II Chronicles. Cyrus, who, by 550 B.C., had welded the Medes and the Persians into a dual monarchy, finally conquered Babylon in October, 539 B.C. **The word of the LORD by . . . Jeremiah.** It was in 605 B.C. that Jeremiah had prophesied the seventy-year captivity of Judah (Jer 25:12; cf. 25:1). And it was this prophecy that caused Daniel to pray for the deliverance of his people in the year of Babylon's fall (Dan 9:2).

2. The LORD . . . hath charged me to build him an house at Jerusalem. Nearly two hundred years earlier, Isaiah had prophesied that Cyrus would be God's chosen instrument for liberating the Jewish exiles and initiating the restoration of the Temple (Isa 44:28–45:7; 45:13). It is not necessary to assume that the liberator was a true believer (cf. Isa 45:4–"I have surnamed thee though thou hast not known me"). The famous cuneiform Cyrus Cylinder records this prayer of the Persian king: "May all the gods whom I have resettled in their sacred cities ask daily Bel and Nebo for a long life for me . . . " Cyrus probably recognized the God of Israel as one of the most important deities, especially if Daniel showed him the prophecies of Isaiah (Jos *Antiq.* 11.1.1). This decree was filed in Ecbatana, where Darius I discovered it twenty years later (Ezr 6:2).

B. Preparations for the Journey. 1:5-11. Thousands of godly Jews heeded the summons of Cyrus and made preparations for the long journey. And many of the vessels that Nebuchadnezzar had taken from the Temple were handed over to the Jews to be restored to Jerusalem.

6. And all they that were about them strengthened their hands. Only about 50, 000 Jews returned (cf. 2:64,65). The majority decided to remain in Babylonia, where many were well settled (Jer 29:4-7). Thus, they were in a position to help those who did return. Gentiles, too, probably gave gifts (cf. Ex 12:35,36).

7. The vessels of the house of the LORD. Some vessels were taken to Babylon in 605 B.C. (Dan 1:2), some in 597 B.C. (II Kgs 24:13), and the rest in 586 B.C. (II Kgs 25:14,15; Jer 27:16-22). Those which Cyrus did not send back at this time were restored to the Temple by Darius I about 518 B.C. (Ezr 6:5). However, the furniture of the Temple, including the ark of the covenant, was destroyed in 586 B.C. (Jer 3:16; II Kgs 25:13). **8. Sheshbazzar, the prince of Judah.** Even as Daniel was known in Babylon officially as Belteshazzar (Dan 1:7), so Zerubbabel was probably known as Sheshbazzar. We know that Zerubbabel laid the foundation of the Temple (Ezr 3:8; 5:2; Zech 4:9); but in an official letter to Darius, "Sheshbazzar" is said to have done this (5:16). Zerubbabel was a grandson of King Jehoiachin (Jeconiah; I Chr 3:17-19) and an ancestor of Joseph (Mt 1:12). The fact that I Chr 3:19 calls him the son of Pedaiah instead of Shealtiel (Ezr 3:2) suggests that Shealtiel died childless and Pedaiah contracted a levirate marriage with his brother's widow. **11. Five thousand and four hundred.** The 2,499 vessels listed in 1:9,10 may have been the largest or most important ones.

C. Those Who Returned. 2:1-70. The list is divided into eight groups: Zerubbabel and his companions (vv. 1,2); Jewish families (vv. 3-19); Palestinian towns (vv. 20-35); priests (vv. 36-39); Levites (vv. 40-42); Nethinim (vv. 43-54); Solomon's servants (vv. 55-58); those with uncertain genealogies (vv. 59-63). The section ends with a list of totals (vv. 64-67), and a brief statement of their arrival and the gifts they gave to the Temple (vv. 68-70).

2. Which came with Zerubbabel: Jeshua, Nehemiah . . . According to Neh 7:7, there are twelve in this group of leaders. **Jeshua,** or Joshua, was the high priest (3:2), grandson of the high priest Seriah, whom Nebuchadnezzar slew at Riblah (II Kgs 25:18-21; cf. I Chr 6:14). The **Nehemiah** listed here is not, of course, the same as the famous governor of eighty years later.

3-19. Many of these names appear again in Ezra 8 and 10 and Nehemiah 10. Thus, we have here not the names of individuals living at this time, but of families that were old and well established. Some members of these families returned with Zerubbabel in 536 B.C., and the rest came later with Ezra. **20-35.** Most of these towns appear elsewhere in the OT.

36-39. Jedaiah is probably the name of a family head in the high-priestly family of **Jeshua,** who descended from Eleazar, the third son of Aaron. **Immer** is the name of the third order of priests (I Chr 24:14). **Pashur** is possibly of the family of Malchijah, the fifth order of priests (I Chr 24:9; cf. I Chr 9:12; Neh 11:12). **Harim** is the name of the third order of priests (I Chr 24:8). **40-42.** Three classes of Levites are mentioned: (1) regular Levites, who assisted the priests; (2) singers; and (3) porters, or doorkeepers. Only 341 Levites returned, as compared with 4,289 priests. Ezra found a similar reluctance to return on the part of the Levites of his day (Ezr 8:15). This is not easy to explain.

43-54. The Nethinims were probably descendants of the Gibeonites, whom Joshua made subject to taskwork (Josh 9). **55-58. The children of Solomon's servants** were doubtless the descendants of his prisoners of war. They were like the Nethinim and were counted with them (v. 58).

59-62. Three families of common people (vv. 59,60) and three families of priests (vv. 61,62) could not prove their relationship to the nation through genealogical records, and were therefore excluded officially, although permitted to accompany the true Jews on this journey.

63. The Tirshatha. This was a Persian title, possibly meaning "his excellency." It here refers to the governor, Zerubbabel. In Neh 8:9 the same title is applied to Nehemiah. **Till there stood up a priest with Urim and with Thummim.** In Ex 28:30, the Urim and Thummim are designated as part of the high priest's ceremonial dress. They were used in some way to determine the will of God. But it seems that God's will could no longer be determined in this way after the departure of the Shekinah glory in 592 B.C. (Ezk 8–11). Zerubbabel's earnest hope (and that of all godly Jews) that this tragic situation would not long continue was, of course, not fulfilled, and the problem of the six families was left unsolved.

64-67. This total of 42,360 is identical with that of Neh 7:66; but the actual numbers in Ezra 2 come to only 29,818, and the numbers in Nehemiah 7 total only 31,088. In the transmission of OT numbers, changes and omissions sometimes occur through repeated copying; perhaps that is the explanation of this discrepancy. **Singing men and singing women** (v. 65). Non-Israelites who were hired for festivities and lamentations, in addition to Levitical singers.

68-70. They came to the house of the LORD. An interesting expression, suggesting that it had continued to be in Jerusalem even after its destruction in 586 B.C.! Cf. Jer 41:5; Hag 2:9 (ASV). **Threescore and one thousand drams of gold.** See notes on parallel passage, Neh 7:70-72. **All Israel in their cities.** Cf. Ezr 2:2b. It is certain that all twelve tribes were represented in this expedition, for refugees from the northern tribes had been pouring into Judah for centuries before the Babylonian captivity.

II. Temple Building Begun. 3:1–4:24.

A. The Altar and the Foundation. 3:1-

13. Soon after reaching the Promised Land, the Jews made provision for offering sacrifices. The following spring the foundation for the second Temple was laid, with great ceremony and mixed emotions.

1. And when the seventh month was come. This was the first day of the month (v. 6), the Feast of Trumpets (Num 29:1-6), a foreshadowing of Israel's final regathering. Assuming a two-year delay in the beginning of the journey from Babylon after Cyrus' decree, this would have been September 25, 536 B.C. The laying of the temple foundation the following spring would thus have brought to an official close the seventy-year captivity predicted by Jeremiah, from 605 to 535 B.C. (Jer 25:1-12). **3. Fear was upon them because of the people of those countries.** Therefore, they were fully aware of their need of God's protection. Contrast the paganism of II Kgs 17:24-34. That their fears were not exaggerated may be seen in the following chapters of Ezra. **4. They kept also the feast of tabernacles.** This feast lasted from the fifteenth to the twenty-second of the seventh month, just two weeks after the Feast of Trumpets. Cf. Num 29:13 ff. The Day of Atonement, on the tenth day of the seventh month, is not mentioned in this chapter.

7. To bring cedar trees from Lebanon to the sea of Joppa. Compare Solomon's gathering of materials, more than 500 years earlier (II Chr 2:16 and context). **According to the grant . . . of Cyrus.** The full terms of this grant are found in 6:3-5.

8. Now in the second year . . . in the second month. May-June 535 B.C. See notes on Ezr 3:1. **Levites, from twenty years old and upward.** Whereas twenty-five was the minimum age for tabernacle service for Levites (Num 8:24; 4:3), the age was only twenty for temple service (I Chr 23:24; II Chr 31:17). There were 24,000 Levites appointed to oversee the work of Solomon's Temple (I Chr 23:4), whereas now there were only 341 altogether! (Ezr 2:40-42) **9. Jeshua . . . Kadmiel . . . Judah . . . Henadad.** For **Judah** substitue the ASV marginal reading, *Hodaviah*. Thus, the first three names here are the same as in 2:40, and represent special Levitical families placed in charge of the temple workmen.

10. The priests in their apparel with trumpets, and the Levites . . . with cymbals. This was the same order observed when the ark was brought to Jerusalem in David's time (I Chr 16:5,6; cf. Num 10:8). **11. And they sang together.** *One to another* (ASV), antiphonally. The very psalm sung on this occasion (cf. Ps 136:1) suggests that they were thinking in terms of Jeremiah's great prophecy (Jer 33:11). **And all the people shouted with a great shout.** Their joy was overwhelming, for the prayers and hopes of decades of captivity were now being fulfilled before their very eyes.

12,13. But many . . . wept with a loud voice; and many shouted aloud for joy. Fifty years had passed since the first Temple had been destroyed, and many of the older men who had seen it wept now because of the sad contrast in size and grandeur of design. And what a contrast this was to the glorious Millennnial Temple prophesied by Ezekiel, the Jews of this period knew all too well! When work on the second Temple was renewed in 520 B.C., there were still some of these old men living who wept again (Hag 2:3).

B. Opposition to the Work. 4:1-24. No sooner had the foundation been laid than the Jews' troubles began. First came the temptation to compromise their testimony. When they had successfully resisted this, active opposition began, and it continued intermittently from the days of Cyrus to the days of Artaxerxes.

1. The adversaries of Judah and Benjamin. These two tribes are mentioned in particular because they now constituted the majority of the nation, and it was largely in their old territories that the remnant now lived. **2. Since the days of Esar-haddon.** Isaiah had prophesied that the northern ten tribes would cease to be a distinct people within sixty-five years. Since he prophesied this in 734 B.C. (Isa 7:8), it was fulfilled by 669 B.C., within the reign of the Assyrian king, Esar-haddon (680–668 B.C.), who was responsible for transplanting foreigners into Samaria (II Kgs 17:24). These foreigners intermarried with Israelites, and it was their descendants who now approached Zerubbabel saying, **"We seek your God, as ye do."** This proposal was the more dangerous since it came under the guise of true religion (II Cor 11:15; cf. II Cor 6:17).

3. We ourselves together will build. That is, the people of Jehovah, as contrasted with "the people of the land" (v. 4). Zerubbabel clearly saw the impossibility of accepting pagans on an equal basis with true Jews in the building of Jehovah's Temple. These Samaritans revealed their true character when, after further rejections, they built their own temple on Mount Gerizim (Jn 4:20-22).

4. Weakened the hands of the people of Judah. The prophet Jeremiah was accused of doing this in his day (Jer 38:4). **5. Hired counsellors against them.** Could this have been in the court at Shushan (Susa)? If this was 535 B.C., then probably Daniel was no longer living, and there was no influential Jew interceding for the nation at the Persian court. **All the days of Cyrus king of Persia, even until the reign of Darius king of Persia.** This means the remaining years of Cyrus (535–530 B.C.), the reign of Cambyses (530–522 B.C.), the short reign of Smerdis (522 B.C.), and until the second year of Darius I (521/520 B.C.). After the parenthetical history of opposition (vv. 6-23), the present history is resumed (v. 24).

6. Now begins a parenthesis in the main story, which tells of similar opposition to the Jews in the days of Xerxes (486–465 B.C.) and Artaxerxes (464–423 B.C.). Since **Ahasuerus** (Heb., *'ăḥashwērôsh)* is mentioned, in verse 6, after the Darius of verse 5, and has the same name as the king of the Book of Esther, it should have been obvious to the older commentators that this was Xerxes (see ASV margin). **An accusation.** The same root word in Hebrew as for Satan, "the accuser" (I Chr 21:1; Job 1:6). This written accusation to Xerxes in 486 B.C. is referred to nowhere else in the OT.

7. Bishlam, Mithredath, Tabeel were probably Samaritans who hired two high Persian officials—Rehum the chancellor and Shimshai the scribe (v. 8)—to write the letter of 4:11-16 to Artaxerxes accusing the Jews of rebuilding the walls of Jerusalem. **Tabeel** *(God is good)* may be the same as Tobiah *(Jehovah is good)* in Neh 2:19. **Written in the Syrian tongue.** This was Aramaic, the commercial language of the Fertile Crescent during the first millennium B.C. Not only is the letter of 4:11-16 written in Aramaic, but also the entire section of Ezra from 4:8 through 6:18. It is very similar to the Aramaic of the Elephantine papyri. **9. Apharsathchites.** Cf. 5:6. Keil believed these were a race specially devoted to the Persian king, who took a prominent position among the settlers in Syria. Some of the other races are difficult to identify, though most of them probably came from the regions of Babylonia, Persia, and Media (cf. II Kgs 17:24). **10. The great and noble Asnapper.** The great Assyrian king Ashurbanipal (668–626 B.C.), who completed the transplanting ot peoples into Samaria that Esar-haddon (v. 2) had begun a year or two earlier. **And at such a time.** Literally, *and so forth.* This abbreviation of the customary lengthy salutation appears again in 4:11, 17; 7:12.

12,13. The enemies of the Jews here profess great concern for the welfare of the Persian king. Their report of the progress on the walls (v. 12) is obviously exaggerated, in the light of verse 13. Nevertheless, it seems clear that some effort had been made to rebuild the walls of Jerusalem, possibly through Ezra's en-encouragement (see note on v. 23). The building of the Temple is not under consideration in this letter, for it had been completed in 515 B.C. (6:15). **The rebellious and the bad city.** Cf. 4:15. Jerusalem had certainly proved to be such under the tragic reigns of Jehoiakim (II Kgs 24:1) and Zedekiah (II Chr 36:13). And as far as the Assyrians were concerned, it was so in the days of Hezekiah and Manasseh (II Chr 32;33).

14. We have maintenance from the king's palace. Literally, *We eat the salt of the palace* (ASV). They were in the king's pay. **15. The book of the records of thy fathers.** See Esther 6:1, where Darius' father, Xerxes, consults "the book of the record of the chronicles." These may have included chronicles of Assyrian and Babylonian as well as Persian history.

20. There have been mighty kings also over Jerusalem. While David and Solomon were Jerusalem's greatest kings, such monarchs as Asa, Jehoshaphat, Uzziah, and Hezekiah had certainly left their mark upon ancient Near Eastern history. **21. Until another commandent shall be given from me.** This final clause left the door open for the king to change his mind, as we find in Nehemiah 2! Truly this was providential, for the laws of the Medes and Persians changed not!

23. Made them to cease by force and power. It is clear that the Samaritans took full advantage of this decree, and even went to the extreme of partially destroying the walls that had been built, and burning the gates. It was news of this disaster that so shocked Nehemiah and forced him into mourning and prayer (Neh 1:3,4). We may thus date this decree at about 446 B.C. Ezra's relation to the entire crisis is not indicated in Scripture, although he was certainly in favor of walls being built for the city (Neh 12:36). **24. Then ceased the work**

of the house of God. This follows the parenthesis of 4:6-23, and harks back to verse 5, with the additional information that it was in the second year of Darius that work on **the house of God** (not the city walls) was resumed (5:2). Older commentators, thinking that 4:24 had to follow 4:23 chronologically, were forced to interpret Ahasuerus in 4:6 as Cambyses, and Artaxerxes in 4:7 as Smerdis!

III. The Building Completed. 5:1–6:22.

A. Work Resumed. 5:1-5. After fifteen years of stagnation, the work on the Temple was resumed under the impetus of powerful preaching from Haggai and Zechariah. Even Tatnai's challenge did not stop the work.

1. The prophets, Haggai . . . and Zechariah. The name of Haggai's father is omitted here and likewise in his book. Zechariah's grandfather was Iddo, his father being Berechiah (Zech 1:1). Haggai's ministry began on August 29, 520 B.C. (Hag 1:1), but Zechariah did not begin his ministry until October-November. **2. Began to build the house of God.** Work on the Temple was renewed only three weeks after Haggai began preaching! This was September 20, 520 B.C. (Hag 1:14,15). **Zerubbabel** is highly honored in the book of Haggai and in Zechariah 4, while **Jeshua** is honored in Zechariah 3 and 6.

3. Tatnai, governor on this side the river. This was the Persian satrap for the entire region west of the Euphrates. From 539–525 B.C., not only this region, but Babylonia as well, was ruled by Darius the Mede. **Shethar-boznai** was probably Tatnai's aide or secretary, as Shimshai later was to Rehum (4:9). **To make up this wall.** The wall of the Temple is referred to here (cf. 5:8). **4.** See the ASV for the Jews' answer to Tatnai. Verses 9,10 contain Tatnai's full question, which explains the answer of 5:4. But the full answer of the Jews to Tatnai's challenge is found in verses 11-16. **5. The eye of their God was upon the elders.** A clear evidence of God's providence. (For a similar and more frequent phrase, see 7:6.) Since it probably took a year to hear from Darius again, it would have been a severe blow to the Jews to stop their work in the meantime.

B. Tatnai's Letter to Darius. 5:6-17. Tatnai, the Persian satrap, then wrote to Darius the king, telling of his challenge and the Jews' answer, and asking for a verdict on the basis of Cyrus' decree.

8. The house of the great God. This letter is concerned exclusively with the Temple, in contrast to the letter of 4:12-16, which was written about seventy years later (see notes). **11-13.** The letter now quotes the Jews' answer to Tatnai, in which they relate the history of their Temple from its completion in 960 B.C. to its destruction in 586 B.C., and Cyrus' decree for rebuilding it in 538 B.C.

16. The same Sheshbazzar . . . laid the foundation of the house of God. Cf. 1:8; 5:14. Another name for Zerubbabel, because Zerubbabel laid the temple foundations in 3:8-10. **Since that time even until now hath it been in building.** The Hebrew wording here does not preclude interruptions in the work (E. J. Young, *An Introduction to the OT*, p. 373). The point is, that there had been no official "cease-work" decree from the Persian court (contrast 4:23) from the days of Cyrus to the present. **17.** Even if Cyrus' decree was found, and was favorable, Tatnai probably hoped for a reversal from Darius, the founder of a new branch of the Achaemenid dynasty (see notes on 6:1,2).

C. Decrees of Cyrus and Darius. 6:1-12. Darius not only succeeded in discovering Cyrus' decree concerning the Jews and their Temple, but made one of his own, ordering Tatnai to help the Jews in their work and threatening those who altered the decree.

1,2. The house of the rolls . . . in Babylon. . . . at Achmetha. Keil points out that the vast complexity of the Persian Empire and the general confusion that accompanied the shift of royal power from the line of Cyrus to the line of Darius in 521 B.C. help to explain why some earlier decrees would have been forgotten. But it is a tribute to the efficiency of the Persian administration that records were safely filed in an elaborate network of archives centering in **Babylon** and reaching to branch libraries as far distant as **Achmetha** (Ecbatana), capital of the old Median empire. **The rolls** (v. 1) should be translated *archives* (ASV). But **a roll** (v. 2) means a papyrus or leather scroll (different Hebrew word), instead of the usual clay tablet. Possibly all the ancient scrolls were stored in the library at Ecbatana because the air was not so hot and humid there as it was in Babylon.

3. For an explanation of the differences between this decree of Cyrus and that of Ezra 1, see E. J. Young (*op. cit.*, p. 372). While that was a public proclamation, this was a more detailed official counterpart for the archives. **The height thereof threescore cubits.** The porch of Solomon's Temple was twice this height (II Chr 3:4).

8. Moreover I make a decree. Not only did Darius warn Tatnai to leave the Jews alone because of Cyrus' decree, but he also added one of his own which must have stunned Tatnai and his companions. **Of the tribute beyond the river . . . expenses be given unto these men.** Cf. 6:4. This probably cut into Tatnai's own pocketbook, for he took his share from the tribute. **10. Offer sacrifices . . . unto the God of heaven, and pray for the life of the king.** Darius could easily say this without abandoning his polytheism. Praying for kings is implied in Jeremiah's command to Jewish exiles (Jer 29:7). Carl F. Keil (*The Books of Ezra, Nehemiah, and Esther*, p. 87) shows that this was done in later centuries too (I Maccabees 7:33; 12:11; Jos *Antiq.* 12.2.5). **11. Let timber be pulled down . . . let him be hanged thereon.** Keil cites Herodotus (III. 159) as saying that Darius impaled 3,000 Babylonians after conquering their city. Therefore this was no idle threat! **Let his house be made a dunghill.** Cf. Dan 2:5; 3:29; II Kgs 9:37.

D. The Temple Finished. 6:13-22. With the help of secular rulers and godly prophets, the Jews finished their Temple within five years, and dedicated it to Jehovah with great joy. A month later, multitudes gathered in Jerusalem to celebrate the Passover and the Feast of Unleavened Bread.

14. The commandment of Cyrus, and Darius, and Artaxerxes king of Persia. Ezra is careful to add the name of his own king, Artaxerxes, because he helped in the maintenance of the Temple (7:15, 16,21). **15. The third day of the month Adar.** That was March 12, 515 B.C., four and a half years after the work was begun in earnest. While the Temple was being built, the events of Zechariah 7 occurred. **17.** Solomon offered more than two hundred times as many oxen and sheep at the dedication of his Temple! (I Kgs 8:63)

19. The passover. This was April 21, 515 **B.C.,** just five weeks after the Temple had been dedicated. Beginning with this verse, the text is again in Hebrew. **20. The priests and the Levites were purified together.** As one, without exception. Levites replaced heads of families (Ex 12:6) and slaughtered Passover lambs for both laity (who might be unclean) and priests (who were too busy). Cf. II Chr 35:11, 14,15. **21.** Two groups of Jews are mentioned here, those who had returned from Babylon, and those who had remained in the land, mixed with the heathen population (II Kgs 17:33). **22. The king of Assyria.** Since the Persians now ruled the former Assyrian territories, it could be said that Darius was king of Assyria, even as Cyrus was king of Babylon.

IV. Ezra's Journey to Jerusalem. 7:1–8:36.

A. Ezra Introduced. 7:1-10. Ezra's family connections and personal characteristics, as well as a brief summary of his great journey, are now set forth.

1. Now after these things. Between chapters 6 and 7, fifty-eight years intervene, during which time the events of the Book of Esther occurred. This might explain Artaxerxes' favorable attitude toward Ezra. **Ezra the son of Seraiah.** Seraiah was high priest in 586 B.C. (II Kgs 25:18). But Ezra must have descended from a younger son of Seraiah, because he is not called "son of Jozadak," as Jeshua is (Ezr 3:2; I Chr 6:14); and therefore his immediate ancestors were not in the high-priestly line. **3. Azariah, the son of Meraioth.** To shorten the list, six names have been dropped out between these two (I Chr 6:7-11).

6. This Ezra . . . was a ready scribe in the law of Moses. Scribe. Hebrew *soper* earlier meant a "secretary." But by Jeremiah's time scribes were already Bible teachers (Jer 8:8), and that is the meaning here. **7-9.** The nine-hundred-mile journey took four months—March 27 to July 24, 457 B.C. **10. For Ezra had prepared his heart.** See II Chr 12:14; 19:3; 30:19, for similar expressions.

B. Letter of Artaxerxes to Ezra. 7:11-28. Artaxerxes wrote a letter in Aramaic to Ezra, giving him permission to take Jewish volunteers, silver and gold, and temple vessels back to Jerusalem. Also, he made ample provision for temple supplies and ministers, and gave Ezra authority to appoint magistrates and judges.

14. His seven counsellors. Artaxerxes' supreme court (cf. Est 1:14; Herodotus

III, 84). **To enquire concerning Judah and Jerusalem.** It seems that Ezra held a position at the Persian court corresponding to that of Secretary of State for Jewish affairs.

18. **And whatsoever shall seem good to thee.** Could Ezra have interpreted this to include permission to rebuild the walls of the city? **And to thy brethren.** His fellow priests. **20-22.** Artaxerxes followed the examples of Cyrus and Darius (cf. 6:4,8). The maximum amounts to be given were **an hundred talents of silver** (about $100,000), **an hundred measures** *(cors)* **of wheat** (625 bushels), **an hundred baths of wine** and also of oil (580 gallons).

25. **Judge all the people that are beyond the river.** That is, Jews ("all such as know the laws of thy God"). **Teach ye them that know them not.** Uninstructed Jews were to be taught the Scriptures. Ezra doubtless suggested to Artaxerxes what the decree should include. The latter provision, in particular, coincided with the scribe's life aim (v. 10).

27,28. Ezra recognized, in this remarkable decree, that Jehovah had turned the king's heart toward His people (Prov 21:1). The beautifying of the Temple was the chief cause for thanksgiving, for the re-establishment of divine worship was the key to revival.

C. The Journey to Jerusalem. 8:1-36. About 1,500 priests and heads of houses started out with Ezra from Babylon. In addition to these, Ezra obtained some Levites and Nethinim from Casiphia. He entrusted the temple treasures to twenty-four priests and Levites. After a time of prayer and fasting, the company began the long journey to Jerusalem. Four months later they arrived at the city, and deposited their treasures at the Temple. They offered sacrifices on the altar and delivered Artaxerxes' commissions to the proper authorities.

2. **Gershom . . . Daniel.** These heads of priestly houses were descendants of the third and fourth sons of Aaron respectively (see v. 24, n.). Strangely, no total is given for the priests, nor for the family of **Hattush,** a descendant of King David.

3-14. This list of genealogies is also to be found among the seventeen genealogies in Ezr 2:3-15, except for **Joab** (v. 9). *Of the sons of Zattu* and *Bani* probably should appear in 8:5,10 (LXX and I Esd), matching the same names in 2:8, 10. The fact that the same names appear eighty years apart shows that they are the names of families, not of individuals living in the days of Zerubbabel and Ezra. Some members of these families returned with Zerubbabel, but other members did not return until Ezra's day.

15. **There abode we in tents three days.** Since they finally left the river Ahava (location unknown, probably a canal) on the twelfth day (v. 31), they must have traveled nine days from Babylon to get there (cf. 7:9). **None of the sons of Levi.** Only 341 Levites returned with Zerubbabel, compared with 4,289 priests (2:36-42). **17. Iddo the chief at the place Casiphia.** This must have been a settlement of Levites and Nethinim. Iddo was probably a Levite. **18-20. A man of understanding.** Probably a proper name, Ishsechel, a descendant of Mahli, Levi's grandson (Ex 6:16,19). **Sherebiah** and **Hashabiah** are mentioned again in Ezr 8:24 (see note).

21-23. **Then I proclaimed a fast.** For other OT examples of fasting to obtain answers to prayer, see Jud 20:26; I Sam 7:6; II Chr 20:3; Joel 1:14. This time, no pillar of cloud appeared to lead the pilgrims back to the Holy Land; but the hand of their God was upon them (Ezr 8:22). **I was ashamed to require . . . soldiers and horsemen.** Ezra gave a good testimony in this way. But the fact that Nehemiah did have an escort (Neh 2:9) only proves that our lives and circumstances before God are never identical. **He was intreated of us.** Ezra thus looks back upon a safe and successful journey.

24. **Sherebiah, Hashabiah, and ten of their brethren.** These are obviously Levites (vv. 18,19), making twelve priests and twelve Levites. None of these twelve priests are named here, but two are named in verse 2. **25-27.** See Artaxerxes' decree, 7:14-16. The silver, gold, and precious vessels were worth about $3,000,000. Little wonder, then, that Ezra proclaimed a fast to seek God's protection for the trip!

31,32. They left Ahava on April 8, 457 B.C., and arrived at Jerusalem on July 24 (7:9). Nine hundred miles in four months was about seven miles a day. This was a good average, for there were "little ones" (v. 21), as well as much equipment to be carried. **The hand of our God was upon us.** Cf. Ezra's testimony, 8:22. **Abode there three days.** Cf. Neh 2:11. **35,36.** What a joy it was for these Jews to offer sacrifices on the true altar of God! Among them were priests and Levites who had never seen Jerusalem or its Temple. **Unto the king's lieutenants, and to the governors.** These were the satraps and rulers of districts surrounding Judah. Judah at this time, and for many decades afterward, was counted as part of a larger governmental area.

V. The Great Reformation. 9:1–10:44.

A. The Tragic Report and Ezra's Prayer. 9:1-15. When Ezra was advised by the Jewish rulers concerning the mixed marriages that had been entered into in recent years, he collapsed in grief, and his deep distress brought conviction of sin to the hearts of many. His great prayer contained no requests for pardon, but it did provide the proper atmosphere for confession and forsaking of sin on the part of the congregation. He contrasted God's faithfulness with the disobedience of Israel, for which the nation deserved extinction.

1. Now when these things were done. It must have taken several months for the events of 8:36 to be accomplished, for we are now in the month of December (10:9). **The princes came to me.** All classes of the nation were involved in this recent sinful trend; but since the princes had led in this sin (9:2), they and not the priests came first to Ezra. Five of the seven Canaanite nations are listed here (Deut 7:1; Acts 13:19), as well as three others. These pagan peoples in the land had escaped deportation by Nebuchadnezzar. **2. The holy seed have mingled themselves.** Cf. Ex 19:5; Isa 6:13.

3. Plucked off the hair. Tearing of garments was a sign of deep affliction (Lev 10:6; Josh 7:6); but plucking out a portion of the hair and beard was an expression of violent wrath or moral indignation (Isa 50:6; Neh 13:25). Ezra fully realized that because of the holiness of God, such grave sin could only lead to another period of captivity. **4. Every one that trembled at the words of the God of Israel.** Cf. 10:3; Isa 66:2,5; Ps 119:120,161. A man's attitude toward God's Word is one of the ultimate criteria of his spirituality.

8. And now for a little space. Literally, *for a little moment*. Eighty years in the Holy Land seemed like a short time compared with the centuries of sufferings under the Assyrians and Babylonians (cf. Neh 9:32). **A nail in his holy place.** Cf. Isa 22:23. The Temple was a nail that upheld the community. **That our God may lighten our eyes.** Cf. Ps 13:3; I Sam 14:27,29. **9. For we are bondmen** (ASV). No well-taught Jew thought that the Millennial Age had dawned when Zerubbabel's remnant returned to Palestine (cf. Isa 14:1-3). **To give us a wall in Judah and in Jerusalem. Wall** here is figurative, like "nail" in 9:8. The Hebrew word *gâdēr* means a wall or fence of a vineyard, built for its protection (Isa 5:2,5). Since the kings of Persia protected them, they were in this sense a 'wall' between Judah and her enemies.

B. The Abandonment of Mixed Marriages. 10:1-17. Ezra's prayer of confession produced the desired effect, and many gathered to him to confess their sin. A proclamation was now issued, that all Jews must report to Jerusalem within three days. However, the complexity of the problem and the inclement weather necessitated a delay in the judicial proceedings. Finally, the guilty Jews were brought to court and were forced to put away their foreign wives.

1. Casting himself down before the house of God. While casting himself down in the court of the Temple, he was still on his knees (9:5). **The people wept very sore.** The Jews were touched to tears by the sins of the nation, seen now in an entirely new light. Ezra accomplished far more by loving heart-concern than he ever could have done by mere force.

6. The chamber of Johanan the son of Eliashib. Josephus (*Antiq.* 11.5.5) states that Joiakim (Neh 12:10) was high priest when Ezra arrived in Jerusalem. His son, the Eliashib of this verse, was high priest in Nehemiah's day (Neh 13:4,7). Since Neh 12:10 states that Johanan (Jonathan) was Eliashib's grandson, we may say that the Johanan of our verse was a younger brother of Joiada, Eliashib's son. In honor of his brother, Joiada named his own son Johanan, too. It is quite reasonable to suppose that the grandson of the high priest Joiakim would have had a chamber in the Temple in Ezra's day. **8. All his substance should be forfeited.** Literally, *devoted.* This probably meant not destruction, as of an idolatrous city (Deut 13:12-17), but appropriation for the benefit of the Temple (Lev 27:28).

9. On December 8, 457 B.C., vast multitudes of Jews, unable to crowd into the small city (cf. Neh 7:4), gathered in the open space in front of the water gate

at the southeastern corner of the temple court (Neh 3:26; 8:1,3,16; 12:37) to hear Ezra's solemn message (Ezr 10:10,11). **Trembling because of this matter, and for the great rain.** Two factors created much discomfort among the people: an overwhelming fear of God's wrath upon the nation; and the pouring rain that characterizes the month of December in Jerusalem. **15. Only Jonathan . . . and Jahaziah . . . were employed about this matter.** Better, *stood up against this matter* (ASV). The opposition of these two men and their two supporters may have been based upon sympathy for the homes that were now threatened with division. If so, they were not looking at the matter from God's viewpoint, and their opposition fortunately failed.

17. And they made an end . . . by the first day of the first month. Parker and Dubberstein *(Babylonian Chronology 626* B.C.–A.D. *75)* have shown that there was an intercalary month in this year, so that the examination actually lasted four months instead of three, and ended on April 15, 456 B.C. This was about a year after Ezra's departure from the river Ahava.

C. List of Those with Foreign Wives. 10:18-44. Seventeen priests, ten Levites, and eighty-six men of the congregation of Israel were found guilty, and each put away his foreign wife, after offering a ram for his trespass.

18. All four orders of priests are represented here, proving true the statement of the princes (9:1; cf. 2:36-39). **19. They gave their hands . . . they offered a ram of the flock for their trespass.** They entered into a solemn agreement, ratified by pledging the right hand (Prov 6:1; Ezk 17:18), that they would put away their foreign wives. See Lev 5:14-16 for the command to offer a ram for the trespass offering.

44. Some of them had wives by whom they had children. This is mentioned to show how thoroughly the separation was carried out, being far more grievous than parting with childless wives. "Doubtless an adequate provision was made for the repudiated wives and children, according to the means and circumstances of the husbands" (Robert Jamieson, *Commentary on Ezra* in JFB). A comparison with Neh 10:30 (twelve years later) and Neh 13:23 (about thirty years later) shows that the evil was not permanently eliminated. Long association with heathen neighbors made such clear-cut separation a difficult thing for untaught Jews. But Ezra was God's man for the hour to preserve, at least for that generation, the identity and true testimony of the nation for the ultimate fulfillment of God's purposes.

BIBLIOGRAPHY

(for Ezra, Nehemiah and Esther)

ADENEY, WALTER F. "Ezra, Nehemiah, and Esther," *The Expositor's Bible.* London: Hodder and Stoughton, 1893.

CROSBY, HOWARD. "Nehemiah," in Vol. VII of *A Commentary on the Holy Scriptures.* Edited by John Peter Lange. Grand Rapids: Zondervan Publishing House, reprint, n.d.

JAMIESON, ROBERT, FAUSSET, A.R., and BROWN, DAVID. *A Commentary Critical, Experimental and Practical on the Old and New Testaments,* II, 581-650. Grand Rapids: Wm. B. Eerdmans Publishing Company, reprint, 1948.

KEIL, CARL F. *The Books of Ezra, Nehemiah, and Esther.* Grand Rapids: Wm. B. Eerdmans Publishing Company, reprint, 1950.

MACDONALD, A. "Esther," *The New Bible Commentary.* Edited by Francis Davidson. Grand Rapids: Wm. B. Eerdmans Publishing Company, 1953.

OLMSTEAD, A. T. *The History of the Persian Empire.* Chicago: The University of Chicago Press, 1948.

PARKER, RICHARD A. and DUBBERSTEIN, WALDO H. *Babylonian Chronology 626* B.C.–A.D. *75.* Providence, R.I.: Brown University Press, 1956.

PRITCHARD, J. (ed.). *Ancient Near Eastern Texts Relating to the Old Testament.* Princeton: Princeton University Press, 1950.

SCHULTZ, F. U. "Ezra" and "Esther" in Vol. VII of *A Commentary on the Holy Scriptures.* Edited by John Peter Lange. Grand Rapids: Zondervan Publishing House, reprint, n.d.

TULAND, C. G. "Hanani-Hananiah," *Journal of Biblical Literature,* June, 1958, pp. 157-161.

WILSON, ROBERT DICK. "Ezra-Nehemiah," *International Standard Bible Encyclopedia,* Vol. II. Grand Rapids:

Wm. B. Eerdmans Publishing Company, reprint, 1946.

Wright, J. Stafford. *The Date of Ezra's Coming to Jerusalem*. London: The Tyndale Press, 1947.

———. "Ezra" and "Nehemiah," *The New Bible Commentary*. Edited by Francis Davidson. Grand Rapids: Wm. B. Eerdmans Publishing Company, 1953.

Young, Edward J. *An Introduction to the Old Testament*. Grand Rapids: Wm. B. Eerdmans Publishing Company, 1949.

NEHEMIAH

INTRODUCTION

Title. Like Ezra, the Book of Nehemiah is named after its main character. See the Introduction to Ezra for a discussion of the relation of the Book of Nehemiah to the Book of Ezra, and of these two canonical books to the apocryphal book of Esdras A.

Date and Authorship. The fact that the narrative is written in the first person singular in many places is evidence that the book was written by Nehemiah himself. The places where he is mentioned in the third person (8:9; 10:1; 12:26,47) can be explained in harmony with his authorship. For example, 12:26 and 12:47, which seem to look back to "the days of Nehemiah," are both used in conjunction with the days of someone else. For uniformity of style, it was better to use the third person than to say, "in the days of X and in my days." Furthermore, perhaps Nehemiah had retired from the governorship, and was here looking back on his administration.

Serious objection to the unity of the book has been raised by some because of the mention, in the same chapter, of Jaddua (12:11,22) as the great-grandson of the high priest Eliashib, and of Darius the Persian (12:22). Arguments in favor of dating Jaddua toward the end of the fifth century B.C., and of identifying Darius the Persian as Darius II (423–404 B.C.), are set forth in the notes on 12:22.

The historicity of the book has been well established by the discovery of the Elephantine papyri, which mention Johanan (12:22,23) as high priest in Jerusalem, and the sons of Sanballat (Nehemiah's great enemy) as governors of Samaria in 408 B.C. We also learn from these papyri that Nehemiah had ceased to be the governor of Judea before that year, for Bagoas is mentioned as holding that position.

Historical Background. Artaxerxes I, whom Nehemiah served as cupbearer, was the son of Ahasuerus (Xerxes), who took Esther to be his queen. The Feast of Purim (Est 9:20-32) was instituted on March 8, 473 B.C., only eight years before Artaxerxes I became king. In the spring of 457 B.C., Ezra led an expedition of Jews back to Jerusalem with the blessing of Artaxerxes; and by the following spring, he had completed the examination of those in Judea who had married foreign women (see notes on Ezra 10).

One of the by-products of the revival under Ezra seems to have been an effort on the part of the Jews to rebuild the walls of Jerusalem. This in turn provoked the wrath of Rehum and Shimshai, who wrote an accusation against them to Artaxerxes (Ezr 4:7-16). The king commanded the work to cease until a further decree should be issued (Ezr 4:21). Rehum and Shimshai, upon receiving this decree from the king, hurried to Jerusalem and "made them to cease by force and power," presumably breaking down the wall that had been started and burning the gates (Ezr 4:23; Neh 1:3). It was the news of this fresh disaster that shocked Nehemiah and brought him to his knees before God.

The Book of Nehemiah covers a period of at least twenty years, from December, 445 B.C., to about 425 B.C., when Nehemiah returned from Babylon to cleanse Jerusalem, and the province, of various evils that had crept in during his absence since 432 B.C. The careers of Ezra and Nehemiah overlap, as may be seen in Neh 8:1-9 and 12:26. It is quite probable that Malachi prophesied during the governorship of Nehemiah, for many of the evils he denounced are found to be prominent in the Book of Nehemiah.

It must be said, in conclusion, that no portion of the Old Testament provides us with a greater incentive to dedicated, discerning zeal for the work of God than the Book of Nehemiah. The example of Nehemiah's passion for the truth of God's Word, whatever the cost or consequences, is an example sorely needed in the present hour. May the prayerful study of this book lead more of God's people today to "earnestly contend for the faith which was once delivered unto the saints."

OUTLINE

I. Nehemiah's arrival in Jerusalem. 1:1–2:20.
  A. Tragic news from Jerusalem, and Nehemiah's prayer. 1:1-11.
  B. The granting of Nehemiah's request. 2:1-8.
  C. Nehemiah's survey of the walls, and his report. 2:9-20.
II. The building of the wall. 3:1–6:19.
  A. The workmen and their tasks. 3:1-32.
  B. The opposition of enemies. 4:1-23.
  C. Reforms of Nehemiah as governor. 5:1-19.
  D. The wall finished despite intrigues. 6:1–7:4.
III. Civil and religious reforms in Jerusalem. 7:5–10:39.
  A. List of Jews who returned with Zerubbabel. 7:5-73.
  B. The reading and observance of God's Law. 8:1-18.
  C. A public confession and covenant. 9:1–10:39.
IV. Lists of inhabitants. 11:1–12:26.
V. Dedication of walls and organization of temple services. 12:27-47.
VI. Nehemiah's final reforms. 13:1-30.

COMMENTARY

I. Nehemiah's Arrival in Jerusalem. 1:1–2:20.

A. Tragic News from Jerusalem, and Nehemiah's Prayer. 1:1-11. Nehemiah hears that Jerusalem's walls and gates have been destroyed, and in great remorse he confesses to God the sins of Israel and prays for deliverance for His people.

1. Nehemiah the son of Hachaliah. This distinguishes him from others of the same name (Ezr 2:2; Neh 3:16), though nothing further is known of his father, nor do we know his tribe. **In the month Chisleu, in the twentieth year.** This was December, 445 B.C., the twentieth year of Artaxerxes (2:1). **In Shushan the palace.** In 478 B.C., Esther became Xerxes' queen in this palace (Est 2:8-18); and in 550 B.C., Daniel was carried there in a vision (Dan 8:2). **Hanani, one of my brethren.** Probably a blood brother (cf. 7:2). **3. The wall . . . is broken down, and the gates thereof are burned.** C. F. Keil *(The Books of Ezra, Nehemiah, and Esther)* and others insist that this refers to the destruction of 586 B.C. But why would Nehemiah have been so shocked about that news? More likely, it was a recent destruction (see *Historical Background,* and notes on Ezr 4:23).

4-11. For four months (2:1), Nehemiah prayed to God "day and night," (1:6) on behalf of His people. **And will bring them unto the place** (v. 9; cf. Deut 12:5,11,14). Here Nehemiah is praying not for more exiles to return to Palestine, but for the protection of those already there. Only through God's supernatural protection could the city survive and be restored. **I was the king's cupbearer.** This was a high and trusted position in the Persian court, for it was the cupbearer's duty to taste the king's wine to see that it was not poisoned. "The cupbearer . . . in later Achaemenid times was to exercise even more influence than the commander-in-chief" (A. T. Olmstead, *The History of the Persian Empire,* p. 217).

B. The Granting of Nehemiah's Request. 2:1-8. Nehemiah's sadness in the king's presence provokes a crucial question, which leads to Nehemiah's request for permission to go to Jerusalem to rebuild the walls. The king grants not only this request, but also his request for letters of introduction to western governors and for materials to build the gates of the city, palace, and castle.

1. In the month Nisan, in the twentieth year of Artaxerxes. Although this was the first month, it was still Artaxerxes' twentieth year (cf. 1:1), because his official year began in the seventh month—Tishri (October). **Wine was before him.** This was probably a private banquet, for the queen was present (v. 6). **2. Why is thy countenance sad? . . . Then I was very sore afraid.** Nehemiah had reason to fear, for being sad in the king's presence was a serious offense in Persia (cf. Est 4:2). Furthermore, he knew that his request might greatly anger the king. **4. So I prayed to the God of heaven.** This brief, silent prayer, backed up by weeks of fasting and petition (1:4-11), brought about one of the most astonishing reversals of royal policy in all history.

5. That thou wouldest send me unto

. . . the city . . . that I may build it. Doubtless Nehemiah knew of the recent decree of Ezr 4:21, with the possibility left open for a further decree concerning Jerusalem. He now asked the king to reverse the first decree. **6. The queen also sitting by him.** This was Damaspia. Remembering Esther's testimony, she probably influenced Artaxerxes to favor the request of this Jew. **I set him a time.** Possibly a short time, later extended; for he remained in Jerusalem twelve years (5:14), and then returned to the king for several years (13:6).

7,8. The letters to the western governors and to Asaph, which the king granted to Nehemiah, probably included his appointment as governor of Judah (5:14). The issuing of these letters, with authority to rebuild Jerusalem and its walls, is almost certainly the decree to "restore and build Jerusalem" which was to begin the seventy weeks of prophetic years of Dan 9:24-27. **The king's forest.** The Hebrew word for **forest** is literally *paradise,* meaning a "park or orchard" (Song 4:13; Eccl 2:5). **The palace which appertained to the house.** This was the castle that protected the Temple and overlooked the northwest corner of its courts. Hananiah was the governor of this castle (Neh 7:2). Hyrcanus I (134–104 B.C.) built an acropolis here (Jos *Antiq*. 15.11.4), and still later Herod rebuilt it and named it *Antonia.* **The house that I shall enter into.** This was to be the governor's palace.

C. Nehemiah's Survey of the Walls, and His Report. 2:9-20. After traveling to Jerusalem with an armed escort, Nehemiah makes a secret night inspection of the broken walls. He challenges the Jews to rebuild the walls, and answers the insults of enemies.

9. Now the king had sent captains . . . with me. Nehemiah's official position called for a military escort (see notes on Ezr 8:22). These soldiers remained in Jerusalem for his protection (Neh 4:23).

10. Sanballat the Horonite. He was probably from Upper or Nether Beth-horon, about eight miles northwest of Jerusalem. An Elephantine papyrus mentions his sons as being governors of Samaria in 408 B.C. **Tobiah the servant, the Ammonite.** He may have been an ex-slave in Ammon, or possibly a servant of the Persian king (see note on Ezr 4:7). **It grieved them exceedingly.** Nehemiah resorts to irony to describe their attitude.

12. I arose in the night . . . neither told I any man. It was wise, with enemies on every hand, to keep his plans secret until he could ascertain the true magnitude of the task. To avoid exciting attention, his companions walked, while he rode a horse or mule. **13-15.** Beginning at the valley gate in the southwest corner of the city wall, he moved eastward and then up the Kidron Valley **(by the brook).** Here his path was broken by collapsed walls, and he was forced to dismount. Circling the city, he entered again by the same gate. **16. The rest that did the work.** Probably those who had worked on the recently destroyed walls of Jerusalem.

17. Ye see the distress that we are in. Nehemiah refrained from assigning blame for the situation, and included himself in the general plight. **Come, and let us build . . . that we be no more a reproach.** Rebuilt walls would end forever the exposed condition of their city, which constantly invited attacks and reproaches from their enemies. **18. Then I told them of . . . the king's words that he had spoken unto me.** What a climax this must have been to his speech! None in Israel could deny the direct providence of God in reversing Artaxerxes' decree of Ezra 4:23. The effect was immediate and wholehearted: **So they strengthened their hands for this good work.** This was August 1, 444 B.C., for the wall was finished fifty-two days later, on September 21 (Neh 6:15).

19. Geshem the Arabian. (Cf. 6:1,2, 6). Probably the governor of Dedan (Olmstead, *op. cit.,* pp. 295, 316), or the chief of some Arab tribe living south of Jerusalem (cf. 4:7). **They laughed us to scorn . . . will ye rebel against the king?** Cf. 4:1. They sarcastically challenged the Jews to build a wall powerful enough to resist the Persian army, against which they were obviously rebelling! (cf. 6:6) **20. The God of heaven, he will prosper us . . . but ye have no portion . . . in Jerusalem.** For its impressive gravity, Nehemiah's reply is comparable to that of Zerubbabel (Ezr 4:3). Only by such uncompromising vigilance could the theocracy be perpetuated.

II. The Building of the Wall. 3:1–6:19.

A. The Workmen and Their Tasks. 3:1-32. Beginning at the northeast corner of the city, and moving in a counterclockwise direction, Nehemiah lists in this chapter eight different gates and their attached sections of wall, together with the men who repaired them. In order, these were: the **sheep gate** (northeast corner); the **fish gate** (north); the **old gate** (northwest corner); the **valley gate** (southwest corner); the **dung gate** (south); the **fountain gate** (southeast corner, near the Pool of Siloam); the **water gate** (east, near Ophel); and the **horse gate** (east, near the Temple).

1. Then Eliashib the high priest rose up (cf. Ezr 10:6; Neh 12:10). In later years this old high priest (Jeshua's grandson, and therefore probably in his eighties now) caused much trouble for Nehemiah (13:4). Where was Ezra at this time? Possibly he had made a trip back to Babylon but returned in time for the revival of the seventh month (8:1-18) and the dedication of the wall (12:36c). **They sanctified it, and set up the doors of it.** Perhaps they dedicated this gate first, in order to sanctify the entire enterprise. On the other hand, 6:1 states that the doors were not set up until later.

5. Their nobles put not their necks to the work of their Lord. It is better to translate *lord,* referring to Nehemiah. Tekoa was the home town of the prophet Amos.

26. The Nethinims dwelt in Ophel. Ophel is now known to be the hill immediately to the south of that on which the Temple was built. It was also known as Zion, and was the site of the Jebusite stronghold that David captured and made his capital (II Sam 5:6-10).

B. The Opposition of Enemies. 4:1-23. When Sanballat and his allies find that ridicule is not enough to stop the work, they actively conspire against Nehemiah's workmen. Many of the Jews are discouraged, and others fear for their homes and families. But Nehemiah sets up a continual guard so that the work may go forward without delay.

2. Will they fortify themselves? will they sacrifice? In other words, "With their utterly inadequate materials and manpower, do they actually expect to carry through this project? And what is the use of offering sacrifices? God can't help them anyway!" (cf. Isa 36:7,15). **Revive the stones . . . which are burned?** Limestone is softened by fire and loses its durability (Keil, *The Books of Ezra, Nehemiah and Esther, in loc.).* **5. Cover not their iniquity.** Let them not go unpunished (cf. Ps 85:2,3). **Before the builders.** These enemies were blaspheming God in the hearing of the builders, to discourage them (cf. Neh 6:5; II Kgs 18:26,27).

7. The Arabians, and the Ammonites, and the Ashdodites. The Arabs were led by Geshem and the Ammonites by Tobiah (2:19). The Ashdodites, who belonged to the Philistine race, were probably easily aroused by Sanballat to fight their old enemies, the Jews. **8. Conspired all of them together to come and to fight against Jerusalem.** It was now obvious that it would take more than ridicule (v. 2) and foxes (v. 3) to stop the work! Therefore they planned to attack, as in Ezr 4:23, "by force and power." But the attack had to be secret **(conspired)** because of Artaxerxes' favorable decree. **9. We made our prayer . . . and set a watch.** Under the circumstances, prayer and watchfulness were an excellent combination, blending faith and responsibility.

10,11. We are not able. The combination of discouragement from overwork and fear of invasion plots was almost too much for God's people. **12. The ASV is better here: They said unto us ten times from all places, Ye must return unto us.** Jews in outlying towns (3:2,5,7) wanted their workmen to quit the wall-building project and help defend their families against the threats of their enemies.

13,14. Be not ye afraid of them. Apparently Nehemiah brought these Jews and their families into the city. He placed them in open spaces behind the wall, and supplied them with weapons so that they could protect their families as well as the city. **15. Our enemies heard that it was known.** The enemies must have abandoned their plan to attack when they saw the alerted Jewish guards on the wall. The crisis now past, work on the wall could continue.

16. The half of my servants wrought in the work. These were probably official servants that pertained to Nehemiah as governor (4:23; 5:10,16). **Habergeons.** Leather coats covered with thin plates of metal. The rulers were **behind all the house of Judah.** In case of attack, each ruler was prepared to lead his people against the enemy. **17,18.** The meaning seems to be that each of the burden-bearers carried a weapon in one hand, while each builder used both hands but kept a sword girded by his side. **He that sounded the trumpet.** To sound the alarm in case of danger (cf. v. 20). **21. Half of them held the spears.** Half of those mentioned in 4:16.

22. Let every one . . . lodge within Jerusalem. Apparently not all workers had been remaining in the city at night. Walking back to their villages not only took valuable time, but left the city exposed to night attacks. **23. None of us put off our clothes.** Nehemiah's own servants and his Persian bodyguard set the example of vigilance. The last phrase is obscure in the Hebrew. Keil translates: **each laid his weapon at the right;** that is, when he slept, his weapon was ready at hand.

C. Reforms of Nehemiah as Governor. 5:1-19. This parenthetical chapter describes how Nehemiah succeeded in stopping the practice of usury, which resulted in extreme poverty and even bondage for many Jews. Throughout his first twelve years as governor, he was an example of unselfishness and generosity toward his fellow Jews.

1. Then there arose a great cry of the people (ASV). It is possible that this occurred during the fifty-two days of wall building, because of the interruption of normal trade; but the calling of a great assembly (v. 7) and the wording of verse 14 suggest a later period, in spite of the position of the chapter. **2-5. There were that said.** This phrase divides the complainers into three classes: (1) large families without property; (2) families with property, which were in the process of mortgaging it; and (3) those who were borrowing money to pay tribute by pledging their crops, and being unable to repay, were forced to sell their children into slavery. For the laws on loans, pledges, and Hebrew debt slaves (who had to be released after six years, or on the year of jubilee), see Ex 21:2-11; Lev 25:10-17,39-55; Deut 15:7-18.

7. Ye exact usury, every one of his brother. "The lending of money, etc., at interest is not regarded in the Bible as wrong in itself (Deut 23:19,20; Matt 25:27), but it was forbidden as between one Israelite and another (Ex 22:25), since the money was borrowed for the relief of distress and not for the development of trade" (J. Stafford Wright, *New Bible Commentary*). **8. Will ye even sell your brethren?** Nehemiah and others who honored the Law had redeemed their Jewish brethren who had been sold to heathen masters. But these usurers had sold their brethren to the heathen in defiance of the Law! (Lev 25:42) **9. Because of the reproach of the heathen.** The constant scrutiny and hatred of enemy nations constitute a powerful motive for blameless and consistent living.

11. Nehemiah appealed to the wealthy Jews to restore immediately the property they held in pledge (v. 5 c) and also to cease exacting from their Jewish debtors **the hundredth part of the money** (probably 1 per cent a month, or 12 per cent a year, like the Roman "centesima"). Thus their "brethren" would find it possible to start paying off on the principal.

12,13. Took an oath of them. Like Ezra before him (Ezr 10:5), Nehemiah insisted upon confirming verbal promises by an oath administered by priests. This time it is emphasized by a graphic symbolic act of warning against transgressors (cf. Acts 18:6), and confirmed by the "Amen" of the entire congregation, most of whom doubtless benefited by this overdue reform.

14. I and my brethren have not eaten the bread of the governor. Just before the close of his first administration as governor of Judea (cf. 13:6), Nehemiah recalled that for twelve years (444–432 B.C.), because of the prevailing poverty (v. 18), neither he nor his household demanded their rightful salaries from the people. Though wealthy, the governor had sacrificed much for Israel. **15. But the former governors . . . were chargeable unto the people.** These were probably Persians who didn't fear God (cf. 15 c). We may be sure he was not including Zerubbabel in this indictment of former governors! **Forty shekels of silver.** "This (like the interest of vs. 11) is probably to be reckoned for the month. The former governors had received their table and 480 shekels a year as salary. The 480 shekels would be only $360 in amount of silver; but this would represent in value a large official salary in that day" (Howard Crosby, *Lange's Commentary on the Holy Scriptures, in loc.).*

16. Neither bought we any land. Nehemiah did his share of work on the wall, and gained no mortgages of land through loaning money and grain (v. 10). **17.** Nehemiah regularly entertained 150 table guests, besides those Jews who came from surrounding nations and as yet had no place to live in the city. All this was at his own expense. Queen Jezebel entertained 400 prophets of Asherah "at her table," i.e., provided for their support (I Kgs 18:19). **18. One ox and six choice sheep.** Contrast I Kgs 4:22,23, where it is recorded that Solomon served thirty oxen and one hundred sheep daily. Times had definitely changed! **19. Think upon me, my God, for good.** Cf. 13:14,22,31.

D. The Wall Finished Despite Intrigues. 6:1–7:4. Failing to trap Nehemiah into coming up to Ono for a conference, Sanballat sends an open letter to Jerusalem accusing Nehemiah of claiming kingship. He also tries to frighten Nehemiah into fleeing into the Temple. But in spite of false prophets and false brethren, the wall is finally finished, to the dismay of the enemy; and special guards are set over the city.

2. One of the villages in the plain of Ono. Trying to appear impartial by leaving the choice of village to Nehemiah, Sanballat and Geshem tried to lure the governor twenty miles northward to certain death or kidnapping. **3,4. I am doing a great work.** Nehemiah saw his task in its true light. His presence in Jerusalem was desperately needed for the completion of the wall, to say nothing of the futility and obvious danger of a trip to Ono, which lay seven miles east of Joppa.

5. An open letter. To discourage the workmen, this letter of accusation against Nehemiah was made public. Possibly it was written on papyrus and was posted or read aloud in a public gathering place in Jerusalem. **6,7.** Sanballat, who was supported by Gashmu (the same as Geshem the Arabian, 2:19), accused Nehemiah of claiming kingship and hiring prophets to support his claims. Perhaps prophets like Malachi were at this very time preaching about Messiah the King, and their messages were purposely twisted by Sanballat to bring Judah into trouble with the Persians. The purpose of the letter was to force Nehemiah to come for an interview to Ono to clear himself of suspicion.

10. As though in fear of Sanballat, the false prophet Shemaiah invited Nehemiah to his home to reveal a plot against the governor's life. He wanted Nehemiah to know that God had revealed Sanballat's plot to him and that the fateful hour would strike that very night. The only real hope, he said, was to flee into the Temple for refuge. **11-13.** But this exposed Shemaiah's treachery, for Nehemiah knew that God could not have led him to break the Mosaic injunction against laymen entering the Temple (Num 1:51; 18:7). Such a cowardly act and ceremonial crime would, at the very least, have permanently destroyed his testimony in Israel. Once again, Satan had overstepped himself.

14. The prophetess Noadiah, and the rest of the prophets. So soon after the Captivity was the land again cursed with false prophets! (See Ezk 13 for God's denunciation of false prophets and prophetesses during the Captivity period.) The plot of 6:10-13 was doubtless only one of many that added to the burdens of an already burdened leader. As in Jesus' day, false religious leaders were the most determined and unscrupulous enemies of God's true servants.

15,16. In fifty and two days. The work was finished between August 1, and September 21, 444 B.C. This may seem like an extremely short time; but there were thousands of zealous workmen, the wall had not been completely destroyed (it was mainly a task of repairing breaches; see 6:1), and the gate of Ephraim, which is not mentioned in chapter 3, may not even have been damaged. Nevertheless, it was indeed a tremendous accomplishment, in which the Jews' enemies perceived the hand of God.

17-19. In concluding his account of plots and intrigues, Nehemiah tells of Tobiah's alliance with Jewish nobles through his marriage with a daughter of **Shechaniah the son of Arah** (Ezr 2:5), and the marriage of his son **Johanan with the daughter of Meshullam** (Neh 3:4,30). Later, even the high priest entered into an alliance with him (13:4-8). Keil suggests that Tobiah and his son (having genuine Jewish names) were probably descendants of the northern tribes while being related also to naturalized Ammonites (2:10). **And Tobiah sent letters to put me in fear.** Apparently, some Jewish nobles demonstrated their alliance with Tobiah by delivering to Nehemiah some of his threatening letters, like that of verse 6.

7:1,2. When the wall was finished, Nehemiah set up doors in the various gates (cf. 6:1). He appointed Levitical singers and porters—whose work was usually that of caring for the Temple and the gates of its courts (26:12-19)—to help stand guard at the city gates ("while they stand by, let them shut the doors, and bar them"—v. 3). Then he put his brother Hanani (1:2) and Hananiah, the governor of the castle (on the north side of the Temple, 2:8) in charge of the city.

3. Every one in his watch, and every one to be over against his house. During the night the inhabitants of Jerusalem were to keep watch over the city, presumably one group occupying posts at various parts of the wall and the other standing by their own homes to watch certain sections of the city. **4. Now the city was large and great: but the people were few therein.** Although vast crowds assembled in Jerusalem on special occasions (8:1; Ezr 10:9), for several generations Jews had avoided making their homes in a city without walls. See notes on 11:1,2.

III. Civil and Religious Reforms in Jerusalem. 7:5–10:39.

A. List of Jews Who Returned with Zerubbabel. 7:5-73. Now that the wall is completed, Nehemiah lays immediate plans for populating the city with pure Jews. The register of those who returned with Zerubbabel becomes his basis for determining purity of genealogy. Except for verses 70-72, the register is identical with that of Ezr 2:1-70.

70. Five hundred and thirty priests' garments. Literally, *thirty priests' garments, and five hundred.* Because of the analogy of verses 71 and 72, and because of the unusual word order, the phrase, "pounds of silver," should probably be added to the end of this verse. If this supposition is correct, then Zerubbabel ("the Tirshatha"), some of the chiefs of the fathers, and the rest of the people gave a total of 41,000 drams (darics) of gold, 4,700 pounds of silver, 97 priests' garments, and 50 basins. This agrees with the round numbers of Ezr 2:69, except for the drams of gold, which are exactly 20,000 less than in Ezra.

B. The Reading and Observance of God's Law. 8:1-18. On the first day of the seventh month, Ezra reads the Law to the people. The people weep because of sin, but are reminded by their leaders of the joyous character of this day. The following day the leaders find in the Law that all Jews should observe the Feast of Tabernacles; so that feast is universally celebrated and with great solemnity.

1. The chapter should begin with the last sentence of 7:73: "And when the seventh month came, the children of Israel were in their cities." Ezra 3:1 begins the same way, after the list of those who returned from Babylon; but the occasion, of course, is quite different. **The street that was before the water gate.** The **street** (ASV, *broad place)* was near the southeast corner of the Temple near Gihon Spring in the Kedron Valley. **They spake unto Ezra the scribe.** Possibly Ezra had been in Babylon during the period of wall construction. But he was the appropriate person to read the Law of God on this occasion, since Nehemiah was a layman.

2. The first day of the seventh month. This was the Feast of Trumpets, which in 444 B.C. fell on September 27. Only a week before, the wall had been completed (6:15). The Feast of Trumpets was the most sacred of the new moons, and commenced the final month of religious festivals (Lev 23:23-25; Num 29:1-6). **3. From the morning until midday.** This would have been about six hours, with Ezra's reading of the Law alternating with instructive lectures on the Law by the Levites (vv. 7,8).

4. Ezra the scribe stood upon a pulpit of wood. This is the first mention of a pulpit in the Bible. Behind him stood six (priests?) on his right hand and seven on his left (compare v. 7, where thirteen Levites are said to have participated). **8. So they read . . . distinctly.** The word **distinctly** (Heb., *m*[e]*pōrōsh)* suggests not only an exposition of the Law, but also, possibly, a translation of it into Aramaic (cf. Ezr 4:18).

9. This day is holy unto the LORD your God; mourn not, nor weep. The clear exposition of God's Word (probably portions of Deuteronomy) powerfuly convicted the people of sin and brought forth tears of repentance. But the only day of the year which God had specifically set aside for weeping and sorrow was the Day of Atonement (tenth day of the seventh month). Therefore, their true strength was to be found in **the joy of the LORD** (v. 10). **12. To make great mirth.** Notice the sudden change in emotions from 8:9 to 8:12! Also, cf. Est 9:19.

13-18. The detailed study of the Law of God caused many of the leaders to come to Ezra the next day for further instruction, especially concerning the proper observance of the Feast of Tabernacles (fifteenth to twenty-second of the seventh month). The Jews had observed this great feast for centuries (I Kgs 8:65; II Chr 7:9; Ezr 3:4); but now they realized, from a more careful study of Lev 23:42, that "*all* that are Israelites born shall dwell in booths." Presumably in past centuries this point had been neglected; so now, for the first time since the days of Joshua the son of Nun, **all the congregation . . . sat under the booths** (v. 17). Probably the inhabitants of the city built their booths by their own homes, the priests and Levites built in the temple courts, and non-resident laymen in the open places (v. 16).

C. A Public Confession and Covenant. 9:1–10:39. Soon after the Feast of Tabernacles, the people gathered to hear the Word of God again, and to confess their sins to God in a solemn public ceremony conducted by certain Levites. Afterwards, all classes of Israelites entered into a covenant to keep the Law of God, especially with regard to separation from the heathen and the support of the Temple.

1. Just one month after the completion of the wall (6:15) and two days after the Feast of Tabernacles (8:18), the people set aside their mood of joy and gladness in order to acknowledge before God in a public manner the depths of their sins and their sorrow for them (cf. Joel 2:15-17). **Sackclothes** were penitential garments made of hair. **Earth upon them.** They put earth on their heads as a sign of deep mourning (I Sam 4:12). **3. One fourth part of the day.** For three hours God's Word was read publicly, following which the people joined in a great confession of sin led by the Levites (vv. 5-37). **5. Stand up and bless the LORD your God.** The Levites now exhorted the people to join them in the confession of sin which follows.

36. Behold, we are servants this day. This sad confession, like that of Ezr 9:9, affords clear proof that the leaders of post-Exilic Judaism did not regard their return from Babylon as final fulfillment of such prophecies of Israel's restoration to the land as Isa 11:11-16; 14:1,2. **38. And because of all this we make a sure covenant.** This written covenant, to which each leader was asked to affix his personal seal, is set forth in detail in 10:29-39. It was simply a renewed effort to keep their part of the Sinai covenant.

10:1-8. Nehemiah the governor and twenty-two priests are listed first. See notes on 12:1-9. **9-13.** Of the Levites, Jeshua, Binnui, Kadmiel, and fourteen of their brethren are mentioned. Individual Levites signed in the names of their families, for two of these names appear in 7:43. **14-27.** Here forty-four chiefs of the people are listed. Of the thirty-three families that returned from Babylon (Ezr 2), only thirteen are found in this list. Perhaps further subdivisions of families were made during the intervening years.

30,31. Three points in the oath are here stressed: (a) no intermarriage with heathen (Deut 7:3); (b) no commerce on the Sabbath or other holy days (Amos 8:5); (c) faithful observance of the seventh year, the year of release (Ex 23:10, 11; Deut 15:1,2).

32. The rest of the chapter deals with support of the Temple. **The third part of a shekel.** This was a revival of the Mosaic precept that every man over twenty years old had to pay one half shekel for the support of the Tabernacle (Ex 30:13; cf. Mt 17:24). Perhaps the poverty of the people at this time called for a slightly lowered tax rate. This was in addition to the contributions guaranteed by Artaxerxes (Ezr 7:20-22). **34.** Lots were cast to determine the correct order in which the various families would contribute temple supplies. **The wood offering** was for the continual altar fire (Lev 6:12; cf. Neh 13:31). **At times appointed year by year.** The order was settled several years in advance. **38,39. And the priest . . . shall be with the Levites, when the Levites take tithes.** The Levites, who received tithes, as well as other Jews, were responsible for the support of the priests (Num 18:26-29) and the porters and singers (from among the Levites) who ministered in the Temple. Note how this gracious system of mutual support soon disintegrated and had to be restored by Nehemiah (13:10-14).

IV. Lists of Inhabitants. 11:1–12:26.

Nehemiah's account of how he sought to populate Jerusalem with pure Jews in accordance with the list of those who returned from Babylon (7:4 ff.) having been interrupted by the narrative of the special services of the seventh month (chs. 8–10), is now resumed (11:1,2). Then follows a list of those who dwelt in Jerusalem (11:3-24); a list of the other towns where Jews lived (11:25-36); a list of priests and Levites who returned with Zerubbabel (12:1-9); and a list of high priests, priests and Levites in later years (12:10-26).

1,2. As was stated in 7:4, Jerusalem had few permanent inhabitants, probably because of the dangers of living in an unwalled city (especially after the disaster mentioned in Neh 1:3). Here we are told that those who did live in Jerusalem were mostly princes. Doubtless Nehemiah had taken occasion, during the revival of the seventh month, to encourage others to move into the capital city. The lot was accepted as Jehovah's will in this matter, and those heads of families who willingly acquiesced were blessed by the people. Jerusalem is called **the holy city** because the Temple was there (Isa 48:2).

3-24. The total number of men living in Jerusalem, exclusive of the Nethinim, was 3,044. If this was one-tenth of the total number of men living in Judea (v. 1), the population had increased considerably during the previous century; for the 50,000 who returned from Babylon with Zerubbabel (Ezr 2:64-67) apparently included women and children.

25-36. Heads of houses are not named for the country districts, but only for the towns in the former territories of Judah (vv. 25-30) and Benjamin (vv. 31-35). Strangely, the towns of Jericho, Gibeon, and Mizpah, though listed in Nehemiah 3, are omitted here.

12:1-9. We have here the names of twenty-two priests and eight Levites who returned with Zerubbabel. Since fifteen of these priests are listed among those who sealed the covenant in Nehemiah's day, we must conclude that they sealed the covenant in the name of their families (10:3-9). In Ezra 2:36-39, only four priestly families are named as having returned with Zerubbabel.

10,11. A genealogy of post-Exilic high priests is given here to provide a comparative chronology. Thus, 12:1-9 lists priests and Levites in the days of Jeshua, while 12:12-26 lists priests and Levites in the days of his high priestly successors. **Jonathan** is the same person as the Johanan of verses 22,23. For comments on **Jaddua,** see verse 22. **12-21.** The sons of priests listed in verses 1-7, who lived in the days of Joshua's successor, Joiakim. **Of Iddo, Zechariah.** This is the famous prophet (Ezr 5:1).

22. In the days of Eliashib, Joiada, and Johanan, and Jaddua . . . to the reign of Darius the Persian. It has frequently been assumed that this Jaddua was the high priest who lived at the time of Alexander the Great (Jos *Antiq*. 11.8.4), and that Darius the Persian was Darius III (335–331 B.C.). But even if Josephus is right that a Jaddua was high priest in Alexander's time (and he is far from trustworthy in his chronology of this period), we are still left with the distinct possibilities that there were two high priests named Jaddua, or that the Jaddua of Neh 12:11,22 lived to be about 100 (the high priest Jehoiada died at the age of 130; II Chr 24:15).

It is quite probable that Nehemiah knew Jaddua as a young man, if not as high priest. There are two lines of evidence to support this. First, the high priest Eliashib must have been over ninety years old when he entered into an alliance with Tobiah (Neh 13:4-9) after Nehemiah's departure for Babylon in 432 B.C., for his grandfather, Jeshua, was high priest in 536 B.C. (Ezr 3:2). Therefore, in 432 B.C. Joiada could have been nearly seventy, Johanan (Jonathan) over forty, and Jaddua twenty. Secondly, Nehemiah expelled from Jerusalem one of Joiada's sons for marrying a foreigner (Neh 13:28), thus demonstrating that Johanan, who was Joiada's eldest son, could have been married long enough to have a twenty-year-old son, Jaddua.

Eliashib lived to such a great age that the four contemporary generations in his high-priestly house are mentioned together in verse 22. This is supported by the fact that "in each of the other lists of the same chapter, the times of only one high priest are mentioned, and at the close of the list, vs. 26, it is expressly stated that the (previously enrolled) Levites were chiefs in the days of Joiakim, Ezra, and Nehemiah" (Keil, p. 147). Furthermore, it is important to observe that the latest date mentioned in the book is the high priesthood of Johanan (v. 23). The fact that Johanan's father Joiada did not retain his high priesthood down into the fourth century B.C. has been proved by the Elephantine papyri, which mention Johanan as being the high priest in 408 B.C. Therefore Nehemiah, who could have lived (even if not as governor) until about 400 B.C., and who might even have seen Jaddua become high priest sometime after 408 B.C., could well have written everything in this chapter and in the book. In the light of these considerations, we may conclude that **Darius the Persian** was almost certainly not Darius III (335–331 B.C.), but rather Darius II (423–404 B.C.). The verse tells us that the Levites were registered during the lifetime of Eliashib; whereas the priests were registered after Eliashib's death, in the days of Darius the Persian (423–404 B.C. See R. D. Wilson, ISBE, II, 1084).

26. In the days of Nehemiah the governor. Cf. 12:47. It has been claimed that this proves that Nehemiah must have died before the book was finished. "But in reply we may note that the phrase is in each instance used in conjunction with the days of someone else, Jehoiakim (v. 26), Zerubbabel (v. 47). Hence, it would seem natural for Nehemiah to employ a similar phrase with reference to his own time" (E. J. Young, *Intro. to the O.T.*, p. 378. See also above, *Date and Authorship*).

V. Dedication of Walls and Organization of Temple Services. 12:27-47.

For the dedication of the city wall, Levites, especially the singers, are brought from surrounding villages. Two great processions move from the southwest corner of the wall, and encircle the city, one led by Ezra and the other followed by Nehemiah. Meeting at the Temple, they offer sacrifices and rejoice greatly. The Temple services are then set in order, and its workers are faithfully supported.

27. The story now resumes from 11:2, although no exact date is given for the events about to be recorded. The various time indications might even lead one to date the dedication service seventeen or more years after the completion of the walls! (cf. 13:4 with 13:1; and 13:10,11 with 12:28-30) **They sought the Levites out of all their places.** According to 11:18, only 284 Levites actually lived in Jerusalem at this time. **28,29.** Members of the three Levitical companies of singers (11:17; 12:25 a) receive special mention here because of the importance of music for this great occasion (v. 27 b). **The villages of Netophathi.** About fifteen miles southwest of Jerusalem (I Chr 9:16). **30. The priests and the Levites purified themselves.** By the offering of blood sacrifices (II Chr 29).

31-37. Speaking in the first person again, Nehemiah tells of the **two great companies** that he gathered at the southwest corner of the city wall (presumably at the Valley Gate) for the purpose of encircling the city and giving public thanks to God on the day of dedication. The first company was led by Ezra and moved eastward and then northward. For both groups the order of procession seems to have consisted first of Levitical singers "that gave thanks" (v. 31), followed by princes (vv. 32,33), then the priests with trumpets (v. 35; cf. 41), and finallv Levites with stringed instruments (v. **36**).

38-43. The second company moved northward and then eastward to the temple area, followed by Nehemiah. The various gates follow the same order given in chapter 3, except for **the gate of Ephraim** and **the prison gate,** which are not mentioned in that chapter (possibly because they were not originally destroyed and did not have to be rebuilt). However, in 3:25 mention is made of "the court of the prison," probably at the southeast corner of the temple area. The two companies seem to have met at the broad place before the water gate (v. 37; cf. 8:1), and from there they entered the Temple to offer their sacrifices (v. 43). Regarding the tremendous joy of this occasion, cf. II Chr 20:27; Ezr 3:13; 6:22.

44-47. At that time (ASV, *on that day*). This phrase (cf. 13:1) refers not only to the dedication day, but possibly also to the entire subsequent administration of Nehemiah, which was characterized by reform movements (Keil, *op. cit.*, p. 152). This might help to explain the phrase, "before this," in 13:4. **The treasures.** The various offerings listed afterward. **The tithes.** One tenth of the nation's crops went to the support of the Levites. **The Levites that waited.** A technical verb in Hebrew meaning "ministered" (Deut 10:8). **The commandment of David and of Solomon** (v. 45). Cf. II Chr 8:14. **The Levites sanctified them unto the children of Aaron.** The people paid tithes to the Levites, who in turn paid tithes of these tithes to the priests (Neh 10:38; cf. Num 18:25-32).

VI. Nehemiah's Final Reforms. 13:1-30.

The climax of dedication day reforms came with the separation of Israelites from the mixed multitude. During Nehemiah's long absence from Judah, many abuses had crept into the life of the nation, such as Eliashib's alliance with Tobiah, failure of the people to support the Levites, breaking of the Sabbath, and intermarrying with the heathen. But with God's help, Nehemiah valiantly cleansed the nation of these abuses, and established proper religious observances once again.

1-3. On that day. Presumably the same day as in 12:44, and thus the day of dedication. **The Ammonite and the Moabite.** Separation from heathen nations was the first point emphasized in the covenant the people had made earlier (10:30). Descendants of mixed marriages with these two nations were excluded from the congregation of Israel to the tenth generation. It was needful that the Jews be reminded of this law, for Tobiah was an Ammonite (2:19), and he was already forging strong alliances with prominent Jewish families through marriage (6:18; cf. 13:4-9). **Hired Balaam against them.** It was a Moabite king who had hired Balaam to curse Israel (Num 22:2-6). **The mixed multitude** (v. 3). Cf. Ex 12:38. Descendants of mixed marriages with Egyptians and Edomites were permitted full membership in Israel after the third generation (Deut 23:7,8).

4-9. And before this. See notes on 12:27; 12:44. **Eliashib the priest . . . was allied unto Tobiah.** The word **allied** can mean *nigh of kin* (Ruth 2:20), and may refer to a family tie with Tobiah through Meshullam, a priest (Neh 6:18; cf. 3:30). During Nehemiah's absence, Eliashib had turned over to Tobiah **a great chamber** in the forecourt of the Temple (vv. 5,7-9), where the tithes and offerings of the nation were to be stored (12:44). There Tobiah had a furnished room (v. 8), or even a suite of rooms (note the plural in v. 9), whenever he visited Jerusalem. **In all this time was not I at Jerusalem** (v. 6). In the year 432, B.C., after governing Judah twelve years (5:14; cf. 2:6), Nehemiah had returned to King Artaxerxes. **King of Babylon.** Since most of the Jews were still in Babylon, and the king himself was probably there at this time, Nehemiah uses the more restricted title (see note on Ezr 6:22). **After certain days.** Nehemiah must have been away for several years, for the abuses he found on his return had had time to spread far and wide in Judah (Neh 13:10,15,23). Since Artaxerxes died in 423 B.C., Nehemiah may have returned to Jerusalem about 425 B.C. It is quite possible that Malachi was prophesying during this time (compare 13:12 with Mal 3:8-10).

10-14. Fled every one to his field. In spite of the oath of 10:35-39 (cf. 12:47), the Levites (and presumably many priests as well) were deprived of their rightful support (I Cor 9:8-14). For that reason they had to forsake their temple duties in order to earn their living on farms (Neh 12:29). **Then contended I with the rulers** (v. 11). It was the duty of the heads of the community to see that tithes, etc., were regularly brought to the Temple (cf. 17,25). **I gathered them together, and set them in their place.** That is, the Levites were gathered from their villages and were set once again to the performance of their duties.

15-18. While touring the outlying districts of Judah, Nehemiah found men desecrating the Sabbath by busily preparing for sales during the following week in Jerusalem (Amos 8:5). He waited until they came to Jerusalem to sell their products, and then **testified against them.** Even worse, merchants of Tyre sold dried fish and other products to Jews in the province and in Jerusalem on the Sabbath, leading the Jews to violate the oath they had taken (Neh 10:31 a). **Did not your fathers thus?** (v. 18) Nehemiah doubtless had in mind the clear warning of Jer 17:21-27, which went unheeded, to the subsequent sorrow of the whole nation.

19-22. At sunset, just before the Sabbath, Nehemiah commanded the main gates to be shut. Presumably during the day of the Sabbath people were permitted to enter and leave the city, but Nehemiah's own guardsmen (4:23) watched the gates to keep merchants out. **I will lay hands on you** (v. 21). When they defied this measure by setting up bazaars just outside the gates, he put an end to this desecration of the Sabbath by threats of violence (cf. v. 25). After the crisis had passed, it seems that he replaced the special guard with Levites (v. 22), who kept the gates and sanctified the Sabbath by consecrating it as a holy day above ordinary days.

23-27. Journeying to the very frontiers of the province of Judah, Nehemiah discovered Jews who long since had married women of surrounding nations, especially those of **Ashdod** (a city in Philistia), **Ammon,** and **Moab.** This was in spite of the reforms which had been initiated by Ezra about thirty years before, and in spite of the more recent decisions of 10:30 and 13:1-3. Children of these unions could not even speak pure Hebrew. Nehemiah, reacting to this challenge with characteristic zeal, **contended with them,** and **smote certain of them** (Deut 25:2), and **plucked off their hair** (Isa 50:6), and **made them swear by God** that they would not intermarry with foreigners. In the light of Ezr 10:19, he probably insisted also that these unholy alliances should be dissolved. Though seemingly harsh, such measures were absolutely necessary, as subsequent history has proved. The sad case of **Solomon** (cf. Neh 12:45) is effectively brought into use at this point. Although he was unique among kings (II Chr 1:12; I Kgs 3:12) and beloved of God (II Sam 12:24), nevertheless foreign wives proved to be his downfall (I Kgs 11:1-8).

28,29. One of the sons of Joiada . . . was son-in-law to Sanballat. We know from 12:22,23 that Johanan was the eldest son of Joiada and the father of

Jaddua. Johanan appears in the Elephantine papyri as high priest in 408 B.C. Therefore, the one who married a daughter of Sanballat must have been a younger brother of Johanan. This is an important fact, because it shows that Johanan must have been old enough at this time to have sons of his own, of whom the eldest was Jaddua. See note on 12:22. **I chased him from me . . . . because they have defiled the priesthood.** This sin deserved special mention, for it was committed against greater privileges. By marrying the daughter of a foreigner, this son of the high priest Joiada had brazenly defied God's covenant of holiness with the Aaronic priesthood (Lev 21:6-8,14,15), and thus richly deserved banishment from the nation. Jos (*Antiq.* 7,8) tells of a certain Manasseh, brother of the high priest Jaddua, in the days of Alexander the Great, who married a daughter of Sanballat. When the Jewish authorities excluded him from the priesthood, Sanballat established for him a new temple and worship on Mount Gerizim in Samaria. It is true that such a rival temple was later established (cf. Jn 4:20), but Josephus was confused in trying to connect this with the episode recorded in Neh 13:28.

30,31. Nehemiah summarizes his great contributions to the spiritual well-being of his nation. Negatively, foreigners were removed from positions of honor in Israel; and positively, the priests and Levites were reinstated in their proper occupations, and the various offerings for the Temple were resumed. **Remember me, O my God, for good.** Cf. 5:19; 13:14,22. This prayer was wonderfully answered by the Lord, for Nehemiah's memoirs form a permanent part of the Word of God.

BIBLIOGRAPHY

For bibliography see under *Ezra*.

ESTHER

INTRODUCTION

Title. The book is named after its principal character, Esther. This is a Persian name and means *star.* Her Hebrew name was Hadassah, *myrtle* (see 2:7).

Date and Authorship. It is quite certain that the book was written after 465 B.C., for the reign of Xerxes (486–465 B.C.) is spoken of in the past tense (10:2). But the author shows too intimate a knowledge of the events of Xerxes' reign and of the furnishings of the palace in Shushan (which was destroyed by fire about 435 B.C.) to permit a date for the book after the time of Artaxerxes I (464–424 B.C.). Although Josephus thought that Mordecai wrote the book, it seems that 10:2,3 excludes this possibility. Nevertheless, the author must have been a Jew who lived in Persia at the time of the events narrated and who had access to the official chronicles of the kings of Media and Persia (2:23; 9:20; 10:2). Purely Persian words and names appear in the book, and its Hebrew style closely resembles that of Ezra, Nehemiah, and Chronicles.

Historicity and Purpose. In spite of the objections that have been raised against the historicity of the book, it gives a perfectly credible account of events that could have occurred during the reign of Xerxes. The statement regarding the extent of Xerxes' dominion (1:1; 8:9) agrees with statements in Herodotus (*Histories* 3.97,98; 7.9), and it was true of no other Persian king. The great feast of the third year of Xerxes' reign (Est 1:3) harmonizes with the date given by Herodotus (7.8) for the planning of the Persian king's expedition against Greece. The description of his palace (Est 1:6) has been confirmed by archaeological discovery. The taking of a new wife in his seventh year (2:16) fits Herodotus' description of the new interest he manifested in his harem after the disastrous Greek campaign (9.108, 109).

The Feast of Purim, which is mentioned in II Maccabees 15:36 as being observed about 160 B.C., could hardly have been established for no reason at all. The most logical explanation is that it was instituted in commemoration of the events described in this book. The Jews have always accepted the Book of Esther as canonical.

When we turn our attention to the purpose of the book, the question immediately arises as to why all references to prayer, worship, Jerusalem, the Temple, and the name of God are omitted, with the exception of some hints of prayer and providence (Est 4:14; 4:16; 9:31). Some have conjectured that it was too dangerous to worship Jehovah openly in those days and therefore all references to him were carefully excluded from the book. But this tends toward a low view of the inspiration of Scripture. It seems better to conclude that "since these Jews were no longer in the theocratic line, so to speak, the *Name* of the Covenant God is not associated with them. The Book of Esther, then, serves the purpose of showing how Divine Providence overrules all things; even in a distant, far country, God's people are yet in His hands. But since they are in this distant, far country, and not in the land of Promise, His Name is not mentioned" (Edward J. Young, *An Introduction to the Old Testament*, p. 349).

Historical Background. As far back as 722 B.C., Israelites from the northern tribes were transplanted as captives to "the cities of the Medes" among other places (II Kgs 17:6). Furthermore, after the conquest of Babylon by Cyrus in 539 B.C., some of the Jews who had been transported to Babylonia by Nebuchadnezzar probably moved eastward to Shushan and other cities in Medo-Persia, as Mordecai did (Est 2:5,6). But of the millions of Jews who had been dispersed throughout the Near East, only about 50,000 chose to return to the Promised Land with Zerubbabel and Joshua in 536 B.C. (Ezr 2:64-67).

According to Ezra 6:15, the second Temple was completed in 515 B.C., in the sixth year of Darius I. It was just thirty-two years later that Xerxes, the son of Darius I, "made a feast unto all his princes and his servants" (Est 1:3). The events of this book cover a period of ten years, from the great feast of Xerxes (483 B.C.) to the Feast of Purim (473 B.C.). Sixteen years after the first Feast of Purim, Ezra led his expedition back to Jerusalem (Ezr 7:9). Thus, the events of this book fit in between the sixth and seventh chapters of the Book of Ezra.

OUTLINE

I. Vashti divorced. 1:1-22.
II. Esther made queen. 2:1-23.
III. Haman's plot against the Jews. 3:1-15.
IV. Esther's decision. 4:1-17.
V. Esther's first banquet. 5:1-14.
VI. Haman humiliated before Mordecai. 6:1-14.
VII. Esther's second banquet. 7:1-10.
VIII. Mordecai's counterdecree. 8:1-17.
IX. The Jews victorious, and Purim instituted. 9:1–10:3.

COMMENTARY

I. Vashti Divorced. 1:1-22.

On the last day of a seven-day feast in Shushan the palace, King Xerxes called for Queen Vashti to appear before his drunken nobles to show her beauty. Her refusal provoked the king's wrath, and he followed the advice of Memucan, one of the chief princes, that she be divorced by a public decree. This punishment, the men reasoned, would warn all wives throughout the empire to honor their husbands.

1. In the days of Ahasuerus. This can be none other than Xerxes (486–465 B.C.; cf. Ezr 4:6), the son of Darius I, who attempted to conquer Greece in 481 B.C. He completely failed in this objective as a result of crushing defeats at Salamis (480 B.C.) and Plataea (479 B.C.). **This is Ahasuerus which reigned, from India even unto Ethiopia.** In order to avoid possible confusion with the father of Darius the Mede, who had the same name (Dan 9:1), the author points to the vast territory over which this Xerxes ruled (cf. 8:9; 10:1). The **India** referred to was the territory corresponding to the province of Punjab in West Pakistan today, the region west of the Indus River to which Alexander's forces came in their conquests. Herodotus tells us that both India and Ethiopia were subject to Xerxes (3.97,98; 7.9). **Over a hundred and seven and twenty provinces.** This has been confused with the twenty satrapies listed by Herodotus for Darius I (3.89-94) and the one hundred and twenty satraps appointed by Darius the Mede (Dan 6:1). The word **provinces** (Heb. *m^e^dînâ)* refers to the smaller governmental units of the empire, such as the province of Judah (Neh 1:3), whereas Herodotus was referring to the larger units, such as the fifth satrapy, which included all of Phoenicia, Palestine, Syria, and Cyprus. But the Book of Daniel speaks of neither of these territorial units, for it merely states that Darius the Mede "set over the kingdom a hundred and twenty satraps" (Dan 6:1, ASV; cf. John C. Whitcomb, *Darius the Mede,* pp. 31-33).

2. Shushan the palace. Shushan (or *Susa)* was one of the main capitals of the Persian Empire, the others being Ecbatana (Ezr 6:1-2) and Persepolis. To this city Daniel was once carried in a vision (Dan 8:2); and later Nehemiah served there as Artaxerxes' cupbearer (Neh 1:1; 2:1).

3. In the third year of his reign, he made a feast. This feast (literally, *a drinking feast)* took place in the year 483/482 B.C., and it was certainly the one referred to by Herodotus (7.8), in which Xerxes laid plans for the great invasion of Greece. **The power of Persia and Media, the nobles and princes.** In the days of Cyrus, Media was mentioned before Persia (Dan 6:8), but now Persia was far more prominent in the dual monarchy. **Power** represents the military, while **nobles and princes** represent the civil rulers. **4,5.** During the 180 days

Xerxes discussed war plans with his subordinates and overawed them with the opulence and grandeur of his court. After this, a seven-day feast was held (vv. 3 and 5 probably refer to the same feast) for **all the people that were present in Shushan the palace,** including the leaders from various provinces who had come for the 180 days of planning (Keil, *in loco*). **The court of the garden of the king's palace.** The grounds or park surrounding the palace.

6. The meanings of some of these words are obscure, but the ASV gives the general sense. White and blue cotton hangings (the royal colors; cf. 8:15) were fastened to marble pillars by means of silver rings. Also, there were gold and silver couches (cf. 7:8) upon floors made of inlaid stones of various colors. This strikingly beautiful palace burned to the ground toward the end of the reign of Artaxerxes, the son of Xerxes, about 435 B.C. (A. T. Olmstead, *The History of the Persian Empire*, p. 352). **7,8. Vessels of gold . . . diverse one from another.** Great variety in drinking vessels was a Persian luxury. **According to the state of the king.** *According to the bounty of the king* (ASV; cf. I Kgs 10:13). **The drinking was according to the law; none did compel.** Usually the king pledged his guests to drink a certain amount, but now they could drink as much or as little as they desired.

9-12. On the last day of the feast, the inebriated king (Jud 16:25; II Sam 13:28) sent his seven chamberlains (or eunuchs; cf. Est 1:12,15), who constituted his means of communication with the harem, to fetch Vashti. Persian queens usually ate at the king's table, but not necessarily at great banquets. Fearing for her dignity in the midst of such a drunken group (Herodotus, 5.18), she utterly refused to obey the summons.

13,14. Wise men, which knew the times . . . the seven princes. Perhaps seven was a sacred number in Persia (cf. 1:10; 2:9; Ezr 7:14). These wise men may have been astrologers or lawyers. It was from these leading families that Persian kings were to find their wives (Herodotus, 3.84). **16-20.** Memucan, one of the seven princes (v. 14), seized the opportunity to transform a private affair into a public and national crisis, doubtless because of a previous conflict between the queen and the princes. The wives of ordinary citizens would defy their husbands (v. 17), and the wives of the seven princes would even "this day" (v. 18) demand equality through a desire to emulate their queen. **That it be not altered** (v. 19). Cf. 8:8; Dan 6:9. Doubtless they did not want Vashti to return to power and punish them for giving this advice!

21,22. Sent letters into all the king's provinces . . . according to the writing thereof. The Persian Empire boasted an efficient postal system, but communication was complicated by the scores of languages spoken throughout the empire. **That every man should bear rule in his own house, and that it should be published according to the language of every people.** The meaning is somewhat obscure, but presumably "the rule of the husband in the house was to be shown by the fact that only the native tongue of the head of the house was to be used in the family" (Keil; cf. Neh 13:23). The mention of this point in the decree presupposes that the facts concerning Vashti were also mentioned.

II. Esther Made Queen. 2:1-23.

When Xerxes longed for Vashti again, it was proposed that a new queen be chosen for him from among the most beautiful virgins in the land. Esther, a young Jewess who had been reared by her cousin Mordecai, was among those brought to the house of the women. Xerxes loved her more than any other and chose her to be his queen. Soon afterward, Mordecai discovered a plot against the king. Through Esther the matter was reported to Xerxes, and the criminals were executed.

1. After these things . . . he remembered Vashti. Since Esther became queen in December, 479 B.C. (2:16), and more than a year must have elapsed between the decree of 2:3 (cf. 2:12) and her marriage, the king's desire for Vashti must have become known while he was still engaged in the great campaign against Greece (481–479 B.C.). **2-4.** Realizing that the restoration of Vashti would spell doom for them (see note on 1:19), the princes abandoned the precedent of providing a queen from among their own daughters, and suggested that the king choose a new queen from among the most beautiful virgins in the empire. **Hege the king's chamberlain** [eunuch], **keeper of the women.** Cf. 2:8,15. Only eunuchs had access to "the house of the women" (v. 9). **Let the maiden which pleaseth the king be queen** (v. 4). In this way, his desire for Vashti would be lessened. The princes were well aware of the weakness of Xerxes' character (Herodotus, 9.108-113) and took full advantage of it for their own purposes.

5-7. A certain Jew, whose name was Mordecai . . . . brought up Hadassah, that is, Esther, his uncle's daughter. The true hero and heroine of the book are now introduced. Mordecai, of the tribe of Benjamin, was the great-grandson of a man named Kish, who had been carried off to Babylon with King Jeconiah (Jehoiachin) in 597 B.C. Upon the death of his uncle Abihail (2:15), Mordecai took his uncle's orphaned daughter into his own home and brought her up. "Assuming that Hadassah is from *hadhas,* myrtle, and that Esther is *sitar,* the Persian for star (Sanskrit *sta'na;* Akk. *istar),* we have here an early example of the later Jewish practice of giving two names—a Hebrew and a Gentile name, such as, John Mark, Joses Justus, etc." (A. Macdonald, "Esther," *The New Bible Commentary,* p. 382).

8-11. Esther was brought also . . . to the custody of Hegai . . . . and the maiden pleased him (vv. 8,9). Esther's personal feelings in this matter are not recorded, but we may assume that she trusted Jehovah and was therefore blessed by him (somewhat like Joseph and Daniel). Unlike Joseph and Daniel, however, she did not identify her nationality, and may therefore have partaken of ceremonially unclean food. Why Mordecai charged her to keep her nationality secret (v. 20) is not easy to determine. Perhaps he feared for her safety (v. 11). Or possibly he was granted by the Lord a special premonition of coming trouble for Israel and the part Esther might play in delivering her people (4:14).

12-15. After an entire year of preparation, the turn of each maiden came to go to the king. For this visit she could have any ornaments, jewelry, or apparel that she wanted. Esther revealed a unique spirit in that she was not concerned to please the king by the "outward adorning of plaiting the hair, and of wearing of gold, or of putting on of apparel," but by "the ornament of a meek and quiet spirit, which is in the sight of God of great price" (I Pet 3:3,4). It is not surprising, therefore, that Esther **obtained favour in the sight of all them that looked upon her,** and that she won the heart of the king.

16-18. In the month of December, 479 B.C., just four years after his divorce from Vashti, Xerxes made Esther his queen. During those four years, the emperor had hurled one of the greatest armies of ancient history against the Greeks, only to suffer humiliating and crushing defeats at Salamis and Plataea. Esther afforded him a measure of the consolation that he so greatly needed. **He made a release to the provinces** (v. 18). This was either a remission of taxes or a remission of labor (a holiday).

19-23. When the virgins were gathered together the second time. The purpose of this second gathering is not explained, but it must be remembered that Xerxes (like Solomon) was a polygamist and was constantly adding to his harem. It was during this second gathering, however, that Mordecai discovered a plot against the life of the king. Two eunuchs, Bigthan and Teresh, who may have had access to the king through the virgins mentioned in 2:19, and who may possibly have been enraged at Vashti's divorce, plotted to kill the king. It is interesting to note that Xerxes finally did die by assassination (Olmstead, *op. cit.,* p. 289). Providentially, Mordecai was the one who foiled the plot, for the record of his good deed was placed in the royal chronicles and later became the means of his exaltation (6:1-3). **They were both hanged on a tree** (v. 23). They were probably either crucified or impaled alive (cf. 7:10).

III. Haman's Plot Against the Jews. 3:1-15.

Mordecai refused to bow before Haman, whom Xerxes had elevated to the second position in the kingdom; and consequently Haman's wrath was aroused against Mordecai's nation. By means of the lot *(Pur),* the fateful day was determined for the destruction of the Jews, and Haman promised to the king all their confiscated property. Haman sent letters to the entire empire in the king's name, announcing the day of the Jews' destruction.

1-6. According to 3:7, the events of this chapter occurred in 474 B.C., more than four years after Esther became queen (cf. 2:16). By now, Haman, the Agagite, had become the king's favorite, and before him every knee had to bow (cf. Gen 41:43). It was customary for Jews to bow before their kings (II Sam 14:4; 18:26; I Kgs 1:16). But when Persians bowed before their kings, they paid homage as to a divine being. The Spartans refused to bow before Xerxes for this reason (Herodotus, 7.136). He

had told them that he was a Jew (v. 4). Since his loyalty to Jehovah was the basis for his refusal to bow before Haman, he had to divulge his nationality at last. At the time, this must have seemed disastrous to Mordecai; but God ultimately brought greater blessing through it, for he delights not in silent witnesses (cf. 8:17). **Haman sought to destroy all the Jews** (v. 6). Discovering that Mordecai's refusal to bow was based upon religious motives, Haman realized that nothing less than a nation-wide pogrom would finally solve this problem.

7. Early in April, 474 B.C., Haman had the astrologers and magicians cast the lot to determine which day of the year would bring destruction to Israel (*Pur* is an Old Persian word meaning "lot"). The ancients placed great confidence in astrology and divination, but little did they realize that when "the lot is cast into the lap . . . the whole disposing thereof is of the Lord" (Prov 16:33). God's overruling was particularly evident in this case, for as they cast the lot concerning each subsequent day of the year, it fell upon the thirteenth day of the twelfth and last month, allowing time for Haman's plot to be overcome and a counterdecree to be issued!

8-11. Haman revealed his extreme subtlety by the proposition he made to the king. Realizing that Xerxes was completely egotistical, Haman gained permission to exterminate the Jews by convincing him that they were defying his laws and that their confiscated property would bring vast wealth to his treasuries. The uniqueness of Israel's laws and customs has always caused offense to ungodly Gentiles (Num 23:9; Acts 16:20, 21). But it was hardly true that they refused to keep the laws of the nations in which they lived, except in the case of doing homage to a mere creature (cf. Dan 3:12; 6:10). Haman was correct, however, in his assumption that the Jews had much wealth. Many were able to give generously to their brethren who returned to Palestine (Ezr 1:4). "Thirty-eight Hebrew names . . . occur on 730 account tablets belonging to Murashu and sons, a family of bankers at Nippur (Babylonia) in 464–404 B.C." (D. J. Wiseman, *Illustrations From Biblical Archaeology*, p. 76). **Ten thousand talents of silver** (v. 9). This would be approximately $15,000,000 in modern currency. Herodotus (3.95) claimed that Darius I received nearly 15,000 talents a year in revenue. **The king took his ring from his hand, and gave it unto Haman** (v. 10). In ancient times the signet ring was very important, for it was equivalent to one's signature. With this ring, Haman was able to send letters in the king's name (3:12). Later, the ring was given to Mordecai (8:2,8). **The silver is given to thee, the people also, to do with them as it seemeth good to thee** (v. 11). Possibly to avoid the appearance of greed, Xerxes offered the money to Haman. The king's utter indifference to the fate of millions of his subjects has found modern parallels in Hitler, Stalin, and Khrushchev.

12-15. On the thirteenth day of Nisan (April 17, 474 B.C.), scribes were called to prepare copies and translations of the decree for distribution throughout the empire. **The letters were sent by posts** (v. 13). Herodotus wrote: "Nothing mortal travels so fast as these Persian messengers. The entire plan is a Persian invention; and this is the method of it. Along the whole line of road there are men (they say) stationed with horses, in number equal to the number of days which the journey takes, allowing a man and horse to each day; and these men will not be hindered from accomplishing at their best speed the distance which they have to go either by snow, or rain, or heat, or by the darkness of night. The first rider delivers his dispatch to the second, and the second passes it to the third; and so it is borne from hand to hand along the whole line, like the light in the torch-race, which the Greeks celebrate to Hephaestus" (8.98). **The thirteenth day of the twelfth month.** This would have been March 7, 473 B.C., nearly a year later. **To take the spoil of them for a prey.** All who helped to exterminate them would gain spoil, but a portion would be turned over to Haman. **The city of Shushan was perplexed** (v. 15). Doubtless the Jews had many friends in this capital city (cf. 8:15), who were stunned by this shocking example of irresponsible despotism. Perhaps the decree was published so soon in order to encourage the Jews to flee and to leave their property behind (Keil).

IV. Esther's Decision. 4:1-17.

Mordecai's great mourning provoked the curiosity of Esther, who then learned from him of the decree and of his desire that she appeal to the king. When she protested that this might prove fatal to her, Mordecai insisted that this was her responsibility to God. She promised to go to the king if Mordecai would join her in a three-day fast.

1-3. Mordecai perceived all that was done (v. 1). Not only did he know what was publicly announced and have in his possession a copy of the decree (v. 8), but he also knew of the agreement between Haman and the king and the exact amount of money that had been promised (v. 7). This aggravated his grief, for he probably realized that it was the divulging of his nationality (3:4) that had brought Haman's wrath upon his people. **Put on sackcloth with ashes.** The token of overwhelming grief (Job 2:12; Dan 9:3). **None might enter into the king's gate clothed with sackcloth** (v. 2). The king would not tolerate sorrow or tragedy in his presence (cf. Neh 2:1,2).

4-8. Learning of Mordecai's mourning, Esther sent appropriate raiment to him so he could enter the court (cf. v. 2). **But he received it not.** He wanted to impress upon Esther the gravity of the situation and have the opportunity of communicating with her. **Then called Esther for Hatach** (v. 5). It is possible that Hatach was a Jew who knew of the relationship between Esther and Mordecai. At least he soon learned, for among other things Mordecai told him to charge Esther to make request before the king **for her people** (v. 8).

9-12. There is one law . . . to put him to death (v. 11). From early times, Median kings had refused entrance to the throne room to unannounced persons in order to enhance their dignity and to protect themselves (Herodotus, 1.99; 3.118). But any who desired an audience might ask to be announced (Herodotus, 3.140). However, Esther had not been called for thirty days and doubtless feared that the king's temporary lack of interest in her would jeopardize the success of her formal request for an audience. The only other possibility was to appear at the entrance of the court unannounced and hope for a gracious response from the king. This was to Esther an impossibly dangerous plan under the circumstances.

13,14. Think not with thyself that thou shalt escape. Mordecai reminded her of the dangerous position in which she herself stood, especially because her refusal to help God's people in this hour of crisis would bring God's judgment upon her and her family, while relief and deliverance would **arise to the Jews from another place** (v. 14). Mordecai knew the promises of God and the history of Israel too well to doubt this for a moment. As a matter of fact, God may very well have raised her to be Queen of Persia because of the crisis that he knew would arise through the wrath of Haman! This passage is a key to the basic meaning of the entire book, namely, to demonstrate the unfailing providence of God in behalf of his people Israel. Mordecai's implications were quite clear and his plea was irresistible.

15-17. Fast ye for me . . . three days (v. 16). Prayer to God is not mentioned here, but it is quite obviously implied (cf. Joel 1:14). **I also and my maidens will fast likewise.** Possibly they were Jewish maidens or else proselytes whom Esther had taught to pray. **If I perish, I perish.** This is not a blind fatalism or a hopeless resignation (cf. Gen 43:14), but rather a confidence in God's will and wisdom (cf. Job 13:15; Dan 3:17,18).

V. Esther's First Banquet. 5:1-14.

The king graciously received Esther, and she in turn invited him and Haman to a private banquet. At the banquet the king offered to grant any request she might have; she asked that they come to another banquet the next day. Haman was overjoyed at the special invitations, but was chagrined at Mordecai's refusal to bow before him. Haman's wife and friends suggested that he obtain permission from the king to hang Mordecai on the gallows which he would build.

1-4. On the third day. The third day of the fast, which probably lasted over forty hours (4:16). **She obtained favour in his sight** (v. 2). A remarkable evidence of the fact that "the king's heart is in the hand of the LORD, as the rivers of water: he turneth it whithersoever he will" (Prov 21:1); especially in view of Est 4:11. **It shall be even given thee to the half of the kingdom** (v. 3). Probably surprised at her unannounced appearance, he thought her request must be an urgent one. Even though this expression was hyperbole, it was never thought to be a light promise (cf. 5:6; 7:2; Mk 6:23; and Herodotus, 9.109).

5-8. My petition and my request is . . . I will do to morrow as the king hath said (vv. 7,8). Esther's purpose in inviting the king and Haman to a private banquet, in the first place, was to accuse Haman of plotting to destroy her people (cf. 7:6). But now, perhaps sensing that she did not yet have sufficient influence with the king to make such a bold accusation, she postponed her request and invited them to another banquet the following evening. This, of course, was providential, for the intervening events, as recorded in chapter 6, provided the necessary background for her accusation at the second banquet.

9-14. Then went Haman forth that day joyful and with a glad heart: but . . . he was full of indignation against Mordecai. An interesting example of the deceived sinner, glorying in self and hating God and God's people. Although Esther's attendants knew of her relation to Mordecai (cf. note on 4:4-8), Haman obviously did not. This ignorance proved to be his undoing. **The multitude of his children** (v. 11). Haman had ten sons (9:7-10). To have many children was considered to be a great honor not only in Israel (Ps 127:3-5) but also in Persia (Herodotus, 1.136). **Let a gallows be made of fifty cubits high . . . that Mordecai may be hanged thereon** (v. 14). Haman ordered the workmen to construct in his own courtyard (7:9) a seventy-five-foot gallows, in order that it might be seen from afar, probably even from the palace. Construction began that very night because Haman was supremely confident that the king would grant his request and thus enable him to enjoy Esther's second banquet with complete peace of mind.

VI. Haman Humiliated Before Mordecai. 6:1-14.

Unable to sleep that night, the king had the official chronicles read to him, which told of Mordecai's unrewarded loyalty in exposing a plot against the king. When Haman arrived at the court to ask for Mordecai's death, he was asked what honors should be bestowed upon a favorite of the king. Thinking of himself, he suggested very elaborate exaltation, only to be told that he had to do these honors to Mordecai the Jew. When he arrived home, his wife and friends warned him that if Mordecai was indeed a Jew, he could not prevail against him; his own doom was surely sealed.

1-3. On that night could not the king sleep. Possibly it was anxiety with respect to Esther's request or overindulgence at the banquet of wine that kept Xerxes awake that night (cf. Dan 6:18). But above all, it was the providence of God, for apart from this, the king would never have heard the account of Mordecai's deed as recorded in "the book of records of the chronicles" (cf. 2:23).

4-9. Who is in the court? His carpenters having worked all night to finish the gallows, Haman arrived at the court early in the morning to ask the king's permission to have Mordecai hanged. But before he could make this request, the king summoned him to the throne room to answer an important question. Apparently the king wanted to consult any statesman he could find, and Haman happened to be the most available man at that moment! **More than to myself** (v. 6). This is a clear illustration of the text: "Pride goeth before destruction, and an haughty spirit before a fall" (Prov 16:18; cf. 11:2; 18:12). Haman immediately began to list those honors which would be most highly esteemed in the Orient, as though he had often meditated on this possibility and was ready to give an answer if the king should ever ask him! **Royal apparel . . . which the king useth to wear** (v. 8). Not an ordinary robe of state, but a costly garment which the king owned and had actually worn (cf. I Sam 18:4). **On the head of which a royal crown is set.** The crown was to be set on the horse's head, for in Assyrian and Persian sculptures ornaments may be seen on the heads of horses (Keil). **Bring him . . . through the street . . . and proclaim before him** (v. 9). Compare the similar honor accorded to Joseph in Egypt (Gen 41:42).

10. Do even so to Mordecai the Jew. Doubtless the king had discovered that Mordecai was a Jew from conversation with his courtiers concerning the good deed he had done (6:1-3). But being a fickle and forgetful monarch, he had failed to connect this fact with the decree he had recently issued commanding the extermination of the Jews! (cf. 3:11)

13,14. Haman's friends, who had formerly acted as his counselors (5:14), now acted as **wise men** *(magi)*, for they predicted his downfall. **If Mordecai be of the seed of the Jews . . . thou shalt not prevail against him** (v. 13). The sudden change in Mordecai's fortunes made them realize, with a superstitious awe borne of careful observation of God's providential care for his people since the days of Cyrus, that Haman's preliminary fall would not stop short of total destruction. **Hasted to bring Haman unto the banquet.** His spirit crushed, Haman went to

Esther's second banquet as a sheep to the slaughter.

VII. Esther's Second Banquet. 7:1-10.

Esther asked the king for the preservation of her people from destruction and boldly accused Haman of being the adversary. The king went into the garden enraged at this discovery, and returned to find Haman pleading with Esther for his life. Accusing him of attacking the queen, he ordered Haman to be hanged on the same gallows he had built for Mordecai.

1-6. We are sold, I and my people (v. 4). Emboldened by Mordecai's sudden change of fortune, Esther finally identified herself with the people of Israel who had been sold (3:9; 4:7) **to be destroyed, to be slain, and to perish** (the same wording as in 3:13). **If we had been sold for bondmen . . . I had held my tongue, although the enemy could not countervail the king's damage.** Literally, *although the enemy is not equal to the damage of the king.* Although the Hebrew wording is not altogether clear to us today, it probably means that the punishment of Haman would involve far less financial loss to the king than would the destruction of thousands of Jews. By contrast, however, Esther would have remained silent if the Jews had been sold as slaves, for this would doubtless have brought much initial profit to the king (F. U. Schultz, "Esther," in *Lange's Commentary*). **Who is he . . . that durst presume in his heart to do so?** (v. 5) This is the response for which Esther and Mordecai had been praying. The king, learning for the first time that his queen was a Jewess, was overwhelmed by the thought that she and her people had been sold unto destruction by an unalterable decree. To be sure, he had originally consented to Haman's plot without much deliberation (3:10,11); but it is difficult to imagine that he didn't know who had been responsible for initiating this pogrom only two months before (cf. 3:7; 8:9). Perhaps he purposely refrained from turning upon Haman in order that the utter wickedness of the deed itself might be emphasized first. **The adversary and enemy is this wicked Haman** (v. 6). Esther carefully built up her case before finally naming Haman.

7. While the enraged king went into the garden to regain control of himself, Haman pled with Esther for mercy, realizing that he could now find no favor from the king apart from her intercession. The day before, he had led a Jew in triumphal procession through the streets of the city, and now he was pleading with a Jewess for his very life! A similar reversal will take place at the inauguration of the Millennium (cf. Isa 14:1-3).

8. Will he force the queen also before me in the house? (v. 8) Desperate for his very life, Haman fell at Esther's feet as she reclined upon the gold and silver couch (ASV; cf. 1:6). The Persians as well as the Greeks and Romans reclined at meals, and the Jews did so in later years (cf. Jn 13:23). When Ahasuerus returned from the garden, he poured his wrath upon Haman and attributed to him the worst of motives for thus approaching the queen. The king certainly did not think that Haman was actually attacking Esther, but in the heat of his anger he spoke out in this manner to show the servants how he now felt toward Haman. **As the word went out of the king's mouth, they covered Haman's face.** This **word** was not the question he had just asked, but a command to execute Haman, which is not actually recorded in the text. The ancients sometimes covered the heads of those about to be executed.

9,10. Harbonah was one of the seven eunuchs whom the king had sent to bring Vashti to the great banquet (1:10). **Behold also, the gallows . . . which Haman had made for Mordecai.** The eunuchs had probably listed the various crimes of Haman in order to keep in step with the king's wrath against him, and concluded by pointing to the seventy-five-foot high gallows in Haman's courtyard, which could be seen clearly from the palace. Following the suggestions of his courtiers, as usual, the king ordered Haman to be hanged upon his own gallows.

VIII. Mordecai's Counterdecree. 8:1-17.

Haman's property and position were now given to Mordecai by Xerxes and Esther. But the king was unable to reverse his decree against the Jews; so he empowered Mordecai to issue a new decree to counteract the first. This was quickly done, and the Jews were now permitted to defend themselves on the thirteenth of Adar, the date which Haman had originally set for their destruction. This produced great rejoicing everywhere and many became Jewish proselytes.

1,2. Now that she had revealed her nationality to Xerxes (7:4), Esther was happy to present Mordecai to the king as her guardian and cousin. The king had already delighted to honor Mordecai for exposing the plot against his life (6:6); so it was perfectly natural for him to give the Jew his signet ring (cf. 3:10; 8:8) and to appoint him chief minister of the empire (cf. Gen 41:42).

3-6. In spite of Haman's death and Mordecai's exaltation, the Jews were still doomed to destruction by an irreversible decree. Therefore Esther's task was not yet completed. In 8:3 the general contents of her petition are outlined, but in 8:5,6 her actual words are given. **Let it be written to reverse the letters devised by Haman . . . for how can I endure to see . . . the destruction of my kindred?** (vv. 5,6) Esther was desperately concerned for the fate of Israel now, as may be seen by the fourfold introductory formula she used, which emphasized her personal relationship to the king. Not fully understanding the intricacies of Persian law, she appealed directly to the heart of the king for mercy upon Israel and for the reversal of "the letters devised by Haman," being careful not to put blame upon the king for his part in Haman's deed.

7,8. Behold, I have given Esther the house of Haman. . . . the writing . . . may no man reverse. Anxious to show Esther that he did love her, he began by reminding her of the favors he had already shown her. But he added that no one, not even the king of Persia himself, had the power to reverse the laws of the Medes and Persians (compare the similar plight of Darius the Mede in Dan 6). Nevertheless, Mordecai had the full right to issue a counterdecree in the king's name, which would be just as irreversible as the one issued by Haman.

9,10. The official letters were now prepared in the same way as those which Haman had sent forth (3:12-15). The date was June 25, 474 B.C., a little over two months after the first decree was issued, allowing more than eight months for the Jews to prepare their defenses (v. 9). **Posts on horseback, and riders on mules, camels, and young dromedaries.** *Posts on horseback, riding on swift steeds that were used in the king's service, bred of the stud* (ASV). Special emphasis is placed here upon the speed with which Mordecai's letters were sent out, some of them perhaps overtaking those of Haman.

11-14. Four main ideas seem to be set forth in Mordecai's decree: (a) the Jews were to gather into groups by the thirteenth of Adar; (b) they were to defend their lives; (c) they were to kill those who attacked them; and (d) they were to take the spoil of their attackers. The **power of the people** (v. 11) refers to their military forces. **Hastened and pressed on by the king's commandment** (v. 14). It has often been observed that this serves as a remarkable illustration of missionary work today. God's death sentence hangs over a sinful humanity, but he also has commanded us to hasten the message of salvation to every land (cf. Prov 24:11,12). Only by a knowledge of, and a response to, the second decree can the terrible effects of the first decree be averted.

15-17. Having issued the decree, Mordecai clothed himself in royal apparel of blue and white (the royal colors of Persia; cf. 1:6), a great crown of gold, and a robe of fine linen and purple. These were probably his own official robes as prime minister rather than the special attire that was granted to him on his previous day of exaltation (6:8). His appearance in the city reinforced the joy that had been produced by the decree (contrast the sorrow produced by Haman's decree, 4:3). **The Jews had light, and gladness, and joy, and honour** (v. 16). *Gladness and joy, a feast and a good day* (ASV). This feast was in anticipation of the Feast of Purim, which was first celebrated eight months later (9:17-19). **Many of the people of the land became Jews** (v. 17). The verb **became Jews** occurs only once in the OT. In fact, we find little evidence of Gentiles becoming proselytes in significant numbers until NT times (cf. Acts 2:10; Mt 23:15). **The fear of the Jews fell upon them.** Israel had now begun to experience one of the greatest deliverances of God since the Exodus, and the lesson was obvious to many (9:2,3; Ex 15:16; Deut 11:25).

IX. The Jews Victorious, and Purim Instituted. 9:1–10:3.

When the fateful day arrived, the Jews successfully defended themselves with the aid of government officials and slew five hundred men in Shushan, including the ten sons of Haman. Esther obtained permission for the Jews to defend themselves a second day as well, and three hundred more enemies were slain in Shushan. In the provinces, seventy-five thousand enemies were slain. The Feast of Purim was then established by special letters to commemorate this tremendous deliverance. A second letter confirmed the first and provided for a fast as well. Mordecai's greatness and his love for Israel were recorded in the chronicles of the kingdom.

1-4. Finally, on March 7, 473 B.C., the fateful day arrived, and the Jews gathered into compact groups within the various cities to await their attackers. **It was turned to the contrary** (v. 1). An obvious reference to the providence of God, and yet the name of God still does not appear! **To lay hand on such as sought their hurt** (v. 2). In this context the phrase **lay hand on** means to kill (cf. 2:21; 3:6; 6:2). **All the rulers of the provinces . . . helped the Jews; because the fear of Mordecai fell upon them.** (v. 3). The tenor of the second decree made it perfectly clear to Persian officials that the king, to say nothing to Mordecai, his prime minister, now favored the Jews. To have joined in the attack against the Jews now would surely have brought wrath upon them. Perhaps they remembered the fate of those rulers who had opposed the true wishes of Darius the Mede in a somewhat similar situation (Dan 6:24).

5-10. Nevertheless, there were many Persian citizens who took full advantage of the first decree to attack their hated Jewish neighbors. Deprived of full government support and faced by a zealous and newly encouraged people, they were totally defeated. In Shushan itself five hundred Persians, plus Haman's ten sons, were slain. All these sons of Haman, with the possible exception of Adalia, had Persian names (see *Lange's Commentary, in loco,* for the root meanings of the names). **On the spoil laid they not their hand** (v. 10). Cf. 3:13; 8:11; 9:15,16. The Jews refrained from taking advantage of their rightful privilege, in order that the purity of their motives might be made evident to all.

11-16. What have they done in the rest of the king's provinces? (v. 12) Apparently the king rejoiced to hear that the Jews had gained such a tremendous victory in Shushan, and he expected reports of even greater victories from the provinces (see ASV). **Let it be granted to the Jews which are in Shushan to do to morrow also according unto this day's decree** (v. 13). Apparently, Esther heard of a Persian plot to attack the Jews on the following day as well, and therefore she asked permission for the Jews to defend themselves again. The king granted this request and issued a new decree permitting the Jews to kill their enemies in Shushan on the fourteenth of Adar as well, for Mordecai's decree had specified only one day for the Jews to defend themselves in this manner (8:13). This additional decree was obeyed (v. 15), and three hundred more Persians were slain in Shushan. Thus, the decree of 9:14 does not refer primarily to the impaling of the dead bodies of Haman's sons (14 b; cf. Deut 21:22,23). In the meantime, the Jews in the provinces had killed seventy-five thousand of their enemies on the thirteenth of Adar.

17-28. Provincial Jews began to observe the fourteenth of Adar as a holiday, while those in Shushan observed the fifteenth. As on our Christmas day, gifts were exchanged (cf. Neh 8:10,12; Rev 11:10), and the poor were cared for (v. 22). **And Mordecai wrote these things, and sent letters unto all the Jews** (v. 20). Apparently after several years had passed, Mordecai reviewed the events relating to their victory and decreed that there should no longer be two distinct holidays (the fourteenth in the provinces and the fifteenth in Shushan) but that both days should be observed as the Feast of Purim (vv. 26-28). In fact, many Jews had already begun to observe both days (v. 23).

29-32. This second letter of Purim. This was not the letter of 9:20, but a new letter described in 9:30-32, in which a period of fasting and prayer (**the fastings and their cry,** v. 31), in addition to the days of joy, was to be observed in memory of the anxious days of prayer which had preceded God's deliverance. Presumably Esther and Mordecai had been observing such a time of fasting for several years now (cf. 4:15-17), and they thought it best to make it a national custom. **And it was written in the book** (v. 32). Not the book of Esther itself, but the book in which Mordecai had written his record of events (v. 20) and which served as one of the basic sources for the book of Esther.

10:1-3. Xerxes died in 465 B.C. Looking back over his reign shortly afterward, the author emphasizes the stupendous power and wealth of this king (v. 1) in order to show the marvelous providence of God in elevating a despised Jew to a position of honor in such an empire.

Speaking peace to all his seed (v. 3). This does not refer to Mordecai's own children, but to Israel, his race (cf. II Kgs 11:1).

BIBLIOGRAPHY

For bibliography see under *Ezra*.

JOB

INTRODUCTION

Title. The name of both the book and its hero, *'iyyôb*, appears in extra-Biblical texts as early as 2000 B.C. Its monosyllabic English form, *Job*, derives from the Vulgate (i.e., Latin) version.

Literary Genre. The central core of the book is poetry, set like a gem within a prologue and an epilogue of epic prose. Such ABA structures are found elsewhere in ancient literature. For example, Hammurabi placed his laws within a prologue and an epilogue of poetry. And an Egyptian work, *The Eloquent Peasant*, frames the peasant's nine semipoetic protests within a prose prologue and an epilogue.

Along with Proverbs, Ecclesiastes, and, in a sense, the Song of Solomon, Job belongs to the Wisdom *(ḥokmâ)* genre, a type of writing amply illustrated in a variety of forms in ancient Near Eastern literature. Within the canon of Old Testament Scripture, the distinctive contribution of the Wisdom books is that they expound the relevance of the foundational covenant revelation through Moses to the great issues of man's life in this world, more specifically, of man's life apart from the peculiarly theocratic context of Israelite history. There are many formal similarities between Job and various extra-Biblical Wisdom pieces; e.g., dialogue style, and motifs like the problem of suffering and the longing for death. Nevertheless, in its essential teaching, Job differs altogether from the non-Biblical Wisdom literature because it represents the unique message of redemptive revelation, the wisdom of God which makes foolish the wisdom of men. Even in its literary structure, considered as a whole, it is unique — a masterpiece universally acclaimed.

Closely related to the literary form is the question of historicity. Certainly Job was a historical person (cf. Ezk 14:14,20; Jas 5:11), and his actual experience was substantially as recorded in this book. Nevertheless, the magnificent poetry of the several discourses has compelled general assent to the conclusion that the treatment of the account here is not literal but free. Moreover, the semipoetic epic style of the prologue and epilogue (with their strophic structure and refrains), though it does not require the view that the narrative is legendary, suggests the possibility of a free, figurative treatment of some details.

Authorship and Date. Discussions of the authorship of Job by most modern critics are complicated by the critics' doubts as to the unity of the book as we have it. The evidence is not primarily external, for though the LXX text of Job is about one-fifth shorter than the Masoretic text, its omissions are clearly secondary. The sections that have been most widely regarded as additions to an original basic work are the prologue and the epilogue, the poem on wisdom (ch. 28), the Elihu material (chs. 32–37), and part or all of the Lord's discourses (chs. 38–41). Also, chapters 24–27 are regarded as seriously disarranged. However, strong defense of the integrity of our present text is found in the masterly structural unity of the whole and the rich interrelationships of all the parts.

The question of date has received every possible answer, which indicates the difficulty of determining the time precisely. The date of the *writing* of the book is not to be confused with the date of the *history* narrated. The man Job apparently lived in early, patriarchal times. We note, for example, the longevity of Job, as well as the not inconsiderable practice of true religion (attended by special supernatural revelation) outside the bounds of the Abrahamic covenant, and the early economic and political developments reflected in the book. The question regarding the dating of the book, then, is: How long was the story of the patriarch Job transmitted — whether orally or at least partially in writing — before the anonymous Israelite writer, under divine inspiration, transformed the tradition into the canonical book of Job. The majority of negative critics favors an Exilic or post-Exilic date, their judgment being influenced by the way they construe the interdependence of Job, Isaiah, and Jeremiah—and by their dating of the pertinent Isaiah passages. The most extreme dating (2nd century B.C.) seems to be decisively contradicted by fragments of Joban manuscripts included among the Dead Sea finds, especially those in the old Hebrew script. The grandeur and spontaneity of the book and its deeply empathic re-creation of the sentiments of men standing early in the progress of revelation point to the early pre-Exilic period, before the doctrinal, especially, the eschatological, contribution of the prophets. Many conservative scholars have favored a date in Solomon's time, that being the great age of Biblical Wisdom literature (cf., e.g., the similarities of Job to Psalms 88 and 89, which are from the Solomonic age; cf. I Kgs 4:31).

Theme. Through the medium of the problem of theodicy, the book of Job sounds anew the central religious demand of the Covenant. It calls men to unreserved consecration to their sovereign Lord. And this way of the Covenant, this consecration to the transcendent, incomprehensible Creator, it identifies with the way of wisdom. Thereby it presents the Church with its proper testimony to redemptive revelation before the wisdom schools of the world.

OUTLINE

I. Desolation: The trial of Job's wisdom. 1:1–2:10.
  A. Job's wisdom described. 1:1-5.
  B. Job's wisdom denied and displayed. 1:6–2:10.
    1. The enmity of Satan. 1:6-12.
    2. The integrity of Job. 1:13-22.
    3. The persistence of Satan. 2:1-6.
    4. The patience of Job. 2:7-10.

II. Complaint: The way of wisdom lost. 2:11–3:26.
  A. The coming of the wise men. 2:11-13.
  B. The impatience of Job. 3:1-26.

III. Judgment: The way of wisdom darkened and illuminated. 4:1–41:34.
  A. The verdicts of men. 4:1–37:24.
    1. First cycle of debate. 4:1–14:22.
      a. First discourse of Eliphaz. 4:1–5:27.
      b. Job's reply to Eliphaz. 6:1–7:21.
      c. First discourse of Bildad. 8:1-22.
      d. Job's reply to Bildad. 9:1–10:22.
      e. First discourse of Zophar. 11:1-20.
      f. Job's reply to Zophar. 12:1–14:22.
    2. Second cycle of debate. 15:1–21:34.
      a. Second discourse of Eliphaz. 15:1-35.
      b. Job's second reply to Eliphaz. 16:1–17:16.
      c. Second discourse of Bildad. 18:1-21.
      d. Job's second reply to Bildad. 19:1-29.
      e. Second discourse of Zophar. 20:1-29.
      f. Job's second reply to Zophar. 21:1-34.
    3. Third cycle of debate. 22:1–31:40.
      a. Third discourse of Eliphaz. 22:1-30.
      b. Job's third reply to Eliphaz. 23:1–24:25.
      c. Third discourse of Bildad. 25:1-6.
      d. Job's third reply to Bildad. 26:1-14.
      e. Job's instruction of the silenced friends. 27:1–28:28.
      f. Job's final protest. 29:1–31:40.
    4. The ministry of Elihu. 32:1–37:24.
  B. The voice of God. 38:1–41:34.
    1. The divine challenge. 38:1–40:2.
    2. Job's submission. 40:3-5.
    3. The divine challenge renewed. 40:6–41:34.

IV. Confession: The way of wisdom regained. 42:1-6.

V. Restoration: The triumph of Job's wisdom. 42:7-17.
  A. Job's wisdom vindicated. 42:7-9.
  B. Job's wisdom blessed. 42:10-17.

COMMENTARY

I. Desolation: The Trial of Job's Wisdom. 1:1–2:10.

A. Job's Wisdom Described. 1:1-5.

The fear of the Lord, which is the beginning of wisdom, was the hallmark of Job. The wellspring of his life and character was the covenantal religion of faith in the Christ of promise, "who of God is made unto us wisdom" (I Cor 1:30; cf. Isa 11:2).

1. Job's homeland, Uz, lay somewhere to the east of Canaan, near the borders of the desert that separates the eastern and western arms of the Fertile Crescent. It was an area of towns, farms, and migrating herds. **Perfect and upright** (AV), does not denote sinless perfection (cf. Job's recognition of his sins; e.g., 7:20; 13:26; 14:16ff.) but straightforward integrity, specifically, covenant fidelity (cf. Gen 17:1,2). There was an honest harmony between Job's profession and his life, quite the opposite of the hypocrisy of which he was presently accused by Satan and later by his friends. **One that feared God.** In the OT "the fear of the Lord" is the name for true religion. Job's piety was the fruit of a genuine commitment to his Lord, before whom he walked in reverence, resolutely rejecting what He proscribed.

2,3. True wisdom finds expression in the vigorous prosecution of God's creation mandates to replenish and subdue the earth (Gen 1:28). Due to the abnormality of history, which results from the Fall, failure often dogs the efforts even of the godly. But Job's undertakings in family, field, and flock had been crowned with the Creator's blessings (cf. Job's description of this period in ch. 29).

4,5. Mindful of his God in good days as in evil, Job faithfully fulfilled his function as priest within his family. No mere formalist, Job perceived the root of sin in the human heart (cf. ch. 31); and no mere moralist, he recognized, as special redemptive revelation had made clear, that there is no remission of sins without the shedding of sacrificial blood. **Burnt offerings,** while symbolic of the Messianic expiation of sin, were also a consecration rite. By means of them Job dedicated the fruits of progress in the area of culture (cf. 1:2,3) to his Creator. Thus human culture reached its proper end in the worship of God.

B. Job's Wisdom Denied and Displayed. 1:6–2:10.

He who is wise unto salvation is aware of the demonic dimension of history, the age-long fury of Satan against "the seed" of the woman (cf. Gen 3:15), that is, Christ and His people. The Adversary charged that Job's godly wisdom was not genuine, that his piety was only a temporary by-product of his prosperity. Put to the test, however, Job bruised Satan under foot by demonstrating that he was ready to serve God "for nought." Since true wisdom, the fear of God, is a divinely bestowed redemptive gift, Satan's charge against Job was actually a defiant denial of the wisdom of God, a challenge to the sovereign efficacy of God's redemptive decree to "put enmity" between the elect and the serpent (Gen 3:15). The primary purpose of Job's suffering, unknown to him, was that he should stand before men and angels as a trophy of the saving might of God, an exhibit of that divine wisdom which is the archetype, source, and foundation of true human wisdom.

1) The Enmity of Satan. 1:6-12.

6,7. That the reader may discover the primary purpose of Job's sufferings and so be in a position to judge accurately where true wisdom lay in the sequel, the veil is withdrawn from the invisible angelic world, depicted here as a royal court with the Sovereign seated on his throne amid his servants. **The sons of God.** This phrase in ancient polytheistic myths denotes divine beings. In the Bible it refers either to men (e.g., Gen 6:2) or, as here, to celestial creatures. **Satan,** literally, *the Adversary,* is among those obliged to render account before the heavenly throne. That, as well as the fact that Satan cannot tempt Job without permission, advertises his absolute subordination, along with all other creatures visible and invisible, to the God whom Job feared.

8-10. God glorifies himself by pointing to Job as a creation of his redemptive grace. **There is none like him in the earth** (v. 8b). This divine endorsement goes even beyond the description in verse 1. But though the hostile accuser can find nothing in Job's outward life to condemn (contrast the situation in Zech 3), he insinuates that the patriarch's apparent devotion is that of calculated self-interest. He is saying, in effect, "Job is a deceiver like me, his true father, the devil." Satan sought to pluck Job out of God's hand, and so he disputed the Lord's claim that Job had been made His son by redemptive grace. The devil hints that, in failing to recognize the fraudulence of Job's piety, God is naive. For who, having been given a world all his own with a fence around it, would not keep up the necessary appearances of loyalty to the giver? The satanic assault on the integrity of Job is thus ultimately an assault on the integrity of God: God has bribed the profane Job to act pious. The opportunity given to Job by his trial, therefore, is not so much to vindicate himself as to justify God.

11,12. In the temptation in Eden, Satan disparaged God to man; here he disparages man to God. But he used the same subtle technique in both instances. He began with an insinuating question, then moved boldly on to outspoken contradiction of the divine word. Remove Job's prosperity, he says, and the piety that rests on it will collapse. God accepts the challenge. Indeed, by directing Satan's attention to Job, in his unfathomable wisdom, he invites the challenge.

That the heavenly scene and the transactions of the heavenly court are not disclosed to Job is in keeping with the fact that this book is not intended primarily to answer the question, Why do the righteous suffer? Rather, the book represents absolute consecration of self to man's faithful Creator-Saviour as true wisdom. A man must continue to fear God even when his world flies apart and life strands him, like Job, in stunned bewilderment on the refuse heap.

2) The Integrity of Job. 1:13-22.

13-19. How unequal the contest seems! Preternatural knowledge and power – with the element of surprise in its favor – arrayed against a mortal! David and Goliath, in comparison, were *equally* matched. Yet Job's steadfast righteousness, like David's heroism, was only the visible index of the power of divine redemption working in and through the servant of God. The strategy of God, like that of Elijah on Carmel, was to make it impossible for Satan to foist on the witnesses a naturalistic explanation of the wonder He was about to perform. The overwhelming advantage God allowed Satan became, in the sequel, the measure of the devil's ignominy and of God's praise.

There was a day (v. 13b). Possibly the banquet weeks were special occasional celebrations; but if there was a continuous succession of weekly rounds of feasting, this was the day when Job had offered burnt offerings. His piety and desolation being thus set side by side, his desolation seems the more unaccountable. Certainly the repetition of the picture of Job's happy family life as the prelude to the record of the strokes that obliterated it serves to set the joyous prosperity and the sudden desolation in sharpest contrast. **The Sabeans** (v. 15). Arab Bedouins. **The fire of God** (v. 16b). Possibly lightning. **The Chaldeans** (v. 17) of this early period, unlike the later empire-builders, were nomadic marauders. The **great wind** (v. 19b). Apparently a desert whirlwind, like that from which God later addressed Job. Note how the unsparing assaults of men on the accumulated fruit of Job's lifetime alternate with the assaults of nature. The messengers were spared only to convey the evil tidings, in overwhelmingly close succession, to their bereaved master.

20-22. And worshipped (v. 20b). Behold, the wise man! Not wise because he comprehended the mystery of his sufferings, but because, not comprehending, he feared God still. **Naked shall I return thither** (v. 21b), i.e., beyond the scene of life under the sun, into the dust (to which Job perhaps pointed). Cf. Gen 3:19. **Blessed be the name of the Lord** (v. 21 c). The remarkable thing is that Job, recognizing that he could not resist the sovereign God, not merely maintained his spiritual composure, but even found in adversity occasion for praise. Perhaps in measuring the greatness of his loss, Job took stock of the abundance which had all the while been entrusted to his stewardship. Moreover, this hour of desolation was a moment of truth for him. Stripped naked of the things of this world, Job was unusually sensible of God's confronting presence. Deep was constrained to cry out unto deep. And how can the adoring redeemed heart respond in the presence of God but with doxology: "Whom have I in heaven but thee? and there is none upon earth that I desire beside thee" (Ps 73:25). Satan prophesied: "He will curse thee" (Job 1:11). But Job blessed God his Saviour. In the Hebrew there is a play here on one root word, Satan using it with the meaning of cursing, and Job with the meaning of blessing.

3) The Persistence of Satan. 2:1-6.

1-3. Summoned again before the throne of the heavenly court to render account, Satan volunteers no report on his temptation of Job. God, however, to magnify His name, declares openly the fact of the tried and true integrity of His servant. **Without cause** (v. 3c). This represents the same Hebrew word as the "for nought" of Satan's question (1:9). God echoes the term to give the lie to Satan's insinuation. It is now obvious that Job does serve God for nought and, therefore, it was for nought that Satan had accused him.

4-6. Skin for skin (v. 4b). A cynical parody of the reverent praise with which Job had responded to his desolation (1:21). Satan insinuates that even Job's doxology, born in the anguish of bereavement, was the calculated response of a shrewd bargainer. Though disappointed that God had not given him anything to keep, Job concealed his bitterness over his losses out of profane concern for his physical well-being: **all that a man hath will he give for his life** (v. 4b). Satan implies that Job, by his doxology had only feigned love for God as the exorbitant but necessary fee for health insurance. **Touch his bone and his flesh** (v. 5b). If God will let Satan touch not merely Job's possessions but also his person, so that there will be no profit left in "the religious deal," Job will weigh back curse for curse. Thus again Satan proceeds from the depreciation of Job's past piety to a prediction that he will prove to be profane. So once again God permits the mystery of affliction to engulf His servant.

4) The Patience of Job. 2:7-10.

7,8. Sore boils (v. 7b). Modern medical opinion is not unanimous in its diagnosis of Job's disease, but according to the prognosis in Job's day, it was apparently hopeless. The horrible symptoms included inflamed eruptions accompanied by intense itching (2:7,8), maggots in ulcers (7:5), erosion of the bones (30:17), blackening and falling off of skin (30:30), and terrifying nightmares (7:14), though some of these may possibly be attributed to the prolonged exposure that followed the onset of the disease. Job's whole body, it seems, was rapidly smitten with the loathsome, painful symptoms. Though Satan had been obliged to spare his victim's life, the sufferer probably thought his death was imminent. **Among the ashes** (v. 8b). The incurable disease was such as to reduce this former prince of eastern patriarchs, reverenced above all others by his fellows, to an outcast from human society. Once renowned as the salt of the earth, he was driven out as its offscouring. His dwelling was in the utter desolation of what was probably the town dunghill.

9,10. The narrative reminds us repeatedly of the temptation in Eden (Gen 3). Job's wife plays a role remarkably like that of Eve. Each woman succumbed to the tempter and became his instrument for the undoing of her husband. Satan had spared Job's wife—as he had spared the four messengers—for his further use in his war on Job's soul. **Curse God, and die** (v. 9b). The blasphemous apostasy to which she urged the sufferer was precisely what Satan had prophesied of Job. Her evil counsel brought this phase of Job's torment to its fiercest pitch and elicited his second decisive response. **As one of the foolish women** (v. 10a). The charitable restraint of Job's reply testifies as convincingly as his doxologies to the genuineness of his piety. He did not call his wife a fool, but he charged her with speaking, in her frenzied despair, like one of that company in whose counsel she would not ordinarily walk. The folly of her behavior brings into sharper relief the wisdom of Job's godly patience. In the Bible, "wisdom" is a religious virtue, and the "foolishness" Job refers to is not lack of intellectual keenness but surly lawlessness and godlessness (cf. Ps 14:1). **Shall we not receive evil?** (10b) The verb means *to receive meekly, patiently*. It is used in an ancient Canaanite proverb: "If ants are smitten, they do not receive (it passively) but they bite the hand of the man who smites them" (Amarna Letters, 252:18). **In all this did not Job sin with his lips** (v. 10c). He did not utter curses against God, as Satan had hopefully prophesied. There is certainly no veiled suggestion that Job had cursed God in his heart. Job's wisdom proved sound; he truly served God for nought but for God Himself.

Satan seduced Adam even while Adam was standing in the integrity of his creation righteousness. From this it might have appeared that Satan could trip up the depraved sons of Adam at will and trample upon them. But herein lies a great wonder of redemptive grace: sinner Job stands triumphant where righteous Adam tragically fell! Thus, for the confounding of Satan and the reassurance of the saints, the Lord gave clear proof that a righteousness more enduring than that of Adam was being provided through the second Adam. This triumph of Job's patience over the Adversary's malice provided a seal, especially for the ages before the Incarnation, of God's promise that He would bestow on the faithful the gift of eternal salvation through the Christ to come.

II. Complaint: The Way of Wisdom Lost. 2:11–3:26.

A. The Coming of the Wise Men. 2:11-13.

The trial of Job's wisdom was by no means over. A new phase of it now began with the aggravation of Job's evil state by spiritual torment. Though Satan does not appear again, he was none the less still present, subtly using Job's well-intentioned comforters as his unwitting accomplices, with more apparent success than had marked his efforts hitherto.

11. After the second crisis of temptation and before the arrival of the friends, there was an interval of some months (7:3), during which Job's spirit was stretched taut by the unrelenting distress in his flesh and the ravages of the foul disease which disfigured him beyond recognition (see chs. 19;30). **Job's three friends.** The cherished companions and counsellors of "the greatest of all the men of the east" must have been princes of their people and sages of renown. Teman in Edom was proverbial for wisdom (Jer 49:7). The Shuhite tribe (cf. Gen 25:2,6) and doubtless Naamah, were located in the east country, land of wise men (cf. I Kgs 4:30).

12,13. Though the friends were aware of Job's calamities, they were unprepared for what they found. Their stunned, week-long silence was like a mourning for the dead (cf. Gen 50:10; I Sam 31:13). Sincere as was their sympathy, their mute presence evidently afforded little comfort. To judge from their subsequent interpretation of Job's wretchedness, their mission of consolation would have misfired even sooner had they spoken. Still, it does seem regrettable that the prolonged silence had to be broken by the cry of the distraught sufferer rather than by a healing word of comfort from a friend.

B. The Impatience of Job. 3:1-26.

Between the heights of spiritual serenity in the prologue and in the epilogue stretches the abyss of Job's spiritual agony. The descent into and ascent out of that abyss are marked by sudden, dramatic changes of spiritual temper. These are described in brief transitional passages (i.e., chs. 3; 42:1-6). The first of these portrays Job's startlingly abrupt plunge from patience to deep despondency.

1. Cursed his day. What turned Job's submissive doxologies into unrestrained imprecations? Had his spiritual resistance been worn away by the endless days and nights of physical distress? Or did the sight of the distinguished companions of his former prosperity recall too vividly the vanished honor and happiness of the past? Or was it that the faces of his friends, aghast with unutterable pity, mirrored too faithfully the ugliness of his present? Is not the clue to be found in the friends' identity as "wise men"? The brooding presence of these philosophical interpreters of life could not fail to start Job philosophizing about his tragic experience. But the more intently he sought an explanation for it, the more anxiously aware he became of the wall of mystery encompassing him. Seeking the Why, he soon had lost the Way. Obsessed by the dread that God had abandoned him, he cursed his forsaken existence. Neither at this point nor later did Job fulfill Satan's prediction that he would renounce God with a curse. By cursing his own existence, however, Job, in effect, ventured to dispute with the Sovereign who decreed it. Whatsoever is not of faith is sin; hence, the need of Job's repentance (cf. 42:1-6) as the way to renewed peace with God.

3-10. Job's inescapable present misery obliterates the memory of his former joyful years as he laments that he was ever born. Let the Almighty not call his birthday into the light (v. 4), but **let darkness and the shadow of death claim it for their own** (v. 5a, ASV). Would that the night of his conception were blotted out of the calendar of time (v. 6), that **leviathan** (v. 8b, ASV; a mythological symbol of the foe of cosmic order) would swallow it into chaos.

11-19. Why? Explosive imprecation yields to piteous lamentation. Why, since he was conceived and born, was he at least not an abortion or stillborn (vv. 11,16)? Even confinement in the dark grave—not yet illumined by the resurrection glory of Christ—seemed a far better state of existence. There Job, outcast and a byword of base men and fools, would share a common lot with kings and princes (vv. 14,15); there all those afflicted by "the wicked" and taskmasters find relief from human troublers (vv. 17-19).

20-26. Why, not having been stillborn but rather welcomed alive and nourished (v. 12), must his wretched life continue? As the complaint draws to a close, Job finally voices his basic problem: Why does God give the light of life **to a man whose way is hid, and whom God hath hedged in?** (v. 23; cf. v. 20) The word Satan had used to describe Job as *hedged about* on every side by the favor of God (1:10), Job now uses for himself as one *hemmed in* by God with darkness and disfavor.

III. Judgment: The Way of Wisdom Darkened and Illuminated. 4:1–41:34.

A. Verdicts of Men. 4:1–37:24.

Because the dialogue of Job and his friends attaches to Job's complaint rather than directly to his calamities, the friends' mission assumes less the air of pastoral consolation than of judicial discipline, and this becomes increasingly so with each successive cycle of speeches. (For the cyclic structure of the dialogue, see the Outline above.) The friends sit as a council of elders to pass judgment on the clamorous offender. The weighing of Job's guilt involves discussion of broader aspects of the problem of theodicy, but always with Job's particular case and condemnation in view. Hence, for Job the debate is not a detached, academic study of suffering in general, but a new, more painful phase of his sufferings. The friends are beguiled by their adherence to traditional theory into aiding and abetting Satan in his hostility to God, and darkening the way of wisdom for God's servant, Job. But the debate serves to silence this wisdom of the world and so prepares for the presentation of the covenantal approach to wisdom, which follows in the discourses of Elihu and the Lord. Again, in Job's appeal from the verdicts of men to the highest court, expressed in his passionate longing to plead his case before the Lord, the debate reaches out to the visible manifestation of God.

1) First Cycle of Debate. 4:1–14:22.

a) First Discourse of Eliphaz. 4:1–5:27.

4:1. As the eldest, apparently, of the friends (cf. 15:10) and thus the possessor of the most seasoned wisdom, Eliphaz is accorded the dignity of precedence in each series of speeches (cf. 42:7). He sets the direction for the counsel of the friends by presenting his theory of sin and suffering and applying it to Job's case. The fundamental, but false, assumption of Eliphaz is that righteousness invariably brings weal and wickedness woe, that there is a direct ratio between sin and suffering. He addresses himself first to Job's despondency (4:2-11), then to his impatience (4:12–5:7), and finally counsels him to repent (5:8-27).

2-11. Who can withhold himself from speaking? (v. 2b) For seven days the wise men had looked on Job's calamities without offering a word of consolation. When Job complained, however, the comforters could not restrain reproof for a moment. Thus for the whole course of the debate their sights were fixed on Job's temporary lapse into impatience, while his earlier prolonged display of patience quite disappeared from their perspective. They reproach Job as though he had given up at the first taste of adversity: it

toucheth thee, and thou art thrown into alarm (v. 5b).

Even as I have seen (v. 8a; cf. 5:3). The authority for Eliphaz' theory is experience. He accepts the traditional view of Eastern sages because his observations of life seem to bear it out. His statistics show, for example, that extreme calamity follows extreme wickedness (vv. 8-11). Only arrogant sinners who make a lifework of sowing sin reap a harvest of death amid calamities. They perish like herbage scorched by the withering blast of desert wind (v. 9), or like a den of roaring lions dispersed by a sudden blow (vv. 10,11). His observation also has confirmed the converse: **Who ever perished, being innocent?** (v. 7a) Though the righteous experience a measure of suffering, they are never **cut off** under affliction. From such observations Eliphaz deduces his law of sin and suffering, and he assumes that it must uniformly and universally govern human history. Unfortunately, Eliphaz' method of constructing the doctrine of providence is unreliable. For true theology rests on the authority of divine revelation, not on limited human observation and fallible speculation. Unfortunately, too, as Job points out later, even Eliphaz' observations and statistics are inaccurate (cf. 21:17ff.).

Vain doctrine can offer only vain comfort. **Is not thy fear of God thy confidence, And the integrity of thy ways thy hope?** (4:6, ASV) Eliphaz does not question Job's essential righteousness. Therefore, thinking to arouse him from his despondency, he assures him that because he is a pious man, he will not perish. But this favorable evaluation of one laid low by disasters is inconsistent with Eliphaz' own theory. To be consistent he must regard Job as the basest son of Belial. For the patriarch's agony is so great that he passionately covets that death from which Eliphaz, declaring it the worst calamity that could befall the ungodly, has pronounced him immune. Later, when Eliphaz has worked out his position more consistently, he charges Job with hypocrisy and criminality. In this first speech, however, unappreciative of the exceptional severity of Job's sufferings, he classifies Job with the generality of moderately sinning, moderately suffering righteous men, and is only astonished that he complains so immoderately.

4:12–5:7. Job had called in question the wisdom of God's providence. Eliphaz counters with the argument that fallen men, whether godly or ungodly, are deficient in wisdom and justice and, therefore, incompetent to criticize Providence (4:12-21). They are, moreover, justly subject to all the woes attending mortality (5:1-7).

4:12-21. Now a word was brought to me stealthily, my ear received the whisper of it (v. 12, RSV). As a supplementary source of his knowledge, Eliphaz refers impressively to a special revelation vouchsafed to him in a hair-raising (v. 15) night vision. His account of the mysterious appearance and voice (vv. 15,16) serves to cast a prophetic mantle about him. (For similar features in theophanies witnessed by Abraham, Moses, and Elijah, see Gen 15:12; Num 12:8; I Kgs 19:12.) The content of the alleged revelation is presented in Job 4:17-21. **Shall mortal man be just before God? Shall a man be pure before his Maker?** (v. 17, ASV marg.; cf. RSV) The AV and ASV translation is also grammatically possible and would provide as suitable a rebuke for the challenge to God's government implicit in Job's complaint. If by comparison with God's wisdom, even the wisdom of angels is imperfect (v. 18), certainly man who lives and dies **without wisdom** (v. 21b, ASV) is not qualified to sit in judgment over God's ways. Analyzing man's inferiority to angels in terms of his mortality, Eliphaz echoes the divine verdict against man's body of dust (v. 19; cf. Gen 3:19). In comparison with angelic life, human life, like that of the moth (Job 4:19,20), is fleeting. Man's death is like the collapse of a tent when its cord is loosed (v. 21, ASV).

5:1-7. If Eliphaz had applied to himself the message of the Lord's transcendent wisdom and man's lack thereof sent him in the night vision, he would not have volunteered so dogmatic an explanation of God's dealings with Job. **Affliction cometh not forth from the dust . . . but man is born unto trouble** (vv. 6a, 7a, ASV; cf. 4:8). Though a servant of God, he insists, Job is still a fallen mortal. His troubles, therefore, did not **spring out of the ground** like a magical harvest, never sown; they are the thorny fruits of his sins. Hence, neither men nor angels can listen sympathetically to his cry (v. 1). **Vexation killeth the foolish man** (v. 2a, ASV). To display resentment against

God's providence is worse than futile; it invites affliction unto death. **I have seen the foolish** (v. 3a). Again Eliphaz' authority is experience. His thoughtless sketch of the cursing of the house, field, and children of the churlish fool (vv. 3-5), reminiscent as it was of Job's recent losses, might well have made Job wonder whether Eliphaz judged him to be such a fool.

8-27. Eliphaz urges the murmuring victim to submit trustfully to God. The core concept of his exhortation is the beatitude of the chastened man (v. 17). He describes the goodness of God's marvelous ways (vv. 8-16), prophesies of the happiness that will follow upon repentance (vv. 18-26), and adds a confident guarantee of the wisdom he has offered (v. 27).

8-16. But as for me, I would seek unto God (v. 8, ASV). The unscarred sage has no doubt how he would act if tempted like Job. His advice is clearly sound; his account of the goodness of God's providence and His special interest in the mourning poor is excellent (see Paul's quotation of v. 13 in I Cor 3:19). But his misinterpretation of Job's extraordinary sufferings and his uncharitable attitude indispose Job to profit from this exhortation.

17. Happy is the man whom God correcteth. Eliphaz recognizes the distinction between chastisement and punishment, and he appreciates the ultimate benefits of God's fatherly chastening. However, his views of the relation of sin and suffering leave no room for other purposes, such as trial and testimony, in the suffering of the righteous. (For further comments on this theme see 33:31-33.)

18-26. Crops and flocks restored (vv. 23,24; ASV, **shalt miss nothing** rather than AV *shalt not sin)*, numerous **offspring** (v. 25), and long life (v. 26)—these are indeed to be Job's happy portion. Eliphaz spoke more truth than he realized, too, in predicting deliverance from **the scourge of the tongue** (v. 21a), as the reader, aware of Satan's slanders and the friends' misjudgments, well knows. The skill of the author is evident in this early anticipation of the actual outcome, presented as it is in the form of a forecast based on such profound misunderstanding. For Eliphaz was mistaken in assuming that renewed prosperity always follows repentance. Suffering is not sent in exact proportion to sin in this life, and neither is prosperity granted in proportion to piety. All depends on God's good pleasure.

b) Job's Reply to Eliphaz. 6:1–7:21.

The presence of the philosophers had set Job to speculating about his fate, and that led to his questioning God's *wisdom* (ch. 3). The pronouncements of Eliphaz concerning the relation of sin to suffering had introduced a theme that was to lead Job to question the *justice* of God; for Job knew that his own extraordinary sufferings could not be accounted for on the ground of extraordinary sins. In this first reply, however, the patriarch does not engage in theological discussion about God's justice, but vents again his inner ferment, the consequence of his sense of estrangement from the God who afflicted him. That had been the undercurrent of Job's original complaint, and the efforts of Eliphaz had only aggravated it. The present speech is, therefore, a continuation of the complaint, with certain new overtones. Beginning on the defensive, Job justifies his original outburst (6:1-13). Then, taking the offensive, he reproves his friends for their pitiless attitude (6:14-30). Finally, turning from his friends to God, he renews his lament (7:1-21).

6:1-13. As the plural forms indicate, this chapter is addressed to all the friends. For they all concurred in the views of Eliphaz, and by glance and gesture had no doubt signified the "Amen" which would presently become vocal in their own speeches. **Oh that my vexation were but weighed** (v. 2a, ASV). Job ignores Eliphaz' insinuations as to the cause of his desolation, and defends the vexation expressed in his complaint. To Eliphaz the complaint had sounded ominous (5:2). But, says Job, if the **rash** (v. 6:3b, ASV) words wrenched from his lips by anguish were placed in the scales, they would easily be overbalanced by his calamities, which were heavier than the sand of the sea. **The arrows of the Almighty . . . the terrors of God** (v. 4). An aloofness, an almost sullen resentment, had been betrayed in Job's complaint by his reluctance to mention God even as the author of his sufferings. The vigorously theistic interpretation of Eliphaz did at least prompt a wholesome change in this regard. Job now frankly expresses his feeling that God is confronting him like an enemy, marshaling hosts of terrors against him. In further defense of his complaint, Job observes that even animals do not complain without reason (v. 5). And it is only natural for a man to reject insipid, loathsome food (vv. 6,7). Then, recalling Eliphaz' description of the death of frail mortals (4:19-21), Job declares that death is precisely what he longs for (vv. 8,9). **I would even exult in pain unsparing** (v. 10b, RSV). Even if he should die the kind of death Eliphaz says is reserved for the ungodly, it would be welcome. Nor would it, in his case, be the death of the ungodly; for contrary to the insinuations of Eliphaz, he had **not denied the words of the Holy One** (v. 10c, ASV). **What is my end, that I should be patient?** (v. 11b, RSV) Job's resources for endurance were spent. In spite of Eliphaz' fair predictions, the future in this world was hopeless.

14-30. Eliphaz has attacked Job's complaint; Job now attacks Eliphaz' "consolation." **My brethren have dealt deceitfully as a brook** (v. 15a). He has not begged favors, such as a great ransom (vv. 22,23)—only the pity a man naturally expects from friends. Yet he has been as bitterly disappointed in his "comforters" as a thirsty desert caravan when it reaches the eagerly anticipated wady—sometimes a rushing, dark torrent—and finds not even a trickle among the rocks (vv. 15-21). **Ye see a terror, and are afraid** (v. 21b, ASV). . . . **And make merchandise of your friend** (v. 27b, ASV). Their pitiless procedure, says Job, is dictated by fear that terrors like his may be visited upon them. If they should show him sympathy, God might misinterpret their concern as criticism of His providence, and He might plague them similarly. To buy God's partiality for themselves, they insinuate that Job must have sinned in proportion to his sufferings. As evidence they point to the rebellious tone of his complaint. But his desperate words uttered under extreme provocation give no proof of his normal attitude and conduct (v. 26). **Return, I pray you** (v. 29a; i.e., "Stop begging the theological question by assuming my guilt, for I am righteous" (v. 30).

7:1-21. In the midst of his replies Job repeatedly turns from his friends and addresses himself to God. The structure of the patriarch's individual speeches thus reflects the over-all course of his inner struggle as, disappointed by earthly friends, he is compelled to look anew to his heavenly Friend and divine Redeemer for understanding.

1-16. Like the days of an hireling (v. 1). Human existence, and Job's life in particular, is like a soldier's hard campaign or a field laborer's weary grind. It is a succession of days of panting for the cool of evening, and restless nights of longing for the morning, a round of misery and hopelessness (vv. 1-6). **Thine eyes shall be upon me, but I shall not be** (v. 8b, ASV). Reverting to the theme of human mortality introduced by Eliphaz, Job builds upon it his renewed complaint. He introduces (vv. 7-10) and concludes (v. 21b) his appeal for relief (vv. 11-21a) with the pathetic prospect of the Deity looking for his faithful servant too late to show him overdue pity. **Am I the sea, or a sea-monster?** (v. 12a, RSV) To judge from the incessant surveillance kept over him, Job says, one would think he was the chaos-monster (a mythological figure, cf. 3:8) threatening the stability of the universe.

17-21. What is man (v. 17a). An ironic twist is given to Ps 8:4 (cf. Ps 144:3). The contrast between divine transcendence and human finitude is exploited to minimize the significance of human action. **If I have sinned, what do I unto thee** (v. 20a, ASV). Actually, of course, God's transcendence magnifies the seriousness of sin; it is the foundation of the meaningfulness of human experience and of all that is. Moreover, this struggle of Job was particularly significant because it had been made the test case for this very truth of the transcendent authority and control of God over history. In Job's temptation the stability of the universe was under attack—as the "sons of God" could have told Job—by the real "dragon" (cf. Rev 20:2) of whom the mythical sea monster was a paganized version. The angels saw the world trembling with every tremor of Job's spirit. For if the redemptive power of God could not preserve Job in the fear of God, not only Job but the world was lost to satanic chaos.

c) First Discourse of Bildad. 8:1-22.

Bildad proves to be as insensible as Eliphaz regarding Job's wretchedness. He spurns the sufferer's defense of his complaint, ignores his criticism of the unsympathetic approach of the friends, and proceeds to give Job more of Eliphaz' counsel in the name of divine justice (vv. 2-7) and venerable tradition (vv. 8-19). Then he awkwardly appends a brief word of cheer (vv. 20-22).

2-7. How long (v. 2 a). Here is no appreciation of the months of patience; only indignation over a few minutes' impatience! **Doth God pervert justice?** (v. 3a, ASV) Of course God was not unjust to Job. But behind Bildad's rhetorical question lay the judgment that Job was reaping a harvest of sin. This issue of God's justice, though doubtless involved in Job's complaint, had not previously been foremost in his thoughts. The patriarch had contemplated his destiny more from the metaphysical perspective of divine transcendence and human finitude. By focusing attention on the judicial aspect, the comforters succeeded only in intensifying their friend's temptation. Job's theodicy was as inadequate as theirs. Reason therefore told him that God must be deeply grieved with him. But his conscience refused to acknowledge transgression commensurate with his suffering. Where then was justice? Where was the good God he had known? **He has delivered them into the power of their transgression** (v. 4b, RSV). An astonishingly heartless but thoroughly consistent application of the friends' thesis! Though the form is conditional, the intent is declarative. **If thou wouldest seek unto God** (v. 5a). Since Job's afflictions have not yet proved fatal, as his children's did, he may entertain hope that he is not, like them, reprobate and that his repentance will be followed by a restoration of blessing surpassing his former prosperity (v. 7; cf. 42:12).

8-19. Enquire . . . of the former age (v. 8). Aware of the limitations of the individual mortal (v. 9), Bildad would bolster the authority of personal observation with traditional lore (vv. 8,10). Between Bildad and Eliphaz there is no essential difference. Each builds on sand—on speculations drawn from the subjectivity of his own consciousness and the relativity of the changing world—rather than on the granite disclosures of the omniscient Creator. Bildad reproduces the proverbial wisdom of the fathers, couched in similes drawn mostly from the lush growth of swamp and garden (vv. 11-19). **So are the paths of all that forget God** (v. 13a). All the similes teach one lesson: the happiness of the wicked is fragile, perishable. If appearances sometimes seem to contradict the traditional theory that suffering is the wages of sin, it is never for long. But why does Bildad allow a warning designed for the ungodly to dominate his counsel to Job?

20-22. The peroration states the application of Bildad's doctrine to the **perfect** and to **evildoers** (v. 20, ASV). The speaker offers some encouragement for Job, but it is brief and perfunctory (vv. 21,22). Though the sufferer finds himself here in the category of the "perfect," he cannot forget Bildad's earlier **If** (v. 6).

d) Job's Reply to Bildad. 9:1–10:22.

Following the general pattern of his previous reply, Job addresses himself first to the friends (9:1-24), then more or less directly to God (9:25–10:22). He opens his rebuttal of Bildad with sarcastic endorsement of his friend's opening (and fundamental) theme (9:2; cf. 8:3) and closes with vehement contradiction of Bildad's closing (and dominant) contention (9:22-24; cf. 8:20-22). Then Job resumes his complaint to God in the mood of reckless defiance to which the counsel of the friends has goaded him. In this speech he plunges into the darkest depth of his imagined alienation from God. Though he approaches blasphemy in his frenzy, he does not turn from God with a curse but wrestles on in prayer. For Satan cannot pluck him from his Father's hand.

9:1-24. Of a truth I know that it is so (v. 2a, ASV). See comments on 8:3. The judicial aspect of the situation now looms large to Job. God appears to him a prosecuting judge. **But how can man be just with God?** (v. 2b, ASV) Though this question is similar in form to Eliphaz' revelation (4:17), its meaning is different. Job is not saying that man, being a fallen mortal, cannot stand in his own integrity before God. He is saying (as the following verses show) that no matter what the righteousness of a man's cause, he is too puny and ignorant to defend it successfully in court before the overwhelming wisdom and power of God. The thought of God's transcendence had led Job to ask why God should bother to afflict a frail man. Now the same thought provokes the question, Why should a frail man bother to contend against God? This question exposes Job's loss of the sense of God's loving-kindness. **The Almighty seems to** confront him like a giant adversary.

Which doeth great things past finding out (v. 10a). Again Job gives a new application to a quotation from Eliphaz (cf. 5:9) by way of answering Bildad. Eliphaz spoke these words as a ground for Job's committing his cause to God (5:8) and illustrated with gracious works of providence (5:10-16). Job repeats them to show how futile it is for him to plead his cause before God. And he illustrates with more ominous examples of the sheer omnipotence of God's cosmic rule (vv. 5-13). In the final illustration Job apparently adopts again the imagery of current mythology, **the helpers of Rahab** (v. 13b, ASV), to depict God's rule over the sea (cf. 26:12). **He cannot answer him one of a thousand. . . . Though I were righteous, yet would I not answer, but I would make supplication to my judge** (vv. 3b, 15). This strikingly anticipates the subsequent theophany (38:3ff.) and Job's response (40:3-5). Yet the preview is again subtly veiled in misunderstanding. For the reality which will prove to be the prelude to joy regained, here seems to Job a dismal eventuality. **I am perfect** (v. 21a, ASV). This section terminates in a crescendo of invective, Job's exclamations becoming almost incoherently staccato. In utter despair of ever establishing his integrity before the irresistible God, who seems bent on breaking him **without cause** (v. 17b; cf. 2:3), Job nevertheless defiantly affirms his uprightness. **He destroyeth the perfect and the wicked** (v. 22b). The assertion of the friends that only the wicked are carried away violently needs correction; Job, however, fails to discern the love of God in the death of the righteous. **He will laugh at the trial of the innocent** (v. 23b), just as, sitting unassailable in the heavens, he will "have in derision" (Ps 2:4, the same word as is here translated **laugh**) the rebels raging against his throne. The friends had condemned Job that God might be righteous—according to their standard. Job, defending himself against their unjustified insinuations, is driven to condemn God that he himself might be righteous (cf. 40:8).

9:25–10:22. The sufferer bewails his sorrows, continuing to interpret them as tokens of divine condemnation. He cannot suppress his longing for a day in court, though he has no hope of being granted such a privilege. Hence, he reasons earnestly with the strange God, the phantom creation of his frenzied doubt.

9:25-35. Now my days are swifter than a post (v. 25a). The opportunity for the Judge to reverse his decision and return Job's prosperity will soon be gone. Job compares the swift passage of his miserable life to those things that are fleetest on land (v. 25), on the sea (v. 26a), and in the air (v. 26b). **Yet shalt thou plunge me in the ditch** (v. 31a). Even if the case came to court and Job proved his innocence as effectively as human skill could (v. 30), the Judge would overpower him with charges of guilt. **There is no umpire between us** (v. 33a, RSV). Here, when Job's faith is at its lowest ebb, there emerges in this complaining negative form the concept of the Mediator, which was afterwards to become for Job a positive conviction. This concept attains its grandest expression in the speech (ch. 19) that marks the crest reached by Job's faith within the course of the debate. For lack of a *daysman*, Job trembles before the omnipotent One, who seems determined to terrorize him into dumbness (vv. 33-35) and find him guilty.

10:1-22. I will give free course to my complaint (v. 1b, ASV). With the bravado of despair Job questions the Judge who condemns him (v. 2). He appeals to God against God—to the nature of the God he had known against the phantom God who contends against him. In particular, Job appeals to God's pride of office as Judge (vv.3-7) and to his Creatorhood (vv. 8-12). Is God subject to human limitations, liable therefore to misread the facts (v. 4) or fail to overtake the guilty (vv. 5,6)? No. He has the qualifications to be judge of all the earth; he is omniscient and omnipotent (v. 7). **Thine hands have made me** (v. 8a). Does the Creator destroy the creature on which he has expended such marvelous skill in the processes of procreation and gestation (vv. 10,11) and such providential care (v. 12)?

The imaginary "trial" of God ends as the reality of pain and ignominy reasserts itself in Job's consciousness. The phantom God has prevailed, it seems, and Job changes abruptly from appeal to complaint and lament (vv. 13-22). **Yet these things thou didst hide in thy heart**

(v. 13a, ASV). God's secret design in the earliest formation and nurture of Job's life was to prepare a prey to be stalked like a lion, mercilessly, relentlessly (vv. 14-16). God's hidden purpose was all the while to make that life miserable at last by witnessing to its guilt with an unending host of plagues (v. 17). **Wherefore then hast thou brought me forth out of the womb?** (v. 18a) The consideration of God's role in the origin of his life brings Job back to the theme of his original complaint (cf. 3:11). **Let me alone** (v. 20b). Cut off, as he feels himself to be, from the *love* of God, the most he can ask, before he slips into the darkness of death, is that God will simply cease paying attention to him for a moment. Nevertheless, it is still to God that Job cries.

e) First Discourse of Zophar. 11:1-20.

Job had reacted to Eliphaz' and Bildad's concentration on his judicial status with increasingly intense protestations of innocence. These in turn provoked the friends to ever more consistent application of their theory, until Zophar now bluntly condemns Job's alleged iniquity (vv. 1-6). He supports his charge by appealing to God's infinity (vv. 7-12), yet he concludes with an assurance of restored prosperity (vv. 13-20).

1-6. Job had insisted that God had afflicted him knowing him to be righteous (v. 4; cf. 9:21; 10:7). That, Zophar points out, contradicts traditional theory, is irreligious, and can not be allowed to stand as the last word. **Should a man full of talk be justified?** (v. 2b) The customary introductory courtesies, dispensed with altogether by Bildad, are thus dispatched by Zophar with such haste and distaste that accusation merges with apology. **But oh that God would speak, and open his lips against thee** (v. 5). Job seems irrepressible in controversy with his fellows; but if he were granted the very thing he himself longs for, an open debate with God (cf. 9:35), he would be silenced. **Know therefore that God exacteth of thee less than thine iniquity deserveth** (v. 6b). More literally, *God causes to be forgotten for thee some of thine iniquity*. In his zeal to contradict Job's complaint that God searches out and mercilessly marks his every sin (cf. 10:6,14), afflicting him out of proportion to his iniquities, Zophar ventures to modify the other two friends' theory of direct ratio—but in the opposite direction from Job! Here is the climax of condemnation in the first cycle. Job 11:6 is pivotal; it concludes the indictment but also introduces the following theme by mentioning the unfathomable wisdom of God (cf. 5:9).

7-12. Canst thou find out the Almighty unto perfection? (v. 7b) By his infinite wisdom God comprehends and controls creation in its height and depth, length and breadth (vv. 8,9). **Who can hinder him?** (v. 10b) If God wills to bring a man into judgment, the man cannot escape. Zophar thus endorses the conclusion Job had earlier drawn from the absolute wisdom of God, namely, that resistance to Him is futile (cf. 9:12; 10:7b). But while Job had also appealed to the divine omniscience for vindication of his innocence (10:7a), Zophar does so to convict Job of guilt: **He seeth wickedness also** (v. 11b). Having openly condemned Job, and being ignorant himself of any direct evidence to substantiate his charge, Zophar finds it convenient to supplement his own ignorance with the omniscience of the Almighty. He would have made better use of his excellent doctrine of the incomprehensibility of God, however, if he had humbly recognized the limitations of his own knowledge of divine providence and had not presumed to understand Job's sufferings to perfection. This truth of God's unsearchable wisdom, though sadly mishandled by Zophar, is the doctrine that should have quieted Job's spirit and silenced his complaints. By reckoning more seriously with it, Job and his friends alike would have recognized that his sufferings were compatible with exemplary piety on one side and divine favor on the other. It is primarily by the proclamation of His incomprehensibility that the Lord Himself later delivers Job from his temptation. Thus again the author of the book employs veiled anticipation. In 11:12 he uses another favorite device, clinching an argument with a proverbial saying. He cites the asininity of vain men as a foil for the infinity of divine wisdom.

13-20. Compare the similar appeals of Eliphaz (5:8ff.) and Bildad (8:5-7,20-22). Contrary to Job's pessimistic opinion (9:28; 10:15), suit for God's favor would be successful (v. 15). At least it would be if preceded by thoroughgoing repentance, extending to heart, hand, and home (vv. 13,14; cf. Ps 24:4). By laying down this condition Zophar manages to insinuate accusation into the midst of consolation. Renewal of God's favor will be accompanied by restoration of prosperity, in which present grief will be forgotten **as waters that are passed away** (v. 16b, ASV). Also, contrary to Job's forebodings of unrelieved darkness (10:21,22), a bright dawning of hope, peaceful security, and honor, as of old, awaits him (vv. 17-19). **But the eyes of the wicked shall fail** (v. 20a). Zophar's growing suspicion of Job suggests the advisability of his seasoning consolation further with warning. He closes by identifying the only hope of the wicked with death, in words clearly resembling Job's description of his own prospects. Zophar's pattern of repentance and restoration was to be worked out; but in a way quite surprising to him.

f) Job's Reply to Zophar. 12:1–14:22. Thoroughly contemptuous of the arrogant ignorance of his counselors, Job subjects them to devastating criticism (12:1–13:12). He declares his righteousness to his friends (13:13-19), then once more appeals directly to God (13:20–14:22). In the midst of this appeal, a new hope dawns in Job's soul—the hope of life beyond Sheol! Though despondency darkens Job's concluding words, it is clear that in this reply to Zophar, his faith has begun its triumphant ascent out of the abyss of despair.

12:1–13:12. Wisdom shall die with you (12:2b). Job's sarcasm suggests how insufferable he found the pretensions of the trio who had all sung the same empty tune. Their words would continue to sting but he would no longer take them seriously as possible solutions to the riddle of his sufferings. **I am not inferior to you** (12:3b; cf. 13:2). The familiar formulae they recited hardly justify their attitude of superiority. **In the thought of him that is at ease there is contempt for misfortune** (12:5a, ASV). In sheer exasperation Job bewails the whole situation. Because of his troubles, a man of godly wisdom is treated like a simpleton or criminal on the basis of a theory that is contradicted by another (equally distressing) fact, namely, that robbers are prospering while he is reduced to such mockery (12:4-6). **Into whose hand God bringeth** (12:6c). Better, *who bring their god in their hand* (ASV marg. and RSV). Lamech-like (cf. Gen 4:23,24; Dan 11:38) they idolize the weapon in their hand.

Ask now the beasts (12:7a). The three friends' doctrine of God's majestic wisdom is common knowledge; all creation teaches it. In 12:11-25 Job demonstrates his familiarity with the concept of divine rule, which his friends thought to teach him. His account of it, indeed, surpasses their own (cf. Ps 107). All the glory and dignity of man's earthly kingdoms are at the mercy of God's sovereign might (Job 12:23; cf. I Cor 1:25). The elemental forces of nature are at his disposal to overturn the earth (Job 12:15; cf. Gen 7). The highest civil and cultic dignitaries are impotent against him (Job 12:17-21,24). Verse 19 mentions *priests* (ASV) and *'ētānîm* (cf. Ugaritic *ytnm*, a temple guild). Job takes special delight in expounding the text: "Hath not God made foolish the wisdom of this world?" (I Cor 1:20), and one need not look far to discover certain wise men he had particularly in mind.

Surely I would speak to the Almighty (13:3a; cf. 5:8). Mounting disgust with human helpers drives Job again to reason with God, but first he delivers a scathing rebuke to the self-appointed legal counsel for God (13:4-12). **And it should be your wisdom** (v. 5b). If they had never broken their seven days' silence, they would not have exposed their stupidity (cf. Prov 17:28). **Will you show partiality toward him, will you plead the case for God?** (13:8, RSV) They have disgraced their dignity by servility. Worse, they have curried God's favor at the expense of truth: **ye are forgers** [lit. *plasterers*] **of lies** (13:4; cf. v. 7). See the similar charge in 6:21,27. **Your memorable sayings are proverbs of ashes, Your defenses are . . . of clay** (13:12, ASV). The weighty maxims by which they falsely condemn Job in order to justify God are as vulnerable to the hammer of truth as clay to a hammer of iron. Their defense of God was an offense to God. They equated a certain providential procedure, falsely assumed to be invariably followed, with divine justice. In effect, they set up an abstract principle as an absolute and so subordinated God to it. **Is it good that he should search you out?** (13:9a) Zophar sought to convict Job of his supposed guilt by haling him before the bar of God's omniscience. The patriarch reminds him and his associate prosecuting attorneys that, in the process of indicting him, they too have come to stand before that Judge; and under such scrutiny their impious motives and false charges cannot escape detection. **He will surely reprove you** (13:10a) is Job's accurate prediction (cf. 42:7ff.). Though Job's confidence in the justice of God is obscured, in his more desperate moments, by his ascription of absolute caprice to the Almighty, he has not lost it altogether.

13:13-19. In the process now of turning from men to God, Job stirs up his courage to face his Judge. **Let come on me what will** (v. 13b). He intends to plead his cause at all hazards, even though it may imperil his life (v. 14). **Behold, he will slay me; I have no hope: Nevertheless I will maintain my ways before him** (v. 15, ASV). This translation follows the Hebrew text, and it suits the context better than the familiar AV rendering – *yet will I trust in him.* The latter depends on the Masoretic marginal suggestion to read *lô* ("for him") instead of *lōʾ* ("not"). The verb in the disputed clause means "wait in patiently eager expectation" (cf. 6:11; 14:14). Job has nothing to look forward to, for he expects God to terminate his life very soon – perhaps all the sooner for the bold plea he is about to make. Nevertheless, he *must* declare his innocence. **This also shall be my salvation** (v. 16a, ASV). This daring desire to come before God is itself a token of a favorable verdict; for the presence of God is the one place shunned above all others by one whose heart condemns him as a hypocrite. **Who is there that will contend with me? For then I would be silent and die** (v. 19, RSV). A triumphant challenge, but unseemly if Job envisages God as well as men. If he could be successfully contradicted, if he could be proved ungodly in reality—and not just according to appearances and theories—, he would die dumb. But that, he knows, is impossible: **I know that I shall be justified** (v. 18b).

13:20–14:22. Then will I not hide myself from thee (13:20b). If granted a fair trial, Job will not, like Adam, flee from God, covered with shame. If only God will desist for a time from oppressing him and refrain from overwhelming him with his terrible majesty (13:21; cf. 9:34, 35), Job will appear before him either as defendant or as complainant (v. 22). If Job can successfully defend his integrity, it will be evident (according to his inadequate concept of human suffering) that God has been at fault in afflicting him so severely. Or, if Job is to succeed in convicting God of such wrong, he must first demonstrate his own integrity. Imagining himself as confronting his tormentor in the coveted trial, the sufferer now demands an explanation of God's hostility (13:23,24). But the judicial scene quickly fades, and the court oratory turns into the customary closing lamentation (13:25ff.).

Thou . . . makest me to possess the iniquities of my youth (13:26b). Compare with this the affirmation of man's universal sinfulness in 14:4. When Job was disputing with his friends, the issue at stake was his general integrity, concerning which he was outspokenly confident. But apparently, in the imagined confrontation with the Judge, that issue yielded to the more penetrating question of the status of a sinner before the perfectly holy One. Job's later response to the actual theophany is foreshadowed here (cf. 40:3-5). Meanwhile, his fearful desolation, not accounted for by the general sinfulness of men, crushes his spirit. **Turn from him, that he may rest, till he shall accomplish, as an hireling, his day** (14:6). Though this lament is expressed in terms of the frailty of all mortals, it is nevertheless personal (cf. 14:3b). Let the common toil and sorrow of mankind suffice for Job (cf. 7:1ff.; Gen 3:17-19). **Till the heavens be no more, they shall not awake** (14:12b). Once laid low in death, man, like a felled tree (14:7-9), has no prospect of standing again on the earth (14:10-12). (For the eternity of the heavens, cf. Ps 72:5,7,17; 89:29,36,37; Jer 31:35,36.) Job does not expect annihilation, but he despairs of anything beyond death except existence in Sheol, which is not real life.

Recoiling from such gloom, he exclaims: **Oh that thou wouldest hide me in Sheol . . . and remember me!** (14:13, ASV) If this longing would come true; if Sheol were only a temporary abode and, indeed, a place of relief from the present inexplicable hostility of God (v. 13); if beyond Sheol there were a resurrection change (v. 14c) springing from renewed compassion in the Creator (v. 15) – so blessed a future would transfigure the present warfare (v. 14b)! The concept of resurrection does not provide the key to unlock the mystery of Job's present suffering, but it does offer a framework for hope. Job's yearning later becomes conviction (19:25ff.), and such a hope is glorious. This ultimate hope of redemption is not, however, the central theme of the Book of Job. The book does, indeed, challenge us to endure, with hope. But it confronts us with an even more profound demand. It sounds the primary and everlasting call for glad consecration, come what may, to the covenant Lord.

But now thou numberest my steps (14:16a, ASV). The curve of Job's spiritual state through the course of the great debate is graphed in reduced scale in individual replies like this, where the climax is not at the end but is followed by an emotional decrescendo. The flame of the patriarch's hope is extinguished, though only for the moment, by his bitter thoughts of the unsparing severity of God, who miser-like hordes up Job's every sin for visitation (14:16,17). **Thou destroyest the hope of man** (14:19c). By incessant affliction, even as a constant force in nature wears away the most durable objects (14:18,19). **Thou prevailest for ever against him** (14:20a). God's hostility culminates in the death stroke, cutting man off from rapport with this world, even from knowledge of his posterity (14:21), shutting him up to himself in death, to the endless dull pain of decomposition and the soul's dreary dirge (14:22).

2) Second Cycle of Debate. 15:1–21:34.

a) Second Discourse of Eliphaz. 15:1–35.

How a round of debate can alienate friends! The genteel Eliphaz forgets even introductory civilities. All is new censorious warning. The philosopher exposes his professional sensitivity to Job's slights (cf. 12:2,3,7ff.; 13:1,2,5,12) by reverting to the relative wisdom of himself and Job each time he introduces a new indictment (cf. vv. 1ff., 7ff., 17ff.).

1-6. Vain knowledge (v. 2a). Literally, *knowledge of wind*. Cf. the parallel **east wind** (v. 2b), i.e., the violent, suffocating desert blast. Job's claims to wisdom are belied by his windy speeches (v. 3). **Yea, thou doest away with fear, And hinderest devotion before God** (v. 4, ASV). Job's brazen outbursts are worse than intemperate, for they depreciate the fear of God, and so undermine religion. **The tongue of the crafty** (v. 5b). Possibly an allusion to the "subtle" (same word) serpent in Gen 3:1. Job's guilt explains his words (v. 5), and his words prove his guilt (v. 6).

7-16. The friends have the advantage over Job in age and hence in wisdom (vv. 7-10; cf. 12:12). His bravado to the contrary, Job has not the antiquity of Adam nor of some primeval beings (v. 7; cf. wisdom personified in Prov 8:22ff.). Neither has he any special, secret knowledge of God's decrees (Job 15:8; cf. the heavenly scenes in the Prologue). Perhaps verse 10 refers particularly to Eliphaz. **Are the consolations of God too small for thee** (v. 11, ASV). A rather charitable description of the friends' counsel, but in line with Eliphaz' alleged special revelation (4:12ff.), which he now echoes (vv. 14-16; cf. 4:17-19). The purpose of the repetition is revealed by a comparison of 15:16 with 4:19. Eliphaz seeks to express his revised estimate of Job as one who lusts disgustingly after sin.

17-35. Unto whom alone the earth was given (v. 19a). In addition to the personal observations of the eldest contemporaries (v. 17; cf. v. 10), Eliphaz invokes the sanction of purest tradition (vv. 18,19) to support his retribution dogma and contradict the Joban heresy that the ungodly often prosper (cf. 12:6). The prosperity of the wicked, with whom Job (by his afflictions) is evidently identified, is merely imaginary (vv. 20-35). **He believeth not that he shall return out of darkness** (v. 22a). His peace is ruined by presentiments of calamity without remedy (vv. 20-24), the tormenting forebodings of a conscience defiled by carnal ease and contempt of God (vv. 25-28). Every promising enterprise he undertakes proves abortive (vv. 29-34), according to the law of retribution (v. 35), which may be delayed but not thwarted. Eliphaz has here sounded the counselors' keynote for the second round of debate.

b) Job's Second Reply to Eliphaz. 16:1–17:16.

As the crisis of faith nears, Job pays little attention to his friends' arguments, except to express his disappointment in a brief introduction (16:1-5). In the remainder of this speech Job seems to be musing aloud and only occasionally addressing his words to God (16:8; 17:3,4) or to his friends (17:10).

16:1-5. Miserable comforters (v. 2b). Literally, *comforters of trouble*. A sarcastic response to Eliphaz' query (15:11). The counsel of the three friends has not merely been irrelevant; but it has also betrayed their ignorance of the comfort of redemptive righteousness.

6-17. Though I speak (v. 6a). It seems useless to Job to continue the lament and the debate, for both man and God are set against him. His fervent protestations of innocence have been and will be interpreted as proof of godlessness. Devoid of inner resources and outer reinforcements (v. 7), he is labeled "sinner" by his impotent wretchedness (v. 8). **He hath torn me in his wrath** (v. 9a, ASV). It seems to Job that God has savagely rent him (v. 9), and given him over to the spiteful rabble, who had once been obliged to respect him (vv. 10,11). God shatters (v. 12a) and batters (v. 14) him, piercing his vitals (vv. 12b,13) and reducing him to a sobbing wreck, prostrate in the dust (vv. 15,16). And all without cause: **Although there is no violence in my hands, And my prayer is pure** (v. 17, ASV; cf. Isa 53:9).

16:18—17:3. The power of God that is made known to a man in his weakness now enables Job to hope against hope. **O earth, cover not thou my blood** (v. 18a). The cry of Job's innocent blood demanding vindication must not be muffled (cf. Gen 4:10; Heb 12:24). **Even now, behold, my witness is in heaven** (v. 19a, ASV). This heavenly witness-avenger is God himself! Job prays to him with tears (v. 20b), that he will **maintain the right of a man with God and with his neighbor** (v. 21, ASV). This paradoxical faith in God to advocate Job's case against God, who now slays him, reappears in the plea: **Give now a pledge, be surety for me with thyself** (17:3, ASV). Let God covenant to establish Job's integrity at the time of judgment.

17:4-9. Verse 4 is transitional. It explains that God must provide Job's pledge because human friends refuse to do so, and it launches a lament over the patriarch's public humiliation. Job's experience cannot but astound righteous men (v. 8). But they (and Job among them) will persevere the more in righteousness, undaunted by the irregular dealings of providence or the slanders of the public. A triumphant confession; it confounds Satan's hopes (cf. 2:5).

10-16. Job's changes in mood are abrupt and extreme. Disdainfully inviting the wisdomless wise men to renew their witless counsel (v. 10), Job concludes with a description of his pathetic plight —on the brink of community with the worms.

c) Second Discourse of Bildad. 18: 1-21.

In his longing for a divine advocate, Job probes far deeper into the mystery of godliness than do his counselors, whose later replies degenerate into irrelevant harangues on the woes of the wicked.

1-4. Resentful of Job's low estimate of his accusers' acumen (v. 3; cf. 17:10; 12:7), Bildad retorts in kind: **Thou that tearest thyself in thine anger** (v. 4a, ASV), like a stupid brute, bellowing the while that God is to blame (cf. 16:9). To judge from the way Job beats himself to death against the established order of creation and providence (in particular, against the law of retribution invoked by the friends), it would seem that he expects the universe to be redesigned just for him (v. 4b, c). The plural forms in verses 2 and 3 are possibly in sarcastic allusion to Job's associating himself with the company of the righteous (cf. 17: 8,9).

5-21. This word-painting, entitled by the artist **the dwellings of the wicked** (v. 21a), is not an exact likeness of its original, but it is sufficiently so for Job to recognize it as his portrait. He beholds his tent-site strewn with brimstone, symbol of God's perpetual curse (v. 15b; cf. 1:16; Gen 19:24; Deut 29:23). He sees himself being consumed by **the firstborn of death** (v. 13b), i.e., deadly disease; being hurried off to **the king of terrors** (v. 14b), death itself; being chased into oblivion (vv. 16-19), a spectacle of horror at which people involuntarily shudder (v. 20).

d) Job's Second Reply to Bildad. 19: 1-29.

Felled by Bildad's brutal judgments (cf. 18:20), Job cannot summon the contemptuous indifference he showed toward the disputants in his previous speech. He is starved for understanding, and he seeks pity from his fellow human beings (19:2-22). But he finds them inhuman still. In his extremity, however, he discovers again the breath of life in the love of God, his heavenly Sympathizer (vv. 23-29).

2-22. Job's introductory plaint leads to further self-defense, along with a description of his desolation (vv. 7-12) and isolation (vv. 13-19). If the friends are so antagonistic that they must prosecute the case against him (v. 5; cf. 22), let them **know now that God hath subverted** Job in his cause (v. 6a, ASV; Bildad used the same verb in 8:3, to which this is a delayed reaction). They are defending injustice. **Mine acquaintance are wholly estranged from me** (v. 13b, ASV). Job's sense of ostracism, aggravated by the debaters' callous handling of him, has become a crushing burden. He is avoided, forgotten, abhorred by all—from nodding acquaintance to closest family intimate (vv. 13-18), and last but not least by his group of counselors (v. 19). Out of this abandonment issues the double **Have pity upon me** (v. 21a). Enough of accusation and false charges! (v. 22) Thus this section comes full circle (cf. vv. 2,3), encompassing Job in dereliction.

23-29. Since his contemporaries disbelieve his personal witness to his integrity, Job wishes it might be committed to writing on a scroll (v. 23) or, more indelibly, on a rock (v. 24). Then it might secure a hearing and possibly a kinder verdict from some future generation. By the inclusion of Job's history in the Scriptures, that wish has been realized beyond his imagining. Job despaired, however, of any fulfillment whatsoever. Besides, what his soul most craved was not human but divine vindication. The look to the future was, therefore, only preliminary to the look unto heaven: **But I know that my Redeemer lives and at the last he shall arise upon the dust** (v. 25). The hope of a heavenly, a divine vindicator which had been gathering strength in Job's soul (cf. 9:33; 16:18ff.) is here perfected. The office of the redeemer (*gô'ēl*) was that of next of kin. It was his responsibility to restore the fortune, liberty, and name of his relative, when necessary, and to redress his wrongs, especially to avenge the shedding of innocent blood. Job is confident that although all earthly kin may disown him (cf. v. 13 ff.), his divine kinsman is prepared to own him and to speak in his favor the last word in the case (cf. Isa 44:6). The heavenly *gô'ēl*, hearing the cry of Job's innocent blood from the dust of his grave (cf. Job 16:18; 17:16), will pursue his defamers (vv. 28,29) and avenge his name.

And after the loss of my skin which is thus destroyed, even from my flesh shall I see God (v. 26). Like English "from," the Hebrew preposition here translated "from" is ambiguous, meaning "in" or "without" (though the latter meaning is not attested elsewhere with a verb of perception). Job still regards death as imminent for his wasted body, rapidly being destroyed by disease (cf. v. 20); but his earlier longing for a return from Sheol to true life (14:13-15) revives now as a firm hope. God will thoroughly fulfill his kinsman's office, even delivering Job from the tyranny of the king of terrors. Hence, Job will witness, as he never could if he were cut off in Sheol (cf. 14:21,22), the intervention of God in the real world for his vindication. However the phrase **from my flesh** is construed, Job still expresses the idea of a renewal of the whole man after death. The emphasis of 19:27 is probably not that Job rather than another will see God (AV), but that Job will behold God as his kinsman, **not as a stranger** (ASV) hostile to him (cf. vv. 11,12). Here are the beginnings of what progressive revelation would ultimately enunciate in the doctrines of the coming of Christ at the end times, the resurrection of the dead, and final judgment. The fact that neither Job nor any other speaker subsequently refers to these exalted convictions is further indication that the author's purpose was not theodicy. This remarkable thrust of faith at the midpoint of the debate served to break the tension for Job, even though his spirit was unable to maintain this sublime level.

e) Second Discourse of Zophar. 20:1-29.

Job has struck such chords of redemptive truth as to thrill angels, but Zophar, having ears, hears not. He is enamored of Eliphaz' song, and he joins in close harmony with Bildad, continuing the ballad of the wicked man. Unfortunately, Zophar is too often content to draw the inspiration for his lyrics from the dunghill where the friends found Job.

I have heard the reproof which putteth me to shame (v. 3a, ASV). At the threat of God's pursuing him to avenge Job's blood (cf. 19:29), Zophar seethes with anger. He hastens to recast the actors, making Job the culprit on whom God wreaks vengeance for his oppression of the poor (v. 19). According to all the friends, the alleged prosperity of the wicked is deceptive, evanescent. Eliphaz stressed the continual inner unrest of the wicked; Bildad pointed to his perpetual desolation; Zophar emphasizes his sudden vengeance at the pinnacle of his rapacious career. While his ambition is in the clouds (v. 6) and **his bones are full of his youth** (v. 11, ASV), when he has just savored sin like a delicate morsel (vv. 12,13,15a), **in the fulness of his sufficiency** (v. 22)—then the Avenger overtakes him (v. 23). Verse 27 is a direct contradiction of Job's hope (cf. 16:18,19; 19:25) and serves, in case there should be some doubt in Job's mind, to identify Zophar's wicked man.

f) Job's Second Reply to Zophar. 21:1-34.

The accusers, blind to Job's transparent sincerity, have denied rather than explained the mystery of his afflictions. But stronger now in hope, Job rises above his disappointment in them and takes the initiative in the debate. His eyes, once opened by his own strange experience to the fallacy of the tidy traditional notion of retribution, perceive that history abounds in "exceptional" cases. After a prefatory request for attention (vv. 2-6), he proceeds to undermine the opposition by exposing the fallacy in their analysis of the fortunes of the wicked (vv. 7-34).

2-6. Let this be your consolations (v. 2b). Their open ears afford more comfort than their open mouths (cf. the similar sarcastic response to Zophar in 13:5). The force of Job's argument should silence them (v. 5).

7-34. Job describes the prosperity of the wicked, first in general terms (vv. 7-16), then in contradiction of the friends' specific representations (vv. 17-26), and finally by way of his self-defense (vv. 27-34).

7-16. Wherefore (v. 7). The apparent inequity of life, though it supports Job's case, troubles him (cf. v. 6) precisely because he recognizes that God governs all (vv. 9b,16a). It is indicative of Job's integrity that even in his misery he would not exchange places with the wicked rich (16b). Job does not, however, appreciate sufficiently the necessity of divine grace for the continuance of the fallen race in this world. Furthermore, he lacks understanding of the evangelical goal of the common grace enjoyed by unbelievers (Rom 2:4; cf. Mt 5:45).

17:26. How oft (v. 17). The patriarch challenges the statistics on which the accusers lean (cf. v. 29). Job himself exaggerates, but he is nearer the truth than his opponents. In 21:19a Job anticipates a possible evasion (cf. 5:4; 20:10) and rebuts it (21:19b-21). The verbs in verses 19b,20 have the force of command; e.g., **Let his own eyes see his destruction** (v. 20a, ASV). **Shall any teach God knowledge?** (v. 22a) The traditional theory constitutes a disguised criticism of God's actual ways (vv. 23-26).

27-34. I know your thoughts (v. 27a). Job recognized his image in their veiled portraits. **Have you not asked those who travel the roads?** (v. 29a, RSV) Though the friends recommend their observations as primeval law (cf. 20:4), they are ivory-tower theorists, out of touch with real life (cf. comments on 4:2-11). **The wicked man is spared in the day of calamity . . . he is rescued in the day of wrath** (v. 30, RSV). The AV would make Job inconsistently endorse his friends' view of the death of the wicked, whereas Job insists that the death of such men is often easy (vv. 13b, 23) and honorable (32,33). Job's estimate of the career of the unrighteous lacks a balancing emphasis (found to an extent in the friends' speeches) on their spiritual unrest during life and perdition hereafter. But by puncturing the balloon of airtight retribution, Job leaves his accusers clinging to falsehood (v. 34).

3. Third Cycle of Debate. 22:1—31:40.

a) Third Discourse of Eliphaz. 22:1-30.

The conclusion inherent in the three friends' theory from the beginning and ever more broadly hinted at is now blurted out unashamedly. This open accusation of Job was their only alternative to capitulation after Job's considered denial that justice is uniformly discernible in God's treatment of men. The lamentable fact is that the friends endorsed Satan's view of Job as a hypocrite. Thinking to defend God, they became Satan's advocates, insisting that he whom God designated as His servant belonged to the devil.

2-11. Since the all-sufficient God cannot be helped or harmed by man's actions, the answer to Job's sufferings cannot be in Him (vv. 2,3). Certainly Job is not being punished for piety: **Is it for thy fear of him that he reproveth thee?** (v. 4a, ASV) From these negative premises Eliphaz draws his positive conclusion in a sad betrayal of truth and brotherhood. **Is not thy wickedness great** (v. 5a). . . . **Therefore snares are round about thee** (v. 10a, ASV). For lack of real evidence Eliphaz finds the key to the precise nature of Job's crimes in his former wealth—its accumulation must have been stained by inhuman abuse of the poor and weak (vv. 6-9). Contrary to this drastic oversimplification of Job's dilemma, the Prologue has, of course, revealed to the reader that the answer was in God, who, though all-sufficient in himself, glorifies himself in his works and had decreed Job's trial for the praise of his redemptive wisdom.

12-20. And thou sayest, What doth God know? (v. 13a, ASV) Presuming to read Job's secret thoughts, Eliphaz puts in Job's mouth blasphemies untrue to the sentiments he has actually expressed (vv. 12-14). The fictitious argument is, then, unsatisfactorily answered by appeal to the unusual divine judgment on the Deluge generation (15ff.; cf. Gen 6:1-7; 8:21,22).

21-30. Eliphaz' last words, urging return to God in hope of peace and blessing, remind us that, in spite of all, he was a friend in the family of faith. Nevertheless, this consolation is vitiated by its Pharisaic spirit and its implicit repetition of the false accusations. In their distorted way these promises were prophetic of the sequel. Note especially 22:30: **He will deliver even him that is not innocent: Yea, he shall be delivered through the cleanness of thy hands** (ASV). Cf. Job's intercession for the friends (42:7-9).

b) Job's Third Reply to Eliphaz. 23:1–24:25.

The patriarch refrains from indignantly denying Eliphaz' unfounded charges, and resumes the theme of his previous speech (ch. 21). This monologue is, therefore, only indirectly a reply to Eliphaz. Job ponders the perplexing absence of discernible justice in God's dealings with himself, a righteous man (ch. 23), and with the wicked (ch. 24).

2-9. Even today is my complaint rebellious (v. 2a, ASV). Job stubbornly refuses to yield to any exhortation to penitence which implies that his sufferings are his just desert (cf. 22:21ff.). **Oh that I knew where I might find him!** (v. 3a) Since he now believes that his divine Avenger lives, his longing to appear before God is more ardent than before, and his confidence in his vindication firmer than ever (vv. 4-7). But he cannot find God to reason with him face to face (vv. 8,9).

10-17. But he knoweth the way that I take (v. 10a). **Knoweth** probably expresses here not mere acquaintance but approval (as in Ps 1:6). **More than my own precept I treasured the words of his mouth** (v. 12b). Job has all along followed the way Eliphaz recommends (cf. 22:22). Yet God inexorably executes against Job all he has foreordained, in apparent disregard of merit or demerit (23:13,14). **Therefore am I terrified at his presence** (v. 15a, ASV) . . . **not because of the darkness or because of my own face which thick darkness covers** (v. 17; cf. ASV marg.). Not dark calamity (cf. 22:11) nor marred visage most dismayed Job but the inaccessibility of God (23:16) and his seeming failure to inform his providential rule with justice.

24:1-12. The burden of this section is found in its opening and closing words: **Why are times not laid up by the Almighty? And why do not they that know him see his days** (v. 1, ASV) . . . **God regardeth not the folly** (v. 12c, ASV). God does not, like Samuel (cf. I Sam 7:16), have a regular judging circuit for preserving order and punishing crime. Cruel and greedy men prey, unchecked, upon the helpless. Job voices, therefore, the plaintive "How long?" of those who are oppressed by the lords of the soil.

13-17. Economic tyrants, such as those just described, often operate within legal technicalities. In addition to them, wanton and violent men overrun the earth. These are murderers, adulterers, thieves (cf. Ex 20:13-15), all lovers of darkness.

18-20. If the point of these verses is the quick, easy death of the wicked and the subsequent cursing of his heritage, unobserved by him, they agree with Job's views in chapter 21. The RSV introduces them with, "You say," so adopting the interpretation that Job here quotes the opposition's view of the certain doom of the wicked in order to answer it (cf. v. 21ff.). Possibly this section represents a corrective modification in Job's earlier analysis of the wicked (cf. 27:7ff.).

21-25. Yet God preserveth the mighty by his power (22a, ASV; for vv. 22,23, see ASV for correction of AV). God allows the lives of the wicked to attain full maturity and to end as other men's lives end (v. 24). **Who will prove me a liar** (25a, ASV). Sure of his facts, Job issues his victory challenge.

c) Third Discourse of Bildad. 25:1-6.

Bildad avoids Job's challenge (24:25). Anxious, however, to say something, he repeats ideas expressed earlier by Eliphaz (cf. 4:17ff.; 15:14ff.) and accepted by Job (cf. 9:2; 14:4). The inept repetition indicates that the philosophers have exhausted their resources of wisdom. Bildad's brief, feeble effort represents their expiring breath. Zophar's subsequent failure to speak is the silence of the vanquished (cf. 29:22).

Job, an insignificant worm of the dust, says Bildad, by comparison with the glorious heavenly bodies (v. 6), may not hope to prove his innocence before God (v. 4), whose awe-inspiring majesty prevails universally (vv. 2, 3), putting to shame even the brightness of moon and stars (v. 5). The speech is reverent but irrelevant.

d) Job's Third Reply to Bildad. 26:1-14.

Job pursues more impressively and to better purpose the theme attempted by Bildad—God's wondrously wise ways (cf. 9:4-10; 12:13-25).

2-4. The patriarch indulges his bent for sarcasm as he turns in disdain from Bildad's useless recitation. **From whom hast thou declared words** (4a. On *'ēt*, "from," cf. Akk. *ittu;* on this use of *'ēt*, with *higgîd*, cf. Mic 3:8). Bildad's ideas were but echoes of Eliphaz', and his use of them to condemn Job was more likely inspired by Satan than by God.

5-14. They that are deceased tremble Beneath the waters and the inhabitants thereof (v. 5, ASV). More remarkable than the awe God instills in beings near his heavenly throne (25:2) is the consternation his wisdom and dominion bring to the shades in Sheol (26:5,6). Whether Job's cosmology actually agreed with ancient concepts or is merely figuratively expressed, it is not presented as necessarily normative revelation. In his survey of the evidences of God's greatness, the speaker now passes from the underworld to this world (vv. 7-13). Though verse 7 might envisage creative action, this section as a whole pictures God's general providential rule of nature. **The north over empty space** (v. 7a, ASV), refers to the northern heavens. **He incloseth the face of his throne** (v. 9a, ASV) means, He veils the heaven with clouds. The qualification in 26:10b is not temporal (AV) but spatial (ASV). **The pillars of heaven** (v. 11), are mountains, their peaks hidden in clouds. **He smiteth through Rahab** (v. 12b, ASV) . . . **His hand hath pierced the fleeing serpent** (v. 13b, ASV marg.). God controls the upper and lower waters to procure favorable climatic order. For the mythological imagery, cf. Isa 27:1; Ugaritic text, Gordon UH 67, I, 1ff. **Lo, these are but the outskirts of his ways: And how small a whisper do we hear of him!** (v. 14a,b, ASV; cf. ch. 28) If Job's friends had recognized the limitations of their knowledge, they would have avoided their misinterpretations. Job's praise of the perfection of God's knowledge contradicts their identification of him with ungodly men.

e) Job's Instruction of the Silenced Friends. 27:1–28:28.

Since Zophar fails to speak, Job continues, now addressing all the friends (cf. plurals in 27:11,12). Aware of his mastery, he assumes the role of teacher (27:11). After once again declaiming his righteousness, with a strong oath (27:1-7), he contrasts his own experience with that of the wicked (27:8-23). Chapter 28 is an artistic introduction to the way of wisdom. Modern critics have argued forcefully that the text from 27:7 on has suffered disarrangement. They contend that the sentiments expressed contradict Job's previous remarks, or, in the case of chapter 28, are incompatible with the sequel. It seems possible, however, to defend the originality of the present textual arrangement, and the following exposition is based upon it.

27:1-7. As God liveth, who hath taken away my right (v. 2a, ASV). This oath remarkably epitomizes Job's spiritual dilemma. On the one hand, it proclaims God the God of truth, and on the other, charges that his treatment of Job is unjust. **Surely my lips do not speak unrighteousness** (v. 4a, ASV, marg.). This is not a vow (AV); it is a declaration that Job's unshakable claim to integrity (vv. 5,6) is true to conscience and fact.

Let mine enemy be as the wicked (v. 7a). The reader of the Prologue appreciates how diabolical was the accusation that Job's piety was not genuine.

8-23. For what is the hope of the godless when God cuts him off? (v. 8a, RSV) No longer driven to reactionary extremes by the pressure of debate, Job achieves a more penetratingly spiritual analysis of the ungodly. They are without God in the world. That means not only that they will suffer eternal perdition (v. 8), but that they have no divine refuge amid present trouble (vv. 9,10; cf. 22b). **Why then are ye become altogether vain?** (v. 12b, ASV) The friends should have recognized by Job's persistent crying to God that their identification of him with the godless was false (cf. 35:9ff.). **This is the portion of a wicked man with God** (v. 13a; cf. 20:29; 31:2). The prosperity of an ungodly family (vv. 14-18) is not passed down through successive generations. As for a wicked individual, prosperity is not his final destiny (vv. 19-23). Job so far modifies his former statement as to agree with his silenced opponents that the prosperity of the wicked is not the dominant trend in the world. But he still recognizes that the wicked may prosper for a season. And any such exception is fatal to the logic of the theory that condemned him.

28:1-28. Some commentators regard this chapter as a hymnic interlude inserted by the author to separate the dialogue from Job's final summing up (chs. 29–31). It is treated here as a continuation of Job's instruction "concerning the hand of God" (27:11a, ASV) and, as such, further demonstrates that his piety is both genuine and fervent.

1-11. As a foil to the following theme of the failure of man to gain true wisdom apart from God (v. 12ff.), there is pictured the success of the daring sons of Tubal-cain (cf. Gen 4:22) in exploiting earth's hidden treasures. Mankind's conquest of the earth, commanded by God at the beginning (Gen 1:28), is marked by phenomenal technological triumphs.

12-19. But where shall wisdom be found? (v. 12a) The next section (20-27) is also introduced by this refrain question. There it receives a positive answer, but here a negative one. In spite of amazing achievements in scientific enterprise (vv. 1-11), men are unable by the techniques or treasures of science to attain wisdom. That supreme prize cannot be obtained by probing or purchase, because it is not, like some precious stones, deposited in earth or sea (vv. 13,14).

20-27. Back of the assumption that man can discover wisdom lies the presupposition that the Creator possesses infinite wisdom. Wisdom is not found in the land of the living (v. 21; cf. 13,14), nor in the realm of the dead (v. 22). The way of wisdom is beyond the unaided ken of man here or hereafter. It is directly visible only to the One who enjoys all-encompassing, all-penetrating perception (vv. 23,24). Note the use of *hearing* and *seeing* for partial and perfect knowledge respectively (vv. 21-27). The Creator perceived wisdom in the beginning, when he was ordaining the laws of the world (vv. 25,26). In fact, the natural creation, with its governing laws, established by God, is an expression and embodiment of wisdom (v. 27; cf. Prov 8:22-31). For wisdom is the word of his will and becomes articulate for man in God's law – natural and moral. Divine law is the form in which God reveals his wisdom to men.

28. The fear of the Lord, that is wisdom. Man's reverent acknowledgment that he and his world are subject to the Creator is so much the lifeblood of human wisdom that it can be identified with wisdom. A man begins to be wise when he ceases to strive for wisdom independently of God and in his own power. He advances in wisdom through meditation on the moral law and investigation of natural law. Apart from a true recognition of divine revelation, whether in the natural creation or in the Word, man's meditation and investigation produce not wisdom but folly. The cultural enterprise not begun and consummated in the cult is vain. And the cult, if it be not the true cult of the Lord, is vanity. The fear of the Lord, covenant consecration, is the beginning and chief part of wisdom.

f) Job's Final Protest. 29:1–31:40.

The engagement with the friends is over; now the encounter with God comes to the fore. In a final monologue Job summarizes his cause. The direct address in 30:20-23 marks it as part of Job's continuing recourse to God. This speech is a reiteration of Job's opening complaint, considerably tempered for having passed through the fires of the great debate. It is a trilogy, consisting of a description of Job's former exaltation (ch. 29), a description of his present humiliation (ch. 30), and a final protestation of innocence (ch. 31).

1-25. Job begins this exposition of his extraordinary history where the Book of Job begins it — in the prosperous **months of old** (v. 2a, ASV). **In the ripeness of my days** (v. 4a, ASV); not *youth* (AV). Job starts with the heart of the matter (as the book also does) — the close covenant bond between himself and God (cf. 1:1). The blessedness of those former days which now stirs such longing in Job was not the paradise-like abundance as such (v. 6), but the friendly favor of God (cf. Ps 25:14), from which that prosperity flowed (vv. 2-5). **When I went forth to the gate** (v. 7a, ASV). Because Job's estate was adjacent to the city, Job was active in civil and judicial affairs. The gate and adjoining "street," or open market place, was the location of the town forum. The eminent role the patriarch had played in council and court seems to him now the most significant aspect of his past (vv. 7-17,21-25), viewed from his present personal struggle for justice. The last word, so grudgingly granted him in the present debate, had always before been his undisputed right (vv. 21-23) as he sat a king among his fellows (v. 25). The irony was that he who had been the celebrated champion of the poor and oppressed (vv. 11-17), the beloved comforter of mourners (v. 25c), was now, in his trouble, denied a fair hearing by friends (cf. esp. ch. 22) and, apparently, by God. **I put on righteousness and it clothed itself with me** (v. 14a, ASV marg.). The righteous cause became incarnate in Job, who, undaunted by despondency or difficulty (v. 24, ASV), wielded the sword of justice to deliver the innocent from predatory men (v. 17a; cf. Isa 11:2-5; Ps 72:12-14). One of the blessings of Job's lost paradise had been his happy hopes of prolonged days in the bosom of his family (Job 29:18), of honor (20a), and of strength (20b) constantly renewed (v. 19). Job presently relates the sad confounding of these hopes (ch. 30).

30:1-31. The repetition of *But now* .... *And now* .... *And now* (vv. 1, 9,16) effectively accents the theme as Job contrasts the bleak, turbulent present with the peaceful past. The king of counselors has become the byword of fools (vv. 1-15). The friendly favor of God has turned into cruelty (vv. 16-23).

1-15. The extremity of Job's dishonor appears in the fact that even the lowest of humanity look down on him. By describing their wretchedness (vv. 1-8; cf. 24:5ff.), the sufferer suggests with skillfull indirectness his own yet worse condition. So devoid of all dignity and reliability was this bestialized breed (vv. 6-8) of starving outcasts (vv. 3-5), that Job, for all his sympathy towards social inferiors (cf. 29:12ff.; 31:15), would not have entrusted even their eldest with responsibilities customarily given to shepherd dogs (v. 1b). **Men whose vigor is gone** (v. 2b, RSV). They lack even the physical stamina to serve as hirelings. **But now** even the juveniles (v. 1a) of this rabble regard Job as the fitting butt of their derisive ditties (v. 9). No show of contempt is too mean for them (v. 10; cf. 17:6, ASV) as with unbridled spite (v. 11b) they devise torments (v. 12ff.) against this ruined bourgeois, now a helpless outcast in their dunghill domain.

16-23. Far more distressing to the patriarch than the cruelty of men is that of God (v. 21a), who seems to stare stonily (v. 20b, ASV) at his pleading victim. God persecutes Job (v. 21b, with physical afflictions continually (vv. 16b,17), humiliatingly (vv. 18,19), mercilessly (vv. 20,21), violently (v. 22, ASV), unto the grave (v. 23). Though Job fails here to pursue the logical implications and to appropriate the comfort of his recently expressed thoughts concerning wisdom, human and divine (ch. 28), it must be remembered that he was not stone but a man of flesh, and still being crushed by the serpent's coils.

24-31. A melancholy cry concludes Job's reflections on his humiliation and dereliction. To cry for help in distress is natural (v. 24, according to ASV and RSV), especially when the calamity is contrary to all expectations (vv. 25,26; cf. 29:15-20). In emotional turmoil (v. 27, ASV), Job wails before the world (v. 28, ASV) like a howling jackal or dolorous ostrich (v. 29, ASV). With death-fever consuming him (v. 30), he plays beforehand a dirge against the day of his burying (v. 31).

31:1-40. Protestation of innocence has been Job's main burden all along. Here, elaborately formulated, it becomes the climax of his peroration. In form, this is a retroactive oath of covenant allegiance (cf. v. 1a). In such oaths the speaker called down curses upon his own head for proved violations of the moral code (cf., e.g., the Hittite Soldiers' Oath, ANET, 353, 354). Even the imagery of the extant samples of such ancient oaths corresponds with Job's (e.g., loss of crops, grinding, breaking of limbs, thistles. See vv. 8,10,22,40). The picture, therefore, is that of the covenant vassal protesting his faithfulness to the various stipulations laid upon him, dumbfounded that his sovereign has visited him with the curses rather than the blessings of the covenant (cf. Deut 28:18,31,35). God seems to Job to have forsaken the suzerain's role as protector, and strangely turned enemy against an obedient vassal.

1-8. Job begins by disclaiming private sins of the heart – lust (v. 1), vain deceit (v. 5), covetousness (v. 7). In this he displays profound insight into the spirituality of God's law (cf. the Sermon on the Mount, Mt 5; 6; 7). His deep concern with the Suzerain's imminent judgment emerges frequently (vv. 2-4; cf. 11,12,14,23,28), most strikingly in his self-maledictions (v. 8; cf. Deut 28:30c, 33). By these references to the penal sanctions of the covenant Job solemnizes his oaths of innocence. Mingled with Job's reverent fear of his Judge is his confident longing to stand before him, eloquently proclaimed in vv. 35-37 and more simply here (v. 6).

9-23. The patriarch also disavows public sins against his neighbors–adultery (v. 9), maltreatment of menials (v. 13), neglect of the social obligation of charity to the needy (vv. 16,17,19-21). Self-maledictions are attached to the first and last "if" clauses in this section. In addition, Job's denials are vigorously enforced: his denial of adultery, by indignant denunciation of such enormity (vv. 11,12); his denial of abuse of servants, by a reckoning with divine investigation (v. 14) and a recognition of common creaturely origin (v. 15); and his denial of uncharitableness, by positive affirmation of the opposite (v. 18) and confession of his fear of God (v. 23).

24-37. The charge of hypocrisy and secret iniquity that the counselors brought against him, for want of evidence of Job's supposed crimes, had already been contradicted by his protestations. It is now directly repudiated by his denial of concealed sin in his relations with God, his enemies, and strangers. Neither the deceitfulness of riches (vv. 24,25) nor the fascination of pagan worship of heavenly bodies (vv. 26,27) had ensnared Job in covert idolatry, the transgression of the most fundamental demand of allegiance to God (v. 28). Secret malice towards foes (v. 29) he firmly denies (v. 30). Household intimates acquainted with his private life can vouch that he has not begrudged hospitality to the passing stranger (vv. 31 [ASV, not AV], 32). Summing up, he forswears any similarity to Adam, who tried to hide his sin (v. 33; cf. 13:20; Gen 3:7-10). Job had no need to fear the open scrutiny of society (Job 31:34) or of God (v. 35ff.). In utter contrast to the fright and flight of Adam at the approach of the Lord, Job passionately desires to confront God (v. 35a; cf. 13:3,22; 23:3-9; 30:20). **Lo, here is my signature** (v. 35b, ASV). Dramatizing the desired audience with God, Job represents the defense he has just offered as a signed and sealed legal document. Then, with consummate arrogance, he declares how he will stride before God as a prince (v. 37b), crowned with the very scroll of his indictment (v. 35c, ASV; v. 36) which will be transformed into an emblem of honor for him by being refuted charge by charge (v. 37a).

38-40. The impious challenge just uttered (vv. 35-37), while answering to the "if like Adam" condition (vv. 33,34), forms so satisfactory a refutation of the entire catalogue of sins and so grandiloquent a conclusion for the whole speech that many scholars regard the anticlimactic verses 38-40 as dislocated. Stylistically, however, the author of Job is fond of the penultimate climax (cf. e.g., 3:23ff.; 14:15ff.). And materially this final sin (vv. 38,39) and imprecation (v. 40) follow naturally the allusion to the fall of Adam (v. 33ff.), for Job here invokes the elementary primeval curse upon the ground (Gen 3:17,18; cf. Gen 4:11,12).

Job's protestations of innocence have kept pace with his deepening perception of the demands of divine holiness. But now his exhibition of remarkable penetration into God's moral requirements exposes an equally remarkable depth of self-righteousness in him. Such blindness to the depravity and deceitfulness of his own heart did not negate the genuineness of the divine redemptive work in Job. But it did constitute a serious spiritual need, to deal with which – as Elihu was presently to point out (ch. 32ff.) – was one purpose of God (even though not the paramount purpose) in appointing Job's sufferings.

4) The Ministry of Elihu. 32:1–37:24.

Elihu, apparently one of a larger audience attending the debate of the masters, now comes forward and presents his theodicy. Introducing him earlier would have marred the dramatic movement of the poem by a clumsy anticipation of the debate's outcome. The younger man was as ignorant as the others of the heavenly transactions related in the Prologue. His interpretation of Job's sufferings is, therefore, not comprehensive. Elihu did, however, perceive the significance of the all-important principle of God's free grace, which the others had slighted. Hence, with this speech, the light of day begins to dawn on the way of wisdom after the long night of debate, pierced by only an occasional gleam of understanding. The princely arrogance of Job is subdued, and thus Elihu serves as one sent before the face of the Lord to prepare the way for His coming in the whirlwind (ch. 38ff.).

The speech of Elihu (32:6—37:24), though marked by several pauses (34:1; 35:1; 36:1), is essentially a unit. Following the apology (32:6-22), the theodicy is developed in answer to particular complaints of Job (quoted in 33:8-11; 34:5-9; 35:2,3; cf. 36:17ff.) and by means of an exposition of God's grace (33:12-33), righteousness (34:10—36:25), and power (36:26—37:24).

32:1-5. The poetical form is briefly interrupted by this prose preface. Elihu's origins are rather fully traced (v. 2a; cf. 1:1; 2:11). **Buzite.** Cf. Gen 22:21. Job's failure to be more jealous of God's honor than his own had aroused Elihu's indignation (v. 2b); note the Lord's concurrence (40:8). What provoked Elihu to instruct his elders was the failure of the friends to answer satisfactorily Job's defiant protests against God. **And yet had condemned Job** (v. 3b). The friends' charge of hypocrisy was a shameful expedient to cover their logical and theological deficiencies. Another possible translation is: **because they had not condemned Job.** That is, they had failed to prove him wrong in his aspersions against divine justice. This agrees well with Elihu's interest in the justification of God. According to a variant ancient textual tradition, verse 3b would read: **and so condemned God.** That is, the friends' silence before the still-protesting Job was tantamount to their condemning God.

6-22. Elihu's preliminary apology for claiming the ears of the audience is here expanded beyond Occidental taste, but that may not reflect on proprieties in the land of Uz (cf. *Iliad* 14:122ff.). **Days should speak** (v. 7a). Deference for the wisdom associated with age had forestalled Elihu's earlier intervention (vv. 6,7,11). Wisdom, however, is basically a matter of divine gift, specifically of God's endowment of the spirit he has breathed into man: **But it is the spirit in a man, the breath of the Almighty, that makes him understand** (v. 8, RSV; cf. Gen 2:7). The inglorious performance of the counselors has demonstrated their lack of wisdom in spite of age (Job 32: 9,12,15,16), while Elihu claims understanding in spite of youth (v. 6b,10). Rebuking them for abandoning the crusade (v. 13, ASV), Elihu undertakes it (vv. 16,17) with new strategy (v. 14), under the compulsion of a spirit bursting with knowledge of the mystery the sages found so perplexing (vv. 18-20), and with fearless devotion to truth alone (vv. 21,22).

33:1-33. The general apology has been directed to the friends. Now introducing his answer to Job's protests, Elihu addresses to him a challenge (vv. 1-7). He cites statements of Job (vv. 8-11) and gives his own reply (vv. 12-30). So the gauntlet is once more thrown down (vv. 31-33).

1-7. Behold, I am toward God even as thou art (v. 6a, ASV). Elihu is a fellow human being, made out of clay (v. 6b) by God's creative breath (v. 4; cf. Gen 2:7). Facing Elihu's challenge, Job cannot, therefore, make his favorite excuse that paralyzing divine terrors rob him of the composure necessary to defend himself (cf. Job 9:34; 13:21).

8-11. Elihu does not misrepresent Job's position. Job had given a nod of assent to his involvement in human sin (cf. 7:21; 13:26). Moreover, his protestations of innocence were justified in so far as they defended his integrity against the cry of hypocrisy and other excessive charges of the friends. Nevertheless, a tendency towards an overestimate of his righteousness is traceable in those protestations (cf. 9:21, ASV; 10:7; 12:4; 16:17; 23:10ff.; 27:5,6; 29:11ff.). And this conceit becomes almost incredibly bald and bold in Job's final words (ch. 31). In 33:10b Elihu quotes 13:24b; in 33:11 he quotes 13:27a.

12-30. When Elihu cites the further complaint of Job that God **giveth not account of any of his matters** (v. 13b;

cf. 19:7; 30:20), it might seem that he has dismissed Job's doubts of God's justice very briefly (vv. 8-12) to return to them later (cf. chs. 34–37). **But** in his answer to the alleged lack of revelation concerning God's ways (vv. 14-30), Elihu incorporates an explanation of the suffering of God's servants, and thus actually begins his defense of divine justice. In OT days God spoke to his people by various special means no longer employed after the completion of the NT revelation (cf. Heb 1:1). Elihu mentions dreams (Job 33: 15-17) and the interpreting angel (vv. 20-30) as special media of revelation. God did not leave his covenant people to grope without the light of authoritative revelation. **If there be for him an angel as an interpreter, one of a thousand** (v. 23). Innumerable angels minister to the heirs of salvation (Heb 1:14; cf. Job 4:18; 5:1; Deut 33:2; Ps 68:17; Dan 7:10; Rev 5:11), one ministry being the interpretation of God's will and ways. Possibly **one of a thousand** suggests not the abundance of such hierophants but the rarity and pre-eminence of his angel-mediator (cf. Eccl 7:28).

To bring back his soul from the pit (v. 30a; cf. vv. 18,24,28). At the heart of such revelation are the principle and purposes of divine grace. Men live under the shadow of **the destroyers** (v. 22b), God's angels of death, because of the Lord's holy displeasure with their sin. But **once . . . twice, yea thrice** (vv. 14,29, ASV) grace intervenes. Sometimes special revelation interposes as a warning to prevent the purposed evil and so deliver from its disastrous consequences (vv. 15-18). Sometimes the revelation comes at the eleventh hour, when a course of sore chastening has brought man to the brink of the pit (vv. 19-22). Then there is remarkable restoration of the blessings of righteousness (vv. 25,26), celebrated by a psalm of confession and thanksgiving (vv. 27,28, ASV). Such deliverances are accomplished by the confrontation of man with **his uprightness**, i.e., the straight, right way for him (v. 23b; cf. v. 16), and by the man's repentance. This process is the **ransom** (v. 24c) which is found if God **is gracious unto him** (v. 24a). In the light of past revelation vouchsafed to God's servants, Elihu labels their sufferings as chastening (v. 19).

31-33. The interpretation of suffering as chastisement is applicable in Job's case (see concluding comments on ch. 31). Eliphaz, too, had suggested chastening as one reason for affliction (5:17), but he regarded chastening as meted out in proportion to sin. Though severe chastening might actually be "blessed," never theless it stigmatized a believer as ranking humiliatingly low in the community of the sanctified! Elihu saw chastening in its redemptive context, as informed and governed by the principle of sovereign grace. Since grace is by its very nature sovereignly free, it may bestow the blessing of chastening most abundantly on the saint who has relatively least need! Elihu does not reflect here upon wicked men, but his discovery that suffering is a working of God's free grace is clearly the key to the unpredictable, seemingly arbitrary variety in their sufferings, and in their prosperity as well. For them, too, suffering is a gracious dispensation warning them away from the eternal pit. Thus Elihu removes the sting from the mystery of the suffering of the righteous and the prosperity of the wicked. Job's heart leaps for joy. But shame fills him as he recalls the railing accusations he has shouted against the God of grace, **and so he holds his peace** (v. 33).

34:1-37. The structure of chapter 33 is repeated: an introductory call to hear (vv. 2-4), quotation from Job's complaints (vv. 5-9), an answer thereto (vv. 10-28), and a closing challenge (vv. 29-37).

2-4. It appears from 34:34 that Elihu calls for the attention of a wider circle of listeners than the three friends.

5-9. Elihu once more sets up as his target Job's complaint that God perverts justice by afflicting him with incurable wounds though he is without transgression. This accurately summarizes much in Job's speeches (for v. 5a, cf. esp. 13:18; 23:10; 27:6; for v. 5b, 27:2; for v. 6, 9:20; 6:14; 16:13; for v. 9, cf. 9:22; 10:3; 21:7ff.; 24:1ff.).

10-28. The perversity of Job's charge is proved by a consideration of the righteousness of God. Elihu begins with a direct denial that God is unjust (vv. 10-12). Logically, this may be begging the question, but that only demonstrates the limitations of human logic. For Elihu's appeal is to the sense of deity in God's image-bearer, and that is the only ultimately sound procedure in declaring God's name. Confirmation of the Creator's perfect justice is found in his omnipotence and omniscience (v. 13ff.). Pure impartiality is the correlate of his transcendence above all possible motivation to show respect to the persons of his creatures (vv. 13-20). It is in God that all flesh lives, moves, and has its being (vv. 13-15); kings and the mighty are no exceptions (vv. 16-20). Moreover, God's ordering of the universe contradicts the charge of injustice in him, for injustice works anarchy, not order (v. 17a). No flaw can arise through ignorance in God's government (vv. 21-28). **He needeth not further to consider a man** (v. 23a, ASV). With one omniscient look God comprehends all the facts in the case, even the secret works of dark ness (vv. 21,22) and veiled oppression of the poor (vv. 24-28).

29-37. To question the benevolent providence of God is folly (vv. 29,30). **For unto God does one say, I have borne (affliction) without offending?** (v. 31). Elihu apparently resumes the thought of verses 5-9 – **the unheard of presumption** (cf. v. 7) of Job's protests to God (cf. v. 6b). **Shall his recompense be as thou wilt, that thou refusest it? For thou must choose, and not I** (v. 33a,b; ASV). Again opportunity is afforded Job to defend his rebelliousness, but he remains silent.

35:1-16. Returning to the idea that God is infinitely exalted above any temptation to tamper with justice (vv. 4-8), Elihu again introduces it by citing the complaint of Job which it refutes (vv. 2,3). He then corrects a distortion of this doctrine of divine transcendence (vv. 9-13), applying the point to Job (vv. 14-16).

2,3. Cf. 34:9. **Thinkest thou this to be right?** (35; 2a) **This** refers not to 2b but to verse 3 (see ASV). Also, 2b is subordinate to 3, thus: To criticize the consequences of righteousness is to assume a righteousness superior to God's.

4-8. Thy companions with thee (4b). The workers of iniquity with whom Elihu associated Job in this complaint of profitless righteousness (cf. 34:8,9). It is evident that men can neither diminish (v. 6) nor increase (v. 7) the glory of him who is exalted above the heavens (v. 5). Therefore, neither fear nor favor can hamper him in his administration of justice. Eliphaz had presented a similar argument for divine justice (cf. 22:2-4), but it was vitiated by his misunderstanding of the administration of that justice. Job, too, had referred to the unchangeableness of the self-contained Creator, but had concluded that it minimized human responsibility (cf. 7:20,21).

9-13. God's transcendent immutability is not equivalent to indifference to human virtue and vice; it is not a distant disinterest in the multitudes who **cry . . . because of the pride of evil men** (v. 12 a,c), as Job had complained (cf. 24: 12). Such prayer rather goes unheeded because **God will not hear an empty cry** (v. 13a, ASV), a mere animal cry (v. 11) for physical relief. **None saith, Where is God my maker, who giveth songs in the night** (v. 10). It is not that God is indifferent to men but that men are indifferent to God. They do not seek God for God's sake, content to sing doxologies in the midst of desolation if only he be their portion. Elihu summons Job to the wisdom of his original response of faith (cf. 1:21).

14-16. If God's judgment tarries (v. 14; cf. 19:7; 23:8ff.; 30:20), and his wrath is restrained the while (v. 15, ASV; cf. 21:7ff.), Job ought not jump to vain conclusions (v. 16).

36:1–37:24. Continuing the theme of God's righteousness, Elihu expounds further the gracious design of the afflictions of the righteous, exhorting Job to be profitably exercised thereby (36:1-25; cf. 33:19ff.). In the closing verses of this exhortation, the appeal shifts to the excellency of God's power (cf. 34: 12ff.), and that becomes the grand subject of Elihu's conclusion (36:26–37: 24), the herald's cry before the advent of the Lord (ch. 38ff.).

36:1-25. Elihu characterizes his theodicy as complete truth (vv. 2-4). Possibly 4b refers to God (cf. 37:16). God's greatness is a greatness of goodness and wisdom (v. 5), of justice bestowed impartially and grace bestowed abundantly on the righteous (vv. 6,7). Here again Elihu might seem to lapse into the approach of the friends, but the difference between them appears in his interpretation of the apparent exceptions to the general pattern observable in divine government (8ff.; cf. comments on 33:12-30). Afflictions call the righteous to more ardent spiritual strivings and thus are an effective means of deliverance from sin and its consequences (vv. 8-10,15). They disappear when their specific purpose is realized (v. 11); and only then (v. 12). Similarly, if the **godless in heart** (v. 13a, ASV) react to a long-suffering God's afflictive warnings with sullen rage (v. 13), they may expect only to be early fatalities of their debaucheries (v. 14). **Let not the great-**

ness of the ransom turn you aside (v. 18b, RSV; cf. 33:24). The overwhelming loss entailed in Job's chastening allured him away from the instruction (lit., *mouth)* of affliction (v. 16a; cf. 15b) into a response of angry judgment and scoffing (vv. 17,18a, RSV). **Will thy cry avail, that thou be not in distress?** (v. 19a, ASV) In Job's angry complaint, with its bitter longing for the night of the grave (v. 20), he spurns the sanctifying work of affliction (v. 21). Let him, therefore, consider the exalted works of God (vv. 22a,25), attend submissively to the instruction he sends (vv. 22b, 23), and so transform complaint into doxology (v. 24; cf. 35:10).

36:26–37:24. Adopting his own counsel (36:24), Elihu utters psalmodic praise to the Lord of creation. The divine rule is illustrated by various atmospheric phenomena: the rain cycle of evaporation and precipitation (36:26-28), fearfully majestic thunderstorms (36:29–37:4), and frosty winter's ice and snow (37:5-13). Each of these is introduced by an affirmation of the incomprehensibility of God's works (36:26,29; 37:5). Elihu observes that the elemental forces once unleashed do not escape God's control; but, like the expertly hurled missiles of warriors in the elite ambidextrous corps (36:32; cf. *Iliad* 21:183; I Chr 12:2), they perform God's bidding (37:12), whether as a curse (36:31a; 37:13a; cf. 1:16, 19) or as blessing (36:31b; 37:13b; cf. 37:7).

The intimate relation thus suggested between God's rule of nature and his rule of history prepares for Elihu's concluding application to Job: If man cannot comprehend God's natural rule, he ought not expect to comprehend God's moral rule. By a series of humbling questions (37:15ff.) Elihu impresses on Job his creaturehood, reminding him that by his finite standards he cannot judge God, all of whose ways are infinitely higher than human thought. Hence the folly of disputing his government (37:19,20,24b). The way of wisdom is to fear him who is incomprehensible and excellent in all his attributes (vv. 23,24a).

His ministry accomplished, Elihu retires from the scene. He has prepared the way of the Lord in the hearts of Job and his friends. From the literary perspective, the Elihu discourse forms an eminently successful transition to the following theophany. The younger man's vivid description of the fury of the elements sets the mood for (perhaps was actually inspired by) the approaching whirlwind vehicle of God. His thematic concentration on natural revelation is continued by the Lord, as is also even the interrogating style of his final exhortation (cf. 38:3ff.). In judging Job's controversy with his friends (cf. 42:7-9), the Lord does not mention Elihu, because the younger man was not a party to the dispute of the older ones, nor had his words been such as to require expiation. Though the Speaker from the whirlwind does not mention Elihu by name, He does not ignore him. For by continuing Elihu's essential argument and endorsing his judgments concerning both Job (cf. 32:2 and 40:8) and the friends (cf. 32:3 and 42:7ff.), the Lord owns Elihu as his forerunner.

B. The Voice of God. 38:1–41:34.

The verdicts passed on Job by men had darkened the way of wisdom until Elihu spoke. That way is now fully illuminated by the Voice from the whirlwind. It is eminently appropriate that the Lord's approach to Job is in the form of challenge. So also he had confronted Satan (cf. 1:7,8; 2:2,3). God challenged both Satan and Job by confronting them with his wondrous works. And since Job himself is the divine work by which Satan was challenged, it is through the success of this challenge to Job that God perfects the triumph of his challenge to Satan. God's challenge to Job proceeds in two stages (38:1–40:2 and 40:6–41:34), with a pause midway, marked by Job's initial submission (40:3-5).

1) The Divine Challenge. 38:1–40:2.

38:1-3. Out of the whirlwind (v. 1). This characteristic vehicle of theophany (cf. Ps 18:7ff.; 50:3; Ezk 1:4,28; Nah 1:3; Hab 3; Zech 9:14) was such as to dramatize the spoken revelation it accompanied. **Who is this that darkeneth counsel** (v. 2). The absurdity of Job's criticism of God's counsel lies in their respective identities. The creature critic of the Creator! **Gird up now thy loins like a man** (v. 3a). The imagery of the divine challenge is drawn from the popular ancient sport of belt-wrestling. The figure is especially suitable in this context because belt-wrestling was also used as an ordeal in court, and it is by ordeal that Job's case is being settled.

38:4—39:30. The ordeal to which the Creator challenges his creature is a test of wisdom. Many of God's questions deal with executive power, but the OT concept of wisdom includes the craftsman's talent. Attention is drawn to the Creator's unsearchable wisdom everywhere displayed—on the earth (38: 4-21), in the heavens (38:22-38), and in the animal kingdom (38:39—39:30), the sequence of narration being, in main outline, the same that this Speaker adopted in Genesis 1. Job becomes increasingly impressed with the immensity of his own ignorance and impotence.

38:4-21. Where wast thou (v. 4a). Job's knowledge of the earth suffers from his spatial and temporal limitations. This section opens and closes with references to Job's nonexistence at creation (vv. 4,21; cf. 12; contrast "Wisdom" in Prov 8:22ff.). Hence his ignorance of how the earth was founded (Job 38:4-7) or the sea bounded (vv. 8-11), of how earth's days are rounded by the cycle of dawn and darkness (vv. 12-15, 19-21). Neither has Job sounded the depth of the sea nor measured the breadth of the land (vv. 16-18).

38:22-38. Canst thou set the dominion thereof in the earth? (v. 33b) To qualify as director and judge of man's life on earth, one must be able to govern the heavenly bodies that rule the earth (cf. Gen 1:14-18). Note the repeated mention of the influence of the atmospheric and astral heavens on earthly affairs (Job 38:23,26,27,33,34,38). But Job has no control over the waters above as to whether, where, when, or how they will precipitate. The lightning will not present itself before him like an obedient servant (v. 35); nor has he the remotest influence upon heaven's seasonal signs (vv. 31,32).

38:39—39:30. Again in this section on animate creation, the purpose is to convince Job of his incompetence for the role of world governor, while magnifying the wisdom of Him who actually is creation's Ruler (cf. 12:7). The creative and providential activity of God embraces wild creatures beyond man's control, just as, in the inanimate sphere, it embraces the wilderness beyond man's acquaintance (cf. 38:26,27). Lions and ravens are not available or likely subjects for man's charities (38:39-41), nor the wild goats for the solicitous care of the animal husbandman (39:1-4). Man cannot bring the elusive wild ass (39: 5-8) and untamable wild ox (39:9-12) under his yoke. Even the stupid ostrich scorns the proud horsemen (39:13-18), while the horse, in turn, scorns the human battle host and the boast of Lamech (39: 19-25; cf. Gen 4:22-24). The final vignette directs Job's eyes on high, toward his Creator's throne—to the raptorial hawk and eagle, waiting to be called by God to His judgment feast, with its prey of rebel men, kings and captains, horses and riders together (Job 39:26-30; cf. Ezk 39:17; Rev 19:17ff.). Here is the ultimate vanity of all the efforts of human wisdom—that man is reduced to food for the subhuman creation. "God hath chosen the foolish things of the world to confound the wise" (I Cor 1:27a). Even the wildlings laugh at man's cultural strivings (vv. 7, 18, 22).

40:1,2. Will the critic contend with the Almighty? (v. 2a) The first "fall" of the wrestling ordeal is about to be decided. God demands that Job admit defeat. This would be still clearer according to a reading reflected in some ancient versions: "Will the contender with the Almighty yield?"

2) Job's Submission. 40:3-5.

Behold, I am of small account (v. 4a, ASV). The Creator's surpassing wisdom has been so effectively impressed on Job that he will not further dispute God's ways as he had once and again (v. 5). Far less will he approach God as a prince (cf. 31:37). Job's practice begins to adorn again the doctrine of wisdom he has confessed (cf. 28:8).

3) The Divine Challenge Renewed. 40:6—41:34.

40:6,7. An aim of belt-wrestling was to strip the opponent of his belt, but a contest was not always terminated by one such "fall." Thus Job is, in a figure, to fasten on the belt again and renew the ordeal. His initial submission (40: 3-5) was good but only the beginning of his repentance. He must recognize not only the unreasonableness but also the sinfulness of criticizing the Almighty.

40:8-14. Hast thou an arm like God? (v. 9a) The redemptive power of God by which he saves his people and judges their enemies is often pictured as an outstretched arm and a mighty hand (cf. v. 14b). Job's criticism of God's government, especially his boast that he will overcome the Lord's imagined opposition to his justification, was, in principle, a usurpation of the divine prerogative of world government, a lusting after godlike knowledge of good and evil (cf. Gen 3:5), a self-deification. Let Job prove his ability to execute the sentence of condemnation against wicked men, whose prosperity seems to him unjust (Job 40:10-13). Then God will worship at the cult of Job, acknowledging that he possesses the divine power of redemptive judgment whereby he can justify and save himself (v. 14).

40:15–41:34. (Heb. text, 40:15–41:26). Since Job obviously cannot ascend the heavenly throne to try his hand at judging the wicked, God proposes a more feasible test. The motif of the deity commissioning an animal champion to battle a human hero is paralleled in ancient mythology. (Cf. Gilgamesh Epic, in which Ishtar sends the bull of heaven against Gilgamesh.) In Mesopotamian art, moreover, the bull of heaven is depicted wearing the wrestling-belt. **Behemoth** (40:15ff.) is commonly identified with the hippopotamus; **leviathan** (41:1ff.; Heb. text 40:25ff.), with the crocodile. These two are found together in Egyptian art. It is not necessary to demonstrate the presence of hippopotamus or crocodile in the Jordan area of old, since *yardēn* (40:23b) is apparently a common noun meaning "river" (cf. the parallel in v. 23a). Many other identifications have been suggested; recently, for example, of behemoth with the crocodile and leviathan with the whale. If behemoth can successfully be identified as a crocodile (cf. 40:17,24a, Heb.), it ought to be considered whether the entire passage describes only one creature, i.e., leviathan. The designation **behemoth,** taken as a plural intensive, "the beast par excellence," would be an epithet like **chief of the ways of God** (v. 19a). Note the similar supreme claims made for leviathan (41:33,34). Certain descriptive details do not fit any real creature. This has led to the view that not zoological creatures are intended but mythological chaos monsters conceived along the lines of stylized hippopotamus and crocodile. Then 40:15ff. would be a symbolic elaboration of the preceding challenge to quell rebellious proud men (40:9-14). Compare the use of the dragon symbol for Satan in Revelation. How appropriate would be an intimation to Job that his wrestlings were with the prince of proud rebels!

Contextually suitable as this mythical interpretation is, the passage is more naturally understood as a picture of real creatures painted with some highly figurative strokes (e.g., 41:19ff.). Note especially that God presents behemoth as one **which I made as I made you** (40:15b, RSV). Here indeed is the point of the passage: Job is to discover from his inability to vanquish even a fellow creature the folly of aspiring to the Creator's throne. The a fortiori conclusion becomes explicit in 41:10b; **Who then is able to stand before me?** The absolute divine transcendence contradicts Job's assumed right of claim against God because it precludes the possibility of Job's having given anything to God: **Who hath first given unto me, that I should repay him? Whatsoever is under the whole heaven is mine** (41:11, ASV).

Since the occasion of this extended demonstration of God's power is his engaging Job in a court ordeal, the demonstration is clearly offered as a defense of God's justice. Accordingly, it is introduced by the question: **Wilt thou also disannul my judgment? wilt thou condemn me, that thou mayest be righteous?** (40:8; cf. 38:2) Not that the attribute of justice can be abstractly deduced from that of omnipotence. Attention is rather directed to the mighty, divine works as compelling witnesses to God—not just to one attribute but to God himself; the God who has revealed himself to man from within and without, by general and special revelation; the living God, infinite, eternal, and unchangeable in his being, wisdom, power, holiness, justice, goodness, and truth; the God whose veracity and justice were the presupposition of Job's trial by ordeal, who swears by himself because he can swear by no greater.

IV. Confession: The Way of Wisdom Regained. 42:1-6.

42:1-6. This confession is the counterbalance to Job's complaint (ch. 3). It acknowledges the sinful rebelliousness which began with that complaint. It is not an admission of sins prior to his sufferings such as would support the friends' accusation. By this unreserved commitment of himself to his Lord, a commitment made while he was still in his sufferings, not having received either explanation of the mystery of the past or promise for the future, Job shows himself a true covenant servant, ready to serve his God for nought. The confession therefore marks Job's final "bruising" of Satan, the final vindication of God's redemptive power.

No purpose of thine can be restrained (v. 2b, ASV). This is not bare resignation under omnipotent pressure, but praise of the living God and a trusting acquiescence in his wise purposes. In 42:3a,4 Job quotes God's words (cf. 38:2,3b; 40:7), directing their convicting light upon himself, and then responds, "I am the man" (42: 3b,5,6). **Things too wonderful for me** (v. 3c). Finite man may not pose as final arbiter, for in God and his ways there is mystery beyond human comprehension. **But now mine eye seeth thee** (v. 5b). For the contrast between hearing and seeing in relation to knowledge, see 26:14; 28:21-27. No form of God had appeared in the whirlwind; but the revelation of the Voice had been a transforming experience, illuminating all other divine revelation, whether general or such earlier, special revelation as had been transmitted to Job. By this new light Job finds again the way of wisdom. **Wherefore I abhor myself, and repent in dust and ashes** (v. 6). Godly hatred of his own defilement is the natural accompaniment of the believer's confrontation with his holy Lord (cf. Isa 6:5). The philosophical Why? has not been answered, but God, by the condescension of his coming, has assured Job of his gracious concern. That is enough for Job.

V. Restoration: The Triumph of Job's Wisdom. 42:7-17.

A. Job's Wisdom Vindicated. 42:7-9.

The Lord works deliverance from Job's evils in the reverse order of their incurrence and in the obverse order of their gravity. Job's false sense of God's estrangement had been the first evil corrected. Now the defamation of Job's name among men is dealt with, and afterwards family and wealth are restored.

Ye have not spoken of me the thing that is right, as my servant Job hath (v. 7c, ASV). If *'ēlay* were translated *unto me*, there would be a clear reference to Job's confession. But even if it is translated *of me*, it seems necessary to think primarily of Job's confession and the friends' lack of such repentance in response to the theophany. For in terms of the theology expressed in their debate, the difference between them was merely one of degree. The words of all of them were in part censurable. Agreeably, the remedy is that Job should mediate for them in offering sacrifice, which was a mode of expressing public repentance in OT times (v. 8). The proportions of the offering were commensurate with the status of the offenders and the solemnity of the occasion (cf. Num 23ff.). Job is vindicated and the friends are rebuffed, but in such a way that the friends are forgiven by Job as well as by God. For the very form of Job's vindication is the privilege of praying for those who have despitefully used him (cf. Ezk 14:14-20). God's vindicatory acknowledgment of Job as *my servant* answered to Job's faith in his heavenly Kinsman and anticipated the eschatological, "Well done, good and faithful servant" (Mt 25:21 ff.). Further, it was the confirmation of God's original boast to Satan (Job 1: 8; 2:3) and so crowns His triumph over the evil one.

B. Job's Wisdom Blessed. 42:10-17.

Religion is not a means to prosperity as an end. But God's creation is good, and the inheritance of the earth promised to the meek is an integral part of the total beatitude of the whole man. As the book of Job itself teaches, in this world piety and prosperity are not invariably companions. But under the government of the righteous Creator, righteous men must ultimately be given beauty for ashes. The life of Job was shaped by God to be a prophetic sign of "the end of the Lord" (cf. Jas 5:11) for the greater encouragement of the righteous in that early period of redemptive revelation when the end was yet very far off (cf. Enoch's rapture, Gen 5:24).

Significantly, the turning point in Job's external circumstances, his deliverance from the hands of Satan, was marked by the act in which he spiritually exemplified the righteousness of God's kingdom (cf. Mt 6:33) and ceremonially typified the Messianic sacrifice which establishes that righteousness (Job 42: 10). The double blessing (v. 10b; cf. Isa 61:7; Zech 9:12) extends to Job's property (Job 42:12) and family (vv. 13-15), for the dead children are still Job's in his hope of immortality (cf. also v. 16b). Possibly the prolongation of his life to patriarchal fullness (vv. 16, 17; cf. Gen 25:7,8; 35:28,29) is a doubling of a previous seventy years (cf. Ps 90:10). It certainly suggests the recovery of health, as the daughters' inheritance among their brothers (Job 42:15b) suggests the restoration of Job's earlier family felicity.

BIBLIOGRAPHY

DAVIDSON, A. B., and LANCHESTER, H. C. O. *The Book of Job (Cambridge Bible)*. Cambridge: The University Press, 1884.

DELITZSCH, FRANZ. *Biblical Commentary on the Book of Job*. Edinburgh: T. & T. Clark, 1869; Grand Rapids: Wm. B. Eerdmans Publishing Co., 1949.

DHORME, P. *Le livre de Job*. Paris: J. Gabalda, 1926.

DRIVER, S. R., and GRAY, G.B. *A Critical and Exegetical Commentary on the Book of Job (International Critical Commentary)*. New York: Charles Scribner's Sons, 1921.

GREEN, W. H. *The Argument of the Book of Job Unfolded*. New York: Robert Carter & Bros., 1881.

TERRIEN, S. *The Book of Job (The Interpreter's Bible)*. New York: Abingdon Press, 1954.

TUR-SINAI, N. H. *The Book of Job*. Jerusalem: Kiryath Sepher, Ltd., 1957.

THE PSALMS

INTRODUCTION

Nature. Among all the books of antiquity, none has made such a powerful appeal to the human heart as *The Psalms*. In no other book of the Bible can one find such varieties of religious experience. Here the heart of Israel is laid bare in manifold expressions of faith, for Israel knew experientially the truth of God's revelation. In the various psalms Israel's insights of former days are united with worship and thus given permanence. The experience of individuals is here linked with the corporate life of Israel. Hence, in the Book of Psalms there is a universal quality which can come only from the combined expression of the spiritual experiences of men in many periods of history and in a variety of circumstances of life. Each man was motivated by his desire to respond to the living God. All were united by their inherent desire to respond by means of their deepest emotions. Every type of religious experience is reflected in the crucible of daily life and projected upon the life of the believer today. There is thus in the Psalms a timelessness which makes this book equally applicable to every age of history.

The term "Psalms" comes from the LXX, which applies the title *Psalmoi* to the collection. One of the major Biblical manuscripts, the Codex Alexandrinus, furnishes the designation "Psalter" by using the Greek word *Psâlterion*. However, the Hebrew Bible uses the designation *Tehillîm*, which means "Praises." In Rabbinical literature this same idea was carried over in the term *Sēper Tehillîm*, meaning "Book of Praises." In both the Hebrew and Greek terms there is the root meaning of playing instrumental music. In time the word took on the meaning of singing to a musical accompaniment, a feature of Israelite worship made popular by the singing of the Levitical choirs. Many of the psalms give evidence of their use by choirs and worshipers as hymns, while others are not suited to such use. However, the collection as a whole attests to the deepest and most passionate yearning of corporate Israel at worship before God.

Titles and Authorship. One of the first things noticed about a particular psalm is the title it bears. How to arrive at a proper interpretation of these titles is one of the most vexing problems posed by this book. At times, authorship is emphasized in the titles, at other times, relationship. The occasion of the psalm's composition is sometimes pointed out. Certain titles make reference to the designated use of a psalm for public worship. Other titles indicate the desired musical effect or setting. Still others describe the basic character of the psalm as (1) a hymn to be sung with musical accompaniment *(mizmôr)*, (2) a song *(shîr)*, (3) an anthem *(maśkîl)*, or (4) a lamentation *(miktām)*.

All but thirty-four of the psalms bear some type of title as a superscription. The thirty-four psalms without titles are referred to as the Jewish "orphans." Among the titled psalms, seventy-three use the inscription *le Dāwid*. This is rendered as "A Psalm of David" in the AV, RV, ASV, and RSV. However, the Hebrew usage may indicate "belonging to David," "connected with David," "concerning David," "for David," "dedicated to David," "in the style of David," or "by David." By no means must these titles be required always to indicate authorship, whether referring to David or others. The LXX adds David's name to fifteen psalms not so designated in the Hebrew. In addition to the seventy-three referred to David (eighty-eight in the LXX), twelve are connected with Asaph, twelve with the Sons of Korah, two with Solomon, one with Ethan, and one with Moses.

Although these titles are not a part of the original text, they are based upon relatively ancient tradition. A comparison between the Masoretic Text and the LXX indicates that the titles antedate the LXX, for some of the musical directions were already unintelligible to the Greek translators, and the titles had not become fixed. Though the superscriptions are not a part of the original text, they are worthy of consideration, for they represent man's first effort to write an introduction to the Psalter.

Structure. Though the book of Psalms may appear to lack a plan, it is not without definite order. While it lacks organization in terms of subject matter, it follows a much more obvious system of organization. It is divided into five sections, representing various collections brought together. According to the *Midrash on the Psalms,* an ancient Jewish commentary, this fivefold division was made to correspond to the five books of the Law. Thus there may have been an original purpose among the editors of the psalm collections to parallel this fivefold response of the people to the fivefold summons by God.

Further evidence of a plan is the presence of a doxology at the end of each of the five books. Psalms 41, 72, 89, 106, and 150 include doxologies for each of the five books. Indeed, Psalm 150 is an over-all doxology, while Psalm 1 is a general introduction to the Psalter. Psalms 2, 42, 73, 90, and 107 serve as introductions to their respective books.

This careful organization gives evidence that the final edition of the entire collection was designed to fit into the scheme of Jewish worship. There is an amazing correlation between the first four books of Law and the first four divisions in Psalms. Since the worshiper in Palestinian Judaism completed the reading of the Pentateuch every three years, it is very probable that the use of the Psalms was scheduled to correspond. According to ancient tradition, it appears that eight portions of the Law were assigned to the Sabbaths in a two-month period, along with suitable portions from the Prophets. N. H. Snaith *(Hymns of the Temple,* p. 18) has shown that successive psalms may well have been used in similar fashion. He has calculated that the book of Exodus was started on the 42nd Sabbath, Leviticus was reached on the 73rd, Numbers by the 90th, and Deuteronomy on the 117th. These Sabbaths correspond exactly with the first chapters in each of the five books of the Psalter. No psalm could be more fitting than Psalm 1 to introduce the forthcoming three-year "meditation upon the Law." Psalm 23, for example, would accompany the reading of the story of Jacob at Bethel.

Collection and Growth. The present organization of the Psalter is the result of a process of growth. Long before the book of Psalms took its present form, minor collections were in circulation. And gradually these smaller collections were added together.

Within the present fivefold arrangement, the bounds of certain smaller collections are still discernible. In addition to the Davidic collections, there are certain groupings assigned to the Sons of Korah and Asaph. In Psalm 72:20, it is stated that "the prayers of David are ended," though other psalms follow which are ascribed to David. Other smaller collections include the Psalms of Ascents and the Hallelujah Psalms. Certain sections also show a decided preference for either *Yahweh* or *Elohim,* pointing toward early existence in specialized collections. The following collections may well have circulated separately, to be later united:

Psalms 3 – 41. A Davidic collection with doxology and preference for *Yahweh* (272 occurrences compared with 15 for *Ĕlōhîm).*

Psalms 51 – 72. A Davidic collection with doxology and preference for *Ĕlōhîm* (208 occurrences compared with 48 for *Yahweh).*

Psalms 50, 73 – 83. Levitical guild collection ascribed to Asaph.

Psalms 42 – 49. Levitical guild collection attributed to the Sons of Korah.

Psalms 90 – 99. Sabbath Psalms closely connected with regular Sabbath worship.

Psalms 113 – 118. Hallel of Egypt Psalms, connected in worship with the Passover Feast (cf. Ps 136).

Psalms 120 – 134. Songs of Ascents or Degrees, probably sung by the pilgrims journeying to the Temple.

Psalms 146 – 150. Hallelujah Psalms sung at festivals.

T. H. Robinson *(The Poetry of the Old Testament)* and others have suggested that a threefold division preceded the final fivefold form. These three books, 1-41, 42-89, 90-150, may well have been redivided into the present form to make them correspond to the divisions of the Law. Whether this theory can be proved or not, a proper understanding of the composite nature of the book of Psalms is essential. Through the gradual process of collection, rearrangement, and revision, God preserved this treasure of Israel's response to his revelation.

Dating. A precise system of dating for the book of Psalms is impossible. Those responsible for the final edition of the Psalter, as well as previous collectors, endeavored to provide a hymnbook for their own generation. In times of stress and difficulty, they sought to revive the vigor of the past to serve the needs of their own day. The process of revision and adaptation makes many of the psalms appear to be later than they were in their original form. N. H. Snaith (*Twentieth Century Bible Commentary*, p. 235) says: "Few Psalms are either pre-exilic or wholly post-exilic. Some Psalms may contain elements varying in date by more than a thousand years." Some scholars have followed Duhm in making the majority of the psalms originate in Maccabean times. However, the trend today among such scholars as Gunkel, Snaith, Patterson, Oesterley, and others is toward earlier dates. The phrase, "The Hymn and Prayer Book of the Second Temple," may still be applied to the over-all collection because of the final editing after the Exile. Yet much of the Psalter is pre-Exilic, with some elements originally pre-Davidic. This recognition of early and late material makes the book of Psalms even more valuable as a record of the entire history of Israel's response to God as his Chosen People.

While it is important in interpretation to know the exact historical background and date of a passage, it is less imperative in the Psalms than in other Old Testament sections. Because of the universality of its truth, the book suffers less from lack of this knowledge than may be expected. Its timeless message makes it applicable in the pre-Exilic period, the post-Exilic period, and in our present age. However, this timelessness should not keep us from discovering the historical background wherever possible. Literary style, historical allusions, language, theological ideas, and other internal evidences should be examined, because any passage gains in reality when the background is properly understood. Even though such gains in reality are desirable, dogmatism in assigning authors, dates, and circumstances is out of place because of the timeless message of the book. It must be remembered that history has a way of repeating itself again and again.

Poetic Form. The Hebrews have given to the world a heritage of simple and childlike poetic expression. Their poetic utterances came from the heart rather than from a desire for artful excellence. Since Hebrew is a pictorial language, every word is graphic and vivid. The verbal roots portray visible action, while the usage provides room for strong imagination. There is in the language an intense emotional quality well fitted to display burning religious passion.

Although Hebrew poetry lacks rhyme and is weak in metrical system, it has compensatory features. Instead of these basic fundamentals of English verse, Hebrew employs two main distinguishing characteristics—accentual stress (rhythm) and parallelism. According to F. C. Eiselen (*The Psalms and Other Sacred Writings*), rhythm is "the harmonious repetition of fixed sound relations." An accentual pattern of two, three, or four beats to the line makes possible this harmonious repetition. Several unaccented syllables between the beats make a regulation of short and long syllables. This form of regulation depends upon rhythm within clauses and rhythmical balance between clauses. The result is a simple but pleasing rise and fall of the voice which can express animated spirit, calm assurance, excitement, lamentation, or other emotional qualities.

The second main distinguishing characteristic of Hebrew poetry is the balance of form and sense called *parallelism*. The poet states an idea; then he reinforces it by means of repetition, variation, or contrast. Three major types of parallelism are found throughout the Psalter:

1. Synonymous. The second line repeats the first in slightly different words (cf. Ps 1:2).
2. Antithetic. The second line shows sharp contrast with the first (cf. Ps 1:6).
3. Synthetic. The second line completes the first by supplementing the original thought (cf. Ps 7:1).

Three lesser types help to add richness and variety to Hebrew expression:

1. Introverted. The second line is parallel to the third and the first to the fourth (cf. Ps 30:8-10; 137:5,6).
2. Climactic. The second line completes the first by bringing the thought to a climax (cf. Ps 29:1,2).
3. Emblematic. The second line continues the thought of the first by raising it to a higher realm or using a simile (cf. Ps 1:4).

There are other factors which explain the effectiveness of parallelism. At the heart of the matter is the reader's expectation and satisfaction. The first line should always raise a sense of expectation, while the succeeding lines should satisfy that expectation. The poet can gain variety by changing the degree of expectation raised or the method of satisfying it by using contrast to show the unexpected. The parallelism is sometimes complete, sometimes incomplete, with one element missing; and at other times there is a compensatory element added to bring a better sense of satisfaction. Not only parallelism but patterned rhythm produces this expectation-satisfaction sensation. G. B. Gray *(The Forms of Hebrew Poetry,* 1915) has given names to the two basic types of rhythm. "Balancing rhythm" produces a certain satisfaction because the number of accentual stresses is equal (3:3 or 2:2). "Echoing rhythm" produces a different sensation by giving the second line fewer stresses than the first (3:2). The most frequently used form of the latter is the *Quinah* metre, used in laments and dirges.

In addition to parallelism and rhythm, two other elements affect Hebrew poetry. These are not distinguishing characteristics, for they are present in all poetry. The first is the emotional quality which produces a *heightened expression.* Special power-packed words or phrases can produce this effect. The use of a profuse number of gutturals can display harshness. Sharp sibilants can express victory or grief over defeat. Onomatopoetic words can easily suggest the message. The second element is the *mnemonic value* of the poem, which helps the reader to remember it. Rather than using rhyme, the psalmist occasionally employed an acrostic arrangement. Each line or a set number of lines would begin with successive letters of the Hebrew alphabet. Psalm 119 is an excellent example, as each line in an eight-line section begins with the same letter. All twenty-two letters of the Hebrew alphabet are used in successive sections. Such an artificial device made it easier for people to commit these psalms to memory. Actually, only eight or nine psalms are so constructed in their entirety. Each of these is proverbial in nature and would suffer from some detachment of thought if it were not for this alphabetical arrangement.

In basic style Hebrew poetry is vastly different from modern poetry. However, the Hebrew pattern has close affinity with that of the Near East. There are numerous similarities in style between the poetry of Israel and that of Egypt and Mesopotamia. Yet the most marked similarities are evident in a comparison of Hebrew psalms and Ugarit poems. The poetry of Ugarit is basically the Canaanite-Syrian type. Canaan and Syria were in close contact with Israel throughout pre-Exilic history. The main similarities concern metaphors, phrases, rhythm, and parellelism—all matters of literary style and phraseology. Religiously and theologically, the differences outweigh all the similarities.

Classification. Any cursory comparison of the poems in the Psalter reveals that they have not been grouped by subject matter. The subjects, covered or alluded to, run the gamut of human experience. Although the various topics are too numerous to list, five dominant themes can be recognized:

1. Realization of God's presence.
2. Recognition of a need for thanksgiving.
3. Personal communion with God.
4. Remembrance of God's part in history.
5. Sense of deliverance from enemies.

There have been many attempts to classify the psalms according to a preconceived standard. Mowinckel and others have centered on the *content,* developing elaborate topical subdivisions. Others have attempted to uncover the basic *mood* of the author of each psalm. Still other authors have relied upon the *type* of each psalm as a criterion for classification. This began simply as a threefold division into hymns of praise, prayers, and songs of faith. Recently Gunkel has done valuable work in further identifying these types or categories. His basic premise is that the psalms were originally cult songs used in the worship of Israel. He thus classifies each according to the "regular recurring formulae" of each particular type. Gunkel recognizes five main types as follows:

1. Hymns of Praise
2. National Laments
3. Royal Psalms (including Messianic Psalms)
4. Individual Laments
5. Thanksgivings of the Individual

To these he adds a number of minor types represented by a few psalms each:

6. Songs of Pilgrimage
7. Thanksgivings of the Nation
8. Wisdom Poems
9. Torah Liturgies
10. Mixed Types

These categories represent the final and latest scheme by Gunkel (cf. N. H. Snaith in *Twentieth Century Bible Commentary,* p. 235ff.). Previously, Gunkel had included other minor types, such as: "Blessings and Curses," and "Prophetic Psalms" (cf. John Patterson, *The Praises of Israel,* p. 32). We may add to these classifications the category of Messianic Psalms.

As tempting as it is to discover a system of classification, there is a certain indefiniteness about the Psalter which defies absolute classification. This lack of definiteness is caused by the timeless and universal characteristics of the collection. Actually, each method of classification gives a different view of the Psalms, making possible an understanding of the many facets available.

Abiding Value. The Psalter is first a living testimony to Israel's faith. The individual psalms give evidence of the thought and feeling of countless Hebrew worshipers. They echo the aspirations and hopes of men and women in every era of Israel's history. They reflect the hardships and struggles of God's people. They show the pilgrimage from doubt to certainty in these critical centuries of God's leading. They point always toward the conquest of despair by means of faith in the living God. The history of Israel would be lacking indeed without these evidences of faith's response to God's revelation.

Secondly, the Psalms form an important background for Jesus' ministry. He learned them in his Jewish home at his devotions. At his baptism, his mission was stated in the words of a psalm. On the cross, a psalm came to his mind in his last moments there. The Psalms are quoted more frequently in the New Testament than any other book of the Old Testament. There are about a hundred direct references or allusions to the Psalter in the New Testament. Phrases and verses are carried over to explain the character and message of Jesus as the Messiah.

In the third place, the book of Psalms has proved to be an indispensable source of devotional material. Christians around the world have been aided in their personal approach to God in worship. Psalm 51 voices the thoughts of the repentant sinner. Psalm 32 shows what joy a forgiven man can experience. Psalm 23 expresses the sense of trust common to all children of God. Psalm 103 pours forth the praise of God which every believer should express. Other psalms satisfy basic devotional needs, enriching the personal experience of any seeking person.

Finally, the Psalter has become the hymnbook of the ages. No other book of hymns has been used so long by so many people. It is read, chanted, or sung every day of the year. Samuel Terrien says of it: "No other book of hymns and prayers has been used for so long a time and by so many diverse men and women" (*The Psalms and Their Meaning for Today*, p. vii). In an age of informality, the Psalms provide an indispensable language for worship. In the words of Luther's "A Mighty Fortress Is Our God," Watts' "Jesus Shall Reign," and his "O God, Our Help in Ages Past," the message of the Psalter sounds around the earth.

OUTLINE

The present organization of the book clearly indicates its own appropriate outline:

Book I. Psalms 1–41.
Book II. Psalms 42–72.
Book III. Psalms 73–89.
Book IV. Psalms 90–106.
Book V. Psalms 107–150.

COMMENTARY

BOOK I. Psalms 1–41

The first book in the fivefold division of the Book of Psalms appears to have been once in a separate Davidic collection. The name Lord, Hebrew *Yahweh,* occurs 272 times, while the more general *'Elōhîm* is found only 15 times. The psalms are varied in content, but the moral teaching is simple and direct. Evident throughout this division is a positive faith in the justice of God. Psalm 1 serves as an introduction to the entire Psalter, while Psalm 2 introduces the collection in Book I. The fact that some manuscripts list Psalm 3 as the first psalm makes the introductory character of 1 and 2 more apparent. It is further possible that 1 and 2 were originally joined as one psalm, beginning and ending with "Blessed." All except 1, 2, 10, and 33 are connected with David in the title annotations.

Psalm 1. The Two Ways of Life

This psalm presents in sharp contrast two extremes—the truly righteous way of life and the basically wicked way. The contrast introduces in a didactic manner the two categories of men to be described throughout the Psalter. The psalmist continues the antithesis by showing the present and future destinies of each group.

1-3. The Way of the Godly Man. **Blessed is the man.** The Psalter opens with a strong interjection, *O the happinesses of the man* who follows God's plan. The verbs, **walketh, standeth, sitteth,** describe the characteristic steps of the wicked which the righteous avoid: accepting the principles of the wicked, participating in the practices of outright sinners, and finally joining with those who openly mock. Note the threefold parallel between the three verbs and their modifying clauses. The shift is then made from the negative refusal to the positive delight. Such a man meditates or muses constantly on God's teaching. As a result, he becomes more and more like a "transplanted tree," with roots in eternal realities. Constant vitality is assured and ultimate success is certain because he has put his trust firmly in God.

4-6. The Way of the Ungodly Man. **The ungodly are not so.** An abrupt change now occurs with the words **not so.** The sharp contrast is intensified by the use of this frequent term for the wicked, which stands as the exact antithesis of the term, **the righteous.** Unlike the firmly established tree, the ungodly is swept away by the wind. The picture is that of a threshing floor on a hill-top, where the wind clears away the chaff and leaves the grain. In parallel construction, the two classes (**ungodly** and **sinners**) are promised no part in the vindicated company of the righteous. While God *regards* or concerns himself with the way of the righteous, the wicked merely drift on to ultimate destruction.

Psalm 2. The Victory of God's Messiah

This is basically a royal psalm, with highly dramatic qualities and great poetical power. Included in its structure is an oracle of the Lord which has occasioned various interpretations. Gunkel connects it with a festival celebrating the coronation of a Judean king. If such was the original setting, the psalm has been thoroughly adapted to wider Messianic hopes. Even as Psalm 1 deals with the two ways for an individual's life, Psalm 2 sets forth the two ways for nations and peoples.

1-3. The Rebellion of the Nations. **Why?** In prophetic style, the psalmist begins with two rhetorical questions. The point of the questions is to demonstrate the absurdity of those who would rebel against the decree of the Almighty. Their rebellion against God's people and king is regarded as an attack against God himself. Basically, this antagonism is aimed at Jehovah's rulership through his **anointed** (one).

4-6. The Answer of God. **He . . . shall laugh . . . then shall he speak.** A bold anthropomorphism draws a sharp contrast between the worried little kings and the supreme Ruler who puts them **in derision** (root idea, "to stammer"). His laughter changes quickly to burning anger as he informs these rebellious ones that he has already installed his king with full divine approval.

7-9. The Plan for the Anointed. **The Lord hath said.** The oracle by God's anointed is declared as God's decree. The declaration, **Thou art my Son,** parallels the "my king" of God's answer. The phrase is applied to Jesus at his baptism (Mk 1:11). The term, **begotten,** is part of an Oriental formula for adoption used in the Code of Hammurabi. Note that two promises are given to God's anointed —dominion and victory. Although the psalmist probably thought of the **Son** as the chosen ruler (II Sam 7:14), in the light of the NT we see the Messiah as truly the Son of God.

10-12. The Admonition to the Kings. **Be wise . . . be instructed.** The choice is laid before the kings, along with the admonition to be wise and straighten up in making their decision. The choice of wisdom goes beyond mere acceptance of the decree. They are to serve the Lord with the awe and reverence due him. The kissing of royal feet and hands was a symbol of homage. Even as the way of the wicked shall perish in Psalm 1, so shall the way of those who refuse to do homage.

Psalm 3. A Morning Prayer of Confidence

The basic characteristics of an individual lament are exhibited in this psalm, the sequel to which is found in Psalm 4, where a sense of relief is evident. Because of the expression of sublime trust in God's protection, this psalm has been a favorite of many people facing peril. Verse 5 clearly identifies it as a morning prayer.

1,2. The Psalmist's Plight. **They . . . that trouble me.** The enemies of the psalmist are becoming more numerous than they have ever been before. Physically, he is in grave danger. And besides, his spirit is weighed down by his adversaries' taunts to the effect that he is beyond the help of God. These disheartening comments are similar to those directed toward Job (Job 2:11-13).

3,4. His Helper. **But Thou, O Lord.** In the midst of his troubles he remembers again that God is **a shield** to protect him, **my glory** to restore his dignity, and **the lifter up of my head** to give him new courage. The verbs in verse 4 should be frequentative: *Whenever I call, He answers!*

5,6. His Confidence. **I laid me down and slept.** The knowledge that God is his helper and protector makes this sleep possible. Upon awaking, he realizes that it is God who has sustained him. With his confidence increased by this experience, he is certain that no number of foes can make him afraid.

7,8. His Prayer. **Arise, O Lord.** The power and deliverance of God are invoked by this petition, as the psalmist seeks active intervention. He is either recalling what God has done on previous occasions or using a prophetic perfect. The latter foresees an end as clearly certain and so speaks of it as complete already. The last verse adapts the psalm to public worship, and may indicate a lack of selfishness in the whole private prayer.

Psalm 4. An Evening Prayer of Relief

The circumstances surrounding this psalm are similar to those of Psalm 3. However, here the lament becomes a song of trust to express the psalmist's relief. The serenity of tone throughout is the result of an experience of God's help in the past. Even as God gave rest in the previous experience (Ps 3), there is assurance that he will provide that same peaceful rest again. Verse 8 connects this song with evening prayer.

1. Urgent Appeal to God. **Answer me . . . be gracious . . . hear my prayer** (RSV). There is here a threefold request to God, who has proved himself to be righteous and capable of deliverance. Past experience leads the psalmist to believe that God will again meet his deepest needs.

2-5. Wise Counsel for Fellowmen. **O ye sons of men.** These men had slandered the reputation of the psalmist; they had loved vain schemes, and thrived on falsehood. In quietness they should meditate on their needs and sin not. They should speak to their own consciences and be silent. Even as the psalmist calls, "O God of my righteousness" (v. 1), he demands this same righteous motive in their sacrifices. The logical parallel is that of trust in the One to whom they offer these sacrifices.

6-8. Serene Trust in God. **Thou hast put gladness in my heart.** Many individuals were discontented and pessimistic, lacking the gladness which the psalmist knew. In contrast to these pessimists, the author knows that God's help in the time of need causes more gladness than bumper crops. He closes with the picture of peaceful sleep possible to one who knows God's care by personal experience.

Psalm 5. A Morning Prayer, Preparatory to Worship

There is in this psalm an atmosphere of strife between the righteous and the wicked, such as is frequently found in the Psalter. The situation is similar to that of Psalms 3 and 4 in that in both there are dangerous foes all about. The psalm may have been used by the priests in their preparation for morning sacrifice or by the individual as he prepared for worship.

1-3. An Invocation to God. **Give ear . . . consider . . . hearken.** The preparation for worship must always include the individual's cry to God. Not only his words but his meditation (lit., *whispering)* is a part of this invocation. In parallel form, the time is specified, probably connecting the speaker's prayer with the morning sacrifice.

4-9. A Lesson in Contrast. **Wickedness . . . worship.** There is a double contrast in these verses: the attitudes of the righteous and wicked toward sin and worship are contrasted, as well as the different responses of God toward the two groups. The psalmist recognizes that God cannot tolerate sin nor sojourn with the evil man. Therefore, God will not allow the **foolish** (lit., *arrogant)* to stand in his presence. He considers the **workers of iniquity** detestable. The end destined for those **that speak lies** (ASV) is utter destruction, and **the bloodthirsty and deceitful man** (ASV) is an abomination that God abhors. While these wicked men deal in treachery, the psalmist prostrates himself before God, praying for divine guidance.

10-12. A Prayer for Retribution. **Destroy thou them.** The prayer continues with a plea for justice upon these enemies. As those who rebel against God, they must be held guilty, allowed to fall, and cast down completely. In contrast to the threefold fate of the wicked ones, those who trust in God share in unending joy. They are to **rejoice,** to **shout for joy,** and to **exult in God.**

Psalm 6. A Cry for Relief

Here is a vivid picture of a man in dire distress because of a severe illness. Although the psalmist refers to his enemies, he is primarily crying out for relief from his malady. His mention of divine wrath shows that he conceives of his suffering as resulting from sin. While used among Christians as one of the seven Penitential Psalms, this may have been a penitential liturgy in the temple worship as well.

1,2a. Prayer for Cessation of Punishment. **Rebuke me not . . . neither chasten . . . have mercy.** These expressions show a recognition of the disciplinary side of suffering. The writer does not deny his guilt, not claim innocence. His punishment must cease before his emaciated body can be restored. All he can do is cast himself on the mercy of God.

2b-5. Prayer for Recovery. **Heal me . . . deliver my soul . . . save me.** The sufferer clearly realizes that deliverance must come from without, for he is thoroughly inadequate. He bases his plea upon the seriousness of his suffering, the mercy of God, and the fact that God will lose his thanksgiving if he goes to Sheol.

6,7. Description of His Condition. **Groaning . . . tears . . . grief.** The nature of his illness is somewhat obscured by the characteristic Oriental expressions. However, there can be no doubt that his grief is real and his suffering intense. Like Job, he has to endure the insults of his enemies in addition to his wretchedness.

8-10. Answered Prayers. **The Lord hath heard.** Twice the psalmist uses this phrase to indicate that a new era has arrived. He predicts that all his enemies shall turn back because God has taken command.

Psalm 7. A Prayer for Justice

Like many other psalms, this is first of all the lament of an individual. There is an element of self-righteousness in the psalmist's appeal. This may be due to the nature of the religious strife which occasioned the bitter persecution. However, there are corporate aspects which point to the possibility that several psalms have been combined into this one. If the individual is taken as representative of the nation, the unity of the psalm is preserved.

1,2. Prayer for Deliverance. **Save me . . . deliver me.** This appeal is based upon the speaker's personal trust in God. The fierce attack of the enemy also appears to be personal, as indicated by **my soul.**

3-5. Protestation of Innocence. **O Lord . . . if I have.** The author was certain that he was not deserving of his persecution. He was willing to put the protest in the form of an oath and an offer to accept any deserved reward for punishment.

6-8. Prayer for Judgment. **Arise, O Lord.** A bold figure of waking God is used to point up the necessity of immediate judgment. There is here a combination of personal vindication and the eschatological idea of a world judgment.

9-13. Confidence in the Righteous Judge. **The righteous God trieth the hearts and reins.** The outcome is assured by the very nature of God. The upright are preserved, while the wicked suffer God's wrath every day. God's action of judgment upon the unrepentant is figuratively stated in terms of earthly combat.

14-16. Nature of the Wicked. **Iniquity . . . mischief . . . falsehood.** These words characterize the adversary, who has fallen by his own devices. He is covering himself with the shroud of his evil desires.

17. Concluding Vow. **I will praise.** This characteristic doxology illustrates the assurance of the psalmist that the cause of righteousness will triumph.

Psalm 8. Man's Dignity and God's Glory

This psalm is a hymn which reaches a height of majesty seldom realized by finite man. There is a development of thought from the grandeur of God's throne in heaven to the lowest beasts of the earth. Man is pictured at the center of God's creation. The poem is artistically set inside a refrain at the beginning and end. This refrain acts as a beautiful introduction and conclusion. The questions of Psalm 8 are cited in Heb 2:6ff. in describing the humiliation and exaltation of Christ.

1,2. The Glory of God. **How excel-**

lent thy name. The introduction carefully identifies that "name" as **Jehovah, our Lord** *('Adôn)*. "Magnificent" or "majestic" would be a better translation than **excellent.** The phrase **babes and sucklings** may be a figure of man in his weakness. The sincere praise of these "babes" is set in sharp contrast to the scheming of God's enemies.

3,4. Man in Contrast. **When I consider thy heavens . . . what is man?** The night scene calls forth this praise of God's glory in the heavens. When man *('enôsh,* frail man) is compared with all of the expanse above, how insignificant he seems. He is truly just the son of mankind *('ādām,* generic man).

5,6. The Place of Man. **Little lower than the angels.** This would be better translated "little lower than divine" or "little less than divinity." Three things designate man's position: his relation to divinity, his dignity (glory and honor), and his dominion.

7,8. Illustrations of Man's Dominion. **All sheep . . . oxen . . . beasts . . . fowl . . . fish.** These lesser forms of life illustrate "all things" of the previous verse. The creatures of earth, air, and sea are included in this obvious reference to the creation story of Genesis 1.

9. Doxology. **How excellent is thy name.** The refrain calls man back to the majesty of God lest he become absorbed in thoughts of personal grandeur. Man has dignity, but God alone is majestic.

Psalm 9. Praise for Destruction of the Enemy

Evidently this psalm was originally joined to Ps 10, as shown in certain Hebrew manuscripts, the LXX, the Vulgate, and in another Latin version by Jerome. The two psalms form an acrostic using the letters of the Hebrew alphabet. The presence of *selāh* at the end of Ps 9 and the lack of a title on Ps 10 bear this out. The first psalm is highly national, while the second is strongly personal.

1-3. The Reason for Thanksgiving. **I will praise . . . shew forth . . . be glad . . . rejoice . . . sing.** All of this is wholehearted thanksgiving because the psalmist's enemies have been condemned by God. Sitting on his throne, God has passed judgment so that there is no doubt about the outcome.

4-8. A Vision of Final Judgment. **He shall judge the world in righteousness.** This is an eschatological picture of the final judgment, visualized as present. Mowinckel believes this to be a psalm used at the Feast of Tabernacles in a symbolical enthronement celebration.

9-12. The Exhortation to Praise. **Sing praises.** Since God will bless those that trust him, the psalmist seeks those who will join him in sincere praise. The natural sequel to praising God's name is to declare his doings.

13,14. An Appeal for God's Favor. **Have mercy upon me.** In the midst of national appeal a personal note is inserted. This lament is unusual within an expression of thanksgiving, but it may be natural for one expressing such sincere gratitude.

15-20. The Certainty of Judgment. **The Lord is known** *by* **the judgment.** The idea, previously introduced, of a world judgment to come is continued, as the writer declares that doom will surely overtake the wicked. The psalmist adds a request that nations may be brought to realize that they are only men!

Psalm 10. A Plea for Action

While this psalm has literary and textual affinity with the preceding one, the mood here is entirely different. The enemy is no longer the wicked of the nations but the wicked within Israel. The calamity has been caused by the misuse of power on the part of ungodly men of power. The mood is one of lament rather than of thanksgiving.

1,2. The Statement of the Plea. **Why . . . Why?** The frequent question beginning with "why" always describes a situation of frustration and forsakenness. The psalmist shows his own impatience and despair. After all, the persecution of the poor by the proud wicked leaders has reached an unbearable limit. His plea is that the wicked may reap what they have sown.

3-11. The Basis of the Problem. **The wicked boasteth.** This long list of grievances begins with the pride mentioned in the previous verses. The singular is used collectively of the many in Israel who have given no thought to God. Each condition is ethically oriented to Israel's way of life, and the whole passage reminds one of the writings of Isaiah, Micah, and Jeremiah.

12-18. The Call for Intervention. **Arise, O Lord . . . lift up thine hand.** This intense appeal for direct action by God is followed by arguments to strengthen the force of the appeal. The faith of the psalmist does not waver as he concludes that the Lord is King forever.

Psalm 11. The Assurance of Faith

A grave peril confronts the psalmist as enemies seek his life. His desperate situation gives rise to deep thought and noble expression of his confidence in the Lord. His words of assurance flow in a poem of true lyric quality. The circumstances are strikingly similar to those of several episodes in David's life.

1,2. Faith versus Expediency. **Trust** or **flee.** The advice of well-meaning friends is to take the way of expediency. "Flee to the mountain, where there are plenty of hiding places," is the worldly idea of how to find safety. Even in the face of the drawn bow of the enemy, the speaker affirms that his trust is in the Lord. Instead of taking the easy way out, he will take the way of faith.

3-7. The Foundation of Faith. **If the foundation be destroyed.** The psalmist knows that fleeing would only undermine his basic faith. After all, God is in his holy temple, his throne is established in heaven, and his eyes behold what goes on down here. Therefore, the punishment of God shall come upon the wicked even as it did upon Sodom, while the upright shall behold God's face.

Psalm 12. A Prayer for the Faithful

This psalm depicts another dark hour of persecution, when society is falling apart. While lamenting a situation in which lying and falsehood prevail, the author is likewise expressing his utmost confidence in God, who is still worshiped by the faithful minority. Gunkel treats this psalm in a liturgical sense, making it corporate. Whatever the final usage, there could well have been an original individualistic basis for its composition.

1-4. The Prayer of the Faithful. **Help, Lord.** The writer is speaking for the faithful, godly men who have been abused by the loudmouthed ones who speak idle flattery and indulge in double talk. Like Elijah, the psalmist speaks of himself as the only one left who has not joined these braggarts.

5. The Answer of God. **Saith the Lord.** This verse takes the form of an oracle from the Lord answering the sincere prayer of the faithful. God promises his help, which will result in complete safety.

6-8. The Response of the Worshiper. **Pure words.** In contrast to the talk of the loudmouthed ones, God's words are as pure as the finest silver. What he has promised, he will perform. His trustworthiness is assured and proclaimed as a response of worship.

Psalm 13. From Doubt to Trust

Expressed in this brief psalm are the deepest longings of a troubled soul. Although a personal enemy is behind the scenes, the psalmist is wrestling with his own doubts as to God's divine activity on his behalf. Since sickness is not alluded to, the problem is probably mental, very likely fear. In its structure this psalm is an excellent example of the lament of an individual, being carefully divided into three brief stanzas of two verses each.

1,2. His Problem of Doubt. **How long . . . ?** The fourfold repetition of this phrase clearly shows the writer's intense suffering. He is wearied by his enemy but even more distressed by God's seeming unconcern. He feels God-forsaken in the time of his greatest need.

3,4. His Prayer for Assistance. **Consider . . . hear . . . lighten mine eyes.** In the midst of doubt and dejection, he prays for God to understand his problem and bring back the brightness in his eyes. Not only does he fear physical death, but he knows how his enemies, in their godlessness, will boast concerning the downfall of a friend of God.

5,6. His Relief in Trust. **But I have trusted.** Although no spoken answer is recorded, a real relief comes over this troubled soul. His trust is based upon God's loving-kindness, his rejoicing upon God's salvation, his singing upon God's bountiful care. He has found true peace by utter trust in God.

Psalm 14. Judgment for Denying God

Here we have a good example to show how the Psalter developed. Except for minor textual variations (esp. v. 6) it is identical with Psalm 53. Since the latter is from a later collection and substitutes *Elohim* for *Yahweh,* Psalm 14 is considered to be the earlier form. In both psalms the speaker views the depraved condition of men with the true prophetic spirit.

1-3. The Depravity of the Fool. **No God.** The use of the word *fool (nābāl)* indicates not a theoretical atheist but a practical atheist, who lives as if there were no god. For all practical purposes God does not enter into his thinking. The words **corrupt, abominable,** and **filthy** all point to the depravity of such an individual, who is clearly pictured as typical of Israel in this age.

4-6. The Corruption of the Priesthood. **No knowledge.** These who lack knowledge of God are perhaps the priests, who eat the shewbread and should call upon God. Instead they are becoming **workers of iniquity** (cf. Hos 1:4-6). Instead of leading God's people, they devour them. The **generation of the righteous** obviously refers to **my people,** while **the poor** have a special place of refuge in God.

7. The Hope of Deliverance. **Oh that . . . !** This appended prayer may have been added for liturgical purposes. Or it may express the psalmist's one glimmer of hope in this dark period. To bring **back the captivity** may mean simply to "restore the fortunes." Regardless of when this verse was composed, it serves as a fitting conclusion.

Psalm 15. The Guest of God

This Wisdom psalm is a commentary on man's duty to God and to his fellowman as set forth in Deut 6:5 and Lev 19:18. It deals with the moral and ethical qualifications which admit a worshiper to the presence of God. The early custom of challenging the fitness of a worshiper may be reflected here. Perhaps the priest asked the questions in verse 1, the worshiper responded with an answer such as is given here, and the priest closed the challenge with the final promise of verse 5b. Some interpreters refer the question to the worshiper, with the answer and promise as the usual reply of the priests to the worshipers entering the Temple. The former seems preferable.

1. The Pertinent Question. **Lord, who . . . ?** The person who is to come into God's presence must face squarely this twofold question. The practice of pitching tents on Mount Moriah may have been allowed to pilgrims in certain periods of Israel's history. However, the parallel questions emphasize that God's standard must be met if a man is to be God's guest.

2-5b. The Acceptable Answer. **He that.** The matters of integrity and righteousness relate to man's duty to God, while truthfulness and the remaining virtues refer to man's duty toward his neighbor. By combining the similar **uprightness** and **integrity** (AV, *righteousness*), it is possible to discover an ethical decalogue in the phrases of this section.

5c. The Priestly Promise. **He that doeth.** The one who meets God's standard must be one who **doeth these things.** Such a person not only knows what God expects of his guest, but puts these principles into practice. The note of stability gives a proper climax to the psalm.

Psalm 16. The Joy of Loyalty

This song of trust is a wholehearted profession of the joy that comes from faithfulness and loyalty. The author lived in a day when apostasy and idolatry were extensive. Against this background he contrasts his supreme happiness with the plight of those who have slipped into idolatry. His great hope amplifies his present trust in God. The psalm is ascribed to David by Peter (Acts 2:25) and by Paul (Acts 13:35,36) when they refer to its prophecy of Messiah's resurrection.

1-4. Joy in Service. **Preserve me, O God.** This prayer is not for deliverance from an enemy but for the continuance of the happiness he has already found. His delight is in the saints, while his trust is in God. Contrasted with this is the state of multiplied sorrows which is the lot of those who have sought other gods.

5-8. Joy in Faith. **Inheritance . . . lot . . . lines.** These figures all refer to the allotment of land by lots whereby the Levites received no specific apportionment. Along with the figure of the writer's cup of happiness, these add up to a truly **goodly** heritage because God is his choicest possession. His stability is based upon God's constant leadership.

9-11. Joy in Hope. **Therefore.** On the basis of his present joy, the psalmist uses phrase after phrase to show the basis of his joyous hope. His **heart, liver** (rather than *glory*), and **flesh** all respond to the thrill of this hope. Verse 10a does not present a clear-cut reference to an afterlife, because the first phrase can be better translated, "For thou wilt not abandon my soul to Sheol"; but verse 10b must refer to someone other than the psalmist in saying, "Neither wilt thou allow thine Holy One to undergo corruption." Verse 11 points to a continuance of the happy life which he has already come to know in the presence of the Lord.

Psalm 17. The Vindication of the Righteous

The psalmist here laments his unjust treatment at the hands of his enemies. The cause of his problem is not known, only that he is innocent of the charges brought against him. God is clearly his last court of appeal, his only hope. His absolute confidence in God is shown throughout, but especially in the final verse.

1-5. An Appeal for Justice. **Hear the right.** The psalmist prays first that God will **hear, attend,** and **give ear** to his side of the case, which he presents, he declares, with lips free of deceit. His cry is only for a just sentence from the One who knows his innocence. God has **proved, visited,** and **tried** him, and will continue to find him guiltless.

6-12. An Appeal for Mercy. **Shew thy marvelous lovingkindness.** The speaker repeats his cry, this time with direct reference to his enemies. He requests that God will demonstrate his loving-kindness, keep him safe, and hide him from those who rise up against him. He describes his enemies in terms that point up the contrast between them and himself.

13-15. An Appeal for Deliverance. **Deliver my soul.** The next step is naturally the actual deliverance of this sufferer and the attendant destruction of the wicked enemy. The psalmist calls for decisive action to **disappoint** and **cast down** the enemy in open vindication of himself. **When I awake** may refer to the next morning after this experience or to a vision of God beyond the sleep of death.

Psalm 18. The Victor's Gratitude

Like Psalm 14, this psalm can be compared with another passage, in this case II Samuel 22. The psalmist repeatedly voices his thanksgiving and his confidence in God.

1-3. An Opening Hymn of Praise. **I will love . . . I will call.** This praise is based upon a full realization of what God means to him. These figures show God as a defending helper, not as the instigator of aggression.

4-19. A Picture of God's Deliverance. **He delivered me.** When the psalmist, in his distress, called on the Lord for help, the earth shook, the Lord thundered, and deliverance came. In graphic figures like those describing the theophany when the Law was given at Mount Sinai (Ex 19:16-18; 20:18,21; 24:16-18), the power of God is set forth.

20-30. The Basis of This Deliverance. **According to my righteousness.** Deliverance is here clearly regarded as a reward for righteousness, cleanness of hands, faithfulness, and uprightness. This is a comparative rather than an absolute evaluation of self. All of this is made possible by trust in God.

31-45. A Picture of Deep Gratitude. **It is God that girdeth me.** Credit for the victory is explicitly given to God, who made every step possible. He prepared the way, taught, trained, and led into battle.

46-50. A Concluding Hymn of Praise. **Let the God of my salvation be exalted.** All honor and praise is due unto God alone.

Psalm 19. God's Glory Above and Within

This psalm is clearly divided into two distinct sections, which suggests that it may be a composite of two poems. The first section (vv. 1-6) uses a general Semitic name for God *('Ēl),* while the second uses the special covenant name *(Yahweh).* In subject matter, style, and form the two sections differ. However, the union has been skillfully made; the psalmist's exaltation of the revelation of nature is fused with his exaltation of the law of God into one glorious hymn of praise.

1-6. The Testimony of the Heavens. **The heavens . . . the firmament . . . the sun.** Each of these has its part in making known the mystery of God's glory. In constant revelation by day and by night the expanse of the heavens reveals the excellence of God's creative work. The sun appears as the greatest member of the heavenly choir, running its appointed course of witness. While similar figures abound in Akkadian literature describing the sun-god Shamash (ANET, pp. 91, 116, 179, 387-389), the psalmist clearly regards the sun as an agent of God in revealing His glory.

7-10. The Testimony of the Torah. **The law of the Lord.** The psalmist here uses six names to describe the whole of God's inner revelation. The word *tôrâ* (law) embodies more than a written list of precepts; it includes all of God's teaching. Using adjectives and participial phrases, the psalmist describes the excellence of God's revelation, which surpasses even gold or honey.

11-14. The Personal Application. **Cleanse thou me.** The moral teaching of God, which serves as a warning, can lead a person to the desired reward. Meditating upon God's teaching acts as a mirror to make visible the inner man. Therefore, the psalmist closes by requesting the strength to overcome all types of sin and be found acceptable.

Psalm 20. Supplication for Victory

In both structure and content this royal psalm is very closely linked with

Psalm 21. The latter acts as a sequel of thanksgiving for answered prayer. The king is the central figure, while his victory occupies the attention of his subjects. It may well have been arranged for antiphonal singing, with the congregation or the Levitical choir acting as a chorus in verses 1-5 and 9. A priest or Levite may have voiced the words of assurance in verses 6-8. Complete confidence in God is expressed throughout.

1-5. A Prayer for the King. **The Lord hear thee.** Although the prayer is addressed *to* the king, it is also an act of intercession *for* the king. This describes a vital step in the preparation for battle, as the king presented his sacrifices to the Lord and received the assurance of God's blessing.

6-8. An Oracle of Assurance. **Now know I.** After an interval, possibly the time during which the sacrifices were offered, the speaker's response of confidence issues in the form of a prophetic oracle. The use of the prophetic perfect tense gives the necessary divine assurance to the king and worshipers. The army is now prepared to go forth in the **name of the Lord.**

9. Closing Chorus. **Save, Lord . . .** This is more literally stated in the LXX as *O Lord, save the King and answer us when we call.* It may have been sung by the whole congregation or by the Levitical choir.

Psalm 21. Thanksgiving for Victory

This royal psalm acts as the natural sequel to Psalm 20, since supplication becomes thanksgiving because of the recent victory. The same antiphonal arrangement may have been used in its adaptation for temple worship. Some commentators have suggested that the occasion was the birthday (cf. v. 4) or the coronation of a king (cf. v. 3).

1-7. Thanksgiving for Answered Prayer. **The king shall joy.** The congregation or temple choir addresses a prayer of gratitude to God for his signal victory. Each verse contributes to the list of things which God has done for and through the king. All of these blessings are directly related to the king's utter trust in God.

8-12. Confidence in the Future. **Thine hand shall.** The words are now addressed directly to the king but still in an attitude of worship. The thanksgiving is continued in terms of anticipated victories until finally all enemies will be destroyed.

13. Closing Doxology. **Be thou exalted.** Again the chorus joins in a final expression of heart-felt gratitude and united praise, returning to the picture of strength in verse 1.

Psalm 22. Triumph in Suffering

This psalm is the first of those sometimes called Passion Psalms. The use of the opening cry by Christ on the cross and the amazing phraseology of verses 6-8 and 13-18 have made this psalm especially important to Christians. There is within the psalm a strange mixture of praise and complaint. There is no reference to sin as the cause of the trouble, no plea of innocence, no claim of righteousness, and no vengeance. Therefore the words are peculiarly appropriate of the suffering Messiah, although in their primary meaning they are based on some experience of the psalmist.

1-18. His Personal Suffering. **My God, my God, why . . . ?** This initial appeal is stated in a question of only four words in the Hebrew *('Ēlî 'Ēlî lāmâ 'ăzabtānî).* These words were quoted by Jesus on the cross in Aramaic. Note that the psalmist does not lose faith even while describing his intense suffering and persecution. He feels forsaken by God but knows that God is near. After recalling the trust of his forefathers and their deliverance, he describes the contemptuous action by his enemies.

19-21. His Plea for Deliverance. **Be not thou far from me.** This idea occurs for the third time in an open plea for God's aid. **Haste thee to help, deliver,** and **save** all point to the urgency of his need.

22-26. His Public Thanksgiving. **I will declare.** This vow forms a transition from his description of suffering to his expression of praise. His desire is now to acknowledge publicly his dependence upon God and to proclaim his own personal deliverance.

27-31. His Joyful Anticipation. **All the ends of the world.** In hope, the psalmist sees the circle widen to include all mankind and future generations. His personal hope encompasses the nation and then the world. In accord with the highest hope of Israel, the turning of mankind to God in worship (cf. Isa 40:7; Phil 2:10) is based upon *what he* (the Lord) *has done.*

Psalm 23. My Shepherd

As a song of trust, this psalm has no peer. It is impossible to estimate its effect upon man through the centuries. Grief, sadness, and doubt have been driven away by this strong affirmation of faith. Peace, contentment, and trust have been the blessings upon those who have come to share the psalmist's sublime confidence. While the language is simple and the meaning clear, no one has been able to exhaust the message of the poem or improve upon its quiet beauty.

1-4. God as the Personal Shepherd. **The Lord is my shepherd.** A long experience of trusting God lies behind these words. The rich corporate relation of Israel to God is appropriated as an individual realization. The picture of a faithful shepherd is the epitome of tender care and continuing watchfulness. The sheep instinctively trust the shepherd to provide for the morrow. The most distinctive feature of this extended metaphor is the wise leading of the shepherd. He leads into rest and reviving, into the struggles of life, and through the dangerous places. The shepherd thus provides for the needs of life and protects from the fear of danger.

5-6. God as the Gracious Host. **Thou preparest a table.** The writer introduces a secondary metaphor to further express his trust. The scene changes to show the psalmist as the guest of honor at God's house, enjoying the warm hospitality characteristic of the East. He is under God's protection. His head is anointed with perfumed oil. His every need is completely satisfied. On the basis of this trust, every moment of his life will be filled with God's richest blessings. The greatest blessing will be an intimate fellowship with God through continued worship of Him.

Psalm 24. An Inaugural Anthem

This is one of the most majestic and stately hymns of the entire Psalter. Because of several abrupt changes in subject matter, many have judged that this psalm is made up of selections from three poems originally independent (vv. 1,2; 3-6; 7-10). While this may be so, the psalm is now an appropriate unit. The occasion has been associated with the Feast of Tabernacles, an annual New Year's festival, the dedication of the Temple, and the bringing of the ark to Jerusalem. It is very likely that this psalm, like many others, was used antiphonally.

1,2. The Processional Chorus. **The earth is the Lord's.** This emphasis upon the sovereignty of God over the habitable earth and all creatures is worthy caution against limiting God to one city or one temple. These words were probably sung on many occasions by groups approaching the city of Jerusalem.

3-6. The Prerequisites of Worship. **Who shall ascend . . . shall stand?** A recognition of the Creator. God as sovereign over all the earth must not be approached lightly. The moral requirements for approaching God are carefully set forth by questions similar to those of Psalm 15. The same high standards of ethical conduct are demanded, with special emphasis upon the character of the worship. The questions and answers were probably chanted by priests or Levites, while verse 6 may have been used as a chorus.

7-10. The Divine Entrance. **Lift up your heads, O ye gates.** The lintels or tops of the portals are pictured as being too low for the divine king to enter. **The King of glory shall come in.** The summons to the gatekeepers symbolizes the truth that the presence of God is to be evident. Then the challenge to identify this King is chanted by another group or by an individual on the city wall. The powerful answer may well have been the response of the congregation clearly identifying this King as the Lord. After the second summons and challenge, the response rings clear – **The Lord of hosts** *(Yahweh Ṣᵉbāʾôt),* **He is the King of glory.**

Psalm 25. An Acrostic Prayer for Help

This psalm, the supplication of an individual, uses the letters of the Hebrew alphabet as a framework. It is difficult to recognize here a logical order of thought because of the necessity of beginning each verse with a subsequent letter of the alphabet. There are only three places in our present text (vv. 2,5,18) where the acrostic breaks down. The style is simple, straightforward, prayerful, and humble.

1-7. A Prayer for Protection. **Unto thee, O Lord.** The basis of this petition for protection is the psalmist's simple trust in God. Though his enemies have not triumphed over him, they are a constant threat. He appeals to God's mercy and loving-kindness, which have been revealed in history.

8-10. A Meditation upon the Character of God. **Good and upright is the Lord.** These and other characteristics of God are discerned from his response in history. Because of his justice, righteousness, loving-kindness, and truth, he will guide and teach men in these same paths.

11-14. A Meditation upon Man's Relation to God. **The secret of the Lord.** After a brief prayer for pardon, the psalmist reflects on the secret of man's proper relation to God. This he discovers to be the **fear of the Lord** – that reverential and trustful relation referred to frequently in Proverbs.

15-22. A Prayer for Deliverance. **Turn thee unto me.** Using graphic verbs (**pluck, turn, bring, look, forgive, consider, keep, preserve**), the writer prays for God to deliver him. A fitting conclusion to the psalm is found in the broadened view of verse 22, where God is petitioned to **redeem** the nation as well as the speaker himself. If this verse is taken as an integral part of the original psalm, it forms a climax for the thought. If, however, it is taken as an addition, it serves to adapt the psalm for corporate use.

Psalm 26. A Worshiper's Prayer

That there was conflict between religious groups in Israel is evident from this lament. Some commentators suggest that a pestilence is involved in the background. However that may be, the psalmist's protests regarding his integrity point to a society in which the ungodly have ascendancy. This psalm, although more individual than corporate, could well be used by a pious group in the time of affliction.

1-7. A Protest of Innocence. **Judge me, O Lord.** The psalmist is so sure of his integrity that he seeks divine judgment; he asks that God **examine, prove,** and **try** him. He claims to have walked in the truth, to have avoided any contact with renegade Jews, and to have participated regularly in worship. All of this stands in sharp contrast to the conduct of his enemies.

8-12. A Prayer for Vindication. **Gather not my soul with sinners.** His plea is not that he may avoid death, but that he may avoid being grouped with the ungodly, whom he has so carefully avoided in life. In this prayer for special treatment, he prays for God to **redeem** and **be merciful** to him because he is going to continue to walk in integrity, stand firmly, and bless the Lord publicly.

Psalm 27. A Song of Trust

The marked contrast between verses 1-6 and 7-14 has led most commentators to designate this psalm as a composite. Both the content and the spirit of these sections are vastly different. The mood changes from joyful confidence to anxious fear. However, two elements tie together these dissimilar parts – similar enemies and trust in God.

1-3. Unconditional Trust. **The Lord is my light and my salvation.** These exultant words introduce a scene of serenity. Nowhere else in the OT is the Lord referred to as **my light.** Because the psalmist has found God as **light, salvation,** and **strength,** there is no cause for fear or terror. His serenity is not conditioned by outward circumstances but is unconditional.

4-6. Life's Greatest Desire. **One thing have I desired.** The one thing desired cannot be equated with the Temple, as many commentators suggest. It must refer to a basis for the three-part wish. That basis or common denominator is most likely the presence of the Lord, which the psalmist desires and seeks. The realization of this presence comes from dwelling in God's house, beholding his beauty, and inquiring in his Temple. This same presence results in safety in the time of trouble.

7-14. A Cry of Anxious Fear. **Hear, O Lord.** These words shift the mood entirely from triumph to deep distress as they introduce a new situation and occasion. Even though the psalmist has been forsaken and rejected, his trust does not fail. From the depths of despair, he calls himself back to the patience required in waiting for God to work out his will.

Psalm 28. An Answered Prayer

This psalm, like many other laments, deals with the strife between those of traditional faith and those affected by alien influences. The psalmist is deeply afraid he will suffer the fate which must overtake his wicked antagonists. That he views his prayer as answered is obvious from the change in verse 6.

1,2. Appeal To Be Heard. **Be not silent. . . . Hear.** The psalmist appeals to God both to hear him and to answer. To a Hebrew, the lack of an answer often seemed to indicate that God would not hear the petition. The urgent nature of the speaker's cry is emphasized by his fear that he will die if God does not answer.

3-5. Prayer for Intervention. **Draw me not away. . . . Give them according to their deeds.** His first prayer is for protection against his godless foes. However, his emphasis quickly changes to a plea for retribution upon these enemies.

6,7. Thanksgiving for Answered Prayer. **Blessed be the Lord.** The cause of this outburst of praise is to be understood as God's response to the appeal of verses 1 and 2. This thanksgiving may have been added later by the psalmist. Or it may be the expression of an inner confidence that God has truly heard and is no longer silent.

8,9. Application for the Nation. **The Lord their strength.** The fact that God is the psalmist's strength finds application for the nation and the king. This may well be a later addition designed to adapt the individual's expression of faith for corporate worship.

Psalm 29. God's Glory in the Storm

In awe-inspiring poetry, this hymn of praise points to the thunderstorm as another evidence of God's glory. Notes of assurance are constantly intermingled with the phrases descriptive of God's omnipotence. Seldom does any psalmist exhibit more graphic poetical power than the one who wrote this nature psalm. The close parallels in terminology with Canaanite poems from 1400–1300 B.C. discovered at Ugarit in Syria indicate that this psalm is at least as old as David, but the psalmist is careful to recognize Yahweh alone as the true God.

1,2. The Call to Worship. **Worship the Lord.** The whole heavenly host is exhorted to **ascribe unto the Lord glory and strength.** This worship is to be accomplished **in holy array** (RSV; rather than *in the beauty of holiness,* AV). Many commentators believe that in using the term *b^{e}nê 'ēlîm* (AV, *O ye mighty),* which might be translated as "sons of God," the author is summoning the angels. But others believe that the people of Israel, as the sons of God, are being addressed (cf. Deut 14:1; Ps 82:6).

3-9. The Seven fold Voice. **The voice of the Lord.** Seven times this phrase is used to express the thunder of the storm. It is not God's anger but his majestic power which makes the storm move. It begins out over the Mediterranean Sea with power and majesty. It then moves in over the mountains to the north of Palestine and over the wilderness to the south. The description of the effect upon trees, mountains, wilderness, and animals is followed by the chorus of "glory" which comes from man's worship.

10,11. Conclusion. **The Lord will bless.** While God sits over all in **glory** (v. 9), he grants to his people the two things they most need – **strength** and **peace.**

Psalm 30. Praise for God's Healing

This psalm relates the experience of one who has just escaped death by being delivered from a serious illness. His remarkable recovery produces joyful thanksgiving and causes him to reflect on the lessons he has gained from his suffering.

1-3. Praise for Recovery. **I will extol thee, O Lord.** The psalmist's object is, clearly, to exalt the Lord because he has been saved from Sheol and the grave. He gives full credit to God for his deliverance. There are, however, foes in the background who rejoice to see a righteous man suffer.

4,5. A Call to Remembrance. **Sing . . . give thanks.** Because of his personal experience with God, the psalmist calls on **the saints** to join him in praise. These are the like-minded ones who are bound to the Lord in covenant relation. They are urged to give thanks **to the memorial of his holiness.** The phrase **in his favor is life** may also be translated *his favor is for a lifetime*. This rendering contrasts the moment of God's wrath with a lifetime of his favor.

6-10. Suffering in Retrospect. **I shall never be moved.** Prior to his sickness, he had boasted, in a spirit of self-sufficiency. His pride collapsed with the crush of illness. However, the sickness had the effect of opening his eyes to his dependence upon God, so that he cried for mercy and healing.

11,12. Renewed Praise. **I will give thanks unto thee for ever.** No longer silent, the psalmist wants everyone to know of the change in his life – from mourning to dancing, from sackcloth to gladness, from silence to praise.

Psalm 31. A Prayer of Surrender

Here, again, is the strong complaint of an individual against the unmerciful treatment of his enemies. The general nature of his sufferings (esp. vv. 1-8) makes this psalm the voice of many worshipers through the centuries. The seeming change in tone in verse 9 and the fact that relief has already come have led many commentators to suggest composite authorship. However, the latter section seems to describe an intensified problem on the part of the same author.

1-8. A Trustful Appeal. **In thee . . . my trust.** It is in God that the psalmist has taken refuge. Upon this basis he can appeal in faith for deliverance and security. Jesus' use of verse 5 on the cross has made this entire psalm sacred and memorable.

9-18. An Intensified Appeal. **Have mercy upon me.** While the preceding verses describe the mercies of the past, these verses set forth the extreme need of the present. This section has several striking parallels with the experiences of Jeremiah. The psalmist has become a **reproach** and **a fear** to his friends. He is a forgotten man who is cast away as a broken vessel. In this state of loneliness and despair, his only friend is God, and his only hope is surrender to God's mercy.

19-24. A Spirit of Gratitude. **Oh how great is thy goodness.** The recollection of past mercies and the assurance of continuing help calls forth words of praise and blessing. This trust in God prompts him to exhort others to **love** the Lord and **be of good courage.**

Psalm 32. The Joy of Forgiveness

The psalmist, in this second one of the seven Penitential Psalms, clearly speaks of his own personal experience. There is only a secondary sense in which the application may be made corporate. The true nature of sin is forcibly realized while the joyous freedom of pardon is a past and present reality. The didactic purpose of the psalmist indicates that the poem has affinity with the Wisdom psalms.

1,2. The Blessedness of Forgiveness. **Blessed.** Literally, *O how happy.* Joy comes to the sinner because God has completely pardoned him. Note the four words for sin: **transgression** means willful disobedience or rebellion; **sin** refers to missing the mark or aim; **iniquity** implies twistedness or perversity; **guile** suggests self-deception in this context. Each of these is an aspect of moral offense and is cared for in God's mercy and forgiveness.

3,4. The Burden of Guilt. **When I kept silence.** His previous silence was actually a refusal to acknowledge his sin before God. Whether sickness was involved or not, the psalmist recognized that God's chastening was being felt. There was no relief, day or night, as long as he refused to confess his sin before the Lord.

5. The Relief of Confession. **I acknowledged . . . thou forgavest.** This was undoubtedly a process rather than an instantaneous act. He first began to acknowledge, did not hide, and finally said, "I will confess." Note the emphatic position of **thou** as the writer shifts the emphasis to what God does.

6-11. The Wisdom of Experience. **For this.** Because of the availability of God's forgiveness, the psalmist exhorts men to pray in like manner. On the basis of his own profound experience, he becomes an instructor, a teacher, and a guide, using the language of a sage. Verse 8 seems to be a quotation from one of the songs of deliverance mentioned in verse 7, so that it is God who guides and instructs the believer.

Psalm 33. A Call to Congregational Worship

This psalm corresponds to the nationalistic psalms of Book V. At first glance it appears to be out of place in Book I, but it is placed here as an answer to the invitation of verse 11 in the preceding psalm. The answer translates the personal experience into a national hymn of thanksgiving. The presence of twenty-two verses suggests a relation to the Hebrew alphabet, although there is no acrostic arrangement.

1-3. The Call to Worship. **Rejoice . . . praise . . . sing . . . play.** The response of the righteous takes the form of public worship. The nature of the accompaniment to be used, as to kinds of instruments and intensity of sound, is clearly stated. The occasion demands a new song or a fresh composition.

4-9. Praise of the Lord's Word. **The word of the Lord.** The actual praise begins with a listing of God's moral attributes as evidenced in history. **Uprightness, faithfulness, righteousness, justice,** and **lovingkindness** all describe him. Praise continues as the writer describes the creative power of God's word. The word is thus viewed as an expression of the Lord's thought, will, and action.

10-12. Praise of the Lord's Counsel. **The counsel of the Lord standeth for ever.** In contrast to the futile counsel of the heathen, God has chosen and guided his chosen people.

13-19. Praise of the Lord's Watchfulness. **The Lord looketh.** God looks, beholds, and considers all that men think or plan. He understands the plots of evil men and his all-seeing eye recognizes the needs of his people.

20-22. The Final Chorus of Praise. **Our soul waiteth.** The rejoicing of the entire psalm is based upon the waiting, trusting, and hoping of the assembled worshipers.

Psalm 34. The Goodness of the Lord

This song of praise is an acrostic, similar in structure to Psalm 25. It is indeed striking that both psalms omit the letter *Waw* and add an extra *Pe* at the end. In regard to content, both are songs of thanksgiving, similar in thought to the book of Proverbs.

1-3. His Invitation to Praise. **O magnify the Lord with me.** The resolution to praise God continually is the basis for seeking others to magnify and exalt the Lord. This invitation is directed toward those who are humble and teachable.

4-6. His Testimony of Deliverance. **I sought . . . he heard . . . and delivered.** Out of his firsthand experience, the psalmist illustrates the basis for this sincere praise. Following the LXX and various manuscripts and versions, verse 5 would be better translated, **Look upon me and be lightened, and your faces will not be ashamed.**

7-10. His Assurance of Blessing. **O taste and see.** The only way that others can know the blessings is by putting God to the test. The psalmist says, "Try him and see." The true blessings come only to those who **trust, fear,** and **seek** the Lord.

11-22. His Lesson for Disciples. **Come, ye children . . . I will teach you.** His experiential knowledge has given him the right to teach others. Those addressed as children are again the humble and teachable disciples of any age. The style is the didactic question and answer method of the wise men. The theme is retribution as interpreted by orthodox Judaism.

Psalm 35. A Plea for Vengeance

The psalmist here offers further evidence that God is the court of appeals for the persecuted in Israel. It appears that two incidents or two series of incidents are described. Verses 1-10 refer primarily to physical acts, whereas the remaining verses suggest a law court scene. The poem is clearly divided into three cycles, each ending in a vow of thanksgiving. The psalmist appears as the defendant throughout, but constantly recommends the punishment for his foes.

1-10. The First Appeal for Judgment. **Plead my cause, O Lord.** In the language of warfare, the psalmist pleads for justice on his own terms. He expresses his resentment by asking that his enemies be completely defeated, discredited, and caught in their own pitfalls. He ends this cycle with a vow that he will really rejoice in the Lord.

11-18. The Basis of Further Appeal. **They rewarded me evil for good.** This appears to belong to another occasion, although it may be a sequel to the first appeal. The enemies are here former friends who have turned on the writer and rejoiced over his ill fortune. They employed false witnesses and mocked him, while he only returned good for their evil. Again he closes the cycle with a vow that he will publicly praise God if God will only deliver him.

19-28. The Second Appeal for Judgment. **Judge me, O Lord.** The psalmist pleads first that his enemies may no longer taunt him or speak evil of him. Then he appeals for a final judgment on the case so that his enemies will receive the treatment of shame and dishonor which they afforded him. Once again he closes the cycle with a vow of thanksgiving.

Psalm 36. A Lesson in Contrast

Two sharply defined pictures, one of godlessness and the other of godliness are presented here. The style varies with the contrast in themes. The psalmist uses rough poetic form and language to describe evil, and smooth form and beautiful language for the description of God. Although some commentators suggest that two poems have been joined together in this psalm, that is neither clear nor necessary. The language and thought of the conclusion in verses 10-12 revert to the pattern of the first section.

1-4. The Hideousness of Evil. **No fear of God.** This appears to be the substance of an oracle which describes in essence the evil enemy of the psalmist. The manuscripts and versions differ as to whether the oracle is directed to the heart of the psalmist or to that of the wicked man. There is also a question as to the subject of **flattereth** in verse 2. It may be the wicked man, transgression, or God. The first seems to be preferable if the oracle is designed to reach the heart of the psalmist, while the second possibility fits best if verse 1 refers to the heart of the wicked. The obvious fruits of denying God are stated in verses 3,4.

5-9. The Gloriousness of God. **Thy mercy . . . thy faithfulness . . . thy righteousness . . . thy judgments . . . thy lovingkindness . . . thy light.** In a beautiful and melodious flow of words, these various attributes of God are likened to different phenomena of nature and then to human experience. In addition, God is spoken of as "the fountain of life." Every aspect of God's glory is spiritually oriented to produce one of the most spiritual pictures of God in the Psalter.

10-12. The Triumph of Love. **O continue thy lovingkindness.** After a brief prayer for the continuance of God's dealings with the righteous, the psalmist envisions the actual overthrow of the wicked.

Psalm 37. A Vindication of Providence

This psalm is related to the Wisdom literature by its distinctively didactic character. The major problem for the psalmist is the inconsistency connected with the prosperity of the wicked. Although tempted to doubt God's goodness, the author quiets his own mind and his hearers' by appealing to patience and trust. The organization is alphabetic, similar in many ways to the acrostic in Psalms 9 and 10.

1-11. Counsel for the Wise. **Fret not thyself because of evildoers.** The opening verse sets forth the basic maxim for a mature outlook: Don't fret or be envious about those who seem to prosper though wicked. Instead, the wise man will **trust, delight in, commit** himself **unto, rest in,** and **wait patiently for** the Lord. Herein is the positive cure for indignation and envy.

12-20. Doom for the Wicked. **His day is coming.** In the preceding passage the scene was set for this proclamation of woe by the declaration that the wicked have just **a little while** (v. 10). The various calamities are carefully catalogued.

21-31. Reward for the Righteous. **Shall inherit the earth.** The **meek** (v. 11), the **blessed** (v. 22), and the **righteous** (v. 29) are the terms applied to the recipients of the promised reward. The personal illustration in verse 25 is a unique departure from the formalized style of the psalm as a whole.

32-40. Contrasts of Retribution. **When the wicked are cut off, thou shalt see it.** While the wicked now watch for an opportunity to trap the righteous, in the future the righteous will have their chance to watch. The end of the upright is **peace,** but the end of the wicked is destruction.

Psalm 38. The Lamentation of a Sufferer

Although this psalm is a personal lament, it is also classed as one of the seven Penitential Psalms. The writer complains of a serious bodily affliction aggravated by mental anguish and the desertion of loved ones. He accepts the fact that his suffering is merited retribution for his sins. Forsaken and dejected, he looks to God as his last and only hope.

1-8. The Suffering of Sin. **No soundness in my flesh because of thine anger.** The psalmist does not contend with God or claim innocence. He pleads for mercy, that his burden may be lightened. His suffering is clearly **because of my sin.** The seriousness of his ailment is indicated by the description of a skin disease comparable to that of Job.

9-14. The Suffering of Persecution. **Stand aloof . . . lay snares . . . speak mischievous things.** These words describe the treatment of his former friends. His **loved ones, friends,** and **kinsmen** all keep their distance. His enemies take advantage of his distress and weakened condition. This phase of his suffering is also similar to Job's circumstances in that friends desert him or fail to sympathize properly with him.

15-22. The Hope of Deliverance. **For in thee, O Lord, do I hope.** The author has not attempted to refute his enemies because his hope is in God alone. After repeating his confession of sin, he voices again his petition for mercy.

Psalm 39. An Appeal for Strength

This appears to be a sequel to the preceding psalm. However, the author need not be the same in each case, since it is the arrangement of the psalms within the collection that gives this continuity. Although penitential in character, this poem has not been included among the seven Penitential Psalms. There are certain affinities to the experience of Job in the suffering of the psalmist as well as a parallel to the book of Ecclesiastes in the view of life.

1-3. A Resolve of Self-control. **I will keep my mouth.** Because of the stroke of God mentioned in verse 10, the psalmist is sorely tempted to complain against God. Like Job, he must restrain the temptation to charge God with foolishness. The presence of the wicked suggests an outside source of temptation and the possibility of doing great harm to the cause of the righteous by public complaining.

4-6. A Prayer for Understanding. **Lord, make me to know.** The object of his prayer is knowledge to enable him to understand the frailty and vanity of life. He gives vent to his feelings and thoughts concerning the vanity of human aims. He hopes to be led back to a quiet confidence in God which will dispel these vain thoughts.

7-13. A Request for Mercy. **And now, Lord. . . . Deliver me.** On the basis of his present hope in God, he can ask that God will **deliver, remove thy stroke, hear,** and **spare.** In tone, these requests are quite different from his former thoughts. His recognition and confession of his sins has given a sense of humility not possible previously.

Psalm 40. A New Song of Praise

Here is yet another good illustration of the method of compiling which has produced our present Psalter. A reading of the psalm soon shows the sudden change from praise for answered prayer to petition for immediate deliverance, verse 12. That a new psalm begins here is verified by the use of verses 13-17 as Psalm 70. Although the latter may have drawn from this psalm in its present form, the separate identity of verse 12 is obvious.

1-3. An Experience of Answered Prayer. **I waited . . . he inclined . . . and heard.** After a period of waiting, the psalmist was rescued from great trouble. The problem may have been illness or another situation where death seemed imminent. This experience has given him a new song which will inspire trust in God.

4,5. The Theme of the Song. **Many . . . thy wonderful works.** Although the psalm begins like Psalm 1 with a beatitude, the theme of God's goodness is uppermost in the psalmist's praise. His wonderful deeds and thoughts are too great to be described and too numerous to be counted.

6-11. The Response to the New Song. **I delight to do thy will.** It is the new song and the experience behind it that leads the psalmist to look beyond the sacrificial system. The four basic sacrifices and offerings of verse 6 are unacceptable to present true gratitude and praise. The depth of the writer's experience is shown in his open proclamation of the nature and work of the Lord. The author of Hebrews quotes these words as applicable to Christ (Heb 10:5-7).

12-17. The Petition for Deliverance. **Make haste to help me.** Verse 12 appears to be a connecting link to join these two poems and to serve as an introduction to the appeal for help. Almost every phrase in this section is found in other psalms as well as in Psalm 70. This use of other sources stands in sharp contrast to the originality of verses 1-11. However, the great need of the psalmist is no less real. After pleading for immediate attention, he requests that his enemies **be ashamed, confounded, driven backward, put to shame,** and **desolate.** He further requests that seekers of God may rightly rejoice and magnify the Lord. Realizing his own inadequacy, he is confident that God considers him and will prove to be his helper and deliverer.

Psalm 41. Thanksgiving for Healing and Vindication

An individual who has just recovered from a serious illness here expresses his thanksgiving. It is not pure thanksgiving in that he is influenced by the Wisdom school in the opening verses and reverts to a lament in describing his desperate situation. However, the danger is now past and recovery is assured.

1-3. Meditation upon God's Deliverance. **Blessed is he that considereth the poor.** This beatitude corresponds to the "Blessed are the merciful" of the Sermon on the Mount. Such a man is delivered, preserved, blessed, and strengthened by God. The psalmist recognizes himself as an illustration of his case in point.

4-9. Prayer for Restoration. **I said, Lord . . . heal.** His appeal includes a plea for mercy and for actual healing. Note that a confession of sin makes the prayer complete. His enemies have taken great delight in viewing his afflictions. Even a close friend has turned on him, as Judas Iscariot betrayed his Master and Friend (cf. Jn 13:18; Acts 1:16).

10-12. Prayer for Vengeance. **Raise me up, that I may requite them.** This is not a prayer that God will punish those who took advantage of him. He asks for strength to do it himself! It is only through such a victory that he can feel sure of God's favor.

13. Benediction. **Blessed be the Lord.** This subscript marks the close of Book I of the Psalter.

BOOK II. Psalms 42–72

The second book in the fivefold division of the Psalms appears to be a part of a larger collection, i.e., Psalms 42–83, which uses the name *'Ělōhîm* instead of *Yahweh* for the most part. The former is used 164 times and the latter only 30 times in Book II. Within the larger collection, several smaller collections are observable: one connected with the Levitical family called the Sons of Korah; one associated with David; and one referring to Asaph. Besides these collections Book II also includes one anonymous psalm and one ascribed to Solomon.

Psalms 42, 43. Longing for God

Here are two poems so closely connected in content and style as to defy separation. The occurrence of the same refrain in 42:5; 42:11; and 43:5, the fact that Psalm 43 is without a title, and the internal form of the two psalms all point to one original composition. The division probably was made after the Elohistic collection, 42–83, began to be circulated. The psalmist is despondent because he cannot make his usual pilgrimages to the Temple. He seems to live in the northern section of Palestine, where he is constantly taunted by enemies who do not share his longings for God. The entire poem is one of great poetic beauty, constantly mingling longing and hope.

42:1-5. The Nature of His Longing. **My soul thirsteth for God.** Even as the **hind** (not *hart)* cannot disguise her thirst, neither can the psalmist hide his passion for **the living God.** His heathen enemies taunt him with remarks about the indifference of his God. The hardest thing for him to endure is the remembrance of the days when he was able to lead pilgrimages to the great festivals. The refrain in verse 5 is the beautiful formula of trust with which he allays his despondency.

42:6-11. The Depths of His Despair. **Deep calleth unto deep.** Again the psalmist becomes downcast and voices despair, which is more plaintive than before. Although he attempts to pray and recall how measureless is God's loving-kindness, he still feels forsaken. Mixed with his longing for the Temple is his remembrance of the constant barbs of his enemies. He gains renewed strength by repeating his formula for inner peace.

43:1-5. The Prayer for His Restoration. **Judge me, O God, and plead my cause.** Despairing again, the psalmist lays his case before God. Two desires alternate here – the desire for freedom from persecution and the desire to go to the Temple. **Light** and **truth** are the personified forces which he requests to lead him even as he has led pilgrims in the past. The repetition of the refrain echoes a confident hope that God will answer his prayer.

Psalm 44. A Plea for Justice

This psalm, national in scope, is permeated with a deep sense of self-justification. The serious calamity alluded to and the attendant humiliation are not viewed as resulting from sin but are taken as ground for rebuking God. The spirit of disrespectful rebuke is found nowhere else in the Psalter. No other psalm makes such claims of national fidelity to God. There is presented here another side of Israel's heart life. The abiding value lies in the emphasis upon God's power to help.

1-3. The Blessings of the Past. **We have heard.** By oral tradition, as well as in the sacred Scriptures read publicly at the religious festivals, the mighty deeds of God in times of old have been preserved. This sense of history is frequently seen because God is best known by what he has done.

4-8. The Assurance of the Present. **In God we boast.** It is by God that all victories are possible. The personal illustration of the bow and sword amplifies the argument of the psalmist.

9-16. The Abandonment of Israel. **But thou hast cast off.** Their only hope does not go out into battle with them. God is thus blamed for their recent defeat. The psalmist uses cutting sarcasm in saying that God made a bad bargain in selling his people to the enemy for nothing.

17-22. The Claim of Faithfulness. **Yet have we not forgotten thee.** The claim is repeated over and over that the nation has remained faithful. At no time in Israel's history was this literally true. The psalmist must have in mind a comparative fidelity based on generalities.

23-26. The Request for Justice. **Awake . . . cast us not off for ever.** The concept of God sleeping on the job is out of place, even in poetical expression. This is similar to the sarcastic words of Elijah on Mount Carmel concerning Baal. However, the psalm closes with the request that God **redeem us for thy mercies' sake.**

Psalm 45. The Marriage of a King

This is one of several royal psalms which relate to many phases of kingly life. Its secular nature is at once recognized. However, the event is idealized and spiritualized by a court attendant who is obviously moved by this solemn occasion. The hopelessness of identifying the king or the period in history gives a more idealized significance to it. Later Jewish interpreters made it Messianic, as did early Christian writers (cf. Heb 1:8, 9).

1. Dedication of the Song. **Touching the king.** Because his heart is overflowing, the psalmist dedicates this song of his own composition to the king.

2-9. Eulogy of the Groom. **Thou art fairer.** His appearance is handsome; his speech is graceful; his bearing is majestic; his rule is righteous; his military might is powerful; his spiritual choices are right; his garments and court are regal. If verse 6a refers to a human king, it might be translated, **Thy throne is like God's.** In Heb 1:8,9 the words are applied to Christ, in accord with the literal sense, "Thy throne, O God."

10-12. Advice to the Bride. **Hearken, O daughter.** Fatherly advice is appropriate for a young princess, to help her find her proper place in the royal family. She must be submissive to the king as well as loyal to his people.

13-15. Entrance of the Bride. **She shall be brought unto the king.** The bride is not described in detail; but, instead, emphasis is placed on the scene of the processional march. Her clothing and attendants are fitting for the occasion.

16,17. Anticipation for the Marriage. **Thy children . . . thy name.** Two wishes are set forth as assured results. There will be princes to bless this union and carry on his name. The psalmist promises to make that name to be remembered for all generations. The name represents the character, reputation, nature, and attributes of a person.

Psalm 46. A Mighty Fortress

This and the next two psalms form a trilogy of praise. The likelihood that the same historical situation provided the background for all three has caused much speculation as to the event itself. Although some great deliverance seems to be understood, the particular occasion cannot be identified. The pronounced apocalyptic elements are used by the psalmist to encourage the people in their current crisis.

1-3. Our Refuge. **God . . . our refuge and strength.** These words express the dominant theme of the psalm, a theme which inspired Luther to write "A Mighty Fortress Is Our God." The idea of a world-wide catastrophe was drawn from the writings of the prophets. It furnishes the background for assuring the people that God will be present whatever the outward circumstances. The refrain found in verses 7 and 11 may originally have appeared also between verses 3 and 4.

4-7. Our Deliverer. **God shall help her.** In contrast to troubled waters, there is a life-giving river which supplies Jerusalem, for God is in her midst (cf. Ezk 47). Again, in the picture of the final battle of the ages, reference is made to the apocalyptic view. Deliverance is certain because the **Lord of hosts is with us.**

8-11. Our Peace. **He maketh wars to cease.** The outcome of the apocalyptic battle is triumph and the end of warfare. The beautiful phrase, **Be still, and know that I am God,** carries the idea of refraining from vain strivings and lack of confidence. The refrain is repeated in order to show the triumph of this confidence in God.

Psalm 47. A Victorious King

This second psalm in the trilogy that expresses confidence in God amplifies the thought expressed in 46:10 and 48:2. According to the Talmud, Psalm 47 was used in later Judaism on the Jewish New Year's Day. As a result of the work of Mowinckel, many commentators regard Psalms 47, 93, 95–100 as celebrating the enthronement of Yahweh as the King of all the earth. There is no direct evidence that such a festival took place in pre-Exilic days. But these psalms become more meaningful when viewed against the background of such a celebration. In its prophetic aspect this psalm finds its fulfillment in the future reign of Christ on earth.

1-4. The Call for Rejoicing. **O clap your hands . . . shout.** In an eschatological vein, all peoples are called upon to rejoice. The description of the divine sovereignty introduced in Psalm 46 reaches a new height here. The psalmist, like the prophets, here envisions the action of the future as occurring in the present. He sees all nations subdued, while Israel stands in a unique relation to God because of her inheritance.

5-9. The Call for Praise. **Sing praises.** There is a slight shift here from jubilant rejoicing to more formal praise. The cue for the shift to praise is seen in verse 5. The future victory of the Lord is again set forth as present in order to give confidence in its absolute certainty.

Psalm 48. A Holy City

The trilogy begun in Psalm 46 with emphasis on confidence in God is here concluded with a similar note of confidence. The concepts of God as Refuge in Psalm 46 and of God as King in 46 and 47 are both incorporated in this psalm. The eschatological features are continued here but in lesser degree. The fact that there is some historical background for the trilogy becomes more apparent. The psalm was undoubtedly used in connection with a prominent festival as first-time pilgrims were shown the city.

1-8. City of Our God. **The city of our God.** The two themes within this section – the greatness of God and the glory of his city, complement one another. Not only is the Lord great, he is the **great King** and exceedingly worthy to be praised. The close connection of this psalm with the preceding ones suggests that perhaps it is the apocalyptic Jerusalem as the center of the Messianic kingdom that is described. However, it is possible that the siege by Sennacherib in 701 B.C. is referred to in verses 4-8 (cf. Isa 37:33-37).

9-14. Praise of Our God. **For this God is our God.** While the psalm begins with praise "in the city of our God," it is raised to praise **unto the ends of the earth** in verse 10. After the worship in the Temple was concluded, the pilgrims undoubtedly joined in joyful procession around the city. Each sacred place reminded them that God would guide them even as he had guided their fathers.

Psalm 49. The Folly of Earthly Wealth

Psalm 49 is a moral lesson designed for all peoples. There is an avowed didactic purpose throughout, in keeping with the purpose of Wisdom writers. Never does the psalmist address God, and only twice does he mention Him by name. His purpose is to present **a** meditation on the riddle of life.

1-4. Call to Attention. **Hear . . . give ear.** The call is not restricted to any class or nationality. It is universal in scope; the psalmist is speaking to mankind. He uses four words frequently employed by the Wisdom school: **wisdom, understanding, parable,** and **dark saying.** His use of the harp to accompany his words is interesting, because this was not the usual practice in instruction of this sort.

5-12. Wealth and the Present Life. **Wherefore should I fear.** The psalmist deals in a different way with the age-old problem of the prosperity of the wicked. He says, Why worry? With this premise he goes on to discuss the problem with a confident rather than a pessimistic attitude. He never accuses God of injustice, but continually points to the fate of those who trust in their wealth. All must come to the end of life and all must leave their wealth behind. Following the LXX, 11a reads better: **Their graves are their houses forever.** Verse 12 is a refrain, emphasizing that man without discernment will go the way of all beasts.

13-20. Wealth and the Fate of Man. **Like sheep they are laid in the grave.** Those who trust in their wealth and honor will share a common fate. They will be led into Sheol by the shepherd, Death. Verse 15 is one of the clearest evidences of a hint of immortality in the OT. This is not a general promise but a prediction regarding the personal fate of the psalmist in contrast to that of the wicked man of wealth. **He shall take me.** The same verb is used here as is employed to describe the special cases of Enoch and Elijah. The refrain of verse 12 is used again as a closing thought.

Psalm 50. The Nature of True Worship

This didactic psalm is closer to the prophetic tradition than to the Wisdom emphasis. The opening utterance of God, the emphasis upon spiritual religion, and the straightforward denunciation of the wicked point to a prophetic background. Acceptable worship and social morality are the two dominant themes. These correspond to the two main divisions of the Ten Commandments – man's relation to God and man's relation to his neighbor.

1-6. The Summons by the Judge. **The mighty God . . . hath spoken.** In a prophetic theophany, God comes to gather and judge Israel. This manifestation takes place out of Zion rather than out of Mount Sinai. Notice that the judgment is to be upon **his people,** although other peoples are to listen. In fact, heaven and earth are to act as silent witnesses.

7-15. The Message to the Worshiper. **Hear, O my people.** God is speaking to the formalistic worshiper and the one who trusts ritual. The judgment is not upon sacrifice as such but upon the wrong motives involved. It is made clear that God is not dependent upon the sacrifice of his people. He most desires heartfelt thanksgiving, proper payment of vows, and sincere prayer.

16-23. The Message of the Wicked. **But unto the wicked, God saith.** This judgment is upon the hypocrites within

Israel who claim to keep the law of God in outward observance, but use the keeping of the law as justification for their evil deeds. Even though God has kept silence by delaying punishment, the time of reproof has come.

Psalm 51. A Cry for Forgiveness

This is the fourth and most profound of the Penitential Psalms. The depth of individual experience, the sense of sin, and the plea for forgiveness are unsurpassed in any other psalm. This is the first psalm in another collection bearing David's name, Psalms 51–70. Opinion is greatly divided as to the occasion suggested by this confession. To some it has a corporate significance; to some it arises from the well-known experience of David; to others it describes a worshiper who goes to the Temple for pardon and cleansing. The addition of verses 18 and 19 seems to adapt a purely individual plea to the requirements of corporate worship. Whether David composed the poem or not, his experience seems to have occasioned it.

1,2. A Cry for Mercy. **Have mercy on me, O God.** The psalmist neither pleads innocence nor shifts the blame to someone else. Since he knows that he does not deserve forgiveness, he pleads first for mercy, based on God's loving-kindness. In line with this mercy, he asks that his transgressions or **rebellions** be wiped out and his iniquity or **twistedness** be washed away.

3-6. A Confession of Sin. **For I acknowledge my transgressions.** Here the psalmist emphasizes the fact that he knows and is constantly aware of his sin, and acknowledges that his sin is more than sin against man. At the same time he recognizes the universal tendency toward sin but does not excuse himself on this basis. The depth of his confession is apparent in his desire to open up the inward and hidden parts of his being.

7-12. A Plea for Cleansing. **Purge me . . . wash me.** The verbs are extremely significant in carrying forward the plea. The psalmist begins (vv. 7-9) by asking for external cleansing. Purging with hyssop and washing are related to ritual acts. With the plea for a newly created heart and a renewed steadfast spirit, his emphasis shifts to inward cleansing.

13-17. A Vow of Consecration. **Then will I teach.** This vow to testify to others gives evidence of the writer's pardon and changed nature. The psalmist's view of sacrifice is essentially prophetic and very similar to that of the author of Psalm 50. His sense of sin and guilt requires more than burnt offerings; hence he offers his broken spirit and contrite heart.

18,19. A Prayer for Restoration. **Do good . . . build . . . then.** This emphasis upon works as a means of making sacrifices acceptable appears to be a liturgical addition by a priestly writer or editor.

Psalm 52. The Fate of an Arrogant Sinner

In this individual lament, presented in the direct manner of the prophets, there is no appeal for God's help, only confidence that God will bring a retributive fate. Although a particular individual is addressed throughout, a class of men may be referred to, with the prophet as the example of a righteous man.

1-4. The Character of the Opponent. **Thou lovest evil.** This denunciation is directed toward an arrogant tyrant whose tongue seems to be his weapon. His greed, treachery, and falsehood all stem from this razor-like tongue.

5-7. The Retribution of God. **God shall likewise destroy thee.** This is the pronouncement of the psalmist, still directed toward the arrogant tyrant. The destruction is described in verse 5 in three stages—God will *snatch, tear away,* and *uproot* (RSV). Although these verbs are rendered as a prayer in the LXX (*May God destroy,* etc.), the future usage seems better, since the psalmist is certain that the righteous will observe this destruction.

8,9. The Trust of the Psalmist. **I trust in the mercy of God.** While the tyrant trusts in his riches, the psalmist has the stability of absolute trust in God. The green olive tree may have stood in the temple courtyard, or the psalmist may be emphasizing his strength in the Lord with two figures—**like a green olive tree** and **in the house of God.**

Psalm 53. The Judgment for Denying God

This psalm is actually another version of Psalm 14. The only significant change is that the content of 14:5,6 is here strengthened and compressed into one verse. It is possible that both of these psalms are adapted versions of an original poem. However, 53 may be simply a version of 14, adapted for some historical crisis. (For outline and comments, see on Ps 14.)

Psalm 54. A Prayer for Assistance

Though this is the appeal of a troubled man, in the characteristic form of an individual lament, the language and content are so general as to make it adaptable for the needs of any who are oppressed by godless men.

1-3. Prayer in a Perilous Situation. **Save me, O God.** This appeal for help is based upon God's revealed character (**his name**) and his revealed power (**his strength**). The adversaries are called **strangers** *(zārîm)* according to the Masoretic Text, while certain manuscripts designate them as proud or insolent men *(zādîm)*. Psalm 86:14 seems to quote verse 3 of this psalm, using the latter spelling. The most important characteristic of these men, however, is their utter disregard of God.

4-7. Praise for an Assured Deliverance. **I will praise . . . for he hath delivered.** Since the psalmist has complete confidence in God as his helper, he is sure that God will give suitable punishment to his enemies. His certainty is such that he can vow to give a freewill offering and promise to praise the name of *Jehovah*.

Psalm 55. A Protest Against the Wicked

Basically this is a lament of an individual oppressed by enemies and deserted by friends. However, some commentators consider that the original lament has been adapted for a national situation. Indeed, many scholars believe that two poems have been combined into one psalm. Verses 12-14, 18b-21, and 23 are most in question. However, no agreement can be reached as to which verses were once a separate poem.

1-8. Complaint of the Psalmist. **I mourn in my complaint.** In keeping with the form of a poetic lament, the writer appeals for God's attention to his restless condition. He is slandered, oppressed, mistreated, and hated. The constant threat to his life causes pain, fear, trembling, and horror. In words of lyric beauty, he expresses his desire to fly away to the wilderness, where he may be able to escape persecution.

9-15. Denunciation of the Wicked. **Destroy O Lord, divide their tongues.** This section opens and closes with a plea for vengeance. The division of tongues is reminiscent of God's judgment upon the builders of the Tower of Babel (Gen 11:5-9). **Violence, strife, mischief,** and **sorrow** are all descriptive of the wickedness inside the city walls. The thing hardest to bear, the psalmist finds, is the treachery of a close friend who had worshiped with him.

16-23. Confidence Through Prayer. **Evening . . . morning . . . noon.** His persistence in prayer is rewarded by personal peace and by confidence in the affliction of his adversaries. The confusion between singular and plural has suggested to some interpreters that verses 20,21 should follow verses 12-14, or form a separate original poem. However, the intensity of wrath may have caused the psalmist to shift from the group to his chief foe without clear transition. The trust of verse 22 brings the assurance of the closing verse.

Psalm 56. The Triumph of Faith

Here, again, an individual voices his lament over his treatment by his enemies. The distress of the psalmist, prompted by the malicious plots of crafty men, makes fear inevitable. However, his trust in God overcomes all fear.

1-4. The Plea for Help. **Be merciful unto me.** This plea is often repeated by the devout worshiper in Israel. It seems that the psalmist's enemies are warriors rather than religious antagonists. They trample him under foot. Yet, the inevitable fear is conquered by trust in God.

5-11. The Appeal for Vengeance. **In anger cast down the people, O God.** After describing the treachery of his enemies, the psalmist calls for divine aid. He has conquered fear, but God must conquer the oppressors lest they escape judgment. The writer is certain that God will answer his prayers and give vengeance. This assurance leads into a repetition of the expression of trust, a kind of refrain, found in verse 4.

12,13. The Vows of Victory. **Thy vows are upon me.** Since victory has already come or is envisioned as assured, the psalmist recalls his obligation of praise and thanksgiving. Perhaps he vowed a vow during his trouble. Since God has fulfilled his part in delivering from oppression and death, the rest is up to the psalmist.

Psalm 57. A Prayer for Protection

The same person who wrote Psalm 56 may possibly have also written this lament of an individual. In spirit, content, style, and situation the two psalms are similar. Both begin with the same appeal and both use a striking refrain as a division of structure. Verses 7-11 of this psalm form a striking hymn that is repeated in Psalm 108. It is possible that two poems were united to fashion this psalm in its present form.

1-5. A Prayer for Protection. **Be merciful to me, O God.** The psalmist's request is not for vengeance or destruction but for God's watchcare and mercy. Since his trust in God is so implicit, he is taking refuge in the confidence that God's mercy and truth will suffice.

6-11. A Resolution of Thanksgiving. **My heart is fixed . . . I will sing and give praise.** After a brief reminder of his present situation and the assurance that his enemies will suffer self-destruction, the psalmist makes his steadfast resolution. His praise is universal and it arises from the two grounds of confidence named in verse 3 – God's mercy and his truth. The psalm closes with the prayerful refrain exalting the universal sovereignty of God.

Psalm 58. A Protest Against Injustice

This is the lament of an individual indignant over the lack of justice in the world. He sees tyranny and oppression as the rule in society rather than the exception. He is especially concerned with the perversion of justice by earthly rulers or judges. It is difficult, however, to determine whether he refers to the leaders of Israel or to foreign rulers (cf. Ps 82).

1-5. A World of Injustice. **In heart ye work wickedness.** The whole problem of injustice in the affairs of men is here recognized as due to innate wickedness. The term translated **congregation** *('ēlem)* in verse 1 is obscure. Some commentators read instead – *O ye gods ('ēlîm),* and find here an expression of sarcasm directed at the unjust judges. This emendation parallels Psalm 82 but is not supported by the MSS or LXX. In verses 3-5 direct reference is made to these wicked men as innately wicked and untamable.

6-11. A Call for Vengeance. **Break their teeth, O God.** With blistering language the psalmist creates a series of brief metaphors dealing with lions' teeth, streams, a snail, miscarriage, and thorns. Each of these is spoken as an imprecation against his unjust enemies. Thus there is here a sevenfold curse in the form of prayer. Verses 10,11 show the confidence of the psalmist in realistic terms. He feels sure that the righteous, whom he represents, will see and rejoice in the utter destruction of these unjust enemies.

Psalm 59. A Prayer for Rescue

Though this psalm is basically the lament of an individual, it has overtones which adapt it to national use as well. There are points of similarity with Psalms 55 and 58. The picture of oppression is again dominant, as is the vindictive attitude of the writer. Contrary to the normal pattern of an individual lament, refrains are evident. Verses 6,13, although not completely identical, act as a recurrent thought. Verses 9,10 are likewise repeated in similar thought pattern in verse 17.

1-5. Prayer for Protection. **Deliver me . . . defend me . . . Deliver me . . . save me.** The seriousness of the psalmist's plight is evident in this fourfold outcry. After describing his enemies' activity and pleading innocence, the psalmist pleads that God will rise up against the **heathen,** i.e., the *nations.* The reference to punishing the nations seems to apply the experience to a national emergency.

6-9. Defiance of the Enemy. **They make a noise like a dog.** The sharp words and taunts remind the psalmist of scavenger dogs searching for food at night. However, he is confident that God will laugh the enemy to scorn and come to his defense.

10-13. Plea for Vengeance. **Slay them not . . . scatter them.** Because of his trust that God will *meet* (AV, **prevent) him,** he prays for a gradual punishment upon his enemies. He does not want them destroyed immediately but rather made an example to the people. The shift to **consume them** in verse 13 shows his ultimate desire for them.

14-17. Contrasts of Fate. **Let them make a noise . . . But I will sing.** Verse 7 is repeated to set up this vivid contrast. While the wicked search in vain all night like scavenger dogs, the psalmist vows that he will sing aloud in the morning. Verses 9,10 serve as a basis for the closing refrain of assurance.

Psalm 60. A Plea for Ultimate Victory

Because of the evident disaster facing the nation, and because of the frequent plurals, this psalm should be classed as a national lament. Public complaint is voiced at the beginning and at the end of the psalm, and a separate oracle of God is placed in the middle. The psalm ends on a note of confidence. Verses 6-12 are repeated by the author of Psalm 108.

1-5. A Dire Circumstance. **O God, thou hast cast us off.** The situation is worse than mere military defeat and disaster, because it is interpreted as God's forsaking his people. The seeming displeasure of God is graphically described as causing earthquakes and making the people reel as if from drunkenness. The conclusion is drawn that God has given them his banner but led them into defeat. The plea of verse 5 is transitional, introducing the promise of God.

6-8. A Prophetic Oracle. **God hath spoken.** The answer is expressed in terms of a previous promise by God. The references to widespread geographical areas seem to express God's universal power and ownership rather than describe a historical situation.

9-12. A Confident Hope. **Through God we shall do valiantly.** Although public complaint continues in spite of the heartening oracle, hope begins to emerge. God is their only hope to win the battle. The plea for help brings with it an assurance of ultimate victory.

Psalm 61. Prayer for a King

This psalm is the earnest lamentation and appeal of one who is away from Jerusalem. **The end of the earth** need not refer to a remote area, because the distance is magnified by the yearning to be back home. Although an enforced exile may be the lot of the psalmist, it is not required by this phrase.

1-4. A Petition for Personal Restoration. **Hear my cry, O God.** In despair the psalmist pleads for the sense of God's presence and protection. He desires to experience the safety of a rock that is too high for him to climb without God's help. Because of God's past blessings, he finds assurance for the present and hope for the future.

5-8. A Prayer for Royal Blessing. **Thou . . . hast heard.** The writer expresses deep confidence that his prayer for the welfare of the reigning king will be answered. Verses 6,7 can be viewed as a statement of his previous prayer or translated as a present request – **Prolong the king's life. . . .** Note that the writer prays for three things – for prolonged life, for an extended reign, and for the blessings of mercy and truth. His confidence that God will answer makes him determine to pay daily vows of thanksgiving.

Psalm 62. An Unshakable Faith

There is an element of lamentation in the opening verses of this outstanding song of passive trust, and a didactic purpose in the closing verses. However, the dominant note of trust and confidence is evident throughout. The author is a man of authority whose position is threatened. Though his opponents are from various walks of life, he views them all as utterly worthless.

1-4. The Only Salvation. **From him my salvation.** The key to the serene confidence is probably tied up with the Hebrew particle, *'ak,* which occurs six times in this brief psalm, three times as the first word of a stanza. The particle may be translated "surely," "but," "alone," or better, "only." *Only* for God does he wait, while *only* God is his rock, salvation, and defense. His persecutors are scheming against him all the time.

5-8. The Only Hope. **My expectation from him.** The words of verses 1 and 2 are slightly altered to form an introduction to this stanza. The writer calls himself to calm remembrance of the key to his peace. Again it is *only* God upon whom he waits and in whom he trusts. In this stillness of humble resignation he adds hope or expectation to the certainty of salvation.

9-12. The Only Strength. **Strength belongeth unto God.** Although he begins the stanza with the same Hebrew particle, *'ak,* it is not until verse 12 that he presents the basis of this phase of his inner peace. His enemies trust in oppression, robbery, and riches, but he has received the twice-spoken oracle describing God as the only strength and mercy worth having.

Psalm 63. A Thirst for God

Like the preceding psalm, this is a song of trust, based upon a close relation to God. The psalmist is obviously in exile or banished from his home. His deep desire to share in public worship is partially satisfied by his fellowship with God in meditation. This song is an excellent example of the highest type of personal and spiritual worship in Israel.

1-4. Longing for God. **My soul thirsteth . . . my flesh longeth.** After positively identifying his life with God, the psalmist expresses his deepest desire. The whole of his being yearns for communion with God. His life is as dry as a thirsty desert without this fellowship. God's loving-kindness is more important to him than existence itself and causes life-long praise.

5-8. Remembering Past Mercies. **When I remember thee.** Recalling his experiences of worship, he likens the soul satisfaction of nightly meditation to **the marrow and fatness** of the sacrifices. In the stillness of the three night watches, he praises and rejoices because God has been near as his Helper.

9-11. Hoping for Retribution. **They shall fall.** The enemies of the psalmist here come into view for the first time. This is not an imprecatory prayer against them, but a quiet confidence that righteous retribution will result. The speaker feels sure that they will die by the sword, their bodies will lie unburied for jackals to eat, and they will find themselves in Sheol.

Psalm 64. An Appeal for Assistance

The familiar plea for help is heard again in this individual lament. The plight of the psalmist is desperate, although there is no reference here to physical harm. His enemies scheme and slander secretly rather than coming out in open opposition. After enumerating and describing their wicked deeds, the psalmist expresses his certainty that God will judge them rightly.

1-6. The Petition for Protection. **Hear my voice . . . preserve my life.** The appeal begins with the request that God will hear his **complaint** (not *prayer*) and will act to give him protection from fear. He describes the machinations of his conspiring enemies in a series of metaphors normally used to portray the hunting of wild animals.

7-10. The Certainty of Judgment. **But God.** The change is swift and abrupt to a statement of prophetic authority. The psalmist declares that the evil deeds of the enemies shall turn back on them. Then men will recognize the hand of God at work. The sorrow of heart finally turns to gladness when the writer considers the fate of the righteous.

Psalm 65. A Hymn of Thanksgiving

As a thanksgiving psalm this is a remarkable review of God's gracious dealings with the children of men. A spirit of universalism breaks the bounds of narrow nationalism in Israel. This hymn was closely connected with a thanksgiving festival at the Temple, either composed for or inspired by such an occasion.

1-4. Praise for God's Favor. **Praise waiteth for thee.** As evidenced by the ancient versions, this can better be rendered *praise is seemly* or *fitting*. Praise is voiced for God's answer to prayer, his forgiveness of sin, and his spiritual favor. The universal note is strong in that **all flesh** is included.

5-8. Praise for God's Power. **By terrible things in righteousness.** God's deeds are pictured as awe-inspiring and righteous, even to men at the ends of the earth. His dominion in creation and his power to still storms are but two illustrations of his sovereignty over the earth.

9-13. Praise for God's Harvest. **Thou visitest the earth, and waterest it.** The aforementioned praise leads up to the primary praise because of the harvest season. It is clearly God who watered the earth, prepared the seed, and made ready the soil. All this brought about a record harvest – **Thou crownest the year.** There is such happiness that the **hills,** pastures, and valleys join in the **rejoicing.**

Psalm 66. A Song of Deliverance

Psalm 66 is both nationalistic and individualistic in its presentation of thanksgiving. Verses 1-12 relate to the nation but also reach out to the world, while verses 13-20 refer to the personal life of the psalmist. Some commentators see here two distinct psalms which have been joined. However, the corporate experience of the nation forms an excellent background for the individual experience of the author.

1-4. The Call for Praise. **Make a joyful noise . . . make his praise glorious.** The psalmist takes in the whole world in one sweep as he sounds the call and gives the proper words for the expression of true praise.

5-12. The Testimony of History. **Come and see.** The events of the exodus from Egypt and Israel's early history were awe-inspiring enough to call forth the praise of God by the peoples of the earth. More recent evidences of deliverance are also included to justify this universal call to praise.

13-20. The Experience of the Psalmist. **Come and hear.** Those who fear God are called to witness the payment of the writer's vow in the Temple. His offerings and sacrifices are supplemented by his public testimony of what God has done for him.

Psalm 67. Hymn for a Harvest Festival

This brief psalm of thanksgiving is

remarkable for its beauty, its simplicity, and its world outlook. The occasion for its use is probably to be seen in verse 6, where the climax is expressed in terms of harvest thanksgiving. The hymn may well have been a part of the music for the Feast of Pentecost or the Feast of Tabernacles.

1,2. The Purpose in God's Blessings. **That thy way may be known.** The familiar priestly blessing of Num 6:24-26 is adapted for use in the first person in order to present the basis of Israel's greater mission. God's gracious dealings are viewed as the means by which all people are led to turn to God. Israel is to be the witness by which the knowledge of God is spread abroad.

3,4. The Call for Universal Praise. **Let the people praise thee.** The refrain in verses 3 and 5 appears to be introductory, because of the presence of the *selâ* at the end of verse 4 and because of the general thought development. This call for joyful praise is based upon God's vindication and guidance of the nations. This is a striking universalistic note.

5-7. The Hope of Continued Blessing. **God shall bless us.** The psalmist repeats the meaningful refrain to correspond to the introductory pleas of verses 1 and 3. The declaration that **the earth has yielded its increase** (RSV) appears to be an obvious connection of the psalm with the joyous harvest festivals. Verse 7 amplifies the thought of verse 1 expressing hope for God's continued blessing in order that Israel's mission may be completed.

Psalm 68. God's Victorious March

This psalm is composed of such diverse elements as to defy classification. Verses 1-18 are basically an ode, while verses 19-35 resemble more closely a hymn. Several commentators have recognized a great number of forms, classifying it as a medley of songs and hymns. The dominant theme appears to be God's march as victor both past, present, and future. The background of the material is to be seen in the totality of Israel's history, rather than in a specific deliverance.

1-6. God's Appearance as Leader. **Let God arise.** This may be a plea or a reference to his appearance ("God ariseth!"). The basis for this language is found in the ancient signal for lifting up the ark (cf. Num 10:35). The righteous are to rejoice at his appearance while the wicked will melt away.

7-18. God's March As Deliverer. **When thou didst march through the wilderness.** The picture is still that of a leader out in front of his people, delivering them by special acts of mercy. The march begins with the deliverance from Egypt and ends with God dwelling in Zion. Cf. Eph 4:8ff., where Paul applies verse 18 to the ministry of the risen Christ.

19-23. God's Presence as Saviour. **The God of our salvation.** Even as God performed acts of deliverance in the past, he is still an ever-present helper who blesses daily and continues to deliver.

24-27. God's Procession as King. **They have seen thy goings, O God . . . my King.** The scene is an actual procession of a festival occasion celebrating the victory and enthronement of God as King. Benjamin and Judah represent the southern tribes, while Zebulun and Naphtali represent the northern tribes.

28-35. God's Exaltation as Lord. **Kings bring presents unto thee.** The deliverances of the past and the blessings of the present point to the future triumph of God. God is called upon to command his strength in a final act of power. After the assertion of ultimate victory, all the nations are called upon to exalt God as Lord through praise.

Psalm 69. A Prayer for Retribution

An individual in the depths of despair and agony here laments his case. His persecution is viewed as a result of his religious convictions. With fervor he pleads for retribution upon his persecutors. Because of his worried state of mind, his mood changes often. However, his despair becomes triumph and his complaint becomes praise after he voices his innermost feelings.

1-6. The Basic Complaint. **Save me. . . . I sink in deep mire.** After crying out for help in one brief phrase, the psalmist describes his plight. The words **waters, mire, deep waters,** and **floods** are all used to show the extreme nature of his trouble. His enemies are numerous, hateful, and powerful. He is greatly concerned that his reproach not injure other devout men who look to him as an example.

7-12. The Underlying Cause. **Because for thy sake.** It is because of his loyalty, faithfulness, and zeal that he has suffered. He appears to have fought against the liberal and popular forms of religious expression in his day. For all this, he has become the laughing-stock of the community and the jest of the drunkards.

13-18. The Intensified Appeal. **My prayer is unto thee.** In terse and rapid pleas, he asks for deliverance and vindication. His previous complaint is repeated but becomes secondary to his request for immediate assistance.

19-28. The Bitter Imprecation. **Pour out thine indignation upon them.** Each of these requests for retribution is based upon God's entering into the bitter indignation of the psalmist. These are God's enemies as well as his. The fierce climax is reached in the plea that they be completely obliterated from the book of the living (cf. Ex 32:32; Phil 4:3; Rev 13:8; 20:15). The Gospel writers may well have had verse 21 in mind as they depicted the passion of Christ (Mt 27:34; Mk 15:23; Jn 19:29).

29-36. The Assured Deliverance. **Let thy salvation, O God, set me on high.** The vow of thanksgiving which follows seems to presuppose an answer to this request for deliverance. It is interesting to note that the psalmist's views on sacrifice may account for some of his opposition. The psalm closes on a note of intense praise as heaven and earth are invited to join in the chorus.

Psalm 70. A Cry for Immediate Help

This psalm is an individual lament which also occurs as part of Psalm 40. Here the name for God has been changed from *Yahweh* to *Elohim,* and some slight variations in wording are evident. Its presence as a separate psalm may indicate that it was found in both of the basic collections already mentioned, or that it was detached from Psalm 40 for liturgical use in the Temple. (Cf. Ps 40:13-17 for added notes.)

Psalm 71. The Confidence of an Aged Saint

Here is the lament of an individual who has suffered great adversity in his many years upon earth. Persecutions, sickness, calamities, and trials have added gray hairs to his head. Yet he has maintained his close relation to God since childhood. His appeal for help once more is based upon the blessings of past experience. His desire is to live long enough to teach the present generation something of what life has taught him.

1-3. His Confidence in God. **In thee, O Lord, do I put my trust.** These words are drawn by the psalmist from Psalm 31 as an expression of his deep confidence in God. He knows God to be his **refuge** and **rock of safety.**

4-13. His Appeal for Deliverance. **Deliver me, O my God.** Although his enemies are quick to take advantage of his weakness, God has **stayed** or *braced* him since birth (cf. Ps 22:9,10). These enemies, who believe that God has forsaken him, are rebuffed for their wrong interpretation of his affliction. His appeal is based solely on his trust in God's power and willingness to deliver him.

14-16. His Hope in God. **But I will hope continually.** The turning point of the psalm is seen here, as appeal changes to hope and praise. The past gives way to the future.

17-21. His Testimony of Revelation. **Thou hast taught me.** On the basis of God's special teaching, he has been able to teach others. Now he asks for more time in order to show forth God's strength, power, and righteousness (vv. 18,19).

22-24. His Vow of Praise. **I will also praise thee.** The psalmist promises to praise with voice, instruments, lips, tongue, and his whole being. He is inwardly assured that he will be vindicated even as he requested (v. 13).

Psalm 72. Blessings on the King

This is the prayer of a loyal subject who desires God's richest blessing upon a young king. All of the hopes of the nation rest on this king, who is God's representative. The description was inspired by Solomon's reign or accession, but it may have been applied to more than one king in its historic use. There is throughout a picture of an ideal king, and thus the psalm has Messianic significance.

1-7. Prayer for Justice and Righteousness. **Give the king thy judgments, O God.** This prayer begins rightly with a plea for the two most important royal characteristics—justice and righteousness. It is on the basis of God's judgment that the king can act justly. The phrase, **the king's son,** probably refers to the new king as young, and parallels the first line of the verse. The verbs translated as futures may express prophetic confidence or be better rendered as prayers, i.e., *may he judge* or *let him judge.*

8-14. Prayer for Dominion and Peace. **He shall have dominion.** Again this plea may better be translated, *May he have dominion.* On the basis of the king's justice, righteousness, and dominion, there will be peace for his subjects. The verbs in verses 12-14 are properly indicatives ("he spares . . . saves . . . redeems," etc.), and mark out the public rewards arising from his ideal characteristics.

15-17. Prayer for Fame and Blessing. **His name shall endure . . . and men shall be blessed in him.** This section is also a prayer, better rendered *may he live* and *may his name endure.* The psalmist prays that the king's fame (his name) may endure long after he has died, even among the other nations which he rules.

18-20. Doxology of Praise, and Conclusion. **Blessed be the Lord God.** These verses were added as a concluding doxology to Book II of the Psalter. Verse 20 is an editorial note which originally separated the preceding collection from the psalms connected with Asaph, which follow. A number of the manuscripts do not include verse 20 here.

BOOK III. Psalms 73–89

The third major division in the Psalter, which is much shorter than the previous two books, includes only seventeen psalms. The first eleven are connected with the name of Asaph, who was one of the chief musicians under David's rule. The other two chief musicians of David were Heman and Ethan, each of whom is connected with a psalm in this book. One psalm is referred to David, while the remaining four psalms are associated with the sons of Korah. Again it is not necessary to attribute authorship to those connected with these titles. Just as the sons of Korah formed a Levitical guild, so Asaph's sons continued to occupy places of musical leadership.

Psalm 73. The Trial of Faith

Here is yet another approach to the problem of the prosperity of the wicked. Although the psalmist is troubled by his own suffering, he is more perplexed by the lack of punishment of the wicked. This psalm goes deeper into the problem than do Psalms 37 and 49, and the author finds peace in spiritual fellowship with God. It may be classified as a song of trust, with overtones that link it with the Wisdom writers. The didactic purpose is evident throughout, but it is interwoven with the confession of a man whose faith has been sorely tested.

1. His Conclusion. **Truly God is good.** The psalmist states first the confident conclusion which came from his supreme test of faith. He uses the Hebrew particle *'ak,* which can be translated in many ways – "now," "truly," "surely," "only," "after all." Here and in verses 13 and 18 it is probably best translated *surely.*

2-12. His Problem. **I saw the prosperity of the wicked.** Contrasted with the writer's general conclusion is his pilgrimage in the valley of doubt, introduced by the emphatic **as for me.** He was in danger of complete apostasy because of his envy toward prosperous wicked men. He describes their arrogant bearing, their freedom from suffering, their overbearing pride, and their mockery of God.

13-22. His Struggle. **Verily, I have cleansed my heart in vain.** This is not his conclusion as stated in verse 1, but a statement of his temptation during his struggle with doubt. He refused to parade his doubts lest he influence others adversely. Though he wrestled with his questions, he found no relief until he went to the Temple. There he regained his spiritual balance, as he received insight into the end reserved for the wicked.

23-28. His Victory. **Nevertheless, I am continually with thee.** Now the writer has found a complete victory over his doubts. His foolishness is a thing of the past, because God is his guide and strength. The phrase, **afterward receive me to glory,** may well refer to a hope beyond life; the same verb here translated "thou shalt receive me" is used for the experiences of Enoch (Gen 5:24) and Elijah (II Kgs 2:10; cf. Ps 49:15). However, the psalmist emphasizes the sense of God's nearness as he experiences it in his present circumstances.

Psalm 74. An Appeal for Vindication

This psalm is the expression of national lament by Israel in the wake of extreme disaster. The feeling is widespread that God has forsaken and forgotten his people. The destruction of the city and the Temple suggests the occasion of the Babylonian conquest. This is the only time known when the Temple was burned to the ground. The conditions are similar to those described in the book of Lamentations.

1-3. The Nation's Appeal. **Remember thy congregation.** The psalmist voices the basic appeal to God to remember His relationship of love with Israel. Even though the Divine wrath is evident in the present tragedy, it is incomprehensible to the psalmist that the Lord, as Israel's Shepherd, could forsake His sheep. Therefore, he pleads for God to take the giant steps necessary to redeem His people.

4-11. The Nation's Plight. **Thine enemies roar.** Instead of being filled with rejoicing worshipers, the temple area is filled with roaring enemies. In place of the emblems of the tribes, the standards of the enemy are seen. The patient, quiet work by which the Temple was built has been nullified by the ruthless axes and hammers of the invaders. The questions introduced by **how long** and Why express the heightened nature of the lament, and relate the basic appeal to the specific disaster.

12-17. The Nation's King. **For God is my King of old.** It is Israel's supreme King whose power is pictured here. Using symbolic language and descriptive terminology drawn from the mythology of the Canaanites, the psalmist insists that it is God who has won the mighty victories of the past. While the figures of speech are derived from ancient creation stories, the psalmist is applying them to God's displays of power in the Exodus and the wilderness wanderings.

18-23. The Nation's Prayer. **Arise, O God, plead thine own cause.** The former appeal is raised to a higher level with this impassioned plea. This is not merely Israel's cause, but God's cause as well. Therefore, the psalmist prays that God will watch over His defenseless people, remember the covenant of love, and keep an eye on the roaring enemies.

Psalm 75. The Gratitude of the Nation

While the opening of this psalm is an expression of national thanksgiving, and the conclusion is related to an individual, the central portion is difficult to classify. Some commentators suggest that verse 1 has been added to an individual's prayer for victory in order to adapt the psalm for public worship. Although this may have been the case, the psalm exhibits careful poetic arrangement as well as definite progression of thought.

1. The Invocation of Israel. **Unto thee . . . we give thanks.** Behind this terse statement of gratitude there appears to lie an actual, historical deliverance. The reality of a recent manifestation of power gives confidence that God's revealed nature (his **name**) is close at hand.

2,3. The Response of God. **I will judge uprightly.** This oracle from God gives the basis for the pronouncements which follow. It is at **the appointed time** (v. 2; *mô'ēd,* not "the congregation," AV) when God will take his place on the judgment seat. His control of the universe assures that the judgment will be sure.

4-8. The Warning of the Psalmist. **I say unto the arrogant . . . to the wicked.** The arrogant and wicked are reminded that power to **lift high** is not found in the east, west, or south. God alone can **lift up** or **put down** (v. 7, ASV) for he it is who executes judgment and causes the wicked to drink the cup of his wrath (Ps 11:6; Rev 14:10).

9,10. The Triumph of the Righteous. **But I will declare for ever.** Speaking as Israel's representative, the psalmist vows endless praise. With these vows comes the assurance that the arrogant will fall from their self-elevation, while the righteous will gain their rightful place.

Psalm 76. A Song of Victory

This song is closely related to Psalms 46, 48, and 75 in its celebration of a military victory. Many commentators seek the common background for these four pieces in the defeat of the Assyrians in 701 B.C. Even though some historical event may have inspired the original poem, the present psalm seems to have been adapted for temple worship.

1-3. The Fame of God. **In Judah . . . in Israel . . . in Salem . . . in Zion.** The reputation of God has been spread far and wide because of his victories. Jerusalem is the center of his fame because his battle headquarters are located there.

4-6. The Might of God. **Thou art more glorious.** The Lord has proved himself in battle to be mightier than all his foes. He easily conquers the **stouthearted** and the **men of might.** He is glorious and majestic, more majestic even than **the everlasting mountains** (cf. LXX).

7-9. The Judgment of God. **Thou, even thou, art to be feared.** The thought goes beyond the battle scene as God takes his seat in heaven. He is the judge **to be feared,** who strikes man with terror. All of the earth stands still as the Lord saves the oppressed peoples, of whom Israel is representative.

10-12. The Homage Due God. **Vow, and pay unto the Lord your God.** This call for praise and offerings is based upon the bold assertion that the Lord can turn even man's most dangerous passion into a means of glory. The last ounce of his enemies' wrath can only add to God's glory, as he girds it upon himself (ASV; not *restrain,* AV).

Psalm 77. Remembering God's Works

Lament is intermingled with praise in this psalm. The opening verses (1-9) are the lamentations of an individual, who may represent the nation in affliction. The later verses (10-20) are words of praise which clearly complement the opening section. Verses 16-19 express a different mood and exhibit a different style and rhythm from the rest of the psalm.

1-3. His Perplexity of Spirit. **I cried unto the Lord . . . my spirit was overwhelmed.** Between these clauses the psalmist's deep anguish and anxiety are graphically portrayed. His outstretched hand (not sore, AV) sought God, but found no comfort. His meditations and musings only overwhelmed his spirit.

4-9. His Search for Answers. **My spirit made diligent search.** Worry and anxiety still ruled his life so that he could not sleep. He counted the days of the past, instead of sheep. Finally, he voiced the six questions that puzzled as well as troubled him. He could not understand why a God of mercy and compassion should remain silent and inactive.

10-15. His Solution in History. **I will remember the works of the Lord.** Recalling the wonders of God in past days brings hope for the psalmist. God has proved himself to be one who does glorious deeds; he has shown his strength, and has redeemed the children of Israel. The unspoken request is that God may so act again.

16-19. His Confidence in God's Power. **The waters saw thee . . . they were afraid.** These verses, which act as a hymn within a hymn, differ greatly in mood and form from the rest of the poem. Although the dominant note of this section is God's power over nature in general, the position of the passage, between verses 15 and 20, relates it to the deliverance at the Red Sea.

20. His Assurance of God's Leadership. **Thou leddest thy people.** This verse voices again the thought of verse 15, with the forceful implication that God can do it again.

Psalm 78. Wisdom from History

Here is a good example of the didactic purposes of the Wisdom writers. God's wonderful acts of deliverance, blessing, and guidance are recalled to serve as a lesson for the psalmist's generation. The teaching is directed toward the inhabitants of Judah, illustrating God's choice of Jerusalem and the Davidic line as recipients of his promises instead of the tribe of Ephraim, which disqualified itself by rebellion (vv. 9-11,57,60,67,68).

1-11. The Warnings of the Past. **I will utter dark sayings of old.** The didactic purpose of the psalmist is clearly stated. A general statement stressing the responsibility of the 'fathers' to teach the children, and the danger of apostasy serves as an introduction to the many illustrations from history which follow.

12-39. The Experiences of the Wilderness. **Marvelous things did he. . . . and they sinned yet more.** The works of God are described in detail: the crossing of the sea, the guidance of the cloud and the pillar of fire, the provision of water, manna, and quails. Even in the face of these constant blessings, the people kept on sinning and tempting God. But in spite of their sin, God demonstrated his compassion and understanding by forgiving them.

40-55. The Deliverance from Egypt into Canaan. **They remembered not his hand.** The same tragic story is repeated. This time the emphasis is placed upon the plagues as illustrations of God's deliverance. Although only seven of the ten plagues are cited and these are not in the same order as in the Book of Exodus, they serve as graphic reasons for faithfulness to God. The psalmist tells how God led His people into Canaan and how they provoked Him by turning aside to idolatry as soon as they had taken the land.

56-72. The Choices of God for Israel. **He forsook . . . awaked . . . chose.** The subjection of Israel during the period of the Judges is pointed out as evidence of abandonment by God. Then, in bold language, the psalmist suggests that the Lord awoke to the need of Israel. The rejection of the northern tribes brought the assurance of God's choice of Judah. The establishment of Jerusalem as Israel's center of worship and David as king marked the southern tribes as undisputed leaders of God's people.

Psalm 79. A Prayer for Vengeance

This psalm is the collective lament of the community of Jerusalem in a time of national disaster. The description of the defiling of the Temple and the devastation of the city points to a serious destruction, such as the Babylonian conquest in 586 B.C. There is here close affinity to the background of Psalm 74, where the Babylonian destruction seems most appropriate. The Jews have long connected these two poems for use on the fast day which commemorates the two destructions of Jerusalem, in 586 B.C. and in A.D. 70.

1-4. The Grief in Jerusalem. **The heathen are come.** The city of Jerusalem is described as being in a real state of emergency. Gentiles have desecrated the Temple, laid the city in ruins, and left the dead unburied. All of this devastation and slaughter has resulted in scorn and ridicule on the part of Israel's Gentile neighbors.

5-8. The Plea for Mercy. **How long, Lord?** This frequent cry of the distressed is followed quickly by the second question, "Will it be forever?" The bitter hurt of the psalmist is evident in his begging God to wreak vengeance on the godless even before he asks Him to extend His **tender mercies** to His people.

9-12. The Prayer for Help. **Help . . . deliver . . . purge . . . for thy name's sake.** The psalmist not only recognizes his forefathers' sin but confesses the sin of his own generation. He stresses not selfish desire, but the glory of God's name. After all, God's name has been abused in the defilement of the Temple and in the derision by the heathen. The psalmist calls upon God to pay them back seven fold for their scoffing.

13. The Vow of Praise. **We will show forth thy praise.** If God will answer the prayer for help, his people will fulfill a double vow. They determine to praise God by giving continual thanks and by publicly declaring his praise.

Psalm 80. A Plea for Restoration

Here is another expression of national lament in a time of distress. The psalmist has sincere interest in the Northern Kingdom either as an outsider or as an inhabitant of that area. The former is probably the case, for the distress appears to be associated with the Exile. The irregular recurrence of a refrain, in verses 3,7, and 19, with an abbreviated form in verse 14, makes the structure of the psalm difficult to explain.

1-3. The Cry to the Shepherd. **Give ear, O Shepherd of Israel.** Although the phrase, **Shepherd of Israel,** is not used elsewhere in the OT, the figure occurs frequently. The three tribes, Ephraim, Benjamin, and Manasseh, were all descended from Rachel and represent the Northern Kingdom. The cry is designed to call God into action to restore his people.

4-7. The Plight of the Flock. **Thou feedest them with the bread of tears.** As in Psalms 74 and 79, the psalmist cries out, **How long . . . ?** He wants to know how much longer God is going to keep on fuming in anger. Although the Lord is not mentioned as shepherd in these verses, the metaphor is continued in the reference to his feeding them with tears.

8-13. The Nurture of the Vine. **Thou hast brought a vine out of Egypt.** Another metaphor is used here to show how God nurtured his chosen people. After transplanting the vine from Egypt to Canaan, the Lord caused it to cover the hills and spread out from the Mediterranean to the Euphrates. With verse 12, the past nurture is compared with the present rejection. The vine has been ravaged by man and beast as they have passed by.

14-19. The Appeal to the Husbandman. **Return . . . and visit this vine.** Since God planted and cared for the vine, he should continue to look down on it and visit it. It is God's wrath which has caused the vine to be burned, and hence the people are in danger of annihilation. If God will revive and restore his people, they will worship him. The last occurrence of the refrain is heightened by the use of the covenant name for God. **The man of thy right hand.** The psalmist prays for help for God's people Israel, depicted as the man of God's right hand. Ultimately, of course, the Messiah became the fulfillment of this prayer (cf. the use of the phrase, "Son of man," in the Gospels, and references to Christ as being at the right hand of the Majesty on high – Heb 1:3; 8:1; 10:12; Acts 7:56).

Psalm 81. A Warning from Experience

A hymn of praise opens this psalm, and a prophetic utterance concludes it. The abrupt change at the end of verse 5 has suggested to many commentators that fragments of two psalms are joined together here. However, this view is not imperative, for a solemn festival would be a logical time for such a recital of God's relation to Israel. The special term for festival, the blowing of the trumpet, the references to the new moon and to the full moon probably give the poem double reference to the Feast of Trumpets and the Feast of Tabernacles.

1-5. A Festival Summons. **Sing . . . make a joyful noise.** This call is a graphic picture of the opening ritual for a great festival. The call was probably vocalized by a priest, who summoned the people to join their voices in joyful singing, the Levitical choir to share with psalms and instruments, and the priests to sound the horns. The **time appointed** in verse 3 is better translated *full moon.*

6-10. A Divine Testimony. **I removed his shoulder from the burden.** In terse statements, the deliverances of the Exodus are recounted by a prophet who acts as God's spokesman. Since God has always satisfied the needs of Israel, He promises to continue to fill their mouths if only they will open them in complete trust.

11-16. A Divine Lament. **But my people would not hearken.** The prophetic utterance continues as a lament over Israel's ingratitude. The cry of verse 13 intensifies the grief of the lament. How different things would have been if only Israel had walked in God's ways! Then she would have had victory and blessings instead of defeat and misery.

Psalm 82. The Final Authority

A scene of judgment upon injustice is set forth in this didactic poem. The proper interpretation of the entire psalm rests on the identity of the second *'Ĕlôhîm* in verse 1. Some commentators translate it literally as **gods** and relate it to a concept of subordinate gods in a heavenly council. Others translate it *angels* and connect it with a less polytheistic concept. Still other interpreters translate it as *judges* and make it refer to the unjust men in authority. The last interpretation seems preferable.

1. The Supreme Judge. **God standeth . . . he judgeth.** The scene is a vision of the assembly over which God presides. This may be identified with the nation of Israel (cf. Neh 13:1, where we find the synonymous phrase, *qᵉhal ha'elohîm*). Thus God takes his stand in his nation and judges among the human judges appointed over Israel.

2-4. The Corrupt Judges. **How long will ye judge unjustly.** The arraignment involves the assembled judges of the nation; the indictment concerns the unjust decisions they have pronounced. The basic problem involves the judges' favoring influential men in the courts. These unjust authorities are admonished to cease their partiality, do justice, and defend the oppressed.

5-7. The Just Sentence. **Ye shall die . . . and fall.** Since these judges lack understanding, the essential quality of justice, judgment is unavoidable. They were given god-like functions as judges, but now they must fall like all men who pervert justice.

8. The Sovereign Judge. **Arise, O God, judge the earth.** The psalm closes with an appeal to God to complete his work as the Sovereign Judge of all nations. He must take possession as well as pass judgment before true justice can endure.

Psalm 83. Judgment upon the Nations

Psalm 83 is a typical national lament in a time of great danger. Since the enemies of Israel are automatically the enemies of God, the name of God (Yahweh) is at stake. The occasion cannot be identified with certainty, because at no period in Israel's history has such a confederation of nations existed. The psalm may refer to an event unrecorded elsewhere in Israel's history, or it may list tribal groups which merely gave moral support in a time of crisis.

1-8. An Appeal for Action. **Keep not thou silence, O God.** In the Hebrew this is a strong plea for activity, repeated in a threefold manner. God's silence must be broken because these nations are his enemies as well. They are making a loud noise about their conspiracy to blot out the name of Israel. Most of these peoples named were nomadic tribes dwelling south and east of Israel. Philistia and Tyre are exceptions; they occupied territory west and north respectively. The majority of these were traditional foes of Israel.

9-18. A Prayer for Vengeance. **Do unto them.** In a blistering imprecation the psalmist appeals for the utter destruction of these would-be foes. He uses the defeat of the Canaanites and Midianites as an illustration of the type of destruction he desires. The severity of his prayer is lessened in verses 16-18 when he inserts a moral basis of conversion and expresses a desire that others may learn from their destruction.

Psalm 84. A Joyful Pilgrimage

This is the song of a pilgrim whose goal is almost reached. There is throughout a sense of peace and communion which transcends the ritual and other outward features of worship. While the poem reflects the sentiments of pilgrims of any age, it appears to come from the period of the monarchy at a time when the Temple was still standing.

1-4. The Longing for God's House. **My soul longeth, yea, even fainteth.** After exclaiming, **How lovely are thy dwelling places,** the psalmist shares his intense longings, which are about to be satisfied. His whole being yearns for fellowship with God. He envies the birds that live in the temple precincts. He recognizes how fortunate are those servants who live within the temple buildings.

5-8. The Pilgrimage to God's House. **Blessed is the man whose strength is in thee.** The happiness of the permanent dweller is reflected in the pilgrim. He has a special sense of God's strength and has **in his heart the highway** to Zion. As he passes through the waterless valley, where only balsam trees can grow, a change takes place. The parched valley is transformed into a place of springs as the pilgrim receives and transmits the blessings of God.

9-12. The Joy of Worship in God's House. **For a day in thy courts is better than a thousand.** After breathing a short prayer for God's anointed king, the psalmist describes the joy of joining others in the service of worship. One day in the place of worship, he feels, would be worth more than a thousand days anywhere else. He would rather be the humblest servant in the Temple, or get no further than the door, than have a permanent place where wickedness abounds. **A sun and shield.** God, like the chief heavenly body in the physical realm, is the sole source of all our spiritual power, energy, and light. He is our protection, and He bestows needed grace in this life and glory in the life to come. **Blessed,** or *happy*. Happiness is again emphasized for the one who has taken refuge in God through spiritual worship.

Psalm 85. A Cry for Pardon

Though basically a national lament, this psalm has a strong prophetic element as well. The first section (vv. 1-3) appears to refer to the return from captivity, but these verses are idealized beyond the known situation of those days. The psalmist uses this ideal picture to show the sharp contrast with the present and the assurance for the future.

1-3. The Ideal of Forgiveness. **Lord, thou hast been favourable.** The pictures of God's favor, restoration, forgiveness, and cessation from wrath set forth the ideal of a perfect relation to God. The verbs in these verses, although translated as past tenses, are probably prophetic perfects, indicating that the psalmist views the events they forecast as certain of fulfillment.

4-7. The Reality of the Present. **Turn us . . . cause thine anger toward us to cease.** The present situation stands in bold relief when viewed in relation to the prophetic ideal. God's anger is still evident and appears to be unending. The psalmist appeals to God to **restore, revive, show** loving-kindness, and **grant** deliverance.

8-13. The Answer of Hope. **I will hear what God the Lord will speak.** In prophetic fashion the psalmist pauses to hear God's message in answer to the prayer of the people. He is certain that it will be a message of peace. By means of vivid personifications, he describes how real is God's salvation. The union of God's **mercy** or covenant love and our **truth** or faithfulness, of His **righteousness** and our **peace** of heart, of **earth** and **heaven** are certain when God and men meet. As a result of this encounter, God will provide for men's needs and lead them in right paths. For us today, the meeting-place can only be at the foot of the cross.

Psalm 86. A Prayer for God's Favor

In Psalm 86 we recognize the sincere prayer of an individual who is in personal distress. The general nature of his distress makes the message apply to any person in trouble. It is this lack of specific detail that has led several commentators to view the psalm as corporate rather than individual. While this is basically a personal meditation, the author at times identifies himself with his community.

1-5. A General Plea for Help. **Bow down . . . hear me.** In general terms the psalmist sets forth his needs. Each plea carries with it the reason why God should answer it. He cries for God to **hear** because of his needy condition, to **keep** because of his pious nature, to **save** because of his continual prayer, and to **gladden** because of his sincere devotions. His faith is based upon the fact that God is a "forgiver," who shows mercy and pardons.

6-10. A Confident Hope in a Response. **Give ear . . . for thou wilt answer me.** The majesty and power of God make this confidence possible. While the other nations have their own gods, none of them can do the mighty works of the Lord. His greatness will eventually cause these nations to worship Him who is God alone.

11-17. A Prayer for Guidance and Protection. **Teach me . . . unite my heart.** It is God's teaching that will enable the psalmist to walk in truth. He desires unity of purpose that he may worthily praise and glorify the name of the Lord. With the humility of a slave or a handmaid's son, he asks for God's merciful protection and requests some sign of divine favor toward him.

Psalm 87. The City of God

The psalmist sings a song in praise of Zion as the center of worship for the world. The abrupt, terse style, which identifies the psalm with prophetic oracles, also renders several phrases obscure and difficult. The pronounced universalism points to the author's contact with the major prophets. The mention of Egypt and Babylon together as world powers suggests the period of the Exile as the occasion of composition of the poem.

1-3. The Glories of Zion. **Glorious things are spoken of thee.** These glories include the facts that God himself founded Zion, that he chose her in preference to every other place where Israelites dwell, and that she is in reality the **city of God.** Further glorious things are referred to in the verses which follow.

4-6. The Citizens of Zion. **This man was born there.** These words act as a refrain in this prophetic utterance. The Egyptians (**Rahab**), the Babylonians, the Philistines, the Phoenicians (**Tyre**), and the Ethiopians are all to become citizens of Zion. The certainty of this edict is assured by God's registering them in his census of the nations as "born in Zion." The concept of the future Jerusalem as the mother of all peoples is developed in Isa 60; 66:7-13,20,23; and referred to in Gal 4:26 and Heb 12:22.

7. The Rejoicing in Zion. **All my springs are in thee.** The musicians are instructed to sing, **All my fountains are in thee. Thee** is feminine, referring to Zion. The psalmist exults in addressing the sacred city as the mother or cradle of Israel's future generations. For *ma'yān*, "springs," in the sense of wife or mother, the source of offspring, see Prov 5:16; Song 4:12,15; Isa 48:1.

Psalm 88. The Darkness of Despair

This lament and prayer of an individual completely engulfed in gloom and despair ends without an answer or even a glimmer of hope. Although some interpreters view the psalm as a corporate sequel to portions of the book of Lamentations, the personal aspects are too intense for such a national interpretation. The psalmist cannot be located in history, but this does not affect the interpretation, for his suffering has a timeless quality.

1,2. His Appeal. **Let my prayer come before thee.** In the midst of his suffering he demonstrates his faith by this direct appeal to the **Lord God of my salvation.** This is not his first plea to God but the continuation of a prayer which begins in the day and runs on into the night.

3-8. His Complaint. **My life draweth nigh unto the grave.** His trouble is so serious that he is as good as dead. Nothing is left for him but the grave and Sheol. His most descriptive term for Sheol is **the pit** (v. 4), a place of darkness where the dead are cut off from God's hand. He seems to feel that the Lord no longer remembers him, since he is counted with the dead.

9-12. His Urgency. **Lord, I have called daily upon thee.** He is certain that he will pass beyond God's help when he actually goes to Sheol. Therefore, God must act immediately if He is going to show His wonders, loving-kindness, faithfulness, and righteousness.

13-18. His Desperation. **But unto thee have I cried.** His petition becomes more impassioned with each outcry. Now in a spirit of desperation, he asks the ever-recurring question, **Why . . . ?** Having prayed continually for relief since his youth, only one conclusion is left: "It is all the result of God's wrath." He makes no further request, but leaves his burden with the Lord. How different is the NT hope in life with Christ beyond the grave (cf. Phil 1:21,23; II Cor 5:1-8).

Psalm 89. An Appeal to God's Promises

This psalm is basically a lament by an individual who speaks for the nation. The actual lament is prefaced by a lengthy introduction, which consists of a hymn of praise and an oracle. These divergent elements have suggested to some commentators that this piece is a composite of two or three original poems. While it is possible that the author incorporated existing poems, the subject matter is arranged in a logical manner. The hymn and oracle both present the basis for the lament.

1-4. God's Limitless Loving-kindness. **Mercies . . . faithfulness . . . covenant.**

In this beautiful introduction the psalmist presents the themes which he will develop. The Lord has shown his *loving-kindness* (v. 1, ASV) in his acts of deliverance. His **faithfulness** is the guarantee of his continued loving-kindness. His **covenant** gives binding power to these important attributes.

5-18. God's Incomparable Faithfulness. **For who in the heaven can be compared unto the Lord?** The incomparableness of God both in heaven and among his saints within Israel is set forth as a plea to God and a comfort to the people. The reference to Rahab (v. 10) employs a term from an ancient Near Eastern legend to speak of God's victory over Egypt at the Red Sea (cf. Job 9:13; Ps 74:13-15; 87:4; I Sam 30:7; Isa 51:9,10). The other allusions are used here to intensify the picture of God's power in creation, his victory over all opposition, and his dominion over heaven and earth.

19-37. God's Sworn Promise. **Then thou spakest in vision.** The motif of the covenant with David now becomes central, though it is still connected with God's loving-kindness and faithfulness (cf. vv. 24,28,33). The psalmist first deals with the divine promise to David. The former promise to the nation as God's firstborn in his estimation (Ex 4:22) is now focused on the king; the epithet of verse 27 is extended to all the Davidic succession, culminating in Jesus, God's anointed one (Messiah). Then the emphasis is shifted in verse 29 to the working out of the promise through the seed of David. While he appeals to God's sworn testimony that the covenant will stand, he recognizes that punishment must come upon David's seed for their unfaithfulness (vv. 30-32).

38-51. God's Shattered Covenant. **But thou hast cast off and abhorred.** The emphatic **But thou** marks a sharp contrast between the promises of God and the present situation. The covenant has been made void, the city walls are broken down, the land is spoiled, the battle lost, and the throne cast down. The shortening of the king's youth may refer to Jehoiachin, who was only eighteen when carried away captive. After setting forth the present plight of the nation, the psalmist turns to his appeal in verse 46. The transitoriness of human life, God's power to save, and his former loving-kindness are all linked to the covenant with David as reasons for immediate restoration. While no hope is expressed, the enthusiasm of the former sections would suggest a positive expectation of hope.

52. Closing Benediction. **Blessed be the Lord for evermore.** This benediction is not a part of the psalm itself, but a doxology added as a formal close to Book III.

BOOK IV. Psalms 90–106

The fourth major division in the Psalter is actually a part of a larger collection embracing Psalms 90–150. The break at Psalm 106 seems to be made for convenience, since the same dominant thought continues in Psalm 107. While the psalms in Book I were primarily personal and those in Books II and III were generally national, the remainder of the Psalter is basically liturgical. The emphasis is upon the worship of God's people as they offer their thanksgiving and praise in a form suitable for temple worship. The covenant name for God, *Yahweh,* predominates. It occurs in every psalm in Book IV and is absent from only two in Book V.

Psalm 90. Our Help in Ages Past

Although this may well be the meditation of an individual, its purpose is clearly to voice the petition of a corporate group. The author looks back on a long period of history to arrive at his concept of God's wrath. In view of man's frailty and brevity, he pleads for restoration to God's favor.

1-6. Man's Life Contrasted with God's Eternity. **Lord, thou hast been our dwelling place.** The psalmist begins by citing his confidence in God's everlasting nature (cf. Deut 33:27). Truly **all generations** have found this to be true. The Lord is immortal; man is mortal. The Lord is above time; man is ever time-conscious. The Lord is from everlasting to everlasting; man, like grass, is short-lived. The similes of verses 4-6 emphasize not merely the brevity or frailty of life, but man's dependence upon the Eternal. Man is surely at God's disposal, returning to dust at His command and being swept away as by a flood.

7-12. Man Consumed by God's Wrath. **For we are consumed by thine anger.** The psalmist now interprets the reason for man's transitory nature and his suffering. He realizes from history and personal experience that God's face is as the light of the sun in its power to probe into the depths of man's being. Compared with God's timelessness, a lifetime of seventy or eighty years seems pitifully short. Furthermore, this span of years is filled with sorrow and suffering. Out of this pessimistic view of life comes the plaintive cry for teaching and wisdom to help a man discern the true meaning of life.

13-17. Man Seeking for God's Favor. **Return, O Lord . . . satisfy us.** The appeal introduced in verse 12 is continued throughout the poem. The writer desires God to grant his people happiness in proportion to the suffering they have endured under His wrath. The psalm closes with a plea that God's loveliness or graciousness (his **beauty**) may be the basis of the Lord's preparing and establishing (cf. Eph 2:10) all the daily tasks ahead (viz., **the work of our hands**; cf. Deut 2:7; 14:29; 16:15; 24:19).

Psalm 91. The Security of Trust

In this companion poem to Psalm 90 the psalmist sings a noble song of trust, but he has a didactic purpose as well. The prophetic oracle at the close adds a note of authority to the confidence expressed throughout. The depth of trust and the quiet confidence suggest that this is the meditation of an individual. However, its possible use as an antiphonal song adapts it for congregational use.

1,2. Divine Protection. **He is my refuge and my fortress.** The writer opens with a powerful presentation of his theme — the security of the one who trusts completely in God. **The secret place** may better be translated *the shelter,* which meaning better parallels the concept of *the shadow*.

3-8. Divine Providence. **Surely he shall deliver thee . . . cover thee.** The basic idea of protection is expanded to include many acts of providential care as well as active deliverance. Because of the references to pestilence and disease, many commentators treat the entire psalm as a polemic against the use of magic formulae for warding off demons. Indeed, the Talmud suggests that the psalm be used in the case of demonic attacks. The **terror by night** may refer to the night demon Lilith, while the **arrow . . . by day** may describe the devices of the wicked demons. The **pestilence . . . in darkness** may have affinity with the demon Namtar, while the **destruction . . . at noonday** may refer to a one-eyed demon also mentioned in Rabbinical tradition. Even if these ideas were absent from the author's thoughts, they were very much a part of the psalm in its actual Jewish use. The **snare of the fowler** is a reference to traps set by adversaries (cf. Ps 124:7). **Noisome pestilence** is literally, *death of destructions,* perhaps referring to a violent death. The psalmist was conscious of God's care amid the varied circumstances of life.

9-13. Divine Reward. **Because thou hast made the Lord . . . thy habitation.** The psalmist, reverting to his main theme, carries forward the idea of reward alluded to in verse 8. The man of faith is assured that God will send guardian angels to protect him from plagues and stumbling. Satan quoted these words in tempting Jesus (Mt 4:6; Lk 4:10). According to the Talmud, every man has two ministering angels beside him during his entire life.

14-16. Divine Promise. **Because he hath set his love upon me.** The authority behind the idea of reward is heightened by the oracle from God. The promise includes the blessings of deliverance, exaltation, answer to prayer, long life, and victory. These blessings and more are promised to the one who has come to love and trust God.

Psalm 92. A Hymn of Gratitude

An individual with great confidence in the righteous judgment of God here expresses his thanksgiving. His confidence goes beyond theory or formal theology, for it is derived from personal experience. The use of the psalm as a hymn for the weekly observance of the Sabbath is attested by ancient Jewish sources. The notation in verse 3 of the instruments to be used shows that it was probably designed for corporate worship.

1-4. The Delight of Praise. **It is a good thing to give thanks . . . to sing praises.** The psalmist expresses his personal delight in the services of the Temple. After enumerating the instruments involved, he clearly sets forth the basis of public praise. It is God's wondrous **works** that make the worshipers glad.

5-8. The Sovereignty of God. **O Lord, how great are thy works.** The sovereign, sublime nature of God as expressed in his works and his thoughts is set in contrast to the lack of comprehension of the **fool** and the **brutish** man. In comparison to the sure destruction of these men who lack perception and understanding, God stands immovable **on high for evermore.**

9-15. The Certainty of Judgment. **Thine enemies shall perish. . . . but my horn shalt thou exalt.** The writer's enemies are again viewed as God's enemies, too. The psalmist is certain that God will bring true retribution, for he feels at one with the Lord, that he is inseparable from the vindicating triumph of God's righteous cause. He closes with a beautiful description of the happy lot of the righteous, who are transplanted into the household of the Lord (v. 13). Following the pattern of antiquity, he gloats over this certain destruction, but returns quickly to a description of the happy lot of the righteous.

Psalm 93. The Everlasting King

The emphasis upon the enthronement of Yahweh as King gives this psalm close affinity with Psalms 47 and 96–99. For this reason, these six poems are usually called Royal Psalms or Enthronement Psalms. Mowinckel and others have done extensive research in an attempt to reconstruct an actual enthronement ceremony in connection with the New Year's celebration. These psalms would take on increased meaning and significance if it could be shown that they were used in such a ceremony. However, positive evidence of such a practice is indeed slight.

1,2. God's Kingship. **The Lord reigneth.** These opening words can better be translated, *Yahweh is King* or *has become king*. He has robed himself with majesty, has girded himself with strength, and is ready for action. The psalmist hastens to state that the Lord's rulership is not a new thing, but has been **established of old** (cf. Jud 8:23), while God himself is **from everlasting.**

3,4. God's Might. **Mightier than the noise of many waters.** It is God's might that assures the permanence and immutability of his rule. Raging storms and pounding waves cannot shake his everlasting throne. The Lord's supremacy in creation is probably alluded to here, as well as his victory over heathen powers.

5. God's Government. **Thy testimonies are very sure.** God's kingship and might are evidenced by his moral laws or decrees. Permanence and immutability characterize the holiness God imparts to his house.

Psalm 94. A Plea for Vengeance

Although this lament embraces the whole community, it is pervaded by a deep personal element. Some writers consider the psalm to be composite, but there is little justification for denying its basic unity. Its position between two joyous psalms sets it out in sharper contrast. While it is possible that foreign oppressors are in view, the author is mainly concerned over those leaders in Israel who oppress the righteous.

1-7. The Judge Sought. **Shew thyself. . . . lift up thyself.** The psalmist appeals to the Lord as the God of **vengeance** and **judge of the earth,** as the One having the power to punish and the right to effect retribution. The big question is not whether God can avenge wrongs done, but **how long** it will be before he brings about justice.

8-11. The Unwise Rebuked. **Understand, ye brutish . . . ye fools.** These two epithets classify the oppressors as cruel and lacking in common sense. The direct address (v. 8) drives home the point that God is aware of all that goes on in the world.

12-15. The Righteous Vindicated. **Blessed is the man.** Happy is the man who is educated by God. He will have strength for the difficult days and assurance of ultimate vindication.

16-23. The Judgment Realized. **Who will rise up for me against the evildoers?** From his experience with God, the psalmist answers his own question: God will surely give the vengeance he seeks (cf. v. 1).

Psalm 95. A Call to Worship

This psalm combines a hymn and a prophetic oracle for group worship. The latter section has the distinctly didactic purpose of reminding the worshipers of their forebears' failures, lest they fall into the same errors. The hymn section was undoubtedly designed as a processional to be sung as the congregation gathered for Sabbath worship. Along with the other psalms in this group (95–100), it seems to have been composed for use in the services of the Second Temple.

1,2. The Call Announced. **O come, let us sing.** This summons was probably sounded by a Levitical choir as the procession to the Temple began. The happy worshipers quickly joined in by making a joyful noise of praise in exuberant Oriental style.

3-5. The Lord Described. **A great God, and a great King.** The basis for the summons of verses 1 and 2 is declared in true hymn style. The greatness of Yahweh as King and Creator and Shepherd is beautifully expressed. The menace of foreign beliefs makes necessary a clear statement of the nature of God as a preparation for worship.

6,7. The Call Repeated. **O come, let us worship.** The processional has now reached the temple gates. The joyful singing gives way to the more solemn acts of worship, such as bowing down and kneeling before God. The emphasis upon God's sovereignty over his cosmic creation gives way to a reminder to the worshipers of his special relation to Israel.

8-11. The Warning Voiced. **Harden not your heart.** The reminder of Israel's sin in wilderness days serves as a warning to those waiting to enter the Temple. God's **rest** refers historically to entrance into the Promised Land, which was denied to those who doubted. Here the worshipers are exhorted to keep their hearts tender before the Lord lest he reject them also.

Psalm 96. The Glory of God

Here is a hymn of praise which closes on an eschatological note. The striking universalism running throughout demonstrates the enlarged outlook of the exiles as they returned from captivity. The LXX identifies the occasion as the time "when the house was being built after the captivity." The frequent quoting of other psalms (9,29,33,40,48,95,98,105), the universalism, and the concept of the "nothingness" of the gods all tend to confirm the LXX designation of the occasion.

1-3. Israel's Mission of Praise. **O sing . . . declare his glory among the heathen. A new song** was needed to express praise for Israel's deliverance from captivity. The people are exhorted to sing unto God and bless him, making known his salvation with new outbursts of praise every day.

4-6. God's Glorious Nature. **Great, and greatly to be praised.** As in the previous psalm, the people are exhorted to praise God, because the great God is worthy of great praise. **Honour . . . majesty . . . strength . . . beauty,** though here personified, are still related in thought to God's characteristics.

7-9. Mankind's Duty of Praise. **Ye kindreds of the people.** In keeping with Israel's universal mission, all the nations are called to praise God. They are invited to give due praise, bring their offering, enter the sacred precincts, and worship God. Note that they must worship in the proper attire – **holy array** (RSV), and in the proper attitude – **fear** or *reverence*.

10-13. God's Righteous Rule. **The Lord reigneth.** The literal translation of this phrase is: *Yahweh is King* or *is become King*. Perhaps this refers to a ceremonial enthronement which may have been a part of the New Year's celebration. However, the main emphasis is eschatological; God is pictured as King of the nations and Judge of the earth.

Psalm 97. The Sovereignty of God

In this hymn of praise the theocratic principle of God's kingship is acclaimed. An eschatological note predominates in the first half of the psalm, which is then applied to the people. The entire hymn may have been designed as a commentary on the last verse of the preceding psalm, or it may have been placed in its present position because of the close relationship in thought. Though almost every phrase that appears here had already been used by other writers, the skill of this psalmist in weaving the phrases together is evident throughout.

1-6. The Manifestation of the King. **The Lord reigneth.** Again the idea is, "*Yahweh is become King.*" All those who will benefit are called to rejoice in the truth of this eschatological dominion. Mystery and awesome majesty characterize the King's coming. However, the righteousness of God's government undergirds all of this awesome display of power.

7-12. The Effect upon Mankind. **Confounded. . . . glad.** The manifestation of God as King makes evident a sharp contrast. Those who worship idols are put to shame, while the worshipers of the Lord are made glad. With this contrast in mind, the conclusion follows that Israel has a distinct duty to God. Those who rejoice at the coming of the King must even now love the Lord, hate evil, rejoice, and give thanks.

Psalm 98. Praise by All Nature

Psalm 98, a hymn of praise, echoes the thoughts of many other psalmists. It is an integral part of the collection that emphasizes God's kingship (Ps 95–99). The reference to God as **the King** in verse 6 and the eschatological note in the concluding verses connect it with the preceding psalms. All nature is here summoned to join in acclaiming God's praise.

1-3. Praise to the Deliverer. **O sing unto the Lord a new song.** This new song, although drawn from previous sources, is occasioned by some recent deliverance. God has done marvelous things, won the victory, and brought deliverance. All of this is based upon the declaration of his righteousness to the nations and the remembrance of his mercy and truth to Israel.

4-6. Praise to the King. **Make a joyful noise unto the Lord. . . . the King.** Since all the earth has seen how God has delivered Israel, all men are called to join with the Israelites in worshiping him. This is a call for universal participation, in keeping with the broad outlook of Isaiah 40–66.

7-9 Praise to the Judge. **Let the sea roar. . . . for he cometh to judge the earth.** Although this stanza continues the appeal of the preceding stanza, a new element is here introduced. God the King comes as the Judge of the earth. Since all creation is to be judged, all created things must join in praise. The psalm closes with the prediction that the judgment will be characterized by **righteousness** and **equity.**

Psalm 99. The Holiness of God

The emphasis in this hymn of praise is on the sublime nature of God, expressed by his holiness. While the hymn is based upon the concept of God's kingship, there is less of the eschatological in this than in the four preceding psalms. The refrain in verses 3,5, and 9 expresses strongly the distinctive teaching on God's holiness.

1-3. The Holy God is Sovereign. **The Lord reigneth.** Again the translation should be: *Yahweh is King* or *is become King*. God is pictured as enthroned upon the mercy seat, between the cherubim, the place of his earthly manifestation in the Temple. He is also represented as taking his place upon his earthly throne in Zion, a concept that relates this psalm explicitly to an enthronement celebration. Such a manifestation of the Eternal causes trembling of man and nature, but issues in praise to His name.

4,5. The Holy God is Righteous. **Judgment . . . equity . . . righteousness.** Not only is God sovereign in his rule of the world; he is righteous in his judgment of men. He does not wield his power in an arbitrary way but according to his just and righteous nature. Again, this righteousness is summed up in the words of the refrain, **Holy is he** (ASV).

6,9. The Holy God is Faithful. **They called . . . he answered.** Moses, Aaron, and Samuel are cited as great intercessors of the past. This is the only place in the OT where Moses is classed as a priest, although he did perform some priestly functions and had access to the Tabernacle. While God answered the prayers of these spiritual giants for Israel, he still found it necessary to punish his people for their persistent evil-doing. The final call for exaltation and worship is occasioned by the Lord's faithfulness and is based upon his holiness.

Psalm 100. The Essentials of Worship

A double call to worship characterizes this brief but eloquent hymn of praise. The psalm was undoubtedly used as a processional hymn and appears to have been written for this purpose. Verses 3 and 5 give a concise statement of the doctrine of Judaism.

1-3. A Joyful Procession. **Make a joyful noise unto the Lord.** This first call to worship may well have been rendered by a choir outside the Temple precincts. Prime essential for such worship is a knowledge of God; that is, a recognition that the Lord is God, Creator, and Shepherd of his people Israel. And this knowledge leads to joyful praise, gladness, and singing.

4,5. A Thankful Entry. **Enter into his gates with thanksgiving.** This second call to worship may well have been the invitation by a choir within the Temple precincts. The worshipers, approaching the gates, were invited to continue their worship by entering the gates and then the courts. The further essentials of worship are thanksgiving, praise, prayer, and additional knowledge of God's character. The Lord's attributes of goodness, love, and faithfulness must be recognized by worshipers in any period of time.

Psalm 101. A Royal Code of Ethics

This is best classified as a royal psalm, since it is a declaration of principles by which a ruler intends to rule. These principles, or resolutions, are expressed in the form of promises to God, and therefore addressed to him. Though no king is mentioned in the body of the psalm, the nobility of expression certainly fits the personality and character of David. As an ideal for kingship, it could have been used by many rulers in Israel, whatever the occasion of its composition.

1-4. Personal Resolutions. **I will sing of mercy and judgment.** The guiding principles of mercy and judgment form the basis for the resolutions. After declaring his determination to choose the way of uprightness or integrity, the speaker voices his longing for closer fellowship with God. He resolves to abstain from wickedness and apostasy. Not only does he hate the work of apostates, but he promises to refuse to know, or entertain any evil thought (v. 4).

5-8. Official Intentions. **Whoso privily slandereth . . . him will I cut off.** In keeping with the guiding principles of mercy and judgment, the speaker sets forth his intentions as to what kind of people he will show favor and what kind he will shun or destroy. Only the faithful and those who walk in integrity will know his favor. Slanderers and wicked-doers he will destroy, and he will deny his favor to the proud, to the deceitful, and to liars. In so doing he will cleanse the royal court, the royal city – Jerusalem, and the entire land.

Psalm 102. A Prayer for Help

Though basically the lament of an individual, this psalm has a corporate element as well. For this reason, commentators are divided as to its original intent. A distinctly personal appeal is followed by a plea for the nation. Then the psalmist reverts to his own problem again, facing it in the light of his assured hope for the nation.

1-11. The Suffering of the Psalmist. **Hear my prayer, O Lord.** The psalmist's deep sense of urgency makes this cry especially poignant. He needs an answer immediately. He is suffering from a disease that has produced mental anxiety, and his enemies have taken advantage of his condition. All of this suffering, he believes, is due to God's wrath.

12-22. The Restoration of the Nation. **But thou, O Lord, shalt endure for ever.** In contrast to the psalmist's transitory nature (v. 11), God endures. It is upon this truth that Zion's restoration is based. The suggestion of some that this section is a separate psalm inserted by the compiler is not warranted. It is evident that the solution of the speaker's problem is intimately tied in with the solution of that of his nation (cf. vv. 12,26,27).

23-28. The Assurance of the Psalmist. **They shall perish, but thou shalt endure.** Though the speaker reverts to his suffering and weakness, he gains assurance from his nation's hope in the Lord. Even when the entire creation has passed away, God will endure. Verses 25-27 are referred to Christ the Lord in Heb 1:10-12 (cf. Heb 13:8). In the meantime, His eternity guarantees deliverance and permanence for the psalmist's people.

Psalm 103. A Hymn of Thankful Praise

This hymn of praise is without a peer in all the world's literature. It appears to be the expression of an individual, though some commentators find here a corporate voice. The psalmist seeks first to stir his own spirit to offer praise and thanksgiving to God, then the spirits of others. His words are untouched by sorrow, complaint, or sadness. The manner of expression and the depth of insight are remarkable for one living prior to the coming of Christ.

1-5. Praise for Personal Blessings. **Bless the Lord, O my soul.** The psalmist first addresses an exhortation to himself. In the term translated **soul** *(nepesh)* as well as in the parallel expression – **all that is within me**, he refers to his entire being. He now stirs his inner self to remembrance as he counts his many blessings. Note the strength in the verbs – forgives, heals, redeems, crowns, satisfies, and renews.

6-10. Praise for National Blessings. **The Lord executeth righteousness and judgment.** God is not only righteous and just in himself, but he actively engages in acts of righteousness and justice for oppressed peoples. Just as the Lord has crowned the psalmist with **lovingkindness** *(ḥesed,* v. 4), he has proved himself in Israel's history to be **plenteous in loving kindness.** This is best seen in his being slow to anger and in his punishing his people less severely than they deserve.

11-14. Praise for Forgiving Love. **So great is his mercy.** Adding illustration to illustration, the psalmist seeks to convey an adequate description of God's loving-kindness. He does not know how far it is from earth to heaven, but he knows that even that vastness could not contain God's mercy. He does not know how far east is from west, but he knows that God's love has removed our sins even farther. The most beautiful and intimate illustration is that of God as the Father who has compassion upon man in his weakness and frailty.

15-18. Praise for Eternal Love. **From everlasting to everlasting.** The continuance of God's loving-kindness stands in the sharpest contrast possible to man's transitoriness. The extension of this loving-kindness to man is conditioned by man's responding to the covenant and commands of God in a proper attitude of fear or reverence.

19-22. Call for Universal Praise. **Bless the Lord, ye his angels. . . . hosts . . . ministers.** After stating the principle of divine kingship, the psalmist calls for praise by the chorus of the whole universe. The purpose of the praise is to declare **all his works in all places,** both in heaven and on earth. The psalmist closes by taking his place in the anthem of the ages.

Psalm 104. The Creative Power of God

Here is a hymn of praise similar in certain respects to the preceding one. The opening and concluding phrases of the two psalms are almost identical, setting forth an attitude of thanksgiving and praise. While the previous hymn emphasized God's relation to history, this one pictures God's relation to creation. It offers interesting parallels to Persian, Babylonian, and Egyptian thought (cf. "Hymn to Aten," ANET, pp. 369-371). Even more important are the parallels with Genesis 1 and Job 38–41.

1-4. God's Greatness in Creation. **Thou art very great.** After calling his whole being to praise, the psalmist pictures the Lord as clothed in the wonderful majesty of his creation. Light appears as his robe; the heavens are spread out as a canopy; his abode is supported by pillars; clouds, wind, and angels are created for his use.

5-9. God's Formation of the Earth. **The foundations of the earth.** The Near Eastern concepts of cosmology are evident here as well as throughout the psalm. The earth is firmly established *upon her bases* (AV marg.) or pillars (v. 5); the mountains and valleys are formed; the seas are divided and fixed as to their bounds.

10-18. God's Provision for His Creatures. **He sendeth the springs.** One of the greatest needs in ancient Palestine was an adequate supply of water. The psalmist praises God for making provision for springs and rain so that all forms of life, animal and vegetable, may be sustained. He praises Him, too, for the blessings of food, wine, oil, trees, hills, and rocks.

19-23. God's Ordering of the Heavens. **The moon . . . the sun.** These two celestial bodies are singled out for attention because they are indispensable in the ordering of seasons and days. While the wild animals thrive on darkness, man's labor is mainly accomplished in the hours of daylight.

24-30. God's Providence. **In wisdom hast thou made them all.** The psalmist pauses to marvel at the Divine wisdom displayed in all God's wondrous creations. The marvels of the sea and the mystery of life are pointed out as illustrations of God's providence.

31-35. God's Glory in Praise. **The glory of the Lord shall endure for ever.** The psalmist vows that he will sing praise to God as long as he has life. His desire that evil be eradicated is in keeping with his concept of the goodness of God's creation (cf. Gen 1).

Psalm 105. The Wonders of the Past

Again the psalmist sings a hymn of praise, this time emphasizing the wondrous acts of God within the covenant relation. Psalms 105 and 106 are companion pieces in that history is searched in both. In the former, God's acts are emphasized; in the latter, Israel's acts of disobedience are recited. Both poems show affinity with Psalm 78, in which the two themes are interwoven.

1-6. The Call for Thanksgiving. **Give thanks . . . call . . . sing . . . talk . . . glory . . . rejoice. . . . seek. . . . remember.** The psalmist's detailed instructions reveal what it means to praise the Lord. It is clear that the hymn was designed for congregational use.

7-15. The Covenant with the Patriarchs. **He hath remembered his covenant.** The special feature of the covenant singled out is the promise that Canaan was to be Israel's inheritance. The rest of the psalm demonstrates the working out of this aspect of the covenant. Note the unusual use of **mine anointed ones** and **my prophets** to refer to the patriarchs.

16-25. The Experiences of the Sojourn. **Moreover he called for a famine.** Also unusual is this reference to God as the direct cause of the famine that brought Israel's family into Egypt. The psalmist is primarily emphasizing God's part in all that occurred: He called a famine, sent a man (Joseph), tried him, allowed him to be raised to power, increased his people, and stirred up hatred for Israel among the Egyptians. In keeping with general OT thought, the psalmist ignores secondary causes.

26-38. The Deliverance from Egypt. **He sent Moses . . . Aaron.** The writer places special emphasis upon the plagues as signs of God's power. He moves the ninth plague to the head of the list, inverts the order of the third and fourth, and omits the fifth and sixth.

39-45. The Realization of the Promise. **For he remembered his holy promise.** After recalling how God guided Israel in the wilderness, the psalmist draws his conclusion: Each of God's wondrous acts was brought about because the Lord remembered and kept his promise, first given to Abraham. The climax comes in the fulfillment of the promise that Canaan, **the lands of the nations** (AV, *heathen)*, with all the fruits of previous labor, should belong to Israel

Psalm 106. The Long-suffering Nature of God

The continuous rebellion of Israel is emphasized in this sequel to Psalm 105. While beginning as a hymn (vv. 1-5), the poem continues as a national lament or confession. The sadness of the lament section is offset, to a certain degree, by the picture of God's long-suffering mercy in dealing with his people.

1-6. Praise and Confession. **Praise . . . give thanks. . . . we have sinned.** In hymnic fashion the author issues a call to praise, followed by an expression of beatitude, a personal prayer, and a confession of national sin. Note that the present generation is included along with the past generations.

7-33. Murmuring and Disobedience. **Our fathers understood not.** Here, as frequently in the Psalms, the Exodus and the period of wandering through the wilderness provide illustrations of the way the children of Israel misunderstood God. They murmured for food (vv. 13-15); they rebelled against Moses and Aaron (vv. 16-18); they apostatized in making a golden calf (vv. 19-23); they refused to accept God's leadership in the incident of the spies (vv. 24-27); they joined in Moabite worship (vv. 28-31); and they involved Moses in their murmuring at Meribah (vv. 32,33).

34-36. Backsliding and Unfaithfulness. **Thus were they defiled with their own works.** In contrast to God's faithfulness, shown by the mighty works he performed in Israel's behalf, his people repeatedly proved unfaithful after entering Canaan. Mingling with the inhabitants, they learned new modes of sin. Not only did they serve idols, but they joined in the abomination of human sacrifice. God's compassion notwithstanding, punishment was repeatedly necessary.

47,48. Prayer and Doxology. **Save us. . . . Blessed be the Lord.** The lengthy confession leads to a request for mercy and restoration. The doxology appears to be an integral part of the psalm, while also serving as a concluding doxology for Book IV.

BOOK V. Psalms 107–150

The fifth book in the fivefold division includes several smaller collections or groups of psalms. The Psalms of Ascents (120–134) and the Hallelujah Psalms (111–113, 115–117, 146–150) are evidently the nucleus around which the other psalms were grouped together. Prior to the fivefold division, there was probably a threefold arrangement in which Books IV and V were one large collection. An over-all liturgical purpose is evident throughout, resulting in a deep sense of public worship, which culminates in the closing words of Psalm 150: "Let everything that hath breath praise the Lord. Hallelujah!"

Psalm 107. The Song of the Redeemed

Psalms 105,106, and 107 constitute a trilogy of praise and thanksgiving, in spite of the book division here. The different character of verses 33-42 has suggested to many that this passage was added later. The differences in content and style make this suggestion plausible although not mandatory.

1-3. The Call to Thanksgiving. **O give thanks unto the Lord.** The recipients of this call are **the redeemed of the Lord.** Isaiah 62:12 uses this term to apply to the captives returning from Babylon, but a wider usage of the term may well be meant.

4-32. The Reasons for Thanksgiving. **They wandered. . . . cried unto the Lord. . . . and he led them forth.** The psalmist uses four vivid illustrations of God's deliverances to reinforce his call to thanksgiving. After each incident he repeats the call in the form of an interjection. This fourfold refrain keeps central the theme of thanksgiving. God's care over lost travelers (vv. 4-9), over captives (vv. 10-16), over the sick (vv. 17-22), and over seafarers (vv. 23-32) calls for thankful remembrance. In each instance, the author describes the helpless condition of those in trouble, their cry to God, and the deliverance He gives.

33-42. The Providence of God. **He turneth rivers into a wilderness. . . . wilderness into a standing water.** These verses describe the blessings and curses apparent in God's rule of nature and mankind. They may serve as a general conclusion drawn from the more particular situations described in verses 4-32. However, the illustrations given are quite different from those of previous passages. This fact, plus the lack of any note of thanksgiving, the didactic purpose, the emphasis upon wisdom in the closing verse, and the lack of any refrain, certainly suggests that these verses were designed for a separate occasion.

Psalm 108. A Prayer for God's Help

In this psalm are combined a hymn and a lament, both of which are found in other psalms. Verses 1-5 occur also in Ps 57:7-11, while verses 6-13 are found in Ps 60:5-12 with only minor variations. Since the divine name *Yahweh* is used in verse 3 rather than the *'Ădōnāy* of Psalm 57, the present psalmist undoubtedly drew his material from the two earlier works. Perhaps the combination was formed to meet the needs of a new historical situation. (Cf. the previously mentioned psalms for further comments.)

Psalm 109. A Plea for Vengeance

Contrary to the views of some commentators, this psalm is clearly the lament of an individual rather than the voice of the nation. The personal character of the thought and expression is too strong for corporate significance. The imprecations in verses 9-20 make the poem unadaptable for worship purposes. The theory of some interpreters that these imprecations are the taunts of the psalmist's enemies is not convincing. There is a *righteous* indignation against evil (cf. Mt 23:13ff.); and the psalmist was assured that his foes were enemies of God.

1-5. His Appeal for Help. **Hold not thy peace.** In one terse statement the writer makes his appeal, and immediately he begins to voice his complaint. His enemies have been extremely vocal, while God has been silent. They have slandered him unjustly **with a lying tongue.** They have rewarded his love and goodness with hatred and evil.

6-20. His Plea for Retribution. **Let him be condemned.** The psalmist envisions a law court in which a wicked man is to be judged. The speaker sets forth the details of the sentence which the accused deserves. At the death of the accused someone else will take his office, and many difficulties will beset his wife and children. Worse than the speaker's desire for the death of his enemy is his wish that his enemy's family may come to an end and the father's name be forgotten within one generation. In verse 20, all of the speaker's adversaries are included in the foregoing imprecations.

21-31. His Prayer for Deliverance. **But do thou for me . . . deliver thou me.** The psalmist prays that God will have mercy upon him in his sick and needy condition, and vindicate him, so that his enemies may realize that God's hand has delivered him. After another outburst of imprecation, he closes with the confident promise that he will have opportunity to praise God for answered prayer.

Psalm 110. The Promise of Victory and Dominion

This is properly a royal psalm with Messianic overtones throughout. The psalmist is uttering a divine oracle with the authority of a prophet. He addresses the oracle to his king and gives him assurance of victory. Men from Abraham to Simon of Maccabean times have been suggested as the historical recipient of the message. Yet Jesus' use of verse 1 clearly authorizes our finding here a wider significance than the primary meaning of the psalm in OT history (cf. Mt 22:41-45).

1-4. The Oracle of the Lord. **The Lord said.** The term used is a prophetic formula, "Oracle of the Lord." It is nowhere else employed in the Psalter, but it is frequently used by the prophets. While some commentators limit the extent of the oracle to verse 1, it seems better to extend it through verse 4. The Messianic king is commanded to occupy the position of highest honor and share the divine rule until his enemies are completely vanquished (cf. Josh 10:24; I Kgs 5:3). The term *footstool* is used by David (I Chr 28:2). The king rules from Zion, and all foes are submissive to him. The oracle is addressed to **my Lord** *('Adōnî)*, a title of respect used for a king or superior. This king is to be honored and protected by divine blessing. His rule is to be universal. His subjects are to be willing volunteers. All of this is made certain by the use of a prophetic oath declaring the king's priesthood by divine appointment. The Messianic ruler serves a priestly as well as a royal office. In this he is likened to Melchizedek, the priest-king of Salem (Gen 14:18), whose ministry typified that of Jesus (cf. Heb 6:20–7:24).

5-7. The Victory of the Priest-King. **The Lord at thy right hand.** The scene changes now to the battlefield, where the Lord at Yahweh's right hand will shatter all his foes. The vivid language and the prophetic perfect tenses are designed to show clearly the completeness of the victory. The subject changes in verse 7 to the anointed king, whose head will be lifted in triumph. The frequent NT application of this psalm to Christ gives it special importance for the Christian interpreter.

Psalm 111. God's Wonderful Works

Here is a hymn of praise carefully designed as an acrostic poem. The twenty-two short lines begin with successive letters of the Hebrew alphabet. While this serves as an excellent mnemonic device, it greatly restricts the choice of words for a given line. This hymn is closely connected with Psalm 112 in form, language, and subject-matter. The two psalms are introductory to the *Hallēl* collection, which properly begins with Psalm 113.

1. The Annunciation of Praise. **I will praise the Lord.** The psalmist declares his intention to praise God **with a whole heart** as an act of public worship. This probably signifies that the message was delivered in the temple services by a solo voice.

2-4. The Greatness of God's Works. **The works of the Lord are great. . . . honourable and glorious.** The author thus describes God's works in general, then speaks of the Lord's eternal righteousness, his graciousness, and his compassion, attributes revealed most fully in his mighty acts. Note that man responds to evidences of God at work by seeking for further evidences and by remembering those works already performed.

5-9. The Verity of God's Care. **The works of his hands are verity and judgment.** God's provision of manna and quail demonstrated that he was mindful of the covenant. His **works** in the conquest of Canaan showed his intention to fulfill his covenant promise to Abraham. The **verity** of God's works is made known by his faithfulness.

10. The Beginning of Wisdom. **The fear of the Lord.** The psalm closes with a familiar maxim of the Wisdom writers. This kind of **fear** is best understood as *reverence* and *awe* that pervade every area of life. It is the beginning of true religion in that insight and understanding follow. It is also the consummation, for it is never replaced in true religious expression.

Psalm 112. Portrait of a Righteous Man

The concluding thought of Psalm 111 is more fully developed here, in keeping with the emphasis of the Wisdom literature. While 111 declares God's wonderful works, 112 describes the righteous man who has learned what it means to fear God. In its acrostic construction as well as in its subject-matter, this didactic psalm is a companion to the preceding one.

1-3. His Blessedness. **Blessed is the man.** In language reminiscent of Ps 1:1, the happiness of the God-fearer is set forth. A man who fears the Lord naturally finds delight in keeping the divine commandments. His children become heirs of his spiritual and material blessings. Note that the phrase, **his righteousness endureth for ever,** is applied to God in the preceding psalm.

4-6. His Character. **Gracious, and full of compassion, and righteous.** These terms are also used in Psalm 111 in the author's description of God. This is an application of the eternal truth that a devout man becomes more and more like the object of his worship. His prosperity will be lasting and his name long remembered because of his godly character.

7-10. His Permanence. **His heart is fixed.** His utter trust in God has given a sense of stability that the wicked cannot know. The truth that **his righteousness endureth for ever** here stands in sharp contrast to the fate of the wicked.

Psalm 113. The Condescension of God

This hymn of praise is the first psalm in a collection known in the Talmud as "The Hallel of Egypt." The designation comes from the repeated use of the Hebrew exclamation *Hallelujah* (**Praise ye the Lord**), and from the reference to the Exodus in 114:1. This collection (113–118) was included in the worship of Judaism on festival occasions.

1-3. Praise to His Name. **Praise the name of the Lord.** The psalmist opens with an appeal to the servants or worshipers of the Lord. By **name** the writer means not a mere appellation, but the character of God's revealed nature and the manifestations of his person. Note that the praise is to be both unending (v. 2) and universal (v. 3).

4-6. Praise for His Incomparableness. **Who is like unto the Lord?** The incomparable nature of the Lord is pictured in the twofold aspects of his transcendence and his immanence. These two aspects are not set in contrast but treated as complementary. While supreme over the nations of the earth and the hosts of the heavens, God humbles himself to consider the needs of mankind.

7-9. Illustrations of His Condescension. **He raiseth up the poor.** The element of God's condescension, set forth by the psalmist in verse 6, deserves further illustration. The **poor, the needy,** and the **barren woman** are singled out as beneficiaries of God's special providence. These instances are cited as representative of all God's generous deeds toward the children of men.

Psalm 114. The Wonder of the Exodus

The power of Hebrew poetry at its best is illustrated by this lyric. The terse expression, the dramatic vividness, the excellent parallelism, and the imaginative exaggeration mark the psalm as a poetic masterpiece. The arrangement of the material into four stanzas of two verses each adds balance to the poem's heightened expression. The final "Hallelujah" of Psalm 113 undoubtedly once stood at the beginning of this psalm, as attested by the LXX.

1,2. The Birth of Israel. **When Israel went out of Egypt.** In concise language, the psalmist presents his theme as the Exodus and the subsequent settlement in Canaan. God brought His people out of a land of strange language into their home. The parallel reference to Judah and Israel points to a time when the Temple was the center of worship and the northern area was considered a part of God's dominion.

3-6. The Effect upon Nature. **The sea saw it, and fled.** With poetic imagination, the psalmist describes the effect of God's works on nature. The **sea, the Jordan,** the **mountains,** and the **hills** were witnesses to his power in overcoming all obstacles that threatened to hinder the progress of Israel. The statements of verses 3,4 become Why? questions in verses 5,6. The answers are clearly implied in the further emphasis upon the awesomeness of God's power.

7,8. The Admonition to Nature. **Tremble, thou earth.** The recognition of God's wondrous acts and the effect of his presence should make all creation tremble. The conclusion to be drawn is that, even as God brought forth water in the wilderness, he will provide for the needs of his people.

Psalm 115. Glory to His Name

This psalm is basically a hymn of praise designed for use in the temple worship. The presence of a complaint (vv. 1,2) does not nullify the hymnic qualities, but gives a historical basis for its original composition. That it was used in the worship of the feast celebrations is known from various sources. In fact, Psalms 115–118 were sung at the conclusion of the Passover meal, just before the worshipers returned to their homes. The hymn appears to have been designed originally for antiphonal use.

1-8. A Contrast of Power. **Our God. . . . their idols.** The burden of the psalm is seen in the question by Israel's Gentile enemies, **Where is now their God?** In appealing for help, the psalmist does not seek glory for his nation but recognition by the heathen of the glory due to the name of Yahweh. The impotent idols and their feeble worshipers stand in sharp contrast to God's power and glory.

9-11. An Exhortation to Trust. **O Israel, trust thou in the Lord.** This threefold appeal for trust was probably voiced by a priest; and very likely a choral response followed each appeal. The nation, the priests, and the devoted God-fearers are all addressed in turn.

12-15. An Assurance of Blessing. **The Lord hath been mindful of us.** Remembrance of God's previous blessings gives assurance for the present and the future. Note that blessing is assured for each of the groups singled out in the previous exhortation.

16-18. A Chorus of Praise. **We will bless the Lord . . . for evermore.** The Lord who created both the heavens and the earth has reserved the heavens for his domain. To man he has given the earth and the right to praise him here and now. In the thinking of most writers, death ends the opportunity for further worship. Hence the urgency of the exhortation, **Praise ye the Lord.**

Psalm 116. A Song of Personal Thanksgiving

This hymn of thanksgiving is strikingly personal from beginning to end. Its use in this Hallel collection in connection with the main feasts probably indicates that it was associated with the payment of individual vows. The LXX divides this psalm into two separate poems, making a division after verse 9. The presence of frequent Aramaic expressions points to a post-Exilic setting.

1-11. Praise for Deliverance. **I love the Lord, because . . .** Out of the depths of trouble and sickness the psalmist called and the Lord answered. From this experience of answered prayer, he came to know God as **gracious, righteous,** and **merciful.** He now knows by experience that God preserves, helps, deals bountifully, and delivers. In the midst of his exultation he recalls that previously he had clung to his faith even when he had said, "I am greatly afflicted" (v. 10). In his consternation or alarm *(haste,* AV) he had said, "All men are liars," i.e., deceitful for not fulfilling their promised help. His quoting of Ps 31:22 in verse 11 probably indicates that now he has learned to rely on God in the face of human frailty.

12-19. Expressions of Gratitude. **What shall I render unto the Lord?** The speaker's realization of God's blessings gives birth to his desire for more concrete expression of gratitude. He promises to offer a drink offering (**take the cup of salvation**), worship (**call upon the name of the Lord**), pay vows, and offer a thanksgiving sacrifice. This is not the usual order of such sacrifices and offerings. The psalmist's humility and sense of dedication are seen in verse 16. As a servant, yea a trusted servant (**son of thine handmaid**), he expresses his dependence upon God.

Psalm 117. A Shout of Praise

This is the shortest hymn of praise recorded in the Psalter. In some MSS it is attached to the preceding poem and in other MSS to the following one. However, both the Hebrew Text and the LXX treat it as an entity. The two verses contain a complete act of praise. The first verse, employing strict parallelism of form, sets forth a universal call to praise. The second verse, which is in similar form, completes the call by expressing the reasons for rendering praise. Truly universal, the call includes all nations and all peoples. The concept of God is equally lofty, as his mercy and truth are singled out for mention.

Psalm 118. Thanksgiving for Deliverance

As a processional and a jubilant expression of thanksgiving, this song of praise serves as a fitting conclusion to the Hallel collection. Clearly designed for antiphonal use, it employs solo voices, choruses, and congregational refrains. Verses 5-21 are quite individualistic in content, suggesting that verses 1-4 and 22ff. were added to adapt the original psalm for collective use.

1-4. The Invocation to Praise. **O give thanks unto the Lord.** This call to thanksgiving and praise was the signal for beginning the procession to the Temple. The leader or priest presented the call, while a chorus or the congregation answered with the refrain. Note that the same threefold division is found in Ps 115:9-11 (Israel, house of Aaron, and God-fearers), while the refrain comes from Psalm 136.

5-21. The Deliverance of God. **I called . . . the Lord answered me.** The theme throughout this passage is one of rejoicing that God has given deliverance and victory. In actual use, this passage, because of its individualized nature, called for a solo voice. The single voice represented the personified nation in general and the assembled worshipers in particular. With verses 19-21, the procession had undoubtedly reached the temple gates and was demanding entrance.

22-29. The Application for Worship. **This is the Lord's doing.** These verses abound in words well known from their NT application. Verse 22, describing the chief cornerstone, was probably a proverb of that day referring to Israel, rejected by the great empire-builders as unworthy to fit into their plans. But the divine mission of Israel became focused and fulfilled in its greatest representative, the Messiah. Thus Jesus appropriated its imagery for his own ministry (cf. Mt 21:42; Mk 12:10; Lk 20:17; Acts 4:11; Eph 2:20; I Pet 2:7). The priestly benediction of verse 26 found expression six times in the Gospels because of its distinct application to the mission of Christ.

Psalm 119. The Torah of the Lord

Essentially a didactic poem, this psalm takes the form of a personal testimony. Although the poem contains allusions to persecution and shows certain characteristics of laments, its main purpose is to glorify the *Tôrâ* (God's law or teaching). The psalmist directs almost every verse to God, using many forms of petition. At the same time, he uses some synonym for the law in all but seven verses. The synonyms are: law, testimonies, precepts, judgments, commandments, statutes, sayings, word, way, and path. Possibly in employing ten terms to describe God's Torah, he was following the lead of Ps 19:7-9, where six such synonyms for the *law* are used.

The acrostic principle is highly developed in this psalm, employing all twenty-two letters of the Hebrew alphabet. Each stanza is composed of eight lines, which begin with the letter characteristic of that stanza. This artificial yet artistic arrangement makes for a certain monotony in the great repetition of words and phrases. However, this mechanical monotony is overcome by the intensity of the psalmist's own devotion to God's teachings.

1-8. The Blessing of Obedience. **Blessed . . . who walk in the law of the Lord.** The theme of the psalm is here set forth clearly. Note that most of the ten synonyms for the law are used in this first strophe.

9-16. The Way of Cleansing. **Wherewithal shall a young man cleanse his way?** The question and answer are in keeping with the emphasis of the Wisdom writers. The answer to the problems of youth in any period of history is to heed God's Word by meditating on it (v. 15) and committing it to memory (v. 11) and by testifying concerning it to others (v. 13).

17-24. The Delight of Experience. **Thy testimonies are my delight.** This delight is based upon his past experience with God in times of persecution. A note of sorrow and desire runs through this strophe, but the section ends in delight.

25-32. The Strength in Understanding. **Quicken. . . . teach. . . . make me to understand.** The peril confronting the psalmist makes him call for strength and comfort. He realizes that the quickening he desires comes from an understanding of God's teachings.

33-40. The Need for Guidance. **Teach me . . . and I shall keep it.** In phrase after phrase, the speaker pleads for God's guidance in ordering his life and in refraining from folly.

41-48. The Courage for Witnessing. **Let thy mercies come.** This appeal for help is not selfish; it is inspired by a desire to have **wherewith to answer him that reproacheth me.** The speaker further declares that he will witness to kings without being ashamed.

49-56. The Source of Comfort. **Remember the word unto thy servant. . . . this is my comfort.** In the time of affliction, God's teachings have been his stay and **the songs in the house of my pilgrimage.**

57-64. The Resolution of Faithfulness. **I have said that I would keep thy words.** Thinking upon his ways brought him to the point where he could turn his feet unto God's testimonies. His gratitude is evident in his promise to arise at midnight to thank God.

65-72. The Discipline of Affliction. **It is good for me that I have been afflicted.** Having gone astray before his affliction, the psalmist now sees a beneficent purpose in his suffering.

73-80. The Justice of Retribution. **Let the proud be ashamed.** After voicing again his desire for understanding, he pleads for God's blessings upon himself and shame upon his enemies. His end desire is that he may strengthen the faith of others.

81-88. The Hope in Darkness. **My soul fainteth . . . I hope in thy word.** In a succession of sobs, he expresses his hope and determination in his darkest hour. With each plea for comfort he reiterates his desire to be faithful.

89-96. The Triumph of Faith. **Unless thy law** [had been] **my delights, I should then have perished** (v. 92). The hope of the preceding strophe becomes an assured victory here. He affirms that he will never forget God's precepts since **with them thou hast quickened me.**

97-104. The Rapture of Enlightenment. **O how love I thy law!** Without the usual petitions, the psalmist describes how his study of the divine law has made him wiser and more understanding than his enemies, his teachers, and the aged. The emphasis is here upon the law itself, the source of knowledge rather than on native intelligence.

105-112. The Light of Life. **Thy word is a lamp . . . a light.** His pilgrimage through life is under the guidance of God's teachings. He thus vows to follow the light wherever it may lead and whatever dangers may be involved.

113-120. The Inspiration of Loyalty. **Thou art my hiding place and my shield.** The sharp contrast drawn between faithless men and the psalmist emphasizes the loyalty of the latter. This loyalty gives him a sense of safety and the inspiration to face the future.

121-128. The Time of Intervention. **It is time for thee, Lord, to work.** After declaring that he has diligently followed the right, the psalmist appeals for action on God's part. So completely have his oppressors disregarded God's law that only divine judgment is left for them.

129-136. The Wonder of Illumination. **Thy testimonies are wonderful.** The greatest wonder is the inner light that gives understanding even to the unlearned man. The psalmist is brokenhearted over those who do not keep God's law.

137-144. The Challenge of Righteousness. **Righteous art thou, O Lord.** The concept of God's nature as righteous finds emphasis here in verses 137,138, 142, and 144. Because the Lord is righteous, his judgments and testimonies, also, are everlastingly righteous.

145-152. The Assurance from Prayer. **I cried . . . hear me, O Lord.** Recalling the many times he has prayed unceasingly for divine help, he cries again for God's quickening power. Then he reaffirms his faith in the Lord's nearness and the verity of His teaching.

153-160. The Consciousness of Need. **Consider mine affliction, and deliver me.** The severity of the speaker's affliction and his understanding of his personal need are clearly shown in the repetition of **quicken me** in verses 154,156, and 159. The enduring nature of God's righteous judgments is his hope and assurance.

161-168. The Peace in Love. **Great peace have they which love thy law.** Even in the presence of potent enemies, the psalmist has an inner peace that grows out of his love for God's way. Note the absence of any petition, as in verses 97-104.

169-176. The Determination of Steadfastness. **My lips shall utter praise.** The psalmist sums up his message by pleading for further spiritual help, while declaring his intention to stand fast upon the foundation of God's teachings.

Psalm 120. The Sojourn of the Pilgrims

Psalm 120 begins a new collection that extends through 134. Each lyric in this group is designated by a term variously translated "A Song of Degrees" (AV), "A Song of Ascents" (ASV), and "A Pilgrim Song." Various theories as to the meaning of the term relate it to the return from Babylon, the fifteen steps from the women's court to the men's court, the climactic parallelism in these poems, and the journeys of pilgrims. The most likely theory is that this collection arose as a hymnbook for pilgrims coming up to the Temple for the great feasts. The fact that 120, 124, 125, 130, 131 are not explicitly related to a pilgrimage points to their incorporation into the collection from other sources. Most of these psalms fit into the pattern of life in post-Exilic society, although some may have first had a pre-Exilic origin.

1,2. A Cry for Deliverance. **Deliver my soul, O Lord.** The psalmist finds himself in the wretched plight of one who has to associate with men given to falsehood. His appeal for deliverance is based upon God's past answers to him in times of similar trouble. Many understand that there is some reference here to the slanderous opposition of Sanballat and Tobiah to Nehemiah's rebuilding the walls of Jerusalem (Neh 4; 6).

3,4. A Plea for Retribution. **What shall be given unto thee?** The deceitful tongue and its owner are singled out for judgment. The answer to the rhetorical questions is based upon the nature of the alleged offense. Sharp arrows and hot coals will provide fitting retribution.

5-7. A Lament for Peace. **Woe is me . . . I am for peace.** The poet's basic complaint is that he finds it necessary to sojourn among bloodthirsty and barbaric enemies. **Mesech** in Asia Minor and **Kedar** in the north Arabian desert south of Damascus are used symbolically to represent barbaric powers.

Psalm 121. The Helper of the Pilgrims

The intense assurance of those journeying up to Zion is reflected in this pilgrim song. They here express a deep sense of trust in God without a murmur of complaint or word of petition. The song was probably used as an antiphonal hymn, although the exact voices or parts used cannot be identified with certainty.

1,2. The Source of Help. **From whence cometh my help?** Looking up to the hills around Zion, one of the pilgrims voices a question which sets the mood for all that follows. The question does not express doubt but introduces the affirmation that contains the theme of the psalm, namely, that his helper is Jehovah the Creator.

3-8. The Promise of Protection. **The Lord is thy keeper.** All verses except verse 6 employ the Hebrew word *shāmar* to emphasize this idea of God's guardianship. Unlike the sentry who occasionally slumbers, or Baal, who has to be awakened (cf. I Kgs 18:27), the Lord never slumbers or sleeps. The psalmist employs climactic parallelism throughout, building up each new phrase from the thought in the preceding phrase. Note that the conclusion applies to the pilgrims in that God preserves them in every phase of their journey, seeing them safely home.

Psalm 122. The City of the Pilgrims

This poem is oriented around the visit of a pilgrim to Jerusalem. By indicating that the journey is accomplished, it acts as a sequel to the two preceding psalms. Some interpreters hold that the speaker has returned home and is reminiscing about his recent pilgrimage. Although this is possible, it is more likely that he is still in Jerusalem, about to leave for home.

1,2. Joy in Pilgrimage. **I was glad when they said . . . let us go.** The psalmist recalls with what joy he responded to the invitation to join a group of pilgrims. Now the journey is complete and he can say, **Our feet have stood within thy gates, O Jerusalem.** The future tense of the AV is not appropriate in the light of the following verses.

3-5. Impressions of Jerusalem. **Jerusalem . . . compact together.** While the city undoubtedly was fully built up within massive walls, the emphasis here seems to be upon its function in unifying the people. The verb *ḥābar*, translated "compact," refers primarily to close human associations. The going up of the tribes accentuates this togetherness and the attendant sense of fellowship.

6-9. Prayer for Jerusalem. **Pray for the peace of Jerusalem.** Before leaving, the pilgrim exhorts his companions to pray for the prosperity and peace of the city, because here is the house of the Lord. There is an excellent play on words in the Hebrew, not evident in any English translation.

Psalm 123. The Plea of the Pilgrims

This is an intense lament by an individual who speaks for his people. The change from the singular to the plural pronoun at the end of verse 1 suggests an antiphonal arrangement in actual use as a pilgrim song.

1,2. The Eye of Hope. **Unto thee lift I up mine eyes.** The psalmist refers to eyes four times in these verses, in order to emphasize the fact that the pilgrims are seeking God's favor. Just as the servant and the maiden look to their superiors for favor, so those in the band of pilgrims wait for God's mercy.

3,4. The Plea for Mercy. **Have mercy upon us, O Lord.** The measure of their need is indicated by the reiteration of this cry for mercy. The previous mention of servants and masters, coupled with the contempt for **those that are at ease**, suggests either the widespread servitude of Israel during the Exile or the dispersion during post-Exilic days.

Psalm 124. The Deliverer of the Pilgrims

Here the community at large expresses thanksgiving. While the original purpose was undoubtedly to praise God for a particular act of deliverance, the place of the poem in this pilgrim collection indicates a general use as well. Because travelers were constantly subject to danger, the words of this psalm would have given them assurance and strengthened their trust.

1-5. Deliverance by God. **If it had not been the Lord.** The repetition in verses 1 and 2 is liturgical; the congregation (later the pilgrims) repeated the words of the leader. Note that the effective use of conditional clauses as a triple apodosis (vv. 3-5) completes the double protasis (vv. 1,2). **If** it had not been for the Lord, **then** the end would have been certain and complete.

6-8. Thanksgiving to God. **Blessed be the Lord.** The psalmist further employs figures of speech to describe the narrow escape and to heighten the expression of gratitude. The last verse refers to the act of calling upon **the name of the Lord** in prayer, recognizing him as the source of help.

Psalm 125. The Security of the Pilgrims

This song of trust emphasizes the confidence of the faithful in Israel. Like the preceding psalm, this one was not designed as a pilgrim song but has been included in the collection. The actual use in pilgrimages can be envisioned from the references to the mountains round about Jerusalem, which come into view after a long and arduous journey.

1-3. A Statement of Confidence. **They that trust . . . as Mount Zion. . . . As the mountains . . . so the Lord.** Not only is God's presence symbolized by the hills around Jerusalem, but also those who trust in the Lord are immovable like the rock of Zion. If foreign rule did remain permanently, a general departure from the faith would occur, even among the righteous. The danger of apostasy is too great even for the righteous to bear.

4,5. A Prayer for Favor. **Do good, O Lord.** The psalmist prays for God's favor upon the faithful, whom he identifies as the **good** and **upright.** In contrast to these individuals, the unfaithful renegades are abandoned to their just fate. The psalm closes with the simple prayer, **Peace upon Israel.**

Psalm 126. The Restoration of the Pilgrims

Psalm 126 is the lament of the community over disappointed hopes past and present. Although there is an obvious reference here to the return from the Exile, the conditions are not those pictured in early post-Exilic society. The psalmist deals with the ideal conditions expected and with the disillusionment experienced for many years.

1-3. The Ideal of Restoration. **We were like them in a dream.** The hope of a glorious restoration was idealized to the point of being too good to be true. The phrase, **turned again the captivity,** may be translated *restored the fortunes.* However, the context seems to demand a picture within the Exile. There was singing and laughter – like that on V-Day – when the Edict of Cyrus was made known. The exiles joined in a chorus of praise reiterating the words of the observers from other nations.

4-6. The Plea for Fulfillment. **Turn again our captivity, O Lord.** The beautiful ideal of restoration envisioned by the prophets and sung about by the exiles was not fully realized by those who returned to the homeland. Conditions were anything but glorious and ideal (cf. Hag 1:10,11; 2:19). Therefore, the plea is now made for completion of the ideal. Even as the farmer sows in anxiety and reaps in joyful singing, Israel will realize the restoration ideal. Christian workers have often made an application of verses 5 and 6 to the ministry of soul winning.

Psalm 127. The Dependence of the Pilgrims

The didacticism of this psalm is characteristic of the teachings of Wisdom literature. Here the emphasis is placed upon the futility of human effort without God's help. Although the original didactic purpose was general, this psalm found special application as a folk song of the pilgrims.

1,2. A Dependence upon the Lord. **Except the Lord build . . . keep.** Man's utter dependence on God is illustrated by reference to basic human endeavors. Building a house and watching over a city cannot succeed (according to divine standards of success) if God is not included in man's plans and efforts. Even the diligent man who works from early morning until late evening cannot hope for success without God's blessings and sanction.

3-5. A Heritage from the Lord. **Lo, children are an heritage of the Lord.** The concept of the necessity of dependence upon God is carried over into the building of a family (cf. Gen 30:2). A recognition that children are God's gift is the basis for building a successful home. Joy and protection are pictured as the results of fruitfulness in the bearing and rearing of children. Especially important are the sons of a man's youth, who can protect him and plead his cause, in his old age, against his adversaries in the local court of justice inside the city gate.

Psalm 128. The Home Life of the Pilgrims

Like the preceding psalm, this one is didactic in character, and thus vitally connected with Wisdom literature. The basic Wisdom teaching, "the fear of the Lord is the beginning of wisdom," is the starting point for the psalmist. He then applies this truth to the ideal home situation. Although not designed as a song for pilgrims, the psalm probably found its way into the collection as a folk song which met the needs of all pilgrims.

1-4. Blessings upon the Home. **Blessed is every one that feareth the Lord.** The psalmist begins by stating that happiness is the lot of the one who has learned to fear the Lord and walk in His ways. It is well with him because he eats the products of his labor rather than losing them in the time of drought or sharing them with oppressive overlords. His wife is likened to a fruitful vine, while his children are compared to the tender shoots of the olive tree. This picture of contentment, joy, prosperity, and fruitfulness illustrates how the God-fearer finds perfect happiness.

5,6. Blessings upon the Community. **Thou shall see the good of Jerusalem.** A vital part of the blessing enjoyed by one who fears God comes from beyond the limits of his home – **out of Zion.** The corporate nature of Israel's society is seen in the adaptation of this psalm for public worship. Like Psalm 125, this one closes with the brief prayer, **Peace upon Israel.**

Psalm 129. The Plea of Suffering Israel

This is a lament of the community, with overtones of confidence and trust. The characteristics of a song of trust are present, but they are overshadowed by the complaint and appeal of the lament. Reviewing past troubles brings the psalmist confidence, while his appeals regarding the future result give him assurance of relief.

1-4. Israel's Past Afflictions. **Many a time have they afflicted me.** The long history of Israel's troubles is compressed by the psalmist into one statement. From the time of the Exodus (Israel's **youth**) onward, the nation had suffered severe affliction from numerous foes. Two metaphors are used to illustrate this affliction: the marks of a whip upon their backs are likened to the furrows made by a plow; and the cords of their oppressors are likened to the ropes used to harness oxen. However, the Lord manifested his righteousness by cutting the cords and delivering his people.

5-8. Israel's Future Hope. **Let them all be confounded.** In an imprecation upon those that hate Zion, the speaker expresses the desire that the enemy may be put to shame and turn homeward. Then a lengthy simile is employed to request that the evil plans of the enemy be thwarted. The grass which grew on the dirt rooftops withered quickly because the soil was too shallow for its roots. It could not be grasped by the reaper nor bound into sheaves. It was not even worth the customary greeting of those passing by.

Psalm 130. The Redeemer of the Pilgrims

Here an individual voices a penitential prayer as his personal plea for forgiveness. The closing plea for others in the household of Israel does not make the entire psalm corporate, but rather emphasizes the personal nature of the speaker's appeal. However, since the psalmist's troubles and despair were shared by the nation, the psalm became appropriate for the bands of pilgrims in post-Exilic society.

1,2. The Cry of the Penitent. **Out of the depths have I cried.** The speaker is more probably using a present tense here, as the remainder of the prayer shows. He is still calling **out of the depths** when the psalm closes, but has clearly expressed his assurance and hope.

3,4. The Assurance of Forgiveness. **But there is forgiveness with thee.** The universality of sin is forcefully presented in the statement that no one could be justified if God marked down every sin rather than blotting sins out. The only hope comes in God's forgiveness, which in turn quickens the feeling of awe in the forgiven sinner.

5,6. The Expectancy in Hope. **I wait for the Lord . . . and in his word do I hope.** The sense of expectancy is strongly emphasized by the repetition of phrases. The speaker's whole being (his **soul**) is engaged in diligent waiting. He waits for the Lord even as the sentinel on the walls awaits the relief of the morning change of watch.

7,8. The Application to Israel. **Let Israel hope in the Lord.** The psalmist's thoughts turn to others who need to share his enthusiastic confidence. In view of the loving-kindness and abundant redemption of the Lord, he can assert that God will redeem Israel **from all his iniquities.**

Psalm 131. The Composure of the Pilgrims

Though essentially a song of trust, this beautiful literary composition reads like a confession. The picture of humble resignation to God's leading exemplifies a deep sense of personal discipline. While some interpreters treat this psalm as a corporate expression, the final plea for Israel suggests that an individual voice speaks consistently throughout. It was only natural that a beautiful expression of humility like this should become a folk song of the pilgrims.

1,2. A Spirit of Humility. **Lord, my heart is not haughty.** After a long struggle, the psalmist has been weaned from his presumptuous desires and his excessive pride. He can now declare himself free of the former attitudes of haughtiness and unbridled ambition. He has calmed or composed his soul or inner self so that he is now like a weaned child upon his mother's lap, no longer fretting after her milk.

3. A Desire for Israel. **Let Israel hope in the Lord.** As in the preceding psalm, here the writer expresses his desire that others in Israel may come to know his inner peace.

Psalm 132. The Assurance of the Pilgrims

Unique among the songs in the pilgrim collection, this one appears to have been included because of its nature as a processional hymn, which may well have been rendered antiphonally. It is basically a song of Zion, connected in thought with David's bringing the ark of the covenant to Jerusalem.

1-10. The Prayer of the Congregation. **Lord, remember David.** Although David's afflictions are mentioned first, the emphasis of this prayer is upon his intention to find a suitable place for the ark. Since the historical narratives mention no oath in this connection, the psalmist may be drawing from an independent tradition. Verses 6,7 were probably rendered by a group of pilgrims as they re-enacted the search for the ark, its discovery in Kirjath-jearim **(the fields of the wood)**, and its entrance into Jerusalem. The prayer is concluded in verse 10 with a plea for God to show favor to each successive king in the line of David.

11-18. The Response of the Lord. **The Lord hath sworn. . . . hath chosen.** These verses act as a liturgical response quoting from two separate oracles of the Lord. The first oracle (vv. 11,12) is the promise to David that his royal line will continue as long as his descendants are faithful (cf. II Sam 7:12-16). The second oracle (vv. 14-18) is introduced by the statement in verse 13 that **the Lord has chosen Zion.** Because of this divine choice, there will be spiritual and material blessings for Zion and the line of David, while there will be shame upon Israel's enemies. Since, when a man died without children, his family line was stopped, his lamp was said to be put out; therefore a lamp symbolized offspring. Thus God ordained a series of descendants of David, to culminate in Messiah the Light of the world (cf. I Kgs 11:36; 15:4).

Psalm 133. The Brotherhood of the Pilgrims

In this short didactic poem we have a beautiful expression of family solidarity, in keeping with the emphasis of the Wisdom writers. The suggestion of many commentators that the psalm mirrors Nehemiah's efforts to increase the population of Jerusalem is intriguing. However, the psalm must have more significant connection with the spirit of fellowship and brotherly harmony at the great feasts.

1. The Premise Stated. **Behold, how good and how pleasant.** The writer begins with a proverbial statement concerning the benefits of brotherly solidarity. The emphasis is upon the pattern of ancient Hebrew life, in which married sons, with their children, continued to live with their parents. A wider application, however, is evident in the family and tribal reunions on the feast occasions.

2,3. The Principle Illustrated. **Like the precious ointment . . . as the dew.** The psalmist employs two comparisons to illustrate the principle embodied in his basic premise. Even as the anointing oil upon the high priest's head symbolized his consecration, so this spirit of brotherly love permeated the nation and symbolized its consecration. Even as dew upon vegetation symbolizes fertility and growth, the sense of true brotherhood revived and quickened the devotion of the nation as a whole.

Psalm 134. The Benediction upon the Pilgrims

Here is a fitting conclusion for the collection of folk songs used by the pilgrims. In its benedictory nature this psalm corresponds to the benediction at the end of each book within the Psalter. The position of the song in the collection and the reference to night service suggest that it was sung at the close of evening worship. The Feast of Tabernacles is the most likely occasion.

1,2. The Call to the Priests and Levites. **Behold, bless ye the Lord, all ye servants.** That the regular ministers of the Temple are addressed is generally recognized. However, the voice of the call is variously ascribed to the high priest, a Levitical choir, or the gathered pilgrims. The last explanation gives more reason for inclusion of the psalm in the collection, since the pilgrims actively participate. The temple ministrants are called to lift up their hands in an attitude of prayer and bless the Lord.

3. The Response by the Priests. **The Lord . . . bless thee.** The answer to the call is given in a shortened form of the priestly blessing found in Num 6:22-26. The people are reminded that God is Creator and that his blessings flow forth **out of Zion.** This may well have been used as the final act before the pilgrims returned to their homes.

Psalm 135. A Mosaic of God's Works

This hymn of praise is a mosaic of quotations from other psalms and various books of the OT. The main emphasis is upon those works of God which illustrate his power in nature and history. That the psalm was designed for temple worship in an antiphonal pattern is evident from its structure. However, there is no unanimity in the division into voices. Undoubtedly, there were solo parts, Levitical choruses, and congregational responses.

1-4. The Initial Call to Praise. **Praise ye the Lord.** Similar phrases are repeated as an emphatic liturgical call to praise. As in the preceding psalm, those who **stand in the house of the Lord** are undoubtedly the priests and Levites. The Lord's goodness and his choice of Israel are given as initial reasons for praise.

5-14. The Greatness of Yahweh. **For I know that the Lord is great . . . above all gods.** The **I** is emphatic, indicating personal knowledge, and possibly the shift to a solo voice in actual temple use. The use of the name *Yahweh* is here important, because it is Israel's covenant God who is contrasted with the gods of the heathen. He is described as the God of Nature (vv. 5-7), doing whatsoever he pleases in heaven, in earth, in the seas, and in all deep places. He is further described as the God of History (vv. 8-14), leading his chosen people out of Egypt and through the conquest of Canaan.

15-18. The Impotency of Idols. **The idols of the heathen.** This section is quoted almost verbatim from Ps 115:4-8. However, the words are especially appropriate here to set in sharp contrast the omnipotence of the Lord and the uselessness of all idols.

19-21. The Final Call to Praise. **Bless the Lord.** The call to praise in Psalms 115 and 118 is expanded by the addition of **O house of Levi** and a concluding verse. The nation as a whole, the priests, the Levites, and the God-fearing worshipers may all have had their own antiphonal parts, but ended the psalm in chorus.

Psalm 136. God's Enduring Mercy

This hymn of thanksgiving greatly resembles Psalm 135 in content. It is, however, much more liturgical, having an antiphonal refrain that appears in every verse. The fact that the psalm is easier to read and understand without the refrain suggests that it originally stood without this repetition in verses 4-25. Yet the refrain gave it a distinctive character and a prominent place in Jewish worship. In the Rabbinical writings, it was designated as "the Great Hallel" (sometimes in conjunction with Ps 135). The term **Hallelujah** at the end of the preceding psalm probably should stand at the beginning of this psalm, as evidenced by the LXX.

1-3. The Call to Thanksgiving. **O give thanks unto the Lord.** The psalm opens with a threefold invitation to join in thanking God for his goodness and mercy. It is addressed by the leader or choir to the congregation. The refrain was probably sung throughout by the entire group of worshipers. The brevity of the refrain is especially evident in the three words of the Hebrew *(for forever his lovingkindness)*. The three terms for God – **Yahweh, God of gods,** and **Lord of lords** – are interesting in light of the emphasis in the preceding psalm on the impotency of idols and the omnipotence of God.

4-9. The God of Creation. **Wonders . . . heavens . . . earth . . . lights.** In concise statements the wonders of creation are made to testify to God's loving-kindness and goodness. Each time **to him** is used, it is the object of **O give thanks.**

10-25. The God of History. **To him that smote Egypt.** Each event, from Egypt to Canaan, witnesses to the way God manifests his loving-kindness within the scope of Israel's history.

26. The Doxology of Thanksgiving. **O give thanks unto the God of heaven.** The opening call is here repeated but with a different term for God. This term would be especially fitting if the emphasis were first on the creative wonders of God alone.

Psalm 137. The Song of the Exiles

A deep spirit of revenge is clearly evident in this community lament. The opening verses evoke a deep sympathy for the captives, while the final verses give vent to their indignation experienced when they witnessed the desolation of their land. While it is not certain where the psalmist was when he wrote this song, he appears to have been one of the exiles who returned to Jerusalem in 538 B.C. His first view of Jerusalem may well have prompted his imprecations against Edom and Babylonia.

1-3. Sorrows of the Exile. **By the rivers of Babylon . . . we wept.** The voice of the psalmist sobs with pathos as he describes the heartbreak of captivity. The exiles undoubtedly had special places along the Euphrates or its canal system where they would mourn their condition. When asked to sing for the amusement of their captors, they would answer by hanging their lyres on the willows that lined the river banks.

4-6. Love for Jerusalem. **How shall we sing the Lord's song.** After all, how could they sing the sacred songs of the temple services for the amusement of those in a foreign land? That would have been to desecrate holy things and to commit treason against Zion. The psalmist would rather have lost his ability to play the lyre and sing than to have forgotten the sanctity of Jerusalem.

7-9. Hatred Toward Enemies. **Children of Edom. . . . daughter of Babylon.** The intensity of the psalmist's emotions is seen in his hatred toward his enemies as well as in his love for Jerusalem. He singles out Edom for her conduct in aiding the enemy against Jerusalem (cf. Ezk 25:12-14; 35; Ob 10-14). Then Babylon becomes the object of the psalmist's impassioned imprecation. Such ruthless slaughter as depicted in verse 9 usually was practiced in sacking ancient cities (Isa 13:16; Nah 3:10) and was used against Israel (II Kgs 8:12; Hos 13:16).

Psalm 138. Wholehearted Thanksgiving

This piece begins as a hymn of thanksgiving but later becomes a song of trust. Even though the speaker is in the midst of troubles, he begins not with a lament but with grateful acknowledgment of God's blessings. Many of the ideas and phrases of this piece are reminiscent of other sections of Scripture, especially Isa 40–66. Several manuscripts of the LXX connect this psalm with the time of Haggai and Zechariah.

1-3. Praise for Strength. **I will praise thee with my whole heart.** The psalmist has experienced a recent answer to his prayers for help. Because of God's gift of spiritual strength, he engages in wholehearted worship. The phrase, **before the gods,** has been variously interpreted, because the LXX uses *angels* and the Targum has *judges*. However, **gods** seems to be the best translation because of the subsequent reference to **the kings of the earth.** Since they now serve their various gods but will in future worship the true God, the psalmist challenges the power of these "gods" (cf. Ps 95:3; 96:4,5; 97:7).

4-6. Worship by Kings. **All the kings of the earth shall praise thee.** The praise of the individual is envisioned as ultimately becoming universal. There is a striking relation here to the Edict of Cyrus, in which the conquering king praises Yahweh (along with the gods of the other displaced peoples). Note that God's glory is especially revealed in his condescension toward the lowly.

7,8. Assurance of Deliverance. **Though I walk in . . . trouble, thou wilt revive me.** The speaker expresses a deep confidence that God will fulfill his promises and complete the deliverance of Israel. Although the whole psalm is spoken by an individual in a very personal manner, he is voicing thanksgiving and assurance for his nation as well.

Psalm 139. The Personal Concern of God

Here an individual who has had an intimate knowledge of and experience with God offers his personal prayer. From the standpoint of OT theology, this is the climax of thought in the Psalter on God's personal relationship to the individual. The psalmist does not engage in abstract philosophy or speculative meditation; he merely describes his humble walk with God and shares his experiential knowledge of the Lord.

1-6. The Omniscience of God. **O Lord, thou hast searched me, and known me.** The psalmist is convinced by experience that God knows everything about him. He realizes that God's perfect knowledge goes behind his individual acts to his motives and purposes. While he stands in awe at his own understanding of divine omniscience, he knows that full comprehension is beyond human understanding.

7-12. The Omnipresence of God. **Whither shall I go from thy spirit?** By means of two rhetorical questions, the psalmist shows that he can never move beyond the reach of God's personal concern. He does not contemplate trying to do so, but uses this method of presenting his thoughts. The four suppositions which follow express the extremes of the universe and reinforce his basic premise.

13-18. The Foreknowledge of God. **My substance was not hid from thee.** Two ideas are involved in the psalmist's thought here: the wondrous way in which he was created, and the way God knew all that was going on in the process. He seems to emphasize the latter as he sees the hand of God ordering his entire life. This is actually another glimpse of the omniscience of God in the marvelous processes of creation and procreation. Again the speaker stands in awe at the incomprehensible nature of God's thoughts.

19-24. The Problem of Evil. **Surely thou wilt slay the wicked.** This surprising change of tone and outlook is regarded by some interpreters as a later addition. However, the intensity of conviction apparent in the earlier verses is seen again here. God, who has such minute knowledge of man, cannot overlook flagrant sinners. The psalmist closes with the personal plea that God will **search, try, know, see,** and **lead** him. His goal is the **way everlasting,** the way of life and peace, as compared with the way of ruin and destruction for the wicked.

Psalm 140. A Plea for Preservation

An individual who has suffered bitter persecution from the ungodly within Israel utters this lament. It is closely related to Psalms 141–143, reflecting the same general conditions and employing similar language, form, and thought patterns. And it may possibly reflect the beginnings of party strife in Israel, although the groups cannot now be identified by name.

1-8. His Appeal for Help. **Deliver me, O Lord.** Through three stanzas (vv. 1-3; 4,5; 6-8) the psalmist makes his appeal for God's help. He pleads: **deliver me, preserve me, keep me, grant not . . . the desires of the wicked.** He uses very descriptive terms to describe these enemies in order to portray vividly his own danger. The singular designations are to be understood collectively, as shown in the use of plural verbs. The four traps which the enemies set are probably to be interpreted in a figurative sense here.

9-11. His Desire for Retribution. **Let the mischief of their own lips cover them.** The deep bitterness of the psalmist becomes more apparent in these verses. While he employs figurative language in expressing his desires regarding his enemies, it is clear that he wants all of their evil plans to turn upon them. He will not be satisfied with less than their complete destruction.

12,13. His Confidence in the Lord. **I know that the Lord will maintain the cause of the afflicted.** The psalmist is convinced that the righteous, in contrast to the wicked, shall have cause for rejoicing, because God champions those who, like the psalmist, are oppressed.

Psalm 141. A Cry for Protection

This psalm is another lament by an individual who has suffered at the hands of the powerful ungodly in Israel. His prayer is not the usual form of lament, where deliverance from enemies is sought. It is more spiritual in that he seeks God's help to overcome the temptations about him.

1,2. His Appeal for an Answer. **Lord, I cry . . . make haste . . . give ear.** The psalmist begins with an urgent plea for God to hear and answer his prayer. The reference to **incense** and **evening sacrifice** suggests the meal (AV "meat") offering, which was accompanied by prayer and presented both morning and evening.

3-5. His Prayer for Strength. **Set a watch, O Lord, before my mouth.** Passing over the circumstances of his complaint, the psalmist prays for strength to overcome temptation. He seeks power to guard his speech, keep his heart pure, avoid the practices of the wicked, refrain from sharing in their luxurious indulgences, and welcome reproof from the righteous.

6-10. His Confidence in Retribution. **When their judges are overthrown.** The historical circumstances behind verses 6,7 are taken for granted. It appears that the speaker expects to be proven right when these judges are punished. Verse 7 either refers to a slaughter of the psalmist's friends or should be translated *their bones* rather than **our bones.** Whatever the original meaning behind these verses, the psalmist is looking to God to continue to strengthen him, while he is certain that the wicked man will receive retributive justice by falling into his own trap.

Psalm 142. A Supplication for Deliverance

Here is the prayer of a devout individual who is facing intense persecution. It follows the normal pattern of a personal lament. The psalmist voices his appeal, makes his complaint, states his petition, and closes with a note of confidence. In this fervent prayer, he makes no appeals for revenge and voices no vindictive imprecations.

1,2. The Appeal. **I cried unto the Lord with my voice.** The verbs in verses 1-5 should be translated as present tense, since the context shows that the psalmist is not recounting a previous appeal. His great need is made obvious by the terms **cry** and **pour out,** as well as by his emphasis upon crying aloud with his voice.

3,4. The Complaint. **They privily laid a snare for me. . . . no man cared for me.** The psalmist realizes that God has known his condition from the beginning. For this reason, he merely states the fact of his trouble and describes his sense of dejection.

5-7. The Petition. **Deliver me. . . . Bring my soul out of prison.** Appealing again for attention to his needs, the psalmist declares that God is now his only refuge. The reference to a **prison** may represent an actual confinement or a state of distress. Vowing to praise God for his deliverance leads him to express his confidence that others will join him in this thanksgiving.

Psalm 143. A Prayer for Guidance and Deliverance

Again an individual in dire trouble utters this very personal prayer. His persecutors have all but taken his life. While seeking deliverance, his greatest desire is for God's direction and guidance. Since he comes as a repentant sinner, this psalm is classed as one of the Penitentials (cf. Ps 6, 32, 38, 51, 102, 130).

1-6. The Appeal of the Penitent. **Hear my prayer . . . and enter not into judgment.** After pleading for attention, the psalmist implies his guilt in God's sight. He does not plead innocence but casts himself on the mercy of God. His complaint, tersely stated, as in the preceding psalm, indicates a bitter persecution. He has been pursued, crushed, and made to dwell in darkness like unto death. However, remembering God's mighty works of the past gives him courage to appeal for further manifestations of power.

7-12. The Plea for Action. **Hear me speedily, O Lord.** In rapid-fire petitions, the psalmist expresses the urgency of his need for help. He seeks a speedy answer, an expression of God's loving-kindness, direction for life, deliverance from his persecutors, instruction in God's will, and destruction of his enemies. As a penitent **servant,** he feels certain that retribution will be accomplished.

Psalm 144. Triumph in War and Peace

Beginning as a hymn of praise, this psalm shifts to the lament pattern after verse 4. Many commentators have raised serious questions as to its unity. Verses 12-15 appear to have once been a part of an unknown psalm. In fact, the entire psalm is a compilation of citations from other psalms (cf. Ps 8, 18, 33, 39, 104).

1-4. Past Blessings Acknowledged. **Blessed be the Lord my strength.** The psalmist opens with a hymn of praise for God's aid to him as a warrior. He has come to know the Lord personally, for he calls him **my rock, my lovingkindness, my fortress, my refuge, my deliverer,** and **my shield.** The contrast between God's greatness and man's insignificance impresses the psalmist. Using the familiar words from Psalm 8, he confesses humility before introducing his petition for help.

5-8. Present Deliverance Sought. **Bow thy heavens, O Lord, and come down.** This prayer for a manifestation of God's power in the form of a theophany is drawn from several verses in Psalms 18 and 104. The psalmist is requesting that God intervene in the struggles with his enemies, because they are guilty of false charges and breaking of treaties.

9-11. Future Praise Vowed. **I will sing a new song unto thee, O God.** Following many quotations from old songs, the psalmist vows to give thanksgiving in a new form when the victory is won. After making this vow and expressing himself as confident of victory, he repeats the appeal of verses 7,8.

12-15. Peace and Prosperity Pictured. **Sons as plants . . . daughters as cornerstones.** As indicated above, this appears to be quoted from an unknown psalm. The picture is an idealized view of family life in a community **whose God is the Lord.** The sons are vigorous as young plants; the daughters are tall and stately; the barns are full; the flocks are prolific; and the oxen are strong. Such are material blessings expected in such an ideal society.

Psalm 145. Praise for God's Greatness

This hymn of praise is both a triumphant expression of faith by an individual and a call to men to glorify the greatness of God. It carries a note of universal appeal too seldom present in expressions of the faith of Israel. The psalmist uses an acrostic framework, beginning each verse with a letter of the Hebrew alphabet. Only one letter is missing, the *nun,* which should come between verses 13 and 14. The psalm serves as an introduction to the final collection of praises (Ps 145–150).

1,2. The Promise of Praise. **I will extol . . . bless . . . praise.** The purpose of the psalmist is clearly shown in his promise to praise God **every day,** yea, **for ever and ever.** His personal relationship and his universal outlook are seen in his initial address to **my God, O king.**

3-20. The Greatness of God. **Great is the Lord, and greatly to be praised.** Verse 3 is the theme of his praise. Although this greatness is unsearchable, the psalmist does an admirable job of illustrating it. His hope is constantly that others will bear witness to God's greatness. In the verses that follow he emphasizes God's greatness in terms of his mighty works, his glory and splendor, his great goodness, his gracious compassion, his tender mercies, his glorious and everlasting kingdom, his providential care, his righteousness, his holiness, and his availability for those who call upon him in truth and with fear. This understanding of God's nature is a high-water mark in the Psalter.

21. The Doxology of Praise. **Let all flesh bless his holy name for ever and ever.** After repeating his promise of personal praise, the speaker opens the invitation to all flesh. His desire includes all mankind and extends as long as the world endures.

Psalm 146. Praise for God's Help

This is the first of five similar hymns of praise, all beginning and ending with *Hallelujah*. This small collection has served as a short hymnal to be used daily in the worship of the Synagogue. Like most of the psalms in this final Book, the present form of these psalms reflects post-Exilic circumstances, thought, and language.

1,2. The Vow of Praise. **While I live will I praise the Lord.** In language similar to that of the preceding psalm, the vow of praise is set forth in absolute terms.

3,4. The Powerlessness of Man. **Put not your trust in princes.** Because of his own experiences, the psalmist pleads with men not to depend on the favors of noblemen (cf. Prov 19:6). He realizes that no lasting help can come from one whose breath and thoughts vanish while his body goes back to dust. The exact circumstance to which the psalmist refers cannot be identified. However, such a conclusion could be drawn from any time in Israel's history.

5-10. The Power of God. **Happy is he . . . whose hope is in the Lord.** The one who has the Lord as his helper and his hope is truly blessed. This hope is based upon God's creation of the universe, his loving care of man, and his everlasting reign. The special emphasis upon God as the champion of the needy and the oppressed suggests that the psalmist was a member of such a group within the society of his day. Note the fivefold emphasis placed upon the name Yahweh in verses 7-10.

Psalm 147. Praise for God's Providence

The outpouring of gratitude, as in this psalm, has always been a vital part of Israel's worship. This is truly a hymn of praise from beginning to end without a word of complaint or a single petition. A logical development is difficult to discover because three psalms are here compressed into one (vv. 1-6, 7-11, 12-20). These separate elements are partly evident in the LXX, where verses 12-20 are listed as a different psalm.

1-6. His Goodness to Israel. **The Lord doth build up . . . he gathereth together.** After a brief call to praise, the psalmist declares how good the Lord has been to his people. Verses 2,3 undoubtedly refer to the restoration following the Exile. Each thing that God has done is linked up with his greatness, his power, and his understanding.

7-11. His Providence over Nature. **Who covereth the heaven with clouds.** The thought is extended beyond the borders of Israel to encompass all creatures. The Lord's provision of rain and food is especially important in a land where skies are cloudless from April to October. The psalmist realizes that God's favor is not based upon physical strength in man or beast.

12-20. His Care for Jerusalem. **For he hath strengthened the bars of thy gates. Jerusalem** and **Zion** are used as parallel terms in descriptive personification, symbolizing God's people who dwell and worship within. The blessings of protection, peace, and prosperity are set forth as present realities. The psalm closes with a reference to Israel's unique relationship to God as his Chosen People.

Psalm 148. Praise by All Creation

The third hymn of praise in the closing collection is a call for a universal chorus of praise by everything in heaven and on earth. The closing verse undoubtedly refers to the return from exile and indicates the reason and occasion for such world-shaking praise.

1-6. The Call to the Heavens. **From the heavens . . . in the heights.** Using the language of the ancient Near-Eastern cosmology, the psalmist seeks praise from the heavenly beings and the heavenly phenomena. Verses 5,6 are a response or a refrain which was probably sung by a choir in an antiphonal manner. God's creation of the heavenly objects and his sustaining of them are reason enough for praise.

7-12. The Call to the Earth. **From the earth.** The psalmist begins with the depths of the earth and refers to all forms of life, inanimate and animate. Note that man, as the crown of creation, is reserved until the last. Verses 13,14 act as a second response, signifying the basic reasons for this praise. God's glory and the redeeming of his Chosen People are judged to be sufficient reasons.

Psalm 149. Praise for God's Triumph

This hymn of praise makes special reference to the celebration of a recent victory. Many interpreters understand the closing verses to be eschatological rather than historical. However, the first four verses are clearly related to a present reality of God's deliverance. Although the event cannot be identified precisely, the purpose of the original composition is evidently to thank God for victory at the time of the warriors' return.

1-4. The Summons to Praise. **Sing unto the Lord a new song.** The scene is a great assembly of the **saints** or godly ones at the Temple. The importance of the occasion is seen in the need for a new song to celebrate the new victory of their armies. Verse 3 with its mention of dancing brings out clearly the spirit of rejoicing and joy requested in verse 2. The victory itself is an indication that God's favor and salvation have been poured out on his oppressed people.

5-9. The Song of Victory. **Let the saints be joyful . . . let them sing aloud.** The pious ones are pictured as rejoicing in triumph and singing on their beds because safety is now their reward. The picture of the warriors praising God with "two-mouthed" (AV, *two-edged)* swords in their hands is symbolic of the victories achieved in his name. Figuratively. God's saints today are to wield the sword of the Spirit, which is the word of God (Eph 6:17; Heb 4:12).

Psalm 150. Praise in Its Universal Climax

This final hymn of praise measures up to its position of honor as the doxology for the whole Psalter. Every phrase in the psalm seems to build upon the preceding thought in preparation for the climax, which comes suddenly as an outburst of mighty praise from the host of heaven and earth.

1. The Place Specified. **In his sanctuary . . . in the firmament.** The **sanctuary** may have reference to God's heavenly habitation or the earthly Temple. While the former meaning is parallel to **the firmament,** the latter idea would have much more significance for the assembled worshipers.

2. The Reasons Advanced. **His mighty acts . . . his excellent greatness.** His mighty acts in creation and history have been the theme of many psalms. His greatness has been a recurring theme in these final hymns of praise (cf. Ps 145, 147).

3-5. The Instruments Enumerated. **With the sound of . . .** The psalmist seems to have arranged these instruments in random order. It is likely that each was sounded when it was mentioned and continued to play through the end of the Hallelujah (cf. W. O. E. Oesterley, *The Psalms,* p. 589ff., for a description of the instruments involved).

6. The Choir Assembled. **Let everything that hath breath.** Not merely the priests and Levites nor merely the congregation, but all the creatures of time and space which have breath are included in this choir of choirs. The Psalter ends, but the melody lingers on as the worshipers continue to chant, *Hallelujah,* **Praise ye the Lord.**

BIBLIOGRAPHY

ALEXANDER, JOSEPH A. *The Psalms Translated and Explained.* 2 vols. 6th ed. New York: Scribner, Armstrong & Co., 1873.

BRIGGS, CHARLES A., and BRIGGS, EMILIE G. *The Book of Psalms (International Critical Commentary).* 2 vols. Edinburgh: T. & T. Clark, 1907.

CHEYNE, T. K. *The Book of Psalms.* London: Kegan Paul, Trench, Trubner & Co., 1904.

CLARKE, ARTHUR G. *Analytical Studies in the Psalms.* Kilmarnock: John Ritchie, Ltd., 1949.

COHEN, A. *The Psalms* (The Soncino Books of the Bible). Hindhead, Surrey: The Soncino Press, 1945.

DAVIES, T. WITTON. *The Psalms, LXXIII–CL (The Century Bible).* Edinburgh: T. C. & E. C. Jack, 1906.

DAVISON, W. T. *The Psalms I–LXXII (The Century Bible).* Edinburgh: T. C. & E. C. Jack, n.d.

DELITZSCH, FRANZ. *Biblical Commentary on the Psalms.* Translated by Francis Bolton. 3 vols. Grand Rapids: Wm. B. Eerdmans Publishing Co., Reprint, 1949.

PSALMS

Eiselen, Frederick C. *The Psalms and Other Sacred Writings*. New York: The Methodist Book Concern, 1918.

Gunkel, Hermann. *Die Psalmen*. Göttingen: Vanderhoeck and Ruprecht, 1926.

James, Fleming. *Thirty Psalmists*. New York: G. P. Putnam's Sons, 1938.

Kirkpatrick, A. F. *The Book of Psalms*. 3 vols. *(The Cambridge Bible for Schools and Colleges.)* Cambridge: The University Press, 1902.

Leslie, E. A. *The Psalms*. New York: Abingdon Cokesbury, 1949.

Leslie, E. A., and Shelton, W. A. "Psalms," *Abingdon Bible Commentary*. New York: Abingdon Cokesbury, 1929.

Maclaren, Alexander. *The Psalms*. New York: Funk & Wagnalls Co., 1908.

McCullough, W. Stewart, and Taylor, William R. "The Book of Psalms," *The Interpreter's Bible*. Vol. 4. New York: Abingdon Press, 1955.

McFadyen, John E. *The Psalms in Modern Speech and Rhythmical Form*. London: James Clarke & Co., 1926.

Morgan, G. Campbell. *Notes on the Psalms*. New York: Fleming H. Revell Co., 1947.

Mowinckel, Sigmund. *Psalmenstudien*. 6 vols. Kristiania: Dybwad, 1921–1924.

Oesterley, W. O. E. *A Fresh Approach to the Psalms*. New York: Charles Scribner's Sons, 1937.

———. *The Psalms*. London: Society for the Promoting of Christian Knowledge, 1939.

Patterson, John. *The Praises of Israel*. New York: Charles Scribner's Sons, 1950.

Patton, John H. *Canaanite Parallels in the Book of Psalms*. Baltimore: Johns Hopkins University Press, 1944.

Perowne, J. J. Stewart. *The Book of Psalms*. 2 vols. London: G. Bell & Sons, 1892.

Peters, John D. *The Psalms as Liturgies*. New York: G. P. Putnam's Sons, 1922.

Robinson, Theodore H. *The Poetry of the Old Testament*. London: Gerald Duckworth, 1947.

Simpson, David C. *The Psalmists*. London: Oxford University Press, 1926.

Snaith, Norman H. "The Psalms," *Twentieth Century Bible Commentary*. New York: Harper & Brothers, 1955.

———. *Studies in the Psalter*. London: Epworth Press, 1926.

Terrien, Samuel. *The Psalms and Their Meaning for Today*. New York: The Bobbs-Merrill Company, 1952.

Walker, Rollin H. *The Modern Message of the Psalms*. New York: Abingdon Cokesbury, 1938.

PROVERBS

INTRODUCTION

The Teaching of Proverbs. The essence of the Book of Proverbs is the teaching of moral and ethical principles. The peculiarity of this book is that it is largely given over to teaching by contrasts. Especially noteworthy are chapters 10–15, where almost every verse is divided by the word "but."

In the first section, chapters 1–9, there is also a use of contrast—between good and evil. The good in this section is denominated by several words—wisdom, instruction, understanding, justice, judgment, equity, knowledge, discretion, learning, counsels—but especially wisdom, which occurs seventeen times in this portion and twenty-two times in the rest of the book. What amounts to a text for the book is the well-known statement of 1:7, "The fear of the Lord is the beginning of wisdom," which is repeated near the end of the section (9:10). This statement reappears verbatim (with the clauses reversed) in the alphabetical Psalm 111:10, and in almost identical form as the climax of chapter 28 of Job, which describes in highly poetic form the search for wisdom.

Peculiar to this section of Proverbs is the personification of wisdom as a woman. This is first seen in 3:15. Actually, in 3:15-18 the pronouns referring to wisdom could be translated "it" as well as "she," but the personification is accepted because of later references. Proverbs 7:4 opens the way for the personification, "Say unto wisdom, Thou art my sister." It is complete in chapters 8 and 9, where Wisdom invites fools to partake of her feast. Only in Proverbs and only in this first part is wisdom thus personified.

It is essential to the understanding of this first part to recognize this personification. Since "wisdom" in Hebrew is a feminine noun, it therefore is naturally and readily personified as a woman. More important, the author here is contrasting "wisdom," the virtuous woman, with the harlot, the strange woman. And just as wisdom stands for all virtue, so probably the strange woman typifies and includes all sin.

The contrast is a studied and artistic one. Wisdom cries in the streets (8:3). Her invitation is, "Whoso is simple, let him turn in hither" (9:4). In contrast, the foolish woman, who invites to stolen waters and whose guests are in the depths of hell (9:17,18), issues the identical invitation, "Whoso is simple, let him turn in hither" (9:16). Wisdom calls the simple to forsake sin; the harlot calls him to its indulgence.

This section, Proverbs 1 to 9, therefore contrasts sin and righteousness. The words "wisdom," "instruction," "understanding," etc., used throughout this passage, do not mean merely human intelligence and skill; but rather they are contrasted with that which is evil. Wisdom as here used is therefore a moral quality. It should be observed that this is a special usage. In most of the Old Testament, wisdom is mere skill or sagacity. Even in Ecclesiastes, where wisdom is also emphasized, it is merely human intelligence and therefore is included with folly as vanity (Eccl 2:12-15). Only in Job 28 and in certain psalms (37:30; 51:6; 90:12; 111:10) is the Proverbs concept of wisdom noticeable. Even the wisdom for which Solomon was famed in the historical books is not exactly this wisdom. He was famous for his skill in natural science (I Kgs 4:33) and jurisprudence (I Kgs 3:16-28) and for his high intelligence (I Kgs 10:1-9). Proverbs adds to the concept of mental acumen the moral rectitude that alone makes intelligence worth while.

In the second section, the Proverbs of Solomon, 10:1–22:16, the teaching is presented almost exclusively by the single verse treatment. Through chapter 15, the teaching is by contrast, indicated by a "but" in the middle of nearly every verse. Thereafter there are parallels of thought more often than contrasts.

This section covers a wide range of subjects and defies outline. The viewpoint, however, is fairly consistent. Solomon is contrasting wisdom and folly. And, as in Section I, this is not intelligence versus stupidity; it is moral wisdom versus sin. In this section wisdom is never personified, but the same synonyms for it as occur in Section I are used here—understanding, righteousness, instruction.

The fool also has his parallels: the scorner, the slothful, the froward. The following sections (see Outline) continue in this vein. As Toy points out (Crawford H. Toy, ICC on *Proverbs*, p. xi), the ethics of the book are very high. Honesty, truthfulness, respect for life and property are insisted upon. Men are urged to extend justice, love, mercy to others. A good family life, with careful training of children and high status of women, is reflected.

As to religious outlook, the Lord is understood to be the author of morality and justice, and monotheism is presupposed. The references to the Law and prophecy (29:18), priesthood and sacrifices (15:8; 21:3,27) are scarce, however. The author speaks in his own right, inculcating principles of right conduct as from the Lord.

Authorship. The name of Solomon occurs in three parts of the book—1:1; 10:1; and 25:1. There is thus a claim of Solomonic authorship for the major sections, indeed for all sections except Parts III, 22:17—24:22; IV, 24:23-34; and VI, 30:1—31:31. This claim is disputed by critical scholars. Toy (*op. cit.* p. xix), who denies the Mosaic authorship of the Pentateuch and holds that Isaiah and the prophets did not write the books attributed to them, rather naturally gives no credit to Solomon here. On the grounds of many internal indications, he assigns the book a post-Exilic date. Driver (S. R. Driver, *Introduction to the Literature of the Old Testament*, 4th ed., pp. 381ff.) holds that parts of the book are pre-Exilic, but little if any of it is by Solomon. Pfeiffer (Robert H. Pfeiffer, *Introduction to the Old Testament*, pp. 649-659) goes over the internal characteristics of Proverbs thinking to date various strata. Because Wisdom literature in Egypt about 1700—1500 B.C. was purely secular, he concludes that the religious strata in Proverbs must derive form the fourth century B.C. After reconstructing to his own satisfaction the history of thought in Israel, he dates Proverbs relative to that development. His conclusion is that the book was finished after 400 B.C. and sometime before the end of the third century.

W. F. Albright ("Some Canaanite-Phoenician Sources of Hebrew Wisdom" in *Wisdom in Israel and the Ancient Near East*, ed. by M. Noth and D. W. Thomas, p. 13) studies the similarity of the language to Ugaritic, and argues that the book in "its entire content" is probably pre-Exilic, but that much of it was orally transmitted until the fifth century. He holds that a Solomonic nucleus is probable. See also an article by one of Albright's students, Cullen I. K. Story, "The Book of Proverbs and Northwest Semitic Literature," JBL, LXIV (1945), 319-337. Charles T. Fritsch (*The Book of Proverbs,* IB, Vol. IV, p. 775) on like grounds holds a very similar opinion. Oesterley (W. O. E. Oesterley, *The Book of Proverbs,* p. xxvi) would place most of the book in pre-Exilic times, but dates Section I, 1:1—9:18, and Section VI, 30:1—31:31, in the third century "and quite possibly later still."

The fact is that the closest attention to these internal evidences can not date the book or its collections. Granted that secular proverbs may have preceded religious, or single-line aphorisms the more developed varieties, still the development to the complex and religious may well have been full-blown already before Solomon's day. Granted that Jeremiah opposed wise men in his day (Jer 18:18), this proves nothing about dating. He also opposed priests and prophets and kings, but that does not prove these offices to be post-Exilic! The most promising approach on dating by internal criteria is that of Albright in his comparison of Ugaritic words and forms.

Our external evidence is not so complete as we might wish it to be, but it should not be totally dismissed. Proverbs 15:8, for example, is quoted with the formula, "It is written," in the Zadokite Document (col. XI. line 20; C. Rabin, *The Zadokite Documents*, p. 58). This shows that the book was regarded as canonical in the second century B.C. Solomon's production of "proverbs and parables" is referred to in Ecclesiasticus 48:17, dated about 180 B.C. There is as yet no external evidence previous to this. Oesterley claims a case of borrowing from Proverbs by the *Story of Ahikar* in the fifth century (see the Commentary at 23:14). One's opinion of the dating of the book will be heavily weighted by the view he holds of other books. If one holds that the Pentateuch was not written until 400 B.C. and the prophets were largely post-Exilic, he will deny that Solomon wrote Proverbs. If, however, the pre-Exilic dating of Pentateuch, Psalms and Prophets be allowed (as by this author), there seems to be no valid reason to deny the traditional ascription to Solomon of the sections that bear his name.

Fritsch *(op. cit.,* p. 770) objects to the traditional glorifying of Solomon's wisdom when "he made so many foolish mistakes throughout his life in every realm." This seems to be a harsh judgment upon Israel's most brilliant king. That he made mistakes in his long reign of forty years is clear; but archaeology testifies to Solomon's skills in architecture, ability in administration, and discoveries in engineering in connection with his copper foundry at Ezion-geber. True, in his old age he became oppressive (I Kgs 12:10), but his later decline should not blind us to his early brilliance. More critics object to Solomon's character because of his many wives. Close attention to the texts, however, (and they are our only sources) shows that they do not picture Solomon as a creature of lust. As an important king over an area that included many petty kings of city states, Solomon doubtless concluded numerous treaties. Surely in many cases such treaties were sealed by Solomon's marrying the petty king's daughter, as was the ancient custom and as was the case in the alliance with Egypt (I Kgs 9:16,17). Solomon's marriages were doubtless largely political arrangements. His error lay not so much in lust as in allowing his politically important wives to bring their heathen worship into the city of God (I Kgs 11:7-9).

The authors of the other sections of Proverbs (III, 22:17–24:22; IV, 24:23-34; VI, 30:1–31:31) are totally unknown to us. See remarks in the Commentary. We can not, therefore, be dogmatic as to their dates except to say that there is no need to place the final editing of the book after the traditional close of the Biblical period—about 400 B.C.

Collections in Proverbs. Toy *(op. cit.,* pp. vii, viii), and others following him, have argued that the appearance of the same line or verse in various parts of the book shows different authorship for those parts. Toy lists over fifty correspondences, some, however, not very close. He inadvertently omits 15:13 and 17:22. Most of these parallels are noted in the Commentary section of this treatment. Toy has not given sufficient attention to the obvious fact that in many cases a portion of a verse is repeated with variations that likely are significant. Such repetitions prove nothing as to collections of proverbs of different authorship. Sometimes, also, the repetition comes within a section held by Toy to be a unified collection, as 14:12 and 16:25. Here Toy is forced to suggest the existence of subcollections. Furthermore, there is a similar repetition in an Egyptian work held to be of unified authorship (cf. Commentary on 22:28). Apparently Toy's contention is based on a fallacious assumption. It is clear that there are several distinct collections in Proverbs, as the titles show; but the internal evidence of these parallels is insufficient to disprove Solomon's authorship of those portions ascribed to him.

Proverbs and other Wisdom Literature. Just as the writing of poetry in ancient times was not limited to the Hebrews, so the literary form of Proverbs is not uniquely Hebrew. It should not surprise us to discover that there were collections of proverbs in ancient Egypt and Mesopotamia. Several such pieces may be named, but two are of special importance—the *Story of Ahikar* and the *Wisdom of Amen-em-Opet,* which must be considered below in some detail.

One of the oldest of these Wisdom pieces is the *Instruction of Ptah-Hotep,* of about 2450 B.C. in Egypt. Few parallels to it in the Book of Proverbs are alleged, but the style of writing is proverbial and the thoughts are similar in some cases. For instance, it commands obedience of sons, humility, justice, caution at the table of a noble, listening rather than speaking, etc. Obviously such pious advice is old and was the common property of the East. Parallels between such materials and Proverbs prove nothing as to the origin of our book. Similar observations apply to the *Instruction of Ani* and other early Egyptian literature. Some pieces of Mesopotamian literature may be mentioned. The so-called Babylonian Job, entitled *I Will Praise the Lord of Wisdom,* reminds us somewhat of the Biblical Job in its story of a man in great sickness who is cured by the gods. There is also a *Dialogue about Human Misery,* sometimes called the Babylonian Ecclesiastes. The similarity of the words to the Biblical Ecclesiastes is quite minor, but it includes a few proverbial sayings.

Various Babylonian tablets from the eighth century or before include proverbs counseling one to recompense good for evil, not to speak hastily, not to enter into another's quarrel, etc. Again, since these principles of morality are very general, their presence in these tablets proves nothing about the origin of the Book of Proverbs, except that it should naturally be considered against its background. Just as Moses could draw on the laws of Hammurabi, and David used some of the forms of Canaanite poetry, so Solomon and his successors had a wealth of background material for illustrative purposes. In all these cases, however, the common ancient material was molded by the Hebrew author, who was inspired by the Spirit of God to write His revelation for His people. (All of these writings can be conveniently seen in the collection edited by James B. Pritchard, *Ancient Near Eastern Texts Relating to the Old Testament*, 2nd. ed.)

Of more consequence for our study is the *Story of Ahikar*, a tale from Mesopotamia embellished with many proverbs. The story has long been known, as portions of it occur in early Christian authors. But in 1906 eleven papyrus sheets containing the story were turned up in excavations of the Jewish colony at Elephantine, Egypt. This copy is from about 400 B.C. Ahikar was a counselor of the kings Sennacherib and Esarhaddon in Assyria, about 700 B.C. He adopted his nephew, who by deceit persuaded the king to execute Ahikar. But the official executioners, being friendly to the doomed man, hid Ahikar a while, then reinstated him when the king's wrath cooled off. Two-thirds of the booklet is composed of Ahikar's sayings, which present a number of parallels with Proverbs. W. O. E. Oesterley in his *The Book of Proverbs* (pp. xxxvii-liii) lists thirty-three parallels, which is probably a somewhat exaggerated number. Story *(op. cit.*, pp. 329-336) also presents important comparisons. For the most part these parallels are general. For instance, Ahikar cautions men against looking at a bedizened and painted woman or lusting after her in their hearts, as this is a sin against God (cf. Prov 6:25, etc.). Also he urges a father to subdue his son while he is young, else he will rebel when he is stronger (cf. Prov 19:18). It is doubtful, however, that there is any direct connection between the proverbs of Ahikar and those of the Bible. Furthermore, the proverbs of Ahikar lack the moral tone of the Book of Proverbs. They do not have the contrast of the wise man versus the sinner which is so characteristic of Proverbs. They are more secular. The Book of Proverbs, however, does occasionally use this secular backdrop to develop its moral teaching. Actually it is quite difficult to be sure—if there is dependence—which piece is the debtor. The *Story of Ahikar*, though the scene is laid in Assyria, was current among the Jews and later among the Christians. Our best copy is from a Jewish source. The proverbs of *Ahikar* could as easily have been influenced by the Book of Proverbs or by the general Jewish reservoir of proverbs as the other way around (see the Commentary on 23:14 for a probable case of borrowing by *Ahikar* from Proverbs).

Some feel that the case is different with the Egyptian *Wisdom of Amen-em-Opet*. This remarkable collection of proverbs has even more parallels to the Biblical book than does *Ahikar*. Its date is uncertain. The papyrus is later than the composition, but is itself not datable. F. Ll. Griffith did the principal work on the translation of the Egyptian. Oesterley reports Griffith's date for the book as seventh to sixth century B.C. and H. O. Lange as even later. Oesterley himself assigns the work to the eighth century or later *(The Wisdom of Egypt*, pp. 9,10). Albright favors an earlier date, about 1100–1000 B.C. *(op. cit.*, p. 6). If this date be sustained, any thought of derivation must be from an Egyptian original. John A. Wilson (ANET, p. 421), in his translation of the work, does not commit himself in regard to the date.

The nature of the parallels is to be observed. Oesterley, in his discerning study, notices that the *Wisdom of Amen-em-Opet* is very un-Egyptian. It has high ethics and a high conception of God—pointing toward monotheism of a sort. He declares that "the like is not to be found elsewhere in Egyptian literature of pre-Christian times" *(op. cit.*, p. 24). Parallels are found by Oesterley with several Old Testament books besides Proverbs, e.g., Deut 19:14; 25:13-15; 27:18; I Sam 2:6-8; Ps 1; Jer 17:6ff. These passages are not particularly significant, however, for most of them deal with themes also appearing in Proverbs, where the parallels are numerous—over forty being listed by Oesterley *(The Book of Proverbs*, pp. xxxvii–liii). The parallels occur with various parts of

Proverbs, but are particularly striking with the portion 22:17–23:14. All but five of these verses are paralleled in *Amen-em-Opet*.

Most striking of all, the Egyptian book is divided into thirty chapters (of considerable length) and concludes with an exhortation to give heed to these thirty chapters. This section in Proverbs, expanding it to include 22:17–24:22, is said to contain thirty sayings (Oesterley, *op. cit.*, p. 192). The introductory words of this section in Proverbs are, "Have not I written unto thee *excellent things*" (22:20). This can with more justification be read with very slightly different vowels, "Have not I written unto thee *thirty*." It must be admitted that the discovery of just thirty sayings in these sixty-nine verses is a bit arbitrary. And the thirty sayings are not nearly so long as the thirty chapters of the Egyptian book. Still, the parallel is striking. Oesterley (*The Wisdom of Egypt*, p. 105) points out the curious fact that the section Prov 22:17–23:12 has parallels to all but three verses in scattered parts of the Egyptian work. But the other parts of Proverbs, which have fewer parallels, have them in general with chapters X and XXI of *Amen-em-Opet*. He argues quite plausibly from this that the usage as regards borrowing differs in the different sections of the two books. Neither work borrowed directly from the other. In some sections, both borrowed from a common reservoir of proverbial sayings. But from the peculiar character of the Egyptian work, he argues that the fountain of both lay in the background of Hebrew wisdom and theology.

We can perhaps go a little further. Much has been made of the reading, "Have not I written to thee *thirty* things." It is clear that the thirty sayings in this section of Proverbs are not copied from the Egyptian thirty. Actually, the last half of the section in Proverbs has no parallels at all with the Egyptian book. The "thirty" of Proverbs may have been modeled after the Egyptian "thirty," but in any case, it was not slavishly borrowed. Rather, we should see here another example of the characteristic use of numbers in Wisdom literature. Well-known examples are the climactic references to "three things . . . yea, four" too difficult to understand (Prov 30:18ff.) or "six things . . . yea, seven" (6:16-19). Such references can be matched in the Ugaritic literature. Baal is said to hate two sacrifices, yea, three (C. H. Gordon, *Ugaritic Literature*, p. 30). Baal captures sixty-six towns, yea, seventy-seven cities (*ibid.*, p. 36). Later, seventy-seven brothers, yea, eighty-eight are mentioned (*ibid.*, p. 55). Many other examples could be given. Apparently in the sayings of *Amen-em-Opet* and in Proverbs 22:20 we have two examples of a literary use of the numeral thirty that probably could be multiplied if our sources of ancient Egyptian and Hebrew Wisdom were more complete. As to the detailed comparisons of Proverbs with the Egyptian sayings, see notes on the verses in the Commentary.

We should also mention the two apocryphal books, Ecclesiasticus of about 180 B.C., and the Wisdom of Solomon, likely a bit later. These books, of great interest in themselves, are modeled in some ways after Proverbs. But they are later, and show a further development in the personification of wisdom and in other matters. They borrow from our Book of Proverbs, not vice versa, and therefore extensive reference to them is not necessary for our present purposes.

OUTLINE

I. Solomon's tribute to wisdom, the fear of the Lord. 1:1–9:18.
   A. Introduction. 1:1-7.
   B. The righteous woman, Wisdom, versus the evil woman. 1:8–9:18.
II. Solomon's miscellaneous single-verse proverbs. 10:1–22:16.
   A. Contrasting proverbs. 10:1–15:33.
   B. Proverbs largely parallel. 16:1–22:16.
III. The Words of the Wise, thirty sayings. 22:17–24:22.
   A. Sayings paralleled in Egyptian Wisdom. 22:17–23:12.
   B. Sayings with no parallel in Egyptian. 23:13–24:22.
IV. The Words of the Wise, Appendix. 24:23-34.
V. Proverbs of Solomon, edited by Hezekiah's men. 25:1–29:27.
VI. Final appendices. 30:1–31:31.
   A. The Words of Agur. 30:1-33.
   B. The Words of Lemuel. 31:1-9.
   C. Alphabetical poem on the virtuous woman. 31:10-31.

COMMENTARY

I. Solomon's Tribute to Wisdom, the Fear of the Lord. 1:1–9:18.

A. Introduction. 1:1-7. Author and Subject. Some commentators have taken this portion to be an introduction to the entire book, but as various other sections also have author data, probably this is to be taken to refer to the first section alone.

1. The proverbs. The root from which this word comes is used both in Hebrew and in other Semitic languages to express comparison. A derivative in Akkadian means "mirror." From such usage, the word comes to include both a reproachful remark (Ps 69:11), and a prophet's message (e.g., Num 23:7,18). It is translated "parable" sixteen times in the OT. In the book of Proverbs it is used mainly in the titles (1:1,6; 10:1; 25:1) to denominate the comparisons and contrasts used to express the moral teaching of the book. **Of Solomon.** See the discussion of authorship in the Introduction to the book.

2-4. Wisdom . . . instruction, etc. There are here five synonyms for **wisdom.** These include **righteousness** (ASV) and **equity,** which are virtues rather than skills. The emphasis is upon moral wisdom or right conduct. **The simple.** This word, used fourteen times in Proverbs, four times elsewhere, designates the opposite of a moral man. It does not mean a simpleton in our sense of the term, but a sinner, a rascal. Proverbs has a message of morality for the wicked. It is not just a *Poor Richard's Almanac* of good advice for people of low intelligence or lazy habits. This introduction cautions us against taking the book in a secular sense. It is a book of Christian principles.

7. The fear of the Lord. A common expression in the Psalms and elsewhere, this phrase is used fourteen times in Proverbs. Illustrations of the usage occur in Ps 115:11 – "Ye that fear the Lord, trust in the Lord," and Isa 11:2,3, where the fear of the Lord is named as a characteristic of the Messiah. Such fear includes awe before the Almighty (Ps 2:11 – "Serve the Lord with fear and rejoice with trembling"). Job 28:28 is practically a definition – "The fear of the Lord, that is wisdom, and to depart from evil is understanding." Proverbs 8:13 is to the same effect – "The fear of the Lord is to hate evil." **The beginning of knowledge.** Not the "chief" or "sum," as the Hebrew root might suggest, for Prov 9:10 uses a word specifically meaning the "start" or "beginning." Rather, the first step in morality is our relation to God. **Fools despise wisdom.** "Fool" occurs eighteen times in Proverbs; seven times elsewhere. Also the usage differs. In Isa 35:8, "fool" obviously means "simpleton," as is true in our English usage. But in the specialized usage of Proverbs, "fool" means a sinner. Proverbs 14:9 is illustrative – "Fools make a mock at sin." The clause means that sinners deride holiness. The Greek LXX well renders **fools** by *ungodly*.

B. The Righteous Woman, Wisdom, Versus the Evil Woman. 1:8–9:18. In this section the method of teaching by contrast is beautifully illustrated. In major sections, personified Wisdom is set off against sin (see Introd., *The Teaching of Proverbs).*

11. Lay wait for blood . . . for the innocent. The motive, it develops, is robbery, but this gang openly suggests murder for gain.

12. Alive as the grave. The expression is found in Num 16:30,33; Ps 55:15. The former passage says that Korah and his company were swallowed alive by the opening earth. The latter expresses the curse that men may go down "quick," i.e., "alive," into the grave. These men of Prov 1:11-14 would murder with dispatch. They would bring **whole,** i.e., healthy men down to death. **The grave.** Hebrew *she'ôl*. The present writer believes that this term simply means "grave." It is used nine times in Proverbs, three times to refer to the results of adultery. Cf. 5:5; 7:27; 9:18, where it is made parallel with "death" and "the dead." At least in 1:12, the emphasis is simply on murder. There is here no concern with the afterlife of the victims. This is not to deny that there was a belief in the afterlife and in resurrection among the Hebrews, but merely to say that this much discussed word may have a more simple meaning than is sometimes given it. (See R. Laird Harris, "The Meaning of Sheol in the Old Testament," *The Evangelical Theological Society Bulletin,* Vol. IV (1961), No. 4.)

16. Their feet. Identical with Isa 59:7.

Possibly Isaiah quotes from this, or possibly it was a common expression. See comments on 30:5 for other quotations found in Proverbs from elsewhere in the OT.

22. Simple ones. Obviously those who are in sin. The word *scorners* is used in Ps 1:1 parallel with *ungodly* and *sinners*. Cf. commentary on 3:34. **25. But ye.** This should be *and ye*. Verses 24 and 25 give the reason as a protasis; the apodosis or conclusion is in verse 26. When we refuse the invitation of the Lord, there comes a time when the door of grace is shut. **32. The turning away.** The *waywardness* of sinners (so Berkeley Version). The word usually refers to apostasy, a turning away from God.

2:1. My son. Thirteen times in the first seven chapters this address occurs. It assists in showing the unity of this section, 1:1–9:18. **6. The Lord giveth wisdom.** The essentially religious nature of the exhortation is here illustrated.

13. Ways of darkness. Verses 12-15 speak of evil in general. This is aptly typified by the expression, **ways of darkness.** It still is true that crime flourishes in the dark. The contrast is expressed in 4:18,19, where the path of the just is compared to light and the way of the wicked to darkness (a different Heb. word from that of 2:13, however). The ethical figure of light and darkness occurs also in Isa 5:20; Ps 43:3; and in a few other places where the contrast is less clear. It is not common in the OT, but is found in the Dead Sea Scrolls and in the NT.

16. The strange woman . . . the stranger. These two expressions obviously refer to the "loose" woman (so RSV). The words basically mean "alien" and "foreigner" (so Berkeley), but in Proverbs it is clear that immorality is implied. Elsewhere in the OT this is not so. Ruth calls herself a "stranger" (Ruth 2:10). These expressions when used in Proverbs are euphemistic for *zônâ*, "a harlot," a word seldom used in this book. **17. Guide of her youth.** Her husband (so Berkeley). **The covenant of her God.** Probably an interesting reference to the divine sanction of the marriage vows.

18. Her house inclineth unto death. The translation is difficult in detail, but the meaning is clear from the parallel: the wages of sin is death. The same thought in very similar words is repeated in 5:5; 7:27; 9:18. Closest is 7:27, which says that her house is the road to Sheol, going down to the chambers of death; i.e., adultery is fatal. It is difficult to take **her house** as the subject of **inclineth** in 2:18, however, as "house" is masculine and the verb *shûaḥ* is feminine. Toy (*The Book of Proverbs,* ICC., *ad loc.*) therefore derives it from a similar verb with the same consonants, *shāḥāḥ,* "to be bowed down." This is possibly correct. **The dead.** Hebrew, *repāîm,* translated by some as *shades* (so RSV and Berkeley). This translation is not necessary. The word cannot give us a theology of the underworld. Its etymology is uncertain. It is used several times in Ugaritic (C. H. Gordon, *Ugaritic Handbook,* glossary) and is there made parallel with "deities." This usage is not very instructive, since it involves Ugaritic theology, which is quite different from that of the Bible. We are thrown back upon the seven other Biblical instances of the use of the word. Three times it is used as parallel to "dead men," twice to Sheol; twice it has no parallel. Instructive is Isa 26:14, 19. In the first verse the plaint is that the dead men, the *repāîm,* shall not live or rise; in the later verse it is promised that they will. The word simply means dead people. As to the state of the dead being shadowy, conscious, or unconscious, this word says nothing. (On this subject cf. the plain teaching of Phil 1:23; Lk 23:43; *et al.*). There is another word spelled the same way which is the name of one of the nations of Canaan, the Rephaims. That word is sometimes translated "giants," but probably not correctly so.

3:1. My law. This phrase and "My commandments" (2:1) and similar words are not to be pressed to refer to the law of Moses. They are the advice of the father-teacher. It is given, however, as the Lord's word. The author implies that he is giving divine commands, as does Paul in I Cor 14:37. Though a practical end is often given in Proverbs, the author urges rectitude for its own sake, not because "honesty is the best policy." **2. Length of days.** A possible allusion to the first commandment with promise (Ex 20:12). **3. Bind them about thy neck.** A similar phrase, but not identical occurs in Deut 6:8. Closer is Prov 7:3: "Write them upon the table of thine heart." **5. With all thine heart.** This precious verse contrasts ordinary human wisdom and the divine wisdom that is the basis of the whole book. **Heart** in Hebrew is used symbolically to represent not so much the seat of the emotions as the seat of intellect and will. In other words, commit your inner self to God. Do not seek to be independent of him. **6. Direct.** Hebrew, *make straight*. The verse promises not so much guidance as enablement for us to go forward.

9. Firstfruits. An interesting reference to the Levitical legislation. In general, Proverbs is silent as to the Mosaic laws (but cf. the verses mentioned in the Commentary at 15:8), although clearly these laws were in force when Proverbs was written – even according to critical opinion which would make both Proverbs and the Levitical legislation post-Exilic The silence of Proverbs in this regard simply shows again that an argument from silence is often fallacious. **10. New wine.** The Hebrew has two words for wine. *Yayîn,* which means fermented wine, is used in the condemnatory passage in Prov 23:31-35. *Tîrôsh,* used here as the fresh product of the pressing, is properly "must," "grape juice." Both words are translated *oinos,* "wine," by the LXX.

11. Despise not the chastening of the Lord. Quoted from Job 5:17, except that in Job the characteristic name *Shaddai,* "Almighty," occurs. Hebrews 12:5,6 quotes verbatim from the LXX (Alexandrinus and Sinaiticus texts), as is usual in Hebrews. The LXX adequately represents the Hebrew. (For other quotations, in Proverbs from the OT, cf. 30:5.)

14. Merchandise. "Profit," or possibly, "value." **15. Than rubies.** Cf. Job 28:18; Prov 8:11; 31:10. **18. Tree of life.** The phrase occurs also in Gen 2:9; 3:22-24; Prov 11:30; 13:12; 15:4; Rev 2:7; 22:2. Genesis is the only satisfactory source for the reference in Proverbs. We should therefore conclude that, as in the Revelation, these verses in Proverbs relate to the narrative of the Fall. There is no evidence for a "primitive sacred tree of life," as Toy supposes. Revelation 22:2 also has reference to a tree of healing by the river of the sanctuary (cf. Ezk 47:12; Zech 14:8). Famous trees in the garden of God, Eden, are mentioned in Ezk 31:8-16. All of these references presume acquaintance with the Genesis narrative. **19. By wisdom . . . founded the earth.** Cf. 8:25-31. The "wisdom" of Proverbs is basically an attribute of God, and is not to be equated with mere earthly maxims of a clever teacher. This wisdom is God's law. In Prov 8, wisdom is personified and called eternal, as God is eternal. Many have found here an adumbration of Christ, which is a possible interpretation, but not sure.

27. Withhold not. Pay wages and pay on time, i.e., treat the laborer honestly and fairly (cf. Lev 19:13; Mal 3:5). Others would broaden the injunction to include all charity. **32. The froward.** The root meaning apparently is *to depart.* This form is used only in Prov 2:15; 3:32; 14:2; Isa 30:12. Its parallel is "crooked." The LXX says *transgressors.* Perhaps "transgressor" or "apostate" gives the meaning best. **34. He scorneth the scorners.** The same root, *lîṣ,* is used in both the noun and the verb. But the meanings probably are a shade different. The verb has the meaning "to deride" (cf. Ps 119:51). The LXX, which is quoted verbatim in Jas 4:6; I Pet 5:5, uses *resist* as a free translation. The noun, however, is limited to Proverbs, Ps 1:1, and Isa 29:20. It is one of the many synonyms for a wicked man. The Greek uses the word *arrogant,* which is a fair representation. Its opposite is *humble* (AV, *lowly)* in the last half of the verse. But there is wide variety in the Greek translation of this root. It evidently has many overtones of wickedness.

4:3,4. My father's son. These verses give an interesting touch. The teacher-father declares that his doctrine is not new. There is no reason why we may not see here the solicitous care of David and Bathsheba for their son Solomon. **7. Wisdom is the principal thing.** The RSV and Berkeley insist on reading here a genitive – *The beginning of wisdom is: Get wisdom.* So also Toy and Delitzsch *(The Proverbs of Solomon,* KD. Reprinted.). But this seems unnecessary. Oesterley *(op. cit.)* and Fritsch *(op. cit.)* would drop the verse, since it is not in the LXX. The same form *beginning* is used four times not in the genitive. The meaning of "chief" or "principal" is well attested. The AV translation can be defended. *The beginning of wisdom is: get wisdom* violates the thought of 1:7 and seems unsuitable. **With all thy getting.** Better, *in all that thou hast acquired.* **Get understanding.** There is not here a progress – Don't stop at wisdom; get real understanding. Rather, as is usual in Proverbs, wisdom and understanding are synonymous. **9. Crown of glory.** The expression is also used in 16:31; Isa 62:3. **12. Not . . . straitened.** The old English *strait* does not mean "straight," but rather, "strict," "narrow" (cf. Mt 7:14). Your steps will be *unimpeded* (Toy).

14. Enter not. Verses 14-27 represent the advice of wisdom – namely, Turn from evil (cf. Job 28:28). **18. The path of the just.** Note the emphatic contrast with "the way of the wicked" (v. 19). **The perfect day.** The precise meaning is debatable. Rashi and many others say *noon* (cited in Julius H. Greenstone, *Proverbs with Commentary*). The general meaning is clear: the just walk in increasing light; the wicked, in darkness (cf. comment on 2:13).

22. Life . . . and health. Cf. 3:8. **23. Keep thy heart,** i.e., the mind which should seek right conduct (cf. 23:26). **Out of it.** Grammatically this could be "out of the heart"; but more likely, "out of keeping the heart in wisdom" is life.

5:3. For the lips. As a honeycomb drops honey, so the strange woman speaks honeyed words; her speech (lit., *palate,* as organ of speech) is, we would say, 'slick.' **Strange woman.** See comment on 2:16. **4. Wormwood.** The Greek translates *gall* as the height of bitterness. The Hebrew *la'ănâ* appears to be a shrub of bitter taste used in the preparation of absinthe and traditionally used as medicine for deworming. **5. To death.** See comments on 2:18. **6. Lest** is difficult and is rendered by the LXX, Delitzsch, and others as a negative. **Ponder** means "weigh" or "make level." The subject could be "thou" or "she." Read, *She does not weigh* (or *consider) the path of life.* The last half can be translated, *Her ways wander* (so RSV). The last verb again could have as its subject "thou" or "she." *She knows it not* (Berkeley and similarly RSV). Jones and Walls ("The Proverbs," *The New Bible Commentary)* favor a slightly attested meaning of the verb, *She is not at rest.* **9. Thine honour unto others.** Proverbs 5:9-14 is aptly called "Rake's Progress" by Jones and Walls.

15. Thine own cistern. Verses 15-17 are highly poetic and beautiful exhortations to fidelity, while 16,17 probably refer to children. In any event, the blessing of marital fidelity is beautifully presented. **19. Let her breasts satisfy thee.** This Hebrew word *dad,* translated "breasts" in the AV, does not bear the connotation expected in this verse as another word, *shad,* would. Certain copies of the LXX and the parallel in Prov 7:18 argue that the word here should be read with another vowel, *dōd,* and translated *Let her love satisfy thee* (so Greenstone and RSV). **21. Before . . . the Lord.** Contrary to Toy, who usually finds in Proverbs the concept of temporal blessings as the incentive for morality, this verse shows that the outlook of the author includes the higher reference to God's holiness as the reason for rectitude. **23. Without instruction.** The Hebrew says, *with no instruction.* Doubtless "for lack of discipline" is meant (so RSV, BV, Jones and Walls, etc.).

6:1. If thou be surety. The practices in regard to lending among the Jews in antiquity are not fully known. Toy imagines that there was no suretyship in the "commercially simple" pre-Exilic life. It would seem, however, that the far-flung enterprises of Solomon, now illustrated by archaeology, and the increase of wealth pictured by Amos and others must have given ample opportunity for making loans and taking surety; although we do not have examples of just this thing in other Scriptures. The rabbinic attitudes are discussed by Greenstone, who remarks that the Hebrew word for "surety" here was used by the Phoenician traders and entered Latin as *arrabo.* He might have added that it is also in Greek *arrabōn* (Eph 1:14. Cf. Zellig S. Harris, *Grammar of the Phoenician Language,* "American Oriental Series," Vol. VIII; Glossary). In brief, the Levitical law forbade lending on interest to poor Israelites (Lev 25:35-37). The idea was that for a poor fellow Israelite, a man should give the needed money outright. The Law required that if a man did lend and take a pledge for collateral, he might not enter his debtor's house to remove the collateral by force. And if a poor man gave his garment as collateral, the lender must restore it to him the same day (Deut 24:10-12). These provisions answer to our minimum personal exemptions. Lending to non-Israelites was permitted, and probably commercial loans were arranged. The author of the article "Usury," in ISBE, remarks that the Pentateuchal regulations do not cover commercial loans; but perhaps he goes too far in saying that commercial loans were practically unknown. Rather, it is probable that the practice of making commercial loans gave rise to the injustices in II Kgs 4:1; Neh 5:1-12. At the year of release all Israelites' debts were remitted (Deut 15:2). This argues for commercial loans being permitted, for other loans were prohibited.

Rates of interest, if we may judge by Neh 5:11, were commonly 1 per cent per month, although they doubtless varied.

Charging such high interest was usury, and those who required it of fellow Jews were condemned. The prophet Jeremiah protests (Jer 15:10) that he has not engaged in such ventures, yet all men hate him – presumably as they hated usurers. The word is translated *extortioner* in Ps 109:11. The very word for "usury," *neshek* (Prov 28:8), implies "bite" or "devour," though milder words are also used. Not to practice usury is an element of righteousness in Ps 15:5; Ezk 18:8, 13,17; 22:12. The practice of a creditor is illustrated in II Kgs 4:1. We can reasonably fill in the details that the husband had a commercial loan which his widow could not pay; or possibly some usurer had loaned to a widow in violation of Lev 25:35-37. The BV and the RSV translate these words by *interest*. It would seem better to translate by "usury," as apparently it is the excesses that are condemned. Because of these excesses, Solomon cautions against becoming surety for "another." He urges one to escape speedily the possibilities of ruin. Sureties are recommended in the post-biblical book, Ecclesiasticus 29:14. When they developed or what form they took, we do not know. It is probable that in the time of Solomon their abuses were such as to call forth the rebuke here recorded (see also Prov 11:15; 20:16; 27:13 – the last two verses practically identical).

6. The ant. Mentioned in the Bible only here and in Prov 30:25, though there probably is no question about the translation. Formerly there was a problem raised about ants storing food (see Toy). A type of ant found in the Near East, however, does this. Ants have social organization, but no ruler corresponding to a queen bee. **Thou sluggard.** This noun is found fourteen times in Proverbs and nowhere else. It is usually defined as "a lazy person." Though the word includes this idea, it may well have other overtones, such as our "ne'er-do-well," which does not mean merely a "failure." The usage in Proverbs argues that "lazy" is not the total connotation. In 15:19, the contrast is an *upright man* – not just a "worker." In 19:15 the parallel is with *remîyyâ,* which is usually rendered *deceit* in the AV and the RSV, but rendered by them *idle* in this place. In Prov 21:25,26 the contrast evidently is a *righteous man* (so AV and Berkeley). The RSV separates the two verses and supplies an extra thought in verse 26. In 26:12-16 there are several verses on the sluggard. Verse 13 is similar to 22:13. Verse 15 is from 19:24. But 26:16, as a final, perhaps climactic verse, says a "sluggard" is wise in his own eyes. We must note that this section of Proverbs 26 was introduced by verse 12, which declares that one wise in his own eyes is worse than a "fool." It is clear that the author is reproaching a "sluggard" not merely with idleness, but with associated sins. We hope to show by many examples that the word "fool" means not a "moron" but a "sinner." So the author of Proverbs here is not merely recommending thrift and diligence; he is apparently condemning a characteristic that combines shiftlessness with shiftiness! **10. A little sleep.** Verses 10 and 11 are exactly paralleled in 24:33,34, except for a couple of vowels (cf. Introd.). In this case both contexts speak of a shiftless man, using different comparisons, but the same conclusion. The saying may have been a well-known epigram. The LXX translates it a bit differently in the two places. The Syriac also differs, but not in the same way as the LXX.

12. A naughty person. Hebrew, *a man of Belial.* **Froward.** Hebrew, *crooked.* **13. Speaketh with his feet.** LXX, *makes a sign with his feet.* The Hebrew *mālal* can mean "speak," "rub," "scrape," "languish," or "wither" (BDB). The meaning "scrape" is poorly attested. The idiom may well refer to some low gesture, like our thumbing the nose. **Teacheth with his fingers.** The word probably means "point," but the connotation is difficult. Possibly another low gesture typical of the wicked man. **14. Frowardness.** A different word from that in verse 12. It is used nine times in Proverbs, elsewhere only in Deut 32:20. The root means *overturn.* It is clear that it refers to some kind of evil, but it is hard to catch the exact intent. The LXX reads *perverted* (so Fritsch). Delitzsch says *malice;* Toy: *evil.* In 8:13 "a perverse mouth" is paralleled with pride and arrogancy. In 23:33 a drunk man is pictured as speaking "perverse things," using this word. **Soweth discord.** Literally, *lets loose strife.* The LXX translation, *causes trouble to a city,* arose from confusing the word with a later derivative. The root is *dîn,* "to judge, whence *mādôn,* "strife." This word, **discord,** with variants, is found twenty-seven times in Proverbs and three times elsewhere. It is part of the peculiar moral vocabulary of the book. The wording of 16:28, a "perverse man lets loose strife," is very similar to that of this verse.

16. Six things . . . yea, seven. These are not seven cardinal sins (Greenstone and Jones and Walls) nor an indefinite six or seven (Toy). Delitzsch strikes it right in saying that the proverb is climactic. The six items are background for the seventh, which receives the emphasis (cf. Job 5:19; Prov 30:18,19). The statement emphatically concludes with what verse 14 had introduced – "letting loose strife."

21. Bind them . . . upon thy heart. Cf. 3:3. **23. Commandment . . . law.** Jones and Walls well remark that this is parental instruction, but that such instruction consisted of the divine law (Deut 6:6,7). **25. In thine heart.** Note well that the OT commandments reach to the internal attitudes of man. Christ's teaching that inner lust was already inner adultery (Mt 5:28) is not an advance upon the OT teaching so much as a rescuing of the OT doctrine from the Pharisaic traditional comments (cf. R. Laird Harris, *Inspiration and Canonicity of the Bible*, p. 53). **30. A thief.** The thought is that there may be mitigating circumstances for thievery, and even restitution greatly assists in removing the blot. But for adultery there is no excuse. It brings a train of evil consequences. No restitution is possible.

35. Ransom. A good example of the meaning of *kōper*, "a payment to pacify." The root is said to mean *cover* (BDB), but it is not so used in the OT, and it is a dubious inference from the Arabic. From the noun for **ransom** a denominative verb, *kipper*, is formed, logically meaning "to give a ransom." This is the verb many times translated "to make an atonement." From this verb a second noun is formed, *kappōret*, "place of atonement." This is the word for the top of the ark called "the mercy seat" in the AV, or *hilastērion* in the LXX. Christ is called our *hilastērion*, or "propitiation," in Rom 3:25.

7:2. Apple of thine eye. *Center of the eye;* therefore the pupil, a symbol of a most precious thing. **5. Flattereth.** Not so much to "flatter" as to use smooth words, i.e., agreeable, seductive words (so Delitzsch and RSV).

7. Among the simple. The silly, the morally unstable. See comment at 1:4 and cf. 9:4 and 16. **10. Subtil.** The Hebrew apparently means "guarded of heart," i.e., secretive, wily (so Delitzsch). The description of the following scene is a classic. As Delitzsch says, "like meets like," the seduction is complete, the excuses are given. But the inspired author gives tersely enough the end product of evil. **11. Loud and stubborn.** Better, *tumultuous and rebellious.* The rebellion is obviously a refusal of God's law and the obligations of morality. **14. I have peace offerings.** The peace offerings were eaten in part by the worshiper. Therefore, at national feasts with thousands present, peace offerings were given by the thousands. The woman does not mean to claim that she has recently worshiped. She is, rather, alluring the young man with the announcement that her refrigerator is full, as we would say. "My husband is away," she says; "the coast is clear. We can have our fling, and no one will know." No one but God! **20. Day appointed.** A rare word. The LXX and Syriac give the sense, *after many days.* Probably the meaning is "at full moon," which was presumably some days off.

22. Straightway. Better, *all at once* (RSV). The man's resistance to sin at last gives way, and his doom is sealed. **Stocks.** The sense is plain, but again the details are difficult. The Hebrew seems to say, "like fetters unto correction a fool (goes)." The word "fetter," however, is rare and elsewhere means anklets. The LXX translates the word for "stocks" by "dog," apparently reading a different text —"like a dog (goes) to bonds." The word "bonds" in the LXX arises from the Hebrew word for "correction," using different vowels. Then the LXX ends the verse with this clause—"as a dog goes to bonds." The word "fool" is understood with different vowels, and it is transferred to the following verse, which reads in the LXX—"A deer shot in the liver with an arrow." The LXX reading of the whole passage differs from the Hebrew only in two words. It is supported by the Syriac and Targum, and should perhaps be adopted.

27. Sheol. See comments for 1:12 and 2:18. We should not lose the solemn thrust of this passage in the details of the exposition. Sin cannot be indulged with impunity; its wages is death. The deceitfulness of sin is an old story, but the ancient Hebrew author here beautifully unmasks its deceit and gives the unvarnished truth. But he does not stop there. There is a cure for sin—it is the voice of Wisdom of chapter 8.

8:1. Doth not wisdom cry? Greenstone

well remarks that we have here not just a discourse on the beauties of family life or on chastity, else the contrast to the harlot would be a dutiful wife. But Greenstone does not follow up his suggestion to show that the contrast is really the basic one of sin versus godliness. It is for this reason that wisdom is personified and so closely paralleled with God himself. Proverbs 8:1-13 gives the exhortation of wisdom; 8:14-31 describes the exalted status of wisdom; 8:32–9:11 presents the invitation of wisdom to profit by her instruction.

5. Simple . . . fools. These are not mental fools, but, as much of the preceding shows, sinners. For **simple,** see comments on 1:4. The word *k^{e}sîl,* "fool," is used forty-nine times in Proverbs, eighteen in Ecclesiastes, three times elsewhere. It is obvious that it is part of what we have called the moral vocabulary of Proverbs. Its use in Ecclesiastes is somewhat different, even as its counterpart, "wisdom," is used differently there. In Ecclesiastes, wisdom is inventive genius, mental ability; folly is pleasure—even noble pleasure in works like architecture, gardening, etc. Both are alike condemned as fruitless. In Proverbs, both wisdom and folly are of a moral sort. Examples of the usage of *(k^{e}sîl)* are: (1) in connection with *'iwwelet,* "folly" of the sinful sort, 12:23; 13:16; 14:8; 15:14; 17:12; etc.; this root is not found in Ecclesiastes. (2) The "fool" *(k^{e}sîl)* is contrasted with the wise man or with wisdom in Prov 3:35; 10:1, 23; 13:20; 14:16; 29:11. (3) The word "fool" is paralleled with "simple" *(petî)* in 1:22; with "scorner" *(lēṣ)* in 19:29; and associated with "evil" *(ra')* in 13:19. This word "fool," or "folly," *'iwwelet,* in Proverbs, obviously connotes moral badness. This must be understood if we are to hold the teaching of Proverbs in focus. It is not a book on intelligence so much as on integrity (see Introd., *The Teaching of Proverbs).*

8. Froward. Not the word used in 2:12 and elsewhere. This root, *pātal,* means "twisted"; therefore it is used for "string," "tie," "wrestle," etc. Here it means morally twisted, the opposite of righteous. **Perverse.** Crooked. **10. My instruction.** The translation of the AV is satisfactory. The Hebrew strictly says, *Receive my instruction and do not (receive) silver.* It is a comparative negative (cf. 9:8; 31:6; and, for another famous example, see Hos 6:6). **11. Than rubies.** Cf. 3:15; 8:10; 16:16; 31:10. **12. Prudence.** Hebrew *'ormâ.* The root means "be wise," and is used in a good sense, as here, and also in a bad sense (Gen 3:1). **Inventions.** This also is used elsewhere in a bad sense (Prov 12:2). Here it is good. **13. To hate evil.** Verses amplifying the concept of "the fear of the Lord" are: 1:7,29; 2:5; 8:13; 9:10; 10:27; 14:27; 16:6; 19:23. Job 28:28, like Prov 16:6, emphasizes departing from evil. Prov 8:13 warns us that true godliness is not all positive. The teaching that sin is hateful is a wonderful and vital truth. In ancient times, as now, only the Biblical revelation stressed this truth.

22. The Lord possessed me. A famous verse. The LXX translates, *The Lord created me,* as does the Syriac. The clear personification of these verses led most of the early Church Fathers to find here a prophecy of Christ. The Arian heretics of the fourth century therefore made much of this verse, speaking of wisdom as a created being. The orthodox party repelled this idea, as Jones and Walls say, "on other grounds." It is curious that the controversy was carried out on the basis of the LXX text. There was little recourse to the Hebrew. The Hebrew uses the word *qānâ.* This verb is used many times in the sense of "buy," "possess," "acquire." Its derivative means "cattle," or practically, "wealth." Only in Gen 14:22 would "make" be a reasonable translation. The RSV has *maker* in Gen 14:22 and *created* here. The BV has *possessor* in Gen 14:22 and *made* here. Albright holds that Ugaritic similarities with Proverbs 8 and 9 are striking, and argues for "create" on that basis *(op. cit.,* p. 7). The deeper question is, What function is here ascribed to wisdom? It seems clear that she is pictured as eternal —having existed even before God created the world. She was not active in creation, but was with God while he created. If wisdom is personified righteousness, then the eternal nature of God is righteous. **The Lord possessed me** simply means, "I was the Lord's." The verbal similarity to John 1:1 has led many to think of an adumbration of Christ. We should compare with Proverbs 8 the teaching of Ecclesiasticus 24, coming from about 180 B.C., and the Wisdom of Solomon 7. Ecclesiasticus is high in his praise of wisdom, but makes her to reside in Israel and equates her with Moses' law. The Wisdom of Solomon also appears to be an extravagant development from the teaching of Proverbs. There seems to be no clear indication that we should find Christ revealed in Proverbs 8. Nor need we be troubled about the translation, *The Lord created me*. Delitzsch remarks, "Wisdom is not God, but is God's; she . . . is not herself the Logos."

23. From everlasting. In several expressions wisdom is said to be eternal: "at the beginning of his way" (v. 22); "when there were no seas" (v. 24); "before the mountains were founded" (v. 25); i.e., before anything was created, there was wisdom. True, wisdom is said to be **brought forth** in this beginning (v. 24). But as this is highly figurative language, there is no reason why verse 22 cannot also, in figurative language, refer to wisdom's creation. It is a poetic declaration of the eternity of wisdom. See Delitzsch for the Nicene interpretations.

24. No depths. Toy makes much of the Hebrews' conception of the world as suggested in 8:24-29. He claims that the Hebrews, like the Babylonians, thought of a subterranean ocean (the **depths**) from which springs arose and in which the **foundations** of the earth were laid. The sky was a solid dome supported on pillars, and rain came through it when the "windows of heaven" were opened (Gen 7:11). All this is an imaginary construction by modern authors who take literally the poetic expressions of various passages and, putting them together, build a crude cosmology which the Bible does not teach. Toy argues that the Hebrews believed rain came through these windows when they were opened. He forgets that windows in an ancient Hebrew house did not close as ours do but were mere slits in the walls. To open a window in a house likely meant to cut out a window. Also, the "windows of heaven" could let down barley and flour (II Kgs 7:2) or other blessings (Mal 3:10). It is obviously a figurative expression which Toy has forced into a crude literalism. Also the assertion that the Hebrews thought of subterranean waters is quite incorrect. The word here used for "depths," *tᵉhôm*, is many times used simply of the sea where Jonah sank (Jon 2:5), or where ships are tossed (Ps 107:26). Also the "waters under the earth," of the second commandment, can not be some unseen subterranean ocean. They are simply the water below shore line. As the Hebrews were forbidden to make images of birds and stars in the sky or animals on land, so they were forbidden to make images of anything in the waters under the earth, i.e., fish living in seas, lakes, and rivers (cf. Deut 4:18). The Bible speaks of no subterranean waters, and the assumed Hebrew cosmology of modern writers is mostly fiction.

27. Set a compass. That is, marked out the circle of the horizon (cf. 26:10; 22:14; Isa 40:22). These verses probably all refer to the circle of the horizon. The use of this phrase should teach us that the other expressions, "the four corners of the earth," the "ends of the earth," were not meant to imply that the earth is square.

30. One brought up. This Hebrew word is used only here and in Jer 52:15. The LXX says: *I was arranging*. The meaning *master workman* (RSV and Berkeley) may be the best. It is based on a tablet found at Taanach which has the root as "wizard," or "craftsman" (W. F. Albright, "A Prince of Taanach in the Fifteenth Century," BASOR, No. 94, (April, 1944), p. 18).

9:1. Wisdom. Here, as in Prov 1:20, the noun is feminine plural, yet used with a feminine singular verb. This usage is well attested from Ugaritic grammar, as Albright has pointed out ("Some Canaanite–Phoenician Sources of Hebrew Wisdom," *Wisdom in Israel and the Ancient Near East*, ed. by M. Noth and D. W. Thomas, p. 9). **Seven pillars.** This has been variously interpreted as a feature of architecture, the liberal arts, seven sacraments, etc. (see Toy). It was even used by T. E. Lawrence as the (irrelevant) title of his book on the Arabian campaign in World War I! Probably it is a round number of perfection, suggesting that Wisdom is fully prepared to satisfy. **2. Mingled her wine.** Just what practice is meant is not clear. The Greeks mingled wine with water in a bowl called a *kratēr*, and the LXX translates, *she has mingled her wine in a bowl*. Revelation 14:10 declares that the wicked will drink the wine of God's wrath unmixed, i.e., undiluted. The apocryphal book II Maccabees 15:39 declares that wine undiluted with water was thought distasteful. The rabbis held that the Passover wine should be diluted with three parts of water (Art. "wine," ISBE; The Mishnah, Berakoth 7:5). Obviously, not all the wine of antiquity was thus diluted or it would all have been nonintoxicating. Wine was also mixed with spices (Isa 5:22). Wisdom's wine is at all events symbolic. **5. Come, eat.** The blessed call often appears as an invitation to a banquet; cf. Isa 55:1; Jn 6:35; Rev 22:17. **Of.** This is a good example of the Ugaritic usage of the preposition *b*, meaning "from" (Story, *op. cit.*, p. 329).

7. A scorner. See notes on 1:22 and 3:34. Here **scorner** parallels "sinner." **8. Reprove not a scorner.** The negative is comparative. It does not treat some men as incorrigible (as Toy), but warns of the rebuff to be expected from a sinner. See 8:10 for another comparative negative. **10. Fear of the Lord.** See comments on 1:7. **The holy.** Better, *the Holy One* (RSV) or *Most Holy* (Berkeley). The noun is plural, but is evidently a plural of majesty (see above, 9:1) and is parallel with **Lord.**

13. Foolish. The feminine abstract form of the noun "fool," which is frequent in Proverbs for the folly of sin (see comments on 8:5). **Clamorous.** See also 7:11, where the word occurs in a similar context. It means "loud," probably with immoral overtones. **18. The dead.** Not the *shades* (RSV) or *ghosts* (BV). The Hebrew word is simply a poetic parallel for the dead. See comments on 2:18. On the whole picture of the harlot, see 7:5-27; 5:3-13, etc. Here the major contrast of wisdom versus sin in the first portion of the book finds its conclusion.

II. Miscellaneous Proverbs of Solomon. 10:1–22:16.

It is our contention that in Proverbs the inspired Word of God is given in a special literary form. Just as David used the vehicle of poetry, so Solomon used the vehicle of Wisdom literature, which teaches largely by contrast. In the first major section (I) the contrast is maintained throughout long passages—e.g., the evil woman is set over against wisdom. In Section II the contrast is expressed in short one-verse units. The great majority of verses in this section have a "but" in the middle of the verse.

The exposition is made more difficult by the isolated nature of these proverbs. There is no immediate context to guide us. Some commentators have concluded that the proverbs follow no plan, but are a motley collection (Greenstone). Toy calls them "detached aphorisms." Delitzsch declares that there is a grouping according to thought, not in a comprehensive plan, but in a "progressive unfolding" that "continuously wells forth." There is a kind of unity in this section, but it comes rather from the language and subject than from the arrangement. A proverb is annunciated, then repeated elsewhere with variations which add to the meaning. The first instance may contrast parts *a* and *b*; the second, *a* and *c*. Even a third may occur, comparing *a* with *d*. Putting all three instances together, we get a fuller definition of the thought expressed in *a*. We would feel it easier if these thoughts were grouped together. The ancients evidently found it more interesting to have these thoughts separated and somewhat concealed. Also, as we have seen, there is a certain unity in the moral vocabulary used. So, many proverbs concern the righteous, the wise, the upright versus the cruel, the foolish, the perverse. Adequate study of one verse may involve concordance study of the whole book—but better, not mere mechanical concordance study so much as a thoughtful musing over the whole outlook of the author. For by repetition, contrast, distinctive vocabulary, and varied consideration of the theme, God, through this author, teaches us that righteousness exalteth anyone, but sin is always a reproach. Again we must insist that this is not a *Poor Richard's Almanac* of pithy, common sense sayings bearing on life's problems; this is a divine collection of sayings pointing out the way of holiness.

A. Contrasting Proverbs. 10:1–15:33.

10:1. The proverbs of Solomon. See Introduction, *Authorship*. **A wise son.** This phrase is used again in 13:1; 15:20. In the latter, 20a is identical with 10:1a. The contrast in 13:1 is with a "scorner" (see comments on 1:22). In 15:20 the contrast is with a "fool" (see notes on 8:5).

2. Treasures of wickedness, i.e., ill-gotten gain. Verse 10:2 b parallels 11:4 b. **3. Soul of the righteous.** Here, as often, **soul** is used for the whole person (cf. Ps 37:3,25). **4. A slack hand.** At first sight, in the English translations, this appears to be merely a recommendation of thrift. But the word **slack** usually means *deceitful*. The difficulty is that its root, *rāmâ*, may mean either "deceive" or "grow loose," though the latter meaning is not well attested. We find the contrast with "diligent" at 12:24 and 12:27. "Slack" is paralleled with "sluggard" in 19:15, which is contrasted with "diligent" in 13:4. "Sluggard" has moral connotations, as we have shown at 6:6. We may therefore conclude that 10:4 means, "The one working with a deceitful hand becomes poor; but the upright hand makes rich." **5. A wise son.** In the English translations this is a proverb opposing laziness. Toy, however, remarks that the verse could as well be reversed—"A wise son gathers in summer," etc. This is the order of the Greek. According to this view, we have here one characteristic of a good man—he is provident—rather than a suggestion that to be provident makes one good!

6. Violence covereth. It is better to turn the phrase around, as do the RSV and the Berkeley. The contrast is better seen in 10:11, where 11 b is identical with 6 b: the mouth of the wicked "conceals violence." **7. The memory of the just is blessed.** This phrase is famous as being used by Jews after mentioning a good man deceased. It is a Hebrew *requiescat in pace,* usually abbreviated to *z s l (zēker saddîq libᵉrākâ).* **8. A prating fool.** The word **fool** ("always morally bad," BDB) and its feminine parallel, "foolishness," are used fifty times in the OT, and forty-one of these occurrences of *'ĕwîl* are in Proverbs. The translation **fool** is misleading in modern English. Some such word as "rascal" would be better. Verse 8 b is repeated in 10 b.

10. Winketh. See comments on 6:13. **11. Violence.** See Verse 6. **12. Love covereth.** Observe the connection between this verse and 17:9; 16:28. In 17:9 the opposite of the man who covers a transgression is the man who magnifies another's fault. Such a man in 16:28 "soweth strife." To stir up strife is the characteristic of hate in 10:12. There are verbal similarities between this passage and 6:14-19, which see. Obviously the meaning here, and in the allusions in I Pet 4:8 and Jas 5:20, is not that if we love others, our love will atone for our sins; but if we truly love others, we will minimize their faults.

14. The fool is near destruction. Jones and Walls nicely remark that **destruction** in this proverb furnishes a catchword for the next verse. Often this happens, and the catchword offers a connection between the proverbs that is totally missed in English. **15. The rich.** This verse alone would be misleading. Neither riches nor poverty is a sacrament in Proverbs. Comparison with 18:11 shows that the rich man *thinks* in his own conceit (or imagination) that his riches are his strength. **19. Multitude of words.** Probably verses 18-21 go together, as 20 and 21 show that it is not loquacity that is condemned, but evil speech.

23. Fool. The remainder of the chapter gives a series of terse contrasts between the wicked and the godly. **Mischief.** Only three places in the AV is *zimmâ* so translated. Elsewhere it is "wickedness," "lewdness," "crime." A rascal thinks sin is fun. **31. Froward.** Here and in verse 32 *perverse* is better.

11:1. A false balance. The same thought is in 16:11. In 20:10 differing weights and measures are called an "abomination to the Lord," and in 20:23 a "false balance" is again condemned. There were various methods of commercial thievery. One was to have a falsely graduated balance. Another was to have shekel weights of varying weight to be used in buying or selling to one's own advantage. These were the "diverse weights." **A just weight.** Hebrew, *a perfect stone.* Stones were used for weights, and it was all too easy to grind them off or chip them down. The law of Moses forbade all such dishonesty (Lev 19:36; Deut 25:15; cf. Ezk 45:10; Amos 8:5, *et al.).* Our governments today have bureaus of weights and measures to maintain standards. In the theocracy of Israel, establishing of such standards fell often to the priests. Therefore we find references to the "shekel of the sanctuary" (Ex 38:26). Weights were especially important, for in the absence of coinage in the early days, silver and gold were weighed for payments. Many shekel weights have been discovered. They average about 11.4 grams for the normal shekel (R. B. Y. Scott, "Weights and Measures of the Bible," BA, XXII (1959), 32-40).

2. Pride. In the Hebrew there is alliteration between **pride,** *zādôn,* and **shame,** *qālôn.* **7. The expectation of the wicked.** Verse 7 a is parallel to 10:28 b. See also 11:23. In Job the term *expectation* (AV, *hope,* Job 14:7) is used of the afterlife (cf. Job 14:7-15). If the wicked man has no hope after death, if his expectation is wrath, whereas the expectation of the righteous is joy, then the author here by faith looks beyond the grave as did Job, David, Daniel, and others.

13. A talebearer. Hebrew, *rākîl,* "slanderer." The statement in 13 a parallels that in 20:19 a, which see. **Concealeth.** See also 10:12, where the same word is used. **14. Multitude of counsellors.** Cf.

24:6 for the same expression. **15. Surety.** See comments on 6:1.

16. A gracious woman. Not in the modern sense of gracious, i.e., cultured and kindly, but literally *a woman of grace*. Possibly verse 16 b is not a mere added statement, but a well-known comparison—"A gracious woman retaineth honor as surely as a ruthless man gets wealth." **17. The merciful man.** Probably a parallel to the "woman of grace" in verse 16. **His soul . . . his flesh**; i.e., himself. There is a reward to goodness. **18. Deceitful . . . reward.** An alliteration, *sheqer* versus *seker*. Such alliterations, catchwords, and repetitions are some of the style features of Proverbs that sometimes explain the order of the material, but are lost in translation. **20. Froward.** *Crooked*. **Upright.** *Perfect, complete* (morally).

22. Jewel of gold. The nose ring often worn by an Oriental woman. How incongruous in the nose of so unclean an animal! But not more so than a woman having beauty without character. **Discretion.** This is doubtless moral perception, as in Ps 119:66. The *good taste* of the Berkeley Version is far too colorless.

24. There is that scattereth. Verses 24-29 may be taken together as treating of liberality—"Give and it shall be given unto you again." This person gives from a heart of blessing (v. 25). The opposite hoards corn—and we may suppose there were many black marketeers in times of siege and famine—and gets a curse for a blessing. The error lies not in *having* riches but in *trusting* in them (v. 2).

25-31. The righteous will flourish (cf. Ps 1:3; 52:7,8; 92:12-14; Jer 17:8). This thought occurs frequently in Proverbs.

30. Tree of life. See comment on 3:18. **Winneth souls.** The idiom is not clear. Literally it is, *the one who takes souls* (persons) *is wise*. Some interpret, "the wise man wins friends" (Berkeley). Fritsch says *take* means "to destroy." The RSV gives an unnecessary conjecture that lawlessness takes many lives (changing *hākām* to *hāmās*). Delitzsch supports the AV, which is satisfactory, though it may include more than fishing for men. **31. The righteous.** The LXX interprets it that the righteous will be punished for their sin; much more the wicked. This is quoted verbatim in I Pet 4:18. However, the Hebrew can also be understood to mean that the righteous will get a blessing, while the wicked will receive judgment. The Syriac agrees with the LXX, and this interpretation can be accepted.

12:4. Virtuous woman. The phrase is used again in 31:10. The word *ḥayil*, when relating to men, especially soldiers, means "strength." Referring to a wife, it designates the womanly virtues, perhaps "nobility." Proverbs 11:16 speaks of a woman of *grace;* 19:14 refers to a *wise* woman. All of these terms in the context of Proverbs speak of a *good* woman under various aspects. **8. Wisdom.** The word *sēkel* is here contrasted with a "perverse" or "twisted" heart. Elsewhere it is contrasted with "deceiving" (13:15), "sinful folly" (16:22; 23:9). Delitzsch, Toy, and others seem quite wrong in calling it only "intelligence." Moral wisdom or goodness surely is intended.

11. Vain persons. This proverb is repeated almost verbatim in 28:19. The RSV, Berkeley, and Delitzsch translate as *vain pursuits*. But the word is not so used elsewhere. In Jud 9:4; 11:3; II Sam 6:20 it refers to vain persons, rascals. The LXX says *vanities*, perhaps referring to idols. **12. Net of evil.** The word **net** is difficult. The LXX omits it. The Syriac translates it, *to do evil*. It can mean *strong tower* (RSV), hardly *booty* (Berkeley). The root is *to hunt*. Possibly the Syriac gives a clue for a helpful reading —"the desire of the wicked is to hunt evil, taking it in an Aramaic form. **18. There is that speaketh.** Several proverbs begin with this special construction, "There is that . . ." Verses 18-23 have to do with evil speech.

28. No death. Not the usual negative for this Hebrew construction, but it is used similarly in 31:4. The LXX and Syriac make 28 b a contrast to 28 a, "the ways of the wicked are unto death," which is adopted by the RSV, Fritsch, Toy, and others. The reading of the AV, the BV, Delitzsch, Greenstone, and others refers the verse to immortality. But the note in Berkeley that there are "few assertions of immortality in the Old Testament" is unfortunate. Many positive references to resurrection and the future life exist in the Psalms and Prophets, though most are debated by 'liberal' scholars. Cf. Job 19:25-27; Ps 16:10; 17:15; Isa 25:8; 26:19; Ezk 37:10; Dan 12:2; and others.

13:1. A wise son. See comments on 10:1. The verb "heareth" is to be supplied in the first half as in the AV, the LXX, and the Syriac. **4. The soul of the**

sluggard. Soul simply means the individual, the sluggard himself. On **sluggard** as a moral term, see notes on 6:6.

8. Ransom . . . are his riches. The thought is that a rich man attacked or kidnapped can ransom himself. Under Hebrew law a man could not buy his freedom from judgment. **The poor heareth not rebuke.** Cf. 1 b, "The scorner heareth not rebuke." To "hear not rebuke" is characteristic of an evil man. Why say it about the poor? The LXX and Syriac follow the Hebrew. The RSV emends drastically. Possibly we should read *rāsh*, "poor," as *rō'sh*, "chief," and make it parallel to verse 8a. The "chief" ("bigshot," as we say) hears no rebuke; he can always buy his way out of a tight spot. **9. The lamp of the wicked.** See also 20:20; 24:20; Job 18:5; 21:17. It was a popular metaphor. **12. Tree of life.** See comment on 3:18.

14. The law of the wise. The preceding verse mentions the "word" and the "commandment." **Law,** therefore, is the meaning here rather than *teaching* (RSV, Berkeley). This verse is like 14:27 with the "law of the wise" replaced by the "fear of the Lord." It is surely purposive that the author thus recurs to a similar thought with variations. **15. Good understanding giveth favour.** Very similar to 3:4. **Ḥēn, favour** and sēkel, **understanding,** are here so clearly moral terms, coming as the result of God's commandments, that it is difficult to see how Delitzsch can call *sēkel* "fine culture." The BV has, *Ideal understanding lends attractiveness.* The RSV speaks of *good sense.* These translations miss the meaning that contrasts goodness with transgression. **16. Prudent man.** Cf. 8:12. A wise man, an opposite to *kesîl*, "knave." **20. Companion of fools shall be destroyed.** A play on words. In the Hebrew, **companion** and **destroyed** are similar words.

24. Spareth his rod. On the rod of correction, see also 19:18; 22:15; 23:13, 14. "Spare the rod and spoil the child," has become a common saying. We should remember, however, that Proverbs does not recommend brutal beatings. Nor is physical chastisement the only instrument of child training mentioned (cf. 22:6). Indeed, instruction in righteousness and in the fear of the Lord is that without which mere whipping will fail.

14:1. Every wise woman. Not quite the same wording as in 9:1, but here and in 14:2 the mention of the one "fearing the Lord" is doubtless a reference to the first section of the book, 1:1–9:18.

5. A false witness. Repeated with interesting variations in 19:5,9 and 21:28. The wording is close to that of the ninth commandment, but not identical with it.

9. Fools . . . mock at sin. The first half of this verse is difficult, largely because **mock** is used as a finite verb only six times in the OT. Its meaning is not clear. Close to 14:9 is 19:28–"An ungodly witness *mocks* at justice" (RSV). It seems that there is equal reason to translate here with the AV, **fools mock at sin. 12. A way which seemeth right.** This verse is repeated verbatim in 16:25. (On these repetitions cf. Introd., *Collections in Proverbs*). In this case, there is a catchword in verse 12, "its end," which ties it to verse 13. **13. Even in laughter.** Rather than understand this verse to show a pessimism not common in Proverbs, the verse can be joined to the preceding, and read–"The end of the way that seems right to a man is sorrowful and heavy."

20. The poor is despised of his neighbor. This verse does not merely state a common truth, much less approve it. The catchword **his neighbor** in verse 21 shows that to despise one's neighbor thus is sin. **24. Their riches.** The Greek, reading one letter differently, has *The crown of the wise is their prudence* (so also the RSV).

27. The fear of the Lord. This goes with verse 26, as the repetition of "the fear of the Lord" shows. Otherwise the verse is a parallel to 13:14. **31. He that honoreth him.** See comments on 19:17, and compare 17:5. **32. Hope in his death.** As it stands, a real witness to hope in eternity. For **in his death** the LXX and Syriac have *bᵉtummô, in his integrity,* reading the *m* and *t* reversed. This is strong witness against the Hebrew text, and it is adopted in the RSV. Toy argues for it because, he says, the author had no hope in a future life. It is dangerous thus to prejudge a question. See comment on 12:28. But the text *in his integrity* has good support.

15:4. Tree of life. See notes on 3:18.

8. The sacrifice of the wicked is an abomination. The phrase, **abomination to the Lord,** ties together verses 8 and 9. A number of verses are thus associated in the Hebrew. Proverbs 15:8 a is repeated in 21:27 a, where it is added that such sacrifice comes from a wicked heart. This verse is quoted in the Zadokite Documents of the age of the Dead Sea literature (see Introd. under *Authorship*). Toy, representing the older 'liberals,' remarks that sacrifices are mentioned in Proverbs only here and in 7:14; 17:1; 21:3,27, and always with disapprobation (but see also 3:9). He sees here a contrast between the prophetic religion, which called for morality, and the priestly emphasis on ritual. He cites the Sermon on the Mount as part of the prophetic movement, which he sees also in Amos 5:22; Isa 1:11; Jer 7:22; I Sam 15:22; and others. Happily, this one-sided reconstruction of Israel's religion, with its perversion of such texts, is no longer fashionable. Of course the prophets opposed idolatrous sacrifices (Jer 7:18; Amos 4:4, 5; and others) and sacrifice offered in disobedience; but they did not oppose true sacrifice. Indeed, Isaiah calls the coming suffering Servant a "sin offering" (Isa 53:10). Unfortunately the newer 'liberalism' of the so-called Swedish school goes off on another tangent: It indeed unites the prophets and priests, but makes them together the devotees of the Babylonian New Year cult.

11. Hell and destruction are before the Lord. Observe how this verse is connected with, "The eyes of the Lord are in every place" (15:3) and "The ways of man are before the eyes of the Lord" (5:21). **Destruction** *(Abaddon)* is paralleled with *Sheol* here and in 27:20 and Job 26:6. It is paralleled with "death" in Job 28:22 and with "grave" in Ps 88:11. Elsewhere it is used only in Job 31:12 and Rev 9:11. Its root means *perish, die* (BDB). Delitzsch falls prey to the common tendency of scholars to interpret *Sheol* and *Abaddon* by the Greek *Tartarus* and *Hades*. This is fallacious, for the Greek and Hebrew conceptions of the afterlife were as different as their deities. These words do not designate the realm of the dead nor place it in a subterranean cavern. They are simply poetic words for the grave, which, of course, is underground. For *Sheol*, see notes on 1:12 and 2:18.

12. Scorner. A sinner. See notes on 1:22. **13. A merry heart.** A happy heart. Similar to 17:22. This is a secular proverb used apparently as a foil for the next one, regarding "an understanding heart," i.e., a heart of integrity (cf. 12:25). **17. A stalled ox.** An ox in his stall, a fattened ox (RSV, Berkeley). Verses 16 to 18 go together as proverbs against anger. Verse 18a parallels 29:22a.

20. A wise son. See comments on 10:1.

24. Hell beneath. For Sheol, see notes on 1:12 and 2:18. The blessing of the good man saves from premature death. Toy takes it that the wise man is preserved from premature descent to the underworld. Delitzsch makes it a contrast between heaven above and Sheol for the ungodly, in a development of the doctrine of the future life. It is simpler to take it as life versus death.

B. Proverbs Largely Parallel. 16:1—22:16.

16:2. Clean in his own eyes. The same thought appears in 14:12 and 16:25. This verse makes it more explicit that the Lord is the true Judge. The same, with variations, occurs in 21:2. **3. Commit thy works.** This wording is very similar to that of Ps 37:5. And Ps 37:1 is distinctly parallel with Prov 24:19.

4. Even the wicked for the day of evil. This verse has been appealed to in support of an extreme Calvinism. Delitzsch comments that "the wickedness of free agents is contemplated in this plan," but he does not take the verse in the sense of a predestination to evil, which careful Calvinists do not hold. Calvin himself, according to Delitzsch, asserted that predestination to evil would be a "horrible dogma." But in the Bible divine sovereignty is taught side by side with free agency. The celebrated verse, "I make peace and create evil" (Isa 45:7), clearly does not mean moral evil, but calamity. **5. Proud in heart.** Note the interconnection of verses against pride: the haughty spirit and pride before destruction (16:18); pride before destruction, and before honor, humility (18:12); before honor, humility (15:33); all pride is an abomination to the Lord (16:5; cf. also 11:20a).

8. A little with righteousness. See 15:16, 17 for similar wording.

10. A divine sentence. Verses 10-15 point out various duties and functions of kings (Greenstone). The passage begins with an interesting verse that must have pleased King James I in 1611! But the word *qesem,* **divine sentence,** is nowhere else used in a good sense! It means basically *divination,* or *oracle* (LXX). *Inspired decisions* (RSV) and *godly* decision (Berkeley) are too grandiose to fit the Hebrew. Delitzsch reminds us that Israel never thought her kings infallible. The proverb of verse 10 means that true judgment is the duty of kings. That duty is specified and limited in 16:12,13. **11. A just weight.** See exegesis of 11:1. **15. His favour.** The word carries on the idea of 16:13, where the king's delight (the same word) is said to be righteous lips.

16. Better . . . than gold. Cf. 8:10, 11. **18. Pride . . . before destruction.** See note on verse 5.

21. Increaseth learning. Verse 21 b is parallel to 23 b in a conscious association. Evidently the Hebrew sages loved this repetition with artistic variation. **22. Wellspring of life.** For 22 a, cf. 10:11; 13:14; 14:27. For 22b, cf. 14:24.

25. A way that seemeth right. Verbatim with 14:12. Cf. 16:2. **28. A whisperer.** Compare 17:9; 18:8 (which is the same as 26:22). On talebearing, see exegesis of 20:19. As 16:28 a shows, a **whisperer** is not merely one who whispers secrets but a "perverse" man (RSV and Berkeley) who "sows discord" (cf. 6:14,19).

31. Crown of glory. The young have strength for their glory (20:29), and the aged have gray hairs. But this verse makes explicit the condition for the glory of the aged—righteousness. **33. The lot is cast.** Greenstone rightly concludes (versus Toy and Delitzsch) that this is not a special sanction of lots to determine matters, much less to determine the divine will. It is merely a declaration that the lot—the most capricious of human acts—is controlled by the all-powerful God.

17:1. A house full of sacrifices. Plenty to eat. A large part of the peace offering was eaten by the worshiper. See notes on 7:14. **2. A son that causeth shame.** See also 19:26; 29:15. A wise servant, i.e., an upright one, will dispossess a wicked son. Toy interprets this in a purely secular way, entitling it, "Cleverness succeeds"!

3. The fining pot. The crucible used in refining. **5. Whoso mocketh the poor.** Compare 14:31 a, which is very similar, and notes on 19:17. **6. The crown of old men.** See notes on 16:31.

8. A gift. Hebrew, *a bribe*. That bribes are effective is here given as common knowledge (cf. 18:16; 21:14). But the author does not stop there; he condemns their use (17:23). **9. Covereth a transgression.** For a truth similar to this, see 10:12. See 16:28 and the exegesis of 20:19 for the truth of 9 b. A good example of the interlocking of distant verses in Proverbs.

12. A bear robbed of her whelps. The same figure is used in Hos 13:8. In Proverbs there are not as many illustrations from nature as we might expect. **13. Evil for good.** Most commentators take this as showing that Proverbs warns merely against ingratitude. But even evil for evil is also condemned (see 20:22; 25:21,22, quoted in Rom 12:20). **18. Becometh surety.** See exegesis of 6:1.

21. The father of a fool. See exegesis of 10:1 and compare 17:25 for this word "fool" (Heb. *nābāl;* hence Nabal, I Sam 25:25). In Proverbs it is found only here and in 17:7; 30:22. It is one of the many synonyms for "fool." As in Ps 14:1, it does not mean mere stupidity. Psalm 14:1 means, "The rascal hath said in his heart, 'There is no God.' " **22. A merry heart.** Note similarity to 15:13. In this verse also there is a catchword, similar to one in the preceding verse.

23. A gift. That is, a bribe (cf. v. 8). **25. A foolish son.** Cf. 17:21 and see notes on 10:1. Verses 21, 25 both use the word *kesîl*, "fool," in their first part, but show artistic variation in the second half. **27. Excellent spirit.** Better, *calm spirit* (Berkeley and Delitzsch). We may question Toy's dictum that 17:27,28 merely teaches the "value of silence." Rather, as Delitzsch shows and the words **understanding** and **fool** *('ewîl*, "rascal") emphasize, the teaching is against angry talk.

18:1. Separated. This verse is somewhat difficult to understand in detail. Hence, it has been given some strained interpretations. Delitzsch takes the first part of the verse as a condemnation of the "schismatic and the sectary," i.e., of dissenting churchmen, in the modern sense of the term. Hillel, also, according to Greenstone, took it to condemn religious separatism. But this interpretation is unnecessary and disagrees with other Scripture. Paul separated himself from the Pharisees (Acts 19:9) in a way that was surely justified. Obviously, this verse has nothing to do with such questions. The **separated** is the one wrongfully separated from God, seeking his own desire, not the Lord's. Such a man is a sinner. **4. Deep waters.** For 4 a, compare 20:5 a. **5. To accept the person of the wicked.** To show partiality in judgment. Cf. 17:15,16; 24:23; 28:21; Deut 1:17; 16:19; *et al.* **8. Talebearer.** Parallel to 26:22. See note on 20:19. **Wounds.** Used only in these verses. Most modern versions say *dainty morsels,* but the evidence for the reading is slight.

11. A high wall. This term is from the same root as for "safe" in verse 10. This proverb offers a contrast to that in

10, which gives the secret of true safety. A rich man is safe only "in his own imagination." The RSV derives its reading from a different root and thus misses the connection with 18:10. Verse 11 a is parallel to 10:15 a. **12. Before destruction.** Note the similarity between 18:12 a and 16:18 a; between 18:12 b and 15:33 b. See notes on 16:5. **20. The fruit of his mouth.** This verse speaks not of food, but of speech, and warns about what Jones and Walls call the "lethal power of the tongue"!

22. A wife. The LXX supplies a *good* wife, which is understood from 12:4 and 31:10, but need not be expressed.

19:1. Better is the poor. Observe that 19:1a is identical with 28:6a. The contrast in 19:1 is with a perverse man, a fool. In 28:6, the contrast is with a perverse rich man. Not riches per se are condemned, but riches with wickedness. **3. Fretteth against the Lord.** The Hebrew verb means *be angry* or *vexed*. Berkeley *resentful* is good. The LXX says *blames God.* **4. Wealth maketh many friends.** Note the similarity to 14:20. Here the thought is elaborated in 19:6,7. See comments on 17:8,23. The fact of the influence of wealth is stated here, but not approved of; elsewhere the evil use of gifts is condemned. **5. A lying witness.** Almost identical with 19:9.

10. Delight. Better *luxury* (as in most versions). **11. Discretion.** The word *sēkel* refers to wisdom, but that moral wisdom which Proverbs commends. *Prudent* (Berkeley) is better than *good sense* (RSV). **Deferreth . . . anger.** The phrase means to restrain anger, be slow to anger. The noun in Ex 34:6 is "longsuffering."

13. The contentions of a wife. Such proverbs on the contentious woman sometimes evoke humor. The verses of similar wording are 21:19; 25:24; and 27:15. The AV gives the impression that the continual drip of a leaky roof is like a nagging woman. But the Hebrew word for **contentions** does not mean nagging. The sin objected to is clearly anger. The same root is used for "discord" (cf. 6:14, 19). Much is said against anger in men. These verses protest against the same vice in women. **14. Prudent.** Same root as "delight" in 19:10. **15. Slothfulness.** See notes on 6:6.

17. He that hath pity upon the poor. He that is charitable. Proverbs 14:31 a is similar. Charity for the poor is earnestly enjoined in Hebrew law (Deut 15:7 ff.). Many verses in Proverbs recommend this liberality (21:13; 22:9,16; 28:3,8,27; 29:7). The usurer, on the other hand, is condemned because he oppresses the poor (cf. on 6:1).

18. Chasten thy son. See comments on 13:24; 23:13,14. The word **his crying** is derived from the root *hāmâ,* to "murmur," "roar." The word can also be read as from the root *mût,* "to kill." Toy translates, *Set not thy heart on his destruction,* and is followed by Greenstone, the RSV, Berkeley, and others. Delitzsch is similar. The Hebrew literally is *unto his crying* (or *his death) do not lift up thy soul.* The AV translation still seems closer than the others to the Hebrew wording and context. But as the parallel in 23:14 speaks of chastisement as saving the child from death, so perhaps, in compressed expression, this proverb means the same: "Don't avoid chastening and [thus] bring on his death."

24. A slothful man. The proverb of 24 a is repeated in 26:15 in a series dealing with sloth. **26. A son that causeth shame.** See notes on 10:1, and compare 29:15, which repeats this phrase. **27. Instruction that causeth to err.** The words **that causeth** are not in the Hebrew, and Proverbs does not use this word *instruction* of false teaching. Therefore the RSV and the Berkeley correctly take the proverb to mean hearing instruction "only to stray" from it.

20:1. Wine is a mocker. See the commentary on 3:10 on wine. **Strong drink.** Hebrew, *shēkār.* The exact meaning is uncertain. It was not strong drink in our sense of the word; for before distillation was invented by the Arabs, no drink was stronger than about 7-10 per cent. It was intoxicating, as the Scriptural context frequently shows. Toy and Berkeley (footnote) suggest that it may have been a drink fermented from fruit juices. The writer of the article on "drink" in ISBE argues that *shēkār* is the term comprehending all such beverages, including wine. This is argued from Num 28:7,14. The term may at least have included beer. We know that beer was made and used in Palestine, for pottery used for straining beer has been found. No word in Hebrew appears to refer to beer specifically. Wine was forbidden to ministering priests (Lev 10:9) and Nazarites (Num 6:3). It was used as a drink offering, but this was not drunk. "Libation offering" would be more accurate. The word for **mocker** is *lēṣ,* "scorner." As Delitzsch says, the wine is condemned with its effects. We may notice that the condemnation is rather severe. **Deceived thereby.** The word usually means "err" or "lead astray." The BDB argues that it means also "reel" in drunkenness. However, the only evidence for that is Isa 28:7, where the word is used in reference to "erring" through wine and also "erring" in vision. It should not be limited to getting drunk, as Berkeley implies. The passage concerns *any* use of wine, because of its final effects. The LXX says, *But every fool is entangled with them.* See comments on 23:29 ff.

2. The fear of a king. On kings, see 16:10 ff. and 20:8.

4. By reason of the cold. The word does not mean "cold" so much as "fall" or "winter." He does not plow in plowing season. Cf. 10:5. Diligence is a virtue. Note the apostolic rule in II Thess 3:10. **5. Deep water.** Compare the similar verse, 18:4. **6. His own goodness.** The word *ḥesed* means "goodness," "kindness" (BDB), not "loyalty" (RSV). The BV here and the RSV often elsewhere have "steadfast love," which is more curious and strange than wrong. The word includes love, but the steadfastness found in some contexts is due to the steadfastness of the God who loves.

8. A king. See 20:2.

10. Divers weights. Diverse, differing weights. See notes on 11:1. **13. Love not sleep.** On industry, see 6:9-11. **16. Surety.** This verse is identical with 27:13. On sureties, see notes on 6:1.

19. A talebearer. Hebrew, *rākîl*. Proverbs 20:19 a parallels 11:13 a. Proverbs 20:19 b explains the meaning: "Do not go with one of deceiving lips" (read "deceive," not "flatter," for the Hebrew *pātâ*). *Rākîl* elsewhere is translated *slander*. Leviticus 19:16 condemns it. But a **talebearer** is not what children call a "tattletale." Another word, *nirgān,* is used in 16:28; 18:8 (which parallels 26:22); 26:20. Here, too, the emphasis is not on tattling, but on spreading slander and discord. **20. Curseth his father.** A capital offense (Ex 21:17; Lev 20:9). Varying degrees of cursing and filial rebellion were recognized. Doubtless capital punishment was exacted only in extreme cases. But the divine attitude toward the offense is given here and in 30:11 (note context). **Obscure darkness.** The word means *pupil of the eye,* as a symbol for blackness or for the middle of the night. **22. Recompense evil.** The principle set forth here is reinforced in 25:21,22, quoted in Rom 12:20. **23. Divers weights.** Compare verse 10 and see notes on 11:1.

24. Man's goings are of the Lord. The first part of 20:24 is identical with the first part of the more famous verse, Ps 37:23. As Ps 37:1 is also echoed in Prov 24:19, we need not hesitate to call these proverbs quotations (note other quotations in 30:5,6). **26. Scattereth the wicked.** Note the similarity to 20:8 b. Literally, *winnows* the wicked. **Bringeth the wheel over them.** The word **wheel** is often used elsewhere, but its use in punishment is unknown. It may be figurative here. Just as a man winnows grain and brings the threshing wheel over it, so a king punishes evil. **29. The grey head.** See exegesis of 16:31. **30. The blueness of a wound.** Better, *blows of bruising,* i.e., that bruise. These cure a man of evil. **Stripes . . . the inward parts.** It is not that stripes reach the inward parts (Berkeley). Rather, the stripes, like the blows, cleanse the inner man (same phrase as in 27 b).

21:2. Right in his own eyes. Almost identical with 16:2. **3. More acceptable . . . than sacrifice.** The thought is that of I Sam 15:22, but the wording varies somewhat. On sacrifices, see Prov 15:8.

9. Brawling woman. Parallel to 25:24. Actually, anger is the sin condemned. **A wide house.** Apparently a storehouse or granary according to Ugaritic evidence (Story, *op. cit.*, p. 325). **10. The wicked.** There is a play on words. In Hebrew, "wicked" and "neighbor" sound alike. **12. Wisely considereth.** A verse difficult in detail. The AV supplies "God" as subject of the second half. The BV makes the second half passive. Neither treatment is fully justified by the text. Perhaps it would help to divide the verse differently: "The righteous act wisely at home; wickedness overthrows the wicked in ruin." This involves adding a vowel for "wickedness."

13. The cry of the poor. See exegesis of 19:17. **14. A reward in the bosom.** A bribe. See notes on 17:8. **16. The congregation of the dead.** The word is *repā'îm,* "shades," according to Toy (also Berkeley, n.). The idea is certainly not that the wicked "find rest" (Berkeley), but that they "dwell" or "lie down" (Delitzsch). The phrase, *assembly of the dead,* says nothing of the state of existence of their souls. It refers merely to their lying in the grave. See exegesis of 2:18.

18. A ransom for the righteous. An unusual thought and unusual use of **ran-**

som. The LXX has *offscouring,* evidently interpreting the verse to mean that the wicked are but refuse in contrast to the righteous. The general sense of the verse is that the bad and not the good suffer judgment (Toy). In Isa 43:3,4 the word is used of God's judgment on Egypt in order to deliver Israel.

19. A contentious . . . woman. See comments on 19:13. **27. The sacrifice of the wicked.** Verse 27 a is parallel with 15:8 a, which see. **28. A false witness.** Parallel to 19:9 b.

22:1. A good name. Not just reputation in our sense of good name, but good character. **3. A prudent man.** This verse is identical with 27:12. **4. By humility.** That is, the consequence of humility and the fear of the Lord. Cf. the triad in 21:21.

5. The froward. The crooked, perverse. **6. Train up a child.** Not a common word for "educate," but the meaning is clear and the promise a rich one.

7. The rich ruleth over the poor. With 22:1,2 in mind, we see that this clause states a fact, but does not approve of it. Possibly the verse is another warning against borrowing with usury: "As surely as the rich rule over the poor, so the borrower is servant . . ." See exegesis of 6:1, on usury. **8. The rod of his anger shall fail.** The LXX here adds a couplet, "God blesses a cheerful and liberal man, but the folly of his works he shall punish." Possibly II Cor 9:7 alludes to the first half of this verse, but of that we cannot be sure. We need not suppose a different Hebrew text, though that would not be impossible.

14. Strange women. The parallel verse, 23:27, shows that loose women are meant (so RSV).

15. Folly . . . in the heart of a child. As we have seen, folly is not just "stupid tricks, silly sport" (Delitzsch), for which indeed we should not whip our children. Nor does the verse say they are "morally immature" (Toy). It says they are sinners and need punishment. The current theories that children are not naturally bad, but only maladjusted, and that education should lead them to self-expression, find no support in Proverbs.

16. He that giveth to the rich. Giving bribes or gifts is condemned (see notes on 17:8,23). Oppressing the poor is often condemned in Scripture, but giving to the poor is commended in 28:27.

III. The Words of the Wise, Thirty Sayings. 22:17–24:22.

The previous section, 10:1–22:16, had the heading, "The Proverbs of Solomon." It was composed almost exclusively of two-part verses. The present section is composed of longer units, often four-part stanzas, or "tetrastichs" (e.g., vv. 23,23). It is not accurate to say, with Oesterley and Fritsch, that at 22:17 the LXX has the heading, "The Words of the Wise," for in the Greek, "Words" is in the dative case, whereas in a heading it would be in the nominative case. The LXX translation is a bit free, but is substantially like the Hebrew except that it includes two words of verse 18 in 17. The phrase, "Words of the Wise," found in both Greek and Hebrew, does, however, suitably chracterize this section.

A. Sayings Paralleled in Egyptian Wisdom. 22:17–23:12. The parallels in this section to the *Wisdom of Amen-em-Opet* are taken from ANET and may conveniently be located by reference to the table at the bottom of p. 424 in that work. (For a discussion of these parallels and their significance, see Introd., *Proverbs and Other Wisdom Literature.)*

17. Bow down thine ear. The similarity between this verse and the introduction of the Egyptian composition has been much emphasized. But the expressions, "Give ear," "Listen to the words of wisdom," are quite general and are found elsewhere in Psalms and Proverbs.

18. They shall withal be fitted in thy lips. Oesterley and Fritsch hold that the word *withal,* or *altogether,* does not make sense. They suggest the translation, *peg,* because the Egyptian parallel in *Amen-em-Opet* has an obscure word which may mean that. But the word "peg" hardly fits better than "altogether." There is no good reason for alteration. The LXX has *hama,* "together." **19. Even to thee.** Toy and Oesterley object to these words as redundant. But we must not judge the Hebrew by our ideas of redundancy. Greenstone quotes Prov 23:15 and I Kgs 21:19 for very similar phraseology.

20. Excellent things. Older commentators and BDB struggled with this word, which comes from a root for *three.* It is used elsewhere only in the phrase, *yesterday three days,* meaning "formerly." The slight alteration of the vowels suggested by the Egyptian evidence (see Introd.,

Proverbs and Other Wisdom Literature) to read *thirty* is a happy solution. The word, then, is used to refer to the thirty proverbs following in this section. Toy suggests that the mention of writing in this verse is unusual in Proverbs and points toward a late date. Oesterley, arguing for dependence on the Egyptian writing, concludes the opposite! **21. That thou mightest answer the words of truth.** Oesterley compares this with the Egyptian, "to direct a report to one who has sent him," referring it to the proper delivery of a message. But the following verses are not instructions for messenger boys! Indeed, even the Egyptian is obviously of deeper meaning, for it goes on: "in order to direct him to the ways of life." The Hebrew uses a plural—"to the ones sending thee." The LXX probably has the right meaning: "Answer words of truth to them that question thee" (cf. I Pet 3:15).

23. The Lord will plead their cause. This has no parallel in *Amen-em-Opet*. The Egyptian, after all, gives only common sense dicta of morality. Proverbs absorbs these dicta from many sources and makes them the background of its divine instruction.

24. An angry man . . . a furious man. Literally, an *owner of anger . . . a man of wrath*. In 29:22 the phraseology is similar, but reversed: "A man of anger . . . an owner of wrath." The Egyptian parallel is: "Do not associate to thyself the heated man nor visit him for conversation." Several times *Amen-em-Opet* contrasts the "heated" man with the "silent" man; i.e., the impulsive versus the humbly pious (ANET, p. 422, n. 7). **25. Lest thou learn his ways.** The alleged Egyptian parallel, "Lest a terror carry thee off," is not impressive.

26. That strike hands. No parallel is alleged for 22:26,27. On the dangers of suretyship, see notes on 6:1.

28. Remove not the ancient landmark. The Egyptian says, "Do not carry off the landmark at the boundaries of the arable land . . . nor encroach upon the boundaries of a widow." Removing landmarks meant falsifying the survey and stealing land (cf. Deut 19:14 and 27:17). This verse does not teach veneration for historical markers, but respect of property rights. The Egyptian proverb is similar but peculiarly adapted to the Nile Valley. Some have argued (Toy, pp. viii) that repetition of a proverb argues for two collections, since one author would not repeat himself. However, in this collection of the "thirty" this proverb occurs a second time, but with a variant ending (23:10). Interestingly, *Amen-em-Opet* (in the English) also has a repetition of three lines of text (ANET, p. 422, col. 2; p. 423, col. 2). Since such repetition was apparently purposive, it cannot be used to prove that there were two authors. Cf. Introd., *Collections in Proverbs*.

29. A man diligent in his business. Because the Egyptian says, "The scribe who is experienced in his office, he will find himself worthy to be a courtier," and because the word **diligent** is sometimes associated in the OT with scribes, Oesterley and Fritsch assume that a scribe is meant here. But there is no warrant for this limitation. The Egyptians in *Amen-em-Opet* and elsewhere ("In Praise of Learned Scribes," ANET, pp. 432, 434) glorified the work of scribes as a profession superior to all others. The Hebrew exalts diligence in any work.

23:1. To eat with a ruler. It seems superficial to say, with Fritsch and Oesterley, that this concerns good table manners. Rather, it concerns one's relation to royalty. It enjoins fear and caution before a king. The point is that the king's table is not for mere surfeiting, but for conference. We get a picture of a king's feast accompanied by discussion in the *Letter of Aristeas*, lines 236-274 (R. H. Charles, *The Apocrypha and Pseudepigrapha of the Old Testament*, II, 117, 118), where the Jewish envoys to Ptolemy are tested with questions by the king at table. The parallel from *Amen-em-Opet* reads, "Eat not bread in the presence of a ruler . . . look upon the dish that is before thee." The differences are as great as the similarity. In Proverbs the attitude toward the king (cf. also 25:6,7) is the backdrop for the warning of 23:4,5 against seeking uncertain riches, power, or advancement. **2. Knife to thy throat.** Threaten your appetite with death. **5. Set thine eyes.** Literally, *if you make your eyes fly* after riches, they in turn fly away. The alleged Egyptian parallel refers to riches acquired by robbery.

6. An evil eye. Not an eye of evil enchantment as used in superstition. The LXX already erred in this fashion. The phrase occurs in 28:22, which does not greatly clarify, but Greenstone, Toy, and Delitzsch compare 23:6 with 22:9, where the "good of eye" refers to a bountiful man. So here the RSV is correct, *the* *stingy man*. The Egyptian parallel is only approximate. **Do not desire his dainties.** Repeated from 23:3. It should be cut out from verse 3, say Toy and Oesterley, but there is no warrant for its excision. **8. Lose thy sweet words.** Cf. verse 9. The "fool" will despise the wisdom of thy words. This parallel assists in identify-the "fool" of 23:9 with the stingy man of verses 6,7.

10. The old landmark. See 22:28. Here end the parallels to *Amen-em-Opet*.

B. Sayings with No Parallel in Egyptian. 23:13—24:22. Curiously the alleged parallels with the Egyptian stop suddenly, and the last two-thirds of this section of the "thirty" has but one alleged parallel with the thirty chapters of the Egyptian work.

12. Apply thine heart. A new subdivision of the "thirty" is hinted at by these words (cf. the heading of 22:17).

13. Withhold not correction. On the use of the rod, see exegesis of 13:24. **14. Deliver his soul from hell.** This translation of the AV is too specific. The word **soul** very often means simply the person (cf. Ps 107:9 and many other instances in concordances). The word Sheol may mean and often does mean simply the grave (see Gen 42:38; Isa 14:11; and comment on Prov 1:12; 2:18). The parallel expression of 23:13 is "he shall not die." The verse likely does not mean that beating will save the child's soul (Greenstone), but that it will be spiritually beneficial and save him from untimely death (Delitzsch, Toy). Oesterley makes the very interesting observation that this proverb has a parallel in the sayings of Ahikar. But in form, the saying is more like 23:14 in the Elephantine copy of *Ahikar* than in other copies, which presumably give Babylonian originals. He concludes that the Jews in Egypt modeled their *Ahikar* after this verse in Proverbs. This section of Proverbs therefore goes back farther than the fifth century (cf. Introd., *Proverbs and Other Wisdom Literature)*.

15. My son. A new subsection characterized by longer treatment of topics. **16. My reins.** Literally, *kidneys*. The Hebrew language used the kidneys and liver as psychological terms very much as we use the "heart." The Hebrew "heart" more closely approximates our word "mind."

20. Be not among winebibbers. The word *sābā'* occurs only here and in Deut 21:20; Isa 56:12; Nah 1:10. **Winebibber** is not an exact rendering. The word refers not so much to a man's drinking habitually, as to his drinking strong drink (Isa 56:12). Delitzsch defines as "to drink wine or other intoxicating drinks." **21. Glutton.** There seems to be no justification for this translation. The word is used elsewhere in Deut 21:20; Prov 23:20; 28:7; Lam 1:8,11; Jer 15:19; and a derivative is used in Ps 12:8. In five of these cases eating of food is not even suggested by the context. The basic meaning is to be "light," "worthless." It refers more to the riotous nature of a feast than to overeating (cf. Prov 23:20). Apparently overeating per se is not condemned at all.

26-28. My son, give me thine heart. A solemn call to the attention of the hearer. Cf. Prov 5; 7; 9 for condemnation of adultery.

29. Who hath woe . . . sorrow? This section seems to be not just a condemnation of excessive drinking, but an exhortation to avoid drink because of its final fatal consequences. Cf. commentary on 3:10, where a nonintoxicating drink is mentioned. **30. Tarry long.** One word, actually, derived from the common preposition "after." It means "remain behind." It is used in Ps 127:2 to mean "stay up late" in anxiety. It is used in Isa 5:11 in a passage similar to ours to refer to staying up late at night to drink. What an old and common tragedy! **Mixed wine.** See notes on 9:2. **31. Giveth his colour in the cup.** Emphasis upon the allurements of the drink. Literally, *gives its eye*. RSV, *sparkles*. **Moveth itself aright.** Literally, *goes straight*. RSV, *goes down smoothly*.

32. At the last. Emphatic condemnation. "Look not" (v. 31), because of the eventual consequences. You will not slide downhill if you never start down the grade! How forceful is the comparison to a serpent's venom, and how apt! Does the author appear to imply that a little is all right, but you must not go too far? That is not our attitude toward a serpent's venom. **Stingeth.** The meaning of the Hebrew word is uncertain, but the translation "sting" is not appropriate to a snake's bite. This same word is used of a snake's bite in Ugaritic (Story, *op. cit.*, p. 326).

33. Strange women. Not *strange things,* as in the RSV. The word is used in Prov 2:16; 5:3,20; 7:5; 22:14, always of harlots. We have the tragic accompaniments and consequences of drink—immorality, insensibility, irresponsibility. It is not importing extraneous thoughts to remark that not a word is said here of allowance of moderate drinking. Nor can the words from Prov 31:4-7 be fairly alleged for this. That passage mentions excessive drinking to drug the deeply unfortunate. It probably does not excuse such conduct, but only contrasts the situation of a king with that of a criminal: "Others do this; you can not afford to."

If this is the conclusion of Proverbs, how much more careful should we be in our day. The wine and strong drink of Biblical times were more like our light wines and beer. The people had no distillation and so could not make strong liquors. In our day, social drinking much more easily turns into alcoholism. Also, in a mechanized age a single drink can have far worse consequences for others than 23:35 suggests. Why, therefore, should so many cling to a practice that rapidly enslaves and so frequently degrades? Why can not drinking be just as sociable with soft drinks? Or, if the escape provided by alcohol constitutes the value of the social glass, is not the desire to "escape" already the incipient drunkenness against which our author contends? Ecclesiasticus, one of the apocryphal books accepted by Roman Catholics, but not by Protestants, has a differing treatment denouncing drunkenness, but expressly allowing moderate drinking (Ecclesiasticus 31:25-30).

24:1-3. Through wisdom is an house builded. In this portion and the verses following, the thoughts are similar to some in the first section, 1:1–9:18. This may indicate some dependence (cf. 9:1). **5. A wise man is strong.** The LXX, Syriac, and Targum say *is better than a strong man,* which is smoother (RSV reading is similar). **7. Too high for a fool.** In 24:7-9 folly and sin appear again as the standard proverbial contrast to wisdom.

10. Thy strength is small. This involves a play on the words *ṣārâ,* "adversity," and *ṣar,* "small," "compressed." **12. Doth not he know.** Probably this verse joins with the preceding and exposes the flimsy excuses of mortals. The verses insist that we are our brother's keepers. **Shall not he render.** The thought resembles that of Ps 62:12, but the wording is not identical. It reappears in Mt 16:27.

13. My son. Another subsection of this division of the "thirty." **14. Thy expectation.** Cf. 23:18.

17. When thine enemy falleth. The same thought as in 17:5. Oesterley and Fritsch object to the last thought of 24:18 —that if we rejoice not, the Lord will continue to punish our enemies; otherwise he will spare them! Toy, Delitzsch, and Greenstone do not take so strict a view. A similarly strict treatment of Rom 12:20 (quoted from Prov 25:21,22) would have us feed our enemies in order to condemn them more severely! Rather, these expressions give results in such matters, not purposes. **19. Fret not thyself.** This verse is identical with Ps 37:1 except for the last word. For other quotations, see 30:5.

IV. The Words of the Wise, Appendix. 24:23-34.

The main reason for calling this a separate section is that with 24:22, the "thirty sayings" come to an end. Toy and Delitzsch, who wrote before the section of the "thirty" was suggested, speak of this section as an appendix or supplement to that portion, as indeed it probably is. The material is not greatly different. The LXX inserts 30:1-14 before this section.

23. Respect of persons. Cf. 18:5.

26. Kiss his lips. Fritsch, Oesterley, and others remark that kissing the lips is not elsewhere mentioned in the OT. Toy thought the custom came from the Persians. Another argument from silence! It is definitely mentioned in Ugaritic (C. H. Gordon, *Ugaritic Literature,* p. 60).

29. As he hath done to me. This is really a statement of the golden rule (Lk 6:31). It is finely expressed here, but also elsewhere (20:22; 17:13; 25:21, 22). This high ethical principle is not opposed to the Mosaic legislation of an "eye for [an] eye" (Ex 21:24; Lev 24:20; Deut 19:21). This particular Mosaic law was for judges, and it required that the penalty fit the crime. It was probably not intended to be executed literally, and we have no cases of its literal application in the OT. It was and is a principle of justice. Christ (in Mt 5:38) did not contradict this principle of OT law, but did object to the Pharisaic interpretation which allowed a vengeful attitude (see the author's *Inspiration and Canonicity of the Bible,* pp. 50-52). There are parallels to this 24:29 in the Babylonian *Counsels of Wisdom* (ANET, p. 427). After all, it is not the ethics of Christianity that is unique—God has given all men consciences. The ethics of Christianity is the highest, but the unique element is redemption.

30-34. The field of the slothful. See comment on 6:6-11. The last verses of the two sections are practically identical.

V. Proverbs of Solomon, Edited by Hezekiah's Men. 25:1–29:27.

The LXX inserts 30:15–31:9 before this section. 1. The meaning of the heading is obscure. It begins like the headings in 1:1; 10:1, except that **these also** reminds us of 24:23. But what did the **men of Hezekiah** do? Collect, or edit, or recopy? The verb "to copy out" means "to be old" or "to remove." Oesterley and Fritsch claim that the meaning "copy out" is very late. True, it is used in post-biblical times, but our evidence regarding literary activity is not full enough to deny it to earlier times as well. Toy says the reference to Hezekiah has no more value than the titles of the Psalms or headings of the prophetical books! We may add, no less value either. Oesterley quotes the Talmudic tradition that Hezekiah edited Proverbs and Ecclesiastes. He explains away the tradition by asserting that it arose because Hezekiah had a prominent scribe, Shebna, at court! (Isa 37:2) Oesterley forgets that other kings—likely all kings—had scribes (II Sam 8:17; I Kgs 4:3) whose duties were apparently military more than literary. They mustered the army. It is safer just to take this heading at its face value. It appears in the LXX and therefore is older, at least, than 200 B.C.

2-7. Honour of kings. A short section on kings. Note in verses 2 and 3 the repetition of the catchwords translated **search out** and **unsearchable.** Also in verses 4 and 5 the secular proverb on refining is tied with moral maxim by the repetition of **take away.** The ideal king is established in righteousness. Fritsch remarks that the reference to kings argues for a pre-Exilic date.

11,12. A word fitly spoken. The figure of speech is difficult to interpret because our vocabulary of Hebrew fruits is not extensive. Delitzsch says **apples of gold** are oranges; Toy says quinces. More important, the **word fitly spoken** of verse 11 is equal to the **wise reprover** of verse 12. **13. As the cold of snow.** Another beautiful comparison. But it does not mean a snowfall in harvest (Mar.–Sept.), which did not happen and would have been disastrous. It refers to a cool drink from the snowy mountains or a cooling trip to them.

15. Breaketh the bone. Softness accomplishes hard things if you have patience.

16,17. From thy neighbor's house. Verse 16 serves as a backdrop to 17. The two verses are tied together by the verbs **be filled** and **be weary,** which in Hebrew are the same. **18. False witness.** The words of 18 a quote the ninth commandment. For other quotations, see 30:5.

20. Vinegar upon nitre. The chemistry is simple and interesting. **Nitre** is the old English for "soda," which was collected from the alkali lakes of Egypt. It was called "natron" in Egyptian. The reaction causes carbon dioxide gas to bubble up violently. The simile does not emphasize "cheering," as Oesterley says, but rather violence. The RSV follows the LXX "wound," but likely the LXX misunderstood the chemistry. The RSV footnote strangely says, "Heb. *lye.*" This would fit neither the chemistry nor the vocabulary. Egyptian natron was a prominent source of soda until Napoleon, noting its value in his Egyptian campaign, offered a prize for its industrial synthesis. **21,22. Thine enemy.** See notes on 24:17. Quoted in Rom 12:20 in the LXX form, which closely follows the Hebrew.

24. Brawling woman. Parallel to 21:9. A woman of discord. See notes on 19:13.

26. Righteous man falling. The Hebrew verb means *to be moved.* Delitzsch, Oesterley, and Fritsch rightly take it to refer to moral defection.

27. To search their own glory. The verse is hard to understand, though the words as they stand are not difficult. Most writers say the verse is hopelessly corrupt and makes no sense (Fritsch, Oesterley, and Toy). It is about as logical to say that there is an idiom concealed in the compressed expression which escapes us. Greenstone follows the AV. Delitzsch changes some vowels to get, *to search difficult things is honour.* **28. No rule over his own spirit.** Very similar to 16:32.

26:1. A fool. Verses 1-12 constitute a subsection on the subject of fools. See exegesis of 10:8. Moral folly is intended. **4,5. Answer not a fool.** A famous case of apparent contradiction, not real. The balance is due to the artistic contrast of proverbs, not to a mistake. In one sense you should answer a rascal; in another sense, not. These verses caused some early Jewish rabbis to question the canonicity of Proverbs! More sober minds saw through the difficulty. **7. Not equal.** Better, *hang down, be useless.* **8. A sling.** Not the usual word for "sling." Perhaps:

"like one who puts stones in a heap."

10. The great God that formed all. All commentaries admit the difficulty of this verse. The LXX departs widely. "God" is not in the Hebrew. **Formed** can have several meanings, among which a common one is "pierce." **The great** is read *archer* by the RSV, which is possible, but *arrow* is equally possible (cf. Job 16:13). A possibility is, "An arrow pierces all; so is one who rewards a fool and a transgressor." **11. As a dog returneth to his vomit.** Quoted in II Pet 2:22. **12. A man wise in his own eyes.** This attitude of pride is repeatedly denominated sin (3:7; 26:5,16; 28:11). It is even possible that this is a climax line after the whole discussion of a fool; i.e., a man of pride is worse.

13-16. The slothful man. See comments on 6:6. **15. Hideth his hand.** Practically identical with 19:24.

17. Meddleth with strife. The Hebrew text has *'ōbēr mit'abbēr*, "passing by and vexing oneself." The AV, following the Syriac and Vulgate, reads as if the word were *mit'ārēb*. Likely Delitzsch is right in making the "passing by" refer to the dog (so also Oesterley). "Like one taking a passing dog by the ears" is one who vexes himself in another's lawsuit.

22. Talebearer. This verse is like 18:8. See comments on 20:19. **23. Silver dross.** A new word for pottery glaze found in the Ugaritic literature explains this verse. The two words "silver dross," *kesep sigim* should be one word, "like glaze," with the consonants *kspsg* (cf. H. L. Ginsberg, "The North Canaanite Myth of Anath and Aqhat," BASOR, No. 98 (April, 1945), p. 21, and W. F. Albright, "A New Hebrew Word for Glaze in Proverbs 26:23," *ibid.*, pp. 24,25). **24. He that hateth.** Repeated in 26:26 as a catchword expanding the thought.

27:1. Boast not thyself of tomorrow. A common, but solemn, thought. Oesterley gives a parallel from the *Wisdom of Amen-em-Opet* differing somewhat from the quotation in ANET, p. 423 (ch. XIX. 12.13). The general parallel may be allowed, however. **2. Let another man praise thee. Praise** is the same Hebrew word as "boast" in verse 1.

12. The simple. The verse is parallel to 22:3. **13. Take his garment.** Parallel to 20:16. **14. Blessing his friend.** Most writers say this insincere, overly loud blessing is a curse. Possibly also we have here a contrary use of "bless," meaning "curse" (see the lexicons). A morning curse will come home at night!

15. A continual dropping. Very similar to 19:13. **16. Hideth the wind.** The thought is of something impossible. Better, *Whoso treasures her, treasures up wind,* i.e., she is worthless. Toy and Oesterley declare the last of the verse impossible. The Delitzsch reading seems all right, *oil meets his right hand,* i.e., he grasps nothing.

17. Iron sharpeneth iron. The significance of this proverb is well known in education. But it illustrates the fact that the similes chosen in Proverbs may be obscure. **19. As in water.** Probably this refers to reflections in water.

20. Hell and destruction. Hebrew *Sheol* and *Abaddon*. On Sheol, see 1:12; 2:18. Sheol often means merely the grave, here called insatiable. **21. Fining pot.** Refining pot. **22. Bray a fool.** Pound him as when pounding grain in a mortar to grind it.

28:1. The wicked. Though there is no heading here, most writers understand a new subsection. The proverbs in chapters 28; 29 remind us of those in the second section (10:1–22:16), with their frequent contrasts of good and evil.

2. Many are the princes. Their reigns are brief and troubled. **4. Forsake the law.** Toy is right in pointing out that the words imply a codified law, like the law of Moses. He concludes that therefore the verse is late. We could as well argue that the Law is early! **Contend.** They oppose the wicked. Oesterley remarks that "forsaking the law" concords best with the Greek period. As if God's people at other periods were always faithful! **8. Usury.** See notes on 6:1. **9. His prayer shall be abomination.** Because insincere (cf. 20:4).

13. Whoso confesseth. Oesterley argues that this is a late usage of the word (though it occurs in David's psalm of penitence, 32). Toy and Fritsch observe that here forgiveness depends not on sacrifice, but on ethics. This is a good case of arguing from silence. Psalm 32 also omits mention of sacrifice. But David's other psalm of penitence, 51, does enjoin sacrifice in verses 16-19. These verses are cut off by W. R. Taylor (IB, *ad loc.)* as a later appendix. The fact is that God requires both contrition and sacrifice. **14. Mischief.** Trouble, *calamity* (RSV).

17. That doeth violence. Toy, Oesterley, and Fritsch declare the Hebrew impossible. But Greenstone relates the verse to homicide. The root *'shq* appears in

Syriac, and clearly means "accuse." A man accused of the blood of a person shall flee unto the pit (or grave). Let them not support him. The verb *'āshaq* is perhaps chosen to contrast with *'āqash* of verse 18.

21. Respect of persons. Cf. 18:5 for similar references. **22. An evil eye.** Cf. 23:6. **23. Afterward.** Literally, *after me.* Toy, Oesterley, and Fritsch urge its deletion. A simple change of vowel would make it read easily, "A man rebuking another."

25. A proud heart. A similar phrase occurs in 21:4. **26. Trusteth in his own heart.** A conscious contrast to verse 25, "one trusting in the Lord." **28. When the wicked rise.** Parallel to 28:12, with slight variations.

29:4. He that receiveth gifts. The word **gifts** usually refers to the heave offering of the Temple. But it clearly refers to taxes in Ezk 45:13,16; so here it should be taken as taxes that are too heavy, or gifts that are in effect bribes. It is not the usual word for "bribes." **5. A man that flatters.** Cf. 26:28; 28:23. **8. Into a snare.** Better, *Set a city aflame* (so RSV).

10. The just seek his soul. The usage of **seek** does not seem to admit of "seek to help." Therefore, Oesterley and Fritsch call the second line impossible. Delitzsch and Greenstone solve it satisfactorily by making the "they" refer to the wicked—*they attempt the life of the upright.* **11. Uttereth all his mind.** Not so much **mind** as *anger* (so Delitzsch, Oesterley, RSV).

15. Bringeth his mother to shame. Note the parallel in 19:26.

16. When the wicked are multiplied. Multiplied is the same word as is translated "authority" in verse 2, but it is here applied to the wicked. Oesterley remarks, "See note on verse 2, where the same slight corruption of the text occurs." We would rather say, "See verse 2, where Oesterley again slightly forces the text!" It is not logical to assume the same corruption in two verses without good reason.

18. Where there is no vision. This famous verse has often been misquoted because the word **vision** has taken on new meaning since A.D. 1611. The Hebrew (and originally the AV) means "where there is no prophetic vision, the people perish." The RSV is right, *Where there is no prophecy.* The proverb does not refer to the need for high idealism, as it is often taken to do. There is no warrant for Fritsch's comment here and at 13:13 that the Prophets of the OT were already canonized and the Writings were not. (The author's *Inspiration and Canonicity of the Bible*, pp. 138-148, gives the evidence on the canonization of the Writings.) **Perish.** Better, *cast off* restraint (ASV).

22. An angry man. Similar wording in 15:18; 22:24.

24. Bewrayeth. An old English word for "betray," "divulge." Cf. Lev 5:1, which requires confession from partners in guilt.

25,26. The fear of man and of rulers is overcome by the fear of God (cf. 18:10).

VI. Final Appendices. 30:1–31:31.

A. The Words of Agur. 30:1-33. The LXX divides these last chapters into four parts: 30:1-9 is located after 24:22; 30:10-33 and 31:1-9 are found after 24:34; 31:10-31 is at the end of the book. The reference to Agur is difficult to understand. Of Agur, Jakeh, Ithiel, and Ucal (v.1), we know nothing. Furthermore, the time and location of the author are equally obscure. In view of the difficulties of the text, Toy and Oesterley call it hopelessly corrupt. Agur and the other proper names do not occur in the LXX, which begins: "My son, reverence my words, and receive them and repent. Thus saith the man to them that believe in God, and I cease." In this version, the Hebrew words sometimes translated Ithiel and Ucal are probably rendered as common nouns or verbs. The Syriac translates the name Ucal as *prevail* and renders Ithiel only once. The vowels of our present Hebrew text were inserted in late times and apparently served to confuse this section. The original consonants, however, seem to have been very close to what is represented both in the LXX and the Syriac, and in our modern Hebrew.

1. There is no reason to emend the first verse to read — **The words of Agur the son of Jakeh, the oracle which the man saith.** The names **Ithiel** and **Ucal** present more of a problem. The most unusual explanation suggested is that given by Charles C. Torrey ("Proverbs, Chapter 30," JBL, LXXIII (1954), 93-96). He argues that these words are not names but an Aramaic phrase. The letters as they stand in the original, with slightly different vowels, can be translated, "I am not God." They then form

a contrast to verse 2, "For I am more brutish than a man." In favor of Torrey's suggestion is the well-known fact that in 31:2 the Aramaic word for "son" is used three times.

4. What is his name, and what is his son's name? The speaker seeks the answer to the riddle of the universe in words reminiscent of God's challenge to Job in Job 38:4-9. He seeks for God. The question about God's **son** is peculiar. Greenstone denies that the name applies to Israel or Moses or the Logos, but gives no positive suggestion to explain it. Delitzsch suggests that it refers to the mediator in creation, revealed at last as God's Son. He well remarks, "He would not have ventured this question if he did not suppose that God was not a unity who was without manifoldness in Himself."

5. Every word of God is tried. This verse is quoted verbatim from Ps 18:30, substituting the Aramaic form of **God** for "Lord." The idea is that the answer to his search is in God's Word. Cf. other quotations from the OT in 1:16; 3:11; 20:24; 24:19; 25:18; 30:5. **6. Add thou not.** From Deut 4:2. Oesterley and Fritsch are right in calling this a reference to Scripture. Oesterley, however, says much that cannot be supported about the third division of the OT not being complete until Christian times. The Dead Sea scrolls show the OT canon to have been complete in the second century B.C. at least. See exegesis of 29:18.

7-33. Numerical proverbs (cf. Introd., *Proverbs and Other Wisdom Literature*). In these sequences of three things, yea, four, it is probably the climactic fourth that is emphasized. It is the author's contention that in the Beatitudes, also, there is this climactic teaching in the two sets of four blessings: Mt 5:3-6; 7-10; see also Lk 6:20-23,24-26. Jesus' teaching in the Jewish proverbial and climactic method emphasizes the fourth item.

8. Feed me with food convenient for me. The Hebrew is, *appointed for me*.

10. Do not accuse. *Calumniate* (Delitzsch). This proverb is the only one in this section standing alone, says Oesterley. Toy thinks it out of place. But likely, as in 6:14-19, the numerical proverb begins with a thought that is reiterated in the concluding statement. "Do not slander a servant," says verse 10. The climactic item mentioned in verse 14 speaks of one with "teeth as knives."

15. The horseleech. This proverb has occasioned much comment because of the obscurity of the point. Toy and Oesterley conclude that the text is corrupt. Delitzsch repeats in the middle of verse 15 the reference to the grave and barren womb from 16. The LXX assigns three daughters to the leech. Our trouble is in seeking too much. For the numerical proverb, all that is required is a backdrop to set off the climax. Verse 7 refers to two things; cf. notes on verse 17. The two insatiate daughters of the leech in verse 15 simply form a background for the 3 and 4 of 15 and 16. The sage could count!

17. Mocketh at his father. An isolated verse, out of place, say Oesterley and Fritsch. As noted above, it is part of a regular sequence—2 plus 3, yea 4. Mocking the father and despising the mother are the backdrop to the **three** and **four** of verses 18-20.

19. The way of a man with a maid. This **maid** is the famous word *'almâ*, "maiden," used in Isa 7:14; Gen 24:43 (of Rebecca); Ex 2:8 (of Miriam); Ps 68:25; and Song 1:3; 6:8 (where the "virgins" are distinguished from queens and concubines). The word nowhere refers to a married woman. In the case of the girl Miriam, it could hardly refer to a marriageable girl. It means a virgin and a young virgin. The root means "conceal." Probably the word refers to a maiden still kept in her father's house. Toy, Oesterley, Fritsch, and Greenstone take the point of our verse to be not the marvels of courtship, but the mysteries of procreation. But Delitzsch points out that there are other words—"male and female," or "man and wife"—to express this. Here the words are literally, *strong man* and *maiden*. Delitzsch takes the proverb as a reference to sin, immorality concealed. However, the "virgin" seems to be contrasted with the adulteress of verse 20. And adultery as it is repeatedly pictured in Proverbs is never represented as **wonderful** or "past knowledge." There seems to be no good reason why the more romantic view cannot still be held: Wonderful is the way of courtship, issuing at last in the mysteries of love and life begotten.

21-31. Three sets of proverbs on authority and kingship. The point of the first two is not clear, yet each of the three has some reference to the king. Perhaps the first two especially set off the last one.

23. An handmaid that is heir. An upside down situation, like a servant's being king. **25. The ants.** See comment on 6:6-8. **26. The conies.** Not rabbits, which do not live in the rocks, but apparently cliff badgers, peculiar little animals, distantly related to the rhinoceros (ISBE, article, "coney"). Conies are classed as unclean in the Mosaic law (Lev 11:5; Deut 14:7), because they chew the cud. Some have objected that conies are not ruminants and only seem to chew the cud. The description in Leviticus, however, is probably not intended to be a scientific description of ruminants, but only a classification based on the easily observed chewing habits of these cliff badgers. The Hebrew may mean no more than that. **27. Locusts.** Not the cicada or seventeen-year locust, but a type of grasshopper. **28. Spider.** Opinions differ regarding the translation of this word, but Delitzsch gives good argument for the meaning "lizard"—a small animal which you can take in your hands (RSV), and which invades king's palaces.

31. Greyhound. The meaning of the Hebrew word is uncertain. The RSV says *strutting cock*, but Delitzsch's arguments for **greyhound** are reasonable. **Rising up.** The Hebrew word is unknown. The LXX *speaking publicly before his nation* is as good a reading as we can get.

B. The Words of Lemuel. 31:1-9. The LXX omits the name of Lemuel in 1 and 4. The Syriac renders it Muel.

1. Prophecy. This is the word for a prophetic oracle. But it could be the name of a place (RSV, *Lemuel, king of Massa)*. It is difficult to account for the absence of the article with "king," but there are no articles in this section, perhaps because of Aramaic influence. It seems easiest to translate the first part as a title: "The words of King Lemuel, a prophecy, the words which his mother taught him."

2. What, my son? Three times the word "son" is used in the Aramaic form *bar*, as in Ps 2:12. **3. Kings.** Again, an Aramaic form. **4. It is not for kings.** The choice of the negative is peculiar, as in 12:28. The LXX follows a different text, but the Hebrew seems preferable. Delitzsch suggests the translation, "Let it not be . . . ." It is the more difficult reading, and, as is generally agreed, the harder reading is usually preferred.

6. Give strong drink. As mentioned at 23:31, this is not an allowance of moderate drinking, as Fritsch suggests, nor cynical advice (Oesterley). It may recommend alcohol as a drug (Toy). Delitzsch mentions the wine offered at executions by the noble women at Jerusalem on the basis of this verse (cf. Mk 15:23). More likely, however, the verse is a comparative negative (cf. 8:10): Regardless of others, you should not take it. Wine, women, and song are the old debasing trio. A king has a higher responsibility, for which see verses 8,9.

C. Alphabetical Poem on the Virtuous Woman. 31:10-31. The alphabet in this piece is regular, as in Lamentations 1 and Psalm 119. (Lamentations 2; 3; 4 have the letters *Ayin* and *Pe* reversed. Some of the alphabetical psalms have minor irregularities). Since an alphabet was discovered in Ugarit dating from the fifteenth century, alphabetical pieces need no longer be thought of as late.

10. A virtuous woman. Literally, *a noble wife*. The same phrase as in 12:4. Fritsch remarks on the high status of women shown in 12:4; 18:22; 19:14; and other places.

15. Meat to her household. The Hebrew words for **food** and **portion** are unusual, but used in a very similar sense in 30:8. **16. She considereth a field.** Oesterley remarks that this is exaggeration, since "these things were wholly outside a woman's sphere." Can we really be so sure? Do we not tend to judge ancient Israel by modern Arabia? **18. Candle.** The oil lamp of ancient times. Does this refer to a custom of burning lamps all night? The meaning is, she has plenty of oil. Contrast Mt 25:8.

19. Spindle . . . distaff. The RSV reverses these. The word for "spindle" is used only here. "Distaff" in one other case seems to mean "staff." The Hebrew women had no spinning wheel, but rotated doughnut-shaped weights on sticks to form thread. This was their **spindle.** The word now is found in Ugaritic as a woman's instrument, but the context adds little of detail (Story, *op. cit.*, p. 329). **21. Scarlet.** The LXX says *double*, using different vowels. This would fit well because of the mention of cold, but the change is not necessary. The word means good clothing.

26. Wisdom. Her virtues are not mere

industry. Wisdom and kindness and nobility are hers—not the characteristics of a sluggard. These virtues, typical of the Book of Proverbs, are capped by the fact that she "feareth the Lord" (v. 30; cf. 1:7).

The book ends as it begins, with that wisdom which is the fear of the Lord.

BIBLIOGRAPHY

Delitzsch, Franz. *The Proverbs of Solomon.* Grand Rapids: William B. Eerdmans Publishing Company, reprinted, 1950.

Driver, S. R. *Introduction to the Literature of the Old Testament,* 4th ed. New York: Scribners, 1893.

Fritsch, Charles T. "The Book of Proverbs, Introduction and Exegesis," *Interpreter's Bible.* Vol. IV. New York and Nashville: Abingdon, 1955.

Gordon, Cyrus H. *Ugaritic Handbook.* Rome: Pontifical Biblical Institute, 1947.

_______. *Ugaritic Literature.* Rome: Pontifical Biblical Institute, 1949.

Greenstone, Julius H. *Proverbs with Commentary.* Philadelphia: Jewish Publication Society of America, 1950.

Harris, R. Laird. *Inspiration and the Canonicity of the Bible.* Grand Rapids: Zondervan Publishing House, 1957.

Jones, W. A. Rees and Walls, Andrew F. "The Proverbs," *The New Bible Commentary.* Edited by F. Davidson, A. M. Stibbs, and E. F. Kevan. London: Inter-Varsity Press, 1953.

Noth, M. and Thomas, D. W. (eds.). *Wisdom in Israel and the Ancient Near East.* Leiden: Brill, 1955.

Oesterley, W. O. E. *The Book of Proverbs.* New York: Dutton, 1929.

_______. *The Wisdom of Egypt and the Old Testament.* London: Society for the Promotion of Christian Knowledge, 1927.

Pfeiffer, Robert H. *Introduction to the Old Testament.* New York: Harper & Brothers, 1948.

Pritchard, James B. (ed.). *Ancient Near Eastern Texts Relating To the Old Testament.* Princeton, Princeton University Press, 1955.

Story, Cullen I. K. "The Book of Proverbs and Northwest Semitic Literature," *Journal of Biblical Literature,* LXIV (1945), 319-337.

Torrey, Charles C. "Proverbs, Chapter 30," *Journal of Biblical Literature,* LXXIII (1954), 93-96.

Toy, Crawford H. *The Book of Proverbs. (The International Critical Commentary.)* Edinburgh: T. & T. Clark, 1899.

Young, Edward J. *An Introduction to the Old Testament.* Grand Rapids: William B. Eerdmans Publishing Company, 1949.

ECCLESIASTES

INTRODUCTION

Title. The book of Ecclesiastes gets its name from the Greek version, which has the title *ekklēsiastēs,* "assembly." The name in Hebrew is literally *qōhelet*, "one who assembles." This has been taken to mean either (1) "one who collects" wise sayings (cf. 12:9,10), or (2) "one who addresses an assembly," that is, a preacher or speaker, the implication being that one assembles a group for the purpose of addressing it. The general understanding in either case is that it is a technical title to denote an office.

Date and Authorship. Until the nineteenth century it was generally believed that Solomon wrote the book in its entirety. Today most scholars agree that Solomon was not the author, but rather that the work is a product of post-Exilic times. They usually assume, however, that the central figure in the book is Solomon, and that the unknown author used him as a literary device to convey his message. He did not intend to deceive his original readers, and undoubtedly no one was in fact deceived. Lack of certainty concerning authorship does not destroy canonicity of the book.

Purpose. The primary aim of the author is to show from personal experience that all earthly goals and blessings, when pursued as ends in themselves, lead to dissatisfaction and emptiness. The highest good in life lies in reverencing and obeying God, and in enjoying life while one can. Thus the author was a man of faith; he was skeptical only of human wisdom and endeavor.

OUTLINE

I. Introduction. 1:1-3.
   A. The title. 1:1.
   B. The theme. 1:2,3.
II. The theme demonstrated (I). 1:4–2:26.
   A. By human life in general. 1:4-11.
   B. By knowledge. 1:12-18.
   C. By pleasure. 2:1-11.
   D. By the fate of all men. 2:12-17.
   E. By human toil. 2:18-23.
   F. Conclusion: Enjoy life while you can. 2:24-26.
III. The theme demonstrated (II). 3:1–4:16.
   A. By the laws of God. 3:1-15.
   B. By the lack of immortality. 3:16-22.
   C. By evil oppression. 4:1-3.
   D. By work. 4:4-6.
   E. By miserly accumulation of wealth. 4:7-12.
   F. By the transient nature of popularity. 4:13-16.
IV. Words of advice (A). 5:1-7.
V. The theme demonstrated (III). 5:8–6:12.
   A. By wealth that can be enjoyed. 5:8-20.
   B. By wealth that cannot be enjoyed. 6:1-9.
   C. By the fixity of fate. 6:10-12.
VI. Words of advice (B). 7:1–8:9.
   A. Honor is better than luxury. 7:1.
   B. Sobriety is better than levity. 7:2-7.
   C. Cautiousness is better than rashness. 7:8-10.
   D. Wisdom with wealth is better than wisdom alone. 7:11,12.
   E. Resignation is better than indignation. 7:13,14.
   F. Moderation is better than intemperance. 7:15-22.
   G. Men are better than women. 7:23-29.
   H. To compromise is sometimes better than to be right. 8:1-9.

VII. The theme demonstrated (IV). 8:10–9:16.
  A. By the incongruity of life. 8:10-14.
  B. Conclusion: Enjoy life while you can. 8:15–9:16.
VIII. Words of advice (C). 9:17–12:8.
  A. Some lessons on wisdom and folly. 9:17–10:15.
  B. Some lessons on the rule of kings. 10:16-20.
  C. Some lessons on overcautiousness. 11:1-8.
  D. Some lessons on enjoying life. 11:9–12:8.
IX. Epilogue. 12:9-14.
  A. The aim of the preacher. 12:9,10.
  B. A commendation of his teachings. 12:11,12.
  C. The conclusion of the matter. 12:13,14.

COMMENTARY

I. Introduction. 1:1-3.

A. The Title. 1:1. Solomon, although not identified by name, becomes the literary spokesman for the observations and convictions of the author. He is the **king in Jerusalem** who, because of his wealth, wisdom, and worldly concern, has ample opportunity to sample all of life.

B. The Theme. 1:2,3. All of human existence, when lived apart from God, is frustrating and unsatisfactory. All of the pleasures and material things of life, when sought for their own sake, bring nothing but unhappiness and a sense of futility.

2. Vanity of vanities. The word **vanity** means basically "breath" (see Isa 57:13) or "vapor" (see Prov 21:6), like the condensed breath that one breathes on a cold day. It appears to imply here both (1) that which is transitory, and (2) that which is futile. It emphasizes how swiftly earthly things pass away, and how little they offer while one has them (cf. Jas 4:14). This concept is given greater stress by the repeated use of the superlative, **vanity of vanities.** The phrase, **all is vanity,** is literally, *the all is vanity:* that is, the whole thing, the totality of existence is vain. This is to be understood, however, not in reference to the universe, but to all the activities of earthly life, the things "under the sun" of verse 3. The latter context shows this quite clearly. The author is not a complete pessimist; he is merely pessimistic about human existence bringing satisfaction apart from God.

3. What profit hath a man of all his labour. From the root "to remain over," the word **profit** conveys here more the idea of "advantage" than of "gain" (cf. 7:11). If a person looks at life merely in terms of earthly values, there is no discernible advantage to struggle and toil. The author then goes on to prove this by a survey of the various areas of human activity.

II. The Theme Demonstrated (I). 1:4–2:26.

A. By Human Life in General. 1:4-11. Life is an endless and meaningless repetition. Man's labor achieves nothing permanent; only the earth remains forever. The course of human activity is as monotonous and aimless as the processes of nature.

4. One generation passeth away. The Hebrew uses participles here—one generation *is* always *passing* off the scene, and another is always arriving. Man is born merely to be caught up in the tide, and then to pass away. But in contrast, the earth **abideth forever,** a participle again being used to express continuance. Man, who was made from earth, is short-lived and dies, but the material from which he was fashioned continues to remain. This wearisome repetition is also seen in the "sun" (1:5), the "wind" (1:6), and the "streams" (1:7).

8. All things are full of labour. The phrase, **full of labour,** is better translated, *all things are wearisome,* a reference to the fact that **all things** in life are monotonous and futile, that no matter where one looks in nature, he finds the same tiresome, ceaseless round of activity. **Man cannot utter it.** It is impossible to put into words the futility of it all. It never brings real satisfaction to the **eye** or the **ear** of man.

11. There is no remembrance of former things. This gives the reason for the "nothing new" of verse 10, and probably is best translated *former men.* Man is plagued not only by his inability to accomplish anything worth while, but also by the realization that even the memory of his efforts is soon forgotten. This is the complete answer to the question in verse 3, "What profit hath a man?" He gains nothing, not even a memory of his struggle. The world of nature is futile; human activity is also futile.

B. By Knowledge. 1:12-18. The author sought knowledge more than anyone else did, but he found no lasting satisfaction, for the world was still full of problems that could not be solved.

14. Vexation of spirit. The better translation is *striving after wind* or *feeding upon wind*, a reference to the aimlessness and futility of human activity, for one can never lay hold of real satisfaction. **15. What is crooked** (RSV). The writer's quest forced upon him the realization that life is full of paradoxes and anomalies that cannot be solved; and, contrariwise, it is empty of so much that could give it meaning and value.

17. To know wisdom. He sought to determine the standard for what was wise and what was foolish, not merely to see both sides of the question. **18. Increaseth sorrow.** Not only does the search for life's meaning prove frustrating and its goal unattainable, but it also brings mental and spiritual pain. There does not appear to be any consistent standard for life upon which one may base his conduct.

C. By Pleasure. 2:1-11. His intellectual faculties having failed him, the author turned to pleasure as a possible source of complete satisfaction. He provided himself with wine, women, and song, with luxuries and buildings and gardens. And although these brought him pleasures for the moment, they also brought him no enduring satisfaction, for he was always seeking something new to do.

3. Acquainting mine heart with wisdom. The idea is not that he went about acquiring more wisdom. The phrase is better translated, *my heart (mind) conducting itself in wisdom.* The author did not blindly grasp at life's pleasures, but rather he conducted his search for satisfaction with thoroughness and care.

8. Peculiar treasure of kings. Probably the taxes and art objects obtained from subject peoples and nations. The phrase **peculiar treasure** *(sᵉqullâ)* means basically "property," but is used generally of valuable property. Thus Israel is called God's "peculiar people" (Ex 19:5), a people whom God has specially chosen and values.

10. This was my portion of all my labour. There was a certain amount of gain in the sensuous life, for his heart **found pleasure** (RSV) in all his toil. This was his **portion,** his profit from his satiety. But the gain was short-lived, lasting as long as the pleasure was being taken in hand. **11. Then I looked.** Literally, *Then I turned (to consider).* The author stopped in the midst of his sensuous indulgence to take stock of the results. And he concluded that although a certain amount of good can be gained from pleasure, it yields no permanent gain; it is a **vexation of spirit.**

D. By the Fate of All Men. 2:12-17. The author made a comparison between wisdom and folly, and admitted that wisdom has certain uses in that it keeps one from unnecessary suffering. But the gain is only temporary, for both the wise man and the fool die and are forgotten.

14. Eyes are in his head. The wise man can at least see what lies ahead of him, and can choose the path that will give him the most happiness; while the fool must grope his way, getting his happiness by chance. But the advantage is not for long, for **one fate comes to all** (RSV).

E. By Human Toil. 2:18-23. He was disgusted not only with life, but also with toil, for he saw that it is useless. Someday he must leave all the results of his diligent work to someone who might be careless, or perhaps to one who had done nothing to deserve them.

20. Therefore I went about. Better translated, *I turned about*. The verb is used of the physical action of turning the body. It speaks here of a traveler who turns around to view the road he has walked. The verb in verses 11 and 12 is different; it speaks of mental turning. What he saw when he turned caused him to **despair of all the labour** which he had done, for he felt that the road he had traveled had not been worth the effort and discomfort it required. **21. A man that hath not laboured therein.** Not only might the heir be a fool, but there was the distressing possibility that the wealth for which he had labored so carefully might fall into the hands of one who, never having worked for it, would not prize it highly and would squander it.

F. Conclusion: Enjoy Life While You Can. 2:24-26. Even though life's pleasures are temporary, and do not completely satisfy, at least they are real. Thus the best a man can do under the circumstances is to enjoy the fruit of his labor as long as he can.

24. From the hand of God. The will of God is that man should get his pleasure from eating, drinking, and working. Since it appears to the author that under God's providence this is the highest man can enjoy, the author recommends taking life where one finds it. **25. More than I?** The AV implies the idea, "Who can prove this by experience better than I?" But perhaps the best way to read the verse, in light of context, is with the Greek version, *apart from Him* (that is, God). **26. To a man that is good in his sight.** The author is not giving a moral judgment here, for the word **good** merely means "one whom God takes a fancy to," while the **sinner** is one with whom God is displeased. He is giving another reason for his philosophy of life; there is no discernible consistency to the conduct of God.

III. The Theme Demonstrated (II). 3:1–4:16.

A. By the Laws of God. 3:1-15. All of life, including human activity, is part of a determined cycle. Although man longs for something more, he can do nothing about it. He must be content to get what little happiness he can while engaging in this endless round of events.

1. To every thing. Literally, *for the all,* that is, for the whole thing. Everything in nature and in human life is under a set scheme. There is a **season** (an appointed period) and a **time** (a predetermind occurrence) for all that takes place under the sun. Seeming chance events are all part of a huge plan.

3. A time to kill. The killing that takes place in warfare, in self-defense, in judgment is never accidental. This finds echo in modern parlance in the expression, "It was his time to go." **5. A time to cast away stones.** In light of the rest of the verse, the Jewish interpretation seems best, i.e., that this is a metaphor for the marriage act. **7. A time to rend.** This is a reference to the practice of rending one's clothes as a sign of bereavement (see Gen 37:29; Job 1:20). The **time to sew** is when one's grief has subsided. This would then be parallel with the last part of the verse and would suggest that a **time to keep silence** refers to a time of deep emotion (cf. Lev 10:3).

11. Every thing beautiful. Although the word **beautiful** is generally used in the OT with the sense of physical beauty, it appears that this is an allusion to such a concept as that of Gen 1:31 regarding the "appropriateness" of all creation. **Everything** (lit., *the all*) is exactly as God wants it. The phrase **he hath set the world in their heart** has a variety of interpretations. The AV rendering, **world,** is rather harsh in context, and is opposed to the use of the word elsewhere. The preceding verses seem to require that the word be translated in its normal sense of "eternity." The author is suggesting the contrast between *time* (individual occurrences) and *eternity* (continuousness without discernible limits). God has ordered all of life's occurrences according to his will. He has also given men minds that look beyond daily occurrences to the total sweep of life. Yet the human mind has been limited, so that **no man can find out the work that God maketh;** he can never solve all the seeming paradoxes of life. God has given man reasoning power, but he has not given him enough to unravel all mysteries.

15. God requireth that which is past. Literally, *God seeks that which is pursued.* The idea is that God has ordained the continual circle of events in life, so that each has its predetermined season. The picture is of God continually pursuing the things that have passed in order to capture them and cause them to reoccur.

B. By the Lack of Immortality. 3:16-22. Miscarriage of justice in life should be rectified in some future life, but is not; for at death all men return to dust, just like the animals.

16. The place of judgment. In the courts of law, where one might expect the proper administration of justice, there is, instead, **wickedness** and **iniquity. 17. God shall judge the righteous.** The author suggests one solution to the problem—God will someday right the wrongs which have been committed, **for there is a time** which he has appointed for all things. **18. God might manifest them.** Here the author contradicts himself, offering another solution to the difficulty. God is merely demonstrating to men that, despite their intelligence, they do not differ in value from animals. The word **manifest** is often translated "test" or "prove"; that is, men are being subjected to the disciplines of life **that they might see that they themselves are beasts.**

21. Who knoweth the spirit of man that goeth upward. The AV implies a belief on the author's part in some sort of immortality. But the text is perhaps better read, as with the RSV, *Who knows whether the spirit of man goes upward.* The author has claimed in the previous verse that there is no afterlife where injustice can be rectified. Here he adds that even if there were, one has no proof of it; so the best thing for a man to do is to **enjoy his work** (3:22, RSV) while he can.

C. By Evil Oppression. 4:1-3. Because of so much oppression in life, the only happy men are the dead men. The happiest or most blessed are those who have never been born. This is a transitory mood which the writer somewhat contradicts in 9:4.

D. By Work. 4:4-6. Human toil is futile because (1) although the man who works may achieve something in life, his motive is only envy of his neighbor; yet (2) the man who does not work destroys himself, for he cannot subsist on nothing.

5. Eateth his own flesh. This is a metaphorical expression implying starvation (cf. Amos 4:6). The person who does not work uses up all his substance until he has nothing left but his own person upon which to feed. **6. Handful with quietness.** A man should not go to extremes. Work brings some reward (cf. 2:10,24), but too much work, or a total concern with work, can destroy this good. It is better to have a handful of earnings when they are gained with a restful mind, than to procure large gains by worry and vexing toil.

E. By Miserly Accumulation of Wealth. 4:7-12. Wealth often makes a man a miser, so that he withdraws from the company of others. This then deprives him of one of the few joys that life can offer.

8. There is not a second. This is explained by what follows, namely, that the man has no partner or helper. Since the passage is concerned with avarice, the implication is that this is a miser who toils alone so that he will not have to share the profits with anyone. The author then goes on to list the advantages of association with others—assistance in distress, warmth, protection and security (cf. 4:9-12). **12. A threefold cord.** This probably refers to the advantage of companionship, and means that if fellowship with two is good, then fellowship with three is better still. A cord with three strands will stand greater strain than one with only two.

F. By the Transient Nature of Popularity. 4:13-16. Those who seek popularity as their chief goal will find that it brings no real satisfaction, for it is dependent on the fickleness of the people, and thus is insecure.

13. Better is a poor and a wise child. A hypothetical example of what often happens in the rise of a man from poverty to the throne. A king **who will no more be admonished,** that is, take advice, was better off when he was a poor youth. Then at least he was open to learning. Now old age and years in the public eye have blinded him (the author implies) to his incapabilities and the need for wise counsel. **14. Out of prison he cometh to reign.** Often age and experience teach a man nothing. The king who himself was once poor, who arose **out of prison** to the throne, who caused the downfall of another, did not learn the chief lesson of his struggle—popular favor is uncertain and unpredictable. The rendering **he that is born in his kingdom becometh poor** suggests that the king, through his failure to learn the lessons of popularity, may someday become a pauper in his own kingdom.

IV. Words of Advice (A). 5:1-7.

Here are various words of advice on proper worship. The author recommends caution and brevity in one's prayers (5:1-3) and alacrity in the payment of one's vows (5:4-7).

1. Keep thy foot. Make sure you know what you are doing when you go to **the house of God.** In the phrase **be more ready to hear,** the author is not speaking of coming to the Temple to listen to the exposition of the Law, but rather he is cautioning against approaching the worship of God in the wrong way. The word **hear** often has the sense of "obey" in the OT. The contrast is between those who come to God in obedience, that is, out of a background of ethical and moral conduct (cf. Ps 119:101), and those who are **fools,** that is, those who worship with unrepentant hearts. **2. Be not rash with thy mouth.** The emphasis is on conscientiousness in prayers. The "vain repetitions" (Mt 6:7) of many do not accomplish as much as the few words of those who are sincere. **3. A dream cometh through the multitude of busi-**

ness. The author quotes a proverb in support of his previous point. Just as a night of dreams is the result of too much preoccupation with one's business, so nonsensical speech is the result of too many words at worship.

6. To cause thy flesh to sin. The word **flesh** is used here as a metonym for one's whole self or person; the idea is not to let one's mouth get one's self into trouble with God. The **angel** or "messenger" is not the angel of judgment sent by God, but rather the priest whose duty it was to collect what had been vowed (cf. Mal 2:7). **7. In the multitude of dreams.** This difficult proverb is probably an allusion to verse 3, and the author is summing up his point. Just as too much concern over business brings dreams, so too many words spoken at worship bring rash promises and punishment by God.

V. The Theme Demonstrated (III). 5:8–6:12.

A. By Wealth That Can Be Enjoyed. 5:8-20. Here riches are viewed from three angles. Though God may give a man a certain power to enjoy wealth, yet (1) riches are the cause of much greed and injustice among government officials (5:8,9); (2) the gaining of wealth never brings satisfaction, for the more one gets, the more one wants (5:10-12); and (3) riches are an insecure possession, for a man acquires wealth only to pass it on to others (5:13-17). So in 5:18-20 the author gives his oft repeated counsel: Enjoy life while you can.

8. For he that is higher than the highest regardeth. This is not a statement to the effect that God watches all earthly rulers, and will eventually punish them, but rather it refers to the system of government in those days. Each official watched the one beneath him in order to obtain part of the spoils of taxation and graft. Because of this system one should not **marvel** at the oppression and lack of justice. **9. The profit of the earth is for all.** It appears best to read this with the RSV margin, *the profit of the land is among all of them; a cultivated field has a king.* In other words, not only do all the officials get a share of the extortion, but there is no cultivated area which does not fall under taxation.

13. Riches were kept by their owner to his hurt (RSV). This refers to the loss the man sustains by **evil travail** (v. 14), that is, in a bad business speculation. The vanity of wealth lies in the fact that a man may accumulate a great deal, only to lose it in an unfortunate business enterprise, and thus have nothing to leave his son.

20. God answereth him in the joy of his heart. Better translated with the RSV, *God keeps him occupied with joy in his heart*. There are not many enjoyments in life, but such as there are should be sought for the pleasure they will provide. This will then cause life to pass pleasantly by, for God will allow a man to be absorbed by these things, and forget about the difficulties of life.

B. By Wealth That Cannot Be Enjoyed. 6:1-9. One of life's greatest misfortunes is that a man may have riches and not be able to enjoy them, either because of an early death or perhaps because of a spirit of avarice which will not let him be satisfied.

2. God giveth him not power to eat thereof. The next verse, as well as the phrase, **a stranger eateth it,** shows that the picture is of a man who dies early in life before he has had a chance to enjoy his wealth. No son becomes his heir, but rather some stranger benefits by it all. **3. If a man beget an hundred children.** This is the opposite of the previous case. Even if a man has long life and many children, this is no guarantee of the enjoyment of life. He may be so bound up with avarice or worry that he lacks the capacity to feel satisfied. To make the contrast even greater, the author adds, **and also that he have no burial.** That is, if he were to live forever, and still not be able to enjoy life, it would have been better if he had never lived at all.

9. Better is the sight of the eyes. Satisfaction in the things that life affords is better than **the wandering of the desire,** that is, better than a life that can never find fulfillment in its longings.

C. By the Fixity of Fate. 6:10-12. It is ultimately useless to try to change things, and to wish for more than one has. Submission to the fixed order is best, since God has determined things the way they are. Man is powerless even to argue the issue.

VI. Words of Advice (B). 7:1–8:9.

The author has questioned, in 6:12, the possibility of determining ultimate good. Here he admits that there are certain ways of living which are "better" than others. And so he gives his advice about how to find these.

A. Honor Is Better Than Luxury. 7:1. To have a **good name,** that is, a good reputation (cf. Prov 3:4; 22:1), is better than having the luxury of much fine perfume. An honorable life makes a man's day of death better than his day of birth, for at the end he knows he has made something out of life.

B. Sobriety Is Better Than Levity. 7:2-7. Sympathetic understanding of sorrow and death gives one a proper appreciation of life. When one visits the **house of mourning** (v. 4), he is reminded of the brevity of life and therefore of the need for wise living. The phrase, **by the sadness of the countenance the heart is made better** (v. 3), implies a thoughtful serious mind concerned about the problems of life.

C. Cautiousness Is Better Than Rashness. 7:8-10. It is best to take a quiet second look at the past and present before saying that **the former days were better than these** (v. 10). The years have probably obscured difficulties in the past similar to those of the present. It is best to be slow to **anger** (v. 9), and not to make a rash statement for which one will be sorry. The phrase, **better is the end of a thing than the beginning thereof** (v. 8), suggests the wisdom of cautious speech, since only after one has spoken is he able to determine the full effects of his words.

D. Wisdom with Wealth Is Better Than Wisdom Alone. 7:11,12. The author is quick to acknowledge that wealth can provide a man with good things (cf. Prov 13:8), and when this wealth is combined with wisdom, the man has double means for finding life's few pleasures.

E. Resignation Is Better Than Indignation. 7:13,14. This is a summation of much of the author's philosophy of life. Since our lives are in the iron grip of God, both the **day of prosperity** (v. 14), and the **day of adversity** have been determined by him. Therefore, let a man make the best of whatever life may bring.

F. Moderation Is Better Than Intemperance. 7:15-22. Experience has shown that the righteous do not necessarily live longer and happier lives than the wicked (cf. Ps 1:3,4). Therefore the best way to live is moderately. **Be not righteous over much** (v. 16), for this will not guarantee happiness; and **be not over much wicked** (v. 17), for evil may bring a premature death. Therefore moderation is the answer, for **why should you destroy yourself?** That is, Why should you alienate yourself by extreme conduct from the few good things that life can provide?

G. Men Are Better Than Women. 7:23-29. A good example of the **wickedness of folly** (v. 25) is an evil **woman** (v. 26) who lures men into sin. It is difficult enough to find a good man, but a (good) **woman** is almost impossible to discover (v. 28). Although God **hath made man upright,** men have deviated from this condition in going after **inventions,** that is, purposes or devices (perhaps here, devices of women) which have brought corruption and evil into the world. (v. 29).

H. To Compromise Is Sometimes Better Than To Be Right. 8:1-9. In the service of a king who is often arbitrary and **doeth whatsoever pleaseth him** (v. 3 b), the wise action is not to demand one's way in every matter. When the king commands some unpleasant thing, **be not hasty to go out of his sight** (v. 3 a). That is, do not impulsively turn your back on what he wants. There is a time and a place for everything (v. 6).

VII. The Theme Demonstrated (IV). 8:10–9:16.

A. By the Incongruity of Life. 8:10-14. Although, perhaps, generally the righteous are insured of a happy life, while the wicked are cut off; yet even this has its exceptions, so that one cannot depend on morality as a guide for life.

B. Conclusion: Enjoy Life While You Can. 8:15–9:16. Since God's ultimate purposes are unknowable (8:15-17), since there is no afterlife (9:1-10), and since the length of life is uncertain (9:11-16), the wise course of action is to enjoy oneself here and now.

9:1. No man knoweth either love or hatred. This difficult phrase is best taken as referring to God. No man knows whether or not his righteous deeds will gain the love or the hatred of God (cf.

Mal 1:1-3; Rom 9:13). **5. Neither have they any more a reward.** The man who is alive can gain a **reward,** that is, some profit on earth from his labor, and at least is somebody, while the dead person is not even a **memory.**

10. In Sheol (AV, *in the grave).* The Hebrews of ancient times thought Sheol was a pit deep under the earth where the dead abode (cf. Deut 32:22). It is uniformly depicted as the place to which both righteous and unrighteous went after death, and where there were no punishments or rewards (cf. Eccl 3:19, 20; 6:6). It was a "land of forgetfulness" (Ps 88:12) and darkness (Job 38:17), where men existed as shadowy replicas of their former selves (cf. Isa 14:9,10). Here (Eccl 9:10) is one of the strongest statements in the OT about the nothingness of Sheol.

VIII. Words of Advice (C). 9:17—12:8.

A. Some Lessons on Wisdom and Folly. 9:17—10:15. The author here adds a few groups of maxims about the wise use of words (9:17,18; 10:12-14), about wise conduct (10:2-4, 8-11), and about wisdom in general as compared with folly (10:1,5-7,15).

17. The words of wise men are heard in quiet. The quiet speech of a wise man is heeded more readily than the clamorous chatterings of a loudmouth. This proverb seems to have been added to suggest that what was said in verse 16 is not always true.

10:1. Dead flies. If a fly, one of the scourges of the East, becomes engulfed in perfume and dies, its decaying body ruins all the perfume. So a little folly can degrade much wisdom and honor. It may seem insignificant, but it can destroy all the good that wisdom has accomplished. A man may commit one sin, and this can destroy a lifetime of virtue.

5. As an error which proceedeth from the ruler. One of the evils of life is human misjudgment, which can appoint a fool to a place of authority, and ignore those who should rule.

8. He that diggeth a pit. These proverbs are general observations on the dangers of various activities, and therefore on the need for prudence. **11. The serpent will bite without enchantment.** Success in life comes by knowing when to exercise skill. If a charm is to work, it must be used before the serpent bites, else what good is it to know how to charm? Instead of the AV rendering, a **babbler is no better,** read, in terms of the context—"the charmer (lit., *the lord of the tongue)* has no advantage."

15. The labour of the foolish wearieth every one of them. Literally, *wearieth him,* that is, himself. The fool, although he can talk a lot, labors to exhaustion without ever really accomplishing anything. He is too stupid to see the obvious way to accomplish his purpose. This is the import of the last phrase, **he knoweth not how to go to the city;** that which is plain to most is veiled to the fool. This last has its parallel in, "He does not know enough to come in out of the rain."

B. Some Lessons on the Rule of Kings. 10:16-20. The consequences on the life of a nation when it is ruled by a fool are illustrated by the author. Buildings are ruined and money is squandered. Yet a person, if he is wise, will not give thought or voice to criticism.

16. When thy king is a child. The **child** is one who is influenced by advisers (the implication being, unscrupulous advisers), while the **son of nobles** (v. 17), better translated *free man,* is mature and able to do his own thinking. **18. By much slothfulness the building decayeth.** The reference is to the neglect of national affairs by rulers who **eat in the morning** (v. 16), that is, spend their time in idleness when they ought to be working.

C. Some Lessons on Overcautiousness. 11:1-8. Since the future is always unpredictable, even "the best laid schemes of mice and men gang aft a-gley [go oft astray]." Therefore a man must be willing to take risks if he is to achieve any sort of success. The person who waits until he is certain will wait forever.

1. Cast thy bread upon the waters. There is no certain explanation of this proverb. Traditionally, it has been seen as an exhortation to liberality or charity, which one is to **cast** (lit., *send forth)* before others without any immediate realization of gain, but which will return someday to reward its giver (cf. Lk 16:9). But perhaps the verse is to be read, "Cast your bread upon the waters (strange though this may seem), yet you may find it after many days." Read thus, it refers to the uncertainty of this life, in which even an apparently unwise action may yield reward. **2. Give a portion to seven.** Here is another emphasis on the uncertainty of life's outcomes even when wisdom is used. Translate, "Give a portion to seven, or even to eight (that is, be wise in your investments); yet you do not know what evil may happen on earth."

3. If the clouds be full of rain. This is at the heart of the author's argument, and seems to be part of verses 4-6. It is an argument against overcautiousness, in the light of nature's unpredictability and man's inability to change it. **4. He that observeth the wind.** The ideal time for action is always uncertain, but one must act sometime if work is to be accomplished. If one worries about storms before he sows or reaps, no crops will be grown or gathered.

D. Some Lessons on Enjoying Life. 11:9—12:8. Make the most of youthful days, when the pleasures of life can still be enjoyed, instead of waiting until old age, when vitality is gone. Yet God's way, not debauchery, must be the guide to pleasure.

9. God will bring thee into judgment. The author recommends intelligent pleasure. Satisfy your heart's desires, he says, but remember that God has certain requirements for living, and that he punishes excess and abuse of his will. This thought is continued in verse 10 in the words **remove sorrow** and **put away evil.**

12:1. Remember now thy Creator. Perhaps better translated, *Remember then thy Creator,* for the author seems to be summing up what he has just said. **2. While the sun.** The imagery in this and the following verses has led to a variety of interpretations, but the majority of commentators take the passage as an extension of the author's advice to his readers to enjoy their youth. These verses are probably, then, an allegory on the decay of old age and the approach of death. The figures of the **sun,** the **light,** the **moon,** the **stars,** and the **clouds** depict old age as a storm that gathers and obscures the light and the heavenly bodies, so that there is no warmth or brightness, that is, no enjoyment of life.

3. Keepers of the house. Here the writer likens man's body to a house. The **keepers** are the hands and arms, the **strong men** are the legs that become weak, the **grinders** are the few teeth that have not fallen out, and **those that look out of the windows** are the eyes that have grown dim. **4. The doors shall be shut.** The form of the word **doors,** in the Hebrew, is dual, suggesting therefore "two doors" or "double doors," probably referring to the ears that have grown deaf. The **sound of the grinding** refers to the toothless chewing. An old man's inability to sleep is illustrated by the fact that he rises up at the **voice of the bird.** The **daughters of music** are probably musical notes which are heard with difficulty because of the man's impaired hearing.

5. That which is high. This is probably a reference to the shortness of breath which makes any ascent difficult. The man has **fears . . . in the way** because he cannot trust his frail legs when he must wend his way through the narrow, crowded streets. The **almond tree** is perhaps a picture of grey hair. For although the blossoms of the almond are actually pinkish, when seen from some distance a tree in full blossom has a snowy white appearance. The **grasshopper shall be a burden** is better translated, *shall drag itself along,* a picture of the wizened old man who can scarcely move his stiff limbs and bent back. The phrase **desire shall fail** is literally, *the caper berry shall fail;* this berry was an aphrodisiac which stimulated sexual or physical appetite.

6. The silver cord. The figure represents an expensive gold and silver lamp hung from the ceiling. Its chain is snapped so that it comes crashing to the ground. The oil spills out of the broken bowl, and the light is gone. Light is the symbol of life. The **pitcher** and the **wheel** continue the same idea, but from the symbolism of the drawing of water. The pitcher is broken, and so it can contain no more water, that is, life; the wheel is broken, so that water can no longer be drawn. **7. Then shall the dust return to the earth.** Here sketched in bold relief is the common thought of what happens after death: the body returns to that from which it was made (cf. 3:20; Gen 2:7); and the **spirit,** that is, the breath of life, returns to its source (cf. Gen 2:7; Job 34:14,15; Ps 104:29). Man ceases to exist as man.

IX. Epilogue. 12:9-14.

A. The Aim of the Preacher. 12:9,10. The purpose of his wisdom, says the author, has been to communicate it to others. He has attempted to do this effectively and frankly.

10. To find out acceptable words. Better read with the RSV, *pleasing words*. The author sought to make his teaching interesting so as to gain the attention of his hearers, but he never sacrificed frankness or **truth** in order to keep his audience.

B. A Commendation of His Teachings. 12:11,12. Claiming to have received his teachings by direct revelation from God, the author states that therefore his hearers do not need to go elsewhere for truth.

11. As nails fastened. These teachings are truths to which one can affix his life securely. The **masters of assemblies.** The schools of wise men. By the words **one shepherd** the author seems to indicate not some teacher, such as Solomon, but rather God, who is often called by such a title (cf. Ps 23:1). He implies, thereby, that his teachings are God-given. **12. Of making many books there is no end.** Speaking to the general reader as **my son,** the author warns against useless reading and studying. The reader should concentrate on the author's teachings, for they are divinely inspired.

C. The Conclusion of the Matter. 12:13,14. Taking everything into consideration—the experiences and the mental turmoil through which the author has gone—the highest good in life is a proper reverence of God in all of life.

13. Fear God. The foundation of life is **fear** of God, that is, reverence toward him, a proper acknowledgment of who he is, and what he demands of men in everyday life (cf. Prov 15:33; Isa 11:3). **14. Every work into judgment.** Both man's **work** and his **secret thing,** that is, his thoughts, will be judged by God. The heart attitude is important in God's sight, as well as one's public actions.

In reality the author says nothing more in these last verses than he has been saying throughout the book—enjoy life while you can. This can be accomplished only by fearing God; for God is in control, and he can be expected to reward righteousness and punish evil.

The author of Ecclesiastes has often been called a pessimist, but this is not necessarily so. He longed to know more of the answers to the puzzles of life than he had thus far learned, but God in His providence did not choose to disclose them. Yet the author had discovered that life apart from God is futile. A man attains to the 'good life' by reverencing God. That this writer's 'highest good' was primarily physical happiness should not cloud the issue. He lived on the plane of the physical and sensuous; he did not know the higher things. But he never gave up his faith in God. The preacher learned to live with life's paradoxes, having discovered, as did Job, that life will not wait upon the solution of all its problems.

BIBLIOGRAPHY

Erdman, W. J. *Ecclesiastes: The Book of the Natural Man.* Chicago: Bible Institute Colportage Association, n. d.

Hendry, G. S. "Ecclesiastes," *New Bible Commentary.* Edited by F. Davidson, A. M. Stibbs, and E. F. Kevan. Grand Rapids: Wm. B. Eerdmans Publishing Co., 1953.

Leupold, Herbert C. *Exposition of Ecclesiastes.* Columbus: Wartburg Press, 1952.

Rankin, O. S. "The Book of Ecclesiastes," *The Interpreter's Bible.* Vol. 5. New York: Abingdon Press, 1956.

Reichert, V. E. and A. Cohen. "Ecclesiastes," in *The Five Megilloth.* London: The Soncino Press, 1952.

Williams, A. L. *Ecclesiastes. (Cambridge Bible for Schools and Colleges).* Cambridge: University Press, 1922.

Wright, J. Stafford. "The Interpretation of Ecclesiastes," *Evangelical Quarterly,* XVIII (1946), 18-34.

THE SONG OF SOLOMON

INTRODUCTION

Name, Authorship, and Integrity. This book, belonging to the five *megilloth*, or rolls, was annually read by the Jews on the eighth day of the Passover. The heading Song of Songs (1:1) is the literal translation of the Hebrew *Shîr hash-shîrîm*. The repetition of the noun in the genitive plural is the Hebrew way of bringing out the special character of the Song: it is the best or most excellent of songs (cf. Gen 9:25; Ex 26:33; Eccl 1:2).

Although the first verse of chapter 1 can also be read: "The Song of Songs which is *about* or *concerning* Solomon," the traditional view has been to regard King Solomon as the author of the Song. Since the contents of the book is fully in harmony with the great gifts of wisdom which we know Solomon possessed (I Kgs 4:32,33), there is no sufficient ground to deviate from this historic position.

The unity of the book can hardly be seriously challenged. Similar refrains occur in 2:7; 3:5; 8:4; the imagery is the same throughout the book; and the same characters appear again and again.

Interpretation. As to its literary genre, the Song of Solomon is obviously a poem of love. The difficulty is how to interpret it. The following are some of the varied interpretations that have been advanced.

1. *Allegorical.* This was the interpretation common among the Jews from ancient times, and from them it has passed over into the Christian Church. The Jews regarded the Song as expressing the love relationship between God and his chosen people. The Christian Church saw in it reflected love between Christ and the Church. Essentially this view has been advocated by Hengstenberg and Keil.

2. *The dramatic view.* The essence of this view, as advocated by Franz Delitzsch, is that the Song is a drama representing Solomon as having fallen in love with a rustic girl, the Shulamite, whom he takes to his royal palace in Jerusalem. A particular form of this view, the *shepherd hypothesis,* introduces into the Song a third character, a shepherd, to whom the Shulamite girl remains faithful despite the advances of Solomon.

3. *The typical view.* This view, too, holds that in the Song there is portrayed the great love between Christ and the Church, King Solomon being regarded as a type of Christ, and the bride as representing the Church. This view differs from the allegorical in that it tries to do justice to the actual language of the Song without seeking a special meaning in every phrase, as the allegorical view does.

4. *The natural or literal view.* The basic tenet of this view is that the Song is a poem extolling human love. From that point on, because of the inclusion of this book in the canon of Scripture, adherents of this view may differ widely as to the ultimate significance of this song of love. This commentary is construed on the assumption that the natural view is correct. Taking this approach, the canonical significance of the Song of Songs may be stated as follows.

(a) The book is called the "best of songs," and understandably so. This is a song which Adam could have sung in Paradise when the Lord in His wise providence led Eve to him to be his wife. In frank but pure language the book praises the mutual love between husband and wife, and thereby teaches us not to despise physical beauty and married love as being of a low order. Since these are gifts from the Creator to his creatures (cf. Jas 1:17), they are good and perfect in their place and for their purpose. The book presents a strong warning against an unbiblical dualism which holds the physical and material in lower regard than the spiritual, and which exalts the unmarried state as more virtuous than the state of matrimony.

(b) As the counterpart of *(a)*, the Song instructs us not to glamorize physical beauty and idolize the biological aspect of marriage. Notwithstanding the straightforward manner in which physical beauty and attractiveness are described, the love relationship portrayed in the Song is of a lofty character. Nowhere does the description even border on what might be considered lewd and licentious. Thus the Song holds before us the ideal love relationship in marriage. (For the separa-

tion of the two lovers spoken of, see the commentary). The Apostle Paul uses marriage to illustrate the nature of the love between Christ and His Church (Eph 5), but certainly not every marriage reflects this bond of intimate love. Only a marital relationship as pure as that portrayed in the Song can serve this purpose.

(c) The reading of this book, far from raising sensuous thoughts in our minds, should lead us to praise the Creator who created man in His own image, who made the human body beautiful, who awoke in Adam the longing for a companion like himself yet different, and who led the first bride—the very climax of the works of creation—to her admiring bridegroom. The reading of this book should also make us aware of our sinful failures in our attitude toward members of the other sex in general, and in particular our sins of the flesh within marriage. Thus it is that by this book the Holy Spirit will lead sinners to the Christ who is also the Redeemer and Sanctifier of holy wedlock. Seeing and experiencing the purity and holiness of this earthly bond of love will also lead us to better understanding of that love relationship which is heavenly and eternal, namely, the spotlessly pure and indestructible bond of love that exists between Christ and his Church.

OUTLINE

(The book does not present definitely marked divisions. The following is a suggested outline.)

I. The mutual affection of bride and bridegroom. 1:1—2:7.
II. The bride speaking of her bridegroom. Her first dream about him. 2:8—3:5.
III. The bridal procession. The bride's second dream. Her conversation with the daughters of Jerusalem. 3:6—6:3.
IV. The bridegroom's further praise of his bride's beauty. Her desire for him. 6:4—8:4.
V. Final expressions of mutual love. 8:5—14.

COMMENTARY

I. The Mutual Affection of Bride and Bridegroom. 1:1—2:7.

A. Superscription. The Maiden's Expression of Her Love for Her Lover. 1:1-4.

1. For this verse see the Introduction. **2.** The bride speaks first, eloquently expressing her great love and longing for her lover. **Let him kiss me.** Not the expression of mere sensuous desire. In Scripture the kiss is frequently referred to as an expression of a deep and pure love (Rom 16:16; I Thess 5:26; I Pet 5:14). The bride's use of the pronouns *him* and *his* suggests the spontaneity with which this expression of love bursts from her lips. It is not necessary to resort to the translation *you* and *your* as in the RSV; oscillations in the use of persons occur frequently in Hebrew (cf. Deut 32:13-15; Jer 2:2,3; Hos 4:6; Zech 9:13,14). **Wine** is often associated with joy and gladness (Jud 9:13; Ps 104:15; Prov 31:6; Eccl 10:19). It can also express the spiritual joy that comes from possessing the gifts of the grace of God (Isa 55:1; Joel 3:18; Amos 9:13). But better than wine which gladdens the heart is the love of the bridegroom to the bride. **3. Ointment.** Anointing oil was an indispensable item in the Orient. The hot climate made frequent bathing necessary, after which the skin was treated with sweet-smelling oil (cf. II Chr 28:15; II Sam 14:2; Dan 10:3; Mt 6:17). **Thy name.** Not merely as a badge of identification. The name of a person frequently said something specific about him (Ex 2:10). It could even suggest his entire character (Mt 1:21). The bride is speaking of the splendid character of her bridegroom and the esteem in which he is held everywhere. Because of these outstanding characteristics, the maidens (AV, **virgins**) love him. In her boundless admiration for him, the bride cannot but think of other maidens as likewise having a great affection for her bridegroom. The word for maiden (Hebrew *'almâ)* is used of a girl of marriageable age who is still unmarried (Gen 24:43; Ex 2:8; Isa 7:14 and Mt 1:23; Ps 68:25; Prov 30:19).

4. Already the bride is close to her lover, having been brought **into his chambers,** but she desires to be in his immediate presence. **The king** mentioned here is Solomon. Those who interpret typically see in this and similar expressions a reference to Christ. **Let us** (AV, *we will)* **be glad.** The bride wishes to share her joy with others; the reference is to the maidens mentioned in verse 3. These maidens are not mistaken in their affection for the king; he fully deserves it.

B. The Bride to the Daughters of Jerusalem. 1:5,6.

5. Swarthy am I, but comely. Exposure to the sun has tanned the skin of the bride, but she has not lost her loveliness. Even though she is swarthy **as the tents of Kedar,** she is still comely **as the curtains of Solomon. Kedar** was a son of Ishmael (Gen 25:13). The tents of the nomadic tribe descended from him (Jer 2:10; Ps 120:5) were of black or dark brown goatskin. The hyperbolic reference to these tents emphasizes the darkness of the complexion of the girl. The curtains of Solomon must have been very beautiful; and notwithstanding her dark complexion, the bride is still lovely like them. The allegorical significance of "black (so AV) through sin, but comely through grace" is often suggested. **6. My mother's children were angry with me.** The girl is not to be blamed for her present dark complexion. For a reason not mentioned her brothers became incensed with her and put her to keeping the vineyards. They went so far as not even to let her tend her own vineyard. This harsh treatment, however, has not detracted from her loveliness, and it has not prevented the king's conceiving a special love for her.

C. The Girl to Her Distant Lover, and the Reply. 1:7,8.

7. Tell me . . . where you pasture the flock. Genuine love for the lover brings with it constant longing to be in his immediate presence. The Song brings this out by several times representing the two lovers as separated from each other. The king is pictured as a shepherd; certainly a fitting designation. **Why should I be as a veiled woman . . . ?** It was the custom of harlots to veil themselves (Gen 38:14). True love wishes to avoid every appearance of unfaithfulness and impurity. **8. Follow the footprints of the flock, and pasture thy kids.** It is not stated from whom the answer to the girl's query comes. The thought expressed by the answer is that all the bride has to do is to perform the duties that are hers as the bride of the king. These duties she is to perform near the tents of the shepherds, that is, in the presence of others; and such faithful service will confirm her unsullied reputation.

D. Bridegroom and Bride to Each Other. 1:9-17.

9. I have compared thee . . . to . . . horses. The king speaks. Horses were known for their strength and their beauty, and they were often beautifully ornamented. A fine description of a horse is given in Job 39:19-25. Solomon possessed large numbers of horses and chariots (I Kgs 4:26; 10:26), many of which came from Egypt (I Kgs 10:28,29). The comparison suggests the striking beauty of the bride and her excellent personality traits. **10. How lovely are your cheeks among the jewels.** The description given here is continued with still greater detail in chapter 4. The ornaments accentuate the beauty of the cheeks and neck of the bride. **11. We shall make for thee . . .** The king promises his love new ornaments to enhance her beauty even more (cf. Ezk 16:11).

12. The bride begins to speak. The Hebrew may also be translated *While the king was on his couch . . .* The **spikenard,** or nard, was a fragrant plant of Indian origin from which was extracted an aromatic oil, very precious and highly valued (Mk 14:3-5). The sweet smell of the nard is a symbol of the bride's love. **13,14. Myrrh** was a fragrant substance, prepared from a plant which also originally came from India. It was used for various purposes (cf. Ps 45:8; Prov 7:17; Est 2:12). Hebrew women often wore small bags of myrrh between their breasts. Myrrh was among the gifts the Wise Men offered Jesus (Mt 2:11). **Henna** is a plant with fragrant yellow and white flowers. In Palestine it was found especially in the valley of Engedi, an oasis on the western shore of the Dead Sea. These comparisons suggest how highly the bride regards her lover.

15. Thou art fair, my love. The bridegroom resumes speaking, again praising the exceeding beauty of his bride. Apparently it is the sparkling beauty of the bride's eyes rather than her purity and innocence that reminds the lover of doves, for in this passage it is the physical beauty of the bride which is emphasized. The allegorical interpreter will insist that the bride's beauty is a gift of God's grace.

16. The bride replies, calling him beautiful, as he did her. Then she immediately turns to a description of imaginary surroundings which form the proper background for their great love for each other. Since all other details in the immediate context are figurative, it is not necessary here to think of an actual place in the open air or of a booth of leaves constructed on the flat roof of a house.

E. Dialogue Between Bride and Bridegroom Continued. 2:1-7.

1. I am the rose of Sharon. The bride is still speaking. It is difficult to determine which flower the bride refers to. The only other occurrence of the word in the OT is in Isa 35:1. *Crocus* appears to be the best translation. **Sharon** is the Mediterranean coastal plain between Joppa and Caesarea. In the time of Solomon it was a place of great fertility. **2. As the lily among thistles.** The bridegroom speaks. In her humility the bride may think of herself only as a beautiful but humble crocus; he regards her as a lily among thistles. So far as lilies surpass thistles, so far does she surpass other maidens. **3. As the apple tree.** The bride responds in the same vein. As an apple tree which produces delicious fruit surpasses the other trees of the forest, so does her bridegroom surpass other young men. **4.** The king has brought her, a humble country girl, to a banqueting hall. But she need not fear and be bashful in the presence of the young ladies of Jerusalem, for with his love he is protecting her and putting her at ease. (For the thought of protection, see Ex 17:15.) **5.** Overcome with love and admiration for her lover, the bride asks for raisin cakes (**flagons**) and apples to strengthen her physically.

6. His left hand is under my head. This verse can be translated either as expressing a wish or as stating a fact. Both translations fit the context equally well. The first translation makes this verse another cry from the bride for help. According to the second possible translation, the fact related in this verse is the response of the bridegroom to the request of his bride; or it may indicate how close together the two are in the banqueting hall. **7. I charge you.** No real oath is intended by the girl, since the adjuration is by animals. Why these animals are chosen, we do not know. Perhaps they were thought of as best symbolizing the character of pure love. Putting her request in the form of an oath emphasizes her most urgent pleading not to awaken love prematurely, for love is very tender and easily harmed. At its own proper time it will awaken of itself.

II. The Bride Speaking of Her Bridegroom. Her First Dream about Him. 2:8–3:5.

A. The Bride's Song of Love for the Bridegroom. 2:8-17.

8. The voice of my beloved! In well-chosen imagery the bride speaks of the coming of her beloved. Although this section may well have had a historical background in the life of the king, its purpose is to give expression to the bride's deep love for her bridegroom. The imagery is drawn from nature. Gazelles and young harts climb mountains and leap over hills with ease and grace. **9.** By **the wall** must be meant the wall of the house in which the Shulamite dwells. Before this wall the bridegroom, like a gazelle or young hart that is shy and distrustful of men, stands looking through the window and peering through the lattices. He does not come to his bride rudely or even boldly but as one deeply respecting her.

10,11. Winter past . . . rain . . . gone. He calls her to go with him. Here the symbolism of the gazelle and hart is dropped and the imagery of the seasons is introduced. The latter suggests that bride and bridegroom have reached the proper state of maturity for the fruition of their mutual love (contrast v. 7). **12-14.** The picture of the arrival of this time of spring is made more vivid by the enumeration of changes that take place in nature at this season. The urgency of the call of the bridegroom to his bride to join him is evident from the repetition of the words of verse 10: **Arise, my love, . . . , and come away.** She had called him a gazelle and a young hart; he now calls her **my dove,** a term of endearment. The bride reproduces here the words of her bridegroom.

15. These are the bride's own words. **The foxes.** Likely the annoyances and cares that may interfere with and damage their love. Their love is fully blossoming, and nothing should be allowed to disturb it. **16,17. My beloved is mine, and I am his.** The bride is confident that she and her bridegroom belong together. She pictures him here as a shepherd who during the day is feeding his flock and is thus away from her. In the language of spiritual devotion, these words have frequently been applied to the relationship between Christ and his beloved people. **Among the lilies** suggests that the bridegroom carries on his daily duties in surroundings that are in keeping with his character and dignity. **Until the day break.** Or, *until the day cools.* Literally, *until the day breathes,* i.e., until the evening breezes come. The reference is to the end of the day, when the heat, often scorching, is displaced by invigorating coolness. Evening is also the time when the shadows, which exist only when there is sunlight, are disappearing. Verse 17 is the final response, in this section, of the bride to her lover. Throughout the section both are giving expression to their yearning desire for each other. **Mountains of Bether** (AV). Or, possibly, *craggy mountains.* The Hebrew verb may come from a root meaning "to cut in pieces" (cf. Gen 15:10; Jer 34:19). If this etymology is accepted, the words may be translated "craggy" mountains or "mountains of separation," that is, *mountains that separate us* (Berkeley Version).

B. The Bride's Dream of Her Lover. 3:1-5.

1. By night . . . I sought him. The section beginning with this verse records a dream of the bride. True love is not blanked out during sleep but may manifest itself in dreams about the beloved. In the dream related here—a consequence of the bride's constant preoccupation with her lover during waking hours – she seeks him everywhere but cannot find him. **2. In the broad ways I will seek him.** The bride dreams that she arises and goes about the city in search of her bridegroom. **3. The watchmen that go about.** A detail of the dream. The words **to whom I said** (AV) are not found in the Masoretic Text. In a dream, scenes shift quickly; hence the seeming abruptness of the question.

4. I found him. The scene shifts again. No answer from the watchmen is recorded; in a dream such is not necessary. The dream of the girl and her longing for her lover culminate in her finding him and bringing him home to her mother's own room. This chamber, which speaks of intimacy, must have been almost sacred to the young woman. Her leading him to it suggests the tenderness of her affection for him. **5. Stir not up . . . my love, till he please.** Love can be a mighty force in the lives of men and women. Unanswered and unsatisfied it can cause untold pain and great grief to the human heart. But love requited gives unspeakable joy. The Shulamite in her dream experiences both in some degree – both love unsatisfied and love fulfilled. Hence this refrain (cf. 2:7) is not an anticlimax to the reunion of the two lovers in the dream. Rather, it indicates recognition of the fact that because these are the effects which love can have, it must be handled with the utmost care and should not be aroused before its proper time.

III. The Bridal Procession. The Bride's Second Dream. Her Conversation with the Daughters of Jerusalem. 3:6–6:3.

A. The Bridal Procession. 3:6-11.

6. What is this. The section beginning here speaks of the bridal procession (see verse 11). The word **desert** (AV *wilderness*) may mean no more here than the open country as distinct from inhabited villages and cities. The **pillars** (or *columns*) **of smoke** indicate that during the procession much fragrant incense is burned, marking the route of the procession. **Myrrh and frankincense, with all the** [fragrant] **powders of the merchant** (AV). These lend additional dignity and importance to what is seen coming up from the desert.

7. Behold his litter. The arrival of the bridal procession is introduced in the form of a question; this verse gives the answer. In keeping with the royal dignity of the king, his litter is surrounded by strong soldiers from among the best men of Israel. **8. Expert in war.** These are all experienced soldiers, capable of protecting the king and his bride from any dangers to which they may be exposed, especially the dangers of the night. **9,10. A chariot.** Or *a bed,* or *a throne.* A more detailed description of the litter or palanquin which Solomon made for himself. The whole gives the impression of magnificent royal splendor and dignity. **The midst thereof being paved . . .** Possibly, *its interior made from gifts of love.* The daughters of Jerusalem, it seems, provided the material for the interior of the royal palanquin, to show their love for their king. **11. Behold king Solomon with the crown.** The bride is not separately mentioned in this verse; but from the fact that Solomon is wearing the crown given him by his mother, it may be inferred that she is sitting beside him on the royal couch. Because Solomon had many wives (I Kgs 11:3), it is impossible for us to say whether or not what is recorded in this section refers to one specific event in the life of the king. This passage does, however, speak of a wedding day and of the great joy which such a day brings to the bridal couple, a gladness which is witnessed and shared by others.

B. The Bridegroom's Praise of His Bride's Beauty. 4:1-15.

Chapter 4 is a song praising the exquisite beauty of the bride, in imagery best understood and appreciated by the Oriental mind. **1.** For **eyes** as **doves,** see on 1:15. **Mount Gilead,** a mountain range east of the Jordan River, was very well suited for animal husbandry (cf. Num 32:1). Goats, which are often of dark color, trailing down the slopes of the mountain, suggests the dark waves of the girl's beautiful hair. **2.** In recognition of the custom of washing sheep before shearing, some commentators prefer to read this verse: *Your teeth are like a flock of sheep ready for the shearing.* It seems better, however, to translate, *your teeth are like a flock of shorn sheep which have come up from the washing,* because the comparison is intended to bring out the whiteness of the teeth. None of the bride's teeth are missing, as the next comparison indicates. **3. Scarlet** is a bright, rich crimson, obtained from an insect called *kirmiz* by the Arabs *(Westminster Dictionary of the Bible).* The bride's temples can be said to be like a sliced pomegranate, because the inside of this fruit is filled with numerous *ruby-colored* seeds. **4. Like the tower of David.** This tower, though no longer known to us, was apparently well known in those days. The exact rendering of the words translated in the AV **builded for an armory** remains a question. The translation, *built with terraces,* which seems the most plausible, goes back to the Vulgate. The **armoury** (AV), or *terraces,* upon which **there hang . . . shields** (cf. Ezk 27:11) may well suggest jewels worn by the bride, which accentuate the beauty of her neck. **5. Like two young roes.** The breasts of the bride are youthfully tender like fawns of a gazelle. Feeding **among the lilies** suggests the well-formed body of the bride from which the breasts arise.

6. I will get me to the mountain. This verse in which the bridegroom digresses from describing the beauty of the bride is difficult to explain. Some commentators hold that the **mountain of myrrh** and the **hill of frankincense** are symbols for the physical attractions of the girl. A better approach seems to be to read here Solomon's intention to gather these precious aromas with which, in the evening, he will go to his beloved. For **Until the day break,** see 2:17. **7. No spot.** Without blemish. This sums up the beauty and attractiveness of the girl.

8. This verse expresses the great longing of the king for his bride. The words, **from Lebanon,** perhaps indicate that because of his great longing for her, she seems far away and inaccessible. **Amana** is one of the streams that flow eastward from the top of the Lebanon mountains (cf. II Kgs 5:12). **Mount Hermon,** called *Senir* (**Shenir,** AV) by the Amorites (cf. Deut 3:9), is the highest peak of the Lebanon. **9.** To the king the beauty of the bride is irresistible. The designation *my sister* expresses how unspeakably dear she is to him. **10.** Compare 1:3,4. **11.** The fragrance of Lebanon, coming from the cedars and other plants that grew there in abundance, may well have been proverbial (cf. Hos 14:6,7). **12. A garden inclosed.** Since the bride belongs exclusively to Solomon, she resembles a garden that is locked and inaccessible to all but the owner. Also wells and fountains were sometimes sealed to preserve the water, a far from plenteous commodity in the Orient, and to keep it away from others. **13,14. An orchard . . . with pleasant fruits.** The figure of the garden is continued. To the king, the Shulamite, whom he may call his own, is like a garden yielding its owner the choicest fruits. **15. A garden fountain.** As verses 13 and 14 elaborate on the first part of 12, so this verse elaborates on the second part of that verse. To the king his bride is like fountains and streams yielding an abundance of fresh and pure water.

C. The Response of the Bride. 4:16.

The bride calls upon both north wind and south wind to blow upon her, that the wonderful fragrance which the bridegroom has ascribed to her may stream forth from her as from a park full of excellent fruits. Since she herself is this garden, or orchard, she here calls her lover to herself to enjoy the fruits to which he is entitled.

D. The Bridegroom's Reply to His Bride, and a Call to the Two Lovers. 5:1.

1a. Heeding the bride's invitation, the king is now saying that he comes and enjoys the excellent fruits of his garden, his bride. The reunion of the two lovers, so deeply in love with each other, is again in view here. **1b.** It is best not to understand these words as part of the preceding paragraph. Someone (possibly more than one), we do not know who, is speaking here and exhorting the two lovers to delight fully in each other's presence. This call forms the fitting climax to the bridegroom's description of the exquisite beauty of his bride.

E. The Bride's Dream of Longing for Her Bridegroom. 5:2-7.

2. The first statement here suggests that what is about to be related occurred in a dream. The contents of this dream must be understood as forming the introduction to the expressions of love and the description of the appearance of the bridegroom in 5:8-16. In 5:2 the poet is skillfully representing the bridegroom as coming to his bride after having gone a long way through the night, as is evident from the **dew** with which his hair is wet. **3. I have put off my coat.** The bride's excuse for failing to open to her beloved. In the East, whether one walked barefooted or wore sandals, the feet always became soiled so that they required frequent washing. **4. By the hole of the door** (AV). Not *put his hand to the latch* (RSV; Berkeley). In events occurring in a dream one must not press for exactness in detail. Through some sort of hole the bridegroom puts his hand, likely in order to open the door.

Seeing this, the bride is greatly thrilled, and (cf. v. 5) overcoming her reluctance, rises to open the door. Touching the handles of the bar, her fingers and hands drip with the myrrh which the bridegroom has poured on it. **6. My soul had fainted** (AV, *failed)* **when he spoke** gives an additional reason for her failure to open the door immediately; hearing his voice has overwhelmed her. **7.** Instead of finding her beloved, she meets with misfortune. As in the previous dream (ch. 3), so now again she meets with the watchmen. But this time, likely thinking her to be an evil woman prowling the streets at night, they beat her and take away her mantle. Then the dream breaks off.

F. Dialogue Between the Bride and the Daughters of Jerusalem. 5:8–6:3. The dream preceding this section introduces a separation between the two lovers. This separation now becomes the basis for renewed declarations of love and devotedness to the loved partner.

8. Tell him, that I am sick with love. This time it is the bride who gives expression to her deep feeling of love for her bridegroom. Not having been able, in her dream, to find her beloved, she now urgently appeals to the daughters of Jerusalem, if they find him, to tell him of her great love (cf. 2:7; 3:5). **9. What is thy beloved more than another.** This urgent appeal prompts these girls to ask what is 'so special' about her beloved. Their question affords the bride opportunity to describe the striking appearance of the bridegroom. **10. Chiefest among ten thousand.** His appearance is such that among ten thousand he is easily distinguished. **11.** The **head like pure** (AV, *most fine)* **gold** illustrates the nobility that radiates from his head and face. **12.** For **eyes as doves** see on 1:15. The sparkling beauty of the dove is particularly brought out when it sits beside brooks of water. Bathing in milk refers to the white in the eyes. **13. As sweet flowers** (AV). Literally, *towers of herbs.* The RSV, with a slight change in the Hebrew original, translates: *yielding fragrance.* However, **towers** should be allowed to stand, since it refers to the fullness of the cheeks. **14-16. His hands . . . his mouth.** The bride moves on to describe other features of her lover's body, every one of which she finds exceedingly beautiful. Finally, to the girls in Jerusalem she calls out: **Such is my beloved, and such is my friend.**

6:1. In 5:8 the bride urges the girls in Jerusalem to tell her beloved of her great love for him in case they should find him. Now these girls ask, **Whither is thy beloved gone?** This question comes also as a direct sequence to the dream of the bride in which she fails to find her beloved. **2. Down into his garden.** But the bride needs the other maidens no longer. Her bridegroom has gone to his garden. In the light of 4:12-15 and 5:1, where each lover calls the other a garden, it does not seem farfetched to read in this verse that the bridegroom has now returned to her. **3.** Cf. 2:16.

IV. The Bridegroom's Further Praise of His Bride's Beauty. Her Desire for Him. 6:4–8:4.

A. The Lover's Praise of His Beloved. 6:4-10.

4. The city of **Tirzah,** located northeast of the city of Samaria, was the first capital of the northern kingdom till the time of Omri (I Kgs 14:17; 15:21,33; 16:8,15,23,24). If Solomon is regarded as the author of the Song of Songs, he cannot, of course, have known Tirzah as a capital city. It appears that the city must have been a very beautiful one, which would account for its mention here. **Terrible as an army with banners.** Though modern Western minds find it difficult to appreciate this illustration, it indicates the irresistible beauty of the bride. **5. Turn away thine eyes.** The great beauty of the bride confuses the king. For 5 b,6,7, see on 4:1-3. **8.** The total number of Solomon's queens and concubines was greater than that mentioned here (cf. I Kgs 11:3). **9. But among all these women and maidens, the Shulamite** stands out by virtue of her flawless beauty, even as the king is distinguished among ten thousand (5:10). **The choice one** (or, *the dearly beloved* or *darling)* **of her mother. 10.** The words, **Who is she . . . ,** are best regarded as reproducing the words of praise spoken by the queens and concubines.

B. The Bride and Her Admirers. 6:11-13.

11. I went down into the garden. It is difficult to determine who is the speaker here, Solomon or his bride, though it seems best to take the bride as the speaker. She is directing these words to the women admiring her (v. 10), to whom she tells of her going down to the garden of nuts. **12. He had placed me in the chariots of my noble people.** No one has yet been able to provide a satisfactory rendering and interpretation of these words. The bride may be speaking here of the way in which she was unexpectedly and suddenly elevated to queenly dignity. This verse, as well as verse 11, would then be the bride's response to the words of praise extended to her by queens and concubines. **13.** The queens and other women ask the bride to turn around again and again so that they may admire her. It cannot be said with certainty who it is that asks the question, **What will ye see.** This question is plainly a device employed by the poet to introduce his next description of the beauty of the bride. It is not impossible that this question is asked by the women urging the Shulamite to turn again and again. The designation *Shulamite* for the bride is likely derived from the place Shunem (cf. Josh 19:18; I Sam 28:4; II Kgs 4:8). The Mahanaim dance must have been a well-known dance. Mahanaim was a place located on the boundary of the tribe of Gad, not far from the river Jordan.

C. The King Extolling the Beauty of His Bride and Her Love for Him. 7:1-13.

Verses 1-9 constitute an ode in praise of the physical excellence of the bride. Our God, who created the magnificence of nature, with its almost infinite variety, also created the human body in such a way that it is a marvel of his handiwork. Physical beauty and the pure desire of husband and wife (and bridegroom and bride) for each other are God-given gifts to man. It is the perversion of these gifts that is base (cf. Rom 1:26,27), and therefore to be condemned.

The second part of Song 6:13 forms the introduction to the description of the bride given here. **7:1. How beautiful are thy feet.** The king is speaking. Perhaps we may think of the bride as engaged in dancing, in which act her beauty becomes even more strikingly apparent. **2. May it never be lacking mingled wine** (AV, *which wanteth not liquor),* serves to complete the picture, as does the phrase **set about with lilies. 3.** See on 4:5. **4. As a tower of ivory.** The bride's neck is fair and smooth like ivory and slender like a tower. The **pools of Heshbon** suggests the sparkling clarity of the eyes. **Heshbon** was the ancient capital of the Amorites (Num 21:25,26; Deut 2:24). **Bath-rabbim** was a gate of Heshbon. **The tower of Lebanon** was likely a watchtower. The writer must have regarded a prominent nose as very beautiful. **5. Carmel** is the mountain range the summit of which overlooks the Mediterranean sea and the Palestinian land in solitary majesty. **Hair . . . like purple.** The beauty of the bride's hair is such that it has captivated the king. **6.** Of all the things that a person may desire, there is nothing that can compare with this beautiful bride. **7. Thy stature is like a palm tree.** She is like a stately palm tree. **As clusters . . .** Likely clusters of dates are meant. **8,9 a.** The bridegroom expresses his desire to embrace his beloved bride and fully enjoy her love and beauty.

9b. Like the best wine. The response of the bride, who continues the symbolic language employed by her lover. Even while he is sleeping, her love is flowing out to him. **10.** The bride echoes the words in Gen 3:16: "thy desire shall be to thy husband." **11,12. Let us go forth into the field.** The bride urges her beloved to go with her to a place where they can fully enjoy each other's love. **13.** The ancients believed that eating mandrakes would stimulate sexual desire (as well as induce conception; cf. Gen 30:14-16). Hence mandrakes are also called love apples. The plant gave forth a strong smell which was pleasing to people in the East. The choice fruits are an indication of the bride's loving care for her bridegroom.

D. The Bride's Longing To Be Fully One with Her Lover. 8:1-4.

1. As my brother. Obviously the Shulamite does not really want her bridegroom to be her brother; rather, she desires the close and intimate relation only brothers and sisters know. The fact that her descent was much humbler than that of Solomon may form the background of this statement (cf. 1:5,6). If he were her brother, she could also freely kiss him in public without incurring public scorn. **2. I would . . . bring thee into my mother's house.** The intimate fellowship in the family circle is referred to (cf. 3:4). **3.** See on 2:6. Another climax in the book; the bride is close to her lover. **4.** Except for **why should you,** this verse is identical to 2:7 and 3:5. Love should not be stirred up before its proper time, because the love relationship, unless carefully guarded, may cause grief instead of the great joy it should bring to the human heart (cf. 2:7; 3:5). Neither is it necessary to seek to arouse love, for worthy love will awaken of itself in its own time.

V. Final Expressions of Mutual Love. 8:5-14.

A. Lover and Loved One Walking Together. 8:5-7.

5 a. Who is this that cometh . . . ? This question is asked by the poet to set the scene for what follows. For **wilderness,** see 3:6. The two are observed walking together and conversing. The king reminds his bride of how he once found her (perhaps on their first meeting?) sleeping under an apple tree near the house of her mother, and had awakened her. **6,7. Set me as a seal upon thine heart.** These words, uttered by the bride, sum up the theme of the entire Song and constitute its climax. A signet ring or **seal** was worn on the right hand (Jer 22:24), or carried suspended over the heart by a string worn around the neck (Gen 38:18). It was an emblem of authority (cf. Gen 41:42; I Kgs 21:8) and hence a very precious possession. The symbolism is expressive of the bride's irresistible desire to be her bridegroom's most treasured possession.

King Solomon, who composed this Song under the inspiration of the Holy Spirit, here transcends his own practices, for his granting the wish of the Shulamite would have ruled out his polygamy. This expression of fervent and irresistible love from the lips of the bride points to the monogamous character of marriage. Marriage is the union in love of *one* man and *one* woman, and any intrusion by a third party violates the unique relationship between the two. The desire of one who truly loves is so strong that he gives himself completely to the other and desires the same strong, exclusive affection in return. Such a love for another is from the Lord, who put it into man's heart, and it cannot be extinguished. Neither can it be bought. Not even Solomon, with all his wealth, could buy the love of the Shulamite girl. Instead, she gave it to him spontaneously, and her love was overwhelmingly great. Such absolute love is likewise the spiritual ideal between God and his people. We are warned not to serve two masters (Mt 6:24) and to love the Lord our God with all our heart, soul, mind, and strength (Mk 12:30).

B. The Virtuous Life of the Bride. 8:8-10.

8,9. We have a little sister. These verses, apparently spoken by the brothers of the bride, form the introduction to verse 9, where we again hear the bride speak. **She hath no breasts.** She has not yet reached maturity; she is not yet of marriageable age. The figure of **a wall** suggests the virtue of chastity and the ability to keep suitors at a proper distance. The **turret** (AV, *palace)* **of silver** shows what great respect, in that case, the brothers would have for their sister. However, if she would be **a door,** that is, be easy in yielding, then they would take proper measures to defend her so that she would not suffer from her own weakness.

It cannot be said with certainty who the young girl mentioned in this verse is, perhaps a younger sister of the bride; although it is also possible that verses 8 and 9 refer to the bride when she was still a child. **10.** The Shulamite was like **a wall,** protecting her sacred honor. Only to her royal suitor, Solomon, did she surrender herself. Him she did not repel; she offered him peace; that is, she gave herself to him.

C. Words from the Bride. 8:11,12.

11. These may also be the words of the poet himself. He shows how rich Solomon was and how his riches continued to increase. The **thousand pieces of silver** were to be given to the king by each one who took of the fruit of the vineyard. **Baal-hamon** is nowhere else mentioned in Scripture; its location is unknown. **12. My vineyard . . . is before me.** The bride, too, had a vineyard, but unlike Solomon she did not keep the price of the fruit for herself. **Two hundred** pieces of silver she paid to those in charge of the vineyard, but the **thousand** (pieces of silver), which represent the yield of the vineyard, she gave to Solomon. She surrendered not only herself to the king but her possessions as well.

D. Final Expressions of Mutual Love. 8:13,14.

13. The bridegroom utters his final longing words to his spouse. To him she is now like one dwelling in the garden (cf. 2:1). The companions, that is, those who are in her immediate presence, like to listen to her sweet voice. He likewise desires to hear it. **14.** She responds to him in words similar to those she spoke before (cf. 2:17). With these words the Song ends. Perhaps we might think that a more appropriate conclusion would have been to bring the two lovers together in joyful union. But it must be remembered that the Song is not a modern novel or poem of love; it is the Word of God teaching us the beauty and purity of genuine human love, one of the gifts of the Creator to his creatures. This love the Holy Spirit saw fit to picture in terms of mutual desire for fellowship on the part of those devoted to one another. This relationship can indeed be used to depict the love between Christ and His Church, although human love, even in its purest form, can never be more than a shadow of that spiritual relationship. People who truly love each other will always long for one another. But greater yet should be the longing of the Church to be with Christ, her heavenly Bridegroom. The Church is the bride of Christ, and through the Holy Spirit dwelling within her she gives expression to her great longing to be forever with Him in the words: "Come, Lord Jesus, yea come quickly" (cf. Rev. 22:17,20).

BIBLIOGRAPHY

Aalders, G. Ch. *Het Hooglied (Commentaar op het Oude Testament).* Kempen: Kok, 1952.

__________. *Het Hooglied (Korte Verklaring der Heilige Schrift).* Kampen: Kok, 1953.

Delitzsch, Franz. *Commentary on The Song of Songs.* Grand Rapids: Wm. B. Eerdmans Publishing Co., reprinted 1950.

Harper, Andrew. *The Song of Solomon (The Cambridge Bible for Schools and Colleges).* Cambridge: The University Press, 1907.

Hengstenberg, E. W. *Das Hohelied Salomonis.* Berlin, 1853.

Rowley, H. H. "The Interpretation of the Song of Solomon," *The Servant of the Lord.* London: Lutterworth Press, 1952, pp. 189-234.

Schonfield, Hugh J. *The Song of Songs.* New York: The New American Library, 1959.

Taylor, J. Hudson. *Union and Communion.* London: China Inland Mission, 1914.

Yamauchi, Edwin. "Cultic Clues in Canticles?" *Bulletin of the Evangelical Theological Society,* IV (Nov. 1961).

ISAIAH

INTRODUCTION

Date and Authorship. Isaiah, the son of Amoz, was apparently a highly esteemed citizen of Jerusalem, who enjoyed access to the royal court, and was a trusted advisor of King Hezekiah. His ministry extended from the year of King Uzziah's death in 740 B.C. (if not from an earlier date) to the reign of the idolatrous King Manasseh, in whose persecution he was probably martyred. Tradition reports that he was slain by being sawn asunder (cf. Heb 11:37). Apparently he did no public preaching after Manasseh ascended the throne in 698, but confined his message to the written form preserved in chapters 40 through 66. The high point of his political influence came in the crucial year 701 B.C., when the Assyrian invasion threatened to destroy the Kingdom of Judah and remove its inhabitants into slavery and exile. Through his intercession with God, the terrible danger was miraculously removed, and the remnants of Sennacherib's army fled back ingloriously to Nineveh.

Historical Background. It was during this critical period of the latter half of the eighth century that Israel, the Northern Kingdom (the Ten Tribes), suffered a swift and catastrophic decline, after the death of the redoubtable Jeroboam II. Samaria was finally destroyed after a desperate siege in the year 722. The long succession of ungodly kings and the steady dwindling of Biblical faith spelled the downfall of Israel. Judah, under the corrupt and degenerate King Ahaz, seemed ready to follow Israel's dismal example of apostasy, and looked to pagan Assyria for protection and deliverance, rather than to her covenant God, Jehovah. Against this unfaithfulness Isaiah and Micah raised a stern and determined protest. By 726 the government had come under the control of Ahaz' God-fearing son, Hezekiah. He obliterated most of the idolatrous "high places," even those dedicated to Jehovah (contrary to His Law), and promoted Bible-literacy among the people as a whole. A near-fatal illness deepened Hezekiah's piety, and the reform movement continued. But still Judah adhered to the misguided policy of trusting to pagan allies, even though Isaiah earnestly warned against intrigues with Egypt. As the prophet predicted, trust in the worldly power of Egypt (rather than in the protection of God alone) proved well-nigh fatal. Egyptian armies crumbled before the onslaught of Sennacherib's fighting machine, and only divine intervention saved Hezekiah's kingdom from utter ruin. At this time of crisis the king thoroughly repented of his disregard of God's warnings (conveyed to him by Isaiah), and rose to such a height of faith and purity of trust that the Lord found it proper to hear his prayer.

Hezekiah survived this moment of glory by only a few years. Then his young, self-willed son, Manasseh, came to the throne. He lent a ready ear to the worldly-minded nobility, who had long chafed under the religious purity his father had enforced, and in the spirit of "broad-mindedness" gave license for the resumption of idolatry. Step by step he became a convinced idol-worshiper himself, and brutally persecuted those who held true to his father's faith. Doctrinal defection among the people was accompanied by a general breakdown in morals. The king and his nobles, who exploited the populace for selfish gain, filled Jerusalem with bloodshed and rapine. In this atmosphere of corruption and depravity Isaiah was granted a series of marvelous revelations looking forward to the Babylonian conquest of the following century, and beyond to the Restoration period, when the Second Jewish Commonwealth would be established in the Promised Land.

Critical Theories of Authorship, Largely on the assumption that genuine predictive prophecy is impossible, rationalist higher critics have contested the genuineness of Isaiah 40–66 ever since the late eighteenth century. The author of these chapters seemed to know of the fall of Jerusalem (a good century later than Isaiah's death), and also of the restoration to Palestine of the Jewish captives after the fall of Babylon to the Persians in 539 B.C. Therefore this section of "Isaiah" must have been written by an unknown author—the "Deutero-Isaiah"—who lived at least 130 years after the death of the eighth-century prophet.

In support of this position it is argued: (a) that a futuristic standpoint could not have been maintained over such a large number of chapters; (b) that the actual name of the Persian conqueror, Cyrus, who was destined to liberate the Jewish captivity, could not have been foreknown a century and a half in advance of the event. Actually, however, a futuristic standpoint is by no means maintained throughout these twenty-seven chapters; many passages deal with issues contemporary with the historical Isaiah. Secondly, Holy Scripture does not hesitate to foretell specific names when the occasion calls for it. The name of King Josiah was predicted by a prophet of Judah three centuries before his time (I Kgs 13:2), in order to furnish a seal that the coming destruction of Jeroboam's idolatrous altar at Bethel was of the Lord's ordaining. Bethlehem was specifically named as the birthplace of the Messiah seven centuries before his advent (Mic 5:1,2). Moreover, it should be recognized that throughout the sixty-six chapters of Isaiah an extraordinary emphasis is laid upon predictive prophecy as a seal of divine inspiration. Some of the predictions were to be fulfilled soon (such as the deliverance of Jerusalem from Sennacherib by sudden, supernatural means—37:33-35; the defeat of Damascus within three years by Assyria—8:4,7; the destruction of Samaria within twelve years—7:16; the retreating of the shadow on the sundial—38:8). Others were intended for the more distant future (such as the Glory that should come to Galilee with the Messiah—9:1,2; cf. Mt 4:15,16; the devastation of Babylon by the Medes and its eventual total destruction, so as to remain an uninhabited and accursed site forever—13:17,19,20). It should be noted that it was precisely the reign of the wicked Manasseh (696—641 B.C.) which furnished the most serious challenge to the survival of the true faith. It was therefore most appropriate at this time for the covenant-keeping Jehovah to demonstrate his sovereignty and absolute authority by announcing a century or two in advance exactly what steps he would take in judgment upon apostate Judah and upon God-defying Babylon. This test of fulfillment of prophecy would furnish unanswerable proof of the divine authority of Isaiah's message: "Who, as I, shall call, and shall declare it . . . ? and things that are coming, and shall come [to pass], let them (the idols) declare. . . . Have I not declared to thee of old and showed it? And ye are My witnesses" (44:7,8). (Cf. 41:21-23, 26; 42:9,23; 43:9,12.)

It has been supposed that this hypothetical "Deutero-Isaiah" lived and wrote in Babylon as one of the Jewish Captivity around 550 B.C. But this is impossible to reconcile with internal evidence. Isaiah 40—66 shows little familiarity with Babylonian geography, but great familiarity with Palestine. The trees referred to are native to Palestine, but unknown in Babylonia (the cedar, cypress, and oak—44:14; 41:19). The viewpoint is Palestinian, for the Lord is said to send a message off to Babylon (43:14); Israel is described as the seed of Abraham which the Lord has taken from "the ends of the earth" (41:9), or "from the east" or "from a far country" (46:11). The prophet's contemporaries are assumed to be dwelling in Palestine, not in the land of exile. For example: "Is not this the fast I have chosen: to loose the bands of wickedness, and to let the oppressed go free, and that ye break every yoke?" The unavoidable inference is that the Jews were still holding their own law courts and administering justice (or injustice) as an independent nation, rather than being a subject race in a foreign land.

Some of the more recent critics (like Bernhard Duhm) have surrendered the notion that any of Isaiah 40—66 was written in Babylonia, but still insist that it was not composed until the latter part of the Exile or even a century later. But this theory also is controverted by the data of the text itself. The same evils prevailing in the time of Isaiah I are still rampant in the last twenty-seven chapters as well. Hypocrisy is prevalent in religion (cf. 29:13 and 58:2-4); bloodshed and violence are the order of the day (1:15 and 59:3,7); falsehood, injustice, and oppression hold sway unchecked (10:1,2 and 59:3-9). The same degeneracy and moral breakdown prevail in 59:1-8 as characterized the reign of Manasseh, who "filled Jerusalem with innocent blood from one end to the other" (II Kgs 21:16). Most decisive of all is the fact that in Isaiah II idolatry appears as a wide and prevalent evil among the prophet's Jewish contemporaries. "Against whom do ye sport yourselves . . . enflaming yourselves with idols under every green tree, slaying the children in the valleys under the clifts of the rocks?" (57:4,5; cf. 65:2,3 and 66:17, which also speak of contemporary Jewish practice.) It is almost universally recognized by critics of every persuasion that Judah was completely purged of idolatry after the Babylonian captivity. Many other evils and national sins are denounced and dealt with in the post-Exilic records, Ezra, Nehemiah, and Malachi, such as: intermarriage with foreign women, oppression of the poor by the rich, the violation of the Sabbath, and the withholding of tithes. But never once is idolatry referred to in any shape or form, even though in the pre-Exilic records it was much spoken of and sternly denounced as Israel's Number One sin. The only logical conclusion to draw in the light of this evidence is that these anti-idolatrous passages were composed before the Exile. And since they are imbedded in the context of the rest of Isaiah II (so also 44:9-20 and other passages), it is only reasonable to assume that the entire twenty-seven chapters were composed before the fall of Jerusalem in 587. There is not a shred of internal evidence to support the theory of a Second Isaiah, apart from a philosophical prejudice against the possibility of predictive prophecy. At every checkpoint the only place of origin that satisfies the data of the text is Palestine; the only time of composition that squares with the internal evidence is a date prior to the Exile, and more specifically, the reign of Manasseh.

The unity of the authorship of all sixty-six chapters is attested by the prevalence of the characteristic Isaianic title for God – "the Holy One of Israel." This occurs only five times in the rest of the OT, but it appears twelve times in the first thirty-nine chapters of Isaiah and fourteen in the last twenty-seven. Many distinctive phrases and figures of speech which are employed in the first part of the book recur in the second part as well (cf. 35:10 and 51:11; 11:9 and 65:25; 1:11,14 and 43:24). The unity is also certified by NT references, notably in Jn 12:38-41, where John quotes first from Isa 53:1 and then from Isa 6:9, and follows with the comment: "These things (i.e., these two quotations) said Isaiah when he saw His glory and spoke of Him." If the same author did not compose the two parts of Isaiah, then plainly the inspired apostle was in error, and his entire Gospel record is open to suspicion of untrustworthiness.

OUTLINE

(In its main divisions this outline follows the excellent analysis of B. F. Copass in *The Prince of the Prophets.)*

VOLUME I. REBUKE AND PROMISE. 1:1–6:13.

Sermon I. Rebellion confronted with judgment and grace. 1:1-31.
Sermon II. Punishment for sin as preparation for glory. 2:1–4:6.
Sermon III. Judgment and exile in store for Israel. 5:1-30.
Sermon IV. The prophet cleansed and commissioned by God. 6:1-13.

VOLUME II. IMMANUEL. 7:1–12:6.

Sermon I. Immanuel rejected by worldly wisdom. 7:1-25.
Sermon II. Messianic deliverance foreshadowed. 8:1–9:7.
Sermon III. Boastful Samaria doomed to exile. 9:8–10:4.
Sermon IV. World empire crushed; glorious empire to come. 10:5–12:6.
- A. God's instrument for judgment to be judged in turn. 10:5-34.
- B. The Messiah to restore and rule. 11:1-16.
- C. Thanksgiving and triumph of Christ's redeemed. 12:1-6.

VOLUME III. BURDENS OF JUDGMENT UPON THE NATIONS. 13:1–23:18.

Burden I. Fall of Babylon; her king's descent into Hades. 13:1–14:27.
Burden II. Downfall of Philistia. 14:28-32.
Burden III. Downfall of Moab. 15:1–16:14.
Burden IV. Downfall of Damascus and Samaria. 17:1-14.
Burden V. Downfall and conversion of Ethiopia. 18:1-7.
Burden VI. Afflictions of Egypt. 19:1–20:6.
Burden VII. Babylon to be conquered and her idols destroyed. 21:1-10.
Burden VIII. Defeat for Edom; victory for Israel. 21:11,12.

Burden IX. Dedan and Kedar to be routed. 21:13-17.
Burden X. Fall of Jerusalem foreseen; Eliakim to replace Shebna. 22:1-25.
Burden XI. Downfall and enslavement of Tyre. 23:1-18.

VOLUME IV. GENERAL REBUKE AND PROMISE, I. 24:1–27:13.

Sermon I. Universal judgment upon universal sin. 24:1-23.
Sermon II. Jehovah praised as deliverer and comforter of Zion. 25:1-12.
Sermon III. Song of joy over Judah's consolation. 26:1-21.
Sermon IV. Oppressors to be punished but God's people preserved. 27:1-13.

VOLUME V. WOES UPON THE UNBELIEVERS OF ISRAEL. 28:1–33:24.

Sermon I. Judgment of Ephraimite drunkards and Jewish scoffers. 28:1-29.
Sermon II. Disaster ahead for hypocrites. 29:1-24.
Sermon III. Confidence in Egypt versus confidence in God. 30:1-33.
Sermon IV. God, not Egypt, to be Jerusalem's defense. 31:1-9.
Sermon V. Israel's final deliverance, and her spiritual renewal. 32:1-20.
Sermon VI. Punishment of the Treacherous, and Triumph of Christ. 33:1-24.

VOLUME VI. GENERAL REBUKE AND PROMISE, II. 34:1–35:10.

Sermon I. Utter destruction of Gentile world power. 34:1-17.
Sermon II. Blessing on the highway of holiness. 35:1-10.

VOLUME VII. THE VOLUME OF HEZEKIAH. 36:1–39:8.

A. Destruction of Judah averted. 36:1–37:38.
  Scene 1. Jehovah challenged by Assyrian world power. 36:1-22.
  Scene 2. Assyria answered and judged. 37:1-38.
B. Destruction of Judah's king averted. 38:1–39.8.
  Scene 1. Hezekiah's recovery from deadly sickness. 38:1-22.
  Scene 2. Hezekiah's foolish pride and God's rebuke. 39:1-8.

VOLUME VIII. THE VOLUME OF COMFORT. 40:1–66:24.

Section I: The Purpose of Peace. 40:1–48:22.

Sermon I. Sovereign majesty of Jehovah the Comforter. 40:1-31.
Sermon II. God's challenge to idolatrous unbelievers. 41:1-29.
Sermon III. The Servant of Jehovah – individual and national. 42:1-25.
Sermon IV. Witness nation redeemed from Chaldean bondage. 43:1-28.
Sermon V. Israel's witness for God against idols. 44:1-28.
Sermon VI. Coming Gentile deliverer, and conversion of the heathen. 45:1-25.
Sermon VII. Downfall of Babylon and preservation of Israel. 46:1–47:15.
Sermon VIII. God's honor to be upheld by Israel's deliverance. 48:1-22.

Section II. The Prince of Peace. 49:1–57:21.

Sermon I. Messiah to restore Israel and enlighten the Gentiles. 49:1-26.
Sermon II. Sinfulness of Israel and obedience of the Servant. 50:1-11.
Sermon III. Encouragement to trust God, not fearing man. 51:1-16.
Sermon IV. Israel summoned to awake and return to God's favor. 51:17–52:12.
Sermon V. The divine Servant's substitutionary atonement. 52:13–53:12.
Sermon VI. Resultant blessings to Israel and the Church. 54:1-17.
Sermon VII. God's grace towards repentant sinners. 55:1-13.
Sermon VIII. Gentiles to be included in Israel's blessing. 56:1-8.
Sermon IX. Condemnation of the corrupt leaders of Israel. 56:9–57:21.

Section III. The Program of Peace. 58:1–66:24.

Sermon I. False worship contrasted with the true. 58:1-14.
Sermon II. Israel's confession and her rescue by God. 59:1-21.
Sermon III. Radiance and peace of God's redeemed people. 60:1-22.
Sermon IV. The joy-bringing Gospel of the Anointed One. 61:1-11.
Sermon V. Restoration of Zion; destruction of infidel heathen. 62:1–63:6.
Sermon VI. Israel's plea for help, based on past mercies. 63:7–64:12.
Sermon VII. God's mercy reserved for spiritual Israel. 65:1-25.
Sermon VIII. Blessing of true believers in the final age. 66:1-24.

COMMENTARY

VOLUME ONE. REBUKE AND PROMISE. 1:1–6:13.

Sermon I. Rebellion Confronted with Judgment and Grace. 1:1-31.

1. Title: **The vision.** A technical term *(ḥăzôn)* for divine revelation, as something displayed before the mind's eye of the prophet. Actually there is no vision (in the modern sense of the word) in the entire first chapter. **Isaiah.** Hebrew *yᵉsha'-yāhû*, "Jehovah is salvation." **Amoz.** "Strong" or "courageous." **Uzziah.** Also known as Azariah, a good king, who fell into the sin of pride and ended his days as a leper (reigned 767–740 B.C.). **Jotham** (co-regent 750–740, sole king 740–736). Uzziah's godly successor. **Ahaz** (736–716). A wicked and idolatrous king, who led the kingdom astray. **Hezekiah** (co-regent 726–716, sole king 716–698 B.C.). Ahaz' god-fearing son, who promoted religious reform, and paid earnest heed to Isaiah's message, except in the matter of his pro-Egypt policy.

A. Judah's Ingratitude and Rebellion Against God. 1:2-9.

2. The words **heavens** and **earth** imply that the angelic inhabitants of the heavens and the human inhabitants of earth are to serve as condemnatory witnesses against God's covenant people. **The Lord.** This title stands for the covenant name of God, "Jehovah" (or more properly, *Yahweh)*, and is everywhere so given in the ASV. This name is used wherever a covenant relationship is involved. **Rebelled.** The first of five significant terms for sin used in this chapter (cf. vv. 4,13). It signifies that primal sin of man in revolt against God whereby he sought to dethrone God from first place and to substitute himself and his own will as supreme. **3.** The ingratitude of these "believers" debased them below the level of brute beasts, for even beasts recognize and appreciate their owners who feed them and care for them. **Crib.** A feeding trough (not a baby's bed). **Doth not know.** This common verb "to know" is often used in Hebrew to mean the owning and acknowledging of one's husband, wife, parent, or child. Israel was ignorant of God, yet this ignorance was not involuntary, but deliberately chosen by a rebellious and self-willed heart.

4. Sinful. A participle from the verb *ḥāta'*, meaning originally, "miss the mark" (cf. Prov 8:6; Jud 20:16); hence, miss the proper goal of life, miss the way God has ordained. **Laden.** Like a wagon with a heavy load. The load is Israel's **iniquity** – a perversion or twisting aside (from *'āwâ*, "to bend or twist") from the standard of rectitude and duty. **Seed of evildoers.** They were of the spiritual family of those who commit harmful, injurious sin (from *rā'a'*, "be harmful," "be evil"). They were **children that are corrupters,** i.e., who destroyed or caused to putrefy *(hiśhḥîth)* that which was wholesome or perfectly made. Because they had rebelled against God's rightful sovereignty over their hearts, they had **forsaken** or abandoned him altogether, and joined the camp of the enemy, so far as moral life and behavior were concerned. Though they attended church, so to speak, and kept up outward appearances of piety, yet in God's eyes they had deserted him for his foes (vv. 11-15). A church-going hypocrite is a most valued tool of Satan.

They had provoked to anger the **Holy One of Israel.** This name for God is the most significant title employed by the prophet Isaiah. In chapter 6 Jehovah reveals himself in a scene of heavenly glory as the Holy One *(Qādôsh),* i.e., the transcendent God, who is wholly separate from the frailty and finiteness of Creation (his majesty-holiness), and wholly separate from the sinfulness and defilement of man (his purity-holiness). But this Holy One has claimed the family of Abraham, Isaac, and Jacob as his covenant children. He has given himself to them and they have given themselves to him in a covenant undertaken nationally, on their part, and solemnized before Mount Sinai (Ex 19:5-8). Therefore he is the **Holy One of Israel.** Wherever this term appears in Isaiah (twelve times in chs. 1–39, fourteen times in chs. 40–66), it presents his pure and holy love acting to vindicate his covenant rights – either chastening his people when they are disobedient, that they may repent and return unto him, or else defending and delivering them from their heathen foes. Because he is the Holy One of Israel, he could not stand idly by while he witnessed their grievous apostasy **(they are gone away backward).** Rather, he must discipline them, and let them suffer affliction and invasion – as they had already.

5,6. The land of Israel, and more especially the Southern Kingdom of Judah, is figuratively presented as the victim of a brutal assault, left bleeding and half-dead by the wayside. The ancient method of treating an infected wound was to squeeze it together (so render, **they have not been closed**) in order to press out the pus, anoint it with olive oil so that it would continue to drain, and then bind it up with a bandage. None of these things had been done for Judah. **The whole heart is faint** (or better, *sick*). Not only are external afflictions in view here, but also sickness of soul. This malady of head and heart (v. 5) found expression in the stubborn waywardness and disobedience the nation manifested toward God.

7,8. The figurative language of the previous verses is now translated into grim realities, describing the devastation of the land by the marauding Syrians (under King Rezin), North Israelites (under King Pekah), Edomites, and Philistines in 734–733 B.C. (cf. II Chr 28). Jerusalem itself was menaced by these invaders and largely cut off from the surrounding territory by besiegers. Doubtless these verses look forward prophetically to the far more serious investment of Jerusalem by the Assyrians under Sennacherib in 701 B.C. (some scholars refer this whole chapter to that later period). The **cottage** or booth (*sukkâ*) in the vineyard and the **lodge** or overnight shelter (*m*[e]*lûnâ*) both refer to temporary lean-to's or shanties built for the quartering of guards to protect the ripening crops against poachers.

9. Very small remnant or group of refugees (*śārîd*). That is, a remnant of true believers, for whose sake God would spare the whole commonwealth from the total destruction it deserved. (Cf. the complete annihilation of Sodom and Gomorrah, centers of filthy immorality and sexual perversion, in the time of Abraham; Gen 18; 19.) The Lord continued, in subsequent history, to preserve the Hebrew race for the sake of a small minority of sincere believers. In Rom 9:29 Paul quotes this verse with reference to Christian converts from Judaism.

B. The Sinful Subterfuge of Hypocritical Worship. 1:10-15.

10. The backsliding people of Jerusalem and their corrupt rulers (under wicked Ahaz) are here addressed as citizens of Sodom and Gomorrah because they had culpably and wickedly turned their backs on God's special revelation — as did the Sodomites upon general revelation — and the voice of conscience.

11-14. These verses do not represent rejection of the validity of blood sacrifices (as some scholars have argued), for such an interpretation would entail also rejection of prayer (cf. v. 15). Rather, they make clear that even right and proper forms of worship are utterly offensive to the Lord when presented by unrepentant worshipers seeking to bribe him to spare them the punishment they deserve. God does not, and cannot, find acceptable even the most lavish and costly offerings the unrepentant may present at the altar. **12.** When the would-be worshiper has no sincere purpose to abandon his evil ways, his entrance before God at the Temple amounts to an impious **trampling** (RSV) of the holy precincts (a verb used of the violent intrusion of foreign invaders) rather than a properly reverent treading upon the hallowed pavement. **13. Vain oblations.** Literally, *a* (meal) *offering of worthlessness* — worthless because of the carnal motive behind it. **It is iniquity, even the solemn meeting.** Better rendered by construing the previous words as anticipatory (since a **solemn meeting** or *ăṣārâh* was generally held on these solemn holidays). Thus: "As for the festival of the new moon and the sabbath (and) the convoking of a convocation—I cannot stand iniquity and (i.e., along with) a solemn meeting." **14. Your appointed feasts** (*môʿădîm*). Probably the major three of the Hebrew year: Passover and Unleavened Bread in the first month, Pentecost in the third month, and Tabernacles in the seventh month. On these three occasions every male in Israel was to appear before the Lord. But no celebration of these feasts had any spiritual value unless supported by the offering of a completely yielded and obedient heart. **15. Spread forth your hands** (lit., *palms*). In supplicatory prayer the Hebrew extends his hands with the palms upward towards God. How offensive these palms must be if they are stained with the blood of innocent victims they have oppressed or slain! Failure to turn from their sins rendered these worshipers utterly filthy in God's eyes.

C. The Invitation to Choose Between Pardon and Destruction. 1:16-20.

Two things are necessary for those who would approach God for forgiveness and favor: repentance from sin (v. 16), and a life-purpose to walk in the ways of holiness (v. 17). **16. Wash you** does not imply self-amendment by mere human effort or exertion of will-power. Rather, it suggests application of the Lord's gracious promise to cleanse those who come to him in the appointed way of blood sacrifice. This appointed way includes the abandonment of all known sin — **put away the evil of your doings** — with a feeling of hatred towards it and sincere regret at ever having committed it. **From before mine eyes** suggests what heinous effrontery it is for a man to appear, unrepentant, before a God who can see all, even down to the very depths of the guilty soul. **17. Learn to do well.** That is, Learn to live virtuously and uprightly, in accordance with God's holy will, and particularly to be fair toward the weak and oppressed. **Seek judgment.** Have an earnest and consistent purpose to apply the principles of righteousness to concrete situations *(mishpāt)*. A believer's chief concern must be to show real justice and fairness, even towards those who are easily victimized and cannot defend themselves. **Judge the fatherless. Judgment** and **judge** both come from *shāpat*, "to judge." This command signifies: "Bring justice and fairness to bear upon the case of the orphan." **Plead for the widow** employs another legal term, *rîb*, which means "to argue or plead the case of someone." The widow was to obtain her legal rights even against a wealthy or influential litigant. In those days, since a woman could not hold a job in industry, the loss of her husband usually meant the cutting off of her income. Forced to mortgage her property, she soon fell into the toils of wealthy moneylenders, who had no scruples against taking her property or selling her children into slavery for the discharge of the debt.

18. Let us reason together. Another courtroom term. The Lord was saying, "Let us implead one another as plaintiff and defendant at a court of law." The defendants in this case were the guilty Israelites who had repented and shown a will to lead a godly life; as described in 1:16,17. No matter how heinous their sins might be, though they bore the guilty hue of shed blood (and the **crimson** dye of the **scarlet** worm here referred to was absolutely colorfast and indelible), nevertheless the grace of God was able to cleanse them completely and restore them to the snowy whiteness of innocence.

19,20. The destiny of the people depended upon their response to this offer of forgiving grace. If they were **willing** to turn from their wickedness and claim the Lord's gracious promises, and if they were **obedient** (i.e., presented themselves as living sacrifices to do the will of God, making that the chief purpose of their life), then it would be safe and proper for God to bestow his favor upon them. He would signify and seal his favor by bestowing on them the external blessing of material prosperity, safely maintained against invaders. But if they continued to reject his offer of grace and persisted in their rebellion against his rightful sovereignty over their hearts, he would have to unleash the heathen invader upon them to wreak havoc in their midst. **For the mouth of Jehovah hath spoken it** (ASV). This formula is added for the sake of special solemnity. Because it contains the very utterance of the Lord himself, this predictive announcement must surely come to pass; else God was no longer God, and his word was not to be trusted. In this case the fulfillment came in two installments: the Assyrian invasion of 701 B.C. and the Chaldean invasions of 588–587 B.C. The Jews were truly devoured by the mouth of the sword.

D. Jehovah's Sorrow at Judah's Moral Decline. 1:21-23.

21. In transgressing against the covenant relation with the Lord, Israel had committed a sin like that of a wife who becomes unfaithful to her husband. To trample upon the tender ties of marriage is to wound her husband in those areas where he is most sensitive and most vulnerable; hence this is the cruelest wrong that can be perpetrated. There was a time when Israel (back in the days of Joshua and of David) was a faithful wife to Jehovah, and in her affections cleaved to him only. In those days Israel's doctrinal purity was accompanied by moral uprightness and the equal enforcement of the laws for the benefit of all. But when the nation later became more "broadminded," ready to see "the good in all religions," it was but a step to spiritual harlotry, the prostitution of the soul to the false and abominable gods of the heathen. Doctrinal declension was accompanied by moral declension, and murderous gangsters came to dominate the life and politics of the Holy City!

22. Wine mixed with water. Wine was customarily diluted with water before being served at the table. But merchants were obligated to deal honestly with purchasers and sell only a pure, unwatered product. **23. Princes . . . rebellious,** That is, against the sovereignty and law of God. These princes and government officials, who were charged with the duty of upholding the law and protecting the public against crime, were covertly in league with the leaders of the underworld – **companions of thieves.** Those who decided judicial cases had their price; the wealthier litigant in any suit was sure to win the verdict. The poor and defenseless, such as widows and orphans, were not even given a hearing, because they had no money to bribe the judge.

E. Restoration To Follow Chastisement and Repentance. 1:24-31.

24. The Lord of hosts, i.e., of the hosts of mighty angels who wait upon his beck and call. This title of God alludes to his omnipotence and sovereignty. This thought is strengthened by the additional phrase, **the mighty One of Israel,** which alludes to the Lord's miracle-working power (as displayed in his redemptive miracles in the days of the Exodus and the Conquest), which would now be employed against the apostate covenant nation instead of on their behalf. **I will ease me.** Literally, *I will comfort or relieve myself of my adversaries.* That is, he would grant relief to his long pent-up feelings of holy displeasure at the flagrant violation of his covenant and the oppression of the weak in Israel. He would inflict due punishment upon the whole Jewish state, and utterly crush their ungodly leaders.

25. Turn my hand upon thee. Literally, *cause the hand to return upon.* This indicates the special interposition of God to take appropriate and summary action against offenders; or, as here, to deal with them as their spiritual condition demands. Only furnace fire can smelt away alloy and slag from metal that is being refined; hence the fiery trial of suffering and exile is implied in God's promise here. **26. Thy judges as at the first;** i.e., as in the days of Joshua, David, and Solomon. God would not set aside the free will of the nation Israel, but he would nevertheless see to it that his ideal of a godly covenant people would some day be realized. The Israelites, despite their stubborn waywardness, would not permanently frustrate his purpose. He would yet make of Jerusalem **the city of righteousness, the faithful city.** This was to be spiritually fulfilled in the formation of the NT Church (cf. Heb 12:22 – "the heavenly Jerusalem"). But also it will be fulfilled in the glorious city of the Millennium, under the personal rule of Christ.

27. Redeemed; i.e., ransomed or bought back out of bondage. **With judgment.** Rather than by some mode of salvation that by-passes the guilt of sin. A judicial act of inflicting punishment upon all God's foes (and the foes of his chosen people), and also upon the Redeemer, as the representative of sinners, at Golgotha.

28. They that forsake Jehovah (ASV); i.e., even though they be nominal Israelites. Only true, converted believers will partake of Zion's glorious future. The rest will go to the destruction destined for the heathen. **29. They shall be ashamed.** At the Last Judgment, when they will be exposed as fools who have staked their immortal souls upon a lie and sealed their eternal doom; and even in this life, when calamity and retribution flood in upon them, and their false idols prove unable to rescue them. **Oaks** and **gardens** refer to the superstitiously venerated oak groves and the pleasure gardens connected with temples of idolatry, where sex orgies were held in connection with heathen worship (cf. 57:5). **30. That hath no water.** Contrast the flourishing tree by the "rivers of water" in Psalm 1, the leaves of which do not wither. When there is no vital connection with the life and Spirit of God, only decay can result. **31. The worker** (AV, *maker)* **of it.** Better, *his work,* as in the ASV (for the word for "work" may be so spelled in Hebrew, and it makes better sense in this context). The sinner's wicked deeds in this life will furnish the basis for his condemnation and fiery destruction in the end. **None shall quench them.** No human power can avert this fiery punishment for unrepentant sinners, and the punishment will be endless and eternal.

Sermon II. Punishment for Sin as Preparation for Glory. 2:1–4:6.

A. God's Goal for Israel: Spiritual Conquest, Lasting Peace. 2:1-4.

2:2. Mountain of Jehovah's house (ASV). Properly, Mount Moriah (which came to be called Zion), on which Solomon's Temple was built. But the literal Temple was a type of the spiritual temple – the NT Church, or body of Christ (Eph 2:21), the beacon light of divine testimony to the world. The gathering of the nations to Jerusalem in eager faith therefore signifies the conversion of the Gentiles. But since this scene is said to occur **in the last days,** and since we are taught by other Scriptures that the Kingdom of God will finally overcome all the kingdoms of this world, we must therefore look to the time of Christ's return, at the end of our present age, for the ultimate fulfillment of this prophecy. In this verse we are granted a glimpse of God's final goal for Israel and for the human race. **Exalted above the hills.** The Kingdom of God will be exalted above the kingdoms of this world (Dan 2:35). **All nations.** All the *gôyîm*, or Gentile nations, as distinguished from the *'am* or "people" of Jehovah – the Israelites. But these are referred to in verse 3 as **many people**[s], or *'ammîm*.

3. The primary concern of the surviving Gentiles of the 'last days' will be to discover the will of God and to do it. And they will be eager to have others share in the blessing of covenant relationship to God, for they will exhort and encourage one another to come to him. They will seek to learn his ways and to walk in his paths of holiness. **Out of Zion . . . the law. Zion** here represents the one authoritative divine revelation, since it was in Zion that God met with man for his enlightenment and forgiveness, and nowhere else. The **law** or *tôrâ* here signifies "revelational instruction" in the larger sense (since *tôrâ* comes from the verb *hôrâ* or *yārâ*, "to instruct"). The verb **shall go forth** may equally well be translated *goes forth* (present tense). Hence it may aptly be included in what the converted nations will say in the 'last days,' as they realize the unique validity of the Hebrew-Christian revelation.

4. He will judge between the nations (ASV). Jehovah himself (i.e., the Lord Jesus, according to 11:3,4) will impose his righteous rule upon the earth, and compel the nations to practice justice and fairness toward each other. There will therefore be no international strife, no aggressor nations; all countries will dwell together in peace. **Rebuke.** Better, *and he will decide* (i.e., as a judge seated upon the bench), as in the ASV. Since there will be no appeal to arms or violence to settle differences – for all will be governed by Christ's judicial decision –, the weapons of war will be converted into tools of peace and economic productivity. The Millennial kingdom will be characterized by a warless society.

B. Judgment upon Sin to Precede Messiah's Rule. 2:5–4:1.

1) A Nation Ripe for Judgment. 2:5-11.

5. In the light of God's promises of pardon for repentant sinners, and in view of the glorious prospects for the future conversion of the Gentiles, the prophet urged his countrymen to walk in the light and live to please God, trusting Him to perform His word. They were to do this even though it meant running counter to the stream of the times and opposing current and fashionable trends. **6.** Judah had eagerly adopted new ideas from the heathen and embraced many elements of heathen religion and morals. **Replenished from the east.** Literally, *they have become full from the east.* They were filled with ideas and influences from Assyria and Babylon. From their Philistine neighbors on the western coastline, they had adopted a faith in **soothsayers** (*'ōn^{e}nîm* probably meant originally, "those who gather omens from the clouds"). **They please themselves in. . . .** Rather, *they strike hands with* the children of foreigners (ASV), a term used of entering into compacts and making common cause with others. **7.** The successful campaigns and mercantile operations of Uzziah had resulted in considerable economic prosperity in Judah, but this wealth had only encouraged the Jews in materialism and neglect of the God of the Bible. From such carnality of viewpoint it was an easy and natural step to idolatry and to joining with the rest of the world in "worshiping the creature more than the Creator." **9.** Before the most abominable idols – Baal, Ashtoreth, Milcom, Dagon, Hadad, and all the rest – both the upper classes of Judah and the common people bowed in heathenish worship. To allow this sin to go permanently unpunished would have cast the greatest discredit upon God's cause and compromised his glory. Therefore Isaiah prayed him to vindicate his truth by punishing those who had shamelessly trampled upon it.

10. As if assured that Jehovah will surely visit judgment upon all who despise His revealed Word, the prophet exhorts the unrepentant of every generation to run for cover, if they can. For dreadful retribution will surely overtake every nation and every culture that ignores the Bible message. There are overtones here suggestive of the unsurpassable horrors of the Great Tribulation to come. The immediate reference, however, is doubtless to the historical judgments of the Assyrian and Chaldean invasions. Not only Israel and Judah, but all the heathen nations of that age as well were to experience crushing blows of disaster as each successive empire rose and fell.

2) Pride of Man To Be Crushed in the Day of the Lord. 2:12-22.

12. The **day of Jehovah** (ASV). An oft-recurring term in the prophetic books. It refers to God's special intervention in human history to bring nations and empires into catastrophic judgment. As a process, the Day of Jehovah occurs whenever God crushes the pretensions and power of a human society in revolt against him; e.g., the fall of Nineveh and the Assyrian Empire in 612 B.C., the fall of Jerusalem in 587, the fall of Babylon in 539. But as an eschatological occurrence, the Day of Jehovah is that final event towards which all of these earlier and partial judgments prophetically point, that final overthrow of all human power which will precede the second coming of Christ (so II Thess 1:7–2:12; II Pet 3:12; Acts 2:20).

13. Cedars and **oaks.** Symbols of the proud, self-sufficient human leaders of society (as in 10:33,34). **14.** Similarly the **mountains** and **hills** are symbolic of the hilltop citadels and the kingdoms over which they presided (as in 2:2), with the added connotation of human pride and self-reliance in the phrase **that are lifted up. 16. Ships of Tarshish.** A term applied, it seems, to large, especially seaworthy merchant vessels, able to make the voyage to distant Tarshish (probably Sardinia, and secondarily also Spain) – whether or not they were actually engaged in Tarshish trade (as those constructed at Ezion-geber certainly were not; II Chr 20:36). **Pleasant pictures.** Or, as in the ASV, *pleasant imagery*. Probably the beautiful objects of art and skill which these merchant vessels brought to wealthy purchasers.

19. The holes of the rocks. Smaller caves, a traditional hiding place in time of invasion or major calamity (cf. I Sam 14:11). But this seems to refer definitely to the events of Rev 6:15. In view of modern weapons of destruction, the need for taking shelter below ground or in mountain caves to escape an overwhelming destructive force has a very up-to-date ring about it. **20.** The complete collapse of all the defenses and security measures upon which worldlings rely will finally result in their anguished rejection of all the false gods and vain philosophies they have substituted for the one true God.

22. Cease ye from man. Cease putting your trust in man (as contrasted with God, the only true refuge). **Breath . . . in his nostrils.** A reminder of man's frail mortality. Once the breath ceases from the nostrils, a man's life is snuffed out and his power is gone (even though he be a Sennacherib or a Tirhakah).

3) All Classes of Society To Be Humbled and Chastened. 3:1–4:1.

1. Stay is simply the masculine form of the Hebrew word for **staff.** Both words signify *that upon which one leans.* In this case the crops and the rainfall are referred to as the support or foundation of the nation's material well-being. **2,3.** Not only were drought and famine to beset the land of Judah, but also the leading classes of Jewish society would be removed from their posts in the government or the army; and even the skilled craftsmen, responsible for manufactured products, would be taken away. The country would be left without leadership or resources. This sentence was gradually carried out by the successive invasions of Nebuchadnezzar, particularly that of 597 B.C., when "he carried away . . . the mighty of the land . . . and all the men of might, even seven thousand, and craftsmen and smiths a thousand, all that were strong and apt for war" (II Kgs 24:15,16).

4. Children to be their princes. Children not only as regards age (the wicked and degenerate King Manasseh, who reigned from 698 to 642, was only twelve when he began to reign), but more especially as regards prudence and political ability. Such were Jehoiakim, Jehoiachin, and Zedekiah. These kings by their foolish vacillation between Egypt and Babylon, brought their country to complete destruction within twenty years after the death of good King Josiah. **6. Thou hast clothing;** i.e., an outer garment or mantle (*śimlâ*), which would set a man off as comparatively wealthy in that coming day of general destitution. He would, therefore, be entitled to the distinction of ruling over the rest, who would be too poor to own more than an undergarment. **7. An healer.** A *binder up* (i.e., of wounds). A comforter, one who cares for others who are injured or in need. So despised was the nation to become that men would not consider it an honor to rule over it. Those invited to do so would beg off on the ground of their poverty. **8. Jerusalem is ruined.** Literally, *has stumbled and fallen.* Her coming destruction had already been decided upon by God, even though it was not to be consummated until nearly 150 years later.

The eyes of his glory. Probably to be understood (with the RSV) as *his glorious presence*.

9. Rewarded evil unto themselves. Better, *have dealt out evil* (or injury) *to themselves*. **12. Children are their oppressors.** Incompetent, degenerate rulers who had no more skill in government than fickle, shortsighted children, and were influenced by their scheming mistresses. **13-15.** These oppressive rulers and aristocrats might be immune from punishment by human courts for their ruthless exploitation of Jehovah's people; but God himself would bring them to judgment for their unfaithfulness to their trust, which was a personal injury to him.

16-26. The fashionable society women of Jerusalem had given themselves over to flirtation and coquetry, to allure other women's husbands. They had devoted themselves to the latest fads in jewelry, hair style, and dress. They were wholly taken up with self-adornment, having no concern for God's law or their holy mission in life. But all the tawdry baubles for which they had sold their souls were to be stripped away from them in the coming invasions (from Assyria and Babylon). Their nakedness would be uncovered when they were led away as miserable slaves by their conquerors (v. 17). Or they would crouch in some wretched corner, filled with despair and covered with sackcloth and ashes. All their earthly possessions would be destroyed or snatched away from them, and their men would be slain. (The Qumran Isaiah Scroll reads in 3:24: ". . . a girding of sackcloth; surely instead of beauty there shall be shame.") So scarce would be the male population (4:1) after the slaughter of war, that each surviving man would be importuned by several unmarried women to marry them as self-supporting wives.

C. Ultimate Blessedness of Revived Israel Under Messiah. 4:2-6.

2. In that day does not refer to the period just described, except insofar as that Assyrian and Chaldean devastation prefigured the tribulation of the 'last days.' Rather, it refers to the final age, when the Messiah shall come to rule the earth. This is the usual force of the phrase, "in that day," throughout the prophetic books of the OT. **The branch** ***(semah)*** **of Jehovah** (ASV) refers to Christ himself as the descendant of the promised line of David. The same word, literally, *sprout*, is used with reference to Messiah in Jer 23:5; 33:15; Zec 3:8; 6:12. In him will be found the true beauty and glory of Israel (as contrasted with the false and worldly beauty of the society women of Jerusalem). Note that the ultimate prosperity is promised only to the **escaped** ***(p^{e}lētâ)*** **of Israel.** Although the nation as a whole must be rejected for disobedience, the Lord would continue to work out his purpose with the remnant of true believers (as Paul later pointed out in Rom 11:5). Only those who have been sanctified by the new birth and inwardly transformed to mirror forth Christ's holiness will be enrolled (Isa 4:3) as citizens of spiritual Jerusalem. Cleansed of carnality and worldliness, the women of that holy city will stand in complete contrast to those of Isaiah's generation. But this new order will not prevail until God's Spirit shall have purged the city of its wickedness and idolatry by the fires of judgment and of suffering (v. 4). In that future day the presence of Jehovah will once again be granted to Israel as in the days of the Exodus, and the Lord will shield his godly children from all calamities and adversity. (This sermon concludes, as it began back in 2:2, with a glowing picture of the final fulfillment of God's covenant plan for Israel).

Sermon III. Judgment and Exile in Store for Israel. 5:1-30.

A. Evil Yield of the Lord's Vineyard. 5:1-7.

This is the first appearance, chronologically, of the **vineyard** as a symbol of Israel. In the OT the figure recurs in Jeremiah 12:10 and Psalm 80. In the NT it appears in the Parable of the Wicked Husbandmen (Synoptic Gospels), and, with a special adaptation, in Christ's discourse on the vine and the branches (Jn 15). **My beloved** (RSV) perhaps refers, not to God (for this term, *dôd*, is never so applied elsewhere), but to some friend of Isaiah's who had suffered this disappointment in his vineyard. Yet the way in which the prophet becomes identified with this "beloved" in Isa 5:4 indicates a mystical unity between them that best befits the relationship of a prophet to the God whose mouthpiece he is. What inexcusable guilt was Israel's, to produce such evil fruit when God had given them every possible advantage in a fair and fertile land! Their inevitable penalty must be the removal of his protective hedge and their devastation by invaders.

B. The Verdict of the Judge: Guilty on Seven Counts. 5:8-23.

8,9. *Guilty of selfish greed.* By foreclosing mortgages or by forcing sales of land, the wealthy landowners acquired all the adjoining farms to form huge estates. But all these were to be stripped from them: their mansions would be left in smoking ruins, and their fertile acreage would be reduced to near-sterility when foreign invaders had done their grim work.

11-17. *Guilty of frivolous pleasure-seeking and vicious dissipation.* They arose early, not to begin the day with God in prayer, but to begin it with their liquor bottles in drunkenness. And they ended the day with wild drinking parties and jazz bands. Because they ignored God and his holy purpose for their lives, their temporal punishment would be bondage, exile, and famine (v. 13); and their eternal punishment would be destruction in Hades (Sheol) along with all their tawdry possessions. Their fair estates would revert to mere pasturage (v. 17). The justice of God was to find complete vindication in their fate (v. 16).

18,19. *Guilty of cynical materialism.* Like idol worshipers drawing the cart of a great idol in festal procession, these backslidden people dragged along their idol of iniquity, challenging the Holy One of Israel as if he were powerless to intervene in human history and exercise his sovereignty.

20. *Guilty of reversing the standards of morality.* They acclaimed depravity of character as manly strength, and sensuous impurity as true virtue and strength.

21. *Guilty of intellectual pride and self-sufficiency.* They fancied themselves wiser than God or the experience of past generations.

22. *Guilty of alcoholic indulgence.* They measured strength by dissipation and excess.

23. *Guilty of corruption.* They sold their integrity for silver in their discharge of public office, and deprived the innocent poor of their legal rights in cases at law.

C. God's Sentence: Defeat and Devastation by a Foreign Foe. 5:24-30.

As a withered plant, rotten at the root, suddenly crumbles away in a breeze, or as dry stubble roars up in sudden flame at the slightest spark, so quickly would Israel fall. Her spiritual dry rot stemmed from her contemptuous rejection of God's Word (v. 24). Therefore the Lord's **stretched forth . . . hand** (v. 25); i.e., his miracle-working power would be turned against them instead of against their enemies. Their corpses would lie like garbage in their streets. The agents of this vengeance were to be invaders from a distant land (e.g., Assyria or Babylon) – rather than from Syria or the other surrounding lands – , and their attack would be spectacularly sudden. The enemy warriors would be fierce and unsparing, and their armies would engulf Palestine like a tidal wave. (These specifications were fulfilled by Nebuchadnezzar after his victory at Carchemish in 605 B.C.)

Sermon IV. The Prophet Cleansed and Commissioned by God. 6:1-13.

A. The Vision of God in His Holiness. 6:1-4.

Uzziah's death in 740 or 739 B.C. marked the passing of a golden age of spiritual vigor in Judah (at least until the king's sin of presumption ten years before his decease); and his ungodly grandson, Ahaz, was perhaps already exerting an influence in Jotham's government. To the discouraged prophet, as he knelt in prayer at the Temple at Jerusalem, the Lord granted a transforming vision of His glory. He thus assured Isaiah that despite the apparent triumph of wickedness on earth, the Lord Jehovah still reigned omnipotent upon his heavenly throne, adored by the mighty angels of heaven (symbolically represented by the six-winged cherubim). Even the foundations of the earthly Temple trembled at the thunder of the angelic choir, and the sanctuary was filled with the incense smoke of adoring prayer.

B. Confession, Cleansing, and Sanctification. 6:5-7.

How could the prophet's impure lips repeat that angelic song? His conscience was burdened by a sense of personal weakness and failure. He could only confess his helplessness and fallen estate. But God's redeeming grace hastened to meet his need, applying to his lips a coal from the incense altar (originally from the altar of blood sacrifice; cf. Lev 16:12). Isaiah was thus cleansed and equipped for praise, intercessory prayer, and the proclamation of God's word.

C. Response and Commission of the Yielded Believer. 6:8-13.

Every believer is saved to serve; he is

ipso facto from the time of conversion a witness for God. But note that Isaiah was invited by the query, **Who will go for us?** (v. 8). God can use only willing, loving service. Coupled with the thrice-repeated "Holy" of 6:3, this reference to **us** may well point to the trinitarian plurality in God (although it may also include the angels as associated with God in common viewpoint and purpose). Isaiah was thereupon commissioned to preach God's message faithfully and fearlessly, even though his ministry would result in rejection and apparent failure. **9.** Render this, *Keep on hearing* and *keep on seeing,* as the Hebrew syntax demands. Because Israel's rejection of Isaiah's message was foreseen, their hearing of it would be like not hearing at all. And their unwillingness to hearken would result in the judicial blinding of their hearts. (For the sake of vividness their negative response is put into the imperative mood, although of course the prophet would not have quoted these exact words in addressing his people.) **13.** Yet his work was not to be in vain, for after the utter destruction of the Chaldean invasion here foretold (resulting in complete depopulation of the land), **a tenth** of the deported population of Judah would come back – **shall return** (for so this verb should be translated in view of the appearance of Isaiah's son, Shear-jashub – *A remnant shall return* – in the next chapter). That is, a remnant would return to Palestine in faith, trusting in God's promises to establish them there. Nevertheless, even this remnant would be consumed by invasion and warfare (notably in the time of Antiochus IV of Syria). Israel would be perpetuated only by the faithfulness of a still smaller remnant, the **holy seed, who** was to spring out of the stump of the felled tree of Judah. (The terebinth and oak are especially prone to produce such shoots from their stumps.)

VOLUME TWO.
IMMANUEL. 7:1–12:6.

Sermon I. Immanuel Rejected by Worldly Wisdom. 7:1-25.

A. God's People Confronted by Peril. 7:1,2.

Syria and the Northern Kingdom of Israel had formed an alliance against the menace of a revived Assyrian empire, and were determined to bring Judah into their coalition, even though it meant deposing Ahaz and substituting a puppet king, the son of Tabeel (see Albright, "The Son of Tabeel," BASOR #140, pp. 34,35). Marshaling their armies for the successful invasions recorded in II Chr 28, they sent a shiver of fear through the outnumbered forces of Judah, captained by their ungodly king.

B. God's Promise of Deliverance. 7:3-9.

3. Ahaz inspected the city's water supply in preparation for the siege that was to come (probable date, 735 B.C.). God revealed to the prophet the precise thoughts running through the king's mind, and bade him go to meet Ahaz, taking along young **Shear-jashub,** presumably because of the gracious promise contained in his name – *A remnant shall return* (from captivity). **7.** Without prior mention of the king's unrenounced sins, God, through Isaiah, first conveyed to him a promise of practical deliverance, treating him with kindness altogether undeserved. **8. Within threescore and five years shall Ephraim be broken** in pieces. That is, by 669 B.C. (reckoning from 735). Actually, Samaria fell within eleven years (722 B.C.), and her population was deported beyond Assyria. But the settling of non-Israelite colonists by the government apparently did not take place on a large scale until the reign of Ashurbanipal (669–626) – a fact alluded to in Ezr 4:10), where the immigrants refer to the king of Assyria as Asnapper (or Osnapper). With this foreign influx, the Northern Kingdom was truly "broken in pieces" ethnically, and the sparse native Israelites still left in the land were submerged. **9.** A threat to Pekah is implied here, though not made explicit. Note that the Jews **(ye)** had to receive and rest upon this divine promise if they were to **be established,** i.e., derive practical benefit from this judgment visited upon the northern allies. Their failure to do so led to the worsening of their plight as they became subject to Assyria.

C. God's Promise Spurned by Unbelief. 7:10-12.

The Lord offered a confirmatory miracle to bolster Ahaz' faith, inviting him to name it. It could be anything from heaven above to earth beneath. But Ahaz, having made up his mind to put his trust in Assyria, put Isaiah off with a hypocritically pious pretext (alluding to the general prohibition of Deut 6:16).

D. God's Deliverance Reaffirmed and His Deliverer Promised. 7:13-25.

14. A virgin shall conceive. The word for **virgin** here is carefully chosen. Etymologically *'almâ* does not necessarily signify a *virgo intacta* (an untouched maiden). In actual usage in the Hebrew Scriptures, however, it refers only to a maiden chaste and unmarried (so far as the context shows). This well fits the prospective mother alluded to in this situation. Judging from 8:1-4, the typical mother was the prophetess who became Isaiah's wife within a short time after this prophecy was spoken. Therefore she was a virgin at the time this promise was given. She serves as a type of the Virgin Mary, who remained a virgin even after her miraculous conception by the Holy Spirit. The son of this prophetess, correspondingly, is a type of the Messianic Immanuel, as will shortly be explained. **15. Butter and honey** was the standard diet of those who lived in a devastated land that had reverted to pasturage. Such a diet the son of the prophetess was to eat as the result of the coming Assyrian depredations, as well as those of the neighboring nations (cf. II Chr 28). Read with the ASV, **when he knoweth,** rather than with the AV, **that he may know** (the Hebrew can signify either). That is, when he attains the age of legal accountability (doubtless twelve years of age). This would come out to 721, after the destructive campaigns of Shalmaneser V and Sargon. Certainly by 721 Damascus was forsaken (having been captured by Assyria in 732) and likewise Samaria (which fell in 722). **17. Jehovah will bring upon** (ASV) Ahaz and his people, because they refused to trust him, **the king of Assyria;** i.e., the unparalleled oppression and tyranny of the Assyrian Empire.

This coming punishment of Judah is more fully described in the remainder of the chapter. **18. The fly . . . of Egypt, and . . . the bee . . . of Assyria.** A forewarning of the clash of armies (notably at Eltekeh in 701) between the rival powers of Egypt and Assyria. Their troops undoubtedly stripped the whole countryside of Judah for provisions and supplies. **20.** The **razor that is hired** was the future king Sennacherib, who leveled most of Judah to the ground in 701, destroying forty-six cities (according to his own account) and leading captive some 200,000 people. The Assyrians were **hired** in the sense that they were first bribed by Ahaz to intervene in the West (II Chr 28:21). **21,22.** Here again we find **butter and honey** as the food of sparse survivors in a land of ruined fields and orchards and desolated cities. **23.** Naturally in such areas the value of real estate would drop to nothing, and fields would revert to young forest in which wild animals might be hunted (v. 24) or cattle might range (v. 25).

Sermon II. Messianic Deliverance Foreshadowed. 8:1–9:7.

A. Birth of a Child Foreshadowing the Downfall of Judah's Foes. 8:1-4.

God told Isaiah before he had even married his fiancee that he would have a man-child by her, and He bade him inscribe the child's name on a tablet as a matter of public record before two witnesses of reputation. **Maher-shalal-hash-baz,** meaning "hasten to the booty, rush to the spoil," was to betoken the successful Assyrian assault upon Damascus and Samaria. This assault would crush both those kingdoms before the infant boy would be old enough to utter, "Mummy" or "Daddy," i.e., within three years. (This prophecy was fulfilled in the capture of Damascus and the spoliation of Samaria in 732 by Tiglath-pileser III).

B. The Foolish Choice of Worldly Wisdom. 8:5-8.

6. Waters of Shiloah or Siloam. A gentle, healing spring in Jerusalem, typifying the reign of God in the yielded heart of the believer. The God-forgetting people were rejoicing **in** (or better, *with respect to)* Rezin of Damascus and Pekah of Samaria because they had been defeated by Tiglath-pileser. (Hence this part of the chapter must have been written two or three years later than the episode of ch. 7.) **8.** The words **O Immanuel** are very significant here. Isaiah's son was but a type of Immanuel, *God with us.* The birth of the child may have evoked this thankful cry from the parents as they beheld the fulfillment of God's word. But from this time on, Israel became the land of the promised Redeemer, the Messianic antitype of Maher-shalal-hash-baz. Though scourged by Assyrian invasion, it remained the land of promise because of the Messiah.

C. Final Triumph of God's Grace. 8:9-15.

9. Though the pagan people might do their worst in trying to extinguish Israel's light, they must eventually fail, because

"God is with us" (*'immānû'ēl*). **12.** Isaiah and his followers were not to be intimidated by the reproach of their countrymen that they were guilty of **conspiracy** (ASV; rather than AV, *confederacy*) against their country in opposing Ahaz' alliance with Assyria. **13.** No matter how unfavorable present circumstances are, true believers will **sanctify** Jehovah by continuing to regard him as supreme in governing human affairs, and the fulfiller of his promises. They are to fear and revere him only; they are never to fear men. **14.** The apostates of Judah would stumble over his word (which they had spurned) into destruction and damnation.

D. The Faithful Remnant To Trust in God Alone. 8:16-22.

16. Now that Isaiah's prophecy had been made public, it was to be sealed up against the day of its fulfillment, when God would authenticate it by the events of history. **18. The children whom Jehovah hath given** (ASV) were, of course, Shear-jashub and Maher-shalal-hash-baz, with their names of prophetic meaning. (Heb 2:13 indicates that here Isaiah speaks of himself and his children as types of Christ and His blood-bought children, who are signs and wonders from the Lord.) **19.** Familiar spirits and wizards were much consulted in that age when people had lost their faith in the Scriptures. Like spiritualists today, they pretended to have communication with the dead. Hence the appropriateness of the rhetorical question: **On behalf of the living (should they seek) unto the dead?** (ASV; rather than AV *for the living to the dead?*). **20.** Every human opinion, religion, or philosophy is valid only as it agrees with God's Word – the only absolute yardstick of spiritual truth. **21,22.** A description of the tragic disillusionment and despair of those who trust in something other than the Word of God. **There is no morning** (AV, marg.) or dawn of deliverance for them. They shall plunge into the eternal night of perdition with vain and bitter curses upon their lips.

E. Coming Deliverance by a Divine King. 9:1-7.

Verse 1 should be construed as in the ASV: **But there shall be no gloom to her that was in anguish** (i.e., the land of Galilee). **In the former time he brought into contempt the land of Zebulun and . . . Naphtali** (by permitting them first to come under the direct yoke of Assyria; cf. II Kgs 15:29); **but in the latter time hath he made it glorious, by the way of the sea,** etc. (by sending his Son to live in Galilee and carry on his principal ministry there; cf. Mt 4:13-17). **3-5. Multiplied the nation;** i.e., by the addition of the Gentile church, which, in the coming age, would unite with Jewish Christians to carry out Christ's Great Commission and bring in the harvest of the redeemed from all the earth. Compare Christ's statement about the joy of the reapers in Jn 4:36. **4.** In the time to come, all the heathen enemies and persecutors of God's people will be utterly crushed (as the Midianite host was defeated by Gideon long ago). **5. For every boot** (RSV; rather than ASV's *armor*, or AV's *battle*) **of the tramping warrior in battle tumult and every garment rolled in blood will be burned as fuel for the fire.** This refers to the complete destruction of all weapons of oppression – both in the temporal judgments of the fall of empires, and in the Armageddon of the 'last days.'

6. Here we have set forth the character of the Immanuel who will bring this deliverance. He will come into the world as a baby born to the Hebrew people, a gracious gift of God to them. (Contrast the fierce denial of the Moslem faith that God could ever have a son, as enunciated in Sura 112 of the Koran.) He will rule God's kingdom with God's authority. He will be a **Wonder of a Counselor.** That is, as a person of two distinct natures – God and Man – he will truly be a wonder from Jehovah; and as the One who alone has the words of eternal life, he will be a counselor like none other. As **mighty God** (a term clearly applied to Jehovah in Deut 10:17; Isa 10:21; Jer 32:18), he will be the irresistible battle champion (as this word for "mighty" implies) who will obtain the final victory in the arena of history. As **everlasting Father** (lit., *Father of Eternity*), he will be not only lord of eternity but the author of eternal life to the redeemed. As **Prince of Peace** he will bestow what *shālôm*, "peace," implies in its fullest meaning: health to the sin-sick soul; a sound and healthy relation between sinners and God, as well as between sinners and fellow sinners; and a sound condition of universal righteousness and prosperity prevailing over the earth. **7.** As the antitype of King David, and as his descendant and heir, this promised One will rule over the people of God forever and ever (cf. II Sam 7:16).

Sermon III. Boastful Samaria Doomed to Exile. 9:8–10:4.

Even after the disastrous invasion of the Northern Kingdom by Tiglath-pileser in 732 (the year in which he also destroyed King Rezin of Damascus), the Ephraimites still blindly ignored God's last warning. They boasted that they would rebuild their devastated country and make it stronger and more glorious than ever before (vv. 9b,10). But the time was soon coming when even their former allies of Syria and Philistia would join the besieging armies of Assyria to bring about Samaria's final extinction. **14,15.** All the leading classes, who had failed to repent and return to God and who had been unfaithful to their trust, would be totally destroyed, with all their children. **18-21.** Sin bears in itself the seeds of its own retribution and destruction. Along with the agonies of famine there would arise the horrors of civil war between Ephraim and Manasseh, the two main tribes composing the Northern Kingdom (doubtless involving the other tribes as well).

10:1-4. Those unrighteous judges and government officials who abused their power by oppressing their people and inscribing unjust sentences and decrees for their own personal gain would find their iniquities fittingly punished before God's bar of justice. They would lose all their tainted possessions when foreign invaders would strip them of all they had and lead them off as miserable captives into bondage. **Your glory.** Their treasures and valuables they had substituted for God (Israel's true glory).

Sermon IV. World Empire Crushed; the Glorious Empire to Come. 10:5–12:6.

A. God's Instrument for Judgment To Be Judged in Turn. 10:5-34.

5,6. Not by its own human power, but by the sovereign action of God had Assyria attained power to chasten Israel and mete out God's punitive displeasure upon the heathen nations. **9.** The cities here mentioned were all notably powerful and defended by strong forces, but they were helpless before the onward march of Assyria. The victors boasted that they had overcome all these kingdoms themselves and the gods who were worshiped there. Insignificant little Judah with her puny gods, they declared, would easily fall. But such contempt towards Jehovah was to result in the complete destruction of this haughty empire when he was through with it. Human rulers are but instruments in God's hand, and they show utmost folly in boasting against him who uses them for his own purposes. **17.** God is here called the **light of Israel.** His fire of judgment would consume the heathen as fiercely as if their invincible armies were a mere patch of briers. The forest of goodly trees, representing their proud leaders, would be so devastated by this fire that a little child might easily count the number left. (All of this was fulfilled between 612, the fall of Nineveh, and 605, the Battle of Carchemish.)

20-23. While pagan empires would have their day and pass away, the Lord declared, the weak and despised people of God were to live on down through history. By the divine discipline they would be taught to trust in the Lord alone for their salvation. Again the hope of Israel is here placed in the remnant of true believers who would return from captivity. No matter how small a fraction they might be, after the judgments of God had befallen the apostate nation, the future would lie with them. **24-27.** They were to trust in these promises of God and not fear the ruthless conquerors who would seem to be having everything their own way. For these enemies, too, would be quickly destroyed, as were the Midianites by Gideon, or the Egyptians who were drowned in the Red Sea. **28-34.** For the present, the Assyrians would irresistibly proceed from one Jewish stronghold to another (their plan of march is here predicted in detail); but they would some day be lopped off and felled like a mighty tree under the woodsman's axe.

B. The Messiah To Restore and Rule. 11:1-16.

1,2. The Messiah (who will set up the true and godly empire, the counterpart of Assyria's) will be a descendant of the promised line of David, God here declares. After the tree of David has been felled and only the stump left, this *nēser* or **Branch,** a significant Messianic title, will spring up. He will be supernaturally endowed by the sevenfold Holy Spirit of God. Therefore, he will administer a perfectly righteous rule, for no clever litigant or petitioner will ever be able to deceive him by false evidence (v. 3). Furthermore, he will maintain the rights of the defenseless and the poor (especially the meek who are persecuted for their faithfulness to God) as against the wealthy and influential. As a belt holds all the wearer's clothes together in proper place, so God's standard of holiness will be the constant and unifying force in Messiah's rule (v. 5). **6-9.** The condition of Christ's empire will be that of harmony and peace, based upon the true religion. The picture of the fierce predatory animals living peaceably with the weak and defenseless symbolizes the removal of all natural hostility and fear between men. (The references to the **little child,** v. 6, and the **sucking child,** in v. 8, clearly preclude construing the beasts as various types of men.) **9.** The basis for this Eden-like harmony will be the full and adequate knowledge of God that all mankind will then possess, and that even brute creation will reflect (cf. Rom 8:21).

10-16. The Messianic kingdom will be ushered in by a **second** (v. 11) restoration of the Jews (which clearly excludes reference to the return under Zerubbabel in 537 B.C. and yet indicates a national restoration of comparable magnitude). This time the scattered people will come from every geographical direction: east – Assyria, Elam, Shinar; west – the isles of the sea; north – Hamath; and south – Egypt, Pathros or Upper Egypt, and Cush or Ethiopia. Such diverse regions were not involved in the return of 537. Not Jews alone, but the Gentile nations *(gôyim)* also will rally to the standard of the cross (v. 12), to form a Jewish-Gentile Church even in the latter days. Furthermore, in that day there will no more be a cleavage between northern tribes and southern, but the Christian Israelites will constitute one harmonious people. God's people, moreover, will triumph over all the not-yet-converted nations surrounding them (as Philistia, Edom, and Moab surrounded ancient Israel). The natural barriers of the Euphrates and Nile will be removed, and communication between all these formerly hostile regions will be easy and unimpeded when the Prince of Peace rules over them all.

C. Thanksgiving and Triumph of Christ's Redeemed. 12:1-6.

Here we have a beautiful paean of praise expressing the joy of a people completely yielded to God's will and discipline, and completely content with his grace. This song of the Millennial believers furnishes assurance that despite the hindrances presented by the disobedient and backsliding ones of the chosen race, God's perfect plan for that race will be completely realized at the end of human history.

VOLUME THREE. BURDENS OF JUDGMENT UPON THE GENTILE NATIONS. 13:1–23:18.

Burden I. Fall of Babylon; and Her King's Descent into Hades. 13:1–14:27.

A. The Downfall of Babylon. 13:1-22.

1. Burden *(maśśā')* is also rendered *oracle,* as if it signified a mere lifting up of the voice of the prophet (coming from *nāśā',* "lift up"). But judging by its usage, it seems better to understand it as *that which is lifted up – a burden.* That is, a burden of divine judgment which an offender must bear. **2. Nobles.** The chief men of the Babylonians. **3.** The Persians under Cyrus the Great are prophetically called God's **consecrated ones** (ASV) because He ordained them to overthrow Babylon. Note that they were to come **from a far country** (v. 5) rather than from some neighboring region. Persia lay well to the east of Elam, over 350 miles from Babylon. **6.** Here the **day of Jehovah** (ASV) is clearly not eschatological, but refers to the events of 539 B.C. Yet this fall of Babylon is prophetically typical of the overthrow of latter-day Babylon (Rev 14:8), to which the fearful meteoric phenomena of 13:10 more particularly apply (cf. Mt 24:29). This is brought out by the reference to the **world** *(tēbēl)* in 13:11, rather than to the Chaldean Empire alone. But verses **14-16** certainly apply to 539, for the mention of **Medes** in verse 17 makes this clear ("Medes" being a name more familiar in Isaiah's day than "Persians," who were then still unknown to the western Asiatics). **19-22.** In these verses the Lord very definitely predicts for historical Babylon eventual extinction of a most permanent sort. Later history saw the literal fulfillment of this prophecy, for Babylon was completely deserted by the seventh century A.D. Its desolate site has been regarded with superstitious dread by the Arabic-speaking population, **the Arabian** (v. 20), ever since.

B. The Fall of the King of Babylon. 14:1-27.

1,2. The ungodly World Power of Babylon will be crushed, but the people of God will emerge triumphant in the end. They will even subject the heathen nations to themselves (through the spiritual conquest of the Gospel, and through the mighty imposition of Christ's rule in the 'end time'). The Gentiles will aid in the restoraton of Israel to her promised land.

3-11. A song of triumph over vanquished Babylon (both the historical city and the eschatological one). **8. Fir trees** and **cedars.** These are both literal (since they were spared from the deforestation of Chaldean axemen) and symbolic – of the other nations in the forest of mankind. **9. Hell** or *Sheol* (ASV). A name for the general abode of the dead prior to Christ's resurrection. But here it represents the dwelling of the spirits of proud God-defying rulers of former ages. These are represented as welcoming the arrival of the king of Babylon with malicious satisfaction, for all of his brief earthly glory will have been extinguished, even as theirs was.

12-20. Lucifer. The Roman name for the morning star (Heb. *hêlēl*, "the bright one"), which speedily disappears before the far greater splendor of the sun. This title is addressed to the king of Babylon, not so much as a specific human individual (like Belshazzar, for example), but as a representative or embodiment of Satan, who is regarded as the power behind the king's throne. The titanic pride and ambition expressed in verses 13,14 are out of place on any lips but Satan's. The epic poetry of Canaanite Ugarit often refers to the "mountain of the North" or *Sapunu* (equivalent to Heb. *sāphôn* used here) as the abode of the gods. The ignominious downfall of the tyrant of Babylon, prophetically pictured here, whose corpse lies unburied and dishonored, reflects upon Satan, his lord.

21-27. This passage reverts more particularly to the fall of historical Babylon in 539, and the permanent extinction of her power and posterity. As a confirmation beforehand of this promise concerning Babylon, the Lord foretold the more immediate disaster to the armies of Assyria (the suzerain of Babylon at the time) in Palestine (v. 25), which took place upon Sennacherib's invasion of 701 B.C. All these disasters to neighboring nations would demonstrate the irresistible power of the one true God, the God of Israel (vv. 24,27).

Burden II. The Downfall of Philistia. 14:28-32.

The Philistines, in their war against Ahaz, had recently seized four large Jewish cities (II Chr 28:18). But here they are warned of coming retribution from Hezekiah, the **adder** (ASV) of verse 29, and from the later Jewish princes of the Hasmonean dynasty (like Jonathan Maccabaeus, who burned Ashdod and Ashkelon and compelled Gaza to surrender). **31. A smoke out of the north** (ASV) refers to the coming devastations of Sargon (20:1) and Sennacherib (mentioned in his record of the campaign of 701). **32.** Philistia's envoys were therefore to be sent home with the declaration that Judah's true and only safety is to be found in Jehovah her God.

Burden III. The Downfall of Moab. 15:1–16:14.

Here we have a vision of the fearful depredations the Assyrians were to inflict upon the various cities of Moab which are mentioned throughout chapter 15. Even though the Moabites had been implacable enemies of Israel, the prophet could only weep with compassion at the spectacle of the bloody cruelty of the conqueror and the wretched lines of refugees streaming away from their doomed cities. **9. Waters of Dimon . . . full of blood.** A play on words, between Hebrew *dām*, "blood," and **Dimon,** which is perhaps a sinister variation from the more familiar name of Dibon. The **lions** mentioned here may refer to triumphant Judah in a later day, or perhaps to Esarhaddon the Assyrian (who records the subjugation of the Moabite king, Mutsuri), or even to the Chaldeans of a subsequent age.

Chapter 16 presents a related but separate utterance occasioned by the coming flight of Moabite refugees to Sela, the capital of Edom (which was allied to Moab). From their asylum in Edom they are bidden to make submission to the people of God, for Jehovah is their only sure refuge. His throne shall some day be established at David's capital of Jerusalem (a prediction of the second coming of Christ). **16:3.** A summons to Judah to maintain a godly testimony and show compassion on the Moabite refugees. **6-12.** The prophet sets forth the reason for Moab's disaster: her overweening pride (so clearly evidenced in the "Moabite Stone" of King Mesha). He follows with a description of her coming devastation at the hands of Sennacherib (who records the submission of Chemoshnadab, king of Moab). **7.** For **foundations** of Kir-hareseth, read with the ASV, *raisin-cakes.* These were offerings that would no longer be available for idol worship because of the destruction of all the vineyards. **8. Sea.** Possibly the Dead Sea, or else the celebrated pools of Heshbon. Isaiah could not but lament the destruction to be meted out to all the fair and smiling countryside of Moab. In vain her suppliants would besiege the heathen altars of her **high place**[s]; their imaginary gods would be powerless to save them. **13,14. Within three years.** A more precise date for this invasion. The time was doubtless revealed in 704 B.C., and referred to the coming of Sennacherib three years later.

Burden IV. The Downfall of Damascus and Samaria. 17:1-14.

This chapter is contemporaneous with Isaiah 7, and predicts the downfall of the northern coalition in the reign of Ahaz. Tiglath-pileser was to leave Damascus a heap of ruins in 732 B.C.; likewise its vassal cities, like Aroer near Rabbath-Ammon. The glory of Damascus would be removed along with that of North Israel (which had risen to such power under Jeroboam II, 782–753 B.C.). Only a pitifully small remnant of the ten tribes would remain, like the final wheat ears or the last olives left after the harvest has been gathered. **7-11.** A prediction that these last survivors after the tragic events of 722 (when Samaria would fall to Sargon and be deported to Assyria) would repent. They would renounce their graven images and their **groves** (v. 8; a mistranslation of *'ashērîm,* cultic wooden pillars or tree trunks representing the female consort of the deity worshiped on a "high place"). They would turn in faith to Jehovah, **the Holy One of Israel** (v. 7). (Cf. the record of the great Passover celebration in II Chr 30:1-22, in which worshipers from the surviving Samaritans participated. But perhaps the perspective here is also eschatological.) The reason for this coming devastation was, of course, their desertion of the true God, who was their only real strength in resisting heathen conquest.

12-14. A graphic description of the coming invasion by the Assyrian host, with its various contingents of subject-allies under Sennacherib (heir of the conquerors of Damascus and Samaria). God would suddenly rebuke the Assyrians, declares the prophecy, in a night of terrible plague and destruction. So shall he eventually deal with all his foes and the armies they marshal against his cause.

Burden V. The Downfall and Conversion of Ethiopia. 18:1-7.

Under Piankhi the Ethiopians had established the Twenty-fifth Dynasty in Egypt, and Piankhi's son Shabaka (called "So" in II Kgs 17:4) had encouraged Hoshea of Israel in the last unsuccessful revolt against Assyria. Shabaka also leagued with Merodach-baladan of Babylon, and was later an encouragement to Hezekiah to rebel against Sennacherib, who finally crushed the Ethiopian-Egyptian forces at Eltekeh in 701. So's nephew, Tirhakah, led a new Egyptian effort, but was finally crushed by Ashurbanipal in 667. **7.** Here the Ethiopians are identified as coming from the land where the Blue Nile joins the White Nile – **whose land the rivers divide** (ASV) – and as being tall of stature and smooth of skin. They would be pruned away like branches, the prophet says, and their carcasses would fall in battle, to be consumed by the vultures. Yet some day the Ethiopians would pay tribute to God and come to Zion as true believers.

Burden VI. The Afflictions of Egypt. 19:1–20:6.

A. The Subjugation of Egypt. 19:1-25.

1-10. Isaiah sets forth the afflictions of civil war, Assyrian conquest, drought, and devastation which were to befall Egypt in the coming decades. Jehovah would demonstrate his sovereignty to the discredit of the false gods of Egypt. Civil war was to arise as the Libyan Dynasty (XXII) clashed with the Ethiopians and with the Saites of Dynasty XXIV, and thus foolishly prepared the way by internecine conflict for the cruel subjugation of them all by Esarhaddon of Assyria (v. 4). This was to take place in 671, and the Assyrian rule would endure nineteen years. The economic ruin of Egypt would be insured by a prolonged and terrible drought (vv. 5,6), in which the Nile would fail to overflow its banks. **7. Paper reeds.** Rather, *meadows by the Nile* (ASV). Hence there would be no fish to catch and no flax to spin. **10. Foundations** (AV marg.; *pillars,* ASV). Rather, *weavers.* Hence read: *And her weavers shall be crushed, all the workers for hire shall be grieved of soul.*

11-15. The Egyptians had prided themselves on being the wisest and most learned of peoples. But they would prove utterly foolish and incapable as they met the coming blows of disaster, and their clashing leaders would bring them to ruin. **13. Zoan** or Tanis was a northeastern capital near the border of Sinai. **Noph** (ASV, Memphis) lay more to the south at the apex of the Delta. **15.** Every class of society would be thrown into a state of unemployment and want.

16-25. But God still had a bright future in store even for this grossly idolatrous land. First of all, the Egyptians would tremble at the fearsome power of Israel's God as he brought judgment upon them, especially when the avenging armies of Nebuchadnezzar would invade their land in pursuit of the Jews who would take refuge there (cf. Jer 46:24-26). Then they would recognize that Jehovah had intervened in history. Later on, Jewish immigrants would exert a leavening influence upon Egypt. They would establish sizable Hebrew-speaking colonies in at least five of the Egyptian cities, one of which would be Heliopolis. **18.** The word *Heliopolis,* "City of the Sun," has here been deliberately altered, in a play on words, to read **city of destruction.** There would even be an altar erected to Jehovah in Egypt (v. 19; erected by a priest named Onias in the reign of Ptolemy VI), as an earnest of the later conversion of Egyptians to Christianity. God would send them a saviour (Alexander the Great) to deliver them from their Persian oppressors, as a token of that divine Saviour who would free them from Satan's rule. **21,22.** Probably a reference to the Christianization of the land. **23-25.** A forecast of the harmonious relations to be established by the spread of the Gospel to all the lands of the Fertile Crescent prior to the Mohammedan conquest. And this in turn is but a foregleam of that final and more lasting peace that will be established between East and West in the days of the Messiah.

B. Egypt To Be Enslaved by Assyria. 20:1-6.

This oracle was probably revealed somewhat later than that of chapter 19, for it expands upon the prediction made in 19:4. At any rate, the exact year of the fulfillment of the prophecy is given. This was 711 B.C., when King Sargon sent **Tartan** (v. 1, AV; Accadian *tartānu),* his "chief general," to subdue the Philistine city of Ashdod. Azuri, king of Ashdod, was deposed (according to Sargon's *Annals),* and a revolt raised by Iatṇa was suppressed. This prophecy of Egypt's disgrace and subjugation came about forty years before the Assyrian Conquest. Severe chastening was due Egypt because she had pretended to serve as Israel's deliverer and had made promises she could not keep, distracting the Hebrews from a wholehearted trust in God alone.

Burden VII. Babylon To Be Conquered and Her Idols Destroyed. 21:1-10.

1. The wilderness of the sea (ASV). The alluvial plain of Babylonia, laid down by the Euphrates and the Tigris with their various tributaries. Numerous swamps and shallow lakes always built up whenever the drainage canals were neglected or damaged. **2.** The **treacherous destroyer** *(dealer;* AV) here mentioned is Chaldean Babylon, ripe for judgment. **Elam.** Persia. Elam was better known than Persia in Isaiah's day, and was later incorporated into the territory of Persia proper. **3,4.** To a man of Isaiah's sympathetic nature, the vision of bloody carnage in the captured cities of Babylonia, as Cyrus' forces advanced toward the capital, had a deeply disturbing effect, like that of a fearful nightmare. **5.** In prophetic vision he saw the princes of Babylon, careless in their false sense of security, banqueting with Belshazzar. **7. A chariot.** Contingents of cavalry and mounted cameleers formed a characteristic portion of the Medo-Persian armies. **8. He cried, A lion.** Better, *He cried as a lion.* So intense was the prophetic watchman's feeling. **9.** This is the first pronouncement of judgment upon the degenerate and idolatrous world culture which Babylon represents; the last is found in Revelation 14 and 17. **10.** Isaiah foresaw Babylon thoroughly beaten and flailed, like wheat upon a threshing floor.

Burden VIII. Defeat for Edom; Victory for Israel. 21:11,12.

11. Dumah. Edom. Apparently an ominous play on words, according to which the main syllable of the name is fitted to the pattern of a word meaning *silence* (used for the realm of the dead in Ps 94:17; 115:17). Isaiah, as the watchman, announces to the Edomites of Mount Seir that the morning of deliverance is breaking for Israel, but the night of defeat and bondage will soon fall upon Edom. Let the Edomites, therefore, seek Jehovah in repentance and faith.

Burden IX. Dedan and Kedar To Be Routed. 21:13-17.

Allied with the Philistines, these northern Arabs had plundered Jerusalem in the reign of Jehoram (c. 845 B.C.). They were later defeated by Uzziah. But here they are warned of the crushing blows to be administered to them by the Assyrians (such as Sennacherib) and the Chaldeans (such as Nabonidus, who made Tema his second capital).

Burden X. Fall of Jerusalem Foreseen; Eliakim To Replace Shebna. 22:1-25.

A. Worldly-minded Jerusalem To Be Destroyed. 22:1-14.

Jerusalem is located upon two or three hills in the midst of valleys surrounded by dominating mountain ranges. As the scene of the revelations granted to God's prophets, its location is appropriately described as the **valley of vision.** The Jerusalemites, from their rooftops, were to descry the approach of the besieging armies of Babylon. Yet in the face of imminent danger, the Jews would be bent upon giddy pleasure and carnal indulgence. And they would meet with utter disaster. Their king (Zedekiah) would vainly attempt flight from the city. Lamentable destruction was to be meted out to both city and people (v. 4).

5-11. The prophet gives details of the coming siege (589–587 B.C.), in which the subject warriors of Kir would fight in the ranks of the Persians of Elam (cf. 21:2). The physical arrangements for the city's defense (the refortifying of the breeches and the guarding of the precious water supply) would all prove useless, because the Jews would refuse to look to their God, their only true defense against the world. **12-14.** The Lord's urgent call for repentance had only met with cynicism and crass fleshly indulgence. But God's fatherly love cannot be so blatantly disregarded and despised without severest consequences. This oracle most likely refers to the eve of Sennacherib's invasion, when Judah would mistakenly choose to rely on the help of Egypt in meeting the vengeance of Assyria. It took the horrors of the invasion in 701 B.C. to bring Jerusalem back to repentance and a renewed commitment to God.

B. A Corrupt Official Replaced by a Godly Public Servant. 22:15-25.

In the light of the preceding context, it is fair to assume that Shebna, the royal chamberlain, was a leader of the pro-Egypt faction in the councils of state. In the confidence that his position was secured, he had ordered a sumptuous tomb for himself, not realizing that he would be demoted from his office and die a pauper in a far country. (In 701 he was already replaced by Eliakim, according to II Kgs 18:18, though he was still a secretary in government service.) But Eliakim *(God will establish)* was a truly devoted follower of God, and therefore he represents the remnant of true believers who opposed alliance with idolatrous Egypt.

22,23. The key of the house of David refers to the position of high trust and influence Eliakim was to enjoy as Hezekiah's prime minister (Hezekiah being of David's dynasty). His position would be as secure as that of a **nail** or large peg built into the wall of a house, and his glory and prosperity would be passed on to his family and descendants. Many interpret verse 25 as a prediction of Eliakim's eventual downfall. But in view of the **sure place** of verse 23 (which, of course, was made sure by God himself), it seems better to understand this of others besides Eliakim who falsely supposed themselves as securely established as he, but had not given their hearts to Jehovah as he had done, and who therefore must some day be cut off.

Burden XI. Downfall and Enslavement of Tyre. 23:1-18.

Tyre represents the ruthless materialism of a great commercial center. Through Jezebel, daughter of the king of Sidon and Tyre, it had exerted a baneful influence upon Samaria, and carried on a brisk trade in Israelite slaves (Amos 1:9). It was forced to capitulate to Assyria in 664; Nebuchadnezzar razed all but the island city in the sixth century; and Alexander completely demolished the island city in 332 B.C.

1. From **Kittim** (ASV), or Cyprus, would come the melancholy tidings of the fall of Tyre. This would mean ruin for the commerce of Tarshish (located in Sardinia or Spain) and for the Phoenician colonies generally throughout the Mediterranean. **3.** No more would the produce of Egypt – **Shihor** (ASV) being a branch of the Nile – purchase valuable goods in the marts of Tyre. **4. Zidon** was to be involved in the same calamity, and her decimated populace would dwindle away. **8-12.** Jehovah would be the author of this doom (as the fulfillment of this prediction would amply demonstrate), which would serve as a judgment not only upon Tyre but upon the whole world view it represents. **11. Canaan** (ASV; AV, *merchant city*). Originally the name of the red-purple wool dyed from the Phoenician murex, which formed the first basis of trade with other nations. Then the name came to be applied to merchants generally. Even in Cyprus the refugees would find no safety (for this island would become tributary to Assyria and its successors).

13-18. A seventy-year eclipse of Tyre would ensue between Nebuchadnezzar's disastrous siege and the fall of Babylon in 539. The Berkeley Version makes **land of the Chaldeans** (v. 13) a vocative, rightly implying that it was the Tyrians who should be no more; the Assyrians would make their land a place for the wild beasts to roam in. It was presumably the Chaldeans who would fashion the siege-engines. **16.** Having lost her independence, the city would have to pander to the lusts and desires of her conquerors, like a woman of the streets. Under the Persians, Tyre enjoyed a great measure of favor and made a good recovery from the Chaldean suppression. Yet even the Persian Cyrus compelled Tyre and Sidon to contribute materials for the rebuilding of Jehovah's Temple in Jerusalem (Ezr 3:7) – a partial fulfillment of Isa 23:18. Today Tyre is virtually a deserted site, and most probably will continue to serve only as a historical symbol of the coming commercial power and capitalistic materialism of the 'last days.'

VOLUME FOUR. GENERAL REBUKE AND PROMISE, I. 24:1–27:13.

Delitzsch describes these four chapters as an appropriate finale, a closing hallelujah, to the unfolding account of God's righteous dealings with the nations.

Sermon I. Universal Judgment upon Universal Sin. 24:1-23.

The judgment that has been particularized in chapters 13–23 for each of the nations involved with Palestine now is represented as about to be poured out upon the earth as a whole. Verse 4 makes it certain that **earth** here must mean "the whole inhabited world" and not simply the *land* (of Palestine), as *eres* (v. 3) might otherwise be construed. There are just two classes of mankind in view here: the wicked and corrupt society of this world; and the faithful people of God. Without distinction as to class or condition, the wrath of the Almighty is to be poured out upon all the people of the world; and all the delights of sinful pleasure will be snatched away from them. Only the smallest remnant of them (vv. 6,13) will survive the general destruction.

On the other hand, there is to be a company of believers all over the world who will rejoice in this outworking of God's righteous condemnation of sin (vv. 14-16). At present, as Isaiah mournfully recognizes (v. 16b), wickedness seems to triumph and victimize the devout people of God. But a dreadful and inescapable doom awaits every citizen of earth as the world comes to a catastrophic end (v. 19). And the proud rulers of men will be cast into the prison house of Hell to await the final judgment of God (v. 22). Then will the glory of God be revealed (as Christ returns to reign on earth) in such splendor that the light of the sun and moon will pale into insignificance. Jerusalem will be the capital of Messiah's empire, and his faithful followers will bask in his radiance (cf. the twenty-four elders in Rev 4:4; 7:11; 14:3).

Sermon II. Jehovah Praised as Deliverer and Comforter of Zion. 25:1-12.

As spokesman for God's covenant people, the prophet gives expression to adoring praise of the Lord for his marvelous providence and righteous dealings with men. Over the span of the centuries the Holy One enforces his holy law upon all the offenders who transgress it. The strongest of cities may become a destroyed and forsaken ruin if its citizens lack faith in God. But the faithful and obedient will be preserved and protected over the years. Despite testings and misfortunes, they will survive the passage of centuries after the proudest human empires have crumbled to dust. **6. This mountain.** Mount Zion. **All people**[s] doubtless includes Gentile Christians, who will be included in the blessings of spiritual Israel. **Fat things.** Choice dishes prepared with olive oil and marrow from meat-bones, the most desirable items of food to the Semites. **Wines on the lees** (or "dregs") were filtered, and afforded a clear and most flavorful drink. These details of food and drink symbolize the delights and nourishing satisfactions of the Gospel. Perhaps they also symbolize "the marriage supper of the Lamb" (Rev 19:9). **7. The covering.** The veil of spiritual blindness beclouding the souls of unbelievers. **8. In victory.** Probably best construed with the ASV as **for ever** (since *lānesah* means that everywhere else; yet *nesah* does mean "glory" in two other passages in the OT). This promise refers to the ultimate triumph of heaven (cf. I Cor 15:54; Rev 21:4). **10. Moab** here is representative of the obdurately hostile and unbelieving world, whose God-resisting troops will be mowed down in the final destruction. **12. Thy walls.** Moab is addressed directly. All the fortifications of the rebellious world will prove powerless against God.

Sermon III. Song of Joy over Judah's Consolation. 26:1-21.

1. The redeemed saints will come thronging to the gate of Jerusalem at the end of the age, chanting hymns of praise (hence the appropriateness of referring to them as **Judah**, for *Yehûdâ* means "Praise"). **2.** They will be a **righteous nation** because clothed with Christ's righteousness and indwelt by God's Spirit. **3.** Their characteristic evangelical faith will be expressed as complete trust in the sufficiency of God and the perfection of his will. **Perfect peace.** More literally, *peace peace (shālôm shālôm),* which means "a peace that really is peace," rather than the spurious and temporary peace, which is all that man can bestow. **4. Trust ye.** The redeemed will readily testify of the everlasting faithfulness of Jehovah. **6.** The **poor** and **needy.** Here (as often in the Prophets and Psalms) the lowly, persecuted, despised people of God who suffer hardship and discrimination in this life. They will yet see the power and pretensions of the world crushed to the ground. **8. The desire of our soul.** They will be wholly wrapped up in the truth and glory of God. This includes all that he has revealed of his person and will (for all this is implied by **name** in Hebrew usage), especially in his character as Jehovah (the covenant-keeping God of grace), for that is his "memorial name." Their most ardent desire and prayer (v. 9) will be, "Thy kingdom come!" **10. Wicked.** The obstinately sinful, the reprobate who reject faith in the Gospel (cf. "the ungodly" in Ps 1).

12. Thou wilt...thou...hast wrought. The redeemed will confess that they have no righteousness apart from Jehovah himself, and it is he who has performed his own good deeds through them (when they have yielded their members as instruments of his righteousness). **13. Other lords.** Probably false gods rather than foreign rulers. They are regarded as false alternatives to the Lord, which the speakers had in former times wickedly chosen in preference to him. **14.** Now they are **dead,** for their 'life' depended upon their now-vanished devotees; **nor** shall they ever **rise** again, for their cult has been forever abandoned. (Christianity forever abolished the worship of all the heathen gods known to the Israelites.) **15. Increased the nation.** This remarkable *increase* of God's people points to the inclusion of the world-wide Gentile Church; hence also the enlargement of the borders of the Kingdom.

16,19. Poured out a prayer. Israel repeatedly called upon Jehovah in times of deepest distress (compared to the agonies of childbirth) and heartbreaking frustration – (**We have . . . brought forth wind**). **Fallen.** That is, "fallen in combat under our successful onslaught" (rather than referring to parturition, as some scholars interpret it). Judah, the speaker here, refers to the dead saints (v. 19) both as **Thy dead** – speaking to God – and as **my dead bodies** (ASV). This is a most explicit OT prediction of the bodily resurrection of believers. **20,21.** God's comforting invitation to his people. They are to take refuge in him during the grim time of the Tribulation, when he will be punishing the unconverted for their rebellion and for their bloody crimes, which will be brought to light at the Last Judgment.

Sermon IV. Oppressors To Be Punished but God's People Preserved. 27:1-13.

1. Leviathan. A symbolic creature (reflected in the dragon myths of the pagan Semites), representing the arrogant, turbulent world in revolt against God. More particularly it stands for the successive world empires of Egypt, Assyria (associated with the swift-running Tigris), and Babylon (associated with the winding Euphrates). **2.** In the end of the age there will be occasion for a blessed counterpart to the mournful Vineyard Song of Isaiah 5. Redeemed Israel will constitute a **vineyard** which a holy God may properly protect from its foes. **4.** Read with the Berkeley Version: *There is no wrath now with Me. Should I find thornbushes and briers (in it), I would fight them and burn them altogether.* **5. Let him take hold.** Even a thornbush, i.e., an enemy of God's people, will be extended an opportunity for forgiveness and grace. Verse **6** should be rendered with the

ASV: *In days to come shall Jacob take root. . . .* Israel's filling the earth with fruit refers to the spread of Christianity (which is the faith of the true Israel of God).

7-12. God reveals his plan for Israel's future: survival through trial; purgation through suffering; and destruction for all her foes. Translate verse 7 (with Delitzsch): *Hath He smitten it* (i.e., Israel) *like the smiting of its smiter, or is it slain like the slaying of those slain by Him?* That is, God would smite Israel only to chasten her; he would smite her foes to destroy them forever. Read verse 8 (Berkeley): *By driving her, by sending her away, He contended with her. He removed her with His rough blast as in the day of an east wind.* This refers, of course, to the Babylonian captivity. The east wind came in from the hot Syrian Desert. **9.** The prophecy looks forward to Israel's complete abandonment of idolatry. **10. Defenced city.** The apparently impregnable capitals of Israel's conquerors, e.g., Nineveh and Babylon. Their inhabitants were devoid of spiritual understanding; they would receive no compassion (such as would be accorded to exiled Judah. **12. His fruit** (ASV). The regathered and converted remnant of Israel. The **river**. The Euphrates.

VOLUME FIVE. WOES UPON THE UNBELIEVERS OF ISRAEL. 28:1–33:24.

Sermon I. Judgment of Ephraimite Drunkards and Jewish Scoffers. 28:1-29.

A. Doom of the Drunkards of Ephraim. 28:1-8.

The declining Northern Kingdom is set forth as a warning example to the Kingdom of Judah. **2.** Though God's **mighty and strong one,** Assyria, was poised to deliver the final blow of destruction, the Ephraimites continued to trust in the fertility of their soil and in economic prosperity, and to lead a life of libertinism and debauchery – in which even the clergy participated with disgusting excess (vv. 7,8). **5.** In contrast to this evanescent and carnal glory of Ephraim stands the Lord himself, who is Israel's only true glory, and who will some day be recognized as such by the remnant of true believers. He will empower them for righteousness in judgment and for victory in warfare.

B. Judah's Scoffing Answered by God's Messianic Promise. 28:9-22.

Verses **9,10** give us the jeering reply of the pro-Assyrian party of King Ahaz, who resisted the impact of Isaiah's words recorded in the previous paragraph. They scoffed at his remarks as 'Sunday School moralizing,' appropriate for infants but quite irrelevant to grown men who understand the art of practical politics. They dismissed the prophet's teaching as hackneyed **precept upon precept; line upon line. 11-13.** The solemn answer to these jibes. God had offered them security and peace if they would trust in him and submit to him; but they preferred to trust in Assyria (against the Northern Coalition). Therefore they would have to learn of their mistake at the punitive hands of those who spoke a foreign tongue (for the Assyrian language was quite incomprehensible to the Hebrews, though distantly related to their tongue). By the hammer blows of cumulative misfortune and disaster, they would have to learn their bitter lesson **precept upon precept; line upon line. 14,15.** These scoffers are identified as the top officials in the government, who had backed Ahaz' foreign policy of bribing Assyria to engage in a treaty of alliance. Assyria wielded her power in the interests of Hell, and she spread death and destruction in her wake. Yet the Jews had chosen her, rather than God, to be their protector, vainly supposing they would thus escape her devastating might. They had made a compact with a heathen power that regarded inconvenient treaties as mere scraps of paper – **we have made lies our refuge.**

16. In contrast to this supposedly clever diplomacy of power politics, God declares the true basis of Israel's safety: the person and work of the Messianic Redeemer. **Foundation . . . stone** implies that Christ's atonement is the basis upon which Israel and the Church are built; apart from him and his merit, there could be no Church at all. **In Zion.** The appointed place of revelation, the only valid disclosure of the one true God; and of blood sacrifice, the only way of salvation. **A tried stone** (lit., *a stone of testing);* i.e., one with no faults or cleavages. Christ proved equal to the subtlest and craftiest temptations Satan could bring against him. **Precious corner stone.** He is of greater value than the whole world. He alone makes the difference between eternal heaven and eternal hell for the sinner. **Shall not make haste.** Better, *shall* *not be excited* or *alarmed* (cf. I Pet 2:6; ASV paraphrases, following the LXX — "shall not be put to shame").

17. The false foundation of the worldly wise was to be violently swept away in the catastrophe of Assyrian invasion, and Judah's treaty of alliance would prove to be a false refuge. **18. Your covenant with death.** The covenant with Assyria would be annulled when the Assyrian government should turn upon Judah and treat her like a subjugated foe. At this, Judah would join a conspiracy of revolt against Sargon, but more especially against Sennacherib, thus breaking solemn oaths of allegiance to the Assyrian government. **19.** The punitive incursions of the Assyrians would be recurrent and of mounting intensity, until the dreadful campaign of 701. **20. The bed is shorter.** Even with Egyptian aid, Judah's resources would be wretchedly insufficient to meet the pressure of Assyria. **21. Mount Perazim.** The place where David, with God's help, routed the Philistines (II Sam 5:20). But now that power of Jehovah was to be turned against his own covenant children — a **strange act, to** which God was compelled by their disobedience.

23-29. Judah's situation is set forth in a parable. The farmer does not plow for the sake of plowing, but rather to prepare for his intended crop. So also God prepares his garden for the crop he wishes to reap — the crop of righteousness from a holy people. To this end God must employ the cutting and crumbling force of disciplinary judgments, perfectly adjusted to Israel's spiritual needs, just as the farmer (using the intelligence God gave him) uses the proper threshing instruments for each type of grain.

Sermon II. Disaster Ahead for Hypocrites. 29:1-24.

1-4. The careless Jews must be humbled and sobered before God. **Ariel,** signifying *hearth of God,* is a symbolic name for Jerusalem, implying that God's fire of judgment would burn there (as invaders spread fire and devastation up to her very gates). **Let them kill sacrifices** (AV). Rather, *let the feasts come round* (ASV). The Jews were faithful about celebrating the feasts of Passover, Pentecost, and Tabernacles each year, even though with guilty, unrepentant hands. **3. I . . . will lay siege.** Through the instrumentality of the Assyrians in 701. **4. Out of the dust.** Jerusalem was to be brought to abject humiliation and extremity of supplication. **5-8. The multitude of . . . nations . . . shall be as a dream.** The Lord would suddenly disperse and destroy these heathen besiegers. Sennacherib's forces lifted the siege to fight the Egyptians at Eltekeh. It was on their return from that victorious engagement that the devastating stroke of God here predicted fell upon them. The loss of 185,000 troops in one night was like the shattering devastation of a mighty thunderstorm and whirlwind. To the Jews the sudden disappearance of the enemy would be like the fading of a nightmare when the dreamer awakes from his tortured sleep.

9-12. A rebuke to the spiritually blind countrymen of Isaiah. Translate verse **9: Tarry and be amazed; blind yourselves and be blind; they are drunken. . . .** As the drunkard could have avoided his besotted condition by abstaining from liquor, so these who had blinded themselves with the folly of sin and unbelief could have avoided their condition. **10. The Lord . . . hath closed your eyes.** Judicial blinding was the natural result of their initial turning away from God's revealed will. Even the professional prophets had lost contact with God and had no more message from him. **11. A book that is sealed.** The Bible and the oracles of the true and faithful prophets of God remained incomprehensible and irrelevant to the "modern men" of the eighth century, who felt that they had advanced beyond their forefathers' outmoded submission to the authority of God's revelation. Having therefore no absolute authority outside themselves and their reason, they could not make head nor tail of God's message to them through Scripture. Verses **13-16** announce God's sentence of judicial blinding upon all who would deceive with sham piety or feigned submission. A mere **commandment of men** (ASV; *precept,* AV). A mere intellectual principle taught by moral philosophy is no satisfactory substitute for true surrender of heart. Their **fear of me** (ASV), or piety, was a mere artificial form, and sprang from no sincere love of God for his own sake. What knowledge they retained of spiritual truth would be taken from them until they were left with nothing but barren agnosticism or heathen superstition. **15. Hide deep their counsel** (ASV). The Jews were carrying on secret intrigues with pagan allies, to whose military strength they were looking for deliverance, rather than to Jehovah.

16. Turning of things upside down. They were attempting to reverse true values, putting man at the top of the scale and God at the bottom, and supposing that the thing created matters more than the Creator. But God will not be subject to man's puny judgment nor tolerate his behaving as if he existed for his own sake, independently of the divine will.

17-24. A prophecy of the eventual removal of Israel's blindness. **17. Lebanon** probably represents man in his self-pride. The proud will be hewn down; but because of this humiliation, the ensuing repentance will cause the cleared ground to spring up as a fruitful garden or orchard *(karmel)*. But those who now produce the fruits of righteousness may later, through carelessness and neglect, revert to a disordered forest. **18,19.** God promises a revival in Israel, centering in the humble and poor of the Lord's flock. Then spiritual deafness and blindness will give way to a ready responsiveness to the glorious truths of the Gospel, and the result will be a joyous, hymn-singing group of believers. **20,21. All that watch for iniquity.** The ruthless and unscrupulous materialists who dominated the economic and political life of Israel were to meet with their just retribution and be removed from God's commonwealth. **22-24.** The Redeemer will surely bring to pass his perfect plan for Israel, and forge them into a godly and reverent people, after they have repented and opened their hearts to the truth of Christ.

Sermon III. Confidence in Egypt Versus Confidence in God. 30:1-33.

A. Futility of Alliance with Egypt. 30:1-17.

1-5. The Lord here pronounces woe upon those who seek human counsel instead of divine, and follow the dictates of worldly wisdom. The **league** (ASV; *counsel*, AV). A secret alliance with Egypt to throw off the yoke of Assyria (a policy into which Hezekiah was unwisely allured at the death of Sargon in 705 B.C.). **4.** The **princes.** The Jewish nobles included in the embassy to the Egyptian court, which conducted negotiations at Hanes (ancient Egyptian *Hwt-nn'-nsw* – "House of the child of the king" – Heracleopolis) fifty miles south of Memphis, as well as at Zoan (or Tanis) in the northeast of the Delta.

6-17. The Lord here condemns the embassy to Egypt. **6.** The **beasts of the south** (or *Negev*, the southernmost part of Judah, which joins with the desert of Sinai). Those that carried the Jewish envoys and their gifts intended for the king of Egypt (Shabaka). The Negev is, of course, the land where these noisome creatures dwelt. **7. Rahab** (ASV) means "insolent arrogance." **That sitteth still** (ASV). More literally, *they are a sitting;* i.e., they are do-nothings. **8.** Isaiah was to inscribe on a tablet, which was to become a matter of public record, that God was displeased with the Bible-rejecting people of Judah and would utterly crush them for their willful disobedience. **10. Speak . . . smooth things.** Very modern is this demand of the congregation that their clergy temper their messages to the desires and preferences of the people, rather than preach some unpopular doctrine derived from God's Word. **11. Cause the Holy One . . . to cease.** They wished to hear no more of the God of the Bible, but only of a God of unrighteous love who would not seriously disturb them in their pursuit of their own schemes and desires. **13.** The wall of self-will which they had built for their protection would suddenly collapse on them and crush them to death. **14.** God would dash their iniquity (or the wall that symbolized it) into pieces like a pot of earthenware. **15. Ye would not.** Through his prophets God had admonished them to "return" to him; i.e., to repent, and to **rest** or **trust** in him with confidence, for then he would deliver them from the tyrannous yoke of Assyrian overlordship. But instead they put their dependence upon Egyptian chariots, as if horses would insure their victory, rather than the strong arm of the Lord of hosts. In the coming time of trouble, bereft of God's favor, they would not be able to resist even an enemy force which they would outnumber a thousand to one (v. 17), and only a few scattered refugees would survive.

B. Comfort for God's Chastened and Repentant People. 30:18-26.

18. Therefore will the Lord wait. Despite the faithlessness of the nation as a whole, Jehovah would bear with them patiently (rather than inflict final destruction upon them all) until a penitent remnant would turn in faith to him; for he would fain display in them the riches of his kindness and grace. Those persecuted and afflicted believers who looked to him for deliverance would some day see him inflict judgment upon the wicked. **19. The people shall dwell in Zion.** His ultimate purpose for his people is that they may dwell in security and peace in his holy city. Yet he must prepare them and teach them (translate **Teacher** in v. 20, rather than **teachers**) through affliction and trial, giving them sure guidance for each step and deterring them from going astray. Thus through suffering he would bring Israel to despise their false gods, who could not save them from disaster (v. 22), and to utterly abjure idolatry.

23-26. Evidently a description of the glories of the Millennium (since this kind of prosperity has no appropriateness for a heavenly existence). **The day of the great slaughter** (v. 25) refers to Armageddon, when the ramparts of the wicked shall have fallen in ruins. The intensified light of 30:26 is symbolic of glorious deliverance and peace as the kingdom of David is established on earth.

C. Destruction of the World Power. 30:27-33.

27,28. The prophet describes, with rich symbolism, the fearful devastation to be wrought upon the rebellious nations of earth at the last great conflict, a token of which was to be the more immediate destruction of Sennacherib's army. But even as these vials of divine wrath are being poured out upon the wicked world, God's redeemed people will abide in peace and joy, recognizing that he is working out his righteous purposes and vindicating the authority of his holy law before angels and men. The tabrets and harps of 30:32 are the orchestra that would sound the Lord's praise at Jerusalem as his supernatural destruction would fall upon the Assyrian host. **33. Topheth** (ASV). The name of a place of Moloch worship in the Valley of the Sons of Hinnom, just outside the southwest corner of Jerusalem. Here idolatrous Jews, since the days of Ahaz, had carried on abominable infant sacrifice (II Kgs 23:10), utilizing special furnaces for this purpose. Possibly the **king** here mentioned is not the king of Assyria (for Sennacherib met no such end), but rather Moloch, the king-god. A furnace or Topheth of destruction was being prepared for Assyria resembling this sacrificial furnace in the Hinnom Valley. Perhaps this is meant to imply the final judgment of hell-fire.

Sermon IV. God, not Egypt, To Be Jerusalem's Defense. 31:1-9.

1-3. Disaster awaits those who trust in human strength rather than in God. The helpers (v. 3) were, of course, the Egyptians, and the helped were the Jews who concluded an alliance with them against Assyria. **4-9.** God would defend Jerusalem without human aid. First he is compared to a lion, invincible and undismayed by all attackers as he guards his own. Then his watchful care is compared to that of birds who protectively hover over their threatened nests. (**Passing over** in verse 5 is from the same root as *pesah* or Passover.) The summons to repent and put away idolatry (v. 6) is accompanied by an assurance that the besieged Jews in Jerusalem, in the last extremity, as the Assyrians thundered at their gates, would discard their idols and cast themselves wholly upon Jehovah. Verse 8 contains a most remarkable prediction that no human army would shatter the enemy, but rather a direct stroke of God. **9. His rock** (ASV; *his strong hold,* AV); i.e., the Assyrians' strength would pass away from Palestine, fleeing back to Nineveh. The **ensign.** Apparently the Jewish battle standard, which doubtless bore the name of Jehovah upon it.

Sermon V. Israel's Final Deliverance, and Her Spiritual Renewal. 32:1-20.

The destruction of the Assyrian army points prophetically to the final world conflict, which will usher in the rule of Christ, the perfect King of Israel. Christ's kingdom will fulfill God's ideal of a holy commonwealth, administering a perfect righteousness throughout the earth. God's King will provide complete shelter to all who seek refuge in him, and he will satisfy their thirsty souls with living water. (Note how all these blessings are already at hand in the present age for those who are spiritually citizens of his invisible kingdom.) He will bestow upon believers spiritual sight and hearing power that will never fail, and an understanding heart and clear testimony resulting from the complete transformation of the new birth. Under his government and influence, men will no longer be deceived by the prince of lies but will clearly see the difference between moral wisdom and folly, appreciating how fatuous is a life bent upon evil. God's standards of judgment will at last become man's standards.

9-14. The prophet issues a stern warning to the worldly-minded society women of Jerusalem that the devastation of warfare would cut off their income and plunge them into poverty (v. 10). They would be reduced to desperate straits and doleful lamentation as their mansions were destroyed and their ruined estates reverted to wilderness in the wake of Sennacherib's scourge. (Virtually every Jewish city besides Jerusalem was looted and burned in the campaign of 701, and the country districts were laid waste by Assyrian foragers).

15-20. The bright promise held out for the future was that after the utter ruin of the land (and this seems to point forward to the Chaldean invasion, and beyond), the Holy Spirit would be poured out upon God's people. This was to take place at Pentecost, as we now know, and the arid wilderness of unconverted souls would become transformed into fruitful gardens. But in the light of 32:18 it is necessary to see in this also a promise of great revival in the 'latter days.' Along with that gracious outpouring, will come unprecedented prosperity and fertility, even in lands now sterile. And conditions of righteousness and peace will safeguard the products of every man's toil. War will be completely abolished, after the forest of human power and pride has been laid low by the hail of divine judgment. **20.** This seems to apply to the well-watered and fruitful lands at the service of Israel in the latter day, where their cattle may graze unhindered.

Sermon VI. Punishment of the Treacherous, and Triumph of Christ. 33:1-24.

1-6. A prophecy of Jehovah's triumph over the treacherous Assyrians. See II Kgs 18:14-36 for the account of how Sennacherib first accepted Hezekiah's bankrupting indemnity and then demanded unconditional surrender. Verses **2,3** express the appeal of the believing Jews to Jehovah for deliverance in the coming crisis, and their admiration and praise at his special intervention and routing of the Gentile invaders. **4. Your spoil.** The prophet addresses the Assyrians directly as a vanquished foe. Verse **5** is an affirmation of God's glorious sovereignty, which was to be demonstrated in the Assyrian disaster. In his revealed Word and holy Temple he has filled Zion with the blessings of righteousness and justice, manifesting these qualities in his own marvelous dealings with Israel. **6. Wisdom and knowledge.** A reference to the blessings of revival under Hezekiah, especially in the last years of his reign. **Thy** is addressed to the Judah of that generation.

7-12. A picture of Judah's situation when Sennacherib would devastate the land and contemptuously spurn the peace envoys of Hezekiah. The Assyrian's earlier acceptance of indemnity would imply a **covenant** of peace, but this he would break. In Judah's extremity of helplessness, Jehovah would arise to destroy the invader's army and expose his vaunting pride as worthless, and his defiance of God as the occasion for his fiery doom. **Burnings of lime** (v. 12) implies a burning so thorough that only ashes would be left, like the small lump left after lime has been burnt.

13-16. The Lord points out for all observers the moral of His judgment upon Sennacherib. The unconverted sinners of Judah would be thrown into consternation at this proof of God's power, for it implies a threat that their own iniquities would be visited upon them. They would see that only a sincere and upright believer can be secure in the face of the perpetual flame of God's just vengeance — **everlasting burnings** (v. 14). The only true safety is a godly walk that follows the laws of God in practical life. There is no place so secure as the center of God's will. There a believer is surrounded by the Lord's protecting care, and defended against all possible assailants (v. 16).

17-24. This passage, judging from the statement that Jerusalem will be inviolable, is a foreglimpse of the Millennial kingdom. Therefore the **king** of Israel (v. 17) must be Christ in his regal splendor, reigning over a world-wide domain. **18,19.** The Almighty prophesies the complete removal of latter-day "Assyrians" from the scene, after their abortive siege of Jerusalem. The undisturbed quiet of the Holy City indicates a time after the conclusion of the "times of the Gentiles" (cf. Lk 21:24). Jehovah's presence with a Zion obedient and faithful will insure her impregnable defense (v. 21). She will be like a city surrounded by protective moats — impenetrable to enemy ships — and fructifying streams. No mere man is sovereign over Israel, but Jehovah God himself, and this insures her ultimate deliverance. But the invading ship of Assyria (figuratively speaking) will run helplessly aground, with its tackling loosened; and all its contents will become spoil to the Hebrew defenders. Even the lame Jews (v. 23) will be able to clamber aboard and pillage the helpless attacker. There will be no more spiritual sickness in the cleansed and forgiven land of latter-day Israel.

VOLUME SIX. GENERAL REBUKE AND PROMISE, II. 34:1–35:10.

Sermon I. Utter Destruction of Gentile World Power. 34:1-17.

1-7. The judicial wrath of God will be poured out upon all rebellious nations of earth and powers of Satan. Here we have depicted the scene of carnage that will ensue upon the Battle of Armageddon. The army or **host of heaven** (v. 4) seems to refer to angelic powers opposed to God, in collaboration with unconverted mankind (cf. Eph 6:12 – "the spirit-beings of wickedness in the heavenlies"; cf. Mt 24:29; Rev 6:12). Also involved is a removal or alteration of the (lower ?) heavens as now constituted, ushering in "new heavens and a new earth" (cf. Isa 65:17). **5-7.** The prophecy here represents the destruction of heathen mankind under the example of Edom, or Idumea, the nation accursed of God (v. 5). Just as Edom was an estranged brother of Israel (Esau and Jacob being their respective ancestors), even so unbelieving men are estranged and lost brethren of the redeemed. Their slain upon the battlefield will be like sacrificial animals slain at the altar. Hence the appropriateness of the mention of Bozrah, a famous sheepherding center in Edom. The wild oxen (AV, **unicorns)** and bulls are symbolic of conquering invaders, who will wreak bloody destruction throughout the land of the Edomites.

8-15. A description of the coming utter desolation of the Edomite domains, and, by implication, the ruin of all the God-denying civilization of unregenerate mankind. The complete depopulation, and the occupation of the site by beasts and birds of prey quite resembles what was earlier predicted of Babylon (13:21,22). Babylon, Moab, and Edom all represent different phases of the degeneracy of the corrupt culture of fallen mankind. **11. Confusion** and **emptiness.** In Genesis 1:2 the same words, *tōhû* and *bōhû,* are translated "without form and void." The **satyr** (ASV, *wild goat)* and **screech owl** (ASV, *night monster;* Hebrew *lîlît)* may perhaps represent demonic creatures, for demons are fit spiritual inhabitants for such a place. **16,17.** A strong affirmation that these predictions recorded in writing in Jehovah's **book,** i.e., the inspired prophecies of Isaiah, would be literally fulfilled; and these loathesome creatures would be the only permanent inhabitants of Edom.

Sermon II. Blessing on the Highway of Holiness. 35:1-10.

In stark contrast to the future of the unrepentant, God-defying world stands the future of the people of God. **1,2.** The blossoming of desert vegetation symbolizes the inward change that takes place in the redeemed soul. Instead of arid fruitlessness and spiritual death comes the fair bloom of newly blossoming faith and the more matured grandeur of the cedars of Lebanon. The redeemed will, in a measure, reflect the glory of the Saviour who has appeared for their redemption. **3,4. Your God will come.** A comforting assurance to the discouraged and disheartened that the Lord will intervene on the world scene, to make society subject to the demands of righteousness and to rescue his people from their oppressors. **5-7.** A guarantee that the strength of God will replace the feebleness of man. Believers will be able to see God's truth and hear his voice, walk in his ways unhampered, and sing forth his testimony and praise. Rich and satisfying refreshment will be their constant portion, rather than the searing heat and parching thirst of their unregenerate past. Note that **parched ground** (v. 7; *glowing sand)* may have been the Hebrew term for "desert mirage," which mocks the thirsty traveler with a deceitful vision of waters on the horizon. **8-10.** The redeemed people will walk on the **way of holiness,** from which moral filthiness will be excluded, as well as the ravenous lions of Satanic malignancy. On that pathway even the foolish and unwary traveler, once redeemed and born again, may travel without becoming lost. And those who journey to the Holy City by this highway from Babylon, the City of Destruction, will be characterized by a special joy of which the world knows nothing, and will sing a special song of thanksgiving which the unsaved can never utter.

VOLUME SEVEN. THE VOLUME OF HEZEKIAH. 36:1–39:8.

A. The Destruction of Judah Averted. 36:1–37:38.

Scene I. Jehovah Challenged by Assyrian World Power. 36:1-22.

In this gripping account there stands on the one side of the arena the arrogant, ruthless power of the world, with every material advantage on its side. On the other stands the feeble remnant of Judah, having no resource but God himself. Here we are presented with a historical test to demonstrate once and for all whether Jehovah is the one true God, the Sovereign over all the earth.

1. **Fourteenth year** seems to refer to the second reign of Hezekiah, i.e., the additional span of fifteen (plus ?) years added to the king at the time of the deadly illness recorded in Isa 38. The illness would have occurred in 714, or eleven years after the death of Hezekiah's father, Ahaz. Sennacherib had begun his reign in 705, and had spent most of his time since then suppressing rebellions in various parts of his empire. **All the fortified cities** (ASV). Sennacherib's own record lists them as forty-six in number. **2. Rabshakeh.** Not a proper name, but the title of a high court official (originally a royal cupbearer, since the name means "chief wine-pourer"). Note that his challenge is given at the very spot where Isaiah had confronted Ahaz twenty-three years before (cf. Isa 7). **3. Eliakim** and **Shebna.** Cf. 22:15-25. **7.** Very craftily the Assyrian appealed to the idolatrous party in Judah, who were grieved at Hezekiah's reforms. **8. Give pledges.** *Make a bargain with.* He threw into their teeth their pitiful inadequacy in cavalry and chariots. They did not have enough trained men to handle two thousand horses even if Assyria should give them that many. **10.** Sennacherib's blasphemous arrogance in claiming Jehovah's authorization contains within it a disquieting element of truth (cf. 10:5,6). **11.** At this early period Aramaic — the Syrian language — was already becoming the lingua franca of the Near East (replacing Rabshakeh's native Akkadian, which had enjoyed this status in the previous millennium). But the average Jew, untrained for foreign commerce, was ignorant of it. **17.** The Assyrian policy was still to deport rebellious populations, just as it had been in the case of the ten tribes in 721. Note that this is an offer of economic security at the price of liberty, an offer presented by Assyria's counterparts even today. **18-20. Hath any of the gods . . . delivered his land.** The Assyrian king regarded his subjugation of these north Syrian principalities as a triumph over the gods of the various nations. Surely, he reasoned, no god could be any bigger and stronger than the nation that served him. The defeat of Israel could be interpreted as defeat of Israel's God.

Scene II. Assyria Answered and Judged. 37:1-38.

1. Hezekiah **rent his clothes** in token of deepest humiliation and distress. Well he knew how largely he himself was responsible for the terrible blow that had fallen upon his kingdom. He had disregarded God's warnings (cf. Isa 30; 31) and concluded the disastrous alliance with Egypt. Now he could only turn back in penitence to the prophet whose warnings he had ignored. **3. The children are come to the birth.** The situation of Judah resembled the hopeless impasse when a baby lodges in the mouth of the womb and cannot pass through. Death threatens both mother and child. **6,7.** God's first response to Sennacherib's challenge was to foretell that (a) a rumor of enemy attack would move Sennacherib to lift the siege; (b) he would return to Assyria without renewing the siege; (c) he would there be assassinated. **8. Libnah** was less than ten miles north of Lachish and just below the border of Dan. **9. Tirhakah** was not king at this time, but Shabaka. Tirhakah must therefore have been the commanding officer of the Egyptian expeditionary force in 701 B.C. His reign as king of Egypt did not begin until 688. (Or perhaps this Tirhakah was of an earlier generation than the one who became king, since some inscriptional evidence indicates that the latter would have been but a child at this time.) **12. Gozan** was in Padan-aram about 180 miles west of Nineveh. **Haran** was still farther west, about 70 miles. Though *Rezeph* and *Telassar* were in the north Mesopotamian region, their location is not certainly known. The cities named in 37:13 were all in Syria, north of Damascus. **15.** So deep was the king's concern and grief at this insult to the Lord God that he dispensed with any prophetic intermediary and went directly to God. **16. Dwellest between.** Rather, *sittest* (enthroned) *above the cherubim* (ASV). That is, the cherubim of the mercy seat on the ark of the covenant in the Temple. **19.** Under the apparently hopeless circumstances confronting Hezekiah, this forthright assertion of the unique deity of Jehovah and the nonexistence of the gods of the heathen demonstrated a sturdy faith. **20.** He grounded his petition upon the need for vindication of God's glory, not upon his own personal need or that of his people (for he realized that they little deserved divine favor).

21-29. God's second reply, directed to Sennacherib personally this time, as well as to Hezekiah. **23.** Very significant is the title **Holy One of Israel,** for it was at this juncture that Jehovah was about to demonstrate his immeasurable superiority over his creatures, and his self-commitment to Israel, his precious possession. **24.** The **cedars** and **fir trees** of **Lebanon** were the choicest of timber for the woodsman to fell. The Assyrian presumed to fell the choicest of nations, including God's specially chosen people. **26.** How fatuous was Assyria's pride, for her armies had achieved their victories so far only by the ordaining of the God whom they defied. **29.** God would humiliate Assyria by treating her as a wild beast subdued by means of hook (used especially for bulls) and bridle, and compelling her to return home with her objectives not achieved. **30-32.** The Lord appointed a confirmatory sign of the divine authority behind this assurance: the Jews would be free to return to their ruined fields and gather unmolested the aftergrowth; that is, the crop that would spring up from the fallen grains of the previous harvest (the invasion having lasted thus far from spring to autumn). The following year also they would be dependent mostly on spontaneous growth, since their houses, equipment, and livestock would have to be repaired or replaced. The year after that they would engage in normal sowing, plowing, and reaping, for there would be no return of the Assyrian marauders. (This, of course, is the fulfillment to which this "sign" points, rather than to the more immediate destruction of Sennacherib's army.) **31,32.** God gave assurance that the cooped-up refugees behind the walls of Jerusalem would fan out and re-establish their cities and towns (during the 113 years' interval before the fall of Jerusalem to the Chaldeans).

33. After withdrawing to meet the Egyptians at Eltekeh, Sennacherib would not return to renew the siege, but would flee homeward by the shortest route possible. **35.** God's ground for delivering Jerusalem was not the merit of the present generation but rather his covenant promises to David of old. **36.** The usual assumption is that the Lord used a sudden outbreak of rat-borne bubonic plague to accomplish this heavy mortality. Herodotus records a tradition of a plague of field mice that chewed through all the bowstrings of the Assyrians during the Egyptian campaign.

38. This assassination seems to have taken place twenty years later, in 681. The Assyrian spellings of these names were *Adadmilki* and *Shar-usur* (whose crime is referred to in inscriptions of Esarhaddon and Ashurbanipal). The idol's name has not yet been identified in Assyrian records, unless **Nisroch** is a misspelling of Nusku. (Schrader explained it as a participle from *sarāku,* meaning "The Dispenser" or "The Gracious One." This might have been the title of some better-known deity.) The **land of Ararat** (ASV) was central Armenia. Armenian tradition relates that these parricides lived to found influential dynasties in that land.

B. Destruction of Judah's King Averted. 38:1–39:8.

Scene 1. Hezekiah's Recovery from Deadly Illness. 38:1-22.

Verses 5,6 of this chapter show clearly that at the time of Hezekiah's illness the Assyrian threat to Judah's existence would not arise for many years, presumably not until the latter end of the additional fifteen years added to the king's life. Therefore this illness must have occurred long before the events of the preceding chapters. Why was chronological order thus violated in the arrangement of material in this book? Because the prophecy of eventual Babylonian captivity for Judah arose out of Hezekiah's folly in displaying his wealth to the Chaldean envoys. This in turn set the stage for the events of the latter portion of the book (chs. 40–66), which tends to center attention on the Exile and the return to Jerusalem. As for the illness itself, it seems to have been a severe carbuncle or abscess, or even a cancer (see v. 21).

3. With a perfect heart; i.e., with a completely sincere and devoted heart. He made no claim to sinless perfection, nor does the Hebrew *shālēm* carry such a connotation. **8.** In the light of our present information it is impossible to ascertain how many steps or degrees made up this sundial of Ahaz. The markings may have indicated half-hours or even quarter-hours. Nor can we be certain whether this miracle involved an actual reverse rotation of the earth (which might well have occasioned violent geological disturbances), or was caused by some special atmospheric condition involving an unprecedented refraction of the sun's rays.

10-14. The prospect of painful and untimely death plunged Hezekiah into anguish and despair. **12. For mine age** (AV), read *my dwelling* (ASV; from *dôr)*. And for **I have cut off,** read *I have rolled up*. That is, the strip of fabric, now completed, is rolled up into a bolt of cloth. **13. I reckoned** (AV). Rather, *I have smoothed,* or quieted [my soul] *until morning; as a lion, so He breaketh all my bones* (ASV; a proverbial expression for acute mental anguish and distress of soul).

15-20. The theme of the second movement of this psalm is thanksgiving for God's grace. **15.** God had spoken to the king powerfully through this great crisis in his life. **Go softly.** Better, *I shall walk in solemn procession* because of the (former) bitterness of my soul. **16. By these things.** By such divine providences as severe sickness or peril. **Men live;** i.e., attain continued life or are saved (spiritually). **17.** Render with the ASV: *Behold, (it was) for (my) peace* (or well-being that) *I had great bitterness*. By this trial he learned a most valuable lesson. **18. The grave.** More properly, *Sheol* (ASV). The inhabitants of the infernal regions cannot maintain fellowship with God as can those still dwelling upon earth. In Sheol, according to Christian theology, the dead were shut away in a waiting room until the day of Christ's resurrection (or the Day of Judgment). **19.** Naturally it is impossible for fathers, after they are dead, to teach their children about God.

Scene II. Hezekiah's Foolish Pride and God's Rebuke. 39:1-8.

1. In Babylonian, **Merodach-baladan** was *Marduk-apla-iddina,* "Marduk has given a son." In 721 this Chaldean leader seized control of Babylon and was accepted as a vassal by Sargon. This congratulatory embassy of his to Judah in 712 B.C. had the ulterior motive of enlisting Hezekiah in a conspiracy against Assyria. But two years later Sargon captured Babylon, and he made the Chaldean a prisoner in 709. **5.** God had lent these earthly treasures as a trust, but Hezekiah regarded them as his own, and missed a wonderful opportunity of spiritual witness to these pagan envoys. He was giving the glory to himself instead of to God. **6.** This very explicit prediction was fulfilled to the letter in the days of Nebuchadnezzar. All this treasure went as booty to Babylon (instead of to the Assyrian capital, Nineveh, as human foresight might have supposed). **8.** Hezekiah felt the justice of God's rebuke and submissively bowed before it. At the same time he clung to the comforting assurance that at least this Babylonian captivity would not take place in his lifetime.

VOLUME EIGHT. THE VOLUME OF COMFORT. 40:1–66:24.

Section I. The Purpose of Peace. 40:1–48:22.

Sermon I. The Sovereign Majesty of Jehovah the Comforter. 40:1-31.

1-11. The Spirit of God here proclaims divine comfort. There is no clear suggestion in this chapter (nor in Isa 41; 42) as to what had befallen Israel. Neither the Exile nor the restoration to the land is specifically alluded to. It is simply stated that Israel will have endured hard military service (**warfare** in v. 2), and received a double penalty from God for her sins. **1. My people.** The gracious language of a compassionate, covenant-keeping God. **Comfort ye.** A summons to all God's true prophets, from Isaiah's time until the close of the Exile. **2. Speak ye comfortably.** More literally, *Speak unto the heart of Jerusalem;* i.e., to soothe or reassure. **Her iniquity is pardoned.** More literally, *has been atoned for*. **Double** perhaps refers to (a) the temporal punishment of the seventy years of captivity, (b) the eternal punishment visited upon the person of Christ the sin-bearer on Calvary.

3. The implication here is that Jehovah was to return to Jerusalem through the desert route by which the exiles would return from Babylon, and that a fitting preparation for his advent would be the removal of obstacles and the smoothing out of a highway. But from Matthew's application of this verse to the ministry of John the Baptist (Mt 3:3), it is apparent that these geographical features symbolize the arid lifelessness of the unconverted soul. The hills therefore represent the carnal pride of the sinner, and the valleys his moods of carnal hopelessness and self-pity. **5. The glory of Jehovah** (ASV) was to be revealed through (a) Cyrus' liberation of the exiles from Babylonian captivity and their restoration to the land of promise; (b) Christ's liberation of Satan's bondslaves and their adoption into the family of God. **All flesh.** All mankind are to witness this divine intervention on behalf of the redeemed people.

6,7. Taken by himself, man is tragically frail and transient, and his beauty soon fades. His life is devoid of real dignity or meaning. But the eternal and infallible Word of God invests believing mankind with imperishable significance and glory.

9-11. The AV reading here, **O Zion, that bringest good tidings** (i.e., that preachest the Gospel) is preferable to that of the ASV, *Thou that tellest good tidings to Zion.* The latter leaves unexplained what female personage it may be who is to evangelize Zion (for the "thou" is feminine in Hebrew). Jerusalem, the Holy City, is to announce Jehovah's coming to all the other cities of Judah. **10. With strong hand.** ASV, *as a mighty one.* **His work** means His *wages* or *reward,* i.e., benefit to the godly and retribution to the wicked. **11. He shall feed . . . gather . . . carry . . . lead.** A prediction beautifully expounded and lived out by our Lord Jesus Christ.

Verses **12-17** set forth the incomparable majesty of Jehovah as the infinitely great and wise Creator. According to pagan mythology the gods of the heathen were spawned by pre-existent matter. But this God of revelation was eternally pre-existent before creation, and remains transcendent above his creation, utterly unapproachable in wisdom and profundity of thought. This sets the scene for the exposure of idolatry (vv. 18-20) in all its pitiful absurdity. The fashioning of a graven image speaks eloquently of the fact that the heathen god himself was a mere creature of man's imagination. **21.** Even the ancestors of the Gentiles (e.g., Adam and Noah), at the beginning of history, knew of the one true Creator-God. **22.** Note that **circle** *(ḥûg)* is compatible with the notion of the earth as a sphere (or even a discoid). **23.** The great ones of this earth – even a Sennacherib or a Nebuchadnezzar – are mere worthless trash (**vanity**) before the omnipotent Sovereign. They are like unrooted seed that is quickly blown off the ground on which it alights (v. 24). **26.** The grandeur of the starry heavens is a reminder of how puny and infinitesimal man is.

27-31. If then the God of Israel is this omnipotent Creator and Sovereign, his people need never fear that their problems and difficulties are too much for him to handle, or that he is unable to bring their unjust oppressors into judgment (even though Israel's long years of captivity to come might give her that impression). His power to deliver and avenge them is never diminishable through weariness or overstrain. His wisdom in ordering the affairs of men is beyond their comprehension. To his children, who lack both stamina and strength, he liberally grants all they need for their constant progress and spiritual attainment, provided they trustingly wait upon him in expectation and prayer.

Sermon II. God's Challenge to Idolatrous Unbelievers. 41:1-29.

1-7. Jehovah, as Lord over the destiny of nations and men, here declares his omnipotent providence. The **islands** or *coastlands* (v. 1). The Mediterranean lands. **The people** (ASV *peoples*). Mankind in general, as an aggregate of national units. God condescends to reason with them on the basis of that intelligence and conscience in regard to the moral law that he has implanted in their hearts by common grace. **2.** The **one from the east** (ASV; or *place of sun-rising*). The future conqueror of Babylon, Cyrus the Great of Persia (558–529 B.C.). He was to come as God's anointed servant (45:1), a type of Christ, the Liberator of God's people from bondage. Isaiah stresses the evidential value of the coming fulfillment of these predictions regarding Cyrus' irresistible triumph under the blessing of God. **3. Pursued . . . passed . . . had . . . gone.** Translate as present or future time (as in ASV). **4.** The coming downfall of Babylon and success of Cyrus would demonstrate that this God of a despised and exiled little nation is truly the Eternal One, the Ordainer of the destinies of men. **6,7.** The idol manufactured by the heathen is a carnal device designed to give men some sense of security in face of the superhuman forces of life.

8-20. Israel, as the chosen people of the Almighty, is an instrument of his sovereign providence. **8.** The first appearance of the momentous figure of the Servant of the Lord. The Servant is here the believing nation of Israel, as opposed to the unbelieving Gentiles. The significance of the people of Israel lies in the facts that (1) they are descendants of Abraham, God's friend (lit., *My lover*); and (2) they are therefore heirs of the covenant promises (Gen 12:1-3). As an immigrant from Ur in Sumeria, Abraham came from the "ends of the earth" (from the Palestinian standpoint, at least). So the captive exiles were to be gathered back from Babylonia in 537. **10.** Even though no exiled nation had ever before in history been brought back to start life anew in their ancestral homeland, and even though the Gentile government would have no practical means of inducing the Jews to return home, nevertheless God would bring this seeming impossibility to pass. In the words of this verse he sought to strengthen his people so that they would triumph over every earthly power (whether Babylon or Persia, Greece or Rome) that would seek to extinguish their testimony. All these heathen empires were to fall and pass away, whereas Jehovah's people would live on and flourish. (Amazing prediction, amazingly fulfilled!) Not that Israel would ever acquire great worldly power, but her God would be her constant strength. By herself Israel was but a feeble **worm** (v. 14), to be despised and stepped on by the world. But as a yielded instrument in God's hand, she was to be the means of overthrowing the mightiest of the nations and bringing them to ruin. The prayers of the faithful unleash the mightiest forces in human history, and even the invincible armies of Persia, Greece, and Rome would crumble before the decrees of God, leaving the people of God triumphant amid their ruins.

17-20. These verses set forth with rich symbolism the transformation of life that God promised to bring about for spiritual Israel. Both in the generation that was to return from Babylon and in all subsequent generations, he guaranteed that he would supply the physical and spiritual needs of the servant-nation. Even in the most distressing hardships and times of gravest peril, God would abundantly furnish all his people might need, invigorating their souls with sweetest refreshment and appointing for them shady and beautiful gardens and groves for their spiritual delight. The seven species of trees in verse 19 symbolize the perfection of God's work in this connection. **20.** Such gracious provision would mightily strengthen the faith of God's people as they recognized and rejoiced in his faithfulness.

21-29. Turning now to idol-worshiping Gentiles, Jehovah challenges them to prove the reality and power of their idols by the test of prophecy and fulfillment (v. 22). His people charge these false gods with being utterly unable to fore-announce their will and purpose, through their prophets, and then carry it out. But Jehovah here and now (v. 25) declares his purpose to raise up – 150 years later – an irresistible conqueror from the east (making his attack from the north), who would respect God's name and carry out his plan. The imaginary gods of the heathen could accomplish no such feat as this. **27. Behold them**; i.e., behold the fulfillments of my predictions. Render the verse thus: "(As) the first (to say) to Zion, 'Lo and behold them,' I was giving to Jerusalem a messenger of good news" (i.e., Isaiah himself). **28. No man.** No predictive prophet among the devotees of idols.

Sermon III. The Servant of Jehovah – Individual and National. 42:1-25.

1-4. The Messiah-Servant is presented as the tender Prophet (a passage applied to the Lord Jesus in Mt 12:18-20). Clearly the Servant is now an individual rather than the nation of Israel as a whole. God would be **delight**[ed] or "well pleased" with him (cf. Mt 3:17). As the Chosen One, he was to be the federal Head of God's elect people. He would be especially empowered by the Holy Spirit (cf. Isa 11:2). Avoiding all ostentation or self-display, he would carry on a quiet and unassuming ministry (even though multitudes, as we now know, would flock to him out in the fields and hills). Tenderly he would avoid crushing the **bruised reed** (v. 3), i.e., the contrite sinner, or extinguishing the feeble testimony of the weakest believer. He would have a ministry to all nations, bringing to them **judgment** (in vv. 1,4 *mishpāṭ* implies the standards or principles of divine holiness and truth – the true faith of the Gospel). Moreover, this message and standard of his would take permanent root in the world, even in the **isles** or *coastlands* of the west.

5-9. God's twofold mission for his Servant would be: (a) to fulfill his covenant promises to Israel; (b) to bring the light of revelation to the Gentiles. The Creator and Sustainer of life would undertake to uphold and support the Servant in his earthly mission (v. 6). The Servant's Gospel would operate to free all believers from the prison house of sin (v. 7). All the glory for accurately predicting coming events is to be kept by God alone. He will not share it with gods invented by men.

Verses **10-13** represent the Gentiles as singing praise for their deliverance and conversion, and rejoicing with faithful Israel over God's conquest of all his foes, his overthrow of empires and intellectual systems hostile to his authority and truth. The culminating conquest, of course, will be the final conflict of Armageddon.

Verses **14-17** set forth the promise that

God would visit condign judgment upon the heathen and tenderly restore his chastened people. Having restrained himself during their disciplinary sufferings, he would now burst forth in judgment upon the heathen powers symbolized by these mountains and hills, and the various water barriers of Babylonia that would keep the Jewish exiles in captivity (v. 15). **16. The blind.** The backslidden and wayward Jews, who were about to be led through suffering to forsake their idolatries and return to God. For their long night of disgrace and sorrow, the Lord would give them spiritual renewal, and he would smooth out all of the difficulties obstructing their return to Palestine. But the heathen idolaters who clung to their abominations he would discredit and destroy.

18-25. Jehovah here calls attention to the strange and unaccountable blindness of his servant-nation, Israel. Having beheld his miracles of deliverance, the Jews nevertheless remained uncomprehending and obtuse. God's purpose, when he chose Israel, was to exalt and dignify his holy law through a people who obeyed it. But, alas, the Jews had altogether ignored his law; and so they would have to undergo despoliation by their foes and captivity in Babylonia. **24.** God made plain that defeat and exile would come upon his people not because he was unable to protect them, but rather because he had chosen and decreed that they should be thus punished.

Sermon IV. The Witness Nation Redeemed from Chaldean Bondage. 43:1-28.

1-7. The Lord here promises Israel blessed restoration, issuing from his love and operating by redemption. **1. Redeemed thee.** Here, as often elsewhere, the word "to redeem" comes from *gā'al*, "to serve as *gô'ēl*, or kinsman-redeemer." Through Isaiah God made clear that he would treat Israel as members of his own family; he would claim their rights and fulfill their obligations for them. **3.** The ground for these promises of companionship and deliverance through suffering and trial was not any superiority or merit on the part of the Jews, but God's unmerited favor and grace, and his self-commitment as Father to his covenant people. He had granted to the Persians, beforehand, as a reward for their releasing captive Israel from Babylon, the country of Egypt and a portion of Ethiopia as additions to their empire (these being added in the reign of Cambyses, son of Cyrus). **4. Thou.** The people of Israel, precious in the Father's eyes because invested with the perfections of the Lord Jesus, imputed to them by grace. **5.** The scattered exiles will be regathered from every geographical direction. But by implication the coming back to Zion seems to refer also to the gathering in of all the elect (v. 7) into the Church of Jesus Christ, for they include **every one . . . whom I have created . . . for my glory.**

8-13. Here the servant-nation is presented as God's witness to the Gentile world. Restored Israel, cured of her blindness, was to qualify as a witness to the truth and faithfulness of the living God – in contrast to the pagan devotees of idolatry, who could testify to nothing like this in their own gods. It was Israel's responsibility to proclaim Jehovah as the only God there is, and as the only Saviour of sinners. **12.** Never was any heathen deity associated with Jehovah in delivering Israel from foreign tyranny or national peril. Never did the Almighty show forth his power to save except when his people put away their worship of all other gods.

14-21. This passage declares that God would demonstrate his sovereignty by overthrowing the Chaldean Empire and bringing the Jews back to Palestine. He would bring the Chaldeans down from their pre-eminence and make them flee from Babylon before the onslaught of Persia. He was the same God who made a path through the Red Sea for the Hebrews of the Exodus, and drowned the Egyptian chariots that pursued after them. But his coming deliverance was to eclipse even that in glory. For he would conduct the liberated Jews through the parched Syrian Desert, and cause it to put forth streams of water to quench their thirst (probably figurative for the sustaining provision he would grant the pioneers through their early years of privation and suffering). The desert animals that are represented as rejoicing in this water supply may stand for Gentile nations which will benefit from the witness of the restored Jews.

22-28. Ungrateful Israel must first suffer national disaster before these promised blessings could be bestowed. Tiring of God and the old-fashioned religion of the Scriptures, they turned to other gods, new faiths, and pagan allies. Hence, although they maintained the forms of worship, what they really brought to Jehovah was not their sheep, but their unrepentant hearts and unconfessed sins. What the Lord requires is not lavish and expensive offerings, but filial trust in him and submission to his will. Despite the guilt of his people, however, God purposed to cancel out their sins altogether (v. 25), not for any extenuating merit in Israel, but only because of his own loving desire to honor his covenant undertakings. From the standpoint of the laws of justice, the Jews had no case to defend, for even their covenant forefather, Abraham, was guilty of sin (in lying to Pharaoh and Abimelech about his wife's status), and their spiritual leaders had turned against the Lord (v. 27). Therefore they would have to endure national catastrophe and shame (in their captivity in Babylonia). **28. I have profaned.** Rather, *I will profane* (ASV).

Sermon V. Israel's Witness for God Against Idols. 44:1-28.

1-5. Despite Israel's backsliding and apostasy, she was God's chosen people and the object of his unmerited favor. **2.** From the very beginning – **from the womb** – he had appointed her to be his peculiar people, bestowing upon her the title of **Jeshurun** (ASV), *Upright One* (cf. Deut 32:15; 33:5,26) – a token of her eventual conversion to Gospel holiness. Circumstances in the reign of Manasseh (when Isaiah was doubtless granted these revelations) may have seemed to indicate a complete and permanent departure from the faith. But God here explicitly predicts that future Israel was to receive the Living Water and the Holy Spirit himself poured out upon them (pre-eminently at Pentecost, Acts 2). **6-8.** God presents anew His challenge to an idol-worshiping world, asserting his eternal being and his uniqueness as the only true God. Again he points to the testimony of fulfilled predictions (a phenomenon peculiar to the Hebrew Scriptures) as a type of evidence of divine authority no man-invented religion can ever produce. To this fulfillment of prophecy, the Jewish nation stands as witness, furnishing verification to all the world that only Jehovah is God, and there is no security in any but him.

9-20. Jehovah exposes the foolishness of polytheism and the blindness of idolaters to most obvious truth. (This extended exposé was doubtless intended to strengthen the Jews against the allurements of paganism during the long captivity in Babylon.) **9. Their delectable things.** The idols these pagans delighted in, all decked with gold and precious stones. The **witnesses.** The spiritually blinded devotees themselves. **11.** They shall be **put to shame** (ASV), as the dreadful judgment of God closed in upon them, and their cities and empire crashed in ruins, even though they had been faithful **fellows** or companions *(hăbārîm)* of their idol. **15-17.** With merciless sarcasm the Lord points out the arrant folly of making a god out of a substance used for firewood. (John Knox, in decrying the idolatry of the Mass, parodied this passage with devastating effect: "With part of the flour you make bread to eat, with the residue you fashion a god to fall down before"). **20.** The idol-worshiper feeds his soul **on ashes**; i.e., upon degrading and revolting worthlessness. Even so, in the philosophical realm, Bible-rejecting agnostics show a similar blindness to obvious and inescapable laws of cause and effect (e.g., that the mechanism of the universe requires a Mechanic to fashion it). But neither idolaters nor modern freethinkers can answer the all-important question: "How can I be saved?"

21-23. Here is a promise of mercy for the nation that stands for God's truth. The many and grievous sins of the Jews would be canceled out, and they might come to God for forgiveness, since he would act for their redemption (in appointing Messiah as their atonement). At these Gospel tidings the angels of heaven would sing with joy, and also the OT saints who in Sheol awaited Christ's resurrection. Even the nonhuman creation, which eagerly awaits the "manifestation of the sons of God" (Rom 8:19), would share in this triumphal rejoicing.

24-28. Jehovah presents himself (1) as the omnipotent Creator, who has prepared Israel from all eternity as his redeemed people; and (2) as the all-wise Sovereign over history, who overthrows the puny wisdom of the philosophers and savants of this world by exposing the fallacy of all their vain imaginations. Worldlings would never have believed that Jerusalem and its holy Temple would be completely rebuilt seventy years after the Chaldeans had demolished them; yet the city and the Temple were restored exactly as God had foretold. Worldlings, too, would have scornfully rejected the possibility that a repopulated Judah would be rebuilt by descendants of Nebuchadnezzar's deportees; yet Jehovah was to bring even that to pass. Least likely of fulfillment, to the mind of an unbeliever, was the prediction that the Jews would be liberated by a non-Israelite pagan like Cyrus; and yet so it was, 150 years after the Lord predicted it.

Sermon VI. Coming Gentile Deliverer, and Conversion of the Heathen. 45:1-25.

1. His **anointed** is *māshîah* or Messiah. As deliverer of God's people from bondage, as invincible victor over his foes, Cyrus stands as a type of Jesus Christ; and many of the promises to him have a spiritual fulfillment also in the ministry and career of our Redeemer. **The gates shall not be shut.** Remarkably exemplified in the capture of Babylon in 539. By strategem a Persian contingent entered the city on the dry river bed and opened the gates to the main army from the inside. **3. Treasures of darkness.** Even treasure hidden away in secret places (Cyrus secured $630,000,000 worth of bullion from Croesus alone). **4. I have surnamed thee.** Rather, *I do surname thee*, or, *give thee an honorable epithet*, namely, "My anointed one." **6.** Great stress is laid upon the evidential value of naming Cyrus specifically such a long time in advance. The fulfillment of this prediction was to furnish positive proof of the divine authority of this prophecy and the sovereignty of the Revealer, as the only God who exists.

7. Jehovah is the Creator and Sustainer of the physical universe, and of the moral law as well. The **evil** he creates is the antithesis of **peace.** But since the opposite of peace is not sin or moral evil, it is obvious that physical evil, or the calamitous consequences of wrongdoing are here intended. Nowhere does the Scripture ascribe to God the creation or authorship of sin; this originates only from the free moral agency of created beings. **8.** God's ultimate purpose is to form a holy and righteous society. As the physical heavens pour fructifying rain upon the soil, so the spiritual influence of heaven is to produce spiritual fruitage in the hearts and lives of those who inhabit the earth. **9,10.** It is the part of folly to subject God's dealing to man's criticism or condemnation. All human understanding of the issues of right and wrong has originated in him as Creator, and therefore can never surpass him in excellence or validity. A child may not properly call his parents to an accounting, as if he possessed judicial authority over them. How much less may a man be critical of God!

11-13. As the Creator of heaven and earth, as the Lord of history, who brings to pass what he foretells will happen, Jehovah here invites the people of Israel to put their complete trust in him. **11. Command ye me** concerning. . . . Translate, with Delitzsch, *commit to me the care of thy sons*. The verb "to command," used with the accusative of the person and the preposition "concerning," forms an idiom meaning, "commit something to the care of someone." **13. I have raised him up**; i.e., Cyrus the Great, who would subsidize the reconstruction of Jerusalem and its Temple without any monetary or practical inducement whatever.

14-19. The nations that lay to the South of Israel would be overcome by the power of God's truth and thereby compelled to acknowledge the Jehovah of Israel as the only true God. Turning from idolatry (v. 16), they would perceive that only through the special revelation of the Scriptures can God truly be known. (Christianity was for a time, at least, extended to the Sabean regions of South Arabia, v. 14a; there were also Sabeans on the Ethiopian side of the Red Sea.) History, in the long run, will vindicate God's truth entrusted to Israel after all other religions and philosophies have fallen into discredit (v. 14b). Through both OT and NT, God discloses that he had a wise purpose in creating the earth as a place for man to dwell on. **18. In vain.** Rather, *a chaos*. Hence, "I did not create it a chaos," *tōhû* being the word translated "without form" in Gen 1:2. (Yet *tōhû* also means "in vain," as in Isa 45:19.) The Lord has not left the human race to its own hopeless conjectures, but has spoken to his covenant people through the clear and sufficient revelation of the Scriptures, that they may know for a certainty how to come into a saving relationship to him.

20-25. Those Gentiles who were to survive the judgment to be visited on their respective nations are here invited to discard their foolish worship of imaginary and futile gods, and to come in faith to the one true God who alone can bring to pass what he has predicted, and who alone can save from sin and death. All nations are included in this invitation, even those most remote. They are to be saved simply by looking in faith to the Lord, as the only God and Saviour. **23. In righteousness.** In fulfillment of his covenant undertakings. **Every knee shall bow,** whether in the loving submission of faith, or constrained by his overwhelming power (at Christ's second advent). **24. Put to shame** (ASV), because they will discover that they wagered their life upon a lie and therefore must be sent away to eternal damnation. **25. Seed of Israel.** The seed of spiritual Israel, all they that are of faith being reckoned as children of Abraham (Gal 3:7).

Sermon VII. The Downfall of Babylon and Preservation of Israel. 46:1–47:15.

1-12. The helplessness of heathen idols is contrasted with the omnipotence of Jehovah. **1. Bel** (the Babylonian form of the name Baal). The god of the lower atmosphere and of the dry land, a patron deity of Babylon. His name appears in Belshazzar, which means *Bel, protect the king!* **Nebo.** Bel's grandson (being the son of Marduk), the god of writing and education. His name appears in Nebuchadnezzar, meaning *Nebo, protect the boundary!* The helpless images of these gods had to be packed like baggage on the draft animals of the Chaldean refugees as they fled before the Persian invaders. The heathen had to carry their gods, but Jehovah had carried and cared for his people (v. 3) from their infancy as a nation, and had undertaken to care for them until the very end of their national career (at the end of this age). **7.** No matter how costly their substance, graven images are helpless to deliver in a time of real crisis. But the Lord God is abundantly able to save, for he is unlike any deity known in man-made religions. **8-11.** All infidels and skeptics are bidden to face the irrefutable objective evidence of divine prophecy and fulfillment. As Jehovah had predicted the fall of Jerusalem, the seventy years' exile, and the return to the homeland, so all should come to pass, fulfilling the forecast to the letter, and demonstrating that the Scripture speaks the truth of the one true and omnipotent God. **11.** The **ravenous bird** and the **man** who executeth God's **counsel** is, of course, Cyrus of Anshan, the province of Persia. **12,13.** The emphasis here is on God's righteous vindication of his unjustly victimized and oppressed people. This leads to an announcement of the righteousness of salvation (according to which God keeps his covenant promises of deliverance for the seed of Abraham).

47:1-7. This passage presents a song of triumph over vanquished Babylon. Cast down from her imperial power, Babylon was to be reduced to the disgraceful status of a half-naked slave girl grinding meal with the heavy grindstone. The silence and darkness of verse 5 refer to the impotence and obscurity that were ever after to be hers. Babylon would never again attain independence or imperial power (and after 539 B.C. she never did). **6,7.** The Lord explains that he would permit the Chaldean conquest and captivity only for the chastening of apostate Israel. But the pagan victors would go far beyond the bounds of humane decency in their savage maltreatment of their captives. Moreover, they would fail to recognize divine righteousness behind the disaster that would befall Judah. They would suppose they were by their own might the lords over the destinies of nations, and secure forever in their supreme position.

In verses **8-11** Jehovah pronounces doom upon the atheistic humanism of Babylonian culture. Babylon represents the man-centered culture of the unregenerate world: living for carnal pleasures and lusts, abjuring responsibility towards a God of justice, and even—with the self-confidence of megalomania—denying God's existence altogether. Chaldean Babylon (v. 10) combined the practical atheism of the freethinker with astrology, necromancy, and crass superstition. Notice how modern is the credo of the philosophical humanist: "I am, and no (God) besides me." The only fitting judgment for these moral and intellectual degenerates was sudden and appalling destruction, the slaughter of Babylon's armies (v. 9 a), and the abrupt termination of her political power (all of which came to pass in 539 B.C.).

12-15. God challenges the proud world power to avert its destruction. Ancient Babylon prided herself on the accumulated wisdom of her sages and wonder-working savants, especially those who had perfected the science of astrology and claimed the ability to tell fortunes and predict propitious and unpropitious days for every enterprise. (The cuneiform literature is full of this sort of thing.) But the fire of God's judgment was to devour the whole tissue of these 'wise' men's lies and leave only ashes behind. The nations that had admired the brilliance of Babylonian culture would return disillusioned to their own places, leaving Babylon to face the Persians alone.

Sermon VIII. God's Honor To Be Upheld by Israel's Deliverance. 48:1-22.

1-11. God here admonishes the faithless hypocrites among his chosen people. These seemingly pious Israelites practiced idol-worship on the side (v. 5) and yet had the effrontery to invoke the name of Jehovah as their God also, pretending that they were true citizens of his holy city. In order to expose the falseness and emptiness of those other gods to whom they divided their loyalty, God presented them with the proof of his existence as the only true God – the unanswerable objective proof of fulfilled prediction. **3. The former things.** The prophecy of Jerusalem's fall to the Chaldeans and deportation to Babylon. The point here is that this prediction was made a long time – a hundred years – before its fulfillment. No human being, not even a demon-inspired devotee of idols, can accurately and specifically foretell events that far ahead. **6. The new things.** The prophecies of deliverance from bondage and return to the land of Israel, not foretold before Isaiah's generation, lest the Jews should boast that they knew all about these coming events all along (v. 8). God well knew from Israel's very beginning as a nation in the time of Moses that the Jews' piety was largely a sham and that their ears were closed to his call to a life of genuine devotion. But because he had chosen them and put his name upon them, he would refrain, for the sake of his glory, from cutting them off as they deserved. Rather, he would purge them of their idolatry and spiritual impurity by putting them through great suffering and leading them thus to repentance. **10. With silver** is inappropriate, since silver is no agent for purification in metallurgy. Translate rather, **as silver** (lit., *in the quality or capacity of silver);* i.e., with an even hotter flame, spiritually speaking, than that needed to smelt silver ore. **11. Will not give my glory unto another.** That is, either (a) the glory of my possession of Israel, not to be given over to idols or demonic powers; or (b) my glory in the spiritual refinement of Israel is not to be granted unto men, i.e., unto the Jews themselves, as if they were capable of self-perfection.

12-16. Jehovah invites Israel to recognize his sovereign wisdom in using a heathen instrument to deliver them. As eternal Creator, God is the Lord of human history and brings to pass amazing providences beyond all human surmise or ability to predict. It was indeed a marvel that God should call Israel's deliverer, Cyrus, by name 150 years before he was born, and love him as His chosen instrument to smite Babylon and destroy her power. But an even greater wonder is the fact that from the beginning of the human race, God the Son, the "angel of the Lord" (of the OT) and the "Word" or *Logos* (of the NT) has time and again clearly spoken to God's covenant children and revealed the divine will and plan for the future. In verse 16 the preincarnate Christ identifies himself as the one sent by the Father and the Spirit to convey God's prophetic message to the inspired prophet.

17-22. God lovingly remonstrates with perverse and wayward Israel, exhorting his people to return and trust in him, as during the Exodus wanderings. He laments the unnecessary tragedy of their loss of his blessing through self-centered waywardness. **18. Peace . . . as a river.** A constant, abundant, fructifying supply of blessing. **Righteousness.** The implanted righteousness and holiness of God himself, operating within them and through them like vast deep waves, flowing in continual succession. **19.** If Israel had obeyed God, her name would not have been cut off (as it was to be during the Babylonian Captivity) from the Land of Promise. **20.** A summons beforehand to Jews who would be captives in 539 B.C. not to tarry in the pagan soil of Babylon, but to take advantage of Cyrus' permissive edict and return to Judah. They were to bear triumphant testimony before the Gentiles as they celebrated this deliverance and recalled Jehovah's mercies to their fathers in that earlier return from Egypt. **22.** Those who would not flee the defilements of Babylon would never know the peace of God, being spiritually *out of joint* (as *rāshāʿ*, the word for **wicked**, literally implies). Note that this same sentiment, in nearly the same wording, also closes Section Two (57:21) of this eighth Volume.

Section II. The Prince of Peace. 49:1–57:21.

Whereas Section I dealt especially with the Doctrine of God, Section II treats principally of the Doctrine of Salvation. Salvation comes from God only, and through the ministry of the Servant of Jehovah. It includes deliverance from the penalty of sin, and a new life of protection, joy, and peace. It is world-wide in scope.

Sermon I. Messiah To Restore Israel and Enlighten the Gentiles. 49:1-26.

1-7. The Servant's divine commission as Prophet is set forth. Although the Servant is addressed as "Israel" in verse 3, we are to understand this name as applying to him on whom the covenant relationship was based and all the covenant promises rested, the One who in his own person fulfilled God's expectations for a holy people. **1. From the womb.** Doubtless an allusion to the annunciation of the angel to the Virgin Mary (Lk 1:31-33). His words, like a sharp sword, were to pierce the conscience of sinners and administer judgment as well (Rev 19:15). **4.** Christ the Servant would have moments of discouragement, as he met with almost universal misunderstanding, even from his disciples. Yet even then he would find his chief satisfaction in "doing the will of him that sent me" (Jn 4:34). His commission would be twofold: (1) to restore Israel to God, i.e., the Remnant of true believers who would make up the Jerusalem Church of the NT period (as well as the Christian Jews of this present age and of the latter day revival); (2) to bring the light of God's salvation to all the nations of earth. **7.** In his humiliation he would be despised and rejected, even by his own nation, the Jews. But in his exaltation, after the resurrection victory, he would eventually be worshiped as Lord, even by the kings of the heathen.

8-13. The prophet describes the joy of those whom Christ will deliver. **8. In an acceptable time.** An anticipatory reference to the "fullness of time" when the incarnate Christ offered himself to the Father, and was delivered from the malice of demons and men. At the hour of atonement on Calvary, he fulfilled the covenant of grace to Abraham and his seed. On the strength of that coming atonement God would physically restore the exiles to their desolated patrimony in Judah, and would spiritually repopulate the forfeited heritage of Israel by entrusting it to a "nation bringing forth the fruits thereof."

From verse 9 on, the reference is chiefly spiritual and pertains to the deliverance of sinners from bondage by the power of the Gospel, their supply of food and drink for their souls, and their protection from the pressures and heat of temptation and the opposition of the hostile world. Even on the **high places** (v. 9), that is, the bare sandy hills of the semiarid wilderness, God will feed them bountifully. That is, their times of affliction he will use to their spiritual enrichment. The mountainous barriers (v. 11) that he will send their way, when conquered by faith, will prove to be stepping-stones to glory. To the strong nucleus of the first Jewish Christians in Palestine there would be added converts from all the Gentiles, even from so remote a region as China (the most probable identification of **Sinim,** v. 12, although Elam and Syene have also been suggested). Verse 13 shows that the scope of this action is world-wide, and that the Church Age is here in view.

14-26. The Lord offers Israel reassurance in view of her discouragement. In the disgrace and misery of the Captivity, it would be easy for Israel to feel abandoned by God. Hence the encouraging affirmation (vv. 15,16) that God's parental love surpasses that of any human mother. The Chaldean destroyers were to pass away into oblivion, and in time the converted heathen would come to Israel to submit to her God, and to acknowledge Messiah as their Saviour and King. Thus multitudes of new citizens would more than fill in the gaps left by the Jews who were to be slaughtered in the Chaldean, Maccabean, and Roman wars. Spiritual Israel, which after Christ's coming would be Christian Israel, would be filled with joyous incredulity at this tremendous influx of born-again Gentiles. It is very likely Gentile converts who are referred to in verse 22 as flocking to the standard of the cross, and showing tender, loving concern for their Jewish co-religionists. Even Gentile royalty would come under the sway of the Messiah and show a reverent concern for the Holy Land and its people, being proud to serve as protectors and guardians of Christ's Church. **24. Lawful captive** should be construed, *their rightful captives,* or those whom "the mighty" have captured in a fair fight. **25.** These **mighty** and **terrible** ones were, in the first instance, the Chaldeans, but then also the Seleucid Greeks, who would engage in frequent internecine warfare as rival dynasts struggled for supremacy. **26.** These oppressors would become **drunken with their own blood.** Here again the fulfillment of prophecy demonstrates to the world the sovereign power of Jehovah God.

Sermon II. Sinfulness of Israel and Obedience of the Servant. 50:1-11.

1-3. It was no personal inclination that was causing God to put away his covenant wife, Israel, during the Babylonian captivity, but rather the compulsion of

Israel's own incorrigible iniquity and deafness to his appeal. Nor was it because Jehovah owed anything to the Chaldeans that he would sell Judah into bondage. His omnipotence was equal to delivering his people from them or any other foe, when he should find it safe and proper to do so.

4-9. By way of contrast the Lord Jesus is set forth as true Israel, the completely obedient Servant. The tongue **of the learned** (AV). Rather, *of them that are taught* (ASV). That is, the Messiah would speak as one to whom God has taught his true message of comfort for those who are weary of sin. **Morning by morning** characterizes his early-morning trysts with the Father. **5.** Unlike national Israel, the Servant would present to God perfect obedience, and willingness to endure humiliation and persecution for the Father's sake. Verse **7** speaks prophetically of the sublime confidence and majestic calm that our Saviour preserved during his Good Friday sufferings, sustained by his consciousness of being in the will of God (v. 8), and therefore in the right, as against all the slanders and assaults of his foes. He was confident that the Father would bring him victoriously through crucifixion and burial, and that his opponents would be inexorably consumed away by divine judgment (until the final blow of the capture of Jerusalem by Titus in A.D. 70).

10,11. God would send deliverance to trusting believers, but fiery condemnation upon those who rebelled against his sovereignty. Note that the Servant was to speak with an authority that must be obeyed, and that salvation would come to sinners only through faith, through trusting in the God of grace. The word translated **sparks** (ASV, *firebrands*) probably means fire arrows. Those arsonists who would set fire to the camp of the Lord would themselves be consumed by the fire of destruction they had hoped to inflict upon others.

Sermon III. Encouragement To Trust God, Not Fearing Man. 51:1-16.

1-3. Israel was to take comfort for the future from God's faithfulness in the past. Abraham was the rock from which his descendants were hewn – having a rocklike quality imparted to him by God's faithfulness and grace. From that single ancestor God made a great and numerous nation. He purposes in the future to settle them in a latter-day Eden (into which the land of Canaan will be transformed when Israel herself has become spiritually transformed).

4-8. The Lord promises to judge the world and purge it of evil. **4. Law** here means "authoritative instruction." God's standard of righteousness will be set up as a standard for all the nations of the earth, who will submit to Jehovah's authority through conversion, and trust in his strength and grace. His salvation will prove longer lasting than the physical heavens (which are temporal, because material, whereas redeemed souls will dwell forever in God's presence). Since all Christ-rejecting unbelievers are doomed to utter destruction, no believer should ever quail before the menace of the world or the hostility of ungodly men, whose plight is desperate, and their doom sure.

9-11. The believer prays that God may indeed fulfill this promise. **9.** Jehovah's **arm** implies his active, supernatural intervention to deliver his people and punish his foes. **Rahab** *(arrogance* or *raging violence)* is here a mythological monster representing Egypt, which lost its finest chariots in the Red Sea crossing. **11.** As the Israelites of the Exodus burst forth in joyous song at their deliverance (Ex 15), so were the returning deportees from Babylon to do in 537 (this verse being a repetition of Isa 35:10). The ultimate vista is, of course, the bliss of heaven (Rev 15:3; 21:4).

12-16. God again speaks to reassure his trusting people. He points out the folly of fearing mortal man (who can kill only the body) more than the omnipotent Creator, who in the end frustrates the fury of even the fiercest opponents. **14. The captive exile.** Better, *He that is bowed down* (as a wretched slave). Read the rest of the verse as – *shall speedily be loosed; and he shall not die,* etc. The Assyrians and Chaldeans would go down to destruction, and only the once-captive Jews would survive. **15.** The **sea** symbolizes the turbulent, restless, unregenerate world (cf. 57:20). But God has put his inspired Word into the mouth of his covenant people (v. 16); it is the possession of Scripture that gives Israel her importance.

Sermon IV. Israel Summoned To Awake and Return to God's Favor. 51:17–52:12.

17-23. God announces that He considers the Captivity sufficient penalty for Israel, and that a new day of forgiveness has dawned. As the drunkard brings woe upon himself by the poison of liquor, even so would wayward Israel drink the slow poison of disobedience and incur the misery decreed by God's righteous wrath. Bereft of all spiritual leadership among her citizens, the nation would meet with the calamities she richly deserved. And the streets of Jerusalem would be covered with her slain, who would be cornered for slaughter by the armies of Babylon (v. 20). But then would come the turn of Judah's brutal oppressors – who had arrogantly trampled upon her prostrate form – to drink the cup of God's vengeance.

In **52:1-6** God conveys his determination to restore captive Israel for his name's sake and for his glory. By grace he presented them with his perfect power and spiritual beauty as equipment already fashioned and complete, which they had only to put on by faith. He adds the assurance that his holy commonwealth would never again be so defiled by idolatry as it had been under Ahaz, Manasseh, and Zedekiah. His people were confidently to lay hold upon "the glorious liberty of the children of God" (Rom 8:21). **3.** They **were sold** (ASV) into bondage for nothing of any value, only the empty promises of the world. Even so they would be redeemed from Babylonian captivity without paying Cyrus any ransom price. **5. For nought.** Without adequate cause, so far as their conquerors were concerned. The arrogant contempt of the heathen towards Israel's God called for him to live up to his covenant name, "Jehovah, the Holy One of Israel," and to demonstrate by Babylon's overthrow his continuing sovereignty. This fulfillment of prophecy would also confirm the authority of God's holy word.

Verses **7-10** express the joy and consolation that the Gospel brings to God's people. To them the very feet of the messengers are fair, because they bear tidings of the most beautiful thing in the universe – the redeeming love ot God. By bearing to ruined Jerusalem the good tidings that God had procured Israel's release from Babylon, these messengers were to serve as types of the Gospel missionaries of the NT age (Rom 10:15). **Peace,** or *shālôm,* includes reconcilement between God and man, the healing of the sinsick soul, and the spiritual prosperity of a harmonious walk with God. **8. Jehovah returneth** (ASV; *the Lord shall bring again Zion,* AV). A reference to the return of God's favor and also his Shekinah presence, in the Second Temple, at rebuilt and restored Jerusalem.

11,12. This is an exhortation addressed beforehand to the Jews of 537 B.C., who would have to choose between the economic security of their situation in Babylonia and the hazards and hardships of pioneering back in their devastated ancestral land. But the safety and purity of their souls would depend upon their fleeing from this defiling atmosphere, and setting their faces towards fulfilling God's program of redemption. **12. Not . . . with haste.** They would not be escaping refugees as their forefathers were in the Exodus), for they would enjoy the patronage and safe-conduct of the Persian emperor. But far more important than such human guarantees would be the vanguard defense of the Almighty, who would also make up their rearguard **(rereward).**

Sermon V. The Divine Servant's Substitutionary Atonement. 52:13–53:12.

13-15. Here is presented Christ's amazing victory through humiliation. **13. Deal prudently** (from *hiśkîl*). The implication is that he would act with such intelligence as to succeed in his objectives. The words for exaltation are piled upon one another in order to convey the idea that he would be lifted up superlatively high, above all other men, to the height of God himself. The words for be **exalted** and **extolled** are the same as those used in 6:1 of Jehovah enthroned – "high and lifted up." **14.** With the words **at thee** the prophet speaks directly to the divine Messiah, as if beholding him before his mind's eye. Then he turns to the people themselves and resumes speaking of him in the third person. This marring of visage, as we now know, was to be the result of his maltreatment at the hands of Pilate's soldiers. **14,15. Like** (ASV; *as,* AV). . . . **so.** The point of the comparison is this: As astonishing as would be his humiliation, so astonishing would be his exaltation (as described in v. 15). **Sprinkle** is still the best attested rendering of this frequently occurring word, although some have preferred to translate "startle" (which would then be the only occurrence of that meaning for this root in the OT). The sprinkling connotes the bestowal of spiritual cleansing upon the nations so evangelized. **Kings shall shut their mouths** – both from amazement and from their inability to say anything by way of self-justification. **That which had not been told** these Gentile kings would, of course, be the Gospel message of salvation through the cross.

53:1-3. The Servant as viewed by man would be rejected and despised. **1. Report.** Literally, *the thing heard* (i.e., by the prophet from God); hence the prophetic message. **Our report.** The message of Isaiah and his fellow prophets. **The arm of the Lord** is a phrase always used to designate special interpositions in human affairs whereby God delivers his people and punishes his foes. It is especially used in reference to the miracles of the Exodus. Christ, then, was to be God's greatest miracle. **2. Tender plant.** More literally, *a suckling* (used of a baby at its mother's breast, as well as of a shoot from a tree stump). **No form.** More accurately, *no comely form.* **Nor comeliness** *(hādār).* More literally, *majesty* or *splendor.* In other words, the Servant would lack the earthly grandeur that allures the admiration of the world. The we here includes the prophet as he identifies himself with his spiritually blind countrymen. **3. Rejected of men.** More exactly, *lacking men of distinction* (as his supporters). **We hid as it were our faces from him.** More literally, *and* (it was) *like a hiding of face from him.* That is, men would persistently avoid facing the real Christ, preferring a "historical Jesus," who would not trouble them with his cross.

4-6. The Servant as viewed by God would be the vicarious Redeemer. **4. Griefs.** More literally, *sicknesses.* In token of Christ's power to forgive sins, he did heal many of men's physical sicknesses. But since the subject matter here is illness of soul rather than of body, the rendering **griefs** is justifiable. **5. Wounded.** *Transfixed* or *pierced,* a term quite appropriate to crucifixion. **Transgressions.** A noun derived from the root, "to rebel," and implying revolt against the sovereignty of God. **Bruised.** More accurately, *utterly crushed.* **The chastisement of our peace;** i.e., the punishment that brings about our peace, or state of well-being (not a mere unfortunate consequence of man's sin). **6. Like sheep** – being helpless to protect themselves or escape from danger when attacked, and being lost without a shepherd. **Turned every one to his own way.** Each of us has preferred his own way to God's way; this is the essence of sin or of "going astray." **Hath laid on him.** Literally, *caused to alight upon him,* or better still, *caused to meet him* (cf. Num 35:19, where the revenger of blood is authorized to slay the murderer when he "meeteth" him in the way – the same verb being used there as here.) Our transgressions were to "meet" him in the way and slay him as if he were the guilty one instead of us. Note that the remedy was to have just as universal application (**us all**) as the need (**all we**).

7-9. As viewed by man, Messiah's suffering would be a tragic misfortune to the innocent. **7. Opened not his mouth;** i.e., in his own defense, before either Caiaphas or Herod or Pilate. **8. From prison and from judgment.** Rather, *as a result of coercion and a judicial action.* That is, by an unjust trial a judicial murder was to be perpetrated. **Taken;** i.e., taken away to the place of execution. Render the next sentence with the ASV: **And as for his generation, who (among them) considered that he was cut off out of the land of the living for the transgression of my people to whom the stroke (was due)? 9. He made his grave.** Better rendered as impersonal: "One appointed his grave." **The wicked.** The two murderous thieves crucified at either side of him. The **rich man** (ASV). Joseph of Arimathea, in whose burial vault he was interred. **Because he had done no violence.** Probably to be construed as, "*although* he had done no wrong (to others)."

10-12. God sees Messiah's suffering as the redemption of sinners and triumph over death. **10. When thou shalt make his soul an offering.** Addressed to God directly, as the One who alone has the prerogative of appointing Christ's life an offering for sin (Isaiah uses the word for trespass offering – *'āshām* – which involved the payment of 120 per cent damages as well as the presentation of the sacrificial animal itself). **See his seed.** His children by faith, born-again Christians. **Prolong his days.** Does this not refer to a time subsequent to his death and burial? Only his bodily resurrection could serve to fulfill such a prediction as this. **11. By his knowledge.** In the light of the fulfillment, this must be an objective genitive, meaning, *by the knowledge of him* (as Saviour). The verse continues . . . *shall a righteous one, my servant, furnish justifying righteousness unto the many* (i.e., the many for whom he shall die). **12. A portion with the great.** Rather, *with the many,* for it is the same word *(hārabbîm)* as the one translated *the many* in verse 11, and both refer to the same class of people – the redeemed. **The strong.** His followers, who do battle with Satan and his minions in the power of Christ's spiritual weapons. **The spoil.** The booty of precious souls won to Christ through the preaching of the Gospel.

Sermon VI. Resultant Blessings to Israel and the Church. 54:1-17.

1-3. Fruitfulness and enlargement are promised to post-Exilic Israel. Jerusalem was first to become **barren,** in that her population would be cut off and carried away by the Chaldeans. But the time would come (especially after Christ's first advent) when believers in Jehovah would be more numerous than they had ever been before the Exile (when Israel had enjoyed the status of covenant wife in the home that her heavenly husband had provided in Palestine). **Enlarge . . . thy tent** and **lengthen thy** (land-measuring) **cords.** Israel in her NT phase would spread the true faith to all the lands of the Gentiles, whose nations should consequently become "possessed" by Zion's posterity as they were conquered by the Gospel.

4-10. The prophet foretells the gracious restoration of Jehovah's covenant wife, Israel. The **shame** of her **youth** refers to her rebellious murmurings during the Exodus journey, and the apostasies of the time of the Judges and the divided monarchy; her reproachful **widowhood** to the Babylonian captivity. **6. When thou wast refused** (ASV, *cast off*) seems to refer to the seventy years' estrangement between Jehovah and Israel. **9.** The promise here is to be understood in the light of the analogy of the Flood. Just as God promised Noah there would never again be such a deluge, even so he promises restored Israel that she shall never again go into exile. Since the Jews actually were driven into exile again after their revolt against the Romans in A.D. 135, this can only mean that God accounts the Christian Church as true Israel. **10. Kindness.** From *hesed,* rendered by the ASV as *lovingkindness* and by the RSV as *steadfast love*. But since it implies mutual committedness or solidarity between the parties involved in a covenant relationship, it is best rendered *covenant love*.

11-17. The Lord describes the purity and glory of the converted Israel of the future. As the Gospel transforms the lives of Jewish and Gentile converts, they will become as living stones (I Pet 2:5) built up into a spiritual temple, and glowing with the beauty of the Christ who indwells them. But the full glory of this new city of God will be that of New Jerusalem described in Rev 21. The Church will be composed of those "taught by God" (Isa 54:13), as Christ reaffirmed in Jn 6:45. The ultimate freedom from fear and terror points toward Millennial conditions. But all the way from Calvary to Armageddon, the enemies of the Church will fall back in ultimate defeat. **16.** God retains sovereign control over the forces of human warfare and destruction; they can never really get out of hand. **17.** The Lord will impart to redeemed Israel a justifying righteousness that he will ever vindicate as against her foes, whether human or satanic.

Sermon VII. God's Grace Towards Repentant Sinners. 55:1-13.

1-5. The price for admission to eternal life is repentance and faith, plus nothing. Those who would partake of the living water must first feel thirst (repent), and then be willing (have faith) to come to the Saviour (cf. Jn 7:37). **Wine** symbolizes the Gospel as cheering and invigorating the soul; **milk** indicates its nourishing quality (I Pet 2:2). **2. That which satisfieth not.** The mirage of personal happiness based upon earthly advantages and blessings. Only God himself can satisfy the human soul. The **David** of Isa 55:3,4 is the Messianic Son of David, since he is here described as exerting a controlling influence in the coming age. Verse 5 is a prediction that Gentiles will be converted and will join themselves to redeemed Israel because of her God.

6,7. In view of these glowing promises for the future, sinners are urged now to respond to the Gospel invitation while they yet have opportunity. **8-11.** The grace of God surpasses human understanding, but it is guaranteed effectiveness through the faithful and inspired preaching of the Word (**that goeth forth out of my mouth**). **12,13.** When God's Word is heard and obeyed, the redeemed shall be freed from their bondage and enter into joy and peace. All nature about them will share in this exultation at the manifested grace of God. And some day nature will indeed share in the liberty and glory of God's children (Rom 8:21).

Sermon VIII. Gentiles To Be Included in Israel's Blessing. 56:1-8.

Here we have an admonition to believers to maintain the testimony of a godly life. In due season they shall reap, "if they faint not." The loving observance of the Sabbath is especially emphasized as a covenant sign testifying to a saving faith. Gentile converts to the faith of Israel are assured of full and permanent citizenship in God's kingdom. Eunuchs (and by implication all childless believers) who manifest saving faith by their godly life are assured eternal life and a glory far more significant than that of a long line of descendants. Two groups are to be included in the true people of God: Gentile converts and the outcasts of Israel. As contrasted with nominal, insincere believers, they will show cordial love for the Sabbath and cordial adherence to the covenant.

Sermon IX. Condemnation of the Corrupt Leaders of Israel. 56:9–57:21.

9-12. The indictment of the self-seeking, unscrupulous professional prophets of Israel. (This passage reverts to the degenerate moral conditions of Isaiah's own time, such as prevailed in the reign of Manasseh.) These prophets are described as watchmen who fail to watch. They are like dogs that fail to bark to warn men of danger, being interested only in filling their own bellies. Or, like stupid shepherds, they are so wholly preoccupied with self-interest that they do not care for their sheep, but give themselves over to winebibbing.

57:1,2. God expresses indignation at the plight of faithful conscientious believers who were being exploited by the cruel and immoral leaders of Jewish society. A notable example of such a leader was King Manasseh, who "shed innocent blood very much, till he had filled Jerusalem from one end to another" (II Kgs 21:16). Yet these martyrs were actually saved from the horrors of Judah's approaching siege and exile, and had entered into the peace of "Abraham's bosom" (Lk 16:22), there to await Christ's resurrection.

Verses **3-10** describe the abominations of Judah's idol-worship. **3.** The idolaters' degenerate parentage is inferred from their degenerate practices. **4.** They made grimaces of mockery and contempt against Jehovah. **5. With idols.** Rather, *among the oaks* (ASV). They indulged in ritual sex orgies in the oak groves and performed infant sacrifices. **6. Stream.** Better, *valley* (ASV). There they poured drink offerings to their idols. **7.** On their high places were their idol shrines, where they committed spiritual adultery. **8. Enlarged thy bed.** A reference to their worshiping several heathen gods at once. **9.** The **king** is probably the king-god, Moloch (rather than some human king). **10.** Despite the bitterness and bondage ensuing from their ungodly life, the people of Judah were too much infatuated to forsake it.

11-13. These theological compromises they had made under the pressure of heathen powers – though all such powers are puny mortals –, and at the same time they had neglected their longsuffering God. In the coming invasions they would have to look to their helpless idols for a deliverance that would not come. Only true believers would inherit God's Kingdom.

14-21. The prophet tells of the Lord's compassion upon the truly repentant. **Cast ye up** refers to the constructing of a cross-country highway by heaping up a long mound of earth and stones. The **stumblingblock** is an unrepentant and idolatrous heart. Verse **15** presents the classic statement in Scripture of the two dwelling places of God. **Revive**; i.e., to restore life to that which is spiritually dead (lit., *cause to live*). **16.** The **spirit**, namely, of the guilty sinner being rebuked. **17.** This **covetousness** *(besa')* is probably the Hebrew expression that comes closest to English "selfishness." **18.** God's grace is bestowed without the slightest human merit to warrant it.

19. The Lord bestows blessings that inspire human lips to offer adoration and praise – **the fruit of the lips** (cf. Heb 13:15). Men praise him for genuine and perfect peace (here *shālôm* is used, as in Isa 26:3). **Far off** – Gentile converts; **near** – Jewish converts (cf. Eph 2:17). **20. Wicked** here is the word for "ungodly" (Ps 1) or "morally out of joint" *(rāshā')*. The unconverted can never find true peace, but are finally spewed up as foul flotsam on the beach of time.

Section Three. The Program of Peace. 58:1–66:24.

In this third section of Isaiah the emphasis is upon the Holy Spirit as he applies and extends the work of redemption. God's program of grace is outlined to the end of this age and the commencement of the new world.

Sermon I. False Worship Contrasted with the True. 58:1-14.

1-7. The hypocrisy of Israel's piety is here exposed. The prophet is bidden to denounce unsparingly the spurious faith of the Jews, with its sanctimonious pose at worship services and its ostentatious fasting, soon to be followed by the same wrongdoing and ungodliness as before (v. 4). No religious observance has value for Jehovah that is not supported by a godly, law-abiding life, and compassion towards those in need. Righteous behavior, the fruit of saving faith, will insure the dawn of deliverance (v. 8) for unhappy Judah; the righteousness of compassionate love will clear the way before God's faithful army as they make their forward march.

8-14. The Lord promises to restore fellowship and blessing to those who abandon hypocrisy. **9. The putting forth of the finger**; i.e., in (false) accusation of the innocent. **10. Thy darkness be as the noon day**; i.e., "your present state of calamity and distress shall be replaced by the sunshine of God's favor." **11. A spring of water.** The outgoing godly influence of a warm believer who shares his blessings with others. **12.** The new commonwealth (after the Exile) was to be built up by sincere and dedicated believers who meant business with God. They would repair the mischief resulting from the wicked hypocrisy of their forebears. **13.** A most significant evidence of sincere love for the Lord is the delight with which his worshiper hallows the Sabbath for God's service and praise (rather than using it for self-serving and weekday purposes). **14. High places.** Spiritual exaltation and prosperity.

Sermon II. Israel's Confession and Her Rescue by God. 59:1-21.

1-8. This passage describes the appalling moral breakdown of Jewish society — which perfectly accords with what we know of the degeneracy of Manasseh's reign. Isaiah told the people why God did not hear their cry for deliverance from the oppressive yoke of Assyria. **5.** The **eggs** of the **cockatrice.** More properly, the *viper*. The suggestion is that the apostate people were like poisonous serpents that produce evil influences calculated to destroy the unwary who trust them. The webs of evil they spun would by no means cover their nakedness before God's piercing eye in the day of judgment (v. 6). They had consecrated every part of their bodies to wickedness and evil. **8.** Peace with others demands a loving good will of which the ungodly are incapable; nor can they ever enjoy contentment or peace in their own hearts.

9-15a. The grim consequences of this depravity of life are clearly set forth. **9.** Judah had become a victim of Assyrian injustice and oppression, and all her hopes of independence and prosperity were constantly dashed to the ground. **10. At noon day as in the night.** Better, *in the twilight*. God's truth shone brightly upon them, but they were plunged into the darkness of spiritual ignorance and national calamity. The Hebrew word for **desolate places** does not occur elsewhere, but probably should be translated stout or *lusty men* (so the ASV— among whom the enfeebled Jews were but corpses by comparison. **12-15.** This passage has the tone of a heartbroken confession of inexcusable guilt and aggravated wickedness. **15. Maketh himself a prey.** That is, anyone who attempted to lead an honest life made himself a victim of the ruthless cutthroats who dominated Israelite society.

In verses **15b-21** is predicted God's personal interposition to rescue helpless sinners from their guilt and bondage. The standpoint here is Calvary. **16.** Displeased as Jehovah was with the Jews' complete moral failure, he was also distressed at the absence of any qualified human mediator for Israel. The only course left was for him to become the Mediator himself — **His arm brought salvation unto him** — in the person of Jesus Christ, who alone was clad with spotless righteousness impenetrable to Satan's darts. **18.** But the First Advent is here combined with the Second, at which Messiah will come to crush the world power (at Armageddon) and enforce God's holy standards upon all the inhabitants of earth. **19.** The whole world will come to revere Jehovah, and his Holy Spirit will successfully repel all attacks upon his redeemed people. (The very different rendering of v. 19b in the ASV depends upon questionable renderings of two rare words; the AV is to be preferred.) **20. Redeemer** here is *gō'ēl*, "kinsman-redeemer," which involves a blood relationship (into which God could not enter except through the incarnation of Christ). **21.** The true people of God will ever be a witnessing people, faithfully proclaiming the truth of the Gospel in the power of the Holy Spirit.

Sermon III. The Radiance and Peace of God's Redeemed People. 60:1-22.

1-3. The prophet declares that the darkness of the world is to be overcome by the light of Israel. The standpoint is that of Christ's first advent, for he is the Light that was to rise upon the Jews.

And his Church was to be the light, i.e., the reflector of his glorious perfection and love, and the channel for his truth in reaching the heathen. The NT Gospel was to have a powerful attractiveness for the Gentiles such as the OT Gospel never had.

4-9. Here Gentile converts are described as crowding into the Kingdom and presenting all their possessions and talents as thank-offerings to the Lord. Perhaps these converts were to be accounted children of God by adoption, hence Israel's **sons** and **daughters** (v. 4). Or else these may be the dispersed Jews who were to be accompanied and escorted by Gentile Christians as they entered by faith into God's Kingdom. It is quite remarkable that, in origin, all these offered treasures are preponderantly Arabian. Perhaps there is a suggestion here that Islam will some day turn to the Cross. All these immigrants into the Land of Promise resemble flights of **doves** in their swift eagerness and great numbers (v. 8). They are drawn thither by their **hope** (v. 9) or trust in the Lord (a better rendering than *wait for* [AV; ASV], which is inappropriate here). The procession is to be led **first** by the ships from the greatest distance – those from Tarshish.

10-14. Here the Scripture gives us a picture of the glory and peace of Millennial Zion, as Gentile believers join hands with Jewish believers to establish the new theocracy and its glorious capital, Jerusalem. (The earthliness of this setting seems to preclude assigning it to heaven.) The empire of Messiah will be supreme and will brook no opposition or rebellion (v. 12). Apparently (as in Ezk 40–48) a beautiful temple is to be built in Zion (Isa 60:13), to which even the converted descendants of Israel's persecutors will come as worshipers. **15-22.** The glory of the Millennial kingdom is contrasted with the ignominy of the apostate pre-Exilic kingdom of Israel: glory in place of contempt, wealth in the place of poverty (vv. 16,17 a), righteousness in place of injustice (v. 17 b), unending peace instead of bloodshed and war (v. 18), the glory-light of God's favor and presence perpetually (v. 19, a verse which points forward specifically to conditions in heaven; cf. Rev 22:3-5), continuous revival and prevailing godliness in all of society rather than the recurrent apostasies and declensions of OT Israel (Isa 60:21). God's plan for a perfectly righteous and obedient human race will then at last be realized on earth (v. 21 b), as the tiny minority of true believers expands into a great number and a mighty nation (v. 22). (In v. 16 the bold imagery indicates that just as the mother gives up vital energy in giving suck to her child, so the nations and their rulers will yield up their vital energy for the service of the Millennial Church.)

Sermon IV. The Joy-Bringing Gospel of the Anointed One. 61:1-11.

1-3. Christ is here represented as empowered by the Spirit to preach the liberating and life-transforming Gospel (a passage applied to Jesus by himself in Lk 4:18-21). The Gospel is especially intended for the **meek** (i.e., the humble, who recognize their own sin and need of a Saviour) and the **brokenhearted** (who repent of their sins). It is a message of deliverance from bondage, of consolation for sorrow, and of power from God for a new holiness of life – **trees of righteousness, the planting of Jehovah** (v. 3, ASV). This Gospel also promises God's righteous judgment upon all the forces of unrepentant evil – **the day of vengeance of our God** (v. 2).

4-9. A picture of the glory of the new life that will replace the old. The new Israel, charged with the energy of Christ's Gospel, will rebuild the structure of the theocracy that has been ravaged by the dreadful consequences of disobedience and infidelity. **5.** Gentile converts will join in the pastoral work and service of the Kingdom, in willing submission to the Jewish apostles and Jewish Scriptures, and gladly present themselves and all their possessions to the Lord. **7. Double.** The double glory or blessing of (a) membership in God's family, (b) possession of Christ himself as their indwelling Lord and Companion. **8. Robbery** (or *rapacity) in connection with* (rather than *for)* **burnt offering** (ASV needlessly amends to *iniquity)* was what characterized the hypocritical majority of Israel, but it will have no place in the Kingdom. The sincere redeemed Jews will have a commanding and influential position among all mankind in that latter day (v. 9).

10,11. The born-again believer joyfully responds to these gracious promises. He has been clothed with Christ's imputed righteousness and has been adorned with his grace as a bridal pair are adorned for marriage. He rejoices in the Saviour as his chief good, and in the triumph of righteousness in the earth.

Sermon V. The Restoration of Zion; Destruction of Infidel Heathen. 62:1–63:6.

1-5. The beauty of Zion's imputed and imparted righteousness is set forth, and her new status as Christ's holy bride. God will not be permanently thwarted in his plan to create a holy nation, despite Israel's sorry record of failure and backsliding. **4.** In the 'latter day' she will display Christ's righteousness and thereupon receive a new name: **Hephzibah,** *My delight is in her*. And her land shall be called **Beulah,** *Married*. In verse **5** alter the vowel point in *bānāyik,* "thy sons," to *bōnāyik,* "thy builders," a plural of majesty for "Thy Builder" (Jehovah); this avoids the implication of incestuous relationship in the word "sons," and forms a perfect parallelism with the second half of the verse.

6-12. God's persevering grace guarantees that this beauty will be conferred on Israel at Christ's second advent. Faithful and diligent prophets who call to mind God's words (**remembrancers,** ASV) will persist in preaching and prayer until Messiah's earthly kingdom is established. From that time on, no invasions will lay waste the crops of Palestine (a prediction which can only be fulfilled by an earthly Millennium). In verse **10** we have a summons to repentance very similar to that in 57:14. The **standard,** or *ensign,* is the cross of Christ. **12.** The people of latter-day Jerusalem will be the very opposite of what they were in the time of Isaiah and his immediate successors: unholy people, left in bondage to their foes, not sought out by God's delivering grace, but abandoned to the consequences of apostasy.

63:1-6. The divine judgment will be inflicted on the World Power (in contrast to Israel's final blessedness). **1.** Here again (as in 34:5,6) **Edom** typifies the rebellious world as implacably hostile to God's people (Amos 1:11). **Bozrah** in Edom suggests the verb *bāsar,* "to cut off grape clusters, gather the vintage." Christ is pictured as wearing garments stained with blood. This is the blood of those who are to be slain at Armageddon (cf. Rev 19:13), where he will by himself achieve the victory (even as he won it alone on Calvary). In verses **3-6** Christ answers the prophet's question in verse **2. Mine own arm** (v. 5) as in 59:16, signifies the personal interposition of God on the arena of history. The scene here is the same as in Rev 14:18,19. A Christ-rejecting, Gospel-spurning world leaves the Lord no other alternative but to send fearful and terrible destruction when the time of his longsuffering is past.

Sermon VI. Israel's Plea for Help, Based on Past Mercies. 63:7–64:12.

63:7-9. Israel sings a song of thanksgiving for Jehovah's tender love toward his covenant children, all of whose rigors and trials he has shared. **10-14.** The prophet recalls Israel's ungrateful rebellion, which compelled the Lord to chasten his chosen people as if they were his enemies. Omit the italicized **saying** in 63:11; the question beginning **Where** is asked by the prophet as Israel's spokesman. **14. Caused them to rest** (ASV); i.e., during the wilderness journey under Moses and Aaron (the **shepherd**[s] mentioned in v. 11). **15-19.** These verses present the supplication of the repentant backsliders that God would cease from his estrangement and once again show his tender love (even if Abraham and Jacob disowned them because of their infidelity). **18. A little while.** About 800 years by the time of Jerusalem's fall in 587 B.C. (and only 673 years thereafter: from 538 B.C. to A.D. 135).

64:1-7. Isaiah represents the people of Israel as entreating Jehovah to intervene in the world scene and enforce the claims of his holiness and sovereignty. **1.** The imagery is reminiscent of the eruption of Mount Sinai. **2.** The righteous people are grieved at the contempt men show God, with apparent impunity. They recognize that the Lord cannot properly intervene to deliver, unless his people walk in love and obedience (v. 5), whereas the people of Israel (and *a fortiori* the rest of mankind) are defiled with sin; even their pretensions to righteousness (v. 6) are vitiated by a basically self-seeking motive, rather than by supreme love of God (which alone can be the basis of true morality; cf. Deut 6:5). **8-12.** Recognizing their own inexcusable guilt, the repentant Israelites plead only God's gracious covenant promises, and present their devastated land and ruined Temple as arguments for his pity and compassion.

Sermon VII. God's Mercy Reserved for Spiritual Israel. 65:1-25.

1-7. This is a scathing indictment of the hypocritical Jewish nation of Isaiah's day, professing to be a holy and righteous people (v. 5), and yet practicing all the execrable abominations of the heathen. (This description would be altogether inappropriate for post-Exilic Israel, which had abandoned idolatry forever). **1. A nation . . . not called by my name.** The Gentiles (according to Rom 10:20,21), who would some day respond to the Gospel, while the covenant nation remained obdurately Christ-rejecting. Warnings and loving entreaties had proved unavailing; there was no other alternative but the well-deserved punishment of the Babylonian captivity (and of the Roman expulsion from Palestine in A.D. 135).

8-12. Yet this inevitable punishment would be delayed for a time, to prepare a remnant of true believers for future blessing. The grape cluster of verse 8 is composed, largely, of spoiled or shriveled grapes; few grapes in it are round and sweet. For reasons of sentiment, because it is the earliest cluster of the vintage season, the husbandman preserves it from discard. **11. That troop.** Better, *Fortune* (ASV; *Gad* here being the proper noun for the Syrian god of good luck). **That number.** Rather, *M^e^nî,* the god of *Destiny,* – which introduces the grim word play of verse **12; I will destine** (from the same root as *M^e^nî*) **you to the sword** (ASV). **13-16.** The ultimate lot of disobedient Israel is contrasted with that of spiritual Israel. The unbelieving Jews will suffer a famine, thirst of soul, and the torments of hell; but the faithful will enjoy the bounties of heaven forever, and be called by **another name** (v. 15), presumably that of "Christians."

17-25. Here is given a foreview of the Millennial felicity of earth after it has been purged of unbelievers. **17.** The designation **new heavens and a new earth** is applied to the Millennial kingdom only as a stage preliminary to the eternal glories of heaven (the New Jerusalem of Rev 21; 22) – just as Pentecost was to be regarded (Acts 2:17) as ushering in the 'last days,' although it occurred at least nineteen centuries before the Second Advent. **20.** This prediction requires the conditions of an earthly city, where babies are born and older people die (even though the average lifespan is to be much prolonged). This final scene is that of a warless, capitalistic (v. 22) society, in which even predatory animals have become tame and inoffensive (as in 11:7-9).

Sermon VIII. The Blessing of True Believers in the Final Age. 66:1-24.

1-4. Jehovah condemns externalism in worship. The Almighty needs no temples built by man to dwell in nor sacrificial animals for food (what a contrast to the pagan concept!). It is the repentant and believing heart that he requires. A valid sacrifice is a sacramental seal of faith. Apart from faith, the slaying of animals is as abominable to God as murder, or the offering of an unclean beast (v. 3). Those who turn away from his call will find to their sorrow that he will turn away from their call.

5-9. The marvelous deliverance of the repentant remnant is here predicted. The unbelieving majority jeer at sincere Bible believers, challenging their God to display his glory by a miracle of deliverance or of vengeance, if he can. Jehovah's answer to the challenge will come as the Chaldean besiegers tumultuously storm the walls of Jerusalem (v. 6). In the 'last days' (beginning at Pentecost) that remnant was to multiply speedily into a great and numerous people as the Gospel was preached. And without the protracted birth pangs of parturition, the far-flung commonwealth of the Christian Church would spring up all over the Roman Empire within a single generation.

10-14. In the comfort and prosperity of the Millennial age, the whole company of believers will enjoy uninterrupted peace and plenty (**like a river** – v. 12) and will exert an absolutely controlling influence over all the world. The closest and tenderest of relations will obtain between latter-day Israel and her God. A decisive and immediate punishment will be meted out to all the unrighteous and disobedient.

15-17. Idolatrous unbelievers will be consigned to the fires of hell (as is reaffirmed in II Thess 1:7-9). **17. Behind one (tree).** Rather, *behind one person;* i.e., behind the cult leader who heads up idolatrous purification ceremonies (e.g., Jaazaniah, in Ezk 8:11).

18-21. God's glory will be manifested to all the world, that is, to all who have **escape**[d] the destructions of Armageddon, and have gathered together as adherents to the Millennial Church. Apparently there will then be extensive foreign missionary activity. Mentioned are **Tarshish** (western Mediterranean), **Pul** (south of Egypt, perhaps Somaliland), **Lud** (probably Lydia in Asia Minor), **Tubal** (southeast of the Black Sea), and **Javan** (Greece). **20,21.** All the regenerated Jews of the Dispersion will be honorably escorted by their Gentile co-religionists to Palestine. Possibly they will be welcomed as equally holy (**for priests and for Le-**

vites) with the Jews already in the land. Or else **of them** refers to the Gentile believers themselves.

22-24. The establishment of new heavens and a new earth will usher in the final, permanent, and unchanging state of both the redeemed and the damned. Apparently the regular appearance of all mankind in Jerusalem for worship is figurative of religious commitment and allegiance to Jehovah as the one true God. Yet Jerusalem visits would still be a logical possibility for the duration of the Thousand Year period. The faithful will look on the corpses of those who have joined in the final assault of the World-Power on Jerusalem, as they litter the battlefield, and will abominate them and all that they stood for in this life. Note that it is not said that the corpses will lie there forever. The souls of the wicked will be consigned to the eternal torments of hell (as Christ reaffirmed in Mk 9:48).

Thus the majestic trilogy of Volume Eight is brought to a close with a glimpse into the everlasting destiny of all mankind. The atoning work of Jehovah's Servant has laid the foundation for a new Commonwealth, for New Heavens and a New Earth that shall never pass away.

BIBLIOGRAPHY

ALEXANDER, J. A. *Commentary on Isaiah.* Grand Rapids: Zondervan Publishing House, reprinted n. d.

ALLEMAN, H. C., and FLACK, E. E. *Old Testament Commentary.* Philadelphia: Muhlenberg Press, 1948.

ALLIS, O. T. *The Unity of Isaiah.* Philadelphia: Presbyterian and Reformed Publishing Company, 1950.

BENTZEN, A. *Introduction to the Old Testament.* 2 Vols. Copenhagen: G. E. C. Gads Forlag, 1948.

BURROWS, MILLAR. *The Dead Sea Scrolls.* New York: Viking Press, 1955.

DELITZSCH, FRANZ. *Commentary on Isaiah.* 2 vols. Grand Rapids: Wm. B. Eerdmans Publishing Co., reprinted 1949.

DUHM, BERNHARD. *Israel's Propheten.* Tübingen: J. C. B. Mohr, 1916.

FITCH, W. "Isaiah," *The New Bible Commentary.* Edited by Francis Davidson, Alan M. Stibbs, and Ernest F. Kevan. Grand Rapids: Wm. B. Eerdmans Publishing Co., 1953.

KISSANE, E. J. *The Book of Isaiah.* 2 vols. Dublin: Browne and Nolan, 1941.

MOELLER, WILHELM. *Grundriss für Alttestamentliche Einleitung.* Berlin: Evangelische Verlagsanstalt, 1958.

NÄGELSBACH, CARL W. E. *Isaiah (A Commentary on the Holy Scriptures).* Edited by J. P. Lange. Grand Rapids: Zondervan Publishing House, reprinted n. d.

PFEIFFER, ROBERT H. *Introduction to the Old Testament.* New York: Harper and Brothers, 1941.

ROBINSON, GEORGE L. "Isaiah," *International Standard Bible Encyclopaedia.* Edited by James Orr. Vol. III. Grand Rapids: Wm. B. Eerdmans Publishing Co., 1946.

SCOTT, R. B. Y., *et al.* "Isaiah," *The Interpreter's Bible.* Vol. 5. New York: Abingdon Press, 1956.

SKINNER, J. *The Book of the Prophet Isaiah (Cambridge Bible for Schools and Colleges).* Cambridge: The University Press, 1951.

STEINMUELLER, J. E. *Companion to Scripture Studies.* 2 vols. New York: Wagner Press, 1942.

UNGER, MERRILL F. *Introductory Guide to the Old Testament.* Grand Rapids: Zondervan Publishing House, 1952.

YOUNG, EDWARD J. *Introduction to the Old Testament.* Grand Rapids: Wm. B. Eerdmans Publishing Co., 1949.

———. *Studies in Isaiah.* Grand Rapids: Wm. B. Eerdmans Publishing Co., 1954.

———. *Who Wrote Isaiah?* Grand Rapids: Wm. B. Eerdmans Publishing Co., 1958.

JEREMIAH

INTRODUCTION

The Life and Times of Jeremiah. The history of the Kingdom of Judah after the death of Solomon and the division of his kingdom has been seen as four religious declines and three revivals. Josiah (640–609 B.C.) was the last good king. In his reign occurred the well-known revival occasioned by the finding of the scroll of the Law. This was the last revival. After this time Judean history is one of constant political, moral, and religious decline, culminating in the Babylonian exile. This final period of decline was the time of the ministry of the prophet Jeremiah.

This was the period during which the new Babylonian empire arose. During the middle of the Divided Kingdom period, Assyria had dominated the Fertile Crescent. But after the fall of its capital Nineveh, in 612 B.C., the Assyrian Empire disintegrated, and Babylon became the mistress of the civilized world. The vain attempt of the Egyptians to assert their authority in this crisis of empires left its imprint on the Biblical story. In fact, it appears from the Biblical sources that there were two parties at the Jerusalem court. The pro-Egyptian party believed that Egypt was reviving as a world power and should be relied upon by the Jews as a bulwark against Babylonian aggression. The pro-Babylonians saw in the rising star of Babylon an invincible power and urged submission to her as the price of continued national existence. The prophets counseled the nation to look neither to Egypt nor to Babylon, but to trust in God.

Jeremiah began his ministry in Josiah's thirteenth year (626 B.C.), five years after the revival. His ministry continued into the early years of the Exile. He died in Egypt, probably a few years after the destruction of Jerusalem, which occurred in 587 B.C.

Josiah was killed in 609 B.C., at Megiddo, in his abortive attempt to stop Pharaoh-necho, who was on his way to support the tottering Assyrian Empire. Jehoahaz, Josiah's son, succeeded his father in Jerusalem. Necho evidently believed Jehoahaz to be of pro-Babylonian sympathies, for he carried him off to Egypt (after a three-month rule) and made Jehoiakim king (609–598 B.C.). Jehoiakim was a strong ruler and a very wicked man. He tried, on a number of occasions, to silence Jeremiah. During his reign Jeremiah dictated his first book, which the king promptly destroyed (Jer 36). During his reign, also, occurred the battle of Carchemish (605 B.C.), in which Egypt was crushed by the Babylonian crown prince Nebuchadnezzar, who soon afterward became king of Babylon. Then the Babylonian empire was on its way to world domination.

Nebuchadnezzar's victory at Carchemish was followed by a conquest of Palestine, which brought Judah into the Babylonian orbit. A few Hebrews (Daniel among them) were deported to Babylon at this time. Later Jehoiakim rebelled. There followed many troubles for Judah, including possibly another Babylonian capture of Jerusalem. In the middle of this unrest, Jehoiakim died—possibly the victim of a palace coup—after a reign of eleven years.

Jehoiachin, the son of Jehoiakim, succeeded his father on the throne. Jeremiah called this king Coniah and Jechoniah (22:24,28; 24:1; 27:20; 29:2). When Jehoiachin had reigned only three months, the Babylonians attacked Jerusalem (in a belated attempt to crush Jehoiakim's revolt) and carried off Jehoiachin to Babylon (597 B.C.), together with other important Jews and many artisans. After thirty-seven years of confinement there, Jehoiachin was released from prison in Babylon.

In Jehoiachin's place, Nebuchadnezzar appointed Zedekiah, uncle of Jehoiachin. For eleven years he maintained a precarious position as Nebuchadnezzar's vassal on the throne. He was a weak character, yet he protected Jeremiah from the nobles' attempts on his life and welcomed Jeremiah's advice, although he was never able to carry it out. Inevitably he, too, was caught up with the will-o'-the-wisp of independence, and rebelled. In the ninth year of Zedekiah, Nebuchadnezzar began the final siege of Jerusalem; in Zedekiah's eleventh year (587 B.C.) the city was captured and destroyed. Zedekiah, blinded, was carried off to Babylon, together with more of Jeremiah's fellow countrymen.

For the events in Judah after the destruction of Jerusalem, we are dependent almost exclusively on Jeremiah (chs. 40–45). Jeremiah and many of the common people were left in the land under Gedaliah, the Jewish puppet governor. After civil unrest, in which Gedaliah was assassinated, certain Jews, doubtless remnants of the pro-Egyptian party, fled to Egypt, forcing Jeremiah to accompany them there. In Egypt the prophet died.

The death of Jeremiah brings the history of the Hebrew kingdom to an end. The proclamation of Cyrus, permitting the exiles to return to Judah, was the opening signal of the new Second Commonwealth epoch.

Jeremiah: The Man and His Message. Jeremiah the priest was called to the prophetic office at a most unhappy time. Josiah's revival was over and its results short-lived. The final decline was under way. When the prophet was called, it was intimated that his message would be one of condemnation rather than of salvation. Throughout his long ministry of more than forty years, his preaching reflected this theme of judgment. God had risen early and sent his servants the prophets, but Israel would not hear. Now the fate predicted for an apostate nation in Deuteronomy 28–30 was inevitable. Babylon would capture Judah. And it would be best for the people to give in gracefully and so save their lives.

This message, coming to men whose desperate nationalism was all they had to cling to, was completely rejected, and the bearer was rejected with his message. Jeremiah was regarded as a meddler and a traitor; and people, nobles, and kings, alternately, tried to do him to death.

We understand Jeremiah's personality more clearly than that of any other prophet. This is due to the fact that his book is full of autobiographical sections—"Jeremiah's confessions." These outpourings of the human spirit are some of the most poignant and pathetic statements of the tension of a man under divine imperative to be found anywhere in Scripture. They are listed below. They show us a Jeremiah who was retiring, sensitive, and afraid of people's "faces," one whom we should consider singularly unfitted for the work placed upon him. That he tenaciously clung to his assigned task through the succeeding years of rejection and persecution is a tribute both to the mettle of the man and to the grace of God, without which his personality surely would have gone to pieces.

Jeremiah's Confessions.

10:23,24	17:9-11, 14-18
11:18–12:6	18:18-23
15:10-21	20:7-18

The Composition of the Book. The book of Jeremiah is not arranged in chronological order. This commentary states the date of each section or chapter, i.e., the time when the events took place or the prophecy was proclaimed, whenever such a date is known. Why the book was arranged as it is, we do not know. Every outline of Jeremiah is somewhat arbitrary. The one given below seeks to show the unity of the book.

It is impossible, in the present state of our knowledge, to tell the circumstances of the writing of the book. Many modern commentators feel that certain parts of it were written not by Jeremiah but by later writers, whose point of view differed markedly from the prophet's. It is the viewpoint of this commentary that there is good reason to take a conservative attitude toward the authorship of the book—that in its present state it is substantially the work of Jeremiah and his helper, Baruch (cf. Jer 45:1).

It seems likely that the book went through a number of editions, each succeeding one containing additional material. The story of the writing of the first edition, its destruction, and the composition of the second edition, with additions, is told in chapter 36. No doubt there were succeeding revisions. It has long been noted that the Greek translation of Jeremiah as it appears in the Septuagint, made in Egypt before 132 B.C., is much shorter than the Hebrew book, from which our English translations have been made. Further, the Septuagint omits many of the repetitions that are contained in the Hebrew copy, and rearranges the material somewhat. It is not now possible to arrive at any certain conclusion about the relationship of the Septuagint to the Hebrew text, and this commentary, based as it is on the English Bible, follows the Hebrew Jeremiah.

The Foe from the North. Throughout Jeremiah's sermons occur references to a foe from the *north* who would devastate Judah and take her captive. Chapter 4 is typical of these oracles: The foe will destroy like a lion or a whirlwind and leave the land in desolation like the primeval chaos. Who is this destroying enemy? The fulfillment indicates that the northern foe was Babylon. Although Babylon is on the same latitude as Samaria, her invasions of Palestine always came from the north, as the desert which separates the two was impassable. The view that the Scythians are referred to as the northern foe in some places of the book seems not to be held so widely today as it once was, and may safely be rejected.

Sometimes *north* is used of the origin of the conquerors of Babylon (50:3,9, 41; 51:48). This use of the term is difficult to account for. The Persians, who were the principal captors of Babylon, came from the east. Probably here *north* has become an expression for the source of any trouble, arrived at because Israel's troubles for so long a time had come from that direction. Further explanation may be found in the fact that the Medes, located to the north, joined with the Babylonians in capturing Nineveh. See note on Jer 50:11.

The Lachish Letters. Lachish, in the Judean foothills, was one of a series of fortresses maintained for the defense of Jerusalem against attack from the Mediterranean Plain. It was one of the last cities to fall to the Babylonians prior to the final taking and the destruction of Jerusalem (Jer 34:7, note). Interesting light has been shed on these last hectic days of Judah's history by a discovery in the ruins of ancient Lachish. When the city was being excavated (1932 through 1938), there were found in a guardroom of the outer gate twenty-one letters written on broken pieces of pottery. They were written in the ancient Hebrew script, with carbon-iron ink, and date from the time of Jeremiah, when Lachish was undergoing its final siege.

Many of these letters were written by a certain Hoshaiah, a military officer at some outpost near Lachish, to Yaosh, the commander of Lachish. Their language is very like that of the book of Jeremiah. Hoshaiah is constantly defending himself to his superior. Could it be that he was suspected of being ready to defect to the Babylonians? Once he describes one of the princes in words almost like those the princes used against Jeremiah (Jer 38:4). There is mention of "the prophet" whose message is "Beware." Is this a reference to Jeremiah? We cannot be sure. According to the book of Jeremiah, there were prophets aplenty in that troublous time. Another letter mentions the inability of Hoshaiah to see the smoke signals of Azekah, although he could still see those of Lachish. Perhaps by that time Azekah had fallen (cf. Jer 34:7). Although the specific meaning of many of the references of these letters eludes us, the letters throw a vivid light on the disturbed and fearful days just prior to the fall of the Judean kingdom. (For a translation of this correspondence, see *Ancient Near Eastern Texts Relating to the Old Testament*, ed. by James B. Pritchard, 2nd ed.).

Literature on Jeremiah. Commentators on the book may be divided into two groups. The older commentators generally believe prophecy to be of divine inspiration and explain the prophecies on that basis, but are out-of-date in matters of historical background. Of these the best is probably still C. F. Keil, *The Prophecies of Jeremiah*, Edinburgh, 1883, recently reprinted in Eerdmans' *Keil and Delitzsch Commentaries Series*.

A majority of the newer commentaries, naturalistic in approach, regard the prophetic message as originating in the mind of the prophet, whose brilliant intuition is the highest form of inspiration. They usually embody the latest archaeological discoveries and so give a better orientation to the large amount of *historical* material in the book. "Jeremiah" in *The Interpreter's Bible* (1956), with introduction and exegesis by James Philip Hyatt, shows this method at its best.

The chapter entitled "The Doom of the Nation" in *Understanding the Old Testament*, by Bernhard W. Anderson, gives a good summary of the contents of the book placed in their historical setting, together with a sympathetic delineation of the character of Jeremiah.

Edward J. Young in his *Introduction to the Old Testament* arranges the material of the book in its chronological order, and gives a discussion of the problem of authorship from the viewpoint of conservative Christianity.

OUTLINE

I. Oracles against the theocracy. 1:1–25:38.

- A. The prophet's call. 1:1-19.
- B. Reproofs and admonitions, mostly from the time of Josiah. 2:1–20:18.
  1. Israel's neglect of God. 2:1–3:5.
  2. Judah warned by the doom of the Northern Kingdom. 3:6–6:30.
  3. Jerusalem's wrong religion. 7:1–10:25.
  4. Israel rejected for breaking God's covenant. 11:1–13:27.
  5. Prophetic intercession unable to prevent judgment. 14:1–17:27.
  6. Two symbolic sermons and an imprisonment. 18:1–20:18.
- C. Later prophecies. 21:1–25:38.
  1. The issue of the siege. 21:1-14.
  2. An exhortation to king and people. 22:1-9.
  3. The fate of Shallum. 22:10-12.
  4. An oracle against Jehoiakim. 22:13-23.
  5. An oracle against Jehoiachin. 22:24-30.
  6. The Messianic King. 23:1-8.
  7. Against the false prophets. 23:9-40.
  8. The vision of the figs. 24:1-10.
  9. The judgment on Judah and all the nations. 25:1-38.

II. Events in the life of Jeremiah. 26:1–45:5.

- A. The temple sermon and Jeremiah's arrest. 26:1-24.
- B. The yoke of Babylon. 27:1–29:32.
- C. The book of consolation. 30:1–33:26.
  1. The Day of the Lord: Its terror and deliverance. 30:1-24.
  2. The restoration of the nation, and the new covenant. 31:1-40.
  3. Jeremiah's redemption of a field in Anathoth. 32:1-44.
  4. More promises of restoration. 33:1-26.
- D. Some of Jeremiah's experiences before Jerusalem fell. 34:1–36:32.
  1. An oracle to Zedekiah. 34:1-7.
  2. The broken covenant regarding Hebrew slaves. 34:8-22.
  3. The example of the Rechabites. 35:1-19.
  4. Jeremiah's prophecies dictated to Baruch. 36:1-32.
- E. Jeremiah during the siege and destruction of Jerusalem. 37:1–39:18.
  1. Jeremiah imprisoned. 37:1-21.
  2. Jeremiah rescued from a cistern. 38:1-28.
  3. The fall of Jerusalem. 39:1-18.
- F. The last years of Jeremiah. 40:1–45:5.
  1. The administration of Gedaliah and his murder. 40:1–41:18.
  2. Migration of refugees to Egypt. 42:1–43:7.
  3. Jeremiah in Egypt. 43:8–44:30.
  4. Jeremiah's oracle to Baruch. 45:1-5.

III. Jeremiah's oracles against foreign nations. 46:1–51:64.

- A. Oracle against Egypt. 46:1-28.
- B. Oracle against the Philistines. 47:1-7.
- C. Oracle against Moab. 48:1-47.
- D. Oracle against the Ammonites. 49:1-6.
- E. Oracle against Edom. 49:7-22.
- F. Oracle against Damascus. 49:23-27.
- G. Oracle against Kedar and Hazor. 49:28-33.
- H. Oracle against Elam. 49:34-39.
- I. Oracle against Babylon. 50:1–51:64.

IV. Appendix: The fall of Jerusalem, and related events. 52:1-34.

COMMENTARY

I. Oracles Against the Theocracy. 1:1–25:38.

A. The Prophet's Call. 1:1-19.

Jeremiah, in spite of his reticence, was commissioned to proclaim the message that Judah would be destroyed by a foe from the north. God promised to protect him from the anger of his fellow citizens.

1) Introduction. 1:1-3.

1. The words. The Hebrew *dibrê* means not only **words** but "deeds," and is so translated in 5:28. Perhaps both meanings apply here. This book contains the prophet's history as well as his messages. **Priests.** A man might be a priest by birth, but he was a prophet only by divine call. **Anathoth.** A town in the territory of Benjamin, set aside for residence of the priests and Levites (Josh 21:18). It is located two and one-half miles northeast of Jerusalem and is called Anata today.

2. The word of the Lord came. Jeremiah's frequently used statement of prophetic inspiration. **Josiah.** Judah's last good king, who instituted a great reform in the religion of the nation. His **thirteenth year** was 626 B.C.; he still had eighteen years to reign.

3. Jehoiakim came to the throne three months after the death of Josiah. During the intervening months, his brother Jehoahaz reigned, until Pharaoh-necho took him to Egypt (II Kgs 23:30-34; II Chr 36:1-4; Jer 22:10-12). Jehoiakim was an apostate, who revived the paganism his father had abolished, and Jeremiah has nothing good to say for him. He reigned eleven years (609–598 B.C.), during which time Nebuchadnezzar attacked Jerusalem, and forced Jehoiakim to pay him tribute. Later Jehoiakim rebelled. The manner of his death is not known, but Jeremiah's prophecy (22:19, note) seems to indicate that he was to come to a violent end (II Kgs 23:36–24:7; II Chr 36:5-8). **Zedekiah.** Judah's last ruler. Although called **king,** he seems to have been more of a regent, acting in the place of Jehoiachin, his nephew, who, after a three months' reign, was carried to Babylon by Nebuchadnezzar (II Kgs 24:8-16; 25:27-30; II Chr 36:9,10). His reign lasted eleven years (597–587 B.C.) and was brought to an end by the destruction of Jerusalem and the captivity of the Jews (II Kgs 24:18–25:7; II Chr 36:11-21). **Fifth month.** See note on 52:12,13. Cf. II Kgs 25:8,9.

2) God's Call to Jeremiah. 1:4-10.

4. Me. The change from third person (vv. 1-3) to first is not unusual in ancient Hebrew literature. **5. Knew . . . sanctified . . . ordained.** These verbs are roughly synonymous. Jeremiah's task was to be a difficult one; these words assured him of God's choice and support. *Know,* when used of God in Scripture, has an active connotation. **Sanctified.** Set apart to the prophetic office. **Prophet.** The Hebrew term *nābî* seems to mean a "speaker," which is a good characterization of the Hebrew prophet. He was God's spokesman.

6. A child. Isaiah, when called to be a prophet, felt "unclean" (Isa 6:5). Jeremiah, in keeping with his timid nature, expresses his feeling as one of inadequacy. **8. Their faces.** A part used for a whole. The faces of the men of Jerusalem will reflect the animosity of their wicked personalities. **9. Touched my mouth.** To enable him to overcome fear and to speak. **My words in thy mouth.** Jeremiah was given a message to preach. Ezekiel, when he became God's spokesman, symbolically ate a scroll (Ezk 3:2,3). **10.** God's use of four synonyms for destruction and only two for building indicates that Jeremiah's message was to be predominantly one of warning about the coming judgment. **Set.** *Made overseer* (Gen 39:4,5).

3) The Vision of the Almond Tree. 1:11,12.

11. There is here a play on words. **Almond tree** is *shāqēd* and **hasten** is *shōqēd*. The mention of *shāqēd* brings to mind *shōqēd,* which sounds like it. This kind of play on words is frequent in the Hebrew Bible. **12. I will hasten.** Better, *I am watching over* (cf. 31:28; 44:27).

4) The Vision of the Seething Pot. 1:13-16.

13. Seething. Literally, *blown upon;* therefore boiling hot. **Face . . . toward the north.** Better, *facing away from the north.* The pot was turned toward the south. Soon it would overturn, and its scalding contents would flow over Judah.

North. Cf. Introduction, *The Foe from the North.* **14. An evil.** Better, *the calamity*. The Hebrew word often means "misery," "distress," "trouble," as well as "evil." **The land.** That is, Judah. **15. I will call.** *I am in the act of calling.* **Entering of the gates.** The open place outside the city gate was the scene of public business (Ruth 4:1,11); here kings dispensed justice (I Kgs 22:10). The fulfillment of this prophecy is recorded in Jer 39:3.

5) Encouragement to the Prophet. 1:17-19.

17. Gird up thy loins. Cf. 13:1 note. **Dismayed . . . confound.** *Do not be dismayed by them, lest I dismay you before them.* **18. Defenced city.** *Fortified city* (cf. Ezk 3:8,9). **Kings . . . princes . . . priests . . . people.** The various classes of citizens; each group later opposed Jeremiah. **People of the land.** The Hebrew idiom means "the common people."

B. Reproofs and Admonitions, Mostly from the Time of Josiah. 2:1–20:18.

These six sections, which are general and repetitive in character, seem to date from the early part of the prophet's ministry. They may well be typical of his oral preaching.

1) Israel's Neglect of God. 2:1–3:5.

The backsliding of the Hebrew people is here very tenderly described in terms similar to those used in Hosea.

2. Kindness. *Ḥesed* contains the ideas of "love" and "faithfulness." The RSV translates it *devotion.* God's relationship to Israel is often likened by the prophets to that of a husband to his wife (Isa 54:4; Hos 2:2-20; Ezk 16). Here Israel's early days are referred to as a honeymoon. Israel had left Egypt and followed her husband to a strange land (Ex 19:4). Jeremiah does not mean to deny the frequent backslidings of the early days, but he emphasizes here the nation's praiseworthy determination to follow her God into the wilderness. **Wilderness** is defined as **a land . . . not sown.** The *midbār* of the Middle East is not completely desolate, but it is an uncultivated land over which the Bedouins roam to find pasture for their flocks (cf. Joel 2:22; Ps 65:12,13). Here the journey of the Hebrews through the **wilderness** from Egypt to Canaan is referred to.

3. Holiness. *Holy* (cf. Ex 19:5,6). **Firstfruits.** The harvest **firstfruits** were set apart as sacred (Ex 23:19; Lev 23:9-21); so Israel, God's **firstfruits-people** among the nations, was sacred. The **firstfruits** were offered to God and could not be eaten by lay Israelites. So here, those who **devour** Israel shall be guilty. **Offend.** Better, *become guilty* (cf. Gen 12:3). History has proved the truth of this statement.

4. Jacob . . . Israel. The whole Hebrew nation is in view. The prophets frequently ignored the division of the kingdom and the exile of the northern tribes and addressed "the whole family which I brought up out of Egypt" (Amos 3:1). **5. Vanity . . . become vain.** The noun and verb come from the same Hebrew root, which means basically "vapor," "breath," and so, "worthlessness" or "worthless." It is frequently used (as here) as a synonym for idolatry (cf. 10:15; 16:19; and many others).

Israel's ingratitude to her Saviour-God. 2:6-8. **A plentiful country** (v. 7). *A garden land,* cultivated and fruitful, in contrast to the desert through which they had just traveled. **The priests said not . . .** (v. 8).

The defection of the people was caused by their leaders. **Law.** Probably **law** in the broad sense of "instruction in the will of God." **Knew me.** The lack of the knowledge of God is a frequent theme of the prophets (cf. Hos 4:6). What is meant is that the priests had deliberately rejected the God "in the knowledge of whom standeth our eternal life" (cf. Jer 31:34). **Pastors.** Hebrew *rōʿeh* has the basic meaning "shepherd" and here should be translated *rulers.* **Baal.** The Canaanite storm-and fertility-god. **Things that do not profit.** This expression (like *vanity,* v. 5) is often used of idolatry, as here (cf. v. 11).

9. Plead. The idea suggested by this word is that of bringing a suit against a person in a court of law. **10. Isles.** Better, *coast lands,* or *regions.* **Chittim.** *Cyprus,* or possibly the coast lands of the Mediterranean in general. **Kedar.** Probably an Arab desert tribe in the opposite direction from Cyprus (cf. Gen 25:13). The meaning is, "Search east or west." **11. Their glory.** God was Israel's glory (Ps 106:20). **13.** A vivid contrast between a perennial spring of fresh water and a cistern (whose water was brackish at best) now cracked by an earthquake and thus completely emptied.

The results of Israel's apostasy. 2:14-19. As the nation neared collapse, two political opinions were advanced at court. Some counseled a league with Babylon —here referred to as drinking "the waters of the river," and others urged a treaty with Egypt—drinking "the waters of Sihor" (v. 18). Jeremiah describes the destruction which has come to the nation in the recent wars in Palestine. Nothing but enslavement and ruin could follow either course; rather, the people must return to God.

14. Homeborn slave. Slaves were of two types: those acquired by purchase, and those born in the house of the master and so his permanent possession (Ex 21:2-4). **15. Made his land waste.** Already the northern kingdom had been desolated because of the apostasy of its people. **16**. At the same time, the Egyptian armies had begun to ravage Judah. **Noph.** Memphis, an important Egyptian city near modern Cairo (44:1). **Tahapanes.** Modern Tell Defenneh, on the eastern border of the Delta, commanding the road to Palestine (cf. 43:7-9; 44:1). **18. Sihor.** The Nile, symbolizing Egypt (Isa 23:3). **The river.** The Euphrates, meaning Assyria (cf. Hos 7:11; 12:1).

20. The RSV is to be preferred:

For long ago you broke your yoke
and burst your bonds;
and you said, "I will not serve."
Yea, upon every high hill
and under every green tree
you bowed down as a harlot.

Israel's infidelity to her husband-lord is frequently called harlotry. The figure is rendered more forceful because of the cultic prostitution frequently practiced in Baal worship, and probably alluded to here (cf. Ezk 16; Hos 1-3). **High hill . . . green tree.** Cf. 3:6 note.

21. Viniculture was one of the main occupations of the ancient Hebrews. Because the raising and care of grape vines was difficult and hazardous, and the yield uncertain, but the product valuable and desired, the vineyard is frequently used as an illustration in prophetic preaching. Israel is likened to a vine, God to the vine-raiser (Isa 5:1-7; Ps 80:8; Hos 10:1; cf. Jn 15:1-8). **A strange vine.** *A wild vine.* **22. Yet thine iniquity is marked before me.** In other words, "Even though you perform righteousness outwardly, this does not conceal from me your secret iniquity, which cannot be cleansed by physical means." **Nitre** is lye, a mineral alkali obtained from the soda lakes in Egypt, and mixed with oil for washing clothes.

23-25. Jeremiah likens his people to wild creatures in heat. Their desire is so great that any mate that wants them can find them without wearying itself. Here the female pursues the male. **Baalim** (v. 23). *Baals* (cf. 2:8 note). **A swift dromedary traversing her ways.** *A restive young camel interlacing her tracks* (RSV). **That snuffeth . . . turn her away** (v. 24). Better, *In her heat sniffing the wind! Who can restrain her lust?* **Her month.** That is, her time of heat. **25. Withhold thy foot.** "Do not continue to run after and crave idolatry," says God. But Israel replies, "I will continue to follow foreign gods."

26-28. In a future time of trouble, the Lord warns, Judah's much-sought-after gods will be unable to deliver her. **Stock . . . stone** (v. 27). Probably references to the widely used cultic objects, *'ăshērâ,* and *maṣṣēbâ*. The *'ăshērâ* (AV, "grove") is thought to have been a wooden pole that stood in a Canaanite high place of worship. It was a symbol of Asherah, the goddess of fertility. The *maṣṣēbâ* (AV, *pillar* and *image)* was used in connection with the worship of Baal (Deut 12:3). **According to the number of thy cities** (v. 28). Baals tended to be identified with places. There was a Baal of Ekron (II Kgs 1:1-16). Thus each city had a local deity (cf. Jer 11:13).

29. Wherefore . . . plead with me? "Why do you complain that I desert you in your crisis, seeing that you rebel against me?" **31. We are lords.** Better, *We are free;* i.e., We roam at large, without restraint. **33. Why trimmest thou thy way . . . ?** *How well you direct your course to seek lovers! So that even to wicked women you have taught your ways!*

A condemnation of the iniquitous oppression of the poor. 2:34,35. Cf. Amos 2:6-8; 4:1; 5:10-12. **34. Poor innocents.** *Innocent poor.* The latter half of the verse should be related to verse 35 thus: "You did not find them breaking in (which might have justified an act of homicide; Ex 22:2). Yet in spite of all this, you say, 'I am innocent.'" **35. Plead with you.** *Judge you.*

36,37. The Lord here condemns the desperate counsels of the pro-Egyptian party. See note on 2:14-19. **Yea, thou shalt go forth . . .** (v. 37). *From it* (Egypt), *too, you will come away empty, beating your hands on your head in grief* *and dismay* (cf. II Sam 13:19). **Thy confidences.** *Those in whom you trust.*

3:1-5. The translators of the AV understood this paragraph as a plea for Israel to return to God. Many modern commentators believe that this is a message of reproof, not of pleading. It is difficult for a divorced wife to return. Yet Israel carelessly and impudently talked of returning and hoped thus to postpone judgment.

1. Deuteronomy 24:1-4 forbids a man's taking back his divorced and remarried wife, even if her second husband dies or divorces her. **Put away**; i.e., divorce. **Yet return again to me.** Or, *and would you return to me?* **2.** Judah's idolatry, stated under the figure of an animal in 2:23,24, is now described with the more usual term "harlot." **In the ways.** Literally, *By the wayside.* **As the Arabian in the wilderness** lay in wait to seize and plunder the unwary, so did Judah run to idolatry. **3. Showers . . . latter rain.** The early rains (probably referred to here as **showers**) fall in October and November, breaking the summer drought. Then the farmer plows and seeds the land, and the crops begin to grow. The latter rains come in March and April, and bring the crops to fruition. Soon afterward follows harvest. God showed his displeasure with his people by withholding the rain (e.g., 14:1-6; I Kgs 17:1; Amos 4:7,8). **A harlot's forehead.** Cf. English "brazen-faced." **4. Wilt thou not from this time cry unto me . . . ?** Or, *Have you not just now called to me?* **5b. Thou hast spoken and done evil.** *Although you have spoken of returning, you have at the same time done all the evil you could.*

2) Judah Warned by the Doom of the Northern Kingdom. 3:6–6:30.

Jeremiah continues his condemnation of Judah begun in the previous section (2:1–3:5). In addition, he here holds out God's promise of pardon, if only the people will genuinely repent. Captive Israel is here mentioned as a warning to Judah, and her restoration is predicted.

3:6-10. Israel's backsliding and punishment were a warning for Judah, yet she had not repented. **Israel** here means the northern ten tribes, taken captive nearly one hundred years previously (721 B.C.). Her unfaithfulness resulted in captivity, referred to as "divorce" (v. 8; cf. Hos 2:2-13). Judah's pretended repentance (v. 10) is a reference to Josiah's revival (II Kgs 23; II Chr 34; 35), which seems to have been legislated by the king, and did not go very deep into the life of the nation. **6. High mountain . . . green tree.** References to high places, where the Canaanites practiced their Baal worship.

3:11-18. God calls Israel to repentance, and promises her pardon and restoration. The OT prophets refused to recognize the division of the Davidic kingdom as final. They often speak of its reunion and the glorification of the whole nation in the Messianic kingdom.

11. Justified herself. *Shown herself more righteous.* Judah had enjoyed greater privileges (divinely ordained kingship, priestly service), and had had before her the example of captive Israel, and so was the more guilty (Ezk 16:44-63; 23:1-49; Lk 12:48). **12. Proclaim . . . toward the north.** That is, towards Assyria, where Israel had been taken captive, for she was not wholly cast off by God. **Cause mine anger to fall.** Literally, *cause my face to fall* (cf. Gen 4:5; contrast Num 6:26). **13. Hast scattered thy ways to the strangers under every green tree.** They were free with their love for foreign gods on the high places.

14. Am married. Israel should return to her God, who is her Husband and Lord (cf. 31:32). The word *ba'al* means, primarily, "be master," then, "be married." These two ideas are really one to the Semitic mind. **One of a city . . . two of a family.** The doctrine of the remnant, frequently found in Jeremiah (23:3; 32:36-44), is here referred to. Out of God's purifying judgment will come a few refined souls. They will be regathered and will constitute the new Israel, blessed by God (cf. Rom 11:5). **15. Pastors.** *Shepherds* (the original meaning of the English "pastors"); i.e., rulers obedient to God (cf. 2:8,26; 23:4).

16,17. In the future regathering, no longer will the ark be God's throne (Ex 25:22), but Jerusalem itself will be the throne of God as he rules all the nations (cf. Rev 21:22). The covenant symbolized by the ark will be replaced by a new covenant written upon the heart (cf. Jer 31:31-34). The ark disappeared when Jerusalem was destroyed in 587 B.C., and was never replaced. **16. Neither shall that be done any more.** *It shall not be made again.* **17. To the name of the Lord.** That is, to God's presence, which his name signifies. **18.** The captivity of Judah as well as of Israel is here understood. Both will be regathered to Palestine.

3:19–4:4. God calls Israel to return. An antiphonal section, characterized by deep feeling. God's urgings (3:19-22a) are followed by Israel's remorseful reply (3:22 b-25), then more divine urgings and promises (4:1-4).

19. The verse begins with an exclamation, not a question. God thought to set Israel among the sons, but she rejected her Father and Husband. **20. Treacherously.** *Faithlessly.* **23. The multitude of mountains.** Perhaps, "The uproar (wild orgies that accompany idol worship) of the mountains." **24. Shame.** *The shameful thing,* a circumlocution for Baal worship (cf. Hos 9:10).

Verses 1 and 2 of chapter 4 constitute one sentence, 4:1-2a being the condition, 4:2b the result. **1. Then shalt thou not remove.** *And (if) you do not waver.* **2. And the nations.** *Then the nations.*

The coming of the foe from the north. 4:5-31. The coming of the Babylonian armies is here vividly described. The people are counseled to flee for safety to the fortresses (v. 5). Many figurative expressions are used to describe the foe: lion (v. 7), sirocco (v. 11), eagles (v. 13). He comes through northern Palestine, from Dan, through Mount Ephraim to Jerusalem (vv. 15,16). Vividly the prophet states his anguish at the destruction (vv. 19-26).

5. Defenced. *Fortified.* The walled cities to which the rural people went for refuge in time of war. **6. North.** Cf. Introduction, *The Foe from the North.* **7. Gentiles.** *Nations.* **9. Shall perish.** *Shall fail.*

10. Thou hast . . . deceived. A difficult statement. Possibly it means that since God permitted the false prophets to cry "Peace! peace!" (cf. ch. 28), he was thought responsible for the people's deception. Jeremiah makes a number of deeply emotional outbursts of this kind (cf. 20:7, although *deceive* there represents a different Hebrew word).

11. A dry wind. The sirocco or khamsin, which blows in from the desert, bringing almost unbearable heat and dust. **The daughter of my people** is the people of Judah personified as a woman (cf. v. 31). **Fan.** *Winnow.* **Cleanse.** Cf. Mt 3:12. This hot wind cannot be used for threshing, as it would blow away grain and chaff together. **12. Even a full wind from those places shall come unto me.** Better, *A wind too full for this* (threshing) *comes for me.* **15. Dan.** The northernmost place in Palestine. **Mount Ephraim.** The last large section of Palestine to be crossed before one reaches Jerusalem. **16. Watchers.** *Besiegers.*

In verses 19-22 Jeremiah again expresses his painful reactions. **Bowels** (v. 19). Thought by the Hebrews to be the seat of the emotions. **Maketh a noise.** *Is beating wildly.*

23-26. In vivid figurative language the prophet describes the destruction of Judah to be made by the Babylonian armies. Among excavated Judean cities, archaeologists have found that every one which existed in Jeremiah's time was completely destroyed. **Without form, and void** (v. 23). The same words occur in Gen 1:2. Jeremiah is likening the destruction about to come upon Judah to the primeval chaos. **24. Moved lightly.** *Moved to and fro.* **27.** This qualifying statement that the desolation will not be quite complete seems at first out of place. Yet it is not, for the prophets all agree on the preservation of the remnant and the reconstitution of the nation through it (cf. 5:10,18; 30:11; 46:28).

28-31. The statement of destruction is now complete. It closes with a reference to the scarlet harlot, destitute and writhing in pain. For verse 28, see note on 18:8. **Thou rentest thy face with painting** (v. 30). *You enlarge your eyes with paint.* A black mineral powder, antimony, was used to increase the brilliance of the eyes by darkening the edges of the lids. **Thy lovers.** A term of scorn—*thy paramours.* **Bewaileth herself** (v. 31). *Gasps for breath.* **My soul is wearied.** *I am fainting.*

The corruption of Jerusalem. 5:1-9. The prophet is told to search the city for a god-fearing man (vv. 1-3), much as Diogenes in ancient Athens of a later time sought for an "honest man." Finding none among the common people, Jeremiah seeks among the leaders, but they are no better (vv. 4-6). Therefore God can find no ground for pardoning them (vv. 7-9).

1. Broad places. *Squares.* **Judgment.** *Justice.* **Truth.** *Faithfulness.* **2. The Lord liveth.** The fact that they use the name "Jehovah" in their oaths is no proof that they really worship him, for they swear to lies. **3. Upon truth.** *Looking for faithfulness.* **4. Judgment.** The word here (and in v. 5, and II Kgs 17:26, RSV) means "the divine law," i.e., religion. **5. The great men.** Those who have leisure and learning to know God's commandments. **6.** The nation is as defenseless as a man in a forest of wild beasts (cf. 4:7). **Evenings.** Better, *deserts*. **8. Fed horses in the morning.** *Well-fed lusty stallions* (cf. 2:23,24). **9. Visit.** *Punish.*

The call to the destroyer. 5:10-19. Jeremiah, like Isaiah (Isa 10:5-34), sees God beckon to a foreign nation to come and chasten His people.

10. Walls. *Vine-rows.* **Battlements.** *Branches.* The vineyard of Israel will be ravaged (2:21; cf. Isa 5:1-7). **12. It is not he.** *He will do nothing.* **13.** This verse continues the statement of the unbelievers. "The prophets of doom are empty windbags, and their threatening predictions will only come upon themselves." There is a play here upon the word *rûaḥ*, which can mean "spirit" or "wind." The prophets believed that they had the spirit of God; the people replied, "It is only wind!" **17. Which thy sons and thy daughters should eat.** Better, *They shall eat up your sons and your daughters* (to be understood metaphorically). **Impoverish.** *Batter.* **19. Strange gods.** *Foreign gods.*

The cause of the impending calamity. 5:20-31. God the moral governor of the universe must judge his rebellious people.

24. Rain. See on 3:3. **Reserveth . . . the . . . weeks of the harvest.** The harvest season (the latter half of April and May) should be a dry season; rain then harms the crops (Prov 26:1). **26-29.** A rebuke to the wicked rich who oppressed the poor. **26,27.** Birds were snared with a net; men closed the net with cords when a bird came into it. Then the birds were put into a basket (**cage,** AV; cf. Mic 7:2). **28. Shine.** *Are become sleek.* **29. Visit.** *Punish.* **30,31.** A rebuke is ministered to the false prophets and the priests who were subservient to them. **Wonderful.** *Appalling.* **By their means.** *At their beck.*

Jerusalem's destruction threatened. 6:1-8. It will be besieged by the northern foe day and night. The people are to flee from the city for safety, for it will be desolated.

1. The Benjamites, living near Jerusalem, usually fled into it for refuge. The prophet urges that warning signals be placed at points south of Jerusalem, for the foe will come from the north (cf. 4:15). **Tekoa.** A town twelve miles south of Jerusalem, probably chosen because its name permits a play on the word "blow" *(tiqʿû)*. **Beth-haccerem.** A town of Judah, probably modern Ain Karim, four and a half miles west of Jerusalem. The smoke signal here referred to is mentioned in the Lachish letters as a means of communication between cities under siege at the time (cf. Introduction, *The Lachish Letters*).

2. I have likened. *The comely and delicate one, the daughter of Zion, will I cut off.*

3. The invaders are likened to shepherds whose flocks denude the land.

4. Prepare. Literally, *sanctify* war; i.e., offer sacrifices to ensure success.

6. Mount. (Siege) *mound.* **Visited.** *Punished.*

7. Casteth out. Literally, *keeps cool;* i.e., keeps fresh.

The shamelessness of the people in the face of their total corruption. 6:9-15. Israel, like a gleaned vine, will be thoroughly devastated. Children and adults, houses and fields, commoner and noble, priest and prophet will be taken.

9. Turn back . . . baskets. *Like a grape gatherer, pass your hand again over its branches* to find the last grape. **10,11.** Jeremiah expresses his personal reaction to the unbelief of his people. He is identified with God in this crisis, and increasingly it will be clear that since the people have rejected God, they have also rejected Jeremiah. **Abroad;** i.e. playing in the street. All people, even children, will suffer the pains of war. **14.** The prophets and priests assure the people that all is well, even while calamity is hovering over them. **15. Visit.** *Punish.*

The ancient paths rejected by the people. 6:16-21. They would not listen to the true prophets, and so their continued sacrifices do not please God (I Sam 15:22,23).

16. The old paths. The ways of the patriarchs and of the fathers who experienced redemption from Egypt. **17. Watchmen.** In a rural, unfenced land, the watchmen played an important part. The prophets often call themselves **watchmen** (Ezk 3:17; 33:7). **18. What is among them.** *What will happen to them.* **19. Their thoughts.** *Their* (evil) *devices.* **20. Sheba.** Modern Yemen. Ancient source of frankincense, which was used as a part of the sacrificial ritual. **Sweet cane.** Calamus, an aromatic rue, which came from India.

The enemy's cruelty and the incorrigibility of the people. 6:22-30. The coming of the northern armies will bring terror to all; let the people mourn. The prophet has been made by God a tester, to discover how wicked they are.

22. The sides. *The remote parts of the earth* (cf. 25:32; 31:8). **25. Way.** *Road.* **Fear** *(terror)* **is on every side**—a favorite expression of Jeremiah (cf. 20:3 note, 10; 46:5; 49:29). **26. Daughter of my people.** Cf. 4:11 note. **Sackcloth** and **ashes** were signs of deepest mourning (cf. Ezk 27:30). **For an only son.** The most severe bereavement a Hebrew could suffer (cf. Amos 8:10; Zech 12:10). **27. Tower . . . fortress.** The words are difficult to interpret, but the sense is probably, "I have made thee a trier and a tester among my people." The prophet would test the people as a smith tests and refines metal, purifying it. But this people was all dross, could not be refined, and so was rejected (cf. 5:14). **29. Are burned.** Better, *blow fiercely.* With a note of rejection and despair the section ends.

3) Jerusalem's Wrong Religion. 7:1–10:25.

Jeremiah warns against trust in the Temple and its ritual. Jerusalem is no more sacrosanct than was fallen Shiloh (7:1–8:3). The people have resisted all reformation and will surely be punished (8:4–9:22). The true wisdom, which consists in the knowledge of God, is contrasted with idolatry (9:23–10:25).

a) The Temple Sermon. 7:1–8:3.

It appears that chapter 26 gives the historical background of this sermon. The fury it aroused well indicates its cogency. Shiloh, in Ephraim, was the home of the Tabernacle during the time of the Judges. The Bible does not mention the fall of Shiloh. Jeremiah's inference that it was destroyed (7:12,14; 26:6,9) has been confirmed by the recent excavation of the site, which indicated that the city was destroyed by the Philistines about 1050 B.C., probably after the battle of Eben-ezer (I Sam 4).

4. The Temple had become a fetish, as was the ark when Shiloh was destroyed (I Sam 4:3).

5-7. Only the practice of justice and godliness would ensure the divine presence which the Temple symbolized. **Judgment.** *Justice.*

12. Shiloh. Cf. Josh 18:1; 22:12; Jud 21:19; 18:31; I Sam 1:9,24; 2:14; 4:3,4. **14. See what I did to it.** As the ark was only an empty box when Shiloh was destroyed, so now Jerusalem, bereft of the divine presence, will be of no help, and will itself perish. **15. Seed of Ephraim.** The northern kingdom of Israel. **16-20.** Jeremiah was not to intercede for his people (contrast Moses, Ex 32:32; Num 14:13-19), for God was determined to punish them (cf. 11:14; 14:11,12). **Cakes to the queen of heaven** (v. 18). Probably a reference to the Babylonian fertility-goddess Ishtar, goddess of the planet Venus. The **cakes** were probably in the form of the goddess (cf. 44:15-25).

The futility of sacrifices without obedience. 7:21-28. Jeremiah is not saying that God never wanted or commanded sacrifices. He is expressing by strong contrast the relative importance of sacrifice and obedience (cf. I Sam 15:22). The prophets opposed empty ritualism, not the Mosaic ceremonies as such. **Put** (v. 21). *Add.* Burnt offerings were wholly burnt on the altar; parts of the other sacrifices were eaten by the priests and offerers. The idea here is that there is no sanctity in offerings brought by unrepentant men. They are merely **flesh,** and so the burnt offering might as well be eaten too.

Sinful rites in the valley of the son of Hinnom. 7:29–8:3. This valley, immediately south of Jerusalem, was the center of the cult of infant sacrifice. This foreign rite, introduced by Ahaz and Manasseh (II Kgs 16:3; 21:6) was stamped out by Josiah (II Kgs 23:10) but had now revived, probably under Jehoiakim. The valley will become a desecrated waste.

29. Cut off thy hair. A sign of mourning (Mic 1:16; Job 1:20). **30. Abominations;** i.e., idols. **31. Tophet** probably originally meant "fireplace," but was now so pronounced that it rhymed with *bōshet,* "shame" – a circumlocution for an idol. References to **slaughter, bury** (v. 32), **carcases** (v. 33), and **bones** (8:1) all mean that what was now a holy religious site would become a desecrated place, for contact with a corpse rendered unclean. Later this valley seems to have become a city dump, and thus *Gehenna,* the NT word for the place of woe, originated. *Gehenna* is a transliteration of the Hebrew *gê' hinnōm*—"the valley of Hinnom." **33. Fray.** *Frighten.* **34. Then will I cause to cease.** Cf. 25:10 note.

8:1. They (Jerusalem's captors) **shall bring out.** The desecration of graves was a common practice in warfare (Amos 2:1). Frequently, too, dead enemies were left unburied, both as an insult and also in the belief that their spirits would thus have no rest in the nether world. **2. Host of heaven.** Cf. 19:13 note.

b) The Result of Impenitence—Retribution. 8:4–9:22.

Here are a number of prophetic oracles with no common theme.

The unnaturalness of Israel's backsliding. 8:4-7. Those who fall rise again; even the birds come back at a certain season. But Israel is perpetually backslidden. **Judgment** (v. 7). *Ordinance, law.*

The leaders' false claims to wisdom. 8:8-12. The scribes, prophets, and priests claimed to be wise in the law and soothingly predicted that all would be well. **Lo, certainly . . . in vain** (v. 8). Better, *But, behold, the false pen of the scribes has made it into a lie.* This is the first mention of the scribes. They copied and studied the Law (i.e., the Scriptures; cf. 2:8). Already they were beginning to make the law of God void (Mt 15:6). Verses **10-12** are almost identical with 6:12-15. God gives a foreglimpse of the results of defeat in war. **Them that shall inherit them.** Better, *their conquerors* (cf. 49:2). **8:13–9:22.** These verses comprise the *Hapṭārâh* (lesson from the prophets) read in the synagogue on the ninth of Ab, the anniversary of the destruction of the Temple and the end of the Hebrew kingdom (cf. 52:12 note).

Despair of the people at the invasion of foreigners. 8:14-17. **Be silent . . . put us to silence** (v. 14). *Be cut off . . . cut us off.* **Water of gall.** See note on 9:15. **Cockatrices** (v. 17). Adders.

The prophet's lament. 8:18–9:22. Jeremiah, in a moving poem, expresses his sympathy with his stricken people (8:18–9:1), laments the people's treachery (9:2-9), and wails for the destruction of Judah (9:10-22).

19. Strange vanities. *Foreign idols* (cf. 2:5 note). **20. Harvest.** This word *(qāṣîr)* refers to the harvest of the barley, wheat, and spelt in April, May, and June. **Summer** *(qāyiṣ)* really means "summer fruits," i.e., the figs, grapes, and pomegranates, that were harvested in August and September, and the olives, picked beginning in October. Thus Jeremiah reviews the whole harvest season; it was ended, but no fruit had been stored for the winter ahead—**we are not saved. 21. I am black.** In mourning. **22. Balm in Gilead** was resin derived from a tree and used medicinally. It was exported (46:11; 51:8; Gen 37:25; Ezk 27:17).

9:4. Utterly supplant. The Hebrew *ʿāqôb yaʿqōb* is from the same root that occurs in the name "Jacob" (cf. Gen 27:36). **8. Layeth his wait.** *Plans an ambush for him.* **9. Visit.** *Punish.*

10. Habitations of the wilderness. Better, *pastures of the wilderness.* The prophet sees the whole land desolate (cf. 4:23-26). **11. Dragons.** *Jackals.* **12. Declare it, for what the land perisheth.** Better, *Declare it? Why is the land ruined?* **14. Baalim.** Baals (cf. 2:8 note). **15. Wormwood.** A plant having very bitter juice. **Gall.** Poisonous bitter herb (cf. 8:14). The two terms are used together to indicate bitter afflictions. **17. Mourning women;** i.e., professional mourners (cf. Mt 9:23). **Cunning.** *Wise,* skilled in lamenting. **19. Our dwellings have cast us out.** Better, *They* (our enemies) *have cast down our dwellings* (cf. II Kgs 25:9). **21. Without . . . streets.** Better, *Streets . . . squares.* **22. Handful.** The reaper would grasp a handful of standing grain, cut it off, and proceed to the next handful. So death shall reap, inexorably.

c) The True God Contrasted with Idols. 9:23–10:25.

24. Lovingkindness. This frequently used word describes God's faithfulness to his covenant promises. The RSV translates it *steadfast love* (cf. 2:2 note). **Judgment.** *Justice.*

25,26. These verses are difficult to understand. The thought seems to be that circumcision without the true knowledge of God is useless (cf. 4:4). Thus Paul's statement (Rom 2:28,29) is anticipated. **Circumcised with the uncircumcised.** Better, *Circumcised but yet uncircumcised.* **Egypt.** See notes on Jeremiah 46. **Edom.** See notes on 49:7-22. **Ammon.** See notes on 49:1-6. **Moab.** See notes on Jeremiah 48. **That are in the utmost corners, that dwell in the wilderness.** Better, *Who dwell in the desert, that cut the corners of their hair.* A heathen practice (cf. 25:23; 49:32; Lev 19:27).

A vigorous denunciation of idols as nothing. 10:1-16. God, by contrast, is the Maker and Upholder of the universe.

The nothingness of idols. 10:1-5. **Signs of heaven** (v. 2). Such as eclipses and comets. The making of an idol demonstrates its nothingness (vv. 3,4). **Vain.** The Hebrew word means "breath," what is unsubstantial and worthless. It is often used of idols (cf. 2:5 note). **They are**

upright as the palm tree (v. 5). Better, *They* (the idols) *are like a post* (i.e., a scarecrow) *in a garden of cucumbers.*

The majesty of God. 10:6-16. **King of nations** (v. 7). God is the universal King, not a tribal god. **Silver spread into plates** (v. 9). *Beaten silver.* **Tarshish** is a place in Spain or Sicily; a source of metals (Ezk 27:12). **Uphaz** is unknown. Verse 11 is the only one in Jeremiah written in the Aramaic language. Perhaps it was originally a marginal notation, which finally became part of the text. **Every founder . . . graven image** (v. 14). *Every goldsmith is put to shame by his idol.* **Vanity** (v. 15). See on verse 3. **Visitation.** *Punishment.* **Portion of Jacob** (v. 16). While God is the King of the universe (v. 7), he is also the peculiar **portion** *(possession)* of the Hebrew people. **Rod.** *Tribe.*

The coming desolation. 10:17-25. Probably Jerusalem is thought to speak verses 19-21. Cities were often pictured as mothers with children (Ezk 26:6,8). **Tabernacle** (v. 20). *Tent.* **Pastors** (v. 21). *Shepherds* (cf. 2:8 note). **Bruit** (v. 22). *Rumor.* **Dragons.** *Jackals.* **With judgment** (v. 24). *In just measure.*

4) Israel Rejected for Breaking God's Covenant. 11:1–13:27.

"This covenant" (11:3) was made with Israel at Sinai. Its fullest statement is found in Deuteronomy (chs. 29; 30). Many scholars believe that these chapters of Jeremiah have as their background the Josianic reforms which were precipitated by the finding of a book, probably Deuteronomy, in the Temple (cf. Introduction, *The Life and Times of Jeremiah*). Jeremiah supported these reforms, but here sees the revival as superficial, inadequate to put off judgment.

a) The Judeans' Violation of the Covenant. 11:1-17.

3. Cursed. Cf. Deut 27:11-26. **This covenant.** Israel was to obey the Lord and be his people; so the Lord would be their God, and Canaan would be their land (Ex 19:5,6; 24:3-8; Deut 29:1-28). **5. Perform the oath.** Cf. Deut 7:8; 8:18; 9:5. **So be it.** The Hebrew word is our "amen," a term used to indicate affirmation of the curse in verse 3 (cf. Deut 27:15-26). **8. Imagination.** *Stubbornness.* **Will bring.** Better, *brought.* The people had already begun to feel the penalty of the broken covenant.

11. I will bring. Better, *I am bringing.* Josiah's revival having been a failure, God was now in the act of terminating the covenant and bringing the punishment. **13.** The Judeans had as many gods and altars as cities and streets (cf. 2:28 note). **Shameful thing.** See note on 3:24. **14.** See note on 7:16.

15. A difficult verse, evidently a statement of the inadequacy of the temple ritual to forestall the coming doom (cf. 7:1–8:3). Using the LXX, the RSV translates it, *What right has my beloved in my house, when she has done vile deeds? Can vows and sacrificial flesh avert your doom? Can you then exult?* **My beloved.** Israel. **My house.** The Temple. **16,17.** Judah is likened to a destroyed olive tree. The olive was the source of oil for light, cooking, medicine, anointing for the body, and many other uses. It became the symbol of "prosperity and divine blessing, of beauty and strength." Thus it is here an apt picture of the Hebrew people, blessed by God, but now rejected. Paul uses the same figure (Rom 11:17-24).

b) The Plot Against Jeremiah's Life. 11:18–12:6.

Perhaps Jeremiah had not yet moved from Anathoth to Jerusalem when this section was written. It is evident from 12:6 that the question, "Wherefore doth the way of the wicked prosper?" raised in 12:1-6 is to be connected with the plot against the prophet's life (11:18-23). Possibly Jeremiah's kinsmen in Anathoth (they would also have been priests) sought to kill the prophet because of his frequent denunciation of the false trust in ritual. This would explain the location of this section after 11:15-17. This is one of Jeremiah's confessions (cf. Introduction, *Jeremiah's Confessions).*

18. It . . . their doings; i.e. the plot against Jeremiah's life. The prophet seems to mean that God informed him of the plot in time for him to escape. **19. A lamb or an ox.** Better, *a docile lamb.* **20. Reins.** Literally, *kidneys,* i.e., the region of the kidneys, the loins, once thought to be the seat of the affections. **23. Visitation.** *Punishment.* **12:3.** Jeremiah did not have the example of Christ's, "Father, forgive them; for they know not what they do" (Lk 23:34). The prosperity of the wicked was one of the most perplexing problems faced by the OT saints. **4. They said**; i.e., men said.

5,6. God replies to his discouraged prophet. **The swelling of Jordan** (v. 5).

The jungle of the Jordan, the low bottom land through which the Jordan flows, hot, full of thick undergrowth, and inhabited by wild animals (cf. 49:19; 50:44). **Called a multitude** (v. 6). Better, *called aloud.* They had raised the hue and cry against Jeremiah, as though he were a common criminal.

c) Jehovah's Lament over the Destruction of His Land. 12:7-13.

It is the Lord rather than his prophet who weeps over the land in this unusual passage. Many figures of speech—**house, heritage, beloved** (v. 7); **lion** (v. 8); **bird** (v. 9); **vineyard, portion** (v. 10)—are used to describe Israel.

9. Speckled bird. It would be attacked by other birds because of its brightly colored plumage. **10. Pastors.** See note on 2:8. The shepherds are here the kings of foreign nations who had desolated Israel. **12. All high places through the wilderness.** Better, *all the bare heights in the wilderness.* **13. They shall be ashamed of your revenues.** Better, *you shall be ashamed of your harvests.*

d) The Fate of Judah's Enemies. 12:14-17.

They will also be despoiled, but will be restored if they repent (cf. 25:8-14). **Return and have compassion** (v. 15). *Again have compassion.*

e) Parables and Warnings. 13:1-27.

The chapter contains five passages unified by the theme of humiliation and doom for Judah. Possibly this chapter dates from the reign of Jehoiachin (13:18; cf. 22:26).

The parable of the buried girdle. 13:1-11. This parable graphically teaches Israel's former importance to God and her present corruption and rejection.

1. Girdle. Better, *loincloth,* used to brace the hip joints for prolonged exertion, and to hold up the hanging skirts for greater freedom in walking or work. **4. Euphrates.** The distance from Judah to the Euphrates River is at least four hundred miles, regarded as a very great distance in ancient times. Two round trips are mentioned (cf. vv. 4,6). Some scholars believe that not the Euphrates River but a Palestinian town with a similar sounding name is here referred to. Many, however, believe the Euphrates River is meant, but regard the account as a spoken parable, not literally acted out. The truth of the story is not dependent upon Jeremiah's having actually made the journey. Certainly the reference to the Euphrates in 2:18 is not to be taken literally! **11.** Israel, as intimately attached to God as a loincloth (v. 11), has become corrupt and useless. She shall be cast off.

The parable of the jars. 13:12-14. It indicated that God would fill the people with confusion, as when men are drunk; they would dash against each other and be destroyed.

12. Every bottle shall be filled with wine. Probably a common tippler's saying. **Bottle.** The large clay jar used for storing oil, grain, or wine. The largest ones found by archaeologists contain up to ten gallons. **13. Drunkenness.** Not literal intoxication. Here, as elsewhere in the prophets (Jer 25:15-28; Ezk 23:31-34; Isa 51:17,18), the picture of a drunkard is used to symbolize the pathetic condition of the people when taken into captivity.

A warning against pride. 13:15-17. **Give glory** (v. 16). Confess your sinful pride. **Dark mountains.** *Twilight mountains.* A vivid picture. The traveler on the mountain road is first overtaken by dusk, then by thick darkness.

A lament over the king and the queen mother. 13:18,19.

Probably Jehoiachin and Nehushta are referred to (22:26; II Kgs 24:8).

18. Queen. Better, *queen mother.* The Hebrews paid great attention to the mother of the king. Since the kings had many wives, not all with the same status, the identity of the prince's mother was important in the succession to the throne. **For your principalities shall come down, even the crown of your glory.** Difficult; perhaps *for your beautiful crown has come down from your head* (RSV). **19. South.** *Negev,* the southern part of Judah. Only recently has the importance of this part of the land in ancient times been realized. **Shut up;** i.e., under siege.

The shame of Jerusalem. 13:20-27.

The city is as a shepherdess who has forsaken her flock. She, the head of the nation, has led it into sin.

21. Difficult. Perhaps, "What will you say when he (the Babylonian conqueror) shall set as head over you those whom you have taught to be friends to you?" **22. Discovered.** *Removed.* Evidently a reference to the treatment of a harlot (cf. v. 26; Hos 2:3). **Made bare.** Better, *suffered violence*. **Heels** may be a euphemism for "secret parts" and the clause parallel to the previous one. **25. Falsehood.** *Idolatry*. **26.** See note on verse 21.

5) Prophetic Intercession Unable to Prevent Judgment. 14:1–17:27.

A section quite autobiographical, full of the prophet's pessimism concerning the future of his people, and also revealing his communion with God, from which he drew his sustenance.

a) The Drought and the Prophet's Intercession. 14:1–15:9.

The drought described 14:1-6. The rainfall in Palestine is marginal; a single dry year may cause much real suffering. Here the drought is described as first touching the city (vv. 2,3), then the farmers (v. 4), and then even the wild animals (vv. 5,6).

1. Dearth. *Drought*. **2. They are black;** i.e., in mourning. **3. Pits.** *Cisterns*. Much of the water supply in cities was gathered into cisterns during the rainy season. **Covered their heads.** As a sign of mourning (cf. II Sam 15:30). **4. Chapt.** *Cracked*. **Earth.** *Land*. **6. They snuffed up the wind like dragons.** *They panted for air like jackals*.

Jeremiah's intercession for the people. 14:7-9. **Our iniquities** (v. 7). The prophet identifies himself with his people. **For thy name's sake.** An appeal for God to act for the sake of his reputation and grace (cf. Ps 25:11; 79:9; 106:8; 109:21; 143:11). **Stranger . . . wayfaring man** (v. 8). Foreigners and tourists have little real concern for the land through which they travel. Let not God be so. **Astonied** (v. 9). Surprised by an unforeseen attack.

Jeremiah forbidden to pray for the people. 14:10-12. **Visit.** *Punish*.

Judgment on the false prophets. 14:13-16. Compare 6:13,14; 23:9-32.

Jeremiah's further lament and prayer for Judah. 14:17-22. **The virgin daughter of my people** (v. 17). Judah is personified as a **virgin,** which term emphasizes God's selection of his people to be his own peculiar possession, his virgin bride. **Go about into a land that they know not** (v. 18). Better, *Ply their trade through the land* (the 'business-as-usual' attitude) *and have no knowledge* (of the impending doom). **Vanities** (v. 22). See note on 2:5.

God's determination not to relent. 15:1-9. **Moses and Samuel** (v. 1). Two great intercessors. For Moses, cf. Ex 32:11-14; Num 14:13-19. For Samuel, see I Sam 7:5-11; 12:19; Ps 99:6. Yet even they would not be successful now: **Four kinds** of punishment (v. 3). **To be removed** (v. 4). Better, *to be a horror,* i.e., an object of terror. **Manasseh** introduced great idolatry into Judah (II Kgs 23:26; 24:3). Yet usually Jeremiah insists that the people are themselves responsible for their sins and punishment (e.g., 31:29,30). **Repenting** (v. 6). Compare note on 18:8. **I will fan them with a fan** (v. 7). *I will winnow then with a winnowing fork* (cf. Mt 3:12).

b) The Renewal of Jeremiah's Call, and Its Cost. 15:10–16:9.

A deeply revealing confession, showing the prophet's bitterness of soul. God's reply indicates that Jeremiah needed to be careful of his mood and to speak nothing but the truth. He was then encouraged and recommissioned.

The prophet's lament and recommission. 15:10-21. **Earth** (v. 10). *Land*. Verse 11 is difficult to interpret. The meaning seems to be that God will protect the prophet in the coming catastrophe. **It shall be well with thy remnant.** Better, *I will strengthen you for good*.

13,14. These verses occur again, with variations, in 17:3b,4. They are directed to the people of Judah, and predict exile.

16. The sufficiency of the Word of God is graphically stated. Cf. Josh 1:8; Ezk 3:1-3; Rev 10:8-11, where John's experience is very like Jeremiah's. **Called by thy name.** Literally, thy name was *called upon me*. A reference to the prophet's special call by God. The remembrance of this call strengthened Jeremiah to go on. **17. Thy hand.** God's hand was upon Jeremiah—an idiom expressing the divine inspiration, which was the reason for Jeremiah's persecution (cf. Ezk 1:3, and frequently in Ezekiel; I Kgs 18:46; Isa 8:11). **18. Liar.** Better, *deceitful brook*. Jeremiah reproaches God with having failed him, as when a traveler in the dry season discovers that the brook from which he hoped to drink has dried up (cf. Job 6:15-20).

19. If thou return, then will I bring thee again. The idea is, If you repent (of your self-pity), I will restore you. **Take forth the precious from the vile.** The prophet needed to discipline his thought and speech. **Then** he could be God's spokesman **(mouth).** The end of the verse is a command to the prophet not to sink to the level of those to whom he ministered.

20,21. These verses repeat the substance of 1:18,19.

The prophet commanded to remain celibate and avoid social intercourse. 16:1-9. His life was to be a warning of the coming judgment. **2. Wife.** Celibacy was very unusual in ancient Israel. Jeremiah was denied the joy and fulfillment of marriage. Others of the prophets used their married life as signs (cf. Hos 1–3; Isa 8:3,4; Ezk 24:15-27). **Verses** 4,6,7,9 portray the results of war. **5-7.** The ancient Semites made a great show of mourning (cf. 7:29 note; 9:17 note). Self-laceration and shaving of the head (v. 6) were forbidden (Deut 14:1; Lev 19:28), but other mentions seem to indicate their frequent practice (Jer 41:5; 47:5; Isa 22:12; Amos 8:10; Mic 1:16; Ezk 7:18). **7. Tear themselves for them in mourning.** Better, *Break bread for them in mourning.* It was customary for the friends of mourners to provide them with their first meal after the funeral (II Sam 3:35). Probably **the cup of consolation** was a similar custom.

c) Warnings and Promises. 16:10–17:27.

10-13. When the people ask, "Why the exile?" Jeremiah is to point out to them their wickedness. **14,15.** They will experience a second Exodus. See note on 23:7,8.

16-18. Israel is still known to God. **Double** (v. 18). In great measure (cf. Isa 40:2). **Carcasses.** As dead bodies defile, so idols pollute.

19-21. Gentiles will be converted to the Lord. **Lies, vanity, and things wherein there is no profit** (v. 19). Synonyms for idols (cf. 2:5 note).

The nation's sin indelible. 17:1-4. **Table of their heart** (v. 1). Where the new and better covenant will be written (31:31-34). **Horns of your altars.** Where the blood of the sacrifices was smeared (Lev 4:7). **Groves** (v. 2). See note on 2:27. **Green trees . . . high hills.** See note on 3:6. Verses 3,4 repeat the substance of 15:13,14.

Trust in man and God contrasted. 17:5-8. The background of these verses may be the tendency of the last Judean kings to seek for the help of Egypt against the Babylonian threat (cf. 2:18 note). **Flesh** (v. 5). In the OT the term refers to the frailty of human kind. **Heath** (v. 6). The dwarf juniper, which grows in the barren desert and has a gloomy, stunted appearance. **Careful** (v. 8). *Anxious.*

Sin a disease of the heart. 17:9-13. **Heart** (v. 9). In the OT, man's inner being, from which spring his will and action. It may also refer to the reason. **Wicked.** This word at times refers to sickness, and is translated "incurable" (15:18). Here it means "corrupt." **Reins** (v. 10). See note on 11:20. **Written in the earth** (v. 13); i.e., in the ground or dust, rather than in the Book of Life (Ex 32:32).

A prayer for vindication. 17:14-18. Cf. 15:15-18. **Pastor** (v. 16). *Shepherd.* Paraphrase: "I have not abandoned the mission you have given me."

Sabbath observance prerequisite for the return of national glory. 17:19-27. Cf. Isa 58:13,14. **It may seem strange** that Jeremiah, who decries ritual observances, should have been interested in the Sabbath. But the Sabbath is more than a ritual observance. It is a humanitarian institution (Deut 5:14,15) and a sign that God is Israel's Sanctifier (Ex 31:13). These words are not incongruous in Jeremiah's mouth. **Plain** (v. 26). The Shephelah, the low hills and valleys between the Judean hill country and the Philistine Plain. A center of ancient Hebrew agricultural life. **Mountains.** **The** central Judean hill country. **South.** "Negev" (cf. 13:19 note).

6) Two Symbolic Sermons and an Imprisonment. 18:1–20:18.

The parable of the potter and the symbolic action of the broken vessel are good examples of the vivid preaching of the prophets. The rest of the section is concerned with the negative response of the people to Jeremiah's preaching, and the prophet's communings with his God.

a) The Parable of the Potter. 18:1-23.

The potter's work a symbol of God's procedure. 18:1-17. Here is emphasized the conditional character of prophecy. Even Jeremiah's sternest declaration of doom, like Jonah's (Jon 3:4), presupposes an opportunity to repent. This parable also teaches the divine Potter's patience.

2,3. Potter's house. Probably located in the potters' quarter in the southern section of the city, near the Potsherd

Gate and the Valley of the Son of Hinnom (cf. 19:2 note). **On the wheels.** Two stone discs were used. The lower, which was kicked by the craftsman, was attached by an axle to the upper, on which the clay was shaped (Ecclesiasticus 38:29,30 describes the process).

5-11. The homily. Jehovah, the Potter of nations, is sovereign in his work, yet his is a sovereignty that is responsive to the wills of his creatures. Here the analogy breaks down. Human clay is not passive as is that of Jeremiah's potter; and if Israel will repent, God will yet make of her a "vessel unto honor." **Repent** (v. 8). The use of the word **repent** in referring to God does not imply fickleness on the part of the Almighty. When a human word is used to describe the actions of the Divine, the word undergoes a subtle redefinition. God is not a man that he should repent (cf. 4:28; 15:6)–he does not blow hot and cold. Yet he does *relent* when his people turn to him; and this action of relenting is called *repentance* (cf. 20:16; 26:3,13,19; 42:10).

13-17. Virgin of Israel (v. 13). See note on 14:17. Verse 14 is difficult to interpret. It seems to teach the unnaturalness of Israel's apostasy from God. The RSV translates it: *Shall the snow of Lebanon fail from the rock of the field? or shall the cold waters that flow down from afar be dried up?* That is to say, nature pursues her course unchanged, but the nation has unnaturally changed its course. **Vanity** (v. 15). See note on 2:5. **Paths.** *Bypaths.* **A way not cast up;** i.e., not properly constructed, not a highway. **Desolate . . . astonished** (v. 16). These words are from the same Hebrew root. They could be translated *a horror . . . horrified.* **East wind** (v. 17). See note on 4:11. **The back, and not the face.** Because God is departing. The **face** of God symbolizes his favor (Num 6:25,26).

A plot against Jeremiah. 18:18-23. Cf. 11:18–12:6; 15:15-21. The three groups of religious leaders are here mentioned (v. 18), together with the special work of each. **The priest** taught the Law (Mal 2:6) and carried out its ritual commands; the **wise** man (the sage) **dispensed the accumulated wisdom of the ages; and the prophet** mediated the direct *word* of the Lord (the false prophet, who opposed Jeremiah, is meant here). Surely Jeremiah (who rejected all three classes) could not be right! **Smite him with the tongue;** i.e., bring charges against him. For verses 21-23, see note on 12:3.

b) The Broken Vessel. 19:1-15.

This sermon upon a symbolic action naturally follows the parable of the potter. As long as the vessel remained plastic, it could be remade. Once it was baked, however, it could no longer be remolded. If unacceptable then, it would be broken up.

1. Earthen bottle. A clay water decanter, with a narrow neck, named *baqbūq* for the gurgling sound of the water being poured out. **Ancients.** *Elders.* **2. Valley of the son of Hinnom.** The southern boundary of Jerusalem (cf. 18:2 note). **East gate.** Probably, "the Potsherd Gate." **4. Blood of innocents;** i.e., infant sacrifice (cf. 7:29 note). **5. Burn their sons.** Cf. II Kgs 16:3; 23:10; Jer 32:35; and notes on 7:29–8:3. **6. Tophet. See** note on 7:31. **9. Straitness . . . straiten.** *Distress . . afflict.*

11. No way was known for mending a broken bottle; it was discarded and a new one obtained; so Jerusalem would be rejected, her time of repentance having passed. **13. Host of heaven.** *Army of heaven,* an expression used of the stars (e.g., Gen 2:1; Isa 45:12), but here for the worship of the planets or the gods of the planets. Ahaz and Manasseh introduced this pagan cult into Judah (II Kgs 21:5; 23:12), probably from Mesopotamia, where it was practiced from remote antiquity.

c) Jeremiah's Persecution and Complaint. 20:1-18.

Jeremiah in the stocks. 20:1-6. **Pashur** (v. 3). A name of Egyptian origin. There is no play on it here, but only on **Magor-missabib,** which means, "Terror on every side"; cf. **terror** (v. 4). **Strength** (v. 5). *Wealth.* **Labours.** *Prosperity.* **Spoil.** *Plunder.*

The prophet's complaint against God. 20:7-18. One of Jeremiah's most revealing confessions, this prayer shows the terrible personal cost at which he spoke the word that was placed upon him.

7. Deceived. A strong word, used of "seducing" a virgin (Ex 22:16), and of the "lying" spirit that deceived Ahab (I Kgs 22:20-22). Here the prophet, bitter of soul, complains against the divine compulsion, which he calls enticement. **8. Since I spake.** Better, *As often as I spoke.* **10. The defaming of many . . .** A vivid statement of the feeling of a man who believes that all are against him. **Fear on every side.** The Hebrew words are the same as the name *Magor-missabib* (cf. 20:3 note). **Halting.** *Stumbling.* **11. A mighty terrible one.** *A mighty warrior.* **12. Reins . . . heart.** Cf. notes on 11:20; 17:9.

14-18. Jeremiah laments the day of his birth (cf. Job 3). **Cities** (v. 16). Sodom and Gomorrah (Gen 19). **Repented.** See note on 18:8. **The shouting.** *An alarm.*

C. Later Prophecies. 21:1—25:38.

These chapters record oracles concerning the kings of Judah and the false prophets after the time of Josiah. They reflect the growing feeling of doom as the captivity nears.

1) The Issue of the Siege. 21:1-14.

Date: Sometime late in the reign of Zedekiah. Zedekiah is urged to submit to Nebuchadnezzar, for the city will fall.

a) Reply to a Deputation from Zechariah. 21:1-10.

1. Pashur. Not the Pashur of 20:1-6. **Zephaniah the son of Maaseiah.** See note on 29:25. **2. Nebuchadrezzar** had evidently just begun the final attack against Jerusalem (588-587 B.C.) which ended in its destruction. This is the Nebuchadnezzar of the books of Kings and Chronicles. Jeremiah's spelling is nearest to the Babylonian form of the name. **4. Chaldeans.** The name given to the reigning dynasty of the new-Babylonian empire and, by extension, to the Babylonians generally at this time.

8-10. The people would do best to give up to the Chaldeans. Little wonder that Jeremiah was regarded as a traitor. But his was a higher patriotism; godliness was to him the only reason for the nation's being, as well as its only hope of survival. **9. Falleth to the Chaldeans;** i.e., defects to the enemy. **Prey.** *Prize of war.*

b) A Message to the Royal House. 21:11-14.

Verse 12 is typical of the prophets' demand for social justice. Even when the city is in her dying gasp, the concern for human welfare is voiced. It is uncertain against whom verses 13 and 14 are directed.

2) An Exhortation to King and People. 22:1-9.

This section, calling upon palace and city to do justice or become destroyed, is probably an introduction to the succeeding oracles against named kings, and may date from the reign of Jehoiakim.

3-5. See note on 21:11-14. **The spoiled** (v. 3). *Him who has been robbed.* **Gilead . . . Lebanon** (v. 6). Well-wooded regions. **Thy choice cedars** (v. 7). The palace complex in Jerusalem included the House of the Forest of Lebanon; and much cedar from Lebanon was used in building Solomon's palace and Temple (I Kgs 5:6,8-10; 10:27). All was to be burned.

3) The Fate of Shallum. 22:10-12.

No doubt this oracle was made early in the reign of Jehoiakim. The people were not to weep for Josiah, who had recently been killed, nor for his son **Shallum** (the private name of Jehoahaz; I Chr 3:15), whom Pharaoh-necho had deported to Egypt, for he would never return (II Kgs 23:29-35).

4) An Oracle Against Jehoiakim. 22:13-23.

This denunciation of the evil Jehoiakim, made during his reign, is one of Jeremiah's most pointed. It condemns the king for building his palace with forced labor at a time when heavy tribute had to be paid to Egypt (II Kgs 23:35). It concludes (Jer 22:20-23) with a wail over the end of the kings, or possibly over the city of Jerusalem.

13. Him that buildeth his house; i.e., Jehoiakim. **14. Ceiled.** *Paneled.* **15. Father;** i.e., Josiah. **16.** The knowledge of God is a moral matter; intellect is not enough. **19 Burial of an ass; i.e., no** burial, the carcass being left for the beasts and birds (36:30). We are not informed as to the fulfillment of this prophecy (cf. II Kgs 24:6). Perhaps this wicked king was overthrown by a palace revolt and his body cast outside the city gates.

20. The passages. Better, *Abarim* ("regions beyond"), the mountain range (which included Nebo) from which Moses saw the Promised Land (Num 27:12; Deut 32:49). **Lovers.** Perhaps the nations upon whom the kings relied for help, instead of trusting God. **22. Pastors.** *Shepherds.* **Lovers.** Cf. note on 22:20. **23. O inhabitant of Lebanon.** Cf. note on verses 6,7. **How gracious.** Spoken ironically.

5) An Oracle Against Jehoiachin. 22:24-30.

Seldom has any reigning king been so severely castigated in an oracle during his reign as is Jehoiachin here.

24. Coniah. This man, also called Jeconiah and Jehoiachin, succeeded his father Jehoiakim on the throne in 598 B.C. During his reign, early in 597 B.C. Nebuchadnezzar besieged and captured Jerusalem and took Jehoiachin and many important people to Babylon (II Kgs 24:8-17; II Chr 36:9,10). **26. Thy mother.** See note on 13:18. **28. Idol.** Better, *vessel;* i.e., a broken, forgotten pot. **30. Childless.** Coniah would have no son to succeed him on the throne. He did have seven sons (I Chr 3:17). Cuneiform tablets found in Babylon list rations of oil provided "Yaukin (i.e., Jehoiachin) king of the land of Yahud (i.e., Judah)" and his five sons. Though the genealogy of Mt 1 follows the descent of the Messiah through Solomon and Jeconiah, that record of David's lineage indicates only who Jesus' legal father was, not who his real father was. Luke traces the real pedigree backward from Mary, His true parent, through Nathan to David.

6) The Messianic King. 23:1-8.

After the oracles against wicked kings, there is a promise of a righteous one, the Shoot of David. The Davidic tree, cut off to the ground by the captivity, would sprout again, and its shoot would be called "The Lord our Righteousness." Prophet, priest, and king are the three offices of OT times that are typical and prophetic of Christ. The Church has always seen here a prophecy of Messiah, "Great David's greater son," the King of Kings.

1,2. Woe unto the (false) **shepherds** *(pastors,* AV). These are the unrighteous king and rulers of Judah, who have been condemned in chapters 21 and 22. The once-glorious house of David has become wholly degenerate. But this woe, unlike many woes of this book, is but a prelude to the pronouncement of a better hope. **Have not visited them** (v. 2). *Have not attended to them.* **I will visit upon you the evil.** *I will attend to you for the evil.* A play on the word **visit.**

3,4. Israel will be regathered from exile, and be ruled by godly shepherds. Verses 3-8 presuppose the Exile. This is not to say that Jeremiah was not the author of this passage. It is a common feature of the style of the pre-Exilic prophets that after announcing exile, they then go on to predict restoration (cf. Amos 9:11-15; Isa 11:1-16; 44:24–45:13; and many others). **All countries** (v. 3). The prophecy seems to imply not only the Babylonian exile, but a world-wide scattering. **Shepherds** (v. 4). The leaders of the nation after the Exile (Zerubbabel, Ezra, Nehemiah, the Maccabees) who prepared the way for Messiah. **They be lacking.** *Any be missing.*

5,6. The scion of David; repeated in 33:15,16. **Behold, the days come** (v. 5). A formula often used to introduce predictions of the Messianic day. *Unto David;* i.e., of David's line (cf. II Sam 7:8-16; Isa 11; 12; Mt 1:1; 21:9,15; Lk 1:32; Rom 1:3). **Branch.** *Shoot,* a Messianic title (Zech 3:8; 6:12; a different word is used in Isa 11:1). **Judgment and justice.** *Justice and righteousness.* These frequent Messianic attributes shed a ray of hope in despot-ridden ancient times, as they do today.

Judah . . . and Israel (v. 6). All of the Hebrew people were involved, not the southern kingdom only (Ezk 37:19). **The Lord Our Righteousness.** *Jehovah Ṣidqēnû* is perhaps a play on Zedekiah's name *(Ṣidqîyāhû*—"Jehovah is righteous"). The ideal Davidic king will more truly deserve the name. **Righteousness here has** the double meaning of "righteousness" and "salvation" (cf. Isa 46:13; 51:6,8; Rom 1:16,17). God is here seen as Saviour or Deliverer.

7,8. A second exodus (cf. 23:3,4 note).

7) Against the False Prophets. 23:9-40.

Jeremiah was troubled throughout his career by men who pretended to be true prophets but were not (27:16-22; 28; 29:8,9). They preached an easy message of "peace in our time" and were no doubt popular. Here the prophet denounces them.

12. Visitation. *Punishment.* **13. In Baal.** *By Baal.* **15. Wormwood . . .** *water of gall.* See note on 9:15. **16. Make you vain.** *Give you false hopes.* **A vision of their own heart;** i.e., they spoke what originated in their own minds (cf. 17:9 note), but the true prophet speaks the word that God gives him (cf. v. 18).

20. Heart. See note on 17:9. **Consider.** *Understand.* **22. In my counsel.** The same Hebrew word means both *counsel* (Amos 3:7) and, as in this verse, *council.*

The OT in various places pictures a heavenly assembly, presided over by the Lord. The beings making up this assembly are called "holy ones," "spirits," "sons of God," etc. These beings worship God and are under his power (Ps 82; I Kgs 22:19-22; Job 1:1–2:7; Isa 6:1-13). True prophets are, evidently admitted to this council.

23,24. The false prophets cannot hide from God to escape his punishment. **25-32.** Jeremiah seems to be saying that the word of the Lord came to him not by a dream, but by some better way, perhaps while he was completely awake.

33. Burden. A term for a prophetic oracle. The word comes from a Hebrew root meaning "to lift up." God placed the **burden** on the prophet. He bore it to the people. The people are here told not to use the term lightly.

8) The Vision of the Figs. 24:1-10.

In this vision, used as a parable, the prophet states that those who have gone into exile with Jehoiachin will fare better than those left behind in Jerusalem. Given early in the reign of Zedekiah.

1. Carried away captive. Cf. notes for Jeremiah 29. **2. First ripe.** The early crop gathered in June was considered best. A later crop appeared in August. **Naughty.** *Bad.* The same word is translated **bad** later in this verse and **evil** in verse 3. **6.** The exiles will be purified and later return; those left in Jerusalem will be destroyed in the fall of the city. **7.** Cf. 31:33. **8. Give.** Treat. **9. To be removed.** See note on 15:4.

9) The Judgment on Judah and All the Nations. 25:1-38.

This important chapter, significantly dated in Nebuchadnezzar's first year (Jehoiakim's fourth; v. 1), predicts a seventy-year exile for Judah, and then goes on, in apocalyptic style, to call upon the nations to drink God's cup of fury. Daniel was reading this passage when the prophecy of the seventy weeks came to him (Dan 9:2; cf. II Chr 36:21).

a) Judah's Captivity and Babylon's Punishment. 25:1-14.

1. Fourth year of Jehoiakim. 605 B.C. (cf. 36:1; 45:1; 46:2).

9. Families of the north. Cf. Introduction, *The Foe from the North.* **My servant.** The heathen Nebuchadnezzar was unconsciously doing God's will (cf. 27:6; 43:10). So Cyrus is called God's "anointed" (Isa 45:1). **These nations round about.** Much of the Near East was to be captured by the Babylonians. **10.** The sounds of daily human activity would cease. **Candle.** Better, *lamp.* **11. Seventy years.** A round number. If the beginning of Judah's submission to Babylon is reckoned at Nebuchadnezzar's first capture of Jerusalem (605 B.C.; cf. 1:3, note), and the decree of Cyrus permitting the return at 538 B.C., the Exile lasted sixty-seven years.

12. Babylon, after being used by God to punish Judah, will be destroyed for her own sins (cf. Isa 10:5-34). **Perpetual desolations.** See note on 50:12,13. **14. Shall serve themselves of them.** "Shall make slaves of them," i.e., of the Babylonians. The reference is to the Medes and Persians, who overthrew Babylon (cf. introductory note to chs. 50; 51; and 51:11 note).

b) The Nations To Drink the Cup of God's Fury. 25:15-38.

These verses could serve as an introduction to Jeremiah's oracles against the foreign nations (chs. 46–51), and they are connected with these oracles by the LXX. The nations listed in these verses are largely the same as those mentioned in the oracles; only those not mentioned there are commented on here.

15-17. To be given a stupifying potion is to feel the effect of God's wrath (cf. 49:12; 51:7). **Be moved** (v. 16). *Reel to and fro.* **20. Mingled people;** i.e., "foreigners" in Egypt. **Uz.** The land of Job (Job 1:1). It was east of Palestine, probably in Edomite territory (Gen 10:23; 22:21; 36:28; Lam 4:21). **Azzah.** *Gaza.* **22. Isles.** See note on 2:10. **23. Tema** is in northwest Arabia (cf. Isa 21:14; Job 6:19). **Buz** is unknown. **That are in the utmost corners.** See note on 9:26. **25. Zimri** is unknown. **Medes.** See note on 51:11. **26. Sheshach.** *Babylon.* The prophet here uses a cipher that substitutes the last letter of the alphabet for the first, the last but one for the second, etc.

32. Coasts of the earth. See note on 31:8. **34. Shepherds . . . principal of the flock;** i.e., rulers of the nations. **37. Habitations.** (Sheep)*folds.*

II. Events in the Life of Jeremiah. 26:1–45:5.

This section consists mainly of autobiographical and historical material. Jeremiah's relations with the rulers and people became more strained, until finally Jerusalem fell as he had predicted. Still, in all this, a theme of hope emerges with the message of the New Covenant. The section closes with a brief account of Jeremiah's last days.

A. The Temple Sermon and Jeremiah's Arrest. 26:1-24.

Here are given the circumstances surrounding the preaching of the temple sermon which is recorded in 7:1–8:3. The date is early in Jehoiakim's reign.

1) The Preaching of the Sermon. 26:1-6.

3. Repent. See note on 26:13,19; 18:8. **4-6.** A summary of the message recorded in 7:3–8:3. **Shiloh** (v. 6). See notes on 7:12-14. **Curse;** i.e., people will curse others saying, "May you become desolate like Jerusalem."

2) The Arrest and Trial of Jeremiah. 26:7-19.

8,9. The religious leaders appear to have stirred up the people against Jeremiah. **Against.** Better, *about.* Jeremiah was surrounded by a throng.

10. Princes. These were the good court officials who had been appointed to office by Josiah and had survived him. They here defend the prophet (cf. 26:24). **14,15.** Jeremiah's unflinching courage here hardly needs comment. **Meet.** *Right.*

16. People. Contrast verse 8. How easily the mob changes sides!

17. Elders. Evidently these were aged, pious men. The Hebrew term more usually means "rulers."

18. Micah the Morasthite. The writing prophet, from Moresheth, who had lived more than a hundred years before. The quotation is from Mic 3:12.

19. We have no other record of Hezekiah's repentance, but he is known as a reforming king (II Kgs 18:3-6).

3) The Arrest and Execution of Urijah. 26:20-24.

This account of how Jehoiakim vented his spleen upon a lesser adversary suggests his intense hatred of Jeremiah, and gives us reason to believe that he was behind Jeremiah's persecution (26:8).

20. Urijah the son of Shemaiah. Nothing is known of him apart from these verses. **Kirjath-jearim.** A town eight miles west of Jerusalem, on the road leading down to the coastal plain. **21. Afraid . . . fled.** It is not given to all men to stand as Jeremiah did, nor is it always wise to do so. **23. Fetched.** Jehoiakim was still an Egyptian puppet; so extradition was easily arranged.

24. Ahikam the son of Shaphan. One of Josiah's princes (cf. v. 10 note; II Kgs 22:12,14). His son Gedaliah was the ill-fated governor of Judah after the fall of Jerusalem (II Kgs 25:22).

B. The Yoke of Babylon. 27:1–29:32.

Zedekiah, although placed on the throne by Nebuchadnezzar, conspired against him, and kings of neighboring nations gathered to Jerusalem to make united plans for rebellion. No doubt the hopes of the people were aroused. Jeremiah here counsels the foreign kings and Zedekiah to desist, for they cannot hope for success. Perhaps his advice carried weight. At least, it seems that the rebellion did not take place at this time. The events of Jeremiah 27; 28 took place in Zedekiah's fourth year (cf. 25:1 note); those of Jeremiah 29, sometime during the same reign.

1) The Message to Foreign Kings. 27:1-11.

A symbolic sermon; the bonds and yokes would graphically set forth the picture of captivity. A similar symbolic act is recorded in I Kgs 22:11.

1. Jehoiakim. Verses 3,12,20 indicate that Zedekiah was ruling at this time. The Syriac Version and some Hebrew manuscripts read *Zedekiah* here. The LXX omits the verse entirely. Many commentators believe that this verse was erroneously copied by a scribe from 26:1. Certainly *Zedekiah* is correct here.

2. Bonds. *Thongs.* The yokes consisted of wooden bars held together by leather thongs. In 28:10 Jeremiah is still wearing the yoke. **3. Moab.** See note on 48:1. **Ammonites.** See note on 49:1. **Tyrus.** Tyre. **Zidon.** Sidon. See note on 47:4. The small nations of Syria-Palestine frequently revolted against their Mesopotamian overlord, often with Egyptian connivance. They were seldom successful. **5. Meet.** *Right.* **6.** Not only would revolt be unsuccessful; it would be wrong, for God had ordained the Babylonian power for its strange work, and Nebuchadnezzar was God's servant (cf. 25:9 note). **7. Serve themselves of him.** *Make him their slave.* **His son, and his son's son.** An idiom meaning "a very long time."

9. Enchanters. *Soothsayers.* The prolonged national crisis had seen the rise of a throng of quack religious practitioners. The hysterical people, it appears, embraced them wholeheartedly. They told the people what they wanted to hear: "Peace, peace" (6:14).

2) The Message to Zedekiah. 27:12-15.

Zedekiah was a weak, vacillating person, likely to dabble in revolts, and also to draw back at the last minute. The word to him is similar to that given to the foreign envoys. Evidently Jerusalem might have been spared destruction, and the large final deportation avoided, had Zedekiah continued to submit to Babylon.

3) The Message to the Priests and the People. 27:16-22.

All are warned not to be misled by the easy message of the false prophets (cf. 23:9-40 notes).

16. Vessels. In the Temple were storerooms, some of which constituted a treasury for expensive objects that had been given to God. These treasures had been carried off to Babylon when Nebuchadnezzar raided Jerusalem in 597 B.C. (II Kgs 24:13). **19. Pillars.** Of bronze. These stood in front of the Temple (I Kgs 7:15). **Sea.** The bronze wash basin in the temple court (I Kgs 7:23-26). **Bases.** *Stands.* These were objects on wheels mentioned in I Kgs 7:27-36. The metal of these objects, as well as that of the "vessels" referred to in verse 16, was very valuable. **20. Jeconiah.** See note on 22:24. **22. Visit.** *Attend to.*

4) Hananiah's Opposition to Jeremiah. 28:1-17.

This conflict occurred shortly after the events of the previous chapter, for Jeremiah still wore the yoke (v. 10). On the false prophets, see notes on 29:9-32.

1. Hananiah the son of Azur. There are fourteen Hananiahs in the OT; the name means, *The Lord has been gracious.* Nothing is known of **the son of Azur** except what is told here.

2-4. Not content with general predictions of peace, Hananiah predicts the return of the deportees and the treasure within two years. This specific prediction proves to be the means for discrediting him, for of course there was no such return. Fulfillment is a test of true prophecy (Deut 18:22). It is interesting to note that according to the recently published *Babylonian Chronicle,* Nebuchadnezzar was at this time busy putting down a rebellion in Babylon. Probably Hananiah's friends among the deportees in Babylon sent this information to him, thus provoking his optimism to be specific. **Jeconiah** (v. 4). See note on 22:24.

6. Amen. *May it be so* (cf. 11:5 note). Jeremiah is quite willing to have the prediction come true. **7-9.** Evidently Jeremiah had no word from the Lord against Hananiah at this time. So he declared that time would tell—if the prediction came to pass—whether Hananiah was sent by God or not.

10. Yoke. See note on 27:2. **12.** Later Jeremiah received an answer for Hananiah. **16.** Jeremiah made a counter sign (cf. v. 3). Its fulfillment meant not only the discrediting of Hananiah as a prophet, but also his death (v. 17).

5) A Letter to the Exiles. 29:1-32.

The prophets of optimism were busy among the Judeans already exiled to Babylon (those carried away after the 597 B.C. attack on Jerusalem), as well as among those still in Jerusalem. To persuade the deportees to settle in Babylon and be contented there was the purpose of this letter, doubtless written within a few years after 597 B.C.

2. Jeconiah. See note on 22:24. **Carpenters . . . smiths.** Nebuchadnezzar took important leaders as hostages, and also artisans (whom he gathered out of every nation he conquered) to help him rebuild and beautify Babylon. **3. Elasah the son of Shaphan.** Possibly the brother of Ahikam, who protected Jeremiah from Jehoiakim (26:24), and also of Gemariah, in whose room in the Temple Baruch read Jeremiah's scroll (36:10). **Gemariah the son of Hilkiah** is unknown. It is very unlikely that he was Jeremiah's brother (1:1). **Elasah** and **Gemariah** were sent on an official mission to Babylon; its purpose is unknown.

5. The Hebrew exiles in Babylon were not slaves but deportees. Evidently they were free to live as they pleased. In time some became wealthy men of commerce, and others attained to high places at the court. **7.** This most unusual command was made out of regard for the people's welfare. The Jews' adherence to this principle of loyalty to the government of the country in which they live is one of the reasons for their survival in the world until today.

8. Which ye cause to be dreamed. The false prophets flourished by the general encouragement of the people. **10. Seventy years.** See note on 25:11. **11. An expected end.** A future and a hope. Israel had both; but they were not to be realized immediately. First she must undergo purgation by fire (cf. vv. 12-14). **14. Turn away your captivity.** The general meaning of the phrase is "restore your fortunes." Here it means particularly "restore you to your land." **17. Vile figs.** Cf. 24:1-10. **18. To be removed.** See note on 15:4. **I have driven them.** Here, as often in the prophets, a future event is spoken of as though it had already taken place.

21. Ahab the son of Kolaiah . . . Zedekiah the son of Maaseiah. We know nothing about these men or the incident here referred to. **22. Of them.** *Because of them.* **Roasted in the fire.** Another reference to Babylonian use of this punishment occurs in Dan 3:6. **23.** The Babylonians would hardly have put men to death for these reasons. These were sins against God, who delivered the men to Nebuchadnezzar, who probably put them to death for plotting to overthrow the state.

24. Shemaiah the Nehelamite. A Judean leader in Babylon who had written to the priest Zephaniah in Jerusalem, urging him to silence Jeremiah. **Shemaiah** is otherwise unknown. **25. Zephaniah the son of Maaseiah** was a temple official (cf. 21:1; 37:3; 52:24). **26-28.** The text of Shemaiah's letter. **Maketh himself a prophet** (v. 27). How little did Shemaiah understand the divine compulsion that drove the timid Jeremiah to do and utter what was so repugnant to him! **29. Read this letter.** Evidently Zephaniah was in sympathy with Jeremiah.

C. The Book of Consolation. 30:1–33:26.

Much of Jeremiah's work was to proclaim judgment. In this section he looks beyond the nearer judgment to the Day of the Lord, Israel's restoration and salvation, and the New Covenant.

1) The Day of the Lord: Its Terror and Deliverance. 30:1-24.

The Day of the Lord will commence with great distress for Israel, but will eventuate in her regathering and salvation.

a) Introduction. 30:1-3.

The captivity is here taken for granted (cf. 23:3,4 note). There was to be a restoration to the land. **Bring again the captivity** (v. 3). See note on 29:14.

b) Jacob's Trouble. 30:4-7.

In the prophetic vision, the Day of the Lord begins with a time of great trouble for the nations and for Israel (Amos 5:18-20; Isa 2:12-22; 34:1-15; Zeph 1:2–3:8; Zech 14:1-8, 12-15). **Israel and . . . Judah** (v. 4). See note on 2:4. **That day** (v. 7; i.e., the Day of the Lord. Cf. Isa 13:6; Jer 46:10; Lam 2:22; Ezk 30:3; Joel 1:15; 2:1; and the references earlier in this paragraph.

c) Jacob's Deliverance. 30:8-11.

Israel shall be saved out of the trouble, freed from Gentile domination, and returned to her land, where she shall serve God and a Davidic king. This is the second part of the Day-of-the-Lord vision. **Serve themselves of him (v. 8).** See note on 27:7. **9. David their king.** Not the resurrected David the son of Jesse, but a king of the Davidic line (Hos 3:5; Ezk 34:23). Caesar was originally the name of a Roman emperor; it became the title of his successors. Jeremiah has already indicated that Messiah will come from the Davidic line (23:5 note). **10,11.** These verses are repeated at 46:27,28. **My servant Jacob** (v. 10). The idea that Israel is God's servant is more fully developed in Isaiah (e.g., 41:8-14; 43:1-7; 44:1,2).

d) Zion's Seemingly Incurable Wounds To Be Healed. 30:12-17.

14. Seek thee not. *Do not care for you.* **17. Seeketh after.** *Cares for.*

e) Jerusalem To Be Rebuilt and Happy. 30:18-22.

18. Bring again the captivity. See note on 29:14. **Heap.** Hebrew, *tēl*. The same word is used by the Arabs today for the desolate mounds of Palestine, the sites of ancient cities. **Remain after the manner thereof.** Better, *stand upon its rightful site.* **21. Their nobles shall be of themselves.** Better, *their prince shall be one of themselves.* **Prince** and **governor** seem to be used to avoid the more usual word "king." **For who is this that engaged his heart to approach unto me?** *For who would dare of himself to approach me?* This prince is also a priest who has the right to come to God.

23,24. The Lord's storm of vengeance.

2) The Restoration of the Nation, and the New Covenant. 31:1-40.

In preparation for the statement of the New Covenant, first Israel (vv. 1-22), and then Judah (vv. 23-30) is assured of God's love and of his purpose to regather them.

a) **God To Do for Scattered Israel As He Did for the Survivors of the Exodus.** 31:1-6.

1. The purpose of the Abrahamic Covenant (Gen 17:7) will finally be realized. This is the highest blessing God can give.

2. Which were left. *Who escaped.* **In the wilderness**; i.e., in the forty-year wilderness wandering (Ex 14—Deut 34).

3. Lovingkindness. See note on 9:24.

4. Virgin of Israel. See note on 14:17. **Tabrets.** The timbrels or hand drums, used to beat time for dances on occasions of rejoicing (cf. Ex 15:20).

5. Eat them as common things. The Hebrews did not eat the fruit for the first three years. The fruit of the fourth year was given to God. But it could be "redeemed" and eaten as a common thing (Lev 19:23-25; Deut 20:6). This verse means that Israel would be settled and living off the land in a normal condition.

6. Israel would also return to the pure worship of the Lord which became lost to her at the division of the kingdom. **Mount Ephraim** was the center of the Northern Kingdom. **The watchman** probably gave the signal for the pilgrimage.

b) Regathering of the Exiles Predicted. 31:7-14.

They will return, repentant and restored to God's favor (cf. Isa 40:3-5,9,11; 42:5-16; 43:1-21; 48:20-22; 49:8-13).

8. North country. Cf. Introduction, *The Foe from the North.* **Coasts of the earth.** *Farthest parts of the earth.* This seems to indicate a dispersion throughout the whole world.

10. Isles. See on 2:10. **11. Redeemed . . . ransomed.** References to God's deliverance of his people from foreign bondage to the freedom of their own land. The NT usage (probably anticipated in Isa 44:22,23; 62:12) of these words in the sense of deliverance from sin is a very natural extension of the meaning. **12. Flow together.** As in our English expression, "the crowd *streamed* into the city." **Wheat . . . wine . . . oil.** Symbols of the good life (cf. Ps 104:15). **Watered garden.** In dry Palestine, irrigation is the only guarantee of perpetual verdure (Isa 58:11).

c) Rachel and Ephraim To Be Comforted. 31:15-22.

Rachel, the mother of Joseph and Benjamin, from whom the leading tribes in the Northern Kingdom descended, is represented as weeping for the captivity of Israel; but God comforts her with the promise of their restoration.

15. Ramah (v. 16). A town about five miles north of Jerusalem, evidently the place where the captives were massed before being taken to Babylon (40:1). The prophecy represents **Rachel** (AV, *Rahel),* who pled for children (Gen 30:1) and died in sorrow (Gen 35:18,19), as weeping at Ramah to see her descendants carried away. (The place of Rachel's burial is a matter of dispute.) Matthew sees a fulfillment of this verse in the Massacre of the Innocents (Mt 2:17,18).

18,19. Ephraim prays a prayer of repentance. **Ephraim** is a synonym for Israel. **19. I was turned**; i.e., away from God. **Smote upon my thigh.** A sign of great sorrow (Ezk 21:12). **20.** God declares Ephraim forgiven. **Bowels.** Cf. 4:19 note.

21,22. The prophet admonishes Israel to prepare to return from captivity. **High heaps** (v. 21). Used as guide posts. **Turn again.** *Return.* **Go about** (v. 22). *Turn hither and thither* (in uncertainty). **A woman shall compass a man.** This statement is difficult to understand. Commentators differ widely on its meaning. It is hard to know how to translate the verb rendered in the AV **compass.** The view which sees here a prophecy of the virgin birth of Christ is now rejected by most. The RSV translates *"a woman shall protect a man"*; i.e., weak Israel shall become strong enough to protect others. Still others, "a woman shall embrace a man"; i.e., Israel shall return to her husband-God. No interpretation has ever gained the acceptance of a majority of commentators.

d) Judah Also To Be Restored. 31:23-30.

23. As yet. *Yet again.* **Bring again their captivity.** See note on 29:14. **24. Husbandmen.** *Farmers.* In ancient Palestine, farmers and shepherds lived in the towns and went out each morning to the fields and the pastures. A situation of quiet prosperity is meant. **25. Satiated.** *Satisfied.* **Replenished.** *Filled* (with joy). **26.** The prophet appears to say this. But it is strange, for Jeremiah repudiated dreams (23:25-28).

27. Captivity resulted in the decimation of the human and animal inhabitants. In the coming day, God will repopulate the united nation (Ezk 36:8-11; Hos 1:11; 2:23). **28. To build, and to plant.** Cf. 1:10. **29.** A popular proverb (cf. Ezk 18:2-4). **30 For his own iniquity.** A statement of the responsibility of the individual.

e) The New Covenant. 31:31-34.

The concept of the new covenant is Jeremiah's most important contribution to Biblical thought. The OT frequently mentions the covenant God made with Israel (Ex 19:3-8; 24:3-8; Deut 29:1-29), which covenant was the foundation of the Israelites' national and religious life. God makes clear, through Jeremiah, that Israel has failed to keep this covenant (7:21-26; 11:1-13) and predicts that He will make a new one with His people. The new covenant will not be a new law (the old law was still good), but it will produce a new "heart"—i.e., it will confer a new motivation to obey the law of God. Jesus, while instituting the Lord's Supper, declared, "This cup is the new covenant in my blood" (ASV, I Cor 11:25; cf. Lk 22:20). The Hebrews epistle teaches that Christ brought in the new covenant by his perfect and final sacrifice for sin (Heb 7:22; 8:7-13; 10:15-22; cf. II Cor 3:5-14).

31. The days come. An eschatological formula. The Day of the Lord is meant (cf. 30:7 note). **32. Covenant that I made with their fathers.** The covenant made at Sinai, renewed at the Plains of Moab (cf. references in introductory paragraph above). **I was a husband;** i.e., I was faithful to them, even though they were unfaithful to me. **33. In their hearts.** The old covenant was written upon stone (Ex 31:18). Only the new covenant, written upon the heart, can accomplish what the old one sought to bring about: "I . . . will be your God, and ye shall be my people" (Lev 26:12; cf. Ezk 36:25-27). **34. Know me.** This knowledge is intimate, experiential, based on the forgiveness of sins.

f) Israel To Remain Forever. 31:35-37.

The survival of the Hebrew people, long after their neighbors have perished, is hardly explainable on any but supernaturalistic grounds.

g) Jerusalem To Be Rebuilt and Holy. 31:38-40.

38. To the Lord. No mere nationalism is here; the city is dedicated to God, holy (v. 40). **Tower of Hananeel.** At the northeast corner (Neh 3:1; 12:39; Zech 14:10). **Gate of the corner;** i.e., the northwest corner (II Kgs 14:13; II Chr 26:9). **39. Hill Gareb . . . Goath.** Unknown; probably they indicate the southwest and southeast extremities of the city. **40. Valley of the dead bodies.** The Valley of Hinnom (cf. 7:31 note). **The brook Kidron** is the eastern boundary of Jerusalem, and flows into the Valley of Hinnom. **The horse gate** seems to have been at the southeast corner of the city.

3) Jeremiah's Redemption of a Field in Anathoth. 32:1-44.

By this action, which took place during the final siege of Jerusalem, Jeremiah showed his faith in the restoration to Palestine after the captivity. The law of redemption commanded that if a needy Hebrew was about to sell his land to pay for his debts, his near relative should redeem the land—i.e., buy it back for him. Jeremiah's action takes on added significance when it is recalled that Anathoth had already fallen into enemy hands; thus his action would have been meaningless apart from the hope of a restoration.

a) God's Command. 32:1-8.

1. Tenth year. Jerusalem fell the next year. Already it was under siege. **2.** The story of Jeremiah's imprisonment is told in 37:11-21. **7. Redemption.** Cf. introductory paragraph above; Lev 25:23-28. **Anathoth.** Jeremiah's birthplace (cf. 1:1 note).

b) The Redemption of the Land. 32:9-15.

An interesting example of a business transaction of that time.

9. Weighed. Since there was no coined money, payments were made by weighing out precious metal. **Seventeen shekels.** About seven ounces. Probably the field was small. **10. Subscribed the evidence.** *Signed the deed.* **Witnesses** were always important for legal transactions. Cf. an earlier real estate transaction, where no writing was done, Ruth 4:1-12. **Balances.** *Scales.* **11.** Two copies of the deed were made, probably on papyrus. One was rolled up and sealed to prevent tampering, the other left unsealed for ready reference.

12. Baruch. The first mention of Jeremiah's secretary, who wrote much of the Book of Jeremiah under the prophet's direction. **15. Possessed.** *Bought*.

c) Jeremiah's Reaction of Doubt. 32:16-25.

The purchase made, a wave of doubt swept over the prophet, and he prayed in anguish of spirit. His prayer is somewhat similar to the prayer of the Levites reported in Neh 9:6-38.

18. Lovingkindness. See note on 9:24. **20. Signs and wonders in . . . Egypt.** Cf. Ex 7:8–12:36. **Unto this day.** Probably this phrase modifies the statement which succeeds it. **24. Mounts.** (Siege) *mounds*. **Chaldeans.** See note on 21:4. **25.** The prayer breaks off as the prophet feels the incongruity of his "playing at business as usual" when the land is lost to the Babylonians. Yet he will not state his doubt more fully.

d) God's Gracious Reply. 32:26-44.

The Lord comforts and reassures his prophet by telling him that although the city will fall as he has been predicting, there will be a restoration, when people will again buy and sell in the land of Judah.

27. With great kindness God urges Jeremiah to greater faith by taking up the prophet's own statement (v. 17) and asking it of him as a question, as if to say, "Jeremiah, do you really believe what you have said?" **34. Abominations;** i.e., idols. There were idols even in the Jerusalem Temple (cf. Ezk 8:3-11). **35.** See notes on 7:29,31; 19:13. **38-40.** See notes on 31:31-34. **44. Mountains.** See note on 17:26. **Valley.** The Shephelah (cf. 17:26 note). **South.** The Negev (cf. 13:19 note). **Cause their captivity to return.** See note on 29:14.

4) More Promises of Restoration. 33:1-26.

The themes introduced in Jeremiah 31 are here repeated. This chapter records revelations Jeremiah received during the final siege of Jerusalem.

a) Rebuilt Jerusalem To Be Holy. 33:1-9.

2. The maker thereof. Maker of what? Probably the earth is meant. **Lord.** See note on Ex 3:14. **3. Mighty.** *Hidden*. **4. By the mounts . . . by the sword.** Better, *for the mounts . . . for the sword*. Buildings near the wall were destroyed so that the soldiers defending the city might have more space in which to maneuver (cf. 32:24 note). **7. Captivity . . . to return.** See note on 29:14. **As at the first.** Before the kingdom was split after the death of Solomon. **8. I will cleanse them.** Cf. 31:34. **9. It;** i.e., Jerusalem (cf. 32:40-42).

b) Devastated Jerusalem To Revive. 33:10-13.

11. See note on 25:10. **Praise the Lord.** A liturgical refrain used in the temple services (Ps 135:1). **Return the captivity.** See note on 29:14. **12. An habitation of shepherds.** A picture of quiet peace. **13. Mountains.** See note on 17:26. **Vale.** The Shephelah (cf. 17:26 note). **South.** The Negev (cf. 13:19 note). **Telleth.** *Counts*.

c) Davidic Kings and Levitical Priests and Israelites Never To Be Cut Off. 33:14-26.

15,16. These verses repeat 23:5,6, for which see notes. **21.** God's covenant with David is stated in II Sam 7:8-16. See note on 23:5. **24. Two families;** i.e., Israel and Judah.

D. Some of Jeremiah's Experiences Before Jerusalem Fell. 34:1–36:32.

These events illustrate the depths to which king and people had plunged, and thus prepare the way for the account of the destruction of Jerusalem which follows.

1) An Oracle to Zedekiah. 34:1-7.

This warning was delivered in the reign of Zedekiah, while Jerusalem was under attack. It contains the frequently repeated warnings of national defeat, with a promise to the king.

1. Jerusalem. Here, as often in the Bible, the name of the capital city stands for the whole nation, as, e.g., Tyre and Sidon are used for Phoenicia, Damascus for Syria, etc.

5. These words of promise hardly seem to have been fulfilled. Zedekiah's eyes were put out, and he died in a Babylonian prison (39:7; 52:8-11; II Kgs 25:5-7; Ezk 12:13). It seems that this is a conditional promise, dependent upon the king's surrender to the Babylonians. Since Zedekiah refused to obey, his end was a worse one. **Burn odours.** **The burning of incense was a part of the funeral** ceremony.

7. Lachish. An important town in the Shephelah (cf. 17:26 note), twenty-three miles southwest of Jerusalem (modern Tell ed-Duweir). It guarded a valley road that led to Jerusalem, and hence it was important for the defense of the capital. Graphic evidence of its destruction by the Babylonian army has been found by its excavators. (For the Lachish letters, cf. Introduction, *The Lachish Letters.)* **Azekah.** Another Shephelah town important for the defense of a road to Jerusalem. It is modern Tell ez-Zakariyeh, eighteen miles west-southwest of Jerusalem, some eleven miles north of Lachish. Both of these cities would have to fall before Jerusalem could be successfully reduced.

2) The Broken Covenant Regarding Hebrew Slaves. 34:8-22.

During the siege of Jerusalem, the people promised to release their Hebrew slaves, hoping thus to obtain God's favor. But when the Babylonians were temporarily distracted from the siege by the approach of an Egyptian army (37:6-11), and withdrew from the city, the people took their slaves back again, thus earning Jeremiah's castigation.

9. None should serve himself of . . . his brother. Hebrew slaves (usually taken for debt) could be held only six years; on the seventh they must be set free (Ex 21:2; Deut 15:1,12-15). It seems that this law (like that of the Sabbatical year, II Chr 36:21) was seldom kept. In a wave of repentance, all slaves held more than six years were released. Probably, with the city now under siege and the fields outside inaccessible, the slaves were an economic liability, with the owners unable to feed them.

14. Seven years. Actually six years. But here the year of liberation is included (cf. Deut 15:1,12).

18. When they cut the calf in twain, and passed between the parts thereof. An interesting allusion to the manner of ratifying a covenant. A sacrificial victim was cut in half, and the contracting parties walked together between the parts prior to the offering of the sacrifice (cf. Gen 15:9-17). This probably accounts for the fact that the Hebrew verb regularly used for making a covenant literally means *to cut*.

3) The Example of the Rechabites. 35:1-19.

Jeremiah's moral drawn from the strange behavior of the sons of Jonadab the son of Rechab was delivered in the reign of Jehoiakim.

a) The Rechabites' Refusal To Drink Wine. 35:1-11.

The Rechabites were a puritan group, the followers of Jonadab the son of Rechab (II Kgs 10:15,16,23). They followed the desert ideal, seeking to abstain from what to them appeared to be the degenerating influences of settled town life—farming, wine, and houses. The Lord praises them not for their strange ideals, but for the tenacity with which they stuck to what they believed to be right.

2. House of the Rechabites; i.e., the Rechabite clan. **3,4.** The persons here named are unknown, except that **Maaseiah** may have been the father of the priest Zephaniah mentioned in 21:1; 29:25; 37:3. **6. Our father.** Used in the extended Semitic sense of "founder" of the order. **11. So we dwell at Jerusalem.** Probably in tents still. However, it was now impossible to keep their vow absolutely.

b) Jeremiah's Sermon on the Rechabites. 35:12-17.

19. Contrast the curse pronounced upon Jeconiah (22:30). Even today, in Syria and Arabia, there are groups that claim to be Rechabites and that follow the Rechabite rule.

4) Jeremiah's Prophecies Dictated to Baruch. 36:1-32.

This chapter is of great interest in that it gives the only detailed OT description of the writing of a prophetic book. That Jeremiah should have dictated to a secretary was normal for the times. Writing was a specialized skill, often restricted to a professional class. Learned men could read, but (like executives today) scorned to write. The book was dictated in Jehoiakim's fourth year. This 'first edition' of the book was burned; immediately the prophet issued a 'new edition' with additions (v. 32). The odd order of materials in our present Book of Jeremiah may be due to this manner of composition—a short original work, with frequent revisions.

a) The Scroll Written by Baruch. 36:1-7.

2. A roll of a book. A blank scroll, probably of papyrus imported from

Egypt. Our present book form ("codex") originated in early Christian times. **4. Baruch the son of Neriah.** Jeremiah's secretary, thought to have been of a prominent family (32:12,13,16; 51:59). **5. I am shut up.** Better, *I am detained.* We do not know whether it was some ritual impurity or physical restraint from his enemies that kept Jeremiah from going to the Temple himself. **6. Fasting day.** A fast had been proclaimed on account of some now unknown calamity. This would have ensured a crowd to hear the reading.

b) The Scroll Read Aloud by Baruch. 36:8-21.

9. Fifth year . . . ninth month. This was December, 605 B.C. It is believed by some that the king's regnal year was at this time reckoned from the autumn (beginning with the seventh month). If this is so, the king's fourth year had ended only two months before, and no very long time need have elapsed between the writing (cf. 6:1) and the reading of the book. **10. Gemariah the son of Shaphan** was a brother of Ahikam (26:24; 39:14; II Kgs 22:8-14). Evidently this was a pious family of nobles.

11,12. Concerning these princes, see note on 26:10. **17. At his mouth.** Jeremiah is not mentioned here but understood. The nobles were fearful for Jeremiah, but sympathetic with him, and they sought to protect him (v. 19).

c) The Scroll Burned by the King. 36:22-26.

22. Winter-house. Probably a sheltered part of the palace, facing the sun. **Hearth.** Better, *brazier.* The rainy season in the Judean hill country is cool, with occasional light snows, as well as rain. **23. Leaves.** Better, *columns.* A scroll was composed of papyrus leaves pasted together, with the writing on the inner side of the scroll in columns. When a few columns had been read, the king cut them off and burned them.

24. Baruch was struck with the lack of reverence of the men for the scroll. In time past, when Josiah heard the Law scroll read, "he rent his clothes" (II Kgs 22:11). It seems that Baruch regarded Jeremiah's scroll to be equally Scripture with the Law which had so impressed Josiah.

26. Hammelech. Literally, *the king.* But Jehoiakim was probably too young to have an adult son at this time. Perhaps this is an honorific title. **Seraiah.** See note on 51:59.

d) A Second Edition Dictated by Jeremiah. 36:27-32.

30. None to sit upon the throne of David. Jehoiakim's son, the last of his descendants to rule, reigned three months. **Dead body.** The manner of Jehoiakim's death is nowhere stated. On the ground of this verse, it is believed that this wicked king may have died in a palace coup or a popular uprising (cf. 22:19).

32. Many like words. The burning of the first scroll could not destroy the oracles; it only led to more words of judgment.

E. Jeremiah During the Siege and Destruction of Jerusalem. 37:1—39:18.

This section tells of Jeremiah's fortunes during the last days of the Judean kingdom. Chapters 21; 32—34 also give information about this period.

1) Jeremiah Imprisoned. 37:1-21.

There is no reason to believe that the prophet meant to go over to the Babylonians when he sought to leave the city during the brief lifting of the siege.. But his people, to whom he seemed a hateful quisling, so interpreted his action, and therefore he was cast into a dungeon.

1. Zedekiah. See note on 1:3. **Reigned.** The Hebrew expression is unusual: literally, *And Zedekiah reigned* (as) *king.* Zedekiah, uncle of Jehoiachin (Coniah), probably was considered a regent in the place of his nephew, who had been carried off to Babylon. **Whom Nebuchadrezzar . . . made king** refers to Zedekiah, not to Coniah (II Kgs 24:17).

a) Jeremiah's Prediction of the Return of the Chaldeans and the Fall of the City. 37:3-10. (Cf. 21:1-10, where a different situation is referred to.)

3. Jehucal the son of Shelemiah, called Jucal in 38:1, was opposed to Jeremiah. **Zephaniah the son of Maaseiah.** See note on 29:25. **Pray now.** Zedekiah was not a strong-willed, wicked man like Jehoiakim. He was rather a weak, vacillating man, usually led the wrong way by the evil nobles who had come to power during the reign of Jehoiakim. He seems to have had a superstitious respect for Jeremiah, as his request here indicates.

5. Pharaoh. He is named Pharaoh-hophra in 44:30. An alliance with Hophra probably encouraged Zedekiah to rebel. Now Pharaoh came to his aid, but, soon after, the Babylonians defeated the Egyptians and returned to Jerusalem.

b) Jeremiah Imprisoned. 37:11-15.

12. To separate himself thence. The Hebrew is difficult to construe. It is often translated *to receive his portion there*. The portion could not be the land referred to in 32:8, for the events of that chapter had not yet taken place. Probably he was bound for Anathoth. **13. Gate of Benjamin.** A gate on the north side of the city, leading to the land of Benjamin (cf. 38:7). **Captain of the ward.** *Sentinel.* **Irijah.** Otherwise unknown. It is interesting to see how all the characters in the moving drama of Jeremiah's ministry are named, even to a humble sentry. **15. The princes.** See note on 37:3. **The house of Jonathan.** Perhaps the regular prisons were full of political prisoners.

c) Zedekiah's Secret Meeting with Jeremiah. 37:16-21.

16. Cabins. *Cells.* **17-20.** Another dramatic situation, in which the prophet neither flinches nor grovels. **21. Court of the prison.** This was in the palace complex (cf. 32:2). **Piece of bread.** Better, *a loaf of bread.* **Bakers' street.** In ancient cities (and in the Old City of Jerusalem today) each business had its own street or quarter (cf. 18:2 note). **Until . . . the bread . . . were spent.** Because of the scarcity caused by the siege.

2) Jeremiah Rescued from a Cistern by Ebed-melech. 38:1-28.

These events seem to have taken place after those of the previous chapter, near the end of the siege, when, in desperation, the anti-Babylonian clique at court sought to rid themselves of their most vigorous opponent. Zedekiah appears weak, but not unfriendly to the prophet. His final interview with Jeremiah is here also recorded.

a) Jeremiah's Rescue. 38:1-13.

1. Gedaliah the son of Pashur. He may have been the son of the Pashur who earlier beat Jeremiah and put him in stocks (20:1-6). **Jucal the son of Shelemiah.** Cf. 37:3. **Pashur the son of Malchiah.** See note on 21:1. **2.** This verse is almost identical with **21:9. 4. He weakeneth the hands of the men of war;** i.e., Jeremiah is a traitor. The same accusation is made in one of the Lachish letters against certain people in Jerusalem (cf. Introduction, *The Lachish Letters*). **5. He is in your hand.** This reveals Zedekiah's weakness. **6. Dungeon.** Better, *cistern.* Jerusalem was full of cisterns, where water was collected during the rainy season for use during the months when no rain fell (May to October). Jeremiah was thrown into a nearly empty cistern and left to suffocate or starve. **Malchiah the son of Hammelech.** Perhaps the father of the Pashur of verse 1. **Hammelech.** See note on 36:26.

7. Ebed-melech the Ethiopian. Ebed-melech means *servant of the king,* but this man was not a slave. **Eunuch** is too narrow a translation for the Hebrew *sārîs,* which means an "officer" or "palace official." Still, it is to be doubted whether he was an important official. It is in keeping with the melancholy temper of this book that only a despised foreigner cared enough for the prophet to risk trouble in saving him (cf. 39:15-18). **Gate of Benjamin.** See note on 37:13. **10. Thirty men.** The number seems unnecessarily large and the grammatical construction is unusual, as if the number had been changed. One Hebrew manuscript and the LXX read *three men,* which is probably the original number. **12.** This thoughtfulness stands in direct contrast to the venomous hatred shown the prophet by his fellow Judeans.

b) Zedekiah's Final Meeting with Jeremiah. 38:14-28.

17. Thy soul shall live. *Thy life shall be spared.* The basic meaning of ***nepesh*** is "life." The word occurs twice in verse 16, once translated "soul," once "life" (cf. v. 20). **19.** Some Jews had surrendered (39:9; 52:15). The king feared that the Chaldeans might give him to them for torture. **22.** A conquering king always took possession of his defeated enemy's harem (cf. II Sam 16:21,22). The second half of the verse represents the women of the royal harem as speaking an oracle as they are led away.

26. Jonathan's house. See note on 37: 15.

3) The Fall of Jerusalem. 39:1-18.

The capture and destruction of the city are described in greater detail in Jeremiah 52, except that the contents of

39:3,14 are not found there. For comment see notes on chapter 52.

3. A large clay prism found at Babylon, which lists high officials of the Babylonian court, helps us to understand these names. Three persons are mentioned: **Nergal-sharezer** (whose office is) **Shamgar** (meaning unknown); **Nebo-Sarsechim** (whose office is) **Rab-saris** (chief of the eunuchs—a high office); and **Nergal-sharezer** (whose office is) **Rab-mag** (meaning unknown); **Nergal-sharezer** was Nebuchadnezzar's son-in-law and second successor.

9. Nebuzar-adan was a general. This name has been found in several Babylonian lists, with the title "Chief Baker." As the name was a common one in this period, we cannot be sure that the Biblical person is identical with the one mentioned in these lists.

13. See note on verse 3. **14. Gedaliah the son of Ahikam.** Cf. 40:5.

The oracle concerning Ebed-melech. 39:15-18. **While he was shut up** (v. 15). Before the city fell (cf. 38:13). **Ebed-melech** (v. 16). See note on 38:7. **Men of whom thou art afraid** (v. 17). Perhaps Zedekiah's princes, who may well have been planning their revenge against the one who had saved Jeremiah's life.

F. The Last Years of Jeremiah. 40:1–45:5.

Jeremiah's old age was as pathetic as his earlier life. Left to remain in Judah after the fall of Jerusalem, he was taken to Egypt against his wishes, and died in that idolatrous place.

1) The Administration of Gedaliah, and His Murder. 40:1–41:18.

II Kings 25:22-26 gives a summary of these events.

a) Jeremiah's Release When the City Fell. 40:1-6.

It is difficult to reconcile the statement here that Jeremiah was released after being held a prisoner at Ramah with the inference of 39:13,14 that the Babylonian princes freed him from the Jerusalem prison to the custody of Gedaliah. Perhaps the inference is unfounded, and 39:14 takes for granted the Ramah episode.

1. Nebuzar-adan. See note on 52:12. **Ramah.** A Benjamite town a few miles north of Jerusalem. Probably the captives were interrogated and screened there prior to their deportation. **2-4.** This speech, couched in Jewish theological language, is not so unlikely in a Babylonian mouth as it might at first seem. It appears that the Assyrians studied the theology of the people whom they attacked for use in psychological warfare (II Kgs 18:22,33-35). And the Babylonians had surely heard of the strange, quisling prophet within the Jerusalem walls and his seeming pro-Babylonian speeches. Since he had served them so well (as they thought), the Babylonians purposed to let him go free. Jeremiah's proud Hebrew heart must have rebelled at the inference that he was on their side, but he accepted his freedom.

5. Gedaliah the son of Ahikam. A man of high birth, a grandson of one of Josiah's nobles. The Babylonians made him puppet governor of the subjugated and largely desolate province of Judah. A seal from this period, found at Lachish, mentions a Gedaliah who was "over the house"; i.e., a palace governor (cf. Isa 36:3). This may well have been the same Gedaliah mentioned in these verses. **6. Mizpah.** Only a few poor farmers were left (52:16). They settled at Mizpah, near Ramah (cf. 40:1), a place a few miles north of Jerusalem, sometimes identified with Tell en-Nasbeh, recently excavated. This place was not so thoroughly destroyed by the Babylonians that it could not have served as a refuge after the destruction of Jerusalem. There was found there a beautifully carved seal with the name of its owner, "Ya'-azanyahu servant (officer) of the king," perhaps the Jezaniah of II Kgs 25:23 and Jer 40:8.

b) Gedaliah's Governorship. 40:7-12.

Gedaliah was a good ruler and probably had Jeremiah's support. His governorship is believed to have lasted about five years (cf. 52:30 note). It was brought to an end by his assassination. This was carried out by the same desperate group that had goaded Judah on to her fateful resistance to the Babylonians prior to Jerusalem's fall.

7. Forces . . . in the fields; i.e., Jewish military units still uncaptured. **8. Seraiah.** See note on 51:59; cf. II Kgs 25:23. **Jezaniah.** See note on 40:8. **9.** Gedaliah sought to quiet these explosive resistance forces by promising that if they submitted, their lives would be safe. **10. Mizpah.** See note on 40:6. Jerusalem was destroyed in the middle of the summer. There was still time to make wine, gather the late summer fruits (cf. 8:20 note) and olives, and so keep from starving during that first desolate winter. In this they were successful.

c) Gedaliah's Life Threatened. 40: 13-16.

The welfare of the little salvaged community depended on their submission to Babylon and their support of Gedaliah. Johanan knew that Ishmael, sponsored by the Ammonites and probably also by the pro-Egypt party, was seeking to kill Gedaliah, but the latter refused to take the necessary precautions.

d) **Gedaliah Assassinated by Ishmael.** 41:1-3.

Seventh month (v. 1). **October. The** Jews keep a fast to recall this murder. **The seed royal.** Perhaps in addition to being an anti-Babylonian extremist, Ishmael wished to avenge the indignities done to King Zedekiah, his relative.

e) The Massacre of Seventy Pilgrims. 41:4-9.

This brutal slaying, for which no good motive can be given, shows the desperation of Ishmael and his band.

5. Pilgrims from the towns which had been in the Northern Kingdom were on their way to Jerusalem. **Shaven . . . rent . . . cut themselves.** Indications of mourning, probably for the fall of Jerusalem and the destruction of the Temple (cf. 16:5 note). **7. Pit.** Compare note on verse 9. **8. Treasures in the field.** Cisterns in the field were frequently used as storage places. They could easily be covered over and concealed, an advantage at this time of great political unrest. **9. Pit.** See note on 14:3. King Asa had fortified Mizpah against Baasha, king of Israel (I Kgs 15:22). Cisterns to provide water during siege were vital for fortress cities. At Tell en-Nasbeh (cf. 40:6 note) fifty-three such cisterns have been found.

f) The Remaining People Carried Off and Returned. 41:10-18.

Ishmael, who was in league with the Ammonite king (40:14), carried off the Mizpah refugees, intending to take them to the Ammonites. But Johanan, with certain Jewish forces, rescued them, and they went south to a place near Bethlehem.

12. The great waters; i.e., a great pool. Referred to in II Sam 2:13. Gibeon is modern El-jib, some three miles southwest of Tell en-Nasbeh (40:6 note). Recent excavations there have disclosed an involved waterworks system, with a large storage cistern. **14. Cast about.** *Turned around.* **17. Habitation of Chimham.** The place is unknown. **To go to enter into Egypt.** The people feared that even though innocent of anti-Babylon activity themselves, they would suffer for Ishmael's murder of Gedaliah and the Babylonian garrison.

2) Migration of the Refugees to Egypt. 42:1–43:7.

a) Jeremiah Asked To Seek Counsel from God. 42:1-6.

The people feared to stay in Palestine, but hesitated to leave their homeland for the protection of a foreign nation. **Jezaniah the son of Hoshaiah** (v. 1). Not the same as the Jezaniah of 40:8. He may be identical with the Azariah the son of Hoshaiah of 43:2, for the two names have a similar meaning.

b) **The Prophet's Warning Against** Going to Egypt. 42:7-22.

7. After ten days. Even though the request was urgent, Jeremiah had to wait until he was certain that he had the divine reply. He dared not confuse his own desire to stay at home with God's will. **10. Repent.** See note on 18: 18. **20. For ye dissembled in your hearts.** Taken at face value these words seem to say that the Jews asked Jeremiah's advice hypocritically, already having determined their course. But many translate, *For you err at the cost of your lives.* In going to Egypt, you will lose everything (cf. v. 22).

c) Jeremiah Taken Along to Egypt by the People. 43:1-7.

Restless after ten days of waiting, the refugees disregarded Jeremiah's warning and migrated to Egypt. They took Jeremiah and Baruch with them against their will. Evidently Jeremiah died in Egypt.

2. Azariah the son of Hoshaiah. See note on 42:1. **3. Baruch the son of Neriah.** See note on 36:4. There is no evidence in this book to confirm the opinion of the people that Baruch unduly influenced the now elderly Jeremiah. **5. Returned from all nations.** The war that culminated in the destruction of Jerusalem had caused many Jews to scatter for safety to the surrounding nations. Some of these had now returned to their land. **6. Nebuzar-adan.** See note on 52:12. **Gedaliah the son of Ahikam.** See note on 40:5. **Jeremiah.** It seems clear that Jeremiah went unwillingly. Whether force or a sense of duty to his irresponsive fellow countrymen impelled him is not known. **7. Tahpanhes.** See note on 2:16.

3) Jeremiah in Egypt. 43:8–44:30.

Jeremiah's life in Egypt seems to have been an unhappy one. The land was filled with idols; his own people were not sympathetic with him; and he could hardly expect good treatment at the hands of the government when his political attitudes voiced during Judah's last years became known.

a) Jeremiah's Prediction of Nebuchadnezzar's Conquest of Egypt. 43:8-13.

Another symbolic action of the prophet. Our knowledge of the neo-Babylonian empire is quite fragmentary. While we do not have enough extra-Biblical information at the present time to confirm the fact that Nebuchadnezzar actually conquered Egypt, we do know that he invaded it. The fact that this prophecy was left in this book by the next generation argues for knowledge on their part (now lost to us) of a reduction of the land by Nebuchadnezzar.

9. The clay in the brickkiln. Better, *the mortar of the quadrangle* (or *pavement).* Sir Flinders Petrie, who excavated Tell Defenneh, found a large paved area which he believed to be the one referred to here. It was situated in front of what he identified as Pharaoh's house, and was probably used as an unloading and storage area. **10. My servant.** See note on 25:9.

12. Carry them away captives. Idols were frequently carried in the triumphal processions of conquering kings. **Array himself . . . putteth on.** These are translations of the same Hebrew verb. The meaning seems to be that Nebuchadnezzar would have Egypt so completely under his control that he would wrap himself with that land as a shepherd wraps himself in his robe in the cool night. **13. Beth-shemesh.** The Hebrew for "the House of the Sun," ancient Heliopolis, modern Tell Husn, near Cairo. Re, the sun-god, was worshiped there in ancient times. The **images** are obelisks. One of the Heliopolis obelisks is now in Central Park in New York City, another on the Thames Embankment in London. Both are wrongly called "Cleopatra's Needle."

b) Idolatry of the Egyptian Jews Condemned. 44:1-14.

1. Migdol. On the northeastern border of Egypt, probably modern Tell el-Heir, eleven miles south of Pelusium. **Tahpanhes.** See note on 2:16. **Noph** was called *Memphis* by the ancient Egyptians. Located near the apex of the Delta, it was an important center of Egyptian life, having been capital of the nation in earlier days. The god Ptah, the creator god, patron of artisans and sculptors, was worshiped here. **The country of Pathros.** Upper (or southern) Egypt—the land south of the Delta. The fact that some Jews had migrated south shows that they quickly became dispersed throughout the land. A little later there was a colony of Jewish mercenary soldiers at Elephantine, modern Aswan on the Ethiopian border.

7. Against your souls. *Against yourselves.* **14. Such as shall escape.** *Some refugees* (cf. 44:28).

c) The Response of the Jews. 44:15-19.

This blatant confession of trust in the Queen of Heaven is characteristic of the people to whom Jeremiah had preached all his life.

15. Their wives. The women seem to have been especially devoted to the Queen of Heaven, perhaps because she was thought to bring the desired fertility. **Pathros.** See note on 44:1. **17. The queen of heaven.** See note on 7:18. **For then had we plenty.** In the opinion of these women, Josiah's reform, which excluded the previously practiced idolatry (II Kgs 23), was the cause of the nation's downfall. **19. To worship her.** Better, *in her image* (cf. 7:18 note). **Without our men;** i.e., the husbands, too, approved of these sentiments.

d) Jeremiah's Warning Concluded. 44:20-28.

26. My name shall no more be named. Because the Jews in Egypt would perish. Later on, during the Inter-Testamental Period, there was a large Jewish population in Egypt, worshiping the Lord. Perhaps this is an example of the conditional character of judgment prophecy. The Jews repented of their idolatry and were spared.

e) Pharaoh-hophra's Downfall a Sign of Disaster to the Egyptian Jews. 44:29, 30.

Pharaoh-hophra reigned from 588 to 569 B.C. (cf. 37:5 note). Jeremiah said Pharaoh would be captured by his enemies, as was Zedekiah. One of his officials, Amasis, revolting against his rule, finally killed him and succeeded him.

4) Jeremiah's Oracle to Baruch. 45:1-5.

Baruch, like his master, became discouraged in the work. Evidently he was also tempted to seek "great things." Perhaps he aspired to influence Jeremiah (cf. 43:3). At any rate, he is here encouraged and warned. Surely his giving Jeremiah's memoirs to the world has brought him legitimate fame.

1. Baruch the son of Neriah. See note on 32:12. **These words.** Evidently Jeremiah 36 is referred to. Compare the date mentioned in this verse with that in 36:1. **5. Thy life will I give unto thee for a prey.** Although Baruch would suffer, his life would be spared.

III. Jeremiah's Oracles Against Foreign Nations. 46:1–51:64.

The Hebrew prophet characteristically had a word for neighboring nations of the Hebrews as well as for the Chosen People themselves. Jeremiah was ordained "a prophet unto the nations" (1:5) and was set "over the nations and over the kingdoms" (1:10). In the last part of this book are gathered together his prophetic indictments of the Gentiles, given at various times. The Greek Bible places these oracles immediately after 25:13.

A. Oracle Against Egypt. 46:1-28.

1) Superscription. 46:1. This verse forms a heading for the whole section 46:1–51:64.

2) Song on Nebuchadnezzar's Victory over Pharaoh-necho at Carchemish. 46:2-12.

2. In Carchemish. A wealthy commercial city, situated near the ford of the Euphrates in northern Syria. It had been a Hittite center in earlier days and was later dominated by the Assyrians. After the collapse of the Assyrian empire, it became the point where the Egyptian and Babylonian powers frequently clashed. The battle of Carchemish (605 B.C.) was one of the decisive battles of history. The Egyptians sought here to curb the rising power of Babylon and bolster the almost destroyed Assyrian empire. The Egyptians were defeated, and Nebuchadnezzar's pursuit of Necho toward Egypt was brought to an end only by the news of the death of his father Nabopolassar. He hurried back to Babylon to become the new king. From this time the Assyrian empire ceased to exist, and Babylon dominated not only Mesopotamia but all of the Levant.

4. Brigandines. *Breastplates,* i.e., protective armor. **5. For fear was round about.** See note on 6:25. **7. As a flood.** *As the Nile.* The word translated "flood" in the AV is *yᵉʾōr,* an Egyptian loan word meaning the Nile River. It is frequently used in connection with the Egyptian plagues (Ex 7,8). The Egyptian armies are here likened to the Nile during its annual inundation. **8. Flood.** See note on 46:7. **9. Ethiopians, Libyans, Lydians.** Allies of the Egyptians in the battle (cf. Ezk 30:5). The **Ethiopians** (Hebrew *Kush)* occupied the upper Nile region, and seem to have become involved in the Egyptian scene increasingly toward the end of Egypt's greatness (cf. II Chr 14:9-15; II Kgs 19:9; Isa 37:9). The **Libyans** lived west of Egypt, along the Mediterranean. **Lydians.** This term usually refers to a kingdom of Asia Minor. Its meaning here is not clear.

10. The day of the Lord God of hosts. This expression occurs nowhere else in Jeremiah. Here (as in Joel 1:15; 2:1) the **day of the Lord** means the day of God's judgment upon a nation, and does not refer to the judgment preceding the Messianic Day. **11. Balm.** See note on 8:22.

3) Nebuchadnezzar's Devastation of Egypt. 46:13-26. Cf. 43:8 note.

14. For these places, see notes at 43:7; 44:1.

15. The RSV translates this verse: *Why has Apis fled? Why did not your bull stand? Because the Lord thrust him down.* Those who translate thus divide the word for **swept away** (AV) into two words. If this division is correct, this is the only mention in the Bible of Apis, the bull-god of Egypt. The image of this god was often carried into battle, and his influence on the Hebrews is probably seen in the golden calf made by Aaron (Ex 32:4,5) and Jeroboam's similar image (I Kgs 12:28,29).

17. He hath passed the time appointed.

Better, *he has let the appointed time pass by*. Perhaps this means that Pharaoh procrastinated and out of fear let pass by the opportune moment for successful battle. **18. Tabor** and **Carmel** are prominent mountains in northern Palestine. The road to Egypt runs by them. **He** (i.e., Nebuchadnezzar) shall come to Egypt as surely as these peaks stand in Palestine.

19. Daughter; i.e., the Egyptians (cf. v. 11). **Noph.** See note on 2:16. **20. Destruction.** Better, *a gadfly*. A stinging insect will come to plague the fair heifer. **21. Hired men**; i.e., mercenary soldiers.

22. The voice thereof shall go like a serpent. Better, *her sound is like that of a serpent going*.

23. It cannot be searched. *It is impenetrable*. **Grasshoppers.** For the severity of a locust plague, see notes on Joel 1:1–2:27.

25. The multitude of No. Better, *Amun of Thebes*. The god Amun, by this time identified with Re, the sun-god, was worshiped at Thebes (modern Luxor). He was now almost a national god (cf. Nah 3:8). **Them that trust in him**; i.e., Egypt's satellite states. **26. Afterward it shall be inhabited.** Egypt will be restored and not become a perpetual ruin (cf. Ezk 29:13-15).

4) Israel's Salvation. 46:27,28.

The prophets frequently add a favorable oracle concerning Israel after a denunciation of a foreign nation (cf. Ob 17-21). These verses are also found in Jer 30:10,11 (cf. notes there).

B. Oracle Against the Philistines. 47:1-7.

The Philistines inhabited that part of the coastal area of Palestine called the Philistine Plain. Their five cities were Ekron, Ashdod, Ashkelon, Gaza, and Gath. Although David subjugated the Philistines to some extent, during the Divided Kingdom their cities maintained their independence of Judah. On the Assyrian inscriptions they are mentioned as formidable peoples. The many campaigns fought in the Philistine Plain from the Assyrian period through the time of Alexander the Great caused the gradual attrition of the Philistines. Those who were left were conquered by the Maccabees (second half of the second century B.C.) and absorbed into the Hebrew people. Other oracles against the Philistines are found in Amos 1:6-8; Isa 14:28-31; Ezk 25:15-17; Zeph 2:4-7.

1. Before...Pharaoh smote Gaza. Perhaps this occurred during the campaign in which Josiah lost his life at Megiddo (II Kgs 23:29,30). **2. Out of the north.** The Babylonians were a menace not to Judah alone, but to the whole Levant. See Introduction, *The Foe from the North.*

4. Tyrus and Zidon. Tyre and Sidon were the chief Phoenician cities, located on the coast of what is now Lebanon. They were great centers of maritime trade, and vigorously resisted Assyrian and Babylonian conquest. Although friendly with the Hebrews during the United Kingdom, they later became bitter enemies. Some prophetic oracles against them are: Amos 1:9,10; Joel 3:4-8; Isa 23:15-18; Jer 27:1-11; Ezk 26–28. Why Tyre and Sidon are mentioned in connection with the Philistines is not known; possibly they were allies. **The remnant of the country of Caphtor. Caphtor** is usually identified with Crete, the supposed home of the Philistines before their migration to Palestine (Amos 9:7; Deut 2:23).

5. Baldness. Perhaps a figurative statement indicating that Gaza would be razed to the ground. Or possibly it is a sign of mourning for destruction (cf. 16:5 note). **With the remnant of their valley.** This phrase is difficult to understand. The LXX reads, *O remnant of the Anakim,* which represents a change of only one Hebrew letter. The Anakim were aboriginal dwellers in Palestine (cf. Josh 11:21,22). **Cut thyself.** See note on 16:5. **7. The sea shore**; i.e., the Philistine Plain.

C. Oracle Against Moab. 48:1-47.

The Moabites were descendants of Moab, Lot's son (Gen 19:37). They lived in Trans-Jordan, east of the Dead Sea. Close neighbors of the Hebrews, they were frequently in conflict with them; for the Hebrews claimed control over the Moabite territory, and asserted this claim when they were strong. Nebuchadnezzar subjugated the Moabites, who then disappeared as a nation. Other prophetic oracles against Moab are: Isa 15; 16; Jer 9:26; 25:21; 27:3; Ezk 25:8-11; Amos 2:1-3; Zeph 2:8-11. This oracle is longer than the others in this section, and has been noted to contain resemblances to Isa 15; 16. Perhaps the invasion of Moabites (among others) into Judah during Jehoiakim's reign (II

Kgs 24:2) is the background against which the oracle should be understood. Of the many Moabite place names that occur here, only the more significant will receive comment.

1. Nebo. A mountain peak across the Jordan from Jericho. **2. In Heshbon they have devised evil.** A play on words. The verb translated **they have devised evil** sounds like **Heshbon.** This city alternated between Moabite and Israelite control. It contained famous reservoirs (Song 7:4). **Be cut down, O Madmen.** Another play on words. **Madmen** is an unknown place name. **Be cut down.** Better, *be brought to silence.* **5. The going up of Luhith.** *The ascent to Luhith,* a town. **The going down of Horonaim.** *The descent to Horonaim.* **6. The heath in the wilderness** is a symbol of destruction and loneliness (cf. 17:6 note).

7. Chemosh. The national god of Moab (cf. vv. 13,46; Num 21:29; I Kgs 11:7, 33; II Kgs 23:13). Idols were frequently taken captive with the people who worshiped them (cf. Jer 43:12; Isa 46:1,2).

8. Valley. The Jordan Valley, near the Dead Sea. **Plain.** The tableland where the Moabites lived.

11. He hath settled on his lees. Moab was so isolated that it had not experienced the discipline of frequent invasions and captivity. The figure comes from wine-making. The wine would be "fined" by being poured from jar to jar through a strainer. Moab had never been so purified, and was like wine with **lees** or sediment in it. **12. Wanderers that shall cause him to wander.** Better, *tilters who will tilt* (i.e., decant) *him,* carrying out the picture of the preceding verse. But in Moab's case, this straining would be disastrous; for the careless tilters would break the jars, and Moab would perish. **13. Beth-el.** A reference to the worship center made by Jeroboam I at Bethel, a religious stumbling block to the nation of Israel (I Kgs 12:26-33).

18. Dibon. Modern Diban, thirteen miles east of the Dead Sea, near the Arnon River. Here was discovered the famous Moabite Stone. **20. In Arnon.** *By the Arnon* River. A perennial stream that falls into the Dead Sea about halfway between its northern and southern extremities. **21. Plain country.** See note on 48:8. **22. Nebo.** See note on 48:1. **25. Horn.** A symbol of military strength and political power, probably derived from bulls, which push with their horns.

26. Drunken. See note on 25:15. **28. The sides of the hole's mouth.** *The sides of the gorge* (of the Arnon). The Moabites would lead a hunted and precarious existence. **30. Wrath.** *Arrogance.* **His lies shall not so effect it.** *His boastings shall not accomplish* (anything).

32,33. Moab's coming desolation is pictured as that of a ruined vineyard. *More than for Jazer I weep for you, O vine of Sibmah! Your branches passed over the sea* (v. 32, RSV). **Jazer** and **Sibmah** were places near Heshbon noted for their vineyards. **Summer fruits.** See note on 8:20.

34. Zoar. Evidently Lot's city of refuge still existed at this time (Gen 19:20-22). It has been identified with el-Keryeh, southeast of the Dead Sea. **As an heifer of three years old.** Better, *and Eglath-shelishiyeh*—another place name. **35. High places.** See note on 3:6. **36. Pipes;** i.e., flutes used for playing funeral dirges. **37.** For these mourning practices, see note on 16:5.

40. He shall fly; i.e., the destroying enemy shall come. **42. Shall be destroyed.** On Moab's fate, see the introductory paragraph to this chapter. **45.** This verse seems to be dependent on Num 21:28,29; 24:17. The thought seems to be that the Moabite refugees would flee to the fortress of Heshbon, but even there they would be destroyed. **Sihon** (Num 21:21-30) is mentioned to recall the Amorite defeat at Heshbon long before. **46. People of Chemosh.** See note on 48:7. **47. Yet will I bring again the captivity of Moab.** Moab would not completely perish, for a remnant of Moab will be found in the Kingdom of God (cf. 46:26; 49:6,39). **Bring . . . captivity.** See note on 29:14.

D. Oracle Against the Ammonites. 49:1-6.

The Ammonites were descended from Ben-ammi, son of Lot (Gen 19:38). They lived in Trans-Jordan, between the Arnon and the Jabbok rivers, eastward toward the desert. They, like the Moabites, frequently fought the Hebrews. They showed their hostility during the reign of Jehoiakim (II Kgs 24:2), and helped to destroy the refugee community after the fall of Jerusalem (Jer 40:11-14). Other oracles against them are found in Ezk 21:20; 25:1-7; Amos 1:13-15; Zeph 2:8-11.

1. Hath Israel no sons? This is probably a reference to the capture of Trans-Jordan from the Northern Kingdom by the Assyrians in 732 B.C. (II Kgs 15:29). Upon the deportation of the Israelites, the Ammonites moved into the territory of Gad—that part of Trans-Jordan between the Arnon and the Jabbok, near the Jordan. **Their king.** If the vowels of this word are changed, it reads *Milcom,* the god of the Ammonites (I Kgs 11:5,7,33; II Kgs 23:13). The Greek, Syriac, and Latin Bibles support this change.

2. Rabbah. The chief city of the Ammonites, now called Amman, the capital of the Kingdom of Jordan. **Heap.** See note on 30:18. **Daughters.** Nearby villages which lived in dependence upon Rabbah.

3. Heshbon, while only five or six miles from the Ammonite border, was controlled by the Amorite king Sihon when Israel came (Num 21:25-30,34). Later it passed into Moabite hands (cf. 48:2 note). **Ai.** It appears that an Ammonite place by that name (not the Ai captured by Joshua, Josh 8:1-29) is meant. It is nowhere else referred to. **Hedges.** Enclosures for sheep. **Their king.** See note on 49:1.

4. That trusted in her treasures. The verse expresses the confidence of a people living in such a remote, inaccessible land that invasion seemed impossible.

6. I will bring again. See note on 48:47.

E. Oracle Against Edom. 49:7-22.

The Edomites were descendants of Esau, who was also called Edom (Gen 36:1-19). They lived in the land of Seir, or Edom, a very rugged, mountainous country, extending south of the Dead Sea, on both sides of the Arabah, to the Gulf of Akabah. The relations between the Hebrew kingdoms and the Edomites were never happy. The latter rejoiced over Jerusalem's destruction (Ps 137:7), and afterward occupied southern Judah. They were in turn dispossessed by the Nabateans. The Maccabees successfully warred against the Edomites, and forced those who remained to become Jews. Other prophecies against the Edomites are found in Ezk 25:12-14; 35:1-15; Joel 3:19; Amos 9:12; Ob 1-16. Parts of this section closely resemble parts of Obadiah's prophecy.

7. Teman. A tribe of Edomites known for their wisdom (cf. Job 2:11). **8. Dedan** A tribe dwelling south of Edom, known for commercial interests (Ezk 25:13; 27:15,20; 38:13; Isa 21:13; Jer 25:23). Possibly the name still remains as Daidan, in the Arabian desert. **Visit.** *Punish.* **9,10.** Edom would be stripped "clean," with nothing left even for gleaners. **12.** Edom, because of her complicity in Jerusalem's fall (Ob 10-14) was especially guilty (cf. 25:15 note, 28).

16. Clefts of the rock . . . height of the hill. A reference to the high mountain fastness of Edom. **Rock.** *Sela',* the Hebrew name of Petra, the principal city of the Edomites (cf. Ob 3).

19-21. These verses are repeated in 50:44-46, where they are applied to Babylon. Verse 19 is difficult to interpret. It apparently says that Edom's enemy will come up against her from the Jordan Valley, but he will run away from her—it is not stated why. God will make His chosen one ruler over Edom. **He shall come up;** i.e., Edom's conqueror. **The swelling of the Jordan.** *The jungle of the Jordan* (cf. 12:5 note). **Teman** (v. 20). See note on 49:7. **Shall draw them out.** *Shall drag them away.*

F. Oracle Against Damascus. 49:23-27.

Damascus was the chief city of Syria. Little is known about it at the time of Jeremiah. Amos 1:3-5 records a prophecy against it.

23. Hamath. Modern Hamah, on the Orontes river, 120 miles north of Damascus. Originally a Hittite city, by this time it was a part of Syria. **Arpad.** A city near Hamath (cf. Isa 10:9). **Sorrow on the sea.** Syria had no sea coast in ancient times. The expression is a metaphor for restlessness and trouble. **It cannot be quiet.** This is the same Hebrew expression translated *it cannot rest* in Isa 57:20.

25. Damascus was considered one of the most beautiful cities of ancient times. Its springs make it a large oasis in the Syrian desert. **27. Ben-hadad.** The name of several Damascene kings (I Kgs 15:18,20; II Kgs 13:24).

G. Oracle Against Kedar and Hazor. 49:28-33.

This oracle is directed against Arab tribes. **Kedar** and **Hazor** are not mentioned among the nations in the oracle of Jeremiah 25, but verses 23,24 of that chapter seem to refer to the same peoples. Little is known of the early history of the desert peoples to the east of Palestine, whom we now call Arabs.

28. Kedar. An Ishmaelite desert tribe (Gen 25:13; Isa 21:13,16; 60:7; Ezk

27:21. Cf. Jer 2:10 note). **The kingdoms of Hazor.** This can hardly refer to the great fortress Hazor in northern Palestine (Josh 11:1-13; 12:19), for it is here used of a desert area. There is no other mention in Scripture of a desert Hazor. **Shall smite.** Earlier, the Assyrians made campaigns against the Arabs, and Josephus refers to a conquest of Arabia by Nabuchadnezzar. **29. Fear on every side.** A favorite expression of Jeremiah (cf. 6:25; 20:3,10; 46:5).

31. Arise, get you up. A commission to the Babylonians to plunder the desert peoples. **32. That are in the utmost corners.** Better, *who cut the corners* (of their hair). See note on 9:26. **33. Dragons.** *Jackals.*

H. Oracle Against Elam. 49:34-39.

Little is known about Elam in the time of Jeremiah. The land of Elam is located beyond the Tigris River, east of Babylonia. It had been conquered by the Assyrians. The Elamites may at this time have been planning a campaign against Babylon. Ezekiel 32:24,25 also mentions Elam.

35. The bow. The Elamites were famous for their skill in archery (cf. Isa 22:6). **38. I will set my throne;** i.e., I will judge (cf. 1:15). **39.** See note on 48:47.

I. Oracle Against Babylon. 50:1–51:64.

This lengthy oracle has two themes—the fall of Babylon and the return of the Jews from Babylonian exile. To argue that it could not have been written by Jeremiah because of the severity of the language against the Babylonians is to misunderstand the prophet. He was not "pro-Babylonian." As God's spokesman he did indeed urge the submission of the Jews to Nebuchadnezzar, God's punishing servant (27:6). Here, he predicts that the heathen nation of Babylon will itself be punished for her pride and rapacity. Babylon fell in 539 B.C. to the armies of Cyrus the Persian without a battle. Cyrus reversed the old Assyro-Babylonian policy of deportation by issuing a series of decrees permitting captive peoples to return to their homelands. The Jews were permitted to end their exile and rebuild Jerusalem.

2. Bel . . . Merodach. Bel is a title meaning *lord* and seems to have been applied at this time to Marduk, the chief god of Babylon, called in the OT **Merodach.** He was a sun-god and, according to the Babylonian creation myth, the creator of the world. **3. Out of the north.** Evidently an allusion to the Persians, who came from the east. Perhaps by this time **north** had become to the Jews a sinister term for the place of origin of all evil. (Cf. Introduction, *The Foe from the North.)*

4. See notes on 31:7-9. **5. Perpetual covenant.** Cf. 31:31-34; 32:40. **6. Shepherds.** See note on 23:1. **8. He goats** are the leaders of the flock. Let the Jews lead the return of captive peoples to their homes.

9. North country. See note on 50:3. **12,13.** Cyrus did not destroy Babylon when he captured it. Later in the Persian period the city revolted, and Darius Hystaspis captured it and destroyed its walls (514 B.C.), thus beginning its decay. The city continued to decline until well into the Christian era, when it ceased to exist. The desolate ruins remained for archaeologists to uncover in the nineteenth century. **15. Walls.** See note on 50:2. **16. Sower.** Babylon was located in a fertile, irrigated farming land. With the destruction of the central authority, the system of irrigation canals became silted up, so that today the area resembles a desert.

19. The fertility of the land to which scattered Israel was to be restored is set forth here. **Carmel** means *the garden land.* The Trans-Jordan areas of **Gilead** and **Bashan** were known for their pasturage and forests (Deut 32:14; Isa 2:13; Mic 7:14; Zech 11:2). The hills of **Ephraim** contained much good agricultural land.

21. Merathaim . . . Pekod. These names represent plays on words on the names of Babylonian localities. **Merathaim** means *double bitterness,* and is a play on *mât marrâti,* a name applied to southern Babylonia. **Pekod** means *punishment,* and refers to the name of a tribe in eastern Babylonia, the *Puqūdu* (cf. Ezk 23:23). **25. The weapons of his indignation.** Cf. Isa 13:5. **31. Visit.** *Punish.* **34. Redeemer;** i.e., Deliverer from Babylonian captivity (cf. Isa 43:14; Prov 23:11).

36. Dote. *Become fools.* **38. Drought.** See note on 50:16. **39,40.** Travelers say that these words are still true of the ruins of Babylon. The Bedouins avoid them as the haunt of wild animals and evil spirits (cf. Isa 13:19-22).

41. From the north. See on 50:3. **44-46.** See note on 49:19-21. **He shall come**

up (v. 44). Cyrus is referred to. **Swelling of Jordan.** See on 12:5.

51:1,2. God's judgment on Babylon is likened to threshers and the wind that winnows the grain on an Oriental threshing floor (cf. 51:33; Ps 1:4). **The midst of them that rise up against me** (v. 1). The Hebrew is *lēb qāmāy,* a cipher for "Chaldea," used in the same manner as the cipher of 25:26. Translate: "and against the inhabitants of Chaldea." **A destroying wind.** An apt picture of Cyrus. **Fanners . . . fan** (v. 2). *Winnowers . . . winnow.*

3. Brigandine. See on 46:4. **6. Deliver every man his soul.** *Let every man save his life.* **Iniquity.** *Punishment.* **7.** The wine of the Lord's wrath (cf. 25:15-17 note). **10. Our righteousness;** i.e., our vindication or victory (cf. 23:6 note).

11. Make bright. Polishing the arrows would sharpen them. **Medes.** An ancient people living south of the Caspian Sea and east of the northern part of Mesopotamia. They had joined with the Babylonians to destroy Nineveh. Together with the Persians, the Medes (both Aryan nations) overthrew Babylon in 539 B.C. And the Medo-Persian empire succeeded the Babylonian (cf. Isa 13:17-19; 21:2,9; Dan 5:28,31; 8:20).

13. Many waters. A reference to the Euphrates and its many canals (cf. 50:16 note). **14. Caterpillers.** *Locusts* (cf. Joel 1:1–2:27). **15-19.** These verses are repeated from 10:12-16. See notes there.

20-23. These verses may be addressed to Cyrus (cf. Isa 41:2-4).

25. O destroying mountain. Babylon was situated on a plain. **Mountain** here is a symbol for a powerful kingdom (cf. Dan 2:35,44). **27. Ararat, Minni, and Ashchenaz** were peoples north of Babylonia who were conquered by the Medes in the sixth century. They are here summoned to aid the Medes (v. 28) in battle against Babylon. **Ararat.** The land roughly equivalent to Armenia, north of Lake Van. **Minni.** A people near the Ararat kingdom, east of Lake Van. **Ashchenaz** (Ashkenaz). Said to be descended from Gomer (Gen 10:3). **Ashchenaz** is identified by some with the fierce Scythians. **Caterpiller.** See note on verse 14. **28. Medes.** See note on verse 11.

31. At one end. *On every side.* **32. Passages.** *Fords.*

34. Dragon. *Monster.* **My delicates.** *My delicacies.* **36. Dry up.** Cf. note on 50:16. **37. Dragons.** *Jackals.* **39. In their heat.** *When they are inflamed.* This verse succinctly describes the fall of Babylon as recorded in Daniel 5.

41. Sheshach. See note on 25:26. **42. Sea . . . waves.** Figurative language to describe the overflowing enemy armies (cf. v. 25 note). **44. Bel.** See on 50:2. **That which he hath swallowed up;** i.e., the people deported from their homelands to Babylon would return home again.

45. Deliver ye every man his soul. See note on 51:6. **46. And** (beware) **lest your heart faint.** A time of anxiety would precede Babylon's fall. God's people should patiently await the outcome. **48. The north.** See on 50:3. **55. Waves.** See on 51:42.

59-64. An appendix to the oracle against Babylon. Seraiah was to perform a symbolic action in the prophet's place (cf. 13:1-11). **Seraiah the son of Neriah** (v. 59). This **Seraiah** is to be distinguished from the one who helped arrest Jeremiah (36:26), from the high priest of the same name (52:24-27), and also from the Seraiah of 40:8. The Seraiah of this verse was the brother of Baruch, Jeremiah's secretary (32:12). **In the fourth year.** This Babylonian journey is not recorded elsewhere. It has been supposed that Zedekiah went at this time to clear himself of suspicion of complicity in a revolt. It is not unusual for puppet rulers of satellite countries to visit the capital of the empire occasionally. **A quiet prince.** Perhaps this is a title: "quartermaster."

IV. Appendix: The Fall of Jerusalem, and Related Events. 52:1-34.

This chapter is almost identical with II Kgs 24:18–25:30. Material in II Kgs which is omitted here is given in Jer 40:7–43:7 (cf. 39:1 note). Probably this appendix was added to the Book of Jeremiah to show how the prophet's message of doom was fulfilled.

1) The Reign of Zedekiah. 52:1-3.

1. Zedekiah. Cf. Introduction, *Historical Background of the Prophet;* and see on 1:3. **His mother's name.** See note on 13:18. **Jeremiah.** Obviously not the prophet. **2. Jehoiakim.** Cf. Introduction, *Historical Background of the Prophet;* and see on 1:3.

2) The Siege and Fall of Jerusalem. 52:4-27.

7. In desperation Zedekiah and his guard sought to flee through the desolate valleys leading down to the Arabah (**plain,** AV)—that geological fault in which the Jordan and the Dead Sea are located. Crossing the Jordan, they would seek to hide themselves in the desolate reaches of Trans-Jordan. **King's garden.** Located in the south of the city, near the Kidron Valley, which leads down to the Dead Sea. **8. The plains of Jericho.** It is amazing that the king and his entourage succeeded in eluding the siege forces and fleeing so far. **9. Riblah in the land of Hamath.** A city (probably Ribleh on the Orontes River, thirty-six miles northeast of Ba'al-bek) where the Babylonians maintained their field headquarters (II Kgs 25:6,7,21).

12. Fifth month . . . tenth day. According to II Kgs 25:8, these events took place on the seventh day of the fifth month. The Jewish fast of the Ninth of Ab (August) recalls both this destruction of Jerusalem and that by Titus in A.D. 70. **Nineteenth year.** 587 B.C. **Nebuzar-adan.** See on 39:9.

16. Poor of the land. For what happened to these people afterwards, see Jer 40–45.

17-23. The sacred vessels were carried captive to Babylon (cf. I Kgs 6–8).

24. Seraiah. See on 51:59. **Zephaniah.** See on 29:25. **25. Eunuch.** See on 38:7. **The principal scribe of the host.** *The secretary of the commander of the army.*

27. These men were executed for revolt against the empire, for the Babylonians had looked upon Judah as a subject state for some years, at least since 605 B.C.

3) The Three Deportations. 52:28-30. Much of this information is unique to this passage.

28. The First Deportation. This deportation is described in II Kgs 24:12-16. There the number of deportees is given as "ten thousand." The discrepancy is reconciled by some by the supposition that the figure in II Kings is for the number taken from Jerusalem; the number in Jeremiah tells how many arrived in Babylon, the rest having failed to survive the journey. II Kings indicates the eighth year of Nebuchadnezzar as the date; Jeremiah, the **seventh. On this,** compare the note on verse 29.

29. The Second Deportation. This one occurred in Nebuchadnezzar's **eighteenth year;** that is, the time of the destruction of the city (587 B.C.), called the nineteenth year in verse 12. The systems of dating based on the year of the king's reign are very confusing. Sometimes the year in which the king began to reign was accounted his first; at other times (and places) the first full year (i.e., the year which began at the first New Year's celebration after the king's accession) was considered his first year. This fact would seem to explain some of the one-year discrepancies in the chronology of the Babylonian period (cf. v. 28 note).

30. The Third Deportation. Not mentioned elsewhere. It may have been caused by a Babylonian expedition to punish the Jews for the disturbances at the time of Gedaliah's assassination (cf. chs. 40; 41; 40:7 note). **Nebuzar-adan.** See on 39:9.

4) Jehoiachin's Release from Prison. 52:31-34.

This section is repeated in II Kgs 25:27-30 (cf. Jer 22:24-30). After a three-month reign, Jehoiachin was carried captive to Babylon (II Kgs 24:8-17). He never returned. Seals found in Palestine lead us to infer that the Judeans continued to consider him as the reigning king, and Zedekiah (his uncle) merely as a regent. Cuneiform tablets found in Babylon confirm this story of Jehoiachin's pension (cf. 22:30 note).

31. Evil-merodach. The son and successor of Nebuchadnezzar. **Lifted up the head.** The Hebrew expression (here translated quite literally) means that Jehoiachin was looked upon with favor by Evil-merodach and allowed to *see the face of the king*—the literal meaning of the phrase translated **that were near the king's person** (v. 25). To see the king's face (in court) was the greatest favor one in politics could hope to gain (cf. Gen 40:13,20; contrast Est 7:8). **34. A continual diet given him.** This is the ancient way of saying that Jehoiachin lived at government expense; he was pensioned.

BIBLIOGRAPHY

BALL, C. J., and BENNETT, W. H. *The Book of Jeremiah (The Expositors' Bible)*. New York: George H. Doran Co., n. d.

LATSCH, THEODORE. *Jeremiah*. St. Louis: Concordia Publishing House, 1952.

LESLIE, ELMER A. *Jeremiah*. New York: Abingdon Press, 1954.

PEAKE, A. S. (ed.). *Jeremiah and Lammentations (The New Century Bible)*. Edinburgh: T. C. & E. C. Jack, 1910.

SMITH, GEORGE ADAM. *Jeremiah*. 4th ed. Garden City: Doubleday, Doran & Co., 1929.

LAMENTATIONS

INTRODUCTION

The five chapters of Lamentations are five beautiful and solemn elegies, or songs of mourning, expressing the anguish of the Jewish people at the sight of the utter ruin of their city, its Temple, and its population, under the conquering Babylonians in 586 B.C.

Title. The title of this book in Hebrew is the first word of chapters 1, 2, and 4 — *'êkâ,* literally, *Ah, how!* or *Alas!* In the Greek version of the Old Testament, the Septuagint (LXX), the Book of Lamentations is associated with the prophecy of Jeremiah, as it is in our English Bible. But in the Hebrew Bible it is placed among the books that make up the third division of the sacred writings. Our Lord spoke of this threefold arrangement as "the law . . . the prophets, and the psalms" (Lk 24:44).

The Greek title for these poems in the LXX is *thrēnoi,* the plural of *thrēnos,* "a lamentation." This noun comes from the Greek verb *threomai,* to "cry aloud, or lament." The Hebrew term for lamentation is *qînâ,* and the peculiar meter of the poems in this book is called *qînôt* meter. It is the Hebrew equivalent of our English term, "elegiac" meter. So in the Babylonian Talmud the book appears under the title *Qînôt*—"Lamentations." The title of this book in the Latin Bible is *Liber Threnorum*, "The Book of Lamentations." English "threnody" means "lamentation" or "dirge."

Literary Form and Style. The book consists of five beautiful poems, one for each chapter. The first four are dirges, but the fifth is more like a prayer poem. The first four are alphabetical (acrostic) in arrangement, each having twenty-two stanzas (verses in AV, except chapter 3, where each stanza is divided into three verses), and each stanza begins with a letter of the Hebrew alphabet. The fifth chapter also has twenty-two stanzas but lacks the alphabetical arrangement. (Compare the alphabetical arrangement of the sections in Ps 119.) In chapter 1 of Lamentations the verses follow the established order of the Hebrew alphabet, but in chapters 2 and 4 the positions of the letters *ayin* and *pe* are transposed. No satisfactory explanation has been found for this transposition.

In chapters 1 and 2 each stanza has three members, but only the first begins with the appropriate letter of the alphabet. In chapter 3 each stanza has three members, each of which begins with the same letter of the alphabet. Since each member is numbered separately in our English Bibles, we have sixty-six verses for the third chapter. Chapter 4 has stanzas of two members, but here again only the first member starts with the appropriate Hebrew letter. In the first four chapters the elegiac meter is used, wherein the second of the two parallel elements (lines in English poetry) is one beat shorter than the first. This gives, usually, a four-beat verse balanced with a three-beat verse or line. In chapter 5 the normal Hebrew meter is used, with four beats to each verse, or each half of the parallelism.

Threnodies in such "limping meter" were used in Bible times by the mourning women in funeral dirges at wakes for the dead. And so chanting songs set to such plaintive, melancholy cadences seemed an appropriate way to mourn the destruction of beloved Jerusalem, now lying a heap of ruins. Perhaps this helps to explain why these national hymns breathe such exquisite pathos and have been constructed with such conscious art. The Hebrew elegiac verse form is admirably suited to express the national woe. In these patriotic hymns we hear the death wail of smitten Zion.

In style there is much use of parallelism in these poems, much repetition, antithesis, and apostrophe, and a play on words and phrases. Vivid imagery throbs throughout. The reader is thus made to see the suffering and feel the pain of widowed, weeping Zion.

Authorship. Although the book itself does not name its author, II Chronicles 35:25 definitely connects Jeremiah with the lamentation type of literature. Our Book of Lamentations is not the lamentation of Jeremiah over the death of the good king Josiah, as some have suggested. But there are definite points of similarity between Lamentations and the poetical sections of Jeremiah's prophecy. And from ancient times the book has been attributed to Jeremiah. The LXX carries the following note as a superscription to the first verse of the first chapter of Lamentations: "And it came to pass, after Israel was led into captivity and Jerusalem laid waste, that Jeremiah sat weeping and lamented with this lamentation over Jerusalem, and said . . ." Then follows the first verse of the first chapter. Some scholars feel that the Hebraic character of this sentence suggests that these words came from a Hebrew original which is lost to us.

Let it be noted that the same sensitivity to national sorrow is to be found in both Lamentations and Jeremiah's prophecy. In both writings the national calamities are referred to the same causes – national sin, and the vain confidence of the people in weak and treacherous allies, along with the guilt of her false prophets and lax priests. Similar imagery runs throughout both writings. The characteristic phrase, "daughter of," occurs about twenty times in each book. The prophet's weeping, his fears as he appeals for aid to God, the righteous Judge, and his expectation that eventually Jerusalem's enemies will be punished – all are manifestly prominent in both books. These similarities of expression argue identity of authorship. Though a number of outstanding scholars reject the idea that Jeremiah was the author of these poems, many others equally important strongly favor Jeremiah as the author.

The vividness of description argues for the book's having been composed at a time very close to the fall of Jerusalem by one who lived through that terrible catastrophe and wrote while his heart was still sore and each horrible detail was still fresh in his mind. This fact, also, points toward Jeremiah as the most likely author.

The occasion for such a book is most assuredly the destruction of the city of Jerusalem in 586 B.C., and therefore the date of the writing could not have been many months afterward.

Religious Import and Usage. The Book of Lamentations represents the death wail of Jerusalem, pictured as a widowed and disgraced princess. It is interesting to recall that following the destruction of Jerusalem by the Romans in A.D. 70, the arch of triumph built as a memorial of that conquest by the Roman general Titus pictured Judah as a woman weeping and disheveled, seated upon the ground in mourning. Recall also that the daughters of Jerusalem sought to wail such a dirge over Jesus at his death (Lk 23:27-31). Certain portions of Lamentations have been interpreted as applying to the passion of Christ. Indeed the use of these national songs indicates that the Jewish people accepted a religious interpretation of the destruction of their city. The Jews include this writing among the Five Scrolls to be read on important anniversary days. The day set for the reading of Lamentations is the ninth of Ab, which commemorates the burning of the Temple. But always verse 21 of chapter 5 is repeated after verse 22, so that the reading may close on a more positive note. Among Roman Catholics the time appointed for the reading of Lamentations is the last three days of Holy Week. Protestant Christians, one regrets to say, have too often neglected the reading of these solemn poems. Yet in these days of personal, national, and international crises (and disaster) the message of this book is a challenge to repent of sins personal, national, and international, and to commit ourselves afresh to God's steadfast love. Though this love is ever present and outgoing, a holy and just God must surely judge unrepentant sinners.

OUTLINE

"The Sorrows of Captive Zion"

I. The suffering, ruined city of Zion. 1:1-22.
   A. Wretched condition of devastated Jerusalem. 1:1-11.
   B. Lament of the "daughter of Jerusalem." 1:12-22.
II. The suffering, ruined holy place of Zion. 2:1-22.
   A. Jehovah's judgments upon the ramparts and upon his sanctuary. 2:1-10.
   B. Lament of the eyewitness of this judgment. 2:11-19.
   C. Terrors of this day of Jehovah's anger. 2:20-22.

III. The suffering representative of smitten Zion. 3:1-66.
   A. The sorrows God sent his servant. 3:1-18..
   B. The servant's prayer of reassurance. 3:19-42.
   C. The servant's prayer for vindication. 3:43-66.
IV. The suffering people of Zion. 4:1-22.
   A. Horrors of the siege, and the sad fate of Zion's nobility. 4:1-11.
   B. Causes and climax of Zion's catastrophe. 4:12-20.
   C. An apostrophe to haughty and gloating Edom. 4:21,22.
V. Supplications of penitent Zion. 5:1-22.
   A. Zion's plea to Jehovah to regard her affliction and disgrace. 5:1-18.
   B. A final apostrophe to the eternal Sovereign. 5:19-22.

COMMENTARY

I. The Ruined City of Zion. 1:1-22.

A. Wretched Condition of Devasted Jerusalem. 1:1-11. **How doth the city sit solitary.** See Introduction, paragraph 2. **1,2. Princess among the provinces.** No longer foremost among the provinces of the land, Judah sits a tributary widow, bereft of her children and betrayed by friends and allies, lonely and desolate, and weeping bitterly, with none to comfort her (cf. the reverse in Ezr 4:20). **3. Judah is gone into captivity.** Exile and slavery are made worse by the pagan environment. Isaiah's prophecy has come true (Isa 39:5-7; 47:8,9).

4-6. From the daughter of Zion . . . beauty is departed (v. 6). The poet's description is graphic. Her approaches are forsaken, her feasts unattended, her gates (places of assembly) deserted, her priests are in anguish, her virgins have been dragged away, and she herself suffers bitterly. The divine judgment upon her sins has given her enemies the upper hand as they force her children into exile ahead of them. Her princes, like stags without pasture, are quite unable to escape the pursuer. (The sons of Zedekiah were captured and slain in the sight of their father, whose eyes were then put out; Jer 39:4-7). **7. Jerusalem remembered.** The memory of better days only increases Zion's present sorrows, especially when she is mocked by those who watch with delight. **Sabbaths.** Better, *destruction,* as in the Berkeley Version.

8-11. Jerusalem hath grievously sinned. Sin never brings ultimate happiness. Jerusalem, despised and desecrated by those who formerly honored her, turns her back in naked shame, for corruption and carelessness have brought their tragic consequences. Pagans have plundered her temple utensils, and people morally and ceremonially unclean have invaded her sanctuary in defiance of Jehovah's ordinance. Groaning for food, the people trade their valuables for mere sustenance. (Note the two apostrophes to Jehovah in vv. 9,11.)

B. Lament of the "Daughter of Jerusalem." 1:12-22. The disaster at God's hands is severe but deserved, as the speaker acknowledges.

12. The day of his fierce anger. Most moderns want to ignore the severity of the divine nature. They fail to recognize that real goodness is not indulgent of evil. **13-16. From above . . . fire into my bones** (v. 13). The daughter of Judah recounts her sufferings endured at the hand of the Lord – fever in her limbs, a snare for her feet, frustration and faintness all day. God has woven her sins into a yoke of subjugation and slavery. Wine for the feast of Judah's foes is the blood of her men of valor trodden out in the wine press of affliction. Hence Judah weeps, uncomforted and unrevived, for her perishing children over whom her enemies have prevailed.

17-19. My lovers . . . deceived me (v. 19). Zion's hands outstretched for help are unheeded, for the righteous command of Jehovah has made enemies of all her lovers (cf. Lev 15:19-27). Jacob's neighbors, now adversaries, treat Jerusalem as a thing unclean. Zion reaps the reward of her rebellion. Her priests and elders, seeking a bare subsistence, have died of hunger; and her young men and maidens are captives. **20-22. Behold, O Lord; for I am in distress . . . none to comfort me.** Zion's plea for vindication. The sword is in her streets and the silence of death is in every home. May her exultant enemies fare likewise, she prays. "Give them as many groanings and a heart just as sore."

II. The Ruined Holy Place of Zion. 2:1-22.

A. Jehovah's Judgments upon the Ramparts and upon His Sanctuary. 2:1-10.

1-5. How hath the Lord covered the daughter of Zion with a cloud. Zion's God has become Zion's enemy. Jehovah in wrath has destroyed the Temple, **his footstool** (I Chr 28:2), **the beauty of Israel.** The boundaries of Jacob are broken down, the strongholds of Judah leveled, and the kingdom with its princes has been degraded. God has become a consuming fire (Heb 12:29; Deut 4:24) to the land simply by withdrawing his power in the presence of her enemies. And like an archer hunting his prey, he has slain everything of youth, beauty, and rank. His fury has burned like a fire in the tabernacle (tent) of Zion. The divine Adversary has gobbled up Judah, her palaces and fortresses, and multiplied to the daughter of Judah **moaning and mourning** *(wails and woe).*

6-10. Violently taken away his tabernacle. That is, his Temple and its sacred institutions. Tabernacle, assembly, Sabbath, king, and priest—all have been despised and violently demolished. The Lord has discarded his own altar, despised his sanctuary, given into enemy hands the ark of the covenant, and allowed the shout of conquest to resound in the House of Jehovah like the sound of an orgy. In his determination to destroy the wall of Zion, his plumb line of judgment has caused both the ramparts and the walls to totter and fall. Zion's gates are sunken, her bars broken, her nobles exiled; her Law is suspended and no longer taught, and her prophets are without revelation. Hence Judah's elders, in their grief, sit silent on the ground, with dust on their heads and burlap on their loins; while her virgins hang their heads for shame.

B. Lament of the Eyewitness of This Judgment. 2:11-19.

11,12. Mine eyes do fail with tears. A graphic portrayal of protracted emotional distress: eyes exhausted with tears (Jer 9:1; 14:17), sympathies outraged, heart broken at the sight of babies swooning, small children crying for food and drink, and — worst of all — infants breathing out their lives on their mothers' breasts. **13,14. What shall I equal to thee?** The witness of these sufferings is at a loss to find a figure or a situation with which to compare Zion's ruin. It is beyond repair. The false and flattering vision of her prophets (Jer 14:14-16; 23:9-40) failed to show the nation her sin, else she might have been spared her captivity. Here we have the moral cause of her misfortune clearly spelled out.

15,16. All that pass by clap their hands. Zion's enemies mock her ruin. The clapping hand, the wagging head, the hissing breath, accompany the spoken jibes at Jerusalem. The enemies, in their gloating, yell and hiss and clench their teeth as they bless the day of her ruin. This is derision unrestrained. **17-19. The Lord hath done that which he had devised,** i.e., what he foretold he would do. Let Zion wail her distress. She rebelled, and he has let her enemies triumph over her. Verses 18,19 are an apostrophe to the wall of the city: Cry day and night with perpetual tears; lift both hands to Jehovah imploring his mercy upon your languishing children.

C. Terrors of This Day of Jehovah's Anger. 2:20-22. Here we have Zion's fourth apostrophe to Jehovah.

20-22. Consider to whom thou hast done this. "O Lord, do You realize whom You have slain?" Children are victims of cannibalistic mothers; priests lie slain in the sanctuary; youth and age lie unburied in the streets; maidens and young men are victims of the sword. In this pitiless killing, which none escapes, these objects of Zion's affections are devoted to the enemy slaughter. (Compare Josephus' description of the fall of Jerusalem in A.D. 70, *Jewish Wars*, Bk. vii.)

III. The Suffering Representative of Smitten Zion. 3:1-66.

This chapter is the mountain peak of the book. Here Jeremiah bares his heart to the reader, as he frequently does in his prophecy. His life was one long martyrdom, in which he served as both judge and intercessor for people bent on their own destruction. No prophet ever pleaded with a people in more impassioned manner, calling for a national conversion, than did he. And no one, except Jesus, was treated with more national contempt than he. These facts are plainly evident in these sixty-six verses of chapter 3.

A. The Sorrows God Sent His Servant. 3:1-18.

1-3. I am the man. Here the sufferer is identified and his theme stated. He speaks as a representative Israelite, facing the dark and baffling ways of Providence. Jehovah's unsparing onslaught against him he describes in verses 4-18.

4-13. He hath broken my bones. Under the tribulation of Jehovah's constant attack upon him, the poet knows only bitterness and frustration. He suffers physically; his light (Ps 143:3) and freedom are gone; his prayers are rejected. All the while Jehovah seems to lurk in ambush for him – like an animal stalking its prey – and at the same time He seems to blockade all the ways of escape. God has thwarted, mangled, and left him. As a target for Jehovah's bow, his vitals are full of arrows.

14-18. I was a derision to all my people. As an object of public derision, his peace of soul and rest in Jehovah have vanished. He is the butt of his people's jokes, and the theme of their daily satire. His abject condition is like that of one stuffed with bitter herbs, drunken with gall (cf. Jer 23:15), his teeth broken on gravel, and his body covered with ashes. His bliss and prosperity are forgotten and his hope in the Eternal is gone.

B. The Servant's Prayer of Reassurance. 3:19-42.

19-21. This I recall to my mind, therefore have I hope (v. 21). The prophet, pondering his bitter afflictions, realizes how they have humbled his soul. He knows that God remembers the humble and afflicted, and so he expresses hope. Verses 22-39 speak of the poet's reassurance in Jehovah's goodness and his resignation to His sovereign ways. **22-24. His compassions fail not.** The loving-kindness (*hesed,* "steadfast love") of Jehovah is unfailing. It is daily renewed (like the manna of old); hence his people are not consumed, and a remnant remains as a seed for a new beginning. **Great is thy faithfulness** (v. 23). "Jehovah is my dearest treasure," declares my soul, "therefore I *do* hope in him" (v. 24).

25-27. A man should both hope and quietly wait (v. 26). Patient waiting upon Jehovah makes one a partaker of his goodness. **The yoke in his youth** (v. 27). Early discipline begets mature dependability. **28-30. Keepeth silence.** Let the chastened soul submit silently and humbly, for in so doing there is hope. **Mouth in the dust** (v. 29). A confession of unworthiness.

31-33. He doth not afflict willingly (v. 33). Hebrew, *from his heart.* Jehovah will not cast off forever, nor is there any vindictiveness in his heart. He does not delight to bring pain and grief. **34-36. To turn aside the right of a man** (v. 35). The Most High is not like a pagan deity, fickle and imperfect. He does not approve oppression, injustice, or subversion. (Favoritism in the courts then, as now, was all too common.) God is Moral Governor over all.

37-39. Wherefore doth a living man complain? (v. 39) Nothing can happen without the permission of the Most High. Then why should a man complain when punished for his sins? Not suffering, but sin should be lamented. Let us not murmur at God for that which we have brought upon ourselves. **40-42. Let us search and try our ways.** An exhortation to heart-searching, sincere repentance. Let the hands be lifted up in supplication and surrender, and the heart become submissive. **We . . . thou** (v. 42). These words stand in contrast. We, on our part, have sinned and rebelled; and thou, thou therefore hast not pardoned (cf. the Hebrew and Luther's German).

C. The Servant's Prayer for Vindication. 3:43-66. The poet and his people tell of the calamities suffered by reason of Jehovah's wrath.

43-45. Thou hast . . . persecuted us. Wrapped in a cloud of anger which no prayer can penetrate, Jehovah has pursued the people of Judah, slaying without pity, until Zion is but rubbish among the people. **46-48. Fear and a snare** (v. 47). In the presence of her yelling enemies, Zion is terror-stricken, like a hunted animal that can see no way of escape from the trap (pit, snare), while torrents of tears flood the eyes of her intercessor.

Verses 49-54 comprise the poet's lament over the enmity of his own people against him. **49-51. Mine eye . . . ceaseth not.** His tears over their fate will flow unceasingly until Jehovah in heaven takes notice of his grief. **52-54. Mine enemies chased me . . . without cause.** With no excuse for their hate, they have hunted him like a bird and cast him into a well, piling in stones upon him until the water closed over his head.

In verses 55-66 we have the prayer that brought Jehovah to the rescue. It is followed by a confident plea for vengeance upon the poet's foes. **55-57. I called . . . . thou saidst, Fear not.** His prayer of desperation brought Jehovah's presence and comforting precept – **Fear not. 58-60. Thou hast seen** (v. 59). He is now confident that Jehovah has observed his plight and will become his Redeemer, Advocate, and Vindicator. **61-63. Thou hast heard.** He is also sure that Jehovah has heard the insults of his assailants, their plots and daily mutterings as he is the topic of their taunt-song. **64-66. Render unto them a recompense,** i.e., vengeance in keeping with their deeds – blindness of heart, the curse of Jehovah, persecution, and extermination from beneath the heavens.

IV. The Suffering People of Zion. 4:1-22.

In this chapter we have something of an eyewitness account of both Zion's guilt and her punishment. The inspired poet-prophet first describes her fate as a people, then gives the moral explanation for such a fate.

A. Horrors of the Siege, and the Sad Fate of Zion's Nobility. 4:1-11. Verses 1-6 give us the description of the suffering of the royal children. **1,2. The precious sons of Zion** (v. 2). Worth their weight in gold as Zion's precious treasures, they have been thrown out like broken pottery and lie scattered at the beginning of every street. **3-5. They . . . brought up in scarlet embrace dunghills** (v. 5). Even the predatory animals do not treat their young as Zion has been forced to treat hers. Sucklings die of thirst and infants lack bread, while their mothers, like cruel ostriches of the desert, disregard their cries. The royal diet and clothing have given way to famine and the garbage heap.

In verses 7-11 the poet contrasts the former beauty of Zion's princes with the frightful fate they now endure. **7. Her Nazarites.** More correctly, *her distinguished ones.* How innocent, comely, and healthy they were! **8-10. Slain with hunger** (v. 9). Now all beauty has become blackness. Note the reversal of the situation in verse 7. That once fair skin is now black, dry, and shriveled (a picture of unburied bodies in the desert sun). Better the piercing sword than the pangs of hunger and starvation. Some mothers even eat their own children during the famine of the siege. **11. His fury.** Jehovah's consuming anger has burned like a fire to the very foundations of Zion.

B. Causes and Climax of Zion's Catastrophe. 4:12-20. Here the writer comes to grips with the moral explanation of such misfortunes. Verses 12-16 point out that what the heathen thought impossible for Zion – that she could be taken by an enemy – was brought about by the sins of her prophets, priests, and elders. Judah has destroyed herself by sin.

12. Would not have believed. No one on earth, not even her enemies, ever thought Zion's gates would fall before the foe. **13-15. Shed the blood of the just.** Alas, these leaders, guilty of spilling righteous and innocent blood, are now defiled with the blood of men they once avoided. Consequently they themselves are treated as contemptible and unclean. (To touch a dead body meant ceremonial uncleanness.) **16. Respected not the persons of the priests.** Now, as fugitives and vagabonds, the priests are without honor or respect. If Jehovah regarded them as his heritage once, he cares nothing for them now.

17-20. As the end draws near, hope for foreign aid is disappointed, and attempts to escape are frustrated. Even the king is captured, and so all hope of living in a foreign land under his rule is destroyed.

C. An Apostrophe to Haughty and Gloating Edom. 4:21,22. Edom was the "brother" of Judah, descended from Esau and Ishmael. Often the sharpest jibes come from one's kinsfolk. But now Jehovah turns his attention to Edom and foretells her humiliation.

V. The Supplications of Penitent Zion. 5:1-22.

This chapter is really a national prayer to Jehovah, Zion's only hope and help.

A. Zion's Plea to Jehovah to Regard Her Affliction and Disgrace. 5:1-18. Verse 1 opens the theme with Zion's fifth apostrophe to Jehovah. The pitiful plight of Zion merits Jehovah's attention.

2-10. This is a picture of the general suffering of the people from lack of life's necessities: they have lost homes and loved ones; they have to pay inflationary (black market) prices even for water and fuel; they toil without respite at hard labor; they are forced to beg food from their enemies east and west; they suffer the deserts of the fathers' sins; they are enslaved by former servants; in seeking bread they are exposed to the peril of Bedouin raids; and all the while the fever of famine consumes them. These distresses are the usual aftermath of war. **11-13.** Here are noted specific cases of individual sufferings, such as rape, insult, and tasks beyond one's strength.

14-18. General despondency prevails. **Joy . . . turned into mourning** (v. 15). The elders have dropped all business and social gatherings, while the youths have left their music-making. Merriment is turned into mourning. The only crown is one of woe for sins committed. **Our heart is faint** (v. 17). Courage and vision fail because the place of the sanctuary is desolate and overrun by wild animals.

B. A Final Apostrophe to the Eternal Sovereign. 5:19-22. In this stanza the book reaches its conclusion. Note here Zion's sixth and seventh apostrophes to Jehovah.

19. Thy throne. The throne of Jehovah stands immovable. **20. Wherefore?** Why, then, should he forget his people forever? **21. Turn . . . and we shall be turned.** Restore and establish us. God is the only source of true revival. **22. Utterly rejected.** In the Hebrew this is more probably a final query: *Wilt Thou utterly reject us?* In other words: "Surely you cannot cast us off and be angry with us forever!" God will not always chide. Or as another prayed: "In wrath, remember mercy" (Hab 3:2).

BIBLIOGRAPHY

Adeney, W. F. *The Song of Solomon and the Lamentations of Jeremiah (Expositor's Bible).* New York: A. C. Armstrong & Son, 1895.

Calvin, John. "Lamentations of Jeremiah," *Calvin's Commentary, Jeremiah,* Vol. V. Grand Rapids: Wm. B. Eerdmans, reprinted 1950.

Cheyne, T. K. "Lamentations," *Pulpit Commentary.* Vol. 11. Grand Rapids: Wm. B. Eerdmans, reprinted 1950.

Clarke, Adam. "Lamentations of Jeremiah," *Commentary.* Vol. IV. New York: Abingdon-Cokesbury, n.d.

Gordon, Alexander. *The Poets of the Old Testament.* New York: Hodder and Stoughton, 1912.

Gottwald, Norman K. "Lamentations," "*Interpretation,* IX:3 (July, 1955), 320-338.

Keil, Karl F., and Delitzsch, Franz. *Commentaries on the Old Testament, Jeremiah.* Vol. II. Grand Rapids: Wm. B. Eerdmans, reprinted 1956.

Meek, Theophile J., and Wm. P. Merrill. "Lamentations," *Interpreter's Bible.* Vol. 6. New York: Abingdon Press, 1956.

Naegelsbach, C. W. E. *Jeremiah and Lamentations.* Lange's *Commentary on The Holy Scriptures.* Grand Rapids: Zondervan Publishing House, reprint.

von Orelli C. "Lamentations, Book of," *International Standard Bible Encyclopedia.* Vol. III, pp. 1824-25.

Pfeiffer, R. H. *Introduction to the Old Testament.* New York: Harper & Bros., 1941.

Robinson, T. H. *The Poetry of the Old Testament.* London: Gerald Duckworth, 1947.

Schmidt, Nathaniel. "Jeremiah, Book of," and "Jeremiah, Lamentations of," *Encyclopedia Americana* (1947). 16: 20-25.

Selbie, J. A. "Lamentations, Book of," *Dictionary of the Bible.* Edited by James Hastings. III: 20-23.

EZEKIEL

INTRODUCTION

The Times. The data in the book of Ezekiel place the prophet's ministry in the early years of the Babylonian exile, between 593/592 and 571/570 B.C. (1:1,2; 29:17). The prophet Ezekiel, from his Babylonian locale, envisaged the fall and restoration of the house of Israel; while his older contemporary, Jeremiah, in Jerusalem, actually beheld the dying gasps of the kingdom of Judah (Jer 1:1-3).

During much of the eighth and seventh centuries B.C., the ruthless Assyrian power harassed the kingdoms of Israel and Judah. The northern kingdom fell in 721 B.C.; but Judah, though seriously weakened, managed to outlive her oppressor. With the reign of Ashurbanipal (669–633), the Assyrian empire began to decline. Egypt pulled out from under her yoke in 655. Within a few years Assyria was fighting for her life against the Babylonians and Medes. The ancient Assyrian capital, Asshur, succumbed in 614, and the long-mighty Nineveh was utterly destroyed in 612. By 607 the remnants of the Assyrian empire had collapsed.

Taking advantage of the Assyrian decline, Josiah (640/639–609/608), the last great king of Judah, strengthened his kingdom. His brilliant career was cut short by an encounter at Megiddo with Pharaoh-necho II of Egypt, who was attempting to prop up the Assyrian empire as a bulwark against Chaldea (II Kgs 23:29). Shallum or Jehoahaz (Jer 22:10-12; Ezk 19:2-4), who succeeded his father Josiah, was deported to Egypt after a reign of three months, and Jehoiakim, an older son of Josiah, was enthroned by Necho (II Kgs 23:31-35).

The Egyptians under Necho were defeated by Nebuchadrezzar (also called Nebuchadnezzar) at Carchemish on the Euphrates River in 605 (Jer 46:2ff.). The Chaldeans became the new world masters (II Kgs 24:7), with Judah as a vassal state. Jehoiakim (608–597) persecuted the prophets (Jer 7; 26; 36), degraded the spiritual life of the nation (Jer 7:1-15; 13; 16–20; cf. Ezk 8), and showed himself a petty tyrant (Jer 22:13-15,17-19). He revolted against Nebuchadnezzar in 602 and was harried by neighboring states (II Kgs 24:1ff.). He died in disgrace before Nebuchadnezzar's punitive invasion reached Judah (Jer 22:19).

Jehoiachin (Jeconiah or Coniah), the son of Jehoiakim, ruled three months and then surrendered to Nebuchadnezzar (II Kgs 24:8-17; Jer 22:24-30; Ezk 19:5-9). After pillaging Jerusalem, the Chaldean monarch deported several thousands of its upper-class citizens to Babylonia. These Jeremiah compared to "good figs," the hope for the future Israel, in contrast to the "bad figs," the poorest of the people, who were left behind (Jer 24; 29). Included in the company of exiles was Ezekiel, who dates his messages from the year of Jehoiachin's captivity (1:1,2; 3:16; 8:1; 20:1; 24:1; 26:1; 29:1; 29:17; 30:20; 31:1; 32:17; 33:21; 40:1). The "Jehoiachin tablets," published in 1939, refer to "Yaukin the king of Yahud" and his sons (cf. W. F. Albright, "King Joiakin in Exile," BA, V (Dec. 1942), pp. 49-55). He was released from his imprisonment by Amel-Marduk, the son of Nebuchadnezzar, in 560, the thirty-seventh year of his exile.

The nineteenth and last king of Judah was Zedekiah (597–586), a third son of Josiah (II Kgs 24:17–25:7; Ezk 19:11-14), a weak king (Jer 37; 38), who soon broke his oath of fealty to Nebuchadnezzar by joining a coalition of revolting states (Ezk 17:13-15; Jer 27:1-11). This folly brought the avenging Chaldeans to Jerusalem. After a siege of one and a half years (II Kgs 25:1-3), relieved briefly by the rumored coming of Pharaoh-hophra's Egyptian army (Jer 34:3ff.; 37:5-8), the city was destroyed, the Temple plundered and burned, Zedekiah taken prisoner, and a host of exiles deported to Babylon (II Kgs 25:1-21). Jeremiah chose to remain in the land with the wretched survivors under the governorship of Gedaliah at Mizpah. After the latter's treacherous murder, the group, fearing reprisals, migrated to Egypt, against the advice of Jeremiah (Jer 40–44).

The Bible says very little about the exiles, and Ezekiel is especially reticent about them. Some no doubt became serfs or slaves, while others prospered, as the contract tablets from Nippur indicate (see on 1:1). Leaders such as Zerubbabel, Ezra, and Nehemiah arose out of the *gôlâ* (the exiles). Many exiles apparently lived in their own homes (Jer 29:1-7), in various settlements (Ezr 2:59; Neh 7:61), and had an organization of elders (Ezk 3:15,24; 8:1; 14:1; 20:1; 33:31). Some lost their faith; but to those who remained true, Ezekiel became a tower of strength. It is not strange that, upon being uprooted from their land, temple, and sacrifices, they laid emphasis upon fasting, the Sabbath, and circumcision, and that prayer, the reading of Scripture, and psalmody—precursors of the synagogue—were stressed.

The Man. Ezekiel *(God strengthens),* the son of Buzi, was of a priestly family, possibly of the Zadokite line (1:3; 40:46; 44:15). He manifests great familiarity with Jerusalem, where he spent his early years, and with its Temple. In 597 B.C. he was exiled to Babylonia by Nebuchadnezzar, along with King Jehoiachin and the upper classes of Jerusalem. His home was at Tel-abib, the principal colony of the exiles, on the river Chebar or "Grand Canal" (1:1; 3:15), near the city of Nippur, southeast of Babylon. He had a dearly beloved wife but no children (24:16-18). Apparently a person of consideration, his home became the meeting place of the elders of the exiles (3:24; 8:1; 14:1; 20:1).

In response to a magnificent theophany (1:4-28), he was charged to be God's spokesman and watchman to the exiles (chs. 2; 3). His ministry extended from the fifth year of Jehoiachin's exile, 592 B.C., to the twenty-seventh year, 570 B.C. (1:2; 29:17). Before the fall of Jerusalem in 586, he was primarily a preacher of repentance and judgment (chs. 1—24). To a people rebellious, inclined to idolatry, and susceptible to a pagan environment, he brought constant warnings (2:3ff.; 3:4-11; 13; 14:1ff.; 18:2,25; 20:1ff.). He reminded the exiles that the people still living in Jerusalem falsely clung to the inviolability of the Temple and the land (11:1-15), and put far off the day of recompense (12:21-28). To his despairing hearers, after the fall of Jerusalem (24:21ff.; 33:10,17; 37:11), he became a consoler, a herald of salvation, an expositor of the necessity of inner religion, a prophet of the regathering, and the envisager of God's restoration of the Temple, worship, and land to a redeemed and purified Israel (33:11; 34; 36:25-31; 37; 40—48). He pictured judgment falling on the hostile nations led by Gog and Magog (chs. 38; 39), but hinted of the conversion of other peoples, e.g., Sodom and Samaria (16:53ff.), and foresaw many nations taking shelter, like birds, under the goodly cedar, the Messiah (17:22-24).

Ezekiel conveyed his message by such striking methods as allegories (chs. 15; 16; 17:1-21; 19; 21:1-17; 23; 24:1-14), symbolic actions (4:1—5:4; 12:1-7,17-20; 21:18-23; 24:3-5,15-24; 37:15-17), and visions (1:4-28; 2:9—3:3; 3:22,23; 8—11; 37:1-10; 40—48). As for Zechariah, so for Ezekiel, an interpreting angel is prominent in his visions (often in 40—48; e.g., 40:3,4; 43:6,7; 47:1ff.). Apocalyptic imagery appears frequently (7:5-12; 20:33-44; 28:25,26; 34:25-31; 36:8-15,33-36; 38; 39; 47:1-12). Ezekiel's mastery of many styles of prose and poetry shows careful preparation and reflection.

During the last generation, scholars have proposed widely differing theories concerning Ezekiel: that no such person existed but the book is a pseudepigraphon of 230 B.C. (C. C. Torrey); that he lived in the time of Manasseh, was a native of North Israel, and addressed the Assyrian diaspora (James Smith); that all his ministry was in Palestine (Herntrich, Harford); that he exercised part of his ministry in Palestine but after 586 was in Babylonia (Bertholet, Auvray, Van den Born, Oesterley and Robinson); that he had several residences (I. G. Matthews, Fisher, Freedman); and that he was a North Israelite of 400 B.C. (Messel). The inability of scholars to produce a theory superior to the traditional view, plus the strong evidence for it, shows that no change is needed with reference to the residence of Ezekiel. (Cf. Carl G. Howie, "The Residence of Ezekiel," in *The Date and Composition of Ezekiel,* pp. 5-26.)

Attempts have been made to prove that Ezekiel was psychopathic. E. C. Broome, writing on "Ezekiel's Abnormal Personality" (JBL, 65 (1946), pp. 272-292), diagnosed him as afflicted with catatonic or paranoid schizophrenia! Howie has carefully contrasted the so-called evidence for Ezekiel's schizophrenia with the parallels between Ezekiel and other mystics ("Psychological Aspects of Ezekiel and His Prophecy," *op. cit.,* pp. 69-84). He points out how absurd it is for a nonprofessional student of psychiatry to claim success in psychoanalyzing a person who has been dead for 2500 years!

Says Howie: "Ezekiel . . . was a mystic by nature with a sensitive, artistic imagination which brought forth some of the best-known visions and symbolic figures of speech in Biblical literature. . . . He deviated considerably from 'the norm' but was not truly psychopathic. No prophet is 'normal,' else he would not be a prophet. Ezekiel's strangeness or abnormality would seem to be the secret of his greatness" (*Ibid.*, p. 84).

The prophet Ezekiel has been called "the first dogmatist of the Old Testament," "the Calvin of the Old Testament," "the most influential man in the whole course of Hebrew history," "the father of Judaism," "the prophet of personal responsibility," etc. One who seriously studies Ezekiel's book can readily see how such encomiums can apply to this priest, prophet, and pastor.

The Book—Authorship and Unity. The book, except for redactional glosses, has been ascribed by most scholars to Ezekiel in the Babylonian *gôlâ*; but modern scholars frequently challenge the unity and single authorship of the book.

Oeder, in 1771, denied the authenticity of chapters 40—48, and Carrodi (1791) in addition rejected 38; 39. Zunz (1831) placed the book in the Persian period, about 440—400, with chapters 25—28 being dated 332 B.C. Seinecke (1876—1884) regarded Ezekiel as a pseudepigraphon from 163 B.C. Kraetzschmar (1900) and Hermann (1908) held that there were two recensions of the book. Gustav Hölscher, in 1924, propounded the radical view that only messages of doom written in the poetic *qînâ* meter could be attributed to Ezekiel with certainty. Hence, six-sevenths of the work is editorial, he said, only 170 verses out of a total of 1273 having been written by the prophet. C. C. Torrey (1930) regarded the book as a pseudepigraphon dating from 230 B.C., but purporting to be from the time of Manasseh. In support of his views he quoted the uncritical fourth century A.D. Talmud *Baba Bathra* 14b-15a, treated the Babylonian exile as an invention (contrary to the findings of archaeology; cf. W. F. Albright, "The American Excavations at Tell Beit Mirsim," ZAW, 6 (1929), p. 16), and found many late Aramaisms in the book. For a reply, consult Howie, "The Aramaic of the Book of Ezekiel" (*op. cit.*, pp. 47-68). W. A. Irwin (1943) ascribes only 251 verses in poetic form out of chapters 1—39 to Ezekiel. The rest of the prophecy, 80 per cent of the book, he says, is "false commentary," reflecting many additions from a multitude of hands over a long period of time.

It is well to heed the note of caution sounded by H. G. May in his commentary on Ezekiel: "Literary and historical criticism is not an exact science. . . . The subjective element enters in, for in a book like Ezekiel, scholars are influenced by their total concept of the development and characteristics of Hebrew religion and history" (IB, VI, 45).

The historical allusions, the nature of the language used, the evidence that Ezekiel lived before the Solomonic Temple was destroyed are all positive evidences to support the traditional date of the book (cf. Howie, "The Date of the Prophecy," *op. cit.*, pp. 27-46).

The Masoretic Text (MT, the Hebrew text received, preserved, and given vowel points by scribes between the years 600 and 900 A.D.) has many textual corruptions, as indicated in the commentary. Scholars resort to the versions, particularly to the Septuagint (LXX), in attempting to restore the text. The LXX Papyrus Codex 967, the Chester Beatty papyri, containing Ezekiel 11—17 with lacunae, and the John H. Scheide collection, containing most of Ezekiel 19:12—39:29, and dating before Origen's Hexapla of the third century A.D., are especially useful. It is to be hoped that light on the text of Ezekiel will soon be forthcoming from the Dead Sea Scrolls manuscripts and fragments.

The Book—Contents. A brief reference to the contents of the book is in order. There are many similarities between Jeremiah and Ezekiel in turns of language, figures, and ideas. G. Currey exhibits in a synoptic chart a comparison of Ezekiel, Daniel, Zechariah, and the Apocalypse (*Ezekiel* in *The Speaker's Commentary*, pp. 12-16).

Some of the outstanding passages of the book, listed by chapter, are: 1; 2; 3:16-21 (cf. 33:1-9); 8 and 9; 11:19ff. (cf. 18:31; 24:7; 31:31; 32:39; 36:26); 14:14; 15; 16; 17:22-24; 18 (cf. 33); 21:8-17; 21:18-27; 23; 27 and 28; 31; 32:17-22; 34; 36:16-38; 37; 38 and 39; 47.

The chief Messianic passages are: 11:16-20, the Lord, the sanctuary; 17:22-24, the wonderful cedar sprig; 21:26,27, the rightful king; 34:11-31, the faithful shepherd; 36:25-35, the great purification; 37:1-14, the great resurrection; 37:21-28, the great reunion; 38 and 39, the overthrow of Gog; 47:1-12, the life-giving stream out of the Temple.

The fundamental teachings of Ezekiel may be enumerated as follows: (1) Ideas concerning God: his glory, chapters 1; 10; 43; his name, 20:8,9,14,22; 36:22,23; his holiness, 20:41; 28:22-25. (2) Emphasis on individual responsibility, 18:2,5-9, 19,20, an expansion of Jer 31:29,30. (3) Israel's sinfulness at the beginnings of her history, 20:8,9; 23:3ff. (4) Promises of restoration: judgment on the nations, 25–32; 38 and 39; endowment of the land with extraordinary fertility, 36:8, 9,29,30,34,35; a spiritual regeneration, 36:25-27; restoration of the exiles, 37:1-14; the Messianic ruler, 34:11-22,23,24; 37:22ff.; the Lord's return to the regenerated people, 37:26,27; 43:1-12. (5) Organization of the restored community, 40–48. Ezekiel, writing as a priest under the old covenant, pictures the renewed Temple, priests, and sacrificial system as the means whereby God enters into relationship with his redeemed people.

OUTLINE

I. Prophecies against Judah and Jerusalem. 1:1–24:27.
  A. Introduction: The call of Ezekiel. 1:1–3:27.
    1. Superscription. 1:1-3.
    2. The prophet's inaugural vision: A theophany. 1:4-28.
    3. His initiation into the prophetic office. 2:1–3:27.
  B. Overthrow of city and state predicted. 4:1–7:27.
    1. Four symbolic actions concerning Jerusalem. 4:1–5:17.
    2. Oracle against the mountains of Israel, seats of idolatry. 6:1-14.
    3. Dirge over the downfall of Judah. 7:1-27.
  C. The sin and fate of Jerusalem. 8:1–11:25.
    1. Vision of four abominations practiced in the Temple. 8:1-18.
    2. Vision of inhabitants slain by divine avengers. 9:1-11.
    3. Vision of Jerusalem destroyed by fire. 10:1-22.
    4. Vision of the internal condition of the city and the Lord's departure from it. 11:1-25.
  D. Moral necessity of the captivity. 12:1–19:14.
    1. Symbolic actions depicting exile and invasion. 12:1-20.
    2. Prophecy and its abuses. 12:21–14:23.
    3. Parable of the grapevine. 15:1-8.
    4. Allegory of the foundling. 16:1-63.
    5. Parable of the vine and the two eagles. 17:1-24.
    6. God's justice shown in his treatment of individuals. 18:1-32.
    7. Allegory of the two lions and the vine. 19:1-14.
  E. Israel's coming downfall inevitable and necessary. 20:1–24:27.
    1. Review of Israel's unfaithfulness, and her preservation. 20:1-44.
    2. Israel to be punished by God's avenging sword. 20:45–21:32.
    3. Jerusalem's sins to be judged in the smelting furnace. 22:1-31.
    4. Allegory of Oholah and Oholibah. 23:1-49.
    5. Symbols of the final siege of Jerusalem. 24:1-27.

II. Oracles against foreign nations: The universal sovereignty of God. 25:1–32:32.
  A. Ammon. 25:1-7.
  B. Moab. 25:8-11.
  C. Edom. 25:12-14.
  D. Philistines. 25:15-17.
  E. Tyre. 26:1–28:19.
    1. Prophecy of the destruction of Tyre. 26:1-21.
    2. Dirge on the downfall of Tyre. 27:1-36.
    3. Fall of the Prince of Tyre. 28:1-19.
  F. Sidon. 28:20-26.
  G. Egypt. 29:1–32:32.
    1. Desolation and restoration of Egypt. 29:1-16.
    2. Egypt to be given to Nebuchadnezzar as a recompense. 29:17-21.
    3. Destruction of Egypt and her allies. 30:1-19.
    4. Pharaoh's might to be shattered. 30:20-26.
    5. Allegory of the mighty cedar. 31:1-18.
    6. Dirge for Pharaoh, the dragon. 32:1-16.
    7. Dirge on Pharaoh's descent to Sheol. 32:17-32.

III. Prophecies of the restitution of Israel. 33:1–39:29.
  The New Covenant: Purification of Israel, her restoration and eternal peace, and her secular restoration.
  A. The prophet: His function in preparation for the new age. 33:1-33.
  B. The royal house: The selfish shepherds of Israel and the Good Shepherd. 34:1-31.

C. The land: Israel to be restored and made fruitful. 35:1–36:38.
 1. Hostile Edom to be devastated. 35:1-15.
 2. Israel to be exalted and blessed. 36:1-15.
 3. Redemptive principles illustrated. 36:16-38.
D. The people: Resurrection of the dry bones of Israel; reunion of Judah and Israel. 37:1-28.
E. Peace: The Lord to defend Israel against Gog's invasion. 38:1–39:29.
 1. Invasion of Gog and his destruction. 38:1-23.
 2. Resumption of prophecy against Gog. 39:1-29.

IV. Vision of the restored community: The new Temple and the new law. 40:1–48:35.
A. Description of the new Temple. 40:1–43:27.
 1. The new sanctuary with its courts and chambers. 40:1–42:20.
  a. The courts, walls, and porches. 40:1-49.
  b. The Temple and Holy of Holies. 41:1-26.
  c. Chambers for the priests. 42:1-20.
 2. Return of the Lord to the Temple. 43:1-12.
 3. The altar and provisions for the dedication of the Temple. 43:13-27.
B. A new service of worship with an ideal ministry and sacrificial system. 44:1–46:24.
 1. Those who may minister in the Temple. 44:1-31.
 2. Portions of land for the priests, Levites, and the prince; and the dues paid to the prince. 45:1-17.
 3. Offerings to be made at the feasts and other appointed seasons. 45:18–46:24.
C. Israel reorganized according to tribal divisions. 47:1–48:35.
 1. The life-giving stream issuing from the Temple. 47:1-12.
 2. Boundaries and division of the holy land. 47:13-23.
 3. Portions of the tribes, priests, city, and prince. 48:1-35.

COMMENTARY

The book of Ezekiel comprises two portions: chapters 1–24, a series of messages delivered before the fall of Jerusalem, the general burden of which is "doom"; chapters 25–48, delivered after its fall, with the underlying theme of "hope." The book is more appropriately studied under four headings: chapters 1–24, Prophecies of Judgment on Judah and Jerusalem; chapters 25–32, Prophecies Against Surrounding Nations; chapters 33–39, Prophecies of the Restoration of Israel; chapters 40–48, Visions of the New Temple and the New Law for the Redeemed People.

I. Prophecies Against Judah and Jerusalem. 1:1–24:27.

The minatory discourses against Jerusalem and the house of Israel, delivered before the fall of Jerusalem, consist of: an introductory section, detailing the prophet's call (chs. 1–3); symbolic actions and oracles portraying the overthrow of the city and state (chs. 4–7); a group of visions depicting the frightful sins of Jerusalem that call for its destruction (chs. 8–11); symbolic actions, parables, and allegories setting forth the moral necessity of the captivity (chs. 12–19); and a review of Israel's past history which cries out for certain judgment (chs. 20–24).

A. Introduction: The Call of Ezekiel. 1:1–3:27.

1) Superscription. 1:1-3.

1. In the thirtieth year. Since the time of Origen (185–254) this time note has been held to be a reference to the prophet's own age, the age when priests began their ministry (Num 4:3,4), a dating system without parallel in Hebrew history. Other proposed interpretations: thirtieth year of Jehoiachin's age, 585 B.C. (Snaith); thirtieth year after Josiah's reform, 593/592 B.C. (so Targum, Jerome, Hermann, Hölscher, L. Finkelstein); thirtieth year of the current jubilee period (*Seder Olam*, Kimchi, Hitzig); thirtieth year of the neo-Babylonian empire, 606/605 B.C. (Scaliger, Ewald); thirtieth year of Manasseh, 667 B.C. (Torrey); thirtieth year of Artaxerxes III, 328 B.C. (sic! L. E. Browne); various emendations: thirteenth year of Nebuchadrezzar's reign, 592 B.C. (Rothstein, Bertholet); fifth year of Jehoiachin's exile, 595/594 B.C. (Herntrich). Albright and Howie suggest that this was the thirtieth year of the editing of Ezekiel's book, three years after the twenty-seventh year of 29:17, or 567 B.C., and the thirtieth year of Jehoiachin's reign. Compare II Kgs 26:27. All the other dates in the prophecy are reckoned from Jehoiachin's "reign" or captivity, also.

The fourth (month) was mid-June to mid-July, reckoning from the first month, mid-March to mid-April.

Among the captives. *In the midst of the exile,* or *captivity.* The Hebrew word *gôlâ* is a collective noun meaning "exiles," or, in the abstract, "exile."

The river Chebar (Ké-bär) or *N^e^har-K^e^bār* (1:1,3; 3:15,23; 10:15,20,22; 43:3). Probably the *nâru kabari,* "the great river," "the grand canal," an artificial watercourse of the Euphrates. Beginning above Babylon, it flows southeast, passes through Nippur, site of ancient Jewish settlements (and of the wealthy banking house of Murashû and Sons, whose archives [464–405 B.C.] contain many Jewish names), and joins the Euphrates again below Ur. Its modern name is Shatt en Nîl, "the river Nile" (see H. V. Hilprecht, *Explorations in Bible Lands in the Nineteenth Century,* p. 409ff.).

Visions of God here includes visions given by God and visions in which God was seen.

2. King Jehoiachin. The eighteenth, and next to the last, king of Judah, was the son of the petty tyrant, Jehoiakim, and grandson of the godly Josiah. His name, meaning "The Lord establishes," is variously spelled: *Yôyākin,* Ezk 1:2; *Y^e^hôyākîn,* II Kgs 24:6,8,12,15; 25:27 a,b; Jer 52:31 a,b; II Chr 36:8,9; *Y^e^konyā,* Jer 27:20; *Q^e^rê;* 28:4; 29:2; Est 2:6; I Chr 3:16,17; *Y^e^kon Yāhû,* Jer 24:1; *Konyāhû,* Jer 22:24,28; 37:1. Enthroned by Pharaoh-necho of Egypt, he reigned only three months, when he was deported to Babylon by Nebuchadnezzar in the year 597, along with the upper classes (II Kgs 24:8-16). He was released by Amel Marduk (Evil Merodach), son of Nebuchadnezzar in 560, the thirty-seventh year of his exile (II Kgs 25:27). "The Jehoiachin tablets," published in 1939, refer to "Yaukin" and his sons as receiving rations (Albright, BA, V (Dec. 1942), pp. 49-55). Jeremiah (22:20-30) and Ezekiel 19:5-9) appear sympathetic toward him. His grandson Zerubbabel was in the Messianic line (cf. Mt 1:11,12; Ezr 3:8; I Chr 3:17-19).

The fifth year of king Jehoiachin's captivity (June-July, 592) is the first of fourteen date references in the book of Ezekiel (cf. 1:2; 3:16; 8:1; 20:1; 24:1; 26:1; 29:1; 29:17; 30:20; 31:1; 32:1; 32:17; 33:21; 40:1). Ezekiel was the first prophet to date his messages chronologically. (For dates of the period, cf. J. Finegan, "Nebuchadnezzar and Jerusalem," JBR, 25 (1957), pp. 203-205.)

3. Ezekiel *(Y^e^ḥezqē'l,* "God strengthens") **the priest.** Nothing is known of his father Buzi. Other prophets with priestly background were: Samuel (I Chr 6:28; I Sam 7:9; 11:14; 16:2ff.); Jeremiah (1:1); Zechariah (1:7; Neh 12:4,16; Ezr 5:1). **The hand of the Lord was . . . upon him.** An expression describing a condition approaching prophetic ecstasy. (See also 3:14,22; 8:1; 33:22; 37:1; 40:1.) Thirteen Hebrew MSS and the Septuagint, Syriac, and Arabic versions read *upon me.*

2) The Prophet's Inaugural Vision: A Theophany. 1:4-28.

Ezekiel's call came in the form of a theophany, a manifestation of God in the midst of a storm. His vision is described in much greater detail than the theophanies of Moses (Ex 33; 24:9ff.), Amos (7:15), Isaiah (ch. 6), Jeremiah (1:4-10), or Daniel (7:9ff.). He starts from below, describing first the four living beings with the four wings and the four faces, combining human and animal forms to make the throne-car (vv. 4-14), then the wheels within wheels enabling the chariot to move in all four directions without turning (vv. 15-21), and lastly the crystal platform on which was the likeness of a throne, where was seated the likeness of one like fire encircled with rainbow glory (vv. 22-28).

a) The Living Creatures and the Chariot. 1:4-14.

4. For God's appearance in **stormy wind** (ASV; AV, *whirlwind)* and **cloud,** see also Ex 9:24; 19:16; Jud 5:4; I Kgs 19:11; Ps 29; Zech 9:14. **Out of the north.** Ezekiel here is not borrowing the mythological concept of the north as the home of the gods, but may be suggesting God's transcendence. **Fire flashing forth continually.** Literally, *fire taking hold of itself.* **Gleaming bronze** (RSV). Hebrew, *like the eye of ḥashmal.* Used only in 1:4,27; 8:2. Compare Akkadian *elmešu* and Egyptian *hesmen,* "bronze" (G. R. Driver, VT, I (1951), 60-62).

5. Likeness *(d^e^mût)* and **appearance** *(mar'eh)* occur ten and fourteen times in the account. The prophet senses the inadequacy of human speech to describe the ineffable, but he is also careful to avoid anthropomorphism. The **four living creatures** *(ḥayyôt)* are later identified as cherubim (10:15,20).

7. Their legs (rather than *feet;* cf. Gen 49:10; Isa 6:2; 7:20) **were straight,** without knee joints; and **the sole[s] of their feet** were rounded (Targum, Aquila) like calves' feet, to exclude bending and turning. **8.** Each cherub probably had two hands, for **on their four sides** may mean "upon the sides of the four of them."

9. The cherubim, with a pair of outstretched wings touching one another, formed the sides of the chariot, which could move in all four directions, **without turning** (RSV; cf. v. 12). A second pair of wings **covered their bodies** (v. 11). **10.** Each cherub had four faces, **the face of a man in front, . . . the face of a lion, on the right side . . . the face of an ox on the left side,** and **the face of an eagle** at the back (cf. 10:14; Rev 4:7).

12. The Spirit of God directed their movements (cf. v. 20; 10:17), just as he directed Ezekiel (2:2; 3:12,24; 11:24). **13.** Read **and in the midst of the living creatures** (so RV marg., Moffatt, RSV, LXX, and Old Lat.). **Fire, torches** (ASV), and **lightning** flashed forth from their midst (cf. Ex 3:2; 13:22; 19:18; Num 11:1-3; Deut 4:24; II Kgs 1:12). **14.** This verse is omitted by LXX B as a marginal amplification of verse 13. The Hebrew text seems corrupt.

b) The Four Wheels. 1:15-21.

15. The prophet next saw **beside the living creatures** (RSV) wheels. **16. Their appearance was like the gleaming** (lit., *eye)* **of a chrysolite** (RSV; AV, *beryl).* Hebrew, *tarshîsh.* The stone named from Tarshish, or Tartessus, in southern Spain, is probably the ancient chrysolite *(goldstone),* corresponding to our gold-colored topaz, not the pale green aquamarine or beryl. **A wheel in the middle of a wheel.** The most common explanation is that each wheel looked like two wheels cutting each other at right angles to form a compound wheel, which could move in different directions without changing front (v. 17). **18.** The Hebrew text is in disorder. The LXX suggests: **And they had rims** (or, felloes; AV, *rings).* **And I looked at them** (instead of Heb *and terror was to them).* **And their rims were full of eyes,** symbolizing life and intelligence.

19-21. There was a unity between the **living creatures** and the wheels, directed by the Spirit of God. Compare references to the wheels of the throne of "the Ancient of days" in Dan 7:9, and of the bases in Solomon's Temple, I Kgs 7:27-30, and to the chariot in I Chr 28:18. In later times the "Ophannim," wheels personified, stand next to the cherubim and seraphim in the presence of God (Enoch 61:10; 71:7).

c) The Platform, the Throne, and the Divine Appearance Thereupon. 1:22-28.

22. The likeness of the firmament. Hebrew *rāqîa* occurs seventeen times in the Scriptures, in Gen 1; Ezk 1; 10:1; Ps 19:1; 150:1; Dan 12:3. Here the picture is that of a "platform" **spread out above** (RSV) the heads of the living creatures like **crystal** (lit., *as the eye or gleam of ice;* so LXX, Syr, Vulg. Cf. Rev 4:6. Omit "terrible," with LXX).

24. When in motion, the sound of their wings was **like the noise of great waters** (Ps 42:7; Isa 17:12), **like the thunder of the Almighty** (Ps 29, "voice of God," seven times), **a sound of tumult like the sound of a host** (RSV; Isa 17:12; Joel 2:5). **Almighty.** Hebrew *Shadday* is a pre-Mosaic term for God, used chiefly in poetry, or in prose with *El* (God) prefixed (Gen 17:1). The name is of uncertain derivation, but may mean "omniscient, all-knowing," rather than "Almighty," or "of the mountains" (cf. N. Walker, "A New Interpretation of the Divine Name Shaddai," ZAW, 72 (1960), pp. 64-66). **25.** This verse is omitted by nine Hebrew manuscripts, the LXX, and a Syriac manuscript, as a dittography.

26. On the platform was a throne in **appearance of a sapphire** (cf. Ex 24:10). This may be the ancient marble-like, azure stone known as *lapis lazuli.* **27.** The upper part of the human likeness seated on the throne shown like **gleaming bronze** (RSV; lit., *like the eye of ḥashmal;* cf. v. 4), which fire enclosed round about (lit., *like the appearance of fire a house to it round about);* while the lower part, also, was covered by a fiery brightness.

28. The brightness round about the Lord's throne was **as the appearance of the bow that is in the cloud.** This suggests calm after storm. To the Hebrews and to us the rainbow recalls the covenant made with Noah (cf. Gen 9:12ff.; Rev 4:3; 10:1). **The glory of the Lord** *(kᵉbôd Y H W H,* 1:28; 3:12,23; 10:4,18; 11:23; 43:4,5; 44:4; and "the glory of the God of Israel," 8:4; 9:3; 10:19; 11:22; 43:2) in Ezekiel means primarily "an appearance of light and splendor indicating the divine Presence" (Cook, *Ezekiel,* ICC, p. 22). The root idea of *kābôd* is "weight," "heaviness," and conveys the idea of some external, physical manifestation of dignity, pre-eminence, or majesty (cf. Betteridge, "Glory," ISBE, II, 1235 ff.).

In the presence of God, Ezekiel recognized his unworthiness (cf. Gen 32:30; Ex 20:19,20; 24:11; Isa 6:5; Jer 1:6).

From his vision Ezekiel learned that God was not limited to Palestine, but was present in Babylon among the exiles, descending to the earth on cherubim and storm (Ps 18:10; 104:3). The chariot could move swiftly in all directions, symbolized by the number four. The figures facing four directions (vv. 9,10,17) suggest the thought that all parts of the universe are open to the gaze of God. The wings connected the vision with heaven and the wheels with earth. Thus no spot is inaccessible to the divine presence and energy. The omnipresence of God is hereby forcefully conveyed.

The figure seated on the throne speaks of the omnipotence and sovereign rule of God (v. 26). The sovereignty of God is manifested over inanimate creation—wind, cloud, fire, thunder (vv. 4,24), and animate creation—the four living beings (vv. 5,10).

The general human form and various faces of the living creatures express the dignity assigned by God to the various portions of his creation, a reflection of His majesty: man, intelligence; the eagle, swiftness; the ox, strength; the lion, majesty. The rabbis explain the symbolism thus: "Man is exalted among creatures; the eagle is exalted among birds; the ox is exalted among domestic animals; the lion is exalted among the wild beasts; and all of them have received dominion, and greatness has been given them, yet they are stationed below the chariot of the Holy One" (Midrash Rabbah *Shemoth*, § 23, on Ex 15:1). The noise of the cherubim's wings (v. 24) is the testimony of all creation to God (Ps 19:1), while the veiled bodies (vv. 8,11) represent the inability of all creatures to stand in the presence of a holy God (cf. Isa 6:2). The Church Fathers employed the four faces as emblems of the Evangelists. Irenaeus, Jerome, Athanasius, and Augustine vary in their usage. Jerome's, which has the greatest currency, is as follows: the man, Matthew; the lion, Mark; the ox, Luke; the eagle, John. While the Babylonian deities Marduk, Nebo, Nergal, and Ninib were denoted by the ox, man, lion, and eagle respectively (Jeremias), Ezekiel most likely derived his symbolism from the figures in Solomon's Temple (I Kgs 6:23-35; 7:27-37) and from the mercy seat above the ark in the Tabernacle (Ex 25:10-22).

The eyes on the wheels suggest omniscient intelligence (v. 18), while the spirit in the wings and the wheels (vv. 20,21) pictures the pervasive working of God's Spirit seen in the unity and harmony of his works. The divine purity and holiness are exhibited by the fire (v. 27), while the rainbow around the throne illustrates sublime beauty, and perhaps, also, the idea of forgiveness and mercy (v. 28).

This glory was seen by Ezekiel at Chebar (1:4-28), gave him a message at Tel-abib (3:12ff.,22ff.), transported him from his home in the exile to the entrance of the gateway of the inner court of the Temple in Jerusalem (8:4,5), departed from the cherubim in the Temple to the threshold of the Temple (9:3; 10:4), mounted up from the threshold to the eastern gate of the Temple's outer court (10:15,16,18,19), went up from the midst of the city to the Mount of Olives on the east side of the city (11:22,23), but returned to fill the new Temple and cleansed people (43:2-7; 44:4).

3) His Initiation into the Prophetic Office. 2:1–3:27.

In chapters 2; 3, the prophet is commissioned to be a fearless messenger to a rebellious people (2:1-7), is commanded to assimilate as his own God's word or message (2:8–3:3), is endowed with courage to speak to a calloused Israel (3:4-9), is impelled on a mission to the exiles at Tel-abib (3:10-15), is charged with the responsibility of a watchman (3:16-21), and is placed under a restraint of silence and seclusion (3:22-27).

a) The Prophet's Commission. 2:1-7.

1. Son of man *(ben-'ādām)* occurs ninety-three times in Ezekiel, meaning simply "man" or "mortal man." The term expresses creaturely weakness in the presence of God's majesty and power (cf. Dan 8:17). The Aramaic *bar'ĕnosh,* "son of man," of Dan 7:13, is a Messianic title. Jesus' use of the title perhaps was intended to conceal as well as reveal his true nature (Mt 8:20; 11:19; 16:13; Jn 12:34; Mk 2:10,28; 8:31; 9:9,12; 10:45; 14:41, etc.; cf. G. P. Gould, "Son of Man," HDCG, II, 659-665; and J. Stalker, "Son of Man," ISBE, V, 2828-2830).

2. The spirit entered into me. While the word is without the definite article in the Hebrew, this is the Holy Spirit. (For similar usage see 3:12,14,24; 8:3; 11:1,5,24; 37:1; 43:5.) In 11:5 and 37:1

"the Spirit of the Lord" occurs, and in 11:24 "the Spirit of God" (cf. H. B. Swete, "Holy Spirit," HDB, II, 402-411).

3. To the people of Israel. The MT has *sons of Israel;* LXX, *house of Israel.* This is the usual phrase in Ezekiel. **To a nation of rebels.** MT *gôyîm* nearly always means "heathen nations." The word is omitted by the LXX and the Old Latin. It appears in the singular *gôy*, "nation," in the Syriac. Ezekiel's mission was to the nation as a whole, both in Jerusalem and in exile.

4. The Lord GOD. The Masoretic Text has *'Ădōnāy Yahweh.* The ancient Hebrews read *'Ădōnāy*, "Lord," in place of the sacred tetragrammaton *Yahweh* (so called from the four consonants YHWH, vowels not being written in ancient times). When *Ădonay* and *Yahweh* occurred together, the Hebrews read the tetragrammaton as *'Elohîm*, God. In English the tetragrammaton is represented in solid capitals, LORD or GOD. An unusual feature of Ezekiel is the occurrence of the twofold name LORD God over 200 times. A. D. Johnson, Gehman, and Kase, editors of *The John H. Scheide Biblical Papyri: Ezekiel*, claim that only Yahweh, the LORD, should be read in these passages (pp. 48-63).

5. There hath been a prophet among them. Fulfillment is the test of a true prophet. See Deut 18:21,22; Jer 28:9.

6. Though briers and thorns. The two words are *sārābîm* and *sallônîm*. The former is found only here in the OT, and is probably an Aramaic loan word; the latter, of unknown etymology, appears also in 28:24. In Sir 4:2 and in the Aramaic, the root *srb* means "to contradict." The LXX and the Syriac render, "for they will contradict." The Hebrew idiom supports the English reading. **A rebellious house.** "House of rebellion" *(bêt m^e^rî*, as in verse 5). This translation is supported by thirty-two Hebrew manuscripts, as well as by the LXX and the Syriac.

b) The Prophet's Inspiration. 2:8—3:3.

8. Hear . . . Be not . . . rebellious. Cf. Jer 1:7,8,17; Isa 50:5.

9. A roll of a book. In Palestine and Babylonia, skins were ordinarily used for scrolls. The Dead Sea Cave Isaiah scroll (I Q Isa[a]) is of parchment, twenty-four feet long. (Cf. Jer 36; Ps 40:7. See J. P. Hyatt, "The Writing of an Old Testament Book," BA, VI (1943), 41-80).

10. Written within and without. Literally, *it was written* (on the) *face and hinder part*, i.e., on both sides, contrary to usual practice. **Lamentation,** following the reading *qînâ*, "elegy, dirge," of the LXX, the Old Latin and Arabic versions, and the Targum, rather than the unusual masculine plural, *qînîm*, of the MT. **Mourning.** Translated *sigh* (Ps 90:9), and *rumbling* (of thunder; Job 37:2). **Woe.** This translation is arrived at by pointing *hî* of the MT as *hôy*, along with the LXX, and the Old Latin, Arabic, and Syriac versions. Before the fall of Jerusalem in 586, Ezekiel's messages in chapters 1—24 were of doom.

3:1. Eat that thou findest. Literally, *what you find, meet with.* The Lord touched Jeremiah's mouth (Jer 1:9) but gave Ezekiel a scroll to eat. God's immanence and transcendence are illustrated by the modes. **3. Eat.** Literally, *make your belly eat.* **And fill your stomach.** Belly and stomach *(beṭen* and *mē'îm)* are both used of "abdomen," "womb," "inward parts," and figuratively as the "seat of the emotions." The message was given by God but was to be assimilated by the prophet and made his own. Although the words were bitter, the scroll tasted *sweet* because its contents were God's word, and the privilege of being God's messenger is a great joy. Among the passages that illustrate the inspiration of the mind and will through the "eating" of God's word and that speak of the sweetness of that word are: Jer 15:16; Deut 8:3; Ps 19:11; 119:103; Rev 10:9,10. (For inspiration through drinking, cf. II Esd 14:38-41.)

c) The Prophet's Encouragement. 3:4-9.

4. Get thee unto the house of Israel. This and similar passages (e.g., 6:2; 7:2; 12:10,11; 16:2; 21:7; 22:2,3) are held to support a non-Babylonian residence for Ezekiel and a mission to his contemporaries in Jerusalem (cf. Introd.)

5,6. Strange speech and . . . hard language. Literally, *deep of lip and heavy of tongue* (cf. Ex 4:10; Isa 28:11; 33:19; and for a similar use of the genitive of specification, see Ezk 16:26; 17:3,6,7). Calloused Israel is often contrasted with the underprivileged heathen (cf. 5:16,17; 16:4,5,51; Jer 2:10,11; Mt 11:24-27; Lk 4:24-27). **7. All the house of Israel are impudent and hardhearted.** *Strong of forehead and hard of heart* (Literal. Cf. 2:4; Jer 5:3; Isa 48:4).

8. Strong. Perhaps a play on Ezekiel's name, *God strengthens.* Cf. Jer 1:18; 15:20. **9. As an adamant harder than flint** (ASV). Hebrew *shāmîr* is a foreign word, possibly related to the Akkadian *ašmar*, "emery." It is also translated *ada-*

mant and *diamond* (cf. Jer 17:1; Zech 7:12). For opposition between the true prophet and the people, see Amos 7:10-17; Jer 20:7-18; 26:1-24.

d) The Prophet's Mission. 3:10-15.

11. Get you to the exiles (cf. 1:1), "to the sons of" **thy people.** Hebrew *'am*, "people," is used in most cases for the chosen nation. The prophet's mission was to the house of Israel (v. 4), but in actuality it was confined to his fellow exiles. Yet he makes little reference to the circumstances of the exiles.

12. Then the spirit took me up. See also 3:14; 8:3; 11:1,24; 43:5. These are not references to physical levitations, as in Bel and the Dragon, verses 36,39; nor to clairvoyance; but to the mystical experiences of a highly sensitive soul under the exaltation of the Spirit. **And as the glory of the Lord arose from its place.** Since *k* and *m* are easily confused in the paleo-Hebrew script, Hitzig and Luzatto, arrived at this reading by changing *brwk* (bārûk) of the MT to *brwm* (beûm). There is no reference to a heavenly anthem being sung or heard. Rather, the prophet **heard the sound of a great earthquake** (AV, *noise of a great rushing). 13.* **Sound of the wings . . . as they touched one another.** Literally, *kissed.* **That sounded like a great earthquake** (RSV). *And a sound of* (lit.).

14. I went in bitterness. An adverbial accusative (cf. 27:30). Ezekiel, in sympathy with God, felt bitterness and heat of spirit against his people and at his task (cf. Jer 6:11; 20:7-11). Though the chariot had gone, he felt the hand of the Lord impelling him.

15. I came to them of the captivity at Tel-abib. In obedience to God, the prophet went to the principal colony of exiles by **the river of Chebar,** at the ancient *Tilabûbu,* "mound of the storm-flood" (cf. Hilprecht, *Explorations in Bible Lands,* p. 411). For the names of other colonies, see Ezr 2:59; Neh 7:61. The Hebrew phrase, following Chebar, reads, *and who were dwelling there,* or following the *Qerê, and I sat where they sat.* It is lacking in two Hebrew manuscripts and the Syriac. **And I sat there overwhelmed** (ASV). Literally, *showing horror,* an inwardly transitive verb (see G-K, § 53d and § 67cc; cf. Ezr 9:3,4; Dan 9:27; 11:31).

e) The Prophet's Responsibility. 3:16-21.

17. I have made thee a watchman; i.e., one spying, or a sentinel (cf. Jer 6:17; Isa 57:10). The prophet's call to be a pastor, a watchman for the souls of individuals as well as for the nation, is more fully expounded in 18:1-32 and 33:1-20. In the present paragraph four cases are considered – the habitual sinner who is not warned (v. 18), the sinner who is warned but does not repent (v. 19), the righteous man who apostatizes but is not warned (v. 20), and the righteous man who is warned and remains righteous (v. 21). Ezekiel is accountable for the faithful deliverance of God's message, not for its success or failure (vv. 17-19). **Die** (v. 18) and **live** (v. 21) do not come up to the highest NT sense, but refer respectively (1) to perishing in the destruction of the state and being excluded from the restored kingdom of God, and (2) to being preserved and entering into the blessedness of the kingdom.

20. I lay a stumblingblock. This may only mean that the "temptations of the righteous are under God's providential control" *(Dummelow's Commentary).* The Hebrews ascribed temptation to God, recognizing that Satan himself is subject to the divine will (cf. Gen 22:1; Ex 4:21; Jer 6:21; contrast II Sam 24:1 with I Chr 21:1). **21. If thou warn the righteous man.** This follows the versions rather than the MT, *if you warn him, the righteous man.* The second appearance of "righteous man" in the MT is lacking in the LXX, and in the Old Latin and Syriac.

f) The Prophet's Restraint. 3:22-27.

Some scholars understand this section to indicate a pathological element in Ezekiel: that he was afflicted with catalepsy and aphasia (vv. 23,26), and that his countrymen had to bind him with cords after he became demented (v. 25).

However, it is best to regard the various expressions of constraint as figurative for a period of silence and inactivity on the part of the prophet. Possibly Ezekiel prophesied publicly to the exiles after his call and met with opposition. Was this opposition occasioned by hostility after the execution of certain false prophets who had incited the people to rebellion? (cf. Jer 29:21-23; H. L. Ellison, *Ezekiel: the Man and His Message,* p. 31) He was summoned by God to the plain (v. 22), where in glorious theophany the Lord instructed him to cease being a public reprover for a time (v. 26). He was to open his mouth only in his own house to those who consulted him privately (v. 24; 26:8). This intermittent silence prevailed from the beginning of the siege of Jerusalem (24:1,27) until news of the fall of the city was brought to the prophet by a fugitive about two years later. Then Ezekiel spoke freely, and the people realized that God had spoken.

22. The plain. Of Babylonia. Not the place of the vision in 1:1 (cf. 8:4; 37:1,2). **23. The glory of the Lord.** See on 1:28. **25. They shall put bands upon thee.** This refers neither to sympathetic magic nor to the fettering of the "demented" prophet, for no acts of hostility are recorded, but to God's restraining him (cf. 4:8), except as He bade him speak (vv. 26,27).

B. Overthrow of the City and State Predicted. 4:1–7:27.

In this cycle of threats the prophet predicts the fall of Jerusalem and Judah by means of four symbolic acts (4:1–5:17), an oracle against the idolatrous centers of the state (6:1-14), and a dirge over the downfall of the kingdom of Judah (7:1-27).

1) Four Symbolic Actions Concerning Jerusalem. 4:1–5:17.

In 4:1–5:4 there are recorded four symbolic actions setting forth the coming siege of Jerusalem, with its attendant hardships and the captivity following thereupon. The prophets Ahijah (I Kgs 18), Isaiah (Isa 8; 20), Jeremiah (Jer 13; 14; 18; 19; 27; 28; 34; 35; 43; 51) all made effective use of symbolic action; and Ezekiel also employed symbolism: 3:25,26; 4:1–54; 12:3-7,17-20; 21:11,12; 24:3-5,15-24; 37:15-17. Scholars disagree as to whether these symbols were enacted in whole, in part, or not at all. Some are held to be so extraordinary or so ludicrous as to be impossible to carry out. But they would not have seemed ludicrous to Orientals! These symbols are to be regarded as illustrative, not as sympathetic magic. It may be that whereas the intent of the symbols was actually carried out, metaphorical language is used in describing some of their details (cf. 4:3,12; contrast 8:3. The prophet was not carried to Jerusalem literally by the hair of his head, but in a vision). Attempts have been made to reconstruct the chapter so as to give it more logical order—but how can visions be logical?—and these reconstructions are conjectural at best.

a) Symbol of the Siege of Jerusalem. 4:1-3.

In this section the prophet draws on a clay brick the representation of the siege of Jerusalem.

1. Take a brick. Of soft clay, such as Babylonians used to write or draw on with a three-cornered stylus.

2. Fort[s] (AV). *Siegeworks; siege wall* or wheeled watchtower. The word *dāyēq* is probably Aramaic. **A mound** (ASV). To connect the tower with the walls of the besieged city. **Camp**[s]. Or detachments of soldiers. **Battering rams.** Or breakers. For these operations, see 17:17; 21:22; 26:8; Deut 20:20; Mic 4:11; Isa 29:3. See also the relief of Sennacherib's army besieging Lachish (II Kgs 18) on the palace walls at Nineveh in J. B. Pritchard, *The Ancient Near East* (Fig. 101).

3. Take . . . an iron pan; i.e., a plate such as was used for baking. This act was to represent the enemy's stout attacks against the city and to suggest the barrier between God and the people.

b) Symbol of the Duration of the Exile. 4:4-8.

4,5. Lie thou also upon thy left side. For the Northern Kingdom, Israel. When facing the sunrise, left is north and right is south (cf. Gen 14:15; Ps 121:5). **I will lay the punishment . . . upon you.** The emended text is preferable to the MT. Here Ezekiel represents Israel bearing her iniquity rather than vicariously suffering for it. **Three hundred and ninety days.** Equal to the number of years of their punishment. The LXX has "one hundred and ninety days." **6. Lie down . . . on your right side for Judah**; i.e., for the southern kingdom. **Forty days . . . each day for a year.** Same in the LXX.

7. In subject matter this verse seems to belong with verses 1-3.

8. I will lay bands upon thee, and thou shalt not turn thee from one side to another. Not physical bonds, but the divine constraint observed in 3:25; a symbol of the loss of freedom awaiting the people.

Some scholars hold that catalepsy or a prolonged illness is the motif behind this second symbol. It seems best to follow the comments made at 3:25 and find here a similar reference to Ezekiel's being bound spiritually and psychically. When he lay down in the privacy of his house, he lay on his left or right side, in keeping with the divine instructions.

From the fall of Jerusalem in 586 to the first return of the exiles in 538 is 48 years, which may in round numbers represent the duration of the **punishment of the house of Judah** (v. 6). On the 390 (or 190) days there is wide disagreement. The penalties of Israel and Judah would have been concurrent for the last forty years, but what is the *terminus a quo*? From the disruption of the monarchy in

922 B.C. to the return in 538 is 384 years, which is very near to 390 years. Perhaps this could be looked upon as a period of iniquity and punishment for the Northern Kingdom. In the books of Kings the total length of the reigns of the kings of Judah from Rehoboam to Zedekiah is given as 394½ years; but this can hardly be equated with Israel's iniquity or punishment. Others find some mystical similarity to the 430 years of Egyptian bondage by adding 390 and 40! Working from 734 B.C., the ravages of Tiglath-pileser (II Kgs 15:29), to the exile yields 148 years, which would be very near to the 150 years of the LXX in the added phrase in 4:5. From the fall of Samaria in 721 to 538 is 183 years, which is close to the figure of 190 years in the LXX in 4:5,9. Perhaps the numbers are to be taken ideally rather than literally. With the data at our disposal, it appears unwise to dogmatize as to how the 40 and 390 (or 190) years are to be reckoned.

c) Symbol of Scarcity During the Siege. 4:9-17.

9. The prophet was to make a mongrel bread from **wheat, barley, beans, lentiles** (a leguminous plant bearing a small reddish bean; cf. Gen 25:34), **millet** *(dōḥan,* a *hapax legomenon,* probably an Aramaic word; an annual grass which grows and matures without rain, the seeds of which are ground to flour and mixed with other cereals to form breadstuffs for the poor), and **fitches,** or spelt, a kind of wild wheat (cf. II Sam 17:28). **The number of . . . days . . . thou shalt lie upon thy side.** Unless this is looked upon as an intrusion from the previous symbol, the indication is that the second and third symbols were enacted simultaneously. The prophet could not have been literally bound on his side and also have gathered grain and baked bread.

10. Eat . . . by weight, twenty shekels a day. A shekel weighs four tenths of an ounce, avoirdupois. His food allowance was thus about eight ounces a day! **11. Water . . . the sixth part of an hin.** Since a *ḥîn* is about six and four-tenths quarts, his water ration was about a quart a day!

12. Dung. Bread baked on human dung would be revolting and polluting (cf. Deut 23:12-14; Lev 5:3; 7:21). **13. Eat their bread unclean among the nations** (RSV). Foreign nations and their products were considered unclean (cf. Amos 7:17; Hos 9:3,4).

14. Polluted. As a member of a priestly family, Ezekiel had observed the dietary laws (cf. Ex 22:30; Lev 7:18,24; 17:11-16; 19:7; 22:8; Deut 12:16; 14:21). Verse 14 is one of the few recorded prayers in the book. **15.** Ezekiel was permitted to substitute **cow's dung,** which is still used as fuel by the Bedouins and fellahin of Arabia and Egypt.

16. Break the staff of bread. Cf. 12:17-19; 14:13; Lev 26:26. **17. Waste away under their punishment** (RSV). Cf. 24:23; 33:10; Lev 26:39.

d) Symbol of the Destruction of Jerusalem's Inhabitants. 5:1-4.

1. Take a sharp sword; use it as a barber's razor (RSV). *As the razor of* (so the Syriac, Theodotion, Symmachus, Old Latin). **A barber.** The noun is *gallāb,* from the Akkadian *gallābu,* by way of the Phoenician or other Canaanite dialect. A *hapax legomenon.* **Pass it over your head and beard** (RSV). Figurative of sweeping the city clean of its inhabitants (cf. Isa 7:20; Jer 41:5). **Take thee balances to weigh.** "The divine justice is accurate" (A. B. Davidson).

2. Burn with fire. One third of the hair was to be burned, symbolic of the consuming of pestilence and famine; a second third was to be smitten with the sword, as was to be the lot of many inhabitants; and a third part was to be scattered to the wind, a figure of the scattered exiles (cf. v. 12). **3. A few in number . . . in thy skirts,** i.e., of his robe. A reference to the pious remnant. For other allusions to the remnant in Ezekiel, see 6:8-10; 9:8; 11:13. **4. Take of them . . . and cast them into the . . . fire.** Even this tiny remnant was to be subjected to additional trials.

e) Explanation of the Symbols. 5:5-17.

5. Jerusalem . . . in the midst of the nations. This is not to equate Jerusalem with the "navel of the earth" of the later apocalyptic, rabbinical, and Christian writers (cf. Eth Enoch 26:1,2; The Book of Jubilees 8:12,19). Israel, it is true, was located in the midst of the traffic lanes connecting Asia, Africa, and Europe; but more especially was she the center of God's providential choice and care (cf. Ex 19:5,6; Deut 7:6-8; 14:2; 26:19). **6. And she has wickedly rebelled** (RSV). This reading of the MT is preferable to that of the versions, *and she has changed* (Theodotion, Symmachus, Samaritan, Targum, and AV). The root is *mārâ.* For the heinousness of Israel's sin, see 16:47, 48; Jer 2:10,11; 18:13.

7. Because you are more turbulent. Böttcher emends the MT's *hămonkem* (root *hāmâ,* "to roar, be turbulent") to *hamrôtkem* (root *mārâ,* as in v. 6), "because of your showing rebellion." **And . . . in my statutes.** Supported by the LXX, and the Old Latin and Syriac. **Have done.** The "not" (AV, *neither)* of the MT is omitted by about thirty Hebrew manuscripts and the Syriac. **8. In the sight** (lit., *eyes)* **of the nations.** God will vindicate his holiness before the world (cf. 20:9,14,22,41; 22:16; 28:25; 38:23; 39:27). **9. I have not done.** Unparalleled punishments upon Israel from the Lord (cf. Lam 1:12; 2:20; 4:6).

10. The fathers shall eat the sons. Cannibalism (cf. II Kgs 6:24-29; Lev 26:29; Deut 28:53; Lam 4:10). **11. Thou hast defiled my sanctuary.** See chapter 8 for details. **I will cut you down** *('egda').* This RSV translation follows ten Hebrew manuscripts, as well as Symmachus, the Targum, the Vulgate, and the Masoretic Text.

12. A third part . . . shall die. These judgments are referred to in verse 2 (cf. Jer 14:12). **13. I will be comforted.** Strong anthropopathy. "I will comfort myself" by taking vengeance (cf. Isa 1:24). **In my zeal.** God's 'jealousy' incites him to punish his people's careless disloyalty (16:38,42) and to restore them lest the heathen question his power (36:5, 6; 38:19; 39:25-29). The solemn asseveration, "I the Lord have spoken," appears in verses 13,15,17; 17:21,24; 21:17, 32; 23:34; 24:14; 26:14; 30:12; 34:24; 36:36; 37:14; 39:5; and elsewhere in phraseology closely resembling this.

15. You shall be a reproach (RSV). This is the reading of the LXX, the Syriac, the Vulgate, and the Targum, which is in keeping with the rest of the verse. **16. When I loose against you** (RSV). This proposed reading differs only by one letter – *bākem* in place of *bāhem* – from the MT. **17.** "The four sore acts of judgment," **famine, evil beasts, pestilence,** and **sword,** also appear in 14:20. See also Lev 26:22-26; Deut 32:24,25; Rev 6:7,8. The judgments on Israel have significance for the world (Ezk 5:5-8); for Israel (5:13-17); and for the survivors (6:8-10).

2) An Oracle Against the Mountains of Israel, Seats of Idolatry. 6:1-14.

While the prophet denounces Jerusalem in chapters 4–5, in this chapter he denounces the nation.

a) Fate of the High Places. 6:1-7.

2. The mountains of Israel. They formed the chief topographical feature of the land of Israel. The phrase is peculiar to Ezekiel. See also 6:2,3; 19:9; 33:28; 34:13,14; 35:12; 36:1,4,8; 37:22; 38:8; 39:2,4,17. In 36:1-15, the prophet portrays the felicity of the mountains under the new kingdom. **3. The mountains . . . hills . . . rivers . . . and valleys** were physical features different from the flat Babylonian plains. They were also seats of idolatry of many kinds (Amos 7:9; Hos 4:13; Jer 2:20,23; 7:31,32; Isa 57:3-12; Zech 12:11; Mal 2:10,11). The course of idolatry had been checked in Israel by such leaders as Samuel, David, Asa, and Hezekiah. Manasseh re-introduced many types of pagan worship. Josiah engaged in a far-reaching reform in 622 B.C. (II Kgs 23:13-20), but his successors did not continue his work. **High places.** For a description of the high place, see W. F. Albright, *Archaeology and the Religion of Israel,* pp. 92,105-107; G. E. Wright, *Biblical Archaeology,* pp. 113, 114.

4. Incense altars. Not "sun images" of the older versions. See also Lev 26:30; II Chr 14:3; 34:4,7; Isa 17:8; 27:9; Ezk 6:4,6. Small limestone altars, with a horn at each corner, and pottery stands for the burning of incense have been found at Megiddo. An inscribed specimen found at Palmyra in Syria has established the identity of the *ḥammān* (cf. Albright, *op. cit.,* pp. 144-147,215; Wright, *op. cit.,* pp. 113,114). **Your idols.** Hebrew *gillûlîm* occurs thirty-nine times in Ezekiel and only nine times in the rest of the OT. The root means *to roll,* but the specific derivation of this name of contempt is obscure.

5. Scatter your bones. This was one method of defiling altars (cf. II Kgs 23:16). **6. That your altars may be laid waste.** This translation follows the reading *weyēshammû* of Symmachus, the Syriac, Targum, and Vulgate, in place of *weyē'shemû,* "and will be made guilty," of the MT. **7. Ye shall know that I am the Lord.** This statement, with its variants, Ezekiel's most characteristic phrase, appears more than sixty times in the book. The Lord is identified as the true God, the sole deity.

b) A Remnant Spared. 6:8-10.

8. I will leave a remnant. "He seasons judgment with grace" (Flack; cf. on 5:3). **9. When I have broken their wanton heart** (RSV). Reading *shābartî* (so Aquila, Symmachus, Theodotion, the Targum, and the Vulgate) in place of MT, *nishbartî,* "I have been broken." Literally, *their heart which has been committing adultery.* Compare the allegories in Ezekiel 16 and 23. **And blinded their eyes** (RSV).

Some such verb is needed to expand the harsh literal *zeugma*, "broken their heart and eyes." **10. In vain.** Hebrew *ḥinnām* (a *hap. leg.;* cf. Assyr. *annáma*, "in vain"), a substantive used as an adverb, from *ḥēn;* thus, "gratuitously, for nought, in vain."

c) Utter Desolation. 6:11-14.

The repetitions in this paragraph are characteristic of Ezekiel, and they emphasize his function as a watchman.

11. The prophet is to exult at the punishment of the abominations of Israel (cf. 21:14,17; 22:13; 25:6) and to exclaim, **Alas!** or *Aha!* (cf. 25:3; 26:2; 36:2). **12. Far off . . . and . . . near.** Judgment will come not only on Palestine but on idolatrous Jews wherever they be. **He that is besieged**, or better, *preserved* (lit., *watched;* cf. Isa 26:3). The survivors shall die of famine.

13. Under every green tree, and under every thick oak. Literally, *under every luxuriant tree and . . . leafy terebinth.* The terebinth *('ēlâ)* is a deciduous tree with pinnate leaves and red berries *(Pistacia terebinthus),* which often reaches a height of forty feet, and has wide spreading branches. It yields a type of turpentine. The verse refers to the cult of the fertility goddess (cf. Hos 4:13). **Sweet savour.** Hebrew, *odor of soothing*, i.e., tranquilizing odor of ascending sacrifices (Gen 8:21; Ex 29:18,25,41; Lev 1:9). Used with reference to idols, here and in 16:19; 20:28.

14. I will . . . make the land desolate . . . from the wilderness to Riblah (so variants in Ginsberg's Masoretic Bible and in Codex Petropolitanus of 916 A.D.); i.e., from the southernmost boundary to the ideal northern boundary (cf. Num 34:11, 12). The MT and the LXX read *from the wilderness of Diblathah.* There is no such place known, nor would the Moabitish towns mentioned in Num 33:45; Jer 48:22 be logical sites in this context. The name of the town is in the accusative (or *he directive).* Michaelis, pointing out the ready confusion between the letters *d* and *r* in both archaic and square characters, proposed *Riblah,* a city fifty miles south of Hamath, on the Orontes River (see also II Kgs 23:33; 25:20,21; Ezk 48:1).

3) Dirge over the Downfall of Judah. 7:1-27.

Ezekiel 7 is a climax to chapters 4–6. In partly lyrical, partly homiletical fashion, it declares that the time has come for the final punishment of Israel. Four short oracles of doom open the chapter (vv. 1-18) with the recurring theme, "the end has come" (vv. 2-4), "evil has come" (vv. 5-9), "the day has come" (vv. 10, 11), "the time has come" (vv. 12,13). The final scenes of the desolation of the state (vv. 14-27) picture the uselessness of defense (vv. 14-18), the wealth of the city becoming a prey to the invader (vv. 19-22), and the stupefaction seizing all classes of people (vv. 23-27). The city (vv. 13-15), king (v. 27), Temple (vv. 20-22), and enemy (v. 24) are all referred to in enigmatic fashion. The chapter abounds in repetitions, and the Hebrew presents many textual problems.

a) Four Oracles of Doom. 7:1-13.

2. The end is come upon the four corners of the land. This prophecy is restricted to Israel (vv. 1,3,7. Cf Amos 8:2; Jer 19:22). **3. I will send my anger.** Cf. Job 20:23; Ps 78:49. **And I . . . will judge thee.** Literally, *and I will give* (or *put) upon you all your abominations* (cf. vv. 4,8,9; 23:49). Carrying the guilt was part of the punishment. **4. Mine eye shall not spare thee.** Cf. 5:11; 7:9; 8:18; 9:10. While the language of verses 5-9 applies to Judah's fall, it has resemblances to eschatological passages, e.g., 30:3; Joel 1:15; Mal 4:1; Dan 12:1.

5. An evil, an only evil. *Disaster after disaster, evil after evil.* This rendering, found in thirty Hebrew manuscripts and the Targum, is derived from reading *'aḥar,* "after," in place of *'aḥat,* "one," of the MT (lit., *an evil, one evil has come).* Cf. v. 26. **6. The end . . . has awakened** (RSV). An instance of paronomasia, or play on words, *haqqēṣ hēqqîṣ.* Similar paronomasia occurs in Amos 8:2 on "summer fruit" and "end," *qāyiṣ* and *qēṣ (fall fruit . . . Israel will fall)* and Jer 1:11 on "almond" and "watching," *shāqēd* and *shōkēd (an awake tree . . . am awake).*

7. Your doom (AV, *morning).* This rendering of *s^e^pîrâ* assumes a root like the cognate Akkadian *sapâru,* "to destroy," rather than the meaning "diadem" of Isa 28:5, or *morning* of the AV based on Aramaic *saphrâ,* "dawn." **The day . . . is near.** Cf. verse 10. In popular thinking, "the day" meant the victory of Israel over her foes (cf. Isa 9:3; Hos 2:2; Ezk 30:9), but the prophets stressed its aspect of judgment on Israel (Amos 5:18; Isa 2:12ff.; 13:9; Jer 30:7; Ezk 7:19; 13:5; 36:33; Mal 4:1). A later development assigned to "the day of Jehovah" the overthrow of heathenism (Jer 46:10; Ezk 30:2ff.; 38:10,14; 39:8,11,13; Zech

14:3) and the ushering in of the new order, the rule of God (Ezk 39:22; Mal 4:2). **Tumult, and not of joyful shouting upon the mountains** (RSV). *Noise of battle and not* (joyous) *shout of mountains* (lit.). The MT is obscure.

Verses **8,9** are virtually a repetition of 3,4.

10. The day . . . is come. Cf. verse **7. Injustice has blossomed** (RSV). The Masoretic Text has *matteh,* "rod." Substituting other vowel points, one gets *mutteh,* "perverted justice" (cf. 9:9). This parallels **pride hath budded.** These are most likely references to the ruling power in Jerusalem. **11. None of them . . . for them.** The Hebrew text here is uncertain. The suggested rendering of the RSV is as good as any that have been offered. (See T. H. Gaster, "Ezekiel and the Mysteries," JBL, 60 (1941), 299.)

12,13. Property is of little value to either **buyer** or **seller** when exile threatens (Isa 24:2). **13. For wrath is upon all their multitude** (RSV). Reading *ḥārôn,* "wrath" (cf. v. 12b), for *ḥāzôn,* "vision," of the MT. The last half of the verse reads literally, *and a man—in his iniquity (is) his life—they shall not strengthen themselves.* The RSV presents a good conjectural reading.

b) Final Scenes of the Desolation of the State. 7:14-27.

14. Made all ready (ASV). An anomalous form of the infinitive absolute used as a continuation of the preceding finite verb (cf. Isa 5:5. Gesenius—Kautzsch, *op. cit.*, 72z, 113zN). **For my wrath.** Cf. verses 12,13. **15. Sword . . . pestilence . . . famine.** Cf. 5:2,12; 6:12; 33:27; Jer 14:18; Lam 1:20.

16. Like doves . . . mourning. Literally, *murmuring* or *growling* (cf. Isa 38:14; 59:11). The Syriac rendering, *All of them will die each because of his own iniquity,* seems premature in view of the following verses. **17.** Paralysis of strength is depicted here. Cf. 21:7; Isa 13:7; Jer 6:24. **18. Gird . . . with sackcloth . . . and baldness upon all their heads.** These were used to lament disaster (27:31; Isa 15:2,3; Jer 48:37) and to mourn the dead (Gen 37:34; Jer 16:6; Mic 1:16). The Hebrews were forbidden to make tonsures for the dead (Lev 21:5; Deut 14:1; Ezk 44:20).

19. Their gold shall be removed. Literally, *shall be impurity,* i.e., the ceremonial impurity of menstruation (Lev 15:19ff.; Ezk 18:6); or of touching a corpse (Num 19:13,20,21); and here of idolatry (cf. v. 20 and 36:17). Ezekiel "has the N. T. suspicion of money" (Lofthouse, *op. cit.*, p. 92). **Their silver and gold . . . cannot satisfy their hunger** (RSV). Cf. Lam 1:11; 2:11,12,19,20; 4:4,8-10; II Kgs 6:25. It was the **stumblingblock** that caused their ruin (cf. 14:3; 18:30; 44:12).

20. The beauty of his ornament. Better, *their beautiful ornament* (so the Syriac, Symmachus, and the MT). **He set it** (AV). Rather, *they used for vainglory.* Read *śamuhû* (along with the LXX Dold's Old Lat., the Syr., and the Vulg.) for MT *śāmāhû.* **They made their abominable images** (RSV) of silver and gold. Cf. 16:16,17; Hos 2:8; 8:4. **21. And I will give it into the hands of strangers . . . to the wicked.** A reference to the Chaldeans (cf. v. 24; 11:9; 28:10; 30:12; 31:12). **They shall pollute,** i.e., *profane,* the gold of the idols by putting it to common use. **22. My secret (place).** The root means *to hide, treasure up.* Hence it connotes both "secret" and "precious." This is probably an allusion to the Temple (cf. 24:21,25; Lam 2:1). **Robbers.** The Chaldean pillagers.

23. And make a desolation (RSV). The LXX attaches the phrase to the end of verse 22, reading, "and they shall make confusion." The rendering of the MT, *Make the chain* (for the captives), gives little sense. **24. The worst of the heathen.** The Chaldeans (see also v. 21; 28:7; 30:11; Jer 6:23; Hab 1:6,7,13). **Pomp.** *Pride of their strength* (so one Hebrew manuscript, the LXX, Dold's Old Latin, the Arabic, and Ezekiel's usual phrase; cf. 24:21; 30:6,18; 33:28). The MT rendering is *pride of (the) strong.* **Their holy places shall be defiled.** A reference to local shrines. The vowel points for **holy places** present a participial form, "they that sanctify them," which can easily be corrected.

25. Destruction cometh. Literally, *shuddering comes.* **26. Disaster comes upon disaster** (RSV). The Hebrew word *hōwâ*, "disaster, ruin," is different from the word in verse 5, *rāʿâ*, "evil" (cf. Jer 4:20). **The prophet** with his oracles from the Lord, **the priest** with instruction out of the Law, and **the elders** with their counsel on civil matters were alike dumb (cf. Jer 18:18; Lam 2:9).

27. The king . . . prince . . . and people were also helpless. Ezekiel refers to Jehoiachin (17:12), to past kings (43:7,9), and to the future ruler (37:22,24) as **king,** but he does not use the title in regard to the reigning Zedekiah (12:12; 21:25). **Prince** is the designation for the head of the new community (45:7,8,16,17,22;

46:2ff.,16ff.; 48:21,22), of which Jehovah alone is king. It is used of members of the ruling class in 21:12; 22:6. **The people of the land.** Here, the general population of Israel (*'am hā' āreṣ;* 12:19; 33:2; 39:13; 46:3,9). In post-Exilic times the term was used with contempt of the non-Hebrews in Palestine (Ezr 4:4; 10:2, 11; Neh 10:31). In the Mishna it means the vulgar herd, who know not the Law (cf. *Aboth* ii, 5; John 7:49). **And according to their own judgments** (RSV). So twenty Hebrew manuscripts and the Vulgate. The MT has *and in their own judgments.*

C. The Sin and Fate of Jerusalem. 8:1–11:25.

The prophet is transported in the Spirit to Jerusalem, where in vision he beholds and describes four forms of idolatry practiced in the Temple (ch. 8), the slaughter of the idolatrous inhabitants by the divine avengers (ch. 9), the destruction of Jerusalem by fire (ch. 10), and the abandonment of the city and sanctuary by the Lord, together with a prediction of restoration (ch. 11).

1) Vision of Four Abominations Practiced in the Temple. 8:1-18.

In this chapter is described the idolatry and superstition practiced in public and private by all classes. The contrast between a glorious and holy God and this debased worship is striking.

a) The Image of Jealousy. 8:1-6.

1. In the sixth year. This vision is dated fourteen months later than that of Ezekiel's call (1:1,2) about August-September, 591 B.C. **As I sat in mine house, and the elders of Judah sat before me.** The leading representatives of the exile or *gôlâ* are frequently referred to (cf. 11:25; 14:1; 20:1,3). **The hand of the Lord GOD** put Ezekiel into a trance state (cf. 1:3; 11:5).

2. The appearance of fire. The LXX reading **man,** *'îsh,* is preferable to the "fire," *'ēsh,* of the MT and agrees with the description in 1:26,27. **3. The spirit . . . brought me in the visions of God to Jerusalem.** We are clearly told that these were visions (v. 3; 11:24; see 3:12), a kind of "second sight," and not physical levitations (cf. II Kgs 5:26; 6:8-12; Isa 21:6-10). Contrast Bel and the Dragon, verses 33-39, where the angel of God transports Habakkuk bodily from Judah to Babylon by the hair of his head.

To the entrance of the gateway of the inner court (RSV). The inner court was the temple court proper (v. 16; 10:3; I Kgs 6:36; 7:12). The middle court, on a lower level, contained the palace (I Kgs 7:8; II Kgs 20:4). On a still lower level was the great court or outer court, which enclosed the entire palace complex (Ezk 10:5; I Kgs 7:12. See description and plan, W. S. Caldecott, "Temple," ISBE, V, 2932 f). In ancient temples the gateway was a covered building entered by means of an entrance or door (vv. 3,5,7).

The seat of the image of jealousy, not of "jealousy" itself, but (that) "which provokes to jealousy" (cf. 5:13; 16:38, 42; 36:6; 38:19; Deut 32:21). This may have been an image of Asherah, the mother-goddess of the Canaanites, set up by Manasseh (II Kgs 21:7), and subsequently destroyed by Josiah (II Kgs 23:6). Albright holds that the *image* or figured slab (Heb., *sēmel;* used only here and in Ezk 8:5; Deut 4:16; II Chr 33:7, 15), similar to those found in Syria, Asia Minor, and Mesopotamia, was placed in a niche in the wall (see *Arch. and Relig. of Israel,* pp. 165,166,221). Was it because the niche was empty that the women were weeping for Tammuz (v. 14)? **4. The glory of the God of Israel.** See on 1:28.

5. North of the altar gate, in the entrance, was this image of jealousy (RSV). The northern gate was that most frequently used, for the palace buildings were to the south and east. **6.** The **abominations . . . of Israel** were causing Jehovah to withdraw from his **sanctuary** (cf. 11:1,22,23). **Thou shalt see greater abominations.** See verses 13,15.

b) The Secret Idolatry of the Elders. 8:7-13.

7. The door of the court is apparently the outside entrance of the gateway into the inner court (cf. v. 3). **8,9.** He saw a hole in the wall, was told to dig through the wall, and there he saw a door, through which he was commanded to enter.

10. Portrayed (lit., *carved, incised;* cf. 23:14) **upon the wall round about** (emphatic, *round about, round about)* was "every pattern" of **creeping things.** Albright *(op. cit.,* p. 166) sees here a syncretistic cult of Egyptian origin, while others find Babylonian influence, or ancient Canaanite worship suggested. **Idols.** The "block gods" of 6:4. **11. Seventy men.** Probably a round number for prominent citizens of the Exile (cf. Ex 24:1; Num 11:16,24,25). **Jaazaniah.** Apparently a man well known. If this man was the **son of Shaphan,** who had assisted in Josiah's reform (II Kgs 22:3-10; Jer 26:24; 29:3; 36:10-12; 39:14), he had greatly corrupted the faith of his family. **Smoke** or *odor*. The Hebrew word *'āthār* is a *hapax legomenon* and its meaning is surmised from the context and from the versions.

12. In the dark; i.e., secretly. **Every man in his room of pictures** (RSV). **Room** is supported by the LXX, the Syriac, the Targum, and the Vulgate. *In his secret chamber* is the rendering of the LXX, the Syriac, and the Vulgate. *In the chamber of his dwelling,* i.e., "in the Temple," seems to be the Targum's rendition. Perhaps all that is meant is "in his imagination."

Two reasons are given for their practices: **The Lord seeth us not; the Lord hath forsaken the earth.** Cf. 9:9; Ps 94:7.

c) Women Bewailing Tammuz. 8:14,15.

14. Tammuz. This god can be traced back to the Sumerian Dumuzi, the god of the subterranean ocean and a shepherd deity, whose sister-consort, Inanna-Ishtar, descended into the lower world to bring him back to life. In his worship are similarities to that of Egyptian Osiris, the Canaanite Baal, and the Syrian Adonis. Gebal or Byblos, twenty-one miles north of Beirut, was the great seat of Adonis worship. The nightly death of the god, the god's dying before the touch of winter, or the vernal god's dying with the parched summer are variations on the theme of death and resurrection. Mourning for the god was followed by a celebration of resurrection. Human sacrifice, castration, virginity, and sexual union formed part of the cult rites at one time or another (see S. Langdon, *Mythology of All Races: Semitic,* pp. 336-351, and *passim*). Here, Jewish women are seen engaged in the sorrowful rites of the vegetation myth involving worship of Tammuz. There may be allusions to Tammuz in Dan 11:37 and Zech 12:11.

d) Sun Worshipers in the Inner Court. 8:16-18.

16. Within **the inner court of the Lord's house,** near the entrance or **door of the temple . . . between the porch** on the east end of the Temple (I Kgs 6:3) and the **altar** of burnt offering (I Kgs 8:64) **were about five and twenty men.** Their station here suggests that they were priests (cf. Joel 2:17), the twenty-four leaders of the classes of priests (I Chr 24:5 ff.) and the high priest (Keil). These men are called "elders" in Ezk 9:6, but Jeremiah also refers to the "elders of the priests" (Jer 19:1, ASV) or "senior priests" (RSV). In worshiping **the sun toward the east** (RSV), their backs would naturally have been toward the Temple. For references to sun worship, see Deut 4:19; II Chr 14:5; II Kgs 23:5; Jer 44:17 (?); Job 31:26.

17. They have filled the land with violence. The word **violence** can mean wrong done to man as well as to Jehovah (7:23; 12:19; 22:26; cf. 11:1-13). **They put the branch to their nose.** The meaning is uncertain. Some have found a reference to the Zoroastrian use of bundles of myrtle rods, or the sacred twig *barsom* held by the Parsees while praying, or even to phallic symbols. **18. Therefore will I also deal in fury.** Cf. 5:11; 7:4,9; 9:5,10.

2) Vision of Inhabitants Slain by Divine Avengers. 9:1-11.

1. Draw near, you executioners of the city (RSV). The Hebrew abstract noun meaning "visitation" is to be taken in a concrete sense in the plural—"overseers, officers, executioners" (e.g., 44:11; II Kgs 11:18; Jer 52:11). **Every man with his destroying weapon . . .** Better, *with his weapons of destruction in his hand.*

2. And, behold, six men. Supernatural agents in human form. **The higher gate, which lieth toward the north.** This gate is mentioned in 8:14 and perhaps in 8:3,5,7. Cf. II Kgs 15:35; Jer 20:2,10; 36:10. **Each one with his** *shattering weapon* **in his hand. A man . . . clothed in linen.** White garments suggest his divine sanctity and eminence (cf. Dan 10:5; 12:6,7; Rev 15:6). With **a writer's inkhorn.** This occurs only here and in verses 3,5,11. The word seems to be a loan-word from Egyptian. This was a case for reed pens, with an ink container attached, and was carried in the girdle or sash (cf. J. P. Hyatt, "The Writing of an Old Testament Book," BA, VI (1943), pp. 78,79). The appearance of seven angels is common: see Rev 8:2,6; 15:6; Enoch 20:1-8; 81:5; 87:2; 90:21, 22. To explain their number as the equivalent of the gods of the seven planets (including sun and moon) is only conjecture. **Stood beside the brasen altar.** This had been set up by Solomon (I Kgs 8:64; II Chr 4:1), and was later replaced by Ahaz' stone altar (II Kgs 16:14).

3. The glory . . . was gone up from the cherub. Some say, *from the cherubim in the most holy place in the Temple.* The text implies that Jehovah went to the threshold (9:3), while the cherubim and vacant throne waited (10:3) until the Lord remounted and departed (10:18).

4,5. The Lord commanded the man with the inkhorn to **set a mark upon the foreheads** of those who wept over the sin of the city, while the rest were to be slain indiscriminately by the six executioners. Here the word **mark** is *taw* (Eng. "t"), the last letter of the Hebrew alphabet, written in the old form as a cross. Compare the "sign" given to protect Cain (Gen 4:15); the blood on the lintel and doorposts on the night of the first Passover (Ex 12:23); and the sealing of the saints of God (Rev 7:3-8; 9:4; 14:1; 22:4). Origen and Jerome found mystical significance in the mark.

6. The slaughter was to decimate all classes, including **little children** (contrast Jon 4:11), but was **to touch no one upon whom is the mark** (RSV). Ezekiel often stresses the doctrine of personal responsibility for sin (cf. 3:19; 14; 18; 33). Like Elijah, he learned that he was not alone in his faithfulness to God (I Kgs 19:18). **Begin at my sanctuary.** Where the grossest idolatry had been carried on. Neither Ezekiel nor Jeremiah held to the inviolability of the Temple (cf. Jer 7:4ff.; I Pet 4:17). **7. Defile the house.** The Temple was desecrated with the slain. Compare the actual happening, II Chr 36:17,18. See also Rev 14:9-11, where those receiving the mark of the beast (Rev 13:16-18) are subjected to Divine torments.

8. Wilt thou destroy all the residue of Israel. Ezekiel so identified himself with the Lord's wrath against sin that we seldom find expressions of pity in him. See, however, 11:13; 24:15ff. Compare intercessions of Abraham (Gen 18:23-32), Amos (Amos 7:1-6), Jeremiah (Jer 14; 15).

9. The guilt of the land lay in its bloodshed and perversion of justice (ch. 22). The people felt that they could sin with impunity, claiming, **the Lord hath forsaken the earth,** and **the Lord seeth not.** All the prophets reminded Israel that a righteous God wants a righteous people, and that national calamity is a punishment for national sin. **10. Mine eye shall not spare.** See also 5:11; 7:4,9; 8:18; 9:5; Isa 5:25ff.; Amos 1:3,6ff.

11. The man clothed with linen. The recording angel stated that he had done his task, and the ominous silence with reference to the six executioners implied that they had done theirs.

3) Vision of Jerusalem Destroyed by Fire. 10:1-22.

The narrative portion of the chapter comprises verses 2-4,6,7,18,19, and is completed by 11:22-25. The rest of the chapter contains descriptions of the throne-chariot very similar to those in chapter 1. The recording angel receives fire from the cherubim with which to burn the city, and the glory of the Lord departs to the outside eastern gate of the outer court.

1. I looked. Cf. 1:26. The throne was empty (cf. 9:3), and the chariot awaited the Lord's return (10:3,18). **2.** The Lord addressed **the man clothed with linen,** who in this chapter becomes the agent of destruction. **Go in among the whirling wheels** (RSV). Hebrew *galgal,* "a whirl," is used of wagons (23:24; 26:10); of wheels (Isa 5:28; Jer 47:3); and of whirlwinds (Ps 77:18; 83:13). Here the word is singular and collective, describing the whole wheelwork. **Under the cherubim.** The LXX, the Syriac, and the Vulgate have the plural **cherubim** for the singular *cherub* of the MT, but the singular can be used in a collective sense, as is true of "living creature" in verses 15, 17,20. **Coals of fire . . . scatter them over the city.** God purposed the destruction of Jerusalem. Compare the event, as recorded in II Kgs 25:9. Sodom and Gomorrah, also, were destroyed by God (Gen 19:24).

3. The cherubims stood on the south (lit., *the right*) **side of the house;** i.e., the Temple. A **cloud filled the inner court,** betokening the Divine Presence (cf. v. 4; Ex 33:9,10; I Kgs 8:10,11; Isa 6:1). **4. The glory of the Lord went up.** The first half of the verse is a repetition of the act described in 9:3. **5. The sound of the cherubim's wings.** Cf. 1:24. **6. He . . . stood beside the wheels.** Cf. verse 2; and 1:13. **7.** A **cherub** on the side approached by the recorder handed him fire. The account is silent about his scattering it over the city, but this is assumed.

In verses 8-17, there is a renewed description of the throne-chariot, greatly resembling that in chapter 1, but with the added feature that the living creatures are definitely identified as cherubim.

8. A man's hand. Cf. 1:8. **9,10. The wheels.** Cf. 1:16. **11. Without turning.** Cf. 1:9,17. **In whatever direction the front wheel faced** (RSV). Literally, *whither the head turned,* i.e., the front of the chariot. **12. And their rims . . . were full of eyes** (RSV). The MT has,

And all their flesh and their backs and their hands and their wings and the wheels were full of eyes, which seems to confuse the cherubim and the wheels. Backs can be rendered as *rims* (cf. 1:18) and hands as *spokes,* confining the reference to the wheels.

13. This verse is definitely out of place here and would more suitably follow verse 6.

14. And every one had four faces. Cf. 1:10, where each cherub has four faces. In this verse, what may be meant is that the prophet, standing to the north of the chariot and looking at it, saw the one face of each cherub that was turned toward him rather than all four faces of the four cherubim. Thus, at the front of the chariot directly in the line of his vision was the **ox** (in place of the *cherub),* while on the north was the **man,** at the rear of the chariot the **lion,** and on the south, the inner visible face, was the **eagle. 15.** Cf. verses 19,20,22. **Living creature** is a singular noun used collectively here and in verses 17,20.

16. Cf. 1:19. **The same wheels also turned not from beside them** suggests that the wheels did not turn away from beside the cherubim. The preposition *min,* "from," often loses its significance in another language, and is better untranslated, thus bringing the phrase into line with 10:11; 1:9,12,17 (cf. BDB, p. 581, under *min,* 4c). **17. When they stood, these stood.** Cf. 1:21.

18. The glory of the Lord departed from . . . the threshold . . . (cf. 9:3), **and stood over the cherubims,** preparing to leave. **19.** The throne-chariot moved to **the east gate,** apparently of the outer court, paused briefly on the Mount of Olives "on the east side of the city" (11:23), and left completely. Later, in prophetic vision, Ezekiel saw the glory return by the same eastern gate (43:1-4).

20. The living creatures . . . were cherubim, already identified in verse **15. 21,22. Four faces.** Cf. 1:6,8,9,12a.

The etymology of *cherub, cherubim* is still dubious, although Akkadian *karâbu,* "to be gracious, bless," and *karubu,* "intercessor," may be cognate forms. They are emblematic, composite figures representing human nature spiritualized, sanctified, and exalted to be the dwelling place of God. They function in several ways: (a) they guard the tree of life (Gen 3:24), and the ark in Solomon's Temple (I Kgs 6:23-28; 8:7); (b) they engage in adoration of God in connection with the mercy seat in the Tabernacle (Ex 25:18-20; 37:7-9); (c) they support the Lord's throne (I Sam 4:2; II Sam 6:2; II Kgs 19:15; Ps 80:1; 99:1); and (d) personified as the wind and cloud, they form the chariot of Deity (II Sam 22:11; Ps 104:3; I Chr 28:18). These various concepts are present in Ezekiel, especially their function as bearers of the throne of Jehovah. In the book of Revelation they engage in perpetual worship (4:6ff.; 5:6ff.; 6:1ff.; 7:11). When redeemed humanity has entered heaven, these figures typifying humanity, having served their purpose, disappear. (See G. A. Cook, ICC, pp. 113,114, and a thorough discussion of "cherubim" in **P.** Fairbairn, *The Typology of Scripture,* **I,** pp. 215-239).

4. Vision of the Internal Condition of the City and the Lord's Departure from It. 11:1-25.

In chapters 8—10, the prophet denounces syncretism in religion. In this chapter he denounces the false confidence of the leaders of Jerusalem who felt that the city was secure and that its inhabitants were morally superior to the exiles who had been deported to Babylonia in 597 (vv. 1-13). Then he sounds a message of hope for the exiles, stating that God will replace their stony heart with a heart of flesh (vv. 14-21). The divine glory rises from the city and moves to the Mount of Olives; the prophet is "carried back" to Babylonia; and he thereupon relates his vision to the exiles (vv. 22-25). The narrative seems to follow chapter 8, and appears out of place after the events described in chapter 10; but in a vision one is not to expect chronological order.

a) The Flesh and the Caldron. 11:1-13.

1. Ezekiel was transported to the outer eastern gate, where he saw **five and twenty men** (not the same as in 8:16), among whom were Jaazaniah (not identical with the personage in 8:11) and Pelatiah, **princes of the people.** They represent the civil government of Judah.

2. These men gave **wicked counsel,** detrimental to the city. The anti-Babylon party counseled that the nation should revolt against Nebuchadnezzar and form an alliance with Egypt (ch. 17), contrary to God's command (Jer 28:16), and in violation of the oath her ruler had sworn to the Chaldean monarch (II Chr 36:13). This was the party of violence (7:23; 9:9; 11:6; ch. 22).

3. It is not near; let us build houses. If read as a question, "Is not the time near to build houses?" (lit., *is not* [or *not is*] *near the building of houses?),* we get a hint of their counsel which went contrary to the prophets. Then follows a popular saying: **This city is the caldron,** protecting us from the fire: and **we be the flesh,** valuable in contrast to the useless broth cast away, like the exiles in Babylonia. But in Jeremiah 24, exactly the opposite valuation is given to the remnant of Jerusalem and to the exiles in Chaldea.

5. The Spirit of the Lord fell upon me. Only here is this expression used in Ezekiel. The prophet was enabled to prophesy while still in the trance.

6,7. Ezekiel reverses the meaning of the proverb, comparing the **city** to a **caldron** burning with the fires of judgment, and the **flesh** to those slain in the streets (cf. 7:23; 22:25). **8. The sword.** Those in Jerusalem were to share the fate of the exiles. For the antithesis, see 35:6. **9. Strangers . . . judgments.** Cf. 7:21; 5:10. **10,11. I will judge you in the border of Israel;** i.e., far from the so-called protecting city. The terrible judgment on King Zedekiah and the leaders took place at Riblah (see comment at 6:14). Cf. Jer 39:5-7; 52:24-27; II Kgs 25:18-21. **12. I am the Lord.** This verse repeats a number of Ezekiel's phrases. Cf. v. 10; 5:6; 18:9,17.

13. When I prophesied. Ezekiel, enabled by God's Spirit to discern things at a distance and in the future, saw the death of Pelatiah, one of the twenty-five leaders. Thereupon he interceded for the *remnant of Israel* (cf. 9:8).

b) Hope for the Exiles. 11:14-21.

14. The word of the Lord. Cf. 6:1; 7:1; 12:1. **15. Your fellow exiles.** With the LXX, Dold's Old Latin, and the Syriac, read *gāluteka* for MT *ge'ullāteka*, "your redemption, kindred." The exiles and **all the house of Israel,** descendants of the captivity of Samaria in 722/721, had been held in contempt by the inhabitants of Jerusalem, who now laid claim to the land.

16. Although I have scattered them (cf. 20:23; 28:25; 36:19) . . . **yet I have been a sanctuary to them for a while** (RSV; lit., *in small measure).* Not in the sense of asylum, but as One greater than the Temple whose presence sanctifies (cf. Ps 84; 137:4-6; Isa 8:12,13). Even **in the countries where they have gone.** Cf. 12:16; 36:20-22.

17. Therefore . . . I will . . . gather you. The gathering of the exiles is a frequent promise in Ezekiel: 20:34,41,42; 28:25; 29:13; 34:13; 36:24; 37:31; 38:8; 39:27; as well as in the other prophets: Jer 23:3; 29:14; 31:8,9; 32:37; Isa 43:5, 6; 54:7; 56:8; Zech 10:8,9. **And I will give you the land of Israel.** Cf. 20:42; 28:25; 34:13; 37:21; 39:28; and elsewhere. The yearning to be back in the land of Israel, uniting patriotic and religious motives, has characterized Judaism through the centuries. **18.** The returned exiles will remove all the **detestable things** from the land. Pure worship is the condition for renewal of true relations with the Lord (cf. 14:6; 18:30,31).

19. I will give them one heart. Three Hebrew manuscripts and the Syriac read, *a new heart,* as in 18:31; 36:26. The LXX has *another heart*. In the Bible the **heart** is regarded as the seat of man's mental activities, his mind, his will. The **spirit** is regarded as the breath, wind, disposition which animates actions. The two together constitute man's inner being, into which God would instill a new energy. For "the heart of stone," unimpressionable, obstinate, God will **give them an heart of flesh** (cf. 36:26,27; Jer 31:31-33), which would be "sensitive, responsive to God's touch, and obedient to His will" (Bewer). This is God's work, his gift of grace. **20. They shall be my people, and I will be their God.** See also 14:11; 36:28; 37:23,27. Cf. Jer 24:7; 30:22; 31:1,33; 33:28. The community of the future will be composed of converted individuals.

21. As for them whose heart walketh after . . . detestable things. Literally, *and to the heart of their detestable things and their abominations their heart goes.* The smoother reading is obtained with the help of the Targum and the Vulgate.

c) Departure of the Divine Glory. 11:22-25.

The narrative in chapter 10 is completed with this paragraph.

23. The midst of the city. The Temple was on the eastern border of the city, but it was the focus of the city's life. **The mountain . . . on the east side of the city,** across the Kidron valley, or valley of Jehoshaphat, was the Mount of Olives (cf. II Sam 15:30; Zech 14:4). From this mountain Jesus wept over the doomed city (Lk 19:37-44). Cf. Ezk 10:19; 43:1-4.

24. The Spirit . . . brought me in the vision . . . into Chaldea, to the exiles (RSV). See on 8:3. **25.** The prophet related to the elders sitting before him (8:1), **all the things that the Lord had shewed me.**

D. Moral Necessity of the Captivity. 12:1–19:14.

The preceding messages of Ezekiel predict the fall of the nation. In this section (chs. 12–19), the prophet deals with the objections of men who thought the present storm would pass, who saw no calamity ahead, and who held that the Lord would never repudiate his people. By symbolical actions, allegories, and parables, Ezekiel demonstrates the moral necessity of the captivity. He gives two symbolical representations of flight from the besieged city (12:1-20), expostulates with false prophets (12:21–14:23), pictures Israel as a useless vine (ch. 15), and in a detailed allegory recalls Israel's long history of unfaithfulness to her divine bridegroom (ch. 16). He returns to the metaphor of the vine to emphasize Zedekiah's disloyalty (ch. 17), answers objections to divine punishment by an analysis of individual responsibility (ch. 18), and bursts forth into a dirge over the princes of Judah and over Judah itself (ch. 19).

The subject matter of chapters 12–24 may be classified under three categories. I. Unfaithful Israel: the useless vine (ch. 15); the foundling child who became an unfaithful wife (ch. 16); the two unfaithful sisters (ch. 23); a review of Israel's history (20:1-44). II. Sin and Its Judgment: prophecy and its abuses (12:21–14:23); moral freedom and personal responsibility (ch. 18); punishment of Jerusalem necessitated by her sins (ch. 22). III. The End of the Monarchy: two symbolic acts (12:1-20); two eagles and the vine (ch. 17); two lions and the vine (ch. 19); the avenging sword of the Lord (20:45–21:32); the allegory of the rusted caldron (ch. 24).

1) Symbolic Actions Depicting Exile and Invasion (cf. chs. 4; 5). 12:1-20.

a) Symbol of the Exile, and Its Exposition. 12:1-16.

1. The word of the Lord also came unto me ("saying"). This formula occurs six times: here and in verses 8,17,21,26; 13:1. **2.** The exiles in Babylonia are a **rebellious house** (2:3,6-8; 3:26,27). They **have eyes to see** but do not discern the moral meaning in events (Deut 29:3,4; Isa 6:9; Jer 5:21; Mk 8:18; Acts 28:27).

3-7. The prophet was commanded to prepare an **exile's baggage** (RSV; lit., *make thee vessels of exile),* such scanty provisions as exiles might carry in bundles on their shoulders, which he was to bring out **by day in their sight** (lit., *in their eyes).* Then he was to **go forth at even in their sight. . . . Dig through the wall,** perhaps of his own house, **go out through it** (the reading of the LXX, Syriac, Vulgate, and Targum, in preference to the MT *bring out),* carrying the baggage on his shoulder *in the thick darkness* (vv. 6,7,12). He was also to cover his face (lit., *eyes).* In doing this he was to be a *sign* or portent for **the house of Israel.** See also v. 11; 24:24,27; cf. Isa 8:18; 20:3; Zech 3:8.

10. This oracle concerns the prince in Jerusalem. Literally, *the prince is this oracle,* or *burden* (AV). There is a play on words equivalent to, "The leader is this load." Ezekiel nowhere refers to Zedekiah as king. **The house of Israel who are in it** (RSV). Read *b^e^tôkâh* for MT *b^e^tôkām,* "in the midst of them." **11. I am a sign for you.** Literally, *your portent, symbol.* Cf. verse 6. **So shall it be done unto them;** i.e., to the people of Jerusalem.

12. The prince (Zedekiah) **. . . shall bear** ("his baggage" should be supplied as direct object). **He shall dig through the wall** (RSV), following the LXX, and the Syriac. The MT has *they shall dig,* which can refer to Zedekiah's attendants. **And go out through it** (RSV). So the LXX, the Syriac, the Targum. The MT reads *to bring* (supply "him") *through it.* **That he see not the ground.** The LXX has a conflate reading, *that he may not be seen by an eye, and he himself shall not see the land.* Verse 12 refers to Zedekiah's disguising himself, while verse 13 refers to his subsequent blinding at Riblah (II Kgs 25:4-7; Jer 52:8,11).

13. My net . . . snare. See also 17:20; cf. 19:8, referring to Jehoiachin. **Babylon . . . shall he not see it.** Zedekiah, for breaking his oath of allegiance, was blinded and died in captivity in Babylon (cf. 17:1-21). **14. I will scatter . . . his helpers.** So the LXX, Dold's Old Latin, the Syriac, and the Targum. The MT reads *his help,* an abstract noun used in a concrete sense. **And all his bands.** A loanword from the Akkadian, "wings"; then "wing of an army," "hordes"; used metaphorically also in 17:21; 38:6,9,22; 39:4. **Draw out the sword.** Cf. 5:2,10,12. **15. They shall know that I am the Lord.** See 6:10.

16. I will let a few of them escape (RSV). Literally, *I will let remain of them men of number;* i.e., "men few in number." Cf. the idiom in Gen 34:30; Deut 4:27; Ps 105:2; Jer 44:28. See also Ezk

6:8-10. **That they may declare . . . among the nations.** The Lord's preserving the survivors will make clear to the nations that the catastrophe to his people was due not to his impotence but to his justice. He is concerned for the honor of his name. See 14:21-23.

b) Symbol of the Siege. 12:17-20.

18. With this symbol of eating **bread with quaking** and drinking **water with trembling and with carefulness** (i.e., anxiety), compare the symbol expounded in 4:9-17. There the emphasis was on the scarcity of food; here it is on the terror. The word **quaking,** *ra'ash,* is used of an earthquake (3:12; 37:7; Amos 1:1); of the hyperbolical shaking of the earth by forces in war (Isa 9:4; Jer 47:3; Job 39:24; 41:21).

19. The people of the land. The general populace, those left behind, in Judah (cf. 7:27). **That her land may be desolate from all that is therein.** *In order that her land* (i.e., Jerusalem's) *may be desolate from her fullness* (lit.; cf. similar construction in 32:15). **Because of the violence of all them that dwell therein.** See Amos 3:9-11 on the violence of Israel. **20.** Cf. 35:4.

2) Prophecy and Its Abuses. 12:21—14:23.

In this collection of oracles the prophet deals with the popular attitude of contempt toward prophecy (12:21-28), citing the common saying that prophecy is no longer fulfilled at all (vv. 21-25), and that Ezekiel's prophecies refer to the far distant future (vv. 26-28). To these charges Ezekiel replies that the prophecies bear on the present and will be fulfilled. This leads to a discussion of the deceivers of the people, false prophets and false prophetesses (ch. 14). The lying prophets are compared to foxes who find ruins congenial (vv. 1-9); these whitewash the tottering walls the people build; i.e., they flatteringly approve of the futile projects of the people (vv. 10-16). False prophetesses, execrable women who professed to read the future for payment and predicted success for the wicked, are denounced (vv. 17-23). The prophet then turns to the wickedness of those who inquired of God but whose hearts were with their idols all the time (14:1-11). This raises the problem of general responsibility. The presence of a righteous man among a sinful people will not save a land when God brings His judgments upon it (14:12-23).

a) Rebuke Against Contempt of Prophecy. 12:21-28.

22. What is that proverb. The Hebrew word *māshāl* is apparently from a verb meaning "to liken, compare, be equal"; hence, a "comparison" or "similitude." Bentzen and J. Pedersen derive it from a verb meaning "to rule"; hence, a sentence spoken by rulers filled with the power of mighty souls, a winged word, outliving the fleeting moment. Ezekiel often quotes and replies to popular sayings (8:12; 11:3; 16:44; 18:2; 20:32). Time goes on and **every vision comes to naught** (AV, *faileth*); i.e., becomes a dead threat. The failure of prophecy to realize itself became a proverb. Scoffers made light of the threatened judgment. See also Jer 5:13,14; 17:15; II Pet 3:3, 4,9.

23. The fulfilment (ASV; AV, *effect;* lit., *word).* The contents were soon to be realized. The prophets did not ordinarily set definite dates for the fulfillment of their messages because of their moral and contingent character (see on v. 27). **24. Vain vision.** The false prophets spoke contrary to the men called of God, and there was no external way to distinguish the truth from falsehood except that, "He that is of the truth heareth my voice" (Jn 18:37). The pagans made use of **divination,** magic, and mediums to learn the mind of the deity (21:21; Deut 18:9-12). In true prophecy mechanical arts were discarded, for Jehovah spoke to the mind of the prophet. Flattering or smooth *divination* promised immunity from trouble (cf. 13:10,16; Jer 23:16,17; 28:1-17). **25. I will speak.** This verse continues verse 23. Literally, *for I the Lord will speak what word I will speak.*

27,28. To those who said, **The vision . . . is for many days to come . . . far off,** i.e., not of immediate concern, the prophet replied that the divine words were to be put into effect at once. In pronouncing threats, the prophets did not normally date their fulfillment, for such prophecies were moral, contingent threats, which might be averted upon repentance and amendment (see Jonah; Jer 18; 26:17-19; Joel 2:14,18).

b) False Prophets. 13:1-16.

The term *false prophets* is not used in the OT, but historical perspective is right in so designating them. There were two classes of false prophets: those who were representatives of some object of worship other than the true God, e.g., Baal, Moloch (cf. Elijah's contest with the prophets of Baal, I Kgs 18:19ff.); and those who falsely purported to speak in the name of Jehovah (cf. Micaiah's opposition to the prophets of Ahab, I Kgs 22:5-28). The strongest denunciations of these deceivers are by Jeremiah, who opposed them on moral, personal, and political grounds (Jer 23:9-32). During the dying gasps of Jerusalem, Hananiah opposed Jeremiah at home (Jer 28), and Ahab, Zedekiah, and Shemaiah opposed him in Babylon (Jer 29:15-32). Ezekiel in this chapter also exposes the false prophets and the false prophetesses. (See A. B. Davidson, "The False Prophets," *O. T. Prophecy*, pp. 285-308).

2. Ezekiel here refers sarcastically **to the prophets of Israel,** false prophets who **prophesy out of their own hearts,** i.e., their emotions and desires. He discloses the source (v. 3), content (vv. 4,5), and result of their message (vv. 6,7), and the doom of the false prophets (vv. 8,9). **3. Foolish prophets.** A play on words: *nᵉbî'îm nᵉbālîm*, something like "profitless prophets." Folly is primarily a moral rather than an intellectual deficiency. In the book of Proverbs, for example, wisdom is set forth as the "fear of the Lord," and folly as disregard for him and his precepts. The force moving these prophets was **their own spirit** and not the Spirit of the Lord.

4. Ruins were as congenial to them as to gamboling foxes, and they increased the devastation. **5.** They failed to stand **in the breaches,** to stop the invading disaster (cf. 22:30; Ps 106:23). Nor did they build a **wall** of moral and spiritual counsel for Israel in the coming crisis. **The day of the Lord.** Cf. on 7:7.

6. Lying divination. To divine means to obtain an oracle from a god by drawing lots (cf. 21:21). To gain knowledge of secret things by superstitious means was forbidden Israel (Ex 22:18; Num 23:23; Deut 18:10,11), and divining was disparaged (cf. Ezk 13:7,9,23; 21:29; 22:28; Mic 3:6,7,11). **Saying, The Lord saith.** *Oracle of the Lord (nᵉ'um Yahweh)*, the formula of true inspiration (cf. Amos, who uses it 21 times, 2:11,16, etc.). **They expect him to fulfill their word** (RSV). There was no external criterion for true prophecy. "While the true prophet had the witness in himself that he was true, the false prophet might not be aware that he was false" (Jer 23:21,31; A. B. Davidson, *op. cit.*).

9. A threefold punishment of the false prophets is predicted. At the present they have prestige and influence, but in the new kingdom **they shall not be in the assembly of my people** (cf. Gen 49:6; Ps 89:7; 111:1), **nor be enrolled in the register** (i.e., list) **of the house of Israel** (RSV; cf. Ezr 2; Neh 7; Ex 32:32,33; Isa 4:3; Mal 3:16), **neither shall they enter the land of Israel** (cf. Ezk 20:38; Jer 29:32).

10. The false prophets announced **peace,** when **there was no peace.** See Mic 3:5; Jer 6:14; 8:11; 23:17.

The next section reads, literally, *and he* (the people) *is building a party-wall* (*ḥayiṣ*, only here in the OT; a wall of stones loosely piled together without mortar), *and behold them* (the prophets) *daubing it with marly clay plaster*, or *whitewash*. The prophets acquiesced in the people's attempt to defend the city, hiding its weakness by lying prophecies.

11. There is a play on the words **whitewash,** *tāpēl* and **fall,** *nāpal*. Three elements in nature will make the wall to fall (cf. v. 13). **Great hailstones.** Omit the MT *and you*. **13.** Cf. Mt 7:24-27. **Hailstones.** The unusual word *'elgābîsh* (only here and in 38:22) is probably the Akkadian *algamešu*, "crystal," and so, "ice crystals." **14. Will I break down the wall.** The prophets were buried beneath the collapsing walls (cf. Isa 25:12; Lam 2:2; Amos 9:1).

c) False Prophetesses. 13:17-23.

Several godly, gifted women are referred to in Scripture as prophetesses: Miriam (Ex 15:20); Deborah (Jud 4:3,4); Isaiah's wife (Isa 8:3); Huldah (II Kgs 22:14); Anna (Lk 2:36); and the four daughters of Philip (Acts 21:9). In the present paragraph, the prophetesses, or rather sorceresses, were counterparts of the false prophets, forerunners of the modern palmists, fortunetellers, and mediums.

17. Out of their own heart. Cf. verse 2.

18. Who sew magic bands upon all wrists and make veils for the heads of persons (RSV). The puzzling expressions in this verse apparently describe features of "sympathetic magic" whereby the sorceress fastened magic influence upon her inquirers by the tying of knots and the shrouding of the persons in veils varying in length according to their stature. It was believed that like effects like, that a desired result could be obtained by mimicking it, and that things once brought into contact continue to act upon each other after being separated. **In the hunt for souls.** Or *persons* (cf. BDB, p. 660b. So in vv. 19,20; 17:17; 18:4; 22:27). The prophetesses made victims of those who consulted them, hunting down some persons and keeping others alive for their own profit, or keeping their own persons alive.

19. Will ye pollute me . . . ? Better, **And ye have profaned me.** To pollute or profane is the opposite of to sanctify. It is to bring God down to the sphere of the common, the false, the unworthy (cf. 20:39). **With** (not *for)* **handfuls of barley and with** (not *for)* **pieces of bread,** used to obtain the oracles (cf. Jer 44:15-19). **To slay the souls that should not die,** i.e., the righteous; **to save the souls alive that should not live,** i.e., the ungodly (cf. v. 22; Hos 6:5; Jer 1:10). Contrast the work of the true prophet, set forth in Ezk 3:16-21.

20. Magic bands with which (RSV; following Dold's Old Lat., the Syr., Targ., and Vulg. in place of MT *where)* **you hunt the souls,** or persons (omit, with the LXX and the Syriac, MT *for flying ones). Pāraḥ,* "to fly" is an Aramaic word, perhaps a gloss. **And I will let the souls,** or persons, **that you hunt go free.** This is Cornill's emendation, reading MT *'et nepāshîm* as *'ōtān ḥopshîm,* "like birds" (so Ewald), instead of MT "for birds." This may also be an Aramaic gloss as above. **21.** To be hunted. Cf. verses 18,20.

22. Because you have disheartened . . . although I have not disheartened (RSV). The second verb is, literally, *pained.* The verbs are *kā'â* and *kā'ab* respectively. Cornill uses "pained," *kā'ab,* in both places. **By promising him life.** Literally, "so as to keep him alive." Whatever encourages sin is false (cf. Jer 23:22). **23. No more . . . delusive visions** (RSV); i.e., falsehood, as in verse 6. The judgment of diviners is at hand. Cf. 12:24; Mic 3:6,7; Amos 8:11. The issue will be that Jehovah shall be known in truth.

d) Idolatrous Inquirers of the Lord. 14:1-11.

1. Elders of Israel; i.e., elders of the exiles (cf. 8:1; 20:1). These leaders, probably perplexed by Ezekiel's denunciations of the false prophets, came to inquire further about Jerusalem and its future.

3. Have set up their idols in their heart. Note the frequent mention of idols *(gillûlîm)* in the paragraph. Cf. 6:4,5. **Stumblingblock of their iniquity.** Cf. 7:19,20. They have busied their thoughts with idolatry, which causes them to stumble and fall (cf. v. 6).

4. Every man of the house of Israel. A legal formula (cf. Lev 17:3,8,10,13; 20:2). The man whose heart was divided in its allegiance to Jehovah would receive no knowledge through a prophet, but would be answered by Jehovah himself in deeds. **I will answer him by myself.** This translation follows the reading of the Targum and of verse 7, *bî,* instead of MT *bâ,* "coming." **5. That I may lay hold of the hearts of . . . Israel** (RSV). The Lord would call them to account for their idolatry. He cannot tolerate secret faithlessness.

6. Although the prophet had pointed out the self-acting law of divine retribution (v. 4), he here says that God pleads with men to forsake their evil way. **7. Stranger that sojourneth in Israel.** Note Ezekiel's care for the resident aliens (22:7,29; 47:22,23). The proselyte enjoyed equal rights under the law and faced equal penalty (Lev 17:8,10,13; 20:2). **8.** Cf. Lev 17:8-10; 20:3,5,6. **A sign** or warning example (cf. Num 26:10; Deut 28:37,46). And **a byword** i.e., *a proverb* reading the word in the singular with the Syriac and the Vulgate.

9. If the prophet be deceived. This may result not only from self-delusion (13:3,6) and from idolatrous inquirers (v. 7), but **I the Lord have deceived that prophet.** In ancient thought, secondary causes were often overlooked, and events attributed directly to the work of the Lord. See Amos 3:6; Isa 45:7. When a man sins against spiritual light, he brings on himself spiritual blindness. This does not relieve him of responsibility, however, for always the principle of "no other gods before me" obtains. Cf. II Kgs 22:15–23:3.

10,11. The **prophet** and he **that seeketh** alike would be punished, for the double purpose of deterring Israel from unfaithfulness (cf. Isa 4:4); and of restoring her true relations with the Lord (cf. 11:20). The judgments all have mercy in view.

e) The Righteous To Save but Themselves, not a Sinful Land. 14:12-23.

13. The prophet declares that **when the land sinneth,** and God sends one of his four judgments (cf. 5:16,17) against it—famine (vv. 12-14), hurtful beasts (vv. 15,16), sword and war (vv. 17,18), pestilence (vv. 19,20)—though the righteous ancients, Noah, Daniel, and Job, were in that land, they could deliver only themselves. The application to Jerusalem (vv. 21-23) finds no righteous persons within it. And what wicked survivors will escape all four judgments, in apparent exception to the principle enunciated above, will be a grim proof to the exiles of God's righteous judgment on Jerusalem. **By trespassing grievously.** A closer rendering is *by treacherously committing treachery.* See also 15:8; 17:20; 18:24; 20:17; 39:26; Lev. 5:15; 6:2.

14. Noah, Daniel, and Job are cited as examples of righteous men, non-Hebrews, in ancient times. Cf. Gen 6:8; 7:1; Job 42:7-10. Virolleaud, deVaux, and others equate the Daniel of Ezekiel with Dan'el, "righteous judge of the cause of widows and orphans," who is referred to in the Ras Shamra texts of about 1400 B.C. (Aqht, 170; 2 Aqht, V: 7,8. For full discussion, cf. Ginsberg, BA 8 (1945), p. 50: Pére de Vaux, RB (1937), pp. 245, 246; W. H. Morton, "Ras Shamra—Ugarit and Old Testament Exegesis," *Review and Expositor,* 45 (1948), pp. 70-72).

15. Noisome beasts. Literally, *an evil beast* (cf. 5:17; Lev 26:22). **And they** (lit., *it,* sing. collective) **spoil,** or *bereave it.* Cf. Jer 9:10,12. **16. These three men.** Cf. 18:10-13; Jer 15:1-4. **17. A sword.** See also 5:12; 6:3; 11:8; 21:3,4; 29:8; 33:2; Lev 26:25. **19,20. Pestilence.** Cf. 5:17; 38:22.

21-23. *Application to Jerusalem.* **21. My four sore acts of judgment** (RSV). Cf. Jer 15:2,3; Lev 26:22-26. **Four** signifies completeness.

22. A remnant. *Any survivors to lead out sons and daughters* (LXX, Syr., Sym., Vulg.). When these bad figs (Jer 24:8-10; 29:16-20) **come forth unto you** in Babylon, **ye shall be comforted** or reconciled by the justice of God's punishment on Jerusalem.

3) Parable of the Grapevine. 15:1-8. The figure of Israel as a vine or vineyard occurs frequently (Gen 49:22; Deut 32:32; Hos 10:1; Isa 5:1-7; Jer 2:21; Ezk 17:61; Ps 80:8-16). Here reference is to the wild vine of the forest rather than to the cultured vine of the vineyard.

3. Shall wood be taken. If the vine did not bear fruit, its wood could not be used even to make a peg. **4.** If in addition, it has been burned at both ends, **is it useful for anything** (AV, *meet for any work)* except for fuel?

6. Jerusalem is the vine destined for burning (5:2; 10:2,7; 16:38-42). **7. From the fire have they escaped?** Yet the **fire shall devour them.** They will escape the burning city, only to meet another fate (5:4; 11:9; 12:14; 23:25).

4) Allegory of the Foundling. 16:1-63. This allegory, like that in chapter 23, depicts the connection between the Lord and his people in terms of a husband-wife relationship (cf. Hos 2; Jer 2:1-3; 3:1-5). The OT seldom uses this figure or the father-son motif, whereas in Canaanite and other polytheistic religions, the marriage of divinities and mortals, and the physical birth of gods and demigods is prominent. After idolatry had been extirpated from Israel, the NT writers could effectively portray the relationship between God and the redeemed, Christ and his Church, under the symbols of fatherhood and husbandhood (Eph 5:25,26; I Jn 3:1-3).

Possibly Ezekiel took a familiar tale and developed it as an allegory, in keeping with Oriental tastes. A foundling child of dubious origin, Jerusalem, is exposed by the roadside to die. But she is rescued by the Lord, who becomes her benefactor (vv. 1-7). Having grown up to beautiful maidenhood, she is taken in marriage by her benefactor and becomes his royal consort (vv. 8-14). The proud queen proves utterly unfaithful and plays the harlot with Canaanites and other pagans (vv. 15-34). The punishment for this conduct, which is described in verses 35-43, is justified, since her depravity is worse than that of her two sisters, Sodom and Samaria (vv. 44-52). Nevertheless, the Lord makes glorious promises of restoration for the three sisters (vv. 53-58), foretelling that penitent Jerusalem will experience a glorious reconciliation through an everlasting covenant (vv. 59-63).

a) Jerusalem as the Foundling Child. 16:1-7.

2. Her abominations. Especially the worship of Baal and Moloch (vv. 15-22) and alliances with heathen nations (vv. 23-34). **3. The Canaanites.** Referred to in the stele of Amenhotep II (1447–1421), in the El Amarna Letters of about 1370 B.C., and in an ancient Hittite incantation (see ANET, pp. 246, 352, 483, 484). **Amorite** *(Westerner).* Or the Amurru, a powerful Semitic people who invaded the Fertile Crescent about 2000 B.C. Cf. Gen 14:7; 15:16; Num 21:21-30; Josh 24:15. Hammurabi (1728–1686), of the first dynasty of Babylon, was an Amorite. (See G. E. Mendenhall, "Mari," BA, XI (1948), 1-19.) **Hittite.** A non-Semitic people, resident in Asia Minor in the second millennium B.C., with contacts in Canaan from patriarchal to Solomonic times (Gen 23:10-20; 26:34; Josh 1:4; I Sam 26:6; I Kgs 11:1). On Hittite bestiality, consult G. A. Barton, *Archaeology and the Bible,* pp. 423-426. Ezekiel was stressing the heathenism in Israel's background.

4. Salting made the skin drier and firmer, and aided in cleansing. **To cleanse,** (AV, *supple)* **you** *(lᵉmishʿī)* is an unknown expression, but it is suggested by the Akkadian and the Targum. **5.** This baby girl, however, was **cast out in the open field.** Child exposure was practiced at the time of Christ's birth (W. H. Davis, *Greek Papyri of the First Century,* pp. 1-7). **6. Polluted;** i.e., "kicking about." Five manuscripts, the LXX, the Old Latin, and the Syriac omit the second, "and I said . . . , Live," as dittography.

7. To multiply. The LXX and the Syriac read *grow* up in place of MT *and a myriad . . . I made thee.* **Art come to excellent ornaments.** *Arrived at full maidenhood.* The Syriac *in the menses,* or verse 8, in **the time of love,** suggests the meaning, *full maidenhood.* **Thou wast naked and bare;** i.e., "unmarried."

b) The Maiden Married to Her Benefactor. 16:8-14.

8. I spread my skirt over thee. Symbolic of marriage (Ruth 3:9; Deut 22:30). **And entered into a covenant with thee.** Cf. Mal 2:14; Prov 2:17. **9. Washed I thee.** Preparatory ceremonies for the nuptials. Cf. Ruth 3:3. Purification from heathenism and consecration to the Lord. **10. I shod you with leather** (RSV). *Taḥash* (used as a covering for the Tabernacle, Ex 25:5; 26:14), is either an Egyptian loan-word, "leather," or the Arabic *dugong,* a kind of porpoise, whose skin was used for sandals.

11-13. For the bride's finery, see Isa 3:18-24; Gen 24:22,30,47. **12. A ring on your nose** (RSV; AV, *forehead).* See also Jud 8:24; Isa 3:21. **13.** Bountiful food. Cf. Deut 32:13,14; Hos 2:10. **14.** The splendor of Jerusalem in Solomon's time (cf. I Kgs 10; Lam 2:15).

c) The Wife's Shameless Infidelity. 16:15-34.

Her idolatries with the Canaanites (vv. 15-22), and with foreign peoples (vv. 23-29): Egyptians (vv. 26,27), Assyrians (v. 28), and Chaldeans (v. 29). **15.** After settling in Canaan, Israel frequented the Canaanite sanctuaries (cf. 20:28; Jer 2:5-7; 3:1-3). **16.** Gaily-colored tents on the high places (cf. II Kgs 23:7). **17. Images.** Of Baals? Or phallic symbols? (May, IB) **18,19.** Cf. Jer 10:9; Hos 2:8. **20,21.** Child sacrifice. Cf. 20:26,31; 23:37-39. Cf Ex 22:29; Jud 11:39; II Kgs 16:3; 21:6; 23:10; Jer 7:31; 19:5; 32:35. **24.** Objects erected for unlawful worship. **25.** Cf. 23:8,17,30,40.

26,27. Alliance with Egypt. Cf. Isa 30:1ff.; 31:1ff.; II Kgs 18:21. **Lustful neighbors** (RSV); cf. 23:20, euphemism for power of Egypt. **27.** Philistine harassment of Judah in the time of Sennacherib (see ANET, p. 288). **28. With the Assyrians.** Ahaz' and Manasseh's pro-Assyria policy (II Kgs 16:7ff.; 21:1ff.; II Chr 33:1ff.). **29. The trading land of Chaldea** (RSV). Literally, *in the land of Canaan unto Chaldea.* Here the word *Canaan* is used in the sense of "a trader, merchant"; i.e., unto the merchants' land, even Chaldea (cf. 17:4; Hos 12:7; Zeph 1:11; Zech 14:21).

30. How weak is thine heart. "How lovesick is your heart," seems to be the idea. In Aramaic and Akkadian the phrase occurs, "How am I filled with wrath against thee" (Cook, ICC). The deeds of a **brazen harlot** (RSV). Literally, *the work of a woman, an imperious harlot.* **31.** Compare verses 24,25. **Scornest** or "mocked" hire (cf. H. G. May, "The Fertility Cult in Hosea," AJSL, 48 (1932) 89-93). **32-34.** Other harlots take hire; she was different in that she gave hire to strangers (cf. Deut 23:18; Hos 2:19; 9:1). **33.** The words *nēdeh,* "gift" (AV **gifts**), and *nādān,* "marriage gifts" (AV, **gifts**), are *hapax legomena.*

d) The Punishment of the Adulterous Wife. 16:35-43.

The passage interweaves a description of the punishment of an adulteress with a foreview of the destruction of Jerusalem.

36. The Hebrew word rendered **thy nakedness** elsewhere means "copper" or "bronze." It may be an Akkadian loanword—"excess, prodigality." The last part of the verse echoes verses 20,21. **37. All thy lovers.** The nations with which she had become allied; **and all those you loathed** (RSV). Those with whom no alliances had been formed, e.g., the Philistines.

38. Break wedlock. Cf. Lev 20:10; Deut 22:22; Jn 8:5-7. **Shed blood.** Cf. verses 20,36; Gen 9:6; Ex 21:12; Lev 24:17. **Blood in fury.** With a minute change, the reading is, "I will lay on you wrath and jealousy," as in 23:25. **39. Strip . . . thy clothes.** This signifies the exposure of the adulteress. See also 23:26; Hos 2:3,10.

40. A company. A multitude gathered for the trial and stoning of the adulteress (cf. v. 38). **41. Burn thine houses.** Cf. Jud 15:6; 12:1. **In the sight of many women.** To warn them. Cf. 23:10,48. **42. My fury** will be appeased. Cf. 5:13. **43. Thou hast not remembered.** A summary of verses 35-43.

e) Jerusalem's Depravity Compared with That of Sodom and Samaria. 16:44-52.

44,45. As is the mother, so is her daughter. Jerusalem and her sisters resembled their common mother, the Hittite (cf. v. 3). **46. Thine elder** (lit., *greater,* i.e., in political and territorial power) **sister** was **Samaria,** who lived with **her daughters** (dependent towns) to the north (i.e., **left,** as one faces east; Gen 14:15), while her **younger** (i.e., less important) **sister** to the south, or **right** (I Sam 23:19), was **Sodom and her daughters.** Galling comparisons. Cf. Jer 3:6ff.; Isa 1:9.

47. More than they. Jerusalem exceeded the wickedness of her sisters (cf. Mt 10:15; 11:20-24). **48-50.** Sodom's heinous crimes of Genesis 19 are not recounted, but rather her **pride, prosperous ease** (RSV; *abundance of idleness,* AV), and failure to **strengthen the hand of the poor and needy.** Cf. Amos 6:4-6; Est 3:15; Lk 16:19-31. **51,52. Samaria.** Samaria's sins are not named, but she and Sodom appear righteous, relatively speaking, in comparison with Jerusalem (cf. Amos 3:2).

f) Glorious Promises of Restoration for the Three Sisters. 16:53-58.

53. Bring again their captivity. Cf. Jer 12:14-17; 46:26; 48:47; 40:6,39; Isa 19:24. **54-56.** If Samaria and Sodom were punished, how much more did Jerusalem deserve punishment! If Jerusalem was to be restored, it was only just that they who were a byword in her mouth be restored also.

57,58. Jerusalem had become an object of **reproach of the daughters** (i.e., cities) **of Syria** (following many MSS and Syr., read *Edom* instead of MT ***Aram,*** **i.e.,** Syria) and to **the daughters of the Philistines.** The destruction of Jerusalem, here prophetically assumed, causes unholy glee in the Edomites and Philistines (25:12-14,15-17; Ob 10-14; Ps 137:7-9).

g) A Glorious Reconciliation and an Everlasting Covenant. 16:59-63.

59,60. Breaking the covenant. Jerusalem had broken the covenant made in her youth at the Exodus (cf. vv. 8,43). Consequently, she must suffer; but in the day of her repentance, God will give her an everlasting covenant (cf. 37:26; Isa 54:9,10; 55:3; Jer 31:35,36; 32:40; 33:20-22). Samaria and Sodom (as representing the heathen world) are to be included in the new covenant as an act of grace, since the former covenant broken by Israel did not include them. **63. Remember.** Jerusalem will be abashed by memories of her unworthy past "when I purge you," "make atonement for you." The word "atone," *kippēr,* with God as agent, is used (cf. Deut 21:8; Jer 18:23; Ps 78:38).

The fall of Israel was a cause of Ezekiel's outreach to the Gentile world. Even peoples like those of Sodom shall be converted to the Lord, says Ezekiel. Similarly the Apostle Paul declares, "By their (Israel's) fall salvation is come unto the Gentiles" (Rom 11:11,12; ASV). "God hath shut up all unto disobedience, that he might have mercy upon all" (Rom 11:32; ASV).

5) Parable of the Vine and the Two Eagles. 17:1-24.

a) The Allegory. 17:1-10.

2. The prophet propounds **a riddle** (*ḥidâ;* cf. Jud 14:12; I Kgs 10:1) requiring interpretation, or a **parable** *(māshāl;* cf. 24:3; Isa 14:4) containing a similitude or comparison.

3,4. A great eagle. The great broad-winged eagle (*nesher,* often "vulture"; Hos 8:1; Lam 4:19; but here "eagle" is more fitting) with long pinions represents Nebuchadnezzar. The many colors possibly indicate the various nations included in the Babylonian empire. **Lebanon** is the mountain of Israel; the **cedar** is the Davidic house (vv. 12,22). Nebuchadnezzar is represented as carrying off Jehoiachin, king of Judah, to the **land of traffick,** Babylon. **5,6. The seed of the land,** native to the region is Zedekiah. It was planted in **a fruitful field** (the land of Israel), in the vicinity of abundant waters (Deut 8:7; 11:11), where it possessed every natural advantage for growth and fruitfulness. Prosperity is indicated by the fact that the seed **sprouted and became a low spreading vine . . . and brought forth branches and put forth foliage** (RSV).

7,8. Another great eagle. Pharaoh-hophra of Egypt enters the scene (Jer 44:30; 37:7). Though flourishing in good soil, the vine (Zedekiah) sought the agency of another power to supply it more abundantly.

9,10. Ezekiel asks, **Shall it prosper?** Like Isaiah and Jeremiah, Ezekiel opposed an Egyptian alliance (Isa 30:1-5; 31:1-3; Jer 2:36). Cooke (ICC) suggests a transposition of verses 9 and 10. First comes destruction upon the vegetation of Palestine by the east wind and then destruction by the arm of Nebuchadnezzar, whose city, Babylon, lay almost due east of Jerusalem.

b) The Interpretation of the Allegory. 17:11-21.

Ezekiel addresses the interpretation to the **rebellious house** (v. 12), the Jewish exiles among whom he lived. The history of Jehoiachin's deportation and of Zedekiah's oath of fealty (II Chr 36:13; cf. Gen 15:9-18; Jer 34:8-22) is recapitulated.

13,14. Nebuchadnezzar had removed **the mighty** (chief men) **of the land** likely to stir up revolt, that Judah might remain as a state dependent on and friendly to Babylon. **15-17. He rebelled.** Zedekiah broke the covenant with the king of Babylon, as well as that with the Lord (v. 19), and consequently was to die in Babylon with no aid from Pharaoh. **21. And all the pick** (i.e., choice men) **of his** (Zedekiah's) **troops** (RSV, following the Targum and the Syriac) **shall fall** before the Babylonian armies.

c) The Promise of a New and Universal Kingdom in Israel. 17:22-24.

The Lord makes clear that he will not permit his kingdom to be annihilated, but will fulfill his promise to the seed of David.

Nebuchadnezzar broke off a twig from the cedar and brought it to Babylon, and the shoot he planted died. The Lord declares that he himself will pluck off a shoot from the top of the high cedar (the Davidic house; vv. 2,3; Isa 53:2) and plant it on a high mountain, that all may see it (cf. Isa 2:2; 11:10) and find protection under it (Ezk 17:23; cf. Mt 13:31, 32). The establishment of this new and universal kingdom by Jehovah will lead the world to recognize him as the Lord of human life and the Controller of Israel's destiny.

Other kingdoms are likewise called trees. See 31:5,8,14,16,18. For passages in Ezekiel concerning God's kingdom, see 21:27; 34:24ff.; 37:24ff. See also Lk 1:51-55. The lineage of Christ is traced through Jehoiachin (Mt 1:11,12).

6) God's Justice Shown in His Treatment of Individuals. 18:1-32.

Ezekiel begins this passage with Jeremiah's quotation of a current saying (Jer 31:29) that had made its way to the exiles at Tell Abib: "The fathers used to eat sour grapes, and the children's teeth are blunted" (Ezk 18:2).

Jeremiah had described the exiles carried away with Jehoiachin in 597 B.C. as "good figs," while those left behind under Zedekiah were "bad figs" (Jer 24). The Jews of Zedekiah's day probably looked upon themselves as righteous in comparison with the people of Manasseh's era; and so the proverb may convey a tone of self-righteousness.

However, the people were slipping into despair and fatalism. If they were being punished for the crimes of Manasseh (II Kgs 24:3,4) and for the sins of their fathers, why should they struggle? What chance does an individual have in the face of a fate inherited from the past? Why should anyone try to be godly in such an unjust world? (Cf. the hedonism pictured in Isa 22:12,13). Is there any alternative to bleak despair for man? (Ezk 33:10)

Ezekiel had previously thundered wholesale condemnation on the people (cf. chs. 16; 20; 23). Yet God allowed for brands being plucked from the burning. The righteous were marked off from the wicked by a sign (4:4). In the face of imminent judgment, they would deliver their own lives, but no others (14:14, 16,18,20). However, repentance would be possible (14:6,11).

The concepts of social solidarity and group responsibility were old in Israel. Ezekiel's homily or essay in chapter 18 implies the working of the natural sequence of cause and effect amidst the circumstances of human life. God does not hold a man responsible for the circumstances into which he was born, but only for the use to which he puts them subsequently. Hence, a man is free to renounce his past, whether for good or for evil.

Just as a writer can change the course of a narrative by adding new material to the previously written chapters of a book, so, despite a dismal past, the present can become the opportunity for total transformation and can issue in a triumphant future. Forgiveness does not obliterate the past, but relates it in a new way to God, so that we can transform it from a curse to a source of blessing (cf. Allen, IB, pp. 157-161).

Our prophet desires to vindicate divine justice and in doing so assigns new value to the individual in his treatment at the hands of God. God deals with men as individuals, says the prophet. "All souls are mine" (18:4). "I have no pleasure in the death of anyone" (v. 32, RSV). Since each soul is immediately related to God, its destiny depends on this relation. "The soul that sinneth, it shall die"

(v. 4); "So turn and live" (v. 32). Cf. 3:16-21; 33:10-20.

As the representative of God, Ezekiel states that the individual man is not involved in the sins and fate of his forefathers (vv. 1-4). And then he develops the principle of the personal responsibility of the individual in the instance of three successive generations: a righteous father, a wicked son, and a righteous grandson (vv. 5-9, 10-13, 14-18). He restates the principle of individual responsibility (vv. 19,20), and declares that divine forgiveness is available to the repentant sinner, but that the apostate will die in his sins (vv. 21-29). He concludes with an exhortation to repent and be saved (vv. 30-32).

a) All Persons Individually Responsible to the Lord. 18:1-4.

2. Proverb *(māshāl)*. Cf. 8:12; 12:22 23, **The fathers have eaten** (lit., *eat* or *used to eat* **sour** or unripe **grapes** *(bōser)*, **and the children's teeth are blunted** (AV, *set on edge)*. That is, the children suffer the consequences of the sins of their fathers (quoted in Jer 31:29,30). On transmission of guilt, see Ex 34:7; Num 14:18; Deut 24:16; II Kgs 14:6; Lam 5:7. **3.** The use of this proverb, ascribing injustice to God, will stop at once. **4. All souls are mine**; i.e., all persons belong to the Lord alike and individually, and he alone has the authority to judge. **The soul that sinneth, it shall die.** "Live" (vv. 9,17,19) and "die" (vv. 4, 13,18) are used in both a literal and an eschatological sense. "To live" is to enter into the perfect kingdom of the Lord which is about to come (chs. 37; 38) and "to die" is to have no share in it. Ezekiel, like the other OT writers, views this kingdom as an earthly one.

b) Life To Be the Reward of the Righteous. 18:5-9.

In this picture of the righteous man we see the obligations of right living. A general statement about the man's righteousness (v. 6) is followed by the description of his practice of piety, his chastity, and his beneficence (vv. 7,8), as rooted in obedience to the commands of God (v. 9). For similar lists of virtues, see Ps 15; 24:3-6; Isa 58:5-7; Job 31. A good man's outward conduct is a revelation of his inner character, the result of obedience to God.

6. Hath not eaten sacrificial meals to false gods **upon the mountains** nor **lifted up his eyes** in prayer to idols (cf. 6:4). A righteous man abstains from adultery and impurity (Lev 15:19-30). **7,8. Hath restored to the debtor his pledge.** Cf. Ex 22:26; Deut 24:6; Job 22:6, Amos 2:8. **Does not lend at interest** (RSV). Jews were forbidden to take interest from their needy brethren (Ex 22:25; Lev 25:25-37; Deut 23:19) but were permitted interest on loans to foreigners (Deut 23:20). Nor **hath taken any increase**; i.e., more than was lent. **9.** The MT reads, "And my judgments he has kept to do *truth ('emet)*, which the LXX renders, "to do *them*" *(ôtām)*. **He shall surely live.** This contrasts with verse 4.

c) A Wicked Son of a Righteous Father To Incur Death. 18:10-13.

10. If he beget a violent son, **a shedder of blood** (the rest of the verse may be a gloss from Lev 4:2). **11. That doeth not any of those duties.** Those listed in verses 6-9. **13. Shall he then live?** This is the logical conclusion of the question posed in verse 10. **He shall surely die.** Literally, *shall be put to death*, the formula of Ex 21:15; 22:18; Lev 20:9,11. A good father cannot pile up merit for his son.

d) A Righteous Son of a Wicked Father To Merit Life. 18:14-18.

14. The man in the third link of the chain **sees all the sin** of his father and fears (so the LXX, Old Lat., and Vulg.), and avoids his example. **16. Exacts no pledge** (RSV), thus going further than verses 7,12. **17. Withholds his hand from iniquity** (RSV). This translation follows the reading of verse 8 and the LXX. The reading of the MT, *has withdrawn his hand from*, so as not to oppress, *the poor* (cf. 20:22), is tenable.

Hezekiah, Manasseh, and Josiah, the later kings of Judah, aptly illustrate the three cases above, though they comprise four generations.

e) The Principle of Individual Responsibility Restated. 18:19,20.

19. Yet say ye. See also verses 25,29; 33:17,20; Mal 1:2; and frequent occurrences in Malachi. **Why? doth not the son bear the iniquity of the father?** Ezekiel points out that neither son nor father will be held responsible for the other's iniquity, but each person is individually responsible to God.

f) Divine Forgiveness for the Repentant Sinner but Not for the Apostate. 18:21-29.

As a man does not inherit the consequences of what his fathers have done, so the individual, through repentance, can be emancipated from his own past. The wicked man who turns from his evil to righteousness shall live (vv. 21-23). However, the righteous man who abandons his righteousness for evil shall die in his evil (v. 24). To the objection that the ways of the Lord are not just, comes the rejoinder that the ways of the house of Israel are not just (vv. 25-29).

21. The sinner is free to repent and turn from sin and do God's will. Contrast the idea in Hos 5:4; Jer 13:23. **22. In his righteousness.** Cf. verse 24; 33:16. **23. Have I any pleasure at all that the wicked should die?** This question reflects God's mercy and his desire to save all. "The most precious word in the whole Book of Ezekiel" (Kraetzschmar). Cf. verse 32; 33:11; I Tim 2:4; II Pet 3:9.

25. The way of the Lord, the principle on which he acts, **is not equal** *(yittākēn).* Literally, *adjusted to the standard.* A figure from the mercantile exchange (cf. v. 29; 33:17; I Sam 2:3). **26-29.** These verses repeat in shorter form the thought presented in verses 21-25, to emphasize this new concept.

g) Exhortation To Repent and Be Saved. 18:30-32.

31. Cast away. Here Ezekiel refers to man's part in the renewal. In 11:19; 36:25-27, he points out God's part. Cf. Jer 4:4; 24:7; 31:33; Ps 51:7; Phil 2:12, 13. His ministry required both emphases. **32. I have no pleasure in the death of him that dieth** (AV). *I desire not the death of him that is to die;* i.e., that deserves to die (cf. v. 23; 33:11).

Ezekiel, as the appointed watchman of the Lord (3:16-21; 33:1-9), warned and wooed his people, proclaiming the justice of God and also His love toward the repentant sinner. How to harmonize the personal responsibility of the individual and his moral freedom with God's justice in the treatment of every individual is a difficult problem, with which the book of Job and Psalm 73 struggle. Job received not a solution but satisfaction in a fresh vision of God (Job 42:5,6). "The heart has reasons that the reason knows not of," said Pascal. Despite the problems of suffering and sin, trust in a loving Heavenly Father is ever the proper attitude of the believer.

7) Allegory of the Two Lions and the Vine. 19:1-14.

Two laments in elegiac meter *(qînâ),* under the guise of allegory, depict: (1) a lioness, the nation Israel, deprived successively of her two whelps—Jehoahaz, deported to Egypt (vv. 2-4), and Jehoiachin, taken captive to Babylon (vv. 5-9); and (2) a vine and its rods, torn up, planted in a wilderness, and consumed by fire out of one of its own rods; that is, Israel involved in destruction by her own King Zedekiah and exiled to Babylon (vv. 10-14).

a) The Lioness Deprived of Her Two Whelps. 19:1-9.

1. A lamentation *(qînâ;* see also 26:17; 27:2; 28:12; 32:2; Amos 5:1) is a poem in characteristic elegiac meter, in which a longer line, usually of three beats, is followed by a shorter one, usually of two beats (cf. Amos 5:1-3; Lam 1).

2. The nation Israel (or Judah) is pictured as a **mother** of mighty kings, a lioness, in power and majesty. Lions were common in ancient Palestine (Jer 49:19; 50:44; Zech 11:3; Song 4:8; Isa 30:6). Five different words for them are found in Job 4:10,11, three of which occur in this verse. The lion became practically extinct in Palestine after the Crusades. **3. One of her whelps.** Jehoahaz. **Learned to catch the prey;** i.e., became a ruling king. **4. The nations sounded an alarm** (RSV). Read the MT as a causative, *caused a cry to be heard.* Cf. Isa 31:4; Jer 50:29. Jehoahaz was carried to **Egypt** by Pharaoh-necho (II Kgs 23:33,34).

5. Was baffled (RSV; AV, *had waited).* Reading *nō'ălâ* in place of MT *nôḥălâ,* "waited." **Another of her whelps.** Jehoiachin. **6. He prowled** (RSV). *Walked about.* **7. And he ravaged their strongholds** (RSV). This translation follows the Targum instead of MT *and he knew his widows.* Cf. Jer 2:15,16; 4:7; 5:6; 25:37. **8.** [Snares] **on every side.** Cf. 12:13; 17:20, where it is also parallel with "net." **9.** Nebuchadnezzar carried Jehoiachin to Babylon (II Kgs 24:15).

b) The Vine Uprooted and Consumed by Fire. 19:10-14.

10. Another metaphor is introduced here. Israel is compared to a vine. See also Isa 5:1-7; 27:2,3; Ps 80:9; Mk 12:1-9. **In a vineyard** (RSV) appears in two manuscripts, in contrast to MT *in thy blood.* **11. Its strongest rod became a ruler's sceptre** (RSV). So the LXX B, the Old Latin, the Arabic, and verses 12,14. This rod is Zedekiah (or Jehoiachin). **12. But she,** the nation, was **plucked up.** Cf. 17:9,10; 31:12; Amos 9:15. **The east wind,** Babylon, **dried up her fruit. 13.** The nation is now in exile amid conditions where national life cannot thrive. **14. The fire has gone out from its stem**

(RSV). The vine was consumed by fire from one of her own rods. Zedekiah by his rebellion brought destruction on both nation and dynasty (II Kgs 24:20ff.; Jer 52:3). **This** [has become] **a lamentation.** That is, the dirge is finished, and has become history (cf. 32:16).

E. Israel's Coming Downfall Inevitable and Necessary. 20:1–24:27.

Ezekiel reviews the history of the people of Israel whom the Lord kept alive out of regard for his own name (20:1-44). But now regard for his name requires that his avenging sword smite Jerusalem (20:45–21:23 = MT 21:1-37). Moreover, Jerusalem's abominations, like dross, must experience the smelting fires of judgment upon the classes and masses alike (ch. 22). In an allegory reminiscent of that in chapter 16, the Lord dilates upon the infidelity and harlotry of two sisters, Oholah (Samaria) and Oholibah (Jerusalem), to their divine spouse, and the punishment consequent upon their adultery (ch. 23). On the day of the beginning of the siege of Jerusalem (Jer 39:1), Ezekiel relates the allegory of the rusted caldron set on the fire for purging. And by his abstention from mourning at the death of his wife, he becomes a symbol of the people's despair at the fate of their city (ch. 24).

1) Review of Israel's Unfaithfulness, and Her Preservation. 20:1-44.

To the elders of the Jewish community in Babylonia seeking a divine oracle (vv. 1-4), Ezekiel reviews Israel's history, with its recurring rebellions (vv. 8,13,16, 21,28), and its preservation by the Lord because of his regard for his own name (vv. 9,14,17,22,41-44). Israel sinned both in Egypt (vv. 5-9) and on the journey from Egypt to Kadesh-barnea (vv. 10-17). The second generation in the wilderness rebelled against God (vv. 18-26), and the people who entered Canaan were continually faithless to Him (vv. 27-29). The prophet's own generation was as idolatrous as the preceding generations (vv. 30-32). However, God's purpose for His people in the future would involve judgment and hope (vv. 33-44). Israel would be brought into the wilderness a second time, for the purpose of judgment (vv. 33-39). Then, after idolatry had been rooted out and true worship made possible, the Lord would be acknowledged by the nations and by an Israel that loathed her past (vv. 40-44).

a) Introduction: Ezekiel Consulted by the Elders of Israel. 20:1-4.

1. In the seventh year. July-August 590 (591) B.C., eleven months after the last date mentioned (8:1). **The elders.** Cf. 8:1. **3. I will not be enquired of.** Cf. verse 31; 14:3; 36:37. Rather than answering their question relative to the present, God rehearses the relevant lesson of Israel's past. **4. Judge them** (cf. 22:2; 23:6) by letting them **know the abominations of their fathers.**

b) Rebellious Israel Preserved by the Lord's Regard for His Name. 20:5-32.

5-9. *Israel's rebellion in Egypt.* **5.** God's choice of Israel is mentioned only here in Ezekiel. It is mentioned first in Deut 4:37; 7:7,8; 10:15; 14:2; once in Jer 33:24; often in Isa 40–66, e.g., 41:8,9. **Lifted up mine hand,** in taking an oath (see also vv. 6,15,23,28,42; 36:7; 44:12; 47:14). **Made myself known.** Cf. Ex 3:6ff.; 4:28ff.; 6:3. **6. Flowing with milk and honey.** In the Pentateuch this expression occurs fifteen times, e.g., Ex 3:8. Elsewhere it occurs only in Ezk 20:15; Jer 11:5; 32:22. On the beauty of Israel, see Jer 3:19; Dan 8:9. **7,8.** The charge of Israel's idolatry in Egypt (cf. 23:3; Josh 24:14; Lev 18:3) is not alluded to in the Exodus account. **9. I wrought for my name's sake.** This refrain occurs also in verses 14,22. Cf. Jer 14:7,21; Isa 43:25; 48:9,11. The **name** stands for what God is and has shown himself to be. If he had not led his people out of Egypt, the nations would have charged him with weakness (Num 14:13-16; Deut 9:28). His name is **profaned** when men harbor thoughts of him or attribute deeds to him inconsistent with his character as holy and unique (cf. v. 39; 36:20-22). The opposite of "to profane" is "to sanctify." It is to recognize the Lord as the one true God in every area of life, and to live in a manner befitting him.

10-17. *Israel's rebellions in the wilderness.* **11. Statutes and . . . ordinances.** Giving of the Law at Sinai (Ex 19ff.). **12. My sabbaths.** As a sign that the Lord was their God and they were his people (v. 20; Ex 31:13,14; Isa 66:2,4). During the Exile the observance of the sabbath became a distinguishing sign of the Jews as the people of the Lord (see vv. 12,13,16,20,21,24). **I am the Lord that sanctify them;** i.e., have set them apart from other peoples and consecrated them for myself. Out of regard for his name (v. 14) and out of pity for the sinners (v. 17), the Lord spared the second generation.

18-26. *Rebellion of the second generation against God.* **18. Their children in**

the wilderness. See Deut 1:39; Num 14:31,33. **21.** They imitated the sins of their fathers (Num 25:1,2; Deut 9:23,24; 31:27). **23-26.** The sins were punished in two ways: by the threat of dispersion upon entering Canaan (vv. 23,24); and by forcing them to incur punishment (vv. 25,26). **23. Scatter them among the heathen.** Such threats could be averted by repentance (cf. Mic 3:12; Jer 26:16-19; 18; Jonah). **25. I gave them also statutes that were not good.** The Lord is not here speaking of the Law, which was good (vv. 13,21). But the rebellious people were left to a law of another kind (v. 18), working not life but death. "It is part of that universal moral government of the world . . . that the effect of disobedience and the neglect of grace is to lead the sinner on to greater sin" (F. Gardiner in Ellicott's *Commentary*). For the judicial blindness with which God afflicts those who willfully close their eyes, see Acts 7:42; Rom 1:24,25; II Thess 2:11. **26.** God permitted them to fall into the crime of offering **by fire all their first-born** (RSV; cf. v. 31; 16:21; 23:37) **that they might know that I am the Lord.**

27-29. *Israel's rebellion against God upon entering Canaan.* **28.** Canaanite worship on high places and under green trees was adopted by Israel. It was condemned by Amos (4:4; 5:21); by Hosea (6:6; 8:11,13; 9:1); by Jeremiah (2:20; 3:6). **They offered there their sacrifices.** Hebrew *zebaḥ* means animals slaughtered and eaten at feasts, especially peace offerings and thank offerings (Lev 3:1ff.; 7:12-25). **The provocation,** or vexation (omitted by the Syriac) **of their offering.** Hebrew *qorbān,* "offering," refers to both bloody and nonbloody oblations (Lev 1:2,3,10; 2:1,5), such as first fruits (Lev 2:12; 23:10,17). **Soothing odors** (RSV; *rêaḥ nîḥôaḥ).* Odors of flesh, fat, or meal burnt on the altar as pleasant to the Lord (Gen 8:21; Ex 29:18; Lev 1:9). **Drink offerings** *(nesek).* Libations of wine that accompanied meal offerings and peace offerings (Lev 23:13; Num 15:1-12). **29. What is the high place whereunto ye go?** These idol repositories (v. 28) were not fit for the worship of the Lord. "High place," *bāmâ,* is the object of a scornful play on words – *bā',* "go," plus *mâ,* "what."

30-32. *Rebelliousness of Ezekiel's generation.* **30,31.** Ezekiel's contemporaries who, like their fathers, had defiled themselves, could not receive an oracle from the Lord (cf. v. 3). **32. Let us be as the heathen.** One interpretation holds that the exiles were planning to assimilate themselves to their heathen surroundings, but it is not likely that they would have shared such plans with the prophet Ezekiel. A second view claims that the exiles wanted Ezekiel's approval for setting up an altar and temple to the Lord in Babylonia. (Cf. the Jewish temple at Elephantine, Egypt.) More likely the prophet, speaking for Jehovah, was condemning the syncretistic and idolatrous practices of his fellow countrymen in Judah.

c) The Lord's Regard for His Name To Bring Israel Through Future Judgment to Prospects of Hope. 20:33-44.

33-39. *A second encounter in the wilderness* (in contrast to vv. 10-26) *for the purpose of judgment.* **34. Will I rule over you.** The sovereign Vindicator of right and truth speaks. **34. I will bring you out from the people.** As a distinct race, to be dealt with as his own people. **35. Wilderness of the people.** Perhaps not a material wilderness, but a wilderness condition – scattered among the nations. **37. I will cause you to pass under the rod.** A figurative reference to a shepherd's staff, used in counting sheep (Lev 27:32; Jer 33:13). **I will let you go in by number** (so RSV, following the LXX) into the fold. **38. I will purge out from among you the rebels.** The rebels will be separated and not allowed to share in the future restoration. **39. Serve ye every one his idols.** God will give them up to pursue their chosen way to its inevitable end.

40-44. *Idolatry to be rooted out of Israel and true worship made possible.* **40. In the mountain of the height of Israel** (Mic 4:1,2; Isa 2:2,3), **all the** (redeemed) **house of Israel** will be accepted. **41. As a sweet savour** to the Lord. **I will manifest my holiness among you** (RSV). So that the nations may acknowledge the Lord's power and sole deity. See also 28:22,25; 36:23; 38:16,23; 39:27. **42. I am the Lord.** Israel will know the Lord as the God to be honored and served when he fulfills his ancient promises to the fathers in the restoration of the land. **43. Ye shall loathe yourselves.** For their past sins (6:9; 16:61ff.). But they will be brought to repentance by the goodness of God (Rom 2:4). **44. I am the Lord.** The people will see that all through their past the Lord, for his name's sake, dealt with them in grace and not as they deserved (cf. Isa 40:5). Verses 40-44 point forward to chapter 40 and the following.

2) Israel To Be Punished by God's Avenging Sword. 20:45–21:32.

The MT numbers this section chapter 21, while the English version, following the LXX, the Syriac, and the Vulgate, makes it 20:45-49; 21:1-32. Four oracles can be distinguished: (a) A fire shall devour the forest of the south (20:45-49), even the fire of war and sword against Jerusalem and Israel (21:1-7); (b) The "song of the sword," despite textual obscurities, graphically depicts the divine visitation impending over Jerusalem (vv. 8-17); (c) The king of Babylon, the wielder of the sword, is directed by lot at the crossroads to proceed against Jerusalem (vv. 18-27); (d) Ammon, threatening Israel with the sword, will himself be doomed (vv. 28-32).

a) The Devouring Fire of War Against Jerusalem and Israel. 20:45–21:7.

45-59. *The figure of a fire devouring the forests of the south.* **46. Set thy face toward the south.** Three words for **south** occur in this verse—*têmān, dārôm,* and *negeb,* meaning respectively, "right hand," "brilliant" or "midday," and "dry land." All are designations for Israel, which lay south in the path of conquerors advancing from Babylon (cf. 1:4). Note the threefold reference to Israel in 21:2,3. **Preach.** Literally, *drop your word against* (cf. 21:2; Amos 7:16; Mic 2:6,11). **47. Kindle a fire in thee.** This is a figure of destruction (cf. Isa 9:17; 10:17-19; Jer 21:14; Zech 11:1-3; Ps 83:14). **Green tree . . . dry tree.** Cf. 21:3. All alike, righteous and wicked, are to be involved in the national judgment (cf. Lk 23:31). **All faces.** Of spectators, or of the trees. **49. Parables.** Or enigmas. For the word *māshāl,* see 18:2. The people took notice of the prophet's method of speaking, but did not apply his message to themselves.

21:1-7. *The fire of war and the sword directed against Jerusalem and Israel.* **2. Preach.** Cf. 20:46. The words, **Jerusalem . . . holy places** (the Temple and its precincts), and **Israel,** correspond to the three *souths* of 20:46. **3. My sword.** Cf. 21:5; 30:24,25; 32:10. Jehovah will fight on behalf of his people (Josh 5:13-15); defeat Israel's enemies (Deut 32:41, 42; Isa 31:8; Jer 50:35), and judge the ungodly (Jer 25:31; Isa 66:16). The sword drawn against Israel is that of his agent, Nebuchadnezzar (see v. 19; 12:13; 17:20). **I will cut off . . . righteous and the wicked.** The "green" and "dry" trees of 20:47. This instance of corporate solidarity does not prevent the righteous individual's entering into that fellowship with God that transcends death (cf. ch. 18).

6. Sigh . . . with the breaking of thy loins. The loins were regarded as the seat of strength (Job 40:16; cf. Ps 66:11; 69:23; Isa 21:3; Nah 2:10). **Before their eyes.** An acted parable. **9.** The exiles in Babylonia would likewise be heartbroken at the news of Jerusalem's fall (cf. 33:21).

b) The Song of the Sword. 21:8-17.

9-11. *The sword sharpened for the slaughter.* **10. Should we then make mirth?** These words, from here to the end of the verse, are corrupt. Keil's interpretation *(Biblical Commentary on Ezekiel, in loco)* retains the MT: "Shall we rejoice (saying), 'The scepter of my son despises all woods' (i.e., other scepters)." This interpretation sees here a reference to Gen 49:9,10; II Sam 7:14. Cf. verse 27.

12,13. *The agitation of the prophet.* **12. Smite . . . upon thy thigh.** As a gesture of despair (Jer 31:19). **13. It is a trial.** The text is corrupt. Of many reconstructions, Keil's is close to the MT: "For the trial is made, and what if the despising scepter shall not come?" That is, What will happen if that kingdom, Judah, shall be left without a ruler? Cf. verses 10,27.

14,15. *The sword doubled and tripled in intensity for the carnage.* The MT of these verses is difficult, and all translations resort to conjectural emendations. **Clap your hands** (RSV). A gesture of strong emotion (cf. v. 17; 22:13). **16. Go thee one way or other.** An apostrophe to the sword. **17. I will also smite mine hands together.** The Lord exults over the coming vengeance.

c) The King of Babylon, the Wielder of the Sword, To Proceed Against Jerusalem. 21:18-27.

19. Appoint thee two ways. The prophet was commanded to mark on the sand, or possibly on a brick or tile (cf. 4:1), two lines representing two roads which the king of Babylon and his army would follow. These roads come forth from the same land, Babylon, and follow the same route hundreds of miles to the Orontes Valley before diverging. **At the head of the way** (road) **to the city.** Perhaps this refers to Riblah, in the Lebanon country (or Damascus), where the two roads separate. A pointing hand or signpost (cf. I Sam 15:12; II Sam 18:18) was to be erected, indicating direction. **20. Rab-**

bath of the Ammonites (cf. 25:5). In Greco-Roman times this city was called Philadelphia; today it is known as Amman. It is situated at the source of the Jabbok, twenty-five miles northeast of the Dead Sea. Rabbath-Ammon lay on one road and Jerusalem on the other. Both were guilty of conspiracy against Babylon (Jer 27:1-3).

21. At the parting (lit., *mother)* **of the way,** the **king of Babylon** would use three types of **divination.** He would shake **arrows,** one marked for Jerusalem and the other for Ammon, in a quiver or helmet; and the one inscribed "Jerusalem" would be drawn out. He would consult **images,** or *teraphim,* small household gods in human form (cf. Gen 31:19; I Sam 19:13,16). He would look at **the liver** (as the seat of life, filled with blood) for omens, a custom practiced among the Babylonians, Greeks, and Romans. **22. Divination for Jerusalem.** All of the methods would point to Jerusalem as the goal against which the invaders would shout a battle cry, and erect **battering rams, mounds, and siege towers** (RSV). **23.** But to the Jews who had **sworn oaths** of allegiance to Nebuchadnezzar only to break them (17:16-18), the divination would seem false. **24. Ye have made your iniquity to be remembered.** Because of your guilt *(āwôn),* transgressions *(pesha'),* and sins *(ḥaṭṭā't),* **you shall be seized by the hand;** i.e., arrested by enemy officers.

25. The dishonored **wicked prince of Israel,** Zedekiah, had reached his **day** (I Sam 26:10) of punishment (cf. Ezk 21:29; 35:5). **26. The turban** (RSV; *miṣnepet,* "diadem" or "mitre," used elsewhere of the high priest; see Ex 28:4; Lev 8:9) and the **crown** *('ățārâ;* cf. Jer 13:18; II Sam 12:30) of the royal house would be removed. The whole existing state of things would be overturned. **27. A ruin, ruin, ruin I will make it** (RSV). The repetition expresses the superlative degree (cf. Isa 6:3; Jer 22:29). The prevailing condition of things would be overturned, **until he come whose right it is; and I will give it him.** This is Ezekiel's first distinct reference to the personal Messiah, who will have the right to wear the crown and will be a true king. See Gen 49:10, where Ezekiel evidently read *shellô,* "whose it is" (equivalent to *'ăsher lô;* cf. v. 27) in place of *Shîlōh.* On this use of **right,** see Deut 21:17; Jer 32:7,8.

d) Oracle Against Ammon. 21:28-32 (cf. 25:1-7; Amos 1:13-15; Zeph 2:8-11; Jer 49:1-6).

Although Nebuchadnezzar would turn aside from Ammon to Jerusalem (vv. 19, 20), Ammon's doom would be worse than Jerusalem's. **28.** Casting **reproach** upon Israel, they drew the sword against her for conquest. **29. They divine a lie.** The false visions and lies of the Ammonite soothsayers would urge their warriors to lay the sword on **the necks of . . . the wicked,** the princes and people of Israel. **30. Return** your sword to **its sheath,** says the Lord, for in your own land, **the land of thy nativity,** will I judge you. **31.** They would be delivered **into the hand of brutish men** (cf. Ps 94:8), savages from the desert (Ezk 25:4,10), "forgers of destruction." **32.** Ammon was to become as **fuel to the fire,** the lifeblood of the nation poured out in its own land. In contrast to Israel, there would be no future restoration for Ammon.

3) Jerusalem's Sins To Be Judged in the Smelting Furnace. 22:1-31.

From the standpoint of homiletics, this chapter specifies the abominations of which the nation was guilty (vv. 1-12), laments the absence of any voice raised against these sins (vv. 23-31), and announces the fires of judgment upon the nation (vv. 13-22).

a) Catalogue of Jerusalem's Defiling Crimes. 22:1-12.

Four main groups of abominable deeds are treated in this first oracle. (1) Idolatry and irreligion. Forgetfulness of the Lord (v. 12) is at the root of all the sins (23:35). **Idols** (vv. 3,4), despising of **holy things,** profaning the **sabbaths** (v. 8; cf. v. 26; 20:20,21), and eating idol sacrifices **upon the mountains** (v. 9; cf. 18:6) are denounced. (2) Widespread bloodshed occurred throughout the city (see vv. 2-4,6,9,12,13,27). (3) Immorality and incest were common. Men **commit**[ted] **lewdness** (v. 9b; cf. 16:27; Lev 18:17), marrying a stepmother (v. 10; cf. Lev 18:7,8; 20:11ff.). They humbled women who were **unclean in their impurity** (v. 10b, RSV; cf. 18:6; Lev 18:9). They committed adultery with a **neighbor's wife,** and incest with a **daughter in law** and with a **sister** (v. 11; cf. Lev 18:20,5,9). (4) Inhumanity was practiced: **father and mother are treated with contempt, the sojourner suffers extortion . . . the fatherless and the widow are wronged** (v. 7, RSV; cf. Ex 21:17; 22:21,22). There was **slander** leading to bloodshed (v. 9; cf. Lev 19:16). Men took **bribes, usury,** and **extortion** (v. 12; cf. Ex 23:8; 22:25; Lev 19:13). The people did not keep the code of righteousness extolled in 18:5-9.

b) The Lord's Judgment To Be Visited upon the Sinful Nation. 22:13-22.

13-16. *The necessity and certainty of the judgment.* **13. I strike my hands together** (RSV). A gesture of disdain (cf. 21:14,17). **16. Thou shalt take thine inheritance.** Better, *I shall be profaned through you.* Read LXX *w^e^nihaltî bāk* in place of MT *w^e^niḥalt b^e^kā.* The chastisement would be dispersion among the nations, by which the Lord would be profaned. Cf. 20:9; 36:20.

17-22. *Judgment on Israel under the figure of a smelting furnace.* For the figure, see also Isa 1:22,25; 48:10; Jer 6:27-30; Zech 13:9; Mal 3:2,3. Here Israel is the raw material, Jerusalem is the furnace, Jehovah smelts the ore, and Israel comes out as dross! Note the repetition of ideas throughout this paragraph. **18. House of Israel is to me become dross. Dross** was a symbol of worthlessness (cf. Ps 119:119; Prov 25:4; 26:23).

c) Classes and Masses Alike Guilty of Failing to Rebuke the National Vices. 22:23-31.

Beginning at the top of the social scale, Ezekiel indicts princes, priests, potentates, prophets, and people for their complicity in sin.

24. Israel is a land that is not **rained upon.** LXX, *wetted by rain.* A drought lies upon her (cf. 34:26). **In the day of indignation.** Day of Jerusalem's overthrow (cf. v. 31; 21:31).

25. Her prophets. Read, *her princes,* substituting *nāsî'*, "prince," of the LXX for MT *nābî'*, "prophet." These were members of the royal house (cf. v. 6). The prophets are singled out in verse 28. Cf. 19:1; 21:12; 45:8,9; Zeph 3:3. **26. Her priests.** The *kōhen.* Cf. Zeph 3:4. **27. Her princes;** i.e., her potentates or nobles, the *śarîm,* chiefs or leaders of the people. Cf. Jer 26:10; 36:12; Zeph 3:3. **28. Her prophets.** The *nābî'*. Cf. 13:10, 11; 21:28; Zeph 3:4.

29. The people of the land (*'am hā' āreṣ*). The common people. Cf. 7:27; 12:19; II Kgs 25:3,19; Jer 37:2. **30. I sought for a man to . . . make up the hedge, and stand in the gap.** Cf. 13:5; Ps 106:23. The Lord sought in vain for a man to stem the tide of ruin and turn the fortunes of the people, but there was none. Compare Isa 59:15,16; 63:5, where, in the absence of a man, the Lord's arm brought victory. **31.** God's indignation and fiery wrath are poured out upon such a people (cf. vv. 21,22; 9:10; Zeph 3:8).

4) Allegory of Oholah and Oholibah. 23:1-49.

Chapter 23 contains an allegorical portrayal of the history of Samaria and Jerusalem as two sisters unfaithful to their divine spouse. In the allegory of chapter 16, Israel's religious unfaithfulness because of the seductions of Canaanite worship is likened to adultery. The present chapter treats of Israel's political alliances with heathen nations, involving distrust in the power of the Lord, under the figure of harlotry. In a poem exhibiting much repulsive detail (vv. 1-35), the prophet describes (1) the infidelities of Oholah (Samaria) and her punishment (vv. 1-10); (2) the infidelities of Oholibah (Jerusalem; vv. 11-21) and her punishment (vv. 22-35). An appended address (vv. 36-49) pictures the two sisters sinning and receiving judgment contemporaneously. The kingdom of the Lord must be faithful to him rather than rely on pagan alliances. "Already the conception was taking possession of the prophetic mind that the kingdom of God was not a state but what we now call a church" (A. B. Davidson, *Cambridge Bible,* p. 165).

a) Introduction. 23:1-4.

2. The two kingdoms, Israel and Judah, are introduced as sisters (cf. Jer 3:7; Ezk 16:46). **4. Oholah,** *she who has a tent,* and **Oholibah,** *a tent is in her,* were "sisters alike in name and in guilt." For similarly formed names, see Gen 35:18; Isa 62:4. Ewald points out that in the East brothers and sisters often have names very similar, as Hasan and Husein (little Hasan), sons of Ali, son-in-law of Mohammed. **They were mine.** The law forbade taking two sisters in marriage (Lev 18:18). The figure of marriage (cf. Jer 2:2; Hos 2:21,22) is developed at length by Ezekiel.

b) The Infidelities of Oholah, Samaria. 23:5-10.

5,6. Her lovers the Assyrians, warriors (RSV). The AV *neighbours, q^e^rōbîm,* is probably connected with the word *q^e^rāb,* "battle" (Job 38:23; Zech 14:3); or it may be a cognate of the Akkadian *ḳurâdû,* "warriors," to be read *q^e^rôdîm.* **7.** The Black Obelisk of Shalmaneser III (859–824) shows Jehu king of Israel paying tribute, 842 B.C. (cf. Pritchard, ANET, pp. 281-284). Israel entered into a costly alliance with Tiglath-pileser III (745–727), king of Assyria (II Kgs 15:19-29). Verses 8,9 tell of Samaria's intrigues with Assyria and Egypt (see also, Hos 5:13; 7:11; 8:9,10; 12:1). Hoshea's intrigues with Egypt against Assyria led to the overthrow of Samaria (II Kgs 17:3-6). **10. She became famous;** i.e., she became a byword (lit., *name;* cf. v. 48; 16:41; 36:3).

c) The Infidelities of Oholibah, Jerusalem. 23:11-21.

11-13. *Intrigues with Assyria.* **11. When her sister Oholibah saw this.** Samaria's example did not prove a deterrent to Jerusalem, which was guilty of greater excesses (16:47,51; Jer 3:8,11). **12. She doted upon the Assyrians.** Cf. verses 5,6. Ahaz called in Assyrian aid (II Kgs 16:7; 23:11,12; Isa 7:1-25).

14-18. *Intrigues with Babylon.* **Men pourtrayed upon the wall.** The Babylonians decorated the walls of their rooms with carved and colored panels (cf. 8:10; Jer 22:14). **15. Girdles.** Belts or *waistcloths* were part of the Babylonian's clothing (see Isa 5:27; 11:5; also, description of Babylonian noble, Herodotus *Histories* I, 195). **Flowing turbans on their heads** (RSV). *Things wound around,* and fillets hanging down behind. **Looking like officers** (RSV). An "officer" *(shālîsh)* was the third man who occupied the chariot with the king and the driver, a man of high rank. **16. She . . . sent messengers.** The occasion is unknown, though Hezekiah had welcomed an embassy from Babylon about the year 712 B.C. (cf. Isa 39). **17. Her mind was alienated** (lit., *was dislocated;* cf. Gen 32:25). She felt the revulsion of sated passion.

19-21. *Intrigues with Egypt.* **19. Played the harlot in the land of Egypt.** In the time of Isaiah, there was a strong pro-Egyptian party (Isa 30—31; cf Jer 2:18; 37:5ff.; Ezk 29—32). **20. Paramours.** For parallels to the revolting figures of this verse, see Hos 8:9; Jer 2:24; 5:8; 13:27. As a harlot is attracted by sexual potency, so Judah was allured by the military prowess of Egypt.

d) The Punishment of Oholibah. 23:22-35.

Four threats are announced, each beginning with the expression, "Thus saith the Lord God"—verses 22-27,28-31,32-34,35.

22-27. *First threat of punishment.* **23. Pekod, Shoa,** and **Koa** (cf. Jer 50:20; Isa 22:5) are identified as the Puḳûdû, Sutû, and Ḳutû, tribes living east of the Tigris River, near its mouth, all part of the Chaldean empire. **Captains and rulers.** *Officers and warriors,* following the reading of verses 5,6, and 12. **Rulers.** The MT translates *called ones,* which may suggest counselors "called in" to give counsel. **24. Buckler.** A small shield carried on the arm. **And shield.** A large protective device. **I will commit judgment;** i.e., of Jerusalem, to the Chaldeans (cf. I Kgs 8:46). They were to "judge" her according to their own cruel **judgments. 25. Set my jealousy.** Cf. Num 25:11. On mutilation of an adulteress, and others, see the Middle Assyrian Law Code (Barton, *Archaeology and the Bible)* pp. 427-438, especially sections 4,8,9,11-14, 40,41,50-59. On the practice in Egypt, see Diodorus Siculus *The Historical Library* i. 78. Cf. Ezk 12:13; 16:40. **26. They shall . . . strip thee.** Cf. 16:38,39.

28-31. *Second threat of punishment.* **29.** (Fruit of) **thy labour;** i.e., wealth (Jer 20:5; Ps 128:2). **31. Cup.** Jerusalem must drink of her sister's **cup** of punishment (cf. Isa 51:17,22,23; Jer 25:15,16; Hab 2:16).

32-34. *Third threat of punishment.* These verses constitute a poem on the cup of punishment. **34. Pluck out your hair** (RSV). A free rendering of the LXX for the MT *gnaw its sherds.* **Pluck off thine own breasts.** Cf. Jer 25:16; Job 39:24.

35. *Fourth threat.* **35. Bear** (the consequences of) **thy lewdness.** Cf. verses 8,27,44.

e) Judgment of Oholah and Oholibah. 23:36-39. This passage constitutes an appendix with an independent description.

36-39. *The sisters guilty of adultery, idolatry.* **37.** The **blood** of child sacrifices was upon **their hands,** in their worship of idols, especially Moloch (cf. 16:20,21). **38. They have defiled** the **sanctuary** of the Temple and **profaned** the Lord's sabbaths. Cf. 20:12,13; 22:8. **39.** After performing heathen worship, they entered nonchalantly into the house of the Lord. Cf. Mic 3:11; Jer 7:9-11.

40-44. *The harlotry of Israel in foreign alliances.* In these verses the harlot makes elaborate preparations to welcome her paramours. **40.** Women painted their eyelids with powdered antimony or stibium to make them appear large and lustrous (cf. II Kgs 9:30; Jer 4:30; see also the name of Job's daughter, *Keren-happuch,* "horn of eye paint," Job 42:14). **42,43.** These verses are unintelligible in the MT, and the versions do not yield satisfactory readings. Verse **44** is a summary of the preceding verses. Translate, **to commit lewdness** (RSV), following the LXX, in place of MT *women of lewdness.*

45-49. *The adulteress put to death by righteous men.* **Righteous men.** Perhaps the meaning is that the moral sense of the community (not the Chaldeans) would pass judgment on the adulteresses (cf. vv. 24,47; 16:40). **47. Stone them.** Stoning was the punishment for adultery prescribed by the Law (cf. 16:38-40; Deut 21:21). **48. Taught.** Warned by a public example (cf. verse 10; 16:41). **49. Shall be requited** (RSV). So the Targum. **You shall bear the penalty** (RSV). Cf. verse 35; Lev 20:20.

5) Symbols of the Final Siege of Jerusalem. 24:1-27.

a) Allegory of the Rusted Pot Set on the Fire. 24:1-14.

On the day when the siege and capture of Jerusalem began, the Lord gave the prophet an allegory and an acted parable to deliver concerning the siege and ultimate capture of the city. He was to set a rusted caldron (Jerusalem) on the fire, fill it with water, and throw pieces of flesh (the inhabitants of Jerusalem) into it. He was to pile fuel under it to make it boil furiously (the siege and its severities). Then he should pull out pieces of flesh indiscriminately from the kettle (the universal dispersion when the siege was over). He next was to set the empty pot on coals so that its rust and filth might be molten and consumed (the purifying judgments were to continue long after the destruction of the city).

1. Ninth year . . . tenth month . . . tenth day of the month. The day of the commencement of the siege of Jerusalem (II Kgs 25:1; Jer 30:1; 52:4). January 587 (or 588) B.C. During the Exile and till 518 B.C., this day was observed as a fast (Zech 8:19). **3. Utter a parable.** A *māshāl* (cf. 17:2). Verses 3-5 are in poetical form. The prophet's inspiration came often during ordinary pursuits, here apparently while in the course of preparing a meal.

5. Pile the logs (RSV). Read with verse 10, in place of MT *pile the bones.* **Boil its pieces** (RSV). So two Hebrew manuscripts in place of MT *boil its boilings.* **Seethe the bones.** Along with the flesh on them (cf. v. 4). **6. Pot whose rust** or filth **is in it** (RSV). Cf. 22:2. **Let no lot fall upon it.** In 597, were the inhabitants of the city taken captive by lot? It will not be so now. The dispersion will be indiscriminate. **7,8. Blood . . . upon the top of a rock.** The openness of Jerusalem's sin (cf. Isa 3:9) is to be paralleled by the openness of her punishment. Blood uncovered cries out for vengeance (Gen 4:10; Lev 17:13; Deut 12:16; Job 16:18). In verse 8 the Lord is spoken of as appointing this shedding, so as to bring judgment on Jerusalem because of it.

10. Heap on wood. This is paralleled by verse 5. **Empty out the broth** (RSV). So the LXX, by slight change, instead of MT, *spice the spicings.* **Let the bones be burned.** By the powerful action of the heat in boiling. **12. In vain I have wearied myself** (RSV). A slight emendation gives this reading, in place of MT *with toil she hath wearied* (me, or herself). **Its thick rust** (RSV) or *great filth* must be consumed out of the pot. **13. Till I have satisfied** or appeased **my wrath** (RSV). See also 5:13; 8:18; 16:42. **14. I will judge you** (RSV). So two Hebrew manuscripts and various versions. Cf. 23:49.

b) The Prophet's Unnatural Abstention from Mourning. 24:15-24.

The Lord told Ezekiel that his beloved wife would die suddenly, and that he was not to engage in the customary mourning practices. He was thus to be a symbol of the despair of the people at the fate of their beloved city Jerusalem.

16. The desire of thine eyes. Cf. verses 21,25. "The phrase alone reveals there was a fountain of tears sealed up within the breast of this stern preacher" (J. Skinner, ExpB). **With a stroke.** This expression refers to a sudden and fatal disease (Num 14:37), usually a plague (Ex 9:14; II Chr 21:14). **17.** The prophet was to check his natural instincts when the blow fell. For mourning customs, consult Ecclesiasticus 38:17; Isa 20:2; Mic 3:7; Lev 13:45. **Nor eat the bread of mourners** (RSV). So the Targum and the Vulgate. Cf. Hos 9:4, reading *'ônîm* for MT *'ănāshîm,* "bread of men." Cf. Jer 16:7; Tob 4:17. **18,19.** The people, accustomed to consult Ezekiel (8:1; 14:1; 20:1), asked why he did not mourn his wife's death. Contrast 21:12.

21. I will profane my sanctuary. By the action of a heathen foe (7:24; 25:3; 44:7; Dan 11:31). The Lord here looks behind secondary causes. **The excellency of your strength.** The Temple (cf. v. 25). **22,23.** Ezekiel was to tell the people that they would grieve silently, deeply, at the destruction of the Temple (cf. 33:10; Ps 38:8), as he had grieved for his wife. **24. Ezekiel is unto you a sign.** Cf. verse 27; 12:6,11.

c) The Prophet's Ministry Released from Limitations at the City's Fall. 24:25-27.

When tidings come of the city's fall, verifying the prophet's predictions, he is to be "no longer dumb"; the limitations will be removed, and he will be able to speak unrestrainedly to willing listeners before him.

25. In the day. Of Jerusalem's fall. **26. In that day.** When the news of the city's fall reaches Babylonia. **27. Thy mouth be opened to him.** In conversation with the **escaped** one. **Be no more dumb.** Cf. 3:26,27; 33:21,22. He can then be a watchman in the pastoral sense. His prophecies of doom will have been confirmed; he will be free to devote himself to building the new community. **Thou shalt be a sign.** Cf. verses 16-18.

II. Oracles Against Foreign Nations. 25:1–32:32.

The oracles announcing punishment on Israel's hostile neighbors (chs. 25–32) constitute a transition between the prophecies of judgment on Judah and Jerusalem (chs. 1–24), and the predictions of her restoration (chs. 33–39; 40–48). Oracles against foreign nations are grouped together in other prophets also: Isa 13–23; Jer 46–51; Amos 1; 2; Zeph 2:4-15.

Before the ideal state can be realized, enemies must be destroyed and Israel made secure in her land (28:24,26; 34:28, 29). Seven nations, possibly a symbol of completeness, are destined for retribution. Five of them had formed an alliance against Chaldea (Jer 27:1-3). Babylon, the anti-God power of the OT, is not included in the denunciations, perhaps because that nation was the instrument of God's justice (29:17ff.), although Ezekiel knew the character of the Chaldeans (7:21,22,24; 28:6; 30:11,12; 31:12).

The Lord was to mete out chastisement upon Israel's surrounding foes because of their demeanor toward Israel (25:3,8,12,15; 26:2; 29:6) and because of their ungodly pride and self-deification (28; 29:3). Here, as in the foreign oracles of the other prophets, is exhibited the international outlook of Hebrew prophecy, with its stress on the universal sovereignty of God and the moral responsibility of all mankind. "A nation's rank among the peoples depends upon the contribution which it makes to God's purpose for mankind and upon its homage to His universal rule" (Cook, ICC, p. 282).

The nations which fall under the prophet's scrutiny are Ammon, Moab, Edom, Philistia (25:1-7,8-11,12-14,15-17), Tyre (three oracles: 26; 27; 28:1-19), Sidon (28:20-26), and Egypt (seven oracles: 29:1-16,17-21; 30:1-19,20-26; 31; 32:1-16,17-32). The first four oracles are short and prosaic (ch. 25), while the pronouncements against Tyre (chs. 26–28) and Egypt (chs. 29–32) are long, magnificent poems, full of color and fire, well illustrating Ezekiel's varied style. The dates attached to some of the oracles locate this section between 587/586 B.C. (seven months before the fall of Jerusalem, 29:1) and 571/570 B.C. (16 years after its fall, 29:17).

A. Oracle Against Ammon. 25:1-7.

For other denunciations, see 21:28-32; Amos 1:13-15; Zeph 2:8-11; Jer 49:1-6.

Ammon at one time possessed the land between the Arnon and the Jabbok rivers but had been pushed eastward by the Amorites (Jud 11:13; Num 21:21). An implacable foe of Israel through the years (Jud 10–11; I Sam 11; II Sam 10), Ammon is denounced in this oracle for its unholy glee and malice at the destruction of the Temple and the miseries of Israel and Judah (Ezk 25:3,6). Post-Exilic references to Ammon are Neh 4:3; I Macc 5:6.

4. The men of the East. The Aramaean and Arabic tribes east of Ammon (cf. Jud 6:3,33; Isa 11:14; Jer 49:28) were to despoil Ammon. **5. Rabbah.** Its chief city (cf. 21:20), the site of Philadelphia, established by Ptolemy II Philadelphus (285–246), was to become pasture (cf. Isa 17:2; 32:14; Zeph 2:14). **Ye shall know that I am the Lord.** The purpose of these judgments is to make men recognize that the Lord rules men and shapes history (cf. Dan 4:17). The expression in varying forms, starting at Ezk 6:7, occurs about sixty-five times in Ezekiel, and repeatedly in the foreign oracles.

B. Oracle Against Moab. 25:8-11.

Other maledictions are Isa 15–16; 25:10-12; Jer 48; Amos 2:1-3; Zeph 2:8-11.

Moab's territory lay between the river Arnon and the brook Zered, but Moab often laid claim to the land extending to the head of the Dead Sea. It possessed a higher degree of culture than Ammon. (On cities of Moab, cf. Nelson Glueck in AASOR, 18-19 (1937-'39), 72-75; *The Other Side of the Jordan* (New Haven: ASOR, 1940), pp. 134-139. Cf. Gen 19:30-38; Num 22–24; Ruth; Neh 13:1). **8.** Moab saw nothing good or unique in Israel's existence: **The house of Judah is like . . . all the nations** (ASV). **9. Beth-jeshimoth.** Tell el-'Azeimah, two and one-half miles northeast of the Dead Sea

(Josh 12:3; 13:20). **Baal-meon.** Mâ'în, nine miles east of the Dead Sea and four miles south of Medeba (Josh 13:17). **Kiriathaim.** Identified as el Qereiyat, ten miles below Baal-meon and seven miles northwest of Dibon (Josh 13:9; Jer 48:1, 23). The second and third of these cities are mentioned in the "Mesha Inscription," or "Moabite Stone" (ANET, pp. 320,321).

C. Oracle Against Edom. 25:12-14.

For other maledictions, see 35:1-15; 36:5; Isa 34; 63:1-6; Joel 3:19; Amos 1:11,12; Ob; Mal 1:2-5.

Edom displaced the Hurrians in Seir to occupy the rugged country extending from the southern end of the Dead Sea on both sides of the Arabah to the Gulf of Akaba (Gen 14:6; 32:3; 36:20,21,30; Deut 2:1,12; Jud 11:17,18; I Kgs 9:26). Its capital was Sela, probably later the site of Petra. At the fall of Jerusalem, the Edomites pressed into southern Judah (I Macc 4:29; 5:65). From the late fourth century B.C. through the first century A.D., the Nabataean Arabs established a high degree of culture in Edomite territory. The Edomites were subdued by John Hyrcanus in 125 B.C. and incorporated into Israel. Herod the Great was an Idumaean, the Greek and Roman name for Edomite. (See Jos *Ant*. XII. 8. 6; XIV. 1. 3; 7. 3; *Wars* IV. 9. 7. I Macc 5:3. 5.)

12. Because that Edom hath dealt against the house of Judah by taking vengeance, all her territory, **from Teman** (v. 13), probably Tawîlân near Sela in the north, to **Dedan,** in the south (cf. Jer 49:7,8; not the Dedan of Arabia, 27:20; 38:13), would be desolated.

D. Oracle Against Philistia. 25:15-17.

For other maledictions, see Isa 14:29-31; Jer 47; Amos 1:6-8; Zeph 2:4-7; Zech 9:5-7.

The Philistines, from whom the name *Palestine* is derived (Herodotus *Histories* vii. 89), came from Caphtor, or Crete, in the Aegean basin (Jer 47:4; Amos 9:7), and as part of the "sea-peoples" established themselves on the southern coast of Canaan, displacing the Avvim (Deut 2:23). Ever a threat to the Hebrews (Ex 3:17,18; Jud 14–16; I Sam 4–6), their monopoly on iron implements (I Sam 18:19-23) made them particularly formidable. Their pentapolis was under the control of five lords or *serens* (cf. Gr. *tyrannos;* Josh 13:3; I Sam 6:4). They adopted the worship of Dagan, the Semitic grain deity (I Sam 5), and various Canaanite gods. The great "uncircumcised" of antiquity were mighty carousers, as their ubiquitous wine craters and beer jugs suggest (Albright, *Arch. of Pal.*, p. 115). Saul fought against them (I Sam 13–14; 17–18; 31), and David defeated them (II Sam 8:1,12; 5:17-25; 21:15-22). Relations continued hostile between Judah and the Philistines (II Chr 21:16; 28:18; II Kgs 18:8; II Chr 26:6,7), until the Maccabees finally liquidated them (I Macc 5:68; 10:83-89; 11:60,61).

16. The Cherethites (Cretans) were foreign mercenaries, David's bodyguard (II Sam 8:18; 15:18; 20:7). They are here synonymous with the Philistines, and not to be equated with Keret of the Ugaritic tablets (cf. Albright, BASOR, 71 (Oct., 1938), 35-40).

The Philistines were to experience God's **wrathful chastisements** (RSV; *furious rebukes,* AV; v. 17), because they took vengeance with malice of **heart, to destroy it for the old hatred** (v. 15).

E. Oracles Against Tyre. 26:1–28:19.

For other maledictions, see Isa 23; Joel 3:4-8; Amos 1:9,10; Zech 9:3,4.

The antiquity of Tyre is attested to by Herodotus (ii. 44) and the Amarna Letters (cf. Pritchard, ANET, 484). Forced out of Palestine and Syria in the thirteenth and twelfth centuries, the Phoenicians turned their energies seawards and became the greatest mariners and traders of all time, in relation to the known world (cf. Albright, "The Role of the Canaanites in the History of Civilization," in *The Bible and the Ancient Near East*, ed. by G. E. Wright, pp. 328-362, esp. pp. 328,335,340ff.). Ahiram I, king of Tyre (969–936), made pacts with David and Solomon (II Sam 5:11; I Kgs 5:1-18; 9:10-14,26,27). Ahab's queen, Jezebel, the daughter of Ethbaal (Ittobaal I, 887–856), king of the Sidonians, introduced the worship of the Tyrian Baal Melkart, lord of the underworld, of storm and fertility, into Israel (I Kgs 16:31; 18).

Tyre was harassed by Assyrian monarchs, and it yielded to Ashurbanipal (ANET, p. 295). It sought an alliance with Zedekiah against Nebuchadnezzar (Jer 27:3; 28:1). In 588 Pharaoh-hophra attacked Tyre and Sidon (Herodotus ii. 161; Diodorus Siculus, I. 68). Nebuchadnezzar laid siege to Tyre for thirteen years (585–573), but did not take it (Ezk 29:18; Jos *Antiq*. X. 11. 1; *Against Apion* I. 20,21). After a seven-month siege, Alexander the Great finally destroyed the island city in 332, by building a mole out to it from the mainland (Diod. Sic. XVII. 40-46). It was rebuilt in 314. Tyre had contacts with the ministry of Jesus (Mt 15:21-28; Mk 3:8; cf. Mt 11:21, 22), and was the home of believers (Acts 21:3-6). Origen was buried there in A.D. 254, and Eusebius preached there in 323. The Moslems conquered it in 638, and the Crusaders took it in 1124. The city was completely destroyed by the Saracens in 1291. Today it is a little fishing village, *eṣ-Ṣur*.

Ezekiel gives more space to Tyre, "The Venice of Antiquity," than does any other OT writer. In chapters 26—28, the prophet predicts the overthrow of this major sea power at the hands of Nebuchadnezzar (ch. 26); laments the shipwreck of the gallant ship Tyre in a magnificent dirge (ch. 27); and in a taunt song depicts the pride and fall of the prince of Tyre (28:1-19).

1) Overthrow and Destruction of Tyre. 26:1-21.

The chapter contains four oracles, each introduced by "thus saith the Lord" (vv. 3,7,15,19). The traditional Hebrew marginal note at the beginning of the chapter reads "half of the book."

a) The Guilt of Tyre. 26:1-6.

1. In the eleventh year, in the first day of the month; i.e., 586 (or 587) B.C. Verse 2 implies that the oracle came after the destruction of Jerusalem in 586, news of which Ezekiel did not hear until the twelfth year and the tenth month (33:21). Some Hebrew manuscripts and the LXX and Syriac read *eleventh year* in 33:21, which would allow for this prophecy in the eleventh year and the eleventh or twelfth month. **2. The gates of the people.** Jerusalem lay on the toll roads. **Is broken.** She could no longer receive from the caravans the imposts that Tyre coveted.

4. Tyre (*=ṣôr;* and *ṣûr* = "rock"), located on a rocky island of 142 acres, had two harbors connected by a canal, the Sidonian harbor on the northeast and the Egyptian on the south. The island city was 1200 yards offshore from the walled city on the mainland. **6. Her daughters on the mainland** (RSV; cf. v. 8). The line of Phoenician settlements opposite the island city.

b) Her Impending Destruction by Nebuchadrezzar. 26:7-14.

7. Nebuchadrezzar is the form of the name always used by Ezekiel, for *Nabu-kudurri-usur,* "Nebo, protect my boundary." **King of Babylon, a king of kings.** An Assyrian title (cf. Dan 2:37; Ezr 7:12). **From the north.** See also Jer 1:14; 4:6; 6:1, etc. **8,9.** In his attack, Nebuchadrezzar employed: a **fort** or moveable tower; **mound** (AV, *mount); **roof of shields*** (AV, *lift up the buckler),* like the Roman *testudo;* **engines of war,** or battering rams; and **axes,** literally, *swords,* in the sense of tools. **11. Mighty pillars** (RSV; *strong garrisons,* AV; singular, *maṣṣēbâ).* Sacred pillars or monuments (cf. Herodotus ii. 44).

c) Effects of Her Fall upon the Princes of the Sea. 26:15-18.

15. Isles. The shores and islands with which Tyre traded. Many of her colonies and mercenaries feared a threat to their own prosperity in the fall of Tyre. **16. The princes of the sea.** Merchant princes or city-kings. **Lay away their robes, and . . . broidered garments.** Cf. Jon 3:6. Note the elaborate garments of Assyrian kings in sculptures and monuments. **17,18. The lamentation** of the princes. Cf. 27:25b-36.

d) Tyre's Descent into the Underworld. 26:19-21.

19. The deep *(t^ehôm).* The nether sea, virtually a proper name here, as in 31:15; Amos 7:4. Tyre was conquered by the **great waters,** rather than conquering them.

20. Tyre was to descend **into the pit, with the people** dead from **of old** (Ps 143:3; Lam 3:6), to the **low parts of the earth.** Cf. 31:15 for discussion of **pit, low parts,** Sheol. The Scriptures often speak of the place of the dead as in the lower parts of the earth (cf. Eph 4:9), but this does not prove that the writers believed this to be the actual place of the departed spirits. Since men think in concrete terms, it is natural, in view of the burial of the body, to localize this place under the earth. Men on opposite sides of the globe speak of God as "above" them, though they know he is omnipresent (cf. Mk 6:41; 7:34; Lk 9:16; Jn 17:1). **So that you will not be inhabited nor have a place** (RSV; LXX, *and you will not stand,* i.e., exist) **in the land of the living.** This rendering of the vowel points seems to give the sense required rather than the unusual antithesis of the MT, *and I will give glory.*

Nebuchadrezzar either did not conquer Tyre, or he failed to obtain any considerable booty from it (29:18); for its treasures were probably shipped away, as Jerome suggests. Alexander the Great destroyed the city in 332 B.C., and the final destruction of the rebuilt city was the work of the Saracens in 1291 A.D. This may be an example of the conditional nature of some prophecies, a case in which repentance revoked the sentence of doom (cf. the Book of Jonah; Jer 26:17-19, which is an elucidation of Mic 3:12; Isa 38; Jer 11:7-11, a clear exposition of the principle). It is possible that Tyre was spared because of an unrecorded repentance.

2) Lament over the Downfall of Tyre. 27:1-36.

In this splendid poem, introduced within a prose passage, Tyre is represented as a gallant ship manned by sailors from Phoenician cities (vv. 1-9a), richly laden with wares from many nations (vv. 9b-25a), and shipwrecked, to the consternation and lamentation of seafaring men (25b-36).

a) The Construction and Manning of the Ship. 27:1-9a.

2. Lamentation. Cf. 19:1. **3. Entry** (lit., *entrances)* of the sea. Possibly a reference to its two harbors (cf. 26:4). **I am of perfect beauty.** The sin of Tyre was its pride (28:2,5,17).

5,6. The ship's timbers are described. Her **planks** were made of **fir trees from Senir,** the Amorite name for Mount Hermon. **Senir** means *sacred mountain,* and is equivalent to the Sidonian *Sirion.* Her **masts** were made of **cedars from Lebanon.** Her **oars** came from **oaks of Bashan, a** region east and northeast of the Kinnereth, or the Sea of Galilee. Her **deck** (AV, *benches;* lit., *frames;* cf. Ex 26:15, 16; Num 3:36) was made of **pines** (the *te'ashshur,* or *sherbîn,* Arabic, refers to a species of cedar) from **Chittim.** *Kittîyyîm* designated first the people of Kition on the south coast of Cyprus, and then was applied to the islands and coasts of the Mediterranean Sea, especially to Greece (cf. Dan 11:30; I Macc 1:1; 8:5). The Dead Sea Habakkuk Scroll reads *Kittîm* (1:6) for MT *Kasdîm,* "Chaldeans." (Cf. Brownlee, BASOR, 112 (Dec., 1948), 8-18; Ginsberg, *ibid,* 20,21.) The deck was inlaid with **ivory.**

7. Her sails were of **fine linen with broidered work from Egypt** *(shēsh;* cf. 16:10). And her deck **awning** (ASV) or covering was of **blue**-purple and red-**purple** from **Elishah,** probably Cyprus, Alashiya (ANET, p. 29; Amarna Letters 33-40) or Carthage. Phoenicia, from *phoinix,* "purple," was famous for its dyes, obtained from the shellfish murex (cf. Pliny *Natural History* ix. 60; B. Maisler, BASOR, 102 (April, 1946), 7-12).

8. The **mariners** (ASV, *rowers)* of the ship were from **Sidon and Arvad** (far north in Phoenicia; classical Aradus; Ruwād of today). Instead of, **thy wise men, O Tyrus,** read *wise men of Zemer* (Tell Kezel, south of Aradus; cf. Gen 10:18). These served as **pilots.** Literally, *rope-pullers.* **9.** The magistrates (AV, *ancients)* of **Gebal** (Gr. Byblos; Jebeil of today, 21 mi. north of Beirut) acted as ship's carpenters.

b) The Far-flung Trade of Tyre. 27:9b-25a.

A prose section follows. **9b-11.** Her mercenaries. **10. They of Persia.** The first mention of **Persia** *(Pāras)* in the Bible. The *Weidner Tablets* from Babylon, 592 B.C., mention one Persian and four Medes. An embassy of Ashurbanipal was sent to Cyrus, the king of Persia, in 639 (cf. Albright, JBL, 51 (1932), 98,99). **Lud.** Probably Lydia, of western Asia Minor. **Phut** may be Cyrene, in Northern Africa, or more likely Punt or Somaliland (cf. 38:5). **11. Arvad.** Cf. verse 8. Possibly *Ḥelech,* in Cilicia; or Ḥethlon near Hamath. **Gammadim.** Perhaps the Kumidi of northern Syria, mentioned in the Amarna Letters, 116, 129, etc., or the Gomerim from Cappadocia. **They hanged their shields** upon the walls of Tyre (cf. Song 4:4; I Macc 4:57).

12-25. In this section are named places which acted as Tyre's merchants. This is "The Trader's Catalogue." For problems involved in identifying these places, see J. Simons, *The Geographical and Topographical Texts of the Old Testament* (Leiden: Brill, 1959), pp. 455ff.

12. Tyre received from **Tarshish . . . silver, iron, tin, and lead.** The Phoenicians had established a number of Tarshishes, i.e., "smelting plants, refineries." Tartessus in southwest Spain, built in the ninth century B.C., was famed for exports from the mines (Strabo *Geography* iii. 2. 8,9; Diodorus Siculus *Hist. Lib.* v. 35ff. Cf. Albright, in *The Bible and the Ancient Near East,* ed. by G. E. Wright, pp. 346,347). **For your wares** (RSV). Hebrew *'izzābôn,* i.e., "what is left *('āzab)* with the purchaser." The expression occurs also in verses 14,16,22.

13. Javan, Tubal, and Meshech. These are, respectively, the Ionians of Asia Minor, Tabal, and Musku of cuneiform sources, who settled on both sides of the Anti-Taurus range in Asia Minor, remnants of the old Hittite population

(Cooke, ICC, p. 353); or they may be the Tibarenoi and Moschoi, who lived southeast of the Black Sea (Herodotus iii. 94; vii. 78). They trafficked in slaves and bronze. **14. Beth-Togarmah, . . . horses, war horses, and mules** (RSV). Probably Armenia, east of southernmost Halys River, famed for horse-breeding.

15. Dedan . . . ivory and ebony. This **Dedan** (not to be equated with Dedan in verse 20) was likely an Arab tribe inhabiting a part of Edom (v. 16). The LXX B reads *rdn,* "Rhodes," for *ddn,* "Dedan" (cf. Isa 21:13). **16. Edom . . . emeralds, purple, embroidered work** (RSV). The reading is supported by twenty-five manuscripts, the LXX, Aquila, and the Syriac. "Aram" or *Syria* of the MT comes in verse 18.

17. Judah, and . . . Israel . . . wheat. The MT has *wheat of Minnith* [an Ammonite town, Jud 11:33] *and Pannag.* None of the versions has a proper name here. Cornill suggests "wheat and spices" (cf. Gen 37:25). *Pannag* may come from Akkadian *pannigu,* "millet" (Zimmern).

18. Damascus . . . wine of Helbon, and white wool. Helbon, twelve miles north of Damascus, was famed for its wine (Strabo *Geog.* xv. 22). **19. Dan also.** The LXX omits Hebrew *wedan,* "and Dan," and reads *Yawan* ("Javan") as *yayin,* "wine." Along with thirteen manuscripts, the LXX, and the Syriac, it reads *mē'ûzāl,* **from Uzal,** for MT *mᵉ'ûzzāl,* "going to and fro." **Uzal.** Sana', caital of Yemen in southeast Arabia. **Cassia.** An aromatic wood from southern India, an ingredient of anointing oil (Ex 30:24). **Calamus.** A sweet cane, used in sacrifice and in anointing oil (Ex 30:23; Song 4:14; Isa 43:24; Jer 6:20).

20. Dedan . . . saddlecloths for riding (RSV). This is el-'Ulâ, near Têma, southeast of the Gulf of Akaba (cf. Isa 21:13, 14; Jer 25:23). **21. Arabia . . . Kedar.** The nomad Bedouins of northern Arabia and a nomad race in the Syro-Arabian desert (cf. Gen 25:13; Jer 2:10; 49:28). **22. Sheba and Raamah . . . spices.** The former country is located in southwest Arabia, almost 1,200 miles from Jerusalem. It was famous for gold, frankincense, and precious stones (cf. I Kgs 10:1-13; Job 6:19). **Raamah** probably was on the Persian Gulf (Gen 10:7).

23. Haran, ancient city in northwestern Mesopotamia, sixty miles east of Carchemish (Gen 11:31,32; 12:45). **Canneh.** An unidentified place in Mesopotamia. **Eden.** Situated on the middle course of the Euphrates, south of Haran (cf. Amos 1:5; Isa 37:12). **The merchants of Sheba** of the MT is probably a dittography from verse 22. **Asshur** is the city south of Nineveh on the west side of the Tigris, between the Upper and Lower Zab rivers. **Chilmad.** Unknown, though apparently near Asshur. **24. Blue clothes.** Hebrew *gᵉlômîm,* "mantles," is *hapax legomenon* from Aramaic through Akkadian. **Chests of rich apparel.** *Carpets of colored stuff.* Read *(ginzê bᵉrômîm)* explained by Aramaic and Akkadian parallels. **And made secure.** Cf. the Arabic root, meaning, "draw together, make firm." The MT *made of cedar* is unlikely. **In these they traded with you.** In place of MT *in thy market.*

c) Loss of the Ship, with Crew and Cargo. 25b-36.

25b-31. *Consternation of all seafaring men.* **26. The east wind.** As an agent of destruction (cf. 17:10; 19:12; Ps 48:7; Jer 18:14; Acts 27:14). **27.** The cargo comprises **riches, wares** (AV, *fairs),* and **merchandise.** The crew consists of **mariners, pilots, calkers** (carpenters), handlers of the wares, and **men of war. 28. The suburbs**—i.e., the countryside, the common land around a town (Lev 25:34; Num 25:2)—hear the cries of the drowning sailors. **30,31.** Eight signs of grief are enumerated. See also, 7:18; 26:16; Job 2:12; Jer 6:26.

32-36. *Lamentation over the wrecked ship.* **32.** They **take up a lamentation** *(qînâ),* saying: **Who was ever destroyed like Tyre?** (RSV). So the LXX, Syriac, Targum, and Vulgate. **34. Now you are wrecked** (RSV). Read with the manuscripts and the versions. **35. Astonished.** Those who have traded with Tyre will be appalled (cf. vv. 3,6,7; 26:15,18).

Revelation 18:11-20 is patterned after 26:16,17; 27:12ff.

3) The Fall of the Prince of Tyre. 28:1-19.

From the city, the prophet passes to its ruler, as a representative of the genius of the community, the embodiment of the spirit of the proud commercial city. King and people constitute a corporate solidarity, the pride and self-deification of which are doomed. Other instances of "the insanity of prosperity" are Sennacherib (II Kgs 17:33-35); Pharaoh (Ezk 29:3); Nebuchadnezzar (Dan 3:15; 4:30; note particularly the autotheism of Babylon, Isa 47:7-10); Herod (Acts 12:21-23); "the man of sin" (II Thess 2:3,4); and conquerors who rely on their weapons (Hab 1:11,16); and all who today worship the "goddess of getting ahead."

The prophet depicts the punishment of the proud prince (Ezk 28:1-10); and utters an ironical dirge over his fall (28:11-19).

a) Punishment of the Prince of Tyre for His Self-Exaltation. 28:1-10.

2. The prince of Tyre is called a *nāgîd,* "leader," a term used only of Israelite rulers except here and in Dan 9:25,26. Its appearance here suggests that he held his office only at God's appointment. He is designated "king," *melek* in verse 12, illustrating the concept of the Fertile Crescent that the ruler was the representative of the gods, and more than human. Ittobaal II was king of Tyre at this time (Jos *Against Apion* I. 21), but it is the autotheism of Tyre rather than any specific ruler that is denounced. **The seat of the gods** (RSV; not *God,* AV) may refer (1) to an empty throne in the Tyrian temple reserved for the king, (2) to the impregnable situation of Tyre, or (3) to the island as sacred to its own gods.

3. Wiser than Daniel. This may be the Dan'el of the Ras Shamra tablets (cf. on 14:14,20); or the Biblical Daniel (Dan 1:17-20; 2:48; 4:8,9). **4,5.** This wisdom was devoted to the amassing of wealth.

7. Strangers . . . the terrible of the nations; i.e., the Chaldeans. See also 7:21,24; 30:11; 31:12; 32:12; Hab 1:5-10. **8. The pit** *(shaḥat).* Equivalent to Sheol, the realm of the dead beneath the earth (cf. 31:15). From the root *shûaḥ,* "sink down"; so, "hollow place," "cavern." **10. Deaths of the uncircumcised.** For the Phoenicians, who practiced circumcision (Herodotus II. 104), to die like the despised uncircumcised was a great shame (cf. Ezk 31:18; 32:19,21, 24ff.).

b) Lamentation over the Fall of the King of Tyre. 28:11-19.

Ezekiel applies to the king of Tyre a tale current among the Phoenicians. It has only cursory resemblances to the Garden of Eden account in Genesis 2; 3. In the garden of God in Eden there lived with the cherub who kept it an ideal person (the *Urmensch,* or first man), the perfection of wisdom and beauty. Though only a man, in his pride he claimed to be a god. For his sin he was driven out of the garden by the cherub. According to God's word to Ezekiel, the king of Tyre, for a similar offense was to be brought to ruin. Some early Church Fathers interpreted this section as having ultimate reference to the fall of Satan or the Antichrist (cf. Isa 14:4-20). This view is also held by some evangelical groups today.

12. Lamentation. Ezekiel's lamentation over the king of Tyre, though in *qînâ* meter, is irony rather than a dirge. **You were the signet of perfection** (RSV). The MT reads, *You are* (or were) *one sealing up,* or *a sealer-of (ḥôtēm) proportion,* measure, symmetry, i.e., "perfection" *(toknît).* This usage occurs nowhere else in the OT, and the versions vary considerably. One manuscript, the LXX, Syriac, and Vulgate read, *You are* (or were) *the signet-ring* [seal] *(ḥôtam) of proportion,* etc., as in the MT. The Syriac and Vulgate read, *the seal-ring of the likeness (tabnît)* of God. Another proposed reading is: *You were wise to perfection ('atâ ḥākām leṭaklît).*

13. Thou hast been in Eden the garden of God. Note "mountain of God" in verses 14,16. **Eden** is derived from the Akkadian *edinu,* "plain," a place capable of irrigation and fertility. It is also a play on the word *'ēden,* "luxury, dainty, delight" (Gen 49:20; Jer 51:39; Ps 8. See also Ezk 31:9,16). **Every precious stone was thy covering;** i.e., robe. Nine stones of the twelve in the high priest's breastplate are named. See Ex 28:17-30, which is paralleled by Ex 39:10-13. See also Rev 21:19,20. The third row, omitted here, is supplied in the LXX. **Wrought in gold were your settings and your engravings** (RSV). The MT reads, *and* (of) *gold* (was) *the workmanship (melā'kâ) of your tambourines* (the context requires "settings") *and of your sockets* (piercings, *neqeb;* probably, "engravings." Cf. Akk. and Ug.).

14. With an anointed guardian cherub I placed you (RSV). The MT has *You ('at) are a cherub.* Read with the LXX and the Syriac, *With ('et) a cherub.* The MT reads, *anointed* (or "of expansion"; *hapax legomenon) that covers* (overshadows) *and I gave* (placed) *you.* **Holy mountain of God.** Located in the recesses of the north (Isa 14:13). To the Phoenicians this would likely have been Mount Ṣāphôn or Casius, between Antioch and Laodicea. Cf. the Tyrian god, *Baal Ṣāphôn,* "lord of the North." **Stones of fire.** Fiery flashing jewels (cf. Enoch 18:6-9; 24:1; 25:3); or, phenomena attending the divine presence (cf. Ezk 1:13; 10:16). Cf. the garden of jewelled trees in the *Gilgamesh Epic* (IX. v. vi. ANET, p. 89). **15. Thou wast perfect** *(tāmîm,* "sound, unimpaired, innocent") . . . **till iniquity** *('awlātâ,* for the more usual *'āwel)* **was found in thee.** There is no reference to the cherub here, for the Bible does not speak of a fall of the cherubim; and the heavenly beings existed before creation (Job 38:7).

16. By the multitude of thy merchandise. The first part of the verse is probably a gloss from verse 5; 26:12; 27:12, 18, anticipating verse 17. **So I cast you as a profane thing** (RSV). The MT reads, *And I profaned you* (casting you) **out of the mountain of God. And the guardian cherub drove you out** (RSV). This reading follows the LXX *we'ibbedkā* (cf. Gen 3:24), in place of MT, *And I destroyed you (wā'abbedkā), O cherub that covers* (cf. Ezk 28:14).

17. Thine heart. This is direct application of the story to the king, who represents the city (27:3) and its inhabitants (27:8,9). **18,19. Thou hast defiled thy sanctuaries.** The prophet predicts the ruin of Tyre itself. The king desecrated the temples which made Tyre a holy island, bringing about their destruction through his own sin. He fell below the standard of the truth his religion had preserved for him.

F. Oracle Against Sidon. 28:20-26.

Other maledictions against Sidon occur at Joel 3:4-8; Zech 9:2. Sidon (present day Saida, probably connected with the deity *Sid*, from the root *ṣûd*, "to hunt") is located twenty-five miles north of Tyre. It is mentioned in the Amarna Letters (75,85,149, etc.) and by Homer, *Iliad* 7:290. The tribe of Asher did not drive out the Sidonians (Jud 1:31; 10:12). Sidon later became subject to its daughter city Tyre (Jos *Antiq*. IX. 14. 2). It was destroyed by Esarhaddon in 677; with Tyre it became subject to Pharaoh-hophra in 588; it submitted to Cambyses in 526 (Herodotus VII. 89; VIII. 67); it sold cedar for the rebuilding of the Jerusalem Temple (Ezr 3:7); it was destroyed by the Persians in 345; it surrendered to Alexander the Great in 333; and it passed to the Romans in 64. In several NT references it is mentioned in connection with Tyre (cf. introd. to ch. 26), and Paul touched at its port (Acts 27:3).

20-23. Set thy face against Zidon (= Sidon). The Lord's greatness is recognized by the judgments on Sidon. Sidon, and the other nations, had been a "pricking thorn and a painful brier" to Israel (v. 24).

24-26. The house of Israel. The punishment of the nations will result in restoration for the house of Israel. God's providence is clearly marked in these verses. The captivity of Israel among her neighbors (v. 24), will lead to her repentance and restoration (v. 25), to God's judgment on her ungodly enemies, and to peace and prosperity for Israel (v. 26).

G. Seven Oracles Against Egypt. 29:1–32:32.

Other maledictions against Egypt occur at Isa 19; Jer 46; Zech 14:18,19. Egypt's sin was its pride (Ezk 29:3,9b; 30:10) and its leading Israel away from the Lord (29:6-9a).

Israel's involvements with Egypt at this time are discussed in the Introduction to Ezekiel. Since Egypt was a great world power, ruling nations and aspiring to universal dominion (29:15), the prophet treats of it on a cosmic scale. The judgment of Egypt was to be "the day of the Lord" (30:3). The fall of that great nation would be felt throughout the world (32:10), while even creation would shudder (31:15). The world was to know that God is the Lord (30:19,26).

The seven oracles describe in various ways God's judgment on Egypt: (1) Pharaoh as a sea-monster or crocodile is to be cast out to be devoured, and the nation is to be restored to lowly status after forty years (29:1-16). (2) Egypt is to be given to Nebuchadrezzar as a recompense for his futile siege of Tyre (29:17-21). (3) Egypt will be overthrown, together with its allies, wealth, princes, and cities (30:1-19). (4) The arms of Egypt will be broken by the arms of the king of Babylon (30:20-26). (5) In an allegory, Pharaoh, the mighty cedar, is cut down and enters the underworld in disgrace (31:1-18). (6) A lament over Pharaoh, the crocodile of Egypt, destroyed by the king of Babylon (32:1-16). (7) A dirge sung at the descent of Egypt into the underworld (32:17-32).

1) The Desolation and Restoration of Egypt. 29:1-16.

a) The Fate of the Great Sea Monster. 29:1-5.

1. Tenth year, tenth month, twelfth day. January 586 (or 587) B.C., seven months before the fall of Jerusalem. **2. Pharaoh king of Egypt.** Apries or Hophra, of the Twenty-sixth Dynasty (588–569). **3. The great dragon** (*tannîm*, or *tannîn* in many MSS). Cf. 32:2; Isa 27:1; 51:9. Gunkel and others equate this dragon with the mythological *Tiamat* of the Babylonians. It is, also, often associated with Leviathan (Isa 27:1; Job 41:1; Ps 74:14) and with "Rahab" (Isa 51:9; Job

26:12,13. Cf. Barton, *Archaeology and the Bible*, 279-302; ANET, 61-68, 137). Here perhaps the **dragon** is the crocodile, for there are no mythological associations in the present context (cf. A. Heidel, *The Babylonian Genesis)*. **River**, the Nile, *ye'ôr*, is an Egyptian loan-word. The **rivers**, *ye'ôrîm*, are the arms of the Nile in the Delta (cf. vv. 4,5,10). "Egypt is the gift of the Nile," says Herodotus, but Pharaoh boasts, **I have made it** (cf. v. 9. So the Syriac; cf. the LXX).

4. Fish of thy rivers. The population or mercenaries of Egypt. **5. I have given thee for meat to the beasts of the field.** Improper burial was considered a fearful fate in the ancient world, especially to the Egyptians in view of their meticulous care of the dead (cf. 32:4,5; Jer 22:18,19).

b) A Sword To Come upon Egypt. 29:6-9a.

6. All the inhabitants of Egypt shall know. Cf. Ex 2:3,5; Isa 19:6; II Kgs 18:21. **7. To shake** (RSV). So the Syriac, a rendering derived by transposing two letters of the MT, *to cause to stand* **8. A sword.** That is, the Chaldeans. See also verses 10; 32:11,12; Jer 46:13ff.

c) Desolation and Restoration. 29:9b-16.

10. Migdol *(tower)*. Tell el-Heir, twelve miles southwest of Pelusium, the northeast border of Egypt (cf. 30:6; Ex 14:2; Jer 44:1). **Syene.** Egyptian *Sun* (prob. meaning "elephant"), at the first cataract of the Nile, near Assuan, the southern boundary of Egypt (cf. 30:6), near the border of **Ethiopia**, or *Kûsh* (Jos *Wars* IV. 10. 5). **11. No foot of man . . . of beast.** Cf. 32:13,15; 26:20. **Forty years.** The period of Chaldean supremacy, anticipating verse 13. **12. Egypt desolate in the midst** of the Arabian and Libyan deserts on either side (cf. 30:7). The Egyptians were to be scattered (cf. 30:23, 26).

13-16. At the end of forty years Egypt was to be restored but only to the status of a **lowly** (AV, *base)* **kingdom.** Cf. Jer 46:26. **Pathros** *(southland)*. Upper Egypt. See also 30:14; Isa 11:11; Jer 44:15.

2) Egypt To Be Given to Nebuchadrezzar as Recompense. 29:17-21.

17. Twenty-seventh year, first month, first day. March-April 570 (571) B.C. The latest prophecy of Ezekiel. Nebuchadrezzar invaded Egypt in the thirty-seventh year of his reign, 568/567 B.C., but Egypt did not become a part of his empire. **18.** In the arduous siege laid to Tyre by Nebuchadrezzar's army (585–573), **every head was made bald** by carrying loads, **and every shoulder was rubbed bare** (RSV) by the chafing of the weights.

19,20. The booty of Egypt was to become **wages** for Nebuchadrezzar's army. Cf. 30:10,24,25; Jer 43:10,11.

21. In that day. Cf. verses 19,20; 30:9; 24:26,27. **The horn.** Symbolizing Israel's restoration to power (cf. I Sam 2:1,10; Ps 92:10). Psalm 132:17 indicates that the Davidic dynasty is to be restored. **Opening of the mouth.** The verification of the prophet's words to his fellow exiles (16:63), that the divine judgments would be followed by new hope.

3) All Phases of Egypt's Life To Be Punished on the Day of the Lord. 30:1-19.

This section, of an eschatological character, is the only one not dated, but is perhaps chronologically related to 29:1-16. It consists of four oracles, each beginning with, "Thus saith the Lord" (see vv. 2,6,10,13).

a) The Day of the Lord Announced with Reference to Egypt. 30:1-5.

3. The day of the Lord. The *dies irae*, "day of wrath." See also 7:7; Amos 5:18-20; Zeph 1:7,14; Isa 13:6; Joel 1:15; 2:1,2. This is the day of judgment on sin and the final doom of the heathen world, of which Egypt is representative. **4. Foundations.** The political and social institutions in which Egypt's strength lay (cf. vv. 6,8,13,15,17). **5.** The allies of Egypt were to be overthrown. **Arabia** (RSV). This translation follows Symmachus, Aquila, and the Syriac in place of the AV, *the mingled people*. **Libya.** In northern Africa, west of Egypt (cf. Nah 3:9). Read *Lûb*, with the LXX, and the Syriac for unknown *Chûb* of the MT. **Men . . . in league.** Literally, *and the sons of the land of the covenant with them*. A reference to Egypt's allies rather than to Jewish mercenaries in the army of Psamtik II (594–588; see *Letter of Aristeas*, ch. 13).

b) Egypt and Its Allies To Be Destroyed. 30:6-9.

6. Migdol to Syene (RSV). Preferable to AV, *from the tower of Syene*. Cf. 29:10. **7.** Cf. 29:12. **8. Fire.** Figurative of war (cf. vv. 14,16). **9.** Cf. Isa 18:2. The Lord's acts against Egypt were meant to warn the **unsuspecting** (AV, *careless)* **Ethiopians** and the world.

c) The Wealth of Egypt To Be Seized by Nebuchadrezzar. 30:10-12.

10. The multitude of Egypt (cf. 4; 29:19) would be carried off by **Nebuchadrezzar,** first referred to here by name. The reference in 29:17-19 is from a later date. **11. The terrible.** Cf. 28:7; 31:12; 32:12; 7:24. **12. I will make the rivers dry.** Drying up of the Nile arms (cf. 29:3) would be a calamity to Egypt. Cf. Isa 19:5ff. **The hand of the wicked . . . strangers.** Cf. Hab 1:6ff.,12,13.

d) Princes and Towns of Egypt To Be Destroyed. 30:13-19.

Eight principal cities, three in Lower and five in Upper Egypt, are singled out for destruction.

13. Idols and . . . images. The words *gillûlîm,* "logs, blocks," and *'elîlîm,* "not-gods," are used only here in Ezekiel but often in Isaiah. One suggestion is to read *g^e^dôlîm,* "nobles" and *'êlîm,* "chiefs" (LXX).

Memphis (Gr.). Or *Noph* (Heb.), *Mennofri* (Egyptian), near *mit Rahîneh,* ten miles south of Cairo. The home of the fire-god, Ptah, and the Apis bull. **14. Pathros.** Cf. 29:14. **Zoan.** Egyptian *S'nt,* or Greek Tanis. The Hyksos capital Avaris, present day Sân el-Hagar, in the east Delta of the Nile, west of Pelusium. **Thebes.** Or *No,* No-Amon, Egyptian Nēt, capital of Upper Egypt, four hundred miles south of Memphis, home of the sun-god, Amon. **15. Pelusium** (RSV). So the Vulgate. MT *Sîn* (only here in Ezk). Identified as Tell Foramen. It was a frontier fortress on the northeast boundary, in the vicinity of Pelusium, twenty-three miles southeast of Port Said. **16. Pelusium** *(Sin)* to **Thebes** *(No)* is all Egypt from north to south.

17. On, or *Aven.* Egyptian *'nw,* Greek Heliopolis. The present Tell Hasn, or 'Ain Shems, "sun fountain," located about seven miles northeast of Cairo. It was the seat of the sun-god Ra. It was also the home of Joseph's father-in-law (Gen 41:45,50). **Pi-beseth.** Egyptian *Pi Bastis,* Greek *Bubastis.* Present-day Tel Basta, thirty miles north-northeast of Cairo. It was the house of the goddess Bast, to whom the cat was sacred. **18. Tehaphnehes.** Elsewhere *Tahpanhes.* Greek *Daphnae.* Modern Tell Defenneh, on the Pelusiac bank of the Nile. It was an eastern frontier fortress, about thirty miles southwest of Pelusium.

19. Will I execute judgments. The purpose of the judgment was to be the revelation of the Lord and the recognition of his deity.

4) The Arms of Pharaoh To Be Broken. 30:20-26.

20. Eleventh year, first month, seventh day. March-April 586 (or 587), three months after 29:1, and four months before the fall of Jerusalem. In verses 21-23 the Lord is the destroyer of Pharaoh; in verses 24-26, the king of Babylon is His agent. **21. I have broken the arm of Pharaoh.** Probably a reference to a recent defeat of Pharaoh-necho (Jer 37:5-8; 34:21). **22.** The breaking of both Pharaoh's arms, **the strong, and . . . broken,** refers to the army still in Egypt for defense and the one defeated and fleeing.

23. I will scatter the Egyptians. Cf. verse 26; 29:12. **24. Strengthen the arms of the king of Babylon.** This refers to the sword of the Lord in Nebuchadrezzar's hand. Cf. 21:9. **25. They shall know that I am the Lord.** See also verses 8,19, 25.

5) Allegory of the Mighty Cedar. 31:1-18.

In the present chapter, the overthrow of a major *land* power is predicted (in contrast to the *sea* power in ch. 26). Ezekiel again uses allegory, now to describe Pharaoh, representing Egypt, as a mighty cedar, reaching to the clouds, in whose shelter the beasts and birds lodged (vv. 1-9). In the allegory the proud cedar is cut down and despoiled as a warning to the other trees, i.e., nations (vv. 10-14). Nature shudders at the fall of the tree, while the trees in the nether world are comforted at its descent (vv. 15-18).

a) Grandeur of the Cedar. 31:1-9.

1. Eleventh year . . . third month . . . first day. May-June, 586 (or 587), about two months before the fall of Jerusalem.

3. I will liken you to a cedar in Lebanon (RSV). The MT reads, *Behold, Asshur* (i.e., Assyria) *was a cedar.* The chapter has nothing to do with Assyria, nor is there any call to compare Egypt with Assyria. Supplying a missing letter to *'ashshûr,* making it *t^e'ashshûr,* gives the reading, "Behold a sherbin, a cedar in Lebanon." Cf. 27:5. For the figure, see 17:3; Dan 4:10ff. **Its top among the clouds** (RSV). Read *'abôt,* with the LXX, in place of MT *'abôtîm,* "interwoven foliage." This reading applies, also, to verses 10,14.

4. The waters. Of the Nile. **The deep** *(t^e^hôm).* The subterranean source of all springs and rivers (cf. 26:19; 29:3; Hab 3:10). **6. The fowls and beasts,** i.e., the nations, dwelt **under his shadow,** the protection of Egypt. **8,9.** The lofty trees of Eden, **the garden of God,** envied it. Cf. 28:13; Ps 104:16; 31:16.

b) Fall of the Tree and Its Significance. 31:10-14.

10. Thou hast lifted up thyself. The pride of Egypt (cf. 29:3,9) was to fall before the Chaldean might (vv. 11,12). **11. The mighty one** (lit., *a ram*) **of the heathen.** Cf. 17:13. **12. Strangers, the terrible.** Cf. 28:7; 30:11; 32:11,12. **13.** The fallen tree, like the carcass of 29:5, would become prey to beasts and birds.

14. The downfall of the great cedar is to be a warning against pride. The last part of the verse, beginning at, **For they are all delivered unto death,** belongs to the subject matter of the next stanza.

c) Consternation at the Fall of the Cedar, and Its Descent to the Underworld. 31:15-18.

There are a number of references to the underworld in this paragraph (cf. note at 26:20). The nether world (*'ereṣ taḥtît*) is located deep down in the earth (26:20; 31:14,16,18; 32:18,24). **The pit** (*bôr*). A name given to the underworld because the grave was the mouth of it. It designates the entrance to Sheol, and is often a parallel word for it (26:20; 31:14,16; 32:18,23,24,25,29,30). **Hell** or *Sheol* ("place of inquiry" for necromancy; place that insatiably "asks," Prov 20:15,16; "hollow place," "underworld"). The vast burying place in the earth, full of graves (31:15,16,17; 32:21,27. Cf. *shaḥat*, 28:9).

15. I caused a mourning. The world of nature would mourn for Egypt. **Lebanon,** "White," would be clothed in black. **16. Trees of Eden . . . comforted in the nether world** (RSV). Cf. Isa 14:9-11; Enoch 25:4-6. **17. They also went down into hell.** More accurately, *They also shall go down* (prophetic perfect) *to Sheol* (RSV). The allies of Pharaoh were to perish with him (cf. v. 18). Pharaoh would be **brought down with** them, to **lie among the uncircumcised** (RSV). Cf. 28:10; 32:19-21. The Egyptians also practiced circumcision. Cf. ANET, p. 326.

6) Lamentations over Pharaoh and Egypt. 32:1-16.

a) The Monster of Egypt Caught, Slain, and Devoured. 32:1-10.

1. Twelfth year . . . twelfth month . . . first day. February-March, 584 (585) B.C., one year and seven months after the fall of Jerusalem. **2. Lamentation** (19:1). Here, a tragic song with denunciations: "Pharaoh, young lion of the nations, you are destroyed!" **You are like a sea monster** (*tannîm;* cf. 29:3), stirring up trouble among the nations.

4,5. Then will I leave thee. The monster would be slain and his carcass flung out to be devoured. Cf. 29:3-5. **7,8. When I shall put thee out.** Pharaoh is compared to a luminary whose extinction darkens the sky and stars. Cf. 30:18; Amos 5:18,20; Isa 13:9,10; 14:12. **9,10. I will . . . vex the hearts of many people.** Egypt's fall would make a profound impression on the nations. Cf. chapters 30; 31.

b) Devastation of Egypt by the King of Babylon. 32:11-16.

11,12. The sword of the king of Babylon and his warriors would come upon Egypt (cf. 21:19; 29:8; 30:11). **13,14. I will destroy.** A dramatic picture of uninhabited Egypt. Cf. verse 2; 29:11. **14. Then will I cause to sink down their waters.** The mud would settle and the water would become clear, and the rivers would run **like oil,** no more trampled by man or cattle. This is the only comparison of a smoothly flowing stream to oil. **15.** The purpose of the judgment.

16. The lamentation chanted by **the daughters of the nations.** Women were hired as mourners (cf. v. 18; 19:14; Jer 9:16,17).

7) Egypt's Descent to the Nether World. 32:17-32.

17. In the twelfth year, in the fifteenth day of the month (so MT). On the basis of 32:1, it may be assumed that this oracle was dated in the twelfth month, two weeks later.

This oracle contains the most graphic portrayal of the Pit or Sheol in the OT. It is the international abode of the dead, full of graves (vv. 22,23), peopled with nations once vital (vv. 18,29,30); nations are in places of honor or dishonor (vv. 23-25,30); kings on their thrones are surrounded by their subjects (cf. Isa 14:9, 10,18,19); warriors are buried with their weapons under their heads (v. 27); the nations are weak (vv. 20,21; Isa 14:10; cf. also Job 3:17-19). **19.** Egypt would be consigned among the uncircumcised. Cf. 31:18.

22-30. *Six welcoming nations to receive Egypt in Sheol.* The repetition, 24-27, 32, gives a mournful quality to the oracle. Its general theme is, "They that live by the sword shall die by the sword."

22,23. Asshur (i.e., Assyria) would be consigned to the bottom of Sheol. **24,25. Elam** *(highlands)*, mentioned only here in Ezekiel, was located east of the Tigris River and north of the Persian Gulf. Its capital city was Shushan (Susa; Neh 1:1; Dan 8:2). The Elamites were a non-Semitic people.

26-28. Meshech and **Tubal.** Cf. 27:13. **27.** The LXX and the Syriac omit **not,** to read, *they lie with the mighty men,* fallen from of old, having their weapons buried with them. The manner of their death and burial will be in keeping with their life of bloodshed and violence. **29. Edom.** Cf. 25:12-14. The Edomites were circumcised, but here they are to lie with those who were not.

30. The **princes** (or *chiefs, nāshîk,* from *nāshak,* "to install"; cf. Josh 13:21; Mic 5:4; Ps 83:11; Dan 11:8) **of the north** *(Ṣapôn)*; i.e., of the Syrian states bordering Mount Ṣāphôn (cf. 28:14). **The Sidonians,** or Phoenicians in general. Cf. Deut 3:9; I Kgs 16:31. The people of the Syrian states and the Sidonians were circumcised, and so the text should read as in verse 29, "they lie with the uncircumcised."

31,32. Pharaoh shall see them. Pharaoh was to have the miserable comfort of knowing that he was not alone in his fate. Cf. 14:22; 31:16.

III. Prophecies of Israel's Restoration. 33:1—39:29.

The fall of Jerusalem marks a turning point in the ministry of Ezekiel. The hitherto minatory oracles against Judah (chs. 1—24) and her pagan foes (chs. 25—32) now give way to the hortatory messages of a pastor to his shattered people (chs. 33—39). After the collapse of the state (33:21) and the complete prostration of people's minds under their calamities (33:10), the prophet declared that the Lord had not made a full end to Israel (contrast ch. 35). A new era was ahead for her. In moving words, Ezekiel here speaks of the purification, restoration, and peace of Israel (chs. 34; 36:16ff.; 37).

First the prophet is recommissioned as a watchman to prepare his people for the new age (ch. 33). A new government under God's servant David will supplant the old dynasty, whose wicked shepherds (rulers) scattered the sheep (ch. 34). Israel's territorial integrity will be assured by the desolation of Mount Seir and other enemies (ch. 35), while Israel will experience both outward restoration (36:1-15) and inward restoration (36:16-38). The reintegration of the people into one nation under one king, David, is symbolized by the resurrection of the dry bones and the joining of two sticks (ch. 37). The peace of restored Israel will be perpetual, for the Lord will protect her miraculously from the threatened invasion of Gog in the latter days (chs. 38; 39).

A. Function of the Prophet in Preparing for the New Age. 33:1-33.

In this transitional chapter, Ezekiel indicates that the prophet is but the medium through whom the principles of the new kingdom and the mode of entering it are announced. Just as the watchman is to warn the inhabitants of a city concerning danger, so the prophet is to sound out God's warning against sin (vv. 1-9). In response to the people's despair at their chastisements, Ezekiel utters reminders of God's good will and perfect justice (vv. 10-20). The presumptuous survivors of the fall of Jerusalem in Judah will have no future (vv. 21-29), but rather, God's purposes will be worked out through those in exile (vv. 30-33).

1) The Prophet Appointed as a Watchman for His People. 33:1-9.

a) The Parable. 33:1-6.

2. Watchman. Hebrew *sôpeh,* "one who looks out, spies, watches." Cf. II Sam 18:25; II Kgs 9:17,18. **3. Sword.** Cf. 21:1-19. **Trumpet.** See Hos 8:1; Jer 6:1; Neh 4:19,20.

b) Its Application. 33:7-9.

7. I have set thee a watchman. The prophet receives a new appointment as the watchman of the people. Ezekiel's concept of the seriousness of his task has had a profound effect on all God's servants. Cf. Isa 21:6; 56:10; Jer 6:17; Hab 2:1.

2) The Prophet's Message to the Despairing Exiles. 33:10-20.

10. We pine away. Cf. 4:17; 24:23. **11,12.** Two gracious words are granted to the exiles stunned by the feeling of irrevocable doom: (1) God has **no pleasure in the death of the wicked,** but wants him to **turn from his way and live.** (2) The past is not irrevocable for men, for they are free either to repent or to sin. Cf. 18:21-32.

13. On **live** and **die,** see comment at 18:4; cf. 18:24,26. **14.** Cf. 3:18; 18:27. **15. Statutes of life.** "Life" in this and related passages is "the enjoyment of the favor of God and the external prosperity which is the reflection and seal of it" (Davidson, *Cambridge Bible)*. Cf. 18:7; 20:11. **16.** Cf. vv. 18-22. **17-20.** Cf. 18:24-30.

3) News of Jerusalem's Fall, and the Prophet's Message to the Survivors in Judah. 33:21-29.

Jerusalem fell in the eleventh year, fourth month, and ninth day of the reign of Zedekiah (Jer 39:2 parallels 52:5-7 and II Kgs 25:2), and was burned a month later (Jer 52:12-14 parallels II Kgs 25:8-10). **21. Twelfth year . . . tenth month . . . fifth day.** The reading of the MT implies that the fugitive reached the exile one and one-half years after the fall of Jerusalem. Stuernagel holds that Jeremiah's year began in the autumn, while Ezekiel, following the Babylonian reckoning, began the year in the spring. Thus the eleventh year of Jer 39:2 is the same as the twelfth year of Ezk 33:21, and so the news reached Ezekiel in January 585.

E. Auerbach (VT, X (1960) 69, 70, and M. Noth (ZDPV, LXXIV (1958), 133-157) have amassed data to show that in the late monarchy the year began in the spring. Eight manuscripts, the LXX, Lucian, and the Syriac read, *eleventh year*. Dating this oracle in the eleventh year, tenth month, fifth day, permits it to fit in before 26:1, which may have been delivered in the eleventh or twelfth month of the eleventh year. The news would have come about six months after the fall of Jerusalem, i.e., about January, 585 B.C. Cf. Ezra's journey, 108 days (Ezr 8:31; 7:8,9).

22. The prophet had been in an ecstasy **in the evening,** and the Lord opened his mouth by the time the man arrived the next morning (cf. 3:26,27; 24:27). One tradition identifies the messenger with Baruch (Jer 45:5; Baruch 1:2). Ezekiel was now free to devote himself to pastoral work, earlier hinted at. Cf. 16:60ff.; 17:22ff.; 20:33ff.

24. They that inhabit those wastes (lit., *ruins;* cf. II Kgs 25:12,22), who survived the destruction of Jerusalem, *keep saying:* If **Abraham . . . one . . . inherited the land** (Isa 51:1,2), surely they, his numerous descendants, had a stronger right to it (cf. Mt 3:9). **25,26. Say unto them.** The survivors of Jerusalem, so confident of their safety before the fall of the city (11:3-12), are charged with six specific sins (cf. 18:6,10-12,15; 22:6, 9), which disqualified them for any inheritance.

27. Those who are hiding in "ruins," the depopulated countryside, and in **forts and . . . caves** will fall before the three destructive forces of 5:12; 14:13-20. **28. The mountains of Israel** (cf. 6:2,3). **29.** God's visitations on the land will cause the apostate Israelites to recognize Him as the Lord, a lesson usually needed by the heathen (25:7,11,17).

4) An Oracle for the Exiles. 33:30-33.

Since Ezekiel's prophecies had been so remarkably fulfilled, the exiles took interest in him; but their enthusiasm was shallow. **30,31.** In this snatch of Oriental life, the exiles are seen **talking together** (RSV) of Ezekiel, sitting **before** him (cf. 8:1; 14:1; 20:1). They liked his messages of the future restoration and prophecies against the nations but would not obey the moral and religious conditions without which they could have no part in the new era. **32. Love songs** (RSV; "sensuous love," *'āgāb)*. Cf. I Sam 16:17; Ps 33:3; 137:3. **33. When this** (judgment or crisis) **cometh,** they will know they have listened not to a hireling singer but to a prophet of the Lord. Cf. 2:5.

B. The Shepherds of Israel and Their Sheep. 34:1-31.

Because the shepherds or rulers in this allegory have been neglectful and selfish, the Lord will punish them (vv. 1-10). He will himself search out the sheep and be the Good Shepherd (vv. 11-16). He will judge between one sheep and another, protecting the weak from the violent (vv. 17-22). The Lord will set up David as the one shepherd (vv. 23,24), and will make a covenant of peace for the land (vv. 25-31).

1) Judgment on Selfish and Neglectful Shepherds. 34:1-10.

The word shepherd, *rō'eh,* occurs sixteen times in this chapter. **2. The shepherds of Israel.** Rulers, like Jehoiakim and Zedekiah. See 19:1-9; Jer 22:10–23:4; see also Jer 25:34-38; Mic 5:5; Zech 10:2,3; I Kgs 22:17. (Cf. Homer *Iliad* i. 273; ii. 85; Dante, *The Divine Comedy,* "Paradise," xxvii, 55,56; Milton, *Lycidas,* 112ff. On king and god as shepherd in other lit., cf. G. E. Wright, "The Good Shepherd," BA, 2 (1939), 44-48.)

3. Ye eat the fat. Or, the *milk;* i.e., curds (so LXX, Vulg.). **4. Diseased . . . sick . . . crippled . . . strayed . . . lost** (RSV). Five cases of the shepherd's neglect. Cf. verse 16; Jer 50:6; Mt 18:12-14; Lk 15:4; 19:10. **5. Scattered . . . no shepherd.** Cf. I Kgs 22:17; Mt 9:36; Mk 6:34.

8. As I live. Cf. 5:11. **Beast of the field.** The exploiting nations, especially Babylon.

2) The Lord a Good Shepherd to His People. 34:11-16.

The Lord **will . . . search** for his sheep (v. 11); **deliver them** (v. 12); **bring them to their own land** (v. 13); **feed them in a good pasture** (v. 14); and **be the shepherd** (ASV) of his sheep (15,16). Ezekiel, like the Lord, had a pastor's heart. **15.** The Lord identifies himself as the good shepherd. Cf. Isa 40:11; Jer 31:10; Ps 23:1; 30:1; 95:7. In the NT Christ is the good shepherd. See Lk 15:3-7; Jn 10:10-16; Heb 13:20; I Pet 2:25; 5:4; Rev 7:17.

3) The Lord To Protect the Weak from the Violent Sheep. 34:17-22.

17. The Lord will **judge between sheep and sheep** (RSV; *śeh).* That is, between the weak and the leaders, **the rams and the he goats,** who oppress the poor. **18,19.** Callous wrongs of upper classes are pointed out. Cf. Isa 1:23; 3:14,15; 5:8; Hos 4:7-11; 7:1-6; Amos 3:9,10; 4:1,6; Mic 3:1-3.

4) David Installed as Shepherd-Prince. 34:23,24.

Instead of many worthless shepherds, there shall be **one shepherd . . . my servant David. . . . prince** (vv. 23,24). There is here no allusion to a resurrection of David. Rather, the ideal ruler of the future will be like David, a servant of the Lord, bearing universal rule, and securing peace for the people (Isa 55:3,4; Jer 23:5,6). He shall be the Lord's viceroy or prince *(nāśīʾ)* forever. Cf. 37:24,25. Christ as the good shepherd (Jn 10:14-18) and the "Son of David" completely fulfills the promises found in II Sam 7:13; Jer 23:5,6; Mic 5:2-5; Isa 9:6,7; Dan 9:25,26; Cf. Mt 1:1; 22:41-45; Lk 1:31-33; Jn 1:43; 4:25; Acts 2:29-33; 13:22,23, to name but a few. Messianic prophecy denotes all prophecy which treats of the person, work, or kingdom of Christ. By extension it includes those passages which speak of the future salvation, glory, and consummation of God's kingdom even where the mediator is not specifically named. The Messianic times comprise the era which Christ inaugurated and conducts as mediatorial king, whether viewed in its entirety or only in some of its aspects.

5) God's Covenant of Peace for the Land. 34:25-31.

God's covenant of peace will remove from the land all that is hurtful (vv. 25, 28). It will provide **showers of blessing** (v. 26) and restore the productivity of nature (vv. 27,29). And, best of all, it will re-establish the presence of God with his people, the sheep of his pasture (vv. 30,31).

26. Shower . . . in his season . . . showers bringing **blessing.** The common words for rain are: *yôreh,* "the early rain," from the last of October to the first of December (Hos 6:3); *malkôsh,* "the latter rain, spring rain," of March-April (Hos 6:3); *geshem,* "shower," the word used here; and *māṭār,* "rain" (Ex 9:33), both of which are used of the heavy winter rains of mid-December to March. **27.** Cf. Hos 2:22; Joel 3:18; Amos 9:13; Zech 8:12.

31. Ye . . . the flock of my pasture. Cf. Ps 74:1; 79:13; 95:7; 100:3. The LXX B, Ranke's Old Latin, and the Arabic omit *men* **(ye . . . are men,** AV; or *you are Adam).*

C. The Territorial Integrity of Israel Assured. 35:1–36:38.

After the promise of a good shepherd to replace the wicked shepherds who had ruled Israel, there follow three oracles on the security of the land itself. Mount Seir, for its hostility to Israel, was to be rendered a desolation (35:1-15); while the mountains of Israel, which had been ravaged by the nations, would become luxuriantly fruitful (36:1-15). The Lord would do all these things for his people for his name's sake (36:16-38).

1) The Desolation of Mount Seir. 35:1-15.

The present oracle, much more detailed than that in 25:12-14, was called forth by Edom's hostile behavior to Judah after 586. Israel must be cleared of hostile neighbors before the blessings of the new age would begin (36:1-7). The desolation of Mount Seir and the restoration of the mountains of Israel form a striking contrast (35:3,4,7-9,15; 36:1-6,8).

2. Mount Seir *(hairy,* i.e., covered with brushwood). The highlands east of the Arabah, stretching from the Dead Sea to the Gulf of Akaba, were the home of Edom (Gen 36:8,9; Deut 1:2; I Chr 4:42). The Edomites are indicted for: (1) their **perpetual hatred** against Israel (v. 5a; cf. Gen 25:15; 27:41; and references at Ezk 25:12. See N. Glueck, *The Other Side of the Jordan,* pp. 50-113; *Rivers in the Desert);* (2) Delivering **Israel by the force of the sword** at the fall of Jerusalem (v. 5b, cf. Ob 10-14; Ps

137:7,8); (3) planning to possess the territory of Israel after the decimation of its inhabitants (v. 10; cf. v. 12), unauthorized by Nebuchadnezzar or the Lord (36:5).

6-9. Retribution must fall on Edom. **10. These two nations.** Israel and Judah (cf. Jer 33:24). After the fall of Jerusalem, the Edomites gradually penetrated Judah, occupying it as far as Hebron (cf. Ezk 25:12ff.). **Whereas the Lord was there.** The Lord had withdrawn his visible presence from the Temple and the city (10:18; 11:22,23), but he had not renounced his right to the land (36:5). A purified Israel, this prophecy declares, shall return, and Jerusalem will be given a new name (48:35). **14,15.** As Edom rejoiced over the destruction of Judah, so the whole earth will rejoice when the Lord makes Edom desolate. Note the frequent first personal pronouns throughout the chapter, applied to the work of the Lord.

2) The Restoration of the Mountains of Israel: Restoration Outward. 36:1-15.

a) Judgment on the Nations. 36:1-7.

1. The mountains of Israel, denounced for idolatry in 6:1-7, are granted gracious promises in this chapter. **2. The enemy.** Edom and other nations (vv. 3-7). Cf. 35:3,5,10,11. Note that in verses 2-7 "thus saith the Lord" recurs six times. Verses 3-7, 14 all begin with *lākēn,* "therefore." **5. In the fire of my jealousy.** Cf. v. 6; 5:13; 23:25; 38:19; 39:25. **6.** Cf. verses 2,3. **The shame of the nations.** Being scorned by and occupied by them (see v. 2; 34:29). **7. I swear** (RSV). Literally, *I lift up my hand* (cf. 20:5,6).

b) Restoration of Israel. 36:8-15.

In the approaching age of the regeneration, the land will be fruitful (vv. 8,9); populous (vv. 10-12); free from scarcity (vv. 13,14); and free from reproach (v. 15). Cf. Isa 54:1-8.

8. For they (my people Israel) **are at hand to come** from exile. Cf. 4:5,6. **10. All the house of Israel.** Both Israel and Judah (cf. 37:16ff.). **11. As in your former times** (RSV). At the time of the Exodus (Hos 11:1-4; Jer 2:1-3,6,7).

12b,13,14. The mountains, scourged by famine or wild beasts, are compared to beasts of prey and said to devour their inhabitants or to **bereave** their nation (cf. Num 13:32). In Ezk 36:13,14,15, Israel is called a *goy* or nation, the usual designation for the heathen (cf. 2:3). Read the word as a singular, along with the Hebrew marginal *kᵉtîb* and the versions. **15. Shame . . . reproach.** Occupation by hostile neighbors (v. 6), destitution and impoverishment (v. 30).

3) Restoration of the People of Israel: Restoration Inward. 36:16-38.

This section containing a divinely imparted philosophy of history declares that Israel's sins deserved the chastisement of exile (vv. 16-21); but that the Lord will restore Israel, not because of any merit of hers, but to sanctify his name. The glorious accompaniments of the restoration are enumerated (vv. 22-32). In two appendices the Lord foretells that Israel's prosperity and increased population will cause the nations to acknowledge His greatness (vv. 33-36,37, 38).

Verses 16-23 constitute the prophetic lesson or *haphtarah* to the weekly Sabbath reading, Num 19:1–22:1, the *Pārāh,* "The Red Cow."

a) Israel Exiled for Her Sins. 36:16-21.

17. The uncleanness of a . . . woman. A figure for idolatry. Compare 7:19; 18:6. (For the figure, see Lev 15:19ff.) **18. Idols** *(gillûlîm).* Cf. 6:4; 20:7,8; 30:13. **20. Profaned my holy name.** Israel's exiling led to the profanation of the Lord's holy name by the nations. Note the expression "my holy name" in verses 20-23. Cf. discussion at 20:9,14, 22. **The people of the Lord.** Cf. Ex 6:7; Lev 20:24; Deut 4:20; 7:6.

b) Restoration of Israel. 36:22-32.

23. I will sanctify. Or set apart as sacred. The return of Israel after her chastisement will make manifest to the nations that the Lord is the supreme and holy God, and that he desires to reveal himself to all the world. See also verse 36; 29:6; 37:28; 39:7; Mal 1:11; Eph 1:3-10.

The next passage, verses 25-29, though referring primarily to Israel, is used in Christian liturgy, and is dear to the whole church.

25-27. The steps in the redemption of Israel are forgiveness, regeneration, and the gift of the Spirit of God. **25. Then will I sprinkle clean water upon you.** Ezekiel the priest recalls the Mosaic ritual (cf. Ex 30:17-21; Lev 14:5-7,9; Num 19:9, 17-19) which is a picture of forgiveness. See also Ps 51:7; Jer 33:8; Heb 9:13; 10:22. **26. A new heart . . . a new spirit.** God's part in regeneration is stressed here. Cf. 11:19; 18:30-32. See also Jer 31:31-34; Ps 51:10-12. On new things in

God's redemptive scheme, see Isa 42:9, 10; 62:2; 66:22; II Pet 3:13; Rev 5:1; 21:1,5. **27. I will put my spirit within you.** The pouring out of God's Spirit is to be a feature of the coming age (cf. 37:14; 39:29; Isa 42:1; 44:3; Joel 2:28, 29; Hag 2:5; Acts 2:16-21; Rom 8:23; Eph 1:13,14; 4:30).

28-32. The results of Israel's regeneration will be: her permanent occupation of the land (v. 28a); a covenant relationship with God (v. 28b); protection against relapse into idolatry (v. 29a); the abundant supply of every want (vv. 29b,30); and self-humiliation and repentance on account of past sin (vv. 31, 32; cf. Plumptre, *Pulpit Commentary, in loco).* These benefits are of pure grace (v. 22).

c) Effect of Israel's Prosperity on the Nations. 36:33-36.

Israel's restoration will cause those who pass by (v. 34b), of **the nations** (AV, *heathen)* **that are left round about you** (v. 36) to recognize the supremacy of the Lord. **35.** History moves from Eden to Eden. **Cities . . . fortified.** Contrast 38:11.

d) Israel's Increased Population. 36:37, 38.

37a. Ask me to do for them (RSV). God is now ready to hear Israel, in contrast to his attitude in her sinful days (14:3; 20:3,31). **37b,38.** The land will be repeopled **with men like a flock,** numerous as the sheep offered to the Lord at **Jerusalem in her solemn feasts** (Deut 16:16ff.; cf. I Chr 29:21; II Chr 7:4ff.; 29:33; 36:7-9; Jos *Wars* VI. 9. 3).

D. Reintegration of the People of Israel into One Nation. 37:1-28.

By the vision of dry bones coming to life, the Lord, through Ezekiel, proclaims to Israel the coming resurrection of her national life (vv. 1-14). He foretells by the symbolic act of joining two sticks the future union of the two kingdoms under one head, David (vv. 15-28).

1) The Vision of the Dry Bones. 37:1-14.

This portion of the chapter constitutes the *haphtarah* (reading from The Prophets) for the Passover and its Sabbath in the synagogue. The entire church has made use of this passage in public and private worship. A painting of the scene, dating from 244–245 A.D., appears on the remains of a synagogue at Dura-Europos (cf. RB 43 (1934), 117,118).

a) A Vision to Exiles Who Feared National Annihilation. 37:1-10.

1. The spirit of the Lord (cf. 1:12,20; 3:14) takes **Ezekiel,** in a prophetic ecstasy (cf. 1:3; 3:14), to a **valley** (cf. 3:22,23) strewn with the dried **bones** of human bodies. **4.** Ezekiel is told to **prophesy** to the bones the promise of life. **5. I will cause breath to enter into you.** The Hebrew word *rûaḥ* is translated "breath" in verses 5,6,8,9,10, "winds" in verse 9, and "spirit" in verses 1,14. The context usually determines the translation. Breath is a sign of life, identical with wind or air, and becomes, in this prophecy, the living principle itself, spirit.

9. The breath of life is breathed from **the four winds** of heaven (cf. Jer 49:36), a symbol of the universal life-giving Spirit of God (v. 14).

b) Explanation of the Vision. 37:11-14.

11. These bones are the whole house of Israel (both Israel and Judah, vv. 16, 22), whose survivors say, **Our hope is lost.** The prophet frequently quotes sayings of the people (e.g., 11:13; 12:22, 27; 16:4; 18:2; 20:49; 36:20).

12. The figure is altered from those slain on the battlefield to those dead in the grave. **I will . . . raise you from your graves . . .** and **bring you** back, out of the dark places of captivity, **home into the land of Israel** (RSV). See also verses 14,21; 36:24. **14. And shall put my spirit in you, and ye shall live.** The Spirit of the Lord gives life. Cf. verse 10; Ps 104:30. In 36:27,28 He is the regenerating Spirit. Cf. Isa 49:8-12; 61:1.

The prophet is not here speaking of the bodily resurrection, though there are intimations of the doctrine in the OT, particularly in Isa 25:8; 26:19; Dan 12:2. It was "our Saviour Christ Jesus, who hath abolished death and hath brought life and immortality to light through the gospel" (II Tim 1:10).

2) A Symbol of the Reunion of Judah and Israel. 37:15-28.

a) The Two Sticks Joined Together. 37:15-17.

16. A stick. Hebrew *'ēṣ*, "tree, wood, staff" (so vv. 17,19,20). Cf. Zech 11:7. Perhaps a wooden tablet. **For Judah, and for the children of Israel his companions,** e.g., Benjamin, Simeon, Levi. **Joseph** or **Ephraim** represents the northern tribes.

b) Explanation of the Symbol. 37:18-20.

Just as the sticks were united into one,

so Israel and Judah are to be reunited into one kingdom.

c) The Blessings Resulting from Unification. 37:21-28.

Five great blessings are promised here: (1) The people will be brought back home (vv. 21,22). **One nation . . . one king . . . no longer . . . two kingdoms.** The prophets regarded Israel of the north as still living (Hos 1:11; 8:3,4; Jer 3:12-15; Isa 43:5-7; 49:5,6). Note the disposition of the twelve tribes in the new kingdom (ch. 48). (2) They will be purified from idolatry (v. 23; cf. 36:25). (3) David will be installed as king over them (vv. 24,25). He is called **king** ***(melek)*** here and in verse 22, but "prince" in other places. **25.** Cf. 36:28. **Jacob my servant.** Jacob was an ancestor of Israel, as Abraham was (Hos 12:12; Isa 29:22). **Their prince for ever.** Cf. 34:23,24. A David-like ideal ruler, rather than a reference to a resurrected David ruling forever. (4) A covenant of peace will be established (v. 26a). Cf. 34:25. (5) God will dwell in their midst (vv. 26b-28).

26. My sanctuary ***(miqdāsh).*** The Temple as the dwelling place of the Lord, made holy by his presence. **27. My tabernacle** ***(mishkān)*** **shall be with them.** Literally, *over them*, i.e., on higher ground (see 40:2; Isa 2:2; Mic 4:1), protecting them or sanctifying them. **I will be their God.** See also 11:20; 14:11; 36:28. **28. I . . . do sanctify Israel.** God comes down to dwell with man, transforming earth into heaven (cf. 43:7,9; 48:8,10,21). Verses 26-28 lead to the rebuilding of the Temple (ch. 40ff.).

This prophecy, like the preceding one, has not yet been fulfilled historically, for so far, Israel has failed to meet the conditions. Its fulfillment lies in the future ingathering of a converted Israel into the body of Christ. It looks forward to the time when the Tabernacle of God will be with his people (Rev 21:3).

E. The Lord To Protect Israel Against Gog and His Allies. 38:1–39:29.

These chapters describe in apocalyptic manner God's deliverance of his people from an unparalleled invasion by a dreadful foe. Israel has been restored to her land (34:12,13,15,23,27) and converted (36:24-28). God's dwelling is in her midst (37:21-28), and she is living in prosperity and security (38:8,11,12, 14). Her neighboring foes no longer molest her (25–32; 36:36). Then in the far distant future (38:8,16), an invasion previously predicted (38:17; 39:8) is made by nations dwelling in the outskirts of the world (cf. Isa 66:19). They come like a cloud (38:9,16) – Gog of the land of Magog, and his allies, Rosh (?), Meshech, and Tubal (38:2,3), from the uttermost parts of the north (38:15; 39:2), along with Persia, Cush, and Put (38:25), and Gomer and Beth-Togarmah, with their hordes from the north (38:6). The commercial nations, Sheba, Dedan, Tarshish and its villages (38:13), are interested in this invasion, too. Gog comes at the direction of the Lord (38:4-7,16; 39:2,3), as well as at his own initiative, spurred on by his greed (38:10-14). Ezekiel only of the prophets places "that day" (38:10, 14,18,19; 39:11) after Israel has long enjoyed restoration and prosperity in her land. See also Rev 19:11; 20:7.

Israel is miraculously preserved, but Gog's hordes are destroyed by earthquake, internecine strife, plagues, torrential rains, fire, and brimstone (38:19-22), as well as rendered helpless in battle (39:3,4). Their discarded weapons will supply fuel for Israel for seven years (39:9,10). Seven months will be required to bury their corpses (39:11-15), and also their bodies and blood will become a feast for birds and beasts (39:17-20). The outcome of this battle will be that the nations shall know that God is the Lord (38:16,23; 39:6,7,21,23; cf. Isa 45:23), while Israel need nevermore doubt the protection of her God (39:22; cf. 39:25-29).

There are three divergent views of these chapters.

(1) They present a literal description of a future attack on Israel. From Jerome to our day, Gog has been variously identified as the Babylonians, the Scythians, Cambyses king of Persia, Alexander the Great, Antiochus the Great, Antiochus Epiphanes, Antiochus Eupator, the Parthians, Mithridates king of Pontus, Suleiman's Turks, the Turks and the Christians, the Armenian descendants of the Scythians, and a confederation of northern European powers including Russia (Rosh; Meshech and Tubal as Moscow and Tobolsk) and Germany (Gomer).

The following objections to the literal interpretations are raised (cf. Fairbairn, 414-431, esp. p. 421; Keil, II, 432; Faussett, JFB, IV, 348ff.): (a) The impossibility of identifying Gog and Magog with a historical person or place. (b) The improbability of such a conglomerate army forming a military coalition. (c) The disproportionate size of the invading army in comparison to Israel and its products. (d) The problems involved in burying corpses for seven months and using discarded weapons as fuel for seven years. (e) The gross carnality of the scene as being inconsistent with Messianic times.

(2) They are a symbolic description of some future event. Some scholars adopt Hengstenberg's view that this section pictures the final conflict of the nation Israel with unidentified foes. The more traditional interpretation of Hävernick and Keil sees this as the final catastrophic struggle between the Church and the forces of the world, and the triumph of God's truth over all forms of ungodliness. This view allows the narrative to be a source of comfort to Israel and the Church but restricts it to far distant fulfillment.

(3) They constitute a prophetic parable illustrating a great truth rather than referring to any specific historical event.

Ezekiel's illustrations frequently have details that cannot be literally pressed (e.g., 16:46-51,53-56,61) but are part of the drapery of the story. Here the elaborate and weird imagery expresses a great truth. To Israel in Babylon this prophecy gave assurance that, once she was restored to her land, the power of God would protect her from the worst foes imaginable. To the Church suffering at the hands of its most relentless persecutors, this is a promise of God's deliverance. The final triumph of the Messiah at the end time is also implicit in this parable. This view makes the passage pertinent to every period of history. The purpose of apocalyptic writing such as this is the "unveiling" of the future, showing God's Lordship over it. Thus it guides and strengthens the people of God in times of darkness (e.g., Daniel, Revelation. Cf. H. H. Rowley, *The Relevance of Apocalyptic*).

In the synagogue, 38:18—39:16 is the *haphtarah* for Ex 33:12—34:26 and Num 29:26-31 for the Sabbath within the festival of Sukkoth.

The chapters contain seven oracles introduced by the formula, "Thus saith the Lord" (see Introduction below, 38:1,2; also vv. 3-9,10-13,14-16,17-23; 39:1-16, 17-24; conclusion, vv. 25-29).

1) Invasion of Gog and His Destruction. 38:1-23.

a) Introduction. 38:1,2.

2. Gog (in chs. 38; 39; Rev 20:7), not based on Gogaia of the Amarna Letters, nor Gyges, king of Lydia (670—652) but on prophecies handed down. **The land of Magog.** The location of this place is unknown. Perhaps it lay between Cappadocia and Media; or the term may refer to the Scythians (Jos *Antiq*. I. 6. 1). **Chief prince of Meshech and Tubal** (cf. 27:13). Read the MT *n^esî' rô'sh* in apposition, *prince of, head of Meshech and Tubal.* The word *rô'sh* means "head," or "chief." The MT can also be read, "prince of Rosh, Meshech, and Tubal." **Rosh** (ASV) has not been identified. Possibly it refers to some Scythian tribe in the region of the Taurus mountains.

On the last battles with Gog and Magog, see Enoch 56,57; Sibylline Books [Oracles], III, 319,320; II Esd 13; Babylonian Talmud, *Aboda Zara,* 3b; *Berakoth,* 7,8; G. F. Moore, *Judaism,* II, 344, 348. Cf. the bloody battles of Anat, ANET, 136,137.

b) Gog and His Hordes Led Forth by the Lord. 38:3-9.

4. I will turn thee back. The figure is that of turning a wild beast from its meaningless inclinations to fulfill the divine purposes. **5. Persia, Ethiopia** *(Kûsh)*, **Libya** *(Pût)*. Cf. 27:10; 30:5. **6. Gomer** (Gen 10:2). The Gimirrai of the Assyrians; the Cimmerians of the Greeks, living south of the Black Sea, probably in Cappadocia. **Togarmah** (cf. 27:14), in the **uttermost parts of the north** (RSV). Similarly Rome in Ps of Sol, 8:16. **7. Be thou a guard** or leader for invading hosts.

8. After many days . . . in the latter years. An expression used of the eschatological future (cf. introd. remarks on chs. 38; 39). **9.** Gog and his allies **advance . . . like a storm . . . like a cloud** (cf. v. 16; Isa 21:1; Jer 4:13) against a peaceful and prosperous Israel (cf. vv. 8,11,12).

c) Gog's Evil Purpose in the Invasion. 38:10-13.

10. Into thy mind. Man's plans are but part of God's overreaching purposes. See, for example, 39:2; Isa 10:5,6. **12. In the midst** (lit., *navel)* **of the earth.** Cf. 5:5. **13. Sheba and Dedan . . . merchants of Tarshish.** Cf. 27:22,20,12. **And all its villages** (RSV). So the LXX and the Syriac, reading *k^eparîm* instead of MT *k^epîrîm,* "young lions." The cry of the commercial nations may be ironical or perhaps in approval of anticipated gains for themselves.

d) Gog's Coming Determined by the Lord. 38:14-16.

14. When . . . Israel dwelleth safely.

Cf. verses 8,11,12. **16. My people . . . my land.** An attack against the Lord's land is an attack against him.

e) Gog's Destruction. 38:17-23.

17. The prophets . . . which prophesied. This invasion was foretold, either in the preceding prophecy of Ezekiel, or in prophecies no longer extant (cf. 39:8; Zeph 1:14ff.; Jer 3-6; Joel 3; Zech 14). **19-22.** Gog's destruction is accomplished by an earthquake (v. 19) that terrifies all nature (v. 20), by a supernatural panic among his soldiers (v. 21), by pestilence and bloodshed and visitations of nature (v. 22). **23.** Cf. 36:23.

2) Resumption of Prophecy Against Gog. 39:1-29.

This is not a second invasion but a parallel account. Ezekiel often repeats his teaching. Cf. chapters 1 and 10; 2:3-7 and 8:4-11; 3:17-21 and 33:1-19; chapters 16 and 23.

a) Destruction and Burial of Gog's Hordes. 39:1-16.

1. Prophesy against Gog. Cf. 38:2,3. **2. I will . . . drive you forward** (RSV). Cf. 38:4. **4.** Gog falls on the **mountains.** Cf. verse 17; 38:21. **6. The coastlands** (*isles,* AV) also feel the **fire** that smites **Magog.**

7. So will I make . . . known. This expresses the purpose of God through the invasion (cf. 38:16,17,23): the recognition of his holiness by Israel and by the nations. See also verses 13,21,25-28.

9. The **weapons** of the enemy will serve as fuel for Israel for **seven years. 11.** The corpses of Gog will be buried in **the valley of the Travelers** (*hāʿôb^e^rîm*), **east of the sea** (RSV). This place has been equated with Wady Fejjas, one and one-half miles from the south end of Lake Kinnereth (Sea of Galilee), or the Valley of Abarim (*hāʿăbārîm*) in Moab, east of the Dead Sea (Deut 32:48), called **The valley of Hamon-gog** (*multitude of Gog*). **12,13.** All the lay people (note 44:25) will be occupied **seven months** in the burial. The number seven (vv. 9,14) signifies the completeness of the cleansing of the land from its enemies. **14-16. They will set apart men to pass through the land continually** (RSV; lit., *men of continuity*), who will **set up a sign** (*ṣîyûn,* "sign-post, monument") by any unburied bone to help the **buriers to cleanse the land. A city Hamonah** (fem. form, "multitude") **is there** (RSV). So Targum *shām,* "there," in place of *shem,* "name." It is a city of graves (cf. Jos *Life* 54).

b) Birds and Beasts Invited To Feast on Gog's Hordes. 39:17-24.

17-20. *Scavenging by birds and beasts* (cf. Isa 63:1-6; Rev 19:17-21).

17,18. The slaughtering of animals was originally a sacrificial act (cf. Lev 17; Isa 34:6; Zeph 1:8). Here **birds** and **beasts** are invited to a **great sacrificial feast** upon **the flesh of the mighty, and . . . the blood of the princes** (RSV), who are compared to the **fatlings of Bashan** (cf. 27:6), a pastoral region famed for its cattle (Deut 32:14; Amos 4:1). **19.** Ordinarily **fat** and **blood,** the holiest part of the sacrifice, were offered to the Lord (Lev 3:11ff.,17). Here they are eaten by beasts. **20. Horses and riders** (LXX, *rōkēb,* "rider," for MT *rekeb,* "chariot"; but cf. II Sam 8:4, "chariot horses") are the fare for the scavengers summoned to the Lord's table. These horrendous details give force to Ezekiel's prophetic parable.

21-24. *Lessons from the great destruction.*

21. I will set my glory among the heathen. God's great power will be revealed to the nations by the destruction of Gog (38:16,23). **22.** Israel will never doubt his protection **from that day . . . forward. 23,24.** The nations will learn that the people of **Israel went into captivity** and **fell . . . by the sword** not because of the Lord's inability to protect them (36:20), but because of their **iniquity** and treachery, which had caused him to hide his **face from them.** What a lesson to our day of powerful weapons!

c) Conclusion: Restoration of the Fortunes of Jacob. 39:25-29.

In this paragraph, which is not a part of the Apocalypse, the prophet returns to the point of view of chapters 33–37, predicting Israel's restoration.

25. Jealous for my holy name. Cf. 20:9,14,22,44. **26. They shall forget** (*w^e^nāshû,* so *k^e^tîb*) **their shame** (RSV), i.e., reproach (cf. Isa 54:4). *Q^e^rê,* several MSS, and the versions read, *they shall bear* (*w^e^nāśeʾû*) *their shame,* i.e., an inward feeling of unworthiness at the goodness of God (cf. 16:52,54).

27,28. When I have brought them again. Through the history of his people, God reveals himself both to the nations and to Israel. **29. I have poured out my spirit.** Cf. 36:25-31; Joel 2:28; Zech 12:10.

IV. A Vision of the Restored Community. 40:1–48:35.

Ezekiel first treated of the sins which

led to Judah's fall (chs. 1—24), and announced the humbling of her hostile neighbors (chs. 25—32). He then pictured the Lord's glorious restoration of his people to their land (chs. 33—39), their regeneration (36:22-32), and the Lord's dwelling in their midst forever (37:26-28). As a practical seer, under divine direction, the prophet's next concern was to give attention to the organization of the religious life in the restored community (chs. 40—48).

These closing chapters present vast difficulties. The rabbis of the Talmud (*Menaḥot* 45a) remarked that only the prophet Elijah, who will herald the ultimate redemption, will elucidate the discrepancies with the Pentateuchal laws and the terms which do not occur elsewhere. Moreover, said they, had it not been for Rabbi Chanina ben Hezekiah (*Babylonian Talmud, Ḥagiga* 13a), who explained away several of these difficulties, the book of Ezekiel would have been excluded from the Canon of Scripture.

Textual corruptions and the bewildering architectural and ritual details baffle the reader. But the most persistent problem is that of the interpretation of these chapters, on which godly scholars have differed through the years. Were the manifold details of this vision (Ezk 40:2) meant to be actualized at some future date? What part will the bloody sacrifices play in any future economy (40:38-43; 43:18-27; 45:13-17; 46:13-15)? Will the Zadokite priesthood, without a high priest, function again (40:45, 46; 42:13,14; 43:18-27; 44:15-31; 45:18-20; 46:19-24)? Who is the prince and who are his sons (44:3; 45:7-12,13-17, 21-24; 46:1-8,12,16-18)? Who are the downgraded Levites (44:10-14), the uncircumcised foreigners excluded from the sanctuary (44:5,9), and the resident aliens who receive property (47:22,23)? How are the geographical problems relating (1) to the stream issuing from the Temple (47:1-12) and (2) to the apportionment of the land among the twelve tribes (47:13—48:29) to be explained?

The emphasis on ceremonials, forms, and institutions has led to the charge that Ezekiel transformed the ideals of the prophets into laws and dogmas and so became "the father of Judaism." Ezekiel, it is true, believed that the new age required expression of its religious concepts in external concrete form. The post-Exilic Jewish community still needed the Temple, priests, and sacrifices. It is doubtful whether it would have survived without them. Like the eighth century prophets, Ezekiel was interested in righteous living (e.g., chs. 3; 18; 33). The regulations of chapters 40—48 are intended for a regenerated people (cf. chs. 33—37).

The interpretations of the temple vision basically appear under two categories — the literal and the figurative. Herewith is a summary of the principal views regarding the account of the temple in Ezekiel's "political Utopia" or "nomocracy" (government by statute; so Joseph Salvador, quoted in J. Klausner, *The Messianic Idea in Israel*, p. 131) in chapters 40—48.

1) Some hold that it is a description of Solomon's Temple, preserved in order that the returning exiles might rebuild their sanctuary. Actually, the specifications for Ezekiel's Temple are different from and larger than those of Solomon's Temple.

(2) Others say it represents a lofty ideal, a general pattern to guide the returning exiles in their building. The whole section is viewed as a constitution for the post-Exilic theocracy. But nowhere in the post-Exilic books of the OT is there a reference to Ezekiel's Temple, nor is there any hint of it in the work of Zerubbabel and Joshua, Haggai and Zechariah (Ezr 3:8-13; 5:1,2,13-17; cf. 1:2-4; 6:14; Hag 1:2,7-15; 2:1-9; Zech 6:9-15), or Ezra (Ezr 7:10,15,16, 20,27) and Nehemiah (8—9) that this was the kind of temple they were required to build.

(3) Some Jewish commentators have held that King Messiah, at his coming, will complete the Temple and institute the details of the ritual.

(4) There are likewise Christians who hold that a literal Temple, sacrifices, and priesthood will obtain during the Millennium, according to the specifications laid down by Ezekiel.

Among serious objections to this viewpoint, the following may be noted:

(a) The atonement of our Lord Jesus Christ nullified OT sacrifices forever (Heb 9:10-15; 10:1-4,18).

(b) The old system was of a provisional nature, to which believers in Christ are not to revert (Gal 3:23-25; 4:3-9; 5:1; Col 2:16,17; Heb 10:11-14).

(c) All believers, whether Jew or Gentile, are Abraham's seed (Gal 3:7,16, 29), and members of the "Israel of God" (Gal 6:16), a relationship based on faith not on ancestry (Rom 4:11,14,16; 8:17; 9:6-8). Christ has broken down "the middle wall of partition" (Eph 2:11-22), so that the distinctions Jew-Greek, circumcision-uncircumcision, bond-free, male-female convey no superior merit (Gal 3:28; Col 3:11; Eph 3:6; Rom 2:28, 29).

(d) The NT refers to the Church as the New Israel, in which adherents of old Israel may participate by accepting Christ (I Pet 2:3-5,8-10). Promises to old Israel broaden out to include the world-wide Church (Acts 2:39; 10:43ff.; 13:26; 15:14-18; Rom 15:9-12).

(e) Not a specific tribe or family, but all believers are priests and have direct access to God through the blood of Christ (see Heb 8:8-13, as fulfilling Jer 31:3-34; Lk 22:20; Heb 9:26; 10:4-10). It is spiritual worship not ritual that God acknowledges (Jn 4:21-24; Acts 7:48-50).

(f) When John employs these chapters to describe the Church of Christ, he removes the specifically Jewish elements (Rev 21:9—22:5).

To insist upon a literal explanation of the vision does not seem to be necessary. Rejecting a literal interpretation does not preclude the holding of a doctrine of the Millennium.

(5) Still others hold that Ezekiel's Temple is a figure representing the redeemed of all ages worshiping God in heaven. However, many of the earthly details of the vision, e.g., the sin offering, negate the suggestion that this is a portrayal of perfect worship in heaven.

(6) The symbolico-typical, or, more accurately, the allegorical view, was favored by the Church Fathers and the Reformers. They discovered in the prince, the priests, the offerings, the temple measurements, the stream that issued from the sanctuary, the tribal allotments, etc., elements depicting Christ and the spiritual perfections of the Church throughout the Gospel age. This view suffers from the vagaries of subjectivism and robs the passage of significance for Ezekiel's day.

(7) Some see in it merely a prophetic parable. These chapters, they say, set forth great spiritual truth in the language and thought patterns of Ezekiel the priest. They are characterized by the same minuteness of detail observed in his visions (ch. 1), allegories (chs. 16: 23), preaching (ch. 18), and predictions (chs. 26—28; 29—32), thus conveying the sense of divine certitude.

Ezekiel and other prophets conceived of the future ideal life as lived in the body, upon this earth (see on 18:4; cf. Isa 66:20; Jer 33:17,18). True religious perfection, they taught, is to be achieved only through the Lord's personal presence among his people (cf. 48:35b). Thus, to Ezekiel's contemporaries in the Babylonian exile, and to the following generations, the description of the new Temple, worship, and land brought comfort and edification.

The Christian Church, all through her history, draws from these chapters, not minute allegorical or typological details of her life, but the broad general principle of God's presence with his people and the fructifying power of his Holy Spirit. They point the Church, especially in their adaptation in Rev 21; 22, to the consummation awaiting God's people at the *parousia* (second coming) of his Son, who has prepared abiding places for his own in the Father's house. They remind the Church of her pilgrim character in this world, that she looks for "new heavens and a new earth wherein dwelleth righteousness" (II Pet 3:13).

Ezekiel's vision of the restored community embraces a new Temple, to which the glory of the Lord returns (chs. 40—43), a new service of worship, with an ideal ministry and sacrificial system (chs. 44—46), and a new holy land redivided among the tribes on new principles (chs. 47; 48).

A. A New Temple. 40:1—43:27.

The temple area, as described by Ezekiel, consists of three terraces, on the highest of which, facing east, stands the Temple with its annexes, the temple yard, and a large building directly behind it. On a middle terrace are kitchens and chambers for the priests, the court containing the altar of burnt offering, and the inner courts with three elaborate porticos. The lowest terrace, surrounded by an exterior wall, contains the outer courts with three porticos and kitchens and chambers for the people.

1) The Plan of the New Sanctuary, with its Courts and Chambers. 40:1—42:20.

1-4. *Introduction.* The prophet is transported in vision to the temple mountain, where a heavenly guide conducts him on a tour of the Temple, beginning at the east gate of the outer court.

1. Twenty-fifth year . . . in the beginning of the year, in the tenth day of the month. March-April 572 (573) B.C. **2. In . . . visions.** Cf. 8:3; 11:22-25. A very

high mountain. The idealized Mount Zion (cf. Ps 48:2; Isa 2:2; Mic 4:1; Zech 14:10). In visions the natural and supernatural mingle freely. The Temple resembles **structure like** (AV, *frame of)* **a city** (RSV). **3. A man, whose appearance was like . . . brass.** A supernatural character (cf. Rev 21:10-27). **With a line of flax.** For long measurements. **And a measuring reed.** For shorter measurements.

a) Measurements of the Courts. 40:5-47.

5-27. *The outer court and its three gates.*

There is a **wall** surrounding the whole **temple area** (v. 5), **one reed** in thickness and one reed in height (v. 6), pierced by three elaborate **gateways** or porticos on the east (vv. 5-16), on the north (vv. 20-23), and on the south (vv. 24-27). Seven **steps** lead up to these gateways (v. 6; LXX, 22,26) which open on the terrace or platform on which the whole temple area is situated (v. 18).

5-16. *The eastern gate.* **5.** The Hebrew cubit was 17.58 inches or 44.65 centimeters. The long cubit was 20.679 inches, and Ezekiel's **reed** was about 10⅓ feet long.

6. The **gate** *(sha'ar)* of the temple is 50 cubits long (v. 15) and 25 cubits broad (v. 13). It contains an outer **threshold** 6 cubits deep and 10 cubits wide (vv. 6,11); a passageway 13 cubits wide (v. 11) with three **little chambers,** side-rooms or guard-rooms on either side, each 6 cubits square (v. 7), having splayed windows (v. 16), and protected on the side towards the passageway by a **barrier** (RSV) or low wall 1 cubit thick (v. 12); **jambs** or blocks of masonry 5 cubits square between the siderooms, with splayed openings and carvings of **palm trees** in relief (v. 16); an inner **threshold** 6 cubits deep (v. 7); a **vestibule** or *porch* 20 cubits by 8 cubits at the inner end of the gateway, with splayed windows (vv. 8,16); and **jambs,** or *posts* of 2 cubits' thickness (v. 9).

17-19. *The thirty chambers in the outer court.* Passing through the east gateway, Ezekiel and his guide enter **the outward court,** situated on the lower **pavement** or terrace (v. 17). Disposed **round about** the court are thirty **chambers** (for the use of the people and the Levites who worship in the outer court) **upon the pavement,** perhaps ten on the east, north, and south sides, five on each side of a gateway. The pavement is fifty cubits wide, **corresponding to the length of the** outer **gates** (vv. 18,15). The four corners contain the people's kitchens (46:21-24). **19.** From **the inner front** of the outer gate to the **outer** edge **of the inner court** is a **hundred cubits.**

20-27. *The north and south gates.* The details for the north and south gates correspond to those for the eastern gate, with the specific mention of **seven steps** up to the platform (vv. 22,26).

28-47. *The inner court and its three gates.* **The inner court** is located 100 cubits to the interior of the outer gates (v. 19) on a platform eight steps higher than the outer court (vv. 31,34,37). It is entered by means of gates on the south (vv. 28-31), east (vv. 32-34), and north (vv. 35-37) sides. In the vestibule of the east gateway there are arrangements for the manipulating of sacrifices (vv. 38-43). On the eastern sides of the inner north and south gateways are chambers for the priests responsible for the care of the temple buildings and the altar (vv. 44-46). Within the inner court is the altar **court** (v. 47), a square of 100 cubits, situated east of the Temple, in the center of which stands the altar of burnt offering (43:13-27). The priests' kitchens and chambers are situated at the western end of the inner court (42:1-14). The Temple itself is on a platform ten steps higher than the inner court (v. 49).

28-31. *South gate of the inner court.* **28.** From the south gate of the outer court (vv. 24-27), Ezekiel is conducted **to the inner court** through its **south gate.** The gates of the inner court correspond to those of the outer court in all respects except that their vestibules lie at the outer end of the gateway, near to the outer court (vv. 31,34,37). **31. Eight steps** lead from the lowest pavement to the terrace supporting the inner court.

32-37. *The east and north inner gates.* These gates are similar in description to the south gate.

38-43. *The vestibule of the inner east gate, and arrangements for sacrifice.* **38.** A **chamber** is constructed within **the vestibule of the** (RSV) east **gate** (cf. vv. 40, 44; 43:17b; 46:2ff.), where the ministering priests or Levites will wash the burnt offerings. **39.** Within the **vestibule** are four tables, **two . . . on either side** (RSV), on which are prepared the flesh of the **burnt offering** *('ōlâ;* Lev 1, "that which goes up," a beast or fowl wholly consumed on the altar to symbolize the offerer's self-surrender to God), **the sin-offering** *(ḥaṭṭa't;* Lev 4:1–5:13, in expiation of sin), and the **trespass-offering** *('āshām;* Lev 5:14–6:7, in which recompense or restitution is made). **40. On the outside,**

northwards of one going up the entrance of the gateway (Cooke, ICC) are four more tables, constituting **eight tables** (v. 41) for the sacrifices mentioned in verse 39. **42.** There are also **four tables,** or pedestals, of **hewn stone . . . on which** the slaughtering **instruments** [are] **to be laid** (RSV). **43. Hooks** or pegs are **fastened** in the outer wall of the vestibule on which to hang the slaughtered carcasses before flaying.

44-46. *Priests' chambers on the east sides of the north and south gates.* **44.** There are **two chambers in the inner court** (RSV), one (v. 45) on the east **side of the north gate toward the south for the priests** (Levites, 44:10-14) **who have charge of the temple** and the other on the east side of the south gate facing north **for the priests who have charge of the altar** (v. 46). The Zadokite priests.

47. *Measurements of the altar court.* Within the inner court is the altar **court,** a square of 100 cubits **in front** (i.e., on the east) **of the temple,** in which stands the altar of burnt offering.

b) Measurements of the Temple Itself and Its Surroundings. 40:48—41:26.

The eighth century temple at Tell Tainat in Syria and the recently excavated Canaanite temple in Hazor had a threefold division of vestibule, nave, and inner room, similar to the arrangement in the plans of Solomon's and Ezekiel's structures. Ezekiel's Temple stands on a third platform ten steps higher than the inner court (v. 49). It consists of three parts, the vestibule (vv. 48,49), nave (41:1,2), and the Most Holy Place (41:3, 4). An annex of side chambers adjoins three sides of the Temple (vv. 5-11), and behind it there is a large building (v. 12). The dimensions of the Temple (vv. 13-15a) and a brief description of its interior are given (15b-26).

48,49. *The vestibule or porch ('ûlām).* The *vestibule* (cf. I Kgs 6:3) is 20 cubits wide from north to south and 12 cubits deep from east to west. Its *entrance,* 14 cubits wide, has a *sidewall* of 3 cubits on either side. Beside the *jambs,* 5 cubits thick, stand two **pillars** (cf. I Kgs 7:15-22, where these are called Jachin and Boaz).

41:1,2. *The nave* or *Holy Place (hêkāl).* The *nave* is 40 cubits long from east to west and 20 cubits broad from north to south. Its *entrance* is 10 cubits wide, with *sidewalls* of 5 cubits breadth on either side and *jambs* 6 cubits thick (cf. I Kgs 6:5).

3,4. *The most holy place.* Or *inner room (qōdesh haqqodāshîm).* The angel alone goes *into the inner room,* or **most holy place,** *beyond the nave,* which is 20 x 20 cubits. Its entrance, sidewalls, and jambs measure 6, 7, and 2 cubits respectively (cf. I Kgs 6:16; 7:50; 8:6).

5-11. *The side-chambers of the annex.* **Round about** three walls of the Temple are side-chambers for storage purposes in 3 stories, 30 in each story (v. 6; cf. I Kgs 6:5-10). The **outer wall of the side-chambers** is 5 cubits thick (v. 9), and the lowest tier of chambers is 4 cubits wide (v. 5), each story becoming broader, **corresponding to the enlargement of the offset in the wall of the temple** (v. 7). Taking a cue from Solomon's Temple (I Kgs 6:6), the temple walls are probably 6 cubits thick at the first story, with a chamber 4 cubits wide (v. 5), 5 cubits thick at the second story, allowing a five-cubit chamber, and 4 cubits thick at the third story, giving a six-cubit chamber. Ladders, or possibly a circular stairway, connect the stories (v. 7; cf. I Kgs 6:6). Both the Temple and the side building stand on a raised platform 6 cubits high (v. 8), the height of the ten steps of 40:49, and 5 cubits broad (v. 9), which give access to the side chambers on the north and south (v. 11). This, in turn, is surrounded by a narrow courtyard or *separate place* 20 cubits wide (vv. 10,12).

12. *The building (binān) behind the Temple.* The purpose of the large building (90 x 40 cubits, with walls 5 cubits thick) behind or west of the Temple, facing the temple yard ("separate place," *gizrâ,* 41:12-15; 42:1,10,13), is not explained. It is called the *parwārîm* in II Kgs 23:11, where the kings kept horses sacred to the sun, and *parbār* in I Chr 26:18.

13-15a. *The measurement of the Temple.* The Temple from east to west is 100 cubits long (v. 13; jamb of the vestibule, 5 cubits; vestibule, 12; jamb of the nave, 6; nave, 40; jamb of the Most Holy, 2; Most Holy, 20; wall, 6; side chamber, 4; outer wall of side building, 5 = 100). The **breadth . . . of the temple** from north to south, including the yard, is **100 cubits** (v. 14; breadth of Temple, 20; side wall, 6 + 6; side chambers, 4 + 4 and their walls, 5 + 5; raised platform, 5 + 5; yard, 20 + 20 = 100). The yard and west building with its walls are 100 cubits long from east to west (vv. 12,13). The length of the western building from north to south, plus its walls is 100 cubits. There are thus three adjoining squares of 100 cubits: the altar court (40:47); the Temple and the yards on its north and south sides; and the western building with the yard in front of it.

15a-26. *Description of the interior of the Temple*. The three parts of the Temple — nave, inner room, and outer vestibule (15b) — are paneled or wainscotted with wood (or "of *šeḥîp* wood"; Ak. loanword for costly black wood; cf. G. R. Driver, "Notes on Hebrew Lexicography," JTS 23 (1922), 409), **from the ground up to the windows** (v. 16). The windows with recessed or narrowing frames (cf. 40:16) are **covered** or latticed (v. 16). The walls of the inner room and nave are carved with likenesses of two-faced **cherubims** alternating with **palm trees** (vv. 17,18). **The face of a man** and the **face of a young lion** look toward palm trees on either side (cf. 1:6; 10:14, 21; I Kgs 6:29ff.).

The doorposts of the nave [are] squared (RSV) or fourfold (v. 21). **In front of the holy place** (RSV; i.e., Holy of Holies), is an altar-like table of wood, 3 x 2 x 2 cubits, possibly for showbread (v. 22; cf. Ex 25:23ff.; Lev 24:5-9). **The nave and the holy place** (RSV; i.e., Holy of Holies) *each has a double door* (v. 23), *with two swinging leaves for each door* (RSV; v. 24), on which are carved **cherubims and palm trees** (v. 25). An ornamental canopy or cornice of wood is on the outside front of the vestibule.

c) Other Buildings in the Inner Court. 42:1-20.

1-14. *The chambers of the priests*. The buildings containing the priests' chambers are located, it seems, at the west end of the inner court, between the north and south temple yards (vv. 1,10; cf. 41:10,12) and the inner edge of the outer court (v. 3). The chambers on the north are described at length (vv. 1-10a), and those on the south correspond to them (vv. 10b-12). The details are obscure and the text is corrupt. Apparently there are two structures, one running parallel to the temple yard, 100 x 20 cubits in size (v. 2), with a passageway beside it 10 cubits wide (v. 4), on the other side of which, overlooking the outer court, is the second structure, 50 x 20 cubits in size (v. 8). The two structures plus the passageway total a width of 50 cubits (v. 2). The chambers within these structures may be arranged in three stories (v. 6) or in three rows on terraces descending to the outer court. Somewhere below the eastern end of the shorter series of chambers is an entrance, giving access up a flight of ten steps (40:49) from the outer court to the priests' chambers (v. 9).

13,14. *Use of these chambers by the priests*. The chambers will be used by the priests for eating the holy offerings, for depositing them till they are baked in the kitchens (cf. 44:29; 46:20), and for storing the priestly garments when the priests are not on duty (cf. 44:19; 46:20). The section on the cooking places of the priests (46:19-24) could well belong here.

15-20. *The over-all measurements of the temple area*. The entire temple area is a square 500 cubits on each side (v. 20; 45:2), not a 500-reed square, which would be 3000 cubits (cf. Rev 21:13). The purpose of the surrounding wall is to **make a separation between the holy and the common** (RSV; v. 20).

2) Return of the Lord to the House Prepared for Him. 43:1-12.

Some eighteen and one-half years earlier, Ezekiel had seen a vision of the departure of the glory of the Lord from the Temple (10:19; 11:22,23). Now that all things are ready, he sees the glory return (vv. 1-5). The enthroned Lord pronounces that the Temple is his throne and instructs the prophet to teach the people the temple regulations (vv. 6-12).

a) The Return of the Lord. 43:1-5.

1. At the gate that looketh . . . east the prophet sees the visible manifestation of the Lord's presence as he had seen it when he **came to destroy the city** (v. 3; cf. chs. 8—11), and in his inaugural vision **by the river Chebar** (1:28; 3:12,23). **4. The glory of the Lord** entered the east gate, and **the spirit took him up** (v. 5; cf. 2:2; 3:12,14; 8:3) **into the inner court.** The prophet cannot go in through the east gate once the Lord has entered it (cf. 44:2). On the glory of the Lord filling the Tabernacle and the Temple, see Ex 40:34,35; I Kgs 8:11.

b) God's Exhortation to Israel from the Inner Sanctuary. 43:6-12.

The Lord (not the man by his side, v. 6) speaks to Israel through Ezekiel concerning the holiness of the Temple (vv. 7-9). His exhortation forms a conclusion to chapters 40—42; and the temple regulations (vv. 10-12) form an introduction to chapter 44 and the following chapters.

7. The Jerusalem Temple is here represented as the **throne** of God (see also Jer 3:17; 14:21; 17:12. For heaven as God's throne, see Isa 66:1; Ps 2:4; 11:4; Mt

5:34; 23:22). Ezekiel pictures heaven come down to earth (cf. 37:26-28). **Whoredom.** Temple prostitution (II Kgs 23:7); or idolatry (ch. 8). **Carcases of their kings.** The royal sepulchres were on the same hill as the Temple, separated from it only by a wall (II Kgs 21:18, 26). **8.** Formerly the Temple and the palace were contiguous (I Kgs 7:8; II Kgs 20:4, corrected). **Thresholds** and **doorposts** may refer to kings' tombs fashioned like houses (Isa 14:18; Job 17:13).

Verses 10-27 form the synagogue *haphtarah* for Ex 27:20—30:10.

10. Cf. 40:4; 44:5. **12. The law of the** Temple is laid down in chapters 40—42. The whole temple area **upon the top of the mountain** is declared **most holy** (41:4; 45:3; 48:12).

3) The Altar of Burnt Offering and Its Consecration. 43:13-27.

a) Description of the Altar. 43:13-17. Compare the various altars: in the Tabernacle (Ex 27:1-8), in Solomon's Temple (II Chr 4:1); in Zerubbabel's Temple (Ezr 3:2,3; I Macc 4:47); in Herod's Temple (Mishna *Middoth IV*, 1a, 3b, 4. Jos *Wars* V. 5,6; *Letter of Aristeas*, 87).

13. The altar of burnt offering (cf. 40:47), made of unspecified material, possibly stone, consists of four square ledges, diminishing in size, placed one on top of the other. The base is 18 x 18 cubits and one cubit high, with a border at the outer edge one-half cubit high, probably as a gutter to carry off the sacrificial blood. **14.** Upon this rests the lower ledge, 2 cubits high and 16 x 16 cubits square. Next comes the upper or larger ledge, 4 cubits high and 14 x 14 cubits square. **15,16.** On top is the altar hearth, or altar proper, 4 cubits high and 12 x 12 square, with horns one cubit high, projecting from its four corners. The name *hārʾēl* (v. 15), or *ʾărîʾēl*, has affinity with the Akkadian *arallû*, "underworld," or with the "mountain of the gods" (Albright, *Arch. and the Relig. of Israel*, pp. 150-152), and its design is reminiscent of the Babylonian ziggurat (Nielson, *Journal of the Palestine Oriental Society*, 13 (1933), 203 ff.). Its total height, including the horns, is 12 cubits. Steps on its east side enable the officiating priest to face the Temple rather than the sun (cf. 8:16; Ex 20:26).

b) Consecration of the Altar. 43:18-27. The altar is consecrated by the applying of the blood of the sin offering for seven days on its four horns, on the four corners of the upper ledge, and on the rim of the base, to **cleanse** (*ḥiṭṭēʾ*, to remove sin, to "unsin," by applying sacrificial blood to the object), and to **purge** (*kippēr*, "to purge," "to expiate by a ritual act") it (v. 20; cf. Ex 29:12; Lev 8:15). Because objects used in the worship contact defilement from sinful man, blood, as the seat of life, is applied to them to remove uncleanness and to impart holiness (cf. Lev 16:15-20). The sin offering the first day is a bullock (v. 19), and on the succeeding days of the week a he-goat (vv. 22,25). Following the daily sin offering, a bullock and a ram sprinkled with salt are offered as a burnt offering (23,24). Salt, originally added to the cereal offerings (Lev 2:13) and to incense (Ex 30:35), was later placed on burnt offerings (Mk 9:49 marg.; Jos *Antiq*. III. 9. 1). **26. And so consecrate it** (RSV). Literally, *fill its hand*, i.e., confer a dignity, invest with office (cf. Ex 28:41; Lev 16:32; I Chr 29:5). **27. From the eighth day . . . forward** the regular burnt offerings and peace offerings (*shelem*, Lev 3, signifying peace and communion with God; they also include the thank, votive, and voluntary offerings, Lev 7:12, 16a, 16b) can be offered on it.

B. A New Service of Worship. 44:1—46:24.

The following ordinances deal with: (1) who may minister in the Temple (ch. 44); (2) the revenues of the priests, the Levites, and the prince, and the prince's obligations to the Temple (45:1-17); and (3) the festal and daily offerings in the Temple, and the special offerings of the prince (45:18—46:24).

1) Those Who May Minister in the Temple. 44:1-31.

a) The Outer, East Gate Closed. 44:1-3.

Ezekiel, taken by the angel to the outer east gate (v. 1), is informed that the gate will remain shut after the Lord's entrance through it, lest the entrance of a mortal desecrate it (v. 2). The "Golden Gate" in the east wall of Old Jerusalem today is walled up. The walls were built by the Ottoman sultan, Suleiman the Magnificent, in 1542. He closed the gate to prevent festivals commemorating "the recovery of the Holy Cross." The **prince** cannot enter through the gate but is permitted to eat the sacrificial meal in its vestibule (v. 3; cf. Jer 30:21).

b) Restrictions on Service in the Temple. 44:4-14.

4. Glory of the Lord. Cf. 43:3. **5.** Cf. 40:4.

7. Ye have brought into my sanctuary strangers. Foreign slaves or war captives had hitherto assisted in the offering of sacrifice and in performing subordinate tasks (Deut 29:11; Josh 9:23,27; I Sam 2:13; Zech 14:21; Ezr 8:20; 2:43-54). **9. Foreigners** are now excluded as spiritually and physically unfitted (cf. Num 3:10; 16:40; Hag 2:14; Ezr 4:3; Neh 13:7-9,30). The Herodian Temple bore tablets in the outer court warning non-Jews against trespassing on pain of death (Jos *Wars* V. 5. 2; *J. E. XII.* 85). **10. Levites** (cf. 48:11, or Israel, v. 15; 14:11) who in going astray misled the people (v. 12; Jud 17:7-13; 18:18,19; 30; Deut 33:8-11) will be degraded in rank. They will be watchmen at the gateways (cf. 40:7), will assist the people in the outer court, and will slay their offerings and cook their sacrifices (v. 11; cf. 46:24; Num 3:5–4:33).

c) Regulations for the Zadokite Priests. 44:15-31.

15. The Levitical priests, the sons of Zadok (RSV), were descendants of Zadok, a contemporary of David and Solomon (II Sam 8:17; 15:24-29; 20:25; I Kgs 2:27,35) and of Aaron through Eleazar (I Chr 6:50-53). **16.** The faithful priests will minister to God. **Come near to my table.** Cf. Mal 1:7,12. **Keep my charge.** Cf. 40:45,46.

Verses **17-19** describe their garments (cf. Lev 13:47,48; Jer 13:1; Herodotus ii. 37). They are to remove their linen garments before going out, **lest they communicate holiness to the people** (RSV), a ritual sanctity which temporarily disqualified persons for the ordinary duties of life (cf. Lev 6:18,27; Ex 29:37; 30:29; Hag 2:10-12).

20,21. On cutting the hair, see Lev 21:5; 10:6; 21:10. On drinking wine while on duty, see Lev 10:9; Hos 4:11; Prov 20:1 (cf. Jos *Antiq.* III. 12. 2). **22. Neither shall they take for their wives.** Cf. Lev 21:7,13,14. **23,24. And they shall teach my people.** These verses set forth the priests' duties towards the people: ceremonial instruction (cf. 22:26; Lev 10:10; Hag 2:11; Mal 2:7); directions for the administration of justice (Deut 17:8-13; 33:10; I Sam 4:18; 7:15; Hos 4:6); **judgments, laws, statutes** (cf. 5:6; Lev 26:46); directions for keeping the **sabbaths** (cf. 20:12).

25-27. They shall come at no dead person. Regulations are given for the priests' necessary contact with the dead. Mourning was forbidden to them except for the closest blood relations (cf. Lev 21:1-3,11; Num 19:14ff.). **26. After he is cleansed.** Cf. Num 19:14-19. **27. He shall offer.** Cf. Lev 4:3.

In verses **28-31** the maintenance of the priests is provided for. They are to subsist on the offerings, things dedicated to the Lord (Num 18:14ff.; Lev 27:28,29), first fruits (Num 8:13; Deut 18:4), the contributions (*t^{e}rûmâ;* cf. 20:40), perhaps the tithe (Num 15:19; 18:19). **30b. Blessing.** Cf. Mal 3:10. **31. Dead of itself.** Cf. 4:14; Lev 22:8.

2) Portions of Land for the Priests, the Levites, and the Prince. 45:1-17.

a) Sacred Territory of the Temple and Its Surroundings. 45:1-8.

The Temple of Ezekiel, in addition to being on a high hill (40:2) and having walled courts (chs. 40–42), and in addition to being protected by the precautionary measures of 44:4ff., is further guarded against desecration by its location in the midst of sacred territory surrounded by the priests' quarters (48:8-22). **A . . . portion** (*t^{e}rûmâ,* "part lifted off or separated from the whole") of land is made over to sacred purposes (v. 1). The area consists of three parallel strips, running east to west, forming a square 25,000 x 25,000 cubits in size. The center strip, 25,000 x 10,000 cubits, is set apart for the priests and their houses (vv. 3,4). In its midst is a square plot, 500 x 500 cubits for the sanctuary, surrounded by an open space of 50 cubits on all sides (vv. 1,2). North of this is the area for the Levites and their cities, 25,000 x 10,000 cubits (v. 5, LXX; Num 35:2; Josh 14:4). To the south is a section 25,000 x 5,000 cubits, in the center of which is a 5,000-cubit square for the holy city, with farm lands on both sides of it (cf. 48:15-20), the property of all the tribes (v. 6). On both sides of this **holy portion** is the portion of land assigned to the prince, 25,000 cubits wide, extending **from the west border unto the east border** of the land (vv. 7,8). In contrast to the past evil shepherds, the **princes shall no more oppress** the **people** (cf. 22:25; 34:1ff.).

b) Duties of the Princes. 45:9-12.

The **princes** of the future kingdom are **to remove violence** (Amos 3:6; Jer 6:7), **execute . . . justice** (Jer 22:3,15; 23:5), and **cease . . . evictions** (v. 9, RSV; cf. 46:18;

I Sam 8:14; Isa 5:8; I Kgs 21:9). There is to be no revival of the kingship with the power and pomp of old. The prince's main function is to provide the offerings. Through him the unity of the nation will find expression in its worship (45:16,17, 21-25; 46:1-12). He has neither priestly nor autocratic powers. The Lord is the true owner of the land. The prince is to establish a system of correct measures (vv. 10,11) and weights (v. 12; cf. G. A. Barrois, "Chronology, Metrology, etc., of the Bible," IB, 1, 142-164).

c) The Offerings of the People to the Prince and the Prince's Offerings to the Temple. 45:13-17.

The people are to give a specified offering from their grain (v. 13), oil (v. 14), and sheep (v. 15) to the prince (v. 16), who in turn will furnish the various offerings for the **feasts, new moons, sabbaths,** and **all the appointed feasts** (ASV), in order that expiation may be made for Israel (v. 17).

Chapter 45:16–46:18 is the *haphtarah* to Ex 12:1-20.

3) Offerings at the Various Sacred Seasons. 45:18–46:24.

a) Offerings at the Feasts. 45:18-25.

18-20. *Semi-annual cleansing of the Temple.* The sanctuary is to be cleansed semi-annually by the blood of the sin offering on the first day of the first month, March/April (vv. 18,19), and by similar rites "in the seventh month" (Sept./Oct.) on the first day of the month" (v. 21, LXX) **atonement** is to be made **for the temple** (RSV).

21-25. *Offerings at the Feast of Passover and the Feast of Tabernacles.* At the **passover** in the spring (cf. Ex 12:6; Deut 16:1) and the seven days of **unleavened bread** (cf. Ex 13:6,7; Deut 16:8), the **prince** is to provide **for himself** and for **the people** the requisite sin offering, burnt offering, and cereal offering (vv. 21-24). In **the seventh month,** he is to provide similar offerings for **the feast** of booths or *sukkoth,* the great harvest festival (cf. Ex 23:16; 34:22; Deut 16:13ff.).

b) Offerings on Sabbaths and New Moons. 46:1-12.

1-5. *Sabbaths.* The east gate of the inner court, shut during the six working days, is to be open on the Sabbath (v. 1). The prince will enter thereby and worship at its threshold, from whence he can see the sacrifices at the altar (v. 2). At the outside entrance of the gate, the people will worship, looking through it (v. 3). The prince will provide burnt offerings, cereal offerings, and optional offerings (vv. 4,5; cf. Num 28:11-15).

6-8. *New Moon.* Similar offerings are to be provided by the prince for the new moons. **8.** He will go in by the vestibule, **and he shall go forth by the same way.** That is, without setting foot in the inner court. **9,10. When the people of the land shall come.** To avoid confusion, the people coming to the feasts will enter by one gate and go out by the other. The prince will worship with them as one of the ordinary people.

11. At the feasts and the appointed seasons (RSV), the cereal offering is to accompany the burnt offering, as on the Sabbaths. **12.** The free will or **voluntary** offerings are to be prepared by the community. On the continual burnt offering *(tāmîd),* see Ex 29:42; Num 28,29; Deut 8:11-13.

c) The Prince and His Landed Property. 46:16-18.

These verses supplement 45:8,9. **If the prince give**[s] any landed property to his sons, it is to remain theirs (v. 16). If he gives land to his servants, **it shall return to the prince in the year of liberty** (v. 17), probably the Year of Jubilee, every fiftieth year (cf. Lev 25:10; Jer 34:14; Isa 61:1). The prince is not to evict people from their property (v. 18; cf. 45:8,9).

d) Cooking Places for the Sacrificial Meals. 46:19-24.

The kitchens for the priests (vv. 19, 20) are at the west end of the priests' chambers, described in 42:1-14. **Not . . . to sanctify the people.** See 44:19. **21-24.** The kitchens for cooking the sacrificial meals of the people are situated in the four corners of the outer court. In each of these are smaller courts or enclosures, 40 x 30 cubits in size, to house the kitchens, where the Levites (44:10-14) serve the people.

The circuit of the temple buildings is now completed, and a new topic is introduced.

C. A New Holy Land. 47:1–48:35.

After a description of the stream which gives life to the land (47:1-12), the boundaries of the land (47:13-23), and the disposition of the tribes in it are indicated (48:1-35).

1) The Life-giving Stream from the Temple. 47:1-12.

The prophet is brought from the outer court (46:21) to the vestibule of the Temple (40:48,49). There he sees **a stream issuing from below the threshold** of the Temple, eastward, passing south of the altar (v. 1), and south of the outer east gate (v. 2). At 1,000 cubits from the gate, the waters are ankle deep (v. 3), but within 4,000 cubits they have become a **river** *(naḥal)*, deep enough to swim in (vv. 4,5).

Along the banks of the river grow ever-vernal **trees** (v. 7), bearing **new fruit** every month, whose leaves possess **a healing** virtue (v. 12, ASV). The water **goes down into the Arabah,** the depression of the Jordan Valley reaching to the Gulf of Akabah, transforming it, making **the stagnant waters of the** (Dead) **Sea fresh** (RSV; v. 8), and teeming with life (v. 9), like the Mediterranean Sea (v. 10). **Fishers shall stand upon it** [beside the Dead Sea] **from En-gedi** *(spring of the kid,* on the middle of the western shore of the Dead Sea, an oasis of fertility because of its abundant waters; cf. Song 1:14) **to En-eglaim** (v. 10; "spring of two calves" [?]), possibly near modern Ain Feshka, about two miles south of the Khirbet Qumran area, where the Dead Sea Scrolls were found. **The miry places** by the seaside will be left unsweetened, i.e., will be salt marshes (v. 11). The transformation of the land will be due to God's presence (cf. 34:26-30; 36:8-15, 30-36; 37:26-28).

Note the influence of this vision on other writers: Joel 3:18; Zech 13:1; 14:8; Jn 4:14; 7:37,38; Rev 22:1,2; also, Sir 24:34,35; Enoch 26:2,3. To the Christian believer, it speaks of life, healing, peace, and prosperity, all made available through the Holy Spirit.

2) The Boundaries of the Land. 47:13-23.

Compare Num 34:1-12, where the north to south boundaries span about 280 miles. The new land is to be divided equally among all twelve tribes (vv. 13,14).

14-17. *The north boundaries:* **from the great** (Mediterranean) **sea by way of Hethlon** (Heitela, six miles north of Tripoli, or Adlun, between Zarephath and Tyre) **to [the entrance of** (LXX)] **Hamath** on the Orontes (115 miles north of Damascus, Amos 6:2), **to Zedad** (Sadad, southeast of Homs), **Berothah** (belonging to Zobah, II Sam 8:8; or Beraitan near Baalbek), **Sibraim** (Ziphron, between Hamath and Homs, Num 34:9), to **Hazer-hatticon** *(central Hazer* = Hazer-enan?) **on the border of Hauran** (east of the Jordan, south of Damascus).

18. *The eastern boundary.* Cf. Num 34:10-12. RSV: **From Hazer-enan, along the Jordan, to the eastern** (Dead) **Sea, as far as Tamar** (perhaps Kurnub, twenty-five miles southwest of the end of the Dead Sea; cf. I Kgs 9:17).

19. *The southern boundary.* RSV: **From Tamar** to the **waters of Meribath-kadesh** (Kadesh-barnea; Num 27:14; Josh 10:41; etc., usually identified with 'Ain Qadeis, about fifty miles south of Beersheba), **along the brook of Egypt** (Num 34:5; the Wadi el-'arish) **to the great sea** (RSV).

20. *The western boundary:* The Mediterranean Sea to a point opposite the entrance of **Hamath** (probably at the northern end of the plain, *el Biqâ,* between Lebanon and Anti-Lebanon).

The country east of the Jordan is excluded.

21-23. According to the tribes. Resident aliens residing among the tribes are to receive an **inheritance . . . among the tribes** in which they dwell.

3) The Disposition of the Tribes in the Land. 48:1-35.

a) Seven Tribes North of the Sacred Portion. 48:1-7.

Seven tribes—Dan, Asher, Naphtali, Manasseh, Ephraim, Reuben, and Judah—are to have strips of land running from east to west from the northern boundary of the land to the Sacred Portion. The physical and topographical difficulties are overlooked.

b) The Sacred Portion. 48:8-22.

For a parallel description, see 45:1-8a. A strip of land 25,000 cubits wide and reaching from the eastern to the western boundaries of the land is set apart for sacred use. In the center of it is the holy district (vv. 8,9,20; cf. 45:1,2).

10-12. *The priests' portion.* Cf. 45:3,4.

13,14. *The Levites' portion.* Cf. 45:5.

15-20. *The portion of the city.* Cf. 45:6. In the middle of the third strip of the sacred portion, 25,000 x 5,000 cubits in size, is **the city** (v. 15), a square of 4,500 cubits on each side (v. 16), surrounded by a 250-cubit wide strip of **open land** (AV, *suburbs;* v. 17). The 10,000 cubits of land on either side of the city are for agricultural puposes, the produce of which is to go to industrial and agricultural laborers (v. 18). Members of **all the tribes of Israel** are to work in it (v. 19).

21,22. *The prince's portion.* **And the residue shall be for the prince.** Cf. 45:7, 8a. His territory is bounded by Judah on the north and Benjamin on the south.

c) The Five Tribes South of the Sacred Portion. 48:23-29.

Benjamin, Simeon, Issachar, Zebulon, and Gad are allotted sections of land running from east to west, reaching from the temple area to the south boundary of the land.

This allotment does not follow the original settlements of the tribes. The entire nation is here united west of the Jordan. Since the Temple must remain in Jerusalem, seven tribes are located north and five tribes south of it. The Leah and Rachel tribes are located closest to the Temple, while the Bilhah and Zilpah tribes are farthest away.

d) The New City of Jerusalem. 48:30-35.

30-34. The goings out of the city; i.e., the gates of the city. Each side of the city is 4,500 cubits in length, with three gates to a side, each named after a tribe of Israel. On the north are the gates of Reuben, Judah, and Levi (v. 31); on the east, the gates of Joseph, Benjamin, Dan (v. 32); on the south, the gates of Simeon, Issachar, and Zebulon (v. 33); and on the west, the gates of Gad, Asher, and Naphtali (v. 34). Note that Levi is reckoned as a tribe, and Joseph represents Ephraim and Manasseh. Cf. Rev 21:12-21; 7:5-8. **35a. It was round about eighteen thousand measures.** The circumference of the city is 18,000 cubits. In Josephus' day, the circumference of the city of Jerusalem was thirty-three stadia, about four miles (*Wars* V. 4. 3).

35b. The name of the city, from the day that it exists again, **shall be, The Lord is there** *(Yahweh shāmmâ).* Cf. Rev 21:3.

BIBLIOGRAPHY

Cook, G. A. *Ezekiel (International Critical Commentary).* New York: Charles Scribner's Sons, 1937.

Currey, G. *Ezekiel (Speaker's Commentary).* London: John Murray, 1876.

Davidson, A. B. *Ezekiel (Cambridge Bible).* Cambridge: Cambridge University Press, 1892.

Ellison, H. L. *Ezekiel: The Man and His Message.* Grand Rapids: Wm. B. Eerdmans Publishing Co., 1956.

Fairbairn, Patrick. *Ezekiel.* Edinburgh: T. & T. Clark, 1863.

Fausett, A. R. "Ezekiel," *Commentary Critical, Experimental, and Practical of the Old and New Testaments.* Edited by Robert Jamieson, A. R. Fausset, and David Brown. Grand Rapids: Wm. B. Eerdmans Publishing Co., reprinted 1945.

Gardiner, F. *Ezekiel (Ellicott's Old Testament Commentary).* London: Cassell, 1884.

Keil, Carl F. *Biblical Commentary on Ezekiel.* 2 vols. Edinburgh: T. & T. Clark, 1882.

Lofthouse, W. F. *Ezekiel (Century Bible).* New York: Frowde, 1909.

Matthews, I. G. *Ezekiel (American Commentary on the Old Testament).* Philadelphia: Judson Press, 1939.

May, H. G. "Ezekiel," *The Interpreter's Bible.* Vol. 6. New York: Abingdon Press, 1956.

Plumptre, E. H. *Ezekiel (Pulpit Commentary).* 2 vols. New York: Funk and Wagnalls Co., 1913.

Redpath, H. A. *Ezekiel (Westminster Commentary).* London: Methuen, 1907.

Schroeder, J. W. J., and Fairbairn, Patrick. *Ezekiel (Lange's Commentary).* New York: Charles Scribner's Sons, 1873.

Skinner, J. *Ezekiel (Expositor's Bible).* New York: Armstrong, 1896.

DANIEL

INTRODUCTION

Name of the Book. In our English Bibles the title of this portion of Scripture is "The Book of Daniel." In the Hebrew Bible the title is simply, "Daniel," which, in accordance with the custom followed in the Major and Minor Prophets, is the name of the author of the book. As in several other books of prophecy (e.g., Jeremiah and Hosea), the author is also the chief actor in the events recorded. These Old Testament writings bear these names in the very earliest lists and references. Jesus referred to the prophecies of this book as "spoken of by Daniel the prophet" (Mt 24:15; Mk 13:14). Our Lord's testimony is not simply that the book was named after Daniel, but that its prophecies were spoken by him.

The name *Daniel* has been identified in literature of several other ancient languages – Akkadian, Sabaean, Palmyrene, Nabataean (J. A. Montgomery, *A Critical and Exegetical Commentary on the Book of Daniel,* ICC., p. 128), and in the Canaanite literature of Ras Shamra, where a hero named Daniel appears (*Tale of Aqhat,* ANET, 149-155).

Evangelical scholars usually identify the author of our book with the Daniel of Ezk 14:14,20; 28:3, where he is cited, along with Noah and Job, as an example of a righteous man. Those who deny the authenticity of Daniel claim that the Daniel of Ezekiel is "a figure of antique and cosmopolitan tradition, like the Noah-Utnapishtim of the flood story," etc. (Montgomery, ICC, p. 2). The Job and Noah of Ezekiel, however, are Biblical, not cosmopolitan, figures. We may therefore assume that the Daniel in Ezekiel is also the author of our book. (For the meaning of the name, see notes on Dan 1:6.)

Date and Authorship. Since the third century of the Christian Era the date and authorship of Daniel have been a battleground between those who accept the Bible's claims for itself and those who do not. So far as is now known, every Jew and Christian of early antiquity accepted the book as having been written in the Babylonian and Persian periods of the sixth century, in and near the city of Babylon, as the book claims. The New Testament, as well as several non-Biblical works, unquestioningly accepts the genuineness of the book. A Neo-Platonist philosopher, Porphyry (A.D. 233–304), in controversy with Christians, saw that the book accurately relates the story of events that took place between the fifth century and the early second century. Specifically, it tells of the advent of the Medo-Persian and Greek empires, and especially the details of the career of one Antiochus Epiphanes, king of Syria 175–163 B.C., in his conflict with the king of Egypt and with the Jews in Palestine. So Porphyry, denying that the book was written as claimed, asserted that it was written in Palestine by a Jew living in the time of Antiochus, and that what was written as prophecy was really history. He further claimed that the book is accurate as history down to Antiochus, but inaccurate after him. Eusebius of Caesarea, Apollinaris, Methodius, and most notably, Jerome, wrote answers to Porphyry (see *Jerome's Commentary on Daniel,* Prologue).

In modern times the rise of unbelief in church circles has brought about the resurrection of the arguments of both Porphyry and his opponents. As E. B. Pusey wrote, nearly a century ago: "Human inventiveness in things spiritual or unspiritual is very limited. It would be difficult probably to invent a new heresy. Objectors of old were as acute or more acute than those now; so that the ground was well-nigh exhausted" (*Daniel the Prophet,* p. iii).

The basic reason why some scholars deny the genuineness of Daniel is that they have previously rejected the possibility of predictive prophecy (see J.E.H. Thomson, *Daniel* in *Pulpit Commentary,* p. xliii). This, though usually left unstated, is sometimes frankly admitted (e.g., Robert H. Pfeiffer, *Introduction to the Old Testament,* p. 755). Arguments advanced in support of the negative view are chiefly these: (1) The author makes historical blunders. (2) The Hebrew and Aramaic of Daniel are of types much later than the sixth century. (3) Several terms used are Persian and Greek words that a Jewish author of the sixth century could not have known. (4) The position of the book in the third section (Writings or Hagiographa) of the Old Testament indicates late origin, after the prophetic canon was closed. (5) There is no external testimony to the existence of Daniel prior to the second century. (6) The theological ideas of the book are too advanced for the sixth century. (7) The stories are fanciful, unhistorical, and unreal. (8) Apocalyptic literature, of which Daniel is an example, did not arise until "well down in the Hellenistic period" (Montgomery, ICC, p. 80).

Arguments used by modern apologists in support of the genuineness of Daniel are these: (1) the prima facie evidence of the testimony of the book; (2) its reception into the canon, which witnesses to the fact that Jews of the pre-Christian centuries believed in its authenticity; (3) the uniform testimony of the New Testament, including our Lord's own expressed opinion; (4) ancient direct external testimony (including Ezk 14:14,20; 28:3; I Macc 2:59,60; and several passages in Josephus); (5) evidence of the influence of Daniel before 165 B.C.; (6) rebuttal of the negative arguments regarding the ideas and history of the book. These have found especially strong support from archaeology. Most of the historical objections have been silenced by Boutflower and Dougherty (Charles Boutflower, *In and Around the Book of Daniel;* R. H. Dougherty, *Nabonidus and Belshazzar*). Note particularly Montgomery's rather damaging admission (ICC, p. 72, 2nd full paragraph).

Structure of the Book. A superficial examination might yield a division of the book into two main parts, each having six subdivisions of a chapter each: chapters 1–6, the *Histories* of Daniel; chapters 7–12, the *Prophecies* of Daniel. As is usual with such neat outlines, however, this two-part division is more apparent than real. Chapters 10–12, in fact, constitute an important unit by themselves.

The true basis of division must be sought in the fact that Section 1:1–2:4 a is in Hebrew, Section 2:4 b–7:28 is in Aramaic (Syriac, Chaldee), and Section 8:1–12:13 is in Hebrew. This strange use of two languages, mysterious as it may be, is of divine intention and means something. Following C. A. Auberlen (*The Prophecies of Daniel and the Revelation of St. John,* 1857) and S. P. Tregelles (*Remarks on the Prophetic Visions in the Book of Daniel,* 1864) in seeing the shift in languages as the key to the thought structure — insofar as there is a structure —, we observe that the Book of Daniel carries a message of judgment and defeat for the Gentile world, of which the chief representatives at the time of the prophet were Nebuchadnezzar, Belshazzar, Darius, and Cyrus. The appropriate language in this Gentile-slanted portion (2:4 b–7:28) is Aramaic, the diplomatic and commercial language of the epoch. The book bears another message, one of hope and deliverance for God's oppressed but precious holy people, the Hebrews. For the Hebrew-slanted portion the language is, appropriately, Hebrew. This is not to say that Hebrews do not appear in chapters 2–7 nor Gentiles in chapters 8–12. It means only that the basic standpoint changes.

All of Daniel is a book of prophecy. This, from the Biblical standpoint, means merely that its author was a prophet (Mt 24:15; cf. Heb 1:1,2). Hence, while Biblical prophecy includes prediction, it is more than prediction. It may relate to events past, present, or future. It is always presented from a divinely given moral and spiritual point of view. So, the historical and hortatory portions are quite as prophetic as the predictive.

On these grounds the following analysis appears.

Historical Background. Ezekiel and Daniel were written in the Exile, a name customarily given to that period during which the Jews of the Judean kingdom were displaced from their country after the destruction of their temple, capital city, and commonwealth by Nebuchadnezzar. This destruction came in three stages: First, in 605 B.C. Nebuchadnezzar brought Jehoiakim to his knees and carried off hostages, among them Daniel and his three associates (Dan 1:1-6; see below on 1:1). Later, 597 B.C., on another expedition to Palestine, after certain rebellious acts of the Judean kings Jehoiakim and Jehoiachin made punishment necessary, Nebuchadnezzar again made Jerusalem submit. This time he carried off 10,000 captives, among them king Jehoiachin and the young prophet Ezekiel (Ezk 1:1-3; cf. II Chr 36:10; II Kgs 24:8-20). Finally, in 587 B.C., after a long siege, Nebuchadnezzar destroyed the city and the Temple and broke up the entire Jewish community (II Kgs 25:1-7; Jer 34:1-7; 39:1-7; 52:2-11).

Restoration to the land began in 538 B.C., when the victorious Cyrus, king of the new Medo-Persian empire and conqueror of Babylon, in harmony with a general policy of restoring displaced peoples to their lands, decreed that the Jews might return (II Chr 36:22,23; Ezr 1:1-4). Though some Jews remained in exile many years after permission was granted to return (indeed, a majority never returned as residents), the Exile as such, during which residence in Jerusalem by exiles was forbidden, lasted only about forty-eight years. The Temple, however, remained unrestored until about 515 B.C. (see Ezr 6:15), about seventy years after its destruction in 587. Jeremiah's prophecy of "seventy years," however, related to the period of servitude to Babylon (Jer 25:11) and included not only Judah but her neighbors. This was the period from 605 to 538, in round numbers, "seventy years" (cf. Dan 9:1,2, the date of which is 539/538 B.C.).

Many cultural and religious changes were thrust upon the Jews by their exile. Among these were the rise of synagogue worship in lieu of temple worship, and at least a beginning toward adoption of a second language – Aramaic (also called Syriac or Chaldee). A number of evidences lead to the conclusion that Abram's language was originally Aramaic. Biblical notices (Deut 26:5; Gen 31:47) show that the family from which Abram, Isaac, and Jacob sprang spoke Aramaic. Archaeological evidences (e.g., Moabite Stone, Ras Shamra tablets) demonstrate that the Canaanites spoke a language almost identical with Hebrew. So the Jews, ages earlier, even before the settlement in Canaan, had adopted "Canaanite," which, with minor evolution, became Hebrew. In Babylon they found Aramaic the language of commerce. It had also been the language of diplomacy for some time (cf. Isa 36:11,12). So, likely the Jews picked up the Aramaic, really very similar to Hebrew (although not identical with it by any means; see II Kgs 18:26) and were for some time bilingual. This circumstance apparently lies behind the fact that six chapters of Daniel are in Hebrew.

Form of Literature. Daniel is the first great book of Apocalypse. Though *apocalypse* is simply a Greek word meaning "unveiling" or "revelation" and is therefore quite properly a name for all of Scripture, especially the predictive portions, it is customary for theologians and exegetes now to apply it exclusively to a certain type of literature of which Daniel is the only Old Testament example and Revelation the only New Testament example. There are apocalyptical portions in other books (e.g., Zech 1:7–6:8), but no other Biblical books of Apocalypse. No conservative scholar could frame a definition of Apocalypse acceptable to the naturalistic temper of much present-day Biblical scholarship. For rationalists hold that falsely ascribed authorship and dates, as of the non-Biblical Jewish apocalyptic literature of the two centuries immediately before Christ, are of the essence of the Apocalyptic.

Those who view both Daniel and Revelation as authentic and truthful, hold Biblical Apocalyptic literature to be a form of predictive prophecy. It is distinguished chiefly by: (1) The employment of visions reported as seen (rather than digested and summarized, as with most prophecy). (2) Use of symbols predominantly as the vehicle of revelation – either interpreted (as the ram and goat of Dan 8), or left uninterpreted (as the woman clothed with the sun of Rev 12). (3) Prediction of the future of God's people (whether Israel or the Church) in relation to the nations of earth as consummated with the coming of Messiah. (4) Prose style rather than the poetic style characteristic of the other prophetic portions of the Old Testament.

Interpretation of Apocalypse. The special character of Apocalypse requires the best effort of the interpreter and his humble dependence on God. No special hermeneutical rules for dealing with Apolyptical literature have yet been successfully brought forth. Especially great care must be exercised that the rules for interpretation of non-Biblical apocalypse be not uncritically carried over into interpretation of Biblical Apocalypse. After all, only the inspired writings of Daniel and John are true Apocalypses. The others are false; and, however useful in supplying New Testament backgrounds or interesting in themselves to those who enjoy fanciful literature, they are still pseudepigrapha, i.e., spurious writings. They are all conscious imitations of true Apocalypse, of which Daniel is a shining Biblical model.

OUTLINE

Title: Prophecies of the Nations of the World and of Israel's Future in Relation to Them in the Plan of God.

I. The historical introduction. 1:1–2:4 a.
II. The nations of earth—their character, relations, succession, and destiny. 2:4 b–7:28.
  1. Nebuchadnezzar's dream of a great image: A prophecy of "the times of the Gentiles." 2:1-49.
  2. Nebuchadnezzar's trial of the confessors' faith: A lesson in steadfast faith. 3:1-30.
  3. Nebuchadnezzar's vision of the high tree: A lesson in humility. 4:1-37.
  4. Belshazzar's feast: A lesson in sin and its punishment. 5:1-31.
  5. Darius the Mede in the role of religious persecutor: A lesson in faith and prayer. 6:1-28.
  6. A vision of four beasts, the Ancient of Days, and the Son of man: The conflict of Christ with Antichrist. 7:1-28.
III. The Hebrew nation, its relation to Gentile dominion, and its future in the plan of God. 8:1–12:13.
  1. A ram, a goat, and a little horn: Israel in conflict with the Old Testament Antichrist. 8:1-27.
  2. The prophecy of seventy weeks: Israel's future in the plan of God. 9:1-27.
  3. Final vision: Israel through the centuries and at the consummation in the hands of enemies and in the hands of God. 10:1–12:13.

COMMENTARY

I. The Historical Introduction. 1:1–2:4 a.

In this section the chief personalities of the book are introduced, together with the circumstances that placed them in the positions they are later reported to have held.

A. The Setting of the Story and of the Book. 1:1-5.

1. In the third year of the reign of Jehoiakim. According to Jer 25:1, the fourth year of Jehoiakim was the first year of Nebuchadnezzar. Yet the Chaldean is called "king of Babylon" here in Jehoiakim's third year. This is a "prolepsis" (C. F. Keil, *Biblical Commentary on the Book of Daniel)* or "anticipation" (Rose, *The Bible Commentary)* whereby a later title is applied in speaking of a period even before it was actually conferred. A short while later Nebuchadnezzar's father, the king of Babylon, died, and Nebuchadnezzar, rushing home to Babylon ahead of his armies, received the throne (Jos *Antiquities* x. 11. 1.). **Came Nebuchadnezzar.** See Introduction, *Historical Background*. Whether the Hebrew *bā'* should be rendered "went" or "set off" (i.e., left Babylon), or "came," "arrived," is uncertain. Daniel's reportorial standpoint was Babylon; so "went" is possible. The Hebrew word is capable of either meaning. Until recently this verse was the only information available concerning this capture of Jerusalem, except for a brief report from Josephus. However, II Kgs 24:1, as well as II Chr 36:6,7, may possibly refer to it. In the absence of further proof it has become almost axiomatic among irreverent modern critics to deny that such an event ever occurred and to cite this as the author's first "historical blunder." As recently as February, 1956, the ancient documents were first published which now provide full historical support for Nebuchadnezzar's presence in Judah at exactly this time (see JBL, Dec. 1956, Vol. LXXV, Pt. IV, p. 277).

It is distressing to see this new data ignored by recent writers (see B. W. Anderson, *Understanding the Old Testament*, 1957, p. 355; N. K. Gottwald, *A Light to the Nations*, 1959, p. 618; John Bright, *A History of Israel*, 1959, p. 569). Believers, however, need not wait for archaeological confirmation to accept Daniel's word.

2. This is true interpretation of history. **The Lord gave Jehoiakim.** There is "no restraint to the Lord to save by many or by few" (I Sam 14:6). Nor is there restraint to *destroy* by many or by few. Later God's rule over history is made more emphatic (Dan 4:17). Nebuchadnezzar was God's "servant" (Jer 25:9). Similarly, God used the self-exalted dictators of the present century to chastise lands and peoples, and later he destroyed them (cf. Jer 25:12-14). As someone has quaintly said, their self-exalting exploits were hardly more than "exercise to keep them healthy for execution." **Vessels of the house of God.** How the nation's sins brought about gradual impoverishment of Solomon's magnificent temple is seen in I Kgs 14:25,26; II Kgs 14:8-14; 16:8; 18:13-16; 24:8-13; Jer 27:16-22; 52:17-23. For the desecration of temple vessels, see Dan 5; and for their return to Jerusalem, see Ezr 1:7-11.

3. Master of his eunuchs. Eunuch (Heb. *sarîs),* a castrated male. For obvious reasons eunuchs were frequently in charge of royal harems. Sometimes the word, by metaphor, was used simply of an official. There is great possibility that Daniel and his friends may have been emasculated. Again see Isaiah's ominous prediction (II Kgs 20:18). **Of the children of Israel** (Heb. *Mib-bᵉnê yiś-rā-'ēl,* lit., *out from the sons of Israel).* These were originally all the descendants of Jacob or Israel. Later, *Israel* was a name for the ten tribes, so-called, who fell away to Jeroboam (I Kgs 11:13; cf. 12:19). But after the destruction of the "Northern Kingdom," the name Israel reverted to its primitive sense. **And of the king's seed** (lit., *seed of the kingdom).* This refers to the family of David (cf. Isa 7:2,13). For a sample of the spiritual degeneracy of certain of the members of the royal line at about this time, see II Kgs 25:25; Jer 41:1 ff. **And of the princes.** The word **princes** (Heb. *partᵉmîm)* is a Persian term apparently cognate with words for important people in several Indo-European languages. It may have been in common courtly use. This refers to important families not of the Davidic house. The sense of the three terms, **Israel . . . king's seed . . . nobles,** is that selection was to be made of Hebrews, both of royal and of other courtly families.

4. Children in whom was no blemish. This is the first of a series of qualifications set up for selecting men to be trained in the court of Babylon. **Children.** Hebrew *yᵉlādîm* is a word like our own, of indefinite meaning, depending on the age standpoint of the speaker. In an objective report like this, the common estimate of fourteen or fifteen years of age is likely right. Absence of blemish does not eliminate the possibility of their castration. As selected, they would naturally have been without that mutilation. **Well favoured,** i.e., good looking. That which the king would look upon ought to be without deformity and very beautiful. The same combination of words is used of the beauty of Rachel (Gen 24:16; 26:7), Bath-sheba (II Sam 11:3), Queen Vashti (Est 1:11), and Esther (Est 2:2,3,7). **Skilful in all wisdom, and cunning in knowledge, and understanding science.** These three cumulative expressions emphasize native ability and previous instruction. The redundancy of the Hebrew idiom is for emphasis rather than for fine distinctions. This is what the youths already were rather than what they were to become. Usually, intellectual ability is an "early bloomer." **Ability in them to stand in the king's palace.** Natural and acquired talents that would enable these men to stand in attendance before a splendid king in a magnificent building are signified. The boys needed to be humble but neither timid nor dull.

Whom they might teach the learning and the tongue of the Chaldeans. The learning (Heb. *book)* of the Chaldeans means the literature of the people of lower Mesopotamia. Since the archaeological discoveries of the past century have uncovered and furnished the key to translation of that literature, we know how vast was the learning of the Chaldeans. Recent discoveries in the Near Eastern-Aegean regions demonstrate that a large amount of cultural exchange took place between the two areas. And the Philistine neighbors of Israel were apparently of "Greek" stock. With them, the Book of Judges shows, there was cultural exchange. (See G. Bonfante,

"Who Were the Philistines?" *American Journal of Archaeology,* I, 2 (April–June, 1946), pp. 251-262.) **The tongue** (language) **of the Chaldeans** must refer to the Akkadian (Babylonian, Assyrian) language of the day. **Chaldeans** here appears to be used in a broad sense, to designate the inhabitants of the region of Chaldea, which in its widest significance was the whole of Babylonia. The several languages of the region, including the very ancient ritual language, were written on clay in wedge-shaped (cuneiform) characters. This was an ideographic and syllabic system, far different from the alphabetic writing inscribed on papyrus with pen and ink to which the people of Palestine and Syria were accustomed. The foundations of astronomy, mathematics, law, and a dozen other disciplines were recorded in that ancient cuneiform script, together with a lot of magical humbug. If all this learning was to be taught these youths, then three years (cf. v. 5) was none too long for their education.

5. A daily provision of the king's meat, and of the wine which he drank. Neither *dainties* (ASV) nor *rich food* (RSV) is any improvement on the AV **meat.** The word so rendered *(patbag)* is a loan to Hebrew from Old Persian, meaning "appropriation" or "allowance" (Montgomery, ICC, pp. 122-124). It has reference to the fact that these youths were put on government support, sharing with others of the king's official ménage'. There is not even a hint in the Hebrew text that there was anything physically or morally harmful in the food and drink. Wine was quite common to the Jewish diet (see Ps 104:15; Isa 55:1; Neh 5:18, where the same word *yayin* is used). Many injunctions against excessive use of wine, however, do appear in the OT (Prov 20:1; 23:20,30,31); and certain religious orders were forbidden the use of wine (Num 6:1-20; Jud 13:1-7; Jer 35:1-14). Priests were forbidden use of wine immediately previous to service in the Temple (Lev 10:1-9), and kings were discouraged from drinking it (Prov 31:4,5).

B. The Identity of the Chief Character of the Story and His Associates. 1:5-7. Daniel, introduced by name, is the one who throughout the book not only reports events but is himself the subject of most of the narrative in several capacities: interpreter of dreams (chs. 2; 4; 5), friend of sufferers (ch. 3), receptor of revelatory visions and dreams from God (chs. 6–12). In several incidents three Jewish friends are associated with him. Here all are introduced by name. The changing of the names of the youths is very significant. Their education in the highest pagan culture history had yet produced was to be completed by the substitution of names honoring the vile deities of Babylon for those honoring the Holy One of Israel. They were to be weaned from the old religion and culture, and transformed completely, even to *identity,* into Babylonians. For among the ancients a man's name was even more a part of his identity and character than it is among moderns.

7. For he gave unto Daniel the name of Belteshazzar. Daniel means in Hebrew, *God's prince* (or *judge),* whereas the new name **Belteshazzar,** in the language of Babylon, means *Bel's prince.* This name, Belteshazzar (a variant of the name of King Belshazzar, ch. 5), honors one of the chief deities of Babylon (see Isa 46:1; Jer 50:2; 51:44). **Hananiah** means *mercy of Yahweh* (being a variation of the original of the beloved name, John), whereas **Shadrach,** possibly meaning "command of Aku," the moon-god (HDB), may be a somewhat disguised form of *Marduk* (Montgomery, ICC, p. 123), a chief god of Babylon. **Mishael** almost certainly means, *Who is what God is?* whereas **Meshach** (according to competent authority, Fred. Delitzsch) means, *Who is like Aku?* This is regrettably uncertain inasmuch as the name appears nowhere else and its derivation is uncertain. **Azariah** means *Whom Yahweh helps,* or *Yahweh will help,* **whereas Abed-nego** most likely means *Servant of Nebo.*

"A custom . . . of imposing new names when persons entered upon a new condition or new relations in life," Moses Stuart points out, "is extensively developed in the OT: see *Abram* and *Abraham,* Gen 17:5; Joseph and Zaphnath-Paaneah, Gen 41:45; comp. II Sam 12:24,25; II Kgs 23:34; 24:17; also Est 2:7; Ezr 5:14 comp. with Hag 1:14; 2:2,21. So in NT: Mk 3:16,17. These names, thus imposed anew, generally designate something which is intended to honor the persons who receive them, or to honor the god that is worshipped by him who imposes them, or to commemorate some event that is interesting, etc." *(A Commentary on the Book of*

Daniel, p. 9). Extensive discussion of these names will be found in Bible encyclopedias and dictionaries, as well as in Hebrew lexicons.

C. Events Placing the Author in Prominence. 1:8–2:4 a. *A Crisis of Righteousness.* This is described above in verse 5. Verses 6 and 7 intervene to identify Daniel and his friends.

8 a. *A Decision for Righteousness.* **Daniel purposed in his heart.** Native intelligence and courtly ability were matched in this man by steadfast loyalty to principle. **That he would not defile himself.** The defilement (cf. on v. 5) had nothing to do with any harmful elements in the food and drink. It was rather that it was "the king's." The word for **defile** *(gā'al,* a late Heb. word) may mean physical defilement (Isa 63:3, "stain"), moral defilement (Zeph 3:1), or, more frequently, ceremonial defilement (e.g., Ezr 2:62; cf. Neh 7:64). On the relation of food and drink to moral defilement, see Mt 15:11. While commending moderation, the Bible nowhere commands abstinence from any food or beverage on *moral* grounds; the problem was ceremonial or religious. Religion affected all of life for the ancients, as it does for primitive people today—and as it should for all men. Even eating and drinking had ritual and mystic significance. Slaughtering was a religious act to be carried out with proper solemnities. Flesh from the king's table was doubtless slain according to pagan ritual and offered to a god. The Jews were forbidden to eat flesh sacrificed to a pagan god (see Ex 34:15), for it was "serving other gods" in the public eye. Jews faced this problem whenever they ate out of the homeland (Hos 9:3,4; Ezk 4:13,14). A similar situation prevailed with regard to the wine. A further problem was that Levitical procedures were not regarded; i.e., the king's food and drink were not "kosher" (see Lev 3:17; 6:26; 17:10-14; 19:26).

8 b-14. *A Procedure for Righteousness.* **8 b. Therefore he requested,** etc. In case of necessity to sustain life, the ceremonial laws might be set aside (Mt 12:3-5; I Sam 21:6; Num 28:8,9). It was because Daniel had the discernment to recognize the king's purpose in these things to wean him from his holy faith that he resolved not to yield without a battle. He "simply determined . . . by his very food perpetually to recall the remembrance of his country. He wished so to live in Chaldea as to consider himself an exile and a captive, sprung from the sacred family of Abraham" (Calvin, *Commentaries on the Book of Daniel the Prophet, in loco.)* The word for **requested** *(biqēsh,* "seek") cannot be used of mild entreaty. Being a *piel* (or intensive active) form, it is always a forceful word (used at II Sam 2:17; 12:16).

9. Now God had brought. The AV gives the impression that Daniel had previously won the favor of the chief eunuch. The sense of the Hebrew is most naturally rendered as consecutive; i.e., Daniel made request, and thereupon God gave him favor in the eyes of the chief eunuch. Observe that good motives and admirable sentiments are not absent from heathen hearts (cf. Josh 2:1 ff.; contrast Prov 12:10; see Gal 5:22). God raises up defenders for his people in strange ways. **10.** One is reminded of the butler and baker of Joseph's acquaintance (Gen 40). It appears that, though the chief eunuch was willing to help Daniel, he saw no means whereby to do it (see Jas 2:14-18).

11. Melzar. It is not a proper name, rather *the steward.* Hebrew names do not normally carry the article. **Over Daniel, Hananiah, Mishael, and Azariah.** Guided by the Holy Spirit's own point of view, the author does not deign to recognize the new names honoring the pagan gods of Babylon conferred by a timeserving heathen bureaucrat but rather uses the God-honoring names conferred by four pious Jewish mothers.

12. Prove thy servants, I beseech thee, ten days. The word **prove** *(nā-sâ)* is an intensive (piel) and joined with the cohortative *na'* expresses strong entreaty. For Daniel and his friends as well as for the steward the ten-day limit was a test of God's will. If the experiment failed, the young Hebrews were prepared to override their own ceremonial scruples, as the next verse shows. There is no evidence that Daniel knew what the outcome would be. No presumption was involved, as Young supposes (Edward J. Young, *The Prophecy of Daniel, in loco),* for a number of approved examples of such tests are furnished by Scripture. **Ten days.** A favorite round number (1:20; cf. Amos 5:3; Zech 8:23). **Pulse to eat** (lit., *from the zērō'îm and we shall eat).* Though used only here and in 1:16 in the entire Bible, and nowhere in other known literature, the word apparently means vegetables, for it is derived from a word meaning "to sow" (seed). So **pulse** was things grown from seeds planted in soil. No religious ritual of dedication to a god was directly involved in the preparation of vegetables, as it was in the preparation of flesh; and vegetables were not used in pagan ritual as were libations of wine. This is not a proof text for vegetarianism (see Rom 14:1-4).

14. So he consented in this matter. The Hebrew indicates that he gave exact heed to Daniel. **15,16.** *Rewards of Righteousness.* The test was successful, and so Daniel and his friends were spared the embarrassment and emotional tension that offense against their own standards would have caused them.

17. As for these four children. Better, *the lads, four of them.* This emphasizes that all four received certain things, whereas Daniel had special endowments besides. **God gave.** All abilities and endowments, whether natural or acquired, are from him and are to be used for him. **Knowledge.** Hebrew *maddā'*, a rare and late word. Though related to the ordinary verb "to know," it appears to mean "thought," in the sense of secret rational process, as its use in Eccl 10:12 clearly indicates. Perhaps "soundness of mind" or "good sense" conveys the idea. **Skill.** From *haśkel* (a *hiph.* inf. abs.), apparently meaning "insight" or "understanding." **Learning.** Hebrew *sēper,* usually meaning "book," but here, as in 1:4, designating the world of letters, literature. **And wisdom.** Hebrew *ḥakmâ.* Though often designating the proverbial lore of the ancient Near East, it has the larger meaning of any "intelligently arranged body of principles," or, as we should now say, "*science*" (S. R. Driver, *Daniel,* in *Cambridge Bible for Schools and Colleges).* Note that the word "all" qualifies this **wisdom,** showing that it was more than the superstitious lore of the pagan priests that was in mind. Researchers have shown that, in addition to astronomy (an adjunct of pagan worship), architecture, linguistics, agriculture, meteorology, agronomy, and many other sciences were already developed in the land of the two rivers. **Daniel had understanding in all visions and dreams,** or better, *in every kind of vision and in dreams.* This is merely pointing out, ahead of the following narrative, the prominence of Daniel as agent of God's revelation.

19. And the king communed with them; and among them all . . . The entire group, including many besides our special four, had participated in the three years of training, and all had been presented to Nebuchadnezzar. The question is irresistible: What happened to the other young Jews' training in true religion? It is obvious that it "went down the drain" of compromise and apostasy. **None like Daniel . . . therefore stood they before the king.** "The king, by his own personal examination, fixed upon the very individuals whom Providence had distinguished by peculiar gifts which rendered them superior to the other children" (Stuart, *Commentary).*

20. Ten times better than all the magicians. "Probably . . . men acquainted with occult arts in general" (Driver). The obscure word *ḥartummîm,* used also in 2:2,10,27; 4:7,9; 5:11, is thought by authorities to be of Egyptian origin. Outside the book of Daniel it is used only of Egyptian "magicians" (Gen 41:8,24; Ex 7:11,22; 8:7,18,19; 9:11). Some suggest that the word, apparently derived from *ḥeret,* "a stylus," should be rendered *scribes,* i.e., scribes of the ancient religious ritual texts in the archaic tongue of earlier inhabitants of Babylonia, a language unknown to common people in Daniel's time. (And) **astrologers.** There is no conjunction in the Hebrew; so **astrologers** is used appositively. This is a Babylonian word, found in both the Hebrew and the Aramaic portions of Daniel but nowhere else in Scripture. It is better rendered *enchanters,* or *charmers.* These words show what superstitious humbug vitiated knowledge of scientific truth in Babylon.

21. Unto the first year of king Cyrus. A contradiction with 10:1 has frequently been imagined. It is most likely that since the epoch of captivity officially came to an end with the first year of Cyrus (cf. Ezr 1:1ff.), the verse is pointing up the striking fact that the young man Daniel, who was in the first detachment of Jews taken captive from Jerusalem to Babylon (605 B.C.) outlived the long dreary epoch of captivity to see the first detachment of exiles return. This is the most natural understanding of the verse.

In *language* and *first significance,* Dan 2:1-4a, which follows, belongs with chapter 1; for these verses are a part of the introduction to the book. Here the reader is admitted to knowledge of the precise situation that brought Daniel into prominence in Babylon. These verses also serve as prologue to the dramatic prophetic narrative of chapter 2. They are, therefore, treated in this latter connection in the Commentary.

A few remarks on the practical meaning of chapter 1 should not be omitted. For the instruction of a hundred generations, this story presents *the elements of moral heroism*. (1) *Discernment*. The four lads saw precisely what was wrong with eating the prescribed food. Where did they learn it? From pious parents (Deut 6:4-9). (2) *Resistance to evil*. Distance from critical observation did not weaken it (see Mt 10:26-28; Jas 4:7). This resistance to evil also developed in their very early years in godly homes. Children do not *naturally* resist evil; rather they embrace it. They must be taught to hate evil! (see Heb 12: 9-13; Prov 3:11,12; 13:24; cf. Eli's sons, I Sam 2:12-30) (3) *Power to voice disagreement*. Youth is an age of conformity. Hence this incident gives strong evidence of special grace in the lives of these four. (4) *Physical courage*. The prince of the eunuchs was right. His head as well as theirs could have been in danger (cf. Dan 2:5, the lions' den, the fiery furnace.) (5) *Perseverance*. When no help came via the chief eunuch, Daniel tried the steward. (6) *Determination*. His purpose was "in his heart," the very center of his being. It was not a shallow purpose. (7) *Meekness*. Without mock heroics Daniel respectfully "requested" or "besought" his superiors. (8) *Good sense*. The trial suggested was reasonable and feasible. (See also Ezk 28:3; Prov 2:23 in context.)

II. The Nations of Earth—Their Character, Relations, Succession, and Destiny. 2:4b–7:28.

A. Nebuchadnezzar's Dream of a Great Image: A Prophecy of the Times of the Gentiles. 2:1-49. (For inclusion of 2:1-4a herein, see note following treatment of 1:21).

In this portion Nebuchadnezzar is reported to have experienced a frightening dream (v. 1), which is used as a means of testing the ability and willingness of his occult advisers (vv. 2-6). The failure of the main group of "wise men" to reproduce and interpret the dream endangers the lives of all the wise men, including the four Hebrews (vv. 7-12). But Daniel, supported by the successful intercession of himself and his friends, reproduces the dream (vv. 13-23). He reports the dream to Nebuchadnezzar (vv. 24-35) and provides a divine interpretation (vv. 36-45). For reward Daniel is made "ruler" over the province of Babylon, whereupon he secures advancement for his three associates (vv. 46-49). The interpretation of the dream provides the reader with a sketch of the succession of world kingdoms from Nebuchadnezzar's time down to the final outward establishment of Christ's kingdom at his second coming. (For discussion of variant views of this chapter, see note at end of chapter.)

1) Nebuchadnezzar's Frightening Dream. 2:1.

1. In the second year of the reign of Nebuchadnezzar. An apparent contradiction with data of chapter 1 is involved. Nebuchadnezzar is called "king" at the time of the capture of Jerusalem (1:1). Yet after the passing of at least three years (1:5,18), when Daniel is called before Nebuchadnezzar in this chapter, the king is in his second year. Any one of several possible explanations is available. None of them is certainly correct, though several are adequate to account for the facts. It is certain that a truly great writer like the author of Daniel would not have fallen into gross discrepancy. His first readers understood. There is, of course, the possibility of textual corruption, not uncommon with numbers in the OT (Montgomery, ICC, reports several suggestions). Some suggest a different beginning of the epoch than that referred to at 1:1—his reign over the whole empire, or after the sacking of Egypt, etc.

Most recent scholarship takes the apparent discrepancy as a simple matter growing out of Hebrew or Babylonian methods of counting regnal years. Among suggestions of this sort Driver's view (endorsed by Young) is good: "There is not, perhaps, necessarily a contradiction here with the 'three years' of i, 5,18. By Heb. usage, fractions of time were reckoned as full units. Thus Samaria, which was besieged from the fourth to the sixth year of Hezekiah, is said to have been taken 'at the end' of three years (II Kgs xviii. 9,10) and in Jer xxxiv. 14 'at the end of seven years' means evidently when the seventh year has arrived (see also Mk 8:31, etc.). If, now, the author, following a custom which was certainly sometimes adopted by Jewish writers, and which was general in Assyria and Babylonia, 'postdated' the regnal years of a king, i.e., counted as his first year not the year of his accession but the first full year afterwards, and if further Nebuchadnezzar gave orders for the education of the Jewish youths in his accession-year, the end of the 'three years' . . . might be reckoned as falling within the king's second year" (Driver, *Daniel*, CBSC, p. 17). As with most difficulties of this sort, the solution will almost always be resolved once the author's point of view and manner of using words have been ascertained.

Dreamed dreams, wherewith his spirit was troubled, and his sleep brake from him. Nebuchadnezzar was no trembling neurotic easily upset, like a juvenile, by vague impressions. This verse is only the first of several pieces of evidence that the AV is incorrect in suggesting that Nebuchadnezzar had forgotten the dream (v. 5). He was scared precisely because he had *not* forgotten it.

2) The Test by Means of the Dream. 2:2-6.

2. The magicians, and the astrologers, and the sorcerers, and the Chaldeans. On magicians and astrologers, see notes on 1:20. **Sorcerers.** Hebrew *m^ekash-sh^epîm*. Possibly from a Semitic root meaning "to cut"; hence to chop up elements in magical potions, formulae. Hence Greek *pharmakoi*, i.e., pharmacists. Recent scholarship prefers a complementary idea of "incantor of magical sayings, sorcerer." The same root appears in Akkadian for sorcerers or witches. The practice of sorcery is proscribed in the OT (Ex 22:18 [Heb. Bible v. 17, *female witch*], Deut 18:10; Isa 47:9). *Chaldeans.* Not used in the broad ethnogeographical sense of 1:4 but in the narrow professional sense, indicating the priestly class of Babylonian religion. Though used in this sense only in Daniel among Biblical books, it was commonly so used by classical writers, of whom the earliest is Herodotus (*Histories* I, 181, c. 440 B.C.; see Driver, *op. cit.*, pp. 12-16 and Young, *op.cit.*, pp. 271-273). Most authorities agree that the four terms are not used precisely but rather distributively to include *all* classes of royal counselors.

4. Chaldeans. Here, all classes of wise men. **In Syriack.** **Rather, Aramaic,** the language of a Semitic people concentrated in those days chiefly in Upper Mesopotamia and Syria. They are the Syrians of the OT. The idea is not that the Chaldeans spoke Aramaic but that, beginning here, the following portion of Daniel is in Aramaic. Compare the phrase, "in Aramaic," of Ezr 4:7 (see RSV note).

5. The thing is gone from me: if ye will not make known, etc. **Gone from me** is from a rare word of Persian origin, now generally acknowledged to be an adjective rather than a verb, and meaning "sure," or "certain." **Thing.** Better, *word.* "Words" (v. 9) is a translation of the same word. So translate, *the word is certain with me, if ye will not,* etc. The rendering of the ASV is correct here.

The king had not forgotten the dream, but rather, since he did remember it, he reasoned that his wise men, if able to predict the future by interpreting dreams, ought to be able to perform the lesser task of reconstructing the past, i.e., the king's private dream. This interpretation of the passage finds support not only in the king's fright (cf. comments on v. 1) and in the revised translation of 2:5, but also in the fact that the wise men did not fabricate something by way of a "dream" for the king when they saw that their lives were threatened. It would have been worth a try! In all likelihood it was precisely because they knew the king remembered his dream that they made no such attempt (see also on v. 8 below).

3) The Failure of the Wise Men. 2:7-12.

8. Ye would gain the time. Not that they were merely buying delay of the fatal moment of their execution (Driver, *et al.*), or trying to gain an interval in which to think up some way out (H. C. Leupold [*Exposition of Daniel*], *et al.*); but rather, in the sense of the primitive meaning of *'idānā'*, "time," a specified time is meant (cf. BDB). Interpretation of dreams was held to be related to the positions of heavenly bodies. When that particular arrangement of the Zodiac that affected that dream had elapsed, they could claim that divining was impossible (Thomson, *Pulpit Commentary, et al.*).

10. The complaint that the king was unjust in his demand has a sound of justice. But when it is recalled what a gigantic hoax the whole hocus-pocus of ancient astrology, divining, soothsaying, etc., really was, the king's decree, while excessively harsh, in that it included their "houses" (families? v. 5), was not unjust as regards the "wise men" themselves. They claimed occult powers and were frauds, granting a good bit of sincere self-deception. God holds men responsible for willful ignorance (cf. Rom 1:28). **11. The gods, whose dwelling is not with flesh.** The comma after gods makes the following clause non-restrictive, that is applicable to all gods. If the comma is omitted, the clause is read as restrictive, i.e., applying only to a certain class of gods. Perhaps it is best to omit the comma and understand the wise men as claiming to have communication in their "flesh" with certain gods of the pantheon but none with the greatest ones (Marduk), who were able to control or reveal the future.

13. The fact that Daniel and his fellows shared in the decrees of destruction shows that they were included as official advisers. Was it because of the Chaldeans' pride that the Hebrews were not consulted earlier? Or, was it supposed that the youth of the exiles did not allow them any knowledge not common to their elder professional associates?

4) Miraculous Success Through Intercession by Daniel and His Friends. 2:13-23.

Herein Daniel's wisdom and piety are thrown into prominence. The same strength of character demonstrated in chapter 1 is raised a step higher. The value of concerted, importunate prayer in the face of imminent personal danger is both approved and exemplified. Daniel's prayer of thanksgiving (2:20-23) is a timeless model, one of a pair of model prayers in the book (see also 9:3-19; cf. 6:9-11; 10:2-12).

5) The Divinely Reconstructed Dream. 2:24-35.

25. I have found a man. It appears that Arioch was another timeserving bureaucrat who was willing to claim credit for goods he had no part in providing.

28. What shall be in the latter days. This is the scope of the prophecy to be revealed by the dream and its interpretation. It is a mistake to restrict this to the end time. A phrase out of the general prophetic literature, it refers to the future as developing and consummated in the Messianic era. See Isa 2:2; Mic 4:1; Gen 49:1ff. (in context), and Jer 48:47. Because it includes both advents of Christ, as well as the epoch between them, it involves the present age. The inquiring student will be satisfied on this point by comparing Acts 2:17 with Joel 2:28, and Jn 5:18 with Heb 1:1,2.

29. What should come to pass hereafter (lit., *what should be that after this*). **Hereafter** *('ahᵉrê dᵉnâ)* has no reference to life after death, nor to the future in general. But, rather, like the equivalent Greek expression, *meta tauta*, or *meta touto* (Rev 4:1; 7:1), it refers to the future as subsequent to some previously mentioned item in the context. Here that item appears to be the king's thoughts about his own kingdom and its future. Hence, in a sense, the meaning of the dream is limited to what the king could understand. The "thing" which should be "after this" is world dominion in its political aspect. We should expect truth of an external political sort here in this chapter, for God is making truth known on the level of a pagan king's understanding ("maketh known to . . . Nebuchadnezzar," Dan 2:28; "maketh known to thee," v. 29; "that thou mightest know the thoughts of thy heart," v. 30). Any spiritualizing of the message in the direction of the NT church or "spiritual Israel" is clearly out of place here.

The description of the dream and the account of the actions involved are treated in the commentary along with the interpretation of the dream, which follows.

6) The Divine Interpretation of the Dream. 2:36-45.

The dream had been of an impressive, glittering, frightening metallic image in the form of a man.

a) The Head of Gold (vv. 36-38; cf. v. 32).

37. A king of kings. A title customarily applied to Medo-Persian and Babylonian emperors, found not only in the Greek classics but in the records of the countries involved and in Scripture (Ezk 26:7; Ezr 7:12), granted that most of the literature involved is later than the sixth century.

38. And wheresoever the children of men dwell . . . hath he given into thine

hand, and hath made thee ruler over them all. Nebuchadnezzar's power is ascribed to divine providence (cf. Jer 25:9; 27:5,6; 28:14; Dan 12:1). The manner of expression may be hyperbolical, for Nebuchadnezzar was not a universal ruler. It is possible, however, that the reference is to a universal divine grant which Nebuchadnezzar never exercised himself to possess. **Thou art this head of gold.** See Isa 14:4.

b) The Breast and Arms of Silver (v. 39 a; cf. v. 32).

39 a. And after thee shall arise another kingdom inferior to thee. The breast and arms of silver represent the kingdom known to history and Scripture as the kingdom of "the Medes and Persians" (see Dan 5:28, 31; cf. 6:8). It replaced Babylon in 539 B.C. (cf. ch. 5). The duality of the kingdom is obviously represented by the duality of the breasts and arms.

c) The Belly and Thighs (buttocks) of Brass (v. 39 b; cf. v. 32).

39 b. And another third kingdom of brass, which shall bear rule over all the earth. History and Scripture agree that this was the Greek (Macedonian) empire of Alexander and his successors. This interpretation is established by Dan 8:20,21. This kingdom replaced that of the Medes and Persians when Alexander in a series of advances, beginning in 334 B.C., overcame the Medes and Persians.

d) The Fourth Kingdom of Iron (vv. 40-43; cf. v. 33). Though divided into legs of iron, and feet and toes of iron mixed with clay, it is *one* kingdom. It is the form of world dominion known to Bible and history as Rome, and which, through the progressive Westernization of mankind, appears to prevail to the present day. It is referred to historically first (chronologically) at Lk 2:1.

40. Strong as iron. Of all the four metals this is strongest. Considered in the context of its own time, none of the three previous kingdoms was as strong as Rome. And to the present hour government tends more and more to exercise control over every area of human activity. This is a necessary accompaniment of the progressive industrialization of society. **Breaketh in pieces.** Rome fragmented and reassembled—socially, culturally, and politically—all the peoples, institutions, etc., it took over. The only notable exception was Christianity itself as a spiritual movement (albeit truly Romanized in the perversion of the Roman Church). **And subdueth all.** "The empire of the Romans filled the world, and when the empire fell into the hands of a single person, the world became a safe and dreary prison for his enemies. To resist was fatal and it was impossible to fly" (Gibbon). Some see in the two legs a prophecy of the division of the empire into two empires, with capitals at Rome and Constantinople.

41. The kingdom shall be divided. The word *p^{e}lî-ga,* though cognate with a common Hebrew verb meaning "to divide," occurs only here in the OT. Young's suggestion, following Buxtorf, that it be rendered "composite" is good, and seems consistent with the meaning of the prevalent Semitic root.

42,43. In its final stage, this kingdom will be brittle and easily shattered. This is owing to the mixture (in symbol) of the clay with the iron. **They shall mingle themselves.** This clause, a single reflexive participle in the Aramaic, apparently means the clay and iron (as grammatic agreement suggests). I take this to mean that "the seed of men," i.e., common humanity, shall intrude into government *en masse.* The Roman government became a rule of the mob. If modern history is forecast here, the suggestion of the dictatorship of the common man, in socialism, is almost irresistible.

e) The Messianic Kingdom of the Stone (vv. 44,45; cf. 34,35). Interpreters of all schools—reverent Christian, Jewish, rationalistic-unbelieving—agree that this refers to the Messianic kingdom. The grammatical meaning of the verses is not obscure. Disagreement about interpretation is rooted in the varying points of view with which readers approach the passage. Cognizance should be taken here of the two main views held by evangelical Christians. Those who identify Messiah's kingdom wholly with the Church (mainly postmillennialists and amillennialists) see the fulfillment of this prophecy in Christ's first advent. Those who, while recognizing in the Church an aspect of Christ's kingdom (Col 1:13; Jn 3:3; Acts 1:3; 20:25; I Pet 2:9), expect it to be manifested finally on earth only at the Second Advent (chiliasts, premillennialists), see the fulfillment in both advents. They call attention to the fact that the prophecy is of external political dominion as revealed *to the mind of a pagan* king (cf. Dan 2:29, 30 and comments), and so refer the prophecy to the Second Advent and the establishment of a "millennium" (cf. Rev 20).

The chief reasons advanced in support of this view are as follows. (1) The prophecy relates to the political fortunes of important empires of history. The fifth kingdom (Messianic) of this series is apparently no different in this respect from the others. Yet the Church (unless one takes a Roman Catholic point of view), is no political establishment. The Millennium has such a political aspect. (2) According to the dream and its interpretation, the destruction of the fourth kingdom by Messiah is sudden, violent, catastrophic. Just such a destruction is frequently assigned to the inauguration of Messiah's Millennial kingdom (see Rev 19:11 ff.). Insofar as the Church has gained any victory over this present world, it has been in a far different manner. (3) This passage predicts the complete victory of Messiah's kingdom over the kingdoms of the world. Just such a complete victory is assigned to the Millennium (e.g., Rev 19; 20; Isa 2). The Church has not conquered the world and will not do so (Mt 13:24-30, 36-43, II Tim 3:1 ff.). The present age is to end in great apostasy rather than in the victory of the Church (II Thess 2).

7) Reward and Promotion for Daniel and His Friends. 2:46-49.

48. Ruler over the . . . province of Babylon. This province, evidently including the city and its environs, was apparently not a large territory. Perhaps it was the same as the "realm of the Chaldeans" (9:1). **Chief of the governors over all the wise men of Babylon.** "What the particular duties of this office were, we do not know. That Daniel so managed them as to keep clear of divination by sorcery or astrology, and the performance of heathen rites, would seem to be implied by the account of his demeanor which is given in the book of Daniel" (Stuart *Comm.*). **49. The gate of the king.** Cf. Est 2:19,21. An important position of nearest access to the king. There are many ancient and modern examples of such titles for Oriental courtiers. Perhaps the word **gate** should be rendered *court* (cf. BDB).

B. Nebuchadnezzar's Trial of the Confessors' Faith: A Lesson in Steadfast Faith. 3:1-30.

Everything in Daniel 3 suggests clearly that the main purpose of this chapter is directly practical rather than doctrinal. There are no predictions. The narrative simply reports the fortunes of the three friends of Daniel as steadfast confessors of faith (Daniel does not figure in the chapter at all). Hebrews 11:34 cites the story as a lesson in faith. The main incident is the subject of a spurious expansion in an Apocryphal book known as The Song of the Three Hebrew Children.

The actors in the 'drama' are familiar, all having been previously introduced: Nebuchadnezzar (Dan 3:1; cf. 1:1; 2:1); the Chaldeans (3:8; cf. 2:2); the "three Hebrew children" (3:12 ff.; cf. 1:6,7; 2:17,49). Why Daniel was not found in civil disobedience as the three were is best explained by the conjecture that he was absent from the city on some official errand.

In harmony with the didactic character of this narrative chapter, a *homiletical* outline, rather than an *analytical* one, is suggested. The actions herein set forth are: (1) the opposition to faith (v. 1; cf. v. 8); (2) the temptation of faith (vv. 2-15); (3) the demonstration of faith (vv. 16-18); (4) the salvation by faith (vv. 19-30).

1) The Opposition to Faith. 3:1 (cf. v. 8). The *occasion* was the erection of an idolatrous image. The dimensions furnished in ratio, $60 \times 6 = 10 \times 1$, suggest an image set on a pedestal. As to the *location* of Dura, though there are at least three places of that name reported by scholars, only one was in the environs of the city. The image may have been dedicated to some Babylonian deity, though verses 12,14,18 seem to rule this out. Montgomery and Keil argue that it was a symbol of Nebuchadnezzar's empire. The charge of treason (v. 12) supports this. Seiss (Joseph A. Seiss, *Voices from Babylon*) thought it might have been a symbol of Jehovah, since Nebuchadnezzar had seemed to confess His supremacy (2:47,48). There are precedents for Jehovah images (Ex 32; I Kgs 12:25-33; cf. Acts 17:23), but it seems unlikely that this was one. The persons who led the attack (Dan 3:8) were of all people those who should have befriended these Hebrews, since they owed their lives to them. But like all wicked men, they were the op-

ponents of true service of God (cf. Prov 29:25; Mt 10:16-39, esp. v. 28).

2) The Temptation of Faith. 3:2-15. The temptation was *first* to *perversion* of faith. Idolatry is essentially perversion of a proper appetite to see God (Jn 14:6). But faith must always be in the "invisible One" only late in time "made flesh" (see Rom 1:23; I Jn 5:21; Acts 17:29; Ex 20:4-6). The temptation was, secondly, to *compromise* their faith. Advancement in their profession appeared to depend on their conforming to idolatry while artfully concealing their rejection of it (cf. II Kgs 5:15-19). Verse 14 suggests also temptation to *concealment* of faith.

3. The princes, the governors, and captains, the judges, the treasurers, the counsellors, the sheriffs, and all the rulers of the provinces (cf. v. 2). Certain of these terms are Semitic, as was the language of Babylon and both Hebrew and Aramaic; certain others are derived from Persian, the non-Semitic language of the Medo-Persian lords of the kingdom which succeeded in 539 B.C. (cf. chs. 5; 6). It is argued that the Persian words are anachronously used. This does not follow, inasmuch as the narrative was composed by Daniel, who published his work in the *Persian* period. The words then chosen would have been terms best suited to the understanding and custom of his readers. If this book had been composed in the Greek period, in Palestine, as many critics claim, it would have been quite surprising if any Babylonian words had been used.

5. The sound of the cornet, flute, harp, sackbut, psaltery, dulcimer, etc. (cf. vv. 7,10,15). It has been claimed that, since the names for certain of these instruments are Greek, the book must have been composed after Alexander's conquest of the East. Every year, however, historical studies demonstrate more fully that there was an early exchange of culture between Greece and the Orient. These musical instruments of Greek origin simply carried their Greek names with them, as is the case in similar cultural exchanges today, viz., piano, viola, guitar, zither, etc.

3) The Demonstration of Faith. 3:16-18.

16. O Nebuchadnezzar, we are not careful to answer thee. Absence of any flattering titles in the Hebrews' address to the king indicates no disrespect–rather, terse directness. Perhaps the name Nebuchadnezzar should be joined in sense with "the king" and the address begun with "We are not careful. . . . For **not careful** read, *there is no need.* These words express full commitment, and appear to answer the king's question of verse 14, **Is it true . . . ?** or better, *Is it on purpose . . . ?* **17,18. Our God . . . is able to deliver us.** This expresses the *full confidence* of their faith (cf. II Tim 1:12). **And he will deliver us out of thine hand.** This expresses the *full knowledge* of their faith. They did not know *how* God would deliver from the king – whether by death, ushering them into His presence, or by a special act of providence, saving them alive. But dead or alive, they knew they were God's (I Cor 3:21-23; see also Heb 13:6).

4) The Salvation by Faith. 3:19-30.

19. One seven times. Possibly the Aramaic word *ḥad,* rendered **one,** has here the sense of our indefinite article "a" or "an"; hence *a seven.* This would be some familiar kind of seven-fold thing (e.g., the Heb. word for week is seven, as is also the similar word for an oath). This seven would then be, as Zoeckler *(Lange's Comm.)* suggests, a seven of completeness of judicial penalty. See also Lev 26:18-24; Mt 18:21,22.

21. They were bound in their own clothing, for no time was allowed for special preparations. The meanings of the words for the articles of clothing are now almost completely lost. They have been lost since the time of the earliest translations, and the Septuagint (not the better known Greek text of Theodotion) comes from the very epoch when certain critics claim this book was written. If the words were unknown in the first two and a half centuries B.C., then the book must have been written far earlier.

24,25. These words must be interpreted from Nebuchadnezzar's pagan point of view, not from our Christian point of view. **Like the Son of God** (Aram. *da-mê lᵉbar ʾᵉlahîn)* should be *like a son of the gods,* i.e., like a divine being. The king was thinking of the various orders of pagan deities. (A similar case of failure of the AV is at Mt 27:54.) This person may indeed have been the preincarnate Son of God, but if so, Nebuchadnezzar did not know who He was. See also Isa 43:1-3.

The victory of faith was fivefold: (1) They were loosed from their bonds (v.

25). (2) They were protected from harm (v. 27). (3) They were comforted in trial (vv. 24,25,28). (4) Their God was glorified (v. 29). (5) As God's servants they were rewarded (v. 30).

C. Nebuchadnezzar's Vision of the High Tree: A Lesson in Humility. 4:1-37.

The first three verses in the Aramaic are joined mistakenly to chapter 3. In both style and thought they belong with chapter 4. The fact that Nebuchadnezzar speaks in the first person throughout chapter 4, from verse 1 on, indicates a distinct change from the *third* person report of 3:30.

Beginning with a brief salutation (vv. 1-3), followed by the king's own report of circumstances at court (vv. 4-9), he presents the narration of a dream (vv. 10-18), which Daniel interpreted (vv. 19-27), and which was fulfilled in the humiliating experiences of Nebuchadnezzar (vv. 28-33), happily followed by the king's recovery and restoration (vv. 34-37).

1) Salutation by Nebuchadnezzar. 4:1-3. The form of this, as well as of the rest of the chapter, indicates that here is a Babylonian state paper, incorporated by Daniel into Holy Scripture. This shows that inspiration of Scripture is by virtue of the divine authority of the person at whose direction a given word is included. Even an ass' words are included in Scripture (Num 22:28,30) by Moses' authority! Nebuchadnezzar's salutation addressed this document — which no doubt circulated independently before it was placed in Scripture — to his entire realm. It is not too much to hope that some archaeologist may turn it up. Perhaps it already lies unrecognized among some of the thousands of recovered, but still unread, clay tablets.

2) Circumstances in Court. 4:4-9.

4. I Nebuchadnezzar was at rest in mine house. Successful wars and immense construction in Babylon had brought him the rest of accomplishment. (Immense archaeological remains so testify. See bibliography and text of Boutflower, *In and Around the Book of Daniel*, pp. 65-113). **Flourishing in my palace.** Ordinarily used of plants, the adjective **flourishing,** *ra-'anan,* appears often in Biblical Hebrew in descriptions of the luxuriant growth of trees (Ps 92:12) and figuratively of healthy people (Ps 92:14). Outwardly all was prosperous. **5. I saw a dream which . . . troubled me.** The king had a neurosis! Uneasy lies the head that wears a crown. **6,7.** Appeal to his advisors was without avail. This school of pompous quacks should long since have been dismissed.

8. But at the last Daniel came in before me. Was it national pride that made him put off calling Daniel? Perverseness? Depravity? The rest of the verse indicates that though he held Daniel in highest regard, he was still maintaining a thoroughly pagan point of view. The evidence does not demonstrate that *rûaḥ 'elahîn qaddishîn* should be rendered "the Spirit of the Holy God," as some hold, though that translation is possible grammatically, and the parallel with the cognate Hebrew of Josh 24:19 supports it, as well as the Greek of Theodotion and the RSV margin. Seeing that Nebuchadnezzar recognized another as "my god," it is doubtful if he regarded Jehovah as the one holy God. **Holy** here seems to mean simply "divine." **My god** is of uncertain identity. It may mean Bel, as in Belteshazzar, or Nabu, as in Nebuchadnezzar, or Marduk, chief patron god of Babylon and of the whole Babylonian pantheon. See Pharaoh's similar words in Gen 41:38.

Four expressions summarize the circumstances at court: *prosperity* in appearance, *trouble* within the king's heart, *frustration* of his efforts, and pathetic *appeal* to God's prophet.

3) Narration of the Dream. 4:10-18.

10,11. A tree. The most useful of all plants, used for shade, food for man and beast, decoration and beauty, fuel, building material. A common symbol in Scripture (e.g., Jud 9:8 ff.; Ps 1:3; Jer 1:11,12; Ezk 15:1 ff.; 31:3-18). Nebuchadnezzar loved the trees of Lebanon. Extant records tell of his traveling to see them and to bring them as lumber to Babylon (Wady Brissa Inscription. Boutflower, *op. cit., in loco*). Cf. Ezk 31:3-18. **12.** Cf. Mt 13:31,32.

14,16. If any natural psychological suggestion from the king's past lay *behind* his dream, it was likely his experience in Lebanon, where he had personally supervised the felling of cedars for transport to his capital. The felling of a tall tree leaves a tremendous impression on the viewer.

For further details, see comments on interpretation in the section to follow. The important thing here is the statement of purpose, which summarizes the spiritual message not only of this chapter but also of the whole book.

17. Young's remark *(Proph. of Dan., in loco)* that the king speaks here as a pagan seems to be in error. The king is reporting the words of a divine messenger. It is better to say that we have a pagan's apparently exact quotation of the words of a divine messenger. The prophecy here, as in chapter 2, is aimed at a pagan king's level of understanding. **This matter.** Better, *the decree*, or, *the decision*. Authorities agree that this is the language of paganism. Possibly the language of astrological decisions is used (Montgomery, BDB). **By the decree of the watchers . . . holy ones.** Cf. v. 13 – "a watcher, a holy one" (RSV). The two names are for the same divine messengers usually known to Hebrews as angels. They are watchful, holy angels. **The most High.** This name is peculiarly appropriate. The pagan king thus assigned to Daniel's God, with whom he identified Daniel, pre-eminence above all gods. The designation can likewise be understood of God's solitary grandeur as the one true God (cf. I Cor 8:4-6). **The basest of men.** The reference is to men of humble station rather than of evil character.

This verse which solemnly declares God's sovereign providential control over the course of human history is the core of the book of Daniel (cf. Isa 40:15 and context; Prov 21:1; Rom 13:1; Acts 17:24-26).

4) The Interpretation of the Dream. 4:19-27.

19. Daniel . . . was astonied. Better, *perplexed*–not because he had difficulty interpreting the dream but because he had none, and was most reluctant to give bad news to the kindly monarch. **One hour.** Probably an expression like our familiar, "for a minute," meaning a moment. **His thoughts troubled** (i.e., frightened) **him.** For Nebuchadnezzar's sake he was frightened. The king's commiseration of Daniel seems to show in what affection he held his Hebrew counselor, in spite of his failure to invite Daniel to his presence earlier. **To them that hate thee.** Some take this and the following clause to indicate Daniel's desire that the distress predicted of the king might be on his enemies and rivals. It is quite possible to interpret his words as stating simply that the events predicted would give comfort to the king's enemies and rivals, and this last seems the more probable sense.

20-22. The tree . . . It is thou, O king. The king himself, conqueror and proud lord of **all the earth,** is symbolized by the tree. **For thy greatness is grown, and reacheth unto heaven, and thy dominion to the end of the earth.** This statement, especially the second and third parts of it, was not literally true, even though it was the declaration of a prophet. Ancient Semites were fond of hyperbole and used it without its being misunderstood by anyone. Nebuchadnezzar's realm, in fact, was smaller geographically than either the Persian or the Greek or the Roman empire. It was, however, very large and included most of the well known parts of the world.

23. The intent of these words was that the king personally would experience a great disaster, losing his position for a period of **seven times.** The Aramaic is no more specific than the English translation in regard to the length of time involved. Inasmuch as days, weeks, or months would hardly have allowed time for the developments of verse 33b, it seems best to follow most commentators in adopting "years" as the meaning.

26. This assured the king of eventual restoration. **27.** Daniel's advice enjoined the outward signs of repentance (see Joel 1:8,14; 2:17,18), no doubt as signs of inner change (see Joel 2:13). Personal impurity **(sins)** as well as oppression of his subjects and conquered enemies **(iniquities)** needed to be stopped. His repentance might bring on divine "repentance" (see Jer 18; Joel 2:12-14).

5) Fulfillment of the Dream. 4:28-33.

29. Twelve months. There had been some merciful "lengthening of thy tranquillity" (v. 27). **The palace of the kingdom of Babylon.** Ancient authors report, as archaeology confirms, that Nebuchadnezzar, in addition to repairing and enlarging older buildings in Babylon, conducted magnificent building projects of his own. A great street which he had rebuilt for processions stretched before him, as well as many temples and many miles of walls. "Now in this palace, having built up lofty substructures of stone, and planted them with all kinds of trees, giving an appearance very closely resembling mountains, he wrought out and prepared the famous Hanging Gardens, to gratify his wife, who was fond of a mountainous country, having been brought up in Media" (Jos *Against Apion* I. 19).

30. Great Babylon, that I have built. See notes on 4:29. Cf. Isa 14:4 ff. "The setting of the scene and the king's self-complaisance in his glorious Babylon are strikingly true to history" (Montgomery, *op. cit.*, p. 243. Also see standard works on the ancient history and archaeology of Babylon. Some of the best are nineteenth century: e.g., Layard, *Nineveh and Babylon;* Rawlinson's various works; George Smith, *Assyrian Discoveries*. Cf. Boutflower, *op. cit.*, for more recent works, as well as Montgomery, *op. cit.*, p. 243). **31-33. A voice from heaven.** The king's last conscious, clear-minded experience turned his attention upward to God in heaven. In the next section it is indicated that *seven years later*, when he returned to sanity, his first action was to respond by looking upward.

For ancient historical evidence of the historicity of this account, the reader is referred to larger standard works. There is *support*, though not *proof*. Various ancient parallels to Nebuchadnezzar's malady have been drawn. If it was a special divine judgment, no natural parallel is necessary, interesting as it might be. Since the ancients often regarded insane people as "possessed" by a god, the king may have been kept in a park and given deferential treatment. Parallels to the king's physical changes have been found in antiquity in the Ahikar story (ANET, pp. 427-430).

6) Recovery and Restoration of the King. 4:34-37.

34. When the man's **understanding returned,** he praised God! Nothing is more insane than human pride. Nothing is more sober and sensible than to praise God. **35-37.** The restoration of the king should encourage men to hope for brighter days ahead, in the providence of God, no matter how low in chastening the Lord may have brought them.

This chapter shows that the heathen are not exempt from Jehovah's moral rule. Moral laws govern the rise and fall of men whether they are related to God in saving grace or not (see also Amos 1:1–2:3).

D. Belshazzar's Feast: A Lesson in Sin and Its Punishment. 5:1-31.

The purpose of this chapter is to give moral instruction rather than historical information. Verses 1,30,31 supply the only significant historical data. The rest is a lesson in sin and its punishment.

Gobryas (Bab. *Gubaru),* general of Cyrus, was at the gates of Babylon at the very moment of the opening of the king's feast. He had diverted the waters of the Euphrates and was marching his men up the bed of the river into the city, which lay on both its banks. The river gates had been left unguarded. Babylon, stocked with supplies for twenty years, was supposedly secure behind massive walls. Nabonidus (Bab. *Nabunaid),* Belshazzar's father, had been worsted in battle by Cyrus' armies, and he was now besieged at Borsippa, not far away. It was no time for alcoholic foolishness!

1) Pleasure, the Pursuit of the Feast. 5:1-4.

1. Belshazzar. Formerly unknown except through this chapter, the king is now well-authenticated by ancient documents (R. P. Dougherty, *Nabonidus and Belshazzar).* **A great feast.** A sensual affair, as the presence of women among the men, unusual in the ancient East, shows (cf. Est 1:9). **Drank wine before the thousand.** Even at public feasts Oriental kings (at least in Persian times) were screened from public sight. This was license unrestrained by convention.

2. Commanded to bring the . . . vessels. For Nebuchadnezzar to take these vessels out of the Jerusalem temple (1:1-3) was according to accepted practice in war. To remove them from the national repository for a drunken feast was sacrilegious. Nebuchadnezzar, the great king, had *real* military exploits to his credit, and to a degree Nabonidus, the king's father had exploits in peaceful pursuits to his credit. The spineless prince could only perform foolish sacrilegious acts to gain notoriety, if not fame. **4.** Belshazzar's behavior was sensual, unrestrained, wild, and sacrilegious. It was also stupid. Gobryas' armies were already inside the city.

2) A Portent, God's Contribution to the Feast. 5:5,6.

5. In the same hour. God spoke suddenly. Time had run out. **Fingers of**

a man's hand. The portent was mysterious. The supernatural was on display. **Upon the plaister.** In the very wall whereon the national memorials may have been written. Ruthless action! God does not care about our patriotic boasts. The **king saw.** It was striking.

3) Perplexity, the Effect of the Divine Visitation. 5:7,8.

7. Astrologers . . . Chaldeans . . . soothsayers. Once more (cf. 2:2-14; 3:8; 4:6,7) these monumental frauds appeared. Not only did they "know not God" (I Cor 1:21) in their "wisdom" but they knew little else (cf. Dan 5:8). **Scarlet.** Better, *purple,* the color of royalty among several ancient peoples and probably with the Babylonians likewise. **A chain of gold.** Cf. Gen 41:42. **Third ruler.** Of uncertain meaning. Some authorities identify it as a word meaning "adjutant" or "officer." The word *taltî* is, however, almost certainly derived from the Aramaic *tᵉlat* (cf. BDB), and **probably means *third* (ruler or part).** Ordinarily only the father of Belshazzar, the besieged Nabonidus, would have had authority to declare a **third ruler.** But for yet an hour or two Belshazzar was *de facto* if not *de jure* supreme monarch, and felt he could confer this honor. No Jew in Palestine in the Maccabean period (second cent., B.C.) could have thus correctly reconstructed the historical situation, as certain critics claim the writer of Daniel did.

4) Pronouncement of Doom, Daniel's Part at the Feast. 5:10-28.

10. The queen. Not the king's wife, but his mother. In polygamous families the grand lady is the husband's mother (cf. reports of Jewish kings' mothers in the OT). This queen was likely a wife of Nabonidus. Perhaps she had also been a young wife of the noted Nebuchadnezzar (cf. Boutflower, *in loco).*

11. Nebuchadnezzar thy father. Nebuchadnezzar was, of course, not the king's immediate male parent. It is unlikely that Nebuchadnezzar was even his grandfather. Probably **father** in a legal sense only, since Nabonidus would have allied himself by marriage with the family of the great Nebuchadnezzar (Boutflower, *in loco).* The queen's repetitious affirmation of the "father" relationship suggests that it was a point of etiquette at court, not a real fact. This kind of etiquette is not unknown in other parts of the Bible (e.g., I Chr 3:17, where Salathiel, the son of Neri, who descended from David through Nathan [Lk 3:27,31] is called the "son" of Jeconiah).

17. The temporal gifts of a king whose time had run out meant little to a saintly prophet of advanced years.

25. MENE, MENE, TEKEL, UPHARSIN. Textual evidence, as well as the following verses, indicates that there is likely a combination of misunderstanding and textual corruption here. The verse should possibly read, using quotation marks: "And this is the writing that was written, 'Mene, Mene, Tekel' and 'Peres.'" The U of **UPHARSIN** is the Aramaic for "and." The PH is an aspiration of P to accommodate the previous vowel sound. The IN is a plural form, likely introduced by some later scribe who connected the word with Persians, for the ending only pluralizes the word. **Mene** is repeated for emphasis. The three words, **Mene, Tekel,** and **Peres,** as they stand, are passive participles, rightly rendered *counted, weighed,* and *divided.* They are also, when left without vowels, viz., MN, TKL, PRS, the names of three ancient weights that might be paralleled with our terms, a pound, an ounce, half a pound. Further, it is possible that the inscription on the wall was in syllabic cuneiform or in ideograms. None of these modes of writing would have been intelligible without a context. Actually, apart from interpretation, their only value was to secure the king's attention so that Daniel could talk to him.

26,28. (Boutflower, Montgomery, and Young are excellent help here.) It is possible that the words interpreted are names of weights or coins as indicated above. If so, then they are a play on words. *Maneh* (Aram.), a weight of fifty shekels, equivalent to about two pounds (see Ezk 45:12), parallels **mene,** which means divided. *Tekel,* a coin or weight, equivalent to the Hebrew *shekel,* suggests **tekel** in the sense of weighed. *Peres* (a half *maneh)* suggests **Peres,** *divided.* It also ominously suggested Persia, which appears in verse 28. **To the Medes and Persians.** This verse proves conclusively that the author of this book believed the successor of the Babylonian kingdom to be a *dual kingdom,* including two national elements. He was not guilty of supposing the second and third stages of empire (chs. 2; 7) to be Median and Persian respectively, but recognized them as Medo-Persian and Grecian respectively. Unbelieving criticism, which would have the author supposing a Babylon, Media, Persia, Greece succession rather than the true Babylon, Medo-Persia, Greece, Rome succession, is "hung" upon this verse.

5) Punishment, the End of the Feast. 5:29-31.

30. Belshazzar's sacrilege, like that of others (II Sam 6:6,7; Lev 10:1,2; I Cor 3:17), required immediate punishment **in that night.** Details of the siege and fall of Babylon had been prophesied long before by Jeremiah (chs. 50; 51). Thus God was fulfilling Isaiah's prophecy regarding Cyrus (Isa 44:24-28; 45).

E. Darius the Mede in the Role of Religious Persecutor: A Lesson in Faith and Prayer. 6:1-28.

The theme of faith and prayer is developed in a story of religious persecution, a theme first mentioned in Scripture at Genesis 4 and continuing to Revelation 20 (see also Mt 10:16-26; 23:33-36; 24:1-28; Jn 21:18,19; Acts 7; 18:2; I Pet 4:12,13; I Jn 3:12; Rev 1:9; 13).

The chapter begins by explaining what a prominent position Daniel held in Babylon (vv. 1-3). Next there is a report of a plot against his life (vv. 4-9). There follows the exemplary prayer of Daniel (vv. 10,11), then a report of the apparent success of the plot (vv. 11-17). The chapter continues with God's amazing answer to the prayer, and the failure of the plot (vv. 18-28).

1) The Prominence of Daniel. 6:1-3.

1 a. It pleased Darius. The same Darius as that represented in 5:31 as the first ruler of Babylon after the Medo-Persian conquest, a man sixty-two years of age. History tells us of no man named Darius who *at this time* ruled in Babylon. Cyrus (1:21; 10:1) was the Persian king in supreme authority at this time, as the Bible (Isa 44:21–45:5; II Chr 36:22, 23; Ezr 1:1-4), secular historians (Herodotus, Berosus, Xenophon), and archaeological evidences (Nabonidus Chronicle, Cyrus Cylinder, etc.) testify. The truth of the narrative may stand without further support, however. Darius obviously was a subking under Cyrus. The language of Dan 5:31 and especially of 9:1 practically requires this. He was local "king over the realm of the Chaldeans" (9:1, i.e., of Babylonia); whereas, Cyrus was "king of Persia" (i.e., of the empire, 10:1). Whether we are to identify Darius with Cyrus himself, Cyaxares, Astyages, or Cambyses of the secular sources, or with Ugbaru or Gubaru of the contemporary records, cannot as yet be regarded as settled, though a very good case has recently been made for Gubaru (John Whitcomb, *Darius the Mede*). Several of the theories mentioned above are now thought to be most unlikely. Faith can wait for further information. We do know that it was common for kings to have two or more names (e.g., II Chr 36:4,8; cf. Jer 22:24).

1b. An hundred and twenty princes (satraps). These are not the heads of the 127 provinces of the grand empire of Ahasuerus (Xerxes, 486–465 B.C.). No geographical divisions are named. Rather, they are 120 assistants to Darius as governor of Babylon. "King" in Aramaic and Hebrew is a rather elastic term covering any ruler from a petty kinglet (e.g., city kings of the book of Joshua) to Nebuchadnezzar (Dan 1:3), Cyrus (10:1), and Ahasuerus (Est 1:2). **2. Three presidents.** Rather, *overseers.* **And the king should have no damage.** The king was concerned for his own financial and material profit, not for the administration of justice. Ancient pagan monarchs had no true conception of government "for the people" (see I Sam 8).

3. Evidently Daniel, with over fifty years of public service behind him, was a prominent international figure, known for integrity; for he was a foreigner, twice removed from Darius, and a holdover from the enemy administration. This suggests the value of age in positions of high responsibility (Prov 16:10-16). But in Daniel's very prominence lay his peril, because of the envy and jealousy of others.

2) The Plot Against Daniel. 6:4-9.

4. Envy was at work (cf. Prov 27:4; Joseph's brethren, Acts 7:9; Joab, II Sam 20:4-10; Jesus' enemies, Mt 27:18). **5.** Daniel's well-known integrity made him a sure target. It is known in advance what an honest man will do in certain circumstances. Control the circumstances and you control him!

6-9. The strength of the plan lay in taking advantage of Darius' vanity. The address and suggestions of the men all appealed to the king's vainglorious pagan desires. As a man sixty-two years old, he knew that if he was to achieve glory, it was now or never! Their claim that "all" the counselors had been consulted was a lie, for Daniel had not been consulted. **Into the den of lions.** The Persians, being Zoroastrians, held fire to be sacred. Hence for them it would have been improper to cremate or to execute by fire. Zoroastrians (Parsees) continue to the present the exposure of their dead to carrion-eating birds.

3) The Prayer of Daniel. 6:10,11.

God's own estimate of Daniel and his reputation in heaven make his prayers worthy of our attention and emulation (cf. Ezk 14:14; Dan 10:11). The sublimity of his courageous faith is recognized by all who enter sympathetically into the situation. He maintained his pious habits and his beliefs—as **he did aforetime**—in the face of an absolutely impossible predicament—**when Daniel knew that the writing was signed.**

10. When he knew. The prayer, in the first place, was courageous (cf. Hus at Constance, A.D. 1415). **Went into his house . . . and prayed.** It was, secondly, truly pious, without mock heroics in public. There was no parade of religion. Daniel only did what he knew was right (cf. Jas 1:27; Mt 6:5ff.). Thirdly, it was prayer according to Scripture. As Moses, in Deut 28:36-68, had predicted the Jews' captivity, so Solomon's words in II Chr 6:36-39 had prescribed their worship in captivity. Daniel 6:10, 11 must be understood in the indispensable light of these passages.

Eight specific elements of true prayer appear in the comparison. (1) *Faith*. Daniel believed the Word, for he obeyed it and regulated his prayers by it. The prayer of the exiles was to be directed "toward their land," and in facing **toward Jerusalem** Daniel showed respectful faith. (2) *Worship*. Solomon prescribed "toward the city," i.e., Jerusalem (Deut 12:5-7; I Chr 11:4-9; 13:1-14; 15:25-29; II Chr 3:1,2; 5:1-14; 7:1-3. Cf. Jn 4:20-22; Acts 4:12). Daniel could not worship literally in the Holy City, but his posture showed that he wished to do so; and in spirit he did do so. (3) The ground of *atonement by blood*. The "house . . . built for my name" was the center of the sacrificial ritual. Daniel's posture recognized that (cf. Heb 10:19-22). (4) *Humility*. This is indicated by the marked emphasis on the kneeling posture (cf. Lk 18:13,14). (5) *Regularity*. **Three times a day** (cf. Ps 55:16,17). (6) *Petition*. **And prayed** or *and kept on praying*. The word *ṣᵉlā'* means "to bow in entreaty." (7) *Thanksgiving*. **Gave thanks,** etc. (cf. Phil 4:6). (8) *Constancy*. **As he did aforetime.**

11. Then these men assembled, and found Daniel praying. Here, as in verse 6, **assembled** has the sense of tumultous assembly. In the earlier case they mobbed the king with excited suggestions, and in the second they noisily interrupted an aged saintly public servant in his private devotions. Neither act was to their credit.

4) The Apparent Success of the Plot. 6:12-17. Darius found himself bound and gagged by his own law. In this manner he showed that his authority was quite inferior in nature to that of Nebuchadnezzar, whose person was above the law. The government of Darius came nearer to the democratic ideal, but it was less absolute than that of the Chaldeans. In that sense it was inferior, and so fulfilled what had been predicted of it by the silver portion of the image prophecy of chapter 2. Note that the king's fondness for Daniel did not fail, and that Daniel's faith inspired the king to believe also.

5) The Amazing Answer to Daniel's Prayer. 6:18-28. If Daniel prayed for himself, then verses 21-23 describe the answer; if for the king, then verse 16 of the earlier section shows God's work in his heart; if for God's glory, then verses 24-28 give the answer. The king's Zoroastrian faith was the nearest that paganism ever came to Jewish ethical monotheism. This statement reads almost as if he had "come across." God was glorified by the destruction of His enemies, by the king's confession, and by His servant's reward.

F. A Vision of Four Beasts, the Ancient of Days, and the Son of Man: The Conflict of Christ and Antichrist. 7:1-28.

Three important changes begin in this chapter. Up to chapter 7 the material is mainly historical. Henceforth it is mainly predictive. Heretofore Daniel has been God's agent in revelation, interpreting others' dreams. Hereafter, an angel interprets Daniel's own dreams and visions (7:16; 8:15-17; 9:20-23; 10:10-14). Heretofore the author has reported in the third person; hereafter he writes in the first, giving a much more intimate report of his experiences.

A transition from prophecy centered in Gentile nations to Jewish-centered prophecy takes place with the entrance of the "holy people" (rendered "saints" vv. 18,22,25). The Jews are the center of interest to the book's end.

The same succession of kingdoms that was found in chapter 2 appears here—four Gentile empires, then the kingdom of Messiah. The view that chapter 7 describes only events in the Mediterranean area at the close of this present age is ably set forth by G. H. Lang *(The Histories and Prophecies of Daniel)* in premillennial perspective. The view that the four kingdoms are (1) Babylon, (2) Medo-Persia, (3) Greece, and (4) the Greek successors of Alexander, and that the fifth is Messiah's kingdom is defended in reverent but non-millennial perspective by Moses Stuart *(Commentary on Daniel)* and in reverent amillennial perspective by the Roman Catholic work of C. Lattey *(The Book of Daniel).* After the usual historical setting (v. 1), there follow details of a series of visions (vv. 2-14,21,22), the new method of interpreting dreams and visions (vv. 15, 16), the interpretation (vv. 17-20, 23-27), and a concluding personal statement (v. 28).

1) Historical Setting. 7:1.

1. The first year of Belshazzar. About fourteen years before the events of chapter 5. It is likely that Babylonian weakness was already beginning to show through. **Dream and visions.** Not always clearly distinguished. Dreams are experiences in sleep; visions may occur in a waking condition, or, as here, may be successive "scenes" or stages in a dream. **Then he wrote the dream, and told the sum of the matters.** He recorded it immediately (**then** or *thereupon,* or *at that* time, as the Aramaic *'ĕdayin* prefixed by *b* emphatically requires). It was *written,* contrary to current oral-transmission-of-prophecy theories (see Isa 30:8; cf. 8:1,16; Hab 2:2; Rev 1:19; 14:13; 21:5). It was a summary only, for the **sum** (Aram. *head)* or substance of the material was recorded. Similar use of Hebrew *rō'sh* appears at Ps 119: 160 *(sum,* ASV) and 137:6 *(chief).* (See Stuart, *Comm., in loco.)*

2) Details of the Visions. 7:2-14,21,22.

2. The four winds of the heaven. Usage elsewhere indicates that the winds represent God's providential power by which he controls the nations, setting them in commotion or settling them in peace (Rev 7:1-3; Jer 23:19; 49:36; 51:1; Zech 6:1-6, 7:14). *Rûaḥ* may be rendered either "spirit" or "wind," and is here purposely ambiguous. (Note further Dan 4:17; I Tim 2:1,2.) Jerome thought the winds represented angels. **Upon the great sea.** Not just any sea, but, as Lang has ably demonstrated *(Histories and Prophecies of Daniel,* p. 86ff.), the Mediterranean (see esp. Num 34:6,7; Josh 1:4; 9:1; 15:11,12,47; 23:4; Ezk 47:10-15, 19,20; 48:28).

3. Four great beasts came up from the sea. Hence, the beasts, later described, are connected with the Mediterranean area. Likewise, as the prophetic, symbolical use of "sea" indicates, they arise with turmoil, unrest, boisterous talk, etc., accompaniments of so-called diplomacy (Isa 57:20; Jer 6:23; 50:42; 51:42; Rev 17:15; cf. Lk 21:25). Nations, and their rise, are not viewed complimentarily in Scripture (Isa 34:2; 40:15-17; Joel 3: 2; cf. "the world," I Jn 2:15ff.; 5:19; II Pet 3:10). **Diverse one from another.** Each nation has its own special characteristics, though all share in common their brutal, irrational, bestial character. How different this inward view of the prophet from the glittering dignity of the pagan Nebuchadnezzar's dream image!

4. The **lion** symbolizes Babylon here and also in Jer 4:6,7. The **eagle's wings** speak of swiftness, as the lion of strength. These are natural symbols scarcely needing explanation (cf. II Sam 1:23; Jer 49:19-22; Ezk 17:3-24). **5.** The **bear** is an apt symbol of the Medo-Persian kingdom. Strength and ferocity figure in almost every Biblical use of the bear. The ponderous bulk fits the massive Persian armies. Xerxes is said to have moved two and one-half million men to attack Greece. Duality may be suggested by reference to the beast's **side. 6.** The sinewy four-winged **leopard** speaks, without doubt, of Alexander's Grecian (Macedonian) kingdom. Rulership passed from Nineveh (Assyria) to Babylon in 612 B.C.; from Babylon to Persia in 539 B.C., and from Darius III to Alexander in 331 B.C.

7,8. As in chapter 2, the fourth stage of empire is Roman. Since this kingdom must prevail until the destruction of Antichrist (the **little horn)** and the establishment of the eternal, final, visible kingdom of Christ (cf. Rev 19:11–20:4), it must be regarded as prevailing today. The ten-fold form of the final stage, perhaps suggested by the ten toes of chapter 2, is clearly taught here and confirmed by Rev 17:3ff. Later in the chapter the **little horn is identified with** final Antichrist.

9-14. This throne scene is fully elaborated in Revelation, chapters 4–20. Evidently the five verses of Daniel cover the same ground as the seventeen chapters of Revelation. It is a judgment scene wherein the **Ancient of days**—none other than "the high and lofty One that inhabiteth eternity" (Isa 57:15)—takes possession of the earth's kingdoms through **the Son of man**—a name our Lord clearly claimed for himself (Mt 24:30). The dramatic action whereby the beast's kingdom is violently taken away fits the many Biblical predictions of the manner in which our Lord will judge the nations at the close of this age.

21,22. Though separated by details of interpretation (vv. 15-20), these two verses belong to the vision itself rather than to the interpretation. **The saints of the most High . . . the saints possessed the kingdom.** Nothing is more sure than that all saints of all ages will share in Christ's ultimate triumph in his kingdom. But this passage is affirming only a part of that truth. The perspective of the book, the meaning of the words, and the context here limit the application to Daniel's people, Israel, clearly identified in 10:14 (the equivalent Hebrew expression is used). "By the 'people of the saints of the Most High' to whom dominion is to be given (Dan 7:18-27), Daniel evidently could only understand the people of Israel, as distinguished from the heathen nations and kingdoms, which were to rule up till then (2:44); nor have we, according to strict exegesis, a right to apply the expression to any other nation; hence we cannot apply it immediately to the Church . . . The prophet's words refer to the re-establishment of the kingdom to Israel" (C. A. Auberlen, *The Prophecies of Daniel and the Revelation of St. John,* pp. 216, 217).

3) The Method of Interpretation. 7:15,16.

Very strangely, an angel who is himself a part of the vision but likewise a real personal being, later identified as Gabriel, becomes the interpreter here and throughout the remainder of the book (cf. 8:16; 9:21). Though treated briefly by Daniel, this is an important feature.

4) Interpretation of the Visions. 7:17-20,23-27.

Except as noted in remarks at the beginning of this chapter, it is generally agreed that the succession of four Gentile dominions to be followed by the Messianic kingdom is the same here as that contemplated in chapter 2. But beginning at verse 19, the prophecy advances far beyond the dream of Nebuchadnezzar, to give details of prediction concerning final Antichrist and the relations the people of God will have with him in eschatological times.

19. I would know the truth of the fourth beast. This beast is of special interest because it produces the "little horn," Antichrist, and is the final form of Gentile dominion (see vv. 23-25 and cf. comments on 2:40-43). **20. And of the ten horns.** See verse 24. Ten kings shall arise in the final stage of the fourth (Roman) kingdom and shall reign contemporaneously (not successively; cf. Rev 17:12ff. as further explanation). **Of that horn that had eyes, and a mouth,** etc. All interpreters—Jewish, Christian, unbelievers—agree that this is Antichrist. Rationalists who say this was written in the Maccabean era insist that he is Antiochus Epiphanes (about 165 B.C.) and that our author, though mistaken, thought the Messianic kingdom would follow immediately.

24-26. Note herein twelve facts about Antichrist: (1) He will not *create* a tenfold confederacy; he will *absorb* one (v. 24). (2) He will be just **another** king—"another . . . horn" (v. 8), and he will be mortal (Rev 13:2; II Thess 2:9). It will be the Satanic power behind him that will make him significant. (3) He will be obscure at first—"little" (Dan 7:8). (4) His march to power will begin with his conquest of three kingdoms (v. 8; cf. v. 24). (5) Yet something about him will be special (**diverse from the first** [ten], v. 24). See Rev 13:15; II Thess 2:4. Many extraordinary events will be connected with him (Rev 13:16,17; II Thess 2:9,10). (6) He will be very intelligent—"eyes of a man" (Dan 7:8). (7) He will be an orator of ability (v. 8). (8) His appearance will be striking (v. 20; cf. Isa 53:2,3). (9) He will be a blasphemer

(Dan 7:25; cf. Rev 13:5,6). (10) He will seek to make his accession a new epoch (Dan 7:25, **change times**). (11) He will seek to destroy Israel (v. 25a; cf. 9:26,27). (12) His time will be short (v. 25), *a time,* [two] *times, and the dividing* [half] *of time* (cf. Rev 11:2; 13:5; Dan 9:25; 12:7-12).

Evidence for a Premillennial View Herein: (1) Messiah's kingdom follows Antichrist's appearance (here described in personal rather than institutional terms), and destruction. The person has not yet appeared. This appears to make post- and a-millennial schemes identifying the Church with the Kingdom unfeasible. (2) The kingdom of Messiah here follows the Gentile kingdoms; it is at no time contemporary with them. It must, therefore, be still future. (3) The kingdom of Christ succeeds a final form of Gentile dominion which has not yet appeared. (4) The Messianic kingdom is external in aspect here, not a kingdom in men's hearts, as Church-Kingdom theories require. (5) This kingdom is in some sense Israelitish (cf. vv. 7,22,25,27 with 8:24). The "saints" or holy people referred to here are Israel and no other. The Church is not a Jewish kingdom.

III. The Hebrew Nation: Its Relation to Gentile Dominion and Its Future in the Plan of God. 8:1–12:13.

A. A Ram, a Goat, and a Little Horn: Israel in Conflict with the OT Antichrist. 8:1-27. This chapter repeats much of the prediction of chapter 2, and especially of chapter 7. It adds details regarding the Medo-Persian and Grecian periods. After a historical introduction (v. 1), the vision of a ram and a goat is described (vv. 2-14), followed by interpretation (vv. 15-26), and a conclusion (v. 27).

1) Historical Introduction. 8:1. This vision came two years after that of chapter 7 (cf. 7:1). It came when the exiled Jews needed encouragement to believe God really would restore them, as he had promised (Jer 25:11,12).

2) The Visions. 8:2-14.

2. I saw in a vision . . . at Shushan. His presence in Shushan, a city 250 miles east of Babylon, was in vision only (cf. Ezk 8:1-3; II Cor 12:2ff.; contrast Jer 13:1-7). Shushan was later a capital *over* Babylon in the Persian Empire. **The palace.** A structure yet future, a Persian palace, likely (cf. Rev 20; 21; and John's vision of a coming city). It was likely the palace of Xerxes a century later (486–465 B.C.), one of the most magnificent of all antiquity, covering two and one-half acres (cf. works on archaeology). Events of Esther (cf. Est 1:2) took place there.

3. There stood before the river a ram which had two horns. The duality of the Medo-Persian empire is again suggested (cf. pair of breasts and of arms in the image of chapter 2). **The higher came up last.** Though Persia was more prominent in the union, it was the younger kingdom. In 550 B.C. Cyrus, a Persian, builder of Pasargadae, twenty-five miles north of Persepolis, the older capital, rebelled against the Medes, who had been dominant, and became lord of the dual kingdom. This took place at about the time Daniel was prophesying.

4. Two books of Herodotus' *Histories* describe the events summarized here. The Persian Empire suffered no serious set-back until 490, when a determined little army of Athenians at Marathon defeated the forces of Darius (father of Xerxes, the Ahashuerus of *Esther*). A second defeat, this time in a naval battle in the Gulf of Aegina (above Athens), came to Xerxes ten years later. But the **ram** indeed **became great** with a magnificence still remembered and imitated today.

5. An he goat came from the west. Observe that both animals are relatively mild domestic farm animals rather than the ravenous bear and leopard of chapter 7. This seems to be because, as regards Israel, both were in the main relatively mild. As regards one another, they were vicious (see Ezk 34:17 and context, also Zech 10:3). As the metals of the image became progressively stronger, so the buck goat is stronger than the ram of sheep. The clean sweep of Alexander's armies is predicted in the latter part of Dan 8:7. His small swift army, with its devastating phalanx formation, swept through Asia Minor, Syria, Egypt, and finally Mesopotamia (334–331 B.C.). After that his armies advanced eastward to India, then turned back again toward the west.

8. Alexander died in the thirty-third year of his age, of fever and alcohol, at Babylon. In the subsequent twenty years, his winnings were divided into four parts among four of his military successors. Two of the resultant divisions —Egypt under the Ptolemies (the last of whom was the famous Cleopatra) and Syria under the Seleucids, the historic kings of the South and the North, respectively—are of importance as neighbors of the Jews. They figure prominently in chapter 11.

9-14. These verses predict the sad conflict of the Jews, in the second half of the second century B.C. (after their return from exile), with the Seleucid king, Antiochus IV, called *Epiphanes* ("Magnificent") by friends, *Epimanes* ("Madman") by enemies. Many evangelical interpreters see here a type of Antichrist and his conflict with Christ and his people in the end time. This may very well be (see below). The 2,300 **days** is literally, *evening-mornings*, i.e., **evening and morning daily burnt** sacrifices, and so refers to only 1,150 days. It seems to refer to a period in 168–165 B.C. when the Temple was desecrated by pagan sacrifices.

3) Interpretation of the Visions. 8:15-26.

15,16. Gabriel means *hero of God.* (See 9:21; 10:13; Lk 1:19. Cf. Dan 7:16 and note.)

17,18. That a man of Daniel's righteous character should so react demonstrates the moral gulf separating God and the holy beings of heaven from mankind. See also 10:9,15,17; Ex 3:6; Isa 6:5; Ezk 1:28; Acts 9:3,4; Rev 1:17. Daniel had reason to fear death (see Ex 33:20; Jud 13:22).

19. The terms, **the end** and **the indignation** (cf. 11:36), suggest that there is more here than history relating to the time of Antiochus and the Maccabees. This observation lends support to the typical interpretation suggested above. It is not uncommon to find a near, literal view combined with a far, typical view within the scope of a particular prophecy.

23-26. These verses add specific details to the portrait of Antiochus. The Jews could hardly fail to recognize him when he appeared. This prophecy may well have been the very divine means used to carry the faithful through those hard days. Hebrews 11:34-37 memorializes their heroism.

4) Historical Conclusion. 8:27. **Fainted.** Literally, *was done in.* He later went back to work, evidently pondering what he saw.

B. The Prophecy of the Seventy Weeks: Israel's Future in the Plan of God. 9:1–27. This prophecy is unique in Scripture in that it actually sets up a sort of time schedule of coming events. The nearest approach to it is Jeremiah's prophecy of seventy years (see below). The schedule relates to events in the future of the Israelites. After devoting brief attention to the historical setting (vv. 1,2), Daniel proceeds to report an intensive season of prayer (vv. 3-19), followed by the arrival of an angelic mesenger of prophecy (vv. 20-23). The very important prophecy of the seventy weeks comes at the end (vv. 24-27).

1) The Historical Setting of the Prophecy. 9:1,2.

1. In the first year of Darius. That is, 539/538 B.C., sixty-seven years after Daniel's transportation in the summer of 605 B.C.; about fifty-nine years from the beginning of King Jehoiachin's captivity (II Chr 36:9,10; Ezk 1:1 ff.); **a bit less** than fifty years from the final destruction of Jerusalem in 586 B.C. This explains Daniel's interest in Jerusalem (Dan 9:2). He wondered if the time was up. **Made king over the realm of the Chaldeans.** Daniel does not confuse him with Cyrus. He was **made** king, i.e., appointed, and that not over the Medo-Persian empire but over Babylonia only.

2. The number of the years. The reference seems to be to Jer 25:11,12, which says, "when seventy years are accomplished . . . I will punish the king of Babylon." That king had already been punished; so Daniel knew it was time for the **desolations of Jerusalem** also to be ended. **Seventy** is a round number; it was actually sixty-eight. Cf. Lk 21:26.

2) The Exemplary Prayer of Daniel. 9:3-19.

In the appreciation of a poem, play, or painting, the greatest value is to be received by simply taking the creation as a whole. Just so Daniel's prayer should be studied as a whole. The prayer was a providential means of accomplishing what was already determined (see Isa 42:24,25; 43:14,15; 48:9-11; Jer 49:17-20. Cf. Jer 50:4,5,20).

The names of Deity employed are significant. Daniel reminds God that both Jerusalem (Dan 9:18) and the Jews (v. 19) are **called by thy name.** He addresses the Lord as Lord God *(ʾᵃdōnāy ʾᵉlôhîm,* v. 3) and LORD God *(Yahweh ʾᵉlôhîm,* v. 4). See a Bible dictionary on names of God. Daniel's conception of God shows balance between **the great and dreadful God** (v. 4; cf. Isa 6:1 ff.) and a God of **mercies and forgiveness** (v. 9; cf. Ex 20:5,6).

The problems of interpretation here are not difficult. Note what light this chapter casts on prayer (Mt 6:5-18; Lk 11:1-13). Observe: (1) Daniel's prayer was a *persistent,* undespairing interest (Dan 6:1-10; cf. 9:1-3). In sixty-eight years of waiting, the prophet had not lost hope. (2) He had *determination* (v. 3; cf. Lk 9:51). (3) He was *importunate* (Dan 9:3. See also Mt 9:27; 15:22; 17:15; 20:30,31. Cf. Lk 16:24; 17:13; 18:38,39). (4) He showed *humility.* Note how he associated himself with his people in their sins (cf. Lk 18:10-14; II Cor 12:7). (5) He made *confession* (esp. Dan 9:4,5. Cf. Ps 32:5; 51:4; Jas 5:16). (6) He displayed *submission* (Dan 9:14) and engaged in (7) *petition* and (8) *intercession.*

Like Moses (Ex 32:10-14; cf. Ezk 14:14,20), Daniel as intercessor carried on argument with the Almighty, on several grounds: (1) God's people were a reproach among the heathen (Dan 9:16). (2) God was known to be merciful (v. 18). (3) God's reputation was at stake (v. 19).

3) The Angelic Messenger of the Prophecy. 9:20-23. Important to the continuity of the book is the fact that throughout the second half of Daniel the revealer is the same individual (cf. 7:16,23; 8:16; 9:21; 10:5ff. and comments). Note also that here is an *immediate* answer to prayer, whereas in chapter 10 there is a long *delayed* answer, both being in the will and plan of God.

4) The Great Prophecy of the Seventy Weeks. 9:24-27.

(For extended treatment, see R. D. Culver, *Daniel and the Latter Days,* pp. 135-160.) This prophecy is referred to by Josephus: "We believe that Daniel conversed with God; for he did not only prophesy of the future, as did the other prophets, but he also determined the time of their accomplishment" *(Antiq.* X. xi. 7). Jerome reports the Christian interpretations current in his time. They were as various as are ours today, although then, as now, all felt that the prophecy was of Christ. At least one writer (Hippolytus) felt that it reached to the times of the Antichrist of the end time, as is asserted and defended in this commentary *(Jerome's Comm. on Daniel,* trans. Archer, p. 103. See also Froom, *The Prophetic Faith of the Fathers,* I, 277. Hippolytus, "Treatise on Christ and Antichrist," *Ante-Nicean Fathers,* V, 213).

24. Seventy weeks are determined. The Hebrew word for **week** *(shābuʿîm),* "sevens," means "sevens" of years. This interpretation was the common one in antiquity. Daniel had been thinking of a multiple of "seven" of years (9:1,2; cf. Jer 25:11,12). He knew that multiple (seventy years) to be an epoch of judgment for 490 years of violated sabbaths ($490 \div 7 = 70$. See II Chr 36:21). Furthermore, there was a common "seven" of years employed in civil and religious reckoning (Lev 25, esp. v. 8) quite as aptly called a "week" as the seven of days. Not only so, but when weeks of days are intended (Dan 10:2,3), the Hebrew for "days" *(yamîm),* is added to "weeks" *(shābuʿîm).* This apparently indicates a break from the use of chapter 9. More importantly, if any literal meaning is to be attached to the weeks, no period less than weeks of years meets the contextual demands. **Upon thy people and upon thy holy city.** The people are Jews; the city is Jerusalem. "Here I have rendered *al* upon . . . in order to approach nearer the true idea of the Hebrew; for *al* often designates the idea of *on* or *upon* in the sense of what is burdensome, or it is used in what the lexicons style a hostile sense . . . . Plainly it is so here. The seventy weeks comprise the special burden, the trials, the troubles, through which Israel must pass, before the Great Deliverer will make his appearance, or in the language of the remainder of the verse, before sin will be thoroughly subdued and expiated, and righteousness introduced in the full measure often predicted" (Stuart, *Commentary,* p. 268). It is this fact, the Jerusalem-Jewish reference of the prophecy, that renders improbable any of the larger "Church" and "redemption" interpretations.

Six accomplishments of the 490 years are predicted:

(1) **To finish the transgression.** "Finish" (Heb. *lᵉkallēʾ)* means "to complete," not

"to atone," as is sometimes asserted. The kind of transgressions Daniel had been confessing for his people were to come to an end. That has not yet, two and a half millenniums later, occurred.

(2) **To make an end of sins.** Literally, *to seal up*. This word (as in Job 9:7; 37:7) means to bring under full restraint. Cf. the sealing of Satan's prison to restrain him (Rev 20:1-3).

(3) **To make reconciliation for iniquity** *(lᵉkap-pēr 'āwōn)* Calvary's reconciliation will become effective for Daniel's people when again, "in that Day" of Messiah's second advent, they look on Him "whom they have pierced" (Zech 12:10; cf. Rev 1:7) and shall in repentance believe on Him (Jer 50:4,5,17-20).

The first three items of accomplishment are negative. The remaining three are positive:

(4) **To bring in everlasting righteousness.** This will be effected by inward moral transformation (Jer 31:33,34). **(5) To seal up the vision and prophecy** (Heb. *prophet).* When the people cease sinning, the disciplinary oracles of prophets will no longer be needed (Jer 31:34). (6) **To anoint the most Holy** *(most holy place,* ASV marg.). Most commentators, even many amillennialists (e.g., Keil and Leupold), to whom this passage is somewhat of an embarrassment, feel that this refers to a renewed Temple, anointed like the Tabernacle of old, following the results enumerated in the five promises preceding (see Ezk 40:1-7; Isa 4:2-6). The nature of worship in such a temple is problematical in view of the end of the ritual system (see Epistle to the Hebrews; Col 2:14-17). But this problem should not interfere with acceptance of this prediction.

25. From the going forth of the commandment to restore. Though the decree was made in heaven, it would be made manifest on earth in some human king's edict permitting the return and restoration. The preferred view is that of Africanus (second and third centuries) that this refers to the decree of Artaxerxes Longimanus (465–423? B.C.) made in 445/444 B.C. (Neh 2). The language of Daniel fits this better than it fits the decree of Cyrus (Isa 44:28, in context; Ezr. 1:1-4). **Unto the Messiah the Prince**. Opinions are nearly unanimous that this is Christ our Lord. **Messiah** is the Hebrew word meaning *anointed*, rendered *Christos* in Greek and transliterated *Christus* in Latin, from which we derive "Christ." Some official presentation, such as his baptism and the formal beginning of his ministry, or his triumphal entry, appears to be predicted. **Shall be seven weeks, and threescore and two weeks.** This translation best renders the Hebrew and has the weight of centuries of Christian tradition and translation behind it. The reasoning and evidence behind the RSV, which renders this clause quite incomprehensible, is most obscure, though the effect—to make the prophecy focus on Antiochus rather than on Christ—is plain enough. The Berkeley Version is no better. Both seem to destroy the essential reference to Christ in this verse.

As a matter of fact, 7 plus 62 equals 69; 69 x 7 = 483. From 444 B.C. to about 30 A.D., the general period of Christ's ministry is 470 plus years—so close to the specified 483 that without further refinement the correspondence is quite convincing—and as precise in proportion as the 70 years of Jeremiah's prophecy, really only about 68 years. Inasmuch as Christ presented himself officially as "Messiah-Prince" only once (Zech 9:9; cf. Mt 21:5. Contrast Mt 16:20; Lk 9:20,21) at the beginning of his last week, those interpreters who favor the Triumphal Entry for the close of the 69 weeks appear to be on the right track.

(Sir Robert Anderson's work, *The Coming Prince,* which seeks to reduce the prophecy to mathematical precision, is most convincing. In view, however, of the present state of NT studies in relation to the chronology of the life of our Lord and especially the date of the crucifixion, commitment to that view is a most risky matter. Anderson's evidences for the termini *a quo* and *ad quem* are still most respectable even if his mathematics is less than absolute demonstrative proof of inspiration.)

26. And after the threescore and two weeks (ASV). It is most important to observe that certain events are said to be **and after** (Heb. *wᵉ'aḥᵃrê)* **the sixty-two** weeks (plus, of course, the seven, or sixty-nine in all). The Hebrew word does not mean "then" or "at that time," as do certain other words (cf. 12:1). Nor does the prophecy at all place the next event *in* the seventieth week. It places it *after* the sixty-ninth. **Shall Messiah be cut off, but not for himself** (or, *and shall have nothing,* ASV): **and the people of the prince that shall come shall destroy the city and the sanctuary.**

It is agreed by almost all evangelical interpreters that these two events, the cutting off of the Messiah *(Anointed One)* and the destruction of the sanctuary refer to the crucifixion of Christ and the destruction of Jerusalem by the Romans. These two events were separated by a period of nearly forty years (29–70 A.D.). Yet, in the literary order of the passage, they are both *after* the sixty-ninth week and *before* the final "one week" mentioned in the next verse. Thus the very syntax, grammar, and word-meaning indicate a gap in the succession of the seventy weeks.

Other important reasons for supposing a gap here are: (1) Jesus placed the culminating week, with its "abomination" in the times of final Antichrist, just before His second advent (Mt 24:15). (2) Daniel 7:25, which describes what appear to be the very same events as those of 9:27, the seventieth week, is certainly a prophecy of the times of final Antichrist. (3) The period of three and one-half *times* or years (the second half-week of v. 27) is often mentioned elsewhere in Scripture and always in an eschatological setting (Rev 11:2,3; 12:6, 14). (4) The six things to be accomplished in the seventy weeks (see Dan 9:24 and comments) require the second advent of Christ, and the restoration and conversion of Israel.

These considerations show that the idea of a gap in the weeks at this point is a matter of exegesis. Considerations of theology are not primarily involved. It is not this author's opinion that the Church is a mere provisional consideration thrust into this hiatus or gap. Both 'dispensational' and 'covenantal' theologians, doubtless, find more in this prophecy than is properly there. Let us stay by what the passage says. C. F. Keil *(Comm., in loco)* is correct in asserting that the **prince is said to be** ***coming (hābbā')***, because he has already been introduced and discussed in the prophecy of chapter 7 as the final Antichrist. The Romans who destroyed Jerusalem (A.D. 70) were his **people** because they and he belong to the fourth stage (the Roman) of world empire (chs. 2; 7).

27. And he shall confirm the covenant with many for one week *(make a firm covenant,* ASV). The language *(higbîr,* from *gābar,* "be strong") does not signify confirmation of a covenant but causation of a firm covenant. *And he shall cause to prevail* is an excellent translation. The most natural antecedent for **he**, the subject of the clause, is the wicked "prince" of verse 26. This is the nearest noun in grammatical agreement, and it fits the sense. The **many** here, as elsewhere, is a reference to the Hebrew people, the subject of discussion throughout chapter 9 (cf. vv. 2,12,18,19, esp. 24, "thy people . . . thy holy city"). Evidently the covenant is to be made between Antichrist and Israel when the Jews are back in their homeland in the last days. The exact nature of the covenant is unknown.

The evil and destructive events described in the remainder of this verse should be interpreted as summary information concerning the final "time of Jacob's trouble" (Jer 30:7 and context) set forth rather more fully in Dan 12:1 ff.; II Thess 2; Rev 13; 14; and other passages.

C. The Final Vision: Israel Through the Centuries and at the Consummation in the Hands of Enemies and in the Hands of God. 10:1–12:13. The last three chapters of Daniel constitute one unit of prophecy. The "dates" at 11:1 and 12:1 do not announce new oracles, as does similar information at the beginning of other chapters.

Chapter 10 is the record of an introductory vision, corresponding in the structure of the section with the first two verses of chapter 9. Chapter 11, down to verse 35, relates to events of long ago that transpired mainly in the Grecian period after the death of Alexander and culminated with Antiochus Epiphanes' persecution of the Jews. From 11:36 to the end of chapter 12, the prediction is of end-time events.

Throughout this section Daniel is filling in details of the picture sketched in his earlier prophecies. Chapter 2 gave the grand outline; chapter 7 renewed it from another point of view, enlarging upon the final end-time stage of the fourth kingdom and the kingdom of Messiah. The future of the Hebrews ("saints" or "holy people") is barely introduced. Chapter 8 enlarged upon Jewish fortunes in the period of Medo-Persia and Greece, concentrating on Antiochus Epiphanes and the Maccabean conflict. Chapter 9 presented a sketch of the whole future of Israel and Jerusalem. Now this last oracle, chapters 10 to 12, fills in further details of Israel's future, concentrating both on the Antiochus epoch and on the questions of "last things": the Great Tribulation, the resurrection of the dead, final rewards and punishments.

These final chapters also report a marvelous culmination in the growing spiritual experience of God's prophet. First, he only interpreted another's dream by means of a dream of his own (ch. 2). Later, he interpreted further dreams and experiences of Nebuchadnezzar and Belshazzar (chs. 4; 5). Chapter 7 reports visions of his own — truly grand spiritual experiences. The story of chapter 8 reports a spiritual "transportation" whereby he received, in a land far from home, a vision of the future as it would affect his nation. Next is reported actual physical sight of the angelic Gabriel in Daniel's own room. Now the prophet sees with his eyes one like the very Son of God in his physical presence.

1) Circumstances of the Revelation. 10:1-4.

1. The date explains Daniel's mourning. By Cyrus' third year, the work begun on the restoration of the Temple (Ezr 1–3) had been stopped (Ezr 4:4,5). **2,3.** These verses show that old age may be a time of intense spiritual activity and accomplishment (cf. Lk 2:36,37). This was temporary abstinence, not asceticism (see Mk 7:14-23; Acts 10:9-18; I Tim 4:1-5).

2) The Revelation and Its Effects. 10:5-9.

In favor of identifying the **man** of verse 5 with Gabriel, the angel who later talks with Daniel, is the absence of any clear categorical indication otherwise. In favor of identifying the **man** with the preincarnate Christ are: (1) correspondence of language with 7:13; (2) similarities to Ezekiel's vision of Him (Ezk 1:26, in context); (3) similarity to John's vision of Christ (Rev 1:12-20); (4) His standing, later in the vision, "above the waters," set apart, where even angels dare not stand (Dan 12:6, ASV); (5) the manner in which angels appeal to Him as having superior knowledge (12:6).

The effect of this sight on Daniel should make men cautious about seeking or praying for unusual supernatural experiences of the presence of God beyond those experiences ordinarily granted to sincere believers.

3) Strengthening of the Prophet for His Work. 10:10-12,15-19.

Suggestions for the believer's private devotional life: (1) *Fear* is not necessarily detrimental (contrast Rom 3:18). "God wishes our fears to restrain us like a bridle" (Calvin). (2) Prayer may be with *fervor* when the will of God is clear. The angel only confirmed Daniel's knowledge (cf. I Jn 5:14). (3) Deep *humility* is a proper accompaniment of prayer in view of God's sovereignty. (4) Fear, fervor, and humility may be joined with *confidence* or boldness, for one comes to his *own* God in Christ (cf. "thy God," Dan 10:12). See also Heb 11:6; Jas 1:6,7; Heb 4:16. (5) *Expectancy.* Something really happened.

4) The Scope of the Prophecy. **10:14.** See comments on 2:38.

5) The Conflicts of the Angelic Messenger. 10:13,20,21.

In the OT world men believed each nation had its own special god (e.g., Isa 37:38; Dan 4:8; II Chr 28:23). The prophets proclaimed idols to be nothing. There is, however, in other portions of Scripture, occasional information to the effect that evil spirits, not to be identified with the idols, stood behind the whole delusion, gaining pleasure and wicked profit from it (Eph 6:11,12; I Cor 8:4,5; 10:19,20; Jude 9; Rev 12:7; Mt 25:41). See also II Cor 10:3,4; I Tim 4:1-4.

6) The Immediate Future of Israel in Relation to the Nations. 11:1-35.

a) Prophecy of the Medes and Persians (vv. 1,2). The purpose and nature of the angelic strengthening of Darius may only be surmised. Perhaps it had something to do with the benevolent treatment this king of the realm accorded the Jews. The three **kings in Persia** appear to have been: first, Cambyses, Cyrus' son (accession 529 B.C.); second, Pseudo-Smerdis, an impostor (though Olmstead, *History of Persia*, argues that he was a genuine Achaemenid, who reigned briefly in 522 B.C.); and third, Darius I, or Hystaspes, also called, the Great, (522–486 B.C.); a truly great monarch. The fourth, **far greater than they all** was, then, Xerxes, known in Esther as Ahasuerus (486-464 B.C.). The wars of Darius and of Xerxes, by which the Persians infuriated all of Greece, are well known to students of classical antiquity and standard ancient history.

b) Prophecy of the Greeks and Alexander (vv. 3,4). See notes on chapter 8.

c) Prophecy of Syria and Egypt in Conflict with One Another and with the Jews (vv. 5-35). Lack of space forbids tracing in detail the correspondence between Daniel's prophecy and the history of the Syrian Seleucid kingdom (the king of the north) and the history of the **Egyptian kingdom of the Ptolemies** (the king of the south). The prophecy does not give a continuous view; i.e., there are gaps in it. Nor is present knowledge of the Egyptian history of the epoch complete. Even the so-called historical portions of the OT lack the precision required of strict history. We may not, therefore, expect the predictions to be as precise in regard to sequence, chronology, etc., as our curiosity desires.

Egypt (v. 8) is mentioned by name in such a manner as to identify it as the "king of the south" (v. 9); but Syria (actually much larger than Syria, and unrelated historically to the OT kingdom of that name) is left unnamed. This appears to be because Egypt had long been known as a kingdom in Daniel's time, but the kingdom of the Seleucids was not yet in existence. If Daniel had been written in the second century, as some critics say, the kingdom of Syria would almost certainly have been named.

At verse 21 Antiochus Epiphanes (175 –163 B.C.) is introduced as a **vile person.** His wicked persecution of the Jews and desecration of the Temple are described by a contemporary witness in I Maccabees, which ought to be read by every student of Daniel. His action is predicted also at Dan 8:13, and his deeds furnish a kind of pattern for those of the wicked "prince that shall come" (Dan 9:26,27; cf. II Thess 2:4,5; Mt 24:15-21).

In the dreadful days of Antiochus only those who knew **their God** (Dan 11:32) were able to hold up their heads without shame, being enabled by God to **do exploits.** Many died for their faith (vv. 34,35), by their deeds instructing many (v. 33). Their suffering produced unusual character, by God's help (vv. 34,35). They were the separatists of that day, who refused the pagan vices of their Greek lords no less than the beautiful lies of the heathen ritual and religion. They constitute the main link between the Testaments, for their spiritual descendants appear in the Gospels as the Pharisees (whose name means "separated ones"). How sad that their descendants fell from their true principles! Hebrews 11:34-39 memorializes the faithful Jews of that time of tribulation.

d) Prophecy of Israel in Conflict with "the Willful King" (vv. 36-45). Jerome states that in his time this portion of Daniel was applied to Antichrist by "our writers." And to the present day that interpretation is prevalent. The following are the chief reasons for holding that the prophecy shifts from Antiochus to Antichrist precisely at verse 36:

(1) The scope of the prophecy (10:14) demands some eschatological reference, thus making this view of the division a possibility.

(2) Although all prophecy in Daniel down to 11:35 can easily be related to well-known events of ancient history, correspondence can not be continued beyond that.

(3) Verse 36 mentions a king whose period is "the indignation," a technical term drawn from Israel's prophetic literature, usually having reference to eschatological events (e.g., Isa 26:20).

(4) Predictions herein correspond quite precisely with recognized prophecies of final Antichrist (cf. II Thess 2:4 ff.; Rev 13; 17).

(5) A natural literary break occurs before Dan 11:36, observed by both the ASV and the RSV.

(6) The willful king is a new element, separate from either of the two kingdoms whose history is under consideration up to verse 35.

(7) Of decisive force is the connection with the Great Tribulation, the resurrection of the dead, and final rewards, etc. (12:1-3) furnished by the words, "And at that time" (Heb. *ûbeʿēt hahîʾ*, 12:1). The time of these eschatological events is the time of the events of the latter part of chapter 11.

36. This king is the same as the "son of perdition" (II Thess 2:3,4), who is to appear before Christ's second advent (II Thess 2:1,2; cf. Dan 7:11,25). His career will be short, lasting only until the indignation of God is vented upon mankind in the end time.

37. God of his fathers *(ʾelōhê ʾabōtāyw).* Though the phrase may be translated, "gods of his father," surely it is to be interpreted of the Lord God of Israel, for a false Messiah of the Jews could hardly be a Gentile. "God of the fathers" is a familiar designation of the Lord.

Desire of women. Meaning unknown. Interpretations vary from female idols to sexual passion. (See comments on "little horn" of ch. 7.) **38,39. God of forces.** Worship of military power, such as that of the Caesars, Hittites, etc. The two verses describe a monumental fraud, who, while proclaiming himself a god, secretly practices religious quackery with astrologers, fortunetellers, etc.,—a situation not uncommon in history.

40. And at the time of the end. Cf. I Cor 15:24; Mt 28:20; 13:39. **The end** is the end of the events prophesied in this book—the arrival of Messiah's kingdom to replace all these others. From here to the close of the prophecies of Daniel, consummating events are in view (cf. esp. 12:1, "and at that time," etc.). Antichrist's end is set forth elsewhere (Rev 19:11 ff.; Isa 11:4; Ps 2). Observe that throughout this section this willful king is a different person from either "the king of the north" or "the king of the south," who both fight against him. With what nations these two opponents will be identified is difficult to say for certain. Antichrist's success at war is prophesied here (cf. Dan 7:8,20; Rev 17:13). Likely the particular engines of war—whirlwind, chariots, horsemen, ships—are to be interpreted in terms of the engines of that future day. He will have modern weapons. Daniel saw war in terms of his own day, else he would not have recognized it.

41. This describes an attack on Palestine. Perhaps it should be connected with Antichrist's breaking covenant (Dan 9:27). On his failure to capture Edom, Moab, and Ammon, see Isa 11:14. **Many countries.** The word "countries" is not in the Hebrew.

42-44. Correspondence of this section with events leading up to World War II, especially Mussolini's early career, was startling. But the failure of history to justify the prophetic interpretations of that decade should discourage other premature identifications with contemporary powers. This much seems sure: there are to be at least three strong national powers contemporary with Antichrist, the "Roman" king. They will be "of the north" (v. 40), "of the south" (v. 40), and **out of the east** (v. 44).

45. Evidently in Palestine to put an end to the perennial Jewish problem by wiping out the Jews, he himself meets his end (Zech 12:1-14; cf. Joel 3:16; see also Zech 14; Rev 14:17-20; 19). Tregelles *(op. cit.)* applies Isa 14:14 and Ezk 28 to the fall of this man. G. H. Lang *(Histories and Prophecies of Daniel)* applies Ezk 38; 39 at this point.

e) Prophecy Concerning the Great Tribulation of Israel (12:1). Here see Jer 30:4-11. **At that time** (cf. on Dan 11:36). At the same time as the events of 11:36-45. **Michael.** See Rev 12:7; cf. Josh 5:13-15; II Kgs 6:15-17; Isa 37:35, 36; Mt 26:53. This is Israel's time of trouble. Every reference to it uses superlative language (cf. also Mt 24:21). It is a providential chastening by the wicked hands of Antichrist to prepare for Messiah's coming (cf. Jer 30; 31; Ezk 20:33-38. See R. Culver, *Daniel and the Latter Days*, pp. 69-76). Though especially Israel's *tribulation,* it is a time of divine *indignation* over all the earth as well; so others will suffer (Isa 26:20; Dan 11:36; Rev 16:10).

f) Prophecy Concerning the Resurrection of the Dead (v. 2). Like the rest of the prophecy, this verse relates to Israelites. Since Scripture knows nothing of a special resurrection for Israelites, the "first resurrection" predicted in Rev 20:6 will include this company. Daniel 12:2 refers to *righteous* Israel only. Other passages which speak of three stages in resurrection (that of Christ, that of his saints, that of the rest of the dead) are I Cor 15:20-24 (see R. Culver, "A Neglected Millennial Passage from St. Paul," *Bibliotheca Sacra,* April, 1956; C. F. Kling, trans. of D. W. Poor on I Cor 15:20-24 in *Lange's Commentary)* and Rev 20. See also Jn 5:28, 29; Acts 24:15. That this passage describes a selective resurrection is agreed not only by many premillennial scholars but also by some amillennialists (e.g., Keil). See R. Culver, *Daniel and the Latter Days,* pp. 172-176; Tregelles, *Remarks, in loco.*

g) Prophecy Concerning Final Rewards (v. 3). **Wise.** See 11:33,35; 12:10. Cf. Prov 11:30; I Cor 9:19; Jas 5:20; I Pet 2:19-25; 4:12-16. See also I Cor 3:19-23; 9:25; II Cor 5:8-10; Phil 4:1; I Thess 2:19; II Tim 2:5; 4:8; Jas 1:12; I Pet 5:4.

h) Final Prophecies and Instructions (vv. 4-13).

4. Shut up the words, and seal the book. No reference to obscuration of meaning is intended. Parallel usage shows that it has to do with the protection and authentication of the message. See a concordance. **Run to and fro . . . knowledge . . . increased.** Eyes will run to and fro in scanning the prophecy, and understanding of it will grow. The disposition of the book and its future are under consideration.

5. Daniel (like the apostles, Acts 1:3-6) knew that revelation was now at an end. He wondered when all these events would come to pass (cf. Acts 1:7,8). **Other two.** Two angelic creatures, one of whom may have been Gabriel of the previous visions. **6. Upon the waters.** Better, *above the waters* (ASV). Here the gulf that separates creatures (angels) from Creator appears in the vision. The **man clothed in linen** appears to be the preincarnate Son of God himself (cf. Rev 1:13-20). Note that ultimate questions are referred to him.

7. The consummation is to take place when the three and one-half times (3½ years; 1,260 days, 42 months) so frequently mentioned in Daniel's previous prophecies and in the Revelation are run out. This verse is an important base in support of the futurist interpretation not only of Dan 9:27 (seventieth week) but of the main portions of the Revelation. That last one-half week of years is an important consideration in prophecy, because in it take place the chief events of consummation. The majestic oath-taking scene reappears in Rev 10:5-7. Note that the center of the prophetic interest herein is still God's (and Daniel's) precious **holy people.**

8. Daniel was still no expert on prophetic interpretation. There will be no expert until prophecy becomes history (cf. Jn 2:22). **9.** See on verse 4. **10.** See Ps 19:7.

11. This carries prophecy from the middle of the seventieth week of Daniel 9 through the first thirty days of the Millennium to follow, perhaps to the end of some "mopping up" period. **12.** This carries the prophecy sixty-five days beyond the end of the "week." Does it reach to the full establishment of Messiah's reign after sixty-five days of initial preliminary work? The Millennium, if a true administration of heaven's rule on earth in a visible manner, will require time for administrative processes to begin to work.

13. But go thou thy way till the end be: for thou shalt rest, and stand in thy lot at the end of the days. Go thy way. A man of the advanced age of Daniel cannot don an ascension robe and climb to the nearest hilltop to wait for the coming of the Lord. And neither can we. Rather, all must, like Daniel, serve faithfully to the end.

Let us then be up and doing
With a heart for any fate—
Still achieving, still pursuing,
Learn to labor and to wait.
— Longfellow.

Thou shalt rest. In the light of the rest of the Bible, these words mean simply that Daniel, like all true believers, would truly find a kind of **rest** in the grave (cf. Isa 57:2), his spirit rejoicing in the presence of God, where he would "see his face" (Rev 22:4; Lk 16:19-22). The intermediate state, that is, the period between death and the resurrection, is neither one of painful purgatory, as the Roman Church teaches, nor one of unconscious sleep of body and soul. It is rather to "depart, and to be with Christ" (Phil 1:23), "in paradise" (Lk 23:43). It is a time of rest, as we read here, in the bosom of Abraham (Lk 16:22) and a time of comfort (Lk 16:25). **And stand in thy lot at the end of the days.** Neither Daniel nor any other saint will ever lose out in the "world's broad field of battle, in the bivouac of life"—rather, he will **stand** up in resurrection glory. Sown in corruption, reaped in incorruption; brought down in dishonor, brought up in honor; lowered in defeat, raised in victory; buried in sorrow, resurrected in joy, we shall stand to receive our **lot.** There is a "crown of righteousness" laid up which our Lord will give us in that day.

On this calm note of immeasurable joy, the book of Daniel comes to an end.

BIBLIOGRAPHY

ANDERSON, ROBERT. *The Coming Prince.* London: Hodder and Stoughton, 1894.

AUBERLEN, CARL AUGUST. *The Prophecies of Daniel and the Revelation of St. John.* Translated by Adolph Saphir. Andover: Draper, 1857.

BARNES, ALBERT. *Notes on the Book of Daniel.* New York: Leavitt and Allen, 1855. Reprinted by Baker Book House, Grand Rapids.

Boutflower, Charles. *In and Around the Book of Daniel.* London: Society for Promotion of Christian Knowledge, 1923.

Calvin, John. *Commentaries on the Book of Daniel the Prophet.* Translated by Thomas Meyers. 2 vols. Grand Rapids: William B. Eerdmans Publishing Company, reprinted 1948.

Culver, Robert D. *Daniel and the Latter Days.* Westwood, N. J.: Fleming H. Revell Co., 1954.

Dougherty, Raymond Philip. *Nabonidus and Belshazzar,* New Haven: Yale University Press, 1929.

Driver, S. R. *Daniel (Cambridge Bible for Schools and Colleges).* Cambridge: The University Press, 1900.

Ironside, Harry A. *Lectures on Daniel the Prophet.* New York: Loizeaux Brothers, 1946.

Jerome's Commentary on Daniel. Translated by Gleason L. Archer, Jr. Grand Rapids: Baker Book House, 1958.

Keil, C. F. *Biblical Commentary on the Book of Daniel.* Translated by M. G. Easton. Grand Rapids: William B. Eerdmans Publishing Company, reprinted 1949.

Lang, G. H. *The Histories and Prophecies of Daniel.* London and Edinburgh: Oliphants, Ltd., 1942.

Lattey, C. *The Book of Daniel.* Dublin: Browne and Nolan, Ltd., 1948.

Leupold, H. C. *Exposition of Daniel.* Columbus, Ohio: Wartburg Press, 1949.

McClain, Alva J. *Daniel's Prophecy of the Seventy Weeks.* Grand Rapids: Zondervan Publishing House, 1940.

Mauro, Philip. *The Seventy Weeks and the Great Tribulation.* New York: Fleming H. Revell, 1919.

Montgomery, James A. *A Critical and Exegetical Commentary on the Book of Daniel (International Critical Commentary).* New York: Charles Scribner's Sons, 1927.

Pusey, E. B. *Daniel the Prophet.* New York: Funk and Wagnalls, 1885.

Seiss, Joseph A. *Voices from Babylon; or, Records of Daniel the Prophet.* Philadelphia: The Castle Press, 1879.

Smith, R. Payne. *Daniel, An Exposition of the Historical Portion of the Writings of the Prophet Daniel.* New York: Cranston and Curts (n.d.).

Stuart, Moses. *A Commentary on the Book of Daniel.* Boston: Crocker and Brewster, 1850.

Thomson, J. E. H. *Daniel (Pulpit Commentary).* Chicago: Wilcox and Follett Company, 1900, 1944.

Tregelles, S. P. *Remarks on the Prophetic Visions of the Book of Daniel.* London: Bagsters, 1864.

Whitcomb, John C. *Darius the Mede.* Grand Rapids: William B. Eerdmans Publishing Company, 1959.

Wilson, R. Dick. *Studies in the Book of Daniel.* New York and London: G. P. Putnam's Sons, 1917.

________. *Studies in the Book of Daniel, Second Series.* New York: Fleming H. Revell, 1938.

Young, Edward J. *The Prophecy of Daniel.* Grand Rapids: William B. Eerdmans Publishing Company, 1948.

HOSEA

INTRODUCTION

Author. Our knowledge of the life of Hosea, the son of Beeri, is derived exclusively from the book which bears his name. He prophesied to the Northern Kingdom (Israel, or Ephraim) during the time that Isaiah was prophesying in Judah (1:1; cf. Isa 1:1). Another contemporary, Amos (Amos 1:1), was a native of Judah who prophesied in Israel. Hosea, however, was the one writing prophet of the Northern Kingdom to address his own people. Speaking to them with a broken heart, he prophesied their impending exile (Hos 3:4). His prophetic vision looked beyond exile to restoration, when a chastened people would again acknowledge the exclusive claims of the Lord (3:5). Since the fall of Samaria is not mentioned as an accomplished fact by Hosea, it is thought that he ministered for the most part before 722 B.C. Most of his prophetic ministry evidently took place during the quarter century from 750 to 725 B.C. That he lived and prophesied as late as the times of Hezekiah (beginning c. 715 B.C.) is attested in 1:1.

Hosea's Marriage. Israel's unfaithfulness to the Lord is depicted by Hosea in terms of a wife who has turned her back upon a faithful husband in order to follow evil lovers. The imagery is taken from Hosea's own experience, for 1:2 tells us that the Lord spoke to Hosea saying, "Go, take thee a wife of whoredoms." The many interpretations of these strange words largely fall into three categories: (1) Some suggest that the words are intended to present an allegory designed to impart the spiritual lesson of Israel's unfaithfulness, and that Hosea did not actually contract such a marriage. Among scholars who have held that view are Calvin, Keil, von Hoonacher, Reuss, Gressman, Robert Pfeiffer, and E. J. Young. (2) Some insist that Hosea actually married a woman known to him to be a harlot, perhaps a temple prostitute. T. H. Robinson and T. Laetsch defend this viewpoint. (3) Many hold that Hosea married a woman whom he thought to be pure but later learned of her faithlessness. According to this view the expression "wife of whoredoms" (1:2) was used proleptically. At the time of writing the book, Hosea saw that the hand of God had brought about a marriage which, from the human point of view, was marked by unmitigated tragedy. With high hopes, Hosea married Gomer, only to learn of her tendency toward adultery. Separation followed, and 2:2 actually contains a divorce formula—"She is not my wife, neither am I her husband." Still, Hosea's love persisted, and subsequently he remarried her (3:1). This parallels God's dealings with Israel. After vowing faithfulness to the Law of the Lord, Israel went lusting after Baal and the other gods of Canaan until God brought about a temporary rejection (the Exile), after which chastened Israel was returned to God's favor in the land of Judea. This view identifies the "woman" of 3:1 with the "wife of whoredoms" of 1:2. With some variations it has been held by Ehrlich, Marti, W. R. Harper, and G. W. Anderson. The present commentary is written from this viewpoint.

Hosea's Times. Hosea's prophecies were first uttered during the chaotic reign of Jeroboam II, when Israel enjoyed external prosperity but suffered inner corruption. The shrines were thronged with worshipers (Amos 4:4, 5), but the poor were oppressed (Amos 4:1) by a people whose religion was external. During the prosperous days of Jeroboam II judgment seemed remote to the Israelite, yet Assyrian power was soon to be felt in western Asia. The year following Jeroboam's death, Tiglath-pileser III came to the throne of Assyria (745 B.C.). By 732 B.C. Damascus had fallen to the Assyrians, and a decade later Samaria, the capital of Israel, fell and its people were deported. Amos and Hosea prophesied during the closing years of the Northern Kingdom, junt as Jeremiah of Jerusalem prophesied during the last hours of Judah's history.

OUTLINE

I. The prophet's married life. 1:1–3:5
- A. His marriage to Gomer. 1:1-9.
- B. A message of hope. 1:10,11.
- C. Judgment on faithless Israel. 2:1-13.
- D. The restoration of faithless Israel. 2:14-23.
- E. Hosea's redemption of his faithless wife. 3:1-5.

II. Israel's unfaithfulness and consequent judgment. 4:1–13:16.
- A. The guilt of the people. 4:1-3.
- B. The guilt of the priests. 4:4-8.
- C. Punishment for all. 4:9,10.
- D. Immoral cult practices. 4:11-19.
- E. Judgment on kings and priests for leading the people astray. 5:1-7.
- F. Disastrous foreign policies of Ephraim (Israel) and Judah. 5:8-15.
- G. Israel's plea and God's rejoinder. 6:1-6.
- H. The crimes of Israel. 6:7–7:7.
- I. Israel's disastrous foreign policy. 7:8–8:3.
- J. Israel's idolatry and wicked alliances. 8:4-14.
- K. The exile of Israel foretold. 9:1-9.
- L. Israel's ancient apostasy at Baal-peor. 9:10-14.
- M. Israel's apostasy at Gilgal. 9:15-17.
- N. Destruction of the Baal cult prophesied. 10:1-8.
- O. The sin at Gibeah. 10:9,10.
- P. The ruin of Israel. 10:11-15.
- Q. God's love; Israel's ingratitude. 11:1-7.
- R. God's pity for his people. 11:8-11
- S. The sins of Jacob. 11:12–12:14.
- T. The wicked bull worship. 13:1-3.
- U. The gracious God to bring destruction. 13:4-11.
- V. Inescapable ruin. 13:12-16.

III. Israel's conversion and renewal. 14:1-9.
- A. The call to repentance. 14:1-3.
- B. The promise of pardon. 14:4-8.
- C. A parting admonition. 14:9.

COMMENTARY

I. The Prophet's Married Life. 1:1–3:5.

A. His Marriage to Gomer. 1:1-9.

1. Hosea's prophecy begins with the assertion that it has its origin in God: **The word of the Lord . . . came.** The word is divine; it finds expression in a human instrument—the prophet, **Hosea, the son of Beeri.** The name **Hosea** means "deliverance" or "salvation." The prophet's father, **Beeri,** is not mentioned elsewhere in Scripture, although early Jewish writers identified him with Beerah (I Chr 5:6), who was carried into exile by Tiglath-pileser. Hosea prophesied **in the days of Uzziah** and was a contemporary of Isaiah (cf. Isa 1:1). Isaiah, however, lived in Jerusalem and addressed his prophecies largely to the Southern Kingdom (Judah), whereas Hosea prophesied to the Northern Kingdom (Israel or Ephraim).

2. Hosea was told to marry **a wife of whoredom** (ASV) and to be a father to **children of whoredom.** Many commentators hold that he did not actually marry a harlot, but that the description is to be taken allegorically (see Introd.). They interpret Hosea's words as descriptive of a vision which he saw rather than of an event in which he was a participant. There is no hint of allegory, however, in the text, and the words seem actually to describe Hosea's marital life. The harlotry of his wife may well have developed after her marriage to the prophet, however. In retrospect Hosea would think of this marriage as providentially ordained by God, for it provided the analogy which he used in addressing Israel. The prophet charges: **the land**

hath committed great whoredom. As Hosea's wife had proved untrue to him, so Israel was untrue to the Lord. Spiritual adultery is a figure of speech drawn from the Canaanite fertility cult, with its ritual prostitution.

3. Gomer the daughter of Diblaim was the name of Hosea's wife. The name was a common one, and there is no ground for reading into it an allegorical meaning. **4.** Gomer's first son bore the name **Jezreel,** which means *God sows.* It had a twofold significance: (1) After the people of Israel had been scattered because of their sin, God would plant or "sow" them in their own land again. (2) Sins committed in the valley of Jezreel by Jehu would be punished, and Israel would taste defeat. **The blood of Jezreel** is a reference to Jehu's ill-advised attempt to defend the cause of the Lord by murdering all of the Baal-worshipers (II Kgs 10:1-11).

5. In judgment God said, **I will break the bow of Israel.** The bow here represents the might (cf. Gen 49:24) of the Kingdom of Israel, which would soon be ended. A broken bow was a sign of impotence. **6. Lo-ruhamah** *(not pitied).* The daughter of Gomer was given a name designed to tell the people of Israel that they could expect no mercy. As "the unpitied one," she symbolized the plight of the Northern Kingdom, which had sinned against God and was ripe for judgment. **7.** In contrast to Israel's imminent fall, God said, **I will have mercy upon the house of Judah.** Israel fell before the Assyrians (722 B.C.), but when Sennacherib besieged Jerusalem, God intervened to save the city (II Kgs 19:35). **9.** The second son of Gomer bore the name **Lo-ammi,** meaning, *Not my people.* At Sinai Israel had covenanted to be the Lord's people, and He to be their God (Ex 19:1-7). They repeatedly broke that covenant, and here Hosea prophetically declares that they will be rejected. This would not be a permanent rejection (cf. Hos 2:3), but it would result in the Exile and the destruction of the Northern Kingdom as a political entity.

B. A Message of Hope. 1:10,11.

10. According to promise (Gen 15:5, 6), the number of the children of Israel would be **as the sand of the sea.** Hosea had pronounced judgment upon unrepentant Israel, but he held forth the promise of ultimate redemption. The people, although decimated by the enemy, were to be revived numerically and would again be called **the sons of the living God.**

C. Judgment of Faithless Israel. 2:1-13.

2. Hosea was to address Gomer with the words—**she is not my wife, neither am I her husband.** The prophet's wife had separated herself from him, and with a broken heart he recognized that their marriage ties were severed. The words are reminiscent of the formula used in divorce. In like manner God now addresses Israel. **3.** She must put away her adulteries **lest I strip her naked.** This punishment for adultery is attested in Scripture (Ezk 16:38) and in the Nuzi tablets from northern Mesopotamia. The words here apply to Israel, who would become a prey to her enemies when left desolate and naked by her God. **5.** Hosea's wife had said, **I will go after my lovers.** As she looked to her paramours, so Israel looked to Baal and the other Canaanite gods. **7.** After being subjected to disappointment, Gomer, like Israel, will say, **I will go and return to my first husband.** Neither Gomer nor Israel could find satisfaction in infidelity. God here declares that he will bring Israel to the place where she shall see her need of him.

8. God had dealt mercifully with his people: **I gave her corn, and wine, and oil.** All the fruitfulness of the land had its source in the Lord, but Israel forgot him and took his blessings for granted. Corn (i.e., grain), wine, and oil were the material blessings provided by God in Canaan (Deut 7:13). **9.** God, in discipline, declared that he would **take away . . . corn.** By removing the blessing he would bring Israel to the place where she would remember its divine source. Baal was powerless to help; and if the Lord did not provide for Israel, she would be hungry and destitute. As corn (grain) was used for food, so **wool and flax** provided clothing. Faithless Israel would be unclothed because she forgot the Lord. **10.** In judgment God added that he would **discover her lewdness.** Literally, *uncover her lewdness,* i.e., reveal her to her lovers to be the shameful creature she really was. **13. The days of Baalim** were sinful days, during which Israel forgot the Lord and made idolatrous and often lewd practices part of Israelite religious life. God could not sit idly by when his name was thus desecrated.

D. The Restoration of Faithless Israel. 2:14-23.

14. In love God says of Israel, **I will allure her.** God says that he will persuade his people with endearing words to turn from their idols and find joy in him. In Canaan Israel rejected her God. Surrounded by other "lovers" (i.e., Baal and other idols), she felt no need of him. God, however, declares his purpose to remove his people from the land of milk and honey and **bring her into the wilderness,** so that he may **speak comfortably unto her.** Literally, *speak unto her heart.* The grieved lover desired to win back the object of his love. He was going to take Israel to the solitary wilderness, where she could hear his voice without distraction.

15. Vineyards, which speak of prosperity and fruit-bearing, would be given by God to his restored people. **The valley of Achor** is described as a **door of hope.** There, centuries before, Achan had died as the troubler of Israel (Josh 7:25,26). Only through Achor, *trouble,* could Israel come back to fellowship with the Lord and its resultant blessing. God would thus restore the **days of her youth.** When youthful Israel crossed the Red Sea, she had a song (Ex 15:1-19). As she lost her first love, the song was quieted; but Hosea pictures repentant, restored Israel as again singing. **16.** Restored Israel would address God as **Ishi,** literally, *my husband,* a word of tenderness. **Baali** is a synonym of **ishi,** but it contains the word Baal *(master),* the name of a Canaanite deity. For this reason it was associated with idolatry and rejected by Hosea. The Baalim (v. 18) will not be mentioned by restored Israel, who then will be true to her Lord.

18. Ancient Hittite covenants were of two kinds: (1) parity covenants, between equals; (2) suzerainty covenants between a sovereign and his subjects. The **covenant** between God and Israel was of the latter type. The Biblical covenant partakes of the nature of an ordinance **with the beasts of the field.** Nature itself will be at peace with restored Israel (cf. Isa 11:1-9). God adds, **I will break the bow.** The weapons of Israel's enemies will be broken so that they can do Israel no harm. **19.** In love God tells his people, **I will betroth thee.** A second marriage between God and Israel—after she is restored—is pictured as preceded by a second betrothal. This betrothal shall be **for ever;** i.e., it will not, like the first marriage between God and Israel at Sinai, be brought to a violent end. This betrothal is **in righteousness.** The bond between God and Israel is not mere sentiment, but one based upon a right relationship. It is also **in judgment,** or justice, as opposed to arbitrariness. God will deal with his people **in lovingkindness.** Hebrew *ḥesed,* a word which stresses the idea of solidarity and belonging together. God deals with his people in a way consistent with their belonging to him. He likewise deals with them **in mercies,** or compassion, being mindful of their needs. **20.** The betrothal is **in faithfulness,** for God will be faithful to his covenant, and his beloved will learn to respond.

21. God can now answer his people's prayers: **I will hear the heavens,** or *respond to the heavens.* Hosea depicts the plea of Israel for prosperity as going through the heavens to the Lord. The earth will not sigh in vain for the rains of heaven, for **they shall hear the earth,** i.e., the heavens will be sensitive to the plea of a parched earth. All nature works in harmony. **22. The earth shall hear,** i.e., respond to **the corn** (grain), and **the wine, and the oil,** the staple agricultural crops of Palestine. The needs of the crops are discerned by the earth; the earth's needs are discerned by the heavens; and the need of the heavens is discerned by God. In poetic language Hosea thus depicts the God of heaven as the ultimate source of all blessing. God lovingly responds to the needs of the earth, watering it so that it will yield in abundance. The corn, wine, and oil will then respond to **Jezreel** *(the Lord sows),* here representing Israel. **23.** Thereupon God adds, **I will sow her unto me.** Restored Israel will flourish like seed in fertile soil.

E. Hosea's Redemption of His Faithless Wife. 3:1-5.

1. Hosea was urged to **love the woman** who had turned her back upon him for the companionship of others. She was **beloved of her friend,** i.e., her paramour. Hosea was called upon to love an **adulteress,** one who had been unfaithful. She was like the Israelites, who **love**[d] **flagons of wine.** Better, *cakes of raisins* (RSV). They participated in pagan Baal rites which involved the offering of cakes of dried grapes. **2.** Hosea bought his wife back from the slavery into which her sin had led her for **fifteen pieces of silver.** The price of a slave was thirty shekels of silver (Ex 21:32). Hosea evidently paid half in money and half in grain. **3.** As punishment for sins, the prophet says, **Thou shalt abide for me many days.** The verb is sometimes used in the sense of "to live in seclusion" (Lev 12:4; Deut 21:13). Gomer was to lead a quiet, secluded life until Hosea would be free to take her as his wife. **So will I also be for thee** is literally, *and also I to thee*. Hosea appears to be saying that Gomer must be separated from others, and he would not have marital relations with her during the period defined as **many days.**

4. Hosea's experience with Gomer had a counterpart in God's experience with Israel, which would be **many days without a king, and without a prince.** Israel, in exile, would have no civil government but would be governed by strangers. She would also be **without a sacrifice.** The manner and place of sacrifice were particularly stressed in the Levitical law. Israel would be unable to meet these conditions in the land of exile. **Without an image.** Literally *a pillar*, a cult object used in pagan worship but forbidden in the Law (Deut 16:22). Israel's exile would remove her from the familiar temptations of Canaan. **Without an ephod.** The ephod was a part of the high priest's attire (Ex 28:6-14). The root meaning of the word is, "to overlay," and in Gideon's time we read of an ephod which was an idol. It was probably made of wood overlaid with precious metal. **Without teraphim,** or household gods (cf. Gen 31:19, 34; I Sam 19:13,16). Hosea states that the Exile would be a time during which the cult objects so dear to pre-Exilic Israel would be removed.

5. Afterward. After Israel had been removed from their land, their king, and their idolatrous worship, God would restore **David their king,** i.e., the Davidic king, or Messiah, who would rule as rightful King of Israel (cf. Mal 3:1). The dynasty would be revived **in the latter days.** Literally, *in the end of days*. The expression is used to describe the Messianic era, the climax of history, when God's Messiah will rule over all the world.

II. Israel's Unfaithfulness and Consequent Judgment. 4:1—13:16.

A. The Guilt of the People. 4:1-3.

1. Israel had been unfaithful to her covenant with the Lord, with the result that he had **a controversy** with her. God now acts as plaintiff and judge (cf. 12:2; Isa 1). Israel had been guilty of repeated transgression, and the prophet declared that the land had no **truth** or fidelity *('emet)* nor **mercy** or covenant-loyalty *(ḥesed)*, nor **knowledge of God,** in the sense of knowing and obeying his will. **2. They break out** into acts of violence, and **blood toucheth blood.** One murder led to another, and the trail of blood was continuous. Idolatry and crimes of violence are closely related in Hosea's thinking. One who rejects the true God may be guilty of the most shameless atrocities.

B. The Guilt of the Priests. 4:4-8.

4. Israel had rejected the claims of God and was like a **people who strive with the priest,** rejecting the counsel of the God-ordained messenger (cf. Mal 2:7). **5.** The result was that Israel would **fall in the day,** when men normally can see and avoid pitfalls. Hosea was aware of the failure of the spiritual leaders, or prophets (i.e., false prophets). Because they did not hold forth the truth, they would **fall . . . in the night.** They would stumble in darkness. **6.** The result was the destruction of Israel **for lack of knowledge.** The people did not know God and his ways. This was not simply the result of neglect, but a criminal action. They **rejected knowledge,** choosing to resolve their problems by looking to false gods and the powerful nations which worshiped them. The priests had been poor examples, leading Israel into apostasy. For this reason they were rejected in the words **thou shalt be no priest to me. 7.** The priests had been highly honored, but **as they were increased, so they sinned.** That is, *the more they increased, the more they sinned*. **8.** Priests became greedy, and the mercenary spirit which prevailed among them is expressed in the charge, **They eat up the sin of my people. Sin** may refer to the sin offering, referring to the fact that the priests grew wealthy as they greedily seized the offerings which the people brought to the Lord. The sons of Eli (I Sam 2:13-17) were guilty of such sins.

C. Punishment for All. 4:9,10.

9. God's judgment is expressed in the words **like people, like priest.** People and priests alike had transgressed, and judgment could be expected to fall on both groups. **10.** In spite of the rapacity of the priests, Hosea states that **they shall eat, and not have enough.** They shall not be satisfied. Greed will be punished by lack of food.

D. Immoral Cult Practices. 4:11-19.

11. Whoredom and wine and new wine characterize those who reject God's word. Hosea states that they **take away the heart.** They make a man devoid of spiritual understanding. **12.** In their bewilderment, the people sought help from **stocks.** That is, from wooden idols (cf. Isa 40:19-21; Jer 2:27). Similarly they used the **staff,** by which the heathen practiced divination, to foretell the future. **13.** Sacrifices were offered on the **tops of the mountains,** instead of at the sanctuary of the Lord. Licentious nature worship characterized the "high places." This took place under the **oaks and poplars and elms** (or terebinths). The homes of the Israelites would be infected, for **daughters,** and **spouses** (or, rather, *daughters-in-law,* ASV marg.) would adopt the licentious religious practices of the Baal cult. **14.** Ironically the Lord declares: **I will not punish the daughters** and spouses *(daughters-in-law).* He emphasizes the fact that the men are the worst offenders and that they cannot point to the women as the guilty ones.

15. Hosea warns the kingdom of Judah not to follow Israel's sins. Judah is urged not to **offend.** Literally, *become guilty.* She is to avoid the shrines at **Gilgal** and **Beth-aven** *(House of wickedness,* the prophet's designation of Beth-el). Judah should refrain from swearing—(As) **the Lord liveth.** To be guilty of idolatry while swearing by the Lord would be a twofold sin.

16. Israel slideth back as a backsliding heifer. Read, *Israel is stubborn like a stubborn heifer.* Rashi comments: "Like a fattened animal that kicks, so has Israel waxed fat and kicked." **Now the Lord will feed them as a lamb in a large place.** Better, *Can the Lord feed them now as a lamb in a broad pasture?* The question is rhetorical. A stubborn heifer is tied up so that she cannot graze as freely as a lamb. God had to restrict Israel because of her propensity toward evil. **17. Ephraim** *(Israel)* **is joined to idols.** Israel's league with the idols of the land caused God to cry out, **Let him alone.** This is tantamount to saying, "Let him shift for himself." The future would show whether or not the idols could be of help.

18. Their drink is sour. Read instead: *A band of drunkards, they give themselves to harlotry* (RSV). The JPS suggests, *When their carouse is over, they take to harlotry.* When tired of one sin, they turned to another. **Her rulers with shame do love.** The text is difficult. The JPS reads, *Her rulers deeply love dishonor.* Cheyne translates: Her *shields are enamoured of infamy* (CBSC). **19.** Speaking of the impending disaster, Hosea adds, **The wind hath bound her up in her wings.** The wind comes suddenly and violently, bringing destruction. Even so, Israel was to be driven into exile.

E. Judgment on Kings and Priests for Leading the People Astray. 5:1-7.

1. The address, **O priests,** reminds us that the priesthood of Israel had been responsible for leading the people into idolatrous worship at the high places. The king and his courtiers had likewise rejected the message of Israel's prophets; hence the further address, **O house of the king.** The idolatrous shrines at Beth-el and Dan had political implications. They were devised to prevent the people from taking part in the worship at the Jerusalem temple. Hosea cites **Mizpah** and **Tabor** as examples of the idolatry which was practiced throughout Israel. There were several places named Mizpah *(watch tower).* This one is probably to be identified with es-Salt in Gilead. Tabor is the well-known mountain in Galilee (cf. Jud 4:6; 10:17).

2. The revolters were those who had turned aside, hence apostates from the law of God. They are described as **profound to make slaughter.** In this context **profound** must have a literal rather than a metaphorical sense. The translation of these words has troubled Biblical scholars since ancient times. Cheyne suggests, *The apostates are gone deep in corrupting.* With a slight emendation the text reads: "And the pit of Shittim they have made deep." If the latter is the true interpretation, Shittim (Num 25:1; Josh 2:1; 3:1), like Mizpah and Tabor, was regarded as a center for idolatrous worship. God adds, **I have been a rebuker of them all.** Literally, *I am chastisement for them all.* If *mûsār* is translated as a hophal participle, we read, *I am rejected of them all.* This would indicate that the idolatry of Israel resulted in the rejection of Israel's God.

3. I know Ephraim. In this context **know** bears the idea of acquaintance. Ephraim's idolatrous ways were not hidden from God. She was guilty of **whoredom,** turning in faithlessness from the

Lord to Baal and participating in his licentious cult. **4. They will not frame their doings.** The translation of the margin is preferable: *Their doings will not suffer them to turn unto their God.* Israel had rejected the Lord and was sinking deeper and deeper into heathen practices. Sin was a despot, keeping Israel from her only hope—God himself. **They have not known the Lord** is an indictment upon a people whose deeds belied any profession of faithfulness to her God. The word "to know" may here be rendered in the present tense, *They know not the Lord.*

5. The pride of Israel suggests a spirit of arrogance and self-confidence which was to be humbled. This interpretation is suggested by the LXX, the Targum, and the Peshitta. Cheyne suggests that the Lord himself is meant, the one designated as "the pride of Israel" being Israel's God. God, then, is seen to be testifying against Israel because of her sin (cf. Ruth 1:21). **6.** Israel would approach God with sacrificial offerings, **with their flocks and with their herds;** but her sins had so alienated her from the Lord that such external gestures would be meaningless. The prophet warned that the idols would not help Israel in the day of her need, and that the Lord himself would not respond when his people made empty gestures at reconciliation. **7.** The parents had turned from God, and they had **begotten strange children** (cf. 2:4,5), who are depicted as following in their evil ways. **Now shall a month devour them.** The Hebrew word for **month** is normally translated, "new moon." The prophet stresses the imminence of judgment. Instead of joyfully welcoming the new moon, they would be reminded by its arrival of the nearness of judgment at the hands of Assyria. **With their portions** is a reference to the lands allotted to the several tribes. They would be "devoured" by the enemy.

F. Disastrous Foreign Policies of Ephraim (Israel) and Judah. 5:8-15.

8. The cornet . . . the trumpet. Note that these names appear in parallel relationship. Hosea did not mean to stress a difference in the two instruments. The two were probably slight variants of the same instrument. The Mishna states that the *shôpār* (here rendered **cornet**) was sometimes straight and sometimes curved. It was usually a simple ram's horn. A silver trumpet, *ḥaṣōṣrâ,* was prescribed in the Law for certain occasions (Num 10:1-10; 31:6). **Gibeah** and **Ramah** were both high among the mountains of central Palestine. The sound of alarm from these eminences could be heard in both Judah and Israel. **Beth-aven.** Cf. 4:15. **After thee, O Benjamin,** may be a warning addressed to Benjamin by the men of Beth-aven (Bethel). It would mean, "Benjamin, the enemy is behind you."

9. A rebuke in Hebrew thought is a judicial decision. God would render a verdict of "guilty" against idolatrous Israel, and the armies of Assyria would be his instruments for punishing his faithless people. God had **made known that which shall surely be.** The impending judgment had been decreed by God. Therefore it was sure. **10. Them that remove the bound.** The **bound** was the boundary marker or landmark. The removing of landmarks was a crime under Israelite law (Deut 19:14; 27:17; Prov 22:28; 23:10). **Judah** is pictured as awaiting the overthrow of Israel, after which she could cross the frontier and appropriate Israelite territory. God's wrath was about to be poured out **like water.** A swollen stream brings destruction in its wake, and Judah's princes merited judgment.

11. Broken in judgment expresses the concept of war as a judgment of God. The opposing armies are depicted as pleading their cause before the bar of God. Here judgment falls upon Israel. The Judge renders an adverse decision. **The commandment** is difficult to explain here. Israel did not follow God's commandment, but is accused of idolatry. The LXX, Targum, and Peshitta translate "vanity," "idols." The Talmudic tractate Sanh. 56b interprets the passage as a condemnation of idol worship. Jeroboam I commanded Israel to worship calves at Bethel and Dan, and Hosea may be referring to that commandment. The JPS emends the text to read, *He willingly walked after filth.* **12.** God likens the destruction that was to come upon Ephraim to the work of a **moth** and to **rottenness** which eats away at a dwelling. Both operate in silence. The moth comes from without, rot from within. Ephraim was being destroyed as much by her own inner corruption as by the external foes.

13. Conscious of her troubles, Ephraim sought help from **the Assyrian,** asking aid of **king Jareb** *(Contentious),* "the fighting king," perhaps Tiglath-pileser III.

14. God declares that he will be **as a lion,** carrying away Israel and Judah as prey. None is strong enough to challenge the lion in his purposes. **15. Looking** upon idolatrous Israel, God says, **I will go and return to my place** (i.e., heaven), leaving his rebellious people to suffer for their sins. When **in their affliction** they sought God, he would be ready to come to their aid.

G. Israel's Plea and God's Rejoinder. 6:1-6.

1. Afflicted Israel had learned the bitter lessons of disobedience, and her people encouraged one another with the words, **Come, and let us return unto the Lord.** The words contain an implied confession, for Israel had departed from the Lord in her idolatrous practices. The God who had **torn** in judgment could be expected to **heal** in mercy. Israel's wounds could not be healed by Egypt or Assyria (cf. 7:1; 11:3). Only God could bring new life to the wounded nation.

2. God could not only be counted upon to deliver his people, but his aid would come speedily. The prophet states that **after two days will he revive us,** adding the parallel line **in the third day he will raise us up.** Ezekiel used similar language in describing life which would enter dry bones, representing Israel (Ezk 37:1-10; cf. Isa 26:19). The Targum paraphrases Hos 6:2: "He will revive us in the days of consolation which are to come." Calvin interpreted the words as expressive of the hope of Israel during the Exile: "... though they long remained in darkness, and the exile was long which they had to endure, they yet did not cease to hope: 'Well, let the two days pass, and the Lord will revive us' " (John Calvin, *The Twelve Minor Prophets,* I, 218). Pusey, on the other hand, considers the reference to our Lord's resurrection to be the primary one: "What else can this be than the two days in which the body of Jesus lay in the tomb, and the third day on which he rose again . . . " (E. B. Pusey, *The Minor Prophets,* I, 63). The fact that "after two days" and "the third day" serve as an idiom for a short period of time may be demonstrated by Jesus' use of the idiom in Lk 13:32,33. The words should not be applied to the Resurrection in a primary sense, although they may be regarded as typical (cf. Hos 11:1). As God brought his son Israel from the Exile "after three days" (i.e., a brief period of time), so he raised his Son Jesus from the tomb outside the walls of Jerusalem on the third day (literally).

3. Then shall we know continues the thought of verse 1. Those who would return to the Lord from their apostasy would come to know the Lord. They would experience his presence and power in their lives. The verb may be translated as the Hebrew cohortative — "And let us know" — suggesting that calamities had befallen Israel because she was living without the knowledge of God. **His going forth.** His answer to the needs of his people. **Is prepared as the morning.** *Is sure as the morning.* Israel was "in darkness" (Isa 9:1), but the appearance of God to bring relief could be likened to the dawn of a new and glorious day. **4. O Ephraim, what shall I do unto thee?** What means can be employed to bring you back to fellowship with God? **Your goodness** (or *piety)* **is as a morning cloud.** You make efforts at reformation, but they do not avail. The morning cloud is deceptive. It is a dense mass of vapor which the westerly winds of summer bear from the Mediterranean. The sun quickly dissipates them, and they produce no rain in the dry Palestinian summer. Similarly **the early dew** does not remain. Grammatically we should read, *The dew (which) vanishes early.* The dew provides no permanent relief from the summer sun.

5. God, complaining about the conduct of his people, says, **Therefore have I hewed them by the prophets.** God sought to hew Israel into shape by sending prophets. The prophets warned of the consequences of sin (Isa 11:4; 49:2; Jer 1:10; 5:14; I Kgs 19:17). They uttered **the words of** (God's) **mouth. 6.** God repudiates the externalism of religion which characterized many in Israel, with the words **I desired mercy, and not sacrifice. Mercy** *(ḥesed)* is a word which speaks of covenantal affection and loyalty. Laetsch *(The Minor Prophets,* p. 60) and Harper (ICC, p. 286) translate it *love.* Harper adds, "This love is not love for God as distinguished from love for one's fellow-men, but both."

H. The Crimes of Israel. 6:7–7:7.

7. For **like men,** the RV reads, *like Adam.* Israel had transgressed God's commandment as Adam did in Eden. The RSV takes *Adam* as a geographical reference, *At Adam.* The AV **like men**

probably means "like other men." **8. Gilead,** the district east of the Jordan, is cited as an example of particular infamy. The Gileadites were less civilized than the tribes west of the Jordan. Here Gilead is mentioned as a city in which murder was common. **9.** The priests **murder in the way by consent.** Read rather, *murder in the way toward Shechem.* Shechem, situated on the road from Samaria to Bethel, had long been noted for its violence (cf. Jud 9:25,43). **10.** From heaven the Lord says, **I have seen a horrible thing in the house of Israel.** The abomination of Israel would bring judgment, and Judah, too, would surely reap the harvest which she had sown.

7:1. When I would have healed Israel *(when I would* have *restore*[d] *the fortunes of my people* (RSV), the sin of **Ephraim** and its capital city, **Samaria,** became apparent. Specifically, sins of **falsehood** and thievery are mentioned. **2.** The rulers of Israel **consider not in their hearts** that God is judge of their doings. Their consciences had been dulled through constant sinning. Yet **their own doings have beset them about.** They were entangled in their sin and could not escape. **3.** Even **the king** and **the princes** were so depraved as to rejoice in the iniquities which abounded in Israel. The rulers actually profited by the people's sins. The whole body politic was corrupt.

4. Hosea describes an incident in which king and people were involved in a drunken orgy. He begins with the generalization, **They are all adulterers,** stating that evil desires burned within them like the fires of an **oven.** For the baker there was an interval of rest between the time when he **kneaded the dough** and the time when it was thoroughly **leavened.** So Israel would have a brief rest after one indulgence before plunging into yet greater lust and infamy. **5. The day of our king** was some special occasion, perhaps the coronation (so the Targum) or a royal birthday (cf. Mt 14:6). The king participated in the revelry—**he stretched out his hand with scorners** (cf. Prov 21:24; Isa 28:14).

6. They have made ready their heart like an oven. The hearts of the wicked courtiers were burning with intrigue. The Masoretic Text reads *their baker sleepeth.* But the LXX and many recent translations suggest: *Their anger sleepeth all night; in the morning it burneth as a flaming fire.* If we follow the MT, the **baker** may be the assassin who, after a night of sleep, attacked the king. Lehrman identifies the assassin with Shallum (II Kgs 15:10). **7. They are all hot as an oven** seems to characterize the closing decades of Israel. Shallum, who killed Zechariah, was in turn killed by Menahem. Four of Israel's last six kings were murdered.

I. Israel's Disastrous Foreign Policy. 7:8–8:3.

8. With reference to the foreign policy of Israel, Hosea complains concerning **Ephraim** that **he mixeth himself among the peoples; Ephraim is a cake not turned** (ASV). The quest for alliances brought about a situation in which Israel was neither truly Israelite nor truly foreign, but "half-baked," like a pancake cooked on one side only. **9.** The foreign nations, described as **strangers,** had weakened Israel, which already showed signs of age, **gray hairs** appearing on her head. Yet Israel did not heed the sign, but assumed that she was still in the vigor of youth and able to care for her needs. **10. The pride of Israel** (cf. 5:5). Here evidently God, himself, testifies against his people; but they show no disposition to listen.

11. The fickleness of Israel is stressed in terms of **a silly dove,** having no understanding. First it calls **to Egypt,** then goes **to Assyria.** Hosea saw alliances with both Egypt and Assyria as evidence of lack of confidence in the Lord. **12.** In their confused flights, God says, **I will spread my net upon them.** The birds would thus be brought to the ground by God. Israel could find deliverance neither from Egypt nor from Assyria. God humbled her for her rebellion.

13. Woe unto them! Israel fled from God like a bird scared out of its nest, but in doing so she left her only safe abode. The RSV reads, **I would redeem them, but they speak lies against me.** God desired to show mercy to his confused and erring people, but they had hardened their hearts. **14.** When trouble came, **they howled upon their beds** in grief, but still they did not cry unto the Lord. Because they needed food, **they assemble**[d] **themselves for corn and wine,** desiring the gift but not the Giver. A variant reading of some Hebrew manuscripts, followed by the LXX, reads, *they cut themselves,* alluding to the practice of cutting the body as a sign of mourning (Deut 14:1; Lev 19:28; 21:5;

Jer 16:6; 41:5; 47:5; 48:37). **15.** In better days God had **bound** (or *trained)* **and strengthened their arms,** enabling them to stand before the foe; yet Israel rejected his revealed will.

16. They return, but not to the most High may be rendered literally, *They turn – not upward.* Israel turned for help, but not to God. She looked to the broken reed of Egypt for aid. **A deceitful bow** fails to shoot the arrow at the chosen target. So Israel's political moves did not accomplish their aim. The princes had spoken boastful words in defiance of the Lord, but **the rage of their tongue** would be their undoing. They expected help from Egypt, but all they would get would be **derision.**

8:1. Set the trumpet to thy mouth. Literally, *To thy palate the cornet.* The prophet is bidden to warn of the approaching foe. The Assyrian would come **as an eagle.** Hebrew *nesher,* the carrion-eating vulture. The bird of prey is an appropriate symbol of Assyria, which sought to control all of western Asia through a policy of unparalleled cruelty. The foe is described as coming **against the house of the Lord,** i.e., Israel. Israel is thus affectionately designated. Compare, "My servant Moses . . . who is faithful in all mine house" (Num 12:7). Although the Northern Kingdom (Israel) had separated itself from Judah, the two together were still reckoned as God's house.

2. In their distress, Israel would cry, **My God, we know thee.** The word order is: *My God, we, Israel, know thee.* In time of affliction Israel would stress the fact that she had known the Lord. In times of prosperity she had been content to forget. **3. Israel hath cast off** *(spurned,* RSV) . . . the **good.** God, who had been good to Israel through the years of her history, had been rejected, with the result that Israel would have to face the evil of her foes without his aid.

I. Israel's Idolatry and Wicked Alliances. 8:4-14.

4. Israel sought aid from a succession of rulers: **They have set up kings.** Yet the kings of Israel lacked God's blessing and brought the people no lasting good. Kings and princes were of no real help when idolatry was rampant in the land. **5.** Samaria had been devoted to calf (or bull) worship, a fact which led the prophet to say, **Thy calf, O Samaria, hath cast thee off.** The RSV reads, *I have spurned your calf.* And Cheyne (CBSC) suggests, *Thy calf, O Samaria, is loathsome.* The calf at Samaria was probably similar to those set up by Jeroboam at Bethel and Dan (I Kgs 12:28,29), which became an occasion for sin in Israel. **6.** Amazed at the enormity of Israel's sin, Hosea exclaims, **For from Israel was it also;** i.e., the idol, as well as a succession of godless kings, had come from Israel. **The workman made it.** Hence it was vain to worship the work of man's hands. In fact, **the calf of Samaria** was to be destroyed by Israel's righteous God.

7. Israel was to learn the lessons of cause and effect, of sowing and reaping. **They have sown the wind,** that which cannot produce crops, but there would be a harvest, **the** destructive **whirlwind.** Israel's efforts had **no stalk.** They produce nothing but vain hope. Should there come the semblance of a harvest, **strangers shall swallow it up.** The enemy would seize it. Israel would have nothing. **8.** Not only crops, but **Israel,** the nation, **is swallowed up.** The tribes were taken into exile, cast aside as a worthless **vessel,** i.e., a piece of cheap pottery. **9.** Israel in exile is likened to **a wild ass** which wanders from place to place. Asses usually travel together, but a solitary, stubborn ass sometimes obstinately pursues its own path. Turning their back on the covenant love of God, Israel **hired lovers.** She tried by gifts to win aid from Assyria and Egypt.

10. Though Israel had sought to purchase favor from the nations, God would **gather them** (i.e., the Israelites) and send them into exile. **They shall sorrow.** They would become impoverished, because of the burden imposed upon them by **the king of princes,** an expression used only here, which may refer to Tiglath-pileser III, known as "the king of kings." The LXX, followed by the RSV, gives an emended reading – *they shall soon cease from anointing kings and princes.*

11. Israel went through the forms of religion. She **made many altars,** but her multiplying of sacrifices was an abomination to God (cf. Isa 1:11). Hosea says that they are **altars to sin,** i.e., for sinning. The altars were erected in defiance of God, and they became an occasion for further sinning. **12.** God had raised up prophets to Israel who had boldly declared his Law. **The great things** should be read *ten thousands* (RSV) or *never so many things* (JPS). Bewer reads the verse: "Were I to write for him by the ten thousand my directions, they would be counted as those of a stranger."

13. The prophet continues to insist that the sacrifices are a mere form: **They sacrifice flesh,** and, in accord with the Law, they **eat it.** But it had no spiritual merit. The words rendered **for the sacrifices of mine offerings** are problematical. The JPS renders them, *As for the sacrifices that are made by fire,* which is justified on the basis of the fact that the word is used in Rabbinic Hebrew with the sense "to roast." The RSV gives a conjectural meaning, "They love sacrifice." Because of Israel's spiritual decline, Hosea prophesies, **"They shall return to Egypt,** i.e., go into exile. Whether or not Hosea meant that they would literally go to Egypt is debatable. He did assert categorically that they would suffer a future bondage similar to that they had once experienced in Egypt. **14.** Hosea charges Israel with forgetting God, and building **temples** (AV). The alternate meaning of the word, viz., *palaces,* fits better here. Judah is similarly charged with building **fenced cities,** i.e., *fortified cities.* Palaces and fortified cities are not evil in themselves, but they were evidence of a secular trust in things material, which was the counterpart to spiritual decay.

K. The Exile of Israel Foretold. 9:1-9.

1. The heathen nations indulged in orgies during their joyful festivals, but the prophet warned Israel, **Rejoice not.** Israel's neighbors took part in licentious fertility rites, and Israel, following them, had loved **a reward,** literally, *a harlot's hire,* **upon every cornfloor.** The heathen had offered gifts to Baal, the fertility god, to induce him to make the fields fruitful. Israel had followed their footsteps. **2.** The prophet warns that **the floor,** i.e., the threshing floor, and **the winepress** will fail. Efforts to seek blessing from Baal would prove futile, because only the Lord can bring blessing upon the fields.

3. The coming exile is described as a return **to Egypt,** i.e., to the house of bondage. Actually, it was to Assyria that Israel was taken, but the experience is metaphorically compared to the earlier bondage in Egypt (cf. 8:13). In Assyria the Israelites would have to **eat unclean food** (RSV). There would be no offering of first fruits to the Lord (cf. Ex 22:29; 23:19; Lev 23:10-12); hence the food would be esteemed unclean. **4.** In exile there would be no **wine offerings.** Offerings are likened to **the bread of mourners** (cf. Deut 26:14), which, because of its association with death, was considered unclean. Food kept in Jewish homes while the corpse is there is still regarded as ritually unclean. In exile **their bread shall be for their hunger only** (RSV). Not *their bread for their soul* (AV). The exiles would have bread to supply their bodily needs, but they would be cut off from **the house of the Lord;** hence there would be no acceptable sacrifices. **5.** The exiles would be perplexed and troubled on the **solemn day** when **the feast of the Lord** would normally be observed.

6. The prophet depicts the land as it would be after the enemy had come. **Because of destruction** Palestine would be depopulated. Some of the people would go to Egypt (cf. II Kgs 25:26). **Nettles** and **thorns** would grow over their treasure cities **(the pleasant places for their silver)** and their **tabernacles** (i.e., tents – either their dwelling places or tents in which their idols were formerly kept). **7.** The judgment is described as the **days of visitation** and the **days of recompense.** Hosea here seems to quote the remarks of the unbelieving people who would not respond to his ministry: **The prophet is a fool, the spiritual man is mad.** They derided the prophet for his pessimistic message. Some scholars suggest that Hosea is uttering the words in condemnation of false prophets (so Laetsch, *in loco).*

8. The watchman of Ephraim is probably to be identified with Hosea, the true prophet. The verse is difficult as it stands. Bewer suggests the reading, "The prophet is the watchman of Ephraim, the people of my God. The snare of a fowler is on all his ways, enmity in the house of his God." The true prophet faithfully declares the word of God and meets active opposition from the blind leaders of Israel, including her false prophets. **9.** The corruption of Hosea's day is likened to that **in the days of Gibeah** (Jud 19–21) which led to the almost complete annihilation of the tribe of Benjamin. For a time it seemed that Benjamin would be victorious and justice would fail, but God had the last word. So it would be again.

L. Israel's Ancient Apostasy at Baal-peor. 9:10-14.

10. Hosea harks back to Israel's early history. God found his people **like grapes in the wilderness.** The traveler rejoices as he comes upon an oasis with its luscious grapes. So God rejoiced over Israel, who received his Law in the wilderness and vowed fidelity to him. At **Baal-peor** (Num 25) Israel's disposition toward idolatry asserted itself. There they **became detestable like the thing they loved** —viz., Baal (RSV). **11.** Once fruitful, Ephraim would soon find her **glory** flying **away like a bird. Glory** here seems to refer to progeny (cf. 4:7). The result of the departure of this "glory" is specified: **There shall be no birth and none with child and no conception** (JPS). **12.** Should any children be brought up, **yet will I bereave them.** Children who survived infancy would not reach manhood. Woes are pronounced on a people from whom the Lord had departed. His blessing was gone, and they were awaiting his judgment. **13.** Ephraim is likened to ancient **Tyrus** (Tyre), **planted in a pleasant place** (cf. Ezk 27; 28), yet destined to bring forth her children **to the murderer. 14.** In the light of the horrors to come, the prophet prays that God may give **a miscarrying womb and dry breasts!** God's judgments are right, and Hosea prays that the children of Israel may be cut off before they are born, that they may be spared the horrors to come.

M. Israel's Apostasy at Gilgal. 9:15-17.

15. The idolatrous shrine at **Gilgal** (cf. 4:15; 12:11; Amos 5:5) embodied all the evil that had marked Israel's history. The evils perpetrated there, and at similar shrines elsewhere, caused God to say, *I will drive them out of mine house;* i.e., from the land of Canaan, which God had given to them as an inheritance. In strong language God says he **hated them,** and **will love them no more.** As long as Israel continued in her sin, she could not enjoy the blessings of God's love. **16.** The thought of verses 11,12 is taken up in verse 16: "Fruitful" Ephraim would be barren; children born to Ephraim would be destroyed. **17.** Refusal to hearken to God and his prophets would bring upon Israel the judgment of exile. Like Cain (Gen 4:12) they were destined to be **wanderers.**

N. Destruction of the Baal Cult Prophesied. 10:1-8.

1. Israel is described as a **luxuriant vine** (RSV; not *empty* as in AV). The vine was very fruitful, but **according to the multitude of his fruit he hath increased the** (heathen) **altars.** With the increase of wealth and power in Israel, there came an increase in idolatry and its attendant evils. **2.** In trying to serve God and Baal, **Their heart is divided.** Yet God was jealous, refusing to share his glory with another. **Altars** and **images** which were offensive to him must be destroyed. **3.** When Israel saw her cities desolated by the enemy, she would cry out, **We have no king,** i.e., none worthy of the name. Godless rulers had not been able to stay the downward course of the nation. **4. They have spoken words.** Kings and their ministers spoke idle words, **making a covenant** with Assyria and Egypt. Their perverted **judgment springeth up** like the deadly **hemlock** which grows abundantly **in the furrows of the field.**

5. The inhabitants of Samaria, seeing their idols carried off by the enemy, would be filled with fear. **The calves of Beth-aven.** The idols of Bethel. Beth-el means *house of God,* but its idolatrous cult had merited a new name for it—**Beth-aven,** *house of iniquity.* Under the tragic circumstances the **people shall mourn,** and the idolatrous priests **shall wail** (RSV), or *tremble* (JPS). Contrast the AV *rejoice*. The reference is to a ritual dance performed by the idolatrous priests, during which they implored their idol to save them and himself. **6.** The calf would be taken from Bethel **unto Assyria,** where it would be presented to **king Jareb,** or "the fighting king." The JPS designates him "King Contentious" (cf. 5:13). The Northern Kingdom (Israel – Ephraim), filled with shame, would learn at last the futility of setting up a dumb idol as protector of the nation. **7. Samaria,** the capital of Israel, would fall. **Her king is cut off.** Not only did he lose his life, but his death marked the end of Israel as a state. The king is described as **the foam upon the water,** or *like a chip on the face of the waters* (RSV). A helpless fragment of wood is irresistibly carried along by the power of the current. **8.** Hosea states categorically that **the high places of** (Beth-) **Aven** would be destroyed. **The thorn and the thistle,** mentioned at the time of the curse on the ground following Adam's sin (Gen 3:18), would cover the altars of Beth-aven, which would come to symbolize the sinfulness of pre-Exilic Israel. The words of the people, to be addressed to **the mountains** and **to the hills,** are echoed in Lk 23:30 and Rev 6:16.

O. The Sin at Gibeah. 10:9,10.

9. Israel's sin at **Gibeah** (Jud 19) found many echoes in subsequent history. Israel had taken vengeance on the Benjamites for the outrage at Gibeah, but the wickedness perpetrated there entered the life of all Israel. **10. It is my desire.** Read with the JPS, *When it is My desire, I will chastise them.* In God's time punishment would come, and the nations upon whom Israel had relied would be shown to be broken reeds. The words, **when they shall bind themselves in their two furrows,** are difficult to explain. The RSV reads, *when they are chastised for their double iniquity,* perhaps referring to the bulls at Dan and Bethel. The double iniquity may be their rejection of the Lord and the Davidic line (cf. 3:5).

P. The Ruin of Israel. 10:11-15.

11. Israel is likened to a well-trained **heifer** that enjoys the treading of **corn** (grain) which it can freely **eat** (Deut 25:4). No heavy yoke was placed **upon her fair neck,** such as the yokes which frequently wounded the necks of animals in the East. God's kindness was abused, however, and now he would cause Ephraim **to ride,** i.e., to draw a heavy load. The heavy work of the heifer is further described in terms of plowing and breaking clods. Drawing, plowing, and breaking up the soil are laborious tasks compared with the easier work of threshing. **12.** Hosea still holds out hope for his people: **Sow to yourselves in righteousness.** If they would but turn to God, they would find him merciful. If a harvest was to be reaped, Israel must **break up** her **fallow ground.** She could not sow among thorns and hope for a good harvest. Hosea reminds Israel that there is still **time to seek the Lord.** If they did so earnestly, God would respond and **rain righteousness** on them. Although in need of material blessings, Hosea stresses the spiritual "rain" of righteousness, or salvation, which was the prime need.

13. In contrast with the spiritual possibilities of regeneration, Hosea charges that Israel had **plowed** (i.e., plotted) **wickedness** and **reaped iniquity** (or injustice). The lying policy bore sour fruit! **14. A tumult,** the noise of armies, would arise among the peoples who had been the object of Israel's trust. Israelite **fortresses** would be despoiled. **Shalman** may be the Assyrian king Shalmaneser V (727–722 B.C.; cf. II Kgs 17:1-6). The battle at **Beth-arbel** is otherwise unknown. The town is either Irbid in Galilee, or Arbela, twelve miles southeast of Gadara, in Trans-Jordan. **15.** The judgment at Beth-arbel was caused by the sins associated with idolatrous **Bethel. In a morning.** *At dawn*—when better things might be anticipated. **The king of Israel** would be **cut off.** The nation would be carried into exile, and the day of grace ended. True, God would remember his people in the land of bondage, but the Northern Kingdom and its succession of rulers was to come to an end forever with the fall of Samaria (722 B.C.).

Q. God's Love; Israel's Ingratitude. 11:1-7.

1. When Israel was a child. God refers to the early history of Israel, and contrasts it with the subsequent idolatry of his people. **Called my son out of Egypt** (cf. Ex 4:22). God called Israel from Egypt to Canaan and provided protection and sustenance. The words are used of Christ in Mt 2:15. God's son, Israel, was taken from Egypt, yet proved faithless in subsequent history and was threatened by judgment. The only begotten of the Father, the Son, Jesus, was taken from Egypt, grew into perfect manhood, and accomplished the work which the Father had purposed. **2. As they called them.** The more they (i.e., the prophets) called them (Israel), the more they (Israel) obstinately hardened their hearts and refused to obey the Lord. **They sacrificed unto Baalim** (cf. 2:13). The cult objects of the iniquitous Baal worship claimed the loyalty of Israel.

3. I taught Ephraim also to go. Again the Lord refers to Israel's infancy. *Walk* is preferable to **go** in this verse. As a parent, God taught Israel to walk. His protecting care was shown when Israel would stumble, yet Israel showed no discernment: **They knew not that I healed them.** Israel did not realize that the Lord was her healer. She took his blessings for granted, ascribing them to Baal and other deities. **4. I drew them with cords of a man.** God's care for Israel continued as she reached maturity. The illustration is here taken from the animal world. A man may lead his beast with cords suitable for an animal. God used cords suitable for a man—i.e., gentle, humane— in seeking to lead Israel. **They that take off the yoke.** A considerate master lifts the yoke from the neck of his beasts that they may eat more comfortably. God had shown consideration in his dealings with Israel.

5. He shall not return into the land of Egypt. The prophet speaks of judgment, but it would not take the form of renewed bondage in Egypt (cf. Deut 17:16). **But the Assyrian shall be his king.** The Northern Kingdom fell to Assyria in 722 B.C. **6. The sword** is a symbol of war. Hosea depicts the cities of Israel as devastated by war. **Because of their own counsels.** In despair, Hoshea conspired with So of Egypt for deliverance, but this only hastened Israel's defeat (II Kgs 17:4-6). **7. Bent to backsliding from me.** The word rendered **backsliding** is, literally, *turning* or *turning about.* Instead of turning to God, Israel persisted in turning from him. **Though they called them** is a reference to the prophets whose ministry was rejected by Israel.

R. God's Pity for His People. 11:8-11.

8. How shall I give thee up . . . ? The cry is heart-rending. God had loved his people, yet justice demanded that they be punished. Since God could not lightly forget the earlier days of Israel's faithfulness, he decreed judgment with great reluctance. **Admah . . . Zeboim** were cities of the plain which were overthrown along with Sodom and Gomorrah (Gen 19). **9. I will not execute the fierceness of mine anger.** Although judgment would fall upon Israel, in wrath God would remember mercy. Israel was not to be forever cast off, although she would be sorely chastised. **I will not enter into the city** does not seem to fit here. The JPS suggests, *I will not come in fury.* Cheyne prefers, *I will not come to exterminate,* which is parallel to **I will not return to destroy Ephraim. 10. When he shall roar.** The Lord is likened to a lion who roars to summon its young. At the sound of his roar they would come from the west (Egypt, v. 11) and the east (Assyria). **The children shall tremble** implies the thrill of eagerness rather than of fear. The Syriac combines the ideas of haste and trembling.

S. The Sins of Jacob. 11:12–12:14.

12. Ephraim compasseth me about with lies. In the Hebrew text 11:12 becomes 12:1, for it begins a new subject. The Lord is speaking concerning the faithlessness of both Ephraim (i.e., Israel) and Judah. **Judah yet ruleth with God** may be read *Judah is yet wayward toward God* (JPS). In spite of all the prophetic messages addressed to Judah, she continued in her sin! **Is faithful with the saints.** The JPS reads: *And toward the Holy One who is faithful.* The LXX gives an entirely different reading: *Judah is still known by God and faithful with the Holy One.* **12:1. Ephraim feedeth on wind.** Literally, *shepherds the wind.* The RSV reads, *Ephraim herds the wind.* The words depict the futility of running for help to Assyria and Egypt. The **east wind** was the hot, destructive sirocco. It was not only vain to look to the east (Assyria) for help, but also dangerous, for destruction would come from that direction. Israel's foreign policy was such that she could make **a covenant with the Assyrians** while at the same time export olive **oil** to Assyria's rival, Egypt. Such duplicity was made possible by a policy of **lies** which would ultimately trap Israel and bring about her ruin.

2. Not only Israel, but **Judah** also followed a path of deceit and duplicity. Her judgment came later than that of Israel, but Jerusalem was destroyed as violently as was Samaria. **Jacob** here is used of Judah (cf. Ps 77:15). **3. He took his brother by the heel** (Gen 25:26) **. . . and by his strength he had power with God** (Gen 32:22-32). The RSV reads, *In his manhood he strove with God.* **4. He found him in Beth-el** (Gen 28:10-17). He came face to face with God at Bethel. **And there he spake with us.** God, in speaking to Jacob, spoke to all Israelites who could be considered as in the loins of their ancestor (cf. Heb 7:9,10). **5.** The God who addressed Jacob at Bethel is identified as **the Lord God of hosts. His memorial** is another way of saying *his name* (so JPS, RSV. Cf. Ex 3:15). **6.** In remembrance of past mercies, the prophet urges Israel to turn back to her God. Jacob's victories would provide an example of blessings his descendants might enjoy. In turning to God, Israel would be expected to obey his commandments: **Keep mercy and judgment, and wait on thy God continually.**

7. Israel had not only followed the Canaanite in his licentious religion, but also had adopted his wicked business practices. The word **merchant** is identical with the word *Canaan.* As a geographical designation it meant the lowland and was applied to Phoenicia as well as to the other parts of Palestine (cf. Isa 23:11). "Canaanite" thus became a synonym for merchant (Job 41:6; Prov 31:24; Zeph 1:11; Ezk 17:4). The evil reputation of Phoenician traders is reflected in Homer *(Odyssey* XIV, 290, 291). **8,9.** Living like her Canaanite neighbors, Israel had become proud and arrogant. She did not even realize that her life had become marked by sin. God, however, reminded her of the events of the Exodus, the period during which the tribes dwelt in tents. In her subsequent history the Feast of the Tabernacles, for which festival the Israelites erected booths to commemorate their earlier tent life, had become a joyous celebration. The prophet warned, however, that God would make his people again to dwell in **tabernacles** (tents), and that this would mean that their cities would be destroyed and life violently altered.

10. Israel could not plead ignorance, for God had **spoken by the prophets** and **multiplied visions.** In "divers manners" (Heb 1:1) God had spoken through his prophetic spokesmen. Here three are mentioned: words ("I have spoken"); visions ("I have multiplied visions"); and parables ("and used similitudes"). **11. Is there iniquity in Gilead?** Read with the RSV, *If there is iniquity in Gilead, they shall surely come to nought.* II Kings 15:29 tells how Tiglath-pileser's armies despoiled Gilead in the days of Pekah of Israel. The Lord was further insulted by the sacrifice of **bullocks** at the shrine in Gilgal.

12. Verses 3-5 give certain lessons from the life of Jacob which were relevant to the Israel of Hosea's day. These continue in verse 12, where we read that **Jacob fled into the country of Syria, and Israel served for a wife.** Jacob-Israel had labored in the house of Laban to secure for himself a wife. Through all those years God cared for Jacob, and ultimately brought him back to Canaan. This fact would offer a glimmer of hope to the nation which was to go into captivity to Assyria. God had brought the earlier Israel back from Syria (lit., *the field of Aram,* the same in meaning as Padan-Aram). **13.** Again, after a time in a distant land, **by a prophet** (Moses) **the Lord brought Israel out of Egypt.** The God who raised up Moses to be the leader of the Exodus, could raise up yet other prophets during the captivity to bring his people back to their homeland. **14.** Through persistent sin, **Ephraim provoked** (God) **to anger.** The result is that He would **leave his blood upon him.** Ephraim-Israel would bear the consequences of his guilt.

T. The Wicked Bull Worship. 13:1-3.

1. When Ephraim spake trembling should be rendered, *When Ephraim spoke, there was trembling.* The tribe of Ephraim was so influential as to command unquestioning respect in the early days of the Northern Kingdom. Ephraim and all Israel subsequently were weakened through the impact of Baal worship, so that Hosea could here say, **He died.** The death was a spiritual one, but the prophet also foretold national judgment and the victory of Israel's foes. **2.** In their spiritual death **they sin**[ned] **more and more** by making and worshiping **molten images.** Those who would **kiss the calves** as an act of worship were guilty of sin against God (cf. 8:5; I Kgs 19:18; Isa 40:18-20; 44:9-20; 46:6,7). **3.** Because of sin, Israel would **be as the morning cloud,** the night mist which appears as a cloud in the morning but soon is dispersed. Cf. 6:14.

U. The Gracious God To Bring Destruction. 13:4-11.

4. In spite of Israel's sins, God reminds his people of his covenant relationship to them: **I am the Lord thy God from the land of Egypt.** The reference to **Egypt** serves as a reminder of the great events associated with the Exodus. God had been faithful to his people, even during times of their faithlessness. **Thou shalt know no god but me** should be rendered in the present — *Thou knowest no god but me.* The Lord alone had met the needs of his people. All other deities were helpless in themselves and useless to their worshipers. **5.** God reminds Israel, **I did know thee in the wilderness.** As in Ps 1:6, **know** conveys the idea "to take favorable notice of." Those whom God knows he blesses, and Israel had received countless blessings — e.g., manna from heaven, water from the rock — during her wilderness sojourn. Yet, Israel became a murmuring people, rebelling against God, and a whole generation perished without seeing the Promised Land. **6.** God had cared for all the needs of his people, but they soon forgot him. **According to their pasture, so were they filled** should read, *When they were fed, they became full.* When they had eaten to satiety, **their heart was exalted,** and they forgot the source of their blessings, God himself.

7. God, who had been the protector of his people, in judgment became their destroyer. He here likens himself to **a lion,** ready to devour, and **a leopard,** ready to spring upon his unprepared people (cf. Jer 5:6). **As a leopard by the way will I observe them** does not bring out the force of the original, which might better be rendered, *As a leopard by the way will I lurk.* **8.** Continuing his similes from the animal world, God likens himself to **a bear that is bereaved of her whelps,** hence ferocious (cf. II Sam 17:8). The heart of Israel had resisted the loving call of her God; now, however, God likens himself to a charging animal, saying, **I . . . will rend the caul** (enclosure) **of their heart. 9.** God continues to address Israel: **O Israel, thou hast destroyed thyself.** The JPS reads, *It is thy destruction, O Israel.* God had described the path which led to Israel's destruction, but he adds, **but in me is thine help.** The LXX and the Syriac suggest a different reading: *Who can help you?* (So RSV). The JPS renders the verse: *It is thy destruction, O Israel, that thou art against Me, against thy help.* Although there are textual problems here, the meaning is clear: By rebelling against the God who was always ready to help his people, Israel had brought about her own destruction.

10. I will be thy king should read, *Where now is your king . . .* (so LXX, Syr., Vulg., BV, RSV). We then have a rhetorical question, "Where now is your king, to save you . . . ?" The people had earlier said, **Give me a king and princes** (cf. I Sam 8:5), but in the present emergency these rulers had proved futile. The BV and the RSV emend the words **in all thy cities** to *all your princes* because of the reference to kings and princes at the end of the verse. The verse then reads: "Where now is your king, to save you; where are all your princes, to defend you – those of whom you said, 'Give me a king and princes'?" **11. I gave thee a king in mine anger.** The initial reference may be to Saul, but the words are likewise appropriate to the dynastic history of the Northern Kingdom, beginning with Jeroboam I. Kings were repeatedly given and taken away. Laetsch renders the passage: *I have been giving you kings in my anger and have taken them away in my wrath.* Because the kings were subject to God's providential government, they can be described as given of God. But their idolatrous ways and the rejection of the Davidic dynasty by the Northern Kingdom furnish the basis for the statement that they were given in God's anger.

V. Inescapable Ruin. 13:12-16.

12. Ephraim's sin (i.e., the sin of the Northern Kingdom) is described as **bound up** or *wrapped up*. It is ***kept in store*** (RSV), remembered in the courts of heaven, and one day will be dealt with in justice. The AV translation ***his sin is hid*** does not show the force of the words, rendered in the JPS, **laid up in store. 13.** Ephraim – Israel is likened to a travailing woman: **The sorrows of a travailing woman shall come upon him.** As the pangs of childbirth are inescapable, so Israel was to bear the trials which her sins had merited. She is also likened to **an unwise son** who, at the time of birth, does not present himself **in the place of the breaking forth of children** (i.e., at the mouth of the womb). In Hosea's apt illustration, a clever child would be eager **to hasten** from the womb; leaving the womb would usher in a new life (cf. Jn 3:3,4). Israel (Ephraim) could have had a new beginning in a life of obedience, but she chose to tarry in her idolatry.

14. I will ransom them from the power of the grave. The words express the feeling of a father who cannot bear to contemplate the utter ruin of even a faithless son. Judgment must come upon Israel, but beyond the judgment would be deliverance. **The grave** *(shᵉ'ôl)* and **death** are used synonymously of the nether world. Its powers are arrayed against God's people of all ages (cf. Mt 16:18). Yet God will be victor over **Death** and the **Grave.** Paul, in I Cor 15:55, cites Hos 13:14 in describing the triumph of the Christian over death: "O death, where is thy sting? O grave, where is thy victory?" **15.** Turning again to the immediate judgment upon Ephraim (which means *fruitfulness),* Hosea says, **Though he be fruitful among his brethren,** the smiting east wind from the wilderness will bring desolation on the land. The wind from the East seems to be an allusion to the Assyrian who would soon despoil Israel. **16.** With the coming of the Assyrian, **Samaria** would **become desolate.** Or, literally, *Samaria shall bear her guilt.* The kings of Israel had been guilty of atrocities similar to those described here (cf. II Kgs 15:16).

III. Israel's Conversion and Renewal. 14:1-9.

A. The Call to Repentance. 14:1-3.

1. Hosea turned to his people with a plea to **return unto the Lord.** Israel had been faithless, but the prophet still saw hope if she would turn from her sin. Israel had **fallen.** Literally, *stumbled.* Sin had put a stumbling block in the way. **2.** Hosea asks for confession of sin: **Take with you words.** Israel had been headed in the direction of judgment, which could only be averted by a complete turning from sin and idolatry to God and his righteous claims upon the lives of his people; hence the command to **turn to the Lord.** The prayer, **Take away all iniquity**, implies renunciation of sin. The words, **and receive us graciously,** literally read, *and take good.* The JPS renders, *and accept that which is good.* The Psalmist says, "it is good to sing praises unto our God" (Ps 147:1). For **the calves of our lips,** the LXX reads, *the fruit of our lips* (cf. Heb 13:15). Confession of sin, and renunciation of its hold upon the life of Israel would result in blessing, with its attendant praise and thanksgiving. Praise is likened to sacrifice which is offered by the grateful worshiper.

3. One party in the Israelite court looked to Assyria for help, but Hosea insisted **Asshur shall not save us.** To those who looked to Egypt, the source of war horses (cf. I Kgs 10:28; Isa 31:1), the prophet insisted, **we will not ride upon horses.** Israel was tempted to look to one or the other of the rival powers to satisfy her needs, but Hosea sought to remind her that such a policy would result in divine judgment. **The work of our hands** refers to idols which Israel made. Salvation would not come from Assyria, Egypt, or Israel's own efforts and idolatrous inventions (cf. Isa 42:17; 54:17). In the words, **the fatherless findeth mercy**, Israel is depicted as an orphan with no father to provide sustenance. Although exposed to danger from Assyria, from Egypt, and from other foes, Israel in her helplessness could find mercy only in her God.

B. The Promise of Pardon. 14:4-8.

4. When God's people call upon him in genuine penitence, he is ready to come to their aid and **will heal their backsliding.** The Lord's love is motivated by his own grace rather than by any merit in its subject. It is given **freely,** a word suggesting that it is bestowed of God's own free will. Israel had not earned God's love, but he was prepared to give it as a gift. The **anger** of the Lord speaks of his reaction to sin, which always provokes his wrath. In grace, however, anger may be **turned away** and judgment averted.

5. Rain is scarce in much of the Near East, and **dew** is essential if vegetation is to grow. God would enable Israel to flourish: **He shall grow as the lily,** suggesting both beauty and fruitfulness. Several flowers are suggested as the lily. Pliny spoke of the white lily which grows wild in Palestine and "is unsurpassed in its fecundity, often producing fifty bulbs from a single root" (Pliny *Natural History* XXI. 5). The *Anemone coronaria* is also suggested. The words, **roots as Lebanon,** imply stability. It is uncertain whether the cedar trees or the mountains of Lebanon are meant, but in either instance the symbol is one of permanence.

6. The **branches** which **shall spread** are the tender branches or saplings which spring from the root after Israel's vine is cut down (cf. Isa 53:2). Hosea indicates that the root of the tree shall send forth many fresh plants. The fruit of **the olive tree** was a staple in the economy of the ancient East. Jeremiah 11:16 speaks of Israel as "a green olive tree, fair and of goodly fruit." **Lebanon** had the fresh smell of its cedars and of the shrubs which grew on its slopes. **7 a.** Read, **They that dwell under his shadow shall again make corn to grow** (so JPS). God is speaking, and declaring that restored Israel will enjoy such blessing that other peoples will be blessed through association with Israel. They shall plant corn and reap harvests under Israel's shadow.

8. Verse 8 is best understood as a dialogue between Israel and God. Israel asks, **What have I to do any more with idols?** Ephraim (Israel) has learned her lesson, and is ready to renounce idolatry. God replies: **I have heard him and observed him.** God looks with favor on Israel's renunciation of idolatry. Israel again speaks: **I am like a green fir tree.** In her prosperity Israel likens herself to a stately fir, or cypress tree. This boast appears presumptuous, however, and God reminds his people, **From me is thy fruit found.**

C. A Parting Admonition. 14:9.

The question, **Who is wise, and he shall understand these things?"** conveys the idea, "Whoso is wise, let him understand these things." The wise and prudent can be expected to heed the prophet's message. **The ways of the Lord** comprise his Word, or will. **The** term "way" is here used as a metaphor. **The just** can walk in the Lord's way without fear, but **the transgressors** find stumbling blocks along the road, and constantly come to grief.

BIBLIOGRAPHY

BATTEN, L. W. "Hosea's Message and Marriage," *Journal of Biblical Literature*, XLVIII (1929), 257-273.

BEWER, JULIUS A. *The Prophets*. New York: Harper & Brothers, 1949.

BROWN, S. L. *The Book of Hosea (Westminster Commentary)*. London: Methuen & Co., 1932.

CHEYNE, T. K. *The Book of Hosea (The Cambridge Bible for Schools and Colleges)*. Cambridge: The University Press, 1913.

HARPER, WILLIAM R. *A Critical and Exegetical Commentary on Amos and Hosea (International Critical Commentary)*. New York: Charles Scribner's Sons, 1910.

KEIL, CARL FRIEDRICH. *The Twelve Minor Prophets*. Vol. I. *(Keil and Delitzsch Commentaries)*. Grand Rapids: William B. Eerdmans Publishing Co., reprinted 1949.

LAETSCH, THEODORE. *The Minor Phophets*. St. Louis: Concordia Publishing House, 1956.

LEHRMAN, S. M. "Hosea," *The Twelve Prophets (The Soncino Bible*. Edited by A. Cohen). Bournemouth: The Soncino Press, 1948.

MAUCHLINE, JOHN. "Hosea," *The Interpreter's Bible*. Vol. 6. New York: Abingdon Press, 1956.

NYBERG, H. S. *Studien zum Hoseabuch*. Uppsala: Almqvist & Wiksells, 1935.

PUSEY, E. B. *The Minor Prophets with a Commentary*. Vol. I. New York: Funk & Wagnalls Co., 1885.

ROBINSON, H. WHEELER. *Two Hebrew Prophets*. London: Lutterworth Press, 1948.

ROWLEY, H. H. "The Marriage of Hosea," *Bulletin of the John Rylands Library*, XXXIX (1956).

SMITH, GEORGE ADAM. *The Book of the Twelve Prophets*. Vol. I. Revised ed. New York: Harper & Brothers, 1928.

SNAITH, NORMAN H. *Mercy and Sacrifice*. London: Student Christian Movement Press, 1953.

WOLFE, ROLLAND EMERSON. *Meet Amos and Hosea*. New York: Harper & Brothers, 1945.

JOEL

INTRODUCTION

Author's Name and Personal History. The author is termed "Joel the son of Pethuel" (1:1). The Hebrew name *Yô'ēl* (LXX; *Iōél,* Vulg.) means "Yahweh (or Jehovah) is God." Hence, like the name *Micah,* it may indicate a confession of faith on the part of the child's parents.

Joel's personal history is limited to what is suggested in the prophecy itself. Although thirteen other persons in the Old Testament bear the name *Joel,* the prophet cannot be identified with any of them. His message is concerned primarily with Jerusalem and Judah. His references to the land and city suggest that he was a citizen of southern Palestine and probably a resident of Jerusalem (see "Zion," 2:1,15,32; 3:16,17,21; the "children of Zion," 2:23; "Judah" and "Jerusalem," 2:32; 3:1,16,17,18,20; the "children of Judah" and Jerusalem, 3:6, 8,19). He demonstrates a thorough knowledge of the Temple, its services and personnel (e.g., 1:9,13,14,16; 2:14,17). However, his castigation of the priests seems to indicate that he was not a member of their caste.

Date. So far scholars have not been able to agree on the dating of the book of Joel. However, of the various dates proposed, there are two primary suggestions: (1) An early date, during the reign of Joash (or Jehoash) in Judah, about 830 B.C. (2) A post-Exilic date, about 400 B.C.—during the Persian period. There are some logical arguments to support a late date. For one thing, there is no reference in the title verse (1:1) to the ruling king, as in other pre-Exilic prophets. Also, the Northern Kingdom (Samaria) is not mentioned, so evidently it had long been extinct. Joel uses the word *Israel* for Judah, which no pre-Exilic prophet would have done. The term was used only for the ten northern tribes prior to 722 B.C. (the fall of Samaria). The priests, not nobles or kings, were the leaders in the post-Exilic society. The reference in 3:6 to the Greeks (Ionians) indicates a time when the Jews were in contact with them. Also verses 1,2,17 of Joel 3 indicate that the Captivity had already occurred.

On the other hand, arguments for the pre-Exilic date are strong. The prominence of the priests and the absence of the nobles and king are due to the fact that Jehoiada the high priest was ruling for the boy king, Joash. The argument from silence (see on Samaria above) is weightless, for the author was not primarily concerned with the events of the Northern Kingdom. The term *Israel* could be used appropriately of Judah as the rightful heir of the spiritual blessings of Jacob. Intercourse between Greece and Tyre could have occurred at an early date, for Greece is not here referred to as a nation. The Hebrew word *Yāwān* (=Ionian) could refer to a group of isolated bands of slave-traders from a distant country. **Bring back the captivity** (3:1) simply means "restore the fortune" (cf. Job 42:10). There is no description in Joel 3 that will not fit pre-Exilic times. Joel 3:4-6 refers to the same events as are described in the book of Obadiah. The enemies referred to are not countries of the Exile (Assyria, Babylonia, and Samaria), but pre-Exilic countries (Phoenicia and Philistia; cf. II Chr 21:16,17).

Authorship. The book of Joel has traditionally been accepted as the work of one author. However, about 1870 M. Vernes suggested that 2:28–3:21 (in the Hebrew Bible, chs. 3; 4) were not written by the author of 1:2–2:27 (in the Hebrew Bible, 1:1–2:18). Later, he modified his view and admitted that the same author wrote both sections; he still maintained, however, that striking differences exist between the two sections. Other minor attempts have been made to prove that the book is not a literary unit. Nowack, Marti, and others who have successfully questioned the validity of this school of thought contend that Joel is a unit. The higher critical view commonly accepted today is that Joel is the responsible author of the book but that later modifications, expansions, and interpolations may have occurred through the centuries of transmission of the Scriptures.

Style. The style of Joel is classical, resembling that of Amos and Micah.

Whether Joel borrowed heavily from the earlier prophets, or whether he was the well out of which they drew cannot be determined with certainty; but literary affinity is strong. Compare Joel 3:18 with Amos 9:13; Joel 1:4 with Amos 4:9; Joel 2:11 with Zeph 1:14,15; Joel 2:3 with Ezk 36:35 and Isa 51:3; Joel 2:11 with Mal 3:2; Joel 3:10 with Isa 2:4.

Occasion for Writing. The immediate occasion for the writing of the book was the devastation of the land by a double plague of locusts and drought. In poetic strain of matchless elegance and power, the prophet depicts the invasion of the locusts under the figure of an army, suggesting that they are a harbinger of the "Day of the Lord." He summons all classes of the population to repentance, and promises them that if they will meet the conditions of obedience to God, the land will be restored to its former fruitfulness. Also the Spirit of God will be poured out upon all flesh, the covenant people will eventually triumph over all their foes, and an era of universal holiness and peace will emerge.

Teachings. That "the Day of the Lord" is coming, is the central teaching of the book—the day when the Lord will manifest himself in the destruction of his enemies and the exaltation of his friends. This day will be accompanied by great convulsions of the earth and a display of extraordinary phenomena in nature (2:30,31). The attitude of a man's heart and life before the Lord will be the factor that will determine his reaction to that day. It will be a day of terror to the sinner (1:15; 2:11) and a day of blessing to the saint (2:12-14, 19-29). Those who call upon the name of the Lord will be delivered, but the enemies of the people will be annihilated (ch. 3).

OUTLINE

Title verse: The Author of the Prophecy. 1:1.

I. The locust plague as the harbinger of the Day of the Lord. 1:2—2:17.
   A. A threefold calamity: locusts, drought, and conflagrations. 1:2-20.
      1. The invasion of the locusts. 1:2-12.
      2. A call to repentance. 1:13,14.
      3. The terrors of the Day of the Lord. 1:15-20.
   B. The scourge as the forerunner of the judgment day. 2:1-17.
      1. A vivid picture of the coming judgment. 2:1-11.
      2. An exhortation to repentance. 2:12-17.

II. The averting of judgment and bestowal of blessings. 2:18—3:21.
   A. The blessings in the immediate future. 2:18-27.
   B. The outpouring of the divine Spirit. 2:28-32.
   C. Judgment upon the nations. 3:1-17.
      1. The avenging of wrongs committed against the Jews. 3:1-3.
      2. Judgment upon Phoenicia. 3:4-8.
      3. World judgment. 3:9-17.
   D. The blessings following the judgment. 3:18-21.

COMMENTARY

Title Verse. 1:1.

1. Joel means *Yahweh* (or *Jehovah) is God.* **Pethuel.** *Persuaded of God.* In the East the use of one's father's name served as a mark of identification. It was analogous to our use of second names (cf. Hos 1:1; Zeph 1:1; Mic 1:1).

I. The Locust Plague as the Harbinger of the Day of the Lord. 1:2—2:17.

A. A Threefold Calamity: Locusts, Drought, and Conflagrations. 1:2-20.

In the *midst* of a terrible calamity the prophet summons the people to universal mourning. He interprets the present condition as a forerunner (harbinger) of the Day of the Lord (1:2-12). To avert its terrors he calls upon all classes of the populace to turn to God in repentance (1:13,14). He re-emphasizes the present plight and closes with a prayer for deliverance (1:16-20).

1) The Invasion of the Locusts. 1:2-12.

2. Listen to this. A solemn plea to be attentive to what follows (cf. Amos 3:1; 4:1; 5:1). **Old men.** Not the official elders, but the "aged" who transmitted the lore of the past to the next generation. **In the days of your fathers.** Among the people of the East memories of past times were handed down from generation to generation. **3.** The reply to the question of verse 2 is not stated. The answer could only be *NO!* **Tell.** The Hebrew word *săppērû* (an intensive stem) comes from the same root from which "book" is derived. Here the verb means the giving of careful, detailed information. (For the transmission of the record of Divine deliverance and revelation in this manner, see Deut 4:9; 6:6,7: 11:8; Ps 78:5.) Now the same procedure must record this unparalleled calamity.

4. Palmerworm . . . locust . . . cankerworm . . . caterpiller. Literally: *Shearer, swarmer, lapper, devourer* – describing four of the eighty or ninety species of locusts in the East. **5. Awake, you drunkards.** It is high time to awake from the sleep of intoxication! The drunkards represent the luxurious classes, who are here urged to weep and howl because the destruction of the vineyards has cut off their supplies.

6,7. The reason for the plight, i.e., the immense number of the enemies, their horrible weapons, and the awful results of their attack. **Nation** (Heb. *gôy*). The swarms of locusts are like a nation; they devastate the land like an invading army. **Has come upon.** A military term used of the approach of an enemy (cf. I Kgs 20:22; Isa 21:2). **Jaw teeth.** The "eye teeth" or "projectors." The jaws of some locusts are toothed like a saw. With such jaws they can gnaw wood and leather as well as foliage. **Barked** (or *splintered*). This is hyperbolic. The locusts could not splinter the fig tree, but they could reduce each fig tree to the value of a mere splinter. **Stripped.** Literally: **Making bare he has made it bare.** By constant gnawing the locusts stripped off the blossoms, foliage, and bark. **White.** Not the appearance of a burnt countryside, but that of ground covered with snow, due to the whiteness of the trees and the dry herbs.

8. Wail (Heb. *'ĕlî*). This verb is used only here, but the meaning is clear from the Aramaic and Syriac. The form is feminine because the entire community is addressed. **Like a virgin** (Heb. *betûlâ*). Literally, *one who is separated* from all others, one who has not known *any* man (Gen 24:16). **Husband of her youth.** Left a widow before she married. **9.** The justification for the call to universal mourning. **Meal offering and drink offering.** They stand for the daily sacrifice (cf. Num 15:5; 28:7; Ex 29:38). In later Judaism nothing was more dreaded than the suspension of the Thamid (see Dan 8:11; 11:31; 12:11). Josephus felt this breach of daily sacrifice to be the most terrible and unprecedented calamity in the siege of Jerusalem *(Antiq* xiv. 16. 2; *Wars* vi. 2. 1).

11,12. The prophet issues a call to the plowman and the vine dressers. **Be ye ashamed.** The farmers, like the vine, are to be embarrassed. Joel depicts men, crops, and fields as mourning together. Jerome allegorizes here and contends that the husbandmen and vine dressers are priests and preachers. **The fig tree** was native in western Asia and very plentiful in Palestine. It was highly prized and often mentioned along with the vine (cf. Deut 8:8; Jer 5:17). To "sit under one's vine and fig tree" was a symbol of prosperity and security (I Kgs 4:25; Mic 4:4). Figs were dried and pressed into cakes and used for food (I Sam 25:18) and as a poultice (II Kgs 20:7; Isa 38:21). Grapes and figs are referred to by Josephus as the principal fruits of the land *(Wars* iii. x. 8). Also today many houses in the Near East are entirely covered with vines and are hidden almost entirely behind fig trees. **Pomegranate tree.** There are numerous references in Scripture to this tree (e.g., Num 13:23; 20:5; Deut 8:8; I Sam 14:2; Song 4:3, 13). It is a shrub or low tree, from ten to fifteen feet high, with small, dark green foliage. It bears a fruit about the size of an orange, sweet on one variety and acid on the other. The pulp is most refreshing to the taste. The juice of the acid kind was sweetened and used as a beverage (Song 8:2). It was also used in salads.

Palm tree. The palm has existed since prehistoric times over a vast area in the dry warm zone which extends from Senegal to the basin of the Indus–chiefly between the fifteenth and thirtieth degrees of latitude. It is very common in Palestine. The coin struck to commemorate the capture of Jerusalem in A.D. 70 represented a weeping woman (the symbol of the country) sitting under a palm tree; it bore the inscription *Judaea capta.* **The apple tree.** Various suggestions have been offered for the identification of this tree, i.e., quince, citron, orange, apricot, and apple. According to the Song it was a majestic tree suitable to sit under, its branches overshadowing a tent or house, its fruit pleasant to the taste, and its smell desirable, refreshing to the weary. **Withers . . . disappeared** (AV, *is withered away*). Literally, *shows shame.* The same verb occurs in verses 10,11,12. This frequent repetition of the word for "ashamed" is an indirect call to repentance in verse 13. When joy itself disappears, the time for penitence has arrived!

2) A Call to Repentance. 1:13,14.

13. The thought returns to verse 9. The priests are here addressed on the same principle as the drunkards are in verse 5. With the failure of the crops, their ministry would end, for there would be no first fruits, and sacrifices would soon cease. **Put on sackcloth.** The wearing of sackcloth by the priests would add solemnity to the occasion. **Lament.** The word used especially of mourning for the dead – expressive of intense grief (LXX, *Smite yourselves* upon the breasts). **My God . . . your God.** A sharp contrast! The prophet's God called for repentance; the priest's God demanded the drink offering and the meal offering. **14.** Joel appeals to the priests to **call a solemn assembly,** to issue a call for a public religious gathering, in which every one will participate. **The elders.** Though officials, they were subject to the priests in religious matters. **House of the Lord.** The Temple.

3) The Terrors of the Day of the Lord. 1:15-20.

15. The day of the Lord. Man has his day and walks in his own way, but eventually the Day of the Lord must come! In the light of man's sin, the Day of the Lord must be a time of vengeance. **Almighty.** Hebrew *Shadday* is used as a name for God, with distinct reference to the Divine power (used thirty-one times in the Book of Job).

16. Before our eyes. The Judeans are helpless to prevent destruction. **Joy and gladness.** The joy of religious convocation and the presentation of the first fruits. These were to be offered at the Temple with rejoicing (Deut 26:1-11). **18.** Even the irrational animals are represented as crying out in agony. **Groan** *(sob)*. The cattle participate in the sorrow of man. **Perplexed.** *Press themselves,* or *are held guilty.* The poor, innocent, helpless beasts have to bear the guilt of man's sin.

19,20. While the beasts can only sob and suffer, the human souls can cry to the Lord. **Pastures of the wilderness.** (Uncultivated land where sheep graze (cf. Amos 1:2). **Fire . . . flame.** Heat and drought which accompany the plague of locusts.

B. The Scourge As the Forerunner of the Judgment Day. 2:1-17.

The prophet visualizes a more terrible plague coming. In highly poetical terms he depicts the swarms of locusts like a hostile army, coming as the army of the Lord for judgment (2:1-11). But the door of mercy, he says, is still ajar! If the people will turn to their God with contrite hearts, the calamity may be averted (2:12-14). The prophet summons the whole community to assemble for prayer and fasting in the house of the Lord (2:15-17).

1) A Vivid Picture of the Coming Judgment. 2:1-11.

1. Blow the trumpet. An announcement of danger (see Jer 6:17; Ezk 33:3; Hos 8:1). **Tremble.** It is high time to awake from careless indifference. The summons is to acts of penitence in face of the scourge.

2,3. A more effective portrayal of the terror of The Day as indicated by the present calamity. **A day of darkness . . . gloom . . . clouds . . . thick darkness.** Four synonyms used for emphasis, signifying intense, impenetrable darkness (cf. Zeph 1:15; Ezk 34:12). Three of the words are used in Deut 4:11 of the darkness which enveloped Sinai when the Lord descended upon it in fire. The fourth word is applied in Ex 10:22 to the plague of darkness. **Dawn dispersed upon the mountains** (AV, the morning spread upon the mountains). The locust hosts are compared to the dawn, either because of its ruddy appearance, or because the dawn is engulfed by masses of cloud and mist, and so day is shut out. One traveler tells of seeing a swarm of locusts that extended a mile in length and half a mile in width, and appeared in the distance like a black cloud. **Fire devours.** All is lost; the beautiful country has become a wasted desert. The country looks as if it has been scorched, burned up, or reduced to brown ash. **Garden of Eden.** This and Ezk 36:26-35 are the only references to the Garden outside the book of Genesis. Before the destruction, the land was rich in vegetation, pleasant to behold; now it is a desolate wilderness, like Egypt and Edom.

4. The prophet vividly describes the appearance of the hosts and their terrible advance. **As . . . horses.** "In the locust is . . . the face of a horse, the eye of an elephant, the neck of a bull, the horns of a deer, the chest of a lion, the belly of a scorpion, the wings of an eagle, the thighs of a camel, the feet of an ostrich, the tail of a serpent" (an Arab saying, quoted in Pusey's *The Minor Prophets*, I, 174). **5.** The noise which accompanies the advance of innumerable horses is compared to the rattling of chariots—low two-wheeled vehicles used for military purposes. The amazing noise of the locusts can be heard six miles off. It is comparable to the sound of a cataract, a torrent, a rushing wind, or a raging flame.

7. Joel begins his comparison of this host with a well equipped army. The advance is irresistible; there is no confusion in the warriors' ranks; they scale the highest walls; they penetrate the inmost recesses of the houses. **They run** to the assault, ready to charge. **Break their ranks.** Literally, *change not their caravans;* each squadron remains compact, like a regiment in an army.

8. Swords or missile(s). Locusts defy all weapons that men may array against them. They are so numerous that even after millions have been detroyed, the swarms advance as though nothing had happened. It is only through the destruction of their eggs that locusts can be eliminated.

9. Like a thief. The doors are shut, but the invaders pour through the unglazed windows. This image reveals that the prophet is not thinking of an attacking army, but only of the actual locusts. The same image is used in the NT for our Lord's coming (Mt 24:43,44; Lk 12:39; I Thess 5:2; II Pet 3:10).

11. His voice. In the terrific storm depicted in 2:10, the prophet hears the voice of God (cf. I Sam 12:18; Ps 18:14; 46:8). **Who can endure it?** (RSV) Behind and beyond the locusts' ravages, the earthquake, and the storm looms the Day of the Lord, bringing a camp more impregnable, a host more irresistible, and a punishment great and terrible. Who can abide the day of his coming? Apparently *no one!* But there is still hope. The door of mercy is open! If the people will turn to God in a true spirit of repentance, he may yet pardon!

2) An Exhortation to Repentance. 2:12-17.

12. Yet even now (RSV). At the eleventh hour, when destruction appears imminent! **Return to me** (RSV). Forsake your self-chosen paths of rebellion; come to your senses; recognize Me as your God; and follow My instructions. This is the appeal of all the great prophets (e.g., Hos 14:1; Isa 1:2; Amos 4:6). **Return** emphasizes the idea of conversion. **With all your heart.** The seat not only of the emotions, but of all the powers of personality, intellect, sensibility, and will. All of the activities of the human spirit (all thoughts, all affections, and all volitions) are to be centered upon the Lord. The inward change (heart turning) will manifest itself in the outward change of actions.

13. Rend your heart, and not your garments. A demand for moral and ethical religion. Penitence must be heartfelt; it must not be a matter of mere ritual. Joel, like all the true prophets, demands "heart sorrow and a clean life following" (cf. Ezk 36:26; Ps 51:19). Penitence is not an *opus operatum* ("a work performed," i.e., a meritorious work), a tearing of the garment (cf. this expression of grief in Lev 13:45; Jer 36:24), but an inward sorrow, yearning, anguish, and a tearing of the heart! **Gracious.** Literally, *inclined* to pardon the repentant sinner. **Merciful.** Possessing mercy in abundance —equivalent to "full of compassion." **Slow to anger.** Literally, *long as to the breathing of the nostrils* in anger. The Lord does not permit his anger to break forth immediately as an avalanche upon the discovery of sin, but he waits to see if the sinner will repent. **Abounding in loving kindness.** The Hebrew word *ḥesed,* used of (1) the love of God toward man, (2) the love of man toward man, and (3) the love of man toward God.

14. Who knows. Perhaps **he might return and repent.** God is not man that he should repent; he cannot turn or be converted like a man. Yet he has his own Divine ways of both repenting and turning. Although changeless in his attitude toward sin, God may still show mercy on his sinful people. **A blessing.** A new harvest, which will make the meal and drink offerings again possible.

15,16. A solemn assembly. Called first in terror in 1:14 and 2:1, it is *now* summoned in the hope of Divine mercy. All classes and ages of the population are summoned to this great expectant party of repentance! Even the bride and the bridegroom, to whom a year's exemption from public service was allowed, are included (cf. Deut 24:5).

17. Priests . . . ministers. The mediators

between God and the people. **Weep.** In sorrow and repentance as they lead the people. **Between the porch and the altar.** The inner part of the court of the priests (cf. Ezk 8:16). Here Zechariah was standing when he was martyred (II Chr 24:20-22; Mt 23:35). **Spare.** Have mercy and withhold future judgment. **Thy people . . . thy heritage.** The basis of the appeal (cf. Deut 9:25,29). The Lord is intensely interested in their welfare. **Reproach.** Again and again the Almighty is reminded that, if he should forsake Israel and permit her to be destroyed, his power would be questioned. **Where is your God?** A sneer at the covenant relation between the Lord and his people. The only way to avoid the mocking is for God to avert the calamity (cf. Ex 32:12; Ps 79:10).

II. The Averting of Judgment and Bestowal of Blessings. 2:18–3:21.

A. The Blessings in the Immediate Future. 2:18-27.

This is the turning point of the book. Evidently the people responded to the prophet's invitation. The solemn convocation was convened, the people repented, and the Lord forgave them. Consequently, he now promises to remove the locusts and restore the prosperity of the land. Now all will know that God himself dwells with his people.

18. Then. The time is not definitely stated, but it is implied that the people turned to the Lord in penitence of heart. **Jealous . . . compassion.** The jealousy of God is founded upon the covenant (cf. marital relationship between the Lord and his people in Isa 54:5; 62:5; Hos 2:19). His jealousy is aroused when his people spurn his love.

20. The northern army. The Northerner. The terrible locust swarms will be removed and scattered in the desert, the Dead Sea, and the Mediterranean Sea. The prophet visualizes the invasion of the land from the north by the armies of Assyria and Babylon, typified by the locusts. **Great things.** Two subjects are referred to, an immediate one—the locusts, and a more remote one—the Northerner. The locust army is seen as the instrument of the Lord. As terrible and repulsive as the locusts were, they turned the people to God in repentance. The stink of dead locusts is often referred to as intolerable and the cause of plagues. Augustine quotes from Julius Obsequens to show how a vast cloud of locusts, cast into the African Sea, were rolled up putrid on the shore, and a plague broke out killing 800,000 persons.

21. The beasts, men, and all sufferers of chapter 1 are now called upon to cast away their fear and to rejoice. **The Lord hath done great things.** A prophetic perfect (completed action). The prophet is so certain, upon Divine authority, of its happening that he speaks as if it has already occurred.

23. Rejoice in the Lord. In the midst of their rejoicing they are to remember that God's mercy made this possible. **The early rain in just measure** *(hammôreh liṣ^e dāqâ)*. There is no doubt that *môreh* in the last clause of the verse means *early rain.* But the Targum, the Vulgate, and Jewish writers, followed by Keil, Pusey, and others, translate "Instructor in righteousness"—the Messiah. The leader of the Qumran community bore this title. However, the context does not permit this translation, which Calvin termed "a strange exposition." **Early rains and latter rains.** The September-October and March-April rains were necessary for the fertility of the land in Palestine.

24,25. The heavens once again will be opened, the drought will end, the locusts will disappear, the harvest will return, and the Lord's presence will be realized.

26. The result of the bountiful restoration: The Jews will recognize the Lord as their God and praise him for his divine intervention. **Name of the Lord.** Equivalent to the *person* of the Lord (cf. Amos 2:7; Mic 5:4).

27. I am the Lord your God. Every religious leader from the time of Moses insisted that the Lord was the God of Israel (see, e.g., Ex 20:2; Deut 5:6), but the people too frequently forgot it and hence went "whoring after other gods" (Hos 2:5,8). The Lord, in order to bring them to their senses, had to rain down judgment upon them again and again. However, the present blow will cure them once and for all; they will recognize him as their only God. **None else.** The gods who in the past lured away the people are worthless. They possess no power to protect or assist. They add loads rather than lift (see Hos 2:7; Isa 1:29-31; 45:5,6,18).

B. The Outpouring of the Divine Spirit. 2:28-32.

In the Hebrew Bible, verses 28-32 constitute chapter 3. The word **afterward** looks forward far beyond the locust plague and Israel's repentance and restoration. For here the prophet turns from the physical and material to the spiritual and eternal. Through his prophetic vision, Joel rises above the religious experience of the local locust plague to a wider view of history. He dips into the future and sees spiritual revival in Israel and deliverance from all surrounding enemies. His vision thus anticipates a first fulfillment on the day of Pentecost and a final realization in the complete victory of the kingdom of the Lord Christ.

28. I will pour out my spirit. In great abundance (Calvin). The Spirit is the life principle in man (cf. Gen 1:2; Job 33:4), the invisible power to which all external actions are traced, and which endowed Israel's heroes with warlike energy (e.g., Jud 3:10; 11:29). The Spirit produces the prophetic power in its higher and lower forms (I Sam 10:6, 10; 19:20; Isa 61:1). **All flesh.** Not the animals but *all mankind* **shall prophesy . . . dream dreams . . . see visions.** In this coming manifestation of the Spirit, no distinction will be made on grounds of sex, age, or position; but a distinction will be made in the different methods by which the revelation is received and the prophetic gift exercised. That is, their sons, daughters, old persons, and youths will receive the Spirit of the Lord with all his various gifts. **Prophesy.** They will become "organs of Divine revelation" to all nations!

29. Even (AV, *also*). Something extraordinary. In the Messianic Age no distinction will be made between the bond and the free. In Ezk 39:29 and Zech 12:10 the Spirit is promised to Israel, to the king's house, and to the favored inhabitants of Jerusalem. But Joel goes further than these and includes all classes, in the spirit of universalism which also characterizes the book of Jonah.

30. There will be wonderful portents of the approach of the judgment. **Wonders.** Extraordinary phenomena on the earth and in the sky. **Blood . . . fire . . . pillars of smoke.** Terrors of war, bloodshed, violence, and columns of smoke rising from burned cities. Wars on an unprecedented scale will be forerunners of the Day of the Lord (cf. Isa 13:6; Zeph 1:7). Some scholars view these as "abnormal atmospherical phenomena," or results of a nuclear holocaust. **Blood.** The red color of the moon. **Smoke.** Perhaps the smoke clouds filling the air as a result of volcanic eruptions. **Fire.** Lightning, since thunderstorms often accompany earthquakes.

31. The phenomena of the sky. The darkening of the sun and the extinction of the lights of heaven are frequently mentioned in the Scriptures as harbingers of the Day of the Lord or of approaching judgment (2:2,10; 3:15; Isa 13:10; 34:4; Jer 4:23; Mt 24:29; Mk 13:24; Lk 21:25; Rev 6:12).

32. A great and horrible day to the nations (3:2), but the true worshipers of the Lord need have no fear! **Call on the name of the Lord.** Not with a cold ceremonial or heartless repetition of phrases but with spiritual, heartfelt worship. The one who *calls on* the Lord is one who *worships* him. The way of escape is through membership in the true Israel, not Israel according to the flesh, but Israel according to the Spirit. This membership is evidenced by true, wholehearted devotion to the Lord. **Survivors** (Heb., *pᵉlêṭâ*). All who escape (AV, *the remnant*). The remnant in Jerusalem embraces all who believe or shall believe from all nations, kindred, and tongues! The Apostle Peter quoted 2:28-32 after the outpouring of the Holy Spirit at Pentecost as having been fulfilled at that event. However, the outpouring of the Spirit on the Day of Pentecost was simply the beginning. It will be continued until all flesh will be equipped with Divine illumination.

C. Judgment upon the Nations. 3:1-17.

When the great day announced by extraordinary phenomena (2:30,31) really breaks, its terrors will fall *only* upon the foes of Israel. This judgment is twofold: first, to consummate a complete and final separation between the faithful and God's enemies; second, to establish the kingdom of the Lord upon the earth in triumphal glory. This conflict is to be waged in the valley of Jehoshaphat (lit., *the Lord's judgment;* 3:1-3). Perhaps this valley is to be identified with the Kidron. The nations that have exhibited the greatest hostility will suffer the most (3:4-8); regardless of their superior numbers they will be utterly annihilated, and the inhabitants of Jerusalem will experience no harm (3:9-17).

1) The Avenging of Wrongs Committed Against the Jews. 3:1-3.

Verse 1 begins chapter 4 in the Hebrew. **For** connects 3:1 with 2:32. It introduces the prophet's explanation for the deliverance of the Jews alone; the other nations will be destroyed. **In those days and at that time.** Refers *not* back to 2:28, but forward to the time of the deliverance of the Jews (Jer 33:15).

2. Muster all nations. All who have mistreated the people of God. **Valley of Jehoshaphat,** or the valley of Divine judgment. This name is given to the scene of the final conflict because of the meaning of the name—*the Lord judges.* **Scattered . . . carved up.** Two specific charges against the nations: they deported the Israelites; and they divided the land among them.

3. The ignominious treatment of the helpless Jews by the conquerors is pointed out. **Cast lots.** A common custom with the ancient peoples (cf. Ob 11; Nah 3:10; Thucydides *History* iii. 50). This made the captives absolute property of their masters. **Boy.** Since he would be of no immediate use, they exchanged him for a **harlot,** to satisfy their lust. **Girl.** Too young for their purpose; or, after they satisfied their lust, they exchanged her for wine, to indulge in licentious revelry.

2) Judgment upon Phoenicia. 3:4-8.

4. The prophet turns aside momentarily to address the nations who have been especially hostile toward the covenant people. He singles out the special mistreatments, and promises the nations swift and righteous retribution for their crimes. **Tyre . . . Zidon** *(Sidon).* The two principal cities of Phoenicia. Originally Tyre was located on the mainland, but it was transferred, for safety's sake, to a neighboring rocky island. **Territories of Philistia.** This district in southwest Palestine, covering an area about forty miles long and fifteen miles wide, was divided between the five chief cities. The Philistines were exceedingly hostile to the Israelites throughout their checkered history.

5. These nations treated the Lord with utter contempt. They stole his silver and gold, filled their temples with his precious things, and sold his children into slavery. **My silver . . . gold . . . priceless possessions.** These included the things taken from the houses of the rich as well as those taken from the Temple. In ancient times plundering always followed the conquest of a city (e.g., I Kgs 14:26; II Kgs 14:14).

6. The Greeks. Literally, *Ionians,* or Javan (cf. Gen 10:2-4; Isa 66:19; Ezk 27:13,19). Post-Biblical literature frequently mentions the slave traffic of the Phoenicians (cf. Ezk 27:13; I Macc 3:41). However, Greek writers show that the Phoenicians and Greeks enjoyed commercial intercourse at an early period. **Far from their own border.** Hence they had no hope of returning. This was a severe blow to the Jews, for they viewed a foreign country or nation as unclean.

7,8. All that the enemies have done will be recompensed *lex talionis* (i.e., by the law of retaliation). **Them.** The children of Judah and Jerusalem. They will be aroused into activity and returned to their homeland; the blessings of the Lord will make them strong and powerful. The Jews in turn will be used of God to undo the Tyrians, Sidonians, and Philistines—sell them into slavery! **Shebans.** A renowned trading race in Arabia. **For the Lord hath spoken it.** A common formula of asseveration in the OT (e.g., Isa 1:20; 22:25; Ob 18).

3) World Judgment. 3:9-17.

9. Announce this among the nations. The prophet returns to the announcement broken off in verse 3. The nations are urged to equip themselves for conflict and assemble in the valley of Jehoshaphat. There they will muster at the command of the Lord, but they will be annihilated. **Prepare** (lit., *sanctify*) **for war.** Bring the sacrifices, perform the customary religious rites before doing battle. **Arouse.** Wake up the heroes, for this is not time for sleep. **Muster . . . come up.** Technical military terms. **10. Plowshares . . . pruning hooks.** The agricultural (peace) implements are to be turned into weapons of war. **11. Hurry.** On the double! The matter is to be settled speedily. **Surrounding nations.** Not merely the immediate neighbors but all Gentile nations.

12,13. God's reply to the brief petition is that he will take care of his people. **Sit to judge.** Not to listen to additional pleas but to pronounce sentence. The judgment is depicted under a twofold figure—the reaping of grain and the treading out of grapes (see also Rev 14:15,16,19,20). **Ripe.** They are so sinful that they are ready for judgment (cf. Amos 3). **Full.** An added picture of extreme sinfulness. **Vats are overflowing.** The grapes of sin are so numerous and ripe that even before they are artificially crushed, the juice is pressed out by their weight.

14. The picture of judgment begins here. **Multitudes, multitudes.** Literally, *tumults.* That is, great multitudes. The repetition is for emphasis. **Valley of decision.** The judgment will be decisive! The nations are assembled because judgment is ready to burst forth.

15,16. This darkness, symbolical of judgment, as at the crucifixion, could mean that before the great light of God, the lesser lights withdraw. But the reference is more probably to the terror of the wrath of God (see 2:10,31; Isa 13:10; Ezk 32:7; Mt 24:29; Mk 13:24). **The Lord . . . shall roar.** The verb describes the anger of the lion as he springs upon his prey. Under the figure of an angry lion (cf. Amos 1:2; Jer 25:30), the Lord is represented as ready to leap upon the nations. **Utter his voice.** The appearance of God is frequently described in the OT under the imagery of a thunderstorm. **Zion . . . Jerusalem.** The Temple on Mount Zion in Jerusalem is the earthly habitation of the Lord, the base of his operation. The fact that God does not leave the Temple is a favorable sign to his people. **The heavens and earth will tremble.** A severe earthquake will accompany the storm.

17. The present crisis, i.e., the destruction of the nations and the deliverance of Israel, will teach the people of Israel that the Lord is their God. They will now recognize him as supreme (2:27; cf. Hos 2:8; Ezk 28:23). **Jerusalem shall be holy.** Set apart, consecrated entirely to God. **Strangers.** Aliens, citizens of foreign countries, who have no interest in or love for the things precious to the redeemed Jews (cf. Hos 7:9; Jer 30:8).

D. The Blessings Following the Judgment. 3:18-21.

After the judgment upon the nations, Judah, under the care and protective hand of the Lord, will enjoy the fullness of divine blessing. The seat of the former world powers will become a barren waste, but in Judah there will be fertility and peace.

18. In that day. The beginning of the Messianic Age—the day of judgment upon God's enemies and of deliverance for the Jews. A hyperbolical picture of extreme fertility now follows. The territory of Judah was covered with limestone rocks, and the soil yielded only a meagre subsistance in return for the most arduous toil. But in this new age the fertility is pictured in terms of the **mountains** and **hills** themselves shooting forth **wine** and **milk.** Canaan is called "a land flowing with milk and honey" (Ex 3:8). **Water** was rationed out sparingly in Judah. Most of the brooks dried up entirely during the dry seasons. In the new age there will be no more drought. Water will be plentiful for man and beast. **A fountain . . . from the house of the Lord.** A fountain shall come forth from Jerusalem, or from the Temple of the Lord (Ezk 47:1-12; Zech 14:8). **Valley of Shittim.** Literally, valley of Acacias—a dry and thirsty place. This was the name of the last encampment of the Israelites before they entered Canaan (Num 25:1; Josh 3:1). Ezekiel pictures the water flowing eastward across the Jordan.

19. While Judah is prospering, the curse of desolation (cf. 2:3) will fall upon Edom and Egypt because of the crimes they have committed against the Israelites. **Egypt.** The old oppressor. **Edom.** The constant thorn in the side of Israel, who triumphed over and benefited by Israel's calamities (Ps 137:7; Lam 4:22; Ezk 25:12; 35:15; 36:5; Ob 10-14). This violence consisted not only of the shedding of Jewish blood during war, but also of the unprovoked massacre of peaceful Jews living in these lands (Amos 1:11; Ob 10).

20. Whereas the surrounding nations shall become desolate, Judah and Jerusalem shall flourish forever. **Endure.** (AV, *abide).* Literally, sit—a poetical expression for continual habitation and prosperity. **For ever** (Heb. *'ôlām).* An endless period—synonymous with **from generation to generation.** Neither the Romans nor the Turks quite reduced the little country of Judah to desolation. Today the Israelis are rebuilding her cities, rejuvenating her land, and restoring her ancient glory!

21. I will avenge (RSV; cleanse, AV). The judgment upon the nations will be decisive proof of their guilt and of the innocence of the Jewish victims. **I am He Who dwells in Zion.** A reiteration of the greatest of all the promises. With the execution of judgment, the Lord will establish himself forever in Zion. Never again will he forsake his people so that they become a byword among their foes.

In the Book of Joel is portrayed Israel's passage from the City of Destruction to the Celestial City. The bright promise of the closing verses parallels the glorious ending of Matthew's Gospel!

BIBLIOGRAPHY

DEERE, DERWARD W. *The Twelve Speak.* Vol. I. New York: The American Press, 1958.

EISELEN, F. C. *The Minor Prophets.* Cincinnati: Jennings and Graham, 1907.

ELLISON, H. L. *Men Spake From God.* Grand Rapids: Wm. B. Eerdmans Publishing Co., 1958.

PUSEY, B. *The Minor Prophets.* Vol. I. New York: Funk & Wagnalls Co., 1885.

ROBINSON, GEORGE L. *The Twelve Minor Prophets.* New York: George H. Doran Co., 1926.

SMITH, GEORGE ADAM. *The Book of the Twelve Prophets (The Expositor's Bible).* Revised edition. New York: Harper and Brothers, 1928.

SMITH, J., WARD, W. H., BEWER, J. *Joel (International Critical Commentary).* Edinburgh: T. & T. Clark, n. d.

AMOS

INTRODUCTION

The Date and Background. The first verse of the prophecy of Amos, together with 7:10-13, places the prophet in the middle of the eighth century B.C., contemporary with Uzziah of Judah and Jeroboam II of Israel. Uzziah, king of Judah, reigned about fifty years (791–740 B.C.), and was successful in some ways. He defeated the enemies of Judah and strengthened the walls of Jerusalem. The country was prosperous under his leadership, and for a time the influence of Amos was spiritually constructive.

But Uzziah was probably under the influence of Jeroboam, king of Israel. Jeroboam's reign of approximately forty years (793–753 B.C.) was extremely successful, and his influence eclipsed that of Uzziah in practically every area. In his religious leadership, Jeroboam, like the first Jeroboam, the son of Nebat, deliberately encouraged the practices of fertility cults (II Kgs 14:24,25). He did not exclude the worship of Jehovah, but paganized it by adding cultic pillars, images, and teraphim (Hos 2:13,16,17; 3:4; 4:12; 10:2; 11:2). The social life of the nation was characterized by adultery, robbery, and murder. The luxury of the wealthy was built upon injustice and oppression of the poor (Amos 2:6-8; 3:15; 4:1; 5:7-12; 6:3-6; 8:4-6; Hos 4:1,2,11-13; 6:8,9; 12:7,8).

It is generally believed that Amos prophesied about 760 B.C. The period of Amos was a time of political security for Israel, which was reflected in the pride and carelessness of the ruling classes. The struggle with Syria had ended with victory for Israel; Jeroboam had "restored the coast of Israel from the entering of Hamath unto the sea of the plain" (II Kgs 14:25). This mood of carelessness characterized the later years of Jeroboam's reign rather than the early period. The threat of Assyrian power under Tiglath-pileser III (745–727 B.C.; see commentary on Amos 1:14) had not yet developed. The earthquake mentioned in 1:1 does not help in determining more definitely the date of the prophet's ministry.

Life of Amos. Amos was a native of Tekoa, located in the desert of Judah, twelve miles south of Jerusalem. He was a shepherd, who supplemented his income by taking care of "sycomore" (wild fig) trees (1:1; 7:14,15). There is no record of his family. The call of God came to him while he was following the flock. His claim that the Lord called him directly (7:15) puts him in line with all the prophets who experienced a direct revelation from God. Although Amos was a native of Judah, he prophesied in the Northern Kingdom. His preaching aroused such antagonism, however, that he returned to Judah, where he committed his message to writing.

The writing of Amos shows that he was not an untutored rustic, but had a deep knowledge of history and of the problems of his day. His language, rich in figures and symbols, stands with the finest literary style in the Old Testament.

The Message of Amos. The great proclamation at the beginning of this prophecy (1:2) sets the tone of Amos' message. The Lord's voice, like the roar of a lion, will be heard in judgment from Zion. The prophet reveals the spiritual corruption under the religious formalism and material prosperity of the time (5:12, 21). He castigates the leaders for the deterioration of social justice and morality (2:7,8) and points out their total disregard of human rights and personality (2:6). He insists that God's people must seek the Lord and repent, and establish justice if they are to live (5:14,15). But because the people of Israel will not repent, there is nothing left for them but destruction (9:1-8). The Day of the Lord will be an assertion of the claims of God's moral character upon those who have repudiated him. When this is recognized, there will be established the glory of the promised Davidic kingdom; and that day is inevitable (9:11-15). The message of Amos is in large measure a "cry for justice."

OUTLINE

I. Prophecies against the nations. 1:1–2:16.
   A. Superscription and proclamation. 1:1,2.
   B. Indictment of neighboring nations. 1:3–2:3.
   C. Indictment of Judah. 2:4,5.
   D. Indictment of Israel. 2:6-16.
II. Three sermons against Israel. 3:1–6:14.
   A. A declaration of judgment. 3:1-15.
   B. The depravity of Israel. 4:1-13.
   C. A lamentation for Israel's sin and doom. 5:1–6:14.
III. Five visions of Israel's condition. 7:1–9:10.
   A. The devouring locusts. 7:1-3.
   B. The flaming fire. 7:4-6.
   C. The plumb line. 7:7-9.
   D. Ecclesiastical opposition. 7:10-17.
   E. The basket of ripe fruit. 8:1-14.
   F. The judgment of the Lord. 9:1-10.
IV. The promise of Israel's restoration. 9:11-15.

COMMENTARY

I. Prophecies Against the Nations. 1:1–2:16.

A. Superscription and Proclamation. 1:1,2. The superscription (1:1) serves as a title for the whole book and identifies the writer. It places the book in its historical setting. The proclamation (1:2) creates the spirit and mood of the prophecy as a whole.

1. The words of Amos. Sometimes a prophet refers to his prophecy as "the word of Jehovah" (e.g., Joel 1:1; Jon 1:1; Mic 1:1). But in this statement (cf. Hag 1:12) the words of the prophecy are declared to be the words of Jehovah. The divine origin of the words of the prophet is emphasized by the phrase, **which he saw.** The word *hāzāh*, "he saw," usually characterizes the method of the reception of the divine message as supernatural (cf. Isa 1:1). The message was God's and not that of Amos. **Who was among the herdmen.** The Hebrew word for **herdmen** is not the ordinary word for shepherd, *rō'eh*, but *nōqēd*, which means that Amos' sheep were not of the common variety. The word refers to one who cares for dwarfed sheep, with short legs. It helps to account for the Arabic expression, "viler than a naqqad." This breed of sheep is prized for its fine, abundant wool. Aside from this reference in Amos, *nōqēd* is found only in II Kgs 3:4, where it refers to Mesha, king of Moab, and is translated "sheepmaster." Archaeologists have found it in line 30 of the Moabite Stone of Mesha. On the basis of II Kgs 3:4, Jews have insisted that Amos was a wealthy sheep owner, with other interests besides his sheep (cf. Amos 7:14), and that he voluntarily submitted to affliction because of Israel's sins. But this interpretation does not necessarily follow. **Tekoa.** A village in Judah, six miles southeast of Bethlehem and twelve miles southeast of Jerusalem. The country surrounding the hill upon which Tekoa was located was stony but rich in pastures. **Concerning Israel.** Although there are allusions to Judah in the prophecy, the words of Amos were intended for Israel. **Uzziah . . . Jeroboam.** See *Date and Background.* **Two years before the earthquake.** The earthquake referred to was intended as a chronological note. It must have been unusually severe to be mentioned thus, since earthquakes are very common in the area. The prophet Zechariah also refers to this earthquake (14:5). Josephus (*Antiq.* ix 10.4) relates it to Uzziah's sin in acting as a priest (II Chr 26:16).

2. Will roar. The Hebrew verb *shā'ag* describes the roar of a lion as he leaps upon his prey. It expresses the immediacy of the judgment; for when the shepherd hears the roar, he knows that the attack is already taking place, and it is too late to save the sheep. The word reflects the background of Amos, who, as a shepherd, was familiar with the terror of a lion's leap, and used it symbolically of the coming judgment of the Lord (cf. Joel 3:16). This verse is the text of the book. **Zion . . . Jerusalem.** To true worshipers of the Lord, these terms represented the center of the theocracy and of national life. **The habitations . . . shall mourn.** *The pastures shall dry up.* This again reflects the shepherd life of Amos. **Top of Carmel shall wither. Carmel** means *garden land,* and it is the most fertile land in the country. The withering of Carmel indicates how severe the drought would be (cf. Isa 33:9; Nah 1:4).

B. Indictment of the Neighboring Nations. 1:3–2:3. Amos was a prophet to Israel, but he began his preaching with an announcement that judgment was to fall upon the surrounding nations. In this way he was able to show that since the other nations were to be punished, Israel could not expect to escape. Because she had the truth as preached by the prophets of the Lord, she had greater condemnation than the nations that did not have this truth.

3. For three transgressions . . . and for four. The word translated **transgressions** actually means *rebellions,* and the expression has reference to the innumerable evil deeds committed, and to the truth that God is longsuffering and does not act hastily in judgment. **Damascus.** According to the tradition in the area, it is the oldest city in the world, and the Arabs think of it as the world's garden. It was the capital of Syria, the greatest of the Aramaean kingdoms. **I will not turn away.** Or, *I will not intervene.* This is a reference to the fact that in the nature of things, because of the rebellions of Damascus, judgment was inevitable, unless God intervened. **Have threshed Gilead.** The bodies of the victims were torn by the teeth of the threshing sledges.

4. House of Hazael. Hazael, whose coming to the throne was predicted by Elisha (II Kgs 8:7-13), was the founder of the Syrian dynasty that ruled in the time of Amos. He was a contemporary of Joram (II Kgs 8:29), Jehu (II Kgs 10:31,32), and Jehoahaz (II Kgs 13:22). **House of Hazael** is a reference to his royal palace, as indicated by the parallelism in the next part of the verse. **Ben-hadad.** The son and successor of Hazael (II Kgs 13:3,25).

5. The bar of Damascus. Bars were used to lock the gates of ancient cities. By synecdoche they refer to the defenses of a city (Jud 16:3; I Kgs 4:13; Jer 51:30; Lam 2:9). **Plain of Aven.** A valley about a four-hour journey from Damascus. **Him that holdeth the sceptre.** The highest officer. **Eden.** Not the Eden of Gen 2:8, but the summer residence of the king, not far from Damascus. **Kir.** According to Amos 9:7, it was the original home of the Syrians (Aramaeans), and it was to Kir that they were exiled (II Kgs 16:9). Its location is unknown.

6. Gaza. This judgment is against the Philistines in general, but especially against Gaza, the most important of the five Philistine cities (I Sam *:17). Gaza, which lay on a junction of the trade routes, was guilty of trafficking in slaves. Whole communities of Israelites were sold to Edom, the bitterest enemy of Israel. **7. Wall.** A reference to the strength of the city. **8. Ashdod . . . Ashkelon . . . Ekron.** Amos omits Gath of the five important Philistine cities, perhaps because it had lost its influence (II Chr 26:6). **The remnant . . . shall perish.** The destruction will be complete.

9. Tyrus. Tyre, with its island location and two harbors, became very powerful. It was a great trade center (Isa 23:1-3), and it, like Gaza, engaged in traffic in slaves. **Remembered not the brotherly covenant.** A reference to a covenant between Solomon and Hiram of Tyre (I Kgs 5:12), which had spiritual provisions as well as political agreements (I Kgs 5:7), and perhaps also prohibited the sale of Hebrew slaves. Hiram refers to Solomon as a "brother" (I Kgs 9:13), and various passages indicate that for a long period Israel and Tyre enjoyed friendly relations (II Sam 5:11; I Kgs 5:1-12; 16:31).

11. Edom. Scripture traces the enmity between Edom and Israel back to the rivalry between Jacob and Esau, from whom the two nations were descended. The word means *red* (Gen 25:25,30). **He did pursue his brother with the sword.** This is not a reference to any specific instance but a description of the traditional attitude of Edom toward Israel (Num 20:17-21; II Chr 21:8-10; II Kgs 8:20-22). **12. Teman.** Another name for Edom (Jer 49:7; Ob 8,9; Hab 3:3). Used in parallelism with Edom in Jer 49:20. **Bozrah.** One of the important cities of Edom (Isa 63:1; Jer 49:22).

13. Children of Ammon. Descendants of Ben-ammi, son of Lot by one of his daughters (Gen 19:38). They were more nomadic than the neighboring Moabites. **Ripped up the women with child of Gilead.** These crimes perhaps took place when Hazael (Amos 1:3,4) also attacked Gilead (II Kgs 8:12; 10:32,33). **14. Rabbah.** A reference to "Rabbah of the sons of Ammon" (Deut 3:16; II Sam 12: 26-31; Jer 49:2; Ezk 21:20). It was the capital city of the Ammonites. This prophecy was perhaps fulfilled in the Assyrian invasion of Ammon. Tiglath-pileser III (745–727 B.C.), the Pul of II Kgs 15:19, in his inscriptions mentions Sanipu, King of Ammon, in a list of kings who were made to pay tribute to him. Others in the list are Salamanu of Moab, Qaushmalaka of Edom, Mitinti of Ashkelon, Hanno of Gaza, Ahaz of Judah, and Menahem of Samaria. The Assyrian Sennacherib (705–681 B.C.) says that Buduilu of Ammon, Ethbaal of Sidon, Mitinti of Ashdod, and others paid him tribute and kissed his feet.

2:1. Moab. A nation descended from Moab, son of Lot by his elder daughter (Gen 19:37). Moabites were closely related to the Israelites and the Ammonites. **Burned the bones of the king of Edom.** This perhaps occurred in connection with the events recorded in II Kgs 3, when Mesha, the king of Moab, was at least temporarily successful in his rebellion. The event is also described on the Moabite Stone, inscribed by Mesha, who was king of Moab at the time (II Kgs 3:4). **Into lime.** Or, *to powder.* The LXX has *to konia,* which was the fine dust with which a wrestler's body was covered after it had been oiled. This afforded his opponent the advantage of a firm grip. The Vulgate has *to ashes.* The Targum indicates that the king of Moab used the powder to plaster his house. **2. Kirioth.** Perhaps the capital city of Moab, called Kir of Moab in Isa 15:1. It is named on the Moabite Stone as the site of a temple of Chemosh, a god of the Moabites. **3. Judge.** The Hebrew word is *shôpēt*, which sometimes refers to a judge in the usual sense of the term. It is also used of a king (cf. Mic 5:2) who functions as a judge (II Sam 8:15; Jer 21:12), and may be used of a high officer who functions in the place of a king (cf. II Kgs 15: 5).

C. Indictment of Judah. 2:4,5. The prophecies against the neighboring nations lead up to the prophecies against Israel. The prophet's prediction of punishment against the surrounding nations probably aroused a sympathetic hearing from his fellow Jews, at least in the beginning.

4. Judah. The only specific references to Judah outside this judgment are found in 1:2; 6:1; 7:12; 9:11. **5. The palaces of Jerusalem.** Jerusalem, even to the Northern Kingdom, was a symbol of Jehovah, who united the Northern and Southern Kingdoms in worship.

D. Indictment of Israel. 2:6-16. Israel was now to learn that her special relationship to Jehovah did not excuse her from punishment.

6. Sold the righteous . . . and the poor. A picture of the injustice and oppression in Israel. **7. Go in unto the same maid.** A reference to the temple prostitute, who carried on her practices as part of the Canaanite fertility cult ritual with which the Israelites had become involved. **8. Clothes laid to pledge.** These were garments given for security by the poor. They were being held over night by the creditors in violation of the Law (Ex 22: 25,26; Deut 24:12). The Law said that, because the poor needed the garments to sleep in, they should be returned at the close of the day. **Drink the wine of the condemned.** The wine actually belonged to those who had pawned it. The verse presents a picture of ruthless foreclosure against honest debtors.

9. Amorite. A general name given to the people east of the Jordan and the Canaanites west of the river. **11. Nazarites.** The law of the Nazarite is given in Num 6:1-21. **13. I am pressed.** Better: *I will press you in your place, as a cart presseth that is full of sheaves* (ASV). **As a cart presseth.** Israel would experience the grinding pressure that a fully loaded wagon exerts on the ground over which it travels. **16. In that day.** The Day of the Lord, when God's judgment would fall upon Israel. Verses 14 to 16 describe an overwhelming disaster.

II. Three Sermons Against Israel. 3:1–6:14.

A. A Declaration of Judgment. 3:1-15. This part of the book is an expansion of the theme of the first two chapters. Amos begins by showing what a unique relation to Jehovah Israel enjoys. But under the compulsion of his prophetic responsibility, the prophet also speaks the message of condemnation and warns of destruction.

1. The whole family. Amos makes it clear that judgment is to fall upon all of the twelve tribes. **2. You only have I known.** The Hebrew verb translated "to know," when used to express the relation between two people, frequently describes the intimacy of marriage (Gen 4:1). It is

Israel above all nations that God has chosen to enjoy a special relation to him and to perform a particular service to the world. This doctrine is peculiar to the prophets of Israel, and has no parallel among other nations. This, of course, places Israel in a position of special responsibility.

3. Except they be agreed? The ASV has *except they have agreed,* i.e., have made an appointment. **5. Gin.** An old English contraction of "engine," referring to the mechanism that releases the trap. **6. Shall a trumpet be blown.** The trumpet was blown to warn of an attack or as a summons to battle (cf. Ezk 33:3; Joel 2:1). **And the people not be afraid?** The warnings of Amos were to be acknowledged. **Evil.** Not a reference to sin but to calamity and disaster.

7. The Lord God will do nothing. When God sends calamity, he also reveals the purpose of the calamity. **8. The lion hath roared.** The prophet heard the roar in the tramp of the Assyrian army.

9. Ashdod . . . Egypt. Sometimes the prophets point out the moral superiority of pagan nations over rebellious Israel. **The mountains.** Ebal and Gerizim, from which one could look down on Samaria. **Samaria.** Founded by Omri (I Kgs 16:24). **10. Know not to do right.** Have lost all sense of moral direction.

11. An adversary. The king of Assyria. **12. Out of the mouth of the lion.** The statement reflects the background of Amos. The remains of an animal were sometimes produced as evidence (Ex 22:13). The insignificance of what remained served to emphasize the comparison. **Corner of a bed.** The ASV and the RSV have *corner of a couch.* The corner was the place of honor. **In Damascus in a couch.** Or, *on the silken cushions of a bed* (ASV). The picture is that of a council chamber in Samaria where the leaders of the nation rested free from care.

13. House of Jacob. A reference to the ten tribes, as indicated by the mention of Bethel in the next verse. **The Lord God, the God of hosts.** This is the longest form of the name of God in the Bible, and it occurs only here in the OT. It emphasizes in a special way the omnipotence of God for the purpose of magnifying the effect of the predicted judgment. **14. The horns of the altar.** The horns of the altar symbolized power and were sacred to the Israelites (I Kgs 1:50). They were important because the blood of the sacrifice was applied to them (Lev 4:30). To cut them off was an act of desecration.

B. The Depravity of Israel. 4:1-13. Amos accuses the women of being responsible for much of the evil in Israel. Ironically the prophet urges Israel to continue the paganized formal worship at their shrines. God had repeatedly demonstrated his disapproval of Israel's conduct, but with no result. Consequently, punishment was inevitable.

1. Kine of Bashan. Bashan, which lay east of the Sea of Galilee, was famous for its wheat and its pastures, and especially for its fat, sleek cattle (Deut 32:14; Ps 22:12; Ezk 39:18). This is a rebuke of the well-fed women of Samaria, who were responsible, in part, for the injustice in the land because of the demands they made upon the men for the luxuries of life. **2. By his holiness.** God's holiness will be vindicated by his punishment of sin. This is an expression of Amos' ethical monotheism, for holiness describes the essential being of God. **With hooks.** As animals led by hooks or rings in their noses. **Posterity.** Read instead with the ASV, *your residue,* or with the RSV, *even the last of you.* **Fishhooks.** Because the regular hooks would be exhausted by the great number of captives, fishhooks would be used for the others. **3. Breaches.** The women would be taken captive through the openings made by the enemy in the wall of the city. **Into the palace.** Read, instead, with the RSV, *you shall be cast forth into Harmon,* a place of captivity.

4. Transgress . . . multiply transgression. The irony of the statement is intended to show that the more frequently the Israelites visited their shrines, the farther they were from God. Even if they should offer their annual sacrifices (I Sam 1:3,7,21) every morning and their third-year tithe (Deut 14:28; 26:12) every third day (cf. ASV), their sacrifices would be vitiated by their apostasy. **5. With leaven.** Leaven was forbidden in Ex 23:18 and Lev 7:12. **Free offerings** refers to the freewill offering (Deut 12:6, 7), which was the most sincere expression of one's religion. **This liketh you.** Or, *This pleaseth you* (ASV).

6. Cleanness of teeth. Nothing to eat. **7. I caused it.** This phrase places in sharp perspective the fact that it was the power of God that had been revealed in the affairs of the nation. **8. Yet have ye not returned unto me.** This recurring phrase reveals the tenderness of God, who had sought, even in the sternness of judgment, to win his people to a deeper understanding of himself. **9. Palmerworm.** Locust.

10. After the manner of Egypt. A reference to the special severity and destructiveness of the Egyptian plagues.

12. Thus will I do. Amos dramatically predicts the final punishment without actually describing what it will be. **Prepare to meet thy God.** This is not a challenge for Israel to be prepared to endure punishment but a call to repentance (LXX has *call upon thy God).* Every prophecy of judgment is an exhortation to repentance. **13. He that formeth.** Amos again declares that the forces of nature are a revelation of the majesty of God.

C. A Lamentation for Israel's Sin and Doom. 5:1–6:14. Amos exhorts the people to listen to his lamentation over Israel. The prophet emphasizes the need of repentance and specifies some of the sins of which the people were guilty. Since their persistent idolatry had set the pattern of life, punishment in the form of captivity was inevitable.

5:1. Hear ye this word. This introduction to a new discourse was designed to quicken attention and fear in the hearts of the people. **2. Virgin of Israel.** Israel is designated as **virgin** because up to that time she had remained unconquered. The designation points up the contrast between her past and her future. **None to raise her up.** No power would be able to help her. **3. Shall leave an hundred . . . shall leave ten.** The verse describes a terrible slaughter in war, a 90 per cent decimation of the army.

5. Seek not Bethel . . . Gilgal. Centers of corrupt worship. **7. Ye who turn judgment to wormwood.** This is addressed to the leaders. The figure is drawn from a bitter, poisonous herb (Jer 9:15; Deut 29:18). Those who had the responsibility of administering justice produced injustice. **8. Maketh the Pleiades and Orion** (ASV). These constellations are referred to in the OT (Job 9:9; 38:31) as a demonstration of God's creative power. **Calleth for the waters.** The verse refers not only to God's control of the forces of nature but probably to the deluge of Noah. **9. Bringeth sudden destruction upon the strong** (ASV). God's irresistible power destroys that which is the basis of human pride.

10. Him that rebuketh in the gate. The gate of any city was the place where justice was administered (Deut 22:15). A judge or a prophet who rebuked injustice was unpopular (Isa 29:21). **13. The prudent shall keep silence.** The man who understood the nature of Israel's sin realized the futility of speaking out against it. This is in glaring contrast to Amos' direct attacks upon the sinners of his day.

15. The remnant of Joseph. The doctrine of the remnant (i.e., that there will be a saved and purified faithful few, in whom much of OT prophecy will be fulfilled) is prominent in the prophets (Isa 11:11; Mic 2:12; 4:7).

18. The day of the Lord. The day when the God of Israel will reveal himself in mighty power. Some people believed that this day would vindicate Israel against her enemies, but Amos pointed out that the Day of the Lord could mean only destruction for an apostate nation. **19. A bear met him . . . a serpent bit him.** The verse emphasizes the sudden coming of catastrophe when and where it is not expected.

21. I will not smell. Read with the ASV, *I will take no delight.* **22. I will not accept.** An unqualified repudiation of the sacrifices of Israel. **24. Judgment . . . righteousness.** This was not an appeal to Israel to turn to righteousness but a proclamation that the only thing that was left was judgment and destruction.

25. Have ye offered unto me sacrifices and offerings in the wilderness . . . ? The implication is that the Israelites in the wilderness did not offer mere sacrifices and offerings (cf. Jer 7:22,23). They brought something more than formal ceremonies. Amos does not say that no sacrifices were offered in the wilderness. The connection is with what follows. **26. You shall take up Sakkuth your king and Kaiwan your star-god** (RSV). It is impossible at the present time to identify **Sakkuth. Kaiwan** was a Babylonian god sometimes identified with Saturn. The idols would be carried into exile by the idolators. **27. Beyond Damascus.** To Assyria. Stephen uses Babylon instead of Damascus (Acts 7:43).

6:1. At ease in Zion. Amos warns the careless men and women of Judah, as well as those of Israel, that their recklessness will end in disaster. **Trust in the mountain of Samaria.** This is sometimes understood to mean confidence in the great power of the mountain fortress of the city, but it could equally well be understood as a reference to the feeling of security and confidence in their own strength on the part of those who dwelt in Samaria. **To whom.** The judges and leaders of Israel, to whom the people of the nation came for justice. **2. Calneh.** The site is uncertain. **Hamath.** An important city on the Orontes River.

3. Put far away the evil day. They acted as though the day of calamity would not come. **4. Lie upon beds of ivory.** The framework of their couches was inlaid with ivory. **5. Invent to themselves instruments.** At the end of the LXX rendering of the Psalter, David is quoted as saying, "My hands fashioned an instrument, and my fingers fitted together a psaltery" (cf. II Chr 29:26,27). **6. Bowls.** The ordinary cup was not large enough; so, in their self-indulgence, they appropriated vessels customarily used for sacrificial purposes (Ex 38:3; Zech 14:20).

8. Hath sworn by himself. The oath was by his holiness. This expression is used elsewhere only in Amos 4:2 and Jer 51:14. For similar expressions see Gen 22:16; Heb 6:13. **The excellency of Jacob.** This does not refer, as it might seem to do, to what Israel was in herself, but to her cities and palaces, of which she boasted and was proud (cf. Nah 2:2). **9. If there remain ten men.** Those not killed in war would perish in a plague. **10. He that burneth him.** A reference not to cremation but to the custom of honoring the dead by the burning of spices (Jer 34:5; II Chr 16:14; 21:19). **We may not mention the name of the Lord.** When a sole survivor of the plague would be found in a house, relatives and friends would take care to avoid mentioning the name of the Lord because of fear of the judgment of God (cf. Amos 8:3; Hab 2:20; Zeph 1:7).

12. Shall horses run upon the rock? There is a spiritual and moral order in the universe that is just as impossible to ignore as the natural order. It is as senseless to pervert justice as it is to expect horses to run on the rocks or for oxen to plow on rock. **13. A thing of nought.** The people had confidence in that which existed only in their imaginations. **14. Hamath.** On the northern boundary of the land (Num 13:21). **The river of the wilderness.** Better, *the brook of the Arabah* (ASV), which flows into the Dead Sea between Edom and Moab.

III. Five Visions of Israel's Condition. 7:1–9:10.

A. The Devouring Locusts. 7:1-3. A vision of destructive locusts, whose devastating invasion was stopped by the Lord when the prophet prayed.

1. Thus hath the Lord God shewed unto me. This formula introduces all the visions that follow except the fifth (9:1). **He formed grasshoppers.** These were locusts in the larval stage. In 4:9 the Lord says he sent locusts to point out Israel's sin, which was actually a revelation of the mercy of God. Here the mercy of God is revealed in his withdrawing the locusts before they had completely destroyed the corps. The two accounts speak of the same plague and reveal the two sides of God's mercy—in the first instance the active side, and here the passive side. **The latter growth.** The grass that grows after the late rains of March and April. **The king's mowings.** The first cuttings of grass were set aside to feed the king's horses, before the people harvested the main crop. The thought of the verse is that "in the beginning of the shooting up of the latter growth," the locusts were in the larva stage; after "the king's mowings," they were fully developed locusts. Thus Amos warned Israel of a complete destruction of the crops when the summer heat was due to begin.

2. As they were about to make an end of eating. The destruction was not completed. **By whom shall Jacob arise?** Or, *Who will raise up Jacob?* **For he is small.** In spite of his boasts (cf. 6:1), Jacob was small. **3. The Lord repented.** This is an anthropopathic expression (cf. 7:6; Gen 6:7; I Sam 15:35; Jon 3:9). God did not change his mind, as men do, but changed his course of action, which is consistent with his eternal unchangeableness. This was in response to the cry of Amos, "O Lord God, forgive" (7:2). According to some scholars, Amos had in mind an actual plague of locusts; according to others, he was thinking of the attack of the Assyrians.

B. The Flaming Fire. 7:4-6. A vision of consuming fire, whose work of destruction is stopped by the Lord when the prophet prays.

4. The Lord God called to contend by fire. The Lord was now in open conflict with his people (cf. Isa 66:15-18; 3:13; Jer 2:9; Hos 4:1). He would demonstrate his judgment by fire. **Devoured the great deep, and did eat up a part.** The summer heat was so severe that it consumed the subterranean sources of the springs and rivers and so affected the land. The fire symbolizes a more severe punishment than that of the locusts. The first two visions are parallel with the chastisements of Amos 4:6-11.

C. The Plumb Line. 7:7-9. A vision of the plumb line and complete destruction.

7. Upon a wall. *Beside a wall* (ASV) is better. The wall is the kingdom of Israel. **8. I will set a plumbline.** The measuring of the wall is a symbol of the testing of Israel's conduct (cf. II Sam 8:2; II Kgs 21:13). **I will not again pass by them any more.** Or, *I shall not pardon.* In the previous visions God had listened to the plea of the prophet, but now he did not permit intercession. The just punishment had to come. **9. The high places.** The people carried on their worship upon the so-called high places, which were natural hills or artificial mounds. Other nations also used such high places (Deut 12:2; Isa 15:2; 16:12). These high places, with their pagan influence, eventually contributed to the corruption of Israel (I Kgs 12:31-33; 13:32-34). **Of Isaac.** Many varying interpretations of this passage have been offered, but it is clear that Amos uses the name as a synonym for Israel, the nation. **The sanctuaries of Israel shall be laid waste.** The parallelism of this statement with what precedes in the verse is evident. **The sword.** A symbol of the Assyrian army (Amos 6:14).

D. Ecclesiastical Opposition. 7:10-17. Amaziah, the priest of Bethel, accused Amos of being a conspirator against Jeroboam, and ordered him to return to Judah. Amos responded that he spoke by the command of God.

12. And there eat bread. Amaziah told Amos to make his living by prophesying in Judah.

14. But I was an herdman. Amos denied that he was a prophet in a professional sense but said that he was a shepherd and a **dresser of sycomore trees** (ASV). The **sycomore** produces a low-grade fig, which has to be opened with a special instrument to release the excess juice within before it will ripen. **15. The Lord took me . . . the Lord said unto me.** The repetition of the name of God puts into bold relief the fact that Amos prophesied not by the will of man but by the direct call of God, who had made him a prophet.

17. An harlot. Violated by the invading soldiers.

E. The Basket of Ripe Fruit. 8:1-14. Amos had a fourth vision of destruction, representing Israel's readiness for judgment. This vision was the occasion of the discourse that follows.

1. Summer fruit. The word means late summer or autumn fruit and thus fully ripe. **2. The end is come.** A reiteration of the thought of the third vision. Israel was ripe in her sins and the end was now near. **3. Songs of the temple.** Some, with the LXX, interpret **songs** as singing-women rather than songs.

5. New moon . . . sabbath. Sacred days in the sense that ordinary occupations were forbidden. **Ephah small . . . shekel great.** The merchants used small measures to give less than was right, and by using heavier money weights, they cheated in taking too much money for the purchase. **8. As a flood.** Rather, *like the River* (ASV); or, *like the Nile* (RSV). The Hebrew text actually has *like the light,* but scholars are agreed that this is a reference to the Nile. **9. In that day.** The Day of the Lord, which will be characterized by changes in the natural world. **Darken the earth.** This probably refers to an eclipse. **10. An only son.** A description of the most intense sorrow (Jer 6:26; Zech 12:10).

11. I will send a famine. The people would long to hear the words they had so long ignored. **14. The sin of Samaria.** The Hebrew has *the guilt of Samaria,* which is a reference to the idolatrous worship carried on there. Some prefer to read *Ashimah,* the name of the pagan goddess worshiped in Samaria (II Kgs 17:30). **The manner of Beersheba.** Or *the way of Beersheba,* referring to the pilgrimages to the pagan shrine.

F. The Judgment of the Lord. 9:1-10. The fifth vision was of the Lord's executing judgment from which it was impossible to escape. There follows a vivid description of the devastation.

1. I saw. The introduction of this vision differs from those of the first four. Here the Lord himself appeared, and so Amos no longer uses symbols. **By** (AV, *upon,* **the altar.** The destruction began at the center of the idolatry. **2. Dig into hell.** A reference to Sheol, the place of the dead (Isa 14:9), as a place inaccessible. **Climb up to heaven.** Heaven and hell are sometimes used as symbols of total opposition (Job 11:8). **3. Carmel.** A symbol of inaccessibility. **The serpent.** A word used for a monster of the deep (Isa 27:1). **5. Like a flood.** Cf. 8:8.

6. His stories in the heaven. Or, *his chambers in the heavens* (ASV). A picture of the vastness of the universe. **His troop.** Or *vault*. The Hebrew means *bind together*. The first part of the verse is a description of the vast arch of the sky, which seems to be firmly established on the earth. **7. Ethiopians.** Rather, Cushites. **Caphtor.** Generally thought to refer to Crete.

IV. The Promise of Israel's Restoration. 9:11-15.

This last section of the prophecy gives a description of the restored Davidic kingdom. It brings into focus the goal of Jehovah's control of history. The idea that God's will must be done in history was an integral part of the thought of Amos.

11. In that day. The Day of the Lord. **The hut** (AV, *tabernacle*) **of David.** In the punishment of Israel the house of David was reduced to a hut. This is a picture of the coming restoration of Israel, when the throne of David will be re-established (cf. Acts 15:15-17). **12. All the heathen.** Amos' vision of the Messianic kingdom under the throne of David represents it as universal and including the Gentiles.

13. The plowman shall overtake the reaper. A forecast of the Millennial fertility of the land. **14. I will bring again the captivity of my people.** A promise that Israel would be restored to her land, which would be rebuilt and made to prosper. **15. I will plant them upon their land** (cf. Jer 24:6; 32:41; 42:10). Israel's return would be a direct act of God. **They shall no more be pulled up out of their land.** An unconditional promise of permanent possession, which has not yet been fulfilled (II Sam 7:10; Isa 60:21; Joel 3:20). **The Lord thy God.** The final words of the prophecy were the ground of the assurance to Israel that these things would come to pass.

BIBLIOGRAPHY

Cripps, Richard S. *A Critical and Exegetical Commentary on the Book of Amos*. New York: The Macmillan Co., 1929.

Driver, S. R. *The Books of Joel and Amos. (The Cambridge Bible)*. Cambridge: Cambridge University Press, 1934.

Edghill, Ernest Arthur. *The Book of Amos with Notes*. London: Methuen and Co. Ltd., 1914.

Jenkins, Sara Lucile. *Amos, Prophet of Justice*. New York: Association Press, 1956.

Jones, Philip Cowell. *Prophet Without Portfolio*. Philadelphia: Board of Christian Education of the Presbyterian Church in the United States of America, 1959.

Mitchell, Hinckley G. R. *Amos, an Essay in Exegesis*. New York: Houghton Mifflin Co., 1900.

Smith, George Adam. *The Book of the Twelve Prophets*. Rev. ed. New York: Harper & Bros., 1940. Vol. I.

Snaith, Norman H. *The Book of Amos*. London: Epworth Press, 1946. Pt. I.

Watts, John D. W. *Vision and Prophecy in Amos*. Grand Rapids: William B. Eerdmans Pub. Co., 1958.

Weiser, Arthur. *Das Buch der Zwölf Kleinen Propheten*. Göttingen: Vandenhoeck & Ruprecht, 1949. Vol. I.

Wolfe, Rolland E. *Meet Amos and Hosea*. New York: Harper & Bros., 1945.

OBADIAH

INTRODUCTION

Title. The Book of Obadiah neither identifies the prophet (beyond giving his name) nor provides a statement that clearly dates the writing. Approximately a dozen men are called Obadiah elsewhere in the Old Testament, but none corresponds to the prophet whose writing is preserved. His parentage, social status, and occupation in life remain obscure to us. The prophet's name means "Servant of the Lord," or "Worshiper of the Lord." It is a compound of *'ôbed*, "servant," and *yâ*, a shortened form of the four-letter name *yhwh*, pronounced *'ădônāy* by pious Jews, and translated either *Lord* or *Jehovah* in English versions.

Authorship. The first nine verses of this shortest of all Old Testament books closely parallel parts of Jeremiah 49, though the sequence of the material is different (cf. Ob vv. 1-4 with Jer 49:14-16; Ob vv. 5,6 with Jer 49:9,10; Ob vv. 8,9 with Jer 49:7,22). The question is: Which prophet is dependent on the other? The most likely situation is that both writers used an earlier, well-known prophecy. Doubtless the present arrangement in this book is the work of Obadiah. Certainly the entire book is the Lord's oracle (1 a).

Date. The prophecy of Obadiah alludes to a historical situation in which the Edomites were allied with the enemies of Israel and participated in the sack of Jerusalem (vv. 10-14). Jerusalem was plundered by the Philistines and Arabians during the time of Jehoram (II Chr 21:16,17), about the middle of the ninth century. Edom is referred to here as having more than one ally (vv. 7,11). It is known that Edom was allied with the Babylonians and others at the fall of Jerusalem in 587/586 B.C., and participated in the plunder of the city. Probably the prophecy of Obadiah is best dated in that period.

Summary of Message. The emotional tone of Obadiah's prophecy is strong but not bitter enough to justify the charge that it is a hymn of hate. The intense mood of the poem is undergirded by a keen sense of justice. Kinsmen had violated the bonds that hold related tribes together, and had committed terrible crimes. Their sins had to be punished! The Israelites did not undertake to punish the Edomites themselves. Instead, they recognized their God as the Judge of all the nations, and believed that he would execute justice on the basis of the crimes committed (v. 15). God is here regarded as universal in his power, so that no nation can escape his all-seeing eye. God is concerned for the oppressed and will lift them up, restoring what has been taken from them. There is a strong note of hope and comfort in the prophecy. The sovereignty of God is never far from sight, however. He is Judge at the beginning of the book and King at its end.

OUTLINE

I. Superscription. Verse 1 a.
II. Nations arrayed against Edom. Verse 1 b.
III. Public Enemy Number One arraigned. Verses 2-7.
IV. Edom indicted. Verses 8-14.
  A. The Judge's intention. Verses 8,9.
  B. The case against Edom. Verses 10-14.
V. Edom sentenced. Verses 15-20.
  A. Judgment. Verses 15,16.
  B. Vindication. Verses 17-20.
VI. The Lord to be King. Verse 21.

COMMENTARY

I. Superscription. Verse 1a (see Introduction).

II. Nations Arrayed Against Edom. Verse 1b.

The prophecy of Obadiah is cast in the form of a criminal trial. An outlaw is identified, brought to justice, and sentenced. **The Lord God** is the judge who speaks out against the outlaw **Edom. We have heard a rumour . . . and an ambassador is sent.** Previous to the trial, heralds of the Judge have proclaimed the event to the nations, calling them to attend in order to be prepared for battle (cf. Jer 49:14).

III. Public Enemy Number One Arraigned. Verses 2-7.

The divine Judge makes public his own estimate of the criminal who is here called to account.

2. I have made thee small. Edom regarded herself as a superior nation (vv. 3,4), but in God's sight she was insignificant. It would not be accidental that other nations would despise her; it would be the Lord's doing. The force of the Hebrew verb refers not to past action but to a certain, future action. Ironically, Edom wanted desperately to be an equal among the nations, but none regarded her as such.

3. The pride of thine heart has deceived thee. Edom's estimate of herself was inflated out of proportion to her real power. She had come to depend heavily upon the protection of her mountain fortresses. **Clefts of the rock.** The inaccessibility of Mount Seir had made that mountain a refuge for the Edomites many times. It is a granite range, with a width of fifteen to twenty miles, oriented north and south, having cliffs as much as 2,000 feet in height. It's stronghold is a lofty, flat-topped rock called *Sela'* in the Old Testament but more popularly known now as Petra. The stronghold could be approached only through a narrow, rock-walled ravine. Edom had come to believe that no enemy could successfully force its defenses. **4. As the eagle.** The fortress was located so high upon the mountain that it is here likened to an eagle's nest among the stars. Yet the Lord declared that Edom was not beyond His reach. He would bring him down and judge him in the presence of the nations.

5. If thieves . . . if robbers . . . if grapegatherers. By drawing upon common practice, the divine Judge strikingly depicts the end of Edom's power. Thieves and robbers (the Edomites were known as thieves and robbers) ordinarily carried off as loot only that which they deemed valuable. Likewise grapegatherers picked only the ripe grapes. But Edom's stronghold would be torn apart and *all* her possessions would be taken from their hiding places. **7. Men of thy confederacy.** Through trickery Edom would be turned over to the Judge by her own allies. The very ones whom Edom had fed would turn against her.

IV. Edom Indicted. Verses 8-14.

A. The Judge's Intention. Verses 8,9. The Judge declares that he intends to expose the shallowness of Edom's vaunted wisdom and power.

8. The wise men will not be able to acquit Edom. They will be confounded by the strength of the prosecution's arguments. **9. And thy mighty men.** The cleverness and skill of the warrior would not free Edom this time. *Teman* was the main Edomite settlement close by the stronghold, *Sela'*, or Petra. Justice would obtain a clear-cut conviction and win a death sentence.

B. The Case Against Edom. Verses 10-14. The exposure of Edom's sins is devastating and overwhelming.

10. Violence against thy brother Jacob. The ancestral father of the Edomites was Esau, the twin brother of Jacob. Though Jacob had grievously wronged Esau (Gen 25:33; 27:36), Esau had forgiven him (Gen 33:4). Now there was violence instead of forgiveness. **11. Thou stoodest on the other side.** When strangers carried away the descendants of Jacob into exile and captured the Holy City, the descendants of Esau did not come to help Judah against the enemy, but became allies of the invader. Edom participated in the plunder of the city. This situation best fits the events related to the fall of Jerusalem in 587/586 B.C., and the period that immediately followed.

12. But thou shouldest not have looked on the day of thy brother. In verses 12,13,14 there are seven occurrences of this phrase, **thou shouldest not,** or its equivalent. They mark out the specific crimes committed by the Edomites.

A kinsman was obligated by blood ties to aid another who faced danger. Edom refused to aid Jacob (Israel) in his need. See Jud 5:23 for an example of condemnation of kinsmen who failed to give aid in a crisis. **Rejoiced.** Edom had not merely withheld aid, but had actually enjoyed seeing the Israelites go down in defeat. The Edomites had **spoken proudly** or boasted to others about the fact that the Israelites deserved their punishment. They had thus added insult to injury. **13. Entered into the gate of my people.** Edom ceased being a gleeful spectator and began to participate actively in the sack of Jerusalem. This crime is emphasized in this verse by two more parallel statements. **14. Stood in the crossway.** The indictment represents Edom as first standing by, a gleeful spectator, then participating in the looting of the city, then serving at the roadblocks on the escape routes from the fallen city, cruelly arresting the fugitives and delivering them to the invader as slaves. A dastardly deed and worthy of the severest punishment!

V. Edom Sentenced. Verses 15-20.

A. Judgment. Verses 15,16. The prosecution has rested its case against Edom, and the Judge now outlines the basis for punishing the criminal.

15. The day of the Lord. The Day of the Lord is the time of God's judgment of wickedness and vindication of righteousness. God is merciful, but he will not forever tolerate sin. When the sinner, whether individual or nation, completely ignores the rule of God, He will step in to judge and to vindicate (cf. Joel 2:1; Amos 5:18-20; Zeph 1:7,8, 14-18; Ezk 25:12-14; 35:1-15). **As thou hast done, it shall be done unto thee.** The judgments of the Lord will be based upon justice, not upon caprice or vindictiveness. The punishment will not be less than nor more than the crimes committed. (See Hos 8:7 for a picturesque way of stating the same principle.) A sinner's sentence will not be out of proportion to his sins, but he can be assured that he must suffer for his sin.

Historically, Edom came to know the reality of this truth. Soon after this time, Edom was pushed out of her ancient home by the Nabateans, so that she had to move to the west side of the Dead Sea. Hebron was made the capital of her new home in south Judah. The Maccabees, especially John Hyrcanus (c. 125 B.C.), subdued and Judaized the Edomites. They were finally destroyed with the Jews in 70 A.D. by the Roman general Titus.

16. As ye have drunk . . . so shall all the heathen drink. The sorrow attending punishment is sometimes depicted by the prophets as comparable to drinking strong wine. See Jer 25:15-28 for an extended application of this analogy. God would not merely pick out Edom for an example but would equally judge all nations for their sins.

B. Vindication. Verses 17-20. Not only would God punish the wicked; he would also deliver the oppressed from their misery.

17. But upon Mount Zion shall be deliverance. In the destruction of Mount Zion, Israel was punished for her sins; but Israel was also to know deliverance. Back of the judgments of God there is the love of God. Sin must be punished, but God more deeply desires to give deliverance to those who turn to him. The fall of Jerusalem brought the Kingdom of Judah to an end, but God's concern for his people had not ceased. He would bring back a remnant from captivity to Mount Zion. **Shall be holiness.** In the OT, holiness means primarily separation unto God (Deut 7:6; Jer 1:5), but it also means separation from all that is unclean (Lev 20:7; 21:6; 22:9). The delivered people were to be God's people, but they were also to be cleansed from the idolatrous practices that had brought about the destruction of the nation. **House of Jacob shall possess.** The promised land would be returned to the exiles who had come back, and the homes and portions of land which belonged to their fathers would be theirs again.

18. Shall be a fire . . . a flame. In the day of the Lord, the relationship between Israel and Esau would be reversed. **The house of Jacob** and **the house of Joseph** (synonyms for Israel) would be masters over **the house of Esau** (Edom) and would be instruments in God's hands to carry out the divine judgment upon Edom.

19. They of the south shall possess the mount of Esau. Another translation reads: *They shall possess the Negev: that is, Mount Esau.* The boundaries of the Davidic kingdom would be restored in the south and in the **plain of the Philistines,** which would include the cities of Gath, Ekron, Ashdod, Ashkelon, and Gaza. (All of this region except the Gaza strip is now within Israel territory.) Then, toward the north, **the fields of Ephraim** and **the fields of Samaria** would be returned to the repatriated exiles. The tribe of **Benjamin** would move across the Jordan River and repossess Gilead.

20. The Davidic boundaries would be extended by including the Canaanites (Phoenicians) as far north as **Zarephath** (Sarepta in Lk 4:26), now known as Sarafand. It is located between Tyre and Sidon on the Mediterranean coast. **Sepharad.** Most likely Sardis, capital of Lydia in western Asia Minor.

VI. The Lord To Be King. Verse 21.

As the prophecy of Obadiah begins with the Lord dominating the scene, it ends with the proclamation that he is to be King of all. **And saviours.** The LXX reads, *those who have been saved;* but the Hebrew seems to refer to victors, that is, the returned exiles, who will again rule from Jerusalem over the land of Edom. **The kingdom shall be the Lord's.** The returned exiles are to be under a theocratic government ruled by God himself. This was the great vision of Obadiah and other prophets—that the Lord God was to be King over Israel and that he would rule the world from Mount Zion (cf. Zech 14:9-11).

BIBLIOGRAPHY

BEWER, J. A. "Obadiah," *International Critical Commentary*. Edinburgh: T. & T. Clark, 1951.

EXELL, J. S. "Obadiah," *Pulpit Commentary*. Vol. 14. Grand Rapids: Wm. B. Eerdmans Publishing Co., reprinted 1950.

KEIL, C. F. "Obadiah," *Biblical Commentary on the Old Testament*, Minor Prophets. Vol. I. Grand Rapids: Wm. B. Eerdmans Publishing Co., reprinted 1951.

KLEINERT, PAUL. "Obadiah," *Commentary on the Holy Scriptures*, Minor Prophets. Edited by J. P. Lange. Grand Rapids: Zondervan Publishing House, n.d.

SMITH, G. A. "Obadiah," *Expositor's Bible*. Vol. 4. Grand Rapids: Wm. B. Eerdmans Publishing Co., reprinted 1943.

THOMPSON, J. A. "Obadiah," *Interpreter's Bible*. Vol. 6. New York: Abingdon Press, 1956.

JONAH

INTRODUCTION

Title. The book receives its name from the main character of the narrative. Jonah *(dove)* is identified as the son of Amittai. A prophet by this same name, who figures in a short narrative in II Kings 14:25, is said to have come from Gath-hepher, located in Zebulon territory, now known as Galilee. This prophet had predicted the successful conquests of Jeroboam II in the first half of the eighth century B.C. There is little doubt that the prophet of Gath-hepher was the same man as the prophet of this small book.

Date and Authorship. Nowhere in the text is there any statement that the prophet himself wrote the book, although the prayer in chapter 2 is in the first person singular. However, tradition has steadfastly maintained that Jonah was himself the author. In recent years many have held that the book is *about* Jonah rather than *by* him. This view is based on several observations: chapters 1, 3, and 4 are written in the third person; there are late expressions of the Hebrew and Aramaic languages in the book; the large number of miracles recorded precludes a historical basis; and the emphasis upon God's mercy toward foreign people suggests a post-Exilic date. Conservative scholars have consistently held that these factors, in themselves, are not important enough to rule out the prophet's having lived in the eighth century or having written the book then.

Historical Background. Taken as a historical narrative of a prophet active in the time of Jeroboam II, king of Israel, the events of the book would have occurred sometime between 780 and 750 B.C. Jeroboam II had succeeded in re-establishing the power of Israel over most of the territory north of Judea controlled by David and Solomon. In the previous century the Assyrian empire had been a threat along the eastern Mediterranean coast, and had become well known as a cruel and ruthless oppressor. During the reign of Jeroboam II, though the power of Assyria had subsided, it was still to be reckoned with. Nineveh had not yet become the capital of the empire, but Calah, one of the parts of the old city-state complex that included Nineveh, was the capital between 880 and 701 B.C.

There is no Assyrian inscription stating that a revival like that described in this book ever occurred there; but during the time when Queen Semiramis was co-regent with her son Adad-Nirari III (810–782), there was a brief swing toward monotheism. Whether the fruits of Jonah's ministry and this purifying of Assyrian worship are to be identified is difficult to say. There were two severe plagues in Assyria in 765 and 759 B.C., as well as a total eclipse in 763 B.C., all of which were normally regarded by the ancients as evidences of divine judgment and could have prepared the hearts of the people for the preaching of Jonah.

Interpretations of the Book. Much controversy has been stirred up concerning the meaning of the Book of Jonah, and this has brought forth a wide range of views The book has been interpreted as a legend, a parable, a myth, and a prophetic allegory; and it has also been taken as history with Messianic import.

It has been suggested (R. H. Pfeiffer, *Introd. to the OT)* that the book is a fiction based on a possible legendary character whose real name has been lost. According to this view, the unknown author drew his miracles from the stories of Elijah and Elisha (cf. Jon 4:3 with I Kgs 19:4b and Jon 4:5,6 with I Kgs 19:4a, 5a) and the scene of mourning from Joel. The book thus was meant to be only a protest against the narrow nationalism of the Jews, who were under the teachings of Ezra. The psalm of Jonah 2 is the thanksgiving prayer of a man saved from drowning.

The interpretation of the book as a parable (IB) is very similar to the view that it is legendary. According to this second view, the character of Jonah is both an analysis and a criticism of post-Exilic Judaism, and the city of Nineveh represents the vast non-Jewish world that awaits the awakening only the true message of God can bring. The parable seeks to portray the justice and mercy of God toward any man or group who will repent of their sins.

Those who understand the story of Jonah as a myth in Jewish dress fancy they detect similarity between it and an ancient Greek fable. A king of Troy chained his daughter Hesione to a rock on the seashore. He intended her for a sacrifice to Neptune, who, as a shark, would come in with the tide and devour her. However, Hercules fought the monster and destroyed him, and so saved the girl.

According to the long-popular allegorical interpretation (see *Abingdon Bible Commentary*), Jonah is identified with Israel. The true mission of Israel is to declare God's truth to the world, but she has failed to do so. The "great fish" is Babylon, who swallowed the Israelites (took them into exile). The disgorging of Jonah upon the land represents the return of the Jews from exile. Jonah's dissatisfaction over the repentance of the heathen parallels the spirit of Judaism after the return.

Those who have maintained the historical character of the book have held that an actual prophet (Jonah) experienced what is recorded and thus fulfilled, in part, the missionary task of Israel in ancient times. For them (see Unger, *Introd. Guide to the OT*) the factual story has an underlying significance as well—both Messianic and typical. Important passages that support this view are certain statements in the New Testament made by Jesus regarding Jonah as a sign of His death and resurrection (Mt 12:40; Lk 11:30). Those holding this view use these references in a double sense: to verify the historicity of the story and to set forth its typical meaning. The position of this commentary is that the story of Jonah is a historical account.

The Message of the Book. The narrative itself is uncomplicated, fast-moving, and touching. A prophet, Jonah, is told by the Lord to go preach to the Ninevites. Instead, he flees and takes passage on a ship due to sail to the far edge of the world. He secludes himself and goes to sleep. Soon after the ship sets sail, a severe storm stirs up the sea into mountainous waves, and the sailors in terror throw the cargo overboard and frantically pray to their gods. By the casting of lots Jonah is identified as the culprit who has offended Providence. The storm ceases only after Jonah, at his own suggestion, is thrown into the sea. He is swallowed by a great fish. Now truly penitent, he prays earnestly for salvation, whereupon God delivers him unhurt upon the shore.

This time the prophet obeys the command to go to Nineveh, and cries aloud, throughout the city, his briefly worded message of woe. The people of Nineveh, from king to lowest subject, respond with earnest repentance, even putting sackcloth on the cattle. The Lord hears their cry and lifts the threat of destruction. Jonah, however, sees the deliverance of Nineveh only as a negation of his prophecy, and complains to the Lord in prayer. In order to teach the prophet a lesson, God prepares a fast-growing plant to shade him from the sun, but the next night allows a worm to destroy it. Then He sets a hot east wind blowing. As a result, Jonah faints in spirit and wishes for death. The story closes with a declaration that whereas Jonah is concerned for gourds, God is concerned for the salvation of sinful men.

Some of the basic religious teachings of the book are: (a) God feels concern for the heathen and asks His servants to warn them of judgment. (b) In the face of a difficult task, men are most inclined to evade responsibility. (c) God is powerful and can, at will, use the forces of nature for His own purposes. (d) Though God will punish disobedience, He still desires to show mercy. (e) The most unpromising mission fields are often the most responsive. (f) Above all else, God yearns to deal with man in mercy and kindness.

OUTLINE

I. Fleeing. 1:1-17.
 A. The Lord's command. 1:1,2.
 B. A ship to Tarshish. 1:3.
 C. A storm at sea. 1:4-14.
  1. Asleep during a storm. 1:4-6.
  2. The culprit found. 1:7-10.

3. Sailors in distress. 1:11-14.
D. Cast overboard. 1:15-17.
II. Praying. 2:1-10.
A. Cast out. 2:1-4.
B. Brought up. 2:5,6.
C. Paying vows. 2:7-9.
D. Delivered. 2:10.
III. Preaching. 3:1-10.
A. The Lord's second command. 3:1,2.
B. Declaring the message. 3:3,4.
C. Nineveh's repentance. 3:5-9.
1. In sackcloth and ashes. 3:5,6.
2. The king's decree. 3:7-9.
D. Judgment withheld. 3:10.
IV. Learning. 4:1-11.
A. Complaint. 4:1-3.
B. The gourd and the worm. 4:4-7.
C. The wind and the sun. 4:8.
D. The lesson. 4:9-11.

COMMENTARY

I. Fleeing. 1:1-17.

A. The Lord's Command. 1:1,2.

1. Word of the Lord came. There is no indication of how God spoke to Jonah. To the true OT prophets, the *way* God spoke to them was not so important as the *fact* that He spoke. **Jonah.** See Introduction for comment about the prophet. **2. Nineveh, that great city.** Located on the east bank of the Tigris River in Mesopotamia, it had been a dominant city-state from ancient times. A city-state comprised its occupied area and the surrounding territory, including the neighboring villages under its control. In Gen 10:11,12 Rehoboth, Calah, and Resen are mentioned with Nineveh as comprising "the great city." Sennacherib made the city the capital of his empire about 700 B.C., which was some time after Jonah's day. It was more than five hundred miles from Palestine—a long way to travel by foot. **Their wickedness.** The sins of Nineveh are not described here, but the city was widely known as a center of fertility cult worship, and for its cruelty to the victims of warfare.

B. A Ship to Tarshish. 1:3.

3. Tarshish. Perhaps to be identified with a Semitic mining colony located just west of the Rock of Gibraltar at the mouth of the Guadalquivir River (cf. Gen 10:4; Isa 23:1,6,10; Ezk 27:12). In Jonah's mind, to flee to Tarshish was to run as far away from home as possible. **Joppa.** The seaport nearest to the central part of Palestine, and, in ancient times, one of the few places along the eastern coastline of the Mediterranean Sea where a port could be established (cf. I Kgs 5:9; II Chr 2:16). **From the presence of the Lord.** This twice-repeated phrase is to be related to the coming of the word of the Lord to Jonah. Jonah mistakenly thought that by going as far as possible away from Nineveh, he could nullify the Lord's command.

C. A Storm at Sea. 1:4-14. Since storms on the eastern Mediterranean Sea usually do not occur until the late autumn, the sailors must have thought that they had plenty of time to sail to Tarshish without danger (cf. Paul's voyage to Rome centuries later, Acts 27). This storm was out of season, sent by the Lord for a special purpose.

1) Asleep During a Storm. 1:4-6.

4. Lord sent out. Literally, *cast* or *threw upon* the sea. **Tempest.** The word comes from a Hebrew word meaning "to agitate or rage." In those days ships were small and not strong enough to withstand severe storms. **5. Mariners.** These sailors were most likely men from the cities of Phoenicia, for that country was the major seafaring power of the ninth and eighth centuries B.C., and Tarshish was a Phoenician colony. They were the remnants of the old Canaanite culture that was widespread over Palestine before the time of Joshua. Because the men were pagans, believing in many gods, in this crisis each began to pray to his own favorite deity. **Cast forth the**

wares. A heavily burdened ship is easily capsized in heavy seas. A lightened ship would ride the waves better. **Was fast asleep.** Jonah had evidently felt so relieved to be on ship that he immediately found a place to rest his travel-weary body. He had gone down to the most remote part of the lower deck, and lying down, had quickly fallen into a deep slumber. (This is the only place in the OT where a ship is described as having a lower deck and an upper covered deck, both of which facts are clear in the Hebrew text.) **6. The shipmaster came.** The skipper, making careful inspection of his ship, found Jonah. Surprised that this man was so unconcerned, he exhorted him to pray. **Thy God.** Literally, *the God,* a term often used in the OT for the true God of Israel. The captain was so desperate that he was ready to try any god in order to be delivered from the dangers of the storm.

2) The Culprit Found. 1:7-10.

7. The lot fell upon Jonah. Casting lots was a popular form of divination among pagan nations, and still is. The Hebrews sometimes used lots, under God's guidance, to select people for some position or task (see Josh 7:14; I Sam 10:20,21), and even the apostles used the lot in one instance (Acts 1:26). Special stones were probably cast for the lot. **8. Tell us.** Once Jonah had been singled out, he became the center of attention. He was given a close cross-examination. **9. I am an Hebrew.** Jonah frankly told the whole story to the sailors. He witnessed to the fact that he was a worshiper of the great universal God of the world and had disobeyed Him. **10. Men exceedingly afraid.** Like most pagans, these men were superstitious, and they greatly feared that the wrath of God would fall upon them for their failing to worship Him properly.

3) Sailors in Distress. 1:11-14.

11. What shall we do? The sailors were perplexed about how to solve their problem. They had on board a man with whom God was angry, and they were far from any place where he could be put ashore. **12. Cast me forth into the sea.** Jonah finally saw what great calamity he had brought upon the sailors by his disobedience, and, condemning himself, he told them to throw him overboard. **13. Men rowed hard.** The sailors, not willing to treat human life so lightly, put themselves to the oars in one last desperate effort to reach shore in the storm. Their concern for one life stands in marked contrast to the attitude of Jonah, who later admitted that he had fled from the Lord because he did not want to see the Ninevites saved from destruction (4:2). **14. Lay not upon us innocent blood.** These men were not cruel monsters but men religious enough to pray earnestly when in danger. The sailors finally reasoned that since God had sent the storm to punish Jonah, He was not intent on harming them. Hence, they decided that Jonah alone should suffer for his sins and, following his advice, threw him overboard.

D. Cast Overboard. 1:15-17.

15. Sea ceased . . . raging. The passing of the storm seemed to confirm their decision, and they were shaken to the core of their being when they realized how narrowly they had escaped the wrath of the great God. **16. Offered a sacrifice . . . made vows.** The pagans were immediately convinced that the Lord of Israel was the true God. Forsaking their idols, they made a sacrifice of thanksgiving and pledged themselves to Israel's God.

17. Prepared a great fish. Even in punishment, Jonah was not forgotten by God. To be swallowed by a great fish may not seem to the victim an act of divine kindness. But the fish was God's means for bearing Jonah safely ashore. The creature that swallowed Jonah was not a whale. "Whale" is a mistranslation of the Greek in Mt 12:40. We do not know what kind of fish is meant in Jon 1:17. Some hold that the sea dog (shark) is large enough to fit the situation; it has been known to swallow men. The text makes it clear that the fish was *specially* prepared by the Lord. **Three days and three nights.** This need not mean seventy-two hours, since any part of a day or night can be considered a whole according to OT reckoning. A total of forty-nine hours would be adequate to meet a literal interpretation of the expression. This is still a long time for a man to be in a fish. Jesus applied the incident to his own burial. If Christ was buried before sundown on Friday (as is traditionally held) and arose before sunup Sunday morning, then a literal rendering of the "three days and three nights" (i.e., seventy-two hours) was not intended.

II. Praying. 2:1-10.

A. Cast Out. 2:1-4.

1. Jonah prayed. Jonah had not prayed while the storm was raging and the sailors were frantically crying out to their gods. Now he felt the desperateness of his situation.

2. I cried. Obviously the prayer was not written down while Jonah was inside the fish praying. It is in the past tense throughout, in keeping with the fact that it was composed after the experience. **Unto the Lord.** Jonah at least knew to whom to pray. The sailors had their own various gods but forsook them when they found out how powerful the Lord was. Jonah, however, had always known the true God. That was his difficulty. He knew God's concern for man, and yet he had fled. Now that he was in trouble, it was this same understanding of divine love that led him back to God. **He heard me.** According to the Hebrew way of thinking, genuine hearing involved response. For man, hearing God involved obeying Him. For God, hearing man involved delivering him. **Belly of hell.** Nothing more is meant here by the Hebrew than that the inside of the fish was a kind of grave.

3. Thou hadst cast me. In the OT a typical feature of a prayer of supplication is the declaration of the cause and nature of the affliction that gives rise to the prayer. Jonah knew why he had been punished, and recognized the justice of God's dealing with him. **4. Yet I will look again.** However, Jonah saw more than justice; he saw God's love, also, and hopefully pled for mercy.

B. Brought Up. 2:5,6.

5. Waters compassed me. The experience of being swallowed was so horrible that Jonah here returns to a graphic description of it. He had even become entangled with the other material within the fish. **6. Bottoms of the mountains.** Several phrases in this verse are difficult to translate with clear sense. The word **bottoms** seems to refer to the bases or foundations of the mountains in the ocean. The beating of the sea waves on the shore suggests the existence of bars that prevent the sea's encroaching upon the land (cf. Job 38:4-11). **For ever.** Jonah could not see any way out of his trouble, yet he looked to God. **Yet hast thou brought up my life from corruption.** Salvation is an act of God in the face of the impossible, and Jonah, in his words, recognized the concern of God for him personally—**my God. Corruption** would be better rendered *grave*.

C. Paying Vows. 2:7-9. Jonah's deliverance begot in his heart a desire to express gratitude to God in some way.

7. Soul fainted . . . I remembered. When the prophet had all but given up hope, he turned to the Lord for help. This theme is repeated several times in the prayer, because the physical impossibility of deliverance stood in stark contrast to the fact of the divine intervention. This was a source of constant amazement to Jonah. **Thine holy temple.** Ordinarily, prayer was to be offered in the courts of the Temple at Jerusalem. But Jonah knew that God's presence is not limited to any earthly temple and that the Lord is aware of the needs of His children wherever they are.

8. Lying vanities. A descriptive name for the idols and gods of paganism (cf. Ps 31:6; Deut 32:21). In this context, **vanity** does not have the sense of "superficiality" but of "worthlessness." **Mercy.** In context the word refers neither to the act of saving another, nor to the spirit of love for man, but rather to the source of salvation—God himself. Jonah reaffirmed his repudiation of idolatry as a way of worship. **9. Sacrifice . . . with . . . thanksgiving.** In contrast to pagan concepts, the true act of sacrifice is an expression of gratitude to God, rather than an effort to appease his wrath. With the sacrifice, a complete committal to God's will was made. In the words, **I will pay that I have vowed,** the prophet indicated that he was yielding to God's desires for him. He had become certain of one thing: **Salvation** is a gift of God and not an achievement of man.

D. Delivered. 2:10. The inner assurance that God saves by the act of his power was not a fancy nor an abstract idea, but was matched by an actual event. Jonah was delivered from the great fish, and found himself upon land, safe but chastened.

III. Preaching. 3:1-10.

A. The Lord's Second Command. 3:1,2. Now that Jonah had surrendered to God, he was ready for service. The second command was almost identical with the first one (1:2). The content of the proclamation was to be given to the prophet later.

B. Declaring the Message. 3:3,4. This time Jonah's response was immediate.

Following the caravan trail to the area of the upper Tigris River, he arrived at the complex known as **Nineveh, that great city** (v. 2), having been directed in his travels by the Lord.

3. Nineveh was. Some have maintained that the Hebrew verb translated **was** is in the pure past tense, which suggests that at the time of this story the city had been destroyed. We know that the destruction of the city occurred in 612 B.C. The Hebrew language has no true past tense, indeed has no tenses in its verb system. The 'perfect' aspect of the verb may at times be translated into an English past tense, but its sense is much broader. The 'perfect' form may also indicate an act (such as the founding of a city) which has been extended into a state of being. Consequently, all that is intended here is: Nineveh existed in Jonah's day as a great city. **City of three days' journey.** In olden times a city comprised not only its built up area, but also its territory and dependent villages or cities (see comments on 1:2). The descriptive phrase may refer to the circumference of this complex, that is, about sixty to seventy miles. On the other hand, the expression may be only an idiomatic parallelism of "that great city."

4. Began to enter . . . a day's journey. This statement does not mean that Jonah completed a day's journey before he started to preach; it means that he started to preach at the beginning of his visit to Nineveh. A day's journey in open country was about twenty miles, but in an inhabited area the course of such a journey was not likely to lie in a straight line but to weave back and forth through the markets and small streets. **Yet forty days.** Jonah's message was brief, and at first glance it seemed to be unconditional. It was a cry of woe and calamity.

C. Nineveh's Repentance. 3:5-9.

1) In Sackcloth and Ashes. 3:5,6.

5. People . . . believed God. The people of Nineveh took Jonah's words as a message from God and became greatly concerned about their danger. Semitic people in groups have always been easily swayed, and a man of Jonah's appearance and desolate cry probably attracted the multitudes and stirred them deeply. Mob reactions are still common in the Middle East. Here their natural tendency was no doubt heightened by the Spirit of God. **Proclaimed a fast.** In times of danger it was considered proper to refuse food and give full time to supplicating deity until danger was past. **Put on sackcloth.** Sackcloth was regarded as a symbol of humility and utter dependence on God. It was a coarse ugly cloth not fit for normal wear. **6. King of Nineveh.** Not the emperor of the Assyrian empire but the ruler of the city-state. He also joined in the fast by making it official. Having put on sackcloth, along with the others, he began to plead for mercy. **Sat in ashes** (cf. Job 2:8; Jer 6:26; Mic 1:10). A graphic way of declaring that man is nothing in the face of great danger.

2) The King's Decree. 3:7-9.

7. Published . . . the decree. The response of the people was made an act of the state. It has been a common practice among Semitic people to include their animals in their times of mourning and distress. It may seem strange to Western people that the cries of the famished beasts were intentionally added to those of the people; but Orientals regarded this as essential for effective supplication. **8. Beast be covered.** By putting sackcloth on the animals as well as on themselves the Ninevites symbolized the unity of man and nature in the humbling and petition. **Turn . . . away from his evil way.** As is so often the case in times of danger, people who otherwise seem completely indifferent become very conscious of their misdeeds—a sad commentary on man's lack of gratitude for God's blessings in good times. **From . . . violence.** The people of Assyria were noted for their cruelty to other people, especially prisoners of war. The Ninevites were quickened in conscience to realize that their treatment of other people was about to bring disaster upon them.

9. God will turn and repent. These two verbs do not signify that the Ninevites thought God was fickle. They indicate, instead, that these pagans believed the Lord's greatest desire was not to destroy men but to save them. The word **repent,** when used of God, does not denote sorrow for sin. It points rather to a decision on God's part to change his method of dealing with his creatures. Thoroughgoing repudiation of sin by man is pleasing to God, and in response He graciously pours out His love.

D. Judgment Withheld. 3:10. Jonah's message apparently was not an "if" sentence; yet in reality it was conditional, because God's threat of punishment can be set aside when real repentance is in evidence. The Lord's promises of salvation take procedence over his threats. God's love is eternal, but his expressions of wrath serve to quicken man to repentance. In the case of Nineveh, the Lord did not change in his essence; only his way of dealing with man changed. This is the wonder of mercy and love.

IV. Learning. 4:1-11.

A. Complaint. 4:1-3. Jonah had obeyed the Lord by going to Nineveh and preaching God's message, but his heart attitude had not been changed to love. He so hated the Ninevites for their cruelty that deep in his heart he looked forward to their destruction. Now the forty days had gone by, and Nineveh was still standing unharmed.

1. Displeased . . . exceedingly . . . very angry. A typical Hebrew parallelism, expressing the extreme reaction of Jonah to the salvation of the city of Nineveh.

2. I knew that thou art a gracious God. At last the secret was out. Jonah was not ignorant of the character of his God. He had fled to Tarshish not because he was afraid of the Ninevites, but because he did not want them to be saved. He knew that every threat of God was conditional, no matter how stated. God was **gracious,** meaning that He had the welfare of man upon His heart, and passionately desired to lift him from his sin. Even Jonah's own nation could not have come into being if God had not been gracious to the children of Israel at the very beginning (Ex 34:6,7). Any deliverance from slavery, oppression, famine, or destruction is an evidence of God's gracious love toward man (Isa 30:18), and the Lord forgives sins because He is gracious (Hos 14:2). **Merciful.** A companion word with **gracious,** pointing to the love of God which is poured upon the undeserving sinner who repents of his sins. God retains the right to help those who show genuine sorrow for sin and who trust in His kindness. **Slow to anger.** It is not God's first wish to punish the wayward. He endures much of man's wickedness. But when it becomes evident, in any given situation, that men are too proud and headstrong to be guided by easy, agreeable discipline, He begins to teach them the "hard way," by expressing His displeasure toward sin. **Of great kindness.** To the prophet, the love of God is so great that he can only multiply phrases in trying to express it. **Kindness** is a translation of the Hebrew word *hesed,* meaning loyalty to a covenant promise. The expression of kindness is not exhausted when the covenant is broken by the other party, but reaches out after the wayward one to draw him back to an intimate personal relation. God's kindness is so great that He is glad to put aside judgment so that the penitent sinner may re-enter the covenant relation.

3. Jonah did not have in his heart the love of God, and he felt shamed because his prophecy had been nullified by the conversion of those he disliked. The prophet was so downcast that he wished for death.

B. The Gourd and the Worm. 4:4-7.

4. Doest thou well to be angry? The Lord called Jonah's attitude into question. In the light of God's concern for man, how could his servant be so ungodlike?

5. Made him a booth. Though Jonah was aware that a wave of repentance in Nineveh would move God to save the people, he doggedly determined to wait for the destruction he had foretold. Going to higher ground outside the city proper, he set up a booth of branches to shade himself from the sun. Such booths are still used in the open country in the Middle East. A man can be comfortable in their shade even when the sun is blazing hot.

6. The Lord God prepared a gourd. The plant, *palma cristi,* is common in the Middle East. The speed of its growth in this case is declared to be an act of God. Jonah was suffering from so much inner conflict that he reacted with widely contrasting emotions at various times. Whereas before he had been greatly depressed, now he was overjoyed.

7. God prepared a worm. The destruction of the gourd was also an act of God. The worm, striking at the roots, destroyed the plant, and with it, the blessing of its shade.

C. The Wind and the Sun. 4:8. **God prepared a . . . wind.** This final act of the Lord robbed Jonah of his last earthly comfort—the cool shade. The east wind is famous for its searing hot temperature, from which not even the shade of a booth can protect a man. When Jonah could not endure the heat, he cried out the second time for the release of death. The first time he wished for death because of his inner despair; this time he cried to God because of his physical distress.

D. The Lesson. 4:9-11. Obviously, the series of divine actions directed toward Jonah had a purpose. God was striving to point up the absurdity of Jonah's spiritual unconcern for human welfare, by contrasting it with his legitimate concern for his own physical welfare.

9. The question of verse 4 is here repeated. From the content of 4:1-3 one can assume that Jonah's answer the first time the question was put would have been the same as the answer here.

10. Thou hast had pity on the gourd. This was a proper concern and probably a reasonable ground for anger. Yet the plant was only a plant, and Jonah had had nothing to do with its growth or destruction. **11. Should not I spare Nineveh.** The Ninevites were human beings—men, women, and children—objects of God's special creation, and therefore objects of his love. A mere plant, like the gourd, cannot enter into personal fellowship with God; neither can sin corrupt it. Jonah's concern for the gourd was selfish; he was sorry for its destruction because it served his personal comfort. But God's concern for man is unselfish, for He seeks only to give comfort by delivering from sin. No man has the right to question or resent the outpouring of God's love in saving man—any man—from sin and the destruction of sin. The Ninevites needed Him more than others because they had had no one to show them moral distinctions.

BIBLIOGRAPHY

Bewer, J. A. "Jonah," *International Critical Commentary*. Edinburgh: T. & T. Clark, 1951.

Deane, W. J. "Jonah," *Pulpit Commentary*, Vol. 14. Grand Rapids: Wm. B. Eerdmans Publishing Co., reprinted 1950.

Keil, C. F. "Jonah," *Biblical Commentary on the Old Testament. Minor Prophets*. Vol. I. Grand Rapids: Wm. B. Eerdmans Publishing Co., reprinted 1951.

Kennedy, James H., *Studies in the Book of Jonah*. Nashville: Broadman Press, 1956.

Kleinert, Paul. "Jonah," *Commentary on the Holy Scriptures*. Edited by J. P. Lange. Grand Rapids: Zondervan Publishing Co., n.d.

Smart, J. D. "Jonah," *Interpreter's Bible*, Vol. 6. New York: Abingdon Press, 1956.

Smith, G. A. "Jonah," *Expositor's Bible*, Vol. 4. Grand Rapids: Wm. B. Eerdmans Publishing Co., reprinted 1943.

MICAH

INTRODUCTION

Title. The prophecy of Micah receives its title from the name of the prophet himself. The name *Mîkâ* (LXX, *Michaias;* Vulg., *Michaeas)* is an abbreviation for *Mîkāyâ*. The prophet is called by this latter full name in Jer 26:18. The original and fullest form is *Mîkāyāhû*, which means, "Who is like Yahweh?" This fullest form was the name of a prince in II Chr 17:7. It is used of both men and women and it is usually abridged. *Yahu* is an ancient form of the name of the God of Israel, often rendered "Jehovah" (Ex 6:3; Ps 83:18; Isa 12:2; 26:4).

The prophet's name, like those of other prophets, as Elijah, Elisha, Hosea, Joel, Obadiah, and others, is important. Such names coupled with that of God or Yahweh signified the prophet's attitude and allegiance to the true God and, in the case of Micah, was a challenge to false prophets and sinners.

Date and Authorship. The date of the ministry is given in terms of the reigns of Jotham (739–735 B.C.), Ahaz (735–715 B.C.), and Hezekiah (715–687 B.C.), kings of Judah (Mic 1:1). Micah began his work at the time of Jotham and served through the entire reign of Ahaz and perhaps through all of that of Hezekiah. His writings, which show a close relationship to those of Isaiah, were written during the reigns of Ahaz and Hezekiah. Both Micah and Isaiah, though addressing their prophecies primarily to Judah, make it clear that God's judgment will also fall on the Northern Kingdom. That Micah prophesied during the reign of Hezekiah is further attested by Jer 26:18,19.

There are liberal critics who judge the work objectively, using the historico-critical method. To them the book of Micah is just another human production. Forgetting that we have only parts of his messages delivered at different times, that he was deeply concerned over the political and social conditions of his people, and that he was moved by the Spirit of Jehovah, these critics find what they consider glosses and interpolations which they date as late as the post-Exilic period. They reject the supernatural in prophecy, especially the naming of Babylon in 4:10, in spite of the fact that Assyria was the hostile power of the day. In arrangement and in scope chapters 1–5 are similar to Isaiah's prophecies. In chapters 1–3 Micah announces the coming judgment of sin, and in chapters 4 and 5 he proclaims that Israel is to be comforted by forgiveness and restoration. Hence the 'liberals' assign chapters 4 and 5 to a Deutero-Micah of the post-Exilic period.

We hold that the entire work is that of Micah, who prophesied at the time of Isaiah. Micah was not from a large city, as his older contemporary was, but from the small village of Moresheth, which belonged to Gath. He spoke as a man of the people, whose sympathy was with the country folk, and he sought to protect them against the greedy rich and the nobles of the capital cities. Though the prophet lived and prophesied in the Southern Kingdom, he condemned the sins of the Northern Kingdom; and he prophesied and witnessed its fall. Micah's prophecy is not presented in the form of a systematic treatise. This may be due to the fact that it contains a collection of oracles, subsequently written by the prophet or one of his disciples.

The oratorical style and the play on words in chapter 1 are reminiscent of Cicero. In chapters 2; 6; 7 the literary form is that of a dramatic dialogue.

Historical Background. The Assyrian kings of this period were Tiglath-pileser III (745–727), Shalmanezer V (727–722), Sargon II (722–705), and Sennacherib (705–681). Sennacherib led his army into the northern and western parts of Judah, subjugating cities and villages as he advanced, until he reached Jerusalem, which, though subjected to a long siege, was never taken. The prophecy concerning the eventual capture and destruction of Jerusalem points to the later time of Nebuchadnezzar. Assyria conquered the entire Near East except Egypt and Jerusalem. Her armies, however, did not occupy all of these lands; rather, she required them, as subjugated nations, to pay annual tribute.

When a new successor came to the throne of Assyria, the tributary kingdoms would revolt. Consequently, it would fall to the lot of this new ruler to resubjugate all the previously held land by a series of military campaigns. The most difficult campaigns were against the nations closest to Egypt. These border countries, acting as buffer states in bearing the brunt of war, were encouraged by Egypt in an effort to protect herself.

These were days of unrest, insecurity, and hardship, especially for the peasants and villagers. The harassment of the passing armies, which not infrequently overran the small villages and made slaves of their inhabitants, caused a state of fear. The political conditions in both Israel and Judah could not have been worse. The rulers, the wealthy, the conniving priests and prophets in the capital cities, feeling secure within strong fortifications, made the most of their power to oppress the poor. The peasants had no protection either from the Assyrians or from the "grafters" of their own nation. To these wrongs Micah addressed himself, championing the cause of the oppressed. Fearlessly following the leadership of the Holy Spirit, he preached at the risk of his life. Micah's messages reflect the prevailing corruptions. His allusions to the Assyrians show what was the common topic of the day.

OUTLINE

Superscription. 1:1.

I. Approaching judgment of Israel and Judah because of persistent sin. 1:2-16.
- A. The call to attention. 1:2.
- B. Terrible coming of the Lord Jehovah announced and described. 1:3,4.
- C. Sins of the capital city representative of those of the nation. 1:5.
- D. Fearful consequences of this judgment. 1:6,7.
- E. The prophet's reaction and his vision of this judgment. 1:8-16.

II. Doom of corrupt oppressors and false prophets. 2:1–3:12.
- A. Woe upon the land monopolizers. 2:1-5.
- B. False preaching of lying prophets. 2:6-13.
  1. Effort to stop the preaching of the true prophet. 2:6.
  2. False preaching that the Spirit of Jehovah is straitened. 2:7.
  3. Insecurity of citizens due to rule of oppressors. 2:8-13.
- C. Denunciation of the leaders of the people. 3:1-7.
  1. Micah's answer to the false prophets and oppressors. 3:1.
  2. Character of wicked oppressors described. 3:2,3.
  3. Jehovah's refusal to hear their prayers. 3:4.
  4. Character of false prophets. 3:5.
  5. False prophets to be discredited. 3:6,7.
- D. Micah's consciousness of power from the Spirit of Jehovah. 3:8.
- E. Gross sin and crime to bring destruction upon Jerusalem. 3:9-12.

III. Vision of hope through the Coming One. 4:1–5:15.
- A. Final triumph of Jerusalem. 4:1–5:1.
  1. Revival of true religion and return to Jehovah. 4:1,2.
  2. The return to Jehovah to bring peace and prosperity. 4:3-5.
  3. Return of those in captivity promised. 4:6,7.
  4. Jerusalem to be restored to greater splendor and power. 4:8.
  5. Redemption to be preceded by suffering as punishment for sin. 4:9,10.
  6. Enemies to see Jehovah's vindication of his people. 4:11,12.
  7. Final victory foretold, with exhortation to prepare for a coming siege. 4:13–5:1 (4:14 in Heb. text).
- B. Coming mighty leader to be born in Bethlehem and to restore the remnant of Jacob. 5:2-15.
  1. The Messiah to be born in Bethlehem. 5:2,3.
  2. The Messiah's beneficent reign. 5:4-7.
  3. Spiritual Israel to become a great conqueror. 5:8,9.
  4. Spiritual Israel to be deprived of material strength and help. 5:10-15.

IV. Lawsuit of Jehovah. 6:1–7:20.
- A. First complaint of Jehovah. 6:1-5.
- B. Israel's first reply. 6:6-8.
- C. Second complaint of Jehovah. 6:9-16.

D. Israel's second reply — a confession of sin. 7:1-10.
E. Israel's promised blessing to follow judgment. 7:11-13.
F. Final plea for Israel — gathered from many nations. 7:14-17.
G. Doxology: The triumph of grace. 7:18-20.
  1. Jehovah, the God of forgiving love. 7:18.
  2. Jehovah, the God of redeeming power. 7:19.
  3. Jehovah, the God of perpetual faithfulness. 7:20.

COMMENTARY

Superscription. 1:1.

The word of Jehovah (ASV). The message was from Jehovah, and hence had divine authority. This was the usual claim of the Hebrew prophets (cf. Jon 1:1; Ob 1:1). **Was to.** In the sense of "directed to". Thus the word of Jehovah was directed to Micah, given to him to proclaim. **Saw,** i.e., with mental and spiritual vision, not necessarily with physical eyes. This verb means to see subjectively. Micah had spiritual understanding of the message he was to declare.

I. Approaching Judgment of Israel and Judah Because of Persistent Sin. 1: 2-16.

A. The Call to Attention. 1:2.

Hear or listen. Hear with interest, having mental and spiritual perception, and with a view to obedience. This is a customary word used by the prophets to call attention to their messages (cf. Isa 1:2,10; Amos 3:1; Joel 1:2; Hos 4:1). **All people, the earth and her fullness.** The message is directed to all peoples. The earth and her fullness are to stand at attention (cf. Isa 1:2; Deut 32:1). **Cause to hearken.** Literally, *cause to point, to sharpen* (the ears). The people are to be attentive while the message is being proclaimed. **Lord.** The enthroned "Lord" or "Master" over the universe. **Against** or **among you** (ASV margin). If "against," the reference is to Samaria and Jerusalem. If used in the sense of "among," the pronoun refers to all people. In either case Jehovah is speaking concerning the wickedness of the capital cities of Israel and Judah. He is witnessing from *the temple of his holiness.* This temple, the context indicates, is in heaven. "Holiness" primarily means "separation." Heaven itself is separated and consecrated to the purposes of the holiness of Jehovah. The Lord's active holiness goes forth into all the earth, in salvation or in judgment.

B. Terrible Coming of the Lord Jehovah Announced and Described. 1: 3,4. These verses introduce a solemn reason why all peoples should hear the message.

3. Goes forth. The form used indicates that Jehovah is continuously sitting in judgment upon sin and sinners. **He shall come down and shall tread.** The two verbs express repeated action.

4. As the majestic stepping forth of Jehovah touches the tops of the mountains, **the mountains shall be dissolved.** New valleys will be formed as *the hills* (valleys) *split themselves* and, like wax before the fire, pour down like a torrent of water over a precipice. It is to be noted that Orelli *(The Twelve Minor Prophets,* p. 191) prefers *plains* to **valleys.** Others suggest the emendation, *hills,* to avoid the apparent difficulty of "valleys" being cleft. Similar descriptions of such awe-inspiring manifestations of Jehovah occur in Ex 19:18,19; Jud 5:5; Isa 64:1; Hab 3:6.

C. Sins of the Capital City Representative of Those of the Nation. 1:5.

For the transgression of Jacob. Transgression literally means *breaking away* or *rebellion. Apostasy* would be nearer the Hebrew (Cheyne, "Micah," *The Cambridge Bible).* Israel, the Northern Kingdom, had broken away from Jehovah and rebelled against his righteous requirements. **For,** i.e., "because of," the transgression is **all this**—either the witnessing that precedes or the judgments that follow. The phrases may point in both directions. **Sins.** To sin is literally to *miss the mark,* as when a marksman shoots and misses. In the NT the Greek word for sin, *hamartia,* has the same meaning. God had set up a target, and the house of Israel had missed the mark. **What is.** Literally, *Who is.* Rebellion and sin are committed by people. The form of the question demands an affirmative answer. **High places** were locations for idolatrous worship, which was forbidden by the Mosaic law (cf. Deut 13). The prophet charged the two capital cities with being the centers of the nations' sins. This accusation can be made against many capital cities throughout history.

D. Fearful Consequences of This Judgment. 1:6,7.

6. Therefore. Because of the sins of Samaria, Jehovah will do as follows. **A heap,** i.e., a ruin for **plantings of a vineyard.** Wars caused the destruction of the city several times, and this prophecy became literally fulfilled (cf. Isa 21:1-3). Jehovah declares that he will cause Samaria's stones to pour down into the valley, completely uncovering its foundations. Today Samaria is heaps of stone, not only on the hill summit but also in the fields below. Archaeological expeditions have extended the uncovering of the foundations to the very palaces of Omri and Ahab.

7. All her graven stone images, Jehovah foretells, he will cause to be beaten into pieces, in his wrath against idolatry (Ex 20:4). **All her hires;** i.e., wages paid to harlots as the price of their sin. The prophet looked upon the idolatrous civilization of Samaria as the product of the hire of harlots; or upon idolatry as harlotry. Samaria was to be destroyed and the fragments of her images were to be returned to the original usage, the hire of harlots.

E. The Prophet's Reaction and His Vision of This Judgment. 1:8-16.

8. On this account. The prophet declares that he will lament and wail, go stripped or plundered and naked, because of the incurable wounds of Samaria that have come upon his own people, even unto the gate of Jerusalem, the political capital and center of worship. **Therefore I.** The prophet identifies himself with the nation. The literary form of verse 8 produces a solemn impression. Micah begins, **Let me wail . . . with the strength of a jackal.** He will lament until he has exhausted himself, so that his voice will become like the "peeping" of a baby female ostrich (ASV, RSV). Nakedness was the common lot of a captive. In his grief the prophet will go stripped and naked.

9. The idolatry and wickedness of Samaria had so influenced Jerusalem that she was guilty of like sin. The descendants of the house of Ahab (king over the Northern Kingdom, husband of Jezebel) ruled in Jerusalem and led the nation away from Jehovah. The resulting wounds, which could never be cured, had infected the political, social, and religious life of Judah, including the very place of counsel, namely the "city gate." In the Near East, **gate** had come to mean the king's counselors or cabinet, and that meaning persisted even until the fall of the Turkish sultanate in recent years. For centuries the cabinet of Turkey was called "the Sublime Porte." Like sin merits like judgment, whether it be the sin of Samaria or that of Jerusalem.

10. Note, beginning with verse 10, that the listing of the cities shows the route of the invader. Whereas the first five cities are north of Jerusalem, the last five are southwest or south of the city. The prophet, in oratorical style, names the cities according to the sound of their names as well as according to meaning. Not only Jerusalem, but also the surrounding locations would suffer. **In Gath** *(gat)* **do not announce it** *(taggîdû).* **In Beth-le-Aphrah** *(House of dust)* **in dust I have rolled myself.** Both were heathen cities. The prophet dreaded the outpouring of the scorn of these people when they should learn of the sin and consequent punishment of those who were called the people of Jehovah. To roll in dust signified abject and intense mourning.

11. Dweller is feminine in form. Micah foresees the women of these doomed cities pass before the men. In nakedness and shame they will go into captivity, and the men will be powerless to help against the might of the enemy. In 1:6 the prophet introduces the prophecy against Samaria. In 1:11 the punishment upon Judah is without an introductory statement. **The female dweller of Zaanan** *(Outlet)* **shall not go out,** i.e., out of the house. She will be in terror because of the coming invader. **Wailing of Beth-ezel** *(House of Separation)* **shall take away from you his stay or strength.** This town, which was probably fortified, would be expected to help resist the invader. But its people would lament over the suffering of others until their strength would be gone. **12. For** *(kî)* **. . . because** *(kî).* The first *kî* is a particle—"yea" or "indeed." The second gives the reason for the first clause. The female inhabitant of Maroth, Micah says, will painfully wait for **good,** but Jehovah will send **evil** to the gate of

Jerusalem. The invasion of the Assyrians was violence sent as judgment from Jehovah (cf. Isa 10:5).

13. Hitch the chariot to the swift racing steed. The female dweller of Lachish *(impregnable hill)* is so commanded that she may escape the coming invader. Judgment is to come upon Lachish because she was the **beginning of sin** (i.e., of *missing the mark)* of the **daughter of Zion** (Jerusalem). Through her, the **transgression** *(breaking away from God)* of Israel—Baal worship with its accompanying abominations—came to Zion. The use of *Lākîsh* and *rekesh* ("swift steed") close together is a characteristic Hebrew play on words. **14. A parting gift.** Or, a dismissal present, i.e., the return of the marriage portion of a bride, hence a bill of divorcement. The "daughter of Zion" and Moresheth-gath (the prophet's home town) have been united in sin. Now they are to be separated. **Houses of Achzib** *(place of deceit)* will be a **deceitful thing** to the kings of Israel. This town (eight miles north of Moresheth) rather than serving as a defense against the invaders will be helpless or even turn traitor.

15. Yet the one possessing (thee) **I will cause to come to thee.** Jehovah will cause the possessor (the Assyrian invaders) to come and take them captive. **Mareshah,** "hereditary city (of Judah)", now is to become the possession of Assyria. **Unto Adullam shall come the glory of Israel.** The nobility will flee to Adullam, famous for its caves; men who should be in the battle line will be hiding. **16. Make thee bald and cut off thy hair.** This is expressed in the feminine gender. Perhaps Israel as a mother is exhorted to extreme manifestation of grief because her sons, born and reared in luxury *(delicately brought up)*, have gone into captivity. Micah sees the horror as already accomplished.

II. Doom of Corrupt Oppressors and False Prophets. 2:1—3:12.

A. Woe upon the Land Monopolizers. 2:1-5.

1. Woe is pronounced upon those who lie awake at night devising crooked or treacherous methods to gain their selfish ends. When morning breaks they put their schemes into effect, for the power is in their hands. "Might makes right." **2.** They **seize . . . take away . . . oppress.** They take all they **covet**—fields, houses, and inheritance. Nothing renders a people so helpless as to make the plain people, the core of the nation's strength, homeless and reduce them to servitude (cf. Goldsmith, *The Deserted Village).* **3. Therefore** Jehovah will recompense these oppressors according to their doings. He is preparing a halter for their necks. Instead of going about with their heads haughtily lifted, they will be led into captivity with haltered necks.

4. In that day some mourner will bitterly bemoan the ruin (lit., *wail a wail of a wailing)* as he sees the fields divided among the enemy. Therefore there will be no prosperity, no land, and for these unscrupulous wealthy people, no further part in the inheritance of the Lord (v. 5).

B. False Preaching of Lying Prophets. 2:6-13.

1) Effort To Stop the Preaching of the True Prophet. 2:6. **Prophesy ye not . . . they prophesy.** The corrupt leaders, using the false prophets who cater to them, will seek to stop the true prophet from preaching. **Prophesy** is used in a double sense, "to preach" by the true prophets and "to drivel nonsense" by the false prophets.

2) False Preaching That the Spirit of Jehovah Is Straitened. 2:7. **Ought it be said . . . that the Spirit of Jehovah is straitened** (impatient)? **are these his deeds?** The oppressors cannot ascribe the calamities to a God who is accustomed only to punishing. No. To the upright his words are good.

3) Insecurity of Citizens Due to Rule of Oppressors. 2:8-13. Instead of walking uprightly, Jehovah's people are rising up as his enemy. They plunder unsuspecting and helpless society, not only stealing clothing and fraudulently driving women from their homes, but taking from the children (soon to enter captivity) the rights of citizenship and temple worship (vv. 8,9). "Arise," proclaims the prophet, "and go into captivity, for uncleanness completely destroys" (v. 10). The indictment of the prophet is scathing. If a person should come to them preaching in favor of wine and strong drink, these oppressors would be base enough to make him their prophet (v. 11).

Bible students differ as to whether the return from exile is foretold in 2:12,13. Some hold that the abrupt turn from the message concerning the nearer future to one concerning the remote future is often found in the writings of true prophets, and would be expected from one who had hope of ultimate blessing. In this view the **breaker** (v. 13) refers to Messiah, who will lead forth his besieged remnant as their king, even Jehovah, at his second advent. Others feel that this prophecy was put forth by the false prophets who held out a false hope of a speedy return. As regards the Northern Kingdom of Israel, this prophecy has never yet been fulfilled.

C. Denunciation of the Leaders of the People. 3:1-7.

1) Micah's Answer to the False Prophets and Oppressors. 3:1. Micah calls to the rulers of both nations to hear with understanding so as to heed. First attacking the political leaders, he asks if it is not their duty to know justice by experience. The question implies an affirmative answer.

2) Character of Wicked Oppressors Described. 3:2,3. Instead of knowing justice, they are habitual haters of good and lovers of evil. They treat the poor as cannibals do victims in their feasts.

3) Jehovah's Refusal To Hear Their Prayers. 3:4. **Then.** When Jehovah's judgment falls, they will repeatedly cry to him, but he in turn will not answer and will **hide his face from them.** These leaders *chose* to do evil (2:1-3) and were guilty, so Jehovah could not but hide his face from them and let justice take its course.

4) Character of False Prophets. 3:5. When these prophets had plenty to eat **(biting with their teeth)**, they preached **peace.** The implication is that the rich oppressors protected and supported the false prophets. And, if the spokesmen did not get their support, a holy war would be declared against the benefactors.

5) False Prophets To Be Discredited. 3:6,7. The false prophets, Jehovah declares, will not have visions nor be able to divine. This frustration will be as the darkness of night to them. The discredited prophets will **be ashamed** (AV; lit., *turn red);* they will cover their lips; there will be nothing to say. And the people will be left groping in religious darkness.

D. Micah's Consciousness of Power from the Spirit of Jehovah. 3:8.

Micah here contrasts himself with the false prophets. He is full of heroic might, inner strength, even the **Spirit of Jehovah.** He is also filled with zeal for administrative justice instead of love of oppression, and with courage instead of cowardice like that of the false prophets. This zeal and courage find expression in this making known **to Jacob his transgression** *(rebellion)* and **to Israel his sin** *(missing the mark).* Micah, being full of holy passion for the cause of Jehovah, could make the high claim of this verse.

E. Gross Sin and Crime To Bring Destruction Upon Jerusalem. 3:9-12.

Hear ye, I pray thee. Beginning with a compassionate plea, Micah summarizes his charges to the **heads** *(judges),* **rulers, priests,** and false **prophets** (vv. 9-11) who even dare to say, **Is not Jehovah in our midst and evil shall not come upon us?** (v. 11), looking to the people for their nod of agreement. **12.** Because of such leaders—destruction is to come. No longer a city, Zion will be **plowed as a** farmer's **field, a heap** of ruins, and **the mountain of the house** (Mount Moriah) where Jehovah long has been worshiped will be a deserted woodland hilltop.

III. Vision of Hope Through the Coming One. 4:1–5:15.

A. Final Triumph of Jerusalem. 4:1–5:1.

Verses 1-3 are found nearly word for word in Isa 2:2-4. Though Micah and Isaiah were contemporaries (Jer 26:18; Isa 1:1), it is doubtful that the older, Isaiah, would copy from the younger prophet. Further, the verses fit better and are more complete as found in Micah. Some scholars propose a third source from which the Holy Spirit led both men to gain material for their discourses.

1) Revival of True Religion and Return to Jehovah. 4:1,2.

1. In the latter (or *last,* lit. *after)* **days.** After the days of judgment described in the previous chapter. This phrase is commonly used by the prophets to denote the Messianic era (cf. Hos 3:5). C. F. Keil states: "The predicted exaltation of the temple mountain is assigned to the period of the completion of the kingdom of God" *(The Twelve Minor Prophets,* II, 456). **The mountain of the house of Jehovah** shall be spiritually exalted above all mountains. Nations shall **flow** (like a river) **unto it,** of their own desire, for God will be there.

2. They will invite and urge others, and Jehovah will be the teacher. The Hebrew word for **teach** comes from a word meaning "to cast a javelin" or "to shoot as an arrow." It came to mean "to cause to point out," hence "to teach or instruct." The thing pointed out became known as the "torah" or law. This word is used not of the Mosaic law only but of the entire OT; hence the teachings concerning the Messiah are included. All nations shall flow to Jehovah's habitation to learn of the Messiah, for they will desire **His ways and . . . his paths.** Jehovah will teach his purposes and demands, and it will be possible to walk therein because this **law** (Heb. *tôrâ)* shall go forth from Zion.

2) The Return to Jehovah To Bring Peace and Prosperity. 4:3-5.

3. He will judge . . . and decide (lit., *arbitrate).* Jehovah will act as arbitrator between contending peoples, setting right **strong nations from afar.** They will cease to war and will change the implements of battle into the tools of peace. This points back to the determination of peoples to walk in the paths of Jehovah, and to the going forth of the Torah from Jerusalem (v. 2). In Jerusalem, the abode of kings, is found the concept of kingship and authority as well as judgment. Peace is the fruitage of the teaching of the Word of God. **4,5.** No longer learning war, **each man shall sit under his own vine and fig tree, and there shall be no fear** (cf. Zech 3:10). This is possible, since Jehovah, the God of Israel, is the eternal, self-existent one. In contrast to Him, heathen gods are without life, and worship of them will perish. Those who walk in the **name of Jehovah** (v. 5) shall have eternal peace.

3) Return of Those in Captivity Promised. 4:6,7. The oracle of Jehovah is that those in captivity will return, but in the "after" days (v. 1), after suffering and judgment. Jehovah will gather the limping and those cast off, those driven cruelly into captivity, afflicted by God for their sin. These will become a **remnant** (v. 7) spoken of by the prophets (cf. Isa 37:32; 46:3; Jer 23:3; Amos 5:15). The cast-off ones will become Jehovah's own **strong people.** And he will rule over them in Mount Zion from their return even to eternity. (See conclusion of ch. 5 for fulfillment of this prophecy.)

4) Jerusalem To Be Restored to Greater Splendor and Power. 4:8. **The former dominion.** The kingdoms of David and Solomon represent Jerusalem in its glory. Here it is implied that even greater splendor is to come to Zion, to the **tower,** a portion of the Davidic palace, from which the good shepherd, in figure, watches over his **flock.**

5) Redemption To Be Preceded by Suffering as Punishment for Sin. 4:9,10. **No king** will be in Israel. **Like a woman in travail** (v. 10) the house of Jacob must suffer captivity in Babylon. There she will be set free.

6) Enemies To See Jehovah's Vindication of His People. 4:11,12. Scorn will come from the cruel heathen nations desiring Israel's pollution. But these will not have perceived Jehovah's counsels, that he is to gather them to Jerusalem as **sheaves to the threshing floor.** Some hold that the enemies are the Assyrians ("Micah," *The Cambridge Bible,* p. 40), or the army of Antiochus Epiphanes, as described in Daniel and in I and II Maccabees (Cowles, *The Minor Prophets,* p. 200), or the nations gathered at the final great battle of Joel 3; Ezk 38; 39; Zech 12; and Rev 20:8ff.

7) Final Victory Foretold, with Exhortation To Prepare for a Coming Siege. 4:13–5:1.

13. Arise and thresh. Zion will punish with a horn of iron and hoofs of brass. Her foes will be destroyed as grain is trampled by oxen on the threshing floor. The enemies of Zion will think to make gain for their selfish ends, but, in reverse, the gain is to be **consecrated,** *devoted,* to Jehovah.

5:1 (4:14 in the Heb. Bible). Micah abruptly turns to an imminent experience. **Israel,** here meaning Judah, is to marshal her forces for a siege, in which the ruling king, who is judge, will be humiliated. This was fulfilled in part by the siege of Sennacherib in 701 B.C., by Nebuchadnezzar's capture of Jerusalem in 587 B.C. and his smiting of King Zedekiah, and by each succeeding siege until the destruction of Jerusalem in A.D. 70.

B. Coming Mighty Leader To Be Born in Bethlehem and To Restore the Remnant of Jacob. 5:2-15.

1) The Messiah To Be Born in Bethlehem. 5:2,3.

2. Bethlehem (Heb. *House of Bread*) in the district of **Ephratah** was too small to have a place **among the thousands** (or families) **of Judah,** yet was destined to be exalted throughout the world; for the Messiah was to be born in this humble place, in the village of his great ancestor David. **His goings forth** are **from everlasting,** for this future **ruler in Israel** is the eternal "Angel-Jehovah" coequal with Jehovah throughout the OT.

3. She who is in travail refers to Israel in affliction, or the personal mother of the coming One; the latter is preferred. Then, there shall be a return of the **residue** (or remnant) of his **brethren** (fellow Judeans) to Jehovah and home.

2) The Messiah's Beneficent Reign. 5:4-7.

4. He . . . shall feed his flock (ASV). Messiah is to become the shepherd who works in the strength and majesty of Jehovah (cf. Jn 10:11; Heb 13:20; I Pet 5:4). Enemies will be unable to molest, for **his name shall be great to the ends of the earth. 5,6. This man shall be the peace** (cf. Eph 2:14) within men's souls, between men, between nations. **When Assyria shall come.** Assyria was the foe most feared in Micah's day, and it is here used to typify Israel's enemies. In the One who is Peace there is power to raise up leaders who will protect Israel and overcome enemies. Micah points to the victory of the Coming One over world powers.

7. The remnant of Jacob (spiritual Israel) **shall be in the midst of many nations as dew . . . showers.** Jehovah's true people are refreshing and a blessing like the dew—of God—not made or removed by the **sons of men.**

3) Spiritual Israel To Become a Great Conqueror. 5:8,9. Israel shall be **as a lion** from whom **none can deliver,** as a mighty warrior who shall **cut off** his **adversaries** (v. 9). This warfare will be completed when "the One" shall have put all enemies under his feet (I Cor 15:25-28).

4) Spiritual Israel To Be Deprived of Material Strength and Help. 5:10-15. Jehovah proclaims that the time will come when all *war* equipment upon which his people have depended will be **cut off** (vv. 10,11). All man-made religions—with their sorceries, diviners, idols, shrines, and cities devoted to idolatry—by which Israel has been led astray, Jehovah will **pluck up** (vv. 12-14). Israel will then rely on the power and mercy of God as revealed in the One from Bethlehem. Israel and the world must recognize that their dependence is on Him. For the nations which reject Jehovah's message (v. 15) there will be only **wrath** (the prophet implying the acceptance of the message by some; see ASV *which hearkened not*).

In chapters 4 and 5 Micah has clearly developed the teaching of the Abrahamic promise as given to Abraham (Gen 12:1-3; 13:14-18; 15:1-21) and as elaborated in the Patriarchal Covenant (Deut 30:1-20):

(1) Israel because of her sin must undergo punishment: (a) Immediate—i.e., pestilence, drought, etc.; (b) Future—an actual captivity.

(2) Israel is to be saved and have a world-wide service: (a) An actual return is to come, he says (and it did come), though for a remnant only. This remnant is to be the seed of the Kingdom and will become great and world-wide. Such seed is to be produced not by natural birth only (natural Israel was only the vehicle for the realization of the spiritual Kingdom), but by spiritual conversion, as at Pentecost, etc.

To Micah the spiritual kingdom is the universal worship of Jehovah, and the ideal Davidic King is the Messiah.

(b) During the Maccabean period Israel actually existed as a nation, with an Aaronic king as ruler. The spirit of Nationalism was strong, and much emphasis was placed on a coming literal restoration of the Davidic ruler. Contrary to God's missionary purpose (Gen 12:3), the nation at this time was highly isolationist in attitude. Micah foretold that the kingdom to be established is to be universal, eternal, and essentially spiritual.

(3) Chapter 5 foretells the birthplace and characteristics of the coming King. This prophecy was fulfilled in Jesus Christ, who proclaimed a spiritual kingdom, to the disappointment of the Pharisees, Sadducees, and others. The Jews rejected Jesus because they held a materialistic conception of the promised kingdom.

(4) Paul in his letters to the Romans and Galatians taught that there is neither Jew nor Greek . . . in the kingdom; *all are one* and all *in* Christ are Abraham's seed and heirs of the Promise.

IV. The Lawsuit of Jehovah. 6:1–7:20.

Chapters 4 and 5 of the Book of Micah foretell the coming and work of the Messiah. The prophecy extends to the consummation of all things, which Micah saw as being brought about through sin, judgment, and salvation. In these last two chapters the prophet describes the sin of the people, as well as Jehovah's striving with them and His judgment upon them; he also foretells that the people will confess their sin and receive the promised blessings. All this is set forth in the form of a lawsuit. The prophet is represented as the prosecuting attorney for Jehovah, with the mountains and the hills (perhaps symbols of unchangeable justice) as the court and the judges. Jehovah pleads through the prophet; the people reply; the mountains and the hills sit in silent judgment.

A. First Complaint of Jehovah. 6:1-5.

1. Hear ye (with obedience). The prophet calls the court to order; Jehovah demands that his words be heeded. **Contend.** Legal terminology, meaning, "to plead a case in court." Jehovah calls to Micah to arise and plead his case against his people. **2. There is a lawsuit** (controversy) **. . . and he will contend.** Literally, *fully prove.*

3. My people, what have I done. Here is Jehovah's formal plea against his people, which should call to mind his faithfulness and their unfaithfulness. **4,5.** Jehovah does not wait for an answer, but points out his gracious guidance and protection in their past history. He redeemed them from slavery in Egypt, gave them great leaders, and delivered them from Balak and Balaam (Num 22–24). Can they not learn from experience the Lord's **righteousness** (v. 5)? The ways of men may be crooked, but in human history Jehovah exhibits his covenant faithfulness in his "straight" ways.

B. Israel's First Reply. 6:6-8.

With seeming sincerity, Israel replies by way of three specific questions, of increasing intensity. **Can I please Jehovah—**

(1) In ordinary sacrifices of calves? (v. 6)

(2) In sacrifices extraordinary in amount, as "thousands of rams, or with ten thousands of rivers of oil?" (v. 7)

(3) In sacrifice so extraordinary in nature as to be violation of the law of Moses, i.e., of the first-born? (v. 7b; cf. Deut 12:29-31; II Kgs 3:27; Jud 11:30-40)

If salvation could thus be bought, by offering material goods as propitiation for sin, all mankind would be striving for salvation. But true salvation is a surrender of spirit. Israel had forgotten Jehovah's law of the redemption of the first-born (Ex 13:12,13) and the experience of Abraham (Gen 22).

8. What Jehovah requires applies to all men of all time, perpetually and unchangeably:

(1) **To do justly.** That is, to live right in relation to one's fellow man in social, political, and industrial affairs.

(2) **To love mercy.** That is, to exhibit that quality of steadfast loving-kindness which is seen in Jehovah and comes from him.

(3) **To walk humbly with thy God.** That is, to have humility and devotion to God through faith. Such sacrifices—of right attitudes and upright character—are acceptable to Jehovah.

C. Second Complaint of Jehovah. 6:9-16.

9. Jehovah calls out rebuke and warning to the city of Jerusalem. **Wisdom sees** (or fears) **thy name** (i.e., Jehovah) and hence takes warning, for the rod of judgment—Assyria—appointed by Jehovah is soon to fall. **10-13. Are there yet the treasures of wickedness?** The answer is found in charges of dishonesty in business, scanty measures, false balances (v. 11), oppression of the poor by the rich, lying and deceitfulness (v. 12; cf. Jas 4:1-12). This is the old story of corrupt social, financial, and moral conditions—in spite of the warnings of Jehovah. Therefore—desolation.

14-16. Jehovah is not arbitrary in his judgments. They are the natural results of sin, namely: (1) hunger (lit., **thy casting down . . .** etc., meaning "a sinking feeling in the stomach due to lack of food", v. 14); (2) toil, without the power to accumulate possessions, which, if accumulated, would be delivered to the sword; and (3) desolation. Would that the people of Israel had walked as carefully in Jehovah's requirements as they had followed the wickedness of **Omri** and **Ahab!** (v. 16; I Kgs 16–22) In their persistent wickedness, they were moving into the purposes of Jehovah's judgments. He overrules even sin to accomplish his own ends for his glory.

D. Israel's Second Reply—a Confession of Sin. 7:1-10.

This concluding chapter completes

Jehovah's lawsuit with Israel begun in chapter 6. The section is broken in thought, which suggests with what deep emotion Micah voices the reply of the people—their confession and lamentation.

1-4. Jehovah's blessings under the figure of the fruit harvest have passed Israel by, declares Micah, and the nation is now destitute of moral men and standards. Note the parallelism of **godly** *(good man,* AV) with **clusters of grapes** and **upright** with **first ripe figs** (vv. 1,2). Such moral men do not exit, just disappear. All men are bloodthirsty, even against their brothers. The prince continually asks for injustice; the judge is ever ready for a bribe (Heb. "to pay," as in a trade); and the great man speaks his evil desire. **Thus they weave** (Heb. *twist* or *knit;* AV *wrap)* it together (v. 3) into terrible reality. The **watchmen** (v. 4), i.e., the true prophets (cf. Isa 62:6; Ezk 3:16 ff.). The day of Israel's watchmen was the day of Jehovah's **visitation.**

5,6. Society was crumbling at its roots; yea, the enemies of a man were those of his own household. Suspicion, distrust, and enmity prevailed. Considering the modern world, human nature has changed little (cf. Mt 10:34ff.).

7. The stricken nation is represented as turning to the only source of hope—**But, I, unto Jehovah I will intently look and cause** (my soul) **to wait with determination.** For **my God will hear,** "heed and deliver." **8. I shall arise.** The enemy, even Assyria, is warned not to rejoice, for Jehovah will shine in the darkness for those who wait for him. **9,10. Anger** (lit., *boiling indignation).* The nation is willing to bear the wrath of Jehovah because she knows she has sinned. Here is real repentance, and also faith that Jehovah himself will settle the case (of sin) and the sinner will be brought forth to the light, to behold and walk in His righteousness. Israel's enemy will see and hide in shame; worse still, she will suffer punishment. Such is the end of those who scoff at Jehovah.

E. Israel's Promised Blessing To Follow Judgment. 7:11-13.

11,12. A day to build thy walls. Here is prosperity, building and extending the boundaries of Israel. Does this foresee the expansion of the Gospel? Israel (perhaps spiritual Israel) is to be the center or rallying point, and people will come to her from far places because of the blessings of Jehovah upon her, which they desire. Or, may these travelers be Israel's own scattered children?

13. But judgment as **the fruit of their deeds** will come before blessing.

F. Final Plea for Israel—Gathered from Many Nations. 7:14-17.

In this passage Micah prays that Jehovah, the Shepherd, as in the glorious days of old, will feed and guide his people, now dwelling secure in the forest. The answer is a promise of miraculous help, as in the exodus from Egypt. Terror will characterize the heathen nations in the presence of these manifestations of God's power, and they will submit themselves to him in humblest fear and reverence. What a contrast to their boasting and arrogance when they taunted the people of Jehovah (cf. Hos 11:10ff.).

G. Doxology: The Triumph of Grace. 7:18-20.

The prophet begins this doxology with a play on his own name, **Who is like God?** (see Introd., *Title),* and in grateful praise he bursts forth in this matchless description of Jehovah.

1) The God of forgiving love (v. 18): He **pardons** (Heb. *to lift* or *bear sin of another,* with the idea of forgiveness) **iniquity** (Heb. *crookedness)* **and . . . passes over** *(overlooks;* cf. Prov 19:11) **transgression** (Heb. *rebellion).* Loving-kindness is the active quality of his yearning love.

2) The God of redeeming power (v. 19): He will have tender **compassion,** even as a mother for her babe, and will cause to cast into **depths of the sea** *our* (versus **their,** AV) sins (so in LXX, Pesh., Vulg.).

3) The God of perpetual faithfulness (v. 20): He will fulfill the covenant he swore to Jacob and Abraham (cf. Gal 3:29).

Who else is or can be such a God? How graciously he meets and satisfies all human needs! Thus the last words we hear from the prophet's lips are those of this wonderful doxology. Such a doxology was possible only because of his faith in God. God had sworn, and he would fulfill his oath (cf. Heb 6:18-20).

BIBLIOGRAPHY

BARNES, ALBERT. *Notes on the Old Testament*. Grand Rapids: Baker Book House, reprinted 1950.

CALVIN, JOHN. *Commentaries on the Twelve Minor Prophets*. Grand Rapids: Wm. B. Eerdmans Publishing Co., reprinted 1948.

CHEYNE, T. K. *Micah, with Notes and Introduction (Cambridge Bible)*. Cambridge: The University Press, 1885.

COPASS, BENJAMIN A., and CARLSON, E. LESLIE. *A Study of the Prophet Micah*. Grand Rapids: Baker Book House, 1950.

DEERE, DERWARD WILLIAM. *The Twelve Speak*. Vol. 1. New York: The American Press, 1958.

KEIL, C. F., and DELITZSCH, F. *The Twelve Minor Prophets (Biblical Commentary on the Old Testament)*. Edinburgh: T. and T. Clark, n.d.

LANGE, JOHN PETER. *Minor Prophets (Commentary on the Holy Scriptures)*. Grand Rapids: Zondervan Publishing House, reprinted n.d.

MASTERMAN, J. H. B., and BOX, G. H. *Minor Prophets (Study Bible Series)*. New York: Richard R. Smith, 1930.

MORGAN, G. CAMPBELL. *Voice of Twelve Hebrew Prophets*. New York: Fleming H. Revell Co., reprinted 1960.

PUSEY, E. B. *Minor Prophets*. 2 vols. New York: Funk and Wagnalls Co., 1885.

ROBINSON, GEORGE L. *Twelve Minor Prophets*. New York: George H. Doran Co., 1926.

NAHUM

INTRODUCTION

Title. As with every prophetic book in the Old Testament, this one bears the name of its author. **Nahum** (nāḥûm) means "consolation" or "consoler." The nature of the contents of the prophecy is indicated in the title "burden." When used technically among the prophets, it signifies that which is a weight upon the heart of God and also upon the heart of the prophet; that is, a threatening or judgmental message. The sole theme of the book is Nineveh, the ancient capital of the Assyrian Empire.

Date and Authorship. The Book of Nahum is susceptible of dating within the limits of about half a century. From archaeological research it is known that Nineveh fell in 612 B.C. The prediction of Nahum was penned probably shortly before the destruction of the city. Furthermore, in 3:8 the prophet mentions the captivity of No (No-Amon or Thebes, the capital of Upper Egypt) as a historical event. Ashurbanipal of Assyria (668–626 B.C.) brought about the downfall of the Egyptian city in the year 663 B.C. Hence, the book may be dated between 663 B.C. and 612 B.C., probably closer to the latter date. Although nothing is known of Nahum's life, apart from the statement that he was an Elkoshite, no valid evidence has been presented to establish some other person as author of the prophecy. Even the birthplace of the prophet is not known with certainty. Three principal suggestions as to its identity have been advanced. (1) It was a town north of Nineveh. This view is founded on a tradition coming from the sixteenth century. (2) Jerome, translator of the Vulgate version, identified it with a small village in Galilee. It cannot be maintained with certainty that Capernaum (lit., *the village of Nahum)* was named after the prophet. (3) A third view locates Elkosh in the territory south of Judah. It may well be that Nahum was born in Galilee, and later ministered in the south.

Historical Background. Along with the prophets Jeremiah, Habakkuk, and Zephaniah, Nahum was a witness to the Southern Kingdom. The Northern Kingdom had been carried into captivity by Assyria almost a century before (722/721 B.C.). Now it was in the purpose of God to visit that nation which had been the rod of God's anger upon Israel. Nineveh had genuinely repented in the days of Jonah the prophet, but she was now ready for judgment because of her cruelty and cupidity. She was ruthless in warfare and greedy for dishonest wealth. The power that had ruled western Asia for some three centuries was now to be broken by the combined might of the Babylonians and the Medes.

OUTLINE

Chapter I.

I. Title. 1:1.
II. The majestic God of Israel. 1:2-8.
III. God's judgment on Assyria. 1:9-14.
IV. Judah's deliverance. 1:15.

Chapter II.

I. A taunt song upon Nineveh. 2:1,2.
II. The siege of Nineveh. 2:3-7.
III. The doom of Nineveh. 2:8-10.
IV. The reason for Nineveh's fall. 2:11-13.

Chapter III.

I. The portrayal of the overthrow. 3:1-3.
II. The moral failure of Nineveh. 3:4-7.
III. The unheeded warning from No-Amon. 3:8-10.
IV. The hopelessness of Nineveh's condition. 3:11-19.

COMMENTARY

Chapter I.

I. Title. 1:1.

1. The burden of Nineveh. The designation indicates that the prophecy is a weighty message or judicial sentence upon Nineveh (cf. Isa 13:1; Zech 9:1; 12:1). **The vision.** The Hebrew word (cf. Isa 1:1) is a technical term for an authoritative revelation from God.

II. The Majestic God of Israel. 1:2-8.

2. God is jealous. The prophet, recalling God's past zeal on behalf of His people when threatened by the Assyrians, is assured that He will now be no less concerned for their protection and vindication. When the Scriptures speak of God as 'jealous,' they do not use the word in the sense in which it is used of men. Here it means, rather, that God is zealous to maintain his holiness and righteous government in the world (cf. Ex 20:5; Num 25:11,13). God loves his people, and he must rectify the wrongs perpetrated upon them in the deportation of the kingdom of Israel and the invasion of the kingdom of Judah, both by the Assyrian kingdom. **The Lord revengeth.** Three times in this verse the prophet declares that God will take vengeance on his enemies. Solemnity and assurance are given to the pronouncement that at long last the righteous God has determined to move out in judgment against his adversaries.

3. Slow to anger. The fact that the vengeance of God is proclaimed with forthrightness, and repeatedly, is no reason to infer that God's decision has been a hasty one; rather, he is long-suffering. It is folly to imagine that the patience of the Lord stems from a lack of power (see Ex 34:6,7). The Lord cannot be prevailed upon to deal with the guilty as though they were innocent. This would be a denial of his nature. **In the whirlwind and in the storm.** The omnipotence of God is clearly seen in the phenomena of the natural world, those elemental powers which man, even in this day, is powerless to tame or harness (cf. Ex 19:16-18). **The clouds are the dust of his feet.** God uses the clouds of the heavens as man does the dust of the earth. In the cuneiform literature from Ras Shamra (Ugarit) in Syria, the heathen poets speak of their gods as riding upon the clouds. But only the true God is capable of such feats of power and majesty (cf. Ps 104.3).

4. Rebuketh the sea. At God's command, rivers and seas are dried up, as were the Red Sea and the Jordan (Isa 50:2). Our Lord Jesus manifested this power at the Sea of Galilee (Mt 8:26). **Bashan languisheth.** In the land of promise Bashan was famous for its rich pastures, Carmel for its vineyards, and Lebanon for its stately forests. But all could wither through drought at the will of the Lord (cf. Isa 33:9; Hos 14:7). **5. The mountains quake.** Earthquakes, which level mountains and hills alike, are at the command of God; fire also serves his irresistible purpose. Moreover, any scorched earth policy applied involves those who inhabit the region. **6. Who can stand.** If the omnipotent God can so manipulate the forces and phenomena of nature, how can puny man expect to withstand the indignation of the Lord? These rhetorical questions of the prophet suggest their own powerful reply. **Rocks are thrown down.** Volcanic activity responds to the mighty hand of God.

7. The Lord is good. Lest the contemporaries of the prophet be given the wrong impression of God, as though he were forbidding and austere, Nahum now emphasizes three comforting truths concerning him. First, he is innately and inherently good. He can never be associated with the opposite attribute. Second, he is the incomparable refuge for his own in the time of their distress, "a bulwark never failing," as Luther put it in his Reformation hymn. Third, he knows, in the sense of loving, covenant care, all who have reposed faith in him (cf. Ps 1:6; 144:3). **8. Darkness shall pursue his enemies.** God's solicitous care is never to be interpreted as soft sentimentality. The Lord never compromises his truth or his holiness; therefore, his foes will be dealt with in summary fashion. The blow will be a crushing one. This verse anticipates what Nahum discloses concerning Nineveh in the following chapters of the book. Scripture employs the figure of a river overflowing its banks to represent an invading army that overruns a land and spreads desolation in its path (cf. Isa 8:8; 10:5-19). As a matter of historical interest, Ctesias (a Greek historian of the fifth century B.C.) recounts that while a drunken feast was going on in Nineveh, a sudden inundation of the Tigris River swept away the city gates and washed away the foundations of the palace, thus permitting the Babylonian army to enter and burn the city.

III. God's Judgment on Assyria. 1:9-14.

9. What do ye imagine against the Lord? In this portion of the chapter the prophet predicts the overthrow of the Assyrian forces. Nahum's question in his abrupt address implies his astonishment at the audacity of the foreign enemy in their senseless and futile attempt to gain advantage in any matter over the Lord. In brief, the prophet asks, "How can you hope to contend with such a God as Israel has?" (cf. Isa 37:23-29). **An utter end.** The punishment God would mete out to the Assyrian would be such that He would never need to repeat it. It would be an irreparable blow. **10. As thorns.** An agricultural people, like Israel, would easily comprehend the vivid figure of intertwined thorns and fully dry stubble. The former, though outwardly presenting an invincible front, are as powerless to withstand fire as the dry stubble. **Drunken as drunkards.** What made the Assyrian army easier to overcome, was the fact that they were in the midst of their revelings during the siege of the capital. According to the historian Diodorus Siculus *(The Historical Library* 2:26), the king and his courtiers were surprised in the midst of their carousings; and the empire fell.

11. One come out of thee. Although some students of the passage prefer not to identify this person specifically, it is generally held that the one who had devised evil against the Lord was Sennacherib of Assyria (705–681 B.C.), the son of Sargon II (the captor of Samaria). He counseled wickedness (lit., *belial,* "a thing of worthlessness"); it did not succeed under the restraining hand of God (cf. II Kgs 19:22,23). **12. Though they be quiet.** Better, *Though they be complete* (that is, in complete or full strength). In spite of the fact that the Assyrian host was a formidable one (II Chr 32:7), it would be powerless against the people of Israel. Assyria, who had already decimated many peoples, would herself be cut down (lit., *shorn)* in her defiance of the Lord. **He shall pass through.** Rather, he shall pass away. As a matter of fact, the Assyrian king, with 185,000 of his men slain in one night, lifted the siege of Jerusalem and retired to Nineveh (II Kgs 19:35,36; Isa 37:36,37). **I have afflicted thee.** This section of the passage relates to God's dealing with Israel. Though he had permitted the Assyrian force to chasten Israel, he would do so no more (see v. 9, "the second time").

13. Now will I break his yoke. Assyria had succeeded in reducing Judah to a vassal kingdom, required to pay tribute (II Kgs 18:14), but the Lord had determined to liberate his people. The yoke and bonds of the oppressing power were to be broken permanently (see also Isa 14:25). **14. No more of thy name be sown.** The prophet now addresses the king of Assyria, and predicts the tragic end of a God-defying life. The dynasty of Sennacherib was to become extinct, a prophecy fulfilled in the suicide of Sennacherib's great-grandson, Saracus, in the last days of the Assyrian Empire. **The graven image.** Along with the fall of the dynasty would come the end of their temple worship and idolatry. It is known that the Medes, who, with the Babylonians, destroyed the Assyrian Empire, were enemies of idolatry, who gladly demolished the idols of their captives. **I will make thy grave.** The place of Sennacherib's death is set forth in the Scriptures (II Kgs 19:37; Isa 37:38). While the king was worshiping his gods in the temple, his sons assassinated him. **Thou art vile.** When weighed in the balances of divine righteousness, the Assyrian monarch was found vile (lit., *light;* cf. Dan 5:27).

IV. Judah's Deliverance. 1:15.

15. That bringeth good tidings. This verse begins chapter 2 in the Hebrew text; as far as thought connection is concerned, it can equally well be joined to chapter 1. The scene is one in which messengers herald a long-awaited deliverance. The wording parallels that of Isa 52:7. There the prophet was announcing freedom from Babylon; here it is freedom from Assyria. The fall of Nineveh (in 612 B.C.) would be welcome news to the Judeans. Just as God intervened on behalf of Judah and Jerusalem in 701 B.C. and decimated the army of Sennacherib during the reign of godly Hezekiah, so God would soon destroy the Assyrian Empire completely. **Keep thy solemn feasts.** Manifestly, it was impossible to carry on the religious ceremonies of the Mosaic law during the protracted siege of the Assyrian, and it was difficult during subsequent decades. With the lifting of that crisis and oppression, the city of Jerusalem was to return to its normal religious life. **Thy vows.** In the hours of trial many of the godly must have made vows to the Lord. When the trial had passed, these promises were to be executed. **The wicked.** The reference is clearly to the ungodly Sennacherib and his successors on the throne of Assyria (cf. v. 11). They would harass God's people no more. Romans 10:15 applies this passage to the blessed deliverance procured by the Lord Jesus Christ.

Chapter II.

I. A Taunt Song upon Nineveh. 2:1,2.

1. Come up before thy face. In irony and bitter mockery Nahum addresses Nineveh, advising her to put forth every possible effort and to strengthen every fortification in order to withstand the approaching army of the Mede, Cyaxares, and the Babylonian, Nabopolassar. To be sure, all would be unavailing, for the Lord himself had decreed the downfall of Assyria. The sarcasm and mockery serve to bring out the hopelessness of the enemy of Judah in more forceful manner.

2. The excellency of Jacob. By the excellency of Jacob and Israel are meant the land and Temple of God. These, though favored by the Lord, were brought under the divine chastening rod because of Israel's sin. **Marred their vine branches.** In OT passages the heritage of the Lord is likened to a vineyard (cf. Isa 5 with Ps 80:8-16). It had suffered from the ruthless Assyrian, who plundered seemingly at will.

II. The Siege of Nineveh. 2:3-7.

3. Red. In this portrayal of the capture of Nineveh, the mighty men are the forces of the Medes and Babylonians. They were particularly fond of red (see Ezk 23:14). They made their shields red by painting them or by overlaying them with copper. Calvin suggested that they did this to frighten the enemy by the bright color, and to hide the blood of their wounds, so that the enemy might not be given confidence thereby. **Scarlet.** Xenophon claimed that this was a favorite color of the Medes, which they used for their military tunics. **The chariots shall be with flaming torches.** Better, *the chariots flash with steel* (ASV). Some war chariots flashed with steel because scythes were fixed at right angles to their axles to form what were called scythe-chariots. One can easily imagine how terrifying were these weapons, which could cut down all who resisted the progress of the army. **The fir trees shall be terribly shaken.** To inject fir trees at this point yields no good sense to the passage. It is probably better to understand that the prophet is describing the brandishing of the cypress spears (so also ASV, *contra* RSV) by the spearmen in readiness for the conflict.

4. The chariots shall rage in the streets. The Ninevites would not take the invasion of their capital city without bestirring themselves in her defense. The war chariots, summoned to the battle, would rush to and fro in the beleaguered city. The speeding chariots darting hither and thither in the panic would seem like flaming torches as the sun struck them. Their speed, as Nahum saw them in his vision, could best be likened to the flashings of lightning. This is one of the finest descriptions of a siege in literature, if not the finest. It serves no good purpose to see here a reference to the modern automobile, as some do. Such handling of Scripture is not worthy of the serious student of Scripture.

5. His worthies. The Assyrian military leaders, with the king at the head, would call the bravest of the soldiers to the colors. They would respond, strangely enough, at a stumbling pace; they would be caught completely off guard. In their perplexity they would be scant help in the crisis. **The wall.** In ancient times it was of utmost importance to protect the wall of the city; hence the ablest defenders took their places there. **The defence shall be prepared.** For **defence,** read *mantelet* (so ASV). It was some form of movable protection, under cover of which the defenders could make ready their counterthrust.

6. The gates of the rivers shall be opened. This has been taken to mean that the Assyrians, in possession of the water gates which controlled the river Chaser that flowed through the capital, opened them, so that the buildings were inundated and the palace was finally undermined by the flood. It is more probable that, after holding out in their fortified city for two years, the Assyrians witnessed heavy rains that broke down the walls of the city. When the canals of the Tigris River were opened, the palace was destroyed.

7. Huzzab. Interpreters are still divided as to whether this word is to be taken as a proper noun, or is the verb meaning "it is decreed" (so ASV and RSV marg.). No queen of Nineveh is known by this name, nor an Assyrian goddess. The passage is clear if the verb force is allowed. **Led away captive.** As God had determined, the city was to go into captivity, while the handmaids, the people of the metropolis, would lament the fall of their beloved city.

III. The Doom of Nineveh. 2:8-10.

8. Of old. Cf. Gen 10:11. **Like a pool of water.** Some interpreters have taken this statement to mean that the population of Nineveh was a heterogeneous one, like a pool fed from many tributaries, with one objective in mind, to gain wealth. The literal sense is better. The city was like a pool of water in that the dams about the city formed a water barricade. But instead of providing security, they were no help to the people fleeing in panic. **Stand, stand.** The command of the military leaders to hold their positions against the invaders, would avail nothing in the hour of confusion.

9. Take ye the spoil. The Lord is represented as addressing the victors, calling on them to spoil the city of silver, gold, furniture, and all wealth. The flooding of the city was to be temporary, because of Nineveh's elevated situation above the Tigris. Ancient writers confirm that there were great treasuries accumulated in Nineveh, the results of repeated campaigns by the Assyrian empire builders.

10. Empty, and void, and waste. The once influential and wealthy city is pictured as left desolate, plundered, and completely destroyed. The words of the original convey the idea of emptiness. **Heart melteth.** Courage has fled, and none has the heart to continue the struggle. The survivors view with sadness and terror the ruin of their once magnificent city.

IV. The Reason for Nineveh's Fall. 2:11-13.

11. Where is the dwelling of the lions. The prophet, looking ahead, tauntingly asks the proud city where its pride has gone, and where its boasted courage has fled. The figure of the lion indicates the greed of the rulers and people. The comparison is quite appropriate, because lions in different forms, with wings and at times with the head of a man, are frequently seen on the Assyrian sculptures. So literally were the predictions of Nahum fulfilled that for centuries armies marched over the site of Nineveh without realizing what lay beneath their feet. **12. The lion did tear in pieces.** The unprecedented cruelty of the Assyrians was the reason for their fall under the stroke of God. Assyrian relics reveal how rapacious were their monarchs. They could boast that they made the blood of their enemies to flow on the high places of the mountains. One even declared that he dyed a mountain red with his enemies' blood.

13. I will burn her chariots. God's answer to this series of atrocities was that he would cut off Assyria's chariots, a primary reliance of her forces. Since Assyria delighted in burning the cities of other nations (almost every description of a battle included such a declaration), she would be recompensed in kind. **No more be heard.** For years the Assyrian kings had demanded tribute of conquered peoples; now the voice of such messengers would be silenced for ever. The people and their position alike would be destroyed.

Chapter III.

I. The Portrayal of the Overthrow. 3:1-3.

1. The bloody city. Nineveh was founded and maintained on murder, bloodshed, and constant warfare. **Full of lies and robbery.** Within the realm, as well as without, promises were broken and truce-breaking was all too common. Extortion and violence were the order of the day. **The prey departeth not.** She never ceased to live by plundering and rapine. The later history of Assyria is one of almost uninterrupted warfare.

2. The noise of a whip. As in chapter 2, Nahum describes in vivid terms the siege of the city. The reader can all but hear the noise of the whips urging on the horses, the rattling of the wheels of the war chariots, the leaping of the horses, the jostling of the chariots. He can almost see flashing swords, and the glittering spears; and then death—everywhere.

3. They stumble upon their corpses. In this siege there is no time for decent burial, so important in the ancient world; the living stumble over the heaps of the slain. No passage of Hebrew literature surpasses this for vividness of description.

II. The Moral Failure of Nineveh. 3:4-7.

4. The mistress of witchcrafts. Nineveh is compared to a well-favored harlot. Such a figure when used of Israel refers to the Jews' idolatry, because they were in covenant relation with God. In the case of Assyria, the harlotry consisted of trafficking in witchcrafts, the occult. Through her cunning ways she made other peoples subject to her. **5. I will discover thy skirts.** Nineveh had brought disgrace upon herself; now God would manifest it (cf. Isa 47:3; Ezk 16:37-41). **6. Abominable filth.** Refuse, the token of greatest contempt. She would be the gazingstock of all nations. **7. They that look upon thee shall flee from thee.** Those who would behold the desolation of the city would flee in terror, not desiring to partake of her miseries. She would be friendless, the object of both scorn and disgust.

III. The Unheeded Warning from No-Amon. 3:8-10.

8. Art thou better than populous No. Nineveh foolishly had not taken the fate of No to heart. God, who is no respecter of persons, had to treat sin in Nineveh as he had done in No. No-Amon or Thebes, the capital of Upper Egypt, flourished during the reigns of the Pharaohs of the Eighteenth, Nineteenth, and Twentieth Dynasties. Even the Greeks and Romans admired its architecture. The Greeks referred to it as Diospolis, "City of God", because the Egyptian counterpart of Jupiter was worshiped there. **Situate among the rivers.** It was located on both sides of the Nile River. The great Greek poet Homer spoke of it as having one hundred gates. There Amon (or Amun), the chief god of the Egyptians, was worshiped as a figure with a human body and a ram's head.
9. Ethiopia and Egypt were her strength. No-Amon was much better off than Nineveh, for while the latter had alienated her neighboring nations, the former had formed powerful alliances. The Egyptian capital could depend on a supply of strong Ethiopians on her southern border, as well as on the help of the whole land of Egypt. The aid was so large that the prophet terms it infinite. **Put and Lubim.** In both the Vulgate and the Septuagint versions **Put** is rendered *Libya*. However, Put is distinguished from Libya in this passage. Present consensus equates Put with Punt, the present Somaliland in Africa. The Lubim spoken of here are the Libyans (with their capital at Cyrene) of North Africa.
10. Yet was she carried away. In spite of having every geographical and political advantage, No-Amon suffered dismal defeat at the hands of Ashurbanipal of Assyria (cf. Isa 20:3,4). Such atrocities as are mentioned as perpetrated upon the Egyptian city were common in the conquests of that day (see II Kgs 8:12). The fall of No-Amon was recent enough in the time of Nahum to afford an excellent parallel to the judgment soon to be meted out to Nineveh.

IV. The Hopelessness of Nineveh's Condition. 3:11-19.

11. Thou also shalt be drunken. The Lord writes his lessons large on the pages of human history. Nineveh had failed to discern God's warning in the doom of No-Amon. It was not that she would be overtaken in the midst of a drunk orgy, but she would drink to the full the cup of God's wrath. (For the figure, see Isa 51:17,21-23; Jer 25:15-28; Ezk 23:33, 34). **Thou shalt be hid.** The prophecy was fulfilled to the letter. Nineveh disappeared from the scene of history – until 1842, when the French Botta and the English Layard and Rawlinson uncovered the site of the once famous metropolis.
12. All thy strongholds shall be like fig trees. In the time of desperate need Nineveh found that none of her fortifications helped her withstand the onslaughts of the enemy. The ripe fig is easily gathered, and offers no resistance; so Nineveh would be in the hands of her foes. **13. Women.** In their panic the fighting men would afford no more help than terror-stricken women. **The gates of thy land shall be set wide open.** Once the entrances to the city were left open without proper defense, the enemy would find it an easy task to enter and burn the besieged capital.
14. Draw thee waters. Again Nahum turns from the description of the coming downfall to heap scoffing and scorn upon the wicked city. To hold out in a long siege, water was a prime necessity. The prophet advises her to lay in a goodly supply. **Go into clay.** The enemy would doubtless bring battering weapons to the

walls of the city in order to make breaches in it. Thus bricks would be needed at once to repair the holes in the walls. **15. There shall the fire devour thee.** Useless would be all such measures of desperation, for both the fire and sword would bring Nineveh low. Ancient history and modern archaeological findings both attest to the fact that Nahum's prediction came true and the city was destroyed by fire. **Like the cankerworm.** The locust is well known for its destructive power. Nineveh would appear as though it had been overrun by a locust plague. Then by a quick turn the prophet compares the people of Nineveh to a locust horde. Even if they were as numerous as a horde of locusts, they could not escape what the prophet was foretelling.

16. Thou hast multiplied thy merchants. No one could doubt the pre-eminence of the city commercially. She was one of the great trade centers of the ancient world. Her commerce with other nations, especially Phoenicia, was lucrative. **Fleeth away.** What had been heaped up for many years by patient and unremitting toil, would be carried off by the foe.

17. Thy crowned are as the locusts. Of how much help would the great military leaders be in the day of calamity? They are likened to swarms of locusts with wings stiffened by the cold, which, after being warmed by the sun's rays, regain strength and vitality and fly away. Locusts in the Middle East are so destructive that the Hebrew language has almost a dozen names for them. Locusts can fly away without leaving a trace, and this feature is utilized here. **18. Thy shepherds slumber.** The slumber of death was to be the portion of the king's officials and governors. **Upon the mountains.** The people of Assyria would be scattered to the mountains north of their land, with no one to reassemble them.

19. No healing of thy bruise. There would be no redress for the loss and destruction suffered by Assyria. No mention is made of a remnant or survivors. **Clap the hands over thee.** Those who would hear the news of the calamity would rejoice over the fate of the unfeeling empire. They would applaud the retribution that had finally overtaken their oppressor. **Thy wickedness.** The question is addressed to the king as the representative of the kingdom. The rule of the tyrant came to an inglorious end in 612 B.C., according to the Babylonian Chronicle. The prophecy of Nahum thus concludes with a strong statement of moral cause and effect: wickedness and woe, cruelty and calamity, crime and catastrophe.

BIBLIOGRAPHY

ELLICOTT, CHARLES J. (ed.). *Commentary on the Whole Bible*. Vol. V. Grand Rapids: Zondervan Publishing House, 1954.

FAUSSET, A. R. "Nahum," *A Commentary Critical, Experimental, and Practical on the Old and New Testaments*. Edited by Robert Jamieson, A. R. Fausset, and David Brown. Vol. IV. Grand Rapids: Wm. B. Eerdmans Publishing Co., reprinted, 1948.

FEINBERG, CHARLES L. *Jonah, Micah, and Nahum*. New York: American Board of Missions to the Jews, Inc., 1951.

FRASER, A. "Nahum," *New Bible Commentary*. Edited by F. Davidson, A. M. Stibbs, and E. F. Kevan. Grand Rapids: Wm. B. Eerdmans Publishing Co., 1953.

MAIER, WALTER A. *The Book of Nahum, A Commentary*. St. Louis: Concordia Publishing House, 1959.

ROBINSON, GEORGE L. *The Twelve Minor Prophets*. New York: Doran, 1926.

HABAKKUK

INTRODUCTION

The Author. Of Habakkuk, himself, nothing is known except what may be inferred from this book which bears his name. He is described as "the prophet," and it is possible, therefore, that he not only had the gift of prophecy but that he was one of a professional group of prophets. Certain musical notations to the psalm in chapter 3 suggest that he may have prophesied in the Temple, like the men who are mentioned in I Chr 25:1.

It is precarious to say much about the prophet's character on the basis of his writing. His name seems to derive from a Hebrew root meaning "to embrace." Jerome (fifth century A.D.) stated that the prophet was called "The Embracer," either because of his love for God or because he wrestled with God. A rabbinical tradition connects the name with II Kgs 4:16 and says that Habakkuk was the son of the Shunammite woman. This is purely fanciful, of course, and unless it be granted that the prophet's name, like that of Jesus, was given in anticipation of his ministry (Mt 1:21), any conjectures as to its meaning, though interesting, are futile. Habakkuk is mentioned in the Apocryphal legend of Bel and the Dragon as rescuing Daniel from the lion's den a second time. No credence need be given to this or to certain other traditions which state that Habakkuk fled to Arabia when Jerusalem fell and returned to Palestine after the Babylonian exile. The stories do, however, point to the approximate time in which the prophet ministered.

Date. The exact time of the writing of the prophecy has been as much a subject of conjecture as has the person of the prophet. Competent scholarship has suggested dates ranging from 650 B.C. (C. F. Keil, *Commentary on the Minor Prophets*, p. 410) to 330 B.C. (E. Sellin, *Introduction to the Old Testament*, p. 183). For various reasons the first date seems to be somewhat too early, since it occurs in the time of Assyrian domination of Judah; while the latter date is closely associated with the opinion that the invading hosts described in the first chapter of the prophecy are not the Chaldeans but the Greek forces under Alexander the Great. The most satisfactory conclusion seems to be that the prophecy was written at a time when the Chaldeans or Babylonians were beginning to become restive against the Assyrian power and had, perhaps, even begun to show their strength. To place the writing of the book much later than this would be to assume that the prophecy is not really a prediction of the invasion of Judah by the Chaldeans but a reference to what had already taken place and is merely an explanation of the presence of the Babylonians in the westlands as the instruments of the Lord. The best conclusion seems to be that the prophecy was written toward the end of the reign of Josiah (640–609 B.C.), preferably after the destruction of Nineveh by the combined forces of the Babylonians, Medians, and Scythians in 612 B.C. This time seems plausible for two reasons. One is that the prophet seems surprised to learn that the *Chaldeans* are God's choice to punish disobedient Judah; after all, was not good King Josiah pro-Babylonian in his political sympathies in that he sought to hinder Pharaoh-necho's march to fight against the Babylonians in 609 B.C.? The other reason is that the rise of Chaldean power would be sufficiently evident that the prophet's description would have meaning for his hearers. Certainly the book should be dated before 605 B.C., when Nebuchadnezzar made his first invasion of Palestine and took Daniel and others as captives to Babylon.

Problem of Chapter 3. It has sometimes been argued that chapter 3, which is a psalm, was not written by Habakkuk. The musical notations found in the chapter point to its being designed for use in the temple worship. This has led some scholars who prefer to think that the temple worship attained comparative purity and an advanced theology only in the period after the Exile to date the psalm in the post-Exilic period. Further support to the argument seems to be found in the fact that the Habakkuk commentary found among the Qumran Scrolls makes no reference to the third chapter of Habakkuk. This apparent ignorance of Habakkuk 3 may be explained, however, by the fact that the writers of the commentary were attempting to explain the first two chapters not in terms of a Chaldean invasion but in terms of the events of their own day. They did not then find the psalm of Habakkuk germane to their purpose. The use of liturgical annotations in Hebrew poetic literature can scarcely be deciding evidence in favor of post-Exilic origin of any writing. Since some of the oldest of the Psalms bear such annotations, it seems that they were a part of such literature considerably before the Exile.

Uniqueness of the Book. Because the contents of the third chapter provide a triumphant climax to the problems posed in the first two chapters, we have in the whole book a theodicy. The structure of this prophecy is unique in the Old Testament, as is the theological content. In the first two chapters there is a dialogue between the Lord and the prophet, in which the latter not only complains of evil, as do some of the Psalmists, but even challenges the Lord to indicate how He, the Holy One, can tolerate such evil. This dialogue is to be thought of as transpiring in the realm of vision (cf. 1:1 and 2:2). The third chapter is a prayer, in which the prophet begins by asking the Lord to accomplish in history the purpose which he has announced, to make His work live in the midst of the years. Following upon this prayer, Habakkuk is granted a vision of God exerting His power and manifesting His glory in the earth somewhat in the same fashion as He did in the Exodus experiences at Mount Sinai. The result of the vision is mingled fear and confidence on the part of the prophet.

OUTLINE

I. Introduction. 1:1.
II. The prophet's complaint of unchecked violence in Judah. 1:2-4.
III. The Lord's answer: The Chaldean is his instrument of punishment. 1:5-11.
IV. A second problem: The Chaldeans are more wicked than the Judeans. 1:12—2:1.
V. The Lord's second answer: The purpose is certain, and faith will be rewarded. 2:2-4.
VI. Five woes upon iniquity, whether Jewish or Chaldean. 2:5-20.
VII. A vision of Divine judgment. 3:1-16.
VIII. The triumph of faith. 3:17-19.

COMMENTARY

I. Introduction 1:1.

The burden. Many prophetic utterances are described as "burdens," particularly where there is an announcement of an ominous or threatening character. Here the prophet deplores the approaching subjugation and devastation of his own people, so that there is a foreboding aspect as far as they are concerned. At the same time the burden is against the proud Chaldeans, whose might is their god (1:11). **Did see.** The word *ḥāzâ*, "see," a term somewhat technical, indicates that this is a revelation. The Spirit of God impresses the message upon the inner consciousness of the prophets with as much force and vividness as if they had seen something with the physical eye. In I Kgs 22:17 Micaiah says, "I *saw* all Israel scattered . . . "

II. The Prophet's Complaint of Unchecked Violence in Judah. 1:2-4.

2. How long. Apparently the prophet had been distressed for some time about the state of affairs in Judah. Through experience he had found that the people seemed to have no conscience, and undoubtedly he had prayed God to correct such wickedness, for he states that he had cried to the Lord. **Thou wilt not hear.** It should not be assumed that the prophet doubted that the Lord had heard his cry (in the sense that the Lord was aware). He took it for granted that God's hearing would involve God's responding. As yet his prayer had been unavailing (cf. Ps 22:1,2). **Violence.** The reference is to wild or ruthless wickedness. The question is, Who is responsible for it? It is assumed here that it is the violence of the Judeans. There are those who believe that, because the same word is used in 2:8 and 2:17 to describe the Chaldeans, the violence of which the prophet complains was that of the Chaldeans. Since, however, they were to be the means of punishment and were about to be raised up, they cannot be thought of as the perpetrators. Neither was the violence that of the Assyrian overlord who had controlled Judah for some time, since a part of the prophet's complaint is the fact that the **law** is slacked and **judgment** perverted (v. 4). These two words usually have reference in the OT to the Mosaic code, and it seems, therefore, that the violence consisted of the acts of cruelty and injustice which pervaded public and private life in Judah.

3. **Why dost Thou show me iniquity, and at mischief Thou thyself lookest?** The Lord's apparent unconcern with the distressing situation was bewildering to the prophet. God had not only permitted the prophet to see iniquity, but had, Himself, looked upon it and had apparently been indifferent or inactive. What concerned Habakkuk was that since God is holy he could not understand how God can look upon mischief complacently. The prophet's strong expostulation, therefore, is really an expression of faith. His indignation had been aroused by the sight of abounding sin, and his confidence in a holy God told him that God must do something about it. **Strife and contention.** These terms point to animosity between members of the Judean community. The Assyrian overlords did not mingle with the local residents. They merely demanded political subjection and a tax, which was collected from the king. These two words, therefore, support the conclusion that the wickedness of which the prophet was complaining was that of his own people.

4. **The law is slacked.** The law here is the Divine law as expressed in the Mosaic code. The law, as Delitzsch says, is "revealed law in all its substance which was meant to be the soul, the heart, of the political, religious, and domestic life." The two Hebrew verbs translated in the AV **slacked** and **go forth** indicate that the contention in Judah was such that law and order were paralyzed. God's rule was a dead issue. **Judgment.** A judgment is a legal decision based upon precedent or customary law. It, therefore, often means the equivalent of our English common law. The point is that anything which could really be called judgment did not exist and that which went bv the name of judgment was a perversion of it. There was no security in public life for person or property. That such a state of affairs existed during the reign of Jehoakim is indicated in Jer 26:1–27:11. **The wicked doth compass about the righteous.** The righteous man finds himself surrounded by wickedness and godless people. It was a sad condition which presented itself to the prophet's view. God's law was despised everywhere. Even those who ought to have defended the cause of justice and truth were, themselves, given to crookedness. The godly found themselves hopelessly outnumbered and overpowered, so that their testimony was of little use. Surely God could not long endure such things among His people!

III. The Lord's Answer: The Chaldean Is His Instrument of Punishment. 1:5-11.

5. **Behold ye among the nations** (ASV; AV, *heathen*). The prophet has expressed amazement that God should so long permit the faults of Judah to go unpunished. The Lord's answer is that he has an instrument at hand which he is about to use. It will be even more amazing than his forbearance has been. The words are addressed in the plural, since God is speaking not to the prophet alone, but rather through him to all the people. The Apostle Paul, quoting from the LXX on this verse, applies the principle of God's dealings in Habakkuk's day to the situation in the church in his own day (Acts 13:41). No doubt God's work of calling the Gentiles into his church would be just as astonishing as his work of using the Babylonian armies to punish Judah. The language of the verse justifies the conclusion that at the time of the prophecy Babylon was not thought of as the great world power. The prophet's hearers were to look among the nations because it was from among them that there would arise the work of God which would be a just recompense to a sinful people. **Be astonished and wonder** (AV, *wonder marvelously*). There can be little excuse for those who give no heed, for as Calvin remarks, "He tells them twice to see and twice exhorts them to be astonished." **Ye would not believe though it be told.** They would not believe that catastrophe could overtake them by Divine determination. They had a false sense of security, thinking that being the chosen people of

God was purely a matter of external relation. Under the reign of Josiah there had been a return to the prescribed ceremonies of the Temple, but not necessarily a return to the Lord who dwelt in the Temple. Ceremonialism readily becomes a foe of true spirituality. Israel was ever ready to say, "The temple of the Lord, the temple of the Lord, the temple of the Lord, are these" (Jer 7:4).

6. God now begins to describe at length the nation through which he will punish Judah, **the Chaldeans.** While this word usually has reference to the Neo-Babylonian empire, which reached its zenith under Nebuchadnezzar in the sixth century B.C., there are indications that, as a group, the Chaldeans were very ancient. Jeremiah 5:15 describes them as a primeval people or ancient nation. They probably had had a loosely knit tribal organization in earlier times, as many Semitic groups did, and gradually infiltrated into Babylon from the outer fringes of the Mesopotamia Valley. Eventually they gained the ascendancy in the city of Babylon. And Merodach-Baladan, who tried to establish the independence of Babylon from Assyria in the days of Hezekiah, was a Chaldean. The Neo-Babylonian or Chaldean empire was established under the leadership of Nabopolassar, a Chaldean general in the Assyrian forces. The most illustrious monarch of the Chaldeans was Nebuchadnezzar, who is described in Ezr 5:12 as "the Chaldean." **I am raising up.** The Chaldeans were about to be raised up, not merely as a political power, but to perform a special part of the Divine plan. This is the answer to the prophet's question, "How long?" **Bitter and hasty nation.** The two words point to a ferocious and swift campaign. The Chaldeans had not lost these characteristics in Daniel's time, for he saw the Babylonian empire in vision as a lion having the wings of an eagle (Dan 7:4).

7. Their dignity shall proceed of themselves. The coming conqueror would be arrogant and imperious. He would acknowledge no authority higher than himself and, in effect, would deny God. In character and mien the Chaldean empire was to resemble all later world empires.

8. Evening wolves. This expression is found a number of times in the OT (see Gen 49:27; Jer 5:6; Zeph 3:3). Evening wolves are probably those which have hunted all day without success and are the more ravenous as evening draws on. War is to the invader as the seizing of prey is to a wild beast – a savage delight. **They shall fly as the eagle,** or better, perhaps, *as the vulture.* There is some evidence that a careful distinction was not always made between the eagle and the vulture. In Mt 24:28 the words of Jesus are translated, "For wheresoever the carcase is, there will the eagles be gathered together." The eagle is not a scavenger, but the vulture is. Vultures are also known for their ability to see or scent food from great distances. They fly very swiftly to secure it, and in eating it they tear it voraciously.

9. As the east wind. In Palestine the wind from the east blows in from the desert, gathering sand in its path. Such winds were the terror of the inhabitants of Palestine because they blasted the crops and were very destructive.

10. They shall heap dust, and take it. This is, no doubt, a reference to the raising of earthworks by means of which city walls could be overthrown or successfully bridged. Many ancient inscriptions depict such activity.

11. Then shall he change as a wind (AV, *his mind change*). Here the prophet resumes the metaphor of verse 9 and indicates that the advance of the Chaldeans might be stopped locally by such a thing as a stronghold. But, like the wind, he would quickly overcome it, change his direction, and pass on. **But he is guilty, imputing his power unto his god.** A ray of hope shone through the gloom, and, for those who trusted God, there was a real hope. However successful the invader might be, he would be guilty before God, and though he would be God's instrument to punish the guilty in Judah, he, himself, would in due time come under Divine judgment.

IV. A Second Problem: The Chaldeans Are More Wicked than the Judeans. 1:12–2:1.

12. It has been suggested that there was an interval of time between the answer of verses 2-11 and the question of verses 12-17. In this interval, supposedly, the Chaldeans had been in Judah and had proved themselves worse than the people they were sent to punish. They had outraged the laws of humanity. Nothing in the text, however, indicates that any period of time elapsed. The prophet has envisioned the Chaldeans as a swift horde gathering captives as one sweeps up sand. The imagery of verses 12-17 suggests a fisherman using every possible means to gather a rich catch. It may be, then, that the prophet's expostulation arose out of what he believed must surely happen if such a vengeful instrument should be used by God. No doubt Habakkuk was distressed not only over the destruction of Judah, but also because the chastisement which was to come upon the wicked in his own country would fall as equally and inevitably upon the faithful. **From everlasting.** The eternity of God in his dealings with the covenant people from of old is often the ground of confidence for believers (cf. Isa 40:28; Ps 90:2). The accumulation of vocatives, **O Lord my God, mine Holy One** is similar to those expressions of deep trust which are found so often in the Psalms. What is meant by **Holy One** is brought out in verse 13. **We shall not die.** Pusey rightly says that this is the lightning thought of faith. The words of men in moments of crisis often indicate their real and inmost convictions. The use of the pronoun **we** should be understood to point to the remnant, who are called "the righteous" (1:2-13), or those who live by their faithfulness (2:4).

13. Of purer eyes than to behold evil. God cannot regard iniquity with complacency or toleration, let alone favor. It is not only the outrages of the Chaldeans which are described. God is too pure of eyes to behold *any* evil. He could not hold his peace at either the violence of the Chaldeans or that which was found in Judah. It was because the prophet had taken for granted that God is pure by nature that there could be any problem for him at all. One who questions the omnipotence of the Lord, or any other of His attributes, would say that God's justice is irreconcilable with such evil, and therefore, either God is not just, or He is not omnipotent. The prophet, however, asked two questions: Why is it so? How long shall it be so? And it was of God, himself, that he sought an answer. At the same time, the problem remained that the godly portion of the nation would have to suffer when the ungodly were punished.

14. Makest men as the fishes of the sea. Here the Lord is said to do what he permits to be done by others. As a result of God's seeming indifference to destruction, men become like fish caught from the sea by a fisherman who uses every conceivable means – fishhook, net, drag (v. 15) – to increase his catch. One commentator says that this thought is the reverse of that of Jesus, who declared even the sparrows to be under God's care. Only a belief in an absolutely comprehensive Providence can produce a statement such as the prophet makes here, however.

16. They sacrifice unto their net. The reference is probably not to any actual practice, although the Scythians are said to have offered animal sacrifices to a scimitar in honor of their god of war. What is meant is that the Babylonians ascribed divine honors to their weapons and, therefore, to themselves. They worshiped and served the creature more than the Creator.

With 2:1, the prophet's expostulation comes to an end. It was not in skepticism that he had presented his complaint to God, but in faith, for he was now prepared to wait upon the Lord, assured that an answer would come. The assertion sometimes made that Habakkuk is the first example in Scripture of an honest doubter is entirely without warrant. Nothing in the language of the prophecy betrays any element of doubt. Indeed, the prophecy ends on a note of sublime faith. It is one thing to face the problems that confront everyone who believes in a good and omnipotent God and ask why things are so, or how they can be so. It is something quite different to question the Divine goodness or justice, or the very existence of God, simply because one cannot answer these questions.

2:1. Watchtower. Several interpreters understand an actual tower or elevation, citing the examples of Moses (Ex 33:21), or Balaam (Num 22:41), and of Elijah at Sinai (Mt. Horeb, I Kgs 19:8ff.). None of these cases is really comparable to that of Habakkuk, who may be using only a figure of speech. Certainly he must have prepared himself by prayerful meditation to receive the Divine answer. Jeremiah waited ten days for an answer to his inquiry (Jer 42:7). Probably some interval of time elapsed between the expostulation of chapter 1 and the answer received. Habakkuk records only his determination to wait for an answer; he does not tell us when it came.

V. The Lord's Second Answer: The Purpose Is Certain, and Faith Will be Rewarded. 2:2-4.

These three verses contain what is perhaps the most difficult section of the prophecy, both from the standpoint of translation and from that of interpretation.

2. Write the vision. Whether or not the prophet actually wrote the vision on tablets for public reading has been disputed, but it is agreed by all that he was told to record the vision. The purpose of recording is twofold: that he may run who reads; the vision is for an appointed time and must be preserved so that its truth may be proved. **Upon tablets** (ASV). Different kinds of materials were used to make records, since the Jews had contacts with all the Near Eastern cultures. Isaiah and Jeremiah both used scrolls, yet Isaiah was also told to use a tablet (Isa 30:8). It may reasonably be supposed that Habakkuk made a record of his vision on a clay tablet, which he brought to the attention of many persons. **In order that he may run.** The matter was to be made so clear that whoever read it might run and publish it. In Dan 12:4, also, the words "many shall run to and fro" seem to point to a publication of information, since it is added that knowledge shall increase.

3. For the appointed time . . . at the end. The fulfillment of the vision was to take place in God's own good time. Since the same two words are used in Dan 8:19, some have concluded that it is the end time, or latter days, that are meant. Here the words refer to the design of God with respect to the Chaldeans. We may, however, understand that the vision concerns the destruction of ungodly world power, of which Babylon was the existing manifestation, and that only Messiah's day would see a final fulfillment of such a promise. **It hasteth . . . shall not lie** (ASV). God's purposes are hastening to fulfillment, though in human estimation there may seem to be unnecessary delays. John Calvin says: "This is the true sacrifice of praise, when we restrain ourselves and remain firm in the persuasion that God cannot deceive nor lie, though he may seem for a while to trifle with us." **It will surely come.** The Hebrew idiom used here has been translated literally by the Greek version (the LXX), *coming he shall come.* The reference is to the certainty of the event. The writer of the Epistle to the Hebrews, using the LXX, has adapted the text to the promise of the second coming of Christ, an event equally certain in God's plan, though it may seem in the eyes of men to be unduly delayed. Thus we read in Heb 10:37, "he that cometh shall come."

4. A clear understanding of this verse is of great importance to the Christian. Of the OT passages quoted in the NT, this one occurs three times in very vital contexts. It should be noted that where the verse is used in the NT it is represented as an *unchanging principle of the Lord's relation to his people*, not as a prediction of events to take place in the NT dispensation. In Habakkuk, the Divine answer is intended to stimulate the hope and confidence of those who are spiritually the children of God, while it spells the doom of Chaldean world power.

Puffed up (ASV). To say that it is the Chaldean, in distinction from the Jew, who is described is too simple an answer. But since the vision is an answer to the question of 1:12-17, the Chaldean is the one primarily in view.

By his faithfulness (AV, *faith*). One minor problem is: Is it the man who is justified by faith who lives, or is the just man to live by faith? Paul's usage seems to stress the former meaning, though the tenor of his writings allows for the latter. At any rate, the apostle uses the word "to live" with particular force. It does not mean merely to survive, but to live eternally in the grace of God.

A more important question is whether the Hebrew *'ĕmûnâ* should be translated as "faith" or "faithfulness." In most places in the OT where it is used it has the second meaning, for example, in II Kgs 12:15; Jer 5:1. It is, however, worth noticing that the root of this word has already been used in Hab 1:5 in the sense of giving credence to God's word or promise. Moreover, faithfulness, even as an aspect of a man's character, does not occur in the void. Faithfulness must be exercised in relation to someone or something. In this case the individual is to be faithful to God, to God's word and covenant. He must rely firmly upon, or have a deep-rooted trust in God himself. The NT use is in complete agreement with this.

It may be pointed out, also, that it may be best to enrich our idea of the NT meaning of "faith" from the OT. Faith is not mere consent to a proposition about God as revealed in Jesus Christ his Son. It is the opposite of swelling pride, of self-trust. It is humility before God, a readiness to conform to his will. It is a conviction that he cannot lie nor fail (2:3), a reliance in spite of outward circumstances (3:17). A deeply religious man such as Habakkuk can scarcely have failed to think of Abraham and to recall that it was said of him that he believed the Lord and it was reckoned to him for righteousness.

Shall live. Undoubtedly in this prophecy the idea of survival is present. Nevertheless, in view of the spiritual relationships involved, this is not the only idea. The real meaning is well brought out by Abraham's request in Gen 17:18, using the same verb, "O that Ishmael might *live* before thee." To **live** means not only to have security or protection in this life, but to enjoy the loving-kindness of God, which is better than life. It is to be dear to him, the object of his care.

There remain two questions in connection with Paul's use of Hab 2:4 in Rom 1:17 and Gal 3:11. Does not the apostle use the word "faith" in the distinct sense of an antithesis to law-works as a means of acceptance with God? This antithesis is not present in Habakkuk. Moreover, is not the faith of which Paul speaks a faith in the Messiah, of whom no mention is made in Habakkuk?

It must be acknowledged at the outset that Paul had no intention of teaching that justification by faith in Christ was set forth by the prophet. He does teach, however, that a definite principle has been laid down in Scripture with respect to the relationship of man to God and that this principle operates most clearly in the realm of man's legal standing before God. To put the matter in other words, Habakkuk had laid down a principle by which faithfulness, that is, humble, steadfast reliance upon God's word, was declared to be the instrument to bring about the well-being and security of the covenant people. Paul declares that the same instrument is the means of attaining to justification before God. In doing so he does not in any way deflect the idea of faithfulness, or faith, from its true meaning. Indeed, if many modern evangelical preachers would give to the word "faith" the meaning which the Hebrew word bears, there would be less superficiality in the profession and practice of Christianity.

On the other hand, it must also be acknowledged that Paul, in comparison with Habakkuk, enlarges infinitely the scope of the word "live," for he applies it to the life to come, to the sphere of salvation or eternal well-being in distinction from merely temporal well-being. That the apostle is justified in doing so will readily be granted by Christians, since the NT writers employ many forms and figures of the OT with a fullness of meaning far transcending that which they had for the believers of the older dispensation. Finally, the antithesis between the principle of active faith and that of meritorious law-works as a means of salvation is, of course, a part of the apostle's own argument. It is a logical development from the nature of faith itself.

VI. Five Woes upon Iniquity, Whether Jewish or Chaldean. 2:5-20.

5. Wine is a treacherous dealer. The Hebrew word *yayin*, "wine," constitutes a problem because it appears in the text as subject of the verb. The LXX interprets it figuratively as *the conceited man*. Some commentators change the consonants to produce another word, "the oppressor." The Qumran Commentary supports the Hebrew text, however. Probably the meaning is that the conduct of the treacherous dealer is like that which wine produces. We are reminded of the words of Kipling's "Recessional":

"If, drunk with sight of power, we loose
Wild tongues that have not Thee in awe."

Enlargeth his desire as hell *(sh^eôl)*. Sheol, the abode of the departed, is envisioned as a rapacious creature anxious to swallow humanity.

6. All these. The reference is to the nations and peoples mentioned in verse 5. **Parable.** The Hebrew word means a resemblance, from which it takes on the sense of a parable. Since, however, there is no parable in this chapter, the word must be understood as the equivalent of **taunting proverb. Thick clay.** Or *pledges* (ASV; RSV). The word used here occurs nowhere else in Scripture, but the latter translation is the better one. The significance lies in the Hebrew abhorrence of the usurer and in the Levitical laws against taking pledges of greater value than were needed for security. The Chaldean had robbed the poor, hoarding all he could gain in an illegal fashion.

7. That shall bite thee, could more accurately be translated *thy debtors*, thus carrying out the idea of the debtor-creditor relationship. The Chaldean, though acting as the creditor, was really the debtor of all; and his turn would come to be **shaken to and fro,** or vexed (cf. Mt 18:28).

8. The people shall spoil thee. The Babylonians were to be recompensed in the ratio of an eye for an eye and a tooth for a tooth. The law of retaliation which runs through the OT from Gen 9:6 onward is not intended as a rule of revenge but as a principle of justice. Men shall receive the punishment they deserve.

While the Chaldean has been the subject of the first "woe," the woes declared in the remainder of the chapter, verses **9-20,** apply more universally, and certainly include the sins of Judah and Israel. To have confined the Divine condemnation to Israel's foes only would have been to confirm in a sense of carnal security the sinners of whom Habakkuk had originally complained.

9. Getteth an evil gain (ASV). Here the extortionist and the grafter are condemned. Basically, of course, it was not specific acts alone which were wicked, but the aims and tendencies of the soul from which they flowed. **Nest on high.** The eagle and vulture build their nests on high, inaccessible crags. To hope to secure happiness and permanence through dishonest accumulation of power and possessions is to attempt to "set" one's nest "on high." On the other hand, the Lord is the dwelling-place of believers in all generations.

10. Thou hast counselled (AV, *consulted)* **shame.** The Chaldean and others had not actually planned confusion for themselves; rather, God would turn to shame what they had contrived. They had, therefore, sinned against their own souls, though it may have appeared that they had sinned chiefly against others.

12. Buildeth a town with blood. Similar expressions in Mic 3:10 and Jer 51:8 point to the fact that the sins of Judah as well as those of Babylon are involved here. In fact, there may very well be here a reference to the misrule of Jehoiakim (cf. Jer 22:13). Strenuous building activities were usually the efforts of the monarch toward self-glorification. *In blood* [s]. This is a frequent expression meaning blood-guiltiness or strong guilt.

13. Is it not of the Lord. The ultimate cause of the failure of human plans and programs is the sovereign providence of God. It is not restricted in its application to the destruction of Babylon. The terms used are very general and include all who stand opposed to the will of God and his kingdom. The Lord of hosts is not simply the God of battles and, therefore, the one in whom ultimate victory for the Jews is found. He is the Lord of all the hosts of the universe and is able to do his will among the armies of heaven and the inhabitants of earth. **Labour in** *(for)* **the . . . fire.** They will take in hand unprofitable work.

14. The earth shall be filled. Many have considered this verse to be a prediction either of the Gospel era or of the Millennial kingdom of Christ. Unlike Isaiah's prediction, Isa 11:9, which foretells a time when men shall *know God,* being brought into intimate fellowship with him, this verse says that there will be a manifestation of the **glory** of the Lord. The reference is to God's power and majesty as these are displayed in judgment against ungodliness and the foes of his people (cf. Num 14:21-23; Ps 97). As water fills the sea in overflowing abundance, so the glory of God shall be manifested to all men in fullest measure.

15. That giveth his neighbour drink. A comparison with several other OT passages, such as Jer 25:15,16; Isa 51:17; Ps 75:8, shows that this statement is not to be taken literally. The concept is that of inducing a state of humiliation and helpless prostration like that of a drunk person. **Their nakedness.** Sensual lust is used as a metaphor for barbarous lust for power. The use of these figures implies, of course, a strong condemnation of the personal acts which supply the figures.

16. This verse promises that the Chaldean would suffer at the Lord's hand the same kind of shameful exposure which he himself had inflicted on others. **Be as one uncircumcised** (ASV). To be in such a condition was to be an object of scorn to God's people (Jud 14:3; 15:18; I Sam 17:26) and to be unfit to come before God. **The cup of the Lord's hand shall come unto thee.** This is not a conviction that somehow right must prevail, or that injustice will be punished in the natural order of things. It is a philosophy of history in which God judges nations and the downfall of empire is the outworking of his will.

17. Violence of *(done to)* **Lebanon.** Successive monarchs from several nations had cut down the timbers of Lebanon, hunted its wild beasts, and killed its cattle. In this instance Lebanon is a name used to describe Judea, as it is also in Jer 22:6,23; Zech 10:10; 11:1.

18. Teachers of lies. In what sense may idols, which are said to be dumb, be also teachers of lies? As Calvin remarks, they allured simple souls. They were instruments for deluding men. The image, said Matthew Poole, "was the product of his [man's] art and yet the hope of his soul."

19. That saith to the wood, Awake . . . The language is obviously mockery, like that of Elijah in taunting the priests of Baal. A Babylonian inscription to Bel reads, "How long will the lord who sleeps still sleep?"

20. In his holy temple. While scholars of many shades of theological opinion identify the **holy temple** as the sanctuary in Jerusalem, a comparison of Ps 11:4; 18:6,9; II Sam 22:7,10 shows that the expression is used with specific reference to heaven. In view of the fact that all the earth is commanded to be silent before the Lord, this conclusion seems best. **Keep silence.** The Hebrew has a strong imperative, *has!* very like our expression *Hush!* Believers, especially, will possess their souls in quietness and confidence, for God has promised that even though the vision tarry, it will surely come.

VII. A Vision of Divine Judgment. 3:1-16.

This chapter is called by the writer a prayer *(t^e^pillâ)*, though it is universally agreed that the major part of it is the description of a theophany experienced by the prophet. Only verse 2 is a petition. Yet the attitudes of reverent fear, of awe, of faith triumphant over disturbing circumstances are so much in the spirit of prayer that there can be little doubt that the "prayer" includes the whole chapter. The chapter is also called a psalm – though not by Habakkuk – since instructions are given in the heading as to the way it is to be sung, and the subscription tells what instruments are to accompany the singing. Also, the enigmatical *Selah*, which customarily marks periodical pauses, or perhaps changes of tempo, appears three times.

For various reasons, as has already been mentioned in the Introduction, this chapter has been thought to have been written by someone other than Habakkuk. This would mean, of course, that 3:1, which ascribes the chapter to him is incorrect. The fact that the third chapter does not appear in the Qumran Commentary is no real objection. Neither is the argument that this passage does not have the dialogue form of the previous sections. The very nature of the chapter, which is a prayer, precludes the dialogue style. There are some linguistic evidences to confirm the unity of the book as well as the fact that the theodicy is incomplete without this chapter.

1. Upon Shigionoth. The meaning of the word is so uncertain that the safest course is to transliterate it. The Latin Vulgate renders it *pro ignorantiis*, "for sins done in ignorance." There is no suggestion in the prophecy that either the sins of Judah or those of the Chaldeans could be thought of as being committed in ignorance. Probably the word indicates the type of music or the tempo in which the psalm may be sung when used in worship.

2. Thy speech, or *report*. The report is that act of Divine judgment which will likely bring suffering upon Habakkuk and those bound to him by common ties of faith and love. It is the judgment announced in chapter 1.

The rendering of the AV in this verse is not altogether satisfactory. The following translation is suggested:

O Lord, I have heard thy report,
I have feared, O Lord, thy work:
In the midst of the years make it live,
In the midst of the years make it known;
In wrath remember mercy.

Make it live. Though the English versions translate the Hebrew as *revive* or *renew*, the prophet is not asking that God should repeat what was done in the great days of old. The verb is used elsewhere with a causative force, e.g., Gen 7:3; 19:32; Deut 32:39, where the meaning is to preserve alive, or to call into existence. God is asked to put his work, that is, his declared program, into operation, to make it a living action. That such is the case is confirmed by the parallelism, "in the midst of the years make it known." **Thy work** is then the purpose announced in 1:5, together with the judgments pronounced in chapter 2.

In the midst of the years. An older commentator, Bengel, states that this verse points to the birth of Christ and the Christian era. God's work is to be done at a time which divides history, the Old Testament from the New. This proposal has not found ready acceptance. Habakkuk is asking that in the course of the years just ahead God may both chastise and heal.

Some have felt that verses 3-15 describe a theophany, or a manifestation of the Deity to the prophet. Others think that it is simply a poetic recital of the works of God with an Exodus motif, that is, employing the patterns of Divine activity at the time of the Exodus. There is no reason to think that Habakkuk had the kind of theophanic experience given to Abraham. At the same time these verses are more than a poetic celebration.

While the language seems to draw upon the Exodus and subsequent accounts of the dealings of God with Israel, there is also a good deal of originality in the description. The prophet speaks, for example, of mountains as writhing and crumbling and also of a display of brilliant splendor that filled the earth and sky. It is best to think of the entire panorama of cosmic disturbances which are the result of God's presence as being in the prophet's vision.

3. From Teman . . . Paran. Paran was the wilderness area west of the Arabah and near the traditional site of Mount Sinai. Teman was the rocky fortress-capital of Edom, but the name also designates the territory east of Paran. God is represented as approaching in judgment from the district where Israel had not only experienced his redemptive grace but had entered into covenant with him. These were also the districts in which some of the unbelieving generation perished. **His praise. Praise,** here, refers not to that which is uttered by earth's inhabitants, but rather to the excellence of God which deserves the praise of all creation.

4. Horns out of his hand. The Hebrew word "horns" is also used to describe rays of light, which latter meaning seems obvious here. These rays emanated from either side. The center from which the sunlike brightness came was the hiding place of God's power.

5. Pestilence and flame are phenomena which accompany the approach of the Lord as lightning and thunder accompany an approaching storm. Perhaps the prophet saw the animate creation as withering before God, as though smitten by a blighting wind. Behind him the path was charred as though seared by flame.

6. He stood. Jehovah halted his advance so that he might survey the land, to determine the kind and degree of judgment to be administered. God's mere touching of the mountains crushed and shook them. There is an a fortiori argument here. If the very rocks and hills which have defied the ravages of time sink into nothingness at the touch of the Lord's feet, or the glance of his eye, then who shall abide the day of his anger?

7. Cushan. It is commonly assumed that Cushan is Ethiopia. It is, however, more logical to suppose that Cushan was a part of the territory over which the Midianites roamed, and that it was from here that Zipporah, Moses' wife, who is called a Cushite, came.

8. Is the Lord displeased with rivers? The question is a rhetorical one, calculated to turn the mind to the real reason for the Lord's visitation – **salvation.** The Divine salvation constitutes, it may be assumed, the kind of deliverance for which the prophet has prayed in chapter 1. It will include deliverance from the violence and mischief with which the godly are surrounded, so that the law will no longer be "slacked." The salvation is not synonymous with that which is offered in our Lord Jesus Christ, though in several respects it is a foreshadowing of the Messianic work.

9. The oaths of the tribes, even thy word. Of all the clauses in the entire prophecy, this is probably the most difficult to explain. As it stands, it must be an interpolation, meaning that Judah's only hope is in God's covenant promise, particularly of the Sinaitic or Mosaic Covenant. In one small group of ancient manuscripts this phrase reads, "thou dost fill thy quiver with shafts," which makes good sense but does not have support in the best Hebrew manuscripts.

10. The deep . . . lifted up his hands. In his vision the prophet saw huge waves mounting in the sea, and was reminded of the gestures of a terror-stricken man.

11. Sun and moon stood still. The two orbs which give light to the earth and govern its time seemed to stand aghast, along with the rest of creation, at the splendor of the Lord as he appeared in judgment. They looked pale by comparison with the light of God's arrows and his glittering spear.

12. Thou didst march. The Lord marched through the earth as a triumphant conqueror, trampling upon the nations as the peasant **thresh**[ed] his grain by trampling upon it. **13. Salvation of . . .** *(with)* **thine anointed.** The **anointed** must be the faithful remnant among the covenant people. In OT times they were not all Israel who were of Israel (Rom 9:6). God's deliverance is extended to the people who look for the consolation of Israel in the person of her Messianic king.

13. The foundation even unto the neck, or *rock*. Apparently the text should read *rock*. The two words are very similar in Hebrew. The figure is that of the conqueror's tearing away the foundation down to the rock. The house of the wicked is utterly demolished.

16. When I heard. Though the vision had been *seen,* its import had been *heard,* or grasped, by the prophet. Cf. Isa 55:3, *"hear,* and your soul shall live." The prophet knew full well what God's going forth in judgment must mean to himself and the people among whom he lived. The immediate effect upon him was one of tremendous astonishment, as the excitement of the internal organs indicates. The ultimate effect, however, was that of assured faith. As Calvin states, "He who in time anticipates the wrath of God and is touched with fear, as soon as he hears that God the judge is at hand, provides for himself the most secure rest for the day of afflictions."

VIII. The Triumph of Faith. 3:17-19.

17. The mention of the fig tree, the grapevine, the olive, the grain, and flocks covers the entire range of agricultural produce upon which the nation was dependent. Presumably the reason for the failure of the crops would be the Chaldean invasion. Enemy troops not only lived off the land but often deliberately destroyed trees and crops. An early Egyptian chronicle boasts that the Egyptian soldiers had ruined the fruit trees in one of the coastal plains of Palestine.

18. Yet I will exult in the Lord. The ruination so vividly described drives the prophet not to despair but to faith in his Lord.

19. My feet like hinds', i.e., gazelles' **feet.** The gazelle is both swift and surefooted, so that it readily escapes pursuers. The picture is that of one who is supremely confident that he who leads his people into trials is faithful and will with each trial make also a way of escape, that they may be able to bear it.

To the chief musician. This prayer was evidently intended to be used by the Levitical choirs, though the psalm, unlike some others which are found outside the collection, e.g., II Sam 22:2ff., I Chr 16:8ff., was never put in the Book of Psalms.

BIBLIOGRAPHY

Commentaries

Calvin, John. *Commentaries on the Twelve Minor Prophets.* Translated by John Owen. Edinburgh: Calvin Translation Society, 1849.

Davidson, A. B. *Habakkuk (Cambridge Bible for Schools and Colleges).* Cambridge: The University Press, 1896.

Keil, C. F. *The Twelve Minor Prophets.* Vol. II. Edinburgh: T. & T. Clark, 1868.

Laetsch, Theodore. *The Minor Prophets.* St. Louis: Concordia Publishing House, 1956.

Lloyd-Jones, D. Martin. *From Fear to Faith.* London: Inter-Varsity Christian Fellowship, 1953.

Nowack, D. W. *Die Kleinen Propheten (Handkommentar Zum Alten Testament).* Göttingen: 1897.

Taylor, Charles L. "The Book of Habakkuk," *The Interpreter's Bible.* Edited by G. A. Buttrick and others. Vol. 6. New York: Abingdon Press, 1956.

Wade, G. W. "Habakkuk," *Westminster Commentaries.* London: Methuen & Co. 1929.

Ward, William Hayes. *Habakkuk (International Critical Commentary).* New York: Charles Scribner's Sons, 1911.

Introductions

Gottwald, Norman K. *A Light to the Nations.* New York: Harper & Brothers, 1959.

Gray, G. B. *A Critical Introduction to the Old Testament.* New York: Charles Scribner's Sons, 1913.

Pfeiffer, Robert H. *Introduction to the Old Testament.* New York: Harper & Brothers, 1948.

Young, Edward J. *An Introduction to the Old Testament.* Grand Rapids: Wm. B. Eerdmans Publishing Co., 1952.

ZEPHANIAH

INTRODUCTION

Title. The book of Zephaniah receives its name from the prophet whose ministry it records. *S^{e}panyâ* means "the Lord hides" or "the Lord has hidden." The prophet was born during the ruthless reign of Manasseh (692–638 B.C.), who "shed innocent blood very much, till he had filled Jerusalem from one end to another" (II Kgs 21:16). His name indicates a confidence in the power of God to hide (i.e., protect) his worshiper in time of danger.

The Prophet and His Message. Of Zephaniah very little is known. He was probably of royal descent (Zeph 1:1; presumably Hizkiah was King Hezekiah), and prophesied during the reign of Josiah (637-607 B.C.) between the fall of Nineveh and the Babylonian attack upon Judea. Under Josiah the administration of the Law and the worship of the Lord had been revived briefly, but the people still practiced idolatrous customs in secret. The perception of this hypocrisy stirred the young prophet to action. Even though the king joined the prophet in a reform movement, the evil tide rolled on. The increase of wickedness inevitably led to the moment when God would use Nebuchadnezzar as the rod of his anger.

Zephaniah pinpoints the cause of God's judgment by proclaiming the moral degeneration of the people. He makes clear, however, that the door of mercy is open for those who will sincerely repent. The prophet sees the meaning of all this in the light of God's purpose to send his Son, the Lord Jesus, as Israel's Messiah and the Saviour of all mankind.

Authorship and Date. The first verse of Zephaniah (using the usual formula of the writing prophets) indicates that the book constitutes the message which God imparted to the prophet and which the prophet himself recorded. And there is no reason to consider this indication to be an insertion by some unidentified writer in a later day. Though Zephaniah was born during the reign of Manasseh (692-638 B.C.), he did not assume his prophetic office until the early part of Josiah's reign, probably 627–626 B.C. Presumably the prophecy was written not many years thereafter.

Historical Background. The wicked reigns of Manasseh (692–638 B.C.) and Amon (638–637 B.C.) were over. King Josiah (637–607 B.C.) had ascended the throne of Judah. His reform was still several years away, and the apostate conditions which prevailed for more than one-half century during the reigns of Manasseh and Amon had not yet been challenged. In the early part of Josiah's reign (probably c. 627–626 B.C.), Zephaniah began to warn his people of the impending judgment of God, whose anger they had provoked by their behavior. The fate of Samaria in 722 B.C. was a solemn reminder of God's power and justice. With youthful vigor Zephaniah laid the groundwork for the reforms which took place later in Josiah's reign.

OUTLINE

I. Introduction. 1:1.
II. A warning of impending judgment. 1:2-18.
  A. The judgment announced. 1:2-6.
  B. The judgment defined. 1:7-13.
  C. The judgment described. 1:14-18.
III. An exhortation to immediate repentance. 2:1–3:8.
  A. An invitation to repentance. 2:1-3.
  B. A detailed warning of judgment. 2:4–3:8.
    1. The land of the Philistines. 2:4-7.
    2. The land of Moab and Ammon. 2:8-11.
    3. The land of the Ethiopians. 2:12.

4. The land of the Assyrians. 2:13-15.
5. The land of Judah and the city of Jerusalem. 3:1-8.

IV. A promise of future blessing. 3:9–20.
A. The promise of conversion. 3:9-13.
B. The promise of restoration. 3:14-20.

COMMENTARY

I. Introduction. 1:1.

Zephaniah's declaration of his ordination to the prophetic office takes on the familiar form: **The word of the Lord . . . came** to the prophet. A man took up the prophetic office in response to a direct call; the priestly office, which was restricted to the family of Aaron, was passed down from father to son. Zephaniah's father was Cushi; his grandfather, Gedaliah; his great-grandfather, Amariah; and his great-great-grandfather, Hizkiah, in all probability the godly king, Hezekiah.

II. A Warning of Impending Judgment. 1:2-18.

A. The Judgment Announced 1:2-6.

2. I will utterly consume. The destruction was to be certain and complete. Total destruction suggests the horrible consequences of idolatry or spiritual adultery. Some scholars suggest that the judgment pronounced had both imminent and future reference. Its imminent reference, some think, was to the fact that the barbaric Scythians, who had left their homeland north of the Black Sea, were sweeping over western Asia and might be expected to attack Judah at any moment. The ruthless Scythians employed the scorched earth policy with fury and vengeance. **3. I will consume man and beast.** Nothing would escape. Man, beast, the fowls of the air, and the fish of the sea would be subjects of the Lord's wrath. The waters would be infected and the air contaminated.

4. I will cut off the remnant of Baal. Men bowing to Baal, the Canaanite fertility-god, whose worship included acts of ritual prostitution, would be destroyed. **The Chemarims.** These long-robed priests who represented the idols (cf. II Kgs 23:5) were to be completely exterminated. **5. The host of heaven.** Astrology and the worship of the heavenly bodies as practiced by the Assyrians and Babylonians was common among the idolaters of Judah (cf. II Kgs 23:11; Jer 19:13; 32:29; Ezk 8:16). **Malcham.** Molech, a Semitic deity honored by the sacrifice of children.

6. Them that are turned back. Caught in this mesh of apostasy were those who rejected the claims of the God of Israel and became captive to the sensuous, immoral fertility cult. **Those that have not sought the Lord.** Some never had availed themselves of the grace and mercy of the Lord. They were self-centered, self-sufficient, living with total disregard for their spiritual needs.

B. The Judgment Defined. 1:7-13.

7. Hold thy peace at the presence of the Lord. The people had apostatized to the point of no return. Punishment was now inevitable. Their vain cry reminds us of the generation that perished in the Flood when the door of the ark was shut. They had refused to offer a burnt offering to the Lord; now they themselves were to become the sacrifice. **The day of the Lord** is the day of judgment, as in Amos 5:18. The **guests** are the enemies of Judah, and the **sacrifice** is Judah (cf. Isa 34:6).

8. I will punish the princes, and the king's children. After the death of Josiah, Judah hastened toward her doom. The evil reign of Jehoahaz (Josiah's successor) lasted only three months, and the rule of idolatrous Jehoiakim only eleven years. The three-month reign of Jehoiachin was quickly followed by the second deportation to Babylon. Then came the final destruction of Jerusalem during the reign of Zedekiah, who was taken to Babylon as a captive, after his eyes had been put out (II Kgs 25:6,7). **9.** Here reference is apparently made to the king's attendants, who were constantly at his beck and call. They were evidently the corrupt politicians of that day—selling their influence and position for silver. Jewish rabbinical scholars suggest that **those that leap on the threshold** were the Philistines, who, after Dagon fell before the ark, would not step over the threshold when they entered his temple, but, rather, leaped over it. Others hold that they were bandits who broke into people's houses and took what they wanted. They may have leaped over the threshold to avoid provoking the gods who were thought to guard the entrances to the houses.

10. That there shall be the noise of a cry . . . an howling. A prophetic picture is here presented of the attacking enemy coming upon Jerusalem from the north. The fish gate opened into the northern end of the Tyropoeon Valley (cf. Neh 3:3; 12:39). This was the direction from which the news of the approaching Chaldean army would come. The sound of the approach of the enemy is described as a **great crashing from the hills.**

11. Maktesh ("a mortar," "a trough," or "a hollow"). Some commentators identify **Maktesh** with the section of Jerusalem lying in the Kidron Valley, where rice, corn, and other grain was ground in a mortar. The configuration of **Maktesh** may have given rise to its name. Prophetically it is used to depict the way the inhabitants would be beaten and pounded to death, as grain is pounded in a mortar. **All the merchant people are cut down.** More specifically, the merchants and the money changers would be beaten to death without hope, and cut off from all help.

12. Search Jerusalem with candles (lamps). A thorough search, both by day and by night, would be made. None would escape. There would be no corner left unsearched in which sin could escape punishment. **Men that are settled on their lees. Lees** are dregs or sediment deposited from wine or liquor (cf. Isa 25:6). To settle on one's lees meant to become complacent and self-satisfied with one's character and circumstances—perhaps to be in a drunken stupor (cf. Jer 48:11). **13. Their goods.** The things in which they trusted would become a snare to them. Their efforts for material gain would come to nothing. They would not enjoy the fruits of their labor. They would not live in the houses they built, nor harvest the vineyards they planted (cf. Amos 5:11).

C. The Judgment Described. 1:14-18.

14. Is near. After the death of Josiah, judgment approached rapidly. It is here compared to a swiftly moving tempest. While the immediate reference appears to be to the Scythian invasion, ultimate fulfillment will come with the final Judgment, when there shall be "weeping and gnashing of teeth" (Mt 8:12; 25:30, *et al.*).

15. That day is a day of wrath. When the mercies of the Lord are spurned, wrath surely results. **A day of trouble and distress.** All the horrible consequences of judgment: the invasion, attack, confusion, torture—suffering and horror of every kind. It would be a day of darkness. The city would be heavily veiled with the smoke and smell of carnage. **16. Day of the trumpet.** The alarm would be sounded, and couriers would dispatch the terrible news, but to no avail. The nation had crossed the point of no return. Judgment must take its course. The fenced cities would be invaded, and the **high towers** would topple at the touch of the battering rams.

17. Distress upon men. A severe state of suffering, pain, and affliction was to come. In their hopeless despair, men would be crazed. They would grope around for help and salvation, but all hope for deliverance from judgment would be gone. Their sin and apostasy against the Lord had triggered his wrath. Blood would cover the streets like dust, and human bodies would be piled on the trash heap as dung. **18. Their silver nor their gold.** The time had passed when the privileged could bribe their way. Their money would not buy food, because there would be no food. A judgment of fire would consume their earthly possessions. A universal desolation would seize the land.

III. An Exhortation to Immediate Repentance. 2:1–3:8

A. An Invitation to Repentance. 2:1-3.

1,2. Gather yourselves together. Misery loves company. The people of Judah were to assemble themselves so that they might see their own collective corruption. **O nation not desired.** Through their apostasy they had forfeited their right to live. They had divorced themselves from the Lord. **Before the decree bring forth.** The people were invited to a final convocation before the **fierce anger of the Lord** broke upon them with all its fury. The Lord's agents of punishment, perhaps the Scythians, were to bring immediate judgment, and the Babylonians would finish what the Scythians left undone.

3. Seek ye the Lord. One last plea was extended by the Lord through the prophet. **It may be ye shall be hid in the day of the Lord's anger.** It was still possible for the repentant to escape judgment if they would only turn to the Lord. As God had warned the hardened among the people to humble themselves, so he now admonished the meek to seek him that they might escape the general calamity (cf. Ps 76:9).

B. A Detailed Warning of Judgment. 2:4–3:8.

1) The Land of the Philistines. 2:4-7.

4. For Gaza shall be forsaken. Even the neighboring Philistine community was to feel the judgment to come. These people had been harassed by the Egyptians; now the Babylonians would bring complete judgment. To reproduce the assonance of this verse exactly in English is impossible, but the rendition of J. R. Dummelow suggests it: "Gaza shall be a ghastly ruin; Ashkelon a deserted ashheap" *(A Commentary on the Holy Bible, in loco).* **5. The Cherethites.** A people occupying the southern coast of the Philistine country (see I Sam 30:14; Ezk 25:16). The LXX renders this word *Cretans* (Amos 9:7; Deut 2:23). The **Cherethites** were probably related to the Philistines and were immigrants from Crete. All of the Philistine coast would feel the wrath of God. No inhabitants would be left; all would be killed or carried into captivity. The invader would be no respecter of persons.

6. The sea coast . . . dwellings and cottages for shepherds. All permanent buildings would be destroyed. Shepherds would build small shelters and folds from the rubble (Isa 17:2). Population and tillage would disappear from the region. **7. The remnant of the house of Judah.** A small remnant would be left behind after the Babylonian attack. A remnant, kept by God's power in Babylon, returned at the close of the Exile. **Turn away their captivity.** Once again they would be free people (cf. Mic 4:6,7).

2) The Land of Moab and Ammon. 2:8-11.

8. Moab and . . . Ammon . . . have reproached my people. Because these enemies had abused the people of Judah, punishment was to be levied against them (cf. Jer 48:27-31; Ezk 25:8-11). **9. Moab shall be as Sodom . . . the children of Ammon as Gomorrah. Sodom** and **Gomorrah** are referred to as symbols of the Lord's fierce judgment. As those towns were utterly destroyed, so God's judgment was to fall on the cities of Moab and Ammon. The whole countryside would be a bed of thorns, and its perpetual desolation would be comparable to salt pits (cf. Isa 15:1ff.).

10. This shall they have for their pride. A haughty spirit precedes a fall (Prov 18:12). The Ammonites and Moabites had paraded their arrogance before the people of Judah. Now their pride was to be reduced to humility and calamity (cf. Ezk 25:8-11). **11. He will famish all the gods.** The destruction of Jerusalem by the Babylonians demonstrated the futility of trusting in the gods of Canaan. Baal worship lost its hold on the Jews during the Exile.

3) The Land of the Ethiopians. 2:12.

Ye Ethiopians also. They, too, were to become victims of Nebuchadnezzar's onslaught (cf. Jer 46:2,9; Ezk 30:4,5; Amos 9:7).

4) The Land of the Assyrians. 2:13-15.

13. He will . . . destroy Assyria . . . Nineveh. Nineveh was so completely destroyed that its location was lost to the memory of man until rediscovered by archaeologists during the nineteenth century. Nahum gives a graphic description of its total destruction in 612 B.C. (cf. Isa 10:12; Nah 1:2; 2:10; 3:15). **14. Flocks shall lie down in the midst of her.** This prophecy has been literally fulfilled. Sheep graze today on the very site where proud Nineveh once stood. Archaeologists have excavated portions of this great city, including the huge winged figures of bulls with human heads that stood on each side of the main gate and symbolized her power. Today this site is truly the dwelling place of the **cormorant** (a large bird, cf. Lev 11:17) and the **bittern** (a porcupine or lizard, or perhaps a bird).

15. This is the rejoicing city that dwelt carelessly (cf. Isa 47:8,9). Once Nineveh was the proud capital of Assyria—the home town of such emperors as Sennacherib and Esarhaddon. This proud city, the capital of western Asia, where emissaries from all over the eastern Mediterranean area presented their royal credentials for favor—would become a place of desolation and ruin. **Everyone that passeth by her shall hiss and wag his hand.** Both actions are signs of contempt and shame.

5) The Land of Judah and the City of Jerusalem. 3:1-8.

1. Her that is filthy and polluted. As a result of the worship of Baal and Molech,

Jerusalem had degenerated. The religious leaders were living in adultery, and they offered their sons as human sacrifices in order to gain favor from the nature gods (Jer 19:5; 23:13,14; 32:35). Jeremiah had difficulty in finding a righteous man in Jerusalem (Jer 5:1). Her civil and religious leaders were on the side of idolatry instead of being spokesmen for God. **2. She obeyed not the voice.** Jerusalem had been warned. The prophets had pleaded with the people, but all urgings to repentance were ignored. The rupture between the people and the Lord widened with each passing day (cf. Jer 22:21).

3. Her princes . . . are roaring lions. The people in authority and power had no regard for truth and righteousness. Their arrogant roar was like that of a wild beast. **Judges are evening wolves.** The judges tore into shreds any vestige of justice. They slunk in the shadows, ready to take a bribe. They practiced the violence and predatory oppression of wild beasts (Ezk 22:27; Mic 3:9-11). **4. Her prophets are light and treacherous.** The prophets no longer possessed the serious conviction and integrity of holy men. They betrayed the souls of the blind. **Her priests have polluted the sanctuary.** The priests had violated the Law by offering animals with spots and blemishes. The sacrifices were devoid of spiritual content (cf. Jer 23:11,32).

5. The just Lord is in the midst thereof. The Lord was still present, and he was keeping a record of their wickedness. Goodness would be the lot of the righteous, but punishment was sure to come to the wicked (cf. Deut 32:4). **6. I have cut off the nations.** Evidently Syria and Israel are meant here. This was prophetic of what the Lord was in the process of doing. **There is none inhabitant.** Every home would be rooted up. **Surely thou wilt fear me.** The Lord had reason to expect repentance and obedience after the intermittent punishment inflicted upon Jerusalem, but the people persisted in their evil doings. Finally, total destruction came at the hands of the Babylonians.

8. For my determination is to gather the nations. The mercy of the Lord is directed to all peoples and nations. Even Nineveh repented at the preaching of Jonah. But likewise, judgment will come upon all who forsake the Lord. The judgment of fire is always associated with the punishment of nations through war.

IV. A Promise of Future Blessing. 3:9-20.

A. The Promise of Conversion. 3:9-13.

9. Then will I turn to the people a pure language. This is a prophetic reference to the time when the Jews would turn from the blasphemy of idolatry and utter the praises of the Lord (cf. Joel 2:28; Acts 2:16-21). **Pure language** may refer to the form of religious worship they would practice. They had been idolaters; now God promised to restore his worship among them. **10. From beyond the rivers of Ethiopia.** After the judgment the Lord would bring his people back from all the areas of the captivity. Even so remote a land as Ethiopia would experience this act of sovereign grace.

11. Shalt thou not be ashamed. Punishment would end, finally, for those who repented. A remnant would be purged of idolatry and would return. **I will take away out of the midst of thee.** The wicked leaders would meet their fate. **Thou shalt no more be haughty.** False pride would turn into humility. **12. An afflicted and poor people.** The captivity would reduce many of the people to poverty. As a matter of fact, many of the poor people responded to the liberation under Cyrus, while the wealthy stayed behind. The prophecy also looks beyond the return from Babylon to the time when the poor and humble finally received the Messiah—"The common people heard him gladly" (Mk 12:37). **13. The remnant of Israel.** After the Babylonian captivity a cleansed and purified remnant would return. Never again would they bow down to the heathen gods (cf. Mic 4:7).

B. The Promise of Restoration. 3:14-20.

14. Sing, O daughter of Zion. A time of rejoicing would come when the remnant would once again worship in the rebuilt Temple. There will also be a time of rejoicing in the more distant future when Israel will accept her Messiah. **15. The king of Israel, even the Lord, is in the midst of thee.** This is a prophetic anticipation of the day when the King-Messiah will rule. Israel has had no Davidic king actually holding the reins of government since the death of Zedekiah.

16. Fear thou not. In the glorious day of the Messiah, all captivities and national afflictions will be removed. **17. The Lord thy God.** This is the high tide of Zephaniah's prophecy. **The Lord . . . God** is the self-existent, divine Being who will stand in the midst of Israel. **Is mighty.** He is the conquering Hero. This is the character Isaiah gives the Messiah (Isa 9:6). He will save his people. **He will joy over thee.** After saving them, the Messiah will find in the redeemed Israel his ground of rejoicing (cf. Jn 15:11).

18. I will gather them that are sorrowful. A remnant will repent of their sins, and they will again gather in Jerusalem to see its great splendor restored. **The reproach of it was a burden.** Jewish people have not been able to enjoy their religion in the countries of their dispersion because o fthe reproach heaped upon them by their heathen neighbors (cf. Ps 137). **19. Undo all that efflict thee.** Those who have punished Judah will be punished. **20. I bring you again.** They will once again possess their own land and be restored to favor with the Lord. Finally, all nations of the earth will be blessed by the Jews through their Messianic King, the Lord Jesus (cf. Isa 11:12; Ezk 28:25; 34:13; Amos 9:14).

BIBLIOGRAPHY

Bewer, Julius. *The Prophets*. New York: Harper and Brothers, 1955.

Carson, J. T. "Zephaniah," *The New Bible Commentary*. Edited by F. Davidson, A. M. Stibbs, and E. F. Kevan. Grand Rapids: Wm. B. Eerdmans Publishing Co., 1953.

Davis, John A. "Zephaniah," *The Westminster Dictionary of the Bible*. Revised and rewritten by Henry S. Gehman. Philadelphia: Westminster Press, 1944.

Dummelow, J. R. *A Commentary on the Holy Bible*. New York: The Macmillan Company, 1943.

Eiselen, F. C. "Book of Zephaniah," *International Standard Bible Encyclopedia*. Grand Rapids: Wm. B. Eerdmans Publishing Co., 1952.

Jamieson, Robert, Fausset, A. R., and Brown, David. *A Commentary, Critical and Explanatory on the Old and New Testaments*. Grand Rapids: Zondervan Publishing House, 1934.

Laetsch, Theodore. "Zephaniah," *Bible Commentary, The Minor Prophets*. Saint Louis: Concordia Publishing House, 1956.

HAGGAI

INTRODUCTION

Date and Authorship. The author of this book is the only person in the Old Testament with the name *Haggai* (meaning "festive" or "festal"). The name may indicate the faith of the prophet's parents that their son would have the joy of seeing his predictions of restoration fulfilled. It is possible that he was so named because he was born on some feast of the sacred Hebrew calendar. Although he is one of the prophets the details of whose personal life are unknown, he is mentioned by Ezra (Ezr 5:1; 6:14). He was the first of the post-Exilic prophets who ministered to the remnant that had returned from Babylonian captivity. His prophecy is clearly to be dated in 520 B.C., the second year of Darius the king. Haggai was probably born in exile in the early part of the sixth century. His contemporary in the prophetic office was Zechariah (cf. Hag 1:1 with Zech 1:1; see also Ezr 5:1; 6:14).

Historical Background. The prophets before the Exile (586 B.C.) had foretold the fall of the Judean kingdom to the new Babylonian empire. It was also revealed that after seventy years the Lord would restore his people to their homeland (Jer 25:11,12; Dan 9:2). When Cyrus the Persian destroyed the Babylonian power, he favored and promoted the Jews' return to the land of promise to rebuild the sanctuary in Jerusalem. The foundation of the new Temple was laid and the work was begun with high hopes. Soon hostile neighbors employed their devices to stop the work. The work was brought to a halt, but outward opposition to the task was only part of the problem. A state of indifference had seized upon the fifty thousand exiles who had returned with resolve to rebuild the house of God. When Darius Hystaspes came to the Persian throne, the Temple had been untouched for some sixteen years. Haggai (and later Zechariah) was sent by God to awaken the people and bestir them from their lethargy to undertake the work of restoration. It is unfair to Haggai to consider that his messages are solely concerned with matters of building. He does begin from that vantage point, but goes on to speak of the glory of the presence of the Lord Jesus Christ, the future establishment of God's earthly kingdom, the judgment of God on ungodly world powers, and the blessing awaiting the nations that will return to God.

OUTLINE

CHAPTER I.

I. Rebuke of indifference. 1:1-4.
II. Call to serious reflection. 1:5,6.
III. Israel's chastenings from God. 1:7-11.
IV. Obedience of the nation. 1:12-15.

CHAPTER II.

I. Encouragement for building. 2:1-5.
II. Promise of future glory. 2:6-9.
III. Clean and unclean in Levitical matters. 2:10-14.
IV. The application of these truths. 2:15-19.
V. God's future blessing for Zerubbabel. 2:20-23.

COMMENTARY

CHAPTER I.

I. The Rebuke of Indifference. 1:1-4.

1. **In the second year.** Cf. Introduction. The prophet dates all his prophecies, as though he kept a strict diary of all the important events in the rebuilding of the Temple. **First day of the month.** The new moon was a time when the people assembled for worship (as do orthodox Jews today); thus it was an appropriate occasion for the preaching of Haggai's divine message. **Sixth month.** Called

Elul, this month falls about September. The dating of the prophecy in the reign of a Gentile monarch is eloquent testimony that "the times of the Gentiles" had begun (cf. Lk 21:24; Ezr 4:24). As the dates are followed throughout the prophecy, the progress of the work becomes clear. **Zerubbabel.** His name means "born or begotten in Babylon." In the historical accounts he is called Sheshbazzar (see Ezr 1:8; 5:14,16). He was a scion of the Davidic dynasty, the grandson of Jehoiachin (Jeconiah; I Chr 3:17, 19), and was made governor of Judah by Cyrus (Ezr 5:14). **Joshua.** He was the son of Jehozadak, who was high priest at the time of the Babylonian invasion (I Chr 6:15). Thus Haggai's prophecy is addressed to the civil and religious heads of the nation.

2. This people. It is not "My" people but "This" people, in order to show the displeasure of the Lord. **The time is not come.** This was the excuse the people offered for not rebuilding the Temple. According to their way of thinking, the time was not appropriate. Actually, the root of the difficulty lay in them, not in some outward circumstance or time factor. The subterfuge is clear; they did not claim that the work should not be carried on, but that it was not the right hour to do it. One would think that a lapse of about sixteen years would have brought home the need for exertion on their part. But the unwilling heart always finds excuses. It is hardly correct to assume that they were reckoning strictly seventy years from 586 B.C. The impression is rather that they thought a renewal of activity in building would evoke the latent hostility of the Persians and bring them to grief.

4. Is it time for you . . . ? The ASV renders the additional pronoun in the original, *you yourselves*. Haggai asked the leaders whether the hour was inauspicious only as far as the things of God were concerned. Their activity in personal matters (such as building homes) gave an altogether different impression. What a contrast—the desolate and waste Temple of the Lord alongside the finished and ornate private dwellings of the returned exiles! The question of the prophet, with one masterful stroke, laid bare the indifference, selfishness, and disobedience of the nation. **Cieled houses.** These were homes paneled, extensively fitted out. Wainscoting with cedar was to be found in the palaces of kings (see I Kgs 7:7; Jer 22:14). Since expensive timber was not common in Judah, its use was a mark of luxury. **Waste.** Where their hearts were, their treasure was also. Contrast their indifference toward the house of God with the commendable concern of David (II Sam 7:2).

II. Call to Serious Reflection. 1:5,6.

5. Consider your ways. The need of the hour was to consider (lit., *set* their *heart to)* their actions. In the OT the heart commonly represents the thought life. To be thankful one must be thinkful. The call to consider is a favorite one with this prophet. He uses it in verse 7 and then twice in 2:18. It is a charge to self-examination and self-judgment. The Jewish people could easily evaluate the nature of their acts by the results which issued from them.

6. Ye have sown much. They expended themselves to the fullest extent in the time of sowing. They spared no effort to insure prosperity. But their returns in the harvest were altogether disappointing. They should have realized that they could not enrich themselves at God's expense (cf. Lev 26:26; Hos 4:10; Mic 6:14). **Ye clothe you.** Nothing seemed to be in sufficient amount, whether food, drink, or clothing. **Bag with holes.** Wages were so small that they vanished in the face of daily necessities; the workers' earnings were soon gone. There is no contradiction between the description of poverty here and the description of the ceiled, expensive houses of verse 4. As in other societies, the wealthy were found along with the poorer class. That age, as every age in man's history, proved the truth of Mt 6:33. When God is forgotten, all labor is without profit. Materialistic civilizations of this day need to ponder this truth as much as any other.

III. Israel's Chastenings from God. 1:7-11.

8. Go up to the mountain. After another call to serious comtemplation of their condition, the remedy is stated. The people were to betake themselves to the high lands and wooded areas to obtain timber for the Temple. **I will take pleasure.** God promised at the outset that obedience would meet with his approval. In brief, Haggai is declaring, "Obey God, and his blessing and approbation will be yours." **I will be glorified.** Here is proof that God was concerned, as was Haggai, with the spiritual aspects of the rebuilding. Solomon had prayed (I Kgs

8:30) that God might be magnified through the worship of His people. When they neglected this activity of their spiritual life, barrenness resulted. The Babylonian Talmud claimed that five things were lacking in the Temple of Zerubbabel which were found in the first Temple: (1) the Shekinah glory, (2) the holy fire, (3) the ark of the covenant, (4) the Urim and Thummim, and (5) the spirit of prophecy (probably the Holy Spirit). Whatever may have been wanting in the restoration Temple, God unequivocally promised that his blessing would be there.

9. Ye looked for much. Haggai returns to the theme of the disastrous consequences of the indifference of the people in spiritual things. Such neglect had a direct effect upon their temporal concerns. Though they had had high hopes for bumper crops, these expectations were disappointed. There was little to show for the great outlay of their labor. **I did blow upon it.** Even the little that was garnered was of little help to them. God saw to it that it was unfit for consumption or was scattered. The people were thus informed that they were not to attribute the poor returns from the soil to any other cause, such as long neglect of the land during the captivity period, but to the direct chastening of God. **Why?** How was God's providence to be explained? God's chastening must have been predicated upon their deeds. Wherein had they failed? **Ye run.** The reply is clear. In seeking their own fortunes, they had displayed a considerable degree of zeal, had run, as a matter of fact, in furthering their selfish interests, to the utter disregard of the interests of the Lord. A marked contrast is presented between *mine house* and *his own house*.

10. Stayed from dew. The Lord withheld the dew that replaced the rain during the dry months of the summer, so that there was no increase from the land. Thus God manifested clearly that he was the supreme administrator of Israel's food. **11. I called for a drought.** More than once in Israel's history God saw that there was need to bring the nation to a realization of her utter dependence upon him for all the needs of life. Repeatedly the OT teachers and prophets emphasized that in the path of obedience Israel could know the proper balance of the forces of nature for her benefit and blessing. God had warned the people that if they were disobedient, the very heavens would become as brass to them (Deut 28:23). The drought he sent on the land and the mountains affected the *grain* (not **corn**), the new wine, the oil, all the issues of the ground, and all the labor of man and cattle. Famine has ever been a dread scourge in the hand of God. See II Kgs 8:1; Ps 105:16; cf. Deut 11:14; 18:4. Lower creation is always involved in the fortunes of man (Rom 8:19-21).

IV. Obedience of the Nation. 1:12-15.

12. Obeyed the voice of the Lord. Here there is indicated a heartening co-operation between leaders and people. The message of the prophet had its intended effect. The people were quick to evaluate the message of Haggai for what it was—the will of God expressed through his servant. **Their God.** Twice God is so designated. There appears to be an implication here that the nation had now moved into closer conformity with the relationship she sustained to God as his chosen, covenant people. **13. The Lord's messenger in the Lord's message.** With new spiritual insight, the people recognized Haggai as the Lord's spokesman, invested with divine authority. **I am with you.** The message was short, but it could not have been more comforting or strengthening. In the past this message had been used by God to spur men on to mighty accomplishments (e.g., Ex 3:12; Jer 1:8), and it is still the most reassuring of all promises to the servants of the Lord Jesus Christ around the world (cf. Mt 28:20). The turning to the Lord was heartfelt; otherwise this strong word of assurance would not have been given to them.

14. The Lord stirred up. Every good intention and purpose of the people of God emanates from the Lord. It is he who energizes men to will and do of his good pleasure (Phil 2:13). **Spirit.** The threefold use of the term indicates that the battle is won or lost in the realm of the spiritual, not in any favorable or unfavorable outward condition. **They came and did work.** The people began the work of collecting the necessary materials for the structure; the foundations were not laid, however, until three months later.

15. Four and twentieth day. Haggai is careful to give another precise date, so important is the matter upon which his heart is set. There was an interval of twenty-three days between this date and the one given in verse 1. God ever takes note of every feature of the obedience of his children.

CHAPTER II.

I. Encouragement for Building. 2:1-5.

1. In the seventh month, in the one and twentieth day of the month. The second message of the prophet is dated on the seventh day of the Feast of Tabernacles, the final feast of ingathering in the Hebrew calendar (cf. Lev 23:39-44). This feast was marked by much joy (as it is to this day), and the sacrifices of thanksgiving were more numerous on the final day than on any other in the year. However, with the scant harvest and the humble beginnings of the Temple, the contrast with former conditions must have been especially painful. There was need, therefore, for encouragement (cf. Ezr 3:12,13). Often Satan makes his strongest attacks on men just after they have firmly resolved to follow the leading of the Lord. The people stood in need of strong encouragement to guard them from despondency. In the first chapter the need was a message to the consciences and wills of the indifferent people; here there was needed a word of comfort and cheer to the hearts of the awakened nation.

3. Who is left among you . . . ? The words are addressed to the civil and religious leaders and the returned remnant. God was comparing the Temple of Solomon and the one then under construction. Through Haggai he asked the leaders and the people how many of them recalled the glory of the first structure. After the lapse of seventy years of exile, likely there were few left who had seen the former Temple. **As nothing?** The occasion for the question of the Lord is found in the account in Ezr 3:8-13. The record states that at the founding of the second Temple the priests accompanied the ceremony with the singing of psalms and blowing of trumpets. The younger generation, with no means of comparison in this case, exulted over the achievement. But the older men who had known the first glorious Temple wept openly because of the marked contrast between the two sanctuaries. Haggai directed his query to this latter group. From God's viewpoint there was but one house of the Lord in Jerusalem, whether built by Solomon, Zerubbabel, or later by Herod. Hence God referred to the building of Solomon as "this house in her first glory." God's thoughts are not man's, and his judgments are made on the basis of absolutes.

4-2. Be strong. In the threefold address to prince, priest, and people, the Lord commanded all to be strong. God, who had first drawn a vivid contrast between the buildings, now offered the people spiritual undergirding for the performance of their task. His purpose in setting forth the difference was not to discourage them, but rather to bring them to a realization of the magnitude of the work, their inadequacy to accomplish it in their own strength, and the necessity of relying on his sufficiency. The Lord was their strength. Again, the uplifting word was given that the presence of the Lord would be their constant portion.

5. I covenanted with you. If any nation on earth could have been certain of God's trustworthiness in regard to his promises, it was Israel. He had covenanted (lit., *cut a covenant*, speaking with reference to the victims that were divided to ratify a covenant; cf. Gen 15:10) to enter into a permanent relationship with the children of Israel when they left Egypt. The covenant at Mount Sinai is in view (cf. Ex 19:5; especially 33:12-14). Since God had been faithful to that promise through all the centuries past of Israel's history, he could surely be relied upon to uphold his pledged word to the contemporaries of the prophet Haggai. **My spirit remaineth among you.** A pledge of the veracity of the promise was the presence of the Spirit of God then abiding among them. God had not forsaken them, though he had been highly displeased with their indifference to his love and his commands. They had nothing to fear.

II. Promise of Future Glory. 2:6-9.

6. Yet once, it is a little while. The cryptic expression probably means that in but a short time the events set forth would take place. **I will shake the heavens.** This verse and the three following are distinctly Messianic in thought (see also Isa 61:1-3; Dan 9:24-27; Zech 9:9,10). Here the prophet's message blends together details of the first and second comings of Christ, as other OT prophecies often do. The prediction of the shaking of the heavens, the earth, the sea, and the dry land surely speaks of something more than an unusual display of God's omnipotence in the natural realm; the whole atmosphere of the prophecy brings the reader to apocalyptic times. Here God is seen once again intervening sensibly and manifestly in the affairs of men. What may be the thought relation between the statement in this verse and that in verse 5? The prophet encouraged the Jews to prosecute the work on the Temple with all diligence, for, he assured them, their God, the Lord of the nations, would before long show forth his mighty power in Israel's behalf. He would shake the material universe and overthrow earthly, finite kingdoms in order to set up the final and ultimate kingdom on earth, the kingdom of God's dear Son.

7. I will shake all nations. This prediction has been referred to the uprisings and upheavals in the Persian and Greek empires. No one can reasonably deny that these governments were shaken in the past. But the careful reading of the prophecies of Scripture will convince an unprejudiced student that those occurrences were only preparatory steps in the process whereby God will yet dislodge the kingdoms of this world, to replace them by the righteous rule of the Messiah of Israel and the Redeemer of the world (see Heb 12:26,27; Rev 11:15). **The desire of all nations shall come.** Translators have not been in agreement in their rendering of the four Hebrew words of this portion of the verse. The LXX translates them, *the choice things of all the nations shall come.* The ASV prefers *the precious things of all nations,* with the marginal reading—*the things desired* (Heb. *desire) of all nations shall come.* Others have suggested: *the Gentiles shall come with their delightful things,* or *the precious possessions of the heathen.* What meaning is to be given to the passage if these translations are followed? The lack of splendor and outward adornment in the Temple of Zerubbabel would be more than compensated for by the precious gifts that all peoples would yet present to make the Lord's Temple a thing of beauty and glory. Of course, such tribute to the Lord would be given out of true homage to him. It is cited in favor of this interpretation that it does justice to the use of the feminine singular subject and the plural verb.

It is well to remember, however, that from earliest days the majority of Christian interpreters followed the Jewish tradition in referring the passage to the coming of Israel's Messiah. It seems clear to these interpreters that the longing all nations have in common must be their yearning for the Deliverer, whether or not they realize the nature of their desire or the identity of its true fulfillment in the Lord Jesus Christ. Moreover, in Hebrew an abstract noun is often used instead of the concrete; thus a reference to the Messiah is not automatically ruled out on the basis of language considerations. The use of a plural verb does not militate against the Messianic interpretation, for there are instances in which the verb agrees with the second of two nouns.

I will fill this house with glory. It is interesting that every earthly abode of the infinite God was filled with glory (see Ex 40:35 for the Mosaic Tabernacle; I Kgs 8:10,11; II Chr 5:13,14 for the Solomonic Temple). The Temple of Zerubbabel was yet to be filled with the glory of the presence of the incarnate God the Son (Jn 1:14), to say nothing of the glory of the Second Advent (Mal 3:1). The Lord foretells that the nations will be shaken (not redeemed). That shaking began preparatory to the first coming and will be completed at the second appearing (Dan 2:35,44; Mt 21:44). Accordingly, God will fill his house, the Temple of the future, with unprecedented glory.

8. The silver is mine. Lest the remnant continue to be surcharged with concern over the lack of precious metals in the restoration Temple, the Lord pointed to his inexhaustible supply. It has been conjectured that in Solomon's Temple some twenty million dollars' worth of gold was used to overlay the innermost compartment of the sanctuary. But what was that in comparison to the supplies of the One who has all? (Ps 50:12) Yea, more than that, God will beautify it in the coming of his Son. The poor exiles had little with which to decorate the Temple, but God assured them that he would supply the lack.

9. The glory of this latter house. The sense is that the latter glory of the house would far exceed all the former glory. It is vital to realize that in the Scriptures the Temple of God in Jerusalem is conceived of as one entity, existing under different forms in different periods of history. Christ's presence would lend a glory to the second Temple which the first Temple never knew. The view has been presented that the latter glory has reference to the Millennial glory of the Temple seen in Ezekiel, chapters 40 to 48. Since there is a continuity in the Temples of different eras, this position cannot be excluded. Though Zerubbabel's Temple was cleared to the foundations by Herod when he renovated it, his Temple was still considered the second Temple. It is so referred to by all Jewish authorities. **In this place will I give peace.**

Christ accomplished the basis for spiritual peace at Jerusalem (Col 1:20). He grants peace of heart and mind to believers now (Rom 5:1; Phil 4:7). But ultimately he will bring world peace as the Prince of Peace (Isa 9:6,7). Sufficient and more, then, is this answer of God to the unimposing appearances of verse 3. God always reserves the best for last. Only the eye of faith can see it.

III. Clean and Unclean in Levitical Matters. 2:10-14.

10. In the four and twentieth day of the ninth month. The fourth message of the prophecy of Haggai was given two months after the preceding one. It was in the ninth month that the early rain could be expected to water the new crops. Having already experienced scarcity and disappointment in the period before this, the people would have been especially concerned about the produce for the ensuing year. During their former period of disobedience, they had been chastened in temporal matters. Would there be a change now that they had obeyed the command of God through Haggai? This question the prophet now answers.

11. Ask now the priests concerning the law. The people were to seek legal help from the priests of the day. The priests in Israel were the authoritative teachers of the Mosaic Law (see Deut 17:8,9). They were commissioned by God to interpret the Law; the prophets were sent to apply it (e.g., Hag 2:13,14). In verses 11 to 13 the people of Israel are described, indirectly, as they had been in their state of disobedience, a condition not to be repeated.

12. If one bear holy flesh. Two distinct questions are asked. The first is: If a man were carrying holy (sacrificial) flesh, and touched another object, would that object by contact with the flesh become holy or set apart to the Lord? **And the priests answered and said, No.** The answer in the first case is in the negative (cf. Lev 22:4-6; Num 19:11). **13. Shall it be unclean?** The second question was: If a man who was unclean ceremonially by reason of contact with a dead body should touch an object, would the object become unclean because of the man's ceremonial uncleanness? The answer to the second query is in the affirmative. The principle is that moral cleanness cannot be transmitted, according to the Mosaic regulations, but moral uncleanness can be transmitted. Legal impurity is transmitted rather than legal or Levitical purity. A man cannot transmit his health to a sick child, but a sick child can communicate his disease to a man.

14. So is this people. Even though the people had been neglecting the work of the Temple, they had been offering sacrifices on an improvised altar at Jerusalem (Ezr 3:3). These offerings had not been pleasing to the Lord; therefore God had withheld his blessing from the people, as is clearly seen in chapter 1. **That which they offer there is unclean.** Just as the ceremonially unclean Israelite polluted all he touched, so the people in their disobedience transmitted the results of that disobedience to their work, which rendered it unprofitable. As holy flesh could not communicate its consecration to any other object, so the external good works of the people, even the offerings they were careful to present on God's altar, could not suffice to secure the blessing of God and the joy of holiness. All their past labors partook of their spiritual uncleanness. The conclusion is clear: they were not to return to their former disobedient course, but were to forsake it. Here Haggai is interpreting cause and effect from the angle of the Mosaic Law, just as he explained it earlier (1:6, 9-11) from the viewpoint of sowing and reaping. The parallels are clear between "this people," "this nation" here, and "This people" in 1:2.

IV. Application of These Truths. 2:15-19.

15. From before a stone was laid. The people of God were asked to consider their difficult circumstances during the period when they interrupted the work on the Temple. **16. When one came to an heap of twenty measures.** In those days of stringency, when a man came to a heap of grain from which he thought to get twenty measures, he found that, after threshing, it yielded but half that amount. **Pressfat.** The winevat that was supposed to yield fifty measures of wine had only twenty. Expectations were constantly disappointed, for the prospering hand of God was not with them. **17. I smote you.** As in the days of the prophet Amos (cf. Amos 4:9), the Lord smote the fields and vineyards of his people with blasting, a result of excessive drought, and with mildew, a consequence of excessive moisture. The remainder of the work of their hands was destroyed by hail. All nature was arrayed against them. **Yet ye turned not to me.** These tokens of God's displeasure should have been clear enough warnings of further chastenings, but the people were slow to perceive and did not return to God in repentance and trust.

18. Consider now from this day. This verse issues a double exhortation to consider. How little men apply their minds, their thought, to the relationship they sustain to the Lord! Before the twenty-fourth day the people had not given themselves unreservedly to the work, as they should have done. They were to compare conditions before and after their obedience. **19. Is the seed yet in the barn?** The people could easily have checked the truth or falsity of the prophet's conclusions. In doing so they would have discovered before long that there was no seed in the barn, and that the vines and trees had not yielded their produce. **From this day will I bless you.** But now, standing in the place of obedience, Israel was to find all different. The prophet was not speaking as a clever agricultural expert, forecasting good crops, but as the prophet of God pronouncing blessing on faith, prosperity on trust. The God who could withhold blessing could also bestow it upon his faithful people.

V. God's Future Blessing for Zerubbabel. 2:20-23.

20. In the four and twentieth day of the month. On the same day on which he delivered the previous message (v. 10) Haggai delivered his last utterance, a word of personal encouragement to the civil leader, Zerubbabel. **21. Speak to Zerubbabel.** It is possible that Zerubbabel, as the governor and civil leader, had wondered about the previous prediction (vv. 6,7) concerning the revolutions among world powers and kingdoms. He may well have been concerned about how these dealings of God would affect the people over whom he was head. **I will shake the heavens and the earth.** It will be readily seen and acknowledged that the personal message to Zerubbabel merges with the prophetic utterance concerning God's future judgments on the nations.

22. I will overthrow the throne of kingdoms. By some interpreters the passage has been placed in the time of the overthrow and revolt of the subject nations against the Persian Empire. This took place when Darius Hystaspes ascended the throne in 521 B.C. But the prophecy of Haggai looks to the future; it is not speaking of some historic event known to all. Furthermore, there is significance in the use of the singular "throne." It is best to see here, along with many able expositors, a reference to the ultimate overthrow of this world system, dominated by Satan, when the rightful King, the Lord Jesus Christ, returns to take up the reins of government (cf. Rev 11:15). **Chariots.** Nations, then as now, will still be depending on carnal forces and weapons to achieve their carnal objectives, but the Lord will utterly destroy their strength and show of force. **By the sword of his brother.** The destruction begun by the Lord will be brought to a conclusion through the insanity of civil strife (see also Ezk 38:21; Zech 14:13). These events are to be set in the days of the War of Armageddon. By no stretch of the imagination can the events of this verse be twisted to fit into some past conflicts or political movements of once-great empires.

23. In that day, saith the Lord of hosts, will I take thee. The personal note is unmistakable. Zerubbabel was not appointed for judgment, but for a specific mission. God had a special honor reserved for this one of his servants. The promise actually pertains to the office Zerubbabel filled as ruler in Judah; it can not refer to Zerubbabel's own lifetime. In his day the predicted events did not transpire. The meaning is that the Messianic descent was to come through Zerubbabel, of the line of David, just as it did through David himself. David's secure throne is here contrasted with the tottering dynasties of the world. Zerubbabel is found in both genealogies of the Messiah (Mt 1:12; Lk 3:27). Jewish expositors referred this passage in Haggai to the Messiah. In Zerubbabel, then, as the type, is prefigured the person of the antitype, the Messiah. Both were descendants of David; hence the blending in this prophecy. **As a signet.** The signet was an object of worth and care to the Oriental. Its stamp was a mark of honor and authority (see Song 8:6; Jer 22:24). In olden times, when the signet ring was used to sign letters and documents, it represented the owner, who wore it always (cf. Gen 38:18; Jer 22:24). It was his prized possession. Here the signet prefigures the precious Christ. **I have chosen thee.** As other OT worthies took their places in Messiah's line of succession by the sovereign selection of God, so Zerubbabel was honored to be placed in this company to point to the Chosen One of God, the Lord Christ.

BIBLIOGRAPHY

DODS, MARCUS. *The Post-Exilian Prophets*. Edinburgh: T. & T. Clark, n.d.

FAUSSET, A. R. "Haggai," *A Commentary Critical, Experimental and Practical on the Old and New Testaments*. Edited by R. Jamieson, A. R. Fausset, and D. Brown. Vol. IV. Grand Rapids: Wm. B. Eerdmans Publishing Co., 1948.

FEINBERG, CHARLES L. *Habakkuk, Zephaniah, Haggai, and Malachi*. New York: American Board of Missions to the Jews, Inc., 1951.

JENNINGS, A. C. "Haggai," *Commentary on the Whole Bible*. Edited by Charles J. Elicott. Vol. V. Grand Rapids: Zondervan Publishing House, 1954.

MCILMOYLE, J. "Haggai," *The New Bible Commentary*. Edited by F. Davidson, A. M. Stibbs, and E. F. Kevan. Grand Rapids: Wm. B. Eerdmans Publishing Co., 1953.

ROBINSON, GEORGE L. *The Twelve Minor Prophets*. New York: Doran, 1926.

ZECHARIAH

INTRODUCTION

Date and Authorship. Zechariah, a contemporary of Haggai, began his prophetic ministry in 520 B.C. The latest date indicated in the book (7:1) is 518 B.C., the fourth year of Darius Hystaspis. The name "Zechariah" was a common one in the Old Testament, twenty-nine persons having borne it. It means *the Lord remembers.* 'Liberal' scholars, observing certain differences in style and subject matter, have maintained that chapters 9 to 14 were not written by the author of chapters 1 to 8. However, chapters 9 to 14 seem to have been written at a later time, and this may well account for the change in style. The difference in subject matter stems from the fact that in the latter part of the book the prophet is commissioned to disclose the apocalyptic events connected with the coming of Messiah and his earthly kingdom. All internal evidence points to single authorship for the book rather than multiple authorship.

Historical Background. Cyrus, the Persian king, issued a decree (about 538 B.C.) that all who desired to return to Jerusalem to rebuild the Temple were permitted to do so (II Chr 36:22,23; Ezr 1:1-4). About 50,000 exiles availed themselves of this lenient policy. With high purpose they determined to resettle in the land and restore the Temple. In the second month of 536 B.C. they laid the foundation (Ezr 3:11-13). Early in the work the Samaritans, denied any participation in the rebuilding, opposed the project (Ezr 4:5). For almost fourteen years the work ceased. When Darius Hystaspis came to the Persian throne in 521 B.C., Haggai and Zechariah, assuming that the decrees of the former rulers were inoperative, aroused their countrymen to take up the task again. Zerubbabel and Joshua, the governor and high priest respectively, led in the rebuilding. An inquiry by Tatnai, Persian governor for the territory west of the Euphrates, halted the work again, but Darius confirmed the original decree of Cyrus. Unfortunately, by this time a change had come about in the attitude of the Jewish people. They judged that hindrances in the reconstruction indicated that God was not in the work. Haggai and Zechariah sought to awaken the nation from its indifference. The people responded, and the building was completed in 516 B.C., the sixth year of Darius' reign. The chronological data in this prophecy fall within the period of the work on the Temple. Although Zechariah begins with the theme of the restoration of the sanctuary, he touches upon many phases of the spiritual life of the nation, and he treats with remarkable fullness the prophetic events leading up to Messiah's return and reign.

OUTLINE

I. Introduction: The call to repent. 1:1-6.
II. The night visions of Zechariah. 1:7–6:15.
   A. Vision of the horses and riders. 1:7-17.
   B. Vision of the horns and artisans. 1:18-21.
   C. Vision of the surveyor. 2:1-13.
   D. Vision of Joshua the high priest. 3:1-10.
   E. Vision of the golden lampstand. 4:1-14.
   F. Vision of the flying roll. 5:1-4.
   G. Vision of the woman in the ephah. 5:5-11.
   H. Vision of the chariots. 6:1-8.
   I. The crowning of Joshua. 6:9-15.
III. Questions concerning fasting. 7:1–8:23.
   A. The question. 7:1-3.
   B. The lesson from history. 7:4-14.
   C. God's purpose of blessing for Israel. 8:1-23.
IV. The future of the nations, Israel, and Messiah's kingdom. 9:1–14:21.
   A. The first burden. 9:1–11:17.

1. The victories of Alexander the Great. 9:1-8.
2. Messiah's reign of peace. 9:9,10.
3. The victories of the Maccabees. 9:11-17.
4. Blessings through Messiah's reign. 10:1-12.
5. The rejection of the Good Shepherd. 11:1-17.

B. The second burden. 12:1–14:21.
1. The world powers against Jerusalem. 12:1-14.
2. The land and people purified. 13:1-6.
3. The smitten Shepherd and the remnant. 13:7-9.
4. Messiah's visible return to earth. 14:1-5.
5. Messiah's holy kingdom. 14:6-21.

COMMENTARY

I. Introduction: The Call To Repent. 1:1-6.

1. In the second year of Darius. The dating of a prophecy according to the reign of a Gentile monarch evidences that the times of the Gentiles, begun in Nebuchadnezzar's day, were in progress (cf. Lk 21:24).

2. The Lord hath been sore displeased. In emphatic language the prophet declares God's displeasure with the fathers of his countrymen. It was more than their neglect of the building of the Temple that distressed Him; it was their general spiritual outlook. Return from exile alone was not enough to please the Lord; they needed a heart return to the Lord. **3. I will turn unto you.** Their repentance would find God ready and willing to receive and bless.

4. Be ye not as your fathers. Bad example is so infectious that Zechariah had to warn his co-religionists not to imitate the ways of their predecessors. The latter had failed to heed the authentic messages of the prophets of God, and consequently they had reaped a harvest of misery and woe in the Babylonian captivity. **5. Your fathers, where are they?** Fathers and prophets alike were now gone. Man is as grass that withers, but there is an abiding force in the universe (Isa 40:6-8).

6. Did they not take hold of your fathers? Man is mortal, but God's words and statutes are undying. Though the former generation was gone, subsequent events revealed the truth of the message of God in the judgments that befell Israel for disobedience. **So hath he dealt with us.** God fulfilled every prediction to the letter. Zechariah's contemporaries must learn the lessons of history, and decide to obey God implicitly.

II. The Night Visions of Zechariah. 1:7–6:15.

A. Vision of the Horses and Riders. 1:7-17.

7. Upon the four and twentieth day of the eleventh month. All eight night visions were granted the prophet in one night, three months after the first message. They form a unit which finds its key in the first vision.

8. A man riding upon a red horse. In verses 11,12 the man on the red horse is said to be the "angel of the Lord." The Angel of the Lord throughout the OT is designated as God (see Gen 16:7-13; Ex 3:2-6; Jud 13:9-18,22; and others). The Babylonian Talmud interprets: "This man is no other than the Holy One, blessed be He; for it is said, 'The Lord is a man of war.' " **Red horses, speckled, and white.** It has been suggested that the colors of the horses represent the distinctive missions of the horses with their riders. According to usage, red signifies war, in this instance judgment on Israel's foes (cf. Rev 6:4). The fact that the Angel of the Lord is riding on this horse, reveals what the purpose of God was for that hour. Sorrel is a mixture of the other colors. White indicates victory (cf. Rev 6:2). The myrtles represent Israel.

9. The angel that talked with me. This angel is the mediating or interpreting angel, commissioned to explain the visions to the prophet (cf. Rev 1:1; 22:16). He does not introduce the visions, but he clarifies their significance to Zechariah.

10. The Lord hath sent to walk to and fro through the earth. The horses, which symbolize divine activity among the nations of the earth, were sent on a mission of reconnoitering. God is always interested in the affairs of earth, especially as they touch the fortunes of his earthly people, Israel. **11. All the earth sitteth still.** The report of the riders was an unusual one; they brought word that the earth was in a state of peace. Actually, the early years of Darius' reign had been stormy, marked by repeated rebellions throughout his domain; but in this year all was calm again. But God had foretold that the nations would be shaken (Hag 2:21,22). Why the disparity, and how was it to be explained?

12. How long wilt thou not have mercy. The contrast between the tranquil nations and the downtrodden people of God was painful; so the Angel of the Lord interceded for them. He prayed that mercy might be extended to them after their long period of chastisement under the disciplinary hand of God. **These threescore and ten years.** The period has been variously reckoned. One calculation sets the terminal dates as 606 B.C. (cf. II Kgs 24:1) and 538 B.C., the year of Cyrus' decree to rebuild (cf. Jer 25:11; 29:10). In this case seventy years would be obtained either by counting both terminal years, an ancient practice, or by considering seventy to be a round number. Here the seventy years seems to refer to the period from 586 to 516, when the Temple ("my house," v. 16) lay in ruins.

13. Good words and comfortable words. In accordance with their need God answered them with words that foretold good and bore comfort. The remainder of the first vision shows what the consoling words were. The comfort consisted of the Lord's assurance of (1) his continued jealousy for Israel; (2) his great displeasure with the nations; (3) his return to Jerusalem with mercy; (4) the rebuilding of the Temple; (5) the restoration of the ruined city; (6) the prosperity of the cities in the land; (7) the comfort of Zion; and (8) the choice of Jerusalem.

14. I am jealous for Jerusalem. It was comfort indeed for Israel to know that God was still actively concerned and zealous for her welfare. **15. I am very sore displeased with the heathen.** This is the reverse of the concept of God's jealous love for Israel. By the very nature of the case he must be unalterably opposed to all who seek the hurt of his people. **At ease.** The fact that the nations were then enjoying peace did not signify that God's blessing was upon them. **They helped forward the affliction.** It is true that God had commissioned the nations to chastise Israel, but they undertook and carried out the assignment for themselves and not for him. Their evil purpose dominated their actions. They had no thought for God's glory; thus they were carelessly and unfeelingly at ease as well.

16. I am returned to Jerusalem with mercies. Now God's purposes concerning Israel related to their restoration, blessing, and enlargement. **My house shall be built in it.** The mark of God's returned favor to Jerusalem was the rebuilding of the Temple. The Temple was already being built, but it was not finished until the sixth year of Darius (Ezr 6:15). **A line shall be stretched forth.** Before a city was devoted to destruction, a line was stretched over it, as though to limit and define the area of desolation (cf. II Kgs 21:13). Now a line was to be stretched over the city of Jerusalem preparatory to building (cf. Job 38:5). A complete reversal of conditions is indicated thereby.

17. Shall yet be spread abroad. The cities of Judah were to realize a remarkable prosperity. Josephus, the Jewish historian of the first century A.D., claimed that the population of the land had increased greatly by the time of the Maccabees (second century B.C.). **The Lord shall yet comfort Zion.** God's strong consolations for his people would disclose to their understanding hearts the immutability of his choice of them as his own. No one will deny that these predictions were fulfilled in those days of the sixth century B.C., but the larger scope of Scripture shows that they will have their fullest realization in Messianic days.

B. Vision of the Horns and Artisans. 1:18-21.

18. Behold four horns. In the Hebrew canon the second vision begins the second chapter of the book. The English versions follow the LXX and the Vulgate. Neither arrangement affects the sense of the passage. In the Bible the horn is a well-recognized figure for power; horned animals manifest their strength through their horns (cf. Mic 4:13; Dan 8:3,4). Interpreters differ as to the significance of the four horns. It has been suggested that they represent: the four quarters of the earth; the foes of Israel on every side; specific enemies on the fringes of the Promised Land; all the adversaries that Israel encounters until the reign of the Messiah. Taking the broad testimony of Scripture, especially in view of the figures in Daniel and Revelation, a large number of expositors refer the horns to the four world powers of Daniel 2; 7; 8—namely, Babylon, Persia, Greece, and Rome. This is probably the view that is best substantiated. It is not to be denied that in Zechariah's day the third and fourth kingdoms had not yet come into existence, but prophecy is known to gather up in one broad panorama the component elements of the prophetic plan. Compare Isa 61:1-3; Dan 9:24-27; Zech 9:9,10.

20. Four carpenters. The word in the original is employed for any skilled workman, whether in wood, metal, or stone.

21. These are come to fray them. The artisans came purposely to frighten and strike terror into the hearts of the nations that had dealt mercilessly with Israel, leaving them in a prostrate and crushed condition. For every enemy of Israel God has a corresponding instrument of judgment to carry out his punishment upon them.

C. Vision of the Surveyor. 2:1-13.

1. A man with a measuring line. From the analogy of the other visions this is probably an angel in human form. He is not the Angel of the Lord, for he is designated more precisely than that one usually is, and with fuller mention (cf. Ezk 40:3; Rev 11:1,2). **2. Whither goest thou?** The prophet's question gains for him the knowledge that the man with the measuring line intended to measure the city of Jerusalem to determine its exact dimensions. This does not mean that the city of Jerusalem was completely restored at that time. It was being surveyed with a view to completion of that task.

3. Another angel went out to meet him. In order that Zechariah may give the intended message to his contemporaries, the interpreting angel goes to receive the message from another angel delegated for that purpose.

4. As towns without walls. The young prophet is informed that Jerusalem will be so enlarged that it will spread beyond its bounds. Because of the multiplication of men and cattle in her, she will be inhabited as villages without walls. Jerusalem was to experience a population explosion unparalleled in her history. For dwelling safely without walls, see I Sam 6:18; Est 9:19; Ezk 38;39. This population increase did not follow the return from exile; it is related to the distant day indicated in the next verse.

5. A wall of fire. Tangible walls would be lacking in Jerusalem, but the Lord himself would be as an impenetrable wall of fire for her protection. **The glory in the midst of her.** But protection is only part of Israel's need. The return of the Shekinah glory is here promised. The spiritual need of the nation will be met with the return of that glory which Ezekiel saw depart from the city. This prophecy awaits fulfillment in the Millennial day (Ezk 11:23; cf. Hab 2:14).

6. Flee from the land of the north. Some of the exiled Jews, because of the infirmities of age and for other reasons, had chosen to remain in Babylon. The Lord now urgently exhorted them to flee the doomed city. Calamity was again to fall upon that wicked city after her futile attempt to revolt in the reign of Darius. **As the four winds of the heaven.** They were scattered not to all quarters of the globe, but with great intensity, as though by means of the four winds.

8. After the glory hath he sent me. The glory can hardly refer to the time of glory in verse 5, for in that case more particulars would have been given, as in other references to this time of blessing. Furthermore, God will visit judgment on Israel's enemies after he comes to dwell in Jerusalem, not prior to that era. The verse means, rather, that God will send the Messiah for the vindication of his glory by dealing with the nations who have oppressed Israel. **The apple of his eye.** The pupil of the eye is most tender, easily injured, irreplaceable, and carefully protected. So is Israel in God's sight. **9. I will shake mine hand upon them.** With this threatening gesture (cf. Isa 11:15) God will reverse the condition of Israel, so that their masters will become their servants.

10. Lo, I come, and I will dwell in the midst of thee. Zion's joy will be complete in the return of her Messiah in his visible appearing (cf. 9:9; Mal 3:1). **11. Many nations shall be joined to the Lord.** In the hour of his power and glory Messiah will draw many nations to himself. **I will dwell in the midst of thee.** For the third time in this chapter the prophet declares that Messiah will dwell in the midst of his people (cf. 8:20-23). **12. The Lord shall inherit Judah.** The fact that many nations will be blessed in Christ the Lord will not detract from Israel's glory. Israel will continue to be the heritage of the Lord, and the Holy City will still be the place of his abode.

13. He is raised up out of his holy habitation. When the Lord is silent in human affairs, it is as though he were asleep. In his intervention, he is likened to a man awaking to action, or a lion roused from his lair.

D. Vision of Joshua the High Priest. 3:1-10.

1. Joshua the high priest standing before the angel of the Lord. The previous visions have stressed blessing for Israel. But these promises are contingent upon obedience and the cleansing of the nation. The fourth vision reveals that the priestly office of Israel must be reinstated in the favor of God. A polluted priesthood had brought woe upon Israel; it needed purging (cf. Ezk 22:26). Zechariah saw Joshua the high priest, in his official and representative capacity, standing before the Angel of the Lord in the performance of his priestly ministry. Suddenly he found himself the object of the accusations of Satan. If he were cast off, the nation also would be rejected; if he were cleared, the nation would be accepted. **Satan standing at his right hand.** Satan appeared in order to lodge his condemnation (cf. Ps 109:31).

2. The Lord that hath chosen Jerusalem. Messiah called down the rebuke of the Father on Satan, not because Israel was righteous, not because Satan had exaggerated his claims, not because the nation had already suffered in the fire of exile, but because God had made an eternal and immutable choice of Israel out of love for her (cf. Rom 9:16; 11:5). **A brand plucked out of the fire.** The figure is used of Israel, because, although she had been under God's hand of chastening, he still had future purposes of blessing for the world through her.

3. Joshua was clothed with filthy garments. The priesthood was besmirched with the filth of sin. How incongruous, then, that a priest should attempt to stand before the holy Angel of the Lord. **4. Take away the filthy garments.** Joshua was powerless to remedy the condition; he could do nothing to cleanse himself. The removal of the polluted garments symbolizes forgiveness, acceptance, and reinstatement in the priestly office. **5. Let them set a fair mitre upon his head.** This command of the Angel of the Lord involves the complete cleansing and clothing of the priesthood (cf. Ex 28:36-38).

7. Walk in my ways. The basic requirement for God's servants is to exercise care in the matter of personal piety. **Keep my charge.** This relates to the faithful performance of official duties. **Judge my house.** The priests were called upon to pronounce on clean and unclean (Lev 10:10). **Keep my courts.** The courts of the Lord needed to be guarded against defilement. **Places to walk among these that stand by.** The greatest blessing of all would be the granting of access (lit., *walks* or *paths*) among the angels of heaven. Immediate communion with the Lord is indicated.

8. They are men wondered at. Literally, *they are men who are a sign,* typical men, who point to another. **My servant the Branch.** It is clear that the antitype is the Messiah of Israel. Both Servant and Branch are designations in the OT for the Messiah. See Isa 42:1; 52:13; Ezk 34:23,24; Isa 4:2; Jer 23:5. The humanity and humility of the Messiah are emphasized.

9. The stone. This is a third name of Messiah (cf. Ps 118:22; Mt 21:42; I Pet 2:6). **The graving thereof.** The allusion is to all the graces, beauties, and gifts of the Messiah, fitting him for his great work. **I will remove the iniquity of that land in one day.** Here is the climax of the vision and the purpose of the symbol. Israel's iniquity is to be removed once for all through the work of the Messiah. As Joshua and his companions were cleansed, and the nation with them, so Messiah will accomplish all this for his people in the future.

10. Under the vine and under the fig tree. Repeatedly in the OT, when Israel is in proper spiritual relationship with the Lord, material prosperity is granted her (cf. Mic 4:4 with I Kgs 4:25).

E. Vision of the Golden Lampstand. 4:1-14.

1. The angel that talked with me came again. Just as the vision of chapter 3 was meant for the encouragement of Joshua, so the vision of this chapter is intended for the strengthening of Zerubbabel. The civil leader had been thwarted again and again in his efforts to build the Temple.

2. A candlestick all of gold. The prophet was familiar with the lampstand in the Tabernacle of Moses (cf. Ex 25:31-40) and with that in Solomon's Temple, but this golden candelabrum differed from those in four details – the bowl, pipes, olive trees, and golden spouts. There were seven lamps to the lampstand, and seven conduits to each lamp, suggesting an abundant and unstinting supply of oil.

6. Not by might, nor by power, but by my spirit, saith the Lord of hosts. The revelation from God to Zerubbabel was that all his work for God depended not on human strength, power, or prowess, but upon God's Spirit for fruition. By this passage it is known that oil in Scripture is a symbol of the Holy Spirit.

7. Before Zerubbabel thou shalt become a plain. Any mountainous obstacle in Zerubbabel's way would become as nothing before the power of God's Spirit. **The headstone.** The civil leader would see the completion of the structure he had begun. **Grace, grace unto it.** The people of God would call down God's grace and favor upon the completed sanctuary. **9. His hands shall also finish it.** In order that Zerubbabel might have strong and unmistakable consolation for the task, the promise of verse 7 is reiterated.

10. The day of small things. From Ezr 3:12,13 and Haggai 2:3 it is known that in Israel many made unfavorable comparisons between the glorious Temple of Solomon and the structure then being built. The time of their rebuilding is here designated as the day of small things. **The eyes of the Lord.** The eyes of men may have looked with disdain upon the work at hand, but the eyes of the Lord viewed with favor the building activity of Zerubbabel. Furthermore, God's providential care, which takes in the whole earth, was committed to the finishing of the Temple (cf. II Chr 16:9).

14. These are the two anointed ones. The two olive trees at either side of the lampstand represent the anointed ones (lit., *sons of oil*), who were the channels through whom the grace of God was then mediated to his people. The individuals under consideration were Joshua and Zerubbabel, the religious and civil agents of God. Ultimately, the one through whom all religious or spiritual and civil or governmental blessings are conveyed is the Lord Jesus Christ.

F. Vision of the Flying Roll. 5:1-4.

1. A flying roll. A roll or scroll is employed in Scripture for a pronouncement of judgment (cf. Ezk 2:9,10; Rev 5:1 and 10:2 in context). Before Israel becomes the light of the world (chapter 4), she must be judged individually and nationally for sin. **2. The length thereof.** The scroll must have been unrolled in order for its dimensions and contents to be seen. The fact that it was flying indicates that its disclosures were soon to be visited on the wicked.

3. The curse that goeth forth over the face of the whole earth. The Mosaic covenant carried with it a curse upon the transgressor (Deut 27:15-26; 28:15-68). This curse hovered over and threatened the land of the people of Israel, to whom the Law was given (cf. Ex 20:1,2). **Stealeth.** Stealing was a violation of the middle commandment of the second table of the law; swearing falsely by God's name transgressed the middle commandment of the first table. Men who violated these commandments were false to God and man. These two commandments are used representatively for the entire law of Moses.

4. And shall consume it. The curse will not go astray; it will find the guilty and extirpate him, root and branch.

G. Vision of the Woman in the Ephah. 5:5-11.

6. An ephah. The **ephah** was the largest measure in use among the Jews. It is employed here to symbolize the appearance of the wicked in the land; as grains are brought together in a measure, so the ungodly of the land will be gathered together for final disposition. **7. There was lifted up a talent of lead.** This was done in order to permit the prophet to see the contents of the ephah. **This is a woman.** A woman is compared to wickedness in Prov 2:16; 5:3,4. The feminine is used in Hebrew to convey abstract ideas. In the NT, wickedness is headed up in the "man of sin" (II Thess 2:3). **8. He cast the weight of lead.** Evidently this was done to hinder the escape of the woman from the place of her confinement. **9. There came out two women.** They are part of the imagery; two are indicated because of the burden to be carried between them. **11. In the land of Shinar.** The reference is to Babylonia (cf. Gen 10:10,11; 11:2; Isa 11:11). This was the area where men had first united in a widespread rebellion against God. Throughout the Scriptures it represents confusion in spiritual matters, idolatry, moral uncleanness (cf. Rev 17:3-5). In Babylon culminates all that defies God and his righteousness on earth. Godlessness of every sort, including that of Israel, will find its place there.

H. Vision of the Chariots. 6:1-8.

1. There came four chariots. The chariot vision completes the series seen by Zechariah in one night. It concludes in thought what was set forth in the first vision. The chariots evidently put into operation the judgment decrees of the Lord. Since chariots were employed in warfare, the purpose of these in the vision is clear. The number four does not refer to the four world powers of Daniel, for the four geographical notations in this passage do not conform to the monarchies of Daniel 2 and 7. Rather, they stand for God's agents by which he is to pour out judgment on Israel's adversaries. **Between two mountains.** The original employs the definite article, *the two mountains;* that is, Mount Moriah and the Mount of Olives. The chariots ran through the Valley of Jehoshaphat.

2. Red horses. They represent war. **Black horses.** Calamity is probably indicated. **3. White horses.** Victory and joy are symbolized by this color. **Grisled and bay horses.** Possibly plagues and pestilence are indicated by these colors. **5. Which go forth from standing before the Lord.** Each agency went forth to accomplish God's will in regard to its particular objective.

8. Quieted my spirit in the north country. God's wrath was quieted in the **north country,** or Babylonia. (Though not actually north of Israel, Babylonia was reached by traveling in a northerly direction.) It is true that the remnant had been delivered from the rule of Babylon by God's judgment on that country through Cyrus. But though Babylon had been subdued by Cyrus, it revolted in the fifth year of Darius, who summarily devastated and depopulated the country.

I. The Crowning of Joshua. 6:9-15.

10. Of Heldai, of Tobijah, and of Jedaiah. As a sort of postscript to the night visions, the prophet concludes with a symbolic act. Three men had come as a deputation from Babylon to the home of Josiah the son of Zephaniah with a gift from the exiles for the building of the Temple under construction. **The same day.** This is the same day as that of 1:7; that night the prophet was given the series of visions.

11. Crowns. The original indicates *one* splendid crown made up of several circlets, for it was intended for the head of Joshua alone. As in chapter 3 he is typical of Messiah, both in his name and in his office. The Levitical priesthood stipulated no crowning of the high priest. A crown did not pertain to his ministrations or office. A mitre belonged to the priestly office, a crown to the kingly office.

12. Whose name is The Branch. The picture of the Messiah in 6:12,13 has been acclaimed as the most inclusive in the OT. The idea in **Branch** is one of humility and lowliness. **Out of his place.** He will originate, as to his humanity, from his native land; he will not be of foreign extraction. **The temple of the Lord.** This is not the restoration Temple of that hour, for Zerubbabel was promised he would complete it (cf. ch. 4). It is the Millennial Temple of Ezekiel 40 to 48.

13. He shall be a priest upon his throne. In true Melchizedek fashion (cf. Heb 5:10) he shall be a Priest-King (cf. Ps 110:4). The concepts of permanence, security, and a finished atonement are all here. **Counsel of peace shall be between them both.** In one person will be united the priestly and kingly dignities; these two functions will be blended in the Person of the Messiah.

14. For a memorial. The crown was to be kept as a memorial of the godly concern of the deputation (and of those whom they represented) for the things of God.

15. They that are far off. Zechariah now sees the deputation that came from Babylon as representative of the Gentiles who will come in the reign of Messiah to build the Temple of the Lord (cf. Isa 60:10,11).

III. Questions Concerning Fasting. 7:1–8:23.

A. The Question. 7:1-3.

1. In the fourth year. The fourth year of Darius' reign was 518 B.C. The people had labored diligently on the Temple, and the work had made much progress. New homes were built in Jerusalem, and the old scars of destruction were being erased. **2. They had sent unto the house of God.** The city of Bethel had sent a delegation to Jerusalem for two purposes: to entreat God's blessing, and to ask about certain national fasts. **3. Fifth month.**

The question was: With all the marks of new life in the national economy, was it still needful to go on fasting and mourning in the fifth month, as they had done during the days of exile? The fast on the tenth day of the fifth month commemorated the burning of Jerusalem in 586 B.C. (cf. Jer 52:12,13). It is still the greatest fast day of the Jews (except for the Day of Atonement, which has an altogether different purpose in mind). The question would seem to indicate that the fasting was both irksome and burdensome.

B. The Lesson from History. 7:4-14.

5. Did ye at all fast unto me, even to me? With one clear stroke this question tore away all the pretense and hypocrisy in their rites and ceremonies. God had not instituted this fast; neither was it carried out to glorify him. It was done to satisfy the carnal heart and spirit. God was not taken into consideration at all. Then as now God wanted truth in the inward parts. The prophet added the fast of the seventh month in his questioning. Later he adds two other fasts (cf. 8:19). All were connected with the fall of Jerusalem under the Chaldean Nebuchadnezzar. In the tenth month Nebuchadnezzar besieged Jerusalem (II Kgs 25:1); in the fourth month the enemy entered the city (II Kgs 25:3,4; Jer 39:2); in the fifth month the Temple was burned (II Kgs 25:8,9); and in the seventh month Gedaliah, the Jewish governor of Judah, was assassinated (II Kgs 25:23-25). **6. Did ye not eat for yourselves.** In their feasting, as in their fasting, their self-centered outlook was manifest. Whether in the one practice or in the other, they were self-righteous and self-satisfied.

7. Should ye not hear. Why should they trouble themselves about something God had not commanded, when they were so heedless of what he had explicitly charged them again and again through the pre-Exilic prophets? It is far better to offer God obedience than to heap up fasts without number (cf. Isa 58:1-9). The carnal conscience seeks to ease itself by formal ordinances, instead of taking warning from God's visitations regarding departures from his revealed will. Sin was the cause of their fasting. If sin were forsaken, the fasting would no longer be necessary.

9. Execute true judgment. The former prophets had all united in their testimony for practical righteousness in everyday life. God delights in the proper administration of justice. Mercy and compassion between brothers delight the heart of the infinitely merciful Creator. **10. The widow, nor the fatherless, the stranger, nor the poor.** The less fortunate and the unprotected are always the special charge of the Lord; any kindness shown them is especially pleasing to him. **Imagine evil against his brother.** Resentment and hatred in the heart against a neighbor are clearly prohibited. Faith and piety must go hand in hand. Religion without morality is useless and a mockery; morality without true religion or piety is without proper foundation and only temporary at best.

11. But they refused to hearken. Here is a summary of the attitude of Israel through the centuries to the ministry of the prophets as they preached faith, piety, and social justice. **12. Therefore came a great wrath.** When repeated warnings and loving entreaties failed, there remained only the wrath of God for the impenitent. God cannot abdicate as Moral Governor of the universe. His message had been faithfully delivered through the energizing Spirit by the hands, hearts, and mouths of his servants, the prophets (cf. II Chr 36:16).

13. So they cried, and I would not hear. They experienced retribution in kind. When they would not hear God's pleas for obedience, he sovereignly refused to hear their cries of distress, arising only out of the bitterness of their calamities and not out of true contrition. **14. Among all the nations.** Up to that hour they had been scattered primarily to Assyria and Babylonia. If the text is to be permitted to have its full significance and plain sense, it must look on to the world-wide dispersion of the Jews, consequent upon their rejection of their Messiah, the greatest exhibition of their obdurate disobedience to the words of the Lord and his messengers. **No man passed through.** The land that had formerly been a delight was to be forsaken and without inhabitant. Though the enemy accomplished this destruction, Israel is charged with the responsibility therefor, because her sin had been the procuring cause.

C. God's Purpose of Blessing for Israel. 8:1-23.

2. I was jealous for Zion. The line of thought carried on in chapter 7 is pursued further in this passage. Twice God declares his continuing love and concern for Israel (cf. ch. 1). **Great fury.** This love must deal in wrath with those who harass God's people. **3. I am returned unto Zion.** God is so resolved to return to Zion in blessing in the future, that he speaks of it as though done. **A city of truth.** This is the result of the Lord's dwelling in her midst.

4. Old men and old women. The picture is one of peace and security. When Israel is properly related to the Lord in spiritual matters, temporal blessings always follow. **5. Full of boys and girls.** Wars will not intrude to cut short the lives and expectations of youth (cf. Ex 20:12; Deut 33:6,24). Doubtless some of these features were present in Maccabean times, but conditions of that day will not suffice for the full realization of these promises. They await fulfillment in Messiah's reign (cf. Isa 65:20,22).

6. Should it also be marvellous in mine eyes? Though these predictions may appear impossible with man, nothing is too wonderful for the Lord (Gen 18:14; Mt 19:26). **7. From the east country, and from the west country.** Israel must be in the Land of Promise before she can realize God's ultimate purpose for her. Restoration to the land is a basic prerequisite according to the testimony of the prophetic Scriptures. The return will be from all the corners of the earth (cf. Isa 11:11,12; Amos 9:14,15).

9. Let your hands be strong. The words of Haggai and Zechariah were intended to be full of encouragement and hope for the laborers on the Temple.

10. Before these days. Before the people had decided to resume the work of rebuilding, their condition was indeed precarious. Labor was unrewarding, and civil strife accompanied attacks from the enemies without (Hag 1:6, 9-11; 2:16-19). **11. But now.** Their obedience has changed the entire outlook. God has committed himself to bless them and their efforts. **12. To possess all these things.** The blessings of nature will no longer be withheld; they will be granted in full measure.

13. A curse among the heathen. When the Lord's hand was heavy upon them, they were an example among the nations when their name was employed to utter a curse. They were a curse **among** (not *to)* the nations. **Ye shall be a blessing.** Their name will be used in a formula for blessing (cf. Gen 48:20; Mic 5:7; Zeph 3:20). **15. I thought in these days to do well.** If the Lord chastened them for disobedience as he had warned them he would do, will he not all the more bless them in answer to faith? God delights to bless, not to blast.

17. For all these are things that I hate. Again they must be warned how hateful are social and ethical injustices. No substitute for genuine godliness is possible.

19. Cheerful feasts. Zechariah finally comes to the answer to the questions on fasting. God will turn all the fasts into feasts; he will abrogate them in answer to their obedience.

21. Let us go speedily to pray before the Lord. Israel in fellowship with God will be the channel for blessing to all the world (cf. Ps 67; Isa 2:3; 60:3). Nations will thus be drawn to him who would not be drawn otherwise. **23. We have heard that God is with you.** The nations will yearn to know the blessings that Israel will have in their hour of spiritual revival and return.

IV. The Future of the Nations, Israel, and Messiah's Kingdom. 9:1–14:21.

A. The First Burden. 9:1–11:17.

1) The Victories of Alexander the Great. 9:1-8.

The first eight chapters of Zechariah had in view encouragement for the rebuilding of the Temple. The last six chapters deal with events far distant from the prophet's day, and were probably written by him at a much later time. The people of Israel were under Medo-Persian rule (chs. 1 to 8); they were to be under Grecian domination (chs. 9 and 10); Rome was to govern them (ch. 11); and their national history would be consummated in the last days (chs. 12 to 14). The first portion of chapter 9 sketches the conquests of Alexander the Great in the fourth century B.C.

1. The burden of the word of the Lord. A burden is a threatening prediction (cf. Isa 13:1). **Hadrach.** It is the *Hattarika* of the cuneiform inscriptions, a city not far from Hamath on the Orontes. **Damascus.** Alexander conquered a number of Syrian cities, but the chief prize he sought was the important city of Damascus. **Toward the Lord.** Such terror and wonder would the triumphs of Alexander occasion, that the eyes of Israel and men of that day would be turned to the Lord for some supernatural interposition.

2. Hamath. This city, which bordered on Damascus, was also to feel the brunt of the Grecian invasion. **Tyrus, and Zidon.** After Syria, Alexander pressed his campaigns into Phoenicia. What the Assyrians and the Babylonians could not do against Tyre, that is, subjugate it, Alexander accomplished. **4. He will smite her power in the sea.** When the Tyrians fortified themselves on an island, Alexander used the ruins of the old city to build a mole, by means of which he captured the island fortress of Tyre. Then he burned Tyre to the ground and forever destroyed her maritime supremacy.

5. Ashkelon. Four of the cities of the Philistine pentapolis are singled out in this verse and the following (Gath being omitted) as coming under similar judgment. The onward march of Alexander was irresistible. **6. A bastard shall dwell in Ashdod.** The city of Ashdod was to lose its native population during the attack, a mixed people taking their place. It was a policy of Alexander to mingle different conquered nations. **7. I will take away his blood.** The heathen ate their idolatrous sacrifices with the blood (Ezk 33:25). The Mosaic law forbade eating of blood (Lev 17:10,12; cf. Gen 9:4; Acts 15:29). The thought is that the Philistines will be turned from their idolatrous practices and be incorporated into the Jewish commonwealth.

8. I will encamp about mine house. Alexander passed by Jerusalem more than once on his campaigns, and although he scourged the Samaritans, he did the Jews no harm. **No oppressor shall pass through them any more.** By the prophetic law of suggestion Zechariah passes from the deliverance in Alexander's time to speak of Israel's final deliverance from all oppressors.

2) Messiah's Reign of Peace. 9:9,10.

9. Thy King cometh unto thee. Not a ruthless conquerer, but the humble King of Israel now fills the vision and horizon of the prophet (cf. Mt 21:5). **He is just.** Justice is Messiah's first prerequisite for his office of King. It is basic to all world peace (cf. Isa 45:21; Jer 23:5,6; Mal 4:2). **Having salvation.** The just King procures a righteous redemption for his own. Of what use is political peace to a heart out of tune with the living God? **Lowly.** In contradistinction to proud Alexander, the Messiah of Israel comes in great humility, manifested in part by the manner of his travel. Moreover, the ass was the animal of peace (cf. Gen 49:11). Verse 9 was fulfilled to the letter in the first coming of the Lord Jesus Christ.

10. I will cut off the chariot. Zechariah passes over in silence all the centuries between the first and second advents of Messiah to his people and the world. When he returns, he will destroy every instrument of carnal strife. **He shall speak peace.** What disarmament conferences and treaties by the score could never accomplish, he will bring about by an authoritative word to the nations. **To the ends of the earth.** His kingdom of peace will be universal (cf. Ps 72:8). The Bible knows of no limited or contained peace. This passage employs no definite articles in expressing the extent of the King's domain.

3) The Victories of the Maccabees. 9:11-17.

11. Thy prisoners. Another martial scene is presented. But first a word of hope is extended to those still in Babylon, on the basis of the blood covenant made at Sinai. The covenant with Abraham cannot be ruled out, however (cf. Gen 15:9-12, 18-21). For those who return there will be blessing and hope. **12. I will render double.** There will be a large and abundant measure of blessing in place of their former distress.

13. Against thy sons, O Greece. The remainder of the chapter foretells the victories of the Maccabean era (in the second centry B.C.), when, as we now know, the people of Israel were successful in their conflict against Antiochus Epiphanes (cf. Dan 11:32; also Dan 8:9-14).

14. The Lord shall be seen over them. The Lord promises them his personal intervention on their behalf. What historians cannot explain was due to the supernatural work of God. **15. As the corners of the altar.** By a bold and vivid figure Zechariah pictures the vast carnage among the oppressors of Israel.

16. The Lord their God shall save them. Physical victory is only the lesser blessing; spiritual deliverance is assured them. **The stones of a crown.** As a redeemed people they will be the delight of God's heart, as a crown to be worn and gloried in.

17. How great is his goodness. The boundless goodness of God will be manifest in the peaceful prosperity of Messianic times.

4) Blessings Through Messiah's Reign. 10:1-12.

1. Ask ye of the Lord rain. The connection with the previous chapter is a close one. If the blessings of prosperity are to be realized, God must give the increase. This he will do in answer to believing prayer.

2. The idols have spoken vanity. In pre-Exilic times the nation often sought for material benefits from idols, diviners, and false dreamers. **There was no shepherd.** Israel's subsequent condition and scattering were due to such misleading. Instead of material blessing there was an entail of spiritual havoc from following these nonentities. In addition they lost their native kings. **3. I punished the goats.** The sense is that God punished the leaders for their part in leading the nation astray. He showed his desire to care for his people.

4. Out of him came forth the corner. From Judah specifically, just mentioned in verse 3, will come forth King Messiah. The figures used represent the Messiah in his strength, stability, and trustworthiness. Compare Isa 19:13 (ASV); I Pet 2:6; Isa 22:23,24; Ex 15:3; Ps 45:4,5. **Every oppressor.** On the basis of cognate languages alone this must not be made to refer to the Messiah; it rather speaks of the result of his work. Since he is the protector of his people, no oppressor will go forth from their midst. **5. Because the Lord is with them.** Granted that the reference in itself is general, the context places it in Messianic times. Then Israel will consist of invincible warriors for God. The prophets were so full of the Messianic hope that they reverted to it on every possible occasion. True students of history that they were, they saw that every victory was a step in the onward march of God's ultimately victorious purpose.

6. As though I had not cast them off. What grace—to wipe out with one stroke all the dismal past! The Lord knows how to restore the years that the locust has eaten. **7. Their heart shall rejoice in the Lord.** Ephraim, the northern kingdom that had experienced a longer exile than Judah, was to enter into the victory of the Lord also. God promised blessing on a reunited nation (Ezk 37:15-23).

8. I will hiss for them. Jeremiah used the figures of hunting and fishing (Jer 16:16) for the regathering of Israel. Zechariah uses the figure of the beekeeper calling his bees by a whistle. **They shall increase.** As once they multiplied under Egyptian bondage (Ex 1:7), so they will increase again. **9. They shall remember me in far countries.** Here is proof that the prophet is predicting more than the return from Assyria and Babylon, which had already been accomplished in the sixth century B.C.

10. I will bring them again. The lands of Egypt and Assyria, from which God will gather them, stand representatively for all the countries of their dispersion. **11. The deeps of the river shall dry up.** Just as God smote the waters of the Red Sea to enable them to cross dryshod, so he will remove every obstacle to their future restoration.

12. They shall walk up and down in his name. Their entire life and conduct will be controlled by the desire to honor the Lord. Such is the goal of prophecy for the nation Israel.

5) The Rejection of the Good Shepherd. 11:1-17.

The events of this chapter are set in the time of the earthly ministry of the Shepherd of Israel, and his rejection by them, with its consequences in A.D. 70. They speak of the dark hour of Israel's national history.

1. That the fire may devour thy cedars. Zechariah, in dramatic form, portrays the judgment of God as falling on Israel like a mighty conflagration, engulfing, first of all, the mighty cedars of Lebanon in the north. **3. Jordan.** Lebanon, Bashan, and Jordan represent the land in its entire extent. Of course the people will be involved in the destruction of their land; they cannot escape the punishment. Such is the pronouncement of the judgment.

4. Feed the flock of the slaughter. Effect is given first, then the cause. The reason for the judgment is the rejection of Messiah. The prophet representatively takes the place of the coming Shepherd. They are called **the flock of slaughter,** because they had been downtrodden before, and were yet to experience their worst persecutions (cf. Ps 44:22). **5. Whose possessors slay them.** The nations into whose hands they were permitted to fall misused them, were enriched by them, and unfeelingly felt no guilt whatsoever in the matter. **Their own shepherds pity them not.** Israel's own rulers had no more pity on them than their oppressive foreign masters.

6. I will no more pity. The climax of their misery was to come with the decision of God not to pity them. **I will not deliver them.** Whether they should fall by the hand of a neighbor in internecine strife or under the death-dealing stroke of a foreign king, the Lord would not interpose.

7. I will feed the flock. Literally, *So I fed the flock of slaughter*. Zechariah faithfully performed his duty in the role of the coming Messiah, and his ministry was received by the remnant, especially, the poor of the flock. **Two staves.** To carry out his work the shepherd in the East used one staff to ward off wild beasts **(Beauty,** or *Favor)*, and the other to aid the sheep in difficult places, to keep the flock intact **(Bands,** or *Binders)*.

8. Three shepherds. One writer has counted forty different interpretations of these words. There is so little evidence for any one interpretation that dogmatism is ruled out. The reference may be to three classes of leaders in Israel — the prophet, the priest, and the civil magistrate. **Their soul also abhorred me.** There was mutual abhorrence, and they mutually rejected each other.

9. I will not feed you. The Shepherd decided to leave off his ministry to them; his patience had been exhausted. They were to be left to their own fortunes, even to mutual destruction. **10. And cut it asunder.** To symbolize the severance of his relations with them, Messiah broke his first staff. This breaking of his covenant with all the nations **(peoples,** not *people)* made them an easy prey to all their enemies. God's hand of restraint had been removed.

11. The poor of the flock. Only the godly minority realized what events were transpiring before them.

12. Give me my price. The Messiah then sought to reveal the depth of Israel's rejection of him and his ministry; so he asked for their evaluation or appraisal of his labors. But there was no compulsion. He indicated that they could forbear to respond if they wished. **Thirty pieces of silver.** This is one of the most amazing transactions reported in the Bible. They valued him at the price of a gored slave (cf. Ex 21:32). This was far worse than outright rejection (cf. Mt 26:15). They placed Messiah on the level of a worthless slave. **13. Cast it unto the potter.** God commanded Zechariah to show the Divine displeasure with their estimate of his Son. The puny and disgraceful price was to be cast to the potter, whose stock in trade was worth a trifle and could easily be replaced. **In the house of the Lord.** The goodly (with great sarcasm) price was to be cast away in the most solemn and public place of all (cf. Mt 27:3-7).

14. I cut asunder mine other staff. Now the internal bond of the nation was loosed, and the nation was riven by many contending factions. Secular historians amply confirm this prophecy as having been fulfilled at the time of the Judeo-Roman war, which culminated in A.D. 70.

15. The instruments of a foolish shepherd. After the rejection of Christ, the true Shepherd, the people of Israel were scattered throughout the world. When the Lord resumes his dealings with them, it will be in the way set forth here. They rejected the true Shepherd; they must have the rule of the false or foolish shepherd. Morally, this is any one of the many wicked rulers who have plagued Israel through the centuries. The culmination will appear in the counterfeit of Christ who will arise at the end time. (See Dan 11:36-39; II Thess 2:1-12; Rev 13:11-18). **16. I will raise up a shepherd.** By divine permission this wicked one will perpetrate his atrocities on hapless Israel. He will perform no function of a good shepherd, but he will serve *himself* by making merchandise of the flock. **17. His arm.** God's judgment will fall on him with an irremedial blow, specifically on the organ of power and the organ of intelligence (arm and eye).

B. The Second Burden. 12:1–14:21.

1) The World Powers Against Jerusalem. 12:1-14.

1. The burden of the word of the Lord for Israel. The final burden, comprising the last three chapters, is full of vital prophetic truth concerning the consummation of Israel's history. God is presented in the fullness of his power in the realms of heaven, of the earth, and of humanity, so significant are the pronouncements about to be made.

2. I will make Jerusalem a cup of trembling. This siege of Jerusalem by the **peoples** (not *people)* of the earth cannot be the invasion of Nebuchadnezzar nor the siege of Titus (A.D. 70); the prophetic passages compel us to place it before the visible return of Christ to earth. The cup is a familiar symbol of God's wrath. (See Isa 51:17,22; Jer 13:13; 25:15-28; 51:7). The enemies who besiege Judah and Jerusalem will be given a staggering blow that will send them reeling. **3. A burdensome stone.** When the enemies of Israel engage themselves with her, they will do so to their own wounding and crushing.

4. I will smite every horse. Supernatural panic, madness, and blindness will overtake both horses and riders in the attack. Cavalry has always formed a large part of Eastern armies. **6. Like an hearth of fire among the wood.** God will bring about his triumph in a twofold manner: by depriving the enemies of their strength, and by empowering Israel to resist their adversaries. The enemies will be consumed as wood and sheaves are devoured by fire.

7. The Lord also shall save the tents of Judah first. That the deliverance may be acknowledged by all as coming from God, he will rescue the outlying, less heavily defended areas of the land before he delivers the capital city. Neither the royal house nor the inhabitants of the capital city will be able to boast against the least dweller in the less favored sections of the country.

8. Shall be as David. Even the feeble (lit., *tottering* or *stumbling*) one among them will become as irresistible as the unconquered David (cf. II Sam 17:8; 18:3). This is invincible power on earth. **As the angel of the Lord before them.** The descendants of David, as the leaders of the nation, are compared to the preincarnate Christ, the highest level of heavenly power (cf. Josh 5:13).

9. I will seek to destroy all the nations. There is here no intimation of weakness or inability, but rather a speaking after the manner of man.

10. I will pour upon the house of David. When the invading enemy has been destroyed, God will turn to spiritual matters that must be set right in Israel. **The spirit of grace and of supplications.** Ultimately, the reference is to the Holy Spirit. God will pour out on the nation, high and low alike, the spirit of conviction which will compel them to prayer (cf. Ezk 39:29; Joel 2:28,29). **They shall look upon me whom they have pierced.** But will that coming generation pierce the Messiah? By refusing to believe in him they will have aligned themselves with their forefathers who did so in historic times (cf. Jn 19:37). **They shall mourn for him.** This is Israel's future national Day of Atonement. When the One who is greater than Joseph makes himself known to his brethren, they will be heartbroken with grief and contrition. **For his only son.** The most intense private sorrow is indicated in the death of the only son or that of the firstborn. This verse teaches plainly that in the future day Israel will see the pierced Messiah return from heaven. It will be the same Messiah they rejected long ago, bearing the selfsame wounds they inflicted then.

11. The mourning of Hadadrimmon. The historical reference is to the slaying by Pharaoh Necho of Egypt of the godly Judean king Josiah, a calamity of great public significance which occurred at Megiddo (II Kgs 23:29,30; II Chr 35:22-27). **12. Every family apart.** All strata of society will be bowed down with the universal grief, whether king, prophet, priest, or laity. **And their wives apart.** So great will be the sorrow that even wives will not join their husbands in the lamentation; each will face his sorrow alone. The sorrow will transcend the closest earthly ties.

2) The Land and People Purified. 13:1-6.

1. There shall be a fountain opened. This chapter follows in thought immediately upon the events of the previous portion. The fount of Calvary, opened potentially so many centuries ago, will do its work in the nation, removing sin and uncleanness (cf. Rom 11:26,27; Isa 65:19; Ezk 36:25). The nation will be morally cleansed.

2. I will cut off the names of the idols. Idolatry will be so thoroughly uprooted from the nation, when they are purged from sin, that even the memory of the idols will be lost. **The unclean spirit.** This is the spirit of uncleanness behind all idolatry and demon worship—namely, Satan. He stands in contrast to the spirit of grace and supplications, the Holy Spirit (cf. Mt 12:43-45; Rev 13:11-18).

3. Thou shalt not live. False prophecy which accompanied idolatry will not easily be removed from the nation. But should one lay claim to the office of prophet, even his parents will put him to death in their zeal for God. **4. The prophets shall be ashamed.** False prophets formerly boasted of their supposedly exalted position; in the day of Israel's purification no prophet will pride himself on his office.

5. I am no prophet. Should a false prophet be seized upon and interrogated, he will disavow any relationship to prophecy. He will rather claim to belong to the lowly farmer class. **6. These wounds in thine hands?** But the questioner of the false prophet will not easily be put off. On the chest of the false prophet he will see certain tell-tale marks (cf. I Kgs 18:28) which lead to the conclusion that the man is a false prophet. **In the house of my friends.** The prophet will claim that the marks are from chastisements received from parents or relatives in his youth. By no valid interpretation can this passage be referred to Christ. Christ was never a farmer, nor did he claim to be. He could never have asserted that he was no prophet. Under what conditions could he have been so interrogated after he had gone to the cross and received his blessed wounds for our sins?

3) The Smitten Shepherd and the Remnant. 13:7-9.

7. Awake, O sword, against my shepherd. God is addressing the sword to smite his Shepherd, who can be no other than the Lord Jesus Christ (cf. Mt 26:31). Christ's death is seen here as the act of the Father. The sword represents the highest judicial power (cf. Rom 13:4) and may be used symbolically for any means of taking life. As in chapter 11, the Messiah is here seen under the figure of a shepherd. **My fellow.** God speaks of his Shepherd as his Fellow, his Equal. When the word is used in Leviticus (6:2; 18:20; 25:14,15,17; and others), it is equal to *brother*. There is no stronger statement in the OT regarding the unimpeachable deity of Israel's Messiah, the Son of God. **Smite the shepherd.** This was the experience of the cross. It entailed the scattering of the people of Israel, who had brought about the Roman smiting by their rejection of their King. **Upon the little ones.** With tender care he will gather the remnant to him.

8. Two parts therein shall be cut off. Even though the awful deed of Calvary was perpetrated many years ago, nevertheless when God resumes his dealings with Israel in judgment, he will need to cut off two-thirds of the people, the unbelieving, in order to purify the remainder for his glory. **9. It is my people.** Once those of the remnant are purified, they will acknowledge God as their own, and he will recognize them as his people.

4) Messiah's Visible Return to Earth. 14:1-5.

1. The day of the Lord cometh. The prophet reverts to the theme of the world confederacy against Jerusalem already treated in chapter 12. The time is that which precedes Messiah's return to earth. The day is peculiarly the Lord's, because in it he will finally vindicate his justice. **Thy spoil shall be divided in the midst of thee.** Jerusalem is seen as having already experienced the sorrow of defeat. Her enemies in leisurely manner divide the spoil in the midst of the city.

2. I will gather all nations. The result of the invasion was given in verse 1; now the occasion is presented. The Lord sovereignly draws the nations – infected through the centuries with the virus of hatred for Israel, and desirous of dealing them a final death-blow – to the city of the coming King. **The city shall be taken.** It is the familiar picture of a city that has been defeated, its property confiscated, its womanhood violated, and its population demoralized and scattered.

3. Then shall the Lord go forth. When the outlook appears the darkest, the Lord, the "man of war" (cf. Ex 15:3) will come forth to champion their forlorn cause. **4. His feet shall stand in that day upon the mount of Olives.** Words cannot express more plainly the personal, visible, bodily, literal return of the Lord Jesus Christ in power. **The mount of Olives shall cleave in the midst.** East of Jerusalem, this mountain affords a formidable barrier to one seeking escape from the city. The bewildered people will have this way of escape supernaturally formed for them. **5. The Lord my God shall come, and all the saints with thee.** It will be the glorious appearing of the Son of God, the Lord God himself, with his saints and the holy angels. The prophet is so overpowered by the vision that he changes to direct address.

5) Messiah's Holy Kingdom. 14:6-21.

7. At evening time it shall be light. The day of Christ's return will be unusual from the angle of the phenomena of nature. The day will be darkened; and the evening, when darkness should settle down, will see light, the light of the effulgent presence of Christ.

8. Living waters. The land will suffer

no drought, but will have abundant waters to fertilize the entire land. The provision will be ample in both summer and winter.

9. The Lord shall be king over all the earth. Messiah will reign from Zion, but all the earth will rejoice in his benevolent and beneficent rule. **His name one.** His manifested glory will be adored throughout the universe (cf. Isa 54:5; Dan 2:44; Rev 11:15).

10. All the land. The entire Land of Promise will be renovated (cf. the implication of Mt 19:28) for the kingdom of the Lord. **11. No more utter destruction.** Sin, strife, and warfare will be gone.

12. This shall be the plague. This verse is related in thought to verse 3. The Lord will accomplish his victory over the invading forces by smiting them with a supernatural, flesh-consuming plague. **13. A great tumult from the Lord.** Confusion and civil strife will complete the work of devastation. **14. The wealth of all the heathen.** The enemy losses will be counted in lives, wealth, and apparel. **15. The plague.** Sadly enough, the plague that will fall upon man will encompass the lower creation as well.

16. To keep the feast of tabernacles. The nations that survive the war will worship the Lord, especially celebrating the Feast of Tabernacles, the feast of ingathering, joy, and rest. It typifies splendidly the tabernacling of God at that time among his own in Israel and among the Gentiles. **17. Upon them shall be no rain.** Any nation that will not send its delegation to represent it will suffer the loss of rain needed for a good harvest. **18. Egypt.** Though Egypt would appear to be independent of the need of rain, she will suffer also in case of disobedience. The plague will be visited upon her people.

20. Holiness unto the Lord. These words were on the tiara of the high priest of Israel. They will be placed upon the bells of the horses, signifying that that which was used for war and personal purposes will be completely dedicated to the Lord. **21. Yea, every pot in Jerusalem.** Sin brought the distinction between sacred and profane; with sin removed in Messiah's reign, there will be no need for such differentiations. One object will be as sacred as another. **No more the Canaanite.** This is another way of stating that holiness will pervade all. Canaanite (the Phoenician) was a name that implied ungodly practices (cf. Hos 12:7), for these merchants and mariners of the ancient world were unscrupulous. Now all will be holy.

BIBLIOGRAPHY

BARON, DAVID. *The Visions and Prophecies of Zechariah*. London: Hebrew Christian Testimony to Israel, reprinted 1951.

COLLINS, G. N. M. "Zechariah," *The New Bible Commentary*. Edited by F. Davidson, A. M. Stibbs, and E. F. Kevan. London: Inter-Varsity Fellowship, 1953.

DODS, MARCUS. *The Visions of a Prophet*. New York: Hodder and Stoughton, n.d.

ELLICOTT, CHARLES J. (ed.). *Commentary on the Whole Bible*. Vol. V. Grand Rapids: Zondervan Publishing House, reprinted 1954.

FAUSSET, A. R. *A Commentary Critical, Experimental and Practical on the Old and New Testaments*. Edited by R. Jamieson, A. R. Fausset, and D. Brown. Vol. IV. Grand Rapids: Wm. B. Eerdmans Publishing Co., reprinted 1948.

FEINBERG, CHARLES L. *Israel's Comfort and Glory*. New York: American Board of Missions to the Jews, Inc., 1952.

———. *God Remembers: Studies in Zechariah*. Wheaton: Van Kampen Press, 1950.

MEYER, F. B. *The Prophet of Hope: Studies in Zechariah*. New York: Fleming H. Revell Company, 1900.

MALACHI

INTRODUCTION

Author and Title. "Malachi" (1:1) may be an abbreviation of *Malachiah,* a Hebrew personal name meaning, "the messenger of Jehovah." God honored the faith of the parents who thus named their child by making him the last of the prophetic vessels of the Old Dispensation. Tradition tells us that Malachi was a member of the "Great Synagogue" and that he was a Levite born in Supha in Zebulun, but no certain knowledge of the prophet has been preserved.

Date and Historical Background. The conditions set forth in Malachi presuppose the rebuilding of the Temple after the Babylonian captivity, the knowledge of the Law communicated by Ezra (Ezr 7:10,14,25,26), and a later departure from the Mosaic ordinances. Also, there is close affinity between the lax religious conditions of Malachi's day and those with which Nehemiah had to contend when in 433 he returned from Persia to take up his duties as governor in Jerusalem. These evils included: (1) the priests' disregard for the sanctity of the Temple and its ceremonies (Neh 13:1-9); (2) laxity of the people in bringing tithes and offerings (Neh 13:10-13); and (3) the intermarriage of the covenant people with the heathen (Neh 13:23-28). Malachi was concerned about these same evils (1:6–2:9; 3:8-12; 2:10-16). His book was therefore likely written during the third quarter of the fifth century B.C.

Message. What Malachi has to say is based again and again upon the sovereignty of God. God is a father (1:6), a master (1:6), a great king (1:14). He is a heavenly governor (1:7,8). He gives covenants and commandments (2:4,5,10; 4:4). Because he is a sin-hating God, and his people are careless and indifferent and sinful—having defiled the Temple, failed in their worship responsibilities, and joined themselves in marriage to their uncircumcised neighbors – he must mete out judgment (2:2,3,12; 3:1-5; 4:1). But because he is a God of infinite grace, he will exercise loving-kindness if only his people will hear his voice and turn from their wicked ways (3:7,10-12). The dread Day of the Lord shall come (3:2; 4:1,5), but the righteous need not fear, for God cares for his own (3:16,17; 4:2,3). The prophet ever pleads, directly or indirectly, with a people who are rebels against their covenant Head. In loving tones of invitation he urges them to return to the God whom they have forsaken—lest they be destroyed in the day of judgment.

OUTLINE

I. Heading. 1:1.
II. Questions for which God has good answers. 1:2–4:3.
  A. "Wherein hast thou loved us?" 1:2-5.
  B. "Wherein have we despised thy name?" 1:6–2:9.
  C. "Wherefore?" 2:10-16.
  D. "Wherein have we wearied him?" 2:17–3:6.
  E. "Wherein shall we return?" 3:7-12.
  F. "What have we spoken so much against thee?" 3:13–4:3.
III. Conclusion. 4:4-6.
  A. Exhortation to keep the Mosaic law. 4:4.
  B. Promise of "Elijah's" coming. 4:5,6.

COMMENTARY

I. Heading. 1:1.

Most OT prophetic books have headings which identify the author and indicate that what follows is divine revelation. Malachi is no exception to the general rule.

1. **Burden** means "a weighty message"

or "a judicial sentence." Cf. Nah 1:1; Hab 1:1; Zech 9:1. **By Malachi.** See Introduction.

II. Questions for Which God Has Good Answers. 1:2—4:3.

A. "Wherein Hast Thou Loved Us?" 1:2-5. The questions around which the book of Malachi is built are those the prophet puts upon the lips of the apostate Israelites of his day. They may or may not have been voiced, but certainly they were to be found in the people's hearts. The very first question betrays a lack of true piety, an absence of trust. Only hearts of stone could be oblivious to the countless manifestations of God's love for his covenant people. But speaking of the God of their fathers, the Israelites say, in effect, "We have seen no evidence of your love."

2. I have loved you. See Deut 7:8; Jer 31:3; Hos 11:1. **Esau.** A name sometimes used for Jacob's brother and other times for the Edomites. **Jacob's brother.** Esau was the first-born of twins (Gen 25:23-26). **Yet I loved Jacob.** In the exercise of his sovereign good pleasure (Rom 9:10-18), God chose to bestow the covenant promise and blessings upon one who was not the first-born. God's love had been translated into action constantly throughout Israel's history. **3. I hated Esau.** Romans 9:10ff. suggests that the "hating" consisted of God's perpetuating the line of the Chosen People through Jacob rather than through Esau, and giving Esau a position subordinate to that of his brother (cf. Gen 27:37-40). On the other hand, both Esau and his descendants led profane, sinful lives (Gen 26:34; 27:41; Ob 10-14). A holy God cannot but be set against sin and unrepentant sinners. **Laid his mountains and his heritage waste.** The fury of the Chaldean forces, responsible for the destruction of Jerusalem in 586 B.C., may also have been felt by Edom (cf. Jer 25:9, 21); and later the Nabatean Arabs drove the Edomites permanently from their land. **Dragons.** Rather, *jackals.* Esau's heritage became a desert place, the home of jackals.

4. We will return and build. Edom was confident that she could fight against God and return to her former state of prosperity. **But I will throw down.** In judgment, God would send the Nabateans or whatever other power was in the prophet's mind. **The border of wickedness.** Those who witnessed Edom's plight would conclude that God had brought her low because of her wickedness. **Against whom the Lord hath indignation for ever.** From the blows of the conqueror, Edom would never recover. **5. Your eyes shall see.** The indication may be that Malachi's contemporaries would witness the conquest. **The Lord will be magnified.** When the people of Israel should behold Edom in perpetual ruins but Jerusalem rebuilt and restored, they would have to recognize God's love rather than voice their present question, "Wherein hast thou loved us?" **From the border.** Rather, *over the border.*

B. "Wherein Have We Despised Thy Name?" 1:6—2:9. The focus of attention is now a corrupt priesthood. The priests of Malachi's day followed in the train of Nadab and Abihu (Lev 10:1) and the sons of Eli (I Sam 2:12-17). They were administrators of the Mosaic ritual of sacrifice, but their hearts were far from God. Like the people at large, they were apostates. In fact, their disregard for the law of God and their failure to honor him were the very influences that undermined true faith and righteous conduct on the part of Israel.

6. Father . . . master. Honor is due unto the sovereign God. It is as though God said, "If you show respect to earthly fathers and masters, should you not the more honor your heavenly Father (Ex 4:22; Isa 43:6; Jer 3:4; Hos 11:1) and him who is Lord of all?" (cf. Ezr 5:11). **Where is mine honour . . . my fear?** The priests conducted themselves as though God did not exist. **O priests, that despise my name.** The priests not only failed to honor the Lord, but they despised him. **Wherein have we despised . . . ?** The priests were hypocrites, feigning piety but going through the altar ritual without heed either to the letter or to the spirit of the Law!

7. Bread. The Hebrew word ordinarily means "food" but here signifies the flesh of animal sacrifices. **Polluted thee?** Offering polluted sacrifices to the Lord is said to be equivalent to polluting God himself. **The table.** The altar of burnt offering (see Ex 27; 38; Ezk 41:22). **Contemptible.** The priests were irreverent, having only contempt for things sacred. **8. The blind . . . the lame and sick.** Such sacrifices were explicitly forbidden (Lev 22:20-25; Deut 15:21). **Thy governor.** Imperfect gifts presented to an earthly governor would be offensive; it would be a much greater insult to offer blemished gifts to the Governor of the universe. **Will he . . . accept thy person?** The implied answer is, "No."

9. Beseech God. This is irony. God will not hear the prayers of those who dishonor him. **Unto us.** All alike suffer when their representatives offend God. **This hath been by your means.** Though the innocent suffered, the guilt was that of the priests. **10. Who is there . . . ?** A better rendering makes this a plea for someone to close the Temple. *No* worship would be better than contemptible worship. **I have no pleasure in you.** Compare the question in verse 9. **An offering.** The word here refers to sacrifices in general.

11. For. God did not want the worthless sacrifices being offered by the Jewish priests, *because* his majestic greatness, which rendered these sacrifices unacceptable, would indeed bring forth true thanksgiving and praise and adoration, without which all the forms of worship were vain. **From the rising of the sun even unto the going down.** That is, everywhere. **My name shall be great.** This prophecy would be fulfilled only when Christ would be received into Gentile hearts the world around. **Incense . . . and a pure offering.** The thought is not that the Gentiles would carry out the Mosaic ritual of sacrifice, but that in the New Dispensation spiritual worship would be rendered unto Jehovah by the nations (cf. Ps 141:2; Rom 12:1; Heb 13:15).

12. The fruit thereof. The sacrificial offering (cf. v. 7).

13. What a weariness. The priests found their tasks burdensome and distasteful. **Ye have snuffed at it.** They had treated the sacrificial system with contempt. **Torn.** Translate as *torn away,* the idea being that the animal had been torn away from the clutches of a wild beast and so presumably maimed. **Should I accept?** A rhetorical question. Jehovah will not accept such offerings.

14. Cursed be the deceiver. Not only the priest but also the layman bringing the illegitimate sacrifice was guilty. **A male.** Lev 22:18,19 indicates that a male was to be used for a votive offering. **A corrupt thing.** Literally, *a corrupt female.* The point may be that one making the vow intended originally to offer an unblemished male but actually presented a blemished female. The main point is clear, namely that an inferior offering had been substituted for the one required by the law of Moses. **A great King.** The deception was an affront to the sovereignty of God.

2:1. This commandment. Commandment, here, is to be understood in the sense of a threat of punishment (cf. Nah 1:14). **2. If.** God's judgment would be conditioned upon the priests' repentance. **A curse.** God would turn aside the blessings that had been enjoyed by the priests. See also the exposition of 3:9. **Have cursed.** The heavy hand of God had already begun to fall.

3. Corrupt your seed. Translate instead, *Restrain your arm.* God would "tie the hands" of those officiating at the altar, and there would be no fruit from their labors. **The dung of your solemn feasts.** God would not only refuse to accept the multitude of sacrifices at festival time but would accord the priests the most ignominious treatment. **Feasts** is a metonymy for the sacrifices offered on such occasions. **Spread dung upon your faces** is a metaphor for the contempt with which Jehovah would treat the erring priests. **Shall take you away with it.** God's appointed end for sinful priests is likened to the place of discard that received the "dung" of the sacrifices. Only condemnation could await such priests.

4. This commandment. See 2:1. **That my covenant might be with Levi.** God wanted the priests to come to their senses, mend their ways, and make possible the continuation of the covenant with Levi, i.e., the Levitical priesthood. **5. My covenant was with him.** Cf. Num 25:12, 13; Deut 33:8-11. **Life and peace . . . fear.** Through the covenant, Jehovah pledged himself to bestow upon the priests life and peace; in turn, the priests were obligated to serve him with reverence.

6. The law of truth. A primary function of the priest was to instruct according to the moral law, which was based upon truth. **Iniquity was not found.** There had been priests who had faithfully presented the righteous revelation of God. **He walked with me** (cf. Gen 5:22,24; 6:9). The priests of old both spoke God's truth and lived it. **Turn many away from iniquity.** Both by words and by conduct, the priest who walked with God turned many to righteousness (cf. Dan 12:3). **7. Should seek the law at his mouth.** Priests were appointed by God in part to set forth a knowledge of God and his will. **The messenger of the Lord.** In a number of OT passages, the expression apparently refers to a messenger who himself is very God (see Ex 3:2,4; Jud 6:12-14). No higher honor could have been given the priest than that similar words should be applied to him. **8. Have caused many to stumble.** Instead of turning many to righteousness (cf. v. 6), the priests' influence had been just the opposite. **At the law.** Corrupted both by the words of the priests and by their example, the Law could only lead men astray. **Have corrupted the covenant.** By their acts, the priests had nullified the covenant. **9. I . . . made you contemptible.** The priests did not have the respect of a people whose sins they made their own. **Have been partial in the law** (cf. Mic 3:11). In their judicial capacity, the priests had shown respect of persons.

C. "Wherefore?" 2:10-16. More fully stated, the question might read: "Wherefore have we dealt treacherously every man against his brother?" As the priests had destroyed God's covenant with Levi, the people had violated the Lord's more general covenants with their fathers by intermarrying with the heathen and putting away their own wives that they might enter into the new marriages.

10. One father. God was their "father" in that in love he had chosen Israel to be his children. **Hath not one God created us?** God was their father also by virtue of his creative activity. **Deal treacherously.** See the following verses. **Against his brother.** If God is father, his children are brothers and sisters and have a family obligation the one to the other. **The covenant of our fathers** (cf. Ex 19:5, 6; 24:8). God's covenant with Israel prohibited either expressly or by implication the sins about to be mentioned (Ex 34:10-16; Deut 7:1-4).

11. Abomination. The Jews needed to be shocked into the realization that God's anathema was as much upon the transgression about to be specified as upon such gross sins as idolatry and witchcraft. **Profaned the holiness of the Lord.** What was profaned was not the divine attribute of holiness but those who were holy because of their relation to a holy God (see Jer 2:3). **The daughter of a strange god.** The specific sin, now mentioned, is the marriage of an Israelite to a person dedicated to the worship of a heathen god (cf. Ex 34:16; Deut 7:3, 4; Ezr 9:1,2; Neh 13:26,27). **12. The Lord will cut off.** God's punishment would take the form of depriving the sinner of posterity. The proverbial allusion which follows indicates that everyone was included. **And him that offereth an offering.** God would also inflict a like punishment upon anyone who might be moved to offer a sacrifice to expiate the sins of the transgressor.

13. Again. The expression indicates that a second moral offense is included in the "dealt treacherously" of verse 11. **Covering the altar . . . with weeping, and with crying out.** The added transgression was that the Israelites had divorced their own wives so that they would be free to marry heathen women, but this is not indicated until 2:14-16. Here the Israelites are represented as distressed because God's displeasure with their conduct had been made known and their sacrifices were no longer acceptable to him. **14. Ye say, Wherefore? One act** of treacherous dealing had been spelled out. There was another. If they refused to recognize it and questioned what it was, the answer would be enunciated clearly. **Witness between thee and the wife of thy youth.** Since contracts, marriage or other, were consummated with God as witness (see Gen 31:49; Prov 2:17), he deemed guilty the Israelites who had taken to themselves Jewish wives but who now had put them away. **Yet is she thy companion.** Affectionate ties should have persisted as a result of long sharing of common experiences. **The wife of thy covenant.** Marriage is a covenant relationship before God (cf. Prov 2:17).

15. And did not he make one? He refers to "Lord" (v. 14). The topic being treated is the validity of God-prescribed monogamy. Jesus, treating the same subject, taught that God in creation indissolubly joined together man and woman as "one flesh" (Mk 10:2-9). Similarly, Malachi may be saying, "And did not God in creation make one pair to live together as one despite the fact that his control of the spirit of life could have been apportioned otherwise? And why did he make man and woman to be one flesh? It was to the end that his purposes for a godly seed, a covenant people of pure religion, might be realized." Divorce could only defeat God's creative purpose. **Let none deal treacherously.** The call to repentance is obvious. **16. He hateth putting away.** That is, God abhors divorce. The OT nowhere countenances divorce, although it does prescribe what shall be done under given circumstances in which divorce takes place (Deut 24:1-4; see also Mt 19:7, 8). **Covereth violence.** Translate instead, *and violence covers his garment.* The very garment of the guilty Israelite was, in God's sight, stained by his heinous sin (cf. Zech 3:3,4).

D. "Wherein Have We Wearied Him?" 2:17–3:6. The Israelite attitude was reprehensible in God's sight; for the people had become practical atheists, assuming that, if there were a God, he would long since have intervened to exercise judgment against evil and evil-doers. God, however, warned that judgment, though it had tarried, would indeed come.

17. Wherein have we wearied him? Though their religion was but an empty form, Malachi's contemporaries protested against having their piety questioned. **Every one that doeth evil.** The reference is to profane Jews as well as to the heathen. **Is good in the sight of the Lord.** The argument: Since many enjoy material prosperity, although consistently violating moral law, if there be a God, he apparently holds them in favor. **Where is the God of judgment?** The very existence of an omnipotent, righteous God was called in question. The insinuation was that if God existed, he would have acted.

3:1. My messenger. John the Baptist (Isa 40:3; cf. Mk 1:2,3). **Shall prepare the way.** John inveighed against moral decadence and hollow religious formality, thus preparing the way for Christ's emphasis upon regeneration and spiritual worship. He also heralded Christ's coming. **The Lord . . . shall suddenly come.** This is the answer to the question, "Where is the God of judgment?" "God" (2:17), **Lord,** and **the messenger of the covenant** all refer to one and the same divine person. Since the forerunner of this person was John the Baptist, the divine person was none other than Jesus Christ. **To his temple.** In the New Dispensation God's sanctuary, once the Garden of Eden, later the Tabernacle, and after that the Temple, was to be the Church (I Cor 3:16,17; Eph 2:21; I Pet 2:5). **Whom ye seek.** They had professedly been looking for God to show himself. **The messenger of the covenant.** This divine Messenger, the Coming One, represented God's covenant with Israel whereby, in contrast to his judgment upon the nations, he could be expected to bless his chosen people. **Whom ye delight in.** Israel supposedly longed for the appearance of the God of judgment.

2. But who may abide the day of his coming? Covenant-breaking Jews, as well as the heathen, would find the Day of the Lord a day of terrible judgment (Zeph 1:17,18). **Like a refiner's fire.** All that was unworthy would be consumed. **Fullers' soap.** A second metaphor symbolizes the same awful truth. Lye or potash was used in the washing of clothes. **3. Sit as a refiner.** The coming Lord is now represented as the Smelter, who would execute the refining process. **Purify the sons of Levi.** The priesthood itself would be the first object of the Refiner's activities. **Purge,** i.e., "to strain." That which was of value would survive the filtering process. **That they may offer . . . in righteousness.** In the refining process, some priests would come forth with pure hearts, so that their worship would be acceptable before the Lord; others would be sifted out to be cast away.

4. The offering of Judah and Jerusalem. The terminology of sacrifice is not to be understood as teaching that the Mosaic ritual was to be continued after the Lord came. Rather, this terminology is a convenient vehicle for the prophets to use in describing worship under the New Dispensation. When the religious leaders were transformed, true religion would return among the people.

5. I will come. See the exposition of 3:1. **Near to you to judgment.** The refining process would include not only the priests but the people also. **Swift.** Though the Lord might delay his coming, when he came he would come suddenly, unexpectedly. **Fear not me.** The basic sin of those who asked, "Where is the God of judgment?" was their contempt for the God of their fathers. **6. I . . . the Lord, I change not.** The *am* of the AV is best omitted. **Lord,** i.e., "Jehovah," has within itself the concept of unchangeableness, but God's immutability is also spelled out in the **I change not.** It is because a righteous God never alters his attitude toward sin that judgment, however long delayed, will surely be carried out. **Therefore ye sons of Jacob are not consumed.** The unchangeableness of God is also the guarantee of the grace of God. The refining fires will not completely destroy his people.

E. "Wherein Shall We Return?" 3:7-12. This question elicited from God the charge that the Israelites had robbed him in failing to keep the laws of the tithe and the heave offering (*tᵉrûmâ*). But God was gracious. Through the prophet he urged them to rectify the situation and promised copious blessing if they did so.

7. Gone away from mine ordinances. The broken ordinances specifically meant were the stewardship requirements pertaining to the tithe and the so-called heave offering. **I will return.** If the people would repent, they would be restored to his favor. **Wherein shall we return?** They did not concede that they had gone astray.

8. Ye have robbed me. Faulty stewardship was equivalent to defrauding or theft. **Tithes.** For the specific obligation, see Lev 27:30-33; Num 18:20-32; Deut 14:22-29. **Offerings.** The word for "offering," *tᵉrûmâ*, is used for freewill gifts, for gifts of the first fruits, for the half-shekel sanctuary tax, and for portions of sacrifices that were reserved for the priests (Ex 30:13; Lev 7:14; Num 15:19-21; 18:26-29). **9. A curse.** Literally, *the curse*. The punishment mentioned in 2:2 would be visited upon the guilty nation as a whole. **10. All the tithes.** Better, *the whole tithe*. Apparently the Israelites had made a pretense of conforming to the Law, presenting some tithes before God but not all those the Law required (cf. Acts 5:1,2). **Into the storehouse.** Tithes were to be brought and stored in special rooms of the Temple. **Meat,** i.e., "food." The tithe provided sustenance for the Levites (Num 18:24). **The windows of heaven.** The figure (cf. II Kgs 7:2,19) has reference to the pouring out of material blessing in superabundance (cf. Lk 6:38). **Pour you out a blessing.** If the Jews doubted that Jehovah rewards the righteous (cf. Mal 2:17), they were to put the matter to the test.

11. Rebuke the devourer. The sovereign God would bring about the superabundant harvest in part by destroying the locusts and other pests that might damage the crops. **Cast her fruit before the time**. God would also protect the vines from mildew and from blasting. **12. All nations shall call you blessed.** Time would prove that God was God and that he would bless his people with material substance (contrast 2:17).

F. "What Have We Spoken So Much Against Thee?" 3:13–4:3. Essentially a recapitulation of 2:17–3:6, this section has a somewhat different emphasis. Here it is made evident that not all the covenant people had lifted their voices against God to charge him with injustice. The righteous, God-fearing people would find in the Day of the Lord deliverance, victory, and rich blessing.

13. Spoken so much. Was there any point in continuing the forms of the ceremonial law? The concensus of opinion was dangerously close to the conclusion that Jehovah worship might as well be discontinued. Yet the Israelites once more feigned piety and asked, "What have we spoken . . . against thee?" **14. It is vain to serve God.** The serving of Jehovah was put on a dollars-and-cents basis: If material prosperity did not result, one might as well not worship God. **Walked mournfully.** The expression should be understood of going through the outward forms associated with repentance without experiencing true repentance within. **15. We call the proud happy**. The passage probably refers to gross sinners in general, whether Jews or Gentiles, who had prospered materially. **Set up.** Better, *built up*. **Yea, they that tempt.** Translate: *Yea, they have tempted God and have been delivered* (cf. 2:17; Ps 95:9).

16. Then. A godless society with its anti-God conversation drives believers together for mutual encouragement and unified witness. **They that feared.** There were still true believers in Israel. **Often.** The word is not in the original. **A book of remembrance.** In heaven record is made of those who reverence the Lord. For the figure, see Est 2:23; 6:1-3; Ex 32:32; Ps 56:8; 69:28; Lk 10:20; Rev 20:12; 21:27.

17. Mine. The first part of the sentence should read, *And they will be mine, a valued possession* (cf. Ex 19:5). **In that day.** The Day of the Lord (cf. 3:1,2). One might translate: "on the day when I act." The day will come when God will act, when justice will be meted out. **I will spare them.** The Day of the Lord will be a dread day (Zeph 1:15-18), but the righteous have the comforting assurance that he whose day it is will deliver them that are his (cf. Ps 91:7). **18. Return.** Translate as "again," and read: "And you will discern again." History had borne abundant witness to the fact that "whatsoever a man soweth, that shall he also reap" (Gal 6:7); it would continue to do so. Only blind eyes or stubborn obstinacy can account for the thesis that God makes no distinction between the righteous and the wicked in apportioning blessings.

4:1. The day cometh. The Day of the Lord. Ignore the AV chapter division. **Oven.** A fire pot employed for baking. Fire as a symbol of judgment is common in Scripture (e.g., Zeph 3:8). **Stubble . . . root nor branch.** The figure changes. **Stubble** suggests that which will be consumed in a moment of time; the former figure emphasizes the thought that none of the wicked will escape the Judgment.

2. Sun of righteousness. The sun is a symbol of righteousness. In the Day of the Lord the night of wickedness will give way to an administration of affairs in which righteousness, like a sun sending its beams to crowd out every pocket of darkness, will bring reward to the godly, and the wicked will no longer flourish. **With healing in his wings.** Wing-like, the rays of the rising sun suggest the basic figure. As the penetrating rays dispel the darkness, sin and its attendant ills will vanish away. **Grow up as calves.** The word employed probably means "to gambol." As a loosed calf exults in his new-found freedom, so the righteous, no longer downtrodden prisoners in a hostile world, will have their day and experience a like exhilaration. **3. Tread down the wicked.** The picture is one of great rejoicing as perfect justice prevails, with the wicked utterly destroyed and the righteous enjoying the uninterrupted blessings of their covenant God. **The day that I shall do this** (cf. 3:17).

III. Conclusion. 4:4-6.

A. Exhortation To Keep the Mosaic Law. 4:4. Malachi's indictment of the people of Israel was that they had gone away from God's ordinances (3:7). However, they could yet avert the dread judgment of the Day of the Lord if, repentant and converted, they would keep the Law in letter and in spirit.

4. Remember ye the law of Moses. The exhortation is for sinners and saints alike. **In Horeb.** Sinai. **With the statutes and judgments.** Translate, *even statutes and judgments.*

B. Promise of "Elijah's" Coming. 4:5,6. God would send a prophet, spoken of as "Elijah," who would cultivate the moral and spiritual soil to prepare for Christ's coming, and so turn aside the necessity for immediate judgment.

5. Elijah the prophet. The thought is parallel to that of 3:1. Prior to the Day of the Lord a heaven-sent messenger would prepare the way. The parallelism alone warrants the identification of **Elijah** as John the Baptist. However, the Gospels also make it clear that the coming "prophet" was not to be Elijah the Tishbite but one of like spirit and power (Mt 11:14; 17:13; Mk 9:11-13; Lk 1:17).

6. He shall turn the heart of the fathers. John the Baptist was to do this (Lk 1:16,17). Through him, men were to be brought to a unity of faith—to repentance and conversion, and to glad obedience to God's law. The oneness of heart to be wrought by John through the Spirit was to be a cultivated soil which, with the coming of Christ, would produce fruit an hundred fold. **Lest I come and smite the earth with a curse.** The words are related both to the exhortation to keep the law of Moses and to the ministry of John the Baptist. When the Lord should come in judgment, the habitation of a covenant-breaking people would inevitably come under the judgment of destruction. A prophetic ministry in spirit and in power could produce a revival and thus turn aside the fullness of judgment so that hearts everywhere might receive the King; and the final judgment of the Day of Wrath might be postponed until the Lord of the Temple should have filled up the roll of his elect. This indeed happened. "Elijah" *did* come and *did* make ready a people prepared for the Lord, and the Lord Jesus *did* come to his temple. So, although the OT closes with a conditional curse, the NT ends with the unconditional promise of Christ to his own, "Surely I come quickly," together with the answer of those who are his "peculiar treasure": "Even so, come, Lord Jesus."

BIBLIOGRAPHY

Calvin, John. *Commentaries on the Twelve Minor Prophets.* Vol. V. Grand Rapids: Wm. B. Eerdmans Publishing Co., 1950.

Cowles, Henry. *The Minor Prophets.* New York: D. Appleton and Company, 1867.

Dentan, Robert C. "Malachi," *The Interpreter's Bible.* Vol. 6. New York: Abingdon Press, 1956.

HENDERSON, E. *The Twelve Minor Prophets*. Andover: Warren F. Draper, 1863.

KEIL, CARL FRIEDRICH. *The Twelve Minor Prophets*. Vol. II. Translated by James Martin. Edinburgh: T. & T. Clark, 1900.

PACKARD, JOSEPH. *"Malachi," Commentary on the Holy Scriptures*. Edited by John Peter Lange. Grand Rapids: Zondervan Publishing House, n.d.

PEROWNE, T. T. *Malachi (The Cambridge Bible for Schools and Colleges)*. Edited by J. J. S. Perowne. Cambridge: The University Press, 1893.

PUSEY, E. B. *The Minor Prophets*. Vol. II. New York: Funk and Wagnalls Co., 1885.

ROBINSON, GEORGE. *The Twelve Minor Prophets*. New York: George H. Doran Co., 1926.

SMITH, JOHN MERLIN POWIS. *The Book of Malachi (The International Critical Commentary)*. New York: Charles Scribner's Sons, 1912.

FROM MALACHI TO MATTHEW

I. Political Developments

The term, "silent years," frequently employed to describe the period between the Old Testament and the New Testament writings, is a misnomer. Although no inspired prophet arose in Israel during these centuries, and the Old Testament was regarded as complete, events took place which gave to later Judaism its distinctive ideology and providentially prepared the way for the coming of Christ and the proclamation of his Gospel.

Persian Supremacy

For about a century after Nehemiah's time, the Persian Empire exercised control over Judea. The period was relatively uneventful, for the Jews were permitted to observe their religious institutions without molestation. Judea was ruled by high priests, who were responsible to the Persian government, a fact which both insured the Jews a large measure of autonomy and degraded the priesthood into a political office. Jealousy, intrigue, and even murder played their part in the contests for the distinction of being high priest. Johanan, son of Joiada (Neh 12:22), is reported to have slain his brother Joshua in the Temple itself.

Johanan was succeeded as high priest by his son Jaddua, whose brother Manasseh, according to Josephus, married the daughter of Sanballat, governor of Samaria, and established a sanctuary on Mount Gerizim which was to occupy in the affection of the Samaritans a place comparable to the love of the Jews for the Jerusalem Temple (cf. Jn 4:20). Although this sanctuary was destroyed during the reign of John Hyrcanus (134–104 B.C.), Mount Gerizim continued to be regarded as the Samaritan holy mount, as it is today. The details in Josephus' account are not historical, but the establishment of a rival temple about this time is known to have taken place.

Persia and Egypt were engaged in constant struggles during this period, and Judea, situated between the two nations, could not escape involvement. During the reign of Artaxerxes III (Ochus) many Jews were implicated in a revolt against Persia. They were deported to Babylonia and the shores of the Caspian.

During the fifth century B.C. a Jewish colony was located on Elephantine Island, at the first cataract of the Nile River, near modern Aswan. Contrary to the Mosaic law, these colonists built a temple for themselves and worshiped other divine beings (e.g., *Eshem-bethel; Herem-bethel; Anath-bethel)* along with the God of Israel. These deities may actually have been identified with the one God of the orthodox Judaism of the time, but their very existence shows tendencies toward syncretism. Since the Elephantine colonists had dealings with the Samaritans as well as with the Judeans, they do not stand in the main stream of Israel's religious life.

Alexander the Great

Following the defeat of Persian armies in Asia Minor (333 B.C.), Alexander marched into Syria and Palestine. After stubborn resistance, Tyre was taken, and Alexander moved southward toward Egypt. Legend states that as Alexander neared Jerusalem, he was met by Jaddua, the Jewish high priest, who told him of Daniel's prophecies that the Greek army would be victorious (Dan 8). The story is not taken seriously by historians, but it is true that Alexander dealt kindly with the Jews. He permitted them to observe their laws; he granted them exemption from tribute during Sabbatical years; and when he built Alexandria in Egypt (331 B.C.), he encouraged the Jews to settle there and gave them privileges comparable to those of his Greek subjects.

Judea Under the Ptolemies

After the death of Alexander (323 B.C.), Judea was first subject for a time to Antigonus, one of Alexander's generals who controlled part of Asia Minor. It subsequently fell to another general, Ptolemy I (by now master of Egypt), surnamed Soter, or *Deliverer,* who seized Jerusalem on a Sabbath day in 320 B.C. Ptolemy dealt kindly with the Jews. Many of them settled in Alexandria, which continued as an important center of Jewish thinking for many centuries. Under Ptolemy II (Philadelphus), the Jews of Alexandria translated their Law, i.e., the Pentateuch, into Greek. This translation was subsequently known as the Septuagint, from the legend that its seventy (more correctly 72—six from each of the twelve tribes) translators were supernaturally inspired to produce an infallible translation.

The Jews in Palestine enjoyed a period of prosperity in the days of Simon the Just, the ruling high priest, whose character is described in the apocryphal book of Ecclesiasticus (50:1-21). He is reputed to have repaired the walls and fortified the city of Jerusalem and to have built a spacious reservoir to provide water for the city.

Judea Under the Seleucids

After about a century, during which time the Jews were subjected to the Ptolemies, Antiochus III (the Great) of Syria wrested Syria and Palestine from Egyptian control (198 B.C.). The Syrian rulers are known as Seleucids because of the fact that their kingdom, built on the ruins of Alexander's empire, was founded by Seleucus I (Nicator). Most of the earlier rulers bore the names of Seleucus or Antiochus. The seat of government was in Antioch on the Orontes River. During the early years of Syrian rule, the Seleucids allowed the high priest to continue to govern the Jews in accord with their law. Strife broke out, however, between the Hellenistic party and the orthodox Jews. Antiochus IV (Epiphanes) allied himself with the Hellenizing group and appointed to the priesthood a man who had changed his name from Joshua to Jason and who encouraged the worship of the Tyrian Hercules. Jason was displaced in two years, however, by another Hellenist, a rebel named Menahem (Gr., *Menelaus*). When the partisans of Jason contended with those of Menelaus, Antiochus marched on Jerusalem, plundered the Temple, and killed many of the Jews (170 B.C.). Civil and religious liberties were suspended, the daily sacrifices prohibited, and an altar to Jupiter was erected on the old altar of burnt offering. Copies of the Scriptures were burned, and the Jews were forced to eat swine's flesh contrary to their law. A sow was offered on the altar of burnt offering in contempt for the Jewish religious conscience.

The Maccabees

The oppressed Jews were not long in finding a champion. When the emissaries of Antiochus arrived at the small town of Modin, about fifteen miles west of Jerusalem, they expected the aged priest, Mattathias, to set a good example to his people by offering a pagan sacrifice. He not only refused, but he also killed an apostate Jew at the heathen altar, along with the Syrian officer who was presiding at the ceremony. Mattathias fled to the Judean highlands and, with his sons, waged guerrilla warfare on the Syrians. Altnough the aged priest did not live to see his people freed from the Syrian yoke, he commissioned his sons to complete the task. Judas, surnamed "the Maccabee," took the leadership at the death of his father. By 164 B.C. Judas had gained possession of Jerusalem. He purified the Temple and reinstituted the daily offerings. Soon after the victories of Judas, Antiochus died in Persia. However, struggles continued between the Maccabees and the Seleucid rulers for about twenty years. During that time Judas died in battle, and his brother Jonathan assumed command. Ultimately Jonathan was ordained as high priest. When he was murdered (143 B.C.), the last of the sons of Mattathias, Simon, became ruler. Simon was able to gain full independence from Syria, but he, too, was murdered (135 B.C.), by a son-in-law, Ptolemy. The surviving son of Simon, John Hyrcanus, succeeded his father and thereby established a dynasty. Hyrcanus determined to build Judea into a powerful independent state. He conquered Samaria and destroyed the schismatic temple on Mount Gerizim. He also broadened the borders of Judea in the directions of Syria, Phoenicia, Arabia, and Idumaea. During the reign of Hyrcanus, when the pro-Hellenistic Sadducean party gained control, the Jews tended to neglect the orthodox principles of the older Maccabees.

Aristobulus I, the son of Hyrcanus, was the first of the Maccabean rulers to take the title, "King of the Jews." After a short reign he was succeeded by the tyrannical Alexander Jannaeus, who, in turn, left the kingdom to his mother, Alexandra. Alexandra's reign was a relatively quiet one. The Pharisees assumed control, but they persecuted the Sadducees as they themselves had been persecuted in the days of Jannaeus. Alexandra's older son, Hyrcanus II, served as high priest. At Alexandra's death a younger son, Aristobolus (II), dispossessed his brother. Thereupon, the governor of Idumaea, Antipater, espoused the cause of Hyrcanus, and civil war threatened. Consequently Pompey marched into Judea with his Roman legions to settle matters and further the aims of Rome. Aristobolus sought to defend Jerusalem against Pompey, but the Romans took the city and penetrated to the Holy of Holies in the Temple. Pompey did not, however, touch the Temple treasures.

Rome

Mark Anthony supported the cause of Hyrcanus. After the murder of Julius Caesar, and of Antipater (father of Herod), who for twenty years had been virtual ruler of Judea, Antigonus, the second son of Aristobolus, sought the throne. For a time he actually ruled in Jerusalem, but Herod, the son of Antipater, returned from Rome and became king of the Jews with Roman support. His marriage to Mariamne, granddaughter of Hyrcanus, provided a link with the Maccabean rulers.

Herod was both ambitious and cruel. He enlarged and adorned Jerusalem, and began the task of rebuilding the Temple on a grand scale. He rebuilt Samaria and named it Sebaste. Caesarea, on the Mediterranean coast, at the site of the former Strato's Tower, he built as a major seaport and government center.

Herod was one of the cruelest rulers of all time. He murdered the venerable Hyrcanus (31 B.C.), and put to death his own wife Mariamne and their two sons. From his deathbed Herod ordered the execution of Antipater, a son by another wife. In Scripture Herod is known as the king who ordered the death of the innocents of Bethlehem because he feared as a rival One who was born to be King of the Jews.

II. Literature

During the period between the Testaments, much of the literature of the apocrypha was written. The apocryphal books are as follows:

I (or *III) Esdras*. Apocryphal I Esdras (i.e., Ezra) retells the Biblical history from Isaiah to Ezra. It includes the account of a debate in the court of Darius I (Hystaspis) concerning the most powerful force in the world. Zerubbabel is commissioned because of the wisdom he manifests in the discussion.

II (or *IV) Esdras*. Wholly different from I Esdras, II Esdras contains a series of apocalyptic visions assigned to the time of Domitian (A.D. 81–96) by many critics.

Tobit. The story of Tobit describes the life of a pious Jew who remained true to his faith while living in heathen Nineveh. The archangel Raphael guided Tobias, the son of Tobit, who was able to exorcise demons from the girl he subsequently married, and also cure his father's blindness.

Judith. Judith was a beautiful Jewess who, like Jael of old, slew her country's enemy. Judith used her beauty to entice the Chaldean general Holofernes, who had besieged the Jewish city of Bethulia. The story probably dates from Maccabean times.

The Rest of Esther. A supplement to the canonical book of Esther, the apocryphal additions, professedly original documents, include prayers of Esther and Mordecai.

The Wisdom of Solomon. Patterned after the early part of Proverbs, the Wisdom of Solomon contains eloquent praises of wisdom. It stresses the immortality of the righteous and the punishment of the wicked. The origin and folly of idolatry are also presented, along with a resumé of God's care for Israel throughout history.

Ecclesiasticus (The Wisdom of Jesus, Son of Sirach). A fine example of Jewish Wisdom literature. Ecclesiasticus extols the virtues of wisdom and the fear of God. The eulogy of famous men (44-50) is particularly fine. It was written about 180 B.C.

Baruch and the Epistle of Jeremiah. Purportedly written from Babylon in the fifth year after the destruction of Jerusalem, Baruch contains a message from the Jews of the Exile to their compatriots in Judea, including a prayer for them to use in confessing sin and asking mercy of God. The Epistle of Jeremiah warns the exiles against idolatry.

The Song of the Three Holy Children.

The song is placed in the mouths of the Hebrew youths, Shadrach, Meshach, and Abednego, and inserted after Dan 3:23 in the Septuagint.

The History of Susanna. An apocryphal supplement to Daniel, the History of Susanna describes the hypocrisy of two elders. They tried to seduce Susanna, were repulsed by her, and then falsely accused her. She was saved by young Daniel, who pointed out discrepancies in their testimony.

Bel and The Dragon. The story of Bel tells how Daniel demonstrated the fraud of the priests of Bel, who secretly consumed the food left for their idol, thereby deceiving the people. The latter story tells how Daniel killed a dragon that was worshiped as a god in Babylon. Daniel was cast into a den of lions but was miraculously preserved. Habakkuk, brought to the den by an angel, ministered to Daniel.

I Maccabees. The struggles with Hellenism and the period of the Maccabean revolt are described in I Maccabees, a book which gives the history of Judea from the accession of Antiochus Epiphanes (175 B.C.) to the death of Simon (135 B.C.). It is thought to have been written about 105 B.C.

II Maccabees. The second book of Maccabees contains a history of the period between 175 and 160 B.C. parallel to, but independent of, I Maccabees. It is the abridgment of a longer history by one Jason of Cyrene (2:23).

III. Religious Sects

When, following Alexander's conquest, Hellenism challenged the thinking of the Near East, some Jews clung more tenaciously than ever to the faith of their fathers, while others were willing to adapt their thinking to the newer ideas emanating from Greece. Ultimately the clash between Hellenism and Judaism gave rise to a number of Jewish sects.

Pharisees. The Pharisees were the spiritual descendants of the pious Jews who had fought the Hellenizers in the days of the earlier Maccabees. The name *Pharisee,* "separatist," was probably given them by their enemies to indicate that they were nonconformists. It may, however, have been used in scorn because their strictness separated them from their fellow Jews as well as from the heathen. Loyalty to truth sometimes produces pride and even hypocrisy, and it is this perversion of the earlier Pharisaic ideal that is denounced by Jesus. Paul reckoned himself a member of this orthodox group within the Judaism of his day (Phil 3:5).

Sadducees. The Sadducean party, probably named for Zadok, the high priest appointed by Solomon (I Kgs 2:35), denied the authority of tradition and looked with suspicion on all revelation later than the Mosaic law. They denied the doctrine of resurrection, and they did not believe in the existence of angels or spirits (Acts 23:8). They were largely people of wealth and position, and they co-operated gladly with the Hellenism of the day. In New Testament times they controlled the priesthood and the temple ritual. The synagogue, on the other hand, was the stronghold of the Pharisees.

Essenes. Essenism was an ascetic reaction from the externalism of the Pharisees and the worldliness of the Sadducees. The Essenes withdrew from society and lived lives of asceticism and celibacy. They gave attention to the reading and study of Scripture, prayer, and ceremonial cleansings. They held their possessions in common and were known for their industry and piety. Both war and slavery were contrary to their principles.

The monastery at Qumran, near the caves in which the Dead Sea Scrolls were found, is thought by most scholars to have been an Essene center in the Judean wilderness. The scrolls indicate that members of the community had left the corrupt influences of the Judean towns to prepare, in the wilderness, "the way of the Lord." They had faith in the coming Messiah and thought of themselves as the true Israel to whom he would come.

Scribes. The Scribes were not, strictly speaking, a sect but rather members of a profession. They were, in the first instance, copyists of the Law. They came to be regarded as the authorities on the Scriptures, hence exercised a teaching function. Their thoughts were usually akin to those of the Pharisees, with whom they are frequently associated in the New Testament.

Herodians. Herodians believed that the best interests of Judaism lay in cooperation with the Romans. Their name was taken from Herod the Great, who sought to Romanize the Palestine of his day. The policy of the Herodians was political rather than religious, and they were more of a party than a sect.

Roman political oppression, symbolized by Herod, and the religious reactions expressed in the sectarian reactions within pre-Christian Judaism, provided the historical framework into which Jesus came. Frustrations and conflicts prepared Israel for the advent of God's Messiah, who appeared "when the fulness of the time was come" (Gal 4:4).

BIBLIOGRAPHY

BARROW, R. H. *The Romans*. Baltimore: Penguin Books, Inc., 1949.

BENTWICH, NORMAN. *Hellenism*. Philadelphia: The Jewish Publication Society of America, 1919.

BEVAN, E. R. *Jerusalem under the High Priests*. London: Edward Arnold, 1904.

BICKERMAN, ELIAS. *The Maccabees*. Berlin: Schocken, 1947.

BOTTSFORD, G. W., and SIHLER, E. G. *Hellenic Civilization*. New York: Columbia University Press, 1950.

FAIRWEATHER, WILLIAM. *The Background of the Gospels*. Edinburgh: T. & T. Clark, 1908.

FARMER, WILLIAM R. *Maccabees, Zealots, and Josephus*. New York: Columbia University Press, 1956.

GHIRSHMAN, R. *Iran*. Baltimore: Penguin Books, Inc., 1954.

KITTO, H. D. F. *The Greeks*. Baltimore: Penguin Books, Inc., 1956.

LEVISON, N. *The Jewish Background of Christianity*. Edinburgh: T. & T. Clark, 1932.

MARCUS, RALPH. "The Hellenistic Age," *Great Ages and Ideas of the Jewish People*. Edited by Leo W. Schwarz. New York: Random House, 1956.

MOORE, GEORGE F. *Judaism in the First Centuries of the Christian Era*. Cambridge: Harvard University Press, 1927.

OESTERLEY, W. O. E., and Robinson, T. H. *A History of Israel*. London: Oxford University Press, 1932.

OLMSTEAD, A. T. *The History of the Persian Empire*. Chicago: The University of Chicago Press, 1948.

PEROWNE, STEWART. *The Life and Times of Herod the Great*. London: Hodder and Stoughton, 1957.

PFEIFFER, CHARLES F. *Between the Testaments*. Grand Rapids: Baker Book House, 1959.

RIGGS, S. J. *A History of the Jewish People: Maccabean and Roman Periods*. New York: Charles Scribner's Sons, 1908.

SNAITH, NORMAN H. *The Jews from Cyrus to Herod*. New York and Nashville: Abingdon Press, n.d.

TCHERICKOVER, VICTOR. *Hellenistic Civilization and the Jews*. Philadelphia: The Jewish Publication Society of America, 1959.

THE NEW TESTAMENT

THE GOSPEL ACCORDING TO MATTHEW

INTRODUCTION

Author. Abundant early historical testimony ascribes this Gospel to Matthew the publican, also called Levi by Mark and Luke. Modern doubts of Matthaean authorship are the product of hypotheses developed to explain the Synoptic Problem. But these hypotheses cannot alter the testimony of the early church, whose writers quoted this Gospel more frequently than any other. Since Matthew was not particularly prominent among the Twelve, and there was no special tendency to demand apostolic authorship for the Synoptics (e.g., Mk, Lk), no a priori reason exists for ascribing the Gospel to him unless he actually wrote it.

As a former taxgatherer Matthew was well qualified to produce such a Gospel. His business knowledge of shorthand enabled him to record fully the discourses of Jesus. His acquaintance with figures is reflected in his frequent mention of money, his interest in large sums (Mt 18:24; 25:15), and his general interest in statistics (e.g., 1:17).

Composition and Date. The great frequency of citations and allusions to Matthew found in the Didache, Epistle of Barnabas, Ignatius, Justin Martyr, and others attests its early composition and widespread use. The literary connections of this Gospel must be considered in its relations to the other Synoptics, and also to the statement of Papias that "Matthew wrote the words in the Hebrew dialect, and each one interpreted as he could" (Eusebius *Ecclesiastical History* 3.39). Many have explained Papias' statement as referring to an Aramaic original from which our Greek Gospel is a translation. Yet our Greek text does not bear the marks of a translation, and the absence of any trace of an Aramaic original casts grave doubts upon this hypothesis. Goodspeed argues at length that it would be contrary to Greek practice to name a Greek translation after the author of an Aramaic original, for Greeks were concerned only with the one who put a work into Greek. As examples he cites the Gospel of Mark (it was not called the Gospel of Peter) and the Greek Old Testament, which was called the Septuagint (*Seventy*) after its translators, not after its Hebrew authors (E. J. Goodspeed, *Matthew, Apostle and Evangelist,* pp. 105, 106). Thus Papias is understood to mean that Matthew recorded (by shorthand?) the discourses of Jesus in Aramaic, and later drew upon these when he composed his Greek Gospel. Though it is surely possible that Mark was written first, and may have been available to Matthew, there was no slavish use of this shorter Gospel by Matthew, and many have argued for the complete independence of the two books.

The date of Matthew's Gospel must be prior to A.D. 70, for there is no hint in it that Jerusalem was in ruins (all predictions of its destruction being clearly prophetic). Such passages as 27:8 ("unto this day") and 28:15 ("until this day") argue for an interval of some length, but fifteen or twenty years following the Resurrection would be sufficient.

Special Emphases. The testimony of Irenaeus and Origen that Matthew was written for converts from Judaism is corroborated by a study of its content. There is more frequent use of the Old Testament (Robertson's *Harmony of the Gospels* lists 93 quotations in Mt, 49 in Mk, 80 in Lk, and 33 in Jn). Much attention is given to demonstrating that Jesus fulfilled Messianic prophecy and thus was Israel's Messiah, who would establish the promised kingdom. The discourses that Matthew records at length distinguish this Gospel, and emphasize the principles, scope, and movements of the Messianic kingdom (Mt 5–7; 13; 24–25). Thus Jewish Christians (who numbered in the thousands in the early church; Acts 2:41, 47; 4:4; 5:14, 28; 6:1, 7) were given an authoritative explanation that faith in Jesus involved no repudiation of the Old Testament, but was the very goal toward which Old Testament revelation pointed. Of course, these same questions face Gentile converts in proportion to their understanding of the Old Testament. And therefore Matthew's Gospel occupies a place of prominence in Christian thinking which quite justifies its position as the first Gospel in our New Testament.

OUTLINE

I. The birth and childhood of Jesus Christ. 1:1–2:23.
  A. Genealogy of Christ. 1:1-17.
  B. Birth of Christ. 1:18-25.
  C. Visit of the Magi. 2:1-12.
  D. Flight into Egypt and massacre of the infants. 2:13-18.
  E. Residence at Nazareth. 2:19-23.
II. The beginnings of the ministry of Jesus Christ. 3:1–4:11.
  A. The forerunner of Christ. 3:1-12.
  B. Baptism of Christ. 3:12-17.
  C. Temptation of Christ. 4:1-11.
III. The ministry of Jesus Christ. 4:12–25:46.
  A. In Galilee. 4:12–18:35.
    1. Residence established at Capernaum. 4:12-17.
    2. Call of four disciples. 4:18-22.
    3. General survey of the Galilean ministry. 4:23-25.
    4. Sermon on the Mount. 5:1–7:29.
    5. Ten miracles and related events. 8:1–9:38.
    6. Mission of the Twelve. 10:1-42.
    7. Christ's answer to John, and related discourse. 11:1-30.
    8. Opposition from the Pharisees. 12:1-50.
    9. A series of parables on the Kingdom. 13:1-58.
    10. Withdrawal of Jesus following John's beheading. 14:1-36.
    11. Conflict with the Pharisees over tradition. 15:1-20.
    12. Withdrawal to Phoenicia and healing of a Canaanitish woman's daughter. 15:21-28.
    13. Return to the Sea of Galilee and performing of miracles. 15:29-38.
    14. Renewed conflict with the Pharisees and Sadducees. 15:39–16:4.
    15. Withdrawal to the region of Caesarea Philippi. 16:5–17:23.
    16. Instruction of the Twelve at Capernaum. 17:24–18:35.
  B. In Perea. 19:1–20:16.
    1. Teaching on divorce. 19:1-12.
    2. Blessing of the children. 19:13-15.
    3. Interview with the rich young man. 19:16-30.
    4. Parable of the laborers in the vineyard. 20:1-16.
  C. In Judea. 20:17-34.
    1. Another prediction of Christ's death and resurrection. 20:17-19.
    2. Ambitious request of Zebedee's sons. 20:20-28.
    3. Healing of two blind men. 20:29-34.
  D. In Jerusalem. 21:1-25:46.
    1. Triumphal Entry. 21:1-11.
    2. Cleansing of the Temple. 21:12-17.
    3. Cursing of the barren fig tree. 21:18-22.
    4. Questioning of Jesus' authority, and his parabolic answer. 21:23–22:14.
    5. Questioning of Jesus by various groups. 22:15-46.
    6. Jesus' public denunciation of the Pharisees. 23:1-39.
    7. Olivet Discourse. 24:1–25:46.
IV. The Passion of Jesus Christ. 26:1–27:66.
  A. Plot against Jesus. 26:1-16.
  B. The final meal. 26:17-30.
  C. Prediction of Peter's denial. 26:31-35.
  D. Events in Gethsemane. 26:36-56.
  E. Events at the Jewish trials. 26:57–27:2.
  F. Remorse of Judas. 27:3-10.
  G. Events at the Roman trials. 27:11-31.
  H. The Crucifixion. 27:32-56.
  I. Burial. 27:57-66.
V. The resurrection of Jesus Christ. 28:1-20.
  A. Discovery of the empty tomb. 28:1-8.
  B. Appearance of Jesus. 28:9,10.
  C. Report of the soldiers. 28:11-15.
  D. The Great Commission. 28:16-20.

COMMENTARY

I. The Birth and Childhood of Jesus Christ. 1:1–2:23.

A. Genealogy of Christ. 1:1-17. This family line from Abraham to Jesus, proceeding through the kings of the Davidic house, is clearly intended to present the claim of Jesus to the throne of David. Although the throne had been vacant for nearly six centuries, no one could expect serious consideration by the Jews as the Messiah unless he could prove his royal descent. (Lk 3:23-38 presents another genealogy, apparently Mary's, to show the actual blood descent of Jesus, which was also from the Davidic family.)

1. **The book of the generation.** A Hebrew expression variously understood as the title of the whole Gospel of Matthew, the first two chapters, or the first seventeen verses. A similar expression in Gen 5:1 is broad enough to include both genealogy and the narrative that is interwoven (Gen 5:1–6:8). **Jesus** is the historical name; **Christ** (the equivalent of the Heb. **Messiah,** "anointed one") is the title of his office. The two names were not generally used together as a proper name until after the Ascension. **Son of David** and **son of Abraham** relate Jesus to the Messianic promises (Gen 12:3; 13:15; 22:18; II Sam 7:12,13; 22:51).

2. The list begins with **Abraham,** the father of the race to which Matthew was particularly writing, and the first one to whom the Messianic promise was given. **Judah and his brethren.** Although the line of descent came through Judah (Gen 49:10), all the patriarchs were heirs of the Messianic promise.

3-6. **Tamar** (see Gen 38). It was unusual for women to be listed in Jewish genealogies. Yet four women are listed here (though the descent was through the man in each case). Two were Gentiles (Rahab, Ruth); three bore moral blots (Tamar, Rahab, Bath-sheba). Is there not here another evidence of the grace of God in his plan to save sinners? The repetition of the title **David the king** emphasizes the royal character of this genealogy.

7-11. These verses name kings, all of whom are also listed in I Chr 3:10-16. After **Joram** Matthew omits the names of Ahaziah, Joash, and Amaziah, and after **Josiah** he omits Jehoiakim. The omissions are doubtless due to his arbitrary shortening of the list to give three groups of fourteen, perhaps as an aid to the memory. **Son** and **begat** indicate direct descent, but not necessarily immediate descent. **Jechonias,** son of Jehoiakim and grandson of Josiah, was regarded by the Jews in exile as their last legitimate king; and Ezekiel's prophecies are dated from him, although Zedekiah, his uncle, followed him as king.

12-16. **Salathiel** (or Shealtiel) is named as the son of Jechonias (cf. I Chr 3:17). This does not contradict Jer 22:28-30, for the predicted childlessness referred to reigning children. (The naming of Salathiel as the son of Neri in Lk 3:27 is better understood of different persons, rather than the result of levirate marriage.) From this point the names, which do not appear in the OT, must have been derived from Joseph's family records. One would expect descendants of royalty to preserve their lineage. Of **Joseph** it is not said that he "begat" Jesus, a marked change from the preceding expressions, and an obvious indication of the virgin birth, which Matthew subsequently explains. The feminine form of the pronoun **whom** also omits Joseph from involvement in the birth of Jesus. This genealogy makes him Christ's legal father because he was Mary's husband, but nothing more. The remarkable reading of the Sinaitic Syriac Version, "Joseph to whom was betrothed Mary the virgin begat Jesus," cannot be correct, and if intended to deny the virgin birth, contradicts itself in the succeeding verses.

17. **Fourteen generations.** This threefold grouping, arbitrarily constructed (as indicated by omissions), must have been intended as an arrangement for convenience. The three periods of national history are covered – theocracy, monarchy, hierarchy. Matthew's computation presents a problem because he lists only forty-one names. Some would solve it by counting David twice, as the end of the first group and the first name in the second (Matthew himself seems to do this; v. 17). Others count the Captivity as one item in the list. The problem is of no importance per se.

B. Birth of Christ. 1:18-25. The circumstances of the birth are related from Joseph's standpoint, and some of the details had to be derived from him (e.g., vv. 19,20). If he had already died before Jesus' ministry began, as many infer from the absence of further mention, Matthew's information may have come from the brothers of Jesus.

18. Betrothed. Among the Jews, marriage vows were said at the betrothal, and required divorce to end them. Custom decreed an interval, usually a year, before the bride should take residence in her husband's house and physical union be consummated. During this interval Mary **was found with child,** a circumstance usually punishable by death (Deut 22:23, 24). Apparently Mary did not explain her situation to Joseph but chose to leave this delicate matter in the hands of God. She could hardly have expected Joseph to accept her story without some divine authentication.

19. Public example. Rather than make a public accusation of fornication, with perhaps a demand for the full penalty, Joseph resolved to use the lax divorce laws and give Mary the writing of divorcement privately, with the accusation stated in a veiled way. **To put her away** means to divorce, not to break an engagement. How he must have loved her!

20. Thou son of David. This address by the angel (Gabriel? Lk 1:26) is a princely title. Though Joseph was in humble circumstances, he was heir to the vacant Davidic throne. The naming of the **Holy Ghost** as the agent in Mary's conception points clearly to the distinct personality of this Divine Being, and to the full awareness by ordinary Jews of this Person without further explanation.

21. Jesus is from the Hebrew for *Jehovah saves,* and points to the purpose of his coming. **His people** relates Jesus to the Messianic promises made to Israel, although the cross would extend this salvation from **sins** to Gentiles as well.

22,23. The miraculous conception is stated to be the fulfillment of Isa 7:14. Whether there was an earlier fulfillment in Isaiah's day is neither discussed nor suggested. Possibly these words were spoken by the angel and thus were an aid to Joseph's faith. **Emmanuel** was not used as a proper name of Jesus, but describes his person as the Son of God.

24,25. Joseph ended the period of betrothal by taking Mary to live in his home so that Jesus at His birth would be his legitimate son and heir to the throne. However, he **knew her not** sexually prior to the birth. Neither **till** nor **firstborn** necessarily indicates what happened afterward. However, one would naturally infer that the normal relationship of marriage would follow, unless one is committed to defend the perpetual virginity of Mary. Matthew betrays no such inclination.

C. Visit of the Magi. 2:1-12. Matthew, who alone records this incident, shows the contrast in attitudes between the non-Jewish wise men who journeyed far to see Jesus and the Jewish authorities who would not go five miles.

1. Bethlehem of Judea was also called Ephrath (Gen 35:16,19). One must read Lk 2:1-7 to learn how it was that the birth occurred in Bethlehem instead of in Nazareth. **Herod the king,** known as Herod the Great, was the son of Antipater, an Edomite, and was made king by the Romans in 43 B.C. His death occurring in 4 B.C. (our calendars err by at least four years) gives us the latest possible date for the birth of Christ. **Wise men** *(magoi)* originally denoted the priestly caste among the Persians and Babylonians (cf. Dan 2:2,48; 4:6,7; 5:7). Later the name was applied by the Greeks to any sorcerer or charlatan (Acts 8:9; 13:8). Matthew uses the term in the better sense to designate honorable men from an Eastern religion. It is entirely conceivable that these men had made contact with Jewish exiles, or with the prophecies and influence of Daniel, and thus were in possession of OT prophecies regarding Messiah.

2. His star. All attempts to explain the star as a natural phenomenon are inadequate to account for its leading the Magi from Jerusalem to Bethlehem and then standing over the house. Rather, it was a special manifestation used of God both when it first appeared to indicate the fact of Christ's birth, and when it reappeared over Jerusalem to guide the Magi to the place. Since a direct revelation to the Magi is recorded (v. 12), there is nothing improbable in assuming a direct revelation at the beginning to impart the significance of the star.

3-6. When word reached Herod that the Magi were making search in Jerusalem for the King of the Jews, the king consulted the **chief priests and scribes,** two of the groups comprising the Sanhedrin. He was given the prediction in Mic 5:2 which clearly names Bethlehem as the birthplace of Messiah.

7,8. Herod summoned the wise men, under pretense of sincere interest, and requested exact information of the star's first appearance (it was apparently not as yet seen in Jerusalem). His motive, however, was to help him fix the precise date of Jesus' birth, that he might more easily locate and destroy Him.

9,10. The star which they saw in the east now reappeared to act as guide from Jerusalem to Bethlehem.

11. The house (not the manger) in which the Magi found the infant Jesus points to the fact that this visit followed Jesus' birth by a considerable interval, perhaps of months (cf. v. 16). The three **gifts** have given rise to the tradition of three wise men. Tradition even names them: Caspar, Melchior, and Balthasar. But tradition is not necessarily fact. **Gold, frankincense,** and **myrrh** were thought by ancient commentators to show recognition of Jesus as King, Son of God, and one destined to die, respectively.

12. Warned of God. A special divine revelation directed the Magi to avoid Herod on their return.

D. Flight into Egypt and Massacre of the Infants. 2:13-18. Again we are indebted to Matthew alone for this material. Both incidents are related to OT passages. Such correlation of OT and NT passages is characteristic of this Gospel.

13,14. Joseph a second time received angelic instruction (cf. 1:20), and took Jesus and Mary to **Egypt.** The hurried trip seems to have begun the same night the Magi departed. In Egypt, where there was a large Jewish population, the family would have been welcome without undue notice. The apocryphal Gospel of the Infancy relates fanciful miracles occurring there (ch. IV).

15. The death of Herod after a revolting illness is recorded in detail by Josephus (*Antiq.* xvii. 6.5). **That is might be fulfilled** relates this experience to Hos 11:1, a passage referring historically to the deliverance of the Israelites from Egypt. Matthew sees Israel in this prophecy as a type of Jesus Christ, God's unique **son.**

16. Slew all the children. That Herod's murderous act (which included no more than a few dozen infants, because of the smallness of Bethlehem) should have gone unrecorded in other histories is not surprising, because of the king's frequent outrages. He was the murderer of his wife and three sons. Josephus calls him "a man of great barbarity towards all men equally" (*Antiq.* xvii. 8.1). **Two years old and under** shows that Herod was taking no chances of missing his victim. Jesus was not necessarily two years old.

17,18. Rachel weeping for her children. A quotation of Jer 31:15, which depicts the wailing at the time of Israel's exile. That calamity, caused by Israel's sin, eventually brought Herod to the throne, and now this new atrocity. Matthew views both calamities as part of the same picture.

E. Residence at Nazareth. 2:19-23. From Matthew one would suppose that Bethlehem was the original residence. Luke supplements by showing Nazareth to be the former home. Joseph apparently intended to dwell permanently in Bethlehem until his plans were divinely altered.

19-22. They are dead. A reference to Herod, and thus an idiom reminiscent of Ex 4:19. **Archelaus,** son of Herod the Great and his Samaritan wife, Malthace, was as brutal as his father. Thus Joseph needed to be **warned** (or instructed) **of God** as to the next step.

23. Nazareth seems to have been chosen by Joseph himself, within the providence of God. Why Matthew regarded this as a fulfillment of prophecy is difficult to understand. **By the prophets** prevents our seeking only one OT passage, thus making doubtful any play on words based on *nēser,* "branch," in Isa 11:1, although this is the common view. It seems better to understand Matthew as seeing in this residence at little Nazareth, a most unlikely place for Messiah (Jn 1:46), a fulfillment of all those OT prophecies which indicate that Messiah would be despised (e.g., Isa 53:3; Ps 22:6; Dan 9:26).

II. The Beginnings of the Ministry of Jesus Christ. 3:1–4:11.

A. The Forerunner of Christ. 3:1-12. All four Gospels describe John's preparatory ministry, and Luke gives a full description of his remarkable birth (Lk 1:5-25, 57-80).

1. In those days relates to the previous verse, which speaks of Jesus as residing at Nazareth. Precise data are given in Lk 3:1,2. **John the Baptist,** called by this name even by Josephus (*Antiq. xviii.* 5.2), did his preaching near the Jordan River in the northern part of the **wilderness of Judea,** a barren wasteland extending along the west shore of the Dead Sea.

2. Repent means "to change the mind," but implies more than mere change of opinion. As a religious term in Scripture, it involves a complete change of attitude regarding sin and God, accompanied by a sense of sorrow and a corresponding change in conduct. **The kingdom of heaven is at hand** (or *has come near),* the reason John called on men to repent. This title, peculiar to Matthew in the NT, is based on Dan 2:44; 7:13,14,27. It refers to the Messianic kingdom promised in the OT, of which Jesus was about to be presented as king. (The term, "kingdom of

God," often has a wider connotation, but usually in the Gospels the two are used interchangeably.) This Messianic **kingdom of heaven,** although promised as a literal earthly kingdom, nevertheless would be based on spiritual principles, and would demand a right relationship with God for entrance; hence the call to **repent.**

3,4. This is he that was spoken of by the prophet Isaiah (Isa 40:3-5) **definitely** relates the prophecy to John, a fact noted in each Gospel (Mk 1:2,3; Lk 3:4-6; Jn 1:23). **Camel's hair** and a **leathern girdle** is probably intentionally similar to Elijah's clothing (II Kgs 1:8; cf. Lk 1:17; Mt 17:10-13), and was the usual dress of prophets (Zech 13:4). **Locusts.** An allowable and not uncommon food (Lev 11:22).

5,6. John's preaching accorded with the mood of expectancy that had gripped many hearts, and caused a general enthusiasm to hear him, as indicated by **all.** As they came, they **were being baptized** to indicate acceptance of his message. Baptism was practiced by Jews when making proselytes, and for remedial and purifying purposes; and thus the outward form was no innovation by John, although the significance was new. Even the Qumran community observed a ritualistic baptism, though certainly not for the same reason that John baptized (W. S. LaSor, *Amazing Dead Sea Scrolls,* pp. 205,206).

7-10. Pharisees. Members of a prominent religious party. They claimed to be guardians of the Mosaic law and adhered rigidly to the traditions of the fathers. Christ characterized them as hypocrites (Lk 11:44; 12:1). **Sadducees.** A party of religious rationalists, who denied the future life. They were politically powerful, including the priestly aristocracy in their number. John realized that their coming was mere display, not indicative of spiritual change, and likened them to **vipers** fleeing before the onrushing brush fire. Having **Abraham** as their national **father** would not insure them against divine judgment. God was not obligated to them individually to fulfill his promises. **Of these stones.** Perhaps an allusion to Isa 51:1,2, but more likely a reference to the pebbles at John's feet, which could be made to respond to the creative touch of God, as Adam was formed from the dust. By the dramatic figure of the ax . . . lying **at the root of the trees,** John shows that time is running out for his hearers. The woodsman is about to appear.

11,12. John's baptism, a public testimony that the participant had repented, is to be followed by Messiah's, which is with the **Holy Ghost** and with **fire.** Some relegate both terms to Pentecost; others, to the Judgment. In view of verse 12, it seems clear that the baptism with the Holy Ghost refers to Christ's saving believers (**wheat**), and the fire describes judgment upon the wicked (**burn up the chaff**). Compare Mal 4:1 (a chapter which in the NT is applied to John; see Lk 1:17). Thus John looks at Messiah's work from the usual OT standpoint, without regarding the interval between the first and second comings, an interval of which he may have been unaware. **Fan.** A wooden shovel for tossing grain against the wind after threshing. The lighter chaff would be blown away, leaving the grain to settle in a pile.

B. Baptism of Christ. 3:12-17. The coming of Jesus to be baptized by John is set in quiet contrast to the hypocritical coming of the Pharisees and Sadducees (v. 7). All three Synoptists record this baptism, and John's Gospel includes the Baptist's later testimony to it (Jn 1:29-34).

13,14. But John was hindering him. The Greek verb emphasizes the continuing remonstrance. In the light of Jn 1:31-33, it may be asked how John recognized the superiority of Jesus so as to speak thus. We need not infer, however, that these kinsmen were total strangers, but rather that John did not yet know him as the official Messiah until the sign of the descending Spirit should occur (Jn 1:33).

15. Thus it becometh us. Although it was true that the positions of John and Jesus would shortly be reversed, in the present instance (**now**) it was the fitting thing to do. Certainly Jesus was not repenting of any personal sin. Yet, as the Substitute who would provide **righteousness** for sinful humanity, he here identifies himself with those whom he came to redeem, and thus publicly begins his work. Jesus, while on earth, always carried on the religious duties of the righteous Jew, such as synagogue worship, attendance at feasts, and payment of the temple tax.

16,17. The descending **Spirit of God** fulfilled the predicted sign to John that Jesus was the Messiah (Jn 1:33; cf. Isa 11:2; 42:1; 59:21; 61:1). As the Spirit came upon OT prophets for special guidance at the start of their ministries, so now He came upon Jesus without measure. Of course, this relates to Jesus in his humanity. **Dove.** An ancient symbol of purity, innocence, and gentleness (see Mt 10:16). The **voice from heaven** occurred at three key points in Christ's ministry: at his baptism, at his transfiguration (17:5), and just prior to the cross (Jn 12:28).

C. Temptation of Christ. 4:1-11. The most obvious sense of this passage, with its parallels, is that an actual historical experience took place. Viewpoints that deny this do not lessen the difficulties of interpretation. The various tests were directed against the human nature of Jesus, and he resisted in that realm. However, the perfect union of the divine and human natures in his person made the outcome certain, for God can never sin. But this in no way lessened the force of the attack.

1. Led up of the Spirit. An indication of the submission (voluntary) of Christ to the Spirit during his earthly ministry. **To be tempted.** A word meaning *to try* or *test*, sometimes, as here, *an enticement to evil*. The Spirit was leading Jesus in order to bring about this test. **The devil.** The name means *slanderer*, and denotes one of the characteristics of Satan, great opposer of God and God's people. **2. Forty days and forty nights.** The three tests recorded here followed this time period, but other temptations had occurred throughout the period (Lk 4:2).

3,4. If thou be the Son of God does not imply doubt on the part of Satan, but rather forms the basis for his suggestion. The subtlety of the test is evident, for neither bread nor hunger is sinful per se. **Man shall not live by bread alone** (Deut 8:3) was Christ's Scriptural answer. Even wandering Israel was made to see that the source of bread (i.e., God) was more important than the bread itself. Jesus refused to work a miracle to avoid personal suffering when such suffering was part of God's will for him.

5-7. The second temptation occurred on **the pinnacle,** or *wing* of the Temple in Jerusalem, perhaps the porch towering above the Kidron valley. Satan employed Scripture (Ps 91:11,12) to make Christ prove His claim that He abode by every word that came from the mouth of God. **It is written again** pointed to the totality of Scripture as the guide for conduct and basis for faith. **Thou shalt not tempt the Lord** (Deut 6:16; cf. Ex 17:1-7). Such presumptuous action in putting God to the test is not faith but doubt, as Israel's experience had proved.

8-11. The **exceeding high mountain** is literal, but its location is unknown. By some supernatural act Satan showed Christ **all the kingdoms of the world. I will give thee** indicates that Satan had something to bestow; otherwise the test would have had no validity. As the god of this world (II Cor 4:4) and prince of the power of the air (Eph 2:2), Satan does exercise sway over earthly kingdoms although as a usurper and within limits. He offered this control to Jesus in exchange for worship, and thus was offering to Christ that which eventually will be His in a far more glorious fashion (Rev 11:15). The coupling of **worship** and **serve** in Jesus' reply (from Deut 6:13) is significant, for the one involves the other. For Christ to bow before Satan would have been to acknowledge the devil's lordship. Such an offer deserved Christ's direct rebuke. Matthew's statement, **then** Satan **leaveth him,** shows that his order of temptations is the chronological one (contrast Lk 4:1-13). Jesus repulsed the mightiest blows of Satan not by a thunderbolt from heaven, but by the written Word of God employed in the wisdom of the Holy Spirit, a means available to every Christian.

III. The Ministry of Jesus Christ. 4:12–25:46.

Matthew's analysis of Christ's ministry is built upon four clearly noted geographical areas: Galilee (4:12), Perea (19:1), Judea (20:17), and Jerusalem (21:1). With the other Synoptists he omits the early Judean ministry, which occurs chronologically between 4:11 and 4:12 (cf. Jn 1-4). Perhaps Matthew starts with Capernaum in Galilee because that is where his own association with Christ began (9:9).

A. In Galilee. 4:12–18:35.

1) Residence Established at Capernaum. 4:12-17.

12. When Jesus had heard. The imprisonment of John, with its accompanying publicity, made Christ's retirement a practical necessity in the best interests of his work. **13. Leaving Nazareth.** Luke 4:16-31 shows that the reason for the removal to Capernaum was the attempted murder of Christ after a synagogue service. Capernaum became the home of Jesus for the rest of his ministry.

14-16. That it might be fulfilled refers to Isa 9:1,2, from which the geographical terms are rather loosely quoted. **Beyond Jordan,** a somewhat puzzling phrase here, but still best understood as Perea, which, along with Galilee, formed the border area of Israel. This region, more exposed to foreign influences than Judea, had a mixed population, and the spiritual state of the people was usually low. The coming of the **light** of Christ into such an area of spiritual **darkness** had been foretold by the prophet, and his prediction was now fulfilled.

17. Repent. The same message John had preached in Judea was now proclaimed by Jesus in Galilee (cf. 3:2).

2) Call of Four Disciples. 4:18-22. Jesus had previously met some if not all of these men in Judea when John the Baptist was still active (Jn 1:35-42). Now in Galilee that association was renewed and made permanent (cf. Mk 1:16-20; Lk 5:1-11).

18-20. Sea of Galilee. A lake in the Jordan valley 680 feet below sea level, 7 miles wide, 14 miles long, abounding in fish, and subject to sudden storms. **Simon** was casting the net with his brother **Andrew,** who had introduced him to Jesus some months earlier (Jn 1:40,41). The invitation, **Follow me,** called these believers to constant companionship with Jesus. Christ's plans for them called for training that would fit them to reclaim lost men. **Straightway.** The immediate response reveals the great impact of their earlier meeting.

21,22. James and **John,** another pair of brothers, were partners with Simon and Andrew (Lk 5:10). **Mending their nets.** Matthew and Mark agree on this fact, but Luke seems to differ. Rather than assume two incidents, it seems more reasonable to harmonize the accounts in some manner, as S. J. Andrews does (*The Life of Our Lord upon the Earth,* pp. 247,248). Most likely the men were engaged in casting and mending when Christ first approached. Our Lord then made use of Simon's boat, produced the miraculous catch, and called Simon and Andrew to follow him. Upon returning to shore, James and John began to repair the broken net, and Jesus then called them also to follow him.

3) General Survey of the Galilean Ministry. 4:23-25. These verses summarize the events unfolded in the succeeding chapters. Christ's ministry during these days involved **teaching** *(didaskōn),* **proclaiming** *(kērussōn),* and **healing** *(therapeuōn).*

23,24. Synagogues. Local places of worship and religious instruction. For a sample of Jesus' synagogue preaching, see Lk 4:16-30. **Gospel of the kingdom** was the good news Jesus proclaimed that the Messianic king had arrived to set up the promised kingdom. Accompanying this announcement were miracles of **healing,** predicted of the kingdom and thus credentials of the king (Isa 35:4-6; Mt 11:2-6). **Syria.** Here a reference to the region northward. **Possessed with demons.** Scripture here clearly distinguishes demon possession from ordinary physical disease.

25. In addition to those who came to be healed, others from far and wide followed without this motivation. **Decapolis.** A federation of ten independent Greek cities under the protection of Syria, lying east of Galilee. **Beyond Jordan.** The region to the east known as Perea. Thus all of Palestine, and the adjacent areas, came under the influence of this ministry.

4) Sermon on the Mount. 5:1–7:29. This is the same discourse as that recorded in Lk 6:20-49, for the differences can be harmonized or accounted for, and the similarity of the beginnings, endings, and subject matter makes the identification most probable. Furthermore, both accounts record the healing of the centurion's servant as the next event. The objection that Matthew places this discourse before his own call (9:9; contrast Lk 5:27 ff.) is explained by his lack of strict chronological order elsewhere. Here, since Matthew had described Christ's activity in proclaiming the arrival of the Kingdom (4:17,23), it was proper for him to include for his readers a full discussion by Jesus of this subject. Hence the Sermon on the Mount is not primarily a statement of principles for the Christian church (which was yet unrevealed), nor an evangelistic message for the unsaved, but a delineation of the principles that would characterize the Messianic kingdom Christ was announcing. Later, Israel's rejection of her King delayed the coming of his kingdom, but even now Christians, having given their allegiance to the King and having been made spiritually to anticipate some of the blessings of his kingdom (Col 1:13), may see God's ideal in this sublime discourse and will assent to its high standard.

1. Multitudes. A reference to the crowds of the previous verse, and an indication that this discourse was not given till the Galilean ministry was in full swing. Further proof is the advanced level of instruction herein contained. **The mountain.** The unnamed elevation, apparently near Capernaum, on which Jesus found a level place to speak (Lk 6:17). **His disciples.** Luke shows that the Twelve had just been chosen (Lk 6:12-16), and the sermon was directed primarily to them (cf. Lk 6:20). However, some of it was heard by the multitudes (Mt 7:28; Lk 6:17).

a) Characteristics of Kingdom Citizens. 5:3-12.

3. Blessed. *Happy.* A description of a

believer's inner condition. When describing a person in God's will, it is virtually equivalent to "saved." Psalm 1 gives an OT picture of the blessed man, who evidences his nature by the things he does. The Beatitudes, also, are not primarily promises to the individual but a description of him. They do not show a man how to be saved, but describe the characteristics manifested by one who is born again. **Poor in spirit.** Opposite of proud in spirit. Those who have recognized their poverty in spiritual things and have allowed Christ to meet their need have become heirs of the **kingdom of heaven.**

4,5. Mourn (cf. Isa 61:3). A sense of anguish for sin characterizes the blessed man. But genuine repentance will bring comfort to the believer. Since Christ bore the sins of every man, the comfort of full forgiveness is readily available (I Jn 1:9). **Meek.** Mentioned only by Matthew. An obvious allusion to Ps 37:11. The source of this meekness is Christ (Mt 11:28,29), who bestows it when men submit their wills to his. **Inherit the earth.** The earthly Messianic kingdom.

6-9. Hunger and thirst after righteousness. A deep passion for personal righteousness. Such desire is evidence of dissatisfaction with present spiritual attainment (contrast Pharisee, Lk 18:9 ff.). **Merciful** (cf. Ps 18:25). Those who put pity into action can expect similar mercy both from men and God. **Pure in heart.** Those whose moral being is free from contamination with sin, without divided interests or loyalties. To them, as possessors of God's pure nature, belongs the unclouded vision of God, which will reach consummation when Christ returns (I Cor 13:12; I Jn 3:2). **Peacemakers.** As God is "the God of peace" (Heb 13:20) and Christ is "Prince of Peace" (Isa 9:6), so peacemakers in the Kingdom will be recognized as partaking of God's nature, and will be properly honored.

10-12. Persecuted for righteousness' sake. At the establishment of the Messianic kingdom, such wrongs will be set right. And even within that kingdom the presence of men with sinful natures will make evil a possibility, although it will be judged at once. **The prophets.** The OT seers who foretold the kingdom and proclaimed its righteous character met the same opposition (Jeremiah, Jer 20:2; Zechariah, II Chr 24:21).

b) Function of Kingdom Citizens. 5:13-16. **Salt.** A common food preservative, often used symbolically. Believers are a restraint upon the world's corruption. Unbelievers are often kept from evil deeds because of a moral consciousness traceable to Christian influence. **Lost its savor** (ASV). Whether this can happen chemically is disputed. Thomson avows that the impure salt of Palestine may become insipid (*The Land and the Book,* p. 381). However, Christ's illustration may be hypothetical to show the anomaly of a useless believer. **Ye are the light.** Believers function positively to illuminate a world in darkness because they possess Christ, who is the Light (Jn 8:12). Christ's light should shine forth publicly, like the cluster of white stone houses in a Palestinian **city.** It should also be displayed in our individual, private relationships (**candle, lampstand, house**).

c) Standards of the Kingdom Compared to Mosaic Law. 5:17-48.

17-20. Not to destroy. Christ answers the objection that he was flouting the OT by denying any effort to annul or abrogate the Law. **But to fulfill.** Christ fulfilled the OT by obeying the Law perfectly, by fulfilling its types and prophecies, and by paying the full penalty of the Law as the Substitute for sinners. (Consequently, believers, by justification, have Christ's righteousness imputed to them; Rom 3:20-26; 10:4.) **Verily I say.** The first use of this impressive formula by Jesus, indicating a statement of utmost importance. **Till heaven and earth pass.** Though regarded by some as idiomatic for *never,* it is probably an eschatological reference (Mt 24:35; Rev 21:1). **Jot.** Smallest letter of the Hebrew alphabet (*yodh*). **Tittle.** Tiny projection on certain Hebrew letters. Those who are not opposed in principle to God's law but have avoided its lesser requirements will not be cast out of the Kingdom but will have a lesser reward **in the kingdom. Your righteousness.** Distinguished from the righteousness of **scribes** and **Pharisees,** which consisted in mere outward, unspiritual conformity to the Mosaic code, even though scrupulously observed. The believer's righteousness is based upon that imputed righteousness of Christ obtained by faith (Rom 3:21,22), which enables him to live righteously (Rom 8:2-5). Only such may **enter into the kingdom** Christ proclaimed.

21-26. First illustration: murder. Jesus shows how his fulfillment of the Law went far deeper than mere outward conformity. **Whosoever shall kill** marks a traditional enlargement of Ex 20:13, but it still deals only with the act of murder. **The judgment.** The Jewish civil court, as based on Deut 16:18 (see also Josephus *Antiq*. iv. 8.14). **Angry.** The best manuscripts omit "without a cause," although Eph 4:26 indicates that some restriction may properly be inferred. **Raca.** Probably "empty head" (from an Aramaic word meaning "empty one"). **Thou fool.** Since this series calls for epithets progressively more severe, Bruce sees **Raca** as contempt for a man's head, and **fool** as contempt for his character (ExpGT, I, 107). **Gehenna of fire.** Literally a reference to the valley of Hinnom outside Jerusalem, where rubbish, offal, and carcasses were burned, and thus a graphic metaphor for the place of eternal torment. (For its gruesome history, see Jer 7:31,32; II Chr 28:3; 33:6; II Kgs 23:10.) Christ locates the root of murder in the heart of the angry man, and promises that in His kingdom swift judgment will be dealt out before murder can result. **At the altar.** Indication of the Jewish coloring of this address. **Hath something against thee,** i.e., if you have wronged your brother. **First be reconciled** obligates the would-be worshiper to make amends with the offended beforehand to make his gift acceptable (cf. Ps 66:18). **Adversary.** An opponent at law (cf. Lk 12:58,59). Since judgment is on the way, offenders should hasten to square accounts. **Till thou hast paid.** Probably a literal situation in the kingdom. If, however, the **prison** is symbolic of hell, the implied possibility of payment and release applies only to the parable, not to its interpretation. Scripture is clear that those in hell are there forever (Mt 25:41, 46), because their debt is unpayable.

27-30. Second illustration: adultery. Jesus indicated that the sin described in Ex 20:14 lies deeper than the overt act. **Every one that looketh** characterizes the man whose glance is not checked by holy restraint, and who forms the impure purpose of lusting after her. The act will follow when opportunity occurs. **Right eye.** To the man who blames the sin on his eye, Jesus shows the logical procedure to follow. As we amputate diseased organs to save lives, so an **eye** (or a **hand**) so hopelessly affected needs drastic treatment. Of course, Jesus wanted his hearers to see that the real source of sin lies not in the physical organ but in the **heart.** A man's evil heart must be changed if he would escape final ruin in **hell** (Gehenna; see comment on 5:22).

31,32. Third illustration: divorce. Mosaic regulation (Deut 24:1) protected woman from man's caprice by insisting on the **certificate of divorce.** Divorce was, however, a concession to human sin (Mt 19:8). The Mosaic grounds of "uncleanness" had been variously explained, from adultery (Shammai) to the most trivial dislike by the husband (Hillel). In Jewish custom only men could obtain divorces. **Fornication.** Some restrict this term to Jewish custom, as describing unfaithfulness during the betrothal period (cf. Joseph's problem, 1:18,19), and thus find no cause whatever for divorce today. Others see "fornication" as equivalent to "adultery" in this passage, and thus the one cause for divorce allowed by Christ. Certainly there are no grounds beyond this possible exception. **Maketh her an adulteress** (ASV). Understood usually as potential, since she may be forced into another marriage. Since this may not necessarily occur, Lenski treats the difficult passive as ***brings about that she is stigmatized as adulterous*** (*Interpretation of St. Matthew's Gospel*, pp. 230-235), and regards the sin as an unjust suspicion brought upon the injured party.

33-37. Fourth illustration: oaths. The OT basis is Lev 19:12 and Deut 23:21 (cf. Ex 20:7). **Forswear.** Swear falsely, perjure oneself. Jewish abuse of oath-taking caused Jesus to say, **Swear not at all.** It is difficult to find any loopholes in this directive (see also Jas 5:12). Thus no believer should employ an oath to authenticate his statements. Even the state will usually allow an affirmation instead of an oath if requested. **By heaven.** Jews used their ingenuity to classify various oaths, and generally discounted those that did not mention God specifically. Jesus showed that such deceptively subtle reasoning was false, for God is still implicated when men invoke **heaven, earth,** or **Jerusalem;** and even swearing by one's own head implicates the One who holds the power over it. **Let your speech be, Yea, yea** (ASV). A solemn affirmation or denial is sufficient for a believer. **Whatsoever is more than these.** By adding oaths to our statements, we either admit that our usual speech cannot be trusted, or else we lower ourselves to the level of a lying world, that follows **the evil one** (ASV). Cf. Jn 8:44.

38-42. Fifth illustration: retaliation. **An eye for an eye** (Ex 21:24). A judicial principle that made the punishment fit the crime. However, it was not intended to permit men to take vengeance into their own hands (Lev 19:18). **Resist not evil.** Probably, "the evil man." Jesus shows the Kingdom citizens how they should respond to personal injury. (He is not discussing government's obligation to maintain order.) A child of God should willingly suffer loss by assault (v. 39), lawsuits (v. 40), compulsory regulations (v. 41), begging (v. 42 a), and loans (v. 42 b). **Coat.** Undergarment or tunic. **Cloak.** More expensive outer garment, sometimes used as a bed covering (see Ex 22:26,27), and thus could not be held overnight as security for debt (Deut 24:12,13). **Compel thee.** A word of Persian origin, depicting the custom of postal couriers having authority to press persons into service whenever needed (cf. Simon of Cyrene, Mt 27:32). This high standard of conduct should cause all believers to endeavor in so far as possible to live as befits their calling and to long for the day when Christ's righteous rule will make this ideal fully workable in every phase of life.

43-48. Sixth illustration: love of enemies. **Thou shalt love thy neighbor** (Lev 19:18,34) summarizes the entire second table of the Law (cf. Mt 22:39). **Hate thine enemy.** This unscriptural addition missed the heart of the law of love; yet it must have been a popular interpretation. The Manual of Discipline from Qumran contains the following rule: ". . . to love all that He has chosen and hate all that He has rejected" (1 QS I. 4). **Love your enemies.** The love (*agapaō*) enjoined is that intelligent love which comprehends the difficulty and extends itself to rescue the enemy from his hate. Such love is akin to God's loving action toward rebellious men (Jn 3:16), and thus is a demonstration that those who so love are true **sons** of their **Father. Publicans.** Jewish collectors of the Roman taxes, hated by their countrymen because of their flagrant extortions and their association with the despised conquerors. The command **Be ye therefore perfect** is to be restricted to the matter of love in this context. As God's love is complete, not omitting any group, so must the child of God strive for maturity in this regard (cf. Eph 5:1,2). This cannot mean sinlessness, for Mt 5:6,7 shows that the blessed ones still hunger for righteousness and need mercy.

d) Attitudes of Kingdom Citizens. 6:1–7:12. Jesus now contrasts the righteous living he expects with the hypocrisy of the Pharisees and their followers (5:20).

1-4. First example: alms. **Alms.** Verse 1 has **righteousness** in the better texts, and is introductory to the entire discussion. Practical righteousness is in view here. **Before men.** Although we are commanded to let our light shine (5:16), deeds of righteousness must not be done for self-glorification (**to be seen of them**). **Alms** is proper in verse 2 and denotes charitable giving. **Sound a trumpet.** Metaphorical for "publicize." **Hypocrites.** From the Greek word for actors playing a part. **They have their reward in full.** Commercial use of this word indicates full payment with a receipt. Showy righteousness has received its full payment; God will add nothing to it. Those content to do their giving secretly shall be rewarded, not by man's applause, but by their heavenly **Father.** Omit **openly.**

5-15. Second example: prayer. **Standing in the synagogues.** This was the usual manner (Mk 11:25) and place for prayer and is not denounced. But the intent of one who claims that the hour of prayer caught him in a prominent place and who loves such display is condemned. **Enter into thy closet.** Public prayer is not pronounced wrong (Jesus himself prayed publicly, Lk 10:21,22; Jn 11:41,42), but vain display is. Private praying is the finest training ground for public prayer. Omit **openly. Vain repetitions** (i.e., *babbling speech*) are characteristic of pagan (heathen or **Gentile**) praying, as ostentation is of **hypocrites.** Such action regards prayer as an effort to overcome God's unwillingness to respond by wearying him with words. Yet it is not mere length nor repetition that Christ condemns (Jesus prayed all night, Lk 6:12, and repeated his petitions, Mt 26:44), but the unworthy motive that prompts such religious acts.

Jesus proceeds to give an example of a suitable prayer, which is a marvel of broad scope and brevity. Though it was certainly not intended to be recited superstitiously (the very action Christ was decrying, v. 7), and it does not embody all of his teaching about prayer (cf. Jn 16:23,24), yet it can be prayed (not just recited) with sincerity by all true believers. Christians, of course, will realize in view of later revelation that the prayer is possible on the basis of Christ's merits.

Our Father. A form of address not common in OT prayers, but precious to all NT believers. The first three petitions of the prayer concern God and his program; the last four, man and his needs. **Hallowed.** Here the meaning is, "be held in reverence, treated as holy." **Thy kingdom come.** The Messianic kingdom. Not only Jews but all believers in Christ should have a vital interest in its arrival.

Our daily bread. This first request for personal needs employs a term, **daily,** found only once in secular Greek (Arndt, p. 296). Opinions of its meaning vary among "daily," "necessary for existence," and "for the coming day." There is no strong reason to change the AV, ASV, or RSV, however. **Forgive us our debts.** Sins viewed as moral and spiritual debts to God's righteousness. These are not the sins of the unregenerate (only disciples are taught this prayer), but of believers, who need to confess them. **As we forgive.** Forgiveness of sin, whether under Mosaic law or in the Church, is always by God's grace and based on Christ's atonement. However, the case of a believer confessing his sin and asking God's forgiveness while withholding forgiveness from someone else is not only incongruous but hypocritical. A forgiving spirit is made easier for Christians when they consider how much God has already forgiven (Eph 4:32). An unforgiving spirit is sin, and should itself be confessed. **Lead us not into temptation.** Cf. Jas 1:13,14; Lk 22:40. A plea that God, in his providence, will spare the supplicant from needless temptations. The doxology in 6:13 b is a liturgical interpolation from I Chr 29:11.

16-18. Third example: fasting. **When ye fast.** Mosaic law (under which Christ's hearers lived) prescribed one fast annually, the Day of Atonement (Lev 16:29, "afflict your souls"). Phariseeism added two fasts weekly, on Mondays and Thursdays, and used them as occasions for public displays of piety. The true function of fasting, however, was to indicate deep contrition, and the temporary devoting of all one's energies to prayer and spiritual communion. But fasting that requires spectators is mere acting. Jesus instituted no fasts for his disciples, though voluntary fasting appears occasionally in the apostolic church (Acts 13:2,3).

19-24. Fourth example: wealth. A common error of Phariseeism and Judaism in general was the undue emphasis upon material wealth as evidence of God's approval. Jesus explained that **treasures upon earth** are fleeting, being subject to loss from **moth** (cf. raiment, v. 25), **eating** (a more likely translation of *brōsis,* cf. meat, v. 25), and **thieves.** The Kingdom citizen should rather store up **treasures in heaven** by concentration upon righteousness (see v. 33). **The lamp of the body,** that which receives and dispenses the light, **is the eye.** If the **eye,** used here figuratively for one's spiritual understanding, be **single** (opposite of "twofold"), not afflicted with double vision in this matter of treasures—an affliction which is **evil**—then the individual can regard riches in their proper perspective. The impossibility of serving two masters in a slave relationship is a graphic illustration. **Mammon.** Though its derivation is uncertain, it appears to be an Aramaic word for wealth, here personified. Note that Jesus condemns not wealth but enslavement to wealth.

25-34. Fifth example: anxiety. Those without wealth may fall victims to faithless worry. Hence the natural transition. **Take no thought.** Not a prohibition of foresight and planning (cf. I Tim 5:8; Prov 6:6-8; 30:25), but of anxiety over daily needs. **Is not the life more than meat?** Since life itself and the body were provided by God, shall we not trust him to provide that which is less important? Since God provides sustenance for birds that have not ability to sow, reap, and store, how much more can men, who have been provided with these abilities, trust their heavenly Father! **Add one cubit unto his stature.** Food is essential to growth. Yet even here God controls. As a child grows to maturity, God adds much more than **one cubit** (about eighteen inches), but anxiety can only hinder and not help. Some wish to translate **span of life** rather than **stature,** and attempt to find instances of **cubit** as a measure of time. However, the former interpretation fits the passage well. **Lilies.** What particular flowers are denoted by this word is uncertain, but they must have been in bloom on this occasion, since Jesus refers to **one of these. Solomon.** The most magnificent Hebrew king. **Grass of the field.** The lilies just mentioned, the beauty of which is short-lived, and which soon find themselves cut with the grasses and used for fuel for man's needs in the baking **oven** (Jas 1:11). **O ye of little faith.** An expression used four times in Matthew, once in Luke, as an encouragement to growth in faith as well as a gentle reproof. **The Gentiles seek.** A reference to the attention of Gentiles to material things because they know not God as a heavenly Father (cf. 6:7,8). **Seek ye first.** Christ's hearers, who had already given allegiance to the King, must continue seeking (durative verb) the Kingdom by concentrating upon spiritual values and resting their full confidence in God; and God who knew their temporal needs would supply what was necessary. **The morrow will be anxious for itself** (ASV). A striking personification. **Sufficient unto the day is the evil.** This evil is clearly physical, referring to the problems that may arise. It is senseless to add tomorrow's cares to those of today.

7:1-12. Sixth example: judging others. **Judge not.** The present imperative suggests that it is the habit of judging others that is condemned. Though the word **judge** is itself neutral as to the verdict, the sense here indicates an unfavorable judgment. Critics of others must stop short of final condemnation, for men cannot judge motives, as God can (cf. Jas 4:11,12). Believers are not to avoid all judging (cf. 7:6,16), for Christians need to judge themselves and offending members (I Cor 5:3-5,12,13). **That ye be not judged.** The aorist subjunctive form is better understood of God's judgment than of human judgment (cf. 6:14,15). **Mote.** A speck of straw or chaff, or a splinter of wood. **Beam.** A log or plank, used of the main beam of a roof or floor; here it represents a censorious spirit. The illustration is intentionally exaggerated to show the ludicrous position of one who sets himself up to judge others. Such a person is termed **hypocrite,** for he pretends to act as a physician, when he is really ailing himself. This command does not relieve believers from making moral distinctions, however. Those who have heard the Gospel and the invitation of Christ, and by their response have shown their nature to be unalterably vicious (**dogs** and **swine** were particularly repulsive to Jesus' audience), must not be allowed to treat these precious things as cheap (cf. 13:11-15).

The following verses on prayer (cf. Lk 11:9-13) answer the believer's problems arising from the instructions on judging. The need of discerning between dogs and swine while avoiding the beam in the eye demands wisdom from above. Hence Jesus encourages his followers to **ask, seek,** and **knock,** that their deficiencies may be met from the divine supply. The three imperatives are in climactic order, and their durative forms suggest not only perseverance but frequent prayer for any and all needs. There is a certain rough resemblance between a **loaf** (small round cake of bread) and a **stone,** and between a **fish** and a **serpent,** but no father would practice such deception upon a hungry child. **Being evil.** A reference to man's sinfulness (even disciples have this sinful nature). **Good things** is replaced in Lk 11:13 (another occasion) by the **Holy Spirit,** the Bestower of all good. **Therefore.** Verse 12 applies the foregoing instruction. Though evil by nature, we are still acknowledged by God as his children and promised answers to prayer. Hence, rather than judging others, we are to treat them as we would like to be treated. This summary of the OT (**the law and the prophets**) is restatement of the second table of the Law (Mt 22:36-40; Rom 13:8-10), and rests upon the first, for man's relation to God is always basic to his relation to his fellows.

e) Concluding Exhortations to Kingdom Citizens. 7:13-27.

13,14. Enter ye in by the narrow gate (ASV). To those who had already entered by faith into relation with Christ (as well as others who were listening; v. 28), our Lord describes the comparative unpopularity of their new position. The order of **gate** and **way** suggests the gate as the entrance to the way, symbolic of a believer's initial experience with Christ, which introduces him to the life of godliness. The first Christians were called those of "the Way" (Acts 9:2; 19:9,23; 22:4; 24:14,22). Though the mass of mankind is upon the **broad way** that leads to **destruction** (eternal ruin), the other **gate** and **way** are so small as to need **finding.** Yet the same God who provided Christ, who is both gate and way (Jn 14:6), also causes men to find the portal (Jn 6:44). **Life.** Here a contrasting parallel to **destruction** and thus a reference to the blessed state in heaven, though this eternal life begins at regeneration.

15-20. Those who enter upon the narrow way must beware of **false prophets,** who claim to guide believers but really practice deception. **Sheep's clothing** is not to be regarded as prophets' garb, but is an evident contrast to vicious **wolves.** God's people in all ages have needed to beware of deceptive leaders (Deut 13:1; Acts 20:29; I Jn 4:1; Rev 13:11-14). **By their fruits.** The doctrines produced by these false prophets, rather than the works they perform, since outward appearances may not cause suspicion. The test of the prophet is his conformity to Scripture (I Cor 14:37; Deut 13:1-5). **Corrupt tree.** One that is decayed, worthless, unusable. The worthlessness of such a tree calls for its swift removal from the orchard lest it infect the others.

21-23. Jesus solemnly implies his divine Sonship (**my Father**) and his position as Judge (**will say to me in that day**), and warns that false leaders (those who have **prophesied** in Christ's name, **cast out demons,** and performed **many wonderful works**) will be fully unmasked and judged. The mere performance of spectacular deeds (even supernatural ones) is not necessarily divine authentication (Deut 13:1-5; II Thess 2:8-12; Mt 24:24). The judgment to occur **in that day** will determine who **shall enter into the kingdom of heaven** (Mt 25:31-46). Though the specific reference must be to those still living at the establishment of the Millennial kingdom (otherwise they would be among the wicked dead who are not raised until after the Millennium, Rev 20:5), the result is the same to both groups; and thus the warning is pertinent. **I never knew you.** In the intensive sense of *know with favor,* or *acknowledge* (cf. Ps 1:6; Amos 3:2).

24-27. The supreme importance of building upon the right foundation. The man whose house collapsed was at fault not because he failed to labor, but because he did not use the rock. **The rock.** Christ himself (I Cor 3:11) and his teaching. **These sayings of mine.** Chapters 5–7. **Doeth them.** Obedience to the teaching. The sermon is addressed to believers and presupposes faith in Jesus as Messiah. This is not legalism. No works founded upon mere human effort are of any spiritual value, but faith in Christ **the rock** brings about that regeneration which manifests itself in godly living.

28,29. When Jesus had ended these sayings. Lenski notes the correctness of Matthew's psychological observation. As Jesus spoke, the crowds were in rapt attention; but when he ceased, tension relaxed and amazement engulfed them (*Interpretation of St. Matthew's Gospel,* p. 314). **Not as the scribes** calls attention to the fact that the scribes, in lecturing, appealed repeatedly to the opinions of distinguished rabbis and to traditional interpretations. How tedious compared to Christ's authoritative, "I say unto you"! (5:18,20,22, *et al.*)

5) Ten Miracles and Related Events. 8:1–9:38. The narratives of these two chapters are topically arranged, and the order differs somewhat from that of Mark and Luke. However, Matthew's description of the cleansing of the leper as immediately following the Sermon on the Mount must be chronological (cf. 8:1), whereas neither Mark nor Luke is specific as to its time.

8:1-4. Cleansing of a leper. **Leper.** For a description of Biblical leprosy see Lev 13,14, and the Bible dictionaries. In the OT this loathsome disease was made symbolic of sin's effect upon man. (The laws were not primarily hygienic, for one completely covered with leprosy could be pronounced clean; Lev 13:12,13.) **Worshipped him.** The faith in Jesus' power demonstrated by the leper (**If thou wilt;** not "If thou canst") shows his prostrate worship to have been religious, not Eastern courtesy. **Touched him.** An act simultaneous with Jesus' healing statement, and thus not ceremonially defiling. **Tell no man.** Not to avoid publicity, since **great multitudes** witnessed the miracle, but to prevent premature notice from reaching the **priest,** lest he be prejudiced against the man. Christ wanted the cleansing officially pronounced first, so that the explanation would be a **testimony unto them** (i.e., the antagonistic priests). Unfortunately, the man disregarded the caution and thereby caused Christ much inconvenience (Mk 1:45).

5-13. Healing of a centurion's servant. **Centurion.** Luke indicates that he made his appeal to Jesus through Jewish elders and other friends (Lk 7:1-10). Centurions are uniformly pictured in the NT as men of good character (Mt 27:54; Acts 10:22; 27:3,43; *et al.*). This man was probably a Gentile commander in the forces of Herod Antipas, who kept foreign troops (Jos *Antiq*. xvii. 8.3). **Sick of the palsy.** The Greek *paralytikos* denoted paralysis caused by a variety of diseases affecting muscles and organs of the body. **I am not worthy.** This Gentile, perhaps not even a proselyte (though he had built a Jewish synagogue, Lk 7:5) thought it presumptuous to ask Jesus to come to his house. **I am a man under authority.** The meaning is: If this minor officer could issue orders to his subordinates, how much more could Christ, who possesses all authority, give a command that His will be done. **He marvelled.** An indication that the omniscience of Christ's divine nature did not prevent normal human responses. In spite of Israel's wealth of revelation, it was a Gentile whose faith in Christ's authority glowed most brightly. Thus Jesus announces that his Messianic kingdom shall be enjoyed by many who are not Jews. **Shall sit down with Abraham.** The figure of a banquet is often used of the Kingdom (Isa 25:6; Lk 14:15-24). **The sons** (or *children*) **of the kingdom.** Jews, who were the recipients of the prophecies and thus the original heirs, are here told that without true faith mere race is not sufficient qualification for Christ's kingdom. **Outer darkness.** The darkness outside the lighted banquet hall (cf. 22:13). **As thou hast believed.** The man believed Jesus could heal at a distance, and so He did.

14-17. Healing of Peter's mother-in-law and others. **When Jesus was come.** From a synagogue service (Lk 4:38; Mk 1:29). **Sick of a fever.** With guests expected, this illness must have greatly distressed the household. **Ministered unto them.** The healing was complete, without gradual recuperation. The suggestion that Peter's wife was dead, since his mother-in-law did the serving, contradicts I Cor 9:5. **When the even was come.** At sundown, the Sabbath being past, many sick and demon-possessed were brought for healing. **Bare our diseases.** Matthew 9:6 shows that Christ's healing of disease (one of sin's effects) indicated his competence to deal with its ultimate cause. Thus these healings were a partial fulfillment of Isa 53:4 (see ASV and RSV margins), which was completed at Calvary when the sin of man was borne by Christ.

18-22. Interview with prospective followers. The chronological connection of this passage is complicated by the Lukan parallel (9:57 ff.), which places it much later. Perhaps the first interview occurred as Jesus prepared to embark, and Matthew adds the later incident to the same paragraph, whereas Luke groups three similar incidents at the occasion of one of the others. **One, a scribe.** Though few of these religious scholars were favorably attracted to Christ (cf. Mk 12:28-34; contrast Lk 11:53,54), this man offered to become a permanent disciple. Jesus evidently saw in this proposal, however, a failure to estimate fully the rigors of true discipleship. **Son of man.** A title understood by the Jews of Messiah (Jn 12:34), and as equivalent to "Son of God" (Lk 22:69,70). It was Christ's usual designation of himself, apparently derived from Dan 7:13,14. **Suffer me first to go and bury my father.** This man, already a disciple, was asked by Jesus to follow him (Lk 9:59). Having just received word of his father's death, he requested a delay. The suggestion that the man's father was still alive (since Jewish burials occurred on the day of death, and the small delay would not warrant Christ's reply) does not lessen the difficulty, for among the Jews a man's responsibility to an aged parent was as great as his duty to the dead. Jesus saw in the man's hesitation a weakness of allegiance. **Leave the dead to bury their own dead** (ASV). When Christ calls a man for a specific task (Lk 9:60), the disciple must sometimes forego what otherwise he would perform. Those who are spiritually dead are capable of caring for the physically dead.

23-27. Stilling of the storm. **Great tempest.** The word usually used for "earthquake" is employed here, perhaps connoting the turbulence of the water, a violence causing terror even to experienced sailors. Violent storms are not unknown on Galilee (W.M. Thomson, *The Land and the Book*, p. 347). **Why are ye fearful** (*deiloi*) shows their fear to be cowardly, indicative of **little faith.** Had not Jesus commanded this trip to the other side (Lk 8:22)? Yet their turning to him in extremity shows a root of faith which could be developed. **Rebuked the winds and the sea.** Christ commanded not only the winds, but also the sea, which otherwise would have continued billowing for some time.

28-34. Healing of two demon-possessed men (cf. Mk 5:1-20; Lk 8:26-39). **Country of the Gadarenes** (ASV). So called from the city of Gadara to the southeast. Mark and Luke have "Gerasenes" (ASV), from the village named Khersa (Gerasa)—now in ruins on the lake shore—which was perhaps in the district belonging to Gadara. **Two possessed with demons.** The other Synoptists mention only the more prominent one of the two. Demoniacs in the NT are pictured neither as gross sinners nor as victims of insanity (though demonism may produce such effects), but as persons whose minds have come under the control of an evil spirit or spirits. That such phenomena should be especially prominent during the days of Christ's earthly ministry is consistent with Satan's efforts to counteract God's program. Demons knew exactly who Jesus was **(thou Son of God),** were aware that their ultimate doom was sure (**the time,** v. 29), and always gave Christ absolute obedience. The owners of the **herd of swine** were probably Jews, who were thus violating Mosaic law—at least in spirit—in this Jewish territory (under Herod Philip). Hence they brought no legal action against Jesus for the loss. Why this strange request of the demons? Perhaps it was to grasp at one last chance to avoid confinement in the abyss (Lk 8:31; Rev 20:1-3). But the swine, by stampeding into the waters, thwarted whatever purpose the demons may have entertained. **They besought him that he would depart.** This request, arising from fear (Lk 8:37), came from the populace, not just from the owners. Awe-struck but unrepentant, they wanted no more of Christ.

9:1-8. Healing of a paralytic (cf. Mk 2:1-12; Lk 5:17-26). **His own city.** Capernaum (Mk 2:1; Mt 4:13). **Sick of the palsy.** This paralytic was lowered through the roof by four friends because of the density of the crowd (Mk 2:3,4). **Seeing their faith.** This includes the faith of the sick man, since forgiveness of sins is given only to those with faith (though healing was sometimes granted before faith was present). **Thy sins are forgiven** (ASV). In this case, the man's condition seems either to have been the direct result of sin or else to have caused him to reflect most seriously upon his sinfulness. **This man blasphemeth.** The charge by the **scribes** and Pharisees, here seen opposing Jesus in Galilee for the first time, condemned him for taking to himself the prerogatives of God (Lk 5:21). **Which is easier?** An unanswerable question. The statements are equally simple to pronounce; but to say either, with accompanying performance, requires divine power. An imposter, of course, in seeking to avoid detection, would find the former easier. Jesus proceeded to heal the illness that men might **know** that he had **authority** to deal with its cause, thus foreshadowing the atonement. **Had given such power unto men.** Christ's authoritative forgiving and healing regarded as divine gifts to mankind.

9-13. Call of Matthew, and the feast in his house. All the Synoptics record this incident as following the healing of the paralytic. **Matthew.** Also called *Levi* (Mk 2:14; Lk 5:27). **Sitting at the place of toll** (ASV). Capernaum (9:1) was situated near the highway that led from Damascus to the coastal cities, and was thus a favorable spot for collecting duties on goods shipped by road or across the Sea of Galilee. Edersheim describes from rabbinic sources the vexatious taxes that were exacted, and the classifications of taxgatherers, of which Matthew, as a customhouse officer, was of the worst kind (*Life and Times of Jesus,* I, 515-518). **He arose and followed him.** This act marked a complete break with the past; there could be no turning back. His position would be filled by another, and to find new employment would be difficult for a publican. **As Jesus sat at meat in the house.** This feast in Matthew's house (Lk 5:29) was held perhaps some time after his call. To it he invited **publicans and sinners,** his former associates who were living contrary to God's will as revealed in the OT. Doubtless he invited them so that Jesus might win them to himself. To the **Pharisees,** who drew the most rigid distinctions and regarded themselves as **righteous,** Jesus responded that his ministry was needed by **sinners,** just as a **physician['s]** services are needed by the sick. **The righteous.** Jesus used the Pharisees' estimate of themselves to answer their objection. **I will have mercy and not sacrifice** (Hos 6:6). A merciful attitude toward the spiritually needy is far better than the mere formality of religious duties **(sacrifice)** without concern for others.

14-17. This interview with the **disciples of John** must also have occurred at Matthew's feast (note close connection in Lk 5:33). **Pharisees fast oft.** To the one annual Scriptural fast (Day of Atonement) had been added fasts each Monday and Thursday, observed by Pharisees and others, including John's disciples (Lk 5:33). Christ's reply recalled John's own statement (Jn 3:29), likening our Lord's ministry to a wedding feast. **Sons of the bridechamber.** The attendants of the bridegroom who assist him. When Christ the Bridegroom **shall be taken away** by violent death, **then shall they fast.** True fasting results from sorrow (note **mourn**), not from ritual. **A piece of undressed cloth** (ASV). A patch of unsized or unshrunken material, when the whole garment was washed, would shrink and tear away the material to which it was sewed. **New wine,** having not yet fermented, would burst **old wineskins** which no longer had elasticity. Thus Christ and his message were much more than contemporary Judaism patched up or rejuvenated.

18-26. Healing of a woman with hemorrhage, and raising of a ruler's daughter. **Ruler.** One of the synagogue rulers, named Jairus, probably of Capernaum (Mk 5:21,22). **My daughter is even now dead.** Matthew has summarized several details. Mark and Luke record that Jairus first said she was dying, and later was informed by messengers that she had died. **She shall live.** Though his faith was less than the centurion's (8:8), it was nevertheless remarkable. En route to the house of Jairus, Jesus was approached from behind by a woman **suffering from hemorrhage** (or AV, *diseased with an issue of blood*) for twelve years. This ailment was ceremonially defiling (Lev 15:19-30), a fact that may explain her action. **The border of his garment** (ASV). Probably the tassel on each of the four corners of his outer garment, worn by Israelites in accordance with Num 15:38 and Deut 22:12. Again Matthew condenses the account but notes that Jesus made clear to the woman that **faith**, not the tassel, had obtained this cure. Jesus proceeded to the house where death had occurred. Already **the flute-players** (ASV) and other mourners had gathered for the ancient funeral pageantry (Jer 9:17; 48:36). **The maid is not dead but sleepeth.** Compare Jesus' similar statement regarding Lazarus (Jn 11:11,14). The statement is neither a mistaken opinion of Jesus, nor a literal truth that she was merely unconscious, nor an argument that death is soul sleep. Rather it was spoken in the light of what he was going to do. **This news** spread throughout the region, in spite of Christ's warning against publicity (Mk 5:43; Lk 8:56).

27-31. Healing of two blind men. This narrative and the next are peculiar to Matthew. **Thou Son of David.** A Messianic designation. Since at this time Jesus was avoiding public titles that would be regarded as political, he did not acknowledge these blind men until all had entered the house. **According to your faith be it done unto you** (ASV). Cf. 8:13. The recognition of Jesus as Messiah, with its blessed implications to such men as these (Isa 35:5,6), received the blessing asked for. **Spread abroad his fame.** Unable to contain their gratitude, they did not obey Christ's stern warning to be silent.

32-34. Healing of a dumb demoniac. Though demoniacs were often violent and vocal, this one was **dumb** and **was brought to him** by others. Matthew describes the event with a minimum of details, noting chiefly the reaction by the multitudes. **Never so seen in Israel.** This statement may be the impression gained over a period of time, culminating in this latest miracle. The **Pharisees'** accusation of Jesus' league with the **prince of the devils** must have reference to this particular miracle. The charge may not have been made to Jesus directly, since he does not deal with it until it is made again (Mt 12:24-29).

35-38. Another Galilean tour. Opinion divides over whether this paragraph describes a third Galilean circuit (cf. Mt 4:23; Lk 8:1; so A. T. Robertson, *Harmony of the Gospels*), or is a summarization of Christ's activities which began at 4:23 (Lenski; Alford). **Jesus was going about.** The Greek indicates continued action. **Teaching, preaching,** and **healing** reaffirm the activities named in 4:23. **Moved with compassion.** This deep sympathy of Jesus is often named as prompting his miracles (14:14; 15:32; 20:34). Two illustrations picture Christ's concept of the multitudes: shepherdless sheep, and a ripened harvest. **Distressed** (ASV). Wearied, harassed. **Scattered,** or lying down, prostrated from exhaustion and neglect. But Jesus saw the people also as a rich spiritual **harvest,** in need of **laborers** to gather it. The disciples are commanded to **pray for the Lord of the harvest** (Jesus himself; cf. 3:12, where John applies the same figure to Christ) to **send forth** the workers. As so often occurs, those who prayed were themselves sent (ch. 10).

6) Mission of the Twelve. 10:1-42. After an explanatory statement and a listing of the Twelve, Matthew gives Christ's charge to them for their first mission. The message is in three sections, marked by the recurring phrase, "Verily, I say unto you" (vv. 15,23, and 42). a) Instructions for the immediate journey (vv. 5-15). b) Warning of future persecutions, culminated by the Second Advent (vv. 16-23). c) General encouragement for all believers (vv. 24-42).

1. His twelve disciples. This group had been formed some time previously, and now after a time of instruction (Mk 3:14) they were sent on a mission. **He gave them authority.** The right and the ability. Included in these delegated powers was the ability to cast out **unclean spirits** and to heal all kinds of **disease** (note that Jesus clearly differentiated between demon possession and disease). **2. The names of the twelve apostles** are listed three other places (Mk 3:16 ff.; Lk 6:14 ff.; Acts 1:13). Comparison shows that each list has three groups containing the same four names, though not always in the same order. However, Peter is always the first name in group one, Philip is always first in group two, and James of Alphaeus first in group three. Judas Iscariot when included is always last. Matthew lists them in pairs, probably because they were sent out that way (Mk 6:7). **Apostles.** Papyri discoveries confirm the meaning of "a duly-empowered representative of a higher official." **The first, Simon.** Not the first chosen, nor merely the first one in the list, but probably a reference to Peter's prominence in the apostolic circle (cf. 26:40; Pentecost; Cornelius' house; and others). But he was first among equals. The NT knows nothing of a Petrine supremacy over other apostles (cf. Gal 2:11; I Pet 5:1). **3. Bartholomew** is a patronymic of Nathanael (Jn 1:46). **Matthew the publican.** A self-effacing epithet employed only in the author's Gospel. **Thaddaeus** (ASV), also called Lebbaeus (in some ancient texts), is apparently the same as Judas the brother of James (Lk 6:16; Acts 1:13). **4. Simon,** called here by the Aramaic **Cananaean,** meaning "zealot" (cf. Lk; Acts). He apparently had belonged to the fanatical political group of the Zealots. **Iscariot.** Probably meaning "man of Kerioth," Kerioth being a town in Judea.

5. Jesus' order prohibiting any mission to the **Gentiles** or to **any city of the Samaritans** (racial half-breeds who maintained a rival worship and were despised by Jews; Jn 4:9,20) was not due to prejudice (Jn 4) nor was it permanent (Acts 1:8). **6,7.** At present, however, their message announced the Messianic **kingdom of heaven** (see 3:2; 4:23), to which **the house of Israel** was heir. **8.** Included among the miraculous powers given to them was authority to **raise the dead,** although there is no record that such power was employed on this mission. These ministrations were to be performed **freely,** without charge, for their authority had been received in this manner. **9. Provide neither gold.** These instructions apply only to this specific mission of limited duration (cf. Lk 22:35,36). Money was not to be carried in their **purses** (belts, girdles). **10. Scrip.** Knapsack, traveler's bag. They were not to procure extra **coats,** extra **sandals,** nor a **staff** (though they might use the sandals and staff they already had, Mk 6:8,9). Support would come from grateful hearers. **11. Search out who in it is worthy** (ASV). As they proclaimed their message (v. 7), the response would reveal who was spiritually disposed toward them. When hospitality was offered, the disciples were to accept it for the duration of their visit. **12.** They were to give the customary greeting (**salute,** which consisted of the rich *shalom*, "peace"). **13.** If the disciples should discover that their host was **not worthy** but really antagonistic to their purpose and message, their pronouncement of **peace** would not be wasted but would **return** for use somewhere else. **14.** If antagonism forced the abandonment of such a **house** or even of a whole **city,** the symbolism of shaking off the **dust** from their feet would vividly and yet solemnly portray the disciples' freedom from involvement in their opponents' guilt and coming judgment. **15. Sodom and Gomorrah.** Two oft-used examples of doomed cities (Isa 1:9; cf. Gen 18:20; 19:24-28). **Verily I say unto you.** This formula closes each section of this instruction (cf. vv. 23,42).

16. This second portion of the instruction looks beyond the specific mission to future dangers, and even gives a glimpse of eschatological times. **Wolves.** Vicious opponents (7:15; Lk 10:3; Jn 10:12; Acts 20:29). **Wise as serpents and harmless as doves.** "Alone, the wisdom of the serpent is mere cunning, and the harmlessness of the dove little better than weakness; but in combination, the wisdom of the serpent would save them from unnecessary exposure to danger; the harmlessness of the dove, from sinful expedients to escape it" (JFB, III, 81). **17. Councils.** The local courts found in every city (Deut 16:18). **18. Governors and kings.** There is no suggestion that this happened on their first mission; thus with typical prophetic method, Jesus uses the present occasion for treating matters some distance away in time. Agrippa I, Felix, Festus, Agrippa II, Sergius Paulus, and Gallio were some who heard testimony regarding Christ and the apostles. **19,20. Be not anxious. The Spirit** would provide the apostles with their oral testimony (as well as inspire their writings). **21,22.** Persecution of the most heartbreaking kind, even within families, must be expected. Yet there must be no yielding to despair, for deliverance is promised (cf. 24:13). **23. Flee ye into another.** Martyrdom was not to be sought; reasonable care for life was to be taken. Before all the **cities of Israel** should be visited in this way, the **Son of man** would **come.** In the similar context of Mt 24:8-31 the Great Tribulation and the Second Advent are in view. Hence, the "coming of the Son of man" is probably eschatological here also. This would have been more readily understood by the disciples, who would hardly have thought to equate this "coming" with the destruction of Jerusalem in A.D. 70. Here then is a promise of deliverance from the greatest persecution of all.

The concluding portion gives general encouragement for all believers (vv. 24-42). **24,25.** Christ's relation to believers is presented by three figures: **disciple** and **teacher, servant** and **lord, master of the house** and **members of the household.** If Jesus himself received ill-treatment, his subordinates could hardly expect to fare better. **Beelzebub** (better, *Beelzebul* or *Beezebul*) was regarded as "prince of the demons" (Mt 12:24; Lk 11:15), apparently identical with Satan. This spelling occurs nowhere else in Jewish literature outside the NT. Exact explanation is uncertain, though it seems related to "Baalzebub," the god of Ekron (II Kgs 1:16). **26,27. Fear them not.** This encouragement is based on the knowledge that God's ultimate judgment will vindicate believers and deal with persecutors. Thus, in accord with this oft-used maxim of Jesus, that which the Twelve had received privately (**in darkness, in the ear**) must be fearlessly publicized (**in light, upon the housetops**). **28.** To answer the objection that such action would endanger their lives, Jesus reminds them that it is more important to fear him who has authority over the **soul** as well as over the **body,** and can bring both to eternal ruin in **hell** (Gehenna). This clearly is speaking of God, not Satan, for believers are never commanded to fear Satan (but to resist him); nor does Satan destoy men in hell (he himself is punished there). **29-31.** God's providence, which extends even to the smallest details of this world, provides an additional antidote for fear. **Two sparrows.** Familiar birds in Palestine, used occasionally for food. **A farthing** (*assarion*). The Roman *as* or *assarion* was a copper coin, worth about one-sixteenth of a denarius (Arndt). Luke says two of these coins would buy five sparrows (12:6). **Without your Father.** Not only without his knowledge; the thought contextually is that without his providential direction not even such insignificant events can occur. This providence applies even to the minutest parts of our being (**all the hairs of your head**). **32,33.** The prospect of divine judgment may also serve as a deterrent to yielding before persecution. **Whosoever shall confess me** refers to genuine acknowledgment of Jesus as Lord and Saviour, with all that those terms imply. **Before men.** Indicative of a public confession before human interrogators, as contrasted with Christ's acknowledgment of believers before the **Father in heaven. Whosoever shall deny me** (cf. II Tim 2:12). The Greek tense (aorist, constative) refers not to one moment of denial (e.g., Peter's), but to the life in its entirety, which Christ is capable of assessing precisely.

34-39. The foregoing warnings of danger ahead might cause one to wonder why there should be such hazard. Jesus explains that his message, delivered in a rebellious and wicked world, would be met with hostility. **Sword.** A symbol of sharp conflict and division, as shown by examples in verses 35,36. **To set at variance** means literally *to divide in two*. Christ's Gospel has often brought cleavage even within family circles, not through any fault of the Gospel, but because of the rebellious attitude of sinful, unrepentant hearts. The illustration shows such a divided family of five: **father** and **mother,** unmarried **daughter,** married son **(man),** and his **bride,** who lived in the father's home, after Oriental custom. **37.** Heartbreaking as these divisions are, a disciple must not let his natural affections cause any weakening of his attachment to Christ. A time may come when he will be forced to make a choice. **38. His cross.** Though Jesus had not yet mentioned his coming crucifixion, this first reference to a **cross** by our Lord needed no explanation. The Jews had seen thousands of their countrymen crucified by the Romans (Jos *Antiq*. xvii. 10.10). Hence allegiance even to death, if necessary, is demanded if we would be **worthy** or **fit** to be called Christ's followers. **39. He that findeth his life.** *Psychē* denotes that which animates the body and in which the consciousness and spirit reside. "Life" and "soul" are two English attempts to translate this many-sided word. The sense is: He who in persecution saves his life by denying Christ will lose it eventually forever (particularly the soul aspect); but he who loses his life because of devotion to Christ will save his soul eternally.

40-42. To conclude this charge Jesus shows that those who risk persecution shall be appropriately rewarded. **He that receiveth you.** Not as a mere house guest but as a messenger of Christ. Our Lord regards this welcome as if done to himself. **He that receiveth a prophet in the name of a prophet,** i.e., because he is a prophet (God's commissioned spokesman). Those who are not prophets themselves may share their labors and also their reward. **One of these little ones.** The smallest service performed to aid the most insignificant of Christ's servants (cf. Mt 25:40) shall not go unnoticed by our Lord.

7) Christ's Answer to John, and Related Discourse. 11:1-30. Here Jesus answers John's keen question, gives to the crowds a tribute to his imprisoned forerunner, and castigates the cities that rejected Him.

2. On John's imprisonment by Herod at Machaerus, east of the Dead Sea (Jos *Antiq*. xviii. 5.2), see 4:12; 14:1-12. **He sent by his disciples** (ASV). Men who had remained loyal to John, and at this stage felt no reason to leave him. **3. Art thou the Coming One?** A common designation for Messiah (Mk 11:9; Lk 13:35). In view of John's prior pronouncements and supernatural revelation (Jn 1:29-34), to accuse him of doubts concerning Jesus' Messiahship seems most unfair. Rather, since the character of Jesus' ministry semed to lack the judgment aspect that John had predicted (Mt 3:10-12), he may have wondered whether an additional Messianic figure needed to appear, such as Elijah (cf. Mal 4:5; Jn 1:19-21). **4,5. Jesus'** kindly reply called attention to his works, which John would recognize as Messianic credentials (Isa 29:18,19; 35:5,6; 61:1). **The dead are raised up.** Luke describes one such miracle just prior to this interview (Lk 7:11-17). **6. Whosoever shall find none occasion of stumbling in me** (ASV). This encouraging stimulus to John's faith reminded him and all believers that recognition of Jesus as Messiah is characteristic of the spiritually blessed man (Jn 20:31).

7-19. Tribute to John. **7. Reed shaken with the wind.** A wavering person. Christ's obvious intent denied that John was such, and hence one must not ascribe faithlessness to John's previous inquiry. **8. Soft raiment.** Though a rich wardrobe might be expected of a politician's emissary, John's well-known prophetic garb (3:4) bespoke his spiritual mission. **9,10. Much more than a prophet** (ASV). John was not only the last of the OT line of inspired spokesmen, but was also the predicted forerunner of Messiah (Mal 3:1), especially chosen to introduce Messiah to Israel. **11.** Consequently, no human being is greater than John. Jesus here destroys any suspicions of friction between himself and John. **He that is least in the kingdom of heaven is greater than he.** In this statement John seems to be regarded as outside the **kingdom.** Hence the **kingdom of heaven** must still be regarded as the Messianic kingdom announced by both John and Jesus (3:2; 4:17). John, whose ministry was one of preparation, was now imprisoned and soon to die. But those who had responded to the announcement and were now in the circle of Jesus' followers were the nucleus of His **kingdom.** They were being given new truths and privileges, and after national rejection of Jesus, would be baptized into a new spiritual body, the Church (a part of the Messianic kingdom, Col 1:13; Rev 20:6). John was the friend of the bridegroom, but the disciples became the bride (Jn 3:29). When Jesus spoke these words (before Pentecost, Acts 2), **kingdom of heaven** was the most intelligible term he could have used. **12. The kingdom of heaven suffereth violence.** This verb may be regarded either as middle – *violently forces its way* (cf. Lk 16:16), or as passive – *is violently treated.* The latter is more consistent with the next clause. From John's initial announcement of the coming of the Kingdom, the response had been a violent one, whether by vicious opponents (cf. vv. 18,19; 14:3,4) or by enthusiastic supporters. **The violent take it by force** (or, *seize it*). Compare Lk 16:16. Among the most prominent of Christ's adherents were the publicans, harlots, and other open sinners, who flocked to our Lord in great numbers. **13-15.** John was the last of the prophets of the OT dispensation who foretold the coming of Messiah. Included in these OT predictions was the coming of **Elijah** to usher in the great Day of the Lord (Mal 4:5). Though John himself denied that he was the resurrected Elijah (Jn 1:21), Jesus states that if the Jews had fully received Him and His Kingdom, John would have fulfilled the OT prediction (Mt 17:10-13; cf. Lk 1:17). Since this did not occur, John did not fulfill all that was predicted of Elijah; and hence the complete fulfillment is still future. This passage clearly shows the contingent nature of the kingdom offer.

16-19. In marked contrast to this glowing estimate of John was the prevailing sentiment of the crowds toward John and Jesus. **This generation.** The contemporaries of John and Jesus (v. 12). **Like unto children.** This homely parable portrays a scene in the public concourse, where a group of peevish children cannot decide what game to play (cf. Lk 7:31-35). Suggestions that they play wedding **(piped, danced)** and funeral **(mourned, lamented)** prove unappealing; so they play nothing. Similarly, John's ascetic ministry brought the charge that he was **demon**-possessed. But Jesus' habit of contacting sinners and sharing their social customs elicited the vicious and untrue claims that he was **gluttonous**, a **winebibber**, as evil as his companions. However, the **wisdom** of the courses of action of both men was proved (**justified**) by the results.

20-24. Upbraiding of the cities. **Wherein most of his mighty works were done.** No miracles are recorded in the Gospels as having occurred in **Chorazin** or **Bethsaida** (not Bethsaida Julias). Probably these two villages were so close to the larger **Capernaum** that many of the miracles performed at Capernaum were witnessed by inhabitants of all three communities. **Tyre and Sidon.** Prominent Phoenician coastal cities, the objects of divine judgment under Nebuchadnezzar and Alexander (cf. Ezk 26 – 28). **Sackcloth and ashes** (cf. Jon 3:5-8). The common Eastern way of demonstrating grief. Had they been granted the opportunities of these Jewish cities, Jesus says, they **would have repented.** Why such opportunities were not granted must be left with the sovereign purposes of God, who sent Christ first to the house of Israel. Yet the greater spiritual privileges granted Chorazin and Bethsaida made their unbelief more culpable. As for **Capernaum,** which, as Jesus' home, had the greatest opportunity of all, the rhetorical question, **Shalt thou be exalted unto heaven?** (ASV), implies a negative answer. **Thou shalt go down unto Hades**. The state of its inhabitants at the **judgment** will be worse than that of **Sodom,** a city proverbial for wickedness.

25-30. Jesus concludes the discourse with an explanation of men's unbelief, and a gracious invitation. **25. Jesus answered.** The following verses are an answer to the problems raised by the previous discussion. **I thank thee, O Father.** The verb *exomologoumai* describes a confession or full acknowledgment, coupled with praise. **Wise and understanding** (ASV). Spiritual awareness of Christ and his Kingdom is not arrived at through intellect or common sense. **Babes.** Those who, in response to Christ's message, recognize their spiritual helplessness are able to receive his teaching (18:3). The glory of the Gospel is that both the learned and the ignorant may become babes. **26.** The final explanation of human response, however, lies in the **good pleasure** of God (cf. Eph 1:5; Phil 2:13). **27. All things are delivered unto me of my Father.** Jesus claims an authority which distinguishes him from all other persons (cf. Mt 28:18; Jn 13:3). Here that authority is stated as involving the revelation of God to men. **Neither knoweth any man the Father, save the Son.**

The mutual knowledge of the Father and the Son is perfect, but it is limited to them unless revelation is imparted to mankind. **To whomsoever the Son will reveal.** The Son as the image of God is the revealer of the invisible God (Col 1:15); he is the Logos, the expression of the unseen God (Jn 1:1,18). Hence Matthew is in agreement with thoughts more frequently expressed by John and Paul. This shows that the Biblical writers were essentially of one mind regarding the truth that man is dependent upon God's grace in Christ for all spiritual knowledge. **28. Come unto me.** In view of the authority vested in Christ (v. 27), this invitation vibrates with opportunity. **All ye that labor.** Men whose wearisome efforts to achieve spiritual rest have not eased the burden of man-made obligations (23:4). **29,30. Take my yoke.** A Jewish metaphor for discipline and discipleship. "Put your neck under the yoke, and let your soul receive instruction" (Sir 51:26). Christ alone is the Teacher who by his person and work can instruct men regarding the Father, and bring them the **rest of soul** which is the very essence of true spiritual experience, a rest involving removal of sin's guilt and the possession of eternal life. **My burden is light.** The obligations involved in the Gospel are blessed ones, and strength to bear them is supplied with the yoke.

8) Opposition from the Pharisees. 12:1-50. Matthew records a series of incidents showing the nature of Pharisaic hostility.

1-8. Pharisees oppose plucking grain on the Sabbath. **1.** As the group journeyed through the **grainfields,** the disciples exercised their legal privilege of plucking and eating the grain (Deut 23:25). **2.** To the **Pharisees,** who must have been taking a walk through the same fields, the act appeared **not lawful** because it involved a breaking of the **sabbath day.** Rabbinically interpreted, plucking grain was reaping, and thus was work (Ex 20:10). **3,4.** Christ's first reply recalls **David** and the **shewbread** (I Sam 21:1-6). Though divine Law restricted the shewbread to the **priests** (Lev 24:9), extreme human need overruled this regulation, and the rabbis so understood it. **5,6.** A second illustration shows that the law of Sabbath rest was not absolute, for the priests were required by that very law to work on the Sabbath (Num 28:9,10). The argument is, if priests can be guiltless in working on the Sabbath for furthering temple worship, how much more are the disciples guiltless in using the Sabbath for the work of Christ, who is the reality to which the Temple pointed. **7.** Christ's third argument points to Pharisaic misunderstanding of Hos 6:6, **mercy and not sacrifice** (cf. Mt 9:13). God desires proper hearts far more than externals which have become mere formalities. A spiritual understanding of Christ and the disciples by the Pharisees would have prevented their judging these **innocent ones. 8. Lord of the sabbath.** Since Jesus as Son of man is master of the Sabbath day, the disciples who had used the Sabbath in the course of following him were employing it in a proper way.

9-21. Pharisees oppose healing on the Sabbath. (Cf. Mk 3:1-6; Lk 6:6-11.) **9. Into their synagogue.** Luke shows that it occurred on a different Sabbath. **10,11. Is it lawful to heal on the sabbath day?** The OT made no prohibition, but some rabbis regarded it as work. Jesus, however, by pointing to what any individual would have done for an unfortunate **sheep,** makes his own obligation clear. **12.** Since man is incomparably **of more value** (ASV) than a sheep, He must come to his aid. To avoid doing good when such is within one's power is really to do harm (see Mk and Lk accounts). **13,14.** The miracle only enraged the **Pharisees,** who immediately plotted (along with the Herodians, Mk 3:6) **to destroy him.** Thus in Galilee, as recently in Jerusalem (Jn 5:18), murderous hatred was taking definite form. Men who called healing a Sabbath violation felt no qualms about plotting murder. **15. He withdrew himself.** Knowledge of the plot prompted Jesus to avoid open conflict at this time, for his hour was not yet come. He thus transferred his ministrations to other areas (Mk 3:7), and **he healed them all. 16.** However, he cautioned those healed (especially the demoniacs, Mk 3:11,12) not to use the miracles to publicize him as Messiah and so excite the crowds and the opposition. **17-21. That it might be fulfilled.** This gracious, non-provocative ministry of Jesus is shown by Matthew to be consistent with Messianic prophecy (Isa 42:1-4). For as Jesus emphasized the righteous and spiritual aspects of his Kingdom, he did not engage in public haranguing, nor political demagoguery. Neither did he trample on the weak in order to gain his ends. **Smoking flax.** The wick of a lamp in which the oil is about gone – symbolic of those who are feeble.

22-37. Pharisees oppose Christ's demon expulsion. **22. One possessed with a demon.** The demon possession had caused two side effects – blindness and dumbness. The healing removed all three afflictions. **23. Can this be the Son of David?** The negative answer implied by the question reveals that even though the miracle had raised the possibility of his Messiahship (**Son of David,** cf. 1:20; 9:27), the people were predisposed to unbelief. **24.** The vicious charge that Christ's power over demons was derived from a league with **Beelzebul** (see comment on 10:25) was fully known by Jesus and refuted publicly in unanswerable fashion. **25,26.** The simple analogy of a **divided kingdom, city,** or **house** as tending to self-destruction refutes the charge. For in expelling demons, Jesus was assuredly frustrating the works of Satan, and we must credit Satan with a reasonable amount of shrewdness. (Nor can it be allowed that Satan might permit one such expulsion to confuse the issue, for this expulsion was no isolated case.) **27. By whom do your sons cast them out?** Since some of these Pharisees' associates (compare the OT expression "sons of the prophets") claimed the power of exorcism, how illogical to attribute similar effects to different causes. Whether or not the Jews did perform valid exorcisms is not necessary to the argument *(ad hominem).* The fact that the Pharisees claimed it made the argument effective. If, however, Jesus implies that at least some of the Pharisaic exorcisms were genuine, then it must be assumed that the power came from God (otherwise Christ's argument is greatly weakened). **28,29.** Christ's final argument calls attention to his own ministry, particularly to his expulsion of demons, which was evidence enough that the **kingdom of God has come.** The description of Christ's ministry as an entry into a **strong man's house** (Satan's domain) and a spoiling of **his goods** (Christ's power over demons), provides clear proof that the **strong man** (Satan) has **first** been bound. Jesus' victory over Satan at the temptation (4:1-11) demonstrated our Lord's superiority. **30. He that is not with me is against me.** In the conflict with Satan, neutrality is impossible.

31,32. Every sin and blasphemy shall be forgiven unto men. The general principle. Atonement by Christ at Calvary would be sufficient to remit the guilt of all sins, even the most aggravated forms of slander against God (**blasphemy**). One sin, however, is declared unpardonable: **whosoever shall speak against the Holy Spirit.** In view of Jesus' previously stated principle, this unpardonableness cannot be due to inadequacy of the atonement, nor may we infer any peculiar sacredness of the Third Person of the Trinity. Many explain this sin as the attributing of the miraculous works of the Spirit to Satanic power (cf. Mk 3:29,30), and see no possibility of its being committed today (so Chafer, Broadus, Gaebelein). Others, however, regard the accusation of the Pharisees as being symptomatic, and not the sin itself. The following verses point to the corrupt heart as the cause of the sin. The particular function of the Spirit is to bring conviction and repentance, and make men receptive to the invitation of Christ. Hence hearts that hate God and blaspheme Christ (I Tim 1:13) may yet be convicted and brought to repentance by the Spirit. But he who rejects every overture of the Spirit removes himself from the only force that can lead him to forgiveness (Jn 3:36). That such a settled state can be reached in this life is clearly implied by the passage. The OT describes these as sinning "with a high hand" (Num 15:30, ASV); for them no atonement was possible. Men cannot read hearts, and thus cannot judge when others have reached such a state. The real possibility of this sin does not weaken the gospel invitation, "Whosoever will," for by its very nature such will have no willingness to accept. As for the Pharisees of Jesus' audience, it is not stated whether or not they had fully committed this sin, but the warning is clear. Their considerable instruction made their responsibility great; their previous hostility showed their determined unbelief.

33-35. Make the tree good. A passage, similar to 7:16-20, where the speech of men is shown to be indicative of the state of the human **heart. 36,37.** On the **day of judgment** the Lord will consider every man's life in its entirety, even **every idle word** (not necessarily evil) coming from the overflow of his heart. Only the divine Judge is capable of recording, evaluating, and rendering a verdict on such matters.

38-45. Pharisees and scribes demand a sign. **38. We wish to see a sign from you.** They discounted previous miracles. What they wanted was some sensational deed in keeping with their ideas of Messiah (cf. Mt 16:1), a sign that would require no faith, only sight. **39. Adulterous generation.** A description of the nation as spiritually unfaithful in its vows to Jehovah (cf. Jer 3:14,20). To such a nation, the one great sign of the Resurrection is here foretold (and had been suggested even earlier, Jn 2:19-21). **40.** The experience of **Jonah,** who was released from the **belly of the sea-monster,** was typical of the coming interment and resurrection of Jesus after **three days and three nights in the**

heart of the earth. Those holding to the traditional Friday crucifixion explain the time here as idiomatic for parts of three days (Friday, Saturday, Sunday). Those holding to Wednesday crucifixion explain the reference literally as denoting seventy-two hours, from sundown Wednesday to sundown Saturday (e.g., W. G. Scroggie, *Guide to the Gospels,* pp. 569-577). **41.** The Ninevites, having received Jonah and his message after his miraculous deliverance, **repented.** Thus their action places Israel in a much worse light, for nationally she has remained unrepentant, both before and after the Resurrection, even though there was **more than** (AV, *a greater than*) **Jonah here. 42.** Likewise the interest in Solomon's **wisdom** (divinely bestowed) by the **queen** of Sheba (I Kgs 10:1-13) will put into sad contrast at the **judgment** the unbelief of current Judaism. **43-45.** A striking parable, suggested naturally by the occasion (12:22 ff.), pictures Israel's (and the Pharisees') precarious situation. The expelled demon, finding no resting place in the **dry places** (indicated elsewhere as abodes of demons: Isa 13:21; Baruch 4:35; Rev 18:2), returns to his former habitation, which is now more attractive (**swept, garnished**) but **unoccupied.** He re-enters with seven other spirits, and the result is greater degeneration. **So shall it be.** Israel (nationally and individually) had been morally cleansed by the ministries of John and Jesus. Since the Exile, the evils of open idolatry had been removed. Yet, in most cases, the reformation which was meant to be preparatory had stopped short. Israel's house was "empty." Christ was not invited to occupy it. Hence **this wicked generation** will reach an even worse state. A few years later these same Jews faced the horrors of A.D. 66–70. End-time members of this race (*genea*) will especially be victimized by demons (Rev 9:1-11).

46-50. Christ's mother and brethren. **46,47. His mother and brethren.** These brethren are presumably the children of Joseph and Mary, born after Jesus. **Seeking to speak to him** indicates effort was being made, but the crowds were too great (Lk 8:19). Reasons for their concern are obvious. Previously, Jesus' preaching at Nazareth had forced the family to move to Capernaum (4:13; Lk 4:16-31; Jn 2:12). Now he had brought the Pharisees into open and blasphemous opposition. In addition, friends had reported that the strain of this ministry was affecting his health (Mk 3:21). Verse 47 adds little new information, and many ancient manuscripts omit it. **48. Who is my mother?** By this intriguing question Jesus startles the crowd to prepare them for a precious truth. **50. Whosoever shall do the will of my Father.** This "doing" is not some form of work-righteousness, but is man's response to Christ's invitation. "This is the work of God, that ye believe on him whom he hath sent" (Jn 6:29). The spiritual relationship between Christ and believers is closer than the closest of blood ties. This saying offered no disrespect to Mary, nor to his brothers, for at a later time we find them sharing this spiritual relation (Acts 1:14). Yet neither is there any suggestion that the mother of Jesus had special access to his presence.

9) A Series of Parables on the Kingdom. 13:1-58. This first extended series of parables was given on one of the busiest days recorded of Jesus' ministry. Matthew's account lists seven parables, and a concluding one of application. Mark records four, including one not in Matthew. Luke records three, not all together. Two of the parables were interpreted by Jesus (The Sower, The Tares), and a third one partially (The Net); this provides a scheme for understanding the others. **1. The same day.** Matthew alone relates this event to the previous discussion. The crowds being so great (as to prevent even his family from reaching him; 12:46), **Jesus went out of the house** to the **sea side. 2.** Using a **boat** as a platform, he **sat** in the usual manner of teachers and addressed those on the **shore. 3a. Parables.** Plausible narratives used by Jesus to convey spiritual truth through comparisons. Though Jesus was not the inventor of parabolic teaching, his use of the method far surpassed that of all other teachers in effectiveness and depth of truth portrayed.

3b-23. The Sower. **3b. The sower.** The definite article is probably generic. All sowers performed in similar fashion. **4.** As the sower scattered his seed, **some** fell on the parched earth of the path that ran through the field. Such seed lying on the surface would quickly attract the **birds. 5,6. Stony places.** Not ground covered with rocks, but a rock ledge covered with a thin layer of soil. Seed sown here would sprout quickly, for the sun would soon warm the thin crust; but for lack of sufficient **root** and moisture, the plant would shortly become **scorched** and **withered. 7. Among thorns.** Ground infested with thorn roots that plowing had not removed. **8. Good ground.** The fertile soil of Galilee was capable of producing harvests of the magnitude mentioned here (W. M. Thomson, *Land and Book,* p. 83). **9. Who hath**

ears to hear, let him hear. A declaration that this simple story, without preface or explanation, had a deeper meaning.

10-17. In response to the disciples' question, Jesus states his reason for speaking in parables. **10. Why?** Previously he had used parables, but this occasion was obviously different. Now the parables themselves formed the basis of the teaching; they were not mere illustrations. **11. The mysteries of the kingdom of heaven** identifies the content of these parables as being revelation previously hidden pertaining to the Kingdom. The interpretation relates them to the present day. The glories of the Messianic reign were clearly sketched in the OT. But the rejection of Messiah and the interval between his first and second comings was not understood. These parables describe the strange form of the Kingdom while the King is absent, during which time the Gospel is preached and a spiritual nucleus is developed for the establishment of the Messianic reign (Col 1:13; Mt 25:34). The revelation of these **mysteries** in parabolic form was due to the existence of two distinct groups: **to you it is given; to them it is not given. 12. Whosoever hath.** The disciples, having responded in faith to Jesus, already possessed much truth regarding Messiah and his program. Careful reflection upon these parables would enlighten them further. **Whosoever hath not.** The determined unbelievers who had refused the previous teaching of Jesus (cf. chs. 10; 11) were not being given the bare truths to trample under foot (cf. 7:6). Yet there is grace even here, for they were spared the greater guilt of rejecting the plainest teaching, and there remained the possibility that the intriguing parable might arouse curiosity and bring about a change of heart. **13-15.** The settled state of spiritual insensibility among the people is viewed as a partial fulfillment (**is being fulfilled**) of Isa 6:9,10. Matthew's quotation follows the LXX, and emphasizes the obstinate unbelief of the people. (The Hebrew, *make the heart of this people fat*, presents the condition as a judgment from God upon their spiritual hardness.) **16,17.** The disciples, who had responded to Messiah, were beneficiaries of privileges longed for by prophets and righteous men in the OT economy (cf. I Pet 1:10-12).

18-23. Jesus' interpretation of the parable explains the fate of the Word in this age as due, humanly speaking, to the condition of human hearts. **18. The sower.** Not identified, but in conformity with the next parable, it is clearly Christ himself, and those who represent him (13:37). **19. The word of the kingdom** (*word of God,* Lk 8:11), symbolized by the seed, is the message Jesus proclaimed concerning himself and his kingdom. **He that was sown by the way side** (ASV). This is not a mixing of figures, but a viewing of the seed in the soil as culminating in the plant, and thus representative of the individual case. The wayside hearer is the completely unresponsive one, from whom Satan (**the wicked one**), either personally or through his agents (**birds,** v. 4, are often symbolic of evil: Jer 5:26,27; Rev 18:2), soon removes all spiritual impressions. **20,21.** The seed on the rocky ledge describes the case of the shallow, emotional hearer (**immediately with joy**) whose initial enthusiasm is completely withered by the invigorating and necessary sun of **tribulation** or **persecution. 22.** The seed sprouting **among the thorns** depicts the preoccupied hearer whose heart is already full of **care** and worldly interests (the thorns were already in the soil, but not visible at the planting). A divided allegiance prevents the maturing of spiritual values. **23.** The only hearers who are approved are those of the **good ground.** Only here is **fruit** produced (Gal 5:22,23), and fruitfulness is the test of life (Jn 15:1-6). The explanation of how the hearts arrived at these conditions is outside the scope of this parable.

24-30. The Tares. For the interpretation see 13:36-43. **24. The kingdom of heaven is likened unto a man.** Christ characterizes the interregnum by the case of a man who had the following experience. **25,26. While men slept.** At night; the most probable time for this wicked work. Neither here nor in the interpretation is this detail regarded as negligence. **Tares.** *Zizania,* it is generally agreed, denotes darnel (*lolium temulentum*), a noxious plant, practically indistinguishable from wheat until the ear has developed. **27. Whence then hath it tares?** The extent of the useless growth could not be accounted for by chance (e.g., wind-blown seed), but only by deliberate planting. Yet, was it not obvious that the householder had planted good seed? (An affirmative answer is implied.) **28. An enemy hath done this.** Instances of such forthright malice are on record (Alford, *New Testament for Eng. Readers,* pp. 98,99). **29,30. The season of the harvest.** When the differences between the wheat and the darnel were most pronounced, and separation could be done economically by the **reapers.** Hence the tares were first bundled **for burning,** and then the wheat was gathered.

31,32. The Mustard Seed. This parable resembles the first two in that all mention a man, a field, and seed. Consistently interpreted, in each the **man** symbolizes Christ, the **field** is the world, and the **seed** is the Word which tells of Christ and his kingdom. **Mustard seed.** Its smallness was proverbial (cf. Mt 17:20). Yet in this instance it grows until it is **greater than the herbs** (ASV), and it becomes a tree. Instances of unusual growth in Palestine have been noted by travelers, but rarely, if ever, to the extent described here (cf. Mk 4:32). That such growth is regarded as unfavorable is suggested by the **birds** that **lodge in the branches.** In this parable series, birds are agents of evil (13:4,19), as they are frequently in Scripture (Jer 5:26,27; Rev 18:2). History confirms the fact that from the smallest beginning, the church made astounding growth through the proclamation of Christ's message. Yet such unusual growth has provided roosting places for those who are enemies of God, who seek the shade and fruit of the tree for their own interests (even nations like to be called "Christian"). Disciples are warned that the mere bigness of what appears outwardly to be Christ's kingdom is not essentially a contradiction of the Lord's teaching that true believers are a little flock surrounded by wolves (Lk 12:32; Mt 10:16).

33-35. The Leaven. Though some interpret this parable and the preceding as depicting the spreading influence of the Gospel, such explanations violate Jesus' use of these symbols elsewhere, as well as the import of other parables (e.g., The Tares) which show evil existing till the end of the age. **33. Leaven.** A lump of old dough in a high state of fermentation. Leaven in the OT is generally symbolic of evil. In Christ's later uses of this symbol, it refers to evil doctrine of the Pharisees, Sadducees, and Herod (Mt 16:6-12; Mk 8:15). Paul's references (I Cor 5:6,7; Gal 5:9), which certainly regard leaven as evil, seem greatly influenced by Christ's parable. **Three measures of meal.** Apparently a common quantity employed in baking (Gen 18:6). The **woman** (in contrast to the **man** in the other parables) is the opponent of Christ and infuses the kingdom in this age with false doctrine. Elsewhere she is called "Wickedness" (Zech 5:7,8), "Jezebel" (Rev 2:20 ff.), and the "great harlot" (Rev. 17:1 ff.). By this characterization of leaven in the meal, believers are warned to beware of false doctrine which would infiltrate all parts of the kingdom in its interregnal aspect.

34,35. On this occasion Christ spoke publicly **(to the multitude)** in symbolic language alone, without interpretation. Only to the disciples did he explain the symbolism (13:10 ff.; 13:36 ff.). Matthew regarded this as reminiscent of Ps 78:2, and saw in Jesus the most perfect fulfillment of the prophet's function.

36-43. Christ's interpretation of The Tares. For the parable itself see 13:24-30. **36. Declare unto us the parable.** This parable was more involved than The Mustard Seed and The Leaven, and its implication of persisting evil may have conflicted with the disciples' notions. Our Lord's explanation of the symbols shows that major details are important, but some features are merely to give form to the story and are not symbolic (e.g., the men who slept, servants of the householder, binding of the bundles). **38,39. The field is the world.** Not the Church. **Children of the kingdom.** As in the explanation of The Sower, the seed is here regarded as having produced plants (13:19). The springing up of Christ's true followers in this world is counterfeited by the **devil,** whose **children** often masquerade as believers (II Cor 11:13-15). **40-43.** Though efficient removal in the early stages is shown to be impossible (v. 29), at the end **angels** will be delegated to **gather** the tares **out of his kingdom.** Thus the tares in the world are also regarded as being in the Kingdom in some sense. It must be, therefore, in the peculiar form of the Kingdom during the interregnum. Final removal will be done by angels at the **consummation of the age** — the end of Daniel's seventieth week, and the time of the second coming of Christ, when He will establish his glorious reign (Mt 25:31-46; Dan 12:3). It must be observed again that the Church and the Kingdom are not co-extensive, though prior to the Rapture, subjects of the Kingdom are also members of the Church. After the Church is removed at the Rapture, there will be Kingdom subjects on earth during the Tribulation. The statement that the tares will be gathered "first" (vv. 30, 41-43) clearly shows this to occur not at the Rapture (at which time the saints are gathered) but at the end of the Tribulation. For a similar statement, see comment on Mt 24:40-42, where those taken away are judged, and those left enter into blessing.

44. The Hid Treasure. Though the treasure is usually explained as Christ, the Gospel, salvation, or the Church, which a sinner should be willing to sacrifice all to obtain, the consistent use of the **man** in this series as referring to Christ, and the action of hiding again after finding make such views unlikely. Rather, the **treasure hidden in the field** depicts the place of national Israel during the interregnum (Ex 19:5; Ps 135:4). To this obscure nation came Christ. The nation, however, rejected him, and so, by the divine purpose, she was removed from her momentary prominence; even today she remains obscured to outward view as to her relation to the Messianic kingdom (Mt 21:43). Yet Christ gave his very life **(all that he hath)** to purchase the whole field (the world, II Cor 5:19; I Jn 2:2), and thus obtained full ownership by right of discovery and redemption. When he comes again, the treasure will be unearthed and fully displayed (Zech 12,13).

45,46. The Pearl. This parable, similar in its movement to that of the Hid Treasure, is often explained in the same way; but such explanations are vulnerable to some of the same objections. It is consistent, however, to regard the **merchant man** as Christ, who came seeking men and women **(goodly pearls)** who would respond to him and his message. Eventually he gave his life **(all that he had)** to purchase **one pearl of great price** (I Cor 6:20). The **one pearl** depicts that other great company in the Kingdom, the Church, composed of men and women who are made one in the Church (I Cor 10:17; 12:12,13).

47-50. The Net. A parable similar to The Tares, but with a different emphasis. This **net** is the large seine, often left in the water for some time. It depicts the Gospel, which was sent out into the world (**sea** in Scripture often symbolizes the restless nations, Lk 21:25; Dan 7:3,17) by Christ and his apostles. Among the various kinds of **fish** enveloped by the net are some **unusable** ones, which Jesus interpreted as **wicked** men, and which in The Tares are shown to have been put there by Satan (cf. also birds in the branches, v. 32). Not all who seem responsive to the Gospel are genuinely converted.

51-53. Conclusion to the parables. The disciples, who had been given not only the parables but also principles of interpretation (cf. Mk 4:34), indicated their comprehension of this teaching. Jesus then compared their status as informed **scribe**[s] (i.e., teachers and interpreters of God's truth) to that of an efficient head of a household who has a rich storehouse with which to perform his duties. **Things new and old.** Old truths long possessed in the OT and new truths such as those revealed in these parables.

54-58. A visit to Nazareth. Matthew appends this incident to illustrate most poignantly the spread of opposition that had necessitated the parabolic method (13:11-15). This visit, recorded also in Mk 6:1-6, is distinct from an earlier one recounted in Lk 4:16-30 (occurring prior to Mt 4:13). **54. His own country.** Nazareth and its environs. **55. The carpenter's son.** Mark's account (6:3) indicates that some called Jesus "the carpenter," showing that our Lord had learned Joseph's trade. **His brethren.** (For a detailed discussion of whether these are uterine brothers, half brothers, or cousins, see J. A. Broadus, *Commentary on the Gospel of Matthew*, pp. 310-312, or P. S. Schaff in *Lange's Commentary on Matthew*, pp. 255-260.) In the absence of any intimation that these **brethren** are to be regarded in an unusual sense, the common understanding of them as children of Joseph and Mary should be inferred. It seems strongly probable that two of them, **James** and **Judas** (Jude), became writers of NT epistles. **56,57.** Though Christ's mother and brothers had moved to Capernaum (4:13), his sisters had evidently married and remained at Nazareth **(with us)**. Since Christ's boyhood and early manhood had been undistinguished by any miracles (cf. Jn 2:11), his fellow townsmen were unable to account for or to accept this new development. Thus Jesus employs the same proverb as before to explain their response (Lk 4:24). **58. Not many mighty works there.** Only a few healings (Mk 6:5). **Because of their unbelief.** Christ's power did not depend on men's faith (cf. Jn 9:6, 36; Lk 7:11-15). However, unbelief prevented many opportunities for miracles inasmuch as not many people came to him.

10) Withdrawal of Jesus Following John's Beheading. 14:1-36. The interest of Herod in the reports regarding Jesus was viewed by our Lord as the signal to withdraw. Matthew's order, which previously has been often topical, now becomes chronological throughout.

14:1-12. Herod's guilty interest. **1. Herod the tetrarch.** Herod Antipas, son of Herod the Great, and ruler of Galilee and Perea. His ignorance of Jesus prior to this time may have been due to his absence from the country or to his luxurious habits, which hindered his taking interest in religious movements. **2. This is John the Baptist.** This explanation, first suggested by others (Lk 9:7), eventually was adopted by Herod, who attributed the miracles to a **risen** John, though John had performed no miracles when living. **3,4. Herodias.** Daughter of Aristobolus, a half brother of Antipas. She had been married to her uncle, Herod Philip, and had borne him a daughter, Salome. Antipas, however, persuaded her to leave her husband and marry him, though he was already married to the daughter of King Aretas (who escaped to her father, and a war ensued). Such a marriage was adulterous and incestuous. **5. When he would have put him to death.** Herod was torn by mixed emotions (see also v. 9). Pressure from Herodias was balanced by political and even personal considerations (Mk 6:20), and thus final disposition of John had been delayed. **6,7.** The implacable Herodias had not relented, however, and the celebration of **Herod's birthday** provided her opportunity for revenge. Debasing her own daughter by sending her to perform a suggestive dance before Herod and his courtiers, she extracted from this puppet ruler a grandiose promise more fitting for a Persian monarch (Mk 6:23; cf. Est 5:3). **8-11. Being put forward by her mother** (ASV) locates the source of the conspiracy. **Give me here John the Baptist's head upon a platter.** Taking advantage of the opportunity, she made her gory request, which left no room for evasion or delay. This banquet must have been held at Machaerus, where John was imprisoned (Jos *Antiq.* xviii. 5. 2.). **12. His disciples came,** and after burying the headless **body,** they told Jesus. The problem of earlier days (11:2-6) had been satisfactorily resolved, and now John's followers turned logically to Jesus. In all probability they attached themselves to him.

13-21. Feeding the five thousand. The only miracle of Jesus recorded in all four Gospels. It occurred at Passover season (Jn 6:4), thus one year before Christ's death. **13,14. When Jesus heard of it, he departed.** Herod's murder of John and his subsequent notice of the activities of Jesus prompted this withdrawal. Another reason was the return of the Twelve from their mission (Mk 6:30; Lk 9:10), who needed a respite from the crowds and further instruction from Jesus. Soon, however, Jesus surrendered his privacy to minister to the multitude, who had followed **on foot. 15. When it was evening.** The Jews distinguished two evenings, the first beginning about three o'clock, and the second at sundown (cf. Ex 12:6, ASV marg.). The first evening is meant in verse 15; the second in verse 23. Harmonization demands that Jn 6:5-7 be understood as occurring previously. But though Jesus had confronted Philip with the problem earlier in the day, no solution had been reached by the **disciples** except **to send the multitudes away.** And already the **time was past** for locating food and lodging (Lk 9:12) in this sparsely inhabited region. **16-18. Give ye them to eat.** By laying this responsibility upon the disciples, Christ intended to awaken in them an awareness that association with him included provision for every need. Andrew mentioned the lad with **five** barley **loaves** and **two fishes,** but he seemed totally unaware of the divine possibilities (Jn 6:8,9). **19.** Jesus, however, called for an orderly reclining of the multitude upon the **grass,** and after he had **blessed** the loaves and fishes (equivalent to "giving thanks," Jn 6:11), he distributed by the **disciples** to the **multitude. 20. Fragments.** Broken pieces that had not been eaten (not merely crumbs here). **Twelve baskets full.** Small wicker baskets (different from the large hamper-like baskets mentioned in 15:37), used for carrying articles while traveling. They may have belonged to the apostles, and the fragments collected in them may have supplied the apostles' need. **21. Five thousand men, beside women and children.** The nearness of Passover suggests that these may have been gathering in Galilee for the trip to Jerusalem.

22-36. Christ's walking on the water. **22. Straightway he constrained the disciples.** The urgency of this action was due to the attempt by the people to make Jesus king by force (Jn 6:15). **23. Mountain.** A secluded place for prayer, apart from the distractions of the unspiritual crowd. The significance of this situation, similar to that of Satan's third temptation (4:8,9), drove Jesus to prayer, that his purpose might be unswerving. From this **mountain** Christ could also observe the disciples in their boat (Mk 6:48). **Evening.** Cf. comment on verse 15. **24.** Ancient manuscripts vary between **in the midst of the sea** and **many furlongs distant from the land** (ASV marg.). John 6:19 shows the distance from shore to have been from three to three and one-half miles. **25. Fourth watch of the night.** That is, from 3 to 6 A.M. The men had been rowing since some time after sundown and were nearing exhaustion. Rough sea and head winds prevented progress. Though the disciples had witnessed Jesus' power over a storm (Mt 8:23-27), this time he was not with them. The new lesson for them was that Christ's power would sustain them in every appointed task, regardless of whether he was present bodily. **Walking on the sea.** To do this required mastery over gravity, wind, and wave. **26. An apparition.** A spectre or ghost. The frantic disciples gave way to current superstition. Perhaps they felt it was a harbinger of death to them. **27. It is I.** On such a dark, stormy night, the sound of the familiar voice brought reassurance where sight was insufficient.

28-33. Peter's walking on the water is given by Matthew only. **28,29. Lord, if it be thou.** With characteristic impulsiveness he desired to be given a command to **come** to Jesus **on the water.** But to accuse Peter of ostentation is to find more fault than Jesus did. **30. When he saw the wind,** i.e., its effects. Though formerly the wind had been just as strong, Peter's full attention had been centered in faith on Jesus, and the Lord had honored his faith by granting him supernatural power. When the concentration of faith was broken, Peter reverted to the control of natural powers. **31. Jesus stretched forth his hand.** A new display of supernatural power, not just physical rescue by human strength. **Thou of little faith.** The miracle had been granted to show, first, that complete faith in Jesus as the divine Messiah is sufficient for every appointed task, and second, that Jesus' refusal to accept the political proposals of the crowd (Jn 6:15) should not disillusion them. **32,33. Thou art the Son of God.** Equivalent to the Divine Deliverer, the Messiah or Christ. Though such identification had been made earlier by the disciples (Jn 1:41,49), there was an ever increasing realization by the Twelve of what these terms meant.

34-36. They came to the land, unto Gennesaret. A fertile plain several miles south of Capernaum. Since the discourse in the synagogue at Capernaum seems to have taken place on the day following the miraculous feeding (Jn 6:22,59), this paragraph may be a general description of events that covered several days or weeks, before and after the visit to Capernaum. The desire of the sick to **touch the hem of his garment** was probably motivated by reports of the cure of hemorrhage that had previously occurred in this region (9:20).

11) Conflict with the Pharisees over Tradition. 15:1-20. Local opposition from Galilean Pharisees (ch. 12) was now reinforced by a delegation from Jerusalem. Such opposition would increase in frequency and intensity during this final year. **1. From Jerusalem, Pharisees and scribes.** Probably sent from headquarters to check on Jesus and harass him. **2. Why do thy disciples transgress.** Though the charge is oblique, the insinuation is clear that Jesus' teaching is responsible for the breach. **They wash not their hands.** The rabbinic custom (not Mosaic) was not hygienic but ceremonial. Its binding force was popularly considered greater than that of the Law itself, and some rabbis went to absurd lengths to observe it (see Mk 7:4). **3. Why do you also transgress the commandment of God.** An admission that Christ's disciples transgressed the elders' tradition, but the contrast to the **commandment of God** showed the logic of such action. **4-6.** Some traditions actually violated the Law itself. The fifth commandment (Ex 20:12; 21:17) was violated by the callous strategem of calling whatever might have been used for assisting one's parents a gift (to God), and thus beyond the claim of the parents. As if God wants from a man what belongs to his parents! Whether the property eventually was given to God is not discussed, though there are evidences of abuses. **7-9.** To summarize, Jesus cites Isa 29:13, in which **this people** may be regarded not merely as contemporaries of the prophet, but as the nation of Israel throughout her history; or else the denunciation of Isaiah's contemporaries was a typical prophecy of Messiah's contemporaries. **10. And he called the multitude.** The preceding exchange had been somewhat private between Christ and the Pharisees and scribes. **11. Not that which goeth into the mouth defileth a man. Defileth** is literally *makes common,* derived from the Levitical distinction between foods allowed by God and all others, viewed as common, profane, "unclean." By this statement, Jesus is not abrogating the Levitical code (nor should Mk 7:19 be so interpreted), an abrogation not announced till after Pentecost (Acts 10—11), but was stating the principle that moral defilement is spiritual, not physical. Food is amoral (I Tim 4:3-5). Sin lies in the heart of the man who disobeys God and perverts its use. Even the defilement arising to a Jew from eating meat Levitically unclean was caused not by the food itself, but by the rebellious heart that acted in disobedience to God. **12-14.** The **disciples** were apparently disturbed over Christ's offending these influential **Pharisees,** and 15:15 indicates they did not understand fully the import of Jesus' statement. **Every plant.** Doctrine of mere human tradition, such as these Pharisees were demanding. **Shall be rooted up.** A prediction of ultimate destruction of all false doctrine, the symbolism perhaps including the persons holding these teachings (cf. 13:19,38 for similar combining). **Let them alone.** As teachers of spiritual truth, the traditionalists were to be abandoned. They were as **blind** spiritually as those who depended on them. **Pit.** Not a *ditch* (AV) beside the road, but an open cistern in the field.

15. Declare unto us this parable. Peter

referred to the statement of 15:11 (as comparison with Mk 7:15-17 indicates). **Parable** is used here in the sense of "difficult saying." The difficulty lay not in the use of symbols but in the departure from tradition, which had confused moral and ceremonial defilement. **16. Are ye also even yet without understanding?** Christ's amazement, though he had not dealt with this specific subject before (but compare 9:14-17; chs. 5–7), suggests that spiritually enlightened persons should have understood this principle, for it has always been true. **17.** Whatever defilement is attached to foods entering the **mouth** is physical and is removed from the body at the **draught,** i.e., the latrine, or privy. **18,19.** But things proceeding **out of the mouth** are spiritually defiling, for all sinful words and deeds find their source in **evil thoughts,** arising in an evil **heart** (cf. 5:21-48). After **evil thoughts,** violations of the Commandments, from the sixth through the ninth, are listed, concluding with **blasphemies**—abusive speech against God or man. **20. To eat with unwashen hands defileth not.** Thus Jesus summarizes by returning to the original question.

12) Withdrawal to Phoenicia, and Healing of a Canaanitish Woman's Daughter. 15:21-28. The forthright attack by the Pharisees (vv. 1,2), emboldened by the recent execution of John and the opposition of Herod, prompted this second withdrawal. The interview with the woman pictures clearly the historical setting of Christ's ministry, together with the wider aspects of his grace. **21. Withdrew into the parts of Tyre and Sidon** (ASV). Though some dispute the point, it seems clear that Jesus actually left the land of Israel and Herod's jurisdiction (cf. also Mk 7:31, ASV), to stay secluded for a time in Phoenicia. **22. A Canaanitish woman.** By race. Inhabitants of this region are called Canaanites in Num 13:29; Jud 1:30,32,33. Mark 7:26 designates her as Syrophoenician in citizenship. **Son of David.** This Messianic designation by the woman implies some awareness of Jewish religion; yet the passage does not suggest that she was a proselyte. **23. He answered her not a word.** Partly to be explained by Jesus' attempt to remain secluded (Mk 7:24). However, the discussion that follows indicates the focus of Christ's mission, and this procedure of Jesus made the instruction most effective. The fact that Mark omits mention of Christ's silence may indicate that this action was not so startling as one might suppose. **Send her away.** This statement by the impatient disciples may imply that Christ should grant her request and thus dismiss the case, for his reply reveals that an appeal had been made. **26. To take the children's bread and cast it to dogs.** This Gentile woman was acquainted with the Jews' custom of referring to Gentiles as **dogs** and to themselves as God's **children.** The seeming harshness of Christ's expression is softened by the fact that the term denotes not the vicious, wild scavengers that roamed the streets, but **little dogs** *(kunaria)* that lived as pets in people's houses. Jesus told this Gentile what he had told a Samaritan woman, that at this time all were dependent on Israel for Messiah and his blessings (Jn 4:21-23). Jesus had healed Gentiles on other occasions, but here in Phoenicia he had to be careful not to give the impression that he was abandoning Israel (cf. Mt 4:24; 8:5). **27,28. Even the little dogs eat of the crumbs.** The woman accepted fully the divine order, and her faith grasped the truth that applied to her. It was this faith that Christ praised. **Great is thy faith.** The second Gentile to be praised for faith (8:10), and the third instance of Christ's healing at a distance (Mt 8:13; Jn 4:50).

13) Return to the Sea of Galilee (Decapolis, Mk 7:31), and Performing of Miracles. 15:29-38. Mark shows that Jesus proceeded northward in Phoenicia through Sidon, then eastward across the Jordan, and finally southward through Decapolis till he reached the Sea of Galilee. This route suggests that he deliberately avoided the domain of Herod Antipas.

29-31. Healing the multitudes. **29. Sea of Galilee.** Apparently the southeast shore. **30. Multitudes** came. Of the many who were healed, Mark has described the case of a deaf and dumb man (Mk 7:32-37). **31. They glorified the God of Israel.** An indication that these were Gentile environs in which Jesus imparted the knowledge of the true God and the Messianic promises.

32-38. Feeding the four thousand. To claim that this narrative relates the same incident as the feeding of the five thousand is to make this Gospel and Mark mere collections of traditions that have become confused, and to treat the words of Jesus in Mt 16:9,10 as mere invention. The differences in details are numerous, and there is nothing essentially improbable about two miraculous feedings. **32. They continue with me now three days.** What food had been brought was now exhausted. **33. Whence should we have so much bread?** To insist that the Twelve had forgotten the previous feeding is unwarranted. They merely state their personal inability to supply, and refrain from presuming to ask Jesus for another miracle (in view of Jn 6:26). **34-38.** From **seven** loaves and a few **fishes** Christ fed the **multitude of four thousand men** and their families in much the same way as he had fed the five thousand. The uneaten pieces amounted to **seven baskets full.** Here the **baskets** are the larger *spurides,* or hampers, which the disciples may have been using on their recent journey, as compared to the smaller *kophinoi* of 14:20, a distinction maintained in 16:9,10. The seven baskets may have contained more than the twelve on the previous occasion.

14) Renewed Conflict with the Pharisees and Sadducees. 15:39–16:4.

39. Magdala. Better, *Magadan.* The location is unknown. Mark 8:10 has *Dalmanutha,* the location of which is similarly uncertain. The place was apparently on the west shore of Galilee. **16:1. Pharisees and Sadducees came.** Traditional foes, joined by a common hatred of Jesus. Sadducees appear only two other times in the Gospel record: at John's baptism (3:7), and during Christ's last week (22:23). **A sign from heaven.** This request, similar to that in 12:38, minimizes all previous miracles of Jesus, and demands a spectacular display that is unmistakably of heavenly origin. This they asked with the ulterior design of **tempting him,** by making him do what he had formerly refused to do (12:39) or else discrediting him by showing his inability. The part of Christ's reply recorded in 16:2,3 is missing in many ancient manuscripts, but contained by some. The figure is similar to that in Lk 12:54-56. It calls attention to men's ability to forecast the weather from available data, but the complete inability of Christ's contemporaries to read the spiritual **signs of the times.** John's preaching, Jesus' teaching and works, Daniel's prophecy of the seventy weeks—all should have been significant factors to the discerning. **4. The sign of the prophet Jonah.** (Cf. comment on 12:38-40.) A reference to Christ's bodily resurrection. This was the great sign to which he always pointed when pressed (Jn 2:18-22; Mt 12:38-40), to believers a precious proof of their redemption but to unbelievers a portent of coming judgment by the risen Christ.

15) Withdrawal to the Region of Caesarea Philippi. 16:5–17:23. This fourth retirement takes Jesus again to Gentile surroundings, away from the tensions of constant opposition (cf. Bethsaida Julias, 14:13; Phoenicia, 15:21; Decapolis, 15:29; Mk 7:31). During this period, perhaps of several months' duration, occurred the momentous confession of Peter, Christ's detailed prediction of His coming passion, and the Transfiguration.

5-12. Conversation en route. **5. To the other side,** i.e., to the northeast part (Bethsaida Julias, Mk 8:22), en route to Caesarea Philippi (Mt 16:13). **Forgot to take bread.** Rapid departure from Magadan may have caused this oversight, so that only one old loaf could be found in the boat (Mk 8:14). **6. Leaven of the Pharisees and Sadducees.** (On **leaven,** see 13:33.) The permeating evil influence of these determined opponents of Christ is the point involved. **7-11.** Yet the disciples, embarrassed at their oversight, failed to grasp the symbolism. **O ye of little faith.** Jesus knew that their failure to understand was due to their anxiety over provisions, and reminded them of the lessons of trust they should have learned. **12. The teaching of the Pharisees and Sadducees.** Pharisees were legalists and traditionalists, whose emphasis upon ritual was hypocritical and spiritually deadening (Lk 12:1). Sadducees were rationalists, who did not believe in resurrection nor in the existence of spirit beings that cannot be explained naturally (Acts 23:8). They numbered among themselves the priestly hierarchy of Israel. Warning against such subtle rationalistic teachings is still pertinent.

13-20. Peter's confession. **13. The parts of Caesarea Philippi** (ASV). The outlying villages (Mk 8:27). Jesus is not said to have entered the city. **Caesarea Philippi.** About twenty-five miles north of the Sea of Galilee. **14.** The variety of opinions which men held concerning Jesus showed that although many connected him with Messianic prophecy, none regarded him properly. **John the Baptist** was the predicted forerunner (3:1-3; 14:1,2). **Elijah** was to precede the "day of the Lord" (Mal 4:5,6). **Jeremiah** was expected by some to appear and restore the ark he had supposedly hidden (II Macc 2:1-8). **15,16.** After causing the Twelve to dispose of erroneous ideas, Jesus asked their personal opinion. **Thou art the Christ, the Son of the living God.** All doubtless concurred, but Peter rose to the occasion with the unequivocal response. Similar statements had been uttered before, some much earlier (Jn 1:41, 49), but many false notions about the character and purpose of Messiah needed to be removed. Thus the statement by Peter here is not the product of early enthusiasm but of studied reflection and solemn faith. The popular notion of a mere political leader is superseded by the concept of the Messiah as **the Son of God,** the definite article **the** marking him out as unique. **17.** Such spiritual knowledge was not the product of unaided humanity (**flesh and blood;** compare this expression in Gal 1:16; Eph 6:12; Heb 2:14), but of divine revelation. Spiritual truth can be comprehended only by those whose spiritual faculties have been made alive by God (I Cor 2:11-14). Such spiritual discernment was an evidence of Peter's **blessed** spiritual state.

18. Upon this rock I will build my church. There is an obvious play upon the words **Peter** (*Petros,* proper name denoting a piece of rock) and **rock** (*petra,* a rocky mass). The spiritual body, the **church,** mentioned here for the first time, is built upon the divinely revealed fact about Christ confessed by Peter (I Cor 3:11; I Pet 2:4) as men are made aware of and acknowledge His person and work (so Chrysostom, Augustine). Another view common among some Protestants (Alford, Broadus, Vincent) is that Peter (along with the other apostles; Eph 2:20; Rev 21:14) is the **rock,** but without the papal supremacy ascribed to him by unscriptural Romish notions. **The gates of Hades shall not prevail against it. Hades** (equivalent to **Sheol),** the realm of the dead. **Gates.** The entrance to Hades, which is usually death. Christ's Church, which would be inaugurated at Pentecost, would not be at the mercy of physical death, for the Lord's resurrection would insure the resurrection of all believers. More specifically, believers who die before the resurrection go immediately to be with Christ, not to Hades (Eph 4:8, RSV; Phil 1:23; II Cor 5:8). **19. The keys of the kingdom of heaven. Keys** symbolize authority to open. **To thee** relates this promise to Peter alone. It refers to the choice of Peter, as first among equals, for officially opening the **kingdom** (since Pentecost, including the whole sphere of Christian profession; cf. 13:3-52) to Jews (Acts 2:14 ff.) and Gentiles (Acts 10:1—11:18; 15:7,14). Some, however, explain the passage eschatologically, as applying to the reign of the saints over the earth in the Millennium (A. J. McClain, *The Greatness of the Kingdom,* p. 329 f.). **Whatsoever thou shalt bind on earth.** This part of the responsibility was later given to all the disciples (18:18), who were eventually empowered for the task (Jn 20:22,23). If Jn 20:23 be an explanation of the binding and loosing, as meaning remitting and retaining sins, then Acts 10:43 is an instance of its exercise. By the proclamation of the Gospel, announcement is made that acceptance brings loosing from sin's guilt and penalty, and rejection leaves the sinner bound for judgment. **20. Tell no man that he was the Christ.** The populace as yet would only be politically aroused by such disclosure.

21-27. Jesus' prediction of his death and resurrection. **21. From that time forth began Jesus.** Now that Jesus had a nucleus of followers who truly believed in him as Messiah (16:16), he entered upon a period of plain teaching regarding his redemptive work. **Elders, chief priests,** and **scribes** formed the Sanhedrin. **Be killed and be raised again.** Though Christ clearly predicted his resurrection following his death, this consequence failed to register with the Twelve. **Third day.** Equivalent to "after three days," Mk 8:31. **22.** Peter's remonstrance, **Be it far from thee, Lord** (an idiom meaning, "God have mercy on thee and spare thee"), showed his complete failure to recognize in the Jewish Messiah the aspect of suffering (Isa 53). **23. Get thee behind me, Satan.** Similar to Jesus' words to Satan in 4:10, uttered here in a comparable situation. Satan, using Peter as his tool, was again trying to turn Jesus aside from the suffering that was His lot. **Thou mindest not the things of God** (ASV). Peter's divinely revealed avowal (v.16) had briefly displayed the appropriateness of his Christ-given name, but here he shows the presence of carnal weakness. Before Pentecost the Twelve often vacillated between keen spiritual discernment and the grossest carnality. And such is often tragically the case among believers today.

24. At this point Jesus and the Twelve were joined by a multitude (Mk 8:34), even though the Lord had been in relative seclusion. **Let him deny himself,** i.e., renounce or disown himself, as far as being able to merit eternal life is concerned. **Take up his cross and follow me.** A well-known figure of suffering and death (cf. comment on 10:38,39). Here it pictures the conversion of a sinner who must recognize his own spiritual poverty, and then accept Christ (His person and teaching), even though it will mean assuming, in some sense, suffering that would otherwise not occur. **25. Whosoever will save his life shall lose it** (cf. on 10:39). He who is unwilling to assume the hazards involved in being a disciple of Christ will ultimately lose his life eternally. But the converse is also true. **26. If he shall gain the whole world and forfeit his life** (ASV). **Life** is *psychē,* the Greek term covering both English concepts of "life" and "soul." Luke 9:25 uses the word "self." The figure pictures a business transaction in which a man exchanges his very life (including the soul) for this world's attractions. What would such a man use to buy back his *psychē*? **27. The Son of man shall come.** At Christ's second coming, he will settle all accounts. Thus, suffering for Christ, even unto death, will receive its proper reward. **28.** To stress the reality of his **coming** and **kingdom** as an incentive to men to follow him, even in suffering, Christ gave the promise of verse 28. This **coming** of the **Son of man** in his **kingdom** is explained by some as the destruction of Jerusalem and by others as the beginning of the Church. But referring it to the Transfiguration meets the requirements of the context (all Synoptists follow this statement with the Transfiguration, Mk 9:1; Lk 9:27). Furthermore, Peter, who was one of those **standing here,** referred to the Transfiguration in the same words (II Pet 1:16-18). Chafer calls the Transfiguration a "preview of the coming kingdom on earth" (L. S. Chafer, *Systematic Theology,* V, 85).

17:1-13. The Transfiguration. At this strategic moment in the ministry of Jesus, when he had evoked from Peter the true designation of himself (16:16), and had announced his coming death and resurrection, there was granted to three disciples this most remarkable experience.

1. After six days. So also Mk 9:2. Luke's "about eight days" (9:28) counts the termini as well as the interval. **Peter, James, and John.** These former business associates (Lk 5:10) were granted special privileges on two other occasions (Lk 8:51; Mt 26:37). Can it be that they had more spiritual perception at this time than the others? **High mountain.** The traditional Mount Tabor is contextually unlikely. More probable is a location near Caesarea Philippi (16:13), perhaps one of the spurs of Hermon. **2. He was transfigured before them.** The verb *(metamorphoō)* denotes a transformation of the essential form, proceeding from within, and is used in Rom 12:2 and II Cor 3:18 of the spiritual transformation that characterizes Christians as the new nature is manifested in them. Though for believers this transformation is a gradual experience, to be completed when Christ is seen (II Cor 3:18; I Jn 3:2), in the case of Jesus, the glorious form that was usually veiled was briefly displayed. **3. Moses and Elijah,** the outstanding representatives, in Jewish thinking, of the Law and the Prophets, appeared **talking with him** about the coming events at Jerusalem (Lk 9:31). Such conversation showed the disciples that the death of Messiah was not incompatible with the OT. Viewing the Transfiguration as a preview of the Messianic kingdom (16:28), some have seen in Moses (who had died) and Elijah (who had passed from this life without dying) representatives of the two groups that Christ will bring with him to establish his kingdom: dead saints who are resurrected and living saints who have been translated. Likewise the three disciples are seen as representing men living on earth at the time of the Second Advent (L. S. Chafer, *Systematic Theology,* V, 85-94; G. N. H. Peters, *Theocratic Kingdom,* II, 559-561). **4,5. Peter answered,** i.e., responded to the situation. A desire to prolong this experience prompted Peter to offer to erect (**I will make**) three brush **tabernacles,** such as worshipers built for the Feast of Tabernacles. In response, the Divine **voice** came **out of the cloud** acknowledging Jesus as God's **beloved Son,** and commanding the disciples, **Hear ye him.** Moses and Elijah had nothing new to impart (Heb 1:1,2). **6-9.** Frightened by the voice, the disciples were reassured but cautioned at the conclusion of these events. **Tell the vision to no man.** Apparently not even the other apostles were to be informed at this time. The things they had witnessed would only confuse and politically arouse the less perceptive. **10. Why then say the scribes that Elijah must first come?** The presence of Elijah on the mount and the subsequent command to silence prompted the question. If this was the predicted coming of Elijah (Mal 4:5), then surely it was time for public announcement. If not, how could Jesus be Messiah, for that personage was to be preceded by Elijah? **11. Elijah indeed cometh** (ASV). Futuristic present form. Jesus here claims that Mal 4:5 will be fulfilled. **12,13. Elijah is come already.** To the unspiritual Jews who were merely hunting for signs, John himself had said, "I am not Elijah" (i.e., the resurrected OT prophet, Jn 1:21). Yet to those who were spiritually sensitive, John had come "in the spirit and power of Elijah" (Lk 1:17), and men had been directed to Christ by him. Thus Jesus' offer of the kingdom was a valid offer, contingent upon national acceptance, and Israel could not blame the absence of Elijah for her failure to recognize Jesus. God in his foreknowledge knew that Israel, at the first coming of Christ, would not be ready for the final Elijah's ministry, and so he sent John "in the spirit and power of Elijah" instead.

14-20. Healing of a demon-possessed epileptic. Each Synoptist follows the Transfiguration with this account, but the narrative in Mark (9:14-29) is the fullest. **15. Lord, have mercy on my son, for he is**

epileptic (ASV). Literally, *moonstruck* (cf. Latin etymology of "lunatic"). The symptoms are generally regarded as describing epilepsy, produced here by demon possession. **17. O faithless and perverse generation.** In words similar to those of Deut 32:5, Jesus cites the faithlessness of the nine apostles as characteristic of their generation. Their faithlessness consisted in their failure to appropriate fully the power granted them in 10:8. **18.** Jesus by removing the **demon** (the cause) brought about the cure of the illness (the effect). **19. Why could not we cast him out?** This was doubtless their first failure after they had received Christ's authorization (10:8). **20. Because of your unbelief.** Not unbelief in Jesus as Messiah, but doubts as to his words given to them formerly (10:8). **As a grain of mustard seed.** Its smallness was proverbial. The power of faith is illustrated by its ability to remove **this mountain.** (Did Jesus point to the Mount of Transfiguration?) Rather than soften the expression by making "mountain" symbolic of any difficulty, it is best to treat it literally. However, it must be borne in mind that Scriptural faith is a trust in God's revealed Word and will. Hence faith to move a mountain can be exercised only when God reveals that to be his will. Verse 21 is omitted by the best manuscripts, being an interpolation from Mk 9:29.

22,23. Renewed prediction of death and resurrection. **While they were gathering themselves together in Galilee** (ASV marg.). Though manuscript evidence is conflicting, this reading seems best attested and agrees well with Mk 9:30. Because of Jesus' desire for secrecy, the Twelve may have returned by separate routes, and upon meeting again, received this disclosure. **The Son of man shall be delivered up. Delivered up** is less interpretative than *betrayed* (AV), though it may suggest betrayal.

16) Instruction of the Twelve at Capernaum. 17:24–18:35.

24-27. Payment of the temple tax. **24. Capernaum.** The final visit of Jesus to this city of his residence. **Does not your master pay the half-shekel** *(didrachma)*? This ecclesiastical assessment, based on Ex 30:11-16, was originally for the support of the Tabernacle, and was reinstituted after the Exile (Neh 10:32, one-third shekel). Apparently in Jesus' time the Jews followed Nehemiah's annual plan, but charged at Moses' rate. The payment, usually made in the spring, was some months overdue. **25,26. Jesus spake first to him** (ASV), i.e., anticipated him. Recognizing Peter's confusion, arising from loyalty to Jesus' integrity and perhaps anxiety over lack of funds, our Lord shows by illustration that the **children of kings** are exempt from **toll.** Thus Jesus, the Son of God, is not personally obligated to pay tribute for the support of God's house. **27. Lest we cause them to stumble.** For Jesus to have claimed his privilege would very possibly have created wrong impressions among the people, including perhaps disrespect for God's house. The miracle, demonstrating Jesus' omniscience in knowing which fish had the **shekel,** and his omnipotence in causing it to be the first one caught, emphasized the fact of his deity (and thus his right of exemption from the tax), which might have been obscured by the payment he intended to make. **Shekel.** A *statēr*, equal to four drachmas or two half-shekels, and thus sufficient for Jesus and Peter.

18:1-14. Instruction on greatness. **1. Who is the greatest?** The background of this question lay in a dispute among the disciples as they journeyed (Mk 9:33; Lk 9:46). Perhaps it had been kindled by the prominence given to the three at Caesarea Philippi (17:1) or to Peter in the temple tax incident (17:27). **2-4.** Calling to himself a **little child,** he warned the disciples that unless they turned from exalted opinions of themselves, their problem would not be one of relative greatness but of entrance into the **kingdom of heaven** (the Messianic kingdom they looked for him to establish). The absence of pride in position is the aspect of childhood referred to here. To enter Christ's kingdom, a man must realize his personal inadequacy, and his complete dependence on the Lord. He must experience a new birth (Jn 3:3 ff.).

5. One such little child, i.e., a person who, by believing, has become as a little child (cf. v. 6). Verses 5-14 no longer discuss the actual child of the illustration (1-4), but a childlike believer. **In my name.** On the basis of Christ. Welcoming other believers because of Christ (not because of prestige, wealth, etc.) is regarded as done to Christ himself (10:42). **6. Cause one of these little ones which believe on me to stumble. Little ones** also refers to believers. The awful judgment awaiting those who would harm the faith of believers is made dramatic by a comparison. **Millstone.** Literally, *ass stone,* the larger upper stone turned by an ass. **7.** Though it is inevitable that **occasions of stumbling** (ASV) occur, for these are among God's means of disciplining as well as molding the character of believers, the human offender is morally responsible for his guilt. **8,9.** Thus, if necessary, one should take the most drastic measures to avoid offending. (See on 5: 29,30.) **10. These little ones.** Childlike believers (not actual children, except as they may be believers). **Their angels.** Angels who are charged with the care of believers as a group (Heb 1:14). There is not sufficient warrant here for the idea that each individual believer has a particular angel assigned to him. (Acts 12:15 reflects a current opinion of angels, but is not necessarily a truth.) Verse 11 was probably interpolated from Lk 19:10.

12-14. The importance of even the lowliest believer is illustrated by the parable of The Lost Sheep. Since the shepherd is greatly concerned over a single straying sheep, how important is our obligation not to minimize such unfortunate ones. This parable was used on another occasion (Lk 15:4-7) to illustrate the salvation of sinners.

15-20. Instruction on procedure toward offenders. **15.** In spite of the severest warnings, offenses will be committed. Procedures are outlined to show the injured party how to respond. His first responsibility is to go privately to the offender, without waiting for an apology. Such procedure makes it easier for him to obtain a confession. If he is successful, he will gain the offending brother as a friend and restore him to the fellowship of the Lord and the congregation. **16.** If a second overture is necessary, several witnesses should be present at the interview (see Deut 19: 15). **17. Tell it unto the church.** When the offender remains impenitent (and the sin is sufficiently grave as to affect the congregation), the church must consider the matter. The **church** here cannot mean the synagogue, in view of the prerogatives mentioned in 18:18,19. A Christian church is in prospect, as indicated by the implied absence of Jesus (v. 20). Failure to heed the counsel of the **church** must cause the offender to be treated as an outsider **(Gentile, publican).** Of course, such treatment should involve efforts to reach him with the Gospel. **18. Whatsoever ye shall bind on earth** (cf. 16:19). The decision of the congregation in such matters, reached through prayer, the Word, and the Spirit, will be ratified in heaven. See also Jn 20: 23. **19,20.** The promise that prayer will be answered if even **two agree** provides additional proof that the prayerful decisions of the congregation in disciplinary actions will be divinely honored. This promise pertaining to united prayer must be considered in the light of Christ's other teaching on the subject (cf. I Jn 5:14). **There am I in the midst.** A promise of Christ's special presence in the smallest conceivable congregation.

21-35. Instruction on forgiveness. **21 Lord, how oft?** The preceding explanation regarding offenders implied a willingness by the offended to forgive. Peter wondered how far forgiveness should be extended for repeated offenses. **Seven times?** Rabbinic teaching (based on Amos 1:3; Job 33:29,30, ASV) demanded only three. **22.** Jesus, however, lifted the matter beyond the realm of practical computation by requiring **seventy times seven.** Rather than seek a numerical standard, the believer must follow the example of his Lord (Col 3:13).

23. The parable of the unmerciful servant teaches that men who have experienced God's forgiveness are accountable to display forgiveness toward others. This is the standard of the **kingdom of heaven** (see comment on 13:11). The Oriental **king** (interpreted as the heavenly Father; v. 35) is depicted as making a reckoning with his slaves. **24. One,** apparently a satrap with access to vast sums of the king's revenue, was found to owe **ten thousand talents.** (The value of a talent differed at various times, according to the metal involved, but was always comparatively high). **25-27.** However, by prostrating himself before the king, he secured a complete cancellation of the **debt** (Greek, *loan;* viewed graciously instead of as embezzlement). **28-30.** Leaving the king's presence, the forgiven servant proceeded to demand settlement from a **fellow servant** owing him a **hundred pence** (one penny, *denarius,* equaled a day's wages, 20:2), a most insignificant amount compared to the talents. **31-33. Shouldest not thou also have had mercy.** Certainly sinners who have experienced God's forgiveness ought to display a kindred spirit toward others, especially since offenses that men commit against one another are infinitesimal when compared with the enormity of man's debt to God. **34,35. Delivered him to the tormentors.** Herein is the crux of the interpretation. It cannot refer to the eternal ruin of one truly saved, for that would conflict with the clearest teaching elsewhere. Neither can it refer to some nonscriptural purgatory. Yet the fact that the servant had been forgiven the debt makes it unlikely that he was a mere professed believer. However, if we view the torments as temporal evils visited upon unforgiving believers by their **heavenly Father,** the previous difficulties are avoided. **Tormentors** (*basanistai*) is derived from the verb *basanizō,* which is used to describe sickness (Mt 4:24; 8:6), and adverse circumstances (Mt 14:24). Lot "tormented his soul" by contact with evil men (II Pet 2:8). Such torments God may use to chasten and produce a proper spirit among his children (I Cor 11:30-32). Thus the divine forgiveness here is that which we must experience daily in order to enjoy perfect fellowship with our heavenly Father, and it fits well this context in which relations among believers are discussed (vv. 15-20).

B. In Perea. 19:1 – 20:16. Matthew notes the departure of Jesus from Galilee and describes the final journey to Jerusalem. Comparison with Lk 9:51–18:14 indicates another trip to Jerusalem and a ministry lasting some months. Thus a gap of perhaps six months must be inferred in 19:1 between **departed from Galilee** and **came into the borders of Judea beyond Jordan.**

1) Teaching on Divorce. 19:1-12. **1. Beyond Jordan.** From the Greek *peran* **(beyond)** came the name "Perea" for the district on the east side of the Jordan River. **3. Is it lawful for a man to put away his wife for every cause?** The strict school of Shammai held that divorce was lawful only for a wife's shameful conduct. Hillel, however, interpreted Deut 24:1 in the widest possible way, and allowed divorce for every conceivable cause. Thus Jesus was being asked, "Do you agree with the most prevalent interpretation (Hillel's)?" **4-6.** Rather than align himself with either position, Jesus cites the purpose of God in creation (Gen 1:27; 2:24). Since God's purpose called for man and wife to be **one flesh,** any disruption of marriage violates God's will. **7,8. Why then did Moses command?** Their citing Moses (Deut 24:1) and the **bill of divorcement** in opposition to Jesus showed their misunderstanding of that regulation. For the provision was a protection of wives from men's caprice, not an authorization for husbands to divorce at will. **9,10. Except it be for fornication** (cf. on 5:31). If **fornication** be regarded as a general term including adultery (an identification most uncertain in the NT), then our Lord allowed divorce only for the cause of infidelity by the wife. (Among Jews, only husbands could divorce. Mark, in writing for Gentile readers, states the converse also, Mk 10:12.) However, if **fornication** be viewed in its usual meaning, and referred here to unchastity by the bride during betrothal (cf. Joseph's suspicions, Mt 1:18,19), then Christ allowed no grounds whatever for divorce of married persons. Thus he agreed neither with Shammai nor Hillel. Such a high and restricted view of marriage would account for the disciples' remonstrance, **It is not good to marry.** It seems unlikely that the disciples, after having imbibed the ideals of Jesus, would have felt the limiting of divorce to cases of adultery an intolerable burden. **11. All men cannot receive this saying,** i.e., the statement of the disciples. Though at times marriage may not be expedient, not all men are so constituted as to abstain. **12.** Some are incapable of marriage because of congenital defects; others because of injury or restrictions imposed by men. Still others may forego the privilege of marriage in order to devote themselves more completely to the service of God (e.g., Paul, I Cor 7:7,8,26,32-35). This statement certainly casts no reflection upon marriage; rather it concludes a discussion in which marriage was exalted to its original pure state.

2) Blessing of the Children. 19:13-15. The **little children** must have been very small, some perhaps being infants (Mk 10:16). The disciples resented the intrusion and rebuked the parents who had brought them (cf. Mk 10:13; Lk 18:15). Yet Jesus was always interested in the young and the weak. During this delightful moment, he reminded the disciples of a forgotten lesson (18:3). **Of such is the kingdom of heaven.** Since entrance to this Kingdom requires that men become childlike in faith, the disciples would do well to be more gracious to actual children.

3) Interview with the Rich Young Man. 19:16-30. The reader should follow the ASV in this passage, since much assimilation from parallel accounts appears in the AV. **16. What good thing shall I do?** This young questioner (called a "ruler" by Luke) felt sure that **eternal life** was gained by the performance of deeds. **17. Why asketh thou me concerning that which is good? One there is who is good.** Mark and Luke indicate that Jesus had been addressed as "Good Master." Our Lord probed his questioner by making him review how he really estimated Jesus, and then sent him to what God had already revealed in His Law. **18,19.** Jesus cited the sixth, seventh, eighth, ninth, and fifth commandments of the Decalogue, and a summarization of the second table – **love thy neighbor as thyself.** These were not stated as the means of salvation (this was never the purpose of the Law), but were intended to indicate the young man's need. **20. All these things have I kept.** Not the words of one brazenly self-righteous, but of one who thought that conformity in externals constituted keeping of the Law. **21. Perfect.** Com-

plete, mature, without the **lack** which he sorely felt. **Go, sell, give.** Jesus unmasked the young man's problem by demonstrating one of its effects. The exhortation to dispense his belongings quickly revealed how far short he had come in grasping the spirit of God's commandments. **Come, follow me.** Here is the positive invitation to put faith in Christ. **22. He went away sorrowful.** The prospect of abandoning his great possessions was so distressing that he failed to find the goal he sought.

23. It is hard for a rich man to enter (ASV). The difficulty with wealth lies not in its possession (many righteous men in Scripture had wealth – Abraham, Job, Joseph of Arimathaea) but in the false trust it inspires (I Tim 6:17; Mk 10:24). **24. Camel** and **needle's eye** are meant literally, as attested by a similar Talmudic proverb using an elephant. The simile was meant to show an impossibility by naming the largest beast known in Palestine and the smallest of apertures. **25. Who then can be saved?** The disciples apparently subscribed in some measure to the prevailing view that riches indicated divine favor. Hence if rich men were excluded, how could others possibly be saved? Perhaps there was latent the thought that all men are afflicted to some degree with the desire for worldly wealth. **26.** Jesus succinctly avowed that salvation is the work of God. Only God can overrule this false trust in human riches and provide true righteousness.

27. We have left all. What the young man had refused to do (cf. Mt 4:20,22; 9:9). **What then shall we have?** Not necessarily a reflection of a mercenary spirit, but a forthright question that drew an appropriate answer. **28. Regeneration.** The word appears elsewhere in the NT only in Tit 3:5 (of spiritual rebirth of the individual). Here it denotes the rebirth that will occur in society and creation when Messiah establishes his reign (cf. Acts 3:21; Rom 8:19). **Twelve thrones.** Specifically for the Twelve in the Millennium. **29,30.** Any sacrifice made for Christ will be amply rewarded. However, a caution must be observed. **Many** (not all) **that are first shall be last.** This axiom, repeated in 20:16 after an explanatory parable, is true in many senses. Here the context suggests its application to those who had first (in time) established their relation to Christ and might develop an attitude of presumption.

4) Parable of the Laborers in the Vineyard. 20:1-16. This parable illustrates Christ's previous teaching, and enlarges 19:30 (cf. 20:16). **1. Householder.** The master of a **vineyard** needed an increase of workers at harvest time. **Early in the morning.** The first workers were hired at dawn. **2. A penny** *(denarius)* a day. The usual wage for a laborer or soldier. **3-7. Others standing idle.** Not working because no man had hired them. No hint is given that they were lazy. From this group of unemployed in the marketplace, the householder hired additional workers at 9 A.M., 12 noon, 3 P.M., and 5 P.M. Each responded immediately to the opportunity. **8. When even was come.** Cf. Deut 24:15. **9-12.** That those hired first might see what was done, payment was begun with those most recently hired. Each worker received one denarius, regardless of the duration of his service. **13,14.** To one of the murmuring group which had labored longest, the householder explained that the contract had been fully performed. As to the others, the employer's obligation to them was his own affair. **15. Is thine eye evil because I am good?** The sense is, Are you envious (Prov 28:22) because I am generous? **16. The last shall be first.** This statement, repeated from 19:30, shows that the parable continued the previous instruction of the Twelve (19:27-30). The parable teaches that service for Christ will be faithfully rewarded, and that equal faithfulness to one's opportunity will be equally rewarded. However, only God can adequately assess faithfulness and opportunities, and thus human judgments may be reversed. The ASV omits the final clause of verse 16 on textual grounds.

C. In Judea. 20:17-34. Matthew is particularly conscious of geographical movements (4:12; 16:13; 17:24; 19:1; 21:1). Having been east of Jordan in Perea, Jesus and his band now moved directly toward Jerusalem. This section describes events on the journey from Perea to Jerusalem, in the vicinity of Jericho in Judea (v. 29).

1) Another Prediction of Christ's Death and Resurrection. 20:17-19. The third direct and detailed prediction of Christ's passion (cf. 16:21; 17:22,23, plus the bare statement of 17:12). It enlarges upon some of the previous information. For the first time Jesus indicated that his death would be at the hands of the **Gentiles**, who would **mock, scourge,** and **crucify** him.

2) Ambitious Request of Zebedee's Sons. 20:20-28. Mark presents the request as coming from the sons. Matthew shows that they at first asked through their mother, but that later they personally joined

the conversation. **20. Mother of Zebedee's children.** Salome, apparently the sister of the Virgin Mary, as shown by comparing Mt 27:56 with Mk 15:40 and Jn 19:25. **21.** The request for seats of highest honor in Christ's kingdom may have been prompted by his previous revelation about the twelve thrones (19:28). Though it arose from the idea that the kingdom would very shortly be established (Lk 19:11), and betrayed a spirit not altogether humble, it should be noted that it was based on a firm faith that Jesus was the Messiah and his kingdom a reality. Such faith Jesus was willing to purge and nourish. **22,23. Cup.** Here a symbol of Christ's sufferings (cf. 26:39,42). **To be baptized with the baptism.** Broadus explains, "to be plunged in the same sufferings" *(Comm. on Matt.*, p. 417). The assent of these two to the stern demands of Jesus was doubtless sincere. James was the first disciple to die for Christ (Acts 12:2); John suffered variously over the longest period of time. Yet assignment of the positions requested is the prerogative of the Father. **24. Moved with indignation.** A response of the **ten** which may have been aggravated by the procedure of the two in pleading their case through a kinswoman of Jesus. **25-27.** Our Lord's answer showed that though human governments maintain greatness by the authority of various officials forced upon their inferiors, his kingdom would be different. Willingness to serve is the mark of spiritual greatness. **28.** The greatest examplar of this principle is the **Son of man.** The supreme display occurred at Calvary, where he gave **his life** as a **ransom** to God, against whom men have sinned and were subject to penalty. **For many.** Christ's death here is clearly substitutionary, "in the stead of" (*anti*) **many.** (See A. T. Robertson, *Grammar of the Greek New Testament*, pp. 572-574.) **Many** does not seem intended to be restrictive here, but is in contrast to the *one* who died. However, the choice was a happy one in view of the clear teaching elsewhere that not all would avail themselves of the proffered salvation.

3) Healing of Two Blind Men. 20:29-34. Parallel accounts (Mk 10:46-52; Lk 18:35-43) pose problems of harmonization, but this fact prohibits any suggestion of collusion. **29. As they departed from Jericho.** Mark agrees, but Luke places the incident on the approach to the city. The main city of Roman Jericho, occupied by poorer Jews, lay about a mile east of Herod's winter headquarters (also called Jericho), which contained the palace, fortress, and houses of Herod's wealthy friends. (See Lucetta Mowry, BA, XV, 2, p. 34). Thus the miracle could have occurred between the two Jerichos, with Luke understandably thinking in terms of the Herodian city, where his next incident (Zacchaeus) most probably occurred. **30-34. Two blind men.** The other evangelists mention only the more prominent Bartimaeus (cf. the two demoniacs, Mt 8:28). **Thou son of David.** By this title they meant the Messiah. Previously Jesus had prohibited its public use, but now as he approaches Jerusalem, he is ready to claim it (cf. 21:16; Lk 19:40).

D. In Jerusalem. 21:1–25:46. In tracing the movements of Jesus to Jerusalem, Matthew omits the trip from Jericho to Bethany six days before Passover (Jn 12:1), which preceded the Triumphal Entry by one day (Jn 12:12).

1) Triumphal Entry. 21:1-11. The first of a series of visits to Jerusalem during this final week (cf. 21:18; Mk 11:19). **1. Bethphage.** A village apparently between Bethany and Jerusalem, since Jesus had lodged in Bethany the previous night (Jn 12:1,12). Certain location is yet unknown. **Mount of Olives.** The hill east of Jerusalem that offered travelers their first glimpse of the city. **2,3.** The explicit instructions of Jesus regarding the **ass** and **colt** indicate the significance of the event. On other occasions Jesus had usually walked, and here the distance was not more than two miles. **4,5.** Fulfillment of Zech 9:9 was the motivation for this act, although the disciples were unaware of it before the Resurrection (Jn 12:16). Jews generally regarded the passage as Messianic (Edersheim, *Life and Times of Jesus,* II, 736). **6-8.** Both animals were brought (the ass being needed to quiet the previously unridden colt), but all the Evangelists testify that Jesus rode the colt. Some from the multitude spread their garments on the path as a mark of homage to him whom they now acclaimed as King (II Kgs 9:13). Others strewed palm fronds in the way (Jn 12:13). The ass was a lowly beast, and no Jewish king since Solomon had ridden upon one officially. But meekness and lowliness were earmarks of Messiah predicted by Zechariah, and now fulfilled. **9. Hosanna.** A Hebrew expression meaning *Save now*. The shouts of the crowd, employing the phrases of Ps 118:25,26, clearly proclaimed their hopes for Jesus as Messiah, **Son of David.** Previously Christ had shunned all such public displays (although confessing his Messiah-

ship to individuals; Jn 4:26; Mt 16:16-20); but now he had made careful preparations for an unmistakable presentation of himself to the nation. **10,11. Who is this?** The Messianic acclamation prompted this question from those who perhaps did not know Jesus (he had been avoiding Jerusalem during much of his ministry).

2) Cleansing of the Temple. 21:12-17. A similar cleansing of the Temple is recorded at the beginning of Jesus' ministry (Jn 2:13-22), but there is no reason to doubt that there were two such instances. Jesus often repeated his words and deeds. These evil men soon reverted to their wicked ways, for the financial inducements were most attractive. **12. Jesus went into the temple.** This was the day following the Triumphal Entry (Mk 11:11,12). Matthew records events here without the time. **Them that sold and bought in the temple.** The outer Court of the Gentiles contained the stalls where sacrificial animals might be purchased and tables where foreign coinage might be exchanged for shekels of the sanctuary. This mart, a rich source of extortion, was controlled by the family of the high priest Annas. Shortly before the war of the Jews with Rome, popular indignation against these Bazaars of Annas caused their removal (see Edersheim, *Life and Times of Jesus,* I, 367-372). **13. It is written.** Isa 56:7 and Jer 7:11. **Den of robbers.** A refuge for robbers, whose foul practices were protected by the sacred precincts. **14-16.** Matthew alone records the healings that brought renewed Hosannas from the **children** (masculine, *boys)* in the Temple. In responding to the disapproving priests, Jesus employed Ps 8:2 to show that God will get praise to himself, even from those whom men regard as insignificant. **17. To Bethany and lodged there.** The village at the foot of the Mount of Olives (cf. Lk 21:37). Whether he spent the night in a house in town or in the open air is uncertain (cf. Lk 24:50 with Acts 1:12 for interchanging of these names).

3) Cursing of the Barren Fig Tree. 21:18-22. Again Mark (11:12-14,19-25) must be consulted for the chronology. Matthew telescopes both phases of the incident into one. **18. Now in the morning.** According to Mark, this was the morning of the day in which he cleansed the Temple. **19,20. Fig tree.** This common tree of Palestine often symbolized the nation of Israel (Hos 9:10; Joel 1:7). A peculiarity of the tree is that the fruit and leaves usually appear at the same time, with the fruit sometimes coming first. The next crop would be expected in June. This particular tree had put forth foliage in April to such an extent that one would expect it to have produced fruit as well. Here seems to be an instance in which, because of Christ's self-emptying (Phil 2:7), he refrained from using his omniscience in order that his human response might be entirely genuine. **Let no fruit grow on thee.** Spoken with the solemnity of doom. Although there is no statement that the situation should be regarded as parabolic, that seems to be the only reasonable explanation of the incident (for trees have no moral responsibility). It provided a graphic sequel to the earlier parable of Lk 13:6-9 regarding the Jewish nation, unfruitful despite every advantage. **Immediately the fig tree withered away. Immediately** can surely be broad enough to allow for several hours. It was first noticed by the disciples on the next morning, at which time it had withered to the roots (Mk 11:20). **21,22.** To the amazed disciples Jesus explained that such power (for even greater deeds) was available to them through believing prayer. This kind of faith, however, will only ask those things that it knows to be God's will (cf. on 17:20).

4) Questioning of Jesus' Authority, and His Parabolic Answer. 21:23–22:14. **23.** During this third visit to the **temple** on successive days, Jesus was approached by officials from the Sanhedrin (**chief priests, elders,** and scribes, Mk 11:27). **By what authority?** Authorization was usually granted by the Sanhedrin or some eminent rabbi, who bore testimony to the validity of the teaching as being duly received from proper traditional sources (see Edersheim, *Life and Times of Jesus,* II, 381-383). **These things.** A reference to Christ's deeds (cleansing the Temple, miracles) as well as his teaching and his acceptance of the homage due to Messiah. **25-27. The baptism of John.** Representative of the ministry of John. Christ's counterquestion was not an evasion of the Sanhedrin's demand, but served the dual purpose of implying the answer (cf. Jn 5:33-35) and exposing the dishonesty of the Sanhedrin. John the Baptist, whose ministry was popularly recognized as genuinely prophetic, had publicly proclaimed Jesus as Messiah and taught that men should trust Him (Jn 3:26-30; Jn 1:29-37; Acts 19:4). Thus the officials saw clearly the dilemma Christ's question posed for them. If they acknowledged John's divine authorization, they would be obligated to acknowledge what he had taught about Jesus – that He was Mes-

siah. Yet a denial of John would bring public wrath upon them. Such cowardly and dishonest men deserved no further answer.

28-32. Parable of the Two Sons. Matthew alone records the three parables (cf. Mk 12:1, "parables") spoken at this time, evoked by the Sanhedrists' opposition to Jesus' authority. The parable of The Two Sons is interpreted by Jesus as depicting the conflicting responses of the religious outcasts and their leaders toward the ministry of John, which was preparatory to His own. The **son** (actually, *child)* who first said **I will not** but later *repented* **and went** pictures the **publicans and harlots,** religious outcasts who eventually accepted John's message. Many of them became followers of Jesus (Lk 15:1,2). The **son** who said **I go** but **went not** describes the religious leaders who first gave an aloof sort of approval to John (Jn 5:35) but never followed through (Lk 7:29,30). Thus the publicans and harlots, by responding to John, demonstrated their readiness for the Messianic **kingdom of God. The way of righteousness** (II Pet 2:21) describes John's preaching (cf. 22:16, "way of God") in terms suggestive of Noah (II Pet 2:5), and probably denotes the content of his message rather than his personal behavior.

33-46. Parable of the Wicked Husbandmen. This parable further answers the question of Jesus' authority by showing him as the divine Son sent by the Father. Though the main lines of the parable are so clear that the Sanhedrists could not escape their import, one must not attempt to press all the details. The householder certainly represents God the Father; yet his mistaken optimism (v. 37) cannot be predicated of God. Perhaps we should see in the actions of the householder the way God appears to man to act. **33. A vineyard.** Symbol of the theocracy of Israel, familiar to every Jew. Cf. Isa 5:1-7; Ps 80:8-16. Verse 43 equates the **vineyard** with the **kingdom of God,** clearly pointing to the kingdom as mediated to Israel through divinely chosen kings. In the parable the householder is depicted as making every provision for the welfare of the vineyard. **35. Beat one, killed another, stoned another.** For records of the shameful treatment accorded God's emissaries to Israel, see Jer 20:1,2; 37:15; 38:6; I Kgs 19:10; 22:24; II Chr 24:21. **37. Last of all he sent his son.** The extraordinary patience of the householder reveals the utter depravity of the husbandmen. **38. Let us kill him and seize on his inheritance.** Exactly this sentiment had been uttered recently by Jewish leaders (Jn 11:47-53). From this point on, the scope of the parable passes from history to prophecy. **39. Slew him.** A prediction of Jesus' death at the hands of these very men. **40,41.** At this point the Jewish leaders apparently did not grasp the full import of the parable (though they did shortly, v. 45), and so readily answered Jesus' question, pronouncing their own judgment. **42-44.** Jesus' use of Ps 118:22,23 pointed to his ultimate triumph following rejection. The same passage is also quoted in Acts 4:11 and I Pet 2:6,7. As a result of this triumph, the **kingdom of God** will be **taken away** from the possession of these leaders (and the contemporary nation of **Israel,** as shown by the mention of another **nation**). **A nation bringing forth the fruits thereof.** A reference to the Church (called by Peter a "holy nation" in a context where the same OT passage is used; I Pet 2:7-9). With Pentecost came the formation of a new body, the Church, which would be the spiritual nucleus of the Messianic (mediatorial) kingdom. Though these individual Jewish leaders were thus permanently removed from the Kingdom, Rom 9-11 explains that the nation of Israel will once again be brought to the blessings of salvation at the close of the present age of Gentile prominence (Rom 11:25). Today the Church enjoys certain spiritual aspects of the Kingdom in that she has acknowledged Christ as King (Col 1:13), and is being prepared for a share in the coming reign. This aspect of the mediatorial kingdom is described in the parables of Mt 13. **45,46. They feared.** The Jewish leaders were hindered in their plans for Jesus' death (Jn 11:53) by their fear of his popularity with the crowds. The same fear prevented their defamation of John's memory (Mt 21:26).

22:1-14. Parable of the Marriage Feast. Though this parable is similar to that in Lk 14:16-24, the differences in certain details and in the occasion render unnecessary any attempt at making the two identical. Any teacher has the privilege of repeating illustrations and changing details to suit a new situation. **1. In parables,** i.e., parabolically. **2. Kingdom of heaven.** The mediatorial kingdom as depicted in Mt 13:11ff., viewed during the period from Jesus' first coming until the full establishment of the Messianic reign. The **king, his son,** and the **marriage feast** are representative of the Father, Christ (Jn 3:29), and the Messianic kingdom (Isa 25:6; 55:1). If the scene describes a marriage that involved the recognition of the son as heir, then refusal to attend showed disloyalty as well as discourtesy. This accounts for the violent destruction brought upon the rebels by the king's forces. **3-6. To call them that were bidden.** Oriental custom included an initial invitation and a second call at the stated hour. The invited ones, here certainly Israel, refused this call, and when further explanatory entreaties were made, became either brazenly rude or positively murderous. Compare Jewish treatment of John (Mt 21:25), Stephen (Acts 7:59), and James (Acts 12:2). **7. Burned their city.** A prediction of the destruction of Jerusalem in A.D. 70. The Roman army under Titus is regarded in the parable as God's instrument (**his armies**). **8,9. Go ye therefore into the highways** (ASV, *partings of the highways;* RSV, *thoroughfares).* This is usually referred to evangelization of Gentiles (which seems clearly to be intended in Lk 14:23). Here, however, the marriage feast naturally implies a bride as distinct from the guests; yet evangelization of the Gentiles in the church age provides the bride, not the guests. Inasmuch as Christ was explaining to unbelieving Jews about their relation to the Messianic kingdom, perhaps these guests who later responded represent Jews who will respond during the Tribulation. **10. Both bad and good.** Open sinners and morally upright. Both are objects of God's gracious invitation, and many of both groups respond. **11. Wedding garment.** Because absence of this garment excluded the man from the feast, we conclude that the garment represents an absolute requirement for entrance to the Kingdom. Thus it represents the robe of imputed righteousness that God graciously provides to man through faith (Isa 61:10). The custom of kings in providing suitable garments when granting interviews appears to be assumed here, since the culprit is held responsible for his lack, and persons gathered from the highways may not have had proper raiment even if they had had time to clothe themselves. **12. Friend.** Fellow, comrade. A form of address to someone whose name is not known. The man without the wedding garment depicts the person who claims to be ready for Christ's kingdom, but is not. Other parables have depicted him as a tare, and an unusable fish. **13. Outer darkness.** In the parable, this is descriptive of the blackness of night outside the brightly lighted palace (the dinner [*ariston*, v. 4] which began at midday had now run into the night); the darkness and the **weeping and gnashing of teeth** are clearly indicative of the torments of Gehenna (13:42; 25:30,46). **14. Many are called, but few are chosen.** There is a general call of God to sinners which invites them to the joys of salvation (11:28), but which may be resisted and rejected. Comparatively **few** are actually selected for this privilege. Scripture clearly indicates a divine election that brings sinners to God. Yet Scripture also indicates that man is responsible for his indifference (v. 5), rebellion (v. 6), and self-righteousness (v. 12).

5) Questioning of Jesus by Various Groups. 22:15-46. These discussions took place on the same day as the previous parables, one of the busiest days of Jesus' ministry.

15-22. Pharisees' and Herodians' question about tribute. **15. Entangle him.** Entrap, ensnare. **16. Their disciples.** Rabbinical students, sent by their Pharisaic masters. **Herodians.** A group of Jews whose characteristics are not fully known. They apparently advocated the return to rule of the Herodian family (whose rule had ended in Judea and Samaria A.D. 6 with the appointment of Roman procurators). These two groups united in their common hatred of Jesus as a possible Messiah. **17.** After an elaborate introduction (which was certainly not believed by the speakers), their carefully planned question was propounded. **Is it lawful to give tribute unto Caesar?** *Kēnsos* is a Latin loanword, referring to the Roman poll tax imposed upon every Jew. The question presupposed a dilemma: Jesus must either acknowledge servitude to Rome (and thus compromise any claim of Messiahship), or risk being charged with disloyalty to Rome. Our Lord's enemies were so sure of the inflammatory nature of the latter charge that they used it against him a few days later, in spite of his clear denial (Lk 23:2). **19. Show me the poll tax coin** (AV, *the tribute money).* The tax was paid with the *denarius,* equal to a soldier's or a laborer's day-wage. **20,21.** By causing his questioners to acknowledge **Caesar's** image and inscription on the coin, Christ elicited from them the principle of his answer. **Render . . . unto Caesar the things that are Caesar's.** Broadus paraphrases, "You got this from Caesar, pay it back to him" *(Comm. on Matt.*, p. 453). Caesar's coinage represented Caesar's government, with its attendant benefits. For these the subject was obligated to pay (cf. Rom 13:1-7). **The things that are God's.** Here spiritual obligations are regarded as separate, though they are not devoid of relationship. Proper subjection to civil power is part of one's spiritual obligation (I Pet 2:13-15), but a believer must always be finally subject to the will of God (Acts 4:19,20).

23-33. Sadducees' question about the resurrection. **23. Sadducees, which say.** Absence of an article in the better manuscripts suggests the true rendering to be *Sadducees came saying*. Their denial of the resurrection was bolstered by an illustration to prove its supposed absurdity. (Cf. Acts 23:8 for Sadducean tenets.) **24-27. Moses said.** A reference to Deut 25:5 ff. The illustration adduced could conceivably occur among the Jews through the custom of levirate marriage (from the Latin word *levir* meaning "brother-in-law"). Such practice, followed by other ancient peoples as well, had largely fallen into disuse. Hence the case supposed by the Sadducees was no burning issue but a theological conundrum. **28. In the resurrection,** the reality of which the Sadducees derided, **whose wife shall she be?** All seven were equally married to her, and no offspring from any of the unions could cause priority. **29. Not knowing the scriptures nor the power of God.** The error of the Sadducees was their failure to understand the Scriptural teaching regarding the resurrection and the ability God can bring to the situation. Their illustration presupposed that resurrection will restore men to the same form of existence they had before (a view commonly held by the Pharisees), though Scripture nowhere affirms this. They did not credit God with the power to raise the dead to a more glorious state (cf. I Cor 15:40-50). **30. But are as the angels,** i.e., in the matter of marriage. Jesus did not state that the resurrected dead would become angels. Nor does this passage imply that the dearest of earthly relationships will be forgotten in the life to come. Just how these relationships will be affected by the possession of glorified bodies is not explained, but all Scripture supports the view that the resurrected state is one of blessedness and perfect fellowship. **31-33. Spoken unto you by God.** Jesus took his questioners to a direct statement of God himself (not mediated through Moses, as in v. 24). **I am the God of Abraham** (Ex 3:6). Instead of employing some of the more specific passages in the Prophets or the Writings (concerning which Sadducean opinion was doubtful), Jesus cited from the Torah a statement to which he gave the profoundest interpretation. By using the revered covenant name of God, Jesus implied the immortality of these patriarchs. As Plummer observed, "What is dead can have a Creator or a Controller; but only living beings can have a God" *(Gosp. According to St. Matt.*, p. 307).

34-40. A Pharisaic lawyer's question about the great commandment. Consult Mark's account (12:28-34) for additional details, including the interesting aftermath. **34. When the Pharisees had heard.** The discomfiture of the Sadducees produced by Jesus' masterful reply to the resurrection question would have suited the Pharisees. However, a clear-cut victory of Jesus would not have been welcome even to them, inasmuch as they shared the Sadducees' hatred of him. **35. A lawyer.** An expert expounder of Mosaic law. **36. Which is the great commandment in the law?** The ulterior purpose of the lawyer is not fully evident, and it must be noticed that Jesus treated the question forthrightly and then commended the astuteness of the lawyer's response (Mk 12:34). It is often suggested that he wanted to draw Jesus into argument regarding the rabbis' computation of 613 commandments. **37-40.** Our Lord summarized the two tables of the Law in the words of Deut 6:5 and Lev 19:18. Proper regard for God and one's neighbor is the essence of man's duty. All the OT interprets and applies these principles (Rom 13:8). **All thy heart.** In Hebrew thought, **heart** symbolized the whole self, in which the **soul** and **mind,** the animating and reasoning elements, are contained. All-encompassing love for God will cause one to perform every moral duty. But such an unattainable standard merely shows **the** corruption of man's heart.

41-46. Jesus' counterquestion about Messiah. **42. What think ye of the Christ?** Virtually the same question he had asked earlier of the Twelve (16:15). **The son of David.** The Davidic lineage of Messiah was taught by the scribes (Mk 12:35). **43-45.** By pointing his hearers to Ps 110, which was interpreted by the Jews as Messianic (see Edersheim, *Life and Times of Jesus*, App. IX), Jesus showed their inadequate understanding of that Scripture. This psalm of David (the authorship of which Jesus clearly affirms), presents the **Lord** (Jehovah) as speaking to Messiah; and David calls Messiah **my Lord** *(Adonai).* Thus the Jews, who acknowledged Messiah as David's descendant, were confronted by this psalm, where David calls this descendant his "Lord" and superior. The prevailing idea of Messiah as a king who would be merely a political ruler was shown to be inadequate. Furthermore, this psalm was given **in the Spirit** (Holy Spirit, Mk 12:36), the product of supernatural revelation. **46. Neither durst any man . . . ask him any more questions.** Though Mark and Luke comment similarly at slightly different places (Mk 12:34; Lk 20:40), examination shows that each Synoptist placed the comment appropriately for his material. **From that day forth** there were no more interruptions by such questioners.

6) Jesus' Public Denunciation of the Pharisees. 23:1-39. Some of the material in this discourse the Lord had used previously (Lk 11:39 ff.), but now he makes his denunciation at the Temple in Jerusalem, in the stronghold of his enemies.

1-12. Warning against the Pharisees. This portion is directed particularly to the disciples, although in the presence of the multitude. **2. Sit on Moses' seat.** That is, they occupy Moses' position among you as expounders of the Law. **3,4. Wherefore whatsoever they say to you, do.** In so far as their teaching presented what Moses gave, the people were obligated to observe. **Do not ye after their works.** Their **works** included their strained interpretations and perversions of the Law, which enabled them to flout the spiritual import of the OT. Their multitudinous additions to the Law, here designated as **heavy burdens, grievous to be borne,** were part of their **works. They themselves will not move them.** Though rabbinic casuistry could doubtless find loopholes for evading what was unpleasant, this statement probably means that they never lifted a finger to remove any of the burdens (**move** is in contrasting parallel to **lay on**). **5. Phylacteries.** Small cases containing strips of parchment on which were written Ex 13:2-10,11-17; Deut 6:4-9; 11:13-22. The cases were bound with straps to the forehead and to the left arm. The practice arose after the Captivity from an extremely literal understanding of Ex 13:16. Pharisees wore them for ostentation. **Enlarge the borders of their garments.** Tassels worn on the four corners of the outer garment, in accordance with Num 15:38 and Deut 22:12. Jesus wore such tassels (Mt 9:20; 14:36), but the Pharisees enlarged theirs for show. **6,7. Seats** of honor at **feasts** and **synagogues** were objects of Pharisaic desire, along with effusive **greetings** in public places, which drew attention to their high position. **Rabbi.** A title equivalent to *teacher* or *doctor*, and applied by Jews to their spiritual instructors. **8-12.** The next words are addressed specifically to the disciples. Christ's followers should not seek to be called by these titles of **Rabbi, Father,** or **Master,** as did the Pharisees. However, this is not an absolute prohibiting of officials nor the use of appropriate titles, for Paul calls himself "father" of the Corinthians and Timothy his "child" (I Cor 4:15,17). **He that is greatest** clearly shows the validity of differing rank. But a spirit of humility should govern believers, not the self-seeking ambition of the Pharisees, which usurped for itself authority that belongs to God.

13-36. Seven woes upon the Pharisees. Here attention is turned from the disciples to the Pharisees, who formed part of the crowd. **13. Hypocrites!** An epithet stressing the sham of the Pharisees and their scribes. **Ye shut the kingdom of heaven.** As religious leaders and recognized interpreters of Scripture, they should have been the first to respond to Jesus and should have influenced others to follow. Yet those **attempting to enter** (present tense is tendential or perhaps futuristic [Dana and Mantey, *Manual Grammar of the Greek New Testament*, pp. 185,186]) they were preventing by their false leadership. Verse 14 is an interpolation from Mk 12:40 and Lk 20:47. **15. Ye compass sea and land.** A zealous search. **Proselyte.** Not the God-fearing Gentile who stopped short of circumcision (i.e., proselyte of the gate), but the Gentile who had been persuaded to adopt Judaism *in toto*, including all the traditions taught by such Pharisees. **Twofold more a son of Gehenna than yourselves.** Proselytes made by these unspiritual Pharisees (and doubtless added to their sect) would merely add rabbinic traditions to their pagan notions. **16-22.** The third **woe** castigates the Pharisees as **blind guides** and **fools** because of their perversions of truth in oath-taking. It is bad enough that a man's word cannot be trusted apart from an oath. But the Pharisees had taught that there are distinctions in the binding force of various oaths. Oaths that used general references to the **temple** or the **altar** did not obligate the user to perform them, but mention of the more specific **gold of the temple** or the **gift** on the altar were binding. Jesus showed the absurdity of such reasoning by pointing out that the greater (**temple, altar, God**) includes the smaller (**gold, gift, heaven**). In view of such perversity, Christ taught, "Swear not at all" (Mt 5:33-37).

23,24. The fourth **woe** pictures the Pharisees' scrupulous care in minor matters and their neglect of more important duties. The tithing of various herbs was based on Lev 27:30. **Mint, dill,** and **cummin** were garden plants used for seasoning foods. **Judgment, mercy,** and **faith.** These ethical and spiritual obligations (cf. Mic 6:8) are **weightier matters of the law** and thus are of primary importance, although the **other** matters (tithing) were also expected of God's people. By such practice, the Pharisees had scrupulously strained out **the gnat** (the Levitically unclean insect that might fall into the cup), but proceeded to **swallow the camel** (the largest unclean animal in Palestine; Lev 11:4). **25,26.** The fifth **woe** portrays the Pharisees' misplaced emphasis on externals. **Ye cleanse the outside of the cup.** The figure points to the Pharisees' concern for ritualistic purification (rabbinic, not Mosaic) and neglect of the contents of the cup. **Within they are full from extortion and excess** (ASV). The Pharisees supported their mode of living by preying upon others. Conformity to rabbinic ritual could not alter this inner corruption.

27,28. The sixth **woe** describes the hidden influence of the Pharisees. **Whited sepulchres.** Each spring, following the rainy season, graves were whitewashed lest the unwary defile themselves ceremonially by touching them (Num 19:16; cf. Ezk 39:15). This recently performed custom provided a timely illustration of the Pharisees' outward attractiveness but inward defilement. Luke 11:44 uses graves in a slightly different illustration. **29-31.** The seventh **woe** describes the Lord's hearers as partaking of the same nature as their wicked ancestors. By their acts of building and beautifying the tombs of murdered prophets, they supposed they were disavowing those murders. But Jesus stated that their acts proved the very opposite. For by building the tombs, they merely completed what their fathers (spiritual as well as racial) had begun. Their own plotting to murder Jesus (21:46; 22:15; Jn 11:47-53) proved them to be true **sons of them that slew the prophets. 32. Fill ye up then the measure of your fathers.** Compare the similar command to Judas, Jn 13:27. **33. Generation of vipers.** Cf. John's denunciation in 3:7. **34-36. I send unto you prophets.** A similar statement in Lk 11:49 attributes this sending to the "wisdom of God." Thus Jesus, as the very personification of God's wisdom, claims for himself this title (I Cor 1:24). **Prophets, wisemen, scribes.** Terms particularly adapted to his audience. The terms would include also the early Christian witnesses, such as Peter, James, Stephen, and Paul. These persecutions here foretold would fill up the measure of the Jews' guilt, so that divine destruction would come upon that **generation** of the nation. **Abel to Zacharias** includes all the murders recorded in the OT, from the first book (Gen 4:8) to the last in the Hebrew canon (II Chr 24:20-22). The failure of these Pharisees to learn the lessons of history and repent of their wickedness, the same that had characterized their fathers, meant that in God's sight they shared the guilt. Further persecutions would make this indisputably clear. **Zacharias, son of Barachias.** In II Chr 24:20 he is called, "son of Jehoiada the priest," perhaps after an illustrious grandfather who had recently died at the age of one hundred and thirty (II Chr 24:15). Matthew may have had documents that named his father. (For an evaluation of all views, see Broadus, *Comm. on Matt.*, pp. 476,477).

37-39. Lament over Jerusalem. Jesus had expressed similar feelings earlier (Lk 13:34,35; 19:41-44). **37. Thou that killest the prophets.** This link with verse 34 provides an easy transition to Christ's public lament over the rebellious city. **How often would I.** An inadvertent testimony to the authenticity of John's Gospel, which alone records numerous visits of Jesus to Jerusalem. **38. Your house is left unto you desolate.** Cf. I Kgs 9:7; Jer 22:5; 12:7. **House** is variously interpreted as the nation, the city, and the Temple. Inasmuch as Jesus uttered these words as he left the Temple for the last time (24:1), the Temple identification is very attractive. A temple abandoned by Messiah becomes **your house,** not God's. **39. Ye shall not see me henceforth.** The Lord's public ministry was finished. Following the Resurrection, Jesus made appearances only to chosen witnesses (Acts 10:41). **Till ye shall say.** At Christ's second coming the Jews as a nation will recognize their rejected Messiah, and will welcome his return (Rom 11; Zech 12:10).

7) Olivet Discourse. 24:1–25:46. This discussion contains some of the most difficult of Jesus' utterances. The apocalyptic nature of the material resembles some of the prophetic discourses of the OT, where the mingling of historical and typical elements makes interpretation difficult. Some see the fulfillment of most of these predictions in the destruction of Jerusalem, A.D. 70. Others regard the sermon as descriptive of the church age, and of a tribulation through which the Church must pass before Christ returns. The view that sees here our Lord's description of Daniel's seventieth week relies heavily on parallels found in Daniel and Revelation, and accords well with the question of the disciples that called forth the discourse. By this interpretation, Matthew's account deals entirely with events still future. Luke alone (21:12-24) records the intervening church age, introducing after his parallel discussion of eschatological events a section beginning, "But before all these things."

1. The buildings of the temple. The magnificence of Herod's temple was known far and wide. The massive limestone blocks adorned with golden ornamentation made a dazzling sight (Jos *Wars* v. 5.6). **2. Not be left here one stone upon another.** Jesus responded in a mood far different from their nationalistic pride. He predicted the most severe destruction, which occurred A.D. 70 (Jos *Wars* vii. 1.1). **3. Mount of Olives.** The hill overlooking the city and the Temple from the east. **The disciples came to him privately.** With the temple crowds now left behind, the disciples could question him in seclusion. **When shall these things be?** That is, the destruction of the Temple. **The sign of thy coming and of the consummation of the age?** Jewish interpreters of the OT had clearly seen that the coming of Messiah would usher in the "age to come," accompanied by destruction of the wicked. It must be remembered that the Twelve asked in the light of their traditional understanding, and Jesus' answer in this discourse surely assumed this. Thus the **consummation of the age** (ASV marg.) refers to the age of which they were a part and had knowledge. That such an age formed a great part of their thinking appears in Acts 1:6. The age in question was described in Dan 9:25-27 as a period of "seventy weeks," of which only sixty-nine had passed when Messiah was "cut off." Jesus directly implies that this particular time period is involved when he describes in 24:15 an event that Daniel places in the middle of the seventieth week. Hence the Olivet Discourse is primarily concerned with the tribulation of Israel, a period known in Daniel as the "seventieth week" and described also in Rev 6—19, which will culminate in Christ's return.

a) First Half of the Tribulation. 24:4-14. Daniel's seventieth week has two clearly marked halves (Dan 9:27). There is an amazing correspondence between the order of the seals in Rev 6 and the order of events in Mt 24:4-14. Thus these verses must be placed in the first three and one-half years of the Tribulation, after the Church has been raptured. **5. Saying, I am Christ** (cf. Rev 6:1,2; first seal: Antichrist). Though such tendencies may develop during the church age (I Jn 4:3), the specific reference is to the final Antichrist and his associates. There is no record of any person's claiming to be Christ between A.D. 30 and 70. **6. Wars and rumors of wars** (cf. Rev 6:3,4; second seal: warfare). **7. Famines** (cf. Rev 6:5,6; third seal: famine). **Pestilences and earthquakes** (cf. Rev 6:7,8; fourth seal: death for one-fourth of the earth). **8. Beginning of sorrows.** Literally, *of birthpains,* suggesting the travail shortly to be followed by a happier day. **9. Shall kill you** (cf. Rev 6:9-11; fifth seal: martyrs). **11. Many false prophets . . . shall deceive many.** Cf. II Thess 2:8-12. **12. The love of many shall wax cold.** The severity of these calamities will cause the majority of Israel to abandon any pretense of piety. **13.** But the distinguishing mark of the **saved** Jewish remnant will be their enduring in faith **to the end. 14. Gospel of the kingdom.** The good news of salvation in the Messiah, with the emphasis that the Messianic kingdom is about to be established. This message will go into **all the world** during the Tribulation through the efforts of the two witnesses (Rev 11:3-12) and the sealed remnant of Israel (Rev 7).

b) Last Half of the Tribulation. 24:15-28. **15. When ye therefore shall see the abomination of desolation spoken by Daniel the prophet.** The **abomination of desolation** reproduces the LXX rendering of Dan 9:27; 12:11; 11:31, of which the first two are certainly eschatological, while the last predicts the profanation of worship by Antiochus, whose act foreshadowed the final abomination. This event occurs in the middle of the seventieth week (Dan 9:27), and its length is variously described as "42 months" (Rev 11:2; 13:5), "1,260 days" (Rev 12:6), or "time, times, and half a time" (Dan 7:25; 12:7; Rev 12:14). **The holy place.** The Temple, to be restored. This enigmatic **abomination** is connected with worship, and other passages would suggest it to be the idolatrous homage that the Antichrist will demand for himself. See Rev 13:5-8; II Thess 2:1-4. It was clearly future in Jesus' day, thus canceling those views of Daniel that find all the fulfillments in the days of Antiochus. Nor can the reference be limited to the catastrophe of A.D. 70, for Mt 24:21 limits the reference to the greatest of all tribulations (cf. Dan 12:1). **16-20. Then.** The use of this temporal particle here and in 24:21 and 23 puts all the events of this section within the framework of the final three and one-half years. The terrors of persecution under Antichrist will make immediate flight necessary (Rev 12:6,14). No time will be available for preparation. Inevitable hardships are foretold. **Neither on the sabbath day.** A reference to the difficulty of travel (securing lodging, meals, services) on the Sabbath in an area where Jews will be observing such restrictions. This does not necessarily imply that Christian Jews will observe Sabbath worship. Jesus was employing concepts familiar to his hearers, none of whom as yet could know of the change to Sunday.

21. Then shall be great tribulation. The additional description, **not since the beginning of the world,** makes Christ's reference to Dan 12:1 unmistakable. The further notice, **nor ever shall be,** prevents our identification of this with anything less than the final tribulation under Antichrist just prior to the resurrection (Dan 12:2). **22. Except those days should be shortened.** Antichrist's violent measures will be cut short by the sudden appearing of Christ, who will destroy the wicked one (II Thess 2:8). **23-26.** During this intense persecution of Israel, many would-be deliverers will arise, as the Maccabean heroes did in the inter-Testament period. But the **elect** are here warned that the deliverance will not be in any partial or gradual manner. **27.** Rather, with the suddenness and universality of **lightning** (language of appearance, **east . . . unto west**), so shall the **Son of man** come to judge the oppressors. **28. Carcase.** The spiritually dead and decaying mass of the wicked. **Eagles.** The term included birds that feed on carrion; hence, *vultures*, the agents of divine judgment. Cf. Rev 19:17,18.

c) The Coming of the Son of Man. 24:29-31. **29. Immediately after the tribulation of those days.** Cf. on 24:21. No reference is made here to the Rapture of the Church (cf. I Thess 4:16,17). Rather, the words describe the actual return of Christ to end the Tribulation and establish the Messianic reign. **The sun be darkened.** These accompanying astral phenomena are foretold also in Joel 3:15 and Isa 13:9,10. **30. The sign of the Son of man.** Interpreters are not agreed on the identification of this **sign.** Lange's explanation of it as the Shekinah or glory of Christ is followed by many scholars. Whatever its exact form, its appearance will cause the Jews **(all the tribes)** to **mourn** as they recognize their Messiah (cf. Zech 12:10-12). **Clouds of heaven, power,** and **great glory** describe the same scene in Dan 7:13,14; II Thess 1:7,9. **31.** The **angels** who gather **his elect** are the same who are described in 13:30, 41-43 as removing the tares from the wheat, that the wheat might then be gathered into the barn.

d) Illustrations to promote watchfulness. 24:32–25:30.

32-36. The fig tree. A frequent Biblical symbol of the nation of Israel (Jer 24; Joel 1:6,7; Hos 9:10). Jesus also had used this figure previously (Lk 13:6). The peculiar trait of the tree mentioned earlier (21:19, 20) is that fruit and leaves appear at about the same time; when leaves are present, summer is near. Jesus thus associated a revitalized nation with the approach of these eschatological events. **34. This generation shall not pass away.** To explain **generation** (*genea*) here as the lifetime of the disciples obligates one to seek the fulfillment of all these events by A.D. 70. But that is manifestly impossible unless one spiritualizes the second coming of Christ. However, *genea* also can mean "race" or "family," and this yields good sense here. In spite of terrible persecution, the Jewish nation will not be exterminated, but will exist to share the blessings of the Millennial reign. In support of this view, Alford points out that Christians of ancient times continued to expect the Lord's coming even after the apostles and their contemporaries had passed away (*New Testament for English Readers,* p. 169). **35. Heaven and earth shall pass away.** Cf. Rom 8:19-22; I Cor 7:31; Rev 21:1. The truth of these solemn predictions of Christ will not experience the slightest alteration. **36.** The exact moment of fulfillment, however, lies in the authority of the **Father** alone (cf. Acts 1:7). No scheme of date-setting by men is possible. The phrase, **neither the Son** (omitted by AV, but included in ASV and RSV on strong textual evidence), indicates that the perfect knowledge which all members of the Godhead share was part of that which Jesus voluntarily refrained from using during his earthly ministry, except in those instances when such knowledge was needed for his purpose.

37-39. The days of Noah. As the **days of Noah** closed an era with judgment, so shall Christ's return. In an age of great wickedness (Gen 6), men went about their daily living undisturbed by impending doom **(eating, drinking, marrying, giving in marriage).** But the **flood took away** all the wicked, so that only the righteous were left to inherit the earth. Likewise the **coming of the Son of man,** following the Great Tribulation (vv. 29-31) will remove the wicked, in order that the faithful remnant who have come out of the Tribulation may participate in the Millennial blessings (cf. 25:31-46; 13:30,41-43,49,50).

40-42. The two in the field, and the two at the mill. **Then** places this illustration in the same period as the preceding, precisely explained in verse 29 as "after the tribulation." Thus it does not refer to the Rapture of the Church. **Two in the field.** The Second Coming will be so sudden and discriminatory that persons working together will be separated, **one** man (masculine numeral) snatched away to judgment, and **one** man left to enjoy blessing. **Two women grinding at the mill.** This task was regularly performed by women, either mother and daughter, sisters, or female slaves (see Thomson, *Land and Book*, pp. 526,527). **Watch therefore.** Although the emphasis here is upon the coming of the **Son of man** after the Tribulation, the warning is pertinent to all believers, for all are to be watchful and ready for his coming. The delineation of various phases of his coming is revealed later. This encouragement to watchfulness is repeated in 24:44 and 25:13.

43,44. The master of the house. If the household master had been watchful, he could have prevented damage and loss. **Broken up.** Literally, *dug through*, a reference to houses of sun-dried brick in Palestine, comparatively easy to enter. Believers have less excuse for carelessness than this **master,** who had not been forewarned that a thief was coming.

45-51. The faithful servant and the evil servant. **45-47.** The figure depicts a **trustworthy** and **prudent servant** who is placed by his master over the other **domestic servants.** Faithful performance of his duties will bring increased privilege and responsibility when **his lord** returns. **48,49.** In contrast, the **evil servant** is a servant in name only, for he flouts his lord's instructions and assumes the rights of authority for himself. His defection is both doctrinal **(my lord delayeth his coming)** and ethical **(smite his fellowservants, eat and drink with the drunken).** He mistakes the uncertainty of the time of coming for a certainty that it will not be soon. Every believer (whether church age or Tribulation saint) is a servant of God with a definite area of responsibility. **50,51.** The coming of Christ will be sudden and unexpected, and will unmask such hypocrites. **Shall cut him asunder.** The literal meaning, "to cut in two," describes the physical punishment (cf. II Sam 12:31; Heb 11:37), and the following words **(with the hypocrites . . . weeping and gnashing of teeth)** affirm the eternal result.

25:1-13. The Ten Virgins. A beautiful story lifted from contemporary marriage custom, but interpreted by evangelicals in widely varying fashion. Some explain the virgins as the professing members of the Church awaiting the return of Christ. Others apply the parable to the Jewish remnant in the Tribulation. Though the central theme of watchfulness is applicable to either group, this writer feels that the latter interpretation meets the demands of content and context more precisely. **1. Then** places the parable within the framework mentioned in 24:29 and 24:40. **The kingdom of heaven.** Cf. on Mt 3:2; 13:11. **Ten virgins . . . went forth to meet the bridegroom.** Jewish weddings had two phases. The bridegroom went first to the bride's home to obtain his bride and observe religious ceremonies. Then he would take his bride to his own home for a resumption of the festivities. The parable gives no intimation that the virgins (plural) expect to marry the bridegroom. This is not a polygamous wedding. Rather, at the end of the Tribulation, Christ will be returning to earth (his domain) after taking to himself the Church as his bride in heaven (her home during the Tribulation). This understanding is reflected in the Western text of this passage, which says, "to meet the bridegroom and the bride." Cf. also Lk 12:35,36, "when he will return from the wedding." Hence the Church as such is not in view here. Interest centers upon the virgins who wish to participate in the wedding feast, representative of the professing Jewish remnant (Rev 14:1-4). **3. Foolish.** Stupid. **Lamps.** Torches, each having a wick and a space for oil. **No oil with them. Oil,** regularly symbolic in Scripture of the Holy Spirit (Zech 4; Isa 61:1). Here a reference to the possession of the Holy Spirit in regeneration (Rom 8:9). All ten appeared outwardly the same (virgins, lamps, similar activity), but five did not partake of the Holy Spirit, which at this time had been given to Israel that they might be ready for Messiah (Zech 12:10).

5. All slumbered and slept. The parable attaches no blame to this detail. Hence it perhaps pictures the assurance of the remnant as they awaited the bridegroom, rather than their carelessness; but in the case of the foolish virgins, it was a false assurance. **6,7. Trimmed their lamps.** Cleaned the wicks, lighted them, and adjusted the flames. A person going about Oriental streets at night must carry a lighted torch. So the virgins prepared to join the procession as the bridegroom approached. **8. Our lamps are going out.** The foolish virgins, who had provided no oil, saw their dry wicks flicker for a few moments and then die. To insist that they had some oil but not enough contradicts 25:3. The failure to provide any oil at all displays their stupidity. **9. Buy for yourselves.** Language of the parable. The Holy Spirit is a free gift, but may be depicted by such metaphors (cf. Isa 55:1). Each person must obtain his own supply. **10-12.** While the foolish were gone, the bridegroom came, and the feast began. Later the foolish virgins returned, the implication being that no oil could be obtained at such an hour. **I know you not.** A statement similar in import to 7:23. Christ will reject all relationship with persons whose claim is profession only.

14-30. The Talents. A parable similar to that of The Pounds, which had been given a few days earlier at Jericho (Lk 19:11-27). The Pounds illustrated the truth that equal gifts, if used with unequal diligence, may be unequally rewarded. The Talents showed that unequal gifts, if used with equal faithfulness, will be equally rewarded. The preceding parable of The Virgins stressed the need for alert preparation for Christ's coming. The Talents emphasized the need for faithful service during his absence.

14. The elliptical nature of the sentence, which causes English translators to supply various words at the beginning, shows its close connection with the previous material. **As a man going into another country.** The **man** is clearly the **Son of man** (v. 13). **15.** A talent was a unit of coinage of comparatively high value. Here the **talents** were silver (v. 18, *argurion*, "silver money"). Depending upon who issued them, talents ranged in value from $1,625 (Aegina) to $1,080 (Attic). A **talent** was worth much more than a **pound** *(mina)*. **According to his several ability.** The talents represent differing responsibilities to be exercised in accord with each man's capacity. **16,17.** The first two servants, though possessing different amounts of money, were equally diligent and doubled their capital. **18.** The servant who possessed only **one** talent displayed no diligence and was not challenged by his opportunity. **Digged in the earth.** A common hiding place (Mt 13:44). **19. After a long time.** An indication that Christ's return would not be immediate, although the expression is indefinite. In the parable the return was yet within the lifetime of the servants. **20-23.** At their lord's return the first two servants had different sums to present, but both offered increases of 100 per cent and received the same commendation and reward. **Well done, good and faithful servant.** Faithfulness is the virtue being examined. **I will set thee over many things.** Part of the reward consisted in gaining higher responsibilities and privileges with the lord. **Enter thou into the joy of thy lord.** Probably a reference to a believer's sharing Christ's joy, which is His by right of His perfect performance of the Father's will (Jn 15:10,11). **24,25.** The unprofitable servant, however, reveals by his explanation an utterly false view of his master. **A hard man.** Harsh, cruel, merciless. **Reaping where thou hast not sown,** i.e., profiting from the labor of others. **Gathering where thou didst not scatter.** It is not certain whether this clause is parallel in thought to the preceding, or whether it pictures the next stage of harvest, the winnowing. If the latter, then the servant accuses his lord of gathering into his barn that which another's labor had scattered with the winnowing shovel to separate the grain from the chaff. **I was afraid.** He pleads his fear of risk and the necessity of accounting for possible loss. This servant was blind to the fact that his master was a generous, loving man, who wanted him to participate in wonderful joys. **26. Thou knewest.** Perhaps this should be regarded as a question, "Did you know that . . . ?" Without acknowledging the truth of this opinion, the master judges the slave on the basis of his plea, to show the baseness of such an attitude. **27.** If the servant really feared the risk of business ventures, then he should have deposited the talent with the **bankers** so that it would have drawn **interest.** Although Israelites were forbidden to extract interest from each other, they could do so from Gentiles (Deut 23:20). **28,29.** Therefore, the talent was taken from this lazy and rebellious servant and given to the one who was most able to use it profitably. **30. Cast ye the unprofitable servant into outer darkness.** The **weeping and gnashing of teeth** show clearly that this symbolizes eternal punishment (8:12; 13:42,50; 22:13; 24:51). Herein is the crux of the interpretation. If this reckoning is the judgment of the believer's works, then we apparently have a true believer suffering the loss of his soul because of the barrenness of his works. But that interpretation would contradict Jn 5:24. Or, if the unprofitable servant represents a mere professing Christian, whose real nature is thus unmasked, then it appears that the judgment of believers' works and the damnation of sinners occur together, although Rev 20 separates these judgments by 1,000 years. The best solution applies the parable to the Tribulation saints (whether Jew or Gentile) because of the clear association with the preceding verses. This explanation agrees with other Scriptures that at the time of Christ's return, the believing remnant will be gathered to enjoy Millennial blessings, but those then living who have no real belief in their Messiah will be removed (Ezk 20:37-42). Of course, the principle is true for men of all ages that God holds men responsible for their use of his gifts.

e) Judgment of All the Nations. 25:31-46. **31. Then shall he sit upon the throne of his glory.** The same scene as 24:30,31, marking the coming of the **Son of man** to end the Great Tribulation and usher in the Millennium. **32,33. Before him shall be gathered all the nations.** This judgment scene must be distinguished from that of Revelation 20 (Great White Throne), for that follows the resurrection of the wicked at the close of the Millennium. Here the **nations** must mean the persons living on earth when Christ returns. They will be judged as individuals, not as groups (**them,** v. 32, is masculine gender, whereas **nations** is neuter). Such a judgment of living men at the time of Christ's glorious coming is foretold in Joel 3:1,2. It will result in a separation into two groups, with the group compared to **sheep** placed at Christ's **right hand,** the position of honor and blessing. **34.** To these who had been pronounced **blessed** by the **Father,** Christ as the **King** (only use of this title by Jesus) invites, **Come . . . inherit the kingdom** (Millennial). **35-40.** As evidence of the regenerated character of these **sheep**-like persons, Jesus cites their deeds of kindness done to "**my brethren,**" which he treats as done to himself. It seems clear that the **sheep** and the **goats** are distinct from **my brethren.** Hence the interpretation of the **nations** as Gentiles and **my brethren** as the faithful Jewish remnant who will proclaim the gospel of the Kingdom in all the world (24:14; Rev 7:1-8) meets the exigencies of the passage. (That Jesus earlier called all believers his "brethren" does not change the demands of this context; 12:47-50.) These Jewish believers will bring about the conversion of an unnumbered multitude of Gentiles (Rev 7:9-14), who will evidence their faith by their deeds. Their visiting those in prison suggests that danger will be involved in a man's publicly acknowledging Christ and His emissaries during that period.

41. Depart from me, ye cursed. Many have noted the absence of the Greek article with **cursed** (as differing from its use in "ye blessed," v. 34). Thus the participle, being circumstantial rather than substantive, may indicate that the phrase means "Depart from me under a curse" (ASV marg.). Though the righteous have been pronounced blessed by the Father and enter a kingdom prepared for them before creation, the fate of the wicked is not stated in such specific terms of election. The **everlasting fire** was not prepared for them but for the **devil and his angels** (Rev 20:10). Neither do men inherit eternal fire (contrast the righteous, v. 34), but go there by refusing God's grace. **42-45.** Jesus points to the goats' lack of the good characteristics displayed by the sheeplike ones. Sins of omission, not heinous deeds of violence, are chosen as indicative of spiritual state. **46. Eternal punishment** and **eternal life** both employ the same adjective (*aiōnios*). Any attempt to reduce the punishment by restricting **eternal** reduces the bliss of the righteous by the same amount. While **eternal** may imply a qualitative as well as a quantitative concept, the aspect of unending duration cannot be dissociated from the word. It was the regular word for the concept of "eternal," as lexicons attest. Eternal punishment is mentioned in such passages as Mt 18:8; II Thess 1:9; Jude 13; *et al.* Thus at the beginning of the Millennium, a judgment is held, and the wicked are removed, so that only regenerated persons will enter the Millennial kingdom (cf. Jn 3:3).

IV. The Passion of Jesus Christ. 26:1–27:66.

This section, of incalculable importance to every Christian, is filled with dramatic human interest. Yet the details supplied by the Evangelists have caused problems, chiefly chronological, from earliest times. Nevertheless, the factual way in which each Gospel (written by men who were themselves emotionally involved) treats these highly emotional events makes these sublime treatises the more remarkable.

A. Plot Against Jesus. 26:1-16.

1-5. Final prediction of his death. **2. After two days.** Since the Passover was eaten on the evening of Nisan 14 (sundown actually began Nisan 15), this prediction was made on the evening of Nisan 12. **Passover.** The first great feast in the Jewish calendar, commemorating Israel's deliverance from Egypt and the "sparing" (meaning of Heb. root transliterated into Gr. as *pascha)* of their firstborn when God smote the Egyptians (cf. Ex 12). Passover was followed immediately by the seven days' Feast of Unleavened Bread (Nisan 15-21), and the entire festival was often called "Passover." **The Son of man is betrayed.** Cf. predictions in 16:21; 17:22; 20:18. Here Christ first foretells that his death will occur at Passover time. **3-5.** This prediction ran counter to the plans of the plotters, however. Fearful of the crowds in Jerusalem, many of whom were Galilean supporters of Jesus, they agreed not to make any move **during the feast.** They may well have expected to delay action for a full week. But Jesus fixed the time of his death in advance, contrary to their scheming, and overruled so that he would die as the true Passover. **Caiaphas** had functioned as high priest since about A.D. 18. He had previously called for Jesus' death (Jn 11:49,50).

6-13. Anointing at Bethany. Interpreters are not agreed on the chronological connections of this event. In view of Jn 12:1, "six days before the Passover," either Matthew (and Mark) or John has followed topical rather than chronological order. Because neither Mark nor Matthew actually dates the event more precisely than "now when Jesus was in Bethany," it seems best to follow the clear chronology in Jn 12:1. Thus Matthew, having described the conspiracy, now reverts to an earlier event to show the circumstances that prompted Judas to the actual betrayal. Parallels are Mk 14:3-9; Jn 12:1-8 (Lk 7:36-50 relates a different incident).

6. Simon the leper. Doubtless a healed leper who felt much gratitude toward Jesus. **7. A woman.** Mary, the sister of Martha and Lazarus (Jn 12:3; 11:1,2). **Very precious ointment.** Parallel accounts describe the ointment as nard, with a value in excess of 300 denarii. **8,9.** When **the disciples** saw the lavish outpouring of this ointment on the **body** (v. 12) of Jesus (both **head,** v. 7, and feet, Jn 12:3), they grumbled with **indignation,** regarding such use as waste. Matthew singles out no one for particular blame (perhaps ashamed at his own participation). But John cites Judas as the instigator, and shows the hypocrisy of his avowed concern for the poor. **10-13.** Jesus explained that one must be spiritually discerning so as not to miss an irrecoverable opportunity. Deeds of benevolence are good and are always in order (Mk 14:7). But there would never be another opportunity to do what Mary did. **She did it to prepare me for burial** (ASV). It is unwarranted to suggest that Jesus was inventing motives for Mary. He had previously announced his approaching death (Jn 10:11,17,18; Mt 16:21; 17:22; 20:18). Instead of closing her mind to the prediction, as the disciples seemed to do (cf. Mt 16:22), Mary believed it. She apparently realized that when the tragedy struck, there would be no time for customary courtesies. Only if Mary's act is seen as born of her spiritual comprehension can the tremendous praise from Jesus be properly understood. As it happened, this was the only anointing his body received. The women who later came to perform this task found only the empty tomb.

14-16. Conspiracy of Judas. How closely **then** is to be understood with the preceding paragraph cannot be ascertained (Mk merely says "and"). If 26:6-13 be regarded as parenthetical, to explain one of the roots of the betrayal, then the plot of Judas may belong to the same time as verses 1-5. By such a view, the indignation at Simon's house six days before the Passover (Jn 12:1,2) developed into a matured conspiracy during the next four days. **Iscariot.** Man of Kerioth, a town in Judea. **They covenanted with him.** The preferred translation is, *they weighed unto him*. Matthew employs the same word as the LXX in Zech 11:12, to which he seems to be consciously alluding. The LXX uses *histēmi* to translate *shakal,* "to weigh out money" (another instance is I Kgs 20:39 [LXX, III Kgs 21:39]). Thus Judas was paid at this time, a fact which the other accounts neither note nor contradict. **Thirty pieces of silver.** Probably shekels. A comparatively small sum, the valuation of a slave (Ex 21:32).

B. The Final Meal. 26:17-30. Probably no harmonistic problem in the Gospels has been as perplexing as the one presented here. Was this final meal the Jewish Passover? The Synoptics imply that it was. Yet John seems equally clear that the Passover was yet future at the time of the feet-washing (Jn 13:1), meal (13:29), trials (18:28), and crucifixion (19:14,31). Some scholars are content to admit an irreconcilable conflict. Others insist that one account must be wrong. It has also been argued that Jesus ate an anticipatory Passover one day in advance of the legal observance. Reinforcement of this view has recently come to light at Qumran, where discoveries have shown that the Qumran sect always observed Passover on Tuesday night. Thus it is suggested that Jesus ate a Passover on Tuesday (as the Synoptics imply), while orthodox Judaism observed Passover on Friday. (See J. A. Walther, "Chronology of Passion Week," JBL, June, 1958, p. 116 ff.) Against this view stands the great improbability that such a remarkable deviation from orthodox Judaism would pass without some special notice in the Gospels, or that a Passover meal could be properly observed in Jerusalem prior to the traditional time (e.g., lambs were to be slain at the Temple shortly before the Passover meal; cf. I Cor 5:7). A more worthy proposal explains either John or the Synoptics in the light of the other. Both possibilities have been tried, although there are admitted difficulties with either method. The present writer prefers to explain the Synoptics by the clear statements of John, which perhaps were partially intended by him to clarify ambiguous points in the chronology. According to this view, the Last Supper was in no sense the Passover meal; rather, Jesus died at the very hour the Passover lambs were being slain at the Temple (cf. I Cor 5:7). Nevertheless, Jesus gave directions to his disciples to make the usual arrangements for the feast, for two reasons: (1) the disciples would eat it; (2) Jesus did not wish to foretell at this time the exact moment of his death.

17-19. Preparation for the Passover. **17. First day of unleavened bread.** The fourteenth of Nisan, on which leaven was removed from the houses in preparation for the feasts of Passover and Unleavened Bread (cf. Mk 14:12; Lk 22:7). This day began at sundown on the thirteenth, and it is to the opening hours of this day that reference is made. **18,19.** In response to the disciples' question, Jesus sent them to a man at whose house the group would assemble. **I will keep the Passover.** To this statement of general purpose must be added the words of Lk 22:16, ASV, "I will not eat it," in which he later indicates that the general plan will be interrupted. Perhaps he did not wish Judas to know his plans so specifically this far in advance.

20-30. The Last Supper. **20. When even was come.** Later that same evening (early hours of the fourteenth), Jesus joined the disciples at the supper hour (Lk 22:14). **21. One of you shall betray me.** First announcement that the "delivering up" of the Son of man (17:22; 20:18; 26:2) was to be by one of the Twelve. What shock that statement must have caused! **22.** The fact that eleven of the disciples innocently asked, **Lord, is it I?** shows that they realized their own weakness, although their questions were so phrased as to expect a negative answer—"*It is not I, is it?*" **23. He that dippeth his hand with me.** Since the group probably ate from a common dish, this statement did not identify the traitor, except to emphasize the dastardly nature of the betrayal, as occurring among intimate companions. **24. As it is written.** The death of Christ was unfolding as predicted in various OT passages. Yet God's sovereignty over all events never relieves man of responsibility or guilt. **25.** When Judas saw that his silence was cause for suspicion, he also asked, **Is it I, Rabbi?** To him Jesus answered, **Thou hast said.** It does not appear that the others heard this answer amid the general hum of conversation. Whether Christ's explanation to John (and Peter) occurred before or after the indication to Judas cannot be ascertained (Jn 13:23-26). When Judas left shortly, none knew that Satan had energized him so that he would immediately put the plot into operation (Jn 13:27-30).

26. Matthew's account of the consecration of the bread and the wine is similar to Mark's; Luke's resembles that in I Cor 11:23-26. **This is my body.** For full discussion of the opposing views of Romanism, Luther, Calvin, and Zwingli, consult Bible dictionaries. The obvious meaning of the passage prevents our understanding the bread in any sense other than symbolic, for his actual body was also present. (Cf. similar metaphors: Jn 10:7; 15:1.) These symbols were to be reminders to the disciples (Lk 22:19) of their absent Lord, and memorials of the cost of their redemption. **27,28. Drink ye all of it,** i.e., all of you. **The new testament** or covenant was put in force by the death of Christ. The old covenant given by God to Israel required continual sacrifices for sin. But Christ's death provided a perfect sacrifice, and made possible both justification and regeneration (Heb 8:6-13). **Shed for many.** (Cf. 20:28.) Christ's death, while sufficient in itself to care for the **remission of sins** for every person, is here regarded as actually effective only for believers. **29. I will not drink henceforth.** This statement directed the gaze of the disciples ahead to the Father's **kingdom** (the Messianic **kingdom of God,** Mk 14:25) and to a time of joy and fellowship at the great Marriage Supper. **30. When they had sung an hymn, they went out.** Before this occurred, the discourse of John 14 must have been delivered.

C. Prediction of Peter's Denial. 26:31-35. Did this occur before they left the upper room (Jn 13:36-38; Lk 22:31-34) or after (Mk 14:27-31; Mt)? Since it seems impossible to harmonize these accounts without doing violence to two of them, it is more feasible to understand two separate warnings to Peter. **31. All ye shall be offended.** Though only Peter denied Jesus, all eleven forsook him and fled (v. 56). Jesus regarded this as fulfillment of Zech 13:7. **32. I will go before you into Galilee.** This was the great postresurrection meeting mentioned several times (28:7,10,16). It does not preclude other appearances, however, some of them earlier in Judea. **33-35.** Peter's boastfulness in rating his devotion superior to that of the others **(though all men shall be offended)** cast reflection upon them and thus drew forth their own avowals of loyalty. This experience was undoubtedly in Jesus' mind when he later asked Peter, "Lovest thou me more than these?" (Jn 21:15).

D. Events in Gethsemane. 26:36-56.

36-46. The prayer. **36. Gethsemane.**

The name means "oil press," and here describes a garden frequented by Jesus and the disciples. It lay across the Kedron on the Mount of Olives (Lk 22:39; Jn 18:1,2), and doubtless contained olive trees and a press for extracting oil. The spot shown to travelers today must be near the place, although the ancient trees cannot be the originals (Jos *Wars* vi.1.1). **37,38.** Stationing eight disciples together, Jesus took Peter, James, and John farther into the garden. Finally he withdrew even from them to pray alone. The agony of soul he experienced is depicted by **sorrowful, sore troubled** (AV, *very heavy*), **exceedingly sorrowful, even unto death.** He gave commandment to the closest three (as well as, more generally, to all) to **watch,** i.e., to lend strength by their alert presence and sympathy. **39. If it be possible,** i.e., morally possible, consistent with the Father's will. **Let this cup pass from me.** The key to understanding Christ's agony lies in identifying **the cup.** Although any normal human being would shrink from the horrors of crucifixion, martyrs have often faced cruel death without such extreme distress (cf. Lk 22:44). Nor can we adopt the view that Christ feared premature death at the hands of Satan, for the cup came from the Father, not from Satan (Jn 18:11). Furthermore, Christ's life could only be given voluntarily (Jn 10:17,18). **Cup** is used figuratively in Scripture either of God's blessing (cf. Ps 23:5) or of his wrath (cf. Ps 75:8). Hence, the most satisfying explanation of the cup refers it to the divine wrath which Christ would incur at the cross as he became man's sin-bearer. This experience during which God for a time was separated from his Son, gave rise to the awful cry of Mt 27:46. If one man's sin can cause him bitter grief when he feels the estrangement of God, how incomparable must have been the anguish of Jesus, who knew what it meant to assume the guilt of all men. **Not as I will, but as thou wilt.** From beginning to end, Christ's prayer was perfectly submissive to the Father. And the prayer was answered, not by removal of the cup, but by strength to drink (Lk 22:43), and ultimately by resurrection "out of death" (Heb 5:7). **40,41.** Finding the disciples sleeping from the draining effects of prolonged emotion and fatigue, Jesus singled out Peter for particular counsel (perhaps in view of his recent boasts), and urged him to continual alertness and prayer lest events surprise him into yielding to **temptation. The spirit is willing.** Man's spiritual nature illuminated by the Holy Spirit. **But the flesh is weak.** Some think that **flesh** here denotes a constitutional part of man's being which is not sinful if controlled by the spirit (and thus the proverb may be applied to Jesus also); others, that it denotes the sinful nature that all men possess (Jesus excepted). **42-45.** In substance, this prayer was uttered three times; and each time the submission of the Son was entire. Yet it is clear that Jesus knew what the outcome would be. **Sleep on now.** Probably not irony, but a simple statement that their opportunity to be useful in the crisis had passed. **46.** At this moment, however, Jesus noticed the approach of the enemy. **Let us be going.** Not in flight, but to meet them (Jn 18:4).

47-56. The arrest. **47. Great multitude.** A force of Roman soldiers, with their usual **swords,** under command of a chiliarch (Jn 18:12); Jewish temple police under orders from the **chief priests** and **elders,** armed with clubs (Jn 18:12); some of the chief priests and elders (Lk 22:52). **48. He . . . gave them a sign.** Most of the Roman soldiers would not have known Jesus. **49. Kissed him.** The compound form here *(katephilēsen)* suggests an intensive, warm embrace (in contrast to the simpler form mentioned in v. 48). **50. Friend.** Comrade, companion (*hetaire*). The term recognizes their previous association, without the connotation of affection. **For what are you come?** Are these words of Jesus elliptical, to which we must add some verb, as "Do that for which you are come" (ASV)? Or a question, "Why are you come?" Or a sad exclamation, "For what a reason you are come!" Whatever the precise intent, Judas and the soldiers proceeded with their plan. **51. One of them.** Identified by John as Peter. **Drew his sword.** The disciples had two of these short swords (Lk 22:38). **Smote the servant.** John, well acquainted with the high-priestly family, records the servant's name as Malchus (Jn 18:10,15). **His ear.** Cf. Lk 22:51. Peter's rash act, while well-intentioned, seriously compromised our Lord's position, and necessitated a miraculous healing to undo the disastrous effects it might have had at the trial (cf. Jn 18:36). Yet so complete was the miracle that the issue of the mutilation was never raised by Christ's accusers. **52. They that take the sword shall perish with the sword.** Christ and his message were not to be defended nor advanced with carnal weapons. This general principle stated by Jesus is confirmed by human experience. "The sword is visited by the sword in war; the sword of retribution opposes the arbitrary sword of rebellious sedition; and the sword taken up unspiritually in a spiritual cause, is avenged by the certain, though perhaps long-delayed, sword of historical vengeance" (J. P. Lange, *Matthew*, p. 486). **53,54. Twelve legions of angels.** Each Roman legion at full strength contained 6,000 men. Christ refrained from invoking the incomparably superior forces at his command, that the Scriptures which foretold his suffering might be fulfilled. **55,56. As against a robber.** The presence of weapons suggests that they expected a violent defense, as of a bold robber (not the hasty flight of a "thief"). Yet all past experience with Jesus should have belied that notion. Can it be (as Plummer and others suggest) that this amazing reaction of Jesus in attributing these events to fulfilled prophecy marked the point of Judas' turning from devilish plotter to remorseful suicide?

E. Events at the Jewish Trials. 26:57–27:2. Jesus was led first to Annas, the ex-high priest, who still retained much prestige (Jn 18:12-23). After the preliminary hearing, which allowed time for the Sandedrin to gather for this highly irregular night session, Jesus was taken to the Sanhedrin. At dawn, a second Sanhedrin session formally condemned him (Mt 27:1).

57-68. First Sanhedrin trial. **57. Caiaphas the high priest.** Son-in-law of the deposed Annas. It appears probable that Caiaphas and Annas had residences in the same building, perhaps separated by a courtyard. By this time the **scribes, elders,** and **chief priests** had assembled in this extraordinary session. **58. Peter followed,** and gained entrance to the **courtyard** (not AV *palace),* with the aid of John (Jn 18:15,16). **59. Sought false witness.** These Jews knew they had no real case against Jesus; hence they had to use trumped up charges. **60,61.** Yet the charges were so vague and inconsistent that they could not find even two witnesses – the minimum specified by law (Deut 17:6) – who agreed with each other. Finally **two** were produced who misquoted and misapplied a statement of Jesus uttered three years previously (Jn 2:19). **I am able to destroy the temple of God.** The actual statement had attributed the destroying to the Jews; and the reference was to his body, not to the Herodian edifice (Jn 2:21). Perhaps some of Jesus' statements in the Olivet Discourse (24:2) had been crudely garbled by Judas and combined with this statement (Jn 2:19). **62. Answerest thou nothing?** Caiaphas hoped to force the captive into some unguarded statement. Yet the wild charges hurled at Jesus were best answered by this dignified silence (cf. Isa 53:7). **63. I adjure thee.** A formula which informed Jesus that his answer would be regarded as under oath. **The Christ, the Son of God.** Although some dispute the full import of **Son of God,** it seems clear that Caiaphas employed it in the unique sense of deity, since acknowledgment brought the charge of blasphemy. This was the real cause for Christ's condemnation (Jn 19:7), and had been the basis of earlier plots against him (Jn 5:18). Reports of other incidents that supported this claim must certainly have reached the high priest's ears (Jn 1:34,49; 9:35-37; 11:27; Mt 14:33; 8:29; *et al.).* **64. Thou hast said.** An unequivocal confession that he was the divine Messiah. (Jesus' statement under oath does not vitiate the teaching of 5:34, where he legislates for his followers. In his unique position as Son of God, the factors that make an oath objectionable for men are not relevant to him.) **The Son of man sitting on the right hand of power and coming in the clouds of heaven** (cf. Dan 7:13,14; Ps 110:1). A pronouncement that the positions of Jesus and his judges would eventually be reversed. **65,66. Rent his clothes.** An indication of righteous horror, doubtless performed sincerely (although mistakenly). Jewish tradition specified in some detail how such an act was to be done. **Blasphemy.** The charge of greatest religious outrage. Because Jesus openly acknowledged that of which he had long been accused (Jn 5:18), and applied Dan 7:13, 14 to himself, he was pronounced **guilty of death** (i.e., deserving to die), probably by acclamation at this night trial, rather than by formal ballot. **67,68.** The physical violence inflicted on Jesus by his captors (probably the subordinate officers, Lk 22:63) included spitting in his face, striking him with fists, striking him either with rods or with open hands (i.e., slapping), and blindfolding (Lk 22:64) in order to mock his prophetic office.

69-75. Peter's denials. The three denials occurred throughout the stages of the Jewish trials and are variously grouped by the Evangelists. The differences among the narratives argue strongly for independence of composition. Yet essential agreement can be found, and the details admit various ways of harmonization. (See tables in Alford, *NT for Eng. Readers*, p. 199; S. J. Andrews, *Life of Our Lord*, p. 518.)

69. The palace. Rather, the courtyard. **One maid came.** Identified by John as the portress who had admitted Peter (Jn 18:16,17). **71,72. Into the porch.** Probably the vestibule or passage leading to the street. **Another maid.** Mark's "the maid" would suggest the same one previously mentioned (though perhaps he means merely *the* one at the porch); Luke says the interrogator was a man. Thus it appears that the second denial was prompted by the scrutiny of several individuals. **With an oath.** Forgetful of the warning of Jesus against such swearing to establish one's truthfulness (5:34). **73. After a little while.** About an hour (Lk 22:59). **They that stood by.** Particularly, a kinsman of Malchus (Jn 18:26). **Your speech makes you evident** (AV, *bewrayeth thee).* Galilean accents and pronunciation. **74. Began to curse.** To call down a curse upon himself if he were lying. **And to swear.** To invoke heaven as a witness to his words (cf. 5:34-37). **A cock crew.** The second crowing that night (Mk 14:72). **75. Peter remembered** (cf. Mt 26:34). Though dependence upon the flesh had caused his memory of Christ's warnings to fail, the simple crowing of a rooster awakened Peter to the enormity of his sin as a flouting of Jesus' gracious attempts to forestall it. **Wept bitterly.** Contrast the remorseful but unrepentant Judas (27:5).

27:1,2. Second Sanhedrin trial. **When the morning was come.** Jewish law forbade night trials and specified that capital cases must have at least two trials, a day apart. This daybreak session was an effort to bring a semblance of legality to the whole sordid procedure. **Pontius Pilate.** Roman procurator of Judea, who was present in Jerusalem at the Passover festival. His official residence was Caesarea. Rome had reserved to herself the final decision in court cases involving capital punishment and the execution of death sentences.

F. Remorse of Judas. 27:3-10. **3. When he saw that he was condemned.** This would be evident from watching Jesus being taken to Pilate. **Repented himself** *(metamelētheis).* Not the usual NT word for repentance to salvation. Here it indicates remorse, without any apparent commitment of himself to God. His "change of mind" was chiefly toward the money, which he now loathed. Finding the **chief priests and elders** (perhaps still at Caiaphas' house, or en route to Pilate), he tried to return the **silver. 5.** Their refusal caused him (perhaps after an interval of continued reflection) to hurl it **into the sanctuary** *(naos)* of the Temple. **Hanged himself.** This detail and the ensuing ones do not contradict Acts 1:18,19. Several ways of harmonization are possible. **6. It is not lawful.** (Cf. Deut 23:18). This dishonorable money could not enter the temple **treasury** *(korbanas),* although these priests had felt no impropriety in paying it out (26:15). **7,8. The field of the potter.** Apparently some well-known plot of ground. The use of this "blood money" gave its name to the field (cf. Acts 1:19 for another detail that made the name appropriate). **Until this day.** An indication that Matthew wrote quite some time after the event, although not after A.D. 70, when the Romans obliterated most such landmarks. **9,10. Jeremiah the prophet.** This reference by Matthew to a prophecy seemingly spoken by Zechariah (11:12,13) has evoked an array of explanations. Some hold that here **Jeremiah,** the name of the first book in the OT Prophets, is taken to stand for the whole section containing Zechariah (just as the name "Psalms" is applied to the whole section of the Writings because it is the first book; Lk 24:44). A passage in the Talmud *(Baba Bathra* 14 b) supports this order of Jeremiah as the first book, but it must be recognized that Isaiah is usually placed first. Another possibility is that Matthew amalgamated Zech 11:12,13 with Jer 18:2-12 and 19:1-15, and merely cited one of the sources.

G. Events at the Roman Trials. 27:11-31. Matthew selects certain aspects of the trial, but for their connections one must consult the parallel accounts. However, Matthew alone records the interesting details of 27:19,24.

11. Before the governor. Resumption of the narrative interrupted at 27:2. **Art thou the King of the Jews?** A question prompted by the formal charges given Pilate by the Jews (Lk 23:2; Jn 18:28-33). **Thou sayest.** To this answer, which surely indicated assent to the question, Jesus added an explanation of the nature of his kingdom (Jn 18:34-38). This interview occurred within the Praetorium, while the Jews remained outside. **12-14.** To the clamoring Jews, however, who **accused** him upon his reappearance before them, **he answered nothing.** Yet this silence was not taken by Pilate as admission of guilt, but as a most unusual composure, causing him to begin a series of attempts to release Jesus without antagonizing the Sanhedrin.

15. The governor was wont to release unto the people one prisoner. Origin of this custom, whether Roman or Jewish is unknown. **16. A notable prisoner called Barabbas.** One who was guilty of insurrection, robbery, and murder (Jn 18:40; Mk 15:7). Broadus suggests that since the two crucified with Jesus were robbers, they may have been Barabbas' followers, and thus Jesus literally took Barabbas' place *(Comm. on Matt.,* pp. 562,563). Exegesis that plays on the etymology of Barabbas ("son of a father"), or adopts the highly inferior reading "Jesus Barabbas" for allegorizing or homiletical purposes is unwarranted. **18. He knew that for envy.** The ridiculous character of the accusations was evident to Pilate, and the passionate actions of the accusers showed him that personal grievance was involved. It was obvious that such a spiritually minded teacher (Jn 18:36,37) would be opposed by these unscrupulous and materialistic religionists.

19. While he was sitting on the judgment seat. While Pilate awaited the Jews' answer regarding Barabbas, his **wife** sent him a message that interrupted the proceedings. The portent of the **dream** mentioned in the message unsettled Pilate and caused him to delay judgment. We do not know whether the dream was sent directly from God, or is to be explained psychologically as the working of a mind troubled over the plot against Jesus. (Pilate must have known of the plot, for he allowed a chiliarch and Roman soldiers to participate, and his wife may have learned of it from him; Jn 18:12.) The apocryphal *Gospel of Nicodemus* quotes the Jews as responding: "Did we not say unto thee, he is a conjuror? Behold, he hath caused thy wife to dream" (2:3). **20,21.** During this interval the **chief priests** and **elders** influenced the **multitude** to demand the release of **Barabbas** instead of Jesus. The degree of moral and spiritual depravity evidenced by such a choice is almost incredible. **22,23. Let him be crucified.** That is, executed in the Roman fashion, ostensibly as the result of the charges laid against him, and thus as the substitute for Barabbas. **24. He took water.** A Jewish symbolic custom (Deut 21:6-9), the meaning of which is natural and obvious. Yet Pilate's use was mockery, for he had to bear the responsibility for ordering the execution. (Proper use of the symbol was to absolve innocent men from implication in a wrongful death.) **The blood of this righteous man** (AV, *just person*). Was Pilate reflecting the influence of his wife's message as he used her description of Jesus? **25. His blood be upon us and on our children.** The subsequent history of Israel reveals the awful consequences of that cry. These words, so quickly uttered, have not rested easily upon the heads of the original leaders (cf. Acts 5:28), nor upon those of their descendants. **26. When he had scourged Jesus.** This cruel torture was applied upon the bare body by means of a leather whip that had pieces of bone or metal imbedded in its thongs. The scourging preceded the delivery to the soldiers for crucifixion. John indicates that it was not performed as the first stage of the execution, but was another attempt by Pilate to satiate the bloodthirsty crowd and cause them to abandon their demands for crucifixion (Jn 19:1-6). **Delivered him.** Officially ordered the soldiers to execute him.

27. Into the Praetorium. This seems to locate the trial at the Castle of Antonia, since it explains more readily the presence of a whole cohort (600 men, one-tenth of a legion), which is known to have been stationed there. Others identify the Praetorium as Herod's palace. **28-31.** After receiving the order to prepare Jesus for execution, the callous soldiers enlivened their work by the crudest mockery. Stripping Jesus of his own garments, they arrayed him in a **scarlet robe,** perhaps a soldier's cloak, faded to resemble royal purple (Mk 15:17). Substituting **thorns** for a crown, a **reed** for a scepter, and spitting for the kiss of homage, they showed their cruel contempt for the Son of God.

H. The Crucifixion. 27:32-56. **32. Simon.** Of Cyrene. His sons were known to the readers of Mark's Gospel (Mk 15:21). **Him they compelled.** Commandeered for this service (see comment on 5:41). **33. Golgotha.** Aramaic word meaning "skull," equivalent to the Latin *calvaria.* Whether the name was derived from a skull-shaped mound, or from its reputation as an execution place, is unknown. Equally uncertain is its location. The traditional Church of the Holy Sepulchre, while within the present walls of Jerusalem, was outside the old north wall of Jesus' day and could well have been the place. Others argue the claims of Gordon's Calvary, farther to the north. **34. Wine mingled with gall** (cf. Ps 69:21). The intent of this drugged potion was to deaden pain and make prisoners easier to handle, but Jesus, after a taste, refused to drink. **35. They crucified him.** For the technical details of crucifixions, consult Bible dictionaries. It must be noted that the Evangelists sketch the scene in stark simplicity, all the more effective for its restraint. **Parted his garments, casting lots.** John 19:23,24 explains that the soldiers divided the items four ways and gambled for the seamless coat. The final clause beginning, **that it might be fulfilled,** is textually doubtful, probably being an interpolation from Jn 19:24. **36. They watched him.** Part of the soldiers' duty was to prevent premature removal.

37. Over his head his accusation. During the procession to Golgotha, the placard prepared by Pilate (Jn 19:19) was probably paraded at the front or hung around Jesus' neck, according to the usual custom. THIS IS JESUS THE KING OF THE JEWS. (Cf. Mk 15:26; Lk 23:38; Jn 19:19.) The varying accounts are in no way contradictory. John's record is fullest; the others pick out the essential elements. The fact that the title appeared in the three languages may account for some variations in the records (Jn 19:20). **38. Two robbers.** The same description as is applied to Barabbas (Jn 18:40), an indication that Jesus literally took Barabbas' place. **39. Wagging their heads** (Ps 22:17). A sneering, mocking gesture. **40.** The taunts hurled at Jesus for claiming that he could **destroy the temple** and that he was the **Son of God** were based on events at the Sanhedrin trial (26:61,63,64). **41-43.** The **chief priests, scribes,** and **elders** joined in the mocking, not by addressing Jesus directly, but by speaking derisively about him to the crowd. **He saved others.** A statement probably not meant as an acknowledgment of his miracles, but intended to cast strong suspicion upon such claims because of his present inability to **save himself.** Their words were far truer than they knew; for to save others in the spiritual sense for which he had come, he had to voluntarily lay down his own life. Smarting under Pilate's insult to their nationalism, the leaders challenged Jesus' title, **King of Israel,** by demanding a sign and promise. **We will believe him.** Yet previous attitudes and reactions of these men show the falsity of their promise (Jn 12:9,10). **44. The robbers also.** Later one of them changed his attitude toward Jesus (Lk 23:39-43).

45. Jesus was placed upon the cross at 9 A.M. ("third hour," Mk 15:25). After three hours had passed, a supernatural **darkness** enveloped **all the land** from the **sixth** to the **ninth** hour (noon to 3 P.M.). Since Passover occurred at full moon, this darkness could not have been a solar eclipse. It was clearly supernatural in its timing, although God may possibly have employed some providential means to bring it about. Whether **all the land** is restricted to a somewhat local area, or is to be understood as "all the earth" (global) is impossible to determine. **46. My God, my God, why hast thou forsaken me?** (Ps 22:1) The only utterance from the cross recorded by Matthew and Mark. The full import of this cry cannot be fathomed. But certainly its basis lay not in the physical suffering primarily, but in the fact that for a time Jesus was made *sin* for us (II Cor 5:21); and in paying the penalty as the sinner's substitute, he was accursed of God (Gal 3:13). God as Father did not forsake him (Lk 23:46); but God as Judge had to be separated from him if he was to experience spiritual death in the place of sinful men. **47-49.** This outcry prompted the suggestion that Jesus was calling for Elijah, doubtless because of the similarity of sound between **Eli** *(my God)* and **Elias** (Elijah). Though some suggest that the darkness had now caused the more superstitious actually to fear that the predicted Messianic figure might come, succeeding attitudes make this doubtful. Rather, it was a further mocking jibe at his Messianic claims. **Let be.** This sentiment was uttered by the crowds, who wanted the soldier to desist from ministering to Jesus (Mt); and also by the soldier himself, after giving the drink, as telling the crowds to cease objecting to his act (Mk). **50.** Jesus, having his throat refreshed by the vinegar (not the drugged potion of 27:34), **cried again with a loud voice.** All the Synoptics indicate that the death of Christ was not the exhaustion of crucifixion, but a voluntary surrender of his life.

51. Veil of the temple. The curtain dividing the Holy Place from the Holy of Holies (Ex 26:31). This event, symbolic of the permanent opening of God's presence to man by the atoning death of Christ (cf. Heb 10:19-23), could have been reported by the priests who were later converted (Acts 6:7). **52,53.** At Christ's death many graves of OT **saints** were **opened,** and their bodies were resurrected **after his resurrection** (cf. Acts 26:23; I Cor 15:20) This amazing circumstance mentioned only by Matthew raises many questions but cannot properly be denied. The six previous resurrections in Scripture (I Kgs 17; II Kgs 4; 13; Mt 9; Lk 7; Jn 11) were all restorations to earthly existence. Such is not necessarily true of those in Matthew 27. The phenomenon is clearly symbolic of Christ's victory over death as it affects believers. Many see here a visible demonstration that Christ's death and resurrection effected the release from Sheol-Hades of the righteous dead (Eph 4:8,9). What happened to these resurrected saints subsequently is not stated. **54. Truly this man was the Son of God.** Though it is presently popular to explain the centurion's statement in terms of pagan concepts (cf. RSV), it must be noted that his comment was based upon his observation of some remarkable phenomena. And it must be regarded as possible that the man, having been in Jewish surroundings for a time, may now have come to faith. After all, pagans can become Christians. **55,56. Mary Magdalene.** First mention in Matthew. Traditions which give her a dishonorable past are without Scriptural basis. **Mary the mother of James and Joses.** Also called the wife of Cleopas (Jn 19:25). **Mother of Zebedee's children.** Same as Salome (Mk 15:40), and apparently a sister of the Virgin Mary (Jn 19:25).

I. Burial. 27:57-66. **57. When even was come.** Time from 3 P.M. to 6 P.M. (Ex 12:6, ASV marg.). **A rich man.** Cf. Isa 53:9. **Joseph of Arimathaea** was a Sanhedrist (Lk 23:50,51), whose wealth enabled him to own a tomb close to Jerusalem, though he lived elsewhere. **58. Asked for the body.** An act of no little courage, since, not being a relative, he would doubtless need to explain his reasons. **59,60.** Receiving permission, Joseph himself **took the body** from the cross and, assisted by Nicodemus, wrapped it in the usual linen cloth (Jn 19:39,40). **61.** Observing the scene were the two Marys mentioned in 27:56.

62. The day after the preparation (ASV). Usually explained as Saturday (cf. Mk 15:42), viewing the entombment as from Friday night till Sunday morning. However, this **preparation** day was the day before the Passover Feast day (Jn 19: 14,31), which feast may have occurred that year on Wednesday night. Perhaps this accounts for Matthew's not using the term "Sabbath" here, lest it be confused with Saturday. According to this view, the entombment lasted a full seventy-two hours, from sundown Wednesday to sundown Saturday. Such a view gives more reasonable treatment to Mt 12:40. It also explains **after three days** and **on the third day** in a way that does least violence to either. **63,64.** How the Sanhedrists learned of Christ's private prediction is not explained (from Judas, perhaps?). The disciples, by failing to grasp its meaning, had largely forgotten the prediction; but these enemies were taking no chances. They feared that the spreading of a report of a resurrection **(the last error)** would be more disastrous to them than the following Jesus had gained, for a time, as Messiah **(the first** delusion). **65,66.** Obtaining Pilate's order, **Take a guard** (ASV marg.), the Sanhedrists took the additional precaution of **sealing the stone,** probably by connecting it to the tomb by a cord and wax or clay, so that tampering could be detected.

V. The Resurrection of Jesus Christ. 28: 1-20.

Matthew's account of the Resurrection includes fewer details than the accounts of Luke and John. Yet to him alone we are indebted for the report of the soldiers (vv. 11-15) and for the full baptismal formula (v. 19). The substantial agreement of the four narratives, coupled with a wide variety of details and viewpoints, demonstrates their truthfulness and yet their independence of one another.

A. Discovery of the Empty Tomb. 28: 1-8. **1. In the end of the sabbath.** The use of *opse* as an improper preposition for "after" is now clearly recognized (Arndt, p. 606), so that the translation here should be **after the sabbath,** in conformity with Mk 16:1,2; Lk 24:1; Jn 20:1. **Mary Magdalene,** the **other Mary** (27:56,61), and certain other women came at the break of dawn on Sunday to do the anointing of Jesus' body. **2-4.** As they approached, an **earthquake** occurred, and an **angel rolled back** the great **stone** from the entrance. This was not the moment of resurrection, but was rather intended to reveal the empty tomb to the witnesses. The resurrected Christ was not confined by natural barriers (cf. Jn 20:19,26), and must have arisen about sundown on Saturday night (see on 27:62). **5-8.** It seems that Mary Magdalene immediately left to notify Peter and John (Jn 20:1,2), and did not hear the announcement, **He is risen,** which the angel made to the other women. **He goeth before you into Galilee.** The directions for the great public appearance in Galilee as previously predicted (26:32) do not exclude earlier personal appearances to individuals or small groups in Jerusalem.

B. Appearance of Jesus. 28:9,10. **And behold, Jesus met them.** The first clause in verse 9 (AV) must be omitted on textual grounds. This appearance of Jesus came after the women had reported the angel's message to the disciples (Lk 24:9-11). Meanwhile, Mary Magdalene, having informed Peter and John of the empty tomb, followed them to the site, and, remaining there, became the first to see the risen Christ (Mk 16:9; Jn 20:1-18). Now on this second appearance, Jesus gave the women essentially the same directions that the angel had delivered (v. 7).

C. Report of the Soldiers. 28:11-15. Recorded here only. These soldiers had been turned over to the Sanhedrin by Pilate, and so reported to them (27:65,66). Their report resulted in the calling of a Sanhedrin session, at which a large bribe was voted to insure the soldiers' continued cooperation in hiding the truth. The self-contradictory nature of the account they were to circulate (as if *sleeping* soldiers would know what had happened, or that *all* would have been sleeping at once, or that *Roman* soldiers would incriminate themselves in this way) makes its acceptance most incredible. Yet the story was widely disseminated **among Jews** (no article). Matthew, writing particularly for the Jewish viewpoint, gives the sordid details that explain the tale. The promise of the Sanhedrin to **persuade** Pilate if he should take action may mean that a bribe would be offered, or that they would assure the governor that the Sanhedrin was satisfied with the soldiers' performance.

D. The Great Commission. 28:16-20. **16.** This appearance to the **eleven** in **Galilee,** fulfilling previous instruction (26:32; 28:7,10), is doubtless the appearance to "above five hundred" mentioned by Paul (I Cor 15:6). Galilee was the home of most of Christ's followers, and the most likely place for such a crowd to be unmolested by the authorities. **17. They worshipped him, but some doubted.** True acknowledgment of his deity by most (cf. the prior case of Thomas, Jn 20:28); hesitation by a few. Difficulty in understanding these doubters as being among the Eleven after the appearances to them in Jerusalem has led many to identify them as among Paul's five hundred. Yet Matthew, while certainly not excluding the presence of others, can hardly have had such in view here. It is better to accept this as a surprising but honest commentary on the facts, and as further indication that the disciples were not a credulous group, but believed only on the basis of "many infallible proofs" (Acts 1:3). **18. All authority has been given unto me.** The ensuing commission is backed by the authority of him who is God's mediatorial King, with power extending to every realm. **19. Make disciples of all the nations** (ASV). The task of evangelizing, enlisting men under the lordship of Christ. **Baptizing them.** The symbolic rite by which one publicly acknowledges his personal commitment to the Christian message. **The name of the Father and of the Son and of the Holy Ghost.** The full formula to be employed, emphasizing the distinctively Christian character of this baptism as compared to earlier types of Jewish ablutions. **20. Teaching them.** Inculcating Christ's precepts as outlining the proper manner of life for his followers. **Lo, I am with you all the days.** A blessed promise that Christ's presence as well as his authority shall empower his servants to perform this commission.

BIBLIOGRAPHY

ALFORD, HENRY. *New Testament for English Readers*. Chicago: Moody Press, reprinted 1956.

ANDREWS, SAMUEL J. *The Life of Our Lord*. Grand Rapids: Zondervan Publishing House, reprinted 1954.

ATKINSON, BASIL F. C. "The Gospel According to Matthew," *New Bible Commentary*. Edited by F. Davidson, A. M. Stibbs, and E. F. Kevan. Grand Rapids: Wm. B. Eerdmans Publishing Co., 1953.

BROADUS, JOHN A. *Commentary on the Gospel of Matthew*. Philadelphia: American Baptist Publishing Society, 1886.

BROWN, DAVID. "Matthew," *Commentary Critical, Experimental, and Practical of the Old and New Testaments*. Edited by Robert Jamieson, A. R. Fausset, and David Brown. Vol. V. Grand Rapids: Wm. B. Eerdmans Publishing Co., reprinted 1948.

BRUCE, A. B. "The Synoptic Gospels," *The Expositor's Greek Testament*. Edited by W. Robertson Nicoll. Vol. I. Grand Rapids: Wm. B. Eerdmans Publishing Co., n.d.

EDERSHEIM, ALFRED. *Life and Times of Jesus the Messiah*. Grand Rapids: Wm. B. Eerdmans Publishing Co., reprinted 1945.

GAEBELEIN, A. C. *Gospel of Matthew*. New York: Our Hope, 1910.

LANGE, J. P. *The Gospel According to Matthew*. Translated by Philip Schaff. *A Commentary on the Holy Scriptures*. Grand Rapids: Zondervan Publishing House, reprint edition, n.d.

LENSKI, R. C. H. *The Interpretation of St. Matthew's Gospel*. Columbus: Wartburg Press, 1943.

MCCLAIN, A. J. *Greatness of the Kingdom*. Grand Rapids: Zondervan Publishing House, 1959.

PLUMMER, ALFRED. *Exegetical Commentary on the Gospel According to St. Matthew*. New York: Charles Scribner's Sons, 1910.

ROBERTSON, A. T. *A Harmony of the Gospels for Students of the Life of Christ*. New York: Harper & Brothers, 1922.

THE GOSPEL ACCORDING TO MARK

INTRODUCTION

Author. Although the Gospel of Mark in itself is anonymous, sufficient evidence is available to provide positive identification of the author. All available testimony from the early Church Fathers names Mark, the attendant of Peter, as the writer of the book. The tradition concerning the Marcan authorship goes back to Papias at the end of the first century or early in the second, and it is confirmed in the writings of such men as Irenaeus, Clement of Alexandria, Origen, and Jerome, as well as in the second century Anti-Marcionite Prologue. That Mark, the companion of Peter, was the John Mark of Acts 12:12,25; 15:37-39 is not specifically stated, but this has been the consensus of opinion among all but the more radical critics. Such identification is made by Vincent Taylor *(The Gospel According to Mark,* p. 26), Harvie Branscomb *(The Gospel of Mark,* p. xxxviii) and H. B. Swete *(The Gospel According to Mark,* p. xix).

The evidence from the Gospel itself is in agreement with the historical testimony of the early church. It is obvious that the author was familiar with Palestine, and with Jerusalem in particular. He makes geographical references which are correct in fine detail (11:1), thus revealing his personal knowledge of the area. He knows Aramaic, the language of Palestine, as is indicated by his use of Aramaic words (5:41; 7:34) as well as by the evidence of Aramaic influence on his Greek. That he was conversant with Jewish institutions and customs is to be seen in the familiarity with which he refers to such items (1:21; 2:14,16; 7:2-4). These characteristics all point toward a Palestinian Jew as author; and according to Acts 12:12, John Mark fits this description, since his home was in Jerusalem. Furthermore, there are indications in the New Testament that Mark and the Apostle Peter sustained a close relationship to one another. It has been noted that there is a striking similarity between the general outline of Mark's Gospel and the sermon of Peter in Caesarea (Acts 10:34-43), which may point toward Peter as the main source for Mark's material. To this may be added Peter's reference to Mark as his son (I Pet 5:13).

Upon the basis, therefore, of both external and internal evidence, it is possible to affirm confidently that John Mark, the son of Mary, and the attendant of Paul and Peter, was the author of the second Gospel. We first hear of the man Mark in Acts 12:12 in connection with a prayer meeting in his mother's house. As a young man he traveled with Paul and Barnabas as far as Perga on their first missionary tour (Acts 13:5,13). Because he did not continue with the party, but returned home, Paul refused to take him on his second journey (Acts 15:36-41). Instead, Mark accompanied his cousin Barnabas (Col 4:10, ASV) to the island of Cyprus. Much later, he appeared with Paul during his first Roman imprisonment (Col 4:10; Phm 23,24). He was with Peter in Babylon (I Pet 5:13); and Paul, during his second imprisonment, requested Timothy to bring Mark to Rome because he had shown himself to be useful in the work (II Tim 4:11).

Date and Place of Writing. There is no explicit statement in the Gospel itself, nor in the rest of the New Testament, from which we may ascertain a specific date for the origin of the book. In recent years the majority of scholars have placed it somewhere between A.D. 50 and 80, with the preponderance of opinion favoring A.D. 65–70. Our best basis for dating is the information from the Church Fathers. Irenaeus says, "Matthew also issued a written Gospel among the Hebrews in their own dialect, while Peter and Paul were preaching at Rome and laying the foundations of the church. After their departure, Mark, the disciple and interpreter of Peter, did also hand down to us in writing what had been preached by Peter" (Irenaeus *Against Heresies* III. i. 1). The word *exodon,* here translated "departure," is used in Lk 9:31, where it is rendered as "decease" (AV), referring to our Lord's death. The Apostle Peter, also, uses the word in alluding to his own approaching death (see II Pet 1:15). That Irenaeus was placing the writing of Mark after the death of Peter and Paul is corroborated by the Anti-Marcionite Prologue, which plainly asserts, "After the death of Peter himself, he wrote down this same gospel. . . ." Such evidence would seem to require a date after A.D. 67, the probable year of Paul's martyrdom. On the other hand, the fact that the prediction of Jerusalem's destruction (Mk 13) is not set forth as fulfilled may point to a date prior to A.D. 70. The most plausible dating, therefore, would seem to be 67–70.

Although Chrysostom placed the origin of the Gospel in Egypt, there is every reason to look for its birthplace in the city of Rome. That such is the case is explicitly stated by the Anti-Marcionite Prologue and Clement of Alexandria, as well as being implied by Irenaeus.

Readers. It has been an almost unanimous opinion that the second Gospel was directed to the Roman mind. The Marcan habit of explaining Jewish terms and customs points toward Gentile readers (5:41; 7:2-4,11,34). The statements of Clement of Alexandria to the effect that those in Rome who heard Peter preach insisted that Mark provide them with a written account are sufficient basis for believing that the Gospel was penned for Roman Christians. That the readers were Romans may be borne out by the presence of certain Latinisms occurring in the book. That they were Christians is further confirmed by the introduction to the Gospel, in which prior understanding on the part of the readers is assumed. John the Baptist is introduced without any attempt at identification; his imprisonment is referred to as though the readers were already familiar with the fact; the terms *baptize* (1:4) and *Holy Ghost* (1:8) are used without any explanation.

Characteristics. Several striking peculiarities of Mark's account make it unique among the Gospels. The manner of writing has been described as graphic, forceful, and dramatic. A vivid realism characterizes both Mark's style and his unvarnished reporting of the facts. Events are described without alteration or extensive interpretation, and their presentation is marked by an "on-the-spot" quality found in the reports of eyewitnesses. A marked vigor and a note of urgency may be sensed in almost any portion of the writing. The characteristic word of this Gospel of action is *euthys*, which occurs some forty-one times and is translated *straightway, immediately, forthwith, anon*. Greek tenses are used effectively to augment the dramatic and graphic effect of a life story that is already dramatic by virtue of its intrinsic nature. In numerous places words of unusual forcefulness appear, such as "driveth" (1:12), compared with "led," which appears in the other Synoptic Gospels (Mt 4:1; Lk 4:1).

In harmony with these peculiarities is the brevity of the book itself and the concise reports of individual events (cf. Mk 1:12,13; Mt 4:1-11).

Content. The Gospel begins with a brief record of events that opened the public ministry of our Lord, namely, his baptism and temptation. Mark has thus omitted, by design of course, any account of the birth and first thirty years of Christ's life. He also makes no reference to the early ministry in Judea, which is recorded in Jn 2:13–4:3. Without any explanation of the intervening events, the author moves from the temptation to the Galilean ministry. The first period of the work in northern Palestine was marked by tremendous success as crowds flocked to hear the new teacher, with the result that he found it necessary to restrict the gatherings to the country areas (Mk 1:45). People came from Judea and Idumea to the south, from Perea to the east, and from Tyre and Sidon to the north (3:7,8). Almost simultaneously, our Gospel records the beginnings of hostility to Christ on the part of the Jewish leaders. This opposition intensified until it became one of the chief characteristics of the second period of the work in Galilee. As a result of the enmity of these leaders and the superstitious suspicions of Herod Antipas, Jesus began a series of systematic retirements from the region of Galilee, always remaining in the general area and often returning to Capernaum for a brief stay. During these days his main occupation was the training of the disciples. The hour toward which he had been purposefully moving was fast approaching, and it was at this point that he began to prepare his own, by repeated explanations, for the consummation of his earthly work in his death and resurrection.

Following the withdrawals for disciple training, Mark traces Christ's last trip to Jerusalem by way of Perea. In so doing our author has again omitted a sizable block of material. He has passed by the entire later Judean ministry and the greater part of the work beyond Jordan in Perea. In keeping with the characteristic brevity of the Evangelist, he moves immediately into an account of the Passion Week. To this short period Mark devotes almost six of his sixteen chapters, a proportion which is fully justified when one realizes that this is the purposed consummation toward which the life of our Lord had been moving.

OUTLINE

I. The title. 1:1.
II. The preparation for Christ's ministry. 1:2-13.
  A. His forerunner. 1:2-8.
  B. His baptism. 1:9-11.
  C. His temptation. 1:12,13.
III. Christ's ministry in Galilee. 1:14–6:30.
  A. Call of the first four disciples. 1:14-20.
  B. First Galilean preaching tour. 1:21-45.
  C. Development of official opposition. 2:1–3:12.
  D. Appointment of the Twelve. 3:13-19.
  E. Concern of Christ's friends, and accusations of his enemies. 3:20-35.
  F. Parables by the seaside. 4:1-34.
  G. Trip to Gadara. 4:35–5:20.
  H. The woman with a hemorrhage, and the daughter of Jairus. 5:21-43.
  I. Another Galilean preaching tour. 6:1-30.
IV. Christ's withdrawals from Galilee. 6:31–9:50.
  A. Withdrawal to the eastern shore of the lake. 6:31-56.
  B. Discussion of the unwarranted exaltation of tradition. 7:1-23.
  C. Withdrawal to the region of Tyre and Sidon. 7:24-30.
  D. Withdrawal to Decapolis. 7:31–8:9.
  E. Withdrawal to Caesarea Philippi. 8:10–9:50.
V. Christ's ministry in Perea. 10:1-52.
  A. Discussions of divorce, children, and wealth. 10:1-31.
  B. Conversation on the way to Jerusalem. 10:32-45.
  C. The healing of blind Bartimaeus. 10:46-52.
VI. Christ's concluding ministry in Jerusalem. 11:1–13:37.
  A. The entrance into Jerusalem and the Temple. 11:1-26.
  B. Final controversies with the Jewish leaders. 11:27–12:44.
  C. The Olivet apocalypse. 13:1-37.
VII. Christ's passion and resurrection. 14:1–16:20.
  A. Treachery and devotion. 14:1-11.
  B. The Lord's passion. 14:12–15:47.
  C. The Lord's resurrection. 16:1-20.

COMMENTARY

I. The Title. 1:1.

These words stand as a title indicating the content of the book as a whole. The **gospel** here is not the book, but the message, the good news of salvation through Jesus Christ. The facts of the life and death of Christ make up **the beginning of the gospel,** which implies that the apostolic preaching was the continuation. **The Son of God.** To Mark, no less than to John, the deity of Christ is of prime importance, and thus he includes it in the title of his Gospel.

II. The Preparation for Christ's Ministry. 1:2-13.

A. **His Forerunner. 1:2-8. Passing by** the birth and early years of Christ's life, Mark turns at once to the opening events of the Lord's public ministry. As predicted in the OT, Jesus was preceded by a herald sent to prepare men for his appearance. John the Baptist came as the last representative of the old order with the express purpose of introducing the key personality of the new.

2. **As it is written.** This clause is to be connected with verse 4. John's baptism and preaching were in accordance with the Scriptures. This was a formula used to designate "an unalterable contract" (Adolf Deissmann, *Paul, A Study in Social and Religious History*, p. 101). **In the prophets.** The citation here is probably a blending of Mal 3:1 and Ex 23:20.

3. This portion of the quotation is an almost exact reproduction of the LXX reading of Isa 40:3.

4. The word **baptize** means *to dip or submerge* and thus refers to an immersion. This was not an entirely new rite, since Jewish proselyte baptism was a form of self-immersion (G. F. Moore, *Judaism in the First Three Centuries of the Chris-*

tian Era, I, 331-335). John proclaimed the **baptism of repentance,** that is, a baptism characterized by, and signifying, repentance. In the NT repentance has a deeper connotation than its original sense of a change of mind. It has come to refer to an inner change of direction and purpose, a turning from sin to righteousness. Josephus makes it clear that this was the prerequisite for baptism by John *(Antiquities of the Jews* XVIII. v. 2). **For the remission of sins.** The Greek preposition *eis* at times was used with the meaning, "because of." Hence, the meaning may be that John baptized because of the forgiveness of sins.

5. Speaking in hyperbole, Mark depicts the throngs that streamed out from all parts of Judea. **There went out.** The imperfect tense portrays in motion picture fashion the continual procession of folk to be **baptized** (also imperfect tense). The rite was performed **in the river of Jordan,** an expression which is to be taken literally.

7. In verses 7,8 Mark records the core of the Baptist's message. He **preached,** or proclaimed as a herald (*kēryssō*), **the fact** of the coming One. **Latchet.** The leather strap used to fasten sandals. John did not consider himself worthy to attend the Messiah even as a slave.

8. The pouring out of **the Holy Ghost** was expected to be a feature of Messianic times (Joel 2:28,29; Acts 1:5; 2:4,16-21). The whole age between Christ's first and second advents is viewed as being Messianic, marked by the ministry of the Spirit.

B. His Baptism. 1:9-11. The high point in the ministry of the forerunner came when the "one mightier" than he arrived to submit to baptism. This act marked the official opening of Jesus' public ministry.

9. In Jordan. The Greek preposition *eis,* meaning, "in," "into," along with the words, "coming up out of the water" (v. 10), indicate an entrance into the river suggestive of immersion. In answer to the question as to why the sinless Christ was baptized with the baptism of repentance, it should be pointed out that this was a deliberate act of identification with sinners. Furthermore, he was in full sympathy with John's ministry, and to be baptized was the right thing to do (Mt 3:15).

10. Observe the first occurrence of Mark's characteristic **straightway** *(euthys);* see Introduction, *Characteristics.* Mark's word translated **opened** is much more forceful in the original, meaning *to tear apart, rend asunder.* **The Spirit.** Cf. Isa 61:1; Acts 10:38.

C. His Temptation. 1:12,13. Mark, in concise summary, records the temptation of Christ in two verses, whereas Matthew and Luke employ eleven and thirteen verses respectively. It is fitting that the ministry of the Saviour begin this way. He further evinces his solidarity with mankind by submitting to the temptations "common to man" (I Cor 10:13).

12. Immediately. Same word rendered "straightway" in 1:10. The word **spirit,** although not capitalized in the AV, refers to the Holy Spirit as in 1:8,10. The temptation of Jesus was no unavoidable accident. Mark's forceful style is to be observed in the word **driveth,** whereas the other Gospels use "led."

13. See sections on Mt 4:1-11 and Lk 4:1-13 for details of the temptations. That this was a genuine temptation which Christ found necessary to resist may be deduced from Heb 2:18; 4:15. It was a reality, not a farce, and by means of its awful reality Christ became qualified to be our High Priest and our Example in times of temptation. That he would not yield to the tempter's solicitations was assured by the omnipotence of his holy will.

III. Christ's Ministry in Galilee. 1:14–6:30.

A. Call of the First Four Disciples. 1:14-20. Again Mark omits a portion of the life and work of Christ as he moves directly from the temptation to the beginning of the Galilean ministry. After an introductory statement (vv. 14,15), he relates the call of the four fishermen to discipleship.

14. After that John was put in prison. These words suggest that Mark consciously passes over a number of events. See Jn 1:35–4:42. **The gospel . . . of God.** Manuscript evidence is strongly in favor of the omission of the words **of the kingdom.** The message Christ kept proclaiming (*kēryssōn,* durative action) during the Galilean ministry was the good news that comes from God.

15. Mark adds an amplification of the message. **The time is fulfilled.** The season *(kairos)* of preparation, the OT period, had come to its consummation according to the plan of God (cf. Gal 4:4). **The kingdom of God** refers to the sovereignty, the royal reign, of God (Arndt, pp. 134, 135). This divine sovereignty is described as being **at hand,** or better, as having *drawn near.* It was not actually present, but potentially so. The terms of entrance are **repent . . . believe the gospel.** John's was a message of repentance, but here a new and positive note is added. The kingdom in these verses is spiritual and present (cf. Jn 3:3,5; Col 1:13). Elsewhere, Scripture describes the future, eschatological kingdom.

16. Simon and Andrew had previously become acquainted with Christ as Messiah (Jn 1:40-42). It is also probable that John (Mk 1:19) was one of those referred to in Jn 1:35-39 as following Jesus.

B. First Galilean Preaching Tour. 1:21-45. The Galilean ministry is marked by three preaching tours, in which Christ systematically carried his message to every part of Galilee. The first and third of these tours are reported by Mark. In this section the ministry in Capernaum and in the Galilean countryside is described, with greater emphasis being placed on the former. Verses 21-34 are descriptive of one day's activities in the seaside town.

21. Capernaum was an important town on the main road to Damascus, the location of a tax office, the town of the first five disciples whom Jesus called, as well as the headquarters for his Galilean ministry. **Taught.** It was the custom to invite qualified persons to teach in the synagogue.

22. They were astonished. A forceful word, meaning *to strike with intense amazement*. **Doctrine.** It was his manner of teaching, as well as the content, that amazed them, because of its difference from the teaching of the scribes. The latter were students and teachers of the written and oral law, whose manner of teaching was to quote the authoritative statements of the scribes who had gone before. Jesus spoke as one having direct authority from God.

24. Let us alone. Literally, *What to us and to thee?* which means, "What have you to do with us?" The man speaks for himself and the demon within. **I know thee.** He was aware of Christ's true identity as **the Holy One of God**, indicating supernatural knowledge imparted by the demon.

25. Hold thy peace. A strong word meaning *to muzzle*. The force of the command is almost equal to our "shut up." **Come out.** Both imperatives in this verse are calls for instantaneous compliance.

26. Had torn him. The spirit convulsed the man as he left him.

29. Leaving the synagogue, they went to the house of Simon, with whom Andrew, his brother, apparently lived. **James and John** accompanied them, but it is not to be understood that it was also their home. This is probably the house referred to on later occasions which served as Jesus' headquarters and to which he returned from his preaching tours.

30. Lay sick of a fever. Mark pictures Peter's mother-in-law as lying prostrate and burning up with fever.

32. This busy day in Capernaum was a Sabbath (v. 21), which is probably the reason for Mark's careful explanation that the diseased were brought **when the sun did set.** Healing was not to be done on the Sabbath, nor was any load to be carried. **They brought.** The Greek imperfect tense signifies continuing action, meaning that they kept on bringing them one after another. **Possessed with devils.** There is but one devil. The plural, **devils,** in the AV is to be understood as referring to demons. *Daimonizomenous* means "demon-possessed." Cf. 1:34,39.

34. Suffered not the devils to speak. The demons were identifying Jesus as **Christ the Son of God** (Lk 4:41), but he repeatedly refused (Gr., imperfect tense) to let them speak. This knowledge of his person is further evidence that these were not merely cases of mental illness.

35. A great while before day refers to the early part of the last watch of the night, perhaps between three and four o'clock in the morning. His purpose was to spend time in prayer in preparation for the preaching tour that was to take him into all Galilee.

39. No hyperbole is intended in the expression, **throughout all Galilee.** Instead the intent is to supply a brief summary of the first Galilean preaching tour.

40. No doubt the cleansing of the leper (vv. 40-45) occurred on the Galilean tour. **Make me clean.** Leprosy resulted in ceremonial uncleanness (Lev 13:1-3). Notice the leper's faith in Christ's ability.

43. Jesus **straitly charged** the man. Mark's verb carries strong emotion, and is used here in the sense of a very stern warning. It originally meant *to snort in anger*. He **sent him away,** or, more literally, *thrust him out (exebalen;* cf. 1:12).

44. Say nothing . . . but go. He was to go at once to the priest and fulfill the Law's requirements (Lev 14:1 ff.). Until pronounced clean by the authorities, he had no right to resume his normal social relationships. This was to be done **for a testimony.** No witness could have been more striking and authoritative than the priest's declaration of cleansing.

45. The man's failure to comply at once added to Jesus' tremendous popularity as a worker of miracles. Crowds were so large that he found it necessary to hold the gatherings **in desert places,** i.e., uninhabited or wilderness locations. And **they came to him** in streams (*ērchonto,* imperfect tense) from everywhere.

C. Development of Official Opposition. 2:1–3:12. The purpose of the author in this section is to show the development of conflict between Christ and the Jewish officials. The mushrooming popularity of the Lord would naturally arouse their disfavor, since his message, by its very nature, was contradictory to their beliefs and practices. Consequently, in each of the five incidents recorded here, the Pharisees are seen either complaining among themselves or openly raising questions or objections.

1. This return to Capernaum marked the completion of the first tour of Galilee. The expression **after some days** is best taken as referring to the report that he had returned. Hence, the verse should read, "And when he entered again into Capernaum, after some days it was reported that he was at home." The **house** was probably Peter's (1:29), and he may well have relayed to Mark the account which follows.

3. Palsy is better understood as paralysis. The man is called *paralytikon.*

4. Press. An old word for a crowd. An ancient flat-roofed house usually had a stairway to the roof, which would have enabled the bearers to carry the paralytic up without difficulty. **Uncovered the roof.** This was accomplished by digging through the composite of grass, plaster, tiles, and lath, as indicated by Mark's *exoryxantes*—**had broken it up** (AV). The **bed** was a mattress or pallet, such as was used by the poor.

7. If a person accepts the assumption of the scribes that Jesus was mere man, he must arrive likewise at their conclusion. He was speaking **blasphemies.** The basic conflict concerned the deity of Christ.

10. That ye may know. The healing of the paralytic became a proof of the Lord's power to forgive sins and thus of his deity. **Son of man.** This is the title that Jesus chose to use almost exclusively for himself. Its background is to be found in Daniel and in the extra-Biblical apocalyptic literature of the Jews, where it had become a designation of the Messiah (cf. Dan 7:13, 14). **Power.** The Greek word means *authority.*

12. That he arose **immediately** indicates another instantaneous healing, so complete that the man could carry his own pallet. The result was that **they were all amazed.** They were so greatly astonished that they were beside themselves. The verb *existēmi* means "to remove out of place," or "to drive one out of one's senses."

13. The first charge against the Lord in the series of conflicts recorded by Mark was the accusation of blasphemy (2:1-12). A second complaint now is raised in 2:13-17 to the effect that Christ associated with outcasts.

14. Levi the son Alphaeus is the same as Matthew (Mt 9:9; Mk 3:18). **Receipt of custom.** The tax office. Capernaum was located on the road leading from Mesopotamia to Egypt, as well as near the junction of the highway to Damascus. Its situation near the border of Herod Antipas' territory explains the presence there of a tollhouse.

15. Sat at meat. The verb means *to recline at a meal,* the customary manner of eating at that time. **His house.** Cf. Lk 5:29. **Publicans.** A designation for tax collectors. The privilege of collecting taxes was purchased by payment of the total tax fee required by the government. The collector was then free to extract as much as possible from the people through extortion. Usually the actual collection was made by lesser collectors, to which class Matthew probably belonged. These men were despised because of their service for a foreign overlord and their fraudulent practices.

16. The scribes and Pharisees. The Pharisees were a sect of laymen who followed rigorously the precepts of the written and oral law, being meticulous in their attempts to maintain ceremonial purity. They viewed with disdain those who were not as strict as they were in observing the commandments, referring to them as "the people of the land" (cf. Jn 7:49). The class designated as **sinners** here probably included all non-Pharisees.

17. They that are whole. Those who are strong and healthy. Jesus was answering the critics from their own point of view. They assumed that they themselves were righteous, and therefore not in need of help. Jesus speaks as the physician whose duty it is to help the sick.

18. The next incident recorded by Mark is the interrogation concerning fasting (2:18-22). **Used to fast.** The Greek says simply that they *were fasting.* Perhaps the very time of Levi's feast was a fast day, since it was the practice of the Pharisees to fast twice a week, on Mondays and Thursdays (Lk 18:12). The nature of John's ministry and message was in harmony with the observance of fasting.

19. The children of the bridechamber. Literally, *the sons of the bridechamber.*

These were the close friends of the bridegroom who served as his attendants, a figure used here to refer to Jesus' disciples. Christ came to announce glad tidings (cf. 1:14,15); with such a message of joy, fasting was completely incongruous.

21. New cloth. This is cloth which has not been treated by the fuller, not shrunk or sized. **Else the new piece.** A close translation of the original would read *otherwise the filling* (that is, the patch) *takes* (tears) *away from it, the new from the old.* When the unshrunken patch becomes wet, it shrinks and tears away from the older, previously shrunk cloth. Thus it is not wise to attempt to patch the old system with the new.

22. Old bottles. Actually the word refers to wineskins, containers made from the skins of animals. The expansion caused by the fermenting of **new wine** would burst old wineskins because they had already been stretched as much as possible. Thus it is not possible to confine to the structure of the old legalism the vitality of the new experience produced by faith in Christ.

23. The next two occasions for opposition to Christ concern Sabbath practices (2:23–3:6). **The corn fields.** Corn, our maize, was not known to the translators of the AV. They used the term as we use the word "grain." The disciples were picking, not **ears of corn,** but heads of grain, such as barley or wheat.

24. That which is not lawful. It was not the appropriating of the grain to which they objected, for the Law allowed this (Deut 23:25); they were criticizing manual labor on the Sabbath. In their zeal to keep the letter of the Law to its last detail, they viewed the picking of the grain as harvesting and thus as a violation of Ex 20:10.

25. Jesus replied by citing **what David did** one time, as recorded in I Sam 21:1-6. His question expects an affirmative answer. The salient feature of the incident is found in the statement that **he had need.** Christ is declaring that human need supersedes all mere ritual and ceremony.

27. The sabbath was not intended to be a heartless despot that man must serve regardless of the cost to himself; rather it was given to meet man's need for rest.

28. Lord also of the sabbath. Christ was not asserting his freedom to violate the Sabbath law, but rather he was declaring his qualification to interpret that law.

3:1. The second Sabbath controversy recorded by Mark (3:1-6) occurred in **the synagogue,** probably in Capernaum, since 3:7 speaks of a withdrawal **to the sea.**

2. The Lord's critics **watched him** persistently and closely. The verb indicates a malicious lying in wait to trap a person. Practicing medicine on the Sabbath was forbidden by rabbinic tradition unless the sick person was on the verge of death, which was not true in this case. Consequently, if Christ healed the man, the Jews were ready to **accuse Him** as a Sabbath violator.

4. Is it lawful. The question of Jesus harks back to the principle of need that had been set forth in the previous Sabbath encounter. To meet this man's need would be **to do good;** to fail to do so would be **to do evil. They held their peace.** The Greek imperfect tense pictures them as persisting in their silence. To reply would have been damaging. Obviously, it was not lawful to do evil, and to do good would be to heal the man.

6. The **Herodians** were not primarily a religious sect. Instead they were men who were politically devoted to the Herodian family. Consequently, they had no real affinity with the Pharisees, who zealously hated foreign domination; but a common opponent can bring enemies into strange coalitions.

7. The incident recorded in verses 7-12 provides another glimpse of the widespread fame of the Lord, which brought people from far and near to see and hear him. The crowd was composed of persons from every section except Samaria, even including some from areas outside Palestine, such as Tyre and Sidon (vv. 7,8). **The sea** to which **Jesus withdrew** was the Sea of Galilee.

9. Small ship. The more accurate translation today would be *small boat.* The crowd was so large that it was pressing (*thlibō*) upon Jesus, and he was in danger of being crushed. Therefore the boat was to **wait on him** in order that he might get into it if it became necessary to escape the pressure of the crowd.

10. This great popularity developed because **he had healed many.** The eager desire of the sick and afflicted to receive help is apparent in the words **they pressed upon him.** Literally, they *fell upon him,* Mark says, meaning that they approached the Lord eagerly, practically throwing themselves upon him. The verb is durative in force, describing continued action.

11. See comments on 1:24,34.

D. Appointment of the Twelve. 3:13-19. From the beginning of the work in Galilee (1:14) to the choice of the twelve apostles, Jesus had been experiencing remarkable success in reaching the people with his message. He had access to the synagogues, and official opposition was only beginning to solidify. During these days he was gathering around him a group of followers from whom he would select a permanent band of disciples. In contrast, the second period of the Galilean ministry was marked by the presence of the twelve disciples as Christ's appointed assistants. The ministry to the multitudes went on, but there was also an attempt on Jesus' part to begin the instruction of his disciples. His popularity with the common people and the opposition from the leaders continued to develop until finally it became necessary for him to withdraw from Galilee.

13. The choice of the disciples occurred on **a mountain,** probably in the vicinity of Capernaum. It appears that Jesus asked a larger group to accompany him on the journey to the hill country.

14. Out of this larger group he selected **twelve** whom he appointed as his apostles (cf. Lk 6:13). **Ordained.** The Greek verb is better rendered as "appointed" *(epoiēsen;* literally, *he made).* The purpose of the appointment was twofold: that they should be with him (for companionship and training), and that they might go out to preach and to cast out demons (v. 15).

16. For the occasion when Simon was **surnamed Peter,** see Jn 1:42, where the Aramaic, *Cephas,* is used instead of the Greek, **Peter.**

17. **Boanerges.** This side of their personalities may be seen in Lk 9:54.

18. **Andrew.** The brother of Peter (Jn 1:40,41). **Bartholomew.** May be identical with Nathanael (Jn 1:45-51; 21:2). **James the son of Alphaeus** may be the same as James the less (Mk 15:40). **Thaddaeus** is also called Lebbaeus (Mt 10:3) and is the same as Judas the brother of James the less (Lk 6:16). **Simon the Canaanite** is more correctly designated Simon Zelotes (Acts 1:13), or Simon the Zealot. The word **Canaanite** is misleading, for the term found in the better Greek manuscripts is *Kananaion,* a transliteration of an Aramaic term meaning "zealot." Apparently Simon, before becoming a disciple of Christ, was a member of the fanatically patriotic party of Zealots, who were in favor of immediate revolt against Roman overlordship.

19. It is at this point that Matthew and Luke place the Sermon on the Mount. **Into an house.** An expression meaning "to come home." Christ probably returned to Peter's house in Capernaum.

E. Concern of Christ's Friends, and Accusations of His Enemies. 3:20-35. These verses are indicative of the attitudes of friends and foes toward Jesus. Both groups misunderstood him, with the result that his friends became overly concerned for his welfare, while his enemies turned to vicious accusations against him.

20. **They could not . . . eat bread.** Again Mark provides a glimpse of the great crowds that continually came to hear and see Christ. **Bread** is to be understood as referring to food in general.

21. The **friends** who became concerned were actually members of Jesus' family, which is the normal connotation of the Greek phrase, *hoi par' autou.* **It seems that** word came to his mother and brothers in Nazareth concerning his ceaseless activity. Their purpose was **to lay hold on** Christ and take him with them by force, because they felt that he was overwrought and mentally disturbed.

22. When the family arrived at Capernaum, they found the Lord engaged in controversy with **the scribes . . . from Jerusalem.** The discussion was occasioned by the scribes' repeated accusations (Gr., imperfect tense, *elegon)* that Jesus was in league with satanic power. **Beelzebub.** The source and meaning of the word are not certain, but it is obviously used here to refer to the devil, **the prince** of demons (not **devils;** see on 1:32). The accusation was that Christ was empowered by Satan himself and that by this means he cast out demons.

23. Jesus took the initiative and **called** his accusers to come and meet him face to face. The logic he used against these accusers is unanswerable: If it is agreed that demons are Satan's servants, then it is illogical to assert that he is casting out his own servants. This argument the Lord reiterated in 3:24-27, supporting it by a series of illustrations.

27. The **strong man** is intended to represent Satan. To cast out demons is to enter his **house** and **spoil his goods.** Christ was asserting that instead of being in league with Satan, He was engaged in combat against him.

29. Blasphemy **against the Holy Ghost** is the act of slandering, reviling, speaking maliciously against the Spirit. For such a sin there is never any **forgiveness. In danger of.** A more correct translation would be *guilty,* or *bound by,* in the sense of being in its grasp. All of the better manuscripts read *eternal sin* rather than **eternal damnation.**

30. **Because they said.** The statements

of the scribes are to be taken as revealing the nature of this eternal offense. They explained Christ's miracles of exorcism as being accomplished by satanic power, when in reality they were wrought by the Holy Spirit. However, we are not to interpret this passage as teaching that the mere statement against the Spirit is the unpardonable sin, for this would be contrary to the general teaching of Scripture that any and all sins will be forgiven to the repentant soul. The essence of the "eternal sin" is the attitude of heart that underlies the act. In the light of Scripture as a whole, this attitude can only be a fixed, unrepentant state of mind that persists in defiant rejection of the overtures of the Holy Spirit.

31. While Jesus was engaged in this discussion with the scribes, **his brethren and his mother** came and were **calling him.** They apparently had journeyed from Nazareth to take him home with them for the rest and recuperation they assumed he needed (cf. 3:20,21). **Brethren.** See comments on 6:3.

33. Christ seized upon this occasion as an opportunity to point up the importance of being spiritually related to himself.

34. Entrance into God's family is gained by doing **the will of God,** and such obedience begins by hearing, believing, and following God's Son.

F. Parables by the Seaside. 4:1-34. Here a different method of teaching comes to the fore. While Christ had made use of parabolic teaching to a limited extent previously, it was not until this point in his ministry that he began to employ it as a major vehicle of expression. As crowds grew, as opposition intensified, and as superficial followers multiplied, Jesus adopted the parable as a means of instructing his own disciples, on the one hand, and of concealing the substance of his teaching from superficial and antagonistic hearers on the other. On this occasion he used the parables to illustrate certain characteristics of the Kingdom.

1. The setting for the presentation of the first of these parables was **by the seaside,** which presumably refers to the Sea of Galilee. Again the pressure of the crowd forced the Lord to address the people from a boat standing off the shore a short distance.

4. The soil **by the way side** had been compacted by the passage of many feet, so that the seed lay on the surface in plain view, and the birds **came and devoured it.**

5,6. The second area where seed fell was **stony ground,** which is not to be understood as soil containing stones but as rock with a thin covering of soil. The heat from the sun made this ground first a hotbed producing rapid germination and then a furnace that **scorched** and **withered** the tender plant.

8. And the remainder of the seed was sown **on good ground.** It is only reasonable to assume that the great bulk of the seed was sown on this kind of soil, and not a mere 25 per cent, as is sometimes asserted. **That sprang up and increased.** It was not the fruit that sprang up. These two participles refer to the word **other,** and hence it was the seed that was growing.

11. The mystery. In the pagan mystery religions, the initiate was instructed in the esoteric teaching of the cult, which was not revealed to outsiders. On the kingdom of God, see comments on 1:15. The **mystery of the kingdom** in its ultimate development is the full-orbed message of the Gospel (cf. Rom 16:25,26). The purpose of **parables** was to instruct the initiates without revealing the items of instruction to the ones who were **without.** This is in keeping with the Biblical principle that spiritual understanding is restricted to those who have become **spiritual** by properly relating themselves to Christ and his message (I Cor 2:6 ff.).

12. That such was the purpose of Christ's use of parables is further confirmed by a quotation from the OT. The citation is introduced with the Greek conjunction *hina* (**that**), which in this instance cannot have a resultant meaning but must indicate purpose (Alf, I, 333). This verse is a free rendering of Isa 6:9,10, giving the gist, but not reproducing the exact wording, of the prophetic passage.

14. The sower (v. 3) is not identified, but he obviously represents Christ himself and all others who proclaim the Gospel. The seed stands for **the word,** which is, as Luke explains, the word of God, or the message which comes from God.

15. The birds of 4:4 are representative of **Satan,** who comes to those who hear the message and prevents any germination of the seed. These folk merely hear the word, and that is all.

16. Cf. verses 5,6. Some hearers of the word **receive it** with alacrity. The appearance of sincerity and genuine joy is present.

17. The statement that they **have no root** indicates the superficiality of their reception of the word. They **endure but for a time,** or *are temporary,* which is a better translation of *proskairoi.* The heat of the sun (v. 6) illustrates the coming of **affliction or persecution,** which soon becomes a stumblingblock or a snare to them, and they fall away because their experience of the word was not genuine.

19. Cf. 4:7. The **cares** are anxieties and worries concerning the interests of this present evil age (**world** is an inaccurate translation of *aiōn,* which refers to a period of time). The **deceitfulness of riches** has reference to the deceptive nature of wealth, always promising to satisfy and yet never able to fulfill the promise. The third hindrance is the longing or craving for **other things,** a general category including anything else which would choke the word and cause it to become **unfruitful.**

20. Cf. 4:8. The good soil signifies the persons who **hear the word and receive it.** A commentary on the meaning of **receive** is supplied by Mt 13:23 and Lk 8:15. These are people who hear, who understand, who are sincere, and who appropriate the message of the Gospel permanently.

21. The sayings of 4:21-25 are general statements that Christ seems to have used at various times (on v. 21 cf. Mt 5:15; on v. 23 cf. Mt 11:15; 13:9,43; Lk 14:35; on v. 24b cf. Mt 7:2; on v. 25 cf. Mt 25:29). Christ's purpose on this occasion was to emphasize the responsibility incumbent upon the hearer of the parables. He who has been enlightened must in turn enlighten others (Mk 4:21-23). **Candle.** *Lamp* is a more accurate translation. **Bushel.** Not the same as the present-day bushel; comparable to our peck measure. The **candelstick** was in reality a lampstand for the open-bowl oil lamps used in that day.

25. He that hath. The principle set forth in this statement is to be applied specifically to the realm of truth and its appropriation. He who lays hold of truth and uses it will receive more enlightenment, but he who refuses to appropriate truth will lose even the understanding of truth which he once had.

26. The second parable of the Kingdom which Mark records is that of the soil producing spontaneously (vv. 26-29). In reality, it takes up where the Parable of the Soils left off, going on to describe the actual growth of the seed which bears fruit. The aspect of **the kingdom** in view here is the present, spiritual aspect, in its internal reality as well as its external manifestations. This kingdom is extended by the sowing of the **seed** of the word (cf. v. 14).

28. The reason why the earth brings forth **fruit of herself** (*automatē,* "automatically") is that the seed contains life which, when placed in the proper environment, produces growth. The characteristic of the present, spiritual kingdom of grace, as set forth by this parable, is that the message of the Gospel, by its very nature, when sown in men's hearts produces growth and fruitfulness spontaneously.

30. Mark's third parable of the Kingdom concerns the mustard seed (vv. 30-32). The AV points up the true nature of a parable by translating *parabolê* as **comparison.**

31. Here the Kingdom is compared to **a grain of mustard seed.** Much has been written concerning the identification of this plant, but it seems best to take it to be the common black mustard, which has a seed about the size of the head of a pin (Harold N. and Alma L. Moldenke, *Plants of the Bible,* pp. 59-62). Its seed was one of the smallest known to the people of Galilee.

32. The remarkable phenomenon of this particular mustard plant is that, though it is really an herb, it may grow to be ten or twelve feet high, with a stem the size of a man's arm, and become a resting place for the smaller varieties of birds. This parable is a further development of the characteristics of the present, spiritual kingdom of God. The main point here is that the seed of the Gospel message will produce phenomenal growth. From small beginnings, the Kingdom, which had only drawn near in the person of Christ (1:14,15), will, by reason of its own inner and supernatural vitality, grow to tremendous proportions. This does not mean that it will result in world conversion, nor that man by his efforts will bring in the kingdom of God on earth as a Utopian development, nor that the Kingdom and the Church are identical. The parable does, however, picture the kingdom of grace as including multitudes of redeemed persons who through the years have come to swell its ranks to phenomenal size.

G. Trip to Gadara. 4:35–5:20. **Probably** for the sake of privacy and relaxation, Jesus proposed a trip across the lake of Galilee. With the vividness so characteristic of our author, Mark gives a graphic account of the stilling of the storm (4:35-41) and of the freeing of the demonized man whom Christ met on the other side (5:1-20).

37. The **great storm of wind** was typical of the Sea of Galilee, situated in a pocket, as it was, with hills on every side. The rising of the warm air of the day allowed the cooler air from the hills to rush down the ravines onto the lake with twisting, whirlwind action that churned the waters into an angry tempest. Mark's account paints a vivid picture, taking his readers to the very scene of action. **The waves** *kept beating* (Gr. imp. tense) into the boat and *it is already filling* (Gr. pres. tense) with water.

39. In contrast, Mark recounts the command of Christ to the storm. The Greek aorist tense is used to show that he **rebuked** it once (point action), and the **wind ceased** *at once* (Gr. aorist), and a **calm** came immediately (Gr. aorist). There was no necessity for the Lord to repeat his command, for it brought instantaneous obedience. **Peace, be still.** Literally, *Be silent. Be muzzled.* Lenski interestingly translates the perfect tense imperative of Christ's second command, "Put the muzzle on and keep it on" (R. C. H. Lenski, *The Interpretation of Mark's Gospel,* p. 201).

40. Fearful. Christ rebuked them for their cowardly fear, and turned the occasion into a stimulus for faith. He was suggesting that if their confidence had been in God, even though he himself was asleep, they would have had no reason to fear.

41. Feared exceedingly. Literally, *they feared with great fear.* The Greek term used here is not the same as in verse 40. This word can mean "reverential, respectful fear or awe." Notwithstanding all the mighty works the disciples had witnessed, so phenomenal was this miracle that they still wondered who their teacher really was. **What manner of man.** The Greek text has, *Who then is this?*

5:1. The Gadarenes. Greek manuscripts are divided among three names here – Gadarenes, Gerasenes, and Gergesenes. The best evidence favors Gerasenes, a term which some have taken to refer to the well-known Gerasa, twenty miles southeast of the Sea of Galilee. There is good reason, however, to believe that Mark refers to a small town of the same name on the eastern shore, the ruins of which are today called Kersa (cf. Harvie Branscomb, *Mark,* pp. 89,90).

3. This man had his habitual **dwelling** in or among **the tombs,** as the Greek imperfect tense shows. He had reached a stage so extreme that he could no longer be bound by anyone, even **with chains.**

4. The impossibility of restraining the man is emphasized dramatically by vivid terms and tenses. The **fetters** were used on the feet. As often as he had been bound he had pulled **the chains** apart and crushed **the fetters** into pieces. No one **could . . . tame him.** The Greek text indicates that no one had strength enough to tame this wild beast of a man.

5. Throughout **night and day** he was continually (Gr. text) **crying** with screams and shrieks and **cutting himself** with stones. The latter verb is an intensive form, meaning that he was cutting himself up or slashing himself to pieces.

7. Jesus, thou Son of the most high God. A remarkable indication of supernatural knowledge. The afflicted man was aware both of the human name of Jesus and of his Deity, although this, as it appears, was his first encounter with Christ, Such knowledge is proof that the man was not merely insane; he was indwelt by demonic powers who knew the true identity of Christ. **Torment me not.** Matthew 8:29 reads, "Art thou come hither to torment us before the time?" And Lk 8:31 (ASV) provides further light by reporting that they asked him not to send them "into the abyss." The torment of which the demons spoke is the final punishment after the day of judgment; they asked not to be imprisoned in the abyss before that time.

9. The question, **What is thy name?** was addressed to the one unclean spirit (demon) mentioned in verse 8. This same spirit replies in 5:9,10. In contrast, all of the demons speak in verse 12. **Legion.** A unit in the Roman army consisting of more than 6,000 men. **We are many.** The one demon was spokesman for the many that had possessed the man.

10. The significance of the phrase, **out of the country,** is to be seen in Luke's reference to **the abyss** (8:31, ASV). They feared being returned to the place of detention to remain in a disembodied state until the judgment.

12,13. Rather than being disembodied, they begged to be sent **into the swine. Jesus gave them leave.** The question persistently provoked by this passage concerns the ethical propriety of Jesus' action, resulting as it did in the destruction of the property of others. A common answer has been that Jews had no right to own pigs, and that Christ thus rebuked their breaking Mosaic law. But since the region of Decapolis contained a mixed population of both Jews and Gentiles, we have no assurance that the owners were Jews or that this was the purpose of Christ's action. Notice that he did not command the demons to enter the swine; he permitted them. It was the demons, not the Lord, who caused the destruction. The fact that Christ permitted the act makes him no more responsible than God is responsible for evil of any kind because he permits it. The devil's affliction of Job is a case in point (Job 1:12; 2:6,7).

15. They **were afraid,** not of the cured man, but of the remarkable power that had cured him. They were aware of supernatural power in the person of Christ but unaware of his infinite love and mercy.

17. Unknowingly they begged the source of potential blessing and salvation **to depart** out of their country. **Coasts.** The Greek word means *boundary, border,* and in the plural it may refer to the territory surrounded by these boundaries.

18. While Jesus was getting into the boat, the cured demoniac kept begging to **be with him.** He alone, among all his countrymen, saw in Jesus not someone to fear but someone to love.

19. **Jesus suffered him not.** That is, he did not permit the man to go with him. Instead, he commanded him to go to his own people and report to them what **great things the Lord hath done.** A basic principle underlies Christ's command. Man is not delivered from bondage merely for his own enjoyment of God-given freedom, but also that he may give testimony to others concerning the divine Deliverer. In the country east of the Sea of Galilee there was no reason to fear any crisis caused by excessive popularity. Thus the cured demoniac was urged to broadcast his story. **Hath had compassion.** The Greek verb means *to have mercy or pity* on someone.

20. **In Decapolis.** This is the region southeast of the Sea of Galilee in which were located ten cities *(deka,* "ten"; *polis,* "city"), Grecian in organization and culture.

H. The Woman with a Hemorrhage, and the Daughter of Jairus. 5:21-43. Two remarkable miracles are described in the following verses. The healing of the woman with the hemorrhage occurred without any apparent conscious act on Christ's part. The raising of the daughter of Jairus was the second instance in Christ's ministry of the restoration of life to the dead (cf. Lk 7:11 ff.).

22. Jairus was **one of the rulers of the synagogue,** which identifies him as one of the elders who were in charge of the services in the synagogue attended by Jesus at Capernaum.

23. **He besought him greatly.** He kept begging, perhaps repeatedly and desperately. **Little daughter.** All commentators note the diminutive form as a term of endearment. **At the point of death.** A good paraphrase of the Greek text, which indicates that she was in the very last stage of her illness. **I pray thee.** These words were supplied by the translators of the AV. Mark's Greek vividly portrays the anguish of this poor father as he pleads with broken phrases: "My little daughter is lying at death's door – that you may come and . . ."

24. The multitude following Christ kept crowding against him on every side (Gr. imp. tense, *synethlibon).*

25. **An issue of blood.** None of the Gospels specifically describes the nature of this hemorrhage except to say that it was a chronic ailment.

26. Mark is very frank in his comments concerning the woman's experience with **many physicians.** She went to doctor after doctor to be healed. Instead, she suffered many things at their hands, she spent all that she had, and still she grew worse. Luke, the physician, is not so blunt in his description (Lk 8:43).

27. **The press.** The crowd that kept pressing in on Christ.

28. **She said.** "She kept saying" (Gr. imp. tense), probably to herself.

29,30. This healing was unique, not merely because it was instantaneous but because it occurred without any apparent conscious participation by Christ. However, **Jesus immediately** was aware of what had occurred. We are not to assume that touching the garment had a magical effect, but rather that Jesus in omniscience recognized the touch of faith and granted the woman's desire. Or it may be assumed that the healing was not a conscious act of Christ, and that it was God the Father who healed the woman. In that case Jesus, in the limitation of his humanity, was not aware of it until the miracle occurred. **Virtue.** It was "power" (Gr., *dynamin)* that was operative in the healing. The question **Who touched my clothes?** may have been asked in order to reveal the miracle to the crowd, if it be assumed that the healing was consciously done on Christ's part. If not, Christ may also have been asking for his own information.

31. As usual, Mark's graphic use of tenses is enlightening. He reports that **his disciples** kept saying, "You see the crowd continually thronging you . . . ."

32. Evidently the woman was not found with one glance, for Mark says that he kept looking **round about** himself (Gr. imp. tense, mid. voice).

34. **Thy faith.** We see this woman's

faith in action in 5:27,28, a confidence so strong that she did not feel it necessary to arrest Jesus' attention. **Made thee whole . . . be whole.** The first expression literally means *has saved you,* referring to salvation from her physical affliction. The second expression means *to be well, healthy,* and is a present imperative, meaning that she was to continue in health.

35. The question of the messengers, **Why troublest thou . . . further?** indicates that they did not expect a restoration of life. **Master.** The Greek text has *didaskalon,* "teacher."

36. Jesus, ignoring the messengers' remarks, said to the ruler, "Stop fearing! Just keep on believing!" Both verbs are in the present tense in Greek. The report had struck fear into the man's heart, but Christ urged him not to forsake his previous faith.

38. The tumult. Among the Jews mourning for the dead was anything but subdued and respectful. Professional mourners were hired to provide a demonstration of sorrow. Matthew 9:23 (ASV) mentions the flute-players and the crowd which were also making a tumult.

39. The impropriety of the demonstration moved Christ to ask, **Why make ye this ado?** or, more literally, "Why are you making such an uproar?" Christ's statement that the girl was **not dead** but sleeping has been taken by some to mean that she was not really dead but only in a coma. However, Lk 8:55 says that **her spirit came again,** indicating that she had been dead. Christ's reference to death as sleep was intended to suggest that the condition was temporary and that the person would awaken again.

40. The mourners, taking Jesus' figure of speech literally, kept laughing (Gr. imp. tense) him **to scorn.** They knew that the girl was dead, and they were sure that death is permanent. **Put them all out.** Mark's verb is forceful, meaning, *to thrust out.* Christ drove the jeering crowd from the house.

41. Talitha cumi. Transliteration of the Aramaic for, "Little girl, arise." Mark inserts the words, **I say unto thee.**

42. Straightway the girl **arose** (point action) and was walking around (continuous action). **Twelve years.** She was old enough to walk. The parents and disciples were indescribably **astonished** at the miracle, so much so that they were beside themselves with amazement.

43. Jesus commanded **that no man should know** lest the parents should proclaim the news abroad and the widespread excitement should precipitate a crisis before the hour for the Saviour's death had arrived (Jn 12:23,27).

I. Another Galilean Preaching Tour. 6:1-30. Mark records but two of the Lord's three tours of Galilee, the first with the four fishermen (1:35-45), and the third at the conclusion of the Galilean ministry (6:1-30). The second tour occurred shortly after the choice of the Twelve (Lk 8:1-3). The third was different from the preceding two in that the disciples were sent out two by two (Mk 6:7), after which Christ went from town to town preaching and teaching by himself (Mt 11:1). The tour should be viewed as including the visit to Nazareth (Mk 6:1-6). It was also during this time that Herod became exercised concerning the great popularity of the Lord (6:14-16).

1. From thence. That is, from Capernaum. While the place to which Jesus went is not specifically named, it is obvious from the following verses that **his own country** refers to his home town, Nazareth.

3. Jesus is called **the brother of James** and the others, a designation which should be taken literally. There is no Biblical reason whatever for not understanding these four men and their **sisters** to be the children of Joseph and Mary, born some time after Jesus. **James** became the leader of the Jerusalem church (Acts 15:13 ff.) and the author of the epistle that bears his name. **Juda** is the same as Jude, the author of the general epistle of Jude. The townspeople **were offended.** This verb originally meant "to be caught in a trap or snare." They were caught in the snare of their own unbelief, and stumbled when they could have risen to their greatest opportunity.

5. Christ was unable to do any **mighty work** there. However, it was not that he tried to heal some and found himself incapable, but that so few people had faith enough to come to him for healing.

6. Where the Lord Jesus might have expected to find the greatest faith in himself, he found the most persistent **unbelief.** And even though he was the omniscient Son of God, **he marvelled** at his unbelieving acquaintances. **He went.** The Greek imperfect tense describes the action as in process. He was going from village to village, **teaching** in every town. This ministry in Nazareth and in the villages is the first stage of the third Galilean preaching tour.

7. The second stage of the tour was introduced when Jesus called the Twelve and **began to send them forth.** This apparently was the first time they had gone out without Christ, and it therefore constituted an advanced step in their training. **Power.** *Authority.*

8. They were to **take nothing for their journey.** This was designed to train them in the practice of faith in preparation for the time when they would be on their own. **No scrip.** A traveling bag for carrying provisions. **Money.** This term refers to small copper coins. They were not even to take small change. **Purse.** A belt or girdle worn to hold the loose Oriental garments in place; it was also used to carry money.

9. The intention was that they should take no extra wearing apparel. **Coats.** The garment referred to is the undergarment worn next to the skin, rather than a coat.

11. They were to **shake off the dust** not in personal animosity but as **a testimony** to show the seriousness of rejecting the message of the Son of God. The statement concerning **Sodom and Gomorrha** was not in the earliest Greek manuscripts.

13. Anointing **with oil** was a common medical practice (cf. Lk 10:34; Jas 5:14). W. K. Hobart *(The Medical Language of St. Luke,* pp. 28,29) records numerous citations from ancient writers to this effect. Swete *(Mark,* p. 119) says that ritualistic anointing of the sick did not appear until the second century. Thus these healings were a combination of miracle and medicine.

14. The incident recorded in 6:14-29 occurred during the third tour of Galilee (cf. vv. 12,13,30). This **king Herod** was Herod Antipas, son of Herod the Great, and tetrarch of Galilee and Perea. The continuing ministry of Christ and his disciples in Galilee had spread his fame to every part of the region. Here, for the first time, we have evidence that the reputation of Christ had come to the attention of government officials.

15. A common rumor among the people was that he was Elijah returning in fulfillment of Mal 4:5 (cf. Mt 16:14; Jn 1:21), or that he was **a prophet** after the pattern of the OT prophets.

17. The **prison** where John was incarcerated was located at Machaerus, on the eastern shore of the Dead Sea (Jos *Antiquities* xviii. 5.2). The marital relationships of the Herods were scandalous. Herodias was the wife of her half-uncle, Herod Philip I, but she left him to marry another half-uncle his brother, Herod Antipas. Herod Antipas was already married to the daughter of Aretas, king of Arabia, but he sent this wife away.

18. John had said. He was saying it repeatedly (Gr. imp. tense).

19. Herodias had a quarrel against him. Literally, Mark says that she continually had it in for him. She, unlike Herod, felt no attraction to John and his preaching; on the contrary, she kept wanting to kill him.

20. With Herod it was different. In spite of his loose living, he was moved by John's life and message. **Observed him.** Better, he *protected him* and would not allow Herodias to kill him. **He did many things.** The most authentic reading says, *. . . he was perplexed.* The conflict between his admiration for John and the attraction of his sinful relationships kept him in a state of inner confusion. Nevertheless, he **heard** (Gr., *kept hearing)* **him gladly.**

21. Herodias had waited with cunning for **a convenient day** to penetrate Herod's defense of John. The elite of the governmental, military, and social circles were invited (**lords, high captains, chief estates,** respectively).

22. The daughter referred to was Salome, the child of Herodias by her previous marriage. It is estimated that the girl was no more than twenty years old at this time (Vincent Taylor, *Mark,* p. 314). For the daughter of a ruler to entertain nobility in this fashion was entirely out of place. It was the work of a slave, not of a princess. This, however, was Herodias' opportune moment (v. 21), and Herod, under the sway of liquor and sensuality, fell into her trap. **Sat with him.** Rather, *reclined with him* (see on 2:15).

25. The request of Herodias was marked by urgency. She wanted the deed accomplished before Herod could find a way to avoid it. Salome returned **straightway with haste** and asked that her request be granted, not **by and by** (AV), but *at once* (Gr.). **Charger.** An archaic word for a platter.

26. Although the request deeply grieved Herod, he found it impossible to go back on his oaths before such an august group. It was more important to save face than to preserve the life of God's prophet. It was no wonder that afterward his conscience troubled him (vv. 14,16).

27. Herod's palace at Machaerus was also a fortress and as such would have contained a **prison.** Thus the execution scene was not far removed from the banquet room.

28. It appears that Salome remained in the dining hall until John had been executed and they **brought his head to her.** The apparent calmness with which she made the request and then carried the gory dish **to her mother** is indicative of the calloused nature of the girl.

30. Having completed the parenthetical explanation concerning the fate of John, Mark returns to the disciples and the preaching tour. He records nothing concerning the time consumed or the events that happened. He simply reports that the apostles came back together again. The designation, "apostle," is most appropriate here. The word speaks of one sent forth on a mission, and the disciples were returning from such an assignment.

IV. Christ's Withdrawals from Galilee. 6:31–9:50.

The Lord had so thoroughly covered Galilee with his message that Galileans in every walk of life were aware of his ministry. Among many of the common people his popularity stood at such a peak that they were ready to set him up by force as their king. The antipathy of the Jewish religious leaders was dangerously near the boiling point. And Herod himself had now become exercised concerning the popularity of Christ. The situation was shaping up toward a premature crisis, while as yet the ministry of Christ had not been completed. The result was that Jesus made four systematic withdrawals from Galilee, one to the eastern shore of the sea (6:31-56), one to the region of Tyre and Sidon (7:24-30), one to Decapolis (7:31–8:9), and the fourth to Caesarea Philippi (8:10–9:50). During this time Christ was occupied with the training of the twelve disciples in preparation for the time of his death.

A. Withdrawal to the Eastern Shore of the Lake. 6:31-56. This section of the Gospel records the feeding of the five thousand (6:31-44), the miracle of walking on the water (6:45-52), and the healings on the plain of Gennesaret (6:53-56). Instead of being a period of rest and retirement from the crowds, it was a time of continued activity.

31. The **desert place** was probably on the northeast shore of the Sea of Galilee. It was not desert; the expression means "a deserted place, a wilderness." After the stress and strain of the preaching tour they needed to **rest a while.**

33. Many knew him. As people saw them leaving, they recognized (Gr. text) them. That the crowds were able to anticipate where Christ was heading and to precede him there seems to confirm the view that the wilderness place (v. 31) was on the northeast shore of the lake.

34. When Jesus landed (AV, **came out),** it became apparent that he and his men would not be able to enjoy the planned period of rest. Nevertheless his reaction was not one of annoyance; instead he **was moved with compassion.** He saw the people in their need as shepherdless **sheep,** having no spiritual leader (cf. Num 27:17; I Kgs 22:17).

36. Country. Mark's word literally means *fields,* which probably refers to the farms of the countryside.

37. Give ye. The emphasis is on the subject, **ye.** The monetary term used here, **pennyworth,** is the word *dēnariōn,* the Roman denarius worth about eighteen cents at that time (Arndt, p. 178).

40. In ranks. The Greek term meant *a garden bed* (Arndt, p. 705). Mark's picture of the scene is that of groups of people scattered like beds of flowers on the green grass (v. 39). No doubt the variegated colors of the clothing served to create such an impression when seen at a distance.

41. The verbs **had taken, looked, blessed,** and **brake** are all in the aorist tense in Greek, signifying instantaneous action. But the verb **gave** is in the imperfect tense, showing, in contrast, that he kept giving to the disciples. It is at this point that the miracle of a multiplied supply occurred.

43. The astonishing fact was not that the people were merely filled, but that there was a superabundant supply. The **baskets** were large handbaskets used for carrying food. In general, however, they were smaller than the ones used at the feeding of the four thousand (see comments on 8:8).

44. The count of **five thousand** did not include women and children (cf. Mt 14:21).

45. Christ **constrained his disciples,** which is to say that he compelled them to enter the boat (not **ship)** and set sail **unto Bethsaida.** Evidently the place of the miracle was south of Bethsaida Julias (Lk 9:10), and Christ directed the disciples to sail to the town and meet him there. The reason for this abrupt dispersion of **the people,** as given by John (6:14,15), was the danger of a revolutionary attempt to make Jesus king.

47. When even was come. That is,

when six o'clock, the hour of sunset, had arrived.

48. Since it was not yet dark, he could still see them from the land **toiling in rowing. Toiling,** from a verb meaning *to torment* or *distress,* pictures the difficulty of the disciples as they attempted to row into the contrary wind. The **fourth watch of the night** lasted from three to six in the morning. Jesus delayed his coming to their aid from sunset until about 3:00 A.M. The statement that he **would have passed by them** should not pose any problem concerning Christ's sincerity. He was not walking directly toward the boat, so that to the disciples it appeared that he would have passed by if they had not cried out (v. 49). Rather than suddenly entering the boat, Jesus was, no doubt, giving them time to see him.

49. A spirit. This is not the Greek word for "spirit," but a term which means an *apparition.* They thought they were seeing a ghost.

50. Be of good cheer. This verb carries with it the idea of courage, which was probably the thought uppermost in the mind of Christ. The present tense prohibition, **be not afraid,** means *stop fearing.*

51. Without a word from Christ **the wind ceased** (Gr., *became weary)* its blowing. The astonishment that was gripping the disciples was the result of a double miracle. The Greek text omits the words, **and wondered.**

52. Not only had they forgotten that Christ had previously stilled the waves (4:39), but they did not understand (Gr. text) the miracle **of the loaves.** Because **their heart was hardened,** they did not grasp the truth concerning the deity of Christ which the miracles were continually demonstrating.

53. Jesus probably entered the boat somewhere off the shore from Bethsaida Julias, after which they **passed over** to the western shore of the lake again. **Gennesaret** was the name of a plain lying along the shore of the lake south of Capernaum. A small town of the same name was also located in the vicinity.

55. Mark provides a glimpse of the kind of scene that must have appeared many times when Jesus came to an area. The people hurried to bring their sick folk before Christ moved from their neighborhood.

56. Besought him. The repeated requests of person after person are depicted by this verb. This is the second reference in Mark to healings effected by touching Christ's garment (cf. 5:27-29).

B. Discussion of the Unwarranted Exaltation of Tradition. 7:1-23. These verses record the clash between Christ and the Pharisees on the basic issue of the source of authority. Does tradition carry divine authority? Is it equal to, or superior to, the written Word of God? Also involved here is the discussion of the real nature of defilement and cleansing. The setting for this section apparently was the vicinity of Capernaum.

2. Mark's explanation of Jewish customs is noteworthy, indicating as it does that this Gospel was written for Gentile consumption. **Defiled . . . hands.** Hands ceremonially unclean. **They found fault** does not appear in the best manuscripts. The sentence is left incomplete as Mark breaks off to introduce the explanation of verses 3,4.

3. The Pharisees had so extended their influence that the washing of the hands had, in a general way, become the practice of **all the Jews.** The Greek text does not support the use of the word **oft.** Instead it reads *with a fist*, probably referring to the act of rubbing the fist of one hand in the palm of the other when washing. The **tradition of the elders** was the unwritten corpus of commands and teachings of the honored rabbis of the past, a body of 613 rules designed to regulate every aspect of life.

6. Jesus did not mean that Isaiah specifically predicted the practices of the first century Jews, but rather that Isaiah's words concerning the people of his own day were applicable also to the Jews of Christ's day. The quotation is from Isa 29:13, following the LXX with slight alteration. The term **hypocrites** is an epithet well chosen, for it referred originally to an actor who wore a mask and appeared to be what he really was not.

8. The main point of the quotation from Isaiah concerns the substitution of **the tradition of men** for **the commandment of God.** This is not an overstatement, for the Pharisees viewed oral tradition as being more authoritative than the written law of the OT.

10. In 7:9-13 this exaltation of tradition is given specific illustration. The law of **Moses** concerning honor to parents is quoted. The first citation is from Deut 5:16 and is identical with both the Hebrew and the LXX. The second, which is from Ex 21:17, follows the Hebrew text very closely.

11. In contrast Christ cites the rabbinical tradition that sets aside the God-given Mosaic commandment. **Corban** is the transliteration of a Hebrew word meaning **a gift,** as Mark explains for the benefit of his Gentile readers. The word was used to refer to something devoted to God by a vow which was inviolable. If a son declared that the amount needed to support his parents was **Corban,** that vow was unalterable, even setting aside the Mosaic command.

13. The **word of God** is placed in sharp contrast to tradition of men. Notice that Christ viewed the Mosaic law as having been spoken by God. To make **of none effect** is to make void or to nullify. The present tense, **do ye,** speaks of habitual practice.

14. In verses 14-16 the Lord returns to the subject of defilement and cleansing, but here he is speaking not only to the Pharisees and scribes but to the crowd whom **he had called** together. Subsequently Christ discusses the matter with his disciples (7:17-23).

15. Nothing from without a man—that is, nothing physical—can defile him morally or spiritually. In the case under discussion (v. 2), eating with unwashed hands cannot produce spiritual uncleanness. Such defilement is internal in origin. A man is defiled by thoughts that originate in the heart and come out in the forms of words or actions. Herein Jesus explained the spiritual significance of the laws of the clean and unclean (Lev 11). One of the reasons why they were given was to teach this very truth of spiritual defilement, but these Jewish leaders never got beyond the mere externals.

19. The **heart** in Biblical usage is not merely the seat of the emotions but also the place of mental and volitional activity. It refers to the inner, nonphysical man. **The belly** refers to the body cavity that contains the stomach and intestines. After the digestive process is complete, the remainder passes **out into the draught,** that is, into the drain. The AV does not make clear what is meant by the phrase, **purging all meats.** The best explanation is that it should be connected with **he saith** (v. 18). Jesus, by his explanation in 7:18,19, declared all food to be 'clean.' He set aside the Levitical distinction between the clean and unclean (cf. Acts 10:14,15).

20-22. These verses contain Jesus' explanation of what he meant by **that which cometh out of the man.** The **evil thoughts** are to be understood as being evil reasonings or designs, deliberate thoughts. The word for **deceit** carries the more potent connotation of treachery. **Lasciviousness** is uncontrolled and unconcealed immorality. The words, **evil eye,** in any other culture than that of the Jews, could refer to the casting of a spell. Among the Jews, however, it is an expression for envy. In this context **foolishness** is more moral than intellectual.

C. Withdrawal to the Region of Tyre and Sidon. 7:24-30. In this brief section Mark reports a rather lengthy journey of Christ to the region of Phoenicia, where the incident with the Syrophoenician woman occurred.

24. The borders of Tyre and Sidon. An idiomatic expression for the region of Tyre and Sidon. This was the only time, so far as the record goes, when Christ went out of Palestine into strictly Gentile territory. His purpose on these tours outside Galilee was not primarily to minister to the multitudes, but to instruct his disciples, which is the reason why he **would have no man know** that he was there.

26. A Greek. This is the same as identifying the woman as a Gentile. By birth she was a Syrian of the region of Phoenicia. **She besought him.** Mark's use of the Greek imperfect tense pictures the repeated request of the woman. **Devil.** Should be translated *demon*.

27. Jesus used the term **children** to represent the Jews. His mission was first to the Jews in order that they might, in turn, fulfill their duty of becoming a blessing to all nations through the world-wide proclamation of the Gospel. **The dogs.** This was a common Jewish term of reproach applied to Gentiles. However, it is softened by the use of the diminutive form meaning "little dogs" or "puppies." These were the family pets, not the wild dogs of the street.

28. The woman's undaunted reply was the response of faith. **The dogs under the table.** Taking up Christ's diminutive term for dogs, she paints a touching scene of the puppies licking up the crumbs dropped by the children. All she asked was a crumb of the blessings available to the Jews.

29. Jesus recognized in **this saying** of the woman the evidence of genuine faith (cf. Mt 15:28). Already as He spoke the demon had left (Gr. perf. tense) her daughter. The unique feature of this miracle was that it was performed at a distance without any vocal command of Christ.

D. Withdrawal to Decapolis. 7:31–8:9. The return from the region of Tyre and Sidon did not take Christ back to Galilee; instead his route skirted the eastern shore of the lake, leading him into the Decapolis. There Jesus healed the deaf man who had an impediment of speech (7:31-37), and he fed the crowd of 4,000.

31. Mark is the most explicit of the Gospel writers at this point. He tells us that Jesus left the region **of Tyre** and passed through **Sidon** (so the best Gr. MSS) approximately twenty-five miles to the north, going deep into Gentile territory. Then turning south he passed along the eastern shore of the Sea of Galilee into the region of Decapolis (see comments on 5:20).

32. The extent of the **impediment of speech** is debatable. *Mogilalon* may be used of one who is completely mute, but its literal meaning is *speaking with difficulty*. The statement of 7:35 that he spoke plainly seems to indicate that previously he had not been able to speak clearly. However, the exclamation of the people in 7:37 was that he made the speechless (Gr.) to speak.

33. That it was not necessary for the Lord to touch a person in order to heal him had been demonstrated previously (cf. 2:3-12; 3:5; 7:29,30). Here Jesus **put his fingers** into the deaf man's ears to indicate what He was going to do for him and thus to help him to believe. Two other symbolical acts followed. **He spit** and He **touched his tongue.** The text does not say that He applied the saliva to the tongue.

34. He sighed. The word may refer to a groan. Perhaps this was an expression of sympathy or of distress because of the suffering of mankind. **Ephphatha.** An Aramaic word that Mark translates for his Gentile readers.

35. The string of his tongue. The bond (Gr.) which held his tongue was released. **Plain.** He began to speak rightly or plainly.

36. Christ still needed to avoid excessive publicity (cf. on 5:43). However, the people would not be stilled. They kept proclaiming (Gr. imp. tense) the miracle *all the more exceedingly.*

37. Beyond measure. The astonishment of the people exceeded all bounds. Mark uses a very strong word here *(hyperperissōs).*

8:1. The feeding of the four thousand is not given a specific setting other than the general statement that it occurred in a wilderness place (v. 4). **In those days.** The Greek text adds the word "again," probably with reference to the recent feeding of the five thousand.

2. Jesus was moved with **compassion** toward these people just as he had been on the occasion of the feeding of the five thousand (6:34), but here his concern was caused by their physical need rather than by their spiritual condition.

6. Here, as in the feeding of the five thousand, the words **took, gave thanks,** and **brake** are all in the aorist tense in Greek, but the word **gave** is in the imperfect tense, showing that Christ kept giving the bread to the disciples for distribution (cf. 6:41).

8. The sufficiency of the miracle is seen in the statements that they **were filled** and that there was an abundance (Gr.) **that was left.** The word **meat,** inserted by the translators of the AV, refers to food in general. These **baskets** were a different type than those used after the feeding of the five thousand. This is indicated by the distinction made between two kinds in 8:19,20 (Gr. text). The kind of basket used this time was often quite large. It was the kind used to let Saul down over the wall at Damascus (Acts 9:25). Thus the seven hampers of 8:8 probably held more than the twelve provision baskets of 6:43.

E. Withdrawal to Caesarea Philippi. 8:10–9:50. The fourth and last withdrawal from Galilee was northward into the region of Caesarea Philippi. Coming from Decapolis, Jesus crossed to the west coast of the Sea of Galilee, where the Pharisees met him with a request for a sign (8:10-12). He then traveled by boat in a northeasterly direction to Bethsaida Julias (8:13-21), where he healed a blind man (8:22-26). From there his journey took him overland to the vicinity of Caesarea Philippi. Here again, Christ's main activity was that of instructing his disciples concerning such themes as his person, his death and resurrection, their discipleship, and his coming in glory as prefigured by the Transfiguration (8:27–9:13). Here also he cured another demoniac (9:14-29). Following this, Christ returned to Galilee, still continuing the instruction of the Twelve (9:30-50).

10. At the present time scholars cannot pinpoint the town of **Dalmanutha** with any degree of certainty. The context seems to assume a location across the sea from Bethsaida, probably on the western shore (cf. vv. 13,22). Matthew calls it Magadan (Mt 15:39; Gr. text), a place equally unknown to us today.

11. The Pharisees were asking for a sensational sign from God which would prove that Jesus was the Messiah. **Tempting him.** The Greek word *peirazō* means "to test." Rather than attempting to entice Jesus to sin, they were putting him to the test of their unbelieving minds.

12. Such persistent refusal to believe caused Christ to sigh **deeply in his spirit.** The word, appearing here in its intensified form, probably means that he actually groaned as the sense of weariness and grief penetrated to the depths of his heart. The question of Christ is better translated, *Why is this generation continually seeking a sign?* (cf. Jn 2:18; Mt 12:38). Matthew adds an exception to the statement of Christ that **no sign** would be given (Mt 16:4). The sign of Jonah is explained in Mt 12:39,40 as referring to Christ's resurrection, the most significant miracle of all.

15. Jesus **charged them** repeatedly (Gr. imp. tense), showing the urgent need to be continually on guard (Gr. pres. tense, **Take heed, beware**). Leaven is here used to symbolize something with a dangerously pervasive influence. Luke 12:1 explains that **the leaven of the Pharisees** is hypocrisy. The **leaven of Herod** may be the influence of the Herodians, which was a spirit of worldliness, an infectious secularism.

19,20. The disciples had so soon forgotten the lessons inherent in the feedings of the **five thousand** and the **four thousand.** The Son of God does not need to worry about food for thirteen men on a short voyage across the lake. He had but recently demonstrated his power to supply food for more than nine thousand persons.

22. The healing of the **blind man** occurred when Jesus passed through **Bethsaida** Julias on his way to Caesarea Philippi.

23. Jesus **led him out of the town,** probably to avoid excessive publicity (cf. v. 26). Here, as in the case of the deaf man (7:33), saliva was used, not as a healing application, but as an aid to the sightless man's faith.

24. This healing was unique in that it consisted of two stages. After the first healing acts, the man saw people indistinctly as moving objects, like **trees walking.**

25. The second stage of healing was preceded by the touching of the eyes. The Greek text does not say that Jesus **made him look up,** but rather that the man *looked intently*. And when he did so, he began to see all things **clearly.**

26. Again in order to avoid the results of undue publicity, Christ sent the man **to his house.** That He told him not to **go into the town** indicates that he lived elsewhere, perhaps in the surrounding countryside.

27. Going north from Bethsaida, Christ came to **the towns of Caesarea Philippi.** Matthew (16:13) explains that he came into the *parts* (Gr.) or the region of Caesarea. Mark has reference to the villages located in the country surrounding the larger city. This Caesarea, located in the northwest section of the tetrarchy of Philip, was designated Philippi to distinguish it from Caesarea on the Mediterranean coast.

29. Whom say ye. This was the point at which Christ was aiming. The emphasis is on the word "you." "But *you* (in contrast to others), who do *you* say that I am?" **Peter** acted as spokesman for the disciples. His confession of Jesus as **the Christ** is more fully given in Mt 16:16, which adds the words, "the Son of the living God." Jesus is both the promised Messiah and the unique Son of God.

30. Here again Christ commanded silence, probably because of the revolutionary ideas connected with the Messianic concept. Christ was not ready at that time to establish an earthly Messianic kingdom.

31. Instead, at his first coming Christ was to **suffer,** and **be killed,** and **rise again.** Particular attention should be given to the sharp contrast between the glowing confession of Peter and Christ's immediate declaration of suffering and death. Notice that the One who was to die was designated by the Messianic title, **Son of man.** The cross was a necessary aspect of Messiah's work. He **must suffer.**

32. He spake . . . openly. The Greek imperfect tense is used to show that Jesus began and continued to speak of his death. No longer did he refer to it in veiled fashion (cf. Jn 2:19), but from this time on he instructed his disciples **openly** and explicitly concerning the fact. This was the next stage in their training. **Peter took him** aside and rebuked him for speaking in such a manner. In Peter's mind violent death did not harmonize with Messianic dignity.

33. Peter's attempt to dissuade the Lord from going to the cross was similar to the temptation in the wilderness. In this instance, **Satan** with great subtilty, used one of Christ's closest disciples (cf. Lk 4:13, RSV). Notice the similar rebuke in Mt 4:10. **Savourest.** The Greek verb refers to the set of the mind, the direction of thought. Peter's mind was running contrary to the purposes of God.

34. The instruction recorded in 8:34-38 is the natural outgrowth of the fact of Christ's suffering. **Whosoever will come after** Christ must walk the path which he walked, the path of denial and cross-bearing. The **cross** is the symbol of suffering, and self-denial speaks of readiness to suffer for someone else. Christ is the pattern;

the disciple is to keep following him (Gr. pres. imperative).

35. The paradox of these verses is resolved by understanding that the Lord used the term **life** in two different senses. The first expression, **save his life,** has reference to the preservation of physical life from death. The person who is completely devoted to the protection of this life will miss the life that is eternal. On the contrary, the person who is so devoted to Christ that he is willing to **lose his life** is the person who gains true life. He finds that **to die is gain** (Phil 1:21). This is not a description of the way of salvation for the lost, but rather of the philosophy of life for the disciple.

36. Here the contrast is between **world** and **soul.** The latter term is the same as **life** in verse 35. Both are translations of *psychē*. This principle applies on the physical level as well as on the spiritual. What is the value of obtaining all that the world has to offer if a person dies and cannot enjoy it? Or, what is the good of amassing a world of earthly possessions for a few short years if it means the loss of eternal life.

38. When Christ used the expression, **ashamed of me and of my words,** he was drawing a contrast with the attitude of willingness to lose one's life for his sake and the Gospel's (v. 35). **To be ashamed** is to deny Christ in the hour of trial rather than to own him even at the risk of death. It is to take one's stand with this **sinful generation** instead of with Christ. **Adulterous.** Used spiritually to describe unfaithfulness to God. In like manner, when the Lord comes as Judge, he will **be ashamed** and will disown those who have disowned him.

9:1. The chapter division here is unfortunate, since this verse is clearly the conclusion of the discourse recorded in the last part of Mark 8. **Verily** is a term of solemn assurance. It is the Greek word *amēn*, from which our "amen" is derived. **Shall not taste of death.** The original is much stronger–*shall by no means taste of death*. The coming of **the kingdom of God** in this statement has been variously interpreted. However, in the preceding verse Christ speaks of his advent in glory, and in the following verses Mark records the Transfiguration. The coming of the Kingdom may well be identical with the glorious coming of the King (8:38), of which Christ's transfiguration was a foretaste.

2. The **high mountain** was traditionally identified as Mount Tabor in Galilee, but this is too far from Caesarea Philippi. Mount Hermon seems to fit the description more satisfactorily. **Transfigured.** From the Greek *metamorphoō* (source of our word "metamorphosis"), which refers to a change of essential form, not a superficial change of outward appearance. Our Lord's human body was glorified, and it is in this glorified body that he will some day come to establish his kingdom.

3. As snow. Not found in the best Greek manuscripts. A **fuller** is one who treats new cloth, shrinking and cleansing it.

4. Elias is a transliteration of the Greek word for *Elijah*. Why Moses and Elijah were the two chosen to appear is not stated. It is noteworthy that both left this life under unusual circumstances. Furthermore, Moses represented the Law, while Elijah was one of the prophets. Luke's Gospel (9:31) states that the subject of their conversation was the imminent death of Christ, a theme which runs through the OT, both in the Law and in the Prophets.

6. Wist. Old English word for "knew." **Sore afraid.** They were terrified.

9. The charge **that they should tell no man** was in keeping with Jesus' policy of restraint lest the current erroneous Messianic ideas be fanned into flames. After the Resurrection the danger of precipitating a popular uprising would no longer be present. Then the experience on the mount would have spiritual value for the disciples as a confirmation of their faith (cf. II Pet 1:16-18).

11. The question concerning Elijah arose because of the presence of the prophet at the Transfiguration. **The scribes,** in this instance, drew their teaching from Mal 4:5,6. It may have been that the disciples were wondering if the appearance on the mount was the fulfillment of the prediction.

12. This prophecy received confirmation by the Lord, and the tense used (futuristic present) indicates that it shall be fulfilled in the future. Elijah is going to come and restore all things (cf. Mal 4:6) before the Messiah comes. **How it is written.** Most students view the remainder of this verse as a question, "How is it written . . . ?" The coming of Elijah was predicted in the Scriptures. What about the predictions that the Messiah should suffer and be rejected? Christ was attempting to stir the thinking of his followers that they might understand that the Son of man must first suffer before the coming of Elijah and the glorious advent of Messiah.

13. But there was a sense in which Elijah had already come. Matthew 17:13 explains that He was speaking of John the

Baptist. This was not to say that John was Elijah in person, but that he came in the likeness of Elijah (cf. Lk 1:17; Jn 1:21). **Whatsoever they listed.** That is, they did with him what they desired, referring to his death at the request of Herodias.

15. Greatly amazed. The explanations of this amazement can all be reduced to two possibilities. One, they were amazed because of the remaining glow of the Transfiguration on Jesus' face. Two, the amazement was caused by the opportune but unexpected appearance of Jesus at the moment of the embarrassing defeat of the nine disciples. The first view is rendered improbable by the absence of any statement concerning a continuing glow on Jesus' face.

17. The **dumb spirit** was a demon that afflicted the boy with dumbness and deafness (v. 25).

18. Taketh him. The father described the action of the demon in seizing or laying hold on the boy. His reaction appears to have been similar to that of an epileptic fit.

19. It is clear that the disciples were weak because of unbelief. The disappointment of our Lord seems almost to verge on impatience. Suffer. Literally, *How long shall I put up with you?*

20. Tare. This is a strong word meaning that he convulsed the boy with such violence that it seemed he would tear him in pieces. **Wallowed.** The Greek word means *to roll.* The imperfect tense should be translated, *He kept rolling.*

23. If thou canst. In the Greek text an article precedes this whole clause for the purpose of drawing attention to it. It is as though Jesus said, "Consider this clause—**if thou canst.**" The word **believe** does not appear in the best manuscripts. Having called specific attention to the man's **if,** Jesus proceeded to show his need for faith.

24. The anguish that filled the father's heart is portrayed by his immediate response as he **cried out** in almost contradictory ejaculations. He did **believe,** and yet he was acutely conscious of the **unbelief** that struggled with his desire to trust implicitly. His unbelief was not an obstinate refusal to believe; it was a weakness with which the man himself could not deal. Hence his cry to Christ for help.

29. This kind. An indication that there are different types of demons. It seems that the one indwelling this boy was unusually vicious and powerful. From Jesus' previous remark about unbelief (v. 19) and from the statement in this verse concerning the need of **prayer,** it is apparent that the nine disciples had attempted to cast out the demon without relying upon God's power (cf. Mt 17:20). Unbelief and prayerlessness are sure to result in spiritual impotency. Many of the best Greek manuscripts omit the reference to **fasting,** as well as the parallel passage in Mt 17:21. It is to be noted that there would have been no opportunity for the disciples to meet this situation with fasting, but they surely could have trusted and prayed.

31. He taught his disciples. This had been the Lord's main occupation during the withdrawals, and still he continued instructing them (Gr. imp. tense), for they were slow to comprehend (v. 32). The heart of his teaching was his coming death and resurrection.

33. The return **to Capernaum** brought him again to **the house** of Peter, which had been the headquarters for his Galilean campaign. The verb, **asked,** is in the imperfect tense, probably to indicate that Jesus continued to question the disciples concerning their discussion on the road.

34. Instead of replying to Jesus' interrogation, **they held their peace.** Again the imperfect tense shows that they persisted in their silence. They were ashamed to reveal the unworthy subject of their discussion. He had tried to explain his coming death, but their minds were occupied with thoughts of personal greatness in the Messianic kingdom (cf. Mt 18:1).

36,37. The humble act of receiving one **child** in Christ's name is a deed of true greatness. It is this willingness to take the lowly position of service, even to a child in arms, which is the mark of genuine stature; for to do so is to render service to Christ and, through him, to the Father. This involves the humbling of one's self as a little child (see Mt 18:4).

38. Perhaps a desire to change the subject led **John** to speak. Apparently Jesus' remark concerning acts done in his name reminded John of the exorcist whom they had seen and who used the **name** of Jesus. **Master.** This is the word for "teacher." **We forbad him.** They kept on forbidding this unknown miracle worker (imp. tense). Their reason, **he followeth not us,** reveals a basically selfish attitude, an unwillingness to accept anyone except those of their own circle. Scofield calls this sectarianism.

39. Forbid him not. Literally, *Stop forbidding him.* Jesus did not quibble about details. If the man was using Christ's name in a sincere effort to help others, he was not to be hindered. A breadth of spirit that ought to characterize God's people is evidenced here. Our Lord's logic was twofold. First, such a man would not soon turn against Christ after working miracles in His name.

40. The second reason for Christ's prohibition was that since the man was not **against** Christ and the disciples, then to some extent he was on their side.

41. This verse further emphasizes the breadth of attitude displayed in 9:39,40. No one who is seeking to serve the Lord, no matter how seemingly unimportant his service may be, is excluded from Christ's circle. The importance of this principle is seen in the use of the word **verily** *(amēn),* and in the strong double negative which may be translated, . . . **will by no means lose his reward** (RSV).

42. The thought of this verse is linked to that of 9:37 by the term **little ones.** Likewise, verses 42-48 are related, being centered around the idea of offenses. It is possible that the action of the disciples in rebuking the anonymous exorcist (v. 38) may have offended him. This would explain why Christ discussed offenses at this point. The undeveloped faith of the exorcist was not to be hindered but encouraged. Harsh criticism of spiritual immaturity may only serve to drive persons away from the Lord. **Offend.** The Greek word *skandalizō* means to place a snare or trap in a person's way, causing him to stumble. The **little ones** may be taken literally as referring to children that believe, or they may be those who are little in faith or spiritually undeveloped. Probably the latter is the intention of Jesus. The **millstone** was the large flat stone turned by a donkey in grinding grain.

43. Jesus turned from the offense of others to the offense of one's self. It is possible for a person to place a stumbling block in his own way. Undoubtedly the command to **cut . . . off** the offending **hand** is figurative and hyperbolic. The sense of the verse is that anything which causes a person to fall into sin should be removed immediately. These verses are not to be taken literally as commanding an extreme asceticism. It must be remembered that the seat of sin is the soul, not any organ of the physical body. **Enter into life.** The parallel expression in 9:47 is **enter into the kingdom of God.** These terms are the opposites of **hell** and are to be understood as referring to the life of the saved in the eternal kingdom. **Hell** is the translation of the Greek *geenna,* which in turn is a transliteration of the Hebrew *gê hinnōm,* meaning "valley of Hinnom." This was a valley southwest of Jerusalem which was accursed because it had been the scene of Moloch worship. Later it became the site of the city dump, where continual fires burned, reducing the rubbish to ashes. The garbage and refuse deposited there would also have been infested with many worms. In Jewish thought this valley became a symbol of the place of eternal punishment.

48. The language of this verse is taken from the LXX of Isa 66:24. The **worm** that **dieth not** is a figure of speech drawn from the actual valley of Hinnom, where worms were continually at work. It is a picture of the unending torture and destruction of hell.

49. This verse and the following are among the most difficult in the Gospels. First, it should be noted that the second clause of 9:49 was probably a later addition, since it has poor manuscript support. It may have been a marginal attempt to explain this difficult passage. The introductory word **for** *(gar)* would normally tie this statement to the preceding one, in which case it serves to support or explain the former assertion. It may then mean that everyone who enters hell shall be preserved, as salt preserves, through an eternity of torment.

50. Taking up the word **salt,** used in 9:49 in connection with hell, Jesus goes on to say that Christ's followers are to be as salt, letting their influence be felt in the world (cf. Mt 5:13). **Have salt in yourselves.** He commanded the disciples to be permeated with this purifying influence. In order to be a wholesome influence, they must themselves be the possessors of this wholesomeness. **Have peace.** Christ concludes with one last reference to the dispute over greatness recorded in 9:34. Both commands are in the present tense, calling for an enduring practice.

V. Christ's Ministry in Perea. 10:1-52.

With one statement Mark summarizes about six months of Christ's ministry (v. 1). His mention of Judea covers the later Judean period, recorded largely in Jn 7:10–10:39 and Lk 10:1–13:21; the reference to **the farther side of Jordan** has to do with the Perean ministry, the greater part of which is reported in Lk 13:22–19:28. The events of Mk 10:2-52 are in reality the closing events of this Perean period (cf. Lk 18:15–19:28).

A. Discussions of Divorce, Children, and Wealth. 10:1-31. These conversations probably occurred somewhere in Perea. No exact location is given. In 10:2-12 Christ answered the Pharisees' interrogation concerning the legality of divorce; 10:13-16 indicates Jesus' attitude toward children; and 10:17-31 records the coming of the rich young ruler and the resultant discussion of wealth.

1. From thence. Jesus left Capernaum, where he had stopped briefly at Peter's home (9:33). The word **coasts** is better translated *regions.* There is an important textual problem here concerning the expression **Judaea by the farther side of Jordan.** The manuscript evidence favors the reading *Judea and the farther side of Jordan.* At first this appears to be an impossible text, since it seems to have reversed the natural order of Perea and Judea. Coming from Galilee, Jesus would have gone through Perea first, and then through Judea. However, this difficulty is removed by viewing 10:1 as a summary of the later Judean and the Perean periods of Christ's ministry. Following the period of withdrawals, Jesus went first to Judea for three months; then he went to Perea for approximately the same length of time. Thus, the order in Mark's summary—Judea first and then Perea—is correct. **As he was wont.** That is, as was his custom. The verb **taught** (Gr. imp. tense) signifies a continuing occurrence. For examples of this teaching, see such passages as Lk 13:22–18:14.

2. The question put by **the Pharisees** concerned one of the debated subjects of that day. The scribes who followed Hillel held that a man could divorce his wife for almost any cause. The followers of Shammai, on the other hand, insisted that divorce was lawful only in case of adultery. **Tempting.** The same Greek word may mean either "to tempt" or "to test." Their question was put with an ulterior motive in order to test Christ.

4. Suffered. That is, Moses permitted divorce. The Mosaic regulation is found in Deut 24:1. It is to be noted that the Pharisees did not state the condition under which Moses permitted divorce.

5. For the hardness of your heart. The stipulation of Moses was not in reality a command, but a concession because of man's unsatisfactory spiritual condition. It was an attempt to regulate and control divorce rather than to encourage it.

6-8. The statement beginning **God made them** (v. 6) and ending **shall be one flesh** (v. 8) is taken verbatim from Gen 1:27; 2:24 (LXX). The condition which existed in **the beginning** is indicative of God's ideal. He meant marriage to be a lifelong union in all cases.

11. The man, in this case, commits **adultery against her,** not because of the divorce, but because of the remarriage. Although he has gone through the legal divorce procedure, in God's sight he is still married to his first wife. Matthew adds the exception of fornication (Mt 19:9).

13. The events recorded in this verse probably took place in the house (cf. v. 10). **Brought.** They *kept bringing* (Gr. text) the children. The attitude of the disciples seems to have been based on the conception that the Lord's time was too valuable to be wasted on children.

14. The translation, **was much displeased,** is not forceful enough to represent the Greek verb, which means *to be indignant.* Mark's Gospel is unique in its description of the emotions of Christ. **Suffer.** Used in the sense of "permit." Jesus' prohibition literally means, *Stop forbidding them.* The reason he offers for his action is that the kingdom of God is made up of such persons. It is clear that he had the present, spiritual kingdom in mind.

16. The age of these children is suggested by the fact that Jesus **took them up in his arms.** He **blessed them** is a compound verb describing the heart-felt fervor with which Christ uttered the words of blessing (cf. Gen 14:19,20; 27:26-29; 48:15-20).

17. The conversation with the rich young ruler took place as Jesus was leaving the house where he had lodged, probably somewhere in Perea (cf. v. 10). Mark simply states that **there came one running,** but he does not mention that the man was a young synagogue ruler. These facts are provided by Matthew and Luke. **Master.** This is the word for "teacher" *(didaskale).* He conceived of **eternal life** as something to be earned by doing good (Mt 19:16).

18. The question, **Why callest thou me good?** was aimed at leading the young man to consider the true identity of Jesus. It was an indirect assertion of His deity, since goodness or sinlessness is a quality of God alone.

19. Christ cited some of **the commandments** without regard for their order in Ex 20. The command, **Defraud not,** may be intended to represent the tenth commandment, which concerns covetousness. The purpose of calling attention to the Law was to show the young man his inability to gain eternal life by good works.

20. All these have I observed. The young man could truthfully make such a claim, but his righteousness was an external obedience. It was as the righteousness of the scribes and Pharisees (Mt 5:20; cf. Phil 3:6).

21. Beholding him. Jesus looked intently and searchingly at him, and He **loved him.** No doubt He recognized the sincerity of the man's search for something to meet his spiritual need; He saw the potential represented in this upright young leader. Then He went to the heart of the man's problem, his devotion to his wealth rather than to God. Therein lay the **one thing** he lacked. In order to **follow** Jesus, he must remove the obstacle, his love of money. It was not works of charity that would gain for him eternal life; it was becoming identified with Christ.

23. The Lord did not deny the possibility that a rich person can be saved; he merely said that it is difficult. **The kingdom of God** is the present, spiritual kingdom, composed of the regenerated people of God (Jn 3:3,5).

25. The idea that **the eye of a needle,** referred to here, was a small gate through which a camel could enter only on his knees is without warrant. The word for **needle** refers specifically to a sewing needle. Furthermore, Jesus was not talking about what man considers possible, but about what seems to be impossible (cf. v. 27). With man it is impossible for **a camel to go through the eye** of a sewing needle.

29,30. Verily introduces a statement of solemn assurance. The word **wife** is omitted in the better Greek texts. **An hundredfold.** The items enumerated here may be taken literally to refer to such things as the many homes which will be opened to God's servants and the many new relationships in the household of God. Or they may be taken as figuratively describing the manifold spiritual blessings which the Lord heaps upon those who follow him sacrificially. The **world to come,** in the original language, is *the coming age*. It has reference to the eternal state to be ushered in by Messiah's second advent and the events connected with it, such as the Day of the Lord, cataclysmic judgments, the Millennium, and the final assize.

B. Conversation on the Way to Jerusalem. 10:32-45. The discussion recorded in these verses took place somewhere in Perea as Jesus was on his way, for the last time, to Jerusalem. Again he repeated the assertions concerning his death and resurrection (vv. 32-34), attempting by repetition to impress the facts upon his disciples. And again the temptation to seek self-advancement plagued the disciples (vv. 35-45).

32. This journey **to Jerusalem** was, as Jesus knew, the one that would take him to his death. The fact that **Jesus went before them,** walking alone, was a surprising departure from his usual practice of companionship with his disciples. No doubt there was something about his strange aloofness that **amazed** them and made them **afraid.** The tenses used here indicate that this was a continuing situation that went on for some time.

33,34. An advance beyond previous predictions is apparent in the number of details given (cf. 8:31; 9:31). Notice the statement, **we go up to Jerusalem,** which indicates that the fulfillment of these predictions would come during this visit to the city. Yet the disciples still did not understand what Christ was attempting to explain to them (Lk 18:34). Their concept of the Messiah led them to think only in terms of glory and kingship (cf. Mk 10:35-37).

35. Matthew states that **James** and **John** came with their mother and made their request through her (20:20). Matthew also says, **Then came . . . ,** which may indicate that this self-seeking request of the two disciples followed immediately on the Saviour's teaching concerning his death.

37. The **right hand** of a king was the place of honor, and the **left hand** was next in importance. **In thy glory.** Or, **in thy kingdom** (Mt 20:21), which explains that the disciples had in mind the glory of the Messianic kingdom.

38. The Lord, recognizing that they asked in ignorance, began to show them that such rewards must be earned. **The cup** and **the baptism** speak of Christ's suffering, into which the disciple must be able and willing to enter. In Gethsemane he spoke of his death as a "cup" (14:36); in Lk 12:50 the term "baptism" is a figure for suffering and death.

40. The honors of the **right hand** and the **left hand** are not to be passed out to friends as favors. Such reward must go to them **for whom it is prepared,** that is, to the ones who earn it by faithfulness in life and service.

42. This sorry spectacle of selfish ambition became an occasion for the Lord to re-emphasize the nature of true greatness (cf. 9:35). First, he reminded the Twelve of the world's standard of greatness. It is customary for rulers and dignitaries to **exercise lordship** and **authority** over the people.

43. But this must not be the custom among the followers of Christ. In contrast, the one who would **be great** must be a **minister** to his fellows.

45. Jesus himself was the supreme example of one who manifested true greatness. He who was God's Messiah (**Son of man;** see on 2:10) might well have asserted his right **to be ministered unto** by men. Instead he came to serve and **to give his life** for mankind. **A ransom.** This significant word was common in the Greek world of Jesus' day, where it was used to refer to the price paid to free a slave (Adolf Deissmann, *Light from the Ancient East,* trans. L. R. M. Strachan, p. 327 ff.). This was the price demanded by a holy God in order that justice might be satisfied in the forgiveness of sins. As a result of this payment, the believer is freed from sin and Satan. **For many.** The Greek preposition *anti* is more accurately translated *in the place of,* as overwhelming evidence from Greek sources demonstrates (cf. J. H. Moulton and George Milligan, *The Vocabulary of the Greek Testament,* pp. 46,47; Arndt, pp. 72,73; Vincent Taylor, pp. 444,445).

C. **The Healing of Blind Bartimaeus.** 10:46-52. This section tells how Jesus, with his disciples, came from Perea across the Jordan to Jericho in Judea, where he restored the sight of Bartimaeus, the last healing miracle of his public ministry.

46. The **Jericho** of Jesus' day was located about five miles west of Jordan and fifteen miles northeast of Jerusalem. The site of the Canaanite city of Joshua's day lay one mile to the north. There is a difficulty in harmonization here. Matthew and Mark say that the miracle occurred as Jesus **went out of Jericho;** Luke places it as **he was come nigh unto Jericho** (18:35). Perhaps the most plausible solution is that the healing occurred as Jesus left the site of old Jericho and entered the new city of Jericho. The difficulty with this explanation is that there is no evidence that the old Jericho was inhabited in Jesus' time. This problem arises, no doubt, from our lack of complete historical and geographical information. We may be assured that no discrepancy would exist if all the facts were known. Meanwhile, the divergence is a testimony to the independent character of the two accounts.

47. The blind beggar, by calling Jesus the **son of David,** was recognizing Him as Messiah. The belief that the Messiah would be a descendant of David was common among the Jews of that day.

48. Charged him. Many kept commanding (Gr. text) him to be silent. He, however, kept crying (imp. tense) all the more. He refused to be silenced.

49. Be of good comfort. The verb means *to be of good cheer, to be courageous.* It was as though they said, "Cheer up!"

50. The verbs of this verse suggest with what haste Bartimaeus responded to the call. He threw off his cloak, jumped up (**rose,** AV), and **came to Jesus.** This was the opportunity of a lifetime, and it must not be allowed to slip away.

51. Lord. The Aramaic word *rabbouni* used by Mary Magdalene at the Resurrection (Jn 20:16). It was a term of high respect, a strengthened form of "rabbi," combining, in some measure, the meanings of teacher and of Lord.

52. The healing was in response to the man's **faith,** demonstrated, as it was, by his persistent eagerness, by his recognition of Jesus as Messiah, and by the term *rabbouni.* The verb *anablepō* (**receive . . . sight**) means to have sight restored, indicating that the man had not always been blind. **Made thee whole.** The Greek word is *sōzō,* meaning "to save," a term often used in the Gospels to refer to physical healing. It may be paraphrased, "Your faith has healed you."

VI. Christ's Concluding Ministry in Jerusalem. 11:1–13:37.

In this section Mark has recorded the last acts and teachings of the Saviour prior to his passion. All of these events took place in and around Jerusalem. Here occurred the 'Triumphal Entry' and the cleansing of the Temple (11:1-26), the numerous controversies with Jewish leaders (11:27–12:44), and the extended apocalyptic discourse on the Mount of Olives (13:1-37).

A. The Entrance into Jerusalem and the Temple. 11:1-26. From this point on, Christ abandoned the cautious attitude that had caused him to withdraw from areas of tension and possible crisis. Now he challenged the Jewish leaders. In the entry into Jerusalem he openly provoked disapproval and opposition. This 'Triumphal Entry' should be viewed not as the coming of a glorious king, but as the presentation of a Saviour who was soon to suffer.

1. Comparison with Jn 12:1 reveals that Jesus came first to **Bethany,** where he spent the night. Then on the day after the Sabbath he made his entrance into **Jerusalem.** Bethany lay a little less than two miles to the southeast of Jerusalem, not far from the eastern slope of **the mount of Olives.** The location of Bethphage is more difficult, but the best evidence seems to point toward a place at the foot of the eastern slope. Mark's order is the reverse of the direction taken by Jesus, but he is viewing the locations of the towns from the standpoint of Jerusalem, which is mentioned first. John gives reason for believing that Jesus arrived in Bethany on Friday (12:1). Since the journey to Jerusalem was more than a Sabbath day's journey, it is assumed that Christ spent Saturday in Bethany and that the 'Triumphal Entry' occurred on Sunday.

2. **The village** was Bethphage, as Mt 21:1 makes clear. **Over against you.** That is, "opposite you." Whether Jesus knew of the colt by previous observation or by supernatural perception is not made clear.

3. It appears that he expected that the owner of the colt would know who **the Lord** was and would be willing to lend the animal to him. The preferred Greek texts read, *and immediately he will send it here again,* a promise on the part of Jesus to return the animal. Matthew states that there were two animals, an ass and a colt (21:2).

7. The **garments** placed on the colt were outer cloaks or robes, the bright colors of which would give the colt the appearance of bearing the accouterments of royalty.

8. Others spread their robes **in the way,** making a royal carpet for the procession. Still others brought leaves, which they scattered on the path. John describes them as palm branches (12:13).

9. The crowd surrounded the Lord; some **went before** him; others **followed.** And they kept crying (Gr. imp. tense), **Hosanna.** This is a transliteration of a Hebrew expression meaning, *Save, I pray,* coming from Ps 118:25. It had become a term of praise and acclamation, as well as a plea for help. **Blessed be he that cometh . . .** is an exact quotation from the LXX of Ps 118:26. This was one of the Hallel Psalms sung in connection with the Passover festival, and was thus particularly appropriate at this time. That the crowd used the words in a Messianic sense is made clear by the next verse.

10. The people felt that the Messianic **kingdom of . . . David** was about to be established. **Hosanna in the highest** undoubtedly means, "Save, now, thou who art in the highest heavens." It is a cry addressed to God himself.

11. **Jesus entered . . . into the temple.** The word *hieron* refers to the whole temple complex, including the courts and porches. When he **looked round about,** his eyes would surely take in the booths of the money-changers and of the sellers of doves, which were to be the objects of his displeasure on the following day.

12. **On the morrow.** That is, on Monday. After spending the night in Bethany, the Lord set out again for Jerusalem.

13. It was normal for the **fig tree** in the vicinity of Jerusalem to begin to put forth new leaves in the latter part of March or early April, the time of the Passover. This tree was apparently fully leaved out, in which case it should have had ripened figs on it ,although the time of ripe figs was in June. That it was the leaves which caused Jesus to expect fruit is made clear by the Greek word translated **haply** (AV). This is the inferential conjunction *ara,* meaning "therefore." Jesus saw the leaves at a distance and came to see "if therefore he might find fruit."

15. This is the second purging of the Temple, not in any sense to be identified with the first, which occurred at the very beginning of Christ's ministry (Jn 2:13-17). Those who **sold and bought, the money-changers,** and those **that sold doves** were in the employ of Annas and the high priestly family. The animals were sold for sacrificial purposes, and the money-changers exchanged the common currency for the half-shekel necessary to pay the temple tax. Exorbitant rates, however, were charged.

17. Jesus' quotation comes from Isa 56:7, where the prophet declares God's house to be a **house of prayer,** a place set apart for sacred use. Not only did the Lord accuse them of desecrating the Temple by using it for business, but he pointed out that they made dishonest gain from the grossly unfair prices they charged. **Den of thieves.** Taken from Jer 7:11.

20. **In the morning.** This was Tuesday morning, and Christ was returning to Jerusalem again for the day.

22. The only significance of the cursing of the fig tree which the Gospels state is to be found in these verses. Jesus used it as an example of **faith in God.** Any further symbolical meaning is without Scriptural justification.

24. **Believe.** A present tense imperative, calling for persistent, continuing faith. **Receive.** Superior manuscript evidence favors the aorist tense—*you did receive.* In other words, we are to keep on believing that God has already given us our request.

25. **Forgive . . . that your Father . . . may forgive you.** Statements such as these, which make God's forgiveness dependent on our forgiveness have been misunderstood as being legal in nature. However,

Christ does not here address himself to the unsaved but to his disciples, those who have already entered into a saving relationship with himself. The forgiveness of which he speaks is not the initial forensic act of forgiveness which abolishes the guilt of sin. It is rather the forgiveness of a father which restores fellowship. The point here is that a disciple cannot pray effectively if an unforgiving spirit has broken his fellowship with God.

B. Final Controversies with the Jewish Leaders. 11:27–12:44. The debates recorded in this section all took place on one busy day – Tuesday of the passion week. They concerned the following subjects: the source of our Lord's authority (11:27-33); the parable of the vineyard and the husbandmen (12:1-12); a question about taxation (12:13-17); the resurrection (12:18-27); the greatest commandment (12:28-34); the Messiah's relationship to David (12:35-40). The section closes with an account of the widow's gift of two mites (12:41-44).

27. Come again to Jerusalem. This was Tuesday morning. The comments on the withered fig tree (vv. 20-25) were spoken on the way to Jerusalem. **The chief priests.** Technically there was but one high priest, but the term had come to include all the living ex-high priests. In this case, at least Annas, the father-in-law of the high priest, Caiaphas, would have been included.

28. Their questions were two in number: What kind *(poiâ)* of **authority** do you possess? What is the source of **this authority?** By **these things,** the officials referred to Christ's purging of the Temple (cf. Jn 2:18). It was said that the Temple could be cleansed only by the Sanhedrin, by a prophet, or by the Messiah.

30. From heaven. In an attempt to avoid the use of the Divine name, the Jews often employed the term "heaven" when speaking of God.

31,32. By this question Jesus placed these religious leaders on the horns of a dilemma. If John's ministry was of divine origin, then they, as spiritual leaders, should have been the first to **believe him.** If, however, they stated that his ministry was of human origin, they would have reduced John to an imposter, and this would have invoked the displeasure of **the people** against them.

12:1. Parables. That Jesus gave more than one parable on this occasion is seen by a comparison with Mt 21:28-32, where the story of the wicked husbandmen is preceded by that of the two sons. The introduction to the parable, as found in Mk 12:1 is unmistakably drawn from Isa 5:1,2. The fact that the vineyard there was representative of Israel (Isa 5:7) gave the Jewish leaders the clue for interpreting the parable of Jesus. **Hedge.** *The word* used by Mark means *fence;* it may have been a stone fence or wall. The **place for the winefat** was a pit or trough beneath the winepress for the purpose of catching the juice. The **tower** was a combination watchtower and storage place. The husbandmen were farmers, in this case vine growers, used here to represent the religious leaders of Israel, such as those being addressed by Jesus (cf. 11:27; 12:12).

2. The **servant,** as in 12:4,5, represents a prophet whom God sent to Israel.

3. The fact that they **caught** and **beat him** is indicative of the persecution of the prophets of the OT (cf. Mt 23:34,37).

6. One son, his wellbeloved. These words are an obvious description of Christ himself (cf. 1:11; 9:7). The term **reverence** is too strong. *Respect* or *give heed to* is more accurate.

7,8. The plot to **kill him** was a description of the scheming in which the Jewish leaders were engaged at that very time in order to put Jesus to death.

9. The prediction that the owner would **destroy the husbandmen** was fulfilled in A.D. 70, when the Romans under Titus destroyed Jerusalem and put an end to any semblance of self-rule which the Jews had previously enjoyed. The **others** unto whom the vineyard was to be given are further described in Mt 21:43, where Jesus is quoted as saying, **The kingdom of God shall be taken from you, and given to a nation bringing forth the fruits thereof.** This is an obvious reference to the Gentiles and the Church.

10. The question, **have ye not read,** is phrased to expect a positive answer. The quotation in this verse and the next is cited verbatim from the LXX of Ps 118:22,23. **The stone** is Christ, who was rejected by **the builders,** the religious leaders of the Jews.

13. In 12:13-17 **the Pharisees** and the Herodians question Jesus concerning payment of tribute to Caesar. This combination is unusual, for the Pharisees had little in common with the Herodians. The former were unalterably opposed to any foreign overlordship, while the latter were supporters of the foreign government of the Herods. The one group would have objected to the Roman tax; the other would have favored it. The motive of these incongruous conspirators was ulterior. They sought **to catch him in his words** as a hunter catches his prey.

14. Carest for no man. This was intended to be taken in a complimentary sense, meaning that his teaching was not influenced by what friends or foes thought. The **tribute** in question was a poll tax which had to be paid personally into the Roman treasury. **Is it lawful?** They wanted him to answer concerning the rightness or wrongness of the tax in the eyes of God.

15. Why tempt ye me? The Lord perceived the dilemma into which they sought to draw him. They thought that if he answered in the affirmative, the Jewish people, who hated the poll tax, would rise up and reject him and his claims; but if he replied in the negative, he could be charged with opposition to Rome. **A penny.** This coin was the denarius, with which the tax had to be paid.

17. Render. The verb means *to pay back in full*. It assumes an obligation to **Caesar.** For the privileges provided by the Roman government, the people were indebted to help support that government (cf. Rom 13:1-7). By the same token they were also to pay their obligations to God. And there is no incongruity in paying the two debts, for both payments are for the accomplishment of God's will. Such an answer completely dissolved the anticipated dilemma, with the result that the questioners were completely amazed (**marvelled,** *exethaumazon,* an intensified word for great astonishment).

18. The question of **the Sadducees** (vv. 18-27) quite naturally concerned the **resurrection,** which Jesus taught and they denied. For the Sadducees there was no such thing as existence after death. They also denied the reality of angels and spirits (Acts 23:8).

19. Moses wrote. A free statement of the levirate law of marriage is found in Deut 25:5-10. If a man died without children, his brother was to marry his wife, and the first son of that union was then considered the child of the dead husband.

23. The problem which is raised seems unanswerable. **In the resurrection . . . whose wife shall she be . . . ?** The possibility of a resurrection is only assumed by the Sadducees as a basis for their argument. The purpose of the question was to attempt to prove the impossibility of a resurrection by reducing it to an absurdity.

24. Err. The Greek verb means *to lead astray*. They were being led astray (or, they were leading themselves astray) for two reasons. One, they did not understand what the OT Scriptures taught concerning resurrection (cf. vv. 26,27). Two, they underestimated **the power of God** to raise the dead and to resolve all seeming difficulties connected with the idea of a resurrection.

25. With this one statement of fact Jesus swept away their apparent problem. They had erroneously assumed the continuation of marriage relationships after the resurrection. Instead, Christ explained, people will have the same relations as **the angels.** There will be no need for conjugal union nor the reproduction of children.

26. The question, **have ye not read,** expects an affirmative answer, for Christ knew well that these Sadducees were thoroughly familiar with the Pentateuch. He referred specifically to Ex 3:6, quoting the LXX.

27. The truth demonstrated here is the fact of immortality. To be the God of Abraham is to be in fellowship with Abraham. It is therefore not possible to be **the God of the dead,** but only **of the living.** Thus when God spoke out of the burning bush, though the patriarchs had been dead for years, he was still in fellowship with them. The argument of Christ then assumes that since there is life after death, this is sufficient to prove that resurrection will follow. Perfect human existence demands the union of soul with body.

28. The question concerning the chief commandment (vv. 28-34) came from **one of the scribes.** He, no doubt, was a Pharisee, for he approved of Jesus' answer to the Sadducees. There seems to be no ulterior motive in this inquiry (cf. vv. 28,32-34).

29,30. Jesus does not go to the traditions of the scribes for his reply, but to the written Law, to Deut 6:4,5. The quotation is taken from the LXX, with the addition of the words **and with all thy mind.** The **mind** and the **heart** are really one and the same in Hebrew thought. The words, **Hear O Israel; The Lord our God is one Lord,** from the creed known as the "Shema" and recited daily by devout Jews. It asserts the distinctive principle of Hebrew faith, that **God is one.** The meaning of this command to **love the Lord** is that he is to be loved with all man's powers and capacities. This is the foundation and the summary of man's total duty to God.

31. The second commandment is quoted verbatim from Lev 19:18 (LXX). Here, likewise, is the basis and the sum of man's obligation to man. These two commandments are foundational to the teachings of all the Law and the Prophets (Mt 22:40).

34. Discreetly. That is, with intelligence. Christ declared the man to have the kind of spiritual understanding which, if persisted in, would lead him into **the kingdom of God.** The present, spiritual kingdom, which is entered by faith and new birth, is in mind here (cf. Jn 3:3,5). Mark closes his account of this discussion with a strong statement showing how completely Christ had silenced his opponents. **No man** was daring to question him any longer. Never again did they attempt to trap Christ with a theological or legal conundrum.

35. However, Christ had not yet finished with his opponents. He had a question for them concerning the relationship of David to the Messiah (vv. 35-40). The citation of the teaching of **the scribes** represents the standard Jewish view that the Messiah would be a descendant of David.

36. The quotation is taken from Ps 110:1 (LXX), a passage which the Jews had long recognized as Messianic. By his introduction to the passage, Christ affirmed the Davidic authorship as well as the divine inspiration of the psalm. His purpose in using David's words was to press home from the Scripture itself the truth of the deity of the Messiah.

37. The fact Jesus pointed up was that David called **him Lord.** How, then, can the Messiah be both David's exalted Lord and **his son?** Matthew states that no one was able to answer this question (22:46). Yet, standing before them, the incarnate Son of God, Israel's Messiah, was himself the answer personified. He was a descendant of David "according to the flesh" and the Son of God "according to the spirit of holiness" (Rom 1:3,4).

38. Doctrine. Our word "teaching" represents Mark's meaning more accurately. The **long clothing** was the long flowing robe of a wealthy person or a dignitary. The **salutations** are explained in Mt 23:7.

39. The **uppermost rooms** are better described as the seats (couches) of honor at banquets.

40. In spite of their recognition as honorable community leaders, the scribes were actually guilty of the most despicable kind of dishonesty. They made **long prayers** in the homes of widows to cover up the fact that they were engaged in crooked schemes to deprive them of their very **houses.**

41. Located in the temple area known as the Court of the Women, **the treasury** contained thirteen trumpet-shaped chests for the deposit of gifts and the temple tax. It appears that Jesus continued watching the giving for some time and that he observed a number of wealthy persons making gifts (cf. Gr. imp. tense used with the verbs **beheld** and **cast,** second occurrence).

42. Of the Greek synonyms for poverty, Mark chose a word descriptive of the beggarly condition of a pauper in order to characterize this **poor widow.** She gave an amount equal to **two mites** or a **farthing.** A mite *(lepton)* was the smallest of copper coins, normally equal to one-eighth of a cent (Arndt, p. 473). The farthing *(kodrantēs)* was a Roman coin valued at one-quarter of a cent (Arndt, p. 438).

44. The principle enunciated by our Lord on this occasion is that a gift is to be evaluated not by its size, but by a comparison of the gift with the total amount possessed by the giver. A large donation out of abundance may be less significant than a small donation out of poverty. This woman gave the smallest possible gift, but it was more significant than the others, for it was **all that she had.**

C. The Olivet Apocalypse. 13:1-37. The Olivet Discourse occurred on Tuesday after the conclusion of the controversies in the temple courts with the Jewish leaders. It may be broken down into the following divisions: the questions of the disciples (13:1-4); the conditions characteristic of this present age (13:5-13); the coming crisis (13:14-23); the second advent of Christ (13:24-27); instruction concerning watchfulness (13:28-37).

1. In the light of Josephus' descriptions of the Temple, it is not surprising to find one of the disciples exclaiming concerning the **manner of stones** and the **buildings.** Josephus depicts the stones as being thirty-seven by twelve by eighteen feet in size. He further states that the ". . . front was all of polished stone, insomuch that its fitness, to such as had not seen it, was incredible, and to such as had seen it, was greatly amazing" *(Antiq* XV. xi. 3-5).

2. Jesus used the strong Greek double negative construction *(ou mē)* twice in this verse in order to deny that **one stone** would be left **upon another**. It was positively certain that the Temple would be completely destroyed, a fact confirmed by history when in A.D. 70 under Titus the Temple, along with the city, was laid in ruins.

4. These things. An obvious reference to the prediction stated in 13:2. There is reason to believe, however, that the disciples also had in mind the sequence of end-time events. Their second question amplified the first in that it asked for the sign which would indicate that fulfillment was about *(mellē)* to take place. From Matthew we learn that the disciples also asked concerning the sign of Christ's coming and of the end of the age (24:3).

5. Jesus began his answer by picturing the conditions characteristic of this present age (vv. 5-13). The first is the presence of deceivers, against whom the disciple must **take heed** constantly (Gr., pres. imper.).

6. In my name. These words refer to the coming of false messiahs, who will claim the position and authority that belong to Christ alone. The prediction has been fulfilled on numerous occasions. Perhaps the most outstanding personage making such a claim was Bar Cochba (A.D. 132).

8. Wars are characteristic of the entire age, as are **earthquakes** and **famines.** The word **troubles** is omitted by the better Greek manuscripts. All of these conditions are described as **the beginnings of sorrows.** Thus, they are set in direct contrast to the end (v. 7). The word **sorrows** actually means *birth-pains,* a term used by the Jews to describe the afflictions and woes that are to usher in the coming of the Messiah.

9. The disciple is commanded to **take heed,** that is, to be constantly on the alert (Gr., pres. imper.). **Councils.** Literally *sanhedrins.* The arrests and beatings foretold here begin to find their fulfillment in the book of Acts (cf. 4:5 ff.; 5:27 ff.), as do also the appearances **before rulers and kings** (cf. 12:1 ff.; 24:1 ff.; 25:1 ff.). These appearances were to be **for a testimony** to them *(autois),* not against them, as in the AV. Consider Paul's witness to Felix (Acts 24:24,25) and Agrippa (Acts 26).

10. Another feature of the age is the world-wide preaching of **the gospel.** The end (v. 7) cannot come until the evangelistic task has **first** been accomplished. Matthew 24:14 concludes the saying with the statement, **then shall the end come,** referring to the end of the age.

13. In the midst of all the disturbances, the moral declension, and the persecutions, endurance becomes the mark of spiritual genuineness. **The end.** Since the conditions described in 13:5-13 are age-long, "the end" does not here refer to the end of the age, but rather to the end of life or of the trial. **Be saved.** In this context physical deliverance cannot be meant. The promise is that the one who endures shall be saved spiritually. The endurance, however, is not the basis of the salvation. In keeping with the general teaching of the NT, endurance is to be viewed as the result of the new birth (cf. Rom 8:29-39; I Jn 2:19). A person who has been regenerated, and thus endures, will most surely experience the consummation of the salvation experience.

14. Having pointed out some of the salient features of this age, Christ went on to describe the coming crisis (vv. 14-23). The **abomination of desolation** is an expression taken verbatim from Dan 12:11 (LXX). It is also found with slight variations in Dan 9:27; 11:31. Among the Jews the term **abomination** was used to describe idolatry or sacrilege (cf. Ezk 8:9,10,15,16). It seems, therefore, that both Daniel and Christ were speaking of an appalling profanation of the Temple. The first fulfillment of Daniel's prophetic use of the term, some writers claim, was the erection of an altar to Zeus on the altar of burnt offering at the command of Antiochus Epiphanes in 168 B.C. (I Macc 1:54,59). Christ's use of the words had immediate reference to the profanation of the Temple by the Romans (A.D. 70). It must be remembered that the disciples had asked concerning the destruction of the Temple (Mk 13:2,4). Furthermore, the instructions given in 13:14b-18 seem to fit that occasion best. However, the close relation of these conditions to Christ's second advent (vv. 24-27) demands an additional application to the time of the end. The conditions of the days of Antiochus Epiphanes and of the Roman destruction of the Temple were foreshadowings of the days of the Antichrist immediately prior to Christ's return (cf. II Thess 2:3,4; Rev 13:14,15). **Standing where it ought not.** In the holy place (Mt 24:15). The appearance of the appalling profanation would be a sign for dwellers in Judea to **flee to the mountains** in order to avoid the coming siege. The specific reference of this command, as well as of those in verses 15-18, was to the soon-coming destruction of Jerusalem (A.D. 70).

15,16. The need for haste would be so urgent that there would be no time to tarry **to take anything** for the flight.

17,18. It would be a very difficult time for expectant mothers and those with babes in arms. A flight **in the winter** would add to the difficulties of an already difficult situation.

19. This summary description of the tribulations of **those days** certainly applied to the horrors of A.D. 70, as a comparison with Josephus' *Wars of the Jews* (Preface, 4; V, VI) will show. However, there is reason to believe that Christ looked beyond Roman days to the great final tribulation which will precede his second coming. This is suggested by the words **neither shall be,** which are a translation of a strong Greek denial *(ou mē).*

20. It is not possible to limit this verse to the situation in A.D. 70. None of the suggested explanations based on such a limitation is satisfactory. There are elements here that go beyond that time and are more correctly associated with the end of the age. The reference to 'the elect' seems to point to the saved during the days of the Great Tribulation just prior to Christ's return. For their sake God has **shortened the days** of that period of terrible affliction.

22. So bold will these deceivers be that they will aim to lead astray **even the elect.** However, the clause, **if it were possible,** shows that it is unthinkable that they should succeed. On the identification of **the elect,** see Lk 18:7; Rom 8:33; Col 3:12; I Pet 1:2.

24,25. The prophecy now moves on to the Second Advent (vv. 24-27). Christ specifically placed this great event **in those days after that tribulation,** obviously referring to the time described in 13:14-23. This necessitates one of two explanations. Either Christ was to come shortly after A.D. 70 or the afflictions of verses 14-23 have a double reference, both to the destruction of Jerusalem by Titus and to the Great Tribulation at the end of the age. Since the former explanation is impossible, the latter interpretation is viewed as the key to the understanding of the chapter as a whole. The language used to describe the disturbances in the heavens is largely taken from the OT (cf. Isa 13:10; 34:4; Joel 2:10,30,31). While it is best to avoid an extreme literalism here, there is no reason for not understanding these expressions to refer to actual celestial changes that will immediately precede Christ's coming. It is not at all strange that so momentous an event should be introduced in this manner.

26. This is the personal, bodily return of Christ to the earth **with great power and glory,** which is described in such passages as Acts 1:11; II Thess 1:7-10; 2:8; Rev 1:7; 19:11-16. "Against the background of a darkened heaven, the Son of Man is revealed in the Shekinah glory of God . . . " (G. R. Beasley-Murray, *A Commentary on Mark Thirteen,* p. 89). The language used here is drawn from Dan 7:13. **They shall see.** His coming will be visible to all men.

27. At this point the resurrection of the righteous dead and the transformation of the living saints will occur (cf. I Cor 15:51-53; I Thess 4:13-18). Then he **shall gather together his elect,** the redeemed of all ages, past and present. Concerning the word **elect,** see on 13:22. The word *episynaxei,* **gather together,** is the verb form of the noun *episynagōgē,* "gathering together," in II Thess 2:1. They will be gathered to the descending Lord from every part of the earth **(the four winds),** even from the farthest extremities **(uttermost part of the earth** and **of heaven).**

28,29. Having finished the delineation of future events, the Lord turned to a discussion of the need for watchfulness (vv. 28-37). There is no indication that Israel is symbolized here by the fig tree. Instead, the parable is a simple demonstration of the truth that coming events cast their shadows before them. When these things begin to come to pass, we will know that the consummation is very near. The **things** to which Christ refers are the events described in verses 14-25.

30. The most natural explanation of the expression, **this generation,** is that it refers to the generation of people alive when Christ was speaking. During their lifetime all these things were to come to pass in the destruction of Jerusalem in A.D. 70. This event is employed by Christ as a preliminary picture prefiguring, in all its essential characteristics, the end of the age (cf. Mk 9:1).

32. The exact **day** and **hour** of Christ's return are not humanly discernible. In fact, the time is known only by God the Father. The statement that **the Son** did not know the time of the consummation is to be understood in the light of his self-limitation during the days of his humiliation (cf. Phil 2:5-8). He had assumed a position of complete subjection to the Father, exercising his divine attributes only at the Father's bidding (cf. Jn 8:26, 28,29).

33. Take ye heed. This present tense imperative calls for constant alertness. The same is true of the verb **watch,** which means *to keep oneself awake* (Arndt, pp. 13,14). Such watchfulness is necessary because we do not know when these end-time events may break upon us.

35. The disciple is to **watch** continually (Gr. pres. tense). This verb, as well as that in verse 33, means *to be or keep awake*. It calls for constant alertness as over against sleep or drowsiness (Arndt, p. 166; cf. v. 36). **At even . . . midnight . . . cockcrowing . . . morning.** These are the four watches of the night according to the Roman reckoning.

36. Such watchfulness is necessary lest the Lord come when we do not expect him. This is what he means by finding us **sleeping.** To a person who is not watching, Christ's coming will be sudden. One who is on the alert will see the signs of the Lord's return (vv. 28,29) and will not be taken by surprise.

VII. Christ's Passion and Resurrection. 14:1–16:20.

Mark's narrative moves now into the final scenes of Christ's life on earth. These were the events that surrounded his death and resurrection. They were the acts that would accomplish eternal redemption for all people everywhere who would receive it.

A. Treachery and Devotion. 14:1-11. These verses begin with a description of the treachery with which the priests and scribes plotted Jesus' death (vv. 1,2). In contrast, this is followed by a moving account of the devotion of Mary (vv. 3-9). Then, in even sharper contrast, the Evangelist relates the traitorous plot of Judas to betray the Lord (vv. 10,11).

1. After two days. The point from which these two days were figured was probably late Tuesday afternoon, at which time the Jewish leaders were seeking **how they might take him by craft.** This would place the Passover meal on Thursday evening.

3. The time was Tuesday evening; Christ had returned to **Bethany** to spend the night. We know nothing of **Simon the leper** beyond what is given in these verses, although some have mistakenly identified him with Simon the Pharisee in Lk 7:36-50. **Sat at meat.** That is, reclined on a couch at the table. The **woman** of the story was Mary, the sister of Martha (cf. Jn 12:2,3). The **alabaster box** was a flask with a long neck that was broken off in order to use the contents (Arndt, pp. 33,34). **Ointment of spikenard.** The Greek text is best translated *ointment of genuine nard*. The nard plant was used to make perfume. **Very precious.** The cost was approximately fifty-five dollars for a pound (cf. v. 5).

5. Three hundred pence. That is, three hundred denarii. This was a Roman silver coin worth about eighteen cents. **They murmured.** The verb used here expresses strong emotion, originally meaning *to snort*. A more expressive translation would be, *they began to scold her severely*.

8. He explained the true reason for Mary's action. The deed was not merely an act of devotion, but a conscious intention **to anoint** Christ in anticipation of his approaching death and burial. Because Mary had sat at the feet of Jesus and listened intently to his teaching, she had come to understand, even better than the disciples, the truth of his coming death.

10. Judas' reaction to the rebuke of Jesus was traitorous. A complete analysis of the man's motives for going **unto the chief priests** is not possible with our limited knowledge. Luke explains it by saying that **Satan entered** into him (22:3). We know that his love of money was a partial reason for the betrayal (cf. Mt 26:14,15). It is also possible that he had been disillusioned by Christ's failure to rise up against Rome and establish a free Jewish kingdom.

11. The amount of money they **promised to give him** was thirty pieces of silver (Mt 26:15), which would be worth between twenty and twenty-five dollars. **He sought.** Continuing action (Gr. imp. tense). From this time on Judas was constantly looking for the right moment to **betray him.**

B. The Lord's Passion. 14:12–15:47. Mark's account of Christ's suffering and death may be outlined as follows: the events surrounding the last supper (14:12-25); the journey to Gethsemane (14:26-42); the arrest (14:43-52); the trials (14:53–15:15); the crucifixion (15:16-41); the burial (15:42-47). The usual chronology assumes that Wednesday was spent as a day of rest in Bethany and that the events of the section under consideration occurred on Thursday and Friday. It is not explicitly stated that such a day of rest intervened, but a comparison of the Gospel records makes it necessary to assume that it did.

12. The **first day of unleavened bread** may, at first thought, be taken to be the day after the Passover, or Nisan 15 (cf. Lev 23:5,6). However, Mark makes it plain that he is referring to Nisan 14; he says it was **when they killed the passover** (cf. Ex 12:6). It is known that the Feast of Unleavened Bread was regarded as beginning on the day of the Passover (cf. Jos *Antiq*. II. xv. 1). This was Thursday. The Passover lambs would have been killed in the afternoon, and the Passover meal would have been eaten after sundown on the beginning of Nisan 15.

14. Having followed the servant to the house, the disciples were to make their request of **the goodman of the house** (Gr., *master of the house, householder*). Who the owner was is not known. Some have suggested that the home was that of Mark, but this is speculation. The Greek text also reads, *Where is my guest-chamber?* It seems from the use of the pronoun, that the Lord had previously made arrangements for use of the room. **Eat the passover.** Some, on the basis of certain statements in John's Gospel, suppose that the meal was not the Passover, but one prior to the Passover (cf. Jn 13:1,29; 18:28; 19:14,31). However, it is clear that Mark represents Christ as intending to eat the Passover. Furthermore, the statements in John do not necessarily demand the view that the Last Supper preceded the time of the Passover (A. T. Robertson, *A Harmony of the Gospels,* pp. 279-284).

16. Not only did Christ intend to eat the Passover, but Mark specifically states that the disciples **made ready** the Passover. This would include the killing and roasting of the lamb and provision of the other prescribed items.

17. In the evening. The Passover was eaten after sunset on the beginning of the fifteenth of Nisan.

19. The question, **Is it I?** expected an answer in the negative, and may be translated, *It is not I, is it?* So monstrous a crime seemed incredible to the eleven. Matthew says (26:25) that Judas also asked the question, but this was obviously an attempt to hide his treachery.

20. In the dish. To eat together, and especially to partake of the contents of the common bowl, was a sign of warm friendship. In the light of this custom, Judas' planned betrayal is revealed as still more heinous.

21. As it is written. See on 1:2. The OT passage to which Jesus had reference would seem to be one that describes his betrayal, perhaps Ps 41:9. Notice that God's sovereign purpose, expressed in the words, **it is written,** did not at all free Judas of moral responsibility for his act.

22. At the Passover meal the **bread** which Jesus used would have been the unleavened cakes prescribed for the feast. When Jesus said, **This is my body,** he obviously meant, "This symbolizes my body." His physical body was still present with them. This is similar to the symbolical usage which occurs in Jn 6:35; 8:12; 10:9. The same is true of his statement concerning his blood (Mk 14:24).

23. The cup. We have no way of knowing which of the four Passover cups Jesus used. In any case, however, the contents would have been wine mixed with two-thirds water.

24. The new testament. In both Matthew and Mark the best Greek texts omit the word for **new.** However, see Lk 22:20; I Cor 11:25. While the Greek word *diathēkē* may refer to a testament or will, the OT background of Christ's remark demands the translation, *covenant* (cf. Ex 24:8). This is not the term used to express an agreement between equal parties *(synthēkē).* God alone initiated the terms of the covenant, and man could only accept or reject. The blood of Christ is the blood of the new covenant promised in Jer 31:31-34 (cf. Heb 8:6-13). **For many.** While the Greek preposition, *hyper,* may mean "in behalf of," it is used many times to mean "instead of." Taylor says that this is one of the clearest evidences that Jesus viewed his death as vicarious (Vincent Taylor, *Mark,* p. 548).

25. No more. A strong denial meaning that Jesus would by no means any more drink with them during this present age. The **kingdom of God** in this remark is eschatological, probably referring to association in the Millennial kingdom to be established when Christ returns (Rev 20:4-6).

26. The hymn, according to Passover usage, would have been a portion of the Hallel Psalms (Ps 115–118). The journey to the Garden of Gethsemane on **the mount of Olives** and Christ's three sessions of prayer are recorded in 14:26-42.

27. Be offended. The word originally meant *to catch in a trap or snare.* It came to refer, also, to the act of causing someone to stumble. Jesus said, therefore, that the events of that night would take all of them unawares and prove to be a snare or a stumblingblock. **Because of me this night.** Omitted by a number of the most significant Greek manuscripts. **It is written.** See on 1:2. The quotation is taken from Zech 13:7, being freely translated from the Hebrew text.

30. Christ stressed the immediacy of the occurrence — **this day . . . this night.** Also he addressed Peter with the emphatic personal pronoun, **thou.** Of all the disciples, Peter, though he insisted on his loyalty, would **deny the Lord.** No contradiction is to be imagined with the other Gospels concerning the number of times the **cock** was to **crow.** The others merely state the fact that the denial would come before cock-crowing (the third watch of the night; see on 13:35). Mark gives added detail by mentioning the specific number of times that the cock would crow.

31. He spake. Peter repeatedly affirmed his boast (Gr. imp. tense), and he did so emphatically **(vehemently). In any wise.** An excellent translation of the Greek double negative, *ou mē*, which expresses strong denial. With this, all of the disciples kept agreeing (Gr. imp., *elegon).*

33. Sore amazed. A strong word, expressing deep emotional upset and distress. It has been translated in various ways *(to be completely upset, to be terrified, appalled, deeply agitated).* Mark adds to this the expression, **very heavy** *(adēmonein),* which speaks of bewilderment and distress (MM, p. 9).

34. Jesus was distressed and grieved to the very point of **death.** Hence, he asked them to **watch** (Gr., "to remain awake, alert, and watchful").

35. The hour concerning which Jesus prayed was the time when, in the plan of God, he was to suffer and die as an atonement for sin (cf. Jn 12:23,27; 13:1).

36. Abba is the Aramaic word for "father." **This cup** refers to the same things as **the hour** (v. 35). It was the cup of a suffering and death which were more than physical. The agony from which the Lord shrank was the agony of soul resulting from bearing the guilt of a lost world. The suffering was to be spiritual suffering, a separation from God the Father (cf. Mk 15:34). And it was concerning this that Christ prayed asking that the cup might be removed if it was possible for God to accomplish his redemptive purpose by some other means. Nevertheless he was in perfect submission to the Father, desiring his will alone.

38. Here the Lord adds the command to **pray** (Gr., *keep praying)* in order that they might not **enter into temptation.** This danger must be interpreted as specifically referring to the coming testings associated with the Lord's arrest and death.

40. Heavy. Literally, their eyes were *weighted down* with sleep. The old English word **wist** meant *knew.* They had no excuse.

41. He came to them **the third time** after praying once more (Mt 26:44). It is difficult to know in what sense Jesus meant the remark concerning sleeping and resting. Some take it as a question (RSV); others see in it a "kind of sad bitterness" (Ezra P. Gould, *Mark,* pp. 271,272). Now that he had emerged from the darkness of the hour, he no longer needed the assurance that they were in some sense facing the trial with him. This seems to be the thought behind the words, **It is enough. Is betrayed.** The present tense which should be translated *is being betrayed,* signifies that the betrayal was taking place at that very moment.

43. The following verses (43-52) recount the arrest of Christ. The mob was led by **Judas,** who knew that Jesus often retired to the seclusion of Gethsemane (Jn 18:2). The **multitude** included some of the Roman cohort garrisoned in Jerusalem as well as the temple police (Jn 18:3). No doubt the soldiers were armed **with swords** and the temple police with **staves** (clubs). The **chief priests, the scribes,** and **the elders** were the three groups of which the Sanhedrin was composed, indicating that the arresting party had been officially dispatched by that body.

45. Judas, in mock respect, played the part of a loyal disciple, greeting his teacher as **Master** (Gr., *rabbi)* and then kissing him fervently. The Greek verb for the latter act is a strengthened form of the word translated "kiss" in verse 44. By this intensified act of mock devotion Judas only added to his guilt.

48. Christ rebuked them for treating him as though he were an armed robber or highwayman (**thief,** AV).

49. This arrest in an out-of-the-way place under cover of darkness was entirely unnecessary, since he had been **in**

the temple teaching every day. By this protest Christ pointed out the absurdity of their procedures, thus undercutting their reasons for arrest and trial. Yet God had foreseen their actions and predicted the course of events in **the scriptures** (for example, cf. Isa 53:8,9,12). Therefore, regardless of the logic of Christ's protests, the arrest would issue in trial and the trial in execution.

51. A certain young man. The Greek word *neaniskos* was used of men between twenty-four and forty years of age (Arndt, p. 536). No other Gospel records this incident. Consequently we have no further information concerning the person's identity. It has often been suggested, perhaps correctly, that Mark was making a veiled reference to himself. There seems to be no other reason why this insignificant event was included.

52. Naked. The word *gymnos* does not necessarily mean naked; it was also used to describe a person clothed only in an undergarment.

53. Here the account turns to the Jewish and Roman trials of Christ (14:53—15:15). Mark moves immediately to the account of the night trial before the Sanhedrin (vv. 53-65). That the examining body was the Sanhedrin is shown by the presence of **all the chief priests and the elders and the scribes.** The high priest at this time was Caiaphas.

54. Perhaps because he was determined to fulfill his boast of loyalty, **Peter followed** Jesus. However, fear held him at a distance, and as a result he was not able to slip into the house of the high priest with the crowd. Mark's word translated **palace** is *aulēn* and actually refers to a courtyard. John explains (18:15, 16) that another disciple secured an entrance for Peter. **The servants** with whom **he sat** were probably temple police and attendants of the high priest.

55. The word translated **council** is *synedrion,* from which the word "sanhedrin" comes. They carried on a prolonged search *(ezētoun,* imp. tense) for witnesses against Jesus. These members of the Jewish court were acting as prosecutors.

58,59. These persons were speaking of Christ's remark during his early Judean ministry on the occasion of the first cleansing of the Temple (Jn 2:19). The falsity of their witness was evidenced by their misuse of the statement and by their failure to agree.

60. Embarrassed by the disagreement of the witnesses, **the high priest** attempted to involve Christ in the discussion, apparently hoping that his answer would prove his guilt.

61. The question, **Art thou the Christ?** places the personal pronoun in the emphatic position; it may be rendered, *You, are you the Messiah?* It was common for the Jews to use some such term as **the Blessed** when referring to God, in order that they might not become guilty of taking the divine name in vain. Matthew makes it clear (26:63) that the high priest placed Jesus under solemn oath, which made it obligatory for him to answer. He had no way out but to bear witness which would be turned against him.

62. With a forthright assertion, Jesus answered, **I am.** The remainder of his reply is couched in terms taken from Dan 7:13 and Ps 110:1. The **right hand of power** is the right hand of God. Christ assured his judges that the day would come when they would see him as Messiah, exercising the power of deity and coming in judgment (see on 13:26).

63. This was the kind of reply desired by the high priest. He promptly **rent his clothes,** as he was required to do at the sound of blasphemy (cf. H. B. Swete, *Mark,* pp. 359,360). No **further witnesses** were needed, since Jesus had been forced to bear witness against himself, an illegal procedure under Jewish law.

64. The declaration of Christ was interpreted as **blasphemy** because the officials viewed Jesus as a mere man (cf. Jn 10:33). The question of his guilt was put to the whole council, and they unanimously **condemned him to be guilty.** The established penalty for blasphemy was **death** (Lev 24:16).

65. Apparently it was **some** of the members of the Sanhedrin who began to treat Jesus in the shameful manner described. For such highly placed, respected religious leaders of Judaism, the acts of these dignitaries were most degrading. They covered **his face** with a blindfold when they struck him in order to make a mockery of his supernatural knowledge (cf. Lk 22:64). When he was turned over to **the servants** (the temple police), these followed the example of the officials and began to **strike him.** The word *rapisma* refers either to a blow with a rod or to a slap with the palm of the hand.

67. Looked upon him. The word indicates that she fixed her gaze on him. Because of John's intercession for Peter Jn 18:15,16), the maid no doubt was sure that Peter was a follower of Jesus.

68. Peter's denial was strengthened by repetition (**know not, neither understand**). Caught by the unexpected identification, he forgot his boast of loyalty. The **porch** to which Peter withdrew was the forecourt or vestibule leading from the street into the courtyard. Many ancient texts omit the words, **and the cock crew.**

69. The Greek text indicates that this was the same **maid** who had previously accused Peter. However, Mt 26:71 speaks of another maid, while Lk 22:58 states that another person (masculine) addressed Peter directly. It is not necessary to find contradictions among the accounts here. There were evidently two maids, the doorkeeper and another, who pointed Peter out to the bystanders. In addition, a man said to Peter, "You also are one of them."

70. The third accusation came from several persons who stood by. There were probably a number of statements made, as the imperfect tense *elegon* may well show. John 18:26 reveals that one of those making accusations was a relative of the person whose ear Peter had cut off.

71. To curse and to swear. These verbs do not mean that Peter used profanity as the term is understood today. Instead, he called down a **curse** probably upon himself (RSV), if he was not telling the truth, and he placed himself under oath in making his denial.

72. Here the manuscript evidence justifies the inclusion of the words, **the second time** (see on v. 68). The best texts also contain the word "immediately" *(euthys)*. The sound of the cock followed hard on the third denial, striking deep into the consciousness of the fallen disciple. At the same time Peter saw Jesus looking down upon him (Lk 22:61) from a room above the courtyard. **He thought thereon.** The word *epibalōn* has long been a problem of translation here. Probably the RSV rendering, *he broke down,* is best (MM, p. 235; Taylor, *Mark,* p. 576). Whereas *epibalōn* describes the onset of the weeping, the imperfect tense *eklaien,* **he wept,** depicts the continuation of it.

15:1. This verse describes a second meeting of the Sanhedrin very early in the morning. Luke 22:66-71 gives a fuller record of this phase of the Jewish trial. It appears to have been an attempt to make the condemnation legal, since it was illegal to hold a trial at night. At this time the Romans did not permit the Jews to inflict the sentence of capital punishment. Consequently it was necessary to take Jesus **to Pilate,** who was the Roman procurator over Judea.

2. The Roman trial is described in 15:2-15. For a more complete account of the Roman trial see Jn 18:28–19:16. One of the charges was that Jesus claimed to be a **king,** and it was out of this allegation that Pilate's question grew. A claim to kingship was ground for trial for treason. Jesus' reply, **Thou sayest,** is capable of being variously interpreted. However, in the light of Jn 18:34-38 it seems best to understand it as an affirmative answer, which, as John shows, was accompanied by an explanation as to what kind of a king Jesus claimed to be.

3,4. These verses picture **the chief priests** as they threw a barrage of accusations against Jesus. So vicious was the attack that **Pilate** could not understand the calm demeanor of the prisoner (cf. v. 5).

6. The governor had established a practice of releasing **one prisoner** each year at the Passover, perhaps as an attempt to maintain the good will of the Jews. The verbs **he released** and **they desired** (Gr., *asked)* are both in the imperfect tense, showing that these were customary acts; i.e., "He used to release . . . ."

7. The prisoner **Barabbas** was no mere petty thief. He was a robber (Jn 18:40), as well as an insurrectionist and a murderer. It appears that the man was a Jew who had participated in an uprising against Rome, a very similar crime to that of which the Jews were accusing Jesus (Ezra P. Gould, *Mark*, p. 285).

8. Crying aloud. The better ancient manuscripts read *anabas,* "went up" (ASV). The crowd asked Pilate to perform his customary act **(had ever done;** Gr. imp. tense) of releasing a prisoner. It seems that the crowd was requesting the release of Barabbas, since he may well have been a kind of hero to them because of his part in the rebellion against Rome.

11. At this point the crowd might have been tempted to request the release of Jesus, but the priests **moved the people** to ask for Barabbas. The word *anaseiō* means "to incite, to stir up," or more literally, *to shake up,* showing their excited agitation of the mob.

15. Willing to content the people. The Greek expression *(to hikanon poiēsai)* implies that he was willing to satisfy the Jews, even if he had to sacrifice an innocent man to do it. **Scourged.** This act was accomplished with a whip made of strips of leather having rough pieces of metal tied at the ends of the strips. The victim was bent forward over a short post, and the punishment was administered to his naked back. Often the resultant deep gashes opened the flesh to the very bone.

16. It was not yet 9:00 A.M. The trial before Pilate was followed very shortly by the crucifixion (15:16-41). **The soldiers** to whom Jesus was committed were Roman military personnel under the jurisdiction of Pilate. **The hall.** The Greek word is *aulē*, "courtyard," the same as in 14:54, where it is translated "palace" (AV). Mark explains that it was **called Praetorium,** a term which could well refer either to the palace of Herod or to the fortress of Antonia, where the Roman troops were quartered (cf. Arndt, p. 704). At any rate, it seems to refer to the soldiers' barracks. The **band** was a Roman cohort containing approximately six hundred men. However, the figure varied with the situation, and in this instance could have been much less.

19. The three verbs, **smote, spit,** and **worshipped,** are all in the imperfect tense, depicting the repetition of these acts. Soldier after soldier made bitter mockery of Jesus' misunderstood claim to be a king.

21. John 19:17 explains that as the procession set out for the execution, Jesus was bearing his own cross. Shortly, however, the soldiers came upon **Simon** and forced him to carry the instrument of execution. This man's identity was evidently known by Mark's Roman readers, for Mark mentions his sons, **Alexander and Rufus,** as familiar persons. There was a Rufus in Rome when Paul wrote the Epistle to the Romans (16:13).

22. Golgotha is an Aramaic word meaning *a skull*. The place was probably so named by reason of its shape. The traditional site, still favored by many, is at the Church of the Holy Sepulcher. Others insist on the hill known as Gordon's Calvary. In the interests of objectivity we must admit that, at the present time, sure identification of the spot is impossible.

23. Gave. The imperfect tense, *edidoun,* is better translated *they were going to give*. Jesus refused the drink after tasting it and discovering what it was (Mt 27:34). **Myrrh** served as a drug administered to deaden the torture of the horrible death of crucifixion. Jesus, however, refused to allow such a stupifying potion to cloud his senses.

24. The details of the crucifixion are absent from all of the Gospels. It is known from Jn 20:25 that nails were used to fasten the hands to the cross. Crucifixion was recognized as being one of the most cruel forms of execution employed in the ancient world. Often the victim was left on the cross for several days before death relieved his intense suffering. The **garments** of the condemned man were left to the executioners.

25. The time of the crucifixion is placed at **the third hour,** which was the Jewish designation for 9:00 A.M. The trial before Pilate occurred about the sixth hour, according to Roman time, which would be 6:00 A.M. (cf. Jn 19:14).

26. It was customary to use a placard of some kind indicating the name and the **accusation** of the condemned man. Mark gives only the crime of which Jesus was accused. John indicates that **the superscription** also contained the identification, **Jesus of Nazareth** (19:19). There is no contradiction; Mark is merely more concise.

27. The two criminals crucified with Jesus were more than mere petty **thieves.** As in 14:48, *lēstēs* means "robber, highwayman."

29,30. Railed on him. The passers-by kept blaspheming (*eblasphēmoun,* imp. tense) Jesus. **Wagging their heads.** They shook their heads in scornful disapproval. The logic behind their sarcasm was an argument from the greater to the lesser. If he could rebuild the Temple in three days, certainly he could easily **come down from the cross.**

31. The **chief priests** and **the scribes** likewise participated in the mockery, but among themselves. Their oft-repeated sarcasm concerning Christ's inability to save himself was in reality a denial that he could help anybody. If he could not deliver himself from suffering and death, how could he deliver anyone else?

33. Three hours had passed; it was now noon, **the sixth hour.** At the hour of the sun's brightest light, **darkness** came (*egeneto*) **over the whole land.** This could not have been a total eclipse so that the whole earth was darkened, as Lenski argues (Lenski, *Interpret. of Mark*, pp. 713-714), for the Passover occurred at the time of the full moon, when no such eclipse is possible. What caused the darkness is not stated. Certainly the timing of the phenomenon was supernatural. The **ninth hour** was 3:00 P.M. (see on v. 25).

34. Jesus had been on the cross for six hours. His cry was a quotation from Ps 22:1. **Eloi, Eloi, lama sabachthani** is a transliteration from Aramaic, the native tongue of Christ. Mark, as his custom was, gave the meaning of the Aramaic for his Roman readers. This cry of abandonment provides a glimpse into the inner sufferings of Christ on the cross. His greatest agony was not physical; it was rather agony of soul as he bore the guilt of the world's sin. The sense in which God had **forsaken** Christ was that the Father withdrew from communion with the Son. No longer did he evidence his love toward his Son. Instead, Christ had become the object of the Father's displeasure, for he was the sinner's Substitute. Christ became "sin for us" (II Cor 5:21), and a holy God cannot look with favor upon sin.

36. The **vinegar** was a sour wine that quenched thirst more readily than water (Arndt, pp. 577,578). Since this was not a drugged mixture as in verse 23, Jesus received it without protest (cf. Jn 19:29,30). **Whether Elias will come.** There is no reason for assuming that the speakers were sincere in their words. This was no doubt a continuation of the mockery that is so evident in 15:29-32.

37. Gave up the ghost. The Greek word is *exepneusen,* which literally means that he *breathed out* or *expired.* It was not a prolonged struggle, such as the imperfect tense would describe. Instead, the aorist tense depicts a brief, momentary occurrence. He breathed out his spirit and was gone.

38. The veil was the heavy curtain that separated the Holy Place from the Holy of Holies in **the temple** *(naos,* "sanctuary"). For a description see Josephus *Wars of the Jews* V. v. 4. The rent moved **from the top to the bottom,** perhaps pointing to the divine origin of the occurrence. Its timing was significant. Since this was the hour of the evening sacrifice, the rending of the veil could not have happened unnoticed. The significance of the opening of the Holy of Holies is set forth in Heb 9:7,8; 10:19-22.

39. A **centurion** normally had one hundred men under his command. In this instance the officer was in charge of the smaller detachment assigned to the crucifixion. **Over against him.** That is, he stood facing the cross. The centurion's declaration that Jesus **was the Son of God** ought not to be taken in the full Christian sense. In the first place, the article does not appear in the Greek text. It should, therefore, read "a son of God" or, at the most, "God's Son." The pagan background of the Roman officer must not be overlooked. He may well have viewed Jesus as a superhuman being, but that he possessed the full Christian concept of the deity of Christ is unlikely. Furthermore, Luke records that he declared Jesus to be **a righteous man** (23:47). For a forceful presentation of the opposite view, see Lenski, *Interpretation of Mark,* pp. 725-727.

40. Mary Magdalene is not to be confused with Mary of Bethany (Jn 12:1 ff.) nor with the sinful woman of Lk 7:37. She came from Magdala in Galilee, and she had experienced deliverance from demon possession at the command of Jesus (Lk 8:2). The second **Mary** seems to have been the mother of James the son of Alphaeus, one of the disciples (Mk 3:18). **Salome** is described as the mother of James and John, the sons of Zebedee (Mt 27:56).

42. The account of the Passion closes with a description of the burial of Jesus (vv. 42-47). **The even was come.** The evening referred to here must of necessity have been the early evening, between the hour of the evening sacrifice (3:00 P.M.) and sunset (about 6:00 P.M.). The arrangements for burial had to be made before the beginning of **the sabbath** at sundown (cf. Jn 19:31-37). Notice Mark's explanation of the Jewish term, **the preparation,** for his Gentile readers.

43. We know nothing about **Joseph of Arimathaea** except what the Gospels present in connection with this event (cf. Mt 27:57; Lk 23:51; Jn 19:38). **Craved.** That is, he requested *(aiteō)* the body.

46. The **fine linen** was wound around the body of Jesus in strips (cf. Jn 19:40, Gr. text). The **sepulchre** had been **hewn out** of the rock by a stonecutter, a common practice in that vicinity. Matthew states that the tomb belonged to Joseph and that it was new (27:60). The **stone** which was **rolled** before the door was probably a flat, circular slab which rolled in a channel carved out of the rock for that purpose.

C. The Lord's Resurrection. 16:1-20. The last chapter of the Gospel falls into two clearly distinguished sections. The visit of the three women to the tomb occupies 16:1-8. The remainder of the chapter, 16:9-20, forms a summary of the resurrection appearances of Christ, concluding with his ascension.

1. Since **the sabbath** ended at sundown, it appears that the three women mentioned in 15:40 went to one of the shops that had been opened again for the evening and purchased the desired materials. The **sweet spices** *(arōmata)* were in a liquid form, such as perfumed oil, for the women planned to anoint the body of Jesus.

2. Very early. John says that it was still dark (20:1), whereas Mark states that it was **at the rising of the sun.** The apparent conflict is easily resolved if we assume that the women began their journey while it was yet dark and arrived at the tomb just after the sun had risen.

4. When they looked. The word is *anablepō*, meaning "to look up." Perhaps as they approached they were walking with bowed heads.

5. Mark reports that **they saw a young man.** Matthew describes the person as an angel who had removed the stone (28:2-4). And Luke says there were two men in dazzling clothes (24:4). The variety is evidence that these are the reports of several eyewitnesses, each of whom described what impressed her most. The full story would include the appearance of two angels, one of whom rolled the stone away and spoke to the women. **Affrighted.** The word is more accurately translated as *utterly amazed*. Lenski uses the word "dumbfounded" *(Interpret. of Mark,* p. 742).

6. Be not affrighted. It should be rendered, *Stop being utterly amazed.* The angel assured them that Jesus had **risen** and left, in proof of which he called their attention to **the place where they laid him.** John 20:6,7 informs us that the grave cloths (ASV) were still there in their place.

7. Notice how **Peter** is singled out in the arrangement for a meeting in **Galilee.** By this means the fallen disciple was assured that Christ had not rejected him as a result of his denials (14:66-72). Comparison with the other Gospels shows that the disciples did not leave at once for Galilee and that Christ first appeared to Peter (Lk 24:34) and then to the disciples that evening (Lk 24:36). The meeting in Galilee is recorded in Mt 28:16-20.

8. They trembled and were amazed. Mark's original is much stronger. He says, ". . . trembling and astonishment were gripping them." It is no wonder that they **fled from the sepulchre.** The statement that they said nothing **to any man** must be understood in the light of the other Gospels. They said nothing to anyone along the way, for they were afraid and in a hurry to take the news to the disciples (cf. Mt 28:8; Lk 24:9,10).

Textual note, 16:9-20. In the two most trustworthy manuscripts of the Greek NT (the Vaticanus and Sinaiticus) the Gospel ends with 16:8, as it does also in several early versions. Both Eusebius and Jerome state that the ending was missing from most of the manuscripts of their day. In addition, several texts and versions offer a shorter substitute in the place of 16:9-20. By far the greater number of manuscripts have the longer conclusion, but many of them are of a late date and an inferior quality. By the recognized standards of textual evaluation, both the longer and shorter endings must be rejected, and this is the judgment of almost all textual scholars. Lenski is one of the few commentators who argue for the longer ending *(Interpret. of Mark,* pp. 750-755). In addition, an examination of verses 9-20 cannot fail to impress the careful student with the fact that these verses differ markedly in style from the rest of the Gospel. Perhaps the most acceptable explanation is that the end of the original Gospel may have been torn off and lost before additional copies could be made. Perhaps others attempted to supply a substitute ending, the most successful of which was that which now appears in 16:9-20.

9-11. The original account, which is here summarized, is to be found in Jn 20:11-18. Notice the author's emphasis on the unbelief of the disciples (Mk 16:11, 13,14).

12,13. For a more complete record of this event, see Lk 24:13-35. **In another form.** Luke 24:16 says that their eyes were somehow affected so that they did not recognize Christ. Whether Christ had actually changed his appearance we do not know. The **residue** were the eleven disciples in Jerusalem (Lk 24:33).

14-18. This appearence to **the eleven** followed immediately upon the report of the Emmaus travelers (Lk 24:36-49; Jn 20:19-25). Luke and John do not create the impression that Jesus scolded them for **their unbelief and hardness of heart,** but that he recognized how hard it was for them to believe, and he sought to remove their difficulty by offering proofs of his resurrection. **He that believeth and is baptized.** This verse has been used by some to attempt to prove that baptism is necessary for salvation. In the first place, the fact that the statement appears only in this questionable conclusion to the book of Mark should indicate the need for caution in the use of the verse as a proof-text. And then, it should be noted that in the second half of the verse the only basis for condemnation is a refusal to believe. It may therefore be concluded that the only basis of salvation is belief. Such an interpretation is in full harmony with the teaching of the NT as a whole on the subject (cf. Rom 3:28; Eph 2:8,9). The statement concerning casting out demons **(devils)** and speaking with **new tongues** (v. 17) could well have reference to occurrences in the early church as recorded in Acts. Even the words about taking up **serpents** may be an allusion to Paul's experience in Acts 28:1-6. The NT contains no other passage dealing with drinking poison **(any deadly thing)**. Even if this passage were unquestionably genuine, it could not reasonably be used as a basis for the deliberate and presumptuous handling of snakes and drinking of poison which are practiced by certain extreme religious sects.

19,20. This final summary is concerned with the ascension of Christ and the continuing ministry of his followers. The phrase, **after the Lord had spoken,** may seem to imply that Christ's ascension occurred immediately after his appearance to the eleven on the evening of the day of his resurrection (vv. 14-18). However, a comparison with Lk 24:50-53 and Acts 1:1-11 shows that forty days had elapsed since his death. The closing verse of the Gospel could well serve as a very brief summary of the book of Acts. **The Lord . . . confirming the word.** Note the striking resemblance to Heb 2:4.

BIBLIOGRAPHY

Alford, Henry. *The Greek Testament*. Revised by Everett F. Harrison. Vol. I. Chicago: Moody Press, 1958.

Beasley-Murray, G. R. *A Commentary on Mark Thirteen*. London: Macmillan and Co. Ltd., 1957.

Branscomb, Harvie. *The Gospel of Mark (The Moffatt New Testament Commentary)*. London: Hodder and Stoughton Ltd., 1952.

Bruce, Alexander B. "The Synoptic Gospels," *The Expositor's Greek Testament*. Edited by W. Robertson Nicoll. Vol. I. Grand Rapids: Wm. B. Eerdmans Publishing Co., n.d.

Earle, Ralph. *The Gospel According to Mark (The Evangelical Commentary on the Bible)*. Grand Rapids: Zondervan Publishing House, 1957.

Gould, Ezra P. *The Gospel According to St. Mark (The International Critical Commentary)*. Edinburgh: T. & T. Clark, 1948.

Grant, Frederick C. and Luccock, H. E. "The Gospel According to St. Mark," *The Interpreter's Bible*. Vol. 7. New York: Abingdon-Cokesbury Press, 1951.

Lenski, R. C. H. *The Interpretation of St. Mark's Gospel*. Columbus: The Wartburg Press, 1951.

Robertson, A. T. *Word Pictures in the New Testament*. Vol. I. New York: Harper & Brothers, 1930.

Swete, Henry B. *The Gospel According to St. Mark*. London: Macmillan and Co. Ltd., 1953.

Taylor, Vincent. *The Gospel According to St. Mark*. London: Macmillan and Co. Ltd., 1953.

Vincent, Marvin R. *Word Studies in the New Testament*. Vol. I. Grand Rapids: Wm. B. Eerdmans Publishing Co., 1946.

Wuest, Kenneth S. *Mark in the Greek New Testament*. Grand Rapids: Wm. B. Eerdmans Publishing Co., 1950.

THE GOSPEL ACCORDING TO LUKE

INTRODUCTION

The Gospel according to Luke is the most complete account of the life of Jesus that has survived from the apostolic age. It was designed to be a full presentation of the career of the Saviour from his birth to his ascension, and was part of a larger work including the book of Acts, which carried the history forward into the missionary activity of the church as far as the establishment of the Christian community in Rome.

Author. According to the uniform testimony of the church, Luke, a Gentile physician and companion of Paul, was the author of the Third Gospel. His name is not mentioned in its pages, but the consensus of available evidence tends to confirm the tradition.

The close relation of the Gospel to the Acts shows that the two works had a common author, and that whatever clues to his identity can be furnished by the one will apply to the interpretation of the other. Both works were addressed to the same man, Theophilus (Lk 1:3; Acts 1:1). The content of Luke fits perfectly the description of "the former treatise" mentioned in the introduction of Acts (Acts 1:1). The continuity of style and of teaching on the person of Christ, the dominant emphasis on the work of the Holy Spirit, the pervasive interest in ministry to the Gentiles, and the writer's constant awareness of contemporary historical events point to a designed unity.

On this basis, the facts supplied by Acts concerning its author will apply also to the Gospel. The author was a Gentile convert, possibly of the church at Antioch, where Paul served with Barnabas at the beginning of his ministry (Acts 11:25, 26). The writer joined him later at Troas, as his use of the pronoun "we" indicates (Acts 16:10), accompanied him to Philippi, and presumably remained there while Paul visited Jerusalem. When Paul returned to Philippi, Luke went back with him to Jerusalem (Acts 20:5–21:15), where Paul was arrested and placed in protective custody. At the close of Paul's detention in Caesarea, Luke accompanied him to Rome (Acts 27:1–28:15).

Paul speaks of Luke three times in his epistles, calling him "the beloved physician" (Col 4:14; Phm 24), and indicating later that he was the last friend to remain with him in his second imprisonment (II Tim 4:11).

Paul's statement that Luke was a physician is corroborated by the language Luke uses and by the interest he shows in disease and in healing. An outstanding example of his bent of mind appears in the difference between his account and that of Mark regarding the woman with an issue of blood (Lk 8:43; Mk 5:26). He diagnoses the woman's case as incurable, whereas Mark emphasizes the helplessness of the physicians.

Luke's ministry was broad. Doctor, pastor, traveling evangelist, historian, and writer, he was tremendously versatile and active. He had a wide acquaintance with the Christian leaders of the first century, and he seems to have had important special connections also with Roman officials.

Tradition has preserved a few interesting legends about him, though they may not be authentic. According to these stories, Luke was an artist, who painted a picture of the Virgin Mary. He never married, and in his later years retired to Bithynia, where he died. Other legends say that he was martyred in Greece.

Sources. The content of Luke bears a general resemblance to that of Matthew and of Mark because all three of the Synoptic Gospels deal with the common occurrences of the life of Jesus. Probably a large portion of Luke's narrative which coincides with the content of Matthew and Mark may be derived from the narrative preaching of the apostolic missionaries. One widely accepted theory adds that Luke used Mark's Gospel and a special discourse source in much the same fashion as Matthew did. According to his own testimony he knew of other accounts (Lk 1:1,2), but how much he used them is uncertain. A great deal of Luke's material, however, is unique. His story of the events relating to the birth of Christ differs from that of Matthew in viewpoint and in some details. He selects more of Jesus' story parables than do Matthew and Mark, and he puts greater stress on individual characters in his narrative. In the discussion of the Resurrection he introduces the walk to Emmaus, which none of the other Gospels contains in full.

These unique features he must have obtained from eyewitnesses, for he was not personally present at the events he describes. In his introduction he states that he did so (Lk 1:2), and later in the Gospel he mentions persons from whom he could have derived his information. Mary, the mother of Jesus, may have supplied the content of the first two chapters; Mary Magdalene, Joanna the wife of Chuza (Herod's steward), and other women (8:3) could have given him many personal reminiscences. If Luke traveled in Palestine during Paul's imprisonment at Caesarea, he could have interviewed countless people who would have remembered hearing Jesus preach and teach. From the preaching of Paul and of other apostles whom he heard, he could have drawn much of the doctrinal application that appears both in the Gospel and in Acts.

Date. Because of the abrupt ending of the book of Acts, it seems likely that Luke concluded his writing at the end of Paul's two years' imprisonment at Rome. If the Gospel was written previously, as the introduction to Acts indicates (Acts 1:1), it must have been composed, at the latest, prior to A.D. 62, when the Roman imprisonment ended. Perhaps Luke gathered the material for it during his ten years of service with Paul, and then, before leaving Palestine with Paul on the journey to Rome, he sent it from Caesarea to his friend Theophilus. If so, the Gospel could have been written as early as A.D. 58. The allusion to a siege and capture of Jerusalem (Lk 21:20-24) has been interpreted by some to mean that the Gospel must have been written after the fall of the city in A.D. 70. Such a conclusion is not necessary if one considers that the content of the chapter is a prophecy, and that Luke is merely recording the words of Jesus about the future.

The affinity in language between Luke's account of the Last Supper (22:14-23) and Paul's summary (I Cor 11:23-26) may indicate that Luke was repeating the words which Paul himself used on numerous occasions. If so, the composition and publication of the Gospel would be related more closely to the time of Paul than to a period of thirty or more years later.

Place. No clue to the place of publication is given to us. One tradition connects the Gospel with Greece, possibly Athens. Another suggestion would place it in Antioch of Syria, where Luke's friends may have lived. Caesarea seems to be the most likely place of composition, but the Gospel might have been completed and sent to Theophilus from Rome, if not from Caesarea itself.

Destination. Theophilus, to whom the Gospel was addressed, was probably a Gentile of high social standing. Luke salutes him with the title, "most excellent," which he reserves elsewhere in his writings for Roman officials (Acts 24:3; 26:25; AV, *most noble).* Nothing is known of him directly beyond the two allusions in Luke 1:3 and Acts 1:1. He was a Christian convert, interested in knowing more about his new faith than he could learn from mere routine instruction. Luke's two treatises were designed to make him an intelligent believer.

The Development of the Thought. The Gospel of Luke unfolds the career of Jesus as one would present its high lights to an audience through a moving picture. It begins with his ancestry and birth, continues through his earthly ministry to the Passion, and comes to a climax in the Resurrection. Acts continues his work in the church through the Holy Spirit down to Paul's arrival at Rome. The Gospel, then, is devoted to the first half of this progressive presentation of the person of Christ.

The structure of Luke follows the same general order as that of Matthew and Mark, since that is determined by the life of Christ itself. The presentation of the facts is fuller in some respects, but is less topical than Matthew's and is more flowing than Mark's.

Summary of Message. The message of Luke's Gospel can be summarized in Jesus' words to Zacchaeus as Luke records them: "For the Son of man is come to seek and to save that which was lost" (19:10). The character and purpose of Jesus as Saviour are the main theme of this book. The activity and teaching of Jesus in Luke are focused on lifting men out of their sins and bringing them back to life and hope. The miracles, the parables, the teachings, and the acts of Jesus exemplify his redemptive power and will.

The concept of Jesus as Son of man emphasizes his humanity and his compassionate feeling for all men. He was to be "a light to lighten the Gentiles, and the glory of . . . Israel" (2:32). Luke writes as a Gentile Christian, with deep appreciation of God's revelation through the Hebrew people, and yet with a warm sympathy for those who are not included in the first covenant of the Law. His Gospel is truly universal in scope.

OUTLINE

- I. Introduction. 1:1-4.
- II. The announcement of the Saviour. 1:5–2:52.
  - A. The annunciation to Zacharias. 1:5-25.
  - B. The annunciation to Mary. 1:26-56.
  - C. The birth of John. 1:57-80.
  - D. The birth of Jesus. 2:1-20.
  - E. The presentation in the Temple. 2:21-40.
  - F. The visit to Jerusalem. 2:41-52.
- III. The appearance of the Saviour. 3:1–4:15.
  - A. The introduction of John the Baptist. 3:1-20.
  - B. The baptism of Jesus. 3:21,22.
  - C. The genealogy. 3:23-38.
  - D. The temptation. 4:1-13.
  - E. The entrance into Galilee. 4:14,15.
- IV. The active ministry of the Saviour. 4:16–9:50.
  - A. The definition of his ministry. 4:16-44.
  - B. The proofs of his power. 5:1–6:11.
  - C. The choice of the apostles. 6:12-19.
  - D. A digest of his teaching. 6:20-49.
  - E. A cross section of his ministry. 7:1–9:17.
  - F. The climax of his ministry. 9:18-50.
- V. The road to the cross. 9:51–18:30.
  - A. The perspective of the cross. 9:51-62.
  - B. The ministry of the Seventy. 10:1-24.
  - C. Popular teaching. 10:25–13:21.
  - D. The beginning of public debate. 13:22–16:31.
  - E. Instruction of the disciples. 17:1–18:30.
- VI. The suffering of the Saviour. 18:31–23:56.
  - A. The progress to Jerusalem. 18:31–19:27.
  - B. The entry into Jerusalem. 19:28-44.
  - C. The teaching in Jerusalem. 19:45–21:4.
  - D. The Olivet Discourse. 21:5-38.
  - E. The last supper. 22:1-38.
  - F. The betrayal. 22:39-53.
  - G. The arrest and trial. 22:54–23:25.
  - H. The crucifixion. 23:26-49.
  - I. The burial. 23:50-56.
- VII. The resurrection. 24:1-53.
  - A. The empty tomb. 24:1-12.
  - B. The walk to Emmaus. 24:13-35.
  - C. The appearance to the disciples. 24:36-43.
  - D. The last commission. 24:44-49.
  - E. The ascension. 24:50-53.

COMMENTARY

I. Introduction. 1:1-4.

Luke's Gospel is the only one that tells what method the author used in composing it. The content of the introduction is intended to strengthen the reader's confidence in what the Gospel will tell about Christ.

1. Taken in hand. A literal translation of the Greek verb, which means "to attempt," or "to undertake." **Declaration.** The word implies a formal narrative which is a concise summary of facts. **Things . . . most surely believed.** The phrase may mean "things fulfilled," but has the sense of "things that are taken for granted as true," or "the acknowledged facts of the case." **2. Delivered.** Paul uses this same word concerning the oral transmission of the content of the Gospel (I Cor 11:23; 15:3). **Eyewitnesses, and ministers of the word. Eyewitnesses** implies that the informants of Luke had seen Jesus in person and because of commitment to him had become **ministers of the word. Ministers** does not have a professional meaning in the modern sense; it was used of synagogue attendants (Lk 4:20).

3. To me also. Luke was as well qualified to write a Gospel as any others. **Perfect understanding.** Paul uses the same expression to say that Timothy had "fully known" the experiences of his career (II Tim 3:10). This knowledge is the familiarity which a man has with contemporary facts. **From the very first** (Gr. *anothen).* In the one other place where Luke uses the word (Acts 26:5), it means "from the beginning." Luke claims complete familiarity with the life of Jesus. **Most excellent.** A title elsewhere used by Luke only of officials or of the nobility (Acts 23:26; 24:3; 26:25). **4. Know.** The Greek word means *to have full knowledge*. **Instructed** may imply either general oral information, or formal instruction. Luke was writing to confirm what Theophilus had learned by word of mouth.

II. The Announcement of the Saviour. 1:5–2:52.

The first two chapters of the Gospel are concerned with the circumstances of Jesus' birth and indicate clearly that the coming of the Saviour was a direct intervention of God in human affairs.

A. The Annunciation to Zacharias. 1:5-25.

5. Herod, the king. Herod the Great, an Edomite by blood and Jewish by religion, was king over Judea from 37 B.C. to 4 B.C. He was an able ruler, but ruthless and corrupt. **Course of Abia.** There were twenty-four "courses" or divisions of the priesthood, based on the families of the descendants of Aaron, of which the family of Abia (or Abijah) was one (I Chr 24:10). **7. They had no child.** A calamity to a Jewish family.

8. The priest's office. Each member of the course took his turn in serving at the altar of the Temple for a specified period of the year. **9. His lot.** The opportunity to minister at the altar was determined by drawing lots, and usually came only once in a lifetime. **10. The whole multitude of the people were praying.** As the smoke of the incense rose from the altar, the people joined in silent prayer. **11. An angel of the Lord.** No description of angels is given in the NT, but they must have had some distinctive features to differentiate them from men. Their appearance is usually connected with some special divine communication. **12. Zacharias . . . was troubled** by the unexpected appearance of another person in the Holy Place and was apprehensive of what he might announce.

13. The angel said. Note the parallel between the announcement of the birth of John and the announcement of the birth of Samson (Jud 13:3-5). In both cases the parents had despaired of having children, and the promised child was empowered from birth for a special task. **15. Filled with the Holy Ghost. Ghost** is an archaic English word for "spirit." **17. In the spirit and power of Elias.** Elijah was the stern prophet of repentance who rebuked Ahab, the idolatrous king of Israel (I Kgs 21:17-24). John's calling was to arouse the nation, and to make the people ready for the coming of Christ (Mal 4:5,6). **19. I am Gabriel.** The angel's name means *man of God*. He appears to men in order to make special announcements of the purpose of God (cf. Dan 8:16; 9:21; Lk 1:26).

21. Marvelled that he tarried. Since the rite of offering incense usually took a short time, Zacharias' delay may have caused alarm. The people may have thought that the priest had died. **23. The days of his ministration.** The priests served in their course for a limited time, and then were free to return to their homes. Zacharias' home was in the hill country, probably not far from Jerusalem (1:39).

B. The Annunciation to Mary. 1:26-56.

27. To a virgin espoused to a man whose name was Joseph. The Jewish law held espousal or engagement to be as binding as marriage. An engagement was completed after negotiations had been carried on by the groom's representative and the dowry money had been paid to the girl's father. After the betrothal, the groom could claim the bride at any time. The legal aspect of marriage was included in the betrothal; the wedding was merely a recognition of the agreement that had already been established. Joseph had a perfect right to travel with Mary to Bethlehem. **Of the house of David.** By adoptive right as the reputed son of Joseph, Jesus could claim the kingly heritage of the house of David.

28. Highly favoured. The word may be translated, *full of grace,* but it refers to one who is a recipient of favor rather than to the source of grace. **29. What manner of salutation this should be.** To be singled out from all other women for a blessing was disturbing. Mary could not understand why she had been selected for this honor.

31. Thou shalt . . . call his name Jesus. Jesus is the Greek form of the Hebrew *Joshua,* which means, *Jehovah is salvation.* Compare Matthew's account of the annunciation to Joseph (Mt 1:21). **32. The throne of his father David.** David's descendants had reigned over Judah from the United Kingdom to the Exile in one unbroken dynasty. The angel predicted that Jesus would complete this succession. **33. And he shall reign over the house of Jacob for ever.** This reign can be both temporal and spiritual.

34. How shall this be, seeing I know not a man? Mary's question confirms the statement of her virginity in verse 27. Joseph had not yet taken her as his wife. **35. The Holy Ghost shall come upon thee.** In contrast to the pagan legends of antiquity concerning the reputed offspring of gods and men, there was no physical intervention. The Holy Spirit's creative act in the body of Mary provided the physical means for the Incarnation. **36. Thy cousin Elizabeth.** If Mary and Elizabeth were first cousins, Jesus and John the Baptist were second cousins. **38. Behold the handmaid of the Lord.** Mary's unhesitating acceptance showed her devout and obedient character. She was willing to risk disgrace and divorce to comply with God's command.

43. The mother of my Lord. Elizabeth's salutation shows that she was ready to acknowledge Mary's Son as her Lord.

46. My soul doth magnify the Lord. Verses 46 to 56 are called the *Magnificat,* from the first word in the Latin translation. Compare the prayer of Hannah (I Sam 2:1-10). **47. God my Saviour.** Mary was not sinless; she acknowledged her need of a Saviour. **48. Handmaiden** (Gr. *doulē*). Literally, *a female slave.* **49. Hath done to me great things.** Better: *hath done great things for me.* **51. The imagination of their hearts. Imagination** (cf. I Chr 29:18) carries the meaning of "conceit," or the boastful expectations of which they were proud. **54. Holpen.** Old English for "helped."

C. The Birth of John. 1:57-80.

59. To circumcise the child. A Jewish boy was circumcised eight days after birth, at which time a name was usually given him. **60. Called John. John** from the Hebrew *Yohanan,* means "God is gracious." **61. There is none of thy kindred that is called by this name.** Children usually carried family names. In this case the choice of a different name was significant of special expectation for the child. **63. He asked for a writing table.** Wax tablets were used in ancient times for temporary notes.

65. These sayings were noised abroad. Perhaps Luke learned of these facts through talking with some of the people who lived in the hill country.

67. Filled with the Holy Ghost. This phrase is used eight times in the Lukan writings, including two previous occurrences in this chapter (1:15,41). In all eight instances it is connected with equipment for speech or preaching. It implies a special control and preparation by the Spirit for delivering a message from God. **Prophesied.** This word does not apply exclusively to prediction, but may refer to the declaration of God's message for men, whether it relates to the past, the present, or the future.

68. Blessed be the Lord God of Israel. Luke, although a Gentile, connects the heart of the message with the God of the OT. **Visited and redeemed his people.** Zacharias recognized in the birth of John the beginnings of the fulfillment of the coming of the Messiah. **69. An horn of salvation.** The horns of an ox were a symbol of power. Many passages in the OT use this figure of speech, especially in the Psalms (cf. Ps 18:2; 89:24; 132:17; 148:14). **70. His holy prophets.** God has had his representatives in all ages and in all places. Enoch, who was God's messenger before the Flood, was called a prophet (Jude 14). **73. The oath.** The Lord had sworn to Abraham that his descendants would be preserved through the bondage of Egypt, and that they should possess the promised land (Gen 15:13,18). **78. Dayspring from on high. Dayspring,** an old term for sunrise, refers to the rising of the "Sun of righteousness" (see Mal 4:2). The entire passage contains echoes of the last chapter of Malachi's prophecy.

D. The Birth of Jesus. 2:1-20.

1. A decree from Caesar Augustus. Luke is the only one of the Gospel writers who dates his material by the reigning emperor (see also 3:1). **Decree** (Gr. *dogma*). An imperial order. **Caesar Augustus.** The first emperor of Rome, who reigned from 27 B.C. to A.D. 14. **All the world.** This means all the empire, not the entire known world. **Taxed.** Augustus had ordered a census of the empire which would serve as a basis for taxation. The decree was issued about 8 B.C., but probably did not actually go into effect until a few years later. **2. Cyrenius was governor of Syria.** P. Sulpicius Quirinius was made governor of Syria in A.D. 6, and took a census of Judea at that time. There is good evidence that he was twice governor of Syria, and that his first governorship was from 4 B.C. to A.D. 1. The preceding census may have been closing when he first took office.

3. Into his own city. In Judea each man went back to the city of his ancestors, where his family records were kept. **4. Galilee** was the region around the Lake of Gennesaret, or Lake of Galilee. It had a large Gentile population, and from the days of the prophets had been known as "Galilee of the Gentiles" (Isa 9:1). **Nazareth.** A city in the hills of Galilee, located on the trade route that ran from the coastal plain across to Damascus and the East. **Judea.** The province south of Samaria and north of Edom and the desert, bounded on the west by the Mediterranean Sea and on the east by the Jordan River and the Dead Sea. **Bethlehem.** The original home of David's family. **5. Espoused wife.** See on 1:27.

7. Firstborn son. This may imply that Mary had other children later (cf Mk 6:3). **Manger.** A feeding trough for cattle. Joseph and Mary may have taken shelter in the stable. Tradition says that it was a cave in the side of the hill behind the inn.

8. Keeping watch over their flock by night. The exact date of Jesus' birth is unknown; the legendary date of December 25 cannot be traced back farther than the fourth century. **9.** The heavenly visitation was attended with the radiance of the divine glory that was present when God manifested himself (Ex 16:10; 20:18; 40:34; II Chr 7:1; Ezk 1:27,28).

10. Fear not. The angel's word was the usual greeting for men to whom such an apparition would be terrifying (cf. 1:13,30). **All people.** The ASV translates more accurately, *all the people,* meaning Israel. **11. Saviour.** In the OT God was the Saviour of his people (Isa 25:9; 33:22). While the prophets thought of him chiefly as a saviour from political oppression, Luke broadens the concept to make Jesus a Saviour from sin. **Christ the Lord. Christ** means *anointed,* the Messiah of Israel, who was the promised Deliverer. **Lord.** A title that the Greek pagans applied to their kings, whom they hailed as gods. A Christian can apply the title only to Christ (I Cor 8:6). **12. And this shall be a sign.** Literally, *the sign.* **14. Peace, good will toward men.** The ASV follows a different manuscript reading—*among men of his good pleasure.* The peace is not given to men who possess good will toward God, but to men whom he is inclined to favor.

15. This thing which is come to pass. The shepherds did not doubt the reality of the angel's proclamation, but accepted it at face value. **19. Mary kept . . . and pondered them in her heart.** The appearance of the heavenly visitors to the shepherds confirmed the mysterious secret of the Annunciation.

E. The Presentation in the Temple. 2:21-40.

21. And when eight days were accomplished. Jesus, like John, was named according to the message of Gabriel (1:13, 59-63). The circumcision may have taken place in Bethlehem. **22. The days of her purification.** According to the law of Moses, a woman who had a male ch was reckoned unclean for seven days. (the eighth day the child was circumcise , and she remained unclean for thirty-three days afterwards. At the end of that time she presented a sacrifice at the Temple and was ceremonially cleansed (Lev 12:2-6). The sacrifice offered was in proportion to the financial ability of the family. **24. A pair of turtledoves.** The offering of the birds indicates that Joseph and Mary were poor (Lev 12:8). For the presentation of the offering they traveled to Jerusalem, which was only a few miles from Bethlehem.

25. Simeon. Simeon may have been one of the Hasidim, sincere and earnest worshipers of God, who kept the Law in spirit as well as in letter. **Just** expresses his attitude toward men; **devout,** his attitude to God. **Consolation of Israel.** The expected Messiah, who would deliver the Jews from their oppressors. **26. And it was revealed unto him.** A special individual prediction was given to Simeon as a reward for his devotion. **28. Blessed God, and said.** The words of Simeon, like the Psalms of David, were spoken in Hebrew poetry.

32. A light to lighten the Gentiles. Simeon perceived the true purpose of God to reach out to the Gentiles as well as to Israel. Luke, a Gentile, must have been specially interested in his prophecy. **34. This child.** Jesus was not just one more Jewish child, but was pivotal for faith. Those who believed in him rose to new heights; those who rejected him fell into darker despair. **35. Yea, a sword.** Simeon hinted that Mary would suffer deep sorrow because of Him.

36. Anna, a prophetess. In both Old and New Testament times, women were gifted with prophetic powers. Deborah (Jud 4:4) was one of the earliest leaders of Israel, and the daughters of Philip the evangelist prophesied (Acts 21:9). **37. She was a widow of about fourscore and four years.** Anna had lived with a husband seven years before his death. If she was married at the age of twelve, she must now have been over one hundred years of age, unless Luke intended eighty-four years to comprise her total age. Like Simeon, she belonged to the pious remnant of Judaism. **38. Redemption in Jerusalem.** The greatness of Anna's faith is shown by her confidence that this infant was the promised means of national redemption.

40. And the child grew, and waxed strong in spirit. Luke is the sole source of information about Jesus' childhood. All sorts of fanciful legends about our Lord's youth were written and published in the apocryphal Gospels, but none of them appear in the Scriptures.

F. The Visit to Jerusalem. 2:41-52.

42. They went up to Jerusalem. Devout Jews customarily attended the Passover at Jerusalem. Jesus, being twelve years old, was approaching the normal age for being received into Judaism as a "son of the law," which would make him a full member of the religious community. **43. Jesus tarried behind.** Like any normal boy, he may have been intrigued by the sights of the city; it is more likely that he was particularly interested in the teaching of the rabbis.

46. They found him in the temple. His interest shows that he had awakened to the need of understanding the Law. He was listening closely to the leading teachers, who were astounded by the clarity and insight of his replies to their questions. **48. Son, why hast thou thus dealt with us?** Like any true mother, Mary had missed him when the caravan had stopped at the end of the day. She was obviously worried. **49. About my Father's business.** The ASV translates: *Knew ye not that I must be in my Father's house?* Both renderings imply that the youth had a keen realization of his relation to God. He was astounded that Mary and Joseph had not understood that relation, and he reminded them that since God was his true Father, he belonged in God's house.

50. And they understood not. Joseph and Mary did not comprehend the full import of Jesus' words, which were the first recorded sign of his growing independence (cf. Jn 2:4). **51. And was subject unto them.** Jesus' independence was not rebellion. He returned to Nazareth and remained with the family until the beginning of his public ministry. **Kept all these sayings in her heart.** Though she did not understand what he meant, Mary did not forget his words. Perhaps Luke learned of them directly from her.

52. And Jesus increased in wisdom and stature, and in favour with God and man. He was not a prodigy in the sense that he was abnormal. **Increased** (Gr. "increase" is lit., *cut one's way forward)* means that there was growth in his size, consciousness, and comprehension of events. He was perfect in every stage as he attained it. He was free from the flaws that disfigure the rest of men at each stage of growth.

III. The Appearance of the Saviour. 3:1–4:15.

The account of the ministry of John the Baptist, the genealogy, and the temptation of Jesus are intended to give a background for the Saviour whom Luke is presenting. The baptism relates him to contemporary spiritual life; the genealogy affirms his relation to the human race; and the temptation proves his competence to meet the moral problems that confront humanity.

A. The Introduction of John the Baptist. 3:1-20.

1. Now in the fifteenth year of the reign of Tiberius Caesar. Luke, being a careful historian, dates the beginning of the Saviour's career by the year of the reigning emperor. Tiberius was the adopted son of Augustus (2:1). Since he succeeded to the throne in A.D. 14, his fifteenth year would be about A.D. 28 or 29. The other personages named here were ruling in Palestine at the same time. **Governor.** Pontius Pilate, who is mentioned again in connection with the trial of Jesus (23:1-25), was procurator (imperial governor) of Judea from A.D. 26 to 36. He was responsible to the emperor for the welfare of the province. **Tetrarch of Galilee.** A tetrarch was strictly the ruler of one quarter of a given territory. **Herod** was Antipas, a son of Herod the Great, who ruled over Galilee and the territory east of the Jordan River. **Ituraea,** the realm of Philip, another son of Herod the Great, lay to the northeast of Galilee, and east of Mount Hermon. Of **Lysanias** little is known, except that he was monarch of the little kingdom of Abilene on the eastern slope of the Lebanon mountains, northeast of Damascus. **2. Annas and Caiaphas.** Caiaphas was the ruling high priest; Annas, his father-in-law, was high priest emeritus, and wielded a strong influence (Jn 18:13). **The word of God.** The divine call came to John as it did to OT prophets (Hos 1:1; Joel 1:1; Jon 1:1; Mic 1:1).

3. The baptism of repentance. Plummer (ICC, p. 86) says that "repentance baptism" is baptism connected with repentance, an external symbol of the inward change. Repentance means a change of mind or attitude that is not solely emotional, but that involves a reversal of previous thinking and conduct. **For the remission of sins.** The purpose of John's preaching was to bring men into the experience of forgiveness. **4. Make his paths straight.** See Isa 40:3-5. In ancient times there were few paved roads. When a king traveled, his subjects built highways for him so that his chariot would not be mired in mud or in sand. Similarly, John was preparing the way for Jesus by his preaching so that all flesh might see God's salvation. By equating the prophet's words (Isa 40:3), "Prepare ye the way of the Lord [Jehovah]" with John's mission, Luke shows that he ascribes deity to Christ. **6. And all flesh shall see the salvation of God.** The writer makes plain at the outset of Jesus' ministry that He had a universal message. **7. O generation of vipers.** Like his prophetic forebears, John denounced the sins of the people in vigorous language. **8. We have Abraham to our father.** To is equivalent to the modern "as." Jews were singularly proud of Abraham as the head of their race, with whom God had made his covenant. Believing that they inherited the blessing of God through Abraham, they trusted in their descent from him to bring them salvation (Jn 8:33). John the Baptist warned them that God would make the very stones to become descendants of Abraham. **9. The axe is laid unto the root of the trees.** Unproductive trees were cut down for firewood. The nation had not brought forth fruits that God expected, and judgment was imminent.

11. Meat in the AV does not mean flesh alone, as it does today in our vocabulary, but is a general word for food. **12. Publicans** were tax collectors, noted for their rapacity. A certain part of men's earnings was demanded for taxes, but the publicans usually asked more, and enriched themselves by the difference. They were hated by the people, who considered them traitors because they worked for Rome. **14. And the soldiers likewise.** Soldiers were often brutal to civilians, and practiced extortion upon them. **Do violence to no man.** The Greek word for **do violence** *(diaseisete)* means "to shake down," an ancient counterpart of modern slang.

15. Whether he were the Christ or not. Christ is a general term meaning "Messiah." It is a title, not a proper name. **16. Latchet.** A shoelace. **He shall baptize you with the Holy Ghost and with fire.** As baptism with water signifies repentance, so the coming of the Holy Spirit is proof of the presence of God. Fire is a symbol of purification and power. **17. Whose fan is in his hand.** The "fan" was the winnowing shovel, used to throw grain into the air so that the chaff would blow away, while the clean kernels fell back to the threshing floor.

19. Herod the tetrarch. Herod had married Herodias, the wife of his brother Philip. When John reproved him publicly, Herodias was enraged, and demanded that John be imprisoned. Herod arrested him, and finally, at his wife's request, ordered the Baptist's execution.

B. The Baptism of Jesus. 3:21,22.

21. Jesus . . . being baptized. By submitting to the baptism of John, he classed himself with sinners, though sinless himself, and began his redemptive mission. The opening of heaven was the divine acknowledgment of Jesus' sonship. **22. And the Holy Ghost descended.** The dove was a symbol of innocence and harmlessness, a messenger of peace (cf. Gen 8:8,9). **A voice came from heaven.** Compare Luke 9:35; John 12:28.

C. The Genealogy. 3:23-28.

23. And Jesus began to be about thirty years of age, being (as was supposed) the son of Joseph. The genealogy of Jesus disagrees with that of Matthew, which gives the legal line of royal descent. Luke's gives the human line, possibly through Mary, if Joseph is reckoned as her father's son through marriage. Luke carries the line back to Adam to emphasize Jesus' descent from the first father of the human race, while Matthew begins with the covenant heads: Abraham, to whom God promised the land (Gen 12:7), and David, to whom He pledged an everlasting kingdom (II Sam 7:12,13,16). The names in the genealogy differ from the spelling in the OT because they are given in Greek form.

D. The Temptation. 4:1-13.

The account of the temptation of our Lord is given in both Luke and Matthew. Jesus, like Adam (Gen 3:6), was tested in the three areas of physical appetite, worldly ambition, and spiritual attainment, in order that he might be proved competent for his mission. Where the first man failed, he triumphed.

1. Led by the Spirit. The first recorded directive of the Holy Spirit led to testing. **The wilderness.** The traditional scene of the Temptation is a barren territory northwest of the Dead Sea, completely devoid of vegetation or shelter of any kind. **2. Forty days.** A common period for trial (Gen 7:4; Ex 24:18; I Kgs 19:8; Jon 3:4).

3. If thou be the Son of God. The Greek condition used implies that the devil did not doubt that Jesus was the Son of God, but rather assumed that Jesus did possess the right to create. **Bread.** Bread in Palestine was not in the form of oblong loaves, but in flat round cakes. The stones on the ground looked like cakes of bread. **4. It is written.** Jesus did not compose his own answer for the tempter, but drew his reply from the revelation of Scripture. **Man shall not live by bread alone** (Deut 8:3). Man needs bread, but bread is not all he needs. Material gratification of the appetites can never satisfy the deepest longings of the human spirit.

5. All the kingdoms of the world. From the heights of the mountain range one could see the territories formerly occupied by the empires of Egypt, Assyria, Babylon, Persia, Greece, and now Rome. **6. All this power will I give thee.** Christ had come to claim the world as his kingdom, and the devil was offering it to him on "easy" terms. **7. If thou therefore wilt worship me.** By worshiping, Jesus would trade his independence for the kingdoms of the world. If he accepted these terms, he would not actually be the sovereign, because he would be compelled to acknowledge the overlordship of Satan. **8. Thou shalt worship the Lord thy God** (Deut 6:13). He would admit only the authority of God as supreme. He could not compromise.

9. A pinnacle of the temple. One of the battlements or towers (Gr. *pterygion*, "a little wing"), that overlooked the courtyard or perhaps the Kidron Valley. If Jesus had leaped from the battlement and had landed unharmed among the crowds below, they would have hailed him as the Messiah from heaven, and his reputation would have been made instantly. **10. It is written.** In the third temptation the devil omitted part of the verse, which reads, "to keep thee in all thy ways." God had not promised to keep his servant in an act of foolish presumption, but only when he was walking in God's ways (see Ps 91:11,12).

13. For a season. The words imply that the temptation or attack was renewed later. The Saviour lived constantly under the pressure of evil. The devil is a real personality, though not necessarily visible.

E. The Entrance into Galilee. 4:14,15.

Matthew, Mark, and Luke begin Jesus' ministry with Galilee; John records an earlier ministry in Judea (Jn 2:13–4:3). Luke stresses the place of the Holy Spirit in the career of Jesus (cf. Lk 1:35; 3:21, 22; 4:1).

IV. The Active Ministry of the Saviour. 4:16–9:50.

The first part of our Lord's ministry occupied about two and one-half years. It covers the choice of the apostles, the larger amount of his teaching and healing, and comes to its climax in the Transfiguration. Luke was endeavoring to show Theophilus the divine character of Jesus, and the prophetic nature of his mission.

A. The Definition of His Ministry. 4:16-44.

16. Nazareth. Jesus began his ministry in his home town. **Into the synagogue.** During the Babylonian captivity after the destruction of the Temple, the Jewish people instituted synagogues as local centers of worship. Even when the Temple was restored, synagogue worship persisted. Luke notes that Jesus had been accustomed to attend synagogue services regularly on the Sabbath. Members participated in the service, and were frequently asked to read the Scripture and make appropriate remarks. Paul did most of his preaching in synagogues (cf. Acts 13:14,15). **17. The book of the prophet Esaias.** The synagogue followed a regular order of readings. Jesus probably took the passage that was usually read on that day. **18. He hath anointed me.** The passage was taken from Isa 61:1,2, which was a prophecy of the Messianic Age.

20. Book. The writings of the OT were scrolls mounted on handles, which were read by rolling up one side while unrolling the other. **Minister.** After Jesus had read, he rolled up the scroll and handed it back to the assistant who had charge of the Scriptures. Scrolls were costly to make, and were very carefully preserved. **21. This day is this scripture fulfilled.** The reader's opening words of comment must have been a shock to his hearers. They had known him from boyhood and had taken him for granted. When he claimed to be the fulfillment of this Messianic prophecy, they were astounded.

22. The gracious words. Luke does not give a verbatim report of all that Jesus said. He must have expounded the first part of the text, applying it to himself. **Is not this Joseph's son?** The question of the villagers shows that they knew nothing of Jesus' origin, but assumed that he was the son of Joseph and Mary by natural birth. As he strengthened his claims, they wondered what right he had to do so.

23. Physician, heal thyself. The Lord often taught by proverbs or parables. On this occasion he was anticipating the demand of the people that he perform in Nazareth the miracles that he had done in Capernaum. **24. No prophet is accepted in his own country.** In the following verses Jesus pointed out not only that he expected rejection by his own village, but that his greatest ministry might be to the Gentile world.

28. They . . . were filled with wrath. The announcement that he had no ministry for the people of Nazareth because they would not accept him aroused their anger, and they tried to kill him by mob action. **29. The brow of the hill.** Nazareth was built on hills, some of which were quite steep. **30. Passing through the midst of them.** His commanding presence and divine protection took him unharmed through the angry mob.

31. Capernaum. A small city on the shore of Galilee, about twenty-five miles northeast of Nazareth. Jesus carried on an extensive ministry in the synagogue. Luke gives a sample day out of Jesus' career, filled with teaching and healing.

33. A spirit of an unclean devil. *Demon* is a better translation. **Devil** is properly used only of Satan. Demon possession was common in Jesus' day, and was distinguished from insanity (see Mt 4:24). In places where the powers of evil are recognized and worshiped, it is still current. Demons are evil intelligences who seek to gain control of human beings as media of expression. **34. Let us alone.** The evil spirits recognized him and expressed fear and hatred of him. **35. Hold thy peace, and come out of him.** Our Lord never allowed the demons to advertise him. His authority over them was a proof of the validity of the Messianic claims that he had made at Nazareth.

38. Simon's house. The call of Simon was recorded by John (Jn 1:41,42). Luke has not mentioned him before, but takes for granted the reader's knowledge that Simon was already a disciple. His summons to service is given later. **A great fever.** Only Luke uses the adjective **great,** reflecting his medical interest. **40. When the sun was setting.** Sunset marked the end of the Jewish day. With the closing of the Sabbath, it was lawful to carry the sick. So many were brought to the Lord that he must have spent a large part of the night in ministering to them.

42. He departed. Often after a busy day Jesus retired from the crowds in order to pray (see 5:16; 6:12). **43. The kingdom of God.** The realm and rule of God through the Messiah was the subject of the Saviour's preaching. His ethics, his deeds, his redemptive work, and his promise to return all belong within the scope of this subject. The Jewish people of his time expected that the kingdom would mean chiefly a restoration of the independence of Israel. Jesus gave it a much fuller content.

B. The Proofs of His Power. 5:1–6:11.

This next division of Luke continues the proofs of Jesus' power, preparatory to a greater emphasis on public teaching.

1. **Lake of Gennesaret.** Another name for the lake of Galilee. It is a large body of water, about thirteen miles long and eight miles wide, surrounded by hills. In our Lord's day the region around it was heavily populated, and there were numerous cities on its shores. Capernaum and Bethsaida (to the north) were centers of the fishing industry. 2. **Washing their nets.** Cleaning the nets was the regular morning's work after a night of fishing. 3. **He entered into one of the ships.** The lake front provided an auditorium, for there was gently rising land along the shore, and the acoustics were good. In order that he might not be crowded, Jesus borrowed Simon Peter's boat for a pulpit.

4. **Let down your nets for a draught.** The fish came nearer the surface at night to feed; in the daytime they went down to the cooler waters deep in the lake. 5. **Nevertheless at thy word.** Though Peter's experience as a fisherman made him quite sure that they would catch nothing, his words show faith in Jesus. He was ready to believe the Master's word even in matters in which Jesus would not naturally be considered an expert. 6. **Their net brake.** Literally, *their nets began to break*. The catch of fish was so large that neither the nets nor the boats could hold it.

8. **Depart from me; for I am a sinful man, O Lord.** This proof that Jesus knew even more about fishing than Peter did, and the gift of fish, which more than compensated for the futile work of the preceding night, made the disciple see himself in a new light. In contrast with Jesus, whose deity was indicated by this miracle, Peter realized that he was sinful, and felt unworthy to have Jesus with him. 10. **Fear not; from henceforth thou shalt catch men.** Simon and his partners, James and John, had already become disciples of Jesus, but had continued with their business. Now Jesus called them to special service, and they left all to follow him.

12. **Full of leprosy.** The language implies an advanced case. Leprosy was a common disease in the Orient. In its final stages it causes disfigurement of the body, as the various members decay. The Law required the segregation of lepers outside the towns (Lev 13:45,46). **If thou wilt.** The leper did not doubt Jesus' competence to heal; he was uncertain of His attitude. 13. **I will.** Since the disease was usually considered incurable, the sudden healing may have been a surprise to the man and to all who knew him. 14. **Go, and shew thyself to the priest.** The Law provided that cases of leprosy must be inspected by the priests, who acted as a board of health in the Jewish commonwealth (Lev 14:1-32). Jesus wanted the man to go through the proper channels, so that he could be reinstated in the community.

17. **Pharisees and doctors of the law.** The fame of the Teacher had brought to Galilee religious leaders from all parts of the land. They were listening critically to his teaching.

18. **A man which was taken with a palsy.** The case was difficult, and healing would be all the more convincing. 19. **Let him down through the tiling.** Luke describes the house as a Roman dwelling with a tile roof, such as would have been found in the cities familiar to his readers. 20. **Man, thy sins are forgiven thee.** Our Lord began with the man's spiritual need, which was greater than his physical need.

21. **Blasphemies.** Jesus' critics were shocked at his assuming a right that belongs to God alone—the right to forgive sins. The Lord did not say that since he was the Son of God with authority, they were wrong in their assumption. Instead, he proposed a test of that authority. 23. **Whether is easier.** It would be easier to say, "Thy sins be forgiven," because if they were not, there would be no outward evidence. If Jesus had commanded healing, and the man had not been healed, everybody would have known that the healer was fraudulent.

24. **Arise, and take up thy couch.** Jesus made his power to cure a test of his power to forgive. By accomplishing what his critics acknowledged as the more difficult, he showed that he could do what they thought to be easier. **Couch** is a bedroll, not a piece of furniture. 25. **And immediately he rose up.** The cure was complete, and the Lord's critics were silenced. The miracle demonstrated that Jesus could remove the paralysis of both spirit and body.

27. **Levi** is identical with Matthew (Mt 9:9). **Receipt of custom.** Taxes on goods transported along the caravan road were levied by Herod's agents, of whom Matthew may have been one. 29. **Levi made him a great feast.** Matthew, a man of wealth, gave a special dinner for his associates that they might meet Jesus. The Pharisees had rejected the publicans ut-

terly and would have nothing to do with them, but Jesus reached out to them. Forgiveness was for publicans as well as for others. **30. Publicans and sinners** were classed together. The publicans had a reputation for avarice and graft. **32. I came not to call the righteous.** Jesus implied that he could do nothing for the "righteous" Pharisees, who were sure of their own perfection. He wanted to reach those who recognized and acknowledged their need.

33. Why do the disciples of John fast often. The people were puzzled, since Jesus' ethical standards were no lower than those of John and the Pharisees. They wondered why his disciples were not as strict as John's. **34. The children of the bridechamber.** The phrase is a Hebrew idiom, meaning the friends of the bridegroom. While Jesus was with the disciples, there was no reason for mourning. But he intimated (v. 35) that some day he would be taken away from them, and that then fasting would be in order. The figure of the friend of the bridegroom was used by John the Baptist himself in speaking of his relation to the Lord (Jn 3:29).

36. And he spake also a parable. The Lord's parables were illustrations or incidents taken from daily life by which he conveyed spiritual teaching. They revealed truth to those who could discern it, and concealed mysteries from those who were not ready for them. Patched garments were common in Palestine, because the people were poor. New cloth, sewed on an old garment, will shrink when washed, and so will pull apart the older and weaker cloth. **37. Bottles** were not glass containers, but skins of animals used as sacks for liquid. The old wineskins had lost their elasticity, and would not hold the new wine, which might still be in partial process of fermentation. Likewise the new teaching of the kingdom of God could not be contained within the forms of the Law, but must be expressed in new ways. A fresh revelation had come in Christ, which demanded a different form of worship.

6:1. The second sabbath after the first. The phrase is a reference to the usage of the Jewish calendar. It may mean the second Sabbath that came in the sequence after the opening of the religious year at the Passover. Some manuscripts of Luke omit the term entirely. **Corn** in the AV is a general word for grain. **Plucked the ears.** Travelers were allowed to pick grains or fruits for immediate consumption, but not to harvest freely on another man's land (Deut 23:24,25).

2. That which is not lawful to do. The strict interpretation of the Law regarded picking and rubbing out grain as work, which was not allowed on the Sabbath.

3. Have ye not read. Jesus referred to the Scripture for a different illustration from the life of David (I Sam 21:1-6). If David could do in an emergency that which was unlawful, why could not He?

5. Lord . . . of the sabbath. In addition to the authority to forgive sins, Jesus claimed sovereignty over the Sabbath law.

7. And the scribes and Pharisees watched him. Angered by their defeat in argument regarding Sabbath observance and by the claims which they regarded as presumptuous, the scribes and Pharisees were now eager to trap Jesus. **9. Is it lawful on the sabbath days to do good, or to do evil?** Since it was lawful to do good on the Sabbath, and since healing was a good deed, the healing was above criticism. **11. They were filled with madness.** Beaten in argument and discredited before the people, Jesus' opponents were driven to desperation. This verse marks the beginning of Christ's controversy with the Jewish leaders that lasted all during the rest of his career.

C. The Choice of the Apostles. 6:12-19.

12. Continued all night in prayer. The rise of opposition and the problem of choosing the right men as his close associates called for protracted counsel with the Father. **13. Disciples . . . apostles.** A disciple is a learner; an apostle is *one sent,* commissioned to deliver a message. **14-16.** The following list agrees with those in Matthew and Mark (Mt 10:2-4; Mk 3:16-19), except for the name of Judas the brother of James, who may be the same as Thaddaeus in the other two Gospels.

17. And he came down with them, and stood in the plain. Bible students have questioned whether the following text is parallel to the Sermon on the Mount of Matthew 5–7, since the latter was spoken on a mountain. **Plain** really means "a level place," which could have been on the side of the mountain. Or, it is possible that Jesus repeated his teaching on more than one occasion. **19. Virtue.** An archaic translation for a word meaning *power.*

D. A Digest of His Teaching. 6:20-49.

Luke's report of the sermon differs from that of Matthew in several respects. He balances four beatitudes with four woes, instead of giving nine beatitudes. He omits the discussion of the application of the Law, and some of the teaching on prayer. A few parables in this sermon are paralleled elsewhere in Luke. There are no contradictions in the accounts, but only different arrangements of material. The address was gauged particularly for the disciples, although the multitude listened to it.

20. Blessed be ye poor. While traveling with Jesus, the apostles had no visible means of support, and were dependent on gifts. **21. Blessed are ye that hunger now.** Satisfaction comes only to those who have a real desire. Matthew implies that the hunger is spiritual. **Blessed are ye that weep.** Jesus knew that those who were faithful to him would have to share in his sorrows, but he promised them also a share in his triumph (cf. Jn 16:20). **22. Blessed . . . when men shall hate you.** The conflict which had already begun between Jesus and the leaders of the nation involved his followers also (cf. Jn 15:18-25).

27. Love your enemies. Love was the heart of the Saviour's teaching, because it is the essence of the character of God. **29. Unto him that smiteth thee on the one cheek offer also the other.** The Lord was trying to teach his disciples love instead of revenge. They were to follow his example in returning good for evil. **35. Love ye your enemies.** The principle that Jesus inculcated was the one that brought him to earth (cf. Rom 5:8; I Jn 4:10).

38. Good measure, pressed down, and shaken together, and running over. The figure of speech is taken from the practice of the Oriental grain merchant, who fills the basket of his customer as full as possible until the grain runs over the edge.

41. The mote . . . the beam. Perhaps Jesus had had the unpleasant experience of getting a piece of sawdust in his eye when he worked in Joseph's carpenter shop. As a bit of sawdust is to a plank, so is the small offense in the brother's life as compared with the greater offense in one's own life.

48. When the flood arose. Because the hills in Palestine had little vegetation on them, the winter rains produced violent floods that swept away any building in their path. Sand would wash away quickly; the buildings founded on rock would remain. Christ taught that the only secure foundation for enduring life could be found in his teachings and truth. By this exclusive claim he made himself the arbiter of human destiny and the object of all true faith.

E. A Cross Section of His Ministry. 7:1–9:17.

In the section between the appointment of the apostles and the climax of Jesus' ministry at the Transfiguration, Luke gives a series of our Lord's acts and teachings which do not make a connected narrative, but which illustrate the character of his ministry. Miracles of healing and parables that contained a story seem to have interested Luke particularly.

1. Capernaum. After teaching the disciples, Jesus returned to the city. Perhaps his disciples visited their homes while he ministered in the locality. **2. A certain centurion's servant.** The centurions were the backbone of the Roman army. Usually they came up through the ranks to posts of command because of their character. This officer seems to have been different from the usual hard type of Roman military man. He had a genuine affection for his servant, and he loved the Jewish nation, which most of the Romans despised. **3. The elders of the Jews.** His relation with the elders must have been good, else they would not have pled his cause. Perhaps the centurion felt that no Jewish rabbi would do a favor for a Gentile Roman. **5. A synagogue.** The ruins of the synagogue now standing in Capernaum show Roman architecture with Jewish motifs carved on the stones. The synagogue to which Luke alludes was earlier, but this later one may have preserved something of its style.

6. Lord, trouble not thyself. Literally, *Do not skin yourself*. This may be a piece of slang that Luke has preserved. **8. For I also am a man set under authority**. The centurion recognized that just as he had authority vested in him by Rome, so Jesus had authority from God that enabled him to exercise power over disease. **9. Not in Israel.** The insight and faith of the pagan made a refreshing contrast to the unbelief of Jesus' own people, from whom he had a right to expect more.

11. Nain was about ten miles southeast of Nazareth. Near the eastern gate of

Nain, along the road to Capernaum, are rock tombs. Jesus, approaching from Capernaum, may have met the funeral procession coming out of the city on the way to these tombs. **12. A widow.** The lot of a widow in the East was hard, since she could not easily find gainful employment, and so was dependent on her nearest male relatives. **Much people.** There were many witnesses of the miracle who could testify to its genuiness. **13. Weep not.** Loud wailing was conventional at Eastern funerals; in fact, mourners were often hired to supply it. The command to stop weeping, spoken by an utter stranger, may have seemed rude. **14. Bier.** The Greek word denotes either a stretcher on which a corpse was carried, or the coffin itself.

16. And there came a fear. The sudden resuscitation of the corpse must have been terrifying for those in the funeral procession, even though they rejoiced over it. **God hath visited his people.** For many years there had been no prophetic testimony in Israel. The magnitude of this miracle compelled the people to believe that Jesus must be a prophet. **18. The disciples of John.** The ministry of John the Baptist was slowly being eclipsed by that of Jesus. The rumor of this miracle at Nain must have been widely discussed if it penetrated the fortress of Machaerus (see Jos *Wars of the Jews* VII. vi. 2) in the wilderness east of the Dead Sea, where John was a captive. **20. Art thou he that should come? or look we for another?** The long imprisonment discouraged John, and made him wonder whether Jesus was the Messiah after all. **22. Then Jesus answering.** Jesus answered by challenging the messengers of John to observe demonstrations of his power. And he appealed to John not to be **offended** (v. 23) by the way he conducted his ministry. "Offend" (Gr. *skandalizo)* has the meaning of "cause to go astray," or "cause to err," rather than "to displease."

24. The Lord paid his tribute to John by asking three questions of the people. **A reed shaken with the wind?** The reeds in the marshes bend with the wind; they do not maintain any one position. Jesus said that John was a man of convictions, who did not change with every fad. **25. A man clothed in soft raiment?** Ordinary clothing was made of coarse hand-woven materials; only the very wealthy wore imported silks and linens. John was rugged, a man who could endure hardships and who belonged to the common people. **26. A prophet?** Among the Hebrews the prophet was the highest type of leader, since he was commissioned and inspired by God. The people of Nain had called Jesus a prophet, and the same title was applied to him on other occasions (Jn 4:19; 7:40; 9:17).

27. This is he of whom it is written. The quotation from Mal 3:1 is doubly significant. It establishes John as the forerunner of the Messiah, which places him above all the other prophets. **Thee** in the original of the quoted text reads "me," and refers to God, who speaks these words, adding, "and the Lord, whom ye seek, shall suddenly come to his temple, even the messenger of the covenant, whom ye delight in." By implication, then, Jesus is identified with **the Lord** of Malachi, and his deity is affirmed. **28. Not a greater prophet than John the Baptist.** John was the greatest and last of the prophets, and the herald of a new dispensation. **He that is least in the kingdom of God.** John knew only that redemption and the work of the Holy Spirit would be introduced by Jesus (Jn 1:29-34); he did not live to see the work of Christ perfected. Those who live in the era of the kingdom of God have greater privileges and powers than John.

29. Justified God. This word is used by Luke more than by the other Gospel writers. The ordinary people acknowledged the righteousness of God by accepting the condemnation of their sins through John's message, and they expressed repentance by submitting to baptism.

31. Whereunto then shall I liken the men of this generation? Jesus illustrated the behavior of the Pharisees from the games of children which he had probably played as a boy. If someone proposed that they "play wedding," the others would not dance; if one suggested that they "play funeral," the others would not mourn. No matter what was suggested, they would not be pleased. They called John crazy because he abstained from luxuries; they accused Jesus of being a glutton and a reveler because he attended feasts.

36. And one of the Pharisees desired him that he would eat with him. *Invited* would be a better rendering than **desired.** The Pharisee's motives may not have been wholly good; he probably wanted to catch Jesus in some act or utterance.

37. A woman . . . which was a sinner. The intrusion of this woman was intolerable to the respectable Pharisee because of her evil reputation and because she was not an invited guest. **An alabaster box.** Alabaster was a fine translucent stone, used only to make decorative pieces. The box of ointment must have been exceedingly valuable, and was possibly the proceeds of her sin. **38. Stood at his feet behind him.** Guests at dinner did not sit at tables, but reclined on couches with their heads toward the table. It would have been easy for this woman to kneel at the end of the couch on which Jesus lay.

39. This man, if he were a prophet, would have known. The Pharisee expected Jesus, as a wise rabbi and a religious leader, to reject the woman's attention as insulting. The rabbis of that time never talked with a woman in public if they could help it, and if they did, their conduct was exceptional (Jn 4:27). Simon concluded that Jesus was either stupid or lax. **40. And Jesus answering said.** Simon had not said a word audibly, but Jesus read his thoughts, and answered by the parable that follows. The story must have held the attention of the guests at dinner and at the same time made the point unmistakably plain.

41. A certain creditor. As a wealthy man, Simon must have been a creditor himself on numerous occasions. Perhaps Jesus knew he was generous, and used this story to appeal to him personally. **Five hundred pence . . . fifty. Penny** represents the Roman *denarius,* worth about seventeen cents. The first creditor owed about $85.00; the second, $8.50.

42. Which . . . will love him the most? Simon may have taken the story to be simply a conundrum proposed as part of the dinner conversation. **43. I suppose** may indicate that he was a bit hesitant to commit himself, because he felt that Jesus had an ulterior motive in telling the story. There was, however, only one logical answer, and he gave it.

44. Thou gavest me no water. Omission of washing a guest's feet was a serious breach of etiquette, and Jesus could have regarded it as a direct insult. His presence at the dinner, however, was a mark of his willingness to overlook Simon's neglect. **45. Thou gavest me no kiss.** In the East today men frequently greet each other by a kiss on the cheek. It was a common polite greeting of friends in Jesus' time (cf. Rom 16:16; I Cor 16:20; I Thess 5:26). **46. My head with oil.** A touch of perfumed oil would have been a part of the preliminaries to the feast, but Simon had omitted even this inexpensive favor. The woman had used costly ointment. **47. To whom little is forgiven.** Jesus contrasted Simon's lack of courtesy with the devotion of this woman, and implied that Simon had not experienced a deep forgiveness.

48. And he said unto her. Jesus had already said (v. 47) that the woman's sins, which he did not deny, had been forgiven; but to clear her before the public he made a direct declaration. **49.** The same question was asked at the healing of the paralytic (5:21). **50. Saved** can mean "made whole" either in a physical or in a spiritual sense. The latter meaning is intended. This woman cannot be identified with Mary Magdalene, nor with Mary of Bethany, despite the similarity of the latter's act recorded in the account of the dinner at Bethany (Mt 26:6-13; Mk 14:3-9; Jn 12:1-9). The differences between these episodes are greater than the resemblances.

8:1. He went throughout every city and village. Jesus made a systematic tour of Galilee, reaching the masses of the people in preparation for his final appeal to them. **The twelve were with him.** Does this statement imply that previously they had not always traveled with him? Perhaps they spent part of their time in self-support. **2. And certain women.** Luke seems to have been personally acquainted with them. Joanna (v. 3) is not mentioned outside of this Gospel. **3. Which ministered unto him.** Their gratitude to Jesus for healing prompted the gifts that helped to support him and the disciples on the preaching tours.

4. He spake by a parable. This parable is narrated and interpreted by all three of the Synoptic Gospels (Mt 13:3-23; Mk 4:3-25). It is an outstanding sample of the Lord's method of teaching. Usually known as the Parable of the Sower, it could better be called the Parable of the Soils.

5. A sower went out to sow. Mechanized farming was unknown in Palestine. One of the most familiar sights in the rural communities was the farmer scattering seed over the plowed soil. **The way side.** Except for a few main highways there were no paved roads, only tracks through the fields. Wayfarers would beat the ground hard as they walked between villages. **6. A rock** (Gr. *tēn petran,* the rock). Palestine is a very stony country. The seed did not fall on bare rock, but on thin soil covering a ledge of rock. The warmth of the rock would cause the seed to sprout quickly, but the soil would dry out rapidly, and the young shoots would wither. **7. Thorns.** Thorn bushes grew in clumps, and were hard to eradicate. Even if the tops of the bushes were cut away, the roots would remain in the ground. **8. Good ground.** The soil of Palestine is rich, and when properly irrigated will produce large crops.

9. What might this parable be? The problem for the disciples was to discover the application of the facts stated; the facts themselves were simple and familiar. **10. The mysteries of the kingdom of God.** "Mystery" (Gr. *mysterion)* is a fact or truth revealed only to the initiated. The truth of God cannot be understood by those who have no spiritual discernment (I Cor 2:14). The disciples would see new truth through the parables; the others would think of them only as entertaining stories.

11. Now the parable is this: The Parable of the Soils is one of the few that Jesus interpreted. It gives a key both to his methods of teaching and to the mental processes that lay behind them. **The word of God** is the truth of God, whether written or spoken. In this parable the Lord was thinking of his own teaching as given to the crowds. **14. Bring no fruit to perfection.** There may be fruit, but the ears of grain will be scanty and stunted. **15. Honest and good heart.** Two Greek words *(kalos* and *agathos),* both meaning "good," are used. The former connotes beauty; the latter, nobility or uprightness.

16. Candle is properly a lamp (Gr. *lychnon),* a little clay dish in which olive oil and a wick were placed. It gave a very feeble light. Placed under a pot or a piece of furniture, it would give no illumination. It was usually set on a lampstand **(candlestick)** so that its light would radiate in every direction. **17. For nothing is secret, that shall not be made manifest.** Truth is like a light; it cannot be kept secret if it is to be useful. **18. Take heed therefore how ye hear.** The listener has as much to do with the effectiveness of the message as the speaker does.

19. His mother and his brethren. Little is said in the Gospels about Jesus' family. His brothers did not believe in his claims (Jn 7:5). The nature of their errand is not revealed. Possibly they felt that Jesus was making extravagant claims and was embarrassing them by his assertions of authority. **21. My mother and my brethren are these.** He declared that kinship with him is spiritual, not primarily physical.

22. Let us go over unto the other side of the lake. The east side of the lake was largely uninhabited. Jesus wanted to get away from the crowds in order to rest and to talk with his disciples. **23. He fell asleep.** The Saviour was subject to human limitations, and the fatigue of his ministry had worn him out. **A storm of wind** was not unusual on Galilee. The lake lies 680 feet below sea level and is surrounded by hills. As the air on the heights cools toward the end of the day, it flows down through the defiles of the hills to the lake surface and churns it into foam. **They were filled with water, and were in jeopardy.** The high waves dashed into the open vessel, so that it was in danger of sinking. **24. We perish.** The storm must have been unusually violent to frighten experienced fishermen who knew every mood of the lake. **Then he arose, and rebuked the wind.** Jesus had authority over the powers of nature. In the natural course of the passing of a storm, complete calm would not have followed instantly.

26. The country of the Gadarenes. The miracle could hardly have taken place at Gadara, which was seven miles from the lake. A well-attested reading in a number of older manuscripts is *Gergesa* or *Gerasa.* There was a village by the lake opposite Capernaum, the site of which is marked today by ruins called *Khersa,* near which were precipitous rocky slopes and abandoned tombs. The territory belonged to Gadara, and thus could be called "the country of the Gadarenes." The variation in manuscript readings may reflect the confusion of early scribes over the identity of the place, or even differing viewpoints on the part of the Evangelists. The territory along the lake was wilderness.

27. A certain man, which had devils a long time. The demoniac was so dangerous that he had been driven from civilization, and had found refuge in the deserted tombs. **28. What have I to do with thee.** Recognizing Jesus as the Son of God, the demon was overcome by fear of the judgment that Christ might pronounce upon him. **29. He was kept bound with chains and in fetters.** The demon-possessed man required forcible restraint. With supernatural strength he broke his bonds, and escaped.

30. A Roman **legion** comprised about 6,000 men. The expression here may mean only a great number. **31. The deep**

means the abyss of destruction to which all evil spirits are doomed (Rev 9:1; 11:7; 20:1,3). **32. Many swine.** The pigs were raised for sale in the Gentile markets of the Decapolis. Jews would not have purchased or used them. **33. The herd ran violently . . . into the lake, and were choked.** The eastern shore of the lake is so precipitous that if the animals started to run, they would have been unable to stop. Pigs cannot swim well, and so the whole herd was lost.

35. Clothed, and in his right mind. Some have questioned the right of Jesus to permit the destruction of another's property. A choice of values was involved. Which was worth more—the man, or the pigs? **37. Besought him to depart from them.** The people evidently valued their pigs more than they did the man, for they feared further trouble, and urged Jesus to leave. **38. Now the man . . . besought him that he might be with him.** The attitude of the healed demoniac was the exact opposite of that of his former neighbors. **Jesus sent him away.** The Lord did not repudiate him, but gave him a commission to discharge. He became an effective witness to the Saviour's power.

41. And, behold, there came a man named Jairus. No place is named as the setting for the raising of Jairus' daughter, but Capernaum is the most likely location. Verse 40 says that Jesus had **returned,** which implies going back to a place originally left. Jairus may have been one of the elders who came to Jesus to intercede for the centurion's servant (7:3).

43. And a woman having an issue of blood twelve years. Luke makes clear that hers was an incurable case, which defied the skill of all the physicians. **44. Touched the border of his garment.** The **border** was really a tassel (Gr. *kraspedon)* which a rabbi wore on his garment. The outer robe was a large square of heavy woolen cloth, draped over the wearer's back in such a way that the tassel of one corner hung between his shoulder blades. In the throng the woman crept up behind Jesus and touched the tassel. **45. Who touched me?** Jesus felt a flow of power going out from him, and knew that someone had touched him. The question seemed silly to the disciples, since he was being jostled on all sides by the crowd. But the Lord could discern the difference between the casual accidental bodily contacts, and the outreach of faith. **46. Virtue.** See comment on 6:19.

47. And when the woman saw that she was not hid. She had sought secrecy to avoid any possible embarrassment, but when her act was discovered, she was frightened. **48. Daughter, be of good comfort.** Jesus' tact and kindliness gave her reassurance. He confirmed the healing, and sent her away relieved.

49. While he yet spake. The delay had been fatal. The news must have disheartened Jairus, and perhaps aroused in him resentment against the woman who had interrupted the Master's plans. **50. Fear not: believe only.** Christ's power and compassion were unlimited. **51. He suffered no man to go in.** After the notable healing of the woman, Jesus wanted no further publicity. **52. She is not dead, but sleepeth.** He spoke of death as sleep because he was thinking of it as a state from which one will awake. The mourners looked upon it as the end of life (cf. Jn 11:11-14).

55. He commanded to give her meat. He was aware of ordinary practical needs as well as of emergencies. **56. He charged them that they should tell no man what was done.** He did not want the populace to use his miracles as a reason for making him a political figure. He intended that his power should be used to relieve suffering and to help the needy; he wanted to avoid mere showmanship.

9:1. Power and authority. Power is inherent ability; **authority** is the right to exercise it. **2. To preach . . . and to heal.** Their ministry was to be an extension of his. **3. Take nothing for your journey.** Jesus wanted to test their faith by making no elaborate preparations for the journey. Deissmann suggests that the **scrip** (Gr. *pēra)* was the wallet which a beggar carried (LAE, pp. 108-110). Jesus forbade the disciples to beg as representatives of other religions did. **4. There abide.** They were not to go from house to house in search of the most comfortable lodgings, but were to accept whatever was offered. **5. Shake off the very dust.** If their word was refused, they were to indicate their rejection of the city by this emphatic gesture. **6. Every where.** Galilee was thoroughly covered.

7. Herod the tetrarch was the ruler of Galilee who had imprisoned and executed John the Baptist. He had feared John's influence, and he thought that Jesus might be the Baptist's successor. **8.**

Elias. Elijah, the most spectacular of the Hebrew prophets, had ascended alive into heaven, and the prophet Malachi (4:5) had predicted that he would return to prepare the way for the Messiah. **9. Herod. . . . desired to see him.** Herod's conscience and his curiosity made him want to see Jesus, probably with evil intent (cf. 13:32).

10. Desert place. Not a barren waste, but uninhabited country. **Bethsaida** was a small town on the north shore of the lake, east of the inlet of the Jordan River, a moderate distance from the larger cities on the west side of the lake. **12. And when the day began to wear away.** The disciples realized that the crowds were hungry, and that they should be fed before they became faint.

13. Give ye them to eat. Jesus commanded the disciples to estimate their own resources, and to use what they had. **Five loaves and two fishes.** The **loaves** were round cakes, like biscuits; the **fish** were small pickled fish, used as relish. **14. Five thousand men.** If women and children were present, as Matthew hints (Mt 14:21), the crowd may have been as large as ten thousand. **Make them sit down by fifties.** Jesus knew how to organize a crowd. Seating the groups would prevent confusion, and would make serving easier. **16. Then he took . . . and . . . blessed . . . and brake, and gave.** As Jesus broke the bread and fish, he multiplied them, so that he gave the disciples a constant supply of food to transmit to the crowd. **17. Twelve baskets** provided a generous share for each of the disciples. The **basket** (Gr. *kophinos)* was a large container, perhaps the size of a modern bushel.

F. The Climax of His Ministry. 9:18-50.

With this section of the Gospel, Luke brings the ministry of the Saviour to a turning point. In the Galilean ministry, which ended with the feeding of the five thousand, Jesus had come to the peak of his popularity, and with his refusal to become a king (Jn 6:15), he began to lose public support. The confession of Peter and the revelation of the Transfiguration to the inner circle of disciples began the progress toward the cross, which dominates the latter part of this Gospel.

18. He was alone praying. Luke notes that Jesus prayed at every great crisis of his life (3:21; 5:16; 6:12; 11:1; 22:44). **Whom say the people that I am?** The Lord changed the focus of the disciples' attention from his deeds and teachings to himself. **20. But whom say ye that I am?** Having nurtured their faith and having given them ample opportunity to observe him, Jesus wanted a confession of their personal faith, not a random opinion. **Peter answering said, The Christ of God.** Peter's affirmation of faith in Jesus as the Messiah promised in the OT was not based on political pretensions on the part of the Master, nor upon any extravagant claims. Jesus' power and authority were self-authenticating.

21. And he straitly charged them. The Lord did not want to be publicized as the leader of a revolutionary movement. The work of the cross must precede any deliverance of the nation from political oppressors. **22. The Son of man must suffer . . . and be raised the third day.** Must (Gr. *dei)* denotes logical necessity. Christ was obligated to fulfill the purpose of God as revealed in the Scriptures. This concept appears in the preaching of the early church (Acts 2:23,24; 13:17-34; 17:3; 26:22,23). The death of Jesus was a tragedy, but it was not an accident; for he was fulfilling the purpose of God in redemption.

23. If any man will come after me. The disciples followed the Master at his initial call to them (5:11), but at that time they had no idea his career would end at the cross. They were still thinking in terms of conquest and of power (22:24). This appeal was a solemn warning to re-evaluate the cost of being his disciples. **Deny** means exactly what Peter did at the trial of Jesus: he refused to recognize him. **Take up his cross daily.** A voluntary acceptance of the responsibilities and sufferings incidental to being a disciple of Christ. **Follow** (Gr. *akolouteite).* An imperative involving persistent action: "Let him keep on following me." **24. For whosoever will save his life. Life** (Gr. *psychēn)* is *soul,* or *personality.* Jesus demanded the consecration of the whole man to his cause. **For my sake.** He claimed to be the final criterion of all human values.

26. When he shall come in his own glory. In the same discourse, Jesus predicted both the cross and the triumphal establishment of the Kingdom at his second coming. **27. There be some standing here.** These words seemingly require the return of Christ within the lifetime of the apostles, but he did not come. The most logical explanation is that Jesus was speaking of the Transfiguration as a sample of the coming of the Kingdom, given to some of the disciples as a pledge of the future (cf. II Pet 1:11,16-19).

29. The fashion of his countenance was altered. For a short time Jesus resumed the glory which he had left to come to earth. His body and clothing became incandescent with the glow of deity. **30. Two men, which were Moses and Elias.** Both of these men had left the world under unusual circumstances: Moses had been buried by the hand of God (Deut 34:5,6), and Elijah had been taken up in a whirlwind (II Kgs 2:11). They represented the Law and the prophets, subordinate to Jesus, but important witnesses to his work. **31. Spake of his decease.** The work of the cross was of supreme importance to the heavenly counsels. **Decease** is literally *exodus*. Jesus' death was a withdrawal from one sphere and the beginning of a new life in another.

32. Heavy with sleep. The event took place at night. **They saw his glory.** Compare the testimony of John (Jn 1:14). **33. Let us make three tabernacles.** Literally, *huts.* Peter was thinking of a temporary shelter, for he wanted to enjoy the company of the celestial visitors for a time. **34. A cloud.** Not a rain cloud, but the Shekinah which marked the presence of God (Ex 13:21,22; 40:38; Num 9:15; Ps 99:7; Isa 4:5; II Chr 7:1). **35. A voice.** The Father repeated his approval of Jesus at the close of his Son's popular ministry (see 3:22).

37. On the next day. Christ returned from the glory of the Transfiguration to continue his ministry and to die. The first step on the road of humiliation was the embarrassment over his disciples' impotence. **41. O faithless and perverse generation.** The Lord was speaking to the disciples, not to the father. In spite of their privileges and previous experience in ministry for him, they were still powerless.

44. Let these sayings sink down into your ears. Jesus was making a supreme effort to acquaint the disciples with the change in his outlook. **46. Which of them should be greatest.** This is the complement of verse 45. They had not learned to evaluate life in terms of the cross (9:23-26). **47. Jesus . . . took a child.** He used the child as an illustration of unpretentious humility. The child had not attained any place of importance in society, and was typical of the **least** (v. 48) of whom our Lord was speaking.

49. He followeth not with us. The disciples were bigoted. Because this man was not of their company, they were ready to discount his work completely.

V. The Road to the Cross. 9:51–18:30.

This section of Luke's Gospel, which is largely peculiar to him, contains many episodes and parables which are not found elsewhere, and which may have been the results of his personal research. The chronology is difficult; the section seems to be a collection of stories rather than a complete narrative. It does, however, represent the teaching of Jesus in the last year of his ministry, and reflects a period of rejection and tension.

A. The Perspective of the Cross. 9:51-62.

51. That he should be received up. There are two possible interpretations: either Luke used the word **received up** (cf. Acts 1:2) in the broad sense of the entire Passion ministry (including the Ascension); or else he implied that Jesus, instead of returning to the Father immediately at the height of his public career, deliberately chose the way of humiliation that led to the cross. The second alternative has some support in the teaching of Heb 12:2, which says that "in exchange for the joy set before him he endured the cross" (original translation).

52. A village of the Samaritans. The Samaritans were descendants of colonists whom the Assyrian kings had planted in Palestine after the fall of the northern kingdom in 721 B.C. Because of their mixed blood and different religious customs, the Jews hated them. Pilgrims to Jerusalem ordinarily did not go through Samaria. **54. Wilt thou that we command fire to come down.** James and John resented the slight to Jesus, and wanted revenge. **56. For the Son of man is not come to destroy men's lives, but to save them.** Luke's quotation exemplifies the purpose of Jesus to save men, which is repeated at intervals in his Gospel.

58. The Son of man hath not where to lay his head. The rejection at Samaria gave point to this utterance. The Lord of the earth had less that he could call his own than the beasts and the birds. **59. Suffer me first to go and bury my father.** The speaker did not mean that his father had died, but that he was obligated to care for him until he died. **60. Let the dead bury their dead.** The spiritually inert can wait for death; Jesus summoned the spiritually alive to follow him. **62. No man . . . looking back, is fit for the kingdom of God. Looking back** is continued action. A farmer who is plowing must always look forward if he is to plow a straight furrow.

B. The Ministry of the Seventy. 10:1-24.

Only Luke records the mission of the Seventy. Jesus must have had a large following if he could command the services of seventy men for a preaching mission in the cities of Galilee and Judea. Edersheim (Alfred Edersheim, *The Life and Times of Jesus the Messiah*, Vol. II, p. 135) suggests that Jesus sent them out at some point before the Feast of Tabernacles preceding his death. It might be deduced from his language that he had been rejected by the crowds in the Galilean cities (10:13,15), and that he was anticipating leaving the district permanently.

1. After these things. Luke's chronology is indefinite; but he locates these events after the crisis of the Transfiguration. **Two and two.** Jesus had sent out the Twelve in the same way on a previous mission (Mk 6:7). Sending them in pairs strengthened their witness, and made the traveling more pleasant. **Whither he himself would come.** The Seventy were to prepare the people for his last appeal to them. **2. The harvest.** Jesus used this figure often in speaking of the ingathering of believers (Jn 4:35,36; Mt 13:30,39).

4. Carry neither purse, nor scrip, nor shoes. The trip was to be brief, and its urgency demanded haste. They were forbidden to encumber themselves with needless baggage. **Salute no man.** The Lord did not want them to be unfriendly, but the Eastern salutations were so elaborate that they might have wasted a great deal of time in ceremony. **6. The son of peace.** A Hebrew idiom, meaning *a peaceful man.* **Son of** was frequently employed with a noun to emphasize a characteristic. John and James were called "sons of thunder" (Mk 3:17) because of their violent disposition. **7. Go not from house to house.** Jesus wanted his disciples to be messengers, not beggars. They were not to wander about, looking for the most comfortable quarters and the most congenial company.

9. Heal the sick. Christ imparted to the disciples the power to heal as an extension of his ministry. There is no indication that all of them retained this power permanently. **12. In that day.** This phrase was used frequently in the prophetic books of the OT to denote the final day of judgment (Amos 8:9; 9:11; Zeph 1:14; Zech 12:8,11; 13:1; 14:4). **Sodom.** A city of Abraham's time, which was so vile that God destroyed it by an exceptional judgment (Gen 19:13,24). **13. Tyre and Sidon** were Phoenician cities noted for their luxury and debauchery. **Sackcloth.** A rough cloth worn by mourners as a sign of grief.

17. And the seventy returned. Their mission seems to have been successful. The Twelve failed to cure the demoniac boy (9:40); but the Seventy reported that even the demons fled at the mention of Jesus' name. **18. I beheld Satan as lightning fall.** *In the act of falling* would be a fair translation. Jesus implied that the power of Satan was broken, and that the success of these disciples was an evidence of the victory. **19. Power** is authority, the right to command. **20. Rejoice, because your names are written in heaven.** The greatest cause for rejoicing is not the momentary victory over supernatural forces, but the eternal triumph of being enrolled among the citizens of heaven. **Written** may mean inscribed on a public register (cf. Heb 12:23; Rev 3:5; 22:19).

21. Jesus rejoiced. The successful tour of the Seventy encouraged Jesus, for the power of Satan had not been sufficient to keep the revelation of God from these men. **22. No man knoweth who the Son is, but the Father.** This verse has a strong resemblance to the phraseology of Jesus as recorded in the Gospel of John (cf. Jn 5:22,23). Since it was spoken in private, it may indicate that the Johannine discourses were private in nature. Our Lord's public discourses seem to have been given in a different style.

C. Popular Teaching. 10:25–13:21.

25. A certain lawyer. In the Jewish community the 'lawyer' was an expert in the religious teachings of the Mosaic law rather than an advocate in court. **Tempted.** The lawyer was testing Jesus to see what he would say in answering a catch question. **Eternal life** was a current topic of religious debate (18:18).

26. What is written in the law? The Saviour accepted the authority of the OT as the revelation of God. His question implies that the lawyer could have found the answer to his query in the Scriptures had he really searched them. **27. And he answering said.** The lawyer's answer was a composite of two texts—Deut 6:5 and Lev 19:18. The former was a part of the Jewish *Shema,* or creed, which was customarily recited in the synagogue worship. **Heart** (Gr. *kardia)* is the inner life, not necessarily only emotion. **Soul** (Gr. *psychē)* is personality, the conscious being. **Strength** (Gr. *ischui*) is physical strength. **Mind** (Gr. *dianoia)* is the capacity to think. **29. Willing to justify himself.** Realizing that he had been caught by his own words, since he had not kept the Law, the lawyer began to quibble over a definition. Strict Jews would not acknowledge that any non-Jew was a neighbor.

30. A certain man. Although Jesus' story is called a parable, it may well have been a report of an actual occurrence. **Went down from Jerusalem.** Literally true, for Jerusalem is 2,600 feet above sea level, and Jericho is nearly 1,300 feet below sea level. The road is crooked and narrow, winding down through rocky defiles, where robbers could easily hide. **32. A Levite.** Levites served in the Temple. Neither the priest nor the Levite attempted to aid the man. They may have thought that he was dead, and did not wish to defile themselves by contact with a corpse. **33. But a certain Samaritan.** The Samaritans were scorned by Jews because they were descended from Gentile ancestry and because their kind of worship was different from that of orthodox Judaism. They worshiped in Mount Gerizim rather than in Jerusalem, and maintained a priesthood of their own. A small group still survives in the village of Nablus, near the site of ancient Shechem. **34. And went to him.** If the robbers were still lurking in the vicinity, the Samaritan was risking his life. Jesus showed that the Samaritan had the attitude of love which the Law commanded. **35. Two pence.** The equivalent of two days' wages. He was paying the expenses of a perfect stranger, simply because of good will. **36. Which . . . was neighbour.** This question shamed the lawyer into admitting that the true neighbor was not either of the priestly officials of Judaism, but the Samaritan.

38. A certain village. John (12:1) says that the village was Bethany, about two miles from Jerusalem on the road that led to Jericho and Trans-Jordan. Jesus must have visited there frequently as he traveled between Galilee and Jerusalem. **Martha** seems to have been the older sister, who took the responsibility for the household. **39. Heard his word.** The Greek word *(ēkouen)* means that she was continually listening to the Master, or that it was her custom to do so. "Who always used to listen to his teaching" would be a good paraphrase. **40. Cumbered.** The Greek word *(periespato)* means *to be pulled away* or *to be pulled apart*, hence "distracted," "overburdened." **41. Martha, Martha.** On several occasions, according to Luke's account, Jesus repeated a name when he wanted to make some unusually impressive statement (see 22:31; cf. Acts 9:4). **42. But one thing is needful.** Martha thought "many things" were necessary for the Lord's comfort, and was wearing herself out to prepare them. Her company meant more to him than her cooking.

11:1. As he was praying. Neither Luke nor Matthew locates exactly the occasion on which Jesus gave his disciples this model prayer. Matthew includes it in the Sermon on the Mount (Mt 6:9-13).

2. When ye pray, say. He did not intend them to repeat this prayer in parrot-like fashion. Rather, its several petitions were to serve as a guide to right attitude and content. **Our Father.** Jesus used a child's word for **father,** which appears also in Rom 8:15. It is used by modern Hebrews within the family circle, and implies familiarity based on love. God is the Father of all who receive Christ (Jn 1:12). **Hallowed be thy name.** The first petition concerns the honor of God, not the needs of the suppliant. The holiness of God must not be marred by the act of the one praying. **Thy kingdom come.** The rule of God must become universally acknowledged. Jesus would not have told his disciples to pray for the coming of the Kingdom if it had been present. **Thy will be done.** God's will is done in heaven by the angels without hesitation or dissent. The prayer calls for the same kind of obedience from the worshiper.

3. Give us day by day. The Greek is concise and graphic: *Keep giving to us our daily allotment*. **4. Forgive us our sins** is both a plea and a confession. It is an acknowledgment of need, because man is a sinner; and it is a plea for divine grace. **Indebted to us.** Sin is a debt owed to God which man himself can never pay. "In whom (Christ) we have redemption through his blood, the forgiveness of sins, according to the riches of his grace" (Eph 1:7). **Lead us not into temptation.** Temptation does not necessarily mean solicitation to evil, for God never tempts in that sense (Jas 1:13). The prayer asks that the believer may be spared from testing which might force him into evil.

5. Which of you shall have a friend. The following parable was given by Jesus to illustrate the certainty of answer to prayer. In it he placed prayer on the basis of personal friendship with God. **Midnight.** The most dangerous and inconvenient hour for a call. People in our Lord's day seldom ventured out at night for fear of bandits. **6. A friend . . . in his journey is come.** If the friend traveled on foot all day, and did not arrive until midnight, he must have been desperately hungry. Hospitality demanded that he be fed.

7. The door is now shut, and my children are with me in bed. Eastern homes did not have a separate bedroom. Usually the father of the family bolted the door, then unrolled mats on the floor for the children. He and his wife occupied the bed or space nearest the wall. It would have been impossible to reach the outer door without disturbing the children. **8. Because of his importunity.** The persistent knocking of the midnight caller was more troublesome than opening the door and handing out the bread.

9. Ask for what you do not possess; **seek** for what is not apparent; **knock** that obstacles may be removed. These three words epitomize the content of persistent prayer. **10. For every one.** Our Lord promised a complete answer; he made no exceptions. **11. A father.** Jesus indicated a stronger tie between God and man than between friend and friend. God is a father, and bestows His gifts not just because man is persistent, but because He loves His children. He will do no less for them than any earthly father would do for his family. **13. If ye then.** If human beings who are evil can act in a gracious and loving manner, how much more will God do so? **The Holy Spirit.** Matthew, in a parallel passage, says "good things" (Mt 7:11). Luke places special emphasis on the gift of the Holy Spirit.

15. Beelzebub. The Greek text of the better manuscripts reads *Beelzebul*, a rendering of the Hebrew *Baalzebul*, "lord of flies," or "lord of the dwelling." It was the title given to one of the gods of the Philistines, and had been brought over into Judaism as a title of Satan. Since Jesus' enemies would not admit that he came from God, they attributed his power over demons to a superdemonic source. **16. A sign from heaven.** The utter unreasonableness of his enemies is demonstrated by their demand for a sign when they had just witnessed one. **18. If Satan also be divided against himself.** The Lord pointed out that it would be foolish to think that Satan would be undoing his own work. **19. By whom do your sons cast them out?** If his works should be attributed to the power of the devil, could the Jews make a better claim for their own children who exorcised demons? **20. With the finger of God.** A figure of speech for the power of God. Jesus' exercise of God's power proved that he had brought the rule of God among men.

21. A strong man armed. Satan is the strong man who keeps his possessions in his grasp. **22. A stronger than he.** Jesus asserted his superiority over Satan, and his ability to release men from the devil's power. **23. He that is not with me.** Compare this with its opposite in 9:50. In the former instance he was speaking of a man who was unconsciously co-operative with him, while in this instance he was speaking of those who were consciously opposed to him.

24. When the unclean spirit is gone out of a man. Christ used the miracle that he had just performed as an illustration of a spiritual truth. The vacuum left by the banishment of evil must be filled with that which is good, or else the evil will become worse. **Through dry places.** The deserts were supposedly inhabited by evil spirits (see Isa 13:19-22).

27. Blessed is the womb. By pronouncing a blessing on Jesus' mother, this woman was complimenting the Saviour himself. **28. Blessed are they that hear the word of God, and keep it.** The Lord intimated that he desired not compliments but obedience.

29. The sign of Jonas the prophet. The miraculous restoration of Jonah from threatened death, to fulfill his commission to the Ninevites, was typical of the Resurrection. Christ's return from death was as great a proof of His ministry as Jonah's rescue was of his. **31. The queen of the south** was the ruler of Sheba, a country in the southern tip of Arabia. **She came from the utmost parts of the earth.** Since travel was slow and difficult, the long journey of the queen was a proof of her eagerness to meet Solomon (I Kgs 10:1-10). **The wisdom of Solomon.** Solomon would be classed today as a writer, a scientist, a connoisseur of art, a patron of industry, and a statesman. Our Lord claimed that he was **greater** than Solomon. **32. The preaching of Jonas** brought repentance to the pagan inhabitants of the populous and wicked city of Nineveh (Jon 3:5-9; 4:11). Jesus claimed that he was a greater preacher than Jonah. The world did not recognize his greatness of wisdom or of person.

33. A candle. Literally, *a lamp.* **A secret place.** The word (Gr. *kryptēn)* may be translated *cellar* (see Arndt *in loco).* **A bushel** (Gr. *modios,* a word borrowed from Latin). A measure holding about a peck. **Candlestick.** A Lamp Stand. **34. Single.** Unclouded, properly focused, or healthy. **Evil** refers to physical defectiveness.

37. A certain Pharisee besought him to dine with him. Luke records numerous occasions on which the Lord was invited to dinner (5:29; 7:36; 14:1; 19:5; cf. Jn 2:1-11; 12:1,2). He utilized these opportunities to reach men who would not otherwise have listened to him. **38. He marvelled that he had not first washed.** The Pharisees washed regularly before meals as a ceremonial observance. Jesus' neglect to do so seemed to be a direct refusal to keep the Law, and an insult to his host. The Pharisee's reaction may have been spoken, or the Lord may have read his thoughts.

39. Ye Pharisees make clean the outside. The Pharisees were the Puritans of Judaism, who were exceedingly strict about the external observance of the Law. Jesus criticized them drastically for their hypocrisy, for they harbored all kinds of covetousness and cruelty in their hearts. **40. Ye fools.** A term that Christ used seldom, and only of those who were morally perverted, not just mentally obtuse. **41. Give alms of such things as ye have.** If the Pharisees would give generously to the poor, they would not have to worry about ceremonial cleansings. **42. Ye tithe mint and rue and all manner of herbs.** They tithed even the vegetables that grew in their gardens, but failed to meet the larger obligation of love to their fellow men. **43. The uppermost seats in the synagogues.** The front seats in the synagogues were usually reserved for the most important members. **44. Graves which appear not.** Any contact with a corpse or with a grave was a defilement. Even to step on a grave without knowing it they held to be a breach of the Law. Usually graves were painted white so that they would be visible by night as well as by day. Jesus said that the Pharisees, by their example, unconsciously caused other men to break the Law and defile themselves.

47. Ye build the sepulchres of the prophets. The martyrs of one generation become the heroes of the next. It was easier for the children to build monuments to the prophets than for their fathers to obey them. **50. Of this generation.** The rejection of God's messengers culminated in the crime of Jesus' generation, because they refused him. **51. From the blood of Abel unto the blood of Zacharias. Abel** was the first martyr of OT history (Gen 4:8). **Zacharias** was the last (II Chr 24:20-22), according to the order of books in the Hebrew Bible, which, unlike the English Bible, ends with Chronicles. **52. Ye have taken away the key of knowledge.** Jesus accused the experts in the Law of not fulfilling their tasks. They were supposed to enlighten the people by explaining the Law; instead, they had kept them in ignorance.

12:1. The leaven of the Pharisees. Leaven is generally figurative of evil. The effect of fermentation and consequent decay was typical of the insidious operation of sin in the human heart. **3. Closets.** The inner rooms or storechambers of an Eastern house, to which only the privileged few had access. Words spoken in them would not normally be heard by anybody else. **Upon the house tops.** An allusion to the public announcement of news by shouting gossip from one housetop to another.

5. Fear him. This refers to God and not to Satan, for Satan cannot determine the destiny of a human soul. **Fear** implies not cringing dread but healthy respect. **Hell.** a translation of *Gehenna,* a Greek form of the Hebrew *Ge-hinnom,* or "Valley of Hinnom," which lay on the southwestern side of old Jerusalem. In the days of the kings it had been the center of idol worship, and in later reforms it was converted into the city dump. Fires were kept burning constantly there to consume the combustible rubbish. The place was used as a picture of the fate of the lost.

6. Are not five sparrows sold for two farthings. On another occasion Jesus quoted the price of sparrows as two for a farthing (Mt 10:29). They were so cheap that an extra one was thrown in for the price of four, yet Jesus said that the infinite God is concerned with the death of each sparrow. **7. Ye are of more value.** Since God's tremendous compassion for man is parallel with his authority over man's destiny, His concern should evoke love rather than fear.

8. Confess. Jesus was appealing to the disciples to make a public avowal of loyalty to him. **9. He that denieth me.** Here, to deny is not to deprive, as in some uses, but to disown. Jesus claimed the right to commend or to condemn any man in the presence of God. **10. Him that blasphemeth against the Holy Ghost.** The slander against the Holy Spirit is irremediable because it cuts a man off from the only power that can change his inner life. The Holy Spirit is God's messenger to men, on whom believers are dependent for their knowledge of the reality of God's truth. **11. Take ye no thought.** An instruction for martyrs, not for preachers or teachers.

13. Master, speak to my brother. Not justice, but possession was what this man desired. He wanted Jesus to exercise his authority, but did not ask him to inquire into the merits of the case. **14. Who made me a judge.** The Lord refused to make a decision for the personal convenience of one man.

16. The ground of a certain rich man. Again Jesus may have been citing an actual example (cf. 11:30 ff.) to illustrate the principle stated in verse 15. **17. What shall I do.** The landowner was embarrassed by riches, but he did not consider the possibility of utilizing his bumper crops for the benefit of others. **18. Barns.** Greek *apothēkē*, a granary or storehouse.

19. Soul, thou hast much goods laid up for many years. On the assurance of a large crop, the gentleman-farmer was ready to retire. He made several false assumptions: that the soul could be satisfied with goods; that the goods would last for many years; and that he would live to enjoy them. **20. This night thy soul shall be required of thee.** The rich man had not counted on the abrupt summons that called him to face God and to leave the property he had so carefully amassed. **21. Rich toward God.** Jesus implied that wealth could be invested for eternal values (cf. 16:9). **22. Take no thought for your life.** Christ did not commend negligence, but taught that food and clothing are neither man's sole nor primary concern. What man *is* is more important than what he *has*. **25. Stature** (Gr. *hēlikia)* may mean "age" (Jn 9:21) rather than "size." The problem of the rich man was not his height, but the time he had to enjoy the goods.

27. Consider the lilies. These flowers were probably anemones, or windflowers. They grew profusely in the fields of Galilee, coloring them brilliantly with reds and purples, the royal colors. **Solomon in all his glory,** i.e., when dressed in his court costume, was not so splendid as these humble flowers. **28. Tomorrow is cast into the oven.** Wood for fuel is almost unobtainable in Palestine; consequently, dry grass and weeds are used for cooking. The grass has a short life; but if God is willing to clothe it with gorgeous colors, how much more care will he expend on man, whose spirit lives forever!

30. For all these things do the nations of the world seek after. Material possessions are the chief quest of the Gentiles, who (from the Jewish standpoint) know not God. Jesus said that for his disciples these material possessions should have secondary value. **31. But rather seek ye the kingdom of God.** The Master gave his disciples a new objective in life – to work for the kingdom of God.

35. Let your loins be girded about, and your lights *(lamps)* burning. Because the Eastern garb was long and flowing, the wearer had to tuck the skirts of his robe into his belt to allow freedom of motion. Lamps were kindled by live coals, for matches were unknown.

36. When he will return from the wedding. The Oriental groom, after a supper with his friends, went to the house of the bride to claim her. Since the return procession took place late at night, the groom expected his servants to be dressed for work and to have their lamps lighted. The traditional wedding preparation was a symbol of readiness for his return. **39. What hour the thief would come.** The change of figure from the bridegroom to the thief emphasizes the element of unexpected appearance. Paul applied the same figure of speech to the Second Coming (I Thess 5:2).

41. Lord, speakest thou this parable unto us, or even to all? In order to make clear whether he was addressing the disciples exclusively or the entire crowd around him, Jesus spoke the next parable.

43. That servant (Gr. *doulos,* "slave"). A steward was often a slave who was charged with managing his master's household. **45. My lord delayeth his coming.** The parable teaches that skepticism about the Lord's return produces misuse of authority and laxity of conduct. **46. The Lord of that servant will come.** The coming of the Lord will bring rewards to the faithful and judgment to the unfaithful. **Cut him in sunder.** Probably this should be taken literally, for the Roman masters had power of life and death over their slaves. To mismanage an estate would have brought the death penalty. **48. For unto whomsoever much is given, of him shall be much required.** The language suggests degrees of punishment.

49. I am come to send fire on the earth; and how I wish it were already kindled! (original translation) Our Lord realized that his mission was divisive and disturbing. He saw clearly that the cross would be a point of controversy and argument, and wished that his lifting up (Jn 12:32) had already been accomplished. **50. I have a baptism to be baptized with.** Christ was referring to his death (cf. Mk 10:38). He felt that his power would be restricted until the work of the cross could be finished. **51. Nay; but rather division.** Judaism was a family religion, in which the people worshiped by households rather than as individuals. Jesus foresaw that his claims would cut across family life, and would necessitate individual decisions.

56. How is it that ye do not discern this time? Jesus' contemporaries did not realize the importance of his coming, nor the seriousness of rejecting him.

58. The officer. The local constable or sheriff (Gr. *praktori*), who carried out the orders of the court.

13:1. Whose blood Pilate had mingled with their sacrifices. Probably the Galileans, who were fanatical nationalists, had created a disturbance in Jerusalem. Pilate, who was there during the feast, had sent soldiers to intervene. The result was a bloody clash in the temple courts. Such action was entirely in keeping with Pilate's known character. **2. Sinners above all the Galileans.** Any unusual calamity is often interpreted as a special judgment on those affected. **3. I tell you, Nay.** Jesus did not assent to the idea that the victims of Pilate were exceptionally sinful, but said that a similar doom awaited all who were unrepentant. He may have had in mind the imminent fate of the city in the Roman siege of A.D. 70 (cf. 19:41-44; 21: 20-24). **4. Or those eighteen.** He alluded to another recent happening that had been the talk of the town, and he drew a similar application. **6. He spake also this parable.** The fruitless fig tree was symbolic of the Jewish nation. Isaiah (5:2) used a similar parable based on a vine. The owner of the fig tree had every right to expect fruit, and was justly disappointed when there was none. **7. Cut it down; why cumbereth it the ground?** Judgment was the only answer to fruitlessness. **8. Lord, let it alone this year also.** The farmer of the landlord's estate interceded for the tree, that it might have one more chance. Jesus implied that his nation was having its last opportunity to make good before the judgment of God would fall because of its rebellion and unproductiveness.

10. And he was teaching in one of the synagogues on the sabbath. The episode that follows was one of a number recounted in the Gospels concerning our Lord's healing on the Sabbath, which was a recurrent source of contention between himself and the Pharisees. **11. A woman which had a spirit of infirmity.** The woman was a victim of demon possession. Demoniac power sometimes was manifested in violent behavior (8:29) and sometimes by the crippling of a bodily member (11:14). Jesus spoke of the woman as one whom Satan had bound (13:16). **12. He called her.** His action was unsolicited; he took the initiative.

14. The ruler of the synagogue represented the standards of Judaism by his stringent interpretation of the Law. He did not speak directly, but by his pronouncement he condemned Jesus' action. **15. The Lord then answered.** The ruler of the synagogue knew the statute; the Lord knew how to apply the exception. Why should not this woman have relief from suffering on the Sabbath, if the Law provided for the prevention of thirst for animals? **16. Ought not this woman.** Jesus went further than to suggest that the healing was allowable; he asserted that it was obligatory.

18. Unto what is the kingdom of God like? The two parables that follow next parallel Mt 13:31-33, which cites them as part of a series describing the kingdom of God. The interpretations of these have been varied, and there has been considerable controversy over them. It is well to remember that usually each parable was spoken to make only one point, and that details not necessary for the point should not be overstressed. **19. It is like a grain of mustard seed.** The mustard plant was the largest that grew in Palestine. Its tremendous growth in one season from the smallest of the seeds to a shrub the size of a small tree illustrated prophetically the growth of the kingdom from the insignificant beginnings of Jesus' company of disciples into the spiritual realm which became universally recognized. **21. It is like leaven.** The figure here concerns the silent and yet powerful growth of the kingdom among men (cf. 12:1). Jesus did not assert that the world would be converted; he did imply that it would be affected by the kingdom.

D. The Beginning of Public Debate. 13:22–16:31.

22. Journeying toward Jerusalem. With this phrase Luke returns to the theme of 9:51. He built this section of the Gospel on the Saviour's last journey. **23. Are there few that be saved?** So stringent was the Lord's ethical teaching that his hearers were sure that only a few could be saved. **24. The strait gate. Strait** is an old English word meaning *narrow*.

25. When once the master of the house is risen up, and hath shut to the door. The door of an Oriental house was locked at night to keep out marauders, and was not opened again until morning. If any man knocked late at night, he was regarded with suspicion, and was usually turned away. **26. We have eaten and drunk in thy presence.** In the Orient, to eat and drink with a man was a mark of permanent friendship. **27. I know you not whence ye are.** Salvation depends on personal acquaintance with him, not upon knowledge of his reputation. **28. There shall be weeping and gnashing of teeth. There** means "in that place." **30. There are last which shall be first.** The implication is that the hour of judgment will bring many surprises.

31. Herod will kill thee. The Pharisees may only have been trying to scare Jesus out of the country. On the other hand, Herod did have an uneasy conscience, and thought that Jesus might have been John the Baptist risen from the dead (cf. 9:7). **32. That fox.** One of the few contemptuous terms our Lord used. It connotes both slyness and cowardice. **The third day I shall be perfected.** He indicated that he had a definite plan for his life, and that he did not fear Herod's threat. **33. It cannot be that a prophet perish out of Jerusalem.** His reply to the Pharisees meant that he was endangered not by Herod's threats, but by the hostility of their own city.

34. O Jerusalem, Jerusalem. Christ's lamentation over the city was prompted by his love and by his foresight. He was well aware of the fate that awaited it. **35. Behold, your house is left unto you desolate.** The destruction of the temple in A.D. 70 and the later expulsion of the Jews under Hadrian (A.D. 135) overthrew completely the Jewish commonwealth. **Blessed is he that cometh.** A quotation from Ps 118:26 which was applied to the Messiah. Jesus identified himself with the nation's hope.

14:1. He went into the house of one of the chief Pharisees to eat bread (cf. 11:37). **They watched him.** The Pharisees observed (Gr. *paretērounto*) Jesus closely (cf. 6:7) with the motive of trapping him if possible. **2. And, behold, there was a certain man before him.** The presence of this man was unexpected. Perhaps he had come to the feast in hope of healing. **Dropsy.** A swelling of the body caused by the retention of excessive liquid in the tissues. The man's pitiful condition would have been obvious to all. **3. Jesus . . . spake unto the lawyers and Pharisees.** He repeated his question of the previous occasion (6:9). **4. They held their peace.** His critics did not know how to answer. If they had said that healing on the Sabbath was not permissible, they would have condemned themselves; if they had said that it was, they could not have criticized him. **5. Which of you shall have an ass or an ox fallen into a pit.** He had used the same argument on two previous occasions (6:9; 13:15).

7. And he put forth a parable. At this dinner our Lord spoke three parables. The first two (14:7-11,12-14) were evoked by the behavior of the guests and the host; the third (vv. 15-24) was a reply to a comment. **They chose out the chief rooms.** Social position was important in the society of that day, and each guest wanted to occupy as high a place of honor as he could. **Rooms.** A better translation would be *places*. The word refers to the location of the seat, not to the dining hall. **9. The lowest room.** By the time that the guest found the best place and discovered that it was reserved for someone else, the intermediate places would have been filled, and only the lowest would be left. **10. Friend, go up higher.** If the host found an honored guest in a lower place, he would invite him to a reserved seat at the head table. **11. He that humbleth himself shall be exalted.** Christ used the immediate situation to illustrate a general spiritual principle. Plummer says: "Humility is the passport to promotion in the kingdom of God" (ICC, p. 358).

12. Then said he also to him that bade him. Jesus had a word for the host as well as for the guest. **Call not thy friends, nor thy brethren, neither thy kinsmen, nor thy rich neighbours.** The kingdom of God is not a closed society of the wealthy nor an exclusive club for friends. **13. Call the poor, the maimed, the lame, the blind.** Our Lord rebuked the selfish practice of entertaining only those who can return the favor. He wanted his host to see that his wealth gave him an opportunity to aid the indigent and helpless. **14. The resurrec-**

tion of the just. The language used here supports the idea of a double resurrection, one of the righteous, and one of the wicked (cf. Jn 5:29; I Cor 15:23; Phil 3:11; I Thess 4:16; Heb 11:35; Rev 20:5,6), separated by an interval of time.

15. Blessed is he. The guest who made this observation was trying to commend himself to the Master by a pious remark. Jesus used the following parable to show him that the kingdom of God demands real purpose, not casual approval.

16. A certain man made a great supper. The parable would have had interest for all of the guests present, because it dealt with an occasion like their own. **17. And sent his servant at supper time.** According to custom, the invitation was issued some days or weeks in advance, but courtesy required that when the time came, a personal invitation should be extended by the call of a messenger. **18. And they all with one consent began to make excuse.** To refuse an invitation at the last moment was an unpardonable breach of etiquette. **I have bought a piece of ground, and I must needs go and see it.** The excuse was hollow, for no sane businessman would buy land that he had not seen. Or, if he had seen it once, the second viewing could wait, since the transaction had evidently been completed. **19. I have bought five yoke of oxen.** The second excuse was worse than the first. Land would be a permanent possession, and might appreciate in value; but the oxen would be worthless if they were not satisfactory at purchase. The new owner was eager to ascertain how the oxen would work. But since he had already acquired them, another day's delay in the test would not have changed their condition. **20. I have married a wife.** The prospective guest evidently thought this excuse was valid, since it involved the most important event of a lifetime.

21. The master of the house being angry. The refusal of the invited guests was a direct insult. **Go out quickly.** The feast was ready, and there was no time to spare. The host would not wait for the guests who had treated him rudely, but ordered his servants to bring the beggars. **22. And yet there is room.** Since beggars abound in any Eastern city, there would have been no difficulty in gathering a large company of them. **23. Compel them to come in.** Oriental etiquette required that the feast should not begin until all places were filled. The servants were commanded to invite even the travelers in the bypaths of the surrounding country. **24. None of those men which were bidden shall taste of my supper.** Once having refused, they were forever excluded. The application of this parable centers on the rejection of Jesus by his nation. When the chosen guests for the kingdom of God refused to heed the call of the Messiah, he turned to others who normally would not have been invited.

25. And there went great multitudes with him. The next few verses do not relate directly to the feast, but to our Lord's outdoor preaching; yet they are used by Luke as a sequel to the story. This appeal of Jesus explained the nature of the call which he gave to those in "the highways and the hedges." **26. And hate not.** Christ certainly was not commanding men to hate their own families in the sense of bearing them ill will or malice. This is strong language to indicate that devotion to one's family must take second place to devotion to Christ. **27. And whosoever doth not bear his cross.** The cross of the disciple is that particular humiliation or hardship that he would incur by becoming a follower of Jesus. Publicly carrying a cross was the brand of a criminal doomed to execution (cf. 9:23,24). **33. So likewise, whosoever . . . of you.** The Lord asked for intelligent appraisal of the cost of discipleship and for complete renunciation of all claims to one's own life.

34. Salt is good. A similar teaching appears in the Sermon on the Mount (Mt 5:13). The ordinary salt of that time was of poor quality, and quickly lost its flavor when exposed to air.

15:1. Sinners designates the people of the street whom the Pharisees looked upon with contempt because they did not know the Law (Jn 7:49). The three parables in this chapter were spoken particularly for this audience, and illustrate God's interest in them. **2. Murmured.** The Pharisees grumbled because they had no appreciation of Jesus' real motive in wishing to reclaim abandoned persons.

4. Wilderness was simply open pasture. **That which is lost.** A shepherd counted his sheep at the close of each day to make sure that none had strayed. If one was missing, he searched for it immediately. **After.** The preposition (Gr. *epi*) means not only that the shepherd tracked down the sheep, but also that he made contact with it. The word connotes persistence and success. **5. Layeth it on his shoulders.** Unlike most animals, a sheep cannot find its own way back to the fold. The shepherd had to bring it. **6. Lost.** The expression is strong, emphasizing possessiveness—"my sheep, my lost one" (Gr. *to probaton mou, to apolōlos).* **7, Just persons, which need no repentance.** A semi-ironical reference to the Pharisees, who regarded themselves as infinitely better than the publicans and sinners.

8. Either what woman. The second parable would have appealed to the woman who lived most of her life indoors, as the first parable would have appealed to the man who lived outdoors. **Having ten pieces of silver.** Coins were scarcer in Palestine than they are in modern civilization, for much commerce was carried on by barter. These coins were *drachmas,* each worth about fifteen to seventeen cents of American money. They represented the savings of many years. **Light a candle.** Since the poorer Oriental houses did not have windows, a lamp was needed even in daytime in order to inspect the dark corners. **Sweep the house.** The coin could easily have been lost in the dirt of the mud floor. **9. Friends and neighbours.** These words in Greek are feminine, indicating that the woman called together her women friends for a party.

11. A certain man had two sons. This parable has been called the Parable of the Prodigal Son. It could better be called the Parable of the Lost Sons, or The Wonderful Father. **12. The portion of goods that falleth to me.** An heir was entitled to claim his share of an estate during his father's lifetime if he wished to do so. The eldest son could claim two thirds; the other children would divide the rest (Deut 21:17). **His living.** Literally, *his life* (Gr. *ton bion),* since his property was the source of his sustenance.

13. A far country. Many of the wealthier young men of Jesus' time went abroad to Rome or to Antioch for the gay life of the city. **Wasted.** The same word is used of sowing or scattering seed (Gr. *dieskorpisen).* **Riotous** (Gr. *asōtōs).* That is, wasteful. **14. In that land.** The Greek preposition *kata,* translated **in,** implies that the famine was widespread and included the whole territory where the boy was living. **Began to be in want,** or, *began to fall behind.*

15. Joined himself. The expression is strong; literally, *he glued himself* (Gr. *ekollēthē).* Desperation forced him to attach himself to some prominent person for the sake of support. **To feed swine.** The lowest possible humiliation for a Jew. **16. Husks.** The pods of the carob tree, or locust tree, which John the Baptist ate (Mt 3:4). They were long beans, sweet to the taste, and were often part of the diet of poor people. **Gave.** The verb implies a custom or process: "Nobody used to give him anything."

17. Hired servants. Hired servants in Bible times had a harder lot than slaves, because their employment was more uncertain, whereas slaves could be sure of food and shelter. **18. Against heaven.** In obedience to the third commandment, "Thou shalt not take the name of thy God in vain," the Jews substituted other terms for God lest they accidentally blaspheme (cf. Mt 5:34; 26:64,65). **19. Make me.** This petition indicates a complete change in his attitude. When he left home, he said, "Give me . . . ." He left with a selfish demand; he returned with a humble prayer.

20. When he was yet a great way off, his father saw him. The father was eagerly watching for the return of the wayward boy. **21. Father, I have sinned.** The boy never finished the speech he had prepared (cf. vv. 18,19). All the father wanted was the confession.

22. The best robe. The best robe was reserved for an honored guest. **A ring** marked the position of sonship which he had forfeited when he deserted the family circle. **23. The fatted calf.** One animal was usually held in readiness for a special occasion, that honored guests might be served quickly (cf. Gen 18:7). **Be merry** has the connotation of a party. **25. Musick and dancing** were probably supplied by hired entertainers. The return of the younger son was cause for a major celebration.

28. He was angry. The reaction of the older son was jealousy and disgust. He was bitter over what he regarded as an injustice. **29. Lo, these many years do I serve thee.** A modern translation would be: "See here! I have been slaving for you all these years, and . . . ." The language implies self-righteousness, self-pity, and an inward alienation from his father's feeling comparable to the younger son's outer alienation from the family. **A kid** would have been of small value compared to the fattened calf. The son was accusing his father of cheating him out of a small gift, while lavishing extravagant favors on the prodigal. **30. This thy son.** "This son of yours." The older brother was contemptuous, and ready to think the worst of the younger brother.

32. It was meet. By this parable, as well as by the two preceding, Jesus showed God's attitude toward sinners. He did not approve of their rebellious attitude nor of their evil deeds, but he welcomed them back and restored them to favor when they were penitent.

16:1. A certain rich man. This parable, and the one following it, may well have been taken from life. The **steward** was the manager of the household and of the estate. **Wasted his goods.** The same word that was used of the prodigal son (15:13). **4. I am resolved what to do.** Literally, *I know* (Gr. *egnōn).* In Luke's graphic style, "I have it!" He had a sudden clever idea. **They** has no expressed antecedent, but it refers to his master's debtors. The steward's device, while strictly dishonest, was effective.

5. So he called every one of his lord's debtors. As long as he was officially steward, he had the power to set the amount of rental payments; and until he was discharged, his decisions must stand. Even if the owner dismissed him, he could not alter the decisions which the steward had made previously. **6. An hundred measures of oil.** Olive oil was one of the common products of Palestine. A liquid measure was about nine gallons. **7.** A measure (Gr. *korous,* taken from the Heb. *cor*) was a little more than ten bushels. **8. And the lord commended the unjust steward.** While the steward's employer did not approve of his action, he could not help admiring his resourcefulness. **Wisely** means *shrewdly, cleverly.*

9. Make to yourselves friends of the mammon of unrighteousness. Of should be translated *by means of.* **Mammon** is an Aramaic word meaning money or property. The dishonest steward knew that he would have a claim on those whose bills he had arbitrarily reduced. They would appreciate the financial relief, and would be glad to aid him. The Lord implied that earthly property can be used to help others, whose gratitude will ensure a welcome in eternity. **11. If therefore ye have not been faithful.** The use of material wealth is a test of character. Those who cannot use it wisely do not deserve to have spiritual responsibilities entrusted to them.

16. The law and the prophets were until John. Jesus declared that John the Baptist marked the end of an era. The old dispensation of the Law was in force until he began proclaiming the coming of the Messiah and introducing the kingdom of God. **Every man presseth into it. Presseth** involves the idea of violence. Expositors differ as to whether Luke meant that men are crowding to enter the kingdom, or that they are bringing hostile pressure to bear against it (cf. Mt 11:12; see Arndt *in loco).* The former idea is preferable on grammatical grounds. **17. One tittle.** The tittle (Gr. *keraian,* "little horn") was a small projection or "hook" that distinguished one Hebrew letter from another similar to it. Jesus was saying that, even down to its smallest point, the Law would maintain its authority and certainty.

18. Whosoever putteth away his wife, and marrieth another, committeth adultery. The Law stipulated that a man could set aside his wife if he "found some uncleanness in her" (Deut 24:1). While the original provision undoubtedly alluded to moral defects, it had been interpreted with shocking laxity. Rabbi Hillel is said to have taught that a man might divorce his wife for spoiling his dinner (Plummer, in ICC, p. 390). Our Lord's words make permanent monogamous marriage the ideal for believers.

19. There was a certain rich man, which was clothed in purple and fine linen, and fared sumptuously every day. Wool, dyed **purple,** was costly and could be worn only by the wealthy. **Linen,** used for undergarments, was equally expensive. **Fared sumptuously.** Lived gaily. Life for him was one continual party, free from hardship and drudgery. **20. Lazarus.** This is the only parable of Jesus in which a proper name is given. **At his gate.** Lazarus' friends laid him at the rich man's gate as an appeal to his sympathy. **21. Desiring to be fed with the crumbs.** The fragments of food and the "left-overs" were flung to the dogs or given to beggars (cf. Mk 7:28). **The dogs . . . licked his sores.** Dogs were the scavengers of the Oriental streets, and were usually vicious. The beggar was too helpless to drive them away, and so was at their mercy. He may have feared the fate of Jezebel (II Kgs 9:35, 36).

22. The beggar died. No mention of burial occurs, not because the corpse was left exposed, but because he was probably buried in a pauper's grave with no ceremony. **Abraham's bosom.** The guest reclined on Abraham's right side, the place of honor. **The rich man . . . was**

buried. The parable emphasizes that the beggar was carried by angels into paradise; the best that could be said for the rich man was that he was buried.

23. And in hell (Gr. *hades).* This word, equivalent to the Hebrew *sheol,* may mean the unseen world in general, or the place of punishment. Hades contained both Gehenna and paradise. **26. A great gulf fixed.** The gap between hell and heaven is unbridgeable and permanent. **29. They have Moses and the prophets.** The Law contained the revelation of God sufficient for their instruction. **31. If they hear not Moses and the prophets.** Miracles do not in themselves produce faith. Jesus' words were prophetic, for when he rose from the dead, his enemies were no more inclined to accept him than they had been before.

E. Instruction of the Disciples. 17:1–18:30.

17:1. Offences. Those acts that cause others to deviate from the path of right as well as shocking their moral sensibilities. **2. A millstone.** The parallel in Mk 9:42 calls it a millstone turned by a donkey (Gr. *mylos onikos),* which indicates a mill larger than the ordinary domestic one. The Lord's words are unusually severe. **4. Seven times in a day.** Seven offenses in one day would bring the person affected to the point of exasperation.

5. Increase our faith. The apostles could not believe that a habitual offender could be forgiven. **6. Faith as a grain of mustard seed.** The mustard seed was the smallest of all the seeds known to the farmers of Palestine (cf. 13:19). Christ emphasized the vitality of faith rather than its quantity. **This sycamine tree.** Most scholars identify it with the black mulberry tree, though the same word (Gr. *sycaminos)* in the LXX and elsewhere denotes the sycamore. The mulberry tree, cultivated in Palestine for its fruit, could be found almost everywhere. The transplanting of such a tree into the sea seems fanciful; but Jesus was endeavoring to show his disciples that faith knows no impossibilities.

7. By and by. In modern English this phrase means, "in the remote future"; in the English of 1611, i.e., of the AV, it means "immediately," which is the true rendering of the Greek text. **9. Doth he thank that servant.** A slave's work was taken as a matter of course; only that which was done beyond the line of duty called for special commendation.

11. As he went to Jerusalem. Luke resumes the narrative of the last journey (cf. 13:22) on which this section (9:51–18:30) is built. **Through the midst of Samaria and Galilee.** Perhaps *between* would be a better rendering (Gr. *dia-meson).* He followed the border between the two provinces across the Jordan, and down the east side of the river; for the next place mentioned is Jericho (19:1), the point at which pilgrims usually returned to the west side.

12. Ten . . . lepers, which stood afar off. Hebrew law forbade lepers to approach close to anybody else. They were at such a distance from Jesus that he had not noticed them until they called to him. **14. Go shew yourselves unto the priests.** Compare the parallel case in 5:12-14. **As they went, they were cleansed.** All of the ten had faith to obey the Master in spite of appearances. They accepted the healing as accomplished, though they had not experienced it. **15. And one of them . . . turned back.** Gratitude was even rarer than faith. **16. And he was a Samaritan.** The only man of the ten who expressed thanks was a despised Samaritan, from whom the pious Jews expected nothing.

20. When the kingdom of God should come. Both John the Baptist and Jesus had preached that the kingdom of God was at hand. The Pharisees expected that if Jesus was the Messiah, he would introduce his rule with a sudden assertion of power and an outward conquest of the land. He had a different program in mind, and his answer covered the two main points of that program. **The kingdom of God cometh not with observation.** Its initial advent would not be a political coup or the result of some visible movement. **21. The kingdom of God is within you. Within,** Greek *entos,* may mean *among.* A kingdom is not just a territory, nor a system of governmental machinery. Its basic existence is in the unity and loyalty of a people. Jesus asserted that the kingdom of God was already present and needed only to be recognized. He had brought the kingdom with him and was living among them.

22. The days of the Son of man. The Jews used this phrase to denote the Messianic age. **Son of man** was a title of the Messiah employed in Dan 7:13,14. **And ye shall not see it.** The coming of the Messiah would be long delayed. **24. For as the lightning . . . shineth.** As a flash of lightning is immediately apparent from one end of the horizon to the other, so the true Messiah will be evident to all men when he comes to set up his kingdom. He will not arise in obscurity, nor be confined to one locality. **25. But first must he suffer many things.** This verse established beyond doubt that Jesus was speaking of himself, for he elaborated upon the same theme in 18:31-34. His interrogators had no concept of a suffering Messiah, but the **must** in this verse refers to the prophetic Scriptures, as 24:44 indicates. He looked upon his coming death in Jerusalem as a part of his Messianic mission, to be followed later by the revelation of power "in his day" (v. 24).

26. And as it was in the days of Noe. The verse implies an interim of delay between the offenses and the ultimate moment of judgment. **The days of the Son of man.** Retribution would not be immediate, but it would be inevitable. **27. They did eat, they drank, they married.** These things were not in themselves wrong, but the preoccupation of the people with them showed that they were living on a wholly materialistic plane, with no thought of God. The judgment of the flood caught them unprepared. **Until the day that Noe entered into the ark.** The moment of the judgment is coincident with or immediately subsequent to the removal of God's servant. Both in the case of Noah and in the case of Lot (see v. 29), God's people were taken away from the scene of judgment before it occurred.

30. Even thus. Material prosperity and apparent security will prevail at the time of Christ's return. **31. Upon the house top.** The flat roof of the Oriental house, accessible by an outside stairway, was used as a porch, and sometimes for sleeping in the hot season. The man on the rooftop would not have time to enter his house to get his valuables; he should flee immediately. A parallel to this prediction occurred in the siege of Jerusalem. According to Eusebius, the Christians in the city abandoned it during a temporary withdrawal of the Roman invaders, and fled to a village called Pella, where they survived the fall of the city (*Ecclesiastical History* III. v).

34. One shall be taken, and the other shall be left. Verses 34, 35, and 36 are alike in meaning; but each refers to a different time. Men are in bed at night; women grind corn in the early morning just before daylight; and workers are in the field during the daylight hours. Instantaneous action is implied; for the coming of the Lord at one moment would occur at different times of day at different points on the globe. **Taken** is often applied to the saints, but it may refer to the gathering out of offenders to judgment. Compare the allusions to the tares (Mt 13:41,42) and to the vine of the earth (Rev 14:18,19).

37. Wheresoever the body is, thither will the eagles be gathered together. When the disciples wished to know where the persons removed would be taken, Jesus answered by a proverb. **Body** may be translated *corpse* (cf. Mt 24:28, *carcase)*, and **eagles** are really *vultures*, for the true eagle does not eat carrion. The interpretation that the birds represent the saints gathering around Christ is foreign to the meaning of the proverb. It refers rather to the sudden descent of judgments upon a decadent and evil culture.

18:1. And he spake a parable unto them. Much of the preceding discourse is paralleled in Matthew 24, but this parable is unique to Luke. It shows that he was making an immediate application of Jesus' prophecy. Readiness for his return will be conditioned by prayer.

2. A judge. Perhaps the judge was a Roman magistrate, who would have had no personal interest in the needs of Jewish people. **3. Came** (Gr. *ērcheto)* is in the imperfect tense, which implies that she kept appearing frequently in the courtroom of the judge. **Avenge me** (Gr. *ekdikēson)* **of** is not a request for punishment of her adversary, but for a decree that would give protection from his injustices. **4. And he would not.** The verb expresses his state of mind rather than a single act. The widow's persistence wore down the judge's obduracy. **5. She weary me.** Literally, *lest she give me a black eye*. Greek *hypōpiazê* may mean either "to annoy," or "to damage reputation."

7. Elect. Luke uses this word only twice: once of the Messiah (23:35), and once of the people whom he has chosen and called. **8. Shall he find faith on the earth?** The rhetorical question implies that faith will be scarce. Our Lord's words do not predict a general improvement in the spiritual condition of the world before his coming.

9. And he spake this parable. The second parable in this chapter may not have been spoken on the same occasion as the first. If it was, it doubtless bears a special relation to the coming of the Kingdom. The setting of future life pervades the whole chapter (18:16,24,30).

10. Two men went up into the temple to pray; the one a Pharisee, and the other a publican. Jesus used this contrast to illustrate the difference between false worship and true penitence. **11. The Pharisee stood and prayed.** Standing was a common posture for prayer (Mt 6:5; Mk 11:25). But in the case of the Pharisee, it may mean that he sought to be noticed. **With himself** refers to his attitude rather than to his position. He was praying *to* himself or *for* himself, rather than *by* himself. **I am not as other men are.** Undoubtedly his conduct was as good as he said it was. The problem was not with his action, but with his self-righteous attitude. **12. I fast twice in the week.** Fasting was part of the Jewish ritual, but it did not require two days' fasting per week. The Pharisee was exceeding the requirements of the Law. **All that I possess.** A better translation would be, *I give tithes of all that I gain.*

13. Standing afar off. The Pharisee stood in the center of the temple area, where he would be noticed; the publican crept into a corner. **God be merciful** *to me, the sinner.* The verb "propitiate" (Gr. *hilasthēti)*, occurs in Heb 2:17, where it is rendered *make reconciliation.* It implies the offering of a sacrifice that makes a satisfactory basis for forgiving the guilt of the offending person. The publican did not plead his good works, but the sacrifice that had been offered. **The sinner.** The definite article is employed to show that the publican was thinking only of his own sins. He was the greatest of sinners in his own eyes. **14. Justified.** This is the one passage in the Third Gospel where this word has a theological meaning. Luke may have drawn it from the Pauline theology (Acts 13:39; Rom 3:23-26), with which he was quite familiar. It means to reckon as righteous rather than to be righteous. Because of his trust in the sacrifice and his confession of sin, the publican was accepted as right in the sight of God.

15. And they brought unto him also infants. Parents often brought small children to a rabbi to be blessed. The disciples thought that the people were imposing on their Master's time and strength. **16. Jesus called them.** Christ's attitude was contrary to that of the average Jewish adult, who felt that children were unimportant. **17. As a little child.** The children came to Jesus without pretense and without fear. They had complete faith that he would receive them and treat them kindly. Eagerness and expectancy characterize those who receive the kingdom.

18. And a certain ruler. Matthew (19: 16-30) and Mark (10:17-31) narrate this same story. Only Luke calls the inquirer a **ruler.** If he was young, he was probably too young to occupy a place in the Sanhedrin, but he may have belonged to the aristocracy. **Good Master.** The adjective (Gr. *agathos)* connotes moral goodness, nobility of character. **What shall I do.** The question shows that the ruler was dissatisfied with himself and with his moral attainments. He had not found the life of which the Law spoke (Lev 18:5), and was sure that he had overlooked some commandment. **19. Why callest thou me good?** Jesus wanted to know whether the title was an idle compliment, or whether the young man had carefully thought through who He was. **20. Thou knowest the commandments.** Jesus did not quote the first four commandments, which deal with man's relation to God, nor the last commandment, which deals with an internal feeling. He cited only those commandments that are concerned with outward human relations. **21. All these have I kept.** The young man told the truth as far as he knew it. He had observed the code scrupulously, and he felt that he had nothing to regret. Paul said of himself that as "touching the righteousness which was in the law," he was "blameless" (Phil 3:6).

22. Yet lackest thou one thing. The righteousness of the Law was negative. Jesus demanded a complete positive devotion. **Sell all that thou hast.** Jesus always fitted his instructions to the need of the individual. Avarice was this man's peculiar sin, and Jesus demanded action from him that would run exactly counter to his weakness. **23. He was very sorrowful.** Had he not been sincerely interested in Jesus, he would not have been sorrowful, but would have dismissed Him with contempt. He wanted what Jesus had to offer, but not enough to meet His terms. The measure of his sorrow was the measure of his wealth.

24. How hardly. Hardly does not mean "scarcely," as in modern English, but "with what difficulty." **25. It is easier for a camel to go through a needle's eye.** Luke uses the word for a surgical needle (Gr. *belonēs).* Attempts to explain this saying by a confusion between *camel* (Gr. *kamēlos)* and *cable (kamilos),* or by a figurative use of the phrase to mean the small gate in a city wall have not been convincing. Jesus was using a current hyperbolic expression to show how difficult it would be for a man of wealth to accept discipleship with him and to enter the kingdom of God. **26. Who then can be saved?** According to Jewish thinking, prosperity was a sign of the favor of God for those who kept the Law (Deut 28: 1-8). If a man was rich, he must therefore be a good man. Christ's utterance was a shock to his disciples, because they were sure that a wealthy man must be righteous.

VI. The Suffering of the Saviour. 18:31–23:56.

At this point Luke resumes the parallel with the other two Synoptic Gospels, and begins his account of the last days of Jesus' life. The whole section should be viewed in the light of Christ's death, though not all of the content is directly concerned with it. The Passion is the undertone of these parables, miracles, and debates.

A. The Progress to Jerusalem. 18:31–19:27.

31. Behold, we go up to Jerusalem. With this third announcement of his coming death (cf. 9:22,44) Jesus began the last stage of the journey to Jerusalem. **All things that are written.** Luke, as well as the writers of the other Gospels, asserts emphatically that Jesus was living in accordance with the Messianic predictions of the OT. **33. They shall scourge him.** In the hand of a strong man the Roman scourge was a deadly weapon. It consisted of a number of leather thongs set in a wooden handle, each of which was usually loaded with small pieces of lead tied into it at intervals. In a few strokes it could cut a man's back to ribbons. **The third day he shall rise again.** The four Gospels agree that Jesus predicted he would rise on the third day (Mt 20:19; Mk 10:34; Jn 2:19).

35. He was come nigh unto Jericho. The differences between Luke's narrative and those of Matthew (20:29-34) and Mark (10:46-52) have caused considerable argument. Luke says that the miracle took place as Jesus approached Jericho; Matthew and Mark say that it occurred as he left. Mark and Luke assert that one man was healed; Matthew mentions two men. Luke was probably speaking of the Gentile city of Jericho, built by Herod and situated some little distance from the site of the old Jericho that had been the Jewish city. Matthew and Mark had the old city in mind. In other words, the miracle took place between the Old and New Testament Jerichos. A writer could view the event as occurring after Jesus left the one town or before he reached the other. (See J. P. Free, *Archaeology and Bible History*, pp. 294,295.) **36. The multitude.** Plummer (ICC, p. 430) thinks that the crowd consisted of a delegation of pilgrims from Galilee going up to Jerusalem for the Passover.

38. And he cried. The word (Gr. *eboēsen)* means *to cry for help*. **Jesus, thou son of David.** He applied to Jesus a royal title, which involved belief in His Messiahship. **39. They . . . rebuked him.** He was creating a disturbance, and interrupting the Master, who may have been teaching as he was walking along. **He cried.** A different term from the word in verse 38. This one means to utter a loud cry. **40. And Jesus stood.** He halted that he might locate the man and answer his petition.

19:1. And Jesus entered and passed through Jericho. Because of its warm climate, it was a favorite winter resort of the aristocracy. **2. A man named Zacchaeus, which was the chief among the publicans.** Plummer suggests that he was "Commissioner of Taxes" (ICC, p. 433). Since Jericho was a city of much commerce, there was ample opportunity to collect import duty. **4. A sycomore tree.** The word is different from the one in 17:6, and denotes the mulberry fig, a tree quite common in Palestine. It grew to large size, with low spreading branches that could easily be climbed. **5. Jesus . . . looked up.** Ordinarily men are not likely to see what is above eye level when there are interests or distractions around them. Jesus was already aware of the presence of Zacchaeus, and was interested in him. **Come down; for to day I must abide at thy house.** Zacchaeus must have been pleased with Jesus' unprecedented concession in eating dinner with a tax collector, but embarrassed to be found in such an undignified position.

8. And Zacchaeus stood, and said. There is no indication as to *when* Zacchaeus spoke these words. It seems most likely that he did so after the dinner, when he had observed the Lord's demeanor and had heard his words. He was convicted of his sins, and had to act on the conviction. **The half of my goods I give to the poor.** Giving was a new experience for Zacchaeus. Like most tax collectors, he had previously been interested only in taking. **If I have taken any thing.** The type of conditional sentence used here (Gr. *ei . . . esykophantēsa)* implies that he knew well that he had extorted money from others. It could be translated, "Since . . . " The **if** implies an actuality, not a hypothetical case. **Fourfold.** The Law required only the restoration of the principal, with 20 per cent interest (Lev 6:5; Num 5:7), but Zacchaeus imposed upon himself a much severer penalty, comparable to that exacted for robbery (Ex 22:1).

9. This day is salvation come to this house. In this context salvation refers to inner wholeness, the salvation of the soul. **Forsomuch as he also is a son of Abraham.** The covenant of God's blessing had been given to Abraham, and those who claimed it were called "children of Abraham" (Gal 3:7). Salvation had come to Zacchaeus not because of his blood descent, but because of his faith, which was like Abraham's. **10. For the Son of man is come to seek and to save that which was lost.** This text is a summary of the entire message of the Gospel of Luke, which stresses the seeking and saving work of the heavenly Messiah.

11. He added and spake a parable. An awkwardly literal translation, which may go back to Jesus' Aramaic idiom. He added a parable to what he had already been saying. **Because they thought that the kingdom of God should immediately appear.** In spite of Jesus' repeated predictions of the cross, the disciples were still expecting his triumph in the immediate restoration of the kingdom of David. The parable was intended to give them the proper perspective of his plans.

12. A certain nobleman. The parable may have been modeled on the well-known episode of Herod's son, Archelaus, who went to Rome to obtain title to the kingdom which his father, Herod the Great, had left to him. His brother, Antipas, supported by many of the leaders among the Jews, protested the claim, and rejected his rulership. Since the event took place about the time of Christ's birth, it was a well-known story thirty years later (cf. Jos *Antiquities* xvii. 9.3; 11.1). **13. Ten pounds.** This parable is different from the parable of the talents given in Matthew (25:14-30), though there is a close resemblance between the two. In this instance the servants were treated equally, and only ten out of a possibly larger number were tested. A pound was worth 100 drachmas, about $16.50 in American money. **Occupy** (Gr. *pragmateusasthe)* means to engage in business. The servants were expected to invest their funds, and to give an account when their master returned. **14. His citizens hated him.** See comment on verse 12.

15. When he was returned, having received the kingdom. The parallelism of this parable implies that the return brought the right to possess and to develop the kingdom. **17. Have thou authority over ten cities.** The awarding of responsibility over territories implies that the master was parceling out governmental posts, and strengthens the idea that this parable was based on the accession of Archelaus. **18. And the second came.** The man who gained less was not reproved for his smaller profit. He was commended, and was given responsibility equal to his ability.

22. Thou wicked servant. The servant considered himself honest because he returned the pound with no loss; the master called him wicked because he returned it with no gain. **23. Usury** in the Elizabethan English of the AV did not have the connotation of excessive interest. **24. Give it to him that hath ten pounds.** From the standpoint of the servants, the giving of the extra pound to the one who had the most seemed unjust. From the standpoint of the master, he had already lost interest on the pound, and he wanted to invest it where the returns had the prospect of being largest. **27. But those mine enemies.** A distinction is drawn between the reproof of a servant and the execution of an enemy. The judgment of believers for reward and that of the opposing world for condemnation seem to be distinguished here.

B. The Entry into Jerusalem. 19:28-44.

28. He went before, ascending up to Jerusalem. He walked ahead of the disciples, who may have followed reluctantly. They knew very well that their Master was already under sentence by the Jewish leaders (Jn 11:16).

29. When he was come nigh to Bethphage and Bethany. Bethany lay on the southeastern side of the Mount of Olives, halfway up the rocky slope, a bit west of the modern village of *el 'Azariyeh*. Bethphage, of which there is no trace remaining, was a short distance farther up the slope, near the top (see Emil G. Kraeling, *Bible Atlas*, pp. 395-398).

30. The village over against you. Perhaps the road did not pass directly through the village. **A colt tied.** Matthew (21:2) informs us that the animal was a donkey, the common beast of burden for the poorer people of Palestine. Horses were used chiefly by the wealthy, or for purposes of war. Christ's entry into Jerusalem on a donkey was symbolic of his humility and of his peaceful intentions. **31. Because the Lord hath need of him.** Jesus must have had an understanding with the owner that he could use the donkey whenever he wished. **33. The owners . . . said . . . Why loose ye the colt?** They did not recognize the disciples, but they knew Jesus. **35. And they cast their garments upon the colt.** Our Lord had been traveling with a crowd of pilgrims (18:36), who had witnessed the miracle of the healing of Bartimaeus. They were sure that Jesus would claim his Messianic throne in Jerusalem at the Passover season, and so they made a public demonstration of acclaim.

37. The whole multitude of the disciples. The language suggests that more than the Twelve are included here. Jesus had many friends in Galilee, a large number of whom may have been among the pilgrims. Their excitement increased as the city of Jerusalem came in sight. **38. Blessed be the King.** This quotation from Psalm 118 (vv. 25,26) was sung by pilgrims as they ascended the road to the Holy City. The psalm was Messianic, so that the very use of its words indicated the popular estimate of Jesus.

40. The stones would immediately cry out. Christ asserted that his sovereignty must be acknowledged. This firm avowal of his claims made the subsequent action of the leaders of the nation all the more culpable. They could not say that they had rejected him unknowingly.

41. He beheld the city. From the summit of the Mount of Olives it is possible to see the entire city in panorama. Jesus was not excited by the applause of the crowd, because he saw prophetically the miseries that would overtake Jerusalem after his rejection. **43. For the days shall come.** He foresaw the siege and final capture of Jerusalem by the Romans under Vespasian and Titus in A.D. 70. **44. They shall not leave in thee one stone upon another.** With the exception of a few half-buried foundations, there is scarcely a vestige of the Jerusalem of that day now standing.

C. The Teaching in Jerusalem. 19:45–21:4.

45. And [he] began to cast out them that sold. Because pilgrims could not bring with them sacrificial animals or the proper coins for the Temple tax, the priests had provided concessions where these might be purchased. The business had become a source of graft and had introduced an atmosphere of commercialism into the temple worship. Jesus asserted his right over his Father's house by expelling the merchants.

20:1. The chief priests and the scribes. The religious leaders were desperate because Jesus was successfully bidding against them for popular favor. **2. By what authority doest thou these things?** Where did this Galilean prophet obtain either the right or the power to change the administration of the Temple and to perform miracles? If they forced him to make an extravagant claim, they could discredit him with the multitude.

3. I will also ask you one thing. Whenever our Lord's opponents tried to corner him with a dilemma, he by a counterquestion put them in a worse position (cf. Jn 7:53 – 8:11; Lk 20:19-40). **4. The baptism of John.** Did John come on divine authority, or on human authority? **5. They reasoned with themselves.** Jesus had forced the Pharisees either to acknowledge that they had refused to heed a messenger of God, or to expose themselves to popular disfavor. **8. Neither tell I you.** Why should he explain the truth concerning himself when they would not believe the truth about John, who was his forerunner?

9. Then began he to speak to the people this parable. From the Pharisees, whom he had silenced, Christ turned to the multitude, and told a parable similar to one used by Isaiah (5:1-7), to explain God's dealing with the nation. **A certain man planted a vineyard.** The culture of grapes was one of the chief occupations in Palestine, and involved a large investment of time and money. **And let it forth to husbandmen.** By the sharecropping system the landlord usually collected about one third of the crop as rent. **10. He sent a servant.** Rent was collected by an agent. Jesus indicated that God's servants, the prophets, had come to enforce his rightful claims on the people who had used his property. **The husbandmen beat him.** Many of the prophets were mistreated by the people, or even died violent deaths. Elijah was forced to hide (I Kgs 17:1-7), Jeremiah was thrown into a dungeon (Jer 38:6), and legend says that Isaiah was placed in a hollow tree and sawed in two.

13. My beloved son. The last appeal of the owner was to send his son. He expected that the renters would respect the person and authority of his heir. Jesus by this metaphor placed himself far above the prophets, who were only servants.

14. Let us kill him, that the inheritance may be ours. The Pharisees rejected Jesus' claims, thinking that they were the true heirs of God. **15. They cast him out of the vineyard, and killed him.** Christ's prophecy of the outcome of his last week in Jerusalem was a clear contrast to the expectations of the multitude.

16. And shall give the vineyard to others. A prediction of the removal of God's favor from Israel to the Gentiles. **17. The stone which the builders rejected.** This citation from Ps 118:22, the same psalm from which the multitude took their greeting at the entry into Jerusalem, our Lord applied to himself. The early preachers of the NT interpreted it (Acts 4:11; I Pet 2:7) as a clear prediction of Messiah's rejection and subsequent exaltation. **18. Shall be broken.** Those who stumble over Christ injure themselves. **Will grind him to powder.** Those who are judged by him will suffer irreparable loss. The verb means "to winnow grain," or "to tread under foot."

19. The same hour. The priests took action immediately, because they feared that Jesus might incite a popular uprising. **20. And they . . . sent forth spies.** Realizing that they could not legally condemn him to death, they tried to trap him so that they could turn him over to the Roman governor with an incriminating charge.

21. We know that thou sayest and teachest rightly. Their words were pure flattery, though literally true. **22. Is it lawful . . . to give tribute unto Caesar, or no?** The question posed a deadly dilemma. If Jesus said, "No," he could be accused of revolutionary tendencies; if he said, "Yes," he would be regarded as a collaborator with Rome and would lose favor with the public.

24. Show me a penny. The **penny** (Gr. *denarius)* was a silver coin issued by Rome, and was the chief monetary unit. The bronze coins of lower denomination did not carry the emperor's image. **Image and superscription.** The **image** was the likeness of the emperor's face; the **superscription** was the imperial title. **25. Render therefore unto Caesar.** The very fact that the Jews used the coin showed that they acknowledged his rule, for a king's domain was considered to extend as far as his coins were accepted. (See SBK, *Das Evangelium nach Matthaus,* p. 884.) If the Jews thus admitted Caesar as their lord, they could not criticize Jesus. **26. And they could not take hold of his words before the people.** His reply was a marvel of exactness, compactness, and directness. There was nothing in it by which he could be incriminated, yet he had answered their question, and had in addition reminded them of their obligation to God.

27. The Sadducees, which deny that there is any resurrection. The Sadducees, fewer in number than the Pharisees, were the priestly party, more interested in politics than in religion. They adhered strictly to the written law of the first five books of Moses, rejecting traditional elaborations of interpretation. They did not believe in angels, nor in spirits, nor in life after death (cf. Acts 23:8).

28. Moses wrote unto us, If any man's brother die. The case that they cited was built on the Mosaic Law, which they held to be of final authority (Deut 25:5-10). It provided that if a man died childless, his brother should marry the widow and raise a son to succeed to the property of the deceased. The purpose of this law was to preserve families from extinction. In this instance, the case was purely hypothetical. **33. Therefore in the resurrection whose wife of them is she?** The Sadducees had used this as a stock passage for disproving the afterlife. If all seven, one after the other, had the woman to wife in this world, she would, of course, be the wife of all seven simultaneously in the next world. In that case the Law would be promoting in the future life what it condemned in the present life. Such a conclusion would be absurd; therefore, according to their logic, there could be no future life.

34. And Jesus answering said unto them. The Sadducees had the right logic but the wrong premise. They were assuming wrongly that the conditions in the future life would be identical with those here. Jesus asserted that in the age to come there would be neither marriage nor death. **37. Now that the dead are raised.** Having met their negative argument, the Lord presented a positive argument of his own, using the same inferential method. **41. How say they that Christ** *(Messiah)* is David's son? The Messiah was commonly called the son (or descendant) of David (cf. 18:38). **44. David therefore calleth him Lord, how is he then his son?** In Hebrew custom, a son was always in subjection to his father. For David to speak of his son as "Lord" violated proper usage.

21:1. He . . . saw the rich men casting their gifts into the treasury. There were chests in the court of the Temple, where gifts could be deposited. **2. Two mites.** A **mite** (Gr. *lepton)* was half a farthing, and worth about one-fifth of a cent. Two mites made the smallest offering that was acceptable. **4. All the living that she had.** Jesus commended the widow not for the size of her gift, but for the sacrifice involved.

D. The Olivet Discourse. 21:5-38.

7. When shall these things be? There is a double perspective in this discourse: the destruction of the Temple and the establishment of the kingdom at Christ's return.

8. Take heed that ye be not deceived. Many false Messiahs came in the generation immediately following Jesus. **9. The end is not by and by.** He gave fair warning that there would be wars and disturbances of various kinds, but that the end would not be immediate. He expected a period of considerable length to elapse between his removal from earth and his return. **11. And great earthquakes shall be in divers places, and famines, and pestilences.** These predictions may be taken literally as signs of the end. **12. They shall lay their hands on you, and persecute you . . . for my name's sake.** He was speaking prophetically of the Christian community; the persecution would be for his name's sake. The succeeding verses find their counterpart in the narrative of the persecutions in Acts.

20. And when ye shall see Jerusalem compassed with armies. It is possible that some of our Lord's hearers lived to see the siege and capture of Jerusalem in A.D. 70. **21. Then let them which are in Judea flee to the mountains.** Only the flight of the Christians from the beleaguered city delivered them from the fate of the Jewish inhabitants who stayed. During a lull in the attack, the Christians left and went to Pella. Those who remained either died of starvation, or were sold as slaves. **24. Jerusalem shall be trodden down of the Gentiles.** From A.D. 70 until the reconstruction of the nation of Israel, Jerusalem was in the hands of Gentiles. **Until the times of the Gentiles be fulfilled.** Compare with "the fullness of the Gentiles" in Rom 11:25. The phrase implies that God has scheduled a day of opportunity for Gentiles, which will close with Israel's future restoration to favor.

25. And there shall be signs in the sun, and in the moon. If the preceding verses predict the fall of Jerusalem and the final destruction of the Jewish commonwealth, the following verses must deal with the time of the end, and with the signs of Christ's appearing (cf. v. 11). **26. Men's hearts failing them for fear.** The political and social crises, together with the physical disturbances in the world, will be more than men can endure. **The powers of heaven shall be shaken.** The final judgments of God will be attended by a change in the whole physical universe (cf. II Pet 3:10,11).

27. Coming in a cloud. A cloud of luminous glory will bring Christ back to earth, making an unmistakable "sign" of his reality (cf. 9:31,32,34; Mt 17:5; Acts 1:9,11; Rev 1:7). **28. And when these things begin to come to pass.** The language implies a process that will extend over a period of time, giving warning to those who are able to interpret the signs. **Redemption** is deliverance, the completion of the salvation of God (cf. Rom 13:11).

29. Behold the fig tree. A common tree in Palestine, which put out fruit buds very early in the spring. **31. The kingdom of God is nigh at hand.** Jesus showed by these words that the kingdom of God had not been fully realized, and that it would come in the future. These words are complementary to 17:21: "The kingdom of God is within you." **32. This generation.** Matthew (24:34), Mark (13:30), and Luke quote this utterance in substantially the same words. If it means the generation of those living when the words were spoken, then the entire chapter up to verse 25 will have to be interpreted as referring to the overthrow of Jerusalem and the collapse of the Jewish commonwealth. If, however, **generation** means the race of Israel, Jesus was predicting only that the people would survive until his return. Either interpretation is in harmony with Luke's usage of the term.

34. And so that day come upon you unawares. A better translation would be, *come upon you suddenly* (Gr. *aiphnidios).* The Lord did not say that the end would be wholly unannounced; he had already described certain warning signs. He did intimate that it would come more suddenly than might be expected. **36. That ye may be accounted worthy.** An alternate manuscript reading, *that ye might be* *strong enough to,* is slightly preferable. The testing of the last days will require exceptional fortitude.

37. At night he . . . abode in the mount . . . of Olives. During the Passover week the city of Jerusalem was always crowded with pilgrims from all parts of the empire. Christ and his disciples may have slept on the grass among the olive trees in the Garden of Gethsemane.

38. The people came early in the morning. Jesus maintained a regular teaching schedule in the court of the Temple.

E. The Last Supper. 22:1-38.

1. The Passover was the greatest and most sacred feast of the Jewish religious year, celebrating the redemption of the nation from the bondage in Egypt. The passover lamb, whose blood was originally sprinkled on the doorposts to avert the judgment of death (Ex 12:7), was typical of Christ (I Cor 5:7). **3. Then entered Satan into Judas surnamed Iscariot.** The treachery of Judas was the result of a trend in his life. He had never taken an unselfish interest in Jesus. When the Lord made clear that he was not going to claim the throne of Israel but that he expected to die, Judas was disappointed, and resolved to save himself if possible. His attitude gave an opening for Satanic suggestion and control (cf. Jn 13:2,27).

7. The day of unleavened bread. All leaven was rigidly excluded from the Jewish household at the Passover season. **10. There shall a man meet you, bearing a pitcher of water.** It was unusual for a man to carry water, for such work was relegated to the women of the household, or to slaves. Our Lord's charge to Peter and John reads as if he had made previous arrangements for a contact by means of a secret signal. He wanted the place of meeting to remain unknown, so that he might eat with his disciples without being arrested. **12. A large upper room furnished.** The room was already prepared for a feast.

15. With desire I have desired. A Hebrew idiom which intensifies the meaning of the verb (cf. Gen 22:17). **Before I suffer.** He indicated that the entire supper should be interpreted in the light of his death. **16. Until it be fulfilled in the kingdom of God.** There is a connection between the Passover and the kingdom of God. The latter is the fulfillment of God's purpose of redemption, as the former was one of its first manifestations.

19. This is my body. He identified himself with the passover emblems. As the body and blood of the lamb had been the sacrifice that was instrumental in accomplishing the redemption from Egypt, so he would be the sacrifice that would effect redemption under the new covenant. There is no indication in his language that the bread and wine were to be physically transformed into his body and blood. **Which is given for you.** This phrase and the entire succeeding text through verse 20 are omitted in the Western text, which usually amplifies rather than omits. It is possible that these lines did not belong in the original text of Luke (see WH, II, Appendix, p. 64), though there is a close parallel to them in I Cor 11:23-26.

22. And truly the Son of man goeth, as it was determined. The death of the Saviour was part of the divine plan for the redemption of men. **24. And there was also a strife among them, which of them should be accounted the greatest.** The disciples had never lost the desire for a high post in the anticipated kingdom. Their attitude of rivalry toward each other created the situation that caused Jesus to wash their feet, as recorded in John 13. **25. Benefactor** (Gr. *euergetēs)* was a title carried by the Greek kings of Egypt and Syria. **27. He that serveth** (Gr. *diakonos)* was not used of slaves, but of those who performed tasks for the aid of others. **29. I appoint unto you a kingdom.** Jesus did not deny that there would be a kingdom in which his disciples would rule. His affirmation revealed his confidence that his death would not end their hopes, but that ultimately he would see the reward of his sufferings and share it with the disciples. **30. The twelve tribes of Israel.** A similar promise is quoted in Mt 19:28. The disciples would have understood this to mean a literal rule over Israel, restored to national status.

31. And the Lord said, Simon, Simon. Jesus spoke to Simon Peter as the representative of the Twelve. **You.** A plural pronoun. **Sift you as wheat.** Wheat was sifted to remove the dirt and chaff, and to eliminate the broken and withered grains. The temptations of the devil often serve the purpose of revealing strength as well as weakness in believers. **32. But I have prayed for thee.** The singular pronoun indicates that the Lord had a special concern for Peter. He knew the failure impending because of Peter's overconfidence; yet he would not relinquish him, nor depose him from his position of leadership.

36. He that hath no sword, let him . . . buy one. This strange command occurs only in Luke. Jesus said that two swords would be **enough** (v. 38), though these would hardly have been adequate to defend the entire group against an arresting party. Did he mean that the possession of the weapons would technically place him among transgressors, and thus fulfill the letter of the prophecy quoted from Isa 53:12?

F. The Betrayal. 22:39-53.

There is a change of scene between verses 38 and 39. Jesus and the disciples had left the upper room, and had resorted to the Mount of Olives.

40. Temptation. Severe trial rather than solicitation to evil.

42. Father, if thou be willing, remove this cup. All four Gospels refer to the "cup" (Mt 26:39; Mk 14:36; Jn 18:11), though John does not reproduce this prayer. Various interpretations of its meaning have been given: the fear of death, the suffering of death, the possibility of death before he could complete the work of the cross, or the burden of the world's sin. In Revelation 14:10 and 16:19 the "cup" is symbolic of the wrath of God. No one of these interpretations may be final, but the **cup** must stand for the suffering which confronted him. He had done nothing to deserve it, but he had to endure it if he was to finish his work. **Nevertheless not my will.** These words do not express a grudging concession or resignation to fate, but the ready acceptance of the will of the Father as the highest good and the supreme desire of his heart.

43. And there appeared an angel unto him from heaven. Verses 43 and 44 do not appear in the Western text, and may not have been a part of the original writing of Luke. On the other hand, they are well attested by other manuscript tradition, and are not the kind of statement that would have been invented by scribes (cf. note on v. 19). **Strengthening him.** The answer to his prayer was not removal of the cup, but strengthening to bear it. **44. As it were great drops of blood.** Luke does not say that the perspiration was blood; he says that it was like blood. There are a few cases recorded in medical history in which intense mental suffering has been accompanied by the oozing of blood from the skin because of a breakdown of the blood vessels. **45. Sleeping for sorrow.** The disciples were not insensitive to their Master's agony, but were worn out by the physical and emotional tension.

47. While he yet spake. Had Jesus chosen to escape to Perea, he could have been safely out of reach of his enemies by the time Judas had completed his negotiations. His surrender was voluntary. **48. Betrayest thou the Son of man with a kiss?** Judas used the customary Eastern gesture of friendship to mark Jesus as the one to be arrested. **50. Cut off his right ear.** The four Evangelists note that the servant of the high priest was wounded in the scuffle, but only John and Luke mention his **right** ear. Luke must have obtained his information from an eyewitness.

52. The chief priests, and captains of the temple, and the elders. The band that came to arrest Jesus was probably composed of the temple guard, though the language of John (Jn 18:3,12) can be interpreted to mean a Roman cohort. **53. Your hour, and the power of darkness. Darkness** was symbolic of the power of Satan (cf. Eph 6:12). Jesus acknowledged the devil's temporary triumph, but anticipated his own victory.

G. The Arrest and Trial. 22:54–23:25.

54. The high priest's house. Joseph Caiaphas was the legally appointed high priest, but his father-in-law, Annas, being high priest emeritus, was still a powerful figure, and was frequently consulted on affairs of state. John says that Jesus was conducted first to Annas (Jn 18:13). They probably lived in the same palace, so that no long transit was involved between the interviews. **Peter followed afar off.** Luke does not narrate the substance of the interview with Annas; he is chiefly interested in presenting the action of Peter.

55. A fire. Since Jerusalem is 2,600 feet above sea level, in the spring the nights are cold. **59. He is a Galilean.** The Galileans spoke Aramaic with a heavy guttural accent. Peter could not hide his origin. **60. The cock crew.** "Cockcrow" was a Roman division of time, marking the close of the third watch, about three o'clock in the morning. **61. The Lord . . . looked upon Peter.** Just a glance, as he passed by on the way to Pilate's hall, was sufficient to remind Peter of the enormity of his act.

63. And the men that held Jesus mocked him. The treatment of Jesus by the henchmen of the Sanhedrin was wholly illegal. A prisoner was supposed to be held inviolate until he was condemned officially. But our Lord was left to the mercy of an irresponsible guard between the close of the hearing before the priests and his appearance before Pilate.

66. As soon as it was day. According to Jewish law, the Sanhedrin **(council)** could not convene at night. Matthew (26:57,58) and Mark (14:53,55) say that there was a preliminary hearing at the house of the high priest, and that formal sentence was passed early in the morning (Mt 27:1; Mk 15:1). Luke mentions only the latter. The *assembly,* or Sanhedrin, consisted of seventy or seventy-two of the elders and teachers of the nation. It was allowed by Rome to pass judgment on religious and civil issues, but could not inflict capital punishment without the concurrence of the Roman governor.

67. Art thou the Christ? Luke reports two questions asked by the Sanhedrin. This one, if answered in the affirmative, could have been interpreted as a confession of treason, for every messiah was regarded as a potential rebel against the Roman government. **69. Hereafter shall the Son of man sit on the right hand of the power of God.** Jesus claimed Messiahship by asserting that subsequently he would be elevated to the right hand of God. **70. Art thou then the Son of God?** The second question was intended to incriminate Jesus with the people. If he claimed to be the Son of God, he could be charged with blasphemy. **Ye say that I am.** The expression is equivalent to "Yes."

23:1. And the whole multitude . . . led him unto Pilate. Pontius Pilate was the Roman governor of Palestine from A.D. 26 to 36. His official residence was in Caesarea, but he usually visited Jerusalem during the Passover season in order to keep a watchful eye on the crowds there. It seems probable that he had been forewarned of the arrest of Jesus in order that he might be on hand early in the morning for the trial. **2. And they began to accuse him.** The charges the priests brought were calculated to incriminate the prisoner in a Roman court, since violations of the Mosaic law would have carried no weight with Pilate. Their falsity has already been shown by the total presentation of Christ's life and words in this Gospel.

3. Art thou the King of the Jews? The English translation does not give the full force of the Greek sentence: "YOU are the king of the Jews?!" Pilate was astonished that so ordinary-looking a person should claim to be a king. Luke does not give the examination of Jesus in full detail, but only the verdict. **4. I find no fault in this man.** Pilate was not pronouncing on the prisoner's sinlessness, but was simply saying that he had committed no crime that demanded legal action.

5. Galilee was a center of constant turbulence and revolt. **7. He belonged unto Herod's jurisdiction.** Pilate had no direct jurisdiction over Galilee, since it had been made part of the puppet kingdom of Herod. He welcomed an opportunity to send this embarrassing prisoner to another judge. **Who himself also was at Jerusalem.** Herod, as a nominal Jew, was under obligation to attend the Passover feast.

8. And when Herod saw Jesus, he was exceeding glad. The fame of Jesus had come to Herod's ears, and had excited his fears (9:9) and his curiosity. **9. He answered him nothing.** Jesus did not fear Herod, and refused to waste his time on a trifler. To Herod the whole affair was one vast joke. **11.** The **gorgeous robe** was probably one of Herod's cast-off robes, which he put on Jesus to mock his royal claims. **12. Pilate and Herod were made friends.** Pilate's gesture of recognizing Herod's rulership relieved any tension of jealousy between the two officials.

15. Nothing worthy of death is done unto him. Better, *done by him.* Pilate was ready to acquit Jesus on the merits of the case. **16. Chastise him.** Pilate suggested a token scourging to "teach him a lesson." **17. He must release one unto them.** It was the custom of the Roman governor to release one political prisoner at the Passover as a conciliatory gift to the people (see Jn 18:39). **18. Release unto us Barabbas. Bar-abbas** in Aramaic means *son of the father.* **19. Who for a certain sedition . . . was cast into prison.** Barabbas was an outlaw, perhaps a Galilean Zealot who had been caught in an uprising (cf. Jn 18:40).

H. The Crucifixion. 23:26-49.

26. Simon, a Cyrenian. The Jews of Cyrene had a synagogue of their own in Jerusalem (Acts 6:9). Simon had lodged outside the city over night, and was coming in for the day's worship at the Temple. The guard, seizing him, impressed him to carry the cross of Jesus. Usually the prisoner carried his own, but our Lord, worn out by the tensions of the preceding hours, was unable to do so.

27. A great company . . . which also bewailed and lamented him. Only Luke mentions this episode. The action of the trial had taken place before Christ's friends realized what was happening and could organize a protest. **28. Weep for yourselves, and for your children.** The Lord foresaw the destruction of the city and the miseries that would fall upon its inhabitants. **31. For if they do these things in a green tree.** He quoted a current proverb. The application means that if such injustice can be perpetrated against an innocent man in the time of peace, what will befall the people of the city in time of war?

32. Malefactors. Matthew calls them "brigands" (Mt 27:44). **33. The place, which is called Calvary.** The exact site is not known. All landmarks were destroyed in the siege of Jerusalem, and so identification is uncertain. The place of execution was outside the wall of the city, near a main-traveled highway. Opinion is divided today between placing it at the Church of the Holy Sepulcher, or at Gordon's Calvary, just north of the Damascus Gate. Calvary (Lat.) or Golgotha (Aram.) means "skull." Evidently the hill was so named either from the configuration of the land, which looked like a skull, or because bones were strewn about the execution ground. The latter alternative is less likely because of Jewish scruples against unburied bodies.

34. This verse, like one or two others preceding (22:19,43) is absent from some of the best manuscripts. Like several other such disputed texts, it is undoubtedly a genuine utterance of Jesus. It is harder to account for its omission than for its inclusion. **And they parted his raiment, and cast lots.** The clothing of condemned prisoners became the property of the execution squad. Turban, sandals, girdle, cloak, and tunic would have made five items. The fifth, in this instance, the tunic, would either have had to be divided into four parts for equal distribution, which would have rendered it useless, or else assigned by lot.

36. Offering him vinegar. The soldiers drank a cheap sour wine, which was much like grape vinegar. **38. And a superscription.** The crimes of the condemned were listed on a placard, which was hung around his neck or nailed above his head on the cross. The Gospel records of the inscriptions differ (cf. Mt 27:37; Mk 15:26; Jn 19:19), and there may have been slight differences in the wording as it appeared in the different languages. The full inscription was probably, **This is** ***Jesus of Nazareth,*** **the King of the Jews.**

39. If thou be Christ. The better Greek text does not contain a condition. "You are the Messiah, aren't you? [Well, then,] save yourself and us!" The first thief was really sarcastic. **42. Lord, remember me when thou comest into thy kingdom.** The tone of this request is utterly different from the cynical fling of the other brigand. This man showed amazing confidence in Jesus; for he saw him dying on a cross, and yet believed that he would come in a kingdom. **Said** (Gr. *elegen)* is in the imperfect tense, which means that the request was repeated. **43. Paradise** is an old Persian term for a park or a garden, a beauty spot. It became a name for the abode of God (cf. II Cor 12:4).

44. The sixth hour. Time was reckoned from daybreak, about six o'clock in the morning. The sixth hour was noon. **A darkness.** The failure of the sun's light cannot be attributed to an eclipse, which would have been impossible during the full Passover moon. **45. The veil of the temple was rent in the midst.** The veil hung within the Temple, separating the Holy Place, where the priests ministered, from the presence of God in the Holy of Holies. It was made of thick woven material, which a man could not have torn with his own strength. The rending of the veil from the top to the bottom was distinctly supernatural.

46. I commend my spirit. He dismissed his spirit to the Father. His death was conscious and voluntary. **47. The centurion.** See comment on 7:2. This man, a Gentile, accustomed to seeing all kinds and conditions of men, confessed that Jesus was **a righteous man.**

I. The Burial. 23:50-56.

50. Joseph, a counsellor. Joseph of Arimathea was a member of the Sanhedrin, who had not consented to the verdict of death for Jesus. He was a disciple, and may not have been present when the council convened; if he was present, he registered a dissenting vote (v. 51 a). **52. This man went unto Pilate.**

To make a request for the body of a condemned criminal would immediately have put Joseph in a suspicious light. He showed courage to make the request. **53. Wrapped it in linen.** The verb means *to roll tightly, to wrap by winding.* It occurs only here, in Mt 27:59, and in Jn 20:7. The implication is that the body was not just carelessly wrapped in a sheet, but that Joseph, with his assistants, carefully wound it in bandage-like swathes, and deposited it in his own tomb.

54. That day was the preparation. According to general tradition, Jesus died on Friday afternoon, the "preparation" for the Sabbath that began at sunset. The body was, therefore, hastily placed in the tomb, in expectation of completing the burial after the Sabbath had passed. **55. The women . . . beheld the sepulchre.** The women witnessed the burial and noted how the body was laid. They could not have been mistaken later about the location of the tomb nor about the reality of the burial. **56. They . . . prepared spices and ointments.** Spices and unguents of various kinds were used to preserve the body, and were also a tribute of love and of respect to the dead.

VII. The Resurrection. 24:1-53.

Luke's account of the Resurrection differs from the other narratives in content, though it agrees with them in the essential facts. Each of the Gospel writers mentions the visit of the women to the tomb; but the appearance of the Lord to the disciples en route to Emmaus is reported only by Luke. He gives three main episodes of the Resurrection: the announcement to the women, the walk to Emmaus, and the appearance in the upper room. He concludes the Gospel with the ascension from Bethany.

A. The Empty Tomb. 24:1-12.

1. Upon the first day of the week, very early in the morning. The first day commenced on Saturday afternoon. Mark seems to imply (16:1,2) that the women finished the purchase of spices on the preceding evening, and came to the tomb at an hour when they would not be disturbed by others. **2. They found the stone rolled away from the sepulchre.** The tomb was a cave cut into the solid rock, across the entrance of which a circular stone could be rolled to keep out intruders. The women were surprised to find the tomb open. **3. Found not the body.** They knew exactly where to look for it, but it had vanished. All the accounts agree that the tomb was empty on the morning of the first day.

4. They were much perplexed. The women had no inkling of what had happened. Obviously there was no plot on the part of the disciples to remove the body (as the Jewish leaders charged) or these women would have had some hint of it. Perhaps they thought that Joseph and his assistants had moved the body to a safer place. **Two men stood by them.** Matthew (28:2-6) and Mark (16:5) say that an angel within the tomb gave them the news that Jesus had risen. There is no essential conflict; one may have been the spokesman for both. Two witnesses attended Jesus at the Transfiguration (Lk 9:30) and at his ascension (Acts 1:10). Luke may be suggesting that the same two appeared at the Resurrection. **In shining garments. Shining** (Gr. *astraptousē)* means flashing like lightning. **6. Remember how he spake . . . in Galilee.** The discussion at the Transfiguration was "his decease which he should accomplish at Jerusalem" (9:31). And before leaving Galilee, Jesus had given his disciples explicit instructions about the necessity of his coming death (18:31-34).

8. And they remembered his words. When he had first spoken about these things, the minds of the disciples had been preoccupied with other concepts; but the Resurrection put all of his teaching in a new perspective. **9. And to all the rest.** Jesus had with him in Jerusalem a larger group of followers than just the eleven disciples. Joseph of Arimathea, Nicodemus, the women, and many others were undoubtedly included in the group. **10. Mary Magdalene, and Joanna, and Mary the mother of James.** Mary Magdalene was probably so named from the town of Magdala in Galilee, where she had lived. Joanna was the wife of Chuza, Herod's steward (see 8:3). Mary the mother of James is mentioned by Matthew (27:56) and Mark (15:40). **11. Idle tales.** The Greek word *(lēros)* means literally, *nonsense*. The disciples were not ready to believe the first story they heard, but began a critical investigation.

12. Then arose Peter. The entire twelfth verse does not appear in the Western text of Luke, but is included in other manuscripts, and accords with the account given in Jn 20:2-10 (cf. 22:19; 24:34). **The linen clothes** were wide bandage-like strips that were wound around the body. **Laid by themselves.** There was no body in them, but they kept the same position they had when it was there. **Wondering in himself.** Peter could not understand why the cloths should have been left, and how the body could have been extracted from the wrappings.

B. The Walk to Emmaus. 24:13-35.

13. A village called Emmaus. Probably the same as the modern 'Amwas, nineteen miles west and slightly north of Jerusalem. **About threescore furlongs.** The distance given by the conventional text is about eight miles, but two of the older manuscripts say 160 furlongs, which would be about 20 miles. **16. Their eyes were holden.** In several instances Jesus was not readily recognized after the Resurrection.

18. Cleopas was the husband of one of the Marys (Jn 19:25), and was possibly the father of James the Less (Lk 24:10). He may have been Luke's informant. **Art thou only a stranger in Jerusalem.** The event of the death of Jesus was so well known that these two men could not understand how even a casual visitor in the city would not have heard of it. **19. Jesus of Nazareth, which was a prophet.** The words of Cleopas reveal the disciples' estimate of Jesus. They had not come into the full realization of his deity.

21. But we trusted. They were disillusioned. They had expected that Jesus would usher in the Messianic kingdom, and nothing of the sort had happened. **The third day.** The situation was hopeless, for with the arrival of the third day after death, there could be no hope of natural restoration. **22. And certain women.** The bewilderment of the disciples was increased by the report of the women. They could not very well deny the truth of the report; yet there was no positive evidence of resuscitation. **24. And certain of them.** They referred to Peter and John, mentioned above. These confirmed the fact that the tomb was empty. **But him they saw not.** For these men, only the verifiable appearance of Jesus himself would have been convincing.

25. All that the prophets have spoken. A clear testimony to the fact that Christ's coming was predicted in the OT. **26. Ought not Christ to have suffered these things?** Jesus intimated that the events of the past week should have been no surprise to them. The Messiah would logically be expected to suffer and to enter into glory, because the OT had foreshadowed it. **27. And beginning at Moses.** From the first of Genesis to the last of Zechariah there were scattered prophecies of the coming Messiah. Our Lord's exposition of these passages has not been preserved as a discourse, but probably his explanations formed the basis of apostolic interpretations of the OT in the sermons in Acts and in the Epistles.

29. Abide with us. They were extending common courtesy to a stranger who had a longer journey before him, but had no shelter for the night. Because of the dangers of the road, people did not usually travel by night. **31. And their eyes were opened.** Their guest's assumption of the place of the host, and perhaps something in his gestures as he broke the bread revealed his identity.

33. They rose up the same hour. The discovery was so great that they could not wait until morning, but returned to Jerusalem immediately to inform the others of their experience. Their journey to Emmaus may have been a sample of the dispersion that would have taken place had not the disciples been held together in Jerusalem by the hope of further appearances of Christ. **34. The Lord . . . hath appeared to Simon.** No record of this interview with Peter has been preserved, except one allusion in I Cor 15:5. The effect on Peter is mentioned in I Pet 1:3 ff.

C. The Appearance to the Disciples. 24:36-43.

36. Jesus himself stood in the midst. The risen Christ seemed to have the ability to appear and disappear at will. His resurrected body possessed powers that transcended the laws of ordinary matter. **37. They were terrified and affrighted.** Obviously they were not expecting him, nor was this simply a hallucination. **39. Behold my hands and my feet.** The scars that he carried indicated his identity with the man whom they had seen crucified. **Handle me.** A ghost would not have been tangible. **41. While they yet believed not for joy.** Their attitude changed, but still the miracle was too great to be comprehended. **43. And he . . . did eat before them.** Ghosts do not consume food. Peter mentioned this convincing evidence when he presented the Gospel to Gentiles (Acts 10:41).

D. The Last Commission. 24:44-49.

44. And he said unto them. This appearance was not his last, but it is the last Luke records before the Ascension. He has utilized it to bring out the message that Jesus expected his disciples to deliver to the world. **In the law of Moses, and in the prophets, and in the psalms.** These were the three main divisions of the Jewish canon of Scripture. The Prophets included some of the historical books, and the Psalms included other poetical books. **46. It behoved Christ to suffer, and to rise.** These two facts became the heart of apostolic preaching (cf. I Cor 15:3). **47. Repentance and remission of sins** were the doctrines stressed in the preaching at Pentecost (Acts 2:38). **Among all nations, beginning at Jerusalem.** The program outlined by Jesus accords exactly with the theme developed in Luke's second volume, The Acts of the Apostles (Acts 1:8).

49. The promise of my Father. The Lord referred to the Holy Spirit, whose coming had been promised in Joel 2:28, the passage that Peter used at Pentecost. **Tarry ye in the city.** Had the disciples dispersed immediately to their own homes, the movement would have been dissipated, and there would have been no united impact by the Spirit upon the world.

E. The Ascension. 24:50-53.

51. While he blessed them, he was parted from them, and carried up into heaven. The Western text omits "and was carried up into heaven," but comparison with Acts 1:9 confirms the genuineness of the accepted text.

BIBLIOGRAPHY

HISTORICAL BACKGROUND

HAYES, DOREMUS A. *The Synoptic Gospels and the Book of Acts*. New York: The Methodist Book Concern, n.d.

MACLACHLAN, H. *St. Luke, the Man and His Work*. London: Longmans, Green, & Co., 1920.

ROBERTSON, A. T. *Luke the Historian in the Light of Research*. New York: Charles Scribner's Sons, 1923.

COMMENTARIES

GELDENHUYS, NORVAL. *Commentary on the Gospel of Luke (The New International Commentary on the New Testament)*. Grand Rapids: Wm. B. Eerdmans Publishing Co., 1951.

GODET, FREDERIC. *A Commentary on the Gospel of Luke*. Translated from the second French edition by E. W. Shalders and M. D. Cusin. Third edition. New York: Funk & Wagnalls, Publishers, 1887.

MORGAN, G. CAMPBELL. *The Gospel According to St. Luke*. New York: Fleming H. Revell Co., 1931.

PLUMMER, ALFRED. *A Critical and Exegetical Commentary on the Gospel According to St. Luke (The International Critical Commentary)*. Fifth Edition. Edinburgh: T. & T. Clark, 1922.

THOMAS, W. H. GRIFFITH. *Outline Studies in the Gospel of Luke*. Grand Rapids: Wm. B. Eerdmans Publishing Co., 1950.

THE GOSPEL ACCORDING TO JOHN

INTRODUCTION

Character of the Book. Simple in language and structure, this writing is nevertheless a profound exposition of the person of Christ in a historical setting. It has a message for the humble disciple of the Lord and for the most advanced theologian.

Certain similarities between it and the Synoptic Gospels are readily discernible. It presents the same person as its central figure. We read of him as Son of God, Son of man, Messiah, Lord, Saviour, etc. Not many years ago it was the fashion in some circles to conclude that the Jesus of John was the result of a theological process in the early church whereby the man of Nazareth had been elevated to the position of deity. This view is no longer tenable, for further study has brought the conviction that the Christology of the Synoptics and the Christology of John are fundamentally one and the same. A merely human Jesus is as much a stranger to the Synoptics as to John.

As the historical pattern unfolds in the Fourth Gospel, it is seen to resemble in its broad outline the course of events as portrayed in the Synoptics – the preparatory ministry of John the Baptist, the call of certain disciples to learn and serve, the twofold ministry of word and deed (miracle), the same tension between popular enthusiasm for the Lord and opposition from official Judaism, the crucial importance of the person and the authority of Jesus. Likewise, in respect to the closing events of Christ's life on earth, there is the same pattern of betrayal, arrest and trial, death by crucifixion, and resurrection.

To be sure, considerable diversity from the Synoptics is apparent also. Whereas the Synoptics mention only one Passover, and therefore seem to limit the ministry of Christ to one year, John mentions at least three Passovers (2:23; 6:4; 13:1), which suggests that the ministry was spread over three years. In the Synoptics the ministry is located almost in its entirety in Galilee, while John emphasizes the activity of Jesus in Judea and has little to say about the Galilean campaign. In the Synoptics the public teaching of our Lord revolves around "the kingdom of God." The expression is almost absent from the Fourth Gospel, where the discourses are centered largely in Jesus himself, his relation to the Father, and his indispensability to man in his spiritual need (cf. the *I am's*). Certain historical details raise problems. An example is the cleansing of the Temple, placed by John early in the ministry (chapter 2), but put at the close of the ministry by the Synoptic writers. The simplest explanation here is probably the true one – that there were two cleansings. Another example pertains to the call of the disciples, which according to the Synoptists occurred in Galilee. John narrates the call of several men in a Judean setting, at the very inception of the ministry (chapter 1). The problem is eased when one reflects that the very readiness of the Galilean fishermen to leave their nets and follow Jesus is most easily explained on the basis of prior acquaintance and tentative discipleship, such as the Fourth Gospel reveals. It is somewhat disturbing to find Jesus regarded as the Messiah in this Gospel at the very inception of his work (John 1), when the knowledge of the Messiahship seems to come at a much later time in the other Gospels. The two representations are not incompatible, however, for Peter's announcement at Caesarea-Philippi (Mt 16:16) need not be understood as a conviction arrived at then for the first time (cf. Mt 14:33). Truth known before has now deepened through personal experience of the Son of God.

Author. Although the book does not name the writer, he is indicated as 'the beloved disciple' (21:20,23,24) and the close companion of Peter. The testimony of the ancient church is to the effect that this is John, the son of Zebedee (cf. 21:2). Irenaeus is the chief witness. Some scholars have questioned whether one who was unschooled and inexperienced (Acts 4:13) could have written such a work. Time, motivation, and the enablement of the Spirit ought not to be underestimated in evaluating the ability of John and the overcoming of handicaps.

Many moderns prefer to hold that an unknown disciple is the actual author of this Gospel, even though most of the material may well go back to John as its source. But this is a needless exchange of a known for an unknown.

Date and Place of Composition. According to Christian tradition, John spent the latter years of his life at Ephesus, where he carried on a ministry of preaching and teaching, as well as writing. From this point he was exiled to Patmos in the reign of the Emperor Domitian. His Gospel seems to presuppose a knowledge of the Synoptic tradition and for this reason should be placed last in the series, possibly somewhere between 80 and 90. Some have put it even later. The discovery in Egypt of fragments of the Gospel, which have been dated from the first half of the second century, requires the writing of the Gospel within the limits of the first century.

Purpose. On the positive side this is stated in John 20:30,31 as the hope that conviction will be created in the readers that Jesus is the Christ, the Son of God, so that life will come through faith in him. The choice of material is calculated to lead to exactly this conclusion. Subordinate objectives may be allowed, such as the refutation of Docetism, a point of view that denied the true humanity of Jesus (cf. 1:14), and the exposure of Judaism as an inadequate system of religion that crowned its other sins by refusing its promised Messiah (1:11, etc.).

OUTLINE

I. Prologue. 1:1-18.
II. Christ's ministry in the world. 1:19–12:50.
  A. The testimony of John the Baptist. 1:19-36.
  B. The gathering of disciples. 1:37-51.
  C. The wedding at Cana. 2:1-11.
  D. The first visit to Jerusalem and Judea. 2:12–3:36.
    1. The cleansing of the Temple. 2:12-22.
    2. The signs. 2:23-25.
    3. The Nicodemus incident. 3:1-15.
    4. The issues latent in the Gospel message. 3:16-21.
    5. Further witness from John the Baptist. 3:22-30.
    6. The credentials of Christ. 3:31-36.
  E. The mission to Samaria. 4:1-42.
  F. The healing of the nobleman's son. 4:43-54.
  G. The healing of the lame man in Jerusalem. 5:1-16.
  H. Jesus' self-defense. 5:17-47.
  I. The feeding of the five thousand and the discourse on the Bread of Life. 6:1-71.
  J. Jesus at the Feast of Tabernacles. 7:1-53.
  K. The woman taken in adultery. 8:1-11.
  L. The self-disclosure of Jesus. 8:12-59.
  M. The restoration of the man born blind. 9:1-41.
  N. Christ, the Good Shepherd. 10:1-42.
  O. The raising of Lazarus. 11:1-57.
  P. Jesus in Bethany and Jerusalem. 12:1-50.
III. Christ's ministry to his own. 13:1–17:26.
  A. The foot washing. 13:1-17.
  B. The announcement of the betrayal. 13:18-30.
  C. The upper room discourse. 13:31–16:33.
  D. The great prayer. 17:1-26.
IV. The sufferings and the glory. 18:1–20:31.
  A. The betrayal. 18:1-14.
  B. Jesus on trial before the Jews. 18:15-27.
  C. The ordeal before Pilate. 18:28–19:16.
  D. The crucifixion and burial. 19:17-42.
  E. The resurrection appearances. 20:1-29.
  F. The purpose of this Gospel. 20:30,31.
V. Epilogue. 21:1-25.

COMMENTARY

I. Prologue. 1:1-18.

Without delay the writer presents the central figure of the Gospel, but does not call him Jesus or Christ. At this point he is the Logos (Word). This term has OT roots, suggesting there the concepts of wisdom, power, and a special relation to God. It was widely used, too, by philosophers to express such ideas as reason and mediation between God and the world. In John's day all classes of readers would have understood its suitability here, where revelation is the keynote. But the unique feature is that the Logos is also the Son of the Father, who became incarnate in order to reveal God fully (1:14,18).

A. The Pre-existent Logos. 1:1,2. The **beginning** of the Gospel (cf. Mk 1:1) is tied in with the beginning of the creation (Gen 1:1) and reaches beyond it to a glimpse of the Godhead "before the world was" (cf. Jn 17:5). The Word did not become; he **was. With God** suggests equality as well as association. **The Word was God** (deity) without confusion of the persons.

B. The Cosmic Logos. 1:3-5. He was the agent in creation. **By him.** Through him.

3. All things embrace the totality of matter and existence, but viewed here in their individual status rather than as universe. **4. Life is in him,** not simply through him. As the life, the Word communicated **light** (the knowledge of God) to **men. 5.** The **darkness** is primarily moral. Not everyone profits by the light (cf. 3:19). Probably the thought is not identical with 1:9,10; so **the darkness comprehended it not** is a less likely translation than *the darkness has not overcome it* (RSV).

C. The Incarnate Logos. 1:6-18. Included here is a summary of the mission of John the forerunner.

6. Was. Better, *came*. This is John's emergence in history, as **sent from God.** The phrase summarizes the material of Lk 1:5-80; 3:1-6. **7.** John came for **witness** or testimony, which is a leading emphasis of this Gospel (1:15,34; 5:33, 36,37; 15:26,27; 19:35; 21:24). His commission was to witness to **the Light,** which had been shining ever since the Creation and was about to enlighten men with his presence. The witness was designed to cause men to **believe** (the noun "faith" does not occur in this Gospel, but the verb is almost a refrain; cf. 20:31). **9. The true Light** does not make John a false light. It denotes light in the antitypical, ultimate sense—the sun, not a candle. Hence, to revere John unduly after the Light has dawned is wrong (3:30; Acts 19:1-7). The syntax of the verse in the Greek is difficult. *The true light that enlightens every man was coming into the world* (RSV) is the most probable rendering. By his presence among men the Logos would bring an illumination surpassing that which he had been affording men before his coming.

10,11. The Light was real and glowing, but the response was disappointing. Beyond this similarity in the two verses lie studied differences: **was, came; the world, his own; knew not, received not.** Failure to discern the preincarnate Logos is more understandable than the tragic refusal of his own people to receive him when he came among them.

12,13. Not all refused the Light. Those who received him gained **power** (authority, right) to **become** (then and there) **sons** (children) of God. Those who **received** are described as those who **believe on his name** (person). See 20:31. These are two ways of saying the same thing. Believers are further described in terms of what God does for them. They are **born . . . of God.** This is not a natural process such as brings people into the world—not of **blood** (literally, *bloods*), suggesting the mingling of paternal and maternal strains in procreation. **The will of the flesh** suggests the natural, human desire for children, as **the will of man** (the word for husband) suggests the special desire for progeny to carry on a family name. So the new birth, something supernatural, is carefully guarded from confusion with natural birth.

14. Before faith could bring about the new birth, it had to have an object on which to rest, even the incarnation of **the Word,** the Son of God. God, having expressed himself in creation and history, where the activity of the Logos was evident but his person veiled, now revealed himself through the Son in human form, which was no mere semblance, but **flesh.** John could have used "man" but he chose to state the truth of the incarnation emphatically so as to contradict those with Gnostic tendencies. This false view of Christ refused to acknowledge that pure deity could take a material body, since matter was regarded as something evil (cf. I Jn 4:2,3; II Jn 7). **Dwelt.** *Tabernacled.* In combination with **glory** it suggests the personalizing of the bright cloud that rested on the tabernacle in the wilderness (Ex 40:34). The Word incarnate is also the answer to Moses' prayer (Ex 33:18). John has no account of the Transfiguration, for he presents the whole ministry as a tranfiguration, except that the light he speaks of is moral and spiritual (**full of grace and truth**- rather than something visual (cf. Jn 1:17).

15. Further notice (cf. 1:7) is taken of the testimony of the Baptist in the light of Jesus' public appearance. Jesus came **after** John in time but went **before** him in importance, even as He was before him as the Eternal One (cf. 1:1). **16.** The Evangelist confirms the uniqueness of Christ. Not only John the Baptist but **all** believers have partaken of his **fulness** —the completeness of deity (cf. **full** in 1:14). **Grace for grace** pictures one manifestation of grace as piled on another—a fullness indeed. **17.** As Jesus Christ surpassed John (1:15), so does He excel Moses. Both brought something from God, but the one brought **the law** which condemns, the other **grace** which redeems from law. **Truth** suggests the reality of Christ's revelation of God.

18. God is invisible, being Spirit (cf. 4:24; I Tim 6:16). Theophanies do not reveal his essence. But God's only **Son** (here the leading manuscripts have **God** rather than **Son**; cf. Jn 1:1) does. **In the bosom of the Father** recalls **with God** (1:1). The Son's mission was to **declare** (the Greek word gives us our "exegete") the Father. Christ interpreted God to man. Nothing is lost (cf. Heb 1:2,3; Gal 1:15).

II. Christ's Ministry in the World. 1:19–12:50.

A. The Testimony of John the Baptist. 1:19-36. In his burning desire to magnify Christ, John turned an inquiry about himself into a strong witness to the greater One about to manifest himself. Jesus' baptism at the hands of John, not narrated in this Gospel, had already occurred (see 1:26).

19. The Jews. As usual in John, this means leaders of the nation. These **priests** were of the Pharisees (v. 24). Two things prompted the deputation: the strong preaching of John, which captivated the multitudes (Mt 3:5), and his baptizing activity (Jn 1:26). Such a person excited so much concern in these leaders that they asked, **Who art thou? 20.** John read their thoughts. They, like the multitudes (Lk 3:15), were wondering if he could be the promised **Christ. 21.** His denial led to a second question. **Elias** (Elijah) was expected before the coming of the Messiah (Mal 4:5). Though John was not Elijah in person, he was that one in function (Mt 17:10-13). By **that prophet** we are probably to understand the prophet of Deut 18:15,18. By some he was taken to be distinct from the Messiah (Jn 7:40).

22-24. The deputation could not be satisfied with negations. Pressed to reveal his role, John replied in the language of prophecy (Isa 40:3). It was a true identification. John had lived in **the wilderness** and there had lifted up his **voice** to announce the near approach of the kingdom (Lk 1:80; 3:2,3). **25-28.** Such a minor role did not seem sufficient justification for John's administration of baptism. But he defended himself—it was merely **with water.** It proclaimed the presence of sin and the need of a purification which he himself could not effect. The ultimate work of purification (so he hinted) rested with a greater than he, One who was still an unknown to the authorities (1:26). John counted himself unworthy to be His servant. This conversation was held at **Bethabara, east** of Jordan. Leading manuscripts have *Bethany,* not to be confused with the Bethany of 11:1,18.

29. The next day introduces a new situation. The deputation had departed and Jesus appeared on the scene. Yet there was no conversation between him and John. Content with affirming to the Pharisees the greatness of Christ, John now became specific about His person and work. His own ministry was grounded on the fact of sin; that of Christ was concerned with sin's removal. Christ was God's **Lamb.** History (Ex 12:3) and prophecy (Isa 53:7) unite in providing the background for this title. The daily temple sacrifices may be in mind also.

31-34. When Jesus came to John's baptism, the Baptist did not recognize Him (cf. Lk 1:80), but he had received a sign of identification from God—**the Spirit descending from heaven like a dove** and remaining on Him. Along with the sign was given a word concerning the work He should perform with the heavenly equipment thus given—He would baptize with the Spirit. Such a one, John knew, could be no less than **the Son of God.** No one of lesser stature could make such authoritative use of the divine Spirit. John gave three sterling testimonies to Christ's person and work. As the Lamb, His mission was to be one of redemption. As baptizer with the Spirit, He would found tne Church. As Son of God, He would be worthy of adoration and obedience.

35,36. These verses are transitional. They inform us that John had **disciples** and also that he desired to transfer them to Jesus. This was an important part of his work as forerunner, as the remainder of the chapter attests.

B. The Gathering of Disciples. 1:37-51. John's unselfish desire to glorify Christ bore fruit among his own followers. Without any command or suggestion from him in addition to his testimony, **two disciples** followed Jesus. One is identified as **Andrew.** Silence regarding the name of the other points to the writer of the Gospel, who withholds his name out of modesty.

37-42. They followed Jesus. The physical act expressed the intent to follow in a spiritual sense. **What seek ye?** Such a question could be a rebuff, but not when spoken kindly. The counterquestion, **Where dwellest thou?** like their following him, could suggest a deeper sense —What is the secret of your spiritual life and power? His abode could not have enticed them, but the lofty converse that followed lingered as a fragrant memory. Years later John remembered the **hour** of day—four in the afternoon.

41. The meaning of **first** is unclear. No further activity by Andrew is stated. Possibly **first** is intended to suggest that the other disciple (John) likewise sought out his brother James, who appears early in the Synoptic narratives as a follower of Jesus (Mk 1:16-20). **Findeth . . . found.** The narrative is alive with the joy of discovery (cf. Jn 1:43,45). **Messias,** the Hebrew term for "anointed one," has its counterpart in the Greek word **Christ.** Did Andrew dare to call Jesus the Christ because the Baptist had so identified Him to his followers, or because of the hours spent in Jesus' company? **42.** Andrew's personal work began early and with his own kin. The change of name from **Simon** to **Cephas,** the Aramaic for Peter, meaning *stone,* probably denotes a promised change from weakness to stability and strength (Lk 22:31, 32).

43. Again the change of **day** is noted (cf. 1:29,35, in contrast to the absence of such features in the Prologue). This time Jesus does the finding (cf. Lk 19:10), and gives a command to Philip to **follow** (contrast Jn 1:37).

45-51. Philip vindicated Jesus' confidence in him as a disciple by finding Nathanael and breathing to him his conviction that Jesus of Nazareth was the long-awaited One who fulfilled the predictions of **Moses** and the **prophets.** One may witness to the Lord even if his understanding is incomplete or even faulty. **Jesus of Nazareth** revealed himself shortly as the heavenly Son of man (v. 51). Even Nathanael came quickly to perceive that **the son of Joseph** was the Son of God (v. 49). Nathanael's first impulse was to doubt that Nazareth was capable of producing **any good thing,** much less the Messiah (v. 46). This does not necessarily imply that the town had a bad reputation, but rather suggests the inconsequential character of the place. **Come and see.** Experience is better than argument. **An Israelite** without **guile** suggests a contrast to Jacob, who became Israel only by a conversion experience. The same penetration that read the heart of Simon (v. 42) like an open book and pierced to the inner life of Nathanael (vv. 47,48) was now cordially acknowledged in the latter's confession—**Son of God...King of Israel.** The shade of the fig tree, a quiet retreat for a reverent soul, had been silently shared by the discerning Christ. Philip realized that the teacher must be more than he saw in Him. And the end was not yet, for the Saviour promised **greater things.** Jacob was still in the background (v. 51). His vision of angels at Bethel would be surpassed as the disciples (ye) came to see in the **Son of man** the one to whom **heaven** was **open** (cf. Mt 3:16) and the one who, as Mediator, links heaven and earth. **Son of man.** A title denoting a supernatural, heavenly figure in Dan 7: 13 and in the Jewish apocalypses, was Jesus' preferred method of designating himself, according to the Gospels. This name was preferable to "Messiah" because it did not suggest political aspirations along lines of a temporal kingdom such as most Jews were looking for. The glory of the Son (Jn 1:14), seen in part by these early followers (vv. 39, (46), was to unfold more **hereafter.**

C. The Wedding at Cana. 2:1-11. This brief return to Galilee was not marked by public ministry, but involved an incident that bears on the deepening of the disciples' confidence in Jesus, continuing the emphasis of John 1. Some light is thrown on our Lord's relation to his mother and also on his attitude toward social life (cf. Mt 11:19). The turning of the water into wine is noted as his first miracle.

1. The third day seems to relate to 1:43. Two days or more would have been required for the journey to Cana, which was located about seven and a half miles north of Nazareth. John notes the presence of **the mother of Jesus** at the marriage. His avoidance of the name *Mary* here and in 19:26 may be due to a restraint similar to that which hides his own name. He had a special relation to Mary (19:27).

2. It is uncertain whether Jesus timed the journey in order to be present for the marriage or whether the invitation to him and his disciples came after their arrival in Galilee. If the latter is the correct alternative, the depletion of the supply of wine may be readily explained. Other guests may have arrived unexpectedly also. Nathanael, whose home was in Cana, possibly had something to do with the arrangements.

3-5. Mary came to Jesus with the tidings that the wine supply had been exhausted. In his reply, the use of **Woman** does not involve disrespect (cf. 19:26). **What have I to do with thee?** The words indicate division of interest and seem to suggest a measure of rebuke. Mary may have expected Jesus to use the situation to call attention to himself in a way that would have furthered his Messianic program. But his **hour** had not yet come. Later references point to the cross as the focal point of the **hour** (7:30; 8:20; 12:23; 13:1; 17:1). Jesus wanted his mother to understand that the former relationship between the two of them (Lk 2:51) was at an end. She was not to interfere in his mission. Mary wisely did not dispute the matter. If she could not command him, she could instruct the servants to obey his directions. Thus she showed her confidence in him.

6-8. In meeting the emergency, Jesus made use of **six waterpots of stone,** such as the Jews used for **purifying**—the washing of the hands before and after meals, and various ceremonial washings. Each would have held about twenty gallons. When these had been filled, Jesus instructed the servants to **draw out.** This seems to refer to the act of taking water out of the large containers by dipping from them and putting into smaller receptacles. What was drawn was then carried to **the governor of the feast.** Some consider that the **governor** was little more than a butler; others see in him a friend of the bridegroom who was requested to act as a master of ceremonies (cf. Ecclesiasticus 32:1ff.).

9,10. A taste of the wine assured this functionary that it was of superior quality, so much superior that he felt constrained to compliment the bridegroom for treating his guests with unusual consideration, giving them good wine at the end of the feast, when many would be so filled as not to be able to discern whether the wine was good or inferior. The shortage of wine was relieved by Jesus' intervention. The deeper truth is that, symbolically, Judaism is here revealed as deficient (in its stress upon ceremonial washings to the neglect of spiritual matters, and in its depletion, indicated by the empty water jars), whereas Christ brings fullness of blessing of the highest sort (cf. 7:37-39). Moreover, he does it without calling attention to himself, a refreshing example.

11. Beginning of miracles. This statement refutes the apocryphal Gospels which report boyhood miracles by Jesus. The word for **miracle,** which John uses throughout, means *sign,* indicating that the outward act is intended to reveal the purpose behind it, throwing light on the person of Christ or his work. **Glory** in this case is a term calling attention to the potency of Jesus to accomplish a spiritual transformation, as suggested by the changing of water into wine (cf. 11:40). **His disciples believed on him.** In contrast to the ruler of the feast, who was characterized by ignorance (v. 9) and to the servants, who had *knowledge* of the miracle (v. 9), the disciples were moved to *faith.* They alone truly profited by the sign.

D. The First Visit to Jerusalem and Judea. 2:12–3:36.

1) The Cleansing of the Temple. 2:12-22. Even though this is not called a sign, it was a more momentous event than the miracle at Cana, for it bore directly on the mission of Jesus, being a Messianic act of a public nature. Once again Judaism was shown to be deficient, and

even corrupt, for the Father's house was being defiled. Jesus related the incident to his resurrection (vv. 19-21). It revealed the unbelief of the Jews (vv. 18-20) and the faith of the disciples (v. 22). As an event, it should be distinguished from a later cleansing prior to Jesus' death (Mk 11:15-19).

12. This verse is transitional. The importance of Capernaum for Jesus' ministry is stressed in the Synoptic Gospels. He made it his Galilean headquarters—"his own city" (Mt 9:1). The rift with his **Brethren** (brothers) had not yet developed (Jn 7:3-5).

13. The Jews' passover (cf. 2:6). Once again John is intent on exposing the deficiencies of Judaism. The sacred memorial of the deliverance from Egypt was being abused. Since it was Jesus' habit to observe the national festivals, as it had been the habit of Joseph and Mary (Lk 2:41), he went up to Jerusalem.

14-16. Jesus the worshiper now became a reformer. The Sanhedrin was permitting, and probably controlling for its own financial interest, a traffic in sacrificial animals and money changing. This traffic, carried on in the large area known as the Court of the Gentiles, was to the advantage of the pilgrim, since he could acquire his sacrifice here rather than bring it with him. Presumably there was a guarantee that the animal was "without blemish." Various kinds of coinage could be changed at the tables for the Palestinian half shekel required for the annual temple tax. This traffic turned the Temple into a mart of trade. Incensed at the sacrilege, Jesus went into action. Quickly he fashioned a **scourge** out of the ropes lying about the place. With this whip he drove the men (**them**) and the animals out of the temple area and upset the tables of the money changers, sending their coins ringing here and there on the pavement. The doves could not well be driven. It was necessary only that their owners take them out. Such strenuous measures needed justification, and it was found in this, that the **Father's house** had been perverted into a **house of merchandise.** The Lord had come suddenly to his Temple and had purified the sons of Levi (Mal 3:1-3). A deeper lesson than the removal of corruption may have been intended by this expulsion of sacrificial animals, even the anticipation of the day when the Temple and its sacrifices would be gone and the final sacrifice of the Lamb of God be achieved (cf. 2:21; 1:29).

17. The incident recalled to the disciples a passage in a Messianic psalm (69:9)—"Zeal for thy house will consume me" (RSV). A hint may be found here that this zeal, which cost him opposition at the moment, would eventually cost him his life (cf. Jn 2:19).

18-22. Such drastic action quickly brought a demand from **the Jews** (leaders) that Jesus produce an incontestable **sign** to show that he had authority for his conduct. He always resisted such a demand (6:30; Mt 16:1). This time he was content to point to the future. **Destroy this temple.** The figurative character of the utterance is evident, not only from Jn 2:21, but from the utter unlikelihood that the Jews would destroy their own Temple. These words are not to be taken as a command or invitation, but are in the nature of a hypothesis—"If you destroy, I will raise up." **In three days** is equivalent to "on the third day." Taking him literally, the Jews felt that his statement was ridiculous, since the Temple had required forty-six years to build. Herod had begun its reconstruction in 20 B.C. Some work still remained to be done, but the structure was sufficiently complete to be spoken of as built. (For the use of the figure **temple** for the **body,** see I Cor 6:19.) This prophecy helped to promote faith on the part of the disciples, but not until after the resurrection of their Lord from the dead (cf. Jn 12:16).

2) The Signs. 2:23-25. This section is transitional, having specially close connection with the following incident. It is summary in nature, picturing Jesus as performing various signs in Jerusalem that are left undescribed. The important thing is the response, which in this case was not rank unbelief, nor the full confidence in Christ attributed to the disciples, but something that may be called miracle-faith. Its unsatisfactory character is certified by the fact that Jesus **did not commit himself unto** these people, because he knew the human heart and discerned the lack of genuine trust. For somewhat similar instances, note 8:30-59; 12:42, 43.

3) The Nicodemus Incident. 3:1-15. In contrast to the many in Jerusalem who "believed" but to whom Jesus refused to commit himself, Nicodemus looms as one to whom the Lord opened his heart, one who became a true disciple. At the same time the passage em-

phasizes an earlier theme—the limitations of current Judaism—by showing the inability of this leader to comprehend the spiritual truth enunciated by Jesus.

1,2. The **Pharisees** were the religious leaders of the nation. Nicodemus not only belonged to this group, but was a **ruler of the Jews,** a member of the Sanhedrin. He came to see Jesus **by night,** probably out of expediency. The official attitude toward the Nazarene, after the cleansing of the Temple, must have been one of strong opposition. John may be suggesting also the blindness of this man concerning divine things. Nicodemus was ready to concede that Jesus was a **teacher** sent of God, the miracles being witness. This could mean that he was a prophet of greater power than John, who did no miracle. **We know** suggests that others were thinking along similar lines. Whether there is any intended hint that Jesus might be the Messiah is not clear. **3,4.** In the mind of Nicodemus the miracles may well have been indications of the speedy coming of the kingdom of God in a political sense. But Jesus introduced an entirely different concept of the kingdom, with the signs pointing to a spiritual reign of God. To be **born again** is to be born anew, from above. Nicodemus was nonplused. He knew that a man can not be born over again in a physical sense. Perhaps Jesus meant that it is just as impossible for one who is **old** to change his outlook and his ways.

5-8. Jesus now described the new birth in terms of **water** and **Spirit.** Of these two, Spirit is the more crucial (see v. 6). Water may well refer to the emphasis of John the Baptist on repentance and cleansing from sin as the necessary background for, even the negative side of, the new birth. Less natural is any allusion to the Word (I Pet 1:23). The positive ingredient is the injection of new creation life by the regenerating power of the Spirit (cf. Tit 3:5). **Ye must be born again.** This is not merely a personal but a universal demand. The necessity lies in the inadequacy of **the flesh.** This includes what is merely natural and what is sinful—man as he is born into this world and lives his life apart from God's grace. Flesh can only reproduce itself as flesh, and this cannot pass muster with God (cf. Rom 8:8). The law of reproduction is "after its kind." So likewise the Spirit produces spirit, a life born, nurtured, and matured by the Spirit of God. If this spells mystery, let it be recognized that there is mystery in nature also. **Wind** (*pneuma,* the same word as for "Spirit") produces observable effects as it blows, but its source and future movements remain hidden. So the redeemed life shows itself as something effective, though defying analysis by the natural man (cf. I Cor 2:15).

9,10. The perplexity of Nicodemus drew a gentle rebuke from Jesus. Could it be that **a master** (lit., *the teacher*) **of Israel** did not know these things? They were not new (Ezk 11:19). A spiritual kingdom and a spiritual life to match it are not foreign to the teaching of the OT.

11-13. Furthermore, others could testify to the reality of these things—**we speak.** Jesus was pleased to associate his followers with himself. **Ye** (you and others like you) receive not the witness. **Earthly things** are the things already discussed, such as the nature of the kingdom and of spiritual birth and life. **Heavenly things** are matters which the Son of man, by his coming down from heaven, had to reveal as new and distinctive (cf. Mt 11:25-27). The last four words of 3:13 are not contained in the leading manuscripts.

14,15. There is another **must** answering to the imperative of the new birth (cf. 3:7). The lifting up of the Son of man cannot well refer to the Ascension, in view of the elevation of the brazen **serpent** on a pole (Num 21:8), with which it is here compared. The allusion is to the cross (Jn 12:32,33). As men afflicted with the bite of the deadly serpent looked with expectancy and hope toward that which resembled the reptile that had set the virus of death flowing in their veins, so sinners must look in faith to Christ their substitute, who came in the likeness of sinful flesh and for sin (Rom 8:3). The issue of such faith is **eternal life.** Apart from this faith one must **perish.** This is not annihilation but the tragedy of being cut off eternally from God. Apparently Nicodemus took to heart the warning and the challenge (Jn 7:50,51; 19:39,40). At this point, it seems, the words of Jesus cease and those of John resume, judging from the phraseology, which has several analogies to other portions of the Gospel where John is unquestionably responsible for the material.

4) The Issues Latent in the Gospel Message. 3:16-21. Love for sin prompts men to reject the light of Christ, whereas those who welcome the light are ready to put their trust in him.

16,17. John enlarges on the statement of Jesus (3:15), retaining **whosoever, perish, believeth, eternal** (*everlasting* also translates the same Greek word) **life.** The added elements are the love of God and the consequent giving of his Son, who is described as the **only begotten.** This means unique, one of a kind. Sons by adoption do not become members of the Godhead. The breadth of the divine love is emphasized in that its object is the (whole) **world.** Though the coming of Christ involved judgment, as the rest of this section attests, the direct purpose of that coming, resting on the divine love, was not condemnation but salvation (3:17).

18-21. The believer in Christ does not come into judgment for his sins either now or in the future (the verb form is flexible enough to cover both aspects). On the other hand, the one who refuses to believe stands judged by virtue of that refusal. He has decided his own fate. The essential idea in judgment is a distinction, a separation (the root meaning of the word); and the coming of Christ as the light proved a great dividing influence. Instead of responding to the love of God by loving his Son, most men loved the darkness in preference to the light because they were attached to their pattern of life, which was **evil** (wicked). In 3:20 **evil** is a different word, denoting what is morally worthless. The offender knows he is enmeshed in wrong, but refuses to advance into the light of Christ lest his deeds, which he loves, be exposed. On the other hand, the one who comes to the light is described as one who **doeth truth.** He acts in accordance with what he knows to be right (cf. 18:37). This conformity to what he knows to be the truth prepares him to advance into the full light of Christ and be saved. All his works are **wrought in God,** who has been leading him to this climax of faith (cf. 1:47).

5) Further Witness from John the Baptist. 3:22-30. The fact that Jesus and his disciples carried on a work of preaching and baptizing in Judea while John and his followers conducted a similar work in another area led to the suspicion that the two were in competition. John denied this emphatically, gladly taking a role of subordination to Jesus.

22-24. After these things. The Nicodemus episode is ended. **The land of Judea** is named in distinction from Jerusalem, where Jesus had been laboring (2:13—3:21). Jesus' baptizing activity presupposes preaching. His relation to baptism seems to have been only supervisory (cf. 4:2; I Cor 1:14). Aenon and Salim have not been positively identified but are now thought to have been a few miles east of Mount Gerizim, rather than south of Beth-shan in the upper Jordan Valley. **They came.** People generally, who were interested in John's message. John's imprisonment is noted here as something familiar to the readers, since it is reported in all the Synoptic Gospels.

25,26. John's disciples were drawn into an altercation with some Jews (there is good basis for reading *a Jew* here) over the issue of purifying. The writer does not tell us whether this means purification in general as practiced by the Jews, or the baptism practiced by John and Jesus over against those purifyings, or the baptisms of John and Jesus in contrast to each other. Perhaps the last is the most likely, in view of the sequel. **They came.** Probably John's disciples. **He.** Failure to mention Jesus more definitely seems like studied depreciation. John's disciples were concerned over the waning position of their leader. The crowds were now thronging Jesus.

27-30. The Baptist deplored any thought of rivalry between himself and Jesus. His own place, given by God (**from heaven**), was not that of the Christ but that of the forerunner (v. 28). His position was not that of the Bridegroom, who should take the people of God to himself. This was reserved for Another. Rather, he was the friend of the Bridegroom. It was the function of such a man to act as go-between in making the marriage arrangements. His **joy** was vicarious—participation in the happiness of the groom as a new family was formed. John's work was done in launching the work of Jesus. He could baptize only with water, not with the Spirit. He could announce the coming of the kingdom but not enter into it himself. His cause had to fade, in the nature of the case, as that of Jesus increased (v. 30). This was God's plan. And so Jesus, in addition to being superior to Judaism, was superior to the movement that centered about John (cf. Acts 19:1-3).

6) The Credentials of Christ. 3:31-36. Here the Evangelist reflects on the distinctives of Jesus, especially as these set him apart from the Baptist. He has a heavenly origin, which puts him above earthlings and earthly things (cf. 3:13). He bears his testimony to what he sees and hears, a testimony to heavenly things (cf. 16:13). Only regenerate men, those born

of the Spirit, can appreciate his testimony (Nicodemus was in the background of John's thought here). Those who do receive his testimony need no other authentication (cf. I Jn 5:10). Christ declares the words of God (Jn 3:34) as a faithful witness. The fullness of those words, as well as their accuracy, is guaranteed by the unmeasured gift of the Spirit granted to him. The original suggests that through him the same Spirit is given to others without measure (cf. 1:33). Further, the Christ is the special object of God's love and is the custodian of divine riches (cf. 16:15; Mt 11:27). He is the touchstone of eternal life or abiding wrath (Jn 3:36).

E. The Mission to Samaria. 4:1-42.

Samaria, a territory to be avoided if possible by Jews, became the scene of a spiritual triumph: a well, a woman, a witness, the winning of a harvest of Samaritans to faith. Samaritanism as well as Judaism needed the corrective of Christ; it needed to be replaced by new creation life.

1-4. The growing popularity of Jesus, exceeding that of John, began to come to the ears of the Pharisees. To avoid trouble with them at this time, Jesus determined to leave the area and go into Galilee. This is where most of his work was done, according to the Synoptic records. **He must** go through Samaria. Ordinarily in John this word points to a divine necessity, and it may do so here, indicating the need of dealing with the Samaritans and opening to them the gateway to life. Along with this may be the more evident need of reaching Galilee by the most direct route.

5,6. Sychar (very likely Sychem, i.e., Shechem) was a few miles southeast of the city of Samaria and fairly close to Mount Gerizim as well as to the ground given by Jacob to Joseph (Gen 48:22). Jacob left also a well as a legacy (Jn 4:6). This is reported to be about eighty-five feet in depth. Here Jesus, wearied with the journey and the midday (**sixth hour**) heat, paused to rest.

7-10. A woman of Samaria. Not a reference to the city of Samaria, which was too far away, but to the territory of the Samaritans. She came equipped to **draw water.** Since the village of Sychar had water, it is possible that the woman's solitary journey to Jacob's well from day to day indicates a species of ostracism by the other women of the community (cf. 4:18). Jesus broke the silence with a request for a drink. It was a natural request in view of his weariness. It is a poignant reminder of our Lord's humanity. Whether the request was fulfilled or not (the latter seems more probable), it led to conversation. The departure of the disciples was providential, for the woman would not have entered into discussion with Jesus in their presence. Two things amazed the woman: that Jesus would make such a request of a woman, for a rabbi avoided contact with women in public; and particularly that he would speak thus to one who was a Samaritan. In explanation of her amazement, the writer adds the observation that Jews had no dealings with Samaritans. This cannot be taken in an absolute sense, for it is refuted by verse 8. It may point to the bad feeling between the two people. The Jews despised the Samaritans because they were a mixed people in blood and in religion, who nevertheless possessed the Pentateuch and professed to worship the God of Israel. A narrower meaning has been proposed for the woman's saying – "Jews do not make common use (of vessels) with Samaritans." This fits the situation well (D. Daube, *The New Testament and Rabbinic Judaism*, pp. 375-382). In his reply Jesus moved away from his own need to suggest that the woman had one which was deeper, one he was able to supply through **the gift of God.** Some explain this in personal terms as referring to Christ himself (3:16), but it is probably better to make it equivalent to **living water.** John 7:37-39 is the best commentary (cf. Rev 21:6).

11,12. Thinking in terms of the well beneath them, the woman was puzzled. Jesus had no utensil for drawing and the well was deep. At the bottom was the **living** (running) **water** fed by a spring. Could this rabbi hope to conjure up what Jacob secured only by hard toil? He would indeed be **greater** if he could do this.

13-15. Water from the well had to be consumed again and again, but the water Christ dispenses will so satisfy that one **shall never thirst.** Such is the refreshment of **everlasting life.** A parallel may be drawn with the repeated sacrifices of the old covenant and the one-for-all sacrifice of the Lamb of God. Still misunderstanding, but now receptive, the woman asked for such water, that her lot might be easier (4:15).

16-18. Before the woman could receive the gift of living water, she had to be made to realize how desperately she needed it. This gift was for the inner life, which in her case was empty indeed. **Thy husband . . . . no husband . . . five husbands . . . not thy husband.** The dreary history of her marital life was unfolded by Jesus' penetration and by her own admission. It is probable that divorce entered into at least some of the five relationships which preceded the final illegitimate status. Morally, the woman had been going downhill for some time.

19,20. To the woman, Jesus was first a Jew, then one entitled to be called **Sir,** and now a **prophet.** He had looked into her soul. The reference to worship on nearby Mount Gerizim, established in competition to that of the Jews at Jerusalem, may have been a diversionary tactic, but more likely it was an indication of a heart hunger to know the way to God.

21-24. The hour cometh. In the new order that Christ has come to inaugurate, the place of worship is subordinated to the Person. The important thing is that men **worship the Father,** whom the Son has come to declare. By using **ye,** Jesus may be anticipating the conversion of the Samaritan men. The Samaritan worship was a confused thing (cf. II Kgs 17: 33). **Salvation is of the Jews** in the sense that special revelation came to them concerning the right approach to God; and Jesus himself, as the Saviour, came from this people (Rom 9:5). **The hour . . . now is.** Even before the new dispensation is inaugurated in its universalistic character, true worshipers are privileged to worship God as Father **in spirit and in truth. Spirit** seems to glance back at Jerusalem and its worship in terms of letter (the Law), whereas **truth** is in contrast to the inadequate and false worship of the Samaritans. The new kind of worship is imperative because God is **Spirit** (not *a* Spirit).

25,26. The woman's allusion to the Messiah was probably based on Deut 18: 15-18, which was accepted by the Samaritans as Scripture. As the prophet par excellence, the Messiah would be able to **tell . . . all things.** This wistful projection into the future was unnecessary. **I that speak unto thee am he.** It would have been dangerous for Jesus to announce himself in this fashion among the Jews, where ideas of Messiahship were politically colored. Here, apparently, he judged it to be safe. The seed was planted, and just in time, for the conversation was ended by the arrival of the disciples.

27-30. The disciples marveled that Jesus would break convention by talking with the woman (see on v. 9). But reverence for their teacher kept them from open questioning. Unimpeded by her **waterpot,** the woman retired with all speed to the town, her act pledging her purpose to return and proclaiming her determination to have the living water henceforth. She did more than Jesus asked, going not to one man, but to **the men** of the place with the news of her exciting experience. She did not presume to teach them, but put a thought in their minds, phrased tentatively: Is this, perchance, the Christ? The men were sufficiently impressed to go along with her to the well.

31-38. Meanwhile the disciples pressed Jesus to take food, but he declined on the ground that he had nourishment of which they were ignorant. This, he explained, was the doing of God's **will** (v. 34). He had been doing this in their absence, and he had done it in the light of the cross, where he would **finish** God's appointed work (cf. 17:4; 19:30). His ministry was one of both sowing and reaping. **Four months** till **harvest** would be a normal expectation in the natural realm, but by lifting up their eyes the disciples could see a harvest already **white** (the approaching Samaritans), the result of his sowing (4:35). In spiritual work, **sower** and **reaper** are ordinarily different persons, who rejoice together in what their combined efforts have accomplished (vv. 36,37). Here in Samaria and in many other situations the disciples, although not the sowers of the seed, might reap. **Others** may include Jesus and the woman of Samaria. In a sense even Moses may belong here, as being humanly responsible for implanting the seed of Messianic expectation in the heart of the woman.

39-42. Here we learn of the fruit which Christ and the woman were able to gather as sower and reaper. **Many** believed on the Lord because of the woman's testimony. This led to an invitation to stay in their midst, which Christ consented to do for **two days.** During those days, others who had heard the woman's testimony and had been inclined to believe in Jesus became full-fledged believers because of what they received through **his own word,** i.e., from Jesus' own lips (v. 42). **Saviour of the world** – a grateful confession, since it meant that Samaritans as well as Jews could be saved.

F. The Healing of the Nobleman's Son. 4:43-54.

This incident is the only item of ministry reported by John in connection with this visit of Jesus to Galilee. The boy, lying sick at Capernaum, was healed by

Jesus' word when He was at Cana, miles away.

43-45. The meaning of Jesus' **own country** has been much discussed. Possibly the easiest solution is that Galilee as a whole is meant. A lack of honor was to be expected there in contrast to the growing popularity accorded him in Judea (3:26; 4:1). The fact that Galileans who had been at Jerusalem and had seen his miracles there were ready to welcome him does not put them in the class of true and permanent believers (cf. 2:23-25; 4:48). Eventually the Galileans would desert him (6:66).

While at Cana, Jesus had a visit from **a certain nobleman** (*basilikos,* indicating a royal figure or one in royal service). The father's hope of getting healing from Jesus for his son seems to have been based on contact with Galileans who had seen our Lord's miracles at Jerusalem (4:47; cf. v. 45). Having journeyed from Capernaum to Cana, the father made repeated and urgent request (*ērōta)* that Jesus would come down and heal the boy. Jesus expressed fear that the father, like so many others, was so preoccupied with the report of wonders performed that he would not **believe.** More important than the boy's health was the father's faith. The father's reply breathes the desperation of need (cf. Mk 9:22-24). Jesus proved himself worthy of faith and also sympathetic to the suppliant's feelings — **Go thy way; thy son liveth.** His faith developing fast, the man believed **the word** of Christ apart from any visible sign, and went his way satisfied.

51-54. The servants of the nobleman, anxiously watching their master's son in his absence, noted the drastic change in his condition and started out to meet the father with the good news. The nobleman himself, already restful in his faith, was interested now in learning the time of the change. When he compared the time of the departure of the fever with the time of his interview with Jesus, he knew the healing was no accident. He **himself believed.** His faith was confirmed by experience. Faith spread to the entire household (v. 53). At the first Cana miracle the disciples had believed. The **second** miracle from the same spot resulted in a wider circle of faith.

G. The Healing of the Lame Man in Jerusalem. 5:1-16.

Both the time and the place of this miracle have been much disputed. If this feast of the Jews was the Passover, then four such feasts are mentioned in John, making the ministry extend to approximately three and a half to four years, provided John lists them all (the others are 2:23; 6:4; 11:55). Since the best manuscript authorities lack the definite article, some feast other than the Passover is probably intended. The place of the miracle may now be identified with some confidence, following the excavation in 1888 of such a pool as John describes, located in the northeastern part of Jerusalem, near the Church of St. Anne. The various readings in the manuscripts for the name of the pool are bewildering. Beth-zatha (RSV) is well attested. It probably means "House of Olives."

2-4. The five porches or porticoes, now uncovered, sheltered a great company of sick, some **blind,** others **lame,** others **withered,** i.e., paralyzed. They were there in hope of being healed when the water was troubled. While our manuscript tradition is such that the end of verse 3 and all of verse 4 cannot be regarded as part of the original text of John, this portion is an early tradition. J. Rendel Harris found evidence in several places throughout the East of a superstition to the effect that at the New Year an angel was expected to stir the water in certain localities, enabling one person to obtain healing by being the first to get into the water after the disturbance. On this basis he judged the feast of this chapter to have been Trumpets, announcing the New Year (so Westcott. See J. Rendel Harris, *Side Lights on New Testament Research,* pp. 36-69). The remains of the Church of St. Anne include the figure of an angel, testifying to this belief and the custom of seeking healing under these special circumstances.

5-7. There is nothing to indicate the precise nature of the ailment that had gripped this sick man for so many years, except that he could not move without help. It is not at all likely that he remained there all this time. Rather, he was brought when the moving of the water was expected. Jesus **knew.** Since nothing is said of the impartation of knowledge by others, we are to conclude that here, as with Nathanael and the woman of Samaria, Jesus discerned the true state of affairs by his own power of perception. **Wilt thou be made whole?** In this case Jesus took the initiative. The question was not needless, for many who are chronic invalids have no hope of cure. Others use their sickness as a means of eliciting sympathy, hence do not really want to be healed. The sick man had the desire for healing, but lacked the means (v. 7). **8,9.** Three commands by Jesus imply the impartation of strength. The healing was instantaneous. **Bed.** Mattress or pallet.

10-13. Quickly the healing became the subject of dispute, because it had been performed on **the sabbath day. The Jews.** In this case not the common people, but their rulers (cf. 1:19). Apparently they observed the man walking through the streets toward his home, carrying his pallet. This violated the Sabbath rest (Jer 17:21). In his confusion, the healed man could only explain that his benefactor had commanded him to do this very thing (Jn 5:11). He could not identify the healer, for he had not learned his name, and now it seemed impossible to find out, for Jesus had left the scene.

14-16. Because he was not guilty of intentional violation of the Law, the healed man was permitted to go his way. Later on he proceeded to the Temple to give thanks for his healing. There Jesus found him and gave him a message of warning. **Sin no more, lest a worse thing come unto thee.** Physical healing at Jesus' hands may be supposed to include forgiveness of sins (cf. Mk 2:9-12). This forgiveness must not be lightly accepted. The **worse thing** is left undefined, and the warning is the more effective for this reason. Returning to the Jews, the man identified Jesus as the healer, probably not because he had taken offense at Jesus' warning, but because he felt an obligation, as a member of the community, to supply information sought by the authorities. This led the rulers to **persecute** Jesus. To them his guilt as a lawbreaker was plain. He had violated the Sabbath. **These things** are not defined. The verb is "he was doing," as though to suggest there were other similar grievances. The words **and sought to slay him** lack sufficient manuscript authority.

H. Jesus' Self-defense. 5:17-47.

The following discourse deals with the authority of Jesus, which he grounds in his special relation to the Father.

17,18. Since working was the basis for contention, Jesus points to God as a continuing worker. Although the Father rested from his creative activity (Gen 2:2), he must work to sustain the universe. He must work also to bring in the new creation. The meaning seems to be that all the while the Father had been working, the Son had been working too. This was a greater claim than to assert that the Father had been working and now the Son was assuming the burden. The Jews caught the implication: Jesus was asserting that God was his own Father, thus claiming equality with God. This was worse than working on the Sabbath. Such blasphemy called for death (cf. Jn 7:30).

19,20. This discourse continued without apparent interruption from the Jews. No arrogance marked Jesus' claim, which was balanced by complete dependence on and subordination to the Father. This is true sonship, Jesus points out, to learn from the Father and reproduce what is seen (v. 19). The Son's perception is aided by the Father's revelation to him concerning the meaning **of all things** that are done by the Father. To demonstrate the reality of the relationship between the two, **greater works** than **these** (the healing of the impotent man and similar signs) will be forthcoming.

21-24. One of these greater works is the raising of the dead (v. 21). Clearly this is as much a creative act as the original impartation of life. If the Son has power to quicken whom he will, he partakes of the Father's power. **Judgment** is a second sphere in which the divine authority is manifest. This function has been given over to the Son. Note that resurrection and judgment are closely related eschatological functions, of which there were foregleams during Christ's ministry, such as the resurrection of Lazarus and the judgment upon Satan (16:11). Behind this sharing of authority is the design that the Son shall receive honor equally with the Father. To refuse it is to dishonor the Father (5:23). The two themes of (1) life out of death and (2) judgment are now brought together (v. 24); but the resurrection here is spiritual, not physical, namely, participation in **everlasting life.** One must believe on the One who sent the Son, not in the sense of by-passing the Son, but as perceiving that faith in the Father and in the Son are indivisible.

25-30. Jesus enlarges on his power to give spiritual quickening (vv. 25,26). This work belongs to the future, he says, but is also **now** going on (note contrast with v. 28). **The dead** in this case are not in the graves, as in verse 28, but are dead in sin. Their quickening comes through hearing **the voice of the Son of God** (cf. v. 24 – **he that heareth my word;** 6:60; 18:37). In nothing is the Son independent of the Father, even in the fundamental matter of **life** itself (5:26).

Once again Christ sets forth his authority in judgment (v. 27). **Son of man** is used here, as it is in Dan 7:13, in connection with judgment and dominion. It is a technical eschatological term, denoting more than humanity but including it. As Lord of resurrection, Jesus will summon all from their graves (cf. Acts 24:15). In view of Rev 20:4,5, we are to think of a time interval between these two phases of resurrection. The doing of **good** includes having faith in the Son of God, even as doing **evil** includes the rejection of the Son and his claims. **Damnation.** Literally *judgment*. The next verse (Jn 5:30) is transitional, retaining the mention of **judgment** from the recent context and anticipating by its use of the first person of the pronoun the material that follows. The Son alone has this unique relation to the Father.

31-40. In this passage the theme of witness is uppermost. If Jesus were to bear witness to himself, he says, in isolation from the Father's witness, it would be untrue because incomplete and unsupported. He could not expect the Jews to receive it. But his witness is actually not of this sort (cf. 8:18). **Another** bears witness, even the Father. Unfortunately the Jews do not recognize the Father's witness (cf. 7:28; 8:19), and so are incapacitated for recognizing the support it brings to Jesus' claims (5:32). A second witness was John the Baptist, who was sought out by the Jews themselves for his testimony (1:26; 3:26). This witness was in accord with **the truth,** as the descent of the Spirit upon Jesus proved. However helpful such witness may have been in leading others to a right evaluation of himself, Jesus did not rely upon it as necessary to his own awareness of person and mission (5:34). Yet John's word, acknowledged by Jesus, was intended to help these people to **be saved.** Jesus here characterizes John as the **burning** and **shining** lamp. As burning, he gradually faded (3:30), but as shining, he enabled men to see their need of the greater Light (cf. 1:8). As such, his testimony outlived him. **For a season.** John's popularity did not last long. A third witness to Jesus is found in his **works,** which were given to him by the Father to perform, in order to attest his divine mission (v. 36). **Finish.** Nothing tentative or incomplete. The works prepared the way for the work, which we now know was finished on Calvary and which needs no revision.

As a part of the greater witness, our Lord includes the testimony of the Father contained in the Scriptures (5:37-40). This he clearly distinguishes from the Father's immediate testimony to him (v. 32). The inaccessibility of God, due to his spirituality (v. 37) is overcome to a considerable degree through the revelation of himself in the Scriptures of the OT. But that **word** had not taken root in Jesus' hearers. The proof lies in the fact that they had not received him of whom the Word speaks (5:38). **Search** may be either indicative or imperative in this instance, but the sense of the passage favors the indicative. The Jews were in the habit of searching **the Scriptures** because they recognized that these contain the secret of **eternal life.** Acquaintance with the Law was the goal of Jewish piety; so the written Word tended to become an end in itself. But the Scriptures testify of a *person!* The tragedy was that that very Person was now present, and religious men would not come to him for the life they vainly sought in the letter of the Word (v. 40).

41-47. Jesus did not want men to believe in him simply that he might have **honour** from them (v. 41). The Greek word is *doxa,* often rendered *glory.* The basic reason for the lack of response to him and his claims was lack of response to God. They lacked **the love of God,** i.e., love for God. Since Jesus had come in the Father's name, this lack of love for God made it impossible for them to see that he was one with the Father, and receive him. In the event that one should come **in his own name,** not resting, as Jesus did, on the authority of the Father, he would have a ready response (v. 43). This was probably not intended as a prophecy of the coming of any one figure, but was spoken to point up a principle involving sinful human nature. The Jews were guilty of seeking honor and glory from one another (cf. 12:43) rather than from the only God, who is the only source of true and abiding recognition. Jesus' mission was not one of accusation and judgment. This was unnecessary anyway in the case of his hearers, because an accuser existed in Moses. The Jews put unbounded confidence in what Moses wrote (v. 45), but at the crucial point they did not believe at all, for they failed to receive Moses' prophetic announcements regarding the Christ. Here we are to think not simply of individual passages, such as Deut 18:15-18, but of the very incompleteness of revelation apart from One to come, and of the condemnation of the Law, which called for a Saviour. The written revelation and the personal revelation are basically one (v. 47).

I. The Feeding of The Five Thousand and The Discourse on The Bread of Life. 6:1-71.

Some scholars, advocating the view that chapters 5 and 6 have become transposed, have pointed out certain advantages in reversing them. But lack of manuscript evidence for it is a formidable barrier to acceptance of the view.

The miracle before us is the only "sign" recorded in all four Gospels. Mark and Luke speak of Jesus as teaching the multitude prior to the miracle, but John alone records the discourse which Jesus gave on the following day.

1-4. The other side of the sea, in this case, is the eastern shore. Another name for this body of water is the Lake of Gennesaret (Lk 5:1). Attracted by Jesus' miracles, a great crowd followed him around the north shore. This presupposes a ministry of some duration, perhaps several months, in the Galilean area, after the events of chapter 5 located in Jerusalem. **A mountain.** The highlands. Mention of the nearness of the Passover is significant. Since John does not record the institution of the Lord's Supper as a part of his recital of the events of Passion Week, he is probably drawing the attention of the reader to the bearing of the miracle and the discourse on the central sacrament of the Christian faith.

5-7. The nearest town was Bethsaida. It would have been difficult for the people to get bread, due to the distance and the lateness of the hour. Jesus assumed that he and his company would make provision (v. 5). He counseled with Philip about ways and means, knowing in himself what he would do, **but desiring to prove** (test) the faith of his disciples. Philip was a native of Bethsaida (1:44). Two hundred denarii worth of bread, the apostle estimated, would hardly be enough. A denarius equaled about twenty cents and was the usual daily wage of a laborer. A laborer with an average-size family of five probably spent half his daily income for food. Assuming that the family ate three meals a day, we can conclude that a half denarius would have furnished them a day's food or fifteen meals. A whole denarius would have provided two days' rations or thirty meals. Two hundred denarii would have provided one meal for some 6,000 people. In this crowd the men alone numbered about 5,000 (6:10). **8,9.** It proved unnecessary to drain the treasury and cause troublesome delay by seeking to purchase food. Andrew stepped forward with information about **a lad.** The Greek word is used for a wide range of ages. It may indicate a slave also, but this is improbable here. **Barley loaves.** The cheap food of the common people. The loaves were scarcely more than buns. The supply seemed pitifully small for the need.

10,11. Order was necessary for the large operation in view. At Jesus' command, given through the disciples, the people were seated. Mention of grass indicates the spring of the year (cf. v. 4). It helped to make the crowd comfortable. Jesus then gave thanks for the provision (Did he include thanks for the boy's generosity?), then distributed to the disciples, and they to the multitude. In the process of distribution the miracle occurred. The people had **as much as they would** (wished for) both of bread and fish, in contrast to Philip's estimate—"a little." **12,13.** The prodigality of the giving was matched by the stringency of the measures for conserving what was left over. God's gifts are not to be wasted. **Twelve baskets** were needed to hold **the fragments,** and so all of the disciples were kept busy.

14,15. There was no doubt that a **miracle** had been performed. The people saw it and were impressed by it. All had been benefited. They saw that their benefactor was no ordinary person, and concluded that he must be the expected **prophet** (Deut 18:18). Here, as in John 4, the **prophet** seems to be identified with the Messiah, whereas in John 1:20,21 the two are differentiated. In the public mind there was probably no hard and fast line between the two representations. The prophet would become **king** at any rate, if this crowd could have its way. Such a move would at once express their gratitude for the miracle and also insure the harnessing of Jesus' wonder-working power to the nation's needs, both economic and military. The popular expectation of Messiah was about to express itself in dramatic fashion. But he whose kingdom was not of this world (18:36), perceiving the intention, foiled it by withdrawal.

16-21. The Lord who had met the need of the throng now met the need of his disciples, who were caught in a storm at night on the lake. Without Jesus, but apparently expecting him to come to them (v. 17), the disciples headed for Capernaum. To the handicap of the **dark** was now added the distress of high **wind** and wave. Forward progress had brought them about twenty-five or thirty **furlongs** from the shore (each such measure—*stadios*—was about six hundred feet). As the situation grew desperate, Jesus drew near. To the fear of the storm was now added the fear of the apparition. But the voice of Jesus, saying, **It is I; be not afraid,** banished their fears. They welcomed him into the ship and found themselves immediately at the land. The Synoptists tell us that on this occasion Jesus walked on the water. His miraculous power manifested itself also in removing the barrier of distance. Gravity and space alike are under his control. John adds no interpretation to his account. The passage is useful as teaching that despite opposing forces, Jesus will enable his people to achieve the goals he has set for them, including heaven itself.

22-25. The setting for the discourse is given in these verses. Perhaps it was the storm that kept the people from leaving the area of the miracle of the multiplication of the loaves, plus the impression that Jesus was still nearby. The desire to have him as their leader and provider was still strong. Seeing that he had not departed with his disciples, they were perplexed as to his movements. When a search of the area failed to reveal him, and boats arrived from Capernaum, the crowd determined to take shipping and cross the lake in the hope of finding him on the other side. **When . . . ?** (6:25) Jesus was a man of mystery to them.

26-34. Rebuked by the Lord, the people demanded a sign as the basis for faith in him. Even though they had seen the miracle (cf. 6:14), Jesus charged them with not seeing, i.e., not looking beyond the external aspect. They saw only the provision of material sustenance and felt its satisfaction (v. 26). **Meat** (v. 27). A general word for food or eating. Jesus' teaching here had a double edge, for he contrasted food that perishes with food that endures unto **everlasting life,** and also pitted **labor** over against **give** (cf. Isa 55:1,2). Even the food Jesus had provided across the lake was perishable. But he had that to give which would be significant for eternal life. His power to do this rested in the authority which God the Father had vested in him (**sealed** by the divine voice at the baptism and by the bestowal of the Spirit). The warning about labor did not fully "register," for the people demanded to know what they must **do** to work the works of God (v. 28), that is, to perform works acceptable to him. In answer, the Lord pointed to faith as the greatest, the indispensable work (v. 29). This seemed to be an unusual requirement. After all, many had spoken for God in the past and had not called for faith in themselves but only in the One who sent them. So the crowd felt justified in requesting a special sign to support this special claim. To believe him they must have something akin to the bringing down of **bread from heaven** (6:31), in contrast to the miracle across the lake.

In order to avoid misunderstanding, Jesus reminded his hearers that it was not Moses but God who gave the bread in the desert, who also was granting the true bread from heaven. By **true** we are to understand the perfect, that which answers to men's deepest need. Christ identified the bread as **he** (v. 33), one who had actually come down from heaven to give **life** to the world. But the explicit identification with himself was not yet made. The people wanted **this bread,** but apparently still thought of it in material terms, much as the woman of Samaria thought of living water (v. 34).

35-65. This section comprises the discourse proper, interrupted three times by questions and discussion.

35. Jesus now finally identified himself as **the bread of life.** Not only does he have life in himself, but he is able to impart it to others. But this bread is not something external, something apart from himself. One must **come** to him, which is the equivalent of believing on him. For those who come, spiritual hunger will be forever banished. Eating and drinking occur together here, perhaps in anticipation of verse 53. One need never turn from Christ to another for satisfaction.

36. Seeing had not resulted in believing (cf. 6:30). "He Himself was the sign which the Jews could not read. No other more convincing could be given" (B. F. Westcott, *The Gospel According to St. John).* **37.** Even so, the Son was not discouraged, for **all** who were the gift of the Father to him would come, and in coming would find in him no spirit of rejection but rather glad welcome. **38.** This reception was inevitable, for the will of the Father was the delight of the Son. **39,40.** This will was not confined to the call but extended also to the preservation of those who were given to Christ (cf. 17:12). The reunion of **the**

last day will defy the power of death. **41,42.** The offense of the humanity of the Nazarene blinded the hearers. They knew too much about him, including his supposed parentage, to accept the conclusion that he **came down from heaven** (cf. Mk 6:2,3). **43,44.** Those who murmured (as did their fathers in the desert) at the high claim of the Son of man showed that they did not know what it was to have the Father **draw** them. Without such a drawing, an inclination of the heart induced by God, one cannot **come** to Christ. One cannot lean to his own understanding. **45.** The drawing comes through teaching rather than through some mystical process. Here Christ quoted Isa 54:13. If the **all** be emphasized, it removes any element of restriction that may seem to lurk in the idea of drawing as stated in Jn 6:44. **46.** But immediate knowledge of God can come only through the One who has **seen** the Father. This is a leading claim of the Gospel (cf. 1:18). **47,48.** Truths given earlier are emphasized again.

49-51. The Jews had demanded that Jesus bring down bread from heaven. What permanent profit would result? The fathers who ate the manna were **dead,** but those who partook of the bread which is the Son of God would not die (spiritually), for the very life of God was theirs. The **flesh** of Jesus, his actual corporeal existence, was to be given for the life of the world. This pointed to the cross. **52-54.** Still thinking in material terms, the Jews argued with one another over the possibility of Jesus' giving them his flesh to eat (v. 52). Making the matter still more difficult, our Lord indicated that his blood as well as his flesh had to be received if one would have life (v. 53). In view of the OT prohibition against consuming blood (Lev 7:26,27), the offense at Jesus' words must have been heightened. Those words seem to anticipate the significance of the Lord's Supper.

55-58. The following quotation will best summarize the thought: "The Eucharistic food and drink are physically bread and wine, spiritually the Flesh and Blood of the Son of man: the true food and drink because they effect the sacred union of the Son of God with those who believe on Him, and thus communicate eternal life and guarantee immortality. The union of the Father and the Son is thereby extended to embrace the believers also. As the Father communicates life to the Son, so the Son communicates life to those who feed on Him, and will bestow on them immortality" (Hoskyns). The feeding need not be confined to Eucharistic celebration.

59. A fine synagogue has been excavated at Capernaum, which has a pot of manna as one of its decorative motifs. Though this structure comes from a period later than the time of Jesus, a synagogue probably stood on the same spot in Jesus' day.

60-65. This section concerns especially the reaction of **disciples** to Jesus' words. These are to be distinguished alike from "the Jews" of the foregoing context and the Twelve in the following verses. These disciples had been followers, but felt, in view of the teaching, that they could not continue. The **hard saying** refers to the necessity of eating Christ's flesh and drinking his blood. His ascension, which for true believers would confirm his claims, would only add to the offense for those who could not receive his humanity offered for them in death on the cross (v. 62). Even Christ's **flesh,** declared to be so indispensable, would profit nothing except as the Spirit vivified it to the believer. His own **words,** however, partook of the character of spirit, that is, were life-giving. They could save, not in independence of the historic work of the cross, but as pointing to that work and interpreting it. The very resistance encountered by his words among would-be disciples demonstrated that their faith was superficial. Jesus discerned not only the presence of pseudo-faith, but the potential of betrayal on the part of one of his followers.

66-71. The effect of the discourse on the Twelve is now unfolded. This was the parting of the ways for many who had been disciples (6:66). Their departure prompted the question of Jesus to the Twelve as to their intentions (v. 67). Peter, as the rock, stood his ground. His confession is similar to that recorded by the Synoptists in connection with the Caesarea-Philippi incident (Mt 16:16), but in keeping with the discourse it emphasizes that Jesus has **the words of eternal life** (cf. Jn 6:63). Others saw in them only words. Peter saw a fruition unto life eternal, even though he did not yet understand the cross. Another in that company could not so speak, for he was a devil *(diabolos).* The meaning is not that he was an instrument of Satan when Christ chose him, but that he had become such. Judas belonged with the departing throng, but he stayed on. Offended that Jesus refused to be made king, as we gather from closely studying his career, he would one day betray Him in spite for having betrayed the confidence of those who trusted Him to lead them to Messianic victory.

J. Jesus at the Feast of Tabernacles. 7:1-53.

This chapter is thoroughly Christ-centered in the sense that Christ is the subject of much discussion and diverse reaction as well as the theme of Jesus' self-disclosure.

1. After these things. The reference seems to be to the events of the last chapter. Despite the breach with so many former disciples, Jesus found it safer to abide in Galilee than to return to Judea, where there was open hostility. **2.** The period spent in Galilee is bounded by the Passover and the Feast of Tabernacles, an interval of slightly more than six months. Judging from the Synoptics, Jesus spent most of this time in out-of-the-way places, teaching his disciples.

3-9. With the approach of this autumn feast, which drew Jews from far and wide for the joyful festivities, Jesus' brothers professed to see in the occasion a capital opportunity for him to extend his influence. His **disciples** in Judea, perhaps including many Galileans who had been offended or had grown cold in their attitude, could be won over by seeing his **works.** The brothers were a miniature of the great bulk of the nation, not questioning the reality of the works, but failing to **believe** in him. Their counsel was that, whereas Jesus was remaining **in secret,** he needed to be known **openly.** This is substantially what Satan sought to suggest to our Lord in the second temptation. Jesus' season had not arrived (elsewhere often called "my hour"—the time of his manifestation in death). The brethren had no such spiritual regulation of their movements. They did not know the hatred of the world, for they were a part of it. On the other hand, Jesus, as the Truth, had to testify against the **evil** in the world. He could not go to Jerusalem simply to gain popularity. If he went, it would be to expose sin. **I go not up yet.** The word **yet** is lacking in many good authorities, and was probably a scribal addition to avoid contradiction with verse 10. Jesus meant by this refusal that he was not going up on the terms suggested by his brothers. He would go in his own time and way, but would remain in Galilee for the time being.

10-13. When he did go up to the feast, he went unobtrusively, **in secret,** as it were, without any fanfare. Meanwhile **the Jews** (the leaders) kept looking for him among the crowds and asking, "Where is that man?" The people were discussing him also, with some difference of opinion, the judgments wavering between the verdict of **good man** and **deceiver.** Fear of the Jews kept the discussion in hushed tones (7:13; cf. 9:22). **14,15. About the midst of the feast,** i.e., in the middle of the week of festivities, which ended with an eighth day convocation (Lev 23:36). Entering the Temple, Jesus began to teach. The leaders were astonished at his expositions, especially in view of the fact that he had not been trained in the rabbinic schools (contrast Paul, Acts 22:3).

16-18. Apparently it was the content of Jesus' teaching rather than his manner or diction that caused astonishment. Instead of boasting in his ability, Jesus explained that the teaching belonged to the One who had sent him, tracing it directly to God instead of acknowledging his debt to some human teacher as the scribes were accustomed to do. Anyone who had the moral aim of pleasing God (doing His will) would be able to determine whether Jesus' teaching was independent or was a faithful reproduction of the divine. He would detect that Jesus was not seeking his own **glory** but that of the One who sent him. Such a person would be sympathetically attracted to Jesus.

19-24. Jesus charged the Jews with failure to keep the Law. In this respect they were not doing the will of God. How, then, could they receive him whom God had sent? Their murderous intent toward him was in itself a breaking of the sixth commandment. The crowd, taking their stand with the rulers but not knowing their designs, thought Jesus must be mad, tormented by a demon, to imagine that his life was in danger (v. 20). It was in order for the Lord to get at the roots of the animosity of the leaders. The **one work** he had done in Jerusalem that made all men **marvel** but that turned the rulers against him was the healing of the impotent man on the Sabbath (ch. 5). Moses himself, so carefully honored by the Jews, commanded circumcision (although the practice originated with **the fathers** and not with Moses), so that it had to be carried out on the eighth day (Lev 12:3) even if that day was **the sabbath. Therefore** (Jn 7:22) is not entirely clear as to its bearing on the matter. It possibly points to this line of thought—that circumcision on the Sabbath was agreeable to and actually pointed to such a work as Jesus had wrought, since the restoration of a man both physically and spiritually was even more significant than the administering of the sign of the covenant.

25-27. Here we encounter the reflections concerning Jesus of a group which must be distinguished from "the people" of verse 20. These were inhabitants of Jerusalem who knew that the intention of the rulers was to kill Jesus. Yet the fact that Jesus was able to speak **boldly** in public made them speculate as to whether the rulers had reversed themselves and were now concluding that this man was the Christ (v. 26). Further meditation on the problem led them to dismiss this possibility, for Jesus' origin excluded him from consideration (cf. 6:42). The Messiah was to be a man of mystery—**no man knoweth whence he is** (cf. Mt 24:24-26).

28-31. Jesus granted, as a starting point, that his hearers both knew him and whence he was (v. 28). Yet even on the earthly level, they were not properly informed, being ignorant of his birthplace and presumably also of the circumstances behind his birth (cf. v. 52). They were ignorant of him in his divine being, and thereby revealed their ignorance of God who sent him. This rebuke brought a show of displeasure. The men of Jerusalem were ready to lay hands on Jesus, but were providentially prevented from carrying out their design (v. 30). Christ's **hour** is a reference to the time appointed by God for his death. Some in the crowd were not ready to dismiss the possibility that Jesus might be the Christ. But apparently they believed in him only on the basis of the **miracles** and therefore were no different from earlier believers who were such only in name (cf. 2:23-25).

32-36. Always alert to what the man in the street was saying, the **Pharisees** and **chief priests** (Sadducees) sent **officers** to capture Jesus. Such appeared again at the arrest in the garden (18:3,12). They constituted a Jewish police force for the temple area. In the light of this development, Jesus insisted that his **little while** (cf. 16:16) was not dictated by human plots against him but by the consummation of his work and his return to the Father (v. 33). The search of the people for him then would be fruitless. Time was running out for them to seek him aright. **Dispersed among the Gentiles.** Literally, *the dispersion of the Greeks*. It probably means the dispersion of the Jews among the Greeks, making possible a reaching of Greeks themselves in the Jewish synagogues. This is exactly what Jesus did through his Church in later times; so the statement is unconsciously prophetic (cf. 11:52).

37-39. On the last day . . . of the feast. This could have been the seventh day or the eighth. The latter was a kind of adjunct to the feast and also a conclusion to the year's cycle of feasts. If Jesus' reference to **thirst** is consciously connected with the priests' practice of bringing water in a golden pitcher each day from the pool of Siloam and pouring it out at the altar, then Jesus' cry of invitation would have special point on the eighth day, when, it seems, this ceremony was omitted. The thirst of the wilderness journey had its divinely supplied satisfaction, but it recurred. Jesus offered lasting spiritual satisfaction (cf. 4:14). Again Judaism was exposed as inadequate. The thought progresses; for the believer in Jesus, who finds this satisfaction, becomes in turn a means of blessing to others as a conductor of **rivers of living water** (7:38). Any allusion to Christ himself (cf. 19:34) is doubtful. **The scripture** cannot be identified. Some possible passages are Ex 17:6; Isa 44:3,4; 58:11; Ezk 47:1-9; Zech 14:8. An alternative is that John has reference to no Scripture passage but to the consensus of several. The promise of new life in abundance is attributed here to **the Spirit,** who is given to all who believe. But at this time the Spirit had not come in the epochal sense of Pentecost (cf. 14:26; 15:26; 16:7). **Glorified,** i.e., reached the goal of his mission in death, resurrection and ascension. It is the glorified Christ whom the Spirit mediates to men.

40-44. The loud cry and the nature of the words of Jesus led many of his hearers to identify him with the prophet who should come (Deut 18:15; Jn 1:21; 6:14). Others were prepared to think of him as the Messiah. This raised the problem of his origin. To meet the requirement of Scripture, Messiah had to come from David's seed and from David's town, Bethlehem. The people, in their ignorance, thought of Jesus as simply a Galilean. Those who looked on him as a pretender and deceiver were in favor of laying hands on him, but were providentially restrained (7:44).

45-49. The officers who had previously been sent to take Jesus (v. 32) now reported back empty-handed. They, like others (vv. 30,44), were restrained from laying hands on the Son of God, and they could explain their failure only on the ground that no man ever spoke as he did. They sensed something supernatural in him and were powerless to carry out their commission. The answer of the Pharisees is that such men ought to get their guidance from their superiors. So far **the rulers** (members of the Sanhedrin) and **the Pharisees** (the teachers of the people) had maintained a solid front against Jesus. **Have any of the rulers . . . believed?** This remained true, but not for long, since one of the rulers was about to declare for Jesus, or at least defend him. The Pharisees sought to explain popular interest in Jesus on the ground that the people were ignorant of the Law and were therefore cursed (cf. Deut 28:15). Jewish sources indicate that there was often bad feeling between the Pharisees and the *am ha-areṣ* or people of the land.

50,51. However well the Pharisees knew the Law, they were not abiding by it themselves, as Nicodemus had the courage to point out. They had sought to arrest a man in violation of the Law, which required that a man be heard before he could be apprehended in this fashion (Deut 1:16). So the Jews were unfaithful to their own Law, on which they prided themselves (cf. v. 19). Ignoring the exposure by Nicodemus, the Pharisees appealed to sectionalism even as they had just appealed to class. Nicodemus had ventured to talk in defense of a Galilean, as though he were one himself. What had Galilee to offer? It had produced no prophet. In thus excluding Jesus from the ranks of the prophets, the Pharisees revealed their own ignorance, for Jonah at least had come from this section (II Kgs 14:25; cf. Josh 19:13).

K. The Woman Taken in Adultery. 8:1-11.

Manuscript authority is strongly against the genuineness of this paragraph (including 7:53), and the language is hardly Johannine. Yet the story is clearly a true one, which early found a place in the text of the Fourth Gospel.

1. When in Jerusalem Jesus usually bivouacked on the Mount of Olives.

2. As a lad he had visited the Temple to be taught (Lk 2:46). Now he was there to teach, with people crowding around him. **3.** The teaching session was interrupted by the arrival of scribes and Pharisees, who were leading a woman apprehended in adultery. Angered at Jesus' success and frustrated by their inability to get rid of him, these leaders now seized on an opportunity to embarrass him before the people. They embarrassed the woman, too, by placing her **in the midst.**

5. Reminding Jesus of the requirement of stoning for this offense (Deut 22:23, 24), these leaders sought his verdict on the matter. They were **tempting** him by putting him in a dilemma. If he upheld the Law, which was apparently not being applied rigorously in such cases, he could be made to appear heartless. If he advocated mercy, he could be heralded as having too lenient a view of the application of the Law. If the Pharisees had been truly concerned for the maintenance of the Law, they would have brought the male offender also.

6. It is useless to speculate as to what Jesus wrote. Nothing is made of the writing in the narrative. Only what the group **heard** from him (v. 9) is crucial. **7. Without sin.** Not necessarily the sin in question, but sin in general. **9.** Jesus' words had the effect of shifting attention from himself and the woman to the accusers. **Conscience** began to do its work. **Beginning at the eldest.** Their age made them leaders, and their longer experience of sin gave them greater cause for self-accusation. Only two remained – the sinner and the Friend of sinners. Jesus could have cast the stone, for he was sinless; but he was more concerned with the rehabilitation of the sinner than with seeing that the Law was meticulously satisfied. If his word, **Neither do I condemn thee,** sounds too lenient, it is balanced by the sequel, **Go, and sin no more.** The Searcher of Hearts saw that there was penitence in the heart of the woman. All that was needed was a warning for the future.

L. Jesus' Self-disclosure. 8:12-59.

On the side of Jesus' opponents there was the question, "Who are you?" (v. 25), which is the perennial question. From Christ's own standpoint he was the light of the world, yet One who was not of this world, the One who had come to set men free from their sins, the eternal "I AM." At every point he stood in sharp contrast to his objectors. The physical setting was still the Temple (v. 20).

12. I am the light of the world. The background for this statement may reside in the practice of lighting the candelabra in the Court of the Women (where the treasury was located, v. 20) during the

Feast of Tabernacles, and in the glory cloud of the wilderness wanderings which those lights were intended to represent, and also in the creation light (1:4, 9), now conceived in spiritual terms. He is **the light of life.**

13-18. Ready to find fault, the Pharisees objected to such self-testimony and labeled it untrue (v. 13). Self-testimony is often untrue and therefore needs support from others; but in Jesus' case, his witness to himself was true, for he had absolute knowledge of his own origin and destiny. Naturally there was no human witness who could corroborate such matters (v. 14). The Pharisees *judged* (i.e., came to an opinion) on mere fleshly considerations. They were blinded to spiritual truth (cf. I Cor 2:14). On the other hand, when Jesus judges (though he did not come for that purpose primarily – cf. Jn 3:17), it is properly a verdict, and so can stand eternally, for it is **true.** The Father endorses it and shares in it (v. 16). If the testimony of two **men** is true (the Law required at least two witnesses as a safeguard of justice; Deut 17:6), how much more valid is the witness of Christ, who has the Father as witness along with himself (Jn 7:18). The witness of the Father at Christ's baptism and transfiguration are well-known features of the Synoptic record.

19,20. Where is thy Father? In other words, If he is an absentee, we cannot profit from his witness. This is "a supreme formulation of Jewish misunderstanding and unbelief" (E. C. Hoskyns, *The Fourth Gospel*). Actually, failure to perceive the true nature of Christ was a confession of ignorance of his Father (cf. 14:7,9). Friction flared again, but once more Jesus was untouched, because his course had not been completed (v. 20).

21,22. The coming of his **hour** would mean for Jesus that he could go his **way** (back to the Father), but not until he should have dealt with the sin problem. Because the Pharisees would not accept him, they would have to **die** in their **sins.** Their separation would be deepened and sealed. They could not come where he would be at that day. As Jesus' prediction of his departure had previously caused perplexity (7:35), so this time it led to the surmise that he was contemplating suicide (v. 22). His death, however, would not be self-inflicted; these men would help to bring it about.

23. The prospect of ultimate separation focused attention on present contrasts: **beneath . . . above; of this world . . . not of this world.** Jesus declined to speak of heaven as "that world," for the term **world** here emphasizes man in revolt and distance from God. **24.** The sin which accounted for their ignorance and hostility would lead them to a hopeless death unless – they believed in him as the **I am** (cf. Ex 3:14).

25. This was worse, from the Jews' point of view, than the claim of verse 12, for it was the absolute claim of deity. Christ's hearers demanded that he furnish a predicate. **Who art thou?** Since he had made himself sufficiently known, he was content to rest on his previous affirmations. The Greek may possibly mean that from the beginning he was all that he had been affirming (cf. 1:1). **26.** The **many things** he might have said further would all have been true, but they would only have added to the condemnation of their hearers (cf. the many things which Jesus could say to the disciples, which would only add to their perplexity; 16:12). Yet opposition would not shut the mouth of Jesus. He would continue to **speak to the world.**

28. The death of the Son of man, his lifting up on the cross (cf. 3:14; 12:32) would vindicate him in the sense that it would lead to resurrection and exaltation, which in turn would bring the convicting ministry of the Spirit. Some, at least, would come to know that his claim that he was the Eternal had not been idly spoken (Acts 2:41; 4:4; 6:7).

30-32. The claims of Jesus, so simple and so lofty, impressed some of those who were present. **Many believed.** Yet before long they were picking up stones to cast at him (8:59). It is the old story of pseudo faith. In this case, they did not **abide** in his word – which is necessary for true discipleship, and which opens the way to knowing the truth more fully – to the point of being set free through it (v. 32). These compact statements are amplified in what follows.

33. The Jews resented the implication that they were not free. As Abraham's seed they had a standing superior to that of any other people (cf. Gal 4:22). They were sons of the heavenly King. They ignored, in this case, their political bondage to Rome, as being irrelevant. **34.** Their bondage lay deeper than the external relations of life. The committing of sin puts one in the position of being the **servant of sin. 35.** The Son (Christ) abides **in the house** of the Father **for ever** as the true Isaac. Ishmael, though he be Abraham's seed, must go out. So with the arrogant Jews. **36.** The truth which makes free (8:32) is now seen to be personal. The Son, who is the truth (14:6), makes men free (cf. Gal 4:4-7).

37. The Lord was willing to concede that his hearers were the seed of Abraham in the ordinary sense. But their antagonism to him showed that they were not spiritually akin to Abraham, who was a man of faith and obedience. **38.** Their inspiration came from a father other than Abraham, one whose sinister identity Christ soon declared. **39.** Abraham's children should be able to produce Abraham's works. He acted on revelation from God. **40.** Christ had spoken the truth (not simply truth as distinct from error, but the truth about his relation to the Father and the truth about his mission). Instead of receiving it, as Abraham would have done, these Jews sought to kill the Son of man.

41. They did have a father, whom they imitated, whose works they reproduced, but it was not Abraham. The Jews retaliated by a slur: "**We** be not born of fornication." The **we** is emphatic. Underlying this is apparently the charge of illegitimacy leveled at Jesus (this same charge colors Matthew's report of the birth of Jesus). We, the Jews were saying, are those who truly have God for our Father, whatever your claims may be. We go back of Abraham to God himself. **42.** Jesus refuted the claim by the simple fact that their attitude toward him was not one of **love**, of family affection. He knew he had come from God, no matter what they might think.

43,44. The true reason for their failure to receive him was their kinship with **the devil.** He was their father. No wonder they acted as he does (cf. Mt 23:15). His special sins are lying (seen in connection with the temptation in the garden) and murder (in the incitement of Cain to slay his brother – I Jn 3:12). **45,46.** Because they were of the devil, the liar, they would not accept the truth from Christ. Yet they could not convict him of **sin.** That being so, they should have accepted his testimony. **47.** The very failure to accept his word sealed the fact that they were not of God.

48. Smarting under a series of rebukes, the Jews struck back by calling Jesus a Samaritan, i.e., one not worthy of being called a member of the people of God even though he lived on Israelitish territory. A deeper note may be struck here if the intent is to repeat the slur about the birth of Jesus. The Samaritans were mixed stock, born of the commingling of Israelites and foreigners. Seeking to account for Jesus' strong outbursts against them (cf. v. 52), the Jews charged him with having a **devil** (demon).

49,50. Jesus denied the allegation. To say such a thing as this about him was sheer contempt, a dishonoring of him which would be brought into judgment by the Father. **51,52.** Turning to another claim, Jesus promised deathlessness for those who would keep his word. This led to ridicule from the Jews, who interpreted his word physically. They knew that death had claimed the people of God, even Abraham.

53-58. Did Jesus imagine that he was greater than Abraham and the prophets? The answer is twofold. Abraham knew that Another greater than himself was to come. He saw Christ's **day** (was this insight not given most clearly at the offering of Isaac? See Rom 8:32). Did this mean that Jesus had seen Abraham? The Jews rejected this as ridiculous, for Jesus was a man in middle life, at the most (Jn 8:57). This led to the second great claim of Jesus respecting his relation to Abraham. **Before Abraham was, I am** (cf. v. 24). Abraham was not in the beginning with God. **59.** Such assertions sounded blasphemous. Once again **stones** were poised to end such claims, but again the Lord eluded his opponents and went his way.

M. The Restoration of the Man Born Blind. 9:1-41.

This section has affinity with 8:12, for now Christ's claim that he was the light of the world received demonstration. It also has close connection with the following chapter, for 10:21 indicates something of the impression made by this miracle.

1-7. The performing of the sign. Jesus **saw** the man; then the disciples **asked** about him. The interest of Jesus quickened theirs, but from a different standpoint. To the disciples the blind man was the occasion for theological speculation; to Jesus he was a human being to be pitied and helped. The question of the disciples (v. 2) was grounded in the belief that bodily infirmity or suffering was due to sin, whether of parents (Ex 20:5) or of the man himself, presumably on the basis of the soul's pre-existence, which some Jews held. Jesus dismissed the thought of any special sin on the part of the man or his parents and invited consideration of an entirely different approach. God had permitted this condition to demonstrate His glory, as His power would become operative in this case (v. 3). Jesus called the disciples from idle speculation to action. The time for labor (**day**) was all too short. In the better manuscripts the text reads, **We must work.** The Master was linking the disciples with himself. It was their work as well as his, even though he did it unaided (v. 4). The thought anticipates 14:12. Jesus now repeated the majestic claim of 8:12, as though to apply this truth to the miracle about to be performed (v. 5). Anointing the eyes of the blind man with clay was not necessary for the cure, but it served to put the man's faith to a severe test. Would he obey? (cf. Naaman's healing) John suggests a symbolic significance in the name of the pool – **Siloam** *(sent)*. Presumably the name originated because of the "sending" or issuing of the waters from the spring into the pool. In the present circumstance this name bears a higher sense, pointing to Christ as the one **sent** of the Father, a truth repeatedly set forth in this Gospel. Obedience issued in the gift of sight (v. 7).

8-12. Neighbors and passers-by gathered around the restored man. The one who sat and **begged** – a natural occupation for one so afflicted – now looked so different that he created a problem of identification. Who was he? His own affirmation of identity settled the discussion (v. 9). The next question, quite naturally, concerned the manner of the cure. Resisting any temptation to enlarge on the story, the erstwhile blind man repeated the steps faithfully. The third question was equally inevitable. Who had anointed the eyes and given the command to wash? Here no answer could be given (cf. 5:13). More light was to come in this matter (vv. 35-38).

13-17. The group just mentioned decided it had a duty to perform, namely, to take the man to the Pharisees, because of the extraordinary nature of what had occurred. Besides, the cure had taken place on **the sabbath day** (v. 14). Once more the man was obliged to give an account of the miracle. His report was briefer this time, perhaps indicating that he was losing patience at being interrogated so much (9:15). The report created division *(schisma)* among these religious leaders, who were doubtless meeting informally. This element is prominent in John, especially that deeper cleavage, noted so often, between faith and unbelief (1:11,12; 3:36, etc.). One group could see nothing beyond the fact that the Sabbath had been broken. Others among them had difficulty in concluding that a sinner could accomplish such things. But their voices did not prevail. Still, to divert attention from their own perplexity, the Pharisees began questioning the man himself. What did he think of his benefactor? He showed more discernment than the leaders. Surely his friend could be no less than **a prophet** (v. 17). Indeed he was that, a prophet mighty in deed (here) and also in word (4:19; cf. Lk 24:19).

18-23. Instead of Pharisees, Jews are mentioned here, probably not as denoting a different body, but as emphasizing their official position and their hostility to Jesus (as often in this Gospel). These men reckoned that God would not have permitted a miracle on the Sabbath, so there must have been something amiss with the man's account. They thought it would be wise to check with his **parents** (9:18). The parents were positive on two matters: this was their son; he had been born blind. They could venture to agree also that he was now able to see, since the Jews had said this themselves. But beyond this they refused to go, even though they may have known the **means** if not the **who** of the miracle (v. 21). Fear caused them to rest all responsibility with their son to state the case. It was apparently common knowledge that the Jews (rulers) had decided before this time to excommunicate any person who acknowledged Jesus as the Christ, i.e., the promised Messiah.

24-34. The man who had gained his sight was recalled for further questioning. **Give God the praise** (glory). That is, give us the truth. See Josh 7:19. But their opening words revealed that they were not conducting an investigation. Their minds were sealed. They hoped to break the man's testimony. Unable to gainsay the miracle, they persisted in regarding Jesus as a **sinner**. Instead of entering into debate – before, he had countered the charge of sinner with his own estimate that Jesus was a prophet – the cured man turned to safe ground, his own experience. Here he could say, **I know.** Once blind, he was now able to **see.** Others could testify of him the same things – parents, neighbors, friends – but the statement was far more meaningful coming from his lips. The Jews' affirmation of knowledge was bombast, an ex cathedra utterance; this man's confession had the weight of simple truth behind it. Weakly the Jews went back over the same ground about the means by which the miracle was performed (v. 26).

Sensing that the purpose of the questioning was not to learn the facts, the man became impatient. Why did they want a second statement when they did not accept the first (v. 27)? Thoroughly disgusted, he began to do some needling of his own. **Will ye also be his disciples?** Now the Jews began to resort to verbal abuse, accusing the man of being Jesus' disciple, something he had not affirmed at all. Moses had given the Sabbath law, and they were standing under his banner. Jesus was an interloper, a disturber of the religious peace. The real issue was the observance of the Law versus the freedom of Christ's regime. If the Jews had read all of Moses and read him aright, they would not have rejected Jesus (cf. 5:45). As it was, they steadfastly refused to believe that God had spoken through him (9:29). He was an upstart. This attitude seemed unreasonable to the man born blind. It was **marvelous** (remarkable, amazing) that such men, who a few moments before were so confidently saying, **we know,** did not know whence Jesus was—a man who had done something notable. Where, then, was their infallibility in religious matters? From the Jews themselves, doubtless, he had heard the point which now he threw back at them, that God would not hear **sinners.** The argument was sound. Trapped as a result of their own interrogations, the Jews resorted to vilification. The man's former state of blindness proved that he had been **born in sins** (cf. 9:2) and was unfit to **teach** them. When they **cast him out,** they did not formally excommunicate him, but rather expelled him from their presence, which might have led to expulsion from the synagogue later. The man had not confessed Jesus as the Christ, but simply that he was of God.

35-41. Jesus, who first saw the man in his blind condition, then healed him, now **found** him (cf. 5:14). The outcasts met—Jesus, the one cast out long before, and the man who had been so disillusioned by his experience with the leaders of his people. But the meeting was not for the purpose of mutual condolence. **Dost thou believe on the Son of God?** This was both a challenge to faith and an assertion of deity. Some of the best manuscripts read *Son of man* here, which does not materially change the sense, since this denotes the man from heaven (cf. 3:13). The question found the heart of the man open and ready to believe. He simply asked for identification of the One sent from God. It was time for the self-disclosure, much as in the case of the woman of Samaria (4:26). This time the man's use of **Lord** was certainly more meaningful (the RSV has rendered the occurrence in 9:36 by "Sir"). He had thought of his benefactor as a worshiper of God (v. 31); now he was prepared to worship Him (v. 38). This was far more than deference to a great man; it was religious worship. The episode does not close without accenting the division made by Jesus. One saw the light of day and passed on to see the light of life. Others, with supposedly greater knowledge of spiritual things, were nevertheless blind, and their contact with Christ sealed that blindness (v. 39). The boast, **we see,** since it assumed a wisdom that did not include faith in the Son of God, amounted to a confession of blindness due to the **sin** of closing their eyes to him who was the light of the world.

N. Christ the Good Shepherd. 10:1-42.

The setting is still Jerusalem. A connection between the presentation of Christ as the Good Shepherd and the events of the preceding chapter is readily perceived. The Pharisees, acting like hirelings, had no real concern for the sheep, as evidenced by their attitude toward the blind man. When this one had been cast out, Jesus came and welcomed him into His fold.

1-6. The teaching here is called a **parable** (v. 6), but the word differs from the usual term. It denotes a figure of speech. Here Jesus was laying the groundwork for the application of the figure to himself in the section which follows.

1. Sheepfold. An enclosure where the sheep were sheltered for the night, usually adjoining the house. It had a single door. One bent on robbery would try to climb the wall. **2,3.** The one who guarded the door was the **porter,** in contrast to the shepherd, who gained admittance from the porter. There is only one shepherd here. Christ has no rival, though there are undershepherds in his Church. His personal interest in the sheep is attested by his calling them **by name** (cf. 1:43). The presence of other sheep is suggested. Not all those who were numbered among the people of God in that time could be called the Lord's sheep. **Leadeth them out**—in contrast to the act of the Pharisees in expelling the man born blind. Confidence in the shepherd is based on the **voice,** which reveals the person (cf. Gen 27:22). No stranger can get the flock to follow him, even if he succeeds in climbing up into the fold. **6.** Jesus' audience did not catch the import of his teaching (cf. 9:41).

7-18. The Lord explained the figure in terms of his own person and mission.

7. The truth is greater than the forms through which it is conveyed. In real life the shepherd could not be identified with **the door.** But the thought is too valuable to let slip (cf. 14:6). **8. All that ever came before me.** This is not a reference to holy men of the old covenant, but to the Jewish leaders who had gained a hold on the nation before he raised his voice. **Thieves** are those who simply steal. **Robbers** are those who also commit violence (cf. Mt 23:25). **The sheep did not hear them.** A case in point was the blind man, who had turned away from these leaders in disgust.

9. Did Jesus refer to undershepherds of the flock or to all believers? Favorable to the former viewpoint is the fact that entering in has already been used of the shepherd (vv. 1,2). Further, to **go in and out** is a familiar OT expression for the activity of a leader (I Sam 18:16; II Sam 3:25). Nevertheless, the breadth of the language – **any man** – and the words **shall be saved** favor an inclusive reference. In a redemptive sense the word **save** occurs infrequently in John (3:17; 5:34; 12:47). The freedom of the believer, in contrast to his situation in Judaism, seems hinted at in the going **in and out,** and his new satisfaction **(shall find pasture)** was a welcome change from the aridity of the teaching to which he had been subjected. **10.** The work of the Good Shepherd is constructive. **Life** answers to being saved (v. 9), and abundance answers to finding pasture. Nothing in the original warrants the addition of **more** in the translation.

11. Here the central revelation in this whole pattern of thought is given. As **the good shepherd,** Jesus fulfilled the OT representation of Jehovah (Ps 23:1; Isa 40: 11), and also set himself over against the leaders who injured the flock because they were evil in heart. Instead of taking life, this Shepherd was prepared to give his life for the sheep. It is a prophecy as well as an attitude (cf. 9:17). **12.** Of a different sort is **the hireling,** who cares not for the sheep and deserts them in a crisis. To some extent this picture reflects the unfaithful shepherds (leaders) of OT days as they are rebuked in the prophets (see Ezk 34 especially).

14. The care of the Shepherd is bound up with the mutuality of knowledge and affection that characterizes the relation between him and the sheep. **15.** A bond of knowledge exists also between the Shepherd and the Father who sent him. The Son knows the will of the Father (which includes the laying down of the life of the Son for the sheep), and the Father knows the Son, and consequently knows that he can count on his obedience in carrying out this costly mission. **16. Fold.** The same word is rendered sheepfold in 9:1. **Other sheep I have.** The language is sovereign and prophetic (cf. Acts 18:10). **Not of this fold.** Is the reference to the Jews of the Dispersion? Hardly, for they were basically one with the Palestinian Jews. Jesus envisioned the Gentiles who would respond to the Gospel. **One fold.** This is not the same word as used above, and is properly rendered *flock* (cf. one Lord, one body in Eph 4:4, 5).

17,18. The Father loves the Son always (17:24), but he has a special reason for loving him because of his obedience unto death. The death was **a commandment** of the Father (cf. the **must** of 3:14; Mt 16:21). No man could touch the Son until his hour had come (19:11). He would deliver up his spirit to God (19:30). But death could not be the end. With an equal sovereignty of command, the Son would reverse the sentence of death and take up his life again. He could confidently predict his resurrection.

19-21. For the third time in this Gospel we read of division *(schisma)* created by Jesus among his hearers (cf. 7:43; 9: 16). **Many** wanted to dismiss the Lord as demonized and unworthy of being listened to. Others were impressed by the **words** he spoke (doubtless his devotion for the sheep) combined with the recollection of the miracle performed on the **blind** man.

22-30. *Further Discussion over the Identity of Jesus.* Probably an interval of about two months separated this occasion from the preceding. The Feast of Tabernacles belonged to the fall of the year, and the Feast of the Dedication came in the **winter.** This celebration memorialized the cleansing and rededication of the Temple by Judas Maccabaeus after the sacrilege committed by Antiochus Epiphanes. The year was 165 B.C. Jesus was accosted by some of the Jews as he walked in Solomon's porch, located in the eastern portion of the Court of the Gentiles, the largest court in the Temple area, which surrounded the inner courts and the temple proper. Their probing was very direct. **Make us to doubt.** Literally, *lift up our soul.* In other words, Jesus was keeping them in suspense. They wanted a straight answer. Was he the Christ or not?

Our Lord put his finger on the difficulty. It was not lack of information but lack of willingness to believe. His own testimony should have been sufficient; if not, in their case, then his works had a **witness** to bear for him (cf. 14:11). There was no lack of clarity in his case; the trouble lay with them. Evidently they did not belong to him, since they had not been willing to **follow** him. They perceived that his shepherd teaching meant a new order, and they were not prepared to leave the Judaism they knew, to which they clung. Yet the new order offered blessing and security which they could not have known in their Pharisaism. Christ offered **eternal life** as a gift (10:28; cf. v. 10). In saying that they should **never perish** if they belonged to his sheep, Jesus used the strongest form of statement known to the language. This certainty was possible because the life offered was grounded in his gift (Rom 11:29) rather than in human achievement. His own sheep are safe also from alien influences – **neither shall any man pluck them out of my hand.** The sheep belong to Christ because they are the Father's gift to him (10:29). Naturally the Father has a stake in their preservation. Since he is supreme – **greater than all** – it is unthinkable that any power will be able to snatch them away from his protective hand (cf. Rom 8:38,39). The conclusion of the matter is that no separation can be made between the Father and the Son. They are more than collaborators; they are one in essence (the word **one** is not masculine – one person – but neuter, oneness of being).

31-33. For the second time Jesus was menaced with stoning by his opponents (cf. 8:59). The provocation here was his claim of oneness with the Father, amounting to blasphemy in the eyes of the Jews, who denied Jesus' heavenly origin. In meeting their opposition, the Lord did not depend on repetition of his claim or enlargement on it, but turned from his words to his works. They were the easier to understand and appreciate. **Many good works.** Attention had been focused mainly on a few, but these were representative of others which are not reported (20:30). They were good works, as was to be expected if they emanated from the **Father.** Could the Jews seriously mean to stone a man because of **good** works? In answer, the Jews brushed aside all reference to works, which they could not deny, and returned to the issue of Jesus' words, which they felt bound to deny on the ground of blasphemy. To them Jesus was a man who had dared to make himself out to be God. On this ground they sought his death now, and on this ground they would seek it later (19:7).

34-38. In this impasse the one hope of finding a basis for further discussion lay in appeal to the **law** (there are strong manuscript witnesses favorable to the omission of **your**), since the Jews accepted that. Law is used here in the broad sense as referring to the OT Scriptures. The words in question, **Ye are gods,** occur in Ps 82:6, in reference to Hebrew judges. God's **word** had invested them with a certain divinity of status as his representatives. Since the Scripture (with special reference to the passage in question) could not be **broken** so as to enable men to reject the teaching, how could objection be raised against him whom the Father had specially set apart and sent into the world? For Christ to have said less than to affirm that he was the Son of God would have been to speak an untruth. To affirm his sonship was not blasphemy (Jn 10:36). If the Jews could not test his verbal claims, they could at least judge on the basis of the works (vv. 37,38; cf. vv. 25,32). It should be possible to progress through the works to a faith in the person. This is the thrust also in 20:30,31.

39-42. The repeated assertion of oneness with the Father caused a threat of violence once more. It was time for the Lord to depart from the city. He found refuge at Bethany, beyond Jordan, where John had formerly baptized (v. 40). Even in retirement he could not be hid. People remembered what John had said about him, and they were able to note the difference between John's ministry, as devoid of miracle, and that of Jesus, which was marked by signs. Clearly the greater one had come, as John had stated. Unbelief was no longer reasonable. **Many** put their trust in Jesus there. Their faith throws into dark relief the stubborn unbelief of the leaders at Jerusalem.

O. The Raising of Lazarus. 11:1-57.

This account includes the narrative of the sickness, death, and resurrection of Jesus' friend and the reaction of official Judaism to the miracle. It concludes with a notice of the heightened popular interest in this man who was stirring the nation. The One who had proved himself the Light of the world by giving sight to the blind man now showed himself as the Life of men, the Overcomer of death.

1-4. John gives the setting for the miracle – the illness of Lazarus and the communication of this fact to Jesus. Mary and Martha are mentioned as though they were already familiar to the reader (cf. Lk 10:38-42), but Lazarus needs introduction because his name does not appear in the Lucan account. It is of interest that all three of these names occur on ossuary inscriptions of Judea excavated in recent years, showing that such names were common in this period (W. F. Albright, *The Archaeology of Palestine*, p. 244). The writer anticipates his own narrative of 12:1-9 in identifying Lazarus as the brother of that Mary who anointed the Lord (11:2). In conveying the information about Lazarus' illness to Jesus, the sisters showed remarkable restraint, being content simply to state the fact, without making request (v. 3). Yet the mention of Jesus' love for Lazarus was a species of appeal in itself, delicate indeed. **This sickness is not unto death.** Even as he spoke, Lazarus was probably already dead (cf. v. 39). The words belong to a higher plane of meaning, associated with the glory of God, which is also that of the Son. A resurrection would demonstrate that glory (a revelation of divine power) more fully than restoration from a sick bed.

5,6. Jesus' love for the entire family is noted, only to be challenged, in appearance at least, by his own inaction in remaining where he was for **two days,** with no move to return to Bethany. The latter part of the chapter helps to unravel this mystery. By waiting, then coming and raising Lazarus from the dead, Jesus stirred up such opposition as to make his own death certain. This was the measure of his love for the family at Bethany.

7-16. *Discussion between the Lord and his disciples over the Lazarus crisis.* Jesus proposed a return to **Judea**—not Bethany, as though they might visit the family, then return—but Judea, the center of opposition to himself. The disciples caught at this immediately. It seemed foolhardy, like walking into a trap. Jesus had barely escaped a stoning not long before (11:8; cf. 10:31,39). The Master's reply may have gained point by being spoken shortly after dawn. It applied both to himself and to his followers. He could safely go back to Judea as long as he was walking in the light of the Father's will. His enemies could not touch him until his hour had come. Then for a brief time the darkness of spiritual opposition would be permitted to close in upon him (v. 9). As for the disciples, it behooved them not to walk in the darkness of self-will and separation from him. Lacking his light, they would indeed stumble (cf. 9:4,5). **Our friend Lazarus sleepeth.** Not knowing of his death, the disciples interpreted this saying of the Lord literally and found in it ground of hope for his recovery. But Jesus had used "sleep" in a special sense as referring to believers' death (cf. Acts 7:60; I Thess 4:13). He followed this with the blunt announcement that Lazarus was dead (Jn 11:14). Another paradox is the Saviour's saying that he was glad he had not been there. The reason is clear. Had he been there, Lazarus would not have died (no one ever did in His presence); and in that case one of the greatest lessons of faith about to be impressed on the disciples through Lazarus' resurrection would have been impossible (v. 15). The disciples were never so advanced as not to need confirmation and development of their faith. Thomas, called Didymus *(twin),* was the first to respond to Jesus' second proposal to go into Judea (11:15,16; cf. v. 7).

17-19. Four days. Likely Lazarus died shortly after the messenger was sent. Allowing a day for his travel, two days of tarrying by Jesus, and one day for the return, we arrive at this total. The distance from Bethany beyond Jordan to Bethany near Jerusalem was about twenty miles. Since the home was only two miles from the city Jerusalem (v. 18), **many of the Jews** found it possible to come and offer condolences. **Jews** here does not refer to rulers. Their presence was two-edged, however. Having come to Bethany as mourners, some of them returned to Jerusalem as informers (11:46).

20-27. *The meeting between Jesus and Martha.* Both sisters appear in this account in characteristic roles. Martha, ready for action, was the one to welcome Jesus. Mary, absorbed in her grief, sat still. Martha had one regret—Jesus had not been there. What a difference his presence would have made! Yet she voiced no criticism. As already noted, Lazarus was dead when the news of his illness came to Jesus. Martha felt in Jesus a tower of strength. Her words (v. 22) almost defy analysis, however. They are an expression of confidence in him as being in close touch with God and able to get a boon from him; yet immediate resurrection does not seem to have been in her mind (cf. v. 24). In affirming the resurrection of Lazarus, Jesus did not name any time (v. 23). Martha supplied this—**at the last day**; but she said it without enthusiasm, for meanwhile her brother lay in the embrace of death. The Lord now moved to correct Martha's imperfect faith (cf. v. 22) by drawing her attention to his lordship over death. **I am the resurrection and the life.** In this case the revelation of word preceded the revelation of deed. The teaching goes beyond the case of Lazarus and includes all who believe. Two truths are stated here. The believer may die, as Lazarus had done, but by Christ's power will **live,** i.e., experience resurrection. But even more important is the possession of eternal life gained through faith in Christ. Those who have this life can never die in the sense of being separated from the source of life (vv. 25,26). Challenged to believe this, Martha made the very confession for which this book was written (11:27; 20: 31), but she did not understand the implications of her own statement. To her, Christ was not yet the absolute Lord of life and death, a complete Saviour (cf. vv. 39,40).

28-32. *Jesus and Mary.* Martha passed on to Mary quietly (**secretly**) the news that the Master (teacher) had come, probably hoping to make possible a private meeting with Jesus for her sister. But the Jews who were present followed Mary to the place outside the village where Jesus and Martha had met, for they thought at first that she was leaving the house to go to the grave. As token alike of reverence and of her own helplessness, Mary fell **at his feet.** Her opening words were the same as those of Martha. Probably this sentiment had been expressed over and over by the two after the death of their brother.

33-37. *The grief of Jesus.* He **groaned in the spirit.** The Greek word for **groaned,** repeated in verse 38, seems regularly to convey the thought of anger over something. Since Christ could hardly have felt anger toward Mary and the mourning friends, it is probable that his deep emotion was due to his inwardly protesting the havoc sin has brought into the world, with sickness and death and sorrow as its terrible entail. On the way to the tomb, Jesus **wept,** breaking out into tears. This was silent weeping in contrast to Christ's audible weeping over Jerusalem (Lk 19:41). The Jews who were present saw in the weeping a proof of Jesus' great affection for Lazarus, but they saw in it also evidence of his limitation. He had given sight to the blind (Jn 11:9), but death was too great for his powers (v. 37). Perhaps in the second **groaning** there was a mingling of indignation at this shortsighted view of his power.

38-44. *The miracle itself.* This cave at Bethany has been described by one who inspected it in modern times as of the deep rock-cut type. **Take ye away the stone.** Only Christ could raise the dead, but others could participate according to their ability. Martha, shocked at such an order from Jesus, tried to interpose an objection; she thought the body had surely begun to decompose. **Four days** had elapsed since death. Without saying what he proposed to do, Jesus summoned Martha to faith, reminding her of his previous words, apparently harking back to verse 23. But this time he stated the coming event in terms of **the glory of God** (cf. 11:4). The glory here was the power of God in operation, declaring his sovereignty (cf. 2:11). There could be no turning back now; the stone was removed (v. 41). One thing more remained to be done. For the sake of the people (literally, *the multitude)* it had to be made clear that what was about to be done would be done through the community of life and power enjoyed by the Son with the Father—that they might **believe.** This was not a request to be heard but a prayer of thanksgiving for a constant bond of communion and understanding. The hold of death was broken by the voice of authority calling, **Lazarus, come forth.** Christ had declared that the time was coming when all the righteous dead would similarly obey that same authority (cf. 5: 28,29). The Lord left untouched the work of loving hands that had prepared the body for burial, that they might have the thrill of undoing that work and setting Lazarus free. (Recall hunan participation in removing the stone.)

45,46. The miracle resulted in a characteristically varying response. Many of the Jews . . . believed; others went to the Pharisees to report what had taken place.

47-50. *The effect upon the Sanhedrin.* This was one of **many** miracles. The rulers felt completely frustrated. What were they to do? They expressed the fear that all the people would **believe** on him—in the sense of giving him their support and following him as their Messiah. This would certainly bring the Romans down on the Jews with force, as they would interpret such a thing as a political revolution. Then the Jews would lose their **place** (Temple) and **nation.** Under the Romans, since the time of Julius Caesar, they had enjoyed certain privileges as "the nation of the Jews." Exactly the situation they feared did develop as a result of the war of the Jews against Rome, A.D. 66–70. Shaming the group into silence with his censure, "Ye know nothing at all," Caiaphas laid out a course of action that was ruthless but simple: Get rid of the offender. Make him die for the people, so that the whole nation would not perish. **That year.** Not a reference to tenure of office, but to the importance of that year for Israel and the world.

51,52. John wanted his readers to sense the fact that this utterance of the high priest was prophetic. The words, so to speak, were put into his mouth. **He prophesied.** Here is a Balaam who would curse Jesus, but out of the prophecy comes the realization of the purpose of God that Christ should die for the nation in a redemptive, vicarious sense, and even for a larger group, that all the dispersed children of God (in a prospective sense) would be brought together (cf. 10:16). How fitting it was that one who filled the office of high priest should unwittingly set forth the work of Christ as the Lamb who takes away sin!

53,54. The counsel of the high priest solidified the purpose of the council so that, from that time forth, it was fully determined on Jesus' death. On this account Jesus found it wise to retire from the area and go to a place called Ephraim, in a near-desert section. This has been tentatively identified as a place twelve miles or so north of Bethany, near where the high plateau breaks away in rugged terrain leading down to the Jordan valley.

55-57. With the Passover at hand, Jesus could not be absent from the city for long. Since the time was not yet ripe, Ephraim was no substitute for the upper room. Jesus' next doings are cloaked in silence. John shifts our attention to the pilgrims who began to wend their way to Jerusalem. For the most part they were friendly to Jesus, in contrast to the authorities, and exchanged opinions with one another as to whether their hero would dare to brave the opposition of the council by coming to the feast. There must have been many informers if the rulers had any hold at all upon the people (v. 57).

P. Jesus in Bethany and Jerusalem. 12:1-50.

The events included here are: **the** anointing of Jesus by Mary of Bethany (vv. 1-11); the Triumphal Entry (vv. 12-19); the coming of the Greeks (vv. 20-26); Jesus' consciousness of the approaching Passion (vv. 27-36); the unbelief of the people and their rulers (vv. 37-43); Jesus' final public plea for faith (vv. 44-50).

The supper at Bethany is narrated with certain variations from the accounts in Matthew and Mark. **1. Six days before the passover,** i.e., Saturday. The other accounts give the location as the house of Simon the leper. John alone mentions the presence of Lazarus. **2. They made him a supper.** Simon would have felt gratitude for his healing, and the sisters of Lazarus for the raising of their brother from the dead. **3. A pound** *(litra)*, a measure of twelve ounces. **Spikenard. Oil** from a plant grown in northern India, very costly as an import into Palestine. Mary is always associated with **the feet of Jesus** (Lk 10:39; Jn 11:32). **The house was filled with the odour of the ointment.** This answers in its own way to the reported words of Jesus in the Synoptics that in the world-wide preaching of the Gospel this act would be told as a memorial of the woman. The fragrance of the act would have a wide distribution and a lasting effect.

5. Judas estimated the value of the nard at **three hundred pence,** or nearly sixty dollars. **6.** His apparent concern for the poor was a cloak for his own covetousness. He had just missed a chance for theft on a larger scale than usual. Evidently he did not make a regular treasurer's report. **7.** Jesus shielded Mary by cutting short the criticism. **Let her alone.** It appears from the Synoptics that Judas, stung by this rebuke, slipped out and bargained with the chief priests to betray the Master. Jesus saw in Mary's act a deep significance — **against the day of my burying hath she kept this.** However much Mary may have wished to help the poor ordinarily, she had reserved this precious portion for Christ. She anticipated his death. In contrast to the rulers, Mary believed in Jesus' person; in contrast to many who believed in a general way, her faith included the work of the Saviour—his death.

9. Lazarus proved an attraction to many of the people, who came to see him as well as Jesus. These were curious but sympathetic. **10,11.** In contrast, **the chief priests** found in the situation reason to include Lazarus in their dark plotting as one who was enhancing the cause of Jesus. A second murder would not have disturbed their hardened consciences.

The next incident has become traditionally known as the Triumphal Entry, although such a title better fits Jesus' future coming. **12.** It is clear that those who sought to honor the Lord were pilgrims, not residents of Jerusalem. They had come for **the feast** of Passover. **13.** John alone mentions the use of **palm** branches. They are cited by the writer of II Maccabees (10:7) in connection with the rededication of the Temple by Judas Maccabaeus after its desecration by the Syrians. **Hosanna.** A Hebrew term meaning, *Save, I pray* (cf. Ps 118:25). In the NT its use is confined to this incident. At times it was not so much a prayer as an ascription of praise, and such is its use here. Jesus was being saluted as **King of Israel,** who had come with the authority of the Lord (Jehovah). These people were looking to him to establish David's kingdom with power (cf. Mk 11:10). The crowd was filled with Messianic expectation (cf. Jn 6:15).

14,15. Jesus . . . found. The story is given in Mk 11:1-6. John is the only Evangelist who describes the animal as **a young ass** *(onarion).* Jesus' act fulfilled the prophetic word (Zech 9:9). The ass, better than the horse, symbolized the meek and peaceful character of the King of Israel. This in itself declared that Jesus' understanding of the event differed from that of the throng. **16.** Only when Jesus was **glorified,** only when the Spirit had come to instruct and bring the things of Christ to their remembrance (7:39; 14:26), did the disciples view this whole scene in the light of Scripture and the plan of God.

17,18. John informs his readers that no small part of the enthusiasm displayed during the march on Jerusalem was due to the raising of Lazarus. The people who were with Jesus on that occasion **bare record** *(kept bearing witness).* Another group, pilgrims to the feast who had only heard of the miracle, advanced to meet Jesus and hail him as their national hero. **19.** This wave of popularity cast gloom in the camp of the Pharisees. In their pessimism they declared that **the world** (everybody concerned) had gone after Jesus.

20. The movement toward Jesus continued in the incident of the Greeks who expressed a desire to see Jesus. They were representatives of **the world** in a larger sense than that suggested by the Pharisees. It was fitting that the **Greeks** should appear now, on the eve of the Passion. They would profit from the Saviour's death, as would the great host of Gentiles whom they represented. **Worship.** Jewish custom restricted them to the Court of the Gentiles. Soon, in Christ, the middle wall of partition would be broken down. It appears that these men resembled Cornelius of a later time. They could be called God-fearers, but were not proselytes who had joined the congregation of Israel. **21.** Philip is a Greek name. This disciple was a natural point of contact with Jesus. **See Jesus,** i.e., have an interview with him. **22.** Andrew also is a Greek name. This disciple seemed to specialize in bringing people to Christ (1:41; 6:8,9).

23. Without addressing the Greeks directly, Jesus met their need. They would not have to wait long to profit from his mission – **the hour is come. Glorified.** This is explained in the following verse. In John's Gospel glorification begins with death and includes resurrection. **24. Corn.** Grain or seed. Nature provides a parable of Jesus' career. Apart from death his life stands in isolation, with no power of increase. Death is the key to spiritual fruitfulness. **25. He that loveth his life.** The same principle obtains for the disciple. "He who seeks to gather round himself that which is perishable, so far perishes with it: he who divests himself of all that is of this world only, so far prepares himself for the higher life" (Westcott, *op. cit.)* **26. Let him follow.** Serving Christ involves following him, even unto death. This will be rewarded by sharing the glorious future with him, including recognition by the Father. This prospect is open to **any man** (Greek as well as Jew). **27.** By speaking of these things, Jesus was made more acutely conscious of the price he would soon be paying for the fulfillment of his office as Redeemer. **Save me.** This is a touch of Gethsemane distress. Jesus' natural inclination was to be saved from the **hour** that was drawing near. Such a prayer bears eloquent testimony to the awfulness of the hour. But Jesus' commitment was so complete that he had to face it. That was why he came. So the prayer was not prolonged.

28. Another prayer took its place. **Glorify thy name.** The Father would do this as he enabled the Son to face his hour and accomplish his mission. **I have . . . glorified.** The glory of the Son, manifested in life and work thus far, reflected glory on the name of the Father. **Again,** namely, in the Passion, which would issue in resurrection and exaltation. **29. The people,** limited in their understanding, misinterpreted the Father's witness.

31. Jesus' hour would bring not only suffering for him but judgment upon the sinful world that would put him on the cross, and ruin for Satan, who heads up the world system. The expelled Christ would expel the one who drives men to reject Him (cf. Col 2:15). **32.** Christ himself, when in apparent defeat, would actually be in position to draw men to himself by the power of his sacrifice. Glory would triumph over shame. Victory would shine through dark tragedy. **All men,** the Greeks included, would come to know the pull of his redeeming love. **Unto me.** Salvation is unto Christ as well as through him. **33. What** (sort of) **death.** The lifting up answers to crucifixion. Jesus knew he would not die by stoning.

34. The **Christ** *(Messiah)* whom the people had learned to expect from the law (OT in general) **abideth for ever.** How, then, could Jesus as the Son of man fulfill this expectation by being lifted up to die? Such a Son of man did not agree with their Messianic expectations. The hopes they had entertained at Christ's entry into Jerusalem were now dashed. **35,36.** Before the contact with the people was broken, Jesus warned them that the light was going to shine only for a limited time. If they did not receive it, darkness would cover them.

The warning apparently went unheeded. John summarizes the resistance to the light that continued to the end (vv. 37-43). **37.** The miracles had not brought the multitudes to faith in the Lord. Only samples of the miracles out of **many** are found in John. **38.** This lack of faith was in agreement with the prophetic announcement of Isaiah (53:1). Significantly, this is the chapter in Isaiah that gives prominence to the death of Messiah. **39,40. They could not believe.** Their hardness of heart made this inevitable. **Blinded . . . hardened.** This activity of God cannot be viewed as deliberately planned to make faith impossible for those who desire to believe. Rather, this is the answer of God to unbelief. The Lord would have to **heal** them if they **converted** (turned to him), so his faithfulness is not impugned. Judicial hardening is a phase of divine judgment. The quotation is from Isa 6:10. **I should heal.** Christ becomes the subject here. **41. His glory,** i.e., Christ's. Even as Isaiah foresaw His sufferings (cf. v. 38), so he saw His glory (Isa 6).

42,43. Nevertheless prepares the reader for an exception to the generally hardened condition of Israel. The identity of these rulers who "believed" is unknown. Unwillingness to confess Christ, however, throws doubt on the complete genuineness of the faith of these men (cf. 2:23-25). They proved themselves unworthy of divine commendation.

At this point John introduces Jesus' final presentation of himself to the nation. **44,45. Cried,** emphasizing the public character of the teaching and its urgency. Jesus reaffirmed his commission from the Father (12:44) and his oneness with him (v. 45). **46. A light.** Cf. 1:7-9; 3:19; 8:12; 9:5; 12:35. **47,48.** If the words of Christ were rejected now, they would act as judge in the last day. His words would never pass away. **49.** Jesus had said only what the Father had given him to speak. How then could he be guilty of blasphemy or untruth? **50. Life everlasting.** This is found in the spoken word of Jesus, even as it is present in himself as the Word (6:63; 1:1,4,18).

III. Christ's Ministry to His Own. 13:1–17:26.

A. The Foot Washing. 13:1-17.

From the Synoptics we learn how Jesus sent two of his disciples to prepare the upper room for the feast and the fellowship he had planned to have with his disciples (Lk 22:7-13).

1. Now before the feast of the passover. This raises questions. Was the meal in the upper room a fellowship meal, or was it truly the Passover? In two other passages John seems to say that the Passover had not yet come (13:29; 18:28). It is clear from the Synoptics that Jesus and the disciples did eat the Passover. This dating in John may represent a protest against the official Jewish observance of the day, on the ground of following a different calendar, in line with the practice of the Qumran sect (Matthew Black, "The Arrest and Trial of Jesus and the Date of the Last Supper," in *New Testa-*

ment Essays: Studies in Memory of T. W. Manson, ed. by A. J. B. Higgins, pp. 19-33). Another possibility is that the references in Jn 13:29 and 18:28 to the Passover as still future are to be explained as references to the Feast of Unleavened Bread, which was sometimes called the Passover (Lk 22:1). This began immediately after Passover and continued for a week. Even so, the meal referred to here seems to have been held before the Passover, whether it be regarded as a proper observance of the annual feast or not. **Hour.** Viewed here not from the standpoint of suffering but of vindication and return to the Father (cf. 19:30; Lk 23:46). **Loved them unto the end.** Or, at the end (at the conclusion of days of preparation and anticipation). This expression *(eis telos)* may also mean "unto the utmost" (cf. I Thess 2:16).

2. **Supper being ended.** Another reading, widely adopted in modern translations, yields the meaning, *while supper was going on.* The action taken by Jesus to wash the disciples' feet would have been more appropriate then than later. The love of Jesus stands in sharp contrast to the hatred of Satan and Judas. 3. Possessed of the knowledge of his authority, of his divine origin, and of his certain return to the Father, Jesus did not disdain to humble himself to perform a menial service. This is the genius of the spirit of the Incarnation. **4,5.** The materials for washing the feet were present (cf. Lk 22:10), but there was no servant (Jesus had requested complete privacy). One of the disciples might have volunteered, but all were too proud. About this time they were disputing as to which of them should be regarded as the greatest (Lk 22:24).

6. It cannot be determined whether or not Christ came to Peter first of all. What is clear is Peter's sense of the unfitness of having the Lord perform this service on him. The pronouns **thou** and **my** are emphatic. Boldly the disciple said what he was thinking. **7.** In Jesus' reply there is a similar emphasis on **I** and **thou. Now . . . hereafter.** Not a reference to heaven or to the events of the evening, but to the enlightenment of the Spirit later on. **8.** More impressed with the inequity of the situation than with its hidden meaning, Peter insisted that Jesus should **never wash** his feet. But the rejoinder of the Lord lifted the act from one of menial service to one of spiritual significance. To be unwashed by Christ is to be unclean, to have **no part** with him. **9.** The alternative of being sundered from Christ was far worse to Peter than the shame of being ministered unto in this way by his superior. Hence the impulsive inclusion of **hands** and **head.** All other parts were, of course, covered. Peter wanted nothing excluded that could be washed.

10,11. Peter needed to know that the virtue in the washing was not quantitative, for the act was symbolic of inward cleansing. **Washed** (from *louō)* denotes a complete body bath. **Wash . . . feet.** Here the word is *niptō,* appropriate for the washing of individual portions of the body, as in the previous narrative. The washing of regeneration makes one clean in God's sight. This is symbolized in Christian baptism, which is administered only once. Further cleansing of the spots of defilement is not a substitute for the initial cleansing but has meaning only in the light of it (cf. I Jn 1:9). **Ye are clean, but not all.** The reference is to Judas. Jesus **knew** his heart and his plan (cf. 6:70,71). For **clean,** see 15:3. Judas was an unregenerated man.

12. Know ye what I have done to you? The divine side of the act had already been explained in terms of cleansing, but the human side needed to be set forth—the act as symbolic of what disciples ought to do for one another. **13,14.** If their superior, the one who was Lord and Master (teacher), was willing to perform this service for them, surely they ought to do it for one another. Humility is not essentially self-abnegation but losing oneself in service to others. **15. An example.** This rules out any thought of foot-washing as a sacrament. Scripture is silent about the practice save as a loving ministration exercised as a matter of hospitality (I Tim 5:10).

B. The Announcement of the Betrayal. 13:18-30. Judas had been on the Lord's mind even during the foot-washing (vv. 10, 11). Now it was impossible to keep back any longer the disclosure that a betrayal would occur. In great wisdom Jesus succeeded in letting Judas know that He was aware of his intentions and in detaching him from the company. He thus provided the right kind of atmosphere in which to proceed with His teaching.

18. I speak not of you all. Judas could

not be expected to profit by the example given in the foot-washing. **I know whom I have chosen** – Judas included. The Scripture had pre-written the treachery of this man (Ps 41:9). Not all the verse is quoted, for the first half is not applicable. **19.** Any temptation on the part of the other disciples to question the wisdom of Jesus in the choice of Judas was thus precluded, for Christ was not being taken by surprise. When the Passion was over, these men would be able to look back and **believe** in their Lord more firmly than ever. **20.** Judas would not go forth as representative of Christ, but these men would. They bore the Saviour's name and authority. Those who responded would be responding to Christ. This principle is grounded in Jesus' own relation to the Father. **21.** Jesus now revealed the cause of the troubled state of his heart. A betrayer was in the midst—**one of you.**

22. Perplexity about the identity of the betrayer gripped the apostolic circle. Judas had played his part well. He was unsuspected by his fellows. **23.** The 'beloved disciple' occupied a place immediately next to Jesus at the table. He could lean on the Saviour's bosom because of the reclining position customarily used. **24.** Anxious to learn who the betrayer was, Peter, too far away to ask Jesus in person, beckoned John to inquire of the Lord. **25,26.** In response to the whispered question of John, Jesus identified the betrayer, not by name but by indicating that he was the one to whom He would hand the **sop,** a morsel given in token of special favor and friendship. He handed it to Judas. Iscariot probably means "man of Kerioth," a town in Judea.

27. Acceptance of the sop without acceptance of the pleading love that went with it meant that Judas was steeling his heart to do what he had contracted to do—betray the Lord. He had been discovered and resented it. From this hour **Satan** was fully in control. **Do quickly.** Further efforts to dissuade Judas were useless. **28. No man . . . knew.** Apparently Judas was seated next to Jesus, on the opposite side from John. The word of command that dismissed Judas was unconnected with the betrayal in the minds of the others. **29.** Knowing that Judas was their treasurer, they assumed that he was being sent out to make purchases for further feasting or else to share something with **the poor** (Neh 8:10). **30. It was night.** In a writing so sensitive to symbolism and underlying meaning as this Gospel, these words must have special significance. They picture at once the benighted condition of Judas through surrender to hatred of Jesus and also the coming of the hour when the powers of darkness would engulf the Saviour.

C. The Upper Room Discourse. 13:31—16:33. These precious words of Christ were spoken in the light of his impending departure to the Father and had in view conditions under which the Lord's followers would have to carry on without his personal presence (16:4). Three principal strands of teaching are discernible: (1) commands concerning the task set before the disciples, which was a fruit-bearing witness undergirded and permeated with love; (2) warnings about the opposition to be faced from the world and from Satan; and most of all (3) an exposition of the divine provisions by which the disciples would be sustained and made triumphant in the coming days. From time to time the Lord's teaching was interrupted by questions, showing that the disciples lacked understanding at many points.

31-35. *Announcement of the departure and command to love one another.* **31. Now is the Son of man glorified.** With the exit of Judas, the stage was rapidly being set for that series of events that would bring glory to the Son and to the Father. In death Christ would be glorified in the eyes of the Father (cf. I Cor 1:18,24). The Father would see in the death of the cross the fulfillment of his own purpose. Only after the Resurrection would the disciples sense the glorification. **32. God shall also glorify him in himself.** In the resurrection and exaltation of Jesus and in the pouring out of the Spirit upon the disciples, God would make it manifest that the One who was obedient unto death and was now honored for his fidelity, was one with himself, even as he had claimed.

33. Little children. Tender affection is sharpened by the poignancy of farewell. The Jews might **seek** him out of curiosity, and his own out of personal attachment; in either case, however, it would be vain for them to seek him in any physical sense. **34.** There was something, however, to which they could properly devote their energies. **A new commandment . . . love one another.** It was new in that the love was to be exercised toward others not because they belonged to the same nation, but because they belonged to Christ. And it was new because it was to be the expression of the peerless love of Christ, which the disciples had seen in life and would see also in death. **As I have loved you** was at once the standard and the motive power of the love that was to be manifested. **35.** Such love would inevitably be a testimony to the world. It would perpetuate the remembrance of Christ and point to his continuing life, for this quality of love has been seen only in him. Men recognize the blessedness of such love even though they cannot of themselves produce it.

36-38. Peter refused to accept the prospect of separation. He was told that he could not follow Christ then, but he could **afterwards** (cf. Jn 21:19). Ready to follow **now,** Peter was prepared to give up his **life** for his Lord. Such self-assurance called for a sad rebuke. Peter's intended loyalty was to issue in base denial, thrice committed.

Chapter 14 deals largely with specific encouragements to counterbalance the departure of Jesus, the defection of Judas, and the predicted failure of Peter. These are: the ultimate provision of the Father's house; the return of Christ for his own; the prospect of doing greater works; unlimited prayer possibility; the gift of the Holy Spirit; and the provision of Christ's peace.

1. If Peter, the leader of the apostolic group, was going to fail, it is no wonder **hearts** were **troubled.** This word is used of Jesus himself in Jn 11:33; 12:27; 13:21. "He shared the experiences which in us He would comfort and control" (T. D. Bernard, *The Central Teaching of Jesus Christ).* **Believe** is probably an imperative in both cases. Everything seemed on the verge of collapse. A renewed faith in God was necessary. The cause of Jesus seemed faced with defeat; so faith in him was more needful than ever. Every fresh test as well as every new revelation is a summons to faith.

2. My Father's house (cf. 2:16). The Temple at Jerusalem, with its vast courts and numerous chambers, suggests the antitype in heaven. **Many mansions.** Places of *abode.* The same word as in 14:23. **I would have told you.** The disciple is warranted in assuming an adequate divine provision even when it is not stated. **I go to prepare.** As Peter and John had gone ahead to prepare the chamber for the supper, so Jesus was preceding the rest into glory to prepare "the upper room" for his own.

3. I will come again. Grammatically, this is a futuristic present, emphasizing both the certainty of the coming and the impending nature of the event. The coming does not emphasize heaven as such but rather the reunion of Christ and his people. **Where I am** – the most satisfying definition of heaven. This spatial language makes it difficult to interpret the verse as a provision for Christ's continuing presence with his people while they are on earth. The application of the words to the death of the believer is inadequate also, for in that experience the saints of God depart to be with Christ (Phil 1:23). **4.** The best text yields the rendering, **And where I am going ye know the way.**

5. Thomas saw a double problem in Jesus' utterance. Since he, as well as others, did not understand the destination, how could he know the way? **6. The way.** This has special prominence because of the context. It had been somewhat anticipated in the teaching about the door (10:9). **The truth.** Christ as truth makes the way dependable and infallible (cf. 1:14; 8:32,36; Eph 4:20, 21). **The life** (cf. 1:4; 11:25). **No man cometh.** The verb puts Jesus on the side of God rather than on the side of man (he does not say, "goeth"). "No man can attain the Father except by perceiving the Truth and participating in the Life which is revealed to men in His Son. Thus, while being the guide, He does not guide to what is beyond Himself. Knowledge of the Son is the knowledge of God" (Hoskyns).

7. The wording suggests the disciples' failure to know Christ as he really was. In view of this last revelation, however, there could be no excuse for failure to know the Father as well as the Son. Some manuscripts have a different reading – "If ye have come to know me (as ye have), ye shall know my Father also." **8.** Desire for objective experience is strong – **show us the Father** (cf. Ex 33:17). Philip felt he knew God, but not as Father in the intimate sense Jesus meant when He spoke of Him.

9. So long time. It was pathetically late for the request. The Son had been revealing the Father all along (10:30). That lay at the root of his mission (1:18). **10.** Surely Philip must believe that there was community of life between Father and Son. Out of the union of the Son with the Father came **the words** that Jesus spoke. Out of the works which he performed came the demonstration that the Father was dwelling in him and acting through him.

11. The appeal shifted from Philip to the Eleven. **Believe me.** That is, accept my testimony about my relation to the Father. A sufficiently high view of Christ makes his self-disclosure the final evidence. For those that need other evidence, the **works** are there to support the claim. **12. Greater works.** Not to be restricted to the signs such as Jesus wrought in the days of his flesh. The works could not be greater in quality than his, but greater in extent. **Because I go unto my Father.** This is the reason for the greater works. The restrictions imposed on Jesus by incarnation would be removed. His position with the Father would be related to the greater works in two ways: answering the prayers of his own, and sending the Paraclete as the unfailing source of wisdom and strength. The works, then, would not be done in independence of Christ. *He* would answer prayer; *he* would send the Spirit.

13,14. Whatsoever. The scope of prayer. **Ask.** The condition of prayer. **In my name.** The ground of prayer. This involves at least two things: praying in the authority Christ gives (cf. Mt 28:19; Acts 3:6) and praying in union with him, so that one does not pray outside His will. **That will I do.** The certainty of prayer. **That the Father may be glorified in the Son.** The purpose of prayer. **If ye shall ask.** The **if** is on the side of the one who prays, not on the side of Christ.

15. If ye love me. This is the atmosphere in which not only the command to pray but all other commands of the Lord will be honored by his servants. **Keep** is imperative in the AV, but very good manuscript authority calls for a future form – "ye will keep." Love is not primarily a sentimental attachment; it is the dynamic for obedience. **My commandments.** Ultimately, only God can command. Deity was speaking. **16.** These commandments can be kept only in the power of the Holy Spirit, called here **another Comforter.** A better translation at this point would be *helper*. At the time the AV was translated, **comforter** retained more of the original force of "strengthener" than it has today. The word **another** puts the Spirit in the same class with Jesus (cf. Phil 4:13). In the Spirit we have more than an occasional helper – **that he may abide with you for ever.**

17. The Spirit of truth (cf. 15:26; 16:13). He is illuminator as well as helper. His great theme is Christ the Truth (14:6; 15:26). **Whom the world cannot receive.** The world is governed by the senses. Since the Spirit cannot be seen nor comprehended by reason, he remains outside the world's conscious experience (cf. I Cor 2:9-14). **Dwelleth with you.** A constant presence, compensating for the withdrawal of the Lord. **In you.** Not only with them as a presence permeating the corporate body, but dwelling in them individually. **18.** The same subject is continued. **Comfortless.** *Orphans.* The need of the disciples would be met when Christ came to them in resurrection blessing. This would bring with it the coming of the person of the Spirit (20:22). As surely as the Spirit would be with them and in them, so would Christ. It would be impossible to differentiate the two, just as the Son and the Father are indivisible (cf. II Cor 3:17). Christ was not speaking here of his future coming, as in verse 3, but of a coming that would meet an immediate need.

19. For only a limited time would Christ be an object of sight to **the world.** Then would come death, and though it would be followed by resurrection, this would not restore him to the eyes of men (Mt 23:39). It was because these disciples were spiritually alive that they would be able to see him and become partakers of his risen life. **20. At that day** these men would be able to grasp what Jesus had been trying to tell them about his life with the Father, which was a life of interpenetration and communion, and also about their own life, which had now been likewise taken up into the divine and infused with it. **Ye shall know.** *Gnōsesthe* speaks of discovery. Needless to say, this does not entitle the believer to say that he is God or the Son of God. Union is meaningless apart from the separate existence of those who compose it.

21. Jesus returned to the subject of love and the keeping of his commandments (cf. v. 15), but in view of the teaching in verse 20 now included mention of the Father. The keeping of Christ's commandments demonstrates love for Christ. This love invites the answering love of the Father, whose love for the Son is such that he must love all who have love for him. It brings also manifestation of the Son to the believer. What the disciples enjoyed by way of physical manifestation of the risen Lord to themselves following the Resurrection, they were to enjoy also in a spiritual sense throughout the rest of their earthly pilgrimage.

22. Judas . . . not Iscariot. The reputation of the betrayer was so bad that John takes care not to permit any confusion of identification, despite the fact that the other Judas had left the room. This Judas could not understand a manifestation restricted to the chosen few, not that it was impossible (that very thing was occurring at the moment) but that it did not seem to accord with the glory of the Messianic office. If Christ was to come again, why not to the world? He was perplexed by Jesus' statement in verse 19. **23.** "The answer to Judas is, that the manifestation referred to must be limited, because it can only be made where there is that communion of love which proves itself by the spirit of self-denial and submission to the charge of Jesus" (William Milligan and W. F. Moulton, *Commentary on the Gospel of St. John).* This manifestation is not only very personal but it leads to a permanent relation – **make our abode with him.** Observe that the Son feels free to commit the Father to a certain course of action, another clear indication of deity. **24.** Here is the corollary on the negative side to the truth of the last verse. Once more Christ affirmed the unity of the Son's word with that of the Father.

25,26. These things.... all things. The teaching of Christ touching the new conditions of the coming age was suggestive rather than complete (cf. 16:12). This deficiency was to be overcome by the coming of the Holy Spirit. His ministry to believers would be, in the main, to **teach** them (one of the great offices of Christ as well; the two are combined, by implication, in Acts 1:1). **All things** (cf. I Cor 2:13-15). These matters presumably would be based on the person and work of Christ, thus affording a continuation of Jesus' teaching. A part of the Spirit's work, in fact, would be that of recalling what Christ had spoken (cf. 2:22; 12:16).

27. Peace. A frequent word in connection with farewells (cf. Eph 6:23; I Pet 5:14). But this is a legacy rather than merely a conventional touch. **Leave** (*aphiēmi*) is rarely used in this sense. Another example occurs in the LXX of Ps 17:14. **My peace.** A distinctive brand of peace, different from that of **the world,** which would be panic-stricken at such an hour as this, with death so near. The gift of his peace would make his followers unafraid, as he was (cf. 16:33).

28. The Lord had no intention of hiding the fact of his departure, but he reminded them that the sadness of departure was relieved by his promise to come again. **If ye loved me.** Their love was yet incomplete. Love desires the best for the one who is loved. The disciples should have rejoiced in his return to the Father. **My Father is greater than I.** This has nothing to do with essential being, and so does not contradict John 10:30 and other passages. The Father was in position to reward the Son for obedience unto death. There is a hint here that blessings would come from Christ's return to the Father that would benefit his followers; so their joy would not be entirely disinterested. **29.** All the outpoured blessings of the future would corroborate the word of Christ and would increase the confidence and faith of the disciples in him.

30. The prince of this world (cf. 12:31). A reference to Satan. Here the immediate significance seems to be the betrayal by Judas, the tool of Satan, and the arrest of Jesus (cf. Lk 22:53). **Hath nothing in me.** No share in Christ's person or cause (cf. 13:8). There may be a suggestion here of the truth that Satan has nothing in Christ which is rightfully his own, which he can claim or lay hold of for his own interest. Christ is sinless and victorious over evil. **31.** The very thing that Satan was about to effect, namely, the death of Christ on the cross, was the thing which the Saviour was pressing forward to do. But he did it not as the helpless victim of Satan but out of love for the Father, knowing it was the Father's commandment (his expressed will). **Arise, let us go hence.** It is by no means certain that the command was carried out immediately. There is difficulty in supposing that the rest of the discourse could have been spoken in a public place, even in the Temple.

In chapter 15 the following strands of thought are discernible: fruit-bearing through abiding in Christ (vv. 1-11); love as the supreme fruit (vv. 12-17); the hatred of the world for the disciple, as for Christ (vv. 18-25); the divine and human witness to Christ (vv. 25-27).

1. I am the true vine. A contrast is probably intended with Israel, a vine of God's planting which proved unfruitful (Isa 5:1-7). **True.** Real, all that a vine should be in a spiritual sense. Christ is not merely the root or stock, but the whole plant. Included in him are his people. **Husbandman.** Both owner and caretaker. **2. Every branch in me.** To be in Christ is a spiritual fact of incalculable importance. **Beareth not fruit.** This is no would-be follower. As there are suckers that grow out from the plant but add nothing to its usefulness and must be cut away, so an unproductive child of God who persists in his own will may expect to be set aside. God's chastening hand may even remove such a person through death. **He purgeth it.** This applies to the fruitful branch. It is kept clean of any tendency to deadness or to mere growth of the branch as distinct from production of fruit. The object is **more fruit.**

3. Clean through (literally, *because of*) **the word.** Set apart from others by having received God's revelation in Christ. **4. Abide in me, and I in you.** This recalls 14:20. But there the thought relates to position; here it relates to volition, the decision to depend consciously upon Christ as the condition of fruitfulness. Christ's answer is an inward manifestation – **I in you.** A branch detached from the vine is necessarily unfruitful. A vital union is in view. **5.** The vine and the branches are distinguished. From the vine comes the life; from the branches, as a result, comes the fruit. The order is the same here as in 14:20 and 15:4. Our abiding in Christ connects us with the source of life. His abiding in us brings a steady supply of fruit – **much fruit. Without me.** Apart from me, severed from me.

6. It is a known fact that apart from producing grapes the vine has no use except to be burned for fuel (cf. Ezk 15:6). **Men . . . they.** "The indefiniteness of the subject corresponds with the mysteriousness of the act symbolized" (Westcott). Since the subject is the bearing of fruit and not eternal life, the burning is a judgment upon fruitlessness, not an abandonment to eternal destruction. The branch is the potential of possible fruit-bearing, not the person himself. It speaks here of unfruitful works (cf. I Cor 3:15).

7. The **words** of Christ, as well as the person of Christ, may abide in the believer. It is the teaching of Christ that gives rise to the proper kind of praying. When the word of Christ dwells richly within (Col 3:16), one may safely ask what he **will,** and it **shall be done.** The teaching is similar to that in Jn 14:13,14. **8.** Discipleship is a growing, dynamic thing. The more fruit we bear, the more truly are we fulfilling the pattern of **disciples,** those who learn of Christ in order to be like him. God is **glorified** thereby. He is vindicated and rewarded for his investment in the vineyard.

9. The mention of **love** in this connection suggests that this is the chief item in the fruit which the Father is concerned to find in his children (cf. Gal 5:22). But this is not love in a general sense – rather, **my love,** the love of Christ. When he comes in to abide, he brings his love with him, which in turn is the very love enjoyed by Christ from the Father. Christian love becomes thereby divine in character. **Continue ye in my love.** Accept no substitutes. **10.** The enjoyment of the Saviour's love is conditioned on keeping his **commandments.** This is no arbitrary requirement, for Christ has operated under this rule himself in his relation to the Father. The disciple is not above his Lord. **11.** The life of love produces **joy.** Christ had it first, as the result of doing perfectly the Father's will and enjoying his love. This is imparted to his own, and in the process becomes personalized so as to become their joy. Possession may be partial at first, but the goal is to **be full,** leaving no room for fear or dissatisfaction.

The next section begins and ends with the command to love one another. **12,13.** Here is an epitomizing of the Christian's obligation. It is no longer an admonition to keep Christ's commandments in order to abide in his love (v. 10). It is rather an injunction to concentrate on the one commandment to have love for one another. **As I have loved you.** The measure of Christ's love for his own is his self-sacrifice, in which they benefit (cf. I Jn 3:16). Such a standard can be met only as Christ's own love is permitted to flow through the life of his people. The Synoptic announcements of the cross by Jesus emphasize its divine necessity; here the motivation is love. The cross is not something imposed but something embraced – **lay down his life.** Immediate proof of love is the willingness to give advance indication of the purpose to die for those who are **friends.** Death for them in no wise contradicts the purpose to die for a larger circle, even the world itself.

14. Friendship with Jesus does not eliminate the necessity for obedience. **15.** If this necessity seems to make **servants** out of friends, there is a difference. The servant is not taken into the confidence of his lord. Proof of the status of friends, in the case of the disciples, was their admission to the counsels of Christ, including all that the Father had disclosed to the Son. Nothing had been withheld. This does not mean that all had been understood by Jesus' followers.

16. Lest the disciples get the impression that they alone were in the plans of

God, Christ now made clear that they had been granted their privileged position with a view to their declaring the message to others. They had been **chosen,** not with a view to their own pleasure or pride. Rather, Christ **ordained** (appointed) them with service in mind. **Go . . . bring forth fruit.** Previously the fruit meant love. Now it was to mean love in action, the heralding of the message of salvation and the winning of souls. There is a close connection in thought with John 12:24. **Remain.** The same word has been translated *abide* earlier in the chapter. That there would be abiding fruit was a gracious promise in view of the disappointing results during Jesus' own ministry, with many professing an interest in him, only to leave him after a time.

17. This verse is transitional. The disciples had to share love among themselves, for they would not get it from the world. At this point the word "love" all but disappears from the passage, being replaced by "hate" or "hatred" (eight times in as many verses).

18. The **world.** Unredeemed society, estranged from God, held in the grip of sin and the evil one, blind to spiritual truth and hostile to those who have the life of God in them. Hatred would not be visited upon the disciples in a spirit of anti-Semitism, but as a continuation of the hostility and hatred visited upon Christ. The attack would move from the Shepherd to the sheep. As surely as their lives would reflect Christ, so surely would they attract the hatred of sinful men (cf. Gal 4:29). **19.** Hostility is rooted in spiritual dissimilarity. The world is comfortable in the presence of its **own.** It is capable of a certain affection for such. The exclusiveness of the Christian society, a redeemed community within an unredeemed, excites displeasure. Rebuked by the holiness of those who are Christ's (cf. v. 22), the world shows its resentment.

20. The proof of genuineness in discipleship is the correspondence between the reaction of men to the ministry of Jesus' followers and the reaction of men to Christ in the days of his flesh. Some men would **persecute** them; others would keep their word. **Remember the word.** The reference is to Jn 13:16. Acts 4:13 is a powerful illustration of Jesus' teaching here. Having rid themselves of Jesus, as they thought, the rulers were dismayed to find themselves faced by disciples who acted as he did. **21. For my name's sake.** Christ suffered rejection because men did not really know the One who sent him. The disciples were being inducted into the circle of the misunderstood, sharing this distinction with their Lord.

22. This ignorance of Christ's identity and mission was grounded in the **sin** of men. Though Christ had not come to judge but rather to save, yet his very presence and witness stirred up manifestations of sin that otherwise would have remained dormant. Exposed by the Saviour, his enemies had no hiding place. Their one resort was to banish Christ from before their eyes. **They had not had sin.** The culminating sin of unbelief and rejection of the Saviour. **23.** The cost of hating Christ is the condemnation of hating the Father as well. Men cannot treat the Father in one way and the Son in another.

24. The **works** (complementing the word of Christ in v. 22) were of such a character that men had to come to a verdict for or against him. In rejecting him, they **had sin.** It was sin accompanied by hatred which logically involved the Father in whose name the Son had come. **25. Their law.** The very Scriptures which the Jews gloried in rose up to condemn them (Ps 69:4). **Without a cause** *(dōrean).* Such hatred is indefensible. It lacks all ground in the one who is hated. The same word occurs, with the same meaning, in Rom 3:24, where the ground of salvation is presented as being God himself and not the worthiness of man.

Such hatred demands a strong and fearless testimony to the world. John now describes the nature of this witness. **26, 27.** The disciples would not face the world alone. They would have a divine helper, **the Spirit of truth.** He would press home the truth about men's sinful condition and the truth about Christ, the remedy for that sin. The Spirit was to come under a double commission, so to speak, being sent of the Son from the Father, in order to **testify** of Christ (cf. 16:7-13). **Ye also bear witness.** Probably indicative rather than imperative. From the standpoint of association with Jesus, which had given them the knowledge necessary for a valid witness, they were qualified now, since they had been with him **from the beginning** – from the early days of the ministry. Yet, to be effective, their witness had to be joined to that of the Spirit working in them and through them (cf. Acts 5:32).

In chapter 16 the dominant note remains the same – the departure of Christ and the anticipation of what this would mean. The thought moves along the following lines: Christ's warning of coming persecution (16:1-4 a); his departure explained in the light of the coming of the Spirit and his ministry to the world (16: 4 b-11); the Spirit's ministry to believers (16:12-15); comforts to offset the pain of separation (16:16-28); the victory of the Son of God (16:29-33). The theme of persecution had been anticipated by the previous teaching (ch. 15) on the hatred of the world for Christ and his own.

1. These things have I spoken unto you. Primarily the information about the hatred of the world, so that the disciples might be forearmed, but also the reminder that they were witnesses to that very world which would despise them (cf. 15:27). Responsibility stiffens character. **That ye should not be offended.** The word "offended" presents the idea of stumbling because of an obstacle in the path rather than because of an inner tendency to defection. On this account the RSV rendering, *to keep you from falling away,* is not wholly satisfactory. Jesus' usual phrase is, "offended in me" (Lk 7: 23; Mt 26:31).

2. Out of the synagogues (cf. 9:22). A most painful experience to a Jew, whose tie with the nation was strong. Jewish believers in Jerusalem continued to mingle with their countrymen in the Temple after Pentecost, showing their sense of kinship with their people. **Will think that he doeth God service.** The best commentary is the confession of Saul of Tarsus concerning his persecuting days (Acts 26:9-11). He measured his zeal for his own religion by the terrors and ravages he inflicted on the church (Gal 1:13; Phil 3: 6).

3. Ignorance of Christ and his true relation to the Father helps to account for persecution. Such ignorance does not make the persecutor excusable. Paul labeled himself chief of sinners on this very account! (I Tim 1:13-15)

4. When persecution would strike, the memory of Christ's faithfulness in warning of these things would serve to strengthen his servants. To meet such things unprepared would bring dismay. **I was with you.** Christ was their shield against opposition. In the light of his soon going away, the present teaching took on a significance it could not have had before.

It was now in order to think more directly about this departure and about what it would mean for those who remained. **5.** For Christ the going meant a return to the One who had sent him. This aspect of it had not laid hold of the minds of the disciples to any extent. They had not asked, **Whither goest thou? 6.** Instead, they had been preoccupied with their sense of loss. They were in the grip of **sorrow.**

7. It is expedient for you that I go away. The disadvantage in terms of separation and sorrow was to be outweighed by the gain occasioned by the coming of the Comforter (helper). One has only to compare the disciples at the end of Jesus' ministry with these same men after the coming of the Spirit to see how greatly they had advanced in understanding and in the effectiveness of their service. **If I go not . . . the Comforter will not come** (cf. 7:37-39). This is not a sign of hostility or jealousy between the Son and the Spirit. Indeed, the Spirit had come upon Christ to empower him for his work; and soon he would come upon Christ's followers, as though to compensate for the loss of the personal presence of the Lord.

8. He will reprove the world. Reprove may equally well be rendered *convict* or *convince.* The Spirit was to come first to the disciples (see end of v. 7), and through them he would undertake his mission of convicting men. In a sense this ministry correlates with the world's activity of persecution. The world may appear to make inroads on the Church, but there is a counterattack in the work of the Spirit, designed not to harm but to convert, or at least to convict. The Spirit, working through the apostles, produced conviction of sin in the very city where Jesus had been put to death (Acts 2:37).

9. Of sin. For the reason that the sin of the world came to sharp focus in the rejection of Jesus when there should have been acceptance of him, the Spirit makes this the important issue. In their blindness men were calling Jesus a sinner at the very time their own sin was leading them to put him to death. **10. Of righteousness.** The very fact that Christ could solve the sin problem of mankind by his redeeming death revealed his perfect righteousness. Otherwise he would have required a Saviour for himself. The Father is the true judge of righteousness. His readiness to receive the Son back into glory is the proof that he found in him no deficiency (Rom 1:4; 4:25; I Tim 3:16). **11. Of judgment.** When those who crucified Jesus saw that God did not interfere, they imagined that the judgment of God was being pronounced on him. Actually, another was being judged there, even Satan, the prince of this world. Satan rules by means of sin and death. Christ's triumph over sin at the cross and over death at the Resurrection heralded the fact that Satan had been judged. The execution of final judgment is only a matter of time.

At this point the thought moves away from the world. The Spirit's work on behalf of believers comes into view.

12. The discourse was not a complete exposition of the thoughts of Jesus toward his own. Held in reserve were **many things.** It was useless to venture upon them, for the disciples could not **bear them.** They were too immature. These truths would become more real to them as their experience grew. **13.** The communication of these things could be safely deferred until **the Spirit of truth** came, who is a teacher as truly as the Lord himself. **All truth.** Not truth in every realm of knowledge, but truth in the things of God in the narrower sense, which we speak of as spiritual things (cf. I Cor 2:10). **He shall not speak of** (from) **himself.** He would not attempt to initiate the things he would teach, but like the Son (15:15), would pass on to men what was given to him from God the Father. One common source guarantees unity in the teaching. Ultimately believers are taught of God (I Thess 4:9). **Things to come.** The return of Christ and attendant events may be in view, but more immediately the **things to come** were the death and resurrection of Jesus and their effects, the very things over which the disciples had stumbled when Jesus had talked about them.

14. Glorify. Even as Christ was glorifying the Father by his obedience unto death, so the Spirit would glorify Christ by making clear the significance of his person and work. The Spirit's teaching mission would be first to **receive** the deposit of Christ-centered truth, then **show** it to believers. It follows that a ministry, to be Spirit-directed, must be one that magnifies Christ. **15.** Since the things of Christ include the truths concerning the Father and his counsels, when the Spirit communicates the things of Christ, he communicates the whole truth.

Next the Lord dealt with the compensations that should ease the pain occasioned by his departure. These included the promise that the disciples would see him again (v. 16); their joy at seeing him (v. 22); the privilege of prayer (vv. 23,24); increased knowledge (v. 25); and the sustaining love of the Father for them (v. 27).

16. A little while. The phrase occurs seven times in four verses. This refers to the short interval that remained before his burial, when the disciples would no longer **see** him with the eyes of physical sight. The second **little while** designates the interval between his burial and his resurrection, after which they would see him again. Here the word **see** is not the same as in the first occurrence. It conveys here the thought of perception as well as of observation. Something of the meaning of this drama of redemption, which was now so mysterious, would dawn upon these men. The last clause, **because I go to the Father**, does not have sufficient manuscript authority to be retained in the text.

17. The words of Jesus were beyond the grasp of the disciples. Individuals among them had asked questions before this. These men **(some of his disciples),** too timid to voice their perplexity openly, conferred with one another instead of addressing the Lord. In this verse the words, **because I go to the Father,** are genuine. They are easily explained on the basis of Jesus' use of them in verse **10.** This fact of his departure is the all-absorbing concern. **19,20.** Recognizing their burning desire to have an answer to the problem of the **little while** in its twofold application, Jesus offered to supply an answer, yet not the precise answer they were hoping for. But he did indicate what the **little while** would mean for them in each instance. In the former, they would weep while the world rejoiced, for the death of the Saviour would bring utterly different reactions from believers than from the people of the world (cf. Rev 11:10). But the very thing that would bring sorrow would be turned into an occasion of **joy** when the disciples were able to see the cross in the light of the Resurrection, when the second "little while" would break upon them.

21. Jesus drew an analogy from human life for the supplanting of sorrow with joy. A woman's travail pains bring sorrow, but she forgets her pain in the joy of the birth. It may be significant that a **man** is said to be born (rather than a child). Christ in resurrection as the first-born from the dead (Col 1:18) joins with himself the new man, his Church, to which he imparts his risen life. **22.** The joy of reunion would be an abiding experience; the second separation, occasioned by the Lord's ascension, would not affect that joy (Lk 24:51-53).

23. In that day. The Lord was thinking of the conditions that would prevail after his return to the Father. In the intermediate period of the forty days after the Resurrection, the disciples did ask something (Acts 1:6). But when he was taken up, all opportunity for questions such as were now being asked would be gone. This does not mean there would be total lack of communication. The door of prayer would be open. If they would but **ask**, the Father would **give** the answers to their perplexities and would meet their needs. **In my name** (see the comment on 14:13,14). **24. Asked nothing.** Here the word "asked" is used in the sense of making petition rather than framing a question. Due to the presence of Jesus in their midst, asking in his name had been unnecessary. But in the new day that was coming, their **joy** at seeing Jesus again would be maintained by this intercourse of prayer.

25. Proverbs. Not maxims, but obscure sayings. His teaching was often enigmatical to his followers. But a change was coming. "The return of Jesus to the Father inaugurated a new era, in which the Lord speaks to His disciples no longer obscurely but clearly and openly; it is presumed that the readers of the Gospel understand that He speaks to them through the Spirit which they have received" (Hoskyns, *The Fourth Gospel*). **26,27.** In the future, prayer would indeed be in the name of Christ, but not in the sense that the Son would be the means of overcoming some sort of hesitancy or resistance in the Father which otherwise believers would encounter. On the contrary, the Father **loveth** them, and is ready to receive them because of their attitude toward his beloved Son. In contrast to the world, they have loved and trusted the Son as the one sent of God.

28. What the faith of the disciples should encompass is now set forth in its simplest and boldest outline. The first half of the statement had been affirmed more than once by one or more of the group; the second part deals with the burden of this discourse, the going away of their leader. Now he put this departure sharply and clearly – **I leave the world, and go to the Father.**

At this point the discourse was almost concluded. It ended on a double note – the pathetic failure of those Jesus had tried to instruct, and his own triumph, aided by the presence of the Father. **29, 30.** Encouraged alike by the commendation of their faith and by the plain speaking of Jesus concerning his career, the disciples imagined that they were basking in the superior knowledge of the Son of God. **31,32.** A rude awakening was in store for them. They would be **scattered** (at the time of the arrest of Jesus) and he would **be left alone,** yet he would have the help of the Father. **33.** For their protection he provided his **peace** (cf. 14:27), which they would need as they faced the **tribulation** in store for them in the world. This is not only peace amid conflict, but peace which rests in the assurance of a victory now won by their champion over the world. Christ's victory is the objective reality which makes valid the inward gift of his peace.

D. The Great Prayer. 17:1-26. Jesus included himself in this prayer (vv. 1-5), but his chief concern was for his own. In both sections the element of dedication is strongly mingled with petition.

1. Father. Used regularly in Jesus' prayers, six times here. **The hour is come.** The time is undefined, as something well known between Father and Son. It was at once the time for suffering and for glorification. **Glorify thy Son.** Enable him to fulfill his course, accomplishing the salvation for which he came. Plainly Christ did not seek some honor here for his own sake, for in his own glorification through death, resurrection, and exaltation, he sought only to **glorify** the Father.

2. This glorification of the Father includes in it the elevation of the Son to glory and power, where he is head over all things (cf. Mt 28:18). **Power** means authority. Here it has especially in view the granting of **eternal life,** on the basis of Christ's finished work. The beneficiaries are described as those whom the Father has given to the Son. This is the description of the disciples which recurs most often throughout the prayer (vv. 2,6,9,11, 12,24).

3. Eternal life is set forth in terms of knowing God (cf. I Jn 5:20). The Jews did not know God, though they knew much about him. It is the claim of this verse and this whole Gospel that the knowledge of God which brings eternal life comes only through the knowledge of the Son. Since the Father and the Son are one, the knowledge is one. The knowledge of God implies the knowledge of his ways as well as of his person, and so includes the perception of his plan of salvation from sin. **Jesus Christ** (cf. 1:17).

Rare in the Gospels but common in the Epistles.

4. I have glorified thee on the earth. This our Lord explained in terms of finishing the work the Father gave him to do – the revelation of the Father, the exposure of sin, the choice and training of the Twelve, and most of all the death on the cross, which was so certain that it could be regarded as already completed. **Finished** means perfected as well as accomplished.

5. Having spoken of his work on the earth (v. 4), the Son now sought glorification with the Father in the heavenly realm. So the contrast is double, consisting of place and person. **With thine own self . . . with thee.** In thy presence. **Before the world was.** Cf. 1:1,2.

Verses 6-8 are transitional, still dealing with the work of Christ on earth but leading up to the petitions for the disciples.

6. A large part of the work of the Son on the earth had been to make the Father known to the disciples (cf. 1:14; 14:7-9). The success of this process is implied in the fact that these men were God's gift to the Son. Their understanding was not perfect, but it was sure and growing. **They have kept thy word.** Not a reference primarily to their obedience to individual commands or teachings, but to their readiness to receive the Son, his message and mission, in so far as they were able.

7,8. The disciples had advanced to the point of understanding that the character and gifts and labors of Christ must be traced to the invisible God, in whose name he had come. In particular the disciples had laid hold of the revelation of truth in Christ, recognizing it as truly of God. They had thus reached a point of development where it was safe to leave them. In their future work they would be representing one who himself had represented the living God. **Thou didst send me.** This expression reverberates through the prayer (vv. 3,8,18,21,23,25). It was a frequent claim of Christ in his discourses.

Having named the qualifications of the disciples as his representatives in the world, the Lord now interceded for them.

9. I pray not for the world. This does not mean that Christ never prayed for the world (cf. Lk 23:34). But he prayed for the disciples because they were the chosen medium of reaching the world after he himself had left it (vv. 21,23). **10. All mine are thine.** Therefore the concern of the Son to pray for these men and the concern of the Father to hear and answer are alike understandable. The proprietary interest is mutual. **I am glorified in them.** The antecedent of **them** may be the things held in common by Father and Son, or better, the disciples who have been mentioned in the previous verse. It was to the glory of Christ that amid general unbelief and rejection, these men dared to trust and serve him. The word **glorified** is in the perfect tense, suggesting the continuance of their testimony to Christ.

The first specific petition was for the preservation of the disciples from the evil that is in the world (vv. 11-15). This in turn was to serve another purpose, one which is heavily emphasized in the rest of the prayer, namely, that they might be one.

11. Keep. Used in the sense of protective oversight, as in I Jn 5:18. The character of God as entirely dissimilar from evil and therefore interested in preserving his children, is emphasized in the address, **Holy Father.** On the positive side, this preservation would make the disciples **one,** reflecting the oneness between Father and Son. The bond is the holy love of God. This unity is seen in the early church (Acts 1:14; 2:1,44,46). **12.** The best attested Greek text reads, *I was keeping them in thy name which thou gavest to me.* Not only did Jesus keep his own disciples by the authority of the Father, but he kept them by the truth and power of the nature of God, which he himself revealed. **The son of perdition.** The word **perdition** is from the same root as the word **lost.** Jesus was saying that the loss was not a reflection on His keeping power as the shepherd of the flock. Rather, Judas had never really belonged to him except in a nominal, external sense (cf. 13:10,11). The idea in *perdition* is exactly the opposite of *preservation.* **The scripture.** Psa 41:9.

13. And now come I to thee. Herein lay the occasion for the whole prayer and all the requests contained in it. The disciples' need for **joy** was particularly acute in the light of Judas' defection. The disciples needed to realize that such a case did not reflect on the Lord or on themselves. It was not to mar their joy in the possession of true faith and life. If Christ could rejoice even in the midst of such things (**my joy**), they should do so also.

14. The reception of the word of Christ identified these men with him and set them apart from **the world,** which rejected and hated him and therefore had the same attitude toward them. **15.** Despite the unity between Christ and his own, he could not pray that the Father would take them out of the world. To do so would have frustrated the purpose of their call and training. As they labored and witnessed, they needed to be kept from **the evil;** otherwise their witness would have ceased to be pure. The reference may well be to the evil one himself (cf. Mt 6:13; I Pet 5:8). **16.** As regenerated men, the disciples no longer belonged to the world as a realm of spiritual evil, even though they resided in the world as a physical entity.

17. Sanctify them through thy truth. This is the second petition on behalf of the disciples. **Sanctify** means to set apart for God and holy purposes. That which reveals the holy will of God in his **truth,** and specifically that truth as enshrined in the **word** of Scripture. There one learns what God requires and how he enables one to fulfill the requirement. **18.** To be sent into the world by Christ as he was sent by the Father is the highest dignity that can be bestowed on men. **19.** Christ did not need to make himself holy, for he was that. But he did need to devote (**sanctify**) himself to his calling, that the disciples might have not only his example but his message to proclaim, and the power derived from his sacrifice whereby to proclaim it effectively.

20,21. The prayer reaches out to include those who will believe because of the testimony of these men (cf. 10:16; Acts 18:10). Faith is the necessary condition for enjoying the life of God and therefore of coming into that unity which is found first of all in the Godhead and then in the body of Christ, the Church. The unity is basically personal—**in us.** Its effect will be to elicit faith on the part of those in the world (cf. 13:35). **22. The glory.** Doubtless this points to the ultimate heavenly position of the Church, but it includes the privilege of serving and suffering, just as the Father bestowed this commission on the Son. This privilege helps to unify the saints as it is exercised in the light of Christ our forerunner within the veil. **23. Made perfect in one.** To be accomplished not by human effort, but by the gracious extension of the unity of the Godhead to those who belong to Christ. This is not a mechanical unity. Its cement is the love of God bestowed on men, that same love (marvelous to relate) which the Father has for the Son.

24. *The final petition.* **I will.** The spirit of the Incarnation was, Not my will but thine be done. It must be that Jesus was praying in the light of his finished work, which entitled him to express himself in this fashion. His will, to be sure, is not to be thought of as something really independent of the will of God. This petition builds on the last. To participate in the love of God in Christ can only result eventually in sharing the presence of Christ — **with me where I am.** Union leads to communion, a communion of love displayed in a setting of **glory** (cf. v. 5).

25. Righteous Father. He is righteous (1) in excluding the world from that glory, because it has not known him and therefore does not love him, and so can have no place in that final unity, and (2) in including those who have come to know him through the knowledge that Christ has and imparts. **26.** Imparting the knowledge of God means imparting love, for God is love. This is not merely a label or a cold attribute. Christ knew the reality and power of the love of the Father for him and asked that this might brighten and warm the lives of those who were his, with whom his life was now so closely bound up.

IV. The Sufferings and the Glory. 18:1–20:31.

A. The Betrayal. 18:1-14. John's account emphasizes the poise of Jesus and his readiness to be taken, making needless the treachery of Judas on the one hand and the attempted display of loyalty by Peter on the other. Included here is the account of the arrest and the transfer of Jesus to the high priest's house.

1. Following the prayer, Jesus led his disciples across **the brook Kidron.** The word **brook** denotes a stream that flows in the winter. A garden on the eastern side was the destination. Matthew and Mark give the name as Gethsemane. John says nothing about the agony in the garden, though he shows awareness of the prayer struggle that took place there (cf. v. 11). We do not know why he omitted this incident. Perhaps he was seeking to give prominence to the element of confidence in the attitude of Jesus, which had already been expressed in prayer (17:4) and was now seen in his bearing and action. **2. Ofttimes** (cf. Lk 22:39). It may have been the usual thing for Jesus and his company to spend the night there (Lk 21:37). Judas therefore knew where to look for the Lord on this night.

3. Judas, too, had a following when

he entered the garden, but what a contrasting array! The **band** of soldiers (Gr. *speira)* denotes a Roman cohort, normally six hundred men, but not necessarily at full strength on this occasion. They were quartered in the Castle of Antonia, at the northern edge of the temple area (cf. Acts 21:31 ff.). Apparently the Jewish authorities were able to call upon these forces for help in any emergency that threatened the public interest. The city was filled with pilgrims attending the feast, many of whom were sympathetic to Jesus and might have given trouble if they had been nearby when he was being apprehended. **Officers.** These were the temple police who were in the service of the Jewish rulers (cf. Acts 5:22). They bore lights for searching out their quarry and carried weapons for putting down any resistance that might be offered.

4. Knowing all things. This is a strongly marked feature of the Johannine presentation of the Christ, and has special prominence in relation to the events of the Passion (cf. 13:1,3). Nothing took our Lord by surprise. **Went forth.** Cf. 18:1 and the oft-repeated emphasis upon the more epochal going forth of the Son from the Father into the world, e.g., 16:28. **Whom seek ye?** The question served to put the oncoming host momentarily on the defensive and obliged them to state that their single objective was Jesus. This made it easier for him to ask that the disciples be permitted to go their way.

5. By answering, **Jesus of Nazareth,** the crowd indicated that they did not recognize him, due to the semidarkness and their distance from him. **I am he.** Literally, *I am.* This assertion can indicate merely identification, as in 9:9, or it can suggest the mysterious and majestic name of God himself (8:58). Perhaps both elements are fused together in this case. **Judas . . . stood with them.** At last he was in his own element, mingling with the enemies of Jesus. **6.** Nothing miraculous is implied here. The bearing of Jesus, plus the fact that he advanced toward them rather than sought flight, unnerved his captors. Remember that some of these same men had found themselves unable to lay hands on him previously (7:45,46). No doubt the majesty of his last utterance had something to do with their reaction also.

7-9. When the crowd confessed again that their objective was Jesus of Nazareth, he could the more readily ask that the disciples be permitted to leave. Their physical safety on this occasion may be regarded as a token that their spiritual preservation was assured (cf. 6:39; 17:12). **10,11.** Peter's action in resorting to use of the sword is understandable in view of his declaration of loyalty in Jn 13:37. His possession of a sword is explained by Christ's counsel in Lk 22:35-38. The sword was symbolic of days of stress lying ahead, but was not intended for literal use. Hence Jesus' rebuke. John's mention of the name of the servant and his ear is an eyewitness touch. Malchus was not one of the officers but a personal slave of the high priest.

12-14. *The Arrest.* With Jesus himself calling for nonresistance, the band of soldiers, led by their **captain** and assisted by the Jewish officers, took (captured) Jesus and **bound** him. They did not want to risk any slip in their plans. The Synoptists tell about Jesus' appearance before Caiaphas, but say nothing about Annas in this connection. **First** calls attention of the reader to material now being supplied supplementary to the Synoptic accounts. Though Annas' son-in-law, Caiaphas, was the actual high priest at this time, Annas himself was far from inactive. In addition to Caiaphas, Annas had several sons who succeeded him in this office, giving this one family a monopoly on the high priesthood for over half a century. Luke is the only other writer who mentions Annas (Lk 3:2; Acts 4:6). Jewish sources label the regime of Annas as corrupt. The counsel of Caiaphas about Jesus had already been delivered to the Sanhedrin (11:49,50).

B. Jesus on Trial Before the Jews. 18:15-27.

15. Spurred by his declaration of loyalty to the Master in the presence of the disciples, Peter **followed** Jesus. **Another disciple.** This figure, unnamed, may be assumed to be John himself. **Known unto the high priest.** The word **known** is found again in Lk 2:44; 23:49. This connection, to be traced, very likely, through his mother and her family, enabled John to secure admission for Peter to the inner court. **Palace.** Courtyard. **17.** The **girl** who acted as doorkeeper, probably assuming Peter's connection with Jesus because she knew of John's, challenged him to declare himself, and got a denial. **18.** Presently Peter found himself with the captors of Jesus, warming himself by a fire in the courtyard. John interrupts the story of Peter's denial in order to report on the proceedings within, where Jesus was being examined.

19,20. The high priest . . . asked Jesus. Annas is apparently meant. This was not a trial, for the Sanhedrin had not been assembled; rather it was a hearing to get evidence to submit to that body when it was convened a few hours later. The inquiry touched Jesus' **disciples** and **doctrine.** It is not clear that Annas had in mind to prosecute the disciples. More likely he hoped to get a confession that these men were being prepared for revolutionary activity. Jesus ignored the matter. So far as his teaching was concerned, he denied having given secret instruction that might be construed as plotting against the authorities. He had taught **openly,** in public places such as the **synagogue** and **temple.** His teaching was not subversive.

21. Why askest thou me? Jesus implied that the procedure was illegal. There were no witnesses. He was being made to implicate himself by his testimony. **22.** One of the attending **officers** (others were in the courtyard) thought the answer impudent and struck Jesus to make him more docile in his attitude toward the high priest. **23,24.** When Christ pointed out the injustice involved, neither the officer nor Annas could make a defense of the procedure. There was nothing to do but to send the captive to Caiaphas (the AV incorrectly suggests that he had been previously sent).

25-27. The narrative returns to Peter. While Christ was denying the insinuations leveled against him – and justly so, Peter was denying his Lord sinfully. The two questions addressed to Peter were quite different. The first was tentative, as though expecting him to deny that he had a relation to Jesus; whereas the second pinned him down, the very form of the question assuming his guilt. He was now recognized as the one who had wielded the sword in the garden. The crowing of the cock reminded Peter of the Lord's prediction (13:38) and brought home to him his sin of denial. 'Cockcrowing' was the name of the third of the four watches into which the night was divided.

C. The Ordeal Before Pilate. 18:28–19:16.

28. Nothing is said about what took place in the house of Caiaphas. The assumption is that the readers are acquainted with the Synoptic tradition of the nighttime deliberations and the formal decree of the council arrived at in the early morning. **The hall of judgment** (Gr. *praitōrion*, a rendering of Lat. *praetorium*, the headquarters of the governor). See the discussion on 19:13. **That they might eat the passover.** The Jewish leaders, to be ceremonially clean, could not enter a pagan's quarters. They were more concerned with ritual cleanness than with the execution of justice. They were out for blood!

29,30. The Sanhedrin had not prepared a formal indictment against Jesus to submit to Pilate. They expected the governor to take their word for it that this man was a **malefactor,** i.e., a doer of evil. The answer was flippant. Pilate was disliked by the Jews.

31. Judge him according to your law. Pilate was satisfied that the very vagueness of the statement by the Jewish leaders indicated that the case was not one he needed to hear (cf. Acts 18:14). **It is not lawful for us to put any man to death.** All the Jews wanted was a verdict of death, the authority of the governor to cover their own decision against Jesus. The taking away of the right to inflict the death penalty made the Jews realize they were a subject people. This had exceptions, as in the case of a person, even a Roman, who transgressed the barrier that separated the Court of the Gentiles from the inner portion of the temple area. Stephen's death seems to violate John's statement, but it may have been based on the knowledge of the Jews that the governor would not interfere in that case. **32.** Jesus had predicted that he would die by crucifixion, a Roman method of punishment, whereas the Jews used stoning (cf. Mt 20:19).

33. Pilate then took matters into his own hands, questioning Jesus within the Praetorium. John seems to suppose that his readers knew the Synoptic account, which included a charge leveled by the Jews against Jesus to the effect that he had declared himself king of the nation. Pilate was obliged to examine this matter on the grounds of possible revolutionary intent. **Art thou the King of the Jews?** The word **thou** is emphatic, as though Pilate were surprised that the appearance and attitude of Jesus so little fitted the claim of kingship. The prisoner seemed harmless.

34. Before he could answer the question, Jesus needed to know whether it came from Pilate himself as a Roman official or whether it was merely passed on as a bit of hearsay. Perhaps the high priest had discussed the case with Pilate when he asked for Roman soldiers to aid in capturing Jesus. **35.** Pilate, unwilling to be trapped into an admission that he had had anything to do with the situation, put the responsibility on the Jews. **Thine own nation.** Pilate could hardly have felt the pathos suggested by his words (cf. 1:11).

36. My kingdom is not of this world. "He does not say that this world is not the sphere of His authority, but that His authority is not of human origin" (Hoskyns). He was not a menace to the Roman authority. There was no place for the use of force in his kingdom. **37.** Pilate was nonplused. Here was a man who had spoken of his kingdom three times in rapid succession, yet he had none of the outward marks of kingship. **Art thou a king then?** Pilate could hardly believe that anyone would mistake the figure before him for a king. **Thou sayest that I am a king.** Jesus was hesitant to affirm that he was a king, lest Pilate misunderstand the nature of his kingship, which he now explained in terms of **truth.** Christ had come to bear witness to it. **Heareth my voice** (cf. 10:3,16).

38. Pilate saw that Jesus had no concern for politics or affairs of state and was far removed from a warlike spirit, and so he terminated the interview, saying rather disdainfully, it seems, **What is truth?** He was no philosopher nor religionist, but a man of action. Satisfied that the prisoner was not dangerous to Rome, he announced this to the Jews outside. **No fault.** This does not refer to sinlessness in this context, but to innocence of any wrongdoing the Jews had charged against him.

39. Sensing the tenacity of the rulers in their desire to get a conviction, Pilate thought he saw a way to get around them and uphold justice by releasing the prisoner. It was a yearly **custom** at Passover time for the governor to please the crowd by releasing one prisoner whom they requested. Pilate thought that, because Jesus was very popular, the people who had gathered by this time for their annual request would seek his release. **40.** Again John presupposes a knowledge of the Synoptic narrative by his reference to Barabbas. **Robber.** Brigand (cf. Acts 3:14).

19:1-3. At Pilate's order the prisoner was scourged. This was the governor's second expedient, the earlier attempt to secure release having failed because of the preference for Barabbas. Pilate thought the Jews might be satisfied if Jesus were humiliated and made to suffer in this fashion. The Lord had predicted this treatment (Mt 20:19). See also Isa 53:5. **A crown of thorns.** This was mockery on the part of the soldiers, in view of Jesus' alleged kingship. Some have thought that this crown was fashioned from the sharp prongs of the date palm, thus connecting it with the nationalist hopes of the Jews expressed by the waving of palms when Jesus entered Jerusalem. Since the palm was an expression of Jewish hopes for independence even in Maccabean days, this action by the soldiers would have been the harsh answer of Rome to the Jews as a whole. From the Biblical standpoint the thorns may be said to express the curse of sin (Gen 3:17,18), which Christ was bearing for the race. **A purple robe.** Often associated with royalty. Clothed thus, Jesus became an object of sport and abuse by the soldiers.

4,5. Pilate . . . went forth again. He proposed to prepare the way for the showing of Jesus by a grandiose announcement. **Behold, I bring him forth to you.** This was in the spirit of the mockery of the soldiers. He, the Roman governor, would present the one who was reputed to be a king but now certainly could not be confused with a king. **Behold the man!** It is uncertain what Pilate meant to imply here. Some see in the situation a desire to create pity in the hearts of the Jews. But the setting suggests more the thought of scorn. **Man** may mean nothing more than "miserable creature." In any event, Pilate's words, **I find no fault in him,** have a strange ring. If the prisoner was innocent, why was flogging administered?

6. The answer of **the chief priests** was a resounding refusal to be satisfied with punishment of this character, however painful and humiliating. **Crucify, Crucify!** Pilate's reply, **Take ye him,** puts emphasis on the **ye.** In other words, "If there is any crucifying to be done here, you will have to do it." Pilate was dissociating himself from the Jews' desire, but not seriously giving permission to them to put Jesus to death. This was the third time the governor declared himself unable to find any **fault** *(aitia)* in Jesus. The word is used here in the legal sense of a proper ground of complaint.

7. Pilate was standing on Roman law. The Jews put something else over against it. **We have a law.** Emphasis falls on the **we.** Our law requires the death of the prisoner, **because he made himself the Son of God.** The individual passage in the background is Lev 24:16. Jesus had been accused of blasphemy during his ministry (Jn 5:18) and at its close (Mk 14:62-64).

8. The more afraid. Pilate's previous fear had been due to the angry persistence of Jesus' accusers, who would not be denied. Perhaps John is presupposing his readers' knowledge of the dream of Pilate's wife (Mt 27:19). The governor's new fear was that he was dealing with one who in some sense was supernatural – a son of a god. **9.** It began to appear to Pilate that this case had more to it than he had thought at first. So he took the prisoner within the Praetorium for another conference. **Whence art thou?** Not residence but origin and nature were in view. **No answer.** Pilate's spiritual incapacity (cf. 18:38) made reply useless.

10. The silence of the prisoner annoyed the governor. Perhaps he thought that by asserting his authority and advancing the reminder that life or death hung on his verdict, he could make Jesus talk. **11.** The device was only partially successful. Jesus talked, but only to state to Pilate his limitations. **Power.** Authority. Christ may have been affirming the broad truth of the divine control over the state (Rom 13:1 ff.), but the stress falls on the immediate situation. Pilate was powerless to do other than carry out the will of God in this case. **He that delivered me.** Any reference to Judas is hardly natural here. **The greater sin,** i.e., greater than that of Pilate. "The sin of Caiaphas is greater because Pilate's authority is from God; and it was the duty of Caiaphas to know and teach as well as do the will of God. But he, the official representative of Israel, the People of God, has had recourse to this heathen, who holds certain authority from God, in order that power conferred by God for the execution of justice may be employed for the perpetration of injustice" (William Temple, *Readings in St. John's Gospel*).

12. As a result of this verbal exchange, Pilate made renewed efforts to release his prisoner, driven alike by fear of this strange person before him and by the conviction that he was not worthy of death. The Jews, sensing fresh resolution in the governor, used their culminating argument. **Thou are not Caesar's friend.** The reigning emperor was Tiberius, to whom Pilate was responsible. Here was a threat to take the case to the imperial court. Caesar would not have looked lightly upon a situation in which one was known as a **king** without Roman consent. He would have viewed this as treason and might well have charged Pilate with inattention to duty. No doubt the governor feared that if a complaint were made regarding his handling of this case, other irregularities in his administration would come to light.

13. The time for decision had come. **Pilate . . . sat down in the judgment seat.** He had now to render his verdict. Due to the excavations of Père Vincent, **the Pavement** *(Lithostrōton)* is now almost certainly identified as the large paved area that was a part of the Castle of Antonia, at the northwest corner of the temple area. **Gabbatha** probably means "elevated ground." **14. It was the preparation of the passover.** "The hour of the double sacrifice is drawing near. It is midday. The Passover lambs are being prepared for sacrifice, and the Lamb of God is likewise sentenced to death" (Hoskyns). **Behold your King!** Whatever moved Pilate to make this final presentation (probably scorn for the Jews – such a king for such a people!), it was providentially used to draw from the lips of the Jews a complete repudiation of their Messianic hope – **We have no king but Caesar.** If language means anything, the very sovereignty of God over the nation was repudiated. Who was guilty of blasphemy now? **16. Delivered.** The verb is the same as that in verse 11. The Jews were now able to see their will accomplished. Jesus was to be crucified.

D. The Crucifixion and Burial. 19:17-42.

17. Bearing his cross. All the Synoptics state that Simon of Cyrene was compelled to bear the cross. John alone states that Jesus carried it. Luke's account makes room for both. Jesus started, but could not carry it all the way. **Golgotha.** Probably named from its appearance; hence a rounded hill. Its Latin equivalent is Calvary (Lk 23:33). It must have been outside the city (Heb 13:12). **18. Jesus in the midst.** His was the place of central importance, even in death.

19. His position is explained by the **title** affixed over the head of the crucified. Matthew and Mark use the word *aitia,* which John employs three times, in his account of the trial, in the sense of "charge." Pilate found no *aitia* in Jesus that warranted his death, but now he let the world know that here hung Israel's king, as though thereby involving the nation in defiance of Rome and deserving of this harsh rebuke. **20-22.** The very publicity given the title (three languages) as well as the implication behind it, incensed the Jews, so that the chief priests requested that the wording be changed from a fact to a claim. This Pilate refused to do, showing an unyieldingness which sharply contrasts with his weakness during the trial.

23,24. Four soldiers took part in the crucifixion (cf. Acts 12:4). These took as personal spoil the garments of Jesus, dividing them among themselves. Sandals, headdress, outer garment *(himation)*, and girdle were likely distributed, leaving the more valuable **coat** or tunic *(chitōn)* for the casting of lots. Josephus describes the high priest's robe in language similar to that used here *(Ant* III. 161). It has been suggested that in John's eyes this seamless robe may have symbolized the unifying power of the death of Christ as securing the one flock. The soldiers unconsciously fulfilled Scripture by their actions (Ps 22:18).

25-27. Three women, all named Mary, took their station near the cross, sorrowfully contemplating the one who was so dear to them. The Greek text, however, is rather favorable to the mention of four, the mother's sister (Salome, the mother of John) being noted but left unnamed. If so, these four may be intended to present a sort of contrast to the Roman soldiers. Solicitous for his mother, Jesus gave her into the care of the 'beloved disciple.' His own brethren were not believers at this time. The unity of the Church, which the Lord was bringing into being, was to be spiritual rather than natural (cf. Mt 12:50). **His own** (home). If John had a residence in Jerusalem, his acquaintance with the high priest is more readily explained (18:16).

28. I thirst. The physical need of the sufferer asserted itself, the only outward indication he permitted to escape his lips. Even so, he stated a fact rather than voicing an appeal. **30.** The **vinegar** was sour wine. It revived Jesus' strength, enabling him to say (with a loud cry, according to the other Gospels), **It is finished.** The same word *(tetelestai)* has already occurred in verse 28, rendered "accomplished." Emphasis here is not on the ending of the sufferings but on the completion of the mission of redemption. **Gave up the ghost.** Delivered over his spirit (to God).

31. The sabbath day. Only a short time remained before sunset and the coming of another day. No matter what the day, the Law required the removal of victims from the cross on the day of death (Deut 21:22,23). To have disregarded this law at Passover time would have been an especially heinous violation of the Sabbath. The breaking of the legs was designed to hasten death. **33,34.** The soldier, finding that death had cheated him of the pleasure of breaking the legs of Jesus, drove his spear into the side of the Saviour. **Blood and water.** This is quite a credible occurrence in the period immediately after death. **35.** John attaches singular importance to this incident, for he solemnly bears record to it. The death of the Saviour means a life-giving flow: blood for the cleansing from sin and water for the representation of the new life in the Spirit (cf. I Jn 5:6-8). **36,37.** These features of the death of Christ also served to fulfill Scripture (Ps 34:20; Zech 12:10).

38-40. In the hour of Jesus' death two secret disciples found a courage they had not possessed before. Joseph gained from Pilate permission to take down the body from the cross; then Nicodemus came forward to provide the **spices** and **linen** for preparing the body for burial. For more information on Joseph, see Mk 15:43.

41. The sepulcher belonged to Joseph (Mt 27:60). **42.** Burial preparations were hurried because the day was coming to a close. Fortunately, the spot was near to the place of crucifixion. More complete preparation of the body could be made after the Sabbath.

E. The Resurrection Appearances. 20:1-29. The Sabbath rest in Jerusalem is passed by in silence. The body of Christ lay amid the stillness of the tomb. But the "must" of Mt 16:21 includes resurrection as well as suffering and death. The supreme test of the claims of Jesus of Nazareth was at hand.

1. The first day of the week. The day after the Sabbath, or the third day from Christ's crucifixion, according to the usual Jewish method of inclusive reckoning. Jesus' resurrection on this day determined the Christian day of worship (Acts 20:7). **Mary Magdalene.** It was well known that several women came early to the tomb, but John concentrates his narrative on Mary alone. The presence of others is assumed in the "we know not" of verse 2. It was the purpose of the women to anoint the body of Jesus more permanently (Mk 16:1). **The stone taken away.** With the stone in place, Mary would have had the problem of gaining access to the tomb; with the stone removed, she had a problem of another kind. To her mind, the situation had worsened.

2. Mary thought of the leading disciples—Simon Peter and the 'beloved disciple'—and ran to take the word to them. It is of interest that in Mary's eyes Peter, despite his denial, was still the acknowledged leader of the group. John, to a degree responsible for Peter's failure (18:16), had been seeking to comfort him. Mary's report of the opened tomb suggested to the two disciples the same fear that had gripped her heart – someone had taken the body.

3,4. Concern caused the two disciples to break into a run, leaving Mary to come at her own gait. The same concern led John to sprint ahead of Peter, though the two had started together. John may have been the more youthful. **5. Stooping down.** The thought is best represented by our word "peer." Restrained by awe and timidity, John took in the interior of the tomb, but did not enter.

6,7. With his characteristic boldness, Peter did not pause at the entrance to look, but went in, and was thus able to see more clearly than John the disposition of the grave clothes. He noticed that they were not all in a heap, but that the headpiece was neatly wrapped and deposited in a place by itself. If the body had been removed, it was strange that the linen cloths were left behind, and even more strange that the napkin was so carefully arranged. **Wrapped together.** This verb is used of the act of winding graveclothes about the body of Jesus before the burial (Mt 27:59; Lk 23:53). It may signify that the head passed through the napkin, leaving it in its circular shape, or that Jesus deliberately folded it up before leaving the tomb.

8. Emboldened by Peter's entrance, John joined him within, took in the scene, and **believed** that the Lord had risen. This is not said of Peter. **9.** The disciples had not received instruction from Christ relating his resurrection to the OT Scriptures (Lk 24:46). They had Jesus' prediction of resurrection, but did not understand this literally (Mk 9:10). **10. Their own home.** The expression is literally, *to themselves,* meaning that they returned to their own quarters and to their own people. Mary (cf. 19:27) would thus have learned of the empty tomb very soon.

11. Mary Magdalene remained at the spot, hoping for some clue to the whereabouts of Jesus, struggling with her double grief over his death and the disappearance of his sacred form. **She stooped down** (cf. v. 5). **12.** She saw something the two disciples had not seen – **two angels.** Such was the experience of the other women also (Lk 24:22,23). **13.** Ordinarily a vision of angels would have brought a thrill, but Mary was too overborne with grief to feel any other emotion. She turned away before receiving any intimation from them that Jesus was risen (cf. Mk 16:6).

14,15. She was equally uninterested in another form that loomed up before her as she turned away into the garden. Her only concern was to press her search for the body, and there was a chance that this man was the gardener and might have removed it. **16.** Electrified at hearing her name spoken in the familiar voice of Jesus, she burst out, **Rabboni** (Master or Lord). Originally the form meant *my great one,* but the word had come to be used without possessive force. It is not unduly surprising that Mary recognized the voice of Jesus when he spoke her name but not when he first questioned her. Even the familiar can seem strange to us when we encounter it unexpectedly.

17. Touch me not. The Greek calls for a different rendering: *Stop clinging to me.* Apparently Mary's first impulse, in her frenzy of joy, was to grasp the sacred form. Jesus did not rebuke the other women for holding his feet (Mt 28:9), for this was an act of worship; nor did he shrink from inviting Thomas to touch him (Jn 20:27). But Mary needed to be taught that the Lord was not with her on the basis of the old relationship. He was already glorified. He belonged now to the heavenly realm, even though he was willing to tarry for a time to meet with his friends. **I am not yet ascended.** The implication was that Mary would be able to touch Jesus in some sense after the Ascension, i.e., she would touch him by faith in the blessed life of the Spirit. The closeness of that new relationship is attested by the fact that he spoke of his followers as **brethren** (cf. the anticipation of this in Mt 12:49). Even in the intimacy of the new order, however, Christ retained his own special relationship to God the Father. **My Father** is the language of deity; **my God** is the language of humanity.

18. The sense of being useful, of fulfilling Jesus' command to **go** to the disciples, relieved any feeling of hurt Mary may have experienced at the rebuff she had received. Her task is a miniature of that given to the whole Church – to go and tell that Jesus has risen.

19. The disciples, having received the message from Mary, now had their first opportunity, as a group, to see Jesus in his risen state. It was the evening of the resurrection day. **For fear of the Jews.** This was natural in view of their flight from the garden, Annas' inquiry about them (18:19), and the expectation created by Jesus' teaching that if he suffered, they should expect to do so also (Mt 16:24; Jn 15:20). The implication is plain that Jesus passed through the closed doors. He had power to dematerialize his body. **Peace be unto you** (cf. 14:27; 16:33). **20.** The word of peace had relieved fear. Now it was in order to establish identity. **He showed unto them his hands and his side.** According to Luke, even more graphic demonstration was needed in order to bring conviction (Lk 24:37-43). **Then were the disciples glad** (cf. 16:22).

21. The first **peace** (v. 19) was to quiet their hearts; the second was to prepare them for a fresh statement of their commission (cf. 17:18). Nothing had been changed in the plan of the Master for them. **22. He breathed on them.** This recalls the creation of man (Gen 2:7), as though to announce the new creation, resulting not so much from the infusion of the breath of God as from the reception of the Holy Spirit (cf. 7:39). This need not rule out any relation to the Spirit in the days of earlier discipleship any more than it rules out the Spirit's coming upon them at Pentecost. Here the Spirit was the necessary equipment for the task that lay ahead, which is stated next.

23. Christ gave authority to the apostles and possibly to others (cf. Lk 24:33 ff.) to forgive and to retain the sins of men. "Either . . . the disciples must possess unfailing insight into man's heart (such as in certain cases was granted to an apostle, cf. Acts 5:3), or the remission which they proclaim must be *conditionally* proclaimed. No one can maintain the former alternative. It follows, then, that what our Lord here commits to His disciples, to His Church, is the right authoritatively to declare, in His name, that there is forgiveness for man's sin, and on what conditions the sin will be forgiven" (Milligan and Moulton, *Commentary on John)* This scene involves the death of Christ (his wounds presented), his resurrection (declared by his living presence), the resultant commission to go and bear witness to him, the equipment for this task, and the message itself, centering in forgiveness of sins.

24.25. John notes Thomas' absence but does not explain it. Since Jesus did not rebuke Thomas on the score of his losing interest in his discipleship, it is precarious for us to do so. He may have preferred to be alone in his grief over the Saviour's death. The report of the others concerning their meeting with Jesus emphasized that they had seen the wounded hands and side of the Lord. Thomas demanded not only the sight of these, but the actual touching of them as the condition of believing that Jesus was alive from the dead.

26. A week later, with conditions the same as before, including the shut doors, Jesus came a second time and with the same greeting of **Peace. 27.** By his very language the Lord revealed that he knew what Thomas had asserted. Therefore he must have been alive when the doubting apostle spoke those words about the **hands** and the **side. 28.** His misgivings completely removed, Thomas rose to a mighty declaration of faith in response to Jesus' challenge. **My Lord and my God.** He knew he was in the presence of deity. **29. Because thou hast seen me.** There is nothing to demonstrate that Thomas touched the Saviour. The sight of him had been enough. But what about the multitudes who would not have this opportunity of sight? A blessing is pronounced on such, who dare to make the venture of faith (cf. I Pet 1:8).

F. The Purpose of This Gospel. 20:30, 31. The **signs** which dot the narrative of John have climaxed in the greatest of them all, the Resurrection. Lest the reader think otherwise, the writer hastens to note that the signs were **many.** Only a select few are included in this book. Yet it is the writer's expectation that these will enable the reader to believe that Jesus is the Christ (the object of Jewish expectation, based on OT prophecy, when that expectation is not perverted by false views of Messiahship) and the Son of God, revealing the Father by word and deed, culminating in obedience to the Father's will even unto death. **Believe** includes the ideas of faith's initial act and of progressing in faith as well. **Life through** (more literally, *in)* **his name,** i.e., in union with his own person.

Because this seems a natural conclusion to the Gospel, some scholars have concluded that the next chapter was added later, either by John himself or by another. But there is nothing to demand such a view of the closing chapter. It is full of suggestiveness as to how the Lord's continuing presence and power enable the Church to fulfill its ministry in the world.

VI. Epilogue. 21:1-25.

1. The scene of the post-resurrection appearances shifts from Jerusalem to Galilee. **The sea of Tiberias** – another term for the Sea of Galilee (cf. 6:1). **2. Together.** This is accounted for, not on the basis of a common occupation, but on that of their discipleship and of their experience in seeing Jesus risen from the dead. Peter and John were to figure prominently in the incident about to be related.

3. I go a fishing. Peter could not stand inactivity. The sight of his boat and the waters of his beloved Galilee, and perhaps the necessity of keeping body and soul together, dictated his sudden announcement. It is hazardous to conclude that Peter was going back to fishing as a permanent occupation. To be sure, the infinitive of the verb "to fish" is present tense, which may suggest sustained action. But this is offset by the fact that the verb **I go** suggests an expedition rather than a career. Further, the concurrence of the other disciples makes it clear that they understood Peter's purpose to be temporary. In view of the appearances of the Lord to them (cf. 20:21-23), it is unthinkable that they were reverting to fishing as an occupation. **They caught nothing.** This was providential, preparing the way for Christ's intervention.

4,5. Standing on the shore, Jesus spoke but was not recognized. **Children** may be rendered *lads* without doing violence to the meaning. **Have ye any meat?** The form of the question carries the suspicion that they did not have any. **Meat.** Relish eaten with bread, but also used in the sense of fish. **No.** It hurts a fisherman to admit that he has caught nothing. **6. Cast the net on the right side.** The position of the boat remained the same, the fishing gear was the same, the men were the same, with the same skill; but now their empty nets became full, all because of the word of Christ (see Jn 15:5).

7. The miracle brought quick awareness to the 'beloved disciple' that the stranger must be Jesus. **It is the Lord.** Peter's mind must have flashed back to another time on this same lake when at Jesus' word he let down the net and garnered a great catch of fish (Lk 5:1-11). Peter's eagerness to see Jesus in person suggests that he was not conscious of being out of the will of God in going fishing. **Coat.** It would have been improper to greet the Lord without being fully attired. **8.** The other disciples followed in the dinghy. **Two hundred cubits.** About one hundred yards.

9. Jesus' followers were about to be reminded that the one who grants success in Christian work is also sufficient for the daily needs of his own. **Fish.** A single fish. **Bread.** A single loaf. Jesus would make them suffice, as he had done with the loaves and fishes for the multitude.

10. Bring of the fish which ye have now caught. The purpose was not to augment what was already provided. There is no indication that the fish were prepared and cooked and eaten. Christ wanted the men to get the full thrill of their catch. Generously he said, "which ye have now caught," despite their impotence apart from himself. **11.** The fish were counted, which is customary. Their number simply indicates the greatness of the catch. If there is any symbolism connected with the unbroken net, it is to the effect that those who are won through Christ-directed service will not be lost, but will be preserved to reach the heavenly strand.

12. Dine. The word is especially suitable for breakfast, though used sometimes of other meals. It was a solemn occasion, with the disciples feeling a fresh sense of awe in the presence of the Lord. **14. The third time.** Two other appearances to the disciples as a group are recounted in the previous chapter. The remainder of this appearance concerns almost exclusively Peter and John, though the others profited from the teaching.

15. This scene has sometimes been called 'The Restoration of Peter,' but this may be misleading. Peter had already been restored in the sense of receiving forgiveness (Lk 24:34). But the leadership of an erring disciple could hardly have been accepted for the days ahead, either by Peter or his brethren, apart from Christ's explicit indication. **Lovest thou me?** More important than love for men is love for Christ. **More than these.** Some understand **these** to refer to the paraphernalia of fishing. If this were so, Peter could have answered without any evasion and without the use of a different word for **love** than Jesus used. The very fact that Jesus probed Peter's love in the presence of his brethren suggests that the others were involved. Peter had boasted that he would remain loyal even if the others did not (Mk 14:29). **Feed my lambs.** Christ is unwilling to entrust his little ones to one who does not love him.

16. The second round of question and answer brings a somewhat different commission, at least verbally. **Feed my sheep** is literally, *Shepherd* (or *tend) my sheep.*

17. Peter's grief here may be traced to two things. First, the threefold questioning may well have suggested his threefold denial. Second, Jesus abandoned his word for love (*agapaō*) and used the one Peter employed (*phileō*), a word indicative of warm affection but perhaps considered inferior to the other. This distinction is blunted, however, by the fact that elsewhere in John the second word is used in a very high sense (e.g., 5:20). **My sheep** (cf. 10:14,27). They are precious to the Lord; he gave his life for them. Peter needed love to assume the pastoral office.

18. The acceptance of this commission was to prove costly. Early days in Peter's life were times of freedom. One day this freedom would be withdrawn, but only when Peter was **old.** The prophecy assured him of years of service. **Stretch forth thy hands.** Suitable language for crucifixion. Early church tradition supports this manner of death for Peter. **19. By what** (sort of) **death.** He would be honored by suffering death in the same manner as his Lord. The word **glorify** has been used of the death of Jesus also (12:23). **Follow me.** This led to a physical movement, but much more is implied (cf. 13:36). Peter was being summoned to an undeviating, faithful walk, to set his face like flint, even as Jesus had done in view of the approaching cross.

20. John followed also, without an invitation. Peter noticed it and commented on it. **21.** Being a friend of John, Peter was curious as to what future the Lord had in view for **this man. 22.** The answer of Jesus had one purpose, to rebuke Peter for being distracted over John's future. It was enough for him to be concerned about doing God's will in his own life. This rebuke is suggested by the emphatic **thou,** which is absent from verse 19. **23.** Jesus' words, however, were readily misconstrued as an assurance that John would live on until the Lord's return. The **if** was easily forgotten. John himself corrects this false impression.

24. This. A reference to **that disciple** in verse 23, i.e., John. **Testifieth.** This may point to John's oral testimony of the things contained in the Gospel, in distinction from the fact that he also **wrote** them. **We know.** The identity of these persons who here add their witness to the veracity of John is unknown. Likely they were men associated with John in Ephesus, possibly elders of the church.

25. The thought is an extension of what has already been stated in 20:30. **I suppose.** This is awkward after the plural **we know** of the previous verse. Some think John's secretary permitted himself this closing word. Again we are reminded that our Gospel records are not intended to be full accounts of the activity of our Lord in the days of his flesh.

BIBLIOGRAPHY

BARRET, C. K. *The Gospel According to St. John.* London: S.P.C.K., 1955.

DODD, C. H. *The Interpretation of the Fourth Gospel.* Cambridge: The University Press, 1953.

BERNARD, T. D. *The Central Teaching of Jesus Christ.* New York: Macmillan and Co., 1892.

HOSKYNS, E. C. *The Fourth Gospel.* Edited by F. N. Davey. London: Faber and Faber, Ltd., 1940.

MILLIGAN, WILLIAM and MOULTON, W. F. *Commentary on the Gospel of St. John.* Edinburgh: T. and T. Clark, 1898.

RIGG, W. H. *The Fourth Gospel and Its Message for Today.* London: Lutterworth Press, 1952.

TEMPLE, WILLIAM. *Readings in St. John's Gospel.* London: Macmillan and Co., Ltd., 1950.

WESTCOTT, B. F. *The Gospel According to St. John.* London: John Murray, 1896.

THE ACTS OF THE APOSTLES

INTRODUCTION

Title. The title as we know it was not attached to the original book but belongs to the second century A.D. The Gospel of Luke and The Acts are two volumes of a single work (see Commentary *in loc.*), and whatever title was originally prefixed to the Gospel served for both books. When the second volume began to circulate independently, this title was used to designate its contents.

Author. Neither the Gospel nor The Acts names their author, but he was most probably Luke, a friend and companion of Paul. The clue to authorship is provided by the three "we" sections, where the narrative is in the first person plural (Acts 16:10-17; 20:5–21:18; 27:1–28:16), suggesting that the author was Paul's companion on these three occasions, and is using his travel diary as his source. Some have suggested that this travel document was written by an unknown companion of Paul and incorporated into Acts by a later unknown author. But the uniformity of style between this travel narrative and the rest of Acts and the retention of the first person plural make this most unlikely. Church tradition uniformly identifies Luke as Paul's companion, and the data of The Acts support this tradition.

Date. The date of Acts is linked with the problem of its abrupt ending (see Commentary *in loc.*). We do not *know* when it was written, but a date shortly after the conclusion of the narrative is likely. If so, Acts was written about A.D. 62.

Sources. Aside from his own travel diary, Luke may have used written sources, especially for the earlier chapters of his work. As a companion of Paul, he was in a position to gather firsthand information from the apostle. Furthermore, since Luke was in Palestine during Paul's Caesarean imprisonment (21:18; 27:1), he had ample opportunity to gather information about the early days of the church from eyewitnesses.

Purpose. Luke wrote to assure Theophilus as to "the certainty of those things, wherein thou hast been instructed" (Lk 1:4). Theophilus was probably a Gentile convert to Christianity, and Luke wrote to give him a greater knowledge of Christian origins than he already possessed. This included the story of the life, death, and resurrection of Jesus (the "Gospel"), and the establishment and extension of the church.

Strictly speaking, Luke did not write a *history* of the early church. This is not to suggest that his narration is unhistorical or inaccurate. However, the task of a "historian" is to give a comprehensive narrative of all of the important facts. This, obviously, Luke did not attempt. He tells us nothing about the churches in Galilee (Acts 9:31) or about the evangelization of Egypt or Rome. His story is not The Acts of the Apostles, for only three of the original twelve appear in his narrative—Peter, James, John; and the latter two are only mentioned. The book of Acts is The Acts of Peter and Paul. Furthermore, Peter is practically dropped from the story after the conversion of Cornelius, and we are left wondering what became of him. Again, Luke gives no explanation of the rise of elders in the church (11:30), of how James came to a place of leadership in the Jerusalem church (15:13), of what Paul did in Tarsus after his conversion (9:30; see 11:25), and of many other important historical matters. Furthermore, he passes over some events with a few words (18:19-23) but relates other events in great detail (21:17–26:32). In other words, Luke is telling a story, not writing a "history." His story is that of the main outlines of the extension of the church from Jerusalem to Rome via Samaria, Antioch, Asia, and Europe; and in this story, only Peter and Paul played outstanding roles. The ministry of the other apostles elsewhere in the eastern world was not important to Luke.

Two themes underlie the story of this expansion: the rejection of the Gospel by the Jews and its reception by the Gentiles; and the treatment of the early church by local and Roman officials. Luke's main purpose, therefore, in his two-volume work (Luke-Acts) is to explain to Theophilus how it came about that the Gospel which began with the promise of the restoration of the kingdom to Israel (Lk 1:32,33) ended with the Gentile church in Rome, distinct from Judaism.

Furthermore, Judaism was a religion recognized by Rome. The new religious fellowship that arose within Judaism and yet was not simply a sect in the older religion received the same recognition from Rome as did Judaism. Thus the Christian church became established in the Roman world as a legitimate religion distinct from Judaism.

Acts and the Epistles. The greatest problem in the history of the study of Acts has concerned its trustworthiness in comparison with the epistles of Paul. Luke does not refer to the epistles of Paul, and it is not always easy to correlate Paul's movements, as reflected in his epistles, with Luke's record. The greatest problem is: How can the events of Gal 1:16–2:10 be correlated with the Lukan narrative? Equally good scholars have felt that the visit of Gal 2:1-10 refers to (a) the famine visit of Acts 11:27-30 and (b) the council visit in Acts 15. Many scholars have felt that the narrative of Acts suffers in comparison with the epistles.

A second aspect of the problem is posed by the contrast between the portrait of Paul in Acts and that reflected in the missionary's own epistles. The Paul of Acts appears to be a flexible, reasonable person who was willing to compromise his principles for the sake of expediency (see 16:3; 21:26); while the Paul of the epistles is an inflexible person of unbending convictions (Gal 1:8; 2:3). The older Tübingen school of criticism built its theory of the history of the primitive church around a supposed conflict between Pauline and Judaistic Christianity, and held that The Acts reflects a late stage in the history of the conflict, when a synthesis was being achieved between the two contradictory viewpoints.

It is obviously impossible to deal in any detail with these problems, but they stand in the background of the study and often enter directly into the commentary.

OUTLINE

THE ESTABLISHMENT AND GROWTH OF THE CHURCH

I. Beginnings of the church. 1:1–2:47.
   A. Preparation: The post-resurrection ministry and ascension of Jesus. 1:1-14.
   B. Choice of Matthias. 1:15-26.
   C. Coming of the Holy Spirit. 2:1-41.
   D. Life of the primitive church. 2:42-47.

II. The church in Jerusalem. 3:1–5:42.
   A. A typical miracle and sermon. 3:1-26.
   B. First opposition from Jewish leaders. 4:1-37.
   C. Death of Ananias and Sapphira. 5:1-16.
   D. Second opposition from Jewish leaders. 5:17-42.

III. Extension of the church in Palestine through dispersion. 6:1–12:25.
   A. Choice of the seven. 6:1-7.
   B. Occasion of the dispersion: Ministry and matyrdom of Stephen. 6:8–8:3.
   C. The Gospel in Samaria. 8:4-25.
   D. Conversion of the Ethiopian eunuch. 8:26-40.
   E. Conversion of Saul. 9:1-31.
   F. Peter's ministry in Palestine and the first Gentile converts. 9:32–11:18.
   G. Establishment of a Gentile church at Antioch. 11:19-30.
   H. Persecution by Herod Agrippa I. 12:1-25.

IV. Extension of the church in Asia Minor and Europe. 13:1–21:17.
   A. First mission, Galatia. 13:1–14:28.
   B. Problem of the Gentile church, and council in Jerusalem. 15:1-35.
   C. Second mission, Asia Minor and Europe. 15:36–18:22.
   D. Third mission, Asia Minor and Europe. 18:23–21:17.

V. Extension of the church to Rome. 21:18–28:31.
   A. Rejection of the Gospel by Jerusalem. 21:18–26:32.
   B. Reception of the Gospel in Rome. 27:1–28:31.

COMMENTARY

I. Beginnings of the Church. 1:1–2:47.

A. Preparation. The Post-resurrection Ministry and Ascension of Jesus. 1:1-14.

1,2. The first two verses constitute a brief introduction that ties Acts to the Gospel of Luke. The introductory verses of the Gospel (Lk 1:1-4) are meant to serve both for the Gospel and for Acts; Acts 1:1,2 is a kind of secondary introduction that looks back to Lk 1:1-4. **The former treatise.** The Gospel of Luke. Acts is the second part of a two-volume work, Luke-Acts. The Gospel contains all that Jesus **began both to do and teach;** Acts traces the continued ministry of the ascended Christ through the Holy Spirit working in the apostles. We do not know who **Theophilus** was, whether a Christian who needed further instruction or an interested pagan (see Lk 1:3).

2. This reference to the Holy Spirit sounds the chief theological note of The Acts—the work of the Holy Spirit.

3. Our Lord's post-resurrection ministry of forty days had a twofold objective: to provide a positive demonstration of the reality of his resurrection, and to give further explanation of his teaching about the **kingdom of God.** We may therefore expect this theme to reappear in the apostles' ministry. The good news about the kingdom of God was the content of Philip's message in Samaria (8:12), of Paul's preaching and teaching in Ephesus (20:25), and of Paul's message to both Jews and Gentiles in Rome when he finally reached that city (28:23,31).

4. The command of Lk 24:49 is here repeated. Since the ministry of the apostles was to be the work of the Holy Spirit, they were to wait in Jerusalem until the promise of the coming of the Holy Spirit—given by the Father in the OT (Joel 2:28; Ezk 36:27) and confirmed through the Son—should be fulfilled. The word translated **assembled together** is of uncertain meaning and may also be rendered "eating with" or "lodging with."

5. The ministry of John the Baptist, baptizing men **with water,** was preparatory for the coming of Messiah. The greater reality, the baptism of **the Holy Spirit,** would shortly take place.

6. This verse expands the last words of verse 3. To the Jews of the first century, the **kingdom** of God meant an earthly, political kingdom for Israel. At one point in our Lord's ministry, the people were prepared to take Jesus by force and compel him to become their king (Jn 6:15). However, Christ's mission was not to bring the kingdom in earthly splendor but to bring it in spiritual power. This was a difficult lesson for the disciples to learn. During the forty days, one of their main questions was whether Jesus would soon establish this earthly kingdom through Israel.

7. Jesus replied that the answer to this question was no present concern of theirs. **Times** and **seasons** probably refer to the time which must elapse before the final establishment of God's kingdom, and to the character of the events that will accompany its establishment. The Father has determined these events **by his own authority** (RSV). This does not mean that God is through with Israel; Romans 11:26 says that all Israel shall be saved. The NT tells us almost nothing about the time and manner of the future salvation of Israel.

8. Rather than devoting themselves to questions about the final establishment of the Jewish kingdom, the apostles were to have a different concern. The Holy Spirit was to come upon them and to give them supernatural power, in the strength of which they would be witnesses of Christ throughout all the world. This verse is a table of contents of the book of Acts: **in Jerusalem** covers chapters 1–7; **in all Judea, and in Samaria** covers chapters 8:1–11:18; and **unto the uttermost part of the earth** covers 11:19 to the end of the book.

9. The **cloud** that received Christ upon his ascension was not merely a cloud of condensed vapor but was a symbol of the Shekinah glory which represents the glorious presence of God (Ex 33:7-11; 40:34; Mk 9:7). The ascension of Christ meant that he had broken off visible fellowship with his disciples on earth, and, still bearing his resurrected body, had entered into the invisible world of God's dwelling.

10. White is the color of angels' garb (Mt 28:3; Jn 20:12).

11. The angels informed the apostles that this experience was no repetition of the Transfiguration (Lk 9:27-36). Jesus had left them, but one day he would return to the earth in the same visible, glorious way in which he had departed. The expectation of the bodily return of Christ is central in Christian faith.

12. The Ascension had taken place from the **Mount of Olives,** which stands directly east of Jerusalem, about three thousand feet away. This was the distance permitted to a Jew to walk on the Sabbath day without breaking the Sabbath rest.

13. This upper room may have been the scene of the Last Supper (Lk 22:12) and was possibly located in the house of Mary, the mother of Mark (Acts 12:12). For other lists of the Twelve, see Mt 10:2 ff.; Mk 3:16 ff.; Lk 6:14 ff. **Simon Zelotes.** Simon the Cananaean. **Zelotes** *(the zealot)* may refer to the fervent character of Simon, but it more likely indicates that he belonged to a nationalistic party among the Jews that advocated open rebellion against Rome.

14. His brethren. Jesus' half-brothers (Mt 13:55), who did not believe in him before his death (Jn 7:5) but who were brought to faith by his resurrection. A resurrection appearance to James is recorded in I Cor 15:7. **The women** may designate either the wives of the disciples or the women mentioned in Lk 8:2; 24:10.

B. Choice of Matthias. 1:15-26. The apostolic college had been broken by the defection of Judas, and the apostles felt the need of choosing a man to take his place.

15. Peter now emerged as the natural leader among the 120 believers, who are called **brethren** *(disciples,* AV, is the reading of an inferior text). **Names** (AV) is a Semitic expression meaning persons (RSV) or individuals. **16.** Peter reminded the company that Judas' betrayal of Jesus was not an unforeseen tragedy but was in the providential purposes of God and therefore foretold in the OT (see v. 20).

18,19. These verses are a note inserted by Luke into his record of Peter's remarks to explain to his readers Judas' fate. According to Mt 27:7, the high priests bought this field; but apparently they did so in the name of Judas, since the money was legally his. **Falling headlong** should possibly be translated *swelling up,* and refers to a fatal rupture. Augustine interprets this passage to mean, "he fastened a rope around his neck and, falling on his face, burst asunder in the midst." **Aceldama.** An Aramaic word meaning *field of blood.*

20. Peter quoted freely from Ps 69:25; 109:8. **Bishopric** means *office of overseer,* in a nontechnical sense.

21,22. The qualifications for Judas' successor in the apostolic college were two: he must have been a companion of Jesus, and he must have been a witness of Jesus' resurrection. There is no reference to ordination in these verses. **23.** We have no other information about these two equally qualified candidates.

24-26. Such a choice by the casting of lots had an OT precedent (Prov 16:33), but it occurs nowhere else in the NT and is not normative for Christian practice. **That he might go to his own place.** Judas experienced the fate he deserved for his incredible treachery. Judas' place was filled not because he had died but because he had defected. When James, the brother of John, was executed (Acts 12:2), his place was not filled. The **Lord** to whom prayer was addressed (1:24) was probably the ascended Jesus, for he who had chosen the original twelve (v. 2) was now asked to choose another. **Lord** is the usual word in the Greek OT to designate God; it was used from the earliest days of the Church to designate the ascended Jesus.

C. Coming of the Holy Spirit. 2:1-41. There is a real sense in which the Church had its birthday on the day of Pentecost, when the Holy Spirit was given to men in a new way to bring believers in Jesus together into a new relationship.

1. Pentecost, meaning *fiftieth,* is the Greek word for the Feast of (seven) Weeks described in Lev 23:15-22, which celebrated the conclusion of the harvest.

2. All the 120 disciples were gathered together in one body and **in one place**—probably the upper room (1:13). **With one accord** is the reading of an inferior text. The **sound from heaven** was **like** [that of] **a rushing mighty wind.** It was not a wind; it sounded **like** a wind. *Pneuma* can mean both wind and spirit; and wind is a symbol of the Spirit's power and also of his invisibility (Jn 3:8). What was seen was not actually tongues of fire but **tongues like fire. 3.** The visible sign was something that could only be likened to a flame of fire that **divided** into separate tongues which rested upon the individual disciples. Many understand this to be the fulfillment of John's promise of baptism with fire (Lk 3:16). However, no fire was present at Pentecost but something **like** fire; and the context in the Gospel suggests that the baptism of fire is the judgment of those who reject Messiah—the burning of the chaff with unquenchable fire.

4. As the Holy Spirit was given to men, the disciples were baptized (1:5) and at the same time **filled with the Holy Spirit.** The baptism of the Spirit is described in I Cor 12:13. It is the work of the Holy Spirit to join people of diverse racial and social backgrounds into one body—the body of Jesus Christ, which is his Church. In the strict sense of the word, Pentecost was the birthday of the Church. This baptism of the Spirit was never repeated. It was later extended to believers in Samaria (Acts 8), to the Gentiles (chs. 10; 11), and to the disciples of John the Baptist (19:1-6). The filling of the Spirit was often repeated, but not the baptism with the Spirit.

5. The disciples had now apparently moved down from the upper room to an open place in the city, possibly within the temple area, where a crowd assembled. The **devout men** were Diaspora Jews, who had been scattered throughout the Mediterranean world but who had returned to the Holy City to live.

6. The **other tongues** (v. 4). Not the language of religious ecstasy. By a miracle the language of the apostles was translated by the Holy Spirit into many diverse languages without a human translator. This phenomenon is not the same as the *glossolalia* or gift of tongues in I Cor 12; 14, which were unintelligible until interpreted. Possibly the Holy Spirit acted as interpreter at Pentecost, so that various language groups heard their own tongue without the mediation of a human interpreter. **7.** It was an amazing thing that these men whose accent showed them to be Galilean Jews appeared capable of speaking many foreign languages. **9-11.** These countries formed a circuit around the entire Mediterranean Sea. Most of these peoples could speak the popular Greek of the Hellenistic world, but they also spoke their native tongues (cf. 14:11). **Strangers of Rome. Jews** and Gentile converts **(proselytes)** from Rome, who were only temporarily residing in Jerusalem.

12,13. All of the hearers were **at a loss** (*in doubt*, AV) to understand what was happening. The accusation of drunkenness suggests that an ecstatic element as well as foreign languages was present in this first gift of tongues. **14.** A large crowd had assembled because of this commotion (v. 6), probably in the outer court of the temple area. Peter offered an explanation of what had occurred before their eyes and then moved on to a proclamation of the Gospel, which was embodied essentially in the announcement of the Messiahship of Jesus.

15. Peter first disposed of the suggestion that the disciples were drunk by pointing out that it was only nine o'clock in the morning and therefore too early for people to have become drunken. **16.** It was not spirits but the Holy Spirit that had taken possession of them. Peter quoted Joel 2:28-31, which foretells the outpouring of the Holy Spirit upon Israel in the Messianic era. It is important to note that a prophecy which in Joel was addressed to the nation Israel now had its fulfillment in the Christian church. However, in God's redemptive purpose, Israel is also to be included in the fulfillment of this prophecy (Rom 11:26).

17. The last days is not found in the prophecy of Joel but was added by Peter under divine inspiration. In the OT this phrase designates the Messianic era of the kingdom of God (Isa 2:2; Hos 3:5). The age of the Gospel is therefore one stage in the realization of the blessings of the Messianic age. In the OT era, the Holy Spirit was given primarily to people who occupied official positions in the theocracy of Israel—kings, priests, and prophets. The new mission of the Holy Spirit was to rest upon **all flesh,** that is, upon all of God's people and not only upon the official leaders. The promise that this new outpouring of the Spirit would result in a new manifestation of **prophecy, of visions,** and of **dreams,** was fulfilled in the experience of the apostles and prophets of the NT era. It was the Jewish belief that the Holy Spirit, who had inspired the OT prophets with their message, had been silent during the Inter-Testamental Period. Peter asserted that the Holy Spirit had now become active again in a new manifestation of God's redemptive purpose. This is seen in the last words of Acts 2:18, where Peter added to the prophecy of Joel the statement, **and they shall prophesy.** This new manifestation of prophecy was not so much foretelling the future as forth-telling the meaning of God's redemptive work through Jesus the Messiah.

19,20. The last half of this prophecy from Joel was not fulfilled in Peter's day as was the outpouring of the Spirit. The **day of the Lord.** The day of Christ's coming in glory to establish his kingdom in the world with power and glory. This final consummation will be attended by a judgment that will fall upon the earthly order, and out of the cosmic catastrophe will emerge a new redeemed order of nature and the world (Rom 8:21). The last days are thus distinguished from the Day of the Lord.

21. This outpouring of the Holy Spirit will bring about a great day of salvation, and whoever **calls on the name of the Lord shall be saved. Lord** in Joel refers to God, but Peter and the early church applied this to the exalted Jesus.

22,23. Peter reviewed the life and death of Jesus to show that it was no mere accident but occurred within the redemptive plan of God. In spite of the fact that God had attested Christ by **miracles and wonders and signs . . . in the midst of** the Jews, they had turned him over to the **hands of lawless men** (RSV), the Romans, who ignored God's law, to have him **crucified and slain.** While neither the Romans nor the Jews were absolved from guilt, the death of Jesus had taken place in accordance with the **definite plan** (RSV) **and foreknowledge of God.**

24. Although human judges had put Jesus to death, a higher court had raised him from the dead, since it was impossible that the Messiah should remain under the power of death. **25-28.** Peter next proved that the death of the Christ was a part of God's redemptive plan by showing that it was foreseen in the OT Scriptures. He quoted from Ps 16:8-11, a passage which in its own context refers to David and his hope of salvation from death. Even in death, David expected to behold the face of the Lord. He therefore could submit to the experience of death in hope that God would not **abandon his soul to Hades** (Sheol), the abode of the dead after death, nor permit him to **see the corruption** of the grave. Since God is the God of the living, in spite of the fact that the OT has no full revelation of life after death, David was confident that God would show him the **ways of life** and bring him into the fullness of joy in the Divine presence even after death.

29. The apostle made it clear that these verses could not refer to David, since David in fact died and experienced corruption. Indeed, his **grave** could be seen south of the city of Jerusalem. The psalmist, therefore, must have referred to David's greater son, the Messiah. **30,31.** Hence the psalmist spoke prophetically of one of **his descendants** (RSV), the Christ, who would be seated **on David's throne.** In these words of David, Peter found a prophecy of the resurrection of Christ. **32.** The resurrection of the Messiah, foreseen by the psalmist, could now be attested by the experience of the apostles.

33. Jesus had not only been raised from the dead; he had also been **exalted at the right hand of God** (RSV cf. v. 34) and had from this exalted position **poured out** upon his people the gift of the Holy Spirit foretold by Joel. **34,35.** Peter again quoted from the Psalms (110:1) to show that the exaltation of Christ was also in the prophetic Scriptures. The Lord God had said to David's Lord, the Messiah, that he should sit at God's right hand until all of his enemies were subdued. From these verses we must conclude that Christ is even now enthroned in the heavens and in a real sense is exercising his Messianic reign (Rev 3:21).

36. The heart of the Gospel is this: that Jesus, raised from the dead and exalted at the right hand of God, has been made both **Lord and Messiah.** His Messiahship means Lordship; he reigns at the right hand of God as Lord and King. The fulfillment of the Messianic office is realized in a new and unexpected way. The Lordship of Christ was the cardinal doctrine of primitive Christianity. Jesus entered into the exercise of his Lordship by virtue of his exaltation (Phil 2:9-11), and salvation is to be found in confessing Jesus as Lord (Rom 10:9).

37 Peter's hearers were both convinced and convicted. They were **cut to the heart** (RSV) by the realization that they had put to death God's Messiah, and they therefore asked what they might do to be delivered from this awful guilt.

38. Peter replied that God's mercy could forgive even this sin. A twofold response was required: **to repent** and **to be baptized in the name of Jesus the Christ.** To repent would mean to turn rightabout-face from their sinful ways and confess faith in Jesus as their Messiah. Baptism would be the public evidence of this repentant spirit. The result would be the **forgiveness of** their **sins** and the reception of the **gift of the Holy Spirit.** The reception of the Holy Spirit is not dependent upon baptism, but it follows baptism, which is the outward and visible sign of a penitent spirit. In the early church, converts were baptized without delay. So being baptized and receiving the Spirit were practically simultaneous.

39. This new age of Messianic blessing, Peter explained, would bestow the Holy Spirit not only upon such leaders as prophets, priests, and kings, but upon all who would repent, upon their descendants, and even upon those outside the family of Israel, even all whom God should call to salvation. **The gift of the Holy Spirit.** The gift of the Spirit himself, not some gift which the Spirit bestows.

40,41. The apostle thereupon exhorted his hearers to save themselves from **this crooked generation,** which had put Jesus to death, by accepting his plea to repent and his testimony that Jesus was their Messiah. The result was that some three thousand received his word and were baptized upon profession of their faith and were added to the fellowship of the little circle of believers. There is no indication that the apostles laid hands on these new converts in order that they might receive the Holy Spirit.

D. Life of the Primitive Church. 2:42-47. Luke now gives a brief sketch of the life and character of the early Christian community.

42. The **apostles' doctrine** or *teaching*. The teaching of the Lord, together with the proclamation of the life, death, and resurrection of Jesus and its meaning for man's salvation. This teaching was an authoritative tradition in the early church and later found embodiment in our New Testament. These early believers found delight in **fellowship** with one another, particularly in the **breaking of bread** (which probably consisted of a fellowship meal, together with the Lord's Supper) and in regular times of united prayer. **43.** The character of the early Christian community aroused in the people a sense of awe, that was reinforced by many miracles performed by the apostles.

44,45. So devoted to one another were those in the first Christian fellowship that wealthy believers sold their possessions to help care for the necessities of the poor members. Christian love manifested itself in a social program of material support for the poor. This Christian sharing seems to have been limited to the early years of the Jerusalem church and was not extended into new churches as the Gospel was carried beyond Judea.

46. The believers were still Jews continuing daily worship of God in the Temple in accordance with the Jewish practice. There was no thought of withdrawing from Judaism and establishing a separate movement. Their Christian fellowship manifested itself particularly in fellowship meals, conducted in various homes. Joyfulness and generosity of heart were two of the outstanding characteristics of the early Christians.

47. Not all the Jews received the witness to the Messiahship of the resurrected Jesus, but even those who rejected it looked upon the early Christian fellowship with great favor. The result was that the Lord was daily adding to the new fellowship those who received the witness, and the Christian community received them as fellow believers.

II. The Church in Jerusalem. 3:1–5:42.

The primitive church at first showed no inclination to embark upon a mission of world-wide evangelization. The first Christians were Jews living in Jerusalem as Jews who had found in Jesus the fulfillment of OT prophecy. Luke selects several episodes illustrating these early years.

A. A Typical Miracle and Sermon. 3:1-26. The healing of the lame man was one of many such miracles, but it was of singular importance because it provided the occasion for a typical sermon that illustrates the content of the apostolic preaching to the Jews. This in turn led to the first opposition from the Jewish leaders.

1. Peter and **John,** the brother of James, are frequently mentioned as the two leading apostles in the early church. The disciples continued to engage in Jewish worship of God in the **temple.** The **ninth hour,** or 3:00 P.M., was a time of prayer accompanying the evening sacrifice.

2. The apostles proceeded through the vast Court of the Gentiles to the gate called **Beautiful,** which led into the Court of the Women, where they found a lame man who was laid there day after day to beg. **6-8.** Peter had no money to offer him, but he gave him something far better—strength for his crippled legs and feet. The healing was instantaneous; and the healed man accompanied the apostles into the Temple, leaping into the air in joy over his new-found strength, and shouting out praises to God. **9,10.** His shouts drew a crowd of people, who were amazed to behold the man whom they had daily seen at the Beautiful Gate now jumping up and down with joy.

11. Peter used this miracle as another occasion to bear witness to the saving power of Jesus. Apparently, after the service of prayer and sacrifice, Peter and John, together with the lame man, proceeded to the covered colonnade on the eastern side of the Court of the Gentiles, which was called **Solomon's porch** (AV) or *portico* (RSV). Here the crowd gathered and Peter addressed them.

12. Peter first disclaimed any credit for the miracle. It was not through the apostles' **power** or **godliness** that the invalid had been healed.

13. It was the God of Israel, the God who had given the promises to the fathers, who had performed this miracle. The man had been healed because God had **glorified his servant Jesus** by his resurrection and ascension. **Son** (AV) is better translated *servant* (RSV), for the word refers to the servant of the Lord prophesied in Isa 52:13–53:12. Jesus could only be glorified after he had been **delivered up and denied** by the Jews before the Roman governor, **Pilate.**

14. The Holy One and the **Righteous One** were titles sometimes used to describe the Messiah. What an unthinkable crime that the Jews should demand the release of a murderer and criminal to put to death the Holy and Righteous One! **15. Prince of life.** Better, *Author of life.* Peter designated Jesus as the source and origin of life. Him the Jews tried to destroy, but God reversed their verdict by raising him from the dead. **16.** The structure of this verse is awkward both in English and in Greek, but its meaning is clear. The name of Jesus did not possess a magical power, but **faith in his name** brought healing.

17. The monstrous crime of murdering Jesus can be forgiven, for Peter admits that the Jews and their rulers did not realize that they were putting to death God's Messiah. **18.** The OT does not foretell a suffering Messiah, although it does predict a suffering servant of the Lord (Isa 53). After his resurrection, Jesus showed the disciples that these prophecies referred to his passion. **Christ.** Not a proper name here but the title meaning *Messiah.*

19. Peter now challenged the Jews to repent of their sins and to turn to God. **Be converted** (AV). *Turn around* from sin to God. This would mean reversing their verdict about Jesus and confessing him as God's Messiah. The result would be the **blotting out** of their sins and the enjoyment of the **times of refreshment** promised by the OT prophets.

20. The conversion of Israel will mean the return of the Messiah. It is the purpose of God to bring salvation to Israel before the coming of God's kingdom (Rom 11:26), and Peter pled with Israel to receive this salvation.

21. Jesus' death, resurrection, and ascension are not the end of his redemptive work. He is to come again in power and to establish a new order free from evil and sin. This restoration will include the redemption of nature (Rom 8:18-23) as well as the perfecting of human society when God's will is done on earth as it is in heaven. **The times of refreshing** are a present blessing; the **establishing of all that God** spoke . . . **by his holy prophets** is a future blessing; but both are the result of the redeeming work of the Messiah.

22,23. These days of which Peter speaks were foretold as far back as **Moses,** who prophesied that God would raise up another prophet like himself (Deut 18:15-19), who would bring the word of God to his people with authority. The threat contained in verse 23 is combined from Deut 18:19 and Lev 23:29. **24,25.** These days of redemption that Peter was proclaiming were the constant theme of the prophets from the time of Samuel. The Jews were the sons of the prophets and of the covenant made with Abraham and were therefore the natural heirs of these Messianic promises.

26. While the promise of Abraham included the Gentile peoples, the blessings of the Messiah have been offered to the natural heirs of the covenant **first,** to turn them from their iniquities. **Son** (AV) is the word found in 3:13, meaning *servant* (RSV). **Raised up** refers to the historical appearance of Jesus rather than to his resurrection.

B. First Opposition from Jewish Leaders. 4:1-37. One of the main purposes of Acts is to show that the Jews who rejected and crucified Jesus continued their rebellion against God by rejecting the gospel of the resurrected and ascended Jesus proclaimed by the apostles. This chapter describes the beginning of this opposition, which culminated with the plots of the Jews to kill Paul on his last visit to Jerusalem (23:12-15; 25:1-3).

1. Such a large crowd gathered in Solomon's Porch that the temple police intervened. **The priests** belonged to a Jewish party called the **Sadducees.** They disagreed with the Pharisees over the interpretation of the Law and also denied the doctrine of resurrection and of the existence of angels and demons. The **captain of the temple** was a high officer next in authority to the high priest and had responsibility for the preservation of order in the Temple.

2. The Sadducees were **annoyed** (RSV) because Peter and John persistently proclaimed that Jesus had been raised from the dead and announced on the basis of his resurrection the hope of resurrection for men. The Pharisees believed in a future resurrection. The apostles declared that God had now provided a new ground for this hope.

3. Since it was late in the day, the temple police, under the direction of the priests, seized the two disciples and put them in prison for the night. **4.** Luke inserts the comment that these events had great effect upon the people, and many believed, so that the number of believers reached five thousand.

5,6. The next morning the Sanhedrin assembled. This was the highest court of the Jews, and was composed of **rulers** or priests, **elders,** and **scribes. Scribes.** The professional students and teachers of the OT. Their disciples were called Pharisees. At this time **Caiaphas** was the presiding high priest and president of the Sanhedrin. His father-in-law, **Annas,** was the former high priest and a sort of elder statesman. The term **high priest,** or better *chief priest,* can be applied to various members of the families from which the high priests came. We know nothing about **John** or **Alexander.**

7. Peter and John were brought before the Sanhedrin and challenged to say by what authority laymen like themselves acted as they had. **8-10.** Peter experienced a fresh enduement of the Spirit for his defense. He pointed out that he had done nothing but good to a crippled man. The former cripple was standing with Peter and John, and Peter declared his healing in the name of Jesus Christ of Nazareth, not by any **power** resident in the apostles themselves.

11,12. Peter was presumably defending himself, but he now turned from defense and began to proclaim the Gospel. He quoted from Ps 118:22, asserting that Christ was the **stone** which the **builders** of the Jewish nation **rejected** but which God had made the most important stone in the building. Furthermore, he said that there was salvation in Him alone; and that if the Jews rejected the saving power of His name, there would be no other way for them to find salvation. Destruction must fall on both them and the nation. **Head of the corner** may designate either the keystone in the foundation or the top corner at the juncture of two walls. **Salvation** here probably refers to life in the age to come.

13. Such speech amazed the Sanhedrin. **Unlearned and ignorant** does not refer to their intelligence or literacy but to the fact that they were not schooled in the tradition of the scribes but were, in fact, laymen. It was an uncommon thing for unschooled laymen to speak with such effectiveness and authority. The rulers already knew that Peter and John were disciples of Jesus, but they now recalled the fact that Jesus, too, although he was unlearned in the scribal traditions (Jn 7:15), had nevertheless amazed the people with the authority with which he spoke (Mk 1:22). Something of this same authority was now reflected in his disciples, and the miracle which had been performed upon the lame man made it difficult to deny the effectiveness of this authority.

15-17. The two disciples were now sent out while the members of the Sanhedrin deliberated. Though Peter and John had broken no law, they were gaining a dangerous popularity. The Sanhedrin decided that the only possible action was to threaten them and to command them to preach no more in the name of Jesus. The Sanhedrin took no steps whatsoever, as F. F. Bruce has pointed out *(Commentary on the Book of Acts),* to disprove the central assertion of the apostles' preaching—that Jesus had been raised from the dead. The preaching of the apostles could easily have been frustrated had their proclamation of the Resurrection been proved false. The body of Jesus had vanished so completely that the Sanhedrin was utterly helpless to refute their message.

18. When Peter and John were recalled into the Sanhedrin, they were not punished but were commanded to break off all preaching in the name of Jesus. **19,20.** The apostles answered that when they were required to choose between the will of God and the decree of men, they had no choice but to obey God.

21. The apostles had gained such popularity that the Sanhedrin dared not risk stirring up the anger of the people by punishing them. Furthermore, the Sadducees did not have the support of the people as did the Pharisees, and they had to be careful of public opinion.

22. The wonder of the miracle lay in the fact that this man was over forty years old.

24. A prayer meeting followed, in which the believers did not ask God to deliver them from future trouble and persecution but praised him because he is the ruler over all. They addressed him as **Sovereign Lord** (RSV), not simply *Lord* (AV). **25,26.** The Christians experienced the persecution predicted in Ps 2:1-3. The rulers opposed both God and his **Anointed** One or *Messiah.* **27.** The believers again referred to Jesus as the

holy Servant who was also the Anointed One. To them **Herod Antipas,** tetrarch over Galilee and Perea, represented the kings of the earth. **Pontius Pilate,** Roman governor of Judea, represented the rulers. The other opponents in the psalm they identified as the Romans **(Gentiles)** and the **people of Israel. 28.** Back of these evil acts of wicked men, they knew, lay the **predetermined plan** of God. **29,30.** The Christians did not pray for safety or protection but that, in the face of opposition, they might be faithful in proclaiming God's word.

31. The response to their prayer was a fresh infilling of the Holy Spirit, which was manifested in their fearless proclamation of the word of God. This was not, however, a fresh baptism of the Spirit.

32. Verses 32-37 contain another summary of the character of the early Christian fellowship similar to that in 2:42-47. One of the outstanding characteristics of this Spirit-filled church was unity, a sense of oneness that manifested itself in the sharing of material resources. **34.** To meet the needs of poor Christians, the more wealthy believers sold their lands or houses and brought the money to be used for the common welfare. **35.** The apostles supervised this ministry of love, which was carried out not on the basis of equality but on the basis of personal need. **36,37.** One Christian is singled out for special attention: **Joseph,** a Jewish Christian from the island of Cyprus, who had relatives in Jerusalem (cf. 12:12; Col 4:10). His surname, **Barnabas** may mean either *son of consolation* or *son of encouragement* or *exhortation*. Such surnames were often given to people to indicate their character.

C. Death of Ananias and Sapphira. 5:1-16. This incident shows us that the primitive church was not free from internal problems. Luke does not try to gloss over the situation but relates the event with black colors.

1,2. Sapphira in the Aramaic tongue means *beautiful*. Like Barnabas, she and her husband sold a **piece of property.** Ananias, with his wife's **knowledge** (RSV), determined upon the plan of bringing only part of the money to the apostles, but pretending that they were giving all. **3.** We are not told how Peter recognized this deception; it was probably by divine illumination. Peter charged Ananias not with deceiving him but with attempting to deceive the Holy Spirit. The Holy Spirit is obviously a person, and verse 4 shows that the Holy Spirit is also God.

4. The program of sharing wealth in the early church was a purely voluntary one and not compulsory. While the land remained in Ananias' possession, it was his alone to dispose of as he chose; and even after he had sold it, the money was his to do with as he pleased. Ananias' sin did not consist in his keeping back the money, but in his pretending a complete consecration to God while deliberately keeping back part of the money. This was the sin of an insincere consecration, for it meant lying to God.

5. When faced with the enormity of his sin, Ananias was completely overcome and immediately fell down and **breathed out** his life. We are not told what caused this stroke. Certainly Peter did not invoke his death. Whether or not Ananias expired from emotional shock, it was a judgment of God upon hypocritical consecration. **6.** In ancient times in the Orient, since decomposition of dead bodies began almost immediately, burial followed death without delay.

7. Sapphira must have been removed from the scene by some distance, else the news of her husband's death would have reached her sooner. **9.** Peter charged her with complicity in trifling with God. To **tempt** God (Ex 17:2; Deut 6:16), that is, to see how far one can go in presuming upon God's goodness, is a fearful sin. This was one of the temptations that our Lord faced (Mt 4:7). **10.** The same fate that struck Ananias overtook Sapphira, and she fell down and expired. There is no reason to believe that Ananias and Sapphira were not saved persons. Their physical death was a divine judgment upon them which did not involve the question of their salvation. The very fact that they were believers determined the enormity of their sin. They were pretending to "surrender all" but were deliberately holding back from God. This is a sin that can be committed only by a Christian.

11. This event brought great awe and fear of God into the church and exercised a purifying influence. Here for the first time in Acts the word for church, *ekklēsia*, appears. It means, *called out*, and refers to the calling out of Greek citizens from their homes to the public assembly for civic purposes. The word is taken over by the Greek OT and used of Israel as the people of God. Its use in the NT therefore indicates that the

Church is the new people of God. The word is never used of a building. It designates both the church at large (5:11; 9:31; 20:28) and local congregations of believers (11:26; 13:1).

12. The early Christians did not have their own building for worship but met in Solomon's Porch, which bordered the east side of the vast temple area.

13,14. The death of Ananias and Sapphira had such a purifying influence that no one dared for purely human reasons to unite with the new fellowship. However, the church was held in high regard by the people. Only those who experienced a genuine, saving work of God dared to unite with the church; but there were great numbers of such believers.

D. Second Opposition from Jewish Leaders. 5:17-42. The popularity of the believers brought them again to the attention of the high priest and the Sadducees. One of the central motifs of Acts is the rejection of the Gospel by the Jewish nation. This section traces a further step in rejection and persecution by the Jewish officials.

17. Sect means simply *party* and carries no unfavorable connotations, as does the modern word. **18.** This time all the apostles were seized and put into prison overnight to await a hearing before the Sanhedrin in the morning. **19,20.** The apostles were supernaturally released during the night and were encouraged to continue witnessing to the people about the way of life and salvation. **This Life.** An unusual designation of the Christian message.

21. Early in the morning the Sanhedrin or **council** (which is also called the **senate**), consisting of both Sadducees and Pharisees, assembled and sent for the apostles to appear before them. **22,23.** The guards went to the prison and found everything undisturbed, the doors locked and sentries alert; but the apostles had completely vanished. **24.** The **captain of the temple** police was a member of the Sanhedrin. **Chief priests.** Heads of the several high priestly families and priests who had previously held the office of high priest and who continued to retain the title. These officials of the Sanhedrin apparently felt that the Christians had won converts within the circle of the temple guards, and it looked as though this new movement would grow out of hand.

25. In the midst of the deliberations, word came to the Sanhedrin that the apostles were again publicly **teaching the people** in the Temple. **26.** The **captain** of the police, with his subordinates, persuaded the apostles to accompany the guard peaceably to the Sanhedrin. The captain dared not use violence in taking the apostles for fear of violent reaction from the people, who highly regarded these preachers and healers.

27,28. The apostles accompanied the police from the temple area to the meeting place of the Sanhedrin. The high priest charged them with two offenses: first, they had disobeyed the earlier injunction of the Sanhedrin to discontinue their teaching in the name of Jesus. Second, they were trying to bring against the Sanhedrin public blame for the crucifixion of Jesus. The apostles, of course, had no such intention, but their preaching of the cross gave this impression.

29. Peter replied that such an injunction from the Sanhedrin really confronted them with the choice of obeying men or obeying God. **30.** In such a situation, only one choice was possible, especially since God had raised Jesus from the dead, whom the Jewish leaders had slain. By the expression, **God of our fathers,** Peter showed that he still regarded himself as a Jew. The early church did not break fellowship with the Jews but existed as a fellowship within Judaism. **31.** While the Jews had inflicted upon Jesus the degradation of the cross (Deut 21:23), God had bestowed upon him the highest honor by making him a **Prince** (AV) or *Leader* (RSV) and **Saviour. Prince** is the same word translated "Author" in Acts 3:15.

32. The apostles' proclamation was grounded in the fact that they had witnessed the things of which they spoke. Furthermore, they did not speak merely as private individuals, but their witness was empowered by the Holy Spirit, who spoke through them. The Holy Spirit had been given not only to the apostles but to all who would obey him.

33. These words of Peter cut the priests to the quick and angered them. The word translated **cut** means *to saw in two.* The Sadducean wing of the Sanhedrin immediately laid plans to put the apostles to death. **34.** Their evil purpose was frustrated by a scribe and **teacher of the law** *(doctor,* AV) named Gamaliel. Josephus, the Jewish historian, tells us that the party of the Pharisees was small in number but commanded such popularity and influence among the people that the Sadducees dared not take any action that the Pharisees opposed. The influence of Gamaliel's advice reflects this situation. Furthermore, Gamaliel was one of the most noted rabbis of the time. Saul of Tarsus had been his disciple (22:3), and he was widely known as the greatest teacher of the Law in his day.

35. Gamaliel warned the Sadducees, who were bent upon taking action without the support of the Pharisaic majority, against rash action.

36. He cited recent historical events to remind them that there had been other movements among the Jews that amounted to nothing, and that therefore they should have no fear of this new group who proclaimed Jesus to be Messiah. Josephus says that there were many such movements in those days of unrest. Gamaliel recalled one Theudas, who claimed to be a person of great importance and who persuaded some four hundred Jews to follow him. This movement was crushed and Theudas slain. We know nothing else about this man. About A.D. 45, a magician by the same name led a large number of Jews to the Jordan River, promising that he could separate the waters so that they could walk across the river on dry ground. The Roman governor, Crispus Fadus, sent horsemen and crushed the movement. This false messiah, however, was a different person from the one mentioned by Gamaliel.

37. Another insurrection was made by **Judas of Galilee.** When Herod Archelaus, one of the sons of Herod the Great (Mt 2:1,22), was deposed from the governorship of Judea, the country was placed under a Roman governor; and a **census** was held to determine the amount of tribute to be exacted from the people for Rome. This Judas stirred up a religious and nationalistic revolt on the grounds that God alone was Israel's king and He alone had the right to rule over the Jewish people. This movement was the beginning of what later became the Zealots; but the revolt under Judas was crushed by Rome.

38,39. Gamaliel counseled the Sanhedrin to trust God's providence. If God was in the movement, it would prosper; otherwise it would fail.

40. Gamaliel's influence was so great that he carried the decision of the Sanhedrin. A minor punishment of beating was inflicted, probably with thirty-nine blows (II Cor 11:24), for disobeying the Sanhedrin's earlier command.

41,42. The apostles were by no means discouraged, for they considered it an honor to suffer for the name of Jesus. They continued their activities of **teaching and preaching of Jesus as the Messiah,** both publicly in the Court of the Gentiles **in the temple** and in their Christian gatherings in their private homes.

III. Extension of the Church in Palestine Through Persecution and Dispersion. 6:1 – 12:25.

Up to this point, the apostles had given no evidence of a purpose to carry the Gospel into all the world but had stayed in Jerusalem witnessing to the Jews. Luke now relates the beginnings of expansion of the church throughout Judea and Samaria, which was occasioned by the persecution that arose around Stephen. This expansion was accomplished not by the vision and purpose of the church but by the providential act of God in scattering the believers. To explain this persecution, Luke first relates how Stephen came into a position of prominence as one of the seven.

A. Choice of the Seven. 6:1-7. The church in its earliest days had no formal organization and no officials or leaders except the apostles. The numerical growth of the church and the rise of problems in its internal fellowship required the beginnings of organization and the choice of additional leaders or ministers.

1. Jews who were natives of Palestine spoke primarily Aramaic; but Jews who had lived in the Mediterranean world outside of Palestine spoke Greek and often did not know Aramaic. Many of these Diaspora Jews returned to Jerusalem to live, and some of them were converted and came into the church. A contention now arose between the Greek-speaking Christians **(Grecians)** and the Aramaic-speaking Christians **(Hebrews)** because it appeared that favoritism for the latter was being shown in the distribution of food to the **widows.** Widows were persons without any means of support, who were provided with the bare necessities of life by the Christian community.

2. The twelve apostles called together the entire church and pointed out that this responsibility for the care of the poor had become such a burden that they found themselves devoting most of their time to this material ministry and neglecting the ministry of the Word. Such neglect was **not right.** **3,4.** They recommended that the distribution of food be placed under the direction of seven Spirit-filled men of **good reputation.** The apostles would then be free to devote themselves to the ministry of prayer and of preaching and teaching the Word.

5. Stephen was among the seven men chosen. All seven had Greek names and apparently were drawn from the Greek wing of the church. **6.** The church at large selected these seven men, but the apostles approved the selection and appointed them to their office. The seven were then ordained to their office by the imposition of the apostles' hands. This laying on of hands was an OT custom (Gen 48:13 ff.; Lev 1:4; Num 27:23), which was also practiced by the Jews when men were admitted to the Sanhedrin. It was taken over by the early church for the ordination of these leaders. A preliminary qualification, however, was that the seven be filled with the Holy Spirit. Aside from the apostles, these seven were the first officials in the church. By tradition they have been designated deacons; but they are not so designated in the text.

7. The solution of this problem added to the effectiveness of the Christian testimony, and even many **priests** believed.

B. Occasion of the Dispersion: Ministry and Martyrdom of Stephen. 6:8–8:3.

8. Stephen was immediately marked out as a man of outstanding endowments and power.

9. He was bearing witness to the Messiahship of Jesus in the Jewish synagogues in Jerusalem, particularly in one that was attended by *Freedmen* (RSV; **Libertines,** AV) who had formerly lived in the four places named. A synagogue was composed of ten or more Jews who met together for the reading and interpretation of the Scriptures. An exaggerated tradition says there were 480 synagogues in Jerusalem. **10,11.** This ministry of Stephen apparently led to a formal debate. When the Jews were unable to overcome the earnest leader in debate because of his **wisdom** and the power of the Spirit (RSV), they secretly instigated (RSV) witnesses who testified that he had spoken blasphemous words against the law of Moses and against God.

12. The faithful "deacon" was brought before the Sanhedrin to defend himself against these charges. **13-15.** Stephen's alleged blasphemy against God was defined as blasphemy against the Temple. He had apparently been teaching that the Jewish Temple was no longer necessary for the true worship of God. He was now charged with teaching that Jesus of Nazareth would destroy the Temple and pervert the practice of the law of Moses. This charge was not a pure fabrication, but a clever misrepresentation of what Stephen had actually taught.

7:1. The **high priest** and president of the Sanhedrin was still Caiaphas, who had presided at the trial and condemnation of Jesus.

2. The speech of Stephen that follows is not really a refutation of the charges leveled against him but rather a positive affirmation of his witness to Jesus Christ and to the Gospel. Stephen did not attempt to show that the charges against him were false. On the contrary, he set forth his conviction that the Temple and the land of Palestine were not necessary for the true worship of God. He outlined a brief sketch of Israel's history to show: (a) that God blessed their fathers even though those men did not live in the land of Palestine; (b) that during much of her history Israel did not worship God in the Temple; (c) and that even the possession of the Temple did not save Israel from being rebellious and disobedient against God. The purpose of this speech was to show from Israel's history that the possession of the Temple had been neither a necessity for nor a guarantee of the true worship of God. And this served to substantiate Stephen's main point that now that Messiah had come, the Jewish worship in the Temple in Jerusalem was superseded.

God's call to **Abraham** did not come in the Promised Land but when he was far away in **Mesopotamia.** Stephen related a divine visitation while Abraham was still in Mesopotamia, as a result of which he went first to **Haran,** where he lived for some time, and then later journeyed from Haran to Palestine. Genesis 11:31,32 does not record this earliest divine visitation; but Gen 15:7 and Neh 9:7 both indicate that God's call came originally to Abraham in Ur of the Chaldees in Mesopotamia.

5. Although Abraham dwelt in the land of Palestine, he did not actually possess the land, but held it only as a promise from God to him and to his descendants. Abraham's blessing, therefore, was not dependent upon possession of the land but upon the promise of God.

6,7. Abraham's descendants did not at once possess the land but spent four hundred years in captivity outside Palestine. **Four hundred** is a round number (cf. Gal 3:17, where the period is 430 years). **8.** God entered into covenant with Abraham and his descendants, giving the sign of circumcision as a seal of the agreement. This covenant blessing, Stephen implied, was not dependent upon the existence of the Temple but upon the promises and faithfulness of God.

9,10. Even when the patriarchs sold **Joseph into Egypt,** God did not forsake him because he was outside the land, but brought to him a wonderful deliverance, making him governor **over Egypt** and the **house** of Pharaoh.

11-15. When a great famine came to both Egypt and Palestine, God gave Joseph foresight to lay aside reserves of grain in **Egypt** as the means of preserving the patriarchs. Jacob and his family migrated to Egypt, where they were preserved by Joseph. The number **seventy-five** follows the account in the Septuagint or Greek translation of the OT; the number seventy in Gen 46:27 and Ex 1:5 is that of the Hebrew text. These two texts reflect two ways of numbering Jacob's family.

16. Although the patriarchs died in Egypt, their bodies were brought back to Palestine and were buried in the land God had promised to Abraham and his seed.

17-43. Stephen had been accused of blasphemy against Moses. By recounting the story of Moses and the giving of the Law, he showed that the possession of the Law did not preserve Israel from rebellion against God.

17. As the time approached when God had promised to bring the patriarchs out of Egypt to give them the land of Canaan, the people had no inclination to leave Egypt, where they were becoming numerous and prosperous. **18,19.** God thereupon raised up another **king** in Egypt who did not continue the practice of favoritism to Joseph and his family, but who treated the Israelites deceitfully, compelling them to destroy all of their infants by exposure.

20,21. Moses, who was born at this time, was **attractive** in the eyes of God. When after three months his parents had to **cast** him **out, Pharaoh's daughter adopted him** (RSV) and brought him up as her own son in the royal family. **22.** As the son of Pharaoh's daughter, Moses received the finest education available in Egypt, and he became a young man of eloquence and of vigorous action.

23. After coming to manhood, Moses determined to leave the palace of Pharaoh to visit his people. Apparently, during these forty years he had had no contact with his people but had lived as an Egyptian in the house of Pharaoh.

24,25. When he saw one of his Israelite kinsmen being afflicted, he moved to his defense, and striking the Egyptian, killed him. Moses thought that his kinsmen would recognize him as one of their own sent by God to bring to them deliverance; but they did not recognize this fact.

26. The next day, when Moses found two of his kinsmen fighting with each other, he tried to reconcile them by pointing out that they were brothers and therefore should not fight together. **27,28.** The aggressor strongly rejected Moses' overture of peace. He accused him of meddling and of wishing to compound the murder that he had committed against the Egyptian on the preceding day.

29. When Moses realized that he was known as a murderer of an Egyptian in defense of the Israelites, he fled from Egypt and **became an exile** in Midian in northwest Arabia. Here he married and fathered two sons.

30. It was here in Mount Sinai, far from the Promised Land and without any temple, that God gave to Moses the wonderful revelation of Himself. **31,32.** At first Moses did not understand what the burning bush meant. Then God spoke to him, revealing Himself as the God of the patriarchs. The voice of the Lord filled Moses with a trembling fear, so that he dared not look upon the burning bush. **33.** This desolate spot in the wilderness was made a holy place because God appeared there. Accordingly He commanded Moses to remove his shoes as a token of reverence. Wherever God appears and speaks to men, there is holy ground.

34. God assured Moses that He had not forgotten His people even though they were in Egypt, and that He would soon fulfill His covenant promises and deliver them. **35.** God reversed the judgment of Moses' kinsmen. They scorned him because they thought he was trying to act as a **ruler** and a **judge;** God made Moses a **ruler** and **deliverer** of his people from Egypt. **Deliverer** carries the idea of redeemer.

36. This redemption was accomplished by a display of mighty power in **Egypt** and in the crossing of the Red Sea and in the forty years traveling from Egypt to the Promised Land.

37. Moses' experience only foreshadowed that of a greater One who was to come after him. For Moses had predicted the coming of another prophet, to whom Israel should give heed (Deut 18:15, 18,19).

38. Israel under Moses' leadership was a type of the Church. The Greek word for church, *ekklēsia,* is used in Deut 18:16 to describe Israel as the congregation of God. **The angel.** The particular angel of the Lord who represents God and makes His presence real to men. Moses also received living oracles from God, that is, the OT Law (Ex 20). All of these blessings the people of Israel enjoyed from the hand of God while they were yet in the wilderness outside of the land and without a temple.

39. In spite of these blessings from the hand of God, the Israelites would not obey the Lord but rejected Moses and desired to turn back to Egypt. **40.** When Moses was in the mountain, the people demanded that Aaron make idols for them to worship. Instead of worshiping God their Creator, they worshiped a golden calf which they themselves had fashioned (Ex 32:16,18). They gave as an excuse that Moses had disappeared and they did not know what had become of him.

41. Stephen was under accusation of blasphemy against Moses. His recital of history showed that the very ancestors of his accusers had themselves failed to keep the law of Moses and had rejected the divine order of worship for the worship of idols.

42. This tendency toward idolatry, reflected throughout the entire course of Israel's history, came to its climax with the Babylonian captivity, when Israel imitated her neighbors by worshiping the planets of the heavens as though they were deities (Deut 4:19; 17:3; II Kgs 21:3,5; 23:4,5; Jer 8:2; 19:13; Zeph 1:5). God abandoned Israel to this pagan idolatrous worship. Stephen quoted from Amos 5:25-27 to illustrate Israel's apostasy. The difference between the passage in Amos and that in Acts in our English versions is due to the fact that Stephen quoted from the Greek translation of the OT, which at this point deviates from its Hebrew original. Stephen indicated that the sacrifices offered to God were only external forms and possessed no spiritual reality (cf. Isa 1:10-14, where God rejects the sacrifices of his people because they do not come from obedient hearts).

43. Moloch and **Rephan** were two deities associated with the stars. The idolatry of the Jews' worship of the calf at Sinai and their formal, unspiritual worship of God through sacrifices in the wilderness led finally to their worship of pagan star deities. Because of this apostasy, God brought upon them the judgment of captivity **beyond Babylon.**

44,45. Israel's apostasy occurred in spite of the fact that God had given to them a clear witness. In the wilderness, God had commanded Moses to build a **tabernacle** or tent, which should be a witness to the presence of God in their midst (Ex 25:9, 40; 26:30; 27:8). The patriarchs brought this Tabernacle with them into the Promised Land under the leadership of Joshua. (The Gr. trans. of *Joshua* is **Jesus**). God drove out the nations from the land (the Gr. word means both **Gentiles** and nations), that Israel might possess it.

46,47. For many years after coming into the land, Israel had no temple but continued to worship God at the Tabernacle. **Tabernacle** in this verse is a different word from that in 6:44. David, a man after God's own heart, desired to provide a dwelling place for God; but this privilege was deferred until the time of Solomon. **48-50.** Stephen now declared emphatically that the **Most High** cannot be limited to structures made by man, because He fills all the world, and there is no sort of house which can contain Him.

51,52. If the Temple is not necessary for the worship of God, neither is it a guarantee that men will worship God rightly. Stephen accused those who worshiped in the Temple of being stiff-necked and **uncircumcised in heart and ears,** of resisting the Holy Spirit, and of betraying and murdering the **Righteous One,** thus following the example of their rebellious forefathers. Stephen had been accused of blaspheming the law of Moses. His answer was that it was not really he who was guilty of this sin but the Jewish people, who from the times of Moses had transgressed God's Word. He was accused of blaspheming God by setting aside the Temple. His answer was that Israel's history itself proved that the Temple was only a temporary institution and was not essential for the true worship of God.

54. When Stephen accused the Jews of blasphemy, they were filled with uncontrollable rage. **Gnashed with their**

teeth. A sign of anger (Job 16:9; Ps 35:14).

55,56. Stephen was untroubled by the anger of the Sanhedrin. At this moment, God granted him a vision of the open heavens with the **Son of man standing** at His right hand. Stephen's words were, in effect, an assertion that the claim of Jesus recently made before this same judicial body to be the heavenly Son of man was not blasphemous, as the Sanhedrin had claimed, but was the very truth of God (Mk 14:62). Stephen claimed indeed that Jesus had now become the Son of man at the right hand of God.

Jesus is usually pictured seated at God's right hand (Ps 110:1; Heb 1:13). It is possible that he is here represented as rising from his throne to receive this martyr. The name **the Son of man** does not designate Jesus' humanity; it is a Messianic title, based upon Dan 7:13,14, and designates the Messiah as a heavenly, supernatural being. This is the only place outside the Gospels where the title is applied to Jesus.

57-59. It is not altogether clear whether Stephen's martyrdom was the result of a formal execution or of a lynching. A legal execution required the approval of the Roman governor, and since this was not secured, Stephen's death looks like a lynching. However, the mention of formal witnesses as required by the Law (Lev 24:14; Deut 17:7) suggests a legal execution. It is possible that the Sanhedrin executed Stephen without securing the official approval of Pilate. Stephen was led out of the city to the place of execution and stoned. The **witnesses** were the official executioners. **Saul,** who later became the Apostle Paul, was an observer of the execution and stood over the shed garments of the executioners. Saul is suddenly introduced into the narrative without explanation.

59,60. Dying, Stephen addressed the exalted Jesus as God Himself, praying Jesus to receive his spirit. His dying word was a prayer for forgiveness for his executioners. **Sleep** is a common Biblical metaphor for death.

8:1. Saul was consenting. Some have felt that these words indicate that Saul was a member of the Sanhedrin. This is not necessarily true. However, since he was from Cilicia, he was undoubtedly a member of the synagogue that debated with Stephen (6:9). Up to this time the church had shown no inclination to take the Gospel into all the world but had remained in Jerusalem. God used the persecution that followed the death of Stephen as the providential means of spreading the Gospel outside Jerusalem. The believers of the Jerusalem congregation were scattered everywhere, but the apostles were able to remain in the city to give stability to the church.

3. The moving spirit in this persecution was Saul (see Gal 1:13,23; I Cor 15:9; Phil 3:6). He was convinced that this new movement which proclaimed a crucified criminal to be the Messiah could not possibly be of God. For the OT pronounced a curse upon anyone who was hanged upon a tree. This was Scriptural proof, so far as Saul was concerned, that Jesus was a pretender and this new movement blasphemous.

C. The Gospel in Samaria. 8:4-25. Luke first records the extension of the Gospel to Samaria. The Samaritans were descendants from a mixture of the remnant of Israel with foreigners who were settled in Samaria by the conquering Assyrians when the upper classes were taken into exile (II Kings 17). The Samaritans had erected a rival temple upon Mount Gerizim (see Jn 4:20). Because the Jews regarded the Samaritans as both racial and religious half-breeds, violent racial prejudices had to be overcome before the church could become a truly universal people.

5. The city of Samaria. It is not clear whether **Samaria** is meant to designate a city or the country. Usually, the word in the NT designates the territory rather than the city. The city of Samaria had been rebuilt by Herod the Great as a Greek city and called Sebaste, in honor of the Roman emperor. Philip's message in Samaria was **the Messiah** (AV omits the definite article) that is, that Jesus was the Christ.

9-11. Before Philip came to Samaria, a magician by the name of **Simon** had practiced his magical arts, claiming "to be somebody." The people were deceived by his tricks and attributed to him the **power of God which is called Great. Great** was a word used by Greeks to designate the Jewish God.

12. The message of our Lord had been the gospel of the kingdom of God (Mt 4:23; 9:35). He had told his disciples to preach the gospel of the kingdom in all the world (Mt 24:14). Philip went to Samaria **gospeling concerning the kingdom of God.** The phrase is exactly the same except that the verb is used instead of the noun and the preposition is inserted. The gospel of the kingdom of God and the name of Jesus Christ are here interchangeable ideas.

14-17. The **apostles at Jerusalem** maintained a supervisory relationship over the entire church, and they therefore sent Peter and John to Samaria to investigate this new development. (John and his brother James had once asked Jesus whether they should not call down fire from heaven upon a certain Samaritan village; see Lk 9:52 ff.). It became evident to Peter and John that the gift of the Holy Spirit received at Pentecost had not been extended to the Samaritan converts. They had received the baptism of water but not the baptism of the Spirit. It was obvious to the two apostles that the faith of the people was genuine. They therefore laid their hands upon the converts, and the Holy Spirit came upon them. The meaning of this event has been a subject of controversy, but it must be pointed out that on the day of Pentecost and in the household of Cornelius (Acts 10), the Holy Spirit was given without the laying on of hands. Therefore it is arbitrary to select this one event and make it normative for Christian experience, and to insist that there is a special baptism of the Spirit that is bestowed subsequent to saving faith by the laying on of hands of those who have already received the experience. The significance of this event lies in the fact that these people were **Samaritans.** Here is the first step in which the church burst its Jewish bonds and moved toward a truly world-wide fellowship. The imposition of hands was not necessary for the Samaritans; but it was necessary for the apostles, that they might be fully convinced that God was indeed breaking the barriers of racial prejudice and including these half-breed people within the fellowship of the Church. This was not a new Pentecost but an extension of the one Pentecost to the Samaritan people.

18-24. Simon's desire to buy the gifts of God with money has given to us the word "simony." Peter's answer was, "To perdition with your money, and with you, too . . . unless you repent." It appears that Simon was really converted, but the habits of the old life and the **bond of iniquity** (v. 23) had not yet been broken. Simon was stricken with fear and pleaded with the apostles to intercede for him and seek God's forgiveness (v. 24).

25. Peter and John now engaged in a vigorous evangelistic program that carried them through many villages in Samaria. Then, having completed this tour, they returned to Jerusalem.

D. Conversion of the Ethiopian Eunuch. 8:26-40. Luke now records a further step in the expansion of the church beyond its initial Jewish setting by relating the conversion of the Ethiopian eunuch, who was probably a half-convert to Judaism, although he may possibly have been a Jew.

26. Gaza, formerly one of the five cities of the Philistines, was situated about two and a half miles from the sea. The city was destroyed in 93 B.C. but was rebuilt some thirty-six years later on a new site nearer the sea. **Which is desert** may refer either to the road (RSV) or, more likely, to the site of the older city.

27. Eunuchs were used in Oriental courts to fill positions of high authority. **Candace.** Not a proper name but the title of the royal office. The king of Ethiopia was thought to be the child of the sun and therefore too sacred to exercise the actual functions of governing. The queen mother, who was called **Candace,** exercised the rule. This eunuch was probably a God-fearing Gentile or half-convert to Judaism, who had gone to Jerusalem on a pilgrimage. As a eunuch, he could never have belonged to the OT people of God (Deut 23:1), but such persons are to receive the Gospel.

28. Riding in a covered chariot, probably drawn by oxen, he was reading from the Greek translation of the prophet Isaiah. **30.** The ancients commonly read aloud, and Philip heard the eunuch reading from Isaiah. **32,33.** The passage of Scripture was Isa 53:7,8. It describes one who suffered in silence, to whom justice was denied, and who was slain.

34. Before the coming of Christ, the Jews did understand that this was a Messianic passage and that the sufferings of the servant were a prophecy of the sufferings of their Messiah. Later some interpreted the suffering servant to refer to the prophet and others to the people of Israel. **35.** Philip showed the eunuch that this was a prophecy of Jesus. This goes back to our Lord's own teaching that he had come to serve and to give his life a ransom for many (Mk 10:45).

36. Northeast of Gaza is a wadi or valley where there is running water. Philip's explanation had apparently included a challenge to believe on Jesus and to be baptized, for the eunuch asked that Philip baptize him. **37.** This verse in our English versions is not found in the oldest Greek texts. It was added to our text at an early time and reflects the primitive Christian practice of baptizing men immediately upon confession of faith in Jesus Christ. **38.** One of our earliest post-Biblical Christian writings, the Didache (c. A.D. 125), says that baptism should be performed in running water if it is possible.

39,40. We do not know what became of the eunuch, but tradition says that he became a missionary among his own people. Philip visited **Azotus,** the old city of Ashdod, some twenty miles north of Gaza, and then journeyed north along the coast, preaching the Gospel in the various cities, probably including Lydda and Joppa (9:32 ff.). He then came to **Caesarea,** where he apparently settled down, for he was living there at a later date (21:8). Caesarea was a Gentile city and the official residence of the Roman procurators of Judea.

E. Conversion of Saul. 9:1-31. The account of Saul's conversion is inserted into the narrative of the extension of the Gospel in Palestine. The record of the ministry of Peter, who had gone through Samaria preaching the Gospel (8:25), is resumed at 9:32. As the Gospel moved out toward the Gentile world, God prepared a chosen vessel to be the main instrument in this mission. Therefore Luke breaks his narrative to relate Saul's conversion, and also to explain the end of the persecution of the church.

1. Saul's conversion is also related in 22:4-16 and 26:12-18. Although Saul was born and reared in the Gentile city of Tarsus in Cilicia (22:3), he had studied in Jerusalem at the feet of Gamaliel, one of the outstanding Jewish rabbis of the day (5:34 ff.). He was known as a brilliant student (Gal 1:14) and a zealous Pharisee (Phil 3:5). Now Saul played the role of the most zealous representative of the Jews in persecuting the church. The violence of his persecution is described in Acts 26:10,11. His aim was to compel Christians to deny their faith on penalty of imprisonment and even death. We do not know how common martyrdom was in this persecution.

2. The **high priest,** president of the Sanhedrin, had jurisdiction over Jews throughout Palestine. Saul secured from the priest letters of extradition to the **synagogues at Damascus** to bring any Christians who had fled there back to Jerusalem in bonds. There was a Jewish community in Damascus of some ten to eighteen thousand people. **The Way.** A phrase used to describe the Christian faith (19:9, 23; 22:4; 24:14, 22).

3,4. The flash of light appeared to Saul near midday (22:6; 26:13), but the light was brighter than the sun. The voice from the midst of the light spoke to Saul in the Hebrew, or Aramaic, dialect (26:14). Although most Jews who lived in the Dispersion spoke Greek, Saul's parents spoke Aramaic and taught him this language (Phil 3:5). This was the language of instruction in the rabbinic schools in Jerusalem. The voice informed Saul that in persecuting the Christians, he had been persecuting Christ.

5. At first Saul did not understand the meaning of this experience. He asked the identity of the voice. **Lord** in Greek idiom often means "sir" (16:30; 25:26); but here it indicates a reverent and awestruck response. The voice identified itself as that of the glorified Jesus. The words in the AV, **It is hard for thee to kick against the pricks,** are not found in this passage in the oldest Greek texts, but have been introduced here from 26:14.

7. Saul was accompanied by a caravan. The statement in this verse that the men heard a voice but saw no one appears to contradict 22:9 and 26:14, where it is said that they did not hear the voice. There are two possible solutions to this problem. The Greek construction in 9:7 is different from that in 22:9. The former statement may mean that they heard a sound and the latter verse that they did not understand its content. A second possibility is that 9:7 refers to Saul's voice speaking to the light; the men heard Saul's voice but they did not hear the voice speaking from the light to Saul (22:9).

9. The experience was so unsettling that for three days Saul could neither eat nor drink.

10,11. We know nothing about **Ananias** except what this passage tells us. Verse 13 indicates that he was apparently a resident of Damascus and not a refugee from Jerusalem. We do not know how the Gospel came to Damascus nor how Ananias was converted. The book of Acts does not give us a complete history of the early church, but relates only the most important events of its growth. The **street called Straight** ran through the heart of Damascus and may still be seen today.

13. A report of the ravages wrought

by Saul against the Christians in Jerusalem had come to Damascus. **Saints.** A common NT word for believers. **15,16.** Suffering is to be looked upon not as the exception in the service of Christ, but as the normal thing.

17. Ananias' obedience was immediate and complete. The reception of the Holy Spirit through the laying on of Ananias' **hands** was an exceptional experience and not the normal thing (cf. 8:17). With the word **brother,** Ananias welcomed Saul into Christian fellowship. **18.** A flaky substance like **scales** fell from Saul's eyes, and he immediately regained his sight and was baptized.

19,20. The **certain days** that Saul spent in Damascus is a very indefinite note of time. Immediately after the vision of Christ, Saul went away to Arabia for some two or three years (Gal 1:15 ff.). The short ministry in Damascus may have taken place either before or after Saul's sojourn in Arabia. There were numerous synagogues in Damascus, and in them Saul proclaimed **Jesus** (RSV) as **the Son of God.** This is the first time this phrase occurs in Acts. It can designate the Messianic king as the object of God's favor (II Sam 7:14; Ps 2:7). This Messianic use of the **Son of God** is illustrated by the question of the high priest to Jesus (Mk 14:61). Probably the term here has the Messianic significance, for Acts 9:22 says that Saul's preaching proved that **Jesus was the Messiah.**

21,22. The transformation in Saul completely amazed his hearers. **Proving.** Literally, *putting together;* that is, putting together the OT prophecies with their fulfillment to show that Jesus was **the Messiah.** Saul's training in the OT as a rabbi now stood him in good stead.

23,24. The **many days** include between two and three years after Saul's conversion (Gal 1:18). "Three years" in Jewish reckoning may refer to a period of more than two full years. Comparison of this verse with II Cor 11:32 tells us that the Jews made a plot with the representative of King Aretas of Arabia. It is possible that the Nabataean kingdom of Aretas extended at this time so far as to include Damascus; but it is more likely that Aretas had a representative in the person of an ethnarch who ruled over the many Nabataeans living in Damascus. When Saul's ministry in Damascus incurred the animosity of both the Jews and the Nabataean authorities, they joined forces to watch the gates in an effort to capture him as he left the city.

25. One of the Christians owned a house built into the **wall** of Damascus. Saul was lowered through a window in the wall in a large woven **basket,** and thus escaped the plot.

26. When Saul returned to Jerusalem, he could not rejoin his former Jewish associates; and the few Christians who remained in the city (8:1) suspected that his profession of faith might be merely a front to further his persecution of the church. **27.** Barnabas had either known Saul previously or he was a man of great discernment, for he recognized Saul's sincerity and introduced him to **the apostles.** The only apostles in Jerusalem at this time were Peter and James, the Lord's brother (Gal 1:18,19). James had been included in the apostolic circle.

28,29. Saul now busied himself with a Gospel ministry in Jerusalem. His ministry did not yet extend beyond the capital city into Judea (Gal 1:22-24). He addressed himself primarily to the Greek-speaking Jews or **Hellenists**—the same group to whom Stephen had previously witnessed (Acts 6:9). The Hellenists attempted to kill Saul as they had earlier brought about the death of Stephen.

30. Saul escaped with his life only through the help of his Christian brethren, who took him down to the seaport city of Caesarea, whence he sailed to his home city of Tarsus, in Cilicia. We now lose sight of Saul until 11:25; but he was unquestionably busy in Tarsus preaching the Gospel, although there is no record of this ministry.

31. Luke next describes the growth, both numerical and spiritual, of the **church** in all **Judea** and **Galilee** and **Samaria.** The plural **churches** (AV) is incorrect. The Church is one even though there are many local churches. Here is the first reference to churches in Galilee. We do not know when or how they were founded.

F. Peter's Ministry in Palestine and the First Gentile Converts. 9:32–11:18. Luke's narrative at this point reverts to the story of the extension of the Gospel throughout Judea through the ministry of Peter. Peter was last mentioned in 8:25, when he, with John, returned from Samaria to Jerusalem. Now we are told that Peter had engaged in a traveling ministry throughout Judea, preaching to the Christians who had been scattered in the various towns. It would be of great interest to have a complete record of Peter's ministry. In Lydda, he found a group of Christians who had probably fled there in the dispersion caused by the persecution in Jerusalem. Philip had already evangelized this region (8:40). Here Peter healed the paralytic Aeneas.

35. The story of Aeneas' healing spread throughout the city of **Lydda** and throughout the plain of **Sharon,** which bordered the seacoast, and resulted in the conversion of many people. This area was populated in part by Gentiles; Luke is tracing the extension of the church from the Jewish Jerusalem community to the Gentile converts.

36. Joppa. A city on the seacoast, some ten miles northwest of Lydda. **Tabitha.** An Aramaic word meaning *gazelle.* **Dorcas.** Greek for the same. She was greatly beloved by the Christians for her good works and acts of charity. **37.** The Jewish ceremonial laws of purification required the **washing** of a dead body. It was placed in an upper room in anticipation of burial. **39. Widows,** who were among the most needy persons in the ancient world, were the particular objects of Tabitha's charity. They were probably wearing garments Dorcas had made for them.

43. Jews considered the business of tanning skins an unclean trade, since it involved handling dead bodies. It is significant that Peter, good Jew that he was, stayed with a man engaged in such a business.

10:1. Luke now records a very important final step in the extension of the Gospel to the Gentiles. Its importance is indicated by Luke's twice recording Peter's visit to Cornelius. This step raised some difficult problems as to the terms of social intercourse between the Jewish and the Gentile Christians and the terms of the admission of the Gentiles into the church. This question became the theme of the conference in Jerusalem in Acts 15.

A **centurion** was an officer in the Roman army who commanded a hundred men and was similar in rank and function to our noncommissioned officers. **Cornelius** commanded the **Italian cohort.** A Latin inscription has been preserved which indicates the presence in Syria of the "second Italian cohort of Roman citizens" in A.D. 69.

2. A few Gentiles became converts to Judaism and accepted all Jewish practices, including circumcision. A larger number stopped short of circumcision but accepted the Jewish belief in God, synagogue worship, the ethical teachings of the OT, and some of the Jewish religious practices. These people, who were called **God-fearers,** were familiar with the OT in the Greek version as it was read in the synagogues. Devout God-fearers provided the most fertile soil in which the Gospel took root. Cornelius was such a "semi-proselyte." His **devout** character was manifested by his liberal **alms** to the people and his regular **prayers** to God.

7. Cornelius chose two trusted servants and a soldier who was a God-fearer like himself to go to Joppa to bring Peter.

9. Joppa is some thirty miles from Caesarea. The three messengers left Caesarea early in the morning and arrived in Joppa about noon.

Meanwhile, God was preparing Peter to receive them. About twelve o'clock **Peter** went up to the flat housetop to seek a quiet place **to pray. 10.** Since it was mealtime, he desired to eat and probably called downstairs to the house below to have food prepared. As he continued to pray, he fell into a state of ecstasy and saw a vision. **11.** In the vision he saw some kind of object, like a **great sheet,** lowered by the four corners from the opened heavens to the earth. **Vessel.** A Greek word that can designate almost any kind of useful material object.

12. In the sheet he beheld the three kinds of creatures described in Gen 6:20 —**four-footed animals, reptiles, and birds. Wild beasts** (AV) is not in the best texts. **13,14.** When commanded to **kill** some of these animals and **eat,** Peter replied that to do so would mean violating the Jewish ritual law against eating **unclean** foods. Leviticus 11 contains these laws. Animals that did not chew the cud and did not have cloven hooves were designated as unclean and were not to be used for food. Furthermore, clean animals had to be prepared in such a way that the blood did not remain within the carcass. Although Peter was a Christian, he was also a good Jew, who did not violate Jewish dietary rules.

15. The voice from heaven told him that God had now abolished these regulations about clean and unclean foods. Jesus had in effect taught the same thing (Mk 7:14-23) by teaching that foods which enter a man's body from without cannot defile his heart. The expression in Mk 7:19 b, "This he said, making all meats clean," is probably a word that Mark received from Peter. The apostle was learning for himself the true meaning of Jesus' teachings.

23,24. The next day Peter set out for Caesarea accompanied by the three messengers and six Jewish Christians from Joppa (11:12). At the house of Cornelius Peter found that the centurion was expecting him, and had gathered together his relatives and close friends.

27-29. Peter explained to Cornelius and his company that Jewish law made it "taboo" for a Jew to **associate with** or **visit** people of **another nation.** However, God had now so lifted Peter out of his Jewish scruples that he could no longer look upon any man as ceremonially common or unclean and therefore unfit for social fellowship. God had made his will so clear to Peter that he had accompanied the servants of Cornelius without any objection, a thing he would not have done as a Jew.

34. The apostle understood the significance of the vision given to him on the rooftop. He realized that the distinction between clean and unclean foods had an application to human beings, and that, contrary to Jewish belief, no people were to be thought of as unclean in the sight of God. God **shows no partiality** to any one people. A person who fears God and does what is right, whether he be Jew or Gentile, is accepted by God. This was a great lesson for a Jew to learn, and it marks a definite step in the extension of the church from a Jewish fellowship to a universal basis.

36. Peter preached the Gospel to Cornelius, pointing out that although God sent his Word first to Israel, Jesus is indeed Lord of all men. **37,38.** Peter's proclamation of the Gospel included a brief summary of Jesus' ministry in Judea and Galilee, his anointing as Messiah at the time of his baptism, his good works, healings, and exorcism of demons. **39-41.** It is notable that Peter says little about the meaning of Christ's death, and that he proclaims no doctrine of the atonement. The Gospel consists of the facts of Jesus' death and resurrection. Jesus' resurrection was not a publicly attested fact but was witnessed by chosen men and is confirmed particularly by the fact that these witnesses ate and drank with Jesus after his resurrection from the dead. **42,43.** The Gospel includes an announcement of the coming judgment of both the living and the dead by the resurrected Jesus, and the offer of the forgiveness of sins to all who will believe in him.

Peter's sermon is our first example of preaching to the Gentiles. It contains very little reflection upon the meaning of the person of Christ, no emphasis upon his pre-existence, incarnation, and deity, nor on the atoning character of his death. It is indeed a "primitive Christology," and consists primarily of the proclamation of the facts of Jesus' death, life, and resurrection, and the appeal to believe on him for the forgiveness of sins.

44. On the day of Pentecost, Peter had exhorted his hearers to repent, to be baptized for the forgiveness of sins, and to receive the Holy Spirit (2:38). At Caesarea, this order of events was changed, and the **Holy Spirit fell** upon Cornelius and his family before they were baptized. This was not a new Pentecost but an extension of Pentecost to include the Gentiles.

45. The **believers of the circumcision** refers to the Jewish Christians who had accompanied Peter from Joppa. Their astonishment was due to the fact that they had not understood that the Gospel was to be extended to the Gentiles. Although they were Christians, they were still Jews, and their Jewish prejudices had to be broken down.

46. The gift of tongues was given on this occasion that there might be no doubt whatsoever that God had given to the Gentiles the same gift he had bestowed upon Jewish believers. **47,48.** Peter at once recognized that the Gentiles should be brought into the fellowship of the church, and he therefore commanded that Cornelius and his family be baptized in the name of Jesus Christ. Baptism in water followed baptism in the Spirit. Peter did not immediately return to Jerusalem but remained with Cornelius for some time, probably instructing him in the things of the Lord.

Chapter 11. It is surprising that in a short book Luke would devote so much space to a second recital of the conversion of Cornelius. This indicates that Luke considered this event one of the most important in the life of the early church.

1-3. News of the reception of the Gospel by the Gentiles reached the apostles and the Jewish Christians in Judea. Peter was apparently called to Jerusalem, and some of the Jewish Christians there disputed with him over the propriety of entering into such fellowship with Gentiles as to eat with them. It is likely that the expression, **those of the circumcision,** has a somewhat different connotation than the same phrase in 10:45. While the Jewish Christians in Jerusalem were discussing the significance of the salvation of the Gentiles, there emerged one party who later took the position that Gentiles must keep the Jewish law in order to be saved (15:1). This conservative party criticized Peter, for they recognized that a Jew who had table fellowship with Gentiles was in effect setting aside Jewish practices, and thereby ceased to be a Jew. They were not prepared to approve such a course of action; they believed that Jewish believers should not give up their Jewish practices.

4-15. By way of reply Peter related to the Jerusalem church the story of his vision of the sheet from heaven, his visit to Caesarea, and the coming of the Holy Spirit upon the Gentiles as upon the Jews on the day of Pentecost (v. 15).

16. This was the third gift of the Holy Spirit. The first was to the Jewish church in Jerusalem on the day of Pentecost (ch. 2); the second was to Samaritan believers (8:17); and now the third was to Gentiles. Undoubtedly Peter's experience in Samaria prepared him for this ministry to the Gentiles. **17. The gift** of tongues made it clear that God had given the same gift to the Gentile believers as he had to Jewish believers when they believed on the Lord Jesus Christ. To refuse Gentiles baptism would have been to refuse to accept God's work and would in effect have been to withstand God.

18. Peter's recital satisfied the circumcision party for the time. But the question of the status of the Gentile Christians in the church was destined shortly to arise again and to create a serious problem.

G. Establishment of a Gentile Church at Antioch. 11:19-30. This section marks a new stage in the extension of the church from a Jewish fellowship in Jerusalem to a universal community. Previously, Luke related the inclusion of the Samaritans in the church and the conversion of the single Gentile family of Cornelius. Now he describes the beginnings of the first independent Gentile congregation in Antioch, which was to become the "mother church" of the Gentile mission in Asia and Europe. The narrative resumes the events of 8:4 and the persecution of Saul.

19. Phoenicia is the narrow strip of land bordering the Mediterranean. It extends north of Caesarea some 120 miles and includes Tyre and Sidon. The preaching of the Gospel was still limited to Jews, for the early church was very slow in realizing the universal character of the Gospel mission.

20. Some of the believers who had come from the island of **Cyprus** and **Cyrene** in North Africa (cf. 13:1) came to Antioch and launched the Gospel in a new direction. Antioch was the third largest city of the Roman Empire and the residence of the Roman governor of the province of Syria. While a large Jewish colony existed in Antioch, the city was primarily Gentile and Greek. The cult of the pagan deities, Apollo and Artemis, whose worship included ritual prostitution, had headquarters near by. Antioch was notorious for its moral degradation.

Grecians or **Greeks** (RSV) in this context refers to pure Greeks rather than to Greek-speaking Jews. The Gospel preached to the Gentiles proclaimed not primarily the Messiahship of Jesus but his Lordship. Messiahship was a Jewish concept that would not have been meaningful to Gentiles who had no Jewish background.

22. This new venture was immediately successful, and the mother **church in Jerusalem** sent **Barnabas** to supervise and confirm the new church as Peter and John had superintended the new work in Samaria (8:14-17). Barnabas, as his name suggests, was gifted in providing encouragement to new Christians, and he exhorted the new converts that **with purpose of heart** they would be faithful and would persevere.

25,26. Barnabas soon realized that the growing church needed additional guidance, and his mind turned to **Saul** of **Tarsus,** who had undoubtedly been engaged in missionary work in the vicinity of his home city (9:30; Gal 1:21). After some difficulty, he found Saul and brought him to Antioch, where they spent **a whole year** working in the church. The word **Christians** occurs in the NT only here, in 26:28, and in I Pet 4:16. The word is formed with the Latin suffix which designates "follower or partisan of" (cf. "Herodians" in Mk 3:6). There is no adequate reason to think that the term was used in derision. It simply means people who follow Christ.

27. The growing importance of the church in Antioch is illustrated by the ministry rendered to the mother church in Jerusalem at a time of famine. **Prophets** are mentioned in 13:1; 15:32; 21:9,10. They were not ordained official leaders but laymen who declared the will of God or future events under direct inspiration of the Holy Spirit. See I Cor 14:29-39. Prophets ranked next to apostles in the early church (I Cor 12:28; Eph 2:20; 3:5; 4:11; Rev 22:9).

28. Agabus appears again in 21:10. **The days of Claudius.** Roman historians refer to several famines during the reign of Claudius (A.D. 41–54), while Josephus, the Jewish historian, mentions a severe famine in Judea in A.D. 46.

30. Elders. Here is the first mention in Acts of these Christian officials. Luke gives no hint as to how the office of elder came into existence or by what means elders were chosen. A group of elders ruled over each Jewish synagogue, and it is probable that the Christian church adopted the Jewish pattern. Probably the believers constituted a number of house congregations in several homes, and the elders may have been the leaders of these several congregations (see Acts 15:6,23). Many scholars think that this famine visit was the journey mentioned in Gal 2:1-10. The "revelation" of Gal 2:2 may refer to the prophecy of Agabus. If this is so, fourteen years (Gal 2:1) had intervened since Saul's first visit to Jerusalem, and he was already a mature Christian and an experienced leader. The problem of whether the visit referred to in Gal 2:1-10 is the famine visit of Acts 11 or the council visit of Acts 15 is one of the most difficult problems in NT history.

H. Persecution by Herod Agrippa I. 12:1-25. Luke interrupts the flow of his narrative to record an event that had occurred a few years earlier. Since Herod died in A.D. 44, the famine mission must have occurred about A.D. 46. The Jerusalem community had met early opposition by the Jewish religious leaders, but the Christians were popular with the people. Violent persecution had arisen against Stephen and the Hellenistic wing under the leadership of Saul. Now for the first time, Luke records persecution from the ruling authorities in Palestine. It came not from Roman rulers but from a Jewish king.

1. Herod the King was Agrippa I, grandson of Herod the Great, who was king of all Palestine when Jesus was born. During our Lord's ministry, Herod Antipas, son of Herod the Great, was ruler over Galilee, while Judea was governed by Roman procurators. Between 41 and 44 A.D. Herod Agrippa was king over both Judea and Galilee. After his death in A.D. 44, the whole of Palestine again became a Roman province under Roman procurators.

2. The death of **James** was the first martyrdom of an apostle and marked a new attitude of hostility on the part of the Jewish people toward the church. At first, the Jews held the Christians in high honor (5:13). Persecution by the Sanhedrin had been spearheaded by Saul. Now the king of the Jews, with popular support, directed persecution against the apostles. James thus fulfilled the prophecy of Jesus in Mk 10:39.

3. Herod is known to have followed a policy of catering to Jewish desires, and the popular response at his execution of James led him to seize **Peter** also. The **days of unleavened bread,** the seven days following the Passover, were holy days, when an execution would not be fitting. **4.** Properly speaking, the **Passover** (AV *Easter* is incorrect) introduced the days of unleavened bread, but Luke uses the two terms interchangeably (Lk 22:1). Peter was guarded by four relays of four soldiers, one squad for each three-hour watch of the night. **5. Prayer . . . without ceasing.** The Greek word may mean either *continuing* prayer or *earnest* prayer. The same word is used in Lk 22:44 of Jesus' prayer in Gethsemane.

6. Peter was chained to two soldiers, and two others stood at the doors. Although the apostle expected to be executed on the next day, he was able to sleep soundly. **7,8.** The **garment.** The mantle or cloak worn over the ordinary clothing. **9.** Peter thought that he was experiencing a vision or a dream and could not believe that it was real. **10.** Peter and the angel passed two gates, each guarded by a soldier. The third gate, which led from the prison to the city, opened automatically. Possibly Peter was imprisoned in the Tower of Antonia, a military installation at the northwest corner of the temple area. One text refers to seven steps leading down to the city.

11. Peter now **came to himself,** for he had been walking as though in a trance. For the first time, the true significance of what had occurred came home to him. **12.** He first hurried to the place where the Christians were gathered in prayer. This **house of Mary** was one of the chief meeting places of the church. "Churches," or buildings erected for Christian worship, are not known in the NT. **John Mark** (12:25; 13:5,13; 15:37-39; Col 4:10; Phil 2:1; II Tim 4:11) is here introduced for the first time. Good tradition relates that he later became Peter's interpreter in Rome and that his Gospel is based on Peter's preaching. He was probably one of the sources of Luke's information.

14-16. Although the believers had

been praying fervently for Peter's release, they were amazed when their prayers were answered. When the maid who answered Peter's knock, recognized the apostle's voice, she rushed back to the assembled church, leaving Peter standing at the locked gate. The believers thought that **Rhoda** was imagining things or that she had seen Peter's guardian **angel** (Mt 18:10; Heb 1:14). When Peter was admitted, his friends broke into excited questions, and he had to motion them to be silent.

17. James, the brother of Jesus, had become the acting head of the Jerusalem church, but he was not with the assembled church at this time. The **brethren** may be the elders of 11:30 who shared the rule of the church with James. After reporting his escape to the church, Peter "went underground," and Luke no longer traces his activities. However, the tradition that he went to Rome is refuted by Acts 15:2, for Peter was present at the council in Jerusalem.

19. The words translated **put to death** may mean "led off to prison"; but Roman law prescribed that if a prisoner escaped, the penalty due him should be inflicted on his guard. **Caesarea** was the Roman capital of the province of Judea; but **Judea** is used here not of the Roman province but of the dwelling place of the Jews.

20. Although **Tyre** and **Sidon** were free cities, they were dependent for their food upon the grain of Galilee in Herod's kingdom. For some unknown reason Herod was angry with these two cities. And so, to make peace with him, they presumably bribed Blastus to intercede with the king and gain a hearing for them. **21.** The **set day,** according to Josephus, was a feast in honor of the Emperor. To receive the delegates from Tyre and Sidon in state, Herod arrayed himself in robes made entirely of silver. **22,23.** Pagans commonly attributed divine attributes to their rulers. Josephus relates that after delivering this oration, Herod was struck down with a violent pain in the stomach and was carried to the palace, where, after five days of suffering, he died. His death occurred in A.D. 44, and Judea was then placed under Roman governors, two of whom (Felix and Festus) appear in the later narrative of Acts.

24,25. Luke now resumes his story of the church in Antioch (see 11:30).

IV. Extension of the Church in Asia Minor and Europe. 13:1–21:17.

Chapter 13 brings us to the second half of Acts. In the first half, Jerusalem is the center of the narrative, and the main theme is the extension of the church from Jerusalem throughout Palestine. Now Jerusalem drops into the background, and Antioch becomes the center of the narrative because it sponsored the extension of the church in Asia and Europe. This extension was accomplished by three missions by Paul, each beginning and ending in Antioch.

A. First Mission: Galatia. 13:1–14:28.

The first mission carried the Gospel from Antioch to Cyprus and to the cities in the southern part of the Roman province of Galatia.

1. The church in Antioch was characterized by many outstanding Christians. **Niger.** A Latin word meaning *black,* here used as a nickname. It apparently describes the dark complexion of **Simeon** and suggests that he was of African origin. He may have been the Simon of Cyrene mentioned in Mk 15:21, who carried Jesus' cross. The adjective describing **Manaen** means *foster brother* and was applied to boys of the same age as royal children who were brought up in the court. The title was retained after the boys reached adulthood. **Herod,** whose playmate was Manaen, was Herod Antipas, who ruled over Galilee and Perea between 4 B.C. and A.D. 39. **Prophets** were enabled to give new revelations of God's will by direct inspiration of the Holy Spirit. **Teachers** were gifted in the interpretation of (OT) Scripture.

2. The utterance of the **Holy Spirit** came probably through a prophet. **3.** The call to this mission came from the Holy Spirit; the church recognized and confirmed the divine call. The laying on of hands does not constitute ordination but separation to a special task and approval of the mission.

4. Seleucia. The port of Antioch. Here Barnabas and Saul took ship for **Cyprus,** a large and important island. Possibly the evangelistic mission was begun in Cyprus because the island was Barnabas' home.

5. Salamis. The eastern port of Cyprus and its largest city. Jews were so numerous that there were several synagogues. It was Paul's custom to preach the Gospel "to the Jew first" (Rom 1:16); but the Gospel usually took root among the Gentiles who attended the Jewish synagogues. **John Mark** accompanied the apostles. **Minister** or *attendant* has been thought by some scholars to designate one whose function was to instruct the converts in the Gospel and in the Christian life.

6. Paphos. The official capital of the province. Bar-Jesus means *son of salvation*. He was a **false prophet** not because he gave false predictions but because he falsely claimed to be a prophet. It was a common practice for rulers to have magicians and astrologers in their retinue. **7. Sergius Paulus** was the proconsul of the province. Rome had two types of provinces—those under the emperor and those under the senate. The former, like Judea, were governed by procurators appointed by the emperors, while the latter were governed by proconsuls. In 22 B.C., the status of Cyprus was changed from imperial to senatorial province, as Luke correctly indicates.

8. Elymas. Another name for Bar-Jesus, probably a Semitic word bearing a meaning similar to the Greek *magos*, which means "sorcerer" or "magician." Elymas sensed that if the proconsul accepted the message of Barnabas and Saul, his own position would be impaired, and he therefore attempted to turn the proconsul from his faith.

9. Saul is the Semitic form, **Paul** the Greek. Of the several reasons suggested for the introduction of the Greek name, the most likely is that as Paul now assumed the position of leadership in the Gentile mission, the Greek form of his name was more appropriate, and Luke so designates him. **10.** Instead of "son of salvation," Elymas was **a son of the devil. 11.** The word translated **mist** is used by medical writers to describe an inflammation of the eye that gives it a cloudy appearance.

13. The missionaries turned from Barnabas' native land of Cyprus to the country bordering Paul's native land. **Pamphylia.** A district on the coast of Asia Minor. **Perga.** A city situated about twelve miles inland. For some unexplained reason, John Mark forsook Paul and Barnabas and returned to Jerusalem. Paul considered this desertion inexcusable, for later when Barnabas wished Mark to accompany them on another trip, Paul refused to take him (15:37,38), and separated from Barnabas over this issue. Mark's desertion may have been due to some change in their missionary plans of which he did not approve. Others have suggested that he was jealous because Paul was outshining his cousin Barnabas. There is no reason to think that the basis of the difference was doctrinal.

14. Paul and Barnabas headed inland over the Taurus mountains and entered the southern part of the Roman province of Galatia. **Antioch.** The most important city of that part of Galatia. It was not situated in **Pisidia,** as the AV translates, but was near the region of Pisidia and had come to be designated **Pisidian Antioch.**

Many scholars, following the researches of William M. Ramsay, conclude that these cities of southern Galatia were those to which Paul wrote the letter to the Galatians. Other scholars have felt that **Galatia** designates the northern part of the province of Galatia, where the Galatian people of Gallic extraction lived. However, this "North Galatian" theory is beset by more problems than the "South Galatian" theory. It is probable that the Galatian epistle was addressed to the churches of Antioch, Iconium, Lystra, and Derbe. Sir William Ramsay speculated that Paul had been seized with malaria on the low-lying seacoast of Perga and was ill when he arrived in Antioch. Although this cannot be proved, it is an interesting possibility. As his custom was, Paul first went to the synagogue of the Jewish colony in Antioch on the Sabbath day.

15. A Jewish synagogue service consisted largely of prayers, a reading from the **law** and one from the **prophets,** and an exposition of the reading, which might be given by anyone in the congregation. The **rulers of the synagogue** were not "clergymen" but persons charged with the superintendence of the synagogue and its worship. Their office gave them authority to invite some one person to deliver the sermon. In accordance with this procedure, the two visitors were invited to give a word of exhortation. The main truths of Paul's sermon are as follows: 1. Jesus is the fulfillment of the history of God's dealings with Israel. 2. The Jews in Jerusalem rejected him, but in crucifying him they fulfilled God's purpose. 3. God fulfilled his promise to the fathers by raising Jesus from the dead. 4. The blessings of forgiveness and justification, which the Law could not provide, are now offered in Jesus' name to the Jews of the dispersion.

16. The synagogue congregation was composed of two groups: **men of Israel,** i.e., Jews; and **God-fearers**—Gentiles who worshiped God and attended the synagogue without accepting all of the demands of the Jewish law (cf. 10:2).

17. Paul first cited some of the highlights in the history of Israel to show that the God who had led Israel through the centuries had now sent Jesus to be the Son of David of prophecy. The heart of the Biblical faith is that God has acted redemptively in history, first in Israel and then in Jesus Christ. The birth of Israel as a nation began with the deliverance from Egypt. With a **high arm** means with a display of power. **18. Suffered their manners** may mean either that he put up with their conduct or that he nourished them like a father. **19. The seven nations** are mentioned in Deut 7:1. The 450 years can hardly be intended to designate the period of the Judges, as the AV suggests, but probably includes the period of the sojourn, the wandering, and the distribution of the land during the period of the Judges.

21,22. The OT does not mention these **forty years,** but Josephus refers to them. **David** was the man after God's own heart and was obedient to his will, but God promised through the prophets to raise up a greater successor to David (Ezk 34:23; 37:24; Jer 23:5,39). The expectation of a Davidic king was a live hope among the Jews of the first century (see the pseudepigraphical Psalms of Solomon 17:23 ff.).

23. However, the promised Son of David had appeared as a **Saviour** rather than as a king; the word **Jesus** means Saviour (Mt 1:21). **Raised** does not refer to the Resurrection but to the historical appearance of Jesus the Saviour. **26,27.** The promised salvation was fulfilled in the death of Jesus. The Jews in Jerusalem unknowingly fulfilled the Scripture because they failed to understand its true meaning and condemned Jesus to death. When the Sanhedrin had wanted Jesus' body removed from the cross before the beginning of the Sabbath (Jn 19:31), he had been buried by Joseph of Arimathea and Nicodemus (Lk 23:50 ff.; Jn 19:38 ff.).

30,31. The resurrection of Jesus, the central theme in the early proclamation and foundation of the Church, was attested by many witnesses whose witness still could be heard (RSV).

32,33. Jesus, Paul declared, was the fulfillment of the OT promise; the Messianic hope given to the fathers was fulfilled in him. **He hath raised up Jesus** probably designates Christ's appearance in history rather than his resurrection from the dead. **Again** is not in the text. However, the historical appearance of Jesus included his resurrection from the dead, as the following verses indicate. **Thou art my Son** (Ps 2:7) does not refer to Jesus' deity so much as to his Messiahship. Part of this quotation was heard at Jesus' baptism (Mk 1:11) and indicated the entrance of Jesus into his Messianic mission. "Sonship" in Biblical thought is a many-sided concept and can designate Messiahship without in any way minimizing the reality of Christ's deity.

34,35. Prediction of the resurrection of Christ is found in Isa 55:3 and in Ps 16:10. Because David died, the promise of Ps 16:10 could not refer to him but must refer to his promised descendant. **36,37. David served his own generation by the will of God** can also be translated, *David served the will of God in his own generation.* David's career was limited to his own generation, for he died and saw corruption; the career of Jesus cannot be limited to any one time but belongs to all ages.

38,39. From Jesus' death and resurrection two blessings result—**forgiveness** and **justification.** Two interpretations of 13:39 are possible: while the Law justifies from some things, Christ justifies from all things; or, though the Law justifies from nothing, Christ justifies from everything. The latter rendition is the more natural, although many scholars have preferred the former and have found here a teaching differing from Paul's doctrine of justification. **40,41.** Paul concluded with a warning from Hab 1:5. If God's people did not repent, a great tragedy would befall them.

42. This new and thrilling message created great excitement. After the synagogue service, many of Paul's hearers showed themselves ready to accept his message. The proper text has no reference to **Jews** and **Gentiles** (AV) but only to **the people** (RSV). **43. Religious** or *devout* **proselytes.** An unusual expression that ought to indicate full converts to Judaism. However, from the context, it seems to refer to the "God-fearers" or Gentile half-converts to Judaism who accepted the Gospel.

44,45. During the week, the report of Paul's sermon spread throughout the city, and on the next Sabbath the synagogue was filled with Gentiles to hear Paul's word. Such a crowd of Gentiles in the synagogue provoked the Jews to envy, and they refuted his message and reviled his person. **Blaspheming** does not mean to blaspheme God but to revile men.

46. Paul replied that it was the divine order that the Gospel should be offered first to the Jews that they might accept it and in turn evangelize the Gentiles. However, since they rejected the word of God and thereby judged themselves unworthy of the life of the age to come, Paul must himself turn to the Gentiles. Here **the word of God** includes much more than the Scriptures; it designates the proclamation of the gospel of the death and resurrection of Jesus. **Eternal life** is here the future possession rather than the present experience. The one, however, includes the other.

47. A prophecy from Isa 49:6, originally referring to the servant of the Lord, is here applied to the apostles, who were to bring light to the Gentiles. **48. Ordained to eternal life.** The primary significance of this reference to predestination is not theological but historical. As the Gospel moved out from its Jewish environment to the Gentile world, many **ordained to eternal life** received it and believed. This, however, does not involve minimizing the teaching of foreordination to life. Here is one of the recurring themes of Acts: At every new and strategic step the Gospel is rejected by the Jews but received by Gentiles.

50. The Jews not only rejected the Gospel; they initiated active steps to frustrate Paul's ministry. Among the God-fearers (cf. note on 10:2) attending the synagogue were **women of high standing.** These the Jews influenced to bring pressure on their husbands to drive Paul and Barnabas out of the area. Here is an authentic touch of local color; women did not exercise such influence in cities of Greece as they did here in Asia. **51,52.** Jesus had commanded his disciples to shake the **dust from their feet** when they were rejected (Lk 9:5; 10:11), thus indicating the breaking off of all intercourse. Among Jews such an action was equivalent to calling a man a heathen.

14:1,2. Iconium was the easternmost city of the district of Phrygia and lay in the Roman province of Galatia. Here the experience of Jewish opposition and Gentile faith was repeated. **3.** However, since it took a while for the opposition to become effective, the apostles were able to preach the word for a long period of time. This indefinite note of time is typical of Luke's method of writing. At a few points he gives us distinct chronological references; but it is impossible from Luke's record to create a precise chronological table of Paul's travels and ministry. **4,5.** The hostile Jews succeeded finally in inciting a riot and stirring up the rulers. And so Paul and Barnabas had to leave Iconium.

6. While Luke is often indefinite as to chronological references, he is often very definite in his geographical notes. This statement that **Lystra** and **Derbe** belonged to the region of **Lycaonia** implies that Iconium lay outside Lycaonia. Other writers of about Luke's time placed Iconium in the district of Lycaonia. Many scholars assumed that at this point Luke was inaccurate. Ramsay tells how this reference caught his attention and how careful examination vindicated Luke's statement. This was the beginning of Ramsay's change in attitude toward Acts, and he became one of the most vigorous and learned proponents of the accuracy of the book (see *The Bearing of Recent Discovery on the Trustworthiness of the New Testament*, chapter III).

11. In their excitement, the people fell into their native *Lycaonian* tongue, and Paul and Barnabas could not understand what was happening. Much of the Mediterranean world was bilingual, the people speaking the general language, Greek, and also their native dialect. **12.** The two visitors were thought to be two gods. *Zeus* was the chief god of the Greek Pantheon, and *Hermes* was the herald of the gods. **Jupiter** and **Mercurius** (AV) are the Latin equivalents for the Greek names of these gods, but the Greek terms ought to be used. Since Paul was the spokesman of the two, the people called him Hermes; while Barnabas, the more silent partner who stood in the background, they called Zeus, the father of the gods. Legends existed that told of other occasions when these two gods visited people of this area.

13. Before the city probably refers to the temple located outside the city. The priest of Zeus prepared oxen adorned with woolen decorations to offer sacrifice to their unexpected visitors. The **gates** probably refer to the gates of the city near the temple. **14.** Although the apostles could not understand the Lycaonian dialect, the actions of the priests soon indicated their purpose to sacrifice, and the apostles strongly protested. **They tore their clothes.** A Jewish gesture of horror at blasphemy (Mk 14:63).

15-17. Paul urged the people to worship the living God rather than His emissaries. This sermon given to a purely pagan audience contrasts strikingly with the sermon delivered at Antioch in the Jewish synagogue. Before pagans can appreciate the mission of Jesus, they must recognize the oneness of God. Paul's sermon rests largely upon the evidences of natural theology which point to the existence of a Creator and Sustainer. Although God allowed men to go their own way, he provided for them a witness unto himself in granting the rains and harvest times to satisfy the human appetites. **18.** Paul barely succeeded in persuading the people that he and Barnabas were not indeed divine beings.

19. No reference is made to a Jewish synagogue in Lystra, but probably such a synagogue existed, for **Jews from Antioch and Iconium** were able to raise up such opposition against Paul that he was **stoned** and dragged out of the city as dead. Paul refers to this event in II Cor 11:24,25. **20.** The abruptness of these words suggests that a miracle took place. It is difficult to conceive of a man's undergoing such a stoning without receiving severe physical injury. "The marks of Jesus" (Gal 6:17) may well be the scars inflicted by these stones. **Derbe.** A frontier city of the province of Galatia.

21. No opposition in Derbe is recorded. **The apostles made many disciples.** This is the meaning of **taught** (AV). The apostles retraced their steps through the cities of Galatia. **22.** The kingdom of God is here the future eschatological realm established by the return of Christ in glory. The very structure of things decrees that in this age the church must expect **tribulation** as it looks forward to the glory of the future kingdom. **The faith** is a synonym for the Gospel.

23. The apostles established a formal leadership in the several churches by the selection of **elders,** after the pattern of the Palestine churches (see note on 11:30). The method of choice is not clear, for the Greek word may describe either an election by the congregation or an appointment by the apostles. It does not designate formal ordination, as the AV suggests. The language suggests that there were several elders in each local church; but the church in a given city may have consisted of a number of house congregations with an elder ruling over each group.

24,25. Pisidia. The southernmost region of the province of Galatia. **Pamphylia.** A small province between Galatia and the Mediterranean Sea, of which **Perga** was the capital and **Attalia** the chief seaport.

26-28. The apostles now returned to **Antioch** in Syria, whence they had been sent upon this missionary venture. It is significant that no report was sent to Jerusalem. The church in Antioch had become independent of the mother church. They **abode long time;** this is one of Luke's characteristically indefinite notes of time. Probably the missionary journey in Galatia lasted about a year and the apostles now stayed in Antioch another year.

B. Problem of the Gentile Church, and Council in Jerusalem. 15:1-35. The success of the Gentile mission now brought to a head the most important problem in the early church—that of the relationship between Jewish and Gentile believers and the terms of admission of Gentiles into the church. In the earliest days, the church consisted of Jews, and the Gentile mission was not foreseen in spite of our Lord's commission. Philip took the Gospel to the Samaritans, and Peter, after being prepared by God, overcame his Jewish scruples and took the Gospel to Cornelius, entering into full fellowship with Gentiles. The establishment of a Gentile church in Antioch and the success of the Gentile mission in Galatia now focused attention upon a problem that had to be solved.

In the Jerusalem church existed a party which insisted that unless Gentiles were **circumcised after the custom of Moses,** they could not be saved and received into the church. Verse 5 indicates that these were converts from among the Pharisees, who were the strictest sect of the Jews. This party looked upon Christianity as a movement within Judaism. They retained all of the practices and customs of the Law, simply adding the gospel of the death and the resurrection of Jesus as the promised Jewish Messiah. It is apparent that no Jewish believers gave up their Jewish practices when they became Christians. However, Pharisee converts insisted that Gentiles must also become Jews in order to become Christians.

This problem had already been raised in the church. If, as seems likely, Gal 2:1-10 describes the famine visit of Acts 11:27-30 [For a statement of the alternative position, that Gal 2:1-10 describes an aspect of the council meeting of Acts 15, see under Gal 2:1 ff.—Editor.], then the leaders at Jerusalem had approved in principle Paul's mission to the Gentiles and did not insist upon circumcision for Gentile converts. Peter was in agreement with this policy; for some time later, when he came to Antioch, he showed that he had learned the lesson taught him by his vision from heaven, and freely entered into table fellowship with Gentile converts (Gal 2:11,12). Two different churches now existed: the Jewish church in Jerusalem, in which Jewish Christians were free to continue the practice of the OT Law, but as Jews and not as Christians; and the Gentile church in Antioch, where none of the Jewish ceremonial requirements were practiced. Peter approved of Gentile freedom from the Law; and when he was in a Gentile environment, he laid aside his Jewish practices for the sake of Christian fellowship.

The "right wing" party in Jerusalem saw something which was not evident to Peter: that the growth of the Gentile church must mean the inevitable end of the Jewish church. As intercourse increased between the two churches, Jewish Christians would have to follow Peter's example and lay aside their Jewish practices. Therefore, when certain men came from James to Antioch (Gal 2:12), they accused Peter of forsaking the Law and pointed out to him that his course of action meant the end of Judaism. Peter had not realized the consequences of his action. Therefore he withdrew from table fellowship with the Gentiles to reflect upon the situation. This immediately caused a breach in the church at Antioch. Paul recognized at once the implication of Peter's withdrawal; it meant nothing less than two separate churches—one Jewish and the other Gentile. Either Jewish Christians would have to lay aside Jewish practices and eat with Gentiles, or Gentiles would have to accept the entire law of Moses; otherwise there would be a divided church. Paul was quite willing for Jews as Jews to practice the law of Moses. But he insisted that when Jewish Christians came into a Gentile church, they must lay aside their Jewish scruples and enter into free fellowship with Gentiles. A divided church was unthinkable, and for Gentiles to accept the Law meant the end of salvation by grace. Paul's viewpoint apparently prevailed, but those of the Jewish party in Jerusalem were not satisfied. They came to Antioch again and insisted that Gentiles be circumcised to become Christians.

2. This caused such dissension that the church at Antioch found it necessary to have the issue decided in Jerusalem. Therefore a delegation was appointed to go to the **apostles and elders** and achieve a settlement of the question. **3.** We know nothing about the churches in **Phoenicia.** It was not Luke's purpose to relate a full history of the early church but only to trace the main lines of its rise and development.

4,5. The church in Jerusalem welcomed the delegation and listened to their story of the success of the Gentile church in Antioch and the Gentile mission in Galatia. Then criticism was voiced by converts from the Pharisees, who maintained their position that Gentile converts must become Jews and accept the law of Moses. **6.** This led to a formal conference of the **apostles and elders** with the delegation from Antioch. Verses 12,22, however, show that the church as a whole participated in the decision.

7-9. Paul's rebuke of Peter in Antioch (Gal 2:11) had been effective. So now Peter, as leader of the apostles, reverted to the position taken after his mission to Cornelius – that God had accepted the Gentiles as Gentiles by faith alone and not on Jewish terms. **10,11. A yoke** in Jewish thought does not necessarily mean a burden but designates an obligation. Here Peter asserts that Jewish legalism was an obligation and a burden that the Jews were unable to bear. In contrast to the burdensomeness of the Law, salvation is through grace both for Gentiles and for Jews. When Jews keep the Law, it is not as a means of salvation.

12. The assembly next listened to the report of Barnabas and Paul as they related the wonderful works of God among the Gentiles.

13-16. The last and decisive word was spoken by **James,** the brother of the Lord, who had come to assume a position of leadership among the elders and apostles in Jerusalem. He referred to Peter's mission to Cornelius and showed that the Gentile mission was in God's plan by quoting a passage from Amos 9:11,12. Some Bible students have seen in this quotation God's program for the end of the age. **After** the Gentile mission God will build again the **tabernacle of David** by restoring the fortunes of the Jewish nation (Acts 15:16). The result of the restoration of Israel at the end of the age will be a further salvation of the Gentiles (v. 17). This interpretation sees here three stages in God's program: 1. The calling out of a people for his name (the church age); 2. The restoration and salvation of Israel; 3. The final salvation of the Gentiles.

However, the quotation from Amos was cited to illustrate and give Scriptural support for the mission of Peter to the Gentiles (v. 14). Verse 15 refers to Peter's mission to Cornelius. **And to this,** i.e., that **God first visited the Gentiles, to take out of them a people for his name,** agrees the prophecy in Amos. If the salvation of **the residue of men** (v. 17) refers to an event at the end of the age, the quotation from Amos has nothing to do with the present visitation of the Gentiles. But James quoted the OT for precisely this purpose – to show that the present salvation of the Gentiles is in God's predicted purpose and that the Gentiles should therefore be freely accepted into the church. **A people for his name** (v. 14). The usual OT word designating Israel as the true people of God. The Gentiles were now included **in this people.** The rebuilding of **the tabernacle of David** therefore must refer to the salvation of the believing Jewish remnant, the "Israel within Israel" (see Rom 9:8; 11:1-5). Scripture elsewhere makes it clear that promises to Israel are fulfilled in the Church. "They which are of faith, the same are the children of Abraham" (Gal 3:7). "He is a Jew, which is one inwardly; and circumcision is that of the heart, in the spirit and not in the letter" (Rom 2:28,29). This does not mean that Israel as a nation has no future. Romans 11 clearly affirms that all Israel shall be saved; God yet has a future for national Israel. However, this was not James' concern; he was citing Amos to prove that the successful mission to the Gentiles is in the purpose of God and was predicted by the OT.

19. James therefore rendered the judgment that they should no longer **trouble** the Gentiles by demanding that they accept circumcision and the law of Moses.

20. There remained another problem, that concerning fellowship between Jew and Gentile. Gentile practices were strongly offensive to Jews and to Jewish Christians. Therefore, as a modus vivendi and an expression of Christian charity, James recommended that Gentile Christians abstain from certain practices that would offend their Jewish brethren. **Pollutions of idols** is described in 15:29 as **meats offered to idols.** Often meat purchased in the market places had been sacrificed in pagan temples to heathen deities. The eating of such meat was offensive to sensitive Jewish consciences, for it smacked of taking part in the worship of the pagan deity. **Fornication** may refer either to immorality in general or to religious prostitution in pagan temples. Such immorality was so common among Gentiles that it merited special attention. **Things strangled.** Meats from which the blood had not been properly removed. Such meat was considered a delicacy by many pagans. **Blood** refers to the pagan custom of using blood as a food. The last two requirements involved the same offense, for the Jew who believed that "the life is in the blood" (Lev 17:11) regarded the eating of any blood particularly offensive. This decree was issued to the Gentile churches not as a means of salvation but as a basis for fellowship, in the spirit of Paul's exhortation that those who were strong in faith should be willing to restrict their liberty in such matters rather than offend the weaker brother (Rom 14:1 ff.; I Cor 8:1 ff.).

21. Abstinence of Gentile Christians from practices offensive to Jews was required by the fact that Jews were to be found **in every city,** and whether in the Palestinian or in the Diaspora **synagogues, Moses . . . is read . . . every sabbath day** and the requirements of the Law strictly observed.

22. Judas called Barsabbas. Apparently a brother of Joseph called Barsabbas (1:23). **Silas.** The *Silvanus* of I Thess 1:1; II Cor 1:19; I Pet 5:12, who later became Paul's companion.

23. The salutation of the letter designates two groups and not three: either **the apostles and elders, brethren;** or **the apostles and elder brethren. 24. Subverting your souls** is too strong a translation; *upsetting your minds* is better. The Jerusalem church as a whole did not back the position of the extreme Judaizing party.

31-33. The decision of the Jerusalem church and the letter to Antioch apparently solved the problem. After an interval of some time, Judas and Silas returned to Jerusalem, while Paul and Barnabas remained in Antioch.

34. This verse in the AV does not appear in the most ancient texts.

C. Second Mission: Asia Minor and Europe. 15:36–18:22. Luke now records the preparations for what we call the second missionary journey. After an indefinite period of time, Paul determined to revisit and to confirm the churches already established. An unfortunate rupture occurred just then between Paul and

Barnabas. **Barnabas** wanted to take along John Mark, who had accompanied them on the first journey but had forsaken them when they had reached the mainland of Asia Minor, and had returned to Antioch. Paul regarded this as such a serious evidence of instability that he refused. The result was that Paul and Barnabas parted company. **Barnabas** and **John Mark sailed to Cyprus** to visit the churches established on the first missionary journey. Paul sent to Jerusalem for **Silas**, who had recently visited Antioch and in whom the apostle recognized a man of great promise.

41. Instead of traveling by ship, Paul and Silas set out by land toward Galatia. We know nothing about the establishment of **churches** in **Syria** and **Cilicia**, but we know from 15:23 that such churches existed. Possibly they were the result of Paul's work before he was brought to Antioch.

16:1. At **Lystra**, Paul selected **Timothy**, who had apparently been converted on the first mission, to be his traveling companion and one of his most important assistants. It was to this Timothy that Paul, toward the end of his life, wrote two of his last epistles. Timothy was of mixed parentage: his **father** was a **Greek** and his mother a **Jewess.** His mother, too, must have believed in Christ when Paul visited Lystra on his first journey; but his father, if he was still living, did not become a believer. We learn from II Tim 1:5 that the mother was named Eunice and that she had been a godly woman. **2.** Since Paul's first visit, Timothy had gained a good reputation among the believers in Lystra and Iconium.

3. Because Timothy was half Jew, to make him acceptable as a traveling companion to the Jews to whom they would minister, Paul **circumcised** him. Although the young man had been brought up by his mother in the faith of the OT (II Tim 3:15), the Jews looked upon him as the uncircumcised son of a Greek. On the other hand, Gentiles would have regarded him as a Jew because of his religion. As a man professing adherence to the Jewish religion but who remained an uncircumcised Gentile, Timothy would have been offensive to the Jews Paul met in city after city and to whom he first preached the Gospel. Paul circumcised him as an act of expediency and not of religious principle. No conflict exists in the fact that Paul steadfastly refused to circumcise Titus (Gal 2:3); for Titus was altogether a Gentile, and there was no cultural reason to circumcise him. Timothy was circumcised therefore not as a Christian but as a Jew. This is an application of the principle that Paul expressed in I Cor 9:20: "And unto the Jews I became as a Jew, that I might gain the Jews; to them that are under the law, as under the law that I might gain them that are under the law." Where no essential principle was involved, Paul applied the principle of expediency and of conciliation in a way that many later Christians cannot understand or appreciate. It was probably at this time that Timothy was set aside for his mission by the elders in Lystra (I Tim 4:14).

6-8. These verses can be interpreted in two ways, depending on whether one follows the "North Galatian" or the "South Galatian" theory; and the interpretation depends upon the meaning of the word **Galatia.** (a) **Galatia** can refer to the northern part of the Roman province of Galatia, where the people of Gallic extraction lived. If so, Paul passed through the **region of Phrygia** (the cities of Iconium and Antioch) and planned to go directly westward to the great cities of the province of Asia. When the **Holy Spirit** forbade him to travel toward Asia, he turned north to Galatia, i.e., to the northern part of the Roman province. Then he traveled westward toward **Mysia,** which is the northermost part of the province of Asia, and attempted to go into the province of **Bithynia,** which lies between Galatia and the Black Sea. When he was hindered in this plan, he passed by **Mysia** and came to **Troas** on the Aegean Sea. There is one difficulty with this "North Galatian" theory: It seems strange that Luke gives no account of the formation of such important churches as those to which the Galatian epistle was written, and there is no positive evidence that such churches existed.

(b) Therefore it is easier to follow the "South Galatian" theory, which understands **the region of Phrygia and Galatia** not as two separate regions but as a single area—*Phrygian Galatia.* This would have been the southern part of the Roman province of Galatia, in which the region of Phrygia was located and which included the city of Antioch. According to this view, after visiting Derbe and Lystra, Paul entertained the purpose of moving through Phrygia and Galatia directly westward to the great cities of Asia. When the Holy Spirit showed by some undesignated means that this was inadvisable, Paul journeyed through

Phrygian Galatia and then turned northward toward **Mysia** and **Bithynia.** When he approached Mysia, he tried to go into Bithynia, but again the Holy **Spirit** hindered him in this purpose. Consequently, he passed by **Mysia** and came to the seaport of **Troas.**

9. At **Troas** God revealed his purpose by sending a man who said, **Come over into Macedonia, and help us.** Such a request eliminates any problem as to how Paul recognized him as a man of Macedonia; his plea indicated his native country.

10. Here is the first of the famous "we" sections in Acts, where the narrative changes from the third person to the first person plural. The reason for this literary phenomenon has been vigorously debated, but the easiest explanation is that at this point the author of the record joined Paul and became his traveling companion. If this is the correct explanation, Luke joined Paul's company in Troas and traveled with him to Philippi (v. 16 is the end of this first "we" section), remaining in Philippi when Paul continued on his way.

11,12. Paul took ship from **Troas** and sailed to the island of **Samothrace** and the next day to **Neapolis,** which was the port of **Philippi,** a city lying ten miles inland. Macedonia was divided into four parts or **districts,** and Philippi was the chief city of one of these four districts. It was also a Roman **colony.** This word is a transliteration of the Latin term. "Colonies" were cities made up largely of Roman citizens and located at strategic points throughout the empire, which enjoyed special privileges, such as self-government, freedom from imperial taxation, and the same rights as citizens in Italy. Such a city was a little Rome far from the motherland.

13. Apparently there was no Jewish colony or synagogue in Philippi. Ten men were sufficient to constitute a synagogue. There was, however, an unofficial meeting place of a group of Jewish women and a number of God-fearers outside the city by the river. According to the best text, **where prayer was wont to be made** should be *where we supposed there was a place of prayer*. The word for *a place of prayer* is used in Jewish writings as a synonym for "synagogue." **We sat down.** The normal position for a Jewish teacher.

14. Lydia may be a proper name, or it may mean "the Lydian," designating the region in which Thyatira was situated. This area was famous for the manufacture and use of **purple** dye, and Lydia had brought this business to Philippi. This woman was a Gentile who had accepted the highest elements in Judaism. **15.** As a woman of means, Lydia had a family and servants, who followed her example in professing faith and being baptized. The phrase **household** may or may not include small children.

16. A spirit of divination. Literally, *a python spirit*. The priestess of Apollo at Delphi was called *python,* and the word was extended to soothsayers. A person having a python spirit was thought to be inspired by Apollo, who was associated with oracles. This girl was demon-possessed, and her uncontrolled utterances were regarded as the utterances of a god. Her owners made money for themselves by using her to tell fortunes. Just as a demon had recognized Jesus as the Holy One (Mk 1:24), so this demon recognized the divine power in Paul and his companions. **17. The most high God.** A designation used by pagans to indicate the supreme Jewish deity. **The way of salvation.** A common expression in Hellenistic religion, and a matter of great concern to many pagans.

19. Paul and Silas were seized not because they were preaching the Gospel but because they had disrupted a profitable business. Luke and Timothy for the time drop out of sight. Luke was concerned to trace the relations of Roman officials with the emissaries of the Gospel and to show that hostility came from other than official sources. **20.** The government of a Roman colony was vested in two **magistrates,** sometimes called "praetors." The Greek word translated "magistrate" is the equivalent of the Latin *praetor*.

21. Roman law permitted Jews to practice their own religion, but it forbade the propagating of foreign religions among Roman citizens. Paul and Silas were not recognized as Christians but as Jews who transgressed the prerogatives that Roman law allowed them.

22,23. No careful investigation was made of these charges. Mob action was roused, to which the magistrates yielded. Paul and Silas were stripped of their clothing and beaten. Verse 35 refers to the **sergeants** (AV) or *police* (RSV). This word designates lictors who attended the magistrates. Each lictor carried a bundle of rods with an axe inserted among them, symbolizing the power to inflict capital punishment. Paul and Silas were now beaten by the rods carried by these lictors. Paul tells us that he suffered this indignity on three different occasions (II Cor 11:25). This is the only such incident that Luke records. Paul and Silas were then locked up in the **inner prison** with their feet securely fastened in wooden stocks. The stocks could be so adjusted as to force a man's legs wide apart in a painful position.

26. Ramsay says that anyone who has seen a Turkish prison would not wonder at the effect of this earthquake. The door was sprung open and the stocks loosened from the walls. **27.** When the jailer was awakened and discovered the prison doors open, he assumed that the prisoners had fled. He determined to follow the only honorable course of action left to him and commit suicide. **28.** Although there was no light, Paul from the inner prison could see the outline of the jailer in the doorway, and he understood what the man was about to do. His call saved the jailer's life.

30. It is not clear what the jailer meant by his question about salvation. Had he listened to the preaching of Paul and Silas? Had he heard the fortuneteller declare that these men proclaimed the way of salvation? In any case, God blessed his modicum of faith, and he and his household were baptized. **34.** A Roman jailer was free to treat his prisoners as he desired so long as he produced them upon demand. This jailer now received Paul and Silas as his guests.

35. In the morning the magistrates decided that the beating and the night's imprisonment were sufficient punishment for these two Jewish troublemakers. So they sent the lictors to the prison with a command that Paul and Silas should be released and ushered out of town.

37. Because Roman citizens were immune from certain forms of punishment, Paul now pointed out that his legal rights as a Roman citizen had been flagrantly violated. He and Silas had been punished without proper legal procedure, **uncondemned.** Paul insisted that the magistrates now treat them with the courtesy due to Roman citizens if they wished them to leave town. Paul doubtless took this position not for self-vindication but that the small Christian community in Philippi might not be left with a shadow hanging over it.

38,39. The magistrates were smitten with deep concern for their improper conduct, for it could conceivably have disqualified them from holding office. They therefore **apologized** (RSV) to Paul and Silas; and although they realized that they could not expel these Roman citizens from the city, they begged them to depart. **40.** The apostles accepted the apology, and after visiting the believers in the house of Lydia and encouraging them, they took their leave. Timothy accompanied Paul and Silas, but Luke remained in Philippi. He appears in 20:5 at the beginning of the second "we" section.

17:1. Paul, Silas, and Timothy journeyed westward along the great military road called the Via Egnatia. The fact that they **passed through Amphipolis** and **Apollonia** indicates that Paul was following the definite plan of planting the Gospel in strategic cities. He did not aim simply to preach the Gospel wherever he could find an audience. Rather, he was a missionary statesman with a program for establishing churches in key centers from which the surrounding countryside could be evangelized. **Thessalonica.** The chief city and capital of the province of Macedonia. In the epistle later written to the Thessalonian church, Paul indicated that the Gospel was sounded forth from them not only in Macedonia and in Achaia but in every place (I Thess 1:8).

2. The apostle followed his usual custom of preaching the Gospel first in the Jewish synagogue. This he did for **three** consecutive **sabbath days.** In the Thessalonian correspondence, he recalls that he engaged in his trade of tent-making that he might not be a burden to the believers (I Thess 2:9; II Thess 3:7-12). The three weeks, therefore, is not meant to indicate the extent of Paul's mission in Thessalonica.

3. Paul's method of preaching consisted of **opening** the OT and **proving** that **the Messiah must suffer and rise from the dead;** and that the Messiah is in fact **Jesus,** whom he was proclaiming. **Alleging** (AV). Literally, *setting alongside*. Paul cited OT Scriptures and set alongside of them the historical fulfillment in Jesus of Nazareth. The Jews did not know how the Messiah could be both a conquering king and a suffering servant, and they therefore were not accustomed to apply the predictions of suffering to the Messiah.

4. As usual, a few Jews were **persuaded** (RSV; a better translation than AV *believed*), and they cast their lot with Paul and Silas. But most of the converts came from the fairly large group of God-fearing Gentiles.

5. The Jews went among the loafers hanging around the streets and stirred up a mob. **Lewd** (AV) simply means "wicked" or "evil." **Jason,** the Greek equivalent for Joshua, was apparently a believing Jew who had opened his house to Paul and Silas. The mob attacked Jason's house, intending to drag Paul and Silas out to trial. **People.** The general assembly of Greek people.

6. Jason had gotten wind of the mob and had removed Paul and Silas to safety. Instead of the evangelists, therefore, Jason and several brethren were brought before the city officials. **Rulers of the city.** Literally, *politarchs.* Since this term was long unknown in Greek literature, Luke was accused by some scholars of a gross inaccuracy. Inscriptions have now been found, however, which show that this term was the correct technical designation of city magistrates in cities of Macedonia. A list of such politarchs has been found engraved in a stone in an arch coming from the first century A.D. in Thessalonica.

7. Jason was charged with harboring men whose religious teaching had seditious political implications, for they proclaimed that **Jesus** was a **king** who would be a rival to the Roman emperor. **King.** The common Greek word to designate the Roman emperor (Jn 19:15; I Pet 2:13,17). This incident illustrates why the epistles of Paul as well as the Acts have relatively little to say about the kingdom of God. Much has been made of the fact that Paul almost never designates Jesus as King but rather calls him Lord. It has sometimes been said that Jesus is King of Israel but Lord of the Church, and that these two are entirely different concepts. This incident suggests that Paul laid little emphasis upon the kingship of Jesus and the kingdom of God because these ideas, familiar and precious to Jews, were subject to misunderstanding by Romans and suggested a rival political power. Such sedition was the charge brought against Jesus by Pilate (Lk 23:2). Rome was tolerant of many things but not of suspected sedition. Therefore Paul proclaimed Jesus to the Gentiles as Lord—a religious concept that was both familiar and acceptable to them and carried no political implications.

8,9. The politarchs were disturbed by this charge, but since Paul and Silas were not to be found, they settled the matter by making Jason and his companions responsible that no further breach of the peace should occur, and took a bond from them which would be forfeited in case of further trouble. This is probably the satanic hindrance to which Paul refers in I Thess 2:18, which made it impossible for him to return to Thessalonica and continue his ministry.

10,11. Beroea was some fifty miles to the west of Thessalonica. At this point Paul and Silas left the main military road and headed southward toward the province of Achaia. Here the Jews were not so prejudiced as those in Thessalonica. They showed openness of mind to test Paul's message by the OT Scriptures in order to decide whether or not it was true.

13-15. When hostile **Jews of Thessalonica** came to Beroea and stirred up opposition, some of the brethren accompanied Paul down to the seacoast and then to **Athens. As it were.** Rather, *as far as.* **Silas** and **Timotheus** did not accompany Paul to Athens but remained behind in Beroea under instructions to rejoin Paul as soon as possible in Athens.

16. Athens was not a city of great political or commercial importance, but it was the world's most famous intellectual center. Even young men of Rome often went to Athens for their university training. Paul's missionary strategy did not include the evangelizing of Athens. But as he waited there for Silas and Timothy, he was deeply moved by the evidence of **idolatry** he saw. The famous temples in Athens were works of art unsurpassed for beauty, but Paul saw behind the beauty the darkness of idolatry. **17.** Therefore he **argued** in the synagogue with the **Jews** and **devout** God-fearers, and he also engaged in discussion those whom he happened to meet in the market place.

18. Followers of the two most influential schools of philosophy of that day heard his message. The **Epicureans,** named after their founder Epicurus (341–270 B.C.), believed that the gods existed but had no interest whatsoever in the welfare of men. The chief end of life, the Epicureans held, was pleasure, which was to be sought in a happy and tranquil life, free from pain or trouble or fear, especially the fear of death. The **Stoics,** founded by Zeno (c. 300 B.C.), believed that God was the world's soul which indwelt all things, and that the happy life was that lived in accordance with nature. Since God was in all men, all men were brothers. Many Stoics were men of high moral principle. To these philosophers, Paul sounded like a **bab-**

bler. This word, which is literally *seed-picker,* was used to describe one who picked up scraps of undigested knowledge. **Jesus and the resurrection.** To the Greek ear, **Jesus** and *Anastasis* **(resurrection)** might sound like the names of a god and a goddess.

19. Areopagus may designate either the hill of Mars (v. 22, AV), which was situated between the market place and the Acropolis, or the council, which met in ancient times on Mars' Hill. Verses 22, 33 make the latter more probable. This council was not a trial court but a group of men who supervised religious and educational matters. Paul appeared before this council to give an account of his "philosophy," apparently to enable them to determine whether he should be permitted to teach in Athens. **21. The Athenians** and the **foreign residents** were noted for their curiosity, being eager to know "the last new idea" (Lake and Cadbury). **22. Mars' Hill** is the same word translated **Areopagus** in 17:19 and should be so rendered. Standing in the midst of this council, Paul attempted to make a point of contact by observing that they were **very religious.** This is a better translation than *too superstitious,* although both meanings are possible.

23. Devotions means *objects of worship.* No inscription has been found with the words **To an unknown God.** However, Greek writers tell us that altars to "unknown gods" were to be seen in Athens, and "if there were two or more altars each bearing an inscription 'to an unknown god,' these could well be referred to comprehensively as 'altars to unknown gods'" (F. F. Bruce, *Commentary).* In their religious zeal, the Athenians did not wish to omit from their worship any deity with whom they might not be acquainted. Paul asserted that there was indeed one whom they did not know, and this one he would declare to them.

24,25. Since this God is the creator of all things, Paul explained, and Lord of heaven and earth, he cannot dwell in any structure erected by men. Neither does he stand in need of anything that human service or worship can provide, for he himself is the source of all life.

26. Since God is the Creator, all men spring from a common source (AV **blood** is not in the best texts), and all men are dependent on him. He has provided them with the earth for a dwelling place and the **seasons** to supply their sustenance. This is the same thought that appears in 14:17 in the speech to the Greeks at Lystra. **Times** (AV) is the same word translated *seasons* in 14:17. **27.** The goodness of God manifested in the created world should lead men to seek God (see Rom 1:20).

28. The Lord is both a transcendent God who cannot be identified with his creation, and also the creating and the sustaining One, upon whom all men are dependent for their very physical life. The apostle illustrated this by words that appear to come from a Cretan poet named Epimenides. He then referred to the poet Aratus from his own country, Cilicia. Paul meant that all men are God's offspring in the sense that they are His creatures and dependent on Him for life. There is a Biblical doctrine of the universal fatherhood of God and brotherhood of man resting upon the fact of common creation rather than upon a spiritual relation, as this passage indicates. **29.** Since God is the creator of men, he must at least be greater than men. Therefore to identify the Deity with something man has made or imagined is the height of folly and the depth of sin (see Rom 1:22,23).

30,31. God **overlooked** (not *winked at,* AV) these **times of ignorance,** but has now given to men full knowledge of himself. Romans 3:25 refers to this patience of God for "the sins done aforetime," and Acts 14:16 alludes to the same patience. But God's patience will not last forever; because of the full knowledge now disclosed in Christ, he commands men to repent, and he has **appointed a day** when he will **judge the world in righteousness** by the man in whom this new light has come. The **pledge** *(assurance)* of this is provided by the resurrection of Jesus from the dead.

It has often been maintained that in Athens Paul attempted the intellectual approach and tried to be a philosopher among the philosophers rather than preaching the simple gospel of Jesus Christ. This is not a valid criticism, for the heart of the early Christian proclamation was the resurrection of Jesus Christ, and this was Paul's central emphasis in Athens. No message could have been more unpalatable to Greek philosophers than that of bodily resurrection from the dead and a day of judgment. A message of personal immortality in a disembodied state would have been acceptable, but the assertion of bodily resurrection was "untactful." Paul did not water down his gospel; he proclaimed the truth that struck at the very heart of Greek philosophy.

32-34. Some ridiculed Paul's message; others were willing to discuss it further. This ended the hearing, and Paul **went out from among** the council men. He was not altogether without success, for some **joined him,** confessing faith in Christ. One believer was a member of the Areopagus itself. But there were few converts in Athens. Not only is there no reference to a church in Athens, but "the firstfruits of Achaia" (I Cor 16:15) were in Corinth and not in Athens. There is no adequate reason to feel that Paul's failure was due to a false method that he later abandoned; it was due rather to the character of the Athenians themselves. Paul had not planned any evangelistic or missionary program in that city.

18:1. The apostle **left Athens** for **Corinth,** where he awaited the arrival of Timothy and Silas from Macedonia. Corinth was the capital of the Roman province of Achaia. It was situated on an isthmus commanding the sea routes to east and west as well as the land routes to north and south. It was a prosperous commercial center, famous for its cosmopolitan character, and notorious for its immorality. According to Strabo, the temple of Aphrodite had a thousand religious prostitutes. The reputation of Corinth is illustrated by the fact that the verb "to act like a Corinthian" was used of practicing fornication, and the phrase "Corinthian girls" designated harlots. Little wonder that the Corinthian church was later plagued by problems of immorality.

2. Suetonius *(Life of Claudius* 25.4) tells us that the Jews were indulging in constant riots at the instigation "of Chrestus," and Claudius therefore banished them from Rome in A.D. 49. It is possible that *Chrestus* (meaning "the useful one") is a Roman misunderstanding of *Christus,* a term that was meaningless to Romans. If so, this means that the gospel of Christ was being preached in the Jewish synagogues in Rome and was meeting such strenuous resistance that Claudius ordered all Jews to leave the city. It is not clear whether **Aquila** and **Priscilla** (called Prisca in the epistles of Paul) were believers before they left Rome. Since nothing is said of Paul's preaching the Gospel to them, they probably had become Christians in Rome. We know nothing about the origin of the Roman church. These two Jews came to Corinth and set themselves up in their trade. **3. Tentmakers.** Either manufacturers of heavy cloth from goats' hair, from which tents and other articles were made; or "leather workers" (Lake and Cadbury). It was customary for Jewish rabbis not to receive pay for their teaching, and therefore Paul, who had been reared as a rabbi, had learned the trade of tentmaking. The apostle did not at once launch into the evangelization of Corinth but joined Aquila and Priscilla in practicing his trade during the week. **4.** The Sabbaths he devoted to preaching in the **synagogue.** An inscription has been found in Corinth dating from the early first century, which reads, "Synagogue of the Hebrews."

5. Paul apparently planned to return from Corinth to Macedonia and continue his ministry in Thessalonica and Beroea after the arrival of Silas and Timothy. The Epistles tell us more about the movements of these two than does Acts. Paul had left them in Beroea with instructions to join him in Athens as soon as possible (17:15). They did, in fact, join Paul in Athens (I Thess 3:1), apparently bringing word that it was not safe for him to return to Macedonia. He therefore sent Timothy back to Thessalonica and Silas to some other city in Macedonia, possibly Philippi. Now Silas and Timothy joined him again in Corinth; and when they reported that Paul could not return to Macedonia, he devoted himself with fresh vigor to the evangelization of Corinth. **Pressed in the spirit,** according to the best texts, should be translated either *was constrained by the word,* or *was occupied in preaching.* Paul's message was that **Jesus was the Messiah.**

7. Next door to the Jewish synagogue was a house owned by one **Titus Justus,** a Gentile "God-fearer" (cf. note on 10:2) who attended the synagogue. He opened his house to Paul to preach the Gospel when the apostle left the synagogue. **8.** The conversion of **Crispus, the ruler of the synagogue** (see 13:15) together with his family must have been a blow to the Jews and given a great impetus to Paul's mission. The baptism of Crispus is mentioned in I Cor 1:14.

9-11. Apparently Paul had not been sure that it was the Lord's will for him to devote himself to evangelizing Corinth. But God now reassured him by a **vision,** urging him **not to be silent** and assuring him that his mission would be attended with divine blessing and success. Paul therefore spent more time in Corinth than was his custom, teaching the word of God for a year and a half

12. At the end of this period of time, a new **proconsul** came to the province of **Achaia,** of which Corinth was the capital city. Such provinces were under the supervision of the Senate and were governed by proconsuls, who filled a two-year term. **Gallio.** The brother of the philosopher Seneca. This provides the one relatively certain date in Paul's career, for Gallio arrived in Corinth in July of either 51 or 52, probably the former. Paul had already been in Corinth for a year and a half. **The Jews** seized the opportunity to try the mettle of this new proconsul, hoping that he might yield to their pressure. An unfavorable verdict from a Roman governor against Paul would have been effective not only in Corinth but throughout the entire province. Therefore they instigated a riot and brought Paul before Gallio's **judgment seat,** accusing the evangelist of propagating a religion that was **contrary** to the Roman **law.** Roman law recognized Judaism as a legitimate religion. The Jews accused Paul of teaching a new religion that was contrary to Judaism and therefore contrary to Roman law.

14-16. Gallio recognized that Paul was guilty of no **wrongdoing or vicious crime** (RSV). And the apostle's message, so far as he could tell, was only a variant form of Judaism and of interpretation of the Jewish law. Therefore he refused to render judgment against Paul and turned the accusers away.

17. The following incident reveals that there existed strong anti-Jewish feelings among the people. **Sosthenes** had succeeded Crispus as **ruler of the synagogue,** and the people set upon him and **beat him** in the presence of Gallio. That **Gallio cared for none of these things** does not mean that he was indifferent to spiritual values but that he deliberately *paid no attention* (RSV) to this mob action, which was technically a breach of the peace.

18. Paul now stayed in Corinth an indefinite period of time (**many days**), beyond the year and a half. Before leaving Corinth, he assumed a Nazarite vow (see Num 6:1-21) which was an OT act of thanksgiving or of dedication to God. During the period of the vow, the devotee allowed his hair to grow uncut, and at the end of the period he cut his hair. It is significant that while Paul steadfastly refused to permit the Law to be imposed on Gentiles, he himself, as a Jew, continued to practice many of its demands. As he came to **Cenchrea,** the eastern port of Corinth, on his way to Syria and Palestine, the time of his vow elapsed, and he therefore **cut his hair.**

19-21. Aquila and **Priscilla** separated from Paul at Ephesus and took up residence there. Paul engaged in a short ministry in the synagogue but refused to tarry. The words, **I must by all means keep this feast that cometh in Jerusalem,** are lacking in the majority of texts; but apart from this explanation, the reason for Paul's haste in returning to Palestine is unexplained.

22,23. These two brief verses summarize a long journey from Ephesus to Palestine and return. The **church** that Paul greeted was most certainly the church in Jerusalem, although this **city** is not mentioned. However, **Antioch** had sponsored the mission, and he spent some time in that city.

D. The Third Mission: Asia Minor and Europe. 18:23–21:17. Paul returned to Asia on what we call his third missionary journey, first traveling through the Phrygia-Galatia region, which he had visited on his second missionary journey (16:6).

24,25. Luke now interrupts his record of Paul's travels to relate an incident that took place in Ephesus. Jewish pilgrims who came to Jerusalem during the days of our Lord's ministry heard John the Baptist preach that the Messiah was soon to come. They recognized in the person and the works of Jesus the fulfillment of the OT Messianic prophecies. Such pilgrims would carry back home a report of the preaching of John and the life and ministry of Jesus, although they would not know of his death and resurrection and the coming of the Holy Spirit at Pentecost. The eloquent **Apollos** had accepted this good news about Jesus; and since he was **mighty in the Scriptures,** he was able to present the Messiahship of Jesus effectively to Jews.

26. When Priscilla and Aquila met him in Ephesus, they enlightened him **more accurately** about the Christian gospel, which included Christ's death and resurrection and the coming of the Holy Spirit. Quite likely, Apollos was now baptized by Aquila in the name of Christ. **27,28.** When he wished to go to Achaia, Aquila and Priscilla sent letters of recommendation for him, and he was able to reinforce Paul's work in Corinth, refuting the Jews by proving that **Jesus**

was the Messiah. That some of the Corinthian Christians formed a party claiming Apollos as their leader (I Cor 1:12; 3:4) was probably not due to any improper conduct on his part.

19:1. Paul traveled from Galatia to Ephesus, following the higher road, which was more direct than the trade route that followed the valleys through Colosse and Laodicea. In **Ephesus** he found **disciples** who had the same partial knowledge of Jesus as Apollos had had. There is no good reason for rejecting the usual meaning of disciples: believers in Jesus.

2. The apostle recognized that the disciples' knowledge of Jesus was incomplete. He therefore asked, **Did you receive the Holy Spirit when you believed?** (RSV) The Greek participle is *having believed*, and it is capable of being translated either *since ye believed* (AV) or *when you believed* (RSV). Since the Holy Spirit was usually received at the time of belief in Christ, the latter is preferable. Their answer must mean that they had heard no distinctively Christian truth about the Holy Spirit, for any one familiar with the OT would have heard about the Holy Spirit. **3,4.** These disciples had not heard about Pentecost. They knew only the message of John the Baptist—that men should receive a baptism of repentance in anticipation of the coming One, **Jesus.** The word *Christ* (AV) is not found in the best texts.

6,7. This does not describe a new Pentecost but an extension of the Pentecostal experience to include all believers. No special significance is to be sought in the imposition of Paul's hands for the bestowal of the Spirit. This experience, like that of Peter and John in Samaria (8:16,17), is designed to illustrate the oneness of the Church. Since believers are baptized by one Spirit into one body (I Cor 12:13), there can be no such "splinter groups" as these disciples of John outside the Church. It is beside the point to debate whether or not these disciples were Christians before Paul met them, even as it is futile to question whether the apostles were saved before Pentecost. They were disciples of Jesus but with an incomplete knowledge of the Gospel.

8,9. Ephesus was the capital of the Roman province of Asia, where the Roman proconsul resided. It was the chief Asian city in the promotion of emperor worship. It was also an important commercial and trade center, with a busy seaport, and it enjoyed great prosperity. Paul's message in the **synagogue** about **the kingdom of God** can hardly refer to the establishment of the kingdom at the second coming of Christ. The Christian gospel announces that the blessings of the kingdom of God have come to men in advance in the person of Jesus the Messiah (see Col 1:13). Most of the Jews accepted Paul's message in Ephesus; only **some** *(divers,* AV) **were hardened** and did not believe. However, this handful had such influence over the **congregation** (RSV) that Paul turned aside from the synagogue and engaged a school or lecture room belonging to one **Tyrannus.** One text says that Paul taught from 11 A.M until 4 P.M., when business was ordinarily suspended. He practiced his trade during the morning and preached the Gospel during the heat of the day. **The Way.** A technical phrase for Christianity in the early church.

10. During these **two years** Ephesus was the center for the evangelization of the entire area, and from it churches were established in Colosse, Laodicea, and Hierapolis (Col 2:1; 4:13). Probably the other churches mentioned in Rev 2:3 were brought into existence at this time. **12.** The **handkerchiefs or aprons** were articles of clothing used in Paul's trade.

13. Luke cites one illustration to show the effectiveness of Paul's ministry in Ephesus. **Traveling Jewish exorcists** were common in the ancient world. In antiquity, the **name** of a person or of a deity was thought to have special power that could control the person concerned if the name were used in the right way. These Jewish exorcists, witnessing the miracles done by Paul in the name of Jesus, attempted to use the name in the practice of their magical spells. **14-16.** No **high priest** by the name of **Sceva** is known. It may be that these **seven** Jews made a false claim to the priesthood and Luke merely reports their claim. Such a claim would be effective, for priests would certainly know how to use the divine name most effectively. The name of Jesus could not be used magically, and the demon recognized that these Jews had no right to use it.

18,19. The fate of the seven Jews led to the conversion of many other magicians. **Confessing and divulging their practices** (RSV) means that they forsook their magic, for it was believed that magical secrets lost their potency when they were made public. Other magicians brought their scrolls inscribed with magic spells and charms and burned them publicly. A number of such magical papyri have been discovered. The volumes burned at Ephesus were worth at least ten thousand dollars.

21. Luke next relates Paul's purpose for his future ministry. **Purpose in the spirit** may refer either to Paul's spirit (AV) or to the leading of the Holy Spirit (RSV). The apostle planned to revisit the churches in **Macedonia** and **Achaia** to collect money for the needy saints in **Jerusalem** (II Cor 8; 9; Rom 15:25 ff.). After taking this collection to Jerusalem, he intended to visit **Rome.** He did not plan an extended ministry there, but wished to visit the Roman Christians on his way to Spain (Rom 15:24,28). It was his policy to preach the Gospel where it had not been heard, and not to build upon another man's foundation (Rom 15:20).

22. Paul sent **Timothy** and **Erastus,** two of his associates, ahead into **Macedonia,** intending to follow them shortly. Luke does not mention Timothy between the time he rejoined Paul at Corinth (18:5) and this point; but he had been with the apostle in Ephesus. Neither does Luke record events that took place between Paul and the Corinthian church while the missionary was in Ephesus. Paul had previously sent Timothy to Corinth to deal with certain problems in the church (I Cor 4:17; 16:10,11). In addition, the older missionary himself had paid a flying visit there as is reported in II Cor 12:14; 13:1.

23. Paul's decision to leave Ephesus was hastened by a riot that arose about **the Way** (RSV). Ephesus was the seat of the worship of the great goddess **Artemis** *(Diana* in AV, vv. 24,27,28, is an inaccurate use of the Latin equivalent for the Greek Artemis). Artemis was not the traditional Greek goddess of this name but the ancient mother-goddess of Asia Minor, commonly known as Cybele. The temple of Artemis, the foundations of which have been uncovered, was one of the seven wonders of the ancient world.

24-27. A profitable **business** was carried on by a guild of silversmiths who made and sold miniature silver shrines containing likenesses of the goddess. Paul's ministry was so effective that the sale of shrines was falling off. Therefore one **Demetrius** called a meeting of guildsmen and pointed out that the trade of the silversmiths was in danger of **coming into disrepute** (RSV) and that if the evangelists were not stopped, the goddess Artemis herself might be **deposed from her magnificence** (RSV). The worship of Artemis is known to have been practiced in at least thirty-three places in the ancient world.

28-30. The mob spirit of the silversmiths spread like a contagion throughout the city and gave rise to a public demonstration in the open-air **theatre.** The ruins of this theater have been uncovered; it could hold over twenty thousand people. Since Paul was not at the moment available, the crowd seized two of his associates; and when the apostle purposed to go out to face the crowd, other disciples would not let him do so.

31. Asiarchs. Provincial officials who supervised and promoted the cult of the worship of Rome and the emperor. Only one person filled the office at a time, but the title was retained in an honorary capacity by previous office holders. Paul had a number of friends among these **Asiarchs** (AV *chief of Asia* is a poor translation) who begged him not to **venture into the theater** (RSV).

32. Meanwhile complete confusion reigned in the theater, so that most people did not know the reason for the gathering. **33,34.** Some of the **Jews** in the crowd felt that they were in danger of being blamed for the riot. Therefore they put forward a man named **Alexander** to make a speech and clear them of guilt. But their spokesman was shouted down, and chaos prevailed.

35. Order was finally restored by the **town clerk,** the executive officer of the city assembly. As the liaison officer between Ephesus and the Roman governor, he was responsible for such a riotous gathering. When he had **quieted** (AV, *appeased)* the people, he reminded them that Ephesus was not in danger of being degraded, for it was famous throughout the world as the **temple keeper** (AV *worshiper* is inadequate) of Artemis. **The image which fell down from Jupiter** is the translation of a single Greek word meaning literally *from the sky,* and probably refers to a meteorite in which the worshipers of Artemis thought they detected a likeness of the goddess and which they worshiped in the temple.

37,38. These men, he said, had done nothing **sacrilegious** (the word literally is *robbers of temples)* nor **blasphemous.** Furthermore, there were regular court days (AV, **the law is open**), and there were **proconsuls** (AV, *deputies)* who were appointed to handle such matters. The silversmiths should **bring charges**

(AV, *implead)* against one another through these regular channels. **39.** Other matters should be settled in the **regular assembly,** not in an irregular gathering. **Assembly** is the Greek word *ekklēsia,* which designates the regular gathering of Greek citizens.

40,41. The silversmiths feared the loss of their business. The town clerk pointed out that their real danger lay in the possibility of their being accused by the Romans of **rioting,** since no reason could be given to justify the confused gathering. These words quieted the mob and dispersed the assembly.

20:1. The purpose of Paul to revisit **Macedonia** and Achaia, stated in 19:21, was now carried out. The apostle's departure from Ephesus is reflected in II Corinthians. When he arrived at Troas, a great opportunity to preach the Gospel presented itself to him, but his concern for the troubles in the Corinthian church did not give him freedom of spirit to take advantage of it. Paul had previously sent Titus to Corinth to deal with the serious problems among the believers there, and he expected to meet his fellow worker in Troas. The failure of Titus to arrive as expected burdened Paul's heart, and he therefore left Troas and headed for Macedonia to meet his helper (II Cor 2:12,13). When Titus finally came from Corinth, he brought the good news of improved conditions in the church (II Cor 7:5-16). At this time Paul wrote the second letter to Corinth, sending it in advance of his own arrival by the hand of Titus and another brother (II Cor 8:17-19).

2,3. Luke passes over all of these activities without a word. After visiting the churches in Macedonia, Paul arrived in **Greece,** or Achaia, and there spent **three months,** probably in Corinth. During this time he wrote the Epistle to the Romans, informing the believers in Rome of his purpose to visit Jerusalem and then to come to Rome (Rom 15:22-29). Luke fails to mention one of the main reasons for Paul's final journey to Jerusalem: the delivery of a generous collection of money which the saints in Macedonia and Achaia had made to aid the poor (Rom 15:25-27; II Cor 8; 9). As Paul was about to take ship from Corinth to Syria, he learned of **a plot** by the Jews to kill him on this voyage. He changed his plans and, traveling by land through **Macedonia,** retraced his steps. **4. Into Asia** (AV) is from an inferior text; Paul's companions journeyed with him to Jerusalem. This party consisted of official representatives from the several churches that were sending money to the saints in Jerusalem.

5. Here begins a second "we" section, which continues to 20:15 and is resumed in 21:1. Luke had been left in Philippi on Paul's second journey (16:16). He now rejoined the apostle at Philippi and continued with him to Jerusalem. The rest of the party went on ahead and met Paul at Troas. **6.** The apostle tarried at Philippi to observe the week of **unleavened bread** and then sailed with Luke to **Troas** to join the rest of the party.

7. The missionaries gathered with the believers at Troas **on the first day of the week** to preach and to celebrate the Lord's Supper. This is the earliest clear reference to the Christian practice of observing Sunday as a day of worship. The first Christians, as Jews, probably continued to observe the Sabbath as well as the first day of the week. We are not told when or how the practice of Sunday worship arose in the church. **8,9.** The meeting was held in an upper room on the **third floor.** Illumination was provided by many smoky **lamps,** which made the air both stuffy and smoky. **They** (v. 8, AV) should read *we.* **11. Broken bread** refers to the breaking of the bread of the Lord's Supper. **Eaten** refers to the *agape* or love feast, a fellowship meal that accompanied the Lord's Supper.

13-15. Luke and the other members of the party now took a ship from Troas around a promontory of land to **Assos,** while Paul traveled by **land** (AV, *afoot).* The apostle embarked with the rest of his party at Assos and sailed to **Mitylene,** the chief town of the island of Lesbos. From Mitylene, they sailed between the mainland and the islands of **Chios** and **Samos** until they came to **Miletus.**

16,17. Because Paul desired to reach **Jerusalem** by **the day of Pentecost,** he had taken a ship from Troas that stopped at Miletus but did not go to **Ephesus.** He did not wish now to visit Ephesus, for he did not have the time to become involved with the problems and the life of the church there. But since his ship was lying over in Miletus for several days, there was time to send to Ephesus and have the leaders of the church come to him for a brief visit.

18-35. Paul's sermon to the Ephesian **elders** is of great significance because it reflects the simplicity of the primitive church organization. Luke calls the Ephesian leaders **elders** or *presbyters* (v.

17), while Paul calls them **overseers** (AV; *guardians*, RSV; v. 28). This word is *episcopoi*, later translated "bishops" (Phil 1:1; I Tim 3:1,2; Tit 1:7). **Presbyter** has a Jewish background, while **overseer** has a Greek background. It is clear that these two terms designate the same office of presbyter-bishop. Only at a later time does the bishop become a ruler distinct from the presbyters. Paul summarized his ministry in Ephesus by saying that he had testified **the gospel of the grace of God** (v. 24), **preaching the kingdom of God** (v. 25), two phrases which are here synonymous and interchangeable. Usually in the book of Acts the kingdom of God refers to the eschatological realm of salvation (14:22). But in this passage, the **kingdom of God** is the summary of Paul's entire message in Ephesus and refers to the present blessings of redemption in Christ.

22. Paul was going to Jerusalem under divine compulsion. The RSV is probably correct in translating **bound in the Spirit,** rather than following the AV, which refers only to Paul's inner compulsion. **23.** The Holy Spirit had disclosed to Paul, possibly through the utterances of prophets (see 21:1-14), that **bonds** (the word often refers to the bonds of imprisonment) and afflictions lay ahead.

28. This verse presents a difficult textual problem. The best text and the most natural translation is that of the AV, which speaks of **the church of God, which he hath purchased with his own blood.** In this context, however, **God** refers to the Father, and nowhere does Scripture refer to the blood of God. Therefore important ancient texts read, *the church of the Lord* (RSV). This, however, is a decidedly inferior reading; **the church of God** must be preferred. It is possible to translate, *which he hath purchased with the blood of his Own,* as the margin of the RSV suggests (see Bruce, *Commentary*).

29,30. Paul predicted that troubles would come to the Ephesian church from two sources: **fierce wolves** would enter the church from without, and false teachers would arise from their own midst to turn disciples away from the faith. The growth of heresy at Ephesus is reflected in I Tim 1:3-7.

33-35. Paul reminded the Ephesians of his custom of making tents not only to support himself but to provide for the needs of others with him. He quoted a saying of the Lord which is not recorded in any of our Gospels, about the blessedness of giving. Very few authentic sayings of Christ have thus survived outside of our Gospels. The main objective of giving in the early church was to provide for the needs of poor brethren rather than to support the preaching of the Gospel, as is the case today.

36-38. The expectation of the Ephesian elders **that they should see his face no more** need not be understood as a hard and fast prophecy that Paul would never again visit Ephesus. The Pastoral Epistles indicate a further ministry after his release from imprisonment at Rome. It does, however, like 20:22,24, reflect the expectation that serious troubles and possible death lay ahead for Paul.

21:1,2. Paul and his party resumed their trip by boat, sailing between the islands and the mainland. **Cos** and **Rhodes.** Two islands where they anchored overnight. Rhodes was also the name of a city located on the island of the same name. **At Patara,** a city on the mainland, they found a ship that would sail directly across the sea to **Phoenicia,** leaving the island of Cyprus on their left. Apparently favorable conditions enabled them to make a rapid voyage, for after this point, Paul no longer appeared to be in haste to reach Jerusalem by Pentecost.

3-6. When they landed at Tyre, Paul had a bit of leisure, for seven days were required for the ship to **unload its cargo.** Disciples had come to Phoenicia as a result of the persecution following Stephen's death (11:19), and Paul now **sought out the disciples** in Tyre (RSV). In this church were prophets who disclosed **through the Spirit** that Paul faced serious dangers in Jerusalem. They therefore sought to dissuade him from his purpose. However, when Paul persisted, the entire church accompanied him to his ship, and after prayer on the seashore, the evangelist and his party embarked.

7. Continuing the journey, they sailed to **Ptolemais,** the southern port of Phoenicia, where Paul spent one day with the believers in that city.

8. Arriving at **Caesarea,** the apostle was entertained by **Philip,** who had gained a reputation as an evangelist. Philip, one of the seven chosen to supervise the ministry to the widows in the early church (6:3 ff.), had evangelized Samaria (8:5 ff.), the Ethiopian eunuch (8:26 ff.), and the coastal plain (8:40). He was last seen in Caesarea (8:40) and apparently made his permanent home in that city. He is called **Philip the evangelist** to distinguish him from Philip the apostle.

9. Philip's **four daughters** were endowed with the gift of prophecy. The fact that they were **unmarried** is only an interesting detail and carries no necessary religious significance.

10,11. Paul, no longer under pressure to reach Jerusalem, spent several days with Philip. **Agabus,** a prophet from Jerusalem (11:27,28), following the example of OT prophets, symbolically acted out the fate that he foresaw for the apostle in Jerusalem, and predicted that he would be delivered **into the hands of the Gentiles. 12,13.** Again the believers tried to dissuade Paul from going to Jerusalem. He replied that it was not important to him whether he lived or died, but their tears were in danger of "softening his will" (F. F. Bruce).

14. Paul's friends then acceded to the will of the Lord. There is no reason to think that Paul went to Jerusalem in violation of the will of God. We are to understand the several prophetic forecasts not as prohibitions from the Holy Spirit but as forewarnings of what lay ahead. As a result of these prophecies, Paul's friends tried to dissuade him from risking his life; but the apostle remained steadfast in accomplishing his course and in fulfilling the will of God in spite of personal danger. **15.** The expression, **we took up our carriages,** is one of the most picturesque archaisms of the AV. The Greek word means simply to make preparations, and it might best be translated *when our preparations were completed.*

16. The Greek of this verse is a bit obscure and may be translated either **bringing us to the house of Mnason . . . with whom we should lodge** (RSV); or **brought with them one Mnason . . . with whom we should lodge** (AV). If the former is correct, Mnason lived somewhere between Caesarea and Jerusalem (a journey of sixty-five miles), and there the party spent the night. It is equally likely, however, that Mnason, a disciple from the earliest days (**an old disciple** has no reference to his age) but a Hellenistic Jew, owned a house in Jerusalem, where he planned to entertain Paul and his party. Paul was accompanied by Gentile Christians, and it was not clear how these Gentiles would be welcomed by the Jewish Christians in Jerusalem. The lodging provided by Mnason promised to avoid tensions that might arise because of associations between Jewish and Gentile believers.

V. Extension of the Church to Rome. 21:18–28:31.

Luke has related the extension of the church from Jerusalem through Judea and Samaria until a semi-independent Gentile church was established in Antioch. From Antioch the Gospel was carried by Paul on three missions through Asia and Europe. Evangelistic and missionary work was undoubtedly being carried on during this time by other apostles. We have, for instance, no account of the evangelization of Egypt, with its great center, Alexandria. Luke is concerned only to trace the main outlines of what he considers to be the most significant line of expansion—toward Rome. There remains only the need to record Paul's mission of taking the Gospel to Rome.

It is evident that it was not Luke's purpose to record the initial evangelization of Rome nor the beginnings of the church there, for he tells how Christian brethren welcomed Paul upon his arrival at the capital (28:15). We know that Paul had written a letter to the church at Rome (Rom 1:7), but Luke gives us no record of how the Gospel originally came to the Imperial City.

Since Luke's purpose was not to describe the initial evangelizing of Rome, it possibly was to show that although Paul first preached the kingdom of God to the Jews, he turned to the Gentiles when the Jews rejected his message (28:24-31). The geographical extension of the church was not Luke's main interest; it was rather **the movement of redemptive history from the Jews to the Gentiles.** In keeping with this purpose, Luke devotes considerable space to the record of Paul's last visit to Jerusalem, not because the visit was important in itself, but because it showed the final rejection of the Gospel by Jerusalem.

A. Rejection of the Gospel by Jerusalem. 21:18–26:32. **18,19.** Paul was received in Jerusalem by James, the brother of the Lord, who had become the leader of the Jerusalem church (15:13), and by the **elders.** Apparently none of the apostles was in Jerusalem at this time. Paul was cordially welcomed by the leaders of the church, to whom he related the success of the Gospel among the Gentiles. He made a statement to the effect that Gentile believers were introduced to the Christian life on the basis of faith alone apart from the keeping of the Jewish law. The leaders of the Jerusalem church heartily approved of this procedure.

20,21. Although the leaders of the Jerusalem church were delighted with Paul's report, they had a word of caution for him. They told him that there were thousands of believing **Jews** who even as Christians continued to be **zealous for the law** of Moses, and that these had been informed that Paul not only preached to Gentiles a gospel of grace entirely apart from the Law, but also taught the Jews of the dispersion to **forsake Moses** and to neglect **circumcision** and the observance of the OT customs. This meant that Paul urged Jews to abandon Judaism and cease to be Jews, i.e., to become Gentiles.

22-24. James and the Jerusalem elders realized that this report was not true and that Paul permitted Jewish believers as Jews to continue in the Law. But they felt that something must be done to show the Jewish Christians that this report was false. **The multitude must needs come together** (AV) is not in the best texts. They suggested that Paul submit himself to the Law to prove to the Jews that he did not advocate the abolishment of the Law for Jewish Christians. There were **four** Jews who had taken a Nazarite **vow**. This ordinarily lasted thirty days, but they had incurred some defilement that had placed them in a condition of ceremonial impurity for **seven days** (v. 27). At the end of this period, they would shave their heads and offer certain sacrifices of purification to God. The elders suggested to Paul that he identify himself with these four and practice the common Jewish custom of paying the expenses for the sacrifices. This would prove to the Jewish church that Paul himself accepted the Jewish customs.

25. James assured Paul that this would not mean a modification of the decision rendered in the Jerusalem council that the Gentiles should be free from the Law but should only **abstain from** certain things that would give particular offense to their Jewish Christian brethren.

26. Paul accepted the counsel of the elders and for several successive days (the verb is in the imperfect tense) went into the Temple with the four Jews to offer a purifying sacrifice for each of them.

There is no fundamental inconsistency between Paul's willingness as a Jew to observe the Law and his inflexible insistence that Gentile believers should not be brought under the Law, since they stood under grace. As a new creature in Christ Jesus, neither circumcision nor uncircumcision could have any vital importance to Paul (Gal 6:15). The evangelist considered such religious practices a matter of indifference, for the world had been crucified to him and he to the world (Gal 6:14). He himself said that if a man was converted as a Jew, he was to remain a Jew (I Cor 7:18), for circumcision in itself means nothing. Jewish Christians might keep the Law as Jews, not as Christians. But when efforts were made to impose the Law on Gentile Christians as a basis of salvation, Paul objected and insisted upon complete freedom from the Law. Undoubtedly if Jewish believers had desired to give up the practice of the Law, Paul would not have resisted them. Paul's position of letting expediency determine principle in certain areas is so delicate a matter that many have not understood him and have accused him unnecessarily of radical inconsistency.

27-29. Apparently Paul's course of action satisfied the Jewish Christians, but it aroused the enmity of a group of unbelieving **Jews from Asia** who had come to Jerusalem to worship at the feast of Pentecost. These men had known Paul in Asia, and they had seen him in Jerusalem in the company of **Trophimus,** a Gentile convert from Ephesus. Now when they saw the apostle in the court of Israel, where only Jews were permitted, they leaped to the conclusion that he had taken Trophimus into the temple court with him. The temple area included a vast court of the Gentiles in which non-Jews were free to come and go. Between this outer court and the court of Israel was a low parapet with inscriptions warning Gentiles not to venture into the court of Israel on pain of death. Two of these inscriptions have been found. The Asian Jews assumed that Paul had thus profaned the Temple and **defiled the holy place.**

30. A mob spirit quickly spread through the crowd, and Paul was dragged out of the court of Israel into the court of the Gentiles. Then the **gates** separating the two courts **were shut** to prevent further rioting within the sacred precincts.

31. Northwest of the temple area was the Tower of Antonia, which housed a cohort of Roman soldiers under a military tribune. This tower was connected with the temple court by two flights of stairs, by which quick access could be had in case of trouble. A **cohort** consisted of a thousand men. Now as Paul was about to be killed by mob action, word came to the **chiliarch** (AV, *chief captain;* RSV, *tribune)* of the garrison that a riot was occurring. **32.** He took a band of at least 200 men with their **centurions** and intervened just in time to save Paul's life. **33.** He **arrested** Paul, taking him into protective custody, and commanded that he be chained to two soldiers for safekeeping.

34. When the tribune tried to determine the cause of the riot, the shouts of the crowd were so contradictory that he could not find out what had happened. He therefore commanded that Paul be carried up the steps into the **barracks** (RSV). *Castle* (AV) reflects the old English idea of a military fortification. **35.** But by the time they reached the **steps** leading to the Tower of Antonia from the temple area, the mob had become so violent that the soldiers had to pick up Paul and carry him.

37. As they came to the head of the stairs, Paul surprised the tribune by speaking to him in Greek.

38. Some three years before this time, an Egyptian Jew had stirred up a **revolt** by leading four thousand men out to the Mount of Olives, promising that the walls of the city would be leveled before them and that they would be able to overthrow the Roman garrison. The supporters of this revolt were called **assassins** (RSV; *murderers,* AV; literally, *sicarii)* because each carried a knife *(sica)* concealed in his garments with which he might assassinate political opponents. This revolt had been crushed by the Roman procurator Felix, but the Egyptian had escaped. The tribune for some reason identified his captive with that Jewish rebel.

39,40. When Paul assured the tribune that he, as a Jew, had a right to enter the temple precincts and that he was a citizen of the important city of Tarsus, the officer permitted him to try to quiet the mob The apostle stood at the head of the stairs overlooking the court of the Gentiles, while the soldiers stood below him on the stairs. When Paul had captured the attention of the mob, he began to speak to them in the native **Aramaic** dialect, which was the common Jewish language of both Palestine and western Asia.

22:1,2. Many Jews of the Diaspora could speak only Greek; and so when the apostle unexpectedly addressed the crowd in their own dialect, he captured their attention.

3. Paul attempted to win their sympathy by assuring them that he perfectly understood the Jewish faith. Although he was born in Tarsus, he had been **brought up** in Jerusalem at the feet of Gamaliel, who was one of the most famous rabbis of the time. He had thus been educated according to the **strict manner of the law** of the Jews and had been as **zealous toward God** as they themselves.

4,5. He further tried to win Jewish sympathy by reminding the crowd that, as a zealot for the Law, he had persecuted the followers of **this Way.** He reminded them that the **high priest and the whole council of the elders** (the Jewish Sanhedrin) could support his testimony, for they had given him letters of extradition to the Jewish brethren in Damascus to arrest Jewish believers who had fled to that city.

6-16. The apostle told the Jews what had turned him from his zeal for the Jewish traditions (cf. the earlier account of his conversion, Acts 9). He emphasized that his commission from the risen and ascended Christ had come to him through a Jewish believer who was a **devout man according to the law,** and who had a good reputation among the Jews in Damascus. Ananias had told him that **the God of our fathers,** that is, the God of Israel, had chosen him to **know his will,** to **see the righteous One** (see 3:14; 7:52 for this title), and to be a witness to all men of what he had experienced. Ananias then exhorted Paul to be baptized in token of the washing away of his sins, calling upon the **name of the Lord.**

17-21. Paul told of a confirmation of this call given to him through a vision after he had returned to Jerusalem (9:26). Since Paul was not concerned to give a complete account of his experience, he omitted all mention of the three years he spent in Arabia (cf. Gal 1:17,18). He related another aspect of his experience in Jerusalem that Luke did not record in his earlier account. Acts 9 says that Paul was sent away from Jerusalem by the brethren to escape a plot to kill him (vv. 28-30). Here Paul tells us that he had left Jerusalem in response to a word from the Lord. While he was praying in the Temple as a faithful Jew, God had warned him in a **trance** that Jerusalem would not receive his message and that he therefore should **get quickly out of Jerusalem.** Paul protested that the

Jews' knowledge of his earlier zeal and sincerity in persecuting the Christians would convince them of the reality of his conversion. The Lord replied that he should leave Jerusalem, for he would be sent **far away unto the Gentiles** (RSV). The word *martys* (v. 20), translated **thy martyr** (AV), should be translated *thy witness* (RSV). *Martys* means "witness," and it only gradually came to designate a witness who sealed his witness with his blood.

22,23. The mob **listened to him** until he mentioned the Gentiles. The word **Gentiles** set the spark to the tinder of the Jews' wrath, and they began to shout for the captive's death, to **wave their garments** (RSV), and to throw **dust into the air** as a gesture of anger.

24. The **tribune,** realizing that he could gain no accurate information from the mob, decided to try to extort a confession from Paul by torture. Though scourging was a legal procedure with slaves, a free man could not legally be scourged. **25.** As they **tied** Paul up and were about to scourge him, he asked if it was lawful to scourge a Roman citizen who had not even received a fair trial.

26-28. Roman citizenship could be obtained by birth from parents who were Roman citizens, or by purchase with money, or as a gift from the Roman government. After the abuse he had just suffered, Paul presented a rather sorry spectacle; and perhaps the words of the tribune implied that such a person must have obtained citizenship very cheaply. Paul replied that he did not buy citizenship but was born of parents who were already citizens. We do not know how his parents became citizens, but it is usually supposed that citizenship was given them as a reward for some service rendered to an earlier Roman ruler.

29. Upon these words, the soldiers who were about to torture Paul at once **drew back from him.** The tribune was stricken with **fear** because he had initiated an illegal procedure against a Roman citizen. **30.** He decided that the proper course of action would be to ask the Jewish Sanhedrin to conduct a hearing and to determine if adequate grounds existed for legal procedures against Paul.

23:1. Paul began his defense before the Sanhedrin by claiming that he had acted in **good conscience before God,** not only in these affairs for which he was being accused but throughout his entire life. **2. Ananias** was the high priest about A.D. 48–58. He was reputedly a very greedy, insolent, overbearing man. Angered by this bold claim of Paul, he commanded some who stood near the apostle to **strike him on the mouth. 3.** Jesus in his trial had also been struck in the face (Jn 18:22) and had challenged the propriety of this blow.

With indignant words Paul now challenged this irregular conduct from a member of the Sanhedrin, accusing those who claimed they were enforcing the Law of actually violating the Law themselves. **Whited wall** suggests a tottering wall whose precarious position has been disguised by a generous coat of whitewash (Bruce, *Commentary).* The meaning is that although he held a high position, Ananias was bound to come to grief. In fact, Ananias was assassinated some eight years later.

4,5. When Paul was rebuked for speaking in such strong terms to **God's high priest,** he apologized, saying that he **did not know** that this man **was the high priest.** No explanation is given as to why Paul did not recognize the high priest, who usually presided over regular meetings of the Sanhedrin and therefore would be easily identifiable. Possibly this was not a regular session of the Sanhedrin and the high priest therefore was not occupying his usual position or wearing his official robes. Possibly Paul did not see from whom the command came to strike him. Some have thought that his words were ironical and mean that Paul did not think that a man who acted in this way could be the high priest.

6. This arbitrary and illegal conduct of the high priest made Paul realize that he could not expect a fair hearing from the Sanhedrin. Therefore he resorted to a strategem to divide his opposition. The Sanhedrin was composed of **Pharisees** and **Sadducees,** who differed on important points of doctrine. The Pharisees, who had developed an elaborate tradition based on the entire OT, believed in bodily resurrection and in an elaborate hierarchy of angels and demons in the spirit world. The Sadducees rejected the later developments in Jewish theology, denying both the doctrine of resurrection and the angelology and demonology. As a Pharisee, Paul had believed in the doctrine of resurrection. As a Christian, the teaching of resurrection took on new significance for him because it was linked inseparably with the resurrection of Jesus Christ. To Paul's mind, the Sadducean denial of resurrection would make Christianity utterly impossible, "for if the dead are not raised, neither hath Christ been raised" (I Cor 15:16). The early Christians had met their first opposition from the Sadducees when they proclaimed in Jesus the doctrine of resurrection from the dead (4:1,2). Now Paul asserted that he was a Pharisee, that the fundamental question at stake was that of the resurrection of the dead, and that it was really because of this doctrine that he was on trial.

9. This served to divide the assembly. The **scribes,** i.e., the students of the Law, who belonged to the **Pharisees' party,** supported Paul to the point of suggesting that the two visions he had experienced near Damascus and in Jerusalem might have been the visitation of **a spirit or an angel.** The words, **let us not fight against God** (AV), are found only in the later Greek texts and were inserted in echo of Gamaliel's words in 5:39.

10. We may assume that the opposition to Paul from the orthodox Jews had been headed up by the priestly Sadducees because of the charge against Paul of polluting the Temple (21:28). Now that Paul had won the sympathy of the Pharisees, order gave way to chaos, and the prisoner was in danger of suffering bodily harm from the opposing elements in the Sanhedrin. Therefore the Roman tribune ordered the soldiers to intervene and to bring Paul to the Tower of Antonia (**castle,** AV).

11. These experiences made Paul feel that his worst forebodings of sufferings in Jerusalem (20:22-24) were likely to be realized. That night he was granted a reassuring vision in which he learned that he would not be killed in Jerusalem but would finally reach **Rome.**

12,13. Paul's fanatical opponents now contrived another way of trying to do away with him. A group of over forty **Jews** conspired together and **bound themselves by a solemn oath** that they would either kill Paul or starve to death. The extent of their fanaticism can be understood when we realize that the execution of this plot would certainly have meant the death of many of them at the hands of the strong Roman guard who protected Paul. However, this risk did not deter these fanatics.

14,15. In order to gain the co-operation of those **priests** and **elders** who had opposed Paul, they informed them of the plot. The priests were to summon a meeting of the council, which would ask the tribune to bring Paul a second time before the Sanhedrin under the pretense that they desired to determine the facts of the case more exactly. The conspiring Jews would waylay Paul and the Roman guards between the Tower of Antonia and the Council House and would kill him. Though this plot failed, these oath-bound Jews did not actually starve to death, for scribal casuistry had ways of relieving men from such an oath.

16. We know almost nothing about Paul's family. It is usually assumed that the apostle's words in Phil 3:8 that he had "suffered the loss of all things" mean that when he became a Christian, his family disinherited him. Paul never refers to any members of his family. We know, however, that he had a nephew, the **son** of a **sister,** who somehow learned of this plan of **ambush** (RSV). How he obtained this information we can only guess. However, he had such a warm feeling for Paul that he brought the word of the plot to the prisoner in the Tower of Antonia. Paul at once sent him to the tribune with his information.

23,24. The tribune, realizing that he had an explosive situation on his hands, determined to solve the problem by sending Paul under heavy guard to the Roman procurator in the capital at Caesarea. **The third hour of the night** was between 9:00 and 10:00 P.M. The word translated **spearmen** has not been found elsewhere, and its meaning is uncertain. Literally it means, *holding by the right.* This was an unusually strong guard, but the tribune was taking no chance that his prisoner might be assassinated and the responsibility fall on him. **25-30.** His letter to the procurator **Felix** explains his reason for sending Paul. For the first time we are given the name of the tribune, **Claudius Lysias. The governor** or **procurator** Felix is addressed as **most excellent** (AV) or *his Excellency* (RSV). This was the usual form of address for members of the Roman equestrian order and also for governors in certain provinces. It is the same title given to Theophilus in Lk 1:3. The tribune's explanation makes it appear that he recognized Paul as a Roman before he rescued him from the Jews (v. 27). Verse 28 suggests that the hearing before the Sanhedrin was not a formal trial but a preliminary investigation to determine the nature of the case. Lysias of course makes no reference to the fact that he had nearly scourged Paul.

31. Antipatris was some thirty-five to forty miles from Jerusalem. A forced march brought Paul with his heavy guard to this point by morning. **32,33.** Now the immediate danger of assassination was over, and the four hundred foot soldiers and spearmen returned to Jerusalem, while only the seventy cavalrymen accompanied Paul the remaining distance to Caesarea.

34. Antonius Felix was the governor or **procurator** of Judea between A.D. 52 and 58. Our historical sources refer to him as an evil man. Tacitus says that "with all manner of cruelty and lust he exercised the functions of a prince with the mind of a slave" (*Histories* 5.9). His period of office in Palestine was characterized by a growing spirit of insurrection, and he governed with a ruthless and heavy hand.

In a case such as this, he had to determine the province from which the prisoner had come, for an accused man might be tried either in his own native country or in the country in which the crime had been committed. Since **Cilicia** was a Roman province, it was proper for a Roman governor to carry out the examination without consultation with any native prince. When Jesus appeared before the procurator of Judea, Pontius Pilate, the procurator, sent him to Herod Antipas, who ruled over Galilee, from which Jesus had come. In the case of Paul, no such external consultation was found necessary.

35. Felix committed Paul to custody in **Herod's palace** (Gr. *praetorium*, RSV). Herod the Great had made Caesarea his capital for all Palestine and had built a palace in this city. This royal residence had been taken over by the Roman governors and made their residence and the seat of the administrative activities.

24:1. Tertullus was a common name in the Roman world. This Tertullus was an **advocate** or attorney (AV, *orator; RSV spokesman* is too colorless) familiar with Roman legal procedures, who provided professional counsel for **Ananias** and the **elders.** As the representative of his clients, he **made his charges** (AV *informed* is too colorless) to the governor against Paul.

2. Tertullus' use of the first person plural in his speech may indicate either that he was himself a Jew or merely that he was associating himself with his clients. The expression **our law,** if genuine, would suggest that he was in fact a Jew. Tertullus introduced his speech with customary expressions of flattery to the governor. According to the best texts, he recalled **reforms** that Felix had introduced on behalf of the Jews (RSV). **3.** The word translated **most noble** Felix is the same word used in 23:26 and Lk 1:3, and should be translated *most excellent* Felix. **4. Clemency.** Better, *kindness, moderation,* or *gentleness*. In fact, Felix was noted for his ferocity rather than for his gentleness.

5,6. Tertullus alleged a threefold accusation against Paul: 1. He was a pest who created dissension among the Jews throughout the world. 2. He was the ringleader of the sect of the Nazarenes. 3. He tried to profane the Temple. The word translated a **mover of sedition** (AV) may refer merely to dissensions among the Jews, but it may also carry a veiled hint that Paul was a leader of Jewish movements that were seditious against Rome. If so, this charge was entirely without foundation, for in every instance when Paul had appeared before Gentile rulers, he had been exonerated of any seditious tendency.

This is the only place in the NT where the followers of Jesus are called Nazarenes. The term continued to be a designation for Christians in Semitic speech, and it is used today in Hebrew and Arabic. **Sect** is the word used by Josephus to designate the various parties within Judaism, such as the Pharisees and Sadducees. The Christians were not yet recognized as a separate group but were regarded as a party within Judaism. Tertullus toned down the earlier charge (21:28) that Paul had actually defiled the Temple and alleged merely that he had attempted to do so. Actual conviction of defiling the Temple would have provided adequate ground for legal execution.

6b-8a. These words are not in the oldest texts, but they may well be authentic. Tertullus alleged that the Jewish Sanhedrin was handling Paul's case in perfectly legal fashion, when the Roman tribune, Lysias, without justification, intervened and by force took Paul out of their hands. This is, of course, a serious distortion of the facts; but Lysias was not present to give his side of the story.

10. Paul introduced his defense with a very modest compliment to Felix, implying that the governor's experience in ruling the Jews for so long a time would assure the accused a fair trial.

11-13. The apostle flatly denied the charge of stirring up dissension. **14,15.** He admitted that he was a follower of **the Way**, but he claimed that this was the true fulfillment of the OT faith and was founded on the hope of the resurrection. **Heresy** (AV) is the same word translated "sect" in 24:5, and should be so translated. It designates no "heretical" tendencies but only a legitimate party within Judaism. Nowhere in his epistles does Paul affirm the **resurrection** of both **the just and the unjust,** although his doctrine of the judgment of the unjust must imply it. In his epistles, Paul is primarily concerned with the resurrection of those who are in Christ. There is no necessity to conclude that Paul here suggests that the resurrection of all men will occur at a single time. I Cor 15:23,24 suggests that the resurrection of those who are in Christ occurs before "the end," when the final resurrection will occur.

17,18. Here is the one clear reference in Acts to the purpose of Paul's visit to Jerusalem, which occupies so large a place in his epistles. The evangelist had brought a collection from the Gentile churches to the impoverished Jewish Christians in Jerusalem.

19-21. Paul claimed that no proof had been brought of any wrongdoing on his part and that the only real charge brought against him was a doctrinal one concerning the resurrection of the dead. This was a matter in which a Roman court would have no interest or jurisdiction.

22,23. Felix already had a **rather accurate knowledge** (RSV) of this new sect in Judaism called **the Way.** Perhaps he had obtained this knowledge from his wife Drusilla (see v. 24). However, the statements of Tertullus and Paul embodied conflicting testimony, and therefore he adjourned the hearing until Lysias, the Roman tribune, should come to Caesarea, at which time he promised to **decide the case** (RSV). Paul was placed in a custody that allowed him considerable **liberty** and permitted his friends to minister to his needs. Luke does not inform us whether Lysias came to Caesarea and whether the promised hearing was conducted.

24. Drusilla was the youngest daughter of Herod Agrippa I (see 12:1). She had been married to the King of Emesa, a small state in Syria, but Felix had persuaded her to leave her first husband to marry him. The governor desired to improve his knowledge about the Way, and he therefore had Paul tell him further about **faith in Christ Jesus. 25.** Paul adapted his message to the situation, emphasizing the ethical implications of the Way. His message of **righteousness and self-control and coming judgment** understandably alarmed Felix, who dismissed the hearing until a later time.

26. The governor fully realized that there was no case against Paul and that he should be dismissed. Although accepting a bribe for the release of a prisoner was forbidden by Roman law, it was a common practice and quite consistent with Felix' character. The procurator, therefore, retained Paul as a prisoner and conversed with him frequently, hoping for a bribe.

27. At the end of two years, the governor was recalled to Rome by the emperor Nero under accusation by the Jews of bad administration. **Porcius Festus** succeeded him as procurator of Judea. Though Felix knew that justice required Paul's dismissal, he left him in prison because he saw that he could thereby ingratiate himself with the Jews. While this two-year incarceration must have been very trying to Paul, one redeeming feature was that throughout this entire time Luke was in Palestine with the apostle. Quite certainly Luke used this time to gather information about the life and ministry of Jesus and to compile notes about the life of the early church. This material later appeared in the Gospel of Luke and in the Acts.

25:1. Festus was a far more honorable and fair ruler than Felix. But by this time Palestine had become a hotbed of seething unrest, and he died in office without being able to settle the troubled conditions.

Festus came first to Caesarea, the capital of his province. However, since Jerusalem was the religious capital, he felt it advisable to make an early visit to that city to try to establish good relations with the leaders of his new subjects.

2,3. The Jewish rulers thought they saw in this visit an opportunity to put pressure on a new and inexperienced governor. They therefore **asked** as **a favor** that he send the prisoner Paul to Jerusalem. Perhaps the same forty Jews who had earlier entered into a plot now again plotted to kill Paul en route to Jerusalem. **4,5.** Festus saw no reason to grant this favor. He intended shortly to return to Caesarea, and he invited **the men of authority** (RSV) or men of ability (AV, *them . . . which . . . are able)* to accompany him on his return and to accuse Paul in the capital.

6,8. Some ten days later, when the hearing was held in Caesarea, the Jewish leaders made **serious charges** (RSV) against the apostle for which they could bring no tangible proof whatever. Paul categorically denied that he had committed any offense against the Law, against the Temple, or against Caesar.

9. As a newcomer to Palestine, unfamiliar with Jewish affairs, Festus did not grasp the point of this argument (see v. 20). The accusations and the defense flatly contradicted each other. However, affairs were so unstable in Palestine that it seemed feasible for him to try to gain the good will of the Jewish leaders. They had previously urged that Paul be brought to Jerusalem for trial; Festus therefore suggested to the prisoner that the trial be transferred to Jerusalem to the scene of the alleged crimes.

10. This plan seemed utterly unreasonable to Paul. It was at Jerusalem that he had had to be rescued from a plot against his life, and it seemed the course of folly to risk such danger again. Although Paul had not been convicted of crime, Festus appeared willing to conciliate the Jews at the apostle's expense, and Paul doubtless feared what might be the end of such a conciliatory course. One course of action for avoiding this danger was open to him as a Roman citizen, i.e., appeal to Caesar. He was confident that in Rome he would receive a fair trial; but before the inexperienced Festus, he feared the influence of the Jews. **11.** This verse suggests that real danger of death at the hands of the Jews awaited Paul in Jerusalem. The apostle asserted that he was quite willing to suffer the death penalty if he was convicted of wrongdoing. Death penalty, however, had to be imposed by Roman justice; it could not be imposed by the Jews. Therefore Paul appealed to Caesar.

12. The council (AV). Not the Jewish Sanhedrin but the circle of advisors who accompanied Festus. Apparently appeal to Caesar did not function automatically; but Festus, with the support of **his council**, granted this request.

13. Before Paul could be sent away, a native king, **Agrippa,** came to Caesarea to greet Festus as the new Roman governor. Herod Agrippa II was the son of the first persecutor of the church (ch. 12). When Agrippa I died, his kingdom was not bestowed upon his son but was placed under Roman governors. In A.D. 53 Agrippa II was given the former tetrarchy of Philip, and also Abilene, a small area north of Palestine. Later, certain towns in Galilee and Perea were added to his domain. In addition, he was entrusted with the important function of the supervision of the temple treasure in Jerusalem and with the appointment of the high priest. This gave him a large influence in Jewish affairs, and his interests thus overlapped with those of Festus. **Bernice,** sister of Herod, had been wife of an uncle, Herod of Chalcis. Her husband had died, and she was now living with her brother in Caesarea Philippi.

14-21. While Agrippa was in Caesarea, it occurred to Festus that here was an admirable opportunity to get help in formulating the report he must send to Caesar explaining Paul's case and the reason for his appeal to the emperor. Agrippa, who was familiar with the Jewish religion, would be able to analyze accurately the nature of the problem Festus could not understand. Therefore he outlined the case, indicating that the accusations seemed to involve no real crimes (v. 18) but only **disputations** about fine points of the Jewish religion (**superstition** is the root of the same word used in Acts 17:22) and about one Jesus whom Paul affirmed to have come back to life from the dead. The word translated **hearing** (v. 21, AV) later became a technical word for a legal decision. **Augustus** (AV) is a misleading translation. The word, which is a translation of the Latin *Augustus,* means "the revered" or "august one"; it was applied to all of the Roman emperors. Augustus was the first Roman emperor; at this time the emperor was Nero. The best modern equivalent for Augustus would be "his majesty."

23. A further hearing was therefore set up before Festus, Agrippa, Bernice, and an advisory council consisting of the **military tribunes** and the **principal men of the city. 24-27.** Festus explained the purpose of this hearing. He had found no reason why he should accede to the demands of the Jewish leaders that Paul be put to death; but since the prisoner had appealed to the emperor, Festus had to compose a letter to explain the character of the charges that he did not understand. **Lord** (v. 26) is here applied to the emperor. This title was used in the Roman provinces of Asia to designate the emperors and carried a divine connotation. The emperor Caligula (A.D. 12–41) was the first to call himself *Dominus,* and the practice later became common.

26:1. When Agrippa granted Paul permission to speak for himself, the apostle **stretched forth the hand** in a gesture of salutation to the king, and **made his defense** (RSV).

2,3. He expressed his gratification that he was able to make his defense before King Agrippa, because the king was an expert in Jewish customs and questions. Although Agrippa had received his throne from Rome and was pro-Roman in sympathy, he also understood the Jews and had a reputation for promoting Jewish interests so far as this was possible. Paul, therefore, believed he could convince Agrippa that his message was but the true fulfillment of the hereditary Jewish faith. The apostle outlined his upbringing, first in his **own nation,** in Tarsus of Cilicia, and then later at Jerusalem. (The AV omits an important connective between **nation** and **Jerusalem.**) All of the Jews knew that Paul was reared in **the strictest party** of the Jewish **religion,** that is, that he was a Pharisee.

6-8. A central doctrine in the faith of the Pharisees was that of the resurrection. The promise that God had made to the fathers was bound up with this hope in resurrection; and now it was because of this very hope which the Pharisees themselves entertained that Paul stood accused by Jews. To anyone who knew the promise given to the fathers, Paul said, it should not seem incredible that God raises the dead. The position of **by Jews** (v. 7) is very emphatic, suggesting that it is an utterly amazing thing that Jews who have hope in the resurrection should accuse Paul for entertaining this very hope.

9-11. Paul explained how he was brought to associate his faith in Jesus with the resurrection. He had not always been of this persuasion, for he was formerly convinced that he ought to oppose the name of Jesus of Nazareth. This account describes in greater detail than the earlier accounts Paul's persecution of the early church. The fact that some Christians **were put to death** is nowhere else mentioned in Acts. Paul's method was to **try to make them blaspheme** the name of Christ and thus renounce their faith. The tense of the Greek word indicates that Paul failed in his attempt. *Compelled them to blaspheme* (AV) says too much. To call Jesus accursed meant to renounce Christian faith.

12-14. This is the only one of the three accounts of Paul's conversion that contains the words, **it is hard for thee to kick against the pricks. It is hard** means "it is painful" rather than "it is difficult." **Pricks.** Goads, used to prod beasts of burden. This was a proverbial saying, found in Greek and Latin but not at that time in Hebrew or Aramaic. It probably indicates that Paul had not been altogether at ease in his conscience in his persecution of Christians. We are not to think that Paul was under a great conviction of sin, for he elsewhere tells us that he persecuted the church in ignorance (I Tim 1:13). However, deep in his mind was the nagging conviction that possibly Stephen and the other Christians were right; and the Lord now showed him that this was a divine pressure.

16-18. Before Herod there was no need to refer to Ananias as there had been earlier (22:14), when Paul was appealing to orthodox Jews. Paul therefore attributed his call directly to the Lord without mention of the human agency. His experience had convinced him that Jesus, whom he had persecuted, was alive, and had sent him both to **the people,** i.e., to the Jews, and also to **the Gentiles.** Paul laid before Agrippa the crucial issue: his message was not only for Israel but also for the Gentiles; both were to be enlightened, to turn **from darkness to light** and **from the power of Satan to God.** Thus they would receive **forgiveness of sins** and an inheritance **among those who are sanctified** by faith in Christ. This verse, which is the summary of Paul's message, is very similar to Col 1:12-14.

19,20. These verses are designed to give not a chronological outline but merely a rough summary of Paul's whole missionary career. Paul preached repentance and conversion first in Damascus, then in Jerusalem, then throughout the country of Judea, and also to the Gentiles, as he was commissioned to do. There is a problem in harmonizing this statement with Gal 1:22, which says that Paul was unknown personally to the churches of Christ in Judea. Possibly the correct text should have read, "in every land to both Jews and Gentiles" (see Bruce, *Commentary*, following Blass).

21. Festus had been unable to understand the basic reason for the animosity of the Jews against Paul. Paul explained that he had been proclaiming the fulfillment of the promise made to the fathers as including the Gentiles as well as the Jews. For this reason the Jews caught him in the Temple and tried to kill him. "Knowing the Jews as he did, perhaps Agrippa understood why they would cherish such animosity towards a former rabbi who would offer Gentile believers spiritual privileges on the same footing as the chosen people" (F. F. Bruce).

22,23. Paul concluded by insisting that his message embodied nothing except that which Moses and the prophets had foretold: namely, that **the Messiah must suffer** and that He **should be the first that should rise from the dead** and should proclaim light both to the Jews and to the Gentiles. This explains why Paul previously placed such emphasis upon the Resurrection. The traditional Jewish hope of resurrection had now taken a new turn because of the resurrection of Christ. The resurrection of the Messiah was not an isolated event, but the beginning of the resurrection itself. Christ was "the firstfruits of them that sleep" (I Cor 15:20), "the firstborn from the dead" (Col 1:18).

24. To the Roman Festus, this line of thought was one which no sane man could pursue. Paul was obviously a man of extensive learning, but he must be insane to harbor such ideas of resurrection from the dead.

25-27. Paul replied that he was quite sane and was speaking **the sober truth.** He then appealed to King Agrippa to vouch for the sobriety and the sanity of what he had just said. He reminded Agrippa that the death and resurrection of Jesus had not **escaped** his notice, for they were **not done in a corner** where no one would behold them. When anyone compares these events with the prophets, he must be convinced of the soundness of Paul's position; and Paul therefore appealed directly to the king, **Do you believe the prophets? I know that you believe.** This appeal placed Agrippa in an uncomfortable dilemma. As a representative of Rome and a colleague of Festus in the administration of government, he did not wish to appear to Festus to share Paul's insanity, and therefore it would have been unpleasant to agree with Paul and admit that he believed the prophets. On the other hand, to deny that he believed the prophets would have seriously impaired his influence with the Jews. Agrippa therefore parried Paul's appeal with the response, **In short, you are trying to make me play the Christian.** The Greek phrase is very difficult and literally translated says, *In a little you are persuading me to make a Christian. In a little* may mean either, "in a little time" or "in brief." *To make a Christian* may mean either to become a Christian or to play the role of a Christian. The translation of the AV is certainly incorrect; Agrippa was not on the point of becoming a Christian. His remark may be a sarcastic parry of Paul's appeal: "In a short time, you think to make me a Christian!" (RSV). However, the rendition suggested above (that of F. F. Bruce) makes Agrippa brush aside Paul's appeal by replying that Paul is not going to make Agrippa play the role of a Christian and try to persuade Festus of the correctness of his prisoner's position.

29. Paul took Agrippa's light comment seriously and replied solemnly, **whether in short or at length** (literally, *in a little or in a great deal)* he wished that all men who heard him might become Christians as he was—with the exception of the chains he was wearing because he was a Christian.

30-32. When Paul ended his defense, Festus, Agrippa, and Bernice, together with their advisors, withdrew to deliberate on the matter. It was obvious that Paul had violated no law and deserved neither death nor imprisonment. He deserved only to be set free; but since he had appealed to Caesar, the legal processes had to be carried out and the appeal carried through. We are to suppose that Festus, with the aid of Agrippa, composed the letter to the emperor explaining the charges of the Jews and recommending Paul's dismissal.

B. Reception of the Gospel in Rome. 27:1–28:31. Luke now relates Paul's journey from Palestine to Italy and his reception in Rome. The fact that Luke tells in detail about this trip shows how important it was for his purpose. The motif of the journey, in Luke's account, is not the initial evangelization of the Roman capital but the rejection of the Gospel by the Jews in Rome and its acceptance by the Gentiles. This brings to a climax one of the central motifs of the entire book—the rejection of Israel and the rise of the Gentile church.

27:1,2. The account of Paul's journey begins with the third "we" section. The last "we" reference was 21:18, when Paul, accompanied by Luke, arrived in Jerusalem; and we must assume that during the two years of Paul's imprisonment, Luke was in the area of Caesarea. Luke now accompanied Paul, along with **Aristarchus** of Thessalonica (see 19:29; 20:4), who had come with the apostle from Thessalonica to Jerusalem. The Roman authorities delivered Paul to a centurion named Julius. The band called **the Augustan cohort** has not been identified with any certainty. The centurion was responsible for the safe delivery of Paul and some other prisoners. The point of embarkation is not mentioned, but it was probably Caesarea. Here they found a coasting vessel from **Adramyttium,** a port of Mysia lying south of Troas in Asia Minor. The course of this ship called for it to sail to the ports along the coast of Asia en route to its home port.

3. The first port of call was Sidon of Phoenicia. The centurion **Julius treated** Paul with special kindness, and gave him liberty to go ashore while the ship was unloading and also to visit his friends, who constituted the Christian community in that city, and receive their ministrations.

4. Since the prevailing summer winds blew from the west or the northwest, the ship sailed between **Cyprus** and the mainland rather than directly into the wind. **5.** It was now necessary to leave the coast and to sail across the open sea westward below **Cilicia** and **Pamphylia. Myra** of Lycia was a port of call for large ships, especially grain ships, sailing between Egypt and Rome, which found it impossible to sail directly across the sea because of the northwesterly winds. **6.** At **Myra** they changed ships, leaving the coasting vessel and taking a grain ship that was sailing from **Alexandria** to **Italy.** Egypt was the chief source of supply of grain for Rome, and the transportation of grain between Alexandria and Rome was an important business conducted under the supervision of the state.

7. The voyage from Myra into the face of the westerly winds was difficult. But after several days they arrived **with difficulty** at **Cnidus** on a promontory at the southwest tip of Asia Minor. From this point, they had the choice of waiting for a more favorable wind and sailing directly westward, or else sailing southward toward Crete. Since **the wind did not allow us to go on** (RSV), the writer says, they chose the latter alternative and sailed southward around **Salome** at the eastern end of Crete and then coasted along westward under the island.

8. After sailing along the coast **with difficulty** *(hardly passing it,* AV) they came to a port called **Fair Havens** midway in the island. **9.** West of Fair Havens the coast of Crete falls off abruptly to the north, so that from that point a ship would be completely exposed to the northwest winds. The sailboats used in the ancient Mediterranean world were not large or sturdy enough to face the winter storms. The dangerous season for sailing began about September 14, and after November 11 all sailing came to an end for the winter. **The fast** to which Luke refers is the Day of Atonement, which **fell** at the end of September or early in October.

10,11. Paul, who was an experienced traveler (II Cor 11:25 says he was shipwrecked three times), advised against continuing the journey at this time lest there be much loss of life as well as of cargo. His advice was opposed by the **captain** *(master,* AV) who was in control of navigation and was the **owner of the ship.** The **centurion** in charge of the prisoners, being the highest official on ship, ranked as the commanding officer; and he **followed the advice** *(believed,* AV) of the shipmaster and owner rather than that of Paul, and decided not to stay at Fair Havens.

12. Fair Havens was not a suitable harbor to winter in, since it was quite exposed. Apparently the advice of all on shipboard was sought, and **the majority** advised that they sail from Fair Havens **on the chance** that they might reach the harbor of **Phoenix,** which lay further west in Crete, facing **southwest and northwest.**

13. Leaving Fair Havens, they were favored by a gentle **south wind** and were able to follow close along the shore of the island. **14.** Suddenly, however, the gentle breeze turned into a **tempestuous wind** blowing from the **northeast. Euroclydon,** meaning "northeaster," is a hybrid word, partly Greek and partly Latin. **15.** At this point they were not far from their destination of Phoenix; but when the ship could not **head into the wind** because of its violence, they had to surrender to the wind and be driven by it.

16. As they came opposite a small island called **Cauda** (other manuscripts read *Clauda),* they found it necessary to pull on board the small **boat** that was carried in tow behind the ship. By this time, this little boat was so waterlogged, that it was secured only with difficulty.

17. Measures were then taken to **undergird the ship.** The nature of this operation is not clear, but it perhaps consisted of running ropes underneath the boat to strengthen it. The ship was now being driven toward the southwest in the direction of Cyrene. Off the north African shore was a dangerous quicksand called **Syrtis** (RSV), and since the sailors feared that they would be driven across the sea onto these shoals, they **lowered the gear** (RSV). This may mean that they *struck sail* (AV), or it may mean that they let out a sea anchor to slow their speed, or that they set storm sails. Nevertheless, they were driven on by the wind.

18. By the next day, the tempest had not weakened, and it was therefore necessary **to throw the cargo overboard** (literally, *they made an ejection*). **19.** When the storm did not abate on the next day, they threw overboard all extra **tackle** and gear.

20. Since sailors were entirely dependent upon the sun and stars for navigation, hope was at last abandoned of being saved, since they had no idea where they were and where they were being driven by the tempest.

21-26. The combination of seasickness, pitching decks, and soaked provisions had caused them to go **long without food.** *Long abstinence* (AV) should not be understood to denote a deliberate fast. Finally, Paul offered a word of encouragement which he prefaced with the all-too-human reminder, "I told you so." He informed the crew and the passengers that an angel of God had appeared to him and assured him that he would escape this peril to **stand before Caesar,** and that his traveling companions would be saved along with him.

27. Experts have figured that it would take exactly fourteen days to drift the distance indicated in the narrative. **Up and down** (AV). Inaccurate. They were drifting *across the sea of Adria*. Adria does not refer to the Adriatic Sea but is a term commonly used of the entire eastern Mediterranean. Something now led the sailors to believe that (lit.) *some land was approaching*. Probably the sound of breakers resounded through the darkness and warned that they were approaching the land. **28.** Soundings indicated that the water was growing increasingly shallow.

30. Some of the sailors decided to escape from the ship to the shore by a small boat rather than risk falling upon the rocks. Therefore, **under pretext** of casting anchors from the **bow,** they undertook to flee the ship. **31,32.** Paul detected the plan and warned the **centurion** and the soldiers that safety lay in staying with the ship. The sailors' plan was frustrated when the soldiers cut away the ropes of the boat and thus **let it fall away.**

33-36. At daybreak, Paul advised the crew and passengers to break their involuntary fast and eat some food, that they might be strengthened by it, and he assured them that no one would perish in the landing that lay ahead. He then set the example by giving thanks to God and eating a substantial meal. All were encouraged and followed his example. **38.** After all had eaten their fill, they cast the rest of the cargo of wheat into the sea to lighten the ship in preparation for the landing.

39. When daylight came and they were able to see the shore, they did not recognize the land. But they observed a bay with a beach, where they planned to bring the ship ashore. **40.** Therefore they **cast off the anchors and left them in the sea** (RSV; this is a far more probable translation than that of the AV). **Rudders.** Two large steering oars on each side of the boat, which would have been lashed tight during the storm. Now these rudders were freed, a small **foresail** was raised to the wind (not *mainsail,* AV), and the ship headed toward the shore.

41. However, the men did not reach the shore, for the ship ran aground on a narrow strip of submerged land separating two stretches of deeper water (the Greek is, **a place of two seas**). The bow of the ship was stuck fast in this shoal, but the force of the waves against the stern was breaking the ship in two.

42,43. The soldiers guarding the prisoners wished to follow the traditional Roman discipline and kill their charges rather than risk the escape of any of them. But the centurion, who had become favorably disposed toward Paul and did not wish to see his death, forbade their doing this. Rather, he ordered all to escape to the shore either by swimming, by floating on planks, or by being carried on the backs of some of the crew (the Greek is, **on some of those from the ship; those** may be either neuter or masculine). Thus all safely reached the land.

28:1. After coming ashore, they discovered that the island was called **Melita** (AV; modern *Malta,* RSV) lying about a hundred miles directly south of Sicily. Melita (the Canaanite word for "refuge") was inhabited by people of Phoenician extraction. **2.** From the Roman and Greek point of view, every one who spoke a foreign language was called a barbarian.

Barbarous people (AV) has no reference to fierce character or primitive culture, but merely indicates that their language (Phoenician) was not Greek or Latin. Since it was raining and cold, these natives showed **no usual kindness** by building a fire so that the chilled and soaked travelers might warm themselves.

3. A large fire for such a large company needed constant replenishing with fuel, and Paul set about gathering wood for the flames. In one bundle was a poisonous snake, stiff from the cold; and as the apostle stood by the fire warming his hands, the **viper,** revived by the heat, crawled away from the flames and sank its fangs into Paul's hand. **4.** The natives interpreted this event in terms of their own superstition. They concluded that Paul actually was a murderer; and although he had escaped death in the sea, the goddess of justice, *Dike,* had now wrought a proper fate upon him. **5,6.** When Paul shook the snake off into the fire without injury, the natives decided that they had been completely wrong. Instead of a victim of the gods, he was himself a divine being who could not be hurt by ordinary human misfortunes.

7. The chief man of the island. The leading official. The word used has been found in two inscriptions as a title for an official in the island. We do not know whether this **chief man** was a native official or a representative of Rome. This Publius had an estate in the neighborhood, where he entertained Paul and his companions for three days, showing them gracious hospitality.

8. Dysentery and fever were common on the island of Malta. **9,10. Healed** in 28:9 is a different word from that in 28:8, and might better be translated *were cured* or *were treated.* It suggests not miraculous healings but medical treatment, probably at the hands of Luke the physician. Verses 10 and 11 suggest that this medical ministry lasted throughout the three months stay at Malta, so that when Paul and Luke left the island, they were **honored with many honors,** and their ship was loaded with everything they needed for the remaining journey.

11. The shipwreck had taken place during the first half of November. **Three months** later, or the middle of February, would still be considered early for safe sailing, but apparently an early spring had come. They found a ship sailing from Alexandria to Italy, which had spent the winter in the island. Ancient ships took their names from their figureheads. This ship had as its figurehead or **sign** (AV) the *Dioscuri,* a term meaning the "sons of Zeus," designating the two brothers, Castor and Pollux, who were regarded as the patron deities of sailors. **12.** Sailing directly north, they came to **Syracuse,** the most important city of Sicily, located on the southeastern side of the island.

13. From Syracuse, since the winds were not favorable, it was necessary to **make a circuit** or tack back and forth in order to reach Rhegium on the toe of Italy. The quaint archaism of the AV, *fetched a compass,* has nothing to do with instruments of navigation. Here the party waited for a more favorable wind, and when the south wind arose on the next day, they easily came to Puteoli, on the bay of Naples, the regular port of arrival for grain ships coming from Alexandria.

14. Apparently Julius, the centurion in charge of the prisoners, had official business that detained him in Puteoli, and he permitted Paul to accept the invitation of Christian brethren in the city to spend the seven days with them. Similar permission had been granted in Sidon (27:3).

15. News of Paul's approach reached Rome during these seven days, and Christian brethren came down the Appian Way to meet Paul and Luke and to accompany them back to the city. The word rendered **to meet** is the same word used of the 'rapture' of believers **to meet** the Lord in the air at his second coming (I Thess 4:17). It is a term regularly used of the official welcome tendered by a delegation who went out to meet a visiting official and accompany him into the city. The **Forum of Appius** is some forty-three miles from Rome, and **Three Taverns** is about ten miles nearer. Both were stopping places on the Appian Way, with inns where travelers might lodge.

16. The statement, **the centurion delivered the prisoners to the captain of the guard,** is found in only a few of the ancient texts and is probably not authentic. Paul was not locked up in prison but was placed under the guard of a soldier who was responsible with his life to present the prisoner at the proper time. Paul was chained by the wrist to the soldier (see v. 20) but was permitted to maintain his own dwelling and to exercise a large measure of freedom. This is the last of the "we" sections. However, since Luke is mentioned in Paul's correspondence written from Rome (Phm

24; Col 4:14), it is clear that he remained with the prisoner in Rome.

17-20. There were a number of Jewish synagogues in Rome, but since Paul was a prisoner, even though he enjoyed some freedom, it was not convenient for him to visit them. Therefore he called the leaders of the Jews together that he might present his case to them. He claimed that he had violated none of the Jewish customs and as an innocent man was delivered prisoner into the hands of the Romans. In spite of the fact that the Romans had wished to release him, the Jews had opposed their decision, and so Paul had felt that his only way of escape was to appeal to Caesar. However, Paul did not desire to make any accusation against the Jews for their treatment of him. He was a prisoner only because of **the hope of Israel.** By this, he meant that his Christian faith was the true fulfillment of the hope of God's people.

21,22. The Jewish leaders declared that they had received neither letters nor emissaries from Jerusalem charging Paul with any evil. Furthermore, they implied that they were not familiar with the **sect** to which Paul belonged but had only heard that it was strongly criticized everywhere. F. F. Bruce *(Commentary on Acts)* logically suggests that at this point the Jewish leaders were telling less than the whole truth. It would have been impossible for them to have been unfamiliar with the Christian church in Rome, since we know from Paul's letter to the Romans that a vigorous church existed there (see also 18:2). Furthermore, it was highly unlikely that word would not have reached the Roman Jews from Jerusalem, because constant communication was sustained. However, it was apparent that no sound case could be registered against Paul, and the Jews therefore felt it the better part of wisdom to dissociate themselves entirely from Paul's case and thus avoid incurring the wrath of the Roman government.

23. Some time later, the Jews came together again in the house where Paul was staying to listen to his opinions. Paul's message consisted of testifying **the kingdom of God, persuading concerning Jesus.** The **things concerning Jesus** and **the kingdom of God** are clearly synonymous concepts. Paul undertook to show that the things about Jesus and the kingdom of God were the true fulfillment of the law of Moses and the prophets and that the ancestral faith of Israel had found its fulfillment in the Christian faith.

24-27. The reaction of the Jewish leaders at Rome to Paul's message was the same as he had everywhere met. Some believed, but the majority rejected his message. Seeing this, Paul quoted from Isa 6:9,10, which describes the dullness and the spiritual hardness of God's people. Their plight is hopeless, and they are unable to turn to God to be healed.

28. The book of Acts comes to a climax with this statement: *The salvation of God is now sent to the Gentiles, who will listen to the message.* The last eight chapters of the book of Acts—over a quarter of the book—are devoted to a record of Paul's experiences in Jerusalem and of his journey to Rome. The question rises: Why did Luke devote so much space to these events when his earlier narrative passed over other equally important events with the barest summary? The answer must be that one of Luke's major purposes was to show that just as the Jewish nation rejected Jesus as her Messiah and sent him to a cross, so the leaders of the Jews, both in Jerusalem and in Rome, confirmed their apostate character by rejecting the greatest figure of the apostolic church and his gospel. On the other hand, everywhere Paul went, he was received by the Gentile worshipers in the synagogues and was extended the protection of the Roman authorities. This keynote of the obdurate character of Israel and the responsiveness of the Gentiles is summarized in Acts 28:25-28. These words stand as a formal pronouncement of the divine displeasure for the rebelliousness of Israel. Henceforth the Gospel was to find lodging among the Gentiles. Israel's rebellion was complete.

30,31. The ending of The Acts leaves the thoughtful reader with many unanswered questions in his mind. Paul lived in Rome for two whole years, not confined in prison but permitted to maintain **his own hired dwelling** under the custody of a Roman soldier. This did not permit him complete freedom of activity but did enable him to receive all who wished to converse with him and hear his message. Luke again summarizes Paul's ministry in Rome with the two phrases **preaching the kingdom of God, and teaching those things which concern the Lord Jesus Christ.** The obvious conclusion is that the good news about the kingdom of God is synonymous with the things which concern the Lord Jesus Christ. This is the same message he had preached to the Jewish leaders when they came to him upon his arrival in Rome (v. 23).

We are left with the questions: How did Paul's imprisonment end? What was the outcome of his appeal to Caesar? Was he found guilty and executed, or was he found innocent and dismissed; or was the case dismissed by default? The natural implication of 28:30 is that after the two years, the apostle was released from detention. Tradition tells us that he was executed in Rome about or shortly after A.D. 64. This leaves an interval of some two or three years between the end of Acts and Paul's death. The three Pastoral Epistles which claim to have been written by Paul reflect a ministry of traveling and preaching that cannot be fitted into the narrative of the book of Acts. In spite of arguments against the authenticity of the Pastoral Epistles, the most likely conclusion is that Paul was released after the two years of imprisonment, engaged in a further ministry, which is reflected in these letters, and finally suffered a second imprisonment in Rome, which is reflected in II Timothy.

The rather abrupt ending of the book of Acts has been variously explained. Some have maintained that Luke had intended to write a third volume to record the trial and release of Paul and his subsequent missionary travels, but for some reason was prevented from carrying out his purpose. Another possible explanation is that Acts was written during the two-year imprisonment, for we know from Phm 24 and Col 4:14 that Luke was with Paul during this interval in Rome. It is likely that Luke had gathered material for his narrative about the early church during the two years of Paul's detention in Caesarea and composed the book of Acts during these two years in Rome. In this case, the narrative ends as it does because it had caught up with history, and at the moment there was nothing more to record.

It is probable that the letters to the Philippians, Ephesians, and Colossians, and that to Philemon were written by Paul during his Roman detention. However, some scholars have felt that these "Prison Epistles" were written either from an imprisonment in Ephesus which is not mentioned in Acts, or possibly from the Caesarean imprisonment.

BIBLIOGRAPHY

BLAIKLOCK, E. M. *The Acts of the Apostles (Tyndale Commentaries)*. Grand Rapids: Wm. B. Eerdmans Pub. Co., 1959.

BRUCE, F. F. *Commentary on the Book of the Acts (The New International Commentary)*. Grand Rapids: Wm. B. Eerdmans Pub. Co., 1954.

JACKSON, F. J. FOAKES, and LAKE, KIRSOPP. *The Beginnings of Christianity*. 5 vols. London: Macmillan and Co., 1933–1943.

RACKHAM, R. B. *The Acts of the Apostles (Westminster Commentaries)*. London: Methuen and Co., 1908.

THE EPISTLE TO THE ROMANS

INTRODUCTION

Original Readers. One gains help in understanding the letters or epistles of the New Testament by learning as much as possible about the people who first received these writings. This is surely true regarding the letter to the Romans. Although most of the first eleven chapters of the book seem quite general, in the last five chapters the reader is made aware of a particular community with particular needs. Then we realize that the teaching of the first eleven chapters, though universal in outlook, contains certain emphases which Paul felt were especially needed by believers in Rome (the right basis of judgment of those who did not know the Jewish law, the relation of the Gentiles to Abraham and the patriarchs, etc.).

The apostle addresses his letter to believers — "To all those who are in Rome, beloved by God, called to be saints" (1:7). Paul's practice in writing to churches was to have the word "church" in the salutation (cf. I Cor 1:2; II Cor 1:1; Gal 1:2; I Thess 1:1; II Thess 1:1) or the word "saint" as the designation of those addressed (Eph 1:1; Phil 1:1; Col 1:2). The address here is a variation of the second of these procedures. The greeting in Romans does not imply a strongly knit church organization, and chapter 16 gives a picture of small groups of believers rather than of one large group.

Were these believers predominantly Jewish or Gentile? This question must be answered in the light of what Romans explicitly says. It is true that a good deal of the content relates to the Jewish people — God's dealing with them in the past, the present, and the future. But the readers are addressed in a manner which leaves no doubt that they were predominantly Gentile (see 1:5,6; 1:13; 11:13; 15:15,16). There probably were Jewish Christians in the church, but they constituted a minority.

It seems pertinent to ask how the church at Rome was founded. Unfortunately there are no documents from the first century that provide the answer. A number of suggestions have been made. It has been asserted that the "strangers of Rome, Jews and proselytes," who witnessed the coming of the Holy Spirit (Acts 2:10) may have returned to the city and established a nucleus of believers there. However, the Christians after Pentecost did not immediately feel themselves distinct from Judaism nor begin to start local churches in distinction from the synagogues. Hence, the beginning of a Christian church in Rome right after Pentecost is unlikely. Others believe that the church in Rome was founded by missionaries from Antioch (cf. Hans Lietzmann, *The Beginnings of the Christian Church*, trans. Bertram Lee Woolf, pp. 111, 133, 199). Since Antioch was a missionary center, this is certainly plausible. But the best suggestion seems to be that the church was founded and enlarged by converts of Paul, Stephen, and the other apostles who traveled to the imperial city either on business or to live there.

When did Peter and Paul arrive at Rome? If one compares the statements in the early Church Fathers with the New Testament evidence, it seems unlikely that either apostle reached Rome before A.D. 60, several years after Romans was written. If Peter had been at Rome when Paul wrote this epistle, Paul certainly would have sent him greetings. Paul's longstanding desire to preach in Rome (Rom 1:11-13) and his policy of not building upon another man's foundation (15:20) make it seem unlikely that Peter was even in Rome before the time of the writing of Romans.

Authorship and Date. There is almost universal agreement that Paul was the author of this epistle. This is based on statements in chapters 1 and 15, on the style and argument put forth in the intervening chapters, and on the testimony of all from ancient times who quote the epistle.

The only questions raised regarding authorship concern chapter 16 and the doxologies. In 16:3-16 there is a long list of persons to whom greetings are sent. Priscilla and Aquila are mentioned in 16:3-5, but Acts 18:18,19 declares that Paul left them in Ephesus. Because of this, some have concluded that Romans 16, containing these names, originally was addressed by Paul to Ephesus. Epaenetus is mentioned in 16:5, where he is referred to as the first fruits of Asia (i.e., of Asia Minor). This also is assumed to support the conclusion that this section was written to Ephesus. But the evidence does not demand this conclusion. Priscilla and Aquila traveled a great deal. Since they originally came from Italy (Acts 18:2), it would not be strange for them to return. The fact that Epaenetus was the first convert of Asia Minor does not prove that he lived there all of his life. One of Paul's consistent practices was that he did not send greetings by name to individuals in places where he personally had ministered (cf. I Cor, II Cor, I and II Thess, Phil, Eph [Ephesus and Asia Minor], and Gal). But in Romans and Colossians he does greet persons by name. In these places where he had not been he could include everyone he knew, in order to establish rapport. Or if he made a selection, the purpose would be evident, so that no one would feel slighted.

In the Authorized (King James) Version of Romans, there are five doxologies or benedictions – 15:13; 15:33; 16:20; 16:24; 16:25-27. In each of these, either God or Christ is besought to do something, to be with the readers, or to provide the readers with grace. The first (15:13) concludes the section in which Paul sets forth the ethical conduct of a Christian and the need for Christians to live in harmony and understanding with each other. The second (15:33) ends a section where Paul tells of his travel plans and his bringing of a collection to Jerusalem, and asks prayer in regard to this collection and his coming to the Romans. The third (16:20) follows a warning against those whose actions and speech are contrary to that which they have been taught. Paul assures his readers that God, who brings peace, will soon crush Satan under their feet. Meanwhile, Paul expresses his earnest desire that the grace of the Lord Jesus may be their portion. The fourth in the Authorized Version (16:24), not having good manuscript evidence behind it, is omitted in all modern versions based upon a better Greek text. The last (16:25-27) is the most interesting of all because it is found in various places in the ancient manuscripts. The Alexandrian textual family, and the Manuscript D from the Western textual family have this rather long doxology at the very end of chapter 16. This is where it belongs. Some other manuscripts place it after 14:23. A few put it both after 14:23 and at 16:25-27. One manuscript, G, omits this doxology altogether. The papyrus manuscript, P^{46}, puts it after 15:33.

Some scholars have tried to show that the content of this last doxology stamps it as having been composed in the second century as a liturgical formula of conclusion (cf. John Knox, "Romans," *The Interpreter's Bible*, IX, 365-68). Dr. Hort, almost a century ago, carefully compared its phrases with phrases in Paul's earlier and later epistles and found a remarkable number of similarities (F. J. A. Hort, "On the End of the Epistle to the Romans," in *Biblical Essays*, compiled by J. B. Lightfoot, pp. 324-329). Hence there is good evidence to support Paul's authorship of this final doxology beyond the fact that it is found at or near the end of Romans.

But why should this doxology at the end of Romans appear in different places in the various manuscripts? A number of factors may have played a part. Origen, in his commentary on the Epistle to the Romans, declares that the heretic Marcion (who flourished A.D. 138 – 150) cut away all of Romans from 14:23 to the end. Followers of Marcion would produce copies that stop at this point. Also, the section headings—terse phrases describing the content—are absent from the last two chapters in two manuscripts of the Vulgate—Codex Amiatinus and Codex Fuldensis. The omission of these chapters from public reading would have influenced the placing of the doxology. Again, Paul, or the Christians at Rome immediately after his death, may have shortened the epistle in order to circulate it to other churches. The very fact that we have so many early manuscripts of Romans permits us to see some of these deviations and to note what the best manuscripts have done. Whether we consider the manuscripts of highest quality (the most important) or their total quantity, most of them include all of Romans except 16:24, which was clearly not a part of the original text.

This letter was written by Paul on his third missionary journey. Since the apostle spent three months in Greece

(Acts 20:3) and he recommends Phoebe, the deaconess from Cenchrea (eastern seaport of Corinth) who probably carried the letter to Rome, it is very likely that the letter was written from Corinth. But it is possible that another Grecian city, such as Philippi, was the place. Dates for the epistle have ranged from A.D. 53 to A.D. 58. The years 55 or 56 seem to be the most likely dates for the letter.

Occasion and Purpose for Writing. The apostle planned to leave Greece and go to Palestine with the collection he had gathered from the Gentile churches. Paul wanted this collection to be presented to the poor saints at Jerusalem by him personally along with representatives from the Gentile churches. He felt that this gesture by the Gentiles would show their love for their Christian brothers in Palestine and demonstrate the unity of the church. He then intended to go to Rome. From Rome he wanted to go to Spain. Before Paul turned his back for a time on his westerly goals, he penned this mighty letter to the Romans and sent it westward.

What kind of a writing is Romans? It is a letter to a group (or groups) of believers in Rome. The fact that it expresses mighty, profound, and sublime thoughts about God does not invalidate the classification of this book as a letter. Paul had prayed for the readers unceasingly (1:9,10) and longed to have fellowship with them (1:11). He wanted them to pray for him because of the dangers that threatened (15:30-32). Hence Romans is not a systematic doctrinal treatise. Paul's thoughts are developed logically, but he surely does not try to present all of his doctrinal teaching. Nor is Romans a controversial essay—a polemic for Pauline Christianity against Jewish Christianity. The *unity* and *oneness* of believers is central in the metaphor of the olive tree in Romans 11.

Romans is a letter of instruction touching upon those main truths of the Gospel that Paul felt were needed by those in Rome. Since the needs of Gentiles were similar whether they were in Rome or Colosse, there is a universal note in the teaching. Romans is a summary of key truths that Paul taught in the churches where he spent some time proclaiming the Gospel. One reason this epistle has had such wide influence is that God guided his servant to present these superb thoughts in a letter so that scholar and layman alike could lay hold of truths that would shape their eternal destiny.

Unfolding of the Thought. Paul begins with some preliminary comments to prepare the reader for all that he intends to write (1:1-17), and so establishes excellent rapport between himself and his readers. Then he launches forth into the subject of the importance of righteousness in man's relations with God (1:18–8:39). He first graphically points out that man is not righteous, then carefully answers the question: How does a man become righteous before God? He re-enforces this with a discussion of how a man should live who has become righteous before God. Being a Jew, Paul looked at mankind as divided into two classes—Jew and Gentile. As a Christian, how should he look at these two divisions? He answers this when he surveys the plan of God for Jew and Gentile (9:1–11:36). Here he lays a distinct basis for a Christian philosophy of history. Then, coming to the area of application, he gives specific exhortations for Roman Christians concerning their outlook, attitude, and action (12:1–15:13). In conclusion he shows his deep interest in the Roman believers (15:14–16:27). They were in his territory and he intended to visit them. Until that was possible, he had to send greetings by mail, give a final warning, and commit them to God, who alone could establish them.

In studying Romans, we must not forget the whole of which each individual passage is only a part. To tear a passage out of its context is always harmful; in Romans it may bring a complete reversal of Paul's meaning.

OUTLINE

I. Opening affirmations of Paul, the apostle. 1:1-17.
  A. Identity of the writer disclosed. 1:1.
  B. The Gospel identified with Jesus Christ. 1:2-5.
  C. Readers addressed. 1:6,7.
  D. Paul's interest in the Romans, part of a larger concern. 1:8-15.
  E. Nature and content of the Gospel summarized. 1:16,17.

II. Righteousness—the key to man's relationship to God. 1:18—8:39.
  A. Righteousness as the necessary status of men before God. 1:18—5:21.
    1. Man's failure to attain righteousness. 1:18—3:20.
      a. Default of the Gentiles. 1:18-32.
      b. Default of the man who judges in contrast with God's righteous judgment. 2:1-16.
      c. Default of the Jew. 2:17-29.
      d. Objections to Paul's teaching on man's default. 3:1-8.
      e. Default of all mankind before God. 3:9-20.
    2. Righteousness attained by faith, not by legalistic works. 3:21-31.
    3. Righteousness by faith in the life of Abraham. 4:1-25.
      a. His righteousness attained by faith, not by works. 4:1-8.
      b. Abraham made the father of all who believe by his faith prior to circumcision. 4:9-12.
      c. Realization of the promise brought by faith, not by law. 4:13-16.
      d. God, Master of death, the object of faith for both Abraham and the Christian. 4:17-25.
    4. Centrality of the righteousness by faith in individual lives and in the framework of history. 5:1-21.
      a. Effects of the righteousness by faith upon the recipients. 5:1-11.
      b. Effects of Adam's disobedience and Christ's obedience. 5:12-21.
  B. Righteousness as the manner of Christian living before God. 6:1—8:39.
    1. Fallacy of sinning that grace might abound. 6:1-14.
    2. Fallacy of sinning because believers are under grace, not law. 6:15—7:6.
      a. Allegiance, fruit, destiny. 6:15-23.
      b. Annulment and new alignment caused by death. 7:1-6.
    3. Questions raised by the struggle against sin. 7:7-25.
      a. Is the Law sin? 7:7-12.
      b. Is that which is good the cause of death? 7:13,14.
      c. How can the conflict within be resolved? 7:15-25.
    4. Victory through the Spirit connected with the purpose and action of God. 8:1-39.
      a. Deliverance from sin and death by the activity of Father, Son, and Spirit. 8:1-4.
      b. The mind-set of the flesh versus that of the Spirit. 8:5-13.
      c. Guidance and witness of the Spirit. 8:14-17.
      d. Completion of redemption awaited by creation and believers alike. 8:18-25.
      e. Intercessory ministry of the Spirit. 8:26,27.
      f. Purpose of God for those loving him. 8:28-30.
      g. Triumph of believers over all opposition. 8:31-39.

III. Israel and the Gentiles in the plan of God. 9:1—11:36.
  A. Concern of Paul for his own people, Israel. 9:1-5.
  B. God free, righteous, and sovereign in his dealing with Israel and with all men. 9:6-29.
    1. God's choice of Isaac rather than the other sons of Abraham. 9:6-9.
    2. God's choice of Jacob rather than Esau. 9:10-13.
    3. God's mercy toward Israel and hardening of Pharaoh. 9:14-18.
    4. God's control over vessels of wrath and mercy. 9:19-24.
    5. God's testimony in Hosea and Isaiah to an extension and limitation of his saving work. 9:25-29.
  C. Failure of Israel and success of the Gentiles. 9:30—10:21.
    1. Attainment by Gentiles of what Israel missed. 9:30-33.
    2. Israel's ignorance of God's righteousness. 10:1-3.
    3. Connection between the righteousness of faith and the object of faith. 10:4-15.
    4. Good tidings rejected. 10:16-21.
  D. Situation of Israel in Paul's day. 11:1-10.
  E. Israel's prospects for the future. 11:11-36.
    1. Degree of blessing from Israel's fall and fullness. 11:11-15.
    2. Individual Gentile's lack of grounds for boasting. 11:16-21.

3. Goodness and severity of God disclosed by his response to belief and unbelief. 11:22-24.
4. Salvation for the people of Israel. 11:25-27.
5. God's mercy to all magnified by his action in history. 11:28-32.
6. Excellence and glory of God—the Source, Sustainer, and Goal of all things. 11:33-36.

IV. Attitude and conduct expected of Christians at Rome. 12:1—15:13.
A. Consecration of body and mind. 12:1,2.
B. Humility in the use of God's gifts. 12:3-8.
C. Character traits to be exemplified. 12:9-21.
D. Submission to governmental authorities to be accompanied by a loving, upright manner of life. 13:1-14.
E. Tolerance necessary for those with strong and weak consciences. 14:1—15:13.
1. Differences of opinion over food or special days. 14:1-6.
2. Judgment by the Lord, not by one's brother. 14:7-12.
3. Removal of stumbling blocks. 14:13-23.
4. The strong to help the weak rather than please themselves. 15:1-3.
5. Glory brought to God by endurance, consolation, and harmony. 15:4-6.
6. Ministry of Christ designed for both Jew and Gentile. 15:7-13.

V. Items of personal interest and care for the readers. 15:14—16:27.
A. Paul's reason for writing boldly to mature readers. 15:14-16.
B. Supernatural confirmation of Paul's pioneer missionary work. 15:17-21.
C. Travel plans: Jerusalem, Rome, Spain. 15:22-29.
D. Specific requests for prayer. 15:30-33.
E. Recommendation of Phoebe. 16:1,2.
F. Particular greetings to individuals and groups. 16:3-16.
G. Dangerous character of those who teach false doctrine. 16:17-20.
H. Greetings from Paul's associates in Corinth. 16:21-23.
I. Establishment of believers by the sovereign God of history. 16:25-27.

COMMENTARY

I. Opening Affirmations of Paul, the Apostle. 1:1-17.

The length of the introduction shows that Paul attached great importance to this letter. Observe the spirit of dedication that permeates these opening lines. Note also how quickly he shifts from one thought to another.

A. Identity of the Writer Disclosed. 1:1. The word for **servant** really means a *slave*. For Paul, this expression said that he belonged to Jesus Christ. He was Christ's property, and, as such, he had a divinely appointed task to perform. **His call** to be an apostle came to him clearly in Damascus (Acts 9:15,16; 22:14,15; 26:16-18). He was **in a state of being set apart** unto the Gospel of God. In Galatians Paul traces this call back to his birth (Gal 1:15), but here in Romans he stresses the purpose for his being set apart: for **the good news** which God had brought into being. Paul had a divine Master, a divine office, and a divine message.

B. The Gospel Identified with Jesus Christ. 1:2-5. In these verses the Gospel is viewed in two dimensions – the historical and the personal.

2. Historically, God had **proclaimed** this **good news in advance,** by special agents, **his prophets.** The record of what they proclaimed is found **in the holy scriptures.** The latter is a technical designation for all the parts of Scripture, the Scripture as a whole.

3. God's good news is about his Son. Paul stresses first his humanity: **who was born from the seed of David as far as his physical descent was concerned.** Here is a stress upon his birth. He **became** man.

4. Next he stresses the quality of his being as Son of God: **who was powerfully declared to be Son of God by the resurrection of the dead.** In every instance where Paul uses the word "dead" after the word "resurrection," the Greek word "dead" is in the plural. Sometimes he explicitly means a resurrection of individuals (cf. I Cor 15:12,13,21,42). But here in Rom 1:4 and also in Acts 26:23 he is referring to the resurrection of

Jesus Christ. Yet the term "dead" is in the plural. Hence in the resurrection of this individual there is implicit the resurrection of all who will be raised by him. But explicitly in Rom 1:4 Paul is referring to the victory of Christ over death (cf. 6:9). The use of the plural here is a stylistic trait of the writer.

In accordance with the Spirit of Holiness. The resurrection from the dead was a fact proclaimed by Christians. But the powerful declaration of Jesus as Son of God by his resurrection was the work of the Holy Spirit in illuminating the full meaning of the historical fact. Some scholars take "spirit of Holiness" to be a strengthened form of "the Holy Spirit" (see Arndt, *hagiōsynē*, p. 10). Others take the phrase to refer to Christ's human spirit, which was characterized by great holiness – "in relation to the (his) spirit of holiness" (see Sanday and Headlam, ICC, p. 9; cf. Arndt, *pneuma*, 2, p. 681). Another view equates "holiness" here with Deity or God. But the Spirit of God, according to this view, is not the Holy Spirit but the Creative Living Principle, God operative in human affairs (see Otto Procksch, TWNT, I, 116: "Christ's Deity becomes clear by the resurrection in which the new creation shows itself according to the Principle of . . . Deity."). **Being born** (1:3; AV, *was made)* asserts origination. **Being declared** (v. 4) asserts the designation of what is. Hence the human and the divine are contrasted in these two verses. One must decide whether the phrase, *pneuma hagiōsynēs* (Spirit of Holiness, spirit of holiness, Creative Principle of Deity), modifies the declaration, or describes the person of Christ, or conveys the idea of the activity of God in the world. The first interpretation, which certainly appears to be the best, calls for the translation, "Spirit of Holiness."

5. Through the Son Paul had received **grace** and his **apostleship.** The phrase, **for his name** (AV), should be tied to apostleship—an apostleship, literally, *on behalf of his name.*

C. Readers Addressed. 1:6,7. It is clear from these verses that the "Romans" addressed were among the Gentiles. Twice Paul stresses the fact that they were **called.** They were called to be **saints.** The idea behind the word "saint" is not that of someone cut off from all association with others but of one who is *consecrated to God.* The impact on society of a group of believers who are consecrated or dedicated to God ought never to be minimized. The words **grace** and **peace** represent a Christian formula of greeting in letters (see Rom 1:7; I Cor 1:3; II Cor 1:2; Gal 1:3; Eph 1:2; Phil 1:2; Col 1:2; I Thess 1:1; II Thess 1:2; Tit 1:4; Phm 3; I Pet 1:2; II Pet 1:2; I Tim 1:2; II Tim 1:2; II Jn 3). **Grace** *(charis)* is here used in place of a common Greek expression, *chairein*, which means "greetings." **Peace** has a Hebrew and Aramaic parallel, *shalōm*, which carries the complex idea of prosperity, good health, and success. But this Christian greeting stresses what God has done in the lives of believers. Yet the student must always remember that this is a formula of greeting – not an independent reference to grace and peace. The phrase must be taken as a whole: **May grace and peace be to you from God our Father and from the Lord Jesus Christ.**

D. Paul's Interest in the Romans Part of a Larger Concern. 1:8-15. Paul tells his readers about his longstanding desire to visit them. Such a visit, he felt, would help not only the Romans but also himself. Rome, with its cross section of humanity, epitomized the various kinds of people to whom the apostle had an obligation.

8. I thank my God. The frequency of thanksgivings at the beginnings of Paul's epistles is a testimony to Paul's closeness to God and his cheerful outlook *(eucharisteō*, "to give thanks": Rom 1:8; I Cor 1:4; Eph 1:16; Col 1:3; I Thess 1:2; II Thess 1:3; Phm 4; *charin echō*, "to be grateful, thankful": I Tim 1:12; II Tim 1:3). Note that thanks as well as petitions are rendered to God **through Jesus Christ.** The object for thanksgiving is specifically stated.

9. Observe the stress here on the inward aspect of service – **whom I serve in my spirit** (ASV). God, who knew the inward man, would testify to Paul's interest in the Romans.

10. Not only did the apostle mention the Romans frequently in his prayers, but he prayed always about coming to them. Here one sees that although Paul earnestly prayed to be in **the will of God** in this matter, he was not sure, at the time of writing, whether it was God's will for him to go to Rome. Here are his own words: **praying whether now at last I may perhaps succeed in coming . . . to you.** God had not said "No"; so Paul continued to pray.

11. The **spiritual gift** was what Paul desired to impart to the Romans for their strengthening. This was not some special gift, such as Paul lists in Rom 12:6-8, but rather a growing knowledge of various truths of God that would enable them to be better Christians.

12. Encouragement or comfort would come to Paul as well as to his readers if he could visit them. Even this great evangelist, who perhaps has never been equaled in spiritual stature, says plainly that he needed the encouragement that comes in Christian fellowship. Thus we dare not underestimate the importance of Christian fellowship for Christian growth. The mutual faith is simply the fact that both Paul and his readers were Christians. Observe how the pronouns make this faith personal – **your** faith and **mine.**

13. The last phrase in this verse should be tied to the verb "purposed." I **purposed** to come in order **that I might have . . . fruit among you . . .** The readers in Rome were Gentiles, and Paul hoped to have the same results from ministering to them as he had had with other Gentiles he had visited.

14,15. The apostle saw himself as a debtor to those who spoke Greek and to those who did not **(Barbarians).** This is a language-cultural division of mankind. The second pair of contrasts in 1:14 deals with intellectual learning and achievement. A **wise** man is one with a trained intellect. An **unwise** man or *unintelligent* man discloses his foolishness in what he does. Representatives of all of these classes were found in Rome. To all of these Paul felt impelled to proclaim the good news. Hence he speaks of his eagerness **to proclaim good tidings** there. It is important to note that he expected to reach all these classes as he ministered to Roman believers – **to you who are in Rome also.** Hence, although Christianity found most of its adherents among members of the lower strata of society (cf. I Cor 1:26-29), there was a compelling urgency to reach all classes of men.

E. Nature and Content of the Gospel Summarized. 1:16,17. In these verses one finds three factors: (1) Paul's attitude toward the Gospel; (2) the nature of the Gospel; and (3) the content of the Gospel. These verses indicate that the good news of the Christian faith is not a system of philosophy or a code of ethics.

16. In contrast to a series of abstract ideas, the Gospel or good news is dynamic. Paul was not ashamed of the Gospel. The phrase **of Christ** (AV) is not found in the best manuscripts and should be omitted. Paul was not ashamed of the Gospel because this good news is God's power, the purpose and goal of which is to bring about deliverance or salvation. A man obtains such salvation when his constant individual response to the Gospel is trust and belief – **to every one in the process of believing.**

The Greek word *pisteuō* is a profound word. Belief in the content of the Gospel is only part of its meaning. Above this it means trust or personal commitment, to the extent of handing over one's self to another person. Though belief does involve response to a truth or a series of truths, this response is not mere intellectual assent but rather wholehearted involvement in the truth believed. To believe in Christ is to commit oneself to him. To trust Christ is to become totally involved in the eternal truths taught by him and about him in the NT. Such total involvement brings moral earnestness, a dedication and consecration apparent in every aspect of life. Note that although the salvation spoken of here is to the Jew first, the Gentile experiences the same salvation.

17. Therein. In the Gospel the righteousness is revealed which God bestows, produces, imputes. The rest of Romans tells more about what is involved in this righteousness. Here Paul stresses that righteousness is **from faith to faith.** This righteousness (which God brings into being) comes to the Christian only because of faith. As the believer becomes increasingly aware of all that God's righteousness signifies, he must still commit himself if he is to receive God's righteousness.

The order of words in the last part of the verse is this: **the just by faith shall live.** Here one sees the danger of following the Greek word order too literally. It might imply that a man being just in some other way could not live even if he met the requirement of being just! Faith is put first for emphasis to show that faith is essential for a man to be just. Greek *dikaios,* **just,** may also be translated *upright* or *righteous;* hence the rendering: **the just** *(upright, righteous)* **shall live by faith.** Does the living referred to here describe the temporal sequence of life immediately ahead or does it refer only to eternal life? Bauer in the lexicon translated and edited by Arndt and Gingrich asserts that "the dividing line between the present and the future life is sometimes non-existent or at least not discernible" (Arndt, *zaō*, 2. b., p. 337). He would translate this clause: **he that is just through faith will have life.** How great is the role of faith in a man's being just, in the life he now lives, and in the life which is to come!

II. Righteousness – The Key to Man's Relationship to God. 1:18–8:39.

Here Paul grapples with great issues of life. How can a man be righteous in the sight of God? How is man affected by the action of Adam and of Christ? How should a man who is righteous live? How can he live in this way?

A. Righteousness as the Necessary Status of Men before God. 1:18–5:21.

Righteousness is necessary for men. This necessity is grounded in the nature and being of God.

1) Man's Failure To Attain Righteousness. 1:18–3:20.

The reason why righteousness is so important is that man does not have it. First, he must be made aware that he does not have it. Throughout the ages there have been those who felt that God ought to be pleased with their character. In these chapters Paul proceeds to show the shallowness of such an outlook.

a) Default of the Gentiles. 1:18-32.

18. The righteousness and wrath of God both express divine action toward man. Righteousness is God's response toward faith or trust; wrath is his reaction to **godlessness** and **unrighteousness.** Both clearly **reveal** the response of God. What does a godless or unrighteous man do? He **holds down** or *suppresses* **the truth** (present participle) in the sphere of unrighteousness where he is living. He wants to avoid the truth about what he is and about what he is doing. So he foolishly tries to get rid of the truth.

19. The truth comes to man in his sphere of unrighteousness. **Because what can be known about God.** Here is the assertion that God is knowable. **Is manifest in them.** This could also be translated *is visible to them* (Arndt, *phaneros,* p. 860; *en,* IV, 4. a, p. 260) or *is manifest among them.* The context certainly favors the latter two. Why is God knowable? He acts. God has **made known** or *revealed* (AV, *shewed)* what can be known about himself to men. This revelation is a self-disclosure that God may carry out in any way he pleases.

20. The invisible things of him. This phrase refers to God's invisible nature or attributes. **From the creation of the world are clearly seen.** Paul makes a bold assertion here. From the time that God brought the world into being, his invisible attributes – characteristics which declare him to be God – are perceived clearly. By whom and how are they perceived clearly? **Being understood in the things that are made. In** is a better translation than the *by* of the AV. The invisible attributes of God are understood by men, who can engage in rational reflection and understanding. What is the basis for their understanding? It is **in the things that are made** *(poiēma).* The word *poiēma* means "what is made," "work," or "creation." Bauer translates it: *in the things that have been made* (Arndt, *kathoraō,* p. 393) or *by the things he has created* (Arndt, *poiēma,* p. 689). The noun is in the plural. In classical Greek the word is used in the plural to refer to works, to poems, to fiction, deeds or acts – i.e., anything made or done (LSJ. p. 1429). The word *poiēma* is found thirty times in the LXX. Except for one occurrence, it translates the Hebrew word *ma'aśeh,* "deed," or "work." In the one exception it translates the Hebrew *pō'al,* "doing," "deed," or "work." Therefore, it is clear that the things which God has created are said to testify to his invisible nature.

To what aspect of the invisible nature of God do they testify? Paul is specific —to **his eternal power.** In creation the everlasting or perpetual power of God is seen. As man's skill in exploring space and in analyzing the structure of the atom grows, so he ought to grow in his awareness of God's power. **And Godhead.** The Creator who has shown such unlimited power is the supreme Being with whom men must reckon. By observing his work, men are confronted with the living God. As a result, **they are without excuse.**

21-23. Paul enumerates the things men put in the place of the living God. What a tragic list of substitutions! **Because, although they knew God.** Here are men who were brought face to face with God's works and with God, so that they knew him. But they did not respond to this knowledge as they should have. They did not **glorify** (praise, honor, magnify) him as God; neither did they **return thanks** to him. These failures show what should be man's chief end: to glorify the Lord for what he is and to return thanks for what he has done.

The thoughts of these Gentiles turned to worthless things. **Their senseless mind was darkened.** To reject God, to turn away from the light, naturally brings darkness. This darkness came into their inner being—the mind, reasonings, emotions, etc. In their idolatry, i.e., in their creating substitutes for the being of God, they actually thought they were wise. Worthless thoughts quickly brought worthless objects of worship.

24,25. Verses 24,26,28 all repeat the same solemn phrase: **God handed them over unto.** The Lord hands men over to the consequences of that which they have chosen for themselves. When men choose an evil manner of life, they also choose the consequences such a manner of life brings. This is proof that God has established a moral universe. **In the desires** *(lusts,* AV) **which originated from their hearts** (or, *which their hearts produced,* v. 24). The word translated "desire" may refer to that which is either good or bad. Here it is obviously an evil desire. The translation "lust" conveys the idea of sensuality, which fits into the context of uncleanness. Notice that God hands men over to the very things which they desire. As a result their bodies are dishonored among them. Idolatry consists in worshiping and serving the creature (v. 25); in sensuality man worships and serves himself.

26,27. Uncleanness always generates more uncleanness. Here is a divine judgment in which God handed the Gentiles over to **disgraceful passions.** Women are charged with homosexuality in verse 26 and men in verse 27. Paul uses straightforward language to condemn perversion of sex from its rightful place in the marriage relationship. He regards the union of the sexes in marriage as a natural relationship (AV, *natural use).* But here women exchanged natural sex relations for that which is contrary to nature. The men did the same thing. Paul pictures the depravity and degradation of men inflamed with sensual desire for each other. This is followed by the note of judgment. **In themselves . . . that recompense . . . which was necessary.** Paul does not go into detail as to the exact nature of the judgment—the psychological and physical consequences. But the nature of the penalty is said to correspond to the enormity of the sin.

28-32. Those who did not see fit to have God in their knowledge were handed over by God to a reprobate mind. The Greek word has the meanings: "base," "unqualified," "worthless," "not standing the test," or "unapproved." Here is a mind with no stabilizing point on which inward harmony may be built. Such a mind can produce only that which is **improper** (AV, *not convenient)* or *those things which are not fitting.* The list in verses 29-31 shows that such a mind is at odds with itself and with its fellow men. Anarchy and chaos come from a mind that removes God from its knowledge. In some good manuscripts **fornication** (AV, v. 29) is not found. **Whisperers** (AV) are gossipers or secret slanderers. **Backbiters** (AV) are those who seek to ruin or defame someone's character—vilifiers of character. The man who ruins other people's reputations himself becomes repulsive. Note the unlovely combination set forth in verse 31: **Senseless, faithless, unloving, unmerciful. Implacable** is not found in the early, good manuscripts. Remember that the people described here had opportunity to know the requirements of God. Further, they knew that death is the penalty of evil action. Yet they not only sinned with pleasure but applauded others who were sinning. Their sin had reached a point where they received a vicarious satisfaction in the sinful deeds of others.

b) Default of the Man Who Judges in Contrast with God's Righteous Judgment. 2:1-16. The man Paul thinks of as judging is not named as a Jew or Gentile. It is likely that Paul had the Jew in mind, since the man who was judging had experienced God's goodness and forbearance in a distinct way. The Lord's recompense to each individual will be according to the man's works—not according to his privileges. God will judge fairly, whether a man lived under the Mosaic Law or apart from it.

1-4. The word **judge** *(krinōn)* occurs three times in verse 1. It means here to pass unfavorable judgment by criticizing or finding fault. The man who is inexcusable is the one who has great power of criticism but no self-discipline. The **judgment of God is rightly upon those doing such things. Such things.** The actions of the critic are identical with the actions of those whom he criticizes. The catalogue of sins in Romans 1 is fairly inclusive. Envy, gossip, and strife are looked upon as faults in others, but the critic may excuse these things in himself as "a rightful sense of need," "a simple statement of fact," or "a courageous stand for the truth." Paul appeals to the man's conscience: **Do you really imagine . . . that you will escape the condemnation of God** (i.e., the sentence pronounced by him)? The translation **despise** (v. 4) may be too strong for *kataphroneō* in this context. It seems better to render it: **Or do you entertain wrong ideas about** (Arndt, p. 421) God's goodness, forbearance, patience? The word **repentance** involves much more than a turning away from a former practice. It involves the beginning of a new religious and moral life (see Arndt, pp. 513,514). Hence God's goodness in not bringing immediate punishment is no evidence that the Lord is indifferent to the sin. Far from it! By divine goodness he wants to lead men to a new way of life. To have wrong ideas about this is to rest in a false complacency. The judgment of God is sure.

5-11. The Almighty examines man's conduct and judges him accordingly. A man whose heart is hard and impenitent stores up divine anger or wrath for himself. **God's anger** stored up in heaven is the most tragic stockpile a man could lay aside for himself. Observe the note of individual judgment in verse 6. What is the mood or outlook of those who seek for glory, honor, and immortality? With an outlook characterized by **a perseverance in doing what is right** (v. 7), these contend for the goals listed. The outcome is that they receive from the Judge eternal life. Those who because of strife are disobedient to the truth and obey unrighteousness receive anger and wrath. Works are always central in the NT picture of judgment. They are an outward indication of an individual's inward trust or commitment. The Lord, of course, looks at both the inward and the outward. But the outward activity reveals the inward conviction. One needs only to compare the verb form in 2:9—**that constantly doeth evil**—with that in 2:10—**that constantly worketh the good**—to see that actions disclose convictions (or the lack of them). This does not mean that those who constantly do the good have a full understanding of God. But apart from a trust in God, which demands some knowledge, men will not carry out constantly and with determination that which God has said to be good.

12-16. Since there is no partiality with God, how does he treat those who sin apart from the law and those who sin under the law? The answer lies in the phrases—**shall perish** and **shall be punished** (v. 12). Both those living under the law and those living apart from the law are said to have sinned. The aorist tense here *(have sinned*, AV) stresses wholeness of action. It summarizes all the sins the individual has committed during his life. For the sum total of such sins, men who have not had the opportunity of living under the Mosaic law **shall perish.** Likewise, for the sum total of their sins, those who have lived under the law **shall be punished.** Although different language is used to describe God's judgment, this judgment is sure and fairly dispensed, whether the Mosaic law plays any part in the judgment or not. As far as judgment is concerned, what counts is performance, not the being aware of this or that statute. The **doer** of the law **will be justified;** i.e., *be acquitted, be pronounced righteous.*

At this point a profound question arises: Are the doers of the Law limited to those who know and carry out the Mosaic law? In 2:14 Paul answers "No" to this question and shows why. The Gentiles who have not the Mosaic law may **do by nature the things contained in the law.** The phrase **by nature** *(physei)* has been interpreted to mean "by following the natural order of things" (see Hans Lietzmann, *Der Brief and die Römer,* also *Handbuch zum Neuen Testament.* Excursus on Rom 2:14-16). But the context here does not make the same stress as in 1:20. Hence it seems much better to take **by nature** to mean "instinctively." What is involved in this type of response? When Gentiles do instinctively the requirements of the Law, they **are law** (2:14). These show **the manifestation of the law written in their hearts.** Such Gentiles have an internal norm or standard put in their hearts by God. This internal standard is the basis both for the response of their conscience and for their reasoning. The **conscience** (v.15) is an automatic intellectual response to a given standard. In contrast, **reason** engages in reflection. The **thoughts** resulting from such reflection represent a weighed value judgment in contrast to the automatic intellectual response of conscience. The consciences of many associated individuals bring about a mutual witnessing together. Similarly the combined value judgments of the group are circulated. The resulting decisions sometimes reproach the individuals of the group and sometimes speak in their defense. Although Paul does not describe the full content of this internal standard, he asserts that it exists. We do know that both the conscience and the reason can decide that certain action is bad and other action is good. Gentiles reacting correctly to this standard are thus not altogether without law. They are obedient doers of the law which God put in their hearts. It would seem best to connect 2:16 with 2:13: "The doers of the law will be justified . . . in the day in which God will judge the secrets of men."

This passage may shed some light upon the eternal destiny of those who have never heard the Gospel. How will God deal with such people in the day of judgment? These verses seem to indicate that he will observe their actions just as he will observe the actions of those who knew the Law, and those who have heard the Gospel, and that he will judge all accordingly. Then, does not obedience to this internal standard nullify the principle of salvation by faith? No. Faith is essential for those who obey the internal standard and for those who obey the Law or the Gospel. But how much richer and fuller is our knowledge of God as revealed through his Son! A seeking for **glory, honour,** and **immortality** (v. 7) could be mere selfishness. But a seeking of these things with a determination to do what is good (v. 7) means that the seeker is aware of a standard of goodness. If this standard were a mere abstraction, how very difficult it would be to persevere in goodness. But if the standard is God himself—even though imperfectly perceived (and who of us perceives God perfectly?), faith or committal to him will lay the basis for constant perseverance in that which is good. Why then should we eagerly take the Gospel to those who have never heard it? First of all, because God has commanded us to do so (Mt 28:19,20; Acts 1:8). Secondly, it is essential because of who God is that every individual be confronted with the knowledge of God (Isa 11:9; Hab 2:14; Isa 45:5,6; 52:10; 66:18,19; II Thess 1:8) and have opportunity to commit himself to Him, and to increase in knowledge of Him (Jn 14:7; 17:3; II Cor 2:14; Tit 1:16; I Jn 2:3-6; 5:19,20; Phil 3:8-10; II Pet 3:18). Finally, it is essential because of who Christ is—the climax of God's revelation (Heb 1:1,2).

Since Christ is the supreme revelation of God, and since the NT is the record that confronts men with Christ, other methods of divine revelation are seen to be only fragmentary. This is especially true of two methods discussed in Romans 1;2: (1) the testimony of the things which are made (1:20); (2) the internal standard put in the hearts (2:14,15). Nevertheless, these are divinely chosen channels the existence and function of which Paul invites his readers to consider seriously.

c) Default of the Jew. 2:17-29. Here Paul vividly pictures the Jew's opportunities, and points out how even these did not bring the Jew to a life of obedience and fellowship with God.

17-20. The failure of the Jew was the more conspicuous because of his privileges and confidence. He **relied upon** the Law. He **boasted** (gloried, prided himself) in God. He knew God's will. He **accepted as proved by testing the things that really matter** (or those things which are essential). He could do this because he was orally instructed in the Law. He had heard the rabbis discuss the crucial points. Because of such a background, the Jew had confidence. He could give help and instruction to the rest of men because he was certain that he had **the embodiment** of knowledge and of truth in the Law (v. 20).

21-24. Paul presses home to the Jew his defeat by asking if his practice conforms to his teaching (2:21,22). **You, who teach another, teach yourself don't you?** (v. 21) Why, of course, he did. In the other three questions: **Do you steal? Do you commit adultery? Do you rob temples?** Paul does not say what kind of answer he expects. But he points out that the Jew, by transgressing the very Law of which he was so proud, dishonored God—the One who gave the Law. The name of God was blasphemed among the Gentiles because of the way the Jews acted. The last phrase—**just as it has been written**—does not refer to a particular OT passage that speaks of the sins of the Jews as causing God's name to be blasphemed. Rather, Paul seems to have put together Isa 52:5 and Ezk 36:21-23.

25-29. Here the apostle points out what it means to be a true Jew. He shows that a Gentile who keeps (the word *phylassō* may also be translated *observe,* or *follow*) **the requirements of the law**

(v. 26) is a true Jew. The rite of circumcision declares only that a man is a Jew providing he practices the Law. For a Jew to become a transgressor of the Law is really in God's sight to become uncircumcised. Not only is a Gentile a true Jew if he observes the requirements of the Law, but he who is physically uncircumcised will sit in judgment over the Jew who has the physical qualifications but nothing by way of obedience (v. 27). This is an assertion of Paul, not a question. In verse 27 Paul stresses that the Jew whom the Gentile will judge is one who is a transgressor of the Law **though provided with the written code and with circumcision** (cf. *dia*, Arndt, III, 1, c, p. 179). Here is the tragedy of one who had an objective written law and the outward sign of God's covenant with his people, but who yet had never laid hold of the reality. In a final parting word to the Jew, Paul stresses that it is not in externals but rather in the inward condition of the heart that a man is a true Jew, i.e., a child of God (v. 29). True circumcision is a heart kind of circumcision (cf. Lev 26:41; Deut 10:16; 30:6; Jer 4:4; 9:26; Acts 7:51). This true circumcision is not in the sphere of legality – a written code – but rather in the sphere of the spirit, i.e., the area of the will.

d) Objections to Paul's Teaching on Man's Default. 3:1-8. Paul is speaking mostly about objections from Jews. But the idea that God's righteousness is exalted by man's sin could come from any opponent of Paul's teaching.

1-4. What is the **advantage** of the Jew? What is the **use** of circumcision? These questions seem to be taken from Paul's experiences in proclaiming the Gospel. Paul's answer is: "Much in every respect" (v. 2). He reminds his questioner that to the Jews were committed **the oracles of God.** In classical Greek the word *logion* ("oracle") is used mostly of short sayings originating from a divinity (Arndt, p. 477). In Acts 7:38 the word is used of the revelations that came to Moses. In Heb 5:12 it is used in connection with the initial elements belonging to the oracles or sayings of God. The passage in Hebrews refers to a collective whole. Peter says that if any man speak who has received grace, he is to speak as the very oracles or sayings of God (I Pet 4:11). In Rom 3:2 the stress is on the promises of God to the Jews. In all contexts the "oracles" involve oral proclamation, and refer to the living voice of God and the truths which God spoke to men. God entrusted these truths to the Jews over long periods of time. The Jews collected them, and they are **recorded** throughout the OT. But the word *logion* itself stresses the particular utterance of God. The fact that all of these utterances came to the Jews was certainly to their advantage.

Paul begins verse 3 with a question: **What then is the situation?** The Jews had these vital truths of God. But how did they respond? **Since some became unfaithful, their unfaithfulness will not nullify the faithfulness of God, will it?** Paul quickly replies: **By no means** *(far from it)*. The word *some* does not necessarily mean a small part. The contrast is between "part" and "whole." Not only is God faithful but also he is true. In support of this the apostle quotes Ps 51:4: "In order that you may be proved to be right in your words and may win when you are accused." God is faithful, true, and victorious, although the Jews, in large part, may have become unfaithful.

5-8. The translation **commend** is not satisfactory for *synistēmi*. The word really means to *demonstrate* or *bring out*. If our unrighteousness – that of Jew and Gentile – brings out the righteousness of God, what then? **God who inflicts wrathful punishment is not unrighteous, is he?** Paul tells us that he is speaking from a human point of view. Then he replies, **By no means** (v. 6). Paul is so concise in the beginning of verse 6 that the full force of his answer is lost. **For otherwise,** if the Lord does not inflict wrathful punishment, **how will God punish the world?** The fact that the divine righteousness shines more brightly against the dark background of man's unrighteousness has nothing to do with the Lord's righteousness in judging and the condemnation that must come. God must judge, condemn, and punish because he is a holy being. As a holy being he *must* deal with every violation of holiness. Paul asserts here the *must* without going into the why. In verse 7 he puts the objection of his questioner in a little different form, but it is the same objection. **But if by my lie the truthfulness of God has shown itself to be supremely great, to his glory** (cf. *perisseuō*, Arndt, p. 656), **why am I indeed still punished as a sinner?** Previously he dealt with the argument that the righteousness of God stands out clearer against the background of human sin. Here he attacks the argument that the truth of God becomes clearer when contrasted with human falsehood. At this point Paul mentions the current caricature of his teaching concerning salvation by grace: **Let us do evil, that good may come** (v. 8). To those who respond in this way, Paul's only comment is: **Whose condemnation is deserved.** These two false arguments are based on the idea that the Lord needs sin in order to demonstrate that he is God. He needs nothing of the kind. Since he is God, he will in the presence of sin show himself to be what he is. But how much more glorious to see what and who he is in the sphere of eternal fellowship with him than in banishment from his presence, with all the consequences thereof.

e) Default of All Mankind Before God. 3:9-20. Paul concludes that this teaching agrees with the OT and the role of the Law, which is to bring about the consciousness of sin.

9. What then? (AV) ought to be expanded into: **What then are we to conclude?** Before giving that conclusion, Paul asks one more question. If this question – **Are we better than they?** (AV) – concerns the Jews with whom Paul has been dealing in the first part of chapter 3, the verb *proechometha* ought to be translated: **Are we** (Jews) **excelled?** That is, Are we Jews in a worse position than the Gentiles? To which Paul answers, **Not at all.** But if the question refers to the whole argument begun in 1:18, then taking *proechometha* to be in the middle voice, the translation should be: **Can we** (the readers) **hold anything before ourselves for protection?** The verb *proechō* in the middle means "to hold before oneself" (see LSJ, p. 1479). The question would then be: Do we have anything in ourselves to shield us from God's wrath? Paul's answer is: **Not at all. Because we have already charged that both Jews and Greeks are all under sin.** The sinner has no means within himself to deal with sin. He is **under sin,** i.e., under the power, rule, command, control of sin. He needs help from without. His own resources cannot set him free.

10-18. In these verses Paul quotes a number of OT passages: 3:10-12 from Ps 14:1-3; 3:13 a,b from Ps 5:9; 3:13 c from Ps 140:3; 3:14 from Ps 10:7; 3:15-17 from Isa 59:7,8; 3:18 from Ps 36:1. The apostle does not quote from the Hebrew text but from the Greek version of the OT, the Septuagint (LXX). Sometimes he quotes it exactly; other times he paraphrases or abridges it; occasionally he is quite free in his handling of the wording (see Sanday and Headlam, *The Epistle to the Romans,* ICC, pp. 77-79). But the thought of the OT is adequately conveyed. All these quotations come from the Psalms except one passage—Isa 59:7. In their original context not all of these verses stress the universality of sin. The first (Ps 14:1-3) does. The next three (Ps 5:9; 140:3; 10:7) deal with the condition, attitude, and conduct of the wicked. The passage from Isaiah (59:7,8) deals with the unrighteousness of Israel. Psalm 36:1 sets forth the wicked man's lack of respect for God. Hence this collection of OT quotations illustrates the various forms of sin, the undesirable characteristics of sinners, the effect of their action, and their attitude toward God. This is the same picture that Paul himself has been painting.

19,20. Whatever *(as many things as)* **the law says.** The word **law** here must refer to the various quotations Paul has just made. Since these come from the Psalms, except for the Isaiah passage, Paul does not here refer to the Mosaic law. These quotations come from "the Writings" and "the Prophets"—two major divisions of the OT—indicating that Paul means by **the law** the whole of the OT. Hence the OT speaks to **those who are subject to the law** (Arndt, *en,* 5. d., p. 259). This includes both Jews and Gentiles—any who take seriously the message of the OT. The teaching of the OT is such that **every mouth is closed**—has no defense to make—and **that all the world has become accountable to God.** In verse 20 Paul seems to return to the narrower and more frequent concept of law—the Mosaic law. By the works which the Mosaic law prescribed, **no person will be acquitted.** Paul has shown the failure of both Jew and Gentile. Therefore, the verdict of no acquittal is an important part of the picture. If the Law and what it prescribes does not bring acquittal, what does it bring? **Through the law is the consciousness** (cf. Arndt, *epignōsis,* p. 291) **of sin.** The word **sin** is in the singular. The Law makes man aware of the defects of his nature, character, or being. By virtue of what he is, man acts as he does. The Law makes man aware that he is not what he ought to be. To bring men to this recognition is a great task. Since Paul assigns to the Law such a task, he surely does not minimize law.

2) Righteousness Attained by Faith,

Not by Legalistic Works. 3:21-31.

If man has failed to attain righteousness, and if righteousness is necessary before God, then how is a man to attain righteousness? How can God be righteous when he acquits a man and declares him righteous? Paul has just made the problem more acute by showing that all men are sinners. So if God declares any man righteous, he is declaring one to be righteous who is unrighteous. Paul's answer shows God's wisdom and involvement in the matter of human sin.

21. The righteousness of God. Paul means the righteousness bestowed by God. Such a righteousness is **apart from the law** in the sense that it is not a righteousness deserved or achieved by keeping the Law. Apart from the Law the righteousness of God **has been revealed.** Here is righteousness sent by God and revealed by God. Though distinct from any righteousness sought by keeping the Law, it is testified to **by the law and the prophets.** The latter phrase means the whole OT (Mt 5:17; 7:12; 11:13; 22:40; Lk 16:16; Acts 13:15; 24:14; 28:23). That God would reckon faith as righteousness is not foreign to the OT (see Rom 4).

22-24. If righteousness is bestowed, upon whom is it bestowed? This righteousness is realized through the efficient cause—faith, which has for its object, Christ. It is a righteousness **to all those in the process of trusting.** The present participle makes it clear that this is a lifelong committal to Christ seen in the day-by-day response of trust (see on 1:16). It is trust and only trust that is required. **There is no difference** between Jew and Gentile so far as sin is concerned (3:23). **Because all sinned** (see 2:12). This sin refers to the involvement of all men—both Jew and Gentile—in transgression. The tense brings together the individual personal transgressions into a collective whole.

All men manifest their involvement in Adam's departure from right by **constantly falling short of the glory of God. Falling short** means to lack or to be without. What is it that men fall short of and lack? The **glory of God** includes the splendor or radiance of God—the outward manifestation of what God is. Majesty and sublimity are also part of the glory of God. Majesty involves power. Sublimity involves a superior and elevated position — that of the One who is supreme. Yet the glory of God is not only to be *seen* by those who believe (Jn 11:40), but it is *received* and *made a part of* those who believe (II Cor 3:18) and is their destiny (I Thess 2:12; II Thess 2:14). It is not only ascribed to God by the great multitude in heaven because of his victory over sin (Rev 19:1), but it also characterizes the Holy City, the eternal dwelling place of God with his people (Rev 21:11,23). Men are constantly lacking God's glory because the continual practice of sin denies all that the glory of God means.

The righteousness of God which has been revealed, and which God bestows upon all those who are believing or trusting means that these **are acquitted** or **freely pronounced righteous** (Rom 3:24). How can this be? It is **by means of God's grace.** God is favorably disposed to do this, not because of any merit in men but because he is gracious and chooses to manifest his grace towards men. But can God do this simply by a decision of his will without any objective action on his part? Paul would answer, "No." Therefore, he adds the phrase, **through the redemption that is in Christ Jesus.** Men can be acquitted (pronounced righteous) because God has acted. He has provided **redemption.** Originally the word meant *the buying back* of a slave or captive, *the making him free* by the payment of a ransom (Arndt, *apolytrōsis,* p. 95). Here redemption refers to the release provided by Christ from sin and its consequences. This redemption or release is **in Christ Jesus.** To be in Christ is to belong to him and to be a part of all that he has done and brought into being through his redemptive work. Paul now proceeds to show just what this work involved.

25,26. This work is an objective transaction, a particular act of God which involved the person of his Son. It was a necessary act. The necessity was not imposed upon God from without, for then he would not have been God. It was imposed upon him from within, by virtue of his own nature. **Whom** (Christ Jesus) **God displayed publicly as a means of propitiation in his blood through faith.** Here Paul brings together God and Christ, the work accomplished, and man's response to this work. God publicly displayed Christ as a means of propitiation in or by his blood. The death of Christ was a fact to be observed by all. But the atoning aspect—that which propitiates sin—was the giving up of his life. This is seen in the fact that his blood was shed or poured out. These details are given not to arouse sympathy but to show the reality of this death. God was the offerer. Christ was the sacrifice. Human sin was covered, i.e., blotted out forever. Yet for this propitiation to be effective in the life of the individual, faith must be present. The faith or trust is in God, first of all, but it also involves what he has done. He took sin into his his own being (II Cor 5:21), dealt with it there objectively, and by doing this **gave proof of his righteousness.** But did God **let go unpunished the sins which happened** before Christ's death? The objective, public death of Christ at Calvary proves that the Lord did not let these sins go unpunished. We know that he was dealing with human sin there—with the past sins of mankind as well as with those presently being carried out, and those yet to be committed—because he declared it through his apostles and prophets. These past sins were done **in the sphere of God's forbearance** (Rom 3:25). The Lord did not forget these sins, although he did not deal with them immediately.

God's action in the cross was more than a vindication of himself in regard to past human history. It was also **the proof of his righteousness in the present** (3:26). The Lord must be just or righteous now as he declares righteous the one who believes in Jesus. He did not pass a law that he who believes in Jesus would be declared righteous simply because He said so. Rather, He acted. The Father, Son, and Holy Spirit entered into the arena of human sin. The Almighty laid the basis upon which he could forgive sin, and upon which he could declare sinners righteous and still himself be righteous.

27-31. Now Paul proceeds to the results of God's saving work in Christ at the cross. He contends that **boasting** is **eliminated.** How? **By what kind of a law?** By what kind of system, principle, code, or norm could boasting be eliminated? By **a system of works?** Oh, no. Such a system engenders pride. Rather, it is by a **faith kind of system.** A work-centered life is a self-centered life. But the law or code of faith brings about a God-centered life. Christianity is regarded here as a new law—a code of life with faith at its center. This idea of the word *law* is found in Rom 3:27; 8:2; Jas 1:25; 2:8,9; 2:12. The essence of **the law of faith** is that **a man is declared righteous by means of faith apart from the works of the law** (Rom 3:28). The Lord is the one who declares men righteous. He is the God both of the Jews and of the Gentiles (v. 29). He declares the Jews to be righteous **because of** *(ek)* faith, the Gentiles **through** or **by** *(dia)* faith. In both instances faith is the cause of God's declaration. So both Jew and Gentile find acceptance with God in the same way—through a personal committal to him, a personal trust in him. This fact does not mean that the Law is nullified. Rather, **the law is confirmed** or **made valid.** It is confirmed in its role of making men conscious of sin (v. 20). The law confronts men not only with their sin but with the Lawgiver as well. When men trust God, the Law-giver, they are at the place where law was meant to bring them.

3) Righteousness by Faith in the Life of Abraham. 4:1-25.

Paul's argument that we are declared righteous by faith was not something new. The object of faith for Paul was Christ. The clear presentation of faith in Christ as the way to righteousness makes the new covenant an everlasting covenant. But the old covenant did embody the principle of being declared righteous by faith. Who could better serve as an example than Abraham? He was the father of the Jewish people. So Paul looks carefully at his life.

a) His Righteousness Attained by Faith Not by Works. 4:1-8. **1.** Paul represents a Jew as raising the question: **What shall we say that Abraham, who physically is our forefather, has found?** These questions that Paul often raises probably are those put to him as he traveled from city to city. **2.** Assume for the moment that Abraham was justified by works; he could then boast. His boast, however, would not be in God but in himself. **3.** The testimony of the Scripture is the final authority to settle any point at issue. Abraham believed or trusted God. This belief or trust **was credited to him as righteousness** (Arndt, *dikaiosynē*, 3, p. 196; *eis*, 8.b., p. 229). Here Paul is quoting Gen 15:6.

4,5. To one working, his pay is credited not as a favor but as due. Wages earned have nothing to do with unmerited favor. **To one not working but trusting the one who pronounces righteous the godless, his faith or trust is credited to him as righteousness.** Here in a nutshell is the Pauline doctrine of justification by faith. Constant trust or committal to God is the first and sole requirement of the man who is declared righteous. This to the Jews was a scandal of no mean proportions. To them it was unthinkable that God should acquit a guilty, godless man. Two things were overlooked by Jews who objected to this as being a libel upon the being of God. First of all, the Jews rejected Jesus as the Messiah, and, therefore, they disregarded the redemptive transaction involving God and Christ. Secondly, they failed to see the significance of belief or trust on the part of one who was godless. Such trust shows that the man is no longer without God but is rather a person who has committed himself to all that God is, to all that God has done, and to all that God will do.

6-8. David also speaks of how blessed (fortunate) is the man **to whom God credits righteousness apart from works.** In so doing he confirms the earlier assertions made about Abraham. In the quotation from Ps 32:1,2, it is clear that righteousness is credited to a man, is put to his account. This same individual is pictured as having his lawless deeds forgiven and his sins covered. The Lord does not put sin to his account. In place of a debt which he can never pay, he has righteousness put to his account which he did not earn. How can a man be righteous in God's sight? God bestows His righteousness upon the one who trusts him (Phil 3:9). The OT asserts that God does this. The NT shows more clearly how he can.

b) Abraham Made the Father of All Who Believe by His Faith Prior to Circumcision. 4:9-12. If Abraham is a test case, how was his faith related to the rite of circumcision? He was the first to participate in this rite, and it became the sign of God's covenant with His people. This question was sure to come up in any discussion Paul had with the Jewish people. **9,10.** The apostle insists that the crediting of faith as righteousness took place prior to Abraham's circumcision. In fact, circumcision is looked upon in the Scriptures as **confirming the righteousness which belonged to the faith Abraham had while in uncircumcision** (v. 11). Hence circumcision was a sign to Abraham of the righteousness that God bestowed upon him because of his trust. Since the faith and the bestowal of righteousness occurred before circumcision, Abraham is the father of the Gentiles who believe but who do not have this religious symbol. The order in Abraham's case – faith and then righteousness credited to him – made it unmistakably clear that righteousness could be reckoned to the Gentiles who believed. The fact that circumcision was a sign of the righteousness imparted to Abraham because of his faith makes Abraham the father of Jews also, who – like him – receive circumcision, exercise faith, obtain a righteousness which God bestows, and regard circumcision as the sign of this faith and righteousness. **12.** Note that Abraham is not the father (in a vital, spiritual sense) of those who have only the external sign; but rather he is the father of those who walk in the faith that he had before he had any external sign. The Jews were to walk in the footprints of Abraham, the man of faith, not in the footprints of one who legalistically carried out a rite that God demanded of him.

c) Realization of the Promise Brought by Faith, Not by Law. 4:13-16. **13.** Paul asserts that it was **not through the law** that the promise came to Abraham or to his seed. What promise does Paul have in mind? It is the promise that **he** (Abraham) **should be the heir of the world.** This exact language is not found in the OT, but certainly Paul is speaking here of Abraham's being the father of a great posterity (Gen 15:5,6; 22:15-18). The great number of his seed – as the stars of the heaven and as the sand along the seashore (Gen 22:17) – was understood by the Jews to refer solely to his physical descendants. But in Rom 4:11 Paul says that Abraham is the father of those who believe among the Gentiles – "those believing in a state of uncircumcision." Hence Abraham is the heir of the world because he is the father of believers. This promise is **through the righteousness which faith bestows.** Of course, faith does not really bestow the righteousness. God bestows it on the ground of faith. **14.** What if we assume that those of the Law are heirs? **Faith is in a state of being invalid. The promise is in a state of being nullified.** Whenever the choice becomes either faith or law, then to choose law (legalism) as the basis of inheriting the world and pleasing God means the abandoning of faith and the promise based thereon. **15. The law produces** or **brings about wrath.** It does this by setting forth God's standard of conduct. Men who disregard this standard and act as they please place themselves directly under God's wrath. **Where there is no law,**

neither is there transgression (ASV). One is not usually charged with speeding if the state has no speed limit, if there are no posted limits along the road, and if there appears to be nothing unreasonable or improper about one's driving. The word **transgression** *(parabasis)* refers to an overstepping, a violation of specifically stated commandment. The role of the Law, then, is to make clear what God demands of men.

16. The promise is from faith. The **it** of the AV should be clearly designated as the promise. The promise has its source in faith in order to make clear that the content of the promise is **a favor,** not an earned, merited payment. Furthermore, the promise becomes certain **to all the seed.** Paul makes clear that the seed is not to be equated with those who lived under the Law. Rather, the seed refers to those who, like Abraham, believe God – to those who share Abraham's faith. If this is the definition of the word **seed,** then **Abraham** is truly **the father of us all.**

d) God, the Master of Death, the Object of Faith for Abraham and the Christian. 4:17-25. In this section the reader sees the God in whom Abraham believed. He also learns what obstacles and difficulties Abraham overcame because of his firm trust. Both Abraham and the Christian share the same conviction: God gives life to the dead.

17. A year before Isaac was born, God reappeared to Abraham, re-emphasized His covenant with him that he should be the father of many nations, and changed his name from Abram to Abraham (Gen 17:1-5). The apostle quotes the phrase, **I have made thee a father of many nations.** Paul pictures Abraham, at the time this declaration was made, as standing **before the God whom he trusted.** Two important things are said about the God in whom Abraham trusted: (1) He is **the one who brings the dead to life.** Abraham experienced this power in the birth of Isaac (cf. Rom 4:19). Paul was thinking of the Father especially as the one who raised up Christ (cf. v. 24). (2) He **calls the things which do not exist as if they did exist.** This is the Lord's power to create. It could also be translated: *God calls into being what does not exist as* (easily as he calls) *that which does exist.* No mortal can comprehend the divine creative power. The bringing of animate and inanimate objects into existence and their maintenance is God's activity. The nature of the objects may be discussed – mind, matter, energy–but the why and how of their existence can be known accurately only to the extent that the Lord reveals them. **18.** Because Abraham knew such a God, he was able, **contrary to all human expectations, in hope to believe.** His faith was directed to the purpose and goal of his being the father of many nations. **19.** There were two great obstacles to his achieving this goal. He was physically incapable of fathering a child. His wife Sarah was physically incapable of conception and childbearing. **Because Abraham was not weak in faith, he looked at with reflection** *(considered)* **his own body in a state of being impotent** (v. 19). The AV has: *He considered* **not** *his own body now dead.* But this negative is not supported by the best manuscripts. Hence Paul pictures Abraham as fully facing the difficulty. He was about one hundred years old. He further considered the deadness of Sarah's womb. **20. But he was not at odds with himself over the promise of God because of unbelief.** The word translated "to be at odds with oneself" (*diakrinō*) could also be translated "to doubt" or "to waver." For the patriarch, there was no uncertainty because of unbelief. In the face of these obstacles Abraham **was strengthened because of faith** or *trust.* Note here the effects of unbelief and belief. Unbelief puts one at variance with himself; belief brings strength to meet the obstacle. Abraham gave glory to God as he was strengthened. **21.** He was convinced that **what God had promised** He was able to do. The verb "to promise" is in the perfect tense. This means Abraham had been in a state of possessing the promise, so great was his conviction that the promise would be realized. **22.** This was the kind of faith credited to Abraham as righteousness. **24.** The crediting of faith as righteousness was not for Abraham's benefit alone. The written record of this fact was **because of us.** Righteousness will be reckoned to those **who are in the process of trusting in the One who raised up Jesus our Lord from the dead.** There is a difference between Abraham and the Christian. Abraham believed or trusted God (v. 3). The Christian trusts the same God, but He is now known as the God who raised up Jesus Christ from the dead (v. 24). In this the Lord has revealed himself as acting on man's behalf in a most unusual way. **25.** The center of his action is Christ, who **was handed over because of our trans-**

gressions. The verb "to hand over" is in the passive, meaning that it was God who did the handing over (cf. 8:32). The same word is used of Judas and his betrayal of Christ. But although Judas was the human instrument who handed Christ over to the soldiers, and although Judas' sin was very great, it was God's purpose that Christ be handed over into the hands of sinners. (The word "to hand over," *paradidōmi,* is used in a number of interesting contexts. For a word study of this term see F. Buchsel, *TWNT*, II, 171-175; Karl Barth, *Church Dogmatics,* Vol. II, Part 2, *The Doctrine of God,* pp. 480-494). When we see that "our" transgressions necessitated Christ's being put to death, the death of Jesus appears in a different light. A detached observer might conclude that Christ died and rose again. But one who has committed himself to God says: "Jesus was handed over because of *my* transgressions." The plural pronoun **our** shows Paul's identification with his Roman readers. **He was raised because of our vindication.** The verb is again passive. God raised Christ from the dead. The resurrection here is said to be essential to our being declared righteous. The resurrection signaled not only Christ's victory over death but also his living to testify that he had completed the redemptive work laid out by God (the work for which he became man), and that he lives to plead the cause of those who believe in him and his saving work.

4) Centrality of the Righteousness by Faith in Individual Lives and in the Framework of History. 5:1-21.

In the first part of this chapter Paul examines the meaning of righteousness by faith for believers. What do they have? What should they do? How did God meet them and what is their future? Then he turns to a comparison of the effects of Adam's departure from God with the effects of Christ's reconciling work. The importance of righteousness in the last half of the chapter is made clear by the occurrence of the term in 5:17,18,19, 21.

a) Effects of the Righteousness by Faith upon the Recipients. 5:1-11. **1.** The participle speaks of action which has occurred. **Having been declared righteous by faith.** This has been the theme from 3:21 through 4:25. From this theme, certain conditions and responses follow. The main verb forms in 5:1,2,3 may be translated: "we have peace . . . we boast in afflictions . . ." Or these verbs can be translated as exhortations: "Let us enjoy the peace we have . . . let us boast (glory) in the hope . . . let us boast (glory) in afflictions . . ." The verbs are all in the present tense and express constant activity. The **peace** a believer has is **peace with God.** This is an objective state for the one who is declared righteous. It is **through our Lord Jesus Christ.** Christ's redemptive work provided an atonement, a covering for the sin of the one declared righteous by faith. Such an one has been reconciled to God. Therefore the hostility and animosity between God and believers are gone. Instead there is blessed peace.

2 a. There is also fellowship – **through whom we have had the approach** or *access.* The wonder of being declared righteous consists in this open access to the presence of God. *Prosagōgē* can be translated "approach," "access," or "introduction" (see LSJ, p. 1500). But the idea of "introduction" goes hand in hand with "access" or "approach." One who came to see a king needed both access – the right to come, and an introduction – the proper presentation. The right or access is fundamental, the introduction more a matter of protocol. Hence the stress here ought to be on **access.** The access is **into this grace in which we have taken our stand. This grace** is the unmerited favor of God to declare righteous those who have put their trust in Jesus.

2 b. The translation **and rejoice in hope** (AV) fails to make clear to the reader that the same verb is used here as in 5:3 – "we glory in tribulations." Hence 5:2 really means: **And we are boasting (glorying) in the hope of the glory that God will manifest or display.** Hope plays a vital part in the life of believers, for it has to do with all that God has promised to do for them in Christ.

3,4. But this hope becomes clearer in the day-by-day pressures of life. The believer glories in tribulations because he knows they will bring clearer vision of what lies ahead – hope with conviction in it. The order of these verses is significant – **tribulation, endurance, character,** and then **hope.** Testing brings the response of endurance. Endurance produces character. The outcome of all of this is hope. **5. Hope does not disappoint.** Even though hope does center in God's future action (8:24,25), it has an important present possession—**God's love,** i.e., the love which God imparts, **is being poured out in our hearts through the Holy Spirit he gave to us.** The abundance of this love in the heart of justified men, and its outreach, are said by Christ to be the distinguishing trait of Christians (Jn 13:34,35).

This love, poured out in our hearts, with the hope that does not disappoint, has its supreme example in God's love for us (Rom 5:6-8). **6. Indeed, while we were still weak** [moral weakness], **at the right time Christ died for the godless.** There are rare examples of a person's dying for an upright man. That someone might dare to die for the good man because of the impact of his life is very plausible. But that God should demonstrate his love for us in that while we were sinners Christ should die **for us** is not only amazing but almost incredible. Four times in this section the preposition *hyper* occurs (vv. 6,7,7,8). It has such broad meaning that no one English word can convey it. It really involves in one unit the ideas of "for the benefit of," "on behalf of," and "instead of." If these ideas are put into the English word "for," then the full significance of Christ's death "for" us begins to dawn.

9. But Paul quickly shifts the scene from our former state as sinners to the **now.** If God loved us when we were sinners, if Christ died for us then, much more now, having been declared righteous by his blood, we shall be saved through him (Christ) from God's future wrath. Note that the ground for justification is Christ's blood. This future salvation is from God's wrathful punishment, spoken of in II Thess 1:9 as "an eternal destruction from the face of the Lord and from the glory of his strength." **10.** Those now justified are said to have been reconciled to God **while** they were **enemies.** The basis for this reconciliation is explicitly stated — **through the death of his Son** (ASV). We were reconciled by his death when we were enemies. This being true, the apostle concludes, much more is it true that **we shall be saved in** or **by his life.** Elsewhere Paul points out that the one who is joined to the Lord is one spirit (I Cor 6:17), i.e., he shares Christ's resurrected life and spiritual power. He also says: "When Christ, our life, shall appear, then shall ye also appear with him in glory" (Col 3:4). We shall be saved by Christ's life because we share this life. We belong to Christ. The writer of Hebrews stresses that Christ lives to make intercession for us (Heb 7:25). The intercessory life of Christ in glory plays a vital role in the salvation of believers. But the context here seems to put the stress on the believers' sharing in Christ's death and resurrected life. Believers will be saved (fut.) by their present and future participation in Christ's life.

11. The boasting or glorying in God by which the believer affirms his devotion to God is through the Lord Jesus Christ. Through him **we have now received the reconciliation** (ASV). God is the one who is active in reconciliation (II Cor 5:18,19), and men are said to be reconciled (Rom 5:10; II Cor 5:20), i.e., they are acted upon by God. Thus believers are said to receive reconciliation. They are recipients of a relationship of peace and harmony brought about by God.

b) Effects of Adam's Disobedience and Christ's Obedience. 5:12-21. This is one of the most difficult passages in the book of Romans, because Paul is so concise. The apparent repetition is only because of frequent mention of Adam and Christ — and those influenced by their action. Actually, Paul carefully develops his argument. He uses the argument *a fortiori* (with stronger reason, more conclusively): If Adam's sin resulted in this, how much more will Christ's redemptive work do this. Although Christ's redemptive work is far more potent than Adam's transgression, as the apostle shows, this does not mean that all men will be saved. For men to reign in life they must **receive** the abundance of grace and the righteousness that God makes available (v. 17).

12-14. *Universality of Sin and Death.* **12. Through one man sin entered into the world and through sin, death.** The man is Adam. The tense of the verb indicates a distinct historic entrance. **World** refers to mankind (a common use of the word in Romans; cf. 1:8; 3:6; 3:19; 5:12,13). **Death passed through to all men because all sinned.** Physical death came to all men but not because they were all in the process of individually sinning. All men did sin (except for infants dying in infancy) experientially. But Paul is not talking about that here. The sin of the **all** is centered in that of the **one man** Adam. **Because all sinned.** Paul asserts that all men sinned when Adam sinned, but he does not explain how. Yet much has been written on the question of how. Paul's concept of racial solidarity seems to be a universalizing of the Hebrew concept of family solidarity. A tragic picture of family solidarity is seen in Josh 7:16-26, where Achan is discovered as the cause of Israel's defeat at Ai. He had appropriated for himself some of the spoil from Jericho contrary to the Lord's specific command (Josh 6:17,18). Achan blamed no one else – "I saw . . . I coveted . . . I took" (Josh 7:21). But in the administration of the punishment, not only Achan but also all his property, his sons, his daughters, his oxen, his asses, his sheep, his tent were destroyed. Everything connected with Achan was blotted out of Israel. Another example of family solidarity is found in Abraham's paying tithes to Melchizedek (Gen 14:18-20). The writer of Hebrews regards Levi as also paying tithes to Melchizedek although he was not born until approximately 200 years later. He regards Levi as being still in the loins of his father when Melchizedek met him (Heb 7:9,10). In the same sense Adam was both the individual and the race. His posterity are looked upon as acting with him because they are *his* posterity. As sons of Adam they constitute *Adam's* race.

13. From Adam's time to that of the Mosaic law, sin was in the world. It was present in men's acts and in their nature (i.e., in the principle of rebellion found in them). **But sin is not charged to an account while there is no law.** Adam's sin was charged to his account and to that of his posterity because he broke an explicitly stated command of God. Men from Adam to Moses without such explicit laws could not have sin charged to their account in the same way as Adam had. They did not have definite, specific statutes, such as those later given in the Mosaic code. **14.** But these men shared in the effect of Adam's sin, because death reigned from Adam to Moses even **over those who did not sin in the likeness of Adam's transgression.** Looking at these men from the standpoint of racial solidarity, Paul sees men from Adam to Moses as involved both in Adam's initial sin and in its consequences. Those in this group who did not sin in breaking a specifically given command still died. Adam is called in this verse **the type of the one about to come.** Paul is not saying that there were no God-given commands known to men between Adam and the Law (cf. Gen 26:5). He does assert that an absence of a code of law – of a divinely given norm – affects the way sin is reckoned against men.

15-17. *Contrasting Results of Diverse Actions.* Paul points out the differences between Adam and Christ.

15. The transgression of the **one** (Adam) is contrasted with the grace of God and the gift in the sphere of grace which the one man Christ bestows. **The many died** because of the transgression of Adam. Since death passed through to all men (v. 12), it is clear that the phrase **the many** means "all men." **Much more.** The grace of God and the gift which is in the sphere of grace that Christ provides have abounded to the many. "The many" is the same group who were affected by Adam's transgression and therefore died. God's grace and the gift in the sphere of Christ's grace abound to all men. The gift is righteousness (see v. 17). Adam's act brought death. Divine grace abounds to those affected by Adam's act.

16. The verdict of condemnation stemming from one transgression is contrasted with the gracious gift that came into existence because of many transgressions. **Now the verdict indeed was from one transgression unto condemnation.** The verdict refers to God's sentence. The word for **condemnation** involves the ideas of "punishment" and "doom." So we ask: Condemned to what? The answer is, to divine punishment and doom. The seriousness of this condemnation cannot be overstated. **The gracious gift is because of many transgressions unto acquittal or justification.** The outcome of Adam's one transgression was condemnation. Many transgressions brought God's gracious gift into operation, and its outcome or goal is acquittal. How powerful must be this gracious gift when it is directed toward such an end!

17. The reign of death, because of the trespass of the one, is contrasted with the reign in life – on the part of those who receive the abundance of grace and the gift of righteousness. **Death reigned through the one.** Adam transgressed God's commandment that he must not eat of the tree of the knowledge of good and evil (Gen 2:17). This command was a test of man's obedience to God. With the coming of sin into man's experience, death also came. Death became king. It reigned supreme. Adam's action brought the reign of death. **Much more.** Here again is man's action; but this time it is man's action simply in response to what God has done. **Those who are receiving the abundance of grace and the gift, i.e., righteousness.** Here we see man obliged to make a response toward the action of God. The abundance of grace has to do with all that God has accomplished and promised to do in Christ. The gift is defined here as **the righteousness.** This is the righteousness bestowed by God on the basis of faith (Rom 1:17; 3:21,22, 26; 5:17,21; 9:30; 10:3). Those who are receiving God's abounding favor toward them in Christ and the righteousness which he provides **will reign in life through the one man, Jesus Christ.** Because of what the one man, Jesus Christ, accomplished, death no longer reigns, but **men reign in life.** Why are there not as many who reign in life as there were under the reign of death? Because the abundance of grace and the gift of righteousness were rejected by many rather than received.

18,19. All men are affected by the one transgression (Adam's) and the one righteous deed (Christ's atoning death and resurrection). **So then** *(as a result then).* Paul is now ready to summarize his argument briefly. **As through one transgression the verdict came to all men unto condemnation.** The subject, **the verdict** (AV, *judgment),* must be supplied here from verse 16. The verb **come** is a satisfactory translation of the Greek verb *egeneto,* which should be supplied. **Thus also through the one righteous deed the gracious gift came unto all men unto the acquittal that brings life.** For the translation **one righteous deed,** see Arndt, *dikaiōma,* 2, p. 197. Romans 4:25 gives evidence that Paul conceived of Christ's death and resurrection as a unified whole. The subject, **the gracious gift** (AV, *the free gift),* must be supplied here from 5:16. This gracious gift comes to all men **for the purpose of** *(unto)* **acquittal that brings life** (see Arndt, *dikaiōsis,* p. 197). In both parts of this verse the same phrase occurs – **unto all men.** Through one transgression the verdict or sentence of judgment came **to all men.** So through one righteous deed the gracious gift of redemption (see Arndt, *charisma,* 1, p. 887) came **unto all men** for the purpose of acquittal that brings life. Paul asserts clearly that the effect of Christ's righteous deed extends just as far as the effect of Adam's transgression.

19. Now just as through the disobedience of the one man the many were appointed (AV, *were made)* **to be sinners, in this manner also through the obedience of the one the many will be appointed** (AV, *shall be made)* to be righteous. The disobedience of Adam is contrasted with the obedience of Christ. In the preceding verse Paul employs the vocabulary and setting of a law court – condemnation on the one hand and acquittal on the other. He retains this legal language in this verse as well. The verb *kathistēmi,* rendered by the AV as **be made,** is part of this language of law. In what sense *were the many* **made sinners,** and in what sense *will the many be* **made righteous?** The legal language suggests the following meanings: "appoint," "put down in the category of," "constitute," "establish." Because of Adam's disobedience, the many were appointed by God to be sinners. They were put down in the category of and constituted to be sinners. Because of Christ's obedience, the many will be appointed to be righteous. The verb is future because Paul was thinking of the future generations of believers who by trusting Christ will be declared righteous. Has the apostle changed the extent of **the many** in either side of this comparison? No, because he is showing in what categories God puts men when he views them in terms of the *actual* effect of Adam's disobedience and the *potential* effect of Christ's obedience. Paul is not teaching, as 5:17 shows, that all men will be saved. But in verse 19 he does assert that Christ's obedience encompasses all those affected by Adam's disobedience.

20,21. *The Reign of Sin Versus the Reign of Grace.* Here Paul concludes the argument he began in 5:12 on the question: Which is the more powerful—sin or grace?

20. The writer reminds us that although righteousness by faith is central in human history, the Law has an important place. The Law came **in order that the transgression might abound** (increase in number, multiply). **But where sin abounded.** The words **transgression** and **sin** are both personified here to make evil a distinct foe and not a mere abstraction. **Grace did much more abound.** Or, *was present in greater abundance.* Grace is much more powerful than sin. Yet when believers see what tremendous power sin has, they forget this truth.

21. Just as sin reigned in the sphere of death, grace abounds **in order that grace might reign through righteousness.** Sin is connected with death in this verse just as it was in 5:12. Grace reigns through the righteousness that God bestows. The fact that the righteousness of Christ is bestowed upon those who believe means not only that they are declared righteous but also that they belong to the reign and the triumph of grace. **Unto eternal life through Jesus Christ our Lord.** Grace reigns with a goal in view—eternal life. Eternal life is a quality of life; it is living by God's life and for God.

Believers have this life now. But eternal life means not only living by God, and for him, but in an environment that he has made perfect – free from all sin. Hence eternal life is the believer's destiny as well as immediate reality. How will this life be achieved? It will be achieved through a person – **through Jesus Christ our Lord.**

B. Righteousness as the Manner of Christian Living Before God. 6:1–8:39. Thus far Paul has stressed that God is righteous or just (cf. 3:26) and that he bestows righteousness on those who believe (cf. 3:22). To the question as to how men become righteous before God, he has replied: "Not by works but by trust in God" (cf. 4:1-8). But the one who has the righteousness that God bestows must live a righteous life. Paul now shows what this means. First, he eliminates some wrong ideas regarding his teaching about grace. Next, he shows that in the struggle against sin, the believer must not condemn law. Then he pictures sin as a powerful tyrant that cannot be defeated by human effort alone. Paul concludes this section by pointing out how victory can be attained.

1) Fallacy of Sinning That Grace Might Abound. 6:1-14.

1. If grace is so powerful, could not a man remain in sin and still experience the delivering power of grace?. **2.** Paul's answer is emphatic: **By no means.** The one trusting Christ has identified himself with the Lord Jesus in His death. **We who died in reference to sin**. Verse 10 makes it clear that Paul is here speaking of Christ's death. But he uses the first person plural – *We* have died to sin. This is a past experience. Such being the case, how can we still live in sin when we have already died to it?

3-5. Having said that the believer died with Christ, Paul now refers to the ordinance of baptism. Here the apostle follows his familiar pattern of asserting a truth and then illustrating it. **3. As many as were baptized unto Christ Jesus were baptized unto his death.** The phrase for "to be baptized unto" *(baptizein eis)* can also be translated *to be baptized in* or *with respect to*. It is used in the sense of being baptized with respect to the name of someone (cf. Acts 8:16; 19:5; I Cor 1:13,15; Mt 28:19; see Arndt, *baptizō*, p. 131). The ordinance of baptism is focused upon the death of Christ–its meaning and outcome. But Paul here points to the implications of baptism with reference to the Romans' way of life. **4. Through baptism, therefore, we were buried together with him in respect to his death.** "Being buried together" stresses the reality of Christ's death. Christ died, and the believer really died with him. **Just as Christ was raised from the dead through the glory of the Father.** This is a comparative clause. The resurrection brought to the Lord Jesus a new manner of life. In a similar way **we also should live in newness of life**. Since we were identified with Christ in his death, we are identified with him in his resurrection. For the Saviour, the resurrection meant a new manner of life. We were buried with Christ in order that we, like him, should **live** in newness of life. The translation to *walk* (AV) *in newness of life* carries with it the day-by-day living in the ordinary routines of life. **5. Since we have become united with** (MM, p. 598) **the likeness of his death, we certainly shall be united with the likeness of his resurrection.** The word **likeness** is used with two words in the English rendering of this verse – **death** and **resurrection.** Though it occurs only once in the original text, it is clear that Paul meant it to apply to both death and resurrection. Some have wanted to supply a "him" in this verse – "Since we have become united with him in the likeness." But **his** death and resurrection makes it clear, nevertheless, that Christ is central here. The word **him** is not found in the text, and good sense can be made out of the text without it. The emphasis in the verse falls on the word **likeness** *(homoiōma)*. To sin in the likeness of Adam's transgression (5:14) means to sin in a similar way, i.e., to break a specific command. It does not mean to sin the same sin. So the word may have the meanings of "representation," "copy," "facsimile," and "reproduction." (For an excellent treatment of the word and the various interpretations given to it in this context, see Johannes Schneider, TWNT, V, 191-195.) Since believers have had a death like Christ's, they will certainly have a resurrection like his. This does not mean that they will have the identical resurrection of Christ; rather, they will have a resurrection like his. In baptism believers are united with the representation of his death. To be united with the likeness of Christ's resurrection is a future hope that they are sure of. Both of these facts (baptism and resurrection) point to a changed manner of life between these two events — the walking in newness of life.

In verses **6-10,** as in verse 2, Paul points to the historic event of Christ's death. **Our old man.** The earlier or unregenerate man before he became a renewed, changed, transformed man. This unregenerated man was crucified with Christ **in order that the sinful body might be done away with.** The body is stressed here because of the role it plays in the man's carrying out of his sinful desires. **In order that we should not be in constant slavery to sin.** Sin is personified here. As a tyrant, it holds men in abject slavery.

Now the one who died has been set free from sin. A dead person cannot act in the daily events of life. One who has died to sin does not respond to the pattern of sinful living. **8. And since we died together with Christ.** Our dying with Christ is the basis for our belief that we will be raised with him. **9.** Christ's death was in reference to sin. His victory over death is permanent. This occurred once for all. **10.** Since the time of his death he lives solely for God, i.e., for God's advantage and glory. And he lived solely for God before his death. But when Jesus had accomplished the redemptive work that centered in his death, his living for God had a new outlook. He had dealt with the sin question once for all. He had conquered death. With sin and death defeated, he could live for God with these experiences behind him.

All of this had certain consequences for believers (6:11-14). **11. We are to keep reckoning** or *considering* **ourselves to be dead indeed to sin and living for God.** The fact that we must continue to reckon ourselves dead to sin shows that the possibility of sinning is ever present. But our reckoning is more than negative. We reckon ourselves to be alive (to be constantly living) for God. The phrase **in your mortal body** is made equivalent to **yourselves** (in v. 13). **Let not sin keep on reigning** in you, i.e., in your person, **with the result that you obey its evil desires.** If we are in Christ, we have the power to dethrone the sin in our lives. If a believer allows sin to reign, he obeys the evil desires that sin generates. **13. Stop handing over your members as weapons** (or *tools)* **of unrighteousness to sin.** When the tyrant, sin, reigns in the hearts of men, sinners freely hand over their hands, feet, eyes, and mind to the cause of unrighteousness. In place of this constant dedication to evil, Paul urges: **Hand over yourselves once for all to God . . . and your members as weapons of righteousness.** Why should we hand over ourselves to God? Because those in Christ are living as having risen from the dead. We died with Christ. Hence we see life from a new perspective. We have dedicated ourselves to God. The self, of course, includes every member or part of us and every activity we may engage in. All that goes to make up the human personality will be either actively serving unrighteousness or actively serving righteousness. In whose service are our members employed? **14.** The abounding of grace is of such a nature that sin does not **lord it over** believers. We are not **under law** but **under grace.** Those in Christ are not under the regime of the Mosaic law as the means of attaining salvation. We are under the grace of God and of Christ. The whole of the OT — the Law, the Prophets, and the Writings (e.g., Psalms) — certainly brings the knowledge of sin (Rom 3:20; 5:20) when understood in the light of Christ's teaching and the teaching of the apostles after his death and resurrection. The OT also teaches Christians great truths about God. Paul regards what Christ taught and Christ himself as law. "Always bear one another's crushing weights, and in this fashion you will fulfill **the law of Christ**" (Gal 6:2). "I became to those without law as without law [to the Gentiles as a Gentile], though I do not reject God's law but *I am subject to the law of Christ* in order that I might gain those without law [the Gentiles]" (I Cor 9:21).

2) Fallacy of Sinning Because Believers Are Under Grace, Not Law. 6:15–7:6.

When we are under grace, we have a new owner. This fact changes all of a believer's conduct. Our status under grace is like that of a woman married to another man after the death of her husband. It involves a whole new manner of life. Thus, by analogy, Paul shows why being under grace never allows a believer to be indifferent to sin.

a) Allegiance, Fruit, Destiny. 6:15-23.

Here Paul appeals to what his readers know. He reminds them of their former lives and the fruit they bore. He tells them the outcome of their new dedication. He contrasts the eternal results of two different kinds of allegiance.

15. Should a man commit a sinful act because he is not under law but under grace? Paul replies: **By no means. 16.** He reminds his readers that they are slaves to that one to whom they hand themselves over. If they hand themselves over to sin, the outcome is death. If they become slaves of obedience to God, the outcome is righteousness. The handing over is looked upon here as a constant process or allegiance.

17. They were formerly slaves of sin. Then there came a break with that bondage. **You obeyed from the heart the pattern of teaching unto which you were given over.** The pattern of teaching, of course, is Christianity. They were given over to it to learn its content. They responded with obedience – obedience that came from the depths of their being. This brought a decisive change. They were freed from sin. They became slaves to righteousness. Both sin and righteousness are personified, and this figure of speech – being a slave to sin or righteousness – helps us understand just what is at stake. **19. I speak in human terms because of the weakness of your flesh.** This human analogy is necessary, Paul says, because of the poor judgment of those who become willing instruments of sin. The man under the control of sin is "in the flesh." Formerly Paul's readers had presented their members as slaves to uncleanness and to one sinful deed after another. This proved their constant devotion to various forms of wickedness. **In this manner hand over your members once for all as slaves to righteousness for consecration.** With the same abandon with which men dedicated themselves to evil, they should now hand over their members as slaves to righteousness. The outcome is **consecration** or **holiness.** Consecrated to whom? To God. Holiness is the product of consecration to God. **20.** Paul contends that when the readers belonged to sin, they certainly did not have righteousness as their master. **21. What fruit did you have then?** (Note change in question from AV.) When you were slaves of sin, what fruit did you have? You had fruit in those things **of which you are now ashamed.** Sinners produce bad fruit (see Mt 7:16-20). **Now the end of those things is death. By death** Paul here means eternal death (see Arndt, *thanatos,* 2, b, p. 352; Rom 1:32; 6:16, 21,23; 7:5; II Cor 2:16; 7:10; II Tim 1:10; Heb 2:14 b; I Jn 5:16; Rev 2:11; 20:6,15; 21:8).

22. Being free from sin means being a slave to God. The immediate fruit produced is consecration. The final outcome of belonging to God is eternal life. **23. Now the compensation paid by sin** (for services rendered to it) **is death.** Paul changes the analogy slightly here. Sin pays wages to those working for it. The wages paid is death. **But the gracious gift of God is eternal life in Jesus Christ our Lord.** God's gracious gift of deliverance from sin, his transforming of the sinner's whole being, is **eternal life.** Eternal life is a new kind of life. The sinner realizes this as an unmerited favor. This kind of life, this quality of existence, is found in only one person – **in Jesus Christ.** The last phrase – **our Lord** – is Paul's way of saying that the Lord belongs to us as we belong to him. We have made him our Lord by our act of commitment. His lordship extends to the manner of our living.

b) Annulment and New Alignment Caused by Death. 7:1-6. **1. The law,** says the apostle, **lords it over** *(rules over)* **a man as long as he lives.** Paul lays down this axiom both for the sake of the illustration that he is about to use and to show that this is the nature of law. Its requirements remain in force as long as one lives under the regime of law. **2. The married woman is in a state of being bound by the law to the living husband.** In the first verse Paul says that he is speaking to those who know law. Since the majority of the Romans were Gentiles, the law here is not the Mosaic Law in particular but merely the legal principle that a married woman is bound to her husband. Paul's handling of this particular command is certainly in the light of his Jewish background in the Mosaic law. **If the husband dies, the woman is discharged from** *(is released from)* **this particular commandment about her husband.** Death brings annulment of the whole former relationship regarding her marriage. **3. While her husband lives, she will be called an adulteress if she belongs to a different husband.** The translation "to belong to" (cf. Arndt, *ginomai,* II, 3, p. 159) has the force of *being married to.* But after the death of her husband she may re-enter the marriage state without being charged with adultery. The living one (the wife) is free to belong to another.

4. When Paul applies the illustration to the relationship of an individual to the Law and to Christ, it is the one who dies (the believer who died with Christ) who is released from the Law and is free to belong to Christ. **You were put to death to the disadvantage of the law through the**

body of Christ. The phrase **through the body of Christ (ASV)** refers to the believer's identification with Christ in his physical death. In 6:6 Paul has already said that our unregenerate person has been crucified with Christ. This death deprived the Law of its power over us and had as its end our **belonging to another – to the one who arose from the dead.** Here is the new alignment. We now belong to Christ, so that we may bring forth fruit to God. To translate the phrase, *eis to genesthai humas heterô*, "in order that you should be married to another," is certainly all right. It is part of Paul's analogy and agrees with his use of the comparison with marriage elsewhere (II Cor 11:2; Eph 5:25,29).

5. To be **in the flesh** means to be under the control and domination of sin. **The sinful passions,** which the Law made conspicuous by reminding men of God's standards, **were constantly at work** in their members. Dominated by these sinful passions, men brought forth fruit to the advantage of death. Death here is personified. It means eternal death (see 6:21). **6. But now having been discharged from** *(released from)* **the law.** The Law was powerless to remove sinful passions. Being released from the Law is here made equivalent to being released from being in the flesh. **Because we died** [in regard to that] **in which** (referring to the Law) **we were held fast.** While under the Law, the believer died with Christ. He died to the Law's claim requiring condemnation. Paul speaks of this death to the Law in Gal 2:19. Being discharged from the Law opens a new relationship with a new attitude. The relationship is that of **constantly being a slave** to God. This means that we serve God, fully aware that we belong to him. He owns us because he redeemed us. We serve **in a new spirit, not in the old letter.** Or better, in newness of Spirit in contrast to the old legal code. In place of a legalism that enforces statutes, there is a spirit of love and dedication.

3) Questions Raised by the Struggle Against Sin. 7:7-25.

Here Paul unfolds his own inward struggles. He does not tell this as an interesting piece of autobiography, but because he knew that his readers had the same struggles. Paul controlled by sin did things that Paul controlled by God did not wish to do. Paul controlled by sin was not his true self but his false self. Nevertheless it was the same self. Paul was guilty when he was controlled by sin and holy when he was controlled by God. As a Jew he knew God's will (Phil 3:6; Acts 22:3; 26:4,5). To the extent that he carried out God's will, he was controlled by God. This did not make him a believer in Christ or a Christian. But it did make him aware of the struggle between doing right and doing wrong. When he became a Christian, the struggle was intensified. Every believer, aware of the righteousness that God bestows, and of righteousness as the manner of Christian living, can say when he reads this passage, "This is my experience." Paul also stands representatively for those Jewish people—the people of the Law—who passed from a place of complacency under the Law to a condition of concern with the deep struggles to which it gave rise, and then to a position of composure and victory in Christ.

a) Is the Law sin? 7:7-12. **7.** If, when a man becomes a Christian, he is released or discharged from the Law, does that mean there is something wrong with the Law? Paul answers: **By no means.** The Law showed him (and it shows us) just what sin is. For example, Paul says: **I would not have felt guilty** [in] **desiring that which is forbidden if the law were not saying: you** (sing.) **shall not desire that which is forbidden.** The longing for that which is evil becomes apparent when the commandment declares: This evil thing is forbidden. Then the sinner wants it. **8.** The apostle tells how sin took the commandment **as a base of operations** and wrought in him **desire of every kind** (for that which is forbidden). **Now without law, sin is dead.** Paul does not say that sin is not committed without law. He is saying that without law sin is not apparent to us. It takes a carpenter's level to make clear how far from straight a board really is.

9. Indeed I was alive without the law at one time. But when the commandment came, sin became alive and I died. The apostle here is talking about his own consciousness of sin. When he was a lad, the content of the Law did not really reach him. He did not understand the true purpose of law. This lack of understanding is not confined to children. An adult like the rich young ruler can assert confidently: "I have guarded (ASV, *observed)* all these things from my youth" (Mk 10:20; cf. Mt 19:20; Lk 18:21). **10.** But there came a day in

Paul's life when the particular commandment, "You (sing.) shall not desire that which is forbidden," hit him right between the eyes. He knew he was desiring the forbidden. Paul became conscious of sin, and he knew that he was spiritually dead. This particular commandment ("Thou shalt not covet") not only made clear the sinfulness of desiring that which is forbidden but also told him how to live. It reminded him that he was not living the right way. **11.** Sin had deceived him. As he understood the commandment, the extent of sin's deception became clear to him. The commandment made Paul see that sin had brought about his death. Sin first **deceives** and then **kills.** This order shows how tricky sin is and what is its objective—the eternal ruin of individuals.

b) Is that which is good the cause of death? 7:13,14. Paul asks this question about himself. He answers emphatically: **By no means.** God put things together in such a way that sin brought death through that which is good. **In order that sin through the commandment might become sinful to an extraordinary degree.** Because man is a sinner, he does not believe that sin is really what it is. The Law shows clearly what it is and what it intends to do.

Both the readers and the writer knew that **the law is caused by or filled with the** (divine) **Spirit** (see Arndt, *pneumatikos,* p. 685). The word *pneumatikos* can also be translated *pertaining* or *corresponding to the* (divine) *Spirit (ibid.).* Here is Paul's great tribute to the Law. It is caused by or filled with the Spirit of God. Paul condemns law only on one ground—legalism. He resists that view which regards law as a lien upon the being of God—by which God is obligated to do this or that for man (e.g., to save him) because man has kept certain statutes. In contrast to the Law, which is filled with or caused by God's Spirit, Paul sees himself as belonging to the flesh. He was one who was **in a state of being sold as a slave under the sovereignty of sin.** The apostle surely did not mean that he was entirely fleshly (see vv. 16,18,22). He did mean that he knew what it was to be under the domination of sin. Paul's battle was not a few isolated conflicts but a continual warfare.

c) How can the conflict within be resolved? 7:15-25. In this section the writer vividly paints the contest within his own soul. He uses some expressions to describe his own person as serving self or sin. He uses others to describe himself as serving God. The conflict arises because he wants to serve God but finds himself serving self and sin.

15. I do not know what I am doing. This is a statement of one who is baffled. But he is not ignorant as to what is wrong. The problem is how to overcome what is wrong. **Because I am not doing this which I wish to do; but what I hate, this I am doing. 16.** Here is a person who has knowledge. He shows that he **agrees with the law that it is good** when he says he hates his actions that are contrary to law. Thus it was not Paul's true self that was doing evil but the sin dwelling within him (v. 17). Here the writer identifies his true self with "I" *(egō).* When he says that it is sin that is doing the evil, Paul is not waiving responsibility, but simply recognizing that it is sin that causes his self to become false.

18. Because I know that in me (that is, in my flesh) dwells no good thing. The phrases **in me** and **in my flesh** describe Paul as under the control of sin. The absence of good in the sphere of the flesh is another way of saying that oil and water do not mix. Where the flesh is powerful, the will to do good becomes powerless. **Now the wishing** or *willing* **to do is present with me but the doing the good, no.** Paul meant that he was in the process of willing but not in the process of doing. **19. Now, I am not doing good which I wish to do, but evil which I do not wish to do, this I am doing.** In doing of good, Paul felt he was making no achievement. But in the area of evil he was aware of his activities. **20.** This being true, he again concludes, as in verse 17, that it is no longer the **I** who is doing it, but **the sin dwelling in me.**

21. Hence the writer concludes that when he wills **to do good, evil is present with him.** His desire to do good is met by a vigorous opponent that he calls **the law** or **the principle.** Here it is sin that is called a law or principle because of the regularity of its action. **22.** On the encouraging side, Paul declares: **I joyfully agree with** (see Arndt, *synedomai,* p. 797) **the law of God according to the inward man.** Here is Paul's inner response to God's law as a child of God. The phrase "the inward man" occurs only three times in Paul's writings —Rom 7:22; II Cor 4:16; Eph 3:16. In the second and third of these passages, Paul speaks of the renewal of the inward man and the strengthening of the inner man. Here in Rom 7:22 one finds a spiritually healthy response to the law of God.

23. At the same time, Paul saw **a different law in his members.** His true self, the inward man, agreed with the law of God. But another law (the law of sin) brought the "me" into captivity, making him a prisoner, But before making Paul a prisoner, the law of sin **was at war** with **the law of his mind.** This law of his mind, together with the inward man, represents Paul's true self controlled by the being of God. Paul says that his true self was **being brought into captivity** to the law of sin in his members. If Paul had stopped here, he would have been at variance with his statement in 6:14. But he did not stop here. He asserts that sin in the members is a powerful force (and no one should try to deny that fact). **24.** The thought that sin could make him captive causes him to cry out: **Wretched man that I am! Who will set me free from the body characterized by this spiritual death?** The body is the scene of this contest. Sin living in the members brings spiritual death to the body, and man becomes aware that he needs outside help. Paul cries out not for deliverance from the body as such, but for deliverance from the body characterized by this spiritual death—the doing of that which is evil in opposition to his desire to do that which is good. **25. Thanks be to God through Jesus Christ our Lord.** Filled with emotion, the apostle does not round out a full reply to his question. He stresses the One to whom thanks should be rendered, emphasizing who the Deliverer is. The full statement would have been: "Thanks be to God; deliverance comes through Jesus Christ our Lord." In Romans 8 he tell more about this deliverance. But here he merely summarizes the argument of 7:7-25. With his **intellect** or **mind** he constantly serves the law of God. But with his **flesh** (the self controlled by sin) he serves the **principle** of sin.

The following expressions characterize Paul under the control of sin: "the sin dwelling in me" (vv. 17,20); "the law" (v. 21); "a different law in my members" (v. 23); "the law of sin which is in my members" (v. 23); "in me, that is, in my flesh" (v. 18); "in or with the flesh" (v. 25). The following expressions designate Paul under the control of God: the emphatic "I" with the pronoun expressed (vv. 17,20); "the inward man" (v. 22); "the law of my mind" (v. 23); "in or with my mind" (v. 25).

4) Victory Through the Spirit Connected with the Purpose and Action of God. 8:1-39.

No one can appreciate the meaning of victory until he knows the nature of the opposition and the kind of struggle involved. In Romans 8 Paul shows what God has done to bring the Christian to victory over sin. He points out what God is now doing and what the believer must do. He examines the purpose of God and the crisis felt by both creation and the believer. He stresses the relation of the Spirit to the believer and the interrelation of the Spirit with Christ and the Father. He paints a glorious picture of the destiny of those who love God and shows that nothing can separate them from God's love. When a believer becomes occupied with himself, he can rise no higher than Rom 7:25. When he sees what God has done and is doing for him, he must respond in the language of 8:37-39.

a) Deliverance from Sin and Death by the Activity of Father, Son, and Spirit. 8:1-4. **1. Therefore** goes back to the last verse of 7:25. Since the deliverance comes through Jesus Christ, there is no **condemnation** (involving punishment or doom) **to those who are in Christ Jesus.** Those in Christ are not condemned, because Christ was condemned in their stead. There is no punishment for them, because Christ bore their punishment. **2.** But how about this contest with sin that Paul has been discussing? **Now the law,** i.e., **the Spirit of life in Christ Jesus freed you from the law,** i.e., **from sin and death.** Both the Spirit and sin and death are called **the law** because of the constancy of their influence and action. **3. Law** here refers to the Mosaic Law, and the reader sees that God did what the Law could not do. The Law was up against *an impossibility.* It prescribed a way of life that men who were in the flesh could not follow. Legalistically, they might give the appearance of doing so, but they could never fulfill the terms of all that God demanded. God sent his son **in the likeness of sinful flesh.** The word **likeness** is important, for it signifies that Christ came in flesh like ours, and was **true** man, but not a **sinful** man. This is the difference between Christ and those whom he came to save: He was free from sin both in nature and in act. God **condemned sin in his flesh.** The phrase could be translated *in the flesh,* but the context favors **his flesh.** Here the word **flesh** refers to Christ's true humanity. **4.** In this verse **flesh** refers to men who are living under the control of sin. Sin as a rebellious force against God was condemned in the flesh of Christ. God pronounced judgment on sin in the flesh of Christ **in order that the requirements of the law might be fulfilled in us who are not walking** *(living)* **in accordance with the flesh but in accordance with the Spirit.** The word translated **requirements** is in the singular. It means the complete requirement of God. God dealt with sin in the death of his Son so that those in Christ might understand the complete requirement of God as it is expressed in the Law. Those who realize this purpose of God live in accordance with the Spirit, not in accordance with the flesh.

b) The Mind-set of the Flesh Versus That of the Spirit. 8:5-13. **5.** In 8:4 the picture is of those who **live** in accordance with the flesh or Spirit. Here the stress is on those who **are** in accordance with the flesh or with the Spirit. In one group are those occupied with all the particulars that go into a sinful life. In the other group are those occupied with all that goes into life under the direction and power of the Spirit. **6. Now the mind-set of the flesh is death, but the mind-set of the Spirit is life and peace.** The flesh—the principle of rebellion within man—produces a certain pattern and way of thinking. Likewise, the Holy Spirit produces a certain pattern and way of thinking. The translation **mind-set** stresses the direction and the outlook of the mind. **Spiritual death** is made the equivalent of the mind-set of the flesh. **Life and peace** are equated with the mind-set of the Spirit. **7,8.** The mind-set of the flesh is hostile to God, unwilling to subject itself to his law. Persons with such a nature cannot please God.

In verses 9-11 the apostle shows what makes the difference between those in the flesh and those in the Spirit. **9.** His readers are "in the Spirit." He assumes that **the Spirit of God dwells** in them. The **if so be that** (AV) gives a false impression. Actually, the writer leaves no doubt in his statement. If one does not have **the Spirit of Christ,** he does not belong to Christ. Those who belong to Christ do have the Holy Spirit. The fact that the Spirit is called the Spirit of God and then the Spirit of Christ shows that the Father and the Son are related to the Spirit in the same way. **10.** Not only is the Spirit said to dwell in the believers—**you,** but **Christ is in them.** For the believer to have the Spirit of Christ within is to have Christ himself within (cf. 8:16,17). Paul is speaking of the reality of God in the life of a Christian. Although filled with God in this fashion, he says, **the body is dead because of sin; but the Spirit is life because of righteousness.** Here the term **body** means the man under the control of sin—the idea usually expressed in "flesh." The false self is dead or useless because of sin. This self cannot be effective for God. But the spirit—the true self—is living because of the righteousness which God bestows. Of course, there are not two separate selves. When the self becomes false, it acts in accordance with the flesh. When the self is true, it acts in accordance with the Spirit.

11. The presence of the Spirit of God in believers guarantees that the God who raised up Christ from the dead will quicken the mortal bodies of believers **through his Spirit dwelling in** [them]. The role of the Holy Spirit in the resurrection of believers is a neglected theme. A mortal body is a body capable of dying. A body made alive by the Holy Spirit becomes immortal. The transition from mortality to immortality is the work of the Spirit.

12. Believers are in the Spirit, and the Spirit dwells in them. Through him they will have glorified bodies. These facts lead to one certain conclusion. **So then, brothers, we are under obligation, but not to the flesh, to live according to its demands** (see Arndt, *opheiletēs,* 2b, p. 603). **13.** Assuming that you live according to the flesh, Paul tells his readers, you are about to die. This is a spiritual death. But assuming that by the Spirit you keep putting to death the evil deeds (cf. Col 3:9) of the body, you will live. Both "ifs" in 8:13 assume the actuality of the thing stated. The conclusions logically follow. Their solemnity corresponds to the seriousness of the action in the "if" clauses. Since spiritual death here is viewed as climactic—the final banishment from God's presence—the life referred to must be the glorified life that awaits the believer.

c) Guidance and Witness of the Spirit. 8:14-17. **14. Sons of God** are defined as those who are led by the Spirit of God. The Spirit does the leading. The verb is in the present tense and in the passive —**as many as allow themselves to be led** (cf. Arndt, *agō*, 3, p. 14). **15.** The phrases **spirit of bondage** and **Spirit of adoption** are parallel. A better rendering would be: the *state of mind that belongs to slavery* and *the state of mind that belongs to adoption*. The outcome of the former is fear; the outcome of the latter is the ability to pray and to address God as Father. The word *Abba* is an Aramaic word put into Greek letters and then transliterated into English. It means "Father." The bringing together of both Jew and Greek (Gentiles) in Christ is seen in these opening words of address in prayer.

16. The Holy Spirit bears witness together **with our human spirit** that we are children of God. This really means that the Spirit bears witness with our very self (see I Cor 16:18; Gal 6:18; Phil 4:23). This witness is directed to every aspect of our personality that goes into the making of our self. The Spirit's testimony is to the person. **17.** It is noted that the believer is an **heir of God** and a **fellow heir of Christ.** We are heirs of all that God has to bestow, which means that we are fellow heirs with Christ, to whom the Father has given all things. But to be a joint heir with Christ means to be a fellow sufferer with Christ. The tense is present: **since indeed we are suffering together.** Suffering was the role that God had appointed for Christ (Lk 24:26,46; Acts 17:3; 26:23; Heb 2:9,10). It is also the God-ordained experience for believers in Christ (Mt 10:38; 16:24; 20:22; I Thess 3:3; II Thess 1:4,5; II Cor 1:5; Col 1:24; II Tim 3:12; I Pet 1:6; 4:12). Those who are fellow sharers with Christ in suffering will also be fellow heirs with him in glory (Rom 8:17). The experience of suffering precedes the experience of glory.

d) Completion of Redemption Awaited by Creation and Believers Alike. 8:18-25. How should one view the sufferings of the present? They are to be viewed in the light of **the glory that is about to be revealed in us** (v. 18). The sufferings are not to be compared with the coming glory, for they are not at all equal in intensity or value. **19.** Not only is glory to be revealed to believers, but believers themselves are to be revealed. Paul says that this event is **the eager expectation of the creation.** The word **creation** (AV, *creature*, except in v. 22) found in 8:19-22 refers to all of God's creation below the human level, here personified to make clear the tensions and dislocation found in creation because of sin. Sin brought distortion not only into man's relation with God but into the universe in which he lives. **20. Creation was made subject to frustration against its own will.** Tornadoes, hurricanes, earthquakes, drought, floods are just a few evidences of the imbalance of nature. Paul says that nature was reduced to this state by God. Although the Lord brought this about, he did it **in hope,** i.e., with a definite hope for a future day when the frustration will be removed. **21. Because the creation itself also will be set free from the slavery to deterioration.** God has promised that the very creation which has been enslaved to deterioration and corruption will be set free from this condition. Its new condition is described as **the glorious freedom which belongs to the children of God. 22.** How different this is from the present situation—both for creation and for God's children. Creation groans and suffers agony together with the men who dwell upon the earth. **23.** Not only creation, but also believers who **have the first fruits of the Spirit** groan within themselves. **First fruits** here may mean the blessings and changes that the Spirit has already produced in the lives of believers. Or it can mean that the Spirit himself is looked upon as the first fruit (cf. II Cor 1:22; Eph 1:14). In the light of the context, the former interpretation seems best. The **groaning** of a believer has nothing to do with complaining. Rather, it is his sighing to himself because he lives in a sinful world. **The adoption** for which the believer awaits refers to **the redemption of our body,** its release from sin and finiteness, the pressure of which we constantly feel as long as we have our mortal body.

24. Now we are saved for the hope. The hope for which God saved us is deliverance from a body put under pressure by sin, and from a state of mortal finiteness in which we await the day when, clothed with immortality, we shall see God. What is hope? Paul says it is a confident expectation of promised blessings not now present or seen. This hope is not a wish for something too good to be true and unlikely to occur. The object or blessing hoped for (here, the redemption of the body) is real and distinct but not yet present. **25. But since we are hoping for what is not seen, with** *(dia;* see Arndt, III, 1, c, p. 179) **patience** (or *fortitude)* **we are eagerly awaiting it.** The redeemed body will be a glorified body, free from all sin. With such a hope before him, the believer awaits its realization with fortitude.

e) Intercessory Ministry of the Spirit. 8:26,27. **26. Likewise,** the Spirit helps our weakness. The weakness referred to is our inability to analyze situations and pray intelligently about them. We know this is the weakness referred to because of the next phrase. The Spirit is said **to plead** or *intercede* **with sighs too deep for words** (see *alalētos,* Arndt, p. 34). Sometimes we cannot pray because words cannot express the needs we feel. The Spirit's response of **sighs too deep for words** shows how God through his Spirit enters into our experiences. **27.** God the Father who investigates the hearts [of men] **knows what is the mind-set of the Spirit.** God knows the total response of the Spirit to any situation or issue. The intercession he makes on behalf of the saints is **in conformity with the being of God.** These words certainly declare that communication of thought and knowledge of each other is shared by two members of the Godhead—Father and Spirit (i.e., the Holy Spirit).

f) Purpose of God for Those Loving Him. 8:28-30. **28.** Paul begins with a basic axiom: **We know.** Then he states this truth: **To those loving God, he** (i.e., God) **works all things together for good.** Paul puts the phrase "to those loving God" first so that there will be no mistake about who are involved in "God works all things together for good." It is for those who continually express love for God both in attitude and action. These are further defined as **those who are called ones in accordance with** (God's) **plan** or *purpose.* The call and election are put side by side in II Thess 2:13,14; II Pet 1:10. The call may be focused upon the eternal destiny (II Thess 2:14) or on the earthly life of freedom and holiness (Gal 5:13; I Thess 4:7).

29. Because whom he knew beforehand or *foreknew.* The pronoun **whom** is plural, not singular. Paul is thinking of a group here—composed of individuals to be sure—but nevertheless a group of individuals who constitute a corporate whole. This is identical with the apostle's procedure in Eph 1:4, where he says: Just as he chose **us** (plural) in him (i.e., in Christ). Christ is the Elect or Chosen **one** (see Lk 9:35 [ASV; RSV]; 23:35; I Pet 2:4,6); and believers—those who belong to God—are elect or chosen **ones** in him (i.e., in Christ). The verb **foreknow** has as its basic ingredient knowledge. This group of individuals, the members of this corporate whole, are foreknown in what sense? They are foreknown as having a distinct place in God's plan or purpose (Rom 8:28). They have a role to play in God's plan. What is their destiny? **Whom** (pl.) **he knew beforehand, he decided upon beforehand to be conformed to the image of his son** (v. 29). God's decision here is that those composing this group shall be like his Son in form and appearance. The number is not small. God decided this beforehand in order that his Son might be the first-born **among many brothers.** The term **firstborn** means the one highest in rank or position. That Christ is supreme or first Paul makes very clear in Col 1:18: "And he is the head of the body, the church, [he] who is (the) beginning, (the) first-born from the dead; that he might come to have the first place in everything." The headship is over and in the midst of many brothers —those who receive the abundance of grace and the gift, i.e., righteousness (Rom 5:17). Christ's rank as first-born shows that he stands as the exalted head of the new humanity—as the second Adam (Rom 5:12-21; I Cor 15:22).

The stress in this section (Rom 8:28-30) lies upon the action of God—his plan and the accomplishment of his plan. **30.** The verbs: **he called, he acquitted** (or *justified)* and **he glorified** have to do both with the plan (eternal counsel of God) and the carrying out of this purpose. Because God has a plan, or purpose—to sum up all things, to bring all things together in Christ, things in the heaven and things upon earth (Eph 1:10, 11), he is able to work all things together for good to those loving him. Paul's emphasis here is on what God does for the many brothers. The only human response mentioned is that of love for God.

g) Triumph of Believers over All Opposition. 8:31-39. **31,32.** Paul now begins to point out the implications of his teaching. God became involved in man's dilemma in order to accomplish his plan. He

handed over his Son on behalf of us all. Christ was handed over for our benefit, on our behalf, and in our stead. God could not spare his Son and carry out his plan of redemption. So he handed him over to death that we might be redeemed. Paul draws certain conclusions from this action by God. With Christ he **will** graciously give us **all things,** though we may not have all of them right now. **33,34.** No one can bring any charge against God's chosen or elect ones or condemn them, because God and Christ have participated in this divine action of handing over Christ.

35,36. Formidable obstacles cannot separate us from the love Christ extends to us. These difficulties are: **affliction, distress, persecution, famine, lack of clothing, danger, or sword** (i.e., violent death). The apostle quotes Ps 44:22 to show what difficulties the people of God have. **37.** His conclusion is that in all these difficulties **we are winning a most glorious victory through the one who loved us.** The meaning here is: "We are in the process of winning." In the external pressures of life we can be gaining the victory through the one who loved us. We are winning not through our own strength or brilliance but through Christ. **38,39.** Paul broadens out the experiences, the personalities, and the things that confront the believer: **death** or **life, angels** or **angelic rulers, space above the horizon** or **space below it,** or **any created thing.** Then he emphatically declares that none of these things shall be able to separate us from the love God manifests, this love that is in Christ Jesus our Lord. The power of God's love is a theme that can never be exhausted.

III. Israel and the Gentiles in the Plan of God. 9:1–11:36.

Paul looks at the plan of God as it relates to the two divisions of mankind that he, as a Jew, saw – Israel or the Jewish people and the Gentiles.

A. Concern of Paul for His Own People, Israel. 9:1-5.

1,2. This chapter begins with an array of proof that Paul had **great grief** and **unceasing pain** in his heart with reference to his own people. Here is the proof: he speaks truth in Christ; he is not lying; his conscience testifies for him in the presence of the Holy Spirit. The apostle told this because he knew how the Jews maligned him (see, e.g., Acts 21:28 – an event that occurred after he wrote Romans but indicative of how the Jews felt.) **3.** So deeply did Paul feel about his people that he here employs the language of an unattainable wish (potential imperfect in Greek): **I could wish that I myself would be under a curse** (and thus separated) **from Christ for the sake of my brothers, my fellow countrymen with respect to earthly descent.** The language here sounds like that of Moses when he pleaded that God would blot him out of His book (Ex 32:31,32).

Paul now lists the blessings that belonged to his fellow countrymen. **4.** They were Israelites to whom belonged **the adoption**—i.e., a people whom God made his own (cf. Isa 43:20,21). They had **the glory.** This could be either the honor of being God's people or the glory of God that appeared in the midst of his people (Ex 24:16,17). The word **covenants** is in the plural because God spoke to his people about his covenant relation with them on a number of occasions. It might also be rendered *decrees* or *assurances.* To them also belonged **the legislation,** i.e., the Mosaic law, and **the service** or *worship* **of God**—the ritual of the Tabernacle and the Temple. They had the promises of God, especially the Messianic promises. **5.** The fathers—Abraham, Isaac, and Jacob—also belonged to them. But the most important blessing was that Christ, with respect to his flesh, came from Paul's fellow countrymen, the Israelites. But this one (Christ), who on the human side came from Israel, was much more than a fellow Israelite; he was **God over all, blessed forever.** (For evidence that this last clause refers to Christ, see Sanday and Headlam, *Epistle to the Romans,* ICC, pp. 232-238). Knowing Christ's exalted place only increased Paul's anguish over the blindness of his people. They had refused such a Messiah. These lines are not a doxology to God, for that does not fit the train of thought. Rather, the lines show how exalted Christ is, which fits the train of thought perfectly.

B. God Free, Righteous, and Sovereign in His Dealing with Israel and with All Men. 9:6-29. From 9:6 to the end of chapter 11 Paul discusses a profound question: *How could God reject his elect people?* He points out to what extent the people have been rejected, why they have been rejected, the existence of a remnant, and what plans God has for the future of his people, Israel. In 9:6-29 the writer is answering an argument of his Jewish opponents that went like this: "We have circumcision as a sign (cf. Gen 17:7-14) that we are God's elect people. Members of God's elect people will not perish. Therefore, we will not perish." Rabbinical evidence shows that this was the attitude of most Jews in Paul's day. Hermann L. Strack and Paul Billerbeck have prepared a *Commentary on the New Testament* in which they bring together parallels from the Talmud and Midrashim that shed light on the NT. In Vol. IV, Part 2, they have devoted an entire excursus (#31) to the subject of Sheol, Gehenna [place of punishment], and the Heavenly Garden of Eden (Paradise). The following quotations include names of tractates of the rabbinical writings from which their ideas about these places are drawn, as well as indicate the location in Strack-Billerbeck.

> Rabbi Levi has said: In the future (on the other side—what the Greeks called the spirit world) Abraham sits at the entrance of Gehenna and he allows no circumcised ones from the Israelites to enter into it (i.e., Gehenna). [Midrash Rabba Genesis, 48 (30ª, 49) SBK, IV, Part ii, p. 1066]

In this same context the question is asked: How about those who sin excessively? The answer is: They are returned to a state of uncircumcision as they enter Gehenna. The next quotation deals with the question of what happens after death to an Israelite.

> When an Israelite goes into his eternal house (=grave), an angel is sitting over the heavenly garden of Eden, who takes each son of Israel who is circumcised for the purpose of bringing him into the heavenly garden of Eden (paradise). [Midrash Tanchum, Sade, waw, 145ª, 35; SBK, IV, Part ii, p. 1066]

Again the question is raised: How about those Israelites who serve idols? As above, the answer is: They will be returned to a state of uncircumcision in Gehenna. Here is a quotation that looks at the Israelites as a group:

> All Israelites who are circumcised come into the heavenly garden of Eden (paradise). [Midrash Tanchuma, Sade, waw, 145ª, 32; SBK, IV, Part ii, p. 1067]

It is clear from these quotations that most Jews believed and taught that all circumcised Israelites who have died are in paradise and that there are no circumcised Israelites in Gehenna.

To the claim that the Lord could not reject his elect people, Paul first of all replies by emphasizing God's freedom, righteousness, and sovereignty. God *acts* freely, *acts* in righteousness, and *acts* sovereignly because he *is* free, righteous, and sovereign in his own eternal being.

1) God's Choice of Isaac Rather Than the Other Sons of Abraham. 9:6-9.

6. But it is by no means as if the word of God had come to failure. The present state of the Jews does not indicate that the divine promise has been rescinded. Not all those who are descended from Israel are really Israel. The promises of the Lord at any one period of history may actively involve as many of his people as he decides. **7.** In the case of Abraham's children, God made a choice. **In** *(through)* **Isaac you are to have your descendants** (cf. *Kaleō,* Arndt, 1. a, p. 400). **8.** Here a distinction is made between the children of the flesh, those born of Hagar and Keturah (Gen 16:1-16; 25:1-4), and Isaac, born according to promise. **That is, not the children of the flesh are thereby children of God, but the children of the promise are looked upon as seed.** The AV is unsatisfactory in verse 8. Paul puts the negative first to make clear that the children of the flesh do not automatically become children of God. Isaac was born because of promise. God chose through him to bring blessings to all of mankind.

2) God's Choice of Jacob Rather Than Esau. 9:10-13.

Paul's Jewish contemporaries might have replied: "We are children of Isaac; hence, we can be certain that God will not reject us." **10,11.** But Paul shows that God made a choice between Isaac's two sons, even before the sons were born or had done anything good or bad. Such a choice occurred **in order that the purpose or plan of God which operates by selection might continue not from works but from the one who calls.** God's selection was not based upon legalistic works but upon himself and his plan for the world. **12,13.** What did this selection involve? **The older will be in subjection to the younger.** Since this selection occurred before the twins were born (Gen 25:23), Paul was certainly thinking of two individuals here. In the quotation from Mal 1:2,3, which looks back to God's dealings with Jacob and Esau, the emphasis falls upon nations. What began in the lifetime of the founders of these peoples continued among their children. The selection had to do with the roles these two groups were to play in history. The Lord showed his love for Jacob by making the patriarch's descendants the channels through whom He spoke His oracles and made known His truth. God **hated** Esau in the sense that He did not make Esau's descendants channels of revelation but rather, as Malachi says: God "made his mountains a desolation and gave his heritage to the jackals of the wilderness" (Mal 1:3). In looking back upon Esau's history, Malachi also uses the word "hate" because of God's severity in dealing with Esau. The historical situation of both individuals and peoples certainly affects their eternal destiny. But **election** in Rom 9:10-13 is not selection for eternal salvation or damnation. Rather, it is selection for the roles God has called individuals and nations to play in their earthly life.

3) God's Mercy Toward Israel and Hardening of Pharaoh. 9:14-18.

14. Therefore, what shall we say? There isn't unrighteousness with God is there? By no means. The fact that God's selection is not based upon human works does not make the Lord unrighteous. He is free, righteous, and sovereign. **15.** These qualities are seen in his action toward Moses and Pharaoh. His declaration to Moses—**I will have mercy upon whomever I am having mercy and I will have compassion upon whomever I am having compassion** (Ex 33:19)—came *after* Israel's sin of the golden calf. At that point Israel could not possibly have deserved God's mercy. Such idolatry as theirs deserved only wrath. **16.** The "it" supplied by the AV refers to the mercy or compassion. **Mercy and compassion therefore do not belong to the one willing or the one running but to God who constantly has mercy.** That is, no one has a claim on God's mercy. God also pours out his wrath as he sees fit. **17.** The verb "to raise up" is better translated in this verse: **For this very reason I cause you to appear.** God brought Pharaoh upon the scene of history in Egypt for the purpose of showing His power and proving that His name would be proclaimed in all the earth. Pharaoh would still have been his own stubborn self if God had placed him in some obscure settlement up the Nile. But God put him over all Egypt in order to carry out His own purpose and plan. **18.** In looking back over these two cases of Moses and Pharaoh, Paul concludes: **Therefore, then, he shows mercy to whom he wishes and he hardens whom he wishes.** God was free and sovereign in the hardening of Pharaoh's heart, but He was not arbitrary.

A study of the Exodus narrative shows that Pharaoh hardened his own heart before God hardened it. And even after God hardened it, Pharaoh still had power to harden it further.

The Lord clearly predicted that he would harden Pharaoh's heart: "I will harden (*ḥāzāq*, piel, "make rigid, hard; harden") his heart" (Ex 4:21; cf. 14:4); "I will make hard (*qāshâh*, hiphil, "make hard, stiff, stubborn") the heart of Pharaoh" (Ex 7:3). But not until 9:12 does the record of Exodus say that God actually hardened the king's heart: "And Jehovah **hardened** (*ḥāzāq*, piel, "make rigid, hard; harden") the heart of Pharaoh."

The Scriptures have much to say about the fact that Pharaoh's heart was "growing hard," and about Pharaoh's "making his heart heavy, dull, unresponsive," even before they state that God hardened Pharaoh's heart. The phrase, "Pharaoh's heart grew hard," means that Pharaoh's moral character (see BDB, p. 525) grew hard. Moral character is a most important aspect of one's person. Hence, in a real sense Pharaoh grew hard as the result of his own activity. "And the heart of Pharaoh **grew hard**" (*ḥāzāq* qal, "grow stout, rigid, hard"; see Ex 7:13,22; 8:19 [Heb. text 8:15]). "The heart of Pharaoh is **hard**" (*kâbēd*, adj., "heavy," "dull," "hard"; see Ex 7:14). "The heart of Pharaoh **became hard**" (*kâbēd*, qal, "be heavy, insensible, dull, hard"; see Ex 9:7). "Pharaoh **made heavy** (or *dull, unresponsive;* all possible translations of *kâbēd*, hiphil) his heart" (see Ex 8:15 [Heb. text 8:11]; 8:32 [Heb. text 8:28]). After all this activity on the part of Pharaoh, "Jehovah **hardened** (*ḥāzāq*, piel, "make rigid, hard; harden") the heart of Pharaoh" (see Ex 9:12). But Pharaoh had the power to continue what he had been doing: ". . . he [Pharaoh] sinned more, and he **made heavy** (or *dull, unresponsive;* all possible translations of *kâbēd*, hiphil) his heart, he and his servants. And the heart of Pharaoh **grew hard**" (*ḥâzaq*, qal, "grow stout, rigid, hard"; see Ex 9:34 b,35 a).

Then Jehovah completed his judicial punishment of Pharaoh. "And Jehovah hardened (*ḥāzāq*, piel, "make rigid, hard"; "harden") the heart of Pharaoh," (see Ex 10:20,27; 11:10; 14:8). "And Jehovah said unto Moses: 'Go unto Pharaoh because **I am making heavy** *(dull, unresponsive;* all possible translations of *kâbēd,* hiphil) his heart and the heart of his servants' " (see Ex 10:1).

So the conclusion that God hardens whom he wishes is based upon his righteousness as well as upon his freedom in dealing with Pharaoh.

4) God's Control Over Vessels of Wrath and Mercy. 9:19-24.

Paul has been directing his argument to the Jews, who thought that, because they had circumcision and were members of God's elect people, the Lord was duty-bound to grant them earthly prosperity and eternal bliss. The apostle has stressed the divine sovereignty and freedom as a corrective to this erroneous Jewish view. The Lord is duty-bound only to his own righteous being – not to claims put upon him by those who misunderstand his being and action.

19. At this point, Paul imagines that one of his opponents is saying: "Look what your argument leads to. The Lord hardens a man like Pharaoh and then finds fault with him. That doesn't make sense." The question is: **Why does he still find fault? Who can resist his will?** Paul's answer is phrased in terms suited to the man who makes the objection rather than in terms of an intellectual analysis of the man's counterargument. Paul writes (v. 20 a): **O man, on the contrary, who are you who answers back to God in this way?** A real knowledge of the true God makes such an objection preposterous. Paul turns to an illustration (vv. 20b,21): **What is moulded will not say to the moulder, why have you made me in this fashion, will it? Or, the potter has the right over the clay, doesn't he, to make from the same lump one vessel for honor and another for dishonor?** This illustration of the potter had been used very effectively by Jeremiah centuries before (Jer 18:4-6). Paul stresses the complete control of the potter over the clay in terms of that for which the vessel is to be used. A vessel is honored or dishonored by the use to which it is put (cf. Arndt, *timē,* 2, b, p. 825). One pot may be intended for carrying water and another for carrying away refuse. The same material is used for both. But they are to be made for different functions, and so the potter gives each one a shape that accords with its intended function.

Paul now applies this principle. He does this in one long sentence that extends from Rom 9:22 to 9:24. If a potter may do what he wants with his vessels, certainly God may do what He wants with His vessels. Although Paul is still stressing God's sovereignty and freedom, he carefully avoids picturing the Lord as having the same relationship to the vessels of wrath as he does to the vessels of mercy. **Now if God, although he wished to show his anger and make known his power, bore patiently** *(endured)* **with much forbearance the vessels of wrath made ready** *(prepared)* **for destruction and** [if he did this] **in order that he might make known** *(reveal)* **the riches of his glory to vessels of mercy, which he prepared beforehand for glory, us whom also he called not only from the Jews but also from the Gentiles** [how can you (sing.; cf. v. 19) bring any objection against God's justice?] In the concessive clause beginning with "although," Paul certainly has in mind Pharaoh and others like him. The words **to show his anger and make known his power** are merely a variation of the language he used in verse 17: "in order that I might show in you my power." Paul was very eager to emphasize God's patience and forbearance with the vessels of wrath. **22.** These are described as **made ready** *(prepared;* see *katartizō,* LSJ, II, pass., p. 910) **for destruction.** Some Bible students, taking the participle to be in the middle voice, have translated: *those who have been in a state of preparing themselves for destruction.* Others have regarded the participle as passive and have said: *those who have been in a state of being prepared by God for destruction.* But the context certainly favors the passive without confining the agent to one being or thing. **23.** God is specifically connected with the preparing beforehand (active voice) of the vessels of mercy. But when it comes to the vessels of wrath, the student finds this indefinite passive. What operates on man to put him in a state of being **made ready** *(prepared)* for eternal destruction? The answer is complex. It includes his own sinful acts and rebellious nature. It involves his environment, which makes sin enticing, as well as the judicial judgments of God (cf. 1:24,26,28). These factors influence certain vessels to become vessels of wrath, i.e., objects that are in a state of being prepared for destruction. God specifically prepared beforehand vessels of mercy for glory, and he also revealed to them the riches of his glory. **Glory** refers to the radiance of the being of God. The outpouring of God's bounty means riches untold to the recipients. Who are these vessels of mercy? In 9:24 Paul defines the **us** as those whom God has called not only from the Jews but also from the Gentiles. The Lord's freedom, power, and sovereignty on the one hand are placed over against his forbearance, his revelation of the riches of his glory, and his preparation beforehand of the vessels of mercy (vv. 22-24). The destiny of those thus prepared is glory (cf. 8:30).

5) God's Testimony in Hosea and Isaiah to an Extension and Limitation of His Saving Work. 9:25-29.

The **us** in verse 24 refers to those whom God has called, not only from the Jews but also from the Gentiles. The writer now turns to the OT to show that it supports such a call.

25,26. Paul quotes Hos 2:23; 1:10, passages originally addressed to the ten tribes. The words **not my people** and **not beloved** were spoken to the ten tribes because of their departure from the Lord. They had become like the Gentiles. God promised the ten tribes that one day they would be called sons of the living God in the very place where they had been called "not my people." The apostle takes this quotation from the LXX and applies it to the Gentiles.

27,28. The writer turns to the testimony of Isaiah about Israel and quotes from Isa 10:22,23. He uses the LXX, which in Isa 10:23 is quite different from the Hebrew text. But on the main point for which Paul is quoting this passage, the Hebrew and LXX agree. Only a remnant **will be saved** (LXX), will *turn back,* (Heb text), *shall return* (AV), i.e., turn back to God. Paul develops this theme further in Romans 11. Difficulty has been found in interpreting Rom 9:28 because of the language and textual variation. The words "in righteousness: because a short work" of the AV are not found in the best texts. Here are two possible ways of translating and interpreting this verse (see Arndt, *suntemnō,* p. 800). (1) **The Lord will act by accomplishing his word and by shortening or cutting off.** The shortening can be construed as fulfilling the promises to a limited degree or as shortening the nation into a remnant. (2) **The Lord will act by closing the account and shortening** [the time]. This means that God will not prolong indefinitely the period of his long-suffering, but that his judgment will come. In Paul's context here, the second interpretation seems the better.

29. Finally, in completing the OT picture of God's saving action, Paul quotes Isa 1:9 from the LXX. Where the LXX has "left us seed," the Hebrew text has "a very small remnant." If God had not left some, the nation Israel would have been blotted out.

C. Failure of Israel and Success of the Gentiles. 9:30—10:21.

Paul now takes up the relation of Israel and the Gentiles to righteousness, faith, and salvation. He shows that this is a crucial matter because the Jews believed that since they were marked by circumcision as God's elect people, the Lord could not reject them.

1) Attainment by Gentiles of What Israel Missed. 9:30-33.

30,31. Since God has called **us,** Christians (v. 24), from both Jews and Gentiles, **what shall we say then** about the attainment of righteousness by the Gentiles and Israel? The answer: We say or declare **that the Gentiles, who were not striving for righteousness attained righteousness, that is the righteousness which is because of faith. But Israel, although pursuing law that would produce righteousness, did not attain to law producing righteousness.** Paul is very concise here. Nevertheless, notice that in verse 30 the word **righteousness** occurs three times. Believing Gentiles had found the key to man's relationship with God—righteousness. They had found the righteousness that God bestows because of faith or trust (cf. 3:21-26). Israel had pursued the principle of law (the Mosaic code was Israel's most treasured embodiment of this principle) in order to obtain righteousness, but they never attained to that righteousness.

32. Why did Israel not attain to righteousness? Tragically the reply comes: **because not from faith but as by works** [they sought after righteousness]. Faith or trust is important because of the object (Christ) believed and trusted. Israel rejected the object. **They rejected** (or *stumbled at)* **the stone which causes men to stumble.** In the warning note of Isa 8:14, Jehovah is the stone of stumbling to the majority of those in both houses of Israel. In the NT it is Christ who is the stone of stumbling (here and in I Pet 2:6-8). **33.** Most of Paul's quotation in this verse is from the promise of Isa 28:16. But the apostle takes the language of warning from Isa 8:14—**a stumbling-**

stone and rock of offence – and inserts this warning in the middle of the positive teaching about the stone in Isa 28:16, and then completes the verse. The last clause of Rom 9:33–**And the one trusting in him will not be disappointed**–introduces a ray of light into an otherwise dark picture. Such a positive response, however, was not that of Israel as a whole, for Israel stumbled at the stone that God placed in Zion.

2) Israel's Ignorance of God's Righteousness. 10:1-3.

1. The apostle again expresses his concern for his people. In place of **for Israel** the best texts have *on behalf of* them. Paul prayed on behalf of them **for salvation**–i.e., that they would appropriate this salvation for themselves. **2.** Their zeal for God was not backed up with knowledge–**in accordance with** *(real)* **knowledge** (see Arndt, *epignōsis,* p. 291). **3.** In the minds of Jewish readers a new question would naturally arise: Why were so many of Israel rejected in spite of their having the covenant of circumcision as a sign that they were members of God's elect people? Paul answers: **Now being ignorant of the righteousness which God bestows and seeking to establish their own, they did not subject themselves to the righteousness of God.** There are two contrasts in this verse. First, the Israelites sought to establish their own righteousness. Note their self-confidence in this. Secondly, they would not subject themselves to what God had provided–their wills were unyielded. Having stumbled at the stone of stumbling (Christ), they knew nothing of God's gift of righteousness.

3) Connection Between the Righteousness of Faith and the Object of Faith. 10:4-15.

In verse **4** two things are stressed: (1) what Christ is; (2) who is benefited by what Christ is. **To every one in the process of trusting, Christ is the goal and termination of the law with respect to righteousness.** The word **end** (AV)–*telos* –seems to combine the ideas of both goal and termination (see Arndt, *telos,* 1, a.b. c., p. 819). We cannot say, merely, that Christ is the goal and termination of the Law. Rather, he is the goal and termination of the Law **with respect to righteousness.** Before Christ came, believers in God were in a tension. That is, they were promised life on condition that they live in a way that was unattainable by them. **5.** Although Paul, in quoting Moses, changes Lev 18:5 somewhat from both the Hebrew and Greek texts, he gives substantially the sense of the verse. **The man who practices** [the righteousness that the Law demanded] **will live by it** (feminine pronoun, referring to righteousness). In the Greek text of Lev 18:5, the Jewish believer is commanded to guard all the ordinances and judgments. Though the one who trusted God did his best to fulfill the righteous demands of the Law, he was also aware of his failures. This inconsistency caused tension. Hence he faithfully presented his sin and trespass offerings. For this reason, the Jewish believer could not take Lev 18:5 as a legalistic guarantee of eternal life, but only as a promise of God involving a man's fellowship with Him. He could not take it as a legalistic prescription. To take this verse as such would have made the tension intolerable. Christ broke this tension. By his life and death he revealed the perfect righteousness of God, bestowed by the Father on the basis of faith in the Son. This was the goal to which the Law pointed. It terminated the tension brought about by the promise of life to man for doing what man could not do. Since man could not live as God demanded, salvation under the Old Covenant as well as under the New had to be by faith.

In Rom 10:6-8 Paul quotes Deut 30:12-14, interspersing his own comments and phrases as he quotes. In the OT passage, the "it," in the questions concerning ascending or descending to bring "it" to men, refers to the commandment "to love the Lord thy God." It was this commandment of God that was in the heart and mouth of the Israelite. **6,7.** But Paul takes the language of Deuteronomy and applies it to the righteousness that comes from faith. He refers the ascending and descending to Christ. **8.** The word that is in the mouth and in the heart is **the declaration about the faith.** Paul is not saying that Moses in Deuteronomy predicted that righteousness was to come by faith. Rather he says, "Righteousness by faith must speak in this way" (10:6). The compatibility of the two covenants is shown by the fact that this righteousness finds the language of the OT so suitable.

9. Confession with the mouth and belief in the heart refer to the believer's outward and inward responses. His inward conviction must find outward expression. When he confesses that Jesus is Lord, he is asserting Christ's deity and His exaltation, and the fact that he, the believer, belongs to Him. A man's belief in the Resurrection shows that he knows God acted and triumphed in the cross. The man who confesses that Christ is Lord and has such a belief or conviction will attain salvation. **10.** This trust or belief is a constant activity and refers to righteousness; the confession is also a constant activity and refers to salvation. These confessed and believed truths are constant, lifelong convictions.

12. Since such confession and belief are the essentials for salvation, Paul's next statement is pertinent and almost self-evident. In the matter of obtaining salvation, there is **no distinction** (or *difference)* **between Jew and Greek.** Christ who is **the same Lord of all is in the process of being rich** (and *generous)* **to all who are calling upon him.** The NT writers made the name Lord *(kyrios)* one of their favorite titles of Jesus (see Arndt, *kyrios*, 2. c., pp. 460,61; Foerster, *TWNT*, III, 1087-94). Paul takes the OT quotation that speaks of Jehovah as Lord and applies the term to Jesus (cf. vv. 13 and 12). To call upon the name of the Lord means to call upon Jesus. Thus prayer to Jesus is explicitly referred to by this language.

14,15. The connection between the righteousness of faith and the object of faith is simple. Belief in the object of faith (Christ) brings the righteousness of faith to the believer. When men trust Christ, they call upon him. This leads Paul to questions about calling upon the name of the Lord There can be no *calling* without *belief* or *trust*. There can be no *belief* or *trust*, without *hearing*. There can be no *hearing* without *preaching*. There can be no *preaching* unless preachers have a *commission*. Note that reaching men for God begins with the commission of the messengers. Then through preaching, hearing, and trusting, men are brought to call upon the name of the Lord. The beauty of the feet of the messengers refers to their eagerness to carry the good tidings. The quotation from Isa 52:7 refers to the report of messengers that Jehovah had redeemed Jerusalem. Paul applies these words to the good tidings about Christ—the Gospel.

4) Good Tidings Rejected. 10:16-21.

16. Although good tidings are proclaimed, this does not mean that the hearers obey the good tidings. Paul quotes Isaiah as asking: "Lord, who has believed our preaching?" (cf. Isa 53:1) **17.** The apostle draws the conclusion that **faith** comes from **preaching** (the things heard). And **preaching** comes to be **through the message** *(command, order, direction)* **of Christ.** The AV has **God, but** the better manuscripts have **Christ. 18.** Since Israel has had both the messengers who proclaim good tidings and the good tidings themselves, why haven't the Jews obeyed? The apostle deals with two excuses that might be put forth. **It was not that they did not listen, was it?** No, they listened all right. He quotes Ps 19:4, which originally dealt with the universal proclamation of God's glory and power by the works of nature. He applies the words of this psalm to the Gospel—**their voice went forth into all the earth, and their words unto the extreme limits of the inhabited earth.** The second excuse deals with a failure of knowledge. **19. It was not that Israel did not know, was it?** No, they knew all right. Moses was the first to say that God would use an unintelligent nation or people to make the Jews jealous and angry (cf. Deut 32:21). The Jews had not only listened to the message about Christ but knew that God would deal with other peoples besides themselves. **20.** Paul quotes the prophet Isaiah as affirming this (Isa 65:1,2). Actually, the two verses quoted from Isaiah refer to disobedient Israel. But in Rom 10:20 the writer applies Isa 65:1 to the Gentiles. In Rom 10:21 he applies Isa 65:2 to Israel. Applying the language of Isa 65:1 to the Gentiles is similar to applying Hos 2:23 and 1:10 (cf. Rom 9:25, 26) to them. The apostle represents God as saying to the Gentiles: **I have let myself be found by those not seeking me; I revealed myself to those not inquiring after me. 21.** In contrast, the Lord implores Israel—He stretched forth his hands **to a disobedient and obstinate people.**

D. Situation of Israel in Paul's Day. 11:1-10.

1. Although Paul has just described the disobedience and obstinacy of his people, he now declares: **God has not repudiated his people, has he? By no means.** Because Paul himself was an Israelite, the idea that God should reject His people was abhorrent to him. By **his people** Paul means national Israel. **2a. God did not repudiate his people**

whom he foreknew. The phrase **his people** emphasizes God's previous choice or selection. The verb **foreknew** indicates that the Lord knew beforehand that Israel would be disobedient and obstinate (cf. 10:21). God foreknows the sins of his people, but he does not directly decree them (see Jas 1:13).

2b-5. By showing that there is a remnant of Israelites who are faithful, Paul proves that God did not repudiate His people. The apostle reminds his readers that there was a godly remnant in Elijah's time, and declares that there is a similar remnant in his own time (Rom 11:5). **Therefore in this same fashion also in the present time a remnant exists** (see Arndt, *ginomai,* II, 5, p. 159) **according to selection by grace** (see Arndt, *eklogē,* 1, p. 242). Grace produces or brings into being this election or selection. **6.** This truth is restated. Selection is by God's grace or favor – not by men's works. Works suggest legalism and nullify grace.

7. What then are we to conclude? We are to conclude that in Israel there is now a faithful remnant and there is a faithless majority. **What Israel kept striving for, this she did not attain to; but those selected attained to it, and the rest were made dull.** An interpreter must ask, What was it that Israel strove for which she did not obtain? Paul has already answered this in 9:32 and 10:3. Israel strove for righteousness. But instead of submitting to the righteousness of God, she sought to establish her own. The selected ones did attain the righteousness that God bestows. **8.** The rest were **made dull.** These were made dull because they failed to submit themselves to the righteousness of God. Here is God acting again in judicial punishment. When a man is confronted with the righteousness of God, but is determined to go his own way, dullness, hardness, and blindness are the outcome. Paul applies the words of the OT to his own generation. His first quotation is from Deut 29:4, with a little of Isa 29:9,10 included. He intensifies this OT passage to emphasize the judicial hardening. God gives a spirit of stupor (cf. Isa 10), eyes for the purpose of not seeing, ears for the purpose of not hearing. **9,10.** Finally, the apostle cites Ps 69:22,23–the LXX translation–in which the psalmist pictures the table of his enemies as desolate, their eyes darkened, and their backs bent under toil. Thus, Paul is saying that although the majority of God's people are presently under divine judgment, the existence of the select minority is proof that the Almighty has not repudiated his people.

E. Israel's Prospects for the Future. 11:11-36.

Here Paul brings to a conclusion his discussion of the place of Israel and of the Gentiles in the plan of God. The purpose of God's action in history is that he might have mercy upon all – both Jew and Gentile. The role of Israel is most impressive whether in rejection or acceptance. Blended together in a sublime picture are the scope of history, the attitudes and response of Israel and the Gentiles, and the wisdom of God in the inter-relations of these two groups. In the metaphor of the olive tree we see the impressive unity of the people of God of both covenants.

1) Degree of Blessing from Israel's Fall and Fullness. 11:11-15.

11. Paul begins with his usual question. **They did not stumble once for all so as to fall into ruin, did they? By no means.** On the contrary, it was by means of Israel's sin (transgression) that salvation came to the Gentiles for the purpose of provoking Israel to jealousy. **12.** What is this sin or transgression? It is the sin of unbelief: **Now if their sin** *(transgression)* **is the riches of the world, and their defeat the riches of the Gentiles, how much more** [will] **their** (the Jews') **fulfilling** (the divine demand) [bring wealth to the world]. Israel's sin (unbelief) and defeat were the means by which God brought blessing to the Gentiles. The apostle argues from the less to the greater; so we can see that the Jews' positive action – the fulfilling of God's demand (see *plērōma,* Arndt, 4, p. 687) – should bring even greater blessing. **13.** The writer reminds the Gentiles that this blessing has come to them – **I am speaking to you** (pl.) **the Gentiles.** Paul magnifies the fact that his ministry is to the Gentiles. **14,15.** He hopes thereby to provoke to jealousy his brothers in the flesh and bring some of them to salvation. **If their rejection is the reconciling of the world, what will their acceptance** (by God) **be except life from the dead?** Note that Paul continues the argument from the less to the greater. The rejection of Israel involved the reconciliation of the world. Both Jew and Gentile have been reconciled to each other and to God in Christ. This is a significant accomplishment. But the acceptance of Israel by God will bring about an even more significant accomplishment — **life from the dead.** This undoubtedly refers to the climax of reconciliation in the return of Christ, the resurrection of the dead, the deliverance of creation from slavery to deterioration or decay (8:21), and the glorious reign of Christ.

2) Individual Gentile's Lack of Grounds for Boasting. 11:16-21.

We must remember that Romans is a letter to a particular group of people at Rome. In verse 13 the writer clarifies this: "I am speaking to you (plural), the Gentiles." But in 11:17-24 he has in mind each individual Gentile reader. In these verses there are eight pronouns and thirteen verbs in second person singular form (the AV shows this clearly: *thou, thee* for singular; *you, ye* for plural). Although the majority of the Israelites had been defeated and rejected, no Gentile could dare to become proud or self-sufficient. Hence, Paul makes the Gentiles, individually, aware of where they stand in relation to Israel. Then in verse 25 he returns to the you (plural) and looks at the believing Gentiles and Israel as two groups.

16. Two metaphors are found here: **the first fruits of dough** and **the whole lump; the root** and **the branches.** The first fruits of dough and the root refer to Abraham and the other patriarchs, Isaac and Jacob (see Paul's stress on "the fathers" in 9:5 and 11:28). The whole lump and the branches refer to God's people Israel, who have come from the patriarchs. The holiness attributed to the part and the whole, the root and the branches, is that of being dedicated, consecrated, set apart to God. This is a legal holiness for the group by virtue of their being God's chosen people.

17-24. Paul develops the second metaphor in verses 17-24. Some of the branches were broken off (v. 17). The individual Gentile as a wild olive branch has been grafted in among the branches of the natural olive tree. Thus this branch, the individual Gentile, **participates in the rich root that belongs to the cultivated olive** (v. 17). But then Paul warns the individual Gentile to stop boasting against the branches. He has no grounds for boasting: **you** (sing.) **are not bearing the root but the root you** (sing; v. 18). The stress here is on the unity that characterizes the people of God from both covenants. The apostle then deals with the argument that the branches were broken off in order that **I** (the Gentile) might be grafted in. **20,21. Quite right, because of unbelief they were broken off and you** (sing.) **have taken your stand** *(you stand firm)* **because of faith. Stop feeling proud, but rather fear. If God did not spare the natural branches, neither will he spare you** (sing.). The difference between the branches broken off and the branch grafted in consists in the presence of faith. Unbelief meant rejection. Faith meant acceptance. Instead of resting proudly in a false sense of security, the individual Gentile is to fear. Genuine fear of God and respect for him constitute the basis of true assurance. God broke off the natural branches because of their unbelief (v. 20). If he did not tolerate unbelief in them, neither will he tolerate it in you.

3) Goodness and Severity of God Disclosed by His Response to Belief and Unbelief. 11:22-24.

22. Therefore. The writer is concluding his extended metaphor of the root and the branches. **Behold, therefore, the goodness and severity of God. On the one hand, to those who fell, severity; but to you** (sing.) **the goodness of God, if you** (sing.) **continue in the sphere of** (God's) **goodness; for otherwise,** (if you do not continue in the sphere of God's goodness) **you** (sing.) **also will be cut off.** Paul urges the individual Gentile to continue in the goodness of God. This, of course, involves his continuing in faith (v. 20), but Paul stresses that God provides for those who trust or believe Him. Hence **to continue in God's goodness** expresses this very well. This goodness will be the portion of the Gentile if he **continues,** *persists, perseveres* (see Arndt, *epimenō,* 2., p. 296) in that goodness. Then comes a causal clause that involves contrast, **otherwise** *(epei,* see Arndt, 2., p. 283. With ellipsis **for** [if it were different], **for otherwise,** Rom. 3:6; 11:6, 22 etc.). As in the other contexts in Romans where this word **otherwise** (Gr. *epei)* appears, the reader, to get the meaning, must reverse the preceding thought and then draw the conclusion. Thus it would read, "Otherwise if you (sing.) do not continue in the sphere of God's goodness, **you** (sing.) **also will be cut off."** These solemn words of the apostle remind us of the words of Jesus: "Every branch in me not bearing fruit, he cuts it out" (Jn

15:2 a); "If anyone does not abide in me, he is thrown away as the branch" (Jn 15:6 a). To make sure this will be an effective warning, the Greek construction shows that Paul does not state whether or not the individual will continue: **If you** (sing.) **continue in God's goodness,** God's goodness will be your portion.

This same Paul wrote in Rom 8:28-30 that God's purpose for those loving him begins with his foreknowledge and foreordination and ends with their glorification. God has not revealed all the aspects of his purpose and all that is involved in his selection. What he has made known centers in the fact that believers are elect in Christ (Eph 1:4). It is very clear that the Lord has acted "for" and "in" those who are "in Christ." But it is equally clear that those "in Christ" must act: they must continue; they must bear fruit. Their action, the writer shows, is just as essential as God's action in bringing them to himself and putting them in Christ. If a teacher minimizes either of these two aspects – God's action or the believers' response – he has departed from the NT. If one thinks that he fully understands the relation between these two factors, he has forgotten that God has left some things to be revealed in the ages to come (cf. Eph 2:7).

23,24. If those from Israel do not continue or persist in unbelief, **they shall be grafted in.** Now Paul stresses God's ability. God is powerful, strong, mighty – able to graft these in again. Since, in the language of the metaphor, the Lord did what was contrary to nature, he can certainly put natural olive branches back into the natural olive tree. **24. Much more** shows Paul's confidence in God's plan.

4) Salvation for the People of Israel. 11:25-27.

25. The mystery of which Paul does not want his readers (note the **your,** pl.) to be ignorant **is that insensibility in part has happened to Israel until the full number of the Gentiles enters in** (comes to enjoy the promised blessing). Unless his readers realize this, they may become wise in their own estimation. **In part.** Characteristic Pauline understatement. The "part" is a very large part, but it is balanced off against the **full number** of Gentiles – those who are foreknown and foreordained by God (cf. 8:28-30).

26. And in this fashion all Israel will be saved. All Israel. National Israel. Compare the parallel **from Jacob** in the next quotation. **All.** Not necessarily every individual, but enough individuals to make the believers in Christ representative of the nation. The phrase **in this fashion** is correlated with the quotation from Isa 59:20,21 and Isa 27:9. The salvation of Israel is directly connected with the personal action of the deliverer, Jesus the Messiah. The **and** *(kai),* which begins verse 26 is a co-ordinating conjunction. This suggests that the work of the Deliverer (Christ) in turning away ungodliness from Jacob and bringing all Israel to salvation goes hand in hand with the entering of the full number of the Gentiles into God's blessing and favor. After this glance into the future, Paul returns to his own day.

5) God's Mercy to All Magnified by His Action in History. 11:28-32.

28. The vast majority of contemporary Israelites, as far as the good news of Christ was concerned, were hostile toward the Roman Christians. But because the Jews were still God's elect people, the Roman Christians were to regard them as beloved because of their fathers. Observe here a group which, though elect, was far from God. Paul's Gentile readers stood in contrasting relation to the Jews. **On the one hand in respect to the gospel they were enemies because of you.** Having rejected the Gospel, most of the Jewish people became hostile to the Christians. Because God had rejected them but showed mercy to the Gentiles, they treated the Gentiles as enemies. **But on the other hand, as far as their** *(the Jews')* **election** *(by God)* **is concerned, beloved because of the fathers.** This refers to the election of the whole Jewish nation and to the fact that the people were beloved because God had chosen their fathers. Election may involve a whole nation, as here; it may involve a remnant, as in 11:5; it may involve a smaller group, such as the Twelve (Jn 6:71). In each of these cases, election concerned a specific task committed by God to the group.

29. Paul teaches the faithfulness of God when he says: **the gifts and calling of God are irrevocable. Gifts.** The privileges Israel enjoyed (cf. 9:4,5). **Calling.** God's declaration to Israel or Jacob that they were his people (cf. Isa 48:12). The Gentiles, who had been disobedient to God, obtained mercy because of, or by means of, the disobedience of Israel. Now, because of the mercy experienced by the Gentiles, the people of Israel are to experience mercy. **32.** Paul's conclusion is that **God imprisoned them all in disobedience in order that he might have mercy upon all.** Each **all** in this verse refers to both Jew and Gentile. God shuts up men for the purpose of setting them free. **Mercy upon all.** Not the salvation of all. Paul's teaching about those who despise the kindness of God also applies to those who despise his mercy (see 2:4).

6) Excellence and Glory of God – the Source, Sustainer, and Goal of All Things. 11:33-36.

God's plan in history enables him to show mercy to both Israel and the Gentiles that he may have mercy upon all. And he is able to make the rebellion of men serve a purpose in his plan. This causes Paul to break out in praise.

33. Depth. God's riches, wisdom, and knowledge are inexhaustible. His **decisions** or *decrees* are beyond man's capacity to fathom. **His ways** – the whole of his conduct – cannot be followed through and tracked out. No man is great enough to observe all of God's actions and to follow them through. The OT quotations (Isa 40:13; Job 41:11) show God's independence from man. **36.** Finally, in one mighty surge of devotion, Paul attributes glory to God for ever, the God who is the Source, Sustainer, and Goal of all things.

IV. Attitude and Conduct Expected of Christians at Rome. 12:1–15:13.

Evidently Paul had been well informed of the needs of believers at Rome. Although most of his exhortations fit any group of believers, many of them show that the apostle was thinking of a particular group as he wrote. The range of these exhortations is amazing. They touch almost every aspect of life. Christian living is simply being a Christian and acting as a Christian should in every part of life.

A. Consecration of Body and Mind. 12:1,2.

1. The language here is from the OT, and reminds us that Jewish believers presented sacrifices to the Lord. But Christian believers, instead of giving something outside themselves, are to offer their own bodies to God as living, holy, and acceptable sacrifices. This type of sacrifice is a spiritual service involving all of their rational powers. **2.** Because of the dedication involved, believers are to **cease being conformed to** this age and let themselves **be transformed by the renewing** of their minds (12:2). Such transformation and renewal is to prove by testing (approve or discover) God's will as to what is good and well-pleasing and perfect.

B. Humility in the Use of God's Gifts. 12:3-8.

3. In introducing the matter of gifts, Paul speaks of **the grace** given to him that enabled him to be an apostle. Then he exhorts each of his readers not to be haughty, i.e., not to think too highly of himself. He resorts to a play on words, using various Greek terms having the word "mind" or "think" as the basic element – **not to be high-minded beyond what is proper to mind** *(think)*, **but to set one's mind for the purpose of being of a sound** *(well-balanced in evaluation)* **mind.** We are to make a self-evaluation as **God has apportioned the measure of faith to each one.** Paul is not here speaking of "saving faith" but rather "a working-for-God faith." "Saving faith" would be no standard for correct self-judgment. Only pride would say: "See how much saving faith I have." But it is a humbling experience to say: "Here is the faith I have for carrying out this or that particular task for God." This can only lead to the prayer, "Lord, increase our faith" (see Lk 17:5). In the account of the heroes of faith in Heb 11, we see that the measure of faith given corresponds to the task to be accomplished.

4,5. The **one body** of which the many are members, while at the same time being individually members of each other, is the Church universal, made up of all believers in Christ. (See I Cor 10:17; 12:12,13,27,28; Eph 1:22,23; 2:15b,16; 4:3-6, 11-13, 15,16; 5:22-30; Col 1:17, 18, 24,25). The symbol of the body describes the Church as an organism, with every member drawing life from Christ (see Col 3:3). Since all the members draw their life from Christ, they all belong to each other. Local groups of believers are the local manifestation of Christ's body, the Church. Such a local group is **body** of Christ but not all of *the body* of Christ (see I Cor 12:27). *The body of Christ* consists of the totality of believers who are joined to Christ, the

Church's head.

6. The grace of God given to individual believers is shown in different gifts. Paul lists the gifts and then tells the way each is to be used. In each case the reader, to get the proper sense, should supply the verb, *let us use,* followed by the particular gift. **Whether prophecy, let us use prophesy in agreement with** or *in a right relationship to* **the faith. Faith** here means the body of faith, belief, or doctrine (see Arndt, *pistis,* 3, pp. 669-670). Prophecy, which is meant to exhort, encourage, and comfort (see I Cor 14:3), must do so in a right relationship to the revealed truth of God. **7.** The word *diakonia,* which in the AV is translated **ministry,** can be rendered *service* if one takes it in a general sense. If one takes it in a particular sense, it refers to **the office of a deacon.** The emphasis here is that these gifts are to be used. Those with gifts for **teaching** and **exhortation** should exercise them. **8. Giving** should be done with liberality. The word *proistēmi,* translated **ruling** (AV), may mean this or it can mean, **give aid.** This is to be done **diligently.** The one who has the gift for **showing mercy** should use the gift with **cheerfulness.** The gifts mentioned here are – (1) prophecy, (2) service or the office of a deacon, (3) teaching, (4) exhorting (possibly comforting, encouraging), (5) giving, (6) ruling or giving aid, (7) showing mercy. Each of these is a special talent for a particular type of activity.

C. Character Traits To Be Exemplified. 12:9-21.

We must meditate on this list if its full force is to strike home. **9. Love** is to be genuine (or sincere, without hypocrisy). Believers are commanded constantly abhor evil and to be attached constantly to the good. **10.** They are to be devoted to one another in brotherly love and they are to outdo one another in showing respect for each other. **11.** They are not to be indolent. They are to be **aglow** (RSV), literally, *boiling,* with the Spirit. They are to be continually serving the Lord. **12.** Believers are to rejoice in the **hope,** i.e., in all that God has promised to do for them in Christ. They are to endure affliction and always be in prayer. **13.** They are to provide for the needs of the **saints** (fellow believers) and to pursue or seek after hospitality. **14.** Believers are to bless their persecutors and stop cursing the rascals. **15.** They are to rejoice with those rejoicing and to weep with those sorrowing. To feel genuine joy for another's success is a mark of true spiritual maturity. **16.** Believers are to live in harmony with each other. Instead of striving after things that are too high for them, they are to accommodate themselves to humble ways and cease being wise in their own estimation. **17.** They are not to return evil in exchange for evil. Rather, they are to be concerned for what is morally good before all men. **18.** As far as that which proceeds from Christians is concerned, if it is possible, they are to keep the peace with all men. **19.** Believers are not to take their own revenge but rather to give the wrath of God an opportunity to work out its purpose (see Arndt, *topos,* 2.c, pp. 830-831). The OT points out that vengeance and recompense belong to God. **20.** Believers are to treat enemies in need as they would treat others in similar circumstances. By feeding them and giving them water to drink, believers heap up burning embers on their heads. This figure seems to mean that the enemy will blush with shame or remorse at such unexpected kindness. **21.** The last character trait mentioned in Romans 12 shows Paul's sense of a contest in the Christian life – "Cease being overcome by evil, but be in the process of overcoming the evil by the good."

D. Submission to Governmental Authorities To Be Accompanied by a Loving, Upright Manner of Life. 13:1-14.

How a Christian faces his responsibilities to government, how he acts toward his neighbor, and how he behaves in his personal life are all matters of great importance.

1,2. Obedience to the state is an ordinance of God. The opening words: **Let every person subject himself to the governing authorities** defines the obligation of the Christian. The rest of the first two verses shows why he has this obligation. **There is no human authority except by God and those which exist have been established by God.** The phraseology stresses both the officeholder and the office. Nothing is said here about form of government. The passage emphasizes government itself and its administrators when these function properly. To resist governmental authority is to resist the ordinance of God. Those who resist will receive condemnation.

3,4. Paul pictures the rulers in the

rightful exercise of their prerogatives. Since rulers in their proper function bring terror to the evil worker – not to the good, the man who does not want to fear the ruler will constantly practice the good work. Paul pictures the man who acts thus as receiving praise from the authority. His description of the ruling authority as a *helper* or *agent* of God seems very strong to us. The one who does evil ought to fear. The authority does not carry the sword without a purpose. Here it is clear that God has ordained force (the sword) to be used by human authorities to prevent anarchy and the tyranny of evil in human society. For the second time in the verse (13:4), the ruler is called the agent of God. Then Paul adds – an avenger who brings (God's) wrath upon the evildoer.

5-7. Two reasons emerge for obedience to governmental authorities, and certain results follow. The reasons for obedience are: (1) God's wrath administered by the ruler will fall upon those who disobey; (2) the Christian's conscience declares that he must obey the ordinances of God. Submission to rulers is one of these ordinances. It involves paying one's taxes, paying customs duties, showing respect to those entitled to respect, and showing honor to those entitled to honor. These are obligations of believers to rulers.

Love is said to be the fulfillment of the Law (13:8-10). **8. Be indebted to no one in anything except the constant loving of each other.** Love is the only debt a believer cannot fully discharge. **8b. Now the one who is in the process of loving is in a state of having fulfilled the law. 9.** Paul shows that the commandments about adultery, murder, stealing, desiring that which is forbidden, and all other commandments that one might mention are summed up in the admonition to love one's neighbor as one's self. **10. Therefore love is the fulfilling of the law.** The commandment about loving one's neighbor as one's self is taken from Lev 19:18. In this OT passage there is found near the close of a series of injunctions a description of how the individual should act in regard to those with whom he lives. Whereas the OT *implies* that love is the fulfilling of the Law, Paul makes this *explicit*. Love clearly shows the believer's positive commitment and active obedience to God.

Upright conduct is essential because of the near approach of complete salvation (Rom 13:11-14). Love is a positive, creative outgoing of one's personality. Certain sins make this love impossible and must be avoided at all costs. **11.** The nature of the present time is such that believers must **be aroused from sleep.** Indifference to sin must be replaced by alertness. The salvation "which is nearer than when the readers first believed" refers to all that Christ will do for believers at his second advent. Certainly Paul hoped that Christ would come during his lifetime. **12.** The contrast between **night** and **day, light** and **darkness** is not only a familiar Biblical theme but is found in the Dead Sea scrolls as well. The people of God know there is a distinct line between evil and righteousness. Yet reminders are constantly necessary. **Therefore, let us lay aside for ourselves the works of darkness and let us clothe ourselves with the weapons of light. 13.** After Paul exhorts the readers to behave decently, as in the day, he lists specific activities that are to be avoided. These are carousings or revelries, and drunkenness, unlawful sexual activities and sensual indulgences, strife and jealousy. **14.** Finally, victory demands that the believer act. He is to clothe himself with the Lord Jesus Christ. He is to stop making provision (forethought) for the flesh to arouse desires for that which God has forbidden.

E. Tolerance Necessary for Those with Strong and Weak Consciences. 14:1–15:13.

In this section Paul is discussing the attitudes that two kinds of Christians have toward each other. In regard to ceremonial matters—eating foods, observing days—the more mature Christian, in Paul's day, saw these things as unimportant. The weaker Christian, who did not yet have a firm standard for his conscience and was "feeling his way along," felt greatly disturbed at the actions of his stronger brother. The conscience is said to be strong if it has a sound standard for judgment and weak if it has an inferior standard.

1) Differences of Opinion over Food or Special Days. 14:1-6.

1. Paul first discusses whether the Christian group should receive into fellowship the one who is weak in knowledge of what it means to be a Christian and how to live as a Christian. The apostle states that such a one is to be received but **not for the purpose of getting into quarrels about opinions** (see

Arndt, *diakrisis,* 1, p. 184). **2.** The weaker Christian was the one who would eat only vegetables. The stronger Christian was the one who believed he could eat all things. **3.** The one who ate was not to be **constantly despising** the one who did not eat. The one who did not eat was not to be **constantly condemning the one who did.** The eating or not eating of certain foods for the Christian is not in itself a moral matter. It is merely a matter of preference. Presently, however, Paul shows that this *may* become a moral matter. **4.** The weaker Christian should not condemn another man's servant; that is the job of his master. Here Paul adds that the master is able to make him stand.

5. Paul next takes up the matter of special days. The weaker Christian **prefers one day above another.** The stronger Christian **holds every day in esteem.** The apostle does not take sides here but merely insists that each one **be fully convinced in his own mind.** This tacitly suggests that each one take thought about the basis for his own opinion.

6. Both groups, whether they observe a day or not, whether they eat or not, are giving thanks to God. Hence there is no question of their devotion to the Lord.

2) Judgment by the Lord, Not by One's Brother. 14:7-12.

7. In giving thanks to the Lord, we are reminded that believers cannot live or die to or for themselves. For them both life and death are focused upon the Lord. In every experience they belong to the Lord. **9.** Christ died and arose so that he might have Lordship over the dead and the living. **10.** If Christ is Lord, then why should the weaker Christian condemn his brother? If Christ is Lord, why should the stronger Christian despise his brother? Both the stronger and the weaker Christians—**we all**—must **stand before the judgment seat of God.** The AV has *judgment seat of Christ,* but all of the best manuscripts here read **God.** In II Cor 5:10, Paul speaks of the "judgment seat of Christ." The shift is of little importance, since Jesus himself told us that the Father judges no one but has given "all judgment to the Son" (see Jn 5:22,23,27,29). God judges men in the sense that he judges them through his Son. **11,12.** Paul quotes Isa 45:23, from the LXX, to show that men must appear before God in judgment, then concludes: Each one of us will give an account of himself [to God]. **To God** ought to be supplied, but it is not a part of the original text.

3) Removal of Stumbling Blocks. 14:13-23.

13. Paul urges his readers to stop condemning each other, and instead, **decide not to be putting an obstacle in their brother's way or a temptation to sin.** In verse 14 the apostle shows that he sides with the stronger Christian. He knows that nothing is unclean of itself. But to the man who thinks that something is unclean, to that one it is. **15.** Nevertheless, food must not be the cause of hurting a brother's feelings (AV, **be grieved**). Such hurt feelings could push a man further and further from Christ. **By means of food do not bring about his ruin [the ruin of] that one on behalf of whom Christ died.** In discussing the word "to bring to ruin" *(apollumi),* Arndt lists Rom 14:15 under the heading, "With reference to eternal destruction" *(apollumi,* Arndt, 1. a., alpha, p. 94). Hence nonmoral issues can become moral if they destroy a man's fellowship with Christ. **16.** Christian freedom is one of the good things of the Christian faith. But a Christian ought not to act in such a way that this good can be blasphemed.

17-19. Note that the kingdom or reign of God is a present reality. It is defined as Christian living: uprightness of conduct, peace or harmony, and joy. This is in the sphere of the Holy Spirit (cf. 8:9) who energizes believers to be **well pleasing to God** and **respected by men.** Instead of engaging in conflict, Paul urges the believers to be pursuing that which makes for the peace and edification of fellow believers.

20,21. For the sake of food, stop tearing down the work of God. Although all things are pure, they become **evil to the man eating with offence.** With offense to what or to whom? If it is with offense to the scruples of another, then it is the stronger Christian who is thought of as doing the eating. If it is with offense to himself, then it is the weaker Christian who is doing the eating. The context in verse 21 favors the former. **Or is made weak** is omitted by many early, good manuscripts.

22,23. Faith. Better, **conviction. You** (sing.), **keep to yourself the conviction which you have before God. Happy is the man who finds no fault with him-**

self in what he approves. But the one who is at variance with himself, if he should eat, he feels condemnation and stays in that state because his eating is not from conviction. And everything which is not from conviction is sin. Here it is made very clear that everyone must have a standard for his conduct. With the right one, there are no qualms of conscience with regard to eating; but with the wrong one, e.g., a standard carried over from a past manner of living, condemnation results. **Conviction** is the assurance that one's standard is right. Without a right basis for judgment the believer may be convicted of sin by his conscience where no sin is really involved. It is highly important that a believer provide the correct standard for his conscience, and that he help his fellow believers to have this standard too. He must shun anything that prevents a fellow believer from getting a correct standard and anything that separates a fellow believer from fellowship with Christ.

4) The Strong To Help the Weak Rather Than Please Themselves. 15:1-3.

1. To bear patiently with the overconscientious scruples – **weaknesses—of those without strength** (Christian maturity) is the obligation of **those who are strong** (in faith). **2.** A believer is to please his neighbor for the neighbor's good and for his edification. **3.** The believer has his example in Christ, who did not please himself. Paul applies the words of David in Ps 69:10 to Christ. The reproaches which fell upon Christ are the evidence that he did not please himself.

5) Glory Brought to God by Endurance, Consolation, and Harmony. 15:4-6.

4. What value does the OT have for the Christian? It has instruction to give to Christian believers. In reading and responding to the OT Scriptures, the Christian learns both **endurance** and **consolation.** Instruction, endurance, and consolation are all essential elements for the Christian who has **hope** (v. 4). The OT can do this because it is a book about God and his people rather than about ideas. **5.** Paul prays that the God who brings endurance and consolation may help his readers live in harmony together, with Christ Jesus as the standard. **6.** The purpose of this harmony is that **with one mind and with one voice** [they] **may glorify the God and Father of our Lord Jesus Christ.** Note that unity of believers is essential if they are to bring glory to God.

6) Ministry of Christ Designed for Both Jew and Gentile. 15:7-13.

7. In concluding the question of the relation of the stronger and weaker Christians, Paul urges that they **receive each other** into their society **just as Christ receives** into fellowship with himself these same people. The outcome of such reception is glory to God.

8,9. For two reasons Christ became **a helper for the circumcision** (i.e., the Jews): (1) to prove that the promises made to the fathers were reliable; (2) to enable the Gentiles to glorify God for his mercy. In sharing the promises made to and through the Jewish people, the Gentiles have come to glorify God (cf. Rom 11:11-36; Eph 3:6, etc.). In becoming a helper to the Jewish people, Christ became a helper to all men. **9 b-12.** Paul then makes four quotations from the Greek version of the OT (LXX). These quotations picture the Gentiles as listening to personal testimony (Ps 18:49), as rejoicing with God's people (Deut 32:4, LXX), as being exhorted to praise the Lord (Ps 117:1), and as being ruled over by the Messianic king and hoping in him (Isa 11:10).

13. After showing what is involved in Christian conduct, Paul concludes with a prayer for his readers. **And may the God who brings hope fill you with all joy and peace in trusting, in order that you may abound in hope by the power which the Holy Spirit bestows.** "Abounding in Christian hope" should be an apt description of every Christian. The Christian looks ahead with a contagious enthusiasm. God has filled him with hope.

V. Items of Personal Interest and Care for the Readers. 15:14–16:27.

Paul's conclusion is long because he wanted to tell his readers about the goals he had as an apostle. He wanted his readers to feel that they had a part in his ministry. Along with his greetings he gives instructions, warnings, and specific teachings. This section surely makes clear that Romans is a letter.

A. Paul's Reason for Writing Boldly to Mature Readers. 15:14-16.

14,15. Though the apostle was confident that the Roman Christians were full of goodness and *in a state of being filled* with Christian knowledge, yet he had written this letter to remind them of certain truths they already knew. Note Paul's modesty. His justification for writing to them **rather boldly on some points** was that he had received special grace for his office. **16.** He regarded his apostleship to the Gentiles as a priestly ministry, in which he ministered or served **the gospel of God as a priest.** The purpose for his ministry was that **the offering up** of the Gentiles might be acceptable because this offering had been consecrated by the Holy Spirit.

B. Supernatural Confirmation of Paul's Pioneer Missionary Work. 15:17-21.

17. Since Paul had received grace as an apostle, and since he ministered the gospel of God as a priest, he could declare: **Therefore, I may boast in Christ of my relation to God. 18,19.** Yet he did not boast in what he had done but in what Christ had accomplished through him by word and deed, by the power of signs and wonders, by the power of the Spirit. His goal was the obedience of the Gentiles – which the Gentiles were rendering even then. Paul looked at his territory thus far as having extended from Jerusalem to Illyricum (also called Dalmatia, a Roman province above Macedonia, extending along the eastern shore of the Adriatic – present day Yugoslavia). **20,21.** His ambition was to preach the Gospel where Christ was not named – i.e., was not known. He carried out the words of Isa 52:15, which refer to kings. But Paul applies them to Gentiles who believed when they heard the good news about Christ for the first time.

C. Travel Plans: Jerusalem, Rome, and Spain. 15:22-29.

22. I have so often been prevented from coming to you. Since Rome was the next step – just across the Adriatic – Paul had often expected to make the journey. **23. Place** (AV). Better, *opportunity.* In the territory where Paul had been he no longer had opportunity to preach Christ where He was not known. **24.** So the apostle hoped to see the Romans on the way to Spain. He announces his plan to visit them and **to be sent forth** by them after he has **enjoyed** their **company for a while.**

25,26. But before Paul could come, he had to complete his immediate project. He had received contributions from believers in Macedonia and Achaia for the poor saints in Jerusalem. He looked upon this collection as part of the Gentiles' spiritual obligation. **27.** As they had shared in the spiritual blessings of Israel, certainly they should now minister to the Israelite Christians from their material things. **28.** The apostle looked upon this fund as a sacred trust. **When I have placed the sum that was collected safely** *(sealed)* **in their hands, I shall come through you to Spain** (see Arndt, *sphragizō*, 2. d., p. 804). Paul mentions this collection in I Cor 16:1 and II Cor 8 and 9. **29.** Note the writer's confidence that he would come in the **fullness of the blessing of Christ.** The word **gospel** (AV) is not found here in the best manuscripts. Paul did come with Christ's blessing, but he came as a prisoner. God fulfilled his desire, but in a way he did not foresee. He knew, however, that the way ahead would be difficult. Therefore he wanted his readers to pray for him.

D. Specific Requests for Prayer. 15:30-33.

30. Paul appealed to his readers either by or through **our Lord Jesus Christ** and **the love which the Spirit produces** that they pray for him. He wanted earnest prayer—**contend along with me in prayer. 31.** He asked them to pray, in the first place, that he might be delivered from the disobedient Jews in Judea. He knew how much the unbelieving Jews in Palestine despised him. Also, he asked the Roman Christians to pray **that the contribution meant for Jerusalem** [might] **be acceptable to the saints.** Paul wanted the believing Jewish Christians to respond to this gesture of Christian love on the part of the Gentile Christians – the collection from all the Gentile churches. **32. Finally,** they were to pray that in joy he might find refreshing with them when he came to them by the will of God. When Paul did reach Rome, he came as a prisoner, with no outward grounds of joy. He could not find refreshing with the Romans, since he was not free to go to them, although they were free to come to him. God's will overruled some of the details of this request, but the request itself was granted. **33.** Since God is the only one who can really bring peace, how natural for Paul to close these prayer requests with a sentence prayer of his own for his readers: **May the God who brings peace be with you all, Amen.**

E. Recommendation of Phoebe. 16:1,2.

1. In recommending Phoebe, Paul tells who she is and where she comes from. She was a deaconess of the church in Cenchrea. Her duties, like those of the deacons, were quite general. Material needs and also spiritual needs of others were met by believers like Phoebe (cf. Acts 6:1-6 with Acts 6:8-15 and 7:1-60). **2.** Paul requests the Romans **to welcome Phoebe in the Lord in a manner worthy of the saints,** and to **help her in whatever undertaking she may have need.** She deserves such a welcome, Paul declares, **because she became a helper of many and of Paul himself as well.** This chapter refutes the idea that the apostle resented women working in the churches or among believers. His tribute to Phoebe is followed by greetings to various people and groups. Among those greeted are eight women. Paul specifically comments on how much work five of these women did (Mary, v. 6; Priscilla, a fellow worker, v. 3; Tryphena and Tryphosa, v. 12; Persis, v. 12). The mother of Rufus was so dear to Paul that he calls her his mother as well (v. 13). Only two women are mentioned without any comment – Julia and the sister of Nereus (v. 15).

F. Particular Greetings to Individuals and Groups. 16:3-16.

The frequency of these names in the catacombs and inscriptions of ancient burial places in Rome and the significance of this information is discussed well by C. H. Dodd, *The Epistle to the Romans,* in *The Moffatt New Testament Commentary;* and William Sanday and Arthur C. Headlam, *The Epistle to the Romans,* in *The International Critical Commentary.* In these commentaries to the book of Romans, see the Introductions as well as the textual comments.

3. Paul starts with two of his dearest friends – Priscilla and Aquila. Ever since Paul had met them in Corinth on his second missionary journey, they had been hard at work in the service of God (see Acts 18:2,18,26; Rom 16:3,4; I Cor 16:19; II Tim 4:19). **4.** Just how they risked their own necks for Paul's life, he does not say. But the fact that not only Paul but all the churches of the Gentiles gave thanks for them shows the extent of their efforts on behalf of Christ. **5 a.** Paul greets the church in their house. This shows that the zeal of these two for Christ was no different in Rome than elsewhere. Household churches are probably also to be found in 16:10,11,14,15. If this is true, then the mention of five household churches makes one realize that Christians in Rome were members of smaller groups rather than of one large assembly.

5 b. Epaenetus is greeted as the first convert of **Asia Minor.** The AV is wrong in its reading, *Achaia.* **7.** Andronicus and Junias were Paul's fellow countrymen, who had been in jail with him at some time. Paul describes them as being prominent among the apostles and as having been Christians before him. This would mean they had been believers for about twenty-five years.

13. Since that which is chosen may be regarded as choice or excellent, **Rufus, the choice one in the Lord,** could also be translated as: *"Rufus, the outstanding Christian* (Arndt, *eklektos,* 2, p. 242).

16. The command to **greet one another with a holy kiss** (cf. I Cor 16:20; II Cor 13:12; I Thess 5:26) or with a kiss of love (I Pet 5:14) shows that warm Christian fellowship was characteristic of the early church. Whatever in modern cultures is symbolic of the deep affection Christians ought to feel toward each other – a kiss on the cheek, a warm handshake, a grasping of both hands, etc. – is the equivalent of the apostolic command.

G. Dangerous Character of Those Who Teach False Doctrine. 16:17-20.

Paul is not saying that false teachers were already present among the Roman believers. But he knew what had happened elsewhere. **17. Now I urge you, brothers, to look out for those making the dissensions and the temptations to sin contrary to the teaching you learned.** The teaching becomes the standard. Here is the authority of the apostolic message. Paul's readers are to **turn away from** those producing dissensions and providing temptations to sin. **18.** Such people, instead of being slaves to Christ, are slaves to their own stomachs. But their manner captivates their audience. **By smooth, plausible speech and false eloquence, they deceive the hearts of the unsuspecting. 19.** Paul wanted his readers to stay wise in reference to the good, but innocent as far as participation in evil was concerned. Hence he gives this warning. **20.** After the warning comes the promise: **the God who brings peace will crush Satan under your feet in a short time.** With final victory on the horizon, the prayer is very pertinent: **May the grace of our Lord Jesus be with you.**

H. Greetings from Paul's Associates in Corinth. 16:21-23.

21. Kinsmen (AV). Rather, *fellow countrymen*. Timothy, Paul's fellow worker, is well known. For the other three, we have no positive identification. Lucius may be the Lucius of Cyrene (Acts 13:1). Jason seems to be the Jason mentioned in Acts 17:5-9. Sosipater looks like the Sosipater of Acts 20:4. **22,23.** The scribe, Tertius, to whom Paul dictated the letter, sends his own greetings. Gaius, who may be the Gaius mentioned in I Cor 1:14. is said to be not only Paul's host but the host for the whole church. This seems to indicate that the church met in his house. The fact that Erastus was the city treasurer shows that the Christian faith reached some people in the upper classes. Quartus, **our brother,** is the last to send greetings.

I. Establishment of Believers by the Sovereign God of History. 16:25-27.

See the Introduction for the discussion of the concluding prayers and doxology in regard to their location in the epistle. **25.** This doxology centers in God's ability or power to strengthen the readers. God's strengthening is **in accordance with Paul's gospel and the preaching about Jesus Christ.** This preaching is being carried on **because of the revealing of the mystery** or *secret*. Three things are said about the mystery or secret: (1) It was **concealed for long ages** or *long ages ago* (v. 25). (2) It **has been revealed now through the prophetic scriptures** (i.e., the OT) **by the command of the eternal God** (v. 26). (3) **It has been made known unto all the nations for the obedience which faith puts into operation** (v. 26). This mystery has to do with God's reaching both Jew and Gentile through the redemption that is in Christ Jesus (see Rom 9; 11; Eph 3:1-7; Col 1:26,27; 2:2,3; 4:3). In the language of Eph 3:6, the mystery consists of the Gentiles' being fellow heirs with the believing Jews, belonging to the same body with them, and being sharers together with them of the promise (cf. Rom 11:11-32).

An account of God's ability and plan precedes Paul's ascription of glory to God. In the very last verse (v. 27) there is a relative pronoun, **to whom,** which, although left out by one good manuscript and a few others, seems to be a part of what Paul originally wrote. But it is very difficult to put it in the text, simply because this whole doxology centers in God. Glory comes to the only wise God through Jesus Christ. This glory is forever and ever. Perhaps the sense of the text may best be seen if we read it thus: **May the glory for ever and ever** [be] **to the only wise God, through Jesus Christ, to whom** [also] **the glory forever and ever** [belongs]. **Amen.** In the original text the phrase **the glory forever and ever** occurs only once. The relative pronoun **to whom** follows Jesus Christ. The phrase **the glory forever and ever** follows the **to whom.** Since the doxology centers in God and this last clause centers in Christ, it seems best to conclude that Paul attributes eternal glory both to God and to Christ. How fitting that Romans should close with the theme, "Glory be to God forevermore!"

BIBLIOGRAPHY

Althaus, Paul. *Der Brief an Die Römer. Das Neue Testament Deutsch.* Herausgegeben von Paul Althaus und Johannes Behm. Göttingen: Vandenhoeck und Ruprecht, 1949.

Godet, F. *Commentary on St. Paul's Epistle to the Romans.* Translated by A. Cusin. New York: Funk and Wagnalls, 1883.

Hodge, Charles. *Commentary on the Epistle to the Romans.* New Edition. New York: A. C. Armstrong and Son, 1890.

LaGrange, P. M. J. *Saint Paul Épitre Aux Romains.* Paris: J. Gabalda et Cie, 1950.

Meyer, H. A. W. *Critical and Exegetical Handbook to the Epistle to the Romans.* Translated by J. C. Moore and E. Johnson. New York: Funk and Wagnalls, 1884.

Murray, John. *The Imputation of Adam's Sin.* Grand Rapids: Wm. B. Eerdmans Publishing Co., 1959.

Philippi, Friedrich Adolph. *Commentary on St. Paul's Epistle to the Romans.* Translated by J. S. Banks. 2 vols. Edinburgh: T & T Clark, 1878.

Sanday, William, and Headlam, Arthur C. *A Critical and Exegetical Commentary on the Epistle to the Romans.* New York: Charles Scribner's Sons, 1915.

Shedd, Russell Philip. "The Pauline Conception of the Solidarity of the Human Race in Its Relationship to the Old Testament and Early Judaism," *Man in Community.* London: The Epworth Press, 1958.

Shedd, William G. T. *A Critical and Doctrinal Commentary upon the Epistle of St. Paul to the Romans.* New York: Charles Scribner's Sons, 1879.

THE FIRST EPISTLE TO THE CORINTHIANS

INTRODUCTION

The City of Corinth. Corinth was a wealthy commercial center, situated on the narrow isthmus that connected the mainland of Greece and the Peloponnesus. Its history may be divided conveniently into two parts. The city, which according to legend was the place where Jason's Argo was constructed, was destroyed by the Roman consul Lucius Mummius Achaicus, in 146 B.C. This ended the first chapter of its history. It was inevitable, however, that a city so favorably located should have a resurrection. Hence, in 46 B.C., the new city was constructed by Julius Caesar and given the status of a Roman colony. It quickly regained its commercial importance and, in addition, became in many ways the leading city of Greece.

The importance of the city must have influenced the Apostle Paul in his missionary endeavors. Being the hub of commerce from the north to the south and from the east to the west and containing a population of mixed character – Roman, Greek, and Oriental – Corinth was a strategic center. In fact, it has been called "the Empire in miniature; – the Empire reduced to a single State" (ICC, p. xiii). A message heralded and heard in Corinth might find its way to the distant regions of the inhabited earth. It is no wonder, then, that Paul was "constrained by the Word" (Acts 18:5) to testify in Corinth. Added to the pressure within from the Lord and from the Word may well have been a pressure from without – the open door in cosmopolitan Corinth.

And finally, Corinth's moral character made it a fertile field for the glorious good news of the Messiah. The old city had contained the famous Temple of Aphrodite, where one thousand sacred prostitutes were made available to its cultists. The same spirit, if not the same temple, prevailed in the new city. The sexually-slanted proverb, "It is not given to everyone to visit Corinth," lived on (cf. MNT, p. xviii). The Greek word *Korinthiazomai*, meaning literally, *to act the Corinthian*, came to mean "to practice fornication" (cf. LSJ, p. 981). "Every Greek," wrote Moffatt, "knew what a 'Corinthian girl' meant" (MNT, *loc. cit.*). The popular Scottish commentator, William Barclay, has said, "Aelian, the late Greek writer, tells us that if ever a Corinthian was shown upon the stage in a Greek play he was shown drunk" (William Barclay, *The Letters to the Corinthians*, p. 3). It is needless to multiply references and illustrations; Corinth was a city noted for everything depraved, dissolute, and debauched. It was providential that Paul was in Corinth when he was writing the Epistle to the Romans. From no other city could he have received more of an incentive to write of the sin of man, and from no other city could he have seen more apt illustration of it. A gaze from Gaius' house may well have been the occasion of the great catalogue of man's wicked deeds set forth in Romans 1:18-32. From this background, then, came Paul's First Epistle to the Corinthians, the epistle of sanctification. It is as if one today were to address an epistle of holiness to a group of believers in Paris, or Singapore.

Origin of the Church. The story of the founding of the church at Corinth is told by Luke in Acts 18:1-17. Paul reached the city on his second missionary journey in A.D. 50, and soon became the first to preach Christ's gospel there. While living and working with Aquila and Priscilla, he began his ministry in the synagogue, a ministry that stretched over eighteen months. A striking insight into the apostle's method of preaching is afforded by the Western text of Acts 18:4, which reads, *And entering into the synagogue every sabbath he discoursed, inserting the name of the Lord Jesus, and tried to persuade not only Jews but also Greeks. Inserting the name of the Lord Jesus* must refer to the application of the Old Testament Scriptures to Christ. In other words, he preached Jesus of Nazareth as the fulfillment of Messianic prophecy. He, therefore, followed the methodology of the Lord himself, who, on the Emmaus Road with the two disciples, began at Moses and all the prophets and expounded unto them in all the Scriptures the things that concerned him (cf. Lk 24:27). The response to Paul's preaching was different from the response to Jesus' teaching. For the most part, the hearts of Paul's listeners did not burn with interest in the truth; they burned with opposition to the truth. And Paul was forced to leave (Acts 18:6). Moving next door to the house of Titus Justus (possibly the Gaius of I Cor 1:14 and Rom 16:23; William Ramsay, *Pictures of the Apostolic Church,* p. 205), Paul continued to preach "in weakness, and in fear, and in much trembling" (I Cor 2:3). And who would not fear under the circumstances? The meeting place of the little assembly was next door to the synagogue! The Lord, however, came to Paul in a vision and encouraged him with the promise that He had "much people" in Corinth (cf. Acts 18:9,10). This promise must have been of great comfort to the apostle in later years, when the believers' moral laxity might have given him reason to doubt the genuineness of the work there. After concluding his ministry in Corinth, Paul returned to Jerusalem and Antioch.

Authorship of the Letter. The external and internal evidences for the Pauline authorship of the letter are so strong that it is really unnecessary to give the subject more than cursory attention. Clement of Rome, writing about A.D. 95, refers the epistle to "the blessed Paul, the Apostle." This is the earliest instance of the quotation of a New Testament writer identified by name (ICC, p. xvii). Ignatius, Polycarp, and others provide abundant additional external evidence. The internal evidences – of style, vocabulary, and content – harmonize with what is known of both Paul and Corinth. This is a genuine product of Paul the Apostle.

Place of Writing. Paul wrote the letter from Ephesus (cf. I Cor 16:8), not from Philippi, as the AV subscription has it.

Date of Writing. The date cannot be fixed with absolute certainty, but it seems probable that the epistle was written during the latter part of Paul's prolonged stay at Ephesus (cf. Acts 19:1 – 20:1). That would put it about A.D. 55.

Occasion of Writing. Before suggesting the occasion of the letter, it would be wise to outline the order of Paul's contacts and correspondence with the Corinthian assembly. Though almost all points in the outline are disputed, defense of them is not within the purpose of this brief introduction.

1. Paul's initial contact was that referred to above, the visit in which the good news was first preached to the Corinthians. According to 2:1, 3:2, and 11:2, it seems that this was the only visit before the writing of the canonical I Corinthians.

2. After this initial visit Paul wrote the church a letter which has been lost (cf. 5:9).

3. When disturbing news came from the believers and a letter requesting information, Paul wrote I Corinthians.

4. Apparently the problems in the church were not solved by the epistle, for the apostle was forced to pay the church a hurried, painful visit (cf. II Cor 2:1; 12:14; 13:1,2).

5. Following this painful visit the apostle wrote the church a third letter of a very severe character, to which he refers in II Corinthians 2:4.

6. The apostle's anxiety for the church was so great that he could not wait in Troas for Titus, the bearer of the severe letter, but hurried on to Macedonia. There he met Titus and learned from him that the letter had produced results; all was well in Corinth. From Macedonia Paul wrote the canonical II Corinthians (cf. II Cor 2:13; 7:6-16).

7. He then followed up this last letter with his final recorded visit to the church (cf. Acts 20:1-4).

The occasion of the writing of I Corinthians may be traced to several things. In the first place, there had come to the apostle from two sources reports of divisions in the church (cf. I Cor 1:11; 16:17). The more serious of the alien elements may have been Judaists (cf. 1:12; 9:1). In the second place, there arrived in Ephesus from the Corinthian church Stephanas, Fortunatus, and Achaicus (cf. 16:17). The trio brought a letter from the believers in which were contained a number of questions for Paul to answer. The questions may be seen in the recurring key phrase, "now concerning" *(peri de;* see 7:1,25; 8:1; 12:1; 16:1,12). In the third place, certain subjects appear to be simply "the spontaneous outcome of the Apostle's anxious thoughts about the Corinthian Church" (ICC, p. xxi).

Chief Characteristics of the Letter. Perhaps the leading feature of this epistle is its emphasis upon the life of the local church. The order and the problems of a primitive church are before the reader. If Romans may be called a theological writing, I Corinthians is certainly a practical one. If in Romans Paul resembles the modern professor of Biblical Theology, in I Corinthians he resembles the pastor-teacher, faced with the care of the church on the firing line of Christian warfare.

On the other hand, the letter is not wholly practical in its emphasis. The most important chapter in the New Testament on the resurrection of Jesus Christ is probably I Corinthians 15, and certainly the most important section in the New Testament on spiritual gifts is found in I Corinthians 12; 13; 14.

And, of course, this great letter is known supremely for its great lyric on love, chapter 13. Here one sees to what heights a man may climb in spiritual writing when borne aloft by the Holy Spirit of God. The genius of the man Paul flashes forth here with indescribable effect.

Finally, it may be of interest to mention that this is Paul's longest epistle.

Plan of the Letter. The Pauline argument is plain and clear, subject following subject in orderly fashion, with the divisions being clearly marked. The following outline is utilized in the exposition.

OUTLINE

I. Introduction. 1:1-9.
  A. The salutation. 1:1-3.
  B. The thanksgiving. 1:4-9.
II. The divisions in the church. 1:10 – 4:21.
  A. The fact of the divisions. 1:10-17.
  B. The causes of the divisions. 1:18 – 4:5.
    1. Cause 1: Misconception of the message. 1:18 – 3:4.
    2. Cause 2: Misconception of the ministry. 3:5 – 4:5.
  C. The application and conclusion. 4:6-21.
III. The disorders in the church. 5:1 – 6:20.
  A. The absence of discipline. 5:1-13.
  B. The lawsuits before the heathen. 6:1-11.
  C. The moral laxity in the church. 6:12-20.
IV. The difficulties in the church. 7:1 – 15:58.
  A. The counsel concerning marriage. 7:1-40.
    1. The prologue. 7:1-7.
    2. The problems of marriage. 7:8-38.
    3. The postscript. 7:39,40.
  B. The counsel concerning things sacrificed to idols. 8:1 – 11:1.
    1. The principles. 8:1-13.
    2. The illustration of the principles. 9:1-27.
    3. The admonition and application to the Corinthians. 10:1 – 11:1.
  C. The counsel concerning the veiling of women in public worship. 11:2-16.
    1. The theological reason. 11:2-6.
    2. The Biblical reasons. 11:7-12.
    3. The physical reason. 11:13-16.
  D. The counsel concerning the Lord's Supper. 11:17-34.
    1. The indignation of Paul. 11:17-22.
    2. The review of past instruction. 11:23-26.
    3. The application to the Corinthians. 11:27-34.
  E. The counsel concerning spiritual gifts. 12:1 – 14:40.
    1. The validity of utterance. 12:1-3.
    2. The unity of the gifts. 12:4-11.
    3. The diversity of the gifts. 12:12-31 a.
    4. The primacy of love over gifts. 12:31 b – 13:13.
    5. The superiority of prophecy, and the public worship of the church. 14:1-36.
    6. The conclusion. 14:37-40.
  F. The counsel concerning the doctrine of the resurrection. 15:1-58.
    1. The certainty of the resurrection. 15:1-34.
    2. The consideration of certain objections. 15:35-57.

3. The concluding appeal. 15:58.
V. The conclusion: Practical and personal matters. 16:1-24.
A. The collection for the poor. 16:1-4.
B. The planned visit of Paul. 16:5-9.
C. Commendations, exhortations, salutations, and benediction. 16:10-24.

COMMENTARY

I. Introduction. 1:1-9.

A. The Salutation. 1:1-3.

The introduction, made up of salutation and thanksgiving, prepares the way for the discussion to follow and, in true Pauline fashion, contains important hints with reference to the burden of the letter.

1. **Called to be an apostle** (Gr., *an apostle by calling*, the force of the verbal adjective) stresses the divine initiative in Paul's summons to office. This phrase, together with the strengthening, **the will of God,** is a designed reference to those in Corinth who may have questioned his right to speak authoritatively (cf. 9:1). **Sosthenes our brother** (lit., *the brother)* may designate the ruler of the synagogue mentioned in Acts 18:17, but this cannot be proved. The definite article may mean nothing more that that he was a well-known Christian. If, however, this is the Corinthian Sosthenes of Luke's account, then the beating he received from the Greeks was a blessing; he became a Christian!

2. The church is **the church of God,** not of Cephas, or Apollos, or even Paul (cf. 1:12). **Sanctified in Christ Jesus** introduces an important doctrine, yet one very much misunderstood. The Greek word *hagiazō* means "to sanctify," not in the sense of "to make holy," but in the sense of "to set apart" for God's possession and use (cf. Jn 17:19). Christians are not sinless, although they should sin less. Biblical sanctification is fourfold: (1) primary, equivalent to the 'efficacious grace' of systematic theology (cf. II Thess 2:13; I Pet 1:2); (2) positional, a perfect standing in holiness, true of all believers from the moment of conversion (cf. Acts 20:32; 26:18); (3) progressive, equivalent to daily growth in grace (cf. Jn 17:17; Eph 5:26; II Cor 7:1); (4) prospective, or ultimate likeness to Christ positionally and practically (cf. I Thess 5:23). The use of the perfect participle here refers to positional sanctification. Christians are saints now, not by human canonization, but by divine operation. Paul's aim in the letter was to bring the Corinthians' practical life into more definite conformity to their position in Christ. **With all that in every place call upon the name of Jesus Christ our Lord, both theirs and ours** does not extend the address to all Christians, but guards against the tendency to confine the teaching to Corinth only (cf. I Cor 4:17; 7:17; 11:16; 14:33, 36), a further confirmation of the oneness of the body.

3. The familiar **grace** and **peace** refer to grace and peace *in* the Christian life. They do not refer to the grace that brings a man *into* that life and the peace that follows thereupon (cf. Jn 1:16; 14:27).

B. The Thanksgiving. 1:4-9.

The thanksgiving is not ironical, nor is it addressed only to a certain part of the assembly. Still less is it simply a courteous attempt "to win friends and influence people," although it is true that "blame comes best on the back of praise" (MNT, p. 7). It is, rather, a truthful estimate of the position of the Corinthians in Christ and forms the basis of Paul's appeal for practical conformity to this. The apostle singles out their gifts of utterance and knowledge for special emphasis.

4. **Grace of God.** That which is responsible for the spiritual gifts mentioned later. 5. **Utterance** probably includes more than the gift of tongues (cf. 12:8-10, 28-30). The Corinthians had a wide assortment of utterance gifts (see 14:26). 7. The result of their enrichment is that they **come behind in no gift.** While the word *charisma,* translated **gift,** has a wide variety of meanings, it probably here refers to spiritual gifts in the technical sense (cf. 12:1 – 14:40). **Waiting,** a strong double compound word, meaning *to await ardently* or *eagerly* (Arndt, p. 82), expresses the believers' attitude as they use the gifts in God's service.

8. **Confirm** was used in Koine Greek as a technical legal term referring to a properly guaranteed security *(ibid.,* p. 138). They have God's guarantee that

they shall be in his presence at Christ's return. **Blameless.** Literally, *chargeless*, or "unimpeachable" (Leon Morris, *The First Epistle of Paul to the Corinthians*, p. 37). "It implies not merely acquittal, but the absence of even a charge or accusation against a person" (W. E. Vine, *Expository Dictionary of New Testament Words*, I, 131; cf. Rom 8:33). **9.** Everything is grounded on the fact that **God is faithful. Fellowship** has as its primary thrust the concept of having a share in, then a common share. Thus, all believers have a share in Christ and, consequently, a share in one another. This is the hinge upon which Paul attacks the party spirit, the climax of the attack being reached in 3:21-23.

II. The Divisions in the Church. 1:10—4:21.

A. The Fact of the Divisions. 1:10-17.

The first major burden of the letter, dissension in the church, is now considered. The apostle will not leave it until he pens the words, "What will ye? shall I come unto you with a rod, or in love, and in the spirit of meekness?" (4:21) The opening verses of the passage (1:10-17) state the facts as reported by servants from Chloe's house. **10. Now** (adversative *de*, "but") introduces Paul's diagnosis. His initial words are an appeal for unity. **Perfectly joined together.** A versatile Greek word, used of the adjustment of parts of an instrument, of the setting of bones by a physician, of the mending of nets (Mk 1:19), as well as of the outfitting of a ship for a voyage. Adjustment with a view to unity is the appeal.

11. For. Introducing the reason for the appeal. **Contentions.** A work of the flesh (cf. Gal 5:20), revealing the presence of divisions.

12. Now this I say. Better, *Now I mean this*. The party of **Apollos** suggests a group who preferred the more polished style and rhetoric of the gifted Alexandrian. There are many modern members of this clique, such as the woman who confessed, "I almost weep every time I hear my minister pronounce that blessed word *Mesopotamia!*" The party of **Cephas** apparently doubted Paul's credentials, preferring the link with Jerusalem by Peter. The ones who were **of Christ** disdained all connections with the others, thus becoming a party themselves. The following words plainly presuppose the disapproval of this group (cf. ICC, p. 12; II Cor 10:7) by Paul.

13. The interrogations make appeals to the unity of the body of Christ and to the believers' identification with him. Barclay comments on **in the name** (lit., *into the name)* as follows: "To give money into a man's name was to pay it into his account, into his personal possession. To sell a slave into a man's name was to give that slave into his absolute and undisputed possession. A soldier swore loyalty into the name of Caesar; he belonged absolutely to the Emperor" *(op. cit.*, p. 18).

14,16. Paul **thank**[s] **God** for the providence which led him to baptize so few at Corinth. It is clear that he does not here depreciate baptism; he simply puts it in its proper place, as a symbolic act pointing to the real fact of identification with Christ by faith. It is also clear that Paul *did* baptize. **17. For.** The reason he did not emphasize baptism. His primary task was to preach the good news. Could Paul have uttered these words if baptism were necessary for salvation? (cf. 4:15; 9:1,22; 15:1, 2) Hardly. His commission also involved no embellishment of the truth with the flowery speech of the professional rhetorician (cf. ICC, p. 15), thus emptying the Gospel of its content. The rendering **be made of none effect** leaves much to be desired. The verb *kenoō* means "to empty," that is, to deprive of substance. The Gospel's appeal is not to man's intellect, but to his sense of guilt by sin. The cross clothed in wisdom of words vitiates this appeal. The Gospel must never be presented as a human philosophical system; it must be preached as a salvation. **Wisdom of words** (lit., *wisdom of word)* marks the transition to Paul's analysis of the cause of the dissension at Corinth, this love of a false wisdom.

B. The Causes of the Divisions. 1:18—4:5.

In the first place, they have not understood the nature and character of the Christian message, the true wisdom (1:18—3:4). In the second place, their sectarian spirit indicates that they have no real understanding of the Christian ministry, its partnership under God in the propagation of the truth (3:5—4:5).

1) Cause one: Misconception of the Message. 1:18—3:4. First, the apostle shows that the Gospel is not a message

for the intellectual (1:18–25). This truth was amply demonstrated by the fact that the church at Corinth contained few worldly-wise persons (1:26-31) and that Paul preached no such message when in Corinth (2:1-5). Then, the apostle expounds the true wisdom of God, outlining its spiritual character (2:6-12), and its spiritual perception (2:13-16); and concludes with a frank statement that carnality accounts for the divisions (3:1-4).

18. For introduces the reason he did not come in wisdom of word. To the perishing, the cross must always appear to be foolishness. **Preaching** (lit., *word)* is evidently contrasted with **words** (v. 17; lit., *word).* Paul regarded the cross as God's saving instrumentality. **Perish** and **saved** (present tenses, but frequentative, rather than durative) vividly portray the constant stream of the lost toppling into eternity without Christ, and the fewer, but still constant, stream of the saved entering the door of eternal fellowship with Christ. **19,20. For it is written.** An appeal to Scripture for support. Good Pauline practice (cf. Isa 29:14; 19:12; 33:18). The words are God's denouncement of the policy of the 'wise' in Judah in seeking an alliance with Egypt when threatened by Sennacherib.

21. Pleased is more than a statement of willingness; it refers to God's happy purpose and plan (cf. Eph 1:5). **Preaching** refers to the content of the proclamation, not the method of delivery (cf. I Cor 2:4); it is the **message** (AV, *preaching)* which saves, a message designed for those who simply **believe. 22-25.** In paradoxical fashion, Paul claims, the **called** (cf. v. 2) have obtained what the sign-seeking **Jews** and the wisdom-loving **Greeks** (v. 22), or Gentiles (v. 24; the AV has *Greeks* again, but the attestation is weak) were after, **the power of God, and the wisdom of God. Christ crucified** is the secret. Jews and Greeks would not recognize their sin. Christ crucified does; hence, he is the power and wisdom of God. The use of the word **crucified** without the article strongly emphasizes the character in which Paul preached Christ, *as* crucified (cf. 2:2; Gal 3:1). A Christ without a cross could not save.

26. For introduces the "unanswerable *argumentum ad hominem*" (ICC, p. 24). "Why, look at your own ranks, my brothers," is Moffatt's rendering (MNT, p. 19). A glance at their own church would prove Paul's point, for there were **not many** of the wise and mighty among them. **Calling** continues the emphasis on God's initiative in man's salvation. In the Pauline tradition was the famous dying remark of John Allen of the Salvation Army, "I deserve to be damned; I deserve to be in hell; but God interfered!" **27,28.** The threefold **God hath chosen** continues the emphasis. **29.** The purpose of God's methodology is stated negatively here and positively in the last verse of the chapter. As Bengel once said, "Glory not *before* Him, but *in* Him." Jonah was absolutely right in saying, "Salvation is of the Lord" (Jon 2:9; cf. Jer 9:23,24).

30. But introduces the blessed contrast. **Of him** and not of wisdom are the Corinthians **in Christ Jesus.** Here is the only solid ground of boasting. Due to the construction of the Greek sentence, it is clear that wisdom is the dominant word, and that the nouns **righteousness, sanctification,** and **redemption** amplify and explain wisdom. Wisdom here, then, is not practical wisdom, but positional wisdom, God's wise plan for our complete salvation. **Righteousness** is forensic, the righteousness given in justification, or that which Paul expounds in Rom 1:1–5:21. **Sanctification** is used in its immediate and complete sense (cf. I Cor 1:2). Righteousness enables one to stand before God in the court of divine justice, while sanctification equips one to serve him in the temple of divine service. It is that which Paul outlines in Rom 6:1–8:17. **Redemption,** in view of the order of words, is probably the final redemption of the body (cf. Rom 8:23), that which occupies the apostle in Rom 8:18-39. **31. That.** The aim of this work of God is to glorify him in his grace, a purpose gloriously achieved. For the worldly-wise have been brought to nought, and the called who believe now enjoy a sovereignly given salvation sufficient for all the exigencies of time and eternity.

2:1-5. The theme continues, the writer now bringing forward his own witness among the Corinthians. It, too, was not based on worldly wisdom, either in its message (vv. 1,2), method (vv. 3,4), or motive (v. 5). **And I** makes the connection.

1,2. Testimony (internally preferable to *mystery,* the reading of many ancient manuscripts). There is no hint from this passage, nor from Acts 17, that Paul preached the simple message of Christ

crucified because of a sense of failure (as some have suggested) in the philosophical approach at Athens. As a matter of fact, the approach at Athens was not basically philosophical. Paul's sermon began with the Biblical revelation of creation (cf. Acts 17:24) and ended on the note of the Resurrection (Acts 17:31). Moffatt is right in saying: "At Athens he had not been able to start from any belief in resurrection, as he could in a synagogue" (MNT, p. 22; cf. N. B. Stonehouse, *Paul Before the Areopagus and Other New Testament Studies*, pp. 25-27).

3,4. Instead of human persuasion, Paul's method involved the **demonstration of the Spirit and of power.** The word **demonstration** refers to the producing of proofs in argument in court (MM, pp. 60,61). The new life of the Corinthians was a conclusive proof of God's power in them (cf. I Thess 1:5). **5. That** introduces the motive. Paul's simple preaching was designed to prevent the Corinthians' holding a **faith** that rested upon logical and philosophical arguments, a faith at the mercy of other arguments of the same nature. "What depends upon a clever argument is at the mercy of a cleverer argument" (ICC, p. 34). A faith, however, that stands **in the power of God** has a solid and enduring foundation.

2:6-12. Someone might infer at this point that Paul had no use for wisdom and that he held Christian truth to be outside the realm of the intellect. The apostle meets this by pointing out that the Gospel does contain a wisdom, but a spiritual wisdom. The opening words, **but a wisdom we do speak,** make the connection (*sophian,* "wisdom," has the position of emphasis in the Greek text).

6. Perfect, mature in the things of God (cf. 14:20; Phil 3:15), is equated by Paul with **spiritual** (I Cor 2:15). The clause, **but a wisdom we do speak among the perfect,** may be a summary statement of the section The **wisdom** would be the subject of verses 6-12, the *speaking,* or teaching, of it the subject of verse 13 (note the **we speak**), and **the perfect** the subject of the remainder of the section (F. Godet, *Commentary on St. Paul's First Epistle to the Corinthians,* I, 135). **7-9. A mystery.** Not something mysterious, but a divine secret, truth which is undiscoverable apart from divine revelation.

10-12. To us (emphatic position in the Greek text) contrasts believers with the world. To them **God has revealed** his wisdom **by his spirit,** who has been given that believers **might know the things that are freely given by God.**

13. Paul moves naturally to the method of communication. This wisdom, he says, **we speak in words which the Holy Ghost teacheth** – an emphatic declaration that the knowledge of divine truth is not traceable to intellect and mental capacity primarily. Paul traces it to the possession of the Spirit of God, the perfect Teacher and the perfect Judge of doctrine. **The words** have been used as support by proponents of verbal inspiration (a true doctrine). But Paul here writes **we speak,** not *we write,* thus referring to oral presentation. The final clause poses a difficult interpretive problem. **Comparing** (AV) may be correct, for the word means this in its only other NT occurrence (II Cor 10:12). The context, however, is decidedly against this unusual meaning of the word. It may also have the sense of "interpreting," or "explaining" (cf. Gen 40:8; Dan 5:15-17, LXX). The rendering would then be, *explaining spiritual things to spiritual men* (cf. RSV). Or, the usual meaning of the word, "combine," may be the sense, the rendering being, *combining spiritual things with spiritual words* (preserving the reference to *words* just preceding). This appears preferable, and Paul thereby refers to "wedding kindred speech to thought" (ExpGT, II, 783). The apostle received his truth from God and clothed it in language given by God's Spirit. His claim is that his utterance was God-given and Spirit-led.

14. The subjective perception of this truth now becomes the topic. **But** introduces the contrast with **the natural man,** the non-Christian (cf. Jude 19; Rom 8:9). The Greek word rendered **natural** means "dominated by the soul," the principle of physical life. This soulish man does not **receive** (lit., *welcome;* cf. Acts 17:11; I Thess 1:6) divine truth, nor **can he know** it, for it is **discerned** by the Spirit (cf. I Cor 2:10,11). Human ears cannot hear high-frequency radio waves; deaf men are unable to judge music contests; blind men cannot enjoy beautiful scenery, and the unsaved are incompetent to judge spiritual things, a most important practical truth.

15,16. The **spiritual** man has the potentiality to understand **all things.** He is **judged of no man** (who is not spiritual), for the unspiritual do not have the necessary relation to the Spirit to judge the spiritual. This explains why Christians are often enigmas to worldlings, and sometimes enigmas to carnally minded Christians. Much controversy among Christians can be traced to this principle.

3:1-4. The application to the Corinthians' condition, indicated by the change from the first person (2:6-15) to the second (3:1-4), is now made. **And I, brethren, could not speak unto you** makes the connection smoothly.

1. Their immaturity prevented Paul's feeding them meat on his first visit. The Greek word for **carnal** (from *sarkinos)* means literally, *made of flesh,* being the equivalent of the expression, *in the flesh* (A-S, p. 402). Back of *sarkinos* is the thought of weakness (cf. Mt 26:41), as **babes** confirms. At Paul's first visit the Corinthians were weak, for the simple reason that they were new believers. The apostle attaches no blame to those in this condition.

2,3. A serious charge of spiritual inability is made in **neither yet now are ye able** (a very strong expression in the Greek). The reason **(for)** is that they are **still carnal.** An important word change must be noted. **Carnal** here is not *sarkinos,* but *sarkikos,* which means, literally, *characterized by the flesh,* being the equivalent of *after the flesh* (cf. Rom 8:4). Back of it is the thought of willfulness, and Paul does attach blame to those in this condition. Weakness prolonged becomes willfulness. Refusal to respond to the milk of the Word prevents reception of the meat of the Word. **And divisions** (AV) is not a genuine reading, although the thought is in the context (I Cor 3:4).

Paul has described four types of men. The first, *the natural man,* is the man without the Spirit, who needs the new birth (cf. Jn 3:1-8). The second is the *carnal-weak man* (I Cor 3:1), the babe in Christ, who needs growth through reception of the milk of the Word. The third type is the *carnal-willful man,* the older, yet immature, Christian, who needs restoration to fellowship, or the healthy condition conducive to the taking of nourishment, by confession of his willfulness, or sin (cf. I Jn 1:9). The fourth is the *spiritual* or *mature man,* who has responded to the milk and grown into spiritual adulthood, so that he is strong and able to take the meat of the Word (I Cor 2:15; 3:2). This is the man God would have every Christian to be. That Paul equates *the mature man* with *the spiritual man* is evident from a comparison of 2:6 with 2:15 (cf. 3:1; he contrasts **babes** with the **spiritual).** He also states that the wisdom of God is for **the perfect,** but he never uses the term again in the section. Instead, he writes of **the spiritual man** (2:15; 3:1), who has unlimited capacity to **judge all things.** The analogy of the physical life with all of this is its best illustration.

2) Cause two: Misconception of the Ministry. 3:5 – 4:5. The second reason for divisions, misunderstanding of the Christian ministry, is now discussed. Ministers are simply servants; actually, it is God who works (3:5-9). They are responsible for the proper materials as they build in the temple of God, the Church (3:9-17). One must not glory in any one of such men, for they all belong to each believer (3:18-23) and will be judged by God alone (4:1-5).

5. Who. Literally, *what.* This draws attention from the men to their functions (Morris, *op. cit.,* p. 64). Paul and Apollos were nothing more than **ministers,** servants of God. **6.** Paul **planted** and Apollos **watered,** but only God could make the seed grow. **8,9.** In the work Paul and Apollos were *one,* that is, in harmony. However, in the matter of **reward,** distinctions will be made. **Labourers together with God** may mean that they were fellow workers with one another who belong to God, or fellow workers with God. The context favors the former.

10. God's building (v. 9) leads to a discussion of the construction of it. It must be emphasized that Paul had in mind *builders* and *works,* not *believers* and *life; service,* and not *salvation* is the theme. The **grace of God** is the divine enablement given Paul for the planting of the churches. God might have used angels, or even sinners, but to use the "chief" of sinners (cf. I Tim 1:15) was a never ending marvel to the beloved apostle. **I have laid** (aorist tense, emphasizing the event) points to the initial preaching, while **another buildeth** (present tense, indicating the continual building) includes Apollos' work (cf. I Cor 3:6). **11.** One must be careful, for **Jesus Christ** is the one and only foundation (cf. Jn 8:12; 10:9; 14:6; Acts 4:12).

12. There are three types of builders – the wise man (vv. 12,14), the unwise (v. 15), and the foolish, who injures the building (v. 17). Three different results follow. Even among God's laborers two types of labor may be expended, the one solid and enduring, the other perishable and passing (the foolish laborer does not belong to God; v. 17). **13.** The phrase, **every man's work,** looks at individual responsibility. **The day** is the day of the judgment seat of Christ (cf. 4:5; II Cor 5:10), before which only believers appear. **Of what sort it is** indicates that the basis of judgment is *quality* of work, not *quantity,* a comforting thing for those of little gift (cf. I Cor 4:2).

14. Paul does not explain the nature of the reward (cf. II Jn 8). **15. Shall suffer loss.** Loss of reward, not loss of salvation. There are no differences among the Lord's *sheep;* there may be differences among his *servants* (cf. Lk 19:17). **He himself** (emphatic) contrasts the person with his work and pointedly upholds the believer's security. **By fire.** Better, *through fire.* The thought back of it is of one's rushing through fire to safety as the building crumbles (the preposition is local; cf. ICC, p. 65).

16,17. The third class of builder, who injures the building, is the non-Christian professor, who is not a possessor (cf. Gal 2:4; II Pet 2:1-22). **Defile** and **destroy** are renderings of the same Greek word, which is much stronger than **suffer loss** (I Cor 3:15). The **temple** is the local church, but surely the local church as the local manifestation of one true temple of God, the Church Invisible, composed of all true believers in Christ.

18-23. There follows a warning to those who think they are wise (vv. 18-20), and an exhortation to glory in the possession of all things, including Paul, Apollos, and Cephas (vv. 21-23). **Seemeth.** Better, *thinketh.* Each believer belongs to Christ, not to some human servant (rebuke to the followers of Paul, Apollos, and Cephas), and all believers belong to him (rebuke to the Christ party; cf. 1:12). Paul is a master teacher!

4:1-5. The analysis of the causes of division comes to a close here. God's ministers are servants, whose sole responsibility is to be faithful (vv. 1,2). Their judgment belongs only to the Lord (vv. 3,4). Therefore, all judgment must await his coming (v. 5). There was to be no pre-judgment seat judgment!

1. Ministers (different in the Greek from the word in 3:5) conveys the thought of subordination, the word originally referring to one who rowed in the lower tier of a trireme (cf. Lk 1:2). **Stewards** were administrators in charge of large estates; directed privilege is the thought. **2.** Reliability is the one necessary virtue for all servants and stewards, especially in the things of God.

3. Paul repudiates judgment by others, as well as judgment by himself. **Man's judgment** (lit., *man's day)* may glance back to 3:13. It means nothing to Paul that man has his day of judgment now. **4. For** explains his unconcern. **By myself** (lit., *against myself)* is a remarkable claim. Paul experienced unbroken fellowship (cf. 1:9); his practice conformed to his position. He had not failed as a steward. **5. Therefore** (the conclusion) since the Lord alone can judge, judgment must await him. At the proper **time** he will perform it capably and completely, probing into **the hidden things of darkness.** That time is his coming (cf. 1:7). And – wonder of wonders! – **every man** (believer) shall have some **praise from God.**

C. The Application and Conclusion. 4:6-21.

Paul now asks a number of indignant questions to demonstrate the pride of the Corinthian believers (vv. 6-13), and then concludes on a gentler note, reminding them of their relation to him (vv. 14-21). He was their father, and therefore they, the children, were to follow him. Otherwise he might have to use the rod when he visited them (v. 21).

6. I have in a figure transferred is the rendering of a verb which means "to change the outward appearance," the thing itself remaining the same (cf. Frederick Field, *Notes on the Translation of the New Testament*, p. 169). *I have adapted* would be a good translation. **These things** refers to 3:5–4:5, not to 1:10–4:5. Paul and Apollos were simply illustrations of the Corinthian situation. The writer omitted the names of the real culprits to prevent resentment. **Not to think of men above that which is written** is difficult. Perhaps a better rendering is, *not to go beyond that which is written;* or RSV, *to live according to scripture.* The apostle desired them to walk by the Word (cf. R. A. Ward, "Salute to Translators," *Interpretation,* 8:310, July, 1954; C. F. D. Moule, *An Idiom Book of New Testament Greek,* p. 64. A marginal gloss is their solution).

7. For explains why pride is pointless. The pronouns are singular; Paul is addressing the individual. Augustine saw the truth of God's grace through the second question in this verse. **8. Now** (MNT, *already,* p. 48) looks back to **before the time** (v. 5). The Messianic age, to begin after the judgment seat of Christ and his second coming to the earth, had begun for the Corinthians, Paul reproachfully wrote. "They (had) got a private millenium of their own" (ICC, p. 84). The verse affords some evidence for Paul's concept of the Kingdom.

9. The **apostles,** in sharp contrast, were far from entrance into the Kingdom. In fact, they were doomed to death, like the condemned criminals, or prisoners, who fought with wild beasts and seldom survived at the close of pagan festivals and exhibitions. Or, Paul may have had in mind the triumphal procession of a Roman general, at the end of which walked those captured soldiers who were being taken to the arena to fight with wild beasts (cf. 15:32; II Cor 2:14-17). In the arena of the world of men and angels, the doomed apostles were a **spectacle** (the English word *theater* is derived from the Greek word, making a vivid picture). **10-13.** A series of caustic contrasts between the apostles and the Corinthians, designed to admonish the believers. The new dispensation had not begun for the apostles!

14. My beloved sons introduces the tender solicitude of a father for his spiritual children. **15. For.** Paul explains why he may exhort them as a father. **Instructors** were Roman slave-guardians, responsible for general supervision of children until they reached adulthood and could put on the *toga virilis* (cf. Gal 3:24). It is as if the apostle were saying that the Corinthians had many supervisors of their spiritual life, but only one who brought them into that life. The **begotten** introduces a third figure of Paul's relation to them (cf. I Cor 3:6, "planted," and 3:10, "laid the foundation"). He did not bring them into life through good advice, but through the good news, **through the gospel.**

16. Paul was the rare preacher who could say, **Be ye followers of me** (lit., *imitators of me).* Most men must say, "Do as I *say,* not as I *do*" (cf. Barclay, *op. cit.,* p. 46). **17-20.** Timothy was to bring them **into remembrance.** Dr. Johnson remarked that more people required to be reminded than required to be instructed (MNT, p. 51). This is not true, but there is much need for the reminding ministry. **The kingdom of God** (cf. v. 8). The Corinthians' kingdom was a kingdom **in word,** not **in power. 21.** A challenge concludes. Will it be **the rod** of discipline that they will choose, or **love and the spirit of meekness** produced by the restoration of fellowship? The answer lies with them. **The rod** introduces the note of discipline, predominant in the next section of the letter.

III. The Disorders in the Church. 5:1–6:20.

A. The Absence of Discipline. 5:1-13.

It is frequently said that the only Bible the world will read is the daily life of the Christian, and that what the world needs is a revised version! The next two chapters are designed by Paul to produce a Corinthian revised version, so that orthodoxy might be followed by orthopraxy (cf. Roy L. Laurin, *Life Matures,* pp. 103,104). Chapter 5 concerns a known case of incest in the church. The believers, rather than mourning over it, were complacently permitting the matter to go unjudged, perhaps even being proud of their liberty (vv. 1,2; cf. 6:12). Paul expresses his attitude in the matter (5:3-5), urges the church to exercise discipline (vv. 6-8), and concludes with a clarification of the previous letter's instruction (vv. 9-13). **Puffed up** (v. 2) marks a slight connection with the preceding (cf. 4:6,18,19), but the real connection is with what follows (cf. v. 1; 6:9,13-20). Both chapters deal with disorders. The lack of a connective in 5:1 confirms this, and also gives the opening words an explosive force in the ears of the serene Corinthians, coolly relaxing "at ease in Zion."

1. Commonly. Better, *actually* (cf. Arndt, p. 568). The **fornication** was incest, forbidden by the Law (Lev 18:8; Deut 22:22). **Have** (present tense) suggests some sort of permanent union (cf. Mt 14:4). The singling out of the man may suggest that the woman, his stepmother, was not a Christian. The father may have been dead or divorced. **Named.** Omit in view of weak textual attestation. The sin was prohibited by Roman law. **2.** Inflated by false liberty, the church was **puffed up.** A church can never prevent evil absolutely, but it should always practice discipline. **Be taken away from you** refers to ecclesiastical censure and excommunication. **3,4.** Paul had already judged the matter in spirit. His words gave them directions regarding proper action.

5. The substance of his judgment is here. **To deliver to Satan** is difficult (cf. I Tim 1:20). It probably refers to committing the man to the world as belonging to Satan (cf. I Jn 5:19). **Destruction of the flesh** has been taken in the moral sense of the annulment of the fleshly appetites. **Destruction** is too severe for this view, although, of course, discipline is to be remedial. It is probably better to see here the thought of bodily chastisement, to which persistent sin leads, according to NT teaching, not only in this letter (cf. I Cor 11:30), but also elsewhere (cf. I Jn. 5:16,17). The purpose of the action is given in the following clause.

6. The principle back of the need of discipline is here. "Never say by way of excuse that after all it's only one case. Only one, but it will infect **the whole** group (xv. 33)" (MNT, p. 57). Sin always spreads and contaminates if left alone, just as poison, weeds, and cancer do. **7. Therefore.** Decisive action is necessary. **As ye are unleavened** expresses the position of the believers, to which their condition is to correspond. Their cleansing is to be manifested in clean living. **For** explains. The background of the apostle's remarks is the Feasts of the Passover and Unleavened Bread. The Passover (cf. Ex 12:1-28) prefigured Christ as God's Lamb, who would take away the sin of the world by his sacrifice on Golgotha (cf. Jn 1:29). The Feast of Unleavened Bread (cf. Ex 12:15-20; 13:1-10), during which the Israelites were to have no leaven in their homes (leaven referring, of course, to sin typically), continued for the week following the slaying of the lamb. This feast prefigured the life of holiness that should follow the slaying and eating of the lamb, seven days being a complete circle of time. The Passover, then, is typical and illustrative of the work of Christ in dying for his own. This has taken place, so Paul writes **is sacrificed for us** (aorist tense, looking at the event as a once-for-all thing). The Feast of Unleavened Bread is illustrative of the believer's walk in holiness, a continuous thing, and so Paul writes **let us go on keeping the feast** (v. 8; present tense, durative action). And just as a crumb of leaven in the house of the Israelite meant judgment (cf. Ex 12:15), so sin in the believer's life means judgment. Hence the need of discipline.

8. The conclusion **(therefore)** of Paul's exhortation is here. Purity and rectitude were to characterize the believer, not the wickedness of the man and the church in this matter of incest. These godly virtues were to be the food of the Christian's feast.

9. The apostle now clarifies instructions given in a previous letter (see Introduction), a letter now lost. **10,11.** A Christian must have some contact with the world; otherwise he would have to **go out of the world,** a manifest impossibility (at least before the advent of the space age!). The key to understanding the command of verse 9 is the verb **to company with** (vv. 9,11), which means literally *to mix up together with* (cf. Arndt, p. 792). The thought is that of familiar fellowship. The apostle knew that some fellowship with the world must take place in the daily pursuits of life. However, the brother under discipline was to be denied fellowship, and particularly were the believers not **to eat with such an one,** the most obvious act of fellowship.

12. For explains why Paul in the lost letter was not referring to the world, but to brethren, when he spoke of denial of fellowship. He was not concerned with the ones **that** [were] **without;** they were in God's province (cf. A. R. Fausset, in JFB V, 297). The Corinthians, however, were obligated to judge the ones **within. 13.** The **therefore** (AV) should be omitted, which gives the final sentence of excommunication an emphatic summary force (cf. Deut 24:7).

B. The Lawsuits Before the Heathen. 6:1-11.

The discussion of disorders continues. While there is no connecting particle in 6:1, the idea of *judging* clearly links the two chapters. The judicial competency of the church among its members is in view in both. Godet has put it well, " 'Not only do ye not judge those whom you have a mission to judge **(them that are within)**; but, moreover, ye go to have yourselves judged by those who are beneath you **(them that are without)**!' " (*op. cit.*, I, 284). The question of lawsuits is introduced (v. 1) and then met (vv. 2-11). The solution features the threefold occurrence of **know ye not** (Gr., *ouk oidate;* vv. 2,3,9).

1. Dare any of you (very emphatic in the Greek text). What audacity for the *justified* (although Greeks were given to litigiousness) to go before the *unjustified* for justice! (cf. v. 11). **2.** The first point in the rebuttal is the known fact that **the saints shall judge the world,** because of their union with the Messiah, to whom all judgment is committed (cf. Jn 5:22; Mt 19:28). **3.** The second point is the known fact that **we shall judge angels; how much more, then, things that pertain to this life** (cf. Jn 5:22; Jude 6; II Pet 2:4,9).

4. Then introduces an inference, somewhat clouded by a problem of translation. **Set to judge** may be taken as an imperative or as an indicative. If indicative, it may also be declarative or interrogative. Probably the indicative with interrogative force is to be preferred, the sense then being, **Are you setting them to judge who are least esteemed by the church? 5.** A very ironical suggestion that there may not be a **wise man** among the 'wise' Corinthians!

7,8. A better course is suggested. **Fault** may be rendered *defeat,* the point being made that resorting to law against a brother constitutes a loss of case already.

9. Paul's third point is an appeal to "wider principles" (ICC, p. 117). The unrighteous, or unjust, are not qualified to judge; only believers, the just, may judge. The negative is presented first (vv. 9,10), followed by the positive (v. 11). The emphasis in **kingdom of God** rests upon **God;** the unjust have no place in his kingdom. The following catalogue of sins proves that Paul and James are in basic agreement. Both affirm that genuine faith produces good works (cf. Eph 2:8-10), and that the absence of good works indicates lack of faith (cf. Jas 2:14-26). The prevailing moral laxity of the Greeks and Romans may have prompted the apostle's emphasis here upon unnatural vice. For example, Socrates, as well as fourteen of the first fifteen Roman emperors, practiced unnatural vice (cf. Barclay, *op. cit.,* p. 60).

11. The positive appeal is here. **And such were some of you** points to the depths from which the grace of God in Christ had rescued them. **Ye are washed.** Literally, *ye allowed yourselves to be washed* (a permissive middle voice), or, *ye washed yourselves* (a direct middle, stressing the active side of faith; cf. Acts 22:16; Gal 5:24). **Washed, sanctified,** and **justified** reflect the new position of the Corinthians. The mention of sanctification before justification is no problem, since Paul has in mind positional truth (see I Cor 1:2,30). The verbs refer to the same thing with differing emphases, the one stressing the believer's cleansing, the next the believer's new calling, and the final one the believer's new standing. **Justified** stands last, as a fitting climax to the argument about seeking justice before the unjust (vv. 1-8).

C. The Moral Laxity in the Church. 6:12-20.

Paul turns his attention to the moral laxity that polluted the church, apparently caused by the application of the truth of Christian liberty to the sexual realm. The question is: If there are no restrictions in food, one appetite of the body, why must there be in sexual things, another physical desire? Paul's reply, in which he begins with the principle of liberty and applies it to fornication specifically, again features the threefold occurrence of **Know ye not** (vv. 15,16,19).

12. The principle of liberty is stated, with two limitations: (1) expediency (cf. 10:23); (2) self-control. **Lawful** and **power,** from the same root, form a designed play on words: "All things are in my power, but I will not be brought under the power of anything." The indulgence in a habit which has one in its grip is not liberty but slavery.

13. While **meats** are **for the belly and the belly for meats** (necessary for one another), this relation is not true of the body and fornication. The body is designed to glorify the Lord, and the Lord is necessary to the body for this to take place. Paul uses the term **body** here in a broader sense than simply the physical tabernacle. It is almost equivalent to the man's personality, much like the use of the word *somebody,* or *everybody* (cf. MNT, pp. 68,69,71-73; Morris, *op. cit.,* p. 100; Moule, *op. cit.,* pp. 196,197). In verse 19 he appears to equate **body** with **you.** This, of course, is not always Paul's usage (II Cor 12:3). **14.** A further difference between the body and the belly and the body and fornication lies in the fact that the body is destined for resurrection, while the belly is to be brought to nought (v. 13). The permanence of the body has more than theoretical significance. For example, what about the practice of cremation?

15. By reason of the believer's union with Christ (cf. 12:12-27), fornication robs the Lord of that which is his. **Take.** Better, *take away.* **16.** The second reason is expressed here. **What** should be omitted. **Or know ye not** is the preferred reading. Not only is the Lord robbed, but a new union takes place (cf. v. 15; Gen 2:24). The practical proof of this is that a new personality may result from the union. **17. One spirit.** One of the strongest expressions of unity and security in the Word of God. As one author has put it, "The sheep may wander from the shepherd, the branch may be cut off from the vine; the member may be severed from the body . . . but when two spirits blend in one, what shall part them?" (Arthur T. Pierson, *Knowing the Scriptures,* p. 146)

18. Flee (present tense for habitual action). The positive command. Morris suggests, "Make it your habit to flee" *(op. cit.,* p. 102). Someone has said, "While it is often claimed that there is safety in numbers, there are times when there is more safety in exodus!" Joseph's experience comes to mind (cf. Gen 39:1-12). The final phrases, **without the body** and **against the body,** are difficult. Perhaps the meaning is that other sins, such as drunkenness, have effects *on* the body, but fornication is a sin wrought *within* the body and involves a monstrous denial of union with Christ by union with the harlot.

19. The final reason is the fact that the **body is the temple of the Holy Ghost. Your body.** A "distributive" expression, i.e., *the body of each one of you* (cf. Charles J. Ellicott, *Paul's First Epistle to the Corinthians,* p. 107). The body of the individual believer is the Spirit's temple (cf. 3:16). How incongruous it is to hear, as one often does, believers praying for the coming of the Spirit!

20. For introduces the reason believers are not their own. The Spirit occupies that which God has obtained by purchase. One can demonstrate ownership by purchase and by occupancy. Both of these things God has done; hence Christians are not their **own,** but *His own* (cf. Jn 13:1). **Bought** (aorist tense) refers to Golgotha, where the price was paid. The figure is that of sacral manumission, whereby a slave, by paying the price of his freedom into the temple treasury, was regarded thereafter as the slave of the god and no longer the slave of his earthly master. **Therefore glorify,** the logical conclusion, is both negative and positive. Negatively, a believer should eliminate defiling things, such as fornication, and positively he should display the One who had come to dwell within. The terrible price of the priceless blood (cf. I Pet 1:18,19) demanded nothing less than this. **And in your spirit, which are God's** have weak manuscript support.

IV. The Difficulties in the Church. 7:1–15:58.

A. The Counsel Concerning Marriage. 7:1-40.

Having discussed the things that came to him by way of report (cf. 1:11; 5:1), the apostle now turns to matters raised in correspondence (cf. 7:1, *peri de;* see Introduction). The problems of marriage are introduced first. The chapter, after a prologue dealing with general principles (vv. 1-7), contains discussions of the problems of the married (vv. 8-24) and of the unmarried (vv. 25-40).

1) The Prologue. 7:1-7. The apostle sets forth the general principle that, while celibacy is a matter of personal preference (vv. 6,7), yet marriage is a duty for those who do not have the gift of continence (vv. 1,2), a real marriage with due provision for the sexual needs of each partner (vv. 3-5).

1. Now concerning the things whereof ye wrote unto me. The equivalent of our modern formula, *Regarding your letter.* It is possible that Paul had been asked to approve celibacy as a duty for all. He grants the state is **good. 2.** Marriage, however, is a duty for those to whom the evil society and habits of the day might prove too much. This is not a low view of marriage; it is an honest facing of the facts in order **to avoid fornication.** Literally, *fornications,* the plural referring perhaps to the many cases at Corinth (cf. 6:12-20). **3-5.** Genuine marriage, however, is a partnership, a union of two people who become "one flesh" (6:16), and involves mutual obligations, conjugal rights.

6,7. The preceding words were spoken by **concession** (AV, *permission),* not by **commandment.** Marriage is a *may,* not a *must.* The leading of the Lord, one's **gift** from God, is the pre-eminent thing (cf. Mt 19:10-12).

2) The Problems of Marriage. 7:8-38.

The writer now considers specific problems involving the married and the unmarried.

8,9. Addressed first are those who were unmarried at the time Paul wrote, but who had had sexual experience. **Unmarried,** probably widowers, being set over against **widows.** Unmarried men and virgins are dealt with elsewhere (vv. 1,2,25,28-38). **Abide** (aorist tense) is the lifelong and final decision. **10,11.** Paul's next word relates to the maintenance or severance of the marriage bond, in the case of believers' marriages (vv. 10,11) and mixed marriages (vv. 12-16). For believers the rule is, No separation, supported by the Lord's viewpoint, **yet not I, but the Lord** (cf. Mk 10:1-12). In the case of unapproved separation, Paul outlines two possibilities. The wife must **remain unmarried,** present tense, emphasizing the permanent state. Or she should **be reconciled,** aorist tense, emphasizing the once-for-all event, with no further separations.

12. But what of marriages in which one of the parties has become a Christian? Jewish law required the unbeliever to be put away (cf. Ezr 9:1–10:44). Again, the rule is, No separation (I Cor 7:12,13).

14. For. The first reason is that the unbelieving partner and the children of a mixed marriage are **sanctified.** This does not mean that a child born into a home where only one of the parents is a Christian is born "into the family of Christ" (cf. Barclay, *op. cit.,* p. 71). Paul simply means that the OT principle of the communication of uncleanness does not hold (cf. Hag 2:11-13). The union is lawful and confers privilege on the members (cf. ICC, p. 142), privileges such as the protection of God and the opportunity of being in close contact with one in God's family. This might ease the path to conversion for the unbelieving.

15. A second reason for the preservation of the union is found in the fact that God **has called to peace.** A curiously ambiguous situation, however, exists. Some interpreters feel that Paul here encourages the believer to permit the separation in the interests of preserving peace, if the unbeliever desires to depart. There might be war otherwise! On the other hand, Paul's thought may be that separation should be prevented if at all possible, since that would disrupt the peace of the marriage union. The general principle of the context (vv. 10,11) favors the second view, as well as the following verse. Nothing is said about a second marriage for the believer; it is vain to put words in Paul's mouth when he is silent. It is true that the verb "to depart" in the middle voice (it is middle in this verse) was almost a technical term for divorce in the papyri (MM, p. 695,696). This, however, really proves nothing here.

16. For. The third reason for no separation is that the salvation of the other member may be accomplished through preservation of the union. Others understand the statement to mean that separation should be willingly agreed to, since one can never know whether the partner will be converted or not. The general context favors the former view. But it is not easy to determine what Paul meant.

17-24. The apostle now summarizes, indicating that this principle of abiding in one's marital relationship is simply part of a more general principle touching every sphere of life. The rule in everything is to abide in one's calling, unless that calling be immoral. Three times Paul states the principle (vv. 17, 20,24), interspersing the declarations of principle with two illustrations, one religious (cf. Rom 2:28,29) and the other secular. The expression **with God,** which concludes the section, emphasizes the fact that the presence of God makes any secular work a work with God. In a sense, then, every Christian is engaged in "full-time Christian work." In the light of Paul's teaching here, is it not also a questionable thing to "pressure" young people into full-time service for God as missionaries, pastors, etc.? The thing of pre-eminent importance for every believer is to be in the calling of God for him.

25. Now concerning *(peri de)* indicates to the readers that an answer to another part of the church's letter follows. In the remainder of the chapter Paul deals with three groups: (1) the unmarried young (v. 25-35); (2) the parents (vv. 36-38); (3) widows (vv. 39,40). The section is bounded by two statements concerning the author's authority (vv. 25,40). The point of the paragraph is this: Celibacy is desirable, but not demanded.

26-28. It is good for a man so to be. Rather, *It is well for a person to remain as he is* (RSV). The first reason for remaining single is **the present distress,** a phrase probably referring to the pressure of the Christian life in an unfriendly world (cf. v. 28; II Tim 3:12). If the Christian life is difficult in itself, why impose more of a burden upon oneself with marriage? **29-31.** A second reason is suggested by the statement, **the time is short** (lit., *has been drawn together* so as to be short). The apostle refers to the time before the coming of the Lord (cf. Rom 13:11). All of life is to be lived in the light of this great fact. Then shall **the fashion of this world** pass **away** and a glorious new day dawn.

32-35. A third reason is found in these verses. It is expressed negatively in the words **I would have you without carefulness** (v. 32), and positively in the words **that ye may attend upon the Lord without distraction** (v. 35). A highly involved textual problem is posed by the words connecting verses 33 and 34. This may find its solution in modifying the words, **There is difference also between a wife and a virgin** (v. 34), to "Parted also by a similar division of interests are the married and the unmarried woman" (ICC, pp. 150,151). The point of the apostle is clear: Marriage is a distracting thing. This he states definitely at the end of verse 35. The words **that ye may attend upon the Lord without distraction** suggest the Lukan account of the incident of the Lord's visit to the house of Mary and Martha in Bethany. There are also several verbal connections in the Greek text between Luke's account and Paul's words (cf. Lk 10:38-42). It is as if Paul were tacitly saying that marriage makes Marthas out of Marys, thus preventing the choice of "that good part" – occupation with the Lord and his Word.

36-38. Parents are in view here. The passage must be understood in the light of the customs of the day. The father had control of the arrangements for his daughter's marriage. **Behaveth himself uncomely** refers to the withholding of marriage when there is evidence of the lack of the gift of continence. It is doubtful that Paul has in mind here "spiritual marriages," in which people went through a form of marriage and yet lived together as brother and sister (cf. Barclay, *op. cit.*, pp. 74,75; MNT, pp. 98-100). **Standeth stedfast,** i.e., does not think that he is behaving unseemly. **So then** introduces the summary, really a summary of the chapter. One does **well;** the other does **better.** The celibate state is not holier than the married state; celibacy simply has greater utility in serving the Lord. But even in marriage everything, as far as possible, is to be in subjection to His interests. The word **giveth in marriage** (v. 38) always has this sense in the NT (cf. Mt 22:30; 24:38); it never means simply *to marry,* which appears to clinch the interpretation just given as being the true one.

3) The Postscript. 7:39,40. Widows are granted **liberty to be married,** but **only in the Lord,** i.e., to Christians. This seems to indicate clearly that Paul would never have approved of mixed marriages (marriages between believers and unbelievers), a truth which has a wide application today. Paul reverts again to utility, however, when he writes **but she is happier if she so abide** (cf. v. 8). The concluding words appear to indicate that Paul thought his words here had divine approval (the **also** may point to some in Corinth who claimed the Spirit's approval for their unscriptural attitudes); and the fact that they have been preserved in Holy Writ may confirm this viewpoint.

B. The Counsel Concerning Things Sacrificed to Idols. 8:1–11:1.

The *peri de* (AV, *Now as touching)* indicates that a new subject begins here. **Things offered unto idols** were the remainders of animals sacrificed to heathen gods. Whether an animal was offered as a private or a public sacrifice, portions of the meat remained for the offerer. If offered as a private sacrifice, the flesh might be used for a banquet, to which were invited friends of the offerer. If offered as a public sacrifice, the meat left after the magistrates took what they wanted might be sold to the markets for resale to the people of the city. The problems, then, were these: (1) Might a Christian partake of meat offered to a false god in a heathen feast? (2) Might a Christian buy and eat flesh offered to idols? (3) Might a Christian, when invited to the home of a friend, eat flesh which had been offered to idols?

1) The Principles. 8:1-13. Paul first sets forth general principles to guide the believer in these ticklish problems.

1. We all have knowledge may be a quotation from their letter to him. Christians do possess knowledge, but it may be only superficial and incomplete (cf. vv. 2,7). **Knowledge,** in addition, is not sufficient for the solution of all problems, for by itself it **puffeth up. 2. He know-**

eth nothing yet refers to the true knowledge of God. While here, man's knowledge of God is always incomplete (cf. 13:12). **3.** To **love God** brings both a knowledge of God and a sense of God's knowledge of the individual. For example, in a palace everyone knows the king, but not everyone is known by the king. The second stage would indicate personal intimacy and consequent first-hand knowledge (cf. Godet, *op. cit.*, I, 410; Gal 4:9).

4. An idol is nothing in the world probably should be *there is no idol in the world.* An idol cannot really be a representation of God. How could wood or stone represent God's incorruptibility? **5.** The apostle admits, however, that there are those **called gods. 6. But to us** marks a forceful contrast. **Of whom are all things** refers to the first creation; the Father is the source of all (cf. Gen 1:1). **We in him** (lit., *we for him*) refers to the Father as the goal of the new creation, the Church. The Church's function is to glorify him. **By whom are all things** points to the Lord Jesus Christ as the agent of God in creation (cf. Jn 1:3). **We by him** presents him as the agent responsible for the new creation (cf. Col 1:15-18).

7. From here to the end of the chapter Paul expounds the words, **love builds up** (v. 1; AV, *charity edifieth).* This is necessary, for **not in every man** is the knowledge of the one God and one Lord, which enables one to eat idol flesh without harm. **With conscience of the idol** has weak attestation. The preferable reading is *by reason of being long accustomed to idols.* **8.** Paul points out that meat in itself will not bring believers near to God. **Commendeth.** The sense is *bring near.* "It is the clean heart, and not clean food, that will matter; and the weak brother confounds the two" (ICC, p. 170).

9. In the next few verses Paul warns the strong to **take heed** that their **liberty** (lit., *authority,* the exercise of their right) does not prove a stumbling block to the **weak.** In other words, knowledge will not solve the problem (cf. vv. 1-3). **10. Be emboldened** (lit., *be built up)* is ironic. Fine edification this is; it builds up to sin!

11. And (lit., *for)* introduces the reason why the strong believer has become a stumbling block. The sentence should be punctuated with a period, not a question mark. The last clause has great appeal. If Christ loved the brother enough to die for him, then the strong believer ought to love him enough to give up his right to eat certain meat. **Perish** refers to bodily perishing, not eternal perishing. The weak brother, persistently violating his conscience by eating something he thinks he should not, sins and makes himself liable to sin unto death (cf. 5:5; 11:30; I Jn 5:16,17). The tense is present; the process of perishing is going on as long as he persists in eating. **12.** The worst consequence of this matter is that the strong believers **sin against Christ** in sinning against the brethren. The argument is based on the unity of the body of Christ (cf. 12:12, 13,26).

13. Wherefore leads to Paul's conclusion. *Love,* not *light* (knowledge), solves the problem. On moral matters, about which the Word has spoken, the Word is supreme. On morally indifferent matters, such as eating meat offered to idols, liberty is to be regulated by love. Several things must be kept in mind, however. In the first place, the passage does not refer to legalists desirous of imposing their narrow-minded scruples on others. Such are not weak brethren, but willful brethren desirous of glorying in the subjection of others to their tenets (cf. Gal 6:11-13). This is tyranny, and Christianity must always be on guard against this. In the second place, it should be noted in this verse that the decision to follow the path of love rests with Paul, not with the weak. The strong are to yield to love's appeal voluntarily, not because the weak demand it (legalists always demand subjection to their laws). Finally, it is significant that Paul, in dealing with fornication and meat sacrificed to idols, does not appeal to the decree of the Jerusalem Council (cf. Acts 15:19, 20). Instead, he appeals to loftier spiritual concepts, which the Greeks would appreciate.

2) The Illustration of the Principles. 9:1-27. Paul does not diverge from the subject here. Rather, he illustrates the principles just set forth by an appeal to his own experience. As an apostle and one who also possessed Christian liberty, he could claim financial support from those to whom he preached (vv. 1-14). Actually, however, he refused to exercise his rights in order to gain a reward (vv. 15-23). Such a decision demanded personal discipline and privation (vv. 24-27). The Corinthians, of course, were to apply the lesson of self-denial and

discipline to the problem of meat sacrificed to idols.

1. Am I not free? This question precedes the question regarding apostleship in the leading manuscripts. There is an appropriateness in this order, too, for the advance from rights as a Christian to rights as an apostle provides a climactic opening of the section. **Have I not seen Jesus our Lord?** The basis of his qualification for the apostolate (cf. Acts 1:21,22). **Are not ye my work in the Lord?** Words designed to emphasize the genuineness of Paul's work among the Corinthians. **2,3.** The Corinthians were **the seal** of his apostleship. That is, they were the guarantee of spiritual fruit in his labors among them, or, in other words, the proof that God really "gave the increase" (cf. 3:5-7). **Them that examine me.** Those who questioned Paul's apostolic position and office. **This** looks backward (vv. 1-3), not forward (vv. 4-14).

4. Having settled the matter of apostleship, the apostle goes on to argue the authority or right of support, which was derived from the office. Compare 8:9, where the AV's "liberty" is the same word as **right** (AV, *power)* here. **To eat and drink** does not refer to idol meats, but to ordinary food and drink.

5,6. Five grounds for the right of maintenance can be discerned. The first, referred to here, might be called the example of others. **The brethren of the Lord,** who did not believe on him, were now missionaries (cf. Jn 7:5; Mt 13:55). The mention of **Cephas'** wife is interesting. If Peter was the first pope (he was *not,* of course), it is clear that he was a married one! (cf. Mt 8:14) Paul's right included support of his family. **7.** The second, the principle of common right, is presented by means of well-known illustrations — the soldier, the vine-planter, and the shepherd.

8-10. The third ground, the teaching of the Scriptures, is now introduced (cf. Deut 25:4). Paul claims that the OT teaches the right of maintenance for those who preach the Word. His use of Scripture here has often been impugned. It has been said that he shows disdain for the literal sense of the OT (cf. MNT, pp. 116,117). That is not true. All that Paul claims is that the passage in Deuteronomy has a deeper significance than the literal sense. Both senses, the literal and the allegorical (both are *spiritual* senses), are found in this passage. **Doth God take care for oxen?** The literal sense of the question must not be pressed. The Greek construction is such that the answer, "No," is expected. Paul means that God's care is not primarily for animals, but for men. However, God's care for animals is affirmed in many passages in the OT (cf. Ps 104:14,21,27; Mt 6:26). Luther's argument was bolder than Paul's. He said the passage in Deuteronomy was written altogether for our sakes, since oxen cannot read! The word **altogether** here probably has the sense of *doubtless* (ICC, p. 184).

11-13. The right of holy ministry, the fourth ground, is set forth here, and the argument turns on the greater value of the spiritual over the material. **Carnal things** are things for the body, the word **carnal** having here a neutral sense. **This power over you** is the teacher's privilege of partaking of the believers' material things. Apparently certain teachers had exercised their right over the Corinthians. But Paul triumphantly boasts that **we have not used this power.** His taking financial help might have **hinder[ed] the gospel of Christ,** for some might have thought he preached only for this. **Partakers with the altar** alludes to the rights of the priests of the old covenant (cf. Num 18:8-24). **14.** The command of the Lord, a fifth ground, concludes the claim to support from the church (cf. Mt 10:10; Lk 10:7).

15. The apostle now shows how love acted in his case, even though he had a perfect right to support from the Corinthians. He thus contrasts his personal sacrifice with the selfishness of those who were using their liberty in the matter of meats to the detriment of others. **But** marks the contrast, and the change to the first person marks the personal illustration, the illustration of knowledge regulated by love. **16.** The readers are led on to Paul's purpose in preaching without pay — namely, he desired a reward. **Necessity is laid upon me** refers to the call on the Damascus Road, a call he could not refuse.

17. For if I do this thing willingly introduces a supposition that could never be true of Paul. Thus, in his case there could be no reward for preaching, for he preached by necessity. The clue to Paul's argument is found in the expression, **a dispensation of the gospel is committed unto me.** A *stewardship* (AV, **dispensation)** was a work committed to one under an owner. The steward, therefore, was of the class of slaves (cf. Lk 12:42, 43). And a slave received no recompense; he had to work (cf. Lk 17:10). Paul, therefore, had to introduce the idea of preaching without pay. As Moffatt puts it, "His pay was to do it without pay" *(op. cit.,* p. 121). This is the way the apostle gained his reward. Thus, *light* is regulated by *love.* **18. To proclaim the gospel of Christ without charge** was his aim and the means of his reward. This, of course, is not a principle to be applied to all preachers of the Gospel. It is the voluntary choice of one who, although having a right to support, was compelled to proclaim the truth through a supernatural vision of the ascended Saviour.

19. Paul now adds other ways in which, for the sake of others, he refused to exercise his rights. **Free from all** refers to his lack of dependence on others in any way (cf. v. 1).

20. The principle that Paul espoused was mobility in methods, not mobility in morals. After the words **as under the law,** the Greek text adds, **though not being myself under law,** a remarkable statement which emphasizes how completely Paul had broken with the Law of Moses. It is difficult to find a stronger statement of this fact anywhere in his writings. **21. Them that are without law** refers to the Gentiles. **Being not without law to God, but under the law to Christ** is added to prevent misunderstanding. While Paul was not under law, he did not become an outlaw, or lawless. The law of love for Christ is a stronger motivation toward righteousness than the fear of the judgments of Sinai. Those who, while not under the Mosaic Law, walk by the Spirit of God with love toward the Lord Jesus Christ will fulfill the righteous requirement of the Law (cf. Rom 8:3; Gal 5:16-23).

22. The weak are the over-scrupulous referred to in 8:7, 9-12. Paul never strays far from the general subject of meats sacrificed to idols. **I am made all things to all men** expresses his principle. (The verb here is in the perfect tense, not aorist as in verse 20, expressing the permanent result of his past action). It is not the end justifying the means, but adaptability because of love within the Word. *Save* is stronger than **gain** (v. 19). *That I might . . . save some* does not remove salvation from the hands of God; it merely emphasizes the human cooperation of God's servant in the ministry of the truth.

23. For the gospel's sake does not mean in order to advance the Gospel, but because of its preciousness to the apostle. Omit the **with you,** which concludes the verse.

24. Paul's decision demanded personal discipline. When a man refuses to discipline himself by always exercising his liberty to the detriment of the weak, he injures not only the weak, but also himself. This is the burden of the remaining verses (vv. 24-27). The background of the section is the great athletic spectacle, the Isthmian games, held every two years near Corinth. **The prize** indicates that the apostle had in mind service and rewards, not salvation and life (cf. v. 17, "reward"; Phil 3:11-14). **25.** After the illustration in verse 24, there follows the application, containing both a comparison and a contrast. **Is temperate.** *Practices self-restraint* (MNT, p. 125). Paul's point is that athletes who expect to win must train diligently – a truth well illustrated in today's athletic endeavors, whether track, baseball, or some other sport. **A corruptible crown** brings in the contrast. Athletes discipline themselves to win an insignificant prize (in the Isthmian games it was a wreath of pine). How much more ought Christians to win **an incorruptible** one (cf. II Tim 4:8; I Pet 5:4; Rev 2:10; 3:11).

26,27. Paul's conclusion follows, introduced by **therefore.** Paul ran, but **not uncertainly;** he knew where he was going (cf. Phil 3:14). He was not like the little lad learning to ride a bicycle, who proudly shouted to his sister, "I'm moving. I really am moving." The sister, coldly observing his wobbly progress, replied, "Yes, you are moving, but you are not going!" **Beateth the air** is a boxing metaphor. The statement has no reference to shadowboxing, a necessary and legitimate boxer's exercise; it has to do with wild misses during the actual contest. Paul was an accurate puncher, always on the mark. **I keep under my body** is the rendering of the text of a few weak manuscripts. The better attested reading is *buffet,* or *maul* (RSV has *pommel).* The thought, of course, is that of personal discipline. Walking with God demands personal sacrifice, sacrifice of things not necessarily evil, but which prevent the full devotion of the soul to God – such as, pleasures and worldly pursuits. In an age of luxury, like the present time, the words have real significance for the serious-minded servant of Christ. **I have preached to others.** A reference to the custom of having the competitors summoned to the race by a herald (a *kēryx,* derived from the same root as the word **preached).** Paul summoned many to the race of the Christian life through the Gospel. He did not want to become a **castaway** after that. The word has no reference to loss of salvation. It means literally *disapproved.* Clearly the apostle was concerned lest he be rejected by the umpire for the prize. He had no fear of the herald's barring him from participation in the race. All run, but not all receive the prize; Paul wanted to win the prize.

3) The Admonition and Application to the Corinthians. 10:1–11:1. Paul concludes his discussion of meats offered to idols with admonition (vv. 1-13) and application (10:14–11:1). In the application he deals with participation in heathen religious festivals (vv. 14-22), with the eating of meat sold in the market place (vv. 23-26), and with the eating of meat in a private home (10:27–11:1).

1. The AV's **moreover** obscures an intimate connection that exists between chapter 9 and chapter 10. The Greek text has *for.* The writer has emphasized the need of personal discipline and the possibility of failure in the realm of rewards for the undisciplined. To show the reality of the possibility, he uses the nation Israel as an illustration of failure, and with this illustration he admonishes the Corinthians to "take heed" lest they fall also. Israel was **disapproved!** (9:27)

But first Paul must enumerate the Jews' advantages. **All,** repeated five times, emphasizes the universality in Israel of divine blessing, and, when considered with the fact that almost all (Caleb and Joshua excepted) perished, links this section very closely with 9:24. There Paul said, "Know ye not that they which run in a race run **all,** but **one** receiveth the prize?" **Were under the cloud** points to prolonged supernatural guidance (cf. Ex 13:21,22; 14:19; Mt 28:20). **Passed through the sea** points to a supernatural deliverance, the second privilege (cf. Ex 14:15-22; I Pet 1:18-20). **2. Baptized unto Moses,** their third privilege, refers to their union with their leader, who under God provided them with supernatural leadership (cf. Ex 14:31; Rom 6:1-10). **3. Did . . . eat the same spiritual meat.** The eating of the manna, "angels' food" (Ps 78:25), was the nation's fourth privilege. The people partook of supernatural food (cf. Ex 16:1-36; I Pet 2:1-3). **Spiritual** probably has the sense of *supernatural* (cf. ICC, p. 200).

4. The same spiritual drink, a fifth privilege, refers to the events mentioned in Ex 17:1-9 and Num 20:1-13 (cf. Num 21:16). The words **that spiritual rock that followed them** do not mean that Paul believed the rabbinical legend that a material rock followed the Israelites throughout their journey and that Miriam, above all others, possessed the secret of obtaining the water (cf. Godet, *op. cit.,* II, 56). Actually, the apostle says, **that Rock was Christ,** i.e., it was the visible means of the supply of water which came ultimately from Christ. Since the people of Israel obtained this water in the opening years of their wilderness wanderings (Ex 17:1-9) and in the closing years (Num 20:1-13), it is only natural to infer that he, Christ, the Supplier of the water, was with them all along the way. The literal sense of **that Rock was Christ** is no more to be pressed than is the literal sense of "I am the true vine" (Jn 15:1). The **was,** rather than *is,* may, however, point to Christ's pre-existence (cf. II Cor 8:9; Gal 4:4). Supernatural sustenance was Israel's fifth privilege. The parallel with the two ordinances of the Church may be intended.

5. One might think that such privileges must mean success. **But** introduces the sad contrast. Privileged people may experience divine displeasure. **With many** (RSV, *with most)* is an understatement; only Caleb and Joshua survived the displeasure. **Overthrown** may be rendered *strewn,* a vivid picture of a wilderness paved with bodies sated with angel's food and drink (cf. Num 14:29).

6. Examples. Probably the correct rendering of the Greek word *typoi;* not **types** in the technical sense (MNT, p. 131). The first reason for Israel's failure was that they **lusted** (cf. Num 11:4), preferring the food of the world, Egypt, to that of the Lord, the manna. **7.** They also became **idolaters,** the second cause for failure (cf. Ex 32:1-14, 30-35; I Jn 5:21). **8.** The third reason, **fornication,** is a reference to the incident involving Israel and the Moabite women (cf. Num 25:1-9). Immorality is always the natural consequence of idolatry (cf. Ps 115:8). **Three and twenty thousand** is not a mistake, although Moses wrote the number 24,000. Paul's **one day** should be noted. He refers to those slain by the plague in one day, while Moses' figure includes the ones who died later from the effects.

9. Presumption, the fourth reason, is referred to by the words **tempt Christ** (cf. Num 21:4-9; Ps 78:19); they dared God to live up to his promise to discipline if they doubted his Word. This was the sin of "ungrateful suspicion" (MNT, p. 132). **10. Murmured** introduces the fifth reason (cf. Num 16:41-50), and this may be a gentle Pauline allusion to the Corinthians' attitude to their own spiritual leaders in the matter of idol meats (the other four reasons can be linked with this problem).

11. While the events were **examples unto them,** the accounts of the events were **written for our admonition. The ends of the world** (lit., *the ages)* refers to the completion of the ages before the present one. Believers in this age are to reap the benefit of preceding ones (cf. ICC, p. 207).

12,13. Two final words conclude the admonitory section, the one for the self-assured, the strong who have no thought for the conscience of the weak (v. 12), and the other for the discouraged, who feel that the Christian life is so hard that they can never hope to survive its trials (v. 13). **Thinketh he standeth.** Written for the strong man who is using his liberty at the expense of the weak (8:9-13). **Fall.** Not from salvation, but into God's discipline, and thus become disapproved (9:27). **Common to man** is that which is incident to man (the Vulgate has *humana).* God does not treat believers as angels, or as demons, but as men (vv. 1-11). **But.** Better, *and;* the encouragement is continued. **Above that ye are able.** Not above that ye think ye are able! **A way to escape.** Literally, *the way out,* the suitable and necessary one. This is not an escape from temptation, nor simply a hope of strength to overcome in the future, but a present power to endure in the midst of temptation (cf. Heb 2:18), a glorious promise for the sorely tried.

14. Wherefore. *Dioper,* a strong conjunction, used in the NT only here and in 8:13. It introduces the application to the readers. Heathen religious festivals are considered first (10:14-22). **Flee from idolatry.** Literally, *Flee away from.* This command might surprise the ones who prided themselves on their liberty, but Paul commands the use of the way of escape immediately.

16. Partaking of a religious table, whether Christian (vv. 16,17), Jewish (v. 18), or heathen Gentile (vv. 19-21), involves fellowship in the being to whom the worship is directed. Therefore, a Christian must not partake of meat offered to idols in a pagan feast; there is no liberty here. **The communion** (lit., *communion;* there is no article in the Greek text). To partake is to share in, according to Paul. **17.** The apostle explains why **(For . . . for)** partaking signifies a share in, or union with, the deity. **18.** The example of Israel confirms the fellowship of the worshipers with the deity.

19-21. The example of Gentile festivals follows. **They sacrifice to demons** (ASV) does not mean that the idol is a deity after all. Rather, the writer means that, while idols and things sacrificed to them are nothing, yet they are used by demonic forces to lead men away from the true God (cf. Deut 32:17,21).

22. Will the Corinthians **provoke the Lord** *(Christ* here, *Jehovah* in Deuteronomy) **to jealousy** as the fathers did? Can they risk his anger with impunity? (MNT, pp. 136,137)

23. Meat bought in shops is now considered. Paul repeats the general principle of liberty (cf. 6:12), subjecting it to the principle of benefit **(expedient)** and edification. **24.** This is the endeavor that builds up. **Wealth** (AV) is an archaism; *welfare* would be better today. **25,26.** Permission is here granted for eating any meat sold in the market (AV, *shambles).* No troubling of the conscience by the asking of questions about the meat is necessary.

27. Finally, the apostle considers the case of private dinner parties in the homes of unbelieving friends. The believers may **eat, asking no question for conscience sake. 28. But** if a "puritanic fellow guest" (MNT, p. 144) should nudge the believer and say, **This is offered in sacrifice to idols,** then he is to **eat not for his sake that shewed it.** In other words, the believer must voluntarily respect the weaker conscience. The quotation from Ps 24:1 is not in the better manuscripts. **29,30. For.** Paul explains the action. What good is there in his eating if it means his liberty is blamed? How can grace be said for that which offends a brother?

31. Therefore introduces the principle that is all-inclusive in the entire discussion. **The glory of God** is the ultimate aim. **32.** The good of others comes next, whether **Jews, Gentiles,** or **the church of God** (cf. Rom 14:21). Three separate groups are in view. **33; 11:1.** Paul concludes with the example of himself and the Lord. **Please** does not mean to curry favor, but to do that which is for men's **profit** (same root as **expedient,** v. 23). Our Lord is one who "pleased not himself" (Rom 15:3). This climactically concludes the discussion. The correct attitude in the matter, then, is liberty, the liberty of love for the Lord, for the truth, and for one's brother. Neither legality, nor license will do; conditioned liberty is the principle to follow.

C. The Counsel Concerning the Veiling of Women in Public Worship. 11:2-16.

In chapters 11 through 14 Paul turns to and discusses matters that concern primarily the public worship of the church. The section on spiritual gifts (12:1—14:40) was written in answer to a question from the church (cf. 12:1, *peri de).* The opening chapter is the result of personal report (11:18). The first matter for discussion is the veiling, or covering, of the heads of women, and Paul's ruling is that women must cover their heads during the meeting. He regarded the Corinthian innovation (apparently some were present in the meetings bareheaded) as "irreligious rather than indecorous" (MNT, p. 150), thus showing that his objections have nothing to do with social custom. (Some commentators have appealed to social custom in order to do away with Paul's decision here.) The worship meeting alone is in view. The apostle advances several reasons for his viewpoint.

1) The Theological Reason. 11:2-6. Paul first points out that in God's order the woman is under the man. This does not, of course, imply inequality of the sexes (cf. Gal 3:28; Eph 1:3). Subordination does not necessarily involve inequality. Headship is not the same as lordship. The clue to the standing of the sexes is found in the last words of I Cor 11:3. Man is head over the woman as the Father is head over the Son. There are four orders in the Word—personal, family, ecclesiastical, and governmental. Truth relative to each must be carefully distinguished.

2. I praise you. A general word of commendation, which sets the stage for particular failures. **Ordinances** (RSV, *traditions).* Oral teaching.

3. The head of the woman is the man. The theological basis for the wearing of a covering. Man's headship goes back to Gen 3:16. **4.** The man, too, has an order to follow; **his head** must not be **covered.** Men must not preach with their hats on! **5. Prayeth or prophesieth** does not mean that Paul approved these actions by women in public worship. Rather, he was simply referring to what was going on at Corinth unauthorized (cf. 14:34,35). **Her head.** The woman's physical head, not her husband. **6. Let her also be shorn.** A disgrace for a woman. Paul's ironical words to the rebellious. He is saying, "Make the reproach complete, then."

2) The Biblical Reasons. 11:7-12. The facts of creation (vv. 7-9,12,13) and the presence of angels at worship (v. 10) are brought forward.

7. He is (probably, *represents,* as in v. 25) **the image and glory of God.** This looks back to Gen 1:26,27. The male displays the authority of God on earth (cf. MNT, p. 151). **8,9.** The two prepositions **of** and **for** reveal the place of the woman. She has her origin and purpose of life in the man (cf. Gen 2:21-25). Every woman taking a new name at her marriage ceremony tacitly affirms the Pauline teaching. **10. Power,** or authority, means, by an unusual metonymy, sign of authority. The veil is the sign of the man's authority. The word for **angels** in the expression **because of the angels** does not refer to elders (cf. Rev 2:1. The same word refers to angels in I Cor 4:9). Nor does it refer to evil angels (cf. Gen 6:1-4). It refers to the good angels who are present in worship meetings, since they live in the presence of God (cf. I Cor 4:9; Lk 15:7,10; Eph 3:10; I Tim 5:21; Ps 138:1). The insubordination of women in refusing to acknowledge the authority of their husbands would offend the angels who, under God, guard the created universe (cf. Col 1:16; Eph 1:21), and know no insubordination.

11,12. Paul gives the other side of the truth here. The man and the woman are necessary for each other **in the Lord;** in fact, the man must always remember that he exists **by the woman.** And both are **of God.**

3) The Physical Reason. 11:13-16. Impropriety, based upon nature itself, argues for the covering. The word **comely** refers to a necessity founded upon an inner fitness of things (cf. Heb

2:10; Mt 3:15). It is better rendered *proper*.

14,15. The fact of short hair for men and long hair for women is a divine suggestion in **nature itself** that the man and the woman are to heed in their dress in the assembly. The words **her hair is given her for a covering** do not mean that the woman's hair *is* her covering and that she needs no veil, a view vitiating the force of 11:2-14. The word **for** is to be rendered *answering to* (cf. Ellicott, *op. cit.*, p. 208).

16. No such custom, i.e., no custom of women worshiping without coverings. Some say that the custom was peculiar to Corinth, but Paul's words, **neither the churches of God,** argue against this view. Still others insist that the custom is not to be applied today (cf. Morris, *op. cit.*, p. 156; Barclay, *op. cit.*, p. 110). It should be noted, however, that each of the reasons given for the wearing of a veil is taken from permanent facts, lasting as long as the present earthly economy (cf. Godet, *op. cit.*, II, 133). Paul did carry his point, for early church history bears witness that in Rome, Antioch, and Africa the custom became the norm. A final word: In the final analysis, the hat, or veil, is not the important thing, but the subordination for which it stands. The presence of both is the ideal.

D. The Counsel Concerning the Lord's Supper. 11:17-34.

The Lord's Supper, the only act of worship for which Christ gave special direction, receives Paul's attention now. It is connected with the previous section by the fact that both matters concern public worship. It may help in reconstructing the situation to realize that in the early church the Supper was usually preceded by a fellowship meal, called the *Agape,* or Love Feast (cf. Jude 12). Disorders at the *Agape* called forth the apostle's indignation (vv. 17-22), a review of past teaching (vv. 23-26), and a stern application of the truth to the Corinthian assembly (vv. 27-34).

1) The Indignation of Paul. 11:17-22. The fellowship meal was primarily religious, not social, but abuses had made it a disgraceful farce.

17. This refers to the following instruction. Their meetings were **for the worse,** because they were incurring judgment as a result of the disorders (cf. v. 29). **18. Divisions.** Better, *parties.* These existed apparently because the rich, contrary to custom, greedily consumed their more bountiful provisions before all the poor came, so that they would not have to share their food in visible representation of the unity of the body. **19. Heresies.** *Factions,* groups with self-chosen views, is the emphasis and meaning of the word. These existed, Paul remarks somewhat resignedly, in order that the **approved** (cf. 9:27; 11:28) might be recognized.

20. It was a supper, but it was not **the Lord's** (the adjective is emphatic) **supper;** that is, it was not a real reenactment of the Last Supper. **21,22.** The indignant question, **Have ye not houses to eat and to drink in?** was addressed to those who regarded the gathering simply as a social banquet and not as a spiritual fellowship meal.

2) The Review of Past Instruction. 11:23-26. The apostle justifies his rebuke by reviewing the real and true significance of the ordinance, tracing the teaching back to the Lord himself.

23. Paul could not praise them, **for** their conduct disagreed with that which he had received **of the Lord** (RSV, *from the Lord).* He does not make clear whether he received his instruction directly from the Lord or through a source. The latter is probable.

24. The words **take, eat,** and the word **broken,** occurring in the AV, do not appear in the best manuscripts. The bread is distributed first, since it represents the incarnation. Then the wine follows, representing the death that ends the old covenant and establishes the new. One thing is sure: in the words, **this is my body,** Paul is not teaching transubstantiation. The bread certainly was not the Lord's body at the moment he said this, nor is the cup the new covenant literally (v. 25). The word **is** has the common sense of "represents" (cf. v. 7; Jn 8:12; 10:9; I Cor 10:4), "as [the] German has it, not *'das ist,'* but *'das heiszt'* " (MNT, p. 168). **For you** emphasizes the sacrificial aspect. **In remembrance** involves more than just memory; the word suggests an active calling to mind. And the phrase **of me** is wider than *of my death.* The person who did the work is the object of the calling to mind. The present imperative **do** suggests that frequent attendance at the Lord's Supper is a divine command (cf. Acts 20:7).

25. The new covenant reminds the

hearer of the old Mosaic covenant, which could only condemn. The Greek *diathēkē* in contrast to *synthēkē*, the usual OT word for "covenant," emphasizes the initiative of God in it. The new covenant provided an effective remission of sins. **In my blood** points to the sphere and basis of the covenantal blessings. Barclay's suggestive rendering is, "This cup is the new covenant and it cost my blood" (*op. cit.*, p. 114). The repetition of **in remembrance of me** is designed for the disorderly Corinthians; they needed to learn that *fellowship* with Christ, not *food*, was the important thing at the Supper.

26. For introduces the reason the Supper is continually repeated. It is an acted sermon, for it **proclaim[s]** (AV, *shew*) **the Lord's death.** The Supper has both a backward and a forward look, since it is to be observed **till he come** (cf. Mt 26:29).

3) The Application to the Corinthians. 11:27-34. Paul now applies the teaching to the disorderly believers.

27. Wherefore introduces the application, a consequence of the instruction. **Unworthily** does not refer to the person of the one partaking, but to the manner of his partaking. All are unworthy always. **Guilty of the body and blood of the Lord.** Guilty of sin against the body and blood. **28. But** introduces the proper alternative, self-judgment. There must be preparation before participation. **29. For.** The reason that self-judgment, or confession of sin, must precede the partaking is that otherwise the believer makes himself liable to **judgment** (the meaning of *krima;* the AV's *damnation* is misleading). Not **discerning** means not "rightly judging" (ICC, p. 252; the verb is found twice in v. 31). That is, the believer does not recognize the unity of **the body,** the Church (cf. 10:16,17; 11:20,21). **30.** Judgment had already come upon some **for this cause** – abuse of the Lord's Table. Some had committed sin unto death and already slept (the verb *koimaō,* **sleep,** when referring to death, always refers to the death of believers; cf. Jn 11:11,12; Acts 7:60; I Cor 15:6,18,20,51; I Thess 4:13,14, 15; II Pet 3:4). These believers had not lost their salvation, but they had lost the privilege of service on the earth.

31. The preventive is to **judge ourselves** rightly. **32.** Even God's judgment, however, is not eternal; it is designed to be family discipline, a **chastening of the Lord,** to prevent condemnation **with the world.** Here Paul uses the strong *katakrinō,* which does mean **to condemn** eternally. **33. Wherefore.** Concluding words follow, a practical appeal to the Corinthians to remember the unity of the body in their observance of the feast. **34. Condemnation** is incorrect. Read, instead, **judgment** (the word again is *krima,* as in v. 29). **The rest** of the details in connection with the Lord's Supper, Paul says, will be **set in order** at his next visit.

E. The Counsel Concerning Spiritual Gifts. 12:1–14:40.

With the familiar *peri de* (AV, "Now concerning") Paul refers to another question propounded by the Corinthians. The new subject, spiritual gifts, is linked, however, with the preceding section by the common relation to public worship. It is important to distinguish spiritual gifts from spiritual graces and spiritual offices. Spiritual graces are features of Christian character. Every believer is responsible for the development of all of them (cf. Gal 5:22,23). Spiritual offices are positions in the church for the administration of its affairs, whether spiritual oversight of the flock (elders) or spiritual oversight of temporalities (deacons; cf. I Tim 3:1-13). Only certain believers hold spiritual office. Spiritual gifts are divine enablements related to service in the local church, both unofficial and official service. Every believer possesses a spiritual gift, but not all believers possess the same gift (cf. I Cor 12:4-11). The church at Corinth, certainly no dead church, was in danger of abusing its privileges by an overemphasis on certain of the spectacular gifts. The apostle first sets forth the unity and diversity of the gifts (12:1-31 a), next the primacy of love over the seeking of gifts (12:31 b –13:13), and finally evaluation and regulation of the exercise of the gifts of prophecy and tongues (14:1-40).

1) The Validity of Utterance. 12:1-3. Paul gives the church an opening word of admonition to aid them in determining genuine spiritual utterance. The pagan background of the Corinthians would have been no help to them in this matter.

1. Spiritual gifts (lit., *the spiritual things*) does not refer to spiritual men (cf. F. W. Grosheide, *Commentary on* *the First Epistle to the Corinthians,* p. 278, although Grosheide himself does not hold this view); nor simply to **the spirituals** (G. Campbell Morgan, *The Corinthian Letters of Paul,* pp. 145,146). The word **gifts** in verse 4, as well as Paul's words in 14:1 (the neuter gender should be noted), support the supplying of the word **gifts** (AV; RSV). **2,3. Wherefore,** because of their need of instruction, they are to **understand, that no man speaking by the Spirit of God calleth Jesus accursed** (the negative criterion): **and that no man can say that Jesus is the Lord, but by the Holy Ghost** (the positive criterion). The apostle, of course, refers to utterance that comes from the heart (cf. Mt 26:22,25).

2) The Unity of the Gifts. 12:4-11. After the short digression Paul looks first at the unity of the gifts, a unity of source and purpose.

4-6. Gifts. Greek *charismatōn,* connected with the word *charis,* "grace," has been rendered **grace-gifts** not inappropriately. The word is used here in its technical sense of spiritual gifts. Viewed (1) as from the Spirit, they are **gifts;** (2) as from the Lord, **administrations,** or services, to the assembly; (3) as from the Father, **operations,** or supernatural workings. **7. Given to every man** distinguishes gift from office (cf. I Pet 4:10).

8-10. Certain of the gifts are now listed. **8. The word of wisdom,** probably a temporary gift like apostleship, had to do with the communication of spiritual wisdom, such as is contained in the Epistles. It was necessary in the early days when the church possessed no NT. **The word of knowledge** had to do with truth of a more practical character (the practical sections of the Epistles); it, too, was a temporary gift. The Word of God is sufficient now. **9. Faith.** Not to be confused with saving faith, the possession of every Christian. This is the faith that manifests itself in unusual deeds of trust (cf. 13:2). The faith of a George Mueller, or of a Hudson Taylor, would qualify. **Gifts of healing.** Not to be confused with the work of so-called divine healers today. This gift of healing provided restoration of life, which is beyond the power of 'divine healers' (cf. Acts 9:40; 20:9). The Word teaches *divine healing* according to a pattern (cf. Jas 5:14,15); it does not contemplate 'divine healers.' **10. Prophecy.** The gift of *foretelling* and *forthtelling* new revelation from God was also temporary, needed when the canon was incomplete. No further revelation is now needed; the proclamation and teaching of the completed revelation is the task of the church today. **Discerning of spirits** is now done by the Spirit through the Word. **Tongues** and **interpretations** were also temporary (see following discussion), having to do with known languages rather than with ecstatic utterance, although the question of speaking in tongues is a moot one.

11. As he will. The Spirit is the sovereign dispenser of the gifts. The words are a key to the following section, showing those apparently more favored in the gifts that there is no self-merit in them, and those less favored that there is no lack of importance for them (cf. Godet, *op. cit.,* II, 206).

3) The Diversity of the Gifts. 12:12-31 a. Using the illustration of the human body, Paul describes the relation of gifted believers to one another and to Christ in the Church, his body.

12. For introduces the explanation of the unity in diversity and diversity in unity of believers in the body. That Christ gives his name to the body is seen in the words **so also is Christ** (lit., *the Christ).* **13. For** gives the reason for the union, the baptism of the Spirit **into one body. By one Spirit** (lit., *in one Spirit;* cf. Mt 3:11; Lk 3:16; Acts 1:5) expresses the sphere of the union effected by baptism. **One body** is the end to which the act is directed (cf. ICC, p. 272). The aorist tense in **baptized** clearly indicates that the action is a past fact true of **all** believers (even the carnal Corinthians; cf. I Cor 3:1-3), never to be repeated. In fact, the baptism that unites to Christ is not to be sought; it has been wrought already for all. As a consequence of this union with Christ, believers **have been all made to drink into one Spirit.** Union with him necessarily involves the Spirit's indwelling.

14-20. The illustration of the body is developed in these verses, with emphasis upon the diversity of the members for the sake of the apparently inferior ones, who thought their gifts were not important. The key thought is: **The body is not one member, but many** (v. 14), and the members have been **set . . . in the body, as it pleased him** (v. 18). Hence, the seemingly inferior were not to envy the seemingly superior.

21-24. The dependent relation of the

members comes to the fore here. Seemingly superior members (having the more spectacular gifts) must not disdain the seemingly inferior. Actually, Paul says, the **uncomely parts** of the human body have the most attention (by way of clothing), and according to this analogy the seemingly inferior can expect from God the same equalization of dignity in the one body, the Church. In fact, this is just what God has done, for he **has tempered the body together. Tempered** refers to the mingling of two elements so that they become a compound, such as wine and water (A-S, p. 245). The body is a unity.

25. That. The purpose of the unity is (negatively) that there be no **schism** (cf. 1:10; 11:18), or division, **in the body;** and (positively) **that the members should have the same care one for another. 26.** The natural results of the perfect blending of the members are fellow suffering and fellow rejoicing.

27. The body of Christ (lit., *body of Christ;* there is no definite article) does not refer to the local church at Corinth, for there are not *many* bodies, a thought contrary to the context. Rather, it points to the quality of the whole, which each of them individually helps to constitute (ICC, p. 277). **28.** A further listing of the gifts, including several not found in verses 4-11. **First, secondarily,** and **thirdly** refer to rank, but the **after that** and **then** probably do not.

29,30. The questions refer the reader to 12:14,27. And in these verses Paul strikes a deathblow to the theory that speaking in tongues is the sign of the possession of the Spirit, for the answer "No" is expected to each question (cf. Greek). **31. The best gifts** (lit., *the greater gifts*) refers to teaching, helps, etc. Tongues is significantly put at the end of the list. This inferior significance of tongues Paul will develop in chapter 14. In the meantime, he says he will describe a pursuit that is more important than the pursuit of any spiritual gift.

4) The Primacy of Love over Gifts. 12:31 b—13:13. The last clause of chapter 12 has been misunderstood. Many feel that Paul is here showing *how* the gifts are to be ministered, i.e., in love. However, the use of **way** *(hodos)* in the sense of "a road" instead of **way** *(tropos)* in the sense of "manner," and the statement of 14:1, indicate that Paul is, rather, pointing out a path of life superior to a life spent in the seeking and displaying of spiritual gifts. In a sense, then, there is a parenthesis in the argument, but a closely related one. The thought is this: In all your exercise in gifts, be sure to understand their proper place in the over-all scheme of things. Love is the pre-eminent thing (31 b—13:3), containing noble properties (vv. 4-7), and it abides permanently (vv. 8-13). It provides the answer to the age-long question, What is the *summum bonum?*

1. Tongues of men and of angels. Probably the gift of tongues. **Charity.** Better, **love,** but it is a love that includes charity! **Sounding brass** (MNT, *noisy gong*). Paul's point is that power of expression is not determined by diction, phraseology, and style; it is determined by depth of heart. **2.** The apostle ascends from tongues to **prophecy, knowledge,** and **faith** (cf. 12:8-10). **Love** is greater than **faith,** because the end is greater than the means (cf. Lk 9:54). **Nothing.** "Not *outheis,* nobody, but an absolute zero" (A. T. Robertson, *op. cit.,* IV, 177).

3. The thought moves from gifts to acts which seem to be expressions of love, one a great act of philanthropy and the other an act of martyrdom. Instead of **to be burned,** many good manuscripts have, *that I may glory.* But on the whole it seems that the AV rendering represents the genuine reading. There may be an allusion here to the Indian, Zarmano-chegas, who burned himself in public on a funeral pyre and had the inscription put on his monument in Athens, "Zarmano-chegas, an Indian from Bargosa, according to the traditional customs of the Indians, made himself immortal and lies here" (Barclay, *op. cit.,* p. 132). Such exhibitionism, or 'showboating,' as moderns would say, was just egoism. The spirit of self can be introduced into the greatest of human acts. This **profiteth nothing.**

4-7. A description of the nature of love, with its noble properties, follows. One might almost say that love is personified here, since the description is practically a description of the life and character of Jesus Christ. However, the picture is directly related to the Corinthians. The observance of the truths of this chapter, as will be noted in the following remarks, would have solved their problems. **Charity suffereth long, and is kind** may be a summary statement of the section, with the next eight qualities related to longsuffering and the next four to kindness. **Envieth not** (MNT, *knows no jealousy)* is related to the attitude of the brethren who felt that their gifts were inferior (12:14-17). Love would have solved that problem. **Vaunteth not itself.** Literally, does not *play the braggart.* This is related to 12:21-26. **Puffed up** clearly points to the opening section of the book (1:10–4:21).

5. The words **doth not behave itself unseemly** are clearly related to several sections in the book (cf. 7:36; 11:2-16,17-34). **Seeketh not her own** would have been the answer to the problem of meats sacrificed to idols (cf. 8:1–11:1). **Is not easily provoked** is not strong enough; there is no **easily** in the Greek text. A translator with a short temper must have been responsible for the AV rendering! This property of love would have solved the problem of the lawsuits (cf. 6:1-11). **Thinketh no evil.** Or, *plots no evil.* **6. Rejoiceth not in iniquity** suggests the problem of immorality and lack of discipline of it in 5:1-13.

7. Believeth all things does not include gullibility. It means, rather, that the believer is not to be suspicious. If, however, sin is evident, the believer must judge it and support its discipline. From this description of love, it is evident that Moffatt is right in saying, "The lyric is thus a lancet." Paul was probing into the open sore of sin in the Corinthian church with this beautiful description of the one thing, love, that would have met all the believers' problems.

8-13. In the remaining verses the permanence of love is expounded. Love, unlike the gifts of prophecy, tongues, and knowledge, never fails, nor ceases its activity. The AV is weak in verse 8, being guilty of rendering two different Greek words by the same English word **fail,** as well as one Greek word occurring twice by two different English words, **fail** and **vanish away.** Fortunately the sense is not greatly affected by the variations. The point of verse 8 is that there will come a time when the gifts mentioned will be done away with, or cease.

9. The **for** introduces the explanation of why the gifts will pass away. A time of perfected knowledge and prophecy is coming. **10. That which is perfect** cannot be a reference to the completion of the canon of Scripture; otherwise we now, living in the age of the completed canon, would see more clearly than Paul did (v. 9). Even the most self-satisfied and opinionated of theologians would hardly admit that. The coming of that which is perfect can only be a reference to the Lord's second coming. That event will mark the end of the exercise of prophecy, tongues, and knowledge. How then can one speak of these gifts as temporary? The following verse will answer the question.

11. It is extremely important to an understanding of Paul's thought to notice the force of the illustration he introduces at this point. The illustration is designed to show the character of the period between the two comings of Christ. With reference to these particular gifts, it may be likened to the growing up of a person from infancy to manhood. The special and spectacular gifts were necessary in the early stages of the growth of the true church (cf. Eph 4:7-16) for purposes of authentication (cf. Heb 2:3,4) and edification (I Cor 14:3) when there was no NT to give light. They were the 'baby talk' of the church. As history has abundantly verified, with the Word and growing maturity, there came to be no need for such gifts. Today it is questionable that there exists anywhere the Scriptural exercise of the three gifts referred to by Paul in this passage. **I spake** (lit., *was speaking,* or *used to speak)* possibly refers specifically to tongues, **I understood** to prophecy, and **I thought** to knowledge. One cannot be dogmatic about it, however. **I put away childish things** (lit., *have put away,* the perfect tense stressing the results of the action) looks ultimately to the coming of **that which is perfect** (v. 10).

12. For. Paul explains that the present time is the infant stage. **Now** might be rendered *at the present moment* (the word *arti* usually refers to the present time in contrast to past or future time). In the light of the fact that the Corinthians saw only **darkly** and **in part** through the exercise of the gifts, why should they have gloried so in that which was fragmentary?

13. Now *(nuni* refers to time generally without reference to other times, but here it may well be logical and not temporal, being rendered *so then)* **Abideth faith, hope,** and **love.** These virtues outlast the gifts and, consequently, are to be cultivated more earnestly. It is not true that "Faith will vanish into sight, Hope will be emptied in delight," for all abide eternally. How shall faith and hope abide? Godet has hit upon the meaning: "The permanent essence of the creature is to have nothing of its own, to be eternally helpless and poor. . . . It is not once for all, it is continually that in eternity faith changes into vision and hope into possession. These two virtues, therefore, abide to live again unceasingly" *(op. cit.*, II, 261). Love is the **greatest** force in the universe, and its true source and clearest expression is Golgotha. One under the spell of that love cannot help singing, with adoration:

"Were the whole realm of nature mine,
 That were a present far too small;
Love so amazing, so divine,
 Demands my soul, my life, my all."

5) The Superiority of Prophecy, and the Public Worship of the Church. 14:1-36. Apparently a major cause of the disorder in the church involved the misuse of the gift of tongues. The apostle deals with the matter in this chapter. He affirms the superiority of prophecy to tongues (vv. 1-25), then adds directions for the exercise of the gifts (vv. 26-33) and for the regulation of the participation of women in the assembly meeting (vv. 34-36). A résumé and a conclusion follow (vv. 37-40).

No one who has investigated the nature of the gift of tongues would care to be dogmatic about the matter. The present exposition of this chapter follows the view that the gift of tongues was the ability to speak in known languages, not in ecstatic speech. (The AV's *unknown* is not found in the Greek text, which reads simply **tongues,** or **tongue,** as the case may be.) Most modern commentators take the view that the gift involved ecstatic speech (cf. MNT, pp. 206-225; Morris, *op. cit.*, pp. 172, 173, 190-198). There are some factors, however, which cast some doubt on the correctness of this interpretation.

In the first place, it seems clear that the speaking in tongues recorded in Acts was in known languages (cf. Acts 2:4, 8,11). In view of the fact that Luke was a close companion of Paul (he may even have been in Corinth) and wrote Acts after the Corinthian correspondence, it would seem logical for him to note the distinction between the phenomenon in Acts and that in Corinth, if any existed. In other words, I Corinthians should be interpreted by Acts, the unknown by the known, a good hermeneutical principle. Furthermore, the terminology of Paul is identical with that of Luke in Acts, although Luke further defines his terminology. Paul uses the Greek word *glōssa,* meaning **tongue;** Luke uses this word and further defines it as being a *dialektos* (Acts 1:19; 2:6,8; 21:40; 22:2; 26:14), a word which in every case refers to a language of a nation or a region (cf. Arndt, p. 184). It is quite unlikely that the phenomena, described by the two writers in identical terms, would be dissimilar.

Finally, the intent of the gift was that it should be a sign to the Jews (I Cor 14:21,22), as prophesied in the OT (cf. Isa 28:11), as well as a suggestion regarding the method of fulfilling the commission of Acts 1:8. At Pentecost there was inaugurated a work of the Spirit that would reverse the curse of Babel (cf. Gen 11:1-9), when there occurred the confusion of [known] tongues. Thus, there was a double edge in the conferring of the gift. It was a sign to provoke the Jews (in every case of the occurrence of the gift in Acts, Jews were present; cf. Acts 2:4 ff.; 8:17,18; 10:46; 19:6), and a signal of a work of God which would unite the redeemed under the banner of King Messiah in his coming kingdom. To introduce ecstatic language into the picture only serves to introduce confusion in more ways than one. Additional points in support of the thesis that the tongues were known languages are set forth in the exposition of the section.

1. The opening verse, which contains no connecting particle, is a reaffirmation of the content of 12:31 b – 13:13 with a view to transition. **Follow after** (lit., *pursue)* is stronger than **desire.** It appears from this statement that, while spiritual gifts are sovereignly bestowed, they are not necessarily granted in every case at conversion. **Rather** points to Paul's evaluation of prophecy in contrast to tongues. Speaking in tongues does not build up (vv. 2-5), does not benefit without interpretation (vv. 6-15); in fact, only befuddles (vv. 16-19). **2. An unknown tongue** (lit., *a tongue).* The words **for no man understandeth him** refer to speaking in the tongue without an interpreter. **3-5.** The apostle's evaluation is clear. Prophecy is greater than tongues **except he interpret.** In the case of interpretation, the speaking in tongues assumed practically the character of prophecy. (Is this why the two are often connected in Acts? Cf. Acts 10:46; 19:6.)

6-15. The uselessness of tongues without interpretation Paul illustrates with facts drawn from life. **Revelation** precedes **prophesying** and **knowledge** precedes **doctrine** (lit., *teaching).*

7. Distinction in the sounds is necessary in music and in speaking; otherwise there is no understanding. **9. So likewise ye** introduces the application of the illustration. **10,11.** A further illustration in the realm of languages; and the point is, "Speech is useless to the hearer, unless he understands it" (ICC, p. 310). **12. Even so ye** introduces the conclusion of the argument from the illustrations. Edification is the aim of spiritual gifts.

13,14. There should be prayer for the gift of interpretation by the one speaking in tongues. Otherwise **my spirit prayeth, but my understanding** (lit., *my mind)* **is unfruitful.** That is, it gains no fruit in the understanding of the listeners. **15.** To **pray with the understanding also** means to pray so that there is fruit in the understanding of the hearers, as the following verses indicate. Intelligible speech is essential. **16. He that occupieth the room of the unlearned** probably refers to the one who does not have the gift of tongues or interpretation, or perhaps to one who is merely an inquirer (cf. F. F. Bruce, *Commentary on the Book of the Acts,* p. 102; Morris, *op. cit.,* pp. 195,196). The rank and file are referred to.

18,19. Paul's preference is clear. However much he may use tongues outside the assembly (publicly or privately), **in the church** (emphatic in the Greek) he must speak with **understanding** in order to **teach others.**

20-25. Paul has pointed out the superiority of prophecy for the insiders, and now he discusses its superiority for the outsiders.

21,22. The apostle introduces a free quotation from **the law** (the OT is indicated by **law** here) to show that tongues are intended to be a **sign** of God's presence with others than the Jews. In Isa 28:11,12, the place of the quotation, the Assyrians are referred to as the men **of other tongues.** Thus, the gift is designed primarily for the unbelieving. In the Acts this gift is mentioned four times ("saw" in Acts 8:18 seems to suggest that there was some outward sign in Samaria), and in each case Jews were present. It was the intention of God to indicate to this unbelieving group that he was with the new movement. It is quite clear that known languages, such as were used at Pentecost, were the only suitable signs to hard-to-be-convinced Jews. Ecstatic language admits of too many natural explanations, not the least of which is the known historical fact that non-Christian groups have frequently so spoken (MNT, pp. 208,209).

23-25. Paul describes the differing effects of tongues and prophecy on outsiders, indicating the superiority of prophecy. There is no contradiction here with 14:22, as appears at first glance (tongues provide no help to the unbelieving, whereas prophecy seems to be a help to them). In the latter verse, individuals who have heard and rejected the truth are in view, as the comparison with the rebellious Israelites shows, whereas in the following verses first-time hearers are in view (ICC, p. 319). Prophecy leads to a conviction of one's sinful condition, a judgment (lit., *examined),* and a manifestation of **the secrets of the heart.** The result is **worship,** the true object of all ministry (cf. Mt 14:33).

26-33. Instruction for the exercise of the gifts is given here. The section is important because it is "the most intimate glimpse we have of the early church at worship" (Morris, *op. cit.,* pp. 198,199). What a contrast is found here with the formal and inflexible order of service that prevails in most of Christendom today! Barclay, in commenting upon this freedom and informality, points out two facts that emerge here. First, "Clearly the early church had no professional ministry" *(op. cit.,* p. 149). Second, in the service itself "there was clearly no settled order at all" *(ibid.,* p. 150). The early believers did not come to the worship meeting to hear a sermon from one man or simply to receive; they came to give. Much has been lost by the renouncement of these privileges.

26,27. Every one points to free participation, but because such freedom might lead to disorder, Paul counsels **Let all things be done unto edifying.** The speaking is to be **by course** (lit., *in turn).* **28,29.** Tongues were not to be exercised unless an interpreter was present, and at the most only three were to participate. Apparently the directions for prophesying were more lenient. **32,33.** The prophetic impulses are **subject to the prophets,** that is, the ones uttering the prophecies. Self-control must always be present; otherwise **confusion** might result.

34,35. A word for the women is inserted here, possibly because of unwarranted intrusion of some into the worship of the church. They were to **keep silence** (cf. I Tim 2:12). Even if, as some think, women were permitted to pray and prophesy in the early church (cf. 11:5, although it must be remembered that prophecy was a temporary gift), other speaking was not allowed. Paul says nothing about spinsters who have no **husbands at home!**

36. The apostle gives an indignant response to the implied suggestion that Corinth had the right to be different from other churches. The Corinthian believers had no unique authority and place.

6) The Conclusion. 14:37-40. A Resumé and conclusion, opening with a strong statement of authority. **38. Let him be ignorant.** The one ignorant of Paul's words was to be left in his condition. The correct translation, however, may be, *he is ignored,* i.e., by God (based upon a variant reading in good manuscripts). **40. Decently** may refer to the behavior of women and the observance of the Lord's Supper (11:2-34), and **in order** may refer to spiritual gifts (12:1–14:40).

F. The Counsel Concerning the Doctrine of the Resurrection. 15:1-58.

In approaching this chapter it is helpful to have some conception of the Greek view of life. In general the Greeks believed in the immortality of the soul, but they did not accept the resurrection of the body. To them the resurrection of the body was unthinkable in view of the fact that they held the body to be the source of man's weakness and sin. Death, therefore, was very welcome, since by it the soul would be liberated from the body; but resurrection was not welcome, because this would constitute another descent of the soul into the grave of the body. This was the skepticism that Paul faced at Athens (cf. Acts 17:31,32) and that the Christian faces in the modern world. James S. Stewart, Professor of New Testament at the University of Edinburgh, has put the timeless conflict succinctly, "Twenty centuries have echoed the laughter of Areopagus."

1) The Certainty of the Resurrection. 15:1-34. The problem at Corinth developed in the Christian church. The believers had accepted resurrection, at least in the case of Christ; but under the influence of Greek thought, some doubted the bodily resurrection of Christians. Therefore, the apostle wrote to combat the doctrinal weakness. His method is fairly clear. He first considers the certainty of the resurrection, developing the necessary connection between Christ's resurrection and the resurrection of believers (vv. 1-34). He follows with a consideration of certain objections (vv. 35-57). Then he concludes with an appeal (v. 58).

1,2. Moreover introduces the new subject, the resurrection, an integral part of **the gospel. Ye are saved** (Gr., present tense) may refer to continual salvation from the power of sin in the lives of believers, or it may refer to the day-by-day salvation of the inhabitants of Corinth as they received the message and formed part of the church of Jesus Christ. **Believed in vain** does not indicate loss of salvation as a possibility. The apostle means either that a faith that does not persevere is not true saving faith, or that a faith lodged in a purported resurrection of the Messiah would be groundless if the message of Christ's resurrection were untrue. The latter interpretation is probably correct. If Christ was not crucified and resurrected, salvation is impossible.

3,4. First of all (lit., *among the first things)* refers to importance, not time. The substance of Paul's message is contained in the four *that*'s following **received,** and it includes Christ's death, burial, resurrection, and appearances. These things make up the Gospel. **For our sins according to the scriptures** must be understood in the light of passages such as Isaiah 53. The preposition **for** (Gr., *hyper,* which modern grammarians now recognize may denote substitution) suggests his death in our stead. The word **buried,** the only reference to his burial outside the Gospels, with the exception of Paul's words in Acts 13:29 (cf. Acts 2:29), blasts the swoon theory of our Lord's death. He really died. It also leads naturally to the empty tomb, a witness for the Resurrection which has never been effectively refuted. **Rose again,** a perfect tense, implies abiding results. (On the problem of translation in view of the definite time phrase, **the third day,** see James Hope Moulton's *A Grammar of New Testament Greek,* I, 137.)

5. And that he was seen introduces evidence outside the NT Scriptures. **6.** The reference to **the greater part** who **remain unto this present** has immense apologetic value. The resurrection story was undisputed, so far as we know, twenty-five years later! The appearance may be that of Mt 28:16-20. **7.** This **James** was probably the Lord's brother, and this appearance may have brought him to faith in Christ (cf. Jn 7:5; Acts 1:14).

8. One born out of due time (lit., *the miscarriage,* or *abortion)* does not refer to the taunts of his enemies, nor to the fact that he came to Christ before his nation, Israel, which will come to Christ in the future (cf. Rom 11:1-36). The **for** of the next verse explains. Paul regards himself in comparison with the other apostles as a miscarried infant would be regarded among perfectly formed infants, because he was lifted out of his role of persecutor into his office of apostle. The others responded to the loving call of the Saviour, but Paul's call on the Damascus Road had almost the element of force in it. Therefore, he magnifies **the grace of God** which came to him (cf. Eph 3:8; I Tim 1:15).

10. Labored more abundantly than they all is ambiguous. It may refer to the other apostles individually or collectively. The latter may be right, for history seems to support him in this. Under any circumstances the apostle emphasizes that he does not take credit for this personally. **11. So we preach** links the Resurrection with the apostolic message. **So ye believed** links the Corinthians with faith in Christ's resurrection. Taking their faith in the Lord's resurrection as a starting point, Paul will now prove that this logically involves faith in the bodily resurrection of all others who are *in him* (vv. 12-19).

12,13. The fact of Christ's resurrection involves belief in the bodily resurrection. There is no need to debate resurrection, since one has already been raised. It is obvious that Paul's argument turns on the humanity of Christ (cf. I Tim 2:5, "the *man* Christ Jesus"). **14. Vain.** Void of content (Gr., *kenos).* If there was no resurrection, the Gospel was empty of real content. And the Corinthians' faith did not take hold of a real fact; it was all a mirage. **15.** Furthermore, if there was no resurrection, the heralds of the Gospel were **false witnesses** against **God.**

17. Vain renders a different adjective here, meaning "void of useful aim or effect" (Gr., *mataios).* If Christ was not raised, their faith had failed to secure its end or aim, namely, salvation. There could be no assurance that he had not died for his own sin. The Resurrection was necessary to demonstrate the perfection of the character of the Redeemer (cf. Acts 2:24) and to demonstrate the acceptance of the Son's work by the Father (cf. Rom 4:25). As someone has said, the Resurrection is God's "Amen" to Christ's "It is finished." We observe the cross and see redemption effected; we see the Resurrection and know the redemption is accepted. **18,19.** Without resurrection, believers who thought they were dying **in Christ,** with the expectation of resurrection blessedness, really **perished** (emphatic contrast). The bitter conclusion is reached that the denial of the Resurrection constitutes Christians the **most miserable** of men. They suffer here and now for a faith that is only a fiction (cf. Rom 8:18).

20. Paul, having established the fact that Christ arose and that the admission of his resurrection is inconsistent with the denial of the resurrection of the dead, now discusses the fruit and issue of the Lord's resurrection. Assumption departs and the facts come in with his words, **but now is Christ risen.** The word **firstfruits,** derived from the Feast of First fruits in Israel (cf. Lev 23:9-14), suggests the thoughts of an earnest and a sample.

21,22. There is a causal relationship between Adam and death and Christ and life. The apostle's thought moves in the realm of Romans 5. When Paul writes **in Christ shall all be made alive,** he is not teaching universalism (a heresy), nor universal resurrection (a truth, but not taught here), but universal resurrection in Christ. The two **all**'s are not identical in quantity, being limited by the prepositional phrases **in Adam** and **in Christ** (cf. Rom 5:18). The word **made alive** is never used of the wicked in the NT (cf. Jn 5:21; 6:63; Rom 8:11; Gal 3:21; I Cor 15:45, the same context). The chapter contemplates the resurrection of believers only.

23. The **order** of resurrection is now discussed. Christ is first, followed by believers, them **that are Christ's at his coming** for the Church (cf. I Thess 4:13-18).

24. Then, Greek *eita,* covers an interval, just as the closely related *epeita,* **after-**

ward, of the preceding verse, covers a long interval, the interval of the kingdom of Christ on earth. Every Pauline use of *eita* involves an interval. Note that the *epeita* of verse 23 has already covered an interval of at least 1900 years! **The end** refers to the end of the kingdom, as the following verse indicates. **25. For** gives the reason he cannot relinquish the kingdom until the end comes. The Son must reign as man under the Father (cf. Ps 110:1). Following this reign, the mediatorial kingdom will be merged with the eternal kingdom of the triune God. **26.** The annulling of **death** will take place at the Great White Throne Judgment, after the kingdom and final rebellion of Satan (cf. Rev 20:7-15). Here is the Christian answer to the Greek philosophers. They said that there is no resurrection, but Paul says there is no death (cf. ExpGT, II, 928).

27,28. The statement that the **Son also himself** shall **be subject** to God has been thought by some to lower the dignity of the Son of God, as well as, possibly, to cast a reflection on his deity. The subjection, however, is not that of the Son *as Son,* but *as the incarnate Son.* This, of course, does not involve inequality of essence. The son of a king may be officially subordinate and yet equal in nature to his father (cf. Charles Hodge, *An Exposition of the First Epistle to the Corinthians,* pp. 333-335). Paul's point is this: The Son as incarnate Son has all power now (cf. Mt 28:18). When he delivers up the administration of the earthly kingdom to the Father, then the triune God will reign as God and no longer through the incarnate Son. Messiahship is a phase of the Son's eternal Sonship (cf. Moffatt, MNT, p. 249).

29-34. After outlining the positive issues of resurrection (vv. 12-28), the apostle turns now to the negative side. **29. Baptized for the dead** is a difficult expression, which has been given many interpretations, some bizarre and heretical. For example, it is claimed by some that Paul refers to the practice of vicarious baptism, such as is observed by the Mormons, although he did not approve of it (cf. Morris, *op. cit.,* pp. 218-219). The practice, however, is known only as early as the second century, and then among heretics. Others feel that the apostle refers to those who were baptized on the basis of the testimony of some who had died. The preposition *hyper,* rendered **for** in the AV, may mean "with regard to," although this is not the normal meaning. Still others feel that Paul refers to the baptism of young converts who took the place in the church of older brethren who had died. *Hyper* has the meaning "instead of" quite frequently, even in the NT, as II Cor 5:15 and Phm 13 indicate, although it is not the predominant meaning. The Greek expositors explained the expression as "baptized with an interest in (the resurrection of) the dead," but this is unnatural for several reasons (cf. ICC, pp. 359-360). The second and third suggestions are more in line with Pauline theology, but the interpretation remains difficult.

31. I die daily refers to the external perils Paul faced. It was a foolish thing to face them if there is no resurrection (cf. II Cor 1:8,9; 11:23). **32. I have fought with beasts at Ephesus** is commonly thought to be a figurative reference to his persecutions from men (cf. 16:9). **Let us eat and drink** expresses the inevitable result of the denial of the future life – moral decay (cf. Isa 22:13).

33,34. After a subtle warning against association with those who were undermining the believers' faith in the resurrection, Paul tells the believers to **awake to righteousness** (lit., *sober up with righteous resolve)* **and sin not** (lit., *stop sinning).* The inevitable moral results of wrong doctrine are clearly seen here. He charges the Corinthians, who prided themselves on their knowledge, with lack of **knowledge of God.** No wonder he adds, **I speak this to your shame.**

2) The Consideration of Certain Objections. 15:35-57. The apostle deals with objections in this section. Two of them are referred to in the first verse. **How are the dead raised up?** questions the *possibility* of resurrection (not the method), and this objection is answered in verse 36. **With what body do they come?** concerns the **nature** of the resurrection body, and this problem is discussed in verses 37 through 49. The final problem, which is implied, is this: What happens to those who do not die? Paul deals with this in the remaining verses of the section (vv. 50-57). **35,36.** The apostle's simple answer to the first question is that the body **is not quickened** (resurrected), **except it die.** Death, the body's enemy, is really the means to resurrection.

37-41. Illustrating from the natural

world, Paul deals with two common errors. One is to regard the resurrection body the same as the original body, simply re-formed; the other is to regard it as a new body unrelated to the original. The fact is that there is continuity (v. 36), identity (v. 38), and yet diversity (vv. 39-41) between the two bodies. **Not that body that shall be** refutes the notion that the body will be the same body in its physical make-up. **38. His own body.** Just as in the case of the grain, each one preserves his personal identity.

39,40. All flesh is not the same flesh. In the light of the theory of evolution, this is an interesting statement. It is designed to preserve the element of diversity among believers' resurrection bodies. **Celestial bodies** are the sun, moon, stars, etc. **41.** The statement, **one star differeth from another star in glory,** may point to differing rewards among the glorified (cf. ICC, pp. 371,372).

42. So also introduces the Pauline application to the resurrection body. Four particulars are singled out, as the apostle labors to describe the indescribable and express the inexpressible. First, the body will be **raised in incorruption;** there will be no possibility of decay (cf. vv. 53,54). **43.** It will also be **raised in glory** and **raised in power.** There will be no more sin principle within it nor physical weakness. **44.** Finally, it will be **raised a spiritual body.** Apparently a reference to the body's use, not its substance. It will be formed to be the organ of the Spirit.

45. Paul points out that Scripture agrees with what he is saying, for **so it is written.** The two Adams stamp their characteristics on their races. The term, **the last Adam,** was coined by Paul (cf. MNT, p. 263) to indicate that there can be no third representative man, sinless and without human father, as were both Christ and Adam. Had God's last Adam failed, there would have been no other. **Quickening** (lit., *life-giving;* cf. Col 1:17; Phil 3:20,21). **47. The Lord from heaven** looks forward to his coming. **48,49. We shall also bear** is a ringing promise. Many excellent manuscripts have *let us bear,* but the reading is probably the result of an early corruption of the text. **The image of the heavenly** is the final note on the nature of the resurrection body. It is to be like Christ's own glorious body (cf. Lk 24:29-43; Phil 3:21; Ps 17:15).

50. The question Paul has next to answer is one that naturally follows. It is this: But what happens to those who do not die? In what way do they participate in the resurrection of the body? The principle is that there must be a transformation, for **flesh and blood** (he does not say *body)* **cannot inherit the kingdom of God.**

51. Mystery (cf. 2:7). Not all believers will **sleep** (die), but **all** shall **be changed,** i.e., have their bodies transformed. The **all** in the last clause negates the doctrine of a partial rapture of the Church. **52. In a moment.** From Greek *atmos,* "that which cannot be cut," from which is derived the word *atom.* In **the twinkling of an eye.** The fluttering of an eyelid. These phrases emphasize the suddenness of the change. The sounding of **the trumpet** points to the time (cf. I Thess 4:16). **53.** The dead and the living come before the writer here, **corruptible** referring to the dead and **mortal** referring to the living.

54. This glorious transformation in resurrection shall bring **to pass the saying that is written, Death is swallowed up in victory** (a free application of Theodotion's rendering of Isa 25:8). The consummation of Gen 3:15 is reached.

55. From the exultation of the resurrection triumph, Paul taunts death. The better manuscripts have the clauses reversed, with **death** being asked both the questions (Paul never uses *hades;* cf. Hos 13:14). **56.** A short and concise statement of the relation of **death, sin,** and **law,** suggested by the thought of death's **sting** being removed. **The sting of death is sin** because it is by sin that death gains authority over man, and it is by **the law** that **sin** gains its **strength.** Law gives sin the character of rebellion, conscious defiance (cf. Rom 4:15; 7:7-13). The Law, then, stirred up sin, which led to death. Christ, by entering death, overcame sin, so that believers may sing, "He death by dying slew."

57. The apostle leads the thanksgiving of the redeemed to the **God** who initiates and in grace **giveth us the victory. Through our Lord Jesus Christ** points to the divine instrumentality, the work of Christ; and the phrase is a short summary of all that is involved in verses 3-5,20-22. These words, concluding the resurrection argument, answer to the apostle's words elsewhere — "and so shall we ever be with the Lord" (I Thess 4:17).

3) The Concluding Appeal. 15:58.

Therefore introduces the conclusion. As Robertson and Plummer put it, "Let there be less speculation and more work" (ICC, p. 379).

V. The Conclusion: Practical and Personal Matters. 16:1-24.

A. The Collection for the Poor. 16:1-4.

The last chapter of the letter is occupied with practical and personal matters, the first of which is the collection for the poor at Jerusalem. The chapter provides an illustration of the outworking of the great spiritual reality affirmed in 1:9—namely, that believers are called "into the fellowship of his Son Jesus Christ our Lord" (cf. 15:58).

1. Now concerning introduces the subject as one mentioned in the Corinthians' letter to Paul. **2. The first day of the week,** or Sunday, was the day the believers met for worship. This is the earliest mention of the fact (cf. Acts 20:7). Giving was to be systematic. **As God hath prospered him** sets forth the NT measure of giving (cf. Acts 11:29). **By him** is probably a reference to the home; giving was to be private giving. Paul desired the collection to be taken before he came, that pressure might be absent (cf. II Cor 9:5). This system would revolutionize present church customs!

3,4. Paul's carefulness in money matters should be noted. He never appealed for money for himself and did not even desire to handle money for others if there could be the slightest question about it. **If it be meet** (lit., *worthy)*, probably means, "If it is large enough to make it worthwhile for me to abandon other work and go with the gift" (cf. Rom 15:25).

B. The Planned Visit of Paul. 16:5-9.

The apostle desired to spend some time among the Corinthians. Therefore, he planned to pass through Macedonia first rather than go to Corinth at once. This constituted a change in plans, for which he was later criticized by some in the church (cf. II Cor 1:15-17). **5,6. Bring me on my journey** does not involve their giving money to him (cf. 9:15). **7. If the Lord permit.** The apostle's acknowledgement of a will above his own. He held the reins of his life in a loose hand. **8,9. Door.** Figurative for an opportunity (cf. II Cor 2:12; Col 4:3). **Many adversaries** may be a motive for Paul's stay at Ephesus (cf. 15:32; Acts 19:1-41).

C. Commendations, Exhortations, Salutations, and Benediction. 16:10-24.

His planned visit reminds him of two helpers in the ministry to Corinth—Timothy and Apollos.

10,11. If Timothy come allows for possible difficulties along the way (cf. 4:17; Acts 19:22). Timothy was young and apparently somewhat timid (I Tim 4:12; 5:21-23; II Tim 1:6-8; 2:1,3,15; 4:1,2), but he was a faithful worker. It is difficult to conceive of a higher commendation than **he worketh the work of the Lord, as I also do. 12.** Although Paul may have had reason to envy Apollos (cf. 1:12), he was not jealous of the attractive and gifted Alexandrian. Nor did he have ultimate authority over Apollos, for although Paul **greatly desired him to come,** Apollos felt it was not the time to come and did not do so. **His will** refers to Apollos.

13. Here begins a series of exhortations addressed to the church. The **first** four are military words; in fact, **quit you like men** reminds one of the battle cry of the Philistines (cf. I Sam 4:9, AV). Each of the imperatives in this verse and the one in the following verse are in the present tense, expressing actions that are to be continuous. **15,16. The house of Stephanas** (cf. 1:16). **Addicted themselves** (lit., *appointed themselves)* refers to "a self-imposed duty" (ICC, p. 395). **17,18. Stephanas and Fortunatus and Achaicus** were probably the bearers of the Corinthian letter to Paul (cf. 7:1). **My spirit and yours** refers to Paul's refreshment and to theirs when they would hear the report of their representatives upon their return and read this letter.

19-24. Concluding salutations, warning, and benediction. **Aquila and Priscilla,** whether at Rome (Rom 16:3-5) or Ephesus, kept their home as a gathering place for the saints. **20. The holy kiss** (cf. Rom 16:16; I Thess 5:26; II Cor 13:12; I Pet 5:14). An ancient custom. This is an implied exhortation to put away their divisions.

21,22. The apostle takes the pen from his amanuensis and inscribes the final words, the first statement of which comes in like a clap of thunder. **Ana-**

thema. The Greek equivalent of the Hebrew *ḥērem,* meaning "a thing devoted to destruction, the object of a curse" (cf. Rom 9:3; Gal 1:8,9; I Cor 12:3). The word should be followed by a period. The following word, **Maranatha** (Gr. transliteration of an Aramaic expression) may mean "Our Lord, come," or "Our Lord is come" (the Incarnation in view), or "Our Lord cometh" (Second Coming). The context, with its note of warning, decides for the last translation (RSV, *Our Lord, come!).* **23,24.** The note of warning is not the final note, however. Even the benediction of grace is not adequate here; Paul must add the tender **My love be with you all.** His rebukes have been the rebukes of love, and his love extends to **all,** even the wayward and rebellious.

BIBLIOGRAPHY

BARCLAY, WILLIAM. *The Letters to the Corinthians (The Daily Study Bible Series).* Philadelphia: Westminster Press, 1956.

FINDLAY, G. G. "St. Paul's First Epistle to the Corinthians," *The Expositor's Greek Testament.* Vol II. Grand Rapids: Wm. B. Eerdmans Publishing Co., n.d.

GODET, FREDERIC. *Commentary on St. Paul's First Epistle to the Corinthians.* 2 vols. Edinburgh: T. & T. Clark, 1880.

GROSHEIDE, F. W. *Commentary on the First Epistle to the Corinthians (The New International Commentary).* Grand Rapids: Wm. B. Eerdmans Publishing Co., 1953.

HODGE, CHARLES. *An Exposition of the First Epistle to the Corinthians.* Grand Rapids: Wm. B. Eerdmans Publishing Co., reprinted 1950.

IRONSIDE, H. A. *Addresses on the First Epistle to the Corinthians.* New York: Loizeaux Brothers, 1938.

MOFFATT, JAMES. *The First Epistle of Paul to the Corinthians (The Moffatt New Testament Commentary).* New York: Harper and Brothers, 1938.

MORRIS, LEON. *The First Epistle of Paul to the Corinthians (Tyndale New Testament Commentaries).* Grand Rapids: Wm. B. Eerdmans Publishing Co., 1958.

ROBERTSON, ARCHIBALD, and PLUMMER, ALFRED. *A Critical and Exegetical Commentary on the First Epistle of Paul to the Corinthians (The International Critical Commentary).* New York: Charles Scribner's Sons, 1911.

VINE, W. E. *First Corinthians.* London: Oliphants, 1951.

THE SECOND EPISTLE TO THE CORINTHIANS

INTRODUCTION

The Occasion of the Writing. The major matters pertaining to Paul's relations with the church at Corinth are dealt with more specifically in the Introduction to I Corinthians than they are here. The immediate occasion that prompted the writing of II Corinthians centered in certain crises that had arisen in the church after the dispatch of the first letter. To state the known facts concisely, it appears that Paul had sent Titus to Corinth to correct certain abuses and to encourage the believers there to complete their contribution for the poor saints at Jerusalem. Paul, troubled in spirit, had departed from Ephesus and had come to Troas with the expectation of finding Titus. Still more troubled because he did not find Titus in Troas, he departed hurriedly to Macedonia. There Titus, freshly returned from Corinth with encouraging news, met Paul. But things were not what they should have been in the Corinthian church. The encouraging news was all but dissipated by the fact that ominous thunderheads were lying along the horizon of the church life at Corinth. It was necessary for Paul to act quickly and sternly. He had to do three things: (1) present the Gospel more clearly to the Christians; (2) put pressure on them for the completion of their promised contribution; (3) pulverize all opposition by an unparalleled defense of his apostolic ministry and authority. These points form the framework around which all the thoughts in this second letter cluster.

Date and Place of Writing. There can be little doubt that this letter was written on Paul's third missionary journey (A.D. 57)—some months or possibly a year or more after I Corinthians. It was written from Macedonia, probably from Philippi.

The Unity of the Writing. Some modern scholars hold that II Corinthians is not a unified work. (1) They affirm that 6:14–7:1 is an interpolation, because it breaks the sequence of thought. But Paul's movements do not always correspond with modern ideas of development. An author dealing with an actual situation may have reasons for an apparent digression that are utterly unknowable to a modern critic. (2) Again these scholars claim that chapter 9 largely duplicates what is in chapter 8. However, if one will study these chapters carefully, apart from the influence of a preconceived theory, he will find that chapter 9 is anything but a repetition of chapter 8. (3) Most importantly, these objectors claim that the last section (10:1 – 13:14) is so different in tone and thought from the earlier sections (1:1 – 9:15) that it must have belonged originally to some "lost" or "stern" letter that Paul sent to Corinth. The fatal objection to this popular theory is that there is absolutely no manuscript evidence for such a fragmentized or truncated epistle. Moreover, a closer study of this epistle will reveal to the diligent student a unity that is simply amazing. And obviously our knowledge of the total situation at Corinth is so nebulous that no modern scholar can safely affirm that any part of this epistle is either discordant with the rest of the epistle or irrelevant to the actual situation at Corinth.

The Development of the Thought. The progress of thought in this epistle is like the movement of a mighty army advancing over rugged terrain still inhabited by pockets of stubborn resistance. Paul never lays his armor down while such resistance to his ministry exists. His letter is, in fact, an ultimatum calling for total and unconditional surrender to the authority of Christ's apostle. In spite of its ruggedness, this letter is as beautiful in its symmetry as a mountain flower—and it carries far more spiritual fragrance. Our outline attempts to show this symmetry.

Influence. It is perhaps invidious to compare any one of Paul's epistles with another. Each one has its special characteristics that make it great in its field. But in II Corinthians we find certain features that are not so evident in Paul's other writings. As the great evangelist defends his apostolic authority against the subtle and insidious attacks of "the superlative apostles" who sought to free the Corinthians of his influence, he reveals his very soul and adds many details about his life that would otherwise be unknown. But this epistle is a monument to the fact that Paul, vital and inspired, was more than a match for "every high thing that is exalted against the knowledge of God" (II Cor 10:5, ASV).

OUTLINE

I. The conciliation. 1:1–7:16.
  A. Paul's distress reciprocated. 1:1-7.
    1. Salutation. 1:1,2.
    2. Adoration. 1:3.
    3. Agonizing tribulation. 1:4-7.
  B. Paul's desperation relieved. 1:8-14.
  C. Paul's diversion justified. 1:15–2:17.
    1. The plan contemplated. 1:15,16.
    2. The plan criticized. 1:17.
    3. The plan comprehended. 1:18-22.
    4. The plan changed. 1:23–2:4.
    5. The plan chastened. 2:5-11.
    6. The plan consummated. 2:12-17.
  D. Paul's dispensation superior. 3:1-18.
    1. In documentation. 3:1-3.
    2. In dynamism. 3:4-6.
    3. In degree. 3:7-9.
    4. In destination. 3:10,11.
    5. In diagnosis. 3:12-17.
    6. In denouement. 3:18.
  E. Paul's dualism explained. 4:1-18.
    1. The hidden and the open. 4:1,2.
    2. The blinded and the enlightened. 4:3,4.
    3. Slaves and the Master. 4:5.
    4. Darkness and light. 4:6.
    5. The frail and the Mighty. 4:7.
    6. Trials and triumphs. 4:8-10.
    7. Death and life. 4:11,12.
    8. The written and the spoken. 4:13.
    9. The past and the future. 4:14.
    10. Grace and thanksgiving. 4:15.
    11. The outer and the inner man. 4:16.
    12. Affliction and glory. 4:17.
    13. The seen and the unseen. 4:18 a.
    14. The temporal and the eternal. 4:18 b.
  F. Paul's dedication motivated. 5:1–6:10.
    1. Motivated by knowledge. 5:1-9.
    2. Motivated by judgment. 5:10.
    3. Motivated by fear. 5:11.
    4. Motivated by unselfishness. 5:12,13.
    5. Motivated by love. 5:14,15.
    6. Motivated by regeneration. 5:16,17.
    7. Motivated by reconciliation. 5:18-21.
    8. Motivated by time. 6:1,2.
    9. Motivated by suffering. 6:3-10.
  G. Paul's dissuasion urged. 6:11–7:1.
    1. The thesis: Change your attitude toward me. 6:11-13.
    2. The antithesis: Change your attitude toward the world. 6:14-16.
    3. The synthesis: Obey and live. 6:17–7:1.
  H. Paul's delight exemplified. 7:2-16.

1. Paul's high regard for the Corinthians. 7:2-4.
2. Reasons for his high regard. 7:5-16.

II. The collection. 8:1—9:15.
A. The first reason for its completion: the example of the Macedonians. 8:1-8.
B. The second reason for its completion: the example of Christ. 8:9.
C. The third reason for its completion: the requirements of honor. 8:10—9:5.
D. The fourth reason for its completion: the requirements of stewardship. 9:6-15.
1. Principles drawn from nature. 9:6.
2. Principles drawn from God's nature. 9:7-10.
3. Principles drawn from Christian nature. 9:11-15.

III. The credentials. 10:1—13:14.
A. Spiritual armor. 10:1-6.
B. Constructive authority. 10:7-18.
C. Justifiable apprehensiveness. 11:1-6.
D. Reasonable abasement. 11:7-15.
E. Well-known assiduity. 11:16-33.
F. Compensatory affliction. 12:1-10.
G. Sufficient attestation. 12:11-13.
H. Beneficial association. 12:14-18.
I. Warranted anxiety. 12:19-21.
J. Defensible asperity. 13:1-10.
K. A Christian adieu. 13:11-14.

COMMENTARY

I. The Conciliation. 1:1—7:16.

A. Paul's Distress Reciprocated. 1:1-7.

1) Salutation. 1:1,2. **1.** The epithet **apostle**, used extensively in Paul's letters (cf. Eph 1:1; Col 1:1; I Tim 1:1; II Tim 1:1), tersely and trenchantly epitomizes Paul's commission and mission (cf. Gal 1:1). **Saints** is a parallel description of the Christian brotherhood (cf. Rom 1:7; I Cor 1:2; Eph 1:1; Phil 1:1; Col 1:1). The term is always reminiscent of the radical change that has taken place (cf. II Cor 5:17; I Cor 6:11). The territory included in **all Achaia** embraced Athens (cf. Acts 17:34) and Cenchrea (cf. Rom 16:1). **2.** In the protocol of salvation, recognized even in a salutation, **grace** always precedes **peace.** The former is the basis and foundation of the latter; therefore, the order cannot be changed. No man can have **peace** who has not previously experienced divine **grace** (cf. 8:9). The deity of Christ is emphatically affirmed in the salutation and doxology (13:14) of this epistle. The single preposition **from** *(apo)* links together (see ASV) **God our Father** and **the Lord Jesus Christ** in an indissoluble union. The full title of Christ should be duly weighed.

2) Adoration. 1:3. The verbal adjective **blessed** *(eulogētos)*, always applied to the divine persons in the NT (11:31; Mk 14:61; Lk 1:68; Rom 1:25; 9:5; Eph 1:3; Col 1:3; I Pet 1:3), describes the infinite felicity and blessedness existing in the Trinity. Paul here characterizes God (1) according to his internal nature – **blessed;** (2) according to his trinitarian relationship – **the Father of our Lord Jesus Christ;** and (3) according to his attributes – **the Father of mercies, and the God of all comfort.** The word *oiktirmos* means "pity, mercy, compassion"; it is always in the plural in the NT (Rom 12:1; Phil 2:1; Col 3:12; Heb 10:28) – possibly to express the variegated nature of the virtue.

3) Agonizing Tribulation. 1:4-7. **4.** God comforts believers. God's comfort is: (1) active – **who comforteth us;** (2) extensive – **in all our tribulation;** (3) purposive – **that we may be able;** (4) specific – **in any trouble;** (5) reflexive – **by the comfort wherewith we ourselves are comforted. Tribulation** and **trouble** represent the same word *(thlipsis;* elsewhere in this epistle in 1:8; 2:4; 4:17; 6:4; 7:4; 8:2, 13). **5.** Christ comforts believers. The **as . . . so** in the Greek here compares two things of equal rank or nature (as in Lk 11:30; 17:26; Jn 3:14; 14:31; Col 3:13). By **the sufferings of** (the) **Christ** we are to understand the **suffering** of the Messiah, the Anointed One (cf. Lk 24:26,46; Phil 3:10; Col 1:24; I Pet 1:11). The verb **abound** *(perisseuō)* is somewhat typical of this epistle (II Cor 3:9; 4:15; 8:2,7,8,12).

6. The better translation is given in the ASV and the RSV. Note the present passives in the original—*are being afflicted . . . are being comforted.* Whether **afflicted** or **comforted,** the result is always good for God's children. The words, **which is effectual,** translate the present middle participle of *energeō*. In the middle form it always implies some kind of mysterious or supernatural force (cf. 4:12; Rom 12:6,11; Gal 5:6; Eph 3:20; Col 1:29; I Thess 2:13; II Thess 2:7; Jas 5:16). In the active form God is always the subject (cf. I Cor 12:6,11; Gal 2:8; Eph 1:11,20; Phil 2:13). **7.** The eschatological **our hope** (cf. I Thess 2:19) is based squarely on the fact that salvation is **stedfast** *(bebaios,* "reliable, dependable, certain" – Arndt). In **knowing** (i.e., "since we know") Paul states the objective cause of his assurance regarding the Corinthians (cf. I Thess 1:4). The **as . . . so** (as in II Cor 7:14; Eph 5:24) differs only slightly from the construction in verse 5. The word *(koinōnos)* back of **partakers** is used of physical companionship (cf. II Cor 8:23), moral participation (cf. Mt 23:30; I Cor 10:18,20; Heb 10:33), and spiritual union (cf. I Pet 5:1; II Pet 1:4).

B. Paul's Desperation Relieved. 1:8-14.

8. The nature of **our trouble** *(thlipsis;* see v. 4) that took place **in Asia** (i.e., the Roman province of Asia) has been debated at length. Some commentators look upon the mob violence at Ephesus (cf. Acts 19:23-41; I Cor 15:32) as the occasion of this **trouble.** Whatever it was – and the language used here puts it among the most excruciating of human experiences – it was one of those trials that Paul endured for the name of Christ (cf. Acts 9:16; also Ps 69:1ff.; Isa 43:2). **9.** Like Isaac (cf. Heb 11:17-19), Paul had a **sentence of death** hanging over him; and, like Abraham, he could now **trust** anew **in God which raiseth the dead** (cf. Gen 22:1-18). **10.** The verb *(rhuomai)* rendered **delivered** is used elsewhere of Lot (II Pet 2:7,9), Paul (II Tim 4:17), and believers (I Thess 1:10). The use of **out of** (ASV) rather than **from** is justified by the fact that the Greek here uses *ek*, "out of," rather than *apo*, "from." Paul actually went through and triumphantly came "out of" the trouble here described (cf. Rom 8:35-39; also Ps 66:12; 69:14; 144:7). The descriptive **so great** (cf. its use in Heb 2:3; Jas 3:4; Rev 16:18) reveals the utter magnitude of this trial. Paul's deliverance was (1) a wonderful providence – **who delivered us;** (2) a sure prophecy – **and will deliver** (ASV); (3) a bright promise – **on whom we have set our hope that he will also still deliver us** (ASV). The future deliverance was fulfilled in II Tim 4:17.

11. This verse can be variously translated (see ASV and RSV). The basic thoughts are these: (1) the efficacy of prayer in Paul's deliverance; (2) the **gift** granted to the apostle; (3) the consequent thanksgiving rendered **by . . . many . . . persons on our behalf** (ASV). Paul had great faith in intercessory prayer (cf. Rom 15:30,31; Phil 1:19; Col 4:12). The word *charisma* means "a gift (freely and graciously given), a favor bestowed" (Arndt). It is not limited to ministerial endowments (cf. Rom 1:11; I Cor 1:7; I Pet 4:10).

12. The word **rejoicing** *(kauchēsis)* is found seven times in this epistle (7:4, 14; 8:24; 9:4; 11:10,17), but only five times elsewhere in the NT. By **behaved ourselves** (ASV) Paul means that three judges determined his conduct: (1) his **conscience;** (2) God's **holiness and sincerity** (ASV); (3) the **world** and the Corinthians. Spiritual irreconcilables and incompatibles are represented by **fleshly wisdom** (cf. Jas 3:15) and **the grace of God** (cf. I Cor 3:10; 15:10; Eph 3:2,7, 8).

13. Paul was a consistent man, whether dealing with hostile Jews (cf. Acts 26:22) or with recalcitrant Christians. What he wrote in his letters could be easily **read** and *fully known* (so *epiginōskō*, here translated **acknowledge,** usually means; cf. I Cor 13:12, ASV). The Greek phrase *heōs telous* can be translated **unto the end** (AV; ASV) or *fully* (RSV). The fact that the word used here usually designates "the end" (cf. Mt 24:6,14; I Cor 15:24), plus the fact that the next verse refers to the Second Advent, seems to justify **unto the end** as the best translation (cf. I Cor 1:8). **14.** Paul's laudation over the Corinthians was made poignant by the fact that the true motivation of his ministry among them was "fully known" (the same verb as in v. 13) only **in part,** i.e., by some of them (see the same construction in Rom 11:25; I Cor 13:9). The Second Advent is called **the day** (as in I Cor 1:8; 3:13; 5:5; Phil 1:6,10; I Thess 5:2; II Thess 2:2).

C. Paul's Diversion Justified. 1:15–2:17.

1) The Plan Contemplated. 1:15,16. **15.** The word *pepoithēsis,* translated here as **confidence,** is used in the NT only by Paul (3:4; 8:22; 10:2; Eph 3: 12; Phil 3:4). The **second benefit** *(charis,* "grace") sums up the double blessing that would be theirs by his two visits (cf. Rom 1:11). **16.** Paul's contemplated plan included four stages: (1) a direct trip to Corinth; (2) a land trip from Corinth to Macedonia; (3) a return trip to Corinth; (4) a trip from Corinth to Judea. Paul often gave his proposed itinerary (cf. Rom 1:10; 15:22; I Thess 2:18).

2) The Plan Criticized. 1:17. Paul answers the charges made against him—of vacillating and using fleshly methods—(1) by using logic (**therefore**; but in the Greek both *oun* and *ara* are used); (2) by an emphatic negative *(mēti;* cf. Mt 7:16; 26:22,25); (3) by repetition (**yea, yea; and nay, nay**); (4) by the emphasis of order (which can be seen only in the Greek).

3) The Plan Comprehended. 1:18-22. **18. But as God is true** may be taken as an adjuration (AV; ASV; RSV) or as a plain statement ("But God is faithful in that our word which was toward you is not yea and nay"). Paul often appeals to the faithfulness of God as a proof of the truthfulness of the Gospel he proclaimed (cf. I Cor 1:9; I Thess 5:24; II Thess 3:3). **19.** This verse reveals (1) the person, (2) the preaching, (3) the preachers, and (4) the positiveness of the message: all having their unity in Christ. The difference between **was** (aorist of *ginomai)* in **was not** and the **was** (perfect of *ginomai)* in **was yea** should be noted: "became not yea and nay, but in him became (and remains as) yea" (cf. Jn 1:14; Rev 1:17,18). **20.** Read as in the ASV. The **how many soever** (ASV) correctly represents the Greek pronoun used here (see its use in Mt 14:36; Jn 1:12; Acts 3:24; Rom 2:12; Phil 3:5). All of God's promises find their realization and fulfillment in Christ (cf. Rom 15:8,9).

21,22. We should not overlook the references to the Trinity in 1:18-22: (1) the certainty given by God (v. 18); (2) the centrality found in Christ (vv. 18-20); (3) the certification established by the Spirit (vv. 21,22). Paul appeals to a present experience (**stablisheth,** present tense of *bebaioō;* cf. its use in Mk 16:20; Rom 15:8; I Cor 1:6,8; Col 2:7; Heb 2:3; 13:9), which is confirmed by three simultaneous and decisive acts that took place at regeneration – **anointed . . . sealed . . . gave** (ASV; all in the aorist tense). The verb *(chriō)* translated **anointed** is used concerning the anointing of the Holy Spirit (cf. Lk 4:18; Acts 4:27; 10:38; Heb 1:9). The name *Christ* ("The Anointed One") comes from the same root. The **earnest** *(arrabōn;* used elsewhere in the NT only in II Cor 5:5; Eph 1:14) is the initial payment on a purchase: *a guarantee* (RSV).

4) The Plan Changed. 1:23–2:4. **23.** Paul gives a negative reason (**to spare you;** 1:23–2:4a) and a positive reason (**but that ye might know the love,** etc.; 2:4b) why he changed his contemplated plan. **But I call God for a witness upon my soul** (ASV) correctly represents Paul's words (cf. 11:31; Rom 1:9; Phil 1:8; I Thess 2:5,10). The **not as yet** statement could be translated as "no more" – implying that Paul desisted from his visit to Corinth until certain things were corrected there (cf. II Cor 13:2,10). **24.** That the words "to spare you" might not be misunderstood, Paul reminds his readers that he is not seeking ecclesiastical tyranny over their **faith** (cf. 4:5; 11: 20; I Pet 5:3). The word **joy** *(chara)* occurs as often in this epistle (1:24; 2:3; 7:4,13; 8:2) as in Philippians (1:4,25; 2:2,29; 4:1). We can read **by faith** (AV) or *in faith* (ASV; RSV) – the former indicating means; the latter, sphere. **On stand,** see also Rom 5:2; 11:20; I Cor 15:1; I Pet 5:9.

2:1. Paul's "determination" issued from the fact that **sorrow** (ASV) would have characterized his visit if his original plan (cf. 1:15,16) had been carried out. Endless debate has revolved around the words **come again.** The issue is made extremely complex by the fact that only one visit to Corinth is recorded in Acts (18:1-18) prior to this epistle. However, in II Cor 12:14; 13:1 it appears that the apostle's next visit was to be his third one. Some scholars hold that Paul made a second (unrecorded) visit. **2.** The **if** assumes the fact to be true (as in 2:5,9; 3:7,9,11; 5: 14). Paul gets no sadistic delight out of pain he causes his converts: his sadness and joy are contingent on their spiritual state.

3. Which letter are we to understand by **I wrote?** Older commentators generally assumed that our I Corinthians is referred to here; more recent commentators think that Paul is referring to a "stern letter" (now lost or else found in chapters 10–13 of our present epistle) that he wrote after he wrote I Corinthians. These same commentators also assume that an unrecorded visit took place prior to the "stern letter." One cannot be dogmatic on the circumstances surrounding Paul's relation to the church at Corinth.

4. Paul's emotional life is here epitomized in (1) depth – **much affliction and anguish of heart;** (2) its visible expression–**with many tears;** (3) its negative purpose – **not that ye should be grieved;** (4) its positive purpose – **that ye might know the love which I have more abundantly unto you.** The last clause gives Paul's positive reason (see 1:23) for changing his plan (cf. 1:15,16).

5) The Plan Chastened. 2:5-11. **5.** The reference of **any** hinges on the view one takes of Paul's visits and letters to Corinth. According to the older view, the incestuous person of I Cor 5:1-8 is referred to here. More recent commentators hold that a person or party (cf. II Cor 10:7; I Cor 1:12) had recently arisen there to challenge Paul's apostolic authority. The issue will probably never be settled until we possess more than the scanty facts we now have. In **overcharge** (*epibareō*, "to weigh down, burden" – Arndt) we have perhaps a polite understatement of Paul's concern (cf. the same word in I Thess 2:9; II Thess 3:8). **6. The punishment** was **sufficient.** "The punishment is severe enough" (Arndt). But the silence was polite (**such a man**) and ominous (**of many** – implying that a recalcitrant minority still rebelled against Paul).

7. Neither **ought** (AV) nor **should** (ASV; RSV) is required by the Greek. Plummer puts it thus: "So that on the contrary you may rather forgive him" (*A Critical and Exegetical Commentary on the Second Epistle of St. Paul to the Corinthians*). The verb **forgive** (*charizomai;* see its use in II Cor 1:10; 12:13; Rom 8:32; Gal 3:18; Eph 4:32; Col 2:13; 3:13) means "to give freely or graciously as a favor" (Arndt). It should be noted that this was the act of the whole church. The use of **lest by any means** (ASV), which translates *mē pōs* (cf. its use in II Cor 9:4; 11:3; 12:20; I Cor 8:9; 9:27), indicates that the action mentioned was within the range of possibility. **8. Confirm** (*kyroō;* elsewhere in NT only in Gal 3:15) means either "to reaffirm" (Arndt) or "to ratify" (Plummer). Their acceptance of him as a brother restored to Christian fellowship would be the public display of this "reaffirmation."

9. Paul indicates three reasons why he wrote: (1) to prepare them for his visit (2:3); (2) to manifest to them his love (2:4); (3) to test their obedience (2:9). The word **proof** *(dokimē)* is found four times in this epistle (2:9; 8:2; 9:13; 13:3); elsewhere in the NT only in Rom 5:4; Phil 2:22. By **in all things** Paul shows that incomplete obedience is intolerable.

10. Read this verse in the ASV or the RSV. Paul ratifies the action of the Corinthian church in the corporate duty of "forgiving" (cf. Jn 20:23). On **forgive,** see II Cor 2:7. We can read the last statement as **in the person of Christ** (AV), i.e., acting as his representative; or *in the presence of Christ* (ASV; RSV), i.e., acting with him as our witness. **11.** We have (1) a common foe – Satan; (2) a common danger – **get an advantage of us;** (3) a common protection – **we are not ignorant of his devices.** The verb *pleonekteō* (found elsewhere in the NT only in 7:2; 12:17,18; I Thess 4:6) means "to take advantage of, outwit, defraud, cheat" (Arndt). Here we may read: "that we may not be outwitted by Satan" (Arndt).

6) The Plan Consummated. 2:12-17. **12.** From here to the end of the chapter Paul tells us how his changed plan was consummated in trial (vv. 12,13), in triumph (vv. 14-16), and in testimony (v. 17). What an opportunity–**a door!** What a privilege–**for me!** What a responsibility–**opened!** What a relationship–**in the Lord!** Paul's travels were always purposive and evangelistic – **for the gospel of Christ** (ASV). **13.** Paul's disturbed **spirit** demanded his quick departure from Troas. To get news concerning the Corinthian church was his immediate obsession; all else – including the evangelization of Troas – was secondary. Who or what caused these two men – Paul and Titus – to "foul up" their plans is not revealed here. Shall we say that souls were lost in Troas because of somebody's failure? God overruled by granting Paul a ministry there on his return from Corinth (Acts 20:6).

14. The order in the Greek is emphatic: "But unto God be thanks" (cf. 8:16; 9:15). This verse illustrates Rom 8:28. The verb *thriambeuō* should be translated **leadeth us in triumph** (ASV; RSV). This verb is used elsewhere in the NT only in Col 2:15. Paul considers himself as a slave (cf. Rom 1:1) being led triumphantly in the Messiah's conquered host (cf. Eph 4:8; after a victorious military campaign it was customary for Roman emperors to stage a "triumph," during which they paraded captives through the streets of Rome). Note the **always** (*pantote;* cf. II Cor 4:10; 5:6; 9:8) and **in every place** (cf. Acts 1:8; Rom 10:18; Col 1:6,23). The verb (*phaneroō*) translated **maketh manifest** is quite common in this epistle (3:3; 4:10,11; 5:10; 7:12; 11:6). The use of **savour** shows that Paul is continuing the picture of a triumphal procession. The word **knowledge** (*gnōsis*) is used twenty-nine times in the NT; Paul uses it twenty-three times. It is used elsewhere in this epistle in 4:6; 6:6; 8:7; 10:5; 11:6.

15. In the NT, salvation is described as (1) past (aorist tense: II Tim 1:9; Tit 3:5); (2) present (present tense: here and in I Cor 1:18; 15:2); (3) future (future tense: Rom 5:9,10; I Cor 3:5; II Tim 4:18); (4) completed (perfect tense: Eph 2:5,8). The verb **perish** (*apollumi;* cf. its use in II Cor 4:3; Jn 3:16; 10:28; 17:12; 18:9; II Thess 2:10) designates destruction and ruination rather than annihilation. **16.** The same **savour** is wafted to all by the messengers of the Gospel. To some it is fatal; to others it is life-giving (cf. Jn 3:19; 9:39; 15:22; 16:8 ff.; Acts 13:46ff.; 28:25-28). The transition from spiritual death (cf. Eph 2:1) to eternal death (cf. Rev 2:11; 20:14; 21:8) is probably indicated by **from death unto death** (ASV).

17. Paul's testimony is that he does not, like **many** (the false teachers mentioned in 11:4,12-15), **corrupt** (*kapēleuō*, meaning "to trade in, peddle, huckster" — Arndt) **the word of God.** Paul's sincerity is evident in its (1) origin — **of God;** (2) manifestation — **in the sight of God;** (3) sphere of action — **speak we in Christ** (cf. 13:3).

D. Paul's Dispensation Superior. 3:1-18.

1) Superior in Documentation. 3:1-3. **1.** Paul vehemently exposes those who need **letters** of self-commendation (cf. 5:12; 10:12,18; 12:11). His mission and ministry did not need such conceited self-appraisal. **2.** On the contrary, Paul's letter is (1) personalized — **our epistle;** (2) permanent — **written in our hearts;** (3) public — **known and read of all men.** **3.** The genuineness of the Corinthians as **an epistle of Christ** (ASV) is authenticated (1) by their ministry — **ministered by us;** (2) by their supernatural origin — **with the Spirit of the living God;** (3) by their internal testimony — **in fleshy tables of the heart** (cf. Jer 24:7; 31:33; 32:39; Ezk 11:19; 36:26).

2) Superior in Dynamism. 3:4-6. **4.** This **trust** (*pepoithēsis;* see 1:15) is **through Christ.** The use of the definite article before **Christ** ("The Christ"; i.e., "The Anointed One") is quite common in this epistle (1:5; 2:12,14; 3:4; 4:4; 5:10, 14; 9:13; 10:1,5,14; 11:2,3; 12:9). On **through** (*dia*), see 5:18 in the ASV. **5.** Our **sufficiency** (*hikanotēs*, meaning "fitness, capability, qualification"—Arndt) is **of God.** The **of** (*ek*) indicates source (as in 4:7,18; Jn 10:47; 18:36,37. Cf. I Cor 15:10).

6. Follow the ASV translation: **who also made us sufficient as ministers.** The **new covenant** (ASV; cf. Mt 26:28; Heb 8:8,13) requires a "new man" (Eph 2:15; 4:24) who is a "new creature" (II Cor 5:17). This regenerated person has a "new name" (Rev 2:17), observes a "new commandment" (I Jn 2:7,8), sings a "new song" (Rev 14:3), looks for "new heavens and a new earth" (II Pet 3:13; Rev 21: 1) where the "new Jerusalem" (Rev 21:2) is and where all things are "new" (Rev 21:5). The contrast between **the letter killeth** and **the spirit giveth life** is not a contrast between extreme literalism and a free handling of Scripture (as in the allegorical method of interpretation); the contrast is rather between the Law as a system of salvation requiring perfect obedience (cf. Rom 3:19,20; 7:1-14; 8:1-11; Gal 3:1-14) and the Gospel as God's gift of grace in Christ. Even the Law, however, could lead a soul to Christ (cf. Gal 3:15-29); but degenerate Judaism had turned it into a lifeless mass of forms (cf. Isa 1:10-20; Jer 7:21-26). The new age of "grace and truth" (Jn 1:17), already anticipated in the OT (cf. Ezk 37:1-14; 47:1-12), is now fully realized in the dynamic dispensation of grace (cf. Jn 4:23; 6:63; Rom 2:28; 7:6).

3) Superior in Degree. 3:7-9. **7.** Read Ex 34:29-35 for background material. The dispensation of "the letter" is inferior to the dispensation of "the spirit" in (1) essential nature — **death** (cf. Rom 7:5,10,11; Gal 3:10,21,22); (2) outward form — **engraven in stones** (cf. Ex 24:12; 31:18); (3) abiding merit — **which glory was passing away** (ASV). The verb (*katargeō*) in the last clause means "to

abolish, wipe out, set aside" (Arndt); except for two places (Lk 13:7 and Heb 2:14), it is used exclusively in the NT by Paul (e.g., II Cor 3:1,13,14; I Cor 15:24,26; II Tim 1:10).

8. The negative **not** *(ouchi)* expects a strong positive answer (as in I Cor 9:1; 10:16,18). The argument used here is called *argumentum a minore ad majus:* if the lesser of two things be true, how much more shall the greater be true.

9. The old dispensation admittedly had its **glory** (cf. Rom 9:4,5); but the new dispensation must **exceed in glory** (cf. Heb 8:6ff.; 9:11-15). In the OT "everlasting righteousness" (Dan 9:24) was promised as a concomitant of the Messiah's advent (cf. Isa 51:5–8; 56:1; Jer 23:5,6). That **righteousness** was fulfilled by Christ (cf. II Cor 5:21; Mt 3:15; Rom 10:4) and is now imputed to all who believe on him (cf. II Cor 5:21; Rom 3:21-31; 4:1-13).

4) Superior in Destination. 3:10,11. **10.** The new dispensation is superior to the old in that the new is not subject to diminution and demolition. The **glory** of the old was but a reflection of the new; it was a "copy and shadow" (Heb 8:5; 10:1) of the new. **11. The old** "is being abolished" (ASV margin); the new remains. The verbs **done away** and **remaineth** are present participles. Cf. Heb 12:18-28.

5) Superior in Diagnosis. 3:12-17. **12.** The new far exceeds the old in clarity and perspicuity. The use of **such** calls up the inherent quality of the thing to which it is applied (as in Mt 19:14; Jn 9:16; Gal 5:21,23; Heb 13:16). Paul uses the word **hope** in all of his epistles except Philemon. **Plainness of speech** *(parrēsia;* cf. II Cor 7:4) describes the *boldness of speech* (ASV) that characterized the early Christians (cf. Acts 2:29; 4:13,29,31) and Paul (cf. Eph 6:19; Phil 1:20) in their testimony against Jews and Gentiles. The believers were not ashamed of the Gospel, because they knew it had an inner power and vitality that could not be found elsewhere (cf. Rom 1:16,17). **13.** Read this verse in the ASV or the RSV. We have here the reason for the "great boldness" of Christians. Moses *used to put* (the verb is in the imperfect tense) a veil on his face so that the Israelites could not see **the end of the fading splendor** (RSV). In Paul's inspired interpretation of the OT, the evanescent glory that shone from Moses' face after his communion with God becomes typical of the passing glory of the old dispensation.

14. Paul here gives a spiritual application for the physical **veil** on Moses' face. That **veil** now becomes a **veil** that keeps the Jews from understanding the true import of **the old covenant** as they read it (ASV). The word *noēma,* here translated **minds,** is used almost exclusively in this epistle (2:11; 4:4; 10:5; 11:3; cf. Phil 4:7). The cognate verb form *(noeō)* designates "rational reflection or inner perception" (Arndt; cf. its use in Jn 12:40; I Tim 1:7; Heb 11:3). The passive form **were blinded** denotes the judicial blindness that befell Israel when the nation rejected Christ (cf. Jn 12:40; Rom 11:7, 25). Such blindness may be due to God (cf. Rom 11:7,8), Satan (cf. II Cor 4:4), or man himself (cf. Heb 3:8). The clause, **which veil is done away in Christ,** can also be translated as in the ASV or as in the RSV. The verb **is done away** (present passive of *katargeō;* see II Cor 3:7 b) means that this **veil** of spiritual blindness is being removed from the hearts of believing Israelites the moment they "see" Christ as their Saviour (cf. Jn 9:40,41).

15. The Pentateuch was habitually read – **whensoever Moses is read** (ASV) – in the synagogues (cf. Acts 15:21). Paul had no question about its authorship (cf. Acts 26:22; 28:23; Rom 10:5,19; I Cor 9:9). It was even necessary for Christ to "open" the minds of his own disciples regarding the Messianic significance of the OT (cf. Lk 24:25,26,32,44,45). **16.** The **whensoever** (ASV) should be retained here. It is the same indefinite particle as is used in verse 15 (but nowhere else in the NT). The subject of **shall turn** may be either "the heart" or "he" (i.e., the individual Israelite). The verb **turn** *(epistrephō)* often designates conversion (cf. Lk 1:16,17; Acts 3:19; 26:20; I Thess 1:9). Whenever the soul believes, then "the veil is being removed" – the removal of the veil synchronizes with the act of saving faith (cf. Isa 25:7; Zech 12:10).

17. The Lord is the Spirit (ASV). This construction in the Greek, with the definite article preceding both subject and predicate (cf. I Jn 3:4), indicates identity of nature. By **Lord** here we are to understand Jesus Christ (so almost universally in Paul's writings; e.g., II Cor 5:6,8,11; 8:5; 10:8; 12:1,8). Paul is here teaching that Christ and the Spirit have the same essence (cf. Jn 10:30); their persons remain distinct. As announced prophetically (Isa 61:1,2; Joel 2:28-32), the new dispensation was to be characterized by the outpouring of the Spirit. The Lord Jesus sent the Spirit (cf. Jn 16:7). **Where** and "whensoever" (II Cor 3:16) the Spirit regenerates the heart, there is real **liberty** (cf. Jn 8:32; Gal 5:1,13).

6) Superior in Denouement. 3:18. Here is the grand finale. Using Ex 34:29-35 as the background, Paul gives a summary of advantages possessed by the new dispensation: (1) liberty – **with unveiled face** (ASV); (2) intimacy–**beholding . . . the glory of the Lord** (cf. Ex 33:17-23, I Jn 3:1,2); (3) efficacy – **are** (being) **transformed into the same image** (ASV); (4) perfection–**glory to glory** (cf. Isa 66:11,12); (5) supernatural origination–**even as from the Lord the Spirit** (ASV). The last statement, translated erroneously in the AV, equates Christ and the Spirit in the cooperative work of salvation (cf. II Cor 3:17; Jn 7:39; 15:26; 16:6-14).

E. Paul's Dualism Explained. 4:1-18.

1) The Hidden and the Open. 4:1,2. **1.** Note three things: (1) our riches – **we have this ministry;** (2) our reminder – **even as we obtained mercy** (ASV; cf. I Tim 1:13,16); (3) our resource – **we faint not** (cf. the same verb in II Cor 4:16; Lk 18:1; Gal 6:9; Eph 3:13; II Thess 3:13). **2.** The decisive act, **renounced,** is explained by two negative concomitants: (1) **not walking in craftiness;** (2) **nor handling the word of God deceitfully.** The resultant life is described according to its (1) means – **by the manifestation of the truth;** (2) method – **commending ourselves to every man's conscience;** (3) measure – **in the sight of God.** Christians should renounce (as here), repudiate (cf. 6:14-17), and reprove (cf. Eph 5:11) **the hidden things of shame** (ASV; cf. Rom 6:21; I Cor 4:5).

2) The Blinded and the Enlightened. 4:3,4. **3.** The **if** assumes the state to be real. **Our gospel.** The one and only **gospel** (cf. Gal 1:6 ff.). **Is veiled** (ASV). The perfect tense portrays the fixed state. The present participle is correctly rendered by **them that are perishing** (RSV; cf. 2:15). The AV's use of **hid** obscures the implicit reference to 3:13-18; the "veil" that "blinded" the Jewish mind has now become the "veil" that Satan uses to "blind" the **perishing** (RSV). **4.** Satan is here called *the god of this age* (so the Greek; cf. Jn 12:31; 14:30; 16:11; Eph 2:2). The word *image (eikōn)* is twice elsewhere applied to Christ (Col 1:15; Heb 1:3). The verb **shine** *(augazō)* is found only here in the NT.

3) Slaves and the Master 4:5. Paul preached **Christ Jesus as Lord** (ASV). The supreme Lordship of Christ was central in apostolic preaching (cf. the same construction as here in the ASV translation of Rom 10:9; Phil 2:11). The original of **servants** is *slaves.* Paul repeatedly calls himself a "slave" *(doulos;* cf. Rom 1:1; Gal 1:10; Phil 1:1; Tit 1:1). Here he uses the term to describe his relationship to his converts at Corinth.

4) Darkness and Light. 4:6. The versions (AV, ASV, RSV) differ considerably here. The RSV seems to present the original most clearly. Paul goes back to creation (Gen 1:3) for a prototype of his own conversion (cf. Acts 9:3ff.). The God who created the physical light illuminates our minds in our re-creation when we savingly behold **the face of Jesus Christ.**

5) The Frail and the Mighty. 4:7. By **this treasure** Paul reminds us that the Gospel is a valuable jewel (cf. Mt 13:44, 52) committed to him (cf. Eph 3:1,2,7,8). Human nature in its weakness and frailty is pictured in the phrase **earthen vessels** (cf. Acts 9:15). The word **exceeding** *(hyperbolē)* means "excess, extraordinary quality or character" (Arndt). The word is used in the NT only by Paul (II Cor 1:8; 4:7,17; 12:17; Rom 7:13; I Cor 12:31; Gal 1:13).

6) Trials and Triumphs. 4:8-10. These verses may be summarized thus: (1) All the verbs in 8-10 a are present participles and are grammatically related to "we" in 4:7. They explain or illustrate Paul's secret of power in "earthern vessels." (2) These participles seem to go in ascensive order – like a swelling crescendo. (3) They are paradoxical and antithetical – contrasting nature with grace. (4) Moreover, although based on 2:14ff., they step up higher on the ladder that will lead us through 6:4-10 up to the climax in 11:16-23. **Always bearing about in the body the dying of the Lord Jesus** (v. 10). Cf. Rom 8:36; I Cor 15:31; Gal 6:17; Col 1:24. Paul's great desire was that **the life also of Jesus may be manifested in our body** (ASV; cf. Gal 2:20; Phil 1:20).

7) Death and Life. 4:11,12. The thought of verse 10 is repeated, with the significant addition of **for Jesus' sake** (cf.

Acts 9:16; Phil 1:29). The apostle's life was a continuous exposure to death – **we are always being given up to death** (RSV; cf. II Tim 4:6, ASV). On **worketh** *(energeō),* see II Cor 1:6. God's power also worked in Paul (cf. Eph 3:20; Col 1:29).

8) The Written and the Spoken. 4:13. Paul, citing Ps 116:10 (LXX), gives the reason for his speaking. **Having** (ASV) equals "because we have." This verse implicitly teaches that the Holy Spirit is the Author of **faith,** Scripture, and testimony. The **we** is emphatic: Paul, like David, believes and speaks; the two dispensations are united in **faith** (cf. Heb 11: 39,40).

9) The Past and the Future. 4:14. The resurrection of believers is here presented with reference to its (1) Author – **he which raised up the Lord Jesus** (cf. Acts 3:26); (2) time – **shall raise up** (cf. I Cor 15:51,52; I Thess 4:13ff.); (3) cause–**also with Jesus** (ASV; cf. I Cor 15:20-23); (4) purpose – **shall present us with you** (cf. Eph 5:27; I Thess 2:19,20).

10) Grace and Thanksgiving. 4:15. Paul's philosophy (**all things . . . for your sakes**) issues in a purpose (**that**) which finds a plenitude of **grace** that causes **thanksgiving to abound unto the glory of God** (ASV). On **abound,** see 1:5.

11) The Outer and the Inner Man. 4: 16. **Faint not.** See 4:1. **Is decaying** (ASV) **. . . is being renewed** (RSV). The present tense in both verbs indicates simultaneous action. The **outward man** corresponds to the "earthen vessels" of 4:7 and the "earthly house" of 5:1. The seeds of decay and dissolution are in the body from birth. Read Rom 8:18-25 as an extended commentary on this verse. "For here we have no continuing city" (Heb 13:14).

12) Affliction and Glory. 4:17. We have here (1) the disparity, (2) the design, and (3) the denouement. The disparity is threefold: (1) in time – **for a moment** contrasted with **eternal;** (2) in magnitude – **light** contrasted with **weight;** (3) in character – **affliction** contrasted with **glory.** The design is found in **worketh,** a verb *(katergazomai),* which means "to bring about, produce, create" (Arndt). This verb is found seven times in this epistle (5:5; 7:10,11; 9:11; 12:12). The denouement is sounded in the **more and more exceedingly** (ASV), in which Paul almost exhausts the Greek language in his crescendo of superlatives.

13) The Seen and the Unseen. 4:18 a. **While we look** represents the present participle of *skopeō* (a verb that occurs elsewhere in the NT only in Lk 11:35; Rom 16:17; Gal 6:1; Phil 2:4; 3:17). One should not "keep one's eye on what can be seen" (Arndt). Consult Heb 11:1,7. 13-15,26 for the same thought.

14) The Temporal and the Eternal. 4: 18 b. The word **temporal** *(proskairos;* elsewhere in the NT only in Mt 13:21; Mk 4:17; Heb 11:25) defines the ephemeral and evanescent in contrast to the abiding and **eternal.** Eternity is the everlasting *now;* we live in the midst of it, although we cannot see it. In the glorified state we shall know fully (cf. I Cor 13: 12) and see fully (cf. I Jn 3:2). Now we walk by faith.

F. Paul's Dedication Motivated. 5:1–6:10.

1) Motivated by Knowledge. 5:1-9. **1.** Christians can **know** *(oida;* the same verb is used in I Jn 2:21; 3:1,2) the truth about the unseen world (cf. II Cor 4:17, 18). The **if** *(ean;* cf. its use in I Jn 3:2) suggests uncertainty regarding the time but not concerning the fact. The **earthly house** (cf. II Cor 4:7) is called **a tabernacle** – very vulnerable and transitory. The verb **were dissolved** *(kataluō)* means "to tear down, demolish" (Arndt). The body's decomposition signalizes its exit from earth into a far more glorious state above (cf. Phil 1:23; 3:20,21; I Jn 3:2, 14). No philosophy can give the assurance found in **we have** (cf. *echō* in II Cor 3:4,12; 4:1,7,13; 7:1; 9:8 for a treasury of spiritual possessions).

2. Probably **tabernacle** (v. 1) is the antecedent of **this.** The use of **groan** *(stenazō;* cf. its use in Rom 8:23) suggests that there is something distasteful in the present state (cf. Phil 1:23). The adverb **earnestly** translates the preposition *epi* in *epipotheō*–a verb expressing vehemence of desire, as can be seen in such passages as Rom 1:11; Phil 1:8; II Tim 1:4. **3.** The meaning of **being clothed** and **naked** has been debated interminably. Such passages as Jn 11:25,26; I Cor 15: 37-49; Phil 1:21-23; 3:20,21; I Thess 4: 13-18; I Jn 3:1ff.; Rev 6:9; 20:4 must be taken into account in our interpretation.

4. This verse restates and expands the previous verses. The transformation here envisaged is **that what is mortal may be swallowed up of life** (ASV). "Death is swallowed up in victory" (I Cor 15:54). Compare the cases of Enoch (Gen 5:24) and Elijah (II Kgs 2:11). The absolute use of *the life* (so the Greek) must carry some significance here as in the other places where the definite article is used (II Cor 4:12; I Jn 1:2; 2:25; 3:14; 5:12). **5.** The aorist **wrought** (ASV; see 4:17 for the verb) takes us back to God's decrees (cf. Rom 8:30; 9:23; I Cor 2:7-9). **On earnest** see 1:22.

6. The adverb **always** *(pantote)* is found in all of Paul's epistles. It is applied to such things as prayer (Rom 1:9), thanksgiving (I Cor 1:4), work (I Cor 15:58), and obedience (Phil 2:12). Cf. also II Cor 2:14; 4:10; 9:8. The verb *endēmeō* ("to be at home" — Arndt) should be consistently translated (as in ASV) here and in 5:8,9 (the only places where it is found in the NT). **7. Walk** *(peripateō).* A verb often used to describe the Christian's whole life (cf. Rom 6:4; 13:13). In II Cor 1:12 "we behaved ourselves" (ASV) is a comparable expression.

8. The thought of 5:6 is resumed. **Willing rather.** Paul does not mean that he is anxiously courting the opportunity to leave the present life (cf. the faulty rendering in the RSV). The verb translated **willing** *(eudokeō)* simply denotes that which brings pleasurable satisfaction (cf. its use in Mt 3:17; 12:18; 17:5). Cf. Phil 1:23. **9.** The verb **labour** *(philotimeomai;* elsewhere in NT only in Rom 15:20; I Thess 4:11) means "to have as one's ambition" (Arndt). The word **accepted** *(euarestos)* is used in the NT only by Paul (Rom 12:1,2; 14:18; Eph 5:10; Phil 4:18; Col 3:20; Tit 2:9) and in Heb 13:21.

2) Motivated by Judgment. 5:10. This important verse may be summarized thus: (1) the plan — **we must;** (2) the parties — **all;** (3) the presence — **appear;** (4) the place— **before the judgment seat of Christ** (cf. Rom 14:10); (5) the purpose — **that,** etc. The purpose (1) includes all — **every one;** (2) recompenses all — **may receive;** (3) recalls all — **the things done in his body;** (4) discriminates between all — **according to that he hath done, whether it be good or bad.**

3) Motivated by Fear. 5:11. **Knowing** is definitely causal ("since we know"). *Phobos* (as in Acts 9:31; Eph 5:21) should be rendered as **fear** (ASV; RSV). It denotes that reverential awe that should characterize the believer's life in view of his appearance before Christ as Judge. The order and emphasis of the original is like this: ". . . men we are persuading; but to God we have been made manifest, and I hope that in your consciences we have been made manifest." Paul sought to **persuade men** either (1) concerning the coming judgment (II Cor 5:10), or (2) of his own integrity as a minister, or (3) of the need of reconciliation (v. 5:18-21). Only (2) seems to be immediately relevant.

4) Motivated by Unselfishness. 5:12, 13. **12. Commend** *(sunistanō).* "To introduce or recommend someone to someone else" (Arndt). This verb is so characteristic of this letter (3:1; 4:2; 6:4; 7:11; 10:12,18; 12:11) that it occurs here more times than in all the rest of the NT. Evidently some at Corinth gloried **in appearance.** Paul wanted to give his converts a real **occasion** for **glorying** in his **behalf,** as one whose glory is truly **in heart,** i.e., in the inner reality. **13.** Plummer translates correctly thus: "For whether we went mad, (it was) for God; or whether we are in our right mind, (it is) for you." The "went mad" (aorist tense) may refer to some occasion when his enemies charged him with insanity (cf. Mk 3:21; Acts 26:24). It is strange how the world considers a man unbalanced when his life is fully consecrated to the Lord.

5) Motivated by Love. 5:14,15. **14. By the love of Christ** (cf. Rom 8:35; Eph 3:19) let us understand Christ's own love for us. The verb **constraineth** *(sunechō)* normally means "to hold together"; but here Arndt takes it to mean "urge on, impel." **Controls us** (RSV) seems to be justified in the light of the previous verse. Christ's love will keep any believer from insane extremes. Paul's judgment, made once for all at his conversion, was this: "One died for all; therefore, all died." The **for** in **one died for all** teaches substitution (as in Jn 10:15; 11:50,51; Rom 5:6ff.; Gal 1:4). The aorist tense in **all died** identifies the believer with Christ in his death (cf. Rom 6:2-11; Gal 2:19; Col 3:3). **15.** Those who have been redeemed by the One **who for their sakes died and rose again** (ASV) should now live wholly for their Lord, not for self (cf. Rom 14:7ff.; I Cor 6:19,20; I Thess 5:10; Rev 14:1-5).

6) Motivated by Regeneration. 5:16, 17. **16.** Before the crisis of his conversion, Paul knew Christ only **after the flesh** (i.e., as merely another man). After he knew the significance of Christ's death (5:15), he knew neither man nor Christ **after the flesh.** Spiritual insight had changed Paul's center of gravity; eternity had become the yardstick of all measurement. **17.** The believer now becomes a **new creature** (AV; ASV). On **new,** see 3:6. Read *passed away* instead of **are passed away.** The tense is aorist, and thus indicates the definitive change that took place at regeneration. The same verb *(parerchomai)* is used of the catastrophic passing away of heaven and earth at the final conflagration (Mt 5:18; Lk 21:32,33; II Pet 3:10). The perfect tense in **are become new** dramatizes the abiding change introduced by regeneration.

7) Motivated by Reconciliation. 5:18-21. **18. God** is the Author of **all things** (cf. Rom 11:36; Rev 4:11). Read thus: "who reconciled . . . and gave"; both acts belong to God. Reconciliation precedes donation. Sinners are reconciled by the death of Christ (cf. Rom 5:10). The word **ministry** *(diakonia)* is used often in this epistle (II Cor 3:7ff.; 4:1; 5:18; 6:3; 8:4; 9:1,12,13; 11:8). **19.** The comma after **Christ** in the AV is misleading. Read as in the ASV. The basic thought, **God was in Christ reconciling** (ASV), is explained negatively–**not imputing** and positively–**having committed** (ASV). Scripture teaches that there is a non-imputation of sin (Rom 4:8) and an imputation of righteousness (Rom 4:3,6,11, 22; Gal 3:6) to the one who believes in Christ.

20. This verse presents (1) the messengers–**we are ambassadors;** (2) the means–**as though God were entreating by us** (ASV); (3) the mediation– **we beseech you on behalf of Christ** (ASV); (4) the message – **become reconciled** (Alfred Plummer *(op. cit.)*. The **as though** *(hōs)* does not express doubt; the thought could be more accurately rendered *seeing that.* **21.** The Greek runs like this: *The One who did not know sin for us sin was made, that we might become God's righteousness in Him.* The Sinless One became (by imputation) sin for the sinner, that the sinner might become (by imputation) sinless in the Sinless One. Here is the very heart of the Gospel, a verse that stands with Jn 3:16 in importance. In the OT, the imputation of God's righteousness to the believer is taught didactically (Gen 15:6; cf. Rom 4:3,9), prophetically (Isa 53:11; 61:10; Jer 23:6), and typically (Zech 3:1-5).

8) Motivated by Time. 6:1,2. **1.** The participle **working together** (ASV) represents *sunergeō* (a verb that occurs elsewhere in the NT only in Mk 16:20; Rom 8:28; I Cor 16:16; Jas 2:22). There is a true 'synergism' after salvation (cf. Phil 2:12,13). **In vain.** Cf. Gal 2:2; Phil 2:16; I Thess 3:5. Paul always seeks real evidence of the power of the Gospel among his converts (cf. I Thess 2:13). **2.** By a quotation from Isa 49:8 (LXX), Paul reinforces the urgency of **receive** in verse 1. Isaiah's statement referred originally to the Messiah; Paul applies it to believers (cf. Rom 10:15 for a similar application). The **now** *(nun;* cf. its use in Eph 3:5,10; Heb 12:26; II Pet 3:7) ends when the Gospel age is finished (cf. Heb 9:26-28).

9) Motivated by Suffering. 6:3-10. All the participles through 6:10 are to be attached to **we . . . beseech** in 6:1. **The ministry** will "not be vilified" (Plummer) when the minister gives **no occasion of stumbling in anything** (ASV). The negative thought of 6:3 is stated affirmatively in 6:4 a, and then, in 6:4 b-10, expanded antithetically and ascensively by the use (in ASV) of **in** (eighteen times), **by** (three times), and **as** (seven times). Here is a multicolored rainbow glowing with the graces of Paul's ministry. Cf. 2:14ff.; 4: 8-10; 11:16-23.

G. Paul's Dissuasion Urged. 6:11–7:1.

1) The Thesis: Change your attitude toward me. 6:11-13. The verb **is open** represents the perfect tense and thus indicates the abiding state–it stands **open** (cf. the same tense in Acts 10:11; Rev 4:1). The same is true of **is enlarged**– a verb *(platunō)* that occurs elsewhere in the NT only in II Cor 6:13 and Mt 23:5. It is evident that the **Corinthians** did not share these affirmations. **12.** The verb **straitened** is from *stenochōreō,* meaning "to crowd, cramp, confine, restrict" (Arndt). It pungently describes how the Corinthians were "tight" in their affections for the apostle. **13.** As amplified, read thus: "(Grant me) the same requital –as to children I am speaking–do you also open wide (your hearts)." Ill feeling against Paul had given the Corinthians a bad case of spiritual hardening of the heart.

2) The Antithesis: Change your attitude toward the world. 6:14-16.

14. The command may be rendered: "Stop becoming heterogeneously yoked with unbelievers." The principle goes back to the Mosaic legislation (cf. Lev 19:19; Deut 22:10). Christians are "new creatures" (II Cor 5:17); they must not be united spiritually with dead unbelievers (cf. Eph 2:1). The word *(metochē)* translated **fellowship** is found only here in the NT; it means "sharing, participation" (Arndt). The word *(anomia)* back of **unrighteousness** really means "lawlessness" (Arndt). Cf. Heb 1:9 for a similar contrast. **Communion** *(koinōnia)* involves "close relationship" (Arndt), as in marriage or as in spiritual relationship with God (cf. II Cor 13:14; I Cor 1:9; I Jn 1:3,6). The contrast between **light** and **darkness** is especially prominent in NT literature (cf. Jn 1:5; 3:19; Eph 5:7, 11; Col 1:12,13; I Jn 1:6,7; 2:10,11) **15.** The word **concord** *(symphōnēsis)* is found only here in the NT. The holiness and purity of **Christ** cannot harmonize with the wickedness and impurity of **Belial** (a synonym for Satan). Cf. I Cor 10:21. The ASV correctly translates **what portion hath a believer with an unbeliever?** The two are spiritually incompatible. The word *(meris)* back of **portion** (ASV) suggests a deep sharing of things in common (cf. its use in Lk 10:42; Acts 8:21; Col 1:12).

16. The word **agreement** *(sunkatathesis)* climaxes the four previous words that Paul uses to express sinful union between the sons of God and the children of the devil. This word suggests a sympathetic union of mind and will in a plan mutually agreed to. The Temple *(naos)* is the inner sanctuary (as in I Cor 3:16,17; 6:19,20). In periods of apostasy, abominations were practiced in the holy place (cf. II Kgs 21:7; 23:6,7; Ezk 6:3-18). The heathen temple at Corinth was a cesspool of iniquity (cf. Rom 1:18-32). The quotation introduced by **even as God said** (ASV) is a composite drawn from the LXX of Lev 26:11,12; Ezk 37:27 (cf. also Ex 25:8; 29:45; Jer 31: 1). We should note how Paul supports his command (II Cor 6:14 a): (1) by an appeal to five self-evident questions (vv. 14 b-16 a), (2) by an appeal to God (v. 16b), and (3) by an appeal to Scripture (v. 16 b).

3) The Synthesis: Obey and live. 6: 17–7:1. **17. Wherefore** *(dio)* always introduces a logical conclusion (as in 2:8; 4:13,16; 5:9; 12:10). The aorist imperatives in **come out . . . be separate** (RSV) **. . . touch not** underscore the urgency and definitiveness of the act involved. The quotation is from Isa 52:11 (cf. Rev 18:4). The gender of **unclean** is ambiguous; it may be masculine or neuter **(thing).** On separation from evil, see Rom 13:11-14; Eph 5:3-14; I Pet 2:9-12; 4:1-5; I Jn 2:15-17. **I will welcome you** (RSV) introduces the first of three promises (cf. Ezk 20:34). God cannot lovingly entertain those who are knowingly and willingly involved in evil. **18.** The two promises here cited (based on such passages as II Sam 7:8,14; Isa 43:6; Hos 1:10) illustrate how promises originally made to Israel are now applied to Christians. For further illustration of this principle, cf. Ex 19:5 with I Pet 2: 5,9,10; Hos 1:10 with Rom 9:25; Jer 31:31-34 with Heb 8:8-12.

7:1. Here is the conclusion of the apostle's sermonette (6:11 – 7:1). He gives the cause, the command, and the consequence. **Since we have these promises, beloved** (RSV) introduces the cause. **These** is quite emphatic in the original —the **promises** just mentioned. **Let us cleanse ourselves.** The aorist tense makes the act absolutely peremptory and final (cf. I Cor 6:11). On "cleansing from," see Heb 9:14; I Jn 1:7,9; also see Eph 5:26; Tit 2:14. The conclusion, **perfecting holiness,** emphasizes the fact that the process is continuous; for *epiteleō,* "to complete, accomplish, perform" (Arndt) is used here in the present tense. On **fear** in the believer's life, see Acts 9:31; Eph 5:21; Phil 2:12; I Tim 5:20; I Pet 1:17; 3:15.

H. Paul's Delight Exemplified. 7:2-16.

1) Paul's High Regard for the Corinthians. 7:2-4. **2.** Hear the apostle's plea: "Make room for us" (so the Greek). Get rid of your petty peevishness and petulance; give us a place in **your hearts** (ASV). Hear his protestation: "None we wronged; none we corrupted; none we defrauded" (so the Greek order and tense). Cf. I Sam 12:3. Paul lived "soberly, righteously, and godly" (Tit 2:12) among them. No one could prove a case of moral laxness against him. **3. The before** recalls 6:11-13. Three things are latent here: (1) Paul's purpose—"You are in our hearts unto—*eis to*—dying together and living together"; (2) the indissoluble union between Paul and his converts—

to die together and live together (ASV); (3) the priority of "dying" to "living." To place "dying" before "living" may teach us either that one must really "die" before he lives (cf. Jn 12:24; Rom 6:1-14) or, equally probable, that physical death must precede eternal life in glory (cf. Jn 11:25,26; Heb 9:27,28).

4. Paul's objective attitude is expressed in **boldness** (see 3:12) and **glorying** (see 1:12); his subjective attitude is expressed in **I am filled** and **I overflow** (ASV). The "filling" (perfect tense, had become a settled state; the "overflowing" (present tense) was an ever-flowing river. On joy in **tribulation,** see II Cor 1:4; cf. Mt 5:12; Rom 5:3; Jas 1:2,3.

2) Reasons for Paul's High Regard for the Corinthians. 7:5-16. **5.** Verses 5-7 give Paul's first reason: Their regard for him. His "tribulation" (7:4), previously experienced at Ephesus (1:8) and Troas (2:12,13), followed him **into Macedonia.** It was incessant (**no rest**), encircling (**on every side**), external (**without**), and internal (**within**). **6.** Does *tapeinos* (AV, **cast down**) mean *downcast* (RSV) or *lowly* (ASV)? Usage elsewhere in the NT (cf. 10:1; Mt 11:29; Lk 1:52; Rom 12:16; Jas 1:9; 4:6; I Pet 5:5) shows that it means "of low position, poor, lowly, undistinguished" (Arndt). The word **coming** *(parousia)* means both "arrival" and "presence." It often designates the Second Advent (e.g., I Thess 2:19; 3:13; 4:15; 5:23). **7.** Three expressions—**your longing, your mourning, your zeal for me** (ASV)—set forth Paul's revived joy resulting from the arrival of Titus.

8. Verses 8-12 give Paul's second reason: Their response to his letter. Four matters in 7:8 need some clarification: (1) We should translate *metamelomai* as **regret** (ASV; RSV) rather than *repent* (AV). (2) The verb for **made . . . sorry** *(lupeō)* means "to grieve, pain" (Arndt). It does not necessarily carry an overtone of moral fault. (3) Some scholars hold that the **letter** mentioned here is a lost "stern letter"; others hold that our I Corinthians is referred to. Available information does not sanction a dogmatic decision about this. (4) If I Corinthians is meant, Paul's inspiration is in no wise impaired by his stating that, humanly speaking, he regretted that **his letter grieved them, though only for a while** (RSV). **9.** Paul's joy had a negative side—**not that ye were made sorry;** a positive side—**but that ye were made sorry unto repentance** (ASV); an underlying reason—**for ye were made sorry after a godly manner;** and an ultimate purpose—**that ye might suffer loss by us in nothing** (ASV). By **suffer loss** (ASV) Paul is thinking of the eternal damage that might result from his irresponsibility and leniency (cf. I Cor 3:15; Phil 3:8).

10. Follow the ASV or the RSV here. Note the contrasts: (1) **Godly** and **of the world;** (2) **salvation** and **death** (i.e., "the second death"—Rev 2:11; 20:6,14); (3) the two different verbs translated **worketh** — *ergazomai,* "to work" (as in I Thess 2:9), and *katergazomai* (see II Cor 4:17), "to produce" (as in 12:12). **11.** The energy of this verse is almost untranslatable. Their **godly** sorrow **produced** (RSV; cf. v. 10) salvation (cf. Phil 2:12, where *katergazomai* is also used), not death. Paul arranges seven nouns in ascensive order to describe the explosive nature of their repentance. The Corinthians came out **pure in the matter** (ASV).

12. Whatever the wrong or whoever the wronged may have been, the apostle's chief concern in writing his letter to them was that **your earnest care for us might be made manifest unto you in the sight of God** (ASV; cf. 5:11; 11:6). Their obedience was Paul's primary concern (cf. 2:9; 7:15; 10:6).

13. In 7:13-16 Paul gives the third reason: Their reception of Titus. Here we enter the calm after the storm. Note the two perfects (**have been comforted . . . hath been refreshed**—ASV). Paul's joy was intensified by **the joy of Titus.** The **you all** reflects the unity of the church. **14.** Three thoughts are here: (1) Paul's vulnerability — **if I have boasted;** (2) his veracity—**as we spake all things . . . in truth** ; (3) his vindication—**so our glorying . . . was found to be truth** (ASV). On **as . . . so,** see 1:7. This is the only place in the NT where **truth** is a predicate noun after *ginomai* ("to become"). "Our glorying . . . became [cf. Jn 1:14] truth" —as if **truth** became incarnate before them!

15. Note the faculties of human personality: (1) the emotions—**his affection** (ASV); (2) the mind—**whilst he remembereth;** (3) the will—**how . . . ye received him.** The Corinthians had learned **obedience** (cf. Heb 5:8) . . . **with fear and trembling** (cf. Phil 2:12). **16. Have confidence** (AV). *Tharreō* (used elsewhere in the NT only in 5:6,8; 7:16; 10:1,2; Heb 13:6) means here "to be able to depend on someone" (Arndt). **Perfect confidence** (RSV) is perhaps too strong; nevertheless, Paul's optimism here is not altogether irreconcilable with his pessimism in 12:20,21. In brief, Paul felt that, in spite of seemingly insurmountable obstacles, no future emergency could permanently undermine his conviction that things would eventually work out for good.

II. The Collection. 8:1–9:15.

A. The First Reason for Its Completion: The Example of the Macedonians. 8:1-8.

1. In **make known** (ASV; AV, *do . . . to wit*) we have a verb (*gnōrizō*) which occurs twenty-four times in the NT and is used eighteen times by Paul, usually in connection with some important revelation (e.g., Rom 16:26; I Cor 15:1; Eph 1:9; 3:3,5,10; Col 1:27). Paul often uses the verb *didōmi*, "to give," with *charis*, **grace** (cf. Rom 12:3,6; 15:15; I Cor 1:4; 3:10; Gal 2:9; Eph 3:2,8; 4:7). The perfect tense (**hath been given**—ASV) and the preposition **in** (ASV) make the present verse unique. The Macedonian **churches** had already received a deposit of the grace of God. **2. Affliction** (*thlipsis*). See 1:4. Some **severe test of affliction** (RSV) had come upon the Macedonian churches (cf. Acts 16:20; 17:5,13; Phil 1:28; I Thess 1:6; 2:14; 3:3-9). There is a contrast here between **great trial** and **abundance of . . . joy,** between **deep poverty** (lit., "down-to-the-bottom poverty") and **riches of . . . liberality.**

3-5. These verses constitute one sentence, the main element of which is found in **they gave themselves** (RSV) in verse 5. Follow the ASV or the RSV. The "liberality" (8:2) of the Macedonians is expanded thus: (1) they gave sacrificially—**beyond their means** (RSV); (2) they gave willingly—**of their own free will** (RSV); (3) they gave eagerly—**beseeching us with much entreaty** (ASV); (4) they gave spiritually—**first they gave their own selves to the Lord** (ASV).

6. On as . . . so, see 1:5. Cf. Phil 1:6. By **finish** (*epiteleō;* see II Cor 7:1) let us understand that **the same grace** of giving must be "brought to an end" (Arndt). It appears (cf. 8:10; 9:2; I Cor 16:1-4) that the Corinthian church had dillydallied too long about this collection. **7.** They were quite proficient in some graces (**faith . . . utterance . . . knowledge . . . diligence**); but they were quite deficient in one grace (**this grace also**). "One thing thou lackest" (Mk 10:21).

8. The word (*epitagē*) translated **commandment** is used in the NT exclusively by Paul (Rom 16:26; I Cor 7:6,25; I Tim 1:1; Tit 1:3; 2:15). An "order" could not do what the *spoudē* ("eagerness, earnestness, diligence"—Arndt) of the Macedonians would do **to prove** "whatever is genuine in your love" (Plummer).

B. The Second Reason for Its Completion: The Example of Christ. 8:9.

9. Look at the wonderful truths here: (1) a knowledge given—**ye know;** (2) a state relinquished—**though he was rich;** (3) a reason offered—**yet for your sakes;** (4) a state assumed—**he became poor;** (5) a resource tapped—**through his poverty;** (6) an exaltation conferred—**ye . . . might become rich** (ASV). Cf. Phil 2:5-10. Give according to the magnitude of your wealth in Christ Jesus.

C. The Third Reason for Its Completion: The Requirements of Honor. 8:10–9:5.

10. My **advice** is reasonable: it **is expedient** (*sympherō*—a verb meaning "to confer a benefit, be advantageous"—Arndt) **for you**—you who were "such ones" (for so the **who** implies) as **first to make a beginning a year ago** (ASV). Let your performance now catch up with and match your willingness! **11.** The **now** (*nuni;* cf. its use in I Cor 15:20; Eph 2:13; 3:10; Heb 8:6; 9:26) is more emphatic than the regular form (*nun;* cf. its use in II Cor 5:16; 6:2; 7:9). The *nuni* form is used in the NT exclusively by Paul (twenty-two times). The **advice** of 8:10 becomes a command—**perform.** The aorist of *epiteleō* (see 7:1) implies urgency and immediacy. **12.** Follow the ASV or the RSV here. One's financial response must be **according to what a man has** (RSV); harsh legalism has no place in Christian giving.

13. Literally: *For not that* (might become) *relief* (*anesis,* as in 2:13; 7:5) *to others* (Jerusalem saints), (but) *to you affliction* (*thlipsis;* see 1:4). The Jerusalem saints were not to enjoy plush seats while the Corinthians sat on hard benches. Let there be no "fringe benefits" at your expense! **14.** The desired **equality** (supplied by Corinthian **abundance**) will (1) supply their need; (2) make more palatable their supply of your (future) need; (3) produce an ethically satisfactory **equality.** The present passage gives no support either to communism or to works of supererogation. Not even

Rom 15:27 is necessarily involved. Paul is speaking of a temporary disparity in the necessities of life existing at Jerusalem and Corinth. **15.** The apostle cites an incident in Israel's history (Ex 16:18) to support the principle of "equality" (II Cor 8:14).

16. On **thanks,** see 2:14. Literally: *But thanks (be) to God who keeps on giving the same diligence for you in the heart of Titus* (cf. 8:1). **17.** Titus' "heart" (v. 16) responded spontaneously: (1) he **accepted** Paul's **exhortation;** (2) he became very diligent; (3) **of his own accord he went unto you.** The verb **being** (present participle of *huparchō)* underscores real existence in the essential nature of a thing (cf. its use in Acts 2:30; 16:20; I Cor 11:7; II Pet 1:8; 2:19; 3:10).

18. Paul does not further identify **the brother** "whose praise in the gospel is through all the churches" (Plummer). No one can dogmatically assert that Luke is **the brother** here referred to. **19.** We have here (1) the past—**chosen** (by "raising the hand"); (2) the present—**this grace** "which is being ministered by us" (Plummer); (3) the future—"unto the (furtherance of the) glory of God and our readiness." The human and the divine are intermingled here.

20. This verse gives the negative side; the next presents the positive side. With such **abundance** Paul would avoid any cause of **blame** (same word as in 6:3) in the possible mismanagement of this fund (cf. I Thess 5:22). **21.** The verb *(proneō)* rendered **forethought** is used elsewhere in the NT only in Rom 12:17; I Tim 5:8. Paul made ample provision to insure his moral integrity **in the sight of the Lord** and **in the sight of men** (cf. Rom 14:18; Phil 4:8; I Pet 2:12,15,16).

22. A third **brother,** who had been **often tested** (RSV) and was **now much more diligent,** was going along in the party. **23.** Titus is described as Paul's **partner and fellowhelper** (cf. Rom 16:3; Col 4:11; Phm 17). The other two men are called **messengers of the churches, the glory of Christ** (RSV). The word *(apostolos)* rendered **messengers** is elsewhere in the AV translated *apostle* (except in Jn 13:16; Phil 2:25). **24.** Three parties are involved: (1) the Corinthians —**ye;** (2) the "messengers" (v. 23)—**them;** (3) the **churches.** All eyes were on Corinth to see how the Christians there would receive the "messengers." Two things were at stake: **your love** and **our boasting.**

9:1. Literally: *For concerning the ministry* (which is) *unto the saints, unnecessary for me is the* (continued) *writing to you.* Nevertheless, he goes on to write more. **2.** The Christians of Achaia (including the Corinthians) were characterized by **readiness** (ASV), preparation (**hath been prepared for a year past**—ASV), and **zeal.** The verb *(erethizō)* back of **provoked** is used here in a good sense—"stimulate." In the only other NT use (Col 3:21), it has a bad sense—"irritate, embitter" (Arndt).

3. Paul fully believed that means are necessary to secure the end. This verse has many spiritual applications (cf. Acts 27:24,31). **4.** An undesirable contingency is expressed by **lest by any means** (ASV; *mē pōs;* cf. its use in 2:7; 11:3; 12:20). **5.** The threefold use of *pro,* "before," is significant: **go before . . . make up before . . . aforepromised** (ASV). **Extortion** (ASV) and **exaction** (RSV) are too strong for *pleonexia.* It is better translated "greediness, insatiableness, avarice, covetousness" (Arndt).

D. The Fourth Reason for Its Completion: The Requirements of Stewardship. 9:6-15.

1) Principles Drawn from Nature. 9:6. The commensurate proportion between sowing and reaping finds expression in the spiritual realm: "He that soweth on the principle of blessings, on the principle of blessings shall reap" (Plummer; cf. Prov 11:24; Lk 6:38; Gal 6:7,8).

2) Principles Drawn from God's Nature. 9:7-10. **7.** We may summarize thus: (1) the person—**every man;** (2) the proportion—**according as he hath purposed** (ASV); (3) the place—**in his heart;** (4) the perversion—**not grudgingly, or of necessity;** (5) the principle—**for God loveth a cheerful giver.**

8. Very literally: *Now God is able to cause to abound all grace unto you in order that you, always having all sufficiency in all things, might abound unto all good work.* Note the repetition of **all.** On **God is able,** see Mt 3:9; 10:28; Mk 2:7; Eph 3:20; Jude 24. The noun **sufficiency** *(autarkeia)* is used elsewhere in the NT only in I Tim 6:6 (but Paul applies the adjective to himself in Phil 4:11). This word, used by the Stoics, describes **"a perfect state of life in which** no aid or support is needed" (Thayer, *Lexicon).* The word "sufficiency" *(hikanotēs)* in II Cor 3:5 designates "ability or competency to do a thing" (Thayer). The two terms are not identical; a person may have one without the other.

9. The apostle uses the exact construction **as it is written** twelve times in Romans, twice in I Corinthians, and twice in this epistle (8:15 and here). Nowhere else does he use it. The quotation is from Ps 112:9 (LXX). The **righteousness** that endures pertains to reward rather than to salvation (cf. II Tim 4:8; Rev 19:8; 22:11). **10.** Follow the ASV or the RSV. The plenitude in nature **(He who supplies** – RSV) is a guarantee for the plenitude in grace **(shall supply and multiply . . . and increase**–ASV). Cf. Isa 55:10; Hos 10:12.

3) Principles Drawn from Christian Nature. 9:11-15. **11.** The first principle is spiritual enrichment. Literally: *in every thing being enriched unto all liberality* (as in 8:2) *which is such as* (the qualitative relative, as in 8:10) *to produce* (see 4:17) *through us thanksgiving to God.* **12.** The second principle is **thanksgiving.** This **service** *(leitourgia;* cf. its use in Lk 1:23; Phil 2:17,30; Heb 8:6; 9:21) emphasizes the ministerial aspect of the contribution. The verb **filleth up** (ASV) translates *prosanaplēroō,* which means "to fill up by adding to" (A. T. Robertson. Giving for the needs of others multiplies **many thanksgivings unto God** (ASV).

13. The third principle is obedience. The **test of this service** (RSV) brings two benefits: (1) Christians at Jerusalem **will glorify God by your obedience** (RSV); (2) they will thereby know "the sincerity of your fellowship" (Charles Hodge, *An Exposition of the Second Epistle to the Corinthians)* toward all believers.

14. The fourth principle is prayer. Follow the ASV. On **long after** *(epipotheō),* see 5:2. To understand **exceeding** *(huperballō),* consult the other places where it is used (3:10; Eph 1:19; 2:7; 3:19). The phrase **in you** is better translated as *upon you* (cf. the same preposition, *epi,* in 12:9; I Pet 4:14). **15.** The fifth principle is praise. Here we have Paul's "outburst of gratitude for the gift of his Son" (Hodge, *op. cit.).* Cf. Jn 3:16; Rom 6:23.

III. The Credentials. 10:1–13:14.

A. Spiritual Armor. 10:1-6.

1. Note the emphatic **Now I Paul myself** – as if anticipating the defensive role he now assumes against those who would impugn his apostolic authority. On **in presence,** see10:10; I Cor 2:3,4. **2.** Paul says he will act sternly **against some** at Corinth who were imputing worldly standards to him (cf. 13:2,10). **3. Flesh** should not be changed to **world** (RSV). On **walk,** see 5:7; cf. also 12:18. The apostle often uses the language of warfare (cf. Rom 13:12,13; Eph 6:13-17; I Tim 1:18; II Tim 2:3,4).

4. This parenthetic verse – with a possible allusion to the fall of Jericho (Josh 6:1-27) – describes the Christian's **warfare** both positively and negatively. **5.** Here we have a microscopic commentary on the book of Revelation. The military terminology reminds us of Eph 2:2; 6:12. Subjugation and submission are the main thoughts. That **high thing** *that is being exalted* (present passive of *epairō;* cf. *huperairō* in 12:7; II Thess 2:4) **against the knowledge of God** will be devastatingly destroyed. Note the twice-repeated **every** (ASV). On **thought** *(noēma),* see 3:14. All theories that are hostile to the word of God will come to nought.

6. The theological implications of 10:5 would have a practical display at Corinth. Literally: *Having in a ready* (state) *to avenge every disobedience, whenever your obedience shall have been fulfilled.* **Whenever** *(hotan,* as in 12:10; 13:9; I Cor 15:24,27,28) makes the time, but not the act, indefinite. Two parties were at Corinth: one disobedient, the other seeking to obey.

B. Constructive Authority. 10:7-18.

7. Evidently some at Corinth measured a man by **outward appearance** (cf. I Cor 1:12; 3:3,4). The **if** assumes the situation as true (as in II Cor 5:17). The verb **trust** (second perfect of *peithō,* "to trust" —as in 5:11) sets forth an internal persuasion that results in outward conviction (cf. its use in Phil 3:4; II Tim 1:5, 12). No group can be more cocksure than those who are deluded by the devil (cf. II Cor 4:3,4; 11:13ff.). On **as . . . so,** see 1:5.

8. Here we have an **authority** (1) assumed – **for though I should boast,** (2) possessed – **our authority,** (3) received – **which the Lord hath given us,** (4) defined – **for edification,** and (5) justified – **I should not be ashamed.**

9. Notwithstanding sinister insinuations, Paul would not **terrify** *(ekphobeō;* only here in NT) his converts with his **letters. 10.** The subtle implication of the gossip at Corinth was that Paul's **presence** *(parousia;* see 7:6) was somewhat less effective than his **letters.** If natives of Lystra could call Paul Hermes (cf. Acts 14:12), it is likely that the inglorious **contemptible** arose from animosity rather than from actuality. Cf. II Pet 3:15,16. **11.** On **such,** see 3:12; cf. 12:2,3,5. **What we are** (ASV) corresponds to the Greek *(hoioi esmen)*. Paul's words and works corresponded – whether he was absent or present. Let his defamer beware!

12. Paul would not become a member of The Society of Self-Approved Scholars at Corinth. Such men (1) **commend themselves;** (2) measure **themselves by themselves;** (3) **are not wise** *(suniēmi;* cf. its use in Mt 13:13ff.; Acts 7:25,26; Rom 3:11 – they cannot put two and two together). The apostle had no use for the "all scholars are agreed" fetish. **13.** Paul would **not boast** as his opponents did (cf. 10:12). God **apportioned** (ASV) a territory or **province** (ASV) for him to evangelize (cf. Gal 2:7; Eph 3:1-9). In that territory, which included Corinth, he would boast.

14. Paul and his helpers did not presumptuously intrude themselves among the Corinthians. They came (1) by province – **we stretch not ourselves overmuch** (ASV); (2) by priority – **were the first to come** (RSV); (3) by proclamation – **in the gospel of Christ** (ASV). Paul uniformly speaks of the gospel of "the Christ"; i.e., the Anointed One (as in 2:12; 4:4; 9:13; Rom 15:19; Gal 1:7; Phil 1:27; I Thess 3:2). **15,16.** These verses enunciate spiritual principles, such as these: (1) A minister should not **boast** in **other men's labours** or in **things made ready** at **hand.** (2) A church's faith (**as your faith groweth** – ASV) affects a minister's activity. (3) By spiritual growth a church can enable a minister to evangelize **even unto the parts beyond you** (ASV; cf. Rom 15:19-29).

17. Cited as Scripture in I Cor 1:31 (cf. Jer 9:24). In Paul's epistles, the **in** *(en)* in the phrase, **in the Lord,** always expresses an intimate and mystical relation with Christ. The phrase is somewhat like a spiritual trademark (e.g., Rom 16:12,13,22; Phil 4:1,2,4,10; Phm 20). No other NT writer uses it. **18.** Paul infinitely preferred Christ's "Well done!" (Mt 25:21,23) to all the plaudits of self-appointed scholars (cf. II Cor 10:12). On **Lord,** see II Tim 4:8,14,17,18,22.

C. Justifiable Apprehensiveness. 11:1-6.

1. Literally: *Would that ye tolerated me in a little something of folly but ye do indeed tolerate me.* The last clause may be understood somewhat ironically. **Would that** (ASV) expresses a strong emotional outburst (as in Rom 9:3). **2.** Here we have Paul's (1) passion – **I am jealous over you;** (2) position–**I espoused you to one husband** (ASV); (3) purpose – **that I might present you as a pure virgin to Christ** (ASV). The false teachers at Corinth were seeking to woo the church away from Christ. The 'espousal' took place at conversion; the 'presentation' will be consummated at the Second Coming (cf. Eph 5:26,27; Rev 21:2,9; 22:17).

3. Follow the ASV. Paul's perturbation (**lest;** see 2:7) was enhanced by a parallel (**as the serpent beguiled Eve;** cf. Gen 3:4,13) which, in the case of the Corinthians, could cause a similar perversion (**your minds should be corrupted**). The verb **beguiled** represents a compound word *(exapataō)* which conveys the idea of utter or complete deception (cf. I Tim 2:14). On **minds,** see II Cor 3:14. The Greek of the last half reads thus: *your thoughts should be corrupted from the simplicity and the purity that is toward the Christ* (Plummer).

4. The ASV correctly translates the three aorists–**did . . . preach . . . did . . . receive, did . . . accept.** Paul is referring to the time of their conversion (cf. I Cor 15:1,2). We should read **different spirit** and **different gospel** (ASV; cf. Gal 1:6-8). **5.** It appears that by **these superlative apostles** (RSV) – a description by no means complimentary – Paul has in mind the false apostles of 11:13-15. **6.** The apostle admits a deficiency (**unskilled in speaking**–RSV). But he asserts a proficiency **in knowledge** (cf. I Cor 2:6-13; Gal 1:11-17; Eph 3:1-13) and an efficiency in making that **knowledge** "manifest among all men to you-ward" (Plummer; cf. Rom 16:26; Col 1:26; 4:4; II Tim 1:10; Tit 1:1-3).

D. Reasonable Abasement. 11:7-15.

7. Or did I commit a sin (ASV) suggests the seriousness of the charge made against Paul. In **abasing myself** we see the teaching (Mt 18:4; 23:12) and example (Phil 2:8) of Jesus. The "exaltation" of the Corinthians was from the depths of pagan darkness to the heights of fellowship with God (cf. Eph 2:1ff.; I Pet 2:9,10). On **freely** see II Cor 12:14; Acts 20:33-35; I Cor 9:4-18; I Thess 2:9. **8,9.** Paul's righteous indignation against false insinuations prompted him to use strong language in his defense. (1) He took from **other churches . . . wages.** (2) His dire need at Corinth was **supplied** by some Macedonians (cf. Phil 4: 15,16). (3) **His fixed policy was to keep himself from being burdensome** unto them.

10. This verse is a strong statement, with emphasis on **is:** "Christ's truth is in me that this glorying shall not be blocked up against me in the regions of Achaia." The verb **stop** *(phrassō)* is used elsewhere in the NT in Rom 3:19; Heb 11:33. **11.** Paul calls God to witness that he loves the Corinthians even while they impute wrong motives to him (cf. 12:15).

12. This verse has been subjected to various translations and interpretations. Follow the AV and the ASV rather than the RSV (which is almost a paraphrase). Three things are plain: (1) Paul would continue his policy of taking no funds from the Corinthians. (2) This financial policy was motivated by a desire to undermine the false teachers. (3) Having nothing to charge against Paul on this score, these false teachers would **be found even as we,** i.e., judged by the same standards; their boasted superiority would evaporate. **13.** Paul describes his antagonists thus: (1) their character – **false apostles;** (2) their chicanery – **deceitful workers;** (3) their camouflage – **transforming themselves into the apostles of Christ.** On **such,** see 3:12. The verb *metaschēmatizo,* translated **transforming,** differs from the verb *metamorphoō* in 3: 18 as an outward change differs from an inner change.

14. It is no **marvel** *(thauma;* elsewhere in the NT only in Rev 17:6) that Satan *is transforming himself* (the habitual practice indicated by the present middle tense) **into an angel of light** (cf. Gen 3:5; Job 2:1; Isa 14:13ff.; Ezk 28:1-19; Mt 4:8,9; II Thess 2:4). **15.** These Satanic **ministers** partake of their father's perversity (cf. Jn 8:44), parade in his theological paraphernalia, and perish in his predestinated perdition (cf. Mt 7:22,23; 25:41; Rev 20:10,15). How do such men, still with us today, **disguise themselves as ministers of righteousness** (RSV)? (1) By rejecting God's righteousness while insisting on the merit of man's righteousness. (2) By denying the fatal effects of sin on man's original righteousness while insisting that man's nature is still basically righteous. (3) By nullifying the imputed righteousness of Christ (cf. 5:21) while insisting that his death still has some moral effect on mankind. (4) By questioning the absolute righteousness of Christ while insisting that his life, though imperfect, is still worthy of our imitation.

E. Well-known Assiduity. 11:16-33.

16. The word **fool** *(aphrōn)* is uniformly translated "foolish" by the ASV (11:19; 12:6,11; Lk 11:40; 12:20; Rom 2:20; I Cor 15:36; Eph 5:17; I Pet 2:15). It means "mindless" – acting "without reflection or intelligence" (Thayer). **17.** The RSV needlessly introduces here the idea of inspiration. By **not after the Lord** Paul simply means that his forced **boasting** has no basis in the life of Christ. **18.** By **after the flesh** (cf. 5:16) such things as one's ancestry, achievements, and accolades are to be understood (cf. Phil 3: 4). Paul reluctantly resorted to the methods of the **many** that he might save his work at Corinth from utter ruin.

19. Literally: *For gladly you tolerated the senseless,* (you) *being sensible.* The biting irony of these words the sophisticated Corinthians could readily understand (cf. I Cor 4:8-10). **20.** Five verbs, increasing in intensity, express the indignities which the sycophant Corinthians willingly endured at the hands of a false prophet. These men (1) degraded them – **makes slaves of you** (RSV); (2) devoured them – **devour you;** (3) defrauded them—**takes advantage of you** (RSV); (4) derided them – **puts on airs** (RSV); (5) defamed them – **smite you on the face.** The dupes of duplicity are the wildest defenders of the very men who debauch them! Cf. Mk 12:40; I Pet 5:2,3; II Pet 2:10-22; Jude 8-16.

21-31. In these verses we have (1) Paul's provocation (v. **21**) – his unwilling defense of himself against unwarranted calumnies; (2) Paul's pretensions (vv. 22-24 a) – his superiority in all matters of human pride (cf. Phil 3:4ff.); (3) Paul's persecutions (II Cor 11:24b, 25) – his many sufferings for the sake of Christ; (4) Paul's perils (vv. 26,27) – his frequent dangers encountered on his journeys; (5) Paul's perturbations (vv. 28,29) – his uninterrupted **anxiety for all the churches** (ASV); (6) Paul's principle (v. 30)—his paradoxical glorying in his **weakness;** (7) Paul's protestation (v. 31) – his ultimate deference to God's knowledge for the truthfulness of his record.

32,33. The incident recorded here (which, on the surface, looks like an anticlimax) harmonizes beautifully (1) with the account in Acts 9:23-25, (2) with the known facts of ancient history (Aretas reigned from 9 B.C. to A.D. 39), and (3) with the providence of God. Paul remembered this incident at the beginning of his ministry (cf. Gal 1:17) as the dramatic event that set the pattern of his life for all the years that followed.

F. Compensatory Affliction. 12:1-10.

1. Follow the ASV or the RSV. There was a certain "oughtness" *(dei,* as in Eph 6:20; Col 4:4) about Paul's boasting, even though it was **not expedient** *(sumpherō;* see 8:10; cf. same verb in Jn 11:50; 16:7; 18:14; I Cor 6:12; 10:23). This verse expresses Paul's compulsion **(I must needs glory**–ASV), repulsion **(though it is not expedient** – ASV), and impulsion **(but I will come,** etc.–ASV).

2-4. The apostle objectified himself for the purpose of defending his visions and revelations from the false ecstasies of the false teachers. His vision was (1) personal – **I know a man** (ASV); (2) Christian – **in Christ** (therefore, not belonging to either Judaism or paganism); (3) historical – **fourteen years ago** (therefore, dated in history – not a fiction); (4) mysterious – **whether in the body,** etc.; (5) ecstatic – **caught up to the third heaven** (cf. Enoch, Elijah, Ezekiel); (6) revelatory – **heard unspeakable words;** (7) indelible – a "thorn" was placed in his flesh (v. 7).

5. Here and in verses 9,10; 11:30 **infirmities** should be translated **weaknesses** (ASV; cf. 12:9,10). **6.** The thoughts here are mainly two: (1) If Paul wished **to glory** further, he would **not be a fool;** for he spoke **truth** *(alētheia;* cf. its use in 4:2; 6:7; 7:14; 11:10; 13:8). (2) He spared *(pheidomai,* as in 1:23; 13:2) them a further recital of his unique privileges for fear somebody might estimate him to be above what could be seen and heard from him. Paul had no desire to become a "superman" or encourage hero worship.

7. A classic passage. The magnitude of Paul's **revelations** (on **abundance,** see 4:7) caused the Lord to give to him a divine deterrent **(a thorn)** in order to deflate any tendency toward exaltation in pride. Paul needed some reminder that, in spite of his rapture to heaven, he still was a man among men. Our information is too scanty (cf. 1:8) to justify our dogmatizing regarding the exact nature of his **thorn in the flesh.** On **exalted,** see 10:5. **8.** Paul prayed specifically **(for this thing),** entreatingly **(I besought the Lord),** repeatedly **(thrice),** and purposively **(that it might depart from me).** On **Lord,** see 10:17,18.

9. The perfect tense in **he hath said** (ASV) registers Paul's complete acquiescence in Christ's definitive answer. Only here in the NT do we find **my grace** (cf. Phil 1:7 in ASV). The verb *(arkeō),* in the predicate **is sufficient,** indicates that Christ's grace is "possessed of unfailing strength" (Thayer). This verb is sometimes rendered *be content* (Lk 3:14; I Tim 6:8; Heb 13:5). The present passive of *teleō* (cf. the perfect tense in Jn 19:28,30; II Tim 4:17) means *is being* (continually) *made perfect* (cf. Heb 5:9). The verb **may rest** *(episkēnoō)* occurs only here in Biblical Greek. The simple verb *skēnoō* is found in Jn 1:14; Rev 7:15; 21:3. Plummer's rendering, "spread a tent over me," is reminiscent of OT phraseology (cf. Ex 33:22; Ps 90:17; 91:4; Isa 49:2; 51:16). **10.** No one can **take pleasure** *(eudokeō;* see 5:8) in the five adverse things mentioned here unless it be **for Christ's sake** (cf. 5:20; Phil 1:29; Col 1:24; III Jn 7). On **when** *(hotan),* see II Cor 10:6.

G. Sufficient Attestation. 12:11-13.

11. A sudden realization **(I have become a fool!** – RSV) is justified (1) by the forced nature of the apostle's self-vindication; (2) by the superiority of his apostleship; and (3) by his essential humility **(though I be nothing;** cf. I Cor 15:9; Eph 3:8; I Tim 1:15). **12.** The **signs of an apostle** could probably be summarized as (1) a divine call (Gal 1:15, 16); (2) a divine commission (Acts 9:5, 6,15ff.); (3) a transformed life (I Tim 1:13-16); and (4) attesting miracles (Acts 5:12-16). On **were wrought,** see II Cor 4:17. Cf. Acts 2:22; II Thess 2:9; Heb 2:4. **13.** Evidently the Corinthians developed an 'inferiority complex' because Paul **did not burden** (RSV) them financially. He prayed (ironically?) that **this wrong** *(adikia,* meaning "unrighteousness, wickedness, injustice" – Arndt) might be forgiven!

H. Beneficial Association. 12:14-18.

14. Paul gives here his purpose – **to come to you,** preparation – **ready,** precaution–**I will not be burdensome to you,** principle – **for I seek not yours, but you,** and precept–**for the children,** etc. cf. 13:1. **15.** Literally: *But I, I will most gladly spend and be utterly spent out for your* *souls. If more abundantly you I am loving, the less am I being loved?* Paul went beyond the love of parents for their children; but his love was reciprocated in inverse proportion to its intensity!

16-18. The apostle's detractors charged him with **crafty** deception. The subtle insinuation seems to have been that, although Paul was not a **burden** to them as a church, yet he had so maneuvered the collection fund as to get a heavy hand in the till. The apostle answers this scurrilous attack (1) by citing the scrupulously impeccable behavior of the two men he **sent** to Corinth, and (2) by affirming that his standard of conduct was of the same kind as theirs. The questions expect a negative answer. On **being** *(huparchō)*, see 8:17.

I. Warranted Anxiety. 12:19-21.

19. Follow the ASV or the RSV. Paul had not **been defending** (RSV) himself before the Corinthians as his judges (cf. I Cor 2:15). His whole ministry was conducted (1) **before God,** (2) **in Christ** (cf. II Cor 12:2), and (3) **for your upbuilding** (RSV).

20. Here the apostle reveals: (1) his subjective fear – the disparity between his ideal for the Corinthians and their actual condition; (2) his objective fear – the disparity between their estimate of him and his actual deportment, upon arrival, among them; (3) the reasons for both fears: the possible existence among them of eight evils – strife, suspicion, spleen, selfishness, slander, scandalmongering, superegoism, sulkiness! The serpent's hiss (cf. 11:3) could still be heard at Corinth! On **lest by any means** (ASV), see 2:7; 9:4. **21.** This verse graphically illustrates: the perturbation caused by sin —**lest . . . I bewail** (AV); sin's pertinacity —**have not repented**; depravity—**uncleanness and fornication and lasciviousness;** and practice – **which they have practiced** (RSV).

J. Defensible Asperity. 13:1-10.

1. Paul promised that, using a Scriptural method (cf. Deut 19:15; Mt 18:16; Jn 8:17), he would thoroughly investigate every charge (cf. II Cor 13:1). **2.** The ASV brings out clearly the symmetry of Paul's Greek here. The doubt expressed by **if** *(ean;* see 5:1) concerns the time, not the fact, of his visit. Paul had previously spared them (cf. 1:23); now judgment was at hand (cf. I Pet 4:17, 18).

3. Here is the reason why Paul cannot spare them: they are actually seeking a **proof** *(dokimē;* see 2:9) *of the in-me-speaking Christ* (so the Greek). This passage is a definite affirmation of the apostle's inspiration and authority. Rejection of him meant rejection of Christ. This same **Christ** is **powerful in you** (ASV), i.e., among you externally (cf. 11:12) and in you internally (cf. 5:17). **4.** Omit **though** (AV). Follow the ASV. The **through** (ASV) indicates source *(ek;* cf. Gal 3:8). The contrast is threefold: (1) between **weakness** and God's **power;** (2) between Christ's death **(he was crucified)** and his resurrected life **(yet he liveth);** (3) between Paul's human weakness **(we also are weak in him)** and Paul's apostolic power through Christ **(but we shall live with him by the power of God toward you).** By the last statement we are to understand, not the resurrected life in glory, but rather the effectiveness of Paul's ministry as an ambassador of the risen Lord. Cf. I Cor 2:3-5.

5. Here Paul turns on his accusers and puts them through a grueling examination. (1) The men tested – **yourselves** (emphatic). (2) The method of testing—**try . . . prove** (ASV). The present imperatives express repeated action ("keep on . . ."). (3) The criteria of testing. The first is objective: Are you **in the faith?** Do you really belong to "the household of faith"? (Gal 6:10, ASV; cf. Acts 6:7; 14:22) The second is subjective: Is **Jesus Christ** really **in you?** (cf. Rom 8:10; Gal 2:20; Col 1:27) (4) The possible result of the test – **except ye be reprobates.** See next verse. This test was not beyond their ability, for they could "fully know" *(epiginōskō;* see II Cor 1:13,14) these things. **6.** The word *(adokimos)* back of **reprobate** (ASV) designates the opposite of "approved" (cf. 10:18; 13:7). It is used exclusively by Paul (Rom 1:28; I Cor 9:27; II Tim 3:8; Tit 1:16; Heb 6:8).

7. We have here (1) the prayer **(Now we pray** – ASV); (2) the purpose – stated negatively **(that ye do no evil)** and positively **(do that which is honest);** (3) the possibility – stated negatively **(not that we should appear approved)** and positively **(though we be as reprobates).** **8.** By **can do nothing** Paul expresses a moral impossibility. The verb used here *(dunamai)* is often thus used (e.g., Rom 8:8; I Cor 2:14; II Tim 2:13;

3:7; Heb 3:19). On **truth** *(alētheia),* see II Cor 7:14; 12:6.

9. The paradox of Paul's being **weak** while the Corinthians are **strong** causes the apostle to **rejoice** (ASV); but still he continues to **pray for** their **perfecting** (ASV; see v. 11). **10.** Paul's present purpose in writing **(I write these things)** anticipates his imminent coming among them **(being present)**; then he will exercise his delegated power (**the authority which the Lord gave me** – ASV) and his constructive prerogative (**for building up and not for tearing down** – RSV).

K. A Christian Adieu. 13:11-14.

11. The five precepts given here are all in the present imperative ("keep on . . ."). The precepts are: (1) **farewell** *(chairō,* meaning "to rejoice, be glad"; cf. its use in 2:3; 6:10; 7:7,9,13,16; 13:9); (2) **be perfect** *(katartizō,* meaning "to restore to its former position" – Arndt; cf. the noun form in v. 9); (3) **be of good comfort** *(parakaleō;* cf. its use in 1:4,6; 2:7; 7:6,7,13); (4) **be of one mind** (lit., *think the same thing*– as in Rom 12:16; 15:5; Phil 2:2; 4:2); (5) **live in peace** *(eirēneuō;* elsewhere in NT only in Mk 9:50; Rom 12:18; I Thess 5:13; Arndt here uses *keep the peace).* God's **love** (cf. Jn 3:16; I Jn 3:1; 4:9,10) and God's **peace** (cf. Rom 16:20; Phil 4:7; Heb 13:20) are united in a blessed promise of futurity and fruition. **12,13.** The **holy kiss,** later restricted because of abuses, was a symbol of Christian fellowship among the first believers (cf. Rom 16:16; I Cor 16:20; I Thess 5:26; I Pet 5:14).

14. This wonderfully human letter closes with the most sublime of all doxologies. The epistle begins (cf. 1:2) and ends with an affirmation of the deity of Christ that is reminiscent of Mt 28:19. The genitives in this doxology are probably subjective – **the grace** which comes from **the Lord Jesus Christ; the love** which **God** bestows; **the fellowship** which **the Holy Spirit** (RSV) engenders. Thus ends a wonderful epistle!

BIBLIOGRAPHY

DENNEY, JAMES. *The Second Epistle to the Corinthians (The Expositor's Bible).* New York: A. C. Armstrong and Son, 1900.

HODGE, CHARLES. *An Exposition of the Second Epistle to the Corinthians.* New York: A. C. Armstrong and Son, 1891.

MENZIES, ALLAN. *The Second Epistle of the Apostle Paul to the Corinthians.* London: The Macmillan Company, 1912.

PLUMMER, ALFRED. *A Critical and Exegetical Commentary on the Second Epistle of St. Paul to the Corinthians.* New York: Charles Scribner's Sons, 1915.

ROBERTSON, A. T. *The Glory of the Ministry.* New York: Fleming H. Revell Company, 1911.

TASKER, R. V. G. *The Second Epistle of Paul to the Corinthians* (Tyndale New Testament Commentaries.) Grand Rapids, Michigan: Wm. B. Eerdmans Publishing Co., 1958.

THE EPISTLE TO THE GALATIANS

INTRODUCTION

Occasion of the Writing. The Galatian churches had come into being as a result of Paul's missionary labors. Therefore the apostle was especially exercised in spirit when he learned that Jewish Christian agitators had circulated among these Gentile converts seeking to impose circumcision and the burden of the Mosaic law upon them as necessary for salvation (Gal 1:7; 4:17; 5:10). Writing under great stress (as is suggested by the omission of the usual thanksgiving), he met the issue squarely, and thus, in the epistle to the Galatians, gave to the Church a mighty polemic against the Judaizing error.

Recipients of the Letter. These churches were sufficiently close together and enough alike to be addressed as a group. In 3:1 Paul calls his readers "Galatians." In the middle of the first Christian century *Galatia* had more than one meaning. (1) It denoted the area in north central Asia Minor where the Gauls had settled after migrating from western Europe. The principal centers were Pessinus, Ancyra, and Tavium. (2) It also denoted the Roman province of Galatia. This the Romans had organized in 25 B.C. by adding to northern Galatia some territory to the south. The latter included the cities of Antioch, Iconium, Lystra, and Derbe, which were visited by the apostle on his first missionary journey. It is hardly likely that the epistle was addressed to Christians in both North Galatia and South Galatia (cf. 4:14).

The debate regarding the destination of this epistle goes on and on, and may never be settled. Lightfoot espoused the North Galatian theory. Most of the German commentators have continued to maintain this position (e.g., Schlatter, Lietzmann, Schlier), though some have remained noncommittal. Sir William Ramsay argued strongly for the South Galatian position, which has gained wide currency among English-speaking scholars. It has the advantage, if it be the correct viewpoint, of providing us with information about the founding of these churches (Acts 13; 14). On the other hand, Luke uses the term "Galatia" (lit., *Galatic region)* only when describing the progress of the missionaries beyond South Galatian territory (Acts 16:6; cf. 18:23). However, the circumstance that he does not mention *churches* in the North Galatian territory, but only *disciples,* favors the South Galatian theory (see Acts 18:23).

Date and Place of Writing. On the basis of the South Galatian theory, one might conclude that the epistle was written prior to the apostolic council described in Acts 15 (when an official pronouncement was made concerning the relation of Gentiles to the Law). Since Paul and Barnabas visited the churches twice on this first journey, the demands of Gal 4:13 could be considered met (there *first* means *former* of two visits), though it is by no means certain that Paul himself would consider this doubling back as a second visit. Many think that when Paul recounts a meeting with certain apostles in chapter 2, he can not be referring to the apostolic council, since he fails to mention the decree that was there drawn up, which would have been highly advantageous to his argument in the epistle. This argument is not decisive, since the purpose of the decree was not to lay down terms on which Gentiles might be admitted to the Church, but rather to facilitate relations between such Gentile converts and those who were of Jewish origin. So the decree did not bear directly on the argumentation of the letter.

Lightfoot emphasized the similarities between Galatians, Corinthians, and Romans. All deal with the Judaizing controversy to some degree. On this basis Galatians may be assigned to the period of Paul's third missionary journey and either to Ephesus or to Macedonia as its point of origin. This would date the epistle as late as A.D. 56. According to the alternative view, it was written in 48 or 49, probably from Antioch. An intermediate date of about 53, early in the ministry at Ephesus, is attractive. A reasonable interval between the letter to the Galatians and the letters to the Corinthians and the Romans is needed to account for differences in tone and treatment.

Development of the Thought. The first two chapters are devoted largely to setting forth the nature of Paul's apostleship. This explanation was vital to the apostle's gospel, for if his opponents could show that he had not been called and commissioned to preach the truth, then his hearers could justly question his message. Though it pained Paul to be so personal, he had to meet the challenge, which he did by showing that he had an independent apostleship fully on a par with that of the original apostles. He had received his gospel not through human instruction but through divine revelation, and it proved to be in agreement with that of the other apostles.

Next Paul passes to a statement of what the Gospel is (chs. 3; 4). It is a message of grace that calls for faith. The law does not produce faith, but rather works a curse, from which Christ had to redeem men.

Beyond the act of receiving the Gospel, lies the necessity of living it out (chs. 5; 6). Here the power of the cross and the energy of the Holy Spirit are presented as efficacious rather than efforts to keep the Law.

Influence. This letter contains the most emphatic statement of salvation apart from works to be found in Scripture. It revolutionized the thinking of Luther and played a strategic part in the Reformation. Luther declared that he was wedded to this book; it was his Katherine.

In the nineteenth century F. C. Baur made the book pivotal to his theory that the legalistic controversy was so severe as to rock the early church to its foundation. According to him, it affected the entire literature of the New Testament positively or negatively as men wrote in the interest of one viewpoint or the other, or else tried to conceal the fact of divergence between law and grace as means of salvation. Since Galatians exhibits this controversy in unmistakable fashion, its genuineness must be granted. This verdict has remained virtually unchallenged since Baur's day.

OUTLINE

I. Introduction. 1:1-9.
   A. Salutation. 1:1-5.
   B. Theme of the epistle. 1:6-9.
II. Paul's apostleship defended. 1:10–2:21.
   A. A special apostleship affirmed. 1:10-17.
   B. Lack of early contact with the apostles at Jerusalem. 1:18-24.
   C. Failure of later contact to question his apostleship or add to his gospel. 2:1-10.
   D. His independent authority vindicated in the encounter with Peter at Antioch. 2:11-21.
III. Paul's gospel explained. 3:1–4:31.
   A. The argument from experience (of the Galatians). 3:1-5.
   B. The argument from Scripture (the case of Abraham). 3:6-9.
   C. The argument from the Law. 3:10–4:11.
      1. The curse of the Law, from which Christ must deliver. 3:10-14.
      2. The inviolability of the covenant of promise and its priority to the Law. 3:15-18.
      3. The purpose of the Law – temporary in its standing and negative in its operation. 3:19-22.
      4. Sonship not through the Law but through faith. 3:23–4:7.
      5. An appeal not to return to bondage. 4:8-11.
   D. The argument from personal reception by the Galatians. 4:12-20.
   E. The argument from the covenant of promise. 4:21-31.
IV. Paul's gospel practiced. 5:1–6:15.
   A. The Gospel practiced in liberty 5:1-12.
   B. The Gospel practiced in love. 5:13-15.
   C. The Gospel practiced in the Spirit. 5:16-26.
   D. The Gospel practiced in service. 6:1-10.
   E. The Gospel practiced in separation from the world. 6:11-15.

V. Conclusion. 6:16-18.
  A. Closing prayer. 6:16.
  B. Closing testimony. 6:17.
  C. Benediction. 6:18.

COMMENTARY

I. Introduction. 1:1-9.

A. Salutation. 1:1-5. The conventional framework of letter-writing is here utilized but transcended, for the writer was an apostle with authority from the Godhead, and he addressed those who by grace had been delivered from this present age. They, too, were not ordinary men, for they were Christians.

1. **Apostle.** The meaning *sent one* will not suffice here. All believers have some such commission. Paul proceeds to defend his special authority as a Christian teacher, founder of churches, disciplinarian, and corrector of false teaching. **Not from men, neither through man.** The negative **not** sets the tone of the epistle; it is a polemic, an exposure of error in order to portray the truth to better advantage. If the Judaizers had any apostleship, it was from men. Paul's was not. It had a higher source. Nor was it **through** man. No person, apostle or other, had mediated Paul's authority (cf. 1:12). It came instead through the intervention in his life of **Jesus Christ.** The contrast makes Christ more than man. Behind him and on an equality with him stands **God the Father,** presented here as the one who **raised** Christ **from the dead.** It was the risen Christ who appeared to Paul and made him an apostle.

2. The identity of **the brethren** with Paul is unknown. For the location of **the churches of Galatia,** see the Introduction.

3. **Grace and peace** are twin gifts of God, never reversed in their order. The divine favor received makes possible a life of fullness and of harmony with God and fellow believers. These blessings come from the Lord Jesus Christ as well as from God the Father.

4,5. **Who gave himself.** An act of finality, purely voluntary. **For our sins. For** *(hyper)* is usually used of the persons benefited by Christ's work (cf. 3:13). Personal sin is not the only barrier between man and God. Man needs to be freed from his whole position in **this present evil age** (AV, *world*). The Gospel is not a message of improvement but of deliverance. **Age** is a time word and does not refer to nature or to man as such, but to the circumstances of man's life, corrupted as it is by sin and dominated by Satan, the god of this age (II Cor 4:4). Christ, in his redeeming work, acted in conjunction with God, according to his **will** (cf. II Cor 5:19). To God belongs the glory, the praise of saints, forevermore. Without affirming the deity of the Son, the apostle conveys the truth of it by linking Christ with the Father in the apostolic call, in the gift of grace and peace, and in the achieving of salvation.

B. Theme of the Epistle. 1:6-9. Instead of giving thanks to God for his readers, Paul expresses his amazement at their defection. He pronounces no blessing, but instead hurls a warning anathema.

6. **Are removed.** Rather, *are removing yourselves,* going over to another position and thus denying the very terms of the divine call to sonship, which is **in the grace** of Christ. **So soon.** Probably not a reference to recency of conversion, for young converts are the most liable to be swayed by false teaching. If this be interpreted temporally, it means so soon after the false teachers began their work, or so soon after the apostle left the Galatians. Perhaps *manner* is intended—*so readily,* with such an unresisting surrender. The removal was still going on, and so was not complete. There was still hope of turning the tide. But the seriousness of the defection is indicated. It was away from God, who called in grace, and it was unto **another,** i.e., a different **gospel.** Paul uses **gospel** by way of concession. Actually there is not **another,** a second gospel which one may choose and still have the divine message of eternal salvation.

7. While the responsibility for the defection belonged to the Galatians (**removing yourselves**), the explanation for it lay elsewhere, in those who were troubling them (cf. Acts 15:24), namely, the Judaizing teachers who were willing to **pervert** the Gospel by changing it into something quite different. Yet it was not theirs to alter, for it was the **gospel of Christ.** The privilege of declaring it does not include the right to change it.

8. Even, Paul says, if **we** (editorial plural here for Paul, the least likely on earth to change it, because of the circumstances of his call) or **an angel from heaven** (who would be even less likely to alter any divine message; cf. Mt 6:10), should proclaim as the Gospel something contrary to the word given out by us in Galatia, he must become *anathema*, **accursed** of God (cf. I Cor 16:22).

9. Paul had given such warning when in the Galatian churches. In this letter he did so **again.** He was a zealous guardian of the purity of the Gospel. In reiterating his strong statement, the apostle changes from the subjunctive mood of possibility to the indicative mood of actuality – if any man is preaching a different gospel (as the Judaizers are), **let him be accursed.**

II. Paul's Apostleship Defended. 1:10 –2:21.

A. A Special Apostleship Affirmed. 1: 10-17.

10. Since the apostle had spoken so harshly, he felt that it should be clear **now** that he was not seeking to persuade men in the sense of conciliating them or seeking their favor. He was concerned, rather, to be on good terms with **God.** Pleasing men by adjusting the message to suit their desires is inconsistent with being **the servant of Christ.**

11. As Christ's servant, the apostle could only make known the Gospel message. Though he preached it, he did not originate it, nor did any other **man.**

12. Since Paul came late into the apostolic ranks, men might have supposed that he received the Gospel from his predecessors or learned it through a course of instruction. Not so. He came into possession of it by **revelation** from Jesus Christ. This was the very highest authority. How, then, could his message be questioned?

13. Nothing less than direct intervention in Paul's life was required to open his heart to the truth of the Gospel. His pre-Christian manner of life was well known. The word **conversation** (Gr., *anastrophē)* means "life pattern." Everything in Judaism was prescribed. Anyone familiar with Pharisaism could predict what Saul's course of life would be. But in his case there was a special element that had become notorious. He was a persecutor of the Christians (not all Pharisees went this far in showing their devotion to Judaism). As the ravening wolf of Benjamin, he was engaged in laying waste the church, which he afterward recognized was the true congregation of Jehovah.

14. This unusual determination and excess of fury earned for Saul an exceptional reputation in Judaism. He kept advancing in devotion to his faith and its traditions, passing by men of his own age, and giving proof of his zeal by persecuting Christians. Humane considerations meant nothing to him compared with the fulfillment of his calling in behalf of his religion. He regarded his murderous activity as the Jews regarded their stoning of Stephen: It was done in the service of God (Jn 16:2; Acts 26:9-11). Clearly, then, Paul could not have been influenced in favor of the Gospel before his conversion, and he could not have received his message from men, as alleged by the Judaizers.

15. Paul's conversion was effected in line with God's purpose. The apostle, like Jeremiah (Jer 1:5), was set apart for his lifework from birth. His conversion was in the nature of a revelation of God's Son within his soul. This statement is not intended to create speculation as to the psychology of his conversion experience, but rather to certify the reality and depth of that transformation. Paul had been blind to the deity of God's Son. His prejudice against his own countrymen who looked to Jesus as their Messiah was due to his belief that the Nazarene was an impostor, a fraud.

16,17. The ultimate, divine purpose of this revelation within the soul of the apostle was that he should in turn proclaim this knowledge to others, especially to the Gentiles. The reality and sufficiency of his encounter with the risen Lord is seen in the fact that he did not confer with **flesh and blood** (an expression denoting humanity, with special emphasis on weakness and inadequacy) either locally, at Damascus, or in Jerusalem, the center of the church's life, where the **apostles** had their headquarters. If Paul had felt uncertain about his message, a journey to one of these centers would have been natural and necessary. But he was an apostle as truly as were the Twelve, fully in possession of the truth of the Gospel from the Lord himself.

The apostle mentions Arabia not as a place for preaching, because, even though preaching was in view in the call, it is not the subject under consideration at this point. Paul is discussing the *source* of his Gospel. He mentions Arabia in contrast to Jerusalem. No apostle was to be found there. No one was there who could inform him about the Lord and His saving work. It is probable that the new convert journeyed to Arabia to be alone with God, to think through the implications of the Gospel. There is no need to suppose that every aspect of the truth was flashed into his mind at the time of his conversion. From Arabia Paul returned to Damascus. This incidental reference confirms the information gleaned from Acts 9:3 that the conversion occurred near that city.

B. Lack of Early Contact with the Apostles at Jerusalem. 1:18-24. This was not a complete lack, to be sure, as Paul in frankness admits, but the contacts were brief, personal, and quite incidental.

18. How much of the **three years** belongs to Arabia and how much to Damascus we cannot tell, but the interval fortifies Paul's contention. If he had lacked the Gospel at his conversion, he would not have waited that long to be informed about it. **To see Peter.** The verb **see** (in the Greek) is in deliberate contrast to **conferred** (1:16), for the latter suggests conferring with a view to being enlightened on a subject, while the former refers to becoming acquainted with a person or thing. It is sometimes used of sightseeing. The visit was brief (fifteen days).

19. Paul saw no other apostle except James, the Lord's brother. This is the James who became the head of the Jerusalem church (cf. Acts 12:17).

20. The apostle declares himself willing to go on oath that he is telling the truth. No Jew dared to do this if he was about to speak a falsehood, for that would have been equivalent to inviting God to pour out His wrath upon him. The deep solemnity of Paul's declaration is the measure of the distrust of his word that the Judaizers had sown in the hearts of his converts.

21. Paul's next move, necessitated by the opposition to his preaching in Jerusalem (Acts 9:29,30), was to Syria and Cilicia. Obviously he had no opportunity in those remote areas to receive instruction from the apostles.

22. Probably the apostle mentioned the churches of Judea in order to strengthen his argument. It is likely that most of the apostles were in the outlying districts at this period, so Paul's lack of contact with the churches of Judea meant a lack of contact with the apostles ministering there. The Twelve did not supervise the work in Syria; Barnabas was sent there (Acts 11:22-26). During the years when Paul ministered in this region, where he had been brought up, he was quite independent of the other apostles. His further purpose in mentioning the Judean churches was to underscore the greatness of the change his conversion had wrought in him. He now **preached the faith** he formerly had sought to tear down. The change meant peace for the believers in Palestine (Acts 9:31).

C. Failure of Later Contact to Question His Apostleship or Add to His Gospel. 2:1-10.

1. The differences between this later visit and the previous one are quite plain. This time Paul went not alone but in the company of Barnabas, and he went with the deliberate purpose of discussing the Gospel, more specifically the application of the Gospel to the Gentiles. It is not easy to fit this visit into the framework of the narrative of Acts. Those who favor identifying it with the so-called famine visit of Acts 11:27-30 can point to the fact that Barnabas accompanied Paul on that occasion. They hold that Paul was obligated to mention every contact he had with the Jerusalem church. But this reasoning is precarious. The only contacts that required notice were those that might have resulted in a communication to him of the Gospel. Since elders only are mentioned in connection with the reception of the gift by the Jerusalem church, it is unlikely that Paul had contact with the apostles at that time. This was a period of persecution for them (Acts 12:1-3), and so they may have been unavailable for consultation.

If the question of the admission of Gentiles into the Church was settled at the famine visit (which is involved in equating Acts 11 with Gal 2), then it is strange that another conference was necessary for the settlement of the very same question (Acts 15). Furthermore, it would have been highly discourteous for the apostles to insist that Paul should remember the poor (Gal 2:10) when he had just brought the gift of the Antioch church for the relief of the saints in the Holy City. Finally, to identify Galatians 2 with Acts 11 is virtually impossible chronologically. The famine visit took place about the time of Herod's death, which occurred in A.D. 44. By adding fourteen years (Gal 2:1) to the three years of 1:18 and then subtracting the total of seventeen from 44, one arrives at the year 27 as the date of Paul's conversion, which is too early. Even if the fourteen years of Gal 2:1 refer to the conversion rather than to the first visit to Jerusalem, the dating of the conversion is still too early; it leaves no interval between the resurrection of Christ and the conversion of Paul.

The identification of Galatians 2 with Acts 15 has its strength in the fact that the subject of discussion is the same in both cases and in the fact that Peter and James, as well as Paul and Barnabas, are given prominence in both passages. There are difficulties in this identification, to be sure. Acts 15 gives the impression of a large public gathering, whereas Gal 2:2 pictures a private session. A harmonization is possible on the assumption that the friction cited in Acts 15:5,6 may have forced the leaders of the church to dismiss the council temporarily and move into a private session such as is described in Galatians 2. On the basis of the understanding reached there, Peter and James would then quite naturally have taken a leading part and a decisive role in the final public phase of the conference reported in Acts 15:7-21. It is possible that the word **them** (Gal 2:2) is a reference to the church as a whole in contrast to the apostles, with whom Paul and Barnabas proceeded to meet privately. A further difficulty to be faced is the failure of Paul to mention the so-called apostolic decree in Gal 2:1-10, whereas that decree is given considerable prominence in Luke's account (Acts 15:20,28,29; 16:4; 21:25). However, since Paul was concerned with the Gospel in this whole passage, and since the decree did not bear directly on the Gospel but simply provided for harmonious relations between Jewish and Gentile believers, he was not under obligation to include the decree in his argument.

2. Paul's second visit to Jerusalem was dictated by **revelation,** in line with the strong emphasis on the supernatural in the previous chapter. This intimation may have come before the decision of the Antioch church to send Paul, or it may have come afterward and sealed for him the decision of the church (Acts 15:2). He and Barnabas met with **them that were of reputation.** Literally, *those who seemed*, a rather curious term for the apostles. The same expression occurs twice in Gal 2:6 and again in 2:9, where the word "pillars" is added. Perhaps Paul felt that the church was in danger of idolizing these leaders by deferring to them overmuch. Did Paul really have a fear that he was running (pursuing his course of Christian service) **in vain** and had run in vain since his conversion, that he had possibly been wrong about the Gospel and now needed to be set right? By no means. But circumstances forced him to submit his message to the apostles, for only in this way could he hope to shut the mouths of his detractors, the Judaizers, and the mouths of those who had been taken in by their propaganda.

3-5. Now the reason for Paul's bringing Titus along (v. 1) becomes evident. He was to be a test case in the matter of Gentile reception into the Church. If he were **compelled to be circumcised,** the rite could not logically be withheld from other Gentile believers. If he emerged from the conference uncircumcised, all other Gentiles who had put their trust in Christ could enjoy their freedom without fear of successful challenge. Paul seems to say that some pressure was exerted here to have Titus circumcised (cf. Acts 15:5). It is highly unlikely that this pressure came from the apostles, for they stood with Paul (Acts 15:19). The culprits were the **false brethren** who had slipped into the ranks of the believers. They bore the name of Christian but were nevertheless opposed to granting that **liberty** which Paul's gospel proclaimed—freedom from bondage to the Law, including freedom from circumcision. Paul's resistance to these Judaizers was not dictated by stubbornness nor by a sense of superiority. He saw that the circumcision issue involved **the truth of the gospel** (Gal 2:5). To impose on a Gentile the sign of the covenant given to Abraham and his descendants was to set aside the simplicity of saving faith by introducing the necessity of a particular work. If this work had been found necessary for church membership, other works would have been found necessary, too.

6-8. In conference with Paul, the apostles could find no fault with his gospel. They **added nothing** to what he had already received by revelation from the Lord. But they perceived that to him had been committed **the gospel of the uncircumcision.** He was responsible for the Gentiles in a special sense (Rom

1:5). For this reason the Lord did not permit him to labor in Jerusalem (Acts 22:17-21). This special call did not rule out a ministry to Jews when Paul labored in the synagogues, where both Jews and Gentiles (God-fearers) were assembled. Peter, charged with proclaiming the same gospel of grace, was to specialize in reaching the circumcision, the Jews. His Aramaic name, Cephas, is appropriately used here. The success of the two men in their respective spheres attested the divine call to them.

9,10. Paul's privilege as preacher of the Gospel to the Gentiles is called a **grace** (cf. I Cor 15:9,10; Eph 3:2). The Jerusalem leaders recognized this grace by extending the right hand of fellowship to Paul and to Barnabas. This was no mere formality, but a meaningful endorsement of the message of free grace that these two had been proclaiming among the Gentiles. The apostles endorsed also the division of labor that sent one group of evangelists to the Gentiles, the other to the Jews. However, they requested the missionaries to the Gentile world not to so divorce themselves from the Jewish believers—especially those at Jerusalem, who were notoriously **poor** (Rom 15:26)—as to forget their need. The proof of Paul's good faith in acceding to this request was that he raised a substantial fund among the Gentile churches for these people (I Cor 16:1-4), which he and others took to Jerusalem on the occasion of his last visit.

D. His Independent Authority Vindicated in the Encounter with Peter at Antioch. 2:11-21. This is the third occasion on which Paul came into contact with Peter. The first time he simply met Peter; the next time he discovered their unity and equality; this time he was moved to differ with him and rebuke him. This confirms the fact that Paul's purpose throughout the epistle to the Galatians is to demonstrate his independent apostleship.

11,12. He withstood Peter because Peter's conduct gave the false impression that he was renouncing the stand he had taken at Jerusalem. The action of the council in the matter of the decree (Acts 15:28,29) had opened the way for freedom of social intercourse between Jews and Gentiles in the church at Antioch, a freedom that Peter was glad to share. He even ate with the Gentiles (cf. Acts 10:28; 11:3). But the arrival of certain men from James, the acknowledged head of the church at Jerusalem, awoke fear in Peter's heart, for he remembered that the mother church had rebuked him for associating and eating with Gentiles in the house of Cornelius (Acts 11:1-18). It is impossible to know in what relation these visitors stood to James and on precisely what mission they came. Peter **separated himself** from his Gentile brethren by degrees, as the original suggests, perhaps absenting himself from one meal one day, from two the next, and finally cutting himself off altogether.

13. Peter's example influenced others. The word **dissimulation** (AV, *dissembled)* ordinarily rendered *hypocrisy,* means a lack of correspondence between one's external acts or demeanor and his state of heart. In Pharisaism the outward acts were good but the state of heart was often corrupt. In Peter's case, his inward convictions were sound, for he endorsed Gentile equality in the Church, but his conduct belied his convictions. There is a plaintive note here—**even Barnabas,** as though Paul expected more of him than of the other Jewish believers.

14. The statement that Peter was not acting according to the truth of the Gospel needs explanation. He was a Jew and therefore not obliged to live **after the manner of the Gentiles,** as he had been doing in his table companionship. But now, having gone that far and then broken off, he was logically compelling Gentile believers to live as Jews, that is, to adopt circumcision and the dietary laws of the Jews and thus remove all barriers between themselves and men like Peter. But if the Gentile believers did this, they would sacrifice the truth of the Gospel, which had been affirmed at Jerusalem. The church had decided that no such burden of legal compliance was to be laid on Gentile believers. The whole principle of grace was at stake. The logical outcome of Peter's conduct was to make Jews out of Gentile Christians or else force the creation of a Gentile church alongside the Jewish church, which would break the unity of the body of Christ. So the truth of the Gospel was involved.

15-18. Paul extracted from Peter the acknowledgment that the two of them, being native Jews and having enjoyed the special advantages of Judaism, including the possession of the Law, had nevertheless been obliged to come to the place of simply trusting Christ for salvation, just as any poor Gentile had to do. Peter was bound to agree, because of his own commitment to this position (Acts 15:11). The OT itself testifies that justification does not come from **the works of the law** (cf. Ps 143:2). To be justified means to be declared and considered righteous in God's eyes, to be vindicated of any charge of sin incident to failure to keep God's holy law. **The faith of Jesus Christ** means faith *in* Christ (Gr. objective genitive). This lowering of the Jew to the level of the Gentile seemed to involve Christ, making Him a **minister of sin** in that He released man from bondage to the Law, since faith in Christ for both Jew and Gentile on equal terms is the condition of salvation. But Paul rejected the conclusion, for it rested on a false premise, namely, the fancied superiority of Jew over Gentile. Here Paul delicately takes what belongs to Peter and refers it to himself. The real transgressor is not Christ, but the one who, like Peter, builds up again a distinction that has in fact been destroyed. Peter was doing just that by withdrawing from Gentile fellowship, making it appear that Jewish believers were a superior breed.

19-21. The Law had done a service for Paul even if it had not brought him justification. Through the Law he had become dead to that very Law, for the Law had wrought a consciousness of sin which prepared him to accept Christ. It had also brought Christ to the cross in order to redeem those who had broken that Law. Christ was Paul's representative in that death to the Law. The result was a new life **unto God. I am crucified with Christ.** The perfect tense emphasizes both the past event and its continuing effects. This death brought life, yet not the same old life in the feebleness of the natural man, but a life entirely new; not simply divine life impersonally granted, but rather the living Christ himself taking up his abode in the redeemed one. In this arrangement, however, there is no submerging of human personality–**the life which I now live.** The new life is lived on the principle of faith in Christ (cf. 2:16) rather than on that of legal obedience. This faith builds on the fact of the personal love of the Saviour for those on whose behalf he died (cf. Eph 5:2). Not to trust Christ in this way would **frustrate** (set aside) the grace of God. If righteousness could be obtained by law, the death of Christ would be unexplainable; it would be a wasted gesture.

III. Paul's Gospel Explained. 3:1–4:31.

A. The Argument from Experience (of the Galatians). 3:1-5. The apostle here declares that the experience of his readers, starting with faith in Christ crucified and certified by the gift to them of the Holy Spirit, lay completely outside the sphere of the Law. Would they now renounce the perfection of the divine provision, he asks, for the folly of their own efforts?

1. They must have become **bewitched,** victims of an evil spell (cf. 1:7). In view of his dramatic preaching of Christ crucified when he was among them (cf. I Cor 1:23; 2:2), their change in attitude seemed strange. Had they forgotten their first vivid impression? **2,3.** After the reception of Christ came the gift of the Spirit (cf. Gal 4:4-6; Eph 1:13), not at all based on law-keeping as an effort of the **flesh** (cf. Gal 5:18,19). **4. Suffered** probably does not refer to persecution or the burden of law-keeping, but is used in a good sense – *experienced.* This interpretation is favored by the continuing mention of the Spirit in the next verse. **5.** The ongoing work of the Spirit in **miracles,** like his advent into the hearts of the Galatians, depended not on works but on **the hearing of faith,** i.e., a faith response to the Gospel message preached to them.

B. The Argument from Scripture (the Case of Abraham). 3:6-9. The mention of faith invites an excursion into the OT to show that Abraham, the revered patriarch, depended on it for righteousness. Only those with like faith are truly blessed of God. Note the companion treatment in Rom 4:9-12.

6,7. Abraham was justified by faith (Gen 15:6; Rom 4:3; Jas 2:23). The real children of Abraham are not his natural descendants (Mt 3:9), but those who share his **faith. 8.** This was anticipated in the very language of the Abrahamic covenant, which had **all nations** in view. The words **in thee** magnify Abraham as the exemplar of faith. **9.** He was **faithful** in the sense of being full of faith. His justification is available also to the nations. This is their promised blessing.

C. The Argument from the Law. 3:10–4:11.

1) The Curse of the Law, from Which Christ Must Deliver. 3:10-14. Paul, hav-

ing disposed of the Jews' confidence that physical relation to Abraham meant justification, now proceeds to the other refuge of Judaism, the possession of the Law.

10. Faith brings blessing, but the Law produces a curse because of the requirement that one must *continue* to meet its demands faithfully (Deut 27:26). **11,12.** To the practical impossibility of being justified by law is now added the truth that God uses another method anyway—**the just shall live by faith.** Judging from the context, the apostle's use of this quotation (Hab 2:4) is intended to stress the truth that one can become just in God's sight only by faith. On this basis alone can he truly live the life of God. A similar sense is demanded in Rom 1:17. Under law, one must *do* before he can *live* (Lev 18:5). Under the Gospel one gets life from God through faith, then begins to do the will of God in the energy of that faith. It may appear that the apostle excludes all blessing for those living under the Law in pre-Christian days. What about the first psalm? **13.** The Law is both a mirror of the will of God for his covenant people and a taskmaster that brings a curse. But in this point Paul is not discussing this brighter aspect of the Law, for he confines himself to the Law as a means of condemnation (cf. II Cor 3:6-9). The curse of the Law was real. It took Christ to the cross. The inflexibility of the Law's demands is clearly seen in the fact that when Christ took the place of the lawbreaker, though he himself was perfectly holy, he had to endure exactly the same penalty as any other who came under the curse of the Law. The circumstance that Christ died by hanging on the **tree** of Calvary emphasized the element of curse (Deut 21:23).

14. The example of Abraham continues to furnish background for the thought here. The death of Christ operated to bring **the blessing of Abraham** (justification) on the Gentiles. God, having delivered his own covenant people (the Jews) from the curse of the Law, was free from all hindrance in dealing likewise in grace with the Gentiles. The token of acceptance with God is **the promise of the Spirit,** i.e., the promised Spirit (cf. 4:6; Acts 1:4,5). **We** includes both Jews and Gentiles.

2) The Inviolability of the Covenant of Promise and Its Priority to the Law. 3:15-18. By its very nature a covenant is something fixed, not subject to change, even when it is a human arrangement. The promise cannot be set aside by the Law, which came much later.

15. I speak after the manner of men. This is a technical expression, a kind of apology. The immutability of God's arrangements should be beyond debate, but Paul finds it necessary to discuss the matter to make it fully clear to his readers. Even in human arrangements, once confirmed, a party to an agreement cannot, by himself, set it aside as no longer binding, nor can he add to its provisions as one might do with a will.

16. God made **promises** (the same promise was repeated) to Abraham and to **his seed**. But how much is embraced in the word **seed?** Not all the descendants of Abraham were intended (it is not **seeds**), nor are all lines of descent in view. We are instructed to think of **seed** as a collective term. It includes the patriarchs, for the promises were spoken to them. But it also looks on to Christ and includes him, as is shown by 3:19, where he is called once more **the seed,** the one who brought to an end the age of law. This corporate sense of the term **Christ** is found again in I Cor 12:12.

17. The promise to Abraham enjoyed priority over the giving of the Law, since it came 430 years earlier. Paul seems to include here the continuation of the promise to the patriarchs who came later, for the interval between Abraham and the giving of the Law was even longer than this. The essential thing, in line with the truth of 3:15, is the consideration that the Law could not possibly set aside the previous arrangement that God had made and confirmed.

18. Another feature is brought forward. Law does not so condition promise as to change its character, for this would violate the unconditional nature of promise. The **inheritance** (the enjoyment of the blessings of the covenant with Abraham – that a justification like his own would be extended ultimately to all the families of the earth) has nothing to do with **law.** The two things, **law** and **promise,** are fundamentally different. If the inheritance were contingent on law, then the promise would be nullified because of the well-known character of law—that it is a yoke which none can bear. It is an indisputable fact that God gave the inheritance to Abraham by promise. Nothing can change that basic truth.

3) The Purpose of the Law – Temporary in Its Standing and Negative in Its Operation. 3:19-22. The apostle's apparent discounting of the Law leads to a necessary question.

19. If the **Law** did not set aside the promise of God or even condition it, then why was it given? **It was added because of transgressions,** i.e., to give sin the distinctive character of transgression (cf. Rom 4:15; 5:20). **Till.** The Law was to run a certain course, fulfilling its mission of preparing the way for the **seed** – Christ, who is "the end of the law for righteousness" (Rom 10:4). The Law **was ordained by angels in the hand of a mediator.** Not only was the Law temporary, but the very manner of its bestowal indicates its inferior character. It had a double mediation, through **angels** (Acts 7:53; Heb 2:2) and through Moses the lawgiver.

20. The very idea of mediation assumes two parties, and this was true at the giving of the Law. But God is one, and this is emphasized in the covenant with Abraham. God acted sovereignly. He needed no one to stand between him and the patriarch. Paul's point is that mediation is a mark of inferiority in the Law. It shows the deliberate remoteness of God in the whole scene. The mediation of Christ in the present dispensation is not thereby labeled as inferior, for he is not a third party between God and men. God was in Christ reconciling the world.

21,22. The Law is not properly thought of as opposing the promises of God, for it operated in a different sphere. Life could not come by the Law. Those who enjoyed spiritual life in the legal dispensation had it not because of the Law but because of the grace of God, which forgave the sins committed against the Law. Such OT passages as promise life in connection with keeping the commandments of God (e.g., Deut 8:1), are properly interpreted as referring to life in a temporal sense, the enjoyment of God's favor and blessing in this earthly existence. **Righteousness** (a righteous standing before God) was no more possible in terms of law in Moses' day than in Paul's. Further, the Law cannot be opposed to the promises, since it aids their fulfillment by shutting men up to their need of grace and showing them that they must put their trust in Christ (cf. Gal 3:19).

4) Sonship Not Through the Law But Through Faith. 3:23–4:7.

23. Before faith came. The new dispensation of free grace brought men the first opportunity, historically speaking, to put faith in Christ. **24.** The age of law was a time of discipline, the Law serving as a **schoolmaster** (not teacher; in fact, only a teacher's aid, usually a slave whose task it was to insure the safe arrival of the child at the school). Christ is the real teacher, who takes us in hand and shows us the way of God in terms of grace. "A low view of law leads to legalism in religion; a high view of law makes a man a seeker after grace" (J. Gresham Machen, *The Origin of Paul's Religion*, p. 179).

25. The disciplinary function of the Law, in the historic sense, ceased with the coming of Christ. But the Law may still operate in an individual life to create a sense of sin and need, thus preparing the heart to turn to Christ.

26-29. Ye . . . all. Gentiles as well as Jews are welcomed into the family of God **by faith.** And thus they attain their position **in Christ Jesus. Baptized into Christ.** Water baptism brings a person into the fellowship of the Church, but behind this rite lies the more significant aspect of baptism–being set apart by the Spirit for living union with Christ and his body (cf. I Cor 12:13). **Have put on Christ.** The Lord Jesus becomes the secret and the sphere of a new life that is shared with other believers. **All one in Christ Jesus.** Sonship with God involves brotherhood in Christ. There is one new man in him (cf. Eph 2:15). The ordinary distinctions and divisions of life are swallowed up in this relationship. To be in Christ Jesus, belonging to him, makes one a part of **Abraham's seed,** since Christ is that, as already stated in Gal 3:16,19. Sonship makes the believer also an heir (cf. Rom 8:17).

4:1-7. The tension here is between the words **servant** and **son. 1. I say,** i.e., *I mean.* The subject has not changed. The **heir,** until he attains maturity, is treated like a **servant. 2.** There are those who direct and control him–**tutors** (guardians) and **governors** (managers)–until he is free to possess his inheritance at the time appointed in his father's will.

3. Application begins here. The time of childhood was the period of the Law's control, when there was **bondage under the elements of the world.** These are not the physical elements, as in II Pet 3:10,12, nor the heavenly bodies, nor the elemental spirits considered by the ancients to be associated with these bodies (Paul would never have agreed that he was serving such spirits when he lived under the Law). They are elements in the sense of *rudiments*, because they belong to the legalistic religion of Judaism, and not to Christianity, the more mature and spiritual faith. This view of the matter is confirmed by the use of the word **elements** in Gal 4:9.

4,5. The fulness of the time corresponds to "the time appointed of the father" (4:2). It suggests that the disciplinary and preparatory work of the Law required a long period. **His Son.** The appropriate means of bringing many sons into glory. Real sonship is impossible until the Son par excellence appears. Pre-existence is suggested here. **Made of a woman.** This is not a reference to the virgin birth (Mt 11:11). Paul's argument requires a stress on Christ's likeness to us, not on dissimilarity. Through His birth He entered into our humanity. **Made under the law.** Circumcised, presented, reared in terms of the Law's requirements, fulfilling all righteousness. It was necessary that he keep the Law perfectly in order to **redeem** his people from the bondage and curse of the Law and to secure for them **the adoption of sons.** This privilege came to them as a gift of grace and not as the result of a long period of tutelage under the Law.

6,7. This acceptance is attested by the testimony of the Spirit, called here **the Spirit of his Son,** since his mission is to further and apply the work of the Son. He begets in the believer assurance of acceptance with God by His testimony in the heart. Paul uses **Abba,** the Aramaic word for *father,* followed by its Greek equivalent (cf. Mk 14:36; Rom 8:15,16). Sonship rules out servanthood and includes heirship. The Holy Spirit is the guarantee of these future blessings (cf. Eph 1:13,14).

5) An Appeal Not To Return to Bondage. 4:8-11. The apostle turns back once more to consider in direct fashion the Galatians and their situation, as regards legalism and Christian liberty.

8. Before conversion they served beings that **by nature are no gods** (being idols). Such conduct is understandable, because at that time these people **knew not God. 9,10.** They knew him now because he had known them, as shown by his overtures of grace toward them. It is incredible that people with such a history would **turn again** to **weak and beggarly elements** (as contrasted with the Gospel), putting great store by special seasons. Apparently the Judaizers first put forward the more pleasant side of obedience to the Law (the Galatians were actually observing these things when Paul wrote) as less burdensome and offensive than circumcision, which the Galatians had not yet wholly accepted (cf. 5:2). **11.** Paul feared that if this attachment to legalism should continue and increase, it would mean that his labor among them had gone for nothing.

D. The Argument from Personal Reception by the Galatians. 4:12-20. The attitude of these people toward Paul at the time of this writing was in stark contrast to their original appreciation of him as God's messenger.

12,13. A plea to abandon legalism and be as Paul was, enjoying his liberty in Christ, for he had become like them. That is, by abandoning his Jewish distinctives he became, as it were, a Gentile (cf. 2:15-18). However much he was pained now, he recalled that the Galatians did him no injury **at the first,** on his **former** (ASV marg.) visit, but overlooked his **infirmity of the flesh** which caused him to tarry in their midst, an ill man. He did not leave their area until he had acquainted them with the good news of the Gospel. **14.** His sickness constituted a **temptation** for them to think lightly of him and reject him. This they refused to do; instead, they received him as one would receive an angel, or even as they would have received Christ himself.

15,16. Blessedness. They congratulated themselves on being thus favored by an emissary of the Lord. Their gratitude was unbounded; they would have sacrificed their **eyes** for Paul. This is not necessarily proof that the apostle had eye trouble (cf. the Gr. of Acts 23:1). The eyes are probably singled out for mention because of their preciousness. It must be, Paul is saying, that the Galatians' present coolness toward him is due to the fact that he has spoken **the truth.** Alienated from truth by Judaizing error, they had turned against Paul as well as against his message.

17,18. In contrast to Paul's habit of speaking the truth, the errorists had resorted to flattery and fawning attention to win the Galatians. Lest it be thought that the apostle was writing out of rancor and self-interest, he made clear that he was not averse to having another man minister to them rather than himself, provided the ministry was of the right sort—aiding the cause of the truth. How different were the Judaizers, who would **exclude** all who came to minister the Word, seeking to keep their protégés away from the apostle and other heralds of grace!

19,20. Paul's pain and concern were like those of a mother in travail. Yet what he agonizingly sought for was not the new birth of his friends (they were his **children** already in the Lord), but the full forming of the new life in them (Eph 4:13; cf. Phil 3:10). Another visit, he felt, would be highly desirable. It would accomplish more than the pen. Then he could speak softly to them, as a mother to an erring but still beloved child, and thus **change** his **voice,** which now necessarily seemed harsh.

E. The Argument from the Covenant of Promise. 4:21-31. Having called his readers **children,** the apostle proceeded to tell them a story, one with a moral, in the hope that they would see their folly.

21-23. They seemed to desire to be under law. Then let them **hear the law** (the Genesis narrative was part of the Law in the broader sense, which included the whole Pentateuch). One son of Abraham was **born after the flesh**—in the ordinary course of things, with a possible suggestion of human expediency trying to help along God's announced plan. This was Ishmael, born of Hagar. The other, namely, Isaac, the son of Sarah, was given by **promise** from God.

24,25. Which things are allegorized. That is, they are capable of expressing something more than the simple historical account. Paul proceeds to bring out the features that bear on the Galatian situation. **These** (women) answer to the **two covenants,** Hagar denoting the one given on **mount Sinai,** the Mosaic code. As she left the place of blessing in Canaan and went to this bleak area (Gen 21:21), so the Galatians had done in departing from the grace of Christ. Sad to say, more were affected than the Galatians. The Jerusalem of the day was **in bondage with her children**—not the church at Jerusalem, but Judaism as centered in this city.

26,27. But there is another Jerusalem, the one above, which is the **mother** of **all** the children of grace. This is a reference not to the future New Jerusalem of the Apocalypse but to a present spiritual reality, the home of believers. This home answers to the "heavenlies" of Eph 1:3 and "the city of the living God" of Heb 12:22. At this point Paul quotes Isaiah as foreseeing glory and triumph for Israel on the basis of the expiatory work of the Suffering Servant after the barrenness of the days of siege and captivity (Isa 54:1). This change of fortune is put in language that reflects the history of Sarah, who, though barren at first and apparently forsaken in favor of another, came into her own, in God's good time, with a greater progeny than that of Hagar. The church was enjoying a rapid increase in apostolic days, whereas Judaism was largely static and was even losing ground because of the witness of Jewish believers to their faith in Christ.

28-31. The New Testament saints were **children of promise,** as Isaac was. Just as Isaac was subject to persecution from Ishmael (cf. Gen 21:9), so they were subject to persecution from the legalists. The pressure to have Titus circumcised was a case in point (Gal 2:3). Yet the trial did not last, for God commanded the expulsion of **the bondwoman and her son** (Gen 21:10). The Judaizers did not have the authority or the blessing of God. Their work must come to nought.

IV. Paul's Gospel Practiced. 5:1–6:15.

A. The Gospel Practiced in Liberty. 5:1-12. Refusal to be circumcised was a prime token of the enjoyment of this liberty.

1. This transitional statement is not well rendered in the AV. **For liberty Christ set us free** is the apostle's statement of fact, followed by the appeal to stand in that liberty and not be involved again in bondage. In some ways it is easier to live as a slave than to make right use of one's freedom (e.g., Israel in the wilderness wishing to return to Egypt).

2-4. One must choose, Paul says, between **Christ** and **circumcision.** This is not spoken of Jews (cf. Acts 21:21), but of Gentiles, who had no background of circumcision. In their case the rite could only signify a deliberate attempt to create merit by adopting a legalistic position and seeking righteousness by works. In the beginning, circumcision had no such connotation, for with Abraham it was a sign and seal of the righteousness which he already had by faith (Rom 4:11). But in the course of time, it had become a badge of merit. This being so, Christ could not **profit** the recipient of circumcision, who had really placed himself under obligation **to do the whole law,** with a view to bring justified thereby. To assume circumcision meant to leave the ground of grace in Christ **(fallen from grace)** in favor of the lower and impossible ground of self-righteousness. The true believer stands in grace (Rom 5:2).

5. Whereas the legalist is bogged down in insecurity—for he cannot know when he has done enough to satisfy the standard of divine righteousness—those who are justified by faith, who have **the Spirit** as the pledge of their acceptance with God, confidently await **by faith** the consummation **(the hope of righteousness)** in glory (cf. Rom 8:10,11).

6. Having shown faith's upreach in hope, the apostle indicates its outreach in **love.** In Christ one is not advantaged by having circumcision; nor is he who lacks it at a loss. What counts is love, which sums up in itself all that the Law demands (Rom 13:9,10). Justifying faith does not set aside this cardinal consideration of love. On the contrary, faith, operating through love, is the only workable means whereby the demands of the Law may be met.

7-10. The spiritual progress of the Galatians had been arrested. Someone had hindered these converts by alienating them from **the truth.** Elsewhere (1:7; 5:12) a group of legalistic agitators is in view; here, however, an individual is indicated, presumably the leader. This propaganda did not emanate from the One who called and started them on their race (cf. 1:6). The readers had been deceived by listening to false teaching. And let no one of them claim that Paul was overwrought, that he was making too much of the troubles in Galatia. A proverb would emphasize their folly. **A little leaven leaveneth the whole lump.** Perhaps the actual converts to legalism were thus far only few in number. Nevertheless, the believers must be on their guard lest the error spread. If it was honestly faced, it could be stayed. Paul had confidence in a happy issue of the difficulty, not based on his converts or on his own ministry, but on **the Lord.** Nevertheless, a favorable turn of events would not lift the responsibility from the shoulders of him who had led the sheep astray. He must **bear his judgment.**

11,12. "Some may contend," Paul says, "that I am inconsistent in arguing against circumcision." It was known, for example, that he had circumcised Timothy (Acts 16:3). But this was a special case, for the young man was a half-Jew whom his father, a Greek, had not circumcised. If Timothy had gone about with Paul in this condition, it would have created needless opposition among the Jews. No principle was violated in this particular circumcision. The proof that Paul did not **preach circumcision** lay in the fact that he continued to **suffer persecution** (from the Jews). If he had circumcised the Gentiles, these same Jews would have regarded him in a much more friendly light. But if he had preached circumcision, **the offence of the cross** would have **ceased** so far as his ministry was concerned. Grace involves the helplessness of man to participate in his own salvation. This truth counters his human pride. Paul found offense not in the cross but in those who *unsettle[d]* (ASV) his converts – **which trouble you** (AV). His indignation led him to make a strong statement: **I would they were even cut off,** or better, *would mutilate themselves* (RSV). As an emasculated man has lost the power of propagation, so should these agitators be reduced to impotence in spreading their false doctrine. Such is the fervent wish to which the Apostle Paul gives expression here.

B. The Gospel Practiced in Love. 5:13-15.

13. While liberty is inherent in the Christian call to salvation, it must not be converted into license. This is what happens when liberty is viewed as an opportunity for **the flesh** to satisfy its desires. The one effective countermeasure is the service of others **by love.** The thought may be paraphrased as follows: You profess to be very zealous for the Law, which I have told you is bondage. But if you are really seeking bondage, there is a type that is harmless, even beneficial. I commend that to you. Be in bondage to each other to demonstrate love (cf. Rom 13:8). **14.** This is the OT requirement (Lev 19:18), and the NT knows nothing higher. **15.** There was dire need for the exercise of love in the Galatian churches, for Paul implies that there was fighting and bitter strife among them. The sharp antagonism was probably between those who had succumbed to the propaganda of the legalists and those who had not. Paul's sympathies were with the latter group, but he recognized that without love they could not win over those who were of the opposite persuasion. Argument without love results in continuing friction.

C. The Gospel Practiced in the Spirit. 5:16-26. Though not expressed here, freedom (5:1,13) has not been lost from view. "Love is the guard of Christian freedom. The Holy Spirit is its guide" (G. G. Findlay, *The Epistle to the Galations* in *The Expositor's Bible,* p. 347). This section, with its contrast between flesh and Spirit, has been somewhat anticipated by the statement in 3:3. Life in the Spirit is seen now as the effective antidote to the movings of the flesh, the sinful principle that persists in the saints. So there is a legitimate and necessary warfare, in contrast to that hinted at in 5:15.

16,17. Walk in (better, *by)* **the Spirit.** Only in this way can believers rise above the limitations of the flesh and avoid fulfilling its desires. The promise is emphatic—ye **shall not at all fulfill. Flesh** and **Spirit** are opposites, locked in continual combat. If the Christian is walking by the power of the one, he cannot be in the control of the other. The statement, **and these are contrary the one to the other,** is somewhat parenthetical, and the conclusion of the verse depends directly upon the second of the two statements earlier in the verse. Behind the Spirit's resistance to the flesh is the divine purpose that believers should be kept from doing things they (otherwise) would do.

18. To realize the victory over the flesh, one must put himself under the leadership of the Spirit. The Law conducts a man to Christ (3:24). Then the Spirit assumes control and directs the child of God into the fullness of the life in our Lord. This fullness will inevitably result unless the Spirit is limited by sin in the believer (Eph 4:30). Instead of saying, in agreement with the first pronouncements of this section, that to be led by the Spirit means to be delivered from the flesh, the apostle draws an unexpected conclusion. To be led by the Spirit demonstrates freedom from **law.** Adherence to law means the multiplying of transgressions (cf. Gal 3:19) instead of their reduction. Evidently a close bond exists between law and flesh (cf. Rom 8:3).

19-21. The **works of the flesh** can be expected to spawn freely in the atmosphere of legalism. A flash of irony is detectable here in the reference to **works** —"Look at the accomplishments of the flesh!" **First** come the sensual sins. **Adultery** is unlawful intercourse with a married person, **fornication** with one who is unmarried. **Uncleanness** covers all sorts of sexual defilement. **Lasciviousness** denotes brazen boldness in this sort of life. Next, religious sins are enumerated. **Idolatry** is devotion to idols. The Greek word rendered **witchcraft** yields the English term "pharmacy," and basically denotes the administering of drugs and magical potions. But it had come to stand for the whole practice of the magician's art (cf. "sorceries," and ASV "sorcery" in Rev 9:21; 18:23). Still a third class includes temperamental sins. These run the gamut from **hatred,** which is something latent, through **strife,** which is something operative (denoting in this case disputes due to selfishness), and **seditions** (better, *divisions)* and **heresies,** or displays of party spirit (**envyings** may be related to the foregoing as helping to produce divisions, or may equally well be associated with the next item), to **murders,** the climax of wrongly cherished antagonisms. In a fourth class may be put **drunkenness** and **revellings.** The list could be extended—**and such like.** Those who practice such things **shall not inherit the kingdom of God** (cf. I Cor 6:9,10). A believer may fall into such wrongdoing if he walks in accordance with the flesh. Hence the inclusion of this list in its present position in this letter, where the life of the Christian is under review.

22,23. Everything here stands in contrast to the foregoing: **fruit** instead of works; **the Spirit** instead of the flesh; and a list of virtues altogether attractive and desirable in place of the ugly things just cited. The word **fruit,** being singular, as usual in Paul's writings, tends to emphasize the unity and coherence of the life in the Spirit as opposed to the disorganization and instability of life under the dictates of the flesh. It is possible, also, that the singular may be intended to point to the person of Christ, in whom all these things are seen in their perfection. The Spirit seeks to produce these by reproducing Christ in the believer (cf. 4:19). Passages like Rom 13:14 suggest that the moral problems of redeemed men and women can be solved by the adequacy of Christ when he is appropriated by faith.

In the light of Paul's preference for the

singular form of **fruit,** it is not necessary to resort to the expedient of putting a dash after **love** in order to make all the other items depend on this one. Love is crucial (I Jn 4:8; I Cor 13:13; Gal 5:6). **Joy** is conferred by Christ upon his own followers (Jn 15:11) and is mediated by the Spirit (I Thess 1:6; Rom 14:17). **Peace** is the gift of Christ (Jn 14:27) and includes inward repose (Phil 4:6) and harmonious relations with others (contrast Gal 5:15,20). **Longsuffering** relates to one's attitude toward others and involves a refusal to retaliate or work vengeance for wrong received. It is literally *long-spiritedness*. **Gentleness** is better rendered *kindness*. It is benevolence in action, a distinctly social virtue. **Goodness** is an uprightness of soul that abhors evil, a clean-cut honesty of motive and conduct. **Faith,** in this setting, means faithfulness (if it were *faith,* it would stand at the beginning of the list). For a parallel use, see Tit 2:10 ("fidelity"). **Meekness** is based on humility and denotes an attitude toward others in keeping with due denial of self. **Temperance** is better rendered *self-control* (lit., *a holding in with a firm hand),* or control of the self life by means of the Spirit. **Against such there is no law.** "Law exists for the purpose of restraint, but in the works of the Spirit there is nothing to restrain" (J. B. Lightfoot, *Galatians,* p. 213). The same truth is stated elsewhere, e.g., Rom 8:4.

24-26. Those who are truly Christ's must be like him in that they participate in his cross. They have **crucified the flesh.** Ideally, this points to their identification with Christ in his death (2:20). Practically, it emphasizes the need of carrying the cross principle into the redeemed life, since the flesh, with its **affections** and desires is still an ever present reality (cf. 5:16,17). The same tension between divine provision and human appropriation is found regarding the Spirit. We **live** in the Spirit by God's arrangement, by means of the gift of the Spirit at conversion. But we **walk** in the Spirit as a matter of personal volition, taking each step in dependence upon him. If one is walking thus, he will not be desirous of **vainglory**—ambitious for self and frustrated when unsuccessful. "Vaingloryіng challenges competition, to which the stronger-natured respond in kind, while those who are weaker are moved to envy" (Hogg and Vine, *Galatians,* p. 305).

D. The Gospel Practiced in Service. 6:1-10. Christians still have a law to fulfill, the law of Christ. They can fulfill it only in the power of the Spirit, as they serve one another in the fellowship of the Church.

1-5. A man. One of like passions with yourselves and therefore liable to fall. **Be overtaken.** Apprehended, taken by surprise, caught in the act. **Fault** should be more strongly worded. It is a lapse (cf. Rom 5:15). A sinning saint needs restoration as well as divine forgiveness. The one qualified to help him is **spiritual,** i.e., possessing to a notable degree the fruit of the Spirit, especially love (5:22) for the brother in trouble and also **meekness** (5:23), seeing that he himself could some day slip into sin and need the same loving ministration for himself. A true spirit of helpfulness should obtain in other matters also—**bear ye one another's burdens** (contrast Lk 11:46). The law of Moses is described as a burden (Acts 15:10), but **the law of Christ** is not so (I Jn 5:3). His burden is light (Mt 11:30). This sets the disciple free to minister to his fellows (Mk 10:43-45). The warning at the end of Gal 6:1 is carried on in 6:3. Over-evaluation of one's self is self-deception. Let a man put his own work to the test. If he finds anything there to give satisfaction, he can have **rejoicing in himself.** His feeling will be one of gratification and contentment rather than of pride and superiority over his brethren. Each had better evaluate himself aright now, in preparation for the Lord's judgment of him in the coming day, when he must **bear his own burden.** He will be held responsible for his own life and work (Rom 14:12).

6-10. Here the thought returns to bearing one another's burdens, but in the specific area of giving for the support of Christian work (cf. II Cor 11:9; II Thess 3:8). **6. Communicate** means to participate in something along with someone else. The one who is **taught in the word** shares his material goods with the one who teaches him. In this way he participates in the work of the Lord. This is the divine plan. Beware lest any try to set it aside. **7. God is not mocked.** The word for mockery is *turning up the nose*. No man can successfully snub God or evade his decree that, "whatsoever a man soweth, that shall he also reap"—the immutable law of life (cf. II Cor 9:6 in a similar connection). **8.** A selfish Christian **soweth to his flesh,** spending his resources to gratify his own personal desires. He may expect to **reap corruption.** That which might have brought reward by being invested in the Lord's work will be nothing but a decayed mass, a complete loss in terms of eternity. On the other hand, by responding to the Spirit in love and kindness, and gladly participating in the extension of the Gospel by supporting Christian workers, believers will be adding interest to the capital of eternal life. This passage is capable of broader application, in line with the proverbial character of the statement in verse **7.** But **flesh** and **Spirit** suggest primary application to the believer (cf. 5:17,24,25), in line with the immediate context. **9.** The specific issue of giving leads naturally to a consideration of the more general theme of doing good, which by implication is a sowing. The harvest will come **in due season.** One may well **faint** if he expects to see the harvest immediately. **10.** Two spheres of Christian beneficence are suggested—**all** men and **the household of faith.** The latter group is **especially** the obligation of the children of God. If one neglects to care for his own (and believers are the family of God), he is worse than an unbeliever (I Tim 5:8).

E. The Gospel Practiced in Separation from the World. 6:11-15. Paul uses this final section as a means of underscoring some of the emphases of the epistle as a whole, stressing the centrality and sufficiency of the cross, and the division it creates between believers and men of the world.

11. How large a letter is not a good rendering. The apostle is not referring to length (Galatians is not a long letter), but to the size of the letters he used as he took the pen from the hand of the scribe and wrote these closing words himself for the sake of greater effectiveness. He returns to the subject of circumcision and exposes the motives of those who were troubling his readers. **12.** They **desire[d] to make a fair show in the flesh**, in the only realm of life which they knew, since they did not walk by the Spirit. **Constrain** in this case means "seek to compel" (cf. 2:3). Pressure was being exerted. By stressing circumcision, and going among the Gentiles to urge it upon them, the Judaizers were hoping to escape the wrath of unbelieving Jews against themselves for having espoused the cause of Christ. They were afraid of **persecution for the cross of Christ** (cf. 5:11). Men of this type are called "the concision" *(cutting party)* in Phil 3:2. **13.** Having dealt with the real motive of the Judaizers, Paul now reveals their professed motive, which was zeal for the Law. They took one item, an external matter at that, and made it stand for the observance of the Law as a whole. They hoped to gain credit for bringing Gentiles under the Law as a system by forcing them to accept circumcision. They would **glory** in this mark made in the flesh of their converts. **14.** Paul refused to boast in circumcision or in anything else except **the cross** by which (AV *by whom*, i.e., Christ) the world with all its craven motives was banished, crucified to him, utterly separated from his thought and way of life. Paul cared not for comfort or reputation, as the Judaizers did (cf. 1:10). **15.** Why does the apostle here discount circumcision? Because it had been made a mere worldly ceremony by the crucifixion. What truly counts, he declares, is the new life that comes through being **in Christ Jesus.** This amounts to a **new creation.** The word **new** denotes what is superior to the old.

V. Conclusion. 6:16-18.

A. Closing Prayer. 6:16. For those who walk according to the **rule** or canon just laid down, namely, the cross of Christ and the message of grace that centers there, Paul requests **peace** and that merciful loving-kindness which brings a continuance of the grace already received in the Gospel. He seeks the same blessing for **the Israel of God.** While it is possible that this refers to the whole church, in view of the **and,** the more probable reference is to Christian Jews, such as Paul himself. These are the real Israel, as opposed to those who merely bear the name (cf. Rom 2:29).

B. Closing Testimony. 6:17. If the Galatians had been troubled, so had Paul. But if any wished to question his devotion to Christ, let them realize that **the marks** of persecution which he bore in his body, scars suffered for the sake of the Lord Jesus, spoke more eloquently than the body marks (circumcision) which the Judaizers loved to impose on others as a proof of their zeal.

C. Benediction. 6:18. This parting word, with its emphasis on grace, summarizes the message of the epistle as a whole. Nothing could be more appropriate.

BIBLIOGRAPHY

Burton, E. D. *The Epistle to the Galatians (International Critical Commentary).* New York: Charles Scribner's Sons, 1920.

Ellicott, C. J. *Commentary on St. Paul's Epistle to the Galatians.* Andover: Warren F. Draper, 1896.

Findlay, G. G. *The Epistle to the Galatians (The Expositor's Bible).* New York: A. C. Armstrong and Son, 1889.

Hogg, C. F., and Vine, W. E. *The Epistle of Paul the Apostle to the Galatians.* London: Pickering and Inglis, 1922.

Lightfoot, J. B. *St. Paul's Epistle to the Galatians.* London: Macmillan and Co., 1896.

Ramsay, W. M. *A Historical Commentary on St. Paul's Epistle to the Galatians.* New York: G. P. Putnam's Sons, 1900.

Ridderbos, H. N. *The Epistle of Paul to the Churches of Galatia.* Grand Rapids: Wm. B. Eerdmans Publishing Co., 1953.

THE EPISTLE TO THE EPHESIANS

INTRODUCTION

Authorship, Date, and Place of Writing. Few critics have seriously denied Paul's authorship of this epistle. More attack has been leveled against the traditional date and place of writing, as well as against the traditional destination (see below).

Ephesians is in the same chronological group of Paul's epistles as Colossians, Philemon, and Philippians, called collectively "The Prison Epistles" because written during Paul's first Roman imprisonment. Paul evidently arrived in Rome in the spring of 61. The Acts speaks of his living two whole years in his own hired house (Acts 28:30), which would bring him to the spring of 63. He was probably released before the burning of Rome in 64. In Philippians he was expecting such release (1:19-26), a hope to which he refers also in Philemon 22. Ephesians, Colossians, and Philemon were dispatched at the same time by the same messengers (Eph 6:21,22; Col 4:7-9; Phm 12,23,24).

Attempts to place these epistles at an earlier time from some other place of imprisonment, such as Caesarea or even Ephesus (George S. Duncan, *St. Paul's Ephesian Ministry*) have not been successful. There is no good reason for rejecting the traditional place of writing—Rome. This epistle, along with Colossians and Philemon, was probably written in the year 62.

Destination of the Epistle. Because the words **in Ephesus** *(en Ephesô)* do not occur in the original handwriting of Codex Sinaiticus (Aleph) and Codex Vaticanus (B), two of the oldest extant manuscripts of the New Testament, some deny that this epistle was addressed to Ephesus. Another point of difficulty is the fact that an epistle from Laodicea is mentioned in Col 4:16, but there is no mention of Ephesus. Some believe that this epistle may have been a circular letter addressed to a number of different churches. [This is the view most widely held today.—Ed.] It seems more likely, however, that a particular congregation was in view, and there is no strong reason for rejecting the traditional destination—Ephesus (see John W. Burgon, *The Last Twelve Verses of St. Mark*, 1959 edition, pp. 169-187). Even Aleph and B are headed by the title *To Ephesians* (*Pros Ephesious*). Paul had remained a comparatively long time in Ephesus while on his third missionary journey (Acts 19:1–20:1; 20:31). His association with the believers there had been most intimate, as his address to the Ephesian elders shows (Acts 20:17-38).

Contents of the Epistle. This epistle, along with Colossians, emphasizes the truth that the Church is the body of which Christ is the Head. While Paul had mentioned the same truth earlier, in Romans 12 and I Corinthians 12, he develops it more fully here. There is no higher point of revelation than is reached in this epistle which shows the believer as seated with Christ in the heavenlies and exhorts him to live in accordance with this high calling. Actually the epistle falls into two main parts of three chapters each. In Eph 1–3 the apostle tells believers what they are in Christ; In Eph 4–6 he tells them what they are to do because they are in Christ. It has often been suggested that the contents of the epistle can be summarized by the three words *sitting, walking,* and *standing*. By position, the believer is seated with Christ in the heavenlies (2:6); his responsibility is to walk worthy of the calling wherewith he has been called (4:1); and this walk is further seen as a warfare in which he is engaged against Satan and all his hosts and in which he is exhorted to stand against the wiles of the devil (6:11).

OUTLINE

I. The believer's position in Christ. 1:1–3:21.
  A. Salutation. 1:1,2.
  B. All spiritual blessings. 1:3-14.
    1. Chosen by the Father. 1:3-6.
    2. Redeemed by the Son. 1:7-12.
    3. Sealed by the Holy Spirit. 1:13,14.
  C. Paul's first prayer. 1:15-23.
  D. Salvation by grace. 2:1-10.
    1. What we were in the past. 2:1-3.
    2. What we are in the present. 2:4-6.
    3. What we shall be in the future. 2:7-10.
  E. Oneness of Jews and Gentiles in Christ. 2:11-22.
    1. What the Gentiles were without Christ. 2:11,12.
    2. The one body. 2:13-18.
    3. The one building. 2:19-22.
  F. The revelation of the mystery. 3:1-13.
    1. The dispensation of the grace of God. 3:1-6.
    2. The fellowship of the mystery. 3:7-13.
  G. Paul's second prayer. 3:14-21.

II. The believer's conduct in the world. 4:1–6:24.
  A. The worthy walk. 4:1-16.
    1. The unity of the Spirit. 4:1-6.
    2. The gift of Christ. 4:7-12.
    3. The unity of faith and knowledge. 4:13-16.
  B. The different walk. 4:17-32.
    1. Description of the Gentiles' walk. 4:17-19.
    2. Putting off the old and putting on the new. 4:20-24.
    3. Practical application. 4:25-32.
  C. The loving walk. 5:1-14.
    1. Walking in love. 5:1-7.
    2. Walking in light. 5:8-14.
  D. The wise walk. 5:15–6:9.
    1. Being circumspect. 5:15-17.
    2. Being filled with the Holy Spirit. 5:18–6:9.
      a. Rejoicing and thanksgiving. 5:19,20.
      b. Submission in practical relationships. 5:21–6:9.
        (1) Wives and husbands. 5:21-33.
        (2) Children and parents. 6:1-4.
        (3) Servants and masters. 6:5-9.
  E. The Christian walk as a warfare. 6:10-20.
    1. Being strong in the Lord—the whole armor of God. 6:10-17.
    2. Prayer for all saints and for Paul. 6:18-20.
  F. Closing greetings. 6:21-24.

COMMENTARY

I. The Believer's Position in Christ. 1:1–3:21.

A. Salutation. 1:1,2. The salutations of all Paul's epistles are strikingly similar. Although this is the regular epistolary form, there is less of the personal element in Ephesians than in most of Paul's letters.

1. Paul, an apostle of Jesus Christ by the will of God. As in other epistles, Paul emphasizes that he has been appointed by God to the special office of apostle. **To the saints.** In the NT saints are those who are set apart, that is, all believers. **Which are at Ephesus.** See Introduction. **The faithful.** Believing ones (cf. Gal 3:9). The absence of the article before the word **faithful** in the original indicates that the saints *are* the believers. **In Christ Jesus.** An important phrase in this epistle. No matter what the geographical location of the saints, their real position in God's sight is in Christ Jesus. They have been put into a vital union with him so that they are identified with him (cf. Jn 14:20).

2. Grace be to you, and peace. This same greeting is found in all of Paul's epistles, though the word *mercy* is added in the Pastorals. Grace must always precede peace. The Greek word for **grace,** *charis,* is related to the common Greek greeting, *chairein,* but gives to the salutation a distinctively Christian emphasis. **Peace** is the usual Hebrew greeting. **From God our Father, and from the Lord Jesus Christ.** The second **from** is not in the original. There is a very close connection here, which shows the identity of the Father and the Lord Jesus Christ in their essence.

B. All Spiritual Blessings. 1:3-14. The believer is seen as the recipient of **all spiritual blessings.** Hence he has no need to seek additional blessings from God. He must, instead, appropriate the ones that already have been provided. All three Persons of the Holy Trinity are seen to have a part in this provision of the spiritual blessings.

1) Chosen by the Father. 1:3-6. The work of the Father is mentioned first.

3. Blessed be the God and Father of our Lord Jesus Christ. "Almost all St. Paul's epistles begin with some ascription of praise" (Alf). Notice the play on words in the use of **blessed. Who hath blessed us.** We are called upon to bless God, who has already blessed us. But of course God has blessed us by what he has done, while our blessing of him is by words, that is, by our praise of him. He is **the God and Father of our Lord Jesus Christ.** This identifies him as the one true God, not some false or imaginary deity. The only way to know him is through Jesus Christ (cf. Jn 14:6). **In heavenly places.** Although the adjective occurs elsewhere, this phrase occurs only in Ephesians in the NT. It is found five times—1:3; 1:20; 2:6; 3:10; 6:12. The word **places** is not in the original. Here it denotes the spheres or realms of our association in Christ. We are not yet actually in heaven, but our calling is heavenly; the power for our daily living is heavenly; God's provision is heavenly. Note the continual repetition in the epistle of the phrase, **in Christ.** It is only in him that we ever could have received these blessings.

4. As he hath chosen us. This is middle voice in Greek; that is, he chose us for himself. The Scripture has much to say about God's electing love. The doctrine of election is never presented in Scripture as something to be afraid of, but always as something for believers to rejoice in. Note that we are chosen **in him,** that is, in Christ, and that this choice took place **before the foundation of the world.** God's purposes are eternal. **That we should be holy and without blame before him.** This is the purpose for which God has chosen us in Christ (cf. Rom 8:29; Jude 24,25). The phrase **in love** probably belongs with what follows rather than with what precedes; that is, *in love having predestinated us* (Nestle).

5. Having predestinated us. God's choice of us in Christ was for a purpose that is eternal. **Unto the adoption of children.** The word translated **adoption of children** is used five times in the NT (Rom 8:15,23; 9:4; Gal 4:5; and here). It refers to our being placed in the position of sons. It is not the modern idea of adoption, but rather the placing of a child in the position of adult sonship. God's purpose is that all believers should be adult sons in his family, in which Christ is the "firstborn" (Rom 8:29). **According to the good pleasure of his will.** Any attempt to base God's election and predestination upon human merit, whether foreknown or otherwise, is un-Scriptural and futile. The cause of God's choice of us is not to be found in us, but in him alone (cf. Tit 3:5; Eph 2:8-10). The will of God is the determining factor.

6. To the praise of the glory of his grace. Note the threefold use of this expression (cf. vv. 12,14). The three occurrences of this phrase mark off the part each of the three Persons of the Godhead takes in our salvation in giving us the blessings that have come to us. The most important consideration in the universe is the glory of God. The Westminster Shorter Catechism expresses this well in its answer to the first question, "What is the chief end of man?" "Man's chief end is to glorify God, and to enjoy Him forever." **His grace.** "Grace is undeserved, unearned, and unrecompensed" (Chafer). It is God's self-dependent favor bestowed upon sinful men, who deserve only his wrath. **Wherein he hath made us accepted.** More literally, *which he has freely bestowed upon us.* There is another play on words in the original—"His grace which he graced." It is difficult to show this in English. This bestowal is **in the beloved;** that is, in the beloved one—namely, the Lord Jesus Christ (cf. Col 1:13; Mt 3:17).

2) Redeemed by the Son. 1:7-12.

7. In whom—that is, Christ,—**we have redemption.** This is our present possession. **Through his blood.** The Scripture presents the blood of Christ as the infinite purchase price of our redemption (cf. Acts 20:28; I Cor 6:20; I Pet 1:18-20). Colossians 1:14 parallels this verse. **The forgiveness of sins.** The Pharisees rightly observed (for once) that no man can forgive sins but God only (Mk 2:7). The fact that the Lord Jesus Christ forgives is evidence that he is God. **According to the riches of his grace.** Again the emphasis on the utter absence of human merit (cf. Rom 5:21). Note the word **riches.** His grace is not limited.

8. Wherein he hath abounded toward us. God abounds in every respect. He is the infinite One. The **wisdom** of the Lord Jesus Christ is unlimited, and he has abounded in the sense that he has made this wisdom available to us, as the next verse indicates. **9. Having made known unto us.** The explanation of his abounding. **The mystery.** In the NT the word **mystery** (literally, *secret*) indicates something not clearly revealed before, but now made known. **According to his good pleasure which he hath purposed in himself.** Again we see that God is completely self-determining and self-sufficient.

10. That in the dispensation of the fulness of times. The word **dispensation** means "stewardship." It is used in the NT to refer to the different administrations of God's blessings. Evidently **the dispensation of the fulness of times** is the final stewardship committed to men, which will bring the purposes of God to fruition in human history. The purpose that has been referred to is summed up in the expression, **He might gather together in one all things in Christ.** This is a literary remark (Robertson) — "that he might head up everything in Christ" (cf. Col 1:18). **All things** includes the whole creation. Since Christ is pre-eminent in God's purpose in the universe and in the Church, the individual who does not have Christ pre-eminent in his life is entirely out of harmony with the purpose of the Father.

11. In whom also we have obtained an inheritance. There is difference of opinion concerning the Greek here—whether it is active or passive. The latter seems more probable, in which case we could translate it *in whom we have been made an heritage.* We are Christ's inheritance, as he is ours. **Being predestinated according to the purpose of him who worketh all things after the counsel of his own will.** The words **predestinated, purpose, counsel,** and **will** have an intimate connection. There is no clearer or more sublime statement anywhere in Scripture concerning the sovereignty of God. Running throughout the Bible are the parallel lines of God's sovereignty and man's responsibility. We cannot reconcile them, but we can believe both because both are taught in the Word.

12. That we should be to the praise of his glory, who first trusted in Christ. Some believe that **we** here refers to the Jews, because of the expression **first trusted.** This seems likely in view of the contrast between **we** in verse 12 and **ye** in verse 13. **To the praise of his glory.** This marks off the second section in this great triad.

3) Sealed by the Holy Spirit. 1:13,14.

13. In whom ye also trusted. That is, you Gentiles, in contrast to the Jews. **After that ye heard the word of truth.** When you heard the word of truth, or word which consists of truth. This is equated further with **the gospel of your salvation**—the good news which brought you salvation. **In whom also after that ye believed.** Literally, *in whom also when you believed, you were sealed.* This sealing did not take place as something subsequent to salvation but was simultaneous with salvation. The sealing ministry of the Holy Spirit is mentioned several times in the NT (cf. II Cor 1:22; Eph 4:30). A seal indicates possession and security. The Holy Spirit himself is the seal. His presence guarantees our salvation. **That holy Spirit of promise. That** is simply *the* in the Greek text. The word **holy** should be capitalized, for this is the third Person of the Godhead, and the adjective is emphatic in the original. **Of promise.** The Holy Spirit himself is the object or content of the promise that was given.

14. Who is the earnest of our inheritance. That is, the pledge which guarantees that all the rest will follow. **Until the redemption of the purchased possession.** Jesus Christ has purchased us for himself and has given us the Holy Spirit as the pledge that the redemption which has been so wondrously begun will be completed. Again we have the refrain **unto the praise of his glory.** The repetition of this refrain reminds us again of the triune God—Father, Son and Holy Spirit, three Persons, yet one God.

C. Paul's First Prayer. 1:15-23. The prayer that follows is based upon the paragraph just concluded. It is because God has done all of these things for the believer, carrying him from his eternal purpose in the past eternity to the completion of the redemption in the future eternity, that Paul can pray as he does. Note that in contrast to most of our prayers, Paul's intercession was primarily for the spiritual welfare of those for whom he prayed.

15. After I heard of your faith in the Lord Jesus, and love unto all the saints. Sometimes we forget that we should pray as earnestly for people after they are saved, as we do for their salvation. The faith and love of these Ephesian believers was an incentive to Paul to pray for their continued spiritual growth. **16. Cease not to give thanks for you.** Thanks on your behalf; that is, thanks to God for what he had done for the Ephesians. **Making mention of you in my prayers.** Paul did not regard prayer as something vague and indefinite. He remembered them and their needs specifically before God.

17. That the God of our Lord Jesus Christ (cf. v. 3), **the Father of glory.** That is, the Father characterized by glory. **May give unto you the spirit of wisdom and revelation.** Probably this is objective; that is, the Holy Spirit who gives wisdom and revelation. **In the knowledge.** This word indicates full experiential knowledge. **18. The eyes of your understanding being enlightened.** Literally, *the eyes of your heart*. "The heart in Scripture is the very core and center of life" (Alf). **That ye may know.** It is only as God enlightens us that we actually can know what he wants us to know. **What is the hope of his calling.** Hope in Scripture is the absolute certainty of future good. **Riches of the glory of his inheritance in the saints.** Compare with the "riches of grace" in verse 7 (cf. also Deut 33:3,4).

19. The exceeding greatness of his power. The phrases that follow pile up words to denote the almightiness of God **to us-ward.** "No better rendering here could be devised than the *to us-ward* of the AV, which is wisely retained by the [English] RV" (Salmond). **20. Which he wrought in Christ when he raised him from the dead.** Frequently in the OT the standard of God's power referred to is the deliverance from Egypt, especially the crossing of the Red Sea. But here is a much greater standard of power. That very power of God that raised Christ from the dead is available to us, and we can know it in our experience. **And set him at his own right hand.** Probably the various references in the NT to Christ at the right hand of God go back to Psalm 110. **In the heavenly places.** In this second of the five uses of this phrase there is evidently a local sense: the Lord Jesus is literally and bodily in heaven.

21. Far above all principality, and power. All in the sense of "every." Different words are used in the NT for varying ranks and kinds of heavenly beings, both holy and fallen angels. For this exaltation of Christ compare Phil 2:8-11. **In this world.** This is a time word—*in this age*. **22. And hath put all things under his feet.** Again the allusion to Ps 110:1 (cf. also Ps 8:6). This indicates Christ's ultimate complete victory. **Gave him** (cf. Jn 3:16) **to be the head.** This is the first mention in the epistle of Christ as the Head of the Church, a truth that is developed quite fully (see Introduction).

23. Which is his body. While we speak of this as a figure, it is more than that. It denotes the complete union of the Church with the Lord Jesus, the absolute identification of believers with him (cf. I Cor 12:12). **The fulness.** That which is filled. "She [the Church] is the continued revelation of his divine life in human form" (JFB). It can be seen that true prayer includes an abundance of praise. Adoration of our wonderful God should take precedence over our own selfish and self-centered petitions. How different our lives would be if we were to pray like this for one another continually!

D. Salvation by Grace. 2:1-10. In this paragraph the apostle tells about our salvation by God's grace, showing what we were in the past, what we are now, and what we shall be in the future.

1) What We Were in the Past. 2:1-3. The opening statement of this section reminds the Ephesian believers of how desperately they once needed God's saving grace.

1. And you hath he quickened. There is a broken construction here. Note that the words **hath he quickened** are in italics, indicating that they are not in the original. Literally it is, *and you who were dead in trespasses and sins.* Verses 2 and 3, then, are parenthetical, and the main thought is resumed in verse 4. The contrast is between you, dead in trespasses and sins, and God, rich in mercy. The death referred to here is not physical, but spiritual; that is, separation from God.

2. Wherein in time past ye walked. Walking is used in Scripture to refer to daily conduct, manner of life (cf. the later portions of the epistle for the believer's walk). **According to the course of this world.** It is unusual to find the word *aion,* "age," and the word *kosmos,* "world," together—"the age of this world-system." Both of these words have acquired an ethical sense from their usage in the NT. **According to the prince of the power of the air.** This obviously refers to Satan. There is a paradox here in that dead people are represented as walking. Everyone apart from Christ is dead and is walking according to the prince of the power of the air. Satan is further described as **the spirit that now worketh in the children of disobedience;** that is, children characterized by disobedience. Ever since Adam's sin, men have been disobedient children.

3. Among whom also we all had our conversation. The word **conversation** means behavior, manner of life, or conduct. The **we** is in contrast to the **you** of 2:1. **Our flesh.** The term **flesh** in the NT is often used in an ethical sense to refer to the old nature, that which we inherited from Adam. **The desires of the flesh and of the mind.** Apparently the body and the mind are connected, both being a part of the flesh, that is, of the old nature. Many people are accustomed to think of sins of the flesh merely as various kinds of immorality, forgetting that there are also sins of the mind. **The children of wrath.** That is, those who are under wrath, whose destination is wrath, upon whom the wrath of God abides (cf. Rom 1:18; Jn 3:36; see also Heb 10:26,27).

2) What We Are in the Present. 2:4-6. God's Word is full of striking contrasts between man's inability and the Lord's sufficiency.

4. The writer now returns to the statement that was interrupted at verse 2. **But God.** This is the saving contrast. **Rich in mercy** (cf. riches of his grace and glory, 1:7,18). There is no limit to the mercy of God. **For his great love.** Literally, *because of his great love wherewith he loved us.* The Scripture repeatedly indicates that God's love toward us, not our love toward him, is the more important (cf. I Jn 4:9,10). **5. Dead in sins.** This looks back to the statement in 2:1. **Hath quickened us.** Made us alive. **Together with Christ.** There is a compound verb here which is joined with the word **Christ,** to show that our being made alive is in conjunction with his being made alive, that is, in his resurrection. The parenthesis, **by grace ye are saved,** is further explained and amplified in verse 8.

6. And hath raised us up together, and made us sit together in heavenly places in Christ Jesus. The Scripture teaches that we have been identified with the Lord Jesus Christ, not only in his death (Rom 6), but also in his resurrection and in his ascension to the right hand of the Father. The word **sit** is one of the great words in this epistle, indicating the position we have in Christ, as partakers of a finished, accomplished redemption and sharers in a victory. **In heavenly places.** The third use of this expression in the epistle. Because of our position in Christ, we are already potentially in heaven, where he is actually.

3) What We Shall Be in the Future. 2:7-10. The fact that God has made redeemed sinners an eternal object lesson of his grace is amazing but true.

7. That in the ages to come he might show. The Church is to be an eternal demonstration of the grace of God. **The exceeding riches of his grace** (cf. 1:7) **in his kindness** (cf. Tit 2:14; 3:4).

8. For by grace are ye saved. That is, *you have been saved.* God's grace is the source of our salvation. **Through faith.** Paul never says *on account of* faith, for faith is not the cause, only the channel through which our salvation comes. **And that not of yourselves.** The word **that** refers not to grace or to faith, but to the whole act of salvation—"That salvation not of yourselves." **The gift of God.** Cf. Rom 6:23. **9. Not of works.** This is the negative complement of the preceding statement. The Holy Spirit has been very careful to guard this precious doctrine of salvation by grace against all forms of heresy. **Works** in the Scripture are the product or fruit of salvation, not the cause of it. **Lest any man should boast.** There will be no boasting in heaven because there will be no one there who has anything to boast about (I Cor 4:7).

10. We are his workmanship. The **his** is emphatic in the original. **Created in Christ Jesus unto good works.** It is the purpose of our new creation that we should walk. The passage has now come full circle, for this walk is in direct contrast to the walk described in verse 2.

E. Oneness of Jews and Gentiles in Christ. 2:11-22. One of the great truths of this epistle is that Jew and Gentile are united in the body of Christ. That body has already been referred to in 1:23, and the union is described here, with further amplification in chapter 3.

1) What the Gentiles Were Without Christ. 2:11,12. The language in these verses paints a very dark picture of the Gentile position before Christ came.

11. Wherefore remember. Most of Paul's original readers were Gentiles. The apostle here reminds them of their position before they heard the Gospel. **In time past Gentiles.** In the sight of men they were still Gentiles, but not in the sight of God. God looks upon all men as either Jews, Gentiles, or the Church (I Cor 10:32). When one accepts the Lord Jesus Christ, whether he be Jew or Gentile, he is no longer such in the sight of God, but a member of the body of Christ. **Called Uncircumcision.** This was a contemptuous epithet applied by the Jews to the Gentiles. **12. Aliens from the commonwealth of Israel.** In the OT God had a covenant with the nation of Israel and governed that state directly. Those who were not Jews were foreigners or aliens. **Having no hope** and being **without God,** they could know the covenant and promises of the Lord only through Israel. The descriptive expressions become more and more serious.

2) The One Body. 2:13-18. Jew and Gentile have been united in Christ, and the latter is now as near to him as the former.

13. But now. This is emphatic. It indicates a contrast to their previous position. **In Christ Jesus.** Formerly they were **in the world** (v. 12). Their condition was hopeless. Now they are **in Christ,** with all the privileges of heaven. Note several contrasts in these verses—**in the world, in Christ Jesus; sometimes** (ASV, *once*), **now; far off, nigh. 14. He is our peace.** Observe the progress in this section: **He is our peace** (v. 14); **making peace** (v. 15); **preached peace** (v. 17; cf. Col 1:20). **Hath made both one.** That is, Jew and Gentile. **The middle wall of partition** may be here an allusion to the wall separating the Court of the Gentiles and the Court of the Jews in the Temple. An inscription on this wall warned Gentiles of the death penalty for entering the Court of the Jews. Now, in the sight of God, there is no distinction (see Rom 1; 2; 3).

15. The enmity. Perhaps in apposition to "the middle wall of partition." **One new man.** Not an individual but the new creation of which Christ is the Head. **16. Both.** Again a reference to Jew and Gentile. **Having slain the enmity thereby.** That is, by the cross. Verses 17, 18 further amplify this truth of the uniting of Jew and Gentile in Christ. **Far off.** The Gentiles. **Them that were nigh.** The Jews. **18.** Note the emphasis on the word **both** (vv. 14,16,18). Both made one, both reconciled to God, both having access.

3) The One Building. 2:19-22. The figure of the Church as a human body now shades into the figure of the Church as a great building. The human body is also described as a building in various passages (e.g., I Cor 6:19; II Cor 5:1).

19. Now therefore. The logical conclusion of what has been written. **No more strangers and foreigners.** The present position of these Gentiles is entirely reversed from their former condition described earlier in the chapter. **But fellow-citizens with the saints.** In Christ, Jews and Gentiles have a new citizenship (cf. Phil 3:20,21).

20. And are built upon the foundation. The Church, which is the body of Christ, is viewed here as a great building, a temple of God. **The apostles.** Men especially appointed by the Lord Jesus Christ in the beginning of the Church. They had no successors. **And prophets.** Not the OT prophets but the Christian prophets, the NT prophets, some of whom are mentioned and described in the book of Acts and in the epistles. **Jesus Christ himself being the chief corner stone.** Passages such as this and I Pet 2:5 help us to understand the meaning of Mt 16:18. Peter, being an apostle, was one of the foundation stones along with the other apostles and prophets, but the whole structure is built upon Christ. Compare what Paul says in I Cor 3:11.

21. All the building. In this context this translation seems preferable to *each several building* (ASV). "But *every building* here is quite out of place, inasmuch as the apostle is clearly speaking of one vast building, the mystical body of Christ" (Alf). This interpretation is confirmed by the language of the following verse. Israel in the OT had a temple of wood and stone. In contrast to this, the Church is a temple (cf. I Cor 3:16; I Pet 1:2-9). A temple is a dwelling place of God, as verse 22 mentions.

F. The Revelation of the Mystery. 3:1-13. The Apostle Paul was chosen by God to make known and explain at least two great revelations. The first of these was the Gospel itself—good news of salvation through the death and resurrection of the Lord Jesus Christ. The second was the truth of the Church as the body of Christ. In the great Gospel epistles — Romans, I and II Corinthians, and Galatians—Paul develops at length this first revelation. In the epistles of the present chronological group, the "Prison Epistles," he deals to a very large extent with the second of these revelations—the Church as the body of Christ. Chapter 3 forms the climax of the first main division of the epistle, which gives us our position in Christ.

1) The Dispensation of the Grace of God. 3:1-6. Here is the mystery of the Church as the body of Christ.

1. For this cause. Referring to the whole preceding statement. **I Paul.** The writer's repetition of his name shows that he attached seriousness and importance to what he was about to write. **The prisoner of Jesus Christ.** Of course Paul was a prisoner of Christ in the sense that he had been captured by Christ, but that is not the primary thought here. He was a prisoner in Rome at the time he wrote, and it was for Christ's sake that he was a prisoner. **For you Gentiles.** Paul was specifically the apostle to the Gentiles by appointment of the Lord Jesus (cf. Rom 15:16).

2. The dispensation of the grace of God. The word **dispensation** means stewardship. The message of grace was a sacred trust given to Paul in order that he might make it known among the Gentiles. **Given me to you-ward.** It was not given to Paul for him to keep, but that he might give it out, particularly to the Gentiles. **3. How that by revelation he made known.** Paul always insisted upon his direct reception of the Gospel from the Lord Jesus himself, without any human intermediaries (cf. Gal 1:11,12). **The mystery.** See comment on 1:9. **As I wrote afore in few words.** Probably not a former letter but something already written in the present epistle (cf. 1:9 ff.).

4. This verse and the one following shed much light on the NT usage of the word **mystery.** The word means, not something mystical or magical, but a sacred secret which has not been previously revealed; when it is revealed, it is understood only by the initiated—here, those who are saved. **5. Unto his holy apostles and prophets by the Spirit.** Just as holy men of God were inspired by the Holy Spirit in OT times (II Pet 1:20,21), so were the writers of the NT. **6. The Gentiles.** The mystery was not that the Gentiles should be saved—there is much in the OT concerning the salvation of the Gentiles, particularly in Isaiah—but that they should be joined with Jews in one body.

2) The Fellowship of the Mystery. 3:7-13.

7. A minister. Paul was made a servant by God's gift. This is the word transliterated in English as *deacon*—one who serves or waits on tables. Paul never considered his office something high, removing him from other men. He always spoke of himself humbly.

8. Who am less than the least of all saints. In several other places Paul, remembering what he had been before he was saved and what he had done to the church, speaks of himself in this self-abnegating way (cf. I Cor 15:9,10; I Tim 1:15). The expression rendered **less than the least** is an unusual form—a comparative of the superlative. The AV expresses it very well. **Is this grace given.** God's grace was given to Paul not in the main for his enjoyment, but that he might pass it on to others. **That I should preach among the Gentiles.** The Lord Jesus gave this word to Ananias concerning Paul (Acts 9:15). **The unsearchable riches.** Here again the word **riches** comes into prominence with an adjective denoting its limitless character. **9. And to make all men see.** To throw light on **what is the fellowship of the mystery.** Some manuscripts have *stewardship* rather than *fellowship.* **Has been hid from ages in God.** Further confirmation of the definition of "mystery" previously given. **Who created all things.** All that exists—not merely the physical creation or the spiritual creation alone.

10. In heavenly places. The fourth occurrence of the phrase in the epistle. Further indication that heavenly beings are observing the Church and seeing in the Church the unfolding of God's wisdom. Both good and evil angels are evidently amazed at the working of God as seen in redeemed men and women. **11. The eternal purpose.** Cf. Rom 8:29; Eph 1:11. **12. In whom.** That is, in Christ. **Access with confidence.** Apart from Christ we could not draw near. This has been shown in chapter 2. **The faith of him.** Objective genitive; meaning, *faith in Him*. Christ is the object of our faith.

13. My tribulations for you. Compare what Paul says in Acts 20:18-35 about his work in Ephesus; also in II Cor 1:8-11.

G. Paul's Second Prayer. 3:14-21. This is the second prayer of Paul for the Ephesians, and like the former one in Eph 1, it is concerned mainly with their spiritual welfare. Whereas the first prayer centers in knowledge, this prayer has its focal point in love.

14. For this cause. This takes up the thought begun in 3:1. Evidently the main thought in this chapter is the prayer, and 3:2-13 is explanatory. **I bow my knees.** While Scripture does not indicate that any one bodily posture is necessary in prayer, yet the bowing of the knee is indicative of true reverence. **The Father of our Lord Jesus Christ.** Some manuscripts omit the words **of our Lord Jesus Christ.** There is a play on words in the word **Father** in 3:14 and the word translated **family** (which is *fatherhood)* in 3:15.

15. Of whom the whole family. There are two possible explanations of this. Some would translate *every family,* with the idea that the concept of family or fatherhood comes from God. This is true, of course, although less common. Grammatically the other explanation seems to fit in better with the context of Scripture generally; that is, **the whole family.** The expression **in heaven and earth** seems to favor this. That is, the whole family of the redeemed—those who have gone before and those who are still alive here on earth—are under the one Father, who is the Father of our Lord Jesus Christ.

16. According to the riches. Again the abundant reference to what we have from God (cf. 1:7; 2:4; Phil 4:19). **Strengthened with might.** Parallel to the earlier prayer, which said much about God's power. **By his spirit.** The Spirit is the agent of the Godhead in applying our redemption to us. **In the inner man.** That is, our immaterial part, true personality.

17. That Christ may dwell. Not merely to live, but to be at home—to abide. This is what every Christian needs always, not praying that Christ may come in for the first time, for he already indwells every believer, but that he may be at home there in the sense that the believer has given over his whole life to him. **Being rooted and grounded in love.** A mixed metaphor referring to that which is planted and that which is built (cf. Col 2:2, which is somewhat parallel to this).

18. May be able to comprehend with all saints. A knowledge that every believer ought to have. **What is the breadth, and length, and depth, and height.** This sort of knowledge would be continually growing, for we could never measure the dimensions. **19. To know the love of Christ which passeth knowledge.** Some things we cannot know fully; often we have experiences that we cannot understand or explain. However, the same root is used here in the infinitive and in the noun, and the idea seems to be to know that which is essentially unknowable—yet to know it enough so that we can rejoice in it. **Filled with all the fulness of God.** God is infinite and we are finite. This is of course paradoxical, but it is an attempt to convey in language that will mean something to us, the superabundance of grace available to us from our heavenly Father through our Lord Jesus Christ.

20. This fullness is further described in the benediction that brings the first great division of the epistle to a close. **Now unto him.** Of course the verb and predicate are in the next verse. **Able.** There is no limit to what God can do. **Exceeding abundantly above.** Superlatives are piled one upon the other here to impress us with this truth. **All that we ask or think.** How limited we often are in our asking, thinking that God will not do some particular thing for us. He is able to do far more than we can ask; indeed, more than we could ever imagine. And he does it **according to the power that worketh in us.** That is, we have been strengthened by his Spirit. Consequently, this power is being energized in us. **21. Unto him be glory** may be taken as a statement—*unto him is the glory;* or as an imperative sentence—*unto him be the glory.* **In the church.** God's glory is being manifested throughout all eternity in the body which he has redeemed. **Throughout all ages, world without end.** Literally, *to all the courses of the age of the ages.* A very strong expression for eternity. With this prayer and benediction Paul concludes that portion of the epistle that tells us about what God has done for us and about our position in Christ.

II. The Believer's Conduct in the World. 4:1–6:24.

A. The Worthy Walk. 4:1-16. God always joins doctrine and practice, teaching and the practical results of the teaching. In Eph 1–3 he has told us of the riches of his grace and the riches of his glory through Jesus Christ. Now he exhorts us toward a worthy manner of life in this world.

1) The Unity of the Spirit. 4:1-6. God has brought about a wonderful unity which it is the responsibility of believers to maintain in experience.

1. I therefore. As is generally the case in Paul's epistles, this exhortation is made on the basis of the teaching that has preceded (cf. Rom 12:1). **The prisoner of the Lord.** That is, the prisoner for the Lord's sake (cf. Eph 3:1). **Beseech.** This word, which stands first in the original, for emphasis, is an entreaty, an encouragement. God, of course, has the right to command and to demand, but instead he entreats, he beseeches, because he wants willing surrender, willing service. **That ye walk worthy.** The word **walk** is used often in the Scripture for our conduct, our behavior, our manner of life (cf. Introduction). **Worthy.** Not that we ever could deserve what God has done, but that we should walk in a manner befitting what he has done for us. We do not become Christians by living the Christian life; rather, we are exhorted to live the Christian life because we are Christians, that our lives may measure up to our position in Christ (cf. Phil 1:27). **Vocation.** Our calling, which is described as a heavenly calling and a holy calling (cf. Heb 3:1; II Tim 1:9).

2. Lowliness and meekness. These virtues can be produced only by the indwelling Spirit of God. They are totally foreign to the flesh and unfortunately rare in the lives of many Christians. **Lowliness** carries the idea of humility; **meekness** connotes gentleness (see Trench). **Longsuffering** is preserving an even temperament in the face of adversity and persecution. **3. Endeavoring to keep.** God realized that this is not always possible because one person alone cannot keep the unity. Observe that Paul does not request the Christians to make the unity, for only God could make the bond; but it is the responsibility of believers to try to keep it. This is **the unity of the Spirit**. That is, the unity which has been forged by the Holy Spirit himself, and its bond or connection is a peaceable one.

4. One body. The organism composed of the Lord Jesus Christ as the Head and all true believers in him. It is the new creation, the body mentioned earlier in the epistle (1:23). **One Spirit.** The Holy Spirit himself is the life infusing every part of the body. **5. One Lord, one faith, one baptism.** Note the emphasis all the way through on the unity. The one baptism is undoubtedly the baptism of the Holy Spirit—that ministry of the Spirit by which we have been put into the body of Christ (I Cor 12:13).

6. The three Persons of the Godhead are mentioned in these verses in the reverse order to that usually given: **one Spirit** (v. 4); **one Lord** (v. 5), that is, the Lord Jesus; **one God and Father** (v. 6). **Who is above all,** etc. Here we have a threefold relationship of the one God and Father to all who are his. He is **above all.** This expresses his sovereignty, his transcendence. He is **through all,** "expressing the pervading, animating, controlling presence of that one God and Father" (Salmond). **In you all.** This is his constant indwelling in his people—all the Persons of the triune God are said in various passages of Scripture to indwell the believer.

2) The Gift of Christ. 4:7-12. The ascended Lord has given gifts to his Church for its upbuilding.

7. To every one of us. This is limited to believers in him. **Is given grace.** Not saving grace, but grace as a gift to believers—God's favor, unmerited and unrecompensed. **According to the measure.** A measure which is immeasurable.

8. Wherefore he saith. The quotation is from Ps 68:18. The connection is not altogether clear. But in his ascension the Lord Jesus is said to have **led captivity captive;** that is, he captured that which had captured us, and annulled its power. **And gave gifts.** In some passages of Scripture, gifts are mentioned which the Lord gave to individuals; e.g., I Cor 12. Here the gifts are those people of various capacities whom he has given to the church. **9.** The apostle, commenting on the quotation, mentions that the Lord Jesus had to descend first before he could ascend. Some take this to be a reference to the death of Christ and his so-called descent into Hades. It seems more likely, however, that it is simply referring to his coming down from heaven. He descended into **the lower parts** which consist **of the earth**—genitive of apposition (cf. Jn 3:13). **10. Far above all heavens.** Cf. Heb 4:14.

11. And he gave some. The various types mentioned are Christ's gifts to the church. **Apostles.** This was a special office at the beginning of the church. The apostles had no successors. They had a unique work from the Lord Jesus (cf. 2:20). **Prophets.** A prophet was a spokesman for God. As used ordinarily in the Scripture, this term refers to someone who has been given a direct revelation, which he is to pass on to men (cf. 2:20). In the strictest sense of the term this office also was temporary in the church, for there were no more prophets in the technical sense after the completion of the NT. **Evangelists.** Those who proclaim glad tidings—those who preach the Gospel. **Pastors and teachers.** These two terms go together. The first word means *shepherds.* Those who are the shepherds of the flock are also to be teachers. The true pastor should carry on an expository preaching ministry of the Word.

12. For the perfecting of the saints, for the work of the ministry. The two uses of for represent two different prepositions in the original. These gifts were given by God to the Church *for the perfecting of the saints unto the work of the ministry.* That is, it is the business of all the saints—not of a few leaders only—to carry on the work of the ministry. The leaders are for the purpose of perfecting or equipping believers to carry on this work. Most local churches today do not follow this NT idea. It is common practice to let the pastor do the ministering. Sometimes the pastor temporarily may find it easier to do the work himself than to train others to do it. But his job is to train up workers, and in the long run his ministry will be more effective if he does so.

3) The Unity of Faith and Knowledge. 4:13-16. The unity of believers in Christ tends toward a unity in faith and knowledge.

13. The unity of the faith. The faith itself is one body of truth. As we hold to this, we in turn are united to one another. **Unto a perfect man.** A reference not to the individual believer but to the composite man; that is, the body of which Christ is the Head.

14. That we henceforth be no more children. Literally, *babies.* **Tossed to and fro.** Driven by the wind, which is here used, of course, figuratively — *wind of teaching.* **By the sleight of men.** The word translated **sleight** originally meant dice-playing. Then it came to mean trickery of any kind, because of the various tricks that were used to cheat in the game of dice. The only way to be able to detect error is to know the truth; hence, we must come to the knowledge of the Son of God, to Christian maturity. A person does not have to study every counterfeit bill in order to know that some particular bill is counterfeit. He needs only to know the genuine article.

15. But speaking the truth in love. It is possible to speak the truth without speaking it in love. Literally, *holding the truth.* We **may grow up into him.** God wants us to be mature or full-grown, to be adults. We have an absolutely perfect Head, Christ himself.

16. Note the perfection of the body. How intricately the human body is fitted together! It is therefore an apt illustration of the body of Christ. Someone has said that not everyone can be one of the larger members, but the joints are very important too. All parts work together (cf. I Cor 12; Rom 12).

B. The Different Walk. 4:17-32. The Scriptures, in both the Old and New Testaments, emphasize that God's people are to be different from the people of the world.

1) Description of the Gentiles' Walk. 4:17-19. The Gentiles are "as sheep going astray" (I Pet 2:25; cf. Isa 53:6). Believers have a great and good Shepherd to follow.

17. This I say therefore. The Christian's walk is described in various ways in the passage. Here we have a negative description. **Testify.** Protest, exhort, or beseech. **Henceforth.** Their lives are to be different now. **Walk not as other Gentiles walk.** This walk has been described in 2:2. Most of the Ephesians were Gentiles in background. Some manuscripts do not have any word for **other.** Hence, *Walk not as the Gentiles walk.* In the sight of God, believers in the Lord Jesus Christ are no longer either Jews or Gentiles (cf. I Cor 10:32). **In the vanity of their mind.** The word for **vanity** seems to mean perverseness or depravity in this connection. **18. Understanding darkened.** Cf. II Cor 4:4. **Alienated from the life of God.** Cf. 2:12. **Blindness of their heart.** Literally, *hardness* or *dull perception* (cf. Mk 3:5).

19. Past feeling. Cf. I Tim 4:2. **Uncleanness.** Impurity in general. Not merely indulging in impurity but indulging in it with a greedy desire to have more. A graphic statement of the insatiable nature of sinful desire.

2) Putting Off the Old and Putting On the New. 4:20-24. The Christian life is compared to putting off one garment and putting on another. This is not a reference to our position in Christ, but to our experience. It is possible to be a new man in Christ Jesus and yet be living like an "old man"; that is, having on the garment of the "old man."

20. But ye. A contrast with the preceding. **Have not so learned Christ.** This is the grandest subject that one could study. **21. If so be that ye have heard him, and have been taught by him, as the truth is in Jesus.** That which they had learned after hearing of the Lord Jesus Christ should have caused them to improve their lives, for Christians ought to act like Christians, not like pagan non-Christians.

22. According to the former conversation. For **conversation** see note on 2:3. **The old man.** That is, the Adamic nature, that which we are in ourselves. **Corrupt according to the deceitful lusts.** Scripture teaches that in the old nature is no good thing (cf. Rom 7:18). **23. And be renewed.** Cf. Rom 12:2. **24. Put on the new man.** Correlative of the preceding, the product of the new birth. For the conflict between the old and the new, compare Rom 7 and Gal 5:16,17. **After God.** According to God. God is the Creator of the new man.

3) Practical Application. 4:25-32. God in his Word never teaches the truth abstractly, but always makes concrete application.

25. Wherefore. On the basis of what precedes; that is, our standing in Christ. **Putting away lying.** Note the negative and the positive. It is not enough simply to abstain from lying; one must also tell the truth (cf. Zech 8:16). **We are members.** Members not only of Christ but of each other (Rom 12:5). **26. Be ye angry, and sin not.** There is such a thing as righteous anger, although the term is much abused. The apostle is saying that if you are angry, be sure it is the kind of anger that is not sinful. **Let not the sun go down.** "Even a righteous wrath by overindulgence may pass all too easily into sin" (Salmond). **27. Neither give place to the devil.** Cf. II Cor 2:10, 11; Eph 6:10 ff.

28. Rather let him labour. A Christian is not only to refrain from stealing but is to provide for himself and his family through his own work. The Scripture everywhere commends honest toil (cf. I Thess 4:11,12). In fact, the apostle lays down the principle that he who will not work should not eat (II Thess 3:10). **To give to him that needeth.** Here is the basis for genuine Christian charity.

29. No corrupt communication. The word for **corrupt** originally meant *rotten* or *putrid.* Again we see the positive emphasized—**but that which is good.**

30. And grieve not the holy Spirit of God. That which grieves the Holy Spirit is sin. The remedy is confession (cf. I Jn 1:9). Although the Holy Spirit may be grieved, yet he will never leave the believer. He is our seal. We have been sealed by him **unto the day of redemption** (cf. Eph 1:13). He is the guarantee that our redemption will be completed. **31.** Some of the sins that grieve the Holy Spirit are now particularized. While some Christians would classify as sins only those grosser iniquities which even the world recognizes as wrong, God mentions matters of the mind and spirit as well as those of the body.

32. The theme of putting on as well as putting off is prominent throughout the section. Living the Christian life is not just observing a list of prohibitions; it is cultivating positive virtues. **And be ye kind.** The verb here means *keep on proving yourselves to be kind* to one another. **Tenderhearted.** The English translation is very good. The word in the original has been much misunderstood, as is shown by its frequent translation elsewhere as *bowels.* "Heart" is correct. In the classical Greek this word referred to the organs of the upper body cavity; specifically the heart, lungs, and liver, as distinguished from the organs of the lower cavity (see the lexicons). **Forgiving one another.** The only way we can be enabled to forgive is through the forgiveness which we ourselves already have received for Christ's sake. As God's love produces our love, so our realization of God's forgiveness produces our forgiveness of others (cf. I Jn 4:19).

C. The Loving Walk. 5:1-14. Christian living involves not only walking worthy of our calling and walking in a manner different from that of the Gentiles, but also walking in love.

1) Walking in Love. 5:1-7. Because believers are God's "dear children" and have experienced his love, they have a standard to uphold, a path to follow.

1. Be ye therefore. Literally, *become therefore,* or *prove yourselves to be therefore.* **Followers.** Literally, *imitators.* **As dear children.** Just as little children learn to do things by imitating their parents, so we are to be imitators of God. **2. And walk in love.** This is descriptive of our whole manner of life. **As Christ also hath loved us and gave himself for us.** That is, he delivered himself on our behalf (cf. Gal 2:20). **An offering and a sacrifice to God.** Cf. Ps. 40:7, which is quoted in Heb 10:7. **For a sweetsmelling savour.** Reminiscent of the sweet savor offerings of the book of Leviticus, which prefigured Christ's voluntary sacrifice of himself to God.

3. But fornication. General term for sexual immorality. **Let it not be once named among you.** The connection with what precedes is clear. Love will not gossip about the sins of others (cf. I Cor 13:4-8). There is danger of one's experiencing a morbid satisfaction in discussing other people's sins. **As becometh saints.** We are to know what is fitting and proper in our high position. **4. Nor foolish talking, nor jesting.** These words do not preclude spontaneous Christian gaiety and a sense of humor, but they indicate that Christians are not to indulge in empty frivolity. In the Greek they connote the sort of jesting that is vulgar and unclean. The antidote for the Christian is thanksgiving.

5. For this ye know. Cf. I Cor 6:9,10. **Nor covetous man.** It is interesting to see that this type of sinner is included in the same classification with immoral and unclean persons. God's way of distinguishing between sins is not like ours. In his sight all sins are hateful. We must learn to look on sins as he does. **6. With vain words.** That is, empty words, meaningless words. **The children of disobedience.** Literally, *the sons of disobedience* (cf. 2:2, where the same expression is used).

7. Be not ye therefore partakers. The use of the present imperative with this form of the negative *(mē)* indicates the prohibition of something already in progress; literally, *stop becoming fellow partakers with them.*

2) Walking in Light. 5:8-14. Love and holiness (often symbolized by light in Scripture) must not be separated, the apostle explains. The loving walk is also the holy walk.

8. Ye were sometimes darkness. A beautiful expression of the contrast between our past and our present (cf. the same sort of contrast in I Cor 6:9-11; I Thess 5:5). **Walk as children of light.** God always places the fact of our position before us as the basis for our behavior. **9. The fruit of the Spirit.** Some manuscripts read *the fruit of light* (cf. Gal 5:22,23). **10. Proving what is acceptable.** That is, putting it to the test. Acceptability to the Lord is the criterion (cf. II Cor 5:9, where the same expression is used).

11. Do not have fellowship. Again, literally, *stop having fellowship.* **But rather rebuke.** If a Christian is in fellowship with his Lord, his very life will be a reproof to the world. **12. For it is a shame** (cf v. 3 above). Dr. A. C. Gaebelein called public discussion of secret sins the "communion of sinners," as contrasted with the Scriptural communion of saints. **13. Are made manifest by the light.** Cf. Jn 3:19-21; I Jn 1:5-7. **14. Wherefore he saith.** The quotation that follows is difficult to identify. It is possibly a combination of several different references (cf. Isa 26:19; 60:1).

D. The Wise Walk. 5:15–6:9. The apostle next describes how the life of a believer is to be circumspect. He enjoins the Ephesians to be filled with the Holy Spirit and shows them the result of that filling in the practical relations of life.

1) Being Circumspect. 5:15-17. A careful walk depends upon wisdom, which can come only from knowing the Lord's will.

15. See then. That is, look to it in view of what has just been said. **That ye walk circumspectly.** Diligently, carefully. **16. Redeeming the time.** Buying up the opportunity. **Because the days are evil.** Cf. Gal 1:4. **17. Be ye not unwise** (AV). Again the command to stop that which is already in progress—*stop becoming foolish.* **But.** Strong adversative in Greek *(alla).*

2) Being Filled with the Holy Spirit. 5:18–6:9. No believer in Christ is ever commanded to be indwelt by the Spirit. His indwelling is certain and permanent (Jn 14:16,17). Nor is a believer commanded to be baptized with the Spirit. This has already been done (I Cor 12:13). But believers are commanded to be filled with the Spirit. Hence there is individual responsibility; there are conditions to be met if we are to experience the Spirit's control in our lives.

18. And be not drunk with wine. There are repeated warnings in the Scripture against drunkenness (cf. Prov 23:31). **But be filled with the Spirit.** As in most contrasts, there is some point of comparison. A person intoxicated with wine acts in an unnatural manner that is evil; a person filled with the Holy Spirit acts in an unnatural manner that is good. Compare what was said to the apostles on the day of Pentecost (Acts 2:13). **Be filled with the Spirit.** Keep on being filled; be continuously filled with the Spirit. A believer can never obtain more of the Holy Spirit, for he indwells the Christian's life in all his fullness. But the Holy Spirit can get more of the believer; that is, he can exercise complete control of the life that is yielded to him.

a) Rejoicing and Thanksgiving. 5:19, 20. One of the evidences of the filling of the Holy Spirit is that exuberance of life that shows itself in rejoicing and in continual thankfulness to God.

19. Speaking to yourselves. The result of the Spirit's filling is praise and thanksgiving as well as submission in the ordinary relationships of life (vv. 19-21). **Psalms.** This word usually indicates songs set to instrumental accompaniment, as does also the participle translated **making melody** (*psallontes*). **In your heart to the Lord.** Some people are not able to make much melody outwardly. But even they, if they are filled with the Spirit, will be making music in their hearts. **20. Giving thanks always.** No limit on the time (cf. I Thess 5:18). **For all things.** No limit on the extent. Some would restrict this to the blessings mentioned in the epistle, but it seems better to take it in its widest sense (cf. Rom 8:28).

b) Submission in Practical Relationships. 5:21–6:9. Another result of the Spirit's filling, besides praise and thanksgiving, is submission. This is a statement of what we should do in our earthly relationships. "In contrast with pagan self-seeking and self-assertion" (Salmond; cf. I Pet 5:5).

(1) Wives and Husbands. 5:21-33. The first human relationship mentioned, also the most intimate one, in which the filling of the Holy Spirit is to be manifested, is the marriage relationship.

21. One another. Note the mutuality of this submission. **In the fear of Christ.** The NT as well as the OT speaks of fear of God—that is, a reverence toward him that makes one afraid of displeasing him (cf. II Cor 5:11).

22. The apostle now shows the outworking of this mutual submission in the three most common relationships of life—marriage, family, and employment. **Wives, submit yourselves unto your own husbands.** This passage is an expression of God's ideal for marriage. The marriage relationship was designed by him to be symbolic of the spiritual relationship between Christ and the Church. The apostle points this out in verse 32.

23. For the husband is the head. The reason for the subjection of the wife is found in this relationship which God has ordained. **24. But as the church is subject to Christ.** Even though there is a difference between the position of the husband toward the wife and that of Christ toward the Church, yet this does not affect the relation of headship which the husband holds to the wife.

25. Husbands, love your wives. The obligations are not merely one-sided. The husband's responsibility is just as binding as that of the wife. This is not a reference to normal marital love, which would not need to be commanded, but to that volitional love which stems from God and resembles his own love. In contrast to normal sexual desire, which by its nature is self-seeking, this love is unselfish. **As also Christ loved the church.** While human husbands can never attain the degree of love Christ manifested, yet they are exhorted to have the same kind of love, which is demonstrated in the clause that follows, **and gave himself for it.**

26. That he might sanctify and cleanse it. This was his purpose in giving himself to die for the Church. **With the washing of water by the word.** Probably water and word are used synonymously. This clearly cannot be a reference to baptism or baptismal regeneration. Just as water washes the body, so the Word of God washes the heart (cf. Ezk 36:27). **27. That he might present it.** The ultimate object for which Christ gave himself. The word **sanctify** shows the immediate object (cf. II Cor 11:2). **A glorious church.** The adjective is predicative rather than attributive; that is, *that he might present the church as glorious.* **Not having spot.** Further explanation of the word **glorious** as descriptive of the "bride" of Christ.

28. So ought husbands to love their wives as their own bodies. That is, as if they were their own bodies. **Love** which is natural, not merely from a sense of duty. God said, "They [two] shall be one flesh" (Gen 2:24). **29. For no man.** The reason for the preceding statement.

30. For we are members of his body. The thought shifts back and forth between the marriage relationship and the relationship between Christ and the Church. **31. For this cause.** A free quotation from Gen 2:24. It sets forth the Scripture basis of marriage as a natural result of woman's creation. The marriage bond is stronger than that between parent and child, establishing such close intimacy as to be called in the Scripture, *oneness*—unity rather than union. **32. This is a great mystery.** That is, although the explanation of this meaning of the marriage relationship had been intimated in the OT (cf. the Song of Solomon), it was not clearly revealed until the NT was given. Paul directs our thoughts from the marriage unity itself to that which it symbolizes.

33. Summary of the mutual submissiveness God expects in this relationship as a normal result of the filling of the Holy Spirit.

(2) Children and Parents. 6:1-4. The apostle now goes on to another specific relationship, that of parents and children, with the obligations entailed upon both sides.

1. Children, obey your parents in the Lord. *Obedience* is a stronger term than *submission*, which was given as the duty of the wife. **In the Lord.** "The sphere in which it is to move, a Christian obedience fulfilled in communion with Christ" (Salmond). **For this is right.** This is shown to be an eternal principle of God.

2. Honor thy father and mother. Paul shows that the Law had the same injunction. All the Ten Commandments except the fourth are restated and applied under grace. **The first commandment with promise.** That is, a promise is given for obedience. **3. That it may be well with thee.** This must be taken as a continuation of the quotation from the Law and not as a direct application to the believer in the present dispensation. Although the principle is always true, the soon coming of the Lord, rather than long life, is the Christian's blessed hope.

4. And, ye fathers. As before, there is a second side to the responsibility. It is stated at first negatively, and then affirmatively. **But bring them up.** Cf. Deut 6:7. A parallel passage is Col 3:20,21.

(3) Servants and Masters. 6:5-9. A third set of relationships is now discussed —that of masters and servants. Slavery existed as an institution in NT days. It was not the function of the Gospel to overthrow slavery, although a by-product of Christianity has been the gradual abolition of that institution.

5. Servants. Literally, *slaves*. However, the principles apply to any kind of employees and employers. **In singleness of your heart.** In reality and sincerity—not in hypocrisy. **As unto Christ.** Cf. I Pet 2:18; Col 3:22-25. **6. Not with eye-service, as men-pleasers.** An amplification of the foregoing. The word **men-pleasers** occurs in the Septuagint, but is found in the NT only here and in Col 3:22. **Doing the will of God from the heart.** Literally, *from the soul*—that is, with one's whole being. **7. With good will doing service.** A Christian who is a bond servant is to recognize that his primary responsibility is to the Lord Jesus Christ. When he does the work he is expected to do and does it well, he is pleasing the Lord. **8. Knowing that.** This is a causal connective—*because we know* there is a reward for faithfulness in serving Christ. **Whether he be bond or free.** A person's standing in this world has nothing to do with his faithfulness and with the reward for faithfulness.

9. And, ye masters. Here the duties of employers are emphasized. **Do the same things to them.** The positive side, showing the mutuality of the obligation. **Forbearing threatening.** What the masters are not to do. **Knowing.** That is, *because you know*. **That your master.** These masters have a Master of their own. This is the Lord *(Kurios)*. There is no respect of persons with him (cf. Col 4:1). All of these practical relationships flow from the filling of the Holy Spirit, enjoined in Eph 5:18.

E. The Christian Walk as a Warfare. 6:10-20. Throughout this whole division of the epistle a great deal has been said about practical Christian living. In this paragraph the walk of a Christian is described as a warfare, a deadly conflict in which he is engaged against the power of Satan and his hosts.

1) Being Strong in the Lord—the Whole Armor of God. 6:10-17. Because this walk is a warfare, as it is here described, a Christian must be prepared and equipped. This passage on the whole armor of God shows what wonderful provision God has made for his warriors.

10. Finally. Here are the general concluding exhortations of the epistle. **My brethren.** Paul reminds his readers of their relationship in the Lord. **Be strong in the Lord.** The Lord Jesus had said, "Without me, ye can do nothing" (Jn 15:5; cf. also Phil 4:13). **And in the**

power of his might. Three words are used in the verse for **power** or *strength.* First, the imperative verb, *be empowered* or *be enabled,* is used, then the word for *force,* and finally the word for *strength–in the force of his strength.*

11. Put on the whole armour of God. While God has provided this, the individual Christian has the responsibility of putting it on; that is, he must consciously appropriate the power the Lord Jesus Christ makes available to him. **The whole armour of God.** The armor is described in detail, as well as the foes a believer must face. **That ye may be able to stand.** Without this armor of God, the Christian is not able to stand. One who is seated with Christ in the heavenlies and walking in this world must now also take a stand **against the wiles**–the methods or stratagems–**of the devil.**

12. For we wrestle not. The reason that we need the whole armor of God. **With flesh and blood.** The Israelites under Joshua had to fight against flesh and blood in order to conquer the land of Canaan. Ours is a spiritual warfare rather than a physical one. **But against principalities.** Not a comparative, but an absolute negation. Different ranks are seen among the hosts of Satan. It is not possible to make clear distinctions between the various types of foes mentioned here. **Against the rulers of the darkness of this world.** Literally, *the world rulers of this darkness.* **Against spiritual wickedness.** This rendering is unsatisfactory. It is *against spiritual forces of wickedness in the heavenly places.* **High places,** in the AV is the same Greek word translated "heavenly places" elsewhere in the epistle. This is the last of the five occurrences of *en tois epouraniois,* "in the heavenlies."

13. Wherefore. Because our enemies are such as have just been described. **Take unto you the whole armour.** Again the human responsibility is emphasized. **Able to withstand.** Note that the passage speaks both of withstanding and of standing. The former is the ability to win the fight, to hold one's position; the latter shows the result of the conflict.

14. Stand therefore. In this and the following verses the armor is described in detail. All of these things speak in a certain sense of the Lord Jesus Christ himself, who is our defense. **Your loins girt about with truth.** One who has his loins girded is prepared for activity (cf. I Pet 1:13). **The breastplate of righteousness.** Cf. Isa 59:17. **15. And your feet shod.** Much of the language in this section is taken from various passages in the OT (cf. Isa 52:7). **The preparation.** That is, that which prepares us. This would correspond to the shoes or boots. **The gospel of peace.** The good news characterized by peace or resulting in peace.

16. Taking the shield of faith. The genitive of apposition; that is, *the shield which consists of faith* or *is faith.* **Fiery darts of the wicked.** The word **wicked** is singular and undoubtedly masculine rather than neuter–hence, the *wicked one*–that is, Satan himself. The full dress of a Roman soldier is indicated in this passage, and the various parts are applied spiritually. **17. And take the helmet of salvation.** Again, the helmet *which is salvation.* **The sword of the Spirit.** Not the same type of genitive as before; perhaps an ablative of source or origin. That is, *the sword supplied by the Spirit.* **Which is the word of God.** God's word is a piercing sword. Here *hrēma,* "word" as utterance, is used. In a similar passage in Heb 4:12 *logos,* "word" as concept or idea, is used. The Scriptures are both *hrēma* and *logos.* All of the parts of the armor mentioned up to this point are defensive. The sword of the Spirit is the only offensive as well as defensive weapon.

2) Prayer for All Saints and for Paul. 6:18-20.

18. Praying always. The panoply of God must always be worn in connection with believing prayer (cf. I Thess 5:17; Col 4:2). **Prayer and supplication.** The former word is used for prayer in general, the latter for petition. **In the Spirit.** The same Holy Spirit who wields the sword of the Word must also be active in our praying. **For all saints.** Paul would not restrict their praying specifically to himself, although he does mention himself in the next verse. **19. And for me.** That is, for me in particular; this in view of Paul's circumstances at the time. **That utterance may be given unto me.** Even in his imprisonment Paul was not thinking primarily of his own welfare but of his testimony for the Lord Jesus Christ. We read in Acts 28:30,31 of Paul's speaking to all who came to him while he was a prisoner in his own hired house in Rome. **To make known with boldness the mystery of the gospel.** Not that the Gospel is any longer a secret to those who will receive it.

F. Closing Greetings. 6:21-24.

21. But that ye also may know my

affairs. One of the few personal references in this epistle. **Tychicus.** Evidently the bearer of the letter (cf. Col 4:7). **22. Whom I have sent.** Epistolary aorist tense. Paul is sending him, but at the time they read the letter he will have been sent. As in writing to the Philippians, Paul wants them to know how it is with him, and he wants to know about them.

23. Peace be to the brethren, and love with faith. Only God can give these qualities. **24. Grace.** Literally, *the grace;* that is, the grace beside which there is no other. **With all them that love our Lord Jesus Christ.** That is, believers.

BIBLIOGRAPHY

ALFORD, HENRY. "The Epistle to the Ephesians," *The Greek Testament*. Vol. III. Chicago: Moody Press, 1958.

CHAFER, LEWIS SPERRY. *The Ephesian Letter Doctrinally Considered*. Chicago: The Bible Institute Colportage Assn., 1935.

ERDMAN, CHARLES R. *The Epistle of Paul to the Ephesians*. Philadelphia: Westminster Press, 1931.

FINDLAY, G. G. The Epistle to the Ephesians. *(Expositor's Bible.)* New York: A. C. Armstrong & Son, 1903.

HARRISON, NORMAN B. *His Very Own*. Chicago: The Bible Institute Colportage Assn., 1930.

MOULE, HANDLEY C. G. *Ephesian Studies*. London: Hodder & Stoughton, 1900.

PAXSON, RUTH. *The Wealth, Walk, and Warfare of the Christian*. New York: Fleming H. Revell Co., 1939.

SALMOND, S. D. F. "The Epistle to the Ephesians," *The Expositor's Greek Testament*. Vol. III. Grand Rapids: William B. Eerdmans Pub. Co., n.d.

SIMPSON, E. K. *Commentary on the Epistles to the Ephesians and Colossians (New International Commentary)*. Grand Rapids: William B. Eerdmans Pub. Co., 1957.

WESTCOTT, B. F. *St. Paul's Epistle to the Ephesians*. Grand Rapids: William B. Eerdmans Pub. Co., 1950.

THE EPISTLE TO THE PHILIPPIANS

INTRODUCTION

Founding of the Church. In response to the Macedonian call, Paul and his companions had crossed the Aegean Sea from Troas to Neapolis and followed the renowned Egnatian Way some eight to ten miles up and over the coastal range to the city of Philippi. Philippi (named after Philip of Macedon, the father of Alexander the Great) was famous for its gold mines and its strategic location as the gateway to Europe. It was a miniature Rome, a proud Roman colony, exempt from taxation and modeled after the capital of the world. With the conversion of Lydia, the slave girl, and the jailer (Acts 16), it became the "birthplace of European Christianity." Soon Paul moved on towards Thessalonica, leaving Luke behind to care for this flock that held such a special place in his affections.

Authorship. Apart from F. C. Baur and several other German critics, the Pauline authorship has never been seriously doubted. External evidence is both early and strong. Some find allusions to it in the letter of Clement of Rome to the Corinthians (c. A.D. 96). Towards the middle of the second century Polycarp wrote to the Philippians, "Paul . . . when he was absent wrote letters to you" (iii. 2).

Place of Writing. That Philippians was written from prison is quite clear. Just where that prison was is another matter. If we assume that Luke mentions all of Paul's imprisonments, then Rome is the most probable answer. (Philippi is out of the question, and Paul's expectation of a speedy release seriously undermines the Caesarean hypothesis.)

However, in recent times an Ephesian origin has been advanced, and the theory has gained considerable ground. The argument is of many strands, the more important being:

(1) The plausibility of an Ephesian imprisonment (I Cor 15:30-32; II Cor 1:8-10).

(2) Inscriptional evidence of the presence of a detachment of the "praetorian guard" as well as members of "Caesar's household" in Ephesus (A. H. McNeile, *St. Paul*, p. 229, notes 1 and 2) — formerly advanced as irrefutable evidence of a Roman origin.

(3) The affinity of Philippians with Paul's earlier letters, namely, Romans and I Corinthians.

(4) The greater ease with which the frequent communications implied in Philippians could have been conducted (Ephesus to Philippi was a journey of seven to ten days, while Rome to Philippi involved a land journey totaling some eight hundred miles, plus an ocean crossing that would be suspended in winter; cf. Acts 27:12).

(5) Paul's avowed purpose to push on to the west which, if the imprisonment had been in Rome, would have been contradicted by his plans to revisit Philippi (1:25; 2:24) upon release. (For a concise presentation of this position, see the introduction to J. H. Michael's *The Epistle of Paul to the Philippians* in *The Moffatt New Testament Commentary*. Cf. also G. S. Duncan, St. Paul's *Ephesian Ministry*. For an important discussion which gives arguments for the Roman origin and which treats the evidence for the Ephesian origin as indecisive, see C. H. Dodd, *New Testament Studies*, pp. 85-128.)

Fortunately the interpretation of the epistle does not depend upon its point of origin. While the Ephesian hypothesis commends itself with greater force, it makes little difference in our understanding of this remarkable letter from prison.

Assuming an Ephesian origin, the date of composition would be about A.D. 54. (A Roman origin would give a date of 61-62.)

Occasion. The popular view that Philippians was primarily a thank-you letter is unlikely. Would Paul have waited until the very last moment (4:10-20) before expressing his appreciation for the gift from the believers at Philippi? The immediate purpose was to send a note of commendation and explanation along with Epaphroditus so as to head off any criticism that he was returning prematurely from his charge. This, in turn, allowed Paul the opportunity to assure the church of his grateful appreciation for their gift and to correct such minor disorders in the church as pessimism over Paul's continued imprisonment, timidity in the face of pagan hostility, the threat of Judaizers, and (especially) the shadow of disunity that was beginning to fall across the church. While these trends were not yet pronounced, if allowed to continue unchecked they would soon have undermined the cause of Christ at Philippi.

Chapter 3 – Interruption or Interpolation? Because of the unexpected and abrupt change of tone and subject matter at 3:2, many have suggested that Philippians is a composite of two or more of Paul's letters. The fatal weakness of the partition theory is the hopeless difference of opinion among the critics as to where the interpolation ends (3:19? 4:9? 4:20? etc.). A far more natural interpretation is that Paul was interrupted in his writing (perhaps by some depressing news of Judaizing activity), and when he returned, he picked up the new subject without transition.

Characteristics. Philippians is the most personal of Paul's writings. It breathes an air of confidence and strong personal attachment. There is a marked absence of formal doctrine. Even the great Christological hymn in chapter 2 is brought in indirectly to buttress an exhortation to humility. The dominant note of the letter is joy. It reveals the apostle Paul as "radiant amid the storm and stress of life."

Outline. Since Philippians is an extremely personal letter, it resists all attempts to force it into a logical outline. The flow of thought is natural and spontaneous. A descriptive analysis might be:

OUTLINE

I. Salutation. 1:1,2.
II. Thanksgiving and prayer. 1:3-11.
III. The unconquerable Gospel. 1:12-14.
IV. Unprincipled preaching. 1:15-18.
V. Life or death? 1:19-26.
VI. Exhortation to steadfastness. 1:27-30.
VII. An appeal to Christian experience. 2:1-4.
VIII. The supreme example of self-renunciation. 2:5-11.
IX. Continued exhortation. 2:12-18.
X. Plans for reunion. 2:19-30.
XI. An interrupted conclusion. 3:1-11.
XII. The homestretch. 3:12-16.
XIII. A Christian commonwealth. 3:17-21.
XIV. Apostolic advice. 4:1-9.
XV. Appreciation for the gift. 4:10-20.
XVI. Greetings and benediction. 4:21-23.

COMMENTARY

I. Salutation. 1:1,2.

Ancient letters usually began, "A to B, Greetings." While following the conventional pattern, Paul could not help transforming this somewhat vague expression of good will into a meaningful Christian blessing.

1. Paul, who alone was the author, graciously added the name of **Timothy** (who was with him at the time of the writing and may have acted as his secretary). Together they were **servants of Christ Jesus.** *Douloi* literally means *slaves,* but there is no thought of cringing submission here. With cheerful abandon they had given themselves to the service of the One to whom they belonged. The term **saints** does not designate a level of ethical achievement, but persons who **in Christ Jesus** have been set apart unto the new life. Just why **with the bishops and deacons** is added is not clear. It may have been an afterthought, calling attention to those who had supervised (*episcopos* is best translated "overseer") the collection of money sent to Paul as a personal gift (4:10-19). Since the terms "bishop" and "presbyter" are virtually synonymous (cf. J. B. Lightfoot, *St. Paul's Epistle to the Philippians,* p. 96 ff.), and since there were several "bishops" (note plural) at Philippi, it would be unwise to contend for a first century episcopacy on the basis of this verse.

2. Grace unto you and peace. Paul's Christian version of the combined Greek and Hebrew greetings. Not *chairein*, "greetings," but *charis*, "grace" — the spontaneous, undeserved, loving-kindness of God towards men. **Peace** is more than inner composure; it has theological overtones that speak of restored fellowship between man and God on the basis of Christ's reconciling work. These spiritual blessings find their ultimate source in **God our Father and the Lord Jesus Christ.**

II. Thanksgiving and Prayer. 1:3-11.

Paul lifts his heart in gratitude and prayer for the partnership of the Philippian Christians in the work of the Gospel and expresses his deep yearning that they continue to grow in love and discernment.

3. Thanksgiving with joy is an undercurrent that runs through all of Paul's writings. (Only in Galatians is it momentarily eclipsed by the seriousness of the Judaizing menace.) Nowhere does it burst to the surface more expressively than in Philippians. Even in prison Paul's thoughts were directed towards others. In his continuing **remembrance** of them (not isolated instances, as the AV suggests) he gave thanks to God. The singular **my God** betrays a profound and intimate relationship.

4. This verse is parenthetical. **Always in every supplication of mine** goes with what follows rather than paralleling verse 3 (cf. J. J. Müller, *The Epistles of Paul to the Philippians and to Philemon,* p. 40, n. 4). For Paul, to remember was to pray. The nature of his intercession is pointed up by the choice of *deēsis* (a prayer of petition) instead of the more general *proseuchē*. The studied repetition of the word **all** (1:4,7,8,25; 2:17, 26; 4:5) is Paul's gentle reminder that there is no place for partisanship in the Christian community. Intercession is not a burden to be borne but an exercise of the soul to be performed **with joy.**

5. The occasion for the thanksgiving is the Philippians' "sympathetic cooperation towards the furtherance of the gospel." *Koinōnia* is poorly translated by the English word **fellowship.** It comes from a verb meaning "to have in common" and may be defined in the NT as "that Christian corporate life and mutual belonging which grows out of the common sharing of Christ and his benefits" (C. E. Simcox, *They Met at Philippi,* p. 28). Even though the immediate reference may be to the gift of money (*koinōnia* is so used in the papyri), the expression is not exhausted by this one act. The gift is only a symbol of a far deeper concern for the propagation of the Gospel. The desire to share had been characteristic of the Philippians **from the first day.** One gift had reached Paul when he had gone no further than Thessalonica (4:16). **6.** Paul's confidence that their partnership in the Gospel would continue rested upon the faithfulness of God who, having begun a good work, would most certainly bring it to completion. To the convert from paganism the semitechnical terms **began** and **complete** would call to mind the initiation into and ultimate goal of the mystery religions. **Good work.** That total action of divine grace in their midst. The **day of Jesus Christ.** NT equivalent for the OT "day of the Lord."

7. It was right for Paul to think of them in this way because he had them **in** his **heart.** This bond of affection is made evident by their partnership with him both in his **imprisonment** and before the court. (Papyri discoveries show that both *apologia,* **defense,** and *bebaiōsis,* **confirmation,** were legal terms.) They were partakers with him **in grace,** not, *of* his *grace.* To suffer for Christ is a special favor of God. **8. I yearn for you all** reveals a deep sense of Christian family affection. Michael comments that the AV translation **bowels of Jesus Christ** "is as inexact as it is inelegant" (p. 19). *Splagchnos* (lit., heart, lungs, liver, etc.; not intestines) refers metaphorically to the feelings of love and tenderness believed to arise from the inward parts. Paul's affection had a divine origin; in fact, it was actually the indwelling Christ who was loving through him (cf. Gal 2:20).

9. Paul does not disparage the warmth of their affection but prays that their love may abound more and more in **precise knowledge** *(epignōsis)* and **moral discernment** *(aisthēsis).* Love must comprehend with accuracy and apply the truth with discrimination and ethical common sense. **All discernment.** Discernment for all kinds of situations. **10. To approve things that are excellent** (interpreting *ta diapheronta* as "things which transcend") is to give one's entire support to that which through testing has proved to be essential and vital. The result of intelligent love is a right sense of values. This, in turn, enables one to be **pure** (one derivation of *eilikrineis* suggests the meaning of "flawless when tested against the light") and **without offense** to others (taking *aproskopoi* as transitive). This becomes a vital concern in view of the coming **day of Christ.** **11. Filled with the fruit of righteousness.** Discerning love will also result in a bumper crop (note sing., *karpos)* of uprightness. But even this depends upon the righteousness by faith—that which comes through **Jesus Christ.** The goal of all Christian activity is to bring recognition and homage *(epainos)* to the divine perfections *(doxa)* of a redeeming God.

III. The Unconquerable Gospel. 1:12-14.

The Philippians were greatly distressed at the news of Paul's imprisonment. What would happen to the cause of Christ now that the chief apostle was in chains? Paul wrote encouragingly that what might have appeared as a setback was in reality an important advance. Not only had the entire Praetorian Guard learned of Christ, but the local church had been emboldened to proclaim the Gospel openly and fearlessly.

12. Six times in this one letter Paul addresses the recipients as **brethren.** The term denotes a strong sense of unity and spiritual comradeship. The circumstances *(ta kat' eme)* that had befallen Paul had unexpectedly proved to advance the Gospel actively. *Prokopē* **(furtherance** or *advance)* is from a verb used originally of a pioneer cutting his way through brushwood (Souter, *Pocket Lexicon,* p. 216). **13.** The advance had been on two fronts: the Gospel had come to the Praetorian Guard (v. 13), and the Christians had been stirred to more fearless witnessing (v. 14). *Praitōrion* here refers not to the official residence of the governor (thus AV, **palace)** but to the imperial guard (RSV and most commentators; cf. Lightfoot's famous note *op. cit.,* pp. 99-104). Even professional guards could not resist speaking of this remarkable prisoner and the reason for his imprisonment. Soon the entire city **(all the rest,** ASV) knew that Paul was in chains **for** the cause of **Christ.**

14. The majority of the brethren were "infected with the contagion of Paul's heroism" (Rainey in ExpB, p. 52). It is better to take **in the Lord** as representing the sphere of their confidence than to make it modify **the brethren.** The occasion of the confidence was Paul's **bonds.** The end result was that they dared more fearlessly than ever to speak out *(laleō* denotes the sound produced) the **word of God.**

IV. Unprincipled Preaching. 1:15-18.

Not all preached out of pure motives; but in that Christ was being preached, Paul rejoiced.

15. The identity of the **some** who preached Christ from impure motives cannot be established with certainty. However, they were not the Judaizing party (as Lightfoot and Moule contend), because they preached **Christ,** not "another gospel" (cf. Gal 1:6-9). Would it have been like Paul to tolerate one day what he had utterly repudiated the day before? Neither were they the minority implied in Phil 1:14, because they were by no means reticent to preach. More probably the antagonists were a group within the church who, envious of Paul's influence (in prison or out) and stirred by a quarrelsome spirit, had increased their missionary activity with a desire to add to the annoyance of the imprisoned apostle. The **good will** of the others refers to their motives in preaching.

16. The Received Text, following inferior authorities, has transposed verses 16 and 17 to avoid the supposed irregularity of dealing with the two groups of verse 15 in reverse order. **Out of love** refers both to their concern for the progress of the Gospel and to their personal attachment to Paul. *Keimai,* **I am set** *(here),* pictures a sentry *posted* for duty. In the present context it may have the more metaphorical meaning of being *destined* for the **vindication of the gospel.** **17.** The preaching of the second group arose out of **selfish ambition** *(eritheia* was used by Aristotle to denote "a self-seeking pursuit of political office by unfair means," Arndt, p. 309). Their real interest was to win against Paul and in the process to annoy him in prison. *Thlipsis,* **affliction,** literally means *friction.* "To rouse friction by one's chains" is a vivid way of portraying the consternation of a person who cannot rectify a situation because of some limitation which has been placed upon him.

18. But what was Paul's reaction? Regardless of the motive, if Christ was being preached, he rejoiced. Even though the Gospel may have been used as a camouflage for personal gain, it was still "the power of God unto salvation." Michael understimates the apostle when he says that "Paul's spirit was fretful as he wrote" and that 1:18 was "a deliberate attempt . . . to curb his agitated spirit" *(op. cit.,* p. 45). **And will rejoice**

does not belong to verse 18 as expressing a strong determination not to lapse into irritation at the deceptive conduct of his antagonists, but introduces the further grounds for rejoicing given in verses 19,20.

V. Life or Death? 1:19-26.

While the apostle's personal desire was to go home to Christ, the need of the church convinced him that he would soon be released and continue working for their advancement in the faith.

19. Paul believed that the present opposition would work out for good because the Christians were praying. As a result, the **Spirit of Jesus Christ** (the Holy Spirit, not a Christlike spirit) would grant a **bountiful supply** of that which was necessary for the existing emergency. *Sōtēria* is best taken as **deliverance** (RSV) from prison, although many commentators understand it in a wider sense. Some detect a quotation from Job 13:16 (LXX), and interpret Paul's hope of vindication as resting on his consciousness of integrity (cf. Michael, *in loc.).* **20.** *Apokaradokia,* **earnest expectation,** is a striking word, perhaps coined by Paul. Literally it means to *look intently into the distance with outstretched head.* The apostle's expectation was twofold: that he would not be **ashamed** (i.e., be disappointed by the failure of divine help), and that **Christ** would **be magnified** (note the sensitive substitution of the third person passive for the first person active) in his **body** (the natural sphere for the outward expression of the inner man). The emphasis upon **now** implies that the hour of crisis was near. **Whether by life or by death** does not reflect indifference on Paul's part about his fate but concern that in either case Christ be honored.

21. Paul's own life had been so completely taken up into the person and program of his Lord that he could say, **For to me to live is Christ.** Christ was the sum total of his existence. **To die is gain** because in the absence of life's limitations union with Christ will be completely realized. No sense of world-weariness should be read into these words. **22.** The lack of continuity within verse 22 reflects Paul's perplexity. Of the several possibilities, the elliptical construction – **If, however** *(it is granted to me)* **to live in the flesh, this** *(will result in)* **fruitful labor for me**–is preferable. The choice of **flesh** instead of "body" emphasizes the weak and transitory nature of physical life. Paul does not venture to decide between the alternatives (in this context *gnōrizō* means "to make known one's decision"), but will leave it with the Lord.

23. I am immobilized by two opposing considerations. *Synechomai (I am in a strait)* is a strong expression meaning "to be held together." With the addition of *betwixt two,* it means "hemmed in and under pressure from both sides." Contemplating the possibility of either release or the sword, Paul is prevented from inclining in either direction. His personal desire is **to depart** *(analyō* pictures a vessel weighing anchor or a soldier breaking camp; it is a euphemism for "to die") **and be with Christ.** That would be **by far the best**–a doubly strengthened comparative ("a bold accumulation," Moule, *op. cit.)* expressing the surpassing excellence of being with Christ. **24.** The greater obligation is *to continue on in this present life.* The preposition compounded with the simple verb, *epi – menō,* gives it the special thought of persistence. Personal desire gives way to spiritual need.

25. Persuaded of this (i.e., the total thrust of vv. 19-24), Paul **knows** (personal conviction, not prophetic insight) that he shall **abide and remain beside** *(to serve)* **them.** The result will be **joyful progress** (the two nouns can hardly be separated) **in the faith** (both objectively – the creed and subjectively – the believer's apprehension). **26. So that** marks a specific purpose–the giving to them of an abundant **ground for boasting.** Even in English, "boasting" may mean "speaking in exulting language of another." **In Christ** is the sphere of their glorying. **In me** is the occasion, explained by the following phrase as **by my return.**

VI. Exhortation to Steadfastness. 1:27-30.

Lest their boasting lead to carelessness in the conflict against paganism, Paul sounds a note of warning. With unity and steadfastness they were to go on contending for the faith.

27. They were to **live as worthy citizens** of the kingdom of heaven. Paul's use of *politeuomai,* "to live as a citizen," "to fulfill corporate duties," instead of the more usual *peripateō,* "to walk," would be noted and appreciated in a Roman colony like Philippi. The word stresses the effect of the Christian community in a pagan society. **Whether I come . . . or . . . am absent** does not indicate doubt concerning the future but is an attempt to disengage them from undue dependence upon him. The thought of gladiatorial combat runs throughout these verses: They are to **take a firm stand** *(stēkō)*, **join in combat** *(synathleō)*, and not **be frightened** *(ptyreomai*, v. 28). **One spirit** designates a unified offensive; **one soul** (seat of affections) indicates that unity must extend to inward disposition.

28. The verb, *to be* **terrified,** pictures frightened horses about to stampede. The opponents were not the Judaizers but members of a violently hostile element at Philippi. The fearlessness of the Christians was a **clear omen** to the adversaries that their attempts to thwart the Gospel were futile and only led to their own **destruction.** It also revealed to them that God was on the other side (reading **of your salvation,** not *to you of salvation)*. **29. It is given** could be more literally translated, *It has been graciously conferred* (*charizomai* is the verb form of *charis,* "grace"). "The privilege of suffering for Christ is the privilege of doing the kind of work for him that is important enough to merit the world's counterattack" (Simcox, *op. cit.*, p. 61). To suffer **for Christ** (in the interest of his cause) is a favor granted only to those who **believe in him. 30.** Connect with verse 28 a. The Philippians were involved in the same sort of **conflict** *(agōn;* cf. our word *agony)* in which Paul had been (Acts 16:19 ff.) and still was engaged.

VII. An Appeal to Christian Experience. 2:1-4.

In four compact conditional clauses Paul sets forth a powerful motive for harmony in the Christian community.

1. First class conditional clauses **(if)** assume the premise to be true, and the **if** may often be translated *since.* **Consolation in Christ.** Ground for appeal because of being in Christ. **Comfort of love.** The incentive furnished by the bond of love. **Fellowship of the Spirit.** The mutual **concern** effected by God's Spirit. **Tender compassion** (joining the two nouns). An appeal to human kindness. **2.** Paul's joy would be complete if the Philippians would **continue** (note present tense) **in harmony of thought and disposition.** The apostle's earnestness is seen in his almost redundant enlargement—**by having the same love** and **by being knit together in soul** *(sympsychē)*, **considering the one and same thing.**

3. Selfish ambition (cf. 1:17) and **vain conceit** *(kenodoxia* combines the two words "hollow" and "opinion") were the headstrong and treacherous foes of the life of the church. They must give way to **lowliness of mind** (the Greeks took self-assertion so much for granted that a new word had to be coined) and **thoughtful consideration** (verb form, *esteem)* for **others** *(as)* **better than** oneself (not necessarily as essentially superior but as worthy of preferential treatment). Müller describes humility as "insight into one's own insignificance" *(op. cit.*, p. 75). **4.** As humility (v. 3 a) is the antithesis of vain conceit, consideration for others (v. 4) is the antithesis of selfish ambition.

VIII. The Supreme Example of Self-renunciation. 2:5-11.

Paul draws upon an early hymn of the church which eloquently portrays the divine condescension of Christ in His incarnation and death in order to buttress his appeal for self-forgetful and sacrificial living. (For a recent and excellent treatment of this much discussed passage cf. V. Taylor, *The Person of Christ*, pp. 62-79.) The interpretation that follows sees a basic contrast between the two Adams, and understands the "self-emptying" of Jesus in terms of the Suffering Servant (cf. A. M. Hunter, *Paul and His Predecessors*, pp. 45-51, for an able presentation of this approach). If it be remembered that the language of 2:5-11 is that of poetry, not of formal theology, many of the problems raised by kenotic (lit., *emptying)* speculation will correctly appear as irrelevant to the essential teaching of the passage.

5. Let this mind . . . (AV). Better, *Maintain that inner disposition towards one another which was exemplified* (the verb must be supplied) **by Christ Jesus. 6. Being in the form of God** (AV). Better, *Though in his pre-incarnate state he possessed the essential qualities of God, he did not consider his status of divine equality a prize to be selfishly hoarded* (taking *harpagmos* passively). *Morphē,* **form,** in verses 6 and 7 denotes a permanent expression of essential attributes, while *schēma,* **fashion** (v. 8), refers to outward appearance that is subject to change.

7. But he emptied himself. *Ekenōsen* is not intended in a metaphysical sense (i.e., that he gave up divine attributes), but is a "graphic expression of the completeness of his self-renunciation" (M. R. Vincent, *A Critical and Exegetical Commentary on the Epistles to the Philippians and to Philemon*, p. 59). Note the allusion to Isa 53:12, "he hath poured out his soul unto death." Christ emptied himself **by becoming a servant** (the use of *morphē*, **form**, here indicates the reality of his servanthood) **and appearing upon the scene as mortal man.** Unlike the first Adam, who made a frantic attempt to seize equality with God (Gen 3:5), Jesus, the last Adam (I Cor 15:47), humbled himself and obediently accepted the role of the Suffering Servant (cf. the contribution of R. Martin in ExpT, March '59, p. 183 f.). **8.** The act of voluntary humiliation did not stop with the Incarnation but continued to the ignominious depths of death by crucifixion. The omission of the article before *staurou*, **cross**, emphasizes the shameful nature of the death – even a **cross death.** (For the Roman view of crucifixion cf. Cicero *In Verrem* 5. 66). **He humbled himself.** He put aside all personal rights and interests in order to insure the welfare of others.

9. As a consequence, **God highly exalted him** (the Ascension and its concomitant glory) **and graciously conferred upon him the supreme name** (either Lord, *kurios*, the OT name for God; or to be understood in the Hebrew sense of denoting rank and dignity). Verses 9-11 answer to verses 6-8, and are best accounted for in the present context (the interrupted exhortation is resumed at 2:12) as the remainder of a hymn originally quoted for the thrust of its first strophe. **10.** Drawing from Isa 45:23, where the Lord prophesies that universal worship will one day be given him, the author writes that **in the name of Jesus** (not *at*, AV, which might suggest mechanical genuflection at the mention of the name, but **in connection with** all the name represents) **the totality of created rational beings will pay due homage. Those in heaven, on earth, and underground** is an expression of universality and should not be forced to support elaborate theories of classification. **11.** The compound verb for **confess** *(exomologeō)* may mean "confess with thanksgiving"–although this would seem strange if **every tongue** includes the lost as well as the saved. **Jesus Christ is Lord** is the earliest creed of the primitive church (cf. Rom 10:9; I Cor 12:3). The Lordship of Christ is the core of Christianity.

IX. Continued Exhortation. 2:12-18.

Christ's great example of self-renunciation led Paul to admonish his Philippian brethren further.

12. My beloved. A favorite expression (occurring twice in 4:1) that betrays a warm love for his converts. He urges them to **work out** their **own salvation,** especially now in his absence. The passage relates primarily to the community rather than to the individual (cf. Michael, *op. cit.*, p. 98 ff.). **Salvation** is corporate. The Philippians were to carry through *(katergazomai*, **keep on working out,** is continuous present) the deliverance of the church into a state of Christian maturity. **Fear and trembling** seems to be an idiomatic expression for a humble frame of mind (cf. I Cor 2:3; II Cor 7:15; Eph 6:5). **13.** Humility in reference to their deliverance was in place because, in spite of their co-operation, it was **God** (note emphatic position) who created within them both the will and the power (he "energizes"–*energeō)* **to do his pleasure** (or, *to promote the good will*, viz., harmony in the Philippian church).

14. The exhortation against **murmurings and disputings** *(dialogismos* is used in the papyri to denote litigation) reflects as a background the grumblings of the Israelites in their wilderness wandering. (However, to picture Paul as consciously comparing himself with Moses as he delivered his final injunctions is more imaginative than probable.) **15.** By not grumbling they would **become** *(ginomai)* **blameless** (before others) **and innocent** *(akeraios*, lit., *unadulterated* – denoting simplicity of charcter). **Unblemished,** *amōmos*, is used almost invariably in the LXX of sacrificial animals. A **crooked and perverse generation** (an adaptation of Deut 32:5) is a result of moral and intellectual distortion. In this dark world Christians are to **shine as lights** (cf. Mt 5:16).

16. If Paul is continuing the same metaphor, *epechontes*, etc. will be translated **holding forth** (like a torch held out before the bearer) **the word** (that brings) **life;** but if the final clause of verse 15 is parenthetical (Lightfoot) and the apostle is contrasting the Christians with the perverse generation, it will be translated **holding fast. Run** reflects the activity of the stadium. **Labor.** Deissmann sees here the discouragement of having woven a piece of cloth only to have it rejected (LAE, p. 317). Perhaps Herklotz is right in referring to Paul as "the master of the mixed metaphor" (H.G.G. Herklotz, *Epistle of St. Paul to the Philippians,* p. 74).

17. A metaphor built on sacrificial ritual. The **faith** of the Philippians (and all that involves in terms of life and activity) was their **sacrifice and priestly service.** Paul's lifeblood would be a libation poured upon their offering. If that was what the future held, then even in this Paul rejoiced. He would **rejoice with** them *(sygchairō)* because a double sacrifice afforded the opportunity for further fellowship. **18.** They were to adopt the same outlook and join their rejoicing with his.

X. Plans for Reunion. 2:19-30.

Paul hoped to send Timothy before long with the news of the court's decision and then to come himself as soon as possible. In the meantime he would send back Epaphroditus—their messenger to Paul in his distress—to ease the Philippians' concern and restore their cheerfulness.

19. Although the apostle had urged them to take their own affairs in hand (v. 12), he would not leave them without guidance. The purpose of sending Timothy was that Paul might **be cheered** *(eupsycheō,* lit., *to be stouthearted)* by news of them, and vice versa (implied by **I also**). **20. No one.** Not a sweeping condemnation of his fellow laborers. But of those available there was no one who, like Timothy, would be **genuinely** *(gnēsiōs,* lit., *born in wedlock;* thus, "like a brother") concerned for their welfare. **21.** Paul felt a bit like the 'deserted' *Elijah.* **22.** Timothy's **character** *(dokimē,* "approval gained through testing") was well known to the Philippians, because they had observed him (Acts 16) as he labored with Paul **as a son with a father in** (the interest of) **the gospel.**

23. It is **this one** (note emphatic position of *touton),* viz., Timothy himself, whom Paul hoped (his plans were still somewhat unsettled) to send as soon as he could get a clear perspective *(aphoraō,* "to see," means lit., *to look from)* on the outcome of his imprisonment. **24.** However, he was persuaded that **before long** *(tacheōs* is a reasonably flexible term) he, too, would come to them. **In the Lord.** All Paul's plans were conditioned by his relationship to Christ.

25. Epaphroditus *(charming)* is one of the most attractively heroic characters of the NT. He had been delegated to bring the gift of money (4:18) and to serve Paul on behalf of the Philippians. Paul calls him a **brother** (emphasizing the bond of Christian family love), **fellow worker** (a term borrowed from the workshop and stressing the spirit of comradeship), and **fellow soldier** *(systratiōtēs* pictures Christians fighting side by side against the onslaughts of heathenism. Phillips translates, *comrade-in-arms).* **I supposed.** In ancient correspondence it was customary for the writer to adopt the reader's perspective (cf. also **I sent,** v. 28). **26.** Epaphroditus' eager longing for the Christians back at Philippi had turned to distress upon his learning that news of his illness had reached them. The verb for **full of heaviness** (AV) is usually derived from *adēmos,* "not at home," viz., "not inwardly at home"; hence **distraught, beside oneself.** It is used, for instance, to portray the profound consternation of Gethsemane (Mk 14:33). **27.** The apostle affirms the seriousness of the crisis. Epaphroditus' condition had been like death (taking *paraplesion,* **nigh to,** adverbially). But God had had mercy on them both: Epaphroditus had recovered, and bereavement had not been added to Paul's other concerns. **Sorrow upon sorrow** means "wave upon wave of distressing circumstances." **28. Rejoice again.** The AV and RSV are mistaken in taking **again** with the participle **seeing.** Lightfoot (p. 124) translates, *may recover your cheerfulness.* The alleviation of their anxiety would lessen Paul's. Thus he sent Epaphroditus back **more quickly** (or *spoudaiaterōs* may indicate "with greater eagerness"; cf. RSV) than he might have done.

29. Some commentators see a note of apprehension in Paul's "letter of recommendation." Would there not be some at Philippi who would judge that, by returning prematurely, Epaphroditus had deserted his charge? However, the verse need not be taken as an appeal. Moule suggests, "Accept him as my gift to you" (p. 54). **30.** He was worthy of honor because in the fulfillment of his obligations he almost died. **Unto death** reflects an attitude like that of Christ (cf. same phrase in 2:8). And this was in order to complete their service to Paul. The context shows that Epaphroditus' critical condition was due to overexertion rather than to persecution or the hazards of the journey. **Having gambled with his life.** From *parabolos,* "venturesome, reckless." In Alexandria there grew up an association of men known as the *Parabolani.* Among the hazardous duties of this "suicide squad" was the nursing of the sick during epidemics.

XI. An Interrupted Conclusion. 3:1-11.

As Paul begins to bring his letter to a close, some sort of interruption breaks his train of thought. When he returns to dictating, he digresses to warn the Philippians against Judaizers and self-complacent antinomianism. By 4:4 (or 4:8) he has worked his way back to the original theme.

1. Finally. W. S. Tindal is quoted as saying that Paul is "the father of all preachers who use 'finally, my brethren' as an indication that they have found their second wind" (Herklotz, *op. cit.*, p. 16). **The same things.** Those central truths of life and doctrine to which Paul makes repeated reference. In the present context they can refer to his teaching ministry while with them or to prior correspondence of which we have no further information. The theory that one such letter has found its way back into the text and accounts for the abrupt change in style and subject at 3:2 (or 3:1 b?) is by no means necessary to explain what is at most only a "curious digression" (Plummer, p. 66. Cf. "Lost Epistles to the Philippians," Lightfoot, pp. 138-142; Vincent, xxxi f.).

2. The warning is not against three types of people (e.g., heathen, self-seeking Christian teachers, and Jews), but against one kind from three angles: their character (**dogs**), conduct (**evil workers**), and creed (**concision.** Cf. Robertson in *Abingdon Bible Commentary*, p. 1246). According to Mosaic law the dog was an unclean animal (Deut 23:18). In Eastern cities he was a scavenger and usually diseased — a "despised, shameless, and miserable creature" (SBK, I, 722). Paul reverses this term of contempt which had long been applied to the Gentiles by the Jews (cf. Mt 15:27) and says that it is the Christians who are feasting at the spiritual banquet table, while the Jews are those who eat the "garbage of carnal ordinances" (Lightfoot). The dogs are either extreme Judaizers or antagonistic Jews (the line becomes rather thin). With a bitter play on words Paul designates them the **concision** *(katatomē)* rather than the **circumcision** *(peritomē)*. They are "those who mutilate the flesh" (RSV). The verb is used in the LXX of cuttings forbidden by Mosaic law.

3. Not they, but **we are the** true **circumcision.** The new Israel is comprised, first, of those who **worship by the Spirit of God.** That the early church made this claim is most certainly implied in the verse. The AV here follows the inferior reading, which, however, rather happily maintains a contrast between that which is external and that which takes place in the domain of the spirit. Again, true Israel is made up of those who **boast in Christ Jesus. Boast** is a favorite expression of Paul's. He uses it thirty times in his epistles, though it appears only twice elsewhere in the NT. Here the meaning is "to glory" or "to exult." Third, the new Israel is made up of those who **have no confidence in the flesh,** viz., in external privileges.

4. The writer, for the moment, places himself on the same ground as his antagonists to show that even according to their standards, he had superior **ground for confidence** (taking *pepoithēsis* objectively). **5.** Paul sets forth his credentials. **Circumcised on the eighth day.** He was a true Israelite from birth (Ishmaelites, whose Jewish blood was mixed with Egyptian, were not circumcised until they were 13). He was no proselyte, but **of the stock of Israel.** In fact, he belonged to the honored **tribe of Benjamin,** which gave to Israel its first king. In contrast with Greek-speaking Jews (Hellenists), he came from a family that had retained Hebrew customs and spoke the Hebrew (or Aramaic) language. In addition to these inherited privileges, there were matters that had involved his personal choice. In his relationship to the Law he was a **Pharisee** — a "passionate adherent of the strictest religious tradition among the Jews" (Müller, p. 110). **6. Law righteousness.** "Righteousness" that consists in obedience to external commands. **Blameless.** A remarkable claim when one considers the minutiae of Pharisaic legislation.

7. Whatever **gains** (note plural) Paul may have had (the privileges mentioned in vv. 5,6), he counted as **loss** (sing.). They were worse than useless–actually a hindrance–because they had to be unlearned. **8.** Here the writer enlarges the preceding thought and protects it against misinterpretation. He says that he is **counting** (present tense indicates that v. 7 was no isolated and impulsive act of the past) **all things** (not only his former ground of confidence) **as loss** in comparison with the surpassing worth of "experiential knowledge of God" (the key thought of vv. 8-11). He not only counted them as loss, but they were actually confiscated. The AV regards *skybalon* as that rejected by the body, i.e., **dung.** Lightfoot favors a derivation from *es kunas*, "that which is thrown to the dogs," *refuse* (RSV). The motive for this unprecedented *volte-face* was to **gain Christ.**

9. Paul discounted all personal achievement that he might be found in Christ. The parallel clauses contrast works-righteousness, which is based on law, with faith-righteousness, which is given by God. Here is Paul's most concise statement of justification by faith. **10.** The passionate expression of Paul's deepest longings. To **know him** is to experience the power that flows from union with the resurrected Christ and to enter into fellowship with **his sufferings** (all the hardships to be endured for the cause of Christ; cf. Acts 9:16). That these are two aspects of the same experience is indicated by the single article in Greek. **Being conformed** (pres. participle) **to his death** further defines the experience as one of continual dying out to self. **11. If by any means.** An expression of humility, not of uncertainty. The **resurrection from** *(ek,* "out of") **the dead** is the resurrection of believers, not a general resurrection.

XII. The Homestretch. 3:12-16.

Lest he leave the impression of having already arrived, Paul carefully indicated that he was still very much involved in the race of life. This caution against misinterpretation was called forth by the spreading influence of complacent perfectionists in the church at large.

12. That which Paul had not **already attained** was the experience of complete and final knowledge of his Lord (vv. 8-11). **Already perfect** further defines his goal. Perfection here would be full knowledge and perfect conformity. Verse 12 b may be paraphrased, "but I press on strenuously if somehow I may **overtake and lay hold of** *(katalambanō* is used in the papyri of colonists appropriating land) that for which I was **taken captive** (same verb as above) **by Christ Jesus** on the Damascus road." God had a purpose in Paul's conversion, and Paul desired intensely that it might be fully realized in his experience. Many commentators take *eph' hō to* mean "because," which would then stress the *motive* (not the goal) of Paul's exertion (cf. C.F.D. Moule, *Idiom Book*, p. 132).

13. Verses 13,14 enlarge the thought of 3:12. The **not yet** state of Christian perfection destroys complacency and demands strenuous pursuit. **I myself** may imply a contrast with the self-appraisal of others. The metaphor is one of a foot-race. The concise, **but one thing,** expresses "singleness of purpose and concentration of effort" (Michael, p. 160). "I do" is added in the English. **Forgetting what lies behind.** The past accomplishments of his Christian career, which might induce self-satisfaction and a slackening of pace. **Straining forward** graphically portrays a runner who draws upon all his remaining strength and stretches out toward the goal (thus, our homestretch). **14. Mark** *(skopos,* from *skopeō,* "to gaze at"). That upon which the eye has been fixed. Distraction would be fatal. (Some suggest that the metaphor is that of a chariot race.) If ultimate perfection is the aim of the runner (that which keeps him from deviating from his course), it is also his **prize.** The prize belongs to those who respond wholeheartedly to God's **upward call,** (away from self and toward new heights of spiritual attainment) **in Christ Jesus.**

15. To be **perfect.** To be mature. In the mystery religions it designated the fully instructed as opposed to the novices. There is no indication here of "reproachful irony" (so Lightfoot). **Be thus minded.** Have this basic attitude of disposition, i.e., that past success does not remove the necessity for future striving. **If in anything ye be otherwise minded,** Paul adds by way of encouragement. "If you are not quite convinced that this point of view should be applied to *every* area of life, God will reveal **even this unto you." 16.** While the precise meaning of this compressed verse is doubtful, the general idea is clear: "Let us not deviate from those principles that have brought us safely to our present stage of Christian maturity." The condition for future enlightenment is to walk according to present light.

XIII. A Christian Commonwealth. 3:17-21.

The presence of those whose sensual manner of life was undermining the effectiveness of the Gospel led Paul to exhort the Philippians to imitate him and others who also lived as citizens of the heavenly state.

17. They were to join with one another in imitating Paul and the others who, after close inspection *(skopeō;* see on v. 14), proved to be living on the same high plane. *Typos* **(ensample)** was originally the mark left by a blow, and then a "pattern" or "mold." **18.** Those here described were not Judaizers (v. 2 ff.) nor heathen (this would have elicited a different reaction than **weeping**), but antinomian libertines who were in some way connected with the church. They misinterpreted Christian liberty as freedom from all moral restraint. They **are** (not "live as") **the enemies** (note definite article) **of the cross.** They were at enmity with everything for which the cross stands. **19.** Their **end** (better, *destiny*) **is perdition,** the antithesis of salvation. Their **god,** the supreme object of their concern, was **the belly.** The reference is not only to gluttony but to all sensual indulgences. Their supposed liberty was really bondage to shameful lusts, and they were disposed to dwell on sordid and earthy matters.

20. In contrast with these licentious profligates, the mature Christians lived as a colony of heavenly citizens whose temporary abode was on earth. While *politeuma* (the only occurrence in the NT) may indicate the pattern of life followed by a citizen (thus AV, **conversation**), here it means the state to which the citizen belongs (*commonwealth,* RSV). Roman citizens living at the outpost of Philippi would immediately grasp the point. *Apekdechometha* (rather mildly translated as **we look,** AV, or *we await,* RSV) denotes eager expectation. Inscriptions show that *sōtēr,* **savior,** was widely used in the Greco-Roman world to designate kings and emperors. Here it extends the preceding metaphor and reflects the attitude of the primitive church toward the return of Christ.

21. At his appearance Christ will **refashion** (*metaschēmatizō*) our **lowly body,** the body which now clothes our lowly state of mortal existence. Not *vile body,* as if Paul shared the Stoic contempt for all things material. **That it may be conformed** (*symmorphon;* for *schēma* and *morphē,* cf. 2:6) to **his glorious body,** the body in which Christ is clothed in his glorified estate. This transformation requires an act of supernatural power, that very power necessary to bring about universal dominion. *Energia* is used only by Paul and nearly always denotes God in action.

XIV. Apostolic Advice. 4:1-9.

The apostle admonishes two women to drop their differences, shows that prayer is the cure for anxiety, and urges a more noble sphere for the life of the mind.

1. Therefore. In view of your heavenly citizenship and the glorious transformation it will involve. The exhortation to **stand fast** is both a conclusion to chapter 3 and an introduction to what follows. Note the six terms of endearment in this one verse. *Stephanos,* **crown,** was a woven wreath awarded to a winning athlete. It was also used of the garland placed on the head of a guest at a banquet. Thus it signified both triumph and festivity.

2. Euodia (not *Euodias,* AV, which is a man's name) **and Syntyche** were two prominent women in the Philippian church who had lately begun to irritate each other. The repeated **I beseech** indicates Paul's impartiality. **Be of the same mind.** Cultivate harmony of thought and disposition (cf. 2:2). **3.** To help effect the reconciliation Paul appeals to *Syzygos,* who, true to the meaning of his name, was a **genuine yokefellow.** *Syzygos* is best understood as a proper name taken by some convert at baptism. If only an epithet, conjectures as to whom it designates run all the way from Silas to Paul's wife – Lydia? *Synēthlēsan.* **They labored** (fought) **side by side,** is a metaphor from the arena (cf. 1:27). The mention of **Clement** may be added to recall a specific occasion. The reference to **the book of life,** in which are listed the members of the heavenly commonwealth, suggests that Clement and others may have given up their lives on this occasion.

4. *Chairete* was the common expression for farewell. The addition **always** indicates that Paul had its deeper meaning, **rejoice,** in mind. The repetition suggests that conditions at Philippi were such as to make such an exhortation seem unreasonable. Christians can be commanded to rejoice, because their ground for rejoicing is not in circumstances but **in the Lord. 5.** The somewhat elusive *epieikes,* **moderation** (AV), indicates readiness to listen to reason, a yieldingness that does not retaliate. The motive for this "sweet reasonableness" is the imminent return of Christ. **The Lord is at hand.** The watchword of the early church (cf. the Aramaic equivalent, *maran atha,* in I Cor 16:22).

6. The hostility of heathendom (cf. 1:28) would give rise to anxiety. This was to be dispelled by prayer. "To care is a virtue, but to foster cares is sin" (Müller, *op. cit.,* p. 141). **In everything.** Anything sufficient to cause anxiety if not prayed about. **With thanksgiving.** Thankfulness for what God has already done is the proper spirit in which to make new requests. **7.** The **peace of God** is that tranquillity of spirit that God enjoys and only God can give. The phrase, **which passes all understanding,** is usually taken as indicating the utter inability of man's mind to fathom God's peace. More probably it means that God's peace far surpasses all our careful planning and clever ideas as to how we can resolve our own anxieties. **Shall keep.** *Phroureō*, "keep," is a military term meaning "to guard or garrison." With striking metaphor Paul here portrays the peace of God as a sentinel standing watch over the citadel of man's inner life – mind, will, and affections.

8. In this "paragraph on mental health" (Simcox) Paul draws up a list of virtues which might well have come from the pen of a Greek moralist. Two of the eight do not occur elsewhere in the NT, and one occurs only here in Paul's writings. **True.** Belonging to the nature of reality. **Honest.** Worthy of reverence, august. **Just.** In accordance with the loftiest conception of what is right (Michael). **Pure.** Not mixed with elements that would debase the soul. **Lovely.** That which inspires love. **Of good report.** Better than this rather tame translation is *that which has a good ring* (Michael). **If there be any virtue.** Lightfoot paraphrases, "Whatever value may reside in your old heathen conception of virtue" (p. 162), in order to stress Paul's concern not to omit any possible ground of appeal. They are to **take into account** *(logizomai;* AV, *think on)* these virtues of pagan morality. **9.** In addition they are to **keep on practicing** (AV, *do;* the imperative *prassete* is present tense) all the distinctively Christian ethics and morality they have learned from the apostle's life and teaching. Not only the "peace of God" (v. 7) but also the **God of peace** will be with them.

XV. Appreciation for the Gift. 4:10-20.

To borrow Paul's expression, **now at length** he thanks them formally for their gift. While not dependent upon the gift, or even seeking it, he rejoices in that such sacrifices are pleasing to God and beneficial for the giver.

10. If Philippians were actually a "thank you letter," we would expect words of appreciation much sooner. That they appear almost as a postscript lends plausibility to Michael's conjecture that Paul had already paid his thanks and was now clarifying some statement that had evidently caused offense (p. xxi f.; p. 209 ff.). *Anathalō*, "to cause to bloom again," pictures a tree putting on new foliage in the spring. Some, to avoid what seems to be a mild reproach, understand **flourished again** as indicating recovery from a period of dire poverty. The lack of **opportunity** would then be a lack of means. However, it probably means that no one was available for the trip.

11. Paul quickly corrects any false impression that he is complaining of want. *Autarkēs*. **Content.** Better, *self-sufficient*. A favorite term of the Stoics, who conceived of man as possessing the intrinsic ability to resist all external pressures. **12. In any and all circumstances** (no matter how distressing any one might be or how comprehensive the sum of them all) Paul had been **initiated** (a technical term in the mystery religions) into the secret of facing both lack and abundance. **13.** The profound difference between Paul and the Stoics is that while they held themselves to be *self*-sufficient, Paul's sufficiency lay in Another – the One who **infuse[d] strength** in him (AV, *strengtheneth me).*

14. Nevertheless, in unitedly entering into fellowship with his misfortune, the Philippians had done a **noble thing** *(kalōs; ho kalos* is the renowned Greek concept of "the beautiful").

15. The beginning of the gospel. When the Gospel was first proclaimed in Macedonia. **When I departed** probably refers to a gift given **at the time of** departure (cf. Acts 17:14) rather than subsequently (in which case see II Cor 11:9). **Giving and receiving.** The first of several allusions to financial transactions. It may be a gentle reminder that material payment for spiritual goods is not at all out of line (cf. I Cor 9:11). **16.** Almost before he was out of sight (even in Thessalonica; cf. Acts 17) they had **more than once** sent him help.

17. Again he was anxious not to leave the impression that he coveted their material help. What he really desired was "the interest that accumulates in this way to (their) divine credit" (Moffatt). Or, less technically, **fruit** may be that greater "capacity for human sympathy" (Scott in IB, XI, 126) which is the inevitable result of sacrificial living. **18.** *Apechō*. Possibly, "paid in full" (so used in the papyri, MM, p. 57), or "I have all that I could wish for" – in fact, he continues, **even more** *Osmē euōdias,* **an odor of a sweet smell,** is used frequently in the LXX for an offering pleasing to God (cf. Gen 8:21).

19. As *you* have responded to *my* needs, so **my God shall supply** all of **yours.** A tit-for-tat arrangement that offers little comfort for "close" Christians. **In**

glory. Either "in a glorious manner," or eschatologically, "in the glorious future age." **According to his riches.** On a scale commensurate with his wealth. **In Christ Jesus.** In union with the One who mediates God's blessings to man. **20. Unto God and our Father.** Better, *to God, even our Father!* It is the thought of God's fatherly care that gives rise to the doxology. **For ever and ever.** Literally, *unto the ages of the ages* – an endless succession of indefinite periods.

XVI. Greetings and Benediction. 4:21-25.

21. Probably added by Paul's own hand (cf. Gal 6:11). **Saint.** Only here in the NT does *hagios* occur in the singular (fifty-seven times in the plural), and even here it is prefaced by **every** – a strong reminder that Christianity is essentially a corporate affair. Those whom Paul commands to do the greeting are probably the elders of the church, who would read the letter aloud to the congregation.

22. Both Paul's personal companions (**brethren,** v. 21) and the entire church (**all the saints**) send their greetings. **Those of Caesar's household.** Not (as formerly thought) the emperor's family, but all those employed in the service of the government. As these were not confined to Rome, the expression does not argue a Roman origin for the epistle. Synge detects a touch of humor: the English euphemism for a prisoner is "his majesty's guest" (*Torch Series,* p. 49).

23. Grace . . . be with your spirit (note singular). Even in the benediction the central theme of harmony reappears.

BIBLIOGRAPHY

HERKLOTZ, H. G. G. *Epistle of St. Paul to the Philippians.* London: Lutterworth Press, 1946.

KENNEDY, H. A. "The Epistle to the Philippians," *The Expositor's Greek Testament.* Edited by W. Robertson Nicoll. Vol. III. Grand Rapids: Wm. B. Eerdmans Publishing Co., n.d.

LIGHTFOOT, J. B. *Saint Paul's Epistle to The Philippians.* London: The Macmillan Co., 1868 (12th ed., 1896).

MICHAEL, J. H. *The Epistle of Paul to the Philippians (The Moffatt New Testament Commentary).* London: Hodder and Stoughton, 1928.

MOULE, H. C. G. *The Epistle of Paul the Apostle to the Philippians (Cambridge Greek Testament for Schools and Colleges).* Cambridge: The University Press, 1897.

MULLER, J. J. *The Epistles of Paul to the Philippians and to Philemon (The New International Commentary on the New Testament).* Grand Rapids: Wm. B. Eerdmans Publishing Co., 1955.

SCOTT, E. F. *The Epistle to the Philippians (The Interpreter's Bible).* New York: Abingdon Press, 1955.

SIMCOX, C. E. *They Met at Philippi.* New York: Oxford University Press, 1958.

VINCENT, M. R. *A Critical and Exegetical Commentary on the Epistles to the Philippians and to Philemon (The International Critical Commentary).* Edinburgh: T. & T. Clarke, 1897.

Significant works published since this commentary was written:

BEARE, F. W. *The Epistle to the Philippians (Harper's New Testament Commentaries).* New York: Harper & Brothers, 1959.

HUNTER, A. M. *The Letter of Paul to the Philippians (The Layman's Bible Commentary).* Vol. 22. Richmond: John Knox Press, 1959.

MARTIN, R. P. *The Epistle of Paul to the Philippians (Tyndale New Testament Commentaries).* Grand Rapids: Wm. B. Eerdmans Publishing Co., 1959.

THE EPISTLE TO THE COLOSSIANS

INTRODUCTION

The Occasion. First century Colosse, an ancient but declining commercial center some hundred miles eastward from Ephesus, was situated on the Lycus Valley caravan route, near the cities of Laodicea and Hierapolis (cf. Col 4:13). Although an earlier evangelization (by the Galatian Christians?) cannot be excluded, the Colossians may have first heard the Christian message during Paul's Ephesian ministry (c. A.D. 53-56; cf. Acts 19:10).

Paul possibly passed through Colosse on his way to Ephesus, but he was personally unacquainted with the Christians there (cf. Col 2:1). His co-worker, Epaphras, who ministered to this church, visited the apostle and made known to him both the progress of the believers and an erroneous teaching that was subverting them.

Jews had been resident in this province of Phrygia for two centuries (Jos *Antiquities* 12. 147). Evidently less than orthodox, they receive this comment in the Talmud: "The wines and baths of Phrygia had separated the ten tribes from their brethren" (Shabbath, 147b). The accommodation to Gentile practices left its mark on Jews embracing Christianity. In the bordering province of Galatia the infant faith was threatened by legalism, a Judaizing heresy; here, as in Ephesus (cf. Acts 19:14,18), the danger lay in a Jewish-Hellenistic religious syncretism. To meet the former situation Paul had earlier addressed an epistle to the Galatians; to meet the equally grave peril in Colosse he wrote the present letter.

The Heresy at Colosse. In the church of the second century there appeared a heretical movement known as Gnosticism. Some of its basic principles were already known in the first century, not only in the Christian church but in the Judaism of the Diaspora as well (cf. R. McL. Wilson, *The Gnostic Problem;* C. H. Dodd, *The Interpretation of the Fourth Gospel*, p. 97 ff.; Rudolf Bultmann, "Gnosis," *Bible Keywords*, II). This incipient Gnosticism was more a religio-philosophical attitude and tendency than a system, and it could adapt itself to Jewish, Christian, or pagan groups as the occasion required. Nevertheless, certain ideas appear to be generally characteristic of the Gnostic mind: metaphysical dualism, mediating beings, redemption through knowledge or *gnōsis*. All religions, Gnostics held, which are manifestations of one hidden verity, seek to bring men to a knowledge of the truth. This knowledge or *gnōsis* is not intellectual apprehension but the enlightenment derived from mystical experience. Because man is bound in the world of evil matter, he can approach God only through mediating angelic beings. By the aid of these powers and through allegorical and mythical interpretations of the sacred writings, spiritual enlightenment can be achieved and one's redemption from the world of sin and matter be assured.

Naturally and perhaps inevitably some in the early church sought to enrich or accommodate their faith to current religious ideas; converts with an imperfect grasp of Christianity may unconsciously have merged earlier beliefs with Christian concepts. This may well have been the origin of the Gnostic influences that appeared in a number of the Pauline churches. In Corinth, for example, the desire for speculative wisdom (I Cor 1:7 ff.) and the disregard for the body (reflected in the denial of resurrection, in asceticism, and in sexual license; cf. I Cor 15:5,7), represent a Gnostic attitude.

The Colossian heresy combined Jewish and Hellenistic elements. Dietary and Sabbath observances, circumcision rites, and probably the mediatorial function of angels are reminiscent of Jewish practice and belief (Col 2:11,16,18); the emphasis on "wisdom" and "knowledge," the *plērōma* of cosmic powers, and the abasement of the body reflect Greek thought (2:3,8,23). Some Jewish converts probably brought this mixture from a heterodox Judaism and developed it further after they became Christians.

In a strategy used elsewhere, Paul

takes the terminology of the errorists to attack their teaching and, in the process, develops the doctrine of the 'cosmic Christ.' In Christ, the one mediator, dwells all wisdom and knowledge; in his death and resurrection all powers of the cosmos are defeated and subjected to himself (2:3,9,10,15). Any teaching which detracts from the centrality of Christ under the pretense of leading men to maturity and perfection is a perversion that threatens the very essence of the faith. The apostle thus identifies and exposes the root of the error at Colosse.

Origin and Date. Colossians, like Ephesians, Philippians, and Philemon, was written from prison and was delivered with the Epistle to Philemon and (possibly) Ephesians by Tychicus and Onesimus (4:3, 7-9; Phm 12; Eph 6:12). The mass of early tradition fixes its origin in Rome during the imprisonment of Acts 28 (c. A.D. 61–63). Although this view remains dominant, a number of scholars suggest that earlier imprisonments in Caesarea (c. A.D. 58-60) or Ephesus (c. A.D. 55/56) offer a more likely occasion for the writings. Caesarea has few advocates today, but the Ephesian imprisonment theory has attracted considerable attention. It has been most recently argued by G. S. Duncan (*St. Paul's Ephesian Ministry*), who points out that: (1) Second Corinthians (6:5; 11:23), written at the close of the Ephesian ministry, indicates that Paul had been in prison a number of times unmentioned in Acts; if I Cor 15:32 is interpreted literally, as seems most reasonable, at least one of these imprisonments occurred in Ephesus. (2) The visit of Epaphras (Col 1:7; 4:12) and the presence of the runaway slave Onesimus are more in keeping with an Ephesian setting than with far distant Rome. (3) Paul plans a visit to the Lycus Valley upon his release (Phm 22), but according to tradition Paul proceeded westward to Spain after the Roman imprisonment (cf. Rom 15:24). Duncan's arguments have been more persuasive in the case of Philippians, but the view remains a live option for the other Prison Epistles as well. Those continuing to favor the Roman origin consider the arguments for other cities given above as inconclusive, and point to the weight of early tradition and to a more developed theology (especially) in Colossians and Ephesians. Could it have been propounded at such an early date as the Ephesian ministry?

Authorship. The Pauline authorship continues to be denied in some quarters, but the majority opinion is in the other direction. A few students, influenced by the fact that one-fourth of Colossians is found in Ephesians, have viewed the former as an expanded version of genuine Pauline correspondence. The relation between the two letters, however, is adequately and most easily explained as the—conscious or unconscious—working of the mind of the apostle himself as he writes upon similar themes.

Chief objections to Pauline authorship have been these: (1) The thought and emphasis of the letter do not conform to that of Romans, Corinthians, and Galatians; (2) The Colossian heresy could not possibly have developed so quickly. It is a mistake, however, to approach Paul as if his mind were in a strait jacket; changed circumstances offer a satisfactory answer for the change of theme and vocabulary. Recent investigations have shown quite conclusively that Gnosticism, at least in the incipient form appearing in Colossians, was already a potent force in the first century. The unanimous and early voice of church tradition joins the majority of present-day scholars in affirming the genuineness of the letter; one may place considerable confidence in this verdict.

Themes and Development of Thought. The structure of the epistle follows the familiar Pauline pattern, in which a doctrinal section (what to believe) is followed by an exhortation (how to act). In opposing false teaching, Paul emphasizes the exalted nature of the lordship of Jesus Christ and its significance for those who have been joined to Him. As lord of creation, Jesus embodies the fullness of deity; as head of the Church and reconciler of his people, he effectively mediates in his person the redemptive relation of man to God (Col 1:15-22; 2:9). To establish the sole sufficiency of Jesus as Lord and Redeemer (in opposition to the Gnostic substitution of redeeming disciplines and a *plērōma,* or plenitude, of mediating powers), Paul stresses both aspects of Christ's character.

Important in this regard is the concept of the 'Body of Christ,' with which the Colossians undoubtedly were familiar (1:18,24; 2:17; 3:15). This mysterious and unique relationship, which is exclusive of every other, makes anathema any belief or practice that displaces the centrality of Jesus as Redeemer and Perfecter of his people. The 'Body of Christ' is a motif deeply embedded in the substructure of New Testament theology. Some have sought its origin in the thought of Paul, but probably its roots lie in the teaching of the Lord himself (cf. Mk 14:58; Jn 2:19-22; E. E. Ellis, *Paul's Use of the Old Testament*, p. 92). Members of a community conceived of as parts of a body was a metaphor not unknown in the Greek world, e.g., among the Stoics. Paul's use of the figure, however, goes beyond mere metaphor and is to be understood in the framework of the ancient and realistic Hebrew concept of corporate solidarity (see R. P. Shedd, *Man in Community*).

In I Cor 12:12-21 the 'body' (of Christ) is pictured as including the 'head'. Hence a Christian can be described as an eye or an ear as well as a hand. In Colossians and Ephesians, where *Christ* is described as the 'head' of the body, the image, at first, appears to be substantially altered. If so, the diverse imagery is an accommodation to the apostle's desire to emphasize in these epistles the intimate relation of Christ to His people and not simply a long-time development of his earlier concept. In the complex of images Paul uses, each must be understood within its own framework and "a single over-all conceptual analysis will be about as useful for the interpretation of the apostle's writings as a bulldozer for the cultivation of a miniature landscape garden" (A. Farrar, *The Glass of Vision*, p. 45).

It is probable, however, that the divine Head is not a variant image of the 'Body' at all, but rather a complementary image. The concept of Christ as the head *(kephalē)* of the Church is analogous to that of I Cor 11:3: "Christ is the head of every man." More specifically: "The husband is the head of the wife, even as Christ is the head of the church: . . . he is the saviour of the body" (Eph 5:23). The 'head' imagery, as it relates to Christ and the Church, is to be understood in terms of the husband-wife analogy. It expresses Christ's union with the Church, for the husband and wife are 'one flesh.' But, more importantly, it pictures Christ's distinction from, his authority over, and his redemption of his body, the Church (cf. Col 2:10). The definition of the Church as the extension of the Incarnation does not reflect sufficiently this aspect of the Pauline imagery.

In the Pauline writings the Christian's relation to the new age is viewed both as a past event and as a future hope. In the past, Christians were crucified with Christ, raised to new life, translated into his kingdom, glorified, and made to sit with him in heaven (Eph 2:5-7; Col 1:13; 2:11-13; Rom 8:30). Yet Paul, toward the end of his life, expressed his yearning to "know him, and the power of his resurrection, and the fellowship of his sufferings, being made conformable unto his death; if by any means I might attain unto the resurrection of the dead" (Phil 3:10-14). The meaning of these different chronological perspectives, and their relationship, is of central importance for understanding Paul's thought-world (cf. E. E. Ellis, *Paul and His Recent Interpreters*, pp. 37-40). Briefly, we may suggest that the concept of the 'Body of Christ' provides a clue to their meaning. When Paul speaks of Christians having died and risen to new life, he speaks of a corporate reality experienced by Jesus Christ individually in A.D. 30, but mediated to the Christian corporately by the indwelling Spirit. Having been incorporated into Christ's body and destined to be conformed individually to Christ's image, the Christian is now to actualize in his individual life the "in Christ" life into which he has been brought. While the self in its mortality will "put on immortality" only at the *parousia*, the Lord's return, (I Cor 15:51-54), the self in its ethical and psychological expression begins to actualize the new-age realities in the present life: "If ye be dead with Christ . . . why . . . are ye subject to ordinances?" "If ye then be risen with Christ, seek those things which are above." "Ye have put off the old man . . . and have put on the new. . . . Put on therefore kindness . . . " (Col 2:20; 3:1,9,10). The character and mind of Christ and, in the resurrection, his immortal life are to be realized in his Body. Within this framework Paul's 'exhortation' is seen to be intimately related to his theological teaching.

OUTLINE

I. Introduction. 1:1,2.
II. The nature of Christ's lordship. 1:3–2:7.
  A. Thanksgiving for the Colossians' faith in Christ. 1:3-8.
  B. Prayer for their growth in Christ. 1:9-14.
  C. Christ as Lord. 1:15-19.
    1. Lord of creation. 1:15-17.
    2. Lord of the new creation. 1:18,19.
  D. Christ as God's reconciler. 1:20-23.
    1. Reconciler of all things. 1:20.
    2. Reconciler of the Colossian Christians. 1:21-23.
  E. Paul: Christ's minister of reconciliation. 1:24-29.
    1. Sharer of Christ's sufferings. 1:24.
    2. Proclaimer of the Christian mystery. 1:25-27.
    3. Instructor of the saints. 1:28,29.
  F. Paul's concern for the Lycus Valley Christians. 2:1-7.
III. Christ's lordship and the false teaching at Colosse. 2:8–3:4.
  A. The sole sufficiency of Christ. 2:8-15.
    1. Christ: Lord of every power and authority. 2:8-10.
    2. Christ: Source of the Christian's new life. 2:11-14.
    3. Christ: Conqueror of all cosmic powers. 2:15.
  B. The Colossians' practices as a denial of Christ's lordship. 2:16-19.
    1. Fixation upon ritual, a retreat into the old age. 2:16,17.
    2. Subservience to angelic powers, a departure from Christ. 2:18,19.
  C. The Colossians' practices as a contradiction of their corporate life in Christ. 2:20–3:4.
    1. Death with Christ means death to the regulations of the old age. 2:20–23.
    2. Resurrection with Christ demands a "new-age" world and life view 3:1-4.
IV. Christ's lordship in the Christian life. 3:5–4:6.
  A. The Christian imperative: Actualize individually the 'in Christ' reality. 3:5-17.
    1. The character of the old age to be put off. 3:5-9.
    2. The character of the new age to be put on. 3:10-17.
  B. Special precepts. 3:18–4:6.
    1. The Christian home. 3:18–4:1.
    2. Prayer. 4:2-4.
    3. Relation to non-Christians. 4:5,6.
V. Conclusion. 4:7-18.
  A. Commendation of the bearers of the letter. 4:7-9.
  B. Greetings from Paul's co-workers. 4:10-14.
  C. The apostle's greetings and blessings. 4:15-18.

COMMENTARY

I. Introduction. 1:1,2.

1. As in a number of other letters—II Corinthians, Philippians, I and II Thessalonians, Philemon—Paul associates Timothy in the salutation of Colossians, but he reserves to himself the title **apostle.** This term conveys the ideas of mission, authorization, and responsibility. And its NT meaning probably is to be derived from the Hebrew word *shālah,* "to send." (See J. B. Lightfoot, *St. Paul's Epistle to the Galatians,* p. 92 ff.; R. H. Rengsdorf, "Apostleship," *Bible Keywords II,* ed. J. R. Coates.) The substantive *shāliah,* a virtual equivalent of the NT word "apostle," is not uncommon in rabbinical writings. It was primarily a legal term, signifying authorized representation. As in the modern law of agency, the one sent was held to be equivalent to the sender himself. To dishonor the king's ambassador was to dishonor the king (II Sam 10; cf. I Sam 25:5-10,39-42). Although the term, **apostle of Jesus Christ,** has other secondary usages (Phil 2:25; II Cor 8:23), it appears to apply primarily to those directly commissioned as apostles by the risen Lord (cf. I Cor 9:1; 15:8-10). Thus Paul exercised the function of an apostle **by the will of God.**

2. All Christians are **saints** or holy by virtue of their relation to God in Christ; the use of the appellation for a particularly devout person is a later development. Paul uses the ancient Hebrew greeting, **peace,** but alters the customary Greek *chaire,* "hail," to *charis,* **grace,** giving the phrase a distinctively Christian ring.

II. The Nature of Christ's Lordship. 1:3–2:7.

A. Thanksgiving for the Colossians' Faith in Christ. 1:3-8.

An ancient Greek letter opens:

> Apion to Epimachus his Father and Lord, many greetings *(chairein).* Before all things I pray that thou art in health, and that thou dost prosper and fare well continually. . . . I thank the Lord Serapis that, when I was in peril in the sea, he saved me immediately. . . . (Deiss, LAE, p. 169).

In opening his letters (except Galatians) with a thanksgiving, Paul follows this literary custom, but he significantly alters the content.

3-6. Paul gives thanks for the triad of graces present among the Colossians. Their **faith** Christward (and in the 'Christ sphere'), which lies in the past, and their **love** manward, manifest in the present, have for their foundation the **hope** that is to be actualized in the future. By **hope** Christ himself may be meant (cf. 1:27). The three go together: If we have hope only in this life, we are to be pitied (I Cor 15:19), but if our hope resides in **heaven,** where the new age is actualized in the person of Christ, it will manifest itself in love and bring **forth fruit** in the present world (cf. Col 1:13; 3:14; Eph 6:12; Mk 4:20).

7. Only here does Paul designate a co-worker as a **fellow slave** (Gr. *sundoulos)* of Christ; this also may be the sense of "fellow prisoner" in 4:10. **Epaphras,** the **minister** or deacon *(diakonos)* of the Colossians may have been the organizer of this Lycus Valley church. Doubtless the apostle had learned from him about the errors threatening the Christians there, as well as about their **love** for Paul **in the Spirit.** The latter probably refers to the sphere of the Spirit or new age, although *spiritual love* and *love from the Spirit* are possible translations (cf. Rom 8:9; Eph 1:3).

B. Prayer for Their Growth in Christ. 1:9-14.

The prayers of Paul not only provide rare insight into the apostle's faith; they offer valuable lessons for all concerning the meaning of Christian prayer. When compared with the Lord's Prayer, they provide an index to the way Christ's instruction, "after this manner pray ye" (Mt 6:9), was applied in the early church. After the initial thanksgiving, Paul begins a petition that merges into thanksgiving as the prayer moves into a paean of praise to the exalted Christ.

9,10. Pray. See on 4:2. C. Masson *(L' Epître de Saint Paul aux Colossiens)* suggests that **filled with the knowledge** *(epignōsis)* should be understood as "mature with regard to knowledge." There is probably a subtle contrast here with the knowledge *(gnōsis)* of the Gnosticizing advocates: Paul emphasizes neither an abstract intellectualism nor an occult experience of the 'powers,' but a thorough knowledge *(epignōsis)* of God's will in accordance with wisdom *(sophia;* cf. I Cor 1:24-30) and perception. Although in using these terms the apostle may have been influenced by the vocabulary of his opponents, he turns the meaning of the words against the false teachers. He prays that the Colossians may undergo God's psychiatric therapy, which will transform their world and life view (cf. Rom 12:1,2). A mental transformation is prerequisite to, and the basis for, ethical renewal; in turn, as they are **fruitful in every good work,** their **knowledge of God** will be further augmented.

11. To intensify a concept, the apostle reiterates: **Strengthened** . . . **might** . . . **power.** At work in the Christian is no less than the power of Almighty God himself, not at present to exalt, but to give **patience,** fortitude, and endurance. The Stoic philosophers also enjoined these virtues but, like the traditional poker-faced Indian, coupled them with an attitude of complete detachment. Paul means hopeful waiting and suffering with **joyfulness.** This is the Christian distinctive! Joy not rooted in the soil of suffering is shallow (C. F. D. Moule, *The Epistles of Paul the Apostle to the Colossians and to Philemon).*

12-14. God's power has **made us meet** (AV), that is, *qualified us* (RSV), **to be partakers,** i.e., has empowered us (MM) and made us worthy. **Light** and **darkness** are common theological terms used in many religions, and found most recently in the Dead Sea Scrolls. Here Paul seems to be contrasting the realm or sphere of the new age – **light,** with that of the present age, the evil sphere or authority *(exousia)* of **darkness.** Elsewhere this evil sphere is equated with the power of Satan (cf. 2:15; Lk 22:53; Acts 26:18; Eph 2:2).

These verses, which posit a past deliverance and transference into Christ's **kingdom** and a redemption which Christians **have** as a present possession, are the hallmarks of 'realized eschatology,' i.e., that the new age arrived with Christ's resurrection and that Christians enter it at conversion. The relation of the realized kingdom and the future kingdom has been long debated and variously understood. Are they mutually exclusive concepts representing stages of doctrinal development in the minds of NT writers? Since virtually all strata of the NT literature contain both concepts, this solution appears to be forced. Is the present aspect of the kingdom a partial realization of the future fulfillment? Paul seems to regard Christians to be fully within the sphere of the new age in their corporate status in Christ, which is mediated to individuals by the Holy Spirit; the new-age sphere of being, however, will become fully actualized individually only at the parousia, i.e., Christ's return. (See Introduction.)

In later Gnosticism a distinction was made between forgiveness, as an initial stage, and redemption, as the escape of the soul to immortal realms. Paul here speaks of **redemption** which effects the forgiveness of sins. (See Leon Morris, *The Apostolic Preaching of the Cross*, p. 43.)

C. Christ as Lord. 1:15-19.

The startling aspect of the ascriptions in this passage is their application to a young Jew who was executed as a criminal only thirty years previously. Jesus Christ is pictured in phrases reminiscent of the divine Wisdom in the OT (cf. Prov 8:22-30; Ps 33:6), in inter-Testamental literature, and in similar NT passages (cf. Jn 1:1; I Cor 1:30; Heb 1:1 ff.). Here Jesus not merely mediates the creation but is the goal of the whole created order. The awesomeness of this stark contrast is captured by the one who wrote:

Who is He on yonder tree
 Dies in grief and agony?
'Tis the Lord! O wondrous story!
 'Tis the Lord, the King of Glory!
At His feet we humbly fall;
 Crown Him! Crown Him Lord
 of all!

15-17. Image of God reflects upon the Adam-Christ typology (cf. Gen 1:27; Ps 8; Heb 2:5-18), in which Christ is viewed as the first true man who fulfills God's design in creation. Thus to be in the image of Christ is the goal of all Christians (cf. Rom 8:28; I Cor 11:7; 15:49; II Cor 3:18; 4:4; Col 3:10). The divine Son, however, is the archetype, the effluence of God's glory and not, as other men, its reflection (Heb 1:3). It is because man "bears the image of his creator that it was possible for the Son of God to become incarnate as man and in his humanity to display the glory of the invisible God" (Bruce in *The Epistles to the Ephesians and the Colossians* by E. K. Simpson and F. F. Bruce).

Firstborn (prōtotokos) was interpreted by the Arians to mean "first of a kind," i.e., Christ was the first creature. The word can have this meaning (cf. Rom 8:29); but such a reading is not consistent with Paul's theme, which here stresses a Messianic priority and primacy (cf. Ps 89:27): Christ is 'chief' because **in him** (RSV) – the sphere of his domain or perhaps through his instrumentality—the created order came into being (cf. Jn 1:3; Heb 1:2), and **for him** it exists. Whatever cosmic **powers** there may be, they have nothing to offer or deny a Christian; in Christ he has all things (cf. Rom 8:38; Eph 1:10).

18. The terms **head, beginning, firstborn,** express the pre-eminence of Christ in the new creation, which has its birth in his resurrection (I Cor 15:22; Rev 1:5; 3:14). Although the **head** as *locus* of control of the body was not unknown to first century medical writers, the OT meaning of "chief" or "origin" is the sense of the word here. As the **body** of Christ (not 'body of Christians') the **church** is not merely a 'society' but is defined in terms of its organic communion with Christ (see Introduction).

19. As the present cosmos was created in and through Christ, so also is the new creation. Both are inclusive, in Paul's mind, of far more than mankind (cf. Rom 8:22,23). Yet the **fulness** *(plērōma)* of all dwells in Christ. It has been suggested that *plērōma* means here, as in later Gnostic usage, the totality of cosmic powers who mediate redemption to men; all these, says Paul, in opposition to the Gnostic teaching, belong to and reside in Christ. In view of the use of the Greek word in the LXX and elsewhere in Paul's writings, however, this technical meaning is unlikely. The proper interpretation is indicated in Col 2:9, where *plērōma* can only mean the fullness of the powers and attributes of God. In this book Christ is regarded as containing and representing all that God is. Moreover, **fulness,** as "image" (cf. 1:15), is predicated elsewhere of Christians in view of their final glorified state in Christ (Eph 3:19; 4:12,13; cf. Jn 17:22,23).

D. Christ as God's Reconciler. 1:20-23.

20. In Eph 2:14-18 Paul views the peace effected by Christ's **blood** sacrifice as encompassing and unifying Jew and Gentile. Here it is primarily mankind and **all things** in the cosmos (cf. Isa 11:6-9; Rom 8:19-23) that are in view. The fact that God through Christ will **reconcile** the universe was equated by Origen (on Jn 1:35) with universal redemption. Whether the meaning here is "reconciled to God" or (more probably) "reconciled in Christ," that is, brought into a unity that has its goal in Christ, is not certain (cf. Arndt). But Origen's view scarcely does justice to the Pauline teaching (and that of the NT generally) concerning the judgment of God. The Colossians were reconciled through redemption, but Col 2:15 suggests that other evil beings and powers are 'reconciled' through defeat and destruction (cf. I Cor 15:24-28). For some the cross is "a savour of death unto death" (II Cor 2:16).

22,23. Body of his flesh and **present** have sacrificial connotations (cf. Rom 12:1,2) and accent the believer's identity with Christ in his death. **If ye continue.** Here is the "proof of the pudding." Paul addresses his hearers as Christians but always recognizes 'existential' factors which prevent any complacency even for himself (cf. I Cor 9:27; II Cor 13:5). For the apostle, assurance always had to be present tense. And, while God's election is not vacillating, it can be affirmed only in terms of profession (cf. Rom 10:9), conduct (cf. I Cor 6:9), and the witness of the Spirit (cf. Rom 8:9). **To every creature** *(ktisis)* may be a reference, as the context would admit, to the cosmic scope of the proclamation (cf. II Pet 3:9). If Paul is here speaking of the Roman citizenry, he may be allowed a hyperbole inevitable to a "born" evangelist.

E. Paul: Christ's Minister of Reconciliation. 1:24-29.

24. Earlier Paul prayed that the Colossians might endure with joyfulness (1:11); he now affirms this as his own experience. The striking concept that Paul's **sufferings** *(pathēma)*, borne on behalf of the Colossians, **complete what is lacking** (RSV) in Christ's **afflictions** *(thlipsis)* is not limited to this passage (cf. II Cor 1:5-7; 4:12; 13:4; Phil 3:10; I Pet 4:13; 5:9; Rev 1:9). This idea is to be understood from the standpoint of the Hebrew concept of corporate personality illustrated in Jesus' graphic statement concerning his **church,** "Why persecutest thou *me*?" (Acts 9:4). And some interpret Col 1:24 to mean that in God's purpose the corporate Christ, the Messianic community, is destined to suffer a quota of 'birth pangs' in bringing in the Messianic age. Probably more central is the idea that union with Christ involves *ipso facto* union with Christ's sufferings: "If we suffer with him, we shall be glorified with him" (Rom 8:17). The corporate "in Christ" reality (Gal 2:20) is to be actualized in individual Christians; thus Paul can speak even of his own death as a sacrifice (Phil 2:17; II Tim 4:6). It is to be noted, however, that in this context, as elsewhere, the sole redemptive sufficiency is in Christ and his atonement. Christians share Christ's sufferings because they have been redeemed, not as an aid to their redemption. (Thus, in the imitation of Christ, stressed by Anabaptists, "the crown of thorns stands over the crown of glory." See Robert Friedmann, "Conception of the Anabaptists," *Church History,* IX (1940), 358; cf. Walther von Loewenich, *Luthers Theologia Crucis;* Dietrich Bonhoeffer, *The Cost of Discipleship;* Elisabeth Elliot, *Through Gates of Splendor).*

25-27. Paul's dispensation or assignment in God's redemptive plan was, specifically, to make salvation known to the **Gentiles.** In the world of the first century **mystery** *(mystērion)* meant (1) something mysterious, (2) an initiatory religious rite, (3) a secret known only by divine revelation (Dan 2:28-30,47). The broad Pauline usage falls into the last category (cf. I Cor 15:51; Eph 5:32; II Thess 2:7). But in relation to God's redemptive plan, the mystery is the corporate union with Christ, **Christ in you,** by which God gives righteousness and salvation. In Ephesians (3:6) the focus is upon the inclusion of the Gentiles in the Body, and this aspect of the mystery is not absent here.

28,29. The 'doctor of souls' has a **warning** and **teaching** ministry, not self-centered but patient-centered. Paul's goal was to **present every man perfect** *(teleios)* or mature in Christ, always **striving** but also recognizing that the power is **His who worketh in me** (Phil 2:12,13).

F. Paul's Concern for the Lycus Valley Christians. 2:1-7.

Like *teleios* above, several words here – **mystery, wisdom, knowledge, head** (v. 10), dear to the Gnostics, are turned into effective instruments of Christian truth. This transition section moves from a presentation of Christ's Lordship to an attack upon the insidious doctrines which were endangering that Lordship in the Colossian church.

1-3. The conflict. The picture suggested by the Greek is drawn from an athletic contest. The word primarily describes, as does the verse above, the apostle's spiritual warfare in prayer against principalities and powers (cf. Eph 6:12). Paul did not command fire to come down in judgment (Lk 9:54) but, positively, prayed that the *Colossians* and *Laodiceans,* who apparently were threatened with the same heresy, might be **comforted** (v. 2), i.e., strengthened, through exhortation, by ethical renewal **(love)** and spiritual apprehension **(understanding).** Orthodoxy without love is sterile, and love apart from truth becomes "mush"; but together they issue in spiritual apprehension, knowledge **of the mystery of God.** If there is a secret, Paul says, Christ is it – Christ as the embodiment of God's **wisdom** (Moule, *op. cit.),* Christ as the sole mediator of God's gifts to men (cf. Prov 2:3-9).

4-7. As a member of Christ's body present with them **in the spirit,** Paul now makes clear the purpose of the preceding comments. He fears that **enticing words,** i.e., persuasive reasoning *(pithanologia),* will disrupt their **order** and **stedfastness.** These paired words are military terms conveying the thought of an enemy breeching a formerly solid formation of troops. The errorists' appeal to philosophy and wisdom (cf. 2:8,23), is an approach not entirely unknown in the present day. Paul did not answer false reasoning with obscurantism nor with a command to believers to shut their ears, but with a reasoned appeal to them to return to that positive Christ-centered tradition through which they had **received** the Gospel (cf. 2:8). From this starting point the emptiness of the Gnostic reasoning would become apparent to them.

III. Christ's Lordship and the False Teaching at Colosse. 2:8–3:4.

A. The Sole Sufficiency of Christ. 2:8-15.

The apostle begins his argument with a reassertion of the uniqueness of Christ and of the believer's relation to Him. As the head and conqueror of every authority and as the very sphere of the Christian's new-age existence, Christ's place in the Christian life is all-inclusive, and it is exclusive of all others.

8. The Colossian heresy was a "philosophy" **after the tradition** *(paradosis)* **of men** and **rudiments** of the cosmos (cf. 2:20). Paul does not condemn tradition in itself but rather contrasts with this heresy the tradition **after Christ,** which the Colossians had received (2:7). There is then a proper tradition – to which the apostle elsewhere expresses indebtedness (e.g., Rom 6:17; I Cor 11:2,23; 15:3; Phil 4:9) – the essence of which lies in its apostolicity (see on Col 1:1). Apostolic tradition has the status of revelation, for in it the exalted Christ himself speaks through his authorized representatives (cf. Oscar Cullmann, "Tradition," *The Early Church,* pp. 59-99).

9,10. The Greek word for **Godhead** or *deity* is the abstract noun for God (Arndt) and includes not only the divine attributes but also the divine nature (Beng). Opposing the Docetic idea that matter is evil is the Biblical assertion that deity itself has been manifest in **bodily** *(sōmatikōs)* or material reality (Lightfoot; cf. Jn 1:14). Others (e.g., Moule) interpret *sōmatikōs* to mean: (1) one organism of Christ in contrast to the multitudinous *plērōma* of cosmic powers; or, less probably, (2) the Body of Christ, i.e., the Church. The fullness *(plērōma;* cf. note on 1:19) that inheres in Christ infuses those in union with him so as to **complete (peplērōmenoi)** them or bring them to fullness (cf. Eph 1:23). Union with Christ alone is sufficient, for he is **head** of all other authorities; they can add nothing to holiness or to redemption.

11,12. In the NT **made without hands** is a quasi-technical term used of corporate new-age realities in contrast to the institutions and rituals of the old covenant. It refers most often to the Church as God's true temple brought into being in Christ's death and resurrection (Mk 14:58; Jn 2:19-22; Acts 7:48; II Cor 5:1; Heb 9:11, 24). Here it identifies Christ's death and resurrection as the true **circumcision** (cf. Phil 3:3), in which Christians, as Christ's Body, participated. Both concepts are, for Paul, expressions of the corporate reality implicit in the Christian's **faith** – union with the Saviour's death and resurrection. (see Introduction). **Putting off the body of flesh** (RSV). See on 2:15. **Baptism** may refer primarily to Christ's baptism of death (cf. Mk 10:38; Lk 12:50), although Christian baptism is not to be excluded (cf. Rom 6:4). There is no direct analogy between Christian baptism and the 'old age' rite of circumcision. Circumcision here is the death of Christ, by which he wrought severance from the old age, cleansing of sin, and reconciliation to God (cf. Deut 30:6; Jer 4:4; 9:25,26). It is to this that Christian baptism is to be related.

13. For the Gentiles the figure of Christ's death as circumcision had particular significance: their former alienation from the people of God was symbolized in their literal **uncircumcision** (cf. Eph 2:11). However, the use here of **flesh,** i.e., man under sin, to indicate a moral uncircumcision is possible. Resurrection, viewed as a corporate action **together with Christ,** finds its realization through God's gracious forgiveness (cf. Eph 2:1-10).

14. A **handwriting** is a certificate of debt (Deiss, BS, p. 247) and presumably refers to the written Mosaic law. For Gentiles it may include also the law to which their consciences assent (cf. Rom 2:14,15; Ex 24:3; Eph 2:15). This obligation which, unfulfilled, stood **against us** was discharged on **his cross.**

15. Spoiled, or better, *stripped (apekdyomai)* is a compound not essentially different from another Pauline expression, *ekdyō*. The latter, as used in the LXX (and classical Greek) of the defeating or "stripping" of enemies in war, provides a clue to the meaning here.

In OT times captives were stripped of most or all clothing. This action came to symbolize defeat, and for the prophets it signified the judgment of God (cf. Ezk 16:39; 23:26). In the NT this idea moves into the realm of 'last things,' when the righteous will be clothed, in contrast to the wicked, who will stand stripped and naked under God's judgment (cf. Mt 22:11; Rev 3:17,18; 16:15; II Cor 5:3,4). The present verse, picturing Christ as "stripping" **principalities and powers** through his death and resurrection, probably refers, on one hand, to angelic powers (through whom the **handwriting of ordinances** had been given, Gal 3:19) who control human rulers, and on the other hand, to such personified evils as death. Christ died, "that through death he might destroy him that had the power of death, that is, the devil, and deliver them who through fear of death were all their lifetime subject to bondage" (Heb 2:14,15). For the individual, death remains to be destroyed (I Cor 15:25,26); "in Christ" its destruction occurred when, in his triumphant ascension, the Saviour led captive this and all other powers (Eph 4:8). Similarly, stripping or **putting off** *(apekdyomai)* **the body of flesh** (Col 2:11, RSV) may refer to the corporate judgment on the cross of the Adamic **body of flesh,** i.e., the whole man under sin, under judgment, under death. If so, this phrase stands in contrast to the 'body of Christ' (cf. I Cor 15:22; Robinson, *The Body,* p. 31). God's gracious forgiveness (Col 2:13) is to be understood in the light of the meaning of the cross: in it man's debt is cancelled and the powers holding man captive are themselves **openly** defeated and made captive. Realizing this, the absurdity of turning, as an aid to redemption, from the triumphant Christ to the subjected powers becomes apparent.

B. The Colossians' Practices as a Denial of Christ's Lordship. 2:16–3:4.

16,17. Therefore. Paul pounds the table and drives home the conclusions following from his argument. The objectionable observances, which evidently had been imposed by the false teachers, not only flew in the face of Christian freedom (cf. Rom 14; Gal 5) but, as among the Galatians (3:1-12; 4:9,10), threatened to draw them from Christ back into the **shadow** of the former age (cf. Heb 10:1-10). Paul points out that shadowy symbolisms and prohibitions have faded before Christ, the daylight reality. To impose such laws (today we call them by different names) on others as tests of spiritual maturity are most evident signs of Christian immaturity and error. **Body** is usually interpreted as "reality" or "substance," in contrast to the OT 'type' (Lightfoot), but **body of Christ** should not be limited to this. " 'Substance,' 'Church' and 'final perfect sacrifice' may all be ideas which would have crowded into the writer's mind . . ." (Moule).

18,19 The description reflects an athletic contest in which the contestant is disqualified (RSV) or deprived of **reward** because of some impediment (cf. I Cor 9:24; Gal 5:7; Phil 3:14; II Tim 4:7). The false teachers either (1) hindered the Colossians in their Christian race or (2) intimidated them by declaring them disqualified if they did not follow the prescribed course. **Humility,** which in Col

3:12 is a virtue, is here condemned because of the object toward which this submissive attitude and activity is directed. Worship of *the* **angels** *(tōn aggelōn)*. Whatever the mediatorial function of angels in the old age (cf. Gal 3:19), it is now obviated by the indwelling Christ. For Paul, angels may still have had a ministerial function (I Cor 11:10; cf. Mt 18:10; Heb 1:14; II Pet 2:11; Jude 8,9), but the heretical teaching seems to have gone beyond OT and Jewish reverence for angels – even beyond more extravagant rabbinic speculations – to an activity of worship which, like the devotion of present-day Roman Catholics to the Virgin Mary, displaced the centrality of Christ Ernst Percy *(Die Probleme der Kolosser und Epheserbriefe,* pp. 168,169), pointing to the virtual identity of **worshipping of angels** with **humility** (cf. Col 2:23), views Paul as saying: "Your legalistic practices amount to a worship of angels." But something more than this is involved (cf. Bruce).

The basis of the error is the egoistic or **fleshly mind** (see on 2:15) that spends its time elucidating **visions** (RSV) **which he hath seen** (ASV). (A difficult clause. See Bruce, Moule.) Such a mind fails to hold to Christ, the **Head,** from whom the **body,** i.e., the Church, is nourished in true and godly growth. In contrast to the earlier use, **Head** here reflects not *authority* so much as the *origin* or *source* of the Church's health and life.

C. The Colossians' Practices as a Contradiction of Their Corporate Life in Christ. 2:20–3:4.

20-22. The **rudiments** *(stoicheia)* or *elemental spirits* (RSV) are identified (1) with demonic powers to whom have been delegated authority in the cosmos and, therefore, over men (cf. 2:15), or (2) with angelic powers generally who mediated the law and exercised in the old age a certain suzerainty over men. [The reader is referred to the careful discussion in E. D. Burton, *Galatians,* pp. 510-518. Ed.] A few commentators (e.g., Moule) translate the phrase *elemental teaching,* i.e., a Jewish or pagan ritualism that stands over against the freedom of the spirit. On Calvary the Christian died **with Christ** to the old age, and so he must not live as though the **world** *(kosmos)* or its **ordinances** still had a claim upon him (cf. Rom 6). To submit to things which **perish** is to admit that one belongs to the perishing old age, the mortal Adamic race (cf. I Cor 15:45-50); and it is a denial of the new-age life into which, in Christ's risen body, the Christian has been incorporated.

23. Perfection of Christian character through rules is the doctrine of men (cf. Col 2:8). Although observing taboos gives a man a reputation for spiritual **wisdom** and sacrificial **humility,** such taboos in actual practice "do honor, not to God, but to man's own pride" (Phillips' trans.). Phillips, probably correctly, understands **flesh** as "the old man," man in his sinful rebellion, and not merely as a sensual term (cf. 2:18). In contrast, *severity to* (ASV) the **body,** is to be understood literally of ascetic practices.

3:1–3. The Christian has not only died but also **risen with Christ.** In his true existence he resides "in heavenly places." (Eph 2:6). The old age still manifests itself in the individual Christian – he sins, gets sick, dies; the new age remains **hid,** realized only in the body of the Saviour. Nevertheless, in A.D. 30 his old-age existence died, crucified with Christ (cf. II Cor 5:14; Gal 2:20). This demands that the Christian **seek** (in the set of his will) and direct his **affection** *(phroneite,* in the set of his mind) to the new-age reality **above** (cf. Rom 12:1,2). "Above" and "below" (or **on the earth**) in the writings of Paul and John do not primarily indicate spatial contrasts, although this mode of expression naturally is involved in reference to Christ and to heaven. The terms express a crucial contrast in the temporal relationship – the old age and the new age. In A.D. 30 the new age burst into history in Christ's resurrection. But Christ, in whom the new age presently inheres, is above, whereas the world continues in the death grip of the old age. Christians at present exist "above," that is, in the new age, only "in Christ" and through the indwelling Holy Spirit. But their corporate existence in Christ is no less a reality than their individual existence. A Christian's citizenship is in the "Jerusalem which is above" (Gal 4:26), and this demands a continuing transformation of his mind and will to that reality. Conformation to the ritual, the ceremony, the mediatorial 'powers' of the old age is a denial of one's corporate resurrected life with Christ.

4. In the sense in which **Christ is our life,** a Christian even now 'realizes' the consummation of his union with Christ. But in the *parousia,* i.e., when Christ comes again, the Christian will be **with him** not merely in a corporate sense but in individually fulfilled **glory** (cf. Rom 8:18; II Cor 3:18). This is the 'futurist' aspect of Paul's eschatological teaching. **Appear** *(phaneroō),* although not as common as *parousia,* is used in a number of passages to denote Christ's second advent (II Thess 2:8; II Cor 5:10; I Tim 6:14; II Tim 4:1,8; cf. I Pet 5:4; I Jn 2:28; 3:2).

IV. Christ's Lordship in the Christian Life. 3:5–4:6.

In the Pauline pattern (cf. Rom 12:1; Eph 4:1), a transition from the doctrinal indicative mode to the ethical imperative now occurs. There is, of course, no absolute dichotomy in the doctrine-ethics sequence. If Paul is saying anything by this literary form, it is that doctrine is the basis for ethics: What a man believes does determine in substantial measure how he acts.

A. The Christian Imperative: Actualize Individually the 'in Christ' Reality. 3:5-17.

5. Members . . . upon the earth probably refers not to literal bodily organs being used immorally (Moule; cf. I Cor 6:15) but to bodily attitudes and actions as expressive of "the old man" (Bruce; cf. Rom 7:23; 8:13). Thus included (as much as **fornication**) is the sin of **covetousness:** acquisitive desire or self-seeking. Perhaps most needed in modern materialistic American Christendom is a vow to own nothing and a prayer to be delivered from things and from ambition. (The thought is A. W. Tozer's.) To call covetousness **idolatry** is not too strong if we realize that, when we (strongly desire to) *own* a thing, it actually owns a part of us.

6. Wrath *(orgē*; cf. TWNT, V, esp. pp. 419-448) is often associated with anger *(thymos),* occasionally when attributed to God (Rom 2:8; cf. Rev 16:19; 19:15). For man, wrath is not absolutely forbidden, as it was in the Stoic doctrine of *apatheia* (see Eph 4:26; cf. I Cor 14:20; Jn 2:13-17; Jas 1:19,20). Nevertheless, Paul does describe it as characteristic of the "old man" (Eph 4:31; Col 3:8; cf. Rom 12:19).

The concept of God's wrath is not a leftover from a primitive OT ideology. God's wrath is the basis for the fear of God (Heb 10:31; Jas 4:12; Mt 10:28); and it is to be understood not as a momentary emotion but as a settled disposition, a principle of retribution (Rom 1:18; 3:5; 9:22; cf. Jn 3:36; Heb 3:11), not unlike that of an earthly ruler (Rom 13:4,5; cf. Heb 11:27). It is often associated with the day of judgment (Rom 2:5; I Thess 1:10). Far from negating God's love, his wrath confirms it. For without justice mercy loses its meaning. (Cf. R. V. G. Tasker, *The Biblical Doctrine of the Wrath of God.)*

7,8. Cf. 2:6. **Out of your mouth** may refer to all of the sins listed. Expressed sin is contagious, and the control of sin's expression is a long step toward deliverance from it.

9,10. Put off *(apekdysamenoi),* referring to the point of conversion, conveys the ideas of divesting, as of a garment, and of passing judgment upon the old man, i.e., by identification with Christ in his death (see on 2:15). *Neon* **(new)** or, as elsewhere, *kainos* (e.g., Eph 4:24) is interpreted by the following **being renewed** (RSV). That is, the corporate "in Christ" existence is increasingly actualized in the individual Christian (cf. II Cor 3:18; see Introduction). Thus the image of God, which the first Adam failed to realize, is to be fulfilled in the sons of the second Adam (cf. Gen 1:26; Heb 2:5 ff.; Rom 8:29; I Cor 15:45 ff.). This means that believers not merely **put on** new attributes, but are undergoing a psychological transformation which, at Christ's *parousia,* i.e., his second coming, will be seen in its radical and comprehensive character (Rom 12:2; I Cor 15:53). Christians, as the second century Epistle to Diognetus expresses it, belong to a 'new race.' **Knowledge.** See on 1:9.

11. Scythian. The lowest type of barbarian slave. In Christ all distinctions are transcended; at the foot of the cross the ground is level. It is not, however, the leveling of the modern socialist ethic, which may only produce Djilas' 'new class.' It is not a uniformity of status in the present world order, but a change in attitude by which the stigma of being different is loved away. It is "a unity in diversity, a unity which *transcends* differences and works within them, but never a unity which *ignores* or *denies* differences or necessarily seeks to erase them" (E. E. Ellis, "Segregation and the Kingdom of God," *Christianity Today,* I, 12. March 18, 1957, p. 8). Thus the apostle, who declared that in Christ there is "no male or female," "no Jew or Greek," at the same time instructed women to be silent in the churches and observed Jewish rites which he forbade to Gentiles (Gal 3:28; I Cor 11:3 ff.; 14:34; Acts 16:3; 18:18; Rom 14; Gal 5:2,3). See on 3:18ff.

12-14. To the Church, the true Israel, belong the titles given to OT Israel: **elect, holy, beloved** (cf. Rom 2:29; 9:6; Gal 3:29; 6:16; Phil 3:3). The virtues listed here, which emphasize the relations of Christians in a situation fraught with friction, reflect the character of **Christ,** whose example is cited (cf. II Cor 8:9; Mt 6:12). The virtue which sums up, gives meaning to, and cements the rest is **love** (Rom 13:9,10).

15,16. The **peace of Christ** (RSV). That peace which Christ mediates to those in union with him (cf. Jn 14:27; Rom 5:1). It is to **rule** in the sense of arbitrating differences that arise in the **body** (Bruce). Similarly, the indwelling **word of Christ,** i.e., his teaching, exercises a transforming influence on a believer's life.

It has been the testimony of Christians from earliest times that "Christ put a song in my heart." And it is no exaggeration to say that **songs** have taught more theology to new converts than textbooks. In the Pauline church oracular utterance sometimes occurred in hymn form (I Cor 14:15), and a number of NT passages may reflect a hymn origin (cf. Phil 2:5-11; Eph 5:14; E. G. Selwyn, *The First Epistle of Peter,* p. 273ff.). **Grace.** The grace of God (Lightfoot) or the grateful attitude of the Christian (Moule).

17. To live **in the name of the Lord Jesus** obviates the necessity for rules; inward motivation replaces external norms. Thus Christ's Lordship of the whole of life is expressed. His Lordship implies not only a mode of conduct but an attitude toward life: in conscious reflection upon the will of Christ, one's actions become an act of thanksgiving to Christ. External rules, even when good, are not adequate for every situation; the 'rule' of the indwelling Christ is the only sufficient guide (cf. I Cor 10:31; Gal 5:18).

B. Special Precepts. 3:18–4:6.

The present section illustrates how the principles of 'life in Christ' may be expressed in everyday affairs. One sees here not only how a Christian household functioned but also what early Christian society was like. The earliest church included persons of wealth as well as the more numerous poor, masters as well as slaves (3:18–4:1). Besides pointing out the nature of the Christian home, Paul pays particular attention to the central importance of prayer (4:2-4) and the relation of Christian to non-Christian (4:4-6).

The conduct of the household was a much discussed subject in both Jewish and pagan writers (e.g., the apocryphal Ecclesiasticus, 30:1-13; 42:5ff.). And it appears to have been a regular item in the Pauline teaching (cf. Eph 5:22-33; I Tim 6:1-8; Tit 2:1-10). In contrast to Jewish and pagan teaching, Paul emphasizes the mutuality of rights and responsibilities. A second Christian distinctive is the motivation urged upon the reader. Since unity in Christ does not negate the diversity of function and status in the world (see on Col 3:11), the Christian, as much as the pagan, should have concern for proper social order and custom. The Christian, however, is motivated by his relationship to Christ and his responsibility to God (e.g., 3:18, 20, 22-25).

18,19. The wives' submission is to be reciprocated in the husbands' **love.** As Eph 5:28 makes explicit, **love** here denotes not mere affection but an outgoing concern for the wife's whole person.

20,21. All things. The child is even to gain his understanding of God's will through his parents' counsel. In a Christian family it is not proper to suggest a conflict between duty to parents and duty to God (T. K. Abbott, *The Epistles to the Ephesians and to the Colossians). Pleasing in the Lord* (ASV) probably refers to obedience as motivated by love for Christ; it does not limit the child's responsibility to Christian parents. Although in an extreme case a young person may have to choose Christ's will in opposition to that of non-Christian parents (cf. Lk 14:26), this course should be taken only after sober thought and Christian counseling. "Don't overcorrect your children" (Phillips). The purpose of discipline is to develop a Christian man, not to produce a hangdog. "Don't," here, as much as in Christian ethics generally (cf. Col 2:21), must be subordinated to a positive "discipline and instruction of the Lord" (Eph 6:4, RSV).

22,23. Servants – today, employees – are to work not only when the boss is watching, and with the motivation his watching supplies, but to work with **singleness of heart,** i.e., in honest dedication. All service, for the Christian, is primarily **to the Lord,** who judges in all fairness and justice.

24. The faithful 'slave' of Christ receives a son's portion – the **inheritance. Reward** *(exact requital,* Lightfoot) is not, as critics use the term, "pie in the sky by and by." Rather, it is the ice cream reserved for the little girl who, rushing into her father's arms, cries, "See, Daddy, I cleaned up my playroom like you told me to." The real reward is the father's approval; the ice cream is mere trimming – but quite proper trimming. The prayer-song which requests that we "may feast in paradise with thee," is unspiritual only to a Platonist. But motivation is necessary; mercenary-mindedness excludes one from true Christian reward (cf. Acts 8:18 ff.).

25. Receive. That is, get back, whether in the present life or at the day of judgment. God is here viewed as the guarantor of justice (cf. Rom 12:19; II Cor 5:10. On 'just desert' as a proper measuring stick in criminal punishment, compare C. S. Lewis, "The Humanitarian Theory of Punishment," *Res Judicate,* VI, 1953-54, 224-230. Also see commentary on Col 3:6). **No respect of persons** refers to both slave and master, and provides a transition to the next section (cf. Eph 6:9; Lev 19:15).

4:1. The admonition brings to mind the teaching of the Sermon on the Mount: "Forgive us our debts as we forgive our debtors"; "With what judgment ye judge ye shall be judged" (Mt 6:12; 7:2. See on Col 3:11).

2-4. Christian **prayer** *(proseuchē;* cf. Trench) should be characterized by a spirit of thankfulness (see on 1:11). **And watch** *(grēgoreō,* "watchful") adds the thought of awareness or alertness (cf. Mk 14:37,38). Christian prayer is to be marked not by ceremonial stupor nor intoxicating verbosity, but by concern and sobriety (cf. I Pet 5:8). **Watch** *(grēgoreō)* is used frequently with reference to the Christian's attitude toward Christ's return (e.g., Mk 13:33ff.; I Thess 5:6; Rev 16:15). **Door of utterance.** An opportunity or, more probably, an ability to declare the **mystery** clearly (cf. 1:26; Eph 6:19,20).

5,6. Wisdom includes not only the apprehension of and ability to communicate the mystery (1:9) but also the knowledge of how to communicate it successfully. Only thus will the redemptive purpose of this **time,** which God has designated "the opportune season" *(kairos;* cf. O. Cullmann, *Christ and Time,* p. 39 ff., 225), be used effectively. An offensive or insipid manner is not likely to accomplish much. Therefore, in life and **speech** the Christian witness should be appetizing – not to other Christians but to non-Christians.

V. Conclusion. 4:7-18.

A. Commendation of the Bearers of the Letter. 4:7-9.

The bearers of the letter, **Tychicus** and **Onesimus,** would convey information not contained in it and doubtless would interpret it to the recipients, answering any questions they might have. Onesimus, subject of the Philemon correspondence, has been suggested as the collector of the Pauline corpus of letters (cf. John Knox, *Philemon Among the Letters of Paul,* p. 98ff.). Paul's commendation of him here served to ease the return of this runaway slave and to remind the readers that he was now a brother in Christ.

B. Greetings from Paul's Co-Workers. 4:10-14.

Epaphras. See on 1:7. Of the other companions, **Mark** (ASV) and **Aristarchus** are known from Acts (15:36-39; 19:29; 20:4; 27:2). The former, after his lapse on Paul's first mission (Acts 15:36-39), was now restored to the apostle's favor. In spite of the doubts of F. C. Grant *(The Earliest Gospel,* pp. 52,53), Mark is almost certainly to be identified with the companion of Peter (I Pet 5:13) and the author of the Second Gospel. Luke, then, has a personal, as well as a literary, relation to Mark. Since Luke is not included among those of the **circumcision,** it is usually inferred that he was a Gentile–the only NT writer so identified. His identity as a **physician** finds confirmation in the vocabulary of Luke-Acts. **Demas.** Cf. II Tim 4:10,11.

C. The Apostle's Greetings and Blessings. 4:15-18.

15. The '**house**-church' was widespread, both in the Pauline congregations and in general (Acts 12:12; 16:15,40; Rom 16:5,23; I Cor 16:19; Phm 2).

16. Paul's 'Letter to the Laodiceans' has been the subject of much speculation. In the second century an apocryphal epistle was composed to fill the gap; in recent times the letter has been identified with Ephesians (e.g., Lightfoot; so Marcion, A.D. 140) or Philemon (e.g., Goodspeed).

17. The personal note to **Archippus,** who may have been the son of Philemon (Phm 2), is reminiscent of the apostle's charge to Timothy (II Tim 1:6). **In the Lord** identifies Archippus' *ministry* as a 'spiritual gift' rather than merely an organizational function (cf. Rom 12:6-8; I Cor 12:5; Eph 4:12). The concern that Paul voices is ever present in the life of the church: the danger is not a lack of spiritual gifts but spiritual gifts which because of personal sin, organizational pressures, or non-spiritual influences are smothered, warped, and unfulfilled.

18. After dictating the letter, Paul confirmed its genuineness, as was his custom (cf. I Cor 16:21; Gal 6:11; II Thess 3:17; Phm 19), with a greeting in his own hand (cf. Deiss, LAE, pp. 171,172). Referring to his **bonds,** Paul reminds his readers that "he who is suffering on behalf of Christ has a right to speak on behalf of Christ" (Lightfoot). On this moving note the apostle closes his letter.

BIBLIOGRAPHY

ABBOTT, T. K. *The Epistles to the Ephesians and to the Colossians.* Edinburgh: T. & T. Clark, n.d.

DIBELIUS, M. *An die Kolosser, Epheser, und Philemon.* Tuebingen: Mohr, 1953.

HANSON, S. *The Unity of the Church in the New Testament: Colossians and Ephesians.* Uppsala: Almquist & Wiksells, 1946.

LIGHTFOOT, J. B. *St. Paul's Epistles to the Colossians and to Philemon.* London: Macmillan, 1886.

MASSON, C. *L'Epître de Saint Paul aux Colossiens.* Paris: Delachaux et Niestle, 1950.

MOULE, C. F. D. *The Epistles of Paul the Apostle to the Colossians and to Philemon.* Cambridge: The University Press, 1957.

ROBINSON, J. A. T. *The Body.* London: SCM Press, 1952.

SIMPSON, E. K. and BRUCE, F. F. *The Epistles to the Ephesians and the Colossians.* Grand Rapids: Eerdmans Publishing Co., 1957.

THE FIRST EPISTLE TO THE THESSALONIANS

INTRODUCTION

Occasion of the Writing. The church at Thessalonica was a fruit of Paul's second missionary journey (Acts 17:1-9). Miraculously released from imprisonment at Philippi, Paul and his companions, Silas and Timothy, trekked southward and then westward along the great Roman highway to the Macedonian capital and commercial center, Thessalonica. There, in spite of dogged opposition, they founded the second European church. Harassed by the Jews in Thessalonica and Berea (Acts 17:10-15), Paul fled to Athens, where concern for the spiritual welfare of the Thessalonian believers prompted him, at some personal sacrifice, to dispatch Timothy to buttress the church against the waves of persecution (I Thess 3:1-3). Timothy rejoined Paul at Corinth with the welcome report that the Gospel seed had fallen on good soil. Paul then penned I Thessalonians to commend his faithful brethren for their stalwart dedication to Christ and to one another and to encourage them to further progress in love and holiness.

Date and Place of Writing. Thanks to Luke's penchant for historical details, the dates of these letters may be fixed with reasonable certainty. Luke's reference to Gallio, proconsul of Achaia, in connection with Paul's sojourn at Corinth (Acts 18:12) has been illuminated by the discovery at Delphi of an inscription which dates Gallio's proconsulship within the reign of the emperor Claudius. The inscription seems to indicate that Gallio assumed office in the summer of A.D. 51. Since Luke apparently suggests that Paul had stayed in Corinth about eighteen months before Gallio came to power (Acts 18:11), the apostle probably arrived in Corinth early in A.D. 50. Not long after this, Silas and Timothy returned from Macedonia with the report which issued in Paul's writing I Thessalonians (Acts 18:5; I Thess 3:1-6) probably about the middle of A.D. 50. A few months later II Thessalonians followed, in response to reports that certain problems were not yet solved.

Development of the Thought. The first three chapters are personal and reflective. Paul recalls the warm reception the Macedonian believers gave the Gospel and reminds them of the difficult circumstances in which he brought the word of God to them. His vital concern was evidenced by his willingness to part with his needed companion, Timothy, in order to strengthen the oppressed church.

Timothy's positive report lifted the apostle's burden and evoked from him a series of practical exhortations. Aware of the temptations that stalked believers in a pagan culture, the apostle warns them about the menace of sexual impurity and the dangers of strife and factiousness.

Paul's teaching on the return of Christ while at Thessalonica had spawned two special problems: lack of industry in view of Christ's imminent coming and a fear that dead believers would be robbed of the rights of participation in the glories of that grand event. With characteristic directness Paul meets these problems with admonitions to diligence and with a dramatic description of the roles of living and dead saints in Christ's coming. The book concludes (ch. 5) with a challenge to alertness and with some practical advice concerning Christian attitudes and spiritual gifts.

Importance. The early date of these epistles allows us to get a glimpse of the uncomplicated structure of the primitive church. There was no complex organization; the glue that held the believers together was a common faith, love, and hope. An unofficial leadership had arisen within the church, yet the Christians were desperately dependent upon the apostolic circle. In few New Testament writings is there found more forceful testimony to the power of the Gospel, which turned the pagans to God from idols, kept their love warm in the midst of strife, and anchored them in hope in spite of relentless onslaughts of persecution.

In these letters Paul lays bare not so much his subject as his soul. Here the beat of the apostle's warm heart is audible. He compares himself to a gentle nurse (I Thess 2:7), a firm father (2:11), and a homeless orphan (in the Greek of 2:17). He shows himself ready to spend and be spent for the spreading of the Gospel. It is Paul, the *man*, who confronts us, gentle in his strength, loving in his exhortations, dauntless in his courage, guileless in his motives – a man (as Carl Sandburg said of Abraham Lincoln) "of steel and velvet, hard as rock and soft as drifting fog."

The eschatological teachings in these letters enhance their importance. Nowhere else does the apostle deal at such length with the sequence of events at Christ's second coming and the role of dead believers in that advent. Furthermore, only in II Thessalonians 2 does Paul allude to the paragon of evil who will set himself up as God at the end of history – the Antichrist.

OUTLINE

I. Introduction. 1:1.
  A. Author.
  B. Recipients.
  C. Blessing.
II. Personal reflections. 1:2–3-13.
  A. Paul's commendation of the church. 1:2-10.
    1. For their reception of the Gospel. 1:2-5 a.
    2. For their testimony to the world. 1:5 b-10.
  B. Paul's founding of the church. 2:1-16.
    1. Purity of the apostle's motives. 2:1-6.
    2. Extent of the apostle's sacrifice. 2:7,8.
    3. Integrity of the apostle's conduct. 2:9-12.
    4. Reliability of the apostle's message. 2:13.
    5. Result of the apostle's message: persecution. 2:14-16.
  C. Timothy's strengthening of the church. 2:17–3:13.
    1. Paul's concern. 2:17–3:5.
    2. Timothy's welcome report. 3:6-10.
    3. Paul's prayer. 3:11-13.
III. Practical exhortations. 4:1–5:22.
  A. Abstain from immorality. 4:1-8.
  B. Love one another. 4:9,10.
  C. Mind your own affairs. 4:11,12.
  D. Comfort one another with the hope of the Second Coming. 4:13-18.
  E. Live as children of the day. 5:1-11.
  F. Abstain from evil; embrace the good. 5:12-22.
    1. In relation to others. 5:12-15.
    2. In basic attitudes. 5:16-22.
IV. Conclusion. 5:23-28.
  A. Closing prayer. 5:23,24.
  B. Request for prayer. 5:25.
  C. A final salute. 5:26.
  D. Command to read the letter. 5:27.
  E. Benediction. 5:28.

COMMENTARY

I. Introduction. 1:1.

A. Author. **Paul** did not need to defend his apostleship, so firm was his friendship with the Macedonian churches. **Silvanus** (Silas), who had replaced Barnabas on the second missionary journey (Acts 15: 39,40), and **Timothy,** who had joined the company at Lystra (Acts 16:1-3), are mentioned because they were partners in the founding of the church (Acts 17:1-9) and were at Corinth at the time of composition of the epistle. Timothy, though subordinate to the others, was probably especially dear to the Thessalonians because of his mission (I Thess 3:1-10). The mention of Paul's associates serves more to buttress the apostle's authority than to divide it.

B. Recipients. The mode of address, **unto the church,** etc., is unparalleled (though cf. Gal 1:2). The emphasis seems to be on the local assembly rather than on the universal church as it is found in any particular place. **In God the Father** shows the new relationship between the believers and God.

C. Blessing. Paul's characteristic greeting, **grace and peace,** combines Greek and Hebrew salutations enriched with theological significance. God's act of unmerited favor in Christ (**grace**) brings in its wake complete spiritual welfare (**peace**).

II. Personal Reflections. 1:2–3:13.

A. Paul's Commendation of the Church. 1:2-10. The rehearsal of the Thessalonians' reception of the Gospel evokes the apostle's thankful prayer. The Spirit who attested God's election by his convicting power also enabled the Thessalonians to face affliction with such steadfastness and joy that reports of their dynamic conversion, stalwart service, and vibrant hope had sped throughout the Mediterranean area.

1) For Their Reception of the Gospel. 1:2-5a. **2. We give thanks. We** is probably editorial, referring to Paul alone, as in 3:1. **Always.** Whenever he prayed, he thanked God for **all** of them. There was no disloyal group for which he could not give thanks.

3. Without ceasing probably belongs with **making mention** in 1:2. Here, as in 5:17, the word *adialeiptōs* means "without let up." In a non-Biblical papyrus it describes the annoying persistence of a cough. The first reason for Paul's constant thanksgiving is his recollection of the faith, love, and hope of the Thessalonians. This is Paul's first mention of these three graces (cf. 5:8; Rom 5:2-5; and especially I Cor 13:13). The order is logical and chronological: **faith** relates to the past; **love** to the present; **hope** to the future. **Work of faith** – faith has produced good works; **labor of love**–love has led them to fatiguing toil for one another; **patience of hope** – hope in Christ's second coming undauntedly endures in persecution. **In the sight of God** should possibly be limited to the final phrase, **patience of hope,** but may also refer to the other achievements of the church, which was aware of and sensitive to God's presence (cf. 2:19; 3:9,13).

4. A second reason for thanksgiving is the apostle's assurance of the Thessalonians' **election.** Paul's oneness with this Gentile church is shown by the frequent appearance of the word **brethren.** Election stems from God's love (cf. Eph 1:4,5). The believers are called **beloved of God,** the phrase **of God belonging with beloved** rather than with **election,** as in the AV. Note the OT background: Gentiles have joined Israel as objects of God's elective love. **5a.** Proof of their election was the fact that the Spirit drove the Gospel home to their hearts. **Our gospel** reveals Paul's personal commitment to his message. Not mere words, it carries its own divinely supplied **power** (cf. Rom 1:16; I Cor 2:4). Preached by men, it is ratified by the Holy Spirit. This divine unction caused the Gospel to be received **in much assurance,** i.e., with full certainty that it was the word of God.

2) For Their Testimony to the World. 1:5b-10. **5 b. What manner of men.** The apostles practiced what they preached. The Holy Spirit had changed their lives; their lives reinforced their message. **6. Followers.** *Imitators.* Responding to the Gospel in spite of **much affliction,** the new believers followed in the train of the apostles and their Master. Affliction cannot dampen the true joy of the Spirit (Jn 16:33; Acts 16:23-25; Gal 5:22; Heb 12:2; I Pet 2:19-21). **Affliction.** *Tribulation,* the relentless pressure to which a believer may be exposed in a world opposed to Christ.

7. Accordingly, this church became an **ensample** (singular is preferable to plural) a *pattern* or *model* for the believers in **Macedonia** and **Achaia,** the northern and southern provinces, standing for all of Greece. **8. Sounded out.** Like a trumpet or a clap of thunder. **Word of the Lord** has an OT prophetic ring and points to the divine authority behind the message. **In every place.** Probably hyperbole, but the strategic location of Thessalonica enabled the report to spread far and wide, and speedily. Possibly Priscilla and Aquila brought this news from Rome to Corinth (Acts 18:2). **Your faith,** i.e., the report of your faith. This sentence should have ended after **every place,** but Paul rushes on to underscore his statement. He delighted to spread the report, for the Thessalonians were his joy (2:19). But wherever he went, the news had preceded him.

9. They themselves. Probably people in general, wherever Paul went. **What manner of entering in.** Both the welcome reception accorded the apostles and the success of their mission. **Turned to God from idols** indicates the thoroughness of their conversion and the predominantly Gentile nature of the church. **To serve,** in complete subjection like slaves, the

living (not lifeless idols) **and true God** (not false gods, who were shams).

10. To wait *(anamenein)* implies patient, confident waiting for the expected coming. **His son.** The only direct reference to Christ's sonship in I and II Thessalonians, which stress rather his Lordship. The Resurrection was the prelude to Christ's return, and the guarantee of God's power to rescue those who are his and judge those who are not (Acts 17:31). **Delivered** should be present tense, the participle *(ruomenon)* being timeless here —*rescuing*. **Wrath.** God's wrath as in I Thess 2:16, and Rom 3:5; 5:9; 9:22; 13:5. **To come** and **to wait** clearly indicate that Paul refers to God's final judgment. This wrath is God's personal retribution against sin, his holiness in action. Though the final period of tribulation is to be a time of wrath, God's ire will not then be exhausted; for Christ's coming itself will be a display of wrath against the wicked and unbelieving nations (Mt 24:30 Rev 19:11-15).

B. Paul's Founding of the Church. 2: 1-16. Paul recalls the hardships of his visit and the integrity of his motives and conduct. Undoubtedly he was deliberately refuting accusations of the Jews, who were using every possible emotional lever to pry the new converts from the rock of their Christian confession.

1) Purity of the Apostle's Motives. 2: 1-6. **1. For yourselves, brethren.** Paul appeals both to the unquestionable reality of their own experience and to the intimacy of his relationship with them. **Entrance in** *(eisodos)* is the same word translated "entering in" at 1:9. Paul calls the believers to affirm personally what others had said about them. **Was not in vain.** The perfect tense of the Greek verb **was** shows that the results of Paul's ministry were still in effect. He uses an understatement. His mission was anything but fruitless. **2. But.** The Greek word is strong, underscoring the success of the visit in spite of both physical **(suffered)** and mental **(shamefully entreated)** ill-treatment at Philippi (Acts 16:19-40). **We were bold.** This verb virtually always in the NT refers to open, fearless preaching (e.g., Acts 13:46; 18:26). The evangelists' confidence was rooted **in our God,** the source of their courage, power, and message. Opposition dogged their tracks, so that in Thessalonica, as in Philippi, the Gospel was preached **with much contention.** This expression recalls athletic contests where competitive struggle **(contention)** preceded every prize.

3. Our exhortation suggests the urgency of Paul's manner of preaching. **Deceit.** False teachers are deceivers and deceived (II Tim 3:13), but Paul was neither. In a world where religion was often coupled with immorality, he kept himself free from **uncleanness.** As the Master was guileless (I Pet 2:22), so the **servant** could not resort to an atmosphere of guile (**in** contrasted with of deceit) to snare unsuspecting followers. **4. Allowed by God.** *Tested and approved by God.* Paul's singleness of eye (Mt 6:22) was based on the double premise that he was commissioned by God and that only God could test his heart, examine his inner motives (I Cor 4:4). **Heart** in Biblical thought is the seat not so much of emotions as of volition and intellect, the center of moral decision. Paul refutes the Jewish charge that he was preaching an 'easy' message, **pleasing men** by removing the yoke of the Law (see Gal 1:10).

5. Flattering words, standard equipment of demagogues of every era, found no place in Paul's arsenal. Nor did he conceal **covetousness** with the **cloak** of pretended unselfishness. His hearers could vouch for absence of flattery, and **God is witness** that no greed lurked beneath the mantle of altruism. **6.** Paul coveted neither material gain nor the **glory** or praise of men, even though as an apostle, dispatched on his missions by **Christ,** he had a right both to financial aid and to personal respect (I Cor 9:1-14; Gal 6:6; *et al.*). **Burdensome,** i.e., insisting on being supported by the church.

2) Extent of the Apostle's Sacrifice. 2: 7,8. **7. But.** A strong contrast. **Gentle** *(ēpioi).* Many excellent manuscripts have **babes** *(nēpioi),* the idea being that Paul, far from being highhanded, actually became as a child, using baby talk to communicate with the infant church. Whichever reading is preferred, Paul, instead of being a burden, put himself out to help. **As a nurse.** Better, *a nursing mother.* **Cherisheth.** Warmly and tenderly cares for **her** own **children.** Paul maintained a dual relationship to his converts: before God he and they were brethren (I Thess 1:4; 2:1; *et al.);* yet they were his children (cf. 2:11), whom he had brought into the life of faith and for whom he was obliged to care. **8. Affectionately desirous.** A word used only here in the NT, indicating warm affection, longing. The apostles were **willing,** *well pleased,* to share themselves, their very

lives, because of their love for the new converts (cf. I Jn 3:16).

3) Integrity of the Apostle's Conduct. 2:9-12. **9. Labor and travail** are also paired in II Thess 3:8 and II Cor 11:27, where the AV "weariness and painfulness" highlights the emphases of the two words. **Night and day.** Paul probably began his tent-making (Acts 18:3) before dawn in order to be able to take some time off for preaching. **Chargeable.** *Burdensome,* as in 2:6. **10.** Both the Thessalonians, who could judge Paul's actions, and God, who could test his motives (2:4), were **witnesses** to the apostle's sterling conduct. **Holily and justly** stresses the positive quality of Paul's life before God and men. The former (*hosiōs*) probably refers to religious purity; the latter (*dikaiōs*) to moral integrity. **Unblameably** states the same thing negatively. **You that believe.** Only the faithful can judge the faithful. The verdict of unbelievers is frequently too biased to be counted.

11. In another striking simile (cf. 2:7) Paul likens himself to a **father,** charged not with the nursing but with the training of **his children.** Three verbs summarize this ministry: **exhorted** (cf. 2:3), calling to decisive action; **comforted** (cf. 5:14; Jn 11:19,31) – Paul was tenderly appreciative of their hard lot; **charged,** reminding of the solemn nature of Christian duty (cf. "testify" in Eph 4:17).

12. This fatherly counsel had one aim: to encourage the Thessalonians to live **(walk)** worthily of God (cf. Eph 4:1). Better manuscripts read *who calls you* for **who called you.** God's call confronts men continually. The **kingdom** has both present and future aspects. It is God's active sovereignty over those who submit to him; yet this submission is neither as complete nor as extensive as it will be. Both the epistle's eschatological tone and the close connection between **kingdom** and **glory** (linked with one definite article in Greek) indicate the future aspect (as in I Cor 6:9; 15:50; Gal 5:21; II Thess 1:5; II Tim 4:1,18) rather than the present (as in Rom 14:17; I Cor 4:20; Col 1:13). **Glory** is future (cf. Rom 5:2; 8:18), referring to the full revelation of God's majestic character.

4) Reliability of the Apostle's Message. 2:13. For similar thanksgiving see 1:2. Two words are translated **received:** the former (*paralambanō*) means to accept formally and outwardly; the latter (*dechomai*), to receive willingly and inwardly, to welcome. The apostle's message was the **word of God** (repeated for emphasis) not **of man.** Compare the stress on the **gospel of God** (2:2,8,9). **Effectually worketh.** The verb should probably be understood as passive—*is set in operation.* God is the source of the power; the word is his instrument (cf. Rom 1:16; Heb 4:12; Jas 1:21; I Pet 1:23).

5) Result of the Apostle's Message: Persecution. 2:14-16. **14. Followers.** *Imitators,* as in 1:6. The churches of God were geographically **in Judea** and spiritually **in Christ Jesus.** The imitation consisted in their suffering **like things** (*the same things*) from their neighbors as the Judean Christians suffered from theirs. **Countrymen** (*tribesmen*) is used here in a local rather than an ethnic sense; probably both pagans and Jews in Thessalonica persecuted the church.

15. Paul indicts his countrymen with a vigor unique in his writings: they killed the one who was both **Lord,** sovereign over creation and history, and **Jesus,** the human Saviour, kinsman to them (the Greek word order stresses both names; cf. Acts 2:36); they killed or persecuted the **prophets (prophets** may be taken as the object of either verb, but it seems preferable to link it with **persecuted;** cf. Mt 5:12); they **persecuted** or *drove out* the apostles **(us).** Paul may have been recalling the parable in Mk 12:1 ff. **Please not God.** A forceful understatement meaning "to displease." (Cf. II Thess 3:2). **Contrary to all men.** By opposing the Gospel the Jews were working against the good of mankind, which so desperately needs salvation. **16. To fill up,** etc., refers to God's sovereign purpose worked out in the lives of the Jewish persecutors. In continuing their rejection of Christ and increasing their opposition, they heaped sin upon sin. The wording recalls Gen 15:16. Especially pertinent are the words of Christ in Mt 23:31,32. **Wrath.** See note on I Thess 1:10. **Is come** emphasizes the completeness and certainty of judgment. Wrath for them was inescapable. (Cf. Rom 1:24,26,28).

C. Timothy's Strengthening of the Church. 2:17–3:13. Paul explains his involuntary absence and the reasons for Timothy's mission. Grateful for Timothy's report, he prays that God will cause the church to continue to flourish.

1) Paul's Concern. 2:17–3:5. **17. Being taken from you.** Literally, *orphaned, bereft,* reflecting the warm tie between Paul and the church. Compare II Cor

11:28, where the writer numbers among his burdens the *anxiety for* (RSV) *all the churches.* **Endeavored the more abundantly** and **with great desire** are strong attempts by Paul to convey his earnest yearning for fellowship. He even uses the graphic word **desire,** *epithymia,* which in the NT usually connotes lusting or coveting. **18. Even I Paul** points out his personal concern. **Once and again** is, literally, *both once and twice,* meaning "repeatedly." **Satan hindered.** This title stresses the devil's role as adversary of God and His people. How was Paul hindered? By illness (II Cor 12:7; Gal 4:13) or by opposition in Athens that made it impossible for him to leave (I Thess 3:1)? Some think the hindrance was the security taken from Jason *et al.*, that Paul would not return (Acts 17:9). Firmly believing in God's sovereignty, the apostle never minimized the reality of evil, especially as it was summed up in Satan (I Thess 3:5; II Cor 4:4; Eph 2:2; 6:12).

19. Paul's emotional attachment to the Thessalonians becomes almost exuberant. **Are not even ye.** This seems to be a parenthesis within the major question: "What is our hope . . . . in the presence . . . ?" **Crown of rejoicing.** An allusion to the wreath or garland of victory awarded to winners in the games or to distinguished public servants. Paul's **hope, joy,** and only grounds for boasting **(rejoicing)** were the thought of the souls he would present to Christ (cf. II Cor 1:14; 11:2; Phil 2:16). **Coming** (*parousia*) originally meant "presence" or "arrival," but later took on a technical sense referring to the visit of a king or official. New Testament writers frequently use it for Christ's second coming (I Thess 2:19; 3:13; 4:15; II Thess 2:1; Jas 5:7,8; II Pet 1:16; I Jn 2:28; *et al.).* **20.** The writer makes doubly sure that the Thessalonians know the answer to his question. **For** has a confirmatory sense – "truly" or "indeed." **Ye** is emphatic: you alone.

3:1. Could no longer forbear. Could bear up under the strain of separation no longer. Though Paul uses **we** here, as throughout these epistles, it seems probable that the **we** is editorial. **Alone** seems to confirm this. **2. Our brother.** Timothy was Paul's son in the faith (I Tim 1:2); but because of this mission, Paul stresses partnership, not dependence (cf. II Cor 1:1; Col 1:1; Phm 1:1). Manuscript evidence indicates that **minister of God and our fellow laborer** is an expansion of an original statement: either *minister of God* or *fellow laborer of God.* The former has slightly better support, while the latter is more startling (although see I Cor 3:9) and is less likely to be a scribal correction. In either case Paul emphasizes Timothy's fitness to perform his mission.

The concern throughout these epistles is the spiritual rather than the physical welfare of the believers. Timothy's purpose was to **establish** (*strengthen*) and **comfort** (*actively encourage*) them **concerning** (as Milligan notes, *for the furtherance of*) their **faith,** which here is active – the experience of believing.

3. Timothy's purpose is further explained: to prevent their seduction by Jews, who might seize the opportunity afforded by affliction to try to lure the believers from their faith. **Moved** (*sainesthai*) probably retains some of its original meaning, *to wag the tail,* and, therefore, to "beguile" or "flatter." (Arndt, however, prefers *move.*) Afflictions are part and parcel of Christian experience (Jn 16:33; Acts 14:22). Note the **we.** Paul, who had suffered more than his share, here groups himself with the suffering believers. **4.** An essential element in the apostle's message to the Thessalonians was the redemptive suffering of Christ (Acts 17:3). The church was born in suffering (Acts 17:6). Paul bore marks of his shameful treatment at Philippi when he evangelized the Thessalonians. Hence, suffering should not have caught them by surprise. **We told you.** The imperfect tense indicates that Paul had reminded them repeatedly.

5. Compare 3:1. **To know.** *To find out.* **Faith.** See note on 3:2. **Tempter** shows the seductive aspect of Satan's work. The devil tried to use Christ's physical difficulties to defeat him spiritually (Mt 4:3), and he did the same to the Thessalonians. The verb **have tempted** is aorist indicative and shows that the tempter was already at work, while the verb **be** is subjunctive, casting doubt upon Satan's success.

2) Timothy's Welcome Report. 3:6-10. After re-creating his personal anguish over the church's lot, Paul expresses his complete release from this burden at Timothy's return.

6. But now brings out the contrast between Paul's past concern and his present confidence, and indicates that Timothy had just arrived (cf. Acts 18:5). **Good tidings.** The Greek root means "to evangelize" and suggests that Timothy's report was virtually a 'gospel' to Paul's anxious soul. The good news was threefold: (1) **faith** was firm—this had been Paul's principal concern (I Thess 3:5,7); (2) **love** was constant—in spite of the trials which could have frayed the edges of their dispositions; (3) their **remembrance** (recollection) of the apostles was always **good**—despite the reproach and persecution which the evangelists' visit had produced.

7. Comforted, i.e., encouraged (cf. 3:2). Paul's own lot had not been a happy one, even while he awaited news from Macedonia. Persecution at Philippi, Thessalonica, and Berea was followed by loneliness and indifferent response at Athens (3:1; Acts 17:32-34). Such dogged opposition plagued him at Corinth that he had to be divinely reassured (Acts 18: 6-10). No wonder he speaks of **affliction** *(choking pressures)* and **distress** *(overbearing tribulation).* **8. We live.** New vitality had come into Paul's flagging body with the good news of the Thessalonians' faith and remained with him while he wrote (**now**). This would pale, however, unless the Thessalonian believers would **stand fast** in their relation to **the Lord.** The verb form seems to show that Paul confidently expected them to **stand firm.**

9. Paul took no credit for the soundness or growth of the church. It was God who gave the growth (I Cor 3:7). Not boastful but thankful (cf. I Thess 1:2 ff; 2:13 ff.), he rejoiced (cf. 5:18) **before our God,** because He made such joy possible. **10.** Timothy's news relieved Paul's concern but did not lessen his desire to see them (cf. 2:17,18; 3:6), a desire prompted by the strong emotional tie (the wish to **see your face**) and by the need for mending the gaps in their **faith. Perfect** *(katartizō)* means to fit a thing for its full and proper use.

3) Paul's Prayer. 3:11-13. **11. Himself.** Paul's destiny was in God's control. Christ's full title stresses His majesty. **He** is associated closely with God as the recipient of prayer and as the co-subject of the verb **direct,** the singular form of which *(kateuthynai)* yokes the subjects **God** and **Christ** together intimately.

12. The Lord, i.e., Christ. **Abound in love.** Cf. Phil 1:9. Love has the capacity for growing endlessly. It increases in intensity toward an individual and expands to embrace others. Christian love is first directed toward believers (**one toward another**) and then reaches out like God's love **toward all men.** This love can be produced only by the Spirit of God (Col 1:8; Gal 5:22). More than sentiment or warm feeling, Christian love is the selfless desire for the total welfare of others. **Even as we.** God's love had been reflected in the apostle's gracious words and **deeds.**

13. Note the connection between **love** and **holiness.** If love is the Christian law (Gal 5:14), then one's **holiness** (separation to God) is measured chiefly by love. Selfishness blemishes this holiness; so Paul prays that the Thessalonians may live in love and be spotless (**unblameable**) in holiness **before God,** who, being completely holy, is the only adequate judge of holiness. God judges not as a brutal critic but as a loving **Father.** The time of reckoning is the **coming** *(parousia;* cf. I Thess 2:19) of Christ. **Saints.** Literally, *holy ones.* It probably includes holy angels as well as dead believers clothed in bodies "not made with hands" (II Cor 5:1), awaiting the resurrection of their earthly bodies. For other graphic pictures of Christ's coming with his whole heavenly entourage see Mt 24:30,31 and Rev 19:11-14. The OT background is Zech 14:5. According to Rev 19–20 this glorious coming paves the way for the Millenial kingdom.

III. Practical Exhortations. 4:1–5:22.

Paul would not have been true to his pastoral calling nor to his parental concern if he had not seized every opportunity for spiritual instruction. To fulfill the law of love he had to say the needful things. Timothy's report was mainly encouraging, but undoubtedly included certain questions that Paul hastened to settle.

A. Abstain from Immorality. 4:1-8 No temptation faced by the early church was more vexing than that of immorality. The edict of the Jerusalem Council lists fornication with the ceremonial prohibitions placed upon Gentile believers, so generally accepted was this practice among the pagans (Acts 15:29). Paul makes the strongest possible case for morality by grounding it within the will and calling of God and the nature of the indwelling Holy Spirit.

1. Furthermore then. *Finally.* The word marks a major transition in subject matter and suggests that the letter's conclusion is approaching. **Beseech.** *Request.* **Exhort** is stronger (cf. 2:11 and 3:2). **Walk** equals *live,* as in 2:12. The essence of Paul's command is that the Thessalonians should do what they are doing, only more so. **Abound.** See 3:12 and 4:10 "increase" for other uses of *perisseuō.* **2.** Paul's ministry included ethical instruction as well as evangelism. His **commandments** (orders or military commands) were stamped with the authority of **Jesus** who is **Lord,** the exalted Ruler of all of life.

3. After a general word of encouragement, in which he also establishes his authority, the apostle tackles the problem at hand – **fornication.** He begins positively: God both commands and enables your **sanctification.** In contrast with 3:13, where **holiness** *(hagiōsynē)* is viewed as a state, here **sanctification** *(hagiasmos)* is seen as a process—the act of being sanctified, set apart for God's service. **Abstain from.** *Keep completely separate from.* **4.** Amplification of **abstain,** etc. The meaning of **vessel** is difficult. Many commentators and translators (e.g., Moffatt, RSV) interpret **vessel** as "wife," appealing to certain Jewish usage, according to which a wife is likened to a vessel. Milligan, Morris, Phillips, and others understand **vessel** as "body," after the analogy of II Cor 4:7. This rendering seems preferable because it avoids the low view of the woman's role in marriage implied in the former interpretation. If **vessel** means "body," *ktasthai* must mean **possess** (as in AV and certain papyri) rather than the more frequent *acquire.*

5. The sanctification and **honor** in which the believer controls himself contrast directly with the **lust,** etc. In I Cor 7:2,3,9 Paul indicates that marriage gives opportunity to control passions, not to give them unbridled vent. **Lust of concupiscence.** Or, *passion of lust* (RSV). This implies the willful desire to yield to base sexual drives. Paul's definition of **Gentiles** is classic—**which know not God.** It is not superior self-control that separates Christian from pagan, but intimate acquaintance with God (cf. Ps 79:6; Jer 10:25). Hosea and Jeremiah both stress the essentiality of the knowledge of God (Hos 4:6; 6:6; Jer 4:22), involving love and obedience. It is the essence of salvation (Jn 17:3).

6. The social significance of chastity. **Go beyond,** i.e., *overstep* the bounds of human decency and social regulations. **Defraud** or *take advantage of* **his brother.** Not merely his Christian brother but his fellow man. **In any matter.** *In the matter* or *in this matter.* The Greek definite article links this statement with the subject of this paragraph—sexual purity. In this verse Paul gives a practical illustration of both the law of love and the connection between love and holiness stressed in 3:12,13. Judgment day casts its lengthy shadow over all of life. **The Lord is the avenger,** who sees to it that full justice is done.

7. The emphasis is on **called** (cf. 2:12). Salvation is purposeful, and **uncleanness,** moral pollution, is not its purpose. Paul here reiterates the thought of 4:3. The will of God designs that a believer should live in **sanctification** *(hagiasmos).* This is the process (cf. 4:3) rather than the state of being sanctified (cf. 3:13). **8.** To **despise** *(reject, treat as worthless)* the command to purity is to break divine law; for God has placed the Holy Spirit within a believer to make him holy. The emphasis is on **holy:** "It is not for nothing that the Spirit God gives us is called the *Holy* Spirit" (Phillips). Those whom he indwells are called to reflect his holiness. **Unto us** should read *unto you,* with the best manuscripts. The statement is pointedly personal.

B. Love One Another. 4:9,10. A second temptation hounded the early church —factiousness and petty strife. The situation at Corinth exemplifies the primitive believers' battle against their pagan environment (I Cor 3:1 ff.). Christianity sprang up in a land and culture where clan ties were strong and society was more corporate than individualistic. Not so the Greco-Roman culture; hence, Paul's constant emphasis on love.

9. Brotherly love *(philadelphia)* is clan love, the love between members of a family. For early believers, accepting Christ often meant severing family ties. But the Christians joined a new family, for they were now God's sons, and brothers of all believers. **Taught of God.** Both by God's gracious example (Jn 3:16) and by the Spirit, who pours God's love into our hearts (Rom 5:5). **10.** The extensive (**all brethren in all Macedonia**) loving deeds (cf. 1:3) of the Thessalonians were proof that they had learned well God's lesson of love. But there was no room for complacency. Paul tenderly (**brethren**) urges them to **increase** their love **more and more** (cf. 3:12; 4:9,10).

C. Mind Your Own Affairs. 4:11,12. This section should be coupled closely with the previous, for selfless industry is a manifestation of Christian brotherly love.

11. Study. *Philotimeomai* originally meant *be ambitious,* but in the NT (cf. Rom 15:20; II Cor 5:9) it means "to strive eagerly," "aspire." The clause is graphic: *strive eagerly* **to be quiet.** They were to strive for two other goals: **to do,** etc. (mind you own affairs and not somebody else's) and **to work,** etc. Apparently some believers were both meddlesome and lazy. Hope of the imminent Second Coming became an excuse for idleness (cf. II Thess 3:11). Greeks shunned manual labor, and Paul had taught the Thessalonians by word (the Lord was a carpenter) and by example (the apostle was a tent-maker) that the Christian doctrine of *creation* implies the Christian doctrine of *vocation:* God made everything good; therefore, man can perform the most menial tasks knowing that he is in touch with the Creator's handiwork; further, he can do them to God's glory.

12. The double purpose of dedicated industry: to live fittingly or becomingly (**honestly**) before non-Christians (**them that are without,** those outside the pale of salvation); to enjoy the freedom which personal financial sufficiency gives. Their diligence would enhance their testimony with outsiders; their "honorable independence" (Phillips) would help them fulfill the law of love by not sponging on fellow believers.

D. Comfort One Another with the Hope of the Second Coming. 4:13-18. Among the problems brought to Paul's attention by Timothy was the role of the dead believers at Christ's second advent. In Paul's discussions, the emphasis seems to have been on the imminence of the return. But persecution and affliction apparently took their toll of believers' lives. What would be the lot of such? Would death have robbed them of participation in the Grand Event? On the contrary, Paul says, they are to share fully in the glories of that day. Christ's death and resurrection are the guarantee of this. These comforting words of Paul were not intended to give a systematic picture of the last things, but were geared to the problem at hand.

13. I would not, etc. Compare Rom 1:13; 11:25; I Cor 10:1; 12:1; II Cor 1:8, where, as here, the statement introduces a new and important subject. In each instance **brethren** is used to add a note of tenderness. **Asleep.** To be "dead in Christ" (4:16) is to be **asleep,** for Christ by his death and resurrection (4:14) has taken the sting out of death. No allusion to 'soul sleeping' is involved. Paul had in mind the *bodies* of dead believers. **Others.** Rather, *the others,* those outside of Christ (cf. 4:12). **No hope.** This could well be the epitaph of unbelievers. **Hope refers to the Second** Coming, with all its attendant blessings. Sadness and loneliness are death's inescapable companions, but bitter grief and desperate hopelessness should play no role in the emotions of a bereaved believer, because he knows in advance the final chapter of history's plot.

14. If we believe. "And we *do* believe" is the idea conveyed by the Greek construction. **Jesus died.** "Sleep" will not do here. Christ took the full cup of death that he might triumph over it (Heb 2:14,15). **And rose again.** His triumph assures ours (cf. I Thess 1:10). **God** is emphatic here. He who raised Jesus is the Guarantor and Agent of our resurrection. **Sleep in Jesus** is *sleep* **through** *Jesus,* the idea being that through him death is transformed into sleep. **With him.** Paul answers the major question: Dead believers will not miss the *parousia;* God will see to it that they accompany Christ on his triumphal return (3:13).

15. By the word, etc., gives authority to Paul's statements (cf. I Cor 7:10). The source of the **word** is uncertain. Among the possible sources: (1) Mt 24:30,31 and parallel passages; (2) an unrecorded saying of Christ (cf. Acts 20:35); (3) a special revelation from the Lord (cf. II Cor 12:1; Gal 1:12,16; 2:2). **We which are alive.** Paul frequently stresses the imminence of Christ's return (I Cor 7:29; Phil 4:5). Like all believers, he hoped to live to share in the event (I Cor 16:22; Rev 22:20). Without stating that Christ *would* come during his lifetime, he seemed to welcome the possibility (cf. I Cor 15:51 ff.). **Shall not.** *By no means.* **Prevent.** *Come before, precede.*

16. The all-important fact is that the Second Advent centers in the activity of **the Lord himself.** The terse phrases add to the drama: (1) **with a shout,** a *call of command* like that of an officer to his soldiers, probably given by the Lord; (2) **with the voice,** etc., may be an explanation of the **shout;** both **voice** and **archangel** are indefinite in the Greek, and the idea is probably *a voice such as an archangel uses,* as Milligan suggests; (3) **with the trump of God,** *a trumpet dedicated to God's service* (Milligan); in I Cor 15:52 Paul twice mentions a trumpet in connection with the Second Coming (cf. Joel 2:1; Isa 27:13; Zech 9:14 for OT background). These three phrases convey the splendor of the scene and the Lord's majestic authority. **Dead in Christ.** The bodies of dead believers. **First.** Dead believers will precede living ones.

17. We which are alive. See 4:15. **Shall be caught up.** *Snatched up suddenly and forcibly, raptured.* **Together with them.** Members of Christ's body will be reunited with each other as well as with their great Head. **The clouds** add to the mystery and drama of the event (cf. Mt 24:30; Acts 1:9; Rev 1:7). **In the air.** The absolute pre-eminence of Christ is underscored by his using the dwelling place of evil spirits (Eph 2:2; 6:12) for this rendezvous. **With the Lord.** The heart of the passage—endless fellowship with Christ. Where? Does the whole retinue ascend to heaven or return to earth? Any answer given will depend on the total interpretation of NT eschatology adopted. Pre-tribulationists posit an ascension with a subsequent return to earth. Post-tribulationists hold that a descent to earth follows this reunion.

18. To a church struggling to maintain itself in a society that was at best heedless and at worst hostile, these were comforting words indeed. We should note that Paul does not discuss here the relation of the Rapture to the Tribulation.

E. Live as Children of the Day. 5:1-11. The discussion of the participants in the *parousia* leads to questions about the time and the signs of the *parousia*. In response to these, Paul alerts the believers to constant readiness. Vigilance and sobriety are the proper attitudes, while faith, love, and hope are the Christian's arsenal.

1. Paul had undoubtedly relayed personally to the Thessalonians the important words of Christ: "but of that day . . . knoweth no man . . . " (Mk 13:32, 33). Nothing need or can be said about the time of the Second Coming. **Times** (*chronōn*, length of time) signifies the chronological periods which are to elapse before the Second Coming; while **seasons** (*kairōn*, kind or quality of time) refers to the significant events, the pregnant opportunities that transpire during these epochs (cf. Acts 1:7).

2. Yourselves know perfectly. Paul had carefully informed the believers that constant preparedness was the Christian's obligation. **The day of the Lord** must be viewed against its OT background. The term was current in Israel before the time of Amos but was applied only to God's judgment of the Gentiles. In a graphic passage, not unlike I Thess 5:2-4, Amos corrects this misinterpretation, pointing out that a righteous God judges sin wherever it is found—even in Israel (Amos 5:18-20). Cf. Joel 1:15; 2:1,2, 31,32; Zeph 1:14 ff. The day is the time of God's righteous intervention in history, when he will exact his rightful due from mankind. In II Thess 2:2 ff. this day is connected with the great apostasy and the revelation of Antichrist, i.e., the Tribulation period. **Thief,** etc., recalls Mt 24:43 and Lk 12:39. The figure depicts the unexpectedness of the event.

3. The fact that **for** is not found in the better manuscripts indicates that this is to be closely connected with the preceding. **They,** i.e., unbelievers. **Peace and safety** calls to mind OT passages like Amos 5:18,19; Mic 3:5-11; Ezk 13:10, which describe a false sense of peace and security. **Destruction.** To be the object of God's righteous wrath is to be completely and hopelessly destroyed, perhaps by separation from God (II Thess 1:9). **As travail.** This comparison is frequent in the OT (Isa 13:8; Hos 13:13; Jer 4:31) and in the Gospels (ASV, Mt 24:8; Mk 13:8). It is not pain but the suddenness and relentlessness of the day that Paul is stressing. Once labor sets in, there is no escape. **Shall not.** *By no means* (cf. 4:15).

4. But ye, brethren, emphasizes the strong contrast between believers and unbelievers. **Darkness** is more than ignorance; it is the unbelievers' moral and spiritual separation from God (cf. Jn 3:19,20; II Cor 6:14; Eph 5:8; Col 1:12,13). **5.** Having stated what the believers are *not*, Paul turns to what they *are*, and adds **all** to make the statement more inclusive. To be **sons of light** is to be characterized by light. Luke 16:8 and Eph 5:8 contain examples of this Semitic idiom. God, the source of light, is called "the Father of lights" (Jas 1:17). **Children** (sons) **of the day** not only reemphasizes the preceding phrase but recalls the **day** of the Lord. Believers are sons of that day because they share in its glory and triumph.

6. Therefore. Since we are sons of the day. **Sleep.** Not physically but morally and spiritually, as in Mk 13:36; Eph 5:14. **Others.** Cf. I Thess 4:13. **Watch** recalls Christ's injunctions about his coming in Mt 24:42; 25:13, etc. Mental and physical awareness is implied. **Be sober** (cf. II Tim 4:5; I Pet 1:13; 4:7; 5:8) speaks not so much of freedom from drunkenness as of rigidly disciplining *all* of one's life so as to be well balanced in every phase. **7.** Sleeping and drunkenness are habits customarily performed at night. Therefore, they have no place in the lives of sons of the day. There is no need for figurative interpretation here. **8. But let us** (in contrast with the "others") **be sober.** Sobriety must be a believer's habit, since he belongs to the day. Paul frequently speaks of spiritual equipment in terms of the armory (cf. II Cor 6:7; 10:4; Eph 6:13 ff.; the OT source is Isa 59:17). The trinity of virtues (cf. I Thess 1:3) protects the believer against the complacency and despair that characterize the sons of the night. **Hope of salvation** is the eager expectation of being rescued from God's final wrath (1:10) and destined for endless glory and fellowship with God.

9. The reason for this hope (5:8) is that God has destined believers for it rather than for **wrath** (cf. 1:10). **Appointed** (*etheto*), though lacking the definiteness of "predestinated" (Rom 8:29 ff.), nevertheless attributes salvation to "the direct purpose and action of God" (Milligan). **To obtain** implies that the believer has an active response to make. Salvation is made available **by** (through) **our Lord Jesus Christ.** The full title conveys the majesty of Jesus the Messiah. **10.** Salvation includes not only rescue from wrath (1:10; 5:9) but bestowal of life and promise of eternal fellowship. The cost of this legacy must not be taken for granted, as **who died for us** reminds us. **Wake** and **sleep** here are figurative for "live" and "die." The triumphant death of Christ perforates the once heavy line between life and death (4:14,15; cf. also Christ's promise in Jn 11:25,26).

11. Edify. *Build up,* a favorite expression of Paul's for "promoting spiritual growth and maturity" (cf. I Cor 3:9 ff.; 14:4; Eph 2:21 ff.). This metaphor and that of the armor (I Thess 5:8) are reminders that Paul, a citizen of "no mean city," drew his figures of speech largely from urban rather than from rural scenes. **Even as also ye do.** Paul's tact combined forceful exhortation with fervent praise.

F. Abstain from Evil; Embrace the Good. 5:12-22. Paul closes his letter with brief exhortations dealing with social, personal, and spiritual attitudes.

1) In Relation to Others. 5:12-15. The apostle lays down a few guiding principles for believers to follow in relation to their spiritual leaders, fellow Christians, the weak and helpless, and all men.

12. Know here must mean "know the value of," "appreciate." **Labor.** Cf. 1:3; 2:9. Leading an afflicted, struggling church has seldom proved easy. **Over you.** The term used here is apparently not technical but refers to a general, informal type of leadership. However, it is probable that elders (presbyters) are meant (cf. Acts 20:17; 21:18; I Tim 5:17,19). **In the Lord** shows that Paul is speaking of spiritual authority, which involves admonishing or warning, especially where blameworthy conduct is involved (cf. I Thess 5:14; II Thess 3:15). **13. In love** (AV) gives the setting and context for this high esteem; **for their work's sake** gives the reason. The task of maintaining and strengthening the believers is worthy of respect in itself. **Be at peace.** To degrade leadership or to cavil with authority is to sow seeds of strife. The well-being of the Christian community (**among yourselves**) is dependent on cordial cooperation between followers and leaders.

14. Directed to the leaders of the church and to the spiritually mature. **Warn.** Cf. "admonish" in 5:12. **Unruly.** *Out of order*. A military word describing soldiers who fail to remain in the ranks. This disorderliness is probably willful negligence of Christian duty, including the duty to work (4:11,12; II Thess 3:6-15). **Feebleminded.** *Fainthearted* (RSV), i.e., despairing in the face of adverse circumstances. **Support the weak.** Give those who are spiritually frail (cf. Rom 14:1; I Cor 8:9,11) a helping hand. **Be patient toward all.** This sums up the basic attitude that must prevail as one seeks to help the unruly, disheartened, and fragile brethren (cf. Eph 4:2), and thus reflect God's own attitude (Rom 2:4; 9:22; I Pet 3:20). **15.** Vindictiveness and retaliation should find no lodging within the household of faith, for the Master clearly forbade them (Mt 5:43 ff.). **Follow.** *Pursue, set out after.* **Good.** In a kind, helpful, useful sense. **All men** includes unbelievers (cf. I Pet 2:17).

2) In Regard to Basic Attitudes. 5:16-22. In staccato-like statements Paul drives home his final exhortations.

16. Christian joy is not dampened by affliction or other harsh circumstances, because it is rooted in one's unassailable relationship to God (cf. Phil 2:18; 3:1; 4:4). In fact, joy may thrive in tribulation when a believer discerns the glorious purposes of God (Rom 5:3-5; Jas 1:2 ff.).

Such joy is not self-generated but is the Spirit's fruit (Gal 5:22). **17.** Prayer is attitude as well as activity. The attitude of devotion to God can be **without ceasing** (cf. note on 1:3), if the activity cannot. Paul illustrates his own command, for his letters are scented with the fragrance of prayer. **18. Everything.** All circumstances, even hardships and affliction. **This,** though singular, seems to embrace the three commands of 5:16,17,18. God's will includes constant joy, ceaseless prayer, and boundless thanks, attitudes made both necessary and possible **in Christ Jesus.**

19. The Greek construction suggests the translation: *Stop quenching the Spirit*. **Quench** aptly describes the hindering of the Spirit, whose nature has been likened to fire (Mt 3:11; Acts 2:3,4). In light of 5:20, this verse seems to indicate that some cautious believers had questioned the use of spiritual gifts in the church. This situation would be the opposite of that in I Cor 12–14, where we find ungracious zeal to outdo each other in exercising spiritual gifts. It is possible, however, that Paul's statement here is general, forbidding them to check the Spirit's refining and convicting work in their lives (cf. Eph 4:30). **20.** In I Cor 14:1 believers are urged to seek the gift of prophecy, the Spirit-guided public utterances of deep truths. This gift may have been abused; but abuse does not preclude use. The predictive element in Biblical prophesying should neither be overstressed nor minimized. The prophet's task is to tell what God has told him, including things to come. For NT references to a prophetic ministry, see I Cor 12:28 and Eph 2:20; 3:5; 4:11.

21. All things refers primarily to sayings that purport to be prophecies. They must not be accepted with credulity but are to be tested by more objective revelation and especially by the touchstones of Christ's Lordship (I Cor 12:3) and incarnation (I Jn 4:1-3). **Good,** i.e., genuine, not counterfeit.

22. Paul's negative command is actually: *Abstain from every kind of evil. Eidos* (**appearance,** AV) is often used in the papyri of the Greco-Roman period to denote "class," "sort," "kind." It has frequently been noted that while "the good" in verse 21 is singular, **evil** is said to take many different forms. The wording recalls Job 1:1,8; 2:3.

IV. Conclusion. 5:23-28.

A. Closing Prayer. 5:23,24. Paul embraces all his exhortations in a prayer for sanctification, and assures the believers that a faithful God will answer it.

23. The very God of peace is *God himself who alone bestows peace,* a characteristic Pauline title of God (cf. Rom 15:33; 16:20; II Cor 13:11; Phil 4:9; II Thess 3:16). Though human surrender and obedience are necessary, sanctification is essentially a divine work (cf. Rom 15:16; Eph 5:26). **Wholly** (*holoteleis*) implies that no part is lacking; the whole person is to be kept **blameless. Spirit and soul and body** should probably not be interpreted as a definitive analysis of the nature of man. The three words are used to indicate the whole being of a person, "whether on its immortal, personal, or bodily side" (Milligan). Paul prays that they may be preserved (**kept**) from judgment at (**unto**) Christ's coming. **24. Faithful is he** can only refer to God (cf. I Cor 1:9; 10:13; II Cor 1:18; II Thess 3:3; II Tim 2:13; Heb 10:23; 11:11). The only guarantee that any believer will have a worthy report at the final judgment is God's faithfulness. His calling carries with it the successful completion of his purposes (Rom 8:30; Phil 1:6).

B. Request for Prayer. 5:25.

A tender plea revealing Paul's dependence on his **brethren** in Christ (cf. Rom 15:30; Eph 6:19; Col 4:3 ff.; II Thess 3:1 ff.).

C. A Final Salute. 5:26.

A fitting conclusion to a letter filled with expressions of affection. Paul includes **all the brethren,** even those who caused the problems. **Holy kiss.** Its character was completely divorced from the sensual. A pure display of the deep emotion of Christian love, this type of kiss remained a Christian custom until abuse and heathen misunderstanding caused the practice to be curtailed. For other NT references to the **holy kiss,** see Rom 16:16; I Cor 16:20; II Cor 13:12; also I Pet 5:14 ("kiss of love").

D. Command to Read the Letter. 5:27.

I charge. *I adjure you, put you under oath.* Paul wanted to make sure that the letter was read in the hearing of **all the brethren** (**holy** being omitted in the best manuscripts). The language is strong, and the switch to **I** from "we" reinforces the command. Paul may have anticipated some factiousness which would have made fraudulent use of his letter (cf. II Thess 2:2). But it is more likely that his urgent desire for fellowship pressed him to make sure that no one was left out.

E. Benediction. 5:28.

Paul ends as he began — with a prayer for **grace**, i.e., Christ's continued favor. Note that the apostle emphasizes the majesty of Christ by giving his full title — **Lord Jesus Christ.** The **Amen** and the subscription naming Athens as the place of writing, as in the AV, are omitted from the better manuscripts (cf. e.g., the ASV).

BIBLIOGRAPHY

ANDREWS, SAMUEL J. *Christianity and Anti-Christianity in Their Final Conflict*. 2nd ed. Chicago: Bible Institute Colportage Association, 1898.

BAILEY, JOHN W. "I-II Thessalonians," *Interpreter's Bible*. Vol. XI. New York: Abingdon Press, 1955.

BARCLAY, WILLIAM. *The Mind of St. Paul*. New York: Harper and Brothers, 1958.

BICKNELL, E. J. *I-II Thessalonians (Westminster Commentary)*. London: Methuen and Co., 1932.

BRUCE, F. F. "I and II Thessalonians," *New Bible Commentary*. Edited by F. Davidson, A. M. Stibbs, and E. F. Kevan. Grand Rapids: Wm. B. Eerdmans, 1953.

DENNEY, JAMES. *The Epistles to the Thessalonians (Expositor's Bible)*. New York: A. C. Armstrong and Son, 1903.

FINDLAY, GEORGE G. *The Epistles to The Thessolonians (Cambridge Bible for Schools and Colleges)*. Cambridge: University Press, 1900.

FRAME, J. E. *Epistles of St. Paul to the Thessalonians (International Critical Commentary)* Edinburgh: T. and T. Clark, 1912.

HENDRIKSEN, WILLIAM. *Exposition of I-II Thessalonians (New Testament Commentary)*. Grand Rapids: Baker Book House, 1955.

HUBBARD, DAVID A. "Antichrist," *Dictionary of Theology*. Edited by E. F. Harrison. Grand Rapids: Baker Book House, 1959.

MILLIGAN, GEORGE. *St. Paul's Epistles to the Thessalonians*. New York: The Macmillan Co., 1908.

MOFFATT, JAMES. "The First and Second Epistles to the Thessalonians," *Expositor's Greek Testament*. Vol. IV. Grand Rapids: Wm. B. Eerdmans, reprinted 1952.

MORRIS, LEON. *The Epistles of Paul to The Thessalonians (Tyndale New Testament Commentary)*. London: Tyndale Press, 1956.

VOS, GEERHARDUS. *The Pauline Eschatology*. Grand Rapids: Wm. B. Eerdmans, 1952.

WALVOORD, JOHN F. *The Thessalonian Epistles*. Findlay, Ohio: Dunham Publishing Co., 1956.

THE SECOND EPISTLE TO THE THESSALONIANS

INTRODUCTION

Development of the Thought. Grateful for the believers' faith, love, and endurance in persecution, Paul explains the purpose of this persecution, which refines believers for future glory and seals the doom of God's enemies. Christ's coming will reverse the present situation, bringing rest to the afflicted, and separation from God to their troublers.

Despite contrary reports, the Day of the Lord has not yet come (ch. 2). The rebellion and the man of lawlessness will appear first. All forms of worship, true and false, will be replaced by the worship of this lawless one. His day will be short in spite of his deceitful Satanic power. As darkness is dissolved by light, he will be slain at Christ's coming, when his deluded followers also will be judged.

The believers' destiny is different because God has called them to salvation. This sense of calling, coupled with the Spirit's ministry, will hold them firm in troubled times. Paul, too, faces opposition in his ministry and comforts himself and his friends with a reminder of God's loving faithfulness and Christ's patient steadfastness (ch. 3).

Industry, not sloth, is the hallmark of Christian conduct, as Paul had taught by instruction and example. Where there prevailed misinterpretation of the imminence of Christ's advent, or spiritual pride that disdained manual labor, firm but loving pressure should be brought to bear on the unruly. (For discussion of date, occasion of writing, etc., see Introduction to I Thessalonians.)

OUTLINE

I. Introduction. 1:1,2.
  A. Authors. 1:1a.
  B. Recipients. 1:1b.
  C. Blessing. 1:2.
II. Encouragement in persecution. 1:3-12.
  A. Commendation for steadfastness. 1:3,4.
  B. Explanation of the purpose of persecution. 1:5-10.
  C. Intercession for continued spiritual growth. 1:11,12.
III. Instruction concerning the Day of the Lord. 2:1-12.
  A. To come in the future. 2:1,2.
  B. To be preceded by definite signs. 2:3-12.
IV. Thanksgiving and exhortation. 2:13-17.
  A. Praise for their calling. 2:13-15.
  B. Prayer for their comfort and stability. 2:16,17.
V. Confession of confidence. 3:1-5.
  A. Request for prayer. 3:1,2.
  B. Reminder of God's faithfulness. 3:3-5.
VI. Commandments to work. 3:6-15.
  A. Shun the idle. 3:6.
  B. Imitate us. 3:7-9.
  C. Work or do not eat. 3:10.
  D. Exhort the idle. 3:11-13.
  E. Warn and discipline the disobedient. 3:14,15.
VII. Conclusion. 3:16-18.
  A. Blessing. 3:16.
  B. Paul's signature. 3:17.
  C. Benediction. 3:18.

COMMENTARY

I. Introduction. 1:1,2.

This letter begins like I Thessalonians. The only addition is the mention of **God our Father and the Lord Jesus Christ** as the givers of **grace** and **peace** (1:2).

II. Encouragement in Persecution. 1:3-12.

A. Commendation for Steadfastness. 1:3,4. The edge of Paul's gratitude has not been dulled since the writing of the first epistle. He warmly commends the believers for their faith, love, and stability in the midst of ruthless persecution.

3. We are bound conveys Paul's sense of personal debt to God because of the growth of the Thessalonians. **It is meet.** That is, "Your conduct merits such thanksgiving." **Your faith groweth exceedingly.** Concerned in the first letter about their faith (I Thess 3:5,10), the apostle rejoices here at its exceptional growth. Having encouraged them to increase their love (I Thess 3:12), he here notes that it **(charity) aboundeth** among them. In I Thess 1:3 he commends them for their **patience of hope.** Is such a statement absent here because the central problem of this letter is a misinterpretation of the hope?

4. Glory in you. Boast about you. He anticipated his boasting at Christ's coming (I Thess 2:19) by boasting of the Thessalonians among the churches where he labored. **Patience,** i.e., steadfastness, as in I Thess 1:3. **Faith** *(pistis)* sometimes means "faithfulness" (e.g., Rom 3:3; Gal 5:22). Though this meaning would fit well here, it is likely that **faith** refers to the act of trusting, as in II Thess 1:3 and everywhere else in these epistles. **Persecutions** *(diōgmois)* is a specific term, referring to attacks by opponents of the Gospel (cf. Acts 8:1; 13:50), while **tribulations** *(thlipsesin)* are more general pressures (cf. Mt 13:21 and Mk 4:17). The present tense of **ye endure** suggests that this bitter opposition was a present reality.

B. Explanation of the Purpose of Persecution. 1:5-10. Trust and stability in persecution are the evidence of the righteous judgment of God, who is preparing the righteous sufferers for his Kingdom and their opponents for his wrath.

5. Which is a manifest token refers not so much to persecution as to their faith and steadfastness in persecution. This stalwart response is *clear evidence* or a *plain indication* that God's **righteous judgment** will be favorable in their case (cf. II Cor 4:16 ff. and Phil 1:28). Though this righteous judgment will be culminated at the end, it is in operation already (Jn 3:19). Judgment is said to have a definite purpose in the lives of believers: **that ye may be counted worthy.** "It is part of God's *righteous judgment* to use tribulations to bring His own people to perfection" (Morris). **Kingdom.** See note on I Thess 2:12. **For which,** i.e., *on behalf of which.* Cf. Christ's beatitudes in Mt 5:10-12. **6.** Final judgment will bring a righteous reversal of present circumstances: troublers will be troubled, while their victims will receive rest. **Seeing,** i.e., *since indeed* (RSV). **It is a righteous thing.** God's righteousness would be blighted if this sort of wicked opposition were allowed to flourish permanently. **Trouble,** i.e., *bring tribulation upon.*

7. Rest. *A relaxing of the tensions.* **With us** apostles, who were strangers neither to tribulation nor to the longing for **rest. Revealed.** *Unveiled* (cf. I Cor 1:7 and especially Lk 17:30). **Mighty angels** is literally, *angels of his power.* That is, angels who are both symbols of and ministers of his power. See note on I Thess 3:13. The kingdom parables of Christ (cf. Mt 13:41,49; 25:31,32) also connect angels with the Judgment. **8. In flaming fire.** For OT background see Isa 66:15 and Dan 7:10,11. The subject of **taking** *(giving)* **vengeance** *(complete punishment)* is the **Lord Jesus** from II Thess 1:7. The Father has entrusted all judgment to him (Jn 5:22,27). The objects of Christ's wrath are **them that know not God and that obey not the gospel.** Some have suggested that two groups – Gentiles (cf. I Thess 4:5) and Jews – are indicated. More likely this is a blanket reference to all who refuse to act on what they know about God and who, more specifically, reject his revelation in Christ.

9. The nature of the vengeance: they **shall be punished** (*shall pay a penalty*) **with everlasting destruction.** Annihilation is not the thought but rather total ruin, the loss of everything worthwhile. Specifically, it is separation **from the presence** *(face)* **of the Lord,** the true source of all good things. New Testament descriptions of the pangs of hell are numerous: "furnace of fire" (Mt 13:42); "lake of fire and brimstone" (Rev 20:10); "outer darkness" (Mt 25:30), etc. But none is more graphic than this picture of endless, utter exclusion from him who is life, light, and love. **The glory of his power.** The "visible manifestation of the greatness of God" (Morris).

10. When *(hotan)* is *Whenever*. The time is indefinite. **In his saints.** Believers are the sphere in which Christ will **be glorified** when he comes. "He will be glorified in them, just as the sun is reflected in a mirror" (Alf). This is the culmination of a process already begun (Jn 17:10; II Cor 3:18). **To be admired.** This revelation of Christ's glory in believers will be amazing and wonderful to all who behold it. **In that day** is to be connected with **to be admired.** The intervening clause is parenthetical and difficult to relate to the verse. Perhaps the best suggestion is that it is a condensed expression to be rendered as Phillips does: "to all who believe – including you, for you have believed the message that we have given you."

C. Intercession for Continued Spiritual Growth. 1:11,12. Having clarified for the Thessalonians God's sovereign purposes in their persecution and its glorious outcome, the apostle reaffirms his constant, prayerful concern that the dedication of the believers shall match the designs of God.

11. Wherefore. *To this purpose*, relating to the entire section from 1:5-10. **Calling** usually refers to God's initial call to salvation, but the idea here probably includes the culmination of that initial act (cf. I Thess 2:12). **Good pleasure of goodness (his** is not in the Greek text) refers to the Thessalonians, not to God. Paul prays that God will **fulfill** *(carry out to completion)* their delight (**good pleasure**) in **goodness.** *Agathōsynē (goodness)* is never applied to God in the NT (cf. Rom 15:14; Gal 5:22; Eph 5:9). Kindness combines with righteousness in **goodness. Work of faith.** Cf. I Thess 1:3. **With power** describes the manner in which God can fulfill these two petitions.

12. The final petition recalls 1:10. **Name** is the revelation of the whole personality, in keeping with Biblical and general Semitic usage. The believers are to reflect continually that glory which shall be fully revealed in them at Christ's coming. **And ye in him** points up the intimacy of union between Christ and his Church. As Christ reveals his glory in the Church, so the only glory the Church can claim is in him. That such a sharing of glory can take place is due to **(according to)** divine **grace.**

III. Instruction Concerning the Day of the Lord. 2:1-12.

A. To Come in the Future. 2:1,2. Paul plunges into the problem which called forth the letter – the reports that the afflictions endured by the believers were sure signs that the Day of the Lord had already come. This Paul categorically denies.

1. By *(hyper)* **the coming** *(parousia;* see note on I Thess 2:19) should be translated *as regarding the coming* (Milligan). So also **by our gathering together** (cf. Mk 13:27; I Thess 4:17). **2. Soon** here means "hastily," or almost "easily." **Shaken in mind.** Thrown off the course of sound thinking and reasoning. **Be troubled.** The present tense suggests "be kept in a state of agitation or panic." Three upsetting means are suggested: (1) **spirit** – report of a special revelation given to Paul; (2) **word** – a report of a sermon preached by Paul; (3) **letter – a false** epistle. **As from us,** *purporting to be from us* (RSV), probably applies to all three. The gist of these false reports was that the **day of the Lord** *(Christ* does not have good manuscript support) had arrived. The verb *(enestēken)* means "is present" (cf. Rom 8:38; I Cor 3:22; Heb 9:9), not **is at hand. Day of the Lord.** See note on I Thess 5:2.

B. To Be Preceded by Definite Signs. 2:3-12. The day will be initiated by an outburst of rebellion and by the revelation of the man of lawlessness. The vanguard of the Satanic army is on the march, but the dreadful, doomed leader has not yet come into view.

3. Let no man deceive. See Mt 24:4 ff. **By any means.** Those in II Thess 2:2 or others. **That day shall not come** does not occur in the Greek text, but something like it must be supplied. **A falling away,** literally, **the** *apostasy*. The meaning of the word was known to Paul's readers, but we are not so fortunate. *Apostasia* usually means "rebellion," whether in a political or religious sense. The reference here is probably to the marshaling of the powers of evil against the people and purposes of God. Christ and Paul both warned against this final wicked conspiracy (e.g., Mt 24:10 ff.; I Tim 4:1-3; II Tim 3:1-9; 4:3 ff.). Apparently it will be of sufficient scope and intensity to mark itself off from the spirit of general opposition to God (**mystery of lawlessness,** II Thess 2:7) which characterizes the world's attitude. The capstone of the rebellion will be the revelation of the **man of lawlessness. Be revealed** suggests that he is waiting behind the scenes until the time for his public appearance is ripe. In the NT only John uses the term "antichrist" (I Jn 2:18,22; 4:3; II Jn 7), but there can be no doubt as to whom Paul had in mind. **Son of perdition** (cf. Jn 17:12) points both to the nature and to the fate of the lawless one. His actions seal his doom. For **son of,** see note on I Thess 5:5.

4. Antichrist's Work. **Opposeth.** As Satan's minister, Antichrist will carry out his master's work (I Tim 5:14). **All that is called God.** The true, living God (I Thess 1:9) and all false gods. **That is worshipped,** i.e., every object held sacred – temples, shrines, etc. Antichrist will take his place **as God in the temple,** probably the Jerusalem temple, as the close connection between this passage and the description of Antiochus Epiphanes (Dan 11:36 ff.) suggests (cf. also Mk 13:14, where the masculine participle may indicate a person rather than an image). Revelation 13:4-15 describes Antichrist's cult. **Shewing himself.** Better, *proclaiming himself,* in accordance with the Hellenistic meaning of *apodeiknymi.*

5. I told you. The imperfect tense indicates that more than once Paul had discussed these events.

6. What withholdeth and the related **who letteth** (v. 7; i.e., "restrains") are exceedingly difficult to interpret confidently because of Paul's brief treatment. That the Thessalonians knew what he meant is of little comfort to us. Certain observations may be made: (1) The present tense of the two participles shows that the arresting force or person was already in operation. (2) The change from neuter (v. 6) to masculine (v. 7) suggests that the restrainer can be spoken of as a thing or person. (3) The restraining influence will be removed in God's **(his) time,** and Antichrist will be revealed. Dispensationalist interpreters (e.g., C. I. Scofield, L. S. Chafer, and J. Walvoord) have identified the restrainer as the Holy Spirit, a view supported by the fact that the Spirit may be described in both neuter and masculine genders. Removal of the Spirit takes place when the Church, his temple, is raptured (I Thess 4:13-17). However, why would Paul speak of the Spirit in such veiled terms? Furthermore, how can the revelation of Antichrist be a sign to the church that has already been raptured? Many Biblical commentators from Tertullian (c. A.D. 200) on have identified the restrainer as the Roman Empire. The neuter participle would refer to the state; the masculine, to the emperor. This view leans upon Paul's charitable attitude toward government as a means of maintaining law and order so that the church may do its work (cf. Rom 13:1-7; Tit 3:1; I Pet 2:13,14,17). But the Roman Empire has long since faded away, and the lawless one has not yet been revealed. Thus it seems probable that the restraining influence refers to the principle of human government manifest in the Roman state. Human institutions are part of God's program of common grace, whereby he bridles the forces of evil to provide the proper setting for the revelation of his special, redemptive grace. Totalitarian in the extreme (cf. Rev 13:15-17), Antichrist's government is so diabolical in nature and so ruthless in practice that it utterly disqualifies itself for being considered a God-ordained human institution. In **his** (God's) **time** shows that God is in ultimate control.

7. Mystery indicates that the wicked spiritual principle already at work had been revealed to believers (cf. the use of *mystērion* in Mk 4:11; Rom 16:25, etc.). **Iniquity.** *Lawlessness.* Matthew 24:24 and I Jn 2:18 mention Antichrist's forerunners, who are embodiments of this principle of lawlessness. **He who letteth.** See note on 2:6. **Taken out of the way.** Probably by God, although not so stated. **8. Wicked.** Literally, *lawless*—Antichrist's basic characteristic, as "man of lawlessness" and "mystery of lawlessness" (vv. 3,7, RSV) show. No sooner is his unveiling **(revealed)** mentioned than his doom is described. **Consume.** Better manuscripts read *slay.* **Spirit,** i.e., *breath.* See Isa 11:4 for OT background. **Destroy.** *Render useless, make powerless.* **Brightness** (*epiphaneia*) or *manifestation* speaks of the brilliant display of Christ's power at his coming (cf. II Thess 1:7,8; Rev 19:11-21).

9. Antichrist has his **coming** as Christ has His. Satan's **working** *(power in operation)* is Antichrist's dynamic (cf. Rev 13:2). His coming reveals itself in **all power** (to work miracles) and **signs** (significant, meaningful miracles) and **wonders** (amazing their observers). In the Greek, **lying** seems to apply to all three: the miracles are steeped in falsehood. Cf. Acts 2:22; Rom 15:19, etc., for the three words describing miracles. **10. Deceivableness of unrighteousness.** Deceit stemming from unrighteousness. **Them that perish.** The present participle (*apollymenois*) suggests that the process is already in operation (cf. I Cor 1:18). **Received.** Welcomed. **Truth,** i.e., of the Gospel.

11. God shall send indicates God's sovereignty, controlling the destinies not only of his own but of his enemies. Rejected light results in greater darkness, as Mt 13:10 ff. and Rom 1:24-32 demonstrate. Effectively deceived, they trust **the lie,** not **the truth** (2:10,12). Satan's **lie** consists in getting men to believe him instead of God (cf. Gen 3:1 ff.; Jn 8:44). **12. Damned.** *Judged.* The verdict of guilty is implied, not expressed. **Pleasure in unrighteousness.** Not helpless victims, they willingly side with Satan against God and will share their captain's fate (Jn 16:11).

IV. Thanksgiving and Exhortation. 2:13-17.

A. Praise for Their Calling. 2:13-15. In marked contrast with the dark portrait of Antichrist and his followers are the bright prospects of those whom God has called.

13. Bound to give thanks. See note on 1:3. **Beloved.** See note on I Thess 1:4. **From the beginning** seems to reflect the Pauline view of an election prior to creation (Eph 1:4). Some manuscripts read *first fruits* for **from the beginning.** This reading, adopted by some editors (e.g., Nestle, Moffatt), would be fitting, because the Thessalonians were among the earliest of Paul's European converts. **Chosen** *(heilato;* cf. LXX, Deut 26:18) reminds us that believers have joined Israel as God's elect people (cf. I Pet 2:9, 10). **Sanctification** (cf. I Thess 4:3,7) **of the spirit** stresses the Spirit's role in separating believers from Satan's sphere of control to God's (I Pet 1:2). **Belief of the truth** emphasizes the human response of faith to the truth of the Gospel (Rom 10:17). **14. Whereunto** refers to God's act of salvation described in 2:13. **Called.** Cf. I Thess 2:12; 5:24. **Our gospel.** Cf. I Thess 1:5. **Obtaining** (cf. I Thess 5:9) **of the glory** is a further description of the meaning of salvation. See note on 1:10.

15. Traditions. Almost none of the NT existed in written form. The basis of instruction was the authoritative oral record (**word**) of the Gospel events and interpretation (cf. I Cor 11:2,23; 15:3). **Epistle** probably refers to I Thessalonians. The content of the tradition is discernible in the sermons in Acts (2:14 ff.; 7:2 ff.; 13:16 ff., etc.) and the creedal statements embedded in the epistles (I Cor 15:3 ff.; I Thess 1:9,10, etc.).

B. Prayer for Their Comfort and Stability. 2:16,17. Paul, as was his custom, seals his exhortation with a prayer.

16. Compare the very similar phrasing of I Thess 3:11. Note the honor paid to Christ by the position accorded him in this verse. **Consolation** (*paraklēsin*) includes strength as well as comfort. **Good hope** speaks of the worthy character of the believer's confident expectation, as well as of the joyous outcome (cf. I Thess 1:3). **Through grace** reminds us that these and all of God's blessings are undeserved, and it stifles pride (cf. 1:11,12). **17. Comfort and stablish.** Cf. I Thess 3:2. **Every good word and work.** Whatever you do or say.

V. Confession of Confidence. 3:1-5.

A. Request for Prayer. 3:1,2. The request of I Thess 5:25 is repeated, with an added note of urgency due to the militant opposition of faithless men.

1. May have free course is literally *may run,* stressing both the vital, active nature of **the word of the Lord** (i.e., Christ's word) and the urgency with which the apostles desired to spread it (cf. Ps 147:15). **Be glorified.** By being received and obeyed (cf. Acts 13:48; Tit 2:10). **With you.** See I Thess 1:6; 2:13 for their wholehearted reception of the Gospel. **2. Delivered.** See note on I Thess 1:10. **Unreasonable.** *Perverse, improper.* **Wicked,** in an actively, deliberately harmful sense. See Acts 18:6,12 for glimpses of this Jewish opposition. **Have not faith.** An understatement; these men not only refused to believe but threatened all who did.

B. Reminder of God's Faithfulness. 3:3-5. This opposition was marked for failure because a faithful God is stronger than faithless men.

3. See I Thess 5:24. **Stablish.** Cf. I Thess 3:2; II Thess 2:17. **Keep,** i.e., guard, protect. **From evil.** *From the evil one,* Satan (cf. Mt 6:13). **4. In the Lord.** The faithfulness of God helps to assure the obedient response of the Thessalonians both in the present **(ye both do)** and in the future **(will do). Which we command you** seems to refer to the instructions to follow (3:6 ff.).

5. Paul pauses to utter one of his most touching prayers. **The Lord,** i.e., Christ. **Direct** *(kateuthynai,* as in I Thess 3:11) means to "clear the way of obstacles," "open a direct path." **Hearts.** See note on I Thess 2:4. **Love of God.** God's love is a tremendous source of stability and security (Rom 8:37-39). **Patient waiting for Christ.** *The steadfastness of Christ* (RSV). Christ's example of unflagging endurance is a prime source of inspiration to troubled believers (Heb 12:1,2).

VI. Commandments to Work. 3:6-15.

With apostolic authority Paul attacks the problem of laziness which was plaguing the Thessalonian church. Reminding his friends of his own diligence, he commands firm yet loving discipline of the idle.

A. Shun the Idle. 3:6.

We command, as an officer his troops. **Brethren.** Paul's sternness does not throttle his affection. The apostle derived his authority from the **Lord. Disorderly.** Out of rank; cf. "**unruly**" in I Thess 5:14. **Tradition** (cf. II Thess 2:15) includes both Paul's personal example and his written instruction (I Thess 4:11,12).

B. Imitate Us. 3:7-9.

7. Follow. *Imitate, emulate* (Arndt). **Behaved not ourselves disorderly** is an understatement. Paul's example of industry was not only untarnished but brilliant. **8. Eat bread** means to gain a livelihood (cf. II Sam 9:7; Amos 7:12). **For nought.** Without cost. This verse resembles I Thess 2:9 but stresses Paul's example of diligence rather than his integrity of purpose. **9. Power,** i.e., apostolic authority to gain his living from his hearers (cf. I Thess 2:6). **Ensample.** Example, pattern (cf. I Thess 1:7). **Follow.** Cf. II Thess 3:7.

C. Work or Do Not Eat. 3:10.

The imperfect tense of **we commanded** shows that more than once Paul had urged them to diligence with these words: **If any would not work,** etc. **Would not** shows that this is willful inactivity. This saying may be based on Jewish interpretation of Gen 3:19.

D. Exhort the Idle. 3:11-13.

11. We hear. Unhappy news spread as easily as the report of the believers' faith (I Thess 1:8,9). **Disorderly.** Cf. II Thess 3:6,7. The force of the nice pun is brought out by Ellicott (cited in Milligan): "doing no business (**working not at all**) but being busybodies." **12.** Paul addresses the troublemakers. **We command.** Cf. 3:6,10 for similar tone of authority. **Exhort** (cf. I Thess 2:11) adds a note of tenderness but retains the urgency. **By our Lord,** etc. Paul views himself as Christ's spokesman. **With quietness.** In contrast to the disorder frequently noted (3:6,7,11). **Eat.** Cf. 3:8. **13. But ye.** The whole church. Regardless of the conduct of the indolent, **be not weary,** i.e., do not flag or become slack. The aorist tense suggests that they had not yet begun to do so. To do the right thing **(well doing)** is never easy, but it becomes exceedingly difficult under irritating circumstances such as these.

E. Warn and Discipline the Disobedient. 3:14,15.

14. This epistle is Paul's last word on this matter of laziness. Anyone who disobeys is to be a 'marked man' **(note that man)** with whom believers are not to mix **(company).** The purpose of this ostracism was not punitive but corrective, Paul's hope being that the sense of shame would bring the offender into line. Such social pressure is especially effective in a close-knit, clan-like society, such as this company of believers. **15.** Love is to prevail. The idle loafer is not to be considered an **enemy** but a **brother. Admonish.** Cf. I Thess 5:12,14.

VII. Conclusion. 3:16-18.

A. Blessing. 3:16.

Human effort alone cannot bring spiritual well-being **(peace).** This is a gift of Christ, who promised his disciples peace (Jn 14:27; 16:33) and is here called **Lord of peace** (cf. note on I Thess 5:23). **Always by all means.** Continually in any kind of circumstance. **With you all.** Even with the idlers.

B. Paul's Signature. 3:17.

The token. Paul's handwriting at the close of his letters was the sign of their authority (cf. I Cor 16:21; Gal 6:11; Col 4:18). **So I write.** Calling to their attention his style of handwriting, a necessary precaution (cf. II Thess 2:2).

C. Benediction. 3:18.

See note on I Thess 5:28. **All.** This blessing includes even the troublemakers.

BIBLIOGRAPHY

For bibliography see under *I Thessalonians.*

THE FIRST EPISTLE TO TIMOTHY

INTRODUCTION

Authorship. The Pauline authorship of the Pastorals (I, II Timothy and Titus) is contested. However, the *prima facie* evidence of the writings themselves indicates that Paul is the writer, since his name appears in the salutation of each, and autobiographical remarks fit the life of Paul as recorded elsewhere: e.g., I Tim 1:12,13; II Tim 3:10,11; 4:10,11, 19,20.

The basic rule of evidence regarding genuineness of documents was stated long ago by Simon Greenleaf: "Every document, apparently ancient, coming from the proper repository or custody, and bearing on its face no evident marks of forgery, the law presumes to be genuine, and devolves on the opposing party the burden of proving it to be otherwise" *(An Examination of the Testimony of the Four Evangelists*, London, 1847, p. 7).

We have in the Pastorals ancient books, coming from the proper custody, the church. The church always accepted them as Pauline; there is no dissenting voice until modern times. What then does criticism offer to offset the *prima facie* evidence and the unanimous voice of tradition? Alleged marks of non-genuineness or forgery are four: (1) non-Pauline language and style; (2) the opposition of the Pastorals to second-century Gnosticism; (3) discrepancies between the Pastorals and Acts—it is assumed that Paul was put to death at the end of the one and only Roman imprisonment, as recorded in Acts, and hence it is concluded that Paul cannot be the author of the Pastorals; (4) advanced ecclesiastical organization, beyond the time of Paul, reflected in the Pastorals.

These arguments do not overcome the positive evidence. (1) The linguistic argument is inconclusive because psychologically absurd as well as difficult, if not impossible, to prove. Would a forger, seeking to have a book accepted as a work of Paul, introduce non-Pauline vocabulary at the rate of seventeen words per page of Greek text, and refer to incidents and persons which did not enter the known life of Paul? The unhesitating and unanimous reception of the books by the ancient church, under such conditions, would be impossible to explain. Indeed, this unhesitating reception is very good evidence that the epistles were well known to be genuine. The linguistic data may conceivably point to the joint authorship of Luke and Paul (Moffatt, *Introduction to the Literature of the New Testament*, 3rd ed., p. 414), but it is well to remember that at best the dating of literature by limiting a writer's language and style is only conjecture. The readers of Paul's Pastoral Epistles were different from those of any other epistles. Timothy and Titus had been intimately associated with Paul's life and thought for fifteen to twenty years. We should therefore not be surprised if Paul chose to speak in language and style different from that used in addressing churches. Paul was encouraging and exhorting his sons in the faith, not correcting quarreling or wavering churches.

(2) The assumption in this objection is that if the Pastorals refute second-century Gnosticism, they must be second-century documents. Given the clear *prima facie* evidence of Pauline authorship, if there are statements answering later Gnosticism, the inference is that Paul has foreseen such developments, which is not impossible even from the standpoint of mere human sagacity. However, Paul has elsewhere in other epistles claimed, by inspiration, to foresee and predict the future. To deny that he could is to beg the whole question of the possibility of supernatural revelation. Moreover, Paul may not have been fighting in these epistles a Gnosticism as advanced as some have argued.

(3) That the names, places, and incidents alluded to in the Pastorals cannot be fitted into the outline of Acts, is a very good reason for extending the life of Paul beyond the narration of Acts. The Pastorals, then, would be the product of

Paul's fourth missionary journey and a second imprisonment.

(4) The elements of ecclesiastical organization found in the Pastorals are found elsewhere in the New Testament. Some have thought that the ranking of Luke's Gospel as Scripture (I Tim 5:18) is an indication of late date. "By the time the author of the pastorals wrote, either Luke's gospel or some evangelic collection containing Luke 10:7 was reckoned as *graphé*" (*Ibid.*, p. 401f.). This argument also assumes the point to be proved, namely, that the book could not have been inspired and known to be inspired from the time of its writing and reception.

Fuller answers to these arguments have been worked out in the standard conservative commentaries and introductions. See especially Hendriksen, *New Testament Commentary: Exposition of the Pastoral Epistles,* pp. 4-32.

Date. The first letter to Timothy and the one to Titus were written during the period of travel and missionary work between Paul's two Roman imprisonments. A date somewhere between A.D. 61 and 63 cannot be far wrong. The second epistle to Timothy contains the last words found from the apostle; they were written from prison shortly before his martyrdom (4:6-8). We should view them, as Calvin expresses it, "as written not with ink but with Paul's own blood." The date of the apostle's death is generally set sometimes between A.D. 65 and 68.

Occasion and Message. As Moses gave the charge to Joshua, and the Lord to his apostles, so Paul gives the charge to Timothy and Titus. Likewise, as Moses ended with an exhortation to all Israel, and Christ to all the Church, so Paul concludes his charge with the benediction, "Grace be with you" ("you" is plural; I Tim 6:21; II Tim 4:22) and "Grace be with you all" (Tit 3:15). The occasion for writing the epistles was no less than the need to maintain the faith, to insure the continuity of the Church of Jesus Christ. The solemn charge – "That good thing which was committed unto thee, keep by the Holy Ghost which dwelleth in us" (II Tim 1:14) – is the heart of the Pastoral Epistles. Here Timothy and Titus, together with all the Church, are charged to keep "the faith," "the deposit," the written record, by the work of the Holy Spirit. The outworking of this charge is not only the maintaining of the faith through good works and right conduct in the house of God, but also the resisting of that which is false. The more immediate need for the first two epistles—I Timothy and Titus – lay, no doubt, in the fact that many things at Ephesus and Crete needed adjustment. Paul, however, having intended to advise his sons in the faith, determined to advise others at the same time.

Structure and Theme. I Timothy. This first of the Pastoral Epistles falls into a literary pattern that is probably not accidental. In its briefest form, it can be indicated thus: (A) Charge, (B) Praise, (A) Charge. Stated in another way it is: (A) Prose, (B) Poetry, (A) Prose. This simple pattern of a solemn charge in two parts, bound together by a doxology or hymn of praise, is repeated three times—in the introduction, the body, and the conclusion. The epistle summarized according to this pattern offers a greater unity than is generally recognized. In the introduction, following the salutation, we find the charge to Timothy, with a longer explanatory portion (1:3-16) and a briefer concluding word (1:18-20). These two parts are bound together by the terse but weighty doxology of verse 17. The initial part leading up to the doxology includes an outline—only briefly suggested—of the main topics of the epistle. All is so skillfully woven together that the many themes presented only serve to focus attention on Paul's charge to Timothy. Then follows the doxology, which gives solemn weight to the final part of the charge.

At the conclusion of the epistle, there is another charge, again twofold, with its parts bound together by the doxology of verse 16b. Again the same proportions are preserved: the first is a longer section (6:3-16a) with a recapitulation of the principal themes of the epistle; the shorter portion (6:17-21) concludes with the deeply moving appeal, "O Timothy, guard the deposit."

In like manner, the major portion of the epistle (2:1-6:2) is subdivided by a transitional paragraph (3:14–4:5), at the center of which are the lines of the ancient Christian hymn of which Paul is probably the author (3:16). The first section of this major portion deals with official or public aspects of the Church, the House of God, culminating in the memorable lines of the hymn. In the second portion, individual and personal aspects are stressed, paralleling to a remarkable degree the themes stated in the first section. For example, the reference to women in the first part sets forth the principle of masculine leadership in the Church; whereas, the reference to women in the second part, deals with the individual and personal problem of dependent widows. It appears that one section is intended to balance the other. But more important, the whole structure of the epistle is designed to throw into prominence the great hymn of praise at the center, which presents succinctly and beautifully the person and work of Christ.

II Timothy. In Paul's second epistle to his "dearly beloved son," he seems to be following essentially the same literary pattern as in the first. This time it occurs in its simplest possible form, namely, a solemn charge in two parts, bound together by a hymn. All is prefaced with a salutation and thanksgiving, and concluded with personal notes and prayer. Again the whole structure is designed to highlight the great hymn of doctrinal truth which appears at the center (2:11-13). The chief point on which the structure turns is Paul's presentation of the Gospel as a trust to be preserved, cherished, and committed to faithful men. His words gain peculiar solemnity and weight because they were the last to come from his pen; he wrote knowing that his "departure" was "at hand."

Titus. The theme of this epistle is like that of all the Pastorals in emphasizing the connection of doctrine, committed to faithful men, with godliness of life. In this letter, Paul most memorably links grace, as the great doctrine of salvation, to good works in the balancing passages, 2:11-15 and 3:4-8. In the one passage grace appears, in the other, kindness and love appear. Both stress the blessed hope (2:13; 3:7b); both conclude with the emphasis on good works.

Note on Commentary. In the commentary that follows an effort has been made to give not merely explanatory words on a given text, but, far more important, the citation of parallel texts which, if patiently searched out, will give the Scripture's own commentary.

OUTLINE

I. Salutation and introduction. 1:1-20.
   A. Salutation, with special notes of authority and hope. 1:1,2.
   B. Charge to Timothy, presenting principal topics of the epistle. 1:3-16.
      1. Sound versus false teaching. 1:3,4.
      2. The purpose of sound teaching. 1:5-7.
      3. The true doctrine of the Law. 1:8-11.
      4. Paul's testimony and gospel. 1:12-16.
   C. Doxology. 1:17.
   D. Charge and encouragement to Timothy. 1:18-20.
II. Exhortations and instructions to the Church of the living God. 2:1–6:2.
   A. To the witnessing church. 2:1–3:13.
      1. Public prayer as related to the missionary purpose of the church. 2:1-8.
      2. Conduct of women as related to the testimony of the church. 2:9-15.
      3. Qualifications of church officers. 3:1-13.
   B. To the church as pillar and ground of the truth. 3:14–4:5.
      1. Its exalted position as organ of the Gospel doctrine. 3:14,15.
      2. Hymn of praise: Poetic statement of true doctrine. 3:16.
      3. Prophetic warning of false doctrine. 4:1-5.
   C. To the witnessing individual. 4:6–6:2.
      1. To Timothy, as a good minister. 4:6-16.
      2. To men. 5:1.
      3. To women, especially widows. 5:2-16.
      4. To elders. 5:17-25.
      5. To servants. 6:1,2.
III. Conclusion. 6:2d-21.
   A. A solemn charge. 6:2d-15a.
      1. Warnings against false teachers. 6:3-5.
      2. Right attitudes of true teachers. 6:6-10.

3. The motives of the man of God. 6:11-15 a.
B. Doxology. 6:15b,16.
C. Return to the solemn charge. 6:17-21.
1. Right use of possessions. 6:17-19.
2. Final appeal: A summation. 6:20,21.

COMMENTARY

I. Salutation and Introduction. 1:1-20.

A. Salutation, with Special Notes of Authority and Hope. 1:1,2. **1.** Paul's apostolic authority was based on the deity and command of Christ. Compare Gal 1:1: ". . . not from men or through a man but through Jesus Christ and God the Father." The divine authorization is further emphasized (1) by the word **commandment:** it suggests a royal command which is to be obeyed; and (2) by the fact that it is the command of both God the Father and Christ Jesus. In thus linking equally the names of the Father and Christ, as in verse 2, Paul leaves no doubt as to the full deity of Christ (see Warfield, *Biblical and Theological Studies,* Ch. III). God is characterized by the name **Saviour,** an exalted title reminding one of Isa 45:21, and similar passages. Jesus is distinguished by the appellation, **our hope,** a succinct way of tying all eschatology to the person of Christ, for Timothy's encouragement. **2.** Also for Timothy's encouragement, no doubt, the apostle adds the word **mercy** to the ordinary formula of **grace and peace.** Only in the Pastorals does Paul thus depart from his usual custom.

B. Paul's Charge to Timothy, Presenting Principal Topics of the Epistle. 1:3-16. Paul's method, apparently, is to present the problems and topics he wishes to discuss, and then to revert to these topics later in order to add details. Hence he first treats the basic matter of sound doctrine. Paul did not need to expound doctrines in detail for Timothy, but it was necessary to remind him of the strategic importance of doctrine for life, and as the correlate, the necessity for obedience to doctrine. This leads to a discussion of one side of the doctrine of the Law, its relation to the cases of outbreaking, flagrant vice here mentioned. The writer briefly sums up the relation of the Law to the believer in the phrase, "The end of the command is love" (v. 5). Paul then encourages Timothy with a superb testimony and doxology, and gives a solemn charge and illustration of the results of not holding a good conscience.

1) Sound versus False Teaching. 1:3,4. The heretical teaching and attention to myths and endless genealogies produced useless speculations and controversies instead of Gospel godliness. Verses 3,4 form the dependent clause of a sentence the main clause of which is verses 5-7. The relation can be seen by (1) omitting **so do,** which has been supplied by the translator, (2) punctuating with a comma instead of a semicolon after **faith,** (3) omitting **now** of verse 5. The thought would then be: "Just as I exhorted you . . . the end (purpose) of my charge is love. . . ." See comment on II Tim 1:3. **4.** The myths and genealogies were probably Gnostic or proto-Gnostic teachings. Gnosticism had two extremes: asceticism, as in 4:3, and antinomian license, as the context intimates here. Erroneous discourses on law, and Gnostic speculations left plain matters of immorality uncorrected. The **dispensation of God** (ASV; AV, *godly edifying)* is the proper issue of sound teaching, and therefore parallels the "love" of verse 5, and the "good warfare" of verse 18. Love is Paul's summary of religious and ethical duty (Rom 13:10; Gal 5:6). The sound teaching brings *God's ordering* or *God's superintendence* of the life.

2) The Purpose of Sound Teaching. 1:5-7. These verses are the main clause of the sentence mentioned above.

5. Commandment. *Charge* (ASV). The word is the noun cognate to the verb **charge** of verse 3. **Faith** is used in the sense of "the faith," sound doctrine. The charge relates to the sources of love: a pure heart, a good conscience, and sound doctrine. **6. Which.** A plural form referring to the heart, conscience, faith just mentioned. It is when these guides of the moral and ethical life have been impaired either by false teaching or disobedience, that people turn to vain jangling. **7. Teachers of the law.** One word. Used of Gamaliel (Acts 5:34) and of eminent teachers (Lk 5:17). Paul seems to refer to the ambitious pride of the false teachers, and exposes their utter incompetence.

3) The True Doctrine of the Law. 1: 8-11. The apostle takes up the relation of the Law to the lost. Again these verses are one sentence. The connection is: "We know that the Law is good, if one uses it lawfully . . . in accordance with the Gospel." Paul discusses this function of the Law in detail in Rom 7:7-25: "It brings the knowledge of sin and makes sin exceedingly sinful, all with the end of bringing a man to Christ.

9,10. The law is not made for a righteous man. "The Law does not condemn a righteous man." The expression is a relative negative, to be taken in context. It does not mean that the Law has no relation to the righteous; for him, it is a righteous rule which he joyfully obeys in the Spirit. The catalogue of sins here given is not the same as lists given elsewhere. Probably this one contemplated special problems in Ephesus. **11.** With the mention of the Gospel, Paul makes his exultant transition to his testimony of what the Gospel did in his case, emphasizing the things needed to encourage Timothy.

4) Paul's Testimony and Gospel. 1: 12-16. The writer's testimony is in two parts: (1) 12-14; (2) 15,16. These parts run parallel, in that Paul's preconversion condition is stressed; and also in each section the turning point and contrast comes with the words, **"but I received mercy."** The heartfelt doxology of the Introduction to the book (v. 17) comes as a fitting climax to Paul's testimony.

12. It is striking that in all Paul's recorded words only here does he give thanks directly to Christ, and only here does he use the eloquent language appropriate to the deep thankfulness he feels as he recalls his own salvation and call. **Faithful** (cf. I Cor 7:25). The basis of Christ's counting Paul faithful was His mercy. Paul was faithful to the trust he had received (I Tim 1:11).

13. Injurious. A violent, proud, insolent person; the "despiteful" of Rom 1:30. Paul characterizes his lost condition in three terrible words: **blasphemer, persecutor, injurious.** Against this self-condemnation, in dramatic contrast, stands the simple word, "I received mercy." Though Paul persecuted the church in ignorance, thinking he was doing God service (Acts 26:9), he does not minimize his sin. Even sins of ignorance need atonement (Heb 9:7; Lev 5:15-19). The mention of ignorance emphasizes the pitiable, guilty blindness of sin (Eph 4:18; I Pet 1:14). "Paul was deeply penitent for having persecuted the church of God, but apparently he did not lay to his charge the black sin of having carried on the persecution in the face of better conviction" (J. Gresham Machen, *Origin of Paul's Religion,* p. 61).

14. Not a separate sentence, but the completion and climax of the statement begun at verse 12. In his sin, Paul found in Christ mercy, grace, faithfulness, love; and this grace overflowed and abounded exceedingly. **15. Saying.** "Faithful is the message and worthy of full acceptance." The message is not merely a **saying,** but is based on the words of Christ (Lk 19: 10), and is equivalent to the truth of the Gospel. It appears in this form here and in I Tim 4:9. In the simple words, **Faithful is the message** (at 3:1; II Tim 2:11; Tit 3:8, as here in verse 15), Paul underscores his lost condition. **Of whom I am chief.** This is parallel to **blasphemer, persecutor, injurious;** and it is climactic.

16. I obtained mercy. Again Paul gives the dramatic contrast between his unworthiness and Christ's mercy, adding here, **for this cause,** pointing to the explanatory **that** which follows: *that in me as chief might Jesus Christ show forth all his longsuffering* (ASV). Paul purposed his testimony as an encouragement to Timothy, who faced the sin mentioned above, plus false teaching in the church. Paul, in effect, says, "If the Lord saved me, who was worse than any others, none need despair; and you may be assured that my Lord can enable you, too."

C. Doxology. 1:17. To the double testimony just given, the doxology of praise comes as the climax and the welling-up of Paul's deep adoration and thankfulness. God the Father has not been mentioned in the context, so this doxology to God may possibly be taken as directed to Christ or to the Triune God.

D. Charge and Encouragement to Timothy. 1:18-20. The charge is the whole responsibility for the Gospel ministry, in accordance with prophetic utterances given at Timothy's ordination. The details of the charge are given in the rest of the epistle and summed up again at 6:13,14.

18. By them. By the prophecies, by the reminder of responsibility and trust reposed in him, Timothy may be challenged and encouraged to remain fruitful in his difficult task. See notes on II Tim 1:4,5. **19. Holding faith and a good conscience.** The whole Gospel message embraces both doctrine and obedience thereto. The **faith** is what we believe about Christ; **good conscience** is not allowing the conscience to be defiled by sinful practices contrary to the doctrine. See note on II Tim 1:3. **Which.** Refers to the **good conscience.** If true doctrine is not obeyed, it is in effect denied and becomes a "dead faith," and men make **shipwreck.** Reshaping their doctrine to fit their sinful course, they proceed to teach a false doctrine. Hence the words: "There is danger lest faith be sunk by a bad conscience, as by a whirlpool in a stormy sea" (Calvin).

20. Paul cites two specific examples of **shipwreck.** Alexander is probably the Alexander of II Tim 4:14, who opposed the apostolic teaching (see Zahn's detailed discussion in *Introduction to the New Testament,* II, 108-110). Hymenaeus is mentioned at II Tim 2:17 and the heresy specified. **Delivered unto Satan.** This has been interpreted by some to mean the apostolic imposition of some extraordinary chastisement (Acts 5:5; 13:11; Job 2:6 – though God's delivering Job to Satan is not analogous to Paul's dealing with a fornicator or heretic). However, a comparison with I Cor 5:3-5 makes excommunication the more probable meaning. He who does not belong to the Church, the body of Christ, is under the dominion of Satan. Blasphemy is any violation of the third commandment, any light and sinful use of God's name (see *Westminster Larger Catechism,* Questions 112, 113).

II. Exhortations and Instructions to the Church of the Living God. 2:1–6:2.

The topics Paul discusses in this section are readily distinguished, as indicated in the general outline. Not so readily distinguished is the point of view governing the choice of these topics and their order. The key idea of the epistle is the preservation of the faith and witnessing. It is not surprising, then, that at the very center of the letter stands the paragraph that presents the Church as **the pillar and ground of the truth,** as the agency which defends and spreads the Gospel message (see Introduction, *Structure and Theme. I Timothy).* Following this paragraph, at 4:6, comes a natural division. Up to this division Paul appears to discuss aspects of the witness of the whole Church. After it he speaks to individuals and particular classes of individuals, selecting his exhortations with reference to witness and testimony.

A. To the Witnessing Church. 2:1–3:13. In general, the point of view here is the church in its public and corporate aspects: worship and officers.

1) Public Prayer as Related to the Missionary Purpose of the Church. 2:1-8. Paul's first topic is prayer for all, and for all in authority. The universal emphasis is clear from the *all's* in verses 1, 2, 4, 6, and from the apostolic, missionary note of verse 7. Paul does not here enter on a complete discussion of the relation of the Christian to civil authority, but only exhorts that prayer be made for those in authority, that believers may lead a quiet and peaceful life. This is conducive to the larger purpose of bringing salvation to men.

1. Supplications, prayers, intercessions, and giving of thanks. These words for prayer are the same as those found in Phil 4:6 and frequently in the NT, with the exception of **intercession,** which appears only here and in I Tim 4:5 (the cognate verb appears in Acts 25:24; Rom 8:27,34; 11:2; Heb 7:25).

3. This. Refers primarily to the prayer, but must include the contemplated result as well. Each has its place in bringing the message to men. **Saviour.** Repeats the theme of the salvation (1:1) and emphasizes the kindness and love of God to all. The emphasis in this passage is on the universal sufficiency, applicability, and offer of the Gospel. This is shown by Paul's characterizing Christ's giving himself as a witness, and by his stressing his own position of trust as preacher, apostle, and teacher of Gentiles. Verses 3-7 form the expansion of an important background thought in the apostolic exhortation to prayer. The writer's plea for prayer is directed toward missions. It is appropriate that missions should be set on its deepest basis: the genuineness of the offer to all, its applicability, and its sufficiency, as found in the work of Christ. Our prayer is good and acceptable to God because it is a prayer for all men and those in authority, to the end that the Church may witness effectively. God desires that through this witness all men may be saved and may come to the knowledge of the truth. **4. Will have.** *Would have*

(ASV). Not to be interpreted to mean "decreed," since not all men are saved. **5.** An earlier verse (1:1) spoke of "God our Saviour." Here Paul uses the terse formula, "One there is who is God; One also there is who is mediator of God and men, the man Christ Jesus." In Mt 19:17 the order of words and thought is the same. "One there is who is good" (ASV). The predicating of the **good,** and **God,** and **mediator** is exclusive and can be said of only one. Here is the sharpest and most unequivocal assertion of the deity and humanity of Christ. It is also involved in the idea of the one true and perfect mediator that he must be God (cf. Heb 7:22; 8:6; 9:15; 12:24). This one gave himself a substitute-ransom for all. **6. Ransom.** Occurs only here in the NT, but it combines the two elements of Christ's ransom-saying in Mt 20:28; Mk 10:45. The preposition **for** and the noun **ransom** of the Gospel saying are here combined in one word. (See notes on I Tim 2:3 above for light on **a ransom for all.**) **To be testified in due time.** Christ, very God and truly man, gave himself as a ransom for all, *as the witness at the proper time.* In the fulness of time God sent forth his Son.

7. Whereunto I am ordained a preacher, etc. "Unto which (witness) I was appointed a preacher and apostle . . ." Paul's emphatic and earnest exaltation of his office shows the direction of his thought: it is because of this witness to Christ's Gospel, and for its success that he enjoins prayer.

8. Here Paul completes the paragraph on prayer. Earnest lifting up of hands, either literal or figurative, signifies earnest entreaty (Ps 28:2; 68:31; 134:2; 143:6; Prov 1:24). **Without wrath and doubting.** *Without wrath and disputing* (ASV); i.e., united (cf. Mt 18:19).

2) Conduct of Women as Related to the Testimony of the Church. 2:9-15. The **in like manner** probably carried on to women what has been said about men, namely that their lives, too, are to be characterized by prayer and devotion to the Gospel.

9,10. The remarks on women's dress are paralleled by I Pet 3:3-5. The compressed style heightens the contrast between attending to ostentatious dress and attending to good works. The implication is that the opposite of the former is the wearing of modest and appropriate clothing—a species of the genus "good works," the proper accompaniment of a true confession of godliness.

11,12. The remainder of the chapter discusses official relations of women in the church. These two verses must be taken together: women are not to assume either leadership or the teaching office in the church. **13.** To illustrate the principle of masculine leadership, Paul cites the order of creation, as establishing the man's natural headship (I Cor 11:8, 9). **14. Adam was not deceived.** This is to be taken relatively; Adam was deceived, but not so completely as the woman. The same Greek word is used of the woman, but in an intensified form. Adam followed deliberately instead of assuming leadership to repel the tempter's suggestions.

15. She shall be saved in childbearing. Paul's language in this section has echoes of the LXX reading of Genesis 2 and 3; and here he may play on the idea of Gen 3:15,16, to point to the incarnation of Christ. Through this **childbearing** the woman who believes and continues in godliness shall be saved.

3) Qualifications of Church Officers. 3:1-13. **1 a.** The opening words of this section probably belong with the last thought of chapter 2, as is suggested in the ASV margin. All the other occurrences of the saying (I Tim 1:15; 4:9; II Tim 2:11; Tit 3:8) seem to follow or precede weighty statements of Gospel doctrine. It is so here, also, if the **childbearing** of 2:15 be taken to refer to the birth of the Saviour. This seems the preferable interpretation.

Paul then begins a consideration of an elder's qualifications, which he treats in orderly fashion: personally (vv. 2,3), as regards his family (vv. 4,5), as regards the church (vv. 5,6), and as regards the heathen world (v. 7). In the second half of this section the apostle deals with deacons and deaconesses (vv. 8-13), whose qualifications are parallel to those of elders. (For classic discussions of the function and office of elder, see Charles Hodge, *Church Polity,* Index, "Elder"; D. D. Bannerman, *The Scripture Doctrine of the Church,* Part VI, ch. iv; and also Lightfoot's essay, "The Christian Ministry," *Commentary on Philippians,* pp. 181-269).

1. Office of a bishop. One word; it also occurs at Lk 19:44, Acts 1:20, and I Pet 2:12. (The English sometimes reads "visitation.") The cognate verb occurs at Heb 12:15, suggesting that the basic function is a responsibility of every believer. The word **bishop** occurs at Acts 20:28; Phil 1:1; Tit 1:7; I Pet 2:25. The office of elder and bishop are the same; in Tit 1:5,7 both words are used of the same people in successive verses. In Acts 20:28 it is the elders whom the Holy Spirit has set as bishops (AV, *overseers)* in the Church. **If a man desire the office . . . he desireth,** etc. Two words are used for **desire** here. The first is used only here, in 6:10, and in Heb 11:16. A man's earnest desire for the office should be like Abraham's desire for the heavenly country. The other word is used more frequently, but also expresses earnest desire (Heb 6:11; I Pet 1:12; Lk 22:15).

2. Blameless. Irreproachable; the same Greek word is used in 5:7 and 6:14. **Vigilant.** ASV, *temperate.* Originally meant "temperate in use of wine," but here it is to be taken figuratively, since the next verse forbids intemperance. The cognate verb means to be self-controlled or self-possessed. **Sober.** *Sober-minded* (ASV); see also Tit 1:8; 2:2,5. **Of good behaviour.** *Orderly* (ASV); used of women's clothing in 2:9. **Hospitality.** Used in Tit 1:8; I Pet 4:9. A similar noun is used in Rom 12:13; Heb 13:2. **Apt to teach.** Used only here and in II Tim 2:24: in the one place of the elder, in the other of the minister.

3. Not given to wine. *No brawler* (ASV); *not quarrelsome over wine* (ASV margin); *no drunkard* (RSV). **No striker.** Not pugnacious or a bully. Used only here and Tit 1:7. **Not greedy of filthy lucre.** Does not belong in the text at this point because it does not appear in the best manuscripts. It obviously duplicates the **covetousness** at the end of the verse. Perhaps it was taken from the similar list of virtues in Tit 1:7. **Patient.** *Gentle* (ASV) or yielding (Phil 4:5; Tit 3:2; Jas 3:17; I Pet 2:18). **Not a brawler.** *Not contentious* (ASV), as in Tit 3:2. **Not covetous.** *No lover of money* (ASV). Used only here and in Heb 13:5.

4,5. Ruleth. To be at the head of. Leadership and direction are prominent in the word, as indicated in the following clause, and in 3:5. The verb in 3:5 (used elsewhere only in Lk 10:34,35) is explanatory of the **ruleth** of verse 4, with increased emphasis on the tender care implied. **6. Not a novice.** Not newly-converted. Occurs only here in the NT. "But, instead of being a *neophytos,* one of whose behaviour in his new faith little can be known, he must also have a good testimony (not only from those within the church, but) from those without" (C. J. Ellicott, ed., *A Bible Commentary for English Readers,* Vol. VII). **Pride.** Puffed up by too rapid advancement. **Condemnation.** See 3:7.

7. He must have a good report of them which are without. See Ellicott's paraphrase above (v. 6). The same thought is found in Rom 12:17 b, which is quoted from Proverbs. Note the ASV margin: *Let not kindness and truth forsake thee . . . so shalt thou find favor and good repute in the sight of God and man* (Prov 3:3,4). Notice the warning against pride in the same OT context (Prov 3:7), also quoted in Rom 12:16b. **Reproach.** This is a parallel to the condemnation pronounced upon Satan because of pride (see Isa 14:12-15). **Snare.** Used in I Tim 6:9 and II Tim 2:26. Pride was the cause of Satan's fall, and is the snare he sets for men (I Jn 2:16).

8. Likewise. In like manner. The principal thought seems to be that there should be the same kind and degree of gifts and qualifications for deacons as for elders. **Grave.** Honorable, commanding respect. **Not double-tongued.** Truthful. **Not given to much wine.** The Bible testimony is consistently against the use of strong drink. The practical application of the principle in modern society is total abstinence. **Filthy lucre.** Used also in Tit 1:7, and the adverb in I Pet 5:2. A compound word, the two components of which are used separately in Tit 1:11. In I Pet 5:2 the word is opposed to *willingly.* The subject of economic motives is discussed more fully by Paul in I Tim 6:5-10; 17-19 (see below). The truism holds: not money, but love of it, is a root of all kinds of evil. The admonition is particularly relevant to the kind of responsibilities the deacon has.

9. Faith. Here again is th eunion of the doctrinal and practical aspects of Christianity: the faith is to be held in an obedient conscience, not defiled by disobedience. The expression **mystery of the faith** does not mean that there is some esoteric secret known only to the initiated. Paul's usage starts with the appearance of Christ in the flesh, as in verse 16 below. The mystery is not a secret to be kept, but a message to be proclaimed (Rom 16:25; Col 4:3).

10. Proved. Not necessarily by a formal test, but by the approval of the church. The **then** is significant: it appears to mean that candidates are to be approved before taking office, then serve; not to be proved in office.

11. Their wives. *Women* (AV). The context makes this most naturally refer to women who are acting in the capacity of deacons, as deaconesses. The apostle immediately returns to the subject of deacons in general and completes his remarks concerning them. The word **grave** and related words occur frequently in the Pastorals. The same virtue is required of deacons (v. 8) and elderly men (Tit 2:2). **Slanderers.** The Greek word for "slanderer" is *diabolos* (Eng., "devil), the name given to Satan in the NT; he is the slanderer *par excellence*. Here, in II Tim 3:3, and in Tit 2:3, the word is used of men. **Sober.** As in I Tim 3:2 and Tit 2:2. **Faithful.** Believing, believer, or (as in the faithful sayings) trustworthy, faithful. The corresponding noun, **faith,** is enumerated in the fruit of the Spirit in Gal 5:22. The noun, like the adjective, can mean either faith in the active sense, "believing," or that "faithfulness" which produces confidence on the part of others and may help to inspire faith. **12.** See verses 4,5 above; the same words are used.

13. Paul closes this section as he began it in verse 1, with an argument designed to encourage the aspiring church leader. Those who serve well purchase or gain for themselves a good **standing** (ASV). The word **boldness** here probably means "ground of" or "cause for" boldness. Thus it could be parallel to, and explanatory of, the preceding **standing** (which is literally a *step* or *foundation* on which one stands). One who serves well finds the Lord faithful: he purchases for himself a good foundation and ground of boldness in the faith (fulness), which is in Christ Jesus. *They* **that have used the office . . . well.** Probably refers not only to the deacons but to the elders as well.

B. To the Church as Pillar and Ground of the Truth. 3:14–4:5.

1) Its Exalted Position as Organ of the Gospel Doctrine. 3:14,15. Paul makes clear why he thought it important to write to Timothy even though he might be with him again soon. One of the major emphases of the epistle is right conduct as a testimony to the truth. So the behavior of Christians in the government of the Church is of first importance, for the Church is the support and foundation of the truth; that is, in its sphere of testimony to the world. Christ, himself the truth, is the one foundation of the Church (I Cor 3:11). In Heb 3:6; 10:21, the Church is referred to as the "house" of Christ or "of God"; also cf. Eph 2:19,20. **The truth.** Most of the occurrences of this word in the NT are found in the writings of Paul and John. The term is often equivalent to "the gospel" or "the message (Rom 2:2,16; Col 1:5; Gal 2:14), as in this context, where it is clearly parallel to the following verse, which gives the substance of the Gospel.

2) Hymn of Praise: Poetic Statement of True Doctrine. 3:16. **Mystery.** See verse 9 above. **Godliness.** This significant word in the Pastorals and in this period of church history is found in I Tim 2:2; 3:16; 4:7,8; 6:3,5,6,11; II Tim 3:5; Tit 1:1; II Pet 1:3,6,7; 3:11; Acts 3:12; (the verb) Acts 17:23; I Tim 5:4; (the adjective) Acts 10:2,7; II Pet 2:9; (the adverb) II Tim 3:12; Tit 2:12. Its area of meaning emphasizes godly conduct, suggesting reverence and loyalty. This aptly stresses Paul's major emphasis in the Pastorals: sound doctrine and faithful living. The context makes it plain that Paul is referring to Christ when he says: **He who was manifest in the flesh** (ASV). Beginning here and in the remainder of the verse, the lines are in regular pattern, such as poetry or a hymn would furnish. It suited Paul's purpose well to tie his thoughts to something well known and current, since the message would then be remembered better. Many of the references to songs and singing in the NT are in connection with Paul (Eph 5:19; Col 3:16; Acts 16:25; I Cor 14:15). Hence it is not difficult to believe that Paul himself wrote this early Christian hymn, assuming, of course, that these lines (and Eph 5:14 also) are taken from a hymn. All the leading words occur elsewhere in Paul's writings. **Flesh.** Paul frequently emphasizes the humanity of Christ by the use of this word (Rom 1:3; 8:3; 9:5; Eph 5:15; Col 1:22; Heb 5:7; 10:20), so here of the incarnation, in harmony with the doctrine of the Virgin Birth. **Justified.** In the sense of being declared righteous, vindicated (Rom 3:4; Lk 7:29, 35). By the presence of the Spirit in Christ's ministry he was vindicated and proved true in all his claims (Rom 1:4; Lk 4:18,19; 10:21; Mt 12:18, 28; and especially Rom 8:10, 11). **Seen.** Translated "appeared" elsewhere, so here, "appeared to angels." The Spirit's final vindication of Christ was his resurrection: the mention of justification in the Spirit thus leads to his appearance to angels at resurrection, ascension, and entrance into

heaven (I Pet 3:22). **Preached unto the Gentiles.** Preached among the nations (ASV): the expression is a summary of the entire present era of missionary work (Rom 16:26; Col 1:6). **Believed.** A summary of the results of preaching. **Received.** Refers particularly to the Ascension, but includes all the subsequent exhibition of his glory. This is suggested by the historical and logical progressions of the poem: the whole messianic work of Christ is summed up in it.

3) Prophetic Warning of False Doctrine. 4:1-5. Gnosticism, one of whose characteristics was the asceticism here described, flooded the church in the second century, and no doubt was in evidence at the time Paul wrote.

1. The faith. The true doctrine of Christ as against the Satanic teaching. More details about the character and methods of the false teachers are found in II Pet 2 and in Jude. **2,3 a.** Characteristics of false teachers are seen in **hypocrisy, seared conscience,** and false attitudes toward the supports and blessings of this life: marriage and food.

3 b-5. The principles governing the right use of the supports of this life are: (a) God is the Creator and his creation is good; (b) He created food for men, and those who believe and know the truth about eternal salvation will have the right attitude toward the necessities of this life, and will neither deify the created thing nor degrade and despise it, but will accept it thankfully as the Father's wise provision (cf. Mt 6:31-33). **Sanctified.** The things God has provided by his creative word are set apart by his directions for their use (Gen 1:29-31; 2:4,5), and are further sanctified as a testimony of our heavenly Father's faithfulness and care when received with prayer, thankfulness, and understanding (cf. I Tim 6:17).

C. To the Witnessing Individual. 4:6–6:2.

1) To Timothy as a Good Minister. 4:6-16.

6. Put the brethren in remembrance. Implies enjoining and teaching or demonstrating: it includes what is more fully stated in verse 11, **command and teach.** Throughout the section (vv. 6-16), the effect of the Gospel on both Timothy and his people is in view. Timothy himself is to be nourished by the words of the faith and good doctrine. **The faith** is the whole body of truth and knowledge of God. **7.** In contrast to the revelation from God are placed the **old wives' fables** (lit., *myths)* which dominate and confuse the minds and conduct of men. **Refuse.** The same word is used in II Tim 2:23. **Exercise.** This is probably to be taken in a comprehensive sense of all efforts advancing the Gospel. It applies to bodily exercise in the next verse, and to all effort in verse 10.

8. Little. *For a little* (ASV); the reference to the present life and to the life to come suggests that it means "little while," in other words, this life. **Godliness.** This word is used only by Paul and Peter in the NT, and is a comprehensive word for obedience to the Gospel in all areas of life. It implies a basis of sound doctrine (Tit 1:1). See I Tim 3:16. **The life . . . to come.** This and similar expressions are basic in Paul's theology and eschatology. **9. Saying.** Gospel message, word. As in 3:1, here the expression sums up what has been discussed. "Word" in one accepted English sense is "an utterance as implying the faith or authority of the person who utters it" *(Webster's New International Dictionary,* sec. ed.).

10. Trust. Have set our hope on. Setting one's hope on the living God, who is able to make good his promises in this life and the next, is a great motive for a life of toil and conflict in the advancement of the Gospel. **Suffer reproach.** *Strive* (ASV); God's servant is forbidden to "strive" in the sense of II Tim 2:24, where a different word is used, meaning to "quarrel." Here, as in Jude 3, it means to "contend earnestly." **Saviour** (Gr. *Soter).* Used in the sense of "deliverer"; the word can have a wider and a narrower meaning. *Soter* was an epithet of guardian deities, especially Zeus; men offered sacrifice to him after a safe voyage, etc. Paul's conception of God is such that all the blessings, deliverances, and kindly providences which men experience are to be attributed only to him (Mt 5:45). In a special and higher sense, he is the deliverer of those who believe unto eternal salvation.

11. Command and teach. Here Paul takes up and emphasizes his **put the brethren in remembrance** of verse 6, and points forward to the emphatic conclusion of the whole paragraph in verse 16. The form of the verbs emphasizes the progressive and continuous nature of the work.

12. So far from his youth's being a hindrance, Timothy might be an example to believers in **word** (speech), **conversation** (manner of life), **charity** (love), **faith** (faithfulness), **purity** (strictly, "chastity"; but here in the sense of "propriety" or "careful observance of religious duties"). **In spirit** is not in the better texts.

13. Here are emphasized things which demand special attention among the people: **reading** (public reading of Scripture), **exhortation** (comfort, encouragement, admonition, exhortation, the whole area of ministry which would today be described as counseling, but here the context favors the ministry of preaching, expounding the Scriptures), **doctrine** (teaching). **14. Gift.** Teaching and counseling are mentioned together (Rom 12:7,8); teachers are among the gifts of the Spirit to the Church (I Cor 12:28); pastors and teachers are mentioned as a unit (Eph 4:11). This word meaning "gift of grace" can be applied to any gift of God through the Spirit. Here it seems to imply a charge given at ordination. Paul reiterates it and reminds Timothy here and at 1:18. **Presbytery** (used only in Lk 22:66, Acts 22:5, and here) refers to a group of representative spiritual leaders, chosen and proved.

15. Meditate. Practice, cultivate, or take pains with; used only here and in Acts 4:25. **Profiting.** Advancement. **16. Thyself.** The minister needs to be reminded of his own needs in connection with doctrine; in feeding others, he too must seek a blessing. **Continue.** This is one of the basic words used to describe the steadfast walk of a Christian (Gal 3:10; Heb 8:9; Jas 1:25; Acts 14:22; Col 1:23). Basically it is the same as "abide" in John 15 and I John. **Save** is used in the sense of the "work out your own salvation" of Phil 2:12.

2) To Men. 5:1. **Rebuke not.** The violent rebuke or attack is forbidden.

3) To Women, Especially Widows. 5:2-16.

2. Purity. Propriety.

3. Indeed (cf. vv. 5,16). Those who are widows and desolate – alone in the world – should be cared for by the church. The whole discussion should be considered in the light of OT teaching, where care for the widow is emphasized (also cf. Jas 1:27). **4. Nephews.** Grandchildren. **At home.** *Toward their own family* (ASV).

5. Here is a description of the true widow, who may serve the church and be cared for by the church (cf. Lk 2:36,37).

6. Liveth in pleasure. This is the contrasting mention of unacceptable widows; more details are added later. This expression occurs only here and in Jas 5:5 and means voluptuous and indulgent living, which indicates a state of spiritual death.

7. Give in charge. Paul is keenly conscious of the effect on the testimony of a failure at the home level. Hence these things are to be **commanded** (same verb as in 4:11), as Paul himself solemnly charges Timothy (6:13). **8.** Failure to provide is a denial of faith. **Infidel.** *Unbeliever*.

9. Here and in the next verse specific details are given about the qualifications of the widow the church is to support. **Not . . . under threescore years old.** Calvin gives two reasons why Paul does not wish any to be admitted under sixty years of age. First, "Being supported at the public expense, it was proper that they should have already reached old age." Second, there was a mutual obligation between the church and these widows: the church was to relieve their poverty, they were to consecrate themselves to the ministry of the church "which would have been altogether intolerable, if there were still a likelihood of their being married." **Having been the wife of one husband.** "It may be regarded as a sort of pledge of continence and chastity, when a woman has arrived at that age, satisfied with having had but one husband. Not that [Paul] disapproves of a second marriage, or affixes a mark of ignominy to those who have been twice married; (for, on the contrary, he advises younger widows to marry;) but because he wished carefully to guard against laying any females under a necessity of remaining unmarried, who felt it to be necessary to have husbands" (Calvin).

11. Wax wanton. This occurs only here and in Rev 18:7. Such conduct is incompatible with salvation and would suggest that Paul does not consider these "widows indeed." The idea of widowhood may have a wider application than actual bereavement; it may mean separation from a husband. For OT background, see II Sam 20:3 and Isa 54:4-6. Israel is a rejected, adulterous wife and widow because of separation, not because of the death of the husband. Hence these women, who are further described as having set aside their first pledge (faith, promise, I Tim 5:12) and as having turned aside to Satan (v.

15) may be unfaithful wives who have been divorced. **12. Damnation.** Remarriage under conditions of separation for unfaithfulness would bring the condemnation of the Lord (Lk 16:18). **First faith.** First pledge or promise. So leaving one's "first love" (Rev 2:4) may be parallel and equal to spiritual unfaithfulness.

14. Younger women. These are probably the younger widows who are eligible, except for their age, not the ones described in verse 12. **Guide the house.** This verb is used only here in the NT. The high estimate of woman's place and ability is paralleled in the classic passage in Prov 31:10-31. **Give none occasion.** "Pretext" or "opportunity." "Let them, in order to shut the mouth of evil speakers, choose a way of life that is less liable to suspicion" (Calvin). The **adversary** is Satan, mentioned immediately following. **To speak reproachfully.** *For reviling* (ASV). Either, unbecoming behavior is a reviling of the truth by those who live thus and gives Satan occasion for further work against the church; or, such behavior gives Satan an opportunity to revile and so harms the church's testimony. **15.** This is not a separate sentence in the punctuation of Nestle's *Greek New Testament,* but is a specific example of the principle just stated.

16. Man should be omitted. **If any woman that believeth** (ASV). Even a woman might be in a position where it would be her responsibility to care for a widow rather than throw the burden on the church, which is to care for those who are **desolate** *(left alone,* v. 5). The governing principle is stated in verse 8.

4) To Elders. 5:17-25. Paul has already discussed some of the elders' official relationships in chapter 3. Here he deals with more detailed and individual relationships, and his style is marked by frequent imperatives and personal exhortations to Timothy. This is Paul's usual way of handling doctrine in his epistles: first a discussion of principle, and then the practical application, with an earnest exhortation to godly living. So in the present section Paul returns to the subject of elders to give further counsel.

17. Rule well. An important qualification of an elder (3:4,5) is that he govern (direct or manage) properly. This is among the basic gifts for the well-being of the church (Rom 12:8; I Thess 5:12). **Double honor. Honor** has two meanings: "Honor" and "honorarium" or "compensation." Both meanings are doubtless intended here. In the case of those who labor in preaching and teaching, their whole time is thus devoted, and they are deserving of compensation from the church (see I Tim 5:18). The word **double** seems to argue for a sufficient or appropriate recompense, rather than a double amount. In the LXX, in Isa 40:2, the same word is used, and it carries in context the idea of "full equivalent." Note also Paul's parallel usage of **honor** in 6:1, where it is "all" or "full honor." (See William Hendricksen, *New Testament Commentary: Exposition of the Pastoral Epistles,* pp. 180,181.)

18. There are two quotations here: Deut 25:4 and Lk 10:7. **Muzzle the ox.** The content in Deuteronomy 25 deals with equitable relations among men; the verse is an aphorism quoted by Moses to prove a principle, and is so understood by Paul, who discusses the same principle at Rom 13:7 and I Cor 9:7-11, and quotes the same passage from Deuteronomy. **Laborer.** The exact original form of the quotation is found only in Luke. The citation here, **the scripture saith,** shows that Luke's Gospel was in existence and was regarded as Scripture.

19. Before two or three witnesses. The rule of evidence given by Moses (Deut 19:15), and used by the Lord (Mt 18:16). **20. Them that sin** (the Greek implies "those who persist in sin") **rebuke before all,** as Paul himself rebuked Peter (Gal 2:14). A godly man when so admonished publicly will take the lesson to heart (Prov 9:8).

21. Paul here uses the solemn charge, an entreaty, to reinforce the importance of the command against partiality. The same verb is used in II Tim 4:1 and again in II Tim 2:14, where Timothy himself is commanded to entreat others with the same earnestness.

22. Lay hands suddenly. This is often understood as forbidding hasty ordination. However, qualifications and ordination were discussed earlier. Locke suggests (ICC, p. 64) that it refers to the overhasty receiving of an offender back into communion. **Hands** (plural) may also mean "violent measures," "force." Here it would be another caution regarding Timothy's dealing with men who were to be rebuked. He should use no partiality, no violent measures, or unnecessary severity, nor, on the other hand, undue leniency, so as to be a partaker of their sins. **Pure.** This and related words are those generally translated "holy," "sanctify," "saint." Sometimes it has the specific meaning of chastity, but generally seems to refer to the right conduct of the Christian life. The closest parallel to **pure,** as used here, is "clear," as employed in II Cor 7:11. So perhaps here it should read: "Keep yourself clear [of other men's sins]." This discussion of others' sins is resumed and concluded in verses 24,25.

23. Drink no longer water. *No longer drink only water* (RSV). Paul's prohibitions are interpreted by context and sometimes are not absolute. To be a "water-drinker" in common usage seems to imply excessive severity and self-denial. The antiascetic principle is stated in 4:3-5. At that point Paul quickly shifted from general principle to specific, practical advice to Timothy (on bodily exercise, v. 8). So here, in speaking of general principles of avoidance, it is in point to warn against excessive frugality and severity. **Wine** is used for a wide variety of products of the grape; medicinal qualities are implied (Lk 10:34). Paul's prescription for Timothy's ailments is not a general rule of "moderate use" for all and sundry. General Biblical rules still apply (Hab 2:5,15; Prov 20:1; 23:31).

24. This and the next verse are to be kept in the context of **neither be partaker of other men's sins** (v. 22) and that in relation to the office of elder. The principle is: "By their fruits ye shall know them." Connect this with the warning against hasty action (v. 22). Some men's sins are open and lead to the appropriate decision; in the case of others, the evidence will be manifest in time.

25. *So also good deeds are conspicuous; and even when they are not, they cannot remain hidden* (RSV).

5) To Servants. 6:1,2. The context and the comparison with I Pet 2:18 suggest that two classes of masters are here dealt with: the believing and the unbelieving. Paul does not discuss the ultimate question of the right and wrong of slavery, but stresses the obligations resting on the slave, and the opportunity even in that situation to "adorn the doctrine" (Tit 2:10). The character of God and the Gospel teaching will be hurt by wrong conduct. And those who have believing masters are not to fail to give full honor, but are to serve them all the better, since it is a Christian brother who is devoting himself to (or benefiting by) good service.

III. Conclusion. 6:2d-21.

A. A Solemn Charge. 6:2d-15a. **These things teach and exhort.** This is a basic theme in the Pastorals, which appears at 4:11 as well as here. Right teaching was a principal reason for leaving Timothy at Ephesus (1:3).

1) Warnings Against False Teachers. 6:3-5. **Wholesome words.** Healthy, sound, because they promote health. This expression is peculiar to the Pastorals, emphasizing Paul's plea for sound doctrine. **Even the words of our Lord Jesus Christ.** This is another indication (see 5:18) that written Gospel narratives were well known and in circulation. **And to the doctrine.** This **and** could better be rendered **even,** since the words of Christ are the basis and substance of the doctrine which accords with **godliness** (practically a synonym for "Christianity"; see notes on 3:16). For the importance in Paul's writings of the teaching and life of Jesus, see Machen, *Origin of Paul's Religion,* pp. 147-152.

4. He is proud. Used three times in the NT, all three occurring in the Pastorals (I Tim 3:6; 6:4; II Tim 3:4). The word combines the ideas of conceit and folly. The rejection of the evidence of the Gospel is rooted in pride and is the utmost folly. **Knowing nothing.** This is the only time Paul uses this word meaning "to understand." **Doting.** The word is literally "sick," "ailing"; having *a morbid craving for controversy and for disputes about words* (RSV). **Surmisings.** Suspicions, conjectures or guesses. **5. Supposing that gain is godliness.** *Supposing that godliness is a way of gain* (ASV). **From such withdraw thyself.** Omit, as in the ASV.

2) Right Attitudes of True Teachers. 6:6-10. **6. Great gain.** This word appears to have the uniform meaning, "way of gain," "means of livelihood," which yields a better sense here. Paul means to say: "The Christian faith with sufficiency for this life is a mighty way of gain." He has already said (in 4:8, which is parallel and a good commentary) that godliness is profitable in every respect, giving the promise not only for this life but also for the life to come. It is this eschatological emphasis which Paul proceeds to stress in the rest of the epistle. In verses 7,8 the apostle shows the folly of setting one's hopes and desires on this

world, which is temporary. One should be content with food and raiment. In verses 9,10 he develops the thought of the folly of concentrating on the accumulation of wealth as an end in itself. The rendering of Hendriksen *(op. cit.)* seems preferable: *For a root of all the evils is the love of money.* **Which** (referring to money) **while some coveted after, they have erred from the faith.** Love of money is idolatry (Col 3:5; Eph 5:5; I Jn 2:15) and leads away from the true hope of the Christian.

3) The Motives of the Man of God. 6:11-15 a. Paul proceeds to outline the things a Christian should be cherishing. Central are the life to come and the return of Christ.

11. Follow after. Pursue, keep pursuing. Vigor and intensity are suggested both in fleeing things that lead from the faith and in pursuing things pertaining to the faith. Paul has a striking number of these suggestive lists of virtues, no two identical and none exhaustive of the possibilities of the "weightier matters of the law." **Righteousness** may be thought of as a comprehensive name for all the fruit of the Spirit. **Godliness** means "godly faith," "true religion." In Paul, this expression is found only in the Pastorals (see note on 3:16). **Faith** may mean "believing" or "faithfulness." A full realization of **love** means the experience of God's love for us, as well as our loving him and others. **Patience** means "endurance," and **meekness** seems to go back to the Lord's teaching and example (Mt 5:5; 11:29).

12. Fight. Compare the use of the same verb with an intensifying prefix in Jude 3. The later epistles of Paul and others had as one of their purposes to inform and prepare Christians for the rising tide of opposition and persecution which was to come in the ages immediately following. The **good fight** involves holding fast the faith and committing it to others. In this context it is closely related to **holding fast** and **laying hold** of eternal life. The same word translated **fight** is used by the Lord in Lk 13:24 as "strive" in a parallel context. **Called.** Calling is the gracious work of the Spirit in bringing us to faith in Christ. **Professed.** The same word is also translated "confess" (Rom 10:9). This is a basic doctrine in the Lord's teaching (Mt 10:32).

13. I give thee charge. The solemn charge which begins here is one sentence running through the doxology of verses 15 and 16. It characterizes God as the one who gives life to all things (cf. Rom 4:17 for the same emphasis on God's sovereign power and purposes in salvation). Paul had just spoken of eternal life in the preceding sentence; here it is emphasized that God is the one who gives it by effectual calling. Christ is characterized as the one who gave a good confession before Pilate. Just as Timothy had been called to life and had given a good confession, so Paul refers first to the Giver of all life and then to One who gave the good confession before Pilate. The **good confession** is to confess Jesus as Lord (Rom 10:9); such was the Lord's claim before Pilate and others. God and Christ are the witnesses of Paul's charge to Timothy.

14. That thou keep this commandment. Commandment seems to be used here as a comprehensive word for the Gospel, as Christ used it in Jn 12:50 (see also I Jn 3:23; II Jn 6). Keeping the commandment spotless and without reproach means both teaching and living above reproach. **Until the appearing of our Lord Jesus Christ.** Here is the high point of Paul's eschatological emphasis mentioned above (v. 6; cf. also II Tim 4:1, notes). The apostle uses it as the climax of his solemn charge to Timothy and as the transition to his great song of praise to the triune God. **In his times.** This expression is identical with "in due time" in 2:6 and Tit 1:3; *in its own times* (ASV); at the proper time, in the fulness of time as known to God.

B. Doxology. 6:15b,16. The triune God is the one who will reveal the appearing of Christ (cf. I Cor 15:28). God is here characterized by an accumulation of titles and ascriptions of majesty and power noteworthy even in Paul, and, indeed, in the entire Scripture. The ideas are parallel to 1:17 but are more fully expressed. Paul's thought moves from God's manifestations to men as Potentate and King through his sovereign prerogative of immortality, back to his mysterious and inscrutable being, and leads to the final ascription of honor and eternal omnipotent sway.

C. Return to the Solemn Charge. 6:17-21.

1) Right Use of Possessions. 6:17-21. **This world.** *This present world* (ASV). Paul's eschatological horizon has in view the age to come, the new heavens and new earth. **High-minded.** *Proud.* The ex-

pression is a single verb in Greek, combining two elements found in both Rom 11:20 and 12:16. **Trust.** *Have hope set on* (ASV). **Enjoy.** God has given all he has created for blessing and pleasure, which is realized only when possessions are put in the right relation to him; they are a stewardship from him. Two pairs of statements follow (v. 18), indicating how to use wealth. To **do good** and to **be rich in good works** are parallel; to be **ready to distribute** and **willing to communicate** (be liberal or sharing) are also parallels. In thus regarding and using wealth, one lays up a good foundation and lays hold on the life to come. **Laying up in store . . . a good foundation against the time to come** is a commentary on and parallel to Mt 6:19-21. **Eternal life.** "The life which is truly life." The adverb "truly" is used four times in I Tim out of the six times Paul uses it, and is emphatic of truth and real existence.

2) Final Appeal: A Summation. 6:20, 21. With deep emotion and personal appeal Paul begins his final exhortation: **O Timothy** (the interjection is especially frequent in Paul's epistles; see Rom 2:1,3; 9:20; Gal 3:1). He then briefly reiterates the principal themes of the entire epistle: (a) **Keep** the deposit of truth. The whole phrase is the rendering of three words: *guard the deposit*. This is the central message of the Pastorals: Guard the Gospel tradition by life and sound teaching, (b) **avoiding** false doctrine. There are two forms of learning which obscure the Gospel: (1) **profane** (implies blasphemous desecration of holy things) **and vain babblings,** consisting of high-sounding, empty words and speculations used for purposes of ostentation: and (2) **science** (lit., *knowledge)* **falsely so called.** Paul makes it plain that he is able to distinguish solid learning and fact from speculations without evidence, mere myth and fancy, **which some professing** (lit., *promising)* **have erred.** "Some, promising these fictions as truth and reality, leave the pledge and promise of God, which is the faith" (cf. II Pet 2:19). **Grace be with thee.** This is the characteristic ending to all Paul's epistles (II Thess 3:17,18; the briefest form is found here and in Col 4:18). The better text has the plural *you* (ASV), which intimates that the contents were intended for all the churches at Ephesus, and not for Timothy alone.

BIBLIOGRAPHY

(for I Timothy, II Timothy, and Titus)

ALFORD, HENRY. *The Greek Testament.* Vol. III. Chicago: Moody Press, reprinted with revisions, 1958.

CALVIN, JOHN. *Commentaries on the Epistles to Timothy, Titus and Philemon.* Grand Rapids: Wm. B. Eerdmans Publishing Co., reprinted 1948.

HARRISON, P. N. *The Problem of the Pastoral Epistles.* Oxford: The University Press, 1921.

HENDRICKSEN, WILLIAM. *New Testament Commentary: Exposition of the Pastoral Epistles.* Grand Rapids: Baker Book House, 1957.

LOCKE, WALTER. *A Critical and Exegetical Commentary on the Pastoral Epistles.* New York: Charles Scribner's Sons, 1924.

PALEY, WILLIAM. "Horae Paulinae," *Works.* Philadelphia: Religious Tract Society, 1850.

PLUMMER, ALFRED. *"The Pastoral Epistles," The Expositor's Bible.* Vol. 6. Grand Rapids: Wm. B. Eerdmans Publishing Co., reprinted 1943.

SALMON, GEORGE. *An Historical Introduction to the Study of the Books of the New Testament.* 9th ed. London: John Murray, 1904.

WARFIELD, B. B. *Faith and Life.* New York: Longmans Green, 1916.

————— *Inspiration and Authority of the Bible.* Philadelphia: Presbyterian and Reformed Publishing Co., 1948.

————— *The Lord of Glory.* New York: American Tract Society, 1907.

————— *The Person and Work of Christ.* Philadelphia: Presbyterian and Reformed Publishing Co., 1950.

ZAHN, THEODOR. *Introduction to the New Testament.* Vol. II. Grand Rapids: Kregel, reprinted 1953.

THE SECOND EPISTLE TO TIMOTHY

OUTLINE

(For the general introduction to this epistle, see Introduction to I Timothy.)

I. Salutation and introduction. 1:1-18.
  A. Salutation of special authority and affection. 1:1,2.
  B. Thanksgiving for Timothy's faith. 1:3-5.
  C. Reminder of responsibility for the Gospel. 1:6-18.
    1. The gift of God. 1:6,7.
    2. Challenge to endure afflictions incident to the ministry. 1:8-12.
    3. Challenge to hold fast the form of sound words. 1:13,14.
    4. Personal illustrations of loyalty and opposition 1:15-18.
II. The Gospel: A trust requiring faithfulness. 2:1—3:17.
  A. To be diligently committed to others. 2:1-7.
    1. As a soldier. 2:3,4.
    2. As an athlete. 2:5.
    3. As a farmer. 2:6.
  B. To be firmly guarded and cherished. 2:8-26.
    1. The central truth of the Gospel. 2:8.
    2. Paul's example of faithfulness. 2:9,10.
    3. The truth embodied in a "faithful saying." 2:11-13.
    4. The truth rightly handled. 2:14-19.
    5. The truth applied to the life. 2:20-26.
  C. To be recognized as a bulwark. 3:1-17.
    1. Against apostasy. 3:1-9.
    2. In defense of the faithful. 3:10-12.
    3. The inspired Scriptures: Our confidence. 3:13-17.
III. Charge to Timothy, and conclusion. 4:1-22.
  A. The solemn charge. 4:1-5.
    1. God and Christ: Witnesses of Timothy's responsibility. 4:1.
    2. Five imperatives: Preach, Be instant, Reprove, Rebuke, Exhort. 4:2.
    3. Turning from the truth; turning to myths. 4:3,4.
    4. Four imperatives: Watch, Endure, Evangelize, Fulfill. 4:5.
  B. Paul's final testimony. 4:6-8.
    1. Paul's calm facing of death. 4:6.
    2. The testimony of one who has fulfilled his task. 4:7.
    3. The blessed hope undimmed. 4:8.
  C. Conclusion: Final notes of love and concern. 4:9-22.

COMMENTARY

I. Salutation and Introduction. 1:1-18.

A. Salutation of Special Authority and Affection. 1:1,2.

1. The special matters put with great terseness and brevity are: (1) Paul's apostleship from Christ Jesus; (2) that this was through the will of God; (3) that his apostleship was in accordance with God's promise of life in Christ Jesus. In I Tim 1:1 we find the expression, "Lord Jesus Christ, our hope." Here it **is the promise of life which is in Christ Jesus.** In Titus the ideas are expressed more elaborately (Tit 1:2). The supernatural evidence and attestation in Paul's apostleship corresponds to the fact of the promise in the Scriptures. **2.** God the Father and Christ Jesus our Lord are the single source of grace, mercy, and peace. **Mercy** is added only in the Pastoral Epistles, apparently for the encouragement of Paul's **dearly beloved son,** Timothy, and his "own son after the common faith," Titus (see Tit 1:4 and notes on I Tim 1:1,2).

B. Thanksgiving for Timothy's Faith. 1:3-5. Only in Galatians and Titus does

Paul omit the formal thanksgiving or eulogy.

3. **God, whom I serve from my forefathers.** Paul knew of at least two previous generations who were intensely loyal to the faith, paralleling the subsequent mention of two generations of godly forebears in Timothy's case (v. 5). This is ground for encouragement that we are not following fables; the faith has endured and has borne its fruits. **With pure conscience.** See notes on I Tim 1:5,19; 3:9; 4:2. The Greek word is the exact counterpart of the Latin *con-science*, "a knowing with," a shared or joint knowledge. It is our awareness of ourselves in all the relationships of life, especially ethical relationships. We have ideas of right and wrong; and when we perceive their truth and claims on us, and will not obey, our souls are at war with themselves and with the law of God, as portrayed in Romans 7. To have a good, or pure, conscience does not mean that we have never sinned or do not commit acts of sin. Rather, it means that the underlying direction and motive of life is to obey and please God, so that acts of sin are habitually recognized as such and faced before God (I Jn 1:9). **I thank God.** The thing Paul is thankful for is the unfeigned faith in Timothy and his mother and grandmother. The clauses lying between give the other circumstances for Paul's thankfulness. **That,** in II Tim 1:3, is better translated as, *I unceasingly remember*. **That,** in verse 4, is better translated, *so that I am filled with joy*. This last phrase is placed between the ideas of Paul's remembering Timothy's tears and his remembering the unfeigned faith. The tears were tears of love and loyalty to Paul and the Lord, and so were cause for joy and led to the apostle's deep thanksgiving to God for the genuine faith expressed in tears.

C. Reminder of Responsibility for the Gospel. 1:6-18.

1) The Gift of God. 1:6,7. The sequence of thought in verse 5 in referring to **faith,** and the reference to the **spirit** in verse 7 indicate that the **gift** of verse 6 is the Holy Spirit, or some special aspect of his work. This would explain Paul's reference to the conferring of the gift by the laying on of his hands. The Holy Spirit in special manifestations was given by the laying on of hands of the Apostles (Acts 8:17; 19:6). **Stir up.** Use the gift, engaging in appropriate activities of the ministry. **Fear.** Romans 8:15 is the commentary on this thought (cf. Heb 2:15; I Pet 3:14; I Jn 4:18). **Sound mind.** This and related words are especially frequent in the Pastorals (I Tim 2:9, 15; 3:2; Tit 2:2,4-6,12) and are closely parallel to the "minding" of the Spirit of Rom 8:5,6,9.

2) Challenge to Endure Afflictions Incident to the Ministry. 1:8-12. In the Greek text these verses are one continuous movement of thought and one sentence. The four imperatives in this and the following challenge contain the main point of Paul's reminder to Timothy: Be not ashamed (v. 8); Be partaker (v. 8); Hold fast (v. 13); Guard the deposit (v. 14). The exposition of the Gospel in verses 9-12 gives the ground for these exhortations. **The testimony of our Lord** is the Gospel he has given to his Church. **The afflictions** which the propagation of the Gospel entails must be borne in the power of God. **9.** Saving and calling are parallel activities of the Holy Spirit. **Given us. Here,** as always, Paul's reference to predestination is designed to strengthen and comfort. God's eternal purposes will not fail. **10. Manifest.** It is his grace (the gift of life) which was ours in his purpose from eternity, and which has now been manifested in the saving work of Christ. The same word, which implies "stands fully revealed," is used in Rom 3:21 and 16:26. **11. Whereunto** refers to the Gospel, of which Paul was appointed an apostle. **12. Cause.** Because of the Lord's commission. **These things.** Imprisonment and bonds. We can without shame endure any unfair and adverse circumstances if we know that in them all the Lord is keeping our deposit: that is, the Gospel he has entrusted to us. **Persuaded.** This passage closely parallels Paul's exposition of Abraham's experience in Rom 4:21.

3) Challenge To Hold Fast the Form of Sound Words. 1:13,14. The necessity of putting the basic outline of doctrine in concrete, easily remembered form is reiterated by Paul (cf. Rom 6:17) in another imperative (II Tim 1:13): **Hold fast the form of sound words,** or the outline of doctrine. The confession of faith was characteristic of the Church from earliest times, and was soon formulated in the Apostles' Creed. In Christ and in his Spirit are the **faith** (fulness) and **love** to insure our keeping the faith. **14. Good thing** means *good deposit*. The

same word is used in verse 12 and in the LXX at Lev 6:2,4. The Spirit will keep the deposit. The intimate connection of the work of Christ and that of the Spirit are evident here as elsewhere in Paul's writings (Rom 8:9-11; II Cor 3:17, 18).

4) Personal Illustrations of Loyalty and Opposition. 1:15-18. Here are instances of those who helped and those who opposed the great apostle. They serve as warning and encouragement to Timothy. Paul's method was similar in I Tim 1:19,20.

II. The Gospel: A Trust Requiring Faithfulness. 2:1–3:17.

A. To Be Diligently Committed to Others. 2:1-7. An all-important detail in guarding the deposit is to teach it faithfully to others who shall themselves be able to teach.

1. To this end, Paul says, the Christian teacher is to **be strong.** All NT occurrences of this word are in connection with Paul or used by him (Acts 9:22; Rom 4:20; Eph 6:10; Phil 4:13; I Tim 1:12; II Tim 4:17). **Grace** is an all-inclusive word for the power and gifts of the Spirit (see Charles Hodge, *Systematic Theology*, II, 654,655).

The three famous metaphors setting forth the relation of the Christian teacher to the faith are given in this passage: (1) The teacher as a soldier (vv. 3,4). **Endure hardness** is more accurately *suffer hardship with me* (ASV). **Please** is almost entirely a Pauline word in the NT; see the force of the cognate noun in Col 1:10. (2) The teacher as an athlete (v. 5). **Strive lawfully.** This implies both the training for the contest and the rules governing it. **Crowned** is used only here and in Heb 2:7,9 in the NT; the noun is used in II Tim 4:8. The crown is elsewhere defined as "incorruptible" (I Cor 9:25), "of righteousness" (II Tim 4:8), "of life" (Jas 1:12; Rev 2:10), "unfading" (I Pet 5:4). (3) The teacher as a farmer (v. 6). This principle (more fully discussed at I Cor 9:1-14 and I Tim 5:17, 18) may be applied to include remuneration and maintenance, but here the spiritual benefit to Timothy himself is stressed. He should know the blessings of the message he is giving to others (cf. I Tim 4:15,16).

7. Consider what I say. Or, *take note, think it over,* **and the Lord give thee understanding.** *Shall give* (ASV) is correct.

B. To Be Firmly Guarded and Cherished. 2:8-26.

1) The Central Truth of the Gospel. 2:8. The ASV has the correct word order in this verse. **Remember** stresses the continuity of the action: *Be continually remembering.* **Jesus Christ.** In the Gospels this is a rare but direct and solemn designation of Jesus, occurring at Mt 1:18; Mk 1:1; Jn 1:17; 17:3. This last passage is especially significant because the Lord used it of himself. This is the basis of the usage in Acts in the early church. Paul is emphasizing the apostolic message of Jesus Christ risen (see B. B. Warfield, *Lord of Glory*, pp. 184-186). **Raised** (ASV, *risen)* underscores the fact that he rose and now lives. The word is that used most frequently in the Lord's own teaching and in the Gospel accounts of his resurrection. Paul's use of the word here, in I Cor 15:4,12, and elsewhere, carries the testimony back exactly in its earliest form. **From** is properly translated *out from among.* **Dead** is not used figuratively, but literally means *dead people.* All the dead are referred to; Jesus rose as the first fruits, out from them. Paul preached that Christ died and was buried, eliminating any figurative interpretation in **risen** or **dead. Of the seed of David.** The apostle refers to Christ in this way here, in Rom 1:3, and in Acts 13:23. This term has the triple advantage of stressing Jesus' true humanity, his Messianic lineage, and his sovereign authority. For this last point, note especially Rev 3:7; 5:5; 22:16. Paul's usual term for this idea is "Lord." Peter connects these ideas in Acts 2:30,36. Paul uses **my gospel** here as he used **my deposit** in II Tim 1:12. The force of it is that the trust or deposit given to Paul is the Gospel, for which he was responsible and for which he was a competent eyewitness. Paul disclaims originality: these were the facts as known to him and to those from whom he had received them (cf. I Cor 15:3,11; see B. B. Warfield, *The Person and Work of Christ*, pp. 535-546).

2) Paul's Example of Faithfulness. 2:9,10. **Wherein I suffer trouble.** The troubles, opposition, and imprisonment Paul experienced stemmed directly from his unswerving testimony to the Resurrection (see J. O. Buswell, *Behold Him!* pp. 42-

49). The two clauses of verse 10 are parallel to the two corresponding clauses of verse 9: **suffer trouble** answers to **endure all things,** with the added thought **for the elect's sakes. The word of God is not bound** answers to **that they may obtain the salvation.**

3) The Truth Embodied in a "Faithful Saying." 2:11-13.

11a. Paul used **a faithful saying** to introduce matters of great importance (see note on I Tim 3:1). Here he uses it to introduce words taken, most probably, from a familiar hymn (see note on I Tim 3:16). This is the heart of what Paul wanted to say; hence he sets it off in memorable form. The poem has a balanced structure. The first clause and the last receive the emphasis through the conjunction which is here translated *indeed* and *for:*

If indeed we died with him, we shall also live with him;
If we endure, we shall also reign with him;
If we shall deny, he too will deny us;
If we are faithless, he abideth faithful,
For himself he cannot deny.

11b. If we be dead. *Died* (ASV) is correct. Our justification and forgiveness is a death to sin and the curse of the Law. **Live with him** looks to the ultimate goal—eternal life, while including our present walk. **12. Suffer** means *endure* (ASV); the thought is parallel to that in Rom 8:16,17. **Reign** further suggests what is involved in living with Christ. **Deny** is a clear reference to Mt 10:33. There is a double incentive to remain faithful: the hope of reigning with him, and the certainty that if we deny him, he will deny us. **13. Believe not** means to be *faithless* (ASV). This last sentence seems to suggest not an emphasis on his denial, if we deny him, but that if Christians sin, his faithfulness is the ultimate reliance: He cannot deny himself. The thought is similar to that of I Jn 2:1, involving the confession and forgiveness of sin (see the entire sermon "Communion with Christ," Warfield, *Faith and Life,* pp. 415-427).

4) The Truth Rightly Handled. 2:14-19. Empty discussions would unsettle those who heard; but Timothy was to proceed according to the Word, avoiding vanities, remembering the marks of the sure foundation, and seeking, by right conduct, to be useful to the Lord. **14.** Timothy was to give others the same charge Paul was giving him (4:1). The same word is used—**charging them.** It was to be done **before the Lord,** who would then witness to the grave responsibility conferred. **Strive not about words** is one word in the Greek text; the corresponding noun is used at I Tim 6:4. Both forms seem to imply quibbling over words and not seeking truth. **15. Study to show thyself approved.** *Give diligence to present thyself approved* (ASV). **Rightly dividing.** *Handling aright* (ASV), as a master workman would his tool. **16. Vain babblings.** Omit **vain,** as in the ASV. This is a further characteristic of the strifes about words. **They** refers to babblings. **Ungodliness.** Diverting the attention from solid truth would allow error in conduct. **17. Their word** seems to mean the doctrine of those who engage in such discussions. **Canker** is a spreading ulcer. **Hymenaeus** is associated with Alexander in I Tim 1:20, where the reason for his departure from the faith lies in his failure to hold a good conscience. **Philetus** is not mentioned elsewhere; nothing more is known of him. **18. Resurrection.** The Gnostics conceived of resurrection allegorically, as referring to an acquaintance with truth, occurring at baptism.

19. Here the ASV translation is preferable. **Foundation** seems to imply both the foundation and the temple, the church, as in I Tim 3:15; Eph 2:20; Mt 16:18. **Seal.** A mark of ownership and authentication. **Knoweth.** This quotation is taken from the LXX of Num 16:5, with allusions to verses 26,27 of the same passage (cf. Mt 7:23; Jn 10:14). **Every one that nameth the name** means every one who names the name of Christ as his Lord. No one distinct passage is cited in this statement, but the sense of many passages is compressed in it.

5) The Truth Applied to the Life. 2:20-26. The truth of separation from evil is applied in balanced and positive fashion in the rest of the chapter.

20. The **great house.** Probably the church in its visible aspect as seen by the world (cf. I Tim 3:15). The connection of thought seems to be that in the visible church there is false profession, from which one should purge himself. **Honour** is parallel to the expression in Rom 9:21. **21. These.** The dishonorable vessels as well as their doctrines and practices. **Purge** is closely related to the word used by the Lord in Jn 15:2,3, and suggests the same doctrine. **Sanctified** implies continuance of the state of being set apart. **Master's.** *Despot's.* An expressive divine title used in Lk 2:29; Acts 4:24; II Pet 2:1; Jude 4; Rev 6:10. It is closely related to "housemaster" in Mt 10:25; Lk 13:25; 14:21; and especially in Mt 13:27,28. It means absolute owner.

22. Charity. Love. **Pure heart** is an expression very similar to that in the beatitude of Mt 5:8, and repeats the thought of **purge** (II Tim 2:21). **Call on the Lord** is parallel to "nameth the name" (v. 19). The preceding verse calls for separation from evil company; this verse calls for fellowship with the Lord's people and seeking the graces of the Spirit.

23,24. Again false doctrine and unprofitable discussions are mentioned, as in verses 14,16-18. **Strive.** A different word from that used in verse 5. Here it is the verb corresponding to "strifes" of the verse preceding, and is used in a bad sense. **Servant** refers still to the figure of the great house and the servants in it. **Patient.** *Forbearing.* **25,26.** This truth harmonizes with the truth of separation taught above: there should still be the meek attempt to instruct, in hope that God will give them repentance, though they are now in Satan's snare. Pride is indicated as the cause of rejection of truth and falling into Satan's snare (I Tim 6:4; 3:6). **Recover.** "Come to their senses"; parallel to "repentance" of the preceding verse.

C. To Be Recognized as a Bulwark. 3:1-17. As the writer contrasts truth and error, devotion to the Lord on one side, and obedience to sin and Satan on the other, he brings his thoughts to a climax in the detailed description of sins that will characterize a future departure from the faith. With this he contrasts the example of his own experience and the great stronghold of the faithful, the Scriptures. In order that Timothy may be the more encouraged to fight, he makes it clear (v. 9) that the truth of God will prevail.

1) Against Apostasy. 3:1-9. It is noteworthy that the severest opposition is to come from those who have a form of godliness only (v. 5). **1. The last days** probably is not here limited to the eschatological age-end, but includes the Gnostic attack on the Church then developing. **2. Lovers of their own selves** is one word in the Greek, used only here in the NT. It is significant that men should be characterized as lovers of self at the beginning of this passage. Then follows (through v. 5) a list of sins flowing from the corrupted hearts that love self rather than God. Most of the following adjectives are compounded of two parts, so that each has the effect of a compressed sentence, combining subject and predicate.

Covetous. The word used of the Pharisees (Lk 16:14). **Boasters** is used only here and in Rom 1:30 in the NT. **Proud** is also in Rom 1:30, Jas 4:6, and I Pet 5:5. **Blasphemers** is used by Paul of himself in I Tim 1:13. **Disobedient to parents,** as in Rom 1:30 (cf. Tit 1:16; 3:3; Acts 26:19). **Unthankful** occurs only here and in Lk 6:35, but the idea is expressed otherwise, as in Rom 1:21. **3. Without natural affection,** as in Rom 1:31. **Trucebreakers** means *implacable* (ASV), as in Rom 1:31. **False accusers** is generally used of Satan as *diabolos* (cf. Rev 12:10; also I Tim 1:10; Tit 2:3). **Incontinent** is *without self-control* (ASV). **Despisers of those that are good.** *No lovers of good* (ASV). **4. Heady.** *Head-strong* (ASV). **Highminded.** Puffed up (I Tim 3:6; 6:4). This sums up the sins flowing from the love of self and is in sharp contrast to **lovers of God.**

5. The terrifying fact is that such people are professing Christians, who very probably wish to be considered religious and holy. They have, however, only a **form of godliness,** only the external appearance of following Gospel doctrine and practice; the **power** is lacking. Only the Holy Spirit makes profession a reality; the faith without the works and fruit of the Spirit is dead. **Denying,** a strong word, implies knowing and yet decisively rejecting the truth. **From such turn away.** The expression may mean "repel them from you" as a good soldier repels a foe.

6-9. Their true character is shown by their sinful acts. **6. Creep into houses.** Enter families and homes. **7. Ever learning** refers to the women. **Knowledge of the truth** includes knowledge of sin (Rom 3:20) on the one side, as well as the knowledge of the truth, according to godliness, on the other (Tit 1:1); it implies a coming short of salvation (Heb 10:26). The implication here may be that these people do not come to a knowledge of their sinful condition even under the testimony of the church. **8. Jannes and Jambres** are names of two of the magicians alluded to in Ex 7:11,22. There were probably more, and the mention of these is simply a way of designating the magicians of Egypt. The mention of Satan earlier (II Tim 2:26) and the extreme corruption of the people here described, as well as the working of Satanic wonders, suggest a parallel to II Thess 2:9-12. **These** (II Tim 3:8) are not the women of verse 7, but those false teachers who seduce them, who deliberately oppose the truth. **Reprobate** seems clearly to imply a lost condition (cf. II Cor 13:5; Heb 6:8; Tit 1:16). The **faith** equals the Gospel. **9.** Paul's encouraging message is that, as the truth of God prevailed against the tricks of the magicians of Egypt, even so the Gospel will triumph over every kind of error that may arise.

2) In Defense of the Faithful. 3:10-12. The full exposure of the senseless opposition to the truth will be fulfilled completely in the time of the return of Christ. **10.** But Paul uses himself as an illustration of God's ability to deliver even now (cf. 4:17). **11.** He encourages Timothy by recalling events of the first missionary journey. Timothy is first mentioned in the second journey at Lystra, but Paul's remarks refer to the earlier visit. Timothy would have been the more affected by the remarks because he had seen the work at Lystra prosper and endure in spite of opposition. **12. Godly** is the adverb related to "godliness" (3:5; Tit 1:1, and frequently in I Tim). Paul must mean that to **live godly** involves the aggressive kind of witness he gave at Lystra, which roused opposition in addition to winning souls.

3) The Inspired Scriptures: Our Confidence. 3:13-17. As opposition increases, the Scriptures become the believer's reliance, his bulwark. Paul's characterization of this age as one of increasing wickedness is in accord with the picture given by the Lord in the Olivet Discourse. **13. Seducers.** Used in the sense of "wizard," and also of "juggler," or "cheat." In this context the emphasis is on deceit. **14.** In sharp contrast to this opposition of the world and its deceit, Timothy was to continue in the sound Scripture doctrine, in reliance on God. An important element in continuing is **knowing of whom** one has learned. The character of the teacher and witness is important in establishing the truth of the Gospel. Paul would have included himself and Timothy's parents, but the **whom** of the original text could also point to the Scriptures as the highest proof of the truth of the doctrines. **15.** Timothy had a lifetime of acquaintance with the Scriptures to teach him their power.

Paul then gives the reason for this efficacy of Scripture: it is of divine origin. **16. Inspiration of God** is a simple word, meaning, *God-breathed.* It comes with full divine authority because of full truthfulness, and is therefore profitable. The alternative translations of the original as **all Scripture** or *every Scripture* (ASV) are both possible and imply the same thing: If every Scripture is inspired, then all is. The Greek sentence has no verb expressed. Should the adjective "God-breathed" stand with the subject, or be a part of the predication made about the subject? The AV is more accurate than the ASV here, since the ASV seems to admit the possibility, absurd in Paul's case, that there could be Scripture which is not inspired. Warfield's paraphrase relieves the ambiguity: "Every Scripture, seeing that it is God-breathed, is as well profitable . . ." ("Inspiration," ISBE, III, 1474 a). **Doctrine** is emphasized in the Pastoral Epistles (nineteen of the twenty-one occurrences of *doctrine* in the NT are found in Paul's writings, and of the nineteen, fifteen are in the Pastoral Epistles.) **Reproof** is closely related to "reprove" of Jn 16:8. The Scripture is the Spirit's instrument in conviction. **Correction** conveys the idea of improvement. **Instruction in righteousness** indicates training or education that is to be found in the way of righteousness, or in "the faith" (cf. ASV: *instruction which is in righteousness).* The word for **instruction** is found only in Paul; it is translated "nurture" in Eph 6:4. In Heb 12:5,7, 8,11 it is rendered "chastening." **17. Man of God.** Paul had Timothy especially in mind (cf. I Tim 6:11). This is an OT phrase meaning prophet (Deut 33:1; Josh 14:6; I Sam 6:9; I Kgs 12:22; 13:1). **Perfect** and **throughly furnished** (equipped) are from the same root; the ASV has correctly translated it: *complete, furnished completely* (cf. Eph 6: 13-17).

III. Charge to Timothy, and Conclusion. 4:1-22.

A. The Solemn Charge. 4:1-5.

1) God and Christ: Witnesses of Timothy's Responsibility. 4:1. The idea of

charging or commanding the passing on of the testimony is emphasized in outstanding Scriptures: Moses charged Israel (Deut 29:1,10; 30:11,16); Moses charged Joshua (Deut 31:7,8,23); Joshua charged Israel (Josh 23:2,6; 24:1,26,27); Samuel charged Israel (I Sam 12:1-25); David charged Solomon (I Kgs 2:1-9; I Chr 28:2-10,20); Ezra charged Israel (Neh 8—10); Jesus charged the apostles (Jn 13:34; 14-17). **Judge.** The right and ability to judge all men belongs to God alone; Christ clearly claimed it (Mt 7:21,22; Jn 5:25-30). **At his appearing.** The sanction of the charge is the appearing of Christ. The ASV translates correctly: *by his appearing and his kingdom.* God and Christ are the divine witnesses; the appearing and the kingdom are the most solemn of incentives to fidelity. **Appearing** means "manifestation" and is used of both the first coming (II Tim 1:10) and the second (4:1,8; Tit 2:13). **Kingdom** has different phases: judgment (Mt 25:31,34,40); Millennial reign (I Cor 15:24,25); eternal in new heavens and earth (Rev 22:3).

2) Five Imperatives. 4:2. These five terse imperatives, which are matched by four more in verse 5, sum up the work of the ministry: (1) **Preach.** Foremost is the great basic work of delivering the fundamental message, as Paul himself did (I Cor 15:1-11), and Jesus (Lk 5:1; 8:11, 21). (2) **Be instant.** Be ready, be at hand, both when it is convenient and when it is not. (3) **Reprove,** closely related to the idea in **reproof** (3:16; see note), is the same word used in Tit 1:9 ("convince"), 13 ("rebuke"); 2:15 ("rebuke"); I Tim 5:20 ("rebuke"). (4) **Rebuke** is translated *charge* in Mt 12:16; Mk 8:30; 10:48; Lk 9:21. It means to lay a value or charge on. The essential idea is often the implied demand for restitution when error is pointed out. (5) **Exhort** is often translated *comfort* or *beseech.* It is an earnest entreaty in any of life's circumstances, and is possible because of the presence of the Comforter, whose name is a different form of the same word. The phrase, **with all longsuffering and doctrine** (teaching), is not to be taken with the last of the imperatives only, but is to accompany all five commands. Punctuate as in the ASV. Patient teaching is the most solid basis for ultimate success in the ministry (cf. 2:25).

3) Turning from the Truth; Turning to Myths. 4:3,4. **3.** The insistence on faithfulness and sound teaching is the more necessary because of the danger of apostasy in the churches. **Itching ears.** People will wish to hear what satisfies their sinful desires. Isaiah powerfully characterizes the attitude in 30:9-11. **Teachers.** The principle is Hosea's: "like people, like priest" (Hos 4:9; Jer 5:30,31). **Heap** means to multiply, have an abundance of false teachers. **4. Truth.** Very wonderful is the Bible's constant orientation to the **truth,** a comprehensive word for God's revelation, centering in Jesus Christ. **Fables.** Turning from the only basis of life, their hopes and conduct will be built on the sand, on myths (see note on I Tim 4:7). In II Pet 1:16 myths are contrasted with the written truth of God. Therefore, the more urgent is the need for much sound teaching.

4) Four Imperatives. 4:5. These conclude Paul's commands to Timothy. (1) **Watch.** Literally, *abstain from intoxicating drinks,* but in all NT occurrences the idea of watchfulness and alertness is stressed. The parallel expressions linked to it are self-explanatory: "watch and be sober" (I Thess 5:6); "be . . . sober, and watch" (I Pet 4:7); "be sober, be vigilant" (I Pet 5:8). (2) **Endure afflictions.** All three Pauline uses of this word are in II Tim: "endure hardness" (2:3); "suffer trouble" (2:9). Note also the same word compounded with the preposition **with** in 1:8: "partaker (sharer) of the afflictions." (3) **Do the work of an evangelist.** If this is meant to indicate a special office (Acts 21:8), the list in Eph 4:11 is noteworthy, for it is fuller than the parallel list in I Cor 12:28: prophets, evangelists, pastors, teachers are mentioned as compared with prophets, teachers. Probably these functions would overlap; the evangelist might well stand between prophet and pastor-teacher. Timothy's life had included much itinerant evangelism, joined with pastoral and teaching work. (4) **Make full proof of thy ministry.** *Fulfill* (ASV) or "fulfill completely thy ministry" gives the thought. It is the command to teach and evangelize given by the Lord, and as such it stands as the climactic and comprehensive imperative of the whole series (cf. Paul's great text, Acts 20:24).

B. Paul's Final Testimony. 4:6-8. This eloquent and confident testimony touches on the main points Paul has endeavored to say to Timothy: confidence in the grace of Christ; faithful transmission of the faith to others; the steadfast reliance on the blessed hope.

1) Paul's Calm Facing of Death. 4:6. **Ready to be offered** (lit., *I am being poured out*). This verb, occurring only here and in Phil 2:17, is used by Paul in a figurative sense. Literally it is used in connection with a libation or drink offering (Gen 35:14). But Paul was thinking of his imminent death as an offering in the service of Christians and their faith. His whole life had been a sacrifice (Rom 12:1), and now his death would complete the life with a drink offering. **The time of my departure is at hand** is a parallel statement of his approaching death, under a different figure. He uses the same metaphor in Phil 1:23, where the verb of the same root is used. Christ (Lk 9:31) and Peter (II Pet 1:15) spoke of death with a similar figure, using the word "exodus."

2) The Testimony of One Who Has Fulfilled His Task. 4:7. **Fight** is rendered "conflict" (Phil 1:30; Col 2:1), "contention" (I Thess 2:2), "race" (Heb 12:1), "fight" (I Tim 6:12). For Paul it was more than a grim and momentous battle; it was a contest, a race that demanded all the enthusiasm of a fervent, consecrated spirit (cf. Acts 20:24). To have fought the **good** fight implies having won. This fits Paul's figure well, and adds irony: though he appears to be conquered and to be about to die a felon's death, yet he has conquered, for he has finished the course Jesus set before him; he has kept the faith by committing it to faithful men and establishing churches. All those who die in faith (Heb 11:13) will ultimately receive the promise and carry off the prize (I Pet 1:9; 5:4; Heb 10:30). **Course** is used only by Paul in the NT (Acts 13:25; 20:24). The word may mean a lap in a race. Paul may be thinking of the transmission of the faith through the centuries as a relay race: he has successfully finished his course and passed on the faith to others. The figure of the relay race seems to fit the following verse, for not Paul only, but the whole 'team' will receive the prize. **Kept.** *Keep* means not only "guard" but also "observe and do." For a believer to persevere and be faithful unto death is a triumph of grace (Rev 2:10). The **faith** is the whole Gospel testimony, going back to the words of Jesus committed to his followers (Rom 10:17; Heb 2:3, 4; Rev 14:12).

3) The Blessed Hope Undimmed. 4:8. Instead of being depressed, Paul is only the more confident. The greater the trial, the clearer the promise shines. The **crown** which is the prize is described in various ways: it is a crown of "righteousness," "life" (Rev 2:10), "rejoicing" (I Thess 2:19); "glory" (I Pet 5:4). **The righteous judge** may suggest that many of the decisions Paul had received in this life were unfair, but the Lord is the Judge who can make no mistake. **Not to me only.** Paul's thought is not of himself alone, but of all the redeemed. **Love.** "Who have set their love upon." The verb form implies steadfast maintaining of love for Christ's appearing.

C. Conclusion: Final Notes of Love and Concern. 4:9-22. Dwelling on the welfare of individuals is characteristic of Paul (see Rom 16). **9. Diligence.** Paul relied on the loyalty of Timothy. **10. Demas** (Col 4:14; Phm 24) . . . **loved this present world.** The strength of the blessed hope shines through as the apostle sadly mentions one so foolish as to set his affections on the things of this world. **Crescens** is mentioned only here. **Titus** had rejoined Paul since receiving the epistle addressed to him and had gone on to Dalmatia, also known as Illyricum (modern Yugoslavia; cf. Rom 15:19). Paul seems to have sent Titus to new territory, beyond where he himself had gone. **11. Mark** had proved himself in Paul's estimation since the time some twenty years before when the apostle had refused to take him on the second journey (Acts 15:37-39). **12.** Paul probably meant that **Tychicus** was to relieve Timothy, who probably was still at Ephesus, so that Timothy could join the apostle in Rome. This would suggest that Tychicus was the bearer of the letter (see note on Tit 3:12).

13. Cloke. A thick upper garment Perhaps Paul passed through in the summer, when it was not needed, but now winter was approaching. **Carpus** is mentioned only here. **The books.** Probably papyri copies of the Scriptures or Scripture portions. **The parchments.** Perhaps vellum codices, the earliest form of books. **14. Alexander.** Probably the same as the one mentioned in I Tim 1:20 (see note there). **Did.** From a Greek word elsewhere translated *show* (see Tit 2:10; 3:2; Heb 6:11). Alexander "showed" evil to Paul in the sense that he revealed an evil heart in his opposition to the Gospel. Paul's wish, then, is not an expression of personal vindictiveness (in II Tim 4:16 he shows compassion for those who have forsaken him); but, like the imprecatory psalms, it is a prayer for justice for those who reject the Gospel. **15. Be thou ware also.** Paul commands Timothy to avoid Alexander, who has openly attacked the truth.

Zahn argues convincingly *(Introd. to NT*, II, 12-14) that verses **16,17** contain a reminiscence of the earlier trial at Rome alluded to in Philippians. Paul was **delivered out of the mouth of the lion** and resumed his work, so that the preaching might be fully known. **18.** Now, however, in the face of imminent death, Paul was confident of ultimate victory — not that he would escape death, but that God would keep him faithful **unto his heavenly kingdom.** This is a general term for all phases of God's future rule on this earth, and in the new earth. **Amen.** After ascribing glory to God, the seal of sincerity and fervency follows; it serves as a characteristic mark of Paul's whole life: the sincere and wholehearted devotion to the will of God.

Paul concludes with a few personal matters, the benediction and amen. **19. Prisca and Aquila** were the companions whom Paul had first met at Corinth after their expulsion from Rome (Acts 18:18, 19,26). They were at Ephesus when I Corinthians was written (I Cor 16:19) and at Rome when Romans was written (Rom 16:3). Now they had returned to Ephesus. **20. Erastus** is mentioned in Rom 16:23 as city treasurer of Corinth. **Trophimus** was not left at Miletus in the journey of Acts 20:4, since he was at Jerusalem later (Acts 21: 29). Paul is referring to a later occasion. **Winter** explains the request for the cloke of II Tim 4:13. The persons who send greetings are mentioned only here in the NT. **22. Lord Jesus Christ** should be *Lord* only (see ASV). **Thy spirit** is for Timothy, primarily, and the **you** (plural) is for all of Paul's readers, the Christians at Ephesus.

BIBLIOGRAPHY

For Bibliography see under *I Timothy*.

THE EPISTLE TO TITUS

OUTLINE

(For the general introduction to this epistle, see Introduction to I Timothy.)

I. Salutation. 1:1-4.
II. Titus' mission: To set matters in order. 1:5–3:11.
  A. The appointment and need of the teaching elder. 1:5-16.
    1. Qualifications of elders. 1:5-9.
    2. Need for elders to combat error. 1:10-16.
  B. The pastoral work of the teaching elder. 2:1–3:11.
    1. Application of sound doctrine to particular cases. 2:1-10.
    2. Proclamation of sound doctrine: The grace of God. 2:11-15.
    3. Demonstration of sound doctrine: The root and the fruit. 3:1-11.
III. Conclusion, emphasizing good works. 3:12-15.

COMMENTARY

I. Salutation. 1:1-4.

Paul's first utterance in his epistles reveals his point of view and attitude. **1. Servant of God** is put forward here, but coupled with it is the authority of apostleship. In Romans, in II Timothy, and here, the apostle states the two aspects of his office together (Rom 1:1,5; II Tim 1:1-3). Elsewhere he uses one or the other alone. To the Philippians he was a servant; to the Galatians and Corinthians, who needed rebuke and authoritative instruction, he was an apostle. To Titus, who especially needed to be armed with Paul's authority before the Cretans, he is both **servant of God** and **apostle of Jesus Christ. The faith of God's elect** is the body of revealed truth and promise that God's people have cherished through the ages. **Acknowledging.** *Knowledge* (ASV). The idea is parallel to the faith just mentioned; both ideas are governed by the **according to.** Both faith and knowledge have their basis in a factual message that can be known and believed. **Truth** has the implication of "God's faithful revelation," so that Jesus Christ could say, "I am . . . the truth." It is according to **godliness,** a word of frequent occurrence in the Pastoral Epistles (I Tim 3:16, note).

2. Hope is connected with Paul's service and apostleship; he was an apostle of hope, the hope of eternal life, which God **promised before the world began,** to our Saviour Jesus Christ (II Tim 1:9), to be given to us through the message. **3. Due times.** Cf. I Tim 2:6. The eternal purposes come to fruition in the history of this world through **preaching** *(the mes-*
Cf. I Tim 1:1. Paul was an apostle by commandment; by commandment he received his message. **Word** is equivalent
sage, thing preached). **Commandment.**
to the **promise** of the preceding verse. The idea is that God made good his promise; he fulfilled his word in the Gospel. **Saviour** is the great comprehensive word for Deliverer; both God and Christ are so named. **4. Son.** Or, *child* (ASV). A term of affection used by Paul of Timothy, Titus, and Onesimus. **The common faith** was shared by Paul, Titus, and all Christians. The apostle may be using the analogy of inheritance: the faith is an estate or trust belonging to all; Titus is being entrusted with the administration of it. **Mercy** is added only in the Pastoral Epistles (see I Tim 1:2, note). **From** governs both God and Lord: together they constitute the one divine source of all blessings. The ASV correctly omits **Lord:** Christ Jesus our Saviour.

II. Titus' Mission: To Set Matters in Order. 1:5–3:11.

A. The Appointment and Need of the Teaching Elder. 1:5-16.

1) Qualifications of Elders. 1:5-9. **5.** For the possible order of events referred to, see 3:12. Paul left Titus in Crete and may have proceeded toward Nicopolis in Epirus, near Dalmatia (II Tim 4:10), where later Titus joined him and went on to Dalmatia. **Wanting** implies things

left undone. **Every city** suggests an extensive but rapid evangelization of the island, leaving further organizational work to be done. **Elders** or *presbyters* here means the teaching elders or pastors, judging from the context. This commission in Crete did not give Titus dictatorial power to appoint ministers. Rather, as Paul and Barnabas ordained elders (Acts 14:23) who had been chosen by the people, so Titus was to do, keeping in mind the proper qualifications. Paul gives three general qualifications (v. 6), a list of negatives (v. 7), and a list of positive qualifications (vv. 8,9). The whole section is closely parallel to I Tim 3:2-4. **9.** The ASV is preferable in word choice and order: *holding to the faithful word which is according to the teaching, that he may be able both to exhort in the sound doctrine, and to convict* [as in Jn 16:8] *the gainsayers.*

2) Need for Elders To Combat Error. 1:10-16. As verse 9 suggests, doctrine has a double application: exhortation and conviction – to instruct believers, and to convict gainsayers. **10. Unruly.** Used here, in 1:6 and in I Tim 1:9. The suggestion is of willful unbelief and rejection of truth. **Vain talkers** and **deceivers** (cf. related verb in Gal 6:3). Used only here in the NT. **Circumcision.** Unbelieving Judaism seemed to be moving into a more and more complete rejection of the truth. At a somewhat later time John spoke of Jews who were of the "synagogue of Satan" (Rev 2:9; 3:9). **11. Mouths must be stopped.** The principal end of contending for the faith (Apologetics) is to exhort and convict. The evidence should be so clearly presented that rejecters should at least be left without an excuse or answer. In Crete the situation was aggravated by the avaricious Judaizers and other false teachers, who subverted whole households in their desire to win favor and financial gain.

12. The rebuke is severe, but it comes from one of the Cretans' own number. Paul did not object to using fragments of truths gleaned from heathen authors (Acts 17:28; I Cor 15:33). **Slow bellies** equals *idle gluttons* (ASV). **13. This witness is true.** Paul presumably had been on the island for a time and could endorse the statement. Since the Cretans were liars, and were rejecting truth, their message had to be refuted. But also Titus was to **rebuke sharply** (same word as "convince" in v. 9) those professing believers who listened and believed. This makes it clear that Paul here turns his attention from the unbelievers to the professing Christians. **14. Fables.** *Myths.* **Commandments of men** is reminiscent of Mt 15:9, and its source in Isa 29:13. False authority and fear of men is involved in rejection of the truth of God.

15. Here the teaching is parallel to that of I Tim 4:2-5. **All things** is to be taken in context as equivalent to "every creature of God" (I Tim 4:3,4). For those who reject God's sovereignty, and worship the creature, all things are defiled, even their mind and conscience. **16. Profess** (cf. II Tim 3:5). The works are the decisive evidence of the condition of the heart (Mt 7:20; I Jn 4:20). **Reprobate.** Unfit for any good work.

B. The Pastoral Work of the Teaching Elder. 2:1–3:11.

1) Application of Sound Doctrine to Particular Cases. 2:1-10. The instruction of this chapter is addressed to Titus directly in verses 1,7,8,15; but through Titus Paul was instructing the whole church of Crete. His central theme is sound doctrine applied, resulting in good works. (1) To Titus (v. 1) the primary responsibility was to preach and teach the truth, that which was in accord with sound doctrine (*healthful;* see 1:9,13; 2:1; and the adjective in 2:8). The use of this word in the Pastorals, always in connection with doctrine, shows Paul's emphasis on correct teaching. (2) To **aged men** (v. 2), who were actually or potentially teachers, life and doctrine were to stand together. This is an important consideration with each of these classes of people. Additional counsel is given in I Tim 5:1. (3) To **aged** and **young women** (vv. 3-5) considerable emphasis is placed on the foundation of the home. The details are reminiscent of Prov 31:10-31. The honor of the Word of God is the supreme sanction for right conduct.

(4) To **young men** (vv. 6-8) the key virtue singled out for emphasis is soberrmindedness or discretion, as in the case of young women (v. 5). The same emphasis is seen in the exhortations to young men in Proverbs (1:4; 2:11; 3:21; 5:2). To Titus himself the apostle gives the appropriate admonition for a young man and minister (Tit 2:7,8). The constant challenge of properly instructing unbelievers is included. (5) To **servants** (vv. 9,10) two common faults are singled out: **answering again,** contradicting or disputing; and **purloining,** stealing (used

only of Ananias and Sapphira in Acts 5:2,3). **Fidelity** is the word frequently used for faith in the NT.

Paul epitomizes the whole section, indeed the entire epistle, when he points out that good works **adorn the doctrine of God our Saviour.** James said that faith (doctrine) without (good) works is dead, just as the body without spirit is dead also. It is a most ennobling thought that our good works adorn the testimony of our God (Mt 5:16).

2) Proclamation of Sound Doctrine: The Grace of God. 2:11-15. **Grace** (Pastorals: I Tim 1:14; II Tim 1:9; 2:1; Tit 3:7) is always the great key word in salvation. **That bringeth salvation** is all one word, meaning "saving." **All men** sounds the universal, evangelistic note so prominent in the Pastorals. It **appeared** in Jesus Christ (II Tim 1:10). All God's promises and saving work from the beginning of the race have revealed his grace; all his blessings and gifts have been designed to lead men to repentance (Rom 2:4).

12. Teaching. Grace saves, but also teaches and trains in sober and godly living. **Denying.** The same strong decisive rejection that refuses grace (I Tim 5:8; II Tim 2:12; 3:5; Tit 1:16). **Soberly, righteously, and godly.** These three words skillfully reiterate the theme of all the Pastorals. **Present world.** Used once in each of the Pastorals (see I Tim 6:17; II Tim 4:10). These words show the basic orientation of Paul's thought — life consists of this world, as well as the world to come.

13. Paul expresses the rest of the thought by the great event of the world to come: the coming of Christ. **Hope . . . appearing** is one concept, as in the ASV: *the blessed hope and appearing.* **God . . . Saviour** is correctly translated: *"our great God and Saviour Jesus Christ"* (ASV margin). Again two ideas form one concept, much as do the compound divine names of the OT. **14. Who gave himself for us.** The atonement has both the particular reference to the elect and the universal reference to all (see note on I Tim 2:6). **Redeem.** Ransom or deliver by payment of a price (used in Lk 24:21; I Pet 1:18; and here). Purchase is stressed in the atonement (cf. Gal 3:13; Rev 5:9). Deliverance from guilt and condemnation is not foremost here, but rather deliverance from ungodly walk. Thus the peculiar mark of God's people appears—their zeal for good works. **Peculiar** is used in the LXX of Ex 19:5. This and the word translated "peculiar" in I Pet 2:9 both imply a possession or purchase. Good works are the fruit of the Spirit, the seal of God's ownership.

15. These things speak. The grace of God is the basis of good works, but it is essential for the minister continually to proclaim this grace, exhorting and reproving, with the authority of God's Word. Let not our ministry be such as would give men reason to despise us.

3) Demonstration of Sound Doctrine: The Root and the Fruit. 3:1-11. Paul here introduces another paragraph discussing righteous living, which, he declares, should be inspired by the example of our own unworthiness and God's dealing with us in kindness and love. He makes it clear (v. 8) that the intention of Christian doctrine is that believers should demonstrate good works. The grace of God is the root; the good works are the fruit. It is not surprising, then, that we find here another remarkable doctrinal summary (paralleling the one in the last chapter on the grace of God). This gem, this brilliant description of God's goodness to us (vv. 4-7), is placed in the setting of the believer's responsibility to demonstrate good works before men.

Paul's first emphasis falls on civic and public virtues and duties. There is also a brief added note about the government of the church (vv. 9-11) which supplements 1:5-16. **1. Principalities.** Rather, *rulers* (ASV). **Powers.** *Authorities* (ASV). **Obey magistrates** should read, *be obedient* (ASV). The same verb is used in Acts 5:29,32. **2.** The virtues listed are similar to those commanded previously, but are here oriented to the unbelieving world. **3. We ourselves also.** Paul never lost his memory of what he once was, and it moved him to compassion for the lost. **4. Kindness and love** are used only here and in Acts 28:2. Pity is also suggested by the context. These graces appeared supremely in Christ, though they are manifested in all God's natural benevolences (Acts 14:17). This whole passage forms a balance and complement to Tit 2:11-14. **5. Works of righteousness.** The ASV gives it correctly: *Not by works done in righteousness, which* [works] *we did ourselves.* This eliminates all works whatsoever; not only those done by an unsaved man in self-righteousness, but also the works done in true righteousness. Over against all works is the free mercy of God, exhibited in the work of the Spirit. **Washing . . . renewing.** The Holy Spirit renews us in regeneration. These two ideas are closely linked together as two ways of expressing the one work of the Spirit. **6. Shed on us.** Poured out. The symbolism of water is often used of the Spirit. Jesus is the one through whom the Spirit is given (Jn 4:10; 7:37). **Abundantly.** Richly. The Spirit is true riches in that he is the earnest of our inheritance and the source and creator of all blessings. **7. That** gives the result of the gift of the Spirit: "so that in being justified by his grace, we become heirs according to the hope, eternal life."

8 a. Faithful saying. This is one of the noteworthy sayings of the Pastorals (I Tim 1:15; 3:1; 4:9; II Tim 2:11, note). It not only gives weighty emphasis to the doctrinal statement just uttered (vv. 4-7), but it also calls attention to the succinct, powerful restatement of the message of the whole epistle which follows. **Affirm constantly** is one emphatic verb used only in I Tim 1:7 and here. The inculcation of Gospel truth requires patient repetition. **They which have believed . . . maintain good works.** The grace of God, producing faith, comes first; good works should follow: the root and then the fruit. **8b,9. Good and profitable** of verse 8 contrasts with **unprofitable and vain** of verse 9, where the Apostle lists things that distract attention from the truth. These should be avoided, as should also those individuals who, having been admonished by the church, still perversely cling to them. **10. Heretick** is used either in the strict sense or of one causing division. **Admonition** is a most important aspect of church discipline. The noun is used here, in I Cor 10:11, and in Eph 6:4; the verb in Acts 20:31; Rom 15:14; I Cor 4:14; Col 1:28; 3:16; I Thess 5: 12,14; II Thess 3:15. **11. Subverted** connotes "permanently turned," "set on a wrong course." **Sinneth** implies willfully sinning, as in Heb 10:26. **Condemned of himself.** Such a one, who has received knowledge of the truth and stubbornly rejected it, is himself the witness that he has twice rejected an earnest explanation and appeal.

III. Conclusion, Emphasizing Good Works. 3:12-15.

After a few personal notes, Paul gives the final reiteration of the main burden of his letter—that the believers should be careful to maintain good works. **12. Artemas** is not mentioned elsewhere; **Tychicus** appears in Acts 20:4; Eph 6:21; Col 4:7; II Tim 4:12. **Nicopolis** is in Epirus. Titus is instructed to join the apostle there (II Tim 4:10, note). **13. Zenas** appears only here. **Apollos** was an Alexandrian; it is possible that the journey alluded to was to Alexandria by way of Crete. **14. Maintain** may mean "to be concerned with," but as used elsewhere in the Pastorals, it means "to lead or rule." There is the suggestion that Christians should be in the lead in doing good works. **15. Grace.** This is the characteristic conclusion of all Paul's epistles (see comment on I Tim 6:21).

BIBLIOGRAPHY

(For bibliography, see under I Timothy)

THE EPISTLE TO PHILEMON

INTRODUCTION

The Occasion and Theme. Paul wrote this letter on behalf of Philemon's slave, Onesimus, who, after escaping from his master, had been converted under Paul's ministry. A recent conjecture of the noted contemporary writer, John Knox *(Philemon Among the Letters of Paul),* makes Archippus the slave owner (and principal addressee of the letter) and Philemon merely an overseer of the churches in Lycus Valley. The traditional view, however, which considers Archippus the son of Philemon and Apphia, remains the more convincing.

In the providence of God several factors were important in the church's recognition of this letter not merely as the private correspondence of Paul, but as apostolic teaching to be received as Scripture: (1) "The church" is included in the address. (2) The master-slave relationship posed a problem important for the whole of the church, not only for Philemon personally. (Philemon was not the only slaveholder in the Colossian church; cf. *Kyrioi,* Col 4:1.) By returning the slave, who, after absconding, had become a Christian and a servant to Paul, the apostle not only instructs us concerning the principles governing the relations of Christian brothers but reminds us that these principles are not to be realized "by compulsion, but by your own free will" (Phm 14, RSV). In Christ there is a completely new frame of reference that transforms all earthly relationships: brotherhood is the focus upon which all other relationships must be evaluated. Paul does not direct a polemic against slavery, but in the course of the passing centuries, the Christian faith has come to view the practice of slavery as incompatible with the principles Paul here enunciates. For the origin and date of the letter, see Introduction to Colossians.

OUTLINE

I. Introduction. Phm 1-3.
II. Thanksgiving. Phm 4-7.
III. Paul's appeal for Onesimus. Phm 8-21.
IV. Conclusion. Phm 22-25.

COMMENTARY

I. Introduction. Phm 1-3.

1. In contrast to the more usual term, "apostle," Paul's designation of himself as **prisoner for Jesus Christ** (RSV; cf. v. 13) has a direct bearing on the theme of the letter (see on Col 4:18). **2,3.** The addressee was not only this Christian family, but **the church** in their home. It was customary, and sometimes necessary, for the local churches to assemble in the home of one of the members (cf. Acts 18:7).

II. Thanksgiving. Phm 4-7.

4,5. In Paul's prayers the **mention** of Philemon *(sou)* always brought to the apostle's lips a word of thanksgiving. Philemon was characterized by **love and faith:** these attitudes were directed primarily toward *(pros)* Christ but found their outworking in *(eis)* the church (cf. J. B. Lightfoot, *St. Paul's Epistles to the Colossians and to Philemon, in loco).* **6,7.** To be **effectual,** the **communication** or *sharing* (RSV) of **faith** must be *in knowledge (epignōsis;* see on Col 1:9; 2:1-3); i.e., a believer must have proper perception of the **good** that he has in **Christ.** The verse is difficult; compare Moule's discussion (C. F. D. Moule, *The Epistles to Colossians and Philemon).* Philemon's ministry was energized by his apprehension of Christian **love** and truth. Paul rejoices in this and desires that this motivation may influence Philemon's attitude toward his runaway slave. **Bowels** *(splagchna;* cf. vv. 12,20). The inmost feelings, "the very self" (Moule).

III. Paul's Appeal for Onesimus. Phm 8-21.

8,9. Paul refrains from invoking apostolic authority to **enjoin** Philemon to do the **convenient,** i.e., the proper, thing. Rather, he appeals to his friend in **love,** as one who has grounds to be heard: he is Paul, "an ambassador" *(presbytēs)* and now a prisoner for Jesus Christ. Although *presbytēs* means strictly **aged** or old man, here the variant spelling and meaning is probably correct (cf. Eph 6:20). Whether the apostle is distinguishing between apostolic authority and the kind of authority exercisable by other Christian leaders is uncertain. In any case, he does illustrate the most effective way true Christian leadership can function.

10,11. As elsewhere (I Cor 4:15; cf. Gal 4:19) Paul refers to his convert as **begotten** by him. Although a slave in a Christian household, presumably Onesimus did not embrace the Christian faith until as an escapee he came under the influence of Paul. As a Christian, **Onesimus,** i.e., *Useful* (a not uncommon name for a slave in that time and region), who formerly was useless, now lived up to his name. John Knox speculates that Paul may have given the name "Onesimus" to the slave at his conversion (cf. Isa 62:2; Gen 17:5,15; 32:28; Acts 13:9). The custom of giving one a new name at conversion exists among Christians in non-Christian cultures today.

12. The verb translated **sent back** (ASV) can have the technical judicial meaning of "to refer a case," i.e., to allow Philemon himself to judge in the matter of Onesimus' freedom (cf. Lk 23:7,11; Acts 25:21). But the ordinary meaning is more probable here. Paul equates sending the slave with *sending my very heart* (RSV).

13,14. Onesimus had been of considerable help to Paul in his **bonds** or imprisonment for **the gospel.** The apostle desired to retain his services—services which Philemon would have gladly approved. But Paul, being sensitive to the ethics of the situation, refused to presume upon Philemon's love. He wanted his friend to make up his own **mind** and act **willingly,** without being manipulated or forced into a corner. When a man performs some 'Christian service' because friends have made it difficult for him to say *no,* his service is not genuinely Christian. Did Philemon free Onesimus and send him back to Paul? Did the former slave become a minister and, later, bishop of the church at Ephesus (cf. the letter of Ignatius to the Ephesians, 1)? Knox *(in loc.)* and Harrison (P. N. Harrison, "Onesimus and Philemon," AThR, XXXIII (Oct., 1953) think so. While no certain answer can be given to these questions, the supposition raised by them is appealing.

15,16. Season. Literally, *for an hour.* An insignificant loss resulted in an immeasurable gain. **For ever.** *Permanently.* The term is reminiscent of the provision for voluntary slavery in Ex 21:6 (cf. SBK, IV, 746; Lev 25:46). But no longer is the relationship to be viewed in terms of master and servant. To be a Christian is to be a **brother** to other believers. And this is the determinative factor in all other human relationships, whether they be **in the flesh,** i.e., on the natural plane, or **in the Lord,** i.e., on the spiritual plane, in the sphere of the 'new age' (see Introduction to Colossians). Yet, relations on both planes must be carried on simultaneously. Philemon was both brother and master; Onesimus was both brother and slave. Such dual relationships gave rise to difficult problems within the early church. And such problems still complicate the economic and social relations of Christians today (I Tim 6:2; see on Col 3:11).

17. Having related the story and having gently restated some Christian principles, Paul now makes a direct appeal: "**Receive** Onesimus as you would **myself** [cf. Mt 25:40; Acts 9:4]; for your sake I would keep him **in thy stead** [Phm 13], but rather I send him to you in my stead." **Partner** *(koinōnon).* Not only a fellow Christian, but one with whom many experiences had been shared.

18,19. Paul does not mention Onesimus' actual offense, but it seems to have been more than mere escape. Paul's offer to **repay** suggests that a monetary loss was involved—through theft, embezzlement, or perhaps simply careless handling of funds. **Thine own self.** Apparently Philemon also was a convert of the apostle. This gentle reminder was designed to hush any demands for 'justice' and bring Philemon and Onesimus closer together; they had the same spiritual father.

20,21. By showing Christian love to Onesimus, Philemon would **refresh** and bring **joy** to Paul himself. On this note the apostle rests his appeal in **confidence** of a good response. **More than I say.** This may refer to (1) giving Onesimus his freedom or (2) returning him to Paul (cf. vv. 13,14).

IV. Conclusion. Phm 22-25.

22. Paul's **trust** that he will be released from this imprisonment echoes his sentiment in Phil 1:25,26 (see Introduction to Colossians). **Through your prayers.** It is noteworthy that the apostle who is most insistent about the sovereignty of God (cf. Gal 1:15,16; Rom 8:29) is equally convinced that God accomplishes His purposes through human instruments. The apostle does not request prayer; he takes for granted that his "partner" (Phm 17) remembers him in his prayers.

23,24. See on Col 4:10-14,15-17.

25. Your *(hymōn)* **spirit** (cf. Gal 6:18; II Tim 4:22). The plural reference is to the whole group included in the salutation (vv. 1,2). **Spirit** appears to be a term for the whole man—in his 'new age' status or outlook (cf. I Pet 4:6; II Cor 2:13; 7:5; I Cor 2:11-16, Phillips).

BIBLIOGRAPHY

Harrison, P. N. "Onesimus and Philemon," *AThR*, XXXII (October, 1953), pp. 268-294.

Knox, John. *Philemon Among the Letters of Paul.* Chicago: University of Chicago Press, 1935.

Lightfoot, J. B. *St. Paul's Epistles to the Colossians and to Philemon.* London: The Macmillan Company, 1886.

Moule, C. F. D. *The Epistles to Colossians and Philemon.* Cambridge: The University Press, 1958.

Mueller, J. J. *The Epistles of Paul to the Philippians and to Philemon.* Grand Rapids: Wm. B. Eerdmans Publishing Co., 1955.

Radford, L. B. *The Epistle to the Colossians and the Epistle to Philemon.* London: Methuen, 1931.

THE EPISTLE TO THE HEBREWS

INTRODUCTION

Introductory Statement. The student of this epistle must understand its uniqueness. It is like no other New Testament epistle, and it poses problems that are peculiar to itself. In form of construction, in style, in argument, and in relation to other books of the Bible, Hebrews stands apart.

Its history has been one of controversy. It has been ignored, challenged as to its authority, questioned as to canonicity, and studied relentlessly to determine its authorship. More recently, critical analysis has raised questions concerning certain portions of the epistle, notably chapter 13. Whether this chapter was added in whole or in part or whether it was a part of the original letter is a problem currently under study.

Increased interest in the Hellenistic period in relation to the history of civilization has also influenced the study of the Epistle to the Hebrews. Some of the mysteries of the epistle are now being set against the Hellenistic culture of the post-Alexandrian eastern Mediterranean world. Some scholars feel that the persons for whom the Epistle to the Hebrews was written were directly influenced by Hellenistic culture, and perhaps were thoroughly Hellenized. Such a view tends to suggest possible revisions of older views as to the recipients of the epistle and its purpose.

It has been said that the Epistle to the Hebrews is the least known of all New Testament epistles. The close reasoning, the sacrificial and priestly terminology, and the reigning idealism of the author are given as the reasons (Purdy and Cotton, *Epistle to the Hebrews*, Vol. XI, IB). This may be, but one thing seems more certain. The Epistle to the Hebrews is best comprehended when the five books of Moses are familiar ground. The inseparable tie of close reasoning from the Levitical system links the Pentateuch to the Hebrews letter.

The problems posed by the book are challenging. In sum, they concern its authorship, readers, destination, date, reason for having been written, and relationship to first century Christianity, Judaism, and the Hellenistic culture.

Occasion of the Writing—Why Written. The classical formulation for the occasion of the epistle is as follows. Jewish Christians, whether of a single congregation or in larger numbers and of broader geographical spread, were in danger of apostasy from Christ back to Moses. This condition of apostasy was an immediate danger (2:1), based upon unbelief (3:12). Conduct intimated such a possible going back (5:13,14). Neglect of public worship (10:25), weakness in prayer (12:12), a certain instability in doctrine (13:9), refusal to teach others as mature believers ought (5:12), and neglect of the Scriptures (2:1) were other symptoms of spiritual weakness. The danger was that those who were "holy brethren, partakers of the heavenly calling" (3:1) might "fall away" (6:6) or "depart from the living God" (3:12).

To forestall such a development, the author of Hebrews stressed the superiority of Christ in a series of contrasts to the angels, Moses, Aaron, Melchisedek, and the Levitical system. The object of such contrasts was to show the inferiority of Judaism and the superiority of Christ.

As the writer develops his thoughts, he weaves together three concepts. The first is exhortation (13:22); the second is a series of warnings, five in number (2:1-4; 3:7-19; 6:4-12; 10:26-31; 12:15-17); and the third is consolation or assurance, gathered around the thought introduced in the word "consider" (3:1), which reaches its culmination in the phrase, "consider him that endured . . ." (12:3). On the basis of these concepts, the writer argues against the tendency toward apostasy.

The line of reasoning developed by the reader—hearers was attractive. If following Christ brought persecution, and the older way of the Jewish practice did not, why not return to Judaism, retain a religion and at the same time be free from persecution? Attractive options, to be sure. The answer to all this is set forth in the Epistle to the Hebrews, as the superiority of Christ is argued point by point against the claims of Judaism.

More recently, this classical view of Hebrews has been questioned. Alexander C. Purdy, in his introductory comment to the *Epistle to the Hebrews* (IB, XI, 591,592), argues that this traditional view is only inferred. He gives nine reasons against the traditional view and then writes, "As it stands, then, Hebrews is an argument for the finality of Christianity resting on the valid foreshadowing in the Old Testament institution of sacrifice of the fundamental need for access to God, which has been brought out of the shadows for all men, Jew and Gentile alike, in the sacrifice of Christ." The marked Jewishness of Hebrews, according to Purdy, belongs to the form rather than to the actual content of its thought. He then goes on to argue that the author of Hebrews was fighting a Jewish-Christian form of Gnosticism and Hellenism rather than Judaism as such, but acknowledges that his view is still only hypothetical.

If we concede to Purdy that the author of Hebrews was writing against Jewish-Christian Gnosticism centered in a Hellenistic culture, it still seems necessary to face the fact that the main themes of the book have a Jewish character and argument. In fact, Hebrews binds together the Old Testament and the New Testament in the person and work of Jesus Christ. Hebrews might be said to be the logical extension of John 17 in that it serves to correlate the high priestly prayer with the high priestly ministry of Christ. As the prayer of John 17 records our Lord's concern that believers should be active in the world, so it also records the petition, ". . . that thou shouldest keep them from the evil one" (Jn 17:15, ASV). The Hebrews epistle tells of such keeping, under the stresses and strains of persecution and of temptation to apostatize. To encourage such keeping, the author of Hebrews balanced the doctrinal and the hortatory, the pastoral and the practical, the word of consolation and the word of exhortation.

Judaism, a "cradle of convenience" for persecuted Christians of Jewish nationality, was thus opposed by contrast. The writer determined to help these early believers face the options with knowledge of the difference between Judaism and the work of Christ for and in the believer. All of this was designed to convince people under trial of the superiority of Jesus Christ.

At the same time, this letter of encouragement to first century believers contains help for today. No other New Testament epistle so clearly answers the "why" of the sacrifice of Christ, and of the redemption offered through this sacrifice. No other New Testament epistle so clearly links the twofold ministry of Christ as the eternal Son of God and the suffering Son of Man. Sin, guilt, atonement, and forgiveness are more fully comprehended through the Hebrews epistle. This writing also helps the readers gain a better understanding of Old Testament truths or incidents. Also, the difference between Judaism and Christianity becomes clear in the teaching of the Hebrews epistle.

Johannes Schneider has written: "Hebrews is very sober in the appraisal of the actual life of the churches. It knows the dangers which threaten God's people on this earth. Therefore it admonishes to hold fast to the faith and not be disloyal to Christ" *(The Letter to the Hebrews,* p. 8). With its emphasis upon the priestly ministry of Christ, and the privileges of the believer in relation to Christ, and its strong admonitions to develop a virile faith, Hebrews still speaks today.

Date and Destination – To Whom Written. A number of factors regulate the date for the Epistle to the Hebrews. The most important of these factors seems to be the Jewish-Roman conflict after A.D. 68 and the destruction of the Temple in A.D. 70. Nothing is mentioned concerning the conflict, the Temple, or the destruction of Jerusalem. Because of this silence, the letter is considered to have been written before 68 or after 80. The earlier dating is preferable, but must be looked at in relation to the mention of Timothy (13:23) and the mention of "they of Italy" (13:24). Also, the knowledge of Hebrews shown in the Epistle of Clement of Rome to the Corinthians (A.D. 95) has some bearing upon the date of Hebrews and perhaps upon its destination.

The argument for the late date of Hebrews is best stated in the IB, *Introduction,* XI, pp. 593,594. By a combination of reasoned arguments and the use of I Clement as a point of reference, the IB generalizes a date somewhere between the late seventies and the very early nineties, but then concludes that the actual date is uncertain.

In contrast, Canon Farrar, *Cambridge Greek Testament* (hereafter referred to as CGT), representing nineteenth century views, and Gleason L. Archer, in *The Epistle to the Hebrews, A Study Manual,* both argue for a date between A.D. 64 and A.D. 68. The latter writer then narrows this period of time to the actual date of 65 or 66 as the time most reasonable, according to internal and external evidence. All views of the date of the epistle stress the importance of the silence of the letter concerning events at Jerusalem in the sixth decade of the first century.

As for destination, three primary theories have prevailed, each of them pointing to a major city in the Roman and Mediterranean world. Some add a fourth view, which is really a modification of one of the main theories.

(1) Jewish Christians in and around Jerusalem were the recipients of the letter.

(2) It was sent to Jewish Christians who lived in Alexandria. This view tends to be held by those who support the argument for a strong Alexandrian flavor for the Hebrew letter.

(3) It was intended for a congregation of Jewish Christians worshiping in the city of Rome, who were under severe trial and persecution. The "church at Rome" view also tends to hold to the "single congregation" theory, that the original recipients of the letter were a small congregation, or a "house church" in Rome.

(4) A modification of (3). The congregation addressed in Hebrews was small, but it might have been anywhere in the Roman Empire, and not necessarily at Rome.

Cogent arguments are offered for all views; all are beset with significant difficulties. The internal evidence of the letter itself contributes little in resolving the issues between the various theories. Jerusalem is mentioned by implication (13:12) in a manner that would be understood by all Hebrews. The reference to Italy (13:24) is general and therefore gives little actual aid in the question of destination.

One thing is clear. Those to whom this epistle was written were Hebrews by national identity and Christians by profession. As Downer has suggested, Hebrews were in view, and the Hebrew point of view prevails (Arthur Cleveland Downer, *The Principles of Interpretation of the Epistle of the Hebrews,* p. 8). These Hebrew Christians had suffered losses, they had been much under trial and difficulty, they had suffered reproach, loss of privilege, persecution, ridicule, and open hatred from fellow Jews. But these conditions could have prevailed anywhere in the Roman world of the first century.

The fact is that all arguments and theories have ingredients of possibility and impossibility in almost equal measure. Discussion of the problem of destination may be examined at length in Farrar, CGT; A. B. Davidson, *The Epistle to the Hebrews;* Archer, *The Epistle to the Hebrews, A Study Manual;* William Manson, *The Epistle to the Hebrews, An Historical and Theological Reinterpretation;* and IB, XI. As for the present weight of opinion, the "Jerusalem" theory is defended best by William Leonard, *Authorship of the Epistle to the Hebrews: Critical Problem and Use of the Old Testament.* The "Rome" and "single congregation" theory is best defended by William Manson *(op. cit.),* who suggests that the files of correspondence of a Roman congregation first held this letter of exhortation and warning. But even this statement is conjecture.

Authorship – By Whom Written. Who wrote the Epistle to the Hebrews still remains the greatest single problem for the student of this book. The suggested authors are many, and opinions favoring one possible author over another are also many. The Apostle Paul, Apollos, Barnabas, Luke, Timothy, Aquila and Priscilla, Silas, Aristion, and Philip the Deacon have all been proposed for authorship, with supporting arguments. Examination of the tradition of the early church and of the church Fathers, both East and West, proves only that opinions vary.

The epistle itself does not name an author or even hint at one. Two main views have predominated in establishing its authorship. (1) The Pauline authorship. The argument supporting this view is also expanded to include a possible unknown writer who had been instructed and influenced by the Apostle Paul, and so gave Hebrews a distinctly Pauline cast. (2) The Alexandrian tradition and influence, based upon the use of the Old

Testament mainly in a typological manner. The reasoning here traces certain of the analogies of Hebrews to like analogies in the work of Philo of Alexandria. This is a view held by few at the present time. As noted in SHERK, II, 877, the influence of Philo upon the author of Hebrews is discounted by most scholars, while at the same time his influence upon the Alexandrian Fathers is generally acknowledged.

The Pauline authorship argument rests strongly upon the last chapter (13) of the epistle. The personal quality of this chapter is typical of the Apostle Paul, as is the epistolary style. The references to Timothy and to Italy (13:23,24) are seemingly direct links to the apostle. In addition, there is marked similarity between the language of this book and that of recognized Pauline letters (e.g., 1:4; 2:2; 7:18; 12:22); and the Christological argument is like that of Paul elsewhere. Much of this argument is inferential, and the same similarities could be noted of any Christian teacher of the early days of Christianity. In support of the Pauline authorship perhaps no work surpasses the definitive work of William Leonard in his *Authorship of the Epistle to the Hebrews: Critical Problem and Use of the Old Testament*.

Weighing against Pauline authorship are the following considerations: (1) failure of the book to name the Apostle Paul specifically, as is done in the recognized Pauline epistles; (2) the use of language that rises above the Pauline norm in construction, use, and style; and (3) logical development of the argument, which is not characteristically Pauline. The rhythm of Hebrews is rhetorical and Hellenic, and the style, in general, is much more calm and reasoned than the Apostle's style usually is.

As for doctrinal differences, these are evident in (1) the treatment of faith, (2) the eschatological view of chapter 12, (3) the applied use of the Mosaic code, and (4) the concept of the sanctuary. Leonard even points out that the habit of regarding the Old Testament Scriptures as an "arsenal of types" *(op. cit.*, p. 19), is not characteristic of the Pauline literature.

But what is known of the author? He was a man of considerable knowledge of the Scriptures, a Biblical theologian who thought in terms of redemptive history, and a person acquainted with the Greek Old Testament (LXX). Though a Jew, he was thoroughly familiar with Hellenistic culture as well as with Jewish tradition. He was an independent thinker who may have been influenced by the Apostle Paul and by the Alexandrian thinkers. He originated a unique literary form, quite different from that of other New Testament writings.

He was completely devoted to his subject of explaining the relationship of Judaism to Christianity, arguing constantly for the absolute superiority of the latter. Perhaps he was a preacher-teacher, familiar with the speaker-hearer relationship and thus committed to the exhortation-explanation-warning style which he used so effectively. In his use of this method, he exhibits more than passing acquaintance with the thinking of the Apostle Paul.

Notwithstanding all this, the actual identity of the author remains unknown. In conclusion, perhaps Origen (third century) as quoted by Eusebius (fourth century) can hardly be improved on in regard to his statement of the problem:

> The style of the Epistle with the title, "To The Hebrews," has not that vulgarity of diction which belongs to the apostle, who confesses that he is but common in speech, that is, in his phraseology. But that this epistle is more pure Greek in the composition of phrases, every one will confess who is able to discern the difference of style. Again, it will be obvious that the ideas of the epistle are admirable, and not inferior to any of the books acknowledged to be apostolic. Every one will confess to this, who attentively reads the apostle's writings.

Then Eusebius adds, or includes:

> But I would say, that the thoughts are the apostle's, but the diction and phraseology belong to some one who has recorded what the apostle said, and as one who noted down at his leisure what the master dictated. If then, any church considers this epistle as coming from Paul, let it be commended for this, for neither did those ancient men deliver it without cause. But who it was that really wrote the epistle, God only knows (Eusebius, *Ecclesiastical History)*.

Tradition and the Early Church – Acceptance of What Was Written. The first mention of the Epistle to the Hebrews outside of the New Testament appears in the *Epistle to the Corinthians* written by Clement of Rome. Hebrews was known to both the Eastern and Western churches, but seems to have been less well known in the West until after the fourth century. The Alexandrian Fathers were actively interested in the problems of Hebrews, and both Clement of Alexandria and Origen commented upon the epistle and discussed it at length. The title "To The Hebrews" appeared by the end of the second century, and has been commonly used since.

From the outset, Hebrews has been accepted as being in the canon. No ancient authority, except Tertullian, failed to include this epistle in the New Testament canon.

At the end of the fourth century the West became more actively interested in the epistle, with Jerome in his *Epistle 129* plainly stating that he unquestionably accepted Hebrews in the New Testament canon. This view was consistently held by medievalists, and humanist scholarship adopted it. Erasmus, the humanist scholar, and Luther, the Reformationist, both accepted Hebrews as being in the New Testament, though they disagreed as to the author's identity. Post-Reformation scholarship has not challenged the canonicity of Hebrews successfully, but has been more occupied with the question of authorship.

The Argument of the Epistle – Theme of the Writer. The thesis of the writer of Hebrews seems to be captured in two main ideas, which are explained and illustrated in the logic of the argument. The first idea is expressed in the word "consider," used in 3:1 and 12:3. In each instance the admonition is to consider Christ. In 3:1, he is to be considered as the "Apostle and High Priest of our confession," and in 12:3 he is to be considered as the one who endured, as the ultimate example of the faith life. By the term "consider," the writer means reflect, study, examine attentively, think on with care. Note that the believers are reminded to consider Christ himself, and not merely the logical reasons why he should be considered, as set forth in the Hebrew letter.

Through the reasoning of the epistle, the readers are led to "consider him" in his priesthood and sacrifice. The contrasts drawn throughout the letter establish conclusively the superiority of Christ over angels, Moses, Aaron, Melchisedek, the Levitical system, and finally even over the greatest examples of the faith life that the Old Testament records (cf. Heb 11). As the priest of God and as the sacrifice acceptable to him, Christ now speaks from within the sanctuary, guaranteeing to every believer an entrance into the very presence of God, and an immediate hearing for petitions and requests (4:14-16).

The second idea is found in the word **exhortation** *(paraklēsis),* with its companion verb, "I exhort" (13:22). This has been called the informal title of the Hebrews letter. Farrar (CBSC) suggests that all of the information in the epistle is to serve the purpose of exhorting the readers. The persecution, trials, and difficulties would be made easier if these Christians, who were also Jews, would "consider him" (12:3), and "bear with the word of exhortation" (13:22, ASV). The supporting argument to this twofold or two-part theme is then built up by the Christianity-superior-over-Judaism argument to which the exhortation is directed.

The whole purpose of this letter was to inform the discouraged Christians and also to encourage them, and to support both approaches by innumerable examples both of Christ and of those who had successfully lived by faith. Central to the whole, the writer placed the eternity (therefore unchangeableness) of the priesthood of Christ, "after the order of Melchisedek" (ch. 7).

The Author's Ideas and Concepts: Sources and Use. Distinctive form and style (see next section of this Introduction) set Hebrews apart from other New Testament epistles. The author employs method, organization, and technique unlike those of any other New Testament writer. He also expresses ideas and combinations of thoughts and events peculiar to himself. Since the main thrust of the epistle is practical, to achieve practicality, he brings all of his theological concepts into this special frame of reference of exhortation, warning, and comfort. His concentration is upon those theological ideas and concepts he regards as significant. His reasoning in behalf of the readers is that this is what this community of believers needs above all else to make them strong in faith.

He approaches these ideas as a speaker would approach them, building one truth upon another in support of the main arguments. Interspersed are the warnings, which seem particularly designed to impress the hearers (readers) with the consequences of failing to comprehend the truth concerning Christ.

Considerable literary skill is demonstrated by the author. Evidently his background gave him a sense of proportion in literary composition. His Greek is perhaps the best in the New Testament, comparable to that of Luke. Cultural depth and familiarity are also evident. The writer seems to realize and reflect the influence of the Greek way of life (Hellenization) upon Judaism and upon the Mediterranean world.

In actual expressed ideas, the writer bases his theological discussion on the Scriptures and develops it by setting the shadowy realm of earth against the realm of reality, or heaven. The Old Testament or Scriptural source he used was the Greek version or LXX. In some instances the word used in the LXX does not even appear in the Hebrew text as we have it. In proving that the heavenly realm is the realm of reality, the author makes all possible passages apply to Christ. The entire Old Testament, as the writer of the Hebrews uses it, is a continuous exposition revealing the person and work of the Lord Jesus Christ. Access to the heavenly realm and understanding of the heavenly realm are also in Christ.

The author of Hebrews is the only New Testament writer who discusses certain of the subjects he takes up. No other writer, for instance, discusses the significance of Melchisedek (7:1-14). A new estimate of the patriarchs is also supplied in chapter 11. Some aspects of Moses' life are stressed in Hebrews which are not mentioned elsewhere. The subject of repentance is approached differently (12:17), as is the subject of deliberate sin (10:26). Many of the individual concepts of the author have posed problems of interpretation to later generations.

The most highly developed of all the ideas in Hebrews is that of the priesthood of Christ. Unique to the epistle, it is the most important concept to be grasped. In presenting this concept, three "sources" are apparent: (1) The Old Testament institution of the priesthood and sacrifice, or Levitical system; (2) Judaism; and (3) primitive or apostolic Christianity. Whatever other influences there may have been, these three are paramount.

As priest, Christ was divinely called, and is one with humanity (2:14-18; 4:15,16; 5:1-3). He met the needs of the people (2:17,18). He opened the way into the presence of God (10:19,20), and made available the "sanctuary" (AV, *heavens)* and the "throne of grace" (4:14-16). He became the perfect and final sacrifice (10:18). Because of the priestly ministry of Christ, the believer has strength of faith and the privilege of worship. Perhaps no book in the New Testament better sets forth fellowship with God through worship than does Hebrews.

The Christology of Hebrews is rich, but it is mainly set forth in the ministry and function of Christ as priest. Christ is first presented as the revealer of God (1:1) and the agent of creation (1:1-4). The significance of the word *charaktēr* (AV, **express image**) in 1:3 should not be missed. After this preliminary statement or prologue, the Christology flows quickly into the main argument of the priestly ministry of Christ.

The ethical teaching of Hebrews is of the highest standard and fully Christian, though general in the main body of the argument. Only in chapter 13 does the ethical teaching become specific and pointed. Brotherly love (13:1), kindness to strangers (13:2), kindness to the less fortunate (13:3), honorable marriage relationships (13:4), a right attitude toward material wealth (13:5), honor to overseers (13:7,17), doing good (13:16), are there positively enjoined. In these the Christian does not have a choice. Much of the earlier ethical injunction in the epistle is found in the priestly analogy, and therefore is not as readily apparent as in the Synoptics or in some of the Pauline literature.

As for its practical value, Hebrews rests solidly upon the unquestioned premise that Christ meets the needs of all men at all times (including those of modern man). Men come to God through Christ in every age. In this concept is expressed the unity of history as lineal and redemptive, with God through Christ working out man's destiny according to His plan and will. Hebrews does not set up a philosophy of history different from that of the other books of the New Testament.

Form and Style: The Author's Organization and Methods. Only the section from 13:17 to 13:25 qualifies Hebrews as an epistle. But the literary genre of the book constitutes a problem. It begins like a treatise, continues like a sermon, and ends like a letter. The present beginning is the only beginning the book has ever had. In it there are no greetings, salutations, or personal references whatever. Within the literary form, certain habits are constant. In using the Old Testament, the writer may employ a reference either literally, historically, or typologically. His consistency lies only in that his use of the Old Testament text supports his main argument at the point where it is introduced.

It has been suggested that the exhortations and warnings in Hebrews class the book as polemic in nature, with the epistolary ending added as a way of concluding the polemic. If this is true, then the author is amazingly apt at avoiding reference to himself in the polemic. Autobiographical references are non-existent, and the metaphors employed strengthen the polemic without revealing a single clue as to the polemicist.

The opinion has been expressed that the basic literary form of Hebrews follows the Alexandrian patterns set by Philo (see J. Herkless [ed.], *Hebrews and the Epistles General of Peter, James and John;* also IB). The way the author contrasts the heavenly and the earthly realms, the "shadowy" and the real or the realm of the heavenly and the true is thought by some to be a technique "borrowed" from Philo of Alexandria. The IB calls this a "two-story" view of reality, which controls the whole thought of Hebrews (XI, 583).

Other opinions expressed are (1) that the influence of Philo is negligible, or (2) that the theory that he influenced the writer is a false premise entirely. Manson tends to minimize Philo's influence (William Manson, *The Epistle to the Hebrews, An Historical and Theological Reinterpretation).* A. B. Davidson, referring to the author of Hebrews *(op. cit.),* speaks of traces of the influence of "the Alexandrian culture . . . upon his language," but presents no argument favoring this Philonic technique. In one sense, then, the origin of the form of Hebrews remains an open question. (3) Spicq, however *(L' épître aux Hébreux),* notes considerable evidence which he regards as indicative of Philonic background.

What is clear, however, is that the writer systematically establishes a basic set of ideas, upon which he brings to bear Old Testament passages and arguments. To win acceptance of these basic ideas is not his objective, but rather to lead the believers to understand them fully and then act upon them. William Leonard *(op. cit.,* p. 221) identifies seven such ideas: (1) the Sonship of Christ; (2) the priesthood of Christ, the basis for cleansing from sin; (3) the priest at God's right hand, the basis of Christian hope; (4) the promise made to Abraham; (5) the permanence of the promised "Sabbath-rest"; (6) the consequences of apostasy; and (7) the exhortations to virtuous living in light of the future. The IB *(loc. cit.)* lists thirteen such basic ideas, which cover the above seven, but include such additions as the promise of Christ's return, the defeat of Satan, the victory over death, and the promised deliverance of believers from bondage. These ideas are the constants; and, both in form and in the style of presentation, everything is made to refer to one or more of them.

Central to these basic ideas is the one concept of Christ as the perfect priest of God establishing the new covenant both by his priestly work and by his sacrificial death. There is no question about the high Christology of the Epistle to the Hebrews. But despite so much information from the Old Testament to support the Christology and other ideas central to the epistle, the enigma of the epistolary ending from 13:17 on still remains. Four possible solutions of the enigma are suggested: (1) That the author wrote to a specific group and from the beginning had such an ending in mind; (2) That the original letter was sent to a second audience, and that the new ending was added to accommodate this group; (3) That a person other than the author added the present ending when forwarding it to another group; (4) That the ending was added by another person to bolster the concept of the Pauline origin of the entire letter. Of these theories, the first and the fourth are the most reasonable or plausible.

Certain habits of style are also evident. The writer makes it a practice to introduce Old Testament quotations by "God says" (see 4:3; 5:5,6; 8:10), and by "the Holy Spirit says" (3:7). He also introduces parts of his argument some time before he proceeds to develop it fully. And so every larger argument in the epistle has its preliminary statement. At all points he makes reference to the ritual law rather than to the moral law or to the social or visual force of the Law, as on the feast days. Characteristically he employs the name "Jesus" rather than the full title used by the

Apostle Paul. Further, in presenting "Jesus" as the "new and living way," the writer does not stray from the thought nor does he leave the argument incomplete. He seems to be the complete master of himself and of his techniques.

OUTLINE

I. Prologue. 1:1-4.
  A. Christ superior to the prophets. 1:1,2.
  B. Christ, the "imprint" of God. 1:3,4.
II. The main arguments introduced and explained. 1:5–10:18.
  A. Christ "greater than"; the argument for superiority. 1:5–7:28.
    1. Superior to angels. 1:5-14.
    2. The greater salvation, and a warning against neglect. 2:1-4.
    3. Christ as the perfect man. 2:5-18.
    4. Christ superior to Moses. 3:1-6.
    5. The superiority of the rest of Christ over the rest of Israel under Moses and Joshua. 3:7 – 4:13.
    6. Christ as high priest in the order of Melchisedek, superior to Aaron. 4:14 – 5:10.
    7. A rebuke for lack of understanding and for immaturity. 5:11 – 6:20.
    8. The priesthood of Melchisedek. 7:1-28.
  B. Christ, the minister and high priest of the new covenant. 8:1 – 10:18.
    1. The new covenant in relation to the old. 8:1-9.
    2. The better covenant explained. 8:10-13.
    3. The new sanctuary and the perfect sacrifice. 9:1-28.
    4. The new covenant complete, perfect, and at work. 10:1-18.
III. The elements of the faith life.10:19–13:17.
  A. The description of the faith life. 10:19-25.
  B. A description of those who spurn this "new and living way." 10:26-39.
  C. Examples of the life of faith. 11:1-40.
  D. Christ, the supreme example of the faith life. 12:1-4.
  E. The Father's love known through chastisement. 12:5-11.
  F. Christian conduct under the new covenant. 12:12-29.
  G. The Christian life in daily practice. 13:1-17.
IV. Personal epilogue. 13:18-25.

COMMENTARY

I. Prologue. 1:1-4.

The writer breaks the form of letter writing customarily identified with the letters of the NT by giving no salutation or opening sentences of greeting and introduction (see Introd.) He moves immediately to his subject, which is the person and work of the Lord Jesus Christ in relation to the Levitical system and the old covenant.

A. Christ Superior to the Prophets. 1:1,2. The implied question dealt with here is: Who was the last and most authoritative spokesman for God?

1. **In many parts** *(polymerōs)*, or part by part, fragmentarily, and **in many manners** *(polytropōs)*, or many and varied ways, God (Jehovah) spoke in the OT days through **the prophets**, many of whom tell in their writings by what methods he communicated with them. *Prophētais* is an all-inclusive word for all whom God used in OT times. **2. At the end of these days** is the literal rendering of a common Hebrew expression found in Num 24:14, having Messianic overtones. God has spoken **unto us** through one who stands in the relation of a son, having complete authority as a spokesman. In this relationship, Christ is unique and is here so described in the classic sense, as under divine appointment because a **Son.** He is both **heir** and *agent* of creation. **Worlds.** Greek *aiōnes*, "ages," including the world of space (cf. 11:3).

B. Christ, the "Imprint" of God. 1:3,4.

3. Light from light, or *effulgence* (ASV). The shining forth to the world of the very character of God in Jesus

Christ. He is the essential being of God. In the same way **express image** is used, as in Mt 22:20, where it refers to the image on the Roman coin. Christ is *the stamp* or impress of God *(charaktēr);* the essence of God. The whole force of the first two clauses of this verse stresses this one concept.

He is also *creator,* both as the "creative Word" (CGT, p. 31) and as Sustainer – the one **bearing them up** (AV, *upholding all things).* Creation and preservation are by God in Jesus Christ, and the **word of his power.** The word of the Son *is* the power to preserve and sustain, but this creative power resolves itself into the greater ministry of redemption. In making purification, or purging of **our sins,** Christ purged the great mass of the world's accumulated sins and uncleanness, which God sees. In Christ the penalty for sin is fully discharged and cleansing is provided. The idea is found in the words of Cowper's hymn:

There is a fountain filled with blood
Drawn from Immanuel's veins;
And sinners plunged beneath that flood,
Lose all their guilty stains.

Having this power and authority as creator and sin-bearer, Christ occupies the place of authority at the right hand of God. As both high priest and sin-bearer, he can present a finished redemption. His work is completed, and he can, therefore, sit down. As the Son of man he occupies this place by the act of God the Father. This is not a place of repose, but of activity for the divine mediator, high priest, and intercessor. In fulfillment of Ps 110:1, he is Lord of all.

4. The first of the contrasts showing the superiority of Christ is then introduced. The idea of contrast in the thought of **superior** *(kreitōn,* "superior," "becoming superior") is used thirteen times. Angels were important in delivering God's message to men. From the giving of the Law on Sinai to the assistance of angels accorded Daniel and the later prophets, these messengers of God served God, but as subordinates. Christ is superior to the angels in his person, name, function, power, and dignity. As for his name, he alone can save the lost (Acts 4:12), and his is the name above every name (Phil 2:10). By his name his reputation is established, for his is a mighty name.

II. The Main Arguments Introduced and Explained. 1:5–10:18.

A. Christ "Greater Than"; The Argument for Superiority. 1:5–7:28.

The thought introduced in 1:4 is now expanded by a series of seven quotations from the OT. Of these, five show the superiority of Christ.

1) Superior to Angels. 1:5-14.

5. The thought presented is an argument from silence, and the **he** is God. Never did God say to any angel that he was a Son; only to and of Christ did he say that (see Ps 2:7; II Sam 7:14). In both passages the immediate meaning is given an exalted or higher meaning, which imparts to these passages (and others to follow) a typological sense. In Ps 2:7 an anniversary celebration (Heb 1:5 a ff.) is made to speak of Christ. And the words spoken of Solomon in II Sam 7:14 are applied to Jesus the Son as being even more true of him. In this use the typology is correct; for Christ is the antitype, a fact that is true throughout Hebrews in the typological interpretation of the writer.

6. Both Deut 32:43 (LXX) and Ps 97:7 speak of angels worshiping Christ the Son. And the psalmist also speaks of a display of glory (97:6), which corresponds to the **brightness** of Heb 1:3. **7.** Two concepts are presented: (1) that angels are inferior or created beings –**Who maketh**; and (2) that angels are servants, as **winds** and **fire** are servants. The idea is thus re-emphasized that angels worship the Son because they are subordinate to him. Psalm 104:4 is thus presented as evidence of angelic subordination.

8,9. Christ is addressed as God and as king, or sovereign. As promised in the Davidic covenant, here is David's greater Son ruling as king, and his rule is eternal. The qualities of his kingship are justice, righteousness, and hatred of wickedness – qualities which can only characterize a just reign. In this position Christ is **above** or superior to all, and particularly to angels. To this exalted and honored position Christ has been **anointed** rather than appointed, and this anointing is that of *Christus Victor* – the victorious one ruling eternally.

10-12. From Ps 102:25-27. Spoken of Christ the Son, who as the Creator has made the world and who is the unchangeable one in the midst of things that will change. This also portrays a sharp contrast between Christ and angels. They are created material, and serve in the world as messengers of God. Christ is eternal, above the world, as being before it and after it. This argument is drawn from a LXX translation of a psalm not considered Messianic by rabbinic interpreters. So used by the writer, it further illustrates the superiority of Christ. **Thy years shall not fail.** They shall never cease or be discontinued.

13. In contrast to the angels, who were never told to sit at God's right hand, Christ now sits there as ruler and king, the God-man, the unchangeable and eternal Messiah. So he will sit until his ultimate triumph, when his enemies shall be made the **footstool of his feet.** This concept goes back to Joshua, who set his foot on the necks of vanquished kings as the ultimate sign of victory. So the passage gives hope to all believers in all ages that Christ will triumph over unrighteousness.

14. Angels serve, as shown by the inclusive **all;** but theirs is a sacred service or a "liturgic" service *(leitourgika)*, and a service to men *(diakonian)*. Angels are thus **ministering spirits,** who serve those who are **heirs of salvation,** or godly persons. This ministry of angels is implied as still continuing. The word salvation *(soterian)* is reserved by the author for development in another place.

2) The Greater Salvation and a Warning Against Neglect. 2:1-4.

The premise has already been stated in the reference to salvation (1:14). This salvation is by Christ, the exalted and anointed Son. It is therefore infinitely more important to heed God's revelation, **the things which we have heard** *(akousthesin)* or the Gospel. This is a solemn warning, greater than that of Deut 4:9.

1. Therefore relates to the Son as well as to the salvation which he gives. **The things that we have heard.** The Gospel, which provides a fixed point to which believers are referred. Here only is the place of safety. Nothing should be permitted to cause us to **drift past** *(pararyōmen)* this one fixed point of safety. No calamity, influence, force, or circumstance should be tolerated that weakens us with reference to the hope of salvation. A vessel launched unpiloted into midstream is made to **drift past** its landing point on the opposite shore by the currents at work in the stream. So the currents of life work against us unless we **take heed.** This is a warning directed specifically to those for whom the epistle was intended, signifying that the warning was necessary.

2. For if . . . Argument in the rabbinic style, from the lesser to the greater; from the giving of the Law by angels to the greater giving of the Gospel by Christ. The Law was vindicated by severe judgments (Lev 10:1-7; Num 16; Josh 7). It carried its penalties with it, and they were faithfully enacted. **3.** If the message of the Law was so jealously guarded, how much more strictly must the message of the Gospel be guarded. It was spoken by the Lord Jesus Christ, and it was established by those who heard him, who served as first-hand witnesses. And thus this Gospel message was both **steadfast** and **confirmed.** This being the case, how is there a way to **make good our escape** if we neglect this salvation? Escape is impossible because the message is of transcendent excellence and eternal importance. A greater message implies a greater judgment.

4. God himself joins in the witness by **signs** *(sēmeia)*, **miracles** *(terata)* and **powers** *(dynameis)*. These are the confirming evidences by no means to be slighted in weighing the authenticity of the Gospel. These evidences were further extended by the giving of **gifts** to believers by the Holy Spirit. Such signs, wonders, powers, and gifts are faithfully recorded in the four Gospels and in the record in the Acts. The gifts are mentioned in Rom 12; 13; I Cor 7:7; I Cor 12. Not the least of the reinforcing witnesses was the oneness of believers of every racial and national background. The implication is transparent. God was in Christ and in the Gospel, and therefore this message of salvation was to be heeded. To fail to pay attention held the threat of judgment. It is so today.

3) Christ as the Perfect Man. 2:5-18.

Having issued the warning, the writer resumes the theological argument. The subject is the humanity and humiliation of Christ, centered in the phrase, "Thou madest him a little lower than the angels" (v. 7).

5. The world to come *(oikoumenēn tēn mellousan)*. The future world, the inhabited earth of the future; the world future to the generation receiving this epistle and also future to us. This world will not be subject to angels, but it will be subject to Christ in its totality, and also to the redeemed. An entirely new condition will prevail, as Christ, with the saints, will rule in a harmony heretofore unknown.

6-9. A quotation from Ps 8:5-7 introduced by the indefinite **one . . . somewhere** (ASV). This quotation is the proof of the statement concerning "the world that is to be." The quotation establishes the humanity of the Son, who was **made a little lower than the angels** in order to **taste death for every man.** Now he is being exalted and crowned with glory and with honor because in his humanity he bore the humiliation of death (Phil 2:5-8). Because he suffered he is now exalted. Because he temporarily subjected himself to the limitations of humanity, he is now crowned with glory.

10. This meant suffering, and he did suffer. By this suffering his human experience was made complete. He *tasted* of the whole of human life, from birth to death. Thus was Christ perfected through suffering, and therefore he can identify himself with the needs of every man. Because he suffered he is now fully qualified to serve as **captain** (*archēgos*, "leader," 12:2) of man's salvation.

11. As the Son of God sent from the Father *into* humanity, Christ does not hesitate to identify himself with his own. We are his brethren. Jesus Christ, who sanctifies, and believers, who are sanctified, are one. **12,13.** A further illustration of the unity of the Saviour and the saved. This is set forth in pertinent OT passages from Ps 22:22; Isa 8:17,18. These "prove," as it were, that the Lord Jesus Christ and Christians are brothers. And **he is not ashamed to call them brethren** (v. 11). Both of the quoted passages from Isaiah are typologically applied.

14,15. The defeat of Satan and of death testifies that the atoning work of Christ is effectual. But not only is there defeat; there is also deliverance. Though fear can enslave, and the fear of dying has long plagued humanity, Christ has settled the problem by his own death and resurrection. As a man he died. He **partook** of flesh and blood and thus he died, but by his death came deliverance. Therefore, the power of Satan has been rendered inoperative (*katargeō*), and Christ has made an atonement for sin fully satisfying to God (Isa 53:11). What great victory is His! And what great victory all believers have in him! Satan and death are defeated and the fear of death is gone! That man who is free in Christ is indeed the most free of men.

16-18. Here is the first mention of the subject that occupies the central place in the argument of the epistle – the ministry of Christ as high priest. In this office Jesus' humanity is again in view, but here only a hint is given as to the full significance of Christ as high priest. Meanwhile he ministers and succors men by taking them **by the hand** (better than taking on the "nature of," AV). This he can do as their elder Brother and the captain of their salvation. Two words indicate the helping quality in the high-priestly function. These are **compassionate** (*eleēmōn*) and **faithful** (*pistos*). To men Christ is compassionate and to God he is faithful. Indeed, mercy and truth have met together in him. His faithfulness is shown in his being steadfast under the temptation which was a part of his suffering. Now he is able to come to the aid of all who are tempted because he has passed through the same tests and emerged victorious, and as Man he knows our need. **Propitiation for** our **sins.** See I Jn 2:2; 4:10; Rom 3:25; and CGT, p. 55.

4) Christ Superior to Moses. 3:1-6.

A comparison of two demonstrations of faithfulness is now introduced, and for the first time the readers are directly addressed in the phrase **holy brethren.** The parallels in structure between chapters 1 and 2 and chapters 3 and 4 are evident (CGT, p. 56).

1,2. The key to the understanding of Hebrews may rest in the thought of **consider** him. From *katanoēsate*, "observe attentively, fix your thoughts, mark with attention." This same thought appears again in 12:3. In 3:1,2 the emphasis is upon Christ as being faithful; in 12:3 it is upon his having endured. Here the **brethren** are encouraged to look to Jesus as **Apostle** ("messenger"; only here is this title used of Christ in the NT) and **High Priest,** an office that is more and more fully explained to the readers. **Confession** (*homologias*) rather than *profession* (AV). The term relates to believers confessing to Christ as their high priest.

3-5. The common metaphor is that of a **house.** The difference? Christ built the **house;** Moses served in the **house.** As in Jn 1:17, the juxtaposition of Moses and Christ is clearly stated. In the same fashion the juxtaposition of the old covenant and the new covenant is intimated. The emphasis is upon faithfulness, however.

Incomparable in position, Christ is faithful as a **son, over his house** (ASV, v. 6).

6. Whose house are we refers to believers, the company of the redeemed of God, whose faith is a continuing faith. Their faith is manifested in a **joyful confidence** *(parrēsian,* "free speech, outspokenness"; and thus outspoken or cheerful confidence) which becomes a **glorying of our hope** in the Son. Christ is the object as well as the basis of their confidence and their hope. **Unto the end** *(mechri telous).* Until hope becomes reality.

5) The Superiority of the Rest of Christ over the Rest of Israel under Moses and Joshua. 3:7–4:13.

The principle of rest is faith. This was true for the Israelites as they came to Canaan, and it is true for believers today. The *rest of faith* has both a present meaning and a future meaning. Psalm 95:7-11 is used to show how both threat and promise were related to Israel's rest in Canaan. Entrance into the promised land was conditioned on obedience.

7-11. The wilderness generation suffered the consequences of the threat made by God. That they perished in the wilderness was not an accident (see Num 14 and 21). As this psalm indicates, the children of Israel challenged God's sovereign authority by their rebellion in the wilderness (Num 20). The lesson is obvious. True obedience of heart goes beyond merely receiving instructions. One generation of Israelites perished because they rebelled in willful disobedience, and this in spite of a full revelation at Mount Sinai.

12. Here the truth of Ps 95:7-11 is given a present (to the original readers) and pertinent application. Willful neglect and disobedience, **an evil heart of unbelief,** can cause one to fall short or apostatize from God. This warning is made both individual and personal to encourage self-examination. A contrast between the faithfulness of Christ and the faithlessness of apostates is suggested. The apostasy is from the **living God** *(theou zōntos),* who carries out his judgments; therefore the warning is even more pointed. **13-19.** The way to avoid both apostasy and consequent judgment is through daily exhortation. Believers are to warn and admonish one another to hope and confidence in Christ. The later warning against failure to assemble together touches upon the same subject (10:25). Such assembling includes the opportunity for exhortation. Mutual strength comes through such exhortation, which is the effective countermeasure against hardened hearts and sin. This is one specific responsibility believers are to exercise until the coming of Christ.

By so exhorting one another and thus encouraging faith and obedience, Christians show themselves to be **partakers with Christ** in the blessings of the promised rest. The test of a believing heart is **confidence firm unto the end.** The generation in the wilderness failed to enter into the Canaan rest (v. 19) **because of unbelief** *(di'apistian).* Can the warning be more plainly stated?

Notice that the children of Israel that perished in the wilderness left only two spokesmen, only two representatives of their faithless and therefore silent generation – Caleb and Joshua. And it was the *faith* of these two that protected them and that speaks to our hearts even today.

The perished generation failed on two counts – (1) hardness of heart, and (2) unbelief. This led them into error and finally to judgment. Their unbelief was manifested in attitudes still common. They murmured or complained; they set up alternate plans and sought alternate leadership; they openly rebelled against God; they expressed dissatisfaction with God's provision; and, finally, they grudgingly accepted their place in God's plan. The record plainly written in Num 14 – 21 and commented upon in Psalm 95 served the writer of Hebrews well in his repeated warnings against such hardness and unbelief as were evidenced in the perished generation (3:12,13,18, 19; 4:6,7,11).

4:1-10. There is no break between chapters 3 and 4. The example of the wilderness experience is applied immediately to the lives of believers. The heart attitude of the readers is discussed in relation to 'the rest of faith,' a phrase often used in relation to this passage of Scripture. Two basic views prevail with regard to the promised **rest.** The first places the **rest** in the future as a heavenly rest, or entrance into the Kingdom of God (see Gleason L. Archer, Jr., *The Epistle to the Hebrews: A Study Manual*, pp. 28,29; Charles R. Erdman, *The Epistle to the Hebrews*, pp. 49,50). The second view places more emphasis upon the present rest than upon the promised rest of the future, though the latter is not disregarded. This 'rest of faith' is spoken of as a "full surrender," which is considered a unique experience (Erdman, *Ibid.)*. This second position emphasizes the present reality of 'the rest of faith' as a ceasing from our works which puts the believer into a closer relationship to Christ.

1,2. The promised **rest** is still available. The promise of God was not used up on the wilderness generation. Only the failure to remain steadfast in faith limits entering into this rest. This is the direct application of the warnings against unbelief in the previous statements. **We are those who have been "gospeled"** (AV, *unto us was the gospel preached)* resolves itself into a statement difficult to translate because of variant readings, but not difficult to understand. The faith of the believer exercised in relation to the promise of God guarantees the rest. (For a discussion of the variant readings of *sugkekerasmenous tē pistei tois akousasin,* see Alf and ExpGT on Heb 4:2 b.)

3,4. Downer suggests a twofold rest *(Principles of Interpretation).* Here the writer discusses spiritual repose for the persecuted and harassed believers to whom this letter is addressed. This is a present personal experience — **we which have believed do enter into rest** *(eiserchometha,* "we enter into"). This is the word of encouragement to troubled Christians. The second, or sabbath rest, is then introduced by the clause, **God did rest the seventh day from all his works.** This is the *sabbatismos* of verse 9, the *sabbath rest.*

5-10. God has provided **rest,** and this rest is to be occupied or entered into. Unbelief blocks entrance into God's rest, while faith opens wide the entrance; and so this rest is available only to true Christians. Joshua did not give this rest to his generation only; therefore the promised rest is still open. **There remaineth therefore a rest to the people of God** appointed for believers today. It is a rest both present and future that depends not upon "works," but upon the faith of the believers. **11.** Here is the "word of exhortation" concerning entering into God's rest (see 13:22) through earnest striving (lit., *give diligence).*

12,13. The offering of *rest* is reinforced by reference to the word of God, that is, reference both to Christ as the living Word and to the revelation, or written word. Five assertions are made concerning the **word of God** *(logos tou theou):* (1) it is *living;* (2) it is the word of power, or creative energy; (3) it *severs,* separating even the closest of relationships; (4) it is a judge of the innermost thoughts; and (5) it is the agency by which God deals directly with the **creature.** In this way the word of God reveals the whole man, particularly in relation to his heart attitudes, and his believing faith, that which will enable him to *enter into rest.* The word of God examines, judges, and admonishes the Christian to holy living and to believing faith.

6) Christ as High Priest in the Order of Melchisedek, Superior to Aaron. 4:14–5:10.

Now the theme first suggested in 2:17 and 3:1 is reintroduced for more extensive discussion. Here the preliminary statement concerning Christ in the sanctuary is made. What will follow will be a constant contrast between the earthly sanctuary or tabernacle and the "true" or heavenly sanctuary, and between the Aaronic or Levitical priesthood and the eternal priesthood of Christ "after the order of Melchisedek." At this point the place and ministry of Christ is explained.

14-16. He is in the sanctuary as our high priest. His right to this position is guaranteed by his death (including the shedding of his blood) and resurrection. He has **passed through the heavens** into the presence of God. He is there not only as the Son of God, but also as the Son of man. In his perfect humanity he is familiar with our needs, cares, temptations, and problems, because he was tempted without succumbing to the temptation. He knows all about sin without having sinned. His final familiarity with sin came when he took our sin upon himself at Calvary.

Now, because he is in God's presence, we can come to God boldly. The **throne of God** (AV, *of grace),* has been changed from a throne of judgment to a throne of mercy because the blood of Jesus has been "sprinkled" upon it. The symbolism is taken from the ark of the covenant in the Tabernacle and from the Day of Atonement (Lev 16). This symbolism and the replacement of the OT practice is explained point by point in the subsequent argument of the writer. For the moment, the author stresses the truth that there is help for the weak, mercy for the wretched, and **strength** (AV, *grace)* **to help,** because Christ our high priest at the throne of God meets our every need. This continual help is available instantly to each Christian, with no formalities save to "call upon the name of the Lord." Perhaps few passages in the NT are so rich as this one in the promise of help and comfort for Christians. Properly understood, this is one of the sublime truths in the Scripture concerning Christ and believers. Here it must be noted that everything relating to Christ as high priest is explained more fully in the passages that follow, up to Heb 10:18; also the comparison with Moses is now concluded.

5:1-10. The qualifications for the office of the high priest are next presented. Aaron serves as the model, since he was first to serve in the office of high priest.

1,2. Chosen from among men to represent man to God. The humanity of the high priest is basic and essential. He is also **appointed,** or *set apart,* to minister both before God and to men. Being a man, he can understand human weakness and minister to the erring and the ignorant. The high priest must deal with sinners as well as represent sinners. He must also offer sacrifice for his own sins as well as for those of the people. The picture is that of one totally involved as a man with the needs of men. **3.** Yet the personal needs of the appointed high priest were not forgotten. As he offered sacrifice for the people, so he offered for himself, representing his own needs to God through the blood of the sacrifice.

4. Aaron, the first high priest, was called of God to this office. He did not seek it nor did he merit it. He was appointed by God. The fate of those who sought to serve in this office apart from God's appointing is sufficiently illustrated by Korah (Num 16:40). **5,6.** So Christ was appointed high priest. The writer quotes Ps 2:7 with the meaning of, "This day I have appointed you to the office of a priest." He was fully qualified to hold the office and did not seek it for himself. He was appointed to this position of **glory** *(edōxasen)* by God the Father.

7-10. Christ's human experience is described here. It was an experience of learning and of limitations. This humiliation (Phil 2:7) was his time of learning to obey in the sphere of man. By this he was made complete. This was the time of his being in the flesh. The specific reference in Heb 5:7,8 is to the hours of agony in Gethsemane. The passage depicts anguish in the words **prayers, supplications, strong crying,** and **tears.** The enemy he faced was death – both physical and, because he was the sinbearer, spiritual, in that he bore the full wrath of God reserved for sinners. His request for deliverance was granted fully in the Resurrection, with its proclamation of death defeated. Through this experience Christ learned obedience as he would not have known it otherwise. Literally, *He learned from the things which he suffered* (v. 8), which is a play on words caught up in the Greek proverb *emathen – epathen.*

Now qualified perfectly as high priest, Christ provides **eternal salvation** *(sōtērias aiōniou,* v. 9), the eternal aspect of which is related to the priesthood of Melchisedek. In contrast to Aaron, Melchisedek is a priest of God eternally, a subject developed fully in chapter 7.

7) A Rebuke for Lack of Understanding and for Immaturity. 5:11–6:20.

Before developing his argument from the Melchisedekian priesthood, the writer again pauses to introduce exhortation and warning, including rebuke.

11-14. This is a strong rebuke. The writer plainly states that his readers are in no condition to receive the teaching he feels obligated to give them. He calls them **immature, backward, untaught,** and **dull of hearing.** Because of this condition, the typology concerning Melchisedek might be beyond their understanding. Jonathan Edwards once preached a sermon on Heb 5:12 entitled: "The Importance and Advantage of a Thorough Knowledge of Divine Truth." He noted that the rebuke in the passage seems to include all the readers addressed in the epistle, that these believers had made no progress either doctrinally or experimentally, that they did not understand Melchisedek, and furthermore, what they should have known, they did not *(The Works of President Edwards,* IV, 1-15).

The writer's conclusion that they were unqualified to be teachers of others seems self-evident. Further, they were actually qualified to receive only elementary truth or **milk.** As **babes** (nēpios, "sucklings"), they could not take stronger food; moreover, they lacked not only knowledge of the truth, but also experience of the truth. But those of **full age** or adulthood *(teloi,* "mature") were like **fully trained athletes** *(gegymnasmena)* ready for the contest because spiritually disciplined. Those so trained were spiritually sensitive and able to discern between truth and error when under instruction. (Throughout the passage the figures of speech are mixed; see Alf, IV, 103.)

6:1-3. The exhortation continues. Having learned already the basic principles concerning Christ, they were not to stop with them but to go on to gain *full stature* and *maturity,* to exhibit full spiritual growth. They were to continue to discern between living truths and lifeless forms, such as were found in Judaism in the washings, baptisms, and rituals. In verse 3 the writer identifies himself with his readers and reveals his own dependence upon God.

4-8. Some had gone on to maturity; others had **fall[en] away.** These are now mentioned to enforce the warning that has just been given—to go on to maturity. Properly, this passage should be interpreted not from within a theological system but from within its own context. First principles learned is the subject. Now the writer speaks of those who, having received such instruction in first principles, had turned away from Christ. They were now enemies of Christ and of the salvation that is in him.

It was the writer's purpose to portray extreme peril so that those tempted to apostasy might have the strongest possible example. The issues were plain: Christ or no Christ, saving faith or unbelief, suffering his reproach or joining his betrayers and murderers. The words used are strong terms. *Hapax phōtisthentas* means **once for all enlightened.** *Tasted* is translated *come to know* in newer lexicons. **Partakers,** from Greek *metochous,* means real sharers (Alf, IV, 109). All these terms indicate a great deal of knowledge and participation on the part of those **once . . . enlightened.** Even miracles were familiar to those now shown to be hostile to Christ.

A somewhat different point of view is possible regarding the passage. It may be rendered, *if they fall away* (cf. the RSV, *if they commit apostasy*). In that case the writer is not thinking of specific instances of apostasy, least of all among the readers (v. 9), but is warning that refusal to progress in the Christian life leads logically to retrogression, of which the ultimate end may be apostasy. If one should go to the extreme of falling away after tasting the heavenly gift, his falling away cannot be classed with ordinary sin, for it involves a repudiation of God's provision in Christ (crucifying the Son of God afresh). Therefore, for him, the hope of renewal vanishes, for God does not have some other cure for sin when Calvary is rejected.

In choosing to reject Christ, the apostates most resembled a field that yields only thorns and thistles, though the rains falling upon it and the farmers tilling were intended to produce beneficial herbs. There can be no mistaking the direct and strong warning to readers tempted to turn away from Christ. Indeed, what was true for these first century believers is still true for believers today.

9-12. But all of the above is not true of those addressed, the writer explains. This is the conclusion of the matter so far as his speaking directly to his readers is concerned. Though he has just spoken in *severe words of warning (houtōs laloumen),* he says he is **convinced of the better things** *(ta kreissona)* of them. God would not **forget in a moment** *(epilathesthai)* all they had done in word and deed in ministering to their Christian brethren, nor that they continued so to minister. This was a sign of their earnestness; now they were to keep this same earnest spirit and attitude all their lives (v. 11). They were to keep before them the splendid example of all who so earnestly persevered (v. 12), and they would enjoy the fulfilled promises of God. They must copy the faith and practices of those who were strong in faith.

13-20. They had the firm guarantee of the covenant made with Abraham, as their assurance. Abraham is introduced here as an example of perseverance. And Abraham persevered because God guaranteed by His own name the covenant He made with him. Having sworn by His own name, God could not then lie to Abraham, because both His authority and His integrity were at stake. God is unchangeable, and we have as strong an encouragement as Abraham had in his day. Our assurance is in Jesus, who is in the heavenly sanctuary already. By oath and by promise those whose hope is in Christ as the **anchor of the soul** will realize their hope of passing through the veil (symbolic, veil of Tabernacle) because Jesus has already **entered for us.**

As the eternal high priest in the sanctuary, Christ fulfills the priestly type of Melchisedek, and the writer returns to the interrupted theme of the person of Christ **after the order of** or *just like* Melchisedek.

8) The Priesthood of Melchisedek. 7:1-28.

Melchisedek is clearly a type of Christ. Everything known about Melchisedek is found in two passages of the OT—Gen 14:17-20 and Ps 110:4. In both instances his position as a priest of God is clear. Also his life story is related entirely in the Genesis passage. Nothing more is known about him, and it is not completely clear that the reference to Salem is to be interpreted as a reference to Jerusalem (Alf, IV, 125). However, there is no mistaking Melchisedek as a type of the eternal or everlasting priesthood of Christ. This thought serves to open up the whole discussion of the Levitical system.

Leonard designates 7:1–10:18 as the heart of the epistle. He speaks of it as a unique section, having few if any parallels in the NT, since it develops a comparative estimate of the priestly mediators of the two covenants (*op. cit.*, p. 32).

The importance of Melchisedek and the significance of the comparison of Melchisedek and Christ has been the subject of much discussion. Opinions about these considerations vary widely. Cotton and Purdy (IB, XI, 660,661) speak of the "Melchisedek speculation," and of the "Alexandrian method of allegorical interpretation," which means, they say, "practically to play fast and loose with historical fact." And yet their comment on the passage goes on to point out clearly that Melchisedek establishes the "validity and dignity of Christ's priesthood," and that Melchisedek is "the prototype of the Son . . . He [the writer of Hebrews] has established proof that Jesus is the Son; he must now show that He is Priest."

A. B. Davidson in his *The Epistle to the Hebrews* (pp. 129, 146ff.) discusses the whole subject of the priesthood of Christ, including the Melchisedek question. He rightly establishes the basic principle. With Melchisedek, the function of the priesthood is not under discussion, but the personnel of the priesthood. The ministry for all priests is essentially the same, being merely extended for the high priest in relation to the Day of Atonement. The writer thus relates Christ to Melchisedek in order to emphasize that *Christ is a priest forever.*

1-3. The historical incident recorded in Gen 14:17-20 is reviewed. The writer indicates that Melchisedek was a king and therefore received tribute of Abraham; but more important, he was **priest of God Most High** (ASV), and therefore received tithes of Abraham. The point of this is made later with reference to Melchisedek's being a priest of God before the Levitical priesthood was established (vv. 4-6). In the parenthetical portion of verses 2, 3, notice is taken of the fact that Melchisedek had no recorded genealogy or succession. Neither is his birth mentioned or his death recorded. His is a record of one **having neither beginning of days nor end of life, but made like unto the Son of God** (ASV). This lack of birth data strengthens the typology of Melchisedek in relation to Christ. Thus Ps 110:4 emphasizes the eternity of the priesthood of Melchisedek, as does *eis tō diēnekes,* "in perpetuity," **continually** (Heb 7:3).

4-14. What does all of this discussion of Melchisedek mean spiritually? **Observe,** or **contemplate** *(theōreite)* the greatness of the one whom Abraham acknowledged to be superior by giving him tithes. The important truth is that the priesthood of Melchisedek was greater than the priesthood of Aaron and the Levites because (figuratively) the later priesthood offered tithes to God through the earlier, or Melchisedekian, priesthood in the person of Abraham. In this way **the less,** i.e., the Levites, **is blessed of the better,** i.e., Melchisedek. The implications are all intended to demonstrate the superiority and eternity of the priesthood of the latter, who functioned as a priest when he blessed Abraham and (figuratively) Aaron and the Levites.

In this sequence the relation of the Levitical priesthood to Christ is discussed (vv. 11-14). Jesus was not of Levi but of Judah. This debarred him from the order of priests under the Law. His humanity related him to the tribe of Judah, and therefore (v. 13) he could not qualify on the human plane to serve before the altar as a priest, for Moses uttered not one word giving Judah priestly authority or function.

15-28. The technical question of whether Christ was/is a priest resolves itself because he is of another order of priesthood. This order is adjudged superior in every point to the Levitical priesthood, and this order is eternal. **16. The power of an endless life** *(akatalytos)* appears in no other place in the NT.

18-20. The Law of Moses referred to in the phrase **disannulling of the commandment,** or *disannulling of a foregoing commandment* (ASV) is abrogated or set aside in that Christ is the priest of God sealed with an oath (Ps 110:4). **22.** Christ is the **surety** or pledge *(engyos)* that God's oath will be kept in the promises and assurances of the new covenant.

23-28. Christ **lives forever** and is not subject to death. The grave has been conquered. He can therefore save **to the uttermost,** completely and to the ultimate, i.e., eternally, whoever calls upon him. In the same fashion his intercession for his own is unceasing. These ministries are guaranteed by his own character (**holy, guileless, undefiled, separated from sinners,** ASV), his function (as the atoning sacrifice), and his relationship.

B. Christ, the Minister and High Priest of the New Covenant. 8:1–10:18.

The new covenant, the Levitical system of the old covenant, and the priestly ministry of Christ are now brought together in the concluding statements of the main argument of the epistle. In summation, direct reference is made to the tabernacle in the wilderness in order that the contrast with the heavenly sanctuary might be introduced. Christ is in the heavenly sanctuary, his presence there being earlier described (4:13-16). He is there as high priest performing priestly service based upon the sacrifice, he being also the sacrifice. Three concepts are thus combined, namely, atoning sacrifice, priestly service, and the heavenly sanctuary.

1) The New Covenant in Relation to the Old. 8:1-9.

Jeremiah mentioned a new covenant centuries before this discussion of its import (Jer 31:31 ff.). In Heb 8:8, both Israel and Judah are named as being the recipients of blessing and divine help in the promised new covenant. The new covenant is clearly contrasted with the old covenant (vv.8,9). It is shown to be inclusive, as well as a **better covenant** because guaranteed by **better promises** (v. 6).

1-5. The new covenant was established by Christ, who is its **minister** *(leitourgos).* He ministers the **holy things** in the **true tabernacle,** which is built by **the Lord** *(kyrios,* evidently the Father, Alf). Here Christ ministers as high priest, having full authority (vv. 1,2). His position in the heavenly sanctuary is in perfect order. He offered to the Father both sacrifices and service. He offered himself as the one acceptable sacrifice (an idea developed more fully in chs. 9; 10), and his service is that of the high priest before God, serving in the sanctuary. In verse 4 there is a possible indication that this epistle was written before the fall of Jerusalem in A.D. 70, in the thought that earthly priests still serve who **offer gifts according to the law.** These serve only in the **copy and shadow** (ASV) given to Moses, who saw the real or true (heavenly) sanctuary on Mount Sinai (Ex 25:40).

6-9. The contrast is then sharpened (v. 6). A better service, or **ministry the more excellent . . . a better covenant** (ASV); and all based on **better promises.** If the old covenant had been satisfactory, God would not have found fault with it nor would he have spoken of replacing it as he did through Jeremiah, the prophet (Jer 31:31 ff.). The prophet reported the giving of the old covenant, the failure of Israel to observe it, and the decision to replace it at some time future to Jeremiah.

2) The Better Covenant Explained. 8:10-13.

The writer appropriates the prophecy of Jeremiah to explain the nature and provisions of the new covenant. Under the new covenant: (1) God puts new laws in the hearts and minds of the people (accomplished by Christ through the new birth, thus establishing the new covenant as a covenant of relationship). (2) He establishes a new relationship with them–**I will be to them a God, they . . . to me a people.** (3) The people have a new function – **teach every man . . . Know the Lord** (v. 11). (4) And God's truth has a new outreach – **all shall know me.** (5) A new cleansing is provided, with sins and iniquities forgiven through Christ, the sacrifice and guarantor of the new covenant (v. 12). The old is replaced by the new, and the old is at the point of completely disappearing (v. 13).

3) The New Sanctuary and the Perfect Sacrifice. 9:1-28.

Familiarity with the functions of the Aaronic priesthood as described in the latter half of Exodus and in Leviticus greatly aids in understanding these verses. The service of the priest in the Tabernacle is described in summary fashion in relation to the various pieces of furniture and their functions. As in the former chapter, the purpose is again to make plain the contrast between the superior service of Christ as high priest in the heavenly sanctuary and Aaron as high priest on earth.

1-10. The old practices are explained as the ordinances of the **earthly sanctuary.** The writer sees to it that his readers do not mistake the location of Levitical priestly service. He names the items of furniture in the Tabernacle and identifies them locationally by **holy place, sanctuary,** ASV, AV *(hagia);* and **holy of holies, holiest of all,** ASV, AV *(hagia hagiōn).* The former was the first room in the earthly Tabernacle, and the latter was the second or inner room. This careful description is important for an understanding of the activities of the Levitical priests and of the high priest in relation to the two rooms. The ministrations of the priests were clearly of greater importance than the furniture, as is indicated by the phrase, **of which things we cannot now speak severally,** or *individually* (ASV, v. 5).

The Levitical priests ministered daily in the Holy Place, but they did not go through the veil into the Holy of Holies. Ceremonial cleansing was obtained for the people as the priests daily ministered at the altar of incense in the Holy Place. Atonement or forgiveness was obtained only once each year, on the Day of Atonement (see Lev 16), when the high priest went through or beyond the veil to the mercy seat carrying the blood of the sacrifice. But these were **carnal ordinances** (Heb 9:10), because the earthly Tabernacle, its furniture and its service, were imperfect. The veil hung between the two rooms of the sanctuary in the Tabernacle bore perpetual witness that the way directly to God was not yet open (see 4:13-16). To this fact the Holy Spirit bore witness (9:8). Also there was a specific time limit as to how long the Levitical priesthood and the earthly Tabernacle were to serve (v. 10). There was to be a **time of reformation.**

11-14. Christ inaugurated this time of reformation by entering as **a high priest** into the heavenly tabernacle, or **greater and more perfect tabernacle,** and presenting his own blood on the heavenly mercy seat as an atonement. An **eternal redemption** was once for all accomplished by the eternal sacrifice of the Son of God. No repetition of this action is necessary or possible. The contrast between the blood of goats and bulls annually offered and the other ceremonial symbols of the Levitical system and the atoning death of Christ is again explained. Of how much greater import is the blood of Christ **who through the eternal Spirit offered himself** *(dia pneumatos aiōniou).* **Through the eternal Spirit** probably means *his eternal Spirit* (ASV marg.), and refers to the consent of his own will in the offering of himself in relation to his position in the Godhead. In this way his was an eternal and not a temporal sacrifice. The exact interpretation of **eternal Spirit** is difficult to determine (cf. Davidson, *Epistle to the Hebrews,* p. 178; CGT, p. 119).

This redemptive and atoning work of Christ satisfies both legal requirements under the Law and personal requirements in a cleansed conscience. It provides internal purity as well as outward and eternal deliverance. This was a particularly important argument in light of the temptation to apostatize on the part of at least some of the readers of this epistle. As sinners delivered and cleansed, they, especially, were obligated to render service to God rather than return to the **dead works** of Judaism.

15-28. The way into the heavenly sanctuary is by atoning death. This is the functional meaning of **mediator of a new covenant.** This is true because a **death** has **taken place,** the death of Jesus Christ upon the cross. A transaction took place there which fully satisfied all redemptive requirements, and this issues in forgiveness and an **eternal inheritance.**

16. This new covenant may be viewed as a testament sealed by the death of him that made it. In OT times the blood of animal sacrifice sealed a covenant to its makers. The death of Christ seals the new covenant. **17.** Here is added argument to strengthen the fact under consideration. The emphasis is upon **testament** *(diathēkē;* cf. Alf) sealed by death and by shedding of blood. This is the only way in which a covenant can be in force. And this is a better covenant. All along through these verses the point made is that death is necessary.

18-22. The blood of animal sacrifices was inseparably linked to the earthly or first Tabernacle. After God gave the promises and instructions to Moses, then Moses took the blood of sacrifices and sprinkled everything symbolically involved in the first covenant. Hence this is called the **blood of the covenant.** By this action these earthly things were cleansed and then maintained as clean and identified with God and his covenant with Israel. This was necessary because there is no remission apart from the blood of the sacrifice. The fundamental truth over which many stumble is the statement of verse 22 that **without shedding of blood there is no remission** (cf. Ex 24:3-8).

23-28. The finality of the atoning work of Christ is explained more fully. **23.** Again, **better sacrifices** is the key. Heaven itself is free from the taint of human sin because the blood of Christ was shed (cf. Moll in J. P. Lange's *Commentary on the Holy Scriptures;* or, Ex 24:3-8).

24-26. Finality. Christ is in the holy place or heavenly sanctuary, appearing there in our behalf (v. 24). He does not go in and come out annually, for his sacrifice is complete (v. 25). He suffered only once; his blood was shed once; and in his suffering and death, sin was once and for all time conquered. This event is identified with **the end of the world** (AV) or *age* (ASV). This time designation and the almost immediate reference to the Second Coming (v. 28) suggest that God's people in the early generations after Christ linked the Lord's death with his return as events close to each other in import, if not in time.

27,28. A physical death precedes judgment. Christ suffered this death, and in so doing he died once and for all. In so doing he took sin upon himself—**the sins of many** (v. 28). And he will come a second time not to bear sin, but to meet sinners whose sins are washed away in his atoning blood. These are the redeemed of God who **wait for him.** Believers will then enter into full salvation and the actual presence of God. Those who know the joy of salvation should also know the hope of the Lord's coming.

4) The New Covenant Complete, Perfect, and at Work. 10:1-18.

How can sins be removed? The old covenant offered a way of forgiveness of sins. Was it satisfactory? Did the method work? These questions form the basis for the final phase of the argument.

1-4. The old covenant failed. It was a mere shadow *(skia)* of the better things to come, an image *(eikōn)* of the real. Because of this, it was ultimately futile in that it never made anyone mature in faith and trust. If it had made perfect believers, it would not have been replaced. The sin problem would have been solved. The fact clearly stated is that yearly offerings and the blood of animal sacrifices cannot take away sin. The vital word in verse 4 is **impossible** *(adynaton).* This is a strong, conclusive, and true statement.

5-10. Psalm 40:7-9 is here used typologically. David is quoted as having spoken of the Messiah and his entrance into the world in human form. The *will* of God for Messiah was to make a full atonement for sin. This necessitated sacrifice and shedding of blood and therefore the **body . . . prepared** so that he might suffer. In suffering and death the will of God was fully accomplished and the second or better covenant was fully established. As a result, believers have been changed because cleansed and sanctified by the **offering of the body of Jesus Christ once for all** (v. 10). By this offering, atonement was made, pleasing a holy God perfectly.

11-13. The ultimate triumph of the Messiah is seen in that he does not come repeatedly, nor does he stand to symbolize an incomplete redemption; but upon offering himself, Christ **sat down on the right hand of God.** Again reference is made to the position occupied by Christ, the place of authority and of priestly service. For believers, he both rules and intercedes, two aspects of the ministry of Christ continually held before those tempted to apostatize back into Judaism and mere legalism and ritual. The rule of Christ will become actual. Meanwhile he patiently waits for the time when his enemies will be vanquished. There will then be no more opposition to Christ or to his rule.

14-18. Jeremiah's covenant prophecy has been fulfilled. Believers in Christ are now perfected, cleansed, purified, fitted for perpetual communion and fellowship with God. The word **perfected** *(teteleiōken)* means "completed." That is, the end in view is achieved; the believer is prepared for entrance into the sanctuary, and his earthly hope of this is assured (cf. ExpGT). This signifies growth and also enjoyment of privileges.

The writer again quotes Jer 31:33 ff., to indicate how the heart of a believer is changed by faith in Christ, and his very nature is transformed. Jeremiah foretold that it would be so as the Holy Spirit spoke through him. Remission of sins is now complete, and what Jeremiah spoke of in prophecy is now reality. Sins are not even remembered, and lives are fully transformed by all that Christ has accomplished in atoning death. The work is done.

III. The Elements of the Faith Life. 10:19—13:17.

Now an exhortation brings to a close the last thoughts of the writer. This closing section is an exhortatory composition with all the thoughts centered in the one word — **faith.** The exhortation is to constancy of faith, with accompanying warnings about the outcome if the life of faith is either rejected or despised. The thought of faith carries through to the personal epilogue with which the epistle finally ends. The thought of an active life of faith seems to be a focal point around which the writer gathers his final arguments and warnings. The thought introduced by **Let us draw near with a true heart in full assurance of faith** permeates all that follows. By description, warning, example, and other means that seem to come to mind, the writer states the case plainly in the phrase, **full assurance of faith.**

A. Description of the Faith Life. 10:19-25.

The life of faith must first be understood. If a teacher finds that the believers' faith is weak, then he must speak much of an assured faith that makes strong, confident believers. This assurance is founded upon the eternal guarantee that Christ has entered into the sanctuary and into the presence of God, making it possible also for every believer to enter into the sanctuary and into God's presence. If this is the privilege of believers, and it is, then believers should take every advantage of the privilege. They should exercise the prerogative of drawing near, because Christ, the Son over God's house and the high priest in eternal (Melchisedekian) generation, has made this possible. In this expansion of 4:13-16, the writer bids us to be bold.

19. Boldness, or confidence. Because of all that the Lord Jesus Christ has done, we have boldness. This is free access **by the blood of Jesus;** the way is already opened. **20, 21.** Here is the means of access, **by a new** *(prosphaton)* **and living way . . . ,** or **consecrated** way. The veil no longer blocks access to God, nor does human nature, symbolized by the reference to flesh *(sarx).* Christ's suffering in the flesh forever removes this barrier. As his body was torn on the cross, so the veil between God and men was torn, giving immediate access to God. And Christ is the **great high priest,** or **great priest,** as in 4:14, doing the work of **a great priest** in the sanctuary.

22. Draw near, bears the idea of coming to God frequently, openly, intimately, and unhesitatingly, but always with a cleansed heart, **true heart; hearts sprinkled** and a fully formed assurance that the way to God is opened to us. The cleansed heart and the fully assured faith are the predominant ideas; the secondary emphasis falls on the triad of cleansed heart, body, and conscience. **23. Confession of our hope** (ASV). An unwavering confession of faith in the living Christ. God undergirds our hope by his own promises, **for he is faithful who promised.** This then speaks of further affirmation based upon faith in the faithfulness of God.

24. With assurance comes concern for others. This is manifested by the willingness of believers to assemble together (v. 25) and also by their willingness both to give and to receive helpful exhortation and instruction. **To provoke.** To stimulate through provocation and encouragement *(paroxysmos, paroxysm).* **Love** and **good works** are to be awakened toward fellow believers. **25.** Assembly and fellowship are two evidences of vital faith. When zeal flags and faith weakens, the desire to fellowship with other believers weakens also. Through such assembly the provocation of verse 24 is possible. When Christians meet together, they exhort each other to fruitful service and unbroken fellowship. The danger of apostasy lurks in the failure of believers to meet together for mutual help *(parakalountes,* "mutual encouragement").

The day. The shortest of all the references to the coming again of the Lord Jesus Christ. A direct reference to the Second Coming. The urgency of the passage concerning exhortation is due to the imminence of this Day of Christ. At this point, some difficulty arises in relation to the fall of Jerusalem. The primary reference of this statement may be to the impending judgment of Jerusalem. But it is evident that the fall of Jerusalem can not completely fufill this promise. So the statement seems to presuppose a second or final judgment as well.

B. A Description of Those Who Spurn This "New and Living Way." 10:26-39.

The exhortation to constancy is continued with a negative application or warning. Alternatives are described in sharp contrast as belief or unbelief, faith and practice or fearful judgment, acceptance or rejection in the light of Calvary.

26. Sin wilfully *(hamartanontōn,* "as long as we are sinning wilfully") and **knowledge** *(epignōsis,* "full knowledge") govern this passage. In this case there is no lack of *understanding* of the truth, just as in the case of false teachers mentioned in II Pet 2:20,21, where the same strong word for **knowledge** is twice used. The basic thought in this climactic warning passage is the same as in Heb 6:4-6. A deliberate rejection of the cross by one who knows the way leaves God with no alternative. When mercy is rejected, judgment must fall.

27-29. Judgment follows. The practice under Mosaic law is cited in order to establish the contrast. This judgment will come upon the **adversaries** of God, and the rejection of verse 26 apparently places the rejectors among those adversaries. This will be **a fearful,** frightful judgment, because the one atoning sacrifice has been rejected.

The threefold charge follows: (1) contempt for Christ in the thought of **trampling under foot;** (2) rejecting the blood-bought covenant as worthless and unholy; (3) despising the person and work of the Holy Spirit.

30,31. From such ultimate condition there is neither remedy nor escape. Only vengeance awaits such persons, declares the inspired writer, quoting Deut 32:35, 36 as supporting evidence. This hopeless apostasy and ultimate and irrevocable rejection leads only to the fiercest judgment from God. Psalm 135:14 is also noted as supporting evidence for these statements.

32-34. Again, the writer draws a contrast. Continuing his exhortation, he describes strong faith and patience under trial and difficulty. He reminds the believers of their early faith and the first blessing of knowing Christ. In the joy of this newly found faith they regarded **afflictions, temptations** *(athlēsis,* such as the struggles of an athlete), **sufferings,** and **reproaches** as nothing. The kind of struggle – whether sympathizing with others under trial or suffering personal loss for Christ – makes little difference. Faith was strong; affliction was welcomed, and confidence in Christ was firm and constant. **A gazingstock.** They were made a theater, or set upon a stage *(theatrizomenoi)* for all to look upon; but they did not waver. In thus encouraging the believers to recall **former days,** the writer personalizes his exhortation.

35-37. Patience, or **confidence,** in the light of the things recalled, should not now be forgotten, or cast away; for this is a confidence based upon assurance, a boldness of vital faith, an assured victory. And this patience is the greatest need. Rather than turning back to an easier way, the believers are to keep both faith and hope high in a steadfast patience, for the reward is certain. To do **the will of God** must be their ruling desire on earth, that their heavenly reward may be the more blessed (cf. Mt 7:21). They must be patient, and carry the load, not cast it off *(hypomenēs).* And they are to remember the words of Hab 2:3, **for he shall surely come and will not delay.**

38-39. Faith is the keynote of this passage. Those who live by faith and die in faith will ultimately rejoice in the final salvation guaranteed in Christ. As Habakkuk admonishes, men are not to **shrink back** (ASV), for then God is obliged to act as described in Heb 10:26-31. True believers will not be guilty of such shrinking back. Their faith is a **faith unto the saving of the soul** (ASV). In his description of the faith of the true believer, the writer has introduced in a quiet manner the next phase of his exhortation.

C. Examples of the Life of Faith. 11:1-40.

Having introduced the faith life as the subject of his final exhortation, and having described it both as to its elements and its opposites, the writer now brings to his argument the example of numerous people who lived such a life of faith. It is as though someone who had followed all the careful reasoning of the author now requested some evidence or proof to substantiate the claims made. Have any persons ever lived like this? Assuredly! Who are they? Heb 11:1–12:4 is the writer's answer.

1-7. He first explains the nature of true faith, giving not so much a definition as a description. Faith is trust in the unseen. It is *not* trust in the unknown, for we may know by faith what we cannot see with the eye. Those to whom the writer was directing his thoughts would now have the added assistance of the record of the heroes of the OT who lived with trust in the unseen, or by faith. Faith is the ultimate assurance and the ultimate evidence that **things not seen** are realities *(pragmata)*. The continuity of men who have believed in **things not seen**, heroes of faith, is unbroken.

By the act of believing, God's children know that the Lord made the worlds by his word. The OT great ones lived by faith. Abel, Enoch, and Noah are mentioned as precise examples of men acting by faith. Also, the generation receiving the exhortation was to live by faith. And each succeeding generation also must live by **things hoped for** until the coming of Christ.

Abel made an acceptable offering, which was a blood sacrifice. And this offering typologically established blood sacrifice as the basis of entrance into the life of faith. The faith life becomes a life only by an atonement made. So Abel continues to speak. Enoch lived a righteous life. His goal was to please God at any cost, and he succeeded; **before his translation he had been well-pleasing unto God** (ASV). This should still be the goal of every true believer, and it is impossible to please God apart from faith. Abel brought an acceptable offering, and Enoch lived a life of unbroken fellowship. Noah believed that God would judge the earth, and this became an incentive for his life of faith. He built the ark as an evidence of his faith. He activated his faith in the light of judgment.

Noah lived to see his faith and practice vindicated. On the one hand, he exhibited his faith by building the ark; on the other, he saw his faith vindicated in his deliverance from the Flood. Thus he joined that glorious company of the just who live by faith through **a righteousness which is according to faith** (ASV).

8-31. The later patriarchs also bore the same witness. Abraham, Sarah, Isaac, Jacob, Joseph, and Moses all exemplify the life of faith. Abraham and Moses serve as the better examples because they played such an important part in the purposes of God in the earth. Abraham exemplifies obedience in the life of faith. When God called him out of Ur of the Chaldees, he became a dweller in tents and a **sojourner,** a spiritual pilgrim, with his eye fixed upon a city as yet unseen.

Later he willingly gave Isaac to God, fully persuaded that the seed of Abraham, through Isaac, predestined to bless the world, would be under no jeopardy if Isaac should die. In faithfulness to His covenant promise of a seed, God would raise him up. Even the birth of Isaac, the son of promise, was an evidence of faith on the part of Abraham and Sarah. For their son was born when they were physically too old for such an occurrence.

13-16. For true believers, to live by faith is to die **in faith.** The faith life is a pilgrimage. Heaven is the only home of faithful believers. It is the **better country** to which those who live by faith are fully committed. And because they are committed to God, God is committed to them. **God is not ashamed of them** (ASV), and he proves this by providing a city or place of habitation for his own (Jn 14:1,2).

17-19. From Genesis 22 we see the faith of Abraham in offering up Isaac on Mount Moriah. The faith of Abraham was tested in at least two ways: (1) he was required to offer to God the best and dearest of his possessions; and (2) he was required to offer to God the son of promise. Abraham's future was assured to him only through Isaac. If Isaac were to die, what of the promise of God to Abraham? In making his offering, Abraham demonstrated in practical fashion his belief that death is no problem to God. Death can be neither barrier nor deterrent to His keeping a covenant promise—**God was able to raise him up, even from the dead. Figure.** Parable, similitude, as though Isaac were actually returned from the dead; a resurrection.

20. Isaac blessed Jacob and Esau in the covenant promise made to Abraham, but still future to Isaac, thus concerning **things to come** (see Gen 27).

21,22. By faith Jacob . . . By faith Joseph. Evidence of the faith of the patriarchs in the promise made to Abraham. Jacob, by blessing the sons of Joseph, perpetuated the promise and evidenced both faith and submission as he worshiped. Joseph demonstrated his faith in the covenant promise to Abraham by requesting that his body **(bones)** be buried in the land of promise (Gen 48; 50).

23-29. In many ways Moses exemplified the life of faith. By faith his parents hid him in defiance of a specific royal command (Ex 1:16-22). He was a **proper** or beautiful child, thus a portent of future blessing from God. Later, Moses himself, by faith, made proper choices. **Son of Pharaoh's daughter.** A phrase symbolic of rank, indicating the rank of prince. Moses chose God's people and the promises of God even though this meant **affliction** and adversity. In this, Moses became the deliverer of a hopeless people (Ex 2). He also chose not to enjoy the **temporary pleasures of sin** (Alf, p. 224). **The reproach of Christ.** Moses seemingly comprehended Messianic truth; hence his choice of faith in the Messiah. This **reproach** was borne by Christ, and it is likewise borne by those who faithfully serve him. This passage suggests that Moses had Christ in view.

Moses also chose to leave Egypt. Again, with Christ in view, he discounted both the riches of the land of his birth and the power and prestige of its Pharaoh, or king. This statement refers to the exodus of Israel from Egypt with Moses as the leader. Moses gave further evidence of his faith by keeping the Passover, thus indicating that deliverance is by the shedding of blood (Ex 12). Notice the reference to faithful continuance—**he endured**—a thought developed more fully in Heb 12:1-4. Furthermore, Moses and the people together by faith witnessed the miracle of the Red Sea—a deliverance for Israel, a judgment upon the Egyptians.

30,31. Jericho fell victim to the faith of Joshua and the children of Israel, and Rahab participated in Israel's blessing by her faith. The memorial to the faith of Rahab is read in Mt 1:5, where she is listed in the genealogy of Christ.

32-38. The writer now resorts to piling up examples, because of the impossibility of taking each case separately. The list is impressive, including some of the Judges, the greatest of Israel's kings—David, and one of her greatest prophets—Samuel.

The list of deeds is equally impressive. In some cases the incidents referred to are well known; in others they are more obscure. In each instance, however, something typical of those who live by faith is brought out. The faith life makes such deeds possible, deeds of valor, might, courage, or perseverance. And these are the kinds of experience that those who live by faith are called upon to endure. All of the history of Israel is encompassed in these few brief sentences. By a careful search of the OT, it is possible to find many of the events mentioned.

39,40. But in spite of all this evidence that men and women of the OT lived lives of faith, the fact remains that they did not know the full blessings of sins forgiven and of fellowship with God through the provisions of Calvary. They lived in anticipation of the new covenant, but without its full provisions. They had a positive and effective witness, **a good report through faith,** or as in the CGT, *having been borne witness to through their faith,* an attestation by God himself.

God unveiled a better plan, or at least a more complete plan, in the generations after the patriarchs and particularly regarding the generations since Calvary. Perfection had to await these generations, **that they without us should not be made perfect** (*teleiōthōsin, teleioō,* "to make perfect, or complete"). The whole of the completed redemption is in view.

Each of the people mentioned in this chapter illustrates some phase or aspect of the life of faith—whether obedience, acting on promises of things to come, separation from the world system (Moses), or some other. But the writer still has not completed his argument concerning the superiority of the life of faith over the practice of Mosaic legalism. One example remains, the Lord Jesus Christ. The final phase of the argument by example culminates in the "consider him" statement of Heb 12:3. Having considered all of these other witnesses, the readers are now to "consider him that endured . . . lest ye be weary and faint in your minds."

D. Christ, the Supreme Example of the Faith Life. 12:1-4.

1, 2. The exhortation is now renewed with vigor because of the examples given in the previous chapter. **Wherefore** includes all the heroes of chapter 11 who, together with us, will be **made perfect.** They are **witnesses,** who, like spectators in a vast arena, watch us progress in the course of the life of faith. **Let us run with patient endurance** (Davidson, *Epistle to the Hebrews,* p. 232) combines exhortations to run and to endure in the light of the example of those who have already run this course faithfully. **Every weight.** The superfluous and unnecessary that might hinder must be cast aside. Each individual must decide what is superfluous. But what is clearly **sin** allows of no individual choice; it must be cast aside immediately upon recognition, as it springs from its ambush to entrap (*euperistatos,* "to ambush, to encircle, to entrap") the unwary. This kind of sin would impede our running, or slow us down; so away with it.

Looking unto Jesus. A reference to the supreme or ultimate example available to us. What did he do? He **endured.** In this he is **leader** or *author,* and **perfecter** or *finisher* **of our faith.** This concept is then expanded in the following passages. In them is set forth the example of patient endurance to which each believer is called – that of Christ himself (12:1). The reward for Christ's endurance is the position of authority and his occupation thereof. In this position his **joy** is complete, and so will our joy be complete when we are in his presence before God. At God's right hand Christ performs all the functions of ruler, high priest, and advocate, yet he came to that place through suffering and endurance, i.e., by way of the cross.

3,4. Consider *(analogizomai,* "compare yourself with," "think over") **him that endured.** A further enlargement on verse 2. **Contradiction** *(antilogia)* is a contrary argument. Christ was literally a contradiction to his enemies, who expressed themselves in open hatred and hostility. **That ye wax not weary, fainting in your souls** (ASV, the best rendering of the text. See CGT, p. 154). The first clause suggests a sudden breakdown in endurance, the second a more gradual relaxation of vigilance.

Ye have not yet resisted unto blood. They had not yet realized the full extent of the struggle. No martyrdom had as yet occurred; no extreme measures, such as wholesale taking of life, had been employed against them. Finally, they were to remember that sin is the antagonist. They were to continue to strive **against sin,** particularly the sin of unbelief, which destroys faith.

E. The Father's Love Known Through Chastisement. 12:5-11.

5-9. The writer uses Prov 3:11 ff. to remind the reader-hearers that chastening is a part of the love relationship, and he also describes this relationship by means of the analogy of father and son. The exhortation begins at the end of the quotation. Sons who are worthy of their sonship must endure or bear chastening. Sometimes we do not understand chastening, but we are still to accept it and endure it as a necessary part of our training. For by it we are acknowledged as true sons, rather than spurious sons (v. 8) or **bastards** *(nothos).*

Since a worthy earthly father corrects his sons, it should not surprise the spiritual sons of God to learn that their heavenly Father chastens them. Such knowledge will help believers to be genuinely **in subjection** or submissive as true sons.

10,11. The illustration leads into a contrast. **They . . . he.** Earthly fathers exercise their fatherly prerogative only for a short time and for immediate ends, but God has both holy lives and eternal ends in view.

Neither in the earthly sphere nor in the heavenly sphere is chastening appreciated at the time, but the final results more than warrant the discipline. In the heavenly or spiritual realm it yields **peaceable fruit, even that of righteousness.** Adversity and chastening, then, are a form of training.

F. Christian Conduct Under the New Covenant. 12:12-29.

The first thing for believers to do is to put away discouragement and complaining in adverse circumstances. The life of faith is not easy, nor does it become easier.

12,13. They are to accept the discipline of adversity and be strengthened through it. They are to be strong in the midst of trial. **Lift up the hands.** Or, *make straight, strengthen,* as one made strong through difficulty. Relaxed hands and **palsied knees,** or *stumbling* knees, do not describe the patient endurance required to finish the course. In so strengthening the hands and knees, any lameness brought on by disuse will be healed. There is a possible suggestion here that joints not firmly held and muscles not properly tensed might suffer dislocation, or a sprain *(ektrapē).* True strength of character is shown in so gathering oneself together in time of adversity.

14,15. Human relationships improve when the nature of adversity is understood. **Follow after peace with all men** (ASV). As one seeking harmony, as one having a peaceful spirit, and as one who desires unity and fellowship among the righteous. **Men.** Better omitted. **And holiness.** The covering or comprehensive term *(hagiasmon,* "sanctification"). **Lord** *(kyrion)* is more probably God than Christ. Certainly one of the essential proofs of new life in Christ lies in the way believers get along with each other.

The antithesis follows. Here is one who comes short, who fails because deep within him is a **root of bitterness** that poisons everything and everyone—**thereby many be defiled.** This root of bitterness is like an infection that spreads through the whole community *(hoi polloi)* of believers. Notice, this describes a breakdown in human relations among believers because one believer has become bitter.

16, 17. Esau serves as the example of the hopelessness of such a condition. By his own choice he became a **profane person,** or lover of the earthly and sensual, so that he lost both birthright and spiritual sensitivity. This latter condition, particularly, is the antithesis of the standard held up in verse 14. Esau exchanged peace and holiness for immediate and earthly pleasures.

When Esau attempted to change his condition, he found it impossible to do so. Whether the blessing of God or repentance was the object of his **tears,** it was too late. Esau was guilty of willful sin, from the consequences of which he found no deliverance. This is the lesson to the Hebrews who were contemplating an act of willful sin in the form of apostasy back to Mosaic tradition. To the writer the illustration-warning seemed obvious.

18-24. The exhortation continues with what Davidson calls "a grand finale to the strain . . . to hold fast their confession." Sinai and Mount Zion are placed in contrast to each other. The setting of the giving of the Law was (1) a mount **that burned with fire,** enveloped in **blackness, darkness, tempest,** and (2) **the sound of a trumpet, and the voice of words.** In this setting Moses was so overcome by the presence of God that he greatly feared and trembled (cf. Ex 19:12 ff. and Deut 9:19).

But ye are come introduces all the blessed realities and personages of the new covenant. Heaven is set against earth, the phenomenal against the superearthly, the glory of Sinai against the infinitely greater glory of the blood-sprinkled way. **Zion . . . the city of the living God,** the **heavenly Jerusalem . . . hosts of angels . . . the church of the firstborn . . . God the Judge . . . just men made perfect . . . Jesus the mediator of a new covenant** (ASV order) – these make a purposely impressive list because of the contrast intended. Again, the thought is transparent. Surely these marvels and blessings far outweigh the temporary respite to be gained through returning to Judaism to escape persecution. Men of faith have this bright hope under the new covenant. Men of faith have already entered that glad company of the **firstborn,** the **just men made perfect** *(prōtotokōn* and *teteleiōmenōn,* "firstborn and perfected," as in Alf and Arndt. See also Davidson, *Epistle to the Hebrews,* pp. 245-250).

25-29. Heed Christ. Do not refuse the voice of Christ speaking through the Gospel. If peril came to those who refused the voice of God at Sinai, how much greater peril must come to those who refuse or reject God's messenger, his own Son (1:2). This refusal is akin to that of the men invited to the "great supper" of Luke 14:16, who "all . . . began to make excuses" *(paraiteomai).* See Lk 14:18, where the same word appears (Arndt).

Judgment is then described, perhaps the last judgment. The earth will be shaken, and the impermanent will vanish in the shaking; only the permanent and eternal will remain – **a kingdom that cannot be shaken** (ASV). This kingdom will be given by God, not conceived by man. Membership in it through faith in Christ ought to result in glad service and reverent worship on the part of all.

The final word is again that of warning. **For indeed our God is a consuming fire** (cf. Deut 4:24). Fire is the final form of judgment (Rev 20:10,14).

G. The Christian Life in Daily Practice. 13:1-17.

The Christian life is sketched out in its bearing on the believer's relations with other people.

1-6. The normal situations are mentioned first. As in the later epistle of I John, **love of the brethren,** or *your brotherly affection* (CGT) is to **continue.** One of the constant evidences of a healthy Christian life is the manner in which Christian brethren get along with one another. Because of the lack of public resting places, hospitality is also enjoined, particularly with reference to **strangers** who know Christ. Matthew 25:35-40 offers the closest parallel to **entertained angels unawares** *(elathon,* "unconsciously").

These social duties or human relations are further expanded to include persons in prison – **them that are in bonds.** The expression **as bound with them** carries the thought of both sympathy and identity. Believers are to share with the prisoner as though they themselves were prisoners. The modern use of "identify" covers the idea. As long as believers are confined in the earthly body, it is possible for each one to suffer either adversity or imprisonment. Therefore, they must be sympathetic.

Then, of course, the closest human relationship, marriage, ought to exhibit to all the graces of the Christian life. If these Hebrews were in Rome or in some of the more notorious cities of the Mediterranean East, they were in a society in which chastity and honor in marriage were commonly disregarded. On the other hand, some religious sects or groups taught celibacy and asceticism. Celibacy is not a safeguard against immorality; but rather honorable marriage is the most wholesome life. Chastity in the bonds of marriage constitutes strong Christian witness. Profligate and licentious people must someday face their sins and practices before God.

As regards money, the writer warns: **Be ye free from the love of money** (ASV). *Aphilargyros* means "not money-loving," rather than *not covetous,* as in the AV. The manner of life (**conversation,** AV) or disposition to be cultivated is contentment with things present, or **such things as ye have.** If the torrents of abuse flung at these Jewish Christians by others more prosperous included references to their lack of prosperity, this came as a very practical and thoroughly NT bit of advice. It is still timely. Instead of taking comfort in possessions, Christians are to derive their comfort from God's own presence and provision, for he neither leaves them nor fails them. Thus **we may boldly say . . . I will not fear. What shall man do unto me?** The last clause is properly a question (ASV). Joshua 23:14 and Psalm 118:6 testify to the faithfulness of God.

7-9. In the Church, especially, all the Christian graces ought to be found. Remember the example, says the author, of those who first taught you Christian truth. They were noted for presenting a true message and a godly example. They spoke God's word and lived holy lives right up to their "exit" or the end of life on the earth. **Imitate their faith** (ASV).

Their example and yours, he continues, is the unchanging person of the Lord Jesus Christ. He is the same; his purposes are the same; his goals are unchanging. **Jesus Christ** [is] **the same yesterday, and to day, and for ever,** thus sustaining and supporting the claims of verse 7. Allegiance to Christ, who is unchanging, should result in clarity of doctrine. Then none will **be carried away,** or turned aside by strange teaching or strange practice in the name of the Gospel. The contradictions of human teachers, externalism, and the embryonic works-righteousness practice of abstaining from certain foods should be avoided.

10-17. We do not now make sacrifice; we have a sacrifice already made for us in Christ; hence **we have an altar.** The OT ordinances as here described no longer avail. When Christ suffered death **outside the gate** on the cross, one of the things accomplished was the setting aside of the Levitical customs. They are now superfluous. The believer's identification is with Christ *outside* or **without the gate.** This means rejection of Judaism on the one hand and rejection by the Jews on the other. For these Hebrew Christians, this was the **reproach** they were to bear.

Because of Christ's death as a sin offering, or **through him,** believers are to demonstrate conduct befitting redeemed ones (vv. 14-17). (1) They are to fix their hope not in the OT ordinances, but in the heavenly city and in the heavenly prospect; (2) they are to give praise and thanksgiving to God, since the fruit of the lips ought to be the overflow of the full heart; (3) they must show benevolence of all sorts or kinds, which God will not forget; and (4) they are to be obedient and submissive. Pleasing God might ultimately be reduced to three fundamental practices or attitudes, all of which are named in this passage—praise, obedience, and submission. These need little comment in light of NT truth. Benevolence naturally follows. In verse 17 submission practically relates to the attitude of believers to their own leaders. With these words of responsibility laid on followers and leaders alike, the writer closes the practical or exhortatory composition that began with 10:19. The rest is personal.

IV. Personal Epilogue. 13:18-25.

With a few personal requests, a subscription and salutations, and a brief benediction, the writer concludes.

18,19. Pray for us. A personal request. The writer asks to be remembered as to

(1) his personal life, testimony, and service; and (2) his desire that he might soon be among them in person. This was a specific prayer request.

20,21. He promises that he, in turn, will pray for them, particularly concerning their obedience to the will of God. This subscription in the form of a prayer should have been a particular blessing to those who heard or who read it. It speaks of:

(1) Comfort, for, in and under persecution, they had access to and fellowship with the **God of peace.**

(2) Hope in Christ resurrected; literally, **brought up from the dead.**

(3) Personal and pastoral care in **our Lord Jesus, that great shepherd of the sheep.**

(4) Doctrine and theology. All of the comfort, hope, and pastoral care is sealed and guaranteed by the **blood of the everlasting covenant.**

Certain personal requests and wishes follow:

(1) **Make you perfect in every good work** (v. 21) or more correctly, *God make up to you,* or *in you, what you lack.* This request conveys the writer's desire that the believers might be fully fitted for their task, having no weaknesses, faults, or lacks. Believers need to be **made complete** *(katartizo).*

(2) To know and to be doing the whole will of God. Because God works in us, we desire to work for him in devoted surrender and obedience.

(3) To please God through Jesus Christ. Only the indwelling Son working in us by the Holy Spirit and through the Word of God can so make us pleasing to God. Let this request be the cry of our hearts.

22-25. Perhaps we have here the key verse of the epistle (see Introd., *The Argument of the Epistle)* as the writer begs his readers to accept his **exhortation.** He expresses the hope that he and Timothy may soon be able to visit them. He sends a general Christian greeting to them, and adds the indefinite **they of Italy salute you,** or *those who are from Italy salute you,* a general statement indicating that friends from Italy known to the writer wished to be included in the Christian greeting.

The closing words are a benediction in the form of a brief prayer, **Grace be with you all. Amen.**

BIBLIOGRAPHY

ARCHER, GLEASON L., JR. *The Epistle to the Hebrews: A Study Manual.* Grand Rapids: Baker Book House, 1957.

BRUCE, A. B. *The Epistle to the Hebrews: The First Apology for Christianity.* Edinburgh: T. & T. Clark, 1899.

DAVIDSON, A. B. *The Epistle to the Hebrews.* Edinburgh: T. & T. Clark, 1921.

DELITZSCH, FRANZ. *Commentary on the Hebrews.* 2 vols. Grand Rapids: Wm. B. Eerdman's Publishing Company, reprinted 1952.

DOWNER, ARTHUR CLEVELAND. *The Principles of Interpretation of the Epistle of the Hebrews.* London: Charles Murray, n.d.

FARRAR, F. W. *The Epistle of Paul the Apostle to the Hebrews (Cambridge Bible for Schools and Colleges).* Cambridge: The University Press, 1883.

——. *The Epistle of Paul the Apostle to the Hebrews.* Cambridge: The University Press, 1896.

HERKLESS, J. (ed.). *Hebrews and the Epistles General of Peter, James and Jude.* London: J. M. Dent, 1902.

LEONARD, WILLIAM. *Authorship of the Epistle to the Hebrews: Critical Problem and Use of the Old Testament.* Vatican: Polyglot Press, 1939.

MANSON, WILLIAM. *The Epistle to the Hebrews, An Historical and Theological Reinterpretation.* London: Hodder and Stoughton, 1951.

MICKELSEN, A. BERKELEY. "Hebrews," *The Biblical Expositor: The Living Theme of the Great Book.* Vol. III. Philadelphia: A. J. Holman, 1960.

MOLL, CARL BERNHARD. "Epistle to the Hebrews," *Commentary on the Holy Scriptures, Critical, Doctrinal and Homiletical.* Edited by John Peter Lange. Grand Rapids: The Zondervan Publishing House, reprint.

NAIRNE, ALEXANDER. *The Epistle of Priesthood: Studies in the Epistle to the Hebrews.* Edinburgh: T. & T. Clark, 1913.

PURDY, ALEXANDER C. and COTTON, J. HARRY. "The Epistle to the Hebrews," *Interpreter's Bible.* Vol. 11. New York: Abingdon, 1955.

SCHNEIDER, JOHANNES. *The Letter to the Hebrews.* Grand Rapids: Wm. B. Eerdman's Publishing Company, 1957.

WESTCOTT, BROOKE FOSS. *The Epistle to the Hebrews.* Grand Rapids: Wm. B. Eerdman's Publishing Company, reprinted 1950.

THE EPISTLE OF JAMES

INTRODUCTION

Authorship. The superscription indicates that the author of the Epistle of James was **James, a servant of God and of the Lord Jesus Christ.** But who was this James? Of the numerous men bearing this name in the New Testament, only two have been proposed as the author of this epistle—James, son of Zebedee, and James, the Lord's brother. The former is an unlikely candidate. He was marytred in A.D. 44, and there is no evidence that he had attained a position of leadership in the church that would warrant his writing a general letter. Although Isidore of Seville and Dante thought him to be the author of the book, this identity has not been widely accepted in any age of the church. The traditional view identifies the author with James, the Lord's brother. The similarity of the language of the epistle with James' speech in Acts 15, the heavy dependence of the writer on Jewish tradition, and the consistency of the contents of his letter with the historical notices in the New Testament concerning James, the Lord's brother, all tend to support the traditional authorship.

Date and Place of Writing. A wide range of opinion prevails on the date of James. Those who accept the traditional authorship usually date it either in the middle forties or early sixties (just before James' death). It has been dated as late as A.D. 150 by those who hold to the "unknown James" or pseudonymous authorship theory.

Although we cannot be dogmatic about the time of writing, a number of factors point toward an early date. The social conditions revealed in the epistle, especially the sharp cleavage between the rich and poor, suggest a date before the destruction of Jerusalem. The eschatology revealed also points to an early date. The expectation of the Lord's return rates in intensity with that found in I and II Thessalonians. There is no suggestion of belief in a delayed return, such as we find in some of the late books of the New Testament; and there are no apocalyptic visions or similar developments, such as those found in late apocalyptic literature. James' readers were living in the active and powerful expectation of Christ's imminent return. There is nothing in the Christian literature of the second century that can match the simple and powerful eschatological teaching of this epistle.

The most crucial passage for dating the book is the famous one on faith and works (Jas 2:14-26). To understand these verses the reader must be acquainted with certain Pauline formulas; yet it is hard to believe that the author of 2:14-26 is refuting Paul. This would involve an almost inconceivable miscomprehension of the Pauline doctrine of justification by faith. The passage is best explained as having been occasioned by a misunderstanding of Paul, not on the part of the author of the epistle, but on the part of his readers. Such misunderstanding would most likely have arisen at the very outset of Paul's public preaching ministry. According to the book of Acts, Paul's first extended public preaching occurred at Antioch (Acts 11:26). This year-long ministry took place before the famine visit to Jerusalem of about 46 (cf. Acts 11:27-29; Gal 2:1-10) and the Herodian persecution of 44. How long it was before the misunderstanding and misapplication of Paul's doctrine of justification by faith came to the attention of James, we do not know. In view of the fact that Jews, both Christian and non-Christian, from all over the Mediterranean world, were constantly moving in and out of Jerusalem, it probably was not long. A date of about 44 for the epistle, during or immediately following the Herodian persecution, would best fit all the known factors.

Although a number of opposing suggestions have been made from time to time, there can be little doubt that James was written from Palestine. Especially in the local coloring suggested, the writer indicates that he is a Palestinian (cf. 1:10,11; 3:11,12; 5:7).

The Recipients of the Letter. The only direct hint in the book which possibly suggests who the readers were is found in the superscription: **James, a servant of God and of the Lord Jesus Christ, to the twelve tribes which are scattered abroad, greeting.** Traditionally the phrase, **the**

twelve tribes, was used to indicate the entirety of the Jewish nation (cf. the noncanonical Ecclesiasticus 44:23; The Assumption of Moses 2:4,5; Baruch 1:2; 62:5; 63:3; 64:3; 77:2; 78:4; 84:3; also see Acts 26:7). But since the entire Jewish nation, no matter how widely it may have been scattered in the Diaspora, could not have been considered to have its entire existence outside of Palestine, it seems best to understand the superscription symbolically. James was writing to the entire church, considered as the New Israel (cf. Gal 3:7-9; 6:16; Phil 3:3), dispersed in an alien and hostile world (cf. I Pet 1:1,17; 2:11; Phil 3:20; Gal 4:26; Heb 12:22; 13:14). There are many indications in the epistle, however, that it is addressed primarily to Jews who are Christians. This may be a further indication of an early date, since the only time in the history of the church when one could address the entire church and be speaking almost exclusively to Jews, was *before* Paul's first mission to the Gentiles—which occurred about 47.

Contents. The Epistle of James is a plea for vital Christianity. Herder caught the tenor of this book when he wrote: "What a noble man speaks in this Epistle! Deep unbroken patience in suffering! Greatness in poverty! Joy in sorrow! Simplicity, sincerity, direct confidence in prayer! How he wants action! Action, not words . . . not dead faith!" (quoted by F. W. Farrar in *The Early Days of Christianity*, p. 324).

In the true spirit of the Wisdom literature, James handles many different subjects. His short, abrupt paragraphs have been likened to a string of pearls—each is a separate entity in itself. There are some logical transitions, but for the most part transitions are abrupt or missing entirely. This phenomenon makes an outline in the usual sense impossible. There follows, however, a listing of the subjects dealt with in the order of their occurrence in the epistle.

OUTLINE

I. Salutation. 1:1.
II. Trials. 1:2-8.
III. Poverty and wealth. 1:9-11.
IV. Trial and temptation. 1:12-18.
V. Reception of the Word. 1:19-25.
VI. True religion. 1:26,27.
VII. Social distinctions and "the royal law." 2:1-13.
VIII. Faith and works. 2:14-26.
IX. The tongue. 3:1-12.
X. The two wisdoms. 3:13-18.
XI. The world and God. 4:1-10.
XII. Judging. 4:11,12.
XIII. Sinful self-confidence. 4:13-17.
XIV. Judgment of the unscrupulous rich. 5:1-6.
XV. Patience until Christ's return. 5:7-11.
XVI. Oaths. 5:12.
XVII. Prayer. 5:13-18.
XVIII. Reclaiming the sinning brother. 5:19,20.

COMMENTARY

I. Salutation. 1:1.

James simply calls himself **a servant of God and of the Lord Jesus Christ.** His readers are **the twelve tribes which are scattered abroad,** a symbolic designation for the Christian church conceived of as the New Israel, its members scattered abroad in an alien and hostile world. Thus James does not have in mind a single congregation but the church at large throughout the Mediterranean world. His salutation *(chairein)* is the typical one found in Greek letters and the same one used in the letter that was sent out from the Jerusalem church over which James presided (Acts 15:23).

II. Trials. 1:2-8.

2. James frequently (at least sixteen times) addresses his readers as **brethren.**

He and his readers were bound together by a common loyalty to Jesus Christ. His first word is one of encouragement—**count it all joy when ye fall into divers temptations.** The RSV renders more adequately, *when you meet various trials.* The word *peirasmos* ("trial") has two meanings. Here it means "external adversities," whereas in verses 13,14 it means "inner impulse to evil," "temptation."

3. The Christian is to be joyful *in* trial not *because of* trial. There was a great need in the early days of the church for teaching along these lines because of the successive waves of persecution. The fruit of trial is **patience** *(hypomonē),* or better, *endurance.* James Moffatt *(The General Epistles,* p. 9) calls it "the staying power of life." **4.** This endurance must be allowed to have its full scope **(perfect work).** It is a process that goes on in the life of a Christian, its goal being perfection *(teleios* is better rendered *maturity).* The writer may have had in mind the words of our Lord recorded in Mt 5:48.

5-8. There seems to be a connection between this paragraph and what precedes. James has been talking about the purpose of trial. He anticipates that some of his readers will say that they cannot discover any divine purpose in their hardships. In that case, he says, they are to ask God for wisdom, i.e., practical insights into life (not theoretical knowledge), and God will grant such a request **liberally** (RSV, *generously),* and will not upbraid or reproach them. There is, however, a condition set down. The request must be made **in faith, nothing wavering** (RSV, *with no doubting).* The man who comes to God with his request must be sure that he wants what he requests. James likens a doubting man to a **wave of the sea driven** to and fro by the wind. Such a man "cannot hope to receive anything from God" (Phillips). He is a **double minded man,** i.e., a man of divided allegiance. He has mental reservations both about prayer itself and about the requests he makes of God.

III. Poverty and Wealth. 1:9-11.

9. This paragraph arises out of James' discussion of trial. Poverty is an external adversity. The poor Christian is to **rejoice** in his new status in Jesus Christ. This relationship has brought him true wealth. He is an heir of God and a joint heir with Jesus Christ!

10,11. A rich Christian, on the other hand, is to rejoice "that in Christ he has been brought down to a level where the 'deceitfulness of riches' (Mk 4:19) and the anxiety to amass and retain them are no longer primary or even relevant considerations" (R. V. G. Tasker, *The General Epistle of James,* p. 43). Furthermore, riches are temporary. They are like the green grass and its flowers, which quickly turn brown under the heat of the Palestinian sun. *Kausōn* **(burning heat)** is used here simply of the heat of the sun and not of the sirocco, the hot desert wind that blows across Palestine from the east (cf. J. Schneider, TWNT, III, 644).

IV. Trial and Temptation. 1:12-18.

12. The reward for faithfully enduring trials is stated in terms both of the present and of the future. The man who endures is truly happy now; but also he **shall receive the crown of life, which the Lord hath promised to them that love him.** The genitive **(of life)** is in apposition to **crown.** The crown consists of life, a gift to all those who love God. Tasker (*op. cit.,* p. 45) pointedly comments that although neither our faith nor our love wins for us eternal life, yet it is "an axiom of the Bible that God has abundant blessings in store for those who love him, keep his commandments, and serve him faithfully whatever the cost may be (cf. Mt. 19:28; I Cor. 2:9)."

13. James now makes the transition from outward to inner trials, i.e., temptations. The word **temptation** (v. 12) carries the idea of luring one into sin. James probably had in mind the Jewish doctrine of the *Yetzer ha ra'*, "evil impulse." Some Jews reasoned that since God created everything, he must have created the evil impulse. And since it is the evil impulse that tempts man to sin, ultimately God, who created it, is responsible for evil. James here refutes that idea. **God cannot be tempted with evil, neither tempteth he any man. 14.** Instead of blaming God for evil, man must take personal responsibility for his sins. It is his own **lust** by which he is **drawn away** and **enticed.** These are primarily hunting and fishing words, used metaphorically here. **15.** When evil desire arises in the mind, it does not stop there. **Lust** gives birth to sin, and sin produces death. "Death is thus the mature or finished product of sin" (Moffatt, *op. cit.,* p. 19). Death is here spiritual death in contrast to the life God gives to those **that love him** (1:12).

16,17. The point the writer makes is that God, instead of being the source of temptation, as some were contending, is the source of all good in the experience of men. James was especially desirous that his readers realize this, and so he addressed them with the tender, **my beloved brethren. Father of lights** is a reference to the creative activity of God. Such a title for God was not unknown in Jewish thought (cf. SBK, III, 752). Although there is considerable question as to the correct reading of the last part of verse 17, the meaning is clear enough: God is completely consistent; he does not change.

In James 1:18 the writer climaxes his refutation of the idea that God is the author of temptation. He has already shown that such a charge is contrary to the nature of God (1:13) and to His consistent goodness (1:17). Now he appeals to his readers' experience in the Gospel. J. B. Mayor *(The Epistle of St. James,* p. 62) aptly states the point of this verse: "So far from God's tempting us to evil, His will is the cause of our regeneration." These early Christians were called **firstfruits** because they were a guarantee of many more to come.

V. Reception of the Word. 1:19-25.

19. There is a possible connection between this paragraph and what precedes. The strong admonition to be **swift to hear, slow to speak, slow to wrath** may be a reference to the readers' accusations against God. Or it may be simply a general statement about hearing and speaking. **20.** When a Christian gives vent to **wrath,** he is incapable of acting justly or righteously; and in addition, he prevents, or at least hinders, the vindication of God's righteousness in the world.

21. Lay apart all filthiness. Since the Word is a seed, it must have good soil in which to thrive. "Have done, then," says James, "with impurity and every other evil" (Phillips). **Superfluity of naughtiness** might suggest that only excess of evil is to be put away. However, Tasker rightly takes **superfluity** to mean "remainder." "Every converted Christian brings with him into his new life much that is inconsistent with it. This has to be laid aside, that he may give himself more completely to the positive work of receiving **with meekness the engrafted** (RV, rightly *implanted)* **word**" *(op. cit.,* p. 51). This word is **able to save** his **soul. 22.** Christianity is a religion of action. As important as it is to listen (cf. 1:19), one must not stop there. Doing must follow listening. To be a hearer only is a form of self-deception.

23,24. The hearing-but-not-doing man is like a person who sees the reflection of his own face in a mirror. "He sees himself, it is true, but he goes on with whatever he was doing without the slightest recollection of what sort of person he saw in the mirror" (Phillips). The tenses in this verse are interesting: **beholdeth** (aorist), **goeth** (perfect), **forgetteth** (aorist). "By the aorists he [James] shows that the impression was momentary, and the oblivion instantaneous; by the perfect he implies a continuing condition of absence from the mirror" (H. Maynard Smith, *The Epistle of St. James,* p. 85).

25. The mirror, which reveals the imperfections of the outer man, is now contrasted with the **perfect law,** the law of freedom, which reflects the inner man. This is the first reference to law in the epistle (cf. 2:8-12; 4:11). James uses the term to denote the ethical side of Christianity, the *didachē,* "teaching." Here he calls the law **perfect.** Compare Ps 19:7: "The law of the Lord is perfect, converting the soul." James, as a Jew, writing to Jews, is deliberately ascribing to *didachē* the attributes of the law. To James it is perfect because it was made perfect by Jesus Christ. **Law of liberty** probably means that it is a law that applies to those who have the status of freedom, not from law, but from sin and self, through the word of truth. The man who looks into this law and makes a habit of doing so *(parameinas)* will become a **doer of the work** and find true happiness **(shall be blessed in his deed).**

VI. True Religion. 1:26,27.

26. The author now moves from the more general "not hearing but doing" to the more specific "not mere worship but doing." The word **religious** *(thrēskos)* means "given to religious observances." In this context it refers to attendance at worship services and to other observances of religion, such as prayer, almsgiving, and fasting. A man who is scrupulous in these observances but fails to control his speech in everyday life deceives himself, and his religion is vain (Moffat, *futile).*

27. "This is not a definition of religion, but a statement . . . of what is better than external acts of worship. James had no idea of reducing religion to a negative purity of conduct supplemented by charity-visiting" (James H. Ropes, *The Epistle of St. James,* p. 182). Since orphans and widows were not provided for in ancient society, they were typical examples of those who needed help. In addition to extending charity, maintaining personal purity is another way in which true religion expresses itself. The **world** here and in 4:4 refers to pagan society opposed, or at least alien, to God.

VII. Social Distinctions and "The Royal Law." 2:1-13.

1. The emphasis on the importance of conduct is continued in this paragraph. Here it is applied to partiality. **My brethren** marks the transition to a new subject (cf. 1:2,19; 2:14; 3:1; 5:1). The AV rightly translates the verb in the imperative (the other possibility being the indicative) in keeping with James' direct manner of writing. It is not certain how the genitive **Lord Jesus Christ** qualifies **faith.** G. Rendall suggests the possibility of regarding the genitive as qualitative, "as defining the particular character of their faith in God. 'The faith in God which has for its support and content our Lord Jesus Christ,' that is the Christian kind of faith in God" *(The Epistle of St. James and Judaic Christianity,* p. 46). It is probably easier, however, to take the genitive as objective – "your faith in our Lord Jesus Christ." Whichever way it is taken, the faith is dynamic faith, trust, directed towards the Lord Jesus Christ. It has nothing whatever to do with the later idea of faith as a body of doctrine to be believed. In the last part of the verse the AV has **the Lord of,** which does not occur in the original. Jesus is here called simply "the glory," an obvious reference to the Shekinah (cf. Jn 1:14; II Cor 4:6; Heb 1:3). The main point of this verse is that it is inconsistent to hold to the Christian faith and at the same time show partiality.

2. The writer now cites an illustration to drive home the point. A wealthy man wearing a **gold ring** and dressed in fine clothing (ASV) and a **poor man** dressed in **vile,** *shabby* (RSV), clothing enter into the Christian assembly (*synagōgē*). The use of this word for the Christian place of meeting has given rise to much conjecture about the author and the readers of the epistle; but as Blackman says, "It must be remembered that the two words *synagōgē* and *ekklēsia* are roughly synonymous, and it is conceivable that *synagōgē* and not *ekklēsia* might have become the Church's regular term for itself. Thus it is possible to take the use of the word here by James as a survival from the time when usage was fluid" *(The Epistle of James,* p. 77). The author uses *ekklēsia* in 5:14. **3.** The rich man is given preferential treatment. He is offered the best seat *(kalōs).* There is a possibility that *kalōs* should be translated "please," as in the RSV. In either case the rich man gets special treatment, while the poor man is abruptly told to stand, or at best, to sit on the floor **under my footstool,** i.e., in a lowly place.

4. The verb translated, **Are ye not then partial . . .?** is passive and should be translated as in the ASV margin, "Are ye not divided?" The division is "between profession and practice, between the profession of Christian equality and the deference to rank and wealth" (Richard Knowling, *The Epistle of St. James,* p. 44). By such action they also reveal themselves to be judges *with* (not **of**) **evil thoughts,** i.e., false-value judges.

5. Those who grant special treatment to the rich fail to take into consideration that **God** has **chosen the poor of this world** *(poor as to the world,* RV) to be **rich in faith, and heirs of the kingdom which he hath promised to those that love him. 6.** Another reason why it is inconsistent to show special favor to the rich is that they have been the very ones who have persecuted the Christians. **Judgment seats** is a reference to Jewish courts allowed and recognized under Roman law. **7.** The climax of James' argument against favoring the rich is that **they blaspheme that worthy name.** It is not the name 'Christian' that is blasphemed but the name of Jesus Christ, the **worthy name by the which ye are called** (ASV, *which was called upon you*).

8. The royal law is connected with the statement in 2:5, where James reminds his readers that God has chosen the poor to be **heirs of the kingdom. The royal law,** then, is for those of God's kingdom. By translating the Greek particle *mentoi* "really," the RSV rightly points out that James thinks that his readers, by showing partiality to the rich, are not fulfilling this law. **9.** For love shows no **respect of persons.** Indeed, partiality is **sin.** The **law** here is not the OT law as such (although Lev 19:15 deals with partiality) but the *didachē,* the whole spirit of which is contrary to partiality.

10. The idea of the solidarity of the

law is found in the rabbinical writings (cf. SBK, III, 755). James adopts this idea but baptizes it into Christ. A. Cadoux writes: "James looks on the law, not as a number of injunctions, but as a personal relationship . . . not like an examination, where nine right answers will secure a pass, despite a wrong one, but like a friendship, where a hundred faithfulnesses cannot be set against one treachery" *(The Thought of St. James*, p. 72). This idea is closely associated with the Christian concept of fellowship with Christ. Transgression of one precept of the Christian rule of faith is a breach of the whole, because it breaks fellowship with the object of faith.

11. The order of the two commandments cited (the seventh before the sixth) is probably due to the order of the LXX in Codex Alexandrinus. If this is the reason, then subtle interpretations of this verse are excluded. It simply buttresses by specific example what the author has said by way of general principle in the preceding verse.

12. James comes now to his summary exhortation. Believers are to speak and act (with special reference towards behavior to the poor) **as they that shall be judged by the law of liberty.** There is a judgment for the Christian, and it will be based on his relation to the Christian ethical standard, the law that free men accept without compulsion (cf. Rom 14:10; II Cor 5:10). **13.** This verse is a warning that God shows no mercy toward those who are merciless (cf. Mt 18:21-35). And conversely *mercy triumphs over judgment* (RSV), i.e., by merciful acts God's judgment is deterred.

VIII. Faith and Works. 2:14-26.

This is the best known and most widely debated passage in the epistle. These were the verses, more than any others, that caused Martin Luther to describe this book as a "right strawy epistle." Most of the difficulties in the interpretation of 2:14-26 have arisen out of a failure to understand that: (1) James was not refuting the Pauline doctrine of justification by faith but rather a perversion of it. (2) Paul and James used the words **works** and **justification** in different senses. These will be discussed in the commentary.

14. The answer which the two questions of this verse expect is a resounding "No!" It is important to note that the faith under discussion is a so-called, or spurious, faith. This is made clear by (1) the statement, **if a man say he hath faith,** and (2) the use of the definite article with the word **faith** in the last clause (RSV, *Can* **his** *faith save him?).* It is only a false faith that does not issue in works and that is incapable of saving. By **works** James does not have in mind the Jewish doctrine of works as a means of salvation, but rather works of faith, the ethical outworking of true piety and especially the "work of love" (cf. 2:8).

15,16. An example is now cited. The "ill clad" (RSV) and hungry person is a **brother or sister,** i.e., a member of the Christian community. The needy brother is sent away with the empty words, **Depart in peace, be ye warmed and filled,** without so much as a hand being lifted to meet his urgent needs. James indignantly asks: "What on earth is the good of that?" (Phillips). The movement from the singular to the plural *(ye)* may indicate that "James assumes that all members of the brotherhood would be responsible for these callous remarks even though only one of them might give utterance to them" (Tasker, *op. cit.*, p. 64).

17. The **faith** under discussion, which is really not faith at all, is not merely useless or unacceptable, but **dead.** A faith that does not concern itself, by active participation, in the needs of others is not faith at all.

18. The difficulties in this verse arise out of the fact that the ancient Greek MSS had neither punctuation nor quotation marks. The objector is introduced by **a man may say,** a form often found in ancient synagogue sermons (cf. A. Marmorstein, "The Background of the Haggadah," *Hebrew Union College Annual,* VI (1929), p. 192). How much of the verse is to be considered as the words of the objector is open to doubt, but it is probably best to include only, **Thou hast faith, and I have works.** James refutes this attempt to separate faith and works by the challenge: **Show me thy faith without thy works.** This he certainly believes to be impossible.

19. Belief in the unity of God *(that God is one,* RSV) was a fundamental article of the creed of the Jews. James holds that such a belief is good. However, if it is lacking in deeds, it arises no higher than the faith of the demons. They, too, are monotheists, but this only makes them **tremble** (RSV, *shudder),* presumably in view of God's judgment (cf. Mk 5:7; Mt 8:29).

20. James reaches a new point in his argument with the words, **But wilt thou**

know. He is now ready to adduce Scriptural arguments to buttress his case for a working faith. Moffatt renders **O vain man** more pointedly, *You senseless fellow*. The ASV and RSV both follow the rendering *barren* rather than **dead,** and rightly so, because the latter is the result of conforming to 2:26. *Argē (barren)* in this context is probably best taken to mean "unproductive of salvation."

21. The Scriptural example given is **Abraham our father.** That he was considered to be the ancestor of all true Christians is clear from Gal 3:6-29. The use of the word **justified** here is not to be confused with Paul's use of the term in relation to Abraham (cf. Rom 4:1-5). Paul points to Abraham's initial justification when he "believed God, and it was reckoned unto him for righteousness" (cf. Gen 15:6). James is referring to an event that took place many years later, when Abraham was instructed to offer up his son Isaac. By this act he demonstrated the reality of the Genesis 15 experience.

22. Abraham's life thus remarkably exemplifies the impossibility of severing faith from works, or vice versa (cf. 2:18). In his case the two went hand in hand. Works brought faith to completion. **23.** In Abraham's act of obedience the **scripture** (Gen 15:6) **was fulfilled. Friend of God** was a title commonly applied to Abraham (cf. Isa 41:8; II Chr 20:7; also the noncanonical Jubilees 19:9; 30:20; Testament of Abraham, *passim*). **24.** This verse is the conclusive reply to the question of verse 14. Bare, unproductive faith, cannot save a man. True faith will demonstrate itself in works, and only such a faith brings justification.

25. James' second Scriptural example stands in marked contrast to Abraham. **Rahab** was a woman, a Gentile, and a prostitute. She was chosen to show that James' argument covered the widest ranges of possibilities (thus the use of *kai* with *hē pornē*, "even though a prostitute"). She, like Abraham, evidenced her justification by action (cf. Josh 2:1-21).

26. The concluding statement to the teaching of 2:14-26, shows that the relation between faith and works is as close as that between the body and the spirit. Life is the result of the union in both instances. When the two elements are separated, death results. "False faith is virtually a corpse" (F. J. A. Hort, *The Epistle of St. James*, p. 45).

IX. The Tongue. 3:1-12.

1. The subject of speech is one of the most prominent in this book (cf. 1:19, 26; 4:11,12; 5:12). This, however, is the classic passage, and it is addressed to *teachers* (the AV's **masters** is misleading). James first warns his readers that they should not be overeager to become teachers, because of the responsibility involved.

2. Because a teacher constantly uses words, there is a particular danger in this area for him. **In many things we offend** (RSV, *make mistakes*), but the most difficult mistakes to avoid are those that involve the tongue. Thus the man who successfully controls his tongue is styled a **perfect** man. Having tamed the most difficult member, he is **able also to bridle the whole body.**

3. "It is with men as with horses: control their mouth and you are masters of all their action" (Ropes, *op. cit.*, p. 229). David, in Ps 39:1, uses the figure of the bridle in relation to control of speech. **4.** This further illustration points out the power of the tongue. It is like the small **helm** (RSV, *rudder*) that controls a great ship. The point of the phrase, **and are driven of fierce winds,** is not clear unless **and** is taken to mean "even." Then the meaning would be that the rudder turns the ship even during fierce storms. The antique **whithersoever the governor listeth** is modernized by the RSV's *wherever the will of the pilot directs*.

5. From the governing or controlling power of the tongue, the author now turns to its destructive power. It may be a **little member,** but it can boast of **great things.** And this is not an empty boast! **Matter** *(hylēn)* probably means *forest* (RSV) here. A small spark can set ablaze an entire forest. **6.** In the punctuation of this verse, it is best to follow the RSV, which places a full stop after **fire.** This eliminates the need for the added **so** in the AV. Tasker (*op. cit.*, p. 76) takes **world of iniquity** (RSV, *unrighteous world*) to mean "all the evil characteristics of a fallen world, its covetousness, its idolatry, its blasphemy, its lust, its rapacious greed." These all find expression through the tongue, and consequently **it defileth the whole body.**

The tongue also sets **on fire the course of nature.** Hort calls this one of the most difficult phrases in the Bible. Although the phrase is probably a technical one, which originated outside of Palestine, James uses it here in a nontechnical sense to mean "the whole of human existence." This tremendous power for evil possessed by the tongue comes straight from **hell** *(Gehenna)*.

7,8. God's command to man (Gen 1:26) to have dominion over the fish of the sea, etc., has been successfully carried out, **but the tongue can no man tame.** But certainly God can tame it! **Unruly** (RSV follows the better reading, *restless)* **evil** though it be and **full of deadly poison,** the Lord has controlled it in the lives of many to bring great blessing to mankind. **9,10.** The tongue is also inconsistent. It is used to fulfill its highest purpose, namely to **bless God,** but it is also used to curse men. Such inconsistency, especially in the case of Christians (**My brethren), ought not so to be. 11,12.** The illustrations of the fountain, fig tree, and vine show that "such incongruity of behavior is a revolt against nature, where everything pursues an orderly course of good or bad" (B. S. Easton, *The Epistle of James,* p. 48).

X. The Two Wisdoms. 3:13-18.

13. Although the entire Epistle of James is Wisdom literature, wisdom *(sophia)* is expressly mentioned only in this passage and in 1:5. It is important that the Jewish (not Greek) idea of wisdom be kept in mind. Hort defines wisdom in James as "the endowment of heart and mind which is needed for the righteous conduct of life" (*op. cit.,* p. 7). **Wise man** *(sophos)* is the technical term for teacher, and **knowledge** *(epistēmōn)* for expert knowledge. By his **good conversation** (RSV's *life* is better) the **wise man** is to demonstrate **his works with meekness of wisdom.** The pride of knowledge has always been the besetting sin of professional teachers.

14. Pride of knowledge in the case of James' readers gave vent to **bitter** jealousy and *selfish ambition* (RSV), which resulted in boasting **(glory not)** and being thus *false to the truth* (RSV). The author does not mean here that the teachers were departing from orthodox doctrine, but rather that by their inconsistent living they were giving a lie to the truth of the Gospel.

15. This "false" wisdom is characterized as **not such as comes down from above** (RSV), i.e., does not have its origin in God (cf. 1:5). Instead it is **earthly, sensual, devilish.** "These three words . . . describe the so-called wisdom, which is not of divine origin, in an advancing series—as pertaining to the earth, not to the world above; to mere nature, not to the spirit; and to the hostile spirits of evil instead of to God" (Ropes, *op. cit.,* p. 248). **16.** The conjunction **for** indicates that what follows is proof for what has just been said. False wisdom produces **confusion** (RSV, *disorder)*—probably a reference to squabbles in the church—and **every evil work.** God is neither a God of confusion (I Cor 14:33) nor sympathetic to evil (I Jn 1:5). Thus "wisdom" that causes such a situation cannot come from God.

17. In contrast is **the wisdom that is from above.** It is the gift of God; it is practical wisdom, wisdom that preserves unity and peace. Because of the attributes ascribed to it—**pure, peaceable, gentle, easy to be entreated** (RSV, *open to reason),* **full of mercy and good fruits, without partiality** (RSV, *uncertainty)* or **hypocrisy** (RSV, *insincerity)*—some commentators have concluded that wisdom here is in reality Christ. In the light of the early identification of Christ with the Wisdom of God, this is not impossible. **18.** The **fruit of righteousness** is probably best taken to mean "the fruit which is righteousness." The statement then is in contrast to 1:20: **The wrath of man worketh not the righteousness of God.** The latter is achieved by peacemakers who sow in peace.

XI. The World and God. 4:1-10.

1. Wars and fightings are suggested by contrast with the preceding **peace.** James had in mind not wars between nations but quarrels and factions among Christians. The source of these is to be found in **your lusts** *(hēdonōn,* which really means *pleasures)* **that war in your members.**

2. The RSV punctuation is to be preferred, which brings out the parallelism of the verse: *You desire and do not have; so you kill. And you covet and cannot obtain; so you fight and wage war.* It is not necessary either to weaken or emend the reading **ye kill.** Ropes rightly says: "James is not describing the condition of any special community, but is analysing the result of choosing pleasure instead of God" (*op. cit.,* p. 255). Thus the force is almost conditional, "If you desire . . . If you covet . . ."

One reason their desires (in this case the legitimate ones) were not being realized was that they did not **ask** God, who alone can fully satisfy human desires. **3.** A second reason is found in the unacceptable motive of those who do ask—**that ye may consume it upon your lusts.** The essential condition of all prayer is found in I Jn 5:14: "If we ask anything according to his will, he heareth us."

4. The AV's **Ye adulterers** is not found in the best manuscripts and so should be omitted. The fact that James addresses his readers as **adulteresses,** after the fashion of the OT prophets who spoke of Israel as the wife of Jehovah (cf. Isa 54:5; Jer 3:20; Ezk 16:23; Hos 9:1, etc.), is strong evidence for both a Jewish author and Jewish readers. To maintain **friendship** with **the world** "is to be on good terms with persons and forces and things that are at least indifferent toward God if not openly hostile to him" (Ropes, *op. cit.*, p. 260), and thus to be at **enmity with God.**

5. A further reason why a Christian cannot be a friend of the world is adduced from Scripture. There are a number of possible translations of the words that follow, but it is in keeping with the context to follow the RSV, which makes God, not **spirit,** the subject of the verb: *He yearns jealously over the spirit which he has made to dwell in us.* God is a jealous God (cf. Ex 20:5; 34:14; Deut 32:16; Zech 8:2; I Cor 10:22), and hence he will not tolerate divided allegiance. No specific OT passage contains the words of this verse, but many passages express a similar sentiment.

6. The difficulties of living wholly for God in a wicked world are many, **but he giveth more grace,** which here seems to mean "gracious help." And this gracious aid God makes available, as Prov 3:34 declares, not to **proud,** self-sufficient persons, but to **humble,** dependent men.

7. The call to **submit yourselves . . . to God** (the first of eight closely following imperatives) follows logically the promise of grace to the humble. Calvin pointedly remarks: "Submission is more than obedience; it involves humility." The devil, the enemy of God, is to be resisted, and when he is, **he will flee from you** (cf. Mt 4:1-11). These are both important steps in avoiding the sin of worldliness.

8. The imperatives continue with **Draw nigh to God.** Close communion with God assures his friendship (**and he will draw nigh to you**), and estranges one from the world. That worldliness is sin is graphically shown by the following imperatives: **Cleanse your hands,** a reference to outward conduct; **purify your hearts,** a reference to inner motives. A **double minded** man is characterized by divided allegiance. And according to this passage, worldliness is basically divided allegiance. Kierkegaard's famous essay, "Purity of Heart Is to Will One Thing," arose out of this verse.

9. Here is a call to repentance in the face of serious sin. **Be afflicted,** i.e., "make yourselves wretched" (cf. Rom 7:24), **mourn, and weep.** These attitudes are more fitting than **laughter** or **joy** (i.e., the frivolity and lightness of the world) in view of the circumstances. **Heaviness** (RSV, *dejection*) "is the downcast, subdued expression of those who are ashamed and sorry" (Moffatt, *op. cit.*, p. 64). **10.** James returns to his initial exhortation in the series (4:7) with the words, **Humble yourselves.** With this is coupled the promise, **and he shall lift you up.**

XII. Judging. 4:11,12.

11. The author again returns to the subject of the abuse of speech. In this passage the interest of the brother and the interest of the law seem to be identified. To speak evil against one's brother or to judge him is to speak evil against the law and to become a judge of the law. **12.** Superiority to the law belongs only to God. He is the one **lawgiver** and judge, and in his hands are the issues of life and death. In view of this, James asks, **Who art thou that judgest another?**

XIII. Sinful Self-confidence. 4:13-17.

13. The attitude of the merchants described here is another expression of the worldliness that brings estrangement from God. The itinerant merchants addressed were Jews who carried on a lucrative trade throughout the Mediterranean world. They are depicted as making careful plans for their business enterprises, declaring, **To day or tomorrow we will go into such a city,** etc. **14.** There is nothing wrong with such planning in itself. However, the planners were ignoring two considerations. The first is the finiteness of human beings, which limits their knowledge—**ye know not what shall be on the morrow.** The second is the uncertainty of life, which James likens to a **vapour,** or a puff of smoke.

15. A Christian man, in making his plans, ought to acknowledge his dependence upon God and say, *Deo volente,*

If the Lord will. 16. But acknowledgment of dependence upon God was not the case among James' readers. Rather, they *boast*[ed] in their *arrogance* (RSV). This braggart talk James denounces as evil. **17.** A concluding warning is sounded for the self-confident merchants. They are Christians. Hence they know that humility and dependence upon God are essential in Christian living. To *know* this and not to *do* it, **is sin.**

XIV. Judgment of the Unscrupulous Rich. 5:1-6.

1. The **rich** addressed here are not Christians but, nevertheless, the warning sounded applies to all men, including Christians. James is consistent with the NT teaching generally in attacking the rich not simply because they are rich, but because they have failed in their stewardship. The weeping and howling are not signs of repentance but expressions of remorse in the face of judgment.

2. Both of the verbs in this verse and the first verb of the following verse are in the perfect tense. Ropes aptly describes them as "picturesque, figurative statements of the real worthlessness of this wealth to the view of one who knows how to estimate permanent, eternal values" (*op. cit.*, p. 284). Wealth is to be used for good purposes, not hoarded.

3. The rust of the hoarded wealth will be a **witness** against the rich, because God meant wealth to be used for the good of mankind. It also will destroy the rich themselves—**shall eat your flesh as it were fire.** The phrase, **for the last days** probably should be changed to *in the last days*. It points to the fact that, though the rich did not realize it, the last days were already present.

4. Another sin of rich men was the cruel defrauding of poor farm laborers. This action was particularly serious because it was explicitly contrary to the Mosaic law (cf. Deut 24:14,15). God, who is here called **Lord of sabaoth,** a title that suggests his sovereign omnipotence, was not oblivious to this injustice. His ears were open to the cries of the poor workmen.

5. A third sin of the rich was their luxury and pleasure. Extravagant living was simply fattening them up for the **day of slaughter.** This phrase is taken from Jeremiah (12:3). In the inter-Testament period (cf. I Enoch 94:9) it took on an eschatological significance, and in this passage it is used of the day of judgment.

6. The **just** man is not Jesus but the poor man (used generically), who has been treated without mercy by the rich. Moffatt (*op. cit.*, p. 70) points out that the word **murdered** had a wider range of meaning in Jewish ethics than it has today. Particularly relevant are the statements in the apocryphal Ecclesiasticus 34:21,22: "The bread of the needy is the life of the poor; whoever deprives them of it is a man of blood. To take away a neighbor's living is to murder him; to deprive an employee of his wages is to shed blood." Here the reference in James is probably to "judicial murders," since the statement follows the word **condemned.** Poor people are haled into court (cf. Jas 2:6) and can do nothing to defend themselves. They are completely at the mercy of the unscrupulous rich men. Despite all of this mistreatment, the poor do not **resist.**

XV. Patience until Christ's Return. 5:7-11.

7. James turns now from addressing the wicked rich to counseling the oppressed poor. His instruction is that the poor should bear patiently their social and economic situation in view of the imminent return of the Lord. There is no suggestion here of the forceful overthrow of the rich. As an example of one who must exercise patience, James cites the case of the farmer who waits for **the precious fruit of the earth.** In Palestine the **early** rain (October–November) came after the crops were planted, and tht **latter rain** (April–May) when they were maturing. Both were crucial for the success of the crops.

8. So the Christian, James says, is not to lose patience in the face of adversities but is to stablish his heart in view of the fact that **the coming of the Lord draweth nigh. 9.** Adversities cause tensions, and these in turn express themselves in human relations. James therefore warns, **Grudge not** (Better, *Do not grumble*, RSV) **one against another.** Such action places them in danger of judgment, and the **judge standeth before the door.**

10,11. In addition to farmers, the prophets are now cited as illustrations of **suffering and patience** (RSV). It is strange that Christ's example is not cited here as it is in I Pet 2:21-23. Job was traditionally considered to be a prophet, and here he is explicitly cited as an example of steadfastness. This is the only place in the NT where Job is mentioned. The main point of the illustration of Job is that "patient endurance can sustain itself on the conviction that hardships are not meaningless, but that God has some end or purpose in them which He will accomplish . . ." (Moffatt, *op. cit.*, p. 74).

XVI. Oaths. 5:12.

It is doubtful whether this verse has any connection with what precedes. **Above all things** is probably best taken as a hyperbole used for emphasis. The subject under discussion is not profanity, but truthfulness. Easton paraphrases the verse: "Abstain from all oaths, for they weaken a man's sense of obligation to speak the truth on all occasions; learn to make a simple 'Yes' or 'No' completely binding" (*op. cit.*, p. 69).

XVII. Prayer. 5:13-18.

13. **Suffering** (RSV; calamity of any sort) calls forth prayer; a joyful heart, praise. **Let him sing psalms** is too limited a translation of *psalletō*.

14. In the case of serious illness, James counsels, the **elders** (a reference to definite officers) of the church should be called. Their prayers were to be accompanied by anointing **with oil in the name of the Lord.** In some cases oil may have therapeutic value, but in most cases its use is best understood as an aid to faith. 15. It is clear from this verse that it is not the oil that heals the sick man, but rather **the Lord shall** raise him up in answer to the **prayer of faith.** This is not to suggest that God always answers believing prayer. All prayer, including prayer for healing, is subject to the will of God. Sometimes, certainly not always, sickness is the result of personal sin. Perhaps this is what is meant by **if he have committed sins.** In any event, the sick man is assured of forgiveness.

16. Prayer, to be most effective, must be intelligent. Thus we find the exhortation, **Confess your faults one to another.** This does not mean that Christians are to indulge in indiscriminate public or even private confessions. And certainly the passage has nothing to do with secret confessions to a priest. Believers are to confess their faults only that they may **pray one for another.** There is no unanimity as to how to render the last part of this verse, but the meaning is clear: a good man has great power in prayer.

17. The example is Elijah, **a man of like nature with ourselves** (RSV). His prayers both brought the drought and caused its end. James seems to be drawing on other sources than the OT, since Elijah's prayers for the drought and its cessation are not mentioned in the OT account. The length of the drought as being three and one half years is also not found in the OT.

XVII. Reclaiming the Sinning Brother. 5:19,20.

The statement, **Brethren, if any of you do err from the truth,** and the two references to bringing him back (cf. RSV) seem clearly to indicate that the man under discussion is a Christian. **Convert** is misleading. If a fellow Christian sees that his brother has left the great doctrines of the Christian faith and the moral responsibilities that spring from these, and is able to bring him back into fellowship with Christ and His Church, the consequences will be twofold: (1) **he shall save a soul** (the sinner's) **from death,** and (2) **shall hide a multitude of sins.** Since the NT teaches the security of the believer in Christ, it is best to take the reference to death as physical death. The early church believed and taught that persistence in sin could cause premature physical death (cf. I Cor 11:30). The sins that are hidden are not those of the reclaiming brother (this suggests the Jewish doctrine that good works offset bad ones) but of the erring man. They are hidden from the sight of God, which is simply another way of saying they are forgiven.

BIBLIOGRAPHY

CARR, A. *Epistle of St. James. (The Cambridge Greek Testament for Schools and Colleges).* Cambridge: The University Press, 1895.

EASTON, B. S. *The Epistle of James. (The Interpreter's Bible).* Vol. 12. New York: Abingdon, 1957.

HORT, F. J. A. *The Epistle of St. James, 1:1–4:7.* London: Macmillan and Co., 1909.

KNOWLING, RICHARD. *The Epistle of St. James. (Westminster Commentaries).* 2nd ed. London: Methuen, 1910.

MAYOR, JOSEPH B. *The Epistle of St. James.* 3rd ed. London: Macmillan and Co., 1913.

MOFFATT, JAMES. *The General Epistles James, Peter, and Judas. (The Moffatt New Testament Commentary).* Garden City, New York: Doubleday, 1928.

PLUMMER, ALFRED. *The General Epistles of St. James and St. Jude. (The Expositor's Bible).* London: Hodder and Stoughton, 1897.

PLUMTRE, E. H. *The General Epistle of St. James. (The Cambridge Bible for Schools and Colleges).* Cambridge: The University Press, 1909.

ROPES, JAMES H. *A Critical and Exegetical Commentary on the Epistle of James. (International Critical Commentary).* New York: Charles Scribner's Sons, 1916.

ROSS, ALEXANDER. *The Epistles of James and John. (The New International Commentary on the New Testament).* Grand Rapids: Eerdmans, 1954.

TASKER, R. V. G. *The General Epistle of James. (Tyndale New Testament Commentaries).* Grand Rapids: Eerdmans, 1956.

THE FIRST EPISTLE OF PETER

INTRODUCTION

The Writer. This letter claims to have been written by the Apostle Peter (1:1). The author also calls himself an elder and a witness of the sufferings of Christ (5:1). He writes with the help of one Silvanus (5:12) and speaks of a dear one, Marcus, as being with him (5:13).

In dealing with any ancient writing, the writer is at the outset assumed to be intelligent and straightforward. His statements of matters ostensibly lying within his knowledge, and particularly any affirmations about himself or his activities, are regarded as reliable. The given literary work is further studied for internal consistency, and the writings of contemporary and later authors are scanned for direct references to this author or his work and for possible allusions to it, quotations from it, or other evidence of their acquaintance with it. The original assumption of genuineness and accuracy is not properly altered unless these further studies reveal very compelling evidence to the contrary.

With reference to the sacred Scriptures, there is for Christian scholars a further important factor operative in their studies. The historic church has always believed firmly that the canonical writings are not only the result of careful reporting by honest men, but that they embody also the element of divine miracle; they are "God-breathed" (II Tim 3:16), and sometimes even transcend the understanding of their human writers (I Pet 1:10-12).

I Peter clearly claims to have been written by the Apostle Peter, and there seem to be no considerations of content or style that refute such a claim. Indeed, it contains statements here and there which are strongly reminiscent of expressions of Peter reported in the Acts. The writer's reference to the Father as judging "without respect of persons" (1:17) recalls Peter's earlier word to Cornelius and the group of Gentiles in his house (Acts 10:34). The allusions to God as having raised Christ from the dead (I Pet 1:21, *et al.)* remind one of the apostle's characteristic resurrection witness in the Acts (2:32; 3:15; 10:40). And the proclamation of Christ as Isaiah's prophetically seen "chief cornerstone" in I Pet 2:7,8 is very similar to Peter's words to the Sanhedrin in Acts 4:11.

Scholars have pointed out similarities to the Pauline writings (Harnack thought I Peter too deeply imbued with the spirit of Pauline Christianity to have been the work of Peter), the relation of the epistle to James, and its undoubted affinity with Hebrews. Still other scholars, notably Dr. Charles Bigg *(St. Peter and St. Jude,* in the *International Critical Commentary),* argue that such similarities may be interpreted as reflecting the borrowing of these other writers from Peter as reasonably as the reverse, that they can well be taken as representing points of view and ways of speaking which were common among the Christians of apostolic times, and that there is nothing here to cast doubt on the individuality of the writer of I Peter or to show that this writer could not have been the Apostle Peter, as claimed in the epistle's opening verse.

The references to persecution and suffering, so prominent in I Peter, have been studied closely by scholars to see how they correspond with what is known from history about the persecutions of the early Christians. Dr. S. J. Case ("Peter, Epistles of," in HDAC) distinguishes three principal waves in the early persecutions: these occurring in the reigns of Nero (A.D. 54–68), Domitian (A.D. 81–96), and Trajan (A.D. 98–117). He follows those scholars who see I Peter as reflecting not only an advanced and severe stage of persecution but one which had spread to the provinces of Asia Minor mentioned in I Pet 1:1.

Referring to Pliny's correspondence with the emperor Trajan regarding the punishment of Christians during Pliny's propraetorship (beginning A.D. 111) of Pontus and Bithynia, two of the provinces to which I Peter is addressed, Case considers this to be the setting that best corresponds to the statements of

I Peter on persecution. To follow such a line of reasoning to its conclusion, placing the writing of this epistle during the reign of Trajan, would make it too late to have been the work of St. Peter. Dr. Case himself, in view of other lines of evidence, does not adopt this conclusion.

Other scholars interpret I Peter as an anticipatory warning against approaching persecution, toward which things were even then moving. Bigg points out that the early persecutions were largely inspired by the Jewish Sanhedrin, but that the Romans were quick to see that here was a way of life incompatible with paganism, and which, from their point of view, must be stopped. The persecution of Paul and Silas in Philippi seems to have been on this basis and without Jewish instigation. The missionaries had impaired the livelihood of the pagan fortunetellers. And Roman law protected the right of each man to make a living without interference.

Dr. Bigg feels that I Peter belongs in this earlier stage of pagan opposition, antedating even the Neronian persecution which followed the burning of Rome (A.D. 64), for which Nero blamed the Christians. Certainly this earlier dating is not impossible nor unreasonable, and it accords best with the epistle's claim to Petrine authorship. This is not to say, of course, that Pliny's letters to Trajan do not contain items that help us greatly in our study of persecution as seen in I Peter.

External evidence strongly supports the genuineness of this epistle. Although Irenaeus (c. 130–216) was the first whom we know to have quoted Peter by name, New Testament scholars have found allusions to I Peter and parallelisms with it in the Epistle of Barnabas (c. A.D. 80), in the work of Clement of Rome (A.D. 95–97), in the *Shepherd of Hermas* (early second century), and in later patristic writings. Polycarp, who was martyred in A.D. 155, quotes from I Peter, although not naming its author.

Eusebius (c. A.D. 324) says that Papias (who wrote c. A.D. 130–140) "used witnesses from the first epistle of John and similarly from Peter" *(Ecclesiastical History* 3.39.17). He counts I Peter among the books received without doubt by the whole church. Moreover, I Peter is found in the Syriac version of the Bible, called the Peshito, and in the Coptic, Ethiopic, Armenian, and Arabic versions. Its external attestation is strong indeed, and bears out the claim of this epistle to the authorship of the Apostle Peter.

The Time and Place of the Writing. The time and the place of the writing of I Peter, granting its Petrine authorship, are closely connected. From 5:13 it appears that the epistle was written from "Babylon." There was an Assyrian refugee settlement by that name in Egypt, where modern Cairo is located. But during the first century it was just a military post, and there is no traditional support for Peter's residence there.

Babylon on the Euphrates is known to have sheltered a Jewish congregation in A.D. 36, and there were Babylonian Jews in Jerusalem at Pentecost. There may well have been a Christian church there subsequently. But toward the end of the reign of Caligula (d. A.D. 41) the Jewish colony in Babylon was scattered by violent persecution and massacre. It seems quite improbable that this epistle was written from there.

There was an early and strong tradition for Peter's residence in Rome during the latter part of his life. This idea was generally held throughout the church prior to the Reformation. It is, perhaps, not impossible that the reformers, in urging Assyrian Babylon as the interpretation of Peter's reference in I Pet 5:13, may have been motivated partly by their opposition to the claim that the Roman papacy had come down from Peter. But the symbolic use of Old Testament names for existing cities was well known in apostolic times. Paul likened Hagar and Mount Sinai to Jerusalem (Gal 4:25). In Rev 11:8 Jerusalem is called "Sodom and Egypt," and in Rev 17:18 it is made clear that the scarlet lady called "Babylon" is a reference to Rome. To the recipients of I Peter, who would have known at once from the bearer whence the letter had come, there would have been no problem about this discreetly veiled reference to Rome.

Peter's arrival in Rome is calculated by Chase *(op. cit.)* to have been about the end of A.D. 63. Lightfoot sets it early in A.D. 64. Paul's coming to Rome as a prisoner had occurred earlier, in A.D. 61 or 62. There is a tradition that Paul was released after two years in Rome, and that II Timothy was written shortly before his execution, later, outside Rome, which is thus dated in A.D. 67 or 68. This second imprisonment is disputed, however, and those who dispute it place the writing of II Timothy about two years after Paul's arrival in Rome and assign a date of A.D. 63 or 64. This would come shortly before Paul's martyrdom, and at about the time Peter is thought to have arrived in Rome. It is interesting to note that Mark, who was summoned to Rome by Paul (II Tim 4:11), was present with Peter when this first epistle was written, as was also Silas, Paul's friend and one-time companion in travel (I Pet 5:12, 13).

This epistle, then, may well have been written from Rome at about the time of the outbreak of the Neronian persecution in A.D. 64. To place it shortly after the beginning of this persecution seems warranted by the epistle's vivid references to the fiery crucible of suffering.

The Message of the Epistle. Written to the Christians in the five provinces of Asia Minor, the epistle addresses its readers as scattered sojourners and foreigners, a figure very familiar to dispersed and downtrodden Israel, but also entirely apt for Peter's many Gentile Christian readers. That he had these Gentile Christians in mind is abundantly clear from the letter. He reminds them that although formerly "not a people," they are now the people of God (2:10). He describes their past life as having been lived in the sinful lusts of the Gentiles (4:3,4).

And why this interest on the part of Peter? Many from these provinces of Asia had heard his sermon at Pentecost (Acts 2:9), and many had doubtless gone back to their home territory as spiritual colonists. Paul had later carried on evangelistic labors in Asia, but to a limited extent only, having been forbidden by the Holy Spirit to work Asia intensively (Acts 16:6-8). Perhaps this was because of the splendid start already made by the Gospel in these parts.

Peter could well recall his Lord's injunctions, "When thou art converted, strengthen thy brethren" (Lk 22:32), and again, "Lovest thou me . . . ? Feed my sheep" (Jn 21:15-17). "When thou art converted," indeed! For the pre-Pentecost Peter, far from being a spiritual rock, was a shifting compound of human loyalty to Christ and treacherous self-interest. "Not the cross!" had been his advice to his Lord (Mt 16:22). And as Jesus went toward that instrument of suffering, in his Father's will, he did so without the company of Peter.

But Pentecost, with the Spirit's mighty filling, had brought a radical change. And now Peter, who had already endured beating and had faced death at Herod's hands, comes forward to encourage and strengthen his dear brethren of Asia to face the impending Calvary which he—perhaps already involved in the cruel Neronian persecution—could see coming upon them.

OUTLINE

Theme: Suffering in the life of the believer.
Key verse: I Peter 4:1.

- I. Comfort and reassurance in suffering. 1:1-25.
  - A. Salutation. 1:1,2.
  - B. Reassurance in the realized facts of Christ's gospel. 1:3-12.
  - C. Reassurance in divinely bought holiness of life. 1:13-25.
- II. The chastened response of practical holiness. 2:1—3:22.
  - A. The negative and positive bases of holiness. 2:1-3.
  - B. The readers' participation in a holy community, the Church. 2:4-10.
  - C. Unimpeachable living, the answer to persecution. 2:11—3:13.
    1. Deference to statutes, officers, fellow citizens. 2:11-17.
    2. Submission by servants, even to injustice. 2:18-25.
    3. Deference of wives to husbands. 3:1-6.
    4. Consideration for wives. 3:7.
    5. Divine love among the saints. 3:8-13.
  - D. Victory in unjust suffering. 3:14-22.
    1. Basic blessedness, freedom from terror. 3:14,15 a.
    2. Respectful apologetic supported by probity of life. 3:15 b-17.
    3. Christ the believer's example. 3:18-21.
    4. Christ the believer's reassurance. 3:22.
- III. The spiritual significance of suffering. 4:1-19.
  - A. Physical suffering a type of death to the flesh life. 4:1-6.
    1. Christ's death the example and empowerment. 4:1 a.
    2. Dying to the sin nature; alive to God. 4:1 b-6.

B. The "crucified life" characterized by divine love. 4:7-11.
C. The fires of persecution seen as purifying. 4:12-19.
IV. Divine love as a guide in church life. 5:1-11.
A. Elders to rule in love. 5:1-7.
B. The devil to be resisted through divine grace. 5:8-11.
V. Closing salutations and benediction. 5:12-14.

COMMENTARY

I. Comfort and Reassurance in Suffering. 1:1-25.

A. Salutation. 1:1,2.

1. **Peter, an apostle of Jesus Christ.** This is a straightforward claim by the epistle to the authorship, humanly speaking, of Peter the apostle. Only one person could have been thus identified. To negate this claim is to mark the epistle as a "pious fraud" and to raise a serious question about how a writing so authored can be depended upon for ethical and spiritual direction. **To the strangers scattered.** The Greek may be rendered, *to the foreign residents of the dispersion.* These were not strangers to Peter, but temporary residents in the provinces of Asia Minor here named by Peter. Their real citizenship was in heaven (cf. Phil 3:20, Gr.). The apostle, writing expressly to comfort these pilgrims, some of whom had no doubt been converted as a result of his sermon at Pentecost, immediately takes knowledge of the separation and even ostracism that marked them among their neighbors. The expression "dispersion" was fraught with poignant meaning for the scattered Jews. Peter adapts this figure to his Gentile readers.

2. **Elect according to the foreknowledge of God.** The Holy Spirit helped Peter, even in his introductory words, to advance a sound basis for encouragement to these Christians who were finding themselves increasingly alone. These were actually the ones who were chosen and preferred by Him whose favor is all-important. As elsewhere in the NT, the doctrine of election is made compatible with personal responsibility, as it is qualified by God's foreknowledge (see Rom 8:29), and is seen as operating in real life through imparted holiness (**sanctification of the Spirit,** II Thess 2:13). The result is **obedience** to God and cleansing from incidental defilement through the continuing **sprinkling of the blood** of Jesus Christ (Heb 12:24). To his dear brethren thus addressed Peter wishes **grace** (the Greek word being suggestive of the Gentile greeting *Chaire!* "Be of good cheer!") and **peace** (reminiscent of the Oriental greeting *Shalom!* "Peace!"). Note, too, the inclusion of reference to all three persons of the Trinity in this salutation.

B. Reassurance in the Realized Facts of Christ's Gospel. 1:3-12.

3. **Blessed be the God and Father of our Lord Jesus Christ.** Beginning properly with this ascription of praise and credit to God, the source of every benefit, Peter begins to build up a picture of the spiritual wealth of his readers, a wealth that remains secure for them despite all tests and indignities. First comes the fact of the new birth, God having **begotten us anew** (Gr.), **in terms of the greatness of his mercy,** with the resultant possession of a **living hope,** this hope and assurance centering about the fully attested and often-proclaimed fact of Christ's **resurrection.**

4. The result of a new birth is a new **inheritance,** which is described as **incorruptible** (indestructible), **undefiled** (unstained), **that fadeth not away** (fresh of color), and **reserved** (kept under watch) **in heaven for you.** To Peter's readers, who had already resigned their part in Israel's earthly inheritance, the promised land of the fathers, and who were also to know the proscription and the spoiling of earthly goods (see Heb 10:34), this thought of the sure inheritance would give comfort and balance. How reminiscent of our Lord's admonitions to his followers to convert their worldly possessions into true riches! (e.g., Lk 12:33,34) 5. **Who are kept by the power of God.** This kept inheritance is "for you the kept (i.e., by a military garrison) ones." The word for **kept** is the same Greek word used by Paul in Phil 4:7—"The peace of God . . . shall keep your hearts and minds." **Through faith.** This is the Christian's response to God's provision (cf. Heb 10:38,39). **Unto salvation ready to be revealed in the last time.**

Here is a salvation now enjoyed, the

full significance of which awaits an ultimate revelation (Gr., *apocalypse).*

6. Wherein ye greatly rejoice, though now . . . in heaviness. Here is the Christian's joy, independent of circumstances, paradoxical to the world. This is why Paul and Silas could sing with lacerated backs. It should be emphasized that this joy is not simply an intellectual anticipation of future possessions but a present appropriation of God's wealth through the Holy Spirit. Joy is one element in the fruit of the Spirit (Gal 5:22). **Through manifold temptations** or testings (Gr., *peirasmos).* These were more than the ordinary vicissitudes of life. Here is a reference to the weight of persecutions even then being felt by the Christians.

7. The trial of your faith. This word for **trial** is closely related to the idea of approval. The end result, not the process, is in focus. This demonstration of the eternal quality of their faith, shown forth brightly as a result of the testings, far excels the gleam of fire-refined gold, perishing in its nature, and will be **found unto praise and honour and glory at** (or *by)* **the appearing** *(revelation)* **of Jesus Christ.** Here is a double significance. Not only will this trying of faith be found rewarding to the Christians at Christ's coming, but it is presently found glorifying to Christ because of his unveiling (Gr., *apocalypsis)* in their suffering (cf. Paul in Gal 3:1). Compare these references to the second coming of Christ in verses 5 and 7 with those in Peter's sermon in the Temple (Acts 3:20,21) and in his message in the house of Cornelius (Acts 10:42).

8. Whom . . . ye love; in whom . . . ye rejoice. Christ personally, realized through faith, is the believer's unspeakable joy (see also Col 1:27). **9. Receiving** (getting) **the end of your faith . . . salvation.** This is not a future but a present reference. In their love of and faith in Christ they have him who is salvation and joy (Jn 17:3).

10. Of which salvation the prophets have inquired. Literally, they *sought out and investigated.* They were intrigued by God's plan of salvation. **11. Searching . . . the sufferings of Christ, and the glory.** The idea of salvation made available through a suffering Messiah was to them, indeed to all the Jews, a mystery (Col 1:26,27). Peter's introduction of the prophecies of glory through suffering must have greatly encouraged his readers. This was the way prohesied in Scripture, the way their Lord had trod, and the way they themselves were now being called upon to traverse. **12. Not unto themselves, but unto us they** (the prophets) **did minister.** An important principle in inspiration. God has sometimes chosen to reveal through the sacred Scriptures mysteries beyond the comprehension of the writers (cf. Dan 12:8,9). Here, then, is a gospel given through the prophets, proclaimed by preachers endued with the Holy Spirit, a wonder to angels.

C. Reassurance in Divinely Bought Holiness of Life. 1:13-25.

13. Wherefore gird up the loins of your mind. He exhorts them to be encouraged in the realization of God's love (cf. Heb 12:12,13). **Be sober.** An injunction to sane appraisal of the facts, without undue emotion and panic (repeated in 4:7; 5:8). **Hope to the end.** The words **to the end** are better translated *perfectly, maturely.* There is a spiritual quality to the Christian's endurance. His is the "patience of hope in our Lord Jesus Christ, in the sight of God" (I Thess 1:3). **The grace that is to be brought** (Gr., *that is being brought).* Doubtless we cannot comprehend this fully. Certainly it includes the redemption of the body (Phil 3:21; Rom 8:23). Compare the statement in verse 5 above. It may be a reference to dying grace ministered divinely to the martyrs.

14. As obedient children. Literally, *children of obedience.* **Not fashioning yourselves.** Actually, "not conforming yourselves" (cf. Rom 12:2) "to your strong desires in your former ignorance" (cf. Eph 2:3). The Christian's desire life has been changed; but unless he is watchful, he may yet be "drawn away with his own desire, and enticed" (Jas 1:14). **15, 16. As he which hath called you is holy.** Christ's imminent return, the believer's precious hope, also is a strong incentive to holiness (I Jn 3:3). For Christ is holy. Recall Peter's embarrassing realization of his own sinfulness and truancy when suddenly confronted by the risen Christ while fishing on the Sea of Galilee one morning (Jn 21:7). This was reminiscent of a similar realization when he had first been called by the Lord (Lk 5:8). **Conversation.** Better, *deportment, manner of life.* **Be ye holy.** This was a commandment very well known to all who knew the Pentateuch (Lev 11:44; 19:2; 20:7; cf. Mt 5:48).

17. If ye call on the Father. Peter speaks to praying people, who call on

God for deliverance from unjust persecution, but who should realize that God himself is a judge. **In fear.** This realization will cause a godly carefulness. The wise man is known by what and whom he fears (Mt 10:28).

18,19. Not redeemed with corruptible things. These were simple and poor folk. For the second time (cf. v. 7) Peter makes a scornful reference to temporal wealth as compared with the priceless heritage of salvation. **From your vain conversation.** More accurately, *from your foolish way of life inherited from your parents.* **The precious blood of Christ.** The word **precious** (Gr., *timios)* is peculiarly Petrine. The sinlessness of the Lamb, the vicariousness of his suffering, provide the basis for a new and heavenly scale of values. **20,21. Foreordained . . . manifest.** Christ's suffering was no emergency. It was God's best plan in view of man's sin. This would have been a comforting thought for saints now hard-pressed themselves. **For you.** Better, *through you.* Christ is actually manifested through them as they trust and hope in the same God who raised him from the dead.

22. Seeing [that] **ye have purified your souls.** Peter appeals to the genuineness of their conversion, an actuality well realized by his readers. They had indeed been changed, **purified.** This change of heart had issued in "unhypocritical brotherly love" (Gr., *philadelphia).* He exhorts them to follow and practice the same principle: **See that ye love one another** *from your heart, earnestly.* **23-25. Being born again . . . by the word of God.** How tenuous a matter regeneration seems to the human mind, resting, as it does, only on God's word. But Peter quotes Isaiah's grand assertion that this seemingly frail, invisible entity–God's word–will outlast all natural phenomena (Isa 40:6-8). And this is the word that gives significance to their faith and to themselves.

II. The Chastened Response of Practical Holiness. 2:1–3:22.

A. The Negative and Positive Bases of Holiness. 2:1-3.

1. Laying aside all malice. There is a negative and purging phase in holiness (Eph 4:22 ff.; Col 3:9 ff.). Here are ugly qualities centering in self-love: **malice,** more exactly, *evil-spiritedness;* **guile,** which hides the unworthy motive it seeks to further; **hypocrisies,** which feign an unfelt righteousness; **evil speakings,** which hurt another to advance one's self.

2. As newborn babes, desire. The Greek words suggest the voracious, hungry impatience of a baby at its mealtime. Peter has been speaking of the word of God as operative in their regeneration (1:23-25). Now he urges the newborn ones to cultivate a healthy appetite for this word, which, while mighty, is *simple* or *unadulterated* (translated, **sincere)** and elementary, like milk. In this way his readers will grow "unto salvation." These latter words, found in some of the best manuscripts, refer to the believer's ultimate deliverance (cf. 1:5,13). **3. If so be ye have tasted.** Here is another reminder of the grace they have already experienced (cf. Ps 34:8).

B. The Readers' Participation in a Holy Community, the Church. 2:4-10.

4. To whom coming, as unto a living stone. Peter is now coming to that grand and comforting assurance that his readers, who are scorned and ostracized as a motley and negligible folk (cf. "foreigners," 1:1) by their neighbors, are members of a holy and glorious community, the Church. He begins rightly with the matter of personal relationship to Christ, Himself rejected as they are, but like them **chosen** *(elect,* cf. 1:1) **of God, and precious** (again this word "precious"; cf. 1:19 and below).

5. Ye also, as lively (living) **stones.** Here is an identity in nature with Christ. The same words are used of the believers as of the Lord. The passage clearly recalls the Lord's words to Peter, "Thou shalt be called . . . a stone" (Jn 1:42); and again, "Thou art Peter *(a stone),* and upon this rock *(rock formation)* I will build" (Mt 16:18). Note that in the present passage Peter makes his Lord, not himself, pre-eminent in this holy building which is the Church. **Are being builded a spiritual house.** Compare Eph 2:19-22. The Church is seen as transcending the glory of the Jewish Temple. The argument in this part of the chapter, to I Pet 2:10, may intimate that the indignities and pressures being experienced by the believers were at the instigation of the Jews, though taken up likewise by the Gentiles, as so often happened in the early days of the church. **An holy priesthood, to offer up spiritual sacrifices, acceptable to God by Jesus Christ.** The offering of Christ is seen as opening the Holy of Holies to all believers and as superseding the Jewish sacrifices. Through Christ, once-sinful man can now make an acceptable offering to a holy God (cf. Rom 12:1,2).

6. It is contained in the scripture. Peter now cites his source, Isa 28:16. It is interesting to note that in this verse in Isaiah the stress is upon the function of the stone as "a sure foundation" (cf. I Cor 3:11). No doubt Peter's feeling for this figure went back to our Lord's use of it (Mt 21:42), following the wording in Ps 118:22,23. Peter himself had used it with the Sanhedrin: "This is the stone which was set at nought of you builders" (Acts 4:11).

7,8. Unto you the believing (Gr) . . . **precious: but unto them which be disobedient . . . a rock of offence.** The noun form of "precious" is here used; literally, *an honor, a thing prized.* Here is a simple representation of Christ as Saviour and Judge. Mercy rejected becomes condemnation. This, again, was Christ's doctrine (Mt 21:44; Jn 12:48). In the present passage the **believing** are contrasted with the **disobedient.** Faith, then, appears as a basic obedience or willingness (cf. "obedient to the faith," Acts 6:7). **Whereunto also they were appointed** (Gr., *set).* The same divine purpose which, on the basis of God's foreknowledge, chose Peter's readers as His own children, has sadly ordained the disobedient to their only alternative.

9,10. But ye are a chosen *(elect)* **generation** (Gr., *genos,* "race, kind"). This is very reminiscent of Christ's own teaching. His reference to the rejected cornerstone was in connection with his parable of the rebellious husbandmen who had slain the son of the owner of the vineyard. At the same time and along with his reference to the rejected stone, he said to the Jewish leaders, "The kingdom of God shall be taken from you, and given to a nation bringing forth the fruits thereof" (Mt 21:43). Peter is now writing to this "nation," whose evident royalty and worth at once mark them as the King's children and reflect credit upon him who called them from the world's darkness to his light. The words translated **peculiar people** literally mean *a people for a gain-making* (Gr., *peripoiēsis).* Sometimes the word indicates the securing of a desired possession ("purchase to themselves," I Tim 3:13; "he purchased through his own blood." Acts 20:28). Sometimes it means a preservation or salvation. In Heb 10:39 it is translated "saving" and contrasted with "perdition." Here is a tremendous word of encouragement. These are a people greatly prized, a people to be saved, a people for a possession. Peter rounds off this doctrine in the words of Hosea (1:6,9; 2:23). These once **not a people**—very probably a reference to their Gentile ancestry—are now **the people of God.**

C. Unimpeachable Living, the Answer to Persecution. 2:11–3:13.

11. As strangers and pilgrims, abstain. Peter sweeps aside the picture of their royalty, turns the page, addresses them once more as pilgrims. He picks up again the thought in 2:11 and bids them "hold themselves away" from carnal desires **which war against the soul.** The figure "to war against" is not that of hand-to-hand fighting, but of a planned expedition against a military objective. We might liken it to Delilah's cool exploitation of Samson's appetites for his destruction. **12. Having your conversation** (way of life) **honest** (the same word is used in "good works" later in the verse). Though a chosen race, they lived among the Gentiles, who were bent to **speak against** them **as evildoers.** Christianity by its very essence opposed the vanities of paganism at every turn. Hence it was in itself a crime, "everywhere spoken against" (Acts 28:22). Like righteous Noah, it "condemned the world" (Heb 11:7). This was the basic explanation for the willingness of the pagans to notice and persecute this insignificant people. And Peter knew that the best answer was probity of life, God-given and wringing unwilling praise from the very enemies of the cross (cf. Jesus' teaching in Mt 5:16). **In the day of visitation** is better rendered *the day of observation* (official inspection or cognizance).

13,14. Submit yourselves to every ordinance . . . to the king . . . unto governors. A Christian is law-abiding, meticulous, and self-disciplined. This doctrine is comparable with Paul's teaching in Rom 13:1-7 and Tit 3:1,2. It is, of course, not to be understood as compelling compliance with evil. Peter's own words to the Sanhedrin answer this: "Whether it be right in the sight of God to hearken unto you more than unto God, judge ye" (Acts 4:19). **15. With well doing . . . put to silence the ignorance of foolish men.** Pliny, in his report to Trajan about the Christians in Pontus and Bithynia, two of the provinces mentioned in 1:1, speaks of the "crimes clinging to the name" of Christian. Although coming at a considerably later time (c. A.D. 112), this is illustrative of the ignorant and unfair way in which a group of people may be assumed to be criminal. The answer of a good life would be the best defense.

16. As free. Spirit-impelled self-control is the only lasting basis of freedom: "If ye be led of the Spirit, ye are not under the law" (Gal 5:18). **But as the servants** *(slaves)* **of God.** The man wholly mastered of God is truly free. God then works in such a one the willing and the doing of His good will. It is this God-implanted love for His way that makes Christ's yoke easy, His burden light.

17. Honour . . . love . . . fear. Here is expressed self-abnegation and willingness to give to each his due. The word for **honor** is related to the word "precious," and suggests the Christian's high regard for human personality. The word for love indicates the divinely given *agapē* of I Cor 13. This was the love with which Christ had twice challenged Peter in Jn 21:15,16, a challenge from which honest Peter swerved with the reply, "I love (Gr., *philo,* "to love humanly") thee."

18-20. Servants, be subject . . . also to the froward. The Spirit-filled man is enabled to meet demands unreasonable, yes, quite impossible on any other basis. "Love your enemies," "turn the other cheek"—these are encompassed only through the complete mastery of him who prayed for his crucifiers, "Father, forgive them." **This is thankworthy.** Reward begins where the reasonable ends. He who serves God without transcendent divine love builds wood, hay, and stubble. **What glory is it . . . ?** Compare Jesus' questions in Lk 6:32-36. **Acceptable with God.** The word **acceptable** is the Greek *charis,* which has a beautiful double force of "grace" and "favor." It can give the sense, "When ye do well, and suffer . . . patiently, this is grace with God" or "this is favor with God."

21-23. Christ also suffered. Here, of course, is the personification of divine love. Here is our pattern. **Who did no sin.** Hence all punishment and indignity to him was without reason. **Who . . . reviled not again . . . but committed himself.** Here is the perfect fulfillment of the principle seen in Rom 12:19,20: "Vengeance is mine . . . saith the Lord. Therefore if thine enemy hunger, feed him." Here is perfect love for God and man. **24. Who . . . bare our sins in his own body.** Peter reminds his readers that this was done for them. **That we, being dead to sins, should live unto righteousness.** He implies that Christ's death was more than an example. By sharing his cross they will share his triumphant life. **By whose stripes . . .** Selwyn *(The First Epistle of St. Peter,* p. 95) calls attention to three strands in St. Peter's thought about the atonement: the paschal lamb "without blemish and without spot" (1:19), the suffering servant of Isa 53, "by whose stripes ye were healed," and the scape goat, "who his own self bare our sins in his own body on the tree." **25. For ye were as sheep . . . but . . .** Peter has been urging upon his readers a sharing of Christ's sufferings. Even as He commanded (Lk 14:27, etc.), they are to follow Him, taking up the cross. But they have already made an initial step in this sharing of the cross; once wayward sheep, they have been converted to the **Shepherd and Bishop** (caretaker) of their souls.

3:1-6. Likewise, ye wives. Leaving the implications of holiness for slaves, Peter addresses the married women. These he directs, **Be in subjection to your husbands** (cf. Eph 5:22; Col 3:18). The rule of divine love is still the background. The husband is recognized as leader in the home, and the wife's **chaste conversation,** her prudent and self-controlled conduct in the home, will win some to Christ. She is not to seek attention by the artificialities of coiffure, jewelry, or ostentatious dress, but to be distinguished by that **meek and quiet spirit** so rare in the world and so prized by God. The wives of the patriarchs are seen as examples of this deportment (v. 5). Apparently gaudy and showy adornment is viewed as contrary to the spirit of self-effacement and modesty toward husbands. The same implication appears in I Tim 2:9-12. Modesty of woman's dress is associated with becoming modesty of deportment. Apparently Christian faith implies a different standard of dress and adornment from the world's. Sara is seen as deferring to Abraham's leadership, **calling him lord** (Gen 18:12). Verse 6 reminds these Christian women that they are adopted daughters of Sara: "Whose children you became, doing good and not being subject to inordinate fear."

7. Likewise, ye husbands. Passing now to the implications of holiness in the husband, Peter enjoins that the marriage relationship be seen in terms of consideration, **according to knowledge.** Here is the opposite of selfishness. **Giving honour unto the wife.** The word for **giving** (Gr., *aponemō)* indicates a deliberate assignment, a purposeful channeling of honor (related to "precious") to the wife, who is in God's grace an equal heir. **That your prayers be not hindered.** Feelings of resentment, growing from selfish conduct in the home, make effective prayer impossible. Effective prayer must be "without wrath" (I Tim 2:8).

8,9. Be ye all of one mind. This recalls the "one accord" of Pentecost, or Paul's injunctions to the Philippians to be "in one spirit" (Phil 1:27) and "likeminded, having the same love, being of one mind, of one spirit" (Phil 2:2), followed closely by his gripping outline of the mind of Christ. Peter's catalog of accompanying graces reads like the gracious self-effacing aspects of the fruit of the Spirit (Gal 5:22,23) or of the "wisdom that is from above" (Jas 3:17).

10-12. For he that will love life. The apostle cites Ps 34:12-16 in substantiation of his teaching that this Spirit-directed and empowered way of self-emptying is really the life of blessing, the outcomes of which are guarded by the Lord, whose **eyes . . . are over the righteous, and his ears . . . open unto their prayers. 13. Who . . . will harm you . . . ?** This reminds us of Paul's postscript to the description of the fruit of the Spirit—"against such there is no law" (Gal 5:23). As a general principle, allowing for exceptions occasioned by the adversary's wrath, people are not punished for doing good. This very principle assures that undeserved suffering will not continue long.

D. Victory in Unjust Suffering. 3:14-22.

14,15 a. But . . . if ye suffer for righteousness' sake, happy *(blessed).* This beatitude, of course, recalls our Lord's beatitude in Mt 5:11,12. Peter then cites God's words to Isaiah (8:12,13), the complete passage reading, "Neither fear ye their fear, nor be afraid. Sanctify the Lord of hosts himself; and let him be your fear, and let him be your dread." This again brings to mind Christ's warning as to whom to fear (Mt 10:28). There was real danger of defection in the face of death. Pliny describes how curtly the alternative was given to the Christians to curse Christ or die, and how not a few turned back. Peter's attitude here is not so quick and confident as it was when he told his Lord, "Though all men shall be offended because of thee, yet will I never be offended" (Mt 26:33).

15 b,16. Be ready always to give an answer. The attitude depicted is one of **meekness and fear,** yet of readiness. This, too, is a Spirit-given quality. Recall Christ's admonition: "Whatsoever shall be given you in that hour, that speak ye; for it is not ye that speak, but the Holy Ghost" (Mk 13:11). Recall the unanswerable apologetics of Stephen (Acts 6:10) and Paul (Acts 24:25; 26:24-28). **Having a good conscience.** As above, probity of life is seen as the basic defense. **17,18. It is better. . . . For Christ also hath once suffered for sins, the just for the unjust.** God-permitted suffering for welldoing is in prospect. Christ is again brought forward as the example (cf. 2:24), the outcome of whose suffering was reconciliation of lost men to God, along with his own vindication through his resurrection by the Holy Spirit's power.

19,20. By which (i.e., the Spirit) **also he went and preached.** Here follows a digression the interpretation of which is obscure. Some scholars, of whom Lange is an example, contend that the only straightforward and natural inference here is that Christ, after his crucifixion, descended into Hades and "proclaimed to these spirits in the prisons of Hades the beginning of a new epoch of grace" (J. P. Lange, *Commentary on the Holy Scripture*, IX, p. 64). He avers that no doubt many were saved because of this second chance. This view raises the difficult question as to why, of all unbelievers, the antediluvians were granted this reprieve, and raises the possibility (which is contrary to the clear teaching of the NT) that other sinners unrepentant at death would have a later chance to believe on Christ. Some take the view that Christ's preaching in Hades was condemnatory, but this is not the usual implication of the Greek word, which means to *herald, announce,* and is often used with the Gospel. John Owen, Calvin's translator and editor (John Calvin, *Commentaries on the Catholic Epistles*, p. 116, note), cites the explanation adopted by Beza, Doddridge, Macknight, and Scott, that the time of the action was in the ministry of Noah, when Christ by the Spirit ("by which") preached through Noah to the wicked who at Peter's later writing were spirits in Hades. And all this while **the longsuffering of God waited,** delaying the flood. The reference to the time spent in building the ark seems to corroborate this interpretation. Reference to the small number of those saved would encourage the "little flock" in Asia.

21. Baptism doth also now save us. The variant *by which* (Gr., *hô*), that is, "by water," is preferred for the beginning of this sentence. We read, then, "by which (water) baptism, as an anti-type, now saves us – not the putting off of the dirtiness of the physical flesh but the asking after" (better than "answers of") "a good conscience toward God." Compare Heb 10:22. The meaning seems to be that water baptism symbolizes spiritual cleansing. The connection of water baptism and the baptism of the Spirit with cleansing is everywhere apparent in the Scripture, relating to the sharing of Christ's death and his resurrection power. Those who believe in baptismal regeneration will perhaps be inclined to make something of the verb **save** here. Others will aver that it is the cleansing of the heart, not the outward ceremony, which saves. **22. Who is gone into heaven.** Resuming the theme of Christ's resurrection, left after verse 18, Peter mentions our Lord's present triumph and recognition as a strong encouragement to the godly who follow their Master in suffering. Selwyn makes a point of the fact that the early Christians often solemnized baptism at Easter time. He feels that the reference to baptism in verse 21, as well as the several allusions to Christ's sufferings, resurrection, and second coming, indicate that I Peter was written as an Easter epistle (*op. cit.*, p. 62).

III. The Spiritual Significance of Suffering. 4:1-19.

A. Physical Suffering a Type of Death to the Flesh Life. 4:1-6.

1 a. As Christ hath suffered . . . arm yourselves . . . with the same mind. Philippians 2:5 uses the verbal form of "mind" and urges, "Be minded the same." The thought here is very similar. A different Greek word is used, suggesting the individuality of both Peter and Paul. Christ is seen as the believer's example and empowerment **for us** in suffering. **1 b, 2. He that hath suffered in the flesh hath ceased from sin.** Peter is now looking at death as encountered by man (cf. Rom 7:1-4), freeing him from all desire and commitment of sin. He immediately drives the spiritual parallel. He who has shared Christ's cross no longer is alive to the pull of sin through the ordinary human desires, but is alive only to the pull of God's will (Gal 6:14).

3,4. The time past of our life may suffice. Literally, *sufficient the bygone time to have wrought the will of the Gentiles.* Then follows a catalog of the ugly sins observable outside of God's grace. This reminds one of Paul's enumeration of the works of the flesh in Gal 5:19-21. **They think it strange . . . speaking evil.** The changed lives of the believers mark them as strange, almost as "foreigners," bringing to the heathen condemnation and a self-defensive and contemptuous defamation of the Christians. **5. Who shall give account.** But it is to God and not to men that such are answerable. And God's judgment will apply both to those now living and to those now dead. Dependent upon one's treatment of verse 6, this judgment may be considered both a vindication of believers and a condemnation of unrepentant sinners. In the OT, particularly in the Psalms, judgment is often seen as vindication for the righteous.

6. The gospel preached also to them that are dead. Some connect this with 3:19,20. Lange sees both passages as referring to a postcrucifixion evangelization of the unbelieving antediluvians by Christ, a further offer of salvation doubtless accepted by many of them. There are various other shades of interpretation. To us there seems to be solid merit in the suggestion of Scott, as modified by John Owen (*op. cit.*, p. 127), whose sense is: "With this end in view (i.e., the final judgment just mentioned) was the gospel preached also to those (martyrs) now dead, that they might be (as they were) judged in the flesh (and condemned to martyrdom) after the fashion of men, but might live in the Spirit according to God." Here, then, is the teaching that, in view of final judgment, the martyred dead are better off than the unbelieving Gentiles of verse 3.

B. The "Crucified Life" Characterized by Divine Love. 4:7-11.

7. The end . . . is at hand. With the focus still on the Judgment, the apostle enjoins an attitude of self-control **(be ye therefore sober),** and calmness (better than **watch)** and recourse to **prayer. 8. Have fervent** (intense) **charity.** Here again is divine love (Gr., *agapē*) as in I Corinthians 13, love which overlooks the sins and wrongs of others. **9.** Here is a love which uses **hospitality . . . without grudging.** Literally, *loving of guests without murmuring.* There is here a giving of self and substance gladly.

10. As every man hath received . . . so minister. The "gift" received is a *charisma,* a grace, which makes its possessors **stewards of the manifold grace of God.** This grace is to be **minister**[ed] (Gr., *diakoneō;* cf. "deacon") to others, the best method also for its continued enjoyment by the original possessor. Here again is loving sharing of spiritual blessings. **11. If any man speak.** The apostle extends the idea of stewardship introduced in verse 10. The speaker in the church must be careful to present God's sayings (Gr., *logia),* not his own. The caretaker (AV, **minister;** Gr., **deacon)** must serve in the strength (better than AV *ability)* which God abundantly supplies. Always the end in view must be **that God in all things may be glorified through Jesus Christ.** Here Peter inserts a benediction, himself giving glory to God as he has just enjoined.

C. The Fires of Persecution Seen as Purifying. 4:12-19.

12. Think it not strange concerning the fiery trial. Peter warns his readers against being taken by surprise, apparently indicating a test more severe than any they had yet experienced. This verse well befits the Neronian persecution, when Christians were nightly burned as torches in the emperor's gardens. Peter, in Rome, feared that soon this virulence would spread to the provinces. **13. Rejoice . . . partakers of Christ's sufferings.** Here was that physical sharing of Christ's cross for which the spiritual sharing (2:24) was an adequate preparation. The admonition to joy recalls Jesus' words in Mt 5:12. **When his glory shall be revealed.** Or, *in the unveiling* (Gr., *apocalypsis) of his glory.* A "better resurrection" (Heb 11:35) was in prospect for them.

14. Reproached for the name of Christ, happy *(blessed).* Here is another beatitude. **The spirit of...God resteth** *(is pausing)* **upon you.** God stands with his martyrs. The Holy Spirit ministers special grace. Recall Stephen's dying radiance (Acts 6:15; 7:55). While men gnash and blaspheme, the martyr's serenity glorifies his God. **15. Let none . . . suffer as a murderer.** Peter warns against sin, which nullifies the witness of suffering. **16. If . . . as a Christian.** Pliny, writing later, speaks of a punishment because of the "name itself" (i.e., "Are you a Christian?"). Under such circumstances, Peter enjoins, **Let him not be ashamed; but let him glorify God in this name** (ASV, better than AV, *on this behalf).*

17,18. Judgment must begin at the house of God. Alluding perhaps to Ezk 9:6, the apostle regards these persecutions as a divinely permitted purging of the suffering believers, and as a harbinger of awful doom to the ungodly (cf. Lk 23:28 ff.). **19. Let them that suffer . . . commit.** Let them rest their case with their Maker, even as did Christ (2:23). To do so betokens the calmness of that divinely implanted love that casts out fear (cf. I Jn 4:18).

IV. Divine Love as a Guide in Church Life. 5:1-14.

A. Elders To Rule in Love. 5:1-7.

1. But this dying grace is also a wonderful principle for living. Peter addresses **the elders.** He calls himself **also an elder, and a witness** (Gr., *martys,* "martyr") **of the sufferings of Christ,** and a sharer of the coming glory. **2-4. Feed the flock.** Does not this recall Christ's words to Peter, "Feed my sheep"? (Jn 21:15-17) Perhaps the ministerial designation "pastor" *(shepherd),* as applied to "elders" may have come from here. **Not by constraint** (forcibly) **but willingly** *(by consent)* **according to God** (added by certain good MSS); **not greedily but with a free will; neither as being lords over** *(lording it over)* **the premises** (more accurate than AV *God's heritage)* **but as examples** *(types)* **of the flock. When the chief Shepherd shall appear.** This recalls our Lord's discourse on the good shepherd (Jn 10:1-16), doubtless heard by Peter. Christ shall bestow upon his undershepherds **the unfading crown of glory** (RSV).

5-7. Likewise, ye younger, submit. The spirit of the elders is to be loving and deferential, an example making it easy and natural for the younger to follow. All are to be **clothed** *(girded about)* **with humility,** and thus to expect God's grace, which is both the cause and the result of **humility.** Peter quotes Prov 3:34 (LXX) in support of this teaching (cf. Jas 4:6), and reinforces his admonition to humility (cf. Jas 4:10). It is the graciously humble who may relax, **casting all your care upon him; for he careth for you** *(it concerns him for you).*

B. The Devil To Be Resisted Through Divine Grace. 5:8-11.

8,9. Be sober *(calm),* **be vigilant** *(watchful)* **. . . your adversary** (opponent in a lawsuit) **. . . as a roaring lion, walketh about, seeking whom he may devour** (closer, *someone to devour).* This passage may well be a veiled reference to Nero or to his amphitheater with its lions. Seen behind all is a personal devil. **Whom resist.** Compare Jas 4:7. Christian determination triggers divine counterforce. And the knowledge that the members of **the brotherhood throughout the world** share **the same kinds of afflictions** tends to make the hard-pressed Christians **stedfast in the faith.**

10. But the God of all grace. Peter has enjoined upon them the graces consistent with their calling. He now commits them to the God of all grace **who hath called us unto his eternal glory by Christ Jesus.** This closing mention of God's call reminds us of his opening thought of their election (1:2). This glory, again, is to be **after . . . ye have suffered a while.** The verbs which follow are simple futures: **shall fit you out completely** (or, make you what you ought to be), **shall fix you firmly** (Christ's word used to Peter, "Strengthen thy brethren," Lk 22:32), **shall fill you with might, shall put you upon a firm foundation.**

11. To him be . . . dominion for ever and ever *(to the ages of the ages).* Peter closes his message with a benediction.

V. Closing Salutations and Benediction. 5:12-14.

12. By Silvanus . . . I have written. Some argue that Silvanus was only the courier, but this statement seems broad enough to suggest the probability that Silvanus – generally agreed to have been the Silas of Paul's second missionary journey – actually served as a secretary in the writing of I Peter. **This is the true grace of God wherein ye stand.** The apostle thus sums up the matter of his encouragement and witness to his readers.

13. At Babylon, elected together with you. Peter here brings greetings from *the fellow elect* (feminine gender) *in Babylon.* The translators of the AV made it "the fellow-elect church." Some think it to have been a greeting from Peter's wife, a noble person who accompanied Peter on his journeys and who, tradition says, was martyred before her husband. She would have been well known to Peter's readers. **And . . . Marcus my son.** Doubtless an indication that John Mark was with Peter at the time.

14. Greet ye one another with a kiss of charity (Gr., *agapē,* "divine love"). **Peace be with you all that are in Christ Jesus.** The letter closes on its keynote of divine love and of peace in Christ, superior to all opposing forces and considerations.

BIBLIOGRAPHY

(for I and II Peter)

BIGG, CHARLES. *A Critical and Exegetical Commentary on the Epistles of St. Peter and St. Jude (The International Critical Commentary).* Edinburgh: T. & T. Clark, 1901.

CALVIN, JOHN. *Commentaries on the Catholic Epistles.* Translated and edited by John Owen. Grand Rapids: Wm. B. Eerdmans Publishing Co., reprinted 1948.

CASE, S. J. "Peter, Epistles of," *Dictionary of the Apostolic Church.* Edited by James Hastings. Edinburgh: T. & T. Clark, 1918.

CHARLES, R. H. (ed.). *The Apocrypha and Pseudepigrapha of the Old Testament in English.* London: Oxford University Press, 1913.

LANGE, JOHN P. *Commentary on the Holy Scriptures.* Translated and edited by Philip Schaff. Grand Rapids: Zondervan Publishing House, reprint, n.d.

MAYOR, JOSEPH B. *The Epistle of St. Jude and the Second Epistle of St. Peter.* London: Macmillan and Company, 1907.

ORR, JAMES (ed.). *International Standard Bible Encyclopedia.* Chicago: Howard Severance Company, 1930. James M. Gray, "Peter Simon"; William G. Moorehead, "Peter, The First Epistle of," "Peter, The Second Epistle of."

SELWYN, EDWARD G. *The First Epistle of St. Peter.* London: Macmillan and Company, 1958.

TENNEY, MERRIL C. "Bible Book of the Month: II Peter," *Christianity Today,* December 21, 1959.

THE SECOND EPISTLE OF PETER

INTRODUCTION

The Writer. At the outset this epistle, using a slightly different wording from that in I Peter, claims to be the writing of Symeon (Symeon appears in some of the better manuscripts; the AV has Simon Peter; cf. Acts 15:14), "a slave and an apostle of Jesus Christ" (II Pet 1:1). Simply and without affectation, the writer again identifies himself with the apostles (3:2). He is acquainted with the Pauline writings and expresses full accord with his "beloved brother Paul" (3:15,16). He refers to Christ's transfiguration with the quiet assurance of an eyewitness. He calls this letter a "second epistle" (3:1). He declares that the violent death predicted for him by his Lord (Jn 21:18) is in early prospect (II Pet 1:13,14). Here then, apparently, is a claim to authorship identical with that of I Peter, and certainly a claim to identity with St. Peter the Lord's apostle.

Are there internal difficulties that compel the honest reader to regard this as a spurious claim? From earliest times critics have called attention to a divergence in style between this epistle and I Peter. There is in II Peter a lack of the simplicity and ease of expression that characterize I Peter. The writer of I Peter was apparently not a Greek (e.g., he makes no use of the particle *an*), but he had an undoubted feeling for the correct use of the language. The style of II Peter does not evince the same familiarity with the language medium. It employs fewer participles than are seen in I Peter and does not use the *men* particle.

This difference in style caused some of the ancients and some of the reformers to question the authenticity of II Peter. Jerome (A.D. 346–420), the translator of the Vulgate version of the Bible, while accepting II Peter along with the other six 'catholic,' or general, epistles *(Epistle to Paulinius)*, at the same time recognized that some scholars have doubted its genuineness because of this variation in style *(Catalogus Scriptorum Ecclesiasticorum).* Elsewhere *(Epistle to Hedibia,* 120) he explains this difference as resulting naturally from Peter's use of different interpreters for the two epistles.

In the same context he mentions Paul's use of Titus as an interpreter and Peter's dictation to Mark of material for the Gospel which was to bear Mark's name. To some with a very literalistic concept of inspiration, the idea of such an editorial function by Silas (I Pet 5:12), impairs the letter's inspiration and authority, despite the clear knowledge that ready scribes have often assisted the inspired writers (Jer 36:2,4; Rom 16:22; and the traditional notes following I and II Cor, Eph, Phil, Col, and Phm). Others have felt that here is no difficulty; the Holy Spirit helped Silas to write as He helped Peter to dictate. The great majority of the historic church have taken the latter attitude.

Another internal matter which has been urged against the Petrine authorship of this epistle is the asserted familiarity of its writer with the Pauline epistles, which, together with his reference to the authority of Paul's writings (II Pet 3:15,16), is taken as an indication that the NT canon had been pretty well established by the time II Peter was written, thus seeming to the holders of this view to make this epistle too late to have been the work of the apostle.

Such a line of reasoning seems gratuitous indeed, for if Peter reached Rome just two or three years subsequent to Paul's arrival as a prisoner, he certainly would have had a natural opportunity to learn of Paul's epistles and might conceivably have had fellowship with Paul himself. Anyway, there seems to be reasonable evidence that Paul's letters were copied and circulated from church to church immediately on their receipt (see Col 4:16).

One further matter of internal study should be considered, namely, the similarity of certain statements in II Peter to statements in Jude. Three of the most important parallelisms follow: (1) II Peter 2:4 and Jude 6 refer to the punishment of the fallen angels, an allusion to a statement in the apocryphal book of Enoch. (2) II Peter 2:11 and Jude 9 speak of the unwillingness of angels to bring a railing accusation against Satan, the Jude statement apparently adding an allusion to the apocryphal *Assumption of Moses,* where Satan is represented as claiming the body of Moses. (3) II Peter 3:3,4 and Jude 17,18 tell of the coming of scoffers in the last days. II Peter refers to this as in the future. Jude refers to it as a present reality, having been prophesied by the apostles, of whom Peter, of course, was one.

Dr. Charles Bigg *(St. Peter and St. Jude,* pp. 216,217), who accepts the Petrine authorship of this epistle, argues convincingly for the priority of II Peter. It is well to keep in mind, too, that there are plausible considerations for the early dating of the epistle of Jude itself. It is assigned a date as early as A.D. 65, and those who set its date as late as A.D. 80 or 90 must reckon with an account of Hegesippus (reported by Eusebius) that two grandsons of Jude were brought before Domitian, who reigned A.D. 81–96, these being described as grown men, horny-handed farmers, at that time. Recall that Jude was a brother of our Lord. The similarities between II Peter and Jude do not seem to require a post-Petrine date for the former.

What, then, of external testimony? This epistle is not quoted directly in the Church Fathers prior to the beginning of the third century, although there are possible allusions in some of the earlier writings. Eusebius *(Ecclesiastical History* 6.14.1), writing about A.D. 324, says that Clement of Alexandria (who died c. A.D. 213) in his *Hypotyposes* had compiled summaries of all the inspired Scriptures, including those whose authenticity was contested, among these the 'catholic' or general epistles.

Origen, who died in A.D. 253, although recognizing the question about II Peter, accepted the book as genuine. Origen's friend and pupil Firmilian, Bishop of Caesarea in Cappadocia A.D. 256, strongly corroborates the Petrine authorship of II Peter when in a letter to Cyprian he speaks of one Stephanus as "gainsaying the blessed apostles Peter and Paul . . . who in their epistles pronounced a curse upon heretics and warned that we shun them" (Cyprian, *Letters,* No. 75). It is in II Peter, not I Peter, that heretics are mentioned.

Eusebius himself, commissioned by the emperor Constantine to prepare fifty copies of the sacred Scriptures, refers to James, Jude, and II Peter as contested but well known to the majority of Christians.

Jerome (c. A.D. 346–420), commenting upon the question of the epistle's authenticity, says that the question arises because of the difference between its style and that of I Peter, and he offers the explanation already noted. He himself accepted II Peter and included it in his Vulgate version of the Bible. It was recognized by the Council of Laodicea (c. 372), and was formally acknowledged as belonging to the canon by the Council of Carthage (397).

This epistle is not found in the Muratorian fragment, a list of the NT Scriptures which dates about the end of the second century. This list is in a somewhat mutilated condition. As we now have it, there is no reference to Hebrews, I or II Peter, James, or III John. It is conceivable that some or all of these may have been included in parts which are missing; but, lacking these, it is certainly clear from the history of the development of the canon that the Muratorian list was not accepted as definitive and final by the church.

Neither was II Peter included in the Syriac Bible called the Peshito. The Old Testament of the Peshito was translated very early. The New Testament is probably the work of Rabbula, bishop of Edessa in Syria from 411–435. This version omits II Peter, II and III John, Jude, and Revelation. It is quite possible that the earliest New Testament of the Syrian church omitted all seven of the 'catholic' epistles.

Some speculate that because of the practical and disciplinary emphasis of these general epistles, they may have been regarded as "un-Pauline" in a region where Paul's name was held in high esteem because of his personal membership in the Antiochean church, and his championing the freedom of Gentile believers from Jewish laws at the Jerusalem council. Others surmise that the inclusion of references to apocryphal writings by some of the general epistles may have caused their rejection by the Christians of the Syrian church, who were particularly allergic to the extremes of Jewish angelology reflected in some of the apocryphal books.

Perhaps some mention should be made of the arguments of the British scholar Joseph B. Mayor *(The Epistle of St. Jude and the Second Epistle of St. Peter)*, who regards I Peter as the work of the apostle whose name it bears but holds II Peter to be spurious.

He bases his opinion upon internal rather than external evidence. After reviewing the external evidence, with its references bearing for and against the acceptance of the epistle as genuine, Mayor summarizes by saying, "If we had nothing else to go upon in deciding the question of the authenticity of II Peter except external evidence, we should be inclined to think that we had in these quotations ground for considering that Eusebius was justified in his statement that our epistle "having appeared useful to many, was respected along with the other scriptures" *(op. cit.*, p. cxxiv; translation ours).

Mayor sets forth a minute study of vocabulary differences and lists 369 words used in I Peter but not in II Peter, and 230 words used in II Peter but not in I Peter. He finds 100 rather solid words (practically all nouns and verbs) used in both epistles. He then, amazingly, seems to set it down as an argument against their common authorship that "the number of agreements is 100 as opposed to 599 disagreements, i.e., the latter are just six times as many as the former" *(op. cit.*, p. lxxiv).

How could one possibly expect any greater vocabulary coincidence in two short epistles, written several years apart with different themes, occasions, and settings? This is argument from silence to a most precarious degree. Certainly two short epistles like these would not begin to tax an intelligent man's vocabulary. The very fact that one-sixth of the words are used in both epistles will certainly appeal to most persons as an argument for, rather than against, a common authorship.

He proceeds to a very scholarly examination of the grammar and style of the two epistles, an area in which their divergence has been a matter of note from earliest times, and on which we have already commented. Mayor's conclusion is moderate: "There is not the chasm between them which some would try to make out" *(op. cit.*, p. civ). Again, "The difference of style is less marked than the difference in vocabulary, and that again less marked than the difference in matter, while above all stands the great difference in thought, feeling, and character, in one word of personality." It should be interjected that differences in subject matter, thought, and feeling do not necessarily reflect a different personality. The same personality, for differing purposes, can write with vastly differing mood and matter.

Mayor, then, seems to place crucial weight upon his judgment as to the difference in feeling between the two epistles—a very precarious sort of thing, since a man's feeling may vary greatly from one occasion to another for any number of reasons. Beginning at page lxxvi of his Introduction, he deals with the matter of reminiscences from the life of Christ which are to be observed in I and II Peter. He observes that II Peter shows fewer of these and that they are "of a far less intimate nature than those in (I) Peter" *(op. cit.*, p. lxxvii). He then proceeds to a discussion in general of the tender spirit of I Peter, contrasting II Peter, which he says "lacks that intense sympathy, that flame of love, which marks I Peter."

Mayor carries this same type of criticism into the references of the two epistles to the Second Coming and to Noah's flood. But is not all this to be expected fully in view of the different purposes of the two epistles? I Peter comforts those who are in suffering; II Peter warns the believers of spiritual perils and exhorts them to holiness. Naturally the tone of the former is tender; of the latter, driving. The amazing thing is that with such differing objectives the appeal is made to the same basic facts—the centrality of Christ and the certainty of his second coming. In this great coming event the suffering believer receives hope, and the potential backslider, warning.

As to the mention of Noah's flood in I Peter (3:20) with emphasis on God's mercy and in II Peter (2:5; 3:6) with emphasis on God's judgment (although II Peter 2:5 also says that God "saved Noah"), this too fits admirably the different purposes just mentioned. And the fact that the same illustration is appealed to in its different facets tends to confirm the identity of authorship of the two epistles rather than the contrary.

Mayor is very fair in setting forth the whole picture. He proceeds to note, without any discounting observations, the agreement of I and II Peter regarding the spoken and written prophetic word, observing that in this they agree closely with the words of Peter in Acts 3:18-21 and of Paul in Acts 26:22,23. He also pays attention to the close correspondence of I and II Peter in their idea of Christian growth (I Peter 2:2; II Peter 3:18). One leaves Mayor's discussion of the authorship of I and II Peter with the feeling that this scholar has corroborated rather than weakened the claim of II Peter to its apostolic authorship.

Why, then, does Mayor reject this claim? One cannot escape the feeling that his position is dictated in large measure by the critical consensus of New Testament scholars and especially by the conclusion of Dr. F. H. Chase, whom he knew personally and quotes frequently, and whose articles on Peter and Jude in HDB he terms "by far the best introduction known to me on the two epistles here dealt with" *(op. cit.*, p. vii).

Suffice it to say that in these considerations there seem to be no compelling reasons for refusing to accept the claims of II Peter to the authorship of the apostle whose name it bears.

The Time and Place of the Writing. The epistle was very possibly written to the Christians in Asia Minor (3:1) when the memory of I Peter was still rather fresh in their minds. If we judge that I Peter was written from Rome about A.D. 64, it seems reasonable to regard II Peter as written from Rome toward the end of Nero's reign, say A.D. 67.

The Message of the Epistle. The specific burden of Peter's heart at this time appears to have been the growth of a spirit of lawlessness and antinomianism in the churches, and also an attitude of skepticism toward Christ's second coming. Some feel that the false teachers described in the epistle were representatives of the Gnostic heresy in its early stages.

But while greatly concerned with the menace of these false teachers, and speaking with some emphasis to this point, the apostle realized that the basic need of his readers was for spiritual upbuilding and strength which would make them superior to such dangers. He, therefore, both opens and closes his letter with encouragement to spiritual conquest, inserting his warnings against the false teachers in the middle chapter of the three.

OUTLINE

Theme: The imperative of spiritual conquest.
Key verse: II Peter 3:18.

I. Peter's readers urged to go forward in grace. 1:1-21.
- A. Salutation and prayer for their spiritual advancement. 1:1,2.
- B. Reminder of the present reality of their spiritual inheritance. 1:3,4.
- C. Challenge to press into its full implications. 1:5-11.
- D. Peter's feeling of responsibility thus to challenge them. 1:12-21.
  1. Because of their need of intensified motivation. 1:12.
  2. Because of the imminence of his departure. 1:13-15.
  3. Because of the complete authenticity of the Gospel. 1:16-21.

II. Peter's warning against the perils of false teachers. 2:1-22.
- A. The inevitability of false teachers. 2:1-3 a.
- B. The judgment of the false teachers. 2:3b-9.
- C. The characteristics of the false teachers. 2:10-22.
  1. Their fleshly self-indulgence and impudence. 2:10-12.
  2. Their perversion of Christian conviviality. 2:13.
  3. Their moral instability. 2:14.
  4. Their crassly selfish motivation. 2:15,16.
  5. Their spiritual barrenness and blight. 2:17-19.
  6. Their basic apostasy. 2:20-22.

III. Christ's second coming an imperative to spiritual conquest. 3:1-18.
- A. Christ's coming in glory previously intimated to the readers. 3:1,2.
- B. The Second Coming an object of skepticism. 3:3-9.
- C. The Second Coming to be catastrophic. 3:10.
- D. An incentive to holy living. 3:11-18 a.

IV. The apostolic benediction. 3:18 b.

COMMENTARY

I. Peter's Readers Urged To Go Forward in Grace 1:1-21.

A. Salutation and Prayer for Their Spiritual Advancement. 1:1,2.

1. Simon *(Symeon)* **Peter, a servant** *(slave)* **and an apostle of Jesus Christ.** This epistle clearly sets forth its authorship by the Apostle Peter. The title, *slave and apostle,* well illustrates Christ's rule: "He that is greatest among you shall be your servant" (Mt 23:11). **To them that have obtained like precious faith with us.** The expression **like precious** (in the original a single word meaning "equally precious") reminds us at once of the use in I Peter of the related words meaning "precious," "in honor," "preciousness or honor"—just one indication of the continuity between the two epistles. Harnack, though denying the Petrine authorship of both I and II Peter, held that the person who wrote II Peter had also authored the opening and closing parts of I Peter. The apostle here assigns great value to faith, and why not? It is the "coin of the realm" in God's kingdom. The writer finds the basis for faith, and its attainment by men in, **the righteousness of God and our Saviour Jesus Christ.** This, of course, is the foundation of the entire ethical universe. It is not a theoretical and juridical righteousness only, but a warm, loving, providential righteousness embracing God's entire redemptive plan. It is only "in the righteousness of God" that faith is possible. And again, it is through this faith, increasingly exercised, that God's righteousness is revealed (Rom 1:17).

2. Grace and peace be multiplied. The same greeting as used in I Peter, a characteristically Christian greeting (see commentary on I Pet 1:2). **Through the knowledge of God, and of Jesus our Lord.** The use here of the Greek word *epignōsis* ("precise and correct knowledge"—Thayer) is of interest. This epistle contains strong warnings against false teachers. Some conclude these to have been Gnostics, and use this as an argument for assigning to II Peter a postapostolic date, say, during the second century, when the Gnostic controversy was at its height. Others, like Bigg, fail to see in the epistle the sure marks of anti-Gnostic apologetic. Perhaps there is a reasonable middle ground. Certainly Gnosticism was a real issue in apostolic times and in Asia Minor, as is witnessed by Paul's Colossian letter, addressed largely to this incipient heresy. A key word in Colossians is the Greek *epignōsis,* "precise and correct knowledge," generally connected with God or Christ (Col 1:9,10; 2:2; 3:10). The Gnostics held to a highly intricate and extra-Scriptural system of doctrine, giving a great deal of attention to angels and to ascetic practices, tending to detract from the godhead of Christ, and withal assuming superior wisdom for their initiates. The Colossian letter from its beginning exalts Christ, the center of "all wisdom and knowledge," fully identified with God. This apologetic was doubtless shared by the other apostles, and may well be reflected here (as in II Pet 1:3,8; 2:20).

B. Reminder of the Present Reality of Their Spiritual Inheritance. 1:3,4.

3. As his divine power hath given unto us all things. Just as Peter opens his first letter, the aim of which was to encourage the Christians in their sufferings, by reminding them of their great spiritual wealth, their stake in remaining true, so he also opens the present epistle, aimed to brace them against plausible false doctrine. Those who are spiritually wealthy have much to lose by revolution and defection. **Through the knowledge of him.** To know Christ is life itself to a Christian (cf. Jn 17:3). **That hath called us.** Again, as in I Peter (e.g., 1:2), the apostle reminds his readers that they are a chosen people. **To glory and virtue** (generally signifying excellence). The original here seems to call for the meaning *by his own glory and virtue*. Either translation is possible and meaningful. It is by Christ's glory and excellence that we are drawn, and again these are the end product of the Christian life.

4. Whereby *(through which,* i.e., through the glory and virtue). The glory and excellence of Christ, reproduced in the characters of the saints, and thus rendered up as an offering to him whose they are, constitute the all-inclusive goal of Christian living. Ours is a goal of character: "We shall be like him" (I Jn 3:2). And in this goal are included all worthwhile things (cf. Mt 6:33). **Are given.** Not the usual word for "give," but a more rich and munificent word, "to endow," "to furnish with an estate." **Exceeding great and precious.** Literally, *the precious and greatest*. Again note the word "precious," so prominent in I Peter. **Promises.** Not the usual term indicating a quiet private agreement, but a heraldic word implying emphatic and public announcement—a very comfortable word for those concerned. **Partakers of the divine nature, having escaped the corruption that is in the world through lust.** On the basis of these publicly declared divine commitments, the believer becomes a sharer of that richest of all treasures, the nature and life of God. "If any man have not the Spirit of Christ, he is none of his" (Rom 8:9). This new life of the Spirit is none other than "Christ in you." It requires a yielding, an obedience, a walk (Gal 5:25). This new life removes us from the living death of bondage to carnal desire (Rom 8:11-13).

C. Challenge to Press into the Full Implications of Their Inheritance. 1:5-11.

5-7. And beside this . . . add. Peter urges these young believers to move on from step to step in divine grace. He tells them to bring to bear on their walk in grace all eagerness. **Add to your faith virtue.** "In your faith provide an ample supply of basic (Christian) excellence." This excellence is the quality of one who diligently practices the basic rudiments and implications of his calling. To virtue, the Christians are urged to add **knowledge.** Here is growth in awareness through study and experience. Next comes **temperance** (self-control). This is the Spirit-aided discipline of the Christian soldier. Then **patience,** the quality of a veteran's ability to see beyond current pressures in view of known resources. In patience the Christian adds **godliness** (Gr., *eusebeia),* a spirit of reverence and deference to God in all matters. In reverence he adds **brotherly kindness** (Gr., *philadelphia).* Deference to God and enduement with his love is the only basis for genuinely altruistic kindness to fellow men. In brotherly kindness, **charity** (Gr., *agapē,* "divine love," as in I Cor 13) is the Christian's quest. It would be amiss to picture these beautiful graces as compartmentalized and attainable only in their order. No, their presentation here seems to observe an order from the more elemental to the more advanced, but they are all of them facets of the Spirit's work in the life of a believer, aspects of the glory of the indwelling Christ, his character shown in the Christian's character.

8,9. If these things be in you, and abound. The word translated *be in* means "to be under one as a foundation or basis." This is implied in regeneration, in the Spirit's presence in the heart. But the matter of "abounding" implies Christian growth and the Spirit's fullness or full control as experienced by believers at Pentecost and since. **Neither . . . barren** (unworking) **nor unfruitful.** The fruit of the Spirit, if we rightly apprehend, is the character of Christ realized in the Christian. In the description of this fruit in Gal 5:22,23, divine love *(agapē)* is mentioned first; and the other graces, seven in number, are subsumed under it. These are closely related in their spirit and tenor to Peter's list above. In Col 3:14 Paul mentions divine love last as the comprehensive summation of the graces, somewhat as does Peter. The Father is glorified as the believer bears much fruit (Jn 15:8). **In the knowledge of our Lord.** Better, *Unto the precise and correct knowledge of our Lord.* This is a statement of the direction in which Christian conquest bears. The alternative is then mentioned. It is blindness and spiritual myopia, and a weakened sense of spiritual reality and life.

10. Give diligence *(make it your business)* **to make your calling and election sure** *(firm).* Here is personal responsibility with reference to God's call and choice of them. **If ye do** *(keep on doing)* **. . . ye shall never fall** *(stumble).* Obedience is not optional in any consideration of Christian safety. **11. An entrance shall be ministered unto you abundantly** *(richly).* Here is an intimation that heaven's society will not be classless. Good stewardship of Christ's riches will bear eternal proceeds. The Christian, endowed with wealth through Christ's provision, invests and saves for future wealth (cf. I Tim 6:19).

D. Peter's Feeling of Responsibility Thus To Challenge Them. 1:12-21.

12. I will not be negligent to put you always in remembrance . . . though ye know . . . and be established. The sense in the Greek is, "I will be intending to remind you always." Even where knowledge and establishment exist, there is need for motivation and exhortation. **13-15. As long as I am in this taber-**

nacle. Christ, in his postresurrection commissioning of Peter, had intimated that the apostle would die a martyr's death (Jn 21:18). This is probably that to which Peter refers in verse 14. A sense of the brevity of his tenure adds weight to his feeling of responsibility for his readers. **After my decease.** Peter's epistles would serve to extend his care and admonition for his brethren.

16-18. We have not followed cunningly devised fables . . . but were eyewitnesses. The authenticity of the apostolic witness urges this reinforcement of it. Peter here speaks of a previous ministry to these people. This may be a reference to his sermon on Pentecost, when some of them had been present, or it may refer to labors among them in Asia Minor. **This is my beloved Son.** This reference to the Transfiguration scene may well have implied a rebuke to the false teachers who, if Colossians describes a parallel situation, were inclined toward the adoration of angels, thus reducing the pre-eminence of Christ. Since only Peter, James, and John were present with Christ on the mount, this also constitutes a reinforcement of the epistle's claim to Petrine authorship.

19-21. We have also a more sure word of prophecy. Taken with what is said in verse 21, the reference of these verses seems to be to the OT Scriptures. It is an amazing assessment of the validity of holy Scripture that Peter declares it to be more dependable than a voice from heaven heard with the natural ear. By implication, here is a rebuke for those teachers who went far beyond Scripture, constructing **cunningly devised** mystical theories. **Holy men of God spake as they were moved by the Holy Ghost,** or *spake from God, being borne along by the Holy Spirit.* This passage strongly recalls the comment on prophetic inspiration recorded in I Pet 1:10-12, another link between the two epistles.

II. Peter's Warning Against the Perils of False Teachers. 2:1-22.

A. The Inevitability of False Teachers. 2:1-3 a.

1-3 a. There shall be false teachers among you. Having just mentioned the prophets who spoke for God, Peter refers to the fact that these faced the opposition of false prophets. He warns the believers (somewhat after the manner of Acts 20:29,30; I Tim 4:1-6; II Tim 3:1-5—though the error here seems to have been in the area of life rather than of doctrine — I Jn 2:18-20; and Jude 3ff.) against false teachers who were perhaps even then known by the apostle to be at work in certain areas of the church. These would deny **the Lord that bought them;** they would gain a following and cast a shadow on **the way of truth.** Their purpose would be mercenary; they would be motivated **through covetousness.**

B. The Judgment of the False Teachers. 2:3 b-9.

3 b. Whose judgment . . . lingereth not. Here seems to be an intimation that these hardened and deliberate heretics had passed the probationary season of possible repentance. Their doom was now inexorable.

4. If God spared not the angels that sinned. Peter, at the very outset of his consideration of the false teachers, sets up a picture of the God of judgment. This is both encouragement to the faithful and warning to any inclined toward apostasy (cf. vv. 7-9 below). **Chains of darkness.** The reading *pits of darkness* (Gr., *sirois* or *seirois* instead of *seirais*) seems preferable. Although Peter seems here to refer to the apocryphal Book of Enoch, with its elaborate discussion of the sin of the fallen angels, their reservation unto judgment, and finally their judgment (this verse seems to reflect Enoch 21), yet there is an absence of that rather wild and questionable theorizing and intrusion of non-spiritual concept which is evident even to the casual reader of Enoch. **5. And spared not the old world, but saved Noah.** Another reference to the severity, as well as to the goodness, of God. **6-8. Turning the cities of Sodom and Gomorrha into ashes . . . delivered just Lot.** Still another illustration of God's judgeship of his creation. This reference to Lot's unhappiness with the developments connected with his choice of Sodom as a residence, because of his basic loyalty to God, whether considered as reflecting ancient tradition or as revelatory, is an interesting supplement to the OT picture of that patriarch.

9. The Lord knoweth how to deliver . . . and to reserve . . . to be punished. While in the supporting instances, Peter shows more interest in God's condemnation of wickedness than in his vindication of righteousness (this because of his preoccupation with the false teachers), in this final recapitulation he adduces first God's mercy to his own, a comfort to the readers. The epistle of Jude parallels very closely the present discussion of false teachers and their punishment. Peter speaks of their activities as being shortly at hand ("there shall be false teachers," 2:1); Jude treats these as present ("there are certain men crept in unawares," Jude 4).

C. The Characteristics of the False Teachers. 2:10-22.

10-12. Them that walk after the flesh . . . and despise government. The picture is one of fleshly self-indulgence and carnal impudence. **Not afraid to speak evil of dignities. . . . Whereas angels . . . bring not railing accusation.** Peter warns against rash and self-confident speech, even as pertaining to evil powers. His reference to the angels is parallel to that of Jude 9, which seems to reflect a contest between Michael and the devil, related in the Assumption of Moses, an apocryphal writing known among the Jews. Peter's reference is discreet, causing some critical scholars to think that II Peter followed here the more specific reference in Jude. Bigg holds the contrary, feeling that Peter's statement was sufficient for his purpose, and that Jude's came a little later and particularized upon it. **Speak evil of the things that they understand not.** Their self-assurance was matched by their ignorance. This recalls the reference in Col 2:18. The characteristic of modern 'liberal' critical teachers which amazes one most is their absolute confidence in their own conclusions, based upon evidence however trivial, and involving tremendously important departures from tenets maintained for centuries by the historic church.

13. Sporting themselves with their own deceivings. Peter speaks of an abuse of Christian conviviality. Always eager for a good dinner, they make of such occasions an opportunity for raucous mirth and continued false teaching. Jude's reference to eating together by Christians as "feasts of charity" (lit., "your loves" or "occasions of love," Jude 12) sets a far different standard.

14-16. Having eyes full of adultery. Here is a picture of moral instability which finds too great a substantiation in the church today. **A heart exercised in covetousness** (ASV) **. . . following the way of Balaam.** It is well known that eagerness for financial remuneration and desire for the large and popular churches have caused many a modern prophet to **forsake the right way** and **to follow the way of Balaam.** And even in evangelical circles, an inordinate concern over financial return, or carelessness in the use of funds, has negated the work of some princes of the pulpit whose words were irresistibly powerful. **The dumb ass . . . forbad the madness.** In the light of eternal outcomes, the sad folly of such a perversion of purpose invites the scorn of even the most simple. Recall that the donkey was permitted to see that which evaded the myopic vision of Balaam "the seer" (Num 22:25).

17-19. Wells without water. The basic condemnation of false doctrine is its utter spiritual barrenness. It is this feature of the movement known as 'religious liberalism' that has caused great numbers of spiritually hungry people to desert coldly formal churches. It has also finally given rise to defection from 'liberalism,' even by intellectuals and scholars. This defection, known as "neo-orthodoxy," is a reactionary movement which, sadly enough, is still unwilling to own the full authority of Scripture. **Promise them liberty . . . servants *(slaves)* of corruption.** Theologians of a half century ago were drinking deep of the heady wine of freedom from the authority of Scripture and even of God. Said Prof. Walter Rauschenbusch, "The worst thing that could happen to God would be to remain an autocrat while the world is moving toward democracy. He would be dethroned with the rest" *(Theology of the Social Gospel,* p. 178). Said Prof. Hugh Hartshorne, "We no longer derive our ethical standards from established authorities, whether of church, state, family, convention, or philosophical system" *(Jour. of Ed. Soc.,* Dec., 1930, p. 202). Today the nation faces a tremendous harvest of increased crime and delinquency. The false teachers described by Peter were themselves examples of spiritual bondage (cf. Jn 8:34).

20-22. Better for them not to have known. This is a solemn assessment of the awful responsibility of apostasy, and it constitutes an implicit warning to the believers to remain steadfast.

III. Christ's Second Coming, an Imperative to Spiritual Conquest. 3:1-18.

A. Christ's Coming in Glory Previously Intimated to the Readers. 3:1,2.

1. This second epistle. Most naturally

taken as a reference to I Peter. **I stir up your pure minds.** Literally, *by a reminder I wake up your pure minds.* The word **pure** (Gr., *eilicrinēs),* while of disputed derivation, probably means "sun-judged," as a vase which, when held up to the sun, reveals no hidden flaws. As such flaws were often concealed by skillful patching with wax, the word is elsewhere (Phil 1:10) translated by the AV "sincere" (Lat., *sine cera,* "without wax"). Some take the word to refer, instead, to a sifting, as of grain.

2. The holy prophets . . . us the apostles. Peter claims a continuity and congruity with the witness of the OT Scriptures, the principal authentication for genuine Christian preaching in the apostolic age, and also with the witness of his fellow apostles. This incidental and unaffected claim to apostleship—as though the writer realized that it was well known to all his readers—is a strong corroboration of the Petrine authorship of this letter. The Second Coming was a subject greatly relished by the apostle. It underlies the exhortation and encouragement of his first letter (e.g., I Pet 1:5,7,10-13; 4:7,13; 5:1,4). He knew that his readers were familiar with this truth.

B. The Second Coming an Object of Skepticism. 3:3-9.

3,4. There shall come . . . scoffers . . . Where is the promise of his coming? It may be questioned whether this is a further reference to the false teachers of chapter 2, or simply a statement that the delay in Christ's return would cause many to abandon and even to scorn the Church's glorious hope.

5,6. Willingly . . . ignorant. Literally, *this escapes the notice of them willing.* A case of judicial blindness. They did not want the thing to be true. **By the word of God.** Peter goes back to the dependability and stability of God's word as demonstrated in creation. Literally, *it consisted in* (or *by) the word of God.* **Whereby** (Gr., *through which things,* i.e., through the word of God and the flood water) **the world that then was . . . perished.** God's judging word, like his creative word, was final. **7. The heavens and the earth, which are now, by the same word are kept in store.** God's promise of fiery judgment upon sinners and upon the world is to be received respectfully. The apocryphal writings prior to the Christian era went into considerable detail about these matters. Our Lord, while on earth, spoke of a fiery destiny for the sinner (e.g., Lk 16:24).

8,9. One day . . . with the Lord. Peter now comes to the point at which he is aiming, namely, that the delay in Christ's return, cited by the skeptics, is no proper basis for doubt as to His coming. This has already been hinted at in his reference to the Noahic flood. It, too, was a long time coming, and its plausibility was quite belittled by the people of those days; but it came, exactly as God had said it would. This is Peter's third reference to Noah (I Pet 3:20; II Pet 2:5), another nice index of the unity of I and II Peter. Peter's comment on the equivalence between one day and a thousand years with God is a beautiful statement of God's eternity, his superiority to time-space limitations (cf. Ps 90:4). And it is exciting to think how such a concept contracts the period of waiting for his return. We accomplish quickly enough our years of this pilgrimage. But then, once "with the Lord" and freed from time-space limitations, it is but a day or two—figured even from apostolic times—until his kingdom comes with all its joys. **That all should come to repentance.** God's waiting is redemptive in its purpose; his basic will is that all might turn from their sin unto him.

C. The Second Coming To Be Catastrophic. 3:10.

10. The day of the Lord will come as a thief. Despite all apparent delay, God's word will again be demonstrated as valid. That day will come. The sudden, never-expected visit of the night burglar was a favorite simile with Christ, taken up by the apostles. **The elements shall melt . . . the earth . . . be burned up.** Here may be another allusion to the Book of Enoch, with its description of the "mountains of the seven metals" and their destruction. There seems to have been a general expectancy among the religious Jews that there would be an ultimate fiery cleansing of the earth. This, of course, looks beyond the reference of Scripture to the Millennium.

D. An Incentive to Holy Living. 3:11-18 a.

11,12. What manner of persons ought ye to be . . . ? Just as in his first epistle (1:14-16), Peter here uses the theme of the Christian's apocalyptic hope as a powerful incentive to holiness. **Looking for and hasting unto the coming of the day of God.** What a picture of "loving his appearing"! (cf. II Tim 4:8) Not like those who dread that awful day, those who, when overtaken, will call for rocks and mountains to hide them from it (Rev 6:15-17), the Christian eagerly awaits it. The words **hasting unto the coming of the day of God** are capable also of the translation *hastening the coming.* . . . Those who help forward God's redemptive work can reasonably feel a partnership in its denouement.

13. We . . . look for new heavens and a new earth, wherein dwelleth righteousness. This had been a theme of the prophets (e.g., Isa 2:4; 11:6-9; Mic 4:1-5); it was **according to his promise.** It was a hope and vision shared by Abraham and the patriarchs (Heb 11:10). It is that which makes Christians of all ages "pilgrims and strangers." Compare Paul's mention of this in Rom 8:19-25. Like Lot in Sodom, the Christian cannot but groan at the prevalence of sin and its results. The name assigned to Jehovah by millennial Israel was Jehovah-Tsidkenu, "The Lord our Righteousness."

14. Wherefore . . . seeing . . . ye look for such things. A repeated urging of the Christian's hope as a motive for careful and holy living. **Be diligent** can be read, *make it your business.* **Peace** and holiness are associated in Heb 12:14. **15. Account that the longsuffering of our Lord is salvation.** Peter urges upon his readers the reasonableness of God's delays, a theme mentioned before, in verse 9. God waits that he may be gracious.

As our beloved brother Paul . . . hath written. Peter knew the Pauline letters, although they were very nearly contemporary with his own. There seems no reason for interpreting this statement as indicating that the NT canon was becoming formalized when this was written. The phrase **our beloved brother** seems to refer naturally to a contemporary. **16. Which they that are unlearned and unstable wrest, as they do also the other scriptures.** Peter refers to those who quibbled about the authority of the Pauline writings as being spiritually illiterate and undependable. The apostle assigns to the letters of this man who was his contemporary and who at times had been critical of him a place among the *other* sacred writings. Compare Paul's own claim that his injunctions *when first written* were the commandments of God (I Cor 14:37; I Tim 6:3).

17. Beware lest ye . . . fall from your own stedfastness. A repeated and final admonition to faithfulness. Their advance knowledge gave them an advantage. Forewarned is forearmed (cf. I Thess 5:4). But there was real danger of their being involved in **the error of lawless men. 18 a. But grow in grace.** Life is never static. One must go forward or he will go backward. Peter closes upon the same note with which he began this epistle (1:5-11), that is, with a challenge to spiritual conquest through **the knowledge of our Lord and Saviour Jesus Christ.** To know him is to live; to grow in that acquaintance is to grow in the Spirit (cf. Phil 3:10).

IV. The Apostolic Benediction. 3:18 b.

18 b. To him be glory both now and for ever. To Christ, the beginning, the process, and the fulfillment of our great salvation, is ascribed eternal praise.

BIBLIOGRAPHY

For bibliography see under I Peter.

THE FIRST EPISTLE OF JOHN

INTRODUCTION

(to I, II, III John)

The Life of John. The apostle's life divides itself into two periods. The first concludes with his departure from Jerusalem some time after the ascension of Christ, and the second continues from that time to his death. John was evidently much younger than Jesus. He may have been born in Bethsaida (Jn 1:44). The son of Zebedee and Salome, he apparently came from a fairly well-to-do family; for they had servants (Mk 1:20), his mother helped with the financial support of Christ (Mk 15:40,41), and John knew the high priest, who was chosen from the upper classes (Jn 18:15). His younger brother was James. Though John probably did not attend the rabbinical schools (Acts 4:13), his religious training in his Jewish home would have been thorough.

Galileans were industrious and hardy men of action and John was no exception. Though artists have pictured him as an effeminate person, the Bible describes him quite differently. He was known as one of the "sons of thunder" (Mk 3:17), who on occasion acted in bigotry (Mk 9:38; Lk 9:49), vindictiveness (Lk 9:54), and scheming (Mt 20:20,21; cf. Mk 10:35). It was the power of Christ that changed this typical Galilean into "the apostle of love."

How long John remained in Jerusalem after Pentecost is uncertain. He was evidently not there when Paul first visited the city (Gal 1:18,19), although he may have been there later as one of the members of the council (Acts 15:6). The evidence that he spent the latter part of his life in Asia Minor, and chiefly at Ephesus, is too strong to be shaken by other conjectures. Justin Martyr (*Dialogue with Trypho,* LXXXI), Irenaeus (Eusebius *Ecclesiastical History* V. xx. 4,5), Polycrates (*Ibid.* V. xxiv. 3), and the strong inference of The Apocalypse that it was written by a church leader in Asia Minor all attest to this fact. Extra-Biblical literature is replete with accounts of John's activities during this period, the most famous stories being about Cerinthus in the bath and a young lad (one of the apostle's converts) who became a bandit and was later restored to the church (cf. A. Plummer, *The Gospel According to S. John, Cambridge Greek Testament,* pp. xvii,xviii).

John is best known as "the apostle of love," but he was also a stern man who even in his later years was intolerant of heresy. Both these aspects of his character, sternness and love, are prominently displayed in the First Epistle. *Intense* is the single word that best describes the man. In actions, in love for the brethren, in condemnation of heresy, John was the intense apostle.

The City of Ephesus. Ephesus, John's home during his later life, is situated in a fertile plain near the mouth of the Cayster River. In Paul's day it was a center of trade, both of the eastern Aegean region and of that which passed through Ephesus from the East. Since the city was the capital of the province of Asia Minor, the Roman proconsul resided there. Democratic assemblies were allowed the people of Ephesus (Acts 19:39). Christianity came to the city about 55 through the ministry of Paul, and he wrote a circular letter to Ephesus and other churches about eight years later. Before John went to the city, many had labored there for the cause of Christ (Aquila and Priscilla, Acts 18:19; Paul, Acts 19:3-10; Trophimus, Acts 21:29; the family of Onesiphorus, II Tim 1:16-18; 4:19; and Timothy, I Tim 1:3).

Morality in Ephesus was low. The magnificent temple of Diana, with its 127 columns 60 feet high surrounding an area 425 by 220 feet, was like a magnet drawing people to the Ephesian cesspool. It was a house of prostitution in the name of religion. And yet in spite of the iniquitous idolatry of that place, it was a Mecca or Rome of religious worship, and the people delighted to call themselves "temple-keepers" of the great Diana (Acts 19:35).

Gnosticism. Gnosticism, a philosophy of existence or being, in its early form was making inroads into the Asia Minor church of John's day. It involved speculations concerning the origin of matter and how human beings can be free from matter. The name is Greek, but its main elements were Greek and Oriental; Jewish and Christian features were added to the mixture. In particular, Gnosticism held that knowledge is superior to virtue, that the nonliteral sense of Scripture is the true meaning and can be understood only by a select few, that evil in the world precludes God's being the creator, that the Incarnation is incredible because deity cannot unite itself with anything material—such as a body, and that there is no resurrection of the flesh. This teaching resulted in Docetism, asceticism, and antinomianism. Extreme Docetism held that Jesus was not human at all but was merely a prolonged theophany, while moderate Docetism considered Jesus the natural son of Joseph and Mary, upon whom Christ came at the time of baptism. Both forms of heresy are attacked by John in the First Epistle (2:22; 4:2,3; 5:5,6). Some Gnostics practiced asceticism because they believed all matter to be evil. Antinomianism, or lawlessness, was the conduct of others, since they held knowledge to be superior to virtue (cf. 1:8; 4:20). John's principal answer to these Gnostic errors is to emphasize the Incarnation and the ethical power of the example of the life of Christ.

The Authorship of the Epistles. The question raised concerning the authorship of First John is whether the John who wrote both the Gospel and the Epistle was really John the son of Zebedee or John the elder. Literature mentions a presbyter John in Ephesus, and some have been led to conclude that John the son of Zebedee was a different person from the John of Ephesus, and that it was the latter who wrote these books (Irenaeus in Eusebius, *op. cit.*, V. viii and xx; Papias in *Ibid.*, III, xxxix; Polycrates in *Ibid.*, V. xxiv; The Canon of Muratori).

The standard argument for the Johannine authorship of the Gospel is based on internal evidence. This argument is in the nature of three concentric circles. (1) The largest circle proves that the author was a Palestinian Jew. This is demonstrated by his use of the Old Testament (cf. Jn 6:45; 13:18; 19:37), and by his knowledge of Jewish ideas, traditions, expectations (cf. Jn 1:19-49; 2:6, 13; 3:25; 4:25; 5:1; 6:14,15; 7:26 ff.; 10:22; 11:55; 12:13; 13:1; 18:28; 19:31, 42), and by his knowledge of Palestine (Jn 1:44,46; 2:1; 4:47; 5:2; 9:7; 10:23; 11:54). (2) The middle circle proves that the author was an eyewitness. This is indicated by the exactness of the details of time, place, and incidents given in the Gospel (cf. Jn 1:29,35,43; 2:6; 4:40,43; 5:5; 12:1,6,12; 13:26; 19:14,20,23,34,39; 20:7; 21:6), and by the character sketches (e.g., Andrew, Philip, Thomas, Nathanael, the woman of Samaria, Nicodemus) which are peculiar to this Gospel. (3) The third circle concludes that the author was John. The method followed is first to eliminate all others who belonged to the inner circle of disciples and then to cite confirmatory evidence to show that only John could have been the author.

The arguments for the common authorship of the Gospel and the Epistle are conclusive. This evidence is built on the parallel passages (e.g., Jn 1:1 and I Jn 1:1), common phrases (e.g., "only begotten," "born of God"), common constructions (use of conjunctions instead of subordinate clauses), and common themes (*agapē*, "love"; *phōs*, "light"; *zōē*, "life"; *menō*, "abide"). Thus the basic question remains: Was the author of both writings John the apostle or John the elder?

Some of the reasons for distinguishing John the apostle from John the elder and thus favoring the authorship of these books by the latter are: (1) an unlettered man (Acts 4:13) could not have written anything so profound as the Fourth Gospel; (2) a fisherman's son would not likely have known the high priest; (3) an apostle would not have called himself an elder, as the writer of the Epistle does; (4) since the writer of the Gospel used Mark as a source, that writer could not have been John, since an apostle would not have used the work of one who was not an apostle. To these arguments the answers which support the case for authorship by John the apostle are not difficult to find. (1) *Unlettered* stands for lack of formal training in the rabbinic schools and does not mean "unlearned"; (2) it must not be assumed that all fishermen were from the lower classes; (3) the Apostle Peter called himself an elder (I Pet 5:1), so why should not John have used the same title? (4) Matthew, an apostle, used Mark as a source, according to the critics, but that is not ordinarily used as an argument against Matthean authorship of the First Gospel. Furthermore, if John the elder is the author of the Fourth Gospel and the same as the beloved disciple, it becomes very difficult to explain why such an important person as John the son of Zebedee is never mentioned in that Gospel. The evidence clearly points to one writer of Gospel and Epistles, John the apostle, the son of Zebedee, who *is* one and the same as John the elder who spent his later years in Ephesus.

Dates and Place of Writing. The dates for the writing of the Epistles are related to the date assigned to the writing of the Gospel. Those who assign a date between 110 and 165 for the Gospel and assume that John was not the author find themselves facing a dilemma. If the Gospel was published that late, allegedly but not actually by John, why did not the hundreds of living Christians who had known John during his later years denounce it as a forgery? Or at least, why did not someone mention that it did not come from John himself? If it was not published until some time between 140 and 165, how could it have been universally accepted by 170, as it was? The fact that the Rylands fragment of John found in Egypt dates from A.D. 140 or earlier requires that the date of the composition of the book be set near the turn of the century or earlier. It is evident in the Gospel that the author is looking back (Jn 7:39; 21:19), which means that since John was the author, the Gospel must have been published between 85 and 90 (although the actual writing may have been done before that time). It was undoubtedly produced at the insistence of the elders of the churches of Asia Minor, who wanted those things which John had been teaching them orally to be put in writing before he died. Since the message of I John seems to presuppose a knowledge of the contents of the Gospel, and since there is no mention of the persecution under Domitian in 95, the First Epistle was probably written about A.D. 90. Second and Third John may also be dated about the same time as the First Letter, i.e., about 90. All the Epistles were written from Ephesus, according to reliable tradition.

OUTLINE

Introduction. 1:1-4.
- A. The Person. 1:1,2.
- B. The purpose. 1:3,4.

I. Fellowship's conditions. 1:5-10.
- A. Conformity to a standard. 1:5-7.
- B. Confession of sin. 1:8-10.
  1. Confession of the principle of sin. 1:8.
  2. Confession of particular sins. 1:9.
  3. Confession of personal sins. 1:10.

II. Fellowship's conduct. 2:1-29.
- A. The character of our conduct: imitation. 2:1-11.
  1. The principle of imitation. 2:1,2.
  2. The pattern for imitation. 2:3-6.
  3. The proof of our imitation. 2:7-11.
- B. The commandment for our conduct: separation. 2:12-17.
  1. The address of the commandment. 2:12-14.
  2. The appeal of the commandment. 2:15-17.
- C. The creed for our conduct: affirmation. 2:18-29.
  1. The necessity for a creed. 2:18-21.
  2. The nature of the creed. 2:22-29.

III. Fellowship's characteristics. 3:1-24.
- A. In relation to our prospect—purity. 3:1-3.
  1. The reasons for purity. 3:1-3a.
  2. The meaning of purity. 3:3b.
- B. In relation to our position—righteousness and love. 3:4-18.
  1. Righteousness. 3:4-9.
  2. Love. 3:10-18.
- C. In relation to our prayer—answers. 3:19-24.
  1. Dependent on confidence. 3:19-21.
  2. Dependent on obedience. 3:22-24.

IV. Fellowship's cautions. 4:1-21.
- A. A caution concerning lying spirits: false prophets. 4:1-6.
  - 1. The existence of lying spirits. 4:1.
  - 2. The examination of lying spirits. 4:2-6.
- B. A caution concerning a loving spirit: false profession. 4:7-21.
  - 1. The ground of love. 4:7-10.
  - 2. The glories of love. 4:11-21.

V. Fellowship's cause. 5:1-21.
- A. Faith in Christ proved by the conduct we exhibit. 5:1-5.
- B. Faith in Christ proved by the credentials we exhibit. 5:6-12.
  - 1. The evidence of the credentials. 5:6-8.
  - 2. The effect of the credentials. 5:9-12.
- C. Faith in Christ proved by the confidence we exhibit. 5:13-21.
  - 1. Confidence in prayer. 5:13-17.
  - 2. Confidence in knowledge. 5:18-21.

COMMENTARY

Introduction. 1:1-4.

Unlike most other NT epistles this one has no salutation at the beginning and no benediction at the conclusion. These four verses of introduction correspond to the opening eighteen verses of the Gospel and three verses of the Revelation. They tell us the writer's subject, namely, the Word, who is life.

A. The Person. 1:1,2. This is **that which** the apostle has to declare.

1. Was. Not "came into existence" but **was** in existence already *(ēn).* **From** [*the*] **beginning.** The absence of the article is idiomatic. Meaning is always determined by the context. In this instance the phrase means a beginning prior to creation, and the meaning is determined by **was with the Father** in verse 2. This is a sweeping claim for the eternity of Christ. **Which we have heard.** Perfect tense, indicating permanent result of a past action. **Seen with our eyes.** John would have us know that the seeing is no figure of speech but a literal fact. **Looked upon, and . . . handled.** The tense is changed to aorist and indicates a special manifestation of Christ. **Handled** is the same word used by Christ in one of his post-resurrection appearances (Lk 24:39). Evidently John is referring to that here. **Word of life. Word** is a name rather than merely the idea of revelation, and **life** indicates work rather than being a name for Christ (though in v. 2 it is practically a name).

2. The **life** which Christ **manifested** was **eternal life** because Christ was **with the Father.** The phrase shows the distinct personality of Christ, who is the life; and the preposition **with** shows the equality of Christ with the Father, as in Jn 1:2.

B. The Purpose. 1:3,4. This is *why* the apostle declares this message.

3. Seen and heard. The Incarnation is the basis for **fellowship. Unto you** (also). Who have not seen and heard. **Fellowship.** This is the purpose *(hina,* "in order that") of John's message and is the theme of the epistle. The word is chiefly used by Paul in the NT, except for this chapter. It is both divine — with God, and human — **with us.** It is proved by exhibiting joy (v. 4) and by generosity (Acts 2:45; Rom 15:26; II Cor 8:4; 9:13; I Tim 6:18). Fellowship is best pictured in the Lord's Supper (I Cor 10:16). **With the Father, and with his Son Jesus Christ.** "Thus two fundamental truths, which the philosophical heresies of the age were apt to obscure or deny, are here clearly laid down at the outset: (1) the distinctness of personality and equality of dignity between the Father and the Son; (2) the identity of the eternal Son of God with the historical person Jesus Christ" (Plummer, *op. cit.*, p. 20).

4. That your joy may be full. Better, *that our joy may be fulfilled.* Fellowship is the basis of joy. The readers' joy depended on it and so did the apostle's. (It is difficult to reach a positive decision, as to the reading, between *our joy* and **your joy.)**

I. Fellowship's Conditions. 1:5-10.

A. Conformity to a Standard. 1:5-7. This section directly contradicts the Gnostic doctrine that moral conduct is a matter of indifference to the enlightened one.

5. Of him. From Christ. **God is light.** No one tells us so much about God as John does. He is spirit (Jn 4:24); he is light (I Jn 1:5); and he is love (I Jn 4:8). These statements concern what God is, not what he does. Thus, light is his very nature. Holiness is the principal idea, and its use here at the beginning of the epistle lays the foundation for the Christian ethics of the letter.

6. If we say. Greek third class condition, but including the writer – a very delicate way to state the possibility. **Walk in darkness.** Out of the will of God, who is light. **Do not the truth.** Truth is not only what one says but what he does.

7. If we walk . . . as he is in the light. God is light; we walk in it. The requirement for fellowship is to let the light reveal right and wrong and then to respond to that light continually. The Christian never becomes light until his body is changed, but he must walk in response to light while here on earth. Two consequences follow – first, fellowship, then cleansing. **Fellowship one with another.** The reference is to our brethren and not to God, as in 3:11,23; 4:7,12; II Jn 5. **And.** The cleansing of Christians is a consequence of walking in the light; the clause is coordinate and indicates a second result of walking in the light. **Blood of Jesus Christ.** In both OT and NT blood stands for death–usually a violent one. **Cleanseth us.** Walking in the light shows up our sins and frailties; thus we need constant cleansing, and this is available on the basis of the death of Christ. The verb is in the present tense and it refers to the cleansing in sanctification. **From all sin. Sin** is singular, indicating the principle of sin, but the addition of **all** (or *every*) shows that it has many forms.

B. Confession of Sin. 1:8-10. The mention of cleansing from sin in verse 7 leads to the thought of this section.

1) Confession of the Principle of Sin. 1:8.

If we say. The second of three false professions in this chapter (cf. vv. 6, 10). **No sin.** The phrase **to have sin** is peculiar to John in the NT (cf. Jn 9:41; 15:22, 24; 19:11). It refers to the nature, principle, or root of sin, rather than to the act. The consequences of not confessing that we have sin are two: (1) **we deceive ourselves,** literally, *lead ourselves astray,* doing for ourselves what Satan endeavors to do for us; (2) **the truth is not in us;** we shut out the light and live in an atmosphere of self-made darkness.

2) Confession of Particular Sins. 1:9.

To admit the truth of verse 8 may not cost much, but to do what is required in verse 9 may. **Confess.** Literally, *say the same thing.* "Having the same medium of vision that God has" (Candlish, p. 49). But it is not mere outward agreement; rather, it includes forsaking, for that is God's attitude for us concerning sin. The confession is to God. **Faithful and just.** Better, *faithful and righteous.* God keeps his word and is just in all his actions, including the way he forgives sins, which is on the basis of the death of his Son. **Forgive . . . cleanse.** Forgiveness is absolution from sin's punishment, and cleansing is absolution from sin's pollution.

3) Confession of Personal Sins. 1:10.

One may admit the truths of verses 8 and 9 in the abstract but never admit being personally involved in sin. **If we say.** This is the third false profession. **Have not sinned** refers to the act of sin, not the state, as in 1:8. **Make him a liar.** Because everywhere God says man has sinned. **His word is not in us.** The word of God in both OT and NT.

Thus fellowship depends on responding to the standard of light and realizing our sinful state. The victorious Christian life is a life of no unconfessed sins; and genuine confession includes forsaking, and thus produces growth.

II. Fellowship's Conduct. 2:1-29.

The writer now deals with the conduct of the believer who walks in the light. There is no break in thought between the chapters.

A. The Character of Our Conduct: Imitation. 2:1-11.

1) The Principle of Imitation – "That ye sin not." 2:1,2. The assurance of forgiveness of sins (1:9) and the statements of its universality (1:8,10) might lead some to take a light view of sin. Therefore, John shows the standard of conduct and the nature of the remedy for sin in order that his readers might not sin.

1. Little children. A term of endearment, not an indication of age. **That ye**

sin not. The aorist tense cannot mean "that ye continue not in sin," but rather "that ye sin not at all." Though this can never be completely true until we see Him (3:2), it should be our aim always. **And if any man sin.** The aorist again shows that it is a particular act of sin. **We have.** John includes himself. **Advocate.** Literally, *one summoned alongside,* especially to serve as a helper – a patron. The word is used in the NT only by John (Jn 14:16,26; 15:26; 16:7; and here). The advocate pleads the cause of the believer against Satan, his accuser (Rev 12:10). He is **Jesus Christ the righteous. Righteous** indicates the particular characteristic of our Lord which gives effectiveness to his advocacy (cf. Heb 7:26). Because he is righteous he can plead with the righteous Father.

2. He. He *himself,* emphatic personal pronoun. **Propitiation.** This is the basis of his advocacy, and although the latter is for believers only, propitiation is for all men. Propitiation means satisfaction (used here and in 4:10 only). Christ himself is the satisfaction (note the present tense). "Christ is said to be the 'propitiation' and not simply the 'propitiator' (as He is called the 'Saviour' iv. 14), in order to emphasize the thought that He is Himself the propitiatory offering as well as the priest (comp. Rom. iii. 25). A propitiator might make use of means of propitiation, outside himself" (B. F. Westcott, *The Epistles of St. John,* p. 44). **For our sins. For** *(peri).* Concerning, not "in behalf of." **But also for the whole world.** There is no limitation on the satisfaction which Christ *is* concerning sin. **World.** *Kosmos* in this case, as in Jn 3:16, means the human race.

2) The Pattern for Imitation – "Even as he walked." 2:3-6.

a) The Word of Christ. 2:3-5. Imitation involves keeping his commandments.

3. Hereby, i.e., **if we keep his commandments. We do know.** We perceive. **That we know him.** Have come to a knowledge of him. **Keep his commandments.** Contrary to Gnosticism, which concerned itself with intellectual attainment, Christianity requires moral conduct. **4. Is a liar.** His whole character is false. Truth as an active principle is not in such a man and hence cannot regulate his whole life. **5.** This verse is the opposite of 2:4 as 2:4 is the opposite of 2:3. **Word.** Wider than **commandments,** covering all of God's revelation of his will. **Love of God.** Probably man's love for God (objective genitive) here as in 2:15; 4:12; 5:3. The opposite (God's love for man, subjective genitive) is seen in 4:9.

b) The Walk of Christ. 2:6.

6. He that saith. To declare oneself on Christ's side binds one morally to imitate him. **Abideth.** A favorite word with John, defined in 3:24 as habitual fellowship maintained by keeping his commandments. **Ought.** Is bound; an obligation represented as a debt (cf. Lk 17:10). **Even as.** *Kathōs,* not merely *hōs,* indicating that the imitation must be exact and in all things. The pattern of Christ as set forth in the NT is everywhere humiliation and self-sacrifice. This should be the focus of the Christian's imitation (cf. Mt 11:29; Jn 13:15; Rom 15:2; Phil 2:5 ff.; Heb 12:2; I Pet 2:21).

3) The Proof of Imitation–Love. 2:7-11.

The life of Christ was one of self-sacrificing love; therefore, the proof of imitating him is exhibited in love. Love is that which seeks the highest good in the one loved; and since the highest good is the will of God, love is doing the will of God.

7. Brethren. Better, *beloved.* First occurrence of the word in this epistle. **Commandment.** To walk as he walked (v. 6) and to love the brethren (vv. 9-11). These are essentially the same. **From the beginning.** This could mean the beginning of the race, or the beginning of the Law (Lev 19:18) or, best, the beginning of the Christian life. **8. Which thing is true.** The best translation seems to be, *A new commandment write I unto you, namely, that which is true.* **Is past.** Better, *is passing away* (present tense). Because the darkness is passing away and the true light is shining, John bids his readers walk as children of light. **The true light.** The revelation of God in Christ.

9. He that saith. This is the fifth time John points out a possible inconsistency between profession and conduct (1:6,8,10; 2:4; cf. 4:20). **Brother.** Fellow Christian, not fellow man (though sometimes in the NT "brother" means fellow man, as Mt 5:22; Lk 6:41). **Is in darkness.** This false profession involves existence in the exactly opposite state from that which is claimed. **10. He that loveth.** This is not mere profession, as in verse 9, but the actual truth. **There is none occasion of stumbling in him.** There is in him nothing likely to cause others to stumble. This follows the general NT meaning of *skandalon*, occasion of stumbling, for it is used of offense caused to others. "Want of love is the most prolific source of offences" (Westcott, p. 56). **11. Is in darkness, and walketh in darkness, and knoweth not.** Darkness is the home and sphere of activity and the blinding agent of the one who hates his brother.

B. The Commandment for Our Conduct: Separation. 2:12-17.

1) The Address of the Commandment. 2:12-14.

The ground of the appeal to separation which follows in 2:15-17 is found in the character and position of those addressed in these verses.

12. Little children. All of John's readers are being addressed, but with special emphasis in this word on the kinship they have one to the other because of the forgiveness of their sins. **For his name's sake.** By believing on the name of Christ (and thus the person for whom the name stands) they experienced forgiveness.

13. Fathers. The address is now made to the older ones in the congregation and those who were prominent by reason of their position. **Ye know** (ASV). You have come to know through abiding in the commandments of the Christian life. **Him that is from the beginning,** i.e., Christ (cf. Jn 1:1-14). **Young men.** The younger ones in the group. **Have overcome.** Perfect tense, expressing the abiding result of past action. Strength, which is characteristic of youth, is necessary for victory in spiritual battles. **The wicked one.** The form could be either masculine (the evil one, i.e., the devil) or neuter (evil). Since the address to the youth is personal, very likely the reference here is also to the personal devil. "The abruptness with which the idea of 'the evil one' is introduced shews that it was familiar" (Westcott, p. 60). **Little children.** The same group as addressed in 2:12, though the word here is *paidia* and the emphasis is on subordination rather than on relationship, as in *teknia* of verse 12. Age distinctions are not apparent in these words as they are in "fathers" and "young men"; hence the reference is to the entire group. **I write.** Literally, *I wrote,* changing to the aorist tense here and in verse 14 from the present tenses in 2:12,13 a. The change has been variously explained. It is probably to be accounted for by a change in John's viewpoint as he wrote. Through 13a he was looking at the letter as still incomplete, and from 13b he viewed it as finished, and so employed these epistolary aorists. **Known the Father.** The use of **Father** in the address to **little children** reinforces the idea of subordination. The term **Father** occurs more often in John's writings than in all three Synoptic Gospels added together.

14. Word of God. The reason the young men could overcome the devil was that the word of God abode in them. They did the will of God as revealed in his word.

2) The Appeal of the Commandment. 2:15-17.

a) The Nature of the Appeal. 2:15 a.

In the addresses of 2:12-14, John reminded his readers of their privileges as Christians. Their sins had been forgiven, they knew Him who is the truth, and they had experienced spiritual victory. In these verses he exhorts them to walk worthy of this high calling by not loving the world nor the things in it. Loving God is incompatible with loving the world.

15. Love not. The command is addressed to all (not to one particular class) and appears abruptly in the text. **The world** *(kosmos,* the opposite of *chaos).* The world is that organized system which acts as a rival to God. It is that "which finds its proper sphere and fulfillment in a finite order and without God" (Westcott, p. 63). Though God loves the world of men (Jn 3:16), we must not love that which organizes them against God. A truly religious man keeps himself from the world (Jas 1:27), since friendship with it is enmity with God (Jas 4:4). The world lies in the lap of the wicked one (I Jn 5:19), and John uses the world as a synonym for darkness (Jn 3:19). The command is not, "Love not too much," but "Love not at all." **Neither the things that are in the world.** Love nothing in the sphere of the *kosmos.* We must use the things in the world, but when we love them in place of God, we abuse their use (I Cor 7:31).

b) The Reasons for the Appeal. 2:15b-17.

15 b. This thought of supplanting God in our affections with the things of the world is stated in the last phrase of the verse. **If any man love the world.** It is the principle of not serving two masters (Mt 6:24; Jas 4:4). Since the world is the same as darkness, it must exclude God, who is light. This is the first reason for not loving the world.

16. The second reason for not loving the world is that the things of the world are not of the Father. **For.** Better, *because.* Verse 16 gives the detailed reasons for the statement of 2:15 b. **Lust of the flesh.** The genitive, **flesh,** is subjective here, as it is normally when used with **lust.** Thus the meaning is not lust for flesh but the flesh's lusts, or those lusts which have their base in the flesh. Flesh used in this ethical sense (as opposed to the material sense, meaning body) is the old nature in man, or his capacity to do that which is displeasing to God. **Lust of the eyes.** The eyes are the gate from the world to the flesh. In the phrase, **lust of the flesh,** the thought is of physical pleasure; while in **lust of the eyes,** the thought is of mental, physical, or aesthetic pleasure. **Pride of life.** The word **pride** occurs elsewhere only in Jas 4:16, where it is translated "boastings." The idea in the word is pretentious ostentation which results from not seeing the real emptiness of the things of the world. **Life.** *Bios,* not *zōē.* The latter means the vital principle of life, while the former means possessions. Thus the "pride of life" is ostentatious pride in the possession of worldly goods. **Is not of the Father. Of,** *ek,* "origin." None of these things originates from the Father but rather from the world.

17. The third reason for not loving the world is that it is transitory. **Is passing away.** Present tense, a process now going on. **The lust thereof.** The lust which belongs to and is stimulated by the world. If all this is passing away, how foolish to fix one's affections on that which is already in the process of dissolution. **But he that doeth.** The Christian is not disturbed. **Doeth.** Not saith, or even loveth, but doeth. **The will of God.** The opposite of all that is in the world. **For ever.** Doing the will of God proves the possession of eternal life, which means abiding forever.

C. The Creed for Our Conduct: Affirmation. 2:18-29.

1) The Necessity for a Creed. 2:18-21.

a) The Last Hour. 2:18 a.

Little children. This is a general address to all of John's readers, regardless of age, by one who has the authority of age and experience. **It is the last time.** The statement arises out of the preceding idea of the passing away of the world. Literally, *a last hour.* The time of this present age which will grow more troublesome immediately preceding the second advent of Christ. A time of trouble and persecution.

b) The Many Antichrists. 2:18b-21.

18 b. Antichrist . . . antichrists. Only John uses the term (here; 2:22; 4:3; II Jn 7). In this verse alone John affirms the presence of many antichrists in his own day and anticipates the coming of the Antichrist in a future day (as described by him in Rev 13:1-10). *Anti* means "opposed" to Christ. Thus, an antichrist is one who opposes Christ under the guise of Christ. Such are empowered by superhuman Satanic forces; they may be part of the Christian assembly outwardly; and they teach false doctrine (2:19; II Jn 7). The presence of antichrists in the world proves that it is a last hour. Since they were present in John's day and have been present throughout church history, the "last hour" must be the entire period between the first and second advents of Christ.

19. They went out from us. They belonged outwardly to the church. **They were not of us.** Never organically united to the body. **Continued with us.** Their very separation from the Christian group proved their false profession, and their departure showed them up as antichrists. Apostasy is possible for those who have never really made Christ their own Saviour. **20. Unction.** Anointing. Even if these antichrists had not separated themselves, believers have within themselves the power to discover them, that is, to discern between truth and error because of the anointing. Anointing designates something for sacred use. The words **Christ** and **anoint** are from the same root; therefore, John seems to be drawing a contrast here between Antichrist and his antichrists on one hand and Christ and his christs (anointed ones) on the other. **Ye know all things.** Particularly the difference between true and false teaching (cf. RSV, **you all know**).

21. I have not written. Epistolary aorist tense, referring to this Epistle (not the Gospel) and particularly to this section concerning antichrists. John states two reasons for writing: because his readers know the truth and because **no lie is of the truth.** These reasons establish a bond of sympathy and point of contact between writer and readers. **Ye know it.**

John appeals to the knowledge they possess. **No lie is of the truth.** Every lie has its origin from the devil and therefore is alien to the truth which the readers know.

2) The Nature of the Creed. 2:22-29.

22. Who is a liar? Literally, *Who is the liar?* Abruptly introduced without any connecting particles. **He that denieth that Jesus is the Christ.** The background of this denial is Gnosticism, not Judaism. If it were Judaism, the denial would be similar to that against which the early apostles preached (Acts 5:42, etc.) – namely, that Jesus of Nazareth was not the Christ of the OT. But the Gnostic heresy against which John is here writing was that Christ came upon Jesus at his baptism and departed before his death. This was the liar's denial that Jesus was truly the God-man. This is the teaching of the antichrist. **That denieth the Father and the Son.** Gnosticism considered Christ and Jesus as two distinct entities. Thus, to deny that Jesus is the Christ is to deny the Son, the God-man. And to deny the Son is to deny the Father, because the Son is the revelation of the Father without whom the Father cannot be known (Mt 11:27).

23. The previous statement is now emphasized. **Hath not the Father.** In verse 22 John says that to deny the Son is to deny the Father. Here he says that to deny the Son is to have not the Father; to deny the Son is to forfeit the right to become a child of God (Jn 1:12) and to possess the Father as a living friend. It is a living relationship that is in view here, not merely a creedal assent. **He that acknowledgeth.** The positive statement of the same truth. The last part of the verse is apparently a genuine part of the original text and should not be italicized (as in the AV) as if it were not genuine.

24. Let that . . . abide in you (AV). In the Greek the sentence opens with emphasis on **you** – "As for **you** . . . ," and contrasts the true believers and the false teachers. **Which ye have heard from the beginning.** That is, the foundational truths of the Gospel. Abiding in them brings abiding in the Son and the Father. **25. This** refers to eternal life, which is the promise. But this is the same as abiding in him in the preceding verse.

26. These things concerning the false teachers. **Seduce.** Lead astray; present participle, indicating habitual effort. **27. And as for you** (ASV). Emphatic position of the pronoun, as in verse 24. **Anointing.** The gift of the Holy Spirit which the believers received when they were converted (cf. v. 20). **From him.** Source of the gift of the Spirit. **Need not that any man teach you.** Because this is the Spirit's work (Jn 16:13 ff.). **As the same anointing teacheth you of all things.** A re-emphasis of the preceding statement. **Teacheth.** Present, continuous teaching of the truth. **Ye abide** (*shall* should be omitted). The verb could be indicative or imperative (as Jn 5:39; 12:19; 14:1; 15:18,27). If indicative, John is merely assuming the truth of the statements he has made concerning his readers. If imperative, he is commanding them to experience these things.

28. Abide. A command to keep His commandments (3:24). **When.** Best texts read *If (ean).* That *if,* does not throw doubt on the fact of his coming but only raises questions as to certain circumstances surrounding his coming; e.g., the time of it. Abiding results in (1) having **confidence** and (2) not being **ashamed. Confidence.** Boldness *(parrēsia);* literally, *freedom in speaking* or *readiness to say anything.* **When he shall appear.** We should be able to have unreserved utterance as we give account of our stewardship to him. **Not be ashamed before him.** Literally, *not shrink with shame from him* as a guilty person surprised at his coming. **Coming.** *Parousia.* The only occurrence of the word in John's writings. Often it is used in connection with judgment which accompanies his return (Mt 24:3,27,37; I Cor 15:23; I Thess 2:19; 3:13; 5:23; Jas 5:7,8).

29. He is righteous. The preceding verse speaks of Christ; thus it seems logical to refer the **he** of this verse to Christ. **Righteous.** Compare 2:1; 3:7. **Every one that doeth righteousness.** The verb is present – "doeth habitually." **Born of him.** Does this mean born of Christ, as would be indicated if the references in verses 28 and 29 a are to Christ? If so, this is the only reference to Christ's work of begetting (though begotten of God and of the Spirit are Scriptural ideas; cf. Jn 1:13; 3:6,8). "The true solution of the difficulty seems to be that when St. John thinks of God in relation to men, he never thinks of him apart from Christ (comp. v. 20). And again he never thinks of Christ in His human nature without adding the thought of His divine nature. Thus a rapid transition is possible from the one aspect of the Lord's divine-human Person to the other" (Westcott, p. 83).

III. Fellowship's Characteristics. 3:1-24.

A. In Relation to Our Prospect – Purity. 3:1-3. The thought of 2:29 – **born of him** – is now developed. "Born of him! That is what awakens John's grateful surprise, and occasions his exclamation, 'Behold, what manner of love!' His discourse now is an expansion of that thought" (Robert S. Candlish, *The First Epistle of John,* p. 227.)

1) The Reasons for Purity. 3:1-3 a, John states two reasons why the Christian ought to be pure. One is related to a past work of God and the second to a future work.

1. Behold. The word is plural – "all of you behold what I have just seen" (2:28). Some take **what manner of** to imply something foreign; i.e., "what kind of foreign or other-worldly love" (cf. Kenneth S. Wuest, *In These Last Days,* p. 142). Others see no such significance in the word as used in the NT (A. Plummer, *The Epistles of S. John, Cambridge Greek Testament,* p. 71). The word does imply astonishment and admiration (cf. Mt 8:27; Mk 13:1; Lk 1:29; II Pet 3:11 for the only other uses in the NT). **Hath bestowed.** Literally, *hath given.* The perfect tense indicates further that the gift is a permanent possession of the child of God. **Sons.** Literally, *born ones* or *children. Huios,* adult son, presents the legal side of sonship (and is used only by Paul of believers). This word *(teknon)* emphasizes the natural side, birth into the family of God. Yet both terms are suitable for expressing adoption (Jn 1:12; Rom 8:14-17). After **sons of God** should be inserted the words *and we are.* **For this cause** (ASV; AV, *therefore)*—because we are children of God—**the world knoweth us not.** The world does not know by experience what sort of people the children of God are. The world cannot have such experiential knowledge because it knows not Christ as Saviour (cf. I Cor 2:14).

2. Now are we . . . and. "The two thoughts of the present and future condition of God's children are placed side by side with the simple conjunction **and,** as parts of one thought. Christian condition, now and eternally, centers in the fact of being children of God. "In that fact lies the germ of all the possibilities of eternal life" (M. R. Vincent, *Word Studies in the New Testament.* II, p. 344). **Like him.** The likeness of the full reflection of the glory of God in the believer. This includes the physical change to a resurrection body as well as the full spiritual change, which includes purity (v. 3), no sin (v. 5), and righteousness (v. 7). The reason for this change is our seeing him at the translation of the church. "The sight of God will glorify us" (Plummer, *Epistles of S. John,* p. 74). **3. Hope in him.** Literally, *on (epi) him,* i.e., hope resting on him.

---

1. Righteousness. 3:4-9.

Characteristics	**Consequences**
a. Does not do sin (4).	a. Is not lawless (4). Does not set at nought Christ's mission (5).
b. Does not sin as a prevailing habit (6).	b. Proves abiding and knowledge of him (6).
c. Does righteousness (7).	c. Is righteous and imitates Christ (7).
d. Does not do sin (8).	d. Is not of the devil and has entered into the victory Christ gives (8).
e. Does not practice sin (9).	e. Is begotten of God (9).
f. Cannot sin (9).	f. Proves being born of God (9).

2. Love. 3:10-18.

Characteristics	**Consequences**
a. Brother love (10)	a. Origin is of God (10).
b. Unlike Cain (11,12).	b. Will not lead to murder (11,12).
c. Hated by the world (13).	c. Not to be surprised (13).
d. Brother love (14)	d. Proof of having passed from death to life (14).
e. No hate (15).	e. Not a murderer and has life (15).
f. Lays down life for brethren (16).	f. Knows love in its essence (16).
g. Shares goods (17,18).	g. Love of God dwells in him (17,18).

Him refers to Christ. **Purifieth.** Present tense, "constantly purifies himself." Personal effort is necessary, but it must be based on resting in our hope (cf. Jn 15:5).

2) The Meaning of Purity. 3:3 b.

The thought behind purity is of ceremonial purification required before appearing in God's presence (cf. Jn 11:55; Heb 10:19 ff.; Ex 19:10). But the idea in the word is not only of outward purification but also of inner cleansing (cf. Jas 4:8; I Pet 1:18,19). Thus, it means that the hopeful Christian should be completely pure, just as Christ was entirely pure. He is ever the standard which John holds before the believer (cf. I Jn 2:6).

B. In Relation to Our Position—Righteousness and Love. 3:4-18. Our position demands a certain practice, and John proceeds to emphasize the characteristics of that practice in two ideas—righteousness and love. Verse 3 is thus explained by expansion and contrast in 3:4-18, and perhaps the best way to follow the writer's thought is to present a chart of these verses. See bottom of page 10.

4. Committeth sin. Literally, *doeth the sin.* The idea is of sinning continually and as completely as possible. **Sin is the transgression of the law.** Literally, *sin is lawlessness.* The terms are interchangeable (because of the use of the article with both words). Sin is lawlessness and lawlessness is sin. Law is used in its broadest concept here and includes natural law (Rom 2:14), the Mosaic law, the law of Christ (Rom 8:2; I Cor 9:21). **6. Abideth . . . sinneth not.** Both words are in the present tense and indicate the habitual character of the person. The person who is abiding in Christ is not able to sin habitually. Sin may enter his experience, but it is the exception and not the rule. If sin is the ruling principle of a life, that person is not redeemed (Rom 6); thus a saved person cannot sin as a habit of life. When a Christian does sin, he confesses it (I Jn 1:9) and perseveres in his purification (3:3). The continuous sinner has not known God and is therefore an unregenerate person.

7. Little children. "The tenderness of the address is called out by the peril of the situation" (Westcott, p. 105). **Deceive.** Literally, *lead astray.* **Doeth.** Present tense; "habitually doeth." **Is righteous.** Righteous deeds spring from a righteous character and are the proof of regeneration. **As.** Christ, as always, is the example.

8. Committeth. Present tense; "he who is continually doing sin." This is his habit of life, not merely a single act. **Of the devil.** Satan is the source of these sinful desires. "Habitual actions again are an index of character, and here, of source" (Wuest, pp. 148,149). **Son of God.** This is John's first use of this title in the *epistle,* and it particularly expresses dignity and authority. **Destroy.** Literally, *loose.* Christ in his death has undone the bonds by which the works of the devil were held together. Satan can no longer present a solid front in his attacks on the Christian.

9. Is born. Perfect participle—past action with results continuing to the present—"has been and remains born" (cf. 2:29; 4:7; 5:1,4,18). **Doth not commit sin . . . cannot sin.** Present tenses, indicating again habitual sinning. **Seed.** The principle of divine life given the one born of God (Jn 1:13; II Pet 1:4). This makes it impossible for the Christian to live habitually in sin. **10. In this** looks back to the preceding verses, though the same teaching is reiterated in the last part of verse 10; that is, "in this life of victory over sin . . ." **The children of God . . . the children of the devil.** This is the only place in the NT where these two phrases stand side by side (cf. Acts 13:10; Eph 2:3). All mankind is apparently of one family or the other; and until one receives Christ, he is a child of the devil (Eph 2:3 and here). **He that loveth not his brother.** "This clause is not a mere explanation of that which precedes but the expression of it in its highest Christian form" (Westcott, p. 109).

12. Love for the brother suggests hate of a brother, and thus the example of Cain is cited. He is said to have belonged to the family of the **wicked one. Slew.** Originally the Greek word (used here and in Rev 5:6,9,12; 6:4,9; 13:3,8; 18:24 only) meant "to cut the throat," and later it meant "to slay with violence." **13. Marvel not.** Literally, *stop marveling.* John's readers evidently could not understand why the world should hate them. **14.** Love means life and hate means death. The test of being born again is not that the world hates us but that **we love the brethren. 15. Murderer.** This is not to be understood figuratively as meaning a murderer of the soul or character, but literally, because of verse 12. God looks on the heart, and the heart that is full of hate is potentially capable of murder. Compare the Lord's teaching in Mt 5:21,22. "He who falls under a state, falls under the normal results of that state carried out to its issue" (Alford, *The Greek Testament,* IV, 474). Should the occasion arise, the person who habitually hates his fellow man would act just as Cain did. Such a person is unsaved.

16. Cf. 2:6. Self-sacrificing love is required of the believer. **17.** Not many are called to lay down their lives for others, but all can follow the instructions of this verse. John suggests "that there is a danger in indulging ourselves in lofty views which lie out of the way of common experience. We may therefore try ourselves by a far more homely test. The question is commonly not of dying for another but of communicating to another the outward means of living" (Westcott, p. 114). **Good.** The necessities of life. **Bowels.** The seat of tender affections; better rendered *heart.*

C. In Relation to Our Prayers—Answers. 3:19-24. The foregoing teaching would naturally raise misgivings in some minds. So John hastens to add that the fruit of love is confidence, and confidence expresses itself in prayer, and confident prayer is answered.

1) Answers Dependent on Confidence. 3:19-21.

19. Hereby. *In this,* i.e., the love of the brethren. **Assure.** Literally, *persuade* or *tranquilize.* Persuade our heart of what? That it need not **condemn us.** Thus the AV **assure** is a correct interpretive translation. **Before him.** It is in God's presence that assurance comes. **20. For if,** i.e., "whereinsoever," balancing the **all things** of the last part of the verse. In what things our heart condemns us, **God is greater . . . .** In examining our brotherly-love life, our hearts may be either too strict or too lenient. But God is greater and knows all things; therefore, we appeal to him for the truth about ourselves, and remember that he is the all-compassionate One. This results in correct judgment and confidence for our hearts. **21.** An a fortiori argument: "If before God we can persuade conscience to acquit us, when it upbraids us, much more may we have assurance before Him, when it does *not* do so" (Plummer, *The Epistles of S. John,* p. 89). **Condemn us not.** Not sinless perfection, but no unconfessed sin in the life. **Confidence.** Literally, *boldness* or *freedom in speaking.*

2) Answers Dependent on Obedience. 3:22-24.

22. Answered prayer is now conditioned on the habitual keeping of commandments and doing the things that please Him. **Keep** and **do** are both in the present tense. **23.** The commandment is to **believe** and **love.** Faith is a work, as in Jn 6:29. **Believe on the name.** Literally, *believe the name.* It means to believe all that Christ is, as represented by his name. Since this is addressed to Christians, it is an exhortation to believe him for all that he provides for the Christian life. **24.** Obedience also results in abiding. **Dwelleth.** This word is translated "abide" in Jn 15. Thus, the sentence is a definition of abiding. To abide is to keep his commandments. And the Holy Spirit bears witness to the fact that Christ abides in us.

IV. Fellowship's Cautions. 4:1-21.

A. A Caution Concerning Lying Spirits: False Prophets. 4:1-6.

1) The Existence of Lying Spirits. 4:1. The mention of the Holy Spirit in 3:24 leads to defining false spirits. This is another example of John's method of using antithesis. **Beloved.** The address of tenderness again reminds the reader that the subject matter is important. **Believe not.** Literally, *stop believing.* Evidently some of his readers were being carried away with Gnostic teaching. **Try.** *Dokimazō,* which means to put to the test for the purpose of approving. This word generally implies testing with the hope that the thing tested will pass, while *peirazō* ("try" or "tempt") generally means to try with the purpose that the thing tried will be found wanting. The reason for testing is simply that **many false prophets** are in the world. False prophets are false teachers (II Pet 2:1) and wonder workers (Mt 24:24; Acts 13:6; Rev 19:20). The test concerns their origin, **whether they are of God.**

2) The Examination of Lying Spirits. 4:2-6.

a) Their Creed To Be Examined. 4:2,3.

2. If a teacher confesses **that Jesus Christ is come in the flesh,** he is a true prophet. He must openly acknowledge (the meaning of **confess**) the person of the incarnate Saviour. This involves the mode of his coming (**in the flesh**) and permanence of the incarnation (perfect tense of **come**). If he had not taken upon himself a human body, he could never have died and been the Saviour. From this verse we are not to suppose that this is the only test of orthodoxy, but it is a major one and it was the most necessary one for the errors of John's day.

3. Negative statement of the truth of verse 2. **Not.** The position of the negative following the relative pronoun requires the translation: "Every spirit who is of such kind as not to confess." **That spirit of antichrist.** The AV rightly supplies **spirit,** though the omission of it in the Greek text indicates a breadth of thought. Such a false prophet is influenced by many forces and spirits, including demonic ones, and all of these reveal the action of antichrist. Superhuman forces are behind these false teachers.

b) Their Crowd To Be Examined. 4:4-6.

4. Ye. In contrast to false teachers. **Them.** The false prophets themselves, not the spirits behind them. **He that is in you.** Undefined as to which particular person of the Godhead John has in mind, though the mention of the Spirit in 3:24 would indicate that the indwelling of the Holy Spirit is referred to. **He that is in the world.** Satan, the prince of the world and the energizing force behind all false spirits and prophets (Jn 12:31). **5. They.** The false teachers. **Speak they of the world.** The world is their source of speech, not their subject matter. The world system headed by Satan is the source of all heresy. **6. We.** Intensive—"As for us, we . . ." **Knoweth . . . heareth.** Both verbs are present, indicating progressiveness. He that is increasing in the knowledge of God continues to hear us. **Hereby.** That is, the apostles speak the truth because God's people hear them, while the false prophets speak error because the world hears them.

B. A Caution Concerning a Loving Spirit: False Profession. 4:7-21.

1) The Ground of Love. 4:7-10.

a) Love is of God. 4:7,8.

7. "The transition seems abrupt, as if the Apostle had summarily dismissed an unwelcome subject" (Plummer, *The Epistles*, p. 99). This is the third section on love (cf. 2:7-11; 3:10-18). **Love is of God.** Origin. **Begotten.** Perfect tense—"hath been begotten and remains his child." **8. Loveth not.** Present participle—"habitually loveth not." **God is love.** The third of John's three great statements concerning the nature of God (Jn 4:24; I Jn 1:5). The absence of the article (God is *the* love) indicates that love is not simply a quality which God possesses, but love is that which he is by his very nature. Further, because God is love, love which he shows is occasioned by himself only and not by any outside cause. The word **God** is preceded by an article, which means that the statement is not reversible; it cannot read, "Love is God."

b) Love is of Christ. 4:9,10.

9. The manifestation of God's love in our case **(toward us)** was in the giving of his Son. **Only begotten.** Not only did God send his Son, but it was his only begotten Son whom he sent. Christ is the only born Son in the sense that he has no brothers (cf. Heb 11:17). **That we might live.** The purpose of the sending of Christ. **10. Herein is love.** Literally, . . . *the love;* i.e., the love which is the nature of God. And such love is unrelated to anything human beings could do, but it is expressed in the gift of Christ. **Propitiation.** Satisfaction.

2) The Glories of Love. 4:11-21.

a) It causes us to love others. 4:11,12.

11. So. If God loved us to the extent of giving his only Son, we **ought** (moral obligation) **to love one another.** False teachers were not concerned with teaching any moral obligations. **12. God** is in the emphatic position. Translate: **God no man hath beheld at any time.** The connection between this thought and the context seems to be this: Since no one has seen God ever, the only way he who is love can be seen is by his children's loving one another and thus showing the family likeness. **His love** could refer to his love for us or to our love for him (Plummer, p. 103) or to his nature (Westcott, p. 152; Wuest, p. 166). It is probably not his love for us. If it is our love for him, this is **perfected** (matured) as we love the brethren. If it is the love which is his nature, that is **perfected** (or accomplishes its full purpose) as believers love one another.

b) It causes us to know the indwelling of God. 4:13-16.

13. Since we cannot see God, he has given us evidence of his presence with us through his Spirit, who dwells within. **Of his Spirit.** Not that we receive part of the Third Person of the Trinity, but that we receive certain of the many gifts of the Spirit. **15. Confess.** Say the same thing; i.e., agree with some authority outside of one's self. **Son of God.** "This confession of the deity of Jesus Christ implies surrender and obedience also, not mere lip service" (A. T. Robertson, *Word Studies in the New Testament,* VI, 234).

16. Love that God hath to (literally, *in)* **us.** Love becomes a force working in us.

c) It causes us to have boldness in the day of judgment. 4:17.

Our love. The text literally reads *the love with us.* It is the love which God, who is love, has produced in us through begetting us and placing his spirit in us. **Boldness in the day of judgment.** The believer who has perfected God's love in his earthly life will be able to approach the judgment seat of Christ without any shame. Such assurance is not presumption, because **as he is, so are we in this world.** The ground of boldness is our present likeness to Christ in this life, and particularly, according to this context, our likeness in love.

d) It casts out fear. 4:18.

The thought of boldness brings to mind its opposite, **fear.** Since love seeks the highest good of another, fear, which is shrinking from another, cannot be a part of love. **Torment.** Better, *punishment.*

e) It proves the reality of our profession. 4:19-21.

19. We love him. The word **him** is not in the best texts, and the verb is subjunctive. Therefore, translate: *Let us love, because he first loved us.* **20, 21.** Our love for our brethren, a visible thing, proves our love for God, an invisible entity. It is easy to say piously, "I love God"; John says that real piety is shown in brotherly love. Furthermore, he drives the point home by declaring in verse 21 that this is a commandment of Christ (Jn 13:34).

V. Fellowship's Cause. 5:1-21.

Believing in Christ is the ground of our fellowship. The word **believe** has occurred only three times so far in the epistle, but it appears six times in 5:1-13. "St. John now traces the foundations of spiritual kinsmanship" (Westcott, p. 176). The fact that the Christian has exercised faith in Christ is proved in three ways, according to the teaching of this chapter.

A. Faith in Christ Proved by the Conduct We Exhibit. 5:1-5.

1) As begotten ones we love the brethren. 5:1-3.

1. The Gnostics denied that Jesus of Nazareth was the Christ. John makes faith in this truth an essential test of being begotten of God. **Him that begat** is God. **Him also that is begotten** is the believer. **2.** The converse of 4:20,21 is here stated. It is equally true to say that he who loves God loves His children, and he who loves God's children loves God. **When.** Literally, *whenever.* **3. Grievous.** Heavy, an oppressive and exhaustive burden. **Love** makes the commandments of God light.

2) As believing ones we live victoriously. 5:4,5.

4. Keeping the commandment to love the brethren is possible because of the **victory** which the Christian has over the world. **Overcometh.** Present tense, implying a continuous battle. **Victory that overcometh.** Here the verb is aorist, indicating the assuredness of the victory. The victory that overcame the world is our **faith. 5.** Our faith is in the fact that **Jesus is the Son of God.** It is the belief in the full deity (Son of God) and true humanity (Jesus) of the God-man. "Our creed is our spear and shield" (Plummer, *The Epistles of S. John,* p. 112).

B. Faith in Christ Proved by the Credentials We Exhibit. 5:6-12.

1) The Evidence of the Credentials. 5:6-8.

6. Water and blood. These have been interpreted to mean (1) the baptism and death of Christ; (2) the water and blood which flowed from Christ's side on the cross; (3) purification and redemption; and (4) the sacraments of baptism and the Lord's Supper. The last two interpretations are symbolical; and there is no call for such interpretations here because **came** is aorist, referring to actual event. The first two make the phrase refer to actual events in the Lord's life. The second is not to be preferred because the order of the words is reversed (cf. Jn 19:34). The first is the most satisfactory explanation. Christ came **through** *(dia,* "by means of") baptism, which marked him off and associated his ministry with righteousness; and through blood, his death, which paid the penalty for the sins of the world. His ministry was also exercised in (the second and third **by** in the verse) the sphere of what his baptism and his death stood for. The Holy Spirit continues to bear witness of this truth. Baptism and death were the two termini of our Lord's ministry.

7. The text of this verse should read, **Because there are three that bear record.** The remainder of the verse is spurious. Not a single manuscript contains the trinitarian addition before the fourteenth century, and the verse is never quoted in the controversies over the Trinity in the first 450 years of the church era. **8.** The three witnesses are **the spirit, and the water, and the blood: and these three agree in one.** "The trinity of witnesses furnish one testimony" (Plummer, *The Epistles,* p. 116), namely that Jesus Christ came in the flesh to die for sin that men might live.

2) The Effect of the Credentials. 5:9-12.

9. A threefold witness is all that is necessary for men (cf. Deut 19:15; Mt 18:16; Jn 8:17). God has given us three witnesses in the Spirit, water, and blood which we must **receive. 10. In himself.** The witness is not only external but also internal. "That which for others is external is for the believer experimental" (Westcott, p. 186). **Made him a liar.** Because the unbeliever makes God out to be a liar about his entire plan of redemption. **11. Record.** Literally, *witness.* The content of the external and internal witness is that God gave his divine Son that men might have eternal life. **12.** A deduction from verse 11. If the Son has life, then he who has the Son also has life. **Life.** Literally, *the life.*

C. Faith in Christ Proved by the Confidence We Exhibit. 5:13-21.

1) Confidence in Prayer. 5:13-17.

13. These things. The whole epistle. **That ye may know.** The conscious knowledge of the possession of eternal life is the basis for the joy of fellowship, which is the theme of the epistle (1:4).

14. Boldness. This is the fourth mention of it (cf. 2:28; 4:17 in connection with judgment; and 3:21,22 and here in connection with prayer). **According to his will.** The limitation is gracious because his will is always best for his children. The promise is that God hears us, and this includes the idea that he also grants the petition (cf. Jn 9:31; 11:41, 42). **15. Whatsoever we ask** is synonymous with the **according to his will** of verse 14. The believer who is in fellowship with God will not ask anything that is contrary to God's will.

16. Prayer is limited not only by the will of God but also by the actions of others. "Man's will has been endowed by God with such royal freedom, that not even His will coerces it. Still less, therefore, can a brother's prayer coerce it. If a human will has deliberately and obstinately resisted God, and persists in doing so, we are debarred from our usual certitude. Against a rebel will even the prayer of faith in accordance with God's will (for of course God desires the submission of the rebel) may be offered in vain" (Plummer, *The Epistles of S. John,* p. 121). **Sin a sin.** Literally, *sinning a sin.* The supposed case is one in which the brother is seen in the very act of sin. **He shall give him life for them that sin not unto death.** The pronouns are ambiguous. The sentence may mean that God shall give the intercessor life, or it can be taken to mean that the intercessor will give the sinner life through his prayers (similar to Jas 5:20). It is difficult to decide which is preferred, for both ideas are Scriptural.

A sin unto death. The translation **a sin** is too definite. There is *sin unto death,* which implies not a single act but acts which have the character of sin unto death. These may not always be outward so that they can be recognized and known, since John says we cannot know what to pray. Neither is the sin unto death the rejection of Christ, for the context is dealing with Christians. It must be similar to the cases cited in I Cor 5 and 11:30. Concerning prayer for such a brother, John is very guarded in what he recommends. He does not forbid intercession nor does he encourage it. Individual fellowship will determine the proper course of action. **17. All unrighteousness is sin.** John warns against the lax thinking that some sins are permissible and others (**unto death**) not.

2) Confidence in Knowledge. 5:18-21.

18. We know. With certain, positive knowledge. **Sinneth not.** Present tense; habitual sinning. "The power of intercession to overcome the consequences of sin might seem to encourage a certain indifference to sin" (Westcott, p. 193). "The condition of Divine sonship is incompatible, not merely with sin unto death, but with sin of any description" (Plummer, p. 125). **Toucheth.** Occurs in

John only in Jn 20:17, and means not a mere superficial touching but a grasping hold of. Satan cannot grasp and hold on to the one begotten of God. **19.** The second fact in our knowledge. **The whole world.** The order of words indicates that **the world** with its thoughts, ways, methods, etc., is meant. **20.** Third fact. **Is come.** The verb *(hēkei* rather than *erchomai)* includes the ideas of his coming at the incarnation and his presence now in believers. **That we may know.** Know experientially through the appropriation of knowledge.

21. Keep. A different word *(phylassō)* from that used in 5:18 *(tēreō)*. It means guard as a garrison does. **Idols.** "An 'idol' is anything which occupies the place due to God" (Westcott, p. 197). Ephesus abounded with idols and idolatrous practices; so the warning was most appropriate.

BIBLIOGRAPHY

ALEXANDER, WILLIAM. *The Epistles of St. John*. New York: George Doran, n.d.

ALFORD, HENRY. *The Greek Testament*, IV, 421-528. London: Rivingtons, 1875.

CAMERON, ROBERT. *The First Epistle of John*. Philadelphia: A. J. Rowland, 1899.

CANDLISH, ROBERT S. *The First Epistle of John*. Grand Rapids: Zondervan Publishing House, n.d.

FINDLAY, GEORGE. *Fellowship in the Life Eternal*. London: Hodder and Stoughton, n.d.

IRONSIDE, H. A. *Addresses on the Epistles of John*. New York: Loizeaux Brothers, n.d.

KELLY, WILLIAM. *An Exposition of the Epistles of John the Apostle*. London: T. Weston, 1905.

LAW, ROBERT. *The Tests of Life*. Edinburgh: T. & T. Clark, 1909.

PLUMMER, A. *The Epistles of S. John. (Cambridge Greek Testament)*. Cambridge: The University Press, 1886.

ROBERTSON, A. T. *Word Studies in the New Testament*, VI, 199-266. New York: Harper & Brothers, 1933.

ROSS, ALEXANDER. *The Epistles of James and John*. Grand Rapids: Wm. B. Eerdmans Publishing Co., 1954.

SMITH, DAVID. "The Epistles of John," *The Expositor's Greek Testament*, V, 151-208. Grand Rapids: Wm. B. Eerdmans Publishing Co., n.d.

STEVENS, G. B. *The Johannine Theology*. London: Richard B. Dickinson, 1894.

VINCENT, MARVIN R. *Word Studies in the New Testament*, II, 303-404. Grand Rapids: Wm. B. Eerdmans Publishing Co., 1946.

WESTCOTT, BROOKE FOSS. *The Epistles of St. John*. Cambridge: The Macmillan Company, 1892.

WUEST, KENNETH S. *In These Last Days*. Grand Rapids: Wm. B. Eerdmans Publishing Co., 1954.

THE SECOND EPISTLE OF JOHN

INTRODUCTION

Neither II nor III John contains any intimation of time or place of writing. In view of this silence and in absence of any evidence to the contrary, it seems probable that the circumstances were the same as those of the First Epistle. The destination of the Second Epistle is enigmatic. Some hold that the phrase **elect lady** (v. 1) is a figurative way of designating the whole church, or at least some particular church group. Such a metaphorical use may be paralleled by Eph 5:22-33 and Rev 21:9. In such a view **elect sister** (v. 13) would refer to John's own congregation. However, "the simplicity of the little letter precludes the possibility of so elaborate an allegory, while the tenderness of its tone stamps it as a personal communication" (David Smith, ExpGT, IV, 162). Others hold that the letter is addressed to an individual lady and her family. Whether or not her name was Kyria is an open question (cf. alternate constructions in III Jn 1 and I Pet 1:1). Whatever her name, she evidently resided near Ephesus and was well known in her community (perhaps her home was the meeting place for the local church). A sister of hers, presumably deceased, had a family resident at Ephesus and connected with John's congregation. Apparently several of the "elect lady's" sons had visited their cousins in Ephesus. Having become acquainted with them, John wrote their mother this letter.

OUTLINE

- I. Introduction. 1-3.
  - A. Author. 1.
  - B. Address. 1.
  - C. Greeting. 2,3.
- II. Warning concerning heresy. 4-11.
  - A. The content of the heresy. 4-6.
  - B. The cause of the heresy. 7.
    - 1. The coming of deceivers. 7.
    - 2. The creed of deceivers. 7.
  - C. The consequences of heresy. 8-11.
    - 1. Examination of self. 8.
    - 2. Examination of others. 9-11.
      - a. Criterion for the examination. 9.
      - b. Consequences of the examination. 10,11.
- III. Conclusion. 12,13.

COMMENTARY

I. Introduction. 1-3.

A. Author. 1.

The elder. See Introduction to I John. Perhaps the informal and more intimate use of **elder** instead of "apostle" lends support to the view that the letter is addressed to an individual rather than to a church. On the word **elder** used with reference to age, see I Tim 5:1,2; I Pet 5:5; and with reference to office, see Acts 11:30; 14:23; 15:4,6,23; 16:4; 20:17; I Tim 5:17,19; Tit 1:5; Jas 5:14; I Pet 5:1.

B. Address. 1.

Elect lady. See Introduction. **Whom** refers to mother and children. **In the truth.** Better, *in truth,* "in all Christian sincerity." **All they . . .** All Christians would love the family if they had the same relationship as John did.

C. Greeting. 2,3.

2. For the truth's sake. Cf. Jn 15:6; 16:6. The Truth (or Christ) and the Spirit make love for the elect lady and her family possible. The Truth is the foundation of love for all believers. **With us.** Emphatic position in clause.

3. Translate: **There shall be with us grace . . .** Unusual mode of greeting, probably suggested by **with us** in the preceding verse. It is a confident assurance of blessing. **Grace.** The favor of God toward sinners. The word occurs elsewhere in John only in Jn 1:14,16,17; III Jn 4; Rev 1:4; 22:21. **Mercy** is the compassion of God for us in our misery. John uses this word only here. **Peace** is the resultant state of wholeness when sin and misery are removed. **From God . . . and from the Lord.** The repetition of **from** *(para)* emphasizes the distinctiveness of the persons of the Father and the Son. **The Son of the Father.** A unique expression apparently connecting the revelation of the Father closely with the Son.

II. Warning Concerning Heresy. II John 4-11.

Truth and love mentioned in verse 3 are now developed. The walk of the lady's children in truth is commended, and loving one another is commanded.

A. The Content of the Heresy. 4-6.

4. Rejoiced. Aorist, perhaps epistolary —"rejoice"; or better, expressing the initial act of joy. **Found.** Perfect tense; what John found continued to be true. **Walking.** *Peripateō,* including every activity of life (cf. I Jn 1:7). **In truth.** The whole character and conduct of their lives was in truth; i.e., in conformity with the whole tone of Christianity. Some, of course, did not walk in truth, and this was the heresy.

5. And now. This introduces a practical exhortation based on verse 4. " 'It is my joy at the Christian life of some of thy children, and my anxiety about the others, that move me to exhort thee' " (Plummer, p. 135). **I beseech.** *Erōtaō,* a personal request, rather than *parakaleō,* a general request (which word is never used by John). **That we love one another.** These words probably depend on **I beseech thee,** the intervening clause being parenthetical.

6. This is love. The love that John refers to consists in this. In verse 5 the commandment is to love; in verse 6 love is obeying His commands. "This is no vicious logical circle, but a healthy moral connexion . . . Love divorced from duty will run riot, and duty divorced from love will starve" (Plummer, pp. 135,136). Love is not merely a matter of feeling; it is the action of doing the will of God. This word would be particularly necessary when writing to a woman, who by nature is more emotional. **In it.** In love, which is His commandment.

B. The Cause of the Heresy. 7.

Some were spreading heresy rather than walking in truth. The heresy consisted in denying the truth of the commandments of the incarnate Christ, and it was due to a denial of the Incarnation. If Christ was not truly human, then there is no basis for Christian ethics (cf. I Jn 2:6). And certainly there is no example of self-denying love if he was merely a phantom or theophany.

7. Deceivers. Those who lead astray. **Confess not.** Not to affirm is the same as to deny. **Is come.** Literally, *coming* (a participle). The emphasis is not simply on the past fact of the coming of Christ in flesh, but also on the continuance of his humanity and even on the future manifestation of the Lord. Christ is never said to come *into* flesh, but *in* flesh; the former would leave room for saying that deity was united with Jesus sometime after his birth. **An antichrist.** Better, *the antichrist.* The one about whom they had already heard. See notes on I Jn 2:28.

C. The Consequences of Heresy. 8-11.

The presence of heretical teaching calls for examination.

1) Examination of Self. 8.

The danger was personal as well as external; therefore, self-examination is called for as well as examination of the heretics.

Look to yourselves. Cf. Mk 13:9. **We lose not.** Better MSS support *ye lose not.* **We have wrought**; i.e., the apostles. **We receive.** Better MSS read *ye receive.* Thus the sentence reads: *that ye lose not those things which we have wrought, but that ye receive a full reward.* The readers are warned to take heed that the deceivers do not undo the work which the apostles and evangelists had done, so that they might receive a full reward. **Full reward.** No element lacking in rewarding of God's people in the life to come.

2) Examination of Others. 9-11.

9. Others should be examined on the

basis of their abiding in the teaching of Christ. **Transgresseth.** Better, *goeth on,* i.e., in the profession of Christianity without the reality of abiding in the doctrine of Christ. **Doctrine of Christ.** That which he taught at his coming. **He hath both the Father and the Son.** The fuller expression in the positive part of the verse shows that, in the negative statement that precedes it, not to have God is also not to have Christ.

10. If there come any. The **if** assumes the case, not merely expresses the possibility. In other words, such people were coming into Christians' homes under a friendly guise (cf. Didache 11). **Unto you.** To the elect lady and her children. **Receive him not . . . neither bid** (say). Present imperatives, forbidding the continuance of what was customary. The injunction is to refuse such ones Christian hospitality. This is a severe measure, particularly when one remembers that hospitality is generally enjoined in the NT. **Neither bid him God speed.** Do not say a greeting of sympathy. **God speed** is a good translation of the broad idea contained in the word *chairein* (cf. Acts 15:23; 23:26; Jas 1:1). **11. Partaker.** One who fellowships. The one who bids God speed actually fellowships in the work of the antichrist. **Evil deeds.** Literally, *his deeds, his* **evil** *deeds*. Emphasis on the evil character of his works.

III. Conclusion. II John 12,13.

The conclusion is very similar to that of the Third Epistle and evidently indicates that the two letters were written at the same time. John has dealt with the main purpose for writing and reserves other subjects for a personal interview.

12. Many things. Perhaps the same subjects discussed in the First Epistle. **13. Elect sister.** See Introduction to II John. The adjective **elect** is used by John only here, in verse 1, and in Rev 17:14.

BIBLIOGRAPHY

For Bibliography, see after I John.

THE THIRD EPISTLE OF JOHN

(See Introduction to II John)

OUTLINE

I. Introduction. 1-4.
   A. Personal salutation. 1.
   B. Personal sentiments. 2-4.
II. The duty of hospitality. 5-8.
   A. The reward of hospitality. 5.
   B. The report of hospitality. 6.
   C. The reasons for hospitality. 7,8.
III. The danger of haughtiness. 9-12.
   A. Haughtiness exemplified. 9.
   B. Haughtiness condemned. 10.
   C. Haughtiness contrasted. 11,12.
IV. Conclusion. 13,14.

COMMENTARY

I. Introduction. 1-4.

This epistle presents one of the most vivid glimpses in the New Testament of a church in the first century. The characters, Gaius, Diotrephes, and Demetrius, are sketched with bold strokes of the apostle's pen. Characteristics of church life are also clearly seen in the epistle. The independence of the believers is outstanding, and their personalities, as well as their doctrinal problems, are patent. This brief and very personal letter shatters the notion that the state of things was ideal, or nearly so, in the first century. Contrariwise, it reveals the problems of a vigorously growing faith.

A. Personal Salutation. 1.

The salutation is brief in contrast with the salutations of other personal letters in the NT. **Elder.** See II Jn 1. This was evidently the usual way John designated himself. **The wellbeloved Gaius.** Since Gaius was one of the most common names of the time, it is impossible to identify him with any other Gaius mentioned in the NT (cf. Acts 19:29; 20:4; Rom 16:23; I Cor 1:14). **Beloved** expresses the common sentiment that others shared about Gaius. **Whom I love in the truth** expresses John's personal feelings. The **I** is emphatic, as if implying that there were some who were hostile to Gaius.

B. Personal Sentiments. 2-4.

2. Above all things. No such meaning for *peri pantōn* is found in the NT or in the LXX. Better rendered *in all things*. It refers to the whole sentence in general. **Prosper.** Only here, in Rom 1:10, and in I Cor 16:2. **Be in health.** Paul sometimes uses the word metaphorically of sound doctrine, but here the sense is of sound physical health, as in Lk 5:31; 7:10; 15:27. It may indicate that Gaius had been ill. The phrase **even as thy soul prospereth** shows that **prosper** and **be in health** refer to temporal blessings, and this verse gives us the authority for praying for such for our friends.

3. Came. Present tense; not on one occasion but on several reports came. **The truth that is in thee, even as thou walkest . . .** The brethren had repeatedly witnessed to Gaius' Christianity, as proved by his doctrine and his walk. The verse may also imply that Gaius had withstood some false teaching. **4.** The literal order is bold: **Greater than these** (tidings of your stand) **I have no joy.** Some manuscripts read *grace* instead of **joy.** The result of these reports was that John might hear that his children were walking (as the habit of their lives) in truth.

II. The Duty of Hospitality. 5-8.

Apparently Gaius had been censured

by some for his hospitality to strange brethren. John approves of his actions and enjoins such hospitality as a Christian duty.

A. The Reward of Hospitality. 5.

Beloved marks a new section. **Thou doest faithfully** *(piston poieis).* Literally, *thou doest a faithful thing,* or *thou makest sure.* That is, any good done for or to the brethren will surely be rewarded (cf. Mt 26:10; Rev 14:13). Hospitality will have its reward. **And to strangers.** The addition of this phrase would indicate that this was the particular point for which Gaius was being taken to task.

B. The Report of Hospitality. 6.

Which have borne witness. Those who had experienced Gaius' hospitality had testified of it before the church, probably at Ephesus, where John was. **Thou shalt do well.** John urges Gaius to continue his good work. **Bring forward.** See Acts 15:3; Tit 3:13, where the idea of supplying provisions for the journey is included.

C. The Reasons for Hospitality. 7,8.

7. Three reasons are given for hospitality. First, these brethren **went forth** for the sake of the **Name,** i.e., Jesus Christ (cf. Acts 5:41; Jas 2:7). Second, they took **nothing** of unconverted Gentiles. The participle is present, indicating that it was their practice to take nothing. **8.** Third, through hospitality Christians can become fellow workers for the truth. **Ought.** Bound to, as in I Jn 2:6.

III. The Danger of Haughtiness. 9-12.

A. Haughtiness Exemplified. 9.

The RSV has, *I have written something to the church,* i.e., a few words. *Ti,* "something," indicates that John viewed his letter lightly. It, of course, has not been preserved. **Unto the church.** The church to which Gaius belonged. But its purpose had failed. **Who loveth to have the pre-eminence among them.** The word occurs nowhere else in the NT. It does not imply doctrinal defection (cf. II Jn 9) but rather proud ambition and the desire to promote personal authority. Plummer makes an interesting suggestion: "Perhaps the meaning is that Diotrephes meant to make his Church independent; hitherto it had been governed by S. John from Ephesus, but Diotrephes wished to make it autonomous to his own glorification" (Plummer, p. 149). **Receiveth us not.** That is, Diotrephes did not receive John's wishes in the matter of hospitality. The improbability that any Christian would have withstood the apostle's authority is one of the internal arguments used against the Johannine authorship of this letter. It is thought to be inconceivable that a Christian would disregard the commandments of a genuine apostle if he were the author. However, Paul's apostolic authority was often challenged.

B. Haughtiness Condemned. 10.

If I come. No doubt because of verse 14 (cf. I Jn 2:28 for similar construction). **I will remember.** Bring these things to his notice and the notice of others. **Prating.** Used only here, though the adjective form occurs in I Tim 5:13. Literally, *to talk nonsense.* **With malicious words.** Diotrephes' talk was both senseless and wicked. His actions included not being hospitable himself, forbidding those who would be, and casting them out of the church. Evidently he had sufficient authority in the congregation to do this excommunicating, of whatever sort it was.

C. Haughtiness Contrasted. 11,12.

11. Beloved again marks the transition. **Follow.** Literally, *imitate.* **Evil.** *Kakos,* "bad." Rarely used by John. **Is of God.** The source *(ek,* "of") of his life is God; i.e., he is a child of God. He imitates his Master (Acts 10:38). **Hath not seen God.** Cf. I Jn 3:6. The question of hospitality is no longer the only specific matter in view, but doing good or evil in general and as the habit of one's life.

12. From the evil Diotrephes John turns to the good Demetrius. All we know of him we learn from this brief mention. It is conjecture that he is the same Demetrius, though now converted, of Acts 19:24. Demetrius' good testimony was witnessed to by three sources: (1) all men, (2) the truth, that is, the standard of Christianity, and (3) John and those with him.

IV. Conclusion. 13,14.

The similarity to the conclusion of II John supports the view that they were written about the same time.

13. I had. Imperfect, referring to the time when he began the letter. **Pen.** Literally, *reed.* **14.** See verse 10.

15. Note the division of verse 14 in the

AV into verses 14 and 15 in the RSV and in editions of the Greek text. **Peace be to thee.** Ordinary blessing which was suitable either for a greeting or for a farewell. **Friends.** It is a question whether John means his friends (thus supply "our" as AV does) or Gaius' (thus supply "thy"). **By name.** The phrase occurs elsewhere only in Jn 10:3. The salutation was to be given to each individual separately. "S. John as shepherd of the Churches of Asia would imitate the Good Shepherd and know all his sheep by name" (Plummer, p. 153).

BIBLIOGRAPHY

For Bibliography, see after I John.

JUDE

INTRODUCTION

Authorship and Date. The Epistle of Jude, the last of the "general" or "catholic" epistles, is declared to have been written by "Jude, the servant of Jesus Christ, and brother of James." Dispute over the authenticity of the claim is as old as Eusebius, who placed this letter, along with Hebrews, under suspicion. However, the soundest historical and internal evidence supports the truthfulness of the text. Matthew 13:55 and Mark 6:3 name Judas (Jude) and James as brothers of Jesus. That James is identified so simply in this epistle is evidence that he was Jesus' brother. Some scholars allege that "Jude" is a borrowed or pen name, but this is open to question. Apart from being the author of this letter, Jude had no special reputation or authority in the early church; therefore little reason existed for a forger to use Jude's name. Though the date of composition cannot be fixed with certainty, it would not be inaccurate to assign it to the latter half of the first century. It is listed in the Muratorian Canon (second century), and mentioned by Tertullian, Clement, and Origen (third century). Although it suffered a diminished status because of its citations from the non-canonical books of Enoch and the Assumption of Moses, its right to inclusion in the canon was universally recognized by A.D. 350.

Purpose. Apparently a general letter to Christians of the first century, the Epistle of Jude warns against the incipient heresy of Gnosticism, a philosophy that distinguished sharply between matter, as being inherently evil, and spirit, as being good. Such a system of thought had serious implications for Christian life and doctrine. It challenged the Biblical doctrine of creation. And it gave rise to the idea that Christ's body was only apparent, not real, for if Christ had had a real body, it would have been evil. In its effect on Christian ethics, Gnosticism prompted two quite different results: on the one hand antinomianism, the belief that one is not under obligation to obey the moral law, and on the other a form of abuse of the body to promote spirituality. Both are opposed by Scripture. It may be inferred from the epistle that the readers were guilty, in varying degrees, of rebellion against authority, irreverence, presumptuous speech, and a libertine spirit. Jude's tone is polemic, for he rebukes false teachers who deceive unstable believers and corrupt the Lord's table.

While no outline is finally authoritative, this epistle falls easily into four sections:

I. Identification, salutation, and purpose. Jude 1-4.
II. Admonitions against false teachers. Jude 5-16.
III. Exhortations to Christians. Jude 17-23.
IV. Benediction. Jude 24, 25.

COMMENTARY

I. Identification, Salutation, and Purpose. Jude 1-4.

1. Jude identifies himself as the writer, describes his relationship to Christ and to James, and defines his readers, all in one short sentence. **Jude,** or Judas, is a popular name in the Hebrew tradition. A frequent Pauline word — **slave,** or *bond servant* — is used, and it speaks of Jude's devotion to Christ. The writer's blood relationship to Jesus is of secondary importance. The sovereignty of God and the centrality of Christ are expressed in the election and preservation of the readers. The verb translated **kept** (ASV) points forward to Christ's return.

2. Jude's trilogy of **mercy . . . peace,** and **love** is distinctly Semitic, and corresponds closely to Paul's "grace, mercy, and peace" (II Tim 1:2).

3. The purpose of the letter is plainly stated, and the polemic point of view indicated. Jude does not harshly demand, but lovingly appeals to these Christians to recall their **common salvation.** The Greek adverb *hapax,* **once for all** (Heb 6:4; 10:2; I Pet 3:18), affirms the finality of the revelation of God in Christ in redemptive history. It is the fixed, nonrepeatable point of our faith. This revelation accomplished its goal, for it was delivered **to the saints.**

4. The occasion for the letter was the intrusion of ungodly persons into the fellowship of the church. These heretics are open to four charges: they entered secretly; they were previously appointed to condemnation; they are ungodly, i.e., irreverent; and they deny Christ as Master and Lord. To deny is positively to disbelieve what Christ testified about himself. Gnostic antinomianism is implied in **licentiousness** (AV, *lasciviousness),* which connotes sexual debauchery.

II. Admonitions Against False Teachers. Jude 5-16.

5. Again the adverb *hapax* is used (cf. v. 3); here it refers to the readers' knowledge of the Gospel. Jude's argument is that a man's *profession* of faith does not establish him as righteous before God. The possibility of lapsing is illustrated by the example of disbelieving Israelites who were saved out of Egypt but subsequently destroyed.

6. A further illustration is the fall of the rebellious angels, who erred from their calling by exalting themselves. Jude's language here may reflect the influence of the book of Enoch, which contains an elaborated description of the disobedient angels. Genesis 6:1-4 provides the original Biblical account.

7. Lastly, Jude cites the history of **Sodom and Gomorrha** to enforce his moral. Throughout Scripture these cities are symbolic of divine judgment executed by fire. So their fate is a foretaste of the fate of professing believers who do not persevere in rightousness.

8. Irreverence is the chief sin of the **ungodly persons** of verse 4. The sense of the word **dignities** (AV), or *the glorious ones* (RSV), is not clear; it may refer to Christian leaders.

9. Jude amplifies his plea for reverence by citing the apocryphal story of Michael and the devil, taken from the pseudepigraphical Assumption of Moses. Although Jude quoted both this book and Enoch, it is not a supportable inference that he ascribed canonical status or historicity to them. The moral that Jude points up is that Michael showed restraint even in his relations with the devil, whereas the false teachers exhibit no reverence for any authority.

10. Lacking the spiritual insight to recognize the "glorious ones," these evil men scoff at them. With irony Jude destroys the Gnostic claim to superior spiritual knowledge by stating that they possess only irrational animal instincts. Dependence upon knowledge gained only by the brute senses leads to sure destruction.

11. Jude pronounces a woe, again employing a triad of historical examples — **Cain, Balaam,** and **Korah.** Cain is typical of unrighteousness, Balaam of the spirit of deceit and covetousness (cf. Num 22—24), and Korah (or Core) of the rebellion of malcontents against duly constituted authority (cf. Num 16). These kinds of sin undermine the spiritual health of the whole church and destroy those who practice them.

12. The author heightens his condemnation of false teachers by turning from Biblical to natural analogies, of which there are five. **Love-feasts** were meals eaten in connection with worship services or the Eucharists, and their intent was to enrich the believers' Christian fellowship and strengthen their sense of union with Christ. Apparently the Gnostic heretics had corrupted such feasts into gluttonous orgies, thereby perverting their purpose. These fed themselves without concern for the spiritual welfare of the Church. **Waterless clouds** is highly descriptive of these men; they carried no spiritual burden, and were blown along as though without weight. Autumn is the time of fruit gathering. But false teachers produce no fruit, and such trees, being doubly dead, are destined for destruction.

13. The lives of the ungodly are like the restless, **raging waves of the sea** that litter the seashores with their refuse. Such lives bring not only future condemnation but present shame and ignominy. Lastly, Jude describes the heretics as **wandering stars.** He implies that theirs is a pointless, useless existence, which will terminate in eternal oblivion. Enoch 18:12-16 may have influenced Jude's thought here.

14,15. A problem arises in these verses because of the quotations from Enoch. Jude says: **Enoch in the seventh generation from Adam prophesied** (RSV). The difficulty is that Jude apparently ascribes this prophecy of apocryphal Enoch to the Enoch of Gen 5. Since there is no Biblical account of any prophecy of Enoch, some claim that Jude either regarded apocryphal Enoch as canonical, or else was guilty of obvious error. However, a solution to the problem rests in the fact that this alleged prophecy is a citation not from a single passage in Enoch, but from several, and it is probable that Jude also quoted the line "the seventh generation from Adam" from Enoch 60:8. Thus Jude did not intend to refer to the Enoch of Gen 5, but referred entirely, even in the introductory line, to words found in the apocryphal Enoch. While the prophecy has no canonical status, its predictions are paralleled and supported by numerous Biblical passages, such as, Mt 25:31-46.

16. After affirming the doom of false teachers, Jude describes their character in three ways. They are grumblers, i.e., furtive complainers; they are malcontents, whose sole guide is their passions; and they are given to noisy boasting, with a view to securing gain for themselves. The language reflects the thought of the Assumption of Moses 5:5.

III. Exhortations to Christians. Jude 17-23.

17. Although this letter was written to Christians, in verses 5-16 Jude defined the errors of false teachers. Now he turns his attention to his readers in a direct exhortation. They will guard themselves from error by recalling the apostles' **predictions** that false teachers would arise in the very church itself. By so doing they will properly "contend for the faith" (v. 3).

18. II Peter 3:3 uses almost identical language. Both passages may look back to a current oral tradition of the teaching of the apostles. **In the last time** sets the tone and points out that at the end of the age desperate lack of spirituality will characterize people. To scoff is to act impiously towards holy things, and **scoffers** (AV, *mockers)* do not obey the law of the Spirit, but follow the law of fleshly passion.

19. Jude continues his indictment against false teachers on two counts: they are divisive, and they are without the Spirit of God. The Greek verb *to separate* suggests setting up lines of demarcation that give rise to a factious spirit. Moreover, it bespeaks a sense of superiority on the part of these false teachers. With fine irony Jude accuses the Gnostics, who regarded themselves as spiritual, of **having not the Spirit.** He affirms that spirituality is a quality of life produced by the Spirit of God, and not by religious exercises known only to the initiated few.

20. Again a direct charge is made to the readers. Purity of life commences with sound doctrine, which is the "faith once for all delivered to the saints" (v. 3). A key to what is meant by **building up yourselves** is given in the following phrase: **praying in the Holy Spirit.** The strong implication is that the truly spiritual are not the exclusive, self-righteous persons (v. 19), but those who pray in the Holy Spirit.

21. Arndt paraphrases as follows: "Keep yourselves from harm by making it possible for God to show his love for you in the future also." The present environment of the Christian is the love of God, and the future expectation is the guarantee of eternal life with Jesus Christ.

22. The Greek text is difficult in Jude 22, 23. In v. 22 the better attested verb is **eleeō,** "to succor," "show compassion." The object of compassion is those who doubt. Thus, in this passage, Jude urges Christians to respond to both the intellectual and the moral doubts of those affected by false teachers. The end in view is not expulsion and condemnation of the doubters but their restoration to fellowship.

23. Zechariah 3:2-4 may have influenced Jude's thoughts here, for he writes of **snatching them out of the fire.** Fire may suggest sensual passion, but more likely it alludes to eternal judgment. It is difficult to know whether the writer intended to draw a sharp distinction between two classes of people by the double use of "some," or simply used the expression in an enumerative sense. However the words are to be understood, the Christian attitude is one of mercy towards the sinner, coupled with abhorrence of his sin.

IV. Benediction. Jude 24,25.

24,25. One of the great and lofty benedictions of the NT is the one at the end of this short epistle. Two comparable Pauline benedictions are Rom 16:25 and I Tim 6:14-16. Vital to all exhortations to believers is the reminder of the infinite resource of God himself, who alone is competent to keep us from falling in this life and to bring us to himself in the last day. He will perfect the work of sanctification so that the believer will be **faultless**, or *without blemish* (ASV). This word looks back to the description of sacrificial animals in the OT. Jude 25 teaches both the oneness of God and the equality of Jesus Christ with God the Father. Thus it militates against the view that the deity of Christ was an invention of the post-apostolic church. God is spoken of as **Saviour** seven times in the NT. Here his saving power is shown in the Person of his Son, whom the Church acknowledges as "Lord," i.e., God. The final ascription of glory, majesty, dominion, and authority is Jude's testimony to the gracious character of God, who wrought our salvation through Christ.

BIBLIOGRAPHY

BIGG, CHARLES. *A Critical and Exegetical Commentary on the Epistles of St. Peter and St. Jude. (International Critical Commentary)*. New York: Charles Scribner's Sons, 1901.

MANTON, THOMAS. *Exposition of the Epistle of Jude*. London: James Nesbet & Co., 1871.

MAYOR, J. B. *Epistle of St. Jude and the Second Epistle of St. Peter*. London: Macmillan and Company, 1907.

MOFFAT, JAMES. *The General Epistles. (Moffat New Testament Commentary)*. Vol. 15. Garden City, New York: Doubleday, Doran and Company, 1928.

REVELATION

INTRODUCTION

Note. At the beginning of this brief commentary on the inexhaustible concluding book of the New Testament Canon, a word is probably in order regarding two features that will be noticed throughout. In the first place, proportionately more space is given to introductory matters than is normally assigned in either a brief or longer treatment of this book. This is done because the writer believes the study of the book of Revelation calls for more preliminary consideration than that of any other book in the Bible. The better a reader has fixed in his mind certain fundamental principles of interpretation, the more readily will he understand these confessedly difficult chapters. In the second place, there is incorporated in these pages a good deal of material from the more important commentaries on Revelation written during the last century, some of the superbly concise and penetrating statements of great scholars of the Christian church concerning subjects touched upon in the book.

There is something almost paradoxical about the book of Revelation. It is a volume of acknowledged difficulty, and yet down through the ages it has been like a magnet, irresistibly drawing to its study Christians of every school of thought, laymen, clergy, and professors. R. H. Charles is right when he opens his *Lectures on the Apocalypse* with this statement: "From the earliest ages of the Church, it has been universally admitted that the Apocalypse is the most difficult book of the entire Bible" (p. 1). Calvin refused to write a commentary on Revelation, and gave it very little consideration in his massive writings. Luther for years avoided its teachings. At the same time, the book has compelled men to give prolonged study to its prophecies, and to go back again and again for a reconsideration of its themes and for a new grasp of its revelations. One testimony will suffice, from the one who is generally acknowledged to have been the most gifted Biblical expositor in the first quarter of our century, G. Campbell Morgan: "There is no book in the Bible which I have read so often, no book to which I have tried to give more patient and persistent attention. . . . There is no book in the Bible to which I turn more eagerly in hours of depression than to this, with all its mystery, all the details of which I do not understand" (*Westminster Bible Record*, Vol. 3 [1912] 105,109).

The Importance of the Book. (1) The New Testament Scriptures would have been incomplete, would have left readers in a more or less depressed mood, had this book not been written and included in the Canon. It is not only the last book in the canonical arrangement of our Bible, but it is the necessary conclusion to God's revelation to men. This truth was brilliantly set forth by T. D. Bernard in his famous Bampton Lectures for 1864, *The Progress of Doctrine in the New Testament:* "I know not how any man, in closing the Epistles, could expect to find the subsequent history of the Church essentially different from what it is. In those writings we seem, as it were, not to witness some passing storms which clear the air, but to feel the whole atmosphere charged with the elements of future tempest and death. Every moment the forces of evil shew themselves more plainly. They are encountered, but not dissipated. . . . The last words of St. Paul in the second Epistle to Timothy, and those of St. Peter in his second Epistle, with the Epistles of St. John and St. Jude, breathe the language of a time in which the tendencies of that history had distinctly shewn themselves; and in this respect these writings form a prelude and a passage to the Apocalypse.

"Thus we arrive at this book with wants which it is meant to supply; we come to it as men, who not only personally are in Christ, and who know what as individuals they have in him; but who also, as members of his body, share in a corporate life, in the perfection of which they are to be made perfect, and in the glory of which their Lord is to be glorified. For this perfection and glory we wait in vain, among the confusions of the world, and the ever-active, ever-changing forms of evil. What is the meaning of this wild scene? What is to be its issue? And what prospect is there of the realization of that which we desire? To such a state of mind as this, and to the wants which it involves, this last part of the teaching of God is addressed, in accordance with that system of progressive doctrine which I have endeavoured to illustrate, wherein each stage of advance ensues in the way of natural sequence from the effect of that which preceded it."

(2) Of all the books of the Bible, this is the one that certainly may be considered as *the* book for the end of the age. And it would seem that in these last thirty years, the Western world itself, including its statesmen, scientists, economists, and essayists, has consciously, or unconsciously, recognized this. This is especially true in regard to the use of the word *apocalypse*. This word has come to stand for an age of upheaval, world conditions fraught with fearful consequences, the unleashing of vast powers which man himself seems unable to control. The author of the book on Revelation in the Moffatt Commentary, Martin Kiddle, refers to "the remarkable relevance" of the message of this book "to the church in our own day. It is only one more example of the divine sanction, and the timeless significance of John's visions. Whenever there is a world crisis, whenever the State exalts itself and demands an allegiance which Christians know they cannot pay without abandoning their very souls, whenever the Church is threatened by destruction, and faith is dim and hearts are cold, then the Revelation will admonish and exhort, uplift and encourage all who heed its message" (p. xlix).

(3) This is supremely the book of one world, and surely now, in the middle of this twentieth century, we are approaching a one-world condition. Frequently in the Apocalypse we come upon such a phrase as "many peoples, and nations, and tongues, and kings" (10:11; 11:9; 17:15), which suggests the universal scope of the vision. When kings are introduced, they are the "kings of the whole world" (16:14; 17:2,18; 18:9; 19:19). Of Satan it is said that he is "the deceiver of the whole world" (12:9). All the nations commit fornication with the harlot (18:3,23). The economic boycott enforced by the beast covers all mankind (13:16,17). In fact, the beast from the sea has given to him "authority over *every* tribe and people and tongue and nation" (13:7); and of him it is said, "*All* that dwell on the earth shall worship him" (13:8). There is great significance in the fact that when the time comes for Christ to assume his rightful place as King of kings and Lord of lords, the word for the government of this world is in the singular, "the *kingdom* of the world" (11:15).

(4) This is pre-eminently a book for a troubled age, for an age in which the darkness deepens, fear spreads over all mankind, and monstrous powers, godless and evil, appear on the stage of history (as they appear in this book). But there is comfort and encouragement here: God knows all things from the beginning, even the tribulations of his own people. However, the ultimate end of this conflict, persecution, tribulation, martyrdom, is determined by Christ, when he, finally, will be victorious. Sin and Satan and all Satan's cohorts will be eternally defeated; and believers will be with the Son of God in glory forever.

(5) Even if all these things were not true, and especially true for our age, we should not forget that this is the only book in the Bible that pronounces a beatitude regarding the hearing, reading, and obeying of its words: "Blessed is he that readeth, and they that hear the words of the prophecy, and keep the things that are written therein" (1:3; 22:7).

(6) Finally, it is in this book that some of the greatest themes of divine revelation are brought to a climactic conclusion. Here the prophecies concerning Christ as King of kings are unfolded in fullness, and are seen coming to pass. Here such words as *tabernacle, temple, paradise, Babylon,* etc., take on their supremely spiritual connotation. Here all the promises of a life in glory are concentrated in the marvelous picture of the Holy City. Here we have the final doom of Satan, Antichrist, false prophets, and all the enemies of God. Here the rebellious kings of Psalm 2 find themselves under the feet of the Lamb of God.

The Author. Through the ages some doubt has been cast upon the authenticity of this book. In this commentary there is not space for presenting and answering the arguments against Johannine authorship, but we should consider the facts testifying to the Apostle John as the writer. (1) Four times in this book the author's name is inserted (1:1, 4,9; 22:8). (2) As early as the first half of the second century, it was the conviction of the Church that John was the author. Justin Martyr frankly states, "And with us a man named John, one of the Apostles of Christ, who in the revelation made to him . . . ." *(Dialogue with Trypho the Jew*, ch. 81). The great historian Eusebius repeatedly assigns this book to John *(Ecclesiastical History* III. xxiv, xxxix); likewise Tertullian *(Contra Marcion* 3:14,24).

(3) Whatever may be the grammatical peculiarities of this book, there are innumerable similarities between the vocabularies of John's Gospel and the Apocalypse. "One important link connecting these writings," Gloag points out, "is the application of the term Logos to Jesus Christ. This term is undoubtedly Johannine; it is not elsewhere employed in Scripture, and yet it occurs in the Apocalypse: 'He is arrayed in a garment sprinkled with blood: and His name is called the Word of God' (Rev. 19:13). So also the word 'the Lamb,' as denoting not merely the emblem or symbol of Christ, but Christ Himself, is peculiar to John; as when in the Gospel it is said, 'Behold the Lamb of God,' and in the Apocalypse, 'I saw in the midst of the throne and of the four living creatures, and in the midst of the elders, a Lamb standing as though it had been slain' (5:6). It is true that the Greek word is different, *ho amnos* being used in the Gospel and *to arnion* in the Apocalypse; but the idea that Jesus Christ is the Lamb is common to both. The word *alēthinos,* 'that which is true,' is used ten times in the Apocalypse, nine times in the Fourth Gospel, four times in the Epistle, and only once in the Pauline Epistles. So also 'he that overcometh' *(nikos),* a favourite expression in the Epistle, is of frequent occurrence in the Apocalypse, as in the conclusion of the Epistles to the Seven Churches and elsewhere throughout the work: 'He that overcometh shall inherit all things' (21:7). The verb *skēnoō,* 'to tabernacle,' only found in the Johannine writings, is used in the Gospel, with evident reference to the Shekinah, of the Logos tabernacling among men (1:14), and is four times employed in the Apocalypse with reference to God: 'Behold the tabernacle of God is with men, and He shall dwell (tabernacle) with them' (21:3)" (P. J. Gloag: *Introduction to the Johannine Writings*, pp. 306,307).

The Date of Composition. There have been two different major convictions concerning the time this book was written. Some have placed it as early as the reign of Nero, in the seventh decade of the first century. But for many reasons it seems that this is too early. The unanimous verdict of the early church was that the Apostle John was banished to the Isle of Patmos by the emperor Domitian (A.D. 81 to 96), some writers placing the exile in the fourteenth year of his reign, A.D. 95. (For the early evidence for this, see, e.g., Revere F. Weidner, *Annotations on the Revelation of St. John the Divine,* pp. xiv-xvii).

The Apocalypse clearly reveals that it was written in a time of great persecution. The persecution under Nero was more or less confined to Rome, but that under Domitian reached to other parts of the Roman empire. Domitian banished men to various places of exile, but Nero did not. Furthermore, the seven churches in Asia here show a mature development, which could hardly have existed as early as A.D. 65. Moreover, we have no evidence whatever that the Apostle exercised any authority over the churches of Asia before the destruction of Jerusalem. With this view agree such writers as Lange, Alford, Elliott, Godet, Lee, Milligan, and others.

Title of the Book. The word *Revelation* is derived from the Latin *revelatio* (from *revelare,* "to reveal or unveil that which has previously been hidden"). This was the title assigned to the book in the Latin Vulgate. The Greek title is *Apocalypse,* taken directly from the first word in the Greek text, *apokalypsis.* In this noun form the word is not found anywhere else in Greek literature, but as a verb it is continually used in the Gospels and the Epistles, in many different ways, especially in reference to some form of divine revelation to man (as of the Son of Man, in Lk 17:30). It is used by Paul in referring to the same coming event (Rom 8:18; I Cor 1:7; II Thess 1:7), and frequently in I Peter (1:7,13; 4:13; 5:1). In the Greek text of Daniel this word is often found referring to the uncovering of secrets, or the interpretation of dreams, or the revelation of God (see Dan 2:19,22,28,

29,30,47; 10:1; 11:35).

The Theme. The Apocalypse is a book of prophecy. In its unfolding of the future, it particularly emphasizes the repeated and increasingly violent worldwide attempts of earthly personalities and peoples, energized and directed by demonic powers and led by Satan, to oppose and prevent the execution of the declared intention of Christ to establish His kingly rule on earth. It makes clear that this conflict is certain to end in the complete overthrow of these evil forces and the establishment of the everlasting kingdom of Christ. This age-long conflict, even involving war in heaven, is made up of a series of plots on the part of the enemies of Christ to defeat the King of kings. Each plot ends in failure, followed by fearful divine judgment. And the long conflict terminates in the final judgment of the Great White Throne, the appearance of the New Jerusalem, and the beginning of eternity.

A Book of Visions. The book of Revelation, above every other book of the Bible, is a record of what the author had revealed to him in visions. All of us know how difficult it is at times to record what we have *seen,* especially when the sight is spectacular. How would anyone adequately describe a glorious sunset, or the majesty of the Alps? The many different Greek verbs meaning, "to see," "behold," or "perceive," occur 140 times in this book, beginning with "what thou *seest* write in a book" (1:11). Immediately afterwards, John says: "I turned to *see* the voice that spoke with me and having turned, I *saw,*" etc. (v. 12). At the beginning of chapter 4, a voice is heard from heaven saying to John, "Come up hither, and I will show thee the things which must come to pass hereafter" (4:1). From this point on, there are numerous paragraphs, right down to the end of the book, beginning, "And I saw."

Not only do we have here a series of visions, but the book is saturated with symbolic language, and these symbols must be given careful consideration. Especially is this true of numbers. First of all, there is the constant repetition of the number *seven.* In regard to the symbolism of numbers in the book, inserted here are the concise and comprehensive summaries of Moorehead and Weidner. "This number [seven] is not only employed to denote so many individual objects," Moorehead explains, "but it enters very largely into the whole plan of the book. Seven is the number of completeness, of perfection, and of dispensational fullness. All readers know that there are four sets of sevens that cover a very considerable section of the book. These are the seven messages to the seven churches (chaps. 2,3). The vision of the seven seals, which embraces 6–8:1 (with an episode between the sixth and the seventh of the series, viz.: vii). The vision of the seven trumpets, 8:2–11:16 (with an episode between the sixth and the seventh, 10–11:13). The vision of the seven vials, 15:5-16. Thus nearly one-half of the book belongs to this fourfold series. . . . It enters into passages where no direct mention of it is made. Thus, in 5:12, seven attributes of praise are ascribed to the Lamb that was slain; the white-robed company in 7:12 worship God with the like number of ascriptions. Chapter 14:1-20 consists of seven parts, viz.: the Lamb with His glorious company on mount Zion: the everlasting gospel: Babylon's fall: the solemn threat against any fellowship with the Beast: happy lot of those who die in the Lord from henceforth: the harvest: the vintage. Besides, the chapter mentions six angels, and One like the Son of Man. The place of honor is given the Son of Man—three angels are on each side of Him, and He is in the midst, presiding over the vast movements. The climax of the series is in the number four, where He sits on the white Cloud. The 'seven spirits before the throne' (1:4) express the infinite perfection of the Holy Spirit. The 'seven stars' in Christ's right hand (1:16) denote the complete authority He has over the churches. The Lamb has 'seven horns and seven eyes' (5:6), which denote the almighty power, the supreme intelligence, and the perfect omniscience with which He is endowed" (Wm. G. Moorehead, *Studies in the Book of Revelation,* pp. 30-32).

"The *half of seven* is used in the Old Testament," says Weidner, "to signify a time of tribulation. It appears in various forms, both in the Old and New Testament. The famine in Elijah's time lasted three and a half years (I Kings 17:1; Lk. 4:25; Jas. 5:17); the same period is the 'time and times, and half a time' of Dan. 7:25 and Dan. 12:7; 'the half of the week' referred to in Dan. 9:27. This same period of time appears in Revelation under the form of forty-two months (Rev. 11:2; 13:5), or 1,260 days (Rev. 11:3; 12:6), or 'a time and times, and half a time' (Rev. 12:14). The *two witnesses* also lay dead 'three days and a half' (Rev. 12:9,11). This *broken number* is therefore a symbol of great significance, and has been taken to be the 'signature' of the broken covenant or of suffering and disaster. . . . *Ten* is the symbolical representation of absolute perfection and complete development, whether referred to God or to the world. It is the 'signature' of a complete and perfect whole. *Ten* is the number of the Commandments; the Holy of Holies was a cube, each side being of ten cubits; *ten* times *ten*, or 100, is the number of God's Flock (Lk. 15:4,7); and the cube of *ten*, or 1,000, is the length of the reign of the saints (Rev. 20:4). The *tenth* generation means 'for ever' (compare Deut. 23:3 with Neh. 13:1). *Ten* is also the number of worldly completion, symbolizing perfect power. The *ten* Egyptian plagues symbolized the complete outpouring of divine wrath; the fourth beast of Daniel had *ten* horns (Dan. 7:7,24); the Red Dragon of the Apocalypse has *ten* horns (Rev. 12:3), as well as the First Beast or Antichrist (Rev. 13:1).

"*Twelve* is emphatically the number referring to the kingdom of God, the 'signature' of God *(three)* multiplied by the 'signature' of the world *(four)*. Lee holds that while *seven* is the sacred number of Scripture, *twelve* is the number of the Covenant People in whose midst God dwells, and with whom He has entered into Covenant relations. *Twelve* are the tribes of Israel: there were twice *twelve* courses of the priests; four times *twelve* cities of the *Levites; twelve* is the number of the Apostles; twice *twelve* is the number of the Elders who represent the Redeemed Church; the woman of Rev. 12:1 had a crown of *twelve* stars on her head; the New Jerusalem has *twelve* gates (Rev. 21:12), the wall of the city has *twelve* foundations (21:14), and the tree of life bears *twelve* names of fruits (22:2)" (Weidner, *op. cit.*, pp. xxxix, xl).

In the symbolism of colors, white is pre-eminently the color of innocence, purity, and righteousness, as well as of spiritual age, maturity, and perfection; black denotes famine, distress, suffering; blood red may, like blood itself, denote war, murder, or sacrificial death; purple is the color of royalty or voluptuous ease; and pale yellow is the color of expiring life and the kingdom of the dead (6:8). (See the excellent treatment of the symbolism of colors in John Peter Lange, *The Revelation of St. John*, pp. 16-18.)

Vocabulary. There are 916 different words in the Greek text of the Apocalypse; of these 416 are also found in the Fourth Gospel; 98 occur only once elsewhere in the New Testament; while there are 108 words that are not found anywhere else in the New Testament. There are numerous words here that speak of authority. For example, the word for *throne* occurs 44 times; *king, kingdom,* and *rule,* 37 times; *authority* and *power* 40 times. The many words translated to *see, to perceive,* etc., occur nearly 150 times. The words meaning *to write,* and the result of writing, i.e., a *book,* are found 60 times.

The Use of the Old Testament in the Apocalypse. This last book of the Bible forms an amazing mosaic, as it were, of Old and New Testament themes. In the appendix to Westcott and Hort's *Greek New Testament* (pp. 184-188), it is estimated that of 404 verses in this book, 265 contain lines which embrace approximately 550 references to Old Testament passages: there are 13 references to Genesis, 27 to Exodus, 79 to Isaiah, 53 to Daniel, etc. Many would agree with the late Professor Briggs that "the eschatology discourse of Jesus [Mt 24:25; Mk 13; Lk 21] is, to our mind, the key to the Apocalypse. This book is the work of a Jew saturated with Old Testament prophecy, under the guidance of the word of Jesus and the inspiration of God. It is the climax of the prophecy of the Old and New Testaments."

This extended incorporation of Old Testament material is seen in large sections, separate verses, and individual phrases. Thus the description of Babylon in chapter 18 has innumerable parallels with Jeremiah 51. The two beasts of chapter 13, with their ten horns which are ten kings, derive directly from the beast visions of Dan 7, 8. The vision of the two olive trees and two candlesticks (ch. 11) is a reframing of a vision of Zechariah (Zech 4). The time periods in the book of Revelation derive from Daniel, as time, times, and half a time (12:14, from Dan 12:7). Many of the judgments of the trumpets are amazingly parallel with the plagues of Egypt, which we shall consider in some detail in the exposition of that passage. Even in the first chapter, verse 6 refers back to Ex 19:6; verse 7 to Dan 7:13 and Zech 12:10,12; verse 14 consists of two passages taken from Dan 7:9,13; 10:5. Verse 15 derives from Dan 10:6; Ezk 1:24; verse 16 from Isa 11:4; 49:2; verse 17 from Isa 44:6; 48:12; and verse 18 from Isa 38:10. Many of the titles of deity used in this book are found originally in the Old Testament: "the Almighty" of 1:8, etc., in Gen 17:1; "Alpha and Omega," as above. (A good chapter on this subject will be found in Merrill C. Tenney's *Interpreting Revelation*, pp. 101-116.)

The Relation of the Revelation to the Olivet Discourse. That there are many lines of thought in the Apocalypse bearing strong resemblance to subjects touched upon in our Lord's Olivet Discourse, all would agree. Some have pressed this too far, it seems to me, and have forced the Revelation into a mold constructed from the threefold division of the Olivet Discourse. The events of the Olivet Discourse may be divided chronologically into three periods — pre-Tribulation, Tribulation, and post-Tribulation. It would be difficult to form a similar outline for the book of Revelation. However, there are many parallel passages, particularly those depicting physical and economic disturbances that are to take place toward the end of the age, e.g., Lk 21:9-11. War, famine, pestilence, and earthquakes appear in the first four judgments of the seals, wars often from Rev 16:12 to the end of chapter 19, and earthquakes in 16:18 and 18:8. The subject of martyrdom, as in Lk 21:12-16, is often introduced into the book, as in Rev 6:9-11; 11:7-10; 13:7,15; 16:6; 17:6; 18:24. The Great Tribulation is referred to in 7:14. False christs and false prophets appear in their final form in chapter 13. The celestial disturbances of Lk 21:25-28 are in Rev 6:12-14 ff. The coming of the Son of Man is announced in Rev 1:7, and is consummated when the Word of God descends from heaven at the time of the battle of Armageddon. (For a chapter on this subject, see my volume, *A Treasury of Books for Bible Study*, pp. 235-242. Some years ago Henry W. Frost wrote an entire book on this subject, *Matthew Twenty-Four and the Revelation*, New York, 1924.)

The Principle of Anticipation. Throughout this book, over and over again the author uses what is known as prolepsis; that is, early in the book he uses a phrase which reappears later, and generally with fuller development. Thus, e.g., Christ is called "the faithful witness" at the beginning (1:5), but he reappears as the Faithful Witness in 3:14; 17:6; 20:4 He is initially assigned the title, "the ruler of the kings of the earth" (1:5). But when we draw near the end of the age, when the prerogatives of this title are actually to be exercised, we find him again so designated (17:14; 19:16). It is announced at the beginning (1:6) that Christ has made us kings and priests; but this reappears at the end of the book (20:6). So likewise the title, "the Alpha and the Omega," is found at the beginning (1:8), and at the end (21:6; 22:13), as well as the title, "the Almighty" (1:8; 19:6,15; 21:22). The command to keep the words of this prophecy is given in the introduction, but this is exactly the command that we find repeatedly at the end of the book (22:7,10,18).

The promises made to believers in the seven epistles of chapters 2 and 3 reappear with amazing reiteration when the great struggles on earth are over, and the children of God are in the resurrection glory of the New Jerusalem. Thus, the promise of "the tree of life" (2:7) is found again at the very end of the book (22:2,14). Deliverance from the second death is promised to the faithful at Smyrna (2:11), and is referred to again at the Last Judgment (20:6,14). "The Spirit" declares, in the fourth epistle, that Christ will rule the nations "with a rod of iron" (2:27); and this is exactly what he is said to do at the battle of Armageddon (19:15). The promise of the "morning star" to those who are faithful (2:28) reappears in 22:16. The idea of walking with Christ "in white" is presented not only to the faithful of Sardis and Laodicea, but to the believers at the end of the age (3:4,5,18; 19:14). The "book of life" (3:5) reappears four times, beginning with the period of tribulation (13:8; 17:8; 20:12,15; 21:27). To the city of Philadelphia there is a fourfold promise (3:12), each phrase of which reappears at the end of the book: "He that overcometh, I will make him a pillar in the temple of God . . . and I will write upon him the name of my God [22:4], and the name of the city of my God [21:2,10], the new Jerusalem . . . [21:2,10], and mine own new name." Finally, the promise to the overcomers in Laodicea, that they would sit down with Christ on his throne, reappears at the beginning of the description of the New Jerusalem (20:4).

Alternating Scenes in Heaven and Scenes on Earth. A fundamental factor in this book, too often passed over by commentators, is of great help in understanding these chapters when it is recognized. That is, many scenes of this book are located in heaven, while the judgments themselves take place on this earth; and the scenes in heaven always precede the earthly events to which they are attached. Thus, the messages to the seven churches are preceded by a vision of the ascended Lord. The opening of the six seals in chapter 6 is preceded by a vision of the Lamb in heaven, worthy to open the book (chs. 4; 5). The judgments accompanying the blowing of the seven trumpets are preceded by a heavenly scene extending from 7:1 to 8:5. The dreadful events of chapters 11; 12; 13 are again preceded by a heavenly scene of instructions to John. The devastations accompanying the seven plagues (chs. 15; 16) are preceded by the announcements of the angels and the showing of "the temple . . . in heaven." And, after the final judgment of chapter 20, the book concludes with a picture of the heavenly home of the redeemed.

I have always felt that there are two great truths to be drawn from this phenomenon. First, what is about to take place on earth, though unknown to man and unexpected by him, is fully known to those in heaven—the ascended Lord, the angels, the twenty-four elders, the living creatures, and the others. Secondly, what is to take place on earth is under the complete control and direction of heaven, so that we may safely say, judging from this book, as well as from other prophetic books in the Scripture, that everything that takes place on this earth only fulfills the Word of God. This principle is remarkably set forth in the preliminary announcements concerning the kings of the earth going forth to make war with the Lamb. Though we read of the ten kings satanically inspired, having one mind and giving their power and authority unto the beast (17:12,13), nevertheless, it is God who "did put in their hearts to do his mind, and to come to one mind, and to give their kingdom unto the beast, until the words of God should be accomplished" (17:17).

The Book of Judgment. From the beginning of this book to almost the very end, we must ever keep in mind the fact that *the book of Revelation is a book of judgment*, therefore, a book involving destruction, havoc, death, pain, tribulation. The very description of the Lord Jesus as he is about to send messages to the churches contains some factors that indubitably speak of judgment—eyes "as a flame of fire," feet "like unto burnished brass," out of whose mouth proceeds "a sharp two-edged sword." The following passages bear especially on this theme of judgment: 6:16,17; 11:17,18; 14:7,10; 16:5,7; 18:8,10,20; 19:2; and 20:11-15.

Canonicity. The Western Church early believed that the book of Revelation should be included in the canonical books of the New Testament, and it was publicly read in the churches. But the Eastern Church seemed reluctant to adopt the same position, and did not agree on the canonicity of the Apocalypse until the fourth century. The Muratorian Canon, compiled about 200, includes the book in its list. By the middle of the third century, the Bishop of Alexandria accepted the book as canonical. It was omitted from the Vulgate Syriac Version. The Third Council of Carthage (397) accepted the book as canonical, and the entire volume appears in the early manuscripts, the Codex Sinaiticus, the Codex Vaticanus, and the Codex Alexandrinus. Luther greatly erred in placing the book of Revelation, along with the epistles of James, Jude, and Hebrews, in an appendix. For centuries the Protestant Church universal and the Eastern and Western Churches have agreed that it is a canonical work. (This entire subject has been treated with great thoroughness in a volume by Ned B. Stonehouse: *The Apocalypse in the Ancient Church*, Goes, Holland, 1929.)

The Four Principal Schools of Interpretation. The book of Revelation is the only large portion of the Word of God concerning which four basic differing systems of interpretation have been developed. The system of interpretation a Bible student adopts will make an enormous amount of difference in what he believes the book teaches.

(1) *The Spiritual Scheme of Interpretation.* From the time of Augustine, there have always been some Biblical scholars who have insisted that the purpose of this book is not to instruct the church regarding the future, not to predict specific events, but simply to teach fundamental spiritual principles. This is the view expressed over and over again by Milligan (W. Milligan, *Lectures on the Apocalypse*), though at times he contradicts his own conviction. He says in one place: "The Apocalypse does deal in a most distinct and emphatic manner with the Second Coming of the Lord." Gloag insists upon the same view: "The book is designed to teach us the spiritual history of the Church of Christ, to warn us of those spiritual dangers to which we are exposed, to inform us of the spiritual trials to which we are liable, to describe the great contest with evil, and to comfort us with the assurance of the final victory of Christ over the powers of darkness." Now all of this is true. The book does teach principles, spiritual principles; it does bear a message of comfort in its assurance of the ultimate victory of Christ. But everything in the book contradicts the view that it does not unfold the prophetic future. The book itself claims to be genuine prophecy. "Evil," as Moorehead says, "ever seeks to concentrate in a person or system; so does good. Revelation shows us evil centralized in the beast and in the false prophet." Certainly the return of Christ is in this book, and that is a prophecy of a future event; likewise, the resurrection of believers and the judgment of the Great White Throne. (This is the view held by most commentators of the Reformed faith, Peters and others.)

(2) *The Preterist Scheme of Interpretation.* This system of interpretation of Revelation insists that the author describes only events taking place on earth in the Roman Empire during his own time, especially toward the end of the first century. This was a view developed principally in the seventeenth century by a Jesuit scholar, Alcazar, in an attempt to reply to the arguments of the Reformers, who insisted that the book predicted the corruption and doom of the Roman Catholic Church, especially in the two chapters devoted to Babylon. Alcazar's view has been adopted by a number of modern writers—Moses Stuart, A. S. Peake, Moffatt, Sir William Ramsay, Simcox, and others. These men hold that the ruler whose deadly wound was healed refers to Nero, and that Domitian was the beast of chapter 13. It is true that the preterist view must be applied in our interpretation of the seven churches. But to say that the remainder of the book refers only to the events of the first century is really to deny its prophetic character, and to force many of its statements into a mold too small to contain them. As Milligan has said, "The whole tone of the book leads to the opposite conclusion. It treats of much that was to happen down to the very end of time, until the hour of the full accomplishment of the Church's struggle, of the full winning of her victory, and of the full attainment of her rest. The Apocalypse bears distinctly upon its face that it is concerned with the history of the Church until she enters upon her heavenly inheritance" (*op. cit.*, p. 41).

(3) *The Historicist Scheme of Interpretation.* In the history of the interpretation of the Apocalypse, probably more great names are attached to this scheme than to any other one view, with the exception of the futurist. According to this conception, the book of Revelation, especially in the prophecies of the seals, the trumpets, and the bowls, sets forth particular events in the history of the world that relate to the welfare of the Church *from the first century down to modern times.* The greatest work based on this theory is the four-volume study by Elliott (E. B. Elliott, *Horae Apocalypticae*), which may be taken as an illustration of this scheme. He says that the trumpet judgments cover the period from A.D. 395 to 1453, that the first trumpet refers to the invasion of the Goths, the third to the Huns under Attila, the fifth to the hordes of Moslems pouring into the West in the sixth and seventh centuries, etc. To take another illustration, Mede, in his famous work, says that the sixth seal predicts the overthrow of paganism under Constantine, that the second vial refers to Luther, the third to events in the reign of Queen Elizabeth I, etc. Many of those who belong to this school insist that the earthquake in 11:19 refers to the French Revolution; others find Napoleon Bonaparte in the book of Revelation, etc., etc.

Now, apart from all other objections to this scheme, it is admitted on every hand that it offers no fundamental principle or criterion of judgment by which we are able to determine exactly what historical events are referred to in a given passage. And this has led to a vast morass of confusion and contradiction among those who hold this view.

Milligan, in a powerful criticism of this whole scheme, says: "We may indeed admit that the events found in it by the historical interpreter would have been instructive or consolatory to the early Christian, if he could have thoroughly apprehended them. But the real difficulty lies in this, that such apprehension was then impossible. . . . While thus useless to the men first addressed by them, the visions of the Apocalypse would, upon this system, have been equally useless to the great body of the Christian Church, even after they had been fulfilled, and their fulfillment recognized by a few competent inquirers. The poor and the unlearned have always known, and will probably always know, little of the historical events supposed to be alluded to. Could it be a part of the Divine plan to make the understanding of a revelation so earnestly commended to us dependent on an acquaintance with the ecclesiastical and political history of the world for many hundred years? The very supposition is absurd. It is inconsistent with the first promise of the book, 'Blessed is he that readeth, and they that hear the words of the prophecy!' . . . The selection of historical events made by the system is in a high degree arbitrary, and cannot be said to correspond to the degree of importance which these events have vindicated for themselves in the course of history" *(op. cit.,* p. 131).

(4) *The Futurist Scheme of Interpretation.* It can hardly be doubted that the Revelation is a book of predictive prophecy. To deny this is to disregard the style, the theme, and the future events of the Apocalypse. Certainly the Second Advent, the final conflict of Christ with the forces of evil, the Millennium, the final judgment, are events still future. The futurist scheme of interpretation insists that, for the most part, the visions of this book will be fulfilled toward the end and at the end of this age. The futurist view was long ago excellently defined as that scheme which "looks for the fulfillment of these predictions, neither in the early presentations and heresies of the church, nor in the long series of centuries from the first preaching of the Gospel until now, but in the events which are immediately to precede, to accompany, and to follow the Second Advent of our Lord and Saviour" *(Lectures on the Apocalypse,* p. 68).

It is strange to find Gloag (in 1891) saying that "this system has not many supporters" *(op. cit.,* p. 372). The fact is, it has a great many supporters, among whom are some of the outstanding Biblical expositors of modern times and some of the most distinguished students of prophecy. Among them are Todd, Benjamin Wills Newton, Seiss, William Kelly, Peters, practically all of those writing within the circumference of the Plymouth Brethren, e.g., S.P. Tregelles, Nathaniel West, A. C. Gaebelein, Scofield, Moorehead, Walter Scott, Alford, and others. Theodor Zahn's notable commentary on Revelation (not yet translated into English) takes the futurist position, and Zahn is recognized as the greatest conservative New Testament scholar of Europe towards the close of the nineteenth century. Simcox, who is no futurist himself, frankly admits "from the time of Tertullian and Hippolytus—not to say Justin and Irenaeus—we have a consistent expectation of the course of events that will precede the last judgment" (G. A. Simcox, *The Revelation of St. John the Divine* in CBSC, p. xliv).

There is, of course, an extreme futurism which must be emphatically rejected. Some futurists go so far as to say that the seven churches of Asia will be reorganized and re-established at the end of the age, at which time the predictions concerning them will be fulfilled—a view wholly unnecessary and unreasonable.

The objection so often heard, that it is strange to have in our New Testament a book which, for the most part, contains matters pertaining to the end of the age, does not hold when one reviews the fundamental factor regarding the basic far-reaching prophecies of the Scriptures, namely, that from earliest times they point to the end of the age for their fulfillment. Is not this true of the very first prophecy of the Bible—"and I will put enmity between thee and the woman, and between thy seed and her seed: he shall bruise thy head, and thou shalt bruise his heel" (Gen 3:15)? Is not this a prophecy of Messianic victory which still awaits its final fulfillment? The extended prophecy of Jacob in Genesis 49 refers to "the last days," as it says. Over and over again in the Book of Daniel, we are told that its prophecies refer to "the end" (7:26; 9:26,27; 11:13,27; 12:8,13).

Does not our Lord's Olivet discourse point directly to the *end* of the age, and Christ's still future Second Advent? (Mt 24:3,14; also his prophetic parables, e.g., Mt 13:39,40) So with Paul speaking to the Thessalonians regarding the man of sin; Peter's account of the apostasy of the last days; Paul's great eschatological prophecy in II Timothy 3, and the whole body of prophecy in the familiar resurrection chapter, I Corinthians 15. All these require a futurist interpretation. It is not unreasonable that the Bible should conclude with a book of prophecies which, for the most part, will be fulfilled at the great final consummation of this age—the end of the revolt against God, and the beginning of that age of righteousness for which all just men long.

Of course, there is some truth in each of these systems of interpretation. The first three chapters must be interpreted historically. There *are* great spiritual principles set forth in the judgments, promises, prophecies, and Messianic victories of this book. For the most part, however, the Apocalypse will be most correctly interpreted if the futurist scheme is adopted.

The Apocalypse and Apocalyptic Literature. When the gift of true prophecy ceased in the Old Testament with Malachi, about 400 B.C., there was developed within the Jewish commonwealth a body of literature a part of which is called apocalyptic. This literature was written in symbolic, pictorial language. It was composed, for the most part, in times of persecution, especially in the days of Antiochus Epiphanes in the second century, as well as in the first century of this era, when the Hebrew people saw the destruction of their holy city. Apocalyptic literature is, principally, eschatological. It concentrates on those future events when the enemies of Israel, and those of our Lord, will be destroyed, and Israel herself will be restored to her former glory.

The Apocalypse of the New Testament is distinctly different, on the whole, from the preceding apocalyptic literature. As George Ladd has well pointed out: (1) The author designates his book as a prophecy (1:3; 22:7, etc.), and the book is thus a product of the prophetic spirit. (2) John does not take the name of some great former prophet of Israel, but uses his own name. (3) John does not retrace history under the guise of prophecy, but looks prophetically into the future himself. (4) John's book, while filled with dark and ominous passages, does not convey the mood of pessimism, as so many of the apocalypses did, but of optimism, for the seer constantly reiterates the great truth that Christ will conquer all enemies, and that the kingdoms of this world will become the kingdom of our Lord and Saviour Jesus Christ. (5) Finally, the Apocalypse presses upon its readers great ethical demands. There is a sense of moral urgency here. Salvation is not something automatically conferred but that which will be given to those who bear the marks of true children of God (G. E. Ladd: "Apocalyptic, Apocalypse," in *Baker's Dictionary of Theology*, 1960, pp. 50-54).

Prolonged Study Needed for the Understanding of This Book. Because of its symbolism, its saturation with Old Testament passages and themes, the various schemes of interpretation that have developed concerning this book through the ages, and the profundity and vastness of the subjects that are here unveiled, I believe that the Apocalypse, above every other book of the Bible, will yield its meaning only to those who give it prolonged and careful study. Professor William Milligan has challengingly reminded us that, "The book is there, and it must either be excluded from the NT, or the Church must continue her struggle to comprehend it until she succeeds in doing so. Consider —1. In the first place, that we start with the supposition—a supposition denied by none of those to whom these lectures are addressed—that the Revelation of St. John is part of the Word of God. This consideration settles the whole question. The simple fact that a book has been given by the Almighty to man constitutes man's obligation to make every effort to understand it. It may be hard to do so. We may be long defeated. Not less is the effort one that we are bound to make; using all the appliances in our power, and watching, if we still feel that we are in darkness, for the first symptoms of light. Nothing is more certain than that, had it not been intended that we should use this book, the exalted Redeemer would not have given it by revelation to His servant John" *(Lectures On the Apocalypse*, p. 4).

Many students, both before and since

Lange, have voiced the same hope he expressed in 1870: "Doubtless, in the future, the importance and influence of this Book will constantly increase with the increasing confusion and gloom of the times, with the increasing danger which they offer to sound and sober faith" (*Revelation*, p. 63).

The Outline of the Book. Many different schemes have been proposed for arranging or classifying the twenty-two chapters of the Apocalypse, some of them quite fantastic. It is my opinion that those schemes which attempt to base an outline upon seven sevens in this book are strained and artificial. Thus, e.g., is Benjamin Warfield's outline: the seven churches (1:1–3:22); the seven seals (4:1–8:1); the seven trumpets (8:2–11:19); the seven mystic figures (12:1–14:20); the seven vials (15:1–16:21); the seven fold judgment of the harlot (17:1–19:10), and the seven fold trumpet (19:11–22:5). All would agree that four of these divisions are inescapable: the seven churches, the seven-sealed book, the seven trumpets, and the seven vials of judgment. But the concept of *seven* is not stated in the other sections. After I had studied this volume for years, there finally opened out to me an outline which, I think, is not strained, and yet is easy to remember. Apart from the prologue (1:1-8) and the epilogue (22:6-21), the book may be logically divided as follows:

I. The letters to the seven churches of Asia. 1:9–3:22.
II. The seven-sealed book and the earthly events it announces. 4:1–6:17.
III. The judgments announced by seven trumpets. 7:1–9:21.
IV. The darkest hour of world history. 10:1–13:18.
V. The seven vials of judgment. 14:1–16:21.
VI. Babylon and Armageddon. 17:1–19:21.
VII. The Millennium; the Last Judgment; the New Jerusalem and Eternity. 20:1–22:5.

Note that these divisions occur in the following sequence of blocks of chapters –3-3-3-4-3-3-3.

The Text. The translators responsible for the epochal King James (Authorized Version of the New Testament used for their authority the Greek text as constructed by Erasmus. For the Apocalypse Erasmus had only one Greek manuscript, a cursive of the thirteenth century, and even this was of inferior quality. For this reason there are many words and passages in the AV that do not rest upon the more ancient and authoritative manuscripts. Since then the great Greek manuscripts of the New Testament, as the Sinaiticus, the Alexandrian, etc., have become known and have been thoroughly studied. Consequently, for all purposes of serious study of the Apocalypse, one must use the RV of 1891, or one of the later versions. (The great value of the now famous Chester Beatty Papyrus of the Apocalypse, probably of the early third century, does not require consideration in our necessarily brief commentary).

COMMENTARY

I. The Letters to the Seven Churches. 1:1–3:22.

1:1-8. Though the exact idea of *letters* to the seven churches is not actually found in chapter 1, in verse 4 we do have the phrase, **John to the seven churches which are in Asia,** and later (v. 11) John receives the command to write what he sees and send it to the seven churches. The location of the seven churches is considered in the commentary on chapter 2.

Chapter 1 contains a rich, almost blinding revelation of Jesus Christ himself. Verses 4-8 present three basic descriptions of Christ. John seems to be describing the Christ he *knows,* for there is no indication that he has been given a special revelation here. This is the Christ of the past, present, and future, as set forth in the phrase, **who is and who was and who is to come** (v. 4, ASV). In the past, Christ was **the faithful witness** and **the firstborn from among the dead;** in the present, he is the one who **loveth us, and loosed us from our sins** (v. 5, ASV); in the future, **he cometh with the clouds**

and every eye shall see him . . . and all the tribes of the earth shall mourn over him (v. 7, ASV). The statement that Christ has made us to be **a kingdom of priests** unto God (v. 6) is from the basic declaration in Ex 19:6, quoted centuries later by Peter (I Pet 2:5,9). The passage referring to the future has a double OT reference: in Dan 7:13 the Son of man is depicted as coming with clouds, and the fact that all shall then see him is declared in Zech 12:10,12. The word here translated **pierced** occurs elsewhere in the NT only in Jn 19:37 (cf. Zech 12:10).

I have always thought that the phrase, **the ruler of the kings of the earth** (1:5), is the key title of Christ for the book of Revelation. Many other kings are referred to in this book: kings of nations that go out to war against the Lamb, the king of the abyss, etc. There is no indication until the end of the book that the kings of the earth acknowledge Christ as King of kings. In fact, the book of Revelation is almost a record of Christ's enforcing this title, and finally assuming the pre-eminence to which the title points.

9-11. We have here the words Christ *spoke* to the apostle, a brief command to record what he is about to see, and instructions for sending the transcription when it is finished. There is little doubt that **the Lord's day** here (v. 10) refers to the day we know as Sunday.

12-19. In this description of the ascended Lord, the Christ John *saw* is seen walking in the midst of the **seven golden lampstands,** which symbolically represent the seven churches (see v. 20). Here as in Dan 7:13, our Lord is called **the Son of man** (Rev 1:13), a title found only once elsewhere in this book (14:14). The various phrases used in describing Christ are taken principally from Dan 7:9,13; 10:5,6; Ezk 1:24. The entire description gives us first an overwhelming impression of omnipotence, and then certain symbols pointing to judgment, as the flame of fire, burnished brass, and a sharp two-edged sword.

Christ identifies himself with the title **the first and the last** (Rev 1:17), a title used of God himself in Isa 44:6; 48:12. Observe what Christ presents as the reasons why those who are his should **Fear not:** (1) He is the First and the Last, and **the Living one;** (2) He was dead, and became alive again; and (3) He has the keys of death and of Hades (vv. 17,18). If he is the First and Last, then he is the Christ of creation in the past, and the one who will bring all things to their divinely ordained consummation at the end. He will abide when all of his enemies have been defeated, and Satan and all his cohorts have been put away forever. The fact that he was dead identifies Christ with the most tragic of all man's experiences. No mere human being can conquer death —but Christ did. As he was dead but is now alive, so we who are his, though we die, will yet be forever alive with him. That he has **the keys of death and of Hades** certainly implies that the destiny of human souls is entirely under the jurisdiction of Jesus Christ.

Verse 19 has been taken by many as indicating a threefold division of the book of Revelation, in which **the things which thou sawest** refers to chapter 1, **the things which are,** to the seven churches in chapters 2 and 3, and **the things which shall come to pass hereafter,** ASV, to the remainder of the book. Actually, this classification does not help much in interpretation. It should be remembered, moreover, that the words here translated **hereafter,** *meta tauta,* occur nine other times in the book of Revelation (4:1; 7:1; 7:9; 9:12; 15:5; 18:1; 19:1; 20:3).

20. We are not absolutely sure what John means by the statement **the seven stars are the angels of the seven churches.** This word translated **angel** occurs seventy-six times in the Revelation. Fundamentally, the word means *messenger.* Some believe this simply refers to some leading person in each church; others say that this implies that each church has its representative angel in heaven. These "angels" are at least the ones through whom these messages are to be conveyed to the seven churches.

The term **Asia** (v. 11) has had various meanings throughout the centuries. In NT times **Asia** was the name of the Roman province located in the westernmost part of what is now Asia Minor. It was the largest and most important of all the Roman provinces of that area, embracing the districts of Caria, Lydia, and Mysia. The seven churches addressed in these letters were all located in the west-central part of this province. Beginning at **Ephesus** in the southwest and moving northward, we come to **Smyrna** and **Pergamum;** turning east and south, we arrive at **Thyatira, Sardis, Philadelphia,** and **Laodicea.** A circle embracing these cities would have a radius of not more than sixty miles. That these letters from the risen Lord should be addressed to churches in Asia is not hard to understand, since that is where John had been living for many years, and no doubt he was well known to the churches of this area. Why these particular churches were chosen, we cannot be sure. Paul spent a long period of time at Ephesus on the third missionary journey (Acts 19; 20:16,17); Lydia was from Thyatira (Acts 16:14); and Epaphras labored at Laodicea (Col 2:1; 4:12-16). However, we know nothing of Paul's labors in six of these seven cities, and four of them appear nowhere else in the NT. Furthermore, we know there were churches existing at the end of the first century in some cities of Asia that are never referred to in the NT. Before Paul had completed his third missionary journey, "all who dwelt in Asia heard the word of the Lord, both Jews and Greeks" (Acts 19:10,26).

All of these letters follow the same sequence. Each begins with a phrase descriptive of the exalted Christ, who is addressing the churches; and each descriptive phrase is found in the preceding chapter in John's account of his vision of the risen Christ. In each letter, with the exception of the ones to Laodicea and Sardis, Christ's first words are those of commendation. This commendation is always followed by some details regarding the condition of the church, leading to a rebuke and warning —with the exception of Philadelphia and Smyrna, which receive no rebuke. Each letter concludes with a promise to those believers who overcome.

Note the many references to things of **Satan:** twice we read of "the synagogue of Satan" (2:9; 3:9); at Pergamum was "the throne of Satan" (2:13); in the letter to Thyatira mention is made of "the deep things of Satan" (2:24); in connection with Smyrna, the warning is given that the devil would cast some of them into prison. In addition, we find references to the curse of the Nicolaitans, the presence of the pernicious teachings of Balaam (2:14), and the rebuke of Thyatira for suffering the presence of one called Jezebel (2:20).

For three reasons I am refraining in this brief survey of the Apocalypse from a detailed examination of each of these letters: In the first place, these two chapters do not present major eschatological problems, while the exact meaning of some of the promises found here, if considered at all, would require extended discussion. In the second place, these letters are more widely used in expository series of messages than any other part of this book, and are somewhat familiar to most Bible students. Thirdly, to discuss the relevant historical data for each of these cities would compel abbreviation in the later treatment of basic problems of prophetic interpretation.

2:1-7. Ephesus was the largest city in Asia. It is the only one of these seven which has a treble place in NT literature: it is given extensive prominence in the Acts (18:18—19:41); to this church Paul wrote one of his epistles; and to it the ascended Lord sent a letter. After commending the church for its labor, patience, and intolerance of pseudo-apostles, the Lord refers to one tragic defect—she had left her **first love** (v. 4).

G. Campbell Morgan relates this passage to Paul's words of warning to the Corinthian church: " 'For I espoused you to one husband, that I might present you as a pure virgin to Christ. But I fear, lest by any means, as the serpent beguiled Eve in his craftiness, your minds should be corrupted from the simplicity and the purity that is toward Christ'. . . . The elements of first love then are simplicity and purity. . . . The love of the Church to Christ is typified by the love of the wife for the husband. What then is the love of Christ to the Church? Unselfish love, love in which there was no single thought of self. What then is the Church's love for Christ? The response of love to the mystery of love, the submission of love to perfect love. First love is the love of espousal. Its notes are simplicity, and purity, marital love, the response of love to love, the subjection of a great love to a great love, the submission of a self-denying love to a love that denies self. First love is the abandonment of all for a love that has abandoned all" (*A First Century Message to Twentieth Century Christians*, pp. 40-42).

8-11. The word **Smyrna** is related to the word *myrrh,* which in turn is symbolic of death. Smyrna's history has been one of successive sackings, fires, destructions. Polycarp, one of the more famous of the earlier martyrs, was Bishop of Smyrna. This city is the only one of the seven still in flourishing condition.

12-17. Of **Pergamum** an ancient writer said it was "given to idolatry more than all Asia." The high hill behind it was adorned with numerous temples, among which was the great temple to Zeus, who was called *Soter Theos*, the Saviour God. Pergamum was the first city in Asia to erect a temple to Augustus. It was famous for its medical schools; and Asclepius, god of health, symbolized by a serpent, was worshiped there. Ramsay says, "Beyond all cities in Asia Minor, it gives the traveller the impression of being the home of authority." How appropriate, then, that here, as we are told, was Satan's throne. A great deal of discussion has arisen over exactly who are meant by the Nicolaitans (here, and in 2:6). In some manner they encouraged some in the church to return to pagan laxity of morals.

18-29. In **Thyatira,** the smallest of these seven cities, the church had allowed a false prophetess to instruct her, leading members into practices of immorality and idolatry. For this reason the Christ who addresses her is described as one coming to execute judgment. To the overcomers of this city Christ promises privileges similar to those he himself exercises (see 12:5; 19:15; 22:16).

3:1-6. In John's day, **Sardis,** once the capital of the ancient kingdom of Lydia, was comparatively insignificant. Even the church there partook of this abasement—**thou hast a name that thou livest, and thou art dead** (v. 1).

7-13. Only the letter to the church at **Philadelphia** contains no word of rebuke. Even today this Asian city has a Christian group. Though so worthy, this church was nevertheless to know a time of severe trial. Note carefully that the word is **trial** here, not *tribulation*. But in the trial the believers were to be divinely kept (see Jn 17:15).

3:14-22. The last letter is to **Laodicea,** which receives no commendation. The unfavorable condition in this church was lukewarmness: the members were **neither cold nor hot** (v. 15). The lukewarm person does not become greatly disturbed at hearing heretical teaching, and is not vigorous in the defense of the truth. This spirit of indifference is the most tragic thing that can happen to a church. The close of this letter is different from the conclusions of the other six in that it makes an application to the individual: **If any man hear my voice, and open the door, I will come in to him,** etc. (v. 20).

Through the centuries, various students have held four different views of the deeper implications of this series of seven letters. First, there is the historical interpretation—that these churches did exist at the time John wrote and bore characteristics such as those here depicted. Secondly, there is the view—no doubt correct—that these churches are not only historic, but are representative of different types of churches down through the ages. Accordingly, they manifest both the good and the tragic characteristics present in churches century after century. The warnings and promises here, then, are for all ages. There is a third, and rather fantastic, view that these prophecies are to be interpreted futuristically; that is, that all these cities are to be literally restored at the end of the age, and then the predictions will be truly fulfilled. A fourth view, held by many, is that these seven churches represent seven successive periods of church history, extending from the first century to the end of this age. I personally do not follow this interpretation, and a study of the writings of its proponents will reveal confusion upon confusion. Virtringa, e.g., identifies the sixth church with the first century of the Reformation, and the seventh with the Reformed church of his own day. Generally, writers who take this view claim that they are in the Laodicean period. The only aspect of this fourth explanation that I think may have some virtue is the interpretation of Laodicea. It seems that lukewarmness and indifference will mark the church at the end of the age, particularly indifference as to the great doctrines of the faith and unwillingness to defend them.

II. The Seven-Sealed Book and the Earthly Events It Announces. 4:1–6:17.

Though there are some eschatological elements in the portrait of Christ in the first chapter, and some predictive elements in the letters to the seven churches, but *not* extending to the end of the age, the truly prophetic portion of the Apocalypse begins with the section we are now about to consider. As noted in the Introduction, the larger part of this section is introductory in nature, for the scene recorded in chapters 4 and 5 is a heavenly one. Actually, predictions of far future events do not begin until chapter

6. John now beholds a door opening in heaven, and hears a voice saying, "Come up hither, and I will show thee the things which must come to pass hereafter." (ASV; on other openings of heaven, see Ezk 1:1; Mk 1:10; Jn 1:51.) Many commentators place the 'rapture' of the Church between chapters 3 and 4 of this book, but inasmuch as the text itself is silent on such a subject, one questions the wisdom of even discussing it here.

4:1-3. Just as the book of Revelation opens with a reference to the throne of God, and the letter to the last of the seven churches closes with a reference to the throne of Christ, so here the first great prophetic vision begins with the statement, **there was a throne set in heaven** (see Dan 7:9). A **throne** is the symbol of government and power. John attempts to record a vision of God similar to that beheld by Moses (Ex 19: 9,19), by Isaiah (6:5), and by Ezekiel (1:26-28). The seer likens what he saw to three stones: the **jasper,** a transparent stone like glass or rock crystal; the **sardius,** red in color; and the **emerald,** green. In the breastplate of the high priest the first and last stones were sardius and jasper (Ex 28:17,20). It has been suggested that these stones stand for holiness, wrath, and mercy. Around the throne was a **rainbow,** which speaks of grace, or, as Hengstenberg says, "of grace returning after wrath."

4,5. The first great heavenly company of this book is now introduced: twenty-four **elders** sitting on twenty-four thrones situated around the throne of God (see also 11:16), arrayed in white garments and wearing **crowns** *(stephanoi)* of gold. *Stephanoi* were crowns bestowed on victors. There have been many identifications of these elders, but most would agree with Govett that they are "councillors of the thrones, conversant with the purposes of the king, and able to impart intelligence to John as the servant of God" (Robert Govett, *Lectures on the Apocalypse, in loco).* Twenty-four as a symbolic number is found only in the Apocalypse, and there only in relation to these elders (5:8; 11:16; 19:4). (For a detailed discussion of the identity of the elders, see G. H. Lang, *The Revelation of Jesus Christ,* pp. 124-136.) From the throne proceeded lightnings, voices, and thunder, and, in addition, John saw seven lamps of fire, which he identifies as symbols of **the seven Spirits of God.** The concept of the seven Spirits of God certainly refers to the perfection and fullness of the activities of the Third Person of the Godhead.

6,7. Before the throne was **a sea of glass** (cf. Ex 24:10), indicating, it would seem, that all that the sea once stood for —storms and treacherous waves, symbolical of agitation among the peoples of the earth—had now been subdued. Another group, **four living creatures,** is introduced—one like a lion, one like a calf, one with the face of a man, and one like a flying eagle (similar to those in Ezk 1:5-14, 15-22; 10:20-22). Swete, with characteristic succinctness, rightly says, "The four forms suggest what is noblest, strongest, wisest and swiftest in animate nature. Nature, including man, is represented before the throne taking its part in the fulfillment of the Divine will and the worship of the Divine majesty" (H. B. Swete, *The Apocalpse of St. John, in loco)* These reappear in Rev 6:7; 7:11; 14:3; 15:7; 19:4.

8-11. With the introduction of the four living creatures, we have the first of twenty hymns, as they might be called, sung by various heavenly groups throughout the book of Revelation. Five of them are in these two chapters prefacing the opening of the seals. The first two are hymns to God: one sung by the living creatures ascribing holiness to God (4:8) and the other by the twenty-four elders acknowledging God as Creator. The opening words of the first hymn remind us of Isa 6:3, technically known in ancient hymnology as the *Trisagion.* The third and fourth are hymns to the Lamb, sung by the two groups just mentioned, acknowledging that the Lamb is worthy to open the book (Rev 5:9,10; 5:11,12). The fifth hymn is sung to both God and the Lamb by "every created thing in heaven, on the earth, and under the earth" (v. 13), and ascribes to them blessing, honor, glory, and dominion.

5:1-5. John adds some details regarding the One sitting upon the throne, who is said to hold in his right hand **a book written within and on the back, close sealed with seven seals** (ASV). Whether this is a book in codex form, like our books today, with the seven seals somewhat equally distributed on the sides, top, and bottom, or a scroll with the seven seals in one continuous line, we are not told. Another voice is heard, that of a strong angel, asking who is **worthy** to open this book (v. 2). The answer is that no one in the universe is worthy. Then one of the elders (v. 5) announces that **the Lion of the tribe of Judah** (Gen 49:9), **the Root of David** (Isa 11:1,10) is **worthy** to open this book, for two reasons: first, he has **overcome,** which would seem to refer to his defeat, while on earth, of Satan and every evil power; and, secondly, by his redemptive work he has purchased us unto God, with his blood (Rev 5:9). Note the universality of the **redeemed** in verse 9.

6,7. It is not without great significance that the redemptive work of Christ is revealed as of pre-eminent importance in the thought of these heavenly creatures and in the program of God to be consummated in this book. The word here translated **slain** (v. 6) occurs only here, in verses 9, 12, and in 13:8. "It is 'blood' even more than 'death' that connotes sacrifice; for one may die without being slain and may be slain without being made a sacrifice" (R. C. H. Lenski, *The Interpretation of St. John's Revelation, in loco).*

8-14. Here the harp is mentioned for the first time (reappearing in 14:2 and 15:2). This idea of **a new song** is found frequently in the OT, as in Ps 33:3; 40:3; 96:1; 98:1; 149:1. Revelation 5:10 is practically a reaffirmation of the truth expressed in 1:6. Here, I think, for the first time we have the concept of the reigning of saints and a kingdom. Carefully note the statement, **they reign**[ed] **upon the earth.**

We are now ready for the actual opening of these seals, but before beginning the study of chapter 6, note—a point often overlooked—that while the seals are opened, that is, stripped from the book, the book itself is never opened. This, of course, leads to many suggestions as to the contents of the book. Simcox says, certainly in error, it is the Book of Life. Irenaeus insisted that it contained "the things of Christ." Swete is safe in saying that its contents cover the unknown future, and he thus calls it "the book of destiny." Milligan says it contains "the whole counsel of God." Only six seals are opened in this chapter; the seventh is not opened until the trumpet judgments are about to be announced (8:1). Of these six seals, the first four form a group; the fifth and sixth stand by themselves. Each of the first four is introduced with a rider on a horse, from which derives the famous phrase, used in many ways in numerous literatures, "the four horsemen of the Apocalypse."

6:1-8. The identity of the first horse will in large part be determined by the identification of the following three. The second horse and its rider are said to **take peace from the earth,** and this, with the words **slay** and **sword,** indicates war. The third horse and its rider surely represent scarcity of food, though not altogether a famine. (The Roman coin *denarius,* here translated **shilling** (ASV), was the equivalent of a man's wages for a day of work. One measure of barley or grain was the average daily consumption of workmen.) The fourth horse and its rider, more dreadful than any of the others, bear the very name **Death.** To them was given authority over the fourth part of the earth, **to kill with sword, and with famine, and with death, and by the wild beasts of the earth** (ASV).

In the light of the meaning of the second, third, and fourth riders, it would seem unreasonable to identify the first rider with the Lord Jesus Christ, who is the rider on the white horse in Revelation 19. When Christ does come, "conquering and to conquer," there will be no subsequent judgments, such as the second, third, and fourth horses represent. Swete is correct in saying of the first horse, "A vision of the victorious Christ would be inappropriate at the opening of a series which symbolizes bloodshed, famine, pestilence." Even Torrance discerns this, though he adopts a strictly spiritual scheme of interpretation: "Can there be any doubt that this is the vision of antiChrist? It so resembles the real Christ that it deceives people, even many a reader of this passage! . . . It applies whenever evil is mounted upon good and wherever spiritual wickedness conquers by borrowing from the Christian Faith" (Thomas F. Torrance, *The Apocalypse Today,* p. 44).

Note that in these first four scenes there are no names of individuals, human or superhuman, no geographical terms, and no specific events. The judgments are, as it were, of a general nature: wars have occurred often on earth, and they are often accompanied by pestilence and by scarcity of food, if not famine conditions. This would seem to be, then, just a preliminary phase of the more terrible judgments to follow.

9-11. The opening of the first four seals forms a unit. In the opening of the fifth seal we have what I would call the first truly difficult problem in the book of Revelation. Here are the souls of men who were **slain for the word of God, and for the testimony which they held.** In other words, these are martyrs, and they ask the risen Lord, **How long . . . dost thou not judge and avenge our blood on them that dwell on the earth?** The reply is twofold. First, they are each given a **white robe** (v. 11), a symbol of the righteous acts of the saints (cf. 19:8), so that even before the end these martyrs in some way have a foretaste of the glory to come. They are told that they must abide as they are **until their fellow servants also and their brethren** are slain. Though it is not specifically said in what period of time these martyrs are to be placed, the sixth seal certainly speaks of tremendous celestial aberrations that have never yet taken place but will occur at the end of this age. Consequently, these, I judge, had suffered martyrdom in the days immediately preceding the Tribulation. Moorehead may be right in saying, " For aught told us to the contrary, they were slain by the order of these riders." The comment of Torrance here is excellent: "After the terrible calamities the powers of the world have brought upon themselves, they try to disown the fact that they are the cause of all the evil and commotion, and so they turn upon God's people and vent their rage upon them as scapegoats" (*op. cit.*, p. 46).

12-17. Events transpiring at the opening of the sixth seal must be placed at the end of this age. This is perhaps the place to consider the question of celestial phenomena, so frequently referred to in the OT and NT Scriptures in passages relating to the end of the age. With the advent of Sputnik, a number of articles were published on this subject, some of which contain some very foolish statements. The subject of celestial disturbances is introduced first by Joel, in texts that clearly point to "the day of the Lord" (1:15; 2:1-11,30,31). One passage in Joel (2:28-32 a) is quoted by Peter in his great Pentecost sermon (Acts 2:16-21). There were no celestial disturbances at that time, so far as we know. These predictions were reiterated by Isaiah, also, in relation to "the day of the Lord" (13:6-10; 24:21-23). Our Lord placed much emphasis upon this particular aspect of eschatology in the Olivet Discourse (Mt 24:29,31; Mk 13:24-26; Lk 21:11,25). All of these statements refer to the period "after the tribulation" (Mt 24:29), with the exception of Lk 21:11, which implies that there will be some celestial disturbances even before the Tribulation itself sets in. It is principally in the Revelation, however, that these disturbances are recorded as taking place. The first is set forth in the passage before us, at the time of the opening of the sixth seal. But this type of phenomenon occurs four times during the trumpet judgments, at the first, third, fourth, and fifth (8:8–9:2). During the pouring out of the fourth vial, the sun seems to be affected (16:8), and during the pouring out of the seventh vial, great stones fall down from heaven on men (16:17-21).

A careful study of these passages seems to reveal that we are not to consider any unusual celestial aberrations before the Tribulation period as having prophetic significance. This is especially true of these devices made by man, important as they are; for the celestial manifestations referred to in the prophetic Scriptures are the result of a direct interference of God himself. On two occasions in the past, men experienced divine judgment in the form of great darkness: at the time of the ninth plague upon Egypt (Ex 10:21-23); and during the last three hours in which our Lord hung upon the cross (Mt 27:45 and parallels).

III. The Judgments of the Seven Trumpets. 7:1–9:21.

7:1-8. The second series of judgments is far more severe and extensive than those introduced by the opening of the seals. Before any of the seven angels sound these seven trumpets, two great multitudes are introduced, one on earth (7:1-8) and the other certainly in heaven, **standing before the throne and before the Lamb** (7:9-17). The first group is identified as 144,000 **sealed out of every tribe of the children of Israel** (v. 4). They are not said to be martyrs. The seal implies that this particular group will be divinely protected in the tribulations about to fall upon the earth.

There has been much disagreement as to who these people are, resulting in four major interpretations of the passage. One is that they should be looked upon in a general way as "representing a continuous process of preservation under the trials and afflictions of all times down to the end." There seems to be nothing in the text to justify such an indefinite designation of these tribal groups. Another view, somewhat similar, identifies these as Christians, the Church – and here many names speak with authority, as Bengel, Alford, Lenski, David Brown, Milligan, etc. Among minor interpretations is the ridiculous one of Albert Barnes that this refers to the ten divisions of the Christian Church. Some sects have claimed identity with these groups, such as the Jezreelites of a former generation.

Finally, there is the literal interpretation, that this is a prophecy concerning the children of Israel at the end of the age. The great prophetic scholar of the nineteenth century, J. H. Todd, summarizes this view in saying: "In strict accordance with the fact revealed in many prophecies, this tells us that at the period referred to in the vision, the Jewish people shall be in existence as a nation, and the majority of them will be still in their unbelief." This is the view held by Godet, Fausset, Nathaniel West, and Weidner.

Fausset adds: "Out of these tribes a believing remnant will be preserved from the judgments that shall destroy all the anti-Christian Confederacy" (JFB). It is significant that the tribe of Dan is here omitted – for which omission many reasons have been suggested–and **Levi** is included. "Since the Levitical ceremonies have been abandoned, Levi is again found on an equal footing with his brethren" (Albert Bengel, *Introduction to the Exposition of the Apocalypse, in loco).* Instead of Ephraim, the name Joseph is used. This I consider the second passage of unusual difficulty in the Apocalypse.

9-17. The other multitude is of a universal nature–certainly not confined to Israel, but from all tribes and peoples now in glory–singing the great hymn to God and the Lamb, together with the angels, the elders, and the four living creatures. These, John is told, are they that have come out of **great tribulation, and have washed their robes, and made them white in the blood of the Lamb** (v. 14). The **great tribulation** can be none other than that referred to in the Olivet Discourse (Mt 24:9,21,29). The entire scene is a heavenly one: The Lamb is presented as their shepherd or ruler; the promise is made that he shall guide them to fountains of waters of life; and, anticipating the detailed later description of the Holy City, they are told that God shall wipe away every tear from their eyes (Rev 21:4).

8:1-6. The trumpet judgments are unfolded in chapters 8 and 9, and, as with the seven seals, the first four belong together. Before any trumpet is blown by one of the angels, we have statements regarding the prayers of the saints (vv. 3,4). Perhaps Todd is right in thinking we can infer from this "that the judgments foretold in this prophecy will be the consequence, in some remarkable manner, of the prayers of saints crying to God to accomplish speedily the number of His elect and to hasten His kingdom" *(op. cit.,* p. 131). There is no reference here to the Roman Catholic doctrine of intercession by angels or saints. The thunder, voices, lightnings, and earthquakes are the symbolic precursors of the divine judgments about to fall upon the earth.

Before considering the judgments themselves, we do well to recall the significance of trumpets in the Holy Scriptures. All these phenomena (except the earthquake) are found in the account of God's descending at Mount Sinai to meet Moses, where we have the first reference to *trumpet* in the Bible (Ex 19:16). The blowing of trumpets called the Israelites together for instruction (Num 10:3,4) or for marching (Num 10:3-7); it summoned them to assemble for war (Jer 4:19; 42:14, etc.), and to return from dispersion (Isa 27:13); it announced release in the year of jubilee (Lev 25:8-10), and here it announces judgment. The trumpet judgments are quite similar to the plagues which God sent upon Egypt at the time of the deliverance of Israel, though they do not occur in the same order.

7-13. The result of the blowing of the first trumpet is the burning up of a third part of the flora of the **earth.** At the sound of the second trumpet, a third part of the **sea** becomes blood, a third of the creatures in the sea die, and a third part of the ships are destroyed (cf. the first plague, Ex 7:20-24). With the blowing of the third trumpet, a great star, burning as a torch, falls upon the **rivers** and **waters** of the earth, turning them to wormwood and causing wide-spread death. The first two judgments affect nature, and man only indirectly, but the third brings about the death of many. The blowing of the fourth trumpet brings about celestial disturbances, so that a third part of the **sun, moon,** and **stars** are smitten, and their light diminished (cf. the ninth plague, Ex 10:21-23). This miraculous eclipse of the sun, moon, and stars is predicted by Amos as a sign of the coming day of judgment (Amos 8:9; see also Joel 2:2, 10). Note that all four of these judgments relate to some disaster falling upon the world of nature. (Weidner, *op. cit.*, has an excellent summary of the various fanciful interpretations of these four trumpet judgments, pp. 343-345). Before the judgments of the next two trumpets, an eagle flying in mid-heaven is heard to cry, **Woe, woe, woe, for them that dwell on the earth.** This is the first time the word translated **woe** appears in the Apocalypse.

9:1,2. To the judgment of the fifth trumpet, which is called the **first Woe** (v. 12), John devotes more space than to all the preceding judgments combined. It is probable that, apart from the exact identification of Babylon in chapters 17 and 18, the meaning of the two judgments in this chapter presents the most difficult major problem in the Revelation. Probably the **star** falling from heaven, to whom was given **the key of the pit of the abyss,** is, as Weidner says, "an evil angel, the instrument of carrying out God's purpose with reference to the ungodly world" (p. 114; so also Alford, and others). The **abyss** is not hell, but the present abode of the devil and his angels, including Hades, where are the souls of the ungodly dead awaiting the last judgment. So dense is the smoke rising from the pit that it darkens the sun and the air (see 6:12; 8:12).

3-10. Also from the abyss come creatures described as **locusts** (v. 3) having great power, who are allowed to torment men (though not to kill them) for a period of five months (v. 5). So intense will be men's suffering that they will seek death, in vain (v. 6). Locusts are used in the famous prophecy of the book of Joel as symbols of invading armies. Men are likened to locusts in Jud 6:5; Jer 46:23; etc.; and in the prophetic Scriptures they are symbols of divine judgment (Deut 28:38,42; Nah 3:15,17; Amos 7:1-3, etc.). It is not possible here to examine each descriptive phrase, but we must come to some conclusion as to what these creatures represent. I personally have not felt I could be more specific than was Milligan, who said—and surely all would agree with this—that the judgment refers to "a great outburst of spiritual evil which shall aggravate the sorrows of the world, make it learn how bitter is the bondage of Satan, and teach it to feel even in the midst of enjoyment that it were better to die than to live."

11. The description concludes with the word that over these creatures is **the angel of the abyss,** called in Hebrew, *Abaddon,* and in the Greek, *Apollyon,* the latter meaning "destroyer." In the Septuagint the word carries this idea in Job 26:2; 28:22; Prov 15:11, etc.; another form is the word translated "destruction" in Mt 7:13 and "destroy" in II Thess 2:8.

13-21. The blowing of the sixth trumpet is identified with the **second Woe** (11:14). We are now taken to a known geographical area on this earth, to the river **Euphrates** (v. 14), which here probably should be taken literally. Four angels bound somewhere along this river are now loosed, *that they should kill the third part of men* (v. 15). This fearful destruction will be brought about by armies of horsemen. Surely we here have come to the days of the beginning of Antichrist. Todd has said, and Weidner and others agree, that "we are probably to look to this region as the scene of this great judgment, which is in exact comformity with the inferences to which we are led by the prophecies of Daniel, where those countries in the region of the Euphrates, once the stage of such mighty empires, are destined to become the scene of the last great struggle between the princes of the world and the people of God."

The result of all this is not a turning to God, or repentance, but a stubborn continuation in the sins that have brought about this judgment, the worship of demons, idolatry, murder, sorceries, fornication, and thefts. In fact, I cannot find any evidence in the Revelation that there will be any great turning to God during the time that these fearful judgments are falling upon men.

IV. The Darkest Hour of World History. 10:1–13:18.

The Angel with the Little Book. 10:1-11.

The tenth chapter presents a pleasant interlude. **Another strong angel** comes down out of heaven with a small **book** in his hand, and as John is about to record what he has seen, he hears a voice from heaven saying, **Seal up those things which the seven thunders uttered, and write them not** (v. 4; cf. Dan 12:9).

Apparently he never did record them, and so we do not know what the thunders said. The angel utters a famous, and more or less enigmatical, statement—**there shall be delay no longer** (ASV); or, as the margin reads, *there shall be time no longer.* Swete translates this, *There shall no more be any interval of time, any further delay.* This declaration, coupled with the one immediately following, **then is finished the mystery of God** (v. 7), convince us that the purpose of this vision, and especially of these utterances, is to prepare us for the final pouring out of God's judgments, the close of the end of the age, and the destruction of the enemies of the Lamb. The **little book** (v. 8) which John is told to take and eat (cf. Ezk 3:1-3; Ps 19:10,11; Jer 15:16) is never opened, and hence its exact nature must be a matter of dispute. But Düsterdieck is quite right, I think, when he says that it "appears to be an inner instruction and interpretation given the seer concerning visions still impending, and which are to continue until the full end. The more important the subjects of the prophecies that now follow, the more natural appears the new special preparation of the prophet" (p. 308).

The Two Witnesses in Jerusalem. 11:1-12. The eleventh chapter of the Revelation has always been to me one of greatest interest. The scene is certainly laid in Jerusalem, which though spiritually called **Sodom** and **Egypt** (v. 8; cf. Isa 1:9,10) is specifically referred to as the place **where also their Lord was crucified.** The events recorded here have never yet taken place, but they will literally occur in "the holy city" at the end of the age.

1,2. John is told to take a reed and **measure the temple of God, and the altar, and them that worship therein** (v. 1), which certainly implies that there will be some kind of temple building in Jerusalem at this time. The statement is made that **the holy city** will be trodden under foot for **forty and two months** (v. 2), a time period found also in 13:5, and equal to the 1,260 days of 11:3, and 12:6. I take this to be the first half of the seven-year terminus of our age, during the last half of which the Great Tribulation will occur, when Antichrist will be exercising universal power.

3-12. Two witnesses now appear, sent of God to prophesy to this city, though what their message is, we are not told. They are likened to the two olive trees and candlesticks (v. 4) portrayed in Zechariah 4. They are given supernatural power, such as Elijah and Moses had (I Kgs 17:1), to slay their enemies, to cause a drought, to turn water into blood, and to smite the earth with plagues at their will (vv. 5,6). When they have finished the work God has assigned to them, **the beast that cometh up out of the abyss shall make war with them, and overcome them, and kill them** (v. 7; ASV). The bodies of these two prophets are placed in the street of this city, and from all over the earth men look upon them for three days and a half day, and enter upon a time of rather universal rejoicing because these men who had tormented them are now, they think, destroyed (vv. 8-10). To the astonishment of their enemies, when three and a half days have expired, God raises them to their feet, calls them into glory, and they ascend into heaven in a cloud (vv. 11,12).

The question is, Who are these **two witnesses?** The answers have been many. The text cannot in any way, I definitely believe, be interpreted as referring to a movement, or, as Lange insists, to the Christian state and the Christian Church (for where is a Christian state today?), or to the OT and NT, or to the Word and the Spirit, or to faithful Christians, as Milligan and Swete believe. I think these witnesses must be regarded as individuals. Many assert that they are Moses and Elijah (Simcox, etc.), others that they are Enoch and Elijah (Seiss, Lang, Govett). But in regard to such views I agree with Moorehead's position: "It is extremely improbable that these saints, after centuries of bliss in heaven, should be dispatched to earth to bear witness to Jews and Gentiles" (*op. cit.*, p. 86). Frankly, I think we gain nothing by prolonged debate as to their identity. They are two witnesses sent by God, and endued by God with great power.

Though written as far back as 1864, Govett's comment upon the peoples, tribes, and nations looking upon these dead bodies (vv. 9,10) is still worth attention: "The word *blepō,* that is, *to look upon,* denotes not merely the nations seeing them but their directing their eyes to this great sight and gazing upon them. 'But how,' it is asked, 'is it conceivable that men all over the earth should be rejoicing in the news when only three days and a half intervene between their death and resurrection? . . .' Is it not perfectly conceivable if the electric telegraph shall then have extended itself at the rate it has done of late years?" (*op. cit.*, pp. 243, 246, 247) Now, with television available, we can understand this passage better.

Lenski's words regarding these enemies of God making merry over the death of the two prophets (v. 10) are especially thought-provoking: "The wicked world cannot let them alone and simply pass on in its obduracy. Even when it is finally and utterly silenced, the obdurate world cannot dismiss the divine testimony. It must talk about it, bring everybody to look at the voiceless lips. Those who spurn the Word *never* get rid of it. Their very rejoicing over its silencing keeps them busy with the Word" (*op. cit.*, p. 346).

13,14. At the ascension of the two witnesses, Jerusalem experiences **a great earthquake,** resulting in the death of seven thousand persons, **and the rest were affrighted, and gave glory to the God of Heaven** (v. 13). We detect no conviction of sin here, merely a sense of fear, which soon passes.

The Seventh Trumpet and the Scene in Heaven. 11:15-18. As with the opening of the seventh seal, when the seventh angel sounds the seventh trumpet, no events directly follow, and no immediate judgment is announced. Rather, with the sounding of this trumpet, we have a scene in heaven, and one of the grandest statements concerning Christ in all the Bible: "The kingdom of the world is become the kingdom of our Lord, and of his Christ: and he shall reign for ever and ever" (v. 15). Note the difference here between the AV translation, "the *kingdoms* of the world," and the more accurate ASV rendering of **kingdom,** singular, as in the Greek text. The whole world now appears under one powerful universal government.

This declaration is followed by a song of praise offered by the four and twenty elders to God the Almighty. This is the only time that the elders are described as prostrating themselves before God. With the announcement that the reign of God through Christ is near at hand, we are given a graphic summary (v. 18) of the events that are about to take place: (1) **the nations** are wroth; that is, there will be an attempted assault upon Christ and his own; (2) the wrath of God is about to descend; (3) the dead will be judged; (4) believers, here divided into three groups – the prophets, the saints, and those that fear His name, will be rewarded; and (5) the destroyers are now to be destroyed. From this, one may surely conclude that as the time nears for Christ to seize his kingly authority over this earth, the hatred of earthly nations for God's people will be intensified, and opposition to the Gospel will increase.

11:19. Most students will agree that 11:19 should be considered as the introduction to what is about to be revealed in chapter 12. Here again, as at the beginning of the passages on the seven seals (4:5) and the seven trumpets (8:5), there are lightnings, voices, thunders, and an earthquake. What John now sees in heaven—a temple of God and **the ark of his covenant** (ASV)—presents a problem in interpretation. This can scarcely be that actual ark of the covenant which was in the midst of Israel during her wilderness journeys (as some insist); for this did not exist even in the time of Christ. The word here translated **temple,** *naos,* means "sanctuary," the innermost part of the temple. When the Holy City descends from heaven, it is explicitly said that there will be no temple there (21:22).

The Woman with the Man Child. 12:1-17.

1-5. Chapter 12 presents another problem in identification—the **woman** seen **in heaven** who was **travailing . . . to be delivered** of a child (vv. 1,2). One thing seems certain—that this child "who is to rule all the nations with a rod of iron" (v. 5) must be the Lord Jesus Christ (see Ps 2:9; Isa 66:7; Rev 19:15). A number of identifications have been suggested for the **woman.** In the period of the Church Fathers, Victorinus said this is "the ancient church of fathers, and prophets, and saints, and apostles" (*Ante-Nicene Fathers,* VII, 355). Many writers say this is Israel, from whom Christ came; while some, as Auberlen, Lenski, etc., interpret it more comprehensively as the Israel of both Testaments. I think we can affirm that this is Israel. The Roman Catholic Church, of course, insists that this is the Virgin Mary, but the Roman Church also says that Mary gave birth to Christ without pain, which is contradicted by this verse (see Isa 66:7). There stands before this woman the great enemy of God, **the dragon** (Rev 12:4), who hopes to destroy Christ. But in this effort he will fail.

6. I personally believe, with Weidner, Walter Scott, and many others, that this verse is anticipatory, and points to Israel's time of tribulation at the end of the age. It is placed here to emphasize the fact that Satan, who hates Christ, and hence His people, will especially persecute Israel as the age draws to a close.

7-9. We are now introduced to what Swete rightly designates as "the supreme attempt on the part of the dragon to unseat the Woman's Son, and to re-establish himself in the presence of God." There are more terms for Satan in this paragraph (v. 9) than in any other single passage in the Word of God: **the great dragon, that old serpent . . . the Devil, and Satan,** and—one of the most dreadful phrases in Scripture—not something Satan boasts of, but something which heaven acknowledges—**the deceiver of the whole world** (see II Tim 3:13; II Jn 7). He is opposed here not by Christ, but by Michael and his angels (Rev 12:7; see Dan 10:13,21; Jude 9), who apparently is the leader of the angelic hierarchy. Satan is cast out of heaven. There may be a reference here to some words of our Lord regarding Satan's falling from heaven (Jn 12:31), though I am convinced that the scene unfolds at the end of this age. Note that Satan is not cast into the abyss, but **down to the earth** (ASV; Rev 12:9), just before Antichrist assumes his temporary and dreadful reign.

10-12. No detail is necessary here on the subsequent song of rejoicing. Emphasis is upon the power of God and the authority of Christ. The brethren **overcame** Satan **because of the blood of the Lamb,** and **the word of their testimony** (v. 11). It is because they have given a faithful testimony even unto death that they are victorious.

13-17. What was referred to in anticipation in verse 6 is stated in more detail here. The time period, **time, and times, and half a time** (v. 14), similar to the 1,260 days of verse 6, is the period of darkest tribulation. The earth's aiding the woman (v. 16) may represent, as Walter Scott says, the governments of the earth befriending the Jew "and providentially (how, we know not) frustrating the efforts of the serpent" (*Exposition of the Revelation of Jesus Christ, in loco).* The reference to the woman and **her seed** (v. 17) recalls the first Messianic prophecy (Gen 3:15).

The Appearance of the Two Beasts. 13:1–18.

1-10. Two dreadful rulers enter the scene in chapter 13, one coming up **out of the sea,** and the other coming up out of the earth. The **sea** here is undoubtedly "a symbol of the agitated surface of unregenerate humanity, and especially of the seething caldron of national and social life out of which the great historical movements of the world arise" (Swete). The first beast, whose horns and diadems represent power, is energized by Satan (v. 2). It is almost unbelievable that **the whole earth** will worship both **the dragon** and **the beast** (vv. 3, 4). There will be much religion on earth, but it will be godless and blasphemous. This first beast is against God (vv. 5, 6); he is satanically energized (v. 2); he is militarily supreme (v. 4); he possesses world-wide power (v. 7); and he persecutes the saints of God (v. 7). Who would deny that the stage of world history is rapidly being set by tendencies that will ultimately lead to the rule and adoration of such a monster? All who do not belong to the Lamb of God will worship the beast.

11-15. While the first beast is undoubtedly a political world power, the second beast (v. 11), as Lee has said, "is a spiritual world power, the power of learning and knowledge, of ideas, of intellectual cultivation. Both are from below, both are beasts, and therefore they are in close alliance. The worldly anti-Christian wisdom stands in the service of the worldly anti-Christian power" (p. 671). The second beast enforces the commands of the first beast, and accompanies his evil work with various forms of miraculous manifestations (vv. 12, 13). The period of the "times of the Gentiles" began with the forced worship of an image set up by a powerful ruler (by Nebuchadnezzar, in Daniel 3); and this period will close with a similar enforced worship, this time on a universal scale.

16,17. The chapter concludes with a prophecy of what might be called economic dictatorship. The text does not say that men will not be able to eat unless they have **the mark . . . of the beast,** but that they will not be able to carry on business without that mark.

18. The concluding verse of this chapter, in which **the number of the beast** is revealed as 666, has given rise to a multitude of interpretations, and to a vast literature. Whole books have been written on this one text. Luther erred in thinking that this is a chronological statement. Adding 666 to the year 1000 gave him A.D. 1666, a year when nothing of prophetic significance occurred. Many have tried to identify this person by discovering names the numerical sum of whose letters is 666. In our language, e.g., X equals 10, L equals 50, and C equals 100. There are similar equivalents for letters in the Hebrew, Greek, and Latin languages. Some have believed, then, that this number so translated refers to the first century Caesar, Nero; others interpret it as *Lateinos,* meaning, "the Latin One." I think we need go no further than to recognize that six is the number of fallen man and thus of incompleteness, and that 666 is the trinity of six. Even in this passage there is a demonic trinity—Satan, the beast **out of the earth** (Antichrist, v. 11), and the beast **out of the sea** (the false prophet, v. 1). (For a tabulation of various interpretations of these two beasts, see Charles Maitland: *The Apostles' School of Prophetic Interpretation* [London, 1849], p. 329.)

Torrance rightly asks: "Do we not see today that image being set up in nation after nation upon the earth by the power of propaganda and lies? . . . Have we not heard the raucous voice of that beast blaring and shouting over the radio, and read his boasts and threats on the pages of the world press? . . . All that can be done apart from Jesus Christ is to give a fresh disposition to unbelief, to give organic or subtle shape to human evil and pride and selfishness. . . . All the time the latent evil in the world is setting up its image and making its imprint upon the persons and minds and deeds of men" *(op. cit.,* pp. 86-89).

Note that these two world rulers are designated as *beasts.* The Russian philosopher, Nicholas Berdyaev, writing on the bestiality of modern man, says: "Movement toward super-humanity and the superman, toward super-human powers, all too often means nothing other than a bestialization of man. Modern antihumanism takes the form of bestialism. It uses the tragic and unfortunate Nietzsche as a superior sort of justification for dehumanization and bestialization. . . . A bestial cruelty toward man is characteristic of our age, and is more astonishing since it is displayed at the very peak of human refinement, where modern conceptions of sympathy, it would seem, have made impossible the old barbaric forms of cruelty. Bestialism is something quite different from the old, natural, healthy barbarism; it is barbarism within a refined civilization. Here the atavistic, barbaric instincts are filtered through the prism of civilization, and hence they have a pathological character. Bestialism is a phenomenon of the human world, but a world already civilized" *(The Fate of Man in the Modern World,* pp. 26-29. For a full discussion of this chapter, see my volume, *This Atomic Age and the Word of God,* pp. 193-221).

V. The Judgments of the Seven Vials. 14:1—16:21.

As there are introductory chapters preceding the judgments introduced by the opening of the seven seals, and by the blowing of the seven trumpets, so here, preceding the last *series* of judgments, we have an introductory chapter.

14:1-5. The chapter opens with a scene on **the mount Zion,** which no doubt stands for heaven—the only reference to Zion in the Revelation. We are introduced to a large company of 144,000, having characteristics which set them apart as unusually dedicated: (1) on their foreheads are the names of the Lamb and of the Father—which shall be true of all the redeemed throughout eternity (22:4); (2) they alone are able to understand the new song sung before the throne by harpers; (3) they have not been defiled with women, for they are virgins—a statement considered later in this study; (4) they follow the Lamb wherever he goes; (5) they are the first fruits unto God; (6) they are without blemish. This is no doubt a select group of God's saints, of which we hear nothing more.

The only real problem here is in verse 4. Many have insisted that this must be taken literally, as Govett, who devotes five pages to the verse. Nowhere in the Scriptures is virginity as such, or celibacy, mentioned as a synonym for holiness, or as making one particularly fit for divine service. The family is a divine institution from the beginning of Scripture. Therefore, I think this must have symbolic significance, similar to Paul's use of these terms in II Cor 11:2,3. Marriage is not defiling (Heb 13:4).

6,7. We now have a description of three successive messages of three different angels. The first has **an eternal gospel,** proclaimed to everyone on earth, consisting of the following admonition: **Fear God, and give him glory; for the hour of his judgment is come: and worship him that made the heaven,** etc. I wholly agree with Swete that this proclamation "contains no reference to the Christian hope; the basis of the appeal is pure theism. It is an appeal to the conscience of untaught heathenism, incapable as yet of comprehending any other." There is no indication here that this message is believed or that, through believing it, any are redeemed.

8-13. The second angel announces the fall of Babylon, which is described in detail in chapters 17 and 18. The third angel utters a judgment upon all those who have worshiped the beast and his image, with an anticipatory statement about the eternal punishment of those who bear the mark of the beast. A century ago the Seventh-Day Adventists seized upon these verses as being fulfilled in their particular convictions regarding the church. They regarded the early Millerite movement as a warning to the church that she is Babylon. Hence, believers should come out of organized Christendom—and the message of the third angel was immediately to follow. Adventists insist that this is a promise that in the last days only those will be acceptable to God who **keep the commandments of God, and the faith of Jesus** (v. 12), and that this is "a call to men to honor the true sabbath of God, the seventh-day sabbath of the Decalogue" (Francis D. Nichol: *The Midnight Cry,* p. 462). Why they particularize the commandment regarding the seventh day, not even hinted at here, and do not incorporate in this scheme the other nine Words of the Decalogue, I do not know.

14-20. The chapter concludes with two scenes that can occur only at the end of the age. The first (vv. 14-16) represents a harvest, a reaping of souls, and apparently a gathering in of the redeemed, to which our Lord refers in Mt 13:30,39; 24:30,31. There has been some dispute over these two scenes, but it seems to me that the second one, which is not a harvest but a vintage scene, must depict the gathering of the unbelieving and wicked ones of the earth. These are anticipatory paragraphs. Govett summarizes this passage correctly in saying, "The Woman's seed furnishes the Harvest, while the Dragon's seed furnishes the Vintage." See also Joel 3:13.

15:1-4. Chapter 15 is still occupied with introductory matters and a scene in heaven. It presents one of the great songs of the book, this time sung, apparently, by those who have triumphed over the evil forces of the last days, who have come off **victorious from the beast, and from his image, and from the number of his name** (ASV; v. 2). This is called **the song of Moses the servant of God, and . . . the Lamb** (v. 3; on the former, see Ex 14:31; 15; Num 12:7; Deut 32). "The song in which Moses celebrated the deliverance from Egypt is now renewed and receives its perfect close when God's people are finally delivered by the Lamb" (Lee). The song is a mosaic of material from Exodus, from the Psalms (86:9; 111:2; 145:17), and from Isaiah (2:2-4; 66:23, etc.).

5-8. John says that he saw **the sanctuary of the tabernacle of the testimony in heaven** (v. 5). This is the last occurrence of the word translated **sanctuary** in this book (cf. 11:19). Out from this most holy place proceed seven angels, with the seven plagues which are now to be poured out upon the earth, **bowls full of the wrath of God** (v. 7). Just before this series begins, we are told that the sanctuary was **filled with smoke from the glory of God, and from his power** (v. 8), which recalls to mind the unapproachableness of God at Sinai (Ex 19:21), and in Isaiah's vision (Isa 6:4,5). The great exegete of a former century, John Albert Bengel, remarked on this passage: "When God pours out His fury it is fitting that even those who stand well with Him should withdraw for a little, standing back in profound reverence till by and by the sky becomes clear again" *(Introduction to the Exposition of the Apocalypse, in loco).*

16:1,2. We are now ready to consider the seven bowls of the wrath of God. The first, comparable to the sixth plague of Egypt, resulted in men who had the mark of the beast being tormented by a **noisome and grievous sore,** not specifically identified. When the second bowl is poured out (cf. the first plague of Egypt), the sea takes on the appearance of **blood as of a dead man,** and all life within it dies (v. 3). Weidner directs attention to the similarity and the difference between this plague and that of the second trumpet (8:8,9): "The judgments of God grow more and more terrible as wickedness increases and the end approaches."

4-11. The third vial of wrath also affects the rivers and fountains of waters, bringing a response from **the angel of the waters** acknowledging the righteousness and holiness of God, and the justification of such terrible manifestations of divine judgment (vv. 5,6). The fourth vial, involving the sun, in some way increases the intensity of heat derived on earth from the sun; and men are scorched with it, as a result of which they blaspheme God (vv. 8,9). The fifth bowl of wrath is similar to the fourth trumpet judgment and the ninth plague of Egypt, in its manifestation of darkness, except that on this occasion it is the kingdom of the beast that is darkened (vv. 10,11). God is now beginning to strike at the very throne of his great enemy, who has been the vital cause for the deception of men, their awful crimes, and their hatred of God.

12-16. In the pouring out of the sixth vial upon the river Euphrates, basically John sees **the kings that come from the sunrising,** or, from the East, driven, as it were, by satanic power to march to **Armageddon** (v. 16) for **the war of the great day of God, the Almighty** (v. 14). This is the only place that **Armageddon** is mentioned by name in the book of Revelation. The battle itself is described in the last part of chapter 19. Moorehead wrote, even before World War I and the modern awakening of Asia, "The vast hordes of Asia will be involved in the decisive and overwhelming battle of the great day of God." The Far East has had deep significance for Western civilization only within the last century, and the same is true for the Near East since the close of the Crusades. What an enormous difference between the powerful China of today, in its communistic, atheistic regime, and the comparatively weak empire we knew at the beginning of this century! The drying up of the **Euphrates River** (v. 12), allowing for the approach of these armies from the East, may or may not be taken symbolically; but it most assuredly cannot refer to the weakening of the Ottoman empire, nor is this the Mississippi River, as some contend. Hengstenberg has accurately commented: "The Euphrates is mentioned here merely in respect to the hindrance it presented to the march of the ungodly power of the world into the Holy Land." These kings are not Jews coming to Palestine for blessing, but pagan kings coming to Megiddo for battle. This passage embraces one of the most dreadful statements in the Bible, i.e., that **unclean spirits** (v. 13), the spirits of demons working miracles, **go forth unto the kings of the whole world, to gather them together unto war** (v. 14). This can mean nothing else than that at the end of the age the rulers of the earth will be demonized. And we are almost compelled to believe, by the events of the last forty years, that already some rulers have been demon-possessed.

17-21. While the seventh seal did not immediately follow the opening of the sixth, and the blowing of the seventh trumpet was postponed for some time, in this chapter the pouring out of the seventh vial promptly follows the pouring out of the sixth. Here the wrath of God is directed toward **the air,** and the declaration of judgment is followed, as others previously have been, by **lightnings, voices, thunders,** and an **earthquake** (vv. 18,19). I cannot help thinking that **the air** here is to be given the same significance it has in Paul's phrase regarding "the prince of the power of the air" (Eph 2:2). (For a further discussion of this, see my volume, *This Atomic Age and the Word of God*, pp. 222-248.) The disturbances in the air culminate in the falling of great hailstones (Rev 16:21), weighing about a talent each (either fifty-seven or ninety-six pounds); and once again men blaspheme God. The statement that at this time **the cities of the nations fell** (v. 19), or, as some translate, *the cities of the Gentiles*, may be, as Weidner suggests, a reference to Mic 5:10-15. Two other cities are named here, **Babylon** and **the great city,** the latter being, according to Milligan, Simcox, Weidner, and many others, Jerusalem.

It has been claimed by some commentators that these three successive septenary series of three judgments are a recapitulation of the same events. That is, the trumpets review what the seals previously set forth, but with greater intensity; and the vials review the same events, characterizing them with even more severity. I have not been able to accept this view. For one reason, the sequence in each series is altogether different, and this alone, it seems, makes the concept of recapitulation impossible. In the following chart I have set forth the sequence of the series of judgments, using the judgment of the vials as a guide. Appearing below the line for the trumpets and seals are phenomena which do not appear in the vial judgments. No attempt has been made to place those below the line in any chronological order, or even to parallel the seals and the trumpets; rather, they have been placed opposite each other to save space.

Nature of the Judgment	Vials ch. 16	Trumpets chs. 8; 9	Seals ch. 6	Plagues of Egypt Ex. 7–10. 12:29-33.
Sores	I. 2			V, VI. 9:1-12
Seas turned to blood	II. 3	II. 8:8, 9		I. 7:20 - 24
Waters turned to blood	III. 4 - 7	II. 8:8, 9		I. 7:20 - 24
Great heat	IV. 8, 9	I. 8:7		
Darkness: Pain	V. 10, 11	IV. 8:12		IX. 10:21 - 23
Kings demon-possessed	VI. 12 - 16			
Lightnings; Voices; Thunders; Earthquakes Great hail stones	VII. 17 - 21	I. 8:7 (hail)	VI. 12-17	(hail) VII. 9:22 - 35
False peace			I. 1, 2	
Locusts		V. 9:1-12		VIII. 10:12-20
War		VI. 9:13-21	II. 3, 4	
Scarcity of food			III. 5, 6	
Death			IV. 7, 8	X. 12:29-33
Bitter waters		III. 8:10, 11		
Martyrs			V. 9-11	

VI. Babylon and Armageddon. 17:1–19:21.

Judgment upon Babylon. 17:1–18:24. One-eighth of the entire book of Revelation, some fifty verses, is devoted to the subject of judgment upon Babylon (14:8-10; 16:17–19:5). Yet, the interpretation of **Babylon** in the Apocalypse has given rise to more differing opinions than any other major passage in this book. In the OT the name *Babylon* takes its origin from *Babel,* which of course has always symbolized revolt against God, and confusion (Gen 10:8-12; 11:1-9). Babylon was the conqueror of the kingdom of Judah, the theocracy (II Kgs 24; 25, etc.). With Nebuchadnezzar, king of Babylon, began the "times of the Gentiles" (Jer 27:1-11; Dan 2:37,38). Babylon occupies a large place in the prophecies of the nations in the OT (Isa 13; 14; 47; Jer 50; 51).

Babylon is set before us in these two chapters under two different aspects. In chapter 17, she is identified with the great harlot, a woman who does not appear as such in chapter 18. The beast with seven heads and ten horns is confined to chapter 17, where alone we find the kings of the earth going out to make war on the Lamb. In chapter 18 Babylon seems to be some city along a great river, crowded with the ships of the merchants of the earth, details that are not present in chapter 17. We should perhaps first look at the text itself and then discuss interpretation.

17:1-12. There are three groups to be identified in this opening paragraph: the **beast,** who has seven heads and ten horns; the **harlot** herself who rides the beast; and those referred to by **many waters,** later said to be "peoples and multitudes, and nations, and tongues" (v. 15). The ten horns, we are later informed, are ten kings (v. 12), certainly contemporaneous; and the seven heads are seven mountains (vv. 9,10), which also represent kingdoms. We must never forget that every federation of kings in the OT, and here, is always opposed to God and the people of God (Gen 15:18-21; Dan 2: 41,42; 7:7,20,24; Ps 2:1-3; 83:1-8; Rev 12:3; 13:1; 16:12-16). This woman, called **THE MOTHER OF THE HARLOTS** (17:5), commits **fornication** with the kings of the earth (v. 2), and for a while dominates them.

To whom or what does this **woman** refer? The majority of commentators, since the time of the Reformation, identify her with the papacy, as Luther, Tyndale, Knox, Calvin (*Institutes,* IV, 2.12), Alford, Elliott, Lange, and many others. The Roman Catholic Church itself identifies this woman with Rome—but of course pagan Rome, now past. She is definitely some vast spiritual system that persecutes the saints of God, betraying that to which she was called. She enters into relations with the governments of this earth, and for a while rules them. I think the closest we can come to an identification is to understand this harlot as symbolic of a vast spiritual power arising at the end of the age, which enters into a league with the world and compromises with worldly forces. Instead of being spiritually true, she is spiritually false, and thus exercises an evil influence in the name of religion.

13-18. The kings of the earth now, having one mind, federate, and give their authority unto this great enemy of God, the beast, and go out to make **war against the Lamb** (vv. 13,14). When this hour is come, the beast, with the power of the kingdoms of the earth, turns upon the harlot, this pseudo-spiritual force, and destroys her (v. 16). That is a very conforting statement in verse 17—"God did put in their hearts to do his mind, and to come to one mind . . . until the words of God should be accomplished."

Chapter 18 seems to have a geographical definiteness not present in chapter 17. Here we have the statement that Babylon has become **a habitation of demons, and a hold of every unclean spirit** (v. 2). Most of the chapter is occupied with a description of the wealth of the city, the merchandise which is brought here for sale, and the grief of the merchants, who have been made rich by this traffic, as they look upon the city now being made desolate by fire. In verses 4-8 judgment is announced; in verses 9-20 we have the lament of kings of the earth; and in 21-24 Babylon's final doom is reported.

We must now return to the problem of interpretation. Some insist upon a geographical identification here. Those who have adopted the historical scheme of interpretation make **Babylon** refer generally to pagan Rome. Some have asserted that **Babylon** here must mean Jerusalem, as Weidner, Kiddle, etc., but this seems utterly impossible. I have read books that defend the view that this city is London or Paris. Even Alford once said, though he admitted he felt this difficulty "unsolved," "Certainly the details of this mercantile lamentation far more nearly suit London, than Rome, at any assignable period of her history" (p. 718). One thing cannot be denied: the muddy Tiber River, flowing through Rome, could never carry the enormous maritime traffic portrayed in chapter 18; moreover, pagan Rome was never famous as a center of exchange and selling of merchandise. Some have contended that this prophecy can only be fulfilled when the city of Babylon is restored. The Scofield Bible specifically repudiates this, but many of its editors personally believed this to be true, as Gray and Moorehead; so also Seiss, Govett, Pember, G. H. Lang, and many others.

Those adopting the ecclesiastical interpretation, as we have noted, make **Babylon** stand for the papacy, and there is much here to support their view. However, I believe that there is more than the papacy implied here. This is apostate Christendom, a world religion that has betrayed Christianity, and is interlocked with the pagan, godless governments of the world. Many believe—and I would agree—that the day is coming when the Roman Church itself will, in some mysterious way, enter into a compromising relationship with atheistic Communism. (A searching treatment of this subject may be found in G. H. Pember, *The Antichrist, Babylon, and the Coming of the Kingdom* [1886].)

The Battle of Armageddon. 19:1-21.

19:1-8. While chapter 19 of this book is generally given the heading, "The Battle of Armageddon," actually the first half of the chapter is devoted to a scene in heaven, where we have the last three songs of the Apocalypse. First, a great multitude is heard singing, **Hallelujah; Salvation, and glory, and power,** because of the judgment upon the great harlot that has now been completed (vv. 1,2). **Hallelujah** is taken directly from the Hebrew and is made up of two words *hallel,* meaning "praise," and *jah,* a basic word for God. Hallelujahs occur at the beginning of Psalms 111 and 112, at the beginning and end of Psalms 146 to 150, etc. This song is repeated a second time. Then the twenty-four elders and the four living creatures fall down before God, also crying out **Amen; Hallelujah** (v. 4).

Finally, John hears voices, which he does not specifically identify (v. 6), singing the last of the songs, beginning with **Hallelujah,** this time not because of the judgment on Babylon, but because **the marriage of the Lamb is come, and his wife hath made herself ready** (vv. 6-8). With this, John is commanded to write the last of the beatitudes of this book, in which is announced that the marriage supper of the Lamb has come (v. 7). The relationship of God and Christ to the redeemed as expressed by the terms of marriage is frequently found in both Testaments (Hos 2:19-21; Ezk 16:1ff.; Ps 45; Mk 2:19; I Cor 6:15-17; Eph 5:25-27). The bridal attire is noticeably different from the attire of the great harlot, for the holy bride wears only glistening white and pure **linen** (Rev 19:8), symbol of the righteous acts of the saints. All that the NT speaks of as relating to Christ the bridegroom and the Church the bride is now consummated.

11-16. This paragraph has always seemed to me almost too overwhelmingly glorious for exposition. Christ is now seen riding upon a white horse, coming down from heaven to "judge and make war." Here he takes the title, **Faithful and True,** which was assigned to him at the beginning of this book (1:5; 3:7,14). The phrase, **in righteousness,** is important. Judgment, throughout the Bible, is always identified with righteousness. This is exactly the phrase used by the Apostle Paul in Acts 17:31. In fact, this is the word used in the first reference to God as the judge of all the earth (Gen 18:25; see also Ps 9:4,8; 98:9; Isa 11:4; etc.). Righteousness, says the lexical authority, Cremer, is "that divine standard which shows itself in behavior conformable to God . . . which corresponds with the divine norm." Our Lord himself said, "My judgment is righteous; because I seek not mine own will, but the will of him that sent me" (Jn 5:30). The description of Christ here (Rev 19:12,13), with eyes **a flame of fire** and garments **sprinkled with blood** (ASV), takes us back to the beginning of the book (1:14; 2:18). The phrase, **sprinkled with blood,** is from Isa 63:3.

Christ now is assigned the great title, **The Word of God** (Rev 19:13). As the Word of God, he made the worlds. It was by rejection of the Word that sin was brought into the world. By the Word of God, salvation is offered to men. Sin and anarchy, godlessness and rebellion, are in one way or another the repudiation of the Word of God. That Word, the Eternal, Omnipotent Word, now descends from heaven to fulfill prophecy, to destroy the enemies of God, to reveal to the universe, once and forever, the folly of resisting Christ and the indisputable pre-eminence of the **King of Kings, and Lord of Lords** (v. 16). We are now introduced to an earthly scene in which the kings of the earth take a prominent part. How strange, how tragic is this situation we now behold, in which it seems that the rulers of the whole world are united in one terrible effort to destroy the anointed of God. How contrary this is to the dreams of men, to the foolish statements of their false prophets, and to their unjustified belief that human society is ever progressing in the areas of peace, goodness, comradeship, and social welfare. We are now to see the fulfillment of Psalm 2.

17-21. I cannot help believing that this battle is to be taken literally, and hence it needs some careful, though brief, attention here. The plain of Megiddo, elsewhere called the plain of Jezreel, or Esdraelon, was famous in Israel's history, both for her defeats and for her victories. Here was the victory of Barak over the Canaanites, when the very stars fought in their courses against Sisera (Jud 4; 5); the victory of Gideon over the Midianites (Jud 7); and likewise the defeat and death of King Saul and his three sons, at the hands of the Philistines (1 Sam 4). Here occurred the tragedy of the defeat and death of King Josiah at the hands of the Egyptians, (II Kgs 23:29,30). Later in history the crusaders were defeated here, in the battle at the Horns of Hattin, A.D. 1187. Here General Allenby, in 1917, won a great victory against the Turks, for which he was honored, later, with the title, Lord Allenby of Megiddo. This great plain, about twelve miles wide, situated in the middle of Palestine, runs from the shores of the Mediterranean to the Jordan

Valley. On this plain, says a great authority, we have "the first battle in history in which we can in any measure study the disposition of troops, and thus, it forms the starting point for the history of military science." This was the battle in May, 1479 B.C., between the Syrian forces and the Egyptians under Thutmose III (see Harold H. Nelson, *The Battle of Megiddo,* pp. 1, 63).

Of this battlefield, George Adam Smith once wrote: "What a plain it is! Upon which not only the greatest empires, races, and faiths, east and west, have contended with each other, but each has come to judgment—on which from the first, with all its splendor of human battle, men have felt that there was fighting from heaven, the stars in their courses were fighting—on which panic has descended so mysteriously upon the best equipped and most successful armies, but the humble have been exalted to victory in the hour of their weakness—on which false faiths, equally with false defenders of the true faith, have been exposed and scattered—on which, from the time of Saul, wilfulness and superstition, though aided by every human excellence, have come to nought, and since Josiah's time the purest piety has not atoned for rash and mistaken zeal" *(Historical Geography of the Holy Land,* p. 409).

Prophecies that probably refer to this coming battle are found as early as 800 B.C. (Joel 3:9-15; see also Jer 51:27-36; Zeph 3:8; and Rev 14:14-20; 16:13-16; 17:14).

The battle is over almost as soon as it begins. Two great enemies of God are now seized, the beast and the false prophet (whose work was outlined in chapter 13), and are **cast alive into the lake of fire** and brimstone (v. 20). (For further treatment of this subject consult: George Adam Smith, *op. cit.,* pp. 379-410; William Miller, *The Least of All Lands,* 1888, pp. 152-212; and articles in various encyclopedias; as well as my own volume, *World Crises in the Light of Prophetic Scriptures,* pp. 96-119).

The word *Armageddon* is now a part of the English language, and is correctly defined by the *Oxford English Dictionary* as "the place of the last decisive battle." Swete, writing before World War I, rightly said, "Those who take note of the tendencies of modern civilization will not find it impossible to conceive that a time may come when throughout Christendom, the spirit of Anti-Christ will, with the support of the State, make a final stand against a Christianity which is loyal to the person and teaching of Christ."

VII. The Millennium; the Last Judgment; the New Jerusalem and Eternity. 20:1—22:50.

The Millennium. 20:1-6. We now approach one of the most debated passages in the Word of God. Throughout the ages this passage has been generally taken to set forth a Millennial period during which Christ will be reigning on this earth. All of us would agree with C. J. Vaughan when he says, "Never did we need more the help of God than in entering upon the interpretation of the chapter now before us." Only here in the Scriptures do we have the phrase, "*the* thousand years," which chronological factor is referred to six times in six verses. The word *millennium* is a Latin word composed of *mille,* "a thousand," and *annum,* "year"; thus, a thousand years, whatever this particular Scripture portion may mean. The passage begins by informing us that during this time Satan is cast into the bottomless pit, where he remains bound for **a thousand years.** This pit is not hell. Satan seems to have no power to resist this act of an angel in binding him. John now sees a great multitude who have not worshiped the beast, sitting upon thrones, and reigning with Christ for **a thousand years.** This is not the place to argue about the Millennium. It certainly seems clear, however, that the OT, over and over again, refers to a great and glorious time to come when peace will prevail on the earth, when the Messiah will reign in righteousness, and when nature will be restored to her original beauty (see, for example, Isa 9:6,7; 11:1; 30:15-33; also chs. 35; 44; and 49; 65:17—66:14, Jer 23:5,6, etc.).

There are four views regarding the Millennium. (1) Some say that this is just a spiritual condition of the redeemed, and must not be given any chronological interpretation, the idea of a thousand being symbolical of fullness and completeness. (2) Some have held the strange view that the Millennium has already taken place, many assigning the beginning of it to the conversion of Constantine. But if the period known as the Dark Ages is to be called the Millennium, then the prophecies in the Bible referring to such a period will never be fulfilled. (3) Some have said that we are now in the Millennium, but once again we insist that if this war-ridden age of anarchy and atheistic communism is the Millennium, then the hopes created by the Word of God for this earth must be abandoned. (4) Finally, many believe that this is an actual prophecy of a thousand-year period, following Armageddon, when Christ will reign on this earth as King of kings. The early church was unanimous in holding this view. Charles *(op. cit.)* who does not accept the Millennium at all, nevertheless admits that "the prophecy of the millennium in chapter 20 must be taken literally."

There is a famous statement on this passage in Alford's *New Testament for English Readers* that has been quoted in many subsequent volumes, but I feel compelled to quote it once again: "It will have been long ago anticipated by the readers of this Commentary, that I cannot consent to distort words from their plain sense and chronological place in the prophecy, on account of any considerations of difficulty, or any risk of abuses which the doctrine of the millennium may bring with it. Those who lived next to the Apostles, and the whole Church for 300 years, understood them in the plain literal sense: and it is a strange sight in these days to see expositors who are among the first in reverence of antiquity, complacently casting aside the most cogent instance of consensus which primitive antiquity presents. As regards the text itself, no legitimate treatment of it will extort what is known as the spritual interpretation now in fashion."

Much discussion has arisen about the brief phrase, **This is the first resurrection** (Rev 20:5). The theory that by the **first resurrection** conversion is meant, a passing from death unto life, i.e., a *spiritual* resurrection, seems wholly out of order in such a passage as this. The *second* resurrection, though it is not so designated, is certainly the one referred to in verses 11-15 of this same chapter. It is not necessary to limit those participating in the *first* resurrection to the groups enumerated in verse 4. The first resurrection may easily be considered as occurring in stages—the dead in Christ, then we who are alive, and then, after a brief period, these martyrs and faithful ones of the Tribulation period.

7-10. At the end of the Millennium, we have a strange episode inserted, the source of which could be nothing but divine inspiration, namely, that Satan will be loosed from his prison, and will go out once more to deceive the nations, assembling them to war (vv. 7,8), and leading them to an attack upon **the camp of the saints . . . and the beloved city** (v. 9). This probably refers to the earthly city of Jerusalem, though some have made it refer to the Holy City, which seems to be most irrational. Scott has a good point here when he says, "No mention is made of how Christ and His people regard this last mad attempt of Satan. All is silent in the camp and city. The apostate nations march into the jaws of death. Their judgment is sudden, swift, overwhelming, and final *(op. cit.,* p. 388). With the destruction of God's enemies, Satan is seized and cast into hell, where he will be forever. The beast and the false prophet have already been consigned to this place of awful doom. No doubt the plural pronoun **they** (v. 10) refers to this trinity of evil.

The question is often asked, How can one account for this last rebellion after the beneficent Millennial reign of Christ? For one thing, it reveals that a thousand years of imprisonment do not alter the evil character of the devil. Furthermore, unregenerate man does not change, and though the whole earth is under the rule of Christ, great multitudes obey him only from fear and not from love.

The Last Judgment. 20:11-14. **One** more great universe-embracing event must take place before there can be eternal peace and righteousness, namely, the judgment of the impenitent dead. This is set forth in the last paragraph of this epoch-crowded chapter. A day of judgment, sometimes called "The Last Day," is referred to more often by our Lord than by all of the apostles and their writings put together (see Mt 10:15; 11:22,24; 12:36; Jn 5:28,29; 6:39-54; 11:24; Heb 9:27; 10:27). Christ is everywhere identified as the judge (see especially Acts 17:31; Jn 5:22-27; II Tim 4:1). Bishop Gore spoke for all the Church when he said, "It seems to me any believer in the God of the prophets, and of our Lord, must believe with them in a Day of God, as bringing the present age of human history to its climax" (*Belief in Christ*, p. 149).

From the judgment for crime exercised by the State, thousands escape every year; in fact, many crimes are not even known to those in authority. But no one will be able to escape this judgment. The dead will be called forth from their graves, and from the sea, from Hades itself (v. 13); and those whose names are not found in the Book of Life will be cast into the lake of fire, which is the second death (v. 14). The records of every human life in this vast assembly will then be produced. Death itself, it seems, is not abolished until the Great White Throne is set up, and human destiny is forever settled. If we believe and embrace with joy the promises of eternal glory that are in this book, we must also believe with equal conviction that this terrible doom of the unrepentant dead is equally true. (For a discussion of the entire matter of judgment, see my book, *Therefore Stand,* the section called, "A Righteous Judgment to Come," pp. 438-466).

The Holy City. 21:1–22:5.

We have now come to the final revelation given to us in Holy Scripture, a glorious climax to all that God has inspired men to write for the edification of his people throughout the ages. In this passage we move from time into eternity. Sin, death, and all the forces antagonistic to God are now forever put away. Most students of the Word are convinced that what we have in this last section (I am not here thinking of the epilogue) is a description of the eternal home of the redeemed in Christ. It is probably not to be identified with heaven, but it must certainly be that to which the Scriptures have previously pointed—the City of God, the New Jerusalem, the Zion that is above. One must not be dogmatic here as to what may be interpreted symbolically and what must be considered literally. Different scholars, with equal devotion to the divine authority of the Scriptures, have different views concerning the hermeneutics of this great passage. Even Lang, normally a literalist, insists upon a strong symbolism here and states that "the reason for the employment of symbols may be that there simply is no other way of creating in our minds any just conception of reality" *(op. cit.,* p. 369).

The Origin and Nature of the City. 21:1-8.

1. This famous description, the equal of which cannot be found in any other literature of the ancient world, begins with John's stating that he saw **a new heaven and a new earth.** There are two Greek words translated **new** in the NT, *neos* and the one used here, ***kainos,*** suggesting "fresh life rising from the decay and wreck of the old world" (Swete). Therefore, this passage does not teach that the heavens and earth are now brought into existence for the first time, but that they possess a new character. (See for other uses of the word, Mt 27:60; II Cor 5:17, etc., and some excellent remarks on these two Greek words in R. C. Trench: *Synonyms of the New Testament,* pp. 219-225.)

As to the statement that there will be no more sea, no one has more sensibly interpreted this affirmation than Swete himself, "The sea belonged to the order which has passed. It has disappeared because, in the mind of the writer, it is associated with ideas which are at variance with the character of the New Creation. For this element of unrest, this fruitful cause of destruction and death, this divider of nations and churches, there could be no place in a world of deathless life and unbroken peace."

2. John now beholds **the holy city . . . coming down out of heaven from God.** As the Jerusalem of old was called "the Holy City," so is the new Jerusalem so designated; only this time the word truly describes the actual character of the abode of the redeemed. Holiness, the great attribute of God, has been the divinely set goal for God's people from the beginning. It is significant that our eternal abode is called a **city,** even in the OT (Ps 48:1,8; Heb 11:16).

C. Anderson Scott, in a remarkable chapter on this aspect of the abode of the blest, has well said: "A city is first the ambition and then despair of man . . . Men are proud of a city; they name themselves by its name; they sun themselves in its power and splendor, and yet in the hands of men, the city has become a monster which devours its children. We can hardly dare to look at the spoil-heaps of *outworn* humanity out of which its wealth has been extracted, at the misery and vice on the top of which most of its comfort and splendor rest. All our effort, legislative, philanthropic, and religious, seems to fail piteously in the attempt to meet the evils inseparably connected with a great city. Yet God prepares for us a city. The instinct to seek a common life, to form a complicated web of mutual sympathy and dependence, which is represented by a city, is after all a true one, and the opportunity for its exercise essential alike to man's true happiness and to the full development of his powers. 'It is not good for man to be alone'; neither is it good for a family to be alone, nor yet for a group of families; and this vision shows us 'the far-off Divine event' as realised in the corporate life of humanity, in a society so vast that none of God's children is left out of it, and yet so compact that it can best be described as the society of those who dwell in one city" *(The Book of Revelation,* pp. 308-310).

That the Holy City comes down **out of heaven** seems to imply that it is not identical with heaven. There is a phrase here that is too often passed over—**as a bride adorned for her husband.** One time in a woman's life she has a right to be extravagant, one time she prepares herself with the greatest care and dresses as elegantly and beautifully and attractively as she can—the time of her marriage. Even young women who have no particular beauty have had it said of them, as they walked down the aisle of a church to the altar for the wedding ceremony, "Isn't she beautiful!" As a bride adorns herself for her husband, so will God adorn and beautify this city for his loved ones. All the beautiful things in the world God has made—sunsets, mountains, lakes, roses, beautiful trees, snowflakes, clouds, waterfalls. What will a city be like made by the Divine Architect! (See also Jn 14:2.) A **holy** city will be one in which no lie will be uttered in one hundred million years, no evil word will ever be spoken, no shady business deal will ever even be discussed, no unclean picture will ever be seen, no corruption of life will *ever* be manifest. It will be **holy** because everyone in it will be holy.

3,4. As in so many other passages in the book of Revelation, we have in verse 3 the perfect consummation and conclusion of the great theme of God—*tabernacling* among men. The Greek word here for **tabernacle** is the same as in the Greek translation of the OT passages describing the Tabernacle, where also we are told that in the Holy of Holies, God would meet with his people (Lev 26:11 ff.). This is the word in its verbal form which is used in John's initial description of the Incarnation: "And the Word became flesh, and dwelt among us (and we beheld his glory, glory as of the only begotten from the Father), full of grace and truth" (Jn 1:14). This time the tabernacle abides; this time there will be no separation between God and his people, a fact that seems to be immediately introduced (Rev 21:3). Here, too, is the assurance of the elimination of five tragic aspects of human life: tears, death, mourning, crying, pain (v. 4). The Bible does not deny the reality of pain and death, but it does give us assurance that the day is coming, by the grace of God, when, for the believer, these will no longer exist.

5. It has been suggested by some that in this verse, for the first time in the Apocalypse, the speaker is God himself. There is certainly great significance in the fact that in this book above all others in the NT, the truth of what is here revealed is emphasized. "God authenticates His own magnificent declaration. He demands our attention, and claims our hearts and unqualified assent" (Walter Scott, *op. cit.,* p. 404). **Faithful and true** characterizes not only the spoken (and written Word), but the Incarnate Word as well (19:9; 21:5).

6,7. Once more we have the title of Christ, **the Alpha and the Omega,** which are the first and last words of the Greek alphabet, indicating that Christ is *before* the universe which was created by him, and will be at the end of all time, for all things will be consummated in him.

8. We now come upon something that we really would not expect to find in this description of the Holy City, namely, an indication of the classes of sinners who will *not* be there but rather will be found in **the lake which burneth with fire and brimstone.** These are dreadful words. If we embrace with enthusiasm and thanksgiving the promises of this book, we must also believe its solemn warnings. Lang calls attention to the phrase, "their part," commenting that "the heart could wish that the vision closed on the radiant heights but instead it sinks to the lowest depths."

A Description of the Holy City. 21:9-23.

12-21. The City has **twelve gates,** on each of which is the name of one of the twelve tribes of Israel, and each gate is guarded by an angel. The wall rests upon **twelve foundations,** which apparently means twelve sections of the foundation, and on each of these is a name of one of the twelve apostles. The length, breadth, and height of the city is twelve thousand furlongs, or about 1,500 miles. This would seem, upon first reading, to be in the shape of a cube, but I certainly would follow Simcox, and many others, in believing that this is a pyramidal structure. The word translated **street,** *plateia,* means literally *a broad place;* from this word derives our word *plaza.* The wall is made of jasper, the city is of gold, the gates of pearl, and the foundations of twelve precious stones. (For a study of the possible population of a city this size, see a remarkable essay in F. W. Boreham's *Wisps of Wildfire,* pp. 202-212).

J. N. Darby rarely said that he did not know what a passage of Scripture might mean, but regarding these stones, he once wrote, "The difference of the stones contains details which are above my knowledge" *(Collected Writings,* Volume V, p. 154). "If we compare the colours of the foundation stones with those of the rainbow," says Govett *(op. cit., in loco),* "we shall find, I believe, a designed resemblance, though, from our ignorance in regard of the precious stones, we cannot come to any very close or satisfactory conclusion. The stones, then, with their colours, and the tints of the rainbow, are as follows:

	1. Jasper, greenish? yellow?
	2. Sapphire, azure.
	3. Chalcedony, doubtful, green and blue.
The Rainbow:	4. Emerald, green.
1. Red	5. Sardius, red.
2. Orange	6. Sardonyx, red and white.
3. Yellow	7. Chrysolite, yellow.
4. Green	8. Beryl, sea-green.
5. Blue	9. Topaz, yellow.
6. Indigo	10. Chrysoprasus, golden-green.
7. Violet (lake)	11. Jacinth, violet.
	12. Amethyst, rose-red."

22,23. John proceeds to tell us that the city has no temple within, and that it is so brilliantly illuminated by the glory of God that it has no need of the light of the sun or moon, though they will still be shining. "So long as men dwell here under the conditions of earthly life, they cannot do without these temples, the place, the time, the thoughts marked off for God, the place where we learn the secret of realising His presence in life, the time when we claim and proclaim His fellowship with Him, the thoughts, which, of set purpose, we direct toward the manifestation of His love in Christ, and of His will in duty. But there is no temple *there;* for the simple reason that none is needed. That which now has to be delimited from the world, and set apart for God—yes, and held with determination and force of will against invading hosts—has there expanded to cover the whole area of human experience and activity. God's presence has no longer to be sought; it is known; it is felt, universal and all-pervading as the light of day" (C. Anderson Scott, *op. cit., in loco.).* Our text does not say that there will not be any sun or moon in eternity, but that we will not *need* the light of the sun and moon, for the very glory of God will illuminate the city. As we need a candle in the night, but not at noon, when the sun is shining, so we do need the sun and moon in our present state of existence, but will need them no more when in the presence of God, who is light indeed.

Those Who Enter the City. 21:24-27.

24-26. The paragraph embracing these three verses is extremely difficult to interpret. Who are these **nations** that walk in the light of the Holy City, and who are the **kings of the earth** that bring their glory into it? Govett is probably right in saying: "By 'the kings of the earth' are meant the kings of the nations. As the nations are now transferred to the new world, so have they kings. Subordination of ranks is a part of God's abiding scheme for eternity. They are called 'kings of *the earth,'* to distinguish them from the kings *of the city.* For there are two classes of kings: those made kings and priests to God by Jesus' blood, who are risen from the dead and dwell with God; and those who are men in the flesh, and live among the nations outside the metropolis. For the citizens are *kings of kings,* and 'they shall reign for ever and ever' (22:5). The kings of the nations, then, sensible of their inferiority, and desirous to appear before God and His risen servants, bring presents."

27. Here is one of the most reassuring, comforting, and hope-filled statements of all the Bible: those will enter the city whose names are **written in the Lamb's book of life.** Two terrible, inescapable factors keep any man from the Holy City—sin and death. It is the Lamb of God who takes away the sin of the world, and it is the Son of God who gives us life instead of death. To be in the Lamb's Book of Life is to be redeemed by the Lamb of God.

The State of Blessedness Prevailing in the Holy City. 22:1-5. It is strange that in chapter 21 there are no descriptive details pertaining to natural phenomena, trees, rivers, etc., such as we find in the description of the original paradise in Genesis 2. Such details are now introduced, reminding us not only of that early chapter but also of Ezk 47:1-12. "Sin drove man from one garden. Grace brings man to an eternal Paradise." Here we have beauty, life in full abundance, the sovereignty of God, health for the nations of the earth, the absence of all curse; **no curse** (v. 3), on man nor on the earth where he lives nor in the city of his habitation, nor on any relationships prevailing among men—Christ has removed the curse and all the consequences of it). Here also is a picture of service, the perfect vision, which is to behold the face of our Lord, and his name stamped upon our foreheads. Here are two more cancellations or final eliminations of things that have troubled and burdened man: the removal of all curse, and the elimination of night forever.

It is not, however, the negative aspects of this passage which most delight our heart, but its positive affirmations. Here the blessedness that God has desired through the ages and made provision for is brought to a climax of perfection: in heaven we shall be serving the Lord (v. 3b); we **shall see his face**; his name will be on our foreheads (v. 4); we shall reign with him forever and ever (v. 5). Here such promises as those found in Mt 5:8; I Jn 3:2; I Cor 15:49; etc., will become the eternal experience of believers. In other words, we shall bear the character of the Lord, we shall serve the Lord, reign with the Lord, and forever rejoice and forever **be satisfied** as we look upon his glorious face. (One of the most profound and satisfying treatments of the Holy City will be found in the work of Govett, pp. 549-610.)

All the glorious purposes of God, ordained from the foundation of the world, have now been attained. The rebellion of angels and mankind is all and finally subdued, as the King of kings assumes his rightful sovereignty. Absolute and unchangeable holiness characterizes all within the universal Kingdom of God. The redeemed, made so by the blood of the Lamb, are in resurrection and eternal glory. Life is everywhere—and death will never intrude again. The earth and the heavens both are renewed. Light, beauty, holiness, joy, the presence of God, the worship of God, service to Christ, likeness to Christ —all are now abiding realities. The vocabulary of man, made for life here, is incapable of truly and adequately depicting what God has prepared for those that love Him.

The Epilogue. 22:6-20. For the closing verses of the Apocalypse, it is not necessary that we give an extended interpretation. Most of these statements here, like the latter part of nearly all the NT epistles, are hortatory.

6-10. The first statement is almost identical with the opening declaration of the Apocalypse (1:1,2), except that there one "servant" is mentioned, John, while here **servants** are mentioned. "The 'spirits of the prophets' are the natural faculties of the Prophets, raised and quickened by the Holy Spirit" (Swete). So likewise in verse 7 we are carried back to 1:3. This command to keep **the words of the prophecy of this book** (see 3:8,16; 14:12, 12:17) emphasizes a truth we are too prone to forget, namely, that the prophetic Scriptures have ethical implications. Prophecies and commandments are here bound together.

11-15. In verse 11 we have a solemn truth, sometimes referred to as "the permanence of character." I must once more at this point bring to my readers the concise and solemn lines of Swete. "It is not only true," he says, "that the troubles of the last days will tend to fix the character of each individual according to the habits which he has already formed, but there will come a time when change will be impossible—when no further opportunity will be given for repentance on the one hand or for apostasy on the other."

The coming of Christ is the pre-eminent theme of both the Prologue and the Epilogue (1:7; 22:7,12,20). By **quickly** (v. 12) is not meant that the Second Advent would occur soon after John completed the writing of this book. Rather, it means that the events of the Second Coming will occur so fast, one event quickly following another, that many will be taken completely by surprise. Verse 13 repeats the title of Christ (1:11; 21:6), which is also ascribed to God (1:8). The classes listed here of those debarred from entering the Holy City, each introduced by the article *the,* are substantially the same as those of 21:8. These verses surely cannot mean that there will still be groups of men *on earth* at this time indulging in these sins.

16. Christ himself now speaks, first simply stating that it is he who has originated the revelations John has recorded. This is the first time the word *church (ekklēsia)* has occurred since the letters to the seven churches. He then assigns a twofold title to himself: he is **the root and the offspring of David,** as was long ago foretold by the prophets (Isa 4:3; 11:1,2; 55:1-5; Amos 9:11,12); and he is **the bright, the morning star** (cf. Rev 2:28). The morning star precedes the full brightness of the sun's light.

17. The threefold invitation, so full of grace, is uttered by (1) the Spirit, (2) the Bride, and (3) those who have heard. This is followed by a specific dual designation of those to whom the invitation is particularly sent—those who are athirst (Jn 7:37), and those that will.

18,19. The book, except for a salutation, closes with one more solemn warning, against adding to or taking away from **the words of the book of this prophecy.** I know of no one who has commented on this more acceptably than Lang: "Revelation of truth is complete, for nothing can lie *beyond* the *eternal* state. While in the strict letter the threats of this terrible warning apply to the Revelation, yet inasmuch as this portion of the Book of God is rooted in, interwoven with, and is the completion of all the Word of God, it becomes impossible to tamper with this final book without maltreating what had been given of God before" *(op. cit.,* pp. 384, 385).

20,21. The three last words are those (1) of Christ: **Yea, I come quickly;** (2) of the Church: **Amen: come, Lord Jesus;** and (3) of John: **The grace of the Lord Jesus be with the saints** (ASV). While this parting formula is similar to what we often find at the conclusion of the NT epistles (Rom 16:20,24; I Cor 16:23; Eph 6:24; II Tim 4:22; Heb 13:25; I Pet 5:12; etc., in the exact form as found here it is used nowhere else. As this age draws to its end, and we behold taking place, in a preliminary way, some of the dreadful consequences of rejecting the Word of God, these three last words become increasingly precious and vital.

BIBLIOGRAPHY

ALFORD, HENRY. *The New Testament for English Readers.* 2 vols. 5th ed. London: Rivington, 1872.

GOVETT, ROBERT. *The Apocalypse Expounded.* London: Charles J. Thynne and Jarvis, Ltd., 1929.

LANG, G. H. *The Revelation of Jesus Christ.* London: Paternoster Press, 1945.

LENSKI, R. C. H. *The Interpretation of St. John's Revelation.* Columbus: Wartburg Press, 1943.

OTTMAN, FORD C. *The Unfolding of the Ages.* New York: The Baker and Taylor Co., 1905.

SCOTT, WALTER. *Exposition of the Revelation of Jesus Christ.* London: Pickering and Inglis, n. d.

SEISS, JOSEPH A. *The Apocalypse.* 3 vols. 10th ed. New York: Charles C. Cook, 1909.

SWETE, HENRY BARCLAY. *The Apocalyse of St. John.* 3rd ed. London: Macmillan and Company, 1909.

ABOUT THE AUTHORS

Charles F. Pfeiffer was a professor of ancient literatures at Central Michigan University. He graduated from Moody Bible Institute and held a B.A. from Temple University, a B.D. from Reformed Episcopal Theological Seminary, a Th.M. from Chicago Lutheran Theological Seminary, and a Ph.D. from Dropsie College for Hebrew and Cognate Learning. He also studied at the University of Chicago's Oriental Institute and New York University. He previously served on the faculties of Gordon Divinity School, King's College, Lancaster School of the Bible, and Moody Bible Institute.

The late Dr. Pfeiffer, as author or editor participated in the production of *The Dead Sea Scrolls, Between the Testaments, The Patriarchal Age, An Outline of Old Testament History, Baker's Bible Atlas, Wycliffe Historical Geography of Bible Lands, The Biblical World,* and *Epistle to the Hebrews.*

Everett F. Harrison received his B.A. from the University of Washington, M.A. from Princeton University, Th.B. from Princeton Seminary, Th.D. from Dallas Theological Seminary and Ph.D. from the University of Pennsylvania. Dr. Harrison served as a missionary in China and as a Presbyterian minister in Pennsylvania, though most of his work was in the classroom. He taught at both Dallas Theological Seminary and Fuller Theological Seminary.

Among numerous literary activities, he served as editor of *Baker's Dictionary of Theology,* as reviser of Alford's *Greek Testament,* and as author of *Introduction to the New Testament.*